Rest easy and save!

AAA Members: Save 10% - 30%* at 57 Days Inn® hotels in Florida.

Just book and save at any of the AAA-approved Days Inn locations listed in this TourBook®. Your room comes with an AM/FM clock radio and hair dryer. You'll also get a free continental breakfast and free *USA Today* newspaper. Not to mention special bonus offers for AAA Members all year long! Pets are welcome at more than 900 Days Inn locations worldwide. For specific locations and reservations, call **1-800-432-9755** or visit **daysinn.com**.

DAYS INN.

There you go.

*Discount off published TourBook rate and may not be combined with any other discounts or special offers. Discounts and amenities vary by property. Some restrictions may apply. ©2002 Days Inns Worldwide, Inc.

hilton.com

doubletree.com

Check in with your card.
Cash in on great savings.

Stay with the Hilton Family of hotels and enjoy our
Stay and Save™ rates with your AAA membership.
We offer members a special discounted AAA rate at
over 700 AAA-approved locations in the US. Choose
from conveniently located properties ranging

from luxury resorts to value-priced
accommodations with all the amenities.
Show Your Card & Save® at any

participating hotel in the Hilton Family. To make
advance reservations, call our dedicated AAA number
at **1-877-655-5694** or your local AAA travel office.

embassysuites.com

hiltongardeninn.com

homewood-suites.com

Florida

Published by:
AAA Publishing
1000 AAA Drive
Heathrow, FL 32746-5063
Copyright AAA 2002

The publisher is not responsible for changes that occur after publication. TourBook® guides are published for the exclusive use of AAA members. Not for sale.

Send Written Comments to:
AAA Member Comments
1000 AAA Drive, Box 61
Heathrow, FL 32746-5063

Advertising Rate and Circulation Information
Call: (407) 444-8280

Printed in the USA by Quebecor World, Buffalo, NY

Florida

 TourBook Navigator

Follow our simple guide to make the most of this member benefit 9-25

Comprehensive City Index
Alphabetical list for the entire book 984

■ Florida

Historical Timeline 32

Fast Facts 35

GEM Great Experience for Members ... 38

Recreation Areas Chart 41

Temperature Chart 45

POINTS OF INTEREST 46-237

    The Florida Keys 60-69

    Fort Lauderdale 70-78

    Jacksonville 88-96

    Miami-Miami Beach 104-126

    Orlando 134-180

    Tampa Bay including
    St. Petersburg and
    Tampa 204-231

MAPS

Florida Orientation 36

Everglades National Park 57

The Florida Keys Destination Area ... 62

Fort Lauderdale Destination Area ... 73

Fort Lauderdale 74

Jacksonville Destination Area 91

Jacksonville 92

Miami-Miami Beach
    Destination Area 108

Fort Lauderdale Hollywood
    International Airport 110

Miami International Airport 110

Miami 113

Miami Beach 114

Orlando Destination Area 138

Orlando International Airport 140

Orlando 144

St. Augustine 189

Sarasota and Bradenton Area 198

Tampa Bay Destination Area 208

Tampa International Airport 210

St. Petersburg-Clearwater International
  Airport 210

St. Petersburg and Tampa 214

LODGINGS & RESTAURANTS 241-963

  The Florida Keys 318-355

  Fort Lauderdale 356-414

  Jacksonville 445-477

  Miami-Miami Beach 500-559

  Orlando 588-752

  Tampa Bay including
  St. Petersburg and Tampa 844-946

Walt Disney World Area
  Orlando 621
  Kissimmee 678
  Lake Buena Vista 714

Tampa-St. Petersburg
  Destination Area 844

St. Petersburg and Beach Area 846

Tampa 856

Featured Information

𝓐𝓐𝓐 *Offices* 964

Driving Distances Map 965

Bed & Breakfast Lodgings Index 966

Country Inns Index 966

Historical Lodgings & Restaurants
  Index 966

Resorts Index 967

Points of Interest Index 968

SAVE Attraction Admission Discount
  Index 983

Comprehensive City Index 984

Photo Credit Index 986

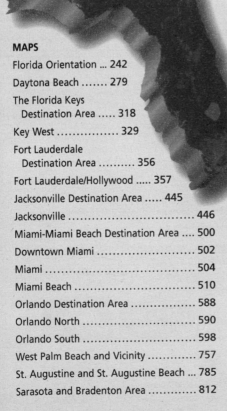

MAPS

Florida Orientation ... 242

Daytona Beach 279

The Florida Keys
  Destination Area 318

Key West 329

Fort Lauderdale
  Destination Area 356

Fort Lauderdale/Hollywood 357

Jacksonville Destination Area 445

Jacksonville 446

Miami-Miami Beach Destination Area 500

Downtown Miami 502

Miami 504

Miami Beach 510

Orlando Destination Area 588

Orlando North 590

Orlando South 598

West Palm Beach and Vicinity 757

St. Augustine and St. Augustine Beach ... 785

Sarasota and Bradenton Area 812

Have you ever celebrated when you've seen your exit sign?

AAA MEMBERS SAVE 10%

Every day should come with a smile. And at Hampton®, we're committed to making you smile. That's why we offer our **Stay and Save**™ rates for AAA members. That's 10% off the best available room rates when you book a room with your AAA card. And with over 1,000 locations nationwide, we're sure to be close to wherever you're traveling. Plus, we'll make sure you start the day right with our free breakfast bar and leave completely satisfied. It's why we have our 100% Satisfaction Guarantee. It's also why you get both Hilton HHonors® hotel points and airline miles for each stay. So book your next trip at Hampton today. Just call **1-800-456-7793** for reservations.

We're with you all the way.

The Hilton Family

See Florida. Stay with us.

WESTIN®
HOTELS & RESORTS

Sheraton®
HOTELS & RESORTS

LUXURY COLLECTION

The Westin Beach Resort, Key Largo
The Westin Diplomat Resort & Spa, Hollywood
The Westin Fort Lauderdale
The Westin Innisbrook Resort, Palm Harbor
Sheraton Bal Harbour Beach Resort, Miami Beach
Sheraton Fort Lauderdale Airport Hotel
Sheraton Gainesville Hotel
Sheraton Suites Cypress Creek, Fort Lauderdale
Sheraton Suites Plantation, Fort Lauderdale — West City
Sheraton Suites Tampa Westshore
Sheraton West Palm Beach Hotel at City Place
Sheraton's PGA Vacation Resort, Port St. Lucie
Sheraton's Vistana Resort, Lake Buena Vista
Sheraton's Vistana Villages, Orlando
Sheraton's Vistana Resort at World Golf Village, St. Augustine
Diplomat Country Club and Spa, Hallandale Beach
Oak Plantation Resort, Kissimmee

6

Crossword Puzzle

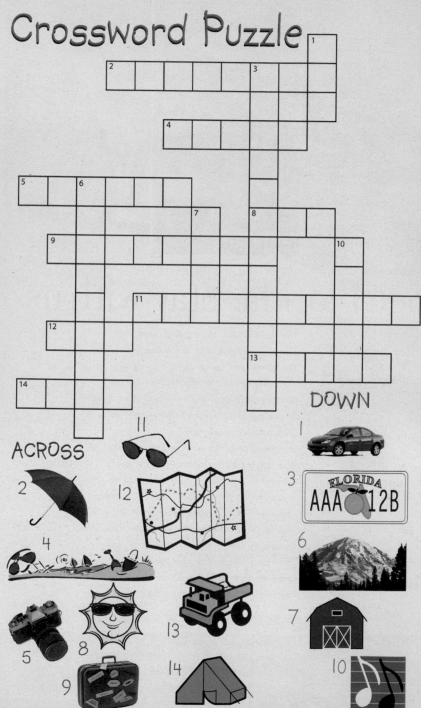

DOWN

ACROSS

2
4
5
8
9
11
12
13
14

1
3
6
7
10

Which two are the same?

Towty is a trademark of AAA

Trust the AAA TourBook® guide for objective travel information. Follow the pages

of the TourBook Navigator to thoroughly understand this unique member benefit.

Making Your Way Through the AAA Listings

Attractions, lodgings and restaurants are listed on the basis of merit alone after careful evaluation, approval and rating by one of our full-time, professionally trained Tourism Editors. Annual evaluations are unannounced to ensure that our Tourism Editors see an establishment just as our members would see it.

Those lodgings and restaurants listed with an 𝐟𝐲𝐢 icon have not gone through the same evaluation process as other rated properties. Individual listings will typically denote the reason why this icon appears. Bulleted recreational activity listings are not inspected but are included for member information.

An establishment's decision to advertise in the TourBook guide has no bearing on its evaluation or rating. Advertising for services or products does not imply AAA endorsement.

How the TourBook is

Organized

Geographic listing is used for accuracy and consistency. This means attractions, lodgings and restaurants are listed under the city in which they physically are located—or in some cases under the nearest recognized city. The Comprehensive City Index located in the back of the book contains an A-to-Z list of cities. Most listings are alphabetically organized by state or province, city, and establishment name. A color is assigned to each state or province so that you can match the color bars at the top of the page to switch from ❶ **Points of Interest** to ❷ **Lodgings and Restaurants.**

Destination Cities and Destination Areas

The TourBook guide also groups information by destination city and destination area. If a city is grouped in a destination vicinity section, the city name will appear at its alphabetical location in the book, and a handy cross reference will give the exact page on which listings for that city begin. Maps are placed at the beginning of these sections to orient you to the destinations.

❸ **Destination cities,** established based on government models and local expertise, are comprised of metropolitan areas plus nearby vicinity cities.

Destination areas are regions with broad tourist appeal. Several cities will comprise the area.

All information in this TourBook guide was reviewed for accuracy before publication. However, since changes inevitably occur between annual editions, we suggest you contact establishments directly to confirm prices and schedules.

Points of Interest Section

Orientation maps
near the start of each Attractions section show only those places we call points of interest. Coordinates included with the city listings depict the locations of those cities on the map. A GEM symbol (🏆) accents towns with "must see" points of interest which offer a *Great Experience for Members*. And the black ovals with white numerals (**22** for example) locate items listed in the nearby Recreation Areas chart.

Destination area maps
illustrate key travel areas defined by local travel experts. Communities shown have listings for AAA approved attractions.

National park maps
represent the area in and around the park. Some campground sites and lodges spotted on the maps do not meet AAA/CAA criteria, but are shown for members who nevertheless wish to stay close to the park area.

Walking or self-guiding tour maps
correspond to specific routes described in TourBook guide text.

City maps
show areas where numerous points of interest are concentrated and indicate their location in relation to major roads, parks, airports and other landmarks.

Lodgings & Restaurants Section

Destination area maps
illustrate key travel areas defined by
local travel experts. Communities
shown have listings for AAA-RATED®
lodgings and/or restaurants.

Spotting maps
show the location of lodgings and
restaurants. Lodgings are spotted with
a black background (**22** for example);
restaurants are spotted with a white
background (**23** for example). Spotting map indexes have
been placed immediately after each map to provide the user
with a convenient method to identify what an area has to
offer at a glance. The index references the map page number
where the property is spotted, indicates if a property is an
Official Appointment and contains an advertising reference
if applicable. It also lists the property's diamond rating, high
season rate range and listing page number.

Downtown/city spotting maps
are provided when spotted facilities are very concentrated.
GEM points of interest also appear on these maps.

Vicinity spotting maps
spot those properties that are outside the downtown or city area. Major
roads, landmarks, airports and GEM points of interest are shown on vicinity
spotting maps as well. The names of suburban communities that have
AAA-RATED® accommodations are
shown in magenta type.

Featured Information Section

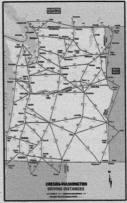

Driving distance maps
are intended to be used only for trip-distance and
driving-time planning.

Sample Attraction Listing

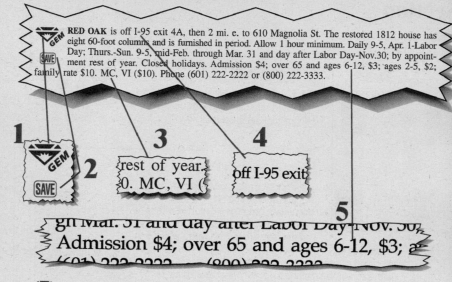

1   This attraction is of exceptional interest and quality and therefore has been designated a AAA GEM—offering a *Great Experience for Members.*

2   Participating attractions offer AAA/CAA, AAA MasterCard or AAA Visa cardholders a discount off the attraction's standard admission; members should inquire in advance concerning the validity of the discount for special rates. Present your card at the admission desk. A list of participating points of interest appears in the Indexes section of the book. The SAVE discount may not be used in conjunction with other discounts. Attractions that already provide a reduced senior or child rate may not honor the SAVE discount for those age groups. All offers are subject to change and may not apply during special events, particular days or seasons or for the entire validity period of the TourBook. Shopping establishments preceded by a SAVE icon also provide discounts and/or gift with purchase to AAA/CAA members; present your card at the mall's customer service center to receive your benefit.

3

AX = American Express	DS = Discover	MC = MasterCard
CB = Carte Blanche	JC = Japan Credit Bureau	VI = VISA
DC = Diners Club		

Minimum amounts that may be charged appear in parentheses when applicable.

4   Unless otherwise specified, directions are given from the center of town, using the following highway designations: I (interstate highway), US (federal highway), Hwy. (Canadian highway), SR (state route), CR (county road), FM (farm to market road), FR (forest road), MM (mile marker).

5   Admission prices are quoted without sales tax. Children under the lowest age specified are admitted free when accompanied by an adult. Days, months and age groups written with a hyphen are inclusive. Prices pertaining to points of interest in the United States are quoted in U.S. dollars; prices for Canadian province and territory points of interest are quoted in Canadian dollars.

Bulleted Listings: Casino gambling establishments are visited by AAA personnel to ensure safety; casinos within hotels are presented for member information regardless of whether the lodging is AAA approved. Recreational activities of a participatory nature (requiring physical exertion or special skills) are not inspected. Wineries are inspected by AAA Tourism Editors to ensure they meet listing requirements and offer tours. All are presented in a bulleted format for informational purposes.

Attraction Partners

These Show Your Card & Save® partners provide the listed member benefits. Admission tickets that offer greater discounts may be available for purchase at the local AAA/CAA club. A maximum of six tickets is available at the discount price.

SeaWorld/Busch Gardens

(SAVE) Save at SeaWorld, Busch Gardens, Sesame Place, Water Country USA and Adventure Island

(SAVE) Save 10% on general admission

Six Flags Adventure Parks

(SAVE) Save $4 per adult on general admission at the gate

(SAVE) Save $12 per adult on general admission at the gate each Wednesday

(SAVE) Save 10% on selected souvenirs and dining (check at main gate for details)

Universal Orlando

(SAVE) Save $4 on a 2-day/2-park pass or $5 on a 3-day/2-park pass at Universal Orlando's theme parks (savings apply to tickets purchased at the gate)

(SAVE) Save 10% on select dining and souvenirs at both Universal Orlando theme parks and at all Universal CityWalk Orlando restaurants (except Emeril's)

Universal Studios Hollywood

(SAVE) Save $3 on a 1-day Universal Hollywood pass (savings applies to tickets purchased at the gate)

(SAVE) Save 10% on selected dining and souvenirs at Universal Studios Hollywood and Universal CityWalk

Gray Line

(SAVE) Save 10% on sightseeing tours of 1 day or less

Restaurant Partners

Landry's Seafood House, The Crab House, Joe's Crab Shack

(SAVE) Save 10% on food and non-alcoholic beverages at Landry's Seafood House, The Crab House and Joe's Crab Shack and 10% on merchandise at Joe's Crab Shack. Savings applicable to AAA/CAA members and up to six people

Hard Rock Cafe

(SAVE) Save 10% on food, beverage, and merchandise at all U.S., Canada, and select international locations

Visit aaa.com to discover all the great Show Your Card & Save® restaurants in your area.

Sample Lodging Listing

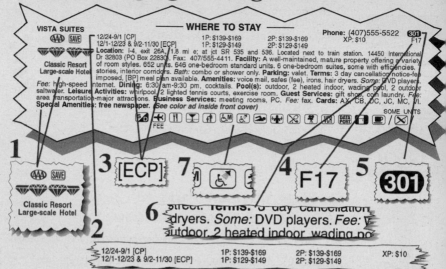

1 **AAA** or **CAA** indicates our Official Appointment (OA) lodgings. The OA program permits properties to display and advertise the **AAA** or **CAA** emblem. We highlight these properties with red diamonds and classification. Some OA listings include special amenities such as free continental breakfast; early check-in/late check-out; free room upgrade or preferred room, such as ocean view or poolside (subject to availability); free local phone calls; and free daily newspaper. This does not imply that only these properties offer these amenities. The **AAA** or **CAA** sign helps traveling members find accommodations that want member business.

▼▼▼ or **▼▼▼▼** The number of diamonds—not the color—informs you of the overall level of quality in a lodging's amenities and service. More diamond details appear on page 16.

Classic Resort Large-scale Hotel or Classic Resort Large-scale Hotel: Diamond ratings are applied in the context of lodging type, or classification. See pages 22-23 for details about our Lodging Classifications and Subclassifications.

Member Values

Discounts normally offered at some lodgings may not apply during special events or holiday periods. Special rates and discounts may not apply to all room types.

SAVE Official Appointment properties guarantee members a minimum 10% discount off the standard room rates published in TourBook guides or the lowest public rate available at the time of booking for the dates of stay, for standard rooms.

SAVE AAA's Show Your Card & Save® chain partners provide AAA's best rates and a satisfaction guarantee to our members: Select from Best Western, Choice Hotels, Hyatt Hotels, Days Inn, most Hilton brands, La Quinta Inn and most Marriott brands. Individual properties appearing in the TourBook guides have been evaluated and approved by AAA. Reservations can be made by calling the AAA member toll-free reservation number 866-AAA-SAVE (have your membership card available), or refer to page 20 for details and a complete listing of participating lodging chains.

S/D Establishments offer a minimum senior discount of 10% off the listed rates. This discount is available to members 60 or older.

ASK Many properties offer discounts to members even though the lodgings do not participate in a formal discount program. The **ASK** is another reminder to inquire about available discounts when making your reservations or at check-in.

To obtain published rates or discounts, you must identify yourself as a AAA or CAA member, request AAA rates when making reservations and have written confirmation sent to you. The SAVE or senior discount may not be used in conjunction with other discounts. At registration, show your membership card and verify the room rate.

The rates listed for approved properties are provided to AAA by each lodging and represent the regular (rack) rate for a standard room. Printed rates, based on rack rates and last room availability, are rounded to the nearest dollar. Rates do not include taxes and discounts. U.S. rates are in U.S. dollars; rates for Canadian lodgings are in Canadian dollars.

2   Rate Lines

Shown from left to right: dates the rates are effective; meal plan provided with rates (see Meal Plan Indicators-if no plan noted, rate includes room only); rates for 1 person or 2 persons; extra person charge (XP); and any applicable family plan indicator.

Rates Guaranteed

AAA/CAA members are guaranteed that they will not be charged more than the maximum regular rate printed in each rate range for a standard room. Rates may vary within the range depending on season and room type. Listed rates are based on last standard room availability. Rates for properties operating as concessionaires for the National Park Service are not guaranteed due to governing regulations.

Exceptions

Lodgings may temporarily increase room rates, not recognize discounts or modify pricing policies during special events. Examples of special events range from Mardi Gras and Kentucky Derby (including pre-Derby events) to college football games, holidays, holiday periods and state fairs. Although some special events are listed in AAA/CAA TourBook guides, it is always wise to check, in advance, with AAA travel professionals for specific dates.

Discounts

Member discounts will apply to rates quoted, within the rate range, applicable at the time of booking. Special rates used in advertising, and special short-term, promotional rates lower than the lowest listed rate in the range, are not subject to additional member discounts.

3   Meal Plan Indicators

The following types of meal plans may be available in the listed room rate:

AP = American Plan of three meals daily
BP = Breakfast Plan of full hot breakfast
CP = Continental Plan of pastry, juice and another beverage
ECP = Expanded Continental Plan, which offers a wider
        variety of breakfast items
MAP = Modified American Plan of two meals daily
See individual listing "Terms" section for additional meal plans that may be offered.

> Check-in times are shown in the listing only if they are after 3 p.m.; check-out times are shown only if they are before 10 a.m.

4   Family Plan Indicators

F = Children stay free
D = Discounts for children
F17 = Children 17 and under stay free (age displayed will reflect property's policy)
D17 = Discount for children 17 and under

5   Lodging Locators

Black ovals with white numbers are used to locate, or "spot," lodgings on maps we provide for larger cities.

6   Unit Types

Unit types, amenities and room features preceded by the word "Some" indicate the item is available on a limited basis, potentially within only one unit.

7   Lodging Icons

A row of icons is included with each lodging listing. These icons represent the member values, member services, and facilities offered by that lodging. See page 19 for an explanation of each icon.

The Lodging Diamond Ratings

AAA Tourism Editors evaluate and rate each lodging based on the overall quality, the range of facilities and the level of services offered by a property. The size, age and overall appeal of an establishment are considered as well as regional architectural style and design.

While guest services are an important part of all diamond ratings, they are particularly critical at the four and five diamond levels. A property must provide a high level of service, on a consistent basis, to obtain and support the four and five diamond rating.

These establishments typically appeal to the budget-minded traveler. They provide essential, no-frills accommodations. They meet the basic requirements pertaining to comfort, cleanliness, and hospitality.

These establishments appeal to the traveler seeking more than the basic accommodations. There are modest enhancements to the overall physical attributes, design elements, and amenities of the facility typically at a modest price.

These establishments appeal to the traveler with comprehensive needs. Properties are multifaceted with a distinguished style, including marked upgrades in the quality of physical attributes, amenities and level of comfort provided.

These establishments are upscale in all areas. Accommodations are progressively more refined and stylish. The physical attributes reflect an obvious enhanced level of quality throughout. The fundamental hallmarks at this level include an extensive array of amenities combined with a high degree of hospitality, service, and attention to detail.

These establishments reflect the characteristics of the ultimate in luxury and sophistication. Accommodations are first-class. The physical attributes are extraordinary in every manner. The fundamental hallmarks at this level are to meticulously serve and exceed all guest expectations while maintaining an impeccable standard of excellence. Many personalized services and amenities enhance an unmatched level of comfort.

The lodging listings with **fyi** in place of diamonds are included as an "information only" service for members. The icon indicates that a property has not been rated for one or more of the following reasons: too new to rate; under construction; under major renovation; not evaluated; or may not meet all AAA requirements. Those properties not meeting all AAA requirements are included for either their member value or because it may be the only accommodation available in the area. Listing prose will give insight as to why the **fyi** designation was assigned.

Guest Safety

Room Security

In order to be approved for listing in AAA/CAA TourBook guides for the United States and Canada, all lodgings must comply with AAA's guest room security requirements.

In response to AAA/CAA members' concern about their safety at properties, AAA-RATED® accommodations must have dead-bolt locks on all guest room entry doors and connecting room doors.

If the area outside the guest room door is not visible from inside the room through a window or door panel, viewports must be installed on all guest room entry doors. Bed and breakfast properties and country inns are not required to have viewports. Ground floor and easily accessible sliding doors must be equipped with some other type of secondary security locks.

Tourism Editors view a percentage of rooms at each property since it is not feasible to evaluate every room in every lodging establishment. Therefore, AAA cannot guarantee that there are working locks on all doors and windows in all guest rooms.

Fire Safety

Because of the highly specialized skills needed to conduct professional fire safety inspections, AAA/CAA Tourism Editors cannot assess fire safety.

Properties must meet all federal, state and local fire codes. Each guest unit in all U.S. and Canadian lodging properties must be equipped with an operational, single-station smoke detector. A AAA/CAA Tourism Editor has evaluated a sampling of the rooms to verify this equipment is in place.

For additional fire safety information, read the page posted on the back of your guest room door, or write:

National Fire Protection Association
1 Batterymarch Park / P.O. Box 9101 / Quincy, MA 02269-9101

Golden Passports

Golden Passports, available in two types, offer a significant savings to individuals who meet certain guidelines.

Citizens or permanent residents of the United States who are 62 and older can obtain Golden Age Passports for a one-time $10 fee. Proof of age is required.

Golden Access Passports are free to citizens or permanent residents of the United States (regardless of age) who are medically blind or permanently disabled.

Both cover entrance fees for the holder and accompanying private party to all national parks, historic sites, monuments, battlefields, recreation areas and wildlife refuges within the U.S. national park system, plus half off camping and other fees. Apply in person at a federally operated area where an entrance fee is charged.

National Parks Pass

The National Parks Pass, valid for 1 year from the month of purchase, allows unlimited admissions to all U.S. national parks. The $50 pass covers all occupants of a private vehicle at parks where the entrance fee is per vehicle. At parks with individual entry fees, the pass covers the pass holder, spouse, parents and children.

As a result of a partnership with the National Park Service, AAA members may purchase the pass for $48, either through AAA's internet site (www.aaa.com) or by visiting a participating AAA office. Members may also phone the National Park Foundation at (888) 467-2757. Non-members may purchase the pass through AAA for the full $50 price.

For an upgrade fee of $15, a Golden Eagle hologram sticker can be added to a National Parks Pass. The hologram covers entrance fees not just at national parks, but at any federal recreation area that has an admission fee. Valid for the duration of the National Parks Pass to which it is affixed, the Golden Eagle hologram is available at National Park Service, Fish and Wildlife Service and Bureau of Land Management fee stations.

Access for Mature Travelers and Travelers with Disabilities

Qualified properties listed in this guide are shown with symbols indicating they meet the needs of the hearing-impaired or offer some accessible features for mature travelers or travelers with disabilities.

 ## Hearing Impaired

Indicates a property has the following equipment available for hearing-impaired travelers: TDD at front desk or switchboard; visual notification of fire alarm, incoming telephone calls, door knock or bell; closed caption decoder; text telephone or TDD for guest room use; telephone amplification device, with shelf or electric outlet next to guest room telephone.

 ## Accessible Features

Indicates a property has some accessible features meeting the needs of mature travelers and travelers with disabilities. Lodging establishments will provide at least one guest room meeting the designated criteria as well as accessible restrooms and parking facilities. Restaurants provide accessible parking, dining rooms and restrooms.

AAA/CAA strongly urges members to call the property directly to fully understand the property's exact accessibility features. Some properties do not fully comply with AAA/CAA's exacting accessibility standards but may offer some design standards that meet the needs of some guests with disabilities.

AAA/CAA does not evaluate recreational facilities, banquet rooms, or convention or meeting facilities for accessibility.

No fees or deposits, even those normally charged for pets, may be charged for service animals. Service animals fulfill a critical need for their owners—they are *not* pets.

Service Animals

The Americans With Disabilities Act (ADA) prohibits businesses that serve the public from discriminating against persons with disabilities. Some businesses have mistakenly denied access to persons who use service animals. ADA, a federal mandate, has priority over all state and local laws, as well as a business owner's standard of business, which might bar animals from the premises. Businesses must permit entry to guests and their service animals, as well as allow service animals to accompany guests to all public areas of a property. A property is permitted to ask whether the animal is a service animal or a pet, and whether the guest has a disability. The property may not, however, ask questions about the nature of the disability, the service provided by the animal or require proof of a disability or certification that the animal is a service animal.

What The Lodging Icons Mean

Member Values
(see p. 14)

AAA or **CAA** Official Appointment

SAVE Offers minimum 10% discount or lowest public rate *(see p. 14)*

SAVE Show Your Card & Save lodging partners

ASK May offer discount

S$D Offers senior discount

fyi Informational listing only

Member Services

⊀ Airport transportation

🐾 Pets allowed

⑪ Restaurant on premises

⑪+ Restaurant off premises (walking distance)

24⑪ 24-hour room service

⏄ Cocktail lounge

⑪ Child care

Accessibility Features
(see p. 18)

Ġᴹ Accessible features

Ġ Roll-in showers

⌕ Hearing impaired

Leisure Activities

🎲 Full service casino

🏊 Pool

⛹ Health club on premises

⛹+ Health club off premises

⌧ Recreational activities

In-Room Amenities

⌧ Designated non-smoking rooms

ᴀᴄ No air conditioning

ᴛᴠ No TV

ᴄᴛᴠ No cable TV

VCR VCR

🎥 Movies

DATA PORT Data port/modem line

☎ No telephones

▤ Refrigerator

▣ Microwave

▢ Coffee maker

Availability

If an in-room amenity is available only on a limited basis (in one or more rooms), the term "SOME UNITS" will appear above those icons.

SOME UNITS

Ġᴹ ⌕ VCR 🎥 ▢ / ⌧ DATA PORT ▤ /

Additional Fees

Fees may be charged for some of the services represented by the icons listed here. The word "FEE" will appear below each icon when an extra charge applies.

SOME UNITS

Ġᴹ ⌕ VCR 🎥 ▢ / ⌧ DATA PORT ▤ /
        FEE FEE   FEE

Preferred Lodging Partners

Show Your Card & Save

AAA. Every Day.

SAVE UP TO 50% ON OVER 1,500,000 ROOMS - When contacting one of the partners listed, you will be given AAA's best rates for your dates of stay. Your valid membership card must be presented at check-in.

SATISFACTION GUARANTEE - If you are not satisfied with any part of your stay, you must provide the property the opportunity to correct the situation during your stay. If the matter cannot be resolved, you will be entitled to recompense for a portion of, or your entire, stay. Satisfaction guarantee varies by chain.

Select the chain you want and have your membership card available when making a reservation and checking in.

| **Visit** | Over 1,100 AAA Offices | **Click** | aaa.com | **Call** | 866-AAA-SAVE |

Making Reservations

When making reservations, you must identify yourself as a AAA or CAA member. Give all pertinent information about your planned stay. Ask about the lodging's pet policy, or the availability of any other special feature that is important to your stay. Request written confirmation to guarantee: type of room, rate, dates of stay, and cancellation and refund policies. At registration, show your membership card. Note: Age restrictions may apply.

Confirm Deposit, Refund and Cancellation Policies

Most establishments give full deposit refunds if they have been notified at least 48 hours before the normal check-in time. Listing prose will note if more than 48 hours notice is required for cancellation. However, when making reservations, confirm the property's deposit, cancellation and refund policies. Some properties may charge a cancellation or handling fee.

When this applies, "cancellation fee imposed" will appear in the listing. If you cancel too late, you have little recourse if a refund is denied.

When an establishment requires a full or partial payment in advance, and your trip is cut short, a refund may not be given.

When canceling reservations, phone the lodging immediately. Make a note of the date and time you called, the cancellation number if there is one, and the name of the person who handled the cancellation. If your AAA/CAA club made your reservation, allow them to make the cancellation for you as well so you will have proof of cancellation.

Review Charges for Appropriate Rates

When you are charged more than the maximum rate listed in the TourBook guide for a standard room, question the additional charge. If management refuses to adhere to the published rate, pay for the room and submit your receipt and membership number to AAA/CAA within 30 days. Include all pertinent information: dates of stay, rate paid, itemized paid receipts, number of persons in your party, the room number you occupied, and list any extra room equipment used. A refund of the amount paid in excess of the stated maximum will be made if our investigation indicates that unjustified charging has occurred.

Get the Room You Reserved

When you find your room is not as specified, and you have written confirmation of reservations for a certain type of accommodation, you should be given the option of choosing a different room or finding one elsewhere. Should you choose to go elsewhere and a refund is refused or resisted, submit the matter to AAA/CAA within 30 days along with complete documentation, including your reasons for refusing the room and copies of your written confirmation and any receipts or canceled checks associated with this problem.

How to Get the Best Room Rates

You'll find the best room rate if you book your reservation in advance with the help of a travel professional or agent at your local AAA/CAA office.

If you're not yet ready to make firm vacation plans or if you prefer a more spontaneous trip, take advantage of the partnerships that preferred hotel chains have arranged with AAA. Phone the toll-free number on the previous page that has been set up exclusively for members for the purpose of reserving with these Show Your Card & Save® chain partners.

Even if you were unable to make a reservation, be sure to show your membership card at the desk and ask if you're being offered the lowest rate available for that time. Many lodgings offer reduced rates to members.

Lodging Classifications

AAA Tourism Editors evaluate lodgings based on classification, since all lodging types by definition do not provide the same level of service and facilities. Thus, hotels are rated in comparison to other hotels, resorts to other resorts—and so on. A lodging's classification appears beneath its diamond rating in the listing.

Large-scale Hotel

A multistory establishment with interior room entrances. A variety of guest unit styles is offered. Public areas are spacious and include a variety of facilities such as a restaurant, shops, fitness center, spa, business center, or meeting rooms.

Small-scale Hotel

A multistory establishment typically with interior room entrances. A variety of guest unit styles is offered. Public areas are limited in size and/or the variety of facilities available.

Motel

A one- to three-story establishment typically with exterior room entrances facilitating convenient access to parking. The standard guest units have one bedroom with a bathroom and are typically similar in décor and design throughout. Public areas are limited in size and/or the variety of facilities available.

Country Inn

Similar in definition to a bed and breakfast, but usually larger in scale with spacious public areas and offers a dining facility that serves at least breakfast and dinner.

Bed & Breakfast

Small-scale properties emphasizing a high degree of personal touches that provide guests an "at home" feeling. Guest units tend to be individually decorated. Rooms may not include some modern amenities such as televisions and telephones, and may have a shared bathroom. Usually owner-operated with a common room or parlor separate from the innkeeper's living quarters, where guests and operators can interact during evening and breakfast hours. Evening office closures are normal. A continental or full, hot breakfast is served and is included in the room rate.

Condominium

Vacation-oriented or extended-stay, apartment-style accommodations that are routinely available for rent through a management company. Units vary in design and décor and often contain one or more bedrooms, living room, full kitchen, and an eating area. Studio-type models combine the sleeping and living areas into one room. Typically, basic cleaning supplies, kitchen utensils and complete bed and bath linens are supplied. The guest registration area may be located off-site.

Cabin/Cottage
Vacation-oriented, small-scale, freestanding houses or cabins. Units vary in design and décor and often contain one or more bedrooms, living room, kitchen, dining area, and bathroom. Studio-type models combine the sleeping and living areas into one room. Typically, basic cleaning supplies, kitchen utensils, and complete bed and bath linens are supplied. The guest registration area may be located off-site.

Ranch
Typically a working ranch with an obvious rustic, Western theme. In general, equestrian-related activities are featured, but ranches may include other animals and activities as well. A variety of guest unit styles is offered in a family-oriented atmosphere.

Vacation Home
Vacation-oriented or extended-stay, large-scale, freestanding houses that are routinely available for rent through a management company. Houses vary in design and décor and often contain two or more bedrooms, living room, full kitchen, dining room, and multiple bathrooms. Typically, basic cleaning supplies, kitchen utensils, and complete bed and bath linens are supplied. The guest registration area may be located off-site.

Lodging Subclassifications

The following are subclassifications that may appear along with the classifications listed above to provide a more specific description of the lodging.

Casino
Extensive gambling facilities are available such as blackjack, craps, keno, and slot machines. **Note:** This subclassification will not appear beneath its diamond rating in the listing. It will be indicated by a dice icon and will be included in the row of icons immediately below the lodging listing.

Classic
Renowned and landmark properties, older than 50 years, well-known for their unique style and ambience.

Historic
These properties are typically over 75 years of age and exhibit many features of a historic nature with respect to architecture, design, furnishings, public record, or acclaim. Properties must meet one of the following criteria:
- Maintained the integrity of the historical nature
- Listed on the National Register of Historic Places
- Designated a National Historic Landmark
- Located in a National Register Historic District

Resort
Recreation-oriented, geared to vacation travelers seeking a specific destination experience. Travel packages, meal plans, theme entertainment, and social and recreational programs are typically available. Recreational facilities are extensive and may include spa treatments, golf, tennis, skiing, fishing, or water sports, etc. Larger resorts may offer a variety of guest accommodations.

Sample Restaurant Listing

WHERE TO DINE

KINGSTON'S RESTAURANT Classic   **Dinner:** $16-$35   **Phone:** 555/987-1600   ⑱

Location: I-459, exit 13 (US 31); adjacent to Riverchase Galleria; in The Wynfrey Hotel. 1000 Riverchase Galleria 35244. **Hours:** 5 pm-10 pm. Closed major holidays; also Sun. **Reservations:** suggested. **Features:** Boasting an upscale atmosphere and excellent American cuisine, the fine dining establishment is the ideal setting for a special, intimate dinner. Its newly renovated dining rooms offer an elegant setting for a truly memorable meal. Dressy casual; cocktails. **Parking:** on-site. **Cards:** AX, DC, DS, MC, VI.

American

1 AAA

American

5 Classic

2 Dinner: $16-$35

3 Cards: AX, DC, DS, MC, VI.

6 ⑱

4

---

1   AAA or CAA indicates our Official Appointment (OA) restaurants. The OA program permits properties to display and advertise the AAA or CAA emblem. We highlight these properties with red diamonds and cuisine type. The AAA or CAA sign helps traveling members find restaurants that want member business.

or The number of diamonds—not the color—informs you of the overall level of quality for food and presentation, service and ambience.

A cuisine type is assigned for each restaurant listing. AAA currently recognizes more than 90 different cuisine types.

2   Prices represent the minimum and maximum entree cost per person. Exceptions may include one-of-a-kind or special market priced items.

3   AX = American Express
CB = Carte Blanche
DC = Diners Club

DS = Discover
JC = Japan Credit Bureau

MC = MasterCard
VI = VISA

4   These three icons are used in restaurant listings. When present, they indicate: the presence of a cocktail lounge, the lack of air conditioning, and/or that the restaurant has a designated non-smoking section or is entirely smoke-free.

5   If applicable, restaurants may be further defined as:

Classic—renowned and landmark properties, older than 25 years, known for unique style and ambience.

Historic—properties must meet one of the following criteria:
- Listed on the National Register of Historic Places
- Designated a National Historic Landmark
- Located in a National Register Historic District

6   These white ovals with black numbers serve as restaurant locators and are used to locate, or "spot," restaurants on maps we provide for larger cities.

The Restaurant Diamond Ratings

AAA Tourism Editors are responsible for determining a restaurant's diamond rating based on established criteria.

These criteria were established with input from AAA trained professionals, members, and restaurant industry experts. They are purposely broad to capture what is typically seen throughout the restaurant industry at each diamond rating level.

These establishments appeal to a diner seeking good, wholesome, no-nonsense eating at an affordable price. They typically provide simple, familiar, and unadorned foods served in a sensible, casual or self-service style. Often quick service and family oriented.

Examples include coffee shops, diners, cafeterias, short order, and modest full service eateries.

These establishments provide for dining needs that are increasingly complex, but still reasonably priced. They typically exhibit noticeable efforts in rising above the ordinary in many aspects of food, service and decor. Service is typically functional yet ambitious, periodically combining informal style with limited self-service elements. Often well-suited to traditional, special occasion, and family dining.

Examples include a varied range of specific concept (theme) and multi-purpose establishments.

These establishments impart an increasingly refined and upscale, adult-oriented experience. This is the entry level into fine dining. Creative and complex menus offer a blend of traditional and trendy foods. The service level is typically semi-formal with knowledgeable and proficient staff. Routinely these restaurants appeal to the diner in search of an experience rather than just a meal.

Examples include high-caliber, chic, boutique, and conventional restaurants.

These establishments impart a luxurious and socially refined experience. This is consistent fine dining. Menus typically reflect a high degree of creativity and complexity, featuring elaborate presentations of market-driven or traditional dishes. A cultured, professional, and highly proficient staff consistently demonstrates a profound desire to meet or exceed guest expectations. Restaurants of this caliber are geared to individuals with an appetite for an elite, fine-dining experience.

Examples include dining rooms associated with luxury lodgings, or exclusive independent restaurants often found in metropolitan areas.

Often renowned, these establishments impart a world-class and opulent, adult-oriented experience. This is "haute cuisine" at its best. Menus are often cutting edge, with an obvious dedication to use of only the finest ingredients available. Even the classic dishes become extraordinary under the masterful direction of highly acclaimed chefs. Presentations are spectacular, reflecting impeccable artistry and awareness. An expert, formalized staff continuously anticipates and exceeds guest expectations. Staff members' unfailing attention to detail appears effortless, well-rehearsed and unobtrusive. Undoubtedly, these restaurants appeal to those in search of the ultimate dining experience.

Examples include renowned dining rooms associated with luxury lodgings, or exclusive independent restaurants often found in metropolitan areas.

The restaurants with [fyi] in place of diamonds are included as an "information only" service for members. These listings provide additional dining choices but have not yet been evaluated.

Savings for all Seasons

Hertz rents Fords and other fine cars. ® REG. U.S. PAT. OFF. © HERTZ SYSTEM INC., 1998/2005-99.

No matter the season, Hertz offers AAA members exclusive discounts and benefits.

Operating in 140 countries at over 7,000 locations, Hertz makes traveling more convenient and efficient wherever and whenever you go. Hertz offers AAA members discounts up to 20% on car rentals worldwide.

To receive your exclusive AAA member discounts and benefits, mention your AAA membership card at time of reservation and present it at time of rental. In addition, to receive a free one car class upgrade, in the United States mention PC# 929714, in Canada mention PC# 929725 and in Puerto Rico mention PC# 929736 at the time of reservation. Offer available through 12/31/04.

For reservations and program details, call your AAA travel office or the Hertz/AAA Desk at **1-800-654-3080.**

Show Your Card & Save

AAA. Every Day.

Hertz ®

exactly.

MEMENTO,OOO,OOO

For the perfect Florida souvenir, pick up
a handful of Scratch-Off games. Or lock
in your lucky numbers weeks down the
road with our "Advance Play" option.
Ask for it when you play Cash 3™, Play 4™,
Fantasy 5™, Mega Money® or Florida Lotto™
and you could end up with the best keepsake
of all – a vacation that never ends.

Florida Lottery.

When you play, we all win.

Florida

Sandy Beaches

Sun and fun are found in abundance along the expansive coast

Theme Park Adventures

Amusements range from water slides to roller coasters

Manatees & Alligators

Placid waters harbor Florida's native creatures

Relaxing in the Keys

Clear water and coral characterize this diving paradise

Journey into Space

Awesome launches light up the sky at Cape Canaveral

a whimsical paradise

W hen you hear the word "Florida," there's a good chance that you conjure a vivid mental picture.

It probably includes swaying palms, sandy beaches and piercing rays of sunlight reflecting off the surface of the surrounding waters.

Perhaps you envision the emerald-green waters that caress the

Gulf beaches at Pensacola. Or the sharks' teeth sprinkled across the sand in Venice. Or the colorful varieties of seashells blanketing the coast on the islands of Captiva and Sanibel. Or the rolling waves lapping at the sugary shore of Ponce Inlet.

Without a doubt, the state's seascapes are spectacular. But Florida boasts an

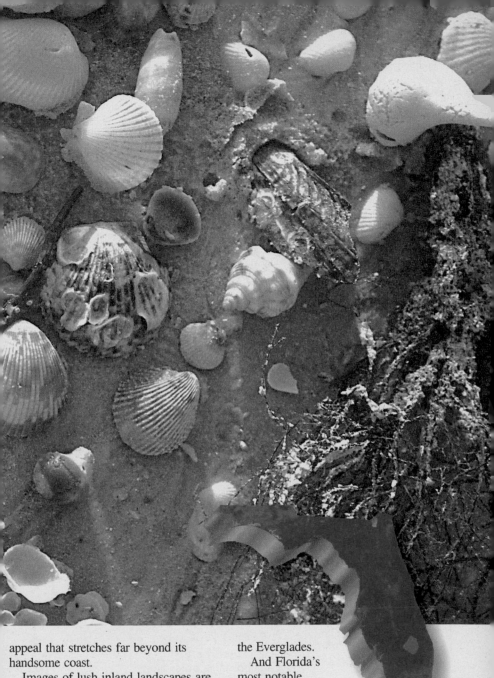

appeal that stretches far beyond its handsome coast.

Images of lush inland landscapes are just as plentiful. Towering pine trees and stolid oaks rise from dense thickets of palmettos in the Apalachicola, Ocala and Osceola national forests. Prairies of sawgrass interrupt mangrove stands and mazes of gnarled cypress roots that emerge from the murky swampland in the Everglades.

And Florida's most notable man-made enticements can't be overlooked: Glittery theme parks encourage young and old to make time for a day of play beneath a sun that almost always shines.

Florida is as close as you can get to seeing the world through the eyes of an artist with a mischievous sense of humor and a wildly creative genius.

The Sunshine State is a place of stunning extremes—a place where the sun shines brighter, the water runs bluer, the slash pines reach higher, the sands feel softer.

It's a place in which the Northerners live way down south around Miami and Fort Lauderdale and where Southern accents ring out from such northern enclaves as Pensacola and Tallahassee.

Strange creatures inhabit the water, the land and the air. Oafish manatees—thought to have given rise to the legend of the mermaid—ply the waters of coastal waterways and placid springs. Garish roseate spoonbills, whose showy pink plumes topped the chapeaus of many a society matron in the early 1900s, grace shorelines once dotted with flocks of flamingos.

Dog-sized Key deer skirt the brush on Big Pine Key. Libidinous lovebugs, known for their mating-while-flying rendezvous, make their impact as they smash two-by-two into the windshields of passing cars.

Exotic plants enliven the landscape with splashes of vivid color—the purple of the spiky pontederia, the fiery crimson of the hibiscus and poinciana, the violet-bluish cast of the Blewit mushroom, the orange, yellow and green of the citrus growing in the state's ubiquitous groves.

They Came with a Dream

This naturally varied canvas has reached out like a beckoning finger to visionaries far and wide.

Juan Ponce de León, who came in search of the legendary Fountain of Youth, blazed a trail for the conquistadores who followed in his footsteps. A pair of Henrys—Flagler and Plant—laid the framework, or rather the railroad tracks, that enabled the state to become a major vacation destination.

Building on that framework: An entrepreneur named Walt Disney, the man who turned a central Florida cow pasture into the home of the rodent with arguably the state's most recognized face—if not surely its most recognized pair of ears.

The stylistic touches left behind by architects of many eras give Florida a rich sense of texture. A Spanish flair prevails in historic

---

Florida Historical Timeline

Juan Ponce de León, searching for the Fountain of Youth, sails around Florida and lands near St. Augustine.

1513

Spanish smuggler Pedro Menéndez de Aviles destroys a French Huguenot colony and establishes St. Augustine, the nation's oldest continuously inhabited settlement.

1565

Gen. Andrew Jackson comes to punish the Indians for attacking the settlers, thus instigating the First Seminole War, which lasts until 1818.

1817

1763

Under the First Treaty of Paris, England gains possession of the region after it returns Cuba to Spain following the Seven Years' War.

1783

The Second Treaty of Paris returns all of Florida to Spain.

1819

Spain sells Florida to the United States.

St. Augustine, where buildings are distinguished by walled patios, stately arches and roofs of burnt-orange clay tile. Ybor City's showier flourishes—wrought-iron balconies, sidewalk cafes and plazas—point to a profoundly Latin influence. Synthetic materials, pastel hues and rectilinear forms characterize the Art Deco hotels along Ocean Drive in Miami's trendy South Beach.

As diverse as the state's architecture are the people who call Florida home. Sharing a place under the sun is a seemingly haphazard mix of retirees, jet setters, refugees and adventurers, of young and old, of "conch" fishermen, business tycoons and developers, and of tourists who came to visit but decided to stay.

Endless Days of Sunshine

One of the state's very few constants is its weather. Florida's climate is sultry, whether you visit in February or August. Its thermostat has but two settings: warm and hot.

For the most part Mother Nature smiles kindly, although she is prone to excess when angered. Hurricanes, tornadoes, floods and fires are among the punishments mercilessly inflicted when she unleashes sporadic fits of fury.

But Floridians take it all in stride. It's considerably easier in a state that simply refuses to take itself too seriously.

As much as Florida is rolling oceans, sawgrass prairies and mangrove and cypress swamps, it is bicycle-riding birds, leaping alligators, and sea lions and walruses masquerading as actors.

As much as you can make a living here growing sugar cane, catching fish or manufacturing semiconductors, you can pull on a tail to perform as a mermaid, choose a sunny sidewalk spot from which to draw caricatures of passersby or stroll through gardens bedecked as a prim Southern belle.

What other state's identity ties so closely to the unabashedly seedy treasures that lurk behind signs of brash neon? Plastic yard flamingos, seashell figurines with glued-on rolling eyes, the simple word "Florida" set amid the chaos of unrestrained tie-dye on a 50/50 cotton blend T-shirt—like no other state, Florida has its kitsch in sync.

It's a place that brings forth smiles and laughter and lets us see things in a different light. A whimsical light. A humorous light.

F lorida achieves statehood.
1845

W alt Disney World opens, bringing with it an explosion of new tourist attractions and thousands of new jobs – along with millions of tourists – to central Florida.
1971

H urricane Andrew devastates the area just south of Miami, cutting a 60-mile swath through the state and leaving behind an estimated $30 billion in damages.
1992

1958
S hortly after the first U.S. satellite, Explorer I, is launched from Cape Canaveral, the National Aeronautics and Space Administration (NASA) is created.

1986
T he space shuttle *Challenger* explodes seconds after liftoff, killing all seven aboard.

2001
G eorge W. Bush is named the 43rd president after Florida's election controversy is resolved by the U.S. Supreme Court.

Recreation

Water, water everywhere, and most is great for play. Recreation is a way of life in the Sunshine State, and what better way to catch some rest 'n' relaxation than to get wet.

Not only is Florida nearly surrounded by ocean and gulf waters, but it also harbors thousands of lakes and hundreds of miles of rivers and canals. The prevalence of boat ramps and the impressive facilities of municipal marinas testify to the popularity of **boating.** Boaters should take caution to watch for endangered manatees in springs and coastal waterways.

To appreciate the beauty of the Everglades' narrow creeks and shallow bays, set out on a **canoeing** adventure. A tranquil weeklong escape awaits serious paddlers who tackle the 100-mile-long Wilderness Waterway. Although the Turner River and Mud Lake Loop trails are considerably shorter, the scenery is no less spectacular. Also worth navigating are the myriad rivers, lakes and ponds of the Apalachicola and Ocala national forests.

Looking for a lazy way to pass the day? Grab a tube and go **river floating** at Coldwater Creek in Blackwater River State Forest or at Ichetucknee Springs, west of High Springs.

In Motion in the Ocean

Surfing is a sure-fire way to beat the heat. The best waves crash on the Atlantic beaches, most notably from New Smyrna Beach south to Sebastian Inlet. Swells occasionally kick up south of Mayport Naval Base near Jacksonville and around Deerfield Beach and South Beach in south Florida.

Off the Miami coast, shipwrecks and other sunken items—such as a Boeing 727 jet lowered to the ocean floor in 1993—function as artificial reefs. Rich coral growth makes **scuba diving** ventures here particularly attractive. **Snorkeling,** especially popular at John Pennekamp Coral Reef State Park in Key Largo, allows for similar encounters with marine life at a more shallow depth.

The nearly 600 varieties of fish that live off the coast lure anglers to cast their lines into the brine. Many marinas provide **saltwater fishing** equipment, bait and guides for deep-sea or offshore charters. Record-size specimens also swim in the state's rivers and lakes, making **freshwater fishing** equally rewarding.

Don't neglect to pick up a license from the county tax collector or a subagent, such as a tackle shop, fish camp or hardware or sporting goods store. Saltwater licenses, required

for all anglers ages 16 to 64, cost nonresidents $6.50 for 3 days, $16.50 for 7 days or $31.50 for 1 year; a resident license costs $13.50 for 1 year. Stamps that allow you to reel in snook and net crawfish cost an additional $2 each. Freshwater licenses cost nonresidents $16.50 for 7 days or $31.50 for 1 year; a 1-year resident license costs $13.50.

Taking to the Terrain

Set out on foot to explore the more than 1,300 miles of **hiking** trails that comprise the Florida Trail; write the Florida Trail Association, 5415 S.W. 13th St., Gainesville, FL 32608, or phone (352) 378-8823, or (877) 445-3352. Supplement your strides with spectacular ocean views by walking along the coastline at Canaveral National Seashore; the Klondike stretch is open only to hikers. Leashed pets are welcomed at Smyrna Dunes Park, at the northern tip of the New Smyrna Beach peninsula.

If you prefer your exertion on the easy to moderate end of the spectrum, catch a breeze while **bicycling** on the relatively flat Florida terrain. Although you won't experience many downhill thrills, you won't grunt through many uphill struggles either. The town of White Springs is near 15 trails, including the looping Gar Pond Trail and the Big Shoals Trail, which passes one of the state's scant white-water stretches on the Suwannee River.

Public and semiprivate courses all over the state make **golf** immensely popular. And there's a good chance you'll work up a sweat just watching a spectator sport. Major and minor league **baseball** and professional **football, basketball, hockey** and **soccer** teams play statewide, while **dog racing, horse racing, jai-alai** and **polo** draw their own crowds.

Recreational Activities

Throughout the TourBook, you may notice a Recreational Activities heading with bulleted listings of recreation-oriented establishments listed underneath. Since normal AAA inspection criteria cannot be applied, these establishments are presented only for information. Age, height and weight restrictions may apply. Reservations often are recommended and sometimes are required. Visitors should phone or write the attraction for additional information; the address and phone number are provided for this purpose.

Fast Facts

POPULATION: 15,982,378.

AREA: 58,560 square miles; ranks 22nd.

CAPITAL: Tallahassee.

HIGHEST POINT: 345 ft., Walton County.

LOWEST POINT: Sea level, Atlantic Ocean.

TIME ZONE(S): Eastern/Central. DST.

MINIMUM AGE FOR GAMBLING: 18.

MINIMUM AGE FOR DRIVERS: 18, unrestricted; 15 with a learner's permit.

SEAT BELT/CHILD RESTRAINT LAWS: Seat belts required for driver, front-seat passengers and back-seat passengers under 18; child restraints required for under 4.

HELMETS FOR MOTORCYCLISTS: Optional for drivers and passengers over 21 provided they meet minimum insurance coverage requirements.

RADAR DETECTORS: Permitted, except in some municipalities.

FIREARMS LAWS: Vary by state and/or county. Contact the Florida Department of State, Division of Licensing, P.O. Box 6687, Tallahassee, FL 32314-6687; phone (850) 488-5381.

HOLIDAYS: Jan. 1; Martin Luther King Jr. Day, Jan. (3rd Mon.); Memorial Day, May (4th Mon.); July 4; Labor Day, Sept. (1st Mon.); Veterans Day, Nov. 11; Thanksgiving, Nov. (4th Thurs.); Dec. 25.

TAXES: Florida's statewide sales tax is 6 percent, with counties allowed to levy up to an additional 1 percent. Counties also may levy on accommodations and meals a Tourist Development Tax or a Tourist Impact Tax of varying increments.

STATE INFORMATION CENTERS: Centers can be found just south of the Florida/Georgia border on US 231 at Campbellton, south of the Florida/Georgia border off I-75 near Jennings, near the Florida/Alabama border off I-10 16 miles west of Pensacola, south of the Florida/Georgia border off I-95 near Yulee, and in the Capitol in Tallahassee.

SPECIAL REGULATIONS: All motorists who drive trucks or pull trailers must stop at road guard agricultural inspection stations. Recreational vehicles and private passenger vehicles without trailers are not required to stop at these stations.

Permanently disabled persons with "handicapped" license plates from any state receive special parking privileges in Florida.

SPECIAL NOTE: Lovebugs are unlovely insects that swarm during daylight hours April through May and September through October, often clogging car radiators and smearing windshields. These insects are extremely sticky and contain an acid which, if allowed to remain on a car, can corrode the finish.

To lessen the problems posed by these insects, place a bug screen over your car's front grille, restrict travel to the early morning or late afternoon hours and drive at slower speeds.

NATIONAL FOREST INFORMATION:
Supervisor's Office
325 John Knox Rd.,
Bldg. F100
Tallahassee, FL 32303-4160
(850) 523-8500
(877) 444-6777 (reservations)

FISHING AND HUNTING REGULATIONS:
Freshwater:
Florida Fish and Wildlife Conservation
Commission
620 S. Meridian St.
Tallahassee, FL 32399-1600
(850) 488-4676
Saltwater:
Florida Fish and Wildlife Conservation
Commission
Division of Marine Fisheries
2590 Executive Center Cir.
Tallahassee, FL 32301
(850) 488-6058

RECREATION INFORMATION:
Department of Environmental Protection
Office of Recreation and Parks
3900 Commonwealth Blvd.
Mail Station 536
Tallahassee, FL 32399-3000
(850) 488-9872

FURTHER INFORMATION FOR VISITORS:
Visit Florida Inc.
P.O. Box 1100
Tallahassee, FL 32302
(850) 488-5607
(888) 735-2872

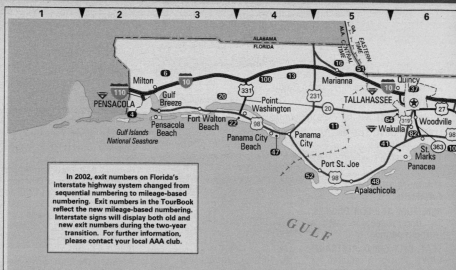

In 2002, exit numbers on Florida's interstate highway system changed from sequential numbering to mileage-based numbering. Exit numbers in the TourBook reflect the new mileage-based numbering. Interstate signs will display both old and new exit numbers during the two-year transition. For further information, please contact your local AAA club.

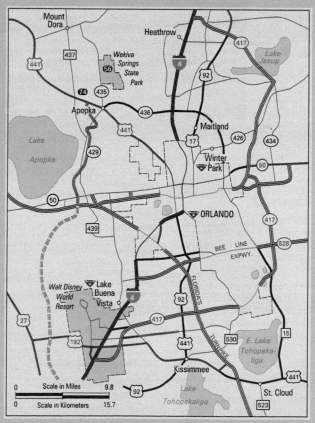

4004-K

ORIENTATION MAP

NOT INTENDED FOR DRIVING.
SEE APPROPRIATE AAA SHEET MAP.

ONLY PLACES LISTED IN ATTRACTIONS
SECTION APPEAR ON THIS MAP.
SEE AAA GEM ATTRACTIONS
SEE CHART OF RECREATION AREAS

Scale in Miles   0   61.8
Scale in Kilometers 0   99.5

Points of Interest Offering A
Great Experience for Members

Dania Beach (G-12)

I.G.F.A. FISHING HALL OF FAME & MUSEUM—A tackle gallery, wetlands exhibit and simulated-fishing stations will lure you to this expansive museum. See p. 77.

Daytona Beach (C-10)

DAYTONA USA—Interactive displays, a movie and trivia games chronicle the city's racing heritage. See p. 53.

Everglades National Park (H-10)

EVERGLADES NATIONAL PARK—Labyrinthine waters creep through salt prairies, hardwood hammocks and stands of mangroves and cypress trees. See p. 57.

Gainesville (C-8)

FRED BEAR MUSEUM—The museum presents a collection of trophies, tools, decorations and weapons Fred Bear collected on his bowhunting adventures around the world. See p. 86.

Jacksonville (B-9)

CUMMER MUSEUM OF ART & GARDENS—Noteworthy gallery features include Meissen porcelain tableware and a formal garden extending to the river. See p. 93.

Kennedy Space Center (D-11)

ASTRONAUTS MEMORIAL SPACE MIRROR—The black granite memorial pays tribute to American astronauts who died in the line of duty. See p. 99.

KENNEDY SPACE CENTER—The center operates as America's center of space operations. See p. 97.

KENNEDY SPACE CENTER VISITOR COMPLEX—The complex features multimedia displays about the American space program, IMAX theaters and actual spacecraft. See p. 97.

U.S. ASTRONAUT HALL OF FAME—The hall of fame honors America's space pioneers and traces the development of space exploration. See p. 99.

Key West (I-9)

CONCH TOUR TRAINS—Narration centers on area history as the trains navigate old and new Key West. See p. 67.

Lake Buena Vista (G-2)

WALT DISNEY WORLD® RESORT—The sprawling complex includes the Magic Kingdom® Park, Epcot®, Disney-MGM Studios, Disney's Animal Kingdom® Theme Park, family water parks and numerous entertainment, shopping and dining facilities. See p. 163.

Lakeland (E-9)

FLORIDA AIR MUSEUM AT SUN 'N FUN—If the aircraft displayed here seem a bit unusual, it is because many are either homebuilt or experimental models (or both). See p. 100.

Lake Wales (E-9)

HISTORIC BOK SANCTUARY—Landscaped gardens surround the marble and coquina stone tower, which contains 60 bronze bells. See p. 101.

Largo (H-7)

PINEWOOD CULTURAL PARK—This 182-acre site features an art museum, botanical gardens and more than two dozen historic buildings representing the early days of Pinellas County. See p. 229.

Miami-Miami Beach (H-11)

THE HOLOCAUST MEMORIAL—The 6 million Jews who died at the hands of the Nazis are remembered here. See p. 112.

MIAMI-DADE CULTURAL CENTER—The center comprises a museum that outlines the history of south Florida; a museum that features the artwork of international contemporary artists; and a library. See p. 114.

MIAMI METROZOO—Animal shows complement cageless environments inhabited by species of African, Asian and European animals. See p. 114.

PARROT JUNGLE—Parrots and other exotic birds thrive in this subtropical flowery paradise. See p. 116.

VIZCAYA MUSEUM AND GARDENS—Opulent furnishings in the impressive 34-room villa represent the renaissance, baroque, rococo and neoclassical eras. See p. 116.

Ocala (C-9)

THE APPLETON MUSEUM OF ART—The museum is a showcase for European, pre-Columbian, West African, Islamic and Asian art as well as antiquities. See p. 130.

FLORIDA'S SILVER SPRINGS—Glass-bottom boats cruise along the clear artesian springs, offering views of underwater life as far as 40 feet below the water's surface. See p. 131.

Orlando (D-9)

DISCOVERY COVE—Swim with the sharks and hug dolphins at this resort-style park geared towards intimate, safe and unforgettable encounters between humans and animals. See p. 142.

SEAWORLD ORLANDO—The theme park lets visitors experience marine life up close through varied displays and shows, such as the one featuring the famed Shamu. See p. 147.

UNIVERSAL ORLANDO—The park features Universal  Studios, where rides and shows are based on popular films and TV shows; Islands of Adventure, with five lands representing legendary characters and super heroes; as well as an entertainment section with restaurants and clubs. See p. 149.

Palm Beach (F-12)

FLAGLER MUSEUM—This Gilded-Age mansion, furnished in original and period pieces, contains historical exhibits. See p. 182.

Palm Coast (C-10)

WASHINGTON OAKS GARDENS STATE PARK—Covering more than 400 acres of Florida coastal scenery, the gardens feature exotic plants from around the world. See p. 182.

Pensacola (B-2)

NATIONAL MUSEUM OF NAVAL AVIATION—Highlights of the museum collection are an NC-4 Flying Boat, a World War II SBD Dauntless and the Skylab Command Module. See p. 185.

St. Augustine (B-10)

CASTILLO DE SAN MARCOS NATIONAL MONUMENT—The Spanish fortress, which features massive diamond-shaped bastions at each corner, defended the city until the mid-18th century. See p. 188.

COLONIAL SPANISH QUARTER—Costumed guides depict the 1740s lifestyle in this quarter of restored and reconstructed buildings. See p. 190.

GOVERNMENT HOUSE MUSEUM—American Indian artifacts, treasure from Spanish shipwrecks and religious items are among the exhibits detailing area history. See p. 191.

HISTORIC OLD JAIL COMPLEX—The complex comprises a museum that depicts Florida's growth; the jail, which displays weaponry and outlines prison life; and narrated trolley tours. See p. 194.

LIGHTNER MUSEUM—Tiffany stained glass, Oriental art and art nouveau works are noteworthy in the Lightner collection. See p. 191.

OLDEST HOUSE—Also known as the González-Alvarez House, the structure is home to two museums: one tracing city history and one devoted to Florida's army. See p. 191.

ST. AUGUSTINE ALLIGATOR FARM—All 23 crocodilian species are represented at the farm, which also features tropical birds. See p. 195.

WORLD GOLF VILLAGE AND HALL OF FAME

WORLD GOLF VILLAGE AND HALL OF FAME—The showcase for this sport honors golfing legends in a hall of fame and along a Walk of Champions; an IMAX theater is part of the complex. See p. 195.

St. Petersburg (E-8)

THE FLORIDA HOLOCAUST MUSEUM—Tolerance and understanding are the lessons taught at this museum commemorating the millions who perished during this tragic period. See p. 212.

SALVADOR DALI MUSEUM—The Spanish artist's creative diversity is captured in works ranging from small impressionistic pieces to gigantic surrealistic montages. See p. 216.

Sanibel (G-9)

THE BAILEY-MATTHEWS SHELL MUSEUM—Seashells from the nearby beaches of Sanibel and Captiva islands as well as locations around the world are displayed. See p. 196.

Sarasota (F-8)

THE JOHN AND MABLE RINGLING MUSEUM OF ART—An extensive collection of pieces by Peter Paul Rubens is the centerpiece of the Italian Renaissance museum. See p. 198.

Sebring (F-10)

HIGHLANDS HAMMOCK STATE PARK—Lush vegetation flourishes in the dense jungle and swampland in this easy-to-explore park. See p. 201.

Tallahassee (B-5)

ALFRED B. MACLAY GARDENS STATE PARK—Colorful azaleas, camellias and Oriental magnolias decorate the grounds of this Southern estate. See p. 202.

Tampa (E-8)

BUSCH GARDENS TAMPA BAY—A late 19th-century African motif punctuates the rides, entertainment, animal exhibits and shows in the park. See p. 217.

THE FLORIDA AQUARIUM—Florida's ecosystem and aquatic habitats are detailed in aquarium exhibits. See p. 218.

MOSI (MUSEUM OF SCIENCE & INDUSTRY)—In addition to a planetarium and an IMAX *Dome* theater, the museum presents displays that explain aspects of science and technology. See p. 218.

Wakulla (B-6)

EDWARD BALL WAKULLA SPRINGS STATE PARK—The clear, deep springs are believed to have been discovered by Ponce de León, who claimed them to be the "fountain of youth." See p. 232.

Winter Haven (E-9)

CYPRESS GARDENS—In addition to being home to more than 8,000 varieties of plants and flowers from around the world, the state's first theme park is popular for its shows and lovely Southern belles. See p. 236.

Winter Park (F-4)

CHARLES HOSMER MORSE MUSEUM OF AMERICAN ART—Most noteworthy in the museum is an extensive collection of works by art nouveau master Louis Comfort Tiffany, whose stained glass gained him fame. See p. 180.

RECREATION AREAS

Name	Map Location	Camping	Picnicking	Hiking Trails	Boating	Boat Ramp	Boat Rental	Fishing	Swimming	Pets on Leash	Bicycle Trails	Skin/Scuba	Visitor Center	Lodge/Cabins	Food Service
NATIONAL PARKS *(See place listings)*															
Biscayne (H-12) 180,000 acres. Scenic.		•	•	•	•	•		•	•			•	•		
Dry Tortugas (I-8) 64,657 acres. Scenic.		•	•		•	•		•	•			•	•		
Everglades (H-10) 1,506,539 acres. Scenic.			•	•	•	•	•	•				•	•	•	•
NATIONAL FORESTS *(See place listings)*															
Apalachicola 565,543 acres. Northwestern Florida.		•	•	•	•	•		•	•	•					
Ocala 383,573 acres. North-central Florida. Horse rental.		•	•	•	•	•	•	•	•	•	•		•	•	•
Osceola 198,484 acres. Northeastern Florida. Horse rentals and trails.		•	•	•	•	•		•							
NATIONAL SEASHORES *(See place listings)*															
Canaveral (D-10) 57,000 acres. East-central Florida.		•	•	•	•			•	•				•		
Gulf Islands (B-2) 137,000 acres. Northwestern Florida.		•	•	•	•	•		•	•			•	•		
ARMY CORPS OF ENGINEERS															
Ortona Lock (G-10) e. of La Belle off SR 80.	80	•	•		•	•		•							
St. Lucie Lock (F-11) 140 acres 8 mi. s.w. of Stuart off SR 76.	81		•			•		•	•						
STATE															
Alfred B. Maclay State Gardens (A-6) 307 acres 5 mi. n.e. of Tallahassee on US 319. Scenic. Horse trails. *(See Tallahassee p. 202)*	37		•	•	•			•	•		•		•		
Anastasia (B-10) 1,035 acres at St. Augustine Beach off SR A1A at SR 3.	1	•	•	•				•	•						•
Bahia Honda (I-10) 524 acres on Bahia Honda Key off US 1 at mile marker 35. Snorkeling tours; kayak rentals.	2	•	•	•		•	•	•	•					•	•
Big Lagoon (B-2) 712 acres 10 mi. s.w. of Pensacola on SR 292A.	4	•	•	•	•	•		•	•						
Bill Baggs Cape Florida (H-11) 900 acres off US 1 on Key Biscayne. Historic. Lighthouse tour.	5		•	•				•	•		•	•	•		•
Blackwater River (A-3) 590 acres 15 mi. n.e. of Milton off US 90. Historic. Canoe rentals.	6	•	•	•					•	•					
Blue Spring (D-9) 518 acres 2 mi. w. of Orange City off US 17/92 on W. French Ave. *(See Orange City p. 132)*	7	•	•	•				•	•			•		•	•
Bulow Plantation Ruins Historic (C-10) 152 acres 9 mi. s.e. of Bunnell off CR 2001 (Old Kings Rd.), between SR 100 and Old Dixie Hwy. Historic. Interpretive center. Canoeing. *(See Bunnell p. 50)*	92		•	•	•	•		•		•					
Caladesi Island (G-7) 653 acres in the Gulf of Mexico w. of Dunedin. Bird-watching, boat camping. *(See Dunedin p. 228)*	8	•	•	•	•			•	•						•
Cayo Costa (G-8) 2,506 acres accessible by boat from Boca Grande or Fort Myers. Bird-watching.	93	•	•	•				•	•				•		
Collier-Seminole (H-9) 6,423 acres 17 mi. s. of Naples on US 41. Historic. Bird-watching. *(See Naples p. 128)*	10	•	•	•	•	•	•	•					•		
Dead Lakes (B-5) 83 acres .5 mi. n. of Wewahitchka on SR 71.	11	•	•	•	•	•		•							
De Leon Springs (C-9) 443 acres 1 mi. s. of DeLeon Springs on SR 181. Canoe rentals.	46		•	•	•	•	•	•	•			•			•
Delnor-Wiggins Pass (G-9) 166 acres 11 mi. n.w. of Naples off SR 846. Shell gathering, turtle watching in nesting season; boardwalks, observation tower.	12		•	•	•	•		•	•	•					
Don Pedro Island (F-8) 115 acres accessible only by boat.	94		•	•				•	•						
Econfina River (B-6) 3,377 acres s. of Lamont at the end of CR 14. Horse trails.	103		•	•	•	•		•		•					
Edward Ball Wakulla Springs (B-6) 2,860 acres .5 mi. e. of Wakulla Springs at jct. SRs 61 and 267. Boat tours, bird-watching; hiking trails. *(See Wakulla p. 232)*	82		•	•					•	•				•	•
Falling Waters (A-4) 155 acres 3 mi. s. of Chipley off SR 77.	13	•	•	•					•						

RECREATION AREAS

	MAP LOCATION	CAMPING	PICNICKING	HIKING TRAILS	BOATING	BOAT RAMP	BOAT RENTAL	FISHING	SWIMMING	PETS ON LEASH	BICYCLE TRAILS	SKIN/SCUBA	VISITOR CENTER	LODGE/CABINS	FOOD SERVICE
Fanning Springs (C-7) 188 acres on US 19/98 on the e. bank of the Suwanee River in Fanning Springs.	104		•	•	•				•	•			•		
Faver-Dykes (B-9) 752 acres 15 mi. s. of St. Augustine off US 1.	14	•	•	•	•	•		•							
Florida Caverns (A-5) 1,280 acres 3 mi. n. of Marianna on SR 166. Bird-watching; horse trails. *(See Marianna p. 103)*	16	•	•	•					•	•			•		
Fort Clinch (A-9) 1,153 acres 2 mi. e. of Fernandina Beach on SR A1A at n. end of Amelia Island. Historic. Bird-watching. *(See Fernandina Beach p. 95)*	17	•	•	•				•	•				•		
Fort Cooper (D-8) 707 acres 2 mi. s. of Inverness off US 41. Historic.	67							•	•						
Fort Pierce Inlet (F-11) 340 acres 3 mi. e. of Fort Pierce on SR A1A. Bird-watching. *(See Fort Pierce p. 82)*	18		•	•	•			•	•	•	•	•			
Fort Zachary Taylor (I-9) 78 acres at the s.w. end of Key West via Southard St. Historic. *(See Key West p. 67)*	88	•						•	•			•			•
Fred Gannon Rocky Bayou (B-3) 357 acres 5 mi. e. of Niceville on SR 20.	20	•	•	•	•	•	•	•	•				•		
Gamble Rogers Memorial State Recreation Area (C-10) 145 acres .5 mi. s. of Flagler Beach on SR A1A.	15	•	•	•	•	•		•	•	•					
Gasparilla Island (G-8) 144 acres 3 mi. s. of Placida on CR 775. Historic. Interpretive center. Lighthouse.	95		•					•	•	•	•				
Grayton Beach (B-3) 365 acres adjacent to Grayton Beach on SR 30A.	22	•	•	•	•	•	•	•	•	•					
Guana River (B-9) 2,400 acres on SR A1A 10 mi. s. of Ponte Vedra Beach. Bird-watching.	105		•	•				•	•						
Highlands Hammock (F-9) 8,133 acres 3.5 mi. w. of US 27 on CR 634. Scenic. Museum. Bird-watching; horse trails. *(See Sebring p. 201)*	23	•	•	•							•		•		
Hillsborough River (E-8) 2,990 acres 6 mi. s. of Zephyrhills off US 301. Living-history program.	24	•	•	•	•		•	•	•						
Honeymoon Island (G-7) 450 acres 3 mi. n. of Dunedin on SR 586, w. of US 19A. Bird-watching.	84		•	•				•	•						
Hontoon Island (C-9) 1,649 acres 6 mi. w. of DeLand off SR 44.	25	•	•	•	•			•						•	
Hugh Taylor Birch (G-11) 180 acres at Sunrise Blvd. and SR A1A in Fort Lauderdale.	26		•	•				•	•						
Ichetucknee Springs (B-7) 2,241 acres off US 27 .5 mi. e. of Hildreth. Scenic. Bird-watching, tubing. *(See High Springs p. 87)*	68		•	•				•	•	•					•
John D. MacArthur Beach (F-12) 760 acres on SR A1A, 2.8 mi. s. of jct. US 1 on Singer Island. Bird-watching. *(See Singer Island p. 201)*	96		•	•				•	•						
John Pennekamp Coral Reef (I-11) 178 nautical miles on US 1 near Key Largo mile marker 102.5. *(See Key Largo p. 65)*	27	•	•	•	•	•	•	•	•			•	•		•
John U. Lloyd Beach (G-11) 244 acres 3 mi. s. of Fort Lauderdale on SR A1A.	28	•	•		•	•		•	•	•		•			•
Jonathan Dickinson (F-11) 10,328 acres 6 mi. n. of Jupiter on US 1. Historic. Scenic. Bird-watching; bicycle rental, horse trails. *(See Jupiter p. 97)*	29	•	•	•	•	•	•	•	•		•			•	•
Koreshan (G-9) 139 acres .5 mi. s. of Estero on US 41. Historic. Bird-watching; canoe rentals. *(See Estero p. 56)*	30	•	•	•	•			•							
Lake Griffin (D-9) 423 acres 1 mi. e. of Fruitland Park off US 27.	31	•	•		•	•		•							
Lake Kissimmee (E-9) 5,027 acres 8 mi. e. of Lake Wales via SR 60, 4 mi. n. on Boy Scout Rd., then 5 mi. n. on Camp Mack Rd. following signs. Living-history program. Bird-watching; horse trails. *(See Lake Wales p. 102)*	32	•	•	•	•		•	•							
Lake Louisa (D-9) 1,790 acres 7 mi. s.e. of Clermont on Lake Nellie Rd. Horse trails.	33		•	•				•	•						
Lake Manatee (F-8) 556 acres 14 mi. e. of Bradenton on SR 64. Bird-watching.	34	•	•	•	•	•	•	•	•	•					

RECREATION AREAS	MAP LOCATION	CAMPING	PICNICKING	HIKING TRAILS	BOATING	BOAT RAMP	BOAT RENTAL	FISHING	SWIMMING	PETS ON LEASH	BICYCLE TRAILS	SKIN/SCUBA	VISITOR CENTER	LODGE/CABINS	FOOD SERVICE
Little Manatee River (E-8) 2,020 acres 5 mi. s. of Sun City off US 301. Equestrian camping; horse trails.	85	•	•	•	•	•		•							
Little Talbot Island (A-9) 2,500 acres 17 mi. n.e. of Jacksonville on SR A1A. Pier.	35	•	•		•			•	•		•				
Long Key (I-10) 849 acres on Long Key at Layton on US 1.	36	•	•	•	•			•	•			•			
Lovers Key (G-9) 267 acres on CR 865, 2 mi. s. of Big Carlos Pass on Lovers Key.	89		•	•	•	•	•	•	•						
Manatee Springs (C-7) 1,075 acres 6 mi. w. of Chiefland on SR 320. Bird-watching.	38	•	•	•	•	•		•	•		•		•		•
Mike Roess Gold Head Branch (B-9) 1,414 acres 6 mi. n.e. of Keystone Heights on SR 21. Bird-watching; bicycle, canoe and paddleboat rentals.	39	•	•	•	•	•	•	•	•	•	•			•	•
Myakka River (F-8) 28,875 acres 17 mi. e. of Sarasota on SR 72. Airboat and safari tram tours, bird-watching; bicycle rentals, hiking and horse trails. *(See Sarasota p. 199)*	40	•	•	•	•	•	•	•	•	•	•		•	•	•
Ochlockonee River (B-6) 392 acres 4 mi. s. of Sopchoppy on US 319.	41	•	•	•	•	•		•	•	•					•
O'Leno (B-8) 6,700 acres 6 mi. n. of High Springs off US 41. Historic. Bird-watching. *(See High Springs p. 87)*	42	•		•	•			•	•	•			•		
Oleta River (H-11) 90 acres at 3400 N.E. 163rd St. in North Miami Beach.	83	•	•	•				•	•			•		•	•
Oscar Scherer (F-8) 1,383 acres 2 mi. s. of Osprey on US 41. Bird-watching.	43	•			•			•	•	•	•				
Paynes Creek (E-9) 400 acres .5 mi. e. of Bowling Green at 888 Lake Branch Rd. Historic. Interpretive center. Bird-watching, canoeing.	99		•	•				•					•		
Paynes Prairie Preserve (C-8) 21,000 acres 1 mi. n. of Micanopy on US 441. Bird-watching, canoeing; horse trail. *(See Micanopy p. 127)*	45	•	•	•	•	•		•		•	•		•		
Ponce de Leon Springs (A-4) 441 acres .5 mi. s. of Ponce de Leon on US 90.	100		•	•				•	•						
Rainbow Springs (C-8) 1,000 acres 3 mi. n. of Dunnellon on US 41. Waterfalls. Tubing.	21	•	•	•				•			•				
Rodman Reservoir (C-9) 10 mi. s.w. of Palatka off SR 19 access roads on the Ocklawaha River. Horse trails.	79	•	•	•	•	•	•	•							
St. Andrews (B-4) 1,260 acres 3 mi. e. of Panama City Beach via SR 392. *(See Panama City Beach p. 183)*	47	•	•	•	•	•		•	•		•	•			•
St. George Island (C-5) 1,833 acres off US 98 via CRs G1A and 300 on St. George Island. Bird-watching.	48	•	•	•	•	•		•	•						
St. Lucie Inlet (F-11) Accessible by boat from Port Salerno on the Intracoastal Waterway. Bird-watching.	87		•					•	•		•				
Sebastian Inlet (E-11) 578 acres 15 mi. s. of Melbourne Beach on SR A1A. Museum. Bird-watching. *(See Sebastian p. 200)*	49	•			•			•	•	•		•	•		•
Suwannee River (B-7) 1,831 acres 13 mi. w. of Live Oak on US 90. Historic.	50	•	•	•	•	•		•							
Three Rivers (A-5) 682 acres 2 mi. n. of Sneads off US 90.	51	•	•	•	•	•		•							
T.H. Stone Memorial (St. Joseph Peninsula) (C-4) 2,500 acres 20 mi. s.w. of Port St. Joe. Bird-watching.	52	•	•	•	•	•		•	•		•	•		•	
Tomoka (C-10) 915 acres 3 mi. n. of Ormond Beach. Museum.	53	•	•	•	•	•	•	•					•		
Washington Oaks (C-10) 400 acres at 6400 Oceanshore Blvd. Interpretive center. *(See Palm Coast p. 182)*	55		•	•				•							
Wekiwa Springs (E-2) 6,396 acres 4 mi. n.w. of I-4, off US 441 near Apopka. Bird-watching; horse trails.	56	•	•	•	•		•	•		•	•		•		•
OTHER															
Alexander Springs (C-9) 30 acres 13 mi. n.e. of Umatilla via SR 19 and CR 445. *(See Ocala National Forest p. 132)*	57	•	•	•	•			•	•	•					•

RECREATION AREAS

	MAP LOCATION	CAMPING	PICNICKING	HIKING TRAILS	BOATING	BOAT RAMP	BOAT RENTAL	FISHING	SWIMMING	PETS ON LEASH	BICYCLE TRAILS	SKIN/SCUBA	VISITOR CENTER	LODGE/CABINS	FOOD SERVICE
Avon Park Air Force Range (E-9) 84,000 acres on SR 64 in Avon Park.	66	•	•	•	•	•	•	•							
C.B. Smith (G-11) 320 acres at Flamingo Rd. and Hollywood Blvd. in Pembroke Pines. Miniature golf, tennis; waterslide.	58	•	•	•	•			•	•	•			•		•
Everglades Holiday (H-11) 10 acres 20 mi. w. of Dania off Griffin Rd. Airboat rides.	71	•	•		•	•	•	•							•
Fort De Soto (F-8) 1,136 acres off I-275 exit 17 at Pinellas Bayway. Historic. *(See St. Petersburg p. 213)*	59	•	•	•	•	•	•	•	•	•	•		•	•	•
Ginnie Springs (C-8) 200 acres 7 mi. w. of High Springs off CR 340. Canoeing. *(See High Springs p. 87)*	72	•	•	•	•	•	•	•				•	•	•	•
Juniper Springs (C-9) 47 acres 28 mi. e. of Ocala on SR 40. Canoeing, kayaking; canoe rental, pool. *(See Ocala National Forest p. 132)*	60	•	•	•			•	•					•		
Kathryn Abbey Hannah (B-9) 450 acres next to Mayport Naval Station off SR A1A in Jacksonville Beach. Canoeing, horseback riding; horse rentals.	73	•	•	•	•		•	•	•	•	•	•	•		
Kelly Park (E-2) 200 acres 6 mi. n. of Apopka on SR 435. Tubing. *(See Apopka p. 160)*	74	•	•	•				•	•		•				•
Lake Dorr (D-9) 10 acres 5 mi. n. of Umatilla on SR 19. *(See Ocala National Forest p. 132)*	61	•	•	•		•	•		•	•					
Lakes Park (G-9) 279 acres 6 mi. s.w. of I-75 exit 131, via Six Mile Cypress. Bicycle rental, jogging trails.	90		•	•		•	•	•	•						•
Maximo Park (I-8) 65 acres in St. Petersburg at 34th St. and Pinellas Point Dr. S. Observation tower, playground.	101		•	•	•	•		•		•					
Okeeheelee (G-11) 1,000 acres in Palm Beach, 6 mi. w. of I-95 on Forest Hills Blvd. Ball fields, water-skiing course.	75		•	•	•	•		•	•		•				•
Olustee Beach (B-8) 15 acres .25 mi. n. of Olustee on CR 231.	63		•	•	•			•	•						
Poe Springs Park (B-8) 202 acres 3 mi. w. of High Springs on CR 340. *(See High Springs p. 87)*	102		•	•	•	•	•	•	•						
Quiet Waters (G-12) 430 acres 2 mi. w. from I-95 via SR 810, then .25 mi. s. on SR 845 in Deerfield Beach. Cable water skiing; canoe, paddleboat and bicycle rentals. *(See Deerfield Beach p. 78)*	69	•	•				•	•	•	•	•				•
Silver Lake (B-5) 25 acres 8 mi. w. of Tallahassee off SR 20.	64	•	•	•	•			•	•		•				
Topeekeegee Yugnee (H-11) 150 acres .5 mi. w. of I-95 on Sheridan St. (SR 822) in Hollywood. Miniature golf; canoe and paddleboat rentals, waterslide.	77	•	•				•	•	•	•	•				•
Tradewinds (G-11) 90 acres at 3600 Sample Rd. in Coconut Creek. Museum. Botanical gardens, horse rental, pony rides and hayrides.	65		•	•			•	•		•	•				
Tree Tops (G-11) 256 acres at 3900 S.W. 100th Ave. in Davie. Canoe, horse and paddleboat rentals.	78		•	•	•			•					•		

Look for our Partners in Savings!

When selecting a AAA Approved lodging, look for properties that participate in our various partnership programs. In addition to actively soliciting AAA business, many of them also offer discounts to AAA members.

- Properties that advertise in the TourBook® guide want to provide members with a more complete picture of their property. Please refer to their ads for more details on what these properties have to offer.

- A red ⟨SAVE⟩ icon in their TourBook guide listing indicates an **Official Appointment** property that offers a minimum 10% discount off published TourBook standard room rates or the lowest public room rate, at the time of booking, for the dates of stay.

- A black ⟨SAVE⟩ icon indicates a chain hotel that participates in the **Show Your Card & Save®** program. These properties offer a satisfaction guarantee and savings up to 50% on more than 1.5 million rooms throughout North America. Please refer to page 20 in the TourBook Navigator section for complete details and a list of participating hotel chains or call **866-AAA-SAVE** to make a reservation.

Florida Temperature Averages
Maximum / Minimum
From the records of the National Weather Service

	JAN	FEB	MAR	APR	MAY	JUNE	JULY	AUG	SEPT	OCT	NOV	DEC
Jacksonville	65/44	67/46	72/50	79/57	85/64	88/70	90/72	90/72	86/70	79/62	71/51	66/45
Key West	76/66	77/66	79/70	82/74	85/76	88/79	89/80	89/80	88/79	84/75	80/71	76/67
Miami	76/59	77/59	79/63	83/67	85/71	88/74	89/75	90/76	88/75	85/71	80/64	77/60
Orlando	70/50	72/51	76/56	81/61	87/66	89/71	90/73	90/73	88/72	82/66	76/57	71/51
Tallahassee	64/41	66/43	72/48	80/56	87/63	90/70	91/72	90/72	87/69	81/58	71/46	65/41
Tampa	71/50	72/52	76/56	82/62	87/67	90/72	90/74	90/74	89/73	84/65	77/56	72/51
West Palm Beach	75/56	76/56	79/60	83/65	86/69	88/72	90/74	90/74	88/75	84/70	79/62	76/57

Points of Interest

AMELIA ISLAND—*see Jacksonville p. 95.*

APALACHICOLA (C-5) pop. 2,334, elev. 17'

Apalachicola is a Hitchiti Indian word meaning "people on the other side." More than 80 percent of the state's oyster crop (10 percent of the nation's total) is cultivated in Apalachicola's more than 6,000 acres of oyster beds.

Apalachicola Bay Chamber of Commerce: 99 Market St., Suite 100, Apalachicola, FL 32320-1776; phone (850) 653-9419.

JOHN GORRIE MUSEUM STATE PARK, 46 Sixth St. at Ave. D, is 1 blk. e. of US 98 on Gorrie Square. Historical and scientific exhibits pertain to the Apalachicola area and to Dr. John Gorrie, inventor of man-made ice, refrigeration and air conditioning. Allow 30 minutes minimum. Thurs.-Mon. 9-5; closed Jan. 1, Thanksgiving and Dec. 25. Admission $1, under 6 free. Phone (850) 653-9347.

APALACHICOLA NATIONAL FOREST

Elevations in the forest range from 10 ft. to 100 ft.

Encompassing 565,543 acres in four northwestern counties, Apalachicola National Forest is the largest of Florida's three national forests. Its varied terrain includes pine flatwoods, hardwood hammocks, swamp rivers, lakes and two wilderness areas, Bradwell Bay and Mud Swamp/New River. Secluded lakes and streams and canoe trails on the Sopchoppy and lower Ochlockonee rivers make this area popular with canoeists. Several lakes have campgrounds and hiking trails. Hunting and fishing also are popular activities.

A portion of the Florida National Scenic Trail, a scenic hiking route through the state, passes through the forest, showcasing a wide variety of plants and wildlife native to the area. Hikers may catch glimpses of such rare and endangered species as Florida alligators, red-cockaded woodpeckers, indigo snakes and southern bald eagles.

Further information about the forest can be obtained at the district headquarters offices in Crawfordville, (850) 926-3561, and in Bristol, (850) 643-2282. *See Recreation Chart.*

APOLLO BEACH—*see Tampa Bay p. 227.*

APOPKA—*see Orlando p. 160.*

ARCADIA (F-9) pop. 6,604

RIVERBOAT TOURS AT THE NAV-A-GATOR, off I-75 exit 31, 3 mi. e. on Kings Hwy., following sign 1 mi. s. on Peace River St. to 9700 S.W. Riverview Cir., offers 2-hour narrated pontoon boat tours of the tranquil Peace River. A ghost town, parks and various wildlife may be spotted. Food is available. Daily at 11, May 1-Oct. 15; at 1, rest of year. Fare $18.95; ages 6-10, $10.95. Reservations are required. AX, DS, MC, VI. Phone (941) 627-3474.

BARBERVILLE (C-9) pop. 400, elev. 44'

[SAVE] **THE PIONEER SETTLEMENT FOR THE CREATIVE ARTS** is just w. of jct. US 17 on SR 40. Guided tours take visitors through buildings from the early 1900s. Many of the houses, stores and barns are Florida originals which have been relocated to the site. During events the settlement features music, crafts and art from the turn of the 20th century. Allow 2 hours minimum. Mon.-Fri. 9-4, Sat. 9-2; closed holidays. Admission $3; ages 5-12, $2. Phone (386) 749-2959.

BIG CYPRESS NATIONAL PRESERVE (H-10)

Big Cypress National Preserve is part of Big Cypress Swamp, which encompasses more than 2,400 square miles of south Florida. These areas are a major source of water for the fragile Everglades and the southwestern part of the state. Big Cypress National Preserve protects this valuable resource and provides sanctuary for varied wildlife, including alligators, herons, egrets, woodpeckers, bald eagles, deer and the endangered Florida panther. Hunting and fishing are permitted under special regulations; licenses are required.

Although referred to as a swamp, the preserve has marshlands, dry prairies, estuarine mangrove

DID YOU KNOW

Of the 50 states, only Alaska has more islands than Florida.

forests and islands of hardwoods. Its most distinctive feature is the broad belts of bald and dwarf pond cypress trees lining the sloughs and wet prairies. Two major highways, Alligator Alley (I-75) and scenic Tamiami Trail (US 41), cross the preserve and make it accessible from both coasts.

Big Cypress Visitor Center, 20 miles east of Ochopee on US 41, presents a 13-minute film about the preserve as well as exhibits about natural resources and native animal and plant life. In winter ranger-led walks and canoe and bicycle tours are offered. Phone (239) 695-4111, ext. 0.

The visitor center is open daily 8:30-4:30; closed Dec. 25. Free. For further information contact the Chief of Interpretation, Big Cypress National Preserve, HCR 61, Box 110, Ochopee, FL 34141; phone (239) 695-1107.

BIG CYPRESS SEMINOLE INDIAN RESERVATION (G-10) pop. 500

[SAVE] **AH-TAH-THI-KI MUSEUM,** 17 mi. n. of I-75 exit 14 on CR 833, tells the story of Florida's Seminole Indians. A short movie details the history of the tribe. Life size figures in native costume depict how the Seminoles hunted, danced, played and lived. Among exhibits are baskets, utensils, clothing and jewelry. A boardwalk traverses the site. Allow 1 hour, 30 minutes minimum. Tues.-Sun. 9-5; phone for holiday hours. Admission $6; over 55, ages 6-17 and students with ID $4. AX, CB, DC, DS, MC, VI. Phone (863) 902-1113. *See color ad.*

[SAVE] **BILLIE SWAMP SAFARI,** 19 mi. n. of I-75 exit 14, gives 25-minute airboat tours and 60-minute "swamp buggy" eco-tours of Billie Swamp Safari Park and Big Cypress. Views of such wildlife as panthers, alligators, snakes, razorback hogs and crocodiles are common. Day and overnight safaris also are offered by reservation. Food is available. Tours depart daily 9:30-5; closed Dec. 25. Airboat tour $12. Eco-tour $20; over 62, $18; ages 4-12, $10. AX, DS, MC, VI. Phone (863) 983-6101 or (800) 949-6101. *See color ad.*

BIG PINE KEY—*see The Florida Keys p. 64.*

BISCAYNE NATIONAL PARK—
see Miami-Miami Beach p. 124.

BOCA RATON (G-12) pop. 74,764, elev. 15'

Long a haven for the wealthy, Boca Raton has become a center for commerce, finance and technology. Strictly enforced regulations help to maintain the city's "small-town" appeal.

The city's oldest unaltered wooden structure, built in 1911 with timber found on the beach, now houses the Children's Museum. The building on Crawford Boulevard features changing exhibits.

The Gulf Stream comes closest to the Florida shore at Boca Raton, making the climate ideal for sports and recreation.

Greater Boca Raton Chamber of Commerce: 1800 N. Dixie Hwy., Boca Raton, FL 33432; phone (561) 395-4433.

Shopping areas: Boca Center, at Military Trail and Town Center Road, offers boutiques, art galleries and restaurants. Mizner Park, on Federal Highway between Palmetto Park and Glades roads, is an outdoor mall with an amphitheater, upscale boutiques, eateries and movie theaters. Royal Palm Shopping Plaza, US 1 and Mizner Boulevard, features boutiques and specialty shops in a Mediterranean setting. Town Center Mall, half a mile west of I-95 on Glades Road, contains 187 stores including Bloomingdales, Burdines, Lord & Taylor, Nordstrom, Saks Fifth Avenue and Sears.

BOCA RATON HISTORICAL SOCIETY, 71 N. Federal Hwy. at Palmetto Park Rd., is housed in the restored 1927 Town Hall, noted for its gold dome. The Mediterranean Revival-style building, designed by Addison Mizner, has such architectural features as cypress millwork, a pecky cypress ceiling, fan-lit windows and a gilded dome. Changing art and history exhibits are shown regularly. Allow 30 minutes minimum. Tues.-Fri. 10-4; closed holidays. Free. Phone (561) 395-6766.

[SAVE] **BOCA RATON MUSEUM OF ART,** just e. of US 1 (N. Federal Hwy.) between Glades Rd. and Palmetto Park Rd. in Mizner Park at 501 Plaza

Real, houses changing exhibits of varied art media. The permanent collection contains 19th- and 20th-century European and American works, including pieces by Edgar Degas, Henri Matisse and Pablo Picasso; contemporary art; graphics and photography; cultural art; and sculpture and ceramics. An outdoor sculpture garden with contemporary works is among the museum's highlights.

Allow 1 hour minimum. Tues.-Sat. 10-5 (also Wed. and Fri. 5-9), Sun. noon-5; closed holidays. Admission $8; over 65, $6; students with ID $4; under 12 free; free to all Wed. 5-9. Admission during special exhibits $12, over 65 and students with ID $7.50. AX, MC, VI. Phone (561) 392-2500.

GUMBO LIMBO NATURE CENTER, 1 mi. n. of Palmetto Park Rd. on SR A1A, has examples of native plants and animals in a variety of habitats, including coastal dune, tropical hardwood hammock, sabal palm hammock and mangrove wetlands. Also featured are outdoor seawater tanks, a boardwalk with a viewing tower and a nature trail. Allow 30 minutes minimum. Mon.-Sat. 9-4, Sun. noon-4; closed holidays. Donations. Phone (561) 338-1473.

[SAVE] **SPORTS IMMORTALS MUSEUM,** 1 mi. n. of Yamato Rd. to 6830 N. Federal Hwy. (US 1), features rotating displays from a collection of more than a million mementos. Among memorabilia are racing helmets, autographed baseballs, uniforms, World Series pins and varied equipment used by sporting greats. Mon.-Fri. 10-6, Sat. 10-5. Admission $5; under 12, $3. MC, VI. Phone (561) 997-2575.

BOKEELIA (G-8) pop. 1,997, elev. 5′

TROPIC STAR **OF PINE ISLAND,** 6 mi. n. of jct. SR 78 and CR 767 at 16499 Porto Bello St., offers full-day narrated cruises through the protected waters of Pine Island Sound to Cabbage Key and a rustic state park on Cayo Costa; a tram carries visitors to the beach on the Gulf of Mexico. Visitors can view porpoises, manatees and birds as well as explore islands accessible only by boat. Picnicking is allowed on Cayo Costa. Allow a full day. Cruises depart daily at 9:30 and return at 4. Fare $25; ages 2-12, $15. State park fee including tram $1. Reservations are required. Phone (941) 283-0015.

BONITA SPRINGS (G-9)
pop. 32,797, elev. 12′

At the edge of Cypress Swamp, Bonita Springs offers good fishing in both the Gulf of Mexico and the Imperial River. Greyhound racing is the focus of attention at The Naples-Fort Myers Greyhound Track; phone (239) 992-2411.

Note: Policies vary concerning admittance of children to pari-mutuel betting facilities. Phone for information.

Bonita Springs Area Chamber of Commerce and Visitor Center: 25071 Chamber of Commerce Dr., Bonita Springs, FL 34135; phone (239) 992-2943 or (800) 226-2943.

EVERGLADES WONDER GARDENS, 27180 Old US 41, was opened in 1936 as a refuge for injured animals. The facility now is home to a large collection of native birds as well as panthers, alligators, Florida crocodiles, flamingos, bears and otters. Otter shows are offered and alligator feedings can be viewed from a swinging bridge above the pit. The grounds include botanical gardens and trees from around the world. A natural history museum also is on the premises. Guided tours are available. Allow 1 hour, 30 minutes minimum. Daily 9-5. Last tour begins 1 hour before closing. Admission $12; ages 3-12, $6. Phone (239) 992-2591.

BRADENTON (F-8) pop. 45,504, elev. 21′
See map page 198.

Nearby Gulf beaches attract visitors to Bradenton (BRAY-den-ton), on Florida's west coast. The Art League of Manatee County, 209 Ninth St. W., displays works of local artists. Classes, demonstrations and workshops are offered September through July; phone (941) 746-2862.

Pirate City, (941) 747-3031, at 1701 27th St. E., is the Pittsburgh Pirates' minor league and spring training facility. The major league team trains here in February, while the Pirates' minor-leaguers play here March through May. The Gulf Coast League plays here June through August, and the Instructional League plays September through October. Visitors can watch the Pirates prepare for the regular season as they battle other major league teams in March at McKechnie Field, Ninth Street and 17th Avenue W.; phone (941) 748-4610.

Bradenton also is the home of Pittsburgh's teams in the Gulf Coast Rookie League and the Florida Instructional League, providing baseball games from June to mid-October; phone (941) 747-3031.

From January through March Bradenton is home to the Royal Lipizzan Stallions from Austria. These world-renowned horses are trained at Colonel Herrman's Ranch on Singletary Road. Visitors are welcome at the training sessions; phone (941) 322-1501 Jan. 2-Apr. 1.

Bradenton Area Convention & Visitors Bureau: P.O. Box 1000, Bradenton, FL 34206; phone (941) 729-9177 or (800) 462-6283.

Shopping areas: De Soto Square Mall, US 41 and Cortez Road, features Burdines, Dillard's, JCPenney and Sears among its 106 stores.

DE SOTO NATIONAL MEMORIAL—
see place listing p. 56.

HUNSADER FARMS is 10 mi. e. of I-75 exit 217 on SR 70, then 3 mi. n. to 5500 CR 675. Geared toward educating children about farming and farm life, the farm features displays of agricultural machinery and equipment and a petting zoo with chickens, cows, ducks, emus, goats, pheasants, pigs and turkeys. Picnicking is permitted. Allow 1 hour minimum. Mon.-Sat. 8-4, mid-Sept. to mid-June; closed major holidays. Free. Phone (941) 322-2168.

MANATEE VILLAGE HISTORICAL PARK is on SR 64, 1 mi. e. of US 41 at jct. Sixth Ave. E. and 15th St. E. The park includes an 1860 courthouse, 1887 church, 1912 settler's house, 1903 general store and 1908 one-room schoolhouse. Other highlights include a replica of a typical Florida barn as well as a boat exhibit, restored smokehouse, turpentine still and working blacksmith shop. Visitors can tour the 1850 Old Manatee Burial Grounds by appointment. Picnicking is permitted. Allow 2 hours minimum. Mon.-Fri. 9-4:30, Sun. 1:30-4:30, Sept.-June; Mon.-Fri. 9-4:30, rest of year. Free. Phone (941) 749-7165.

[SAVE] **SOUTH FLORIDA MUSEUM,** 201 10th St. W., reflects Florida's history from prehistoric times to the present. An extensive collection of artifacts dates from the Paleoindian period to the arrival of Spanish explorers in the early 1500s. Highlights include a mastodon discovered in the Aucilla River, a full-scale replica of a 16th-century chapel and a natural-history gallery with fossils, birds and shells. The 60,000-gallon Parker Manatee Aquarium is part of Florida's manatee rehabilitation network. Discovery Place offers hands-on activities for children.

Allow 1 hour, 30 minutes minimum. Mon.-Sat. 10-5, Sun. noon-5, Jan.-Apr. and in July; Tues.-Sat. 10-5, Sun. noon-5, rest of year. Closed Jan. 1, first 2 weeks in Sept., Thanksgiving and Dec. 25. Admission $7.50; over 59, $6; students with ID $5; ages 5-12, $4. MC, VI. Phone (941) 746-4131.

RECREATIONAL ACTIVITIES

Canoeing

- **Ray's Canoe Hideaway** is at 1247 Hagle Park Rd., Bradenton, FL 34212. Other activities are offered. Mon. and Thurs.-Fri. 9-5, Sat.-Sun. 9-6, during DST; Thurs.-Mon. 9-5, rest of year. Phone (941) 747-3909 or (888) 572-2663.

BROOKSVILLE (D-8) pop. 7,264, elev. 126′

The rolling terrain surrounding Brooksville is rich in limestone, making its quarrying and distribution the city's major industry. The limestone also makes this a fertile agricultural and grazing area, as evidenced by the number of cattle ranches and horse farms. The founding of Brooksville predates the Civil War, and many of its residential streets are lined with turn-of-the-20th-century Victorian homes. Murals on downtown buildings depict historic events.

In the center of town, Hernando Park has an outdoor band shell, a playground and recreational facilities. The park also is the site of arts and crafts shows. Winding through nearby countryside are miles of hiking and biking trails, including those of nearby Withlacoochee State Forest.

Hernando County Welcome Center: 30305 Cortez Blvd., Brooksville, FL 34652; phone (800) 601-4580.

Self-guiding tours: Brochures for a self-guiding walking or driving tour of the historic district are available from the welcome center.

MAY STRINGER HERITAGE MUSEUM is at 601 Museum Ct., 1 blk. n. of jct. SRs 50 and 41. Guides conduct tours of the four-story gabled building, which was built in the mid-19th century. Furnished rooms and a re-created schoolroom depict area history. Also featured is a collection of period medical equipment. Allow 1 hour minimum. Tues.-Sat. noon-3, Sept.-July. Donations. Phone (352) 799-0129.

ROGERS' CHRISTMAS HOUSE VILLAGE is at 103 S. Saxon Ave. The village sits on a hilltop and consists of five turn-of-the-20th-century houses with gardens featuring azaleas and dogwood and magnolia trees. The main house is decorated in a Christmas theme and displays gift items from around the world. Country Cottage, Magnolia House and Little House Under the Oak Tree also feature decorations and gifts. Storybook Land, next to the main house, has animated displays. Daily 9:30-5; closed Dec. 25. Free. Phone (352) 796-2415 or (877) 312-5046.

BUNNELL (C-9) pop. 2,122, elev. 25'

BULOW PLANTATION RUINS HISTORIC STATE PARK, 9 mi. s.e. on CR 2001 (Old Kings Rd.) to 3501 Old Kings Rd., following signs, are the remnants of Bulowville, a territorial period sugar mill and plantation destroyed by Seminoles in 1836. Interpretive center exhibits relate the story of the plantation and its destruction. The 152-acre site features a canoe trail, picnic and playground facilities and the preserved remains of original boat slips. Canoe rental is available. Freshwater and saltwater fishing is permitted with a license.

Allow 30 minutes minimum. Daily 9-5. Admission $2 per private vehicle, $1 for persons arriving by bicycle or on foot. Phone (386) 517-2084. *See Recreation Chart.*

BUSHNELL (D-8) pop. 2,050, elev. 75'

Rural Bushnell, where the Withlacoochee River flows through a cypress swamp as a small stream, features small lakes once fished by American Indians and Spanish explorers. Most are still popular with anglers today, as is Lake Panasoffkee, to the north. Withlacoochee State Forest which covers 113,000 acres in three units, is west of town.

Florida National Military Cemetery, off I-75 exit 309 on SR 476B, is among the largest in the nation. On SR 471 in nearby Webster shoppers enjoy Monday events at the Webster Flea Market, one of the largest flea markets in the country.

Sumter County Chamber of Commerce: 225 S. US 301, P.O. Box 100, Sumterville, FL 33585; phone (352) 793-3099.

DADE BATTLEFIELD HISTORIC STATE PARK, 1.5 mi. e. off I-75 exit 314 or 1 mi. w. of US 301 on CR 603, commemorates the massacre of Maj. Francis L. Dade and his troops, who were ambushed by Seminole Indians the morning of Dec. 28, 1835. Highlights of the 80-acre park include reproductions of the log breastworks used in the battle and monuments to the valor of Dade and his men. A visitor center has exhibits and artifacts, and an interpretive trail marks the military road and battlefield. Picnic facilities are available.

Allow 1 hour minimum. Grounds open daily 8-dusk. Visitor center open daily 9-5. Admission $2 per private vehicle (maximum eight people), $1 per person arriving by bicycle or on foot. Phone (352) 793-4781.

CANAVERAL NATIONAL SEASHORE (D-10)

Canaveral National Seashore lies north of the Kennedy Space Center *(see place listing p. 97).* This 57,000-acre unit of the National Park Service encompasses 24 miles of unspoiled barrier beaches, shallow lagoons and dunes. Alligators, turtles, manatees and a variety of birds are among the abundant wildlife.

Swimming, boating, surf fishing and ranger-led activities can be enjoyed at Playalinda Beach at the southern tip of the seashore and at Apollo Beach at the area's northern end. The Merritt Island National Wildlife Refuge *(see Titusville p. 232)* adjoins the national seashore. An information center at 7611 S. Atlantic Ave. in New Smyrna Beach is open daily; phone (386) 428-3384.

The seashore is open daily 6 a.m.-8 p.m., late Apr.-late Oct.; 6-6, rest of year. Playalinda Beach is closed 3 days before a shuttle launch and reopens the following day. Admission $5 per vehicle. An annual pass is $28. For further information contact the Superintendent, Canaveral National Seashore, 308 Julia St., Titusville, FL 32796; phone (321) 267-1110. For a recorded daily beach report, phone (321) 867-0677. *See Recreation Chart.*

CAPE CORAL (G-9) pop. 102,286, elev. 5'

SAVE **THE CHILDREN'S SCIENCE CENTER,** .5 mi. w. of US 41 at 2915 N.E. Pine Island Rd. (SR 78), offers hands-on exhibits dealing with science, math and technology. Visitors can experiment with optical illusions, mazes, holographs and various inventions. Educational programs for children also are offered. Allow 1 hour minimum. Mon.-Fri. 9:30-4:30, Sat.-Sun. noon-5; closed Jan. 1, Easter, July 4, Thanksgiving and Dec. 25. Admission $5; ages 3-16, $3. MC, VI. Phone (239) 997-0012.

SAVE **SUN SPLASH FAMILY WATERPARK,** off I-75 exit 143, w. 12 mi. on SR 78, then s. 0.5 mi. to 400 Santa Barbara Blvd., offers 12 acres of recreational activities, including giant waterslides, activity and family pools, otter slides, an inner tube river, a children's play area and a game arcade. Food is available.

Allow 2 hours minimum. Sun.-Wed. 10-6, Thurs. 10-9, Fri. 10-6, Sat. 10-9, Memorial Day to mid-Aug.; Sat.-Sun. and Labor Day 10-5, mid-Aug. through Sept. 30; Fri. 11-5, Sat.-Sun. 10-5, mid-Mar. through mid-Apr.; Wed.-Fri. 11-5, Sat.-Sun. 10-5, late Apr.-day before Memorial Day. Days may be added to the schedule during spring break. Phone to confirm schedule. Admission $10.55; over 54, $4.98; under 48 inches tall $7.95; under age 3 free. MC, VI. Phone (239) 574-0557.

CAPTIVA ISLAND—see Sanibel p. 196.

 CASTILLO DE SAN MARCOS NATIONAL MONUMENT—
see St. Augustine p. 188.

CEDAR KEY (C-7) pop. 790, elev. 8′

Due to its location on a small barrier island off the Gulf Coast of Florida, Cedar Key was a strategic point from which blockade runners exported cotton and lumber and imported food and supplies for the Confederacy during the Civil War. Following the war, lumbering and then fishing and shipbuilding formed the town's economic base.

An 1896 hurricane leveled the original town. Now primarily a resort area, the town relies on commercial fishing, crabbing, clam farming, oystering and tourism to sustain its economy. Cedar Key is home to many artists and its surrounding area is popular with bird-watchers.

Cedar Key Area Chamber of Commerce: P.O. Box 610, Cedar Key, FL 32625; phone (352) 543-5600.

Self-guiding tours: The Cedar Key Historical Society Museum (see attraction listing) offers brochures with tours of the historic district.

CEDAR KEY HISTORICAL SOCIETY MUSEUM, on SR 24 at Second St., depicts the town's history through photographs dating to the 1850s. Other displays include Seminole and Timucuan Indian artifacts, minerals and woodworking tools. Allow 30 minutes minimum. Sun.-Fri. 1-4, Sat. 11-5; closed Jan. 1, Thanksgiving and Dec. 25. Admission $1; ages 12-18, 50c. Phone (352) 543-5549.

CEDAR KEY STATE MUSEUM is 1.75 mi. n. off SR 24 following signs to 12231 S.W. 166th Ct. Exhibits contain household articles from the past as well as a Confederate salt kettle and the St. Clair Whitman Shell Collection, said to be one of the most complete collections ever assembled. Displays also relate the history of the area's railroad and fishing industries. Allow 30 minutes minimum. Thurs.-Mon. 9-5. Admission $1, under 5 free. Phone (352) 543-5350.

CHIEFLAND (C-7) pop. 1,993, elev. 40′

LOWER SUWANNEE NATIONAL WILDLIFE REFUGE, 17 mi. s. on CR 347, is home to more than 90 species of birds that make their nests in the refuge's 51,340 acres. Hikers may spot such wildlife as bald eagles, white-tailed deer, wood ducks, blue-winged and green-winged teals and alligators. The .4-mile River Trail offers visitors a view of the Suwanee River and the cypress trees and hardwood swamps that surround it. The refuge is open

Safety at Florida's Beaches

Florida's expansive coastline provides numerous opportunities for fun in the sun, but it also requires an extra degree of caution when taking a dip: A large number of Florida beaches are unguarded. Swimming at an unguarded beach presents a risk to swimmers not only through injury or drowning, but also through the dangers of rip currents, dangerous or poisonous marine animals and other hidden hazards.

However, many Florida beaches are guarded by trained, certified ocean lifeguards. To ensure your safety and that of your family, be sure to swim only when ocean lifeguards are

 present. A list of guarded beaches is available from the United States Lifesaving Association and the Florida Beach Patrol Chiefs Association, 340 S. Ocean Blvd., Delray Beach, FL 33483; phone (561) 243-7352.

daily 24 hours; the refuge office is open Mon.-Fri. 7:30-4. Free. Phone (352) 493-0238.

CHRISTMAS—*see Orlando p. 160.*

CLEARWATER—*see Tampa Bay p. 227.*

CLERMONT—*see Orlando p. 160.*

COCOA (D-10) pop. 16,412, elev. 25'

Cocoa's first families arrived at this site along the Indian River in 1860, and the town was platted beginning in 1882. Although there are differing accounts of the name's origin, records do show that Cocoa was selected in the 1880s when the town's original name, Indian River City, was deemed by postal authorities to be too long for a postmark.

Throughout its early history, Cocoa experienced periodic growth spurts interrupted by such reversals as a catastrophic fire, a freeze that damaged the area's citrus crops and the Great Depression. The town's prospects improved considerably in the latter half of the 20th century thanks to its proximity to the Kennedy Space Center.

The Brevard Museum of History and Science, at 2201 Michigan Ave., offers local history exhibits as well as a hands-on science discovery room for children; phone (321) 632-1830. The museum's grounds include a 22-acre nature preserve with trails. Walking tours of the nearby Cocoa Village historic district depart from the museum regularly.

Cocoa Beach Area Chamber of Commerce: 400 Fortenberry Rd., Merritt Island, FL 32952; phone (321) 459-2200.

ASTRONAUT MEMORIAL PLANETARIUM & OBSERVATORY is 2.5 mi. e. of I-95 exit 201 on SR 520, then 1.75 mi. n. on SR 501 to 1519 Clearlake Rd. Visitors can look through a 24-inch telescope to see objects in the solar system and deep space. The planetarium's International Hall of Space Explorers honors the men and women from around the world who have flown in space. The Science Quest Demonstration Hall features hands-on exhibits relating to space science. Other options include presentations in the planetarium theater, large-format films in the Iwerks Discovery Theatre and a laser show.

Fri.-Sat. 6:30-10:30 p.m. Other days and times vary; phone ahead. Film or planetarium show $6; over 55, $5; under 12, $4. Film and planetarium show $10; over 55, $8; under 12, $6. Laser show $6. Three shows $14. Rooftop observatory free. MC, VI. Phone (321) 634-3732 or (321) 632-1111.

COCOA BEACH (D-11) pop. 12,842, elev. 12'

Long a popular spot with locals, Cocoa Beach also is known for its location at the heart of the Space Coast. Cocoa Beach Pier extends 800 feet into the Atlantic, affording opportunities for fishing, surfing, dining and dancing. An 850-foot promenade leads to the beach and an observation deck overlooking the ocean.

Cocoa Beach Area Chamber of Commerce: 400 Fortenberry Rd., Merritt Island, FL 32952; phone (321) 459-2200.

COCONUT CREEK—*see Fort Lauderdale p. 77.*

COCONUT GROVE—
see Miami-Miami Beach p. 124.

CORAL GABLES—
see Miami-Miami Beach p. 124.

CORAL SPRINGS—*see Fort Lauderdale p. 77.*

CROSS CREEK (C-9) elev. 69'

MARJORIE KINNAN RAWLINGS HISTORIC STATE PARK, on CR 325, 4 mi. w. of jct. US 301 next to the county park, is the restored home of Marjorie Kinnan Rawlings, author of the Pulitzer Prize-winning novel "The Yearling." This area was the setting for several of Rawlings' books. Grounds open daily 9-5. Guided house tours are given Thurs.-Sun. at 10, 11, 1, 2, 3 and 4, Oct.-July; closed Jan. 1, Thanksgiving and Dec. 25. Grounds free. Tours $3; ages 6-12, $2. Phone (352) 466-3672.

CRYSTAL RIVER (D-8) pop. 3,485, elev. 4'

Crystal River denotes both a town and the river that runs through it into Kings Bay. The waters accommodate anglers and scuba divers.

Citrus County Chamber of Commerce at Crystal River: 28 N.W. US 19, Crystal River, FL 34428-3900; phone (352) 795-3149.

CRYSTAL RIVER ARCHEOLOGICAL STATE PARK, 2.5 mi. w. off US 19N on N. Museum Point, preserves the ceremonial mound complex built by American Indians who occupied the site from 200 B.C. to 1400. In addition to temple and burial mounds, there are middens, or refuse mounds, formed in part by the empty shells of the seafood that was an important part of the Indians' diet. The visitor center displays artifacts and information about these pre-Columbian Mound Builders, including an 8-minute videotape interpreting the site's past.

Allow 1 hour, 30 minutes minimum. Grounds open daily 8-dusk. Visitor center open daily 9-5. Admission $2 per private vehicle (maximum eight people), $1 per person arriving by bicycle, motorcycle or on foot. Phone (352) 795-3817.

 CYPRESS GARDENS—
see Winter Haven p. 235.

DADE CITY—*see Tampa Bay p. 228.*

DANIA BEACH—*see Fort Lauderdale p. 77.*

DAVIE—*see Fort Lauderdale p. 77.*

DAYTONA BEACH (C-10)

pop. 64,112, elev. 10′

Daytona Beach was more speedway than beach in the early days of the automobile. Between 1902 and 1935 some 13 speed records were set by Barney Oldfield, Sir Henry Segrave and Sir Malcolm Campbell. The tradition continues at Daytona International Speedway *(see attraction listing)* with such races as the Daytona 500 in February and the Pepsi 400 in July. For ticket information phone (386) 253-7223.

White sand beaches stretch for 23 miles; during the day cars may be driven on some of the hard-packed sand along the water's edge. For safety, beach driving should be done during a low or outgoing tide and never in the water, however shallow.

Drivers should heed signs noting conservation areas. Overnight parking or camping is not permitted on the beach. The beach is not open to motor vehicles from Sea Breeze to International Speedway boulevards and south of the Emelia Avenue beach approach in Daytona Beach Shores to the Beach Street approach in Ponce Inlet, at Lighthouse Point Park in Ponce Inlet or north of the Granada Boulevard beach approach in Ormond Beach. A daily beach access toll of $5 per vehicle is charged February through November. Toll booths are at each approach. The speed limit on the beach is 10 miles per hour. For beach information phone (386) 239-7873.

A wide promenade along the ocean is the center of the amusement area near the fishing pier. Featured are a sightseeing tower and sky ride. The bandshell in Oceanfront Park, at the north end of the promenade, is the setting for events.

A scenic portion of SR A1A extends along the ocean from Daytona Beach north to Fernandina Beach, a distance of 105 miles.

Ocean lovers enjoy sailing, surfing and riding personal watercraft; the Halifax River is a popular boating, water skiing and sailboarding destination. Greyhounds race at Daytona Beach Kennel Club, next to the speedway; phone (386) 252-6484.

Note: Policies vary concerning admittance of children to pari-mutuel betting facilities. Phone for information.

Daytona Beach Area Convention and Visitors Bureau: 126 E. Orange Ave., Daytona Beach, FL 32114; phone (386) 255-0415 or (800) 854-1234. *See color ad & p. 146.*

Shopping areas: Daytona Flea Market, 1 mile west of Daytona Speedway at the junction of I-95 and US 92, provides weekend browsing. Fresh produce, citrus and seafood are available at the Farmers Market, downtown on City Island. Volusia Mall, 1700 International Speedway Blvd. (US 92), features Burdines, Dillard's, JCPenney and Sears among its 120 stores.

ANGELL & PHELPS CHOCOLATE FACTORY TOUR, just s. of US 92 (International Speedway Blvd.) at 154 S. Beach St., offers tours of a working factory where visitors can watch handmade chocolates being created. Allow 30 minutes minimum. Tours are given Mon.-Fri. at 10, 11, 1, 2 and 3. Free. Phone (386) 252-6531.

DAYTONA INTERNATIONAL SPEEDWAY is 1 mi. e. of I-95 exit 261A (southbound) or exit 261 (northbound) on US 92 (International Speedway Blvd.). The track is accessible to visitors for self-guiding tours through the entrance to Daytona USA. Guided tram tours of the racetrack, infield, pit and garage areas are offered by Daytona USA *(see attraction listing)*. Sections of the grandstands are named for well-known racers. The speedway features 10 weekends of racing each year, including stock cars, sports cars, motorcycles and go-carts.

Guided track tours are given by Daytona USA daily 9:30-6 (weather and track schedule permitting). Self-guiding tours free. Phone (386) 253-7223 for tickets, or TTY (386) 947-6700.

DAYTONA USA is 1 mi. e. of I-95 exit 261A (southbound) or exit 261 (northbound) on the grounds of Daytona International Speedway. Visitors enter through a replica of the raceway's famed twin tunnels and are greeted by "The Heritage of Daytona," an exhibit that offers a chronological look at racing history.

Through interactive displays guests can broadcast a race, electronically interact with eight of racing's drivers, test their motor sports knowledge at a six-station trivia game, computer-design their own race

car and participate in a timed pit stop. Visitors can experience the thrill of being in the driver's seat by watching "The Daytona 500," a 14-minute audio-visual presentation that captures the excitement of stock car racing. Viewers exit the theater to step into Victory Lane, where the winning car from the current Daytona 500 is displayed.

Not for the faint-of-heart is Daytona Dream Laps, an exhilarating motion-simulator ride from Iwerks. The Acceleration Alley simulator gives guests the feeling of driving at 200 mph. A 30-minute tram tour of the speedway features stops at Pit Road, the Start/Finish Line, the 31-degree banking on Turn Four and Victory Lane. Food is available.

Allow 1 hour, 30 minutes minimum. Daily 9-7; closed Dec. 25. Extended hours during race events. Speedway tour daily (weather and track schedule permitting) 9:30-6. Admission $16; over 59, $13; ages 6-12, $8. Speedway tour $7, under 6 free. Admission and tour $20; over 59, $17; ages 6-12, $14. MC, VI. Phone (386) 947-6800. *See color ad.*

HALIFAX HISTORICAL SOCIETY AND MUSEUM is 2 blks. s. of US 92 at 252 S. Beach St. Housed in the restored 1911 Merchants Bank building, the museum's displays of artifacts detail local history. Of special interest are the Spanish helmet and sword dating from the age of exploration as well as a scale model of the 1938 boardwalk. Grandma's Attic is a large exhibit containing memorabilia dating to the early 1900s.

Allow 1 hour minimum. Tues.-Sat. 10-4; closed Thanksgiving weekend and Dec. 24-Jan. 1. Admission $4; under 12, $1; free to children under 12 on Sat.; Thurs. afternoon adult admission by donation. Phone (386) 255-6976.

(SAVE) **KLASSIX AUTO ATTRACTION** is .5 mi. s.w. of I-95 exit 261B on US 92 to 2909 W. International Speedway Blvd. The museum features a large assortment of classic automobiles and muscle cars as well as vehicles used in television shows and movies. Also presented are motorcycles and racing memorabilia. Allow 1 hour, 30 minutes minimum. Daily 9-6. Admission $8.50; over 55, $7.50;

ages 7-12, $4.25. AX, DS, MC, VI. Phone (386) 252-3800.

MUSEUM OF ARTS AND SCIENCES is .25 mi. w. of Nova Rd. (SR 5A) and .75 mi. s. of jct. US 92 at 1040 Museum Blvd. Located on a 90-acre plot, the museum features permanent and changing exhibits. Included are railroad and race cars; Coca-Cola memorabilia; furniture from the 18th-20th centuries; paintings; sculpture; African, Chinese and Cuban art; Florida history exhibits; and a skeleton of a giant ground sloth. The museum also maintains a planetarium, library and a sculpture garden.

Allow 1 hour minimum. Museum open Tues.-Fri. 9-4, Sat.-Sun. noon-5; closed major holidays. Planetarium star shows Tues.-Fri. at 2, Sat.-Sun. at 1 and 3 and the first Tues. of each month at 2 and 7. Museum admission $7, students with ID $3, under 5 free. Planetarium admission an additional $3, children $2. Phone (386) 255-0285.

SOUTHEAST MUSEUM OF PHOTOGRAPHY is at 1200 W. International Speedway Blvd., Building 100, on the Daytona Beach Community College campus. The gallery of changing photography exhibits features both early and contemporary selections. Allow 30 minutes minimum. Mon.-Fri. 10-4 (also Tues. 4-7), Sat.-Sun. 1-5; closed holidays. Donations. Phone (386) 254-4475.

A TINY CRUISE LINE departs from the Halifax Harbor Marina "Showdock" at 425 S. Beach St. Narrated cruises along the Halifax River are aboard a replica of an 1890s excursion boat. A 2-hour midday waterway trip offers chances to see dolphins and wildlife. One-hour cruises travel past riverfront estates or historic downtown. Sunset cruises also are available April through September.

Two-hour waterway cruise departs Mon.-Sat. at 11:30. One-hour riverfront estate cruise departs Mon.-Sat. at 2; historic downtown trip departs Mon.-Sat. at 3:30. Fare for 1-hour cruises $10.56; ages 4-12, $6.33. Fare for 2-hour cruise $15.72; ages 4-12, $9.15. Reservations are required for sunset cruises. Phone (386) 226-2343.

DEERFIELD BEACH—

see Fort Lauderdale p. 78.

DeLAND (C-9) pop. 24,904, elev. 27'

The stately oaks lining the streets of DeLand are the result of the arboreal interests and endeavors of Henry A. DeLand, who founded the city in 1876. Another local entrepreneur was Chinese emigrant Lue Gim Gong, who produced highly successful strains of oranges and grapefruit in the late 1800s.

DeLand Museum of Art presents changing exhibits; phone (386) 734-4371. Stetson University, established in 1886 by DeLand and named for hat magnate John Stetson, contains Gillespie Museum of Minerals and Duncan Gallery of Art; phone (386) 822-7000. Both attractions are on N. Woodland Boulevard. A booklet describing a campus walking tour is available at the public relations office.

Bill Dreggors Park on Stone Street is a popular picnic spot; phone (386) 740-5800.

West Volusia Visitors Bureau: 101 N. Woodland Blvd., DeLand, FL 32720; phone (386) 734-0575 or (800) 749-4350.

THE AFRICAN AMERICAN MUSEUM OF THE ARTS, off US 17/92 at 325 S. Clara Ave., presents permanent displays of more than 150 artifacts including masks and carvings, as well as a photo gallery of famous African-Americans and changing exhibits from established and emerging artists. Allow 30 minutes minimum. Wed.-Sat. 10-4. Free. Phone (386) 736-4004.

CULTURAL ARTS CENTER, .5 mi. n. of jct. US 17/92 and SR 44 at 600 N. Woodland Blvd., offers changing exhibits in two galleries. Plays, concerts and children's shows are presented in the 240-seat Sands Theater Center. Allow 30 minutes minimum. Tues.-Sat. 10-4, Sun. 1-4; closed holidays. Donations. Phone (386) 736-7232.

HENRY A. DeLAND HOUSE MUSEUM, 137 W. Michigan Ave., was built in 1886 on land purchased from city founder Henry A. DeLand. The home was built by attorney Arthur George Hamlin, DeLand's first attorney and developer of the Hamlin orange. It is filled with period furnishings and collectibles. An extensive collection of period photographs is on display. Guided tours are available. Allow 1 hour minimum. Tues.-Sat. noon-4; closed holidays. Donations. Phone (386) 740-6813.

MANATEE SEEKER SCENIC RIVER TOUR departs from Pier 44 Marina, 3 mi. w. on SR 44. Two-hour narrated cruises along the St. Johns River offer insights into the history of Florida and the river. Native wildlife such as manatees, alligators, otters, ospreys, bald eagles and egrets may be sighted in their natural environment. Cruises depart daily at 10, 12:30 and 3; closed the last 2 weeks in May and Dec. 20-26. Fare $20; over 65 and ages 6-11, $16; under 6, $10. Ask about multi-child discounts. Reservations are recommended. Phone (800) 587-7131.

DELRAY BEACH (G-12)
pop. 60,020, elev. 20'

A resort community, Delray Beach offers its residents simplicity and a relaxed pace. The city supports a variety of light industries.

Greater Delray Beach Chamber of Commerce: 64 S.E. Fifth Ave., Delray Beach, FL 33483; phone (561) 278-0424.

ARTHUR R. MARSHALL LOXAHATCHEE NATIONAL WILDLIFE REFUGE is on US 441/SR 7, 2 mi. s. of jct. SR 804 (Boynton Beach Blvd.) or 3 mi. n. of jct. SR 806 (Atlantic Ave.). The 147,000-acre refuge is home to endangered and threatened species such as the snail kite, the wood stork and the American alligator. Migrating waterfowl flock in the winter. The refuge offers facilities for fishing, boating and bird-watching. Other features include an observation tower, nature trails, a 12-mile bicycle trail, a 5.5-mile canoe trail and a visitor center with exhibits and a videotape presentation about the area.

Refuge open daily 6 a.m.-dusk. Visitor center open Mon.-Fri. 9-4, Sat.-Sun. 9-4:30, mid-Oct. through Apr. 30; Wed.-Fri. 9-4, Sat.-Sun. 9-4:30, rest of year. Closed Dec. 25. Admission $5 per private vehicle or $1 per person arriving by bicycle or on foot. Phone (561) 734-8303.

[SAVE] **THE MORIKAMI MUSEUM AND JAPANESE GARDENS** are 3.5 mi. w. of I-95 exit 51 on Linton Blvd., 1 mi. s. on Jog Rd., then .5 mi. w. on entrance road to 4000 Morikami Park Rd. Dedicated exclusively to the living culture of Japan, the museum explores modern and traditional Japanese culture and the history of Florida's Yamato Colony, an early 20th-century farming settlement. Two museum buildings house permanent and changing exhibits. On the grounds are a 200-acre park, ponds, Japanese and bonsai gardens and a nature trail. Food is available.

Allow 1 hour, 30 minutes minimum. Tues.-Sun. 10-5; closed holidays. Admission $10; over 65, $9; ages 6-18, $7. Phone (561) 495-0233.

[SAVE] **OLD SCHOOL SQUARE CULTURAL ARTS CENTER AND NATIONAL HISTORIC SITE** is 5 blks. w. of US 1 at 51 N. Swinton Ave., or 1 mi. e. of I-95 on Atlantic Ave. The center consists of the 1913 Delray Elementary and 1925 Delray High School buildings; restored, they now house Crest Theatre, Cornell Museum of Art & History and Vintage Gymnasium. The theater presents lectures and professional music, theater and dance productions from November to April. The museum features rotating regional, national and international exhibits. An outdoor pavilion plays host to special events.

Allow 30 minutes minimum. Tues.-Sat. 10:30-4:30, Sun. 1-4:30, Oct.-Apr.; Tues.-Sat. 10:30-4:30, rest of year. Closed holidays. Admission $5; over 59, $3; ages 6-11, $1. Phone (561) 243-7922.

DE SOTO NATIONAL MEMORIAL (F-8)

De Soto National Memorial is on the south shore of the Manatee River, 5 miles west of Bradenton on SR 64, then 2 miles north on 75th Street N.W. The memorial commemorates the first major European exploration of what is now the southeastern United States.

The expedition began in 1539 when Hernando de Soto and about 600 Spanish soldiers landed somewhere in the Tampa Bay area. Marked by many Indian battles, the expedition covered 4,000 miles to the north and west. De Soto crossed the Mississippi River in 1541 and was buried in it when he died a year later. About half the group survived the 4-year ordeal.

The visitor center contains artifacts and exhibits explaining the expedition's effect on American Indians. A 21-minute film depicting the expedition is shown hourly. Talks by costumed rangers as well as crossbow and arquebus (matchlock musket) demonstrations are given hourly 10:30-3:30, mid-December to early April. There also is a nature trail. Allow 1 hour minimum. Daily 9-5. Free. Phone (941) 792-0458.

DISNEY WORLD, WALT—
see Lake Buena Vista in Orlando p. 163.

DRY TORTUGAS NATIONAL PARK—
see The Florida Keys p. 64.

DUNEDIN—*see Tampa Bay p. 228.*

ELLENTON (F-8) pop. 3,142, elev. 11′

Ellenton, a small community on the northern bank of the Manatee River, offers fine fishing opportunities, nearby white sandy beaches and a climate favorable to agricultural endeavors.

Bradenton Area Convention & Visitors Bureau: P.O. Box 1000, Bradenton, FL 34206; phone (941) 729-9177 or (800) 462-6283.

Shopping areas: Prime Outlets Ellenton, off I-75 exit 224, features more than 130 factory outlet stores, including Mikasa, Nike, Off 5th Saks Fifth Avenue and Samsonite.

GAMBLE PLANTATION HISTORIC STATE PARK AND JUDAH P. BENJAMIN CONFEDERATE MEMORIAL, on US 301, was a prosperous 3,500-acre sugar plantation from about 1845 to the late 1850s. The antebellum mansion is furnished in period. At the end of the Civil War, Judah P. Benjamin, secretary of state of the Confederacy, found refuge here before escaping to England. Picnicking is permitted. Allow 1 hour minimum. Grounds open daily 8 a.m.-dusk. Mansion tours are given Thurs.-Mon. at 9:30, 10:30, 1, 2, 3 and 4. Grounds and visitor center free. Mansion admission, which is only by guided tour, $4; ages 6-12, $2. Phone (941) 723-4536.

EPCOT—*see Lake Buena Vista in Orlando p. 168.*

ESTERO (G-9) pop. 9,503, elev. 11′

KORESHAN STATE HISTORIC SITE, US 41 at Corkscrew Rd. on the banks of the Estero River, was the site of the religious community established in 1894 when Cyrus Reed Teed and his followers, members of the Koreshan Unity, arrived from Chicago. Restored historical buildings and gardens occupy the site. Carry insect repellent. Camping and canoe rentals are available; reservations are recommended. Fireside programs for campers are available by seasonal demand.

Allow 1 hour minimum. Park open daily 8-dusk. Self-guiding walking tours can be taken daily 8-5. Admission $3.25 per private vehicle (maximum eight people), $1 per person arriving by bicycle or on foot. AX, DS, MC, VI. Phone (239) 992-0311. *See Recreation Chart and the AAA Southeastern CampBook.*

EVERGLADES CITY (H-10)
pop. 479, elev. 3′

Because of its location at the northwest corner of the Everglades, Everglades City is a popular point of departure for fishing trips into Everglades National Park. Some hotels will send a box lunch with the angler and also will prepare the day's catch for the evening meal.

Everglades Area Chamber of Commerce: P.O. Box 130, Everglades City, FL 34139; phone (239) 695-3941 or (800) 914-6355.

EDEN OF THE EVERGLADES, 2 mi. s. of jct. US 41 on SR 29, has an elevated boardwalk that winds through a mangrove forest. Forty-five-minute pontoon boat trips tour the waterways of the Ten Thousand Islands area. Airboat rides also are available. Bring insect repellent. Daily 9-5. Admission $17.50; ages 3-10, $8. MC, VI. Phone (239) 695-2800 or (800) 543-3367.

EVERGLADES EXCURSIONS—*see Naples p. 129.*

EVERGLADES NATIONAL PARK BOAT TOURS leave from the park's ranger station .5 mi. s. on CR 29. The Mangrove Wilderness tour cruises past Calusa Indian shell mounds to native mangrove forests, and the Ten Thousand Islands tour cruises through this island group bordering the Gulf of Mexico. Both tours offer bird and wildlife sightings. For reservations and schedule information write P.O. Box 119, Everglades City, FL 34139. Cruises depart at intervals daily 8:30-5. Mangrove Wilderness tour $25; ages 6-12, $12.50. Ten Thousand Islands tour $16; ages 6-12, $8. AX, DS, MC, VI. Phone (239) 695-2591, or (800) 445-7724 in Fla.

MUSEUM OF THE EVERGLADES is at 105 W. Broadway. The museum is housed in a former laundry built in 1927 for workers constructing the Tamiami Trail across the Everglades. Exhibits recount the early history of this erstwhile company town and describe the region's first trading post as well as Seminole Indian culture. The life of Collier County developer and self-made millionaire Barron G. Collier also is highlighted. Allow 30 minutes minimum. Tues.-Sat. 10-4; closed holidays. Donations. Phone (239) 695-0008.

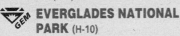 EVERGLADES NATIONAL PARK (H-10)

See map page below.

Elevations in the park range from sea level to 8 ft.

The park's main entrance is reached via SR 9336 from US 1 at Florida City. Everglades National Park, the largest remaining subtropical wilderness in the nation, is a diverse and intricately linked series of habitats sheltering a variety of plants and animals, many of them threatened or endangered. The park contains more than 1.5 million acres of natural habitat, half of them water, including Cape Sable, the southernmost point on the U.S. mainland. From Cape Sable the park extends 45 miles north along the Gulf of Mexico and 30 miles east, including Florida Bay.

The Everglades is essentially a slow-moving freshwater river, 50 miles wide and a few inches deep, fed by Lake Okeechobee. Much of the region is a labyrinth of mangrove waterways and sawgrass marsh dotted with hammocks and salt prairies. Except for the pinelands and the highest hammocks, any spot can become a swamp in the rainy season.

Increased development in southern Florida imperils the area. Canals alternately drain and flood the region to meet the water demands of nearby cities, but in doing so they reverse the natural wet and dry cycles of the Everglades. Although fire occurs naturally in this environment, drought and canal drainage have magnified its destructive impact.

The land areas are not more than 8 feet above mean sea level, and bay bottoms are not more than 16 feet below mean sea level. The Ten Thousand Islands area conceals a strange kind of beauty and tranquility within its tide-swept maze of islets, oyster bars and mud shallows.

Trees and flowers are much the same as those found in Cuba and the West Indies. At least six species of palms grow within the park. The stately royal palm is found in greatest numbers at the Royal Palm Visitor Center. In addition to the tropical and semitropical trees and shrubs, there are at least four species belonging to the temperate zone

and multitudes of ferns, orchids and air plants. Beware of the sawgrass; its sharp barbs can easily slash bare skin and thin clothing.

The park is home to more than 350 species of birds, 60 percent of which leave during summer. Among those that stay are two species found only in the southernmost tip of the Florida peninsula: the Cape Sable seaside sparrow and the great white heron. One species that does proliferate is the mosquito; strong insect repellent is a necessity from May to November and is recommended all year.

The Everglades is among the few remaining places where the manatee, or sea cow, and the rare American crocodile are assured a permanent sanctuary. Along with more than 600 species of fish, alligators, snakes and sea turtles are common. Bottlenose dolphins occasionally are seen. A fishing license is required for all fishing areas, and bag limits are strictly enforced for both freshwater and saltwater fishing.

General Information and Activities

Everglades National Park is open all year. From the headquarters and visitor center at the main entrance, this road continues to Flamingo. The Tamiami Trail (US 41) skirts the park's northern border and leads to the Shark Valley and Everglades City entrances.

Few people really know the waterways of the Everglades. Most of the waters have been charted by the U.S. Coast and Geodetic Survey, and visitors traveling by boat should obtain these charts at area bait and tackle shops before starting their trips. Permits are required for overnight camping and must be applied for in person at ranger stations, no more than 24 hours in advance. As a safety precaution, park officials urge boaters to file trip plans before their departures.

Four marked canoe trails offer 4- to 22-mile round trips from the Flamingo area, and the 99-mile Wilderness Waterway winds between Flamingo and Everglades City. The Shark River is navigable for most small boats. Canoe rentals are available at outfitters in Flamingo and Everglades City; visitor centers distribute trail maps.

Along the main park road between park headquarters and Flamingo are five major boardwalk or blacktop nature trails *(see Points of Interest)*. Flamingo has accommodations, eateries, sightseeing and charter fishing boats, a service station, marina, campground and visitor center which is open November through April. A ranger station on the south side of Everglades City on SR 29 is open daily 7:30-5, Nov.-Apr.; 8-4:30, rest of year; phone (239) 695-3311. *See Recreation Chart and the AAA Southeastern CampBook.*

Sightseeing opportunities are abundant. Boat trips through a portion of the Ten Thousand Islands area leave from nearby cities *(see Everglades City p. 56 and Naples p. 129)*. Other sightseeing trips are available from Flamingo, within the park. Self-guiding bicycle, kayak and canoe trips originate in Flamingo; phone (239) 695-3101.

Boat tours depart from Flamingo Marina. The 2-hour Backcountry cruises leave daily at 9, noon and 1:30, late Dec. to mid-Apr.; schedule varies rest of year. A 1.5-hour Florida Bay Cruise is offered daily at 2:30 and sunset, late Dec. to mid-Apr.; schedule varies rest of year. Boarding is 10 minutes before departure. Boat tours also leave from the visitor center in Everglades City.

Backcountry cruise $16; ages 6-12, $8. Florida Bay Cruise $10; ages 6-12, $5. Reservations are recommended for all boat tours. For further information about all boat tours phone the lodge at (239) 695-3101.

Airboat rides, available outside the park, are offered by private operators along the Tamiami Trail (US 41) west of Miami.

VISITOR CENTERS offer information that can enhance a visit to the park.

Ernest Coe Visitor Center, at the entrance at 40001 SR 9336, has exhibits about the park. Naturalists are on duty daily 8-5. Free. Phone (305) 242-7700.

Flamingo Visitor Center, 38 mi. s.w. of the main park entrance via SR 9336, has natural history exhibits and a marina opening onto Florida Bay. Rentals are available at the marina. Daily 8-5, Nov.-Apr.; staffing is intermittent rest of year. Free with park admission. Phone (239) 695-2945.

Gulf Coast Visitor Center, in Everglades City in the northwest corner of the park, contains natural-history exhibits. Daily 8:30-5. Free. Phone (239) 695-3311.

Royal Palm Visitor Center is 4 mi. inside the park, off the main park road. The center provides park information and, in winter, naturalist-led walks and illustrated talks. Daily 8-4:15. Free with park admission. Phone (305) 242-7700.

ADMISSION to the park is $10 per private vehicle or $5 per person arriving by bicycle, motorcycle or on foot.

PETS are permitted only in the park campgrounds and only if they are leashed, crated or otherwise physically restrained at all times. They are not allowed on developed trails, in the backcountry or in the visitor centers.

ADDRESS inquiries to the Superintendent, Everglades National Park, 40001 SR 9336, Homestead, FL 33034; phone (305) 242-7700.

Points of Interest

ANHINGA TRAIL, beginning at the Royal Palm Visitor Center, follows an elevated boardwalk. During the winter, alligators, snowy egrets, water turkeys and garfish can be seen.

CHEKIKA, 18 mi. n.w. of Homestead off SR 997, offers 640 acres of hardwood hammocks and wetlands with more than 100 species of birds.

GUMBO LIMBO TRAIL, starting from Royal Palm Visitor Center, penetrates the interior of Paradise Key hammock, where many species of native plants can be seen.

LONG PINE KEY AREA, 7 mi. from the entrance station, contains camping and picnic facilities, and nature and hiking trails. *See the AAA Southeastern CampBook.*

MAHOGANY HAMMOCK, 19.5 mi. from the park entrance, is a region of mahogany trees and many other subtropical plants labeled for easy identification. An elevated boardwalk winds through the forest. Following the completion of repairs to the boardwalk, the trail was scheduled to re-open in 2003; phone the Superintendent's office for information about the status of the boardwalk.

MANGROVE TRAIL, 30.5 mi. from the park entrance station at West Lake, extends through a mangrove forest on an elevated boardwalk. The trail, badly damaged by a hurricane in 1960, shows the devastation such storms can cause.

PA-HAY-OKEE OVERLOOK is 12.5 mi. from the park entrance. The overlook consists of a 12-foot tower at Shark River Basin which affords views of the vast sawgrass wilderness.

PINELANDS TRAIL, 6.5 mi. from the park entrance, extends into an area of southern pines, scrub palmetto and related plants.

SHARK VALLEY, off US 41, has several short self-guiding trails that explore the area. Bobcat Hammock Trail passes through a variety of habitats, while Otter Cave Trail leads through limestone formations and a tropical hammock. Self-guiding bicycle trails and bicycle rentals are available. A visitor center is open daily 8:30-5:15. Admission $8 per private vehicle, $4 per person arriving by bicycle, motorcycle or on foot (fee deductible from entrance fee to Everglades National Park). Phone (305) 221-8776.

The Shark Valley Tram Tour departs from Shark Valley off US 41. The 2-hour, 15-mile excursion explores the sawgrass wilderness of Shark Valley and includes a 20-minute stop at the observation tower at the southern end of the valley. Tours operate daily 9-4, Dec.-Apr.; 9:30-3, rest of year (weather permitting). Fare $10.50; over 62, $9.50; under 12, $6. Reservations are required 1 to 3 weeks in advance Nov.-Apr. AX, DS, MC, VI. Phone (305) 221-8455.

FERNANDINA BEACH—
see Jacksonville p. 95.

FLORIDA CITY—*see Miami-Miami Beach p. 125.*

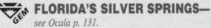 **FLORIDA'S SILVER SPRINGS—**
see Ocala p. 131.

FORT GEORGE ISLAND—
see Jacksonville p. 96.

The Florida Keys

A watercolor sky glows lavender, cobalt, carmine, sienna—another sunset. The street performers pause. The audience applauds.

And then, on with the show. Back to shuffling for a better spot to watch the sword-swallower, kilted bagpiper, painted human "statue" and tip-pleading tightrope walker. Back to dodging oncoming onlookers, observing the people parade and eyeing vendors' wares. Back to the raucous ritual.

End the Beginning

You could only be in Key West, Florida's accessible slice of island spice. The final course in The Florida Keys' full menu of fun.

Imbued with a tropical flavor that extends to its ubiquitous dishes—conch chowder, conch fritters and, of course, Key lime pie—this tiny town at The End of the Road is a slightly sugary, slightly tart, somehow sublime little custard of sights, sounds, tastes and tempos. As impious as eating dessert first, it's perfectly placed to introduce this curving island chain's curious charisma.

Like its sister Keys that Henry Flagler's railroad linked, Key West's influences have been Bahamian, Cuban, military, visionary. Its industries have ranged from shipwreck salvaging to turtle hunting to cigar making to tourism. Its wealth has been vast (in the 1880s, before lighthouses helped treasure-laden ships avoid treacherous reefs) and lost (in the 1930s, after 42 miles of railroad succumbed to storm-tossed seas).

Its Old Town historic district—pedestrian-friendly and architecturally rich—is where wreckers' and shipbuilders' hybrid homes are now high-end bed-and-breakfasts admired for their tin roofs, gingerbread trim, signature shutters and wraparound verandas. Where former hangouts of hard-drinking heroes and hippies are now vacation-photo backdrops for families *and* frat boys. Where fierce, fighting roosters' docile descendents quaintly roam free, legally protected. That's Key West: tradition with a Key lime twist.

But of all its aspects, the self-nicknamed Conch Republic is arguably best known for having perpetuated a simple habit of nightly saluting the blazing horizon, albeit with an atmosphere increasingly more theme park than Thoreau.

In fact, if you strayed there straight from the airport or cruise ship, today's Mallory Square sundown scene could cause culture shock. Amid the pet-toting locals and souvenir T-shirt masses, first-timers tend to feel a bit like bit

players on a crowded movie set. But for those who've been before, or who drove in through all those other quirky Keys, well, you've seen enough to know it's all for real. Surreal as it may be.

Driving the mostly two-lane Road That Went to Sea from Miami to Key West is like backtracking to the days predating endless exit ramps. Through the car windows—interspersed with mangroves, cattails and "passing lane 3 miles" signs—appear pirates posed in full regalia, monster lobsters, towering mermaid cutouts, lots of crusty cannons, a few giant anchors. Conspicuously placed as if to encourage a pull-off photo op, followed by a stop inside the air-conditioned comfort of whatever restaurant or shop sits close by, such oddities lend the landscape an innocent charm.

Then there are the signs: "Seafood" spelled in seashell mosaic; a neon turtle; even a rhinoceros-topped billboard. After many miles of this sort of scenery, one reaches the landlocked concrete buoy emblazoned "Southernmost Point" a little more prepared for Key West's mystique.

But don't think you have to head all the way to that oft-photographed red, yellow and black landmark to have *arrived.* Simply stop at almost any populated Key (taken from the Spanish *cayo,* or "small island") along the way and you'll usually be well fixed with great R & R opportunities. A good number of Florida Keys vacationers do just that, making family traditions out of annual stays at tuck-away campgrounds, easygoing efficiencies, "botels"—lodgings where marinas replace parking lots—or sport-fishing hot spots flush with charter boats, guides and all-inclusive resorts.

Getting There *Is* Half the Fun

In the Upper Keys, where most of the kitsch is confined, Key Largo and the unparalleled John Pennekamp Coral Reef State Park beckon snorkelers and scuba divers. Here, experienced divers can find everything needed to explore the fantastically diverse and extremely fragile reef system several miles offshore. But amateurs aren't left out; many lodgings offer on-site diving instruction. The park's main beach even has a staged shipwreck that especially delights children, who can be heard shouting to shore their discovery of what surely is the long-lost cannon of an unfortunate Spanish galleon.

Anchoring the Upper Keys stretch is sport-fishing-focused Islamorada, boasting one of the region's largest concentrations of charter boats as well as the midwaylike atmosphere of lively Holiday Isle; complete with beach, pools, shops, boardwalk and marina, the resort is famous for appealing to a festive crowd. Nearby, The Museums of Crane Point Hammock offers an educational look at area animals, marine life and ecosystems. If time allows, a kayak jaunt through the Florida Bay "backcountry" can provide a fascinating close-up glimpse of similar sights; rentals are readily available.

(continued on page 64)

Destination The Florida Keys

*B*lame Henry Flagler. He laid the track that became the roadbed that put the Keys in easy reach.

*N*ow, millions visit. Some drop in, some drop out, some just drop anchor. And why not? With its warm breezes, top-notch water sports and weekend way of life, this enigmatic island chain is hard to resist.

Mallory Square, Key West.
The wares and amenities of the southernmost United States town have a distinctive motif. (See mention page 60)

*Southernmost Home,
Key West.*
Only 90 miles from Cuba, this Victorian-era beauty is the southernmost house in the United States.

*P*laces included in this AAA Destination Area:

Big Pine Key................64	Key Largo....................65	Marathon....................69
Islamorada..................65	Key West......................66	Sugarloaf Key..............69

Key West.
This whimsical gator expresses
the Keys' philosophy-don't take
life too seriously.

Key
Largo

Islamorada

Marathon

Florida Keys

*John Pennekamp Coral
Reef State Park,
Key Largo.*
In addition to its
natural wonders, this
scuba diver's delight
also is home to the
serene statue "Christ
of the Deep." (See
listing page 65)

Key West Lighthouse Museum.
Climb the stairs if you dare,
or just enjoy the historical
exhibits and life-size lens that
accompany this 1847 structure.
(See listing page 68)

Marathon, in the Middle Keys, combines residential side roads, numerous fishing tournaments and several resorts ideal for tropical retreats, and the sunset's just as pretty from here.

Once over the Seven Mile Bridge, be sure to visit Bahia Honda State Park. A sandy beach and walkable segment of old bridge—providing incredible views of the new bridge—make this a must-see spot to stretch your legs *and* shift your perspective into "island time."

Back in the car now and heading to the Lower Keys, you're in the homestretch. Be sure to slow for the endangered Key deer in Big Pine Key; it's the law. Then prepare for the sameness of mangroves, scrub, Australian pines and power lines, sights whose monotony instills an antsy appetite for what lies ahead.

The feeling heightens as you close in on Key West proper. You may know you're there by the sound of Navy fighter jets shredding air overhead; Naval Air Station Key West, on nearby Boca Chica Key, is one of the Navy's premier pilot-training facilities. Or by the "T" where U.S. 1 hits Roosevelt Boulevard (and New Town's jumble of condos and commerce commences). Or perhaps it won't fully register till you've reached Old Town itself and done the obligatory "Duval crawl"—head swiveling from T-shirt shop to tavern to tree-shaded courtyard eatery.

However you reach it, once that mile-marker-zero mentality finally hits, you'll know The End of the Road—just like the sunset that closes every Key West day—is only the beginning of the barhopping, souvenir-shopping, conch-fritter-popping party more than a million visitors a year sojourn here to savor. On with the show.

Destinations in this region listed under their own names are Big Pine Key, Dry Tortugas National Park, Islamorada, Key Largo, Key West, Marathon and Sugarloaf Key.

BIG PINE KEY (I-10) pop. 4,200, elev. 5′

Big Pine Key, between Marathon and Key West, is home to the Key deer, a miniature species maturing to the size of a large dog. By the 1950s hunting had almost annihilated this subspecies of the Virginia whitetail. With only 800 of the animals remaining, the deer still is an endangered species.

Many deer have collided with vehicles and been injured or killed. Visitors are asked to observe the speed limit and not pull over to feed or photograph deer, as doing so encourages them to approach the road.

Great White Heron and Key West national wildlife refuges also preserve area bird life. The Key West refuge also provides a safe haven for sea turtle nests. Both are accessible only by boat.

The headquarters for both wildlife refuges—in Big Pine Shopping Plaza, a half-mile north of US 1 on Key Deer Boulevard at mile marker 30.5 at the traffic light—is open Mon.-Fri. 8-5.

Many reefs and their undersea inhabitants are protected in the Florida Keys National Marine Sanctuary, at nearby Looe Key. Characterized by coral reefs and clear water, the sanctuary is a delight to divers. Snorkel and scuba trips can be arranged from Looe Key Dive Center on Ramrod Key at mile marker 27.5; phone (305) 872-2215 or (800) 942-5397.

Lower Keys Chamber of Commerce: P.O. Box 430511, Big Pine Key, FL 33043-0511; phone (305) 872-2411 or (800) 872-3722.

NATIONAL KEY DEER REFUGE, headquarters at mile marker 30.5 on US 1, is a designated sanctuary for the endangered diminutive deer. It encompasses approximately 2,300 acres. Blue Hole, 1.25 miles north of Key Deer and Watson boulevards, is a freshwater pond in a former quarry. It attracts such wildlife as alligators and turtles. A .7-mile self-guiding nature trail begins off Key Deer Boulevard, north of the Blue Hole, and winds through the refuge area. Early morning and evening hours are the best times to view the deer. Daily dawn-dusk. Free. Phone (305) 872-0774.

DRY TORTUGAS NATIONAL PARK (I-8)

Elevations in the land portion of the park are at sea level. Most of the park is water.

The Tortugas are 68 nautical miles west of Key West. The seven Tortugas Keys, or Dry Tortugas Islands, and the surrounding waters in the Gulf of Mexico constitute Dry Tortugas National Park. Discovered by Ponce de León in 1513 and named Las Tortugas for their great number of turtles, the islands are called Dry Tortugas because they lack fresh water.

For centuries the islands were inhabited by pirates who were protected from detection by passing vessels by the rocks and shallow waters. Lighthouses were built on Garden Key in 1825 and on Loggerhead Key in 1856. Discoveries of sunken Spanish treasure ships nearby bear witness to the shipwrecks that occurred along these shoals.

Strategically located between the United States and South America, the Tortugas attract many species of migratory birds. The most noted inhabitant is the sooty tern, which breeds on Bush Key between March and September. Another familiar inhabitant is the sea turtle, four endangered species of which nest in the park.

Access to the park is by boat or seaplane. Seaplanes of Key West Inc., in Key West International Airport, provides daily half- and full-day trips to Fort Jefferson in the park; reservations are required. The 45-minute low-altitude flights allow good views of marine life, shipwrecks and treasure-salvaging operations. Phone (800) 950-2359.

Fort Jefferson was begun on Garden Key in 1846, but after 30 years of construction it was still incomplete. Intended to protect vital shipping access to the Gulf, its 8-foot-thick walls and 450 guns were never tested. During the Civil War Federal troops occupied the fort, but by 1866 the introduction of rifled cannon and the fall of Fort Pulaski had made brick and masonry forts obsolete.

In 1861 Fort Jefferson became a prison for army deserters and in 1865 received the four "Lincoln Conspirators," condemned for their part in the assassination of President Abraham Lincoln. The fort was abandoned in 1874 following a hurricane and a second yellow fever outbreak. The Navy used it as the site for a wireless station in the early 1900s, then as a seaplane base in World War I. In 1935 President Franklin Roosevelt proclaimed the area a national monument.

Dry Tortugas National Park is open daily 24 hours. Fort open daily 9-5. Park free. A fee is charged for camping. A brief audiovisual presentation is available in the visitor center. Camping is permitted on the fort's grassy apron, and its shores lend themselves to swimming and snorkeling. No fresh water, food, fuel, supplies or public telephones are available. For further information contact the Superintendent, Everglades National Park, 40001 SR 9336, Homestead, FL 33034; phone (305) 242-7700. *See Recreation Chart.*

ISLAMORADA (I-11) pop. 6,846, elev. 5′

Islamorada (I-lah-mor-AH-dah) is a fishing haven spread over the islands of Lower Matecumbe Key, Plantation Key, Upper Matecumbe Key and Windley Key. Its purplish appearance from a distance caused the Spanish to call it the "purple isle" *(isla morada).* The wreck of the galleon *Herrera,* 2.5 miles off Whale Harbour Bridge, offers opportunities for underwater exploration and photography.

Indian Key Historic State Park, a half-mile mile southeast of Lower Matecumbe Key, is a 10-acre uninhabited island. This lavish paradise of notorious wrecker Capt. Jacob Housman was destroyed in 1840 when the captain's misuse of power prompted an Indian uprising. The ruins of houses and cisterns are now choked by vegetation planted by physician and botanist Dr. Henry Perrine, who conducted plant experiments at the settlement in 1838. The site is accessible only by private or chartered boat. For information phone (305) 664-2540 or (800) 322-5397.

Lignumvitae Key State Botanical Site can be reached only by private or chartered boat from the marinas at the western end of Islamorada. Because of its high elevation and the sensitive management of former owner William Matheson, the island retains a singular plant community and is a fine example of a West Indian hardwood hammock. Indigenous and introduced trees blossom at various times but are best viewed in spring or early summer.

Matheson House, built of coral in 1919 and furnished in 1930s styles, remains unchanged. A stone wall, possibly built by Spanish explorers as a navigation aid, extends the length of the island. Walking shoes and mosquito repellent are musts. For information phone (305) 664-2540.

Islamorada Chamber of Commerce: P.O. Box 915, Islamorada, FL 33036; phone (305) 664-4503 or (800) 322-5397.

Shopping areas: Bass Pro Shops Outdoor World, 81576 Overseas Hwy., features an Everglades aquarium, wildlife exhibits and sporting several demonstrations.

KEY LARGO (I-11) pop. 11,886, elev. 6′

At 30 miles, Key Largo is the longest of the Florida Keys. Linked to the mainland by the first of 42 bridges along the Overseas Highway—the scenic 113-mile section of US 1 between the Florida mainland and Key West—Key Largo introduces the lifestyle of the keys with its marinas and diving and tackle shops.

Key Largo Chamber of Commerce: 105950 Overseas Hwy., Key Largo, FL 33037; phone (305) 451-1414 or (800) 822-1088.

JOHN PENNEKAMP CORAL REEF STATE PARK, on US 1 at mile marker 102.5, combines a land area with 178 nautical miles of protected ocean waters. Features include a portion of a living coral reef and the underwater, 9-foot bronze statue, "Christ of the Deep," which can be viewed by snorkel or scuba tours. It also is possible to view the statue from a boat if water conditions are favorable.

A boardwalk provides access to a mangrove area. A visitor center displays aquariums and offers films and interpretive programs. Glass-bottom boat, sail-and-snorkel or snorkel tours, which range from 2.5 to 4 hours, are available.

DID YOU KNOW

There are 882 islands in the Florida Keys.

Park open daily 8-dusk (weather permitting). Visitor center open daily 8-5. A 2.5-hour glass-bottom boat tour departs daily at 9:15, 12:15 and 3. A 2.5-hour snorkel tour departs daily at 9, noon and 3. The 4-hour sail-and-snorkel tour departs daily at 9 and 1:30. Visitors must be at the boat 1 hour before departure.

Admission $4 per private vehicle and driver plus 50c per person; $1.50 per person arriving by bicycle, bus or on foot. Glass-bottom boat tours $18; ages 3-11, $10. Snorkeling tour $25.95; under 18, $20.95. Sail-and-snorkel tour $31.95; under 18, $26.95. Reservations are recommended. Phone (305) 451-1202, or (305) 451-1621 for tour information and reservations. *See Recreation Chart and the AAA Southeastern CampBook.*

CASINOS

- **SunCruz Casino**, on US 1 at Holiday Inn Key Largo Resort and Marina at mile marker 100. Afternoon and evening departures available daily; phone for schedule. After each day's first sailing, guests are shuttled out to the ship on a water taxi. Phone (305) 451-0000 or (800) 474-3423, ext. 11.

KEY WEST (I-9) pop. 25,478, elev. 22'

To its rocky shores, sandy beaches and weathered homes reminiscent of a coastal New England town, Key West adds another feature: its subtropical climate, which nourishes lush vegetation, especially palm trees, hibiscus and bougainvillea. Ship carpenters, using wooden pegs instead of nails, built many of the older houses, which are predominantly Bahamian in architecture.

The southernmost city in the continental United States, Key West once served as a base of operation against pirates; today it is the southern terminus of the scenic Overseas Highway (US 1). The prosperity of mid-19th century Key West was based on the thriving salvage business. At one time these enterprises provided the town with the highest per capita income in the nation.

Because of its proximity to Havana, about 90 miles south, the town was later a haven for Cuban political exiles. San Carlos Institute on Duval Street dates from the late 19th century, when it was used as a meeting place for the local Cuban community. City Cemetery on Margaret Street is the gravesite of the victims of the USS *Maine,* whose sinking precipitated the Spanish-American War.

Home at various times to Ernest Hemingway, Tennessee Williams and Robert Frost, Key West remains a popular retreat for artists and writers.

Although turtle hunting was once a major industry, federal laws protecting the endangered reptiles were enacted in the 1970s. The remains of a turtle-canning factory stand behind Turtle Kraals Bar and Restaurant on the harborfront at the north end of Margaret Street.

Donkey Milk House Museum, 613 Eaton St., derives its name from the alley in back where donkeys used to pull milk delivery carts. The restored

1860s home is open by appointment only; phone (305) 296-1866.

Of Key West's many natural attractions, its sunsets are among the most popular. Every night, weather permitting, more than two dozen ·street vendors and performers gather at Mallory Square Dock in Old Town off Duval Street. Jugglers, palm readers, contortionists, musicians and other entertainers vie for the attention and donations of the many spectators who begin gathering about an hour before sunset.

Nature also puts on a daily show in the shady confines of Nancy Forrester's Secret Garden, an environmental earthwork, at 1 Free School Ln., off Simonton Street, where an extensive collection of rain forest plants creates a junglelike atmosphere complete with (caged) parrots; phone (305) 294-0015.

The Caribbean influence extends to the town's cuisine. Along Duval Street and its side streets, imaginative cafes and open-air restaurants serve foods ranging from gourmet specialties to ethnic snacks.

Various types of cruises, including those offering underwater viewing of the denizens of the deep, sailing, snorkeling and reef diving, depart from several private and city marinas. Of particular interest are bed and breakfasts cruises which incorporate snorkeling and gourmet meals. Deep-sea fishing trips leave from City Marina on Garrison Bight off Roosevelt Boulevard. Seaplanes of Key West Inc. provides transportation to Dry Tortugas National Park *(see place listing p. 64),* 68 miles west. Contact the chamber of commerce for more information.

Note: Parking regulations are strictly enforced throughout the city. Motorscooters should be parked in the areas designated for that purpose. There is no street parking available for recreational vehicles; follow signs to designated RV parking areas.

Key West Chamber of Commerce: Mallory Square, 402 Wall St., Key West, FL 33040; phone (305) 294-2587 or (800) 527-8539.

Self-guiding tours: Pelican Path—a route marked with pelican signs—leads visitors through historic Key West. A descriptive brochure outlining the tour and its sights can be picked up at the chamber of commerce.

AUDUBON HOUSE AND TROPICAL GARDENS, 205 Whitehead St., is where John James Audubon stayed while painting the wildlife of the Florida Keys in 1832. Chippendale furniture, a rare collection of porcelain birds and 1820 Staffordshire pottery are among the 18th- and 19th-century furnishings found in the restored home of noted harbor pilot and wrecker Capt. John Geiger. Original engravings by Audubon are displayed. Tours include the house and tropical gardens, which feature exotic native plants. Allow 1 hour minimum. Daily 9:30-5. Admission $9; ages 6-12, $5. AX, MC, VI. Phone (305) 294-2116.

CONCH TOUR TRAINS leave from two depots—Mallory Square and 3850 N. Roosevelt Blvd. The 90-minute, 10-mile tour through old and new Key West features an informative narration about area history. Local points of interest along the tour include Old Town, Hemingway's house, Duval Street, Southernmost Point and the waterfront. Trains depart daily every half-hour 9-4:30. Fare $20; ages 4-12, $10. DS, MC, VI. Phone (305) 294-5161.

DISCOVERY UNDERSEA TOURS departs from the historic Key West Seaport at 251 Margaret St. Offering narrated excursions aboard an 80-foot, glass-bottom vessel, this cruise company takes passengers out to nearby living coral reefs. Twenty windows set at an angle in the hull provide a panoramic view of the reef and its colorful denizens. Food is available. Allow 2 hours minimum. Cruises depart daily at 11:30, 2:30 and dusk, early Apr.-late Oct.; at 10:30, 1:30 and dusk, rest of year. Passengers should arrive 30 minutes before departure. Fare $25; ages 3-12, $16. Sunset cruise $30; ages 3-12, $16. DS, MC, VI. Phone (305) 293-0099 or (800) 262-0099.

DRY TORTUGAS NATIONAL PARK FERRY departs from the Key West Seaport at 240 Margaret St. The ferry service offers a round-trip excursion to Fort Jefferson in the Dry Tortugas aboard a high-speed catamaran with air-conditioned cabins and open decks. Before returning to Key West, passengers spend 4.5 hours within the park during which they can swim, snorkel and take a 45-minute guided tour of the fort. Food is available. Allow a full day. Daily 7:30-5:30; closed Dec. 25. Fare (includes breakfast and lunch) $109; over 62, $99; ages 4-16, $69. AX, DS, MC, VI. Phone (305) 294-7009 or (800) 634-0939.

ERNEST HEMINGWAY HOME AND MUSEUM is at 907 Whitehead St. Hemingway bought the 1851 Spanish colonial-style mansion in 1931. Among works written here is "For Whom the Bell Tolls." The house, set in a lush tropical garden planted by the author, is home to more than 50 cats, descendants of Hemingway's felines. Of interest is the penny embedded in the concrete at the head of the pool—it supposedly was tossed there when Hemingway discovered the pool's $20,000 price tag. Allow 30 minutes minimum. Daily 9-5. Admission $9; ages 6-12, $5. AX, MC, VI. Phone (305) 294-1136.

FORT ZACHARY TAYLOR HISTORIC STATE PARK, at the s.w. end of the island via Southard St. past the Truman Annex, was built 1845-66 as part of Florida's coastal defense system. The cannons within the walls constitute one of the largest collections of Civil War armaments. Swimming, fishing and picnicking on a tropical beach are among the recreational activities available. Guided tours are available.

Allow 3 hours minimum. Daily 8-dusk. Tours are given daily at noon and 2. Admission $2.50 each for first two people in a vehicle, 50c each additional passenger up to eight; $1.50 per person arriving by bicycle, bus or on foot. Phone (305) 292-6713. *See Recreation Chart.*

KEY WEST AQUARIUM, at the foot of Whitehead St. on Mallory Sq., was one of the first open-air aquariums when it opened in 1934. Shark and turtle feedings take place daily, and a touch tank lets visitors interact with the marine life. Guided tours are available. Allow 1 hour minimum. Daily 10-6. Admission $9; ages 4-12, $4.50. Phone (305) 296-2051.

SAVE **KEY WEST LIGHTHOUSE MUSEUM,** 938 Whitehead St., recounts Florida lighthouse history through exhibits featuring historical items, including a complete light assembly. The museum is in the former keeper's quarters. A spiral staircase leads to the top of the 1847 Key West Lighthouse. Allow 30 minutes minimum. Daily 9:30-4:30; closed Dec. 25. Admission $8; over 62, $6; ages 7-17, $4. AX, MC, VI. Phone (305) 294-0012.

KEY WEST SHIPWRECK HISTOREUM, 1 Whitehead St. in Old Mallory Square, is housed in a reproduction of the wreckers warehouse that originally stood on the site. Costumed actors interact with visitors and recreate the events of the wreck and salvage of the *Isaac Allerton,* which sank in 1856. Artifacts from the shipwreck are on display and videotapes are shown. A 65-foot observation tower provides a magnificent view of the Atlantic Ocean and the Gulf of Mexico. Allow 1 hour minimum. Daily 9:45-4:45. Admission $8; ages 4-12, $4. AX, DS, MC, VI. Phone (305) 292-8990.

SAVE **THE LIBERTY FLEET OF TALL SHIPS** departs from Hilton Resort and Marina, jct. Front and Greene sts. The schooner cruises around Key West and allows passengers the chance to steer and sail. Dinner cruises also are available. Cruises depart daily at 11, 2:30 and 6:30, Nov. 1 to mid-May. Fare for 11 and 2:30 cruises $30; under 12, $15. Fare for 6:30 cruise $40; under 12, $20. Reservations are required. DS, MC, VI. Phone (305) 292-0332.

LITTLE WHITE HOUSE MUSEUM, 111 Front St. inside the Truman Annex, is the vacation retreat that Presidents Harry Truman, Dwight Eisenhower and John F. Kennedy used during their administrations. The house has been restored to its 1948 appearance. A 10-minute videotape introduces visitors to Truman, and a 40-minute guided tour gives insight into both his experiences in Key West and his presidency. Allow 1 hour minimum. Daily 9-5. Admission $10; ages 6-12, $5. AX, DS, JC, MC, VI. Phone (305) 294-9911.

MARTELLO TOWERS, on the south side of the island, are reached via SR A1A (S. Roosevelt Blvd.).

The two brick fortifications were begun in 1858 by Union engineers to protect the defenses east of Fort Zachary Taylor.

SAVE **East Martello Museum and Gallery,** 3501 S. Roosevelt Blvd. at the airport entrance, exhibits Key West memorabilia relating to trade and the development of the island, including shipbuilding tools, treasure chests and boat models. The works of Mario Sanchez, a local artist and woodcarver, and metal sculpture by folk artist Stanley Papio are displayed. The citadel, accessible by stairs, provides a scenic overlook. Allow 30 minutes minimum. Daily 9:30-4:40; closed Dec. 25. Admission $6; over 62, $5; ages 7-12, $3. AX, MC, VI. Phone (305) 296-3913.

Key West Garden Center is on a county beach on Atlantic Blvd. and White St. Tropical plants grow among the ruins of the west tower. Tues.-Sat. 9:30-3:15. Donations. Phone (305) 294-3210.

MEL FISHER MARITIME MUSEUM, Greene and Front sts., displays both precious and functional artifacts recovered from the wreckage of two Spanish galleons. While en route to Spain from Havana, the ships sank 40 miles off Key West in a hurricane Sept. 6, 1622. Highlights of the collection include a 77.76-carat emerald as well as gold and silver religious objects. Informative exhibits illustrate techniques of underwater archeology. Allow 1 hour minimum. Daily 9:30-5. Admission $7.50; ages 6-12, $3.75. AX, MC, VI. Phone (305) 294-2633.

OLD TOWN TROLLEY tours leave from Mallory Square downtown or can be joined at any of the 9 stops as the trolley tours the island. The 1.5-hour tours of old Key West provide a narrated introduction to the history, legends and geography of the island. Points of interest along the tour include Key West Aquarium, Duval Street and Ernest Hemingway's house. Frequent departures daily 9:35-4:30. Fare $20; ages 4-12, $10. Tickets include one full loop around the island. AX, DS, MC, VI. Phone (305) 296-6688.

SAVE *STARS & STRIPES*—**KEY WEST,** departing from Land's End Marina at Caroline and Margaret sts., offers trips aboard a 54-foot catamaran. A full-day excursion includes snorkeling and beachcombing as well as undersea viewing through the glass-bottomed hull. A 2-hour sunset cruise offers a full view of Key West's legendary sunsets; complimentary refreshments are served.

Full-day trip departs daily at 9:30. Sunset cruise departs daily; times vary according to season. Boarding is 30 minutes before departure. Full-day fare (includes snorkel gear, instruction and food) $75; ages 7-17, $40. Sunset sail $35; ages 7-17, $17.50. Reservations are recommended. AX, MC, VI. Phone (305) 294-7877 or (800) 634-6369.

SAVE **WRECKERS' MUSEUM/OLDEST HOUSE,** 322 Duval St., is said to be the oldest house in south Florida. The construction of the 1829 house includes horizontal wall boards, a ship's hatch in the roof and the "landlubber's tilt" in the office. Furnished with American antiques, the house contains maritime documents, ship models, undersea artifacts and displays about the history of 19th-century ship wrecking. The garden has a separate cookhouse and an exhibit pavilion. Allow 30 minutes minimum. Daily 10-4. Admission $5; ages 3-12, $1. DS. Phone (305) 294-9502.

MARATHON (I-10) pop. 10,255

Marathon, named for the lament of an East Coast Railroad engineer when told to continue the line still farther, is the commercial and sport fishing center of the Middle Keys.

Marathon Chamber of Commerce: 12222 Overseas Hwy., Marathon, FL 33050; phone (305) 743-5417 or (800) 842-9580.

SAVE MUSEUMS AND NATURE CENTER OF CRANE POINT HAMMOCK, gulfside at mile marker 50, is a historic site. The natural history museum features models of marine life, animals and birds in naturalistic settings, while the children's museum features touch tanks. Also on the site are a model ship's deck, nature trails and an early Bahamian homestead. Allow 1 hour minimum. Mon.-Sat. 9-5, Sun. noon-5. Tours are available upon request. Admission $7.50; over 65, $6; students with ID $4; under 7 free. Phone (305) 743-9100.

SUGARLOAF KEY (I-9)

Sugarloaf Key gained its name from the sugarloaf pineapples once grown in the area. Just north of US 1 at the airport entrance is Bat Tower, an island landmark and a monument to a futile attempt to manipulate nature. Built in 1929 by fishing resort owner R.C. Perky, the tower was to become home to a colony of bats intended to feed on the resident mosquito population; once the bats were released they flew away, and the mosquitoes remained.

This ends listings for the The Florida Keys.
The following page resumes the alphabetical listings
of cities in Florida.

Fort Lauderdale

Honeycombed by rivers, bays, inlets and canals, Fort Lauderdale is a city of islands, where the boat rivals the automobile as a mode of transportation. One-tenth of the city surface is water; 165 miles of navigable waters provide either home or temporary port for boats of all sizes. The Intercoastal Waterway, a canal system reminiscent of Venice, connects downtown office buildings, the galleries and boutiques on Las Olas Boulevard, and the museums, theaters and nightspots of Riverwalk.

Fort Lauderdale is primarily residential; with the exception of the waterfront and beach areas, it does not give the appearance of a resort community. The canals and waterways furnish a striking setting for many beautiful homes, the most lavish of which are east of US 1. However, residential does not necessarily mean sedate— Fort Lauderdale's clubs and discotheques offer a flourishing nightlife.

Although settled in 1838 by Maj. William Lauderdale, the resort did not begin to grow until after its incorporation in 1911. In Fort Lauderdale proper almost all hotels, motels and stores are just west of SR A1A. The beach to the east provides a 3-mile-long strip of sand that has proven to be one of Fort Lauderdale's foremost attractions. Fort Lauderdale Beach Boulevard, the stretch of A1A from Bahia Mar Marina to Sunrise Boulevard, is nationally noted for its integration of urban streetscape and beachfront scenery.

Miles of lagoons, waterways and beaches make Fort Lauderdale one of the most popular areas on the Gold Coast. Water taxis provide a convenient and relaxing way to navigate the inland waterways that wind through the city.

In addition to being a leading resort area, Fort Lauderdale also is an active commercial center. The marine industry and citrus groves play important roles. Port Everglades, 2 miles south, has one of the deepest harbors south of Norfolk, Va. The 10 modern terminals provide facilities for Caribbean-bound luxury liners as well as for the handling of millions of tons of cargo each year.

Approaches

By Car

SR A1A, US 1, Florida's Turnpike (toll), I-95 and US 441 are the major approaches to Fort Lauderdale from the north and I-75/I-595, known as Alligator Alley, is the major western approach. The roads are well-marked; the only trouble drivers might have is with US 1, variously posted as US 1 and Federal Highway. Downtown this route is known as N.E. or S.E. Sixth Avenue.

Getting Around

Street System

The street plan of Fort Lauderdale is a fairly simple grid. Broward Boulevard and Andrews Avenue divide the city into quadrants (N.E., S.W., etc.). Boulevards, courts, drives and streets run east and west; avenues, terraces and ways run north and south.

The speed limit is 25 mph or as posted. Do not try to follow an unfamiliar route during rush hours (7 to 9 a.m. and 4:30 to 6 p.m.) or during lunch time.

Parking

Parking on downtown streets is metered; there are ample lots at rates of 75c per hour. Municipal parking in the beach areas costs $3-$6 per day. No parking is available along SR A1A. Parking along side streets costs 25c-75c per hour.

What To See

SAVE BONNET HOUSE MUSEUM & GARDENS, 900 N. Birch Rd., just s. of Sunrise Blvd., is a 35-acre beachfront estate that was the winter home of two artists, Frederic and Evelyn Bartlett. Built during the 1920s, the estate features lagoons, gardens and an art gallery. Also of note are pieces of artwork and hand-painted ceilings created by the Bartletts. The house is open only by guided 75-minute tours. Allow 1 hour, 30 minutes minimum. Open Wed.-Sat. 10-4, Sun. noon-4, Dec.-Apr.; Wed.-Fri. 10-3, Sat. 10-4, Sun. noon-4, rest of year. Last tour begins 90 minutes before closing. Schedule may vary; phone ahead. Guided tour and grounds admission $9; over 60, $8; ages 6-18, $7. Grounds admission only $5. AX, MC, VI. Phone (954) 563-5393.

INTERNATIONAL SWIMMING HALL OF FAME is 1 blk. s. of Las Olas Blvd., just w. of SR A1A at 1 Hall of Fame Dr. The hall highlights the achievements of notable swimmers and contains aquatic artifacts dating to the 15th century. An art gallery features aquatic art from around the world. The Hall of Fame swimming pools adjoin the museum.

Allow 1 hour minimum. Museum daily 9-7. Art gallery Mon.-Fri. 9-5. Pool daily 8-4 (also Mon.-Fri. 6-8 p.m.); closed during swim meets. Museum and art gallery admission $3; over 55, $1; under 12 free; family rate $5. Pool $3; senior citizens, military and students with ID $1. Parking $1 per hour. Phone (954) 462-6536, or (954) 828-4580 for the pool.

SAVE MUSEUM OF ART, 1 E. Las Olas Blvd., features a permanent collection of 20th-century European and American art including works by Moore, Picasso, Stella and Warhol. The museum also contains an extensive collection of American Impressionist William Glackens' works as well as art from the CoBrA movement and important African, South Pacific and contemporary Cuban art. Photography and videotaping are not permitted.

(continued on page 74)

The Informed Traveler

City Population: 152,397

Elevation: 7 ft.

Sales Tax: The sales tax in Broward County is 6 percent. A tourist development tax of 5 percent is levied on rental accommodations.

WHOM TO CALL

Emergency: 911

Police (non-emergency): (954) 828-5700; sheriff (954) 765-4321.

Fire: (954) 828-6800

Time and Temperature: (954) 748-4444

Hospitals: Broward General Medical Center, (954) 355-4400; Imperial Point Medical Center, (954) 776-8500.

WHERE TO LOOK

Newspapers

The Fort Lauderdale *Sun Sentinel* is published daily. The daily *Miami Herald* is available throughout the city. Many weekly publications supplement these papers.

Radio

Fort Lauderdale radio station WINZ (940 AM) is an all-news/weather station; WLRN (91.3 FM) is a member of National Public Radio.

Visitor Information

The Greater Fort Lauderdale Chamber of Commerce distributes maps, brochures and a variety of other local information Mon.-Fri. 8-5. For further information contact the chamber at 512 N.E. Third Ave., Fort Lauderdale, FL 33301; phone (954) 462-6000.

The Greater Fort Lauderdale Convention and Visitors Bureau, open Mon.-Fri. 8:30-5, is at 1850 Eller Dr., Suite 303; phone (954) 765-4466 or (800)

356-1662, events hotline (954) 357-5700. The Fort Lauderdale Parks and Recreation events hotline is (954) 828-5363.

TRANSPORTATION

Air Travel

The Fort Lauderdale-Hollywood International Airport is between I-95 and US 1, just south of SR 84. Friendly Checker Cab, (954) 923-2302, provides service to the airport from downtown; the fare is approximately $10.

Rental Cars

Hertz, 3030 Holiday Dr. in Marriott Harbor Beach Hotel, (800) 654-3080, and at the airport, (954) 764-1199 or (800) 654-3080, offers discounts to AAA members. Many car rental agencies are listed in the telephone directory.

Rail Service

The Amtrak station is at 200 S.W. 21st Terr. For arrival information phone (954) 587-6692; for reservations and other information phone (800) 872-7245.

Buses

The bus terminal serving the city is Greyhound Lines Inc., 515 N.E. Third St.; phone (954) 764-6551, or (800) 231-2222 for schedule and rate information.

Taxis

Cabs are plentiful. Fares are metered and are $2.75 for the first mile and $2 for each additional mile. The largest company is Yellow Cab, (954) 565-5400; consult the telephone directory for others.

Public Transport

Broward County Transit, (954) 357-8400, provides transportation to all sections of Fort Lauderdale and its outlying areas. Buses also are available between the downtown area and the beach. Free shuttle buses operate downtown on weekdays; for information phone (954) 761-3543.

Destination Ft. Lauderdale

*C*asual and laid-back.
Sophisticated and energetic.
Contradictory terms, but all
appropriate for describing
Fort Lauderdale.

*B*reezy resortwear is perfect
for a day at the beach, a
riverfront stroll or a museum
visit. Or indulge in a little
haute couture, fast-paced jai alai or
Thoroughbred action. Set
your own style and pace in
Fort Lauderdale.

Hendricks Isle waterways, Fort Lauderdale.
Sleek white sailboats serenely sandwiched
between sky and water reflect the dreams
of owners and visitors alike.

*Fort Lauderdale
skyline.*
Legions of high-
rise lodgings seem
to parade down
Fort Lauderdale's
beachfront.

*I.G.F.A. Fishing Hall
of Fame & Museum,
Dania Beach.*
This soaring sword-
fish greets anglers
making their way to
celebrate the sport of
game fishing. (See
listing page 77)

See Vicinity
map page 74

*P*laces included in this AAA Destination City:

Coconut Creek......77	Deerfield Beach.....78
Coral Springs.......77	Hallandale Beach...78
Dania Beach.........77	Hollywood............78
Davie.................77	Pompano Beach.....78

Flamingo Gardens, Davie.
Strutting his stuff and spreading his
splendor, this peacock's finery far
outshines that of his feathered friends.
(See listing page 77)

Allow 2 hours minimum. Tues.-Sat. 10-5, Sun. noon-5; closed holidays. Admission $10; over 64, $8; students ages 19-25 with ID and ages 10-18, $6. Parking is available for a fee in nearby City Garage. An additional fee may be charged for special exhibits. Phone (954) 525-5500.

SAVE MUSEUM OF DISCOVERY AND SCIENCE AND BLOCKBUSTER IMAX THEATER, 401 S.W. Second St., is a hands-on science center featuring seven interactive exhibit areas. Gizmo City offers visitors a chance to play virtual volleyball and explore the Internet. Florida EcoScapes, focusing on the state's native ecology, has live sea turtles, sharks, alligators and an Atlantic coral reef. The Discovery Center offers a scientific playground for young children, while Space Base features a manned maneuvering unit (MMU) ride that simulates a space flight.

No Place Like Home is a cutaway of a house designed to explore issues of construction and conservation. The Sound exhibit illustrates the principles of sound and hearing. Choose Health presents the facts about nutrition, drugs and the human body.

The Great Gravity Clock is a 52-foot-tall kinetic energy sculpture. Traveling exhibits also are featured. The 300-seat Blockbuster IMAX Theater presents films on a five-story screen; headsets enhance the experience. Food is available.

Allow 2 hours minimum. Mon.-Sat. 10-5, Sun. noon-6; closed Thanksgiving and Dec. 25. IMAX shows are presented daily; schedule varies with each film. Museum admission (includes exhibits and one IMAX show) $14; over 64 and students with ID $13; ages 3-12, $12. Museum or theater admission only $9; over 64 and students with ID $8; ages 3-12, $7. Metered parking is available. AX, MC, VI. Phone (954) 467-6637 for museum or (954) 463-4629 for theater.

OLD FORT LAUDERDALE MUSEUM OF HISTORY, 231 S.W. Second Ave., presents exhibitions of artifacts from prehistoric times to the present. The changing exhibits, archives and library offer information about local and regional history. Guided tours, which include the 1907 King-Cromartie House, a museum of pioneer lifestyles, are available. Allow 1 hour minimum. Tues.-Sun. noon-5; closed Jan. 1, Easter, Thanksgiving and Dec. 25. Tours are given Tues.-Fri. on the hour 1-4. Admission (includes guided tour) $5; ages 6-16, $3. Admission (includes tours of museum and King-Cromartie House) $8; ages 6-16, $5. Phone (954) 463-4431.

RIVERWALK, downtown, is a meandering promenade through lush tropical landscaping along the New River. The walkway links attractions, arts and cultural institutions, restaurants and shops. Riverboat cruises are available and evening entertainment is offered year-round. Esplanade Park features an interactive scientific display with a lawn area which contains a human sundial in its center, and "whisper dishes"—satellite-like dishes that amplify whispered messages from 25 feet away. Daily 24 hours. Free. Phone (954) 468-1541.

SAWGRASS RECREATION PARK is 2 mi. n. of jct. I-75 at 5400 US 27N. Thirty-minute airboat tours of the Everglades feature an environmental and historical narration. Guides point out native flora and fauna; alligators sometimes can be seen. Tour guides explain tribal customs and history as visitors are led through a replica of a typical 18th-century Seminole Indian village with clothing, musical instruments and other tribal artifacts. Snakes and alligators are displayed in separate exhibit areas. Fishing guides and boat rentals are available.

Daily 9-5. Admission $15.65; over 60, $14.08; ages 4-12, $7.65. AX, DS, MC, VI. Phone (954) 389-0202, (954) 426-2474 or (800) 457-0788.

SAVE STRANAHAN HOUSE is at Las Olas Blvd. and S.E. Sixth Ave. Owned by one of Fort Lauderdale's founding families, this 1901 building has served as a trading post, restaurant and private home. Guided tours are available. Events are held throughout the year. Allow 30 minutes minimum. Wed.-Sat. 10-4, Sun. 1-4; closed major holidays.

Guided tours are given on the hour. Last tour begins 1 hour before closing. Admission $5; under 12, $2. Phone (954) 524-4736.

What To Do

Sightseeing

Boat Tours

Discovery Cruise Line, departing Port Everglades, offers day-long cruises to Freeport, Grand Bahama Island, where, for additional fees, visitors can scuba or snorkel, fish or golf, or just shop and eat. Food, a sun deck and swimming pool, casino gambling and entertainment are featured aboard ship. Departures daily at 8 a.m., with return arrival at 10:30 p.m. Mon.-Sat., at 9:30 p.m. Sunday; phone to confirm schedule. United States and Canadian citizens must carry proof of citizenship, such as a passport or original birth certificate. Phone (800) 937-4477 in Fla. or (800) 866-8687 out of Fla.

Sightseeing cruises along the Intracoastal Waterway and the New River are available aboard the Water Taxi. The taxis also offer transportation to restaurants, hotels, shops and attractions. For schedules and information phone (954) 467-6677.

JUNGLE QUEEN RIVERBOAT CRUISE, s. side of Bahia-Mar Yacht Basin on SR A1A, offers a 3-hour sightseeing cruise along the New River past luxurious homes and downtown Fort Lauderdale. Dinner/entertainment cruises also are available. Sightseeing cruises depart daily at 10 and 2; closed Dec. 25. Three-hour fare $12.95; ages 2-10, $8.75. Reservations are required. Phone (954) 462-5596. *See color ad.*

RIVERFRONT CRUISES, New River dock at Las Olas Riverfront Marketplace, 1 blk. w. of Andrews Ave., offers a 90-minute cruise along the New River and Intracoastal Waterway to the mansion-lined canals nicknamed "The Venice of America." Cruises depart daily at 10:30, 12:30, 2:30, 4:30, 6:30 and 8:30 (also Sat.-Sun. at 10:30 p.m.). Fare $14; ages 4-10, $8. AX, MC, VI. Phone (954) 267-3699.

Sports and Recreation

Fort Lauderdale has a public beach and excellent inland and ocean **fishing** waters. Many species of fish are caught in the "inside" waters. The Everglades and deep-sea fishing rank with the best in Florida. Fishing boats can be rented at Bahia-Mar and Pier 66. Area piers are good spots for fishing; bait, tackle and food are available.

Boating is another popular sport. There are numerous canals to be explored, and sailing around the barrier islands is a favorite pastime. Most marinas rent boats.

Scuba diving is rewarding along three lines of reefs, where clear water permits views of sea fans, branched coral and tropical fish. Many firms offer instruction and rental equipment; consult the telephone directory.

Water skiing is popular on the city's protected waterways and canals. Instruction is offered by the McGinnis School, 2421 S.W. 46th Ave., (954) 321-0221, and Ski-Rixen at Quiet Waters Park in Deerfield Beach, (954) 360-1315.

The Broward County Brian Piccolo Velodrome in nearby Cooper City consists of two tracks: one for competitive **bicycle racing** and one for recreational riding and **in-line skating**; phone (954) 437-2626.

The Broward County Parks system includes 15 regional parks, 35 neighborhood parks and more than 20 natural areas for outdoor recreation. In addition, community centers offer activities ranging from bridge for beginners to instruction in shellcraft. For more information, phone the Parks and Recreation Department at (954) 357-8100.

The Baltimore Orioles head south each year for **baseball** spring training in Fort Lauderdale; phone (954) 776-1921. **Hockey** comes to sunny South Florida in October when the Florida Panthers of the National Hockey League take to the ice at National Car Rental Center in Sunrise; phone (954) 835-7000, or (954) 835-8326 for tickets.

Golf in the area is excellent. Most courses are semiprivate, with play governed by local regulations. Many hotels have agreements allowing guests to play on certain courses; check with your hotel manager.

Tennis is popular throughout the area; many hotels and motels have their own courts. Supplementing these are the public courts at George English Park, 1101 Bayview Dr., (954) 396-3620; Jimmy Everett Tennis Center, 701 N.E. 12th Ave., (954) 828-5378; and Joseph C. Carter Park, 1450 W. Sunrise Blvd., (954) 828-5411.

Shopping

Broward County shopping is diverse and plentiful. The two-story SAVE Galleria, 2414 E. Sunrise Blvd., features 150 shops including anchors Burdines, Dillard's, Neiman Marcus and Saks Fifth Avenue. In nearby Plantation are SAVE Broward Mall, University Drive and Broward Boulevard, and Fashion Mall at Plantation, 321 N. University Dr.

Offerings in the western suburbs include Coral Square Mall, 9469 W. Atlantic Blvd. in Coral Springs, and SAVE Pembroke Lakes Mall, 11401 Pines Blvd. in Pembroke Pines. South of the city is Oakwood Plaza, 2900 Oakwood Blvd. in Hollywood.

The shops along Las Olas Boulevard between Federal Highway and the beach offer a unique experience. Specialty shops line US 1 at both the north and south entrances to the city.

More than 400 outlet stores, including many upscale and high-fashion retailers, comprise SAVE Sawgrass Mills, 12801 W. Sunrise Blvd. in Sunrise.

True bargain hunters may enjoy the Swap Shop, 3291 W. Sunrise Blvd. The 80-acre flea market features more than 2,000 vendors with wares ranging from brand-name electronics to antiques.

Theater and Concerts

Broward Center for the Performing Arts, 201 S.W. Fifth Ave. on the New River, is the setting for events including ballet, opera, Broadway shows, children's theater and concerts; phone (954) 522-5334 or (954) 462-0222.

Parker Playhouse, in Holiday Park at US 1 and N.E. Eighth Street, offers Broadway shows; phone (954) 763-2444.

War Memorial Auditorium, at 800 N.E. Eighth St. in Holiday Park, seats 2,100 people. Plays, operas, concerts, sports events and exhibitions are presented throughout the year; phone (954) 828-5380.

Broward County supports an opera company, symphony orchestra and ballet, as well as other dance and musical programs. For performance information contact the Arts and Entertainment Hotline, (954) 357-5700, or (800) 249-2787 out of Fla.

Special Events

During January and March artists from across North America show their efforts at the Las Olas Art Fair. Canada Fest and Florida Renaissance Festival are held during February. In mid-February the Seminole Tribal Fair takes place in nearby Hollywood.

March brings the Florida Derby, a thoroughbred racing event at Gulfstream Park in Hallandale Beach. The Fort Lauderdale Spring Boat Show and the Fort Lauderdale Seafood Festival are held in April.

The 2-day Fort Lauderdale Air & Sea Show, featuring demonstrations of military and civilian aircraft along 4 miles of the city's beachfront, takes place in early May. Beginning at 5 p.m. the third Friday in May, the 3-day consumer show and celebration Ocean Fest draws more than 200 exhibitors to Lauderdale-By-The-Sea for diving, treasure hunts, entertainment and seafood. The Pompano Fishing Rodeo and the Cajun/Zydeco Crawfish Festival also are in May.

In July the Florida Philharmonic presents Beethoven by the Beach; the music festival also features lectures and dramatic presentations.

The Riverwalk Fall Arts Show takes place in October at Los Olas Riverfront. The Fort Lauderdale International Boat Show is held in late October and early November. During the Fort Lauderdale International Film Festival in November celebrities flock to town to preview films from around the globe.

Also in November is the Sound Advice Blues Festival, a 2-day event featuring local and nationally known blues artists in the Fort Lauderdale Stadium; and the Hollywood Jazz Festival. Mid-November through January Tradewinds Park dresses up for the Holiday Fantasy of Lights.

On a mid-December Saturday yachts at Port Everglades don holiday lights in preparation for a night's cruise up the Intracoastal Waterway—the spectacular and festive Winterfest Boat Parade. For further event information phone (954) 767-0686.

DID YOU KNOW

Although Stephen Foster wrote about life "way down upon the Suwanee River" in his famous song, he saw neither the river nor even the state in which it flows.

The Fort Lauderdale Vicinity

COCONUT CREEK (G-11)
pop. 29,200, elev. 17'

BUTTERFLY WORLD, in Tradewinds Park South at 3600 W. Sample Rd., includes a breeding laboratory, a butterfly museum and an insectarium with displays of unusual insects and butterflies from around the world. Also featured are a botanical vine walk and an English rose garden. Two-story aviaries present gardens and a simulated tropical rain forest in which butterflies live restricted only by the buildings' screen construction.

Allow 1 hour minimum. Mon.-Sat. 9-5, Sun. 1-5; closed Easter, Thanksgiving and Dec. 25. Last admission 1 hour before closing. Admission $14.95; ages 4-12, $9.95. Park entrance fee on weekends and holidays $1 per person. AX, MC, VI. Phone (954) 977-4400.

CORAL SPRINGS (G-11) pop. 117,549

SAVE **CORAL SPRINGS MUSEUM OF ART,** off SR 868 exit 8, 1.5 mi. e. on Sample Rd., then .5 mi. s. to 2855 Coral Springs Dr., displays paintings, sculpture and mixed-media works by local and regional artists. Allow 1 hour minimum. Tues.-Sat. 10-5, Sun. noon-5. Admission $3, under 18 free; free to all Wed. AX, MC, VI. Phone (954) 340-5000.

DANIA BEACH (G-12) pop. 13,000, elev. 11'

Dania Beach is a winter beach resort. Jai-alai is played year-round at Dania Jai-Alai Fronton on Dania Beach Boulevard, one-half mile east of US 1; for schedule phone (954) 927-2841.

Note: Policies vary concerning admittance of children to pari-mutuel betting facilities. Phone for information.

Shopping areas: Antique hunters will find remembrances of early Americana in the shops along Federal Highway. Bass Pro Shops Outdoor World, jct. I-95 and Griffin Rd. at 200 Gulf Stream Way, features an indoor waterfall and 33,000-gallon aquarium, wildlife exhibits and sporting demonstrations.

GEM **I.G.F.A. FISHING HALL OF FAME & MUSEUM,** off I-95 exit 23, w. on Griffin Rd. (SR 818) to Anglers Ave., then s. to 300 **SAVE** Gulfstream Way, features a tackle gallery, a re-created saltwater marsh and wetland including alligators and turtles, a children's Discovery Room and an 18-minute film. Interactive fishing simulator stations demonstrate the effort required to reel in various species.

Allow 2 hours minimum. Daily 10-6; closed Thanksgiving and Dec. 25. Admission $4.99; over 61, $4.49; ages 4-12, $3.99. AX, DS, MC, VI. Phone (954) 922-4212.

SAVE **SOUTH FLORIDA MUSEUM OF NATURAL HISTORY,** 2.5 mi. e. of I-95 exit 21 on SR 822 (Sheridan St.), then .7 mi. n. on US 1 (Federal Hwy.) to 481 S. Federal Hwy., features a wide array objects. Exhibits deal with dinosaurs; paleontology; minerals; the geology, history and first inhabitants of Florida; shipwrecks and marine archeology; African, Egyptian and Mediterranean cultures; and pre-Columbian ceramics. Karabuni! Discover Africa portrays the relationship between animals and culture, while offering hands-on activities for children. Silk to Samurai explores Asian cultures.

Allow 2 hours minimum. Tues.-Sat. 10-4 (also Sat. 4-6), Sun. noon-6. Admission $9.95; over 65, $8; students with ID $7; ages 4-12, $6. AX, MC, VI. Phone (954) 925-7770.

DAVIE (G-11) pop. 75,720, elev. 5'

BUEHLER PLANETARIUM & OBSERVATORY, on the A. Hughes Adams central campus of Broward Community College, 1 mi. s. of I-595 at 3501 S.W. Davie Rd., offers programs with time and space themes. Allow 1 hour minimum. Main features Fri.-Sat. at 7 p.m. Family features Sat.-Sun. at 1:30 and 3. Star show Wed. at 7 p.m. Phone for Wed. afternoon show schedule. Free sky observing Wed. and Fri.-Sat. 8-10 p.m. Doors to the shows close on time. Main feature tickets $5; family show tickets $4. Star show ticket $2. For information phone (954) 201-6681.

SAVE **FLAMINGO GARDENS,** w. on I-595 to exit 2, then 3 mi. s. to 3750 S. Flamingo Rd., contains trees and plants indigenous to subtropical forests throughout the world. The gardens are home to river otters, alligators, flamingos, American bald eagles and other birds of prey. A 1.5-acre Everglades free-flight aviary features plants from five ecosystems and a large collection of wading birds. Visitors may walk through a tropical jungle or take a 25-minute narrated tram tour through citrus groves, native oak hammocks and the Wray Botanical Gardens. Wildlife shows are presented several times daily.

Allow 2 hours, 30 minutes minimum. Daily 9:30-5:30, Oct.-May; Tues.-Sun. 9:30-5:30, rest of year. Tram tours depart on the hour 11-4. Admission $12; over 65, students and military with ID $9.60; ages 4-11, $6. Tram tour $3; ages 4-11, $2. Phone (954) 473-2955.

SAVE **YOUNG AT ART CHILDREN'S MUSEUM** is off I-595 exit 2 (Hiatus Rd.), then just s. to 11584 W. SR 84. Geared to children 2-11, this hands-on museum includes a recycled-arts center where kids make sculptures from donated materials, a painting center, multicultural "village" and toddler play area. Mon.-Sat. 10-5, Sun. noon-5. Admission $4; over 60, $3.50; under 2 free. MC, VI. Phone (954) 424-0085.

DEERFIELD BEACH (G-12)
pop. 64,583, elev. 16'

QUIET WATERS COUNTY PARK, 401 S. Power-line Rd., is 2 mi. w. from I-95 via SR 810 (Hills-boro Blvd.), then .2 mi. s. on SR 845 (Powerline Rd.). Within its 430 acres this water-oriented park offers canoeing, paddleboating, freshwater fishing, swimming, camping, picnicking, bicycling and a mechanical water ski tow. A fishing license may be required for over 16 years of age. For tow schedule and prices phone (954) 429-0215. Daily 8-7:30, last Sun. in Apr.-last Sat. in Oct.; 8-6, rest of year. Park admission Mon.-Fri. free; Sat.-Sun. and holidays $1 for vehicle driver and per passenger over age 4. Phone (954) 360-1315. *See Recreation Chart.*

HALLANDALE BEACH (H-12)
pop. 31,000, elev. 10'

Primarily a retirement community, Hallandale Beach is the home of Gulfstream Park and the Hol-lywood Greyhound Dog Track. The dog track pre-sents races December through May; phone (954) 924-3200. Gulfstream Park, at US 1 and Hallandale Beach Boulevard, is open for horse racing from early January to mid-March; phone (954) 454-7000.

Note: Policies vary concerning admittance of children to pari-mutuel betting facilities. Phone for information.

HOLLYWOOD (G-12) pop. 139,357, elev. 7'

A resort and residential city between Fort Lau-derdale and Miami, Hollywood is bordered with palm-lined ocean beaches. The city's redeveloped downtown sports an Art Deco touch. Free evening entertainment is offered throughout the year at Young Circle Park amphitheater, downtown, and at the Beach Theater bandshell, on the Hollywood Beach Boardwalk.

The Hollywood Playhouse presents musicals, comedies and dramas October through June; phone (954) 922-0404.

Greater Hollywood Chamber of Commerce: 330 N. Federal Hwy., Hollywood, FL 33020; phone (954) 923-4000 or (800) 231-5562.

ANN KOLB NATURE CENTER is off I-95 exit 21, then 2.8 mi. e. to 751 Sheridan St. The center has nature trails, interactive bird-call displays and an observation tower overlooking a mangrove estuary. An exhibit hall houses a research center and three aquariums. Allow 1 hour minimum. Park open daily 8-7:30, Apr.-Oct.; 8-6, rest of year. Exhibit hall open daily 9-5. Admission $2; ages 6-12, $1.50. Phone (954) 926-2415.

ART AND CULTURE CENTER OF HOLLYWOOD, 1650 Harrison St., is a multidisciplinary art center that presents contemporary visual art exhibits, the-ater performances, lectures, cultural and educational programs and workshops. Allow 1 hour minimum. Galleries open Tues.-Sat. 10-4 (also Thurs. 4-8), Sun. 1-4; closed holidays. Admission $5. Phone (954) 921-3275 for performance information.

POMPANO BEACH (G-12)
pop. 78,191, elev. 13'

Settled in 1880 and named for a local fish, Pom-pano Beach is known for its abundant sunshine and variety of recreational opportunities. Tourism be-came the city's focus in the 1920s after the Dixie Highway was completed. Warmed by the Gulf Stream, Pompano Beach is a popular resort. The city has approximately 20 parks, many of which of-fer tennis, softball, fishing and swimming.

Horse racing takes place at Pompano Park Rac-ing, west of I-95 on Powerline Road (Race Track Road), October through August; phone (954) 972-2000.

Note: Policies vary concerning admittance of children to pari-mutuel betting facilities. Phone for information.

Greater Pompano Beach Chamber of Com-merce: 2200 E. Atlantic Blvd., Pompano Beach, FL 33062; phone (954) 941-2940.

Shopping areas: Pompano Square Mall, 1 Pom-pano Sq. at the corner of Federal Highway and Co-pans Road, counts Burdines, JCPenney and Sears among its 100 stores. SAVE Festival Flea Market Mall, 2900 W. Sample Rd. in Pompano, offers a farmer's market and more than 800 vendors selling bargains Tuesday through Sunday.

This ends listings for the Fort Lauderdale Vicinity.
The following page resumes the alphabetical listings
of cities in Florida.

Ride our waters free.

All that Greater Fort Lauderdale has to offer is now even better with a $50 voucher* your family can use towards a free Everglades airboat tour, Billie Swamp Buggy Tour, water taxi ride, SeaEscape Cruise, glass bottom boat ride or Jungle Queen Riverboat sightseeing cruise. And with special summer hotel rates, there's never been a better time to immerse yourself.

Call 800-22-SUNNY or visit www.sunny.org

Yes! Please send me free Greater Fort Lauderdale information:

☐ Free list of participating "Ride Our Waters Free" hotels[†]

☐ Free Vacation Planner

☐ Free Superior Small Lodgings Guide

#2A025

Name _____

Address _____

City/State/ZIP _____

Phone _____ E-mail _____

*Coupon valid May 15–September 30, 2003. †Available after May 1, 2003

FREE RIDE COUPON

$50

Upon your 2-night minimum hotel
check-in, May 15 - September 30, 2003
present this $50 free ride coupon
for validation*

LAS OLAS

*One voucher per room for use May 15 - September 30, 2003.
Valid with original coupon only at participating hotels.
Not valid with any other offers.

immerse yourself
GREATER FORT LAUDERDALE

Call 800-22-SUNNY or visit www.sunny.org

From a reader of AAA TourBook 2003 (105)

Name _____

Address _____

City/State/ZIP _____

Greater Fort Lauderdale
Convention & Visitors Bureau
P.O. Box 1
Hollywood, Florida 33022

FORT MATANZAS NATIONAL MONUMENT (B-10)

Off SR A1A 14 miles south of St. Augustine, Fort Matanzas National Monument includes the southern tip of Anastasia Island and the northern third of Rattlesnake Island. There is ferry service to the fort from which the monument took its name every hour on the half hour daily 9:30-4:30; to determine if the ferry is operating phone (904) 471-0116. The fort can be seen from the dock on Anastasia Island.

Built of coquina 1740-42 by the Spaniards, Fort Matanzas replaced temporary watch stations that had guarded the southern approach to St. Augustine since 1569. During the 16th century French Huguenots established bases in the area, threatening the Spaniards with territorial encroachment and what the latter considered to be religious heresy. The fort became United States property in 1821.

In 1565 Pedro Menéndez de Avilés set up his headquarters at what later became known as St. Augustine; in a hurricane which scattered the French ships, he captured the enemy base about 35 miles north of St. Augustine. Upon returning to St. Augustine, Menéndez located the shipwrecked survivors of the French fleet some 14 miles south of town, where most of them surrendered and were killed. This engagement led the Spaniards to christen it the site of *matanzas*, or "slaughters."

A small visitor center on Anastasia Island contains exhibits pertaining to the fort's history. Swimming east of SR A1A at Matanzas Inlet is dangerous because of the currents. Grounds open daily 8:30-5:30. Visitor center open daily 9-4:30. Closed Dec. 25. Free. Phone (904) 471-0116.

FORT MYERS (G-9) pop. 48,208, elev. 9′

Majestic royal palms line the streets of Fort Myers, a city with more than 70 varieties of palms and a profusion of exotic flowers and tropical fruit. March through early April Fort Myers is the spring training home of the Boston Red Sox and the Minnesota Twins. The Red Sox play exhibition games at City of Palms Park, 2201 Edison Ave.; phone (239) 334-4700. The Twins play their games at Lee County Sports Complex off Daniels Road and Six Mile Cypress; phone (239) 768-4270 or (800) 338-9467.

Another sporting option is the Florida Everblades, who play their East Coast Hockey League home games at Everblades Arena, at I-75 exit 123 (Corkscrew Road); phone (239) 948-7825. The hockey season is mid-October through April.

The City Yacht Basin area is the town's boating center. Boating is popular on the Caloosahatchee River; a tropical cruise leaves from the yacht basin regularly.

Greater Fort Myers Chamber of Commerce: 2310 Edwards Dr., P.O. Box 9289, Fort Myers, FL 33902; phone (239) 332-3624 or (800) 366-3622.

Shopping areas: Edison Mall, 4125 Cleveland Ave. (US 41), features Burdines, Dillard's, JCPenney and Sears among its 155 stores. Bell Tower Shops, 13499 US 41 S.E., includes Saks Fifth Avenue and upscale boutiques. Royal Palm Square, 1400 Colonial Blvd., offers many boutiques and restaurants. Outlet shoppers will find more than 55 stores at SAVE Tanger Sanibel Factory Stores, between McGregor Boulevard and Summerlin Road. More than 100 shops, including Brooks Brothers, Polo Ralph Lauren and Tommy Hilfiger, can be found at Miromar Outlets, I-75 and Corkscrew Road (exit 123).

BURROUGHS HOME, Fowler and First sts. (SR 80) at 2505 First St., is a riverside home built in

1901 for a wealthy businessman. Of Georgian Revival architecture, the three-story home is furnished with original family pieces. Tour guides portray characters from the history of Fort Myers. Allow 30 minutes minimum. Tours are given on request Tues.-Fri. 11-3, Oct.-May; by appointment only, rest of year. Guided tour $6; ages 6-12, $3. Self-guiding tour $4. Free parking is available at the adjacent Ramada Inn. Phone (239) 332-6125.

[SAVE] **CALUSA NATURE CENTER AND PLANETARIUM** is .5 mi. w. of I-75 exit 136 on SR 884, then n. to 3450 Ortiz Ave. In addition to being home to snakes, turtles, alligators and crocodiles, the center offers a learning area for children, nature trails, an aviary, a reproduction of a Seminole Indian village and planetarium shows.

Allow 2 hours, 30 minutes minimum. Nature center open Mon.-Sat. 9-5, Sun. 11-5; closed Jan. 1, July 4, Labor Day, Thanksgiving and Dec. 25. Planetarium open Fri.-Sun. Planetarium show schedule varies; phone ahead. Admission $5; ages 3-12, $3. Planetarium show $3; ages 3-12, $2. MC, VI. Phone (239) 275-3435.

ECHO is off I-75 exit 143, then 1 mi. e. on SR 78, then n. to 17391 Durrance Rd. ECHO, Educational Concerns for Hunger Organization, is a 45-acre farm demonstrating tropical food plants and techniques useful to farmers and urban gardeners in developing countries. The Global Village is divided into separate areas that represent urban gardens, a rain forest clearing, semi-arid land, hillside farming and tropical lowlands.

Appropriate technologies demonstrated include biogas, turning cow manure into gas for cooking and lighting; a sawdust cooker; and a solar food dryer. Zebu cattle, tropical sheep, goats, turken chickens, ducks, tilapia fish and rabbits also are on the farm. Unusual gardening techniques exhibit the capacity to grow food in unusual locations. The farm is open only by guided tour.

Allow 1 hour, 30 minutes minimum. Edible Landscape Nursery open Mon.-Sat. 9-noon; closed holidays. Guided farm tours are given Tues.-Sat. at 10, Jan.-Mar.; Tues. and Fri.-Sat. at 10, rest of year. Donations. Phone (239) 543-3246.

EDISON-FORD WINTER ESTATES, 1 mi. s.w. on SR 867 at 2350 McGregor Blvd., contains the adjacent winter homes of two of America's most famous early 20th-century industrialists. Another highlight is a banyan tree said to be the largest in the continental United States, a 1925 gift from Harvey Firestone to Thomas Edison. Admission is only by guided tour. A replica of the *Reliance,* Edison's battery-powered boat, offers cruises on the Caloosahatchee River.

Guided 90-minute estate tours depart continuously Mon.-Sat. 9-4, Sun. noon-4; closed Thanksgiving and Dec. 25. River cruises depart every 30 minutes Mon.-Fri. 9-3:30 (weather permitting). Admission (includes both estates) $12; ages 6-12, $6.

River cruise $4. MC, VI. Phone (239) 334-3614. *See color ad p. 81.*

Henry Ford Winter Home has been restored and furnished in the style of the 1920s, using photographs and records of the house. Bought by Ford in 1916 because of its proximity to his good friend Edison, this winter residence of the world's first billionaire features grounds planted with citrus, bamboo and tropical foliage. A garage houses three antique cars in operating condition. Allow 1 hour minimum. *See color ad p. 81.*

Thomas A. Edison's Winter Home is where the inventor spent his "working vacations" from 1886 until his death in 1931. Here he perfected such earlier inventions as the incandescent light bulb, the phonograph, the motion picture camera and the storage battery. He also cultivated a 14-acre tropical garden. Tours include the furnished home, a guest house, the laboratory and workshops, a museum containing a large collection of his inventions and the garden. Allow 1 hour, 30 minutes minimum. *See color ad p. 81.*

[SAVE] **FORT MYERS HISTORICAL MUSEUM** is 1.5 mi. e. of US 41 on Dr. Martin Luther King Blvd., then 1 blk. s. on Jackson to 2300 Peck St. In a restored railroad depot, artifacts depict the history of Fort Myers and southwest Florida, focusing on Calusa and Seminole Indian cultures, Spanish exploration and early settlers. Also displayed is *The Esperanza,* the longest and the last-built Pullman private railroad car. Tues.-Sat. 9-4; closed holidays. Admission $6; over 65, $5.50; ages 3-11, $3. MC, VI. Phone (239) 332-5955.

[SAVE] **IMAGINARIUM HANDS-ON MUSEUM,** 2000 Cranford Ave., contains more than 60 interactive exhibits that allow visitors to explore Southwest Florida's environment as well as topics such as physics, anatomy and the weather. An outdoor area offers walking paths and a lagoon with koi, while aquariums are indoor diversions.

Allow 1 hour, 30 minutes minimum. Mon.-Sat. 10-5, Sun. noon-5; closed Thanksgiving and Dec. 25. Admission $7; over 55, $6.50; ages 3-12, $4. Under 13 must be with an adult. DS, MC, VI. Phone (239) 337-3332.

J.C. SIGHTSEEING BOAT CRUISES, at the foot of Lee St. at the Fort Myers Yacht Basin, offers jungle cruises aboard 80-passenger *The Wofford* and several other cruises, including lunch and dinner cruises, aboard the triple-decked, 600-passenger paddlewheeler *The Capt. J.P.* The boats take passengers by historic sites and lush wooded areas. Exotic birds, manatees, alligators and other tropical fauna can be seen in their native habitat.

Allow 2 hours minimum. Jungle cruises depart Tues.-Thurs. at 10 and 2, Sun.-Mon. and Fri. at 2, Nov.-Apr.; Tues. and Thurs. at 10, Sun. at 2, rest of year. Day and evening cruises aboard the *Capt. J.P.* available daily, late Oct.-April 15. Schedule may

vary; phone ahead. Arrive 30 minutes before departure. Fares for *Capt. J.P.* $15-$76; ages 3-11, $9-$39. Jungle cruise $12; ages 3-11, $6. Reservations are required. MC, VI. Phone (239) 334-7474.

LEE COUNTY MANATEE PARK, off I-75 exit 141, then 1.5 mi. e. to 10901 SR 80, features observation platforms on a canal where manatees sometimes congregate during cooler winter months. Prime viewing season extends November through mid-March; phone ahead for recorded updates. A boardwalk and trail system wind through native plant habitats and a butterfly garden. Pets are not permitted.

Allow 1 hour minimum. Grounds daily 8-8, Apr.-Sept.; 8-5, rest of year. Manatee program daily at 11 and 2, Nov.-Mar. Guided habitat walks are given Sat. at 9, Apr.-Oct. Admission free. Parking 75c per hour, maximum $3. Phone (239) 694-3537.

SEMINOLE GULF RAILWAY departs from Colonial Station, 3.5 mi. w. of I-75 exit 136 on Colonial Blvd. The 105-minute RiverRail Explorer excursion travels north to the Caloosahatchee trestle and back in vintage coaches while a narrator recounts information about railroad history, animals and plant life. Three-hour murder mystery dinner trips also are available year-round.

Sightseeing trips depart Wed. and Sat. at 10 and 12:15, Sun. at 12:15, Dec.-Aug.; closed holidays. Sightseeing fare $13.95; ages 3-12, $8.95; family rate (two adults and two children ages 3-12) $29.95. DS, MC, VI. Phone (239) 275-8487 or (800) 736-4853.

SIX MILE CYPRESS SLOUGH PRESERVE is 4 mi. w. of I-75 exit 21 on Daniels Pkwy., then 1.8 mi. n. on Ben Pratt-Six Mile Cypress Pkwy. While walking along a milelong boardwalk trail visitors can explore the wetland and observe such inhabitants as turtles, wading birds and alligators. Allow 1 hour minimum. Daily 8-8, Apr.-Sept.; 8-5, rest of year. Tours are given daily at 9:30 and 1:30, Jan.-Mar.; daily at 9:30 in Apr. and Nov.-Dec.; Wed. at 9:30, rest of year. Free. Parking 75c an hour or $3 a day. Phone (239) 432-2004.

FORT MYERS BEACH (G-9)
pop. 6,561, elev. 8′

Fort Myers Beach traces its history from 1513, when Ponce de León passed this way. The town includes Estero Island, San Carlos Island and part of the mainland. Recreational activities include golf, tennis, scuba diving, jet skiing, windsurfing, parasailing and fishing. Full- and half-day charter fishing trips provide opportunities to haul in flounder, trout, mullet, pompano, bluefish, snook and tarpon. The catch from a pier or bridge is likely to be a sheepshead. A ferry service, X-Press to Key West, offers daily 4-hour high-speed trips to Key West aboard a 116-foot vessel (weather permitting); phone (239) 765-0808.

A barrier island on the Gulf of Mexico, Estero Island includes seven miles of white sand beaches.

Lynn Hall Memorial Park, south of Matanzas Pass Bridge, offers a public beach area with picnic facilities and hosts outdoor concerts throughout the year. Next to the park is the public fishing pier, frequented not just by anglers but also by porpoises, pelicans and, of course, sea gulls. On the north end of Estero Island, Bowditch Point Park is accessible by foot, bicycle or trolley. On the south end are Lovers Key State Park *(see Recreation Chart)* and Carl Johnson Park.

To facilitate beach traffic, public transportation is provided for a fee; phone (239) 275-8726.

Greater Fort Myers Beach Area Chamber of Commerce: 17200 San Carlos Blvd., Fort Myers Beach, FL 33931-5306; phone (239) 454-7500 or (800) 782-9283.

FORT PIERCE (E-11) pop. 37,516, elev. 16′

Beef, citrus and vegetables from nearby ranching and farming areas find a market in Fort Pierce, which developed on the site of a U.S. Army post established in 1838 as a defense against the Seminoles. Native trees, flowers and colorful birds can be seen along Indian River Drive, which follows the river's west shore toward Jensen Beach.

The world's fastest ball game can be seen at Fort Pierce Jai-Alai, 1750 S. Kings Hwy. (SR 713). Evening and matinee games are scheduled January through April; phone (772) 464-7500 or (800) 524-2524.

Note: Policies vary concerning admittance of children to pari-mutuel betting facilities. Phone for information.

Ball games of a different kind are played at Thomas J. White Stadium in nearby Port St. Lucie. In early February this stadium becomes the spring training site for the New York Mets, and the St. Lucie Mets play minor league baseball here April through September; for further information phone (772) 871-2100.

The Indian River Community College McAlphin Fine Arts Center presents live performances throughout the year; phone (772) 462-4750.

East of Fort Pierce on SR A1A, Fort Pierce Inlet State Recreation Area includes Jack Island, a bird and wildlife refuge accessible by footbridge, as well as recreational facilities *(see Recreation Chart)*.

St. Lucie County Chamber of Commerce: 2200 Virginia Ave., Fort Pierce, FL 34982; phone (772) 595-9999.

FPL'S ENERGY ENCOUNTER, on Hutchinson Island at 6501 S. Ocean Dr. at the St. Lucie nuclear power plant (Gate B), offers interactive displays and exhibits pertaining to energy, electricity and nuclear power. Highlights include an energy treasure hunt, computer games and a nuclear reactor model. Also at the site is a self-guiding nature trail that winds through three habitats of a coastal barrier island—beach/dune, mangrove and a tropical hammock.

Allow 1 hour minimum. Energy Encounter and nature trail open Sun.-Fri. 10-4; closed holidays. Free. Phone (772) 468-4111 or (877) 375-4386.

SAVE **HARBOR BRANCH OCEANOGRAPHIC INSTITU-TION**, 1 mi. n. on US 1 from jct. SR 614 to 5600 US 1N, then e. to visitor center, is devoted to the research and study of the marine environment. Two tours are available, a 90-minute tour of the campus and a 90-minute lagoon wildlife boat trip around the Indian River lagoon.

Allow 2 hours minimum. Facility tours Mon.-Sat. at 10, noon and 2, Thanksgiving-Easter; noon and 2 rest of year. Boat tours Mon.-Sat. at 10, 1 and 3, Thanksgiving-Easter; at 1 and 3, rest of year. Facility tour $12; ages 6-12, $6. Boat trip $19; ages 6-12, $12. Reservations are suggested for boat trips. AX, MC, VI. Phone (772) 465-2400, ext. 517.

HEATHCOTE BOTANICAL GARDENS, between Virginia Ave. and Edwards Rd. at 210 Savannah Rd., showcases varied gardens, including a Japanese garden with bonsai. Flowers and foliage of the subtropics and rain forest, palm trees and herb gardens also are featured. A self-guiding tour is available. Events are held throughout the year. Allow 1 hour minimum. Tues.-Sat. 9-5, Sun. 1-5, Nov.-Apr.; Tues.-Sat. 9-5, rest of year. Closed major holidays. Admission $3; ages 6-12, $1. Phone (772) 464-4672.

MANATEE OBSERVATION AND EDUCATION CEN-TER, 480 N. Indian River Dr., offers indoor educational displays about manatees, and the fragile Treasure Coast ecosystem, as well as aquariums and displays of live animals. Outdoors, the covered observation walkway and the observation tower offer views of the Indian River and potential sightings of manatees in their natural habitat. A garden planted to attract butterflies also is on the grounds. Allow 30 minutes minimum. Grounds open daily 24 hours. Indoor exhibits open Tues.-Sat. 10-5, Sun. 1-4, Oct.-June; closed Jan. 1, Thanksgiving and Dec. 24-25. Donations. Phone (772) 466-1600, ext. 3071.

ST. LUCIE COUNTY HISTORICAL MUSEUM, 414 Seaway Dr. (S. SR A1A), is at the east end of South Beach Bridge. Spanish shipwreck treasures, artifacts from the 1837 Old Fort Pierce and Seminole relics are displayed. The complex also includes a restored 1919 American LaFrance fire engine, a restored 1907 early Florida home, a memorial garden and changing exhibits. Allow 1 hour minimum. Tues.-Sat. 10-4, Sun. noon-4; closed holidays. Admission $4; over 64, $3.50; ages 6-17, $1.50. Phone (772) 462-1795.

UDT—SEAL MUSEUM, 3 mi. n.e. of US 1 at 3300 N. SR A1A, depicts the history and development of the U.S. Navy's UDTs (Underwater Demolition Teams), SEALs (Sea, Air, Land Teams), Naval Combat Demolition Units, Scouts and Raiders through photographs and artifacts. The collection features weapons, equipment and suits used by UDT and SEAL members. A videotape presentation details the arduous training process. Outdoor displays include small landing craft, a helicopter and Apollo training modules.

Manatees

If you see a manatee while in Florida, both you and the manatee are lucky. You would be lucky to see one of Florida's most endangered animals, and the manatee will be lucky simply to exist. Despite protection efforts, the large gray mammals that inspired the legend of mermaids are threatened by human activity, and their future is uncertain.

Also called sea cows, manatees once ranged from North Carolina to Texas but now live almost exclusively in Florida. In winter they gather in the Crystal and Homosassa rivers, near Sanibel Island and Fort Myers, throughout the tip  of the peninsula and along the St. Johns River. Blue Spring State Park in Orange City is a manatee refuge, and the animals are protected by state and federal law.

Manatees can be 8 to 10 feet long and weigh almost 2,000 pounds. They have round bodies, two front appendages, a large round tail and a square, whiskery snout. Since each eats 50 to 100 pounds of vegetation a day, they act as underwater lawnmowers, helping keep waterways open.

Although they have no natural predators, pollution and development can destroy their habitats. Manatees must be near the surface to breathe, but they have poor eyesight and move too slowly to avoid motorboats, the greatest cause of injury and death. Motorboat propellers kill up to 50 manatees per year.

Females take 2 to 3 years to bear and raise a calf, and the population grows slowly. Manatees are bred in captivity at the Miami Seaquarium in the hope that those calves can be released into the wild to benefit future generations of manatees and humans.

Allow 1 hour minimum. Mon.-Sat. 10-4, Sun. noon-4, Jan.-Apr.; Tues.-Sat. 10-4, Sun. noon-4, rest of year. Closed major holidays. Admission $4; ages 6-11, $1.50. Phone (772) 595-5845.

FORT WALTON BEACH (B-3)
pop. 19,973, elev. 18′

Warm Gulf waters and a wide variety of recreational activities make Fort Walton Beach a popular area for family vacations. The sugar white sand beaches have attracted people since 500 B.C., when various Indian tribes conducted ceremonies in the area.

Just north is Eglin Air Force Base, where Gen. Jimmy Doolittle's "Raiders" trained and which is the headquarters of the Air Force Armament Center and home of the climatic laboratory.

Greater Fort Walton Beach Chamber of Commerce: 34 S.E. Miracle Strip Pkwy., P.O. Box 640, Fort Walton Beach, FL 32549; phone (850) 244-8191.

AIR FORCE ARMAMENT MUSEUM is 6 mi. n. of US 98 on SR 85, just outside Eglin Air Force Base's west gate. The museum exhibits nearly 30 restored aircraft including B-52 and B-17 bombers, a SR-71 Blackbird spy plane, an F-16 jet fighter and a Soviet MiG. The armament collection features missiles, bombs and rockets. Noteworthy among an extensive collection of antique pistols are flintlock dueling pistols and Western six-shooters. A videotape depicts the history and development of Eglin Air Force Base. Daily 9:30-4:30; closed federal holidays. Free. Phone (850) 882-4062.

GULFARIUM, 1 mi. e. on US 98, presents the Living Sea, where sharks, moray eels and sea turtles can be seen in their natural habitat through a glass-enclosed tank. Penguins, otters and alligators are featured in separate exhibits. Live shows present the antics of dolphins and sea lions. Daily 9-dusk; closed Thanksgiving and Dec. 24-25. Shows are given at 10, noon, 2 and 4 (also at 6, May 15-Sept. 15). Admission $16; over 55, $14; ages 4-11, $10. MC, VI. Phone (850) 244-5169.

INDIAN TEMPLE MOUND MUSEUM, 139 Miracle Strip Pkwy., depicts 10,000 years of Indian occupation of the northwest Florida coast as well as the history of European exploration and settlement in the area. The museum houses one of the largest collections of Woodland pottery in the Southeast. The temple mound, next to the museum, is topped by a replica temple. The mound was constructed around 1400 A.D.

Allow 30 minutes minimum. Mon.-Sat. 9-4:30, Sun. 12:30-4:30, June-Aug.; Mon.-Fri. 11-4, Sat. 9-4, rest of year. Admission $2; ages 6-17, $1. Phone (850) 833-9595.

GAINESVILLE (C-8) pop. 95,447, elev. 170′

Gainesville was founded in 1854 and named for Revolutionary War general Edmund Gaines. Both an agricultural and educational center, the community is home to the University of Florida and Santa Fe Community College. A map of the University of Florida campus can be obtained from the AAA office at 1201 N.W. 13th St. or by contacting the university at (352) 392-2241.

Opportunities to observe wildlife and geological formations are within a few miles of town. Four miles northwest on SR 232 is the 6,900-acre San Felasco Hammock Preserve State Park; a nature trail on SR 232 (Millhopper Road) at the I-75 overpass enters the area. Ranger-guided weekend activities are offered October through April. Activities include walks, hikes, overnight trips and classes in wilderness orientation; reservations are required. Phone (386) 462-7905.

In nearby Micanopy *(see place listing p. 127)* is the 20,000-acre Paynes Prairie Preserve State Park *(see Recreation Chart)*. The Gainesville to Hawthorne Rail Trail, a 17-mile trail designed for walking, bicycling and horseback riding, extends from Gainesville's Historic Boulware Springs Park at Paynes Prairie through Lochloosa Wildlife Management Area to the town of Hawthorne. Gainesville Raceway, on CR 225, is where to go for automobile racing.

Most Saturday mornings, and by appointment, guided tours leave from the visitors bureau for a trip to nearby Rosewood, site of the 1923 tragedy in which thirty African-American families were driven from their homes and their village destroyed; phone (800) 250-4645.

Hippodrome State Theatre, one of Florida's four state theaters, offers performances in the original Gainesville Post Office. The theater also offers a cinema series and a gallery which displays the work of local artists.

Alachua County Visitors and Convention Bureau: 30 E. University Ave., Gainesville, FL 32601; phone (352) 374-5231. *See color ad p. 435.*

Shopping areas: Among the 175 stores at Oaks Mall, 6419 Newberry Rd., are Belk Lindsey, Burdines, Dillard's, JCPenney and Sears.

DEVIL'S MILLHOPPER GEOLOGICAL STATE PARK is at 4732 Millhopper Rd. (SR 232), following signs. Measuring 120 feet deep and 500 feet across, this sinkhole formed as early as 10,000 years ago. The area is home to plants and animals normally found in the ravines of the Appalachian Mountains. A half-mile walking path circles the sinkhole while a 232-step wooden walkway descends it. An interpretive center houses exhibits about the natural history of the site as well as an audiovisual presentation about sinkholes. Picnic facilities are available.

Allow 30 minutes minimum. Mon.-Fri. 9-5, Sat.-Sun. 9-dusk, Apr.-Sept.; daily 9-5, rest of year. Guided tours depart Saturday at 10. Admission $2 per private vehicle, $1 per person arriving by bicycle, bus or on foot. Phone (352) 955-2008.

FLORIDA MUSEUM OF NATURAL HISTORY, Hull Rd. and S.W. 34th St. on the University of Florida campus, exhibits include a full-size North Florida limestone cave replica and a 14-foot-tall mammoth skeleton. Allow 1 hour minimum. Mon.-Sat. 10-5, Sun. and holidays 1-5; closed Thanksgiving and Dec. 25. Free. Phone (352) 846-2000.

FRED BEAR MUSEUM, 1 blk. w. of I-75 on Fred Bear Rd. at Archer Rd., features natural history exhibits, archery artifacts, bowhunting trophies and items Fred Bear collected on his bowhunting adventures around the world. The many animals displayed include an elephant, lion, kodiak bear, polar bear, brown bear, American buffalo and moose. Indian, Eskimo and tribal African items can be seen as well as ancient tools, weapons, charms and decorations.

Allow 1 hour minimum. Tues.-Sat. 10-6; closed Jan. 1, Thanksgiving and Dec. 25. Admission $5; senior citizens $4; ages 6-12, $3; family rate (two adults and children under 12) $12. Phone (352) 376-2411.

KANAPAHA BOTANICAL GARDENS is 1 mi. w. off I-75 exit 384 (SR 24) at 4700 S.W. 58th Dr. This 62-acre facility features a 1.5-mile paved walkway through butterfly, hummingbird, vinery, bamboo, wildflower, medicinal herb, palm, carnivorous plant and rock gardens. A water lily pond and ferns also are part of the gardens. Demonstrations of a water reclamation facility are presented. Picnic facilities are available. Pets on leash are permitted. Allow 1 hour minimum. Wed. and Sat.-Sun. 9-dusk, Mon.-Tues. and Fri. 9-5. Admission $5; ages 6-13, $3. Phone (352) 372-4981.

SAMUEL P. HARN MUSEUM OF ART, on the University of Florida campus at jct. S.W. 34th St. and Hull Rd., houses a diverse collection of art from varied cultures of the Americas, Asia, Africa and Europe. Permanent exhibits include American paintings, contemporary art and art from West Africa. Changing exhibits also are displayed. Allow 1 hour minimum. Tues.-Fri. 11-5, Sat. 10-5, Sun. 1-5; closed state holidays. Guided tours are given Wed. at 12:30, Sat.-Sun. at 2. Last admission 15 minutes before closing. Free. Phone (352) 392-9826.

UNIVERSITY GALLERY is in the College of Fine Arts at the University of Florida at the intersection of S.W. 13th St. and 4th Ave. The gallery displays contemporary and experimental art, with an emphasis on the works of emerging, mid-career and senior artists. Allow 1 hour minimum. Tues.-Fri. 10-5 (also Tues. 5-8), Sat. 1-5; closed holidays. Free. Phone (352) 392-0201.

GULF BREEZE (B-3) pop. 5,665, elev. 14′

Incorporating miles of bays and lagoons near Pensacola, this peninsula is 1 mile from the Gulf of Mexico. Surrounded by water on three sides, it's a haven for water lovers and offers a variety of recreational activities including swimming, boating, sailing, fishing, diving and golfing.

Gulf Breeze Area Chamber of Commerce: 409 Gulf Breeze Pkwy., P.O. Box 337, Gulf Breeze, FL 32562; phone (850) 932-7888.

THE ZOO, 8 mi. e. on US 98 at 5701 Gulf Breeze Pkwy., is home to more than 700 animals in naturalistic habitats. Highlights include Japanese gardens, Gorilla Island, a children's petting zoo and wildlife demonstrations. Visitors ride the Safari Line train through a 30-acre wildlife park with free-roaming animals. Daily 9-6, Apr.-Sept. (weather permitting); 9-5, rest of year. Closed Thanksgiving and Dec. 24-25 and 31. Last admission 1 hour before closing. Admission $9.95; over 65, $8.95; ages 3-11, $6.95. Phone for train fares. AX, DS, MC, VI. Phone (850) 932-2229.

GULF ISLANDS NATIONAL SEASHORE (B-2)

Stretching west 150 miles from Fort Walton Beach to Ship Island off Gulfport, Miss., Gulf Islands National Seashore covers more than 137,000 acres, 80 percent of which are submerged lands. Most of Florida's portion is accessible by car and includes Naval Live Oaks Reservation; part of Perdido Key; Fort Barrancas and the Redoubt on Pensacola Naval Air Station; the Okaloosa area near Fort Walton beach; and portions of Santa Rosa Island including the Fort Pickens area.

Guided tours of Fort Pickens are offered daily, and tours of restored Fort Barrancas (see Pensacola p. 185) and other forts are offered seasonally. A visitor center at Naval Live Oaks Reservation features a picnic area, interpretive trail and exhibits.

On the bay side of Santa Rosa Island is a recreation area with picnic facilities. Entrance fees are charged at Perdido Key, Fort Pickens and Santa Rosa areas.

For further information contact Gulf Islands National Seashore, 1801 Gulf Breeze Pkwy., Gulf Breeze, FL 32561; phone (850) 934-2600. See Recreation Chart and the AAA Southeastern CampBook.

HALLANDALE BEACH—
see Fort Lauderdale p. 78.

HEATHROW—see Orlando p. 160.

HERNANDO (C-8) pop. 8,253, elev. 50′

TED WILLIAMS MUSEUM AND HITTERS HALL OF FAME is 3.2 mi. w. of jct. US 41 on CR 486 in The Villages of Citrus Hills. Built in the shape of a baseball diamond, the museum houses photographs, artwork, memorabilia and other items from the life and career of Ted Williams, one of baseball's greatest hitters, and other notable players. The museum also features the Hitters Hall of Fame; a theater presents continuous showings of the "20 Greatest Hitters," and the "Up Close Interview with Ted Williams."

Allow 1 hour, 30 minutes minimum. Tues.-Sun. 10-4; closed major holidays. Admission $9; under 13, $1. MC, VI. Phone (352) 527-6566.

HIGH SPRINGS (C-7) pop. 3,863, elev. 69′

High Springs, once a mining and railroad town, now offers antiquing and recreational opportunities in a small-town atmosphere. The downtown business section, representative of old Florida, features antique shops and several historic buildings.

O'Leno State Park, one of the first state parks developed in Florida, is 6 miles north and offers primitive camping, swimming, boating, fishing, nature trails, horseback riding trails, bicycle trails and a playground. For the adventurer, Blue Springs, Ginnie Springs, Ichetucknee Springs, and Poe Springs offer swimming, tubing, canoeing and underwater cave exploration. *See Recreation Chart and the AAA Southeastern CampBook.*

High Springs Chamber of Commerce: P.O. Box 863, High Springs, FL 32643; (386) 454-3120.

RECREATIONAL ACTIVITIES
Canoeing
• **Santa Fe Canoe Outpost**, US 441 at the Santa Fe River Bridge, P.O. Box 592, High Springs, FL 32643. Daily year-round. Reservations are recommended. Phone (386) 454-2050.

HILLIARD—*see Jacksonville p. 96.*

HOBE SOUND (F-11) pop. 11,376, elev. 24′

HOBE SOUND NATIONAL WILDLIFE REFUGE is at 13620 S.E. US 1. Occupying more than 1,000 acres of coastal sand dunes, mangrove swamps, sand pine-scrub oak forests and sea turtle nesting areas, the refuge offers trails, surf fishing, a white sand beach and observation platforms. At the Hobe Sound Nature Center visitors can observe live animals—including snakes, an alligator and a tarantula—as well as shell and taxidermy displays. The beach is on Jupiter Island, accessible from North Beach Road, 1.5 miles north of Bridge Road.

Allow 1 hour minimum. Refuge daily 6 a.m.-dusk. Nature center Mon.-Fri. 9-3; closed holidays. Beach parking $5 per private vehicle. Phone (561) 546-6141 for the refuge or (561) 546-2067 for the nature center.

HOLLYWOOD—*see Fort Lauderdale p. 78.*

HOMESTEAD—*see Miami-Miami Beach p. 125.*

HOMOSASSA SPRINGS (D-8)
pop. 12,458, elev. 6′

[SAVE] **HOMOSASSA SPRINGS WILDLIFE STATE PARK** is on US 19 at 4150 Suncoast Blvd., 6 mi. n. of jct. US 19/98, following signs. Source of the Homosassa River, the freshwater spring emits millions of gallons each hour at a constant temperature of 72 F. Saltwater and freshwater fish inhabit the spring and can be watched through a floating glass observatory. Pontoon boats make scenic shuttle runs from US 19 to the park.

A trail through woodlands and wetlands allows visitors to observe native wildlife, including black bears, bobcats, river otters, alligators, cougars and white-tailed deer. Daily educational programs feature manatees, alligators, a hippopotamus, birds of prey, tortoises and native snakes.

Allow 3 hours minimum. Daily 9-5:30. Last admission 1 hour, 30 minutes before closing. Last boat departs 2 hours, 15 minutes before closing. Admission $7.95; ages 3-12, $4.95. AX, DS, MC, VI. Phone (352) 628-5343.

YULEE SUGAR MILL RUINS HISTORIC STATE PARK is 2.5 mi. w. of US 19/98 via CR 490 and Fish Bowl Dr. Now a ruin, the 1851 mill was built by Florida's first U.S. senator, David Levy Yulee, as part of a 5,100-acre sugar plantation. During the Civil War the mill supplied the Confederate Army with sugar products. Picnic facilities are available. Daily 8-dusk. Free. Phone (352) 795-3817.

INDIAN ROCKS BEACH—
see Tampa Bay p. 228.

INDIAN SHORES—*see Tampa Bay p. 228.*

INVERNESS (D-8) pop. 6,789, elev. 38′

WILD BILL'S AIRBOAT TOURS & WILDLIFE PARK is on SR 44, 6.3 mi. e. of jct. US 41, 9 mi. w. of I-75. Narrated 30- and 45-minute airboat rides on the Withlacoochee River provide sightings of native wildlife, including wading birds, ospreys, eagles, deer and alligators.

Allow 1 hour, 30 minutes minimum. Daily 10-5; closed Jan. 1, Thanksgiving and Dec. 25. Admission $13.95; under 11, $8.95. Extended tour $19.95; under 11, $13.95. Reservations are required. AX, DS, MC, VI. Phone (352) 726-6060 or (800) 833-5769.

ISLAMORADA—*see The Florida Keys p. 65.*

Jacksonville

Jacksonville is in the great double loop of the St. Johns River, the nation's longest north-flowing river. A busy seaport, it is one of Florida's major cultural, financial, industrial, transportation and commercial centers. The city also is a wholesale lumber market and coffee importation port and is home to a naval stores yard.

The city's history began in 1562, decades before the English settled Jamestown, when French Protestants known as Huguenots founded a colony on the banks of the St. Johns River. Named Fort Caroline, the ill-fated settlement was destroyed just 3 years later by Spanish troops from the garrison at nearby St. Augustine, and for the next 200 years Spain controlled Florida.

Spanish rule ended in 1763 when Spain traded Florida to Britain in return for Havana, which the British had conquered the year before. Ownership by Britain lasted only 20 years, but during that time The King's Road between Savannah, Georgia, and St. Augustine was completed. A settlement developed where the road crossed the St. John's River, roughly where downtown Jacksonville is today.

As a result of the 1783 Treaty of Paris which officially ended the American War of Independence, Britain returned Florida to Spain. But despite Spanish ownership, citizens of the new United States of America began settling in northern Florida, and during the War of 1812 both British and American forces made several incursions into the region.

To contend with the threat of American expansionism, Spain struck a deal with the United States in 1819 trading its interests in the Oregon Country and Florida in exchange for recognition of Spanish sovereignty over Texas.

After the United States took formal possession of Florida in 1821, settlers poured into the territory. The next year residents founded Jacksonville and named it after Gen. Andrew Jackson, the first military governor of the territory.

The town prospered as a port of entry until the Civil War, during which it was burned and abandoned several times. A major yellow fever outbreak killed hundreds of citizens in the late 1880s and forced many more to flee. In 1901 tragedy visited the city yet again when a fire destroyed nearly the entire downtown area.

The resurrected town became the leading metropolitan area in Florida for the next 40 years thanks to the railroad and the wealthy tourists who flocked to the city each winter. During these years several movie studios opened in the area, giving Jacksonville the nickname, "the World's Winter Film Capital." Naval bases built during World War II contributed to the city's further

growth, and later, banking and insurance became important parts of the local economy.

City and county governments were consolidated in 1968 which made Jacksonville the largest U.S. city in land area at the time. In 1996 the metropolitan area's population passed the 1 million mark, and today Jacksonville remains a major port, financial center, site of military bases and a health center that continues to grow rapidly.

Approaches

By Car

Two important interstate highways, I-95 and I-10, intersect in the Jacksonville downtown area. I-95 traverses the United States from north to south beginning in Maine and ending in Miami. It is frequently congested as it approaches downtown.

I-10 connects Jacksonville on the East Coast with Los Angeles by way of New Orleans, Houston, San Antonio, Tucson and Phoenix.

I-295 arcs northeast and southwest of downtown, connecting with I-95 both south and north of downtown. I-295 also intersects with I-10 directly west of the city.

A more scenic approach is SR A1A which follows the coastline through Jacksonville. Northeast of the city, SR A1A travels through historic Fernandina Beach.

US 1 is another important route. This highway runs the length of America's east coast, from Lubec, Maine, to Key West, Fla. US 17 approaches from the west and provides yet another route into Jacksonville.

Getting Around

Street System

Like most newer cities, the street system of downtown Jacksonville is a simple grid. Bay Street divides the city north-south, while Main Street is the east-west divider. The city does not adhere to a street naming convention, and thus a road's name (that is, whether it is called a street, avenue or boulevard) does not indicate its compass orientation.

The downtown speed limit is 30 mph. Traffic is most congested 7 to 9 a.m. and 4 to 6 p.m.

Parking

Both on-street parking and several parking garages are available downtown. A parking area under the Main Street bridge is convenient to Jacksonville Landing and other businesses. Parking meters require 25c per half hour.

What to See

ALEXANDER BREST MUSEUM, 6 mi. n. on the Jacksonville University campus at 2800 University Blvd. N., features a permanent collection of decorative arts and pre-Colombian objects, in addition to works by guest artists, faculty and students. Mon.-Fri. 9-4:30. Free. Phone (904) 745-7371.

(continued on page 93)

The Informed Traveler

City Population: 735,617

Elevation: 20 ft.

Sales Tax: The sales tax is 7 percent in Clay and Nassau counties, 7 percent in Duval County and 6 percent in St. Johns County. A 6 percent bed tax is levied in Duval and St. Johns counties; the tourist development tax in Clay County is 2 percent.

WHOM TO CALL

Emergency: 911

Police (non-emergency): (904) 630-0500

Fire: (904) 630-0529

Weather: (904) 741-4311

Hospitals: Baptist Medical Center, (904) 202-2000; Memorial Hospital Jacksonville, (904) 399-6111; St. Vincent's Medical Center, (904) 308-7300; Shands Jacksonville Medical Center, (904) 244-0411.

WHERE TO LOOK

Newspapers

Jacksonville's daily paper, *The Florida Times-Union,* is distributed in the morning.

Radio

Radio station WZNZ (1460 AM) is an all-news station; WJCT (89.9 FM) is a member of National Public Radio.

Visitor Information

Visitor information is available from the Jacksonville and the Beaches Convention and Visitors Bureau, 201 E. Adams St., Jacksonville, FL 32205; phone (904) 798-9111 or (800) 733-2668.

TRANSPORTATION

Air Travel

More than a dozen major and regional carriers serve Jacksonville International Airport, which is about 13 miles north of downtown near the northern junction of I-95 and I-295.

Several taxi and limousine companies serve the airport, although the baggage claim area is served exclusively by Gator City Taxi, (904) 355-8294. Taxi fares to downtown average $22.50.

Rental Cars

Hertz, at the airport, offers discounts to AAA members; phone (904) 741-2151 or (800) 654-3080. For listings of other agencies check the telephone directory.

Rail Service

The Amtrak station is at 3570 Clifford Ln., 5 miles northwest of downtown. For arrival information phone (904) 766-5110; for reservations and information phone (800) 872-7245.

Buses

The main Greyhound Lines Inc. bus terminal is at 10 N. Pearl St.; phone (904) 356-9976. A substation is at 5532 Normandy Blvd.; phone (904) 786-4323. For rate and schedule information phone (800) 231-2222.

Taxis

Major cab companies are Checker Cab Co., (904) 764-2472, and Gator City Taxi, (904) 355-8294. Base fare is $1.25 with a rate of $1.50 per mile.

Public Transport

Jacksonville Transportation Authority operates city buses. Stops include the transfer center at Florida Community College Jacksonville and the South Bank area. Fare for buses on the beaches is $1.35; town routes are 75c. For information phone (904) 630-3100. The Skyway Express, an automated monorail system, provides transportation between the Prime Osborn Convention Center, Hemming Plaza and Jacksonville Landing on the north bank and Dupont Station across the river for 35c; phone (904) 630-3181.

Boats

River taxi service between points along the St. Johns River is available from S.S. Marine Taxi, (904) 733-7782.

Destination Jacksonville

*F*or many visitors heading south Jacksonville is, geographically at least, Florida's unofficial welcome center—and the city is a fine example of what the Sunshine State is all about.

Jacksonville skyline.
A skyline enhanced by contemporary skyscrapers and riverfront marketplaces defines northeast Florida's hub city.

*T*ake beaches for example. Jacksonville and its environs have miles of sand to wiggle your toes in. Add to that an assortment of museums to suit individual tastes, professional sports and abundant recreational activities.

Cummer Museum of Art & Gardens, Jacksonville. Riverfront gardens grace the grounds of this museum, while fine and decorative arts adorn its galleries. (See listing page 93)

Museum of Science and History, Jacksonville. The life-size models in the Atlantic Tails exhibit focus on the mammals that inhabit Florida's waters. (See listing page 93)

Hilliard

Fernandina Beach

Amelia Island

Fort George Island

Mayport

Jacksonville

Jacksonville Beach

See Vicinity map page 92

Jacksonville Zoological Gardens, Jacksonville. The Dark Continent motif of the zoo's entrance prepares visitors for encounters with the rare and exotic. (See listing page 93)

*P*laces included in this AAA Destination City:

Amelia Island..............95	Hilliard......................96
Fernandina Beach........95	Jacksonville Beach.......96
Fort George Island.......96	Mayport.....................96

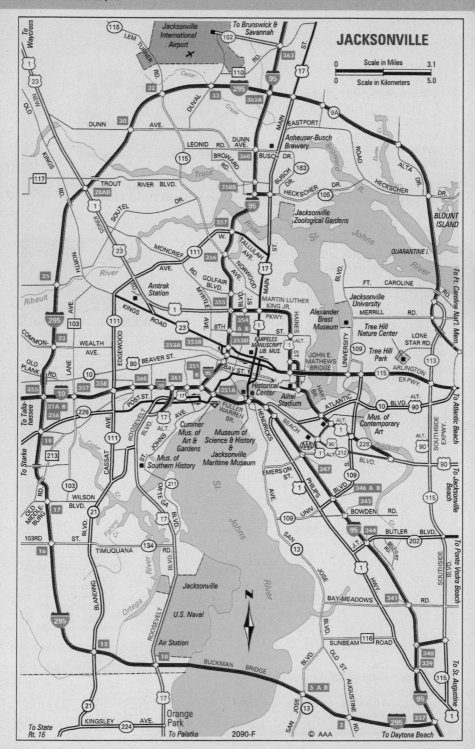

JACKSONVILLE

Scale in Miles 0 — 3.1
Scale in Kilometers 0 — 5.0

Jacksonville International Airport

To Brunswick & Savannah

To Waycross

To State Rt. 16

To Palatka

To Daytona Beach

To St. Augustine

To Ponte Vedra Beach

To Jacksonville Beach

To Atlantic Beach

To Ft. Caroline Nat'l. Mem.

To Starke

To Tallahassee

Anheuser-Busch Brewery

Jacksonville Zoological Gardens

BLOUNT ISLAND

QUARANTINE I.

FT. CAROLINE

Jacksonville University

Alexander Brest Museum

Tree Hill Nature Center

Tree Hill Park

LONE STAR RD.

ARLINGTON

Amtrak Station

MARTIN LUTHER KING JR. PKWY.

KARPELES MANUSCRIPT LIB. MUS.

JOHN E. MATHEWS BRIDGE

Historical Center

Alltel Stadium

Mus. of Contemporary Art

Cummer Mus. of Art & Gardens

Museum of Science & History & Jacksonville Maritime Museum

Mus. of Southern History

FULLER WARREN BR.

BOWDEN

BUTLER

BAY-MEADOWS

SUNBEAM

U.S. Naval Air Station

Jacksonville

BUCKMAN BRIDGE

Orange Park

KINGSLEY

St. Johns River

Ortega River

Ribault River

Trout River

Cedar Creek

© AAA

2090-F

CUMMER MUSEUM OF ART & GAR-DENS, 829 Riverside Ave., contains an impressive array of decorative and fine arts dating from 2000 B.C. Of interest is a collection of early 18th-century Meissen porcelain tableware. Changing exhibits complement the permanent collection. A formal garden, modeled after the gardens of Villa Gamberaia in Florence, Italy, extends from the museum to the river. Art Connections, in the Art Education Center, features an interactive teaching gallery.

Allow 2 hours minimum. Tues.-Sat. 10-5 (also Tues. and Thurs. 5-9), Sun. noon-5; closed major holidays and for 2 weeks in Apr. Admission $6; senior citizens and military with ID $4; students with ID $3; under 6, $1; free to college students with ID Tues.-Fri. after 1:30; free to all Tues. 4-9. Phone (904) 356-6857.

FORT CAROLINE NATIONAL MEMORIAL, 13 mi. e. near jct. Monument and Fort Caroline rds., is within the Timucuan Ecological and Historic Preserve. The memorial marks the site near which French colonial adventurers established a settlement in 1564. A year later Spaniards massacred many of them at Matanzas Inlet. A model of the fort is reached by a quarter-mile path through oak woods. Ribault Monument, half a mile east of the fort, is an obelisk that commemorates the first landing at St. Johns in 1562. A 1-mile trail helps explain the site's history. Trails also lead to other areas within the preserve.

The visitor center, which also serves as the chief interpretive center for the Timucuan Ecological and Historic Preserve, has displays about the area's marine environment, the Timucuan Indian era, early attempts at colonization and a satellite image of present-day northeast Florida. Allow 1 hour minimum. Daily 9-5; closed Dec. 25. Donations. Phone (904) 641-7155.

FORT GEORGE ISLAND—*see place listing p. 96.*

JACKSONVILLE HISTORICAL CENTER, on S. Riverwalk just e. of Main St. Bridge, features displays depicting Jacksonville's history. Mon.-Sat. 11-5; closed Jan. 1, Thanksgiving and Dec. 25. Free. Phone (904) 398-4301.

JACKSONVILLE MARITIME MUSEUM, on the s. bank of the Riverwalk at 1015 Museum Cir., Unit 2, maintains exhibits depicting the origin, development and current impact of the maritime trade upon Florida. The importance of the St. Johns River and the port of Jacksonville are emphasized. Among displays are scale-model ships, paintings and photographs. Mon.-Fri. 10:30-3, Sat.-Sun. 1-5. Free. Phone (904) 398-9011.

[SAVE] **JACKSONVILLE ZOOLOGICAL GARDENS,** I-95 exit 358A, off Heckscher Dr. at 8605 Zoo Pkwy., showcases more than 1,000 animals from around the world on 73 acres. In addition to Great Apes of the World, Birds of Rift Valley and Wild Florida is Australian Adventure, which features koalas, kangaroos, wallabies, lorikeets and a cassowary. A train ride and a play area also are available. Picnic facilities and wheelchairs are available.

Allow 2 hours minimum. Daily 9-5; closed Thanksgiving and Dec. 25. Admission $8; over 65, $6.50; ages 3-12, $5. Ask about the military discount. Train ride $5; ages 3-12, $3. AX, DS, MC, VI. Phone (904) 757-4462.

KARPELES MANUSCRIPT LIBRARY MUSEUM, 101 W. First St. at Laura, has changing exhibits of historic and significant documents. Displays, which rotate between the Karpeles museums, may include letters by Napoleon Bonaparte and George Washington, the musical notations of Ludwig van Beethoven, Wolfgang Amadeus Mozart or Richard Wagner, or such documents as constitutions and treaties. A highlight of the collection is the Emancipation Proclamation signed by Abraham Lincoln. Sprinkles' Museum is an educational, hands-on play area for ages 1 to 10.

Allow 1 hour minimum. Museum open Tues.-Sat. 10-1. Children's area open Wed. and Sat. 10-1. Museum admission free. Children's area $3. Phone (904) 356-2992 for the museum or (904) 632-2386 for the children's area.

KINGSLEY PLANTATION—
see Fort George Island p. 96.

MUSEUM OF SCIENCE AND HISTORY is at 1025 Museum Cir. In this playground for the mind where "do touch" is the rule, visitors can explore far off galaxies in the Alexander Brest Planetarium, view the collection of live northeastern Florida animals, or stroll back through 12,000 years of northeast Florida history.

Mon.-Fri. 10-5, Sat. 10-6, Sun. 1-6; closed Jan. 1, Easter, Thanksgiving and Dec. 25. Admission $6; senior citizens and military with ID $4.50; ages 3-12, $4. AX, MC, VI. Phone (904) 396-6674.

MUSEUM OF SOUTHERN HISTORY is off I-10 exit 358, 3 mi. s. on Cassat Ave., 1.5 mi. e. on San Juan Ave., then just n. to 4304 Herschel St. The museum houses an extensive collection of artifacts, clothing and memorabilia from the Civil War era, in addition to a 3,000-volume research library and genealogical records. Allow 1 hour minimum. Tues.-Sat. 10-5. Admission $1, under 16 free. Phone (904) 388-3574.

TREE HILL NATURE CENTER is across the St. Johns River from downtown via US 90A and the Matthews Bridge. Take US 90A/Arlington Expwy. 4 mi. e. to Arlington Rd., then .5 mi. n. to Lillian Rd., then .5 mi. e. to 7152 Lone Star Rd. The 50-acre nature preserve showcases Northeast Florida's native flora and fauna and encompasses four nature trails, a butterfly garden, a hummingbird garden and a small, pyramidal natural history museum with exhibits of snakes, animal skulls and fossils. Turtle Town is home to the protected gopher tortoise; another exhibit area describes the Florida black bear.

Allow 1 hour minimum. Mon.-Sat. 8:30-5. Admission $1; under 18, 50c. Phone (904) 724-4646.

What To Do

Sightseeing

Industrial Tours

ANHEUSER-BUSCH BREWERY, 111 Busch Dr., offers self-guiding and guided tours. Visitors may view the brewing and bottling processes and then sample products in the hospitality room. Allow 1 hour minimum. Mon.-Sat. 9-4; closed some holidays. Guided tours are given on the hour. Free. Phone (904) 751-8116.

Sports and Recreation

The intricate chain of barrier islands off the coast adjacent to Jacksonville offers more than 50 miles of white sandy beaches that are great for **swimming.** Just 20 miles northeast of the city are the pristine beaches and wild natural beauty of Little Talbot Island State Park and Fort George Island State Cultural Site. The beach communities of the area—Atlantic Beach, Neptune Beach, Jacksonville Beach and, to the south, Ponte Vedra Beach—combine surf and sand with the amenities of hotels and restaurants.

With Jacksonville's access to water, **boating** is a popular pastime in the area. The city operates docks at the following locations: Huguenot Memorial Park, Kathryn Abbey Hanna Park, Metropolitan Park and Southbank Riverwalk.

Fishing can be enjoyed along the St. Johns River and Intracoastal Waterway and in the Atlantic Ocean. Speckled trout, striped bass, bluefish, redfish, flounder and whiting are a few of the fish frequently caught at Little Talbot Island State Park. Saltwater fishing and more than 60 acres of freshwater fishing lakes are available at Kathryn Abbey Hanna Park.

Golf and Florida's balmy climate go together perfectly, and Jacksonville offers more than 50 area golf courses. Courses include Baymeadows Golf Club at 7981 W. Baymeadows Cir., (904) 731-5701; Deerfield Lakes Golf Club off Lem Turner Road, (904) 359-0404; Fernandina Municipal Golf Club at 2800 Bill Melton Rd., (904) 277-7370; Golf Club of Jacksonville at 10440 Tournament Ln., (904) 779-0800; and Jacksonville Beach Golf Club at 605 S. Penman Rd., (904) 247-6184.

Tennis courts can be found throughout the Jacksonville area. The Association of Tennis Professionals (ATP) Tour is headquartered in Ponte Vedra.

Timucuan Ecological & Historic Preserve, 12713 Fort Caroline Rd., offers numerous **hiking** trails through several distinct ecological communities; phone (904) 641-7155. Three self-guiding nature trails are at the University of North Florida Nature Preserve. Bird-watching is a popular pastime along the hiking trails of both Big and Little Talbot islands.

Local fans of professional **football** were given a gift in 1993 when the city was awarded a National Football League franchise. The Jacksonville Jaguars play at Alltel Stadium, One Alltel Stadium Place; phone (904) 633-2000. The Jacksonville Tomcats play arena football in spring and summer at Jacksonville Veterans Memorial Coliseum; phone (904) 358-7825.

The Jacksonville Suns, a farm team of the Detroit Tigers, play AA Southern League **baseball** at Wolfson Park, 1201 E. Duval St.; phone (904) 358-2846.

Greyhound racing takes place at Orange Park Kennel Club from early September to mid-April and at Jacksonville Kennel Club from mid-April through early September. For more information about either track, phone (904) 646-0001.

Note: Policies vary concerning admittance of children to pari-mutuel betting facilities. Phone for information.

Shopping

In addition to major shopping malls, a multitude of small shopping centers and an array of antique stores and flea markets, the city boasts Jacksonville Landing, on Independent Drive along the St. Johns River. This downtown marketplace features shops, riverfront cafes and restaurants. A water taxi takes patrons across the river to the Riverwalk.

Avenues Shopping Mall, 10300 Southside Blvd., has 110 stores including Belk, Dillard's, JCPenney, Parisian and Sears. Orange Park Mall, 1910 Wells Rd., counts Belk, Dillard's, JCPenney and Sears among its 134 stores. SAVE Regency Square, 9501 Arlington Expwy., has 160 stores including Belk, Dillard's, JCPenney and Sears.

Theater and Concerts

The Jacksonville Symphony Orchestra presents performances throughout the year including a guest artist series, an outdoor concert series and smaller group concerts. Times-Union Center for the Performing Arts, 300 Water St., is a state-of-the-art performance venue overlooking the St. Johns River downtown. Its three halls include Robert E. Jacoby Hall, home of the Jacksonville Symphony Orchestra; Moran Theater, which can accommodate large-scale concerts and Broadway touring shows; and Terry Theater, which is used for smaller performances. For more information phone (904) 354-5479.

The Florida Community College at Jacksonville Artist Series brings Broadway productions along with national and international ballet, opera and contemporary dance companies; phone (904) 632-3373.

Located downtown, the lavish Florida Theater was built in 1927 and serves as a performing arts center; phone (904) 355-5661 for information or (904) 355-2787 for tickets.

Special Events

Jacksonville is host to exciting events throughout the year. College football fans celebrate the new year with the Gator Bowl, which is played on the Saturday nearest Jan. 1 and is one of the city's top sporting events.

In March the GATE River Run attracts 9,000 runners for a 15-kilometer race along the city's roads and bridges. Also taking place in March is The Players Championship golf tournament, the Professional Golf Association's premier spring event. In late April, Beaches Festival Weekend is celebrated at SeaWalk Pavilion in downtown Jacksonville Beach.

In May the Kuumba Festival celebrates African-American heritage with parades, music and food at A. Philip Randolph Park. The Greater Jacksonville Kingfish Tournament features prizes, a fish fry, seafood festival and entertainment in July.

The Greater Jacksonville Agricultural Fair in October offers livestock, a petting zoo, horticultural exhibits, arts and crafts, carnival rides and country entertainment.

Ring in the new year during the Gator Bowl New Year's Eve Street Festival on the riverfront in downtown Jacksonville.

The Jacksonville Vicinity

AMELIA ISLAND (A-9)

Miles of Appalachian quartz beaches and towering sand dunes distinguish Amelia Island, a picturesque island off the northeast tip of Florida's Atlantic coast. Formerly a haven for smugglers of slaves, liquor and foreign goods, in the mid-19th-century the island became the site of Florida's first cross-state railroad and, consequently, the state's first resort. The many Victorian buildings in Fernandina Beach, the island's only city *(see place listing),* remain a testament to the island's "Golden Age."

Ironically, another railroad—Henry Flagler's Florida East Coast Railway—soon lured tourists farther south, locking the island in its Victorian atmosphere. Once thought a disaster, this development is now heralded as a blessing, as visitors seek relief from the modern world in Amelia Island's old-fashioned charm and pace.

A popular resort area, the island offers many recreational opportunities including golf, swimming and horseback riding. At the southern end of the island is American Beach, one of the country's last predominately African-American beaches. The town of American Beach was founded in the 1930s, an era during which many beaches were closed to African-Americans.

Amelia Island/Fernandina Beach/Yulee Chamber of Commerce: P.O. Box 472, Fernandina Beach, FL 32035-0472; phone (904) 261-3248 or (800) 226-3542.

RECREATIONAL ACTIVITIES
Horseback Riding

• **Kelly Seahorse Ranch**, 7500 First Coast Hwy., Amelia Island, FL 32034. Rides daily at 10, noon, 2 and 4. Reservations are recommended. Phone (904) 491-5166.

FERNANDINA BEACH (A-9)
pop. 10,549, elev. 10′

Fernandina Beach is the northern terminus for a portion of scenic highway extending 105 miles

south via SR A1A to Daytona Beach. Once called a "festering fleshpot" by President James Monroe because of the pirates and smugglers who anchored here, the town later became Florida's first resort.

This centuries-old town on Amelia Island features a variety of architectural styles. The Victorian district is scattered across 50 blocks, including residential and commercial buildings and a popular shopping area. On Centre Street at Second Avenue is the Palace Saloon, built in 1878 and reputedly the oldest in the state. A hand-carved, 40-foot mahogany bar and hand-painted murals decorate the interior.

The first week in May the town celebrates the local shrimping industry and its early days under the flags of eight nations with the Isle of Eight Flags Shrimp Festival.

Amelia Island/Fernandina Beach/Yulee Chamber of Commerce: P.O. Box 472, Fernandina Beach, FL 32035-0472; phone (904) 261-3248 or (800) 226-3542.

Self-guiding tours: A brochure outlining a tour of the historic district is available from the chamber of commerce.

AMELIA ISLAND MUSEUM OF HISTORY, 233 S. Third St., is in Nassau County's former jailhouse. The second floor of the museum depicts the history of Amelia Island through photographs and artifacts. One-hour guided tours of the first floor exhibit hall depict the island's past and tell of the eight nations whose flags have flown over its harbor. Allow 1 hour minimum. Museum open Mon.-Fri. 10-5, Sat. 10-4; closed holidays. Guided tours are given Mon.-Sat. at 11 and 2. Admission $4, students with ID $2. Phone (904) 261-7378.

FORT CLINCH STATE PARK, 2 mi. e. on SR A1A at the n. end of Amelia Island, comprises 1,153 acres. The brick and masonry fort was begun in 1847 but never completed. Occupied by Federal forces in 1862, it was instrumental in introducing Northerners to Florida's warm climate, which resulted in a tourist boom after the Civil War. The interpretation center traces the history of the fort.

Rangers dressed in Union uniforms carry out the daily chores of garrison soldiers of the Civil War era. Campsites are available; reservations are recommended.

Park open daily 8-dusk. Fort open daily 9-5; candlelight tours are available by reservation Fri.-Sat., early May-Labor Day. Park admission $3.25 per private vehicle (maximum eight people), $1 per person arriving by bicycle or on foot. Fort admission $2, under 6 free. Candlelight tours $3. Phone (904) 277-7274. *See Recreation Chart and the AAA Southeastern CampBook.*

FORT GEORGE ISLAND (A-9)

In the 16th century the Spanish established a blockhouse and the mission San Juan del Porto on Fort George Island. By 1736 Gen. James Oglethorpe had turned the island into a base for forays against the Spanish. About 25 miles northeast of Jacksonville, the island is accessible from the beaches on SR A1A and by ferry from Mayport. The Dames Point Bridge provides access to the island via SR 105.

KINGSLEY PLANTATION, .5 mi. n. of the St. Johns River Ferry on SR A1A, then 2.5 mi. w. on Fort George Rd., is part of the Timucuan Preserve. This 19th-century cotton plantation was operated 1813-39 by Zephaniah Kingsley. It is one of the last remaining examples of the plantation system of territorial Florida. The main lodge and the remains of 23 slave cabins are visible. Interpretive displays reflect 19th-century plantation life. Daily 9-5;

closed Jan. 1, Thanksgiving and Dec. 25. Free. Phone (904) 251-3537.

HILLIARD (A-9) pop. 2,702, elev. 69'

RECREATIONAL ACTIVITIES

Horseback Riding

• **Country Day Stable,** 2940 Jane Ln., Hilliard, FL 32046. Daily 10-5; closed Thanksgiving and Dec. 25. Reservations are required. Phone (904) 879-9383.

JACKSONVILLE BEACH (B-10)
pop. 20,990, elev. 14'

ADVENTURE LANDING, 1 mi. w. of SR A1A at 1944 Beach Blvd., features an uphill water coaster, a wave pool and a pirate play village with 12 slides and more than 200 spray nozzles. Among other amusements are go-karts, laser tag and miniature golf. Amusement park open Mon.-Thurs 11-10, Fri. 11 a.m.-midnight, Sat. 10 a.m.-midnight, Sun. 10-10. Water park open daily 10-8, May 1 to mid-Oct. Admission $19.99, under 42 inches tall $16.99, under 3 free when accompanied by an adult. After 4 p.m. $12.99. AX, DS, MC, VI. Phone (904) 246-4386.

MAYPORT (B-9) elev. 10'

CASINOS

• **La Cruise Casino,** 4738 Ocean St. Mon. 7 p.m.-midnight, Tues.-Sat. 11 a.m.-4 p.m. and 7 p.m.-midnight; Sun. 1-6. Phone (904) 241-7200 or (800) 752-1778.

This ends listings for the Jacksonville Vicinity. The following page resumes the alphabetical listings of cities in Florida.

JACKSONVILLE BEACH—
see Jacksonville p. 96.

JUPITER (F-11) pop. 39,328, elev. 28′

Once the transportation hub of southeastern Florida, Jupiter was the starting point for the Celestial Railroad, which ran through Mars, Venus, Neptune and Juno to Lake Worth. The town since has become a center for recreation and light industry while retaining its quaint atmosphere.

The Montréal Expos and the St. Louis Cardinals both take up residence in Jupiter during spring training. Exhibition baseball games are played in March at Roger Dean Stadium, 4751 Main St.; phone (561) 775-1818.

Jupiter-Tequesta-Juno Beach Chamber of Commerce: 800 N. US 1, Jupiter, FL 33477-4440; phone (561) 746-7111.

FLORIDA HISTORY CENTER & MUSEUM is s. of jct. SR A1A at 805 N. US 1 in Burt Reynolds Park. Regional Florida history is depicted through photographs and memorabilia. Exhibits focus upon conservation of the coastline, pioneer fashions, Spanish contacts and such area inhabitants as Alligator Alice and Trapper Nelson. Highlights of the collection include fossil shells, Seminole Indian artifacts and an iron cannon from a 1659 shipwreck. Changing displays also are featured. Tours of the nearby 1896 DuBois Pioneer Home and 1860 Jupiter Inlet Lighthouse *(see attraction listing)* are available.

Allow 1 hour minimum. Museum open Tues.-Fri. 10-5, Sat.-Sun. noon-5; closed major holidays. Tours of the DuBois home are offered Wed. and Sun. 1-4. Museum admission $5; over 55, $4; ages 6-18, $3. Dubois Home tour $2. AX, MC, VI. Phone (561) 747-6639.

JONATHAN DICKINSON STATE PARK, 6 mi. n. on US 1 in Martin County, comprises 12,000 acres, including the Loxahatchee River. Bald eagles, scrub jays and sandhill cranes are among the birds that thrive amid the park's abundant plant life. Guided tours depart to Trapper Nelson Interpretive Center on the river; it is accessible only by boat. Canoe rentals are available. A 2-hour river tour is available on the *Loxahatchee Queen;* phone (561) 746-1466.

Park open daily 8-dusk. River tours depart daily at 9, 11, 1 and 3. Admission $3.25 per private vehicle (maximum eight people), $1 per person arriving by bicycle, bus or on foot. River tour fare $12; ages 6-12, $7. Phone (772) 546-2771. *See Recreation Chart.*

JUPITER INLET LIGHTHOUSE is .5 mi. n. on US 1, .1 mi. e. on Beach Rd., then .2 mi. s. on Captain Armours Way. Completed in 1860, the lighthouse still guides ships approaching the Florida coast with a beam that is visible from 18 miles at sea. On 45-minute guided tours, visitors can climb 108 feet for a view of the Atlantic Ocean (maximum 15 people per tour). Allow 1 hour minimum. Sun.-Wed. 10-4.

Last admission 45 minutes before closing. Admission, includes climbing tour, $5. Under 48 inches tall not permitted on tour. Phone (561) 747-8380.

◤GEM KENNEDY SPACE CENTER (D-11)

Forty-seven miles east of Orlando via the Bee Line Expressway (toll) or SR 50, the John F. Kennedy Space Center (KSC) is accessible from the mainland off US 1, 6 miles across the SR 405 causeway over the Indian River, or from the beaches across the SR 520 or 528 causeways to Merritt Island, then north on SR 3. The center is located within the 140,000-acre Merritt Island National Wildlife Refuge *(see Titusville p. 232)* and extends some 34 miles along the coast.

Kennedy Space Center is the launch and landing site for the space shuttle, NASA's reusable space transportation system that first flew into Earth orbit when *Columbia* launched in 1981. It is home to two launch pads, one of the world's longest runways and the nation's third-largest building, the Vehicle Assembly Plant. KSC also is the only place in the world where man has launched from Earth and traveled to another planet—the moon.

Cape Canaveral Air Station, east of the space center, was the site of the historic Mercury and Gemini flights including America's first suborbital space flight, taken by Navy Cmdr. Alan B. Shepard Jr. on May 5, 1961, and the country's first manned orbital flight by Marine Lt. Col. John H. Glenn Jr. on Feb. 20, 1962. Cape Canaveral is now the site for unmanned rocket launches.

The most current space shuttle information can be obtained from NASA's shuttle hotline; phone (321) 867-4636 or (800) 572-4636. Missile launches can be viewed from US 1 along the Indian River, especially in Titusville. Good vantage points include the Bee Line Expressway (SR 528) at Bennett Causeway and the Banana River, as well as SR A1A in Cocoa Beach, Jetty Park in Port Canaveral and the coastline south of the Cape Canaveral Air Force Station border.

With the purchase of a $15 Launch Transportation Ticket, visitors parking at the KSC Visitor Complex can board shuttle buses to a restricted viewing site on the NASA causeway. For additional information phone (321) 449-4444, or TTY (321) 454-4198. *See color ad p. 98.*

◤GEM KENNEDY SPACE CENTER VISITOR COMPLEX is 11 mi. e. of I-95 on SR 405.

Built in 1967 to allow the families of NASA astronauts and employees to view space center operations, the modern facility explores the past, present and future of the U.S. space program. The 70-acre complex features multimedia displays and hands-on exhibits, IMAX films, spacecraft and artifacts, encounters with astronauts and behind-the-scenes tours.

Admission to the complex includes a self-paced bus tour of restricted areas, offering a view of the

shuttle launch pads from the four-story LC 39 Observation Gantry. At the Apollo/Saturn V Center, visitors can walk beneath the 363-foot Saturn V rocket and watch footage of Neil Armstrong's history-making walk on the moon. The Firing Room Theater simulates an earth-shaking rocket launch.

Exploration in the New Millennium chronicles the 1976 Mars Viking Lander and features the live-action comedy stage show, "Mad Science—Mad Mission to Mars 2025." Question-and-answer sessions and personal stories are part of Astronaut Encounter, which brings guests face-to-face with men and women involved in the space program. Visitors can also attend live launch status briefings, climb aboard a replica of the Space Shuttle *Explorer* and tour the Rocket Garden, where space equipment traces the program's development.

Two special-interest programs also are available: the NASA Up Close Tour provides access to areas normally limited to astronauts, their families and NASA personnel; and "Dine with an Astronaut" enables visitors to share a meal with a space explorer.

IMAX theaters equipped with 5½-story screens present "Space Station," a 3-D adventure film narrated by Tom Cruise; and "The Dream is Alive," featuring footage taken by astronauts in space. Food is available. Free pet kennels are provided.

Allow 5 hours minimum to see the visitor complex and take the KSC bus tour. To avoid crowds arrive early. Complex open daily 9-5:30; closed Dec. 25 and certain launch days. Bus tours depart continuously 9:45-2:15. KSC admission (includes all shows and exhibits, IMAX films and bus tour) $26; ages 3-11, $16. NASA Up Close Tour $20 (in addition to KSC admission). Phone for "Dine with an Astronaut" schedule and rates. AX, DC, DS, MC, VI. Phone (321) 449-4444. *See color ad p. 98.*

Astronauts Memorial Space Mirror is accessible through the entrance to the Kennedy Space Center Visitor Complex. Dedicated to American astronauts who died in the line of duty, this 60-ton black granite monument is carved with the names of 17 men and women. The mirrored surface is illuminated to reflect each name against the sky. Allow 30 minutes minimum. Daily 9-dusk; closed Dec. 25 and certain launch days. Included in Kennedy Space Center Visitor Complex admission. Phone (321) 452-2887.

U.S. ASTRONAUT HALL OF FAME is s. of jct. SR 405 and US 1 at 6225 Vectorspace Blvd. Dedicated to honoring America's space pioneers, the Hall of Fame traces the development of space exploration through video footage, personal memorabilia and historical artifacts. Simulators let visitors experience aerial acrobatics and astronaut training, squeeze inside a Mercury spacecraft and take a multimedia ride

aboard a space shuttle mock-up. Visitors also may observe children training in space camp. **Note:** At press time the schedule was uncertain; phone ahead.

Allow 3 hours minimum. Daily 9-5, with extended summer hours; closed Dec. 25. Last admission 1 hour before closing. Admission $13.95; over 60, $12.95; ages 6-12, $9.95. AX, MC, VI. Phone (321) 269-6100. *See color ad p. 99.*

KEY BISCAYNE—
see Miami-Miami Beach p. 126.

KEY LARGO—*see The Florida Keys p. 65.*

KEY WEST—*see The Florida Keys p. 66.*

KISSIMMEE—*see Orlando p. 160.*

LAKE BUENA VISTA—*see Orlando p. 163.*

LAKELAND (E-9) pop. 78,452, elev. 227'

Lakeland encompasses 13 lakes providing ample opportunities for fishing, boating and water skiing. The area also offers pleasant surroundings for such sports as golf and tennis. The city is a processing and distribution center for citrus fruits and other agricultural products. A majority of the world's phosphate, the primary ingredient in fertilizer, is mined in the Lakeland area.

The world's largest group of buildings designed by Frank Lloyd Wright is on the Florida Southern College campus at Ingraham Avenue and McDonald Street. The 1938 Annie Pfeiffer Chapel was the first structure here; others were patterned after its theme. Maps for a self-guiding tour are available outside the administration building.

During March the city is the spring-training camp for baseball's Detroit Tigers, and from April through August it is the home of the Lakeland

---

DID YOU KNOW

Saber-tooth tigers, mastodons, giant armadillos and camels once roamed in what is now Florida.

Tigers. Exhibition games are played at Joker Marchant Stadium; phone (863) 688-7911. Ice hockey games, concerts, ballet performances and trade shows are among the entertainment presented at The Lakeland Center, 700 W. Lemon St.

Every spring Lakeland is the site of the 7-day Sun 'n Fun EAA Fly-In, which attracts nearly 650,000 persons from around the world. In addition to 450 commercial exhibitors, there are workshops, forums and daily airshows, and the exhibits and aircraft of the Florida Air Museum at Sun 'n Fun *(see attraction listing).* Dates for the 2003 Fly-In are Apr. 2-8. For Fly-In information phone (863) 644-2431.

Lakeland Chamber of Commerce: 35 Lake Morton Dr., Lakeland, FL 33801; phone (863) 688-8551.

Self-guiding tours: Information about tours of the downtown historic district is available from the chamber of commerce.

Shopping areas: Lakeland Square, on US 98 at I-4, contains Belk Lindsey, Burdines, Dillard's, JCPenney and Sears. Antique lovers can find more than 60 shops and dealers in the city's antiques district, located 2 blocks north of Main Street along Kentucky Avenue and Pine Street.

EXPLORATIONS V CHILDREN'S MUSEUM, 109 N. Kentucky Ave., offers changing hands-on exhibits, materials and activities allowing children ages 2-12 to explore the realms of nature, science, the continents, business and fantasy. The interactive programs are designed to promote learning and cultural growth. Allow 1 hour minimum. Wed.-Sat. 9-4 (also Thurs. 4-5), Sun. 1-4, Mon.-Tues. 9-1; closed holidays. Ages 2-15, $4; over 15, $2. Phone (863) 687-3869.

 FLORIDA AIR MUSEUM AT SUN 'N FUN is at 4175 Medulla Rd. at the Lakeland Linder Regional Airport. The museum houses more than 70 collectible aircraft including many unusual experimental and homebuilt models. Amphibious aircraft, biplanes, gyrocopters, radio-controlled drones, sailplanes, sports planes, ultralights and vintage military planes, along with a collection of aircraft engines, are among the various items on display. Visitors can see aeronautical memorabilia from tycoon Howard Hughes' collection. A library contains several thousand aviation-related books and magazines. Guided tours are available.

Allow 1 hour minimum. Mon.-Fri. 9-5, Sat. 10-4, Sun. noon-4; closed holidays. Admission $8; over 54, $6; ages 8-12, $4. AX, MC, VI. Phone (863) 644-0741.

POLK MUSEUM OF ART, 800 E. Palmetto St. just off Lake Morton Dr., has changing exhibits of contemporary and historical art. The museum's permanent collection includes pre-Columbian artifacts; Oriental ceramics, ivory and fabrics; European ceramics; Georgian silver; and American art of the 19th and 20th centuries. Allow 1 hour minimum.

Mon. 10-5, Tues.-Fri. 9-5, Sat. 10-5, Sun. 1-5; closed holidays. Free. Phone (863) 688-7743.

LAKE WALES (E-9) pop. 10,194, elev. 252'

On North Wales Drive at North Avenue in Lake Wales a bizarre phenomenon occurs: Through optical illusion, cars appear to roll uphill. To experience this mystery, park your car at the bottom of the incline known as Spook Hill and release the brake.

It is said that the Spook Hill mystery stems from a Seminole legend in which Chief Cufcowellax and his tribe settled on Lake Wales. Soon a huge bull alligator moved into the lake and regularly attacked the Indians. Aided by the Great Spirit, the chief stalked the beast and engaged him in a month-long battle, after which the chief rose from the water in victory.

During the battle a small lake, now North Lake Wales, appeared next to the big one. The chief was later buried on the shores of the new lake. Some attribute the Spook Hill enigma to the alligator seeking revenge, while others speculate that Cufcowellax has returned to defend his homeland from encroachment.

Housed in a 1927 mission-style structure that served as a Catholic church for 60 years, the Lake Wales Arts Center at 1099 SR 60 E. provides gallery and performance space for local actors and artists; phone (863) 676-8426. Florida's Natural Grove House Visitor Center on US 27 offers information about the citrus industry and local attractions, as well as a free glass of juice; phone (863) 679-4110 or (800) 237-7805. *See ad.*

Lake Wales Area Chamber of Commerce: 340 W. Central Ave., P.O. Box 191, Lake Wales, FL 33859-0191; phone (863) 676-3445.

Shopping areas: Eagle Ridge Mall, 5 miles north on US 27, has Dillard's, JCPenney and Sears as its anchor stores. Art galleries, antique shops and specialty stores can be found in the downtown Lake Wales Historic District.

THE DEPOT—LAKE WALES MUSEUM AND CULTURAL CENTER, 325 S. Scenic Hwy. (US 27A), is the former 1928 Atlantic Coast Line train depot. A turn-of-the-20th-century Pullman car is the highlight of the center's displays, which include photographs and memorabilia pertaining to local history and the railroad, cattle, citrus and turpentine industries. Also featured are a 1926 restored caboose, a 1944 engine and changing exhibits. The adjacent 1916 Lake Wales depot is restored as a train museum. Allow 30 minutes minimum. Mon.-Fri. 9-5, Sat. 10-4; closed some holidays. Free. Phone (863) 678-4209.

HISTORIC BOK SANCTUARY, 3 mi. n. off CR 17A (Burns Ave.), consists of 200 acres of gardens and grounds, featuring the 157-acre woodland Gardens created by Frederick Law Olmsted, Jr. The marble and coquina stone tower contains 60 bronze bells weighing from 17 pounds to more than 11 tons. Carillon recitals are

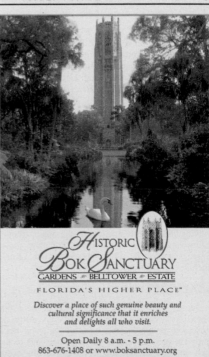

given daily at 3 (some days a recorded recital); selections are played every 30 minutes daily beginning at 10. Special recitals are announced in advance. The bells are best heard at a distance of about 200 yards.

The tower and gardens were dedicated to the American people by founder Edward Bok, a Dutch immigrant. A self-guiding tour leads visitors through walkways graced by thousands of native and exotic plants. Wildlife abounds and is not afraid of the public. Visitors can enjoy the reflecting pool; the large benches overlooking the highest point in central Florida—298 feet; Window by the Pond, a wildlife nature observatory; and the Pine Ridge Nature Reserve, a 1-mile trail showcasing the Long Leaf Pine-Turkey Oak Habitat. Pinewood Estate, a 20-room Mediterranean Revival-style mansion, is open seasonally for tours; the 6-week Christmas at Pinewood begins the day after Thanksgiving.

An audiovisual tour of the gardens and tower is presented in the Education and Visitor Center; the center also houses changing art exhibits and permanent exhibits about Edward Bok, the tower, carillon and the endangered species program. Seasonal guided nature walks depart daily from the visitor center. Picnic facilities and food are available. Gardens open daily 8-6. Last admission 1 hour before closing. Visitor center and other facilities open daily 9-5. Mansion tours daily at 11 and 1:30, Oct. 1 through mid-May. Grounds admission $6; ages 5-12, $2. Phone (863) 676-1408. *See color ad.*

LAKE KISSIMMEE STATE PARK is 8 mi. e. via SR 60, 5 mi. n. on Boy Scout Rd., then 5 mi. e. on Camp Mack Rd. following signs. Wildlife abounds in this part of Florida's Osceola Plain between lakes Kissimmee, Rosalie and Tiger, an area that forms the headwaters of the Everglades. During the ice ages this plain lay beneath the sea; the ancient shoreline and beach dunes still are recognizable in the form of a rise and dips on Camp Mack Road.

Thirteen miles of hiking trails wind through the park. An observation tower provides a good view. Daily 7-dusk. Admission $3.25 per vehicle (maximum eight people), $1 per person arriving by bicycle or on foot. Phone (863) 696-1112. *See Recreation Chart and the AAA Southeastern CampBook.*

Kissimmee Cow Camp, 14248 Camp Mack Rd., is a living-history representation of the area's frontier cattle country days in 1876. Sat.-Sun. and major holidays 9:30-4:30. Admission $3.25 per vehicle (includes park entrance fee).

LAKE WORTH (G-12) pop. 35,133, elev. 19'

Development of Lake Worth began in the 1900s when lakeshore lots were offered as giveaways to those who bought nearby tracts of fruit and truck land. The area became so popular that land to the west intended for development was virtually abandoned until the late 1930s, while the lake settlement

expanded and was named for Gen. William Jenkins Worth of Seminole Indian Wars fame.

A variety of recreational programs is offered throughout the city for visitors and residents alike, including golf, concerts in the park, shuffleboard, tennis and boating. Local theater groups perform at the Lake Worth Playhouse; phone (561) 586-6410. Concerts are held at Watson B. Duncan III Theater on the Palm Beach Community College campus; phone (561) 439-8141.

Lake Worth offers fine fishing. Freshwater varieties are caught in Lake Osborne at the city's western edge and from bridges spanning Lake Worth; saltwater species are snagged from one of Florida's longest municipally owned Atlantic Ocean piers as well as from charter craft for deep-sea and reef fishing. A trackless trolley provides service to the beach, shopping areas, parks and downtown businesses.

A 65-foot mural depicting the construction of King Solomon's Temple occupies one wall inside the Scottish Rite Masonic Temple at 2000 North D St. A video describes the mural and its Biblical subject along with the history of the masons; phone (561) 582-6794.

Lake Worth Chamber of Commerce: 807A Lucerne Ave., Lake Worth, FL 33460; phone (561) 582-4401.

LARGO—*see Tampa Bay p. 228.*

MADEIRA BEACH—*see Tampa Bay p. 229.*

MAITLAND—*see Orlando p. 178.*

MARATHON—*see The Florida Keys p. 69.*

MARCO ISLAND (H-9) pop. 14,879

At the northern tip of the Ten Thousand Islands, Marco Island is reached from US 41 via either SR 92 or 951; both bridges are free. This shell-gatherer's paradise on Florida's southern Gulf Coast has been transformed from a fishermen's retreat into a lively resort community. Golf, tennis, swimming and surfing are among the recreational activities.

Marco Island Area Chamber of Commerce: 1102 N. Collier Blvd., Marco Island, FL 34145; phone (239) 394-7549.

Shopping areas: Prime Outlets at Naples, 5 miles north on SR 951, offers 40 outlet shops representing manufacturers such as Bass Shoes, Dansk, Geoffrey Beene, Liz Claiborne and Mikasa.

MARCO ISLAND TROLLEY TOURS, boarded at most accommodations on Marco Island and Goodland Island, provides a 90-minute narrated tour of the island's historic sites, including seashell mounds built by Calusa Indians. Departures daily 10-4:45. Last boarding at 3:15. Fare (includes an all-day boarding pass) $16; ages 1-12, $7. Phone (239) 394-1600.

SAVE **VANTASTIC TOURS** picks up passengers from area hotels. These narrated tours begin aboard an air-conditioned van that transports visitors to various natural areas where they may see alligators, bald eagles, manatees, ospreys, red-shouldered hawks and turtles among many other specimens of Florida wildlife. Tours include a 1-hour airboat ride across the saw grass wilderness of the Everglades. Allow 5 hours minimum. Tours depart daily at 8 and 1, Oct.-Apr.; at 8, rest of year. Fare $72; ages 4-11, $42. AX, DS, MC, VI. Phone (941) 394-7699 or (866) 826-8687.

MARIANNA (A-5) pop. 6,230, elev. 89′

FLORIDA CAVERNS STATE PARK, 3 mi. n. on SR 166, has extensive limestone caverns with calcite formations, a museum, natural rock gardens and a horse trail (no horse rental). The Chipola River Canoe Trail, part of the Florida Canoe Trail System, begins here. Guided cavern tours cover a lighted passageway.

The park is open daily 8-dusk. Cavern tours are conducted daily 9-4. Park admission $3.25 per private vehicle (maximum eight people), $1 per person arriving by bicycle or on foot. Cavern admission $5; ages 3-12, $2.50. Canoe rental $10 per half-day, $15 per full day. Phone (850) 482-9598 for recorded information. *See Recreation Chart and the AAA Southeastern CampBook.*

MAYPORT—*see Jacksonville p. 96.*

MELBOURNE (E-11) pop. 71,382, elev. 21′

Melbourne's first residents were black freedmen who established a settlement in the area in the 1860s. The town was named Melbourne, after the Australian postmaster's hometown, in 1879. The arrival of the Florida East Coast Railroad in 1894 brought economic growth to the small community.

The introduction of another innovative form of travel—space flight—has led to the development of high-tech and electronics industries, an additional benefit of the city's proximity to the Kennedy Space Center *(see place listing p. 97).*

Melbourne-Palm Bay Area Chamber of Commerce: 1005 E. Strawbridge Ave., Melbourne, FL 32901-4782; phone (321) 724-5400 or (800) 771-9922.

Shopping areas: Melbourne Square Mall, on US 192, 2 miles east of I-95, contains Belk Lindsey, Burdines, Dillard's and JCPenney.

BREVARD MUSEUM OF ART AND SCIENCE, 2 blks. e. of US 1 at 1463 Highland Ave., presents changing exhibits of works by local, national and international artists. Workshops and demonstrations are presented on a regular basis. The Ruth Cote Clemente Children's Science Center offers more than 35 interactive exhibits. Allow 1 hour minimum. Tues.-Sat. 10-5, Sun. 1-5; closed major holidays. Admission $5; over 62, $3; students with ID $2; free to all Thurs. after 1. AX, MC, VI. Phone (321) 242-0737.

SAVE **BREVARD ZOO,** .5 mi. e. of I-95 exit 191 to 8225 N. Wickham Rd., features more than 480 animals representing some 130 species. From shaded boardwalks visitors can view such animals as alligators, giant anteaters, Florida panthers, river otters, giant flying foxes, red wolves and exotic birds. Paws-on is an interactive learning area and petting zoo for children. The Australia exhibit is home to red kangaroos, wallabies, emus, kookaburras and a free-flight aviary where birds can be hand-fed. Asian birds, giant fruit bats and miniature antelope inhabit the Flying Fox Forest.

The Wetlands Outpost explores the native Florida environment on 160 feet of raised boardwalk traversing 22 acres of wetland habitat; 20-minute guided kayak tours also are available. Zoo visitors may kayak the Indian River Lagoon on an extended 4-hour eco-tour; phone for rates and reservations. A train ride and food are available.

Allow 2 hours minimum. Daily 10-5; closed Thanksgiving and Dec. 25. Last admission 45 minutes before closing. Wetlands kayak tours daily 10:30-3:30. Admission $7; over 59, $6; ages 2-12, $5. Train $2. Kayak tour $3; under 11 must be with an adult, and under 5 are not permitted. Train $2. AX, DS, MC, VI. Phone (321) 254-9453.

Miami-Miami Beach

Population:

Miami 362,470   Miami Beach 87,933

Elevation:

Miami 20 ft.   Miami Beach 4 ft.

Popular Spots:

Miami Metrozoo.................. *(see p. 114)*

Vizcaya Museum and Gardens .. *(see p. 116)*

Cultivated from a tropical wilderness, Miami celebrated its centennial in 1996. Even Julia Tuttle and Henry Flagler, the visionaries who saw the potential of this seemingly inhospitable portion of south Florida, would be amazed to see the transformation the area has undergone. The former wilderness is now a thriving, colorful city, young and vibrant despite its 100 years. Mediterranean architecture and a contemporary skyline blend with Art Deco styling, just as the smell of orange blossoms now coexists with the scent of *arroz con pollo.*

Then there are the colors: flamingo pink, lime green, Caribbean blue. The landscape is punctuated with marzipan hues, predominant in the tropical deco of hip Miami Beach. And it is surely the image of a fuzzy orange Miami sun, green palms and azure waters that draw some 11 million vacationers annually to this new Casablanca.

Miami and Miami Beach, interchangeable in the minds of most tourists, in reality are vastly different. Miami is a larger and more diverse metropolis that caters to tourism but also supports light industry. Miami Beach, almost exclusively tourist-oriented, consists mostly of condos and hotels. In fact, squeezed into an area of only 7.5 square miles, sandwiched between the Atlantic Ocean and Biscayne Bay, is a dazzling array of hotels that can accommodate three times the city's usual population.

One of the first to recognize Miami's potential was Julia Tuttle. The Chicagoan arrived in 1891, enchanted by the sunshine and mild ocean breezes. South Florida then was frontier territory and Miami amounted to little more than the ruins of a U.S. army outpost and a few plantations. But the coastal location and commercial promise of the Miami River led to Tuttle's bold prediction—that the area would become one of the world's busiest seaports and a vital link for trade with the Americas and the Caribbean.

Tuttle unsuccessfully tried to persuade millionaire industrialist Henry Morrison Flagler to extend his rail line south from West Palm Beach. Then, in a fateful twist, an 1895 freeze destroyed most of Florida's northern citrus crop. Tuttle sent a bouquet of orange blossoms to Flagler, proof of a frost-free Miami. It was enough to change Flagler's mind: The Florida East Coast Railroad arrived in April 1896, and the city of Miami was incorporated 3 months later.

Among the first of the tourists and Northern transplants was New Jersey businessman John Collins, who had bought, sight unseen, a coconut plantation on one of Miami's barrier islands. Collins sought to link the isles with the mainland by building a bridge, but ran out of money before finishing the project.

Exclusive Fisher Island is named for the businessman who came to Collins' aid. Carl Fisher, inventor of the automobile headlight and owner of the Indianapolis Speedway, traded completion of the bridge for part of Collins' island property—and Miami Beach was born. Dredging Biscayne Bay to build up the narrow, sandy stretch, Collins sculpted

Getting There — starting on p. 110

Getting Around — starting on p. 111

What To See — starting on p. 112

What To Do — starting on p. 117

Where To Stay — starting on p. 517, 526

Where To Dine — starting on p. 525, 540

paradise, constructing golf courses, hotels, tennis courts and polo fields, beginning the halcyon days of winter retreats and sun-splashed resorts.

The first real estate boom was barely in full swing when it rocked out of control. Property sold for mere pennies, hawked on street corners by binder boys who would bind the sale with a slip of paper. Speculation was such that entire communities were designed and auctioned without so much as a brick laid, though there might be an imposing archway leading nowhere.

The whimsical, pastel-painted Art Deco hotels on South Beach today are gentle reminders of a re-awakening city after the dismal Depression era. Created in the streamlined moderne style, lodgings sported the mixture of austere and cheerful favored by designers of the day. Charmed by the look and Miami's affordability, vacationers, retirees and Northern transplants flocked to the area in the 1930s and '40s.

Miami's modern expansion saw a changing social climate and a growth of business opportunities. A second building boom was on, as servicemen who trained in Miami Beach during World War II returned with their families after the war. And the advent and increasing popularity of commercial aviation brought the city its first flush of international sun worshippers.

There were other firsts, such as the bittersweet press reviews of the 1950s when the city made national headlines during the U.S. Senate committee hearings on organized crime. Miami had attracted mafiosi, including the infamous Al Capone. The '50s were, nonetheless, heydays, as Arthur Godfrey and Jackie Gleason televised nationally from Miami studios and high fashion held sway in such stores as Saks Fifth Avenue, Bonwit Teller and Cartier. Few could conceive the turning point of 1959 and its profound implications.

When Fidel Castro overthrew Fulgencio Batista Zaldivar on Jan. 1, 1959, the first Cubans exiled to Miami were the deposed dictator's political and military henchmen. Wealthy Havana citizens and a brain drain of professionals—doctors, journalists, lawyers, conservative politicians—followed, suspicious of Castro's socialist drift. When widespread disillusion with the regime set in, an exodus began, and Miami's Cuban population swelled to 300,000 before the freedom flights ended in 1973.

By sheer numbers, Cuban expatriates transformed Miami; their entrepreneurial skills and desire for a new life formed the basis for a multinational society. Although the changing face of the city brought with it ethnic tensions, industry flourished. The next decade saw Miami's harbor become the world's largest cruise ship port.

Events in Cuba once again changed the face of the city. When Castro opened the port of Mariel,

140,000 Cuban refugees arrived in 1980. Liberty City and other overcrowded areas erupted in violence, and longtime residents, disheartened by the crime and commotion, headed north out of Miami-Dade County.

But Miami surmounted its crisis in a timely and spectacular fashion. The criminal-justice system worked to blot up hard-core criminals, and a $3 billion building boom downtown resulted in the glass skyscrapers and fanciful architecture along Biscayne Bay's boulevards.

Other Spanish-speaking groups also have made Miami their home, and Spanish is heard everywhere. Whether street signs and billboards are in English or Spanish first (nearly all display both) depends on how close they are to "Little Havana," the Latin district centering on S.W. Eighth Street, or *Calle Ocho.*

When producers discovered the city's unpredictable shapes and dazzling colors, Miami became the locale of a new television series. "Miami Vice" premiered in 1984, transforming the city into a cool, hip, hot metropolis. Property values rose, tourism boomed and investors rushed in. When "Miami Vice" ended in 1989, the city's international reputation had been set, and city leaders looked forward to capitalizing on the resulting mystique. They did not, of course, anticipate the devastating results of Hurricane Andrew, which demolished billions of dollars worth of real estate in 1992. But Miami survived.

As the cultural complexion of Miami continues to evolve, Hispanics, Central and South Americans and those of Caribbean heritage are joined by Asians and Europeans, transforming the city's social and economic fabric. Nowhere is this more apparent than in South Beach, where the Art Deco gems of yesterday are now the ultra-hip backdrop for America's Riviera.

Though much of the action is centered around the Art Deco District's refurbished landmarks, sidewalk cafes, nightclubs and beaches, the mainland is thriving as well. Little Havana and Little Haiti are reminders of Miami's cultural heritage, while downtown the highest concentration of international banks in the Southeast adds muscle to Miami's transcontinental economy.

Central to Miami-Dade County's worldwide air, sea and ground transportation networks is the Port of Miami, handling more than 5 million tons of containerized cargo annually. Miami International Airport ranks first among U.S. airports for international cargo, moving more than 1 million tons each year.

As America's new Ellis Island, Miami may very well be the most foreign of U.S. cities. The entrepreneurial spirit, however, that fostered its evolution from swampy wetland to diverse, international metropolis is distinctly American. The intriguing contrasts of hedonism and hardship are unmistakably Miami.

The Informed Traveler

 ## Whom To Call

Emergency: 911

Police (non-emergency): (305) 595-6263 (Miami-Dade County) or (305) 579-6111 (Miami)

Fire: (305) 595-6263 (Miami-Dade County) or (305) 579-6231 (Miami)

Time and Temperature: (305) 324-8811

Weather: (305) 229-4522

Hospitals: Baptist Hospital of Miami, (305) 596-1960; Jackson Memorial Hospital, (305) 585-1111.

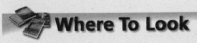 ## Where To Look

Newspapers

Miami's two main papers are the *Miami Herald* (morning) and *Diario Las Americas* (Spanish, afternoon). Miami Beach has the *Miami Beach Sun Post* (weekly).

Radio

Miami radio station WINZ (940 AM) is an all-news/weather station; WLRN (91.3 FM) is a member of National Public Radio.

Visitor Information

The Greater Miami Convention and Visitors Bureau distributes information Mon.-Fri. 8:30-5. Write 701 Brickell Ave., Suite 2700, Miami, FL 33131; phone (305) 539-3000, (888) 766-4264 locally or (800) 933-8448. *Miami/South Florida*, a monthly magazine, lists daily events.

What To Pack

Miami's average annual temperature is a balmy 76 degrees. December through March is delightful, with daytime highs in the mid-70s, comfortable lows around 60 and little rain. Miami is hot and humid the rest of the year. June through September can be sweltering, with daytime temperatures averaging around 90. Ocean breezes temper the heat along the coast.

The sun's ultraviolet rays are insidiously strong, especially when reflected off the water. Wear sunscreen—an SPF rating of at least 15 is recommended—and a hat.

Thunderstorms are common from May through October; carry an umbrella to be prepared for sudden showers. Severe storms and hurricanes are unlikely but do occur; Hurricane Andrew in 1992 is the most recent example. The hurricane season lasts from June through November. *For additional information see temperature chart p. 45.*

Lightweight resort wear is appropriate almost everywhere although there are ample opportunities to dress up. A light sweater is handy in some air-conditioned interiors.

Sales Tax: Miami-Dade County sales tax is 6.5 percent. An additional hotel room tax is 4 percent in Bal Harbour and Surfside and 6 percent in Miami Beach and the rest of Miami-Dade County.

Destination Miami-Miami Beach

*L*inked by causeways and an easygoing lifestyle, Miami and Miami Beach are an energizing mix of natural beauty and contemporary entertainment.

Beach and palm trees, Miami Beach. Miami Beach is known worldwide for its sunny days and sandy beaches.

*S*napshots of swaying palm trees and gently breaking waves share space in vacation albums with souvenir programs from professional sporting events. And reminiscences of exotic bougainvillea and hibiscus linger with memories of performing dolphins and rare wildlife.

See Vicinity map page 113

Miami Metrozoo, Miami. This pink flamingo, whose likeness graces lawns nationwide, looks as if it would be more at home in Miami Beach's Art Deco District. (See listing page 114)

Homestead
Florida City

Miami-Dade Cultural Center, Miami. This downtown destination offers two museums, a library and a spacious, sunny courtyard with interesting art objects. (See listing page 114)

*P*laces included in this AAA Destination City:

Coconut Grove	124	Homestead	125
Coral Gables	124	Key Biscayne	126
Florida City	125	North Miami Beach	126

North
Miami Beach

826

836

874

Coconut Grove

5

● Key Biscayne

Coral
Gables

9336

Miami

*Vizcaya Museum and
Gardens, Miami.*
Allow plenty of time to
explore the 10 acres of
formal gardens and the
34 rooms of this Italian
Renaissance-style villa
built in 1916. (See
listing page 116)

*Miami
Seaquarium,
Miami.*
Flipper and
friends frolic
during daily
performances
at this Miami
landmark.
(Hint: don't
sit too close
if you don't
want to
get wet.)
(See listing
page 115)

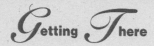

Getting There

By Car

Moving from the coast inland, the major north-south routes are SR A1A, US 1, I-95, US 441 and Florida's Turnpike. The coastal route—SR A1A—is by far the most scenic but is slow. It is the only approach to Miami Beach from the north. US 1 travels through cities and commercial areas. I-95 is a congested four- to six-lane freeway. Two- to four-lane US 441 traverses developed and industrial land with heavy traffic.

From farther north, through the central part of the state, comes Florida's Turnpike (toll), which swings in a wide arc to the west around Miami; it also is linked directly with the I-95 connection into downtown. SR 826 (Palmetto Expressway) provides another western bypass closer to the city limits. SR 836 (Dolphin Expressway) runs east and west, connecting to the turnpike, I-15 and SR 826.

From the west come I-75, US 27 and US 41 (Tamiami Trail), all of which become congested as they approach the city limits.

Seven causeways span Biscayne Bay to link Miami and Miami Beach: Mac-Arthur (US 41 and SR A1A), Venetian (toll), Julia Tuttle (I-195), 79th Street, Broad (96th Street), 163rd Street and William Lehman (SR 856).

Air Travel

Miami International Airport, northwest at Le Jeune Road and N.W. 36th Street, is centrally located 7 miles from downtown. It ranks ninth in the United States and 14th in the world for total passenger traffic, serving approximately 34 million travelers annually. A $5.4 billion airport expansion is expected to be completed in 2010.

Exit the airport on Central Boulevard east to Le Jeune Road (S.W. 42nd Avenue). To go directly downtown, take Le Jeune Road south to SR 836 East. For points north, take Le Jeune Road north to SR 112 (Airport Expressway) and I-95 north. For Miami Beach, take Le Jeune Road north to SR 112, following the signs for I-195 and the 36th Street (Julia Tuttle) Causeway.

Kendall, West Miami and other points west are accessed by taking Le Jeune Road south to SR 836 (Dolphin Expressway). SR 836 crosses northbound/southbound SR 826 (Palmetto Expressway). To reach Coconut Grove and Coral Gables, take Le Jeune Road south.

Taxis offer transportation to hotels but at almost twice the price of limousines, which may not leave the airport until all seats are filled and may stop often to discharge passengers. Some

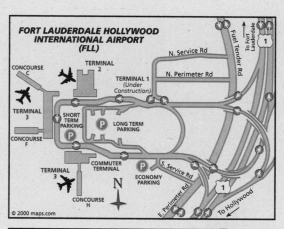

hotels offer shuttles for their guests; the shuttles stop only at departure level airport entrances. Airport limousine service to most locations in Miami-Dade and Broward counties may be charged at a flat rate; return trip rates usually are less.

The Fort Lauderdale-Hollywood International Airport, between I-95 and US 1, just south of SR 84, is a convenient option for those traveling to the northern portions of the Miami-Miami Beach area. The airport is approximately 45-minutes to 1-hour north of Miami via I-95, US 1 or Florida's Turnpike.

Miami and Miami Beach are served by many major car rental agencies. Arrangements should be made before you leave on your trip; your local AAA club office can provide this assistance or additional information. Hertz, (800) 654-3080, or (305) 871-0300 at Miami International Airport, and (305) 534-4661 inside the Fontainebleau Hilton in Miami Beach, offers discounts to AAA members.

Rail Service

The Amtrak Station is at 8303 N.W. 37th Ave. For arrival information phone (305) 835-1221; for reservations and other information phone (800) 872-7245.

Buses

Greyhound Lines Inc. stations are at 4111 N.W. 27th St., (305) 871-1810, in Miami; at 16560 N.E. Sixth Ave., (305) 945-0801, in North Miami. For fares phone (800) 231-2222.

Getting Around

Street System

Negotiating the streets of Miami can be mastered easily despite its sprawling layout. Two helpful points of reference are the city's cluster of skyscrapers, downtown at the geographical center, and Biscayne Bay, always to the east.

Miami is divided into four quadrants: Northeast, Northwest, Southeast and Southwest. Should you be looking for a particular address within the city, the section designation (N.E., N.W., S.E., S.W.) is an important factor.

Flagler Street divides the city north-south, while Miami Avenue is the east-west divider. Avenues, courts and places run north and south; streets and terraces run east and west. Except for the communities of Hialeah and Coral Gables, which have their own numbering systems, all street numbers start at Flagler Street and at Miami Avenue.

Unless otherwise posted, the speed limit is 30 mph in business and residential areas and 55 mph on highways. It is 65 or 70 mph on Florida's Turnpike and other designated highways. Miami has a typical big city rush hour (7 to 9 a.m. and 4:30 to 6 p.m.). Expressway traffic is particularly slow. Right turns on red are permitted after a complete stop,

unless otherwise posted. Left turns on red are permitted from a one-way street onto another one-way street after a complete stop. U-turns are permitted except where otherwise posted.

The primary point of reference in Miami Beach is Collins Avenue (SR A1A), the city's major north-south through street. Along or near this thoroughfare is the famed string of hotels and motels, with the residential area lying west to Bay Road.

In both cities the speed limit is 25 mph or as posted. Motorists should not try to follow an unfamiliar route during rush hours. The lunch hour also is busy.

Directional signs sporting an orange sunburst on a blue background begin at the airport and guide motorists to some of the more popular destinations within the Miami area as well as pointing out the quickest routes to such resort areas as Orlando and Key West.

Parking

Both Miami and Miami Beach have downtown, on-street metered parking, parking lots and garages. Downtown metered street parking is available in Miami at the rate of $1 per hour.

Miami has four municipal parking garages: at 40 N.W. Third, 190 N.W. Third, 90 S.W. First and 100 S.E. Second streets. Rates at the former two are $1.25 per 30 minutes to a daily maximum of $9.50; at the latter two the rates are $2 and $3 respectively per half-hour with daily maximums of $14.50 (on S.W. First) and $21 (at S.E. Second). Some specialty districts, such as Bayside Marketplace, have their own lots and fee schedules. Lot rates vary according to location, but they generally start at about 50c to $1 for the first hour and about 50c for each additional half-hour. Bayside Marketplace charges $2 per hour for parking after 9 a.m.

On-street parking in Miami Beach often is difficult to find. Visiting drivers should look carefully for signs when parking on Miami Beach streets due to the number of areas where parking is restricted.

Metered parking is available throughout Miami Beach at the rate of 25¢ per 15 minutes to half-hour. There are five municipal parking garages: at 42nd Street between Sheridan and Royal Palm avenues; 17th Street between Penna and Meridian avenues; Collins Avenue at 13th Street; at the intersection of Michigan Avenue and Lincoln Road; and Drexel Avenue at 12th Street.

There are also numerous public parking lots in the Miami Beach area. Rates vary by lot and location. Lots with daily rates generally charge $1 an hour. Some lots are served by electronic meters that charge the standard metered rate; these lots offer a daily rate only during events.

Taxis & Limousines

Cabs are plentiful and operate on the meter system. Fares are $1.50 base fee plus $2 per mile and 30c for each minute of waiting. The largest companies are Yellow Cab Co., (305) 444-4444, and Metro Taxi, (305) 888-8888. Consult the telephone directory for others.

Private limousine service is $50 to $75 an hour, with a 2-hour minimum; most companies add a 20 percent driver gratuity.

Public Transportation

The Miami-Dade County Transit Agency links greater Miami with buses, Metrorail and Metromover. Metrorail is an elevated rail system serving

downtown Miami; it also runs north and west to Hialeah and south to Kendall. Metromover is a 4.4-mile elevated rail system that loops around downtown.

Buses operate countywide. The fare is $1.25, plus 25c for a transfer to another bus or to Metrorail; transfers to Metromover are free. Express bus fare is $1.50. Exact change is required. Reduced-fare Golden Passports are available for senior citizens.

Metrorail fare is $1.25; exact change is required. Bus transfers are 25¢; transfers to Metromover are free. Regular Metromover fare is 25¢; there is a $1 fee to transfer from Metromover to a bus or Metrorail. Both trains operate downtown daily 5:30 a.m.-midnight; service on the outer loop ends at 10:30 p.m. Metromover trains arrive every 90 seconds; Metrorail trains arrive approximately every 20 minutes. For schedules and route information about both systems phone (305) 770-3131.

What To See

THE AMERICAN POLICE HALL OF FAME AND MUSEUM, 3801 Biscayne Blvd. (US 1), 2 blks. n. of jct. I-195, displays more than 10,000 items relating to law enforcement. Exhibits include a mock crime scene, execution equipment, specialty cars and replicas of jail cells. A memorial lists the names of U.S. police officers killed in the line of duty since 1960. Allow 1 hour minimum. Daily 10-5:30; closed Dec. 25. Admission $12; over 65, $9; ages 6-11, $6; police officers and family survivors free. MC, VI. Phone (305) 573-0070.

BASS MUSEUM OF ART, 2121 Park Ave. in Miami Beach, features a permanent collection of Old Master paintings and sculpture, contemporary art and architecture. Temporary exhibits in the Art Deco building include contemporary and historical art from throughout the world.

Allow 1 hour minimum. Tues. and Thurs.-Sat. 10-5, Wed. and second Thurs. of the month 10-9, Sun. 1-5; closed holidays. Admission $6, over 64 and students with ID $4, under 6 free. AX, MC, VI. Phone (305) 673-7530.

CARL FISHER MONUMENT is in Fisher Park at Alton Rd. and Surprise Ave. in Miami Beach. The monument, which consists of a bust of Fisher mounted on a large keystone, commemorates the man who helped to establish Miami Beach and who deeded many public beaches and parks to the city.

THE HOLOCAUST MEMORIAL, 1933-1945 Meridian Ave., is dedicated to the memory of the 6 million Jews who suffered and died at the hands of the Nazis during their rule of Germany. The focus of the memorial is a 42-foot-high bronze arm rising from the ground; sculptured people climb it, looking for an escape.

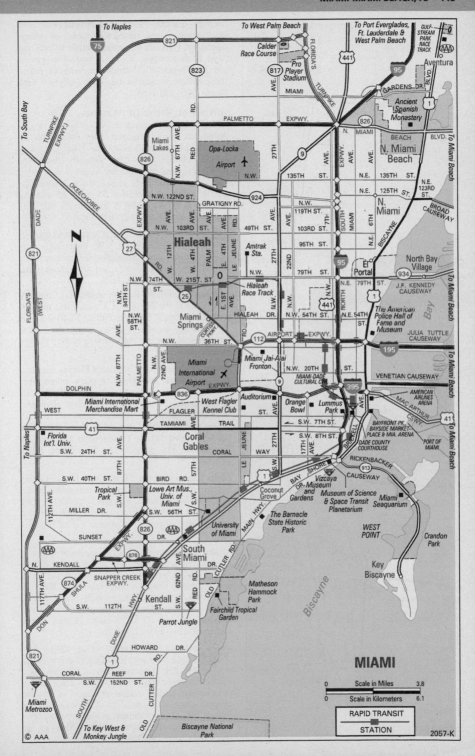

MIAMI

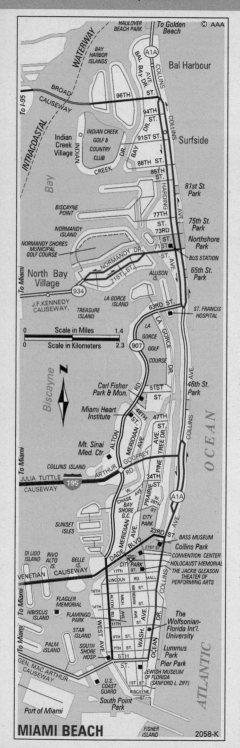

MIAMI BEACH

2058-K

Other features include a memorial wall with black granite panels etched with names of victims; a series of vignettes displaying victims helping victims; a photographic mural; a meditation garden; and the Dome of Contemplation with an eternal flame. Allow 30 minutes minimum. Daily 9-9. Free. Phone (305) 538-1663.

JEWISH MUSEUM OF FLORIDA, 2 blks. s. of Fifth St. at 301 Washington Ave., is housed in a restored Art Deco synagogue. The core exhibit depicts Jewish life in Florida since 1763. Temporary exhibits change three times annually. Films and public programs are presented. Allow 1 hour minimum. Tues.-Sun. 10-5; closed major national and Jewish holidays. Admission $5; over 65 and students with ID $4; under 6 free; family rate $10; free to all Sat. Phone (305) 672-5044.

MIAMI-DADE CULTURAL CENTER, 101 W. Flagler St. at S.W. First Ave., comprises three Spanish-style buildings with arched windows, tile roofs and wrought-iron fixtures surrounding a large plaza.

Allow 1 hour, 30 minutes minimum. Combination ticket to the Miami Art Museum and the Historical Museum of Southern Florida $6. Visitors can get a parking discount at the garages to the west of the center if they get their parking stubs validated at either museum.

Historical Museum of Southern Florida uses artifacts, dioramas, audiovisual displays, photographs and other media to illustrate the past 10,000 years of the region's history and development. Highlights include a replica of a pioneer house and a 1920s trolley car. Mon.-Sat. 10-5 (also Thurs. 5-9), Sun. noon-5; closed Jan. 1, Thanksgiving and Dec. 25. Admission $5; ages 6-12, $2. Phone (305) 375-1492.

Main Library of the Miami-Dade Public Library System offers a lecture and concert series. Mon.-Sat. 9-6 (also Thurs. 6-9 p.m.), Sun. 1-5, Oct. 1-weekend before Memorial Day; Mon.-Sat. 9-6 (also Thurs. 6-9 p.m.), rest of year. Closed holidays. Free. Phone (305) 375-2665.

Miami Art Museum offers two stories of works by international artists, including major touring exhibitions focusing on contemporary art from the 1940s to the present. Tues.-Fri. 10-5 (also third Thurs. of the month 5-9), Sat.-Sun. noon-5; closed Jan. 1, Thanksgiving and Dec. 25. Admission $5, over 65 and students with ID $2.50, under 12 free; free to all Sun. Phone (305) 375-3000.

MIAMI METROZOO is at 12400 S.W. 152nd St. (Coral Reef Dr.), .2 mi. w. of jct. SR 821 (Florida's Tpke.). Metrozoo is a cageless zoo where animals roam in settings similar to their natural habitats. The spacious exhibits cover the continents of Africa, Asia and Europe with such inhabitants as chimpanzees, orangutans, elephants, bongo antelopes, Malayan sun bears and Cuban crocodiles.

Asian River Life is home to small-clawed otters, clouded leopards, Malayan water monitors and blood pythons. Winding paths and tunnels separate the animals from the visitors in this jungle exhibit. Also featured are rare white Bengal tigers, whose island replicates an Asian temple; an African plains exhibit, where giraffes, zebras and ostriches coexist as they do in the wild; and a gorilla family.

Animal shows are presented three times daily. An air-conditioned monorail provides an overview of the zoo's 290 acres. Viewing caves are offered. The Children's Zoo has an ecology theater and a petting zoo. Food is available.

Allow 3 hours minimum. Daily 9:30-5:30. Last admission 1 hour, 30 minutes before closing. Admission $8.95; ages 3-12, $4.75. AX, MC, VI. Phone (305) 251-0400.

[SAVE] MIAMI SEAQUARIUM, 4400 Rickenbacker Cswy., offers shows and presentations as well as numerous marine mammal exhibits. Divers hand feed reef fish and moray eels in a 750,000-gallon saltwater aquarium. Popular shows involve the funny exploits of Salty the Sea Lion and his friends and the graceful beauty of the Pacific white-sided dolphins that perform with Lolita the killer whale. Other features include sharks and endangered manatees and sea turtles. Food is available.

Allow 4 hours, 30 minutes minimum. Daily 9:30-6. Last admission 1 hour, 30 minutes before closing. Admission $22.95; over 55, $20.95; ages

3-9, $17.95. Parking $5. AX, MC, VI. Phone (305) 361-5705. *See color ad.*

[SAVE] MONKEY JUNGLE is 22 mi. s.w. on US 1, then 3 mi. w., or Florida Tpke. exit 11 and then 4 mi. w., at 14805 S.W. 216th St. Visitors embark upon a jungle safari to the wilds of South America, Asia and Africa, where monkeys roam freely above enclosed walkways. The 30-acre reserve is home to more than 400 primates representing 30 species. Habitats include the Camaroon Forest, Parrots of the World and the Amazonian Rain Forest. Among various daily shows is a demonstration of the Java monkey troop's ability to forage and dive for food.

Allow 2 hours, 30 minutes minimum. Daily 9:30-5. Last admission 1 hour before closing. Admission $15.95; over 65, $12.95; ages 3-9, $9.95. AX, DC, DS, MC, VI. Phone (305) 235-1611.

MUSEUM OF SCIENCE AND SPACE TRANSIT PLANETARIUM, s.w. of jct. I-95 and US 1 at 3280 S. Miami Ave., can be reached via the pedestrian overpass from the Vizcaya Metrorail station.

Miami Museum of Science presents national traveling exhibitions spanning topics from archeology to zoology. Permanent exhibits include Smithsonian Expeditions, where visitors trek the paths blazed by early scientists and explorers in search of rare artifacts in the Americas. The outdoor Wildlife Center is a rehabilitation facility for injured birds of prey including American bald eagles, hawks, falcons and owls.

At Miami Seaquarium® dolphins and whales fly. Sea lions sing. Flamingos stroll by. And people have the time of their lives. Just ten minutes from downtown Miami or the Port. You can see dozens of thrilling shows and marine life exhibits. Or take the plunge and swim with our dolphins. For more information, just give us a call at 305-361-5705.

An uplifting experience that's always tons of fun.

Wait'll you see what there is to see!

PRESENT YOUR AAA CARD & RECEIVE 10% OFF REGULAR ADMISSION.

Miami Seaquarium
4400 Rickenbacker Causeway
Miami, Florida 33149
www.miamiseaquarium.com

Daily 10-6; closed Thanksgiving and Dec. 25. Last admission 1 hour before closing. Admission (including Space Transit Planetarium) $10; over 61 and students with ID $8; ages 3-12, $6; half-off admission Mon.-Fri. after 4:30. AX, MC, VI. Phone (305) 646-4200.

Space Transit Planetarium presents multimedia and star shows daily, including demonstrations for finding the current season's constellations and planets in the night sky. Allow 1 hour, 30 minutes minimum. Planetarium open daily 10-6; phone for show schedule. Observatory open Fri. 8-10 p.m. (weather permitting); free star show Fri. at 7:30 p.m. Admission (including Miami Museum of Science) $10; over 61 and students with ID $8; ages 3-12, $6. AX, MC, VI. Phone (305) 646-4270, or (305) 646-4420 for show information.

PARROT JUNGLE is at 11000 S.W. 57th Ave., 11 mi. s.w. at jct. Red Rd. (S.W. 57th Ave.) and Killian Dr. (S.W. 112th St.). This bird sanctuary, wildlife habitat and botanical garden was founded by Austrian-born Franz Scherr in 1936. The Trained Parrot Show highlights some of the park's more talented residents, including parrots, cockatoos and macaws. Dragons and Monsters features a rare albino alligator and other exotic reptiles. Jungle Creatures brings visitors face-to-face with nocturnal animals, and Primate Encounter offers an educational look at orangutans, gibbons and other monkeys. The park also features a lory aviary, alligator and crocodile pools, a playground and petting zoo.

Allow 4 hours minimum. Daily 9:30-6. Last admission 1 hour before closing. Admission $15.95; over 65, $13.95; ages 3-10, $11.95. **Note:** Parrot Jungle is scheduled to move to Watson Island on the MacArthur Causeway (I-395) in early 2003; phone ahead to verify location. AX, MC, VI. Phone (305) 666-7834.

VIZCAYA MUSEUM AND GARDENS, 3251 S. Miami Ave., is an Italian Renaissance-style estate. Formerly the estate of industrialist James Deering, the 10-acre estate is now a museum featuring 34 rooms lavishly furnished with European decorative arts representing the Renaissance, baroque, rococo and neoclassic eras. The once open-air home has been enclosed unobtrusively with glass to protect the valuable furnishings from the weather. The use of cameras within the house is prohibited.

Hedges and walls divide the estate into many small gardens. Extensive formal gardens with pools and fountains contain sculptures from France and Italy. At the foot of the steps leading to Biscayne Bay, an unusual sculptured barge creates an area of calm water.

Allow 2 hours minimum. House open daily 9:30-5. Gardens open daily 9:30-5:30. Closed Dec. 25. Last admission at 4:30. Admission $10; over 61, $8; ages 6-12, $5. AX, MC, VI. Phone (305) 250-9133. *See ad.*

SAVE **THE WOLFSONIAN-FLORIDA INTERNA-TIONAL UNIVERSITY** is at 1001 Washington Ave. in Miami Beach's Art Deco District. Housed in a renovated 1920s Mediterranean-style warehouse, the museum features furniture, paintings, ceramics, architectural models, posters, books and memorabilia that depict the history, art, architecture and design of the late 19th and early 20th centuries.

Allow 1 hour minimum. Mon.-Tues. and Fri.-Sat. 11-6, Thurs. 11-9, Sun. noon-5; closed Jan. 1, July 4, Thanksgiving and Dec. 25. Admission $5, over 54 and students with ID $3.50, under 6 free; free to all Thurs. 6-9 p.m. Phone (305) 531-1001.

What To Do

Sightseeing

Driving Tours

Main and Ingraham highways and Old Cutler Road, south from Coconut Grove, offer scenic drives through Coconut Grove and Coral Gables. Old Cutler Highway passes Matheson Hammock Park and Fairchild Tropical Garden (see Coral Gables p. 125).

South Miami Avenue, between 15th Road and Dixie Highway, is lined with royal poinciana trees. During late May and June the trees are ablaze with red flowers.

An interesting drive in Miami Beach is along Collins Avenue, with its hotels and motels. Also of interest are the magnificent homes and estates, which run the architectural gamut from Spanish-Mediterranean to bold modern. Although not open to the public, these can be seen by driving around some of the private islands accessible from the MacArthur, Venetian, North Bay and Broad causeways.

Walking Tours

There are several opportunities for exploration on foot. Coconut Grove, with its varied architecture and bohemian air, is particularly appealing.

The Art Deco District in Miami Beach is a showcase for the movement's characteristic architectural touches: porthole windows, geometric patterns, rounded corners and glass-block construction as well as walls bathed in fuchsia, turquoise, chartreuse and lavender. The Miami Design Preservation League offers a 90-minute tour of the area Thursdays at 6:30 p.m. and Saturdays at 10:30 a.m. The tour begins and ends at the Art Deco Welcome Center at Ocean Front Auditorium, 1001 Ocean Dr. in Miami Beach; phone (305) 672-2014. The fee is $15. The organization also arranges other Miami Beach area tours and provides audiotapes for self-guided tours.

Little Havana, S.W. 12th Avenue to S.W. 27th Avenue, has open-air markets, music, shops, restaurants and a plaza, all of which reflect the Cuban culture.

Spectator Sports

In addition to year-round sunshine and white, sandy beaches, Miami is blessed with an abundance of professional sport offerings, including four major-league teams. No matter what your preference might be, you'll find a venue and a crowd of like-minded fans ready to cheer on their favorites.

Auto Racing

The 5,000-seat stadium at **Hialeah Speedway,** 3300 Okeechobee Rd., holds weekly stock-car races in five divisions; phone (305) 821-6644.

The **Homestead-Miami Speedway,** 1 Speedway Blvd. in Homestead, has a 1.5-mile oval track that is negotiated by some of the sport's top names. For information phone (305) 230-7223.

Baseball

Fans of the National League **Florida Marlins** passionately support their team during home games at **Pro Player Stadium,** 2267 Dan Marino Blvd., east of 27th Avenue in North Miami; phone (305) 626-7400. The Marlins brought the World Series title home to Miami in 1997. The national pastime also is played locally in the college ranks when the **University of Miami Hurricanes** take the field on the UM campus at **Mark Light Stadium.**

Basketball

The Atlantic division champion **Miami Heat** have been a hot ticket in town since their 1988 debut. During their October to April season, the Heat play at the new **American Airlines Arena**, downtown on Biscayne Boulevard adjacent to Bayside Marketplace; phone (786) 777-4328 for information.

Football

Backed by legions of "dolfans," the **Miami Dolphins** suit up for battle at the 75,000-seat Pro Player Stadium; phone (954) 452-7000 for the Dolphins or (305) 623-6100 for the stadium. The **Orange Bowl** stadium at 1501 N.W. Third St. is home turf for the University of Miami Hurricanes; phone (305) 643-7100. Despite five national championship titles, the 'Canes seldom fill up the stadium, so tickets are not difficult to come by.

Greyhound Racing

The dogs average a swift 40 mph at **Flagler Greyhound Track,** 401 N.W. 38th Ct., from June through November; phone (305) 649-3000.

Horse Racing

Thoroughbreds run to the roar of the crowd December through May at **Gulfstream Park,** 901 S. Federal Hwy. in nearby Hallandale *(see Hallandale Beach p. 78),* about a half-hour drive north from downtown Miami. The scenic track, encircling an artificial lake, is host to numerous major races; phone (305) 931-7223.

The usual March-to-May season is extended at **Calder Race Course,** just south of County Line Road (SR 852) at 21001 N.W. 27th Ave., where the

horses run from late April to early January on a 1-mile course in a glass-enclosed, air-conditioned sports facility. Phone (305) 625-1311 for specific starting and wrap-up dates.

Jai-Alai

In this high-speed, indoor version of lacrosse, players climb the walls to catch and hurl balls *(pelotas)* with woven baskets *(cestas).* Spectators place bets on the evening's players from behind a protective wall of glass. See the action for yourself at America's oldest jai-alai arena *(fronton),* the **Miami Jai-Alai Fronton,** 3500 N.W. 37th Ave.; phone (305) 633-6400.

Note: Policies on admitting children to parimutuel betting facilities vary. Phone in advance for specific information.

Recreation

A wealth of clear blue skies and a climate conducive to outdoor activity any time of the year make Miami a "hot" spot for those in search of fun in the sun. This tropical playground, with an average annual temperature of 76 F, comes equipped with aquamarine waters and more than enough landbased activities to suit all tastes.

Bicycling

Few places offer such diverse cycling environments as Miami. Pedal the hard-packed sands of **Miami Beach** while enjoying the sun and sights, or take the bicycle path that winds beneath a canopy of trees in **Coconut Grove,** where you can hop off and cruise through the neighborhood's colorful downtown area. Slightly more removed is the tropical escape of **Key Biscayne.** Here, on an island just 7 miles long and 2 miles wide, are 12 miles of bicycling trails. Bicycle rentals are available at all of the above locations; helmets are required for those under 17.

Experienced bicyclists desiring more extensive routes can contact the Miami-Dade Bicycle Pedestrian Program, which distributes maps about bicycling and bicycling safety and outlines some of Miami's more than 180 miles of bicycle trails; phone (305) 375-1647. A color-coded map of Miami-Dade County's suitable roads also is available.

Fishing

An abundance of water naturally brings plenty of fishing opportunities, and the popularity of bridge fishing, seen all over Miami, is just a prelude to the opportunities available in a city where fishing is serious business. **South Pointe Park** in south Miami Beach offers excellent surf casting. Although bridge fishing is generally not allowed, it is permitted on the old **Rickenbacker Causeway,** which was left standing for that purpose when the new bridge was constructed for automobile traffic. Several piers in Miami Beach, as well as the **Tamiami Canal,** also are favorites of anglers.

Numerous marinas offer deep-sea fishing excursions, where avid anglers haul in prizes that range from snapper and bonita to big game catches like sailfish, tarpon and bluefish.

Kelley Fishing Fleet, 10800 Collins Ave. at Haulover Marina, provides party boats for half-day or full-day excursions out of Miami Beach; phone (305) 945-3801. Private charter boats abound at Haulover, with many offering 2-, 3- and 4-day fishing trips to the Bahamas; make the rounds and choose the one that suits your needs.

Licenses, required for freshwater fishing, are available at bait and tackle shops, sporting goods and discount department stores, as well as the county tax collector's office in the Miami-Dade County Courthouse, 140 W. Flagler St., Miami, FL 33130. Licenses also are available by mail; phone (888) 347-4356 (a credit card is required).

Golf

More than 30 golf courses provide a wide choice of greens for hackers and seasoned golfers alike. Crandon Park Golf Course, 6700 Crandon Blvd. in Key Biscayne, (305) 361-9129, is recognized by most Florida golfers as the No. 1-ranked public course in the state; it also is among the top public links in the country. All courses listed below offer at least 18 holes and are open to the public.

Sites in the Miami area include Bayshore, 2401 Biarritz Dr. in Miami Beach, (305) 868-6502; Biltmore, 1210 Anastasia in Coral Gables, (305) 460-5364; Don Shula's Hotel and Golf Club, 6842 Main St. in Miami Lakes, (305) 821-1150; Doral Park Golf and Country Club, 5001 N.W. 104th Ave., (305) 591-8800; Golf Club of Miami, 6801 Miami Gardens Dr., (305) 829-8449; International Links Miami-Melreese, 1802 N.W. 37th Ave., (305) 633-4583; Killian Green, 9980 S.W. 104th St., (305) 271-0917; Miami Springs Golf Course, 650 Curtiss Pkwy. in Miami Springs, (305) 805-5180; and Miccosukee Golf & Country Club, 6401 Kendall Lakes Dr., (305) 382-3930.

The two city-owned Miami Beach courses welcome guests, and many hotels and motels have arrangements with private and semiprivate courses that allow guests to play.

Tennis

Miami's balmy climate allows for year-round tennis dates, and nearly 500 public courts cater to the racket. A majority of the hotels and motels in Miami and Miami Beach have private tennis facilities for their guests. Nearly all charge an hourly fee for use by nonresidents.

Best bets include the **Tennis Center at Crandon Park,** 7300 Crandon Blvd. in Key Biscayne, with

hard courts; phone (305) 365-2300. Miami Beach's **Flamingo Tennis Center,** at Jefferson and 11th streets, offers 19 well-maintained clay courts; phone (305) 673-7761. For additional information about public courts phone the Miami-Dade County Parks Department at (305) 755-7800.

Water Sports

Whether you like zipping across its surface or exploring the world below it, everything you need to enjoy the water can be found in Miami, and all of it can be rented—from kayaks, windsurfers and boogie boards to catamarans, sailboats, personal watercraft and scuba equipment.

Many scuba and sail shops offer day-trip packages that include rental equipment and lessons for windsurfing, scuba diving and snorkeling. There are many sunken hulls, reefs and underwater gardens that provide excellent opportunities for photography or exploration. North of Snapper Creek and south of Matheson Hammock Park is one of the better snorkeling sites. Another favorite location is near **Fowley Rocks Light** just south of Key Biscayne.

Boating is popular in Miami. Boats of all sizes and descriptions are for hire, whether for pleasure cruising, fishing or water skiing. **Dinner Key** and waterfront Coconut Grove are pristine and popular sites for launching sailboats. Other locations for sailboat rentals are available around the bay and on

the **Miami River.** Boating events, whose locations and schedules are printed in area newspapers, take place throughout the year.

Powerboat rentals are available from **Club Nautico** at several locations: at Monty Trainer Restaurant, 2560 S. Bayshore Dr. in Coconut Grove, (305) 858-6258; at Crandon Park Marina in Key Biscayne, (305) 361-9217; and at Miami Beach Marina, in Miami Beach, (305) 673-2502. Renters must be at least 21 years of age.

Water skiing and windsurfing instruction and equipment are available throughout the area. Many shops are clustered around the 79th Street Causeway (North Bay). Skiing is good all along the bay.

Personal watercraft also can be rented. Surfing, while not the best in the country, attracts many enthusiasts. Two of the best spots are **South Beach** and **Haulover Beach.**

Some of the most popular white sand beaches in the Miami area are at **Bill Baggs Cape Florida State Recreation Area** and **Crandon Park.** Miami Beach's oceanfront restoration program added 150

to 200 feet to the width of the city's 10.5-mile stretch of beach, southward from 87th Terrace to the south end of Miami Beach.

Shopping

Greater Miami can easily accommodate those with a shop-'til-you-drop mentality. Although big city congestion can mean rare parking spaces and a frenzied atmosphere, such inconveniences are quickly forgotten by those who browse the shops' enticements. And, because of Miami's tourist orientation, the area is a treasure trove of souvenirs, from technicolor T-shirts to opulent *objets d'art.*

Antiques

Miami's tastes in antiques are far from mainstream. Shops are hidden around the region, to be uncovered like sunken treasure. In Coral Gables, fine European furniture, clocks, bronzes and art glass are found at **Alhambra Antiques Center,** 2850 Salzedo St.; **Olde Tyme Shoppe,** 1423 Ponce de Leon Blvd., offers vintage pocket watches, chiming watches, clocks and other unique collector pieces. And, of course, where else would you expect to find a wealth of Art Deco wares but in the heart of the trendy Art Deco District?

Malls

More than 160 specialty shops fill the spacious **Dadeland Mall,** 7535 N. Kendall Dr. in Kendall. Anchored by Florida's largest Burdines department store, Dadeland features JCPenney, Lord & Taylor, Saks Fifth Avenue and The Limited/Express. Also in Kendall, the open-air [SAVE] **The Falls,** 8888 S.W.

136th St., has Miami's only Bloomingdale's department store as well as more than 100 ritzy shops in a lush, tropical setting.

Just west of the airport, **Miami International Mall,** 1455 N.W. 107th Ave., has Burdines, JCPenney and Sears in addition to 140 smaller stores. Off the Palmetto Expressway at the N.W. 103rd Street exit in Hialeah is **Westland Mall.** Burdines, JCPenney and Sears join 100 smaller shops.

At 19501 Biscayne Blvd. in Aventura, a short hop off the William Lehman Causeway (SR 856), **Aventura Mall** is anchored by Burdines, JCPenney, Lord & Taylor, Macy's and Sears. Specialty boutiques are among the mall's 250 shops and restaurants. **Cutler Ridge Mall,** US 1S and Caribbean Boulevard, has Burdines, JCPenney and Sears among its 125 stores.

Specialty Districts

In addition to a multitude of malls, Miami also features upscale and themed shopping districts. The boutique district along **Collins Avenue** in South Beach features Armani Exchange, Banana Republic and Nicole Miller. Continental cafes and the boutiques of Bulgari, Cartier, Gucci, Louis Vuitton, Tiffany & Co. and Ungaro, to name a few, give credence to the internationally renowned status of **Bal Harbour Shops,** 9700 Collins Ave. in Bal Harbour; the shops also claim Florida's largest Neiman Marcus store. In this area it is not just business as usual; gracious transactions and outstanding service are customary in Bal Harbour's elegant setting.

The 50 swanky boutiques in the European-styled **Streets of Mayfair,** 2911 Grand Ave. in Coconut Grove, proffer exclusive gifts, art, antiques and apparel; late-night clubs and trendy restaurants are nestled around the palm trees and waterfalls as well. VIP services for shopping, mailing or wrapping add the extra touch for which Mayfair is known.

Fun, funky and favored for drinks by an after-work crowd, the **Bayside Marketplace,** 401 Biscayne Blvd., is a downtown shopping, dining and entertainment mecca on Biscayne Bay. Designed after the historic Faneuil Hall Marketplace in Boston, the waterfront arcade combines more than 100 specialty boutiques, street performers, restaurants and outdoor eateries, and nightly open-air concerts to create a festive atmosphere. The **Pier 5 Market,** part of the complex, showcases the works of local artisans, entrepreneurs and inventors.

Rustic outdoor push carts, avant-garde clothing stores and lavishly decorated plazas are the hallmarks of **Coconut Grove,** Miami's tropical, pedestrian-friendly shopping and dining village. A smorgasbord of funky import shops, European salons and vintage clothing boutiques, the Grove is centered around Main Highway and Grand Avenue. At its heart is **CocoWalk**, 3015 Grand Ave., a colorful, casual open-air shopping center that includes cafes and trendy nightspots.

Some of the region's finest boutiques, gourmet restaurants and art galleries line the famed **Miracle Mile** in Coral Gables. The neighborhood's central boulevard and an integral part of George Merrick's original city plan, Miracle Mile is actually a half mile, between 37th and 42nd avenues, of small, picturesque 1970s storefronts along a wide, tree-lined boulevard. The significance here is historical as well as commercial.

A unique assortment of art galleries, antique shops and offbeat boutiques provides blocks of inspired browsing along South Miami Beach's **Lincoln Road.** This 7-block pedestrian mall near the north end of the Art Deco District is the center of the city's happening art scene. It is surrounded by the district's two main commercial arteries, Collins and Washington avenues.

Performing Arts

The 1981 development of the National Foundation for the Arts was the springboard for cultural evolution in south Florida. Patrons of the arts enjoy an expanding array of performing arts venues. Included are the handsomely refurbished **Colony Theater** on Lincoln Road in south Miami Beach, (305) 674-1026; the 1,710-seat, Moorish-styled **Gusman Center for the Performing Arts,** 174 E. Flagler Street in downtown Miami, (305) 374-2444; and the Art Deco **Jackie Gleason Theater of the Performing Arts** (known as "TOPA") on Washington Avenue in south Miami Beach, (305) 673-7300.

Dance

Among the professional dance troupes in the Miami area is the **Miami City Ballet,** Florida's first fully professional resident ballet company. Artistic director Edward Villella premiered in the New York City Ballet under George Balanchine; works by Balanchine are included in the company's repertoire. Performances take place October through March at the Jackie Gleason Theater of the Performing Arts and at other venues throughout south Florida; phone (305) 929-7010 for ticket information.

The professional dance company **Ballet Flamenco La Rosa** moves to a flamenco and Latin-style beat; for ticket and schedule information phone (305) 672-0552.

Music

Although Miami does not have a resident symphony orchestra, the void is filled by the **New World Symphony.** Conductor Michael Tilson Thomas created the only advanced-training orchestra in the world as an interim step for young musicians who have completed their academic instruction. For subscriptions, season or single tickets phone (305) 673-3331, or phone the main office at (305) 673-3330.

Lovers of classical music appreciate the high-caliber offerings of the **Concert Association of Florida.** The long-running series features such luminaries as Itzhak Perlman and Andre Watts; phone (305) 808-7446.

Performing primarily at Gusman Center for the Performing Arts downtown, the **Florida Philharmonic** maintains its main office at 3401 N.W. 9th Ave. in Fort Lauderdale. South Florida's premier symphony orchestra presents a full season of concerts, including children's programs; phone (954) 561-2997 or (800) 226-1812 for schedule and ticket information.

Opera

The celebrated **Florida Grand Opera,** 2901 W. Flagler St., which has provided South Florida with operatic performances since the early 1940s, offers five productions annually in the **Miami-Dade**

County Auditorium, at Flagler Street and 29th Avenue; phone (305) 854-7890. Included among those honored during the opera's International Series are Placido Domingo and Luciano Pavarotti. Promising singers make their mark in lead roles during the lower-priced National Series.

Theater

Housed in a lovely Spanish rococo-style palace, **Coconut Grove Playhouse,** 3500 Main Hwy. in Coconut Grove, has been one of Miami's most respected theaters since its inception in 1956, offering star casts in hit shows. Check the local newspapers for rates and schedules or phone (305) 442-4000.

Broadway-bound plays and musical reviews are staged in its 1,100-seat main section; the playhouse also presents productions in the intimate **Encore Room.**

Area Stage Company presents off-Broadway plays throughout the year. **Actor's Playhouse** offers year-round productions for adults and children and is host to the National Children's Theater Festival.

Special Events

On New Year's Day Miami honors the orange with the **Orange Bowl Festival.** The festival is capped that night by the **Orange Bowl** football game. Runners join in the celebration during the **Orange Bowl 5K/10K.** The **Junior Orange Bowl International Youth Festival,** held in December, is a children's counterpart to the Orange Bowl festivities and features arts and crafts shows and competitions in football, tennis, soccer, golf and bowling.

Art Deco Weekend, a 3-day festival in mid-January where South Beach's fanciful architecture takes center stage, celebrates the Miami Beach historic district with a street fair, a 1930s-style ball, a film series, lectures, entertainment and a parade. The **Royal Caribbean Classic** golf tournament beckons devotees of that sport late January to early February.

The February calendar is filled with such events as the **Miami/Coconut Grove Art Festival,** one of the state's largest, offering works in almost every medium; the **Miami International Boat Show** at Miami Beach Convention Center; and the **Mid-Winter Sailing Regatta.** Miami-bound foreign and independent film fans will enjoy the **Miami International Film Festival,** which takes place during 10 days in February at Gusman Center for the Performing Arts. This increasingly important affair attracts more than 45,000 cinema aficionados. In late February or early March, engines and crowds roar during the **Miami Grand Prix,** while galleries of fans hush at the **Celebrity Golf Championship.**

In the jubilant tradition of Rio de Janeiro, 9 days of merrymaking begin with the pageantry of **Carnival Miami,** said to be the nation's largest Hispanic

celebration and Miami's largest event. This weeklong Cuban celebration in early March has parades, concerts, fireworks and entertainment. Festivities culminate in the famous **Calle Ocho,** where more than 1 million people, mostly of Latin American descent, fill a 23-block area along S.W. Eighth Street in the heart of the Cuban district to enjoy music, food and each other's company.

Villa Vizcaya fills with period costumes, food and craft vendors, music and performances at the **Italian Renaissance Festival** in mid-March. In June the **Royal Poinciana Festival** coincides with the blooming of the trees in Bayfront Park. Also in June, the **Miami-Bahamas Goombay Festival** celebrates the city's ties to Caribbean culture with street dances and other entertainment; this event takes place in Coconut Grove.

Handmade arts and crafts, alligator wrestling, food and American Indian music are all part of the festivities that take place in late July at the Miccosukee Indian Village during the **Everglades Music and Craft Festival.** Amid more than 150 exhibits of arts, crafts and novelties, south Florida jazz musicians perform on three stages in mid-September at **Taste of Art and Jazz** in Miami Lakes.

Cultural heritage comes to the forefront at three fall events. At the beginning of October is the **West Indian American Day Carnival,** a celebration of the Caribbean, featuring concerts, arts and crafts, food, costumed galas and street festivals. **Caribbean Carnival,** also in October, is a celebration of the Caribbean people and cultures, featuring concerts, arts and crafts, food, costumed galas and street festivals, all taking place at Hialeah Park race track in Hialeah.

In November the **NASCAR Winston Cup Series Pennzoil 400** and the **NASCAR Busch Series Miami 300** are run at the Homestead-Miami Speedway. The **Harvest Festival,** a popular craft extravaganza the weekend before Thanksgiving, includes historical re-enactments, music, a quilt sale and antique cars.

The **Marion Edwards Jr. Memorial Race** for late-model stock cars is held in December at the Hialeah Speedway. In a zany spoof of the beloved King Orange Jamboree Parade, the **King Mango Strut** in late December features such wacky entries as the Precision Briefcase Drill Team and the Marching Freds. To round out the year the **Big Orange New Year's Eve Celebration and Parade** snakes along Biscayne Bay to kick off a weekend of New Year's celebrations.

The Latin Chamber of Commerce (CAMACOL) sponsors Hispanic festivals throughout the year. For information contact the chamber at 1417 W. Flagler St., Miami, FL 33135; phone (305) 642-3870.

Nightlife

Generally, Miami's native night owls balance a feverish club scene with simple evenings spent dockside. **Sundays on the Bay,** 5420 Crandon Blvd. in Key Biscayne, is one of numerous hot spots where locals enjoy a breathtaking view and live band sounds under the stars; phone (305) 361-6777. **Shuckers,** in the Best Western Bayfront at 1819 79th St. Cswy., is another bayfront bar, adding volleyball and late-night dancing to its casual but raucous atmosphere; phone (305) 866-1570.

Roadhouse-style blues, reggae and salsa are easy to find around town, as is mainstream pop and rock. Gentler souls who desire the sounds of jazz piano or the quiet tempo of a Latin ballad are especially gratified in this city, often finding solace in the cool, lush intimacy of a hotel lounge. Diversity is Miami's strong suit, but there is one exception: Country and folk music fans will have to look hard and be lucky—such acts are infrequently booked at area clubs.

Dance Clubs

The dance club scene in Miami is centered within South Beach's Art Deco District. Clubs—gay and straight—are constantly being reinvented, keeping South Beach at the pinnacle of the city's hot spots. Weekends are jammed with fashionable partyers making the Washington Avenue venues. A current favorite is **Bash,** 655 Washington Ave., for dancing and enjoying tapas on an intimate patio; phone (305) 538-2274.

Crobar, 1445 Washington Ave., is still decorated with remnants of its grand days as a 1930s theater. The spacious interior pulses with techno, alternative and progressive sounds; phone (305) 532-0922. Also popular is the intimate **Groove Jet,** 323 23rd. St.; phone (305) 532-5150.

Entertainment Complexes

The pub-hopping crowd finds a mix of upbeat and laid-back entertainment downtown at **Bayside Marketplace,** 401 Biscayne Blvd., where Hooters, the Hard Rock Cafe, Snapper's Bar and Grill, Bubba Gump Shrimp Co. and Mambo Cafe all serve a happy, loud bunch; phone (305) 577-3344. **Let's Make a Daiquiri,** an outdoor bar, presents

live jazz, rock, reggae and calypso music, along with bay breezes and glimpses of ocean liners as they make their way to and from the Port of Miami; phone (305) 372-5117.

In Coconut Grove locals and out-of-towners rendezvous at **CocoWalk,** 3015 Grand Ave., (305) 444-0777, a multilevel open mall with a combination of popular clubs including Cafe Tu Tu Tango, Fat Tuesdays, Hooters and Cafe Med.

Jazz & Blues

In the Miami area the urban roadhouse of long standing is **Tobacco Road,** 626 S. Miami Ave. Opened in 1912, this one-time Prohibition speakeasy sings the blues downtown, with local and national bands performing nightly; past performers have included Albert Collins, James Cotton and John Lee Hooker. Jazz jams take place on Wednesday nights; phone (305) 374-1198.

You also can enjoy the rhythms of jazz and blues at the upscale **Iguana Cantina,** 3390 Mary St. on the third floor of Streets of Mayfair, (305) 444-5911; performed nightly by both local and national artists at **Satchmo Blues,** 60 Merrick Way in Coral Gables, (305) 774-1883; and at **Upstairs at the Van Dyke,** in Miami Beach, at 846 Lincoln Rd., (305) 534-3600.

Latin Clubs

Snappy rhythms, swirling partners, the click of heels on a parquet floor. . .now that's Miami. At the city's heart is a Latin beat, and the Fontainebleau Hilton Resort & Towers, 4441 Collins Ave., offers **Club Tropigala,** a jungly four-tier cabaret featuring a Latin orchestra several nights a week; phone (305) 672-7469.

Similar smaller venues are scattered throughout the city. A hot spot for Latin and salsa beats is **Alcazaba,** open Wednesday and Saturday at 50 Alhambra Plaza, in the Hyatt Regency Coral Gables; phone (305) 441-1234.

The Miami-Miami Beach Vicinity

BISCAYNE NATIONAL PARK (H-12)

Elevations in the land portion of the park are at sea level. Ninety-five percent of the park is water.

Biscayne National Park, reached via Florida's Turnpike (exit 2, Campbell Drive) and S.W. 328th St. (North Canal Drive), encompasses a huge part of southeast Florida. The park offers a look at an unspoiled part of Florida. Only 4,370 of its 180,000 acres are land; the rest are water, and there is as much to see below its surface as there is above it.

Biscayne National Park has four biological systems: the mainland mangrove forests, Biscayne Bay, the upper Florida Keys and the underwater reefs. Shallow Biscayne Bay, which is between the coast and the northernmost Florida Keys, has clear water and is home to sponges, crabs, dolphins and manatees, endangered mammals that favor the bay's warm waters.

The undeveloped upper Florida Keys are the result of many thousands of years of construction by the tiny animals collectively known as coral. The 20 miles of the park's reefs were formed by more than 100 species of coral and harbor more than 200 different kinds of fish, including brilliantly colored parrotfish, angelfish and wrasses. Moray eels also inhabit many of the underwater crevices.

To preserve the fragile reefs, visitors must anchor boats in the sandy bottoms, not on the coral. Do not touch the coral; doing so will kill it. Also, do not sit or stand on the coral, as it breaks easily and can cause painful cuts. Collecting coral, plants, animals, shipwreck artifacts or any other "souvenir" is prohibited.

The upper keys support other endangered species. Bald eagles, ospreys, pelicans, egrets and other large birds find refuge in the dense vegetation. Arsenicker and West Arsenicker keys are important nesting areas and therefore are closed to the public.

The islands feature many tropical plants that originated from seeds either blown here by West Indian winds or deposited by birds. On the mainland are forests of mangroves, easily recognized by their twisted roots, which trap and filter out sediment that would otherwise harm the water and its inhabitants. The mangrove roots provide excellent hiding places and food sources for young fish—another function vital to the region's food chain.

Biscayne National Park is an undeveloped wilderness. Camping is permitted only on Elliott Key and Boca Chiton Key, which can be reached only by boat. Because the park is accessible primarily by boat, it is helpful to get a tour boat schedule from the headquarters on Convoy Point, reached via Florida's Turnpike (exit 2, Campbell Drive) and S.W. 328th St. (North Canal Drive). The facility is open daily 8:30-5; closed Dec. 25.

Canoe rentals also are available. Reservations are required for all trips and rentals and must be confirmed before departure; phone (305) 230-1100.

For further park information contact Biscayne National Park, 9700 S.W. 328th St., Homestead, FL 33033-5634; phone (305) 230-7275. *See Recreation Chart and the AAA Southeastern CampBook.*

BISCAYNE NATIONAL UNDERWATER PARK INC., whose trips depart from Convoy Point Visitor Center at 9700 S.W. 328th St., offers 3-hour glass-bottom boat tours on a 53-foot vessel and snorkeling and scuba diving excursions on a 45-foot catamaran.

Glass-bottom boat trips depart daily at 10. Snorkeling trips depart daily at 1:30. Scuba diving trips depart Wed.-Fri. 9-1, Sat.-Sun. 8:30-1 (weather permitting). Glass-bottom boat fare $19.95; under 13, $9.95. Snorkeling fare (includes equipment) $27.95. Scuba fare $35. Reservations are required. AX, MC, VI. Phone (305) 230-1100.

COCONUT GROVE (H-11) elev. 10'

THE BARNACLE STATE HISTORIC PARK is at 3485 Main Hwy. Commodore Ralph Munroe, an area pioneer and noted designer of shallow-draft sailing yachts, built the cottage in 1891 and later enlarged it by raising the seven rooms to accommodate another floor underneath. Most furnishings belonged to Munroe, and many of his photographs are displayed. A boat house also is on the property. The cottage may be viewed only by guided tour.

Allow 1 hour minimum. Grounds open Fri.-Mon. 9-4. Free guided tours of the cottage are given at 10, 11:30, 1 and 2:30; closed Jan. 1 and Dec. 25. Park admission $1, under 6 free. Phone (305) 448-9445.

CORAL GABLES (H-11)
pop. 42,249, elev. 11'

A planned community, Coral Gables is noted for its landscaped plazas and parkways, gateways of coral rock and royal poinciana trees. Spanish, Mediterranean and contemporary architecture blend in the downtown area. Many estates are in the older section of the city; modern mansions line the bayfront. Coral Gables House, 907 Coral Way, was the home of founder George Merrick, who named the city after his family home.

The Spanish architecture, lagoons and grottoes of the Venetian Pool, a public swimming pool at 2701 De Soto Blvd., reflect the lavish Coral Gables lifestyle of the 1920s. Also of interest are the Dutch-South African, Chinese and French villages.

Coral Gables is home to the University of Miami.

Coral Gables Chamber of Commerce: P.O. Box 347555, Coral Gables, FL 33234; phone (305) 446-1657.

FAIRCHILD TROPICAL GARDEN is next to Matheson Hammock Park at 10901 Old Cutler Rd. Narrated tram tours take visitors through this 83-acre botanical garden, which features rare tropical plants, palms, flowering trees and vines, exotic orchids and striking vistas. The park features an outdoor exhibit of tropical rain forest plants from around the world. Food is available. Gardens open daily 9:30-4:30; closed Dec. 25. Tram tours depart hourly Mon.-Fri. 10-3, Sat.-Sun. 10-4. Admission (includes tram tour) $8; over 64, $7; ages 3-12, $4. AX, DS, MC, VI. Phone (305) 667-1651.

SAVE **LOWE ART MUSEUM, UNIVERSITY OF MIAMI** is w. of jct. US 1 and Stanford Dr. at 1301 Stanford Dr. Opened in 1952, the museum houses a permanent collection of more than 12,000 objects representing western and non-western art from classical to contemporary. Spanning 5,000 years, the collection includes Greco-Roman antiquities, Italian renaissance and baroque art, pre-Columbian and southwest American Indian pieces and artworks from the Americas, Europe, Asia and Africa.

Allow 1 hour minimum. Tues.-Wed. and Fri.-Sat. 10-5, Thurs. noon-7, Sun. noon-5; closed major holidays. Admission $5, over 65 and students with ID $3, under 12 free. AX, DS, MC, VI. Phone (305) 284-3535.

MATHESON HAMMOCK PARK, 9610 Old Cutler Rd., is a man-made atoll pool separated from Biscayne Bay by a walkway. Trails wind among native shrubs and virgin forest. A boat ramp, bathhouse and picnic areas are available. Daily 6 a.m.-dusk. Admission $4. Parking $4 for automobiles, $10 for recreational vehicles or buses, $8 for boats. Phone (305) 665-5475.

FLORIDA CITY (H-11) pop. 7,843, elev. 6'

Florida City is surrounded by agricultural fields often referred to as the nation's "winter vegetable basket." Snap and pole beans, zucchini and squash are winter crops, while okra, limes, avocados and mangoes grow during the summer. Florida City State Farmer's Market, 300 N. Krome Ave. west of the junction of US 1 and Florida's Turnpike, is a wholesale and retail outlet. The retail outlet is open November through June, the wholesale outlet year-round; phone (305) 246-6334.

Greater Homestead-Florida City Chamber of Commerce: 43 N. Krome Ave., Homestead, FL 33030; phone (305) 247-2332.

Shopping areas: Prime Outlets at Florida City, junction SR 821 (Florida's Turnpike) and US 1 at 250 E. Palm Dr., offers 60 outlet shops including Bass, Mikasa and Nike.

HOMESTEAD (H-11) pop. 31,909, elev. 9'

The center of south Florida's fruit and nursery production, Homestead serves as a gateway to

Everglades National Park *(see place listing p. 57)*, Biscayne National Park *(see place listing p. 124)* and The Florida Keys *(see place listing p. 60)*.

Homestead-Miami Motorsports Complex, 1 Speedway Blvd., offers scheduled races throughout the year. For ticket information phone (305) 230-7223. The city's historic district offers shops and restaurants in a landscaped setting.

Tropical Everglades Visitor Center: 160 US 1, Florida City, FL 33034; phone (305) 245-9180 or (800) 388-9669.

SAVE **CORAL CASTLE OF FLORIDA,** 2 mi. n. on US 1, is built of massive blocks of hand-hewn coral rock. Using primitive tools, Latvian immigrant Ed Leedskalnin worked alone 1923-40 to build the structure and its furnishings. Audiotapes are available for self-guiding tours. Allow 1 hour minimum. Daily 7 a.m.-9 p.m. Admission $9.75; over 62, $6.50; ages 7-12, $5. AX, DS, MC, VI. Phone (305) 248-6345.

FRUIT AND SPICE PARK, 5 mi. w. of US 1 on S.W. 248 St., encompasses 35 acres with more than 500 species of fruit, nut and spice trees from throughout the world. Features include an herb and vegetable garden and a banana grove. Picnic facilities are available. Daily 10-5; closed Dec. 25. Admission $3.50; ages 4-12, $1. Phone (305) 247-5727.

KEY BISCAYNE (H-12) pop. 10,507, elev. 5′

CRANDON PARK, 4000 Crandon Blvd., is reached via the Rickenbacker Causeway over Biscayne Bay; toll $1. A scenic park, it has landscaped picnic areas and a 2.5-mile public beach. Allow 1 hour minimum. Daily 8-dusk. Admission $4 per private vehicle, $6 per bus or recreational vehicle. Phone (305) 361-5421.

NORTH MIAMI BEACH (H-11)
pop. 40,786, elev. 10′

ANCIENT SPANISH MONASTERY (Episcopal) is at 16711 W. Dixie Hwy. Built in 12th-century Spain, the structure was dismantled and shipped to the United States in 1925. The monastery was rebuilt in 1952 and now houses ancient artworks and furniture. Allow 2 hours minimum. Mon.-Sat. 9-5, Sun. 1:30-5; closed Easter, Thanksgiving and Dec. 25. May close for private parties on weekends, so phone ahead. Admission $5; over 65 and students with ID $2.50; under 12, $2. Phone (305) 945-1461.

SAVE **MUSEUM OF CONTEMPORARY ART,** off I-95 exit 13A, then 1.5 mi. e. to 770 N.E. 125th St., offers changing exhibits in various media from sculpture to ceramic tile. Allow 1 hour minimum. Tues.-Sat. 11-5; Sun. noon-5; closed major holidays. Admission $5; over 55 and ages 13-18, $3. AX, MC, VI. Phone (305) 893-6211.

This ends listings for the Miami-Miami Beach Vicinity.
The following page resumes the alphabetical listings of cities in Florida.

MICANOPY (C-8) pop. 653, elev. 100′

The former site of a Timucuan Indian village, Micanopy (MIK-uh-no-pee) is the state's oldest inland town. Many antique, art and curio shops help to create an atmosphere of a small Florida village during the 19th century.

MICANOPY HISTORICAL SOCIETY MUSEUM, off I-75 exit 374 to 81 Library Ln. SW, features antiques, historic photographs and American Indian artifacts housed in an 1880s warehouse building. Guided tours are available. Allow 30 minutes minimum. Daily 1-4. Donations. Phone (352) 466-3200.

PAYNES PRAIRIE PRESERVE STATE PARK, 1 mi. n. on US 441, encompasses 21,000 acres of freshwater marsh, hammocks, pine flatwoods, swamps and ponds. More than 20 miles of trails are available to explore these areas. Visitor center exhibits interpret the natural and cultural history of this important ecological area. An audiovisual program explains the preservation of the basin's natural landscape. A 50-foot observation tower stands near the center of the preserve and a recreation area is at Lake Wauberg. Camping is permitted.

Ranger-led activities are available November through April by reservation; phone (352) 466-4100. Allow 1 hour minimum. Park open daily 8-dusk. Visitor center open Mon.-Tues. 10-4, Wed.-Sun. 9-5. Admission $3.25 per private vehicle (maximum eight people), $1 per person arriving by bicycle or on foot. Phone (352) 466-3397. *See Recreation Chart and the AAA Southeastern CampBook.*

MILTON (A-2) pop. 7,200, elev. 15′

A heavy growth of briars along the Blackwater River elicited Milton's early name, Scratch Ankle. The Blackwater, one of the state's most pristine rivers, has retained its importance to modern Milton as a carrier of recreational canoeists rather than commerce; canoes and tubes can be rented in the area. Blackwater River State Park *(see Recreation Chart)* and Blackwater River State Forest are northeast. Historic old homes date back to the Civil War days. Whiting Field Naval Air Station is north on SR 87.

Santa Rosa County Chamber of Commerce: 5247 Stewart St., Milton, FL 32570; phone (850) 623-2339.

RECREATIONAL ACTIVITIES
Canoeing

• **Adventures Unlimited**, 12 mi. n. on SR 87, then 4 mi. e. following signs to 8974 Tomahawk Landing Rd., Milton, FL 32570. Other activities are offered. Daily 8-6, Mar.-Sept.; 8-4, rest of year. Closed Thanksgiving and Dec. 25. Phone (850) 623-6197 or (800) 239-6864.

MOUNT DORA—*see Orlando p. 178.*

MULBERRY (E-9) pop. 3,230, elev. 140′

Long known as the center of phosphate production in central Florida, Mulberry was founded in 1901. The city today covers about 6 square miles.

MULBERRY PHOSPHATE MUSEUM, 1 blk. s. of jct. SRs 37 and 60 at 101 S.E. First St., features a collection of fossilized remains of prehistoric animals, area memorabilia and exhibits related to the phosphate industry. A phosphate train also is displayed. Allow 1 hour minimum. Tues.-Sat. 10-4:30. Donations. Phone (863) 425-2823.

NAPLES (G-9) pop. 20,976, elev. 9′

Naples quickly is becoming the Palm Beach of Florida's west coast; its Fifth Avenue corridor contains trendy boutiques, art galleries, cozy restaurants and other upscale accouterments. This image is a far cry from the days in 1885 when development began and the area was accessible only by water. The Naples Pier is a relic of that period.

Naples' greatest treasures are not found in the shops and malls—the city has long been famous for its 10 miles of public beaches. Shell gathering and other beachfront activities are available at Delnor Wiggins Pass State Recreation Area *(see Recreation Chart),* 11 miles northwest via SR 846.

Rookery Bay, 5 miles south, is an area of mangrove islands that shelter rare birds and marine life. Maintained as a national estuarine research reserve, it is reached by a half-mile boardwalk that explores the upland areas. The reserve also features The Conservancy's Briggs Nature Center *(see attraction listing page 128).* The mainland portions are accessible from Shell Island Road, off Collier Road in East Naples.

Golfing is popular in the Naples area, as is swamp buggy racing. Swamp buggy races, first held in 1949, are occasionally held off Collier Road at the Florida Sports Park; phone (800) 897-2701.

Philharmonic Center for the Arts, at 5833 Pelican Bay Blvd., presents varied entertainment; phone (239) 597-1900 or (800) 597-1900.

Naples Visitors Center: 895 Fifth Ave. S., Naples, FL 34102; phone (239) 262-6141.

Shopping areas: Among the 140 stores at [SAVE] Coastland Center, 1900 N. Tamiami Tr., are Burdines, Dillard's, JCPenney and Sears. Old Marine Marketplace at Tin City, at the corner of US 41 (Tamiami Trail) and SR 851 (Goodlette-Frank Road), is restored to capture the flavor of pioneer-era Naples. The Village on Venetian Bay, 4200 Gulf Shore Blvd. N., offers boutiques, restaurants and galleries in a Mediterranean setting.

Waterside Shops, US 41 and Seagate Drive, has a wide selection of shops including Banana Republic, Jacobsons and Saks Fifth Avenue. The Third Street South Shopping Area in the historic district of Old Naples, just 2 blocks from the Naples Pier, has more than 100 shops, galleries, restaurants and cafes.

SAVE **CARIBBEAN GARDENS: THE ZOO IN NAPLES** is 1.75 mi. n. via US 41 to jct. Fleischmann Blvd., then .5 mi. e. to 1590 Goodlette-Frank Rd. Founded in 1919, the 52-acre zoo features a self-guiding trail that winds through a botanical garden populated by animals from apes to zebras. Visitors to Safari Canyon can observe natural animal behavior, complemented by wildlife footage and graphics. A 20-minute boat cruise offers views of monkeys, lemurs and apes roaming freely in nine island habitats. Scheduled activities include Alligator Bay Feeding and Meet the Keeper. Picnicking is permitted.

Allow 4 hours minimum. Daily 9:30-5:30; closed Easter, Thanksgiving and Dec. 25. Last admission 1 hour before closing. Admission (including boat cruise) $14.95; ages 4-15, $9.95. DS, MC, VI. Phone (239) 262-5409.

COLLIER COUNTY MUSEUM is at jct. US 41E and Airport Rd., in the County Government Center. Exhibits trace the history of Collier County from the Calusa Indian period to the present. A steam logging locomotive also is featured. Allow 30 minutes minimum. Mon.-Fri. 9-5; closed holidays. Free. Phone (239) 774-8476.

COLLIER-SEMINOLE STATE PARK BOAT TOURS is 17 mi. s. on US 41 at 20200 E. Tamiami Tr. Hourlong tours aboard a pontoon boat take passengers along the Black Water River, which runs through Collier-Seminole State Park. Narration is provided about the early settlements and pioneers of the area as well as the animals and plants that populate the Everglades.

Departures daily at 9:30, 11, 12:30, 2 and 3:30; closed Dec. 25. Departures require a minimum of four adults. Fare $10; ages 6-12, $7.50. MC, VI. Phone (239) 642-8898. *See Recreation Chart and the AAA Southeastern CampBook.*

THE CONSERVANCY—NAPLES NATURE CENTER, off Goodlette-Frank Rd. at 1450 Merrihue Dr., features a wildlife rehabilitation center, nature trails, canoe and kayak rentals. A Museum of Natural History features snakes, a loggerhead sea turtle, a marine conservation station, a videotape presentation and hands-on displays. Among the highlights is a free 45-minute narrated boat tour of a mangrove forest and lagoon.

Allow 1 hour minimum. Mon.-Sat. 9-4:30; closed major holidays. Center $7.50; ages 3-12, $2. Phone (239) 262-0304.

Briggs Nature Center, in Rookery Bay National Estuarine Research Reserve between Naples and Marco Island, offers nature exhibits, canoe rides, boat trips and nature excursions. A .5-mile boardwalk explores a butterfly garden and the upland areas. Admission $4; ages 3-12, $2. Phone (239) 775-8569.

CORKSCREW SWAMP SANCTUARY, on Sanctuary Rd. 16 mi. e. of I-75 exit 111 via Immokalee Rd., is an 11,000-acre wilderness area and wildlife sanctuary of the National Audubon Society. A large colony of American wood storks can nest here from November through April. The sanctuary contains the largest known stand of virgin bald cypress; some trees are said to be more than 500 years old. Alligators can be seen regularly from the boardwalk on the 2.25-mile self-guiding tour.

Allow 1 hour minimum. Daily 7-5:30, Dec. 1 to mid-Apr.; 7 a.m.-7:30 p.m., rest of year. Admission $8; students with ID $5.50; ages 6-18, $3.50. MC, VI. Phone (239) 348-9151. *See color ad.*

DOUBLE SUNSHINE departs from Tin City on US 41. During 90-minute narrated sightseeing cruises of Naples Bay, passengers can enjoy views of mangrove-lined islands as well as dolphins, manatees and such birds as bald eagles and pelicans. Also available are half-day deep-sea fishing trips aboard the *Lady Brett*, and half-day bay fishing trips aboard the *Capt. Paul.*

Sightseeing cruises depart daily at 10, noon, 2, 4 and 1 hour before dusk. Deep-sea trips depart daily at 7:45 and 1. Bay fishing trips depart at 9 and 1. Sightseeing fare $23; under 12, $11.50. Deep-sea

fare $50; under 12, $45. Bay fishing fare $45; under 12, $40. Reservations are recommended. Phone (239) 263-4949.

EVERGLADES EXCURSIONS, departing from hotels in Naples and Marco Island, offers full- and half-day excursions throughout the Everglades. Highlights include a narrated cruise through sawgrass prairies and mangroves, a visit to Everglades City, an airboat ride through the Ten Thousand Islands and a tour of Fakahatchee Strand Preserve State Park and Big Cypress Swamp.

Allow 4 hours minimum. Everglades trips depart daily at 8; closed Dec. 25. Half-day Everglades fare $59; ages 4-12, $49. Full-day fare (including lunch) $89; ages 4-12, $69. Reservations are required. AX, DS, MC, VI. Phone (239) 262-1914 or (800) 592-0848. *See color ad.*

NAPLES DEPOT CIVIC AND CULTURAL CENTER, 1051 Fifth Ave. S. at 10th St., is a renovated 1927 train station which serves as a civic and cultural center. A collection of railroad memorabilia, including an operating Lionel train, is displayed inside the depot; a baggage car stands outside, where a children's train ride is offered. Mon.-Fri. 10-4; phone for Lionel train schedule. Admission $5; children $3. Phone (239) 262-1776.

NAPLES TROLLEY TOURS boards at Old Naples General Store & Trolley Depot, downtown, and at many stops along the route. The area's historic sites, shopping areas and residential sections are highlighted in a narrated 1.75-hour tour, which travels to Naples Pier, Palm Cottage, 5th Avenue S. and Tin City. Daily 8:30-5:30. Fare (includes an all-day reboarding pass) $17; ages 3-12, $8. AX, DS, MC,

VI. Phone (239) 262-7300 or (800) 592-0848. *See color ad.*

THE TEDDY BEAR MUSEUM OF NAPLES, 1.75 mi. w. of I-75 exit 107 at 2511 Pine Ridge Rd., displays almost 5,000 teddy bears, ranging in size from less than 1 inch to larger than life. The collection includes bears made of fabric, marble and bronze as well as antique and limited-edition bears. Teddy bear art and memorabilia also are featured, and teddy bear-making classes are available seasonally. Allow 30 minutes minimum. Tues.-Sat. 10-5; closed major holidays. Admission $8; over 60 and ages 4-12, $6. AX, DS, MC, VI. Phone (239) 598-2711 or (866) 365-2327.

NEW SMYRNA BEACH (C-10)
pop. 20,048, elev. 10'

On this beach north of Cape Canaveral, automobiles may be driven along the stretch of firm white sand from the inlet south to 27th Avenue. Drivers should heed signs noting unsafe areas. Overnight parking or camping are not permitted on the beach. February through mid-November, a daily driving toll of $5 per car is charged; season passes are available for both residents ($20) and nonresidents ($40). Toll booths are at each approach.

The foundations of the Turnbull Ruins/Old Fort, built of coquina, are on N. Riverside Drive between Washington and Julia streets. These ruins, made of walls 3 feet thick, represent a local mystery—it has never been established if the foundation is the unfinished remains of a pre-colonial fort or the incomplete beginnings of a mansion for the Turnbull family. The remains of a large plantation's sugar

mill can be seen at Sugar Mill Ruins, 1050 Old Mission Rd. Built in the early 1800s, the mill was destroyed during the Second Seminole War.

The Atlantic Center for the Arts, 1414 Art Center Ave., features an art gallery and various performances and exhibitions by the resident artists; phone (386) 427-6975 or (800) 393-6975.

New Smyrna Beach Visitors Bureau: 2242 SR 44, New Smyrna Beach, FL 32168; phone (386) 428-1600 or (800) 541-9621.

FLORIDA COASTAL CRUISES' *MANATEE* departs from Sea Harvest Marina between the North and South causeways. Narrated cruises aboard the *Manatee* navigate the protected wetland and scenic mangrove shores along the Intracoastal Waterway. Sights include Ponce de Leon Lighthouse, waterfront homes and native wildlife, such as dolphins. Lunch cruises also are available. Narrated cruises depart daily; times vary. Boarding is 15 minutes before departure. Fare $15; under 12, $12. Reservations are required. Phone (386) 428-0201 or (800) 881-2628.

NORTH MIAMI BEACH—
see Miami-Miami Beach p. 126.

OCALA (C-9) pop. 45,943, elev. 104'

An agricultural and manufacturing city, Ocala (oh-KAL-a) has moss-draped oaks and stately old Southern homes along many of its streets. The surrounding area is considered to be the heartland of Florida's Thoroughbred industry. It is possible to visit some of the horse farms. Particularly scenic segments of two highways approach Ocala: US 301 from Waldo and US 27 from Williston.

Ocala-Marion County Chamber of Commerce: 110 E. Silver Springs Blvd., Ocala, FL 34470; phone (352) 629-8051.

Shopping areas: Paddock Mall, a half-mile east of I-75 on SR 200, features Belk Lindsey, Burdines, JCPenney and Sears.

THE APPLETON MUSEUM OF ART, 4333 N.E. Silver Springs Blvd., houses European paintings, sculpture and decorative arts; contemporary art; pre-Columbian artworks; West African, Islamic and Asian artworks; as well as antiquities. The Edith-Marie Appleton wing features a library, a workshop and additional galleries. Lectures, films and concerts also are offered. Allow 1 hour minimum. Daily 10-6; closed Jan. 1 and Dec. 25. Admission $12; over 54, $10; college students with ID $8; ages 10-18, $5. AX, MC, VI. Phone (352) 236-7100.

E-ONE FACTORY TOURS is .5 mi. e. of I-75 exit 352 on SR 40, .5 mi. s. on S.W. 33rd Ave., then 1 mi. s.w. on S.W. Seventh St. to 1601 S.W. 37th Ave. Guided tours of three factories where fire trucks are manufactured are offered. Tours cover 2 miles of walking and safety goggles are provided; the tour can be noisy and hot during the summer. Shoes with closed toes must be worn.

Allow 1 hour, 30 minutes minimum. Tours offered Mon.-Fri. at 9, 11 and 1 (weather permitting); closed holidays and Dec. 26-31 Admission $6; over 55, $4; fire service members and ages 6-12 free. Children under 6 are not allowed on the factory tour, but may take an abbreviated tour of the Vehicle Delivery Center which includes sitting in the cab of a fire truck and a demonstration of the vehicle's lights and sirens. Phone (352) 861-3524.

FLORIDA'S SILVER SPRINGS, on SR 40, is reputedly the world's largest formation of clear artesian springs. One major spring, 65 feet long and 12 feet high, and more than a dozen minor springs form the headwaters of the crystalline Silver River, part of the inland waterway that links the springs to the St. Johns River and Jacksonville. The springs release more than 550 million gallons every 24 hours.

The narrated Glass-Bottom Boat Cruise offers a clear view of underwater life as far as 40 feet below the surface. During the Jungle Cruise visitors can spot more than 22 species of animals—including zebras, giraffes and ostriches—from six continents. Jeep Safari is a four-wheel adventure through a 35-acre area where sloths, Brazilian tapirs and oryxes roam free. The safari also takes visitors through a 3-foot-deep alligator pond.

Among other features are World of Bears, home to five bear species; Panther Prowl, an outdoor habitat with Florida panthers and western cougars; Big Gator Lagoon; Lost River Voyage; and live animal shows. Concerts are presented on the Twin Oaks Mansion stage seasonally. Free pet kennels are available. Picnicking is permitted only in the picnic area.

Allow 5 hours minimum. Daily 10-5. Last admission 1 hour before closing. All-inclusive admission $32.99; over 54, $29.99; under 48 inches tall $23.99; under age 3 free. Combination ticket with Silver Springs Wild Waters $34.99; over 54, $31.99; under 48 inches tall $25.99; under age 3 free. Parking $5. AX, DS, MC, VI. Phone (352) 236-2121. *See color ad.*

Silver Springs Wild Waters is adjacent to Silver Springs. The water park features a wave pool, waterslide flumes including the Twin Twister; and Cool Kids Cove, a children's play area. Picnic and volleyball facilities are available. Daily 10-7, early June to mid-Aug.; Sat.-Sun. 10-5, late Mar.-early June and mid-Aug. to late Sept. Hours may vary; phone ahead. Admission $23.99; under 48 inches tall $20.99; under age 3 free. Parking $5. Phone (352) 236-2121.

GARLITS' AUTO ATTRACTION is 8 mi. s. on I-75 to exit 341, .25 mi. e. on CR 484, then .25 mi. s. on CR 475A to 13700 S.W. 16th Ave. In addition to displaying 100 antique automobiles in a separate building, the museum traces the evolution of the sport of drag racing through the 50-year collection of "Big Daddy" Don Garlits' drag racing cars and artifacts.

Allow 1 hour minimum. Daily 9-5; closed Dec. 25. Admission $12; over 55 and ages 13-18, $10; ages 5-12, $3. Under 13 must be with an adult. MC, VI. Phone (352) 245-8661 or (877) 271-3278.

OCALA NATIONAL FOREST

Elevations in the forest range from
10 ft. to 125 ft.

With more than 430,000 acres in the central part of the Florida, the forest contains numerous species of vegetation and hundreds of clear lakes and streams. The forest is said to have the world's largest stand of sand pine. Other predominant trees include longleaf, slash and other pines, as well as cypress and hardwoods. In addition to several shorter trails, a well-traveled section of the Florida Trail which winds its way through the forest is popular with hikers. Hunting is allowed by permit.

Developed recreation sites include Alexander Springs, Juniper Springs, Lake Dorr, Fore Lake, Mill Dam, Clearwater Lake, Salt Springs and Silver Glen Springs. Juniper Prairie Wilderness is home to Pat's Island, where parts of the movie "The Yearling" were filmed. Juniper Springs was constructed in 1935 by the Civilian Conservation Corps. Phone (352) 625-2520. *See Recreation Chart.*

Brochures and information on forest recreational opportunities are available at Ocklawaha Visitor Center on SR 40 at SR 315, between Silver Springs and the Ocklawaha River; phone (352) 236-0288. The center is open daily 9-5.

ODESSA—*see Tampa Bay p. 229.*

OKEECHOBEE (F-10) pop. 5,376, elev. 29′

At the crossroads of SR 70, US 98 and US 441, Okeechobee serves as a center for such outdoor activities as boating, fishing, camping and air boat rides. The town also is a commercial center for cattle which is evident in the several festivals and rodeos that take place throughout the year.

Okeechobee Chamber of Commerce: 55 S. Parrott Ave., Okeechobee, FL 34974; phone (863) 763-6464 or (800) 871-4403.

DID YOU KNOW

Harriet Beecher Stowe,
author of *Uncle Tom's
Cabin,* had a winter home
on the St. John's River
1867-84.

LAKE OKEECHOBEE, covering approximately 750 square miles, is the second largest freshwater lake in the continental United States. Its greatest depth is 24 feet, but the water is so shallow in most places that birds can be seen wading a mile from shore. A lighted pier at Lock 7 (US 441 and SR 78) provides day and night fishing. A hiking and biking trail— part of the Florida National Scenic Trail—winds 110 miles along a levee which surrounds the entire lake to protect adjacent rich lands from overflow. Recreational facilities are available.

OLUSTEE (B-8) elev. 140′

OLUSTEE BATTLEFIELD HISTORIC STATE PARK, about 2.5 mi. e. on US 90, marks the site of the largest Civil War battle on Florida soil. Union forces were defeated decisively at the site on Feb. 20, 1864; the battle is re-enacted every February. Highlights include a museum featuring Civil War artifacts. Site open daily 8-5. Museum open daily 9-5. Site and museum free. Phone (386) 758-0400.

ORANGE CITY (D-9) pop. 6,604, elev. 43′

Orange City's early residents were the Timucuan Indians, who lived along the St. Johns River and ate the snails that inhabited the river's sandbars. The mound formed by the accumulation of centuries of snail shells later served as a foundation for the area's first permanent home, the 1872 Thursby House.

Today the residence is preserved in Blue Spring State Park, a winter habitat of the endangered manatee.

Chambers of Commerce of West Volusia: 520 N. Volusia Ave., Orange City, FL 32763; phone (386) 775-2793.

BLUE SPRING STATE PARK, 2 mi. w. off US 17/92 on W. French Ave., contains a spring run that maintains a temperature of 72 degrees Fahrenheit. Manatee season typically is November through mid-March, although the sea cows also can be seen here when they come to escape the cooler waters of the St. Johns River. A manatee-viewing platform and ranger interpretation programs, including a video presentation, introduce visitors to these gentle creatures. Visitors may not swim with or feed the manatees. Canoe rentals are available.

Allow 2 hours minimum. Park daily 8-dusk. Video presentation shown Mon.-Fri. at 1:30, 2:30 and 3:30, Sat.-Sun. at 11, 1:30, 2:30 and 3:30, mid-Nov. to mid-Mar. Admission $4 per private vehicle (maximum eight people), $1 per person arriving by bicycle or on foot. Phone (386) 775-3663. *See Recreation Chart and the AAA Southeastern CampBook.*

St. Johns River Cruises, in Blue Springs State Park at 2100 W. French Ave., offers narrated cruises and nature tours along the St. Johns River. Allow 2 hours minimum. Cruises depart daily at 10 and 1 (also at 3:30, Jan.-Apr.). Fare $14; over 60, $12; ages 3-12, $8. Park admission $4. Reservations are required. AX, MC, VI. Phone (407) 330-1612 or (386) 917-0724.

AAA Travel ... for Those On the Go.

Travel

Going on a trip? Whether you let AAA handle the planning or do it yourself, trust us to steer you right with reliable information and valuable guidance. We'll help you:

- Choose the best **travel route**, whether it's scenic, direct, or somewhere in between.
- Select **accommodations**, from pampered luxury to clean and practical.
- Explore your **dining** options, whether it's a night on the town to a bite on the run.
- Get the inside scoop on **attractions**, from neon lights to natural sights.

Prefer personal assistance? Enjoy the complimentary services of a AAA/CAA auto travel professional at your local club office or by phone. Just tell us what you have in mind and we'll design your route, book your reservations, and offer you exclusive travel materials to enhance your trip.

Rather do it yourself? Choose from a flexible array of travel resources. Use *Traveler*, the Internet TripTik on aaa.com, to create your ultimate route, complete with driving distances and stops at AAA Approved hotels, restaurants, and attractions. Book your stays using the Online TourBook. And explore your destination using detailed TourBook guides and handy sheet maps.

Whichever way you go ... go with AAA Travel! Contact your nearest AAA/CAA service office to speak with a travel professional and pick up valuable travel materials. Or, access AAA's renowned travel services online at www.aaa.com!

Travel With Someone You Trust®

Orlando

City Population: 185,951 Elevation: 111 ft.

Popular Spots:

SeaWorld Orlando................ *(see p. 147)*

Universal Orlando .... *(see p. 149)*

Walt Disney World® Resort ...... *(see p. 163)*

Walt Disney World. It is the dream destination of every young child, the first stop on a Super Bowl champion's victory tour. It conjures up images of azure swimming pools, life-size cartoon characters and a fantasy castle where dreams come true. And it has made the young city of Orlando the world's most popular vacation spot.

Central Florida's Disney story began in the mid-1960s, when entertainment visionary "Uncle Walt" Disney paid a series. of hush-hush visits to the swamplands of southwest Orange County. Secretive property deals soon followed, piquing locals' interest and sparking questions about the mysterious doings south of town. The answer—and instant fame—came in 1971 when the Magic Kingdom became the area's first theme park.

Bolstered by Walt Disney World's phenomenal success, Orlando began a rapid growth spurt. Hotels and restaurants sprang up around the park practically overnight, swiftly followed by a legion of souvenir shops and tourist strips. A diverse mix of people flocked to the area, lured by Disney's magic spell and the promise of easy living in the nation's new vacation capital.

But while Disney is the centerpiece of Orlando's appeal, the City Beautiful offers more than just theme parks. Summer rainstorms and a warm climate promote lush vegetation. Pines, palms and oaks draped with Spanish moss line the streets, and landscaped gardens display many varieties of flowers.

In the midst of the state's lake country, central Florida offers more than 1,200 lakes and dozens of parks in which to hike, lounge, bike or engage in water sports. Even in the throes of rapid growth, the downtown streets, many of them brick, seem clean and friendly, the skies are smog-free and subtropical vegetation graces almost every view.

Of course, success breeds risks along with rewards. New residents arrive by the thousands each year, and as a result, Orlando natives make up less than half the population and the best-known citizens are the mascots of the local theme parks.

Surprisingly, Orlando is no stranger to the boomtown hustle and bustle, having experienced several boom-and-bust cycles in its short but tumultuous past. The city began as a small settlement founded by brothers Aaron and Isaac Jernigan, who in 1843 established a cattle ranch and trading post on what is now Lake Holden.

More than one story explains the origin of the town's name, but the most reliable claims it honors a member of a company of U.S. soldiers and volunteers, Orlando Reeves. One night in 1835 Reeves was at his post as sentry along Sandy Beach—the shores of today's Lake Eola—when he noticed a "log" in the lake. Realizing it was an Indian creeping toward the camp, Reeves gave the alarm to warn his company.

The frontier outpost grew quickly, and by the 1860s cattle ranches and cotton plantations were a common sight. By virtue of its remote location, Orlando was far removed from the ravages of the Civil War. It was very much a Confederate city, however, and so became a haven for displaced Southerners. They came seeking a fresh start among the thriving cattle herds and the thick groves of a new industry: citrus production.

Getting There — starting on p. 140

Getting Around — starting on p. 141

What To See — starting on p. 142

What To Do — starting on p. 153

Where To Stay — starting on p. 612

Where To Dine — starting on p. 619

The first success story belonged to William Harrison Holden, who in 1875 planted a commercial orange grove on the shore of the lake that would later take his name. Countless would-be citrus kings followed his lead, and soon lemons, oranges and grapefruit constituted the area's leading business.

The pioneer period came to a close in 1880 with the completion of the South Florida Railroad, which offered a link to the North. The advent of rail travel was a defining moment for the city: Along with increased commercial opportunities came multitudes of sun-seeking tourists escaping harsh Northern winters.

By 1890 the cowtown had become a real town, with all the trappings of 19th-century success. Stores and businesses prospered along the main thoroughfare, Orange Avenue, and Orlando's first population boom was well under way. Even a minor freeze in 1886—a harbinger of larger disasters to come—had little effect on the growth of the citrus and real estate industries.

Those heady days ended soon enough. Another, more devastating freeze gripped central Florida during the winter of 1894-95, destroying crops and ruining growers' fortunes overnight. A gradual recovery eventually offset the losses, and citrus production continued to be an economic staple through the 1950s. But increasing urbanization and colder winters steadily pushed the industry south into warmer, more rural areas, and Orange County's once-abundant groves now are a distant memory.

In the waning years of the 1920s, growth had escalated to unsupportable levels and the local economy destabilized. A serious fruit fly infestation in 1929 derailed the citrus business, leading to an eerily prophetic crash. As the boom ground to a halt, the Great Depression struck a heavy blow, leaving the city and its residents in dire financial straits.

World War II brought defense manufacturing and related businesses, helping to erase the effects of the Depression. But it was the postwar period that ushered in the region's most dynamic growth. Defense build-ups and the space race—the major fronts of the Cold War—soon became central Florida's primary industries. The Glenn L. Martin Co. (now Lockheed Martin Corp.) opened its first Orlando plant in 1957, bringing in hundreds of workers from the North and creating thousands of jobs for locals. The Kennedy Space Center soon followed, and the resulting economic activity spawned numerous supporting businesses, attracting a tremendous influx of new residents.

These developments were spurred in large part by the area's most rewarding transaction: Walt Disney's purchase of the land where he would build the Walt Disney World Resort. When plans for developing the site were formally announced late in

1965, they fueled yet another land rush. Real estate prices skyrocketed as speculators bought their own piece of the action. In an unprecedented move, the state legislature granted the company the autonomy to rule itself. Disney promptly set up its own government within an area called the Reedy Creek Improvement District, complete with taxing privileges and municipal services.

The Magic Kingdom's price tag topped $400 million at its Oct. 1, 1971, opening. Though Disney himself was not alive to see it, the park quickly exceeded all expectations and remains one of the world's most popular destinations. In fact, Walt Disney World's allure helped make Orlando something of a theme park mecca. In the decades since the first guests walked through the turnstiles, such attractions as SeaWorld Orlando, Epcot, Disney-MGM Studios and Universal Orlando have opened their gates to the visitors thronging Mickey Mouse's hometown. Gone are the quiet days of orange groves and rural simplicity.

Today Orlando is a far cry from the small Southern town it was in the 1840s. The perennial boomtown is well on its way to becoming a major international city. The Orlando International Airport has undergone a series of renovations and expansions that have made it an important transportation center. The Orlando Arena (renamed T.D. Waterhouse Centre in 2000) opened in 1989, mainly to serve as home court for the city's popular NBA team, the Orlando Magic. The area also has attracted new businesses, even as others like Lockheed Martin began to downsize.

With the coming of two major players in the entertainment market, Universal Studios and Disney-MGM Studios, Orlando has emerged as an up-and-coming center for the motion picture industry. Technology also remains a key component in Orlando's business picture. Although defense has taken a big hit, the high-tech fields of software, telecommunications, lasers and electro-optics are filling the gap.

Recent developments indicate that the city's growth shows no signs of ending any time soon. Despite the Navy's decision to close the city's Naval Training Center, Orlandoans are optimistic about plans to convert the site to other, equally productive uses. The University of Central Florida (UCF), founded in 1968, continues to grow and now has one of the region's finest technology programs. Disney's planned residential community, Celebration, is patterned after the progressive village that Walt himself envisioned as the solution to modern urban problems.

The Informed Traveler

Whom To Call

Emergency: 911

Police (non-emergency): (407) 246-2414; Sheriff (407) 737-2400

Fire: (407) 422-7121

Time and Temperature: (407) 646-3131

Hospitals: Florida Hospital, (407) 896-6611; Orlando Regional Health Care System, (407) 841-5111.

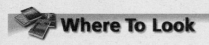

Where To Look

Newspapers

The *Orlando Sentinel* is distributed in the morning. Friday's *Calendar* section summarizes the coming week's events.

Radio

Radio station WWNZ (740 AM) is an all-news/talk station; WDBO (580 AM) is an all-talk/weather station; WMFE (90.7) is a member of National Public Radio.

Visitor Information

Orlando/Orange County Convention & Visitors Bureau distributes a variety of information. The Official Visitor Center on International Dr. is open daily 8-7. Write 8723 International Dr., Orlando, FL 32819; phone (407) 363-5872 or (800) 551-0181.

The Greater Orlando Chamber of Commerce distributes information Mon.-Fri. 8:30-5. Write 75 S. Ivanhoe Blvd., Orlando, FL 32804; phone (407) 425-1234.

A free monthly magazine titled *See Orlando* is distributed at hotels and motels throughout the city.

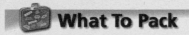

What To Pack

Orlando is as renowned for its warm weather as for its theme parks. The winter months

especially are a relief from colder climates, with lows generally in the 50s and highs in the 70s. Sudden cold snaps lend a certain unpredictability to central Florida winters, but these usually are short-lived.

Summer months tend to be hot and muggy, with temperatures routinely in the 90s. The intense humidity is alleviated many afternoons by brief thunderstorms. These sudden storms are the worst facet of Orlando's weather. (Note: Seek shelter indoors to wait out storms, as lightning strikes and pounding rain pose serious hazards, especially to the uninitiated driver. If you can't pull over safely, turn on your headlights and proceed with extreme caution.)

It is always a good idea to wear sunblock if you will be outdoors for any length of time, as the strong Florida sun can burn unprotected skin even on cool or overcast days. *For additional information see temperature chart p. 45.*

Comfort is the driving fashion force in Florida, and Orlando is a typically casual city. Shorts and sandals are acceptable in all but the most exclu-

sive restaurants. Winters are fairly mild, but cold snaps necessitate sweaters, jackets or light coats from December through February.

A word to the wise: Warm temperatures outside often make for cold temperatures inside, as air conditioners are turned full blast against the summer heat.

Sales Tax: In Orange and Osceola counties the sales tax is 6 percent; in Lake and Seminole counties it is 7 percent. Orange and Osceola counties levy a 4 percent resort tax, while in Lake and Seminole counties the tax is 2 percent.

Destination Orlando

*I*t all started with a mouse—the emergence of Orlando as everyone's favorite vacation destination, that is.

Orlando Philharmonic, Orlando.
There definitely are strings attached to this presentation at the Bob Carr Performing Arts Centre. (See mention page 157)

*O*nce a quiet town surrounded by citrus groves, Orlando was almost overnight transformed into a tourist mecca. Other attractions followed Mickey, and Orlando soon grew into a vibrant metropolitan area with world-class cultural offerings.

*Street parade in The Magic Kingdom®
Park, Lake Buena Vista.*
The only unsmiling face you'll see in this enchanted land will likely belong to Grumpy. (See listing page 169)

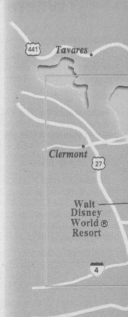

*P*laces included in this AAA Destination City:

Apopka	160	Maitland	178
Christmas	160	Mount Dora	178
Clermont	160	St. Cloud	179
Heathrow	160	Sanford	179
Kissimmee	160	Tavares	179
Lake Buena Vista	163	Winter Park	179

Charles Hosmer Morse Museum of American Art, Winter Park. One of the largest collections of Louis Comfort Tiffany's stained-glass masterpieces graces the museum's galleries. (See listing page 180)

Heathrow

Sanford

Mount Dora

Maitland

Apopka

Winter Park

417

50

Christmas

436

417

528

Orlando

Lake Buena Vista

Kissimmee

192

St. Cloud

60

See Vicinity map page 144

Orange County Regional History Center, Orlando. From gators to space shuttles, the natural and cultural history of Central Florida is symbolized in this dome. (See listing page 147)

Universal Studios, Orlando. Street entertainment includes old time rock 'n' roll at a 1950s era diner. (See listing page 152)

Getting There

By Car

Orlando is laced with busy thoroughfares. Primary among these is I-4, a trans-Florida route that combines direct travel through the city with strategic controlled access. From the Daytona Beach area it forks off I-95 and enters Orlando on the northeast side; from the Gulf Coast it comes from Tampa and St. Petersburg, passing Walt Disney World and entering town from the southwest.

Florida's Turnpike (toll) links Orlando with the resort areas of southeastern Florida. About 35 miles to the northwest it connects with I-75, a major north-south freeway. Florida's Turnpike interchanges with I-4 at the southwestern city limits.

I-4 and Florida's Turnpike form an X across central Florida. Two older routes, US 17/92 and US 441, also cross at Orlando, traversing different portions of the area.

SR 528, more commonly known as the Bee Line Expressway (toll), passes south of the city. It channels traffic between Orlando and the Cape Canaveral area and connects with routes leading downtown.

SR 50 (Colonial Drive) is an east-west route that passes through downtown and connects smaller communities near the Gulf with Atlantic coast areas. To avoid traffic an alternative is SR 408, the East-West Expressway (toll), which links with SR 50 both east and west of downtown. The expressway also connects with the Central Florida Greeneway (SR 417) just south of SR 50. An expansion to the eastern terminus brings the toll road to US 17/92 in Sanford; other eastern and western expansions are planned and sections of the expressway may be undergoing construction.

SR 436 (Semoran Boulevard) swings in a wide northwesterly arc from the airport and Bee Line Expressway southeast of town to US 441 northwest at Apopka and offers an alternative—although often busy—route to I-4.

Air Travel

The Orlando area is served by two airports: Orlando International Airport (OIA), at SR 436 and the Bee Line Expressway, and Orlando Sanford Airport in Sanford, which serves commercial and private aircraft. OIA, about 15 miles from both downtown and the tourist district, is a primary destination for many major domestic and international airlines. Serving more than 27 million passengers in 1999, it is one of

the world's fastest growing major airports. Its three satellite terminals are linked to the main terminal by automated people movers, making it easy to navigate. (**Note:** Orlando's tourist volume often leads to traffic congestion during peak vacation seasons. Allow plenty of transit time—coming and going—between the airport and your destination.)

To reach downtown Orlando, follow Airport Boulevard north as it merges into SR 436. Though heavily traveled, SR 436 offers direct access to central, east and north Orlando via SRs 50 or 408 (toll). To reach the International Drive area, take Airport Boulevard to SR 528 (toll), then head west to SR 482, which intersects International just east of I-4. Take Airport Boulevard south to SR 417 (toll) to go to the Disney resort via SR 536 or to reach Kissimmee via US 17/92/441.

Cab fares from the Orlando airport to downtown or International Drive average $36; limousines are approximately $90 plus a 20-percent tip to downtown and $115 to International Drive; shuttle vans are $13 one way, or $23 round trip; and public transportation is $1. Cab fare to the Disney resort averages $42. Many hotels and motels have courtesy car service.

Orlando is served by several major rental car agencies. Arrangements should be made before you depart especially during peak seasons. Your local AAA club can provide this service or additional information. Hertz, (407) 859-8400 or (800) 654-3080, offers discounts to AAA members.

Rail Service

Amtrak provides train service to four stations in the metro area. Passenger-only trains stop at the stations at 1400 Sligh Blvd. in downtown Orlando and 150 W. Morse Blvd. in downtown Winter Park; Kissimmee's passenger station is at 111 Dakin St. The AutoTrain, which runs south from Lorton, VA,

stops at the Sanford station at 800 Persimmon Ave. Phone (800) 872-7245 for both rail services.

Buses

A Greyhound Lines Inc. terminal, (407) 292-3422 for customer service, (407) 292-3424 for tickets, (800) 231-2222, or (800) 531-5332 for Spanish-speaking persons, is off West SR 50 (Colonial Drive) at 555 N. John Young Pkwy.

Getting Around

Street System

Because much of Orlando's growth occurred during the 1960s and '70s, the city is remarkably car-friendly. Roads are generally in good shape, although construction caused by near-constant expansion is a fact of life around the tourist district and downtown. Points of interest are usually on or near the main thoroughfares, most of which are accessible via I-4. For a small city, Orlando has surprisingly lengthy rush-hour periods, 6:30-9 a.m. and 4-6:30 p.m. Try to avoid traveling on I-4, US 17/92, SR 50 and SR 436 during these times.

Downtown Orlando is basically a grid, with several one-way streets. All street numbering begins at the intersection of Central Boulevard and Orange Avenue, the main strip through downtown. Orange is a one-way road south through the downtown core; its northbound counterpart is Rosalind Avenue. East-west roads accessing important downtown sites include Amelia Street (T.D. Waterhouse Centre), Livingston Street (Bob Carr Performing Arts Center, Expo Center), Robinson Street (Lake Eola), Central (Orlando Public Library, Lake Eola), Church Street (Downtown Farmer's Market) and South Street (City Hall).

International Drive, the heart of the tourist area, is south Orlando's busiest road. A profusion of hotels, shopping centers, outlet stores, restaurants, strolling vacationers and cruising teenagers usually combine to create crowded conditions and frequent delays.

Unless otherwise posted, the speed limit on most streets is 30 mph. Rush-hour traffic, 6:30 to 9 a.m. and 4 to 6:30 p.m., should be avoided. Unless otherwise posted, right turns are permitted on red after a complete stop.

Parking

Metered street parking downtown is available at 75c per hour, but spaces are generally hard to find at peak periods, which are on weekdays and weekend evenings. Downtown parking also is available in an open-air lot underneath I-4 on Garland Avenue between Central Boulevard and Pine Street.

Municipal garages can be found throughout downtown, including at Amelia Street, between Revere Street and Hughey Avenue; Church Street, between Division and Hughey avenues; Pine Street, between Garland and Orange avenues; Central Boulevard, between Garland and Orange avenues; and Central Boulevard, between Rosalind and Magnolia avenues. Rates range $1-$1.50 per half-hour or $12 per day.

Winter Park has free parking along Park Avenue, but spaces can be hard to come by during peak hours. Public lots are located just west of Park Avenue off New England Avenue, Morse Boulevard and Canton Avenue.

Most attractions and shopping centers have ample parking, but parking fees for the major theme parks can run as high as $8 per day. Check with your hotel to see if it offers free shuttle service to the theme parks.

Taxis and Limousines

Local taxis are metered and charge $3.25 for the first mile, $1.75 for each additional mile. Major cab companies are Ace Metro, (407) 855-0564; Checker, (407) 699-9999; City, (407) 422-5151; and Yellow, (407) 422-4455.

Limousine service is available throughout most of the city; the ride from the airport to downtown Orlando or International Drive is about $90 plus a 20-percent tip, and $115 to International Drive.

Public Transportation

Brightly painted buses are a colorful sight in the metro area, thanks to LYNX, the transit authority for Orange, Osceola and Seminole counties, which operates more than 200 buses on 50-plus routes. The main transit station is hard to miss—it is painted bubblegum-pink and is located in the heart of downtown on Central Boulevard between Garland and Orange avenues.

Bus stops, called Links, are marked by fuchsia paw-print signs listing all the routes that are immediately accessible from that stop. The system serves most of the city, including downtown, the tourist district and major shopping centers. Main routes are 4, between south Orlando and Kissimmee; 10, through Kissimmee; 38, downtown to the International Drive area; 41, between SR 436 and the airport; 42, between Dr. Phillips Boulevard and the airport; and 50, between downtown to the Walt Disney World Resort.

I-Ride Trolleys cater exclusively to tourist traffic along International Drive from 7 a.m.-midnight; the wait is 15 minutes. Trolley fare is $1; over 65, 25c; under 13 free with adult. LYNX also offers Lymmo, a free bus service that uses a bus-only lane to transport passengers throughout the downtown area, including stops at city hall and T.D. Waterhouse Centre. Lymmo runs Mon.-Thurs. 6 a.m.-10 p.m., Fri. 6 a.m.-midnight, Sat. 10-midnight, Sun. 10-10.

LYNX fare is $1; transfers are an extra 10c. Exact change is required. Buses run Mon.-Fri. 5 a.m.-12:15 a.m., Sat. 5:30-a.m.-7:15 p.m., Sun. 6:15-6:15; holiday schedules may vary. For additional information about routes and schedules phone (407) 841-8240 or (407) 423-0787.

What To See

DISCOVERY COVE is at 6000 Discovery Cove Way next to SeaWorld Orlando. The park allows visitors to encounter a variety of animals up-close and in a lush island resort setting. Three beautiful lagoons are home to playful dolphins with which guests, under the supervision of trainers, can swim and have their pictures taken. An artificial reef beckons snorkelers with its realistic coral and colorful tropical fish. Nearby, swimmers, protected by clear underwater partitions, come face-to-face with sharks and barracudas. A tropical river allows guests to float through a free-flight aviary where they can hand-feed exotic birds. Stingrays, sloths and anteaters are among the other touchable creatures at the park.

Allow a full day. Daily 9-5:30. Admission, including dolphin swim, $219; without dolphin swim, $119; under age 3 free. Admission to Discovery Cove also includes 7 consecutive days admission to SeaWorld Orlando, one meal and all swim gear. Children under 6 are not permitted to swim with the dolphins. Reservations are required. AX, DS, MC, VI. Phone (877) 434-7268. *See color ad p. 143.*

EPCOT—see Lake Buena Vista p. 168.

GATORLAND is 8 mi. s. of the Bee Line Expwy. (SR 528) on US 17/92/441 at 14501 S. Orange Blossom Tr. Opened as a roadside attraction in 1949, the 110-acre park and wildlife preserve is home to thousands of alligators, crocodiles, snakes and other reptiles. Highlights include a children's water park, a petting zoo, a train ride, an aviary and a breeding marsh with observation tower. Educational wildlife programs, presented several times daily, include the Gator Wrestlin' Show, Gator Jumparoo Show, Jungle Crocs of the World and the Up-Close Encounters Show. Food is available.

Allow 3 hours minimum. Daily 9-6. Admission $17.93; ages 3-12, $8.48. AX, DS, MC, VI. Phone (407) 855-5496 or (800) 393-5297.

HARRY P. LEU GARDENS is at 1920 N. Forest Ave.; I-4 exit 85 to Princeton Ave., s. on Mills Ave., then .5 mi. e. via Virginia Dr. The Leu House Museum, dating from the 1880s, can be viewed by guided tour. The garden's 50 acres feature paved walkways, camellias, one of the largest formal rose gardens in Florida and the Butterfly Garden. A wooded deck overlooks Lake Rowena. Allow 1 hour, 30 minutes minimum. Gardens open daily 9-5; closed Dec. 25. House tours are given daily 10-3:30. Admission $4; ages 5-18, $1. Phone (407) 246-2620.

HOLY LAND EXPERIENCE, off I-4 exit 78 (Conroy Rd.), then just w. to 4655 Vineland Rd., is a living Biblical museum that presents Christian religious history through outdoor exhibits and live musical dramas. Allow 4 hours minimum. Mon.-Fri. 9-5, Sat. 9-6, Sun. noon-6. Admission $22; ages 4-12, $17. AX, DS, MC, VI. Phone (407) 367-2065 or (866) 872-4659.

LAKE EOLA PARK, 3 blks. from the center of town on E. Central Blvd., has stately trees and flowering plants and shrubs. In the center of Lake

Kiss your dreams hello.

Come to Orlando and swim with dolphins, rays and thousands of tropical fish. Relax on pristine beaches.

And discover how close your dreams really are

Purchase your Discovery Cove admission package now at participating AAA Auto Club offices.

For reservations, call 1-877-4-DISCOVERY or visit www.discoverycove.com

DISCOVERY COVE
ORLANDO

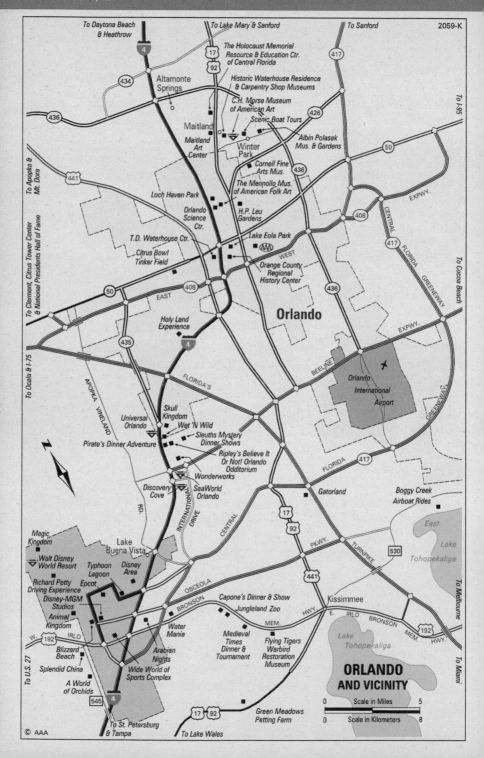

To Daytona Beach & Heathrow

To Lake Mary & Sanford

To Sanford

The Holocaust Memorial Resource & Education Ctr. of Central Florida

Altamonte Springs

Historic Waterhouse Residence & Carpentry Shop Museums

C.H. Morse Museum of American Art

Maitland

Scenic Boat Tours

Maitland Art Center

Winter Park

Albin Polasek Mus. & Gardens

Cornell Fine Arts Mus.

The Mennollo Mus. of American Folk Art

Loch Haven Park

H.P. Leu Gardens

Orlando Science Ctr.

T.D. Waterhouse Ctr.

Lake Eola Park

WEST

Citrus Bowl Tinker Field

Orange County Regional History Center

Orlando

EAST

Holy Land Experience

Skull Kingdom

Universal Orlando

Wet 'N Wild

Sleuths Mystery Dinner Shows

Pirate's Dinner Adventure

Ripley's Believe It Or Not! Orlando Odditorium

Wonderworks

Discovery Cove

SeaWorld Orlando

Gatorland

Boggy Creek Airboat Rides

East Lake Tohopekaliga

Magic Kingdom

Walt Disney World Resort

Lake Buena Vista

Typhoon Lagoon

Disney Area

Richard Petty Driving Experience

Epcot

Disney-MGM Studios

Animal Kingdom

Blizzard Beach

Splendid China

A World of Orchids

Water Mania

Arabian Nights

Wide World of Sports Complex

Capone's Dinner & Show

Jungleland Zoo

Medieval Times Dinner & Tournament

Flying Tigers Warbird Restoration Museum

Kissimmee

Lake Tohopekaliga

To Apopka & Mt. Dora

To Clermont, Citrus Tower Center & National Presidents Hall of Fame

To Ocala & I-75

To U.S. 27

To St. Petersburg & Tampa

To Lake Wales

Green Meadows Petting Farm

To I-95

To Cocoa Beach

To Melbourne

To Miami

Orlando International Airport

ORLANDO AND VICINITY

Scale in Miles   0   5

Scale in Kilometers   0   8

© AAA

TITUSVILLE   COCOA BEACH   MELBOURNE   PALM BAY

THE Ultimate™

FLORIDA

9,614 hotels rooms,
1,400 restaurants, 72 miles
of beach, 24 golf courses,
90 charter boats, 115 parks,
over 100,000 acres of wildlife
refuges,862 retail stores,
23 attractions, 3,000 RV sites,
two gaming ships, over 400
cruises per year, 20 shuttle
and rocket launches per year,
13 museums, one zoo,
one planetarium.

The Ultimate Vacation

Call **800-93-OCEAN**
or visit www.space-coast.com

FLORIDA'S SPACE COAST

Orlando's
Closed Beaches

© 2002

Eola is the colorfully lighted Clinton Allen Fountain. Swan paddleboats, a playground and food are available. Paddleboats available daily 11-dusk; under 14 must be with an adult. Playground open daily 8 a.m.-10 p.m. Park and playground free. Paddleboats $7 per half-hour (three people per boat). Phone (407) 246-2827 or (407) 839-8899 for paddleboat information.

LOCH HAVEN PARK, bounded by Mills (US 17/92) and Orange aves. and bisected by Princeton St., contains three museums and a theater. The Civic Theatre of Central Florida stages productions. *(See What To Do, Theater and Concerts.)* Phone (407) 896-7365.

SAVE **The Mennello Museum of American Folk Art** is at 900 E. Princeton St. next to the Orlando Science Center's parking garage. The museum houses a permanent collection of the works of Earl Cunningham, a prominent 20th-century American folk artist. Traveling exhibits also are featured. Allow 30 minutes minimum. Tues.-Fri. 11-5, Sun. noon-5; closed holidays. Admission $4; over 60, $3; students with ID $1; under 12 free. Phone (407) 246-4278.

Orlando Museum of Art, 2416 N. Mills Ave., maintains permanent collections of American art, African works and artifacts from the Ancient Americas. Discovery Centers offer hands-on activities for children. Changing exhibits also are featured. Allow 1 hour minimum. Tues.-Sat. 10-5, Sun. noon-5; closed holidays. Admission $6; over 55 and students with ID $5; ages 4-11, $3. Phone (407) 896-4231.

Orlando Science Center, 777 E. Princeton St., features 10 exhibit halls with hundreds of hands-on, interactive learning displays. Visitors can journey through the human body, observe life in a Florida cypress swamp and unearth dinosaur mysteries. Large-format films and planetarium shows can be viewed in the eight-story CineDome.

Allow 2 hours minimum. Mon.-Thurs. 9-5, Fri.-Sat. 9-9, Sun. noon-5, Memorial Day to mid-Aug.; Tues.-Thurs. and Mon. school holidays 9-5, Fri-Sat. 9-9, Sun. noon-5, rest of year. Closed Thanksgiving and Dec. 25. Admission to exhibits $9.50; over 54,

$8.50; ages 3-11, $6.75. Exhibits and one CineDome show $12.50; over 54, $11.50; ages 3-11, $9.25. Parking $3.50. Phone (407) 514-2000 or (888) 672-4386.

ORANGE COUNTY REGIONAL HISTORY CENTER, 65 E. Central Blvd., offers permanent and changing exhibits tracing the area's history from Paleo-Indians to the present. In the orientation theater, visitors view a 15-minute audiovisual presentation from rocking chairs on a "Florida back porch."

Other features include a Florida Pioneer Cracker-style cabin, a sample sinkhole and cave, and a re-created Seminole Indian village, as well as interactive displays about Florida industries from cattle to citrus. Changing exhibits also are featured. Allow 1 hour, 30 minutes minimum. Mon.-Sat. 11-5, Sun. noon-5; closed Jan. 1, Thanksgiving and Dec. 24-25 and 31. Admission $7; over 59 and students with ID $6.50; ages 3-12, $3.50. MC, VI. Phone (407) 836-8500.

PIRATE'S DINNER ADVENTURE is .25 mi. s. of International Dr. at 6400 Carrier Dr. Guests at this interactive dinner show enjoy a Caribbean feast while musical comedy, swashbuckling stunts and live-action performances take place aboard a pirate galleon. After the show, guests may attend the Buccaneer Bash dance party or visit the Pirate's Maritime Museum. Shows daily at 8; doors open at 6:30. Phone for matinee information. Admission $43.95; ages 3-11, $26.95. Reservations are recommended. AX, CB, DS, MC, VI. Phone (407) 248-0590 or (800) 866-2469.

RIPLEY'S BELIEVE IT OR NOT! ORLANDO ODDITORIUM is .5 mi. s.e. of I-4 exit 74A (Sand Lake Rd.) at 8201 International Dr. Odd and unusual exhibits and video presentations from around the world are featured in 16 themed galleries that include interactive illusions, human and animal oddities, weird art and dinosaurs and fossils. Allow 1 hour minimum. Daily 9 a.m.-1 a.m. Last admission 1 hour before closing. Admission $14.95; ages 4-12, $9.95. AX, DS, MC, VI. Phone (407) 345-0501 or (800) 998-4418, ext. 3.

SEAWORLD ORLANDO is at 7007 Sea World Dr., at jct. I-4 and SR 528 (Bee Line Expwy.). SeaWorld Orlando is a marine life adventure park featuring sea-themed shows, up-close marine animal encounters, attractions and rides.

Kraken, a "floorless" roller coaster, combines a 15-story ascent with three underground loops—one of them underwater through a mythical serpent's lair. Journey to Atlantis is a water coaster thrill ride that plunges visitors into the middle of a clash for the lost city of Atlantis.

A rocky, simulated helicopter ride transports visitors to Wild Arctic, where beluga whales, walruses and polar bears coexist.

Shows include The Shamu Adventure, a killer whale show featuring an eagle and video host and animal expert Jack Hanna; Clyde and Seamore Take Pirate Island, featuring sea lions, walruses, otters and harbor seals searching for a lost treasure map; Pets Ahoy, which is a showcase for four-legged celebrities adopted from animal shelters; Cirque de la Mer, which blends athleticism, dance, music and special effects into a nontraditional circus; and The Intensity Games Water Ski Show, a performance of wakeboarding, skiing and water stunts.

Key West at SeaWorld features live bands and entertainment, close-up encounters with sea turtles and opportunities to touch and feed dolphins and stingrays. Manatees: The Last Generation? explores the underwater world of the endangered manatee, and Pacific Point Preserve is home to California sea lions and harbor and fur seals. Playful bottlenose dolphins and false killer whales are the focus of Key West Dolphin Fest.

Other features include Shamu's Happy Harbor, a 3-acre children's play area; Penguin Encounter, home to hundreds of Antarctic birds; Dolphin Nursery, with new moms and calves; Tropical Reef, which is a showcase for sea creatures in jewel aquariums; Terrors of the Deep, with sharks and other feared ocean dwellers; and The Anheuser-Busch Hospitality Center, featuring beautiful Clydesdales.

Available for an additional fee are rides on the 400-foot sky tower, the Adventure Express tour, behind-the-scenes tours and educational classes. The 5.5- to 6-hour Adventure Express includes reserved seating and no waiting in line at certain shows and attractions; feeding opportunities; and guide service. Other guided tours also are available. Kennels, strollers, lockers and wheelchair rentals are available.

Allow a full day. Park generally opens daily at 9; closing times vary. Last admission 1 hour before

Travel

Preferred Cruise and Tour Partners

Ask your AAA Counselor about Member Benefits from our partners in travel.

 **Carnival.**
THE MOST POPULAR CRUISE LINE IN THE WORLD®

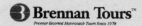 **Brennan Tours**™
Premier Escorted Motorcoach Tours Since 1978

Pleasant Holidays.

 *Celebrity Cruises*

 **contiki**
VACATIONS for 18 to 35 year olds

TAUCK  WORLD DISCOVERY

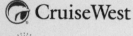 CruiseWest

 CLASSIC CUSTOM VACATIONS®

 **TRAFALGAR TOURS**
THE WORLD'S BEST SELLING ESCORTED TOURS

 **CRYSTAL®** CRUISES

 DISNEY CRUISE LINE.

 **DriveAmerica**

.TRAVEL BOUND

 **Holland America**

 **General Tours.**
Making Travelers Feel At Home All Over The World For More Than 50 Years

 **T**ravel ✈ **I**mpressions
Now more than ever...
...the right choice

 **PRINCESS**
where i belong℠

 GRAND CANYON RAILWAY & RESORT

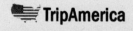 **TripAmerica**

 RADISSON **SEVEN SEAS CRUISES**®
LUXURY GOES EXPLORING™

 **der**
destination europe resources

UNIVERSAL STUDIOS Vacations

 RoyalCaribbean®
INTERNATIONAL
Get out there.℠

 **U·S AIRWAYS**
—————
VACATIONS

 **AAA** Vacations®

 WINDSTAR CRUISES
180° FROM ORDINARY®

closing. Admission $49.95; ages 3-9, $40.95. Adventure Express tours $75; ages 3-9, $70. Guided tours $8.95; ages 3-9, $7.95. Sky tower $3. The Orlando Flex Ticket, a multi-day, multi-park ticket that includes SeaWorld Orlando, Universal Studios Florida, Universal Studios Islands of Adventure and Wet 'n Wild in Orlando and Busch Gardens Tampa Bay, is available at the park. Parking $7 for automobile, $8 for recreational vehicle or camper. AX, DS, MC, VI. Phone (407) 351-3600. *See color ad inside front cover.*

SAVE **SKULL KINGDOM,** off I-4 exit 75A at 5933 American Way, is a haunted castle complete with special effects and robotics as well as night creatures and fiends. Sudden encounters and gruesome scenes await visitors as they make their way through two floors of mazes and caverns. Daily noon-11, July-Aug. and major holidays; Mon.-Fri. 6 p.m.-11 p.m., Sat.-Sun. noon-11, rest of year. Admission $12.50. Not recommended for under 8. AX, CB, DS, JC, MC, VI. Phone (407) 354-1564.

SAVE **SLEUTHS MYSTERY DINNER SHOWS** is 1 blk. e. of International Dr., jct. of Universal Blvd. and Carrier Dr. in Republic Square at 7508 Universal Blvd. Guests become detectives to help solve a crime in these comedy-mystery dinner shows. Allow 3 hours minimum. Shows daily at 7:30; phone for additional seatings. Show times vary; phone ahead. Tickets $41.95; ages 3-11, $24.95. Reservations are required. AX, DC, DS, MC, VI. Phone (407) 363-1985 or (800) 393-1985.

GEM **UNIVERSAL ORLANDO** is off I-4 exit 75A (eastbound) or 74B (westbound), following signs. The complex brings movies to life through rides and shows at Universal Studios, visits the universe of myths, legends and super heroes at Islands of Adventure, and offers CityWalk for shopping, dining and entertainment.

The theme parks, entertainment area and on-site resorts are within walking distance of each other. All shopping, dining and entertainment facilities also are available to day guests. Because of the popularity of the parks, large crowds and long lines can be expected, especially during holiday periods. Strollers, wheelchairs and electric carts can be rented. Kennels are available.

The theme parks open daily at 9; closing hours vary by season. CityWalk open daily 11 a.m.-2 a.m.

A 1-day pass to either Universal Studios or Islands of Adventure is $49.95; ages 3-9, $40.95. Two- and 3-day passes provide unlimited admission to both parks on the same day. Multi-day passes also include early admission to the parks and access to all clubs at CityWalk. Two-day pass $94.95; ages 3-9, $81.95. Three-day pass $109.95; ages 3-9, $96.95. Multi-day passes do not expire until all days are used. The Orlando Flex Ticket, a multi-day, multi-park ticket that includes SeaWorld Orlando, Universal Studios Florida, Universal Studios Islands of Adventure and Wet 'n Wild in Orlando and Busch Gardens Tampa Bay, is available at the park. Check with the attractions or your AAA club for more details. Parking $6;

valet parking $12. Special discounts are available to AAA members. See page 13 for more information. AX, DS, MC, VI. Phone (407) 363-8000. *See color ads starting on p. 150.*

CityWalk, off I-4 exit 75A (eastbound) or 74B (westbound), is an entertainment complex featuring dining in themed restaurants, nightclubs, specialty shopping and movie theaters. Live performances at restaurants and clubs are evening highlights. Daily 11 a.m.-2 a.m. Evening cover charges vary by club. A pass covering evening admission to all clubs is $8.95, or $12 with cineplex admission included. AAA/CAA members save 10 percent on dining and souvenirs at all restaurants except Emeril's. AX, DS, MC, VI. Phone (407) 363-8000.

SAVE **Islands of Adventure,** off I-4 exit 74B (westbound) or 75A (eastbound), following signs, is a theme park that presents five themed islands with rides and shows based on such popular and legendary characters as The Cat in the Hat, Spider-Man, Popeye, The Incredible Hulk, Sindbad and the dinosaurs of "Jurassic Park." The Port of Entry, with food and shops, serves as an introduction to the park.

Experience the worlds of legendary super heroes and villains at Marvel Super Hero Island. Rides include Doctor Doom's Fearfall, a rocket ride 150 feet straight up—and then back down again; The Amazing Adventures of Spider-Man, a high-tech 3-D thrill ride; and the Incredible Hulk Coaster, a high-speed roller coaster adventure.

Meet some of your favorite characters at Toon Lagoon, where rides and shows are based on cartoons and comic strips. Watch out for splashing

A Vacatio

From The Ordi

AAA Gives You *Three Ways to Save!*

SAVE ON UNIVERSAL ORLANDO° RESORT VACATIONS.

AAA members save when they stay at one of Universal Orlando's three magnificently themed on-site hotels. Enjoy the luxurious Portofino Bay Hotel, A Loews Hotel, the exciting Hard Rock Hotel° – both AAA Four Diamond Award° winners – and the exotic new Royal Pacific Resort, A Loews Hotel (not yet rated). *Be sure to ask about exclusive AAA member benefits valued at $50!*

SAVE ON MULTI-DAY TICKETS.

AAA members enjoy the lowest prices on multi-day tickets, the best way to experience both Universal Orlando theme parks — **Universal Studios**° and **Islands of Adventure**.

SAVE ON FOOD AND MERCHANDISE.

Plus, remember to show your AAA membership card and *SAVE 10% OFF* food and merchandise at select shops and restaurants throughout Universal Orlando Resort.

For tickets or Universal Orlando vacations call or visit your AAA office today!

www.universalorlando.com

water on Dudley Do-Right's Ripsaw Falls log flume ride and Popeye & Bluto's Bilge-Rat Barges twisting, churning white-water raft ride.

Jurassic Park, based on the popular motion picture and novel, re-creates the land inhabited by prehistoric creatures. Jurassic Park River Adventure, a raft ride through dinosaur habitats, features a steep water drop, while visitors have an opportunity to create a dinosaur through DNA sequencing at Jurassic Park Discovery Center. Camp Jurassic is an interactive prehistoric play area, and Pteranodon Flyers offers children and their parents a view of the Jurassic Park area from up high.

The centerpieces of the mysterious island the Lost Continent are Dueling Dragons, an inverted double roller coaster, and the Eighth Voyage of Sindbad, an action-filled stunt show.

The whimsical characters of Theodor "Dr. Seuss" Geisel's popular books come to life at Seuss Landing. The Cat In The Hat takes visitors on a couch ride through Dr. Seuss' childhood classic, and a menagerie of the good doctor's characters serve as steeds on the Caro-Seuss-el. The younger set will also enjoy the play area If I Ran The Zoo and One Fish, Two Fish, Red Fish, Blue Fish.

Allow a full day. Park opens daily at 9; closing hours vary according to season. One-day admission $49.95; ages 3-9, $40.95. Parking $8; valet parking under 2 hours $7, more than 2 hours $14. Discounted tickets available at participating AAA offices. Members save 10 percent on in-park dining

and souvenirs (excludes food or merchandise carts, tobacco, candy, film, collectibles, clearance and sundry items). AX, DS, MC, VI. Phone (407) 363-8000.

SAVE **Universal Studios,** off I-4 exit 75A (eastbound) or 74B (westbound), following signs, is a theme park that takes visitors into the worlds of Hollywood, movies and television. The theme park also is a working studio for television and motion picture production, complete with a back lot and sound stages. Realistic street scenes and special sets include Rodeo Drive, Hollywood Boulevard, Pennsylvania Station, Fifth Avenue, Gramercy Park and Fisherman's Wharf.

Men in Black Alien Attack, based on the movie, is a high-tech, interactive ride that gives visitors a chance to save Earth from aliens by zapping the creatures as the ride progresses through the streets of New York. But be warned; these aliens zap back, spinning your vehicle out of control.

The multisensory Terminator 2: 3-D Battle Across Time, offers a 3-D cyberadventure. Visitors hurtle through time and space in Back to the Future. . .The Ride and come face-to-face with a tornado in Twister. . .Ride It Out. Nickelodeon Studios lets you experience games based on Nickelodeon kids shows.

An 8.3 earthquake hurls fire, flood and even a runaway truck at visitors as their surroundings are leveled in Earthquake. . .The Big One, while King

Kong is on the rampage in Kongfrontation. Jaws subjects visitors to an attack by a 3-ton, 32-foot great white shark.

Woody Woodpecker's KidZone, a special area just for kids, features the Curious George Goes to Town play area, Woody Woodpecker's Nuthouse Coaster, E.T. Adventure, A Day in the Park with Barney, Animal Planet Live and Fievel's Playland.

Allow a full day. Park opens daily at 9; closing hours vary according to season. One-day admission $49.95; ages 3-9, $40.95. Parking $8; valet parking under 2 hours $7, more than 2 hours $14. Discounted tickets available at participating AAA offices. Members save 10 percent on in-park dining and souvenirs (excludes food or merchandise carts, tobacco, candy, film, collectibles, clearance and sundry items). AX, DS, MC, VI. Phonc (407) 363-8000.

WALT DISNEY WORLD—
see Lake Buena Vista p. 163.

[SAVE] **WET 'N WILD** is off I-4 exit 75A at 6200 International Dr. This water recreation park contains slides and flumes, a wave pool and a cable-operated kneeboard ride. Among the highlights is Surge, a multipassenger slide that races through 600 feet of curves and the Flyer, a four-passenger toboggan ride. A children's playground offers child-size versions of the park's most popular rides. Food, picnic facilities, locker rooms and showers are available. Bathing suits are required—no shorts, cutoffs or items with metal fasteners, rivets, zippers or buckles are permitted.

Allow 6 hours minimum. Open daily; hours vary according to season. Admission $30.95; ages 3-9, $24.95; over 55, $15.48. Parking $5; recreational vehicles $6. Lockers $5. The Orlando Flex Ticket, a multi-day, multi-park ticket that includes SeaWorld Orlando, Universal Studios Florida, Universal Studios Islands of Adventure and Wet 'n Wild in Orlando and Busch Gardens Tampa Bay, is available at the park. Check with the attractions for more details. AX, DS, MC, VI. Phone (407) 351-1800 or (800) 992-9453.

WONDERWORKS is .8 mi. n. of SR 528 at 9067 International Dr. An upside-down building contains this interactive attraction, which features more than 100 hands-on exhibits and a laser tag arena. Virtual reality technology and simulations enable visitors to experience an earthquake and hurricane force winds, design and ride their own roller-coaster, walk with their own shadow, swim with a shark and feel the power of 2,000 volts of electricity. Food is available.

Allow 1 hour minimum. Daily 9 a.m.-midnight. Admission $16.95; over 55 and ages 4-12, $12.95.

Laser tag is additional. Fee for parking. AX, DC, DS, MC, VI. Phone (407) 351-8800.

Sightseeing

Balloon Tours

[SAVE] Orange Blossom Balloons, (407) 239-7677, and Blue Water Balloons, (407) 894-5040 or (800) 586-1884, offer aerial views of the Orlando area via hot air balloons. The scenic trips include breakfast and champagne.

Bus, Carriage, Limousine or Train Tours

Guided tours are a good way to make the best use of time in Orlando. Gator Tours, (407) 522-5912 or (800) 537-0917, offers day and overnight narrated tours, with pickup at your lodging.

Spectator Sports

From downtown Orlando to Walt Disney World Resort, fans have several venues to choose from when it comes to the city's various professional sports offerings. Orlando's premier sports arena, **T.D. Waterhouse Centre,** 600 W. Amelia St., hosts arena football, basketball and hockey games.

Baseball

Baseball fans can cheer Orlando's minor league team, the **Orlando Rays,** at **Disney's Wide World of Sports**™, Osceola Parkway and Victory Way, April through August. Disney's 200-acre multipurpose sports complex also is the spring training home of the **Atlanta Braves.** For game schedules and ticket information phone (407) 939-1500.

Osceola County Stadium, 1000 Bill Beck Blvd. in Kissimmee, is the site of the **Houston Astros** spring training camp.

Basketball

Orlando basketball enthusiasts root for their home team, the NBA's **Orlando Magic.** Fans can attend games at T.D. Waterhouse Centre, where they can also watch the Women's NBA **Orlando Miracle.** The city's two colleges also have basketball teams. For schedule and ticket information phone the Orlando Magic, (407) 916-2400; Rollins College, (407) 646-2663, in Winter Park; and the University of Central Florida Arena, (407) 823-6006, in Orlando.

Football

The **Citrus Bowl** hosts college football games, including the annual Capital One Bowl and home games for the Division I **UCF Knights.** The city has an arena football team, the **Orlando Predators,** who were league champions in 1998 and 2000; games are played in the T.D. Waterhouse Centre downtown.

Greyhound Racing

Dog racing is a year-round diversion. **Sanford-Orlando Kennel Club,** (407) 831-1600, at 301 Dog Track Rd. in Longwood, holds matinee and evening races.

Note: Policies concerning admittance of children to pari-mutuel betting facilities vary. Phone for information.

Jai-Alai

Played in only a few states, jai-alai is one of Orlando's most unusual offerings. The game is similar to handball, except the athletes field the ball not with their bare hands, but with a curved basket worn on one arm. Pari-mutuel betting adds to the excitement of this fast-paced sport at **Orlando-Seminole Jai-Alai Fronton,** (407) 339-6221, in Fern Park on US 17/92. The live jai-alai season in Orlando is November through June, although the facility is open year-round for televised jai-alai and racing events.

Note: Policies concerning admittance of children to pari-mutuel betting facilities vary. Phone for information.

Recreation

Lengthy summers and mild winters create ideal recreation conditions in central Florida year-round,

and locals make the most of it. The area's many waterways host a wide variety of activities, and drier pastimes abound as well. Phone the Orange County Parks & Recreation Department 24-Hour Parks InfoLine, (407) 836-6280, for more information.

Bicycling

Although bicycling is growing in popularity in Orlando, there are few dedicated bike paths in the city, and traffic is always a concern. Exercise caution and obey all traffic laws when bicycling on the street. If possible, ride in a park—both **Turkey Lake** and **Lake Underhill** parks offer trails—or other specially designated area. Locals enjoy the **Cady Way Trail,** running 3.5 miles from the Fashion Square Mall on SR 50 to Cady Way in Winter Park, as well as the quiet, tree-lined streets of **Rollins College, College Park** and **downtown Orlando.** The **Walt Disney World Resort** offers a variety of trails as well as bicycle rentals.

Fishing

With hundreds of lakes and several rivers to choose from, anglers will have no problem finding a place to cast their lines—bass, bream and catfish are among the available catches. Some favorite spots are **Gaston Edwards Park** on **Lake Ivanhoe** near downtown; **Lake Fairview,** north of College Park; Lake Underhill Park, east of town off Conway Road; **Lake Cane/Marsha Park** and **Turkey Lake Park,** both just off Conroy-Windermere Rd.; **Wekiwa Springs State Park,** on SR 435 in northwest Orange County; and **Lake Tohopekaliga** in Kissimmee, south of US 192. The Walt Disney World complex also affords angling opportunities for tourists and residents alike. A freshwater license is required for those age 16 or older; phone Fisheries Management, (407) 846-5300, for additional details.

Deep-sea fishing is a popular pastime, and charters are available in many beachfront towns. Anglers age 16 and over must purchase saltwater licenses, which are available at many bait and tackle shops, most Wal-marts and Kmarts and at all tax assessors' offices. For further information phone the Florida Marine Enforcement, (800) 342-5367.

Golf

Golf is a way of life for many Orlando residents; an abundance of courses—more than 150—graces the metropolitan area, from the city-bound links of small municipal properties to the spectacular settings of the luxury resorts. All of the following courses offer at least 18 holes and are open to the public year round: Buena Vista, (407) 939-4653, in Lake Buena Vista; Casselberry, (407) 699-9310, 300 S. Triplet Lake Dr.; Celebration Golf Club,

(407) 566-4653, 701 Golf Park Dr.; Dubsdread, (407) 246-2551, 549 W. Par St.; Eastwood Golf Club, (407) 281-4653, 13950 Golfway Blvd.; Hunter's Creek, (407) 240-4653, 14401 Sports Club Way; Mayfair Country Club, (407) 322-2531, in Sanford; MetroWest Country Club, (407) 299-1099, 2100 S. Hiawassee Rd.; Stoneybrook Orlando, (407) 384-6888, 2900 Northampton Ave.; Walt Disney World Golf Complex, (407) 939-4653, in Lake Buena Vista; and Wedgefield Golf and Country Club, (407) 568-2116, 20550 Maxim Pkwy.

Jogging and Walking

Orlando also boasts two scenic, paved recreation trails built on old railway beds. Both provide opportunities for walking and jogging. The 22.5-mile **West Orange Trail** runs between the Lake/Orange county line through abandoned orange groves to Apopka. For information contact the Orange County Parks and Recreation Department at (407) 654-1108. Closer to downtown Orlando, the 3.5-mile Cady Way Trail connects Winter Park to Fashion Square Mall. For information contact the Transportation Planning Bureau (407) 246-2775.

One can walk or jog just about anywhere in central Florida, but the following spots are exceptionally nice. Downtown Orlando features **Lake Eola,** noted for Centennial Fountain, as well as **Langford Park** on Central Boulevard. Just outside downtown are College Park's charming streets and the serene oasis of Lake Ivanhoe's **Gaston Edwards Park. Winter Park** is a good place for a stroll, particularly along popular **Park Avenue** or on the **Rollins College** campus. Other appealing sites include **Mead Gardens** and **Kraft Azalea Gardens and Park** in Winter Park. Due to the relentless Florida sun, early morning and late afternoon are the best times for either activity.

Tennis

Tennis courts are nearly as numerous as lakes in metropolitan Orlando, with more than 800 throughout the area. Many hotels offer court privileges to their guests. The courts at county parks are always open to the general public; for further details phone the City of Orlando Recreation Bureau, (407) 246-2288, or the Orange County Parks and Recreation Department, (407) 836-6200. Some resorts offer public access, including **Cypress Creek Country Club** at 5353 S. Vineland Rd., (407) 351-2187; the **Grand Cypress Racquet Club,** 55 Grand Cypress Blvd., (407) 239-1944; and Kissimmee's **Poinciana Golf & Racquet Resort,** 500 E. Cypress Pkwy., (407) 933-5300.

Water Sports

The abundance of lakes in central Florida—more than 1,200 by some counts—provides endless opportunities for water sports of all kinds, including boating, canoeing, swimming, water skiing and windsurfing. Some of the most popular sites include Lake Ivanhoe; Lake Underhill; and the **Butler Chain of Lakes** and **Winter Park Chain of Lakes.** For information about the Butler Chain of Lakes contact the Orange County Parks and Recreation Department at (407) 246-2238; for information about the Winter Park Chain of Lakes, phone (407) 599-3334; or phone the City of Orlando Aquatics Department at (407) 246-2288.

Just north of Orlando near Apopka is Wekiwa Springs State Park *(see Recreation Chart and the AAA Southeastern CampBook),* where swimming in the crystal clear spring water is popular. The Wekiva River is considered one of the state's best canoeing rivers; canoe rental information is available at the marina, (407) 862-1500.

Boating is a favorite recreation; residents have their choice of several inland waterways to explore. The Butler and Winter Park Chain of Lakes are groupings of connected lakes. The Rollins College campus and beautiful homes line the shores of the lakes in Winter Park's chain, and boat tours are available *(see place listing p. 180).* Another active waterway, the **St. Johns River,** connects nearby Sanford with Jacksonville and boat tours are available *(see DeLand p. 55).* Houseboats can be rented on a daily basis in DeLand, allowing visitors to navigate the river in style.

Shopping

With an influx of tourists from all over the world, Orlando's shopping areas must satisfy a variety of tastes and styles. From high fashion and international selections to famous labels at bargain-

hunter prices, Orlando has them. Weather-related items such as lightweight sportswear and swimsuits are stocked all year, and area citrus products are sold at many roadside stands.

Antiques

The best antiquing downtown is in the **North Orange Avenue Antiques District,** running south from the 2900 block to the 1600 block. This funky strip is lined with stores selling everything from 1930s radios to 19th-century furniture to housewares from the 1950s and '60s. Particularly charming is a little cluster of buildings known as **Ivanhoe Row,** along the 1200 block across from Lake Ivanhoe. The College Park section of **Edgewater Drive** and **Fairbanks Avenue** east of I-4 also have a number of antiques dealers. Pricier items can be found at the shops along **Park Avenue** in Winter Park.

Malls

In south Orlando, the massive **Florida Mall,** 8001 S. Orange Blossom Tr., boasts more than 200 shops and a bustling food court anchored by such major retailers as Dillard's, JCPenney, Saks Fifth Avenue and Sears, and including the Adam's Mark Hotel as well. Bloomingdale's, Chanel, Gucci, Macy's and Neiman Marcus are among the upscale tenants of **The Mall at Millenia,** off I-4 at 4200 Conroy Rd., which includes more than 150 shops, services and restaurants. Northeast of downtown is **Orlando Fashion Square Mall,** 3201 E. Colonial Dr., featuring Burdines, Dillard's, JCPenney, Sears, a second-floor food court and 165 smaller stores, including such mall standards as The Limited and the Gap. SAVE **Altamonte Mall,** 451 E. Altamonte Dr., offers four anchors—Burdines, Dillard's, JCPenney and Sears—along with a food court and two floors containing 175 boutiques from the Banana Republic to the Body Shop.

Sanford's **Seminole Towne Center,** 200 Towne Center Cir., is the northernmost of the area malls. It has about 120 shops, a food court and five department stores: Burdines, Dillard's, JCPenney, Parisian and Sears. East of Orlando is the **Oviedo Marketplace** with Burdines, Dillard's and Sears. West of downtown, SAVE **West Oaks Mall** at Clarke Road and SR 50 in Ocoee is anchored by Dillard's, JCPenney, Parisian and Sears.

Outlets

International Drive is a mecca for bargain hunters. In addition to the abundance of souvenir shops, there are outlet stores scattered along the length of the road throughout the tourist area. Goods run the gamut from shoes to cookware, representing such manufacturers as Corning-Revere, Dansk, Mikasa and Royal Doulton.

Bass Pro Shops Outdoor World, 5156 International Drive, features an indoor waterfall, aquarium, wildlife exhibits, an indoor shooting arcade and sporting demonstrations.

At 8200 Vineland Ave., which connects International Drive and SR 535 (or take I-4 exit 68), is SAVE **Orlando Premium Outlets,** which offers mid-to high-end designer labels and name brands in a Mediterranean village atmosphere. The mall's amenities include a food court, parcel lockers and a currency exchange. Stores include Banana Republic, Bottega Veneta, Coach, DKNY, Louis Feraud, Nautica, Nike Factory, Oilily, Polo Ralph Lauren, Tommy Hilfiger and Timberland.

The largest conglomeration of outlet stores is at the **Belz Factory Outlet World,** off International Drive on W. Oakridge Road. Apparel, electronics, jewelry, shoes, housewares and other items are available from more than 170 vendors; the Annex also offers a food court and a carrousel. Expect to find the likes of Calvin Klein, Easy Spirit, Etienne Aigner, London Fog and Oneida, among many others. Just south is the **Belz Designer Outlet Centre,** 5211 International Dr., a large plaza ringed with discount shops for Ann Taylor, Coach, Cole Haan, Fossil, Lenox, Saks Fifth Avenue and more. The **Kissimmee Manufacturer's Outlet,** 4673 W. Irlo Bronson Memorial Pkwy., features several dozen stores, including Bass and Nike.

Specialty Districts

Large malls aren't the only game in town—there are many interesting boutiques to be found in the area's themed shopping areas and independent districts. The **Winter Park Farmer's Market** fills Saturday mornings with fresh produce, herbs, baked goods and hot coffee in a refurbished train depot at 200 W. New England Ave. One block east is Winter Park's heart and soul, **Park Avenue.** The European-flavored promenade is lined with an eclectic assortment of boutiques, galleries and eateries ranging from the upscale to the funky, making the avenue a favorite for shopping, browsing or just meandering. Especially interesting are the shops in the courtyards and the **Hidden Garden.** Tired shoppers can take a break across the street in **Central Park** or at one of the many charming cafes along the way.

With five restaurants, 60 stores and live entertainment in the courtyard every night, the **Mercado Mediterranean Shopping Village,** 8445 International Dr., is almost a world unto itself. Boutiques in the Spanish-style complex sell a variety of wares, including beachwear, collectibles, casual clothing and imported goods.

Downtown Disney Marketplace is the place to go for international purchases. Here boutiques filled with items from around the world line the shores of Buena Vista Lagoon, and artisans demonstrate their skills for passersby. Also in the Downtown Disney area on Buena Vista Drive is **Planet Hollywood,** where the fascination with all that is Hollywood is captured in souvenirs ranging from designer T-shirts to key chains to leather jackets. Farther south, near the intersection of I-4 and US 192, is **Disney's Town of Celebration,** a planned community with all the amenities of a small town including a downtown area complete with nearly two dozen shops and restaurants.

Yet another shopping destination on International Drive is **Pointe*Orlando,** at 9101 International Dr. near the Orange County Convention Center. This six-building complex features more than 80 shops, restaurants and attractions, including FAO Schwarz, IMAX and conventional theaters, and Wonder-Works *(see attraction listing p. 153),* an entertainment center in what appears to be a three-story, upside-down building.

Flea World, on US 17/92 in Sanford, features merchants, eateries, amusement rides and live entertainment. A half-hour northwest of Orlando, historic Mount Dora is known for its abundance of antiques shops. Hundreds of dealers gather each weekend at **Renninger's Antique Market** on SR 441. Antiques lovers also can search for finds in downtown Sanford.

Kissimmee's **Old Town,** 5770 W. Irlo Bronson Memorial Pkwy., evokes a turn-of-the-20th-century atmosphere with brick walkways, a Ferris wheel, a roller coaster and a wooden train exhibit. More than 70 shops offer an extensive selection of wares ranging from music boxes to magic tricks.

Performing Arts

The strength of Orlando's appeal lies mainly with its family-oriented attractions and entertainment. While this is good news for the folks at Disney and Universal, it has detracted some focus from the city's cultural scene. Arts enthusiasts need not despair, though—local arts groups have begun to expand their presence. Theater offers the most varied slate, with dance and music filling in the gaps.

As the film industry gains a foothold in the area, it is likely that the fine arts will enjoy even greater success, attracting new artists to practice their crafts in the City Beautiful.

Dance

The **Orlando Ballet** is the city's professional dance company. The season, which lasts from September to May, features concerts and programs

ranging from classical to modern. The troupe also stages the Nutcracker ballet every Christmas, accompanied by a live orchestra of local musicians. Performances generally are held at the **Bob Carr Performing Arts Centre**; for information phone (407) 426-1733.

Rollins College brings in some of the dance world's brightest stars, including the Alvin Ailey Repertory and Pilobolus, to the **Annie Russell Theatre** to supplement the **Rollins Dance** student program; phone (407) 646-2145.

Film

Alternative cinema finds a home at the **Enzian Theater,** 1300 S. Orlando Ave., offering filmgoers a varied menu of critically acclaimed American independent and foreign films. The theater itself is unusual—it is set in an old house, with audience seating at tables rather than in an auditorium. For information phone (407) 629-1088.

Music

Despite lacking a full-time professional orchestra, Orlando does have a variety of groups dedicated to making beautiful music. The **Orlando Philharmonic** gives three concert series during the year. Performances are held at the Bob Carr Performing Arts Centre; the **Orlando Museum of Art,** 2416 N. Mills Ave., in Loch Haven Park; and the **John and Rita Lowndes Shakespeare Center,** in Loch Haven Park behind the Orlando Museum of Art; for additional information phone (407) 896-6700. The **Festival of Orchestras,** (407) 539-0245, imports full-size symphonies, featuring such esteemed groups as the Cleveland Orchestra; guests also play at the Bob Carr.

A favorite local event is the Bach Festival, a celebration of masterworks by Bach and other major composers. Held in late February or early March, the program is performed by the **Bach Festival Choir and Orchestra,** which also offers the Festival Concert Series from October through April. The group performs at the **Knowles Memorial Chapel** at Rollins College; phone (407) 646-2182.

Opera

Opera in central Florida is presented by the **Orlando Opera Company,** staging three major works from November through March, as well as special programs during the season. Performances are at the Bob Carr Performing Arts Centre with the venue for the company's operettas being the **Dr. Phillips Center for the Performing Arts** at 1111 N. Orange Ave. For season and ticket information phone (407) 426-1717 or (407) 426-1700 for the box office.

Theater

One of the area's most popular theaters is the **UCF Civic Theatre,** 1001 Princeton St., (407) 896-7365. Another local favorite is the **SunTrust Broadway in Orlando** series, sponsoring touring Broadway shows at the Bob Carr Performing Arts

Centre. Tickets for the biggest hits often require several weeks' notice; phone (800) 448-6322. **Theatre Downtown,** (407) 841-0083, offers avantgarde and mainstream works just north of the city center at 2113 N. Orange Ave. The **Orlando Theatre Project,** (407) 328-2040, puts on a similar mix at **Seminole Community College's Fine Arts Theatre,** 100 Weldon Blvd. in Sanford.

The play's the thing at the **Orlando-UCF Shakespeare Festival,** (407) 447-1700, dedicated to staging the bard's timeless plays in innovative ways. The festival, held each April at the **Walt Disney Amphitheater at Lake Eola Park,** produces additional works throughout the year, from classically-inspired independent pieces to the **PlayLab Series,** a selection of experimental plays, presented at the **Orange County Historical Museum Theatre** at Loch Haven Park, 812 E. Rollins St.

The University of Central Florida features a full season of performances through **Theatre UCF,** (407) 823-1500. Rollins College also mounts a full season, with four productions at the Annie Russell Theatre running the gamut of theatrical genres; phone (407) 646-2145.

Special Events

On New Year's Day two top college football teams test their skills during the **Capital One Bowl** Football Classic. A parade and other related activities precede the big game.

In late January the **Zora Neale Hurston Festival of Arts and Humanities** celebrates the life of the noted interpreter of Southern rural African-American culture. This culture is celebrated further throughout February at varied events during the **Black History Month Festival.**

Orlando's moderate temperatures are ideal for art festivals. Most popular are the **Mount Dora Arts Festival** in early February; the **Downtown Orlando Arts Festival** in early March; the **Winter Park Sidewalk Art Festival** on the third weekend in March; and the **Maitland Arts & Fine Crafts Festival** in mid-April. A pair of **Fiesta in the Park** celebrations take place in April and November on the shores of Lake Eola.

For 10 days in late April and early May, entertainers from around the world converge on downtown Orlando, treating theatergoers to a variety of unusual and cutting edge performances as part of the **International Fringe Festival.** Towards the end of the following month, more than 200,000 ears of corn are eaten during the **Zellwood Sweet Corn Festival,** also a showcase for big-name country musicians.

Two PGA golf tournaments are on Orlando's calendar of events. In March the **Bay Hill Invitational** is held at Bay Hill Country Club, while the **National Car Rental Golf Classic at Walt Disney World** is held at the Palm, Osprey and Magnolia courses at Walt Disney World in October.

In early November the **Walt Disney World Festival of the Masters** is held at Downtown Disney Marketplace. During this 3-day event, major American artists display their works. The city of Winter Park rings in the holiday season with **Christmas in the Park,** which combines a concert by the Bach Festival Choir and stunning outdoor displays of lighted Tiffany windows on loan from the nearby Charles Hosmer Morse Museum of American Art.

Nightlife

Since its renaissance during the 1970s and '80s, downtown Orlando has become a hotbed of hot spots, from crowded dance clubs to alternative coffeehouses. And for those who want a theme to go along with their entertainment, nightspots at the Walt Disney World® Resort and Universal Orlando fit the bill nicely.

The *Calendar* section of the Friday *Orlando Sentinel* has the latest information on all the area nightspots.

Dance Clubs

Orange Avenue is the main strip for downtown dance clubs, and alternative rock is the music of choice. **Independent Bar,** 70 N. Orange Ave., presents alternative music; phone (407) 839-0457. Daring types dance the night away to house music at The **Club at the Firestone,** (407) 872-0066, in the former Firestone Tire and Service Center at 578 N. Orange Ave. The old Beacham Theater, 46 N. Orange Ave., houses **Tabu Dance Club,** (407) 648-8363, a hot spot popular for its mix of disco, high-energy and Top 40 tunes. At the Egyptian-themed **Cairo,** 22 S. Magnolia Ave., music ranges from disco to house; phone (407) 422-3595.

On Disney property in the Wyndham Palace Resort and Spa is the **Laughing Kookaburra Good Time Bar,** (407) 827-3722, also known as "the Kook." International Drive offers **Backstage** at the Rosen Plaza Hotel; phone (407) 996-1719.

Entertainment Complexes

It's always New Year's Eve at **Downtown Disney Pleasure Island,** (407) 934-7781, celebrated every night at midnight with lots of music and fireworks. Baby boomers can indulge their 1970s nostalgia at *8TRAX* while Generation Xers dance the night away to current chart-toppers at *Mannequins Dance Palace.* The *Rock 'n' Roll Beach Club* features live bands covering hits from the '60s through the '90s and *BET Soundstage Club* delivers urban contemporary entertainment. The '30s are the focus of the eccentric players of the *Adventurers Club,*

and a troupe of improvisational players brings down the house at the *Comedy Warehouse.* Top 40 hits are on tap at *Motion,* but jazz aficionados will appreciate the mellower stylings of the *Pleasure Island Jazz Company.*

Downtown Disney West Side features the *House of Blues,* serving up some of America's best-loved music with rock 'n' roll, R&B, country, alternative, gospel and the root of it all—blues. Another Lake Buena Vista hot spot, **Disney's BoardWalk,** (407) 939-5101, offers a dance hall and live band at *Atlantic Dance,* dueling pianos at *Jellyrolls,* and the sports-oriented *ESPN Club.*

At the entrance to Universal Orlando is an eye-catching new entrant in the competition for Orlando's late-night revelers and club hoppers: **CityWalk;** phone (407) 224-9255. If variety is the spice of life, then this place is five-alarm chili *hot.* Reggae rules at *Bob Marley-A Tribute to Freedom,* which is housed in a replica of Marley's former home in Jamaica. Performers sing Motown's classic hits every twenty minutes at the *Motown Cafe,* and jazz mementos line the walls at *CityJazz,* which also features live performances. *Pat O'Brien's* is a carbon copy of the New Orleans landmark; pianos duel it out in the raucous piano bar. Wildly decorated period rooms offer retreats from the pounding beat on the dance floor at *the groove,* while the *Latin Quarter* plays host to Salsa, Merengue, Mariachi and Latin Rock bands. Designed to look like Rome's Coliseum, *Hard Rock Live* is a state-of-the-art theater spotlighting some of the biggest names in music.

Jazz & Blues

Locals make the scene downtown at **The Social,** (407) 246-1419, 54 N. Orange Ave. A few doors away at 100 S. Orange Ave. is the bluesy **Tanqueray's Bar & Grille,** (407) 649-8540, set in the cellar of the 1920s Metcalf Building.

Rock

The **Howl at the Moon Saloon,** (407) 841-4695, at 55 W. Church St., features dueling pianists covering rock standards and a rowdy crowd welcome to join in the fun.

The Orlando Vicinity

APOPKA (E-2) pop. 26,642

ROCK SPRINGS AND KELLY PARK are 6 mi. n. on SR 435. Rock Springs, a half-mile east of the park entrance on Kelly Park Road, discharges 26,000 gallons of clear, 68-degree Fahrenheit water per minute into a spring that is popular for tubing and swimming. Picnic grounds, shelters, bathhouses, tube rentals (outside park), hiking trails and camping facilities are available. Daily 9-7, Apr.-Oct.; 8-6, rest of year. Admission $1, under 6 free. Phone (407) 889-4179. *See Recreation Chart.*

CHRISTMAS (D-10) pop. 1,162, elev. 44'

Every yuletide the town of Christmas receives thousands of pieces of mail, which are stamped with the Christmas postmark and sent on their way. Four miles south on SR 50 is the headquarters of the Tosohatchee State Preserve. The preserve's 28,000 acres of woodlands and wetlands along the St. Johns River offer hiking and bicycling trails, fishing and nature study.

FORT CHRISTMAS MUSEUM is 2 mi. n. of SR 50 on CR 420 (Fort Christmas Rd.). The museum is a reconstruction of a fort begun Dec. 25, 1837, during the Second Seminole Indian War. Two blockhouses contain exhibits about the Seminole Indian Wars and area pioneers. Guided tours of seven restored pioneer houses are available. Picnic and recreation facilities are available. Allow 1 hour minimum. Tues.-Sat. 10-5, Sun. 1-5; closed holidays. Tours given Tues.-Sat. 11-3, Sun. 1-3. Free. Phone (407) 568-4149.

SAVE **JUNGLE ADVENTURES,** 26205 E. SR 50, lets visitors view alligators in their natural habitat. A swamp cruise on board a pontoon boat; a wildlife show including endangered Florida panthers; and alligator feeding demonstrations are featured. An American Indian village re-creates the lifestyle of native Florida Indians. Guided tours are available. Allow 2 hours, 30 minutes minimum. Daily 9:30-5:30. Admission $16; over 60, $12.50; ages 3-11, $8.50. AX, DS, MC, VI. Phone (407) 568-1354.

CLERMONT (D-9) pop. 9,333, elev. 190'

Clermont founder A.F. Wrotnoski named this town of wide, shady streets and rolling hills after his French birthplace. Lake Louisa State Park *(see Recreation Chart),* 7 miles southeast of Clermont on Lake Nellie Road, is one of 13 in a chain of lakes connected by the Palatkahah River.

South Lake Chamber of Commerce: 691 W. Montrose St., P.O. Box 120417, Clermont, FL 34712-0417; phone (352) 394-4191.

CITRUS TOWER CENTRE is 1 mi. n. of the SR 50 jct. at 141 N. US 27. Reached by elevator, the 226-foot-tall tower's observation deck provides a panorama of the surrounding lakes and rolling hills. Food is available. Allow 30 minutes minimum. Mon.-Sat. 9-6, Sun. 11-5; closed Jan. 1 and Dec. 25. Admission $3.50; ages 3-15, $1. AX, DS, MC, VI. Phone (352) 394-4061.

NATIONAL PRESIDENTS HALL OF FAME, just n. of SR 50 at 123 N. US 27, features changing exhibits of memorabilia related to U.S. presidents and their first ladies. Among displays are campaign and inaugural artifacts, first ladies' evening gowns and replicas of china place settings. A miniature re-creation of the White House is frequently displayed. Videotape presentations include a tour of the White House and presidential biographies. Allow 2 hours minimum. Daily 9-5. Admission $9.95; ages 4-11, $4.95. AX, MC, VI. Phone (352) 394-2836.

WINERIES

- **Lakeridge Winery and Vineyards,** 2.5 mi. s. off Florida's Tpke. exit 285 to 19239 US 27N. Mon.-Sat. 10-5, Sun. 11-5; closed Jan. 1, Easter, Thanksgiving and Dec. 25. Phone (352) 394-8627 or (800) 768-9463.

HEATHROW (D-3) pop. 4,068, elev. 50'

Heathrow is the site of American Automobile Association's national office. North of Orlando at I-4 and Lake Mary Boulevard, the Heathrow community includes recreational, commercial and residential areas.

KISSIMMEE (H-3) pop. 47,814, elev. 62'

Kissimmee (Kiss-SEM-mee), or "Heaven's Place" in the Calusa Indian language, is near the

DID YOU KNOW

Except for their cream-colored bellies, alligators are black, not green.

southern terminus of a scenic portion of Florida's Turnpike extending 65 miles southeast from Wildwood. It is more widely known to visitors to the central Florida region as being a near neighbor of Walt Disney World® Resort. Many downtown businesses occupy structures dating from the late 1800s; landscaping and renovations preserve the town's old-time aura.

Area industries include plastics, engineering, electronics and agriculture. The Florida Cattlemen's Association and Tupperware International have their headquarters in town. Kissimmee also attracts the sports-minded with the Osceola County Stadium and Sports Complex, where the Houston Astros conduct spring training during March; phone (407) 933-5400, or (407) 933-2520 for Astros ticket information.

Picnic tables and boat ramps are available at Lake Front Park, .25 mile southeast of US 17/92. Also in this park is the Monument of States, a stone pyramid consisting of stones from various states and 22 countries.

Kissimmee-St. Cloud Convention & Visitors Bureau: 1925 E. Irlo Bronson Memorial Hwy., P.O. Box 422007, Kissimmee, FL 34742-2007; phone (407) 847-5000 or (800) 327-9159. *See color ad p. 687.*

Shopping areas: Old Town, just east of I-4 on US 192, features 75 specialty shops as well as restaurants and amusement rides in a re-created turn-of-the-20th-century setting. Hundreds of classic cars cruise the streets of Old Town every Friday and Saturday night.

AQUATIC WONDERS BOAT TOURS departs from Big Toho Marina, 3 blks. s. of jct. US 192 on John Young Pkwy. to Emmett St., .5 mi. e. to Ruby Ave., then s. to 101 Lakeshore Blvd. Various 2-hour wildlife and nature cruises are offered on Lake Tohopekaliga aboard a 30-foot covered pontoon boat. Fishing trips and evening tours also are available. Departures daily. The maximum passenger capacity is six. Sightseeing fare $18.95-$35; ages 1-11, $12.95-$16. Reservations are required. Phone (407) 846-2814.

[SAVE] **ARABIAN NIGHTS,** off I-4 exit 64A at 6225 W. US 192, is a 1-hour, 45-minute dinner show featuring equestrian acts in an indoor arena. The performances include a Wild West act, Lipizzan horses and a Roman chariot race. A three-course dinner is served during the show. Allow 2 hours, 30 minutes minimum. Performances nightly; occasional noon matinee. Admission $44; ages 3-11, $27. Reservations are recommended. AX, CB, DC, DS, MC, VI. Phone (407) 239-9223, (407) 239-9221 or (800) 553-6116.

[SAVE] **BOGGY CREEK AIRBOAT RIDES** is e. on Osceola Pkwy., just n. on Boggy Creek Rd. (CR 530), then e. 1.5 mi. to East Lake Fish Camp, following signs. The company offers airboat trips through the wetland wilderness around Boggy Creek. Passengers can see eagles, turtles, alligators and other Florida wildlife during the voyage. Allow 30 minutes minimum. Daily 9-5:30. Fare $17.95; ages 3-12, $12.95. MC, VI. Phone (407) 344-9550.

[SAVE] **CAPONE'S DINNER AND SHOW,** 4740 W. Irlo Bronson Memorial Hwy. (US 192), .7 mi. e. of jct. SR 535, presents a musical dinner show based on the 1930s escapades of gangster Al Capone. Allow 2 hours, 30 minutes minimum. Performances nightly at 8. Admission $39.95; ages 4-12, $23.95. Reservations are suggested. AX, DS, MC, VI. Phone (407) 397-2378. *See color ad.*

FLYING TIGERS WARBIRD RESTORATION MUSEUM is 7 mi. e. of I-4 on US 192, then s. to 231 Hoagland Blvd. The museum specializes in the restoration of World War II aircraft. Displays include antique and World War II and Korean War planes, equipment, armaments and memorabilia. Guided tours are available. Allow 1 hour, 30 minutes minimum. Daily 9-6. Admission $9; over 60 and ages 6-11, $8. DS, MC, VI. Phone (407) 933-1942.

GREEN MEADOWS PETTING FARM, 3 mi. e. of I-4 exit 64A on US 192, then 5 mi. s. on Poinciana Blvd., offers guided tours of a 50-acre farm with more than 300 farm animals. The hands-on philosophy encourages learning as visitors milk a cow, ride a pony or hold a chicken. Petting pens with various farm animals are a highlight of the tour. Tractor-drawn hayrides and a train ride are included. Picnic facilities are available.

Allow 2 hours minimum. Daily 9:30-4; closed Thanksgiving and Dec. 25. Admission $16, under 2 free. DS, MC, VI. Phone (407) 846-0770.

JUNGLELAND ZOO is at 4580 W. Irlo Bronson Memorial Hwy. (US 192). The 7-acre zoo is home to lions, tigers, Himalayan bears and 75 other species of rare and exotic animals and birds from around the world. Several wildlife shows are presented two to three times daily: The Magic of the Rainforest features on-stage illusions; Cats of the Wild puts big cats in the center ring; and The Bushmaster's Gator Show lets visitors pose for a photo with a live alligator. Food is available. Allow 2 hours minimum. Daily 9-6. Admission $14.95; over 55, $12.95; ages 3-11, $9.95. MC, VI. Phone (407) 396-1012.

LAKE KISSIMMEE STATE PARK—
see Lake Wales p. 102.

MEDIEVAL TIMES DINNER AND TOURNAMENT, 6 mi. e. of I-4 exit 64A at 4510 W. Irlo Bronson Memorial Hwy. (US 192), is in a replica of an 11th-century European-style castle. A medieval feast is served by staff members costumed in medieval attire. Spectators feast a few feet from the action in the Great Ceremonial Arena, where knights on horseback compete in jousting matches, medieval tournament games and sword fights.

Allow 2 hours minimum. Performances nightly; show times vary. Admission $46; ages 3-11, $30. Reservations made at least 1 day in advance are highly suggested. AX, DS, MC, VI. Phone (407) 396-1518, (888) 935-6878 or (800) 229-8300.

Medieval Life is a permanent re-creation of a medieval village. This 12-cottage hamlet showcases medieval artifacts and costumed artisans working their trades. Allow 1 hour minimum. Open daily 2 hours before dinner show time. Admission free with Medieval Times dinner ticket.

SPLENDID CHINA is 3 mi. w. of I-4 exit 64B on US 192, then s. via Formosa Garden Blvd. to 3000 Splendid China Blvd. The park lets visitors experience Chinese heritage, culture, geography, architecture and lifestyles while viewing more than 60 miniaturized replicas of such landmarks as the Great Wall, the Terra-cotta Warriors, the Forbidden City, Tibet's Potala Palace and the Stone Forest. Other park features include live entertainment and cuisine native to various regions of China. The Mysterious Kingdom of the Orient, a 90-minute live stage show, is offered nightly. Guided tours are offered. Food is available.

Allow 5 hours minimum. Daily 9:30-7. Mysterious Kingdom of the Orient show Tues.-Sun. at 6. Admission $26.99; over 54, $25.30; ages 5-12, $16.99. Mysterious Kingdom of the Orient show $14.95; ages 5-12, $9.95. AX, DS, MC, VI. Phone (407) 396-7111 or (800) 244-6226.

WATER MANIA, .5 mi. e. of I-4 at 6073 W. Irlo Bronson Memorial Hwy. (US 192), is a 36-acre park containing raft rides, waterslides, flumes, a wave pool, a surfing simulator, an inner tube river ride, children's play areas and an arcade. A picnic area, raft rentals, life vests, showers, changing rooms, lockers and food are available. Allow 4 hours minimum. Daily 10-5, mid-Mar. through Sept. 30; Wed.-Sat. 10-5, Oct. 1-late Oct. Admission $19.95; ages 3-9, $16.95. Locker rental $7-$9, with a $3 deposit refund. Parking $5-$6. MC, VI. Phone (407) 396-2626 or (800) 527-3092.

A WORLD OF ORCHIDS is 2.5 mi. w. of I-4 exit 64B on US 192, then 1 mi. s. on CR 545 (Old Lake Wilson Rd.). Exotic orchids are showcased in changing exhibits in an enclosed tropical rain forest setting. Indoor and outdoor gardens feature various varieties of bamboos, palms, ferns and bromeliads. Allow 1 hour minimum. Tues.-Sun. 9:30-4:30; closed Jan. 1, July 4, Thanksgiving, Dec. 25 and the second and third weeks in July. Free. Phone (407) 396-1887.

DID YOU KNOW

The oldest place name in North America is Florida.

LAKE BUENA VISTA (G-2)
pop. 16, elev. 100'

RICHARD PETTY DRIVING EXPERIENCE, off US 192 exit World Dr., following signs to Magic Kingdom, puts race fans in the seat of a Winston-Cup style stock car on a 1-mile, tri-oval track. A ride-along program allows guests 16 and older to ride with a professional instructor at speeds up to 145 mph. A variety of programs for drivers 18 and older includes behind-the-wheel experiences; reservations and a valid driver's license are required.

Daily 8-5; closed Jan. 1 and Dec. 25. Ride-along program $89; riders 16-18 must be accompanied by parent or legal guardian. Driving programs start at $349. AX, DS, MC, VI. Phone (407) 939-0130 or (800) 237-3889.

Walt Disney World.

WALT DISNEY WORLD® RESORT is accessible from US 192, Osceola Pkwy. and several exits off I-4 s. of Orlando, depending on the park destination. Covering 30,500 acres, the complex includes four theme parks: the Magic Kingdom® Park, Epcot®, Disney-MGM Studios and Disney's Animal Kingdom® Theme Park; two themed water parks; 18 resorts; Disney's Fort Wilderness Resort and Campground; five championship golf courses; two luxurious spas; Disney's Wide World of Sports™ complex; and the Downtown Disney® area, a shopping, dining and entertainment district.

Walt Disney's Florida legacy is a land of vision, imagination and innovation. The news that the creator of California's popular Disneyland was going to build a theme park just south of the small town of Orlando was announced in 1966. Drawn to the area by its climate, highway access and inexpensive land, Disney and his "Imagineers" began transforming acres of swamps and orange groves into a magical vacationland that opened in 1971.

Walt Disney World, where childhood dreams and fantasies are brought to life, was an instant success. Other theme parks were soon on the drawing board, and Epcot®, a celebration of technology and world cultures, joined the Magic Kingdom® Park in 1982. Disney-MGM Studios, a natural addition considering Disney's background in animation and television and film production, followed in 1989. Disney's Animal Kingdom® brought both wild and imaginary creatures to the public in 1998.

The resort is in a near-constant state of expansion and modernization. This process may include enhancements to existing attractions as well as new development.

The golf, recreational, shopping, dining and entertainment facilities of the resort also are open to day visitors. Monorail, boat and motor coach transportation are available throughout the resort.

Navigating the Walt Disney World property is greatly simplified by clear, concise road signs. Tram service is provided from parking areas to the main entrance of Disney's Animal Kingdom® Theme Park, Epcot®, Disney-MGM Studios and to the Transportation and Ticket Center near the Magic Kingdom® Park. From the Transportation and Ticket Center, ferries and a monorail transport visitors to the Magic Kingdom® Park.

Disney's FASTPASS[SM] is an easy-to-use computerized system that helps guests avoid waiting in long lines at many attractions. This free service is available for the most popular rides at each of the four theme parks. By choosing the FASTPASS[SM] option, guests are assigned a guaranteed entrance time.

To obtain a FASTPASS[SM], each guest must insert his theme park ticket into the FASTPASS[SM] machine located near the entrance to the chosen attraction. A timed ticket is delivered, printed with a 1-hour window of time during which the guest may return and enter the attraction at a special FASTPASS[SM] entrance with little or no wait. There is no limit as to how many FASTPASS[SM] tickets a guest can use in a visit; however, the guest must first use his or her current FASTPASS[SM] ticket or wait 2 hours before getting another. Park maps list participating FASTPASS[SM] attractions.

Theme parks open generally at 9; closing times vary. Multi-day ticket options provide admission to all four theme parks and other entertainment areas. One-day, One-park admission $50; ages 3-9, $40. AX, DC, DS, JC, MC, VI. Phone (407) 824-4321. *See color ads starting on p. 171.*

DISNEP-MGM STUDIOS **Disney-MGM Studios,** 2 mi. n. of US 192 off World Dr., is a theme park and working production studio featuring attractions, Broadway-style shows and live entertainment, all centered around popular films, television, music and animation. The centerpiece of the park is the 122-foot Sorcerer's Hat, designed to resemble the pointed hat worn by Mickey Mouse in Disney's animated film "Fantasia."

Hollywood and Sunset boulevards re-create the glamorous golden age of Hollywood. Tower of Terror, which begins with a journey through the haunted hallways of the vintage Hollywood Tower Hotel, culminates in multiple 13-story drops in a runaway service elevator. Rock 'n' Roller Coaster Starring Aerosmith is an indoor thrill ride featuring a soundtrack by the renowned rock 'n' roll band. The coaster ride, complete with rock concert lighting, takes visitors on a high-speed trip through the Hollywood Hills.

Disney characters riding in retrofitted classic cars lead a motorcade during the Disney Stars and Motor Cars Parade, while the life and accomplishments of Walt Disney can be experienced interactively at Walt Disney: One Man's Dream. Here guests can see a film about Disney's life, listen to a collection of audio interviews and view Disney memorabilia.

At Who Wants to be a Millionaire-Play It!, guests can participate in a re-creation of the hit TV game show. The game's high-tech set is complete with its signature dramatic lighting. The "fastest finger" determines who will sit in the hot seat, though all audience members can play along using their own keypads.

Fantasmic! is a nighttime water spectacular that takes you inside the dreams of Sorcerer Mickey. The show is a battle of good versus evil in which Sorcerer Mickey's magic creates dancing waters, dazzling lasers, shooting comets, animated fountains, swirling stars, balls of fire and other wonders. Mickey himself conducts the musical score as the presentation lights up the night sky.

Death-defying stunts are the cornerstone of the Indiana Jones™ Epic Stunt Spectacular, inspired by the film "Raiders of the Lost Ark." Sound effects are the focus as Drew Carey stars as an undercover detective in the video presentation Sounds Dangerous—Starring Drew Carey.

A Broadway-style rendition of "Beauty and the Beast" is performed at the Theater of the Stars, where highlights from the animated film about Belle and the Beast's love story are brought to life on stage. Voyage of the Little Mermaid brings the story of Ariel and her colorful undersea world to the stage. The Hunchback of Notre Dame—A Musical Adventure captures the power and majesty of the musical story in a live stage event.

Visitors will feel as if they are bursting into outer space aboard Star Tours, a motion simulator ride based on the movie "Star Wars." Disney-MGM Studios Backlot Tour shows how filmmakers create special-effect movie and television disasters. Riders are taken on a shuttle tour of movie sets, the highlight of which is an explosive journey through Catastrophe Canyon, where fires erupt and a flash flood threatens to tip the shuttle over.

Guests can travel into classic moments from the movies on The Great Movie Ride as well as see Kermit, Miss Piggy and friends in a 3-D misadventure in Jim Henson's Muppet*Vision 3-D.

Visitors can meet Bear in the Big Blue House, Stanley, familiar characters from The Book of Pooh, and Rolie Polie Olie as they sing and laugh with visitors and other Disney Channel characters in Playhouse Disney-Live on Stage!

Park opens daily generally at 9; closing times vary. Admission $50; ages 3-9, $40. AX, DC, DS, JC, MC, VI. Phone (407) 824-4321. See color ads starting on p. 171.

Disney's Animal Kingdom® Theme Park, n. of US 192 on World Dr. then following signs along Osceola Pkwy., offers adventures with creatures from different realms. Entering through The Oasis, a lush area of streams, gardens and waterfalls, visitors can go back in time to encounter dinosaurs, take an African safari amid free-roaming animals, be transported to southeast Asia and come face-to-face with Disney characters in entertaining settings.

At the center of the park in Discovery Island™ is the majestic Tree of Life, which reaches 14 stories high and represents the diversity of animal life through intricate carvings of more than 300 animal life forms. Flamingos, otters, tortoises and deer are among the animals that can be seen from several viewing points. Shown in a theater deep inside the Tree of Life, It's Tough to be a Bug!® is a comical, 3-D, special effects adventure offering a bug's-eye view of the world from the perspective of Flik, the hero of the movie "A Bug's Life."

DinoLand U.S.A.®, devoted to the drama of the Age of Dinosaurs, is entered by walking under a 50-foot-tall brachiosaurus. Here you'll find Chester & Hester's Dino-Rama!, a roadside carnival featuring a dinosaur-themed midway, games and rides, and Primeval Whirl, a time machine-themed coaster that spins riders back through the ages to encounter crazy prehistoric creatures.

TriceraTop Spin enables kids to ride flying dinosaurs, though cautions them to watch out for flying comets.

Also in DinoLand U.S.A., the thrill ride Dinosaur blasts back 65 million years to rescue a dinosaur from the edge of extinction as a deadly asteroid speeds toward Earth.

Nearby is Dino Sue, a replica of the most complete and best preserved Tyrannosaurus rex fossil ever unearthed. The Boneyard is an open-air playground and dig site in which children can maneuver their way through a maze of dinosaur skeletons and help unearth the bones of a giant mammoth.

Africa features a journey into one of the last wild sanctuaries of our planet. Beginning in the modern-day town of Harambe, the Kilimanjaro Safaris® expedition takes you on a chase for poachers through an African savanna where hippos, zebras, gazelles, giraffes and elephants roam freely.

After exiting their vehicle, visitors can traverse the Pangani Forest Exploration Trail and observe a troop of gorillas interacting in this naturalistic habitat; meerkats and tropical birds also inhabit the forestlike area. Another option is the Wildlife Express Train; riders are transported to Rafiki's Planet Watch, where conservation efforts are explained and small animals can be seen up-close.

The land of Asia features a soaking, white-water rafting adventure at Kali River Rapids. Intrepid explorers can dry off while exploring palace ruins along the Maharajah Jungle Trek; expect to encounter tigers, giant fruit bats, gibbons and Komodo dragons along the way.

Costumed actors and storytellers, puppets, stage floats and live animals entertain in Disney's Animal Kingdom. Elaborate puppets, giant animal stilt walkers and drummers join Mickey, Minnie, Donald and Goofy during Mickey's Jammin' Jungle Parade. Festival of the Lion King at Camp Minnie-Mickey combines song, dance and characters from the popular movie.

Other shows include Tarzan Rocks!, an array of stunts and aerial acts in DinoLand U.S.A.®; Flights of Wonder, where talented birds are the show, on the edge of Asia; and Pocahontas and Her Forest Friends, featuring the Indian maiden and her woodland companions at Camp Minnie-Mickey.

Park generally open daily 9-7. Admission $50; ages 3-9, $40. AX, DC, DS, JC, MC, VI. Phone (407) 824-4321. *See color ads starting on p. 171.*

 Disney's Blizzard Beach Water Park, 2 mi. n. of US 192 off World Dr., features a mix of Florida sun and alpine snow. Snow-capped Mt. Gushmore is where you'll find side-by-side racing waterslides and Summit Plummet, where those who dare can plunge down a 90-foot drop at 60 mph.

Tamer offerings include a family raft ride down Teamboat Springs, "icy" bobsled runs, an inner tube run, a chair lift ride, flumes, a wave pool and a children's area. Food is available. Hours vary. Admission $31; ages 3-9, $25. AX, DC, DS, JC, MC, VI. Phone (407) 560-9283. *See color ads starting on p. 171.*

 **Disney's Typhoon Lagoon Water Park,** US 192 w. to World Dr., then e. on Buena Vista Dr., re-creates a tropical village that has just experienced a great storm;

a shipwrecked boat left dangling from Mt. Mayday serves to illustrate the force of the typhoon.

The island paradise features waterslides, a saltwater snorkeling pool, three rafting rides, a meandering stream for tubing, a children's water playground and a large wave pool. Food is available. Hours vary. Admission $31; ages 3-9, $25. AX, DC, DS, JC, MC, VI. Phone (407) 560-9283. *See color ads starting on p. 171.*

Disney's Wide World of Sports™, w. on US 192 to World Dr., then e. on Osceola Pkwy., is a state-of-the-art sports venue where amateur and professional athletes hone their skills and compete in their particular sport. The complex is the spring-training home of the Atlanta Braves.

Guests can test their football skills at the NFL Experience and punt, pass and kick on an interactive playground. Food is available. Admission (includes NFL Experience) $9.75; ages 3-9, $7.50. Admission may increase for special events. Some events may require a separate admission charge. Parking is free. AX, DC, DS, JC, MC, VI. Phone (407) 363-6600. *See color ads starting on p. 171.*

Downtown Disney® Area, w. on US 192 to World Dr. then e. on Buena Vista Dr., is a 120-acre waterfront shopping, themed dining and entertainment complex. The area is a showplace of celebrity restaurants, music venues, a 24-screen movie theater and specialty shops.

In addition to a movie theater, shops and restaurants, Downtown Disney West Side also is home to DisneyQuest®, a five-story indoor interactive theme park where visitors can design and take a simulated ride on their own roller coaster or battle virtual villains. Other options include

the extravagant theatrical production of the Cirque du Soleil® show La Nouba, which is performed only at the Walt Disney World® Resort.

For adult nighttime fun Downtown Disney® Pleasure Island is a shopping, dining and entertainment complex featuring eight themed clubs, including an improv comedy club; a '70s-themed dance club; Mannequins Dance Palace, with a rotating dance floor; the BET SoundStage™ Club, featuring rhythm & blues, soul and hip-hop; a live jazz club; and high-energy dance clubs.

Downtown Disney Marketplace has restaurants and retail options, including the LEGO Imagination Center®, an interactive LEGO playground, and Disney specialty shops.

A $19.95 entrance fee provides admission to Pleasure Island and all clubs after 7 p.m. An annual pass is $54.95. There may be additional charges for special events. Under 18 must be with a parent or legal guardian for admission after 7 p.m. Under 21 not permitted in Mannequins or BET SoundStage Club. DisneyQuest $31; ages 3-9, $25. Cirque du Soleil $67; under 10, $39. AX, DC, DS, JC, MC, VI. Phone (407) 934-7781, or (407) 939-7600 for Cirque du Soleil reservations. *See color ads starting on p. 171.*

Epcot® is 3 mi. s. of the Magic Kingdom® Park off World Dr. The park encompasses Future World and World Showcase—two major areas designed to combine Disney fun and imagination with the wonders of the real world.

Attractions in Future World include the park's symbol, Spaceship Earth, where human communication is explored in a time travel adventure from Earth's earliest days to the present, and Innoventions, which lets guests discover the world's latest technology in a constantly changing, hands-on showcase. Interactive displays include new technologies such as cars of the future, a high-tech home, medical breakthroughs and the future of the Internet.

Universe of Energy features Ellen's Energy Adventure, where Ellen DeGeneres learns all about energy in a dream sequence in an attempt to correctly answer questions on the game show "Jeopardy!".

The Land examines our environment and food resources. A boat ride takes visitors through greenhouses of the future, while Food Rocks is a wacky concert featuring food-shaped performers.

"Honey I Shrunk the Audience," in the Imagination pavilion, has 3-D effects that virtually jump off the screen. Journey into Imagination stars a purple dragon named Figment who shows how our five senses influence our imagination.

Wonders of Life and The Living Seas explore advances in science and technology in a fun and interactive way. Body Wars takes visitors on a virtual reality ride through the human body, while a saltwater aquarium is home to a coral reef inhabited by sharks, rays and dolphins.

Test Track is based on a General Motors automotive proving grounds and takes guests on a thrilling high-speed ride filled with turns, climbs and evasive maneuvers.

World Showcase presents the best of Mexico, China, Norway, Germany, Italy, Japan, France, Morocco, the United Kingdom, Canada and America, all of which can be reached by foot or boat across the World Showcase Lagoon from Future World. Guests can experience the cultures, traditions, holidays, architecture, food and entertainment of all 11 countries.

Visitors to Mexico can enjoy a boat ride on El Rio del Tiempo, while in Norway the Maelstrom boat ride transports guests back to the days of the Vikings. The Circle-Vision 360 film in the China pavilion and the 180-degree film in the France pavilion celebrate each nation's history and culture. Other pavilions spotlight artists performing traditional music, dance and theatrical works. All pavilions are staffed by nationals of that country and bilingual Disney cast members.

IllumiNations: Reflections of Earth features fireworks, original music, lasers and magic every evening.

For daily entertainment schedules visit Guest Relations. Reservations for lunch or dinner at any full-service restaurant should be made at Guest Relations or by phoning (407) 939-3463. Epcot® is connected to the Magic Kingdom® Park by an 8-mile monorail circuit.

Future World opens daily generally at 9. World Showcase opens daily at 11. Closing times vary. Admission $50; ages 3-9, $40. AX, DC, DS, JC, MC, VI. Phone (407) 824-4321. *See color ads starting on p. 171.*

**Magic Kingdom®
Park,** US 192 exit
World Dr. follow-
ing signs, is di-
vided into seven
themed "lands,"
all featuring at-
tractions, enter-
tainment, restaurants and shops. The
park is entered through Main Street,
U.S.A., a representation of a typical
late 19th-century boulevard complete with cafes, shops and horse-
drawn streetcars. Entertainment
schedules and other services are
available at City Hall. Main Street,
U.S.A., also serves as the starting
point for the park's seven lands and
is the site of the Share a Dream Come
True Parade.

The park's centerpiece is Cinderella
Castle, the gateway to Fantasyland.
The adventures in this whimsical land
are based on Disney films. The Many
Adventures of Winnie the Pooh is a
journey into the Hundred Acre
Wood, while hundreds of dolls in in-
ternational costumes perform at It's
a Small World. Join other favorite
Disney characters at the Mad Tea
Party, Dumbo the Flying Elephant,
Snow White's Scary Adventure and
Peter Pan's Flight rides.

At Mickey's ToonTown Fair children
can visit Mickey's house, Minnie's
cottage and Donald's boat, an interactive water fountain. The Barn-
stormer, a children's roller coaster, is
featured at Goofy's Wiseacre Farm.

The futuristic Tomorrowland features Space Mountain, a high-speed
race through the darkness of space;
Astro Orbiter, a rocket to the stars;
Tomorrowland Indy Speedway; The
Timekeeper, a Circle-Vision 360 presentation; and the ExtraTERRORestrial
Alien Encounter, a
sensory thriller
that brings the
audience
face-to-face
with a

frightening space alien. Buzz Light-
year's Space Ranger Spin, an interactive space fantasy, arms guests with
infrared lasers to zap Emperor Zurg's
forces in this ride based on the movie
"Toy Story."

Liberty Square depicts early
America with boat trips on the *Liberty Belle,* Mike Fink Keelboats and
Davy Crockett's Explorer Canoes, and
the Hall of Presidents, where George
W. Bush joins his predecessors in animated conversation. A lively collection of ghosts and ghouls is found in
the Haunted Mansion, and a spirited
musical variety show, Old West style,
takes place at the Diamond Horseshoe Saloon Revue.

Adventureland offers a swashbuckling voyage with the Pirates of the
Caribbean as well as an opportunity
to ride a four-passenger carpet while
trying to avoid water-spewing camels
on The Magic Carpets of Aladdin.
Jungle Cruise journeys through four
continents and encounters "wild"
animals from tropical jungles. The
nearby Swiss Family Treehouse is
home to the shipwrecked Robinsons.
A cast of irrepressible birds conducts
a musical show at The Enchanted Tiki
Room-Under New Management.

Big Thunder Mountain Railroad, a
runaway mine train, is the focus of
Frontierland, which also is the site of
Splash Mountain, a log flume ride
themed after "Song of the South."
Take a ride on a log raft to reach and
explore Tom Sawyer Island, then join
a zany group of singing bears at the
foot stompin' Country Bear Jamboree. Frontierland also is the starting
point for a ride on the Walt Disney
World® Railroad.

Park opens daily generally at 9;
closing times vary. Admission $50;
ages 3-9, $40. AX, DC, DS, JC, MC, VI.
Phone (407) 824-4321. *See color ads
starting on p. 171.*

General Information

Disney's Magic Kingdom® Park, Epcot®, Disney-MGM Studios and Disney's Animal Kingdom® Theme Park open daily generally at 9. Closing times vary between each park, depending on the season.

Large crowds and long lines are to be expected, especially during holiday periods. Individual park maps are available at Guest Relations Information Centers near the entrance of each park.

Parking and Pets

The entrance road leads to parking (fee $6 per day). Free tram service connects the parking area with the Ticket and Transportation Center, Epcot®, Disney-MGM Studios and Disney's Animal Kingdom® Theme Park. Transportation also is available to all guest areas. Kennels—at Magic Kingdom® Park, Ticket and Transportation Center, Epcot®, Disney-MGM Studios, Disney's Animal Kingdom® Theme Park and Disney's Fort Wilderness Resort and Campground—charge a nominal fee to care for and feed pets.

Admissions

• *Park Hopper® Plus Pass provides admission to the four theme parks for the number of days purchased plus a set number of visits to Downtown Disney® Pleasure Island, Disney's water parks and Disney's Wide World of Sports complex. Five days $259; ages 3-9, $208. Six days $289; ages 3-9, $232. Seven days $319; ages 3-9, $256.*

• *Park Hopper® Pass provides unlimited admission to the four theme parks for the number of days on the pass. Four-day pass $199; ages 3-9, $159. Five-day pass $229; ages 3-9, $184.*

• *One-day, One-park ticket covers one day's admission to attractions in one of four theme parks: Magic Kingdom® Park or Disney's Animal Kingdom® Theme Park or Epcot® or Disney-MGM Studios. Admission $50; ages 3-9, $40.*

• *Premium Annual Pass provides unlimited admission to all four theme parks, Disney's two water parks, Pleasure Island and Disney's Wide World of Sports™ complex for 1 year from date of first use, free parking and other benefits. Admission $489; ages 3-9, $416.*

• *Theme Park Annual Pass provides unlimited admission to all four theme parks for 1 year from date of first use, free parking and other benefits. Admission $369; ages 3-9, $314.*

• *Select Park Hopper and Park Hopper Plus passes are available at participating AAA Travel offices.*

Tickets are valid during regular hours. Passes include unlimited use of the Walt Disney World transportation system. No refunds for unused tickets are issued for any reason. Tickets are non-transferrable. Some activities or events may be separately priced. **Prices quoted above do not include tax. Prices and entitlements may change without notice.** AX, DC, DS, JC, MC, VI. For ticket information phone (407) 824-4321 or TTY (407) 827-5141.

"As to Disney artwork/properties: © Disney"

Walt Disney World

THE

DISNEY TOTAL VACATION GUIDE

for Kids and Kids at Heart

Welcome to a place where storybook fantasy becomes everyday reality. It's where elephants fly, teacups dance, and every day ends happily ever after. Everyone in the family can play make-believe throughout seven enchanting lands of fantasy and fun. You'll find classic Disney tales and characters coming to life around every corner in a perfect wonderland for kids of all ages. Enjoy a visit to a land where the possibilities are endless. And so is the magic. Start exploring right now.

▼ ▼ ▼ ▼ ▼ A FEW OF OUR FAVORITES ▼ ▼ ▼ ▼ ▼

The Many Adventures of Winnie the Pooh
Enter the Hundred Acre Wood and bounce along with Tigger. Float through a floody place with Piglet. And dream along with Pooh.

Splash Mountain®
Hop into a hollowed-out log and get ready to scream into the Briar Patch on a five-story drop.

Cinderella's Surprise Celebration
Join Cinderella at her Castle for a magical new show featuring more than two dozen favorite Disney characters.

Buzz Lightyear's Space Ranger Spin
Fire your laser cannon at interactive targets to score as you pilot your own star cruiser and save the galaxy from the sinister Emperor Zurg.

Space Mountain®
Jockey this rocket ship ride through the inky blackness of outer space. Everything's scarier in the dark, especially roller coasters.

DISNEY'S ANIMAL KINGDOM

E xplore an amazing kingdom where imagination roams free and your wildest dreams come true. It's where dinosaurs still walk the earth, storytelling magic is unleashed, and every day comes alive with creatures from our world – and our imagination.

Every adventure leads you to another, and every trail beckons you to come explore. Round up your adventurous spirit and embark into the newest *Walt Disney World* Theme Park. Ahh... yes, this incredible place is many things. Begin your exploration now.

▼ ▼ ▼ ▼ ▼ A FEW OF OUR FAVORITES ▼ ▼ ▼ ▼ ▼

Kilimanjaro Safaris
Climb aboard your safari vehicle for an exciting expedition to a place where animals freely roam through acres of savannah.

Kali River Rapids
Take a raft ride down turbulent waters. Stay alert, there are adventures ahead, along with the very real threat of getting extremely wet.

It's Tough to be a Bug!
Come see Flik and Hopper from Disney/Pixar's "A Bug's Life" in a totally wild 3-D adventure.

DINOSAUR
Journey back 65 million years to save the last dinosaur in this thrill-packed attraction.

Festival of the Lion King
Sing along with all your favorite songs as Simba, Timon, and Pumbaa lead a tribal celebration of music, dance and amazing acrobatic feats.

Primeval Whirl
Take a ride on a prehysterical spinning coaster for a wacky run that sends you through curves, hills and drops.

EPCOT®

Discover the wonders of technology and explore exotic countries from around the globe. There are two amazing worlds at *Epcot*®. In one, you're a part of the excitement as high-tech meets big fun. In another, you'll travel through eleven great nations in a celebration of one-of-a-kind performances, and outstanding cuisine. At night, don't miss the awe-inspiring spectacular, *IllumiNations: Reflections of Earth*, as the art of lasers, music and fireworks soars to new heights. Start the discovery now.

▼ ▼ ▼ ▼ ▼ A FEW OF OUR FAVORITES ▼ ▼ ▼ ▼ ▼

China
Explore the mysteries of the East in an incredible experience that literally surrounds you with the dazzling beauty of China.

Test Track
Buckle up and take the ride of your life through all the hair-raising challenges of an automotive proving ground.

France
Dine in the shadow of the Eiffel Tower at a faithful re-creation of a typical Parisian sidewalk café.

Honey, I Shrunk the Audience
Go on an adventure beyond 3-D with incredible special effects and awesome surprises. You won't believe your size.

Body Wars
Shrink down to the size of a blood cell and take a turbulent ride through the human body.

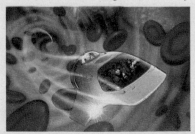

Innoventions– The Road to Tomorrow
See and touch all the incredible technology that will soon be changing our lives.

DISNEY-MGM STUDIOS

Get cast into an exciting day of showbiz! Indulge your fascination with Hollywood glamour here in the place where showbiz is. Thrilling attractions take you everywhere from the top of a haunted hotel to the ultimate Rock 'n' Roll road trip. Spectacular Broadway-style shows bring memorable Disney characters to life. Your whole family will love a chance to step into the bright lights. So come be the star of the fabulous Comedy-Thriller-Action Adventure that is your day.

▼ ▼ ▼ ▼ ▼ A FEW OF OUR FAVORITES ▼ ▼ ▼ ▼ ▼

Who Wants To Be A Millionaire – Play It!
This incredible new attraction gives fans of the TV show the chance to really get into the game.

Playhouse Disney—Live on Stage!
Sing and dance with your pals from Bear in the Big Blue House,™ Rolie Polie Olie and other favorites from the Disney Channel.

Rock 'n' Roller Coaster Starring Aerosmith
Go from zero to sixty in less than three seconds through twists and turns — even upside down.

The Twilight Zone Tower of Terror™
You'll fear every drop as you descend 13 gut-wrenching, faster-than-gravity stories again and again and again.

Fantasmic!
Sorcerer Mickey takes on some wicked villains in one of the most explosive nighttime extravaganzas ever.

DISNEY RESORTS

For the complete *Walt Disney World®* vacation experience, stay in the middle of the magic at a Disney Resort. With a variety to please every taste and vacation budget, Disney Resorts transport you into fantastic places yet keep you as close as possible to the magic of the Theme Parks and more. You'll also enjoy exclusive Guest benefits including complimentary transportation throughout the *Walt Disney World* Resort and one-of-a-kind Disney service.

Find out how to choose the perfect Disney Resort in the accommodations section of this guidebook.

AND EVEN MORE

**Downtown Disney®
Pleasure Island**
Blow off your bedtime for a night of everything from comedy and jazz to R&B and rock 'n' roll on Pleasure Island, an entire island just for adults.

AAA Tip: Disney Water Parks and Pleasure Island are all included with any AAA Vacations® package and Disney's *Park Hopper® PLUS* Ticket. (See next page for details.)

**Disney's Blizzard
Beach Water Park**
There are thrills on every water-slicked slope. Feel the chills of the nation's tallest water slide and reach the peak of exhilaration on attractions for every age.

**Disney's Typhoon
Lagoon Water Park**
The whole family can kick back with a little tropical attitude as you bodysurf in one of the world's largest wave pools and snorkel with real, live sharks.

AAA VACATIONS® PACKAGES

You can save on select Disney Resort accommodations with the AAA Disney *Magic Moments®* savings plan or other special AAA Vacations® packages. Packages include a Disney Resort stay, Disney's *Ultimate Park Hopper* Tickets (see below), and exclusive AAA benefits. To book, simply call or visit your local AAA Travel office. They can help you with all your travel needs.

AAA Vacations® Walt Disney World benefits include:

• **AAA Vacations® Diamond Card** entitles you to special savings on meals, merchandise and recreation at select Disney locations.

• **AAA VIP Lounge** in the *Magic Kingdom®* Park. It's like having a private club in the middle of the magic. What a great place to unwind and enjoy a complimentary beverage.

• **Preferred Parking** in special AAA spaces at all *Walt Disney World* Theme Parks (some block-out dates apply).

• **Preferred viewing** for selected Theme Park fireworks and parades (selected packages only). See your AAA Travel professional for details.

PARK HOPPER TICKETS

Enjoy more of the magic you want — and save money by planning ahead. Disney *Park Hopper®* Tickets offer the flexibility to tailor each day of your vacation any way you want by letting you come and go as you please through all four Theme Parks. And Disney *Park Hopper PLUS* Tickets give you all that, plus Disney's Water Parks, *Downtown Disney®* Pleasure Island, and more.

And now, buying select *Park Hopper®* Tickets before you leave home lets you enjoy special Advanced Purchase Savings. Just stop by any participating AAA Travel office and buy your Disney tickets before you leave for your vacation.

Remember, all AAA Vacations® packages include the *Ultimate Park Hopper* ticket. Exclusively for selected *Walt Disney World®* Resort hotel Guests, this ticket gives you maximum Disney fun and is good from the moment you check-in until midnight of your check-out day.

AAA Tip: Buying your *Park Hopper* Tickets through AAA Travel also entitles you to Preferred Parking in special AAA spaces at the Disney Theme Parks (some block-out dates apply).

Disney Multi-Day Tickets	Ultimate Park Hopper Ticket	Park Hopper PLUS Ticket	Park Hopper Ticket
FOUR THEME PARKS:			
Magic Kingdom®	✓	✓	✓
Epcot®	✓	✓	✓
Disney-MGM Studios	✓	✓	✓
Disney's Animal Kingdom®	✓	✓	✓
AND MORE!		Choose From the Following Options:	
Blizzard Beach Water Park	✓	✓	
Typhoon Lagoon Water Park	✓	✓	
Pleasure Island	✓	✓	
Disney's Wide World of Sports™ complex*	✓	✓	
DisneyQuest® Indoor Interactive Theme Park	✓	Number of Options Varies According to Number of Days on Your Ticket.	

*Admission valid only on event days.

MAITLAND (E-4) pop. 12,019, elev. 91'

HISTORIC WATERHOUSE RESIDENCE AND CARPENTRY SHOP MUSEUMS are .9 mi. n. of SR 423 on US 17/92, then e. to 820 Lake Lily Dr. The 1884 Waterhouse residence is a house museum that highlights the experiences of one of Maitland's pioneer families. Antique tools and woodworking techniques are exhibited at the Carpentry Shop Museum. Allow 30 minutes minimum. Thurs.-Sun. noon-4; closed major holidays. Admission $2, family rate $5. Phone (407) 644-2451.

THE HOLOCAUST MEMORIAL RESOURCE AND EDUCATION CENTER OF CENTRAL FLORIDA is 1.25 mi. e. of I-4 exit 90A at 851 N. Maitland Ave. (SR 414). The center illustrates key events of the Holocaust through chronological displays, photographs and audiovisual presentations. A memorial wall built of Jerusalem stone remembers the 6 million Jews who died at the hands of the Nazis. Allow 1 hour minimum. Mon.-Thurs. 9-4, Fri. 9-1; closed major national and Jewish holidays. Free. Phone (407) 628-0555.

MAITLAND ART CENTER is 1.5 mi. e. of I-4 exit 90A on SR 414 (Maitland Blvd.), .7 mi. s. on CR 427 (Maitland Ave.), then .2 mi. w. to 231 W. Packwood Ave. One of the few surviving examples of "fantasy" architecture in the southeast U.S., this 23-building complex is ornamented with murals, bas-reliefs and carvings in Aztec and Mayan styles.

Walkways wind through courtyards and gardens at the center, which was founded as an artist's colony in the 1930s. In addition to changing exhibits that showcase local, regional and national artists and craftspersons, the center also offers year-round classes and lectures, garden concerts, gallery walks and special events. Guided tours are available.

Allow 1 hour minimum. Mon.-Fri. 9-4:30, Sat.-Sun. noon-4:30; closed major holidays. Donations. Phone (407) 539-2181.

MOUNT DORA (D-2) pop. 9,418, elev. 175'

Established in 1880, Mount Dora—about 25 miles northwest of Orlando—is a mecca for antiques collectors and dealers alike. Equally known as a festival city, Mount Dora is home to top-rated arts and crafts festivals.

Sightseers can take trolley, train or boat trips, rent a bicycle or canoe, or simply stroll along the shore of picturesque Lake Dora. Gilbert Park, with a playground, croquet field and boating facilities, is a popular spot for picnics. The 1,700-foot-long Palm Island Boardwalk is said to be Florida's longest lakeside boardwalk.

Mount Dora Chamber of Commerce: 341 N. Alexander St., Mount Dora, FL 32757; phone (352) 383-2165.

Shopping areas: Boutiques, gift shops and antiques galleries line Mount Dora's downtown streets, and as many as 1,500 antiques dealers gather for the fairs and extravaganzas held at Renninger's Antique Center. There, collectors and window shoppers can find anything from furniture and jewelry to Art Deco items and World's Fair collectibles.

ORLANDO & MOUNT DORA RAILWAY, 2 blks. s. of 5th Ave. (old US 441) at 150 W. 3rd Ave., offers an hour-long, 12-mile scenic round trip to Tavares on an 1850s countryside railroad line. The "Mount Dora Cannonball"—a vintage 1946 diesel locomotive—takes open-window coaches along the shores of Lake Dora, offering views of tropical foliage, wildlife and wetlands. Sightseeing excursions depart Wed.-Sun. at 11, 12:40 and 2:20 (also Sat.-Sun. at 4); closed Thanksgiving and Dec. 25. Fare $12; over 54, $11; ages 4-12, $8. MC, VI. Phone (352) 735-4667.

ST. CLOUD (I-5) pop. 20,074, elev. 63′

REPTILE WORLD SERPENTARIUM, 4 mi. e. on US 192, .5 mi. e. of jct. CR 532, houses snakes from around the world in glass display cases. A walled compound contains turtles and a fenced compound houses alligators. Venom programs are given daily at noon and 3. Allow 1 hour, 30 minutes minimum. Tues.-Sun. 9-5:30, Oct.-Aug.; closed Thanksgiving weekend and Dec. 25. Admission $5.50; ages 6-17, $4.50; ages 3-5, $3.50. Phone (407) 892-6905.

SANFORD (D-10) pop. 38,291, elev. 20′

At the head of navigation on the St. Johns River, Sanford was established as a trading post in 1837. Gen. Henry R. Sanford bought 12,000 acres, including the townsite, in 1871 and established citrus groves.

Amtrak's Auto Train transports passengers and their cars to and from Lorton, Va. To reach the station, take SR 46 (I-4 exit 101C) east to 400 Persimmon Ave.

Sanford/Seminole Chamber of Commerce: 400 E. First St., Sanford, FL 32771; phone (407) 322-2212.

BIG TREE PARK is 6 mi. s. on US 17/92, then 1.5 mi. w. on Gen. J.C. Hutcheson Pkwy., near Longwood. A boardwalk in the 11-acre park leads to The Senator, a 3,500-year-old giant cypress tree that is one of the largest in the United States. The tree is 138 feet high, with a diameter of 17.5 feet and a circumference of 47 feet. Picnicking is permitted. Daily 8 a.m.-dusk. Free. Phone (407) 788-0405.

MUSEUM OF SEMINOLE COUNTY HISTORY is 1 mi. s. on US 17/92, then w. to 300 Bush Blvd. Housed in the former County Old Folks Home built in 1927, the museum's 22 rooms feature displays about early transportation, turpentine, cattle and agriculture. Period rooms feature furniture and artifacts. Allow 30 minutes minimum. Tues.-Fri.

9-noon and 1-4, Sat. 1-4; closed holidays. Free. Phone (407) 665-2489.

[SAVE] RIVERSHIP ROMANCE docks 4 mi. e. of I-4 exit 101C, on SR 46 at Monroe Harbour Marina. Luncheon sightseeing cruises are offered along the St. Johns River aboard a 100-foot, 1940s-style Great Lakes steamer. Dinner/dance cruises also are available. Three-hour luncheon cruise departs Wed. and Sat.-Sun. at 11; 4-hour luncheon cruise departs Mon.-Tues. and Thurs.-Fri. at 11. Three-hour lunch fares start at $35; 4-hour lunch fares begin at $45. Reservations are required. AX, DS, MC, VI. Phone (407) 321-5091 or (800) 423-7401.

THE SANFORD MUSEUM, 520 E. First St., houses exhibits depicting the city's history. Two rooms dedicated to city founder Henry Shelton Sanford include his art collection, books and papers. Tues.-Fri. 11-4, Sat. 1-4; closed holidays. Free. Phone (407) 302-1000.

ZOO ORLANDO AT SANFORD is n.w. on US 17/92, .7 mi. s. of I-4 exit 104. The park contains mammals, birds, reptiles and a children's zoo. Picnic facilities are available. Allow 2 hours minimum. Daily 9-5; closed Thanksgiving and Dec. 25. Admission $8; over 60, $5; ages 3-12, $4. DS, MC, VI. Phone (407) 323-4450.

TAVARES (D-9) pop. 9,700, elev. 66′

CAPTAIN DAVE'S DORA CANAL CRUISES departs from the dock at the intersection of US 441 and Lake Shore Blvd. Captain Dave's offers narrated cruises of Lake Eustis, Lake Dora and the Dora Canal during which passengers can see a variety of local wildlife. Allow 1 hour, 30 minutes minimum. Cruises depart at 10:30, 1 and 3, mid-Oct. to mid-May. Fare $10. Reservations are required. Phone (352) 343-3889.

WINTER PARK (F-4) pop. 24,090, elev. 96′

Moss-draped oaks line the residential streets of Winter Park, a community of beautiful homes and picturesque lakes. The campus of Rollins College features brick streets and Mediterranean-style buildings on the shores of Lake Virginia. The small, private college is at the foot of Park Avenue, a popular shopping district with a varied selection of upscale boutiques, galleries and restaurants.

Winter Park Chamber of Commerce: 150 N. New York Ave., Winter Park, FL 32787; phone (407) 644-8281.

ALBIN POLASEK MUSEUM AND GARDENS is 1.3 mi. e. of US 17/92 at 633 Osceola Ave. (SR 426). Three galleries and the gardens display the sculptures and paintings of the Czech-American artist. Noteworthy is a wooden nativity Polasek created at age 15. Tues.-Sat. 10-4, Sun. 1-4, Sept.-June; closed holidays. Admission $4, seniors $3, students with ID $2, under 12 free. Phone (407) 647-6294.

CHARLES HOSMER MORSE MUSEUM OF AMERICAN ART, 445 Park Ave. N., contains a major collection of works by Louis Comfort Tiffany, a celebrated and influential designer of the late 19th and early 20th century. Many of the stained-glass windows on exhibit were installed at Laurelton Hall, Tiffany's mansion on Long Island. A highlight is the chapel Tiffany designed for the 1893 Exposition at the Chicago World's Fair.

The museum houses works of art and historical documents including works by Tiffany's contemporaries, a collection of American art pottery and American paintings from the late 19th century to the early 20th century. Guided tours are available. Allow 1 hour minimum. Tues.-Sat. 9:30-4 (also Fri. 4-8, Sept.-May), Sun. 1-4; closed major holidays. Admission $3; students over 12, $1; free to all Fri.

4-8 in season, Easter, July 4 and Dec. 24. Phone (407) 645-5311.

CORNELL FINE ARTS MUSEUM, 2.25 mi. e. of I-4 exit 87 at the end of Holt Ave. on the Rollins College campus, displays permanent and changing exhibits of American and European paintings, decorative arts and sculpture. Representative artists include William Merritt Chase, Childe Hassam and Louis Comfort Tiffany. Allow 1 hour minimum. Tues.-Fri. 10-5, Sat.-Sun. 1-5; closed holidays. Free. Phone (407) 646-2526.

SCENIC BOAT TOURS, leaving from the foot of Morse Blvd., provide narrated 1-hour cruises past many of Winter Park's opulent lakeside estates and landmarks. Allow 1 hour, 30 minutes minimum. Departures daily on the hour 10-4; closed Dec. 25. Fare $7; under 12, $3. Phone (407) 644-4056.

This ends listings for the Orlando Vicinity.
The following page resumes the alphabetical listings of cities in Florida.

ORMOND BEACH (C-10)
pop. 36,301, elev. 6'

Charles and Frank Duryea, Barney Oldfield, R.E. Olds, Alexander Winton and others raced cars on the sands of Ormond Beach in the early and mid-1900s, giving the city its reputation as the birthplace of speed.

Ormond Beach Chamber of Commerce: 165 W. Granada Blvd., Ormond Beach, FL 32174; phone (386) 677-3454.

THE CASEMENTS, 25 Riverside Dr., was the winter home of John D. Rockefeller from 1914 until his death in 1937. The house is now a cultural and civic center, with a collection of Hungarian folk art, Boy Scout memorabilia and an exhibit of Rockefeller furnishings and personal items. Changing exhibits are featured. Allow 30 minutes minimum. Mon.-Fri. 9-5, Sat. 9-noon; closed holidays. Tours Mon.-Fri. 10-2:30. Donations. Phone (386) 676-3216.

ORMOND MEMORIAL ART MUSEUM AND GARDENS, 1 mi. e. of US 1 at 78 E. Granada Blvd., contains a 4.5-acre botanical memorial garden with a waterfall, nature trails and turtle ponds as well as changing exhibits of contemporary Florida art and fine crafts. Of note is a collection of symbolic religious paintings by Malcolm Fraser. Allow 30 minutes minimum. Gardens open daily dawn-dusk. Gallery open Mon.-Fri. 10-4, Sat.-Sun. noon-4; closed major holidays. Admission $2; senior citizens and students free. Phone (386) 676-3347.

OSCEOLA NATIONAL FOREST
Elevations in the forest range from
120 ft. to 180 ft.

Osceola National Forest encompasses 187,000 acres near the Georgia border. It is mostly flat country dotted with ponds and swamps. Fishing is available in numerous creeks and rivers. Hunting is permitted, but a special license is required in the Osceola Wildlife Management Area; for information phone the Florida Fish and Wildlife Conservation Commission at (850) 488-4676. Endangered species in the forest include the red cockaded woodpecker and gray bat. Ocean Pond (see the AAA Southeastern CampBook) and Olustee Beach are major recreation areas within the forest. Phone (386) 752-2577. See Recreation Chart.

OSPREY (F-8) pop. 4,143, elev. 10'

HISTORIC SPANISH POINT, 337 N. Tamiami Trail (US 41), is a 30-acre archeological, historic and environmental site on Little Sarasota Bay featuring the remains of a prehistoric living site, a pioneer family homestead and restored gardens from an early 20th-century estate. A nature trail now leads visitors along the bay past a citrus packing house, a restored pioneer home, a chapel, boat-building exhibits, native plants and formal gardens. Visitors can view an archeology display inside a prehistoric shell mound. An orientation video is shown in the visitors center. Guided tours are available. Picnicking is permitted.

Allow 1 hour, 30 minutes minimum. Mon.-Sat. 9-5, Sun. noon-5; closed Jan. 1, Easter, Thanksgiving and Dec. 25. Admission $7; senior citizens $5 on Mon.; ages 6-12, $3. DS, MC, VI. Phone (941) 966-5214.

PALATKA (B-9) pop. 10,033, elev. 28'

Judge Isaac Bronson, one of Palatka's foremost residents, was a member of the 25th U.S. Congress and was responsible for proposing the act by which Florida became a state. His restored home, Bronson-Mulholland House, 100 Mulholland Park, was built in 1854 and is open to the public.

Putnam County Chamber of Commerce: 1100 Reid St., P.O. Box 550, Palatka, FL 32178; phone (386) 328-1503.

RAVINE STATE GARDENS, on Twigg St., is 1.25 mi. s. off SR 20. Formed by water erosion from the St. Johns River, the steep ravines provide a rich environment for wild plants. Two swinging bridges cross the ravines, and nature trails wind through the 59-acre park, which has been landscaped extensively with azaleas and camellias. Picnic facilities, a preschoolers' playground and a fitness trail are available. Daily 8-dusk. The road is closed to traffic at 4 p.m. Admission $3.25 per private vehicle (maximum of eight people), $1 per person arriving by bicycle, bus or on foot. Phone (386) 329-3721.

PALM BEACH (F-12) pop. 10,468, elev. 32'

In 1878 a Spanish brigantine bound from the West Indies to Spain went aground at Palm Beach, spilling its cargo of coconuts along the sandy, barrier island. When Henry Flagler visited the area in the early 1890s, he found a small community of settlers amid a growth of coconut palms. Recognizing the potential of South Florida, he chose Palm Beach for the site of his next luxury hotel and laid out a fashionable resort that has retained the quiet charm and tropical beauty of his original vision.

A scenic portion of SR A1A meanders along the ocean as it extends from Palm Beach south to Fort Lauderdale, a drive of 47 miles.

Also see West Palm Beach p. 233.

Palm Beach Chamber of Commerce: 45 Cocoanut Row, Palm Beach, FL 33480; phone (561) 655-3282.

Shopping areas: Exclusive shops such as Cartier, Gucci and Tiffany line tree-shaded Worth Avenue.

BETHESDA-BY-THE-SEA, S. County Rd. and Barton Ave., is an Episcopal church of modified 15th-century Gothic design. Adjacent are the attractive, formally landscaped Cluett Memorial Gardens. Church and gardens open daily 8-5. Free. Phone (561) 655-4554.

FLAGLER MUSEUM is at Cocoanut Row and Whitehall Way. Original and period furnishings and Flagler family memorabilia grace Whitehall, the opulent 1902 Gilded Age mansion railroad magnate Henry Flagler built for his bride. The 55-room house was hailed as "grander and more magnificent than any other private dwelling in the world."

The house was restored as a museum in 1960. Among the highlights are a marble entrance hall, Louis XIV music room and Louis XV ballroom. The museum also features changing exhibits and special programs. Visitors can see Flagler's private railroad car on the south lawn.

Allow 1 hour, 30 minutes minimum. Tues.-Sat. 10-5, Sun. noon-5; closed Jan. 1, Thanksgiving and Dec. 25. Admission $8; ages 6-12, $3. AX, MC, VI. Phone (561) 655-2833. *See color ad p. 235.*

SOCIETY OF THE FOUR ARTS, Four Arts Plaza just off Royal Palm Way, comprises a library, art gallery, auditorium and sculpture and botanical gardens. Lectures by authors and noted speakers are presented weekly, early December through mid-April. Allow 30 minutes minimum. Gallery open Mon.-Sat. 10-5, Sun. 2-5, Dec. 1 to mid-Apr. Gardens open Mon.-Fri. 10-5 (also Sat. 9-1, Nov.-Apr.). Library open Mon.-Fri. 10-5 (also Sat. 9-1, Nov.-Apr.). Free. Phone (561) 655-7226 or (561) 655-2766 for the library.

One Perfect Gift

PALM COAST (C-10) pop. 32,732, elev. 10'

 WASHINGTON OAKS GARDENS STATE PARK, 6400 N. Oceanshore Blvd., originally was part of Bella Vista Plantation owned by Gen. Joseph Hernandez, a militia general who commanded troops during the Second Seminole War. Extending from the Atlantic Ocean to the Matanzas River, the preserve covers more than 400 acres of Florida coastal scenery. Included are scenic tidal marshes, a scrub community, a beach and a hammock. Coquina rock outcroppings worn into unusual shapes by the sea give the beach area an unearthly appearance. Many species of shorebirds and marine and forest animals make their home in the area.

Formal gardens contain exotic plants from around the world; a history of the area is presented at the Young House. Guided walks are provided on weekends and by request. Picnicking is permitted. Allow 3 hours minimum. Daily 8-dusk. Admission $3.25 per private vehicle. Phone (386) 446-6780. *See Recreation Chart.*

PANACEA (B-6) elev. 5'

GULF SPECIMEN MARINE LABORATORY, just s. of US 98, following signs to 222 Clark Dr., features a 25,000-gallon marine aquarium as well as touch tanks housing sea horses, crabs, rays, sponges, starfish and small sharks. Allow 1 hour minimum. Mon.-Fri. 9-5, Sat. 10-4, Sun. noon-4. Admission $5; ages 2-11, $3. Phone (850) 984-5297.

PANAMA CITY (B-4) pop. 36,417, elev. 33'

Panama City, county seat of Bay County, is a leading port on St. Andrew Bay off the Gulf of Mexico and is the eastern terminus for a scenic portion of US 98 extending 98 miles to Gulf Breeze, just south of Pensacola. Spanish expeditions visited this site 1516-40, but it was not until 1765 that an English settlement was made at St. Andrew, now part of Panama City.

The area also is home to Tyndall Air Force Base and Navy Coastal Systems Station. The city is known for its sugar-white beaches. A marina at the foot of Harrison Avenue includes berths for about 400 boats. Fishing boats can be chartered on St. Andrew Bay.

Bay County Chamber of Commerce: 235 W. Fifth St., P.O. Box 1850, Panama City, FL 32402-1850; phone (850) 785-5206.

JUNIOR MUSEUM OF BAY COUNTY, 1731 Jenks Ave., offers child-oriented hands-on exhibits including Body Works, Hands-On Science, Nature Corner, Imagine Me and Discovery Depot. Highlights include the Pioneer Homestead, a re-created farm from the late 1800s, and a boardwalk nature trail through a swamp and forest area. Allow 30 minutes minimum. Mon.-Fri. 9-4:30, Sat. 10-4; closed major holidays. Admission $3; ages 2-12, $2. Phone (850) 769-6128.

PANAMA CITY BEACH (B-4)

pop. 7,671, elev. 7'

Powdery white sand beaches and emerald waters of the Gulf of Mexico give Panama City Beach its status as a popular shore resort. The Yucatan Current, part of the Gulf Stream, runs close to the shores of Panama City Beach, bringing with it nutrient-rich Caribbean water and blue marlin, sailfish, big bull dolphin (fish), wahoo and tuna. One fishing pier extends 1,600 feet into the Gulf.

Scuba diving locations in the Gulf of Mexico include shipwrecks and almost 50 artificial reefs. Five championship golf courses are in the immediate area.

St. Andrews State Recreation Area *(see Recreation Chart and the AAA Southeastern CampBook)* flanks the pass separating Panama City Beach from Shell Island, the barrier isle guarding the mouth of St. Andrew Bay. The mainland portion of the park, reached via Thomas Drive, contains a restored turpentine still.

The Shell Island segment, an excellent spot for both swimming and shell gathering, is accessible only by boat. Passage is available from the recreation area and Capt. Anderson's Marina, 5550 N. Grand Lagoon Dr., from March 1 through Labor Day. Shuttles to Shell Island also depart from Treasure Island Marina.

Miracle Strip Amusement Park, 12000 Front Beach Rd., and the adjacent Shipwreck Island, a water theme park, are popular family attractions.

Panama City Beach Convention and Visitors Bureau: P.O. Box 9473, Panama City Beach, FL 32417; phone (850) 233-6503 or (800) 722-3224. *See color ad.*

CAPTAIN ANDERSON CRUISES, Capt. Anderson's Marina 5550 N. Lagoon Dr. at jct. Thomas Dr., offers 3-hour sightseeing cruises to Shell Island and a 75-minute sunset dolphin watch aboard the *Capt. Anderson III,* a glass-bottom boat. Dinner/dance, gospel music and deep-sea fishing cruises also are available. Shell Island cruises depart daily at 9 and 1, sunset cruise daily at 5:15, Mar.-Oct. Shell Island cruise $16; ages 6-11, $10; ages 2-5, $7. Sunset cruise $8; ages 2-11, $5. MC, VI. Phone (850) 234-5940 or (800) 360-0510.

SAVE **THE MUSEUM OF MAN IN THE SEA,** .25 mi. w. of jct. SR 79 at 17314 Panama City Beach Pkwy. (US 98), illustrates the history of undersea exploration using dioramas and written records. Highlights include rare and antique diving equipment and related displays. Changing exhibits are featured. Allow 1 hour minimum. Daily 9-5; closed Jan. 1, Thanksgiving and Dec. 25. Admission $5; over 65, $4.50; ages 6-16, $2.50. AX, DS, MC, VI. Phone (850) 235-4101.

THE OCEAN OPRY MUSIC SHOW, 2 mi. w. of Hathaway Bridge on US 98A (Front Beach Rd.), presents a comedy and country music stage show in a 1,000-seat theater. Nashville stars appear October through March. Food is available.

Allow 2 hours minimum. Performances Mon.-Sat. at 8 p.m., June-Aug. (also Sun. performances Memorial Day, July 4 and Labor Day weekends); Tues. and Fri.-Sat. at 7:30 p.m., rest of year. Admission $19.95; ages 5-11, $9.95. Prices vary for special shows. DS, MC, VI. Phone (850) 234-5464 for reservations and schedule.

PENSACOLA (B-2) pop. 56,255, elev. 39′

Although an attempt was made in 1559 by Don Tristan de Luna, permanent settlement at Pensacola was not established until 1698. The town has flown the flags of Spain, France, England, the Confederate States and the United States, and its government has changed hands 13 times.

In 1814 the British used the harbor as a base in their war with the United States, but withdrew when the city was attacked by Gen. Andrew Jackson. Here Jackson completed the transaction by which Spain sold Florida to the United States in 1821. In the city's historic downtown at Plaza Ferdinand VII is the site where the Spanish flag was lowered for the last time. Pensacola was the territorial capital until 1822, and Andrew Jackson was a resident while governor of Florida.

The Seville Square historic district, bounded on the north by Government Street and on the east by Alcaniz Street, is an area of restored 19th-century buildings that now houses shops, restaurants, museums and art galleries.

Pensacola's Naval Air Station is a center for electronic warfare and cartographic training as well as headquarters for the Blue Angels precision flying team.

Gulf Islands National Seashore *(see place listing p. 86 and Recreation Chart)* offers miles and miles of unspoiled sugar-white beaches and emerald waters. Recreational activities include boating, swimming and sun-bathing. Other outdoor activities can be enjoyed on the area's numerous waterways, including the Blackwater and Perdido rivers and Coldwater and Sweetwater-Juniper creeks *(see Milton p. 127)*.

The Wildlife Sanctuary of Northwest Florida, 105 N. S St., cares for injured and orphaned wildlife, including foxes, deer, eagles, egrets, herons, owls, pelicans and hawks; for information phone (850) 433-9453.

West of the city on Dog Track Road, Pensacola Greyhound Track presents dog races Wednesday through Saturday evenings and Saturday and Sunday afternoons. Phone (850) 455-8595.

Note: Policies vary concerning admittance of children to pari-mutuel betting facilities. Phone for information.

Pensacola Convention and Visitors Center: 1401 E. Gregory St., Pensacola, FL 32501; phone (850) 434-1234 or (800) 874-1234.

Self-guiding tours: The convention and visitors center, at the foot of the 3-mile bay bridge, offers free information about tours of the city.

Shopping areas: Cordova Mall, 5100 N. Ninth Ave., contains more than 150 stores including Dillard's and Parisian. University Mall, 7171 N. Davis Hwy., features JCPenney, McRaes and Sears among its 85 stores. Old buildings have been transformed into specialty shops at Palafox Place.

CIVIL WAR SOLDIERS MUSEUM, 108 S. Palafox Pl., offers insights into the daily lives of Civil War soldiers from the North and the South through an extensive display of medical artifacts and life-size camp dioramas. Tues.-Sat. 10-4:30; closed Jan. 1, Thanksgiving and Dec. 24-25. Admission $5; military with ID $4; ages 6-12, $2.50. MC, VI. Phone (850) 469-1900.

[SAVE] **HISTORIC PENSACOLA VILLAGE** is a complex of 10 museum buildings reflecting 450 years of Pensacola's history. Allow 1 hour minimum. Tues.-Sat. 10-4, June 1-Labor Day; Mon.-Fri. 10-4, rest of year. Closed state holidays. Village admission $6; over 65 and military with ID $5; ages 4-16, $2.50. Phone (850) 595-5985.

Dorr House, 311 S. Adams St., is an example of Greek Revival architecture. Built in 1871 by Clara

Barkley Dorr, the widow of a lumber baron, the two-story house is furnished with late Victorian pieces.

Julee Cottage, 210 E. Zaragoza St., was built in 1804 and once belonged to Julee Panton, a free black woman.

Lavalle House, 205 E. Church St., was built by Carlos Lavalle and Marianna Bonifay in 1805 during Florida's second Spanish period. A rare example of French Creole Colonial architecture, the house is furnished to reflect the 1820s Pensacola frontier.

Museum of Commerce, 201 E. Zaragoza St., features a full-scale replica of an 1890s Pensacola street inside a 19th-century warehouse. Printing presses, a hardware store, a toy shop and a horse-drawn buggy collection are among the exhibits.

Museum of Industry, 200 E. Zaragoza St., displays photographs, tools and equipment related to the 19th-century industrial boom in west Florida. Exhibits focus on Pensacola's fishing, brickmaking, railroad and lumber industries.

T.T. Wentworth Jr. Florida State Museum, 330 S. Jefferson St., was built in the Renaissance Revival style in 1907 as Pensacola's city hall. The elaborate building now houses changing exhibits about the region's history, architecture and archeology.

NATIONAL MUSEUM OF NAVAL AVIA-TION, on the Naval Air Station, Pensacola, traces the development of American naval aviation from its beginnings to the present. Among the highlights of the collection are the NC-4 Flying Boat, which in 1919 became the first plane to cross the Atlantic; the only surviving SBD Dauntless from the Battle of Midway; and the Skylab Command Module in addition to more than 170 other historic naval aircraft. Four A-4 Skyhawks are suspended from the ceiling in formation in the Blue Angels Atrium. Bus tours of the flight line feature additional aircraft.

Walk-through displays portray a World War II carrier hangar bay, South Pacific Sea Island forward Marine base and the wartime home front. Other exhibits range from pre-World War I memorabilia to items used by Navy prisoners of war during the Vietnam War.

One wing of the 290,000-square-foot exhibit area showcases a replica of a World War II aircraft carrier island and flight deck with a working elevator. Visitors can take the controls of aircraft trainers and simulators and ride a motion-based simulator. Aviation art and photography also are featured. An IMAX theater presents films every hour. Food is available. Allow 1 hour, 30 minutes minimum. Daily 9-5; closed Jan. 1, Thanksgiving and Dec. 25. Museum free. IMAX movie $6.25; senior citizens, military with ID and ages 4-12, $5.75. Phone (850) 453-2389 or (800) 327-5002. *See color ad.*

NAVAL AIR STATION, PENSACOLA, s. end of Navy Blvd., provides maps and visitor information at the front gate, Building 777. For historical maps and base information contact the public affairs office. The air station is open daily; hours vary. Free. Phone (850) 452-2311.

Fort Barrancas is one of several U.S. forts built by the U.S. Corps of Engineers in the 19th century along northwestern Florida's coastline. A dry moat surrounds the inner walls and makes access to the fort possible only by way of a drawbridge. Allow 30 minutes minimum. Daily 9:30-4:45, Apr.-Oct.; 8:30-3:45, rest of year. Hours may vary; phone ahead. Closed Dec. 25. Tours are given Sat.-Sun. at 2. Free. Phone (850) 455-5167.

PENSACOLA HISTORICAL MUSEUM, in the Arbona Building at 115 E. Zaragoza St., relates the military and maritime history of the town from its early days to the present. Exhibits of local historical items include clothing, silver, bottles, and American Indian artifacts. A resource center maintains genealogical information, maps, government records, photos and manuscripts relating to the area's history. Allow 30 minutes minimum. Museum Mon.-Sat. 10-4:30. Resource center Tues.-Thurs. and Sat. 10-noon and 1-3. Closed holidays. Museum $2. Resource center research fee $5. Phone (850) 433-1559 for museum, or (850) 434-5455 for resource center.

PLAZA FERDINAND VII, S. Palafox St. between E. Government and Zaragoza sts., was part of Pensacola's original Spanish settlement. A statue of Andrew Jackson commemorates the transfer of Florida to the United States.

VETERANS MEMORIAL PARK, at the corner of Bayfront Pkwy. and Romana St., is a half-size replica of the Vietnam Veterans Memorial in Washington, D.C. It contains the names of the Americans lost in Southeast Asia during the Vietnam War. Also on the site are a UH-1M "Huey" helicopter and a memorial to veterans of World Wars I and II. Daily 24 hours. Free. Phone (850) 456-0040.

PENSACOLA BEACH (B-3) elev. 7'

Snow white sand and aquamarine water make Pensacola Beach one of Florida's most beautiful beaches. Bordered by two preserved seashores, the area offers more than 20 miles of beach front covered in sugarlike sand composed of 99 percent pure quartz.

Wide paths parallel beach roads to offer skaters, cyclists, walkers and joggers a place for recreation. Other popular pursuits include fishing, golf and a wide array of water sports.

Pensacola Beach Chamber of Commerce: Visitor Information Center, 735 Pensacola Beach Blvd., Pensacola Beach, FL 32561; phone (850) 932-1500 or (800) 635-4803. *See ad.*

PERRY (B-7) pop. 6,847, elev. 30'

FOREST CAPITAL STATE MUSEUM, 1 mi. s. on US 19/27A/98 at 204 Forest Park Dr., depicts the development of the forest industry. Exhibits illustrate modern forestry, turpentine production, regional wildlife and the cutting of virgin forests, cypress swamps and hardwood hammocks. The adjacent North Florida Cracker Homestead, built in the 1860s, interprets the lifestyle of early settlers. A playground is available. Picnicking is permitted. Allow 30 minutes minimum. Thurs.-Mon. 9-noon and 1-5; closed Jan. 1, Thanksgiving and Dec. 25. Admission $1, under 6 free. Phone (850) 584-3227.

PLANT CITY—*see Tampa Bay p. 229.*

POINT WASHINGTON (B-4) elev. 16'

EDEN STATE GARDENS AND MANSION, in Eden State Park, are 1 mi. n. of US 98 on CR 395. Magnolias, colorful camellias and azaleas, a historic rose garden and live oaks draped in Spanish moss surround an 1898 Greek Revival mansion filled with Colonial, Empire and Victorian furnishings. Two Civil War re-enactments, including a Confederate Christmas, are held throughout the year; phone for information. Forty-five minute guided tours of the mansion are offered.

Grounds open daily 8-dusk. Mansion tours Thurs.-Mon. on the hour 10-3. Admission to grounds $2 per private vehicle. Mansion tour $1.50; under 13, 50c. Phone (850) 231-4214.

POLK CITY (D-9) pop. 1,516, elev. 173'

Incorporated in 1925, Polk City is near the Lake Wales Ridge, the highest ground on the Florida peninsula. Hundreds of thousands of years ago, when most of Florida was underwater, the ridge was part of an island chain that was isolated from the rest of North America. As a result of this isolation, the area today includes sandhill and scrub habitats that are home to a host of rare, threatened and endangered species.

The Water Ski Museum and Hall of Fame at 1251 Holy Cow Rd. contains vintage water ski paraphernalia from the early days of the sport including two pine boards that are said to be the very first water skis ever used; phone (863) 324-2472.

Central Florida Visitors & Convention Bureau: P.O. Box 8040, Cypress Gardens, FL 33884-0009; phone (863) 298-7565 or (800) 828-7655.

FANTASY OF FLIGHT, I-4 exit 44, then .5 mi. n. on SR 559, features vintage aircraft portraying various eras of aviation including the Short Sunderland—purportedly the world's last airworthy civilian four-engine flying boat. A full-scale, walkthrough diorama of a World War II bombing mission aboard a B-17 Flying Fortress is complete with films and audiotapes. Fightertown lets visitors experience an aerial dogfight. Guided tours of the aircraft shop are available. Food is available.

Allow 1 hour, 30 minutes minimum. Daily 9-5; closed Thanksgiving and Dec. 25. Admission $24.95; over 59, $22.95; ages 5-12, $13.95. AX, MC, VI. Phone (863) 984-3500.

POMPANO BEACH—
see Fort Lauderdale p. 78.

PONCE INLET (C-10) pop. 2,513, elev. 10′

FLORIDA COASTAL CRUISES—
see New Smyrna Beach p. 130.

PONCE DE LEON INLET LIGHTHOUSE, just w. of SR A1A (S. Atlantic Ave.) at 4931 S. Peninsula Dr., is a restored 175-foot-high brick structure whose light, reactivated in 1982, guided mariners past the shoals 1887-1970. Visitors may climb to the top of the lighthouse for a panorama of the Daytona Beach area. The keepers' cottages are now museums. The generator building houses tools and lighthouse pictures from around the world. A park with picnic tables is next to the lighthouse.

Allow 1 hour minimum. Daily 10-9, Memorial Day-Labor Day; 10-5, rest of year. Last admission 1 hour before closing. Admission $5; under 11, $1.50. Phone (386) 761-1821.

PORT ORANGE (C-10) pop. 45,823, elev. 20′

SUGAR MILL BOTANICAL GARDENS, 1 mi. w. of US 1 off Herbert St. on Old Sugar Mill Rd., encompasses 12 acres of landscaped grounds surrounding the restored ruins of an 1836 English sugar mill burned by Seminole Indians. A life-size statue of a prehistoric ground sloth and four dinosaur statues are along the garden trails. Guided tours are available. Daily dawn-dusk. Tours are given Wed. 9-3. Donations. Phone (386) 767-1735.

PORT ST. JOE (B-5) pop. 3,644, elev. 5′

CONSTITUTION CONVENTION MUSEUM STATE PARK, 1.5 mi. s. on US 98, preserves the site of Florida's first constitutional convention. Exhibits pertain to this event and other local history. Animated talking mannequins provide 2 minutes of closing remarks at the end of the tour. Allow 30 minutes minimum. Thurs.-Mon. 9-noon and 1-5 Eastern Time; closed Jan. 1, Thanksgiving and Dec. 25. Admission $1, under 6 free. Phone (850) 229-8029.

PUNTA GORDA (F-9) pop. 14,344, elev. 61′

Punta Gorda, the county seat, is Charlotte County's only incorporated community. The old city dock, on the banks of the Peace River, has been transformed into Fisherman's Village, a marina and shopping complex. Across the street, the Visual Arts Center houses several galleries and features revolving exhibits. The area offers cruises, boat rentals and fishing charters.

Octagon Wildlife Sanctuary, I-75 exit 143, provides refuge for injured or unwanted wild and exotic animals; phone (239) 543-1130. Another organization offering assistance to orphaned or injured animals is the Peace River Wildlife Center in Ponce de Leon Park, which attempts to rehabilitate and release native wildlife to their natural habitats; phone (941) 637-3830.

Charlotte County Chamber of Commerce: 326 W. Marion, Suite 112, Punta Gorda, FL 33950; phone (941) 639-2222.

BABCOCK WILDERNESS ADVENTURES is off I-75S exit 164 (southbound), 1 mi. n. on US 17, 15 mi. e. on SR 74, then 6 mi. s. on SR 31; or off I-75N exit 143 (northbound), 3 mi. e. on SR 78, then 9 mi. n. on SR 31, to 8000 SR 31. Visitors get a close look at rare Florida panthers, alligators, snakes, birds, bison and other native fauna and flora during the 1.5-hour swamp buggy tours through a working cattle ranch and the surrounding cypress swamps. Seasonal off-road bicycle tours also are offered. These 3-hour guided rides explore Florida ecosystems; reservations are required. Food is available.

Allow 2 hours minimum. Swamp buggy tours daily 9-3. Fare $17.95; under 12, $9.95. Reservations are required. AX, DS, MC, VI. Phone (800) 500-5583 for reservations. *See ad p. 79.*

[SAVE] **FLORIDA ADVENTURE MUSEUM** is 1 blk. n. of US 17, between US 41N and US 41S at 260 W. Retta Esplanade. This interactive museum houses changing exhibits exploring state and local history, natural history, natural science and military history. Allow 30 minutes minimum. Mon.-Fri. 10-5, Sat. 10-3; closed major holidays. Admission $2; under 13, $1. Phone (941) 639-3777.

KING FISHER CRUISE LINES, 1200 W. Retta Esplanade in Fisherman's Village, offers day cruises to the offshore islands of Cabbage Key or to Cayo Costa State Park. Half-day river and harbor cruises, deep-sea fishing trips, afternoon and evening cruises and seasonal trips, including a Christmas Canal Cruise, also are available. Cabbage Key cruises depart Tues., Thurs. and Sat. at 9. Cayo Costa cruises depart Tues., Thurs. and Sun. at 9. Schedules may vary; phone ahead. Full-day cruises $21.95; ages 3-12, $11. Reservations are recommended. AX, MC, VI. Phone (941) 639-0969.

QUINCY (A-6) pop. 6,982, elev. 187′

Established in 1828, the agricultural town of Quincy owed its early prosperity to the tobacco industry. The Quincy State Bank eventually persuaded its patrons to invest in the fledgling Coca-Cola Co., resulting in economic fortune for both the town and its citizens.

Soldiers from the battles of Natural Bridge and Olustee were treated in Quincy, a medical center during the Civil War. The town also served as a supply commissary for the Confederate Army. In 1868 a fire destroyed more than half the town, leading to an ordinance requiring that all new buildings be constructed of brick.

The 36-block historic district features landscaping, period lighting and Victorian-style buildings. Most structures were built in the late 1880s, although several houses date back to the 1840s.

Gadsden County Chamber of Commerce: 203 E. Jefferson St., P.O. Box 389, Quincy, FL 32353; phone (850) 627-9231.

Self-guiding tours: A brochure outlining a tour of the historic district is available from the chamber of commerce.

ST. AUGUSTINE (B-10) pop. 11,592, elev. 7'

As the oldest, continuously occupied European settlement in the United States, St. Augustine has played varied and prominent historic roles. Juan Ponce de León, in search of the legendary Fountain of Youth, landed in this area Apr. 3, 1513, and took possession of the region for Spain. In 1565 King Phillip II sent Pedro Menéndez de Avilés to colonize the new territory. Menéndez de Avilés arrived in Florida on the Feast Day of St. Augustine and named the landing site after the saint.

Its coastal location made the town both strategic and vulnerable. Pirates sacked St. Augustine in both the 16th and 17th centuries. Military importance soon came to the forefront as England extended its holdings southward down the coast. Spain responded by starting to build Castillo de San Marcos in 1672.

By the time St. Augustine was ceded to England in 1763, it had served as the seat of government for 30 missions as well as for all Spanish possessions in the regions of Florida and coastal Georgia. British loyalists from adjacent states sought refuge during the Revolutionary War.

In 1783 Florida was traded back to Spain. Encouraged by Spanish land grants, many Americans moved onto property vacated by the English. Florida became a U.S. possession in 1821, and during the Second Seminole War in the 1830s, St. Augustine resumed a military role.

The quiet coastal town came to life in the 1880s when Henry Flagler began to develop the area as a winter resort and playground. With a railway link provided from New York, plush hotels were built and leisure activities such as golf and yachting awaited the city's guests.

Still preserving strong evidence of its Spanish origin, the Old City is being restored to a likeness of its colonial days; much of the historic area north of the Plaza de la Constitución is complete. Typical Spanish houses, with walled patios enclosing Old World gardens, line the many narrow streets.

Tolomato Cemetery, also known as the Old Spanish Cemetery, is at Cordova Street between Orange and Saragossa streets. Formerly the site of the Christian Indian village of Tolomato, the cemetery served as a Catholic burial ground 1784-1892 and is the burial site of Augustin Verot, the first bishop of St. Augustine. The cemetery is only open by request; information is available at the rectory

entrance of the Cathedral of St. Augustine on Treasury Street.

South of the city, St. Augustine Beach provides a return to the present. Miles of wide, hard-packed sand beaches afford beach driving, swimming and surfing opportunities. Boating also is popular.

Tours of area attractions by horse-drawn carriage depart from the bayfront area next to Castillo de San Marcos. Costumed guides tell eerie stories about the city and its historic buildings as part of Ghost Tours of St. Augustine; phone (904) 461-4604. [SAVE] St. Augustine Scenic Cruise offers sightseeing cruises departing from St. Augustine Municipal Marina; phone (904) 824-1806 or (800) 542-8316. [SAVE] Gray Line guided bus tours explore the old city, St. Augustine's maritime history and archeology and the World Golf Hall of Fame; phone (888) 275-8902.

The Huguenot cemetery, between the City Gate and the Visitor Information Center, is open to the public anytime the gate is unlocked.

Note: Parking regulations are enforced strictly throughout the city. Yellow curbs are no-parking zones.

St. Augustine, Ponte Verde and The Beaches Visitors and Convention Bureau: 88 Riberia St., Suite 400, St. Augustine, FL 32084; phone (904) 829-1711 or (800) 653-2489. *See color ad p. 190.*

Shopping areas: St. Augustine Outlet Center and Belz Factory Outlet World are both off I-95 exit 318 on SR 16.

The Old City

CASTILLO DE SAN MARCOS NATIONAL MONUMENT, a Spanish fortress, is at Castillo Dr. and Avenida Menéndez. The oldest masonry fort in the United States, it was built 1672-95 of coquina, a soft local shellrock, as part of the defenses along the route of the treasure fleets. For many years the fort was the northernmost point of Spain's New World holdings.

The symmetrical fort has massive diamond-shaped bastions at each of its four corners, and 60 to 77 cannons once occupied the gun deck. Its walls, 12 feet thick at the base, 8 feet thick at the top and 33 feet high, are skirted by a moat on three sides. Part of the "Cubo Line," a palisaded city wall, has been rebuilt. A stairway leads to the gun deck overlooking the Old City Gate, quaint old streets and Matanzas Bay.

Until the mid-18th century this fortress defended St. Augustine; after one unsuccessful siege in 1702, the city was burned. The English acquired the fort and Florida from Spain in 1763 at the end of the French and Indian War. Following Charleston's fall during the Revolutionary War, Gen. Christopher Gadsden, a South Carolina patriot, was imprisoned in the fort; three signers of the Declaration of Independence were imprisoned in the city. Spain regained possession of Florida in 1784 as part of the Treaty of Paris.

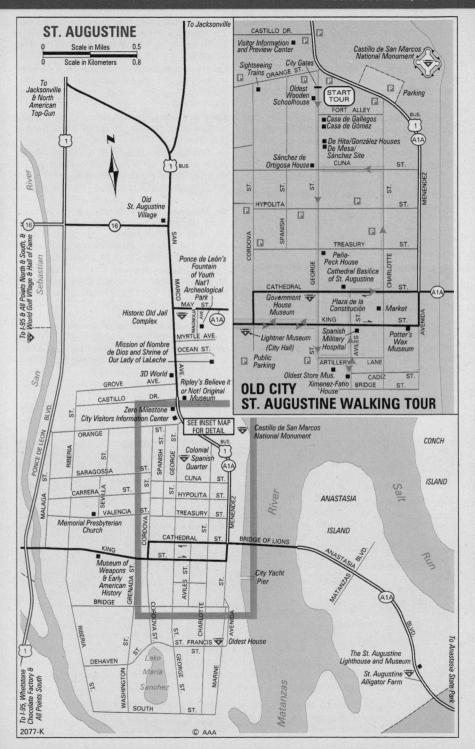

ST. AUGUSTINE

Scale in Miles   0   0.5
Scale in Kilometers   0   0.8

To Jacksonville

To Jacksonville & North American Top-Gun

To I-95 & All Points North & South, & World Golf Village & Hall of Fame

River Sebastian

San Sebastian BLVD.

PONCE DE LEON AVE.

To I-95, Whetstone Chocolate Factory & All Points South

2077-K

Old St. Augustine Village

Ponce de León's Fountain of Youth Nat'l Archeological Park

Historic Old Jail Complex

Mission of Nombre de Dios and Shrine of Our Lady of LaLeche

3D World

Ripley's Believe it or Not! Original Museum

Zero Milestone City Visitors Information Center

SEE INSET MAP FOR DETAIL

Colonial Spanish Quarter

Memorial Presbyterian Church

Museum of Weapons & Early American History

Oldest House

ORANGE ST.
SARAGOSSA ST.
CARRERA ST.
VALENCIA ST.
RIBERIA ST.
SEVILLA ST.
CORDOVA ST.
SPANISH ST.
GEORGE ST.
KING ST.
BRIDGE
RIBERIA ST.
DEHAVEN
WASHINGTON ST.
GRENADA ST.
CORDOVA ST.
AVILES ST.
CHARLOTTE
GEORGE ST.
MARINE ST.
ST. FRANCIS ST.
SOUTH ST.
Lake Maria Sanchez

CUNA ST.
HYPOLITA ST.
TREASURY ST.
CATHEDRAL ST.
MENENDEZ AVE.
AVENIDA

BRIDGE OF LIONS

City Yacht Pier

Castillo de San Marcos National Monument

CASTILLO DR.
Visitor Information and Preview Center
Sightseeing Trains   ORANGE ST.
City Gates
Oldest Wooden Schoolhouse
Castillo de San Marcos National Monument
Parking

START TOUR

FORT ALLEY
Casa de Gallegos
Casa de Gómez
De Hita/González Houses
De Mesa/Sánchez Site

Sánchez de Ortigosa House

CUNA ST.

HYPOLITA ST.
SPANISH ST.
TREASURY ST.

Peña-Peck House
Cathedral Basilica of St. Augustine

CATHEDRAL

Government House Museum
Plaza de la Constitución
Market

KING ST.

Lightner Museum (City Hall)
Spanish Military Hospital
Potter's Wax Museum

Public Parking

ARTILLERY LANE
Oldest Store Mus.
Ximenez-Fatio House
CADIZ ST.
BRIDGE ST.

CORDOVA ST.
SPANISH ST.
GEORGE ST.
CHARLOTTE ST.
MENENDEZ ST.
AVENIDA
MENENDEZ

OLD CITY
ST. AUGUSTINE WALKING TOUR

River

ANASTASIA ISLAND

CONCH ISLAND

Salt Run

ANASTASIA BLVD.

MATANZAS BLVD.

A1A BLVD.

The St. Augustine Lighthouse and Museum

St. Augustine Alligator Farm

To Anastasia State Park

Matanzas

© AAA

N

Upon the acquisition of Florida in 1821, the fortress became part of the U.S. coastal defense system. It also was used as a military prison. Seminole leader Osceola was confined in the fort during the Second Seminole War. The fort's final military use was for imprisonment of some court-martialed American soldiers during the Spanish-American War. It was decommissioned in 1900.

Exhibits trace its history, and cannons are fired Saturday and Sunday from Memorial Day through Labor Day. Metal detectors are prohibited. Allow 1 hour minimum. Daily 8:45-4:45; closed Dec. 25. Admission $5; ages 6-16, $2. Phone (904) -829-6506.

CATHEDRAL OF ST. AUGUSTINE, on Cathedral St. facing the plaza, is the seat of the oldest Catholic parish in the nation. Built in the 1790s, it was reconstructed after a fire in 1887. The original structure forms the nave. Tours daily at 1 and 3. Donations. Phone (904) 824-2806.

COLONIAL SPANISH QUARTER consists of restored and reconstructed buildings that reflect different aspects of Spanish colonial life. The Triay House contains an orientation center with period artifacts and informational displays. Costumed guides demonstrate 1740s crafts and lifestyles; of interest are the blacksmith, woodworker and textile crafts shops. Tickets are available at the Museum Store, 33 St. George St.

Allow 1 hour minimum. Daily 9-6; closed Dec. 25. Admission $6.50; over 62 and military with ID $5.50; ages 6-18, $4; family rate $13. Phone (904) 825-6830.

Casa de Gallegos, 21 St. George St., is a tabby (oyster shell and lime) house typical of the 1750s. Inside the lifestyles of early Spanish settlers are demonstrated.

Casa de Gómez, 23 St. George St., is a typical wooden house occupied by a Spanish soldier and his family in the 1750s.

De Hita/González Houses, 37 St. George St., are good examples of Spanish colonial homes. The González House presents demonstrations of textile arts. The De Hita House offers hands-on learning activities.

De Mesa/Sánchez Site began as a two-room coquina (shell-rock) house in the mid-18th century. Additions and modifications continued until the end of the 19th century. Much information about the area has been gleaned from the excavation.

Spanish Military Hospital, 4 blks. off St. George St. at 3 Aviles St., is a reconstruction of a military hospital of the second Spanish colonial period. Costumed guides re-enact the daily life of patients and staff in the 18th-century hospital. Five exhibit areas illustrate medical practices of the time and include an apothecary with period artifacts. Allow 30 minutes minimum. Daily 9-5; closed Dec. 25. Admission $2.50; under 18, $1. Phone (904) 825-6830.

GEM **GOVERNMENT HOUSE MUSEUM,** 48 King St., illustrates area history through a chronological series of exhibits and presentations. Displays feature an archeological exhibit, American Indian artifacts, treasure from Spanish shipwrecks and military and religious items. Allow 1 hour minimum. Daily 9-6; closed major holidays. Admission $2.50; senior citizens and military with ID $2; ages 6-18, $1. Phone (904) 825-5033.

GEM **LIGHTNER MUSEUM,** at King and Cordova sts., is housed in the former Alcazar Hotel, built by Henry Flagler in 1888. In 1948 Otto C. Lightner, the Chicago publisher and editor of *Hobbies* magazine, converted the empty hotel into a museum to contain his vast collection of art, antiques and other items.

Three floors display furnishings, costumes, Victorian art glass and natural history specimens. One room is devoted to a collection of Tiffany stained glass. Other highlights include Oriental art, art nouveau works and a Victorian village.

Nineteenth-century mechanical musical instruments are demonstrated daily at 11 and 2. The steam baths of the hotel still exist on the second floor. The former indoor swimming pool behind the building, one of the largest of its day, is now an antiques mall. Food is available. Allow 2 hours minimum. Daily 9-5; closed Dec. 25. Last admission 1 hour before closing. Admission $6; ages 12-18, $2. Phone (904) 824-2874.

OLD ST. AUGUSTINE VILLAGE, entrance on Cordova St. at Bridge St., occupies an entire city block. The nine buildings, all in their original locations, range from the 1790 Prince Murat House, through the 1899 Star General Store, to the 1910 William Dean Howells House. Costumed interpreters, various programs and occasional guided walking tours provide a vivid depiction of early Florida. Allow 1 hour minimum. Daily 9-5; closed Dec. 25. Admission $7; over 61, $6; ages 4-11, $5. Phone (904) 823-9722.

GEM **OLDEST HOUSE,** 14 St. Francis St. at the s. end of the seawall, also is known as the González-Alvarez House and is on a site occupied since the early 1600s. The present structure, with coquina walls and hand-hewn cedar beams, dates from the early 1700s. Records dating to 1763 identify Tomás González, an artilleryman at the Castillo de San Marcos, as the owner. Gerónimo Alvarez bought the house in 1790, and it remained in his family for almost 100 years.

During the British period 1763-83, the first of a number of alterations was made which brought the house into its current shape and size, reflecting both Spanish and British architectural styles. The house is furnished to represent its different periods; artifacts unearthed at the site are displayed.

An ornamental garden typifies plants grown by the Spanish, British and American occupants. Within the complex are two museums; one traces the city's history and contains the historical society's gallery, and the other, The Museum of Florida's Army, follows the army's history from 1565 to the present. Guided tours are available.

Allow 1 hour minimum. Daily 9-5; closed Dec. 25. Tours are given daily every half hour. Last admission 30 minutes before closing. Admission $5; over 55, $4.50; students with ID $3. MC, VI. Phone (904) 824-2872.

OLDEST STORE MUSEUM, 4 Artillery Ln., evokes turn-of-the-20th-century life with more than 100,000 items from the store's original stock. Antique vehicles include a steam tractor, a Model T Ford and a Conestoga wagon. Allow 30 minutes minimum. Mon.-Sat. 9-5, Sun. 10-5, June.-Aug.; Mon.-Sat. 10-4, Sun. noon-4, rest of year. Closed Dec. 24-25. Admission $5; ages 6-12, $1.50. Children must be with an adult. Phone (904) 829-9729.

OLDEST WOODEN SCHOOLHOUSE, 14 St. George St., was built 1750-60 of cypress and cedar and is among the nation's oldest. Automated mannequins representing the professor and his students dressed in period clothing relate the school's history and explain the barter system, subjects studied and the use of the dunce cap. Schoolbooks, slates, old maps and other artifacts are displayed. The kitchen, separated from the main building to reduce the risk of fire, is open to the public.

Allow 30 minutes minimum. Daily 9-5; closed Dec. 25. Admission $2.50; over 65 and military with ID $2; ages 6-12, $1.50. Phone (904) 824-0192.

SAVE **PEÑA-PECK HOUSE,** 143 St. George St., was built in the 1740s of native coquina stone. Originally the home of Royal Treasurer Juan Estaban de Peña, Dr. Seth Peck bought the property in 1837. Displays include early Spanish artifacts and Peck family furnishings from the 18th century. Allow 30 minutes minimum. Mon.-Fri. 12:30-4:30, Sat. 10:30-4:30, Sun. noon-4:30; closed Easter, Thanksgiving and Dec. 23-25. Admission $4.50; over 55, $3.50; ages 12-18, $2.50. MC, VI. Phone (904) 829-5064.

PLAZA DE LA CONSTITUCIÓN, bounded by Cathedral, King, Charlotte and St. George sts., was the central square around which the business section of the Old City was built and where the slave market was held. One end overlooks Matanzas Bay and opens into the approach to the Bridge of Lions. Spaniards erected the monument in the center of the plaza in 1813. The public marketplace at the east end is a reconstruction of one built in 1824.

POTTER'S WAX MUSEUM, 17 King St., faces the plaza. More than 170 life-size figures depict historically significant persons and events. In summer visitors may watch the craftspersons at work. Allow 30 minutes minimum. Daily 9-9, June 15-Labor Day; 9-5, rest of year. Closed Dec. 25. Admission $5.95; over 55, $4.95; ages 6-12, $2.75. AX, DS, MC, VI. Phone (904) 829-9056.

SIGHTSEEING TRAINS, 170 San Marco Ave., provides stop-offs at major points of interest, shops and restaurants over a 7-mile tour. Tours depart every 15-20 minutes daily 8:30-5. Fare (good for 3 consecutive days) $12; ages 6-12, $5. Package tours are available. Phone (904) 829-6545 or (800) 226-6545.

XIMENEZ-FATIO HOUSE, 20 Aviles St., is a well-preserved merchant's house and store dating to the Second Spanish Period 1783-1819. The house has been restored to the Territorial Period 1821-45, when it was operated as an inn. Guided tours are offered. Allow 30 minutes minimum. Thurs.-Sat. and Mon. 11-4, Sun. 1-4. Tours are conducted every half-hour. Last tour begins 30 minutes before closing. Donations. Phone (904) 829-3575.

⚠️ Walking Tour: The Old City

See map page 189.

The tour will take 1-2 hours, depending on your pace as well as the number of listed sites you visit and plaques you stop to read along the way. Those attractions appearing in bold type have detailed listings in The Old City section. Even if you decide not to visit a listed site, reading the listing when you reach that point should make the tour more interesting.

The best place to park is at the Visitor Information Center, 10 Castillo Dr., in front of the Castillo de San Marcos. Keep in mind that no automobiles are permitted on St. George Street in the restoration area.

St. Augustine, compact and full of history, is a great place for a stroll. Influenced by the Timucuan Indians and placed under Spanish and English rule before becoming a U.S. territory, the city retains the flavors of its multicultured past. In the early 18th century, the walled city was entered through the City Gates, and this remains a logical place to begin a walk through Old St. Augustine. The Spanish built the wall surrounding the city in 1739 for defense; this gateway connected the wall, which was constructed of palm logs, dirt, cacti and coquina (soft limestone containing shell and coral fragments, quarried locally on Anastasia Island). The pillars, also made of coquina, were added in 1808. Closed at dusk, the gates protected the north end of the city. A replica of the log wall runs from the gates to the **Castillo de San Marcos,** which you can see by looking east toward the water.

The Huguenot Cemetery, just north of the City Gates, serves as a final resting place for many non-Catholics, not solely French immigrants. An outbreak of yellow fever coupled with the fact that the Catholic cemetery inside the city walls would not accept Protestants brought about its founding in 1821.

Begin by heading south on narrow St. George Street, where second-story balconies add interest to simple buildings and whitewashed walls hide courtyards. More than 50 houses and craft shops have been restored or reconstructed on this pedestrians-only lane, where it seems there are always groups of school children on field trips.

The first spot the kids flock to is the **Oldest Wooden Schoolhouse,** on the right at 14 St. George St. The cedar building also served as a guardhouse during the Seminole Wars due to its proximity to the City Gates. If you can beat the crowd, check out its tabby floors (a mixture of crushed oyster shells and lime) and wooden peg construction.

The major part of the restoration area begins as you cross Fort Alley. Note the National Greek Orthodox Shrine, 41 St. George St., dedicated to the Greek colony of New Smyrna, where Greek immigrants were kept as servants. Its St. Photios Chapel is decorated with icons and frescoes depicting Greek Orthodox theology. Gold leaf highlights much of the chapel's artwork, and sounds of Byzantine music fill the halls.

Colonial workers at the reconstructed **Colonial Spanish Quarter** (the entrance is via the Triay House at 29 St. George St.) go about their work as if it's just another day in the mid-18th century. Clad in period dress, gardeners tend to their vegetables; woodworkers repair furniture under a thatched hut; and blacksmiths fashion nails. Note the citrus tree planted by the Spanish to aid in the prevention of scurvy. You might find Señora Gallegos cooking dinner on a fogon (Mediterranean stove) in the two-room **Casa de Gallegos.** Casa de Ribera is decorated with antique furnishings, and **Casa de Gómez** is a Spanish soldier's dwelling with a small store. Other noteworthy structures in the village are the **De Hita/González Houses** and the coquina **De Mesa/Sánchez Site,** where costumed interpreters perform various household chores.

On the west side of the block at the corner of Cuna Street is the Sánchez de Ortigosa House. Nearby are the reconstructed wooden buildings comprising the Peso de Burgo/Pellicer House, occupied by a Minorcan family 1763-83.

Proceed along St. George, enjoying the warm tones of ancient coquina stonework and the glimpses of courtyards between many of the buildings. At 105 St. George is the Sánchez House, a restored coquina and masonry building (now home to a crystal shop); house tours are offered.

As you cross Hypolita Street, look out for the sightseeing tram that shuffles by, accompanied by clanging bells.

Glance down Treasury Street, one of the narrowest streets in the Old City. On the left, the **Peña-Peck House** occupies the corner of Treasury and St. George; built in the 1690s for the Spanish treasurer, it was later occupied by a British doctor whose wife often used the house for high-society get-togethers. The art and furnishings reflect an extravagant lifestyle.

The tower on your left is part of the large **Cathedral Basilica of St. Augustine,** which faces the Plaza de la Constitución. Founded in 1565, the parish holds what are said to be the country's oldest parish records, dating from 1594. The present cathedral was built in 1797 in the Spanish Mission style; following a fire in 1887 it was restored and its adjacent Spanish Renaissance-style bell tower was added. Inside the church, oil paintings are replicas of those found in the Vatican's Pauline Chapel. Victorian stained glass and sculpted marble also adorn the interior. (You might choose to visit the church later, as the route circles back this way.)

Cross Cathedral Street and continue south along St. George. To your left is the **Plaza de la Constitución,** which extends east toward the bay. Established in 1598 by an edict from King Phillip II, it was the hub of the original settlement. In the center is a monument dedicated to the Spanish Constitution of 1812.

The building to your right on the corner of St. George and King streets is the **Government House Museum.** Dating to the 1700s, the site served as the headquarters for Spanish, English and territory governors 1595-1821. It is now home to the St. Augustine Preservation Board and contains interesting artifacts and Spanish treasure.

Turn right at King Street. At Cordova Street, the Casa Monica Hotel will be on your left. This Spanish/Moorish-style structure, one of three hotels owned by railroad magnate Henry Flagler, has a long history. Born as a grand hotel in 1887, it later served as the county courthouse for nearly 30 years before reopening in its present state.

Now look to the right. You can't miss the former Ponce de León Hotel—a huge Moorish-style palace with tall spires, turrets and a red-tiled roof. Built in 1888 by Henry Flagler as part of his grand plan to turn the city into an exclusive winter retreat, the hotel was the country's first major building to be crafted using poured concrete. The interior is posh: It features Tiffany stained glass, imported marble and carved oak. A beautiful courtyard, open to the public, leads to the foyer. Since 1968 the building has served as the main hall of Flagler College, and its ornate rotunda has been converted into what is arguably the fanciest student dining room. Free guided tours are given during the summer.

Across the street from Flagler College is the third of Henry Flagler's hotels—the Spanish Renaissance Revival-style Alcazar Hotel, which also opened in 1888. Its design was based on the royal palace in Seville, Spain. Palm trees, fountains and a statue of Pedro Menéndez front the large building, which shelters City Hall and the **Lightner Museum.** Flagler would be proud—the museum's collection of decorative arts is quite affluent.

If you like, continue 1 block west on King Street to the **Museum of Weapons and Early American History.** Next door is the funky Zorayda Castle, a smaller re-creation of the 13th-century Spanish Alhambra in Granada.

Retrace your steps along King to St. George. At the corner of St. George and King is Trinity Episcopal Church, established in 1830 and said to be the oldest Protestant church in Florida. Turn right onto St. George and make a left on narrow Artillery

Lane to enter the city's oldest section. The **Oldest Store Museum** (originally the C.F. Hamblen Store) dates to the early 1800s; its original wooden shelves are crammed with everything from potions to apple peelers to antique signs. Back in its heyday, shoppers could have eyeglasses made and get their teeth cleaned here.

At Aviles Street, turn right. At the corner of Cadiz Street is the two-story **Ximenez-Fatio House** (it's the one surrounded by the white picket fence). This late 18th-century coquina house has been restored and is furnished to reflect an 1850s boarding house.

Traipse back on Aviles, where galleries and boutiques reside. On the right, at 3 Aviles, is the **Spanish Military Hospital** (once called the Hospital of our Lady Guadalupe), which has displays depicting day-to-day operations of the 18th century.

Head back to the Plaza de la Constitución by continuing north on Aviles. The market building to your right is a replica of the original. Turn right on Cathedral Street and walk for one block to Charlotte Street. From here you can see the statue (on the east end of the plaza) of Juan Ponce de León, who landed in 1513—he points east toward Matanzas Bay and the Bridge of Lions, a Mediterranean-style bridge built in 1927. Tile-roofed towers, arches and lion statues grace the structure, which is on the National Register of Historic Places.

Turn left on Charlotte and proceed north. A three-block walk past boutiques, antiques shops and bed and breakfast inns leads to Cuna Street. Look northeast from the corner of Charlotte and Cuna for a good view of the fort and bay. Turn left on Cuna, where more stores in restored buildings entice shoppers. At St. George, turn right. The City Gates, where you began your tour, is about a block north.

Other Points of Interest

3D WORLD is at 28 San Marco Ave. Theater presentations include "Fantastic Fountains at Saint Augustine," a water and light show, and two 3-D motion-simulator rides. Allow 1 hour minimum. Daily 10-10, June-Aug.; 10-8, rest of year. Admission $10, under 42 inches tall free for water and light show only. AX, DS, MC, VI. Phone (904) 824-1220.

HISTORIC OLD JAIL COMPLEX, 167 San Marco Ave., encompasses the Florida Heritage Museum, The Old Jail and Old Town Trolley Tours of St. Augustine. Daily 8:30-5; closed Easter, Thanksgiving and Dec. 25. Combination rates are available. Phone (904) 829-3800.

Florida Heritage Museum depicts Florida's growth from early Indian cultures through the Flagler era. Personal items and pictures of Henry Flagler are displayed along with a model railroad tracing the route he established between Jacksonville and Key West. Additional exhibits focus on the Florida cracker, Fort Mose, Confederate items, 16th-century Spanish weapons, a life-size sunken ship and its treasures, and a replica of an Indian village. Allow 1 hour minimum. Admission $5; ages 6-12, $4.

The Old Jail contains a large collection of weapons and displays that illustrate prison life in early St. Augustine. Costumed guides portray the sheriff and his deputies. Visitors may tour the family's living quarters, which are in the same building as the prisoners' cells. Newspaper articles and photographs depict the history of the jail. Allow 30 minutes minimum. Guided tours depart every 15 minutes daily 8:30-4:30; closed Easter, Thanksgiving and Dec. 25. Admission $5; ages 6-12, $4.

Old Town Trolley Tours of St. Augustine offers a narrated 1-hour tour of the city with stops at 20 sites. Passengers may reboard the open-air trolleys at their own pace. Tours depart every 15-20 minutes daily 8:30-5. Fare (includes admission to Florida Heritage Museum) $15; ages 6-12, $5. MC, VI. Phone (904) 829-3800.

MEMORIAL PRESBYTERIAN CHURCH is at Valencia and Sevilla sts. Henry Flagler built the Venetian Renaissance structure in 1890 as a memorial to his daughter. Construction was completed in less than a year, although the stained-glass windows took an additional 11 years to complete. Guides provide a brief overview of the church's history. Allow 30 minutes minimum. Mon.-Sat. 9-4:30, Sun. 12:30-4:30. Donations. Phone (904) 829-6451.

MISSION OF NOMBRE DE DIOS is 5 blks. n. of the city gate on San Marco Ave. Pedro Menéndez de Avilés landed here Sept. 8, 1565, and established the first permanent community. A 208-foot stainless-steel cross marks the site of the founding of St. Augustine. The Shrine of Our Lady of La Leche and a small museum are on the grounds. Allow 1 hour minimum. Grounds daily 7-6. Mission, museum and shrine daily 7-6; closed Easter and Dec. 25. Donations. Phone (904) 824-2809.

MUSEUM OF WEAPONS AND EARLY AMERICAN HISTORY, 81-C King St., displays weapons of all types including cane guns, swords, muskets and unusual firearms. Other exhibits include 18th-century shipwreck items, Indian artifacts, a large Civil War display, the only known Confederate Florida flag and artifacts relating to American history. Allow 30 minutes minimum. Daily 9:30-5; closed Dec. 25. Admission $4; ages 6-12, $1. Phone (904) 829-3727.

NORTH AMERICAN TOP-GUN, at the St. Augustine Airport on US 1, offers flights and air-to-air combat training in World War II fighter-type aircraft. Passengers can choose sightseeing, aerobatic or fighter pilot flights, from a 15-minute ride to a 5-hour air-combat mission. A videotape of the flight is offered. Daily 9-5. Fare $190-$1,490. Reservations are required. AX, DS, MC, VI. Phone (904) 823-3505 or (800) 257-1636.

PONCE DE LEÓN'S FOUNTAIN OF YOUTH NATIONAL ARCHEOLOGICAL PARK, e. of SR A1A (San Marco Ave.) on Williams St. to 11 Magnolia Ave., is on the site claimed to be Ponce de León's landing place Apr. 3, 1513. The park contains the Timucuan Indian spring Ponce de León hoped was the Fountain of Youth. A cross of coquina stones excavated in 1909 is thought to be Ponce de León's claiming landmark. Remains of Christian Indian burials and archeological exhibits of early St. Augustine are on the grounds. Additional features include a planetarium with an audiovisual display about star navigation and a two-story globe displaying Spanish discoveries.

Allow 1 hour minimum. Daily 9-5; closed Dec. 25. Admission $5.75; over 60, $4.75; ages 6-12, $2.75. Phone (904) 829-3168 or (800) 356-8222.

SAVE **RIPLEY'S BELIEVE IT OR NOT! ORIGINAL MUSEUM** is at 19 San Marco Ave. Entrepreneur Robert L. Ripley opened his first permanent exhibit of oddities and curiosities here in 1950. Castle Warden, a Moorish Revival mansion built in 1887 for a Philadelphia industrialist and later operated as a hotel by Marjorie Kinnan Rawlings, now houses more than 750 exhibits, from shrunken heads and torture devices to life-size wax figures and unusual works of art.

Allow 1 hour minimum. Daily 9-9, Memorial Day-Labor Day; 9-8, early Mar. to day before Memorial Day; 9-7, rest of year. Admission $9.95; over 54, $7.95; ages 5-12, $5.95. AX, DS, MC, VI. Phone (904) 824-1606.

ST. AUGUSTINE ALLIGATOR FARM, 1.75 mi. s.e. on SR A1A, on Anastasia Island, features a complete collection of the 23 crocodilian species, including rare white alligators. An elevated walkway winds through a rookery and over an alligator swamp. Florida wildlife shows are presented hourly. Allow 2 hours minimum. Daily 9-6, June-Aug.; 9-5, rest of year. Admission $14.25; ages 5-11, $8.50. AX, DS, MC, VI. Phone (904) 824-3337. *See color ad.*

ST. AUGUSTINE LIGHTHOUSE AND MUSEUM is 1 mi. s.e. on SR A1A, then n. on Red Cox Dr. on Anastasia Island. St. Augustine's maritime past is reflected in this working lighthouse and restored keeper's house. Visitors may climb the 219 stairs to the top of the tower for a panoramic view of the city and its beaches. Highlights include exhibits illustrating the lives of lightkeepers and their families and the men and women of the U.S. Coast Guard who were stationed in St. Augustine during World War II. Shipwreck artifacts also are featured.

Daily 9-6; closed Easter, Thanksgiving and Dec. 24-25. Lighthouse tower opens 15 minutes after the museum. Lighthouse and museum $6.50; over 54, $5.50; ages 7-11, $4. Museum only $4; over 54, $3; ages 7-11, $2. Under age 7 and under 4 feet tall are not admitted to the lighthouse tower. Phone (904) 829-0745.

WHETSTONE CHOCOLATE FACTORY, 2 Coke Rd., offers self-guiding tours of its factory. Visitors can see a high-speed molding plant, the packing room and the specialty room where chocolates are made. A 15-minute videotape introduces visitors to the factory. Allow 1 hour minimum. Mon.-Sat. 10-5; closed Thanksgiving and Dec. 25. Prime production times are 10-2. Free. Phone (904) 825-1700, ext. 25, for tour information. *See color ad.*

WORLD GOLF VILLAGE AND HALL OF FAME, .5 mi. w. of I-95 exit 323, is a showcase for the game of golf. In addition to the sport's hall of fame, the complex also consists of the Walk of Champions, an IMAX theater, several golf courses, hotels, a convention center and shopping.

The hall of fame pays tribute to the history of the game and honors the world's greatest golfers. Interactive exhibits allow visitors to test their golfing skills as well as experience the joy of sinking a hole-in-one. Collections of golfing artifacts and videotape presentations help explain the game, while the swing analyzer and putting areas allow visitors to participate. Guided tours are available. Food is available.

Daily 10-6. Admission $10; over 49 and students with ID $8; ages 5-12, $5. IMAX theater $9; over 49, ages 3-12 and students and military with ID $7.

Combination tickets are available. AX, DS, MC, VI. Phone (904) 940-4123.

ZERO MILESTONE is at Castillo Dr. and San Marco Ave. The coquina ball marks the eastern terminus of both the Old Spanish Trail, which linked the missions between St. Augustine and Pensacola, and the first transcontinental highway within the United States. Daily 24 hours. Free.

WINERIES
• **San Sebastian Winery**, 157 King St. Mon.-Sat. 10-6, Sun. 11-6; closed Jan. 1, Easter, Thanksgiving and Dec. 25. Phone (904) 826-1594 or (888) 352-9463.

ST. CLOUD—*see Orlando p. 179.*

ST. MARKS (B-6) pop. 272, elev. 7'

In 1836 a railroad was built to connect Tallahassee with St. Marks. Now dismantled, the Tallahassee-St. Marks Historic Railroad State Trail offers a 16-mile paved trail for bicyclists, hikers, horseback riders and skaters. For additional information phone (850) 922-6007.

ST. MARKS NATIONAL WILDLIFE REFUGE, off US 98 s. of Newport, covers approximately 68,500 acres along the Gulf of Mexico. The refuge borders Apalachee Bay and extends from the Aucilla River west to the Ochlockonee River. Thirty-two miles of the Florida Trail pass through the refuge. Varied wildlife can be observed all year; concentrations of waterfowl can be seen during fall and winter. The refuge is home to the historic St. Marks Lighthouse which was built in 1831, as well as several other historic sites.

Refuge visitor center open Mon.-Fri. 8-4, Sat.-Sun. 10-5. The refuge is open daily dawn-dusk; closed federal holidays. Admission $4 per private vehicle, $1 per person arriving by bicycle. Phone (850) 925-6121.

SAN MARCOS DE APALACHE HISTORIC STATE PARK, off SR 363, 1 mi. s.w. on Old Fort Rd., displays Indian, Spanish and Civil War artifacts. The interpretive center is on the site of a fort built by the Spanish in 1679 at the confluence of the Wakulla and St. Marks rivers and later occupied by English, Confederate and Federal troops. Outside are a military cemetery and the remains of the fort and earthworks. Allow 30 minutes minimum. Thurs.-Mon. 9-5; closed Jan. 1, Thanksgiving and Dec. 25. Grounds free. Museum $1, under 6 free. Phone (850) 925-6216 or (850) 922-6007.

ST. PETE BEACH—*see Tampa Bay p. 230.*

ST. PETERSBURG—*see Tampa Bay p. 204.*

SANFORD—*see Orlando p. 179.*

SANIBEL (G-9) pop. 6,064, elev. 6'

Sanibel is on a resort island of the same name; access to the island is by a toll causeway ($3 access, free egress) from Punta Rassa. This barrier island is known for its lighthouse, lush vegetation, extensive beaches, abundant bird life and, perhaps most of all, seashells. Each tide brings thousands of shells onto the fine sand beaches.

When Ponce de León discovered the southwest coast of Florida in 1513, he named it *Costa de Caracoles,* or "Coast of Seashells." The apparently smooth harbor at the southern end of this chain of islands later was designated on a Spanish map as *Puerto S. Nibel,* south level port. *S.* also is the Spanish abbreviation for *San,* or saint; through an error, subsequent maps designated this harbor as *Puerto de San Nibel.*

The traditional, and less prosaic, explanation of Sanibel's name is that pirate José Gaspar was so charmed by this lovely island that he named it after Santa Isabella, a beautiful queen of Spain.

The many paved trails beneath overhanging trees make bicycling a favorite mode of transportation. Moped and bicycle rentals are available. Public beach parking is limited on Sanibel Island and regulations are enforced strictly. For information about designated parking areas contact the Sanibel Visitors Center.

A bridge connects Sanibel Island with Captiva Island. Some historians believe that the incident that gave Captiva its name was one that was similar to that of Pocahontas. In 1528 Juan Ortiz was captured by the Calusa Indians and held captive on the island. Facing execution, Ortiz escaped to a friendly Indian tribe with help from the chief's daughter. In 1539 he was released to Hernando de Soto and became his interpreter. Visitors can see the remains of the ceremonial shell mounds built by the Calusa.

Sanibel Visitors Center: 1159 Causeway Rd., Sanibel, FL 33957; phone (239) 472-1080.

THE BAILEY-MATTHEWS SHELL MUSEUM, 3075 Sanibel-Captiva Rd., features 30 exhibits of seashells from around the world. Displays are devoted to shells in art and history, shell habitat, rare specimens, fossil shells and common Sanibel-Captiva shells. A children's learning lab features hands-on play areas, games, displays and a tank with indigenous mollusks. A 30-minute slide presentation is given on the hour, and a children's videotape also is shown. Allow 1 hour minimum. Tues.-Sun. 10-4; closed major holidays. Admission $5; ages 8-16, $3. Phone (239) 395-2233 or (888) 679-6450.

CAPTIVA CRUISES departs from South Seas Resort on Captiva Island. Among cruises offered are 1- to 3-hour nature, natural history and sunset cruises, 3-hour shelling trips, 4- to 5-hour cruises to Cabbage Key or Useppa Island, and 5- and 6-hour excursions to Boca Grande or Cayo Costa.

Tours offered daily. Dolphin-wildlife and sunset cruises depart 4 and dusk; shelling trips at 9 and 1; island cruises at 10 and 10:30. Closed Dec. 25. Fare $17.50-$35; ages 4-12, $10-$17.50. Reservations are required. Inquire about policies regarding refunds, inclement weather and minimum number of passengers. AX, MC, VI. Phone (239) 472-5300.

J.N. "DING" DARLING NATIONAL WILDLIFE REFUGE, 1 Wildlife Dr., is named for the editorial cartoonist and pioneer conservationist. The refuge encompasses more than 6,000 acres of wetlands and island uplands. Facilities include canoe trails, a birdwatching tower, a wildlife drive, an interpretive trail and marinas. A list of more than 200 bird species that can be viewed is available from the headquarters at the refuge entrance.

Wildlife Drive open Sat.-Thurs. 7:30 a.m.-30 minutes before dusk. Visitor center open daily 9-5, Nov.-Apr.; 9-4, rest of year. Bailey Tract and walking trails open dawn-dusk. Admission $5 per private vehicle, $1 for pedestrians and bicyclists. Phone (239) 472-1100.

Sanibel-Captiva Conservation Foundation, 3333 Sanibel-Captiva Rd., has guided nature trail tours, a butterfly house, an exhibit with a touch tank, and a reception center with displays about the ecology of area wetlands. Mon.-Sat. 8:30-4, mid-Nov. to mid-Apr.; Mon.-Fri. 8:30-3, rest of year. Admission $3, under 17 free. AX, DS, MC, VI. Phone (239) 472-2329.

SANIBEL HISTORICAL VILLAGE AND MUSEUM, 950 Dunlop Rd., exhibits local artifacts and memorabilia in a 1913 Florida "cracker" house. Early photographs and documents trace the history of Sanibel from its pioneer days, while archeological finds document the prehistory of the island. The 1898 Burnap Cottage, the Rutland House and the Morning Glory Cottage, a 1926 post office, a 1927 tearoom and the 1927 Bailey's General Store and Gas Station have been moved to the site and restored in period. A 1926 Model T pickup truck is displayed.

Wed.-Sat. 10-4, Sun. noon-4, Dec. 1-Easter; Wed.-Sat. 10-1, day after Easter to mid-Aug. and first Wed. in Nov.-Nov. 30. Admission $3. Phone (239) 472-4648.

SARASOTA (F-8) pop. 52,715, elev. 18′

See map page 198.

Although the origin of its name is not clear, the town has been a fixture on Sarasota Bay since the 1700s. The population was augmented by Scottish settlers in the 1880s, and the area became popular as a resort in the early part of the 20th century.

The circus is an integral part of Sarasota's past. In 1927 John Ringling selected the town for his Ringling Brothers and Barnum & Bailey Circus and made it his home. He exerted a major influence on the growth and development of the city because people from all over the world came to Sarasota to star in his show.

Sarasota, including the offshore islands of Casey Key, Lido Key, Longboat Key, St. Armand Key and Siesta Key, is a beach resort and art community. Hotels and residential and commercial areas ring Sarasota Bay, and the islands offer 35 miles of beaches that border the blue waters of the Gulf.

In the mainland section of the city is an array of performing arts groups, including the Asolo Theatre

Company, The Players, Sarasota Opera, the Florida West Coast Symphony, Sarasota Ballet of Florida, the Florida String Quartet, Florida Symphonic Band and several vocal and chamber ensembles as well as an active theater district.

Performing arts facilities include The F.S.U. Center for the Performing Arts *(see attraction listing)*; Van Wezel Performing Arts Hall, 777 N. Tamiami Tr.; the Sarasota Opera House, 61 N. Pineapple Ave.; and the Florida West Coast Symphony Center, 709 N. Tamiami Tr. The Golden Apple Dinner Theatre, 25 N. Pineapple Ave., presents entertainment from drama to musicals.

Since Sarasota is the city where golf was introduced to Florida from Scotland and where the first course was laid out in 1886, it is understandable that the sport remains popular; more than 30 courses are within minutes of downtown.

During March, Ed Smith Sports Complex at 12th Street and Tuttle Avenue is the spring training home for baseball's Cincinnati Reds; phone (941) 954-4101, ext. 5200. Beginning Dec. 1 and throughout spring training, ticket information for Reds games is available at (941) 954-4464. The Sarasota Red Sox, the class A affiliate of the Boston Red Sox, take to the field April through early September; phone (941) 365-4460.

Sarasota Ski-A-Rees presents a free water ski show each Sunday from late January through the end of April at Ken Thompson Park on City Island near the aquarium; phone (941) 388-1666.

Greyhound racing takes place from late December to mid-April at Sarasota Kennel Club on Old Bradenton Road; phone (941) 355-7744.

Note: Policies vary concerning admittance of children to pari-mutuel betting facilities. Phone for information.

Visitor Information Center: 655 N. Tamiami Tr., Sarasota, FL 34236; phone (941) 957-1877 or (800) 522-9799.

Shopping areas: Sarasota Square Mall, 8201 S. Tamiami Tr., includes Burdines, Dillard's, JCPenney and Sears among its 90 stores. St. Armands Circle and the vicinity contain more than 150 shops. Dillard's, Burdines and Saks Fifth Avenue are at South Gate Mall, 3501 S. Tamiami Tr.

ENTERPRISE SAILING CHARTERS depart from Marina Jack Bayfront Birth E19 near jct. John Ringling Blvd. and US 41. The tour company offers excursions in the waters of Sarasota Bay and the Gulf of Mexico aboard a three-sail sailboat that can accommodate up to 12 passengers. A sunset cruise is available. Food is available. Allow 2 hours minimum. Daily 8-8. Fare $35-$55. Reservations are required. AX, DS, MC, VI. Phone (941) 951-1833 or (888) 232-7768.

THE F.S.U. CENTER FOR THE PERFORMING ARTS, 5555 N. Tamiami Tr., is an arts complex whose ornate interior is a reconstruction of a 1903 Scottish opera house. The complex houses the

Florida State University Asolo Conservatory for Actor Training and the professional Asolo Theatre Company. The Asolo Theatre Company offers performances in the 500-seat Mertz Theatre November-June, while student performances are staged in the 161-seat Cook Theatre. Although the schedule varies, tours generally are available Wed.-Sat. at 10 and 11, Nov.-June. For tour information or theater reservations phone (941) 351-8000 or (800) 361-8388.

GULFCOAST WONDER & IMAGINATION ZONE (G.WIZ), 1001 Boulevard of the Arts, encourages learning through hands-on activities. In addition to exploring science, machinery and electricity, visitors can play the laser harp and build a robot. A Kids' Lab area is aimed at preschoolers. Crafts and educational demonstrations are given Saturday afternoon. Picnicking is permitted.

Allow 1 hour minimum. Tues.-Sat. 10-5, Sun 1-5; closed Jan. 1, Easter, Thanksgiving and Dec. 25. Admission $7; over 54, $6; ages 2-18, $5. All children must be with an adult. Phone (941) 906-1851.

THE JOHN AND MABLE RINGLING MUSEUM OF ART is 4 mi. n., just w. of US 41 at Sarasota/Bradenton Airport. The fortune John Ringling derived from his circus and vast real estate investments was well spent on his art

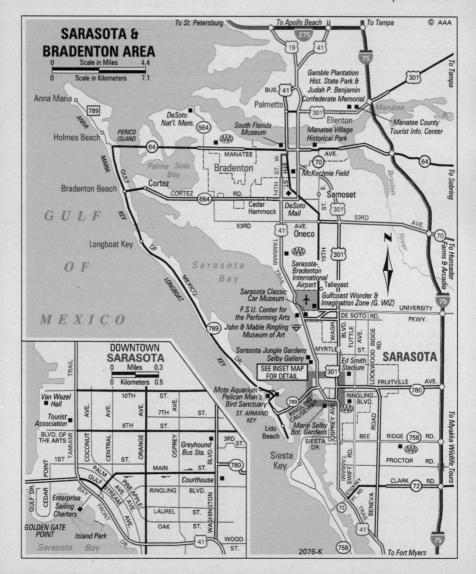

museum and early 1920s estate. The 66-acre complex, decorated with statues and dotted with banyan trees and Cuban laurels, offers flower gardens, sitting areas and a view of Sarasota Bay.

The museum was built in Italian Renaissance style, with an inner garden courtyard studded with reproductions of many world-famous sculptures and dominated by a bronze cast of Michelangelo's "David." The collection of paintings includes works from the 14th to 20th centuries, representing Western European cultures and emphasizing the baroque period.

The museum also has a collection of 17th-century Italian paintings, an extensive Peter Paul Rubens collection, modern works and temporary exhibits. Food is available.

Allow 3 hours minimum. Daily 10-5:30; closed Jan. 1, Thanksgiving and Dec. 25. Grounds free. Admission (also includes The Museum of the Circus and Cà d'Zan) $9, senior citizens $8, under 12 free; Florida students and teachers free with ID. AX, MC, VI. Phone (941) 359-5700.

Cà d'Zan (Ringling Winter Residence) was completed in 1926 at a cost of $1.5 million. The 30-room, terra-cotta mansion resembles a Venetian palace. Marble, tapestries and elaborately carved and gilded furniture dominate the interior. Tour sizes are limited; an admission time is provided with museum entrance.

The Museum of the Circus consists of displays of gilded parade wagons, calliopes, costumes, posters, photographs and a variety of circus memorabilia as well as changing exhibitions.

[SAVE] **MARIE SELBY BOTANICAL GARDENS,** US 41S at 811 S. Palm Ave., occupies 9 acres of lush gardens. The gardens specialize in epiphytes, or air plants. Among plants featured in the varied gardens are orchids, Amazonian bromeliads, carnivorous pitcher plants, cypress trees, water lilies, succulent plants, giant bamboo and banyan trees. The Baywalk Sanctuary Canopy Walk features an elevated boardwalk that winds through a mangrove swamp. Other features include a butterfly garden, a museum of 18th-century through contemporary botanical art and a learning center engaged in rainforest research. Food is available.

Allow 1 hour, 30 minutes minimum. Daily 10-5; closed Dec. 25. Admission $10; ages 6-11, $5. Phone (941) 366-5731, ext. 221.

[SAVE] **MOTE AQUARIUM** is on City Island between Longboat Key and St. Armands Key at 1600 Ken Thompson Pkwy. On view in the aquarium's more than 50 exhibits are manatees, sharks, sea turtles, eels and many of Southwest Florida's plants, fish and invertebrates. Visitors can touch stingrays, horseshoe crabs and other marine life in a 30-foot tank and view three research areas at Mote Marine Laboratory. Boat tours of local waters are available aboard the *Sarasota Bay Explorer.* Food is available.

Allow 1 hour minimum. Daily 10-5. Admission $12; ages 4-12, $8. Additional fee for boat tours. AX, DS, MC, VI. Phone (941) 388-2451 for the museum, (941) 388-4200 for the boat, or (800) 691-6683.

MYAKKA WILDLIFE TOURS, 9 mi. e. of I-75 exit 205 via SR 72, offers narrated tram tours through the wildlife habitats in Myakka River State Park *(see Recreation Chart and the AAA Southeastern CampBook).* Narrated airboat cruises on Upper Myakka Lake interpret the ecology of the lake and offer views of the animals. Binoculars are suggested.

Allow 1 hour minimum. Tram tours daily at 1 and 2:30, Dec. 16-May 31. Airboat cruises daily at 10, 11:30 and 1 (also at 2:30, Dec. 16-May 31). Fare for each tour $8; ages 6-12, $4. Apply for boarding pass upon arrival. Phone (941) 365-0100.

PELICAN MAN'S BIRD SANCTUARY is s. of Longboat Key at s. end of New Pass Bridge at 1708 Ken Thompson Pkwy., off SR 789. Dedicated to the rehabilitation of sick and injured birds, the sanctuary also serves as an education center. A boardwalk winds through the parklike setting, which contains habitats for a variety of birds including pelicans, herons, storks and sandhill cranes. Hawks, ospreys and owls can be viewed in the Birds of Prey Center. Guided tours are available. Allow 30 minutes minimum. Daily 10-5. Admission $4, children $2. Phone (941) 388-4444.

SARASOTA CLASSIC CAR MUSEUM is 3.5 mi. n. at jct. US 41 and University Pkwy., 1 blk. s. of Sarasota/Bradenton Airport. More than 85 vintage and classic vehicles are featured, including four cars belonging to by John and Mable Ringling and John Lennon's Mercedes. Antique cameras and photographs, arcade games and collectibles also are displayed. Guided tours are offered. Allow 1 hour, 30 minutes minimum. Daily 9-6; closed Dec. 25. Admission $8.50; senior citizens $7.65; ages 13-17, $5.75; ages 6-12, $4. AX, MC, VI. Phone (941) 355-6228.

SARASOTA JUNGLE GARDENS is .25 mi. w. of US 41 via Myrtle St., at 3701 Bayshore Rd. Trails wind through a 10-acre tropical jungle of palms, seasonal flowering shrubs and unusual plants. The Flamingo Lagoon harbors flamingos, swans and native waterfowl. Leopards, alligators, wallabies, lemurs, monkeys, cockatoos and macaws are housed along the jungle trails. The Gardens of Christ display hand-carved dioramas depicting the life of Jesus. Children's highlights include a "Kiddie Jungle" playground and a bird posing area; pony rides are available on weekends.

Five wildlife shows, including Birds of Prey, Critters 'n Things, Meet the Keeper, Reptile Encounter and Birds of the Rain Forest, are presented twice daily. Food is available. Allow 2 hours minimum. Daily 9-5; closed Dec. 25. Admission $10; over 62, $9; ages 3-12, $6. AX, DS, MC, VI. Phone (941) 355-5305.

SELBY GALLERY, on the campus of Ringling School of Art and Design on Dr. Martin Luther King Jr. Way, just e. of 2700 N. Tamiami Trail, showcases exhibits by national and international artists and designers. Lectures and films are presented throughout the year. Allow 30 minutes minimum. Mon.-Sat. 10-4; closed holidays and between exhibits. Free. Phone (941) 359-7563.

SEBASTIAN (E-11) pop. 16,181, elev. 19′

In July 1715 several ships were lost in Sebastian Inlet during a hurricane. The 1,500 men, women and children who survived formed a camp to recover for the Spanish Crown the gold and silver that had been lost to the sea. Their efforts were aided by Ais Indians in the area.

Sebastian River Area Chamber of Commerce: 700 Main St., Sebastian, FL 32958; phone (772) 589-5969.

McLARTY TREASURE MUSEUM, 5.25 mi. n. of CR 510 on SR A1A, is at the s. end of Sebastian Inlet State Recreation Area *(see Recreation Chart).* The museum's historical displays include artifacts and a diorama of the 1715 *Spanish Plate Fleet* and the shipwreck salvors' camp, including salvage materials. An audiovisual presentation highlights the modern-day treasure salvaging operations off the coast. Allow 1 hour minimum. Daily 10-4:30. Last

show begins 1 hour, 15 minutes before closing. Admission $1, under 6 free. Phone (772) 589-2147.

SEBRING (F-10) pop. 9,667, elev. 160′

Sebring (SEE-bring) was founded in 1911 by George E. Sebring, an ardent prohibitionist from Ohio; some early deeds contained bans against the use or sale of alcohol on the premises. The Atlantic Coast Railroad reached the town in 1912 and the land boom began. By 1920 there were nine resorts and the area was a popular winter resort for the affluent, and in 1926, the residents numbered 7,000. Following the land bust of 1924-26, the population dwindled to approximately 3,000. The establishment of the B-17 training facility Hendricks Field in World War II began the town's rebirth.

Today Sebring boasts some of the state's largest groves of citrus, lime and avocado trees. Sebring International Raceway plays host to automobile races, including March's grueling 12 Hours of Sebring Endurance Race, part of the American Le Mans Series; phone (800) 626-7223. Medal of Honor Park, on US 27 at the Agricultural Center, is an outside memorial dedicated to veterans.

Sebring Chamber of Commerce: 309 South Circle, Sebring, FL 33870; phone (863) 385-8448.

THE CHILDREN'S MUSEUM OF THE HIGH-LANDS, 219 N. Ridgewood Dr., has a child-size supermarket complete with shopping carts, a scanner

and a cash register. Other hands-on exhibits include a bank and a television station. Children can make music, paint their faces and make huge bubbles using materials provided by the museum. Allow 1 hour, 30 minutes minimum. Tues.-Sat. 10-5 (also Thurs. 5-8); closed Jan. 1, Thanksgiving and Dec. 24-25. Admission $2. Children must be with an adult. Phone (863) 385-5437.

HIGHLANDS HAMMOCK STATE PARK, 3.5 mi. w. of US 27 on CR 634, is a 8,133-acre wilderness of lush vegetation, dense jungle and swamps, all accessible by an excellent system of paved drives and well-marked trails. Trees range in age from more than 400 years to nearly 1,000 years. Ranger-narrated tram tours are available; inquire at the ranger station. Highland Hammocks was Florida's first state park, and was developed by the CCC in the 1930s. The Florida State Civilian Conservation Corps Museum features displays about park history.

Park rangers conduct nature programs on Thursday evenings, November-April. Slide presentations about a variety of topics are offered on Saturday evenings. Food is available during winter months. Park open daily 8-dusk (also open Fri.-Sat. dusk-10 p.m. for camper check-in, Oct.-May). Museum open daily 8-5. Nature walk Mon. at 10, Nov.-Apr. Admission $3.25 per private vehicle (maximum of eight people), $1 per person arriving by bicycle or on foot. Phone (863) 386-6094. *See Recreation Chart and the AAA Southeastern CampBook.*

SINGER ISLAND (F-12)

Known for its wide beaches and proximity to the Gulf Stream a mile away, Singer Island was owned in the 1920s by Paris Singer, son of the sewing machine magnate. He planned to develop the island as Palm Beach had been, but it became the property of one of Singer's ex-wives, who did not appreciate its potential. The island now supports a resort community.

JOHN D. MacARTHUR BEACH STATE PARK is on SR A1A. The park is 1.75 mi. s. of jct. US 1, SR A1A and SR 786 or 3 mi. n. of jct. US 1, SR A1A and SR 708. Sandwiched between the Atlantic Ocean and Lake Worth, the park features nature trails and a 1,600-foot-long footbridge over a cove to sand dunes. Free tram service from the parking lot to the beach front is available daily 10-4. Snorkeling (must have a dive flag—rentals are available), swimming, fishing and picnic sites with a playground also are available. The nature center has exhibits about ecology and area flora and fauna and presents a movie about this ecosystem.

Allow 1 hour, 30 minutes minimum. Park open daily 8-dusk. Nature center open Wed.-Mon. 9-5. Admission $3.25 per private vehicle (maximum eight people), $1 per person arriving by bicycle or on foot. Phone (561) 624-6950. *See Recreation Chart.*

STARKE (B-8) pop. 5,593, elev. 150′

CAMP BLANDING MUSEUM AND MEMORIAL PARK is 8.5 mi. e. of jct. US 301 on SR 16, at the main gate of Camp Blanding. The museum, housed in a refurbished World War II barracks, contains photographs, artifacts and exhibits honoring the camp, which was a major training center during World War II, and those who trained there.

Outdoor exhibits include weapon and vehicle displays as well as monuments and memorials to individuals, groups and divisions who served in World War II and other conflicts during the 20th century. Tours are available. Allow 1 hour minimum. Daily noon-4; closed holidays. Donations. Phone (904) 682-3196.

STUART (F-11) pop. 14,633, elev. 12′

Stuart is known by boating enthusiasts as the eastern terminus of the Okeechobee Waterway, which crosses the state to the Gulf of Mexico. Fishing is excellent in nearby Indian River as well as in the Gulf Stream about 10 miles offshore, where larger species, especially sailfish, are caught.

At nearby Jensen Beach during June and July, approximately 6,000 sea turtles can be observed making their annual nesting journey from ocean to shore and back. The turtles should not be disturbed. The Jensen Beach Chamber of Commerce can make reservations for turtle watches; phone (772) 334-3444.

Stuart/Martin County Chamber of Commerce: 1650 S. Kanner Hwy., Stuart, FL 34994; phone (772) 287-1011.

Self-guiding tours: The chamber of commerce provides a walking tour map of downtown.

ELLIOTT MUSEUM is on Hutchinson Island, 4.5 mi. n.e. of US 1 on SR A1A. The museum houses the many inventions and patents of Sterling Elliott and his son. The Americana Wing contains turn-of-the-20th-century shops, including barber, apothecary and an ice cream parlor. Collectible dolls and toys are displayed. Other galleries house antique bicycles, autographed memorabilia from Baseball Hall of Fame members and vintage cars, including a 1926 Bugatti Grand Prix race car.

Allow 1 hour minimum. Daily 10-4, Oct.-Aug.; closed Jan. 1, Easter, July 4, Thanksgiving and Dec. 25. Admission $6; ages 6-13, $2. Phone (772) 225-1961.

GILBERT'S BAR HOUSE OF REFUGE MUSEUM, on Hutchinson Island, is 4 mi. n.e. via SR A1A, then 1.25 mi. e. through the Marriott Resort. The restored 1875 lifesaving station houses a museum of nautical and marine history. A restored boathouse contains a maritime exhibit. Allow 30 minutes minimum. Daily 10-4; closed July 4 and Dec. 25. Admission $4; ages 6-12, $2. Phone (772) 225-1875.

SUGARLOAF KEY—

see The Florida Keys p. 69.

TALLAHASSEE (B-5) pop. 150,624, elev. 216′

In 1823 two explorers set out to find a permanent seat of government for the newly formed territory of Florida. The site they chose—midway between St. Augustine and Pensacola—was called "tallahassee" (tal-a-HASS-ee) by the Creek and Seminole Indians, a name meaning "old town." The rendezvous point became the state capital.

A convention in 1861 declared Florida an independent nation and a member of the Confederate States of America. In 1865 during the Civil War, Confederate Floridian soldiers repelled Union forces at the Battle of Natural Bridge *(see attraction listing p. 237)* to protect Tallahassee, making it the only uncaptured Confederate capital east of the Mississippi River.

Tallahassee's first state house was a log cabin; two more impressive structures were constructed in later years. The Old Capitol, built in 1845, is now an elegant centerpiece to the Florida State Capitol complex, which was completed in 1977. *(See attraction listings.)*

The oldest building in the city is the Columns, begun in 1830 by wealthy banker William "Money" Williams. It served as the focal point of financial, political and social development in the state's early history and was saved from demolition by being moved to 100 N. Duval St. in 1973.

The Governor's Mansion at Brevard and Adams streets is open for tours during legislative sessions and the Christmas season. Highlights include hollowware from the battleship USS *Florida* and French impressionist paintings. Another historic landmark is Union Bank at 295 Apalachee Pkwy. The oldest surviving bank building in the state, the restored 1841 structure contains displays about the history of Florida banking and the history of the bank and its restoration.

In a region of rolling hills, live oak forests and rivers, Tallahassee has beautiful gardens and large lakes. The city also is noted for its many canopy roads; Miccosukee, Centerville, Meridian and Old Bainbridge are just a few of the sheltered roads. The 419-acre campus of Florida A&M University stands on the highest of Tallahassee's seven hills, and Florida State University is on a 347-acre campus slightly west of downtown. The Flying High Circus offers collegiate performances under Florida State University's big top in April.

Tallahassee Little Theatre presents comedic and dramatic productions from September to July. Both evening and matinee performances are offered; phone (850) 224-8474.

Tallahassee Area Convention and Visitors Bureau: 106 E. Jefferson St., Tallahassee, FL 32301; phone (850) 413-9200 or (800) 628-2866. *See color ad.*

Shopping areas: Among the 150 stores at Governors Square Mall, 1500 Apalachee Pkwy., are Burdines, Dillard's, JCPenney and Sears. Tallahassee Mall, 2415 N. Monroe St., features Dillard's and Parisian among its 100 stores. Antique stores and art galleries line Main Street in downtown Havana, a small town 13 miles north of Tallahassee.

ALFRED B. MACLAY GARDENS STATE PARK, at 3540 Thomasville Rd. 1 mi. n. of I-10 exit 203 on US 319, consists of more than 1,100 acres, including 28 acres of ornamental gardens. The gardens are the focal point of the park. New York businessman Alfred B. Maclay and his wife Louise began the gardens in 1923 on the grounds of their southern estate. The gardens, in bloom January through April, contain colorful azaleas, camellias and Oriental magnolias as well as many native plants. The Maclay House has restored living and dining rooms and serves as a center for information about the Maclays, camellias and the gardens.

Nearly 8 miles of hiking, biking and horse trails run through the park, which also features a picturesque picnic/recreation area with covered picnic shelters, a swimming beach, a boat launch and playground.

Allow 1 hour minimum. Park open daily 8-dusk. Gardens open daily 9-5. House open daily 9-5, Jan.-Apr. Park admission $3.25 per private vehicle (maximum eight persons, $1 extra for every person over the maximum), $1 per person arriving by bicycle or on foot. Garden admission Jan.-Apr. (includes park and house) $3; ages 6-12, $1.50. Garden admission rest of year free. AX, MC, VI. Phone (850) 487-4556. *See Recreation Chart.*

BLACK ARCHIVES RESEARCH CENTER AND MUSEUM is on the Florida A&M University campus, off Monroe St. between Gaines St. and Orange Ave. Housed in the 1907 Carnegie Library, the oldest building on campus, the museum contains artifacts, photographs, manuscripts, art works, oral history tapes and rare maps that document the history and culture of Africans and African Americans. A visitor parking permit is available at the campus police department on Wahnish Way. Allow 1 hour minimum. Mon.-Fri. 9-4; closed holidays. Free. Phone (850) 599-3020.

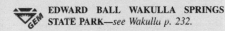 **EDWARD BALL WAKULLA SPRINGS STATE PARK**—*see Wakulla p. 232.*

FLORIDA STATE CAPITOL, 401 S. Monroe St., is a 22-story tower with house and senate chambers on either side, both with public viewing galleries. There is an observation deck on the top floor and a Florida information center just inside the west plaza entrance. Florida's legislature is in session from March through April. Guided tours are available all week. On weekends and holidays visitors must be with a guided tour.

Allow 1 hour minimum. Building open Mon.-Fri. 8-5, Sat. 11-3; closed Jan. 1, Labor Day, Thanksgiving and Dec. 25. Free. Phone (850) 488-6167 for guided tour information.

THE KNOTT HOUSE MUSEUM, 301 E. Park Ave., was built in 1843 as a private home. Restored to its 1930s appearance, this stately house has been restored and is fully furnished with the Victorian pieces acquired by the Knott family when they bought the house in 1928. Colorful stories of William Knott, career politician, and his wife Luella, a poet, musician and community activist, are recounted. Narrated tours are given on the hour Wed.-Fri. 1-4, Sat. 10-4; closed holidays. Free. Phone (850) 922-2459.

LAKE JACKSON MOUNDS STATE ARCHAEOLOGICAL SITE is 2 mi. n. of I-10 at the s. tip of Lake Jackson. The mounds are remains of a ceremonial center that existed A.D. 1200-1500. Six earth temple mounds are within the site. Daily 8-dusk. Admission $2 per private vehicle, $1 per person arriving by bicycle or on foot. Phone (850) 922-6007.

[SAVE] **THE MARY BROGAN MUSEUM OF ART AND SCIENCE,** 350 S. Duval St., houses interactive educational art and science exhibits. The

museum is an affiliate of the Smithsonian Institution. The art exhibitions feature a broad range of works from many cultures and time periods, and include one of the largest collections of artwork by untrained amateurs—often called "outsider" art.

Science exhibitions feature traveling exhibitions and the museum's permanent hands-on collection. Mon.-Sat. 10-5, Sun. 1-5; closed major holidays. Admission $6; over 61 and under 17, $3.50. AX, DS, MC, VI. Phone (850) 513-0700.

MISSION SAN LUIS is off US 90 at 2020 Mission Rd. Marked trails connect re-created dwellings and other structures on this hilly, oak-shaded site, home to a Spanish-Indian village 1656-1704. Tues.-Sun. 10-4; holiday schedule varies. Closed Thanksgiving and Dec. 25. Donations. Phone (850) 487-3711.

MUSEUM OF FLORIDA HISTORY, in the R.A. Gray Building at 500 S. Bronough St., has exhibits depicting Florida's colorful past. Visitors can view a mastodon skeleton and a giant armadillo mannequin from the Pleistocene era, gold and silver from Spanish shipwrecks, the actual flags flown during the Civil War, a partial replica of a Florida steamboat and various artifacts from the changing gallery. Special event tours and educational programs also are featured.

Allow 30 minutes minimum. Mon.-Fri. 9-4:30, Sat. 10-4:30, Sun. and holidays noon-4:30; closed Thanksgiving and Dec. 25. Donations. Phone (850) 245-6400.

THE OLD CAPITOL, jct. Monroe St. and Apalachee Pkwy., has been restored to its 1902 appearance. Self-guiding tours of the building cover the house and senate chambers, the governor's suite, the supreme court and the rotunda. The Florida Center for Political History and Governance explores the political process and individuals who have played important roles in Florida's colorful history. Allow 30 minutes minimum. Mon.-Fri. 9-4:30, Sat. 10-4:30, Sun. and holidays noon-4:30; closed Thanksgiving and Dec. 25. Donations. Phone (850) 487-1902.

TALLAHASSEE MUSEUM OF HISTORY AND NATURAL SCIENCE, 6.5 mi. s.w. at Lake Bradford, depicts north Florida's natural and human history. A trail winds through 52 acres of woodlands, cypress swamp and old fields, which are home to more than 100 indigenous animals. Also on the grounds are a restored 1880s farm complex; the antebellum home of the great-grandniece of George Washington; a one-room schoolhouse; a church; a gristmill and a caboose. Food is available.

Allow 2 hours minimum. Mon.-Sat. 9-5, Sun. 12:30-5. Admission $6.50; over 64, $6; ages 4-15, $4.50. MC, VI. Phone (850) 575-8684.

Tampa Bay
including St. Petersburg, Tampa and Clearwater

Population:
St. Petersburg 248,232   Tampa 303,447

Elevation:
St. Petersburg 45 ft.   Tampa 27 ft.

Popular Spots:

Busch Gardens Tampa Bay .... *(see p. 217)*

The Florida Aquarium .... *(see p. 218)*

Salvador Dali Museum............ *(see p. 216)*

With the world's tourism mecca—Orlando—just 70 miles up the road, it's easy to overlook the cities by the bay as major travel destinations. But Tampa, St. Petersburg, Clearwater and their adjoining communities have a great deal to offer the visitor. And yes, there's a theme park here, too: Busch Gardens Tampa Bay preceded Walt Disney's dream by 12 years.

But there are also some things Mickey and friends don't have. Stretching for almost 35 miles from Crystal Beach south to Fort De Soto Park are the Gulf Coast's broad, graceful, white-sand beaches—some of the prettiest in the country. With varied cultural offerings, water recreation opportunities and savory Spanish- and Cuban-influenced cuisine, Tampa Bay merits a closer look.

Spanish explorer Hernando de Soto apparently agreed when he led a band of men ashore on the southern Pinellas coast in 1539. But de Soto wasn't the first foreign visitor. Fellow countryman Panfilo de Narváez had stopped off 11 years earlier, and some historians believe that Juan Ponce de Léon may have come ashore as early as 1513.

Yet the Timucuan and Tocobega tribes inhabited the area centuries before the first Spaniards arrived. The Pinellas Peninsula takes its name from the Spanish phrase meaning "point of pines," and the city of Clearwater borrowed from the Tocobegan word *pocotopaug,* "clear water." But the name "Tampa" is a cartographic typo. Local American Indians called their village *Tanpa,* meaning "sticks of fire" (an allusion to the lightning so common in central Florida), but the area's first maps read "Tampa."

During the 18th century the bay belonged to pirates who left a decided influence on the area. One of them, the legendary Jose Gaspar, may have pillaged and kidnapped his way to annual celebrity—Tampa's first Gasparilla Pirate Festival was held in 1904, and the weeklong extravaganza continues each February. The area's NFL team, the Tampa Bay Buccaneers, also takes its name from this era.

In 1824 the U.S. Army arrived to establish Fort Brooke. Tampa was chartered within a decade and became the center of the Florida territory's cattle industry due to nearby pastureland and convenient water transportation. The Civil War interrupted growth; the defenseless settlement was shelled by Union troops and ravaged by a yellow fever epidemic in the early 1870s. Prosperity returned when railroad tycoon Henry B. Plant brought his South Florida Railroad to town in 1884. Plant also built several deep-water piers, setting the stage for the city's development as a port.

Getting There — *starting on p. 210*

Getting Around — *starting on p. 211*

What To See — *starting on p. 212*

What To Do — *starting on p. 219*

Where To Stay — *starting on p. 863, 870*

Where To Dine — *starting on p. 867, 887*

Meanwhile, Dr. Odet Philippe arrived on the Pinellas Peninsula in the mid-1830s. Philippe brought with him Bahamian citrus stock and planted the area's first groves at what is now Safety Harbor. Nearby Clearwater took shape after the 1841 establishment of Fort Harrison; the town was incorporated in 1891, 3 years after Russian immigrant Peter A. Demens brought his Orange Belt Railroad through en route to St. Petersburg. Following the 1894-95 freeze (which damaged local citrus groves), Plant took over the railroad and in 1896 built the Gulf Coast's first luxury hotel, the Belleview. Shortly thereafter wealthy winter residents built estates overlooking Clearwater Harbor.

St. Petersburg saw its first influx of homesteaders around 1856. Union blockaders forced inhabitants across the bay during the Civil War, yet farmers and fishermen trickled back to the peninsula following the war, and citrus groves were planted. About the time Plant was making tracks to Tampa, Demens' Orange Belt Railroad arrived. He named the city for his Russian birthplace, and St. Petersburg was incorporated in 1892. Although somewhat isolated, it became a popular winter resort.

Tampa, however, maintained a developmental edge. By 1890 the Ybor City cigar industry was booming. In the early 1900s, sponge beds were found in gulf waters near Tarpon Springs; Greek immigrants arrived by the hundreds to cultivate them. Railroads stimulated the tourist trade, and the area attracted wealthy Northern vacationers. The exclusive Tampa Bay Hotel, now part of the University of Tampa, was built by Plant in an effort to outdo railroad rival Henry Flagler, who was developing a string of luxury properties southward down Florida's east coast. The hotel's 1891 opening was attended by royalty, financial bigwigs and luminaries.

With the outbreak of the Spanish-American War in 1898 came another group of visitors—the U.S. military. Theodore Roosevelt and his Rough Riders set up camp in Tampa and staged their Cuban invasion from the port on Old Tampa Bay.

Tampa's population grew to nearly 16,000 by 1900—after Jacksonville, it was the state's largest city. The cigar industry peaked shortly before World War I, but cigar makers continued to produce high-quality, handmade Havanas. Most of the '20s roared by in a series of successive land booms. During this period O.H. Platt developed Tampa's first subdivision—the stately Victorian homes comprising Hyde Park, west of the Hillsborough River. David P. Davis, meanwhile, reclaimed the land south of downtown known as the Davis Islands. These man-made islands were a showcase of winding streets, substantial homes and ornamental landscaping.

By 1934 two bridges—the Gandy and the Courtney Campbell—linked Tampa with St. Petersburg and Clearwater respectively, establishing the Pinellas Peninsula as a major travel destination in its own right.

(A third, the Howard Frankland Bridge, opened in 1960.) Tampa's MacDill Air Force Base received its first troops in 1940, and the port became an important shipbuilding center during World War II.

Cigars were once the city's mainstay, and brick and frame buildings housing such companies as the Hav-a-Tampa Cigar Factory and the Cuesta-Rey Cigar Factory provided employment for Spanish and Cuban immigrants who labored at long tables handrolling tobacco leaves. Cigars are still produced, but the area business community has diversified. Tourism has the biggest economic impact—visitors spend some $1.9 billion here every year—but varied industries include electronic equipment and biomedical manufacturing, citrus canning, shrimping, paint production, brewing, phosphate mining, transportation and finance and government sectors.

Tampa is the foremost port of Florida's west coast and one of the nation's busiest. The port's strategic location contributes to some 93,000 jobs and $10.6 billion each year to the local economy.

Tampa Bay also is known to some as "Technology Bay." Fifteen percent of Florida's high-tech employees live and work in the bay area at such firms as AT&T Paradyne, General Electric, Honeywell Avionics, Johnson & Johnson, Verizon and Unisys, and the Home Shopping Network's headquarters are in St. Petersburg. The bay area is home to, in whole or in part, nearly 200 of the nation's Fortune 500 companies, and 23 percent of

Florida's biomedical manufacturing takes place in the Tampa metropolitan area.

Architecturally, Tampa admirably records the different periods of its growth. Older stucco homes with flat roofs, patios and wrought-iron balconies show a marked Spanish influence. Scattered throughout the central city are old frame dwellings and compact single-story bungalows surrounded by moss-draped oaks, towering palms and blooming hibiscus.

Tampa's vertical profile was fairly thin before the building boom of the 1980s and early 1990s. The addition of Tampa Convention Center, Tampa Bay Performing Arts Center (TBPAC) and several office skyscrapers heightened the city's once modest business district to a stature worthy of more established corporate centers. Adding an exotic—albeit low-lying—touch to the lofty skyscrapers are the bulbous silver-domed minarets and intricate Moorish accents of the University of Tampa.

The 1990s brought further development. A $110 million expansion enhanced the Tampa International Airport, and next door to the Florida Aquarium on Channelside Drive is the Garrison Seaport Center, a dining, shopping and entertainment complex centered on the new cruise ship terminals; an addition to the complex is the Seaport Street Terminal. A Riverwalk connects Curtis Hixon Park and Washington Street and the Tampa Convention Center.

The Tampa Bay area's blend of big-time industry and leisure pursuits proves to be a combination that works.

The Informed Traveler

 Whom To Call

Emergency: 911

Police (non-emergency): *St. Petersburg:* (727) 893-7780; Sheriff (727) 582-6200. *Tampa:* (813) 231-6130; Sheriff (813) 247-8200.

Fire: *St. Petersburg:* (727) 893-7694; *Tampa:* (813) 227-7015.

Hospitals: *St. Petersburg:* Bayfront Medical Center, (727) 823-1234; St. Anthony's, (727) 825-1100. *Tampa:* St. Joseph's Hospital, (813) 870-4000; Tampa General Healthcare, (813) 251-7000.

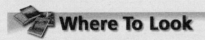 **Where To Look**

Newspapers

The area is served by two daily newspapers, the *St. Petersburg Times* and *The Tampa Tribune*. Several publications with smaller circulations serve local areas; one such paper is the trilingual *La Gaceta*.

Radio

WUSF (89.7 FM) is a member of National Public Radio.

Visitor Information

Visitors to *St. Petersburg* can obtain information, maps and brochures from the St. Petersburg Chamber of Commerce at 100 Second Ave. N., St. Petersburg, FL 33701; phone (727) 821-4715. It is open Mon.-Fri. 8-5. An information center at The Pier is open Mon.-Sat. 10-8, Sun. 11-6; phone (727) 821-6164.

In *Clearwater*, information about the greater Tampa Bay area is available from the Suncoast Welcome Center, which is open daily 8:30-5; it is closed Jan. 1, Easter, Thanksgiving and Dec. 25. Stop in or write 2001 Ulmerton Rd., Clearwater, FL 33762; phone (727) 573-1449. Another source is the St. Petersburg/Clearwater Area Convention

& Visitors Bureau, 14450 46th St. N., Suite 108, Clearwater, FL 33762; phone (727) 464-7200.

For visitors to *Tampa Bay*, information about touring the area is available daily 9:30-5:30 from the Tampa Bay Visitors Center, 615 Channelside Dr., Suite 108-A, or write to the Tampa Bay Convention and Visitors Bureau, 400 N. Tampa St., Suite 2800, Tampa, FL 33602; phone (813) 226-0293.

 What To Pack

Winter temperatures in the Tampa Bay area rarely fall below freezing. Skies are mostly sunny, and humidity is moderate. However, from May into October highs hover around 90 degrees. The "heat index" reading—a combination of heat and the relative humidity—may make it feel more like 100. Afternoon thunderstorms offer relief but can be dangerous, capable of producing high winds, lightning, driving rain, local flooding, occasional hail and, possibly, tornadoes. *For additional information see temperature chart p. 45.*

Even though *Tampa* is more businesslike than *St. Petersburg* and *Clearwater* when it comes to attire, dress tends to be informal. Few restaurants require a jacket and tie, and most nightspots are decidedly casual. When sightseeing, dress for comfort.

Sales Tax: Sales tax is 6.75 percent in Hillsborough County, 7 percent in Pinellas County and 6 percent in Pasco County. An accommodations tax is 5 percent in Hillsborough County and 4 percent in Pinellas County.

Destination Tampa Bay including St. Petersburg, Tampa and Clearwater

Dunedin Historical Society and Musuem.
All aboard for a trip down memory lane.
(See mention page 228)

*T*he Tampa Bay area has all the ingredients for one heck of a vacation.

*T*here are theme and water parks for the active crowd; world-class museums for the culturally inclined; recreational pursuits for athletic types; and shopping and spectator sports for everyone in between.

Tampa Bay Buccaneers. The Bucs bring exciting NFL action to the Tampa Bay area at the Raymond James Stadium. (See mention page 221)

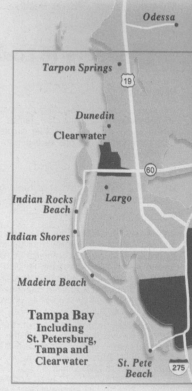

*P*laces included in this AAA Destination City:

Apollo Beach............................227
Clearwater................................227
Dade City.................................228
Dunedin...................................228
Indian Rocks Beach...................228
Indian Shores...........................228
Largo......................................228
Madeira Beach........................229
Odessa....................................229
Plant City................................229
St. Pete Beach..........................230
Tarpon Springs........................230
Thonotosassa...........................231

Tampa Bay
Including
St. Petersburg,
Tampa and
Clearwater

Odessa

Tarpon Springs

Dunedin

Clearwater

Indian Rocks Beach

Largo

Indian Shores

Madeira Beach

St. Pete Beach

Busch Gardens Tampa Bay.
After braving the Congo River Rapids,
these hardy souls may check out the
latest in roller coasters at this African-
themed entertainment park.
(See listing page 217)

Chaise lounges on beach.
Sparkling sand and warm Gulf waters
lure vacationers and inspire soft
dreams of early retirement.

See Vicinity map page 214

St. Petersburg Museum of History, St Petersburg.
No bones about it, this is a mammoth exhibit.
(See listing page 216)

Getting There

By Car

When approaching **St. Petersburg** from the north, take I-75 and US 19. I-75, the fast freeway route, merges with other routes in Tampa and becomes I-275 as it heads for St. Petersburg over the Howard Frankland Bridge. Divided US 19 and two-lane US 19A diverge at Tarpon Springs to offer a choice of slower approaches from the northern Gulf Coast.

Coming from the south on I-75, US 19 and I-275, enter **St. Petersburg** over the mouth of Tampa Bay via the Sunshine Skyway Bridge (toll). Approaching from the east, I-4 provides direct access to the I-275/Howard Frankland Bridge into St. Petersburg.

The major direct route to **Tampa** from the north is I-75, which traverses Florida's north-central lake district: The 62-mile stretch south of Wildwood is especially scenic. It is roughly paralleled by US 301 on the east and US 41 on the west. North of downtown I-75 changes to I-275, which merges with I-4 in mid-city. I-75 bypasses the city proper to the east, rejoining I-275 north of Bradenton.

Driving into **Tampa** from the south, US 41 parallels I-75, the main corridor from the southern Gulf Coast. From Daytona Beach in the east, I-4 angles across central Florida through Orlando, while older US 92 runs parallel from Lakeland. SR 60, a four-lane, divided highway, leads from Lake Wales. Running from the Gulf Coast west of Tampa, SR 60 connects to **Clearwater,** and I-275 travels to St. Petersburg.

Air Travel

Commercial flights entering **Tampa** land at Tampa International Airport. Several commercial airlines and privately-owned planes use St. Petersburg-Clearwater International Airport. Private and corporate planes have access to Albert Whitted Airport in **St. Petersburg.** The Peter O. Knight Airport in Tampa serves general aviation.

Tampa International Airport is on the city's west side along Old Tampa Bay. To reach downtown **Tampa,** take I-275 (Tampa Expressway) north—though you'll actually be traveling east—and take the Ashley Street exit.

Past this exit I-275 turns sharply northward, bisecting the city. Continue along I-275 to reach such destinations as the University of South Florida and Busch Gardens Tampa Bay. Exit to I-4 east if you're heading for Ybor City, Plant City or Lakeland. Or take a cab: United and Yellow cabs provide service from the airport. Average fare to downtown (about 6 miles) is about $17.

To reach downtown **St. Petersburg,** take I-275 south. Cross the bay on the 7-mile Howard Frankland Bridge and proceed another 10 miles or so due

ST. PETERSBURG–CLEARWATER INTERNATIONAL AIRPORT

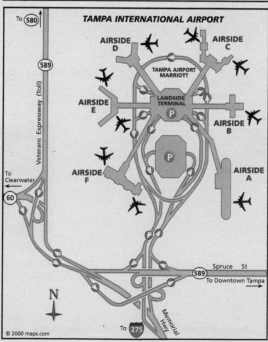

TAMPA INTERNATIONAL AIRPORT

south. From I-275, take I-375 into the northern half of downtown or I-175 into the southern half. Transportation from Tampa International to St. Petersburg is easily acquired. Supershuttle provides transfers from Tampa International to St. Petersburg and other Tampa Bay-area cities; phone (727) 572-1111. Central Florida Limousine, (813) 396-3730, also provides transfers from the airport to most points in Hillsborough and Polk counties.

St. Petersburg-Clearwater International Airport is about 10 miles across the bay from Tampa on SR 686 (Roosevelt Boulevard), near the west side of the Howard Frankland Bridge. Airport traffic exits northwest toward Clearwater or south, providing access to St. Petersburg and Tampa. To reach **Clearwater,** take SR 686 about 3 miles west to US 19, US 19 another 3 miles north to SR 60 (Gulf-to-Bay Boulevard), then SR 60 a mile or so west into town. Downtown St. Petersburg is about 10 miles due south of the airport via I-275. To get to the interstate, exit south from the airport on SR 686 to SR 688 (Ulmerton Road). Go a mile or so east to another segment of SR 686 and take it a mile south to I-275.

Hertz, which offers discounts to AAA members, is at Tampa International Airport, (813) 874-3232; St. Petersburg-Clearwater International Airport, (727) 531-3774; and at St. Pete Beach, (727) 360-1631; or phone (800) 654-3080. Check the telephone directory for other agencies.

Rail Service

Tampa's Amtrak station is at 601 N. Nebraska Ave. in downtown Tampa, behind historic Union Station. Daily service is offered; phone (813) 221-7600 or (800) 872-7245. Buses from **St. Petersburg** to the Amtrak station leave ParkSide Mall, Suite 324, 7200 US 19N; phone (727) 522-9475 for schedule or (800) 872-7245.

Bus service to Union Station also is available via several HARTLine routes; phone (813) 254-4278. In addition, the Pinellas Suncoast Transit Authority (PSRA) maintains two bus routes to the terminal: The 100X runs from Gateway Mall, Ninth Street N. and 77th Avenue, and the 200X runs from Clearwater Mall, US 19 and Gulf to Bay Boulevard. For PSTA schedules phone (727) 530-9911.

Buses

Greyhound Lines Inc. is at 180 Ninth St. N. in **St. Petersburg** and 610 E. Polk St. in **Tampa;** phone (800) 231-2222.

Getting Around

Street System

St. Petersburg's street system is essentially a compass-oriented grid. All avenues, terraces and places run east-west; streets and ways run north-south. Central Avenue (CR 150) is the north-south divider; parallel to Tampa Bay is First Street. Numbering of north-south streets begins at the bay and progresses westward 81 blocks to Boca Ciega Bay on the Gulf.

From I-275, I-375 accesses the northern half of downtown **St. Petersburg** and I-175 the southern half. US 92 (Fourth Street) and SR 689 (Ninth Street) provide downtown access from I-275 as well.

Downtown **Tampa** is bracketed by water and has only a few major access routes. From I-275, take the Ashley Street exit. Also from the north, Nebraska Avenue SR 45 and one-way US 41 Bus. Rte. lead into downtown. Cass Street approaches from the west. From the east, use SR 60 (John F. Kennedy Boulevard).

Tampa also is laid out in a basic grid, with a few geographic variations. US 41 Bus. Rte. (Florida Avenue) divides east from west; John F. Kennedy Boulevard/Frank Adamo Drive (SR 60) separates north from south. Many streets in the downtown area are one way.

Five major east-west thoroughfares support cross-town traffic: SR 582 (Fowler Avenue), SR 580 (Busch Boulevard), US 92/US 41 (Hillsborough Avenue), SR 574 (Martin Luther King Jr. Boulevard), and the South Crosstown Expressway (toll). Three others parallel I-275: on the west, SR 597/SR 580/US 92 (Dale Mabry Highway); through the central city, US 41/SR 45 (Nebraska Avenue); and on the east, SR 583 (56th Street).

Besides I-275, US 19 and US 19 Alt. are the main north-south routes on the Pinellas Peninsula. Congested SR 699 (Gulf Boulevard), lined with shops, restaurants and motels, connects the beach communities from Clearwater Beach south to St. Pete Beach. Running east-west are SR 60 (Gulf-to-Bay Boulevard/Courtney Campbell Causeway) to Clearwater, SR 688 (Ulmerton Road) to the beaches, and SR 694/CR 694 (Gandy Boulevard/Park Boulevard) through the communities of Pinellas Park and Seminole to the beaches.

Generally, downtown speed limits for *Clearwater, St. Petersburg* and *Tampa* are 30 mph or as posted. Unless otherwise posted, a right turn is allowed on a red light after a complete stop. It is best to avoid taking an unfamiliar route during rush hours (about 7 to 9 a.m. and 4:30 to 6 p.m.).

Parking

Clearwater, St. Petersburg and *Tampa* all have limited on-street parking in the downtown business sections and along major thoroughfares. Rates for municipal parking garages start at $1.25 per hour and range from $5.40 to $7 for 6-24 hours. Metered lot parking and use of the Old Fort Brooke at Tampa City Centre parking garage in Tampa cost $1.25 per hour (if using the garage for 6-24 hours, the rate is $7).

Metered parking at the beaches is available on the street and in lots at 25c-$1 per hour; beach parking is not allowed. For additional parking information phone (813) 274-8179.

Taxis and Limousines

Companies include *Tampa*-based United Cab Co., Tampa Bay Cab and Taxi Plus, all at (813) 253-2424; and Yellow Cab Co., (813) 253-0121 in Tampa and (727) 821-7777 in *St. Petersburg.*

Taxis are metered. Most cabs in *Clearwater* and *St. Petersburg* charge $1.50 to enter and $1.60 per mile; most *Tampa* cabs are $1.25 to enter and $1.75 per mile. Limousine service averages $40-$50 per hour in the Tampa Bay area.

Public Transportation

Pinellas Suncoast Transit Authority serves *St. Petersburg* and Pinellas County; for bus fares and schedules phone (727) 530-9911. HARTLine serves *Tampa* and its immediate suburbs; service includes

the TECO Line Streetcar System, which makes 11 stops along a 2.3-mile track between downtown **Tampa** and Ybor City. For HARTLine bus and streetcar fares and schedules, phone (813) 254-4278.

ST. PETERSBURG

See map page 214.

BOYD HILL NATURE PARK, 1101 Country Club Way S., is reached by taking I-275 exit 17, 1.75 mi. e. on 54th Ave. to Martin Luther King St., n. to Country Club Way, then w. 2 blks. This 245-acre preserve on the west side of Lake Maggiore has nature trails and boardwalks. The Nature Center offers interpretive displays, an aquarium and birds of prey exhibits. A 60- to 90-minute guided tram tour is offered daily.

Picnic facilities, bicycle trails, nature trails and guided walks are available; nighttime hikes are offered the second Monday of the month. Allow 1 hour, 30 minutes minimum. Park open daily 9-5 (also Tues. and Thurs. 5-8, during DST); closed Thanksgiving and Dec. 25. Tram tour daily at 10, during DST; at 3 rest of year. Admission $2; ages 3-17, $1. Additional tram tour fee $1. Phone (727) 893-7326.

Lake Maggiore Park, Ninth St. and 30th Ave. S., covers 721 acres around Lake Maggiore. Fishing and picnic facilities as well as bicycle trails are available. Daily dawn-dusk. Free.

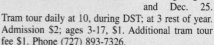

THE FLORIDA HOLOCAUST MUSEUM, downtown at 55 Fifth St. S. at jct. First Ave. S., is one of the country's largest Holocaust museums. Eleven eternal flames, symbolizing the 11 million victims of the Nazis, are part of the three-story building's facade. The 12 sections of the permanent exhibit trace the Holocaust's beginnings in eastern Europe through the establishment of the state of Israel.

The museum's centerpiece is one of the boxcars used to transport Jews and other prisoners to concentration/death camps; the car rests on a section of railroad track from the Treblinka camp. Changing exhibits feature art, photography and artifacts related to the Holocaust, responsibility and human rights. An audiotape tour is included with admission.

Allow 2 hours minimum. Mon.-Fri. 10-5, Sat.-Sun. noon-5; closed Thanksgiving, Dec. 25 and Jewish holidays. Last admission 1 hour before closing. Admission $8; over 60 and students with ID $7; under 18, $3. AX, CB, DS, MC, VI. Phone (727) 820-0100 or (800) 960-7448. *See color ad.*

FLORIDA INTERNATIONAL MUSEUM is at 100 Second St. N. This Smithsonian affiliate presents two permanent and a variety of traveling exhibitions. Permanently displayed are more than 500 artifacts relating to John F. Kennedy and the Kennedy family, as well as a re-creation of the West Wing of the White House. The second permanent exhibition, The Cuban Missile Crisis, examines the culture of the early 1960s and the Cold-War events leading up to October 1962.

Garage parking is available at 218 Second Ave. N. Open Mon.-Sat. 10-5, Sun noon-5. Last admission 1 hour before closing. Admission $12; over 64 and college students with ID $11; ages 6-18, $6. Parking $5. MC, VI. Phone (727) 822-3693 or (800) 777-9882.

FORT DE SOTO PARK is off I-275 exit 17 at Pinellas Bayway; two toll causeways are crossed en route. The 1,136-acre park occupies five keys: Madeleine, St. Jean, St. Christopher, Bonne Fortune and Mullet. Plants and wildlife are protected; pets must be leashed. Daily dawn-dusk. Nature tours begin at various locations Sat.-Sun. at 10. Free. Toll 85c. Phone (727) 582-2267. *See Recreation Chart and the AAA Southeastern CampBook.*

Fort De Soto, on the southern end of Mullet Key, was begun during the Spanish-American War but was incomplete at war's end. Its guns never were fired in battle. There are walkways around the fort area. A pamphlet outlining a self-guiding tour along the Historical Trail is available. A 90-minute guided walking tour of the fort is offered Sat. at 10.

GREAT EXPLORATIONS, on the third floor of The Pier, 800 Second Ave. N.E., offers six pavilions of hands-on exhibits including Explore Galore, which is geared towards children under 7. VETerinary Office puts children in charge of a toy animal's exam, while Touch Tunnel challenges the senses in a pitch-black, 90-foot maze. Other exhibits focus on cultural diversities; touch- and sound-activated art; and international displays. Changing programs and exhibits explore various facets of the arts and sciences.

Allow 1 hour minimum. Mon.-Sat. 10-8, Sun. 11-6. Admission $4; over 55, $2; under 3 free. AX, MC, VI. Phone (727) 821-8992. *See color ad.*

MUSEUM OF FINE ARTS is at 255 Beach Dr. N.E. on the waterfront. French Impressionist paintings and 20th-century photography are among the highlights of the museum collection, which includes works by Paul Cezanne, Paul Gauguin, Claude Monet, Berthe Morisot, Georgia O'Keeffe, Robert Rauschenberg, Pierre Auguste Renoir and Auguste Rodin. Also displayed are ancient Greek and Roman, pre-Columbian, Asian, African and American Indian works and decorative arts, including a gallery of Steuben glass. Special exhibitions also are presented.

Tues.-Sat. 10-5 (also the third Thurs. each month 5-9, Sept.-May), Sun. 1-5; closed Jan. 1, July 4,

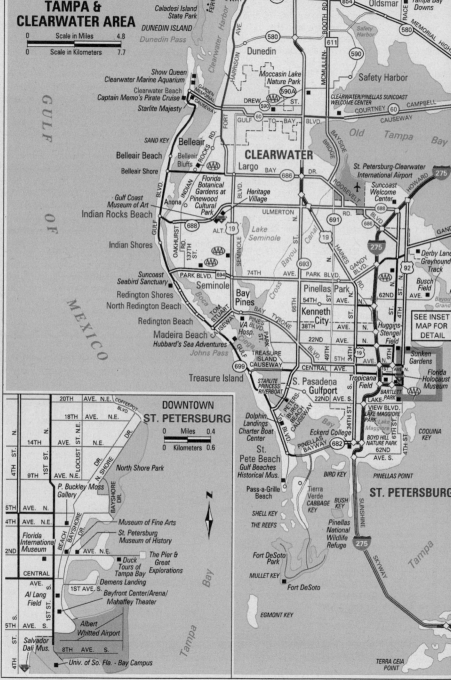

ST. PETERSBURG, TAMPA & CLEARWATER AREA

Scale in Miles   0   4.8
Scale in Kilometers   0   7.7

HONEYMOON ISLAND
To Tallahassee
To Tarpon Springs
Caladesi Island State Park
DUNEDIN ISLAND
Dunedin Pass
Oldsmar
Tampa Bay Downs
DUNEDIN CAUSEWAY
Clearwater Harbor
Safety Harbor
Dunedin
Moccasin Lake Nature Park
Show Queen
Clearwater Marine Aquarium
Captain Memo's Pirate Cruise
Starlite Majesty
CLEARWATER/PINELLAS SUNCOAST WELCOME CENTER
CLEARWATER
Largo
SAND KEY
Belleair
Belleair Beach
Belleair Bluffs
Belleair Shore
Belleair
Florida Botanical Gardens at Pinewood Cultural Park
Heritage Village
St. Petersburg-Clearwater International Airport
Suncoast Welcome Center
Gulf Coast Museum of Art
Indian Rocks Beach
Anona
ULMERTON
Lake Seminole
Derby Lane Greyhound Track
Indian Shores
Busch Field
Suncoast Seabird Sanctuary
Seminole
Redington Shores
North Redington Beach
Bay Pines
Pinellas Park
Kenneth City
Redington Beach
Madeira Beach
Hubbard's Sea Adventures
Johns Pass
VA Hosp.
Huggins-Stengel Field
SEE INSET MAP FOR DETAIL
TREASURE ISLAND CAUSEWAY
CENTRAL
AVE.
Sunken Gardens
Florida Holocaust Museum
Treasure Island
STARLITE PRINCESS RIVERBOAT
S. Pasadena
Gulfport
Tropicana Field
LAKE PARK

DOWNTOWN ST. PETERSBURG

Miles   0   0.4
Kilometers   0   0.6

North Shore Park
P. Buckley Moss Gallery
Florida International Museum
Museum of Fine Arts
St. Petersburg Museum of History
The Pier & Great Explorations
Duck Tours of Tampa Bay
Demens Landing
Al Lang Field
Bayfront Center/Arena/Mahaffey Theater
Albert Whitted Airport
Salvador Dali Mus.
Univ. of So. Fla. - Bay Campus

VIEW BLVD.
LAKE MAGGIORE PARK
BOYD HILL NATURE PARK
COQUINA KEY
Dolphin Landings Charter Boat Center
St. Pete Beach
Gulf Beaches Historical Mus.
Eckerd College
PINELLAS BAYWAY
BIRD KEY
PINELLAS POINT
Pass-a-Grille Beach
SHELL KEY
THE REEFS
Tierra Verde
CABBAGE KEY
BUSH KEY
ST. PETERSBURG
Pinellas National Wildlife Refuge
Fort DeSoto Park
MULLET KEY
Fort DeSoto
EGMONT KEY
SUNSHINE SKYWAY
Tampa Bay
TERRA CEIA POINT

GULF OF MEXICO

Tampa Bay

Old Tampa Bay

Thanksgiving and Dec. 25. Guided tours are offered Tues.-Fri. at 10, 11, 1, 2 and 3; Sat. at 11, 1, 2 and 3; Sun. at 1 and 2. Admission $6; over 64, $5; students with ID $2; under 6 free. AX, MC, VI. Phone (727) 896-2667. *See color ad p. 213.*

P. BUCKLEY MOSS GALLERY, downtown at 190 Fourth Ave. N.E., overlooks a small yacht harbor. The gallery houses an extensive collection of paint-

ings, watercolors, etchings and serigraphs by P. Buckley Moss, a contemporary artist focusing on Amish and Mennonite themes. Allow 1 hour minimum. Mon.-Fri. 10-6, Sat. 10-5, Sun. noon-5, Sept.-May; Mon.-Fri. 10-6, Sat. 10-5, rest of year. Closed major holidays. Free. Phone (727) 894-2899.

THE PIER, extending 2,400 feet into Tampa Bay at the foot of Second Ave. N.E., downtown, is one of the most recognized landmarks on Florida's west coast. The complex is an inverted five-story pyramidal structure that offers fishing, an aquarium and a variety of specialty shops and boutiques, restaurants and entertainment. An information center is on the first floor.

A free trolley runs between the parking lot and the pier. Allow 2 hours minimum. Mon.-Thurs. 10-9, Fri.-Sat. 10-10, Sun. 11-7. Information center open Mon.-Sat. 10-8, Sun. 11-6. Parking $3; $5 for special events. Phone (727) 821-6443.

ST. PETERSBURG MUSEUM OF HISTORY is at 335 Second Ave. N.E. at The Pier. Permanent and changing exhibits reflect the history and pre-history of the Pinellas Peninsula. Galleries include Walk Through Time and Try History On For Size, where mirrors let visitors see themselves in vintage costumes. The First Flight Gallery traces the evolution of commercial aviation. Artifacts include a Tocobaga Indian canoe from the 1500s, a replica of the world's first commercial airliner and a 3,500-year-old mummy.

Allow 1 hour, 30 minutes minimum. Mon.-Sat. 10-5, Sun. 1-5; closed Jan. 1, Thanksgiving and Dec. 25. Admission $5; senior citizens $4; ages 7-17, $2. Phone (727) 894-1052.

SALVADOR DALI MUSEUM, next to the University of South Florida Bayboro Campus at 1000 Third St. S., houses a comprehensive collection of the Spanish artist's works. Dating from 1914-80, Dali's paintings range from small impressionistic works to gigantic surrealistic montages. Sculptures and other objects illustrate Dali's artistic diversity. Guided tours are conducted regularly; phone for schedule.

Allow 1 hour minimum. Mon.-Sat. 9:30-5:30 (also Thurs. 5:30-8), Sun. noon-5:30; closed Thanksgiving and Dec. 25. Admission $10; over 64, $7; students with ID $5; under 10 free. Admission half-price Thurs. 5-8. DS, MC, VI. Phone (727) 823-3767 or (800) 442-3254. *See color ad p. 213.*

SUNKEN GARDENS is at 1825 4th St. N. In the early 1900s, plumber and avid gardener George Turner drained a shallow lake on his property to expose the fertile muck at the bottom, creating a perfect environment in which to indulge his interest in plants. In the 1920s he began charging visitors a nickel to stroll among his garden's lush foliage, and in 1935 he officially opened it to tourists.

Today visitors can follow paths that meander among ponds, waterfalls and a multitude of exotic plants, many of which are labeled. Butterflies, flamingoes, lorikeets, kookaburras and colorful macaws live in the garden; horticultural and wildlife programs are offered throughout the year. Guided tours are available by appointment. Picnicking is permitted. Food is available. Allow 2 hours minimum. Wed.-Sun. 10-4. Admission $7; over 54, $5; ages 3-11, $3. MC, VI. Phone (727) 551-3100.

SUNSHINE SKYWAY connects Pinellas and Manatee counties across lower Tampa Bay. The 15-mile bridge is made up of three smaller bridges and a 4-mile concrete skyway and is a vital link of I-275. There are areas for fishing, picnicking and swimming off the roadway. The central section of the southbound span of the original bridge collapsed into the bay when a tanker hit one of the supports in 1980. The original north section now is home to a three-quarter-mile-long fishing pier.

Open daily 24 hours. Toll $1. Fishing pier $3 per vehicle. There is a separate fishing fee of $2; over 65, $1.50; ages 6-12, $1. Phone (727) 865-0668.

TAMPA

See map page 214.

ADVENTURE ISLAND, .25 mi. n. of Busch Gardens Tampa Bay at 10001 Malcolm McKinley Dr. (40th St.), is a 25-acre tropical water park encompassing slides, water play areas and a beach volleyball complex, all within a Key West atmosphere. Twists, drops, curves and turns can be expected while negotiating the thrill slide Wahoo Run, a tunnel raft ride. Key West Rapids sends rafters cruising down six stories of turns, water mines and pools. Splash Attack is an extensive tree house.

Changing facilities and showers are included with admission; free kennels are available at Busch Gardens. There is an additional fee for locker rental and the games area. Food is available.

Allow 5 hours minimum. Daily Apr.-Aug.; Sat.-Sun., late Feb.-March 31 and Sept.-Oct. Park generally open between 9 and 10; closing times vary. Phone ahead for exact hours. Admission $27.95; ages 3-9, $25.95. The 2-day Bounce Ticket, a combination ticket with Busch Gardens Tampa Bay, is $54.95 for all ages. Parking $5. Under 8 must be with an adult. AX, DS, MC, VI. Phone (813) 987-5660.

AMERICAN VICTORY MARINERS MEMORIAL & SHIP MUSEUM is at 705 Channelside Dr. Berth #271. The memorial, a World War II-era military cargo ship named the SS *American Victory,* is dedicated to the men and women who built, served aboard and protected American merchant vessels. Completed in 1945, the 455-foot-long ship served many roles in its history such as delivering food and machinery to help rebuild Europe as part of the Marshall Plan.

Visitors can take a self-guiding tour of the ship that includes the captain's stateroom and office, cargo hold, engine room, a crew cabin, officers' mess, the aft gun deck, the ship's hospital, the galley, the cabin deck and the bridge deck. Allow 2 hours minimum. Mon.-Sat. 10-5, Sun. noon-5. Last tour begins 1 hour before closing. Admission $6; ages 6-12, $3. DS, MC, VI. Phone (813) 228-8766.

 BUSCH GARDENS TAMPA BAY is at 3000 E. Busch Blvd. (SR 580), 2 mi. e. of jct. I-275 exit 50 or 2 mi. w. of I-75 exit 265. The 335-acre African-themed family-entertainment park offers naturalistic animal habitats, thrill rides, live entertainment, shopping and dining. Nearly 2,700 animals are part of the park's African atmosphere.

Rhino Rally, an off-road safari and wild river adventure, takes guests on an unpredictable journey through the Serengeti bringing them face-to-face with white rhinos, elephants, cape buffaloes, zebras and other African species. The trek, which takes place aboard customized Land Rovers, leads to an encounter with a raging river, shifting the adventure from a safari to a water thrill ride.

Roller coaster thrills can be experienced on Gwazi, a double wooden coaster; Montu, an inverted steel coaster; and the loops and spirals of Kumba. With a world-class zoo as its showcase, Edge of Africa offers an intense safari experience and features naturalistic animal habitats, remote encampments and African villages.

Those who opt for the additional cost of the Serengeti Safari Tour will take a ride on an open,

flat-bed truck past free-roaming giraffes, zebras, antelopes and ostriches. Lory Landing is an aviary populated with tropical birds, including lorikeets, hornbills and touracos. Myombe Reserve: The Great Ape Domain allows visitors to observe lowland gorillas and chimpanzees in a naturalistic setting.

World Rhythms on Ice is a Broadway-style show featuring skaters and special effects. Other entertainment options include the marching brass band Mystic Sheiks of Morocco. Food, free kennels, and stroller, wheelchair and locker rentals are available.

Allow a full day. Park open generally daily at 9; closing hours vary. Phone ahead for exact hours. Admission $49.95; ages 3-9, $40.95. The 2-day Bounce Ticket, a combination ticket with Adventure Island, is $54.95 for all ages. The Orlando Flex-Ticket, a multi-day, multi-park ticket that includes SeaWorld Orlando, Universal Studios Florida, Universal Studios Islands of Adventure and Wet 'n Wild in Orlando and Busch Gardens Tampa Bay, is available at the park. Parking $7 for automobiles, $11 for recreational vehicles and campers. AX, DS, MC, VI. Phone (866) 353-8622. *See color ad inside front cover.*

CENTRO YBOR MUSEUM is at 1600 E. 8th Ave. Located within Tampa's historic cigar-manufacturing district, the museum displays clothing from Ybor City's days as "Cigar Capital of the

World" as well as numerous historic photographs. A 7-minute video recounts the history of Tampa, tracing the area's transformation from quiet swampland to bustling city. Allow 1 hour minimum. Mon.-Sat. 10-6, Sun. noon-6. Free. Phone (813) 241-8838.

THE FLORIDA AQUARIUM, 701 Channelside Dr. on the downtown waterfront, is a three-story, 152,000-square-foot glass-domed aquarium that features more than 10,000 aquatic plants and animals in exhibits related to Florida's ecosystem and aquatic habitats, and those around the world.

Sunshine State highlights include the Florida Wetlands Gallery, which displays a cypress swamp, mangrove roots and a river containing live otters; the Florida Bays and Beaches Gallery, which contains freshwater and saltwater displays; and the Florida Coral Reefs Gallery, which showcases many fish, barracudas and colorful coral reefs. Other plants and animals native to Florida—including alligators and crocodiles—are shown in their natural habitats.

Exotic animals include invertebrates from the world's beaches in No Bone Zone; rare Australian sea dragons in Dragons Down Under; and ocean predators in SeaHunt. Sharks! From Fear to Fascination features a diver in the shark tank.

Also available are behind-the-scenes tours; close-up animal encounters; dive shows; two touch tanks; and audiotape tours. DolphinQuest eco-tours of the bay aboard a 64-foot, 49-passenger catamaran take passengers in search of sightings of the more than 400 bottle nose dolphins in the bay and of manatees. Tours depart daily; phone for schedule.

Food is available. Allow 2 hours minimum. Aquarium open daily 9:30-5; closed Thanksgiving and Dec. 25. Aquarium admission $15; over 60, $12; ages 3-12, $10. DolphinQuest fare $18; over 60, $17; ages 3-12, $13. Combination tickets are available. Parking $4. AX, DS, MC, VI. Phone (813) 273-4000.

KID CITY: THE CHILDREN'S MUSEUM OF TAMPA is next to Lowry Park Zoo at 7550 North Blvd. Children and their families can explore buildings together at this hands-on museum, designed like a child-size city. Visitors can shop for groceries, become a firefighter and drive cars through the streets. A toddler area is for under age 5. Allow 1 hour minimum. Mon.-Fri. 9-5:30, Sat. 10-5:30, Sun. noon-5:30; closed major holidays. Admission $4, under 2 free. Phone (813) 935-8441.

LOWRY PARK ZOO, I-275 exit 48 w. to 1101 W. Sligh Ave., is 41 acres of lush natural habitats comprising five main exhibit areas: The Florida Manatee and Aquatic Center; Native Florida Wildlife Center; Asian Domain; Primate World; and Wallaroo Station Children's Zoo. Visitors can feed the birds in Lorikeet Landing and touch and feed stingrays at Stingray Bay. Manatee Encounter offers a behind-the-scenes look into a manatee hospital. Food is available.

Daily 9:30-5. Last admission 15 minutes before closing. Admission $9.50; over 49, $8.50; ages 3-11, $5.95. AX, DS, MC, VI. Phone (813) 935-8552.

MOSI (MUSEUM OF SCIENCE & INDUSTRY), 4801 E. Fowler Ave., is 3 mi. e. on SR 582 from I-275 exit 51 or 3 mi. w. of I-75 exit 265. One of the largest science centers in the Southeast, MOSI contains more than 254,000 square feet of exhibits including hands-on displays; various demonstrations pertaining to science and technology; health and human body exhibits; and flight and space displays.

The Gulf Coast Hurricane simulates the winds of a hurricane, while the Back Woods, a 40-acre wilderness, offers more than 3 miles of trails to explore. Visitors can follow the life cycle of a butterfly in a free-flight butterfly garden, focus on environmental factors of the state in Our Florida, and learn about space and flight in Our Place in the Universe. The daring can pedal a bicycle along a 1-inch-thick, 98-foot-long steel cable suspended 30 feet off the ground. There also is a special area for children under age 5.

The Saunders Planetarium offers presentations daily; phone for schedule. A high-powered telescope is available on Saturday night. The IMAX *Dome* Theatre features movie presentations projected on a 10,500-square-foot screen.

Allow 4 hours minimum. Open Mon.-Fri. 9-5, Sat.-Sun. 9-7, June-Aug.; opens daily at 9, closing times vary, rest of year. Admission, including the IMAX *Dome* theater, $13.95; over 59, $11.95; ages 2-13, $9.95. AX, DS, MC, VI. Phone (813) 987-6300 or (813) 987-6100.

TAMPA BAY HISTORY CENTER, I-275 exit 44, then 1.5 mi. e. following signs to 225 S. Franklin St., features artifacts, memorabilia, maps, military uniforms and photographs depicting life in the Tampa Bay region from 12,000 years ago to the present. Changing exhibits also are featured. Allow 1 hour minimum. Tues.-Sat. 10-5; closed holidays. Free. Phone (813) 228-0097.

[SAVE] **TAMPA MUSEUM OF ART,** 600 N. Ashley Dr., displays permanent and major traveling art exhibits. Permanent collections include Greek and Roman antiquities as well as contemporary art. Tues.-Sat. 10-5 (also Thurs. 5-8), Sun. 1-5; closed major holidays. Admission $5; over 61, $4; students with ID and ages 6-18, $3; all ages by donation Thurs. 5-8 and Sat. 10-noon. AX, MC, VI. Phone (813) 274-8130.

UNIVERSITY OF SOUTH FLORIDA occupies 1,695 acres on Fowler Ave. in n.e. Tampa. The campus features a contemporary art museum and botanical gardens. Guided campus tours can be arranged. Phone (877) 873-2855.

UNIVERSITY OF TAMPA, 401 W. Kennedy Blvd., was established in 1931 as a private liberal arts-based institution. Today it offers more than 60 fields of study to more than 4,000 students. Encompassing 85 acres, the campus centers on the former Tampa Bay Hotel, a Victorian-style building complete with Moorish revival architecture featuring minarets, domes and cupolas. The hotel was built in 1891 by Henry B. Plant, the transportation magnate who was instrumental in the reconstruction of the South. The administration and classroom building, Plant Hall, served as Theodore Roosevelt's headquarters in the Spanish-American War.

Allow 30 minutes minimum. University tours are given Tues. and Thurs. at 1:30, Sept.-May; closed Jan. 1, Thanksgiving and Dec. 18-25. Free. Phone (813) 253-6220.

Henry B. Plant Museum is housed in the south wing of Plant Hall. Once the Tampa Bay Hotel, the museum displays the Moorish Revival-style building's original collection of decorative arts and furnishings. Exhibits re-create the first-class accommodations and activities of 1891. A video presentation highlights Tampa's Victorian-era lifestyle and tourism, and a live stage performance features character vignettes of the hotel's staff and guests. Museum open Tues.-Sat. 10-4, Sun. noon-4. Stage show Sun. at 2, Sept.-Nov. and Jan.-May. Admission $5; under 13, $2. Stage show free with admission. A fee is charged for the Victorian Christmas Stroll in Dec. Phone (813) 254-1891.

WILDLIFE ON EASY STREET is at 12802 Easy St. Specializing in rare and endangered cats, this 40-acre wildlife sanctuary and rehabilitation center offers guided walking tours of its grounds and facilities. More than 20 cat species live in the sanctuary including Bengal tigers, bobcats, caracals, leopards, lions, lynxes, ocelots and servals. During

the tour visitors have the opportunity to pet one of the cats. Behind-the-Scenes, night, safari and photography tours also are available. Special tours for children under 10 are available by reservation. Allow 3 hours minimum. Tours depart Mon.-Fri. at 9 and 3, Sat. at 9:30, 11:30 and 1:30. Fee $20. Under 10 are not permitted. MC, VI. Phone (813) 920-4130.

YBOR CITY MUSEUM STATE PARK, 3 blks. s. of I-4 exit 1 at 1818 E. Ninth Ave., is in a former bakery with huge brick ovens still intact. Displays depict Ybor City's founding by Vicente Martinez-Ybor as well as the cigar industry, which brought many nationalities to Tampa. An 1895 cigar worker's cottage, furnished in period, is open by guided tour. Allow 30 minutes minimum. Daily 9-5. Admission $2, under 6 free. Phone (813) 247-6323.

What To Do

IN TAMPA BAY

Sightseeing

Balloon Tours

THE BIG RED BALLOON meets in the First Watch parking lot, 11610 N. Dale Mabry Rd. between Stall Rd. and Hudson Ln. in Tampa, for departure to the launch site. Trips offer panoramas of the Tampa landscape. A hot champagne brunch and a history of ballooning are provided. Rides last approximately 1 hour. All pilots are FAA certified.

Trips depart year-round (weather permitting). Fare $175; ages 5-10, $160. Reservations are required. AX, DS, MC, VI. Phone (813) 969-1518.

CRYSTAL MAGIC BALLOON COMPANY meets in the Northdale Shopping Center parking lot on N. Dale Mabry Hwy. at jct. N. Dale Blvd. in Tampa, for departure to the launch site. Flights offer views of the Tampa Bay area, and a champagne brunch is provided. Rides last approximately 1 hour. Both pilots are FAA certified. Trips depart year-round (weather permitting). Fare $150; ages 8-12, $135. Under 45 inches tall not permitted. Reservations are required. AX, DS, MC, VI. Phone (727) 536-3005 or (800) 930-3144.

Note: The mention of the preceding hot air balloon rides is only for information and does **not** imply endorsement by AAA.

Boat Tours

[SAVE] *STARLITE PRINCESS* **RIVERBOAT** boards at the Corey Causeway at 3400 Pasadena Ave. S. in St. Petersburg. The paddlewheel excursion boat offers a variety of sightseeing cruises on scenic inland waterways. Dinner dance cruises also are offered. Two-hour luncheon/sightseeing cruise departs Tues. and Fri.-Sat. at noon. A 3-hour luncheon/sightseeing cruise departs Wed. at noon. Dixieland Jazz cruise departs Sun. at 1. Boarding begins 30 minutes before departure. Closed major holidays.

Two-hour luncheon/sightseeing cruise (meal optional) $11.25; ages 3-12, $8.20. Three-hour sightseeing and Dixieland Jazz cruises (meal optional) $13.80; ages 3-12, $10. Reservations are required. AX, MC, VI. Phone (727) 462-2628 or (800) 444-4814.

Bus Tours

First Class Coach Martz Group bus tours service the Tampa Bay area; phone (727) 526-9086 or (800) 282-8020 for additional information.

DUCK TOURS OF TAMPA BAY depart from the downtown St. Petersburg Pier at 800 2nd Ave. N.E. Narrated tours of St. Petersburg begin on land aboard restored, World War II-era amphibious landing vehicles known as Ducks. After passengers are introduced to the history and architecture of downtown, the bright yellow craft splash into Tampa Bay for a tour of the city's waterfront. Allow 2 hours minimum. Daily 9:30-1 hour before dusk. Fare $18.50; over 54 and military with ID $16.50; ages 3-12, $9.95. Reservations are recommended. DS, MC, VI. Phone (727) 432-3825.

Driving Tours

With its scenic views of Hillsborough Bay, Bayshore Boulevard in *Tampa* is not only a popular hiking area but also a preferred driving route. Among the beautiful residential neighborhoods to explore is Davis Island, built on three man-made islands in the 1920s.

Walking Tours

The 6-mile sidewalk along Bayshore Boulevard in *Tampa,* which skirts the west side of Hillsborough Bay, is an excellent hiking area. The sidewalk is reputedly one of the world's longest continuous walkways.

The Ybor City Chamber of Commerce and Ybor City State Museum offer a guided walking tour of historic Ybor City; the fee is $5. The 2-hour tour departs from Ybor City State Museum Sat. at 10:30. For further information contact the museum at 1818 E. Ninth Ave., Tampa, FL 33605; phone (813) 247-6323.

Spectator Sports

Tampa Bay area fans have the option to root for a home run; slap high-fives after a touchdown; count down the time during a power play; watch dogs chase a stuffed rabbit; or applaud as a favorite horse makes a photo finish. Whatever your pleasure, the following options will have you cheering.

Baseball

Professional baseball is played at several locations. The **Tampa Bay Devil Rays** play major league baseball April through September at **Tropicana Field,** 1 Tropicana Dr. in *St. Petersburg;* phone (727) 825-3250 for general information, or (727) 898-7297 for tickets. The Devil Rays remain in St. Petersburg during the off-season; spring training games take place at Al Lang Field at **Florida Power Park,** 180 Second Ave. S.E.; phone (727) 825-3284 for ticket information. Both the Devil Rays major and minor league teams train at 7901 30th Ave. N.

The **New York Yankees** major and minor league teams call *Tampa* home in the spring. They play at **Legends Field,** N. Dale Mabry Highway and Martin Luther King Jr. Boulevard. The facility's 10,000-seat stadium is a replica of New

York's Yankee Stadium. Play is March to September; for information phone (813) 875-7753.

Two other major league teams hold spring training on the Pinellas Peninsula: the Philadelphia Phillies and the Toronto Blue Jays, both of which have minor league affiliates that play ball locally. In summer the **Clearwater Phillies** train at *Clearwater's* **Jack Russell Memorial Stadium,** north of Drew Street at 800 Phillies Dr., and the **Dunedin Blue Jays** work out at **Dunedin Stadium,** 373 Douglas Ave. in Dunedin. Both teams play a full minor league schedule; phone (727) 441-8638 for the Phillies and (727) 733-9302 for the Blue Jays.

Football

The NFL's **Tampa Bay Buccaneers** play at **Raymond James Stadium** between N. Dale Mabry Highway and N. Himes Avenue; for ticket information phone (813) 879-2827. The stadium also is the setting for the Outback Bowl game, played on New Year's Day. The **Tampa Bay Storm** play arena football from February to June at the **St. Pete Times Forum,** downtown *Tampa* at Channelside Drive and Morgan Street; phone (813) 276-7300.

Greyhound Racing

The *St. Petersburg* Kennel Club's **Derby Lane** track at 10490 Gandy Blvd. features greyhound racing most evenings and weekends from early January to late June; phone (727) 812-3339. **Tampa Greyhound Track,** 8300 N. Nebraska Ave. at Waters Street in the Sulphur Springs section of *Tampa,* does the same July through December; phone (813) 932-4313.

Note: Policies vary concerning admittance of children to pari-mutuel betting facilities. Phone for information.

Hockey

The NHL's **Tampa Bay Lightning** hits the ice at the St. Pete Times Forum October through April. For more information phone (813) 223-6100; for tickets phone (813) 223-1000.

Horse Racing

Horse racing devotees can go to the only Thoroughbred track on Florida's west coast, **Tampa Bay Downs,** 11225 Race Track Rd. in Tampa. The track holds races mid-December to early May. For more information phone (813) 855-4401.

Note: Policies vary concerning admittance of children to pari-mutuel betting facilities. Phone for information.

Recreation

The American Medical Association was on to the bay area's bounty of recreational riches back in

1885, when it named St. Petersburg as an ideal location for a "world health city." Near year-round warmth, broad beaches, a varied system of waterways and some 400 public parks and playgrounds make the region a true haven for outdoor enthusiasts.

Bicycling

Tampa's busy roadways generally are not conducive to safe bicycling; however, scenic, 6-mile **Bayshore Boulevard** is a delightful exception. It offers a breezy ride along the western shore of Hillsborough Bay with pretty water views as a backdrop. **Suncoast Parkway Trail** parallels the toll-road of the same name between the Veterans Expressway and State Road 50, and is generally separated from it by a buffer zone of plants and trees.

The **Friendship Trail Bridge,** once the Old Gandy Bridge connecting *Tampa* and *St. Petersburg,* now serves as an over-the-water recreation trail for bicyclists, in-line skaters and joggers. Phone (813) 289-4400, ext. 303 for information.

Fishing

The central Gulf Coast offers some of the best saltwater fishing in the state. More than 300 species roam these warm waters. Tarpon appear in late spring and early summer, and kingfish run in spring and fall. Sea trout, bluefish, mackerel and grouper are commonly caught, and the waters of Hillsborough County yield bass, bream and perch.

Boats can be chartered for inshore and offshore saltwater and freshwater fishing; make arrangements at **Clearwater Municipal Marina, St. Pete Beach** or **Isla del Sol.** Boats equipped for 30-100 passengers venture into deep Gulf waters; they can be rented for half-day or all-day trips, which cost $20-$40 per person, depending on the amenities offered. For details about what may be caught where and when, pick up a *Guide to Florida Fishing* at local tackle shops.

Lake Thonotosassa, northeast of *Tampa* via SR 582, attracts freshwater fishing enthusiasts. The docks of **Davis Island** and Bayshore Boulevard in Tampa offer ample casting sites. **The Skyway Fishing Pier,** next to the Sunshine Skyway Bridge, extends 3,350 feet into lower Tampa Bay; its northern end has concession stands, showers, picnic tables and parking lots.

Freshwater and saltwater fishing licenses are sold at some tackle shops, sporting goods and discount department stores and at the county tax collector's office. Phone (813) 307-6549 for information.

Golf

With some 50 courses to choose from and weather that allows for year-round play, the bay area is a true golfer's paradise. Some of the public and semiprivate courses in the *St. Petersburg* area are Bardmoor Golf and Tennis Club, 8001 Cumberland Rd. in Largo, (727) 392-1234; Baypointe, 9399 Commodore Dr., (727) 595-2095; Mainlands, 9445 Mainlands Blvd., (727) 577-4847; Mangrove Bay, 875 62nd Ave. N.E., (727) 893-7800; Tides, 11832 66th Ave. N. in Seminole, (727) 393-8483; and Twin Brooks, 3800 22nd Ave. S., (727) 893-7445. East Bay Golf Club of Largo, 702 Country Club Dr., offers night golf until 11:30 p.m.; phone (727) 581-3333.

Tampa area courses include Babe Zaharias, 11412 Forest Hills Dr., (813) 631-4374; Rocky Point, 4151 Dana Shores Dr., (813) 673-4316; and Rogers Park, 7910 N. 30th St., (813) 673-4396. There are several semiprivate courses, such as Northdale, (813) 962-0428, that let visitors play upon payment of greens and cart fees.

Jogging and Walking

Sunny weather encourages both visitors and locals to enjoy the outdoors. The **Pinellas Trail**, a former railroad corridor stretching 37 miles from Tarpon Springs to *St. Petersburg*, provides opportunities for walking, jogging, bicycling and in-line skating. Many entry and exit points exist along the trail. For information contact the Pinellas County Park Department, 631 Chestnut St. in Clearwater; phone (727) 464-3347.

Some 8 miles of nature trails wind through scenic hardwood hammocks at **Hillsborough River State Park,** about 12 miles northeast of *Tampa* via US 301.

Tennis

The **St. Petersburg Tennis Center,** 650 18th Ave. S., features 15 clay tennis courts; phone (727) 823-2225. For additional information phone the Tampa Recreation Department at (813) 274-7529.

In *Tampa* the city-operated facility at **Hillsborough Community College,** west of Raymond James Stadium, has both hard and soft courts; phone (813) 348-1173. There are eight clay courts at **Marjorie Park,** on Davis Island just south of downtown Tampa; phone (813) 259-1664. There are six clay and two hard courts at the **Treasure Island Golf, Tennis and Recreation Center,** 10315 Paradise Blvd.; phone (727) 360-6062.

Water Sports

The Pinellas Peninsula's many beaches, with their attendant pleasures—swimming, skin diving and water skiing—line the slender offshore islands.

While there are two public beaches on the *Tampa* side of the bay—**Ben T. Davis Beach,** along Courtney Campbell Causeway (SR 60) near the airport, and **Picnic Island Park** near Port Tampa—it's the gulf beaches that draw water lovers. Some of the popular island towns are **Indian Rocks Beach, Madeira Beach,** St. Pete Beach, **Treasure Island** and **North Redington Beach.**

Water sports of all kinds, including parasailing, are the focal point at **John's Pass Village and Boardwalk,** 140 128th Ave. in Madeira Beach, (727) 391-7373. The **Tackle Shack** in Pinellas Park offers instruction and rentals for kayaking, sailboating and scuba diving; phone (727) 546-5080 or (800) 537-6099.

Canoeing on area waters is another popular form of recreation. **Canoe Escape,** off I-75 exit 265, then east to 9335 E. Fowler Ave. in Thonotosassa, offers trips of varying distances. Trips weave through streams and creeks adjacent to wooded banks populated with alligators, turtles and birds. Canoers paddle downstream where they are met and shuttled to the point of origin; phone (813) 986-2067.

The Pinellas County park system provides several areas throughout the county where picnicking, boating and swimming can be enjoyed. **Fort De Soto Park,** south of St. Pete Beach, is one of the most developed *(see Recreation Chart and the AAA Southeastern CampBook).*

Picnic Island Park, near the original encampment of Theodore Roosevelt's Rough Riders during the Spanish-American War, beckons boaters, swimmers, picnickers and anglers. The park is south of the Gandy Bridge (US 92) near MacDill Air Force Base and accessible via Commerce Street in *Tampa.*

Other Diversions

One of the world's largest shuffleboard clubs is at **Mirror Lake Recreation Park** in downtown *St. Petersburg*. A daily guest membership is available. The **St. Petersburg Shuffleboard Club,** next to Mirror Lake Recreation Park, provides lawn bowling lanes; phone (727) 822-2083. If you'd rather exercise gray matter than muscles, try the **St. Petersburg Chess Club** any day of the week at 540 4th Ave. N. in Mirror Lake Recreation Park; phone (727) 822-1171. For trapshooting enthusiasts, the **Tampa Bay Sporting Clays** in Land O' Lakes offers 5-stand sporting clays and courses through palmetto and pine woods; phone (813) 995-9282.

Shopping

Tampa Bay's retail front offers a great deal of activity, whether it be expansive malls, factory outlet centers or specialty shopping districts.

Antiques

In *St. Petersburg* the **Gas Plant Antique Arcade,** 1246 Central Ave., offers wares from more than 100 dealers. Unusual shops contain a variety of finds from jewelry to antiques along **Beach Drive.**

An antiques district of sorts centers on the shops along **Euclid Avenue** and **El Prado Boulevard** near south *Tampa's* Palma Ceia neighborhood. And **Antique & Decorative Arts,** 917 N. Franklin St., carries European furniture, glassware, rugs, silver jewelry, porcelain and works of art.

Malls

Want to shop until you drop? *St. Petersburg's* selection of malls can get you started. The four anchors at **Tyrone Square Mall,** Tyrone Boulevard and 22nd Avenue N., are Burdines, Dillard's, JCPenney and Sears. The mall also contains more than 170 other stores and restaurants. Other malls include **Crosswinds Shopping Center,** 66th Street and 20th Avenue N., and **ParkSide Mall,** Park Boulevard and US 19. Downtown St. Petersburg is home to **Baywalk,** 153 2nd. Ave. N., a shopping complex that includes Ann Taylor.

The largest mall on the Pinellas Peninsula is *Clearwater's* **Countryside Mall,** US 19N and SR 580, which features Burdines, Dillard's, JCPenney and Sears, in addition to restaurants and more than 170 boutiques and specialty outlets. Countryside also contains the state's only in-mall ice-skating rink.

Clearwater Mall, US 19N and Gulf-to-Bay Boulevard, has Burdines, Dillard's, Gayfers and more than 120 other stores. If you're heading for the beach and need to pick up a few things, **Seminole Mall,** at the corner of 113th Street and Park Boulevard in Seminole, has a Bealls outlet and some 70 other stores.

There's more shopping across the bay in *Tampa*. **Franklin Street Mall** is in the city center and is open mainly when office workers are downtown.

Citrus Park Town Center, off Veterans Expressway and Gunn Highway, is in west Tampa. One of the area's newer malls, built in 1995, is **Brandon TownCenter,** at the intersection of I-75 and SR 60 on Tampa's east side. The major anchor stores are Burdines, Dillard's, JCPenney and Sears, complemented by 120 specialty shops and boutiques.

[SAVE] **University Mall,** west of the University of South Florida at 2200 E. Fowler Ave., is the region's largest at 1.3 million square feet. The major stores operating here are Burdines, Dillard's, JCPenney and Sears, along with more than 130 specialty shops and restaurants.

Next to Tampa International Airport, [SAVE] **International Plaza** is an upscale, two-story mall with a large restaurant courtyard and approximately 200 stores. It is anchored by Dillard's, Lord & Taylor, Neiman Marcus and Nordstrom, and includes Christian Dior, Godiva and Tiffany & Co. Last but not least, [SAVE] **West Shore Plaza,** off I-275 exit 40A, opened in 1967 and was the first of *Tampa's* enclosed malls. Burdines, JCPenney, Saks Fifth Avenue and Sears anchor the mall, which has more than 130 other stores and an international food court.

Outlets

The area's factory outlets are a good bet for good buys. In *Clearwater,* **Crossroads Mall,** Roosevelt Boulevard and US 19, has Bass Shoes, 9 West, TJ Maxx, Van Heusen and about 60 other stores.

Specialty Districts

The Pinellas side of the bay offers intriguing shopping, much of it with an appropriately waterside theme. At Gulf Boulevard and 128th Avenue in

Madeira Beach is **John's Pass Village & Board-walk,** where a fishing village atmosphere permeates more than 100 stores, boutiques and restaurants. The shopping experience is enhanced by a scenic 1,000-foot boardwalk. The **Wagon Wheel Flea Market,** 7801 Park Blvd. in Pinellas Park, has more than 2,000 vendors and is open Sat.-Sun. 7:30-4.

A bit farther down the peninsula, at 5501 Gulf Blvd. in St. Pete Beach, is **Silas Bayside Market,** a small complex of shops and restaurants in a tropical setting. **The Pier,** at the end of 2nd Avenue N.E. in downtown *St. Petersburg,* has shops, restaurants and a food court, all under one inverted pyramid roof facing Tampa Bay.

The atmosphere is as enticing as the offerings at the bay area's assorted specialty emporiums. Just off Bayshore Boulevard at Swann and Dakota avenues in Hyde Park—a stone's throw from downtown *Tampa*—is **Old Hyde Park Village,** which contains a delightful collection of more than 50 shops, restaurants and cafes. The area offers an Old World charm complemented by a cosmopolitan tempo. Shoppers can settle at a shady outdoor table after perusing the upscale merchandise at the likes of Brooks Brothers, Restoration Hardware, The Sharper Image and Williams-Sonoma.

More eclectic offerings are available in Ybor City, *Tampa's* Latin Quarter just northeast of downtown. Shopping and dining establishments are focused around **Centro Ybor,** between 15th and 17th streets and 7th and 9th avenues. Here and in the surrounding area shoppers may delight in boutiques and specialty stores. A short drive from Ybor City and adjacent to the Florida Aquarium is **Channel-side,** an entertainment and dining complex featuring several boutiques and gift shops.

Performing Arts

Tampa Bay's spectrum of arts encompasses blockbuster Broadway musicals, symphony and chamber music concerts, children's shows and holiday spectaculars. Its keystone is the 300,000-square-foot **Tampa Bay Performing Arts Center** (TBPAC), the largest performing arts facility south

of Washington, D.C.'s Kennedy Center. On the east bank of the Hillsborough River in downtown *Tampa,* the TBPAC plays host to a great variety of cultural events at its venues: the 2,557-seat **Carol Morsani Hall;** 1,000-seat **Ferguson Hall;** 300-seat **Jaeb Theater;** and 150-seat **Shimberg Playhouse.** Phone (813) 229-7827 for schedule and ticket information regarding each of these venues.

Be sure to grab a free copy of the *Weekly Planet,* which is available throughout the city. The publication is filled with local news features; sections on restaurants, theater, film and music; and listings of upcoming events.

Film

Downtown's 1,500-seat **Tampa Theatre,** a restored 1926 movie palace at 711 Franklin St. Mall, is a great spot to catch foreign films, cult movies, Hollywood classics and occasional concerts. Tours of the historic building also are offered; phone (813) 274-8981. **Beach Theatre,** 315 Corey Ave. in St. Pete Beach, shows foreign and offbeat, low-budget films; phone (727) 360-6697.

Music

A full season of symphonic presentations is brought to the Tampa Bay area by the **Florida Orchestra Inc.** and by local dance companies. Performances take place at TBPAC; *Clearwater's* acoustically acclaimed **Ruth Eckerd Hall** in the Richard B. Baumgardner Center for the Performing Arts; and the **Mahaffey Theater** in *St. Petersburg's* Bayfront Center. Phone (813) 286-2403 or (800) 662-7286 for ticket and schedule information.

Works for voice are presented by the **Master Chorale of Tampa Bay,** (813) 258-9468; **Tampa Oratorio Singers,** (813) 247-3866; and **Tampa Bay Arts Inc.,** (727) 865-9004. Performance locations vary.

Free band concerts are held January through March at **Williams Park** in downtown *St. Petersburg.* **Straub Park,** next to the Museum of Fine Arts overlooking the inner harbor, and bayside **Vinoy Park,** near Straub Park, are settings for many events in St. Petersburg.

Theater

Broadway and off-Broadway plays are a big hit in the bay area. Try the **American Stage Theater,** 211 Third St. S. in *St. Petersburg,* for classical and contemporary plays in an intimate setting; phone (727) 823-7529. The **St. Petersburg Little Theater,** 4025 31st St. S., stages six major productions September through June; phone (727) 866-1973.

The **Carrollwood Players,** 4333 Gunn Hwy. in *Tampa,* is a little-theater group presenting a variety of productions; phone (813) 265-4000. TBPAC's Shimberg

Playhouse features local performing companies and improvisational groups, and the cozy Jaeb Theater presents plays and cabaret shows.

The **Tampa Bay Broadway Series** brings the best of Broadway to TBPAC's Carol Morsani Hall. Productions for the 2002/2003 season include "Lord of the Dance," "The Lion King," "The Full Monty," "Aida," "Seussical the Musical," "42nd Street" and "Satchmo." Phone (813) 229-7827.

Special Events

St. Petersburg recognizes its ethnic groups during the **International Folk Fair** in March; offerings include ethnic foods and folk dances.

St. Petersburg's biggest celebration is the **Festival of States,** which is held in early April and pays tribute to the city's winter visitors; waterfront fireworks, an arts festival, music festival, the election of royalty, a ball and a parade fill the agenda.

St. Petersburg also is host to **St. Anthony's Tampa Bay Triathlon,** which takes place in April; **Shakespeare in the Park,** which offers several weeks of professional productions of Shakespeare's works redone in a lighter, humorous mode mid-April to mid-May; and **Tarpon Round-Up,** a popular fishing event held during May and June. To round out the year, the holiday **Lighted Boat Parade** takes place downtown at the waterfront in early December.

Tampa's calendar of events begins with **The Outback Bowl** at **Raymond James Stadium** on Dale Mabry Highway. This New Year's Day event matches college football's Southeastern Conference and Big 10 Conference champions.

But of all the goings-on, the **Gasparilla Pirate Fest** is the biggest, maddest and most colorful of *Tampa's* events. Florida's answer to Mardi Gras, Gasparilla is held the first Saturday in February with the capturing of Tampa by pirates, followed by several parades throughout the city. The festivities continue throughout the month with **Fiesta Day,** a celebration of ethnic diversity in Ybor City, and the 5- and 15-kilometer **Gasparilla Distance Classic** the first weekend in March. The **Gasparilla Festival of the Arts** wraps up the celebration with artists and craftspersons from around the world.

Not to be outdone by "the invasion" and all its associated activities, the **Florida State Fair** in February is the showcase for the state's finest agriculture, handicrafts, arts and industry. A midway, entertainment, shows and exhibits add to the festivities. The **Verizon Classic,** held at TPC of Tampa Bay, tees off in mid-February. The **Best of Tampa Bay,** sponsored by the Tampa Bay Performing Arts Center in April, features culinary creations from the area's top restaurants.

Guavaween, *Tampa's* Latin-style Halloween celebration, includes a street party, satirical parade, contests and entertainment. The event, held in Ybor City in October, takes its name from a succulent tropical fruit and echoes a Tampa nickname: "The Big Guava."

Celebrate another delicious fruit at the **Florida**

Strawberry Festival in Plant City, where visitors can indulge in strawberry shortcakes and enjoy musical performances. Festivities coincide with the fruit's harvest in early March.

Aficionados of performing arts won't want to miss the **Clearwater Jazz Holiday.** The 4-day festival, held the third weekend in October at downtown *Clearwater's* Coachman Park, features performers of national and international acclaim.

Nightlife

Evening options in Tampa Bay range from a romantic stroll along a quiet beach under the stars to a night of dancing, where the musical accompaniment could be mellow jazz, twangy country and western, thunderous rock or just about anything in between.

Comedy Clubs

Give your funny bone a workout at **SideSplitters,** 12938 N. Dale Mabry Hwy. at S.W. Fletcher Avenue in *Tampa.* The club presents local talent and national acts; phone (813) 960-1197 for show times and reservations. Top comic talents can also be found at the **Improv Comedy Club,** 1600 E. 8th Ave. at Centro Ybor; phone (813) 864-4000.

Two **Coconuts Comedy Clubs** can be found in the city; phone (727) 797-5653 (Sunset Point Road and US 19 in the Cinema Cafe) or (727) 360-5653 (6100 Gulf Blvd. in the Howard Johnson, St. Pete Beach).

Country

Country music is popular in the bay area, and several area clubs accommodate the genre by offering live and recorded music. In *Tampa* it's the **Round-Up,** 13918 W. Hillsborough Ave. at Race Track Road, a country & western club with a

3,000-square-foot dance floor, free dance lessons and occasional live concerts; phone (813) 855-1464 or (813) 855-1229.

Dance Clubs

More than a few spots in the bay area specialize in disco- and alternative-style music. At 420 Park Place Blvd. in *Clearwater,* **Joe Dugan's** is a restaurant and DJ dance club; phone (727) 796-7867.

Ybor City in downtown *Tampa* has several nightclubs that pack in the crowds. **Club 1509** is at 1509 E. Eighth Ave.; phone (813) 247-6606. **Pleasuredome,** 1430 E. Seventh Ave., caters to a gay and lesbian clientele on Tuesday nights and attracts people of all persuasions Friday and Saturday. The club features high-energy dancing and occasional concerts; phone (813) 247-2711. Nearby is **Masquerade,** 1503 E. Seventh Ave., in the historic Ritz Theatre. The young, dressed-to-thrill crowd grooves to house, techno, underground and alternative music programmed by guest DJs. Live shows tend toward the latest new bands. Masquerade is open Wednesday through Sunday; phone (813) 247-3319.

Jazz & Blues

Tampa Bay retains an active jazz and blues scene. In *St. Petersburg,* check out the **Ringside Cafe,** 2742 Fourth St. N., (727) 894-8465. **Skipper's Smokehouse,** at the corner of Skipper Road and Nebraska Avenue in north *Tampa,* offers an eclectic lineup of artists covering blues to reggae to funk to world beat. Most shows start at 8 p.m.; phone (813) 971-0666.

Rock

Classic and contemporary rock in addition to Top 40 and reggae—live as well as recorded—all can be heard around town. Near the gulf beaches, try **Cha Cha Coconuts** at The Pier, 800 2nd Ave. N.E. in *St. Petersburg;* phone (727) 822-6655. Alternative bands take the stage in St. Petersburg at **Jannus Landing,** 220 First Ave. N.; phone (727) 896-2276. Another favorite is **Gasoline Alley,** at 17928 US 19 in *Clearwater;* phone (727) 532-0265.

The Green Iguana has two locations: at 4029 S. Westshore Blvd. in south *Tampa* and 1708 E. 7th Ave. in Ybor City; phone (813) 837-1234 or (813) 248-9555, respectively. Ybor City also is home to **Harpo's,** 1805 E. 7th Ave.; phone (813) 248-4814.

Current pop, rock and rap acts are booked into the **Sun Dome** at the University of South Florida, 4202 E. Fowler Ave., and **Expo Hall,** on the Florida State Fairgrounds at 4800 Hwy. 301 N.; phone (813) 974-3002.

The Tampa Bay Vicinity

APOLLO BEACH (E-8) pop. 7,444

MANATEE VIEWING CENTER, is 2.5 mi. w. of I-75 exit 246, Big Bend Rd., at jct. Big Bend (CR 672) and Dickman rds. The center is across the warm-water discharge canal from the Tampa Electric Big Bend power plant, and features an observation platform for winter manatee watching. The education building presents displays and a movie about manatee biological characteristics and habitat as well as displays about coastal water birds, Florida yard landscaping, power plant generation and by-product recycling.

The self-guided nature trail on the tidal flat walkway provides closer glimpses of the plant and wildlife native to the area. The best time to see manatees is when Tampa Bay water temperature is below 68 degrees F. Much of the facility is outdoors, so dress for current weather conditions.

Allow 1 hour, 30 minutes minimum. Daily 10-5, Nov.-Apr.; closed Easter, Thanksgiving and Dec. 25. Free. Phone (813) 228-4289 to verify operating dates.

CLEARWATER (G-7) pop. 108,787, elev. 29'

A resort city and popular retirement community on the Pinellas Peninsula, Clearwater overlooks the Gulf of Mexico. Clearwater Beach, which is part of the city, is connected with the mainland by the Clearwater Memorial Causeway, a landscaped, 2-mile drive. The broad, white sand beach attracts both residents and visitors.

Outdoor entertainment is plentiful. The Clearwater Municipal Marina harbors a large sport-fishing fleet: Boats for deep-sea fishing can be chartered daily. Sightseeing cruises on the Gulf are available. The Dolphin Encounter offers an opportunity to view dolphins and feed seabirds; for schedule and fare information, phone (727) 442-7433.

The Philadelphia Phillies baseball team trains and plays exhibition games at Jack Russell Memorial Stadium from early March to early April; phone

(727) 441-8638. Magicians, jugglers, musicians, and craftspeople gather on Pier 60 daily at dusk for Sunsets at Pier 60.

Broadway shows, orchestral and jazz performances, ballet, opera and children's theater are staged throughout the year at Ruth Eckerd Hall in Richard B. Baumgardner Center, 1111 McMullen Booth Rd.; phone (727) 791-7400.

Clearwater Regional Chamber of Commerce: 1130 Cleveland St., P.O. Box 2457, Clearwater, FL 33755; phone (727) 461-0011.

Shopping areas: Crossroads Mall, 15579 US 19 S., offers a variety of shops. Countryside Mall, 27001 US 19 N., features Burdines, Dillard's, JCPenney and Sears as well as an ice skating rink.

CAPTAIN MEMO'S PIRATE CRUISE, just off SR 60 at Clearwater City Marina, offers 2-hour cruises in the Gulf of Mexico aboard a reproduction of a pirate ship. Cruise departs daily at 10, 2, 4:30 and 7 p.m. Boarding is 30 minutes before departure. Schedule may vary; phone ahead. Fare $28 ($30 for 4:30 and 7 p.m. cruises); over 65 and ages 13-17, $22; ages 2-12, $18. Reservations are recommended. AX, DS, MC, VI. Phone (727) 446-2587. *See ad.*

[SAVE] **CLEARWATER MARINE AQUARIUM,** 249 Windward Passage, is a working aquarium dedicated to public education, marine research and the rescue, rehabilitation and release of injured or sick whales, dolphins, otters and sea turtles. Marine exhibits, underwater viewing tanks and animal care presentations are offered. Allow 1 hour, 30 minutes minimum. Mon.-Fri. 9-5, Sat. 9-4, Sun. 11-4; closed major holidays. Admission $8.75; ages 3-11, $6.25. MC, VI. Phone (727) 441-1790 or (888) 239-9414.

MOCCASIN LAKE NATURE PARK: AN ENVIRONMENTAL AND ENERGY EDUCATION CENTER, 2750 Park Trail Ln., is a 51-acre nature preserve. The interpretive center features wildlife,

plant and energy exhibits. Nature trails wind through upland hardwoods and wetlands to a 5-acre lake. Guided tours are available for a fee with advance notification. Picnicking is permitted. Allow 1 hour minimum. Tues.-Fri. 9-5, Sat.-Sun. 10-6; closed Jan. 1, July 4, Thanksgiving, day after Thanksgiving and Dec. 25. Admission $2; ages 2-13, $1. Phone (727) 462-6024.

SAVE **SHOW QUEEN** departs from Clearwater Beach Marina at 25 Causeway Blvd. The captain gives a historical narration during sightseeing/lunch and dinner cruises along the Clearwater harbor and intracoastal waterway. The open top deck provides opportunities for viewing seabirds and marine life. Afternoon cruises depart Mon.-Sat. at 12:30, Sun. at 1:30 (weather permitting). Sightseeing cruise $9.95; ages 4-10, $5.95. Sightseeing cruise with lunch $17.95; ages 4-10, $7.95. Reservations are recommended. AX, DS, MC, VI. Phone (727) 461-3113.

SAVE **STARLITE MAJESTY** is just off SR 60 at Clearwater Beach Marina. The tri-deck yacht offers 2- and 3-hour sightseeing tours of Clearwater Harbor. Dinner/dance cruises also are available. Two-hour sightseeing tours depart Tues.-Wed. and Fri.-Sat. at noon. Three-hour cruise departs Thurs. at noon. Boarding is 30 minutes before departure. Two-hour sightseeing cruise $11.25; ages 3-12, $8.20 (meals extra). Three-hour cruise $13.80; ages 3-12, $10 (meals extra). Reservations are required for luncheon and dinner/dance cruises. AX, MC, VI. Phone (727) 462-2628 or (800) 444-4814.

DADE CITY (D-9) pop. 6,188, elev. 89′

Originally settled as Fort Dade in the 1840s, the settlement's name was changed to Dade City in 1884. Historic Church Avenue, the restored Old Courthouse, antiques shops, and a lively calendar of events add to the community's quaint atmosphere.

Greater Dade City Chamber of Commerce: 14112 8th St., Dade City, FL 33525; phone (352) 567-3769.

SAVE **PIONEER FLORIDA MUSEUM AND VILLAGE** is 1.5 mi. n. via US 301, then e. on Pioneer Museum Rd. Highlights include a one-room pioneer schoolhouse; the 1860s John Overstreet House; Enterprise Methodist Church; the 1896 Trilby Depot, featuring a 1913 Porter steam engine; Cummers Sons Cypress Sawmill Co. buildings; C.C. Smith General Store; Bromley Shoe Repair Shop; a moonshine still; a natural stream exhibit; and a sugar cane exhibit. The museum's permanent collection displays early farm machinery, vintage carriages, American Indian artifacts, Roseville pottery, textiles, and antique toys and dolls.

Allow 2 hours minimum. Tues.-Sun. 1-5; closed holidays. Admission $5; over 54, $4; ages 6-18, $2. Phone (352) 567-0262.

DUNEDIN (G-7) pop. 35,691, elev. 13′

Dunedin, a name closely resembling the Gaelic word from which Edinburgh is derived, traces its Scottish heritage to the town's early days as a seaport and trading center. Its villagelike image has been preserved in a rejuvenated downtown with boutiques and antiques shops, while subtropical surroundings and almost four miles of waterfront account for its tranquil atmosphere. Home of the spring training camp of the Toronto Blue Jays baseball club, Dunedin Stadium features exhibition games from early March to early April and A league Dunedin Blue Jays throughout the summer; phone (727) 733-9302.

Just off the coast, two barrier islands are available to water and nature enthusiasts. The Gulf beaches of Honeymoon Island State Recreation Area, accessible via Dunedin Causeway, are popular for swimming and sunbathing. Caladesi Island State Park is reached by passenger ferry departing from the recreation area at regular intervals; phone (727) 734-5263. *See Recreation Chart.* Both parks are refuges for endangered birds, including egrets, herons and storks. Between the mainland and the islands outdoor enthusiasts can windsurf, sail catamarans and ride personal watercraft on the protected waters of St. Joseph Sound.

Bicycling, walking, jogging and inline skating can be enjoyed on a portion of the Pinellas Trail that winds through the downtown area.

Transportation memorabilia and historical documents, photographs and artifacts are found at Dunedin Historical Society and Museum, 341 Main St., in the former railroad depot; phone (727) 736-1176.

Greater Dunedin Chamber of Commerce: 301 Main St., Dunedin, FL 34698; phone (727) 733-3197.

INDIAN ROCKS BEACH (H-7)
pop. 5,072, elev. 10′

Indian Rocks Beach is a resort community near the midpoint of Sand Key, a long, narrow island in the Gulf off the Pinellas County coast. It is accessible by SR 688 north of St. Petersburg.

Tampa Bay Beaches Chamber of Commerce: 6990 Gulf Blvd., St. Pete Beach, FL 33706; phone (727) 360-6957 or (800) 944-1847.

INDIAN SHORES (H-7) pop. 1,705, elev. 5′

SUNCOAST SEABIRD SANCTUARY, on the Gulf Coast at 18328 Gulf Blvd., houses and treats injured pelicans, herons, egrets, owls, hawks and other birds. Rehabilitated birds are released into the wild; those with permanent impairments remain at the sanctuary or are sent to other wildlife parks around the world. Educational programs are presented the first Sunday of each month at 2. Daily 9-dusk. Guided tours and lectures are offered Wed. and Sun. at 2. Donations. Phone (727) 391-6211.

LARGO (H-7) pop. 69,371, elev. 50′

Largo is bordered on three sides by water—the Gulf of Mexico circles around the west and south sides, and Tampa Bay is on the eastern border. In 1905 when it became a city, it had 291 residents and covered 1 square mile.

Greater Largo Chamber of Commerce: 151 3rd St. N.W., P.O. Box 326, Largo, FL 33779-0326; phone (727) 584-2321.

Shopping areas: Largo Mall, on the corner of Ulmerton Road (SR 688) and Seminole Boulevard, has more than 75 stores and restaurants.

PINEWOOD CULTURAL PARK is just off Ulmerton Rd. at 125th St. N. This 182-acre site is home to three attractions and the Pinellas County Extension office of the University of Florida. Daily 7-7. Free. Phone (727) 582-2200.

Florida Botanical Gardens is at 12175 125th St. N. Among the many themed areas at this 150-acre garden are those dedicated to herbs, palms, roses and topiaries. Native Florida plants and exotic specimens suited to the local climate are represented in both natural and formal settings. Visitors can wander along paths that wind around ponds bordered by colorful flowers and splashing fountains. Allow 2 hours minimum. Daily 7-6. Welcome Center Mon.-Sat. 8-5. Closed Thanksgiving and Dec. 25. Free. Phone (727) 582-2100.

Gulf Coast Museum of Art is at 12211 Walsingham Rd. Permanent and changing displays of contemporary art include works by Florida artists from 1960 onward and fine contemporary craft media objects from the southeastern United States. Allow 1 hour, 30 minutes minimum. Tues.-Sat. 10-4 (also Thurs. 4-7), Sun. noon-4. Admission $5; over 61, $4; students with ID $3; under 12 free; free to all Thurs. Phone (727) 518-6833.

Heritage Village is at 11909 125th St. N. More than two dozen structures relocated to this 21-acre site depict life during the early days of Pinellas County. A museum in the center of the complex displays maps and photographs of early Pinellas County. Guided tours are available. Open Tues.-Sat. 10-4, Sun. 1-4; closed major holidays. Donations. Phone (727) 582-2123.

MADEIRA BEACH (H-7) pop. 4,511, elev. 6′

Joined to the mainland near St. Petersburg by a free causeway, Madeira Beach offers good swimming and parasailing as well as rentals of personal watercraft. Boats can be chartered from several marinas for fishing in the Gulf of Mexico.

Tampa Bay Beaches Chamber of Commerce: 6990 Gulf Blvd., St. Pete Beach, FL 33706; phone (727) 360-6957 or (800) 944-1847.

Shopping areas: John's Pass Village and Boardwalk, 12901 Gulf Blvd. E., is a shopping area with a nautical theme; it contains more than 100 gift and specialty shops, restaurants and art galleries.

HUBBARD'S SEA ADVENTURES, departing from 150 John's Pass Boardwalk, offers a narrated 1.5-hour sightseeing trip aboard a catamaran. Passengers can view dolphins and a variety of bird life along the way. Deep-sea fishing trips also are available. Allow 2 hours minimum. Sightseeing cruise departs daily at 1, 3 and 5 (also at 6:30, Apr.-Sept.); closed Dec. 25. Fare $11.95; ages 3-11, $6. Reservations are suggested. AX, DS, MC, VI. Phone (727) 398-6577.

ODESSA (E-8) pop. 3,173, elev. 58′

J.B. STARKEY'S FLATWOODS ADVENTURES is at 12959 SR 54. Visitors board a "range buggy," a specially designed open-sided bus, for narrated 2.5-hour tours of this vast working cattle ranch. During the tour, Florida cowboys known as "crackers" demonstrate calf roping and whip cracking and describe how the horses they ride are trained. The tour also includes tracts of wilderness where passengers may see wild turkeys, gopher tortoises, fox squirrels and alligators among other animals. An elevated boardwalk leading to an observation deck provides a view of an alligator hole. Horseback riding tours also are available.

Allow 3 hours minimum. Mon.-Fri. 8-4:30, Sat. 8-1. Admission $15.75; senior citizens $14.75; ages 3-12, $8.75. Reservations are required. MC, VI. Phone (813) 926-1133 or (877) 734-9453.

PLANT CITY (E-8) pop. 29,915, elev. 37′

Plant City was named after Henry Bradley Plant, a wealthy railroad magnate, but the town is best known for its plant crop, the strawberry. The majority of all the winter strawberries in the United States is grown on farms surrounding Plant City. The annual Florida Strawberry Festival draws some 900,000 visitors in early March.

The town is home to the International Softball Federation, the world governing body for softball competition. The Tampa Bay Polo Club plays at Walden Lake Polo Field Sunday afternoons at 2 from early January through late April; admission $4; phone (813) 752-4495.

The Pioneer/Heritage Museum, in the 1914 Plant City High School Community Center at 605 N. Collins St., have several exhibit rooms with period themes such as clothing, furnishings, medical equipment, farm implements and railroading; phone (813) 757-9226.

City Hall: 302 W. Reynolds St., Plant City, FL 33566; phone (813) 659-4200.

DINOSAUR WORLD, off I-4 exit 17, just n. on Branch Forbes Rd., then just w. to 5145 Harvey Tew Rd., features more than 160 life-size fiberglass models of dinosaurs in a tropical outdoor setting. Picnicking and pets are permitted. Allow 1 hour minimum. Daily 9-dusk. Admission $9.75; senior citizens $8.95; ages 3-12, $7.75. AX, DS, MC, VI. Phone (813) 717-9865.

ST. PETE BEACH (I-7) pop. 9,929, elev. 5'

A resort community on Long Key, St. Pete Beach is connected to the mainland by the St. Pete Beach Causeway and the Pinellas Bayway (toll). The town has good swimming beaches, several fishing piers and charter boat operations.

Tampa Bay Beaches Chamber of Commerce: 6990 Gulf Blvd., St. Pete Beach, FL 33706; phone (727) 360-6957 or (800) 944-1847.

Shopping areas: Silas Bayside Shopping Center, 5505 Gulf Blvd., features specialty shops in a tropical setting. The historic Corey Avenue area offers varied shops, and the 8th Avenue Shopping District at Pass-a-Grill Beach offers galleries, shops and restaurants.

DOLPHIN LANDINGS CHARTER BOAT CENTER is at 4737 Gulf Blvd. (SR 699), .5 mi. s. of jct. SRs 693 and 699, in Dolphin Village Shopping Center. The 2-hour dolphin watch cruise on a 37- to 46-foot sailboat affords opportunities for spotting the playful creatures. Other cruises are available, including sunset, snorkeling, fishing and shelling excursions. Allow 2 hours minimum. Dolphin watch departures daily at 9:30, noon and 2:15. Departures require a minimum of two people. Reservations are suggested. Fare $25; under 12, $15. AX, MC, VI. Phone (727) 367-4488.

GULF BEACHES HISTORICAL MUSEUM, 115 10th Ave., is housed in the first church built on the barrier islands. Exhibits portray the history of the area. Guided walking tours are offered on the second and fourth Thursday of the month, October to April. Allow 1 hour minimum. Thurs. and Sat. 10-4, Sun. 1-4; closed major holidays. Free. Phone (727) 552-1610.

TARPON SPRINGS (F-7)
pop. 21,003, elev. 18'

Tarpon Springs became an important center for sponge fishing when Greek divers came to the area in the early 1900s. Although the industry has diminished, the Greek influence still is evident in the remaining sponge boats and in the dock area, where sponge shops and Greek restaurants and bakeries are plentiful. Sponge-diving exhibitions, scenic cruises and deep-sea fishing charters are available from the dock area.

A replica of St. Sophia's in Constantinople, the 1943 Greek Orthodox Cathedral of St. Nicholas, at the corner of Pinellas Avenue (US 19A) and Orange Street, is the center of colorful pageantry during Greek festivals.

The ancient craft of brass rubbing, transferring designs from brass engravings to paper, can be attempted at the Medieval Brass Rubbing Centre on Dodecanese Boulevard; phone (727) 934-6760.

Tarpon Springs Chamber of Commerce: 11 E. Orange St., Tarpon Springs, FL 34689; phone (727) 937-6109.

GEORGE INNESS JR. PICTURES, in the Unitarian Universalist Church at Grand Blvd. and Read St., contains 11 religious paintings by George Inness Jr., son of the American 19th-century landscape artist. The paintings depict his extraordinary treatment of light and use of the green tones that were named after him. Guided tours are available. Allow 30 minutes minimum. Tues.-Sun. 2-5, Nov.-May; closed holidays. Last tour begins 30 minutes before closing. Donations. Phone (727) 937-4682.

SAVE **KONGER TARPON SPRINGS AQUARIUM** is at 850 Dodecanese Blvd. A simulated coral reef, complete with native plants and tropical fish, illustrates life under the sea in a 120,000-gallon tank. Visitors may watch a shark-feeding show, and a tidal pool offers a close look at such sea creatures as starfish and hermit crabs. Allow 30 minutes minimum. Mon.-Sat. 10-5, Sun. noon-5. Admission $4.75; over 55, $4; ages 3-11, $2.75. Phone (727) 938-5378.

ST. NICHOLAS BOAT LINE, .4 mi. w. of jct. Alt. US 19 at 693 Dodecanese Blvd., offers 35-minute, narrated, round-trip cruises through the historic sponge docks of Tarpon Springs. A diver in traditional diving gear provides a demonstration of sponge harvesting. The boat has been used in the filming of several movies and television shows. Allow 1 hour minimum. Departures daily approximately every 45 minutes 10-5; closed Greek Orthodox Easter and Dec. 25. Fare $5; ages 6-12, $2. Phone (727) 942-6425.

THONOTOSASSA (E-9) pop. 6,091, elev. 49'

Fort Foster, on the Hillsborough River in nearby Hillsborough River State Park *(see Recreation Chart),* was used as a battle post and supply depot during the Second Seminole War. Abandoned in 1838 because of disease and the miserable, damp conditions, the fort and the bridge it guarded have been reconstructed on the original site. Canoeing, picnicking and fishing are permitted. Nature trails are on the grounds. Guided tours are available; phone (813) 987-6771.

RECREATIONAL ACTIVITIES

Canoeing

- **Canoe Escape**, off I-75 exit 265, then .5 mi. e. to 9335 E. Fowler Ave. Write P.O. Box 292396, Tampa, FL 33687-2396. Mon.-Fri. 9-5, Sat.-Sun. 8-6; closed Thanksgiving and Dec. 24-25. Last 2-hour trip departs at 2. Phone (813) 986-2067.

This ends listings for the Tampa Bay Vicinity.
The following page resumes the alphabetical listings of cities in Florida.

TARPON SPRINGS—*see Tampa Bay p. 230.*

TAVARES—*see Orlando p. 179.*

THONOTOSASSA—*see Tampa Bay p. 231.*

TITUSVILLE (D-10) pop. 40,670, elev. 18'

Named for founder Col. Henry T. Titus in 1874, Titusville once was a citrus shipping point and commercial fishing port. The establishment of Kennedy Space Center *(see place listing p. 97)* brought the Space Age—and increased tourism—to this small mainland city.

Titusville Area Chamber of Commerce: 2000 S. Washington Ave., Titusville, FL 32780; phone (321) 267-3036.

MERRITT ISLAND NATIONAL WILDLIFE REFUGE, 3.5 mi. e. on SR 402 across the Titusville Cswy., is a habitat for wintering migratory waterfowl. A visitor center offers educational displays, wildlife exhibits and a 20-minute video about the refuge. Behind the center, a boardwalk takes visitors over a pond and through an oak hammock to a freshwater marsh. Special interpretive programs are offered November through March.

Licensed hunting for waterfowl is permitted in season; licensed fishing is available all year. Black Point Wildlife Drive off SR 406 is a 7-mile self-guiding driving tour of major refuge habitats. Oak Hammock Foot Trail off SR 402 identifies the plants of a hammock community; Scrub Ridge Trail off SR 3 provides access to scrub and marsh habitat; and the Manatee Observatory Deck off SR 3 provides views of manatees.

For information contact the Refuge Manager, Merritt Island National Wildlife Refuge, P.O. Box 6504, Titusville, FL 32782. Park daily dawn-dusk. Visitor center Mon.-Fri. 8:30-4:30, Sat. 9-5 (also Sun. 9-5, Nov.-Mar.). Free. Phone (321) 861-0667.

VALIANT AIR COMMAND WARBIRD AIR MUSEUM, 6600 Tico Rd. at the Space Coast Regional Airport, following signs, features such aviation memorabilia as model planes, uniforms, controls from various aircraft and a U.S. Navy flight simulator. A hangar and a ramp contain a changing collection of restored planes in running condition. Allow 2 hours minimum. Daily 10-6; closed Jan. 1, Thanksgiving and Dec. 25. Admission $9; over 60 and military with ID $8; ages 4-12, $5. MC, VI. Phone (321) 268-1941.

VENICE (F-8) pop. 17,764, elev. 13'

As its name implies, Venice has a distinct Mediterranean ambience with Northern Italian influences. The city's location on the Gulf makes it a popular destination for boating, fishing and golfing. Visitors can comb the beaches for fossilized shark teeth, which range in size from one-eighth-inch to 3 inches.

Venice Area Chamber of Commerce: 333 Tamiami Trail S., Suite 225, Venice, FL 34285-2424; phone (941) 488-2236.

VERO BEACH (E-11) pop. 20,362, elev. 17'

Vero Beach plays host to the Los Angeles Dodgers baseball team during spring training. Exhibition games are played at Holman Stadium from March to early April; phone (772) 569-4900. The Vero Beach Dodgers offer games during their regular season from mid-April to early September.

Indian River County Chamber of Commerce: 1216 21st St., Vero Beach, FL 32960; phone (772) 567-3491.

WAKULLA (B-6)

EDWARD BALL WAKULLA SPRINGS STATE PARK, jct. SRs 61 and 267, was known to early Seminole Indians for its plentiful wildlife and was believed to be discovered by Ponce de León in 1513, who claimed it to be the "fountain of youth." The main spring, with a water temperature of 70 F, is considered one of the state's deepest, having been explored to a depth of 300 feet. The maximum flow was recorded in 1973 at 1.2 billion gallons a day; in 1931 the minimum flow was measured at 16.2 million gallons. The average is 576 million gallons of crystal-clear water daily.

A popular "birding mecca," the park offers hiking, bicycle and nature trails as well as swimming opportunities. Narrated river cruises offer glimpses of a variety of animals in their native habitats, while glass-bottom boat tours provide views of fish, marine plants and mastodon bones.

Allow 2 hours minimum. Park daily 8-dusk. River cruises depart daily every half hour 9:45-5, during DST; 9:15-4:30, rest of year (weather permitting). Glass-bottom boat cruises depart daily 11-3 (only when the water has clear visibility). Admission $3.25 per private vehicle (maximum eight people), $1 extra for every person over the maximum. Glass-bottom boat or river cruise $4.50; under 13, $2.25. Phone (850) 224-5950. *See Recreation Chart.*

WALT DISNEY WORLD—
see Lake Buena Vista p. 163.

WARM MINERAL SPRINGS (F-8)
pop. 4,811, elev. 9'

THE SPRINGS is off I-75 exit 191, n. on US 41, .8 mi. e. on Ortiz Rd., then just s. to 12200 San Servando Ave. This warm mineral spring produces 870 million gallons of water yearly. Lockers and food are available. Picnicking is permitted. Allow 2 hours minimum. Daily 9-5; closed Dec. 25. Admission $10; senior citizens $8; ages 1-12, $2. MC, VI. Phone (941) 426-1692.

WEEKI WACHEE (D-8) pop. 12, elev. 34'

WEEKI WACHEE SPRINGS WATERPARK, on US 19 at jct. SR 50, is built around a spring that flows at a rate of 170 million gallons a day and maintains a temperature of 74 F. The Wilderness River Cruise explores the flora and fauna of a typical Florida ecosystem. "Mermaids" perform in an underwater theater.

A natural spring on the Weeki Wachee River features a white sand beach, six flume rides, a river tube ride and a children's play area. Lockers, picnic facilities, food and kennels are available. Allow 6 hours minimum. Park opens daily at 10; closing times vary. Water park is open seasonally; phone ahead. Last admission 1 hour before closing. Admission $16.95; ages 3-10, $12.95. AX, MC, VI. Phone (352) 596-2062 or (877) 469-3354. *See color ad.*

WELAKA (C-9) pop. 586, elev. 28'

WELAKA NATIONAL FISH HATCHERY AQUARIUM, on CR 309, displays reptiles and 22 tanks containing specimens of about 50 species of native freshwater fish. Allow 30 minutes minimum. Daily 8-3. Free. Phone (386) 467-2374.

WEST PALM BEACH (G-12)
pop. 82,103, elev. 21'

Founded in 1894 by railroad tycoon Henry Flagler, West Palm Beach has grown into a center for commerce and business. Fifty miles north of Miami, the city is a popular destination for beach recreation, sport fishing, shopping and cultural activities.

Kravis Center for the Performing Arts includes a 2,200-seat concert hall, a black box theater, a restaurant and an outdoor amphitheater. Performances range from classical to country and feature well-known entertainers; for information phone (561) 833-8300 or (800) 572-8471. CityPlace in downtown West Palm Beach offers a mix of upscale shopping, gourmet dining and entertainment, including dancing fountains choreographed to light and music. Clematis Street is known for its trendy shops, restaurants, theaters and nightlife.

Approximately 15 miles west of town in Wellington, the Palm Beach Polo Grounds is the site of polo matches and horse shows from December through April; phone (561) 798-7000. The Palm Beach Kennel Club, Belvedere Road and Congress Avenue, holds greyhound races year round; phone (561) 683-2222.

Note: Policies vary concerning admittance of children to pari-mutuel betting facilities. Phone for information.

Palm Beach County Tourist Information Center: 8020 W. Indian Town Rd., Jupiter, FL 33478; phone (561) 575-4636.

Shopping areas: Palm Beach Mall, 1 block east of I-95 exit 71, features Burdines, Dillard's, JCPenney and Sears among its 100 stores. The Mall at Wellington Green, 15 miles west at US 441 and Forest Hill Boulevard, features more than 120 stores, including Burdines, Dillard's, JC Penney and Lord & Taylor.

[SAVE] **LION COUNTRY SAFARI,** 15.5 mi. w. of I-95 on US 98/441 and SR 80 (Southern Blvd.), is a 500-acre drive-through wildlife preserve in which giraffes, wildebeests, rhinoceroses, African elephants, lions, zebras, chimpanzees, Aldabra tortoises, Asiatic water buffalo and many other animals roam freely. Visitors must stay in their cars with doors and windows closed. Convertibles are not permitted; rental vehicles are available.

Other park highlights include an amusement park with an animal theater and a petting zoo. A miniature golf course, a carousel, a bird feeding exhibit, paddle boats and a boat ride also are offered. Picnic facilities, food and free kennels are available. Pets are not permitted.

Allow 3 hours minimum. Daily 9:30-5:30. Last vehicle admission 1 hour before closing. Admission $16.95; over 65, $14.95; ages 3-9, $12.95. Rental vans $8 per 1.5 hours. AX, MC, VI. Phone (561) 793-1084. *See color ad.*

MOUNTS BOTANICAL GARDEN, off I-95 exit 69, 2.5 mi. w. on Southern Blvd., then .4 mi. s. to 531 N. Military Tr., features labeled plants lining several walkways as well as a pond with fish, turtles and other wildlife. Allow 1 hour minimum. Mon.-Sat. 8-4:30, Sun. 1-5, holidays 1-5; closed Jan. 1, Thanksgiving and Dec. 24-25. Free. Admission is charged during special events. Phone (561) 233-1749.

NORTON MUSEUM OF ART is .5 mi. s. of Okeechobee Blvd. on US 1, at 1451 S. Olive Ave. The museum is recognized for its permanent collection of European, American and contemporary art; photography; and Chinese art, including ancient bronzes, jades and ceramics. Highlights include 19th- and 20th-century paintings and sculpture by such Europeans artists as Paul Gauguin, Henri Matisse, Claude Monet and Pablo Picasso; and American artists including Edward Hopper, Georgia O'Keeffe and Jackson Pollock. Guided tours are offered daily from October through April.

Allow 1 hour minimum. Tues.-Sat. 10-5, Sun. 1-5 (also Mon. 10-5, Nov.-Apr.); closed major holidays. Admission $6; ages 13-21, $2. AX, DS, MC, VI. Phone (561) 832-5196.

PALM BEACH ZOO is e. of I-95 at 1301 Summit Blvd. in Dreher Park. The zoo is home to more than 500 animals, including a Florida panther, Bengal tigers, giant tortoises and exotic birds. Wallabies and red kangaroos are the highlights of the Australian Outback exhibit. The children's zoo features small animals. Food and picnic facilities are available.

Allow 2 hours minimum. Daily 9-5; closed Thanksgiving. Last admission 45 minutes before closing. Admission $7.50; over 60, $6; ages 3-12, $5. AX, MC, VI. Phone (561) 533-0887 or (561) 547-9453.

SOUTH FLORIDA SCIENCE MUSEUM, 4801 Dreher Tr. N. in Dreher Park, has a variety of permanent and changing exhibits and interactive displays. Galaxy Golf features an 18-hole miniature golf course with a science theme. Dozens of tanks at the McGinty Aquarium display Atlantic and Pacific species of ocean life, including live corals. The Buzz Aldrin Planetarium offers star and laser light shows, and the Gibson Observatory features one of the largest telescopes in the state.

Allow 1 hour minimum. Museum open Mon.-Fri. 10-5 (also Fri. 5-10), Sat. 10-6, Sun. noon-6; closed Thanksgiving and Dec. 25. Planetarium shows daily at 1 and 2 (also Fri. at 7 and 8 p.m.). Laser light shows Fri.-Sun. at 3 (also Fri. at 9 and 10 p.m.). Museum $6; ages 3-17, $4. Fees may change for special exhibits. Planetarium shows $2. Laser light shows $4 (Fri. evening $6.50). Galaxy Golf $4; ages 3-17, $2. Phone (561) 832-1988 or (561) 832-2007.

WHITE SPRINGS (B-8) pop. 819, elev. 125'

Once a health resort, White Springs is built around sulphur springs. Seminole and Timucuan Indians considered the springs sacred and believed their warriors were impervious to attack while recuperating.

STEPHEN FOSTER FOLK CULTURE CENTER STATE PARK, 3 mi. e. of I-75 on US 41, covers 850 acres of wooded land beside the Suwannee River, which the composer immortalized in his song "Old Folks At Home." In the visitor center are animated dioramas depicting Foster's songs. Two other dioramas and period exhibits are in the 200-foot carillon tower; recitals are given daily. An arts and crafts center features "cracker"-style buildings, a two-story craft shop and five studios in which Florida crafts are demonstrated daily. Hiking and bicycling trails and camping facilities are available. Picnicking is permitted.

Allow 4 hours minimum. Park open daily 8-dusk. Buildings open daily 9-5. Admission $3.25 per private vehicle (maximum eight people) or motorcycle, $1 per person arriving by bicycle, bus or on foot. Some events have varying admission charges. Phone (386) 397-2733.

WINTER HAVEN (E-9)
pop. 26,487, elev. 170'

Located 75 miles from both the Atlantic Ocean and the Gulf of Mexico, Winter Haven is surrounded by some of the state's finest citrus groves. Exhibition games for baseball's Cleveland Indians are held in March at Chain of Lakes Stadium; phone (863) 293-3900.

Community theater productions are presented at Theatre Winter Haven, in the Chain of Lakes complex on Cypress Gardens Boulevard; for performance information phone (863) 299-2672.

Fishing is among Winter Haven's popular recreational activities. Spring-fed lakes near the city are connected by canals to form a 30-mile waterway containing numerous game fish. Around Lake Silver, tennis and shuffleboard, an amphitheater, two recreational sport facilities and a beach are available.

Greater Winter Haven Area Chamber of Commerce: 401 Ave. B N.W., P. O. Box 1420, Winter

Haven, FL 33882-1420; phone (863) 293-2138 or (800) 871-7027. *See color ad p. 237.*

CYPRESS GARDENS is 5 mi. s.e. on SR 540. Founded in 1936, Cypress Gardens was the state's first theme park. More than 8,000 varieties of plants and flowers from 90 countries around the world are showcased in the renowned 208-acre botanical garden. Towering cypress trees provide the backdrop for elaborate displays of bromeliads, bougainvillea, hibiscus and other exotic flora. Special areas include the Mediterranean Waterfall, Big Lagoon, Oriental Gardens and the All-American Rose Garden.

The Cypress Roots Museum displays photographs and memorabilia tracing the park's development. When Radios Were Radios is an exhibit of vintage radios and radio equipment from the 1920s through the 1950s. An elaborate model railroad travels across historic America at Cypress Junction, while Southern Crossroads re-creates an antebellum town.

Southern Breeze, a turn-of-the-20th-century paddle-wheel boat, offers daily cruises; dinner cruises are available nightly.

Wings of Wonder is a glass-enclosed, Victorian-style conservatory containing more than 1,000 free-flying butterflies. Gator Gulch is an alligator habitat. Plantation Gardens feature rose, herb and scent and fruit and vegetable gardens, as well as a butterfly garden with plants that attract Florida butterflies.

Five animal habitats and an aviary add to the natural enjoyment. Events, including light shows and floral festivals, are held throughout the year.

Among the park's shows are a fast-action water ski show with world-class, champion athletes; Moscow on Ice; and Do You Know Your Animals?, an educational program featuring parrots, birds of prey and exotic reptiles.

A good way to cool off on those steamy summer afternoons is by visiting Summer Wacky Water Park, which includes water sprays, eight body flumes and a children's pool.

Exotic flowers are showcased in the FloraDome, an indoor garden featuring a waterfall, pond and stream. Floral displays are changed bi-monthly.

No pets are allowed inside the park; a kennel is available at the entrance for a fee. Food is available, as are wheelchair and stroller rentals.

Daily 9:30-5 with extended hours during special seasons. Admission $34.95; ages 6-17, $19.95. DS, MC, VI. Phone (863) 324-2111. *See color ad p. 236.*

WINTER PARK—*see Orlando p. 179.*

WOODVILLE (B-6) pop. 3,006, elev. 39′

NATURAL BRIDGE BATTLEFIELD HISTORIC STATE PARK is a 6-acre site 6 mi. e. off SR 363. The Battle of Natural Bridge was fought Mar. 6, 1865, to prevent Union troops from capturing the Capitol at Tallahassee. Fishing opportunities and picnic facilities are available. Daily 8-dusk. Free. Phone (850) 922-6007.

Planning a trip to Florida?

Check out these three must-have guides created just for Florida travelers! The *Orlando & Florida Spiral Guide*, with its revolutionary design, provides spectacular graphics, engaging text, and witty articles about Orlando and other Florida cities. The *AAA Barrier-Free Central Florida Travel Guide* helps mature travelers and travelers with disabilities to plan a safe, comfortable trip by providing up-to-date accessibility information. The *Orlando Tour Guide* features the convenience of a folding map and the need-to-know details of a travel guide.

Purchase AAA travel publications at participating AAA club offices, on participating club Web sites at www.aaa.com, and in fine book stores.

Enjoy Florida.

We'll take care of the rest.

We have 33 convenient locations.
How may I help you?
Did you enjoy your swim?
How about the free breakfast?
Need a ride to the airport?
Don't forget to book us on-line.
We hope you enjoy your stay.

laquinta.com · 1-800-221-4731

THERE'S A MAGICAL VACATION IN EVERY DIRECTION

No matter where you're headed for your next Disney vacation, every direction points to a magical experience with AAA Travel. Enjoy exclusive benefits when you book a *Disney Cruise Line*® vacation or a AAA Vacations® package to the *Walt Disney World*® Resort, or the *Disneyland*® Resort through AAA Travel. And that means more magic, more fun, more value and more dreams come true. Call or visit your AAA Travel office today.

Ships' Registry: The Bahamas
As to Disney artwork, logos and properties: ©Disney

Splash into savings...

...with Florida Fun Rates!

With Florida Fun Rates at Ramada, you can enjoy more of the Sunshine State for less! From sandy beaches to awesome amusement parks to unique shopping and beautiful natural attractions, you can experience the best that Florida has to offer—all while knowing there's a Ramada property on your way!

So ask for Plan Code LPFL when making your reservations—and you'll be in the swim in no time!

For reservations, call **1.800.2.RAMADA** or visit floridaramada.com

expect our personal **best** RAMADA

RAMADA®

Florida

The Florida
Keys . . . .

Ft. Lauderdale.

Jacksonville . . .

Miami-Miami
Beach . . . .

Orlando . . . .

Tampa Bay
including
St. Petersburg,
Tampa and
Clearwater . . . .

Florida Orientation Map to Destinations

Florida Keys (see p. 320)

Cudjoe Key..............320	Key Largo................323	Long Key................352
Islamorada...............320	Key West 333	Marathon................353
Key Colony Beach........323	Little Torch Key...........352	

Fort Lauderdale (see p. 356)
The Fort Lauderdale Vicinity (see p. 389)

Coral Springs......389	Hillsboro Beach 396	Lighthouse Point...402	Plantation.........405
Dania Beach.......390	Hollywood........396	Margate 402	Pompano Beach....407
Davie.............391	Lauderdale-By-	Miramar 403	Sunrise 410
Deerfield Beach....392	The-Sea 400	North Lauderdale ..404	Tamarac...........412
Hallandale Beach...394	Lauderhill.........402	Pembroke Pines....404	Weston 413

Jacksonville (see p. 445)
The Jacksonville Vicinity (see p. 466)

Amelia Island.............466	Green Cove Springs........469	Orange Park..............473
Atlantic Beach............468	Jacksonville Beach.........470	Ponte Vedra Beach 475
Baldwin...................469	Neptune Beach............472	Yulee....................477

Miami (see p. 500)

Downtown Miami ..513	Miami 517	Miami Beach.......526

The Miami-Miami Beach Vicinity (see p. 543)

Aventura..........543	Florida City........548	Miami Lakes.......553	North Miami Beach .557
Bal Harbour.......543	Hialeah............550	Miami Springs.....554	South Miami.......557
Coconut Grove.....544	Homestead........551	North Bay Village ..556	Sunny Isles.......558
Coral Gables......546	Kendall 551	North Miami.......557	Surfside 559
Cutler Ridge.......548	Key Biscayne 552		

Orlando (see p. 588)

Orlando North.....612	Orlando South.....621

The Orlando Vicinity (see p. 671)

Altamonte Springs .671	Fern Park 677	Lake Mary.........740	Oviedo 747
Apopka...........673	Heathrow.........677	Leesburg..........742	St. Cloud..........747
Casselberry.......674	Howey-In-The-Hills .677	Longwood 743	Sanford...........747
Celebration.......675	Kissimmee 678	Maitland..........744	Tavares 749
Clermont.........675	Lady Lake 714	Mount Dora 745	Winter Garden 749
Davenport 676	Lake Buena Vista...714	Ocoee 746	Winter Park 750

Tampa Bay (see p. 844)

St. Petersburg 863	Tampa............870

The Tampa Vicinity (see p. 896)

Apollo Beach 896	Indian Shores......918	Plant City 926	South Pasadena....937
Belleair Bluffs 896	Largo.............920	Port Richey........927	Sun City Center 937
Brandon 896	Madeira Beach.....920	Redington Beach ...928	Tarpon Springs.....938
Clearwater........899	New Port Richey...922	Redington Shores ..928	Temple Terrace.....939
Clearwater Beach ..906	North Redington	Riverview (Hillsborough	Tierra Verde 939
Dade City 915	Beach............923	County) 928	Treasure Island.....940
Dunedin 916	Oldsmar 924	Ruskin............928	Wesley Chapel 945
Holiday...........917	Palm Harbor.......924	Safety Harbor 930	Zephyrhills........946
Indian Rocks Beach .917	Pinellas Park......925	St. Pete Beach 931	

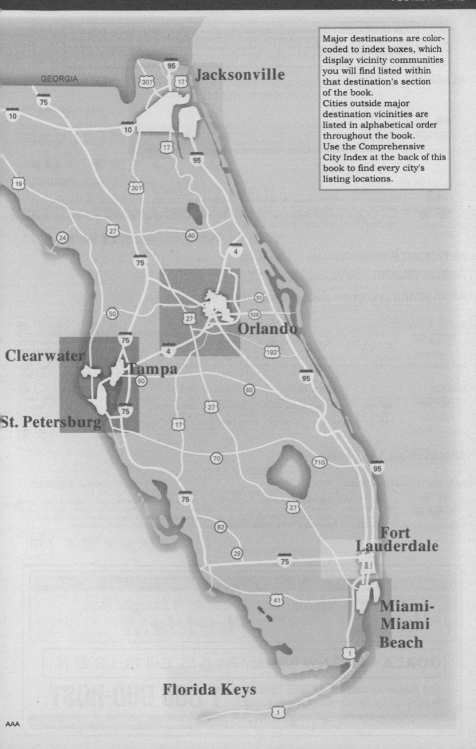

GEORGIA

Jacksonville

Orlando

Clearwater

Tampa

St. Petersburg

Fort Lauderdale

Miami-Miami Beach

Florida Keys

Major destinations are color-coded to index boxes, which display vicinity communities you will find listed within that destination's section of the book.
Cities outside major destination vicinities are listed in alphabetical order throughout the book.
Use the Comprehensive City Index at the back of this book to find every city's listing locations.

In January 2002, exit numbers on Florida's interstate highway system began shifting from sequential numbering to mileage-based numbering. Both new and old numbers will remain posted for 2 years. The exit numbers presented in this publication are the new, mileage-based numbers. For further information, please contact your local AAA club.

ALACHUA pop. 6,098

——— WHERE TO STAY ———

COMFORT INN/FL-339

Small-scale Hotel
Phone: (386)462-2414
All Year — 1P: $65 — 2P: $75 — XP: $5 — F17
Location: I-75, exit 399, just e. 15920 NW US Hwy 441 32615. Fax: 386/462-2220. **Facility:** 62 one-bedroom standard units. 2 stories, exterior corridors. **Parking:** on-site. **Terms:** pets ($10 extra charge, in smoking units). **Amenities:** irons, hair dryers. **Pool(s):** outdoor. **Guest Services:** coin laundry. **Business Services:** fax (fee). **Special Amenities:** free continental breakfast and free newspaper.
SOME UNITS

DAYS INN OF ALACHUA
Motel
Phone: (386)462-3251
All Year [ECP] — 1P: $60-$125 — 2P: $65-$125 — XP: $5 — F12
Location: I-75, exit 399, just w. 16100 NW Hwy 441 32615. Fax: 386/462-3251. **Facility:** 55 one-bedroom standard units. 2 stories, exterior corridors. **Parking:** on-site. **Terms:** 15 day cancellation notice-fee imposed, pets ($5 extra charge). **Amenities:** hair dryers. **Pool(s):** outdoor. **Guest Services:** coin laundry. **Business Services:** fax (fee). **Cards:** AX, DC, DS, MC, VI.
SOME UNITS

ALTAMONTE SPRINGS —See Orlando p. 671.

AMELIA ISLAND —See Jacksonville p. 466.

ANNA MARIA pop. 1,814 (See map p. 812; index p. 816)

——— WHERE TO DINE ———

BISTRO AT ISLAND'S END
Continental
Phone: 941/779-2444 — 65
Location: On north end, jct Gulf Dr and Pine Ave; 3 mi n of jct SR 64. 10101 Gulf Dr 34216. **Hours:** 5:30 pm-9:30 pm, Fri & Sat-10:30 pm. **Reservations:** suggested. **Features:** Enjoy steak, seafood and pasta in a cozy, bistro-style setting. Excellent presentation, quality ingredients and good flavor are all elements of this superb menu. Wet your appetite with Gulf Coast gumbo, then sample the first-rate grilled salmon. Smoke free premises. Dressy casual; cocktails; entertainment. **Parking:** on-site. **Cards:** AX, CB, DC, DS, MC, VI.

SANDBAR
Seafood
Phone: 941/778-0444 — 66
Lunch: $6-$11 — Dinner: $11-$18
Location: 2.8 mi n of SR 64 on Gulf Dr, just w. 100 Spring Ave 34216. **Hours:** 11:30 am-10 pm. Closed: 12/25. **Features:** "Old Florida" is the theme of this popular, casual restaurant overlooking the Gulf of Mexico. Vintage photos set a nostalgic mood, and each table is afforded a wonderful view of the gulf. Enjoy live entertainment nightly on the outdoor dining deck. Casual dress; cocktails. **Parking:** on-site. **Cards:** AX, CB, DC, DS, MC, VI.

APALACHICOLA pop. 2,334

——— WHERE TO STAY ———

BEST WESTERN APALACH INN
Small-scale Hotel
Phone: (850)653-2116
All Year — 1P: $80-$125 — 2P: $90-$145 — XP: $10 — F14
Location: 1.5 mi w. 249 Hwy 98 W 32320. Fax: 850/653-9136. **Facility:** 42 one-bedroom standard units, some with whirlpools. 2 stories, exterior corridors. **Parking:** on-site. **Terms:** cancellation fee imposed. **Amenities:** irons, hair dryers. **Pool(s):** outdoor. **Business Services:** fax (fee). **Cards:** AX, CB, DC, DS, MC, VI. **Special Amenities:** early check-in/late check-out and free continental breakfast.
SOME UNITS

THE GIBSON INN

Historic
Country Inn

All Year 1P: $95-$110 2P: $95-$110 XP: $5 F
Phone: (850)653-2191
Location: On US 98 at west end of bridge. Market St & Ave C 32320 (PO Box 221, 32329). **Fax:** 850/653-3521. **Facility:** Victorian accents and antiques from around the world furnish the individually decorated guest rooms of this restored 1907 inn. 30 units. 28 one-bedroom standard units. 2 one-bedroom suites ($115-$145). 3 stories (no elevator), interior corridors. *Bath:* combo or shower only. **Parking:** street. **Terms:** 18% service charge, pets ($5 extra charge, owner's cats on premises). **Dining:** restaurant, see separate listing. **Business Services:** meeting rooms, fax (fee). **Cards:** AX, MC, VI. **Special Amenities:** free local telephone calls.

SOME UNITS

——— WHERE TO DINE ———

THE GIBSON INN Country Inn

American

Lunch: $6-$10 Dinner: $12-$28 **Phone:** 850/653-2191
Location: On US 98 at west end of bridge; in The Gibson Inn. Market St & Ave C 32320. **Hours:** 7:30 am-11 & 6-9 pm, Fri & Sat-10 pm, Sun 6 pm-9 pm. Closed: Mon. **Reservations:** accepted. **Features:** Located in a historic coastal hotel, the restaurant projects a warm, inviting atmosphere with walls of cypress, candlelight and fresh flowers. The menu features delicious creations like sesame yellowfin tuna coated in seeds and seared in oil. Smoke free premises. Casual dress; cocktails. **Parking:** street. **Cards:** AX, MC, VI.

APOLLO BEACH —See Tampa Bay p. 896.

APOPKA —See Orlando p. 673.

ARCADIA pop. 6,604

——— WHERE TO STAY ———

ARCADIA'S MAGNOLIA HOUSE

Historic Bed
& Breakfast

All Year [ECP] 1P: $85-$95 XP: $35
Phone: (863)494-4299
Location: Just n of SR 70 at jct Dade Ave; downtown. 500 W Oak St 34266. **Fax:** 863/494-4299. **Facility:** Designated smoking area. 4 one-bedroom standard units. 2 stories, interior corridors. *Bath:* combo, shower or tub only. **Parking:** on-site. **Terms:** 7 day cancellation notice, weekly rates available. **Business Services:** PC, fax. **Cards:** AX, DS, MC, VI. **Special Amenities:** free continental breakfast and free local telephone calls.

BEST WESTERN ARCADIA INN

Motel

2/1-3/31 [ECP]	1P: $75-$105	2P: $79-$119	XP: $5 F12
1/1-1/31 [ECP]	1P: $65-$85	2P: $75-$95	XP: $5 F12
12/1-12/31 & 4/1-11/30 [ECP]	1P: $49-$75	2P: $59-$85	XP: $5 F12

Phone: (863)494-4884
Location: 0.6 mi s of SR 70 on US 17. 504 S Brevard Ave 34266. **Fax:** 863/494-2006. **Facility:** 37 units. 36 one-bedroom standard units, some with whirlpools. 1 one-bedroom suite ($79-$149) with kitchen. 1 story, exterior corridors. *Bath:* combo or shower only. **Parking:** on-site. **Terms:** cancellation fee imposed, small pets only ($15 extra charge, with prior approval). **Amenities:** safes, irons, hair dryers. **Pool(s):** outdoor. **Leisure Activities:** covered picnic area and grills. **Guest Services:** gift shop, valet and coin laundry. **Business Services:** fax. **Cards:** AX, CB, DC, DS, JC, MC, VI. **Special Amenities:** early check-in/late check-out and free continental breakfast.

SOME UNITS

——— WHERE TO DINE ———

ARCADIA TEA ROOM RESTAURANT

American

Lunch: $4-$8 **Phone:** 863/494-2424
Location: Just n of jct SR 70; downtown. 117 W Oak St 34266. **Hours:** 11 am-4 pm, Sun-3 pm. Closed: Mon. **Features:** Step into history in these quaint dining rooms decorated with lavish antiques. Fresh, home-cooked entrees are offered at reasonable prices, like the hearty classic liver and onions with real mashed potatoes and savory gravy. Casual dress; beer & wine only. **Parking:** street. **Cards:** DS, MC, VI.

NAV-A-GATOR GRILLE

Seafood

Lunch: $3-$24 Dinner: $3-$24 **Phone:** 941/627-3474
Location: I-75, exit 170, 3.1 mi ne on CR 769, 1.5 mi s on Peace River St. 9700 SW Riverview Cir 34269. **Hours:** 11 am-9 pm, Sun-8 pm. Closed: 4/20, 11/27, 12/25. **Features:** On the Peace River in the DeSoto Marings, the active and loud restaurant is a local favorite. Its menu offers grouper, captain's platter, shrimp, alligator, seafood baskets and many sandwiches. Enjoy deck dining, where you can watch fishermen bringing in their latest catch and marvel at the scenery. Or take a stroll through the small on-site museum. Casual dress; beer & wine only. **Parking:** on-site. **Cards:** AX, DC, DS, MC, VI.

ATLANTIC BEACH —See Jacksonville p. 468.

AVENTURA —See Miami-Miami Beach p. 543.

AVON PARK pop. 8,542

——— WHERE TO STAY ———

ECONO LODGE

Motel

1/16-3/31 [CP]	1P: $70-$150	2P: $70-$150	XP: $5 F18
9/1-11/30 [CP]	1P: $60-$90	2P: $60-$90	XP: $5 F18
12/1-1/15 & 4/1-8/31 [CP]	1P: $60-$70	2P: $60-$70	XP: $5 F18

Phone: (863)453-2000
Location: US 27, 2.5 mi s of jct SR 17 and 64. 2511 US Hwy 27 S 33825. **Fax:** 863/453-0820. **Facility:** 58 one-bedroom standard units. 2 stories, exterior corridors. **Parking:** on-site. **Pool(s):** outdoor. **Guest Services:** coin laundry. **Business Services:** fax (fee). **Cards:** AX, DS, MC, VI.

SOME UNITS

BALDWIN —*See Jacksonville p. 469.*

BAL HARBOUR —*See Miami-Miami Beach p. 543.*

BARTOW pop. 15,340

──────── WHERE TO STAY ────────

THE STANFORD INN
▼▼▼▼
Bed & Breakfast
All Year [BP]   1P: $125-$165   2P: $125-$165   XP: $15   F18
Location: Main St, s on S Broadway to E Stanford St; downtown. 555 E Stanford St 33830. Fax: 863/519-0238.
Facility: Designated smoking area. 6 units. 4 one-bedroom standard units, some with whirlpools. 2 cottages.
2 stories, interior/exterior corridors. *Bath:* combo or shower only. **Parking:** on-site. **Terms:** 7 day cancellation
notice-fee imposed. **Amenities:** *Some:* irons, hair dryers. **Pool(s):** outdoor. **Leisure Activities:** whirlpool. **Business Services:**
fax (fee). **Cards:** AX, CB, MC, VI.

SOME UNITS
(ASK) (SD) 🏊 ✕ 🎥 / 📶 🖥 📺 /

BELLEAIR BLUFFS —*See Tampa Bay p. 896.*

BELLE GLADE pop. 14,906

──────── WHERE TO STAY ────────

TRAVELERS MOTOR LODGE
(AAA) (SAVE)
▼▼ ▼▼
Motel
1/21-5/31   1P: $62-$68   2P: $68-$78   XP: $10   F12
12/1-1/20   1P: $58-$62   2P: $62-$68   XP: $10   F12
6/1-11/30   1P: $52-$58   2P: $62-$68   XP: $10   F12
Location: 1 mi sw on SR 80. 1300 S Main St 33430. Fax: 561/996-6764. **Facility:** 26 one-bedroom standard
units. 1 story, exterior corridors. **Parking:** on-site. **Terms:** cancellation fee imposed. **Cards:** AX, DS, MC, VI.
Special Amenities: free local telephone calls and free newspaper.

SOME UNITS
(SD) 🎥 / 📶 /

Phone: 561/996-6761

BOCA GRANDE

──────── WHERE TO STAY ────────

UNCLE HENRY'S MARINA RESORT
▼▼ ▼▼
Motel
12/1-7/15 & 11/16-11/30   1P: $150-$240   2P: $150-$240
7/16-11/15   1P: $99-$240   2P: $99-$240
Location: North end of Gasparilla Island, 2 mi s of the causeway toll. Located in the Courtyard Shopping Center. 5800
Gasparilla Rd 33921 (PO Box 294). Fax: 941/964-2098. **Facility:** 18 units. 16 one- and 2 two-bedroom standard
units. 2 stories, exterior corridors. **Parking:** on-site. **Terms:** 3 day cancellation notice-fee imposed. **Amenities:** irons, hair dryers.
Pool(s): outdoor. **Leisure Activities:** Fee: boats, marina, charter fishing. **Guest Services:** coin laundry. **Business Services:**
meeting rooms, fax (fee). **Cards:** AX, DS, MC, VI.

Phone: 941/964-2300

SOME UNITS
(ASK) (SD) 🍴 🏊 ✕ 🎥 📺 / ✕ 📶 /
FEE

──────── WHERE TO DINE ────────

JAM'S OF BOCA GRANDE
▼▼▼
Italian
Lunch: $6-$16   **Dinner:** $6-$16   **Phone:** 941/964-2002
Location: Center. 480 E Railroad Ave 33921. **Hours:** 11 am-10 pm. **Closed:** 11/27, 12/25.
Reservations: accepted. **Features:** The restaurant offers a good selection of Italian and American dishes,
as well as sandwiches and pizza. Casual dress; cocktails. **Parking:** on-site. **Cards:** AX, DC, MC, VI.

🍽 ✕

BOCA RATON pop. 74,764

──────── WHERE TO STAY ────────

BEST WESTERN UNIVERSITY INN
(AAA) (SAVE)
▼▼▼▼
Motel
12/25-4/21   1P: $89-$139   2P: $99-$139
12/1-12/24 & 4/22-11/30   1P: $59-$79   2P: $69-$89
Location: US 1, 1 mi n of jct SR 808 (Glades Rd). 2700 N Federal Hwy 33431. Fax: 561/338-9180. **Facility:** 90 one-
bedroom standard units. 2 stories (no elevator), interior/exterior corridors. *Bath:* combo or shower only.
Parking: on-site. **Terms:** [AP] & [ECP] meal plans available. **Amenities:** voice mail, safes (fee), irons, hair
dryers. **Dining:** 11 am-11 pm, cocktails. **Pool(s):** heated outdoor. **Leisure Activities:** whirlpool, exercise
room. **Guest Services:** coin laundry, airport transportation-Fort Lauderdale, West Palm Beach Airports. **Cards:** AX, DC, DS,
MC, VI. **Special Amenities:** free continental breakfast and free newspaper.

Phone: (561)395-5225

SOME UNITS
(SD) ✈ 🍴 🍽 🎧 🏊 🎥 (DATA PORT) 📶 🖥 📺 / ✕ /

BOCA RATON MARRIOTT
(SAVE)
▼▼▼▼
Large-scale Hotel
1/1-4/30   1P: $199-$254
12/1-12/31 & 9/16-11/30   1P: $194-$204
5/1-9/15   1P: $159-$169
Location: I-95, exit 44 (Palmetto Park Rd), 0.8 mi n on Military Trail. 5150 Town Center Cir 33486. Fax: 561/368-9223.
Facility: 256 units. 255 one-bedroom standard units. 1 one-bedroom suite. 11 stories, interior corridors. *Bath:*
combo or shower only. **Parking:** on-site and valet. **Terms:** cancellation fee imposed. **Amenities:** dual phone
lines, voice mail, honor bars, irons, hair dryers. *Fee:* video games, high-speed Internet. *Some:* safes. **Pool(s):** heated outdoor.
Leisure Activities: sauna, whirlpool, exercise room. **Guest Services:** gift shop, valet laundry. **Business Services:** conference
facilities, business center. **Cards:** AX, CB, DC, DS, JC, MC, VI.

Phone: (561)392-4600

SOME UNITS

FEE   FEE

BOCA RATON RESORT & CLUB

▼▼▼▼ ▼▼▼▼

Resort
Large-scale Hotel

1/5-4/30	1P: $270-$750	2P: $270-$750	XP: $33	F16
12/1-1/4	1P: $190-$725	2P: $190-$725	XP: $33	F16
10/1-11/30	1P: $195-$530	2P: $195-$530	XP: $33	F16
5/1-9/30	1P: $155-$530	2P: $155-$530	XP: $33	F16

Phone: (561)395-3000

Location: I-95, exit 44, 1.9 mi e on Palmetto Park Rd to Federal Hwy, s to Camino Real, then 0.5 mi e. 501 E Camino Real 33432 (PO Box 2025). Fax: 561/391-3183. **Facility:** Historic Florida resort built in 1926 on Intracoastal Waterway. Rooms in original Cloister Inn, high-rise tower villas or beach club. Meticulous grounds. 1041 units. 851 one-bedroom standard units. 178 one- and 12 two-bedroom suites ($340-$6200), some with kitchens and/or whirlpools. 3-27 stories, interior corridors. *Bath:* combo or shower only. **Parking:** valet. **Terms:** 14 day cancellation notice-fee imposed, [BP] & [MAP] meal plans available, $9 service charge, pets (in limited units). **Amenities:** dual phone lines, voice mail, fax, safes, honor bars, irons, hair dryers. *Fee:* video games, high-speed Internet. *Some:* CD players. **Pool(s):** 5 heated outdoor. **Leisure Activities:** whirlpool, lifeguard on duty, rental sailboats, recreation programs, jogging, spa, volleyball. *Fee:* marina, waterskiing, scuba diving, snorkeling, charter fishing, golf-36 holes, 34 tennis courts (9 lighted), bicycles, game room. **Guest Services:** gift shop, valet laundry, area transportation. **Business Services:** conference facilities, business center. **Cards:** AX, CB, DC, DS, MC, VI. *(See color ad below)*

SOME UNITS

[icons] FEE ... FEE

COURTYARD BY MARRIOTT

SAVE

Phone: (561)241-7070

1/16-4/1	1P: $179-$209
12/1-1/15 & 10/4-11/30	1P: $129-$159
4/2-10/3	1P: $109-$139

Small-scale Hotel

Location: I-95, exit 45 (SR 808/Glades Rd). 2000 NW Executive Ct 33431. Fax: 561/241-7080. **Facility:** 152 units. 140 one-bedroom standard units. 12 one-bedroom suites ($139-$209). 4 stories, interior corridors. *Bath:* combo or shower only. **Parking:** on-site. **Amenities:** dual phone lines, voice mail, irons, hair dryers. **Pool(s):** heated outdoor. **Leisure Activities:** whirlpool, exercise room. **Business Services:** meeting rooms, fax (fee). **Cards:** AX, DC, DS, MC, VI. *(See ad p 247)*

SOME UNITS

DOUBLETREE GUEST SUITES-BOCA RATON

SAVE

Phone: (561)997-9500

12/18-4/27 [ECP]	1P: $169-$229	2P: $169-$229	XP: $10	F18
12/1-12/20 & 10/1-11/30 [ECP]	1P: $129-$169	2P: $129-$169	XP: $10	F18
4/28-9/30 [ECP]	1P: $109-$149	2P: $109-$149	XP: $10	F18

Small-scale Hotel **Location:** I-95, exit 48 (Yamato Rd), just w. Located in Arvida Corporate Park. 701 NW 53rd St 33487. Fax: 561/994-3565. **Facility:** 183 one-bedroom suites. 4 stories, interior corridors. **Parking:** on-site. **Terms:** cancellation fee imposed, package plans, pets ($50 extra charge). **Amenities:** dual phone lines, voice mail, irons, hair dryers. **Pool(s):** heated outdoor. **Leisure Activities:** whirlpool. *Fee:* massage. **Guest Services:** valet and coin laundry, area transportation. **Business Services:** meeting rooms, fax (fee). **Cards:** AX, CB, DC, DS, JC, MC, VI. *(See ad below)*

SOME UNITS

EMBASSY SUITES-BOCA RATON

SAVE

Phone: (561)994-8200

1/1-4/27 [BP]	1P: $159-$239	2P: $159-$239	XP: $10	F18
12/1-12/31 & 10/1-11/30 [BP]	1P: $99-$169	2P: $99-$169	XP: $10	F18
4/28-9/30 [BP]	1P: $99-$139	2P: $99-$139	XP: $10	F18

Small-scale Hotel **Location:** I-95, exit 48 (Yamato Rd), just w. Located in Arvida Corporate Park. 661 NW 53rd St 33487. Fax: 561/995-9821. **Facility:** 263 units. 261 one- and 2 two-bedroom suites. 7 stories, interior corridors. *Bath:* combo or shower only. **Parking:** on-site. **Terms:** cancellation fee imposed. **Amenities:** voice mail, safes, irons, hair dryers. **Pool(s):** heated outdoor. **Leisure Activities:** saunas, whirlpool, exercise room. *Fee:* massage. **Guest Services:** gift shop, valet and coin laundry, area transportation. **Business Services:** meeting rooms, fax (fee). **Cards:** AX, CB, DS, MC, VI.

SOME UNITS
FEE

FAIRFIELD INN & SUITES BY MARRIOTT

SAVE

Phone: 561/417-8585

12/21-4/15 [ECP]	1P: $119-$129
12/1-12/20 & 4/16-11/30 [ECP]	1P: $89-$129

Small-scale Hotel **Location:** I-95, exit 45, just e, then 1.1 mi n. 3400 Airport Rd 33431. Fax: 561/417-5355. **Facility:** 119 one-bedroom standard units. 4 stories, interior corridors. *Bath:* combo or shower only. **Parking:** on-site. **Amenities:** dual phone lines, voice mail, irons, hair dryers. *Some:* CD players. **Pool(s):** small heated outdoor. **Leisure Activities:** whirlpool, limited exercise equipment. **Guest Services:** valet laundry. **Business Services:** meeting rooms, fax (fee). **Cards:** AX, DC, DS, MC, VI.

SOME UNITS

HAMPTON INN-BOCA RATON

SAVE

Phone: (561)988-0200

12/20-3/27	1P: $169-$199	2P: $179-$209	
3/28-4/30	1P: $129-$169	2P: $139-$179	
12/1-12/19	1P: $119-$159	2P: $129-$169	
5/1-11/30	1P: $89-$119	2P: $99-$129	

Small-scale Hotel **Location:** I-95, exit 48 (Yamato Rd), just w. 1455 Yamato Rd 33431. Fax: 561/988-0203. **Facility:** 94 one-bedroom standard units. 4 stories, interior corridors. *Bath:* combo or shower only. **Parking:** on-site. **Terms:** cancellation fee imposed, [ECP] meal plan available. **Amenities:** dual phone lines, voice mail, irons, hair dryers. *Some:* fax. **Pool(s):** heated outdoor. **Guest Services:** valet laundry. **Business Services:** fax (fee). **Cards:** AX, CB, DC, DS, MC, VI.

SOME UNITS
FEE

HILTON GARDEN INN BOCA RATON

Phone: (561)988-6110

AAA SAVE	12/20-4/24	1P: $139-$199	XP: $10
	12/1-12/19 & 4/25-11/30	1P: $89-$139	XP: $10

Location: I-95, exit 50, just w. 8201 Congress Ave 33487. **Fax:** 561/989-9256. **Facility:** 149 one-bedroom standard units. 4 stories, interior corridors. *Bath:* combo or shower only. **Parking:** on-site. **Amenities:** video **Small-scale Hotel** games (fee), high-speed Internet, dual phone lines, voice mail, irons, hair dryers. **Dining:** 6:30-10 am, 11-2 & 5-10 pm, cocktails. **Pool(s):** heated outdoor. **Leisure Activities:** limited exercise equipment. **Guest Services:** sundries, valet and coin laundry, area transportation-within 2 mi. **Business Services:** meeting rooms, business center. **Cards:** AX, CB, DC, DS, JC, MC, VI. **Special Amenities:** free newspaper. *(See color ad below)*

SOME UNITS

HOLIDAY INN BOCA RATON TOWN CENTER

Phone: (561)368-5200

	1/26-4/12	1P: $129-$179
	12/1-1/25	1P: $89-$139
Small-scale Hotel	8/31-11/30	1P: $79-$139
	4/13-8/30	1P: $69-$109

Location: I-95, exit 45 (SR 808/Glades Rd), just w. 1950 Glades Rd 33431. **Fax:** 561/395-4783. **Facility:** 184 units. 146 one-bedroom standard units. 38 one-bedroom suites ($129-$209). 3-5 stories, interior/exterior corridors. *Bath:* combo or shower only. **Parking:** on-site. **Terms:** cancellation fee imposed. **Amenities:** dual phone lines, voice mail, irons, hair dryers. **Pool(s):** heated outdoor, wading. **Leisure Activities:** whirlpool. **Guest Services:** valet and coin laundry. **Business Services:** meeting rooms, fax (fee). **Cards:** AX, DC, DS, MC, VI. *(See color ad opposite inside back cover)*

SOME UNITS

HOLIDAY INN EXPRESS

Phone: (561)395-7172

AAA SAVE	12/21-4/20 [ECP]	1P: $109-$169	2P: $119-$179
	12/1-12/20 [ECP]	1P: $79-$109	2P: $89-$119
Motel	4/21-11/30 [ECP]	1P: $69-$99	2P: $79-$109

Location: US 1, 1 mi n of jct SR 808 (Glades Rd). 2899 N Federal Hwy 33431. **Fax:** 561/750-7351. **Facility:** 48 one-bedroom standard units. 2 stories (no elevator), exterior corridors. **Parking:** on-site. **Terms:** 7 day cancellation notice, package plans - 6/1-9/30. **Amenities:** irons, hair dryers. **Pool(s):** outdoor. **Guest Services:** valet laundry. **Business Services:** meeting rooms, fax (fee). **Cards:** AX, DC, DS, MC, VI. **Special Amenities:** free continental breakfast and free local telephone calls.

SOME UNITS

HOLIDAY INN-WEST BOCA

Phone: (561)482-7070

▼▼▼

12/1-4/15	1P: $99-$145	2P: $99-$145
4/16-11/30	1P: $69-$79	2P: $69-$79

Small-scale Hotel **Location:** SR 808, w of Florida Tpke, exit 75. Located in Lakeside Centre Shops. 8144 Glades Rd 33434. Fax: 561/482-6076. **Facility:** 97 one-bedroom standard units. 2-4 stories, interior corridors. *Bath:* combo or shower only. **Parking:** on-site. **Amenities:** voice mail, irons, hair dryers. **Pool(s):** heated outdoor. **Leisure Activities:** exercise room. **Guest Services:** valet laundry. **Business Services:** meeting rooms, fax (fee). **Cards:** AX, CB, DC, DS, JC, MC, VI. *(See color ad opposite inside back cover)*

SOME UNITS
(ASK) (S⃠) (†¶) (Y) (E⃠) (≈) (🎦) (DATA PORT) (💻) / (⊠) (🔒) /
FEE

HOMESTEAD STUDIO SUITES HOTEL-BOCA RATON/COMMERCE

Phone: (561)994-2599

▼▼

12/22-4/15	1P: $95	2P: $149	XP: $5	F18
12/1-12/21 & 4/16-11/30	1P: $55	2P: $109	XP: $5	F18

Motel **Location:** I-95, exit 50, just s on Congress Ave to NW 6th Ave. 501 NW 77th St 33487. Fax: 561/994-2792. **Facility:** 115 units. 91 one-bedroom standard units with efficiencies. 22 one- and 2 two-bedroom suites ($99-$149) with efficiencies. 2 stories, exterior corridors. *Bath:* combo or shower only. **Parking:** on-site. **Terms:** cancellation fee imposed, pets ($75 fee). **Amenities:** voice mail, irons. *Some:* dual phone lines. **Guest Services:** coin laundry. **Business Services:** fax (fee). **Cards:** AX, CB, DC, DS, JC, MC, VI.

SOME UNITS
(ASK) (S⃠) (🛏) (E⃠) (🎦) (DATA PORT) (🔒) (💻) (💻) / (⊠) /

THE INN AT BOCA TEECA

Phone: 561/994-0400

▼▼ ▼▼

Property failed to provide current rates

Resort Motel **Location:** I-95, exit 48A (Yamato Rd), 0.5 mi e, then 0.5 mi n. Located in Boca Teeca Country Club. 5800 NW 2nd Ave 33487. Fax: 561/998-8279. **Facility:** 46 one-bedroom standard units. 3 stories, interior corridors. **Parking:** on-site. **Terms:** check-in 4 pm. **Pool(s):** heated outdoor. **Leisure Activities:** saunas, whirlpools, 6 tennis courts, exercise room. *Fee:* golf-27 holes. **Guest Services:** coin laundry. **Business Services:** meeting rooms, fax (fee). **Cards:** AX, DC, MC, VI.

SOME UNITS
(†¶) (≈) (⊠) (🔒) / (⊠) (💻) /
FEE

LA BOCA CASA

Phone: (561)392-0885

(AAA) (SAVE)
▼▼ ▼▼

12/16-4/14	1P: $145
12/1-12/15 & 4/15-11/30	1P: $85

Motel **Location:** On SR A1A, just n of jct Palmetto Park Rd. Located across from the beach. 365 N Ocean Blvd 33432. Fax: 561/367-8127. **Facility:** 19 one-bedroom suites with kitchens. 2 stories (no elevator), exterior corridors. **Parking:** on-site. **Terms:** 3 night minimum stay, 3 day cancellation notice-fee imposed, weekly rates available. **Amenities:** voice mail, irons. **Pool(s):** heated outdoor. **Leisure Activities:** whirlpool. **Guest Services:** complimentary laundry. **Cards:** AX, MC, VI.

(≈) (VCR) (DATA PORT) (🔒) (💻)

OCEAN LODGE

Phone: 561/395-7772

(AAA) (SAVE)
▼▼ ▼▼

2/1-4/16	1P: $100-$125	2P: $100-$125	XP: $10
12/19-1/31	1P: $95-$120	2P: $95-$120	XP: $10
12/1-12/18 & 4/17-11/30	1P: $55-$75	2P: $55-$75	XP: $10

Motel **Location:** On SR A1A, 0.5 mi n of jct Palmetto Park Rd. Located across from the beach. 531 N Ocean Blvd 33432. Fax: 561/395-0554. **Facility:** 18 one-bedroom standard units, some with efficiencies. 2 stories (no elevator), exterior corridors. **Parking:** on-site. **Terms:** 3 day cancellation notice. **Amenities:** voice mail. **Pool(s):** heated outdoor. **Guest Services:** coin laundry. **Cards:** AX, DS, MC, VI. **Special Amenities:** early check-in/late check-out and preferred room (subject to availability with advanced reservations).

SOME UNITS
(≈) (🔒) (💻) / (⊠) /

RADISSON BRIDGE RESORT OF BOCA RATON

Phone: (561)368-9500

(AAA) (SAVE)

◇◇◇◇

12/21-4/15	1P: $269	2P: $279	XP: $10	F17
10/1-11/30	1P: $159	2P: $169	XP: $10	F17
12/1-12/20 & 4/16-9/30	1P: $149	2P: $159	XP: $10	F17

Location: Just w of SR A1A, 1 mi s of jct SR 798 (Palmetto Park Rd). Located across from the ocean. 999 E Camino **Large-scale Hotel** Real 33432. Fax: 561/362-0492. **Facility:** 121 units. 96 one-bedroom standard units. 25 one-bedroom suites ($179-$299). 11 stories, interior corridors. *Bath:* combo or shower only. **Parking:** on-site and valet. **Terms:** 3 day cancellation notice-fee imposed. **Amenities:** video games (fee), dual phone lines, voice mail, irons, hair dryers. **Dining:** 2 restaurants, 6:30 am-10 pm, Fri & Sat-11 pm, cocktails, entertainment. **Pool(s):** heated outdoor. **Leisure Activities:** saunas, rental boats, exercise room. *Fee:* bicycles. **Guest Services:** gift shop, valet parking. **Business Services:** meeting rooms, fax (fee). **Cards:** AX, CB, DC, DS, JC, MC, VI. **Special Amenities:** free newspaper. *(See color ad p 250)*

SOME UNITS

RADISSON SUITE HOTEL BOCA RATON

Phone: (561)483-3600

(AAA) (SAVE)

◇◇◇

12/21-4/14	1P: $249-$269	2P: $269-$289	XP: $10	F18
10/1-11/30	1P: $189-$209	2P: $209-$229	XP: $10	F18
12/1-12/20	1P: $179-$199	2P: $199-$219	XP: $10	F18
4/15-9/30	1P: $169-$189	2P: $189-$209	XP: $10	F18

Small-scale Hotel Location: Florida Tpke., exit 75 (SR 808/Glades Rd). Located in Arvida Pkwy Center. 7920 Glades Rd 33434. Fax: 561/479-2280. **Facility:** 200 one-bedroom suites. 7 stories, interior corridors. *Bath:* combo or shower only. **Parking:** on-site. **Terms:** [BP] meal plan available, small pets only ($100 fee). **Amenities:** dual phone lines, voice mail, honor bars, irons, hair dryers. *Fee:* video games, high-speed Internet. **Pool(s):** heated outdoor. **Leisure Activities:** whirlpool, exercise room. **Guest Services:** valet and coin laundry, area transportation-within 5 mi. **Business Services:** meeting rooms. **Cards:** AX, CB, DC, DS, JC, MC, VI. **Special Amenities:** free continental breakfast and free newspaper. *(See color ad below)*

SOME UNITS

RENAISSANCE BOCA RATON HOTEL

Phone: (561)368-5252

(AAA) (SAVE)

◇◇◇

	1P:	2P:
1/1-4/1	1P: $169-$199	2P: $169-$199
10/1-11/30	1P: $129-$159	2P: $129-$159
12/1-12/31	1P: $110-$159	2P: $110-$159
4/2-9/30	1P: $110-$150	2P: $110-$159

Large-scale Hotel Location: I-95, exit 45 (SR 808/Glades Rd), just w to NW 19th St. 2000 NW 19th St 33431. Fax: 561/750-5437. **Facility:** 189 units. 184 one-bedroom standard units. 5 one-bedroom suites ($225-$375). 5 stories, interior corridors. **Parking:** on-site and valet. **Terms:** package plans - weekends. **Amenities:** high-speed Internet (fee), dual phone lines, voice mail, safes, honor bars, irons, hair dryers. *Some:* DVD players, fax. **Dining:** 6 am-10:30 & 5-10 pm. **Pool(s):** heated outdoor. **Leisure Activities:** whirlpool, limited exercise equipment. **Guest Services:** valet laundry, area transportation-within 5 mi. **Business Services:** meeting rooms, business center. **Cards:** AX, CB, DC, DS, JC, MC, VI. **Special Amenities:** early check-in/late check-out and free newspaper.

SOME UNITS

RESIDENCE INN-BY MARRIOTT-BOCA RATON
Phone: (561)994-3222

[SAVE]

12/1-3/31   1P: $139-$189
4/1-11/30   1P: $69-$119

▼▼▼▼

Motel

Location: I-95, exit 50, just w of Congress Ave. 525 NW 77th St 33487. Fax: 561/994-3339. **Facility:** 120 units. 111 one-bedroom standard units with kitchens. 6 one- and 3 two-bedroom suites with kitchens. 2 stories (no elevator), exterior corridors. **Bath:** combo or shower only. **Parking:** on-site. **Terms:** cancellation fee imposed, [ECP] meal plan available, pets ($75-$100 extra charge). **Amenities:** voice mail, irons, hair dryers. **Pool(s):** heated outdoor. **Leisure Activities:** whirlpools, sports court, basketball, volleyball. **Guest Services:** complimentary evening beverages: Mon-Thurs, valet and coin laundry, area transportation. **Business Services:** meeting rooms. **Cards:** AX, CB, DC, DS, JC, MC, VI.

SOME UNITS

[icons] / [✕] [VCR] /
FEE

SPRINGHILL SUITES BY MARRIOTT
Phone: (561)994-2107

[SAVE]

12/1-4/27 & 11/22-11/30   1P: $99-$179   2P: $99-$179
4/28-11/21   1P: $59-$89   2P: $59-$89

▼▼▼▼

Small-scale Hotel

Location: I-95, exit 48 (Yamato Rd), just w. Located in Arvida Corporate Park. 5130 NW 8th Ave 33487. Fax: 561/994-0226. **Facility:** 146 one-bedroom standard units. 5 stories, interior corridors. **Bath:** combo or shower only. **Parking:** on-site. **Terms:** [ECP] meal plan available. **Amenities:** dual phone lines, voice mail, irons, hair dryers. **Pool(s):** heated outdoor. **Leisure Activities:** whirlpool, exercise room. **Guest Services:** valet and coin laundry. **Business Services:** meeting rooms, business center. **Cards:** AX, DC, DS, JC, MC, VI.
(See color ad p 251)

SOME UNITS

[icons] / [✕] /

TOWNEPLACE SUITES BY MARRIOTT
Phone: (561)994-7232

[SAVE]

12/1-4/27 & 11/22-11/30   1P: $99-$159   2P: $99-$159
4/28-11/21   1P: $59-$89   2P: $59-$89

▼▼▼▼

Small-scale Hotel

Location: I-95, exit 48 (Yamato Rd), just w. Located in Arvida Corporate Park. 5110 NW 8th Ave 33487. Fax: 561/994-2134. **Facility:** 91 units. 66 one-bedroom standard units with efficiencies. 6 one- and 19 two-bedroom suites with kitchens. 4 stories, interior corridors. **Bath:** combo or shower only. **Parking:** on-site. **Terms:** 5 night minimum stay - in season, [ECP] meal plan available, small pets only ($70 fee, $3 extra charge). **Amenities:** video games (fee), dual phone lines, voice mail, irons, hair dryers. **Pool(s):** heated outdoor. **Leisure Activities:** limited exercise equipment. **Guest Services:** valet and coin laundry. **Business Services:** fax (fee). **Cards:** AX, DC, DS, JC, MC, VI. *(See color ad p 251)*

SOME UNITS

[icons] / [✕] /

——— **WHERE TO DINE** ———

ARTURO'S RISTORANTE
Lunch: $14-$20   **Dinner:** $17-$35   **Phone:** 561/997-7373

[AAA]

▼▼▼▼

Italian

Location: On US 1, 1 mi s of jct Yamato Rd. 6750 Federal Hwy 33487. **Hours:** noon-3 & 6-10 pm, Sat & Sun from 6 pm. Closed: 11/27, 12/25; also Super Bowl Sun. **Reservations:** suggested. **Features:** This gem has family working in every facet of the restaurant. You will find all the traditional Italian favorites as well as the house favorites. There are two dining rooms: one is rather on the formal side, while the other has more of a garden feel to it. The restaurant offers an award-winning wine list as well. Dressy casual; cocktails; entertainment. **Parking:** on-site and valet. **Cards:** AX, CB, DC, DS, MC, VI.

[Y] [✕]

BISTRO ZENITH
Lunch: $7-$12   **Dinner:** $11-$21   **Phone:** 561/997-2570

▼▼▼▼

American

Location: Jct of Yamato and Jog/Powerline rds; in Regency Court Shopping Center. 3011 Yamato Rd 33434. **Hours:** 11:30 am-2:30 pm, Fri 11:30 am-2:30 & 5:30-11 pm, Sat from 5:30 pm, Sun 5:30 pm-10 pm. Closed: 5/26, 7/4. **Reservations:** suggested. **Features:** The diverse menu includes fresh seafood, pasta and American comfort foods. Those seated in the dining room get glimpses of the fast-paced kitchen. At night, the lighting is soft with some Art Deco neon accenting the decor. Dressy casual; cocktails. **Parking:** on-site. **Cards:** AX, MC, VI.

[Y] [✕]

CRAB HOUSE SEAFOOD RESTAURANT
Lunch: $5-$14   **Dinner:** $13-$18   **Phone:** 561/750-0498

▼▼ ▼▼

Seafood

Location: Powerline Rd and SW 18th St; in Wharfside Shops. 1.3 mi s of jct Palmetto Park Rd. 6909 SW 18th St 33431. **Hours:** 11:30 am-10 pm, Fri-11 pm, Sat noon-11 pm. Closed: 11/27. **Reservations:** accepted. **Features:** When you're hungry for seafood but don't want to make a trip to the beach, this popular and busy lakefront restaurant fits the bill. Enjoy a drink at the outside bar before sampling varied crab dishes, seafood offerings and raw bar delicacies. Casual dress; cocktails. **Parking:** on-site. **Cards:** AX, DC, DS, MC, VI.

[&M] [Y] [✕]

KATHY'S GAZEBO CAFE
Lunch: $9-$18   **Dinner:** $24-$35   **Phone:** 561/395-6032

▼▼▼ ▼▼

Continental

Location: US 1, 0.5 mi s of Yamato Rd. 4199 N Federal Hwy 33431. **Hours:** 11:30 am-3 & 5:30-10 pm, Sat & Sun from 5:30 pm. Closed major holidays; also Sun 8/7-9/1. **Reservations:** suggested. **Features:** This popular, European-style restaurant features fine dining with generous portions of freshly prepared entrees. Subdued lighting, fresh flowers and comfortable booths enhance the intimate, cozy setting. Patio dining is also offered. Semi-formal attire; cocktails. **Parking:** on-site. **Cards:** AX, MC, VI.

[✕]

LA VIEILLE MAISON Historic
Dinner: $18-$42   **Phone:** 561/391-6701

[AAA]

▼▼▼ ▼▼

French

Location: Just w of SR A1A. 770 E Palmetto Park Rd 33432. **Hours:** 6 pm-9:30 pm; to 10 pm in season. **Reservations:** required. **Features:** This restored Mizner-style mansion with a lovely courtyard is set among lush tropical gardens. Several intimate dining rooms, each tastefully appointed, provide the backdrop for nouvelle and classic French cuisine. An extensive wine list is available. Semi-formal attire; cocktails. **Parking:** valet. **Cards:** AX, DC, DS, MC, VI.

[Y] [✕]

MARK'S AT THE PARK
▼▲▼▲▼ ▼▲▼▲▼

Mediterranean

Lunch: $8-$15   **Dinner:** $15-$30   **Phone:** 561/395-0770

Location: I-95, exit 45 (SR 808/Glades Rd), 2.2 mi e, 0.4 mi s on N Federal Hwy, then e to Mizner Park; opposite fountains. 344 Plaza Real 33432. **Hours:** 11:30 am-3 & 5-11 pm, Fri & Sat-midnight, Sun-10:30 pm. **Reservations:** suggested. **Features:** "New Mediterranean" cuisine reflects the delicate balance of flavors of the different countries of the region. Fresh, local ingredients contribute to the outstanding taste of preparations of fish, poultry, fresh pasta and meat. The atmosphere is modern contemporary, with muted colors accented with mild tones. Soft, indirect lighting lends sophistication. Among seating options are the chef's counter, which offers a view of the kitchen, and an outdoor patio. Dressy casual; cocktails. **Parking:** valet. **Cards:** AX, DC, MC, VI.

⟨&M⟩ ⟨Y⟩ ⟨X⟩

NEW YORK PRIME, A STEAKHOUSE
▼▲▼▲▼

Steak House

Dinner: $20-$39   **Phone:** 561/998-3881

Location: I-95, exit 45 (SR 808/Glades Rd). 2350 NW Executive Center Dr 33431. **Hours:** 5 pm-10 pm. **Reservations:** required. **Features:** Steak, the prime entree, is not to be overlooked on a menu that also includes other meat selections and seafood. The steaks are large, and the lobsters are larger. The dining room is upbeat and bustling. An extensive wine list is offered. Dressy casual; cocktails. **Parking:** valet.

Cards: AX, MC, VI.

⟨Y⟩ ⟨X⟩

ROY'S
▼▲▼▲▼

Hawaiian

Dinner: $20-$30   **Phone:** 561/620-9401

Location: I-95, exit 44, 0.3 mi n of Palmetto Park Rd, then 1.2 mi n. 1901 N Military Tr 34134. **Hours:** 5:30 pm-10 pm, Fri & Sat-10:30 pm. Closed: 11/27, 12/25. **Reservations:** suggested. **Features:** The decor gives a nod toward the Asian influence, with rich Oriental colors and exposed wood beams. Pacific Ocean seafood is prepared in a Hawaiian fusion style. Some hard-to-find bottles make their way onto the noteworthy wine list. Smoke free premises. Dressy casual; cocktails. **Parking:** valet.

⟨&M⟩ ⟨Y⟩ ⟨X⟩

ZEMI
▼▲▼▲▼

American

Lunch: $8-$15   **Dinner:** $14-$36   **Phone:** 561/391-7177

Location: I-95, exit 44, 0.3 mi w of Palmetto Park Rd, 1 mi n on Military Tr; in Boca Center. 5050 Town Center Circle #245 33466. **Hours:** 11:30 am-2:30 & 6-10:30 pm, Fri-11 pm, Sat 6 pm-11 pm, Sun 6 pm-10 pm. Closed major holidays. **Reservations:** suggested. **Features:** The restaurant blends a modern look, an open kitchen in the back and an eclectic menu of American cuisine to appeal to a wide range of palates. Dressy casual; cocktails. **Parking:** on-site and valet. **Cards:** AX, CB, DC, DS, MC, VI.

⟨Y⟩ ⟨X⟩

The following restaurants have not been evaluated by AAA but are listed for your information only.

FLANIGAN'S SEAFOOD BAR & GRILL
[fyi]

Phone: 561/395-4699

Not evaluated. **Location:** 45 S Federal Hwy. **Features:** The family-friendly restaurant is known for its baby back ribs, burgers and seafood.

LEGAL SEA FOODS
[fyi]

Phone: 561/447-2112

Not evaluated. **Location:** 6000 W Glades Rd 33431. **Features:** New England style seafood has arrived, experience the clam chowder and the New England Clam bake as well as other favorites.

BONITA SPRINGS pop. 32,797

--- WHERE TO STAY ---

AMERICINN HOTEL & SUITES
▼▲▼▲▼

Small-scale Hotel

1/21-3/31 [ECP]	1P: $109	2P: $109	**Phone:** (239)495-9255
12/1-1/20 [ECP]	1P: $89	2P: $89	
4/1-11/30 [ECP]	1P: $59	2P: $59	

Location: I-75, exit 116, 0.7 mi s of Bonita Beach Rd on US 41. 28600 Trails Edge Blvd 34134. Fax: 239/495-6448. **Facility:** 87 one-bedroom standard units. 4 stories, interior corridors. *Bath:* combo or shower only. **Parking:** on-site. **Amenities:** irons. **Pool(s):** heated outdoor. **Leisure Activities:** exercise room. *Fee:* game room. **Guest Services:** coin laundry. **Business Services:** meeting rooms, fax (fee). **Cards:** AX, CB, DC, DS, MC, VI. *(See color ad p 871)*

SOME UNITS

(ASK) (S&D) (↑↓) (&M) (&) (⊘) (≈) (♦) (DATA PORT) (🛏) (📠) (🖥) / (X) /

BAYMONT INN-BONITA SPRINGS
(AAA) (SAVE)
▼▲▼▲▼

Small-scale Hotel

2/1-3/31 [ECP]	1P: $90-$130	2P: $90-$130	**Phone:** (239)949-9400
12/16-1/31 [ECP]	1P: $80-$90	2P: $80-$90	
12/1-12/15 [ECP]	1P: $60-$70	2P: $60-$70	
4/1-11/30 [ECP]	1P: $48-$65	2P: $48-$65	

Location: I-75, exit 116, just w. 27991 Oakland Dr 34135. Fax: 239/949-4437. **Facility:** 60 one-bedroom standard units. 3 stories, interior corridors. *Bath:* combo or shower only. **Parking:** on-site. **Amenities:** voice mail, irons, hair dryers. **Pool(s):** outdoor. **Leisure Activities:** whirlpool, exercise room. **Guest Services:** coin laundry. **Business Services:** fax (fee). **Cards:** AX, DC, DS, MC, VI. **Special Amenities:** free continental breakfast and free newspaper.

SOME UNITS

(S&D) (≈) (♦) (DATA PORT) (🛏) (📠) (🖥) / (X) /

BONITA RESORT & CLUB

Phone: 239/992-5198

AAA SAVE / ▼▼▼
Condominium

All Year Wkly   1P: $465-$915   2P: $620-$1140

Location: I-75, exit 116, 7.9 mi w on Bonita Beach Rd/CR 865; from US 41 (S Tamiami Tr), 4.4 mi w. 26101 Hickory Blvd 34134. Fax: 239/992-2649. **Facility:** 26 one-bedroom standard units. 4 stories, interior corridors. **Parking:** on-site. **Terms:** office hours 8:30 am-5 pm, 30 day cancellation notice-fee imposed, daily rates available. **Amenities:** irons. **Pool(s):** heated outdoor. **Leisure Activities:** whirlpool, boating, boat dock, fishing, recreation programs, rooftop sun deck, barbecue grills, bicycles, horseshoes. **Guest Services:** complimentary laundry. **Cards:** MC, VI.

COMFORT INN HOTEL

Phone: (239)992-5001

AAA SAVE / ▼▼▼
Small-scale Hotel

All Year   1P: $92-$98   2P: $92-$98   XP: $10   F18

Location: I-75, exit 116, 2.5 mi w on CR 865. 9800 Bonita Beach Rd 34135. Fax: 239/992-9283. **Facility:** 69 one-bedroom standard units. 3 stories, interior corridors. **Parking:** on-site. **Terms:** cancellation fee imposed, [CP] meal plan available. **Amenities:** voice mail, safes, hair dryers. *Some:* irons. **Pool(s):** heated outdoor. **Leisure Activities:** whirlpool. **Guest Services:** coin laundry. **Business Services:** fax (fee). **Cards:** AX, CB, DC, DS, JC, MC, VI. **Special Amenities:** free continental breakfast and free newspaper.

SOME UNITS

DAYS INN

Phone: (239)947-3366

SAVE / ▼▼
Motel

12/1-3/31   1P: $75-$125
4/1-11/30   1P: $44-$75

Location: I-75, exit 116, just w on CR 865. 28090 Quails Nest Ln 34135. Fax: 239/947-6789. **Facility:** 100 one-bedroom standard units. 1 story, exterior corridors. *Bath:* combo or shower only. **Parking:** on-site. **Terms:** check-in 4 pm, cancellation fee imposed. **Amenities:** hair dryers. **Pool(s):** outdoor. **Guest Services:** coin laundry. **Business Services:** fax (fee). **Cards:** AX, CB, DC, DS, JC, MC, VI.

SOME UNITS

HAMPTON INN

Phone: (239)947-9393

SAVE / ▼▼▼
Small-scale Hotel

12/20-4/26 [ECP]   1P: $109-$149   2P: $109-$149
12/1-12/19 & 4/27-11/30 [ECP]   1P: $59-$89   2P: $59-$89

Location: I-75, exit 116, 3.3 mi w on CR 865 at jct US 41 and Bonita Beach Rd. 27900 Crown Lake Blvd 34135. Fax: 239/947-3966. **Facility:** 91 one-bedroom standard units. 3 stories, interior corridors. *Bath:* combo or shower only. **Parking:** on-site. **Terms:** weekly rates available. **Amenities:** voice mail, irons, hair dryers. **Pool(s):** heated outdoor. **Guest Services:** valet laundry. **Business Services:** meeting rooms, fax (fee). **Cards:** AX, CB, DC, DS, MC, VI. *(See color ad p 566)*

SOME UNITS

FEE

HOLIDAY INN EXPRESS

Phone: (239)948-0699

▼▼▼
Small-scale Hotel

1/26-4/15 [ECP]   1P: $125-$145   2P: $125-$145   XP: $8   F
12/1-1/2 [ECP]   1P: $65-$120   2P: $65-$120   XP: $8   F
1/3-1/25 [ECP]   1P: $75-$85   2P: $75-$85   XP: $8   F
4/16-11/30 [ECP]   1P: $65-$75   2P: $65-$75   XP: $8   F

Location: I-75, exit 116, 0.4 mi to CR 865, 3.2 mi w, then n. 27891 Crown Lake Blvd 34135. Fax: 239/948-0676. **Facility:** 108 one-bedroom standard units. 4 stories, interior corridors. *Bath:* combo or shower only. **Parking:** on-site. **Amenities:** dual phone lines, voice mail, safes, irons, hair dryers. **Pool(s):** small outdoor. **Guest Services:** valet and coin laundry. **Business Services:** fax (fee). **Cards:** AX, CB, DC, DS, JC, MC, VI.

SOME UNITS

HYATT REGENCY COCONUT POINT RESORT & SPA

Phone: (239)444-1234

AAA SAVE / ▼▼▼ ▼▼▼
Resort
Large-scale Hotel

1/1-4/30   1P: $225-$450   2P: $225-$450   XP: $25   F18
12/1-12/31 & 10/1-11/30   1P: $190-$340   2P: $190-$340   XP: $25   F18
5/1-9/30   1P: $125-$225   2P: $125-$225   XP: $25   F18

Location: I-75, exit 123 (CR 850/Corkscrew Rd), 1.9 mi e to US 41/Tamiami Tr, 2.3 mi s, then 1.5 mi e. 5001 Coconut Rd 34134. Fax: 239/390-4344. **Facility:** Water views and balconies enhance most accommodations at this resort decorated with a tropical touch. 450 units. 423 one-bedroom standard units. 27 one-bedroom suites. 18 stories, interior corridors. *Bath:* combo or shower only. **Parking:** on-site and valet. **Terms:** check-in 4 pm, 3 day cancellation notice-fee imposed, $10 service charge. **Amenities:** DVD players, CD players, dual phone lines, voice mail, safes, irons, hair dryers. *Fee:* video games, high-speed Internet. **Dining:** 5 restaurants, 6:30 am-10 pm, cocktails, also, Tanglewood, see separate listing, entertainment. **Pool(s):** outdoor, 2 heated outdoor. **Leisure Activities:** whirlpools, waterslide, jogging, playground, spa. *Fee:* charter fishing, golf-18 holes, golf and tennis instruction, 2 lighted tennis courts. **Guest Services:** gift shop, valet laundry, area transportation-golf course, beach. **Business Services:** conference facilities, business center. **Cards:** AX, CB, DC, DS, MC, VI. *(See color ad p 564)*

SOME UNITS

STAYBRIDGE SUITES BY HOLIDAY INN

Phone: 239/949-5913

▼▼▼
Small-scale Hotel

12/21-4/7   1P: $135-$198
12/1-12/20 [BP]   1P: $84-$119
4/8-11/30   1P: $83-$119

Location: I-75, exit 116, 3.5 mi w on CR 865, then 1.4 mi n on US 41. 8900 Brighton Ln 34135. Fax: 239/949-5914. **Facility:** 106 units. 53 one-bedroom standard units with kitchens. 35 one- and 18 two-bedroom suites, some with kitchens. 4 stories, interior corridors. *Bath:* combo or shower only. **Parking:** on-site. **Terms:** cancellation fee imposed, small pets only ($75 fee). **Amenities:** dual phone lines, voice mail, irons, hair dryers. **Pool(s):** heated outdoor. **Leisure Activities:** exercise room. **Guest Services:** sundries, valet and coin laundry. **Business Services:** meeting rooms, business center. **Cards:** AX, DC, DS, MC, VI.

SOME UNITS

TRIANON BONITA BAY
Small-scale Hotel

			Phone: (239)948-4400	
12/21-4/20 [ECP]	1P: $140-$200	2P: $140-$200	XP: $10	F18
4/21-11/30 [ECP]	1P: $82-$115	2P: $82-$115	XP: $10	F18
12/1-12/20 [ECP]	1P: $85-$105	2P: $85-$105	XP: $10	F18

Location: I-75, exit 123, just w of US 41, 6 mi s of Corkscrew Rd. 3401 Bay Commons Dr 34134. Fax: 239/948-4401. **Facility:** 100 one-bedroom standard units. 4 stories, interior corridors. *Bath:* combo or shower only. **Parking:** on-site. **Terms:** cancellation fee imposed. **Amenities:** voice mail, safes, irons, hair dryers. *Some:* CD players. **Pool(s):** heated outdoor. **Leisure Activities:** exercise room. **Guest Services:** valet laundry. **Business Services:** meeting rooms, fax (fee). **Cards:** AX, DC, DS, MC, VI. *(See color ad p 573)*

SOME UNITS
[ASK] [S/D] [T|+] [Y] [&M] [&] [~~] [*] [DATA PORT] [□] / [X] [VCR] [□] /
FEE

WHERE TO DINE

ROY'S
Pacific Rim

Dinner: $22-$29   **Phone:** 239/498-7697

Location: I-75, exit 116, 3.3 mi w on CR 565 (Bonita Beach Rd), 1 mi n to W Terry St/Bonita Bay Blvd, then w, then just n on S Bay Dr; in The Promenade Shops. 26831 S Bay Dr, Suite 100 34134. **Hours:** 5:30 pm-10 pm. Closed: 7/4, 11/27, 12/25. **Reservations:** suggested. **Features:** An open-air kitchen, from which many interesting aromas arise, greets diners as they enter the dining room. The menu's many entrees—including many seafood dishes not seen on this coast—reflect a Hawaiian fusion style. A large wine list complements the food. Dressy casual; cocktails. **Parking:** on-site. **Cards:** AX, CB, DC, DS, JC, MC, VI.

[&M] [Y] [X]

TANGLEWOOD
Continental

Dinner: $18-$30   **Phone:** 239/444-1234

Location: I-75, exit 123 (CR 850/Corkscrew Rd), 1.9 mi e to US 41/Tamiami Tr, 2.3 mi s, then 1.5 mi e; in Hyatt Regency Coconut Point Resort & Spa. 5001 Coconut Rd 34134. **Hours:** 5 pm-10 pm. **Reservations:** suggested. **Features:** The room's decor is soft, with earthy tones and accents of a tropical plantation home. Continental cuisine is prepared with a Florida twist: fresh local ingredients. The chef changes the menu seasonally to take advantage of the freshest available products. Dressy casual; cocktails. **Parking:** on-site and valet. **Cards:** AX, CB, DC, DS, JC, MC, VI.

[Y] [X]

BOYNTON BEACH pop. 60,389   (See map p. 757; index p. 760)

WHERE TO STAY

ATLANTIC LODGE
[AAA] [SAVE]
Motel

			Phone: 561/732-4446	[68]
12/15-4/15	1P: $66-$70	2P: $70-$80	XP: $10	D12
12/1-12/14 & 4/16-11/30	1P: $34-$44	2P: $45-$50	XP: $8	D12

Location: US 1, 0.8 mi s of jct Woolbright Rd. Located in a quiet area. 2607 S Federal Hwy 33435. Fax: 561/731-0325. **Facility:** 20 one-bedroom standard units, some with efficiencies. 1 story, exterior corridors. *Bath:* combo or shower only. **Parking:** on-site. **Terms:** 14 day cancellation notice-fee imposed, weekly rates available. **Pool(s):** heated outdoor. **Guest Services:** coin laundry. **Cards:** AX, DC, DS, MC, VI.

[S/D] [T|+] [~~] [□]

BOYNTON MOTEL
Motel

			Phone: (561)737-3729	[67]
12/16-4/15	1P: $65-$80	2P: $65-$80	XP: $5	F18
12/1-12/15 & 4/16-11/30	1P: $50-$65	2P: $50-$65	XP: $5	F18

Location: US 1, 0.5 mi s of jct SR 804 and Boynton Beach Blvd. Located in a quiet area. 623 S Federal Hwy 33435. Fax: 561/731-1612. **Facility:** 21 one-bedroom standard units with efficiencies. 1 story, exterior corridors. *Bath:* shower only. **Parking:** on-site. **Terms:** 3 day cancellation notice-fee imposed. **Guest Services:** coin laundry. **Cards:** AX, CB, DC, DS, MC, VI.

[ASK] [S/D] [T|+] [□]

(See map p. 757)

HAMPTON INN & SUITES BOYNTON BEACH

SAVE

12/1-4/30	1P: $129-$199
10/1-11/30	1P: $109-$179
5/1-5/31	1P: $99-$149
6/1-9/30	1P: $79-$134

2P: $139-$209
2P: $119-$189
2P: $109-$159
2P: $89-$149

Phone: (561)369-0018 63

Small-scale Hotel **Location:** I-95, exit 59 (Gateway Blvd), 1.2 mi w. 1475 W Gateway Blvd 33426. Fax: 561/738-5235. **Facility:** 161 units. 146 one-bedroom standard units. 15 one-bedroom suites. 4 stories, interior corridors. *Bath:* combo or shower only. **Parking:** on-site. **Terms:** [CP] meal plan available. **Amenities:** video games (fee), dual phone lines, voice mail, irons, hair dryers. *Some:* fax. **Pool(s):** heated outdoor. **Leisure Activities:** exercise room. **Guest Services:** sundries, complimentary evening beverages: Mon-Thurs, valet and coin laundry. **Business Services:** meeting rooms, business center. **Cards:** AX, DC, DS, MC, VI.

SOME UNITS

(icons)

HOLIDAY INN-CATALINA

All Year   1P: $69-$149   2P: $69-$149

Phone: (561)737-4600 64

Small-scale Hotel **Location:** SR 807 (Congress Ave), 0.3 mi s of jct SR 806 (Gateway Blvd). Located adjacent to Catalina Shopping Center. 1601 N Congress Ave 33426. Fax: 561/734-6523. **Facility:** 152 one-bedroom standard units. 4 stories, interior/exterior corridors. **Parking:** on-site. **Terms:** cancellation fee imposed. **Amenities:** voice mail, irons, hair dryers. **Pool(s):** heated outdoor. **Leisure Activities:** whirlpool, exercise room. *Fee:* game room. **Guest Services:** valet laundry. **Business Services:** meeting rooms, fax (fee). **Cards:** AX, DC, DS, MC, VI.
(See color ad opposite inside back cover)

SOME UNITS

(icons)

HOLIDAY INN EXPRESS I-95

AAA **SAVE**

1/18-6/1	1P: $117	XP: $10	F18
12/1-1/17 & 10/14-11/30	1P: $85	XP: $10	F18
6/2-10/13	1P: $75	XP: $10	F18

Phone: (561)734-9100 66

Small-scale Hotel **Location:** I-95, exit 57, jct SR 804 (Boynton Beach Blvd). 480 W Boynton Beach Blvd 33435. Fax: 561/738-7193. **Facility:** 102 one-bedroom standard units. 4 stories, interior corridors. **Parking:** on-site. **Terms:** [ECP] meal plan available. **Amenities:** video games, irons, hair dryers. **Pool(s):** heated outdoor. **Guest Services:** complimentary evening beverages, coin laundry. **Business Services:** meeting rooms, fax (fee). **Cards:** AX, DC, DS, MC, VI. **Special Amenities:** free continental breakfast and free local telephone calls. *(See color ad below)*

SOME UNITS

(icons)

FEE   FEE

—— WHERE TO DINE ——

MAMA JENNIE'S ITALIAN RESTAURANT

AAA

South Italian

Dinner: $8-$15   **Phone:** 561/737-2407 36

Location: I-95, exit 57, just w on SR 804. 706 W Boynton Beach Blvd 33426. **Hours:** 4 pm-9 pm, Fri & Sat-10 pm. **Reservations:** accepted. **Features:** Generous portions at reasonable prices make the restaurant a good choice if you're seeking an excellent value. Well-prepared homemade dishes—such as baked stuffed lobster, seafood pomodoro and traditional pasta—are served in a casual, family atmosphere. Casual dress; cocktails. **Parking:** on-site. **Cards:** AX, DS, MC, VI.

(icons)

(See map p. 757)

─────── *The following restaurant has not been evaluated by AAA* ───────
but is listed for your information only.

TWO GEORGES HARBOR HUT   **Phone:** 561/736-2717
[fyi]   Not evaluated. **Location:** From S Federal Hwy, e on E Ocean Ave, then n. 728 Casa Loma Blvd.
Features: Seafood specialties. Building has an open side overlooking Intracoastal Waterway. Moderate to
expensive prices.

BRADENTON pop. 45,504   (See map p. 812; index p. 816)

─────── **WHERE TO STAY** ───────

COMFORT INN-BRADENTON   **Phone:** (941)747-7500   [106]
[AAA] [SAVE]   1/15-4/20 [ECP]   1P: $90-$110   2P: $100-$120   XP: $10   F12
               12/16-1/14 [ECP]   1P: $70-$90   2P: $80-$100   XP: $10   F12
▽▽▽▽▽   12/1-12/15 [ECP]   1P: $60-$70   2P: $70-$80   XP: $10   F12
               4/21-11/30 [ECP]   1P: $50-$60   2P: $60-$70   XP: $10   F12
Motel   **Location:** I-75, exit 220 southbound; exit 220B northbound, 0.3 mi w on SR 64. 580 E 66th St Court 34208.
Fax: 941/748-8002. **Facility:** 70 units. 64 one-bedroom standard units. 6 one-bedroom suites ($99-$159),
some with kitchens and/or whirlpools. 2 stories, exterior corridors. *Bath:* combo or shower only. **Parking:** on-site. **Terms:** 7 day
cancellation notice. **Amenities:** irons, hair dryers. **Pool(s):** outdoor. **Leisure Activities:** whirlpool. **Guest Services:** valet and
coin laundry. **Business Services:** meeting rooms. **Cards:** AX, CB, DC, DS, MC, VI. **Special Amenities: free continental breakfast and free local telephone calls.**
SOME UNITS
[S] [T] [✚] [M] [⌂] [⌖] [≈] [♨] [✦] [DATA PORT] [☕] / [✕] [🔒] [▣] /
                              FEE

DAYS INN BRADENTON   **Phone:** (941)746-1141   [115]
[SAVE]   12/1-4/30   1P: $79-$99   2P: $79-$99   XP: $10   F16
               5/1-11/30   1P: $46-$66   2P: $46-$66   XP: $10   F16
▽▽▽▽   **Location:** On US 41, just e of jct 301 Blvd. 3500 1st St W 34208. Fax: 941/745-2382. **Facility:** 130 one-bedroom
Motel   standard units. 2 stories, exterior corridors. *Bath:* combo or shower only. **Parking:** on-site. **Terms:** 3 day can-
cellation notice-fee imposed. **Amenities:** safes (fee), hair dryers. *Some:* irons. **Pool(s):** outdoor. **Leisure Ac-
tivities:** shuffleboard. **Guest Services:** valet laundry. **Business Services:** meeting rooms, fax (fee).
Cards: AX, CB, DC, DS, MC, VI.
SOME UNITS
[S] [T] [≈] [✦] [DATA PORT] / [✕] [🔒] [▣] /

DAYS INN I-75   **Phone:** (941)746-2505   [108]
[SAVE]   12/1-3/31 [ECP]   1P: $75   2P: $75   XP: $5   F11
               4/1-11/30 [ECP]   1P: $40   2P: $40   XP: $5   F11
▽▽   **Location:** I-75, exit 220 southbound; exit 220B northbound, 0.3 mi w on SR 64. 644 67th St Cir E 34208.
Motel   Fax: 941/745-1839. **Facility:** 60 one-bedroom standard units. 2 stories, exterior corridors. **Parking:** on-site.
Terms: [CP] meal plan available. **Amenities:** hair dryers. *Some:* irons. **Pool(s):** outdoor. **Guest Services:**
coin laundry. **Cards:** AX, CB, DC, DS, JC, MC, VI.
SOME UNITS
[S] [T] [≈] [✦] [🔒] / [✕] /

ECONO LODGE AIRPORT   **Phone:** (941)758-7199   [114]
[AAA] [SAVE]   12/1-4/15   1P: $55-$85   2P: $60-$90   XP: $5   F12
               7/1-9/30   1P: $45-$60   2P: $60-$70   XP: $5   F12
▽▽ ▽▽   4/16-6/30   1P: $45-$55   2P: $55-$65   XP: $5   F12
               10/1-11/30   1P: $40-$50   2P: $50-$60   XP: $5   F12
Motel   **Location:** US 41, 2 mi s of jct SR 70. 6727 14th St W 34207. Fax: 941/751-4947. **Facility:** 78 one-bedroom stan-
dard units. 2 stories, exterior corridors. **Parking:** on-site. **Terms:** small pets only ($5 extra charge). **Business Services:** fax (fee). **Cards:** AX,
CB, DS, MC, VI.
SOME UNITS
[S] [🛏] [T] [≈] [✦] / [✕] [DATA PORT] [🔒] [▣] /
                                              FEE FEE

(See map p. 812)

ECONO LODGE I-75

Motel

				Phone: (941)745-1988	113
1/31-4/15	1P: $69-$94		2P: $75-$99	XP: $4	F18
12/1-1/30 & 4/16-11/30	1P: $49-$64		2P: $51-$68	XP: $4	F18

Location: I-75, exit 220 southbound; exit 220B northbound, 0.3 mi w on SR 64. 607 67th St Cir E 34208. Fax: 941/746-9189. **Facility:** 54 one-bedroom standard units. 2 stories, exterior corridors. **Parking:** on-site. **Pool(s):** outdoor. **Guest Services:** coin laundry. **Cards:** AX, CB, DC, DS, MC, VI. **Special Amenities:** free local telephone calls. *(See color ad p 257)*

SOME UNITS

HOLIDAY INN EXPRESS

			Phone: (941)748-6610	107
12/21-4/30	1P: $109	2P: $109		
12/1-12/20 & 5/1-11/30	1P: $79	2P: $79		

Location: I-75, exit 220 southbound; exit 220B northbound, 0.3 mi w on SR 64. 648 67th Cir E 34208. Fax: 941/748-0922. **Facility:** 60 units. 57 one-bedroom standard units. 3 one-bedroom suites ($89-$129) **Small-scale Hotel** with whirlpools. 3 stories, interior corridors. *Bath:* combo or shower only. **Parking:** on-site. **Terms:** [ECP] meal plan available. **Amenities:** dual phone lines, voice mail, irons, hair dryers. **Pool(s):** heated outdoor. **Guest Services:** valet and coin laundry. **Business Services:** business center. **Cards:** AX, CB, DC, DS, JC, MC, VI. **Special Amenities:** free continental breakfast and free newspaper.

SOME UNITS
FEE

HOLIDAY INN-RIVERFRONT

			Phone: (941)747-3727	109
1/13-4/26	1P: $109-$169	2P: $109-$169		
12/1-1/12 & 4/27-11/30	1P: $89-$139	2P: $89-$139		

Small-scale Hotel **Location:** W of US 41 and 301 at south side of Hernando Desoto Bridge via 3rd St W. 100 Riverfront Dr W 34205. Fax: 941/746-4289. **Facility:** 153 units. 96 one-bedroom standard units. 57 one-bedroom suites. 5 stories, interior corridors. **Parking:** on-site. **Terms:** cancellation fee imposed, [AP] & [BP] meal plans available. **Amenities:** dual phone lines, voice mail, irons, hair dryers. **Pool(s):** heated outdoor. **Leisure Activities:** whirlpool, fishing, exercise room. **Guest Services:** gift shop, valet laundry. **Business Services:** conference facilities, fax (fee). **Cards:** AX, CB, DC, DS, JC, MC, VI. *(See color ad opposite inside back cover)*

SOME UNITS
FEE

PARK INN & SUITES

				Phone: (941)795-4633	110
12/1-4/16	1P: $114-$144		2P: $114-$144	XP: $10	F18
4/17-8/31	1P: $84-$114		2P: $84-$114	XP: $10	F18
9/1-11/30	1P: $79-$104		2P: $79-$104	XP: $10	F18

Location: Just s of jct SR 684 (Carter Rd). 4450 47th St W 34210. Fax: 941/795-0808. **Facility:** 130 units. 103 **Small-scale Hotel** one-bedroom standard units. 27 one-bedroom suites ($99-$144), some with whirlpools. 3 stories, interior corridors. **Parking:** on-site. **Terms:** [ECP] meal plan available. **Amenities:** video games, irons, hair dryers. **Pool(s):** heated outdoor. **Leisure Activities:** whirlpool. **Guest Services:** complimentary evening beverages, valet laundry. **Business Services:** meeting rooms, fax (fee). **Cards:** AX, CB, DC, DS, MC, VI. **Special Amenities:** free continental breakfast and free newspaper.

SOME UNITS
FEE   FEE FEE

QUALITY INN & SUITES

				Phone: (941)747-6465	112
12/1-3/31	1P: $65-$95		2P: $65-$95	XP: $5	F16
4/1-11/30	1P: $45-$70		2P: $45-$70	XP: $5	F16

Motel

Location: On US 41, 1 mi s of jct SR 64. 2303 1st St E 34208. Fax: 941/747-1070. **Facility:** 185 units. 159 one-bedroom standard units. 26 one-bedroom suites. 2 stories, exterior corridors. **Parking:** on-site. **Terms:** 1 day cancellation notice, [ECP] meal plan available. **Amenities:** *Some:* irons. **Pool(s):** heated outdoor. **Leisure Activities:** 2 tennis courts, playground, shuffleboard. **Guest Services:** coin laundry. **Business Services:** meeting rooms, fax (fee). **Cards:** AX, CB, DC, DS, MC, VI.

SOME UNITS

SHOREWALK VACATION VILLAS RESORT

		Phone: (941)794-9800	111
2/1-4/15	2P: $135		
12/16-1/31	2P: $109		
4/16-11/30	2P: $92		
12/1-12/15	2P: $89		

Condominium

Location: Just s of jct SR 684 (Cortez Rd) on 47th St W. 4601 46th St Court W 34210. Fax: 941/795-2163. **Facility:** 150 two-bedroom suites with kitchens. 2 stories, exterior corridors. **Parking:** on-site. **Terms:** check-in 5 pm, 14 day cancellation notice-fee imposed. **Amenities:** video library (fee), irons. *Some:* hair dryers. **Pool(s):** 2 heated outdoor. **Leisure Activities:** whirlpools, rental paddleboats, fishing, 2 lighted tennis courts, recreation programs, playground, basketball, shuffleboard. *Fee:* bicycles, game room. **Guest Services:** complimentary laundry. **Business Services:** fax (fee). **Cards:** AX, DS, MC, VI.

SOME UNITS
FEE

——— **WHERE TO DINE** ———

ANNA MARIA OYSTER BAR

Seafood

Lunch: $5-$25   **Dinner:** $5-$25   Phone: 941-758-7880   52

Location: On US 41 at jct 69th Ave. 6906 14th St 34207. **Hours:** 11:30 am-10 pm, Fri & Sat-11 pm. **Features:** Island-style dining is offered in a fun, contemporary setting with lots of nautical touches. The menu has a multitude of choices, ranging from seafood to poultry to meat dishes. Fried shrimp is an outstanding selection. Casual dress; cocktails. **Parking:** on-site. **Cards:** AX, DS, MC, VI.

(See map p. 812)

LEVEROCK'S OF PERICO HARBOR

Lunch: $7-$19   Dinner: $9-$19   Phone: 941/794-8900   54

♦♦♦♦ ♦♦♦♦
Steak & Seafood

Location: On SR 64, on Perico Island, east side of Anna Maria Island Bridge. 12320 Manatee Ave W 34209. **Hours:** 11 am-10 pm, Fri & Sat-11 pm. Closed: 11/27, 12/25; also Super Bowl Sun for dinner. **Features:** Atmosphere abounds at this waterfront destination, where busy boat docks and gorgeous sunsets are among the many sights to see. The seafood Martinique, babyback ribs and puffed seafood pastry with cream sauce are particularly tasty. Casual dress; cocktails. **Parking:** on-site. **Cards:** AX, DC, DS, MC, VI.

☎ ✕

MILLER'S DUTCH KITCH'N

Lunch: $5-$14   Dinner: $5-$14   Phone: 941/746-8253   53

♦♦♦♦ ♦♦♦♦
American

Location: On US Business Rt 41 at jct 35th Ave W; downtown. 3401 14th St W 34205. **Hours:** 11 am-8 pm. Closed major holidays; also Sun. **Features:** Amish cooking and courteous service are the attractions, with simple meals to remind you of home like pan-fried chicken with potatoes and gravy; or come in for a cup of coffee and a slice of one of 20 made-from-scratch pies, like the rich coconut cream. Smoke free premises. Casual dress. **Parking:** on-site. **Cards:** MC, VI.

✕

BRADENTON BEACH pop. 1,482   (See map p. 812; index p. 815)

——— WHERE TO STAY ———

ECONO LODGE SURFSIDE   Phone: (941)778-6671   75

SAVE	2/1-4/25	1P: $136-$205	2P: $136-$205	XP: $10
	12/21-1/31	1P: $109-$169	2P: $109-$169	XP: $10
♦♦♦♦ ♦♦♦♦	4/26-11/30	1P: $105-$162	2P: $105-$162	XP: $10
	12/1-12/20	1P: $99-$155	2P: $99-$155	XP: $10

Small-scale Hotel **Location:** On SR 789, 1.2 mi n of jct SR 684. 2502 Gulf Dr N 34217. Fax: 941/778-0360. **Facility:** 53 one-bedroom standard units, some with efficiencies. 3 stories, exterior corridors. *Bath:* combo or shower only. **Parking:** on-site. **Terms:** 2 night minimum stay - weekends, 3 day cancellation notice-fee imposed. **Amenities:** *Some:* irons, hair dryers. **Pool(s):** heated outdoor. **Leisure Activities:** Fee: game room. **Guest Services:** coin laundry. **Business Services:** fax (fee). **Cards:** AX, DC, MC, VI. *(See color ad p 257)*

SOME UNITS

TORTUGA INN   Phone: (941)778-6611   79

AAA SAVE	2/1-4/30	1P: $125-$319	2P: $125-$319	XP: $10	F7
	12/16-1/31	1P: $115-$305	2P: $115-$305	XP: $10	F7
♦♦♦♦ ♦♦♦♦	12/1-12/15 & 5/1-11/30	1P: $110-$299	2P: $110-$299	XP: $10	F7

Motel **Location:** On SR 789, 0.3 mi n of jct SR 684. 1325 Gulf Dr N 34217. Fax: 941/778-6748. **Facility:** Designated smoking area. 37 units. 21 one-bedroom standard units, some with efficiencies and/or whirlpools. 16 two-bedroom suites with kitchens, some with whirlpools. 2 stories, exterior corridors. *Bath:* combo or shower only. **Parking:** on-site. **Terms:** 14 day cancellation notice-fee imposed, pets ($25 extra charge, in designated units). **Amenities:** video library, irons, hair dryers. **Pool(s):** heated outdoor. **Leisure Activities:** boat dock, fishing, gas grills, lounge chairs, umbrellas. **Guest Services:** coin laundry. **Business Services:** meeting rooms, business center. **Cards:** AX, DS, MC, VI.

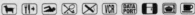

TRADEWINDS RESORT   Phone: (941)779-0010   77

AAA SAVE	2/1-4/30	1P: $149-$289	2P: $149-$289	XP: $10	F7
	12/16-1/31	1P: $99-$240	2P: $99-$240	XP: $10	F7
♦♦♦♦ ♦♦♦♦	12/1-12/15 & 5/1-11/30	1P: $89-$225	2P: $89-$225	XP: $10	F7

Motel **Location:** On SR 789, 0.5 mi n of jct SR 684. 1603 Gulf Dr N 34217. Fax: 941/778-6114. **Facility:** Designated smoking area. 34 units. 33 one-bedroom standard units with kitchens. 1 two-bedroom suite with kitchen. 1-2 stories, exterior corridors. *Bath:* combo or shower only. **Parking:** on-site. **Terms:** cancellation fee imposed, pets ($25 extra charge, in designated units). **Amenities:** video library, irons, hair dryers. **Pool(s):** small heated outdoor. **Leisure Activities:** fishing dock, rod and reels, picnic tables, barbecue area with grills. **Guest Services:** coin laundry. **Business Services:** fax. **Cards:** AX, DS, MC, VI.

BRANDON —*See Tampa Bay p. 896.*

BROOKSVILLE pop. 7,264

------ WHERE TO STAY ------

BEST WESTERN BROOKSVILLE I-75   Phone: 352/796-9481
AAA [SAVE]   1/1-4/15   1P: $75-$89   2P: $79-$99
              12/1-12/31 & 4/16-11/30   1P: $59-$79   2P: $64-$89
Motel   **Location:** I-75, exit 301, just w on SR 50/US 98. 30307 Cortez Blvd 34602. **Fax:** 352/799-7595. **Facility:** 121 one-bedroom standard units. 2 stories, exterior corridors. *Bath:* combo or shower only. **Parking:** on-site. **Terms:** [AP] meal plan available, pets ($20 extra charge). **Amenities:** irons, hair dryers. **Dining:** 6:30 am-10 & 6-9 pm, cocktails. **Pool(s):** outdoor, wading. **Leisure Activities:** playground, exercise room. **Guest Services:** valet and coin laundry. **Business Services:** meeting rooms, fax. **Cards:** AX, DC, DS, MC, VI. **Special Amenities:** free continental breakfast and free room upgrade (subject to availability with advanced reservations). *(See ad below)*

SOME UNITS
[symbols] / [symbols]

DAYS INN   Phone: (352)796-9486
[SAVE]   12/1-3/31   1P: $69   2P: $69   XP: $5   F17
              4/1-11/30   1P: $59   2P: $59   XP: $5   F17
Motel   **Location:** I-75, exit 301, just e on SR 50/US 98. 6320 Windmere Rd 34602. **Fax:** 352/754-8721. **Facility:** 118 units. 104 one-bedroom standard units. 14 one-bedroom suites ($89-$109). 2 stories, exterior corridors. *Bath:* combo or shower only. **Parking:** on-site. **Amenities:** *Some:* irons, hair dryers. **Pool(s):** outdoor. **Guest Services:** coin laundry. **Business Services:** meeting rooms, fax. **Cards:** AX, DC, MC, VI.

SOME UNITS
[symbols] / [symbols]

HAMPTON INN   Phone: 352/796-1000
[SAVE]   1/1-4/15 [ECP]   1P: $74-$84   2P: $79-$99
              12/1-12/31 & 4/16-11/30 [ECP] 1P: $66-$74   2P: $69-$79
Small-scale Hotel   **Location:** I-75, exit 301, just w on SR 50. 30301 Cortez Blvd 34602. **Fax:** 352/796-9170. **Facility:** 75 units. 72 one-bedroom standard units. 3 one-bedroom suites. 2 stories, interior/exterior corridors. *Bath:* combo or shower only. **Parking:** on-site. **Amenities:** voice mail, irons. *Some:* hair dryers. **Guest Services:** valet laundry. **Business Services:** meeting rooms, fax (fee). **Cards:** AX, DC, DS, MC, VI. *(See ad below)*

SOME UNITS
[symbols] / [symbols]

------ WHERE TO DINE ------

PAPA JOE'S ITALIAN RESTAURANT   **Lunch:** $5-$16   **Dinner:** $6-$16   Phone: 352/799-3904
Italian   **Location:** I-75, exit 301, 4 mi w on US 98/SR 50, just s. 6244 Spring Lake Hwy 34601. **Hours:** 11 am-9 pm, Fri & Sat-10:30 pm, Sun noon-8 pm. Closed major holidays. **Features:** This well-established local favorite offers a wide variety of homemade items. Try the seafood pasta loaded with lobster, crab, shrimp, oysters and scallops in a creamy sauce. A deli, capricci and gift shop appeals to after-dinner browsers. Casual dress; cocktails. **Parking:** on-site. **Cards:** AX, DS, MC, VI.
[symbol]

YE OLDE FIRESIDE INN   **Lunch:** $6-$9   **Dinner:** $12-$23   Phone: 352/796-0293
American   **Location:** Just ne of jct SR 50 truck route, on US 41. 1175 S Broad St 34601. **Hours:** 11:30 am-9 pm, Fri & Sat-10 pm, Sun-8 pm. Closed: Mon. **Reservations:** suggested. **Features:** A rustic feel, characterized by three fireplaces and old photographs, is the trademark of this 1908 home. Settle into the relaxed atmosphere to peruse the predominant beef and seafood selections, such as Iowa prime rib, the centerpiece of the menu. Casual dress; cocktails. **Parking:** on-site. **Cards:** AX, MC, VI.
[symbols]

BUSHNELL pop. 2,050

------ WHERE TO STAY ------

CYPRESS HOUSE BED & BREAKFAST
♦♦♦♦
Bed & Breakfast
12/1-4/30 & 11/1-11/30 [BP]   2P: $80-$95
5/1-10/31 [BP]   2P: $70-$85
Phone: 352/568-0909
XP: $10   F16
XP: $10   F16
Location: I-75, exit 309, 2 mi n on CR 476B, just e on 90th Blvd (dirt and gravel road). Located in a rural area. CR 631C 33513. **Facility:** Set on 10 acres, this log home built of cypress features rustic, country decor with modern amenities. Smoke free premises. 5 units. 3 one-bedroom standard units. 1 one- and 1 two-bedroom suites ($75-$95). 2 stories, interior/exterior corridors. *Bath:* shower only. **Parking:** on-site. **Terms:** 7 day cancellation notice, weekly rates available. **Amenities:** video library, irons. *Some:* hair dryers. **Pool(s):** outdoor. **Leisure Activities:** hiking trails, horseshoes. *Fee:* horseback riding. **Business Services:** meeting rooms, fax. **Cards:** AX, DS, MC, VI.

SOME UNITS
🛥 ⊠ ⊠ 📺 ☎ / 📶 VCR 🔌 📠 /

CAPE CANAVERAL pop. 8,829

------ WHERE TO STAY ------

CAPE WINDS RESORT
AAA SAVE
♦♦♦♦
Motel
12/1-4/30 [ECP]   1P: $150-$175   2P: $150-$175
5/1-11/30 [ECP]   1P: $130-$160   2P: $130-$160
Phone: (321)783-6226
Location: Jct SR 520, 1.8 mi n on SR A1A, 0.3 mi e via Taylor Ave. 7400 Ridgewood Ave 32920. Fax: 321/799-2676. **Facility:** 67 units. 33 one- and 34 two-bedroom suites with kitchens. 5 stories, exterior corridors. **Parking:** on-site. **Terms:** 30 day cancellation notice-fee imposed, weekly rates available. **Amenities:** voice mail, irons, hair dryers. **Pool(s):** heated outdoor. **Leisure Activities:** sauna, whirlpool, boogie boards, 2 lighted tennis courts, basketball. **Guest Services:** coin laundry. **Business Services:** fax (fee). **Cards:** AX, DC, DS, JC, MC, VI. **Special Amenities:** free continental breakfast.

🅂🄳 🛥 ⊠ VCR 🄳🄰🅃🄰🄿🄾🅁🅃 🔌 📠 💻

RADISSON RESORT AT THE PORT
AAA SAVE
♦♦♦♦
Small-scale Hotel
2/1-4/27   1P: $149-$169   2P: $149-$169
12/1-1/31   1P: $139-$159   2P: $139-$159
4/28-11/30   1P: $139-$149   2P: $139-$149
Phone: (321)784-0000
XP: $10   F
XP: $10   F
XP: $10   F
Location: SR A1A. 8701 Astronaut Blvd 32920. Fax: 321/784-3737. **Facility:** 284 units. 212 one-bedroom standard units. 72 one-bedroom suites ($159-$179) with whirlpools. 2-3 stories, interior/exterior corridors. *Bath:* combo or shower only. **Amenities:** voice mail, irons, hair dryers. *Some:* dual phone lines, safes. **Dining:** 6:30 am-2 & 5:30-10:30 pm, cocktails. **Pool(s):** heated outdoor, wading. **Leisure Activities:** whirlpool, lighted tennis court, exercise room. **Guest Services:** gift shop, valet and coin laundry, area transportation-cruise ships & beach, car rentals. **Business Services:** conference facilities, business center. **Cards:** AX, CB, DC, DS, JC, MC, VI. *(See color ad p 274)*

SOME UNITS
🅂🄳 🍽 🍸 ♿ ▶ 🛥 ⊠ 📺 🄳🄰🅃🄰🄿🄾🅁🅃 💻 / ⊠ 🔌 📠 /

ROYAL MANSION RESORT
AAA SAVE
♦♦♦♦
Condominium
All Year Wkly   1P: $735-$1785   2P: $735-$1785
Phone: (321)784-8484
Location: Jct SR 520, 2.8 mi n on SR A1A, then 1 mi e via Central Blvd. 8600 Ridgewood Ave 32920. Fax: 321/799-2907. **Facility:** 107 units. 71 one- and 36 two-bedroom suites with kitchens, some with whirlpools. 3 stories (no elevator), exterior corridors. **Parking:** on-site. **Terms:** 7 day cancellation notice-fee imposed. **Amenities:** voice mail, safes (fee), irons, hair dryers. **Pool(s):** heated outdoor. **Leisure Activities:** whirlpool. **Guest Services:** valet and coin laundry. **Business Services:** fax (fee). **Cards:** AX, DS, MC, VI. *(See color ad p 274)*

SOME UNITS
🅂🄳 ♿ 🛥 📺 🔌 📠 💻 / VCR 🄳🄰🅃🄰🄿🄾🅁🅃 /

CAPE CORAL pop. 102,286

——— WHERE TO STAY ———

ART'S MALAGA RESORT
Phone: (239)542-3464

Motel — ◆ (Diamond)

12/15-4/15	1P: $75-$85	2P: $85-$95	XP: $10	F10
12/1-12/14 & 8/1-11/30	1P: $65-$70	2P: $70-$75	XP: $10	F10
4/16-7/31	1P: $50-$55	2P: $60-$65	XP: $10	F10

Location: I-75, exit 136, just e of Del Prado Blvd. 1721 SE 46th Ln 33904. Fax: 239/592-5294. **Facility:** 23 units. 21 one- and 2 two-bedroom standard units. 2 stories, exterior corridors. **Parking:** on-site. **Terms:** 7 day cancellation notice, weekly rates available. **Amenities:** *Some:* irons, hair dryers. **Pool(s):** outdoor. **Leisure Activities:** boat dock, shuffleboard. **Guest Services:** coin laundry. **Cards:** AX, CB, DC, DS, JC, MC, VI.

SOME UNITS

(ASK) (S/D) (✈) (🍴) (⊃) (🖥) (☎) (🔲) (🔳) (🔳) / (⊠) /

CASA LOMA MOTEL
Phone: 239/549-6000

Motel — (AAA) (SAVE) ◆◆

2/1-3/31	1P: $75-$85	2P: $75-$85	XP: $5
12/1-1/31 & 4/1-4/30	1P: $65-$70	2P: $65-$70	XP: $5
5/1-11/30	1P: $50-$55	2P: $50-$55	XP: $5

Location: 1.5 mi n of jct Cape Coral Pkwy. 3608 Del Prado Blvd 33904. Fax: 239/549-4877. **Facility:** 49 units. 48 one-bedroom standard units with kitchens. 1 one-bedroom suite ($80-$130) with kitchen. 2 stories, interior/exterior corridors. *Bath:* combo or shower only. **Parking:** on-site. **Terms:** 7 day cancellation notice, weekly rates available. **Amenities:** *Some:* irons, hair dryers. **Pool(s):** heated outdoor. **Leisure Activities:** boat dock, fishing, sun deck. **Guest Services:** coin laundry. **Business Services:** fax (fee). **Cards:** AX, DS, MC, VI. **Special Amenities:** early check-in/late check-out. *(See color ad below)*

SOME UNITS

(🍴) (📶) (⊃) (⊠) (🔲) / (⊠) (🔳) /

QUALITY INN-NAUTILUS
Phone: (239)542-2121

Small-scale Hotel — (AAA) (SAVE) ◆◆◆

1/15-4/15	1P: $85-$105	2P: $95-$115	XP: $10	F18
12/1-1/14	1P: $70-$90	2P: $75-$95	XP: $10	F18
4/16-11/30	1P: $55-$75	2P: $60-$85	XP: $10	F18

Location: Jct Del Prado Blvd. 1538 Cape Coral Pkwy 33904. Fax: 239/542-6319. **Facility:** 142 one-bedroom standard units. 5 stories, interior corridors. **Terms:** check-in 4 pm, pets ($8 extra charge, on 1st floor). **Amenities:** voice mail, irons, hair dryers. **Pool(s):** heated outdoor. **Leisure Activities:** exercise room, shuffleboard. **Guest Services:** valet and coin laundry. **Business Services:** meeting rooms, fax (fee). **Cards:** AX, CB, DC, DS, JC, MC, VI. **Special Amenities:** free local telephone calls and free newspaper.

SOME UNITS

(S/D) (🐾) (🍴) (Y) (🎧) (⊃) (DATA PORT) (🔳) / (⊠) (🔲) /
FEE

RAINBOW MOTEL RESORT
Phone: 239/542-0061

Motel — (AAA) (SAVE) ◆

1/21-3/31		2P: $89-$95	XP: $5	D12
12/1-1/20		2P: $69-$75	XP: $5	D12
4/1-11/30		2P: $49-$55	XP: $5	D12

Location: 1.2 mi n of jct Cape Coral Pkwy. 3817 Del Prado Blvd 33904. Fax: 239/542-3678. **Facility:** 15 one-bedroom suites with kitchens. 2 stories, exterior corridors. **Parking:** on-site. **Terms:** 7 day cancellation notice-fee imposed. **Amenities:** *Some:* irons, hair dryers. **Pool(s):** heated outdoor. **Leisure Activities:** boat dock, fishing, boat slips, sunset cruises, fishing excursions, gas grills, tiki huts. **Guest Services:** coin laundry. **Cards:** AX, DS, MC, VI.

SOME UNITS

(S/D) (🍴) (⊃) (⊠) (🔲) (🔳) / (⊠) /

——— WHERE TO DINE ———

ARIANI ITALIAN STEAKHOUSE
Dinner: $15-$25
Phone: 239/772-8000

Northern Italian — ◆◆◆

Location: I-75, exit 143, just e of Del Prado Blvd; in Del Prado Mall. 1529 SE 15th Terr 33990. **Hours:** 5 pm-10 pm. Closed: Sun. **Reservations:** suggested. **Features:** Specializing in northern Italian cuisine, the restaurant has a casually elegant dining room attended by thoughtful, well-attired servers. Many fresh pasta dishes are available, as are grilled and roasted meats and fresh seafood. Among favorite choices are lambuco, veal scallopini, salmon, tuna, pork medallions Florentine and chicken breast prepared in varied ways: alla Riveria, marsala mushroom, pizzaiola, Milanese or alla parmigiana. Casual dress; cocktails. **Parking:** on-site. **Cards:** AX, DC, MC, VI.

(Y) (⊠)

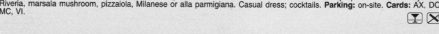

BRIGANDS STEAK & SEAFOOD GRILL   **Lunch:** $5-$9   **Dinner:** $13-$24   **Phone:** 239/540-4665

Location: In Cay West Pavilion. 1708 Cape Coral Pkwy W 33914. **Hours:** 11 am-10:30 pm, Sun from 4 pm.
Closed major holidays. **Features:** This clean dining room with a nautical decor is tucked away in a small
Steak & Seafood   shopping mall. The menu features grilled, fried, broiled or blackened seafood, and other specialties like
prime rib and chicken. Love spicy food? Try the Jamaican jerk chicken. Casual dress; cocktails. **Parking:**
on-site. **Cards:** AX, MC, VI.

IGUANA MIA   **Lunch:** $6-$10   **Dinner:** $6-$15   **Phone:** 239/945-7755
Location: Cape Coral Pkwy, just e of jct SE 10th Pl (Leonard St). 1027 E Cape Coral Pkwy 33904. **Hours:** 11
am-10 pm, Fri & Sat-midnight. Closed: 11/27, 12/25. **Features:** Hop into this lively, yet simple, cantina,
Mexican   where you'll find a good variety of standard favorites such as sour cream chicken, fajitas and beef burritos
with black beans. Frozen margaritas and fried ice cream cool the jalapeno-heated palate. Casual dress;
cocktails. **Parking:** on-site. **Cards:** AX, DS, MC, VI.

CAPE HAZE

——— WHERE TO STAY ———

COLONY DON PEDRO   **Phone:** 941/697-2192
12/15-4/30 Wkly   2P: $1075-$1815
12/1-12/14 & 5/1-11/30 Wkly   2P: $890-$1775
Condominium   **Location:** On Don Pedro Island, access by car ferry from Island Transit Ferry terminal, just w of CR 775. Located in a
remote area. 40 S Gulf Blvd 34224 (7025 Placida Rd, ENGLEWOOD). Fax: 941/697-8441. **Facility:** 30 units. 1 one-
and 29 two-bedroom standard units, some with efficiencies. 2 stories, exterior corridors. **Parking:** on-site. **Terms:** 2 night
minimum stay, 90 day cancellation notice, 60 day 5/2-12/2-fee imposed, daily & monthly rates available. **Amenities:** irons. *Some:*
CD players. **Pool(s):** 2 heated outdoor. **Leisure Activities:** boat dock, fishing, 2 lighted tennis courts. *Fee:* bicycles. **Guest Services:** complimentary laundry. **Cards:** DS, MC, VI.

SOME UNITS

PALM ISLAND RESORT   **Phone:** (941)697-4800
12/19-4/20 Wkly   1P: $850-$2360   2P: $1530-$3090   XP: $25   F6
4/21-11/30 Wkly   1P: $850-$1570   2P: $1400-$2100   XP: $20   F6
12/1-12/18 Wkly   1P: $800-$1500   2P: $1330-$2030   XP: $20   F6
Resort   **Location:** Jct CR 771/775/776, 5 mi s to Panama Blvd, just w to Ferry Landing (Gulf Blvd), 1.1 mi w. 7092 Placida Rd
Condominium   33946. Fax: 941/697-0696. **Facility:** The resort's spacious, one- to three-bedroom condominium villas on
Palm Island can be reached by car ferry from 7 am to 10 pm. 130 one-bedroom standard units. 2-3 stories.
Parking: on-site. **Terms:** 2-3 night minimum stay - in season, 21 day cancellation notice, daily rates available, package plans - seasonal. **Amenities:** irons, hair dryers. **Dining:** noon-9 pm, Fri-9:30 pm, Sat & Sun 7:30 am-10 pm,
cocktails. **Pool(s):** 5 heated outdoor. **Leisure Activities:** whirlpools, rental boats, rental paddleboats, fishing, 11 tennis courts,
recreation programs, playground, exercise room. *Fee:* canoes, sailboats, marina, snorkeling, charter fishing, golf carts, tennis instruction, tennis pro shop, bicycles. **Guest Services:** gift shop, complimentary laundry. **Cards:** AX, DS, MC, VI.
Special Amenities: free local telephone calls. *(See color ad below)*

SOME UNITS
FEE

——— WHERE TO DINE ———

JAM'S OF CAPE HAZE   **Lunch:** $6-$22   **Dinner:** $6-$22   **Phone:** 941/697-2080
Location: 0.6 mi n on CR 775; in Cape Haze Plaza. 8501 Placida Rd 33946. **Hours:** 11:30 am-10 pm. Closed:
1/1, 12/25. **Reservations:** accepted. **Features:** The restaurant offers a good selection of Italian and
Italian   American dishes, as well as sandwiches and pizza. Casual dress; cocktails. **Parking:** on-site. **Cards:** AX,
DC, MC, VI.

CAPTIVA pop. 379

------ WHERE TO STAY ------

SOUTH SEAS RESORT & YACHT HARBOR
Phone: (239)472-5111

	2/7-4/26	1P: $370-$1800	2P: $370-$1800	XP: $20	F16
	12/1-2/6	1P: $350-$1400	2P: $350-$1400	XP: $20	F16
	4/27-5/26	1P: $290-$1300	2P: $290-$1300	XP: $20	F16
	5/27-11/30	1P: $240-$1200	2P: $240-$1200	XP: $20	F16

Resort
Large-scale Hotel
Location: At north tip of Captiva Island. 5400 South Seas Plantation Rd 33924 (PO Box 194). Fax: 239/481-4947. **Facility:** On a secluded site adjoining the gulf and bay, this extensive property offers a variety of room types. 562 units. 263 one-bedroom standard units. 299 one-bedroom suites with kitchens. 1-3 stories, exterior corridors. **Parking:** on-site. **Terms:** check-in 4 pm, 14 day cancellation notice-fee imposed, $8 service charge. **Amenities:** voice mail, safes, irons. *Some:* hair dryers. **Dining:** 7 restaurants, 7:30 am-midnight; 18% service charge, cocktails, nightclub, entertainment. **Pool(s):** 18 heated outdoor. **Leisure Activities:** saunas, whirlpools, rental boats, fishing, recreation programs, aerobic & aqua exercise instruction, salon, playground. *Fee:* canoes, sailboats, marina, charter fishing, aqua bikes, fishing guides, parasailing, sailing & instruction, shelling charters, sightseeing cruises, waverunners, golf-9 holes, 18 tennis courts (5 lighted), bicycles, massage, game room. **Guest Services:** gift shop, valet and coin laundry, area transportation-within resort. **Business Services:** meeting rooms, business center. **Cards:** AX, CB, DC, DS, MC, VI. **Special Amenities:** free newspaper. *(See color ad below)*

SOME UNITS

------ WHERE TO DINE ------

THE BUBBLE ROOM
Lunch: $7-$14   **Dinner:** $14-$27   **Phone:** 239/472-5558

American
Location: Jct Andy Rosse Ln. 15001 Captiva Rd 33924. **Hours:** 11:30 am-2:30 & 5-10 pm. Closed: 12/25. **Features:** The decor is a whimsical mix of Christmas, nostalgia, '30s and '40s memorabilia and Hollywood. Friendly servers efficiently manage their tables. The menu features steak, fresh fish and thick cut prime rib. Portions are generous and the desserts are not to be ignored. Casual dress; cocktails. **Parking:** on-site.
Cards: AX, DC, DS, MC, VI.

CHADWICK'S RESTAURANT
Dinner: $19-$25   **Phone:** 239/472-7575

Seafood
Location: 15.8 mi nw of Sanibel Cswy at north tip of Captiva Island; at entrance to South Seas Resort & Yacht Harbor. Captiva Dr 33924. **Hours:** 5:30 pm-9:30 pm, Sun 9 am-2 pm. **Reservations:** suggested; 2/1-4/30. **Features:** Located at the entrance to the South Seas Resort, it features an extensive themed dinner buffet and a lovely brunch on Sundays. A limited standard menu is also available. Please note the 18% service charge added to each bill. Casual dress; cocktails; entertainment. **Parking:** on-site. **Cards:** AX, CB, DC, DS, MC, VI.

——— *The following restaurant has not been evaluated by AAA* ———
but is listed for your information only.

THE GREEN FLASH BAYSIDE BAR & GRILL   Phone: 239/472-3337
[fyi]   Not evaluated. **Location:** Jct Murmond Ln. 15183 Captiva Dr 33924. **Features:** Located in a lush tropical
setting; you'll find a casual retreat in this dining restaurant with a menu that offers many different dishes
from seafood to chicken.

CARRABELLE pop. 1,303

——— **WHERE TO STAY** ———

THE MOORINGS AT CARRABELLE   Phone: 850/697-2800
▼▼▼   2/1-7/31   1P: $75-$90   2P: $75-$90   XP: $10   F12
12/1-1/31 & 8/1-11/30   1P: $55-$75   2P: $55-$75   XP: $10   F12
Small-scale Hotel **Location:** US 98, just e of bridge. 1000 US 98 32322 (PO Box M). **Fax:** 850/697-3950. **Facility:** 22 units. 21 one-
and 1 two-bedroom standard units. 2 stories, exterior corridors. **Parking:** on-site. **Terms:** weekly rates available, pets ($50 deposit, $10 extra charge). **Pool(s):** outdoor. **Leisure Activities:** marina, fishing. **Fee:** charter fishing. **Guest
Services:** coin laundry. **Business Services:** meeting rooms, fax (fee). **Cards:** AX, DC, DS, MC, VI.

SOME UNITS

(A$K) (S🛏) (🛏) (📡↦) (🏊) (🚫) (📽) (📁) (🖥) (💻) / (VCR) /

CASSELBERRY —See Orlando p. 674.

CEDAR KEY pop. 790

——— **WHERE TO STAY** ———

DOCKSIDE MOTEL   Phone: 352/543-5432
(AAA) (SAVE)   All Year   1P: $55-$77   2P: $55-$77   XP: $7   F12
▼▼▼   **Location:** SR 24, just w on Front St to Dock St, then just w. Located adjacent to public marina & fishing pier. 491 Dock
St 32625 (PO Box 55). **Facility:** 10 one-bedroom standard units. 2 stories, interior corridors. **Parking:** street.
Motel   **Terms:** 3 day cancellation notice. **Business Services:** fax. **Cards:** DS, MC, VI. **Special Amenities:** free
local telephone calls.

(📡↦) (📽) (📁) (💻)

ISLAND PLACE OF CEDAR KEY   Phone: (352)543-5307
▼▼▼   2/1-7/31   1P: $90-$155   2P: $90-$155   XP: $5
12/1-1/31 & 8/1-11/30   1P: $85-$145   2P: $85-$145   XP: $5
Condominium **Location:** On SR 24. 550 First St 32625 (PO Box 687). **Fax:** 352/543-9141. **Facility:** 30 units. 27 one- and 3 two-
bedroom standard units with kitchens. 3 stories (no elevator), exterior corridors. **Parking:** on-site. **Terms:** 2-3
night minimum stay - weekends in season, 3 day cancellation notice-fee imposed. **Amenities:** voice mail. **Pool(s):** outdoor.
Leisure Activities: whirlpool. **Guest Services:** complimentary laundry. **Business Services:** business center. **Cards:** AX, DC,
MC, VI.

SOME UNITS

(📡↦) (🏊) (VCR) (📽) (💻) / (🚫) /

PARK PLACE MOTEL & CONDOMINIUMS   Phone: 352/543-5737
(AAA) (SAVE)   2/1-5/31   1P: $70-$90   2P: $70-$90   XP: $5   F13
▼▼   12/1-1/31 & 6/1-11/30   1P: $65-$80   2P: $65-$80   XP: $5   F13
Location: At A St. 211 2nd St 32625 (PO Box 613). **Fax:** 352/543-8011. **Facility:** 30 units. 22 one-bedroom stan-
Motel   dard units with efficiencies. 8 one-bedroom suites with efficiencies. 3 stories (no elevator), exterior corridors.
Parking: on-site. **Terms:** 2-6 night minimum stay - weekends, small pets only ($7 extra charge).
Amenities: voice mail. **Leisure Activities:** gazebo with grill. **Business Services:** fax. **Cards:** AX, DS,
MC, VI.

SOME UNITS

(🐾) (📡↦) (📁) (🖥) (💻) / (🚫) (VCR) /
FEE

SEAHORSE LANDING   Phone: 352/543-6801
▼▼▼   All Year   1P: $125-$150   2P: $125-$150
Location: Just w on 6th St. 4050 G St 32625. **Fax:** 352/543-6119. **Facility:** 13 two-bedroom standard units with
Condominium kitchens. 2 stories, exterior corridors. **Parking:** on-site. **Terms:** check-in 4 pm, 2-3 night minimum stay -
weekends, 3 day cancellation notice, weekly rates available. **Amenities:** irons. **Pool(s):** outdoor. **Leisure
Activities:** whirlpool, boat dock, fishing. **Guest Services:** complimentary laundry. **Business Services:** meeting rooms, fax.
Cards: AX, MC, VI.

(🏊) (🚫) (🚫) (VCR) (📽) (📁) (🖥) (💻)

——— **WHERE TO DINE** ———

ISLAND HOTEL & RESTAURANT   **Lunch:** $7-$12   **Dinner:** $18-$26   Phone: 352/543-5111
(AAA)   **Location:** Center. 373 2nd St 32625. **Hours:** 6 pm-9 pm; also Sat & Sun 11:30 am-2 pm. Closed: Tues.
▼▼   **Features:** On the National Register of Historic Places, the hotel features a quaint, full-service lounge with
beers from around the world and a "special occasion" dining room. Fresh seafood, including seasonal
American   Florida rock lobster, Cedar Key oysters and stone crab. Shrimp and grouper are specialties. Lamb, pork,
chicken, Angus beef and a few vegetarian dishes round out the menu. Smoke free premises. Casual
dress; cocktails. **Parking:** on-site. **Cards:** DS, MC, VI.

(🍸) (🍴) (🚫)

THE ISLAND ROOM AT CEDAR COVE   **Lunch:** $8-$9   **Dinner:** $11-$28   Phone: 352/543-6520
(AAA)   **Location:** At the Cedar Cove Beach and Yacht Club. 192 2nd St 32625. **Hours:** 5 pm-10 pm, also Fri-Sun 11:30
▼▼   am-2:30 pm. **Reservations:** suggested. **Features:** Adjacent to the public beach and overlooking the bay to
the south, the dining room is on the ground floor of Cedar Cove condominiums. The menu leans toward
Seafood   fish, but preparations are multiregional. Pasta can be ordered Alfredo, primavera, or marinara, and grouper
is particularly good cooked Cajun-style. Crab cakes, oysters, shrimp, lamb, chicken, Angus beef and surf
'n' turf are all featured. Desserts include a Key lime tart, New Orleans bread pudding and creme brulee.
Casual dress; cocktails. **Parking:** on-site. **Cards:** AX, DS, MC, VI.

(🍸) (🚫)

CELEBRATION —See Orlando p. 675.

CHARLOTTE HARBOR pop. 3,647

——— WHERE TO STAY ———

BANANA BAY WATERFRONT MOTEL   **Phone:** (941)743-4441

	1/16-4/15	1P: $54-$64	2P: $54-$92	XP: $6	F12
◆	12/1-1/15	1P: $46-$59	2P: $46-$72	XP: $6	F12
Motel	4/16-11/30	1P: $46-$56	2P: $46-$66	XP: $6	F12

Location: Jct US 41. 23285 Bayshore Rd 33980. Fax: 941/743-4172. **Facility:** 13 one-bedroom standard units, some with efficiencies. 1 story, exterior corridors. *Bath:* shower only. **Parking:** on-site. **Terms:** age restrictions may apply, 3 day cancellation notice-fee imposed, weekly rates available, small pets only. **Amenities:** high-speed Internet. *Some:* irons, hair dryers. **Leisure Activities:** fishing, shuffleboard. **Guest Services:** coin laundry. **Business Services:** fax. **Cards:** AX, DS, MC, VI.

SOME UNITS
(A$K) 🛏 🍴 DATA PORT / ✕ VCR 🛗 📠 /
FEE

CHIEFLAND pop. 1,993

——— WHERE TO STAY ———

BEST WESTERN SUWANNEE VALLEY INN   **Phone:** 352/493-0663

AAA SAVE · All Year [ECP] · 1P: $60-$75 · 2P: $70-$85 · F
◆◆◆

Location: On US 19/98, just n of jct US 129. 1125 N Young Blvd 32626. Fax: 352/493-0663. **Facility:** 60 one-bedroom standard units. 2 stories, exterior corridors. **Parking:** on-site. **Terms:** cancellation fee imposed, small pets only ($10 extra charge). **Amenities:** irons, hair dryers. **Pool(s):** outdoor. **Guest Services:** coin laundry. **Business Services:** meeting rooms, fax (fee). **Cards:** AX, DC, DS, MC, VI. **Special Amenities:** early check-in/late check-out and free continental breakfast.

Small-scale Hotel

SOME UNITS
(S/D) 🛏 🍴 🏊 🎥 DATA PORT 📺 / ✕ 🛗 📠 /

HOLIDAY INN EXPRESS   **Phone:** (352)493-9400

◆◆◆ · All Year · 1P: $65-$99 · 2P: $65-$99

Location: US 19/98, 1.5 mi n of jct US 129. 809 NW 21st Ave 32626. Fax: 352/493-4050. **Facility:** 66 one-bedroom standard units. 2 stories, exterior corridors. *Bath:* combo or shower only. **Parking:** on-site. **Terms:** [ECP] meal plan available. **Amenities:** irons, hair dryers. **Pool(s):** outdoor. **Leisure Activities:** whirlpool. **Guest Services:** coin laundry. **Business Services:** meeting rooms, fax (fee). **Cards:** AX.

Small-scale Hotel

SOME UNITS
(A$K) (S/D) 🍴 ⚙ ❤ 🍳 🏊 🎥 DATA PORT / ✕ 🛗 📠 /

——— WHERE TO DINE ———

BAR-B-Q BILL'S · Lunch: $5-$10 · Dinner: $5-$10 · **Phone:** 352/493-4444

◆ · **Location:** On US 19 at jct NW 19th Ave. 1901 N Young Blvd 32626. **Hours:** 7 am-9 pm, Wed from 11 am, Fri & Sat-10 pm. **Closed:** 11/27, 12/25; also 12/24 for dinner. **Features:** Under live oak trees in the middle of a commercial area, the eatery serves succulent barbecue beef, chicken, pork and turkey. A salad bar with several hot items is also an option. Barbecue meats can be ordered by the pound or as a sandwich or plate. Also on the menu are fried fish, fried or grilled chicken, soup, chili and even hot dogs and knockwurst. Service is casual and folksy, and it seems everybody knows everybody. Casual dress; beer only. **Parking:** on-site. **Cards:** DS, MC, VI.

American

✕

CHIPLEY pop. 3,592

——— WHERE TO STAY ———

SUPER 8 MOTEL   **Phone:** (850)638-8530

◆◆ · All Year [CP] · 1P: $40-$75 · 2P: $45-$75 · XP: $5 · F12

Location: I-10, exit 120, just n. 1700 Main St 32428. Fax: 850/638-9895. **Facility:** 40 one-bedroom standard units. 1 story, exterior corridors. **Parking:** on-site. **Terms:** small pets only ($5 extra charge). **Business Services:** fax (fee). **Cards:** AX, DC, DS, MC, VI.

Motel

SOME UNITS
(A$K) (S/D) 🛏 🎥 / ✕ 🛗 📠 /

CLEARWATER —See Tampa Bay p. 899.

CLEARWATER BEACH —See Tampa Bay p. 906.

CLERMONT —See Orlando p. 675.

CLEWISTON pop. 6,460

——— WHERE TO STAY ———

BEST WESTERN OF CLEWISTON   **Phone:** 863/983-3400

AAA SAVE	1/1-3/31 [CP]	1P: $109-$129	2P: $119-$139	XP: $10	F12
	12/1-12/31 [CP]	1P: $79-$80	2P: $89-$99	XP: $10	F12
◆◆◆	4/1-11/30 [CP]	1P: $69-$79	2P: $79-$89	XP: $10	F12

Location: On US 27/SR 80. Located in a quiet area. 1020 W Sugarland Hwy 33440. Fax: 863/983-3441. **Facility:** 51 units. 50 one-bedroom standard units. 1 one-bedroom suite. 2 stories (no elevator), exterior corridors. *Bath:* combo or shower only. **Parking:** on-site. **Terms:** cancellation fee imposed. **Amenities:** voice mail, irons, hair dryers. **Pool(s):** small heated outdoor. **Guest Services:** coin laundry. **Business Services:** meeting rooms, fax (fee). **Special Amenities:** free continental breakfast and free newspaper.

Motel

SOME UNITS
(S/D) 🍴 🏊 🎥 DATA PORT 🛗 📠 📺 / ✕ /

COCOA pop. 16,412

—— WHERE TO STAY ——

BEST WESTERN

Phone: (321)632-1065

AAA SAVE
$\blacktriangledown\blacktriangledown\blacktriangledown$ $\blacktriangledown\blacktriangledown\blacktriangledown$

2/13-4/30 [ECP]	1P: $89	2P: $89
5/1-9/7 [ECP]	1P: $59-$79	2P: $59-$79
12/1-2/12 [ECP]	1P: $59-$69	2P: $59
9/8-11/30	1P: $59	2P: $59

Small-scale Hotel Location: I-95, exit 201 (SR 520), 0.3 mi e. 4225 W King St 32926. Fax: 321/631-3302. **Facility:** 120 one-bedroom standard units. 2 stories, exterior corridors. *Bath:* combo or shower only. **Parking:** on-site. **Terms:** 7 day cancellation notice, weekly rates available, pets ($6 extra charge). **Amenities:** voice mail. **Pool(s):** heated outdoor. **Leisure Activities:** barbecue grills, covered wood deck, picnic tables, darts, pool table, large screen TV. *Fee:* game room. **Guest Services:** coin laundry. **Business Services:** meeting rooms. **Cards:** AX, DC, DS, MC, VI. **Special Amenities: free continental breakfast and preferred room (subject to availability with advanced reservations).**

SOME UNITS
$\boxed{\text{S}/\text{D}}$ 🐾 🛗 👔 ♿ 🖉 🛥 🎥 / ⊠ 🔲VCR 🔌 🖥 /
FEE

CAMPBELL MOTEL

Phone: 321/636-6111
XP: $5   **F12**

AAA SAVE
$\blacktriangledown$
Motel

All Year   1P: $45-$55   2P: $55-$65
Location: 1.5 mi s of jct SR 528. 1084 N Cocoa Blvd 32922. Fax: 321/636-6111. **Facility:** 18 one-bedroom standard units. 1 story, exterior corridors. *Bath:* combo or shower only. **Parking:** on-site. **Terms:** 7 day cancellation notice. **Cards:** DS, MC, VI. **Special Amenities: early check-in/late check-out and free local telephone calls.**

SOME UNITS
$\boxed{\text{S}/\text{D}}$ 🖉 / ⊠ 🔌 /

ECONO LODGE-SPACE CENTER

Phone: (321)632-4561
XP: $5   **F17**

AAA SAVE
$\blacktriangledown\blacktriangledown\blacktriangledown$ $\blacktriangledown\blacktriangledown\blacktriangledown$

All Year   1P: $49-$150   2P: $50-$150
Location: US 1, just n of jct SR 528. 3220 N Cocoa Blvd 32926. Fax: 321/631-3756. **Facility:** Designated smoking area. 144 one-bedroom standard units. 3 stories, exterior corridors. **Parking:** on-site. **Terms:** [MAP] meal plan available, small pets only ($10 fee). **Dining:** 6:30 am-11:30 & 5-9:30 pm, Fri & Sat-10 pm, cocktails. **Small-scale Hotel Pool(s):** outdoor. **Leisure Activities:** shuffleboard. **Guest Services:** coin laundry. **Business Services:** meeting rooms, fax (fee). **Cards:** AX, CB, DC, DS, JC, MC, VI.

SOME UNITS
$\boxed{\text{S}/\text{D}}$ 🐾 🍽 👔 🖉 🛥 🎥 / ⊠ 🔌 🔌 🖥 🖥 🖥 /
FEE FEE

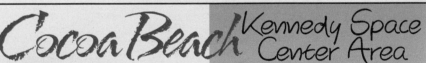

RAMADA INN COCOA BEACH AREA/KSC
AAA (SAVE)

2/10-4/26 [ECP]	1P: $69-$99	2P: $69-$99	XP: $10	F18
12/1-2/9 & 4/27-11/30 [ECP]	1P: $59-$89	2P: $59-$89	XP: $10	F18

Small-scale Hotel

Location: I-95, exit 202 (SR 524), just w. 900 Friday Rd 32926. Fax: 321/636-8661. **Facility:** 99 one-bedroom standard units. 2 stories, exterior corridors. **Parking:** on-site. **Terms:** small pets only ($25 deposit). **Amenities:** voice mail, safes (fee), hair dryers. **Dining:** 7 am-10 pm, cocktails. **Pool(s):** heated outdoor. **Leisure Activities:** boat dock, fishing, jogging, shuffleboard. **Guest Services:** coin laundry. **Business Services:** meeting rooms, fax (fee). **Cards:** AX, CB, DC, DS, JC, MC, VI. **Special Amenities:** early check-in/late check-out and free room upgrade (subject to availability with advanced reservations). *(See color ad p 267)*

Phone: (321)631-1210

SOME UNITS

SUPER 8 MOTEL COCOA BEACH AREA/KSC
AAA (SAVE)

2/10-4/26	1P: $59-$89	2P: $59-$89	XP: $5	F18
12/1-2/9 & 4/27-11/30	1P: $49-$79	2P: $49-$79	XP: $5	F18

Motel

Location: I-95, exit 202, 0.5 mi sw. 900A Friday Rd 32926. Fax: 321/636-8661. **Facility:** 53 one-bedroom standard units. 2 stories, exterior corridors. **Parking:** on-site. **Terms:** small pets only ($25 deposit). **Amenities:** voice mail, safes (fee). **Pool(s):** heated outdoor. **Leisure Activities:** fishing, jogging, shuffleboard. **Guest Services:** coin laundry. **Business Services:** fax (fee). **Cards:** AX, CB, DC, DS, JC, MC, VI. **Special Amenities:** early check-in/late check-out and free room upgrade (subject to availability with advanced reservations). *(See color ad p 267)*

Phone: (321)631-1212

SOME UNITS

——— **WHERE TO DINE** ———

BLACK TULIP

Continental

Lunch: $4-$9   **Dinner:** $14-$20   Phone: 321/631-1133

Location: On SR 520, just e of jct US 1. 207 Brevard Ave 32922. **Hours:** 11:30 am-2 & 5:30-10 pm. Closed: 12/25. **Reservations:** suggested. **Features:** In historic Cocoa Village, this charming and comfortable cafe features classic dishes with innovative touches. For a flavorful lunch, try the traditional chunky gazpacho with the quiche of the day, and finish with the delicious flan from a Brazilian recipe. At night, subdued lighting sets a romantic mood. Daylight is prime time to enjoy dining on the outdoor patio. Smoke free premises. Casual dress; cocktails; entertainment. **Parking:** on-site. **Cards:** AX, DC, DS, MC, VI.

CAFE MARGAUX

French

Lunch: $5-$11   **Dinner:** $16-$26   Phone: 321/639-8343

Location: In Historic Cocoa Village off SR 520, just e of US 1. 220 Brevard Ave 32922. **Hours:** 11 am-3 & 5-9:30 pm. Closed: 12/25; also Tues, Sun & 7/1-7/14. **Reservations:** suggested. **Features:** Bright during the day and romantic at night, the cozy dining areas and outside courtyard terrace are reminiscent of New Orleans. An extensive wine list includes selections to complement a nice variety of seafood, lamb, beef, pasta and mixed grill dishes. Smoke free premises. Casual dress; cocktails. **Parking:** on-site. **Cards:** AX, DC, DS, MC, VI.

COCOA BEACH pop. 12,842

——— **WHERE TO STAY** ———

BEST WESTERN OCEANFRONT RESORT
AAA (SAVE)

4/27-8/14	1P: $79-$209	2P: $89-$219	XP: $10	F18
8/15-11/30	1P: $69-$209	2P: $69-$219	XP: $10	F18
2/7-4/26	1P: $109-$199	2P: $119-$209	XP: $10	F18
12/1-2/6	1P: $69-$169	2P: $69-$179	XP: $10	F18

Small-scale Hotel

Location: SR A1A, 0.8 mi n of jct SR 520. 5600 N Atlantic Ave 32931. Fax: 321/799-4576. **Facility:** 180 one-bedroom standard units, some with efficiencies or kitchens. 2-7 stories, interior/exterior corridors. *Bath:* combo or shower only. **Parking:** on-site. **Terms:** small pets only (in designated units). **Amenities:** video games (fee), voice mail, irons, hair dryers. **Pool(s):** heated outdoor. **Leisure Activities:** sun deck, barbecue grills, playground, exercise room, shuffleboard. **Guest Services:** gift shop, complimentary evening beverages: Tues, coin laundry. **Business Services:** meeting rooms, fax (fee). **Cards:** AX, CB, DC, DS, JC, MC, VI. **Special Amenities:** free newspaper and preferred room (subject to availability with advanced reservations). *(See color ad below)*

Phone: (321)783-7621

SOME UNITS

COCOA BEACH OCEANSIDE INN
AAA SAVE
Small-scale Hotel

All Year [ECP]   1P: $69-$179   2P: $69-$179   XP: $10   F

Phone: (321)784-3126

Location: Just e of SR A1A; 0.8 mi n of jct SR 520. 1 Hendry Ave 32931. **Fax:** 321/799-0883. **Facility:** Designated smoking area. 76 units. 74 one-bedroom standard units. 2 one-bedroom suites ($200-$350), some with whirlpools. 5-6 stories, exterior corridors. **Parking:** on-site. **Amenities:** safes, hair dryers. **Dining:** 2 restaurants, 7 am-11 & 3-11 pm, cocktails. **Pool(s):** heated outdoor. **Leisure Activities:** rooftop observation deck for shuttle launches. **Guest Services:** valet laundry. **Business Services:** fax (fee). **Cards:** AX, DC, DS, MC, VI.
Special Amenities: free continental breakfast and preferred room (subject to availability with advanced reservations).
(See color ad below)

SOME UNITS

COMFORT INN & SUITE RESORT

Phone: (321)783-2221

(AAA) (SAVE)	2/7-4/26	1P: $89-$229	2P: $89-$229	XP: $10	F12
	4/27-8/31	1P: $79-$229	2P: $79-$229	XP: $10	F12
▽▽▽▽▽	12/1-2/6 & 9/1-11/30	1P: $69-$199	2P: $69-$199	XP: $10	F12

Location: SR A1A, 0.3 mi s of jct SR 520. 3901 N Atlantic Ave 32931. Fax: 321/783-0461. **Facility:** 170 units. 80 **Small-scale Hotel** one-bedroom standard units, some with efficiencies. 90 one-bedroom suites, some with whirlpools. 1-6 stories, exterior corridors. *Bath:* combo or shower only. **Parking:** on-site. **Terms:** 14 day cancellation notice-fee imposed. **Amenities:** safes (fee), hair dryers. *Some:* dual phone lines, irons. **Pool(s):** heated outdoor. **Leisure Activities:** whirlpool, poolside grills, pool tables, table tennis, playground, exercise room, shuffleboard, volleyball. *Fee:* game room. **Guest Services:** valet and coin laundry. **Business Services:** meeting rooms, fax. **Cards:** AX, CB, DC, DS, JC, MC, VI. **Special Amenities:** free newspaper. *(See color ad p 269)*

SOME UNITS

COURTYARD BY MARRIOTT COCOA BEACH

Phone: 321/784-4800

(AAA) (SAVE) All Year   1P: $99-$149   2P: $99-$149

▽▽▽▽▽ **Location:** 0.5 mi s jct SR 520. 3435 N Atlantic Ave 32931. Fax: 321/784-4812. **Facility:** 131 units. 119 one-bedroom standard units, some with whirlpools. 12 one-bedroom suites ($139-$179). 7 stories, interior corridors. *Bath:* combo or shower only. **Parking:** on-site. **Terms:** 7 day cancellation notice. **Amenities:** dual **Small-scale Hotel** phone lines, voice mail, irons, hair dryers. **Dining:** 6:30-10:30 am, Sat & Sun-11 am. **Pool(s):** heated outdoor. **Leisure Activities:** whirlpool, exercise room. *Fee:* beach equipment. **Guest Services:** gift shop, valet and coin laundry. **Business Services:** meeting rooms, business center. **Cards:** AX, DC, DS, MC, VI. **Special Amenities:** early check-in/late check-out and free newspaper. *(See color ad p 272)*

SOME UNITS

DAYS INN COCOA BEACH

Phone: (321)784-2550

(AAA) (SAVE)	4/27-8/14	1P: $79-$169	2P: $89-$179	XP: $10	F18
	2/7-4/26 & 8/15-11/30	1P: $79-$159	2P: $89-$169	XP: $10	F18
▽▽▽▽▽	12/1-2/6	1P: $69-$139	2P: $69-$149	XP: $10	F18

Location: SR A1A, 0.8 mi n of jct SR 520. 5500 N Atlantic Ave 32931. Fax: 321/868-7124. **Facility:** 103 one-bedroom standard units, some with efficiencies. 2 stories, exterior corridors. **Parking:** on-site. **Terms:** small **Small-scale Hotel** pets only. **Amenities:** video games (fee), voice mail, irons, hair dryers. *Some:* safes. **Pool(s):** heated outdoor. **Leisure Activities:** barbecue grills, picnic area, sun deck, exercise room. **Guest Services:** coin laundry. **Business Services:** fax (fee). **Cards:** AX, CB, DC, DS, JC, MC, VI. **Special Amenities:** free local telephone calls and free newspaper. *(See color ad below)*

SOME UNITS

DISCOVERY BEACH RESORT & TENNIS CLUB Phone: (321)868-7777

12/16-1/5	2P: $180-$250
2/16-11/30	2P: $110-$250
1/6-2/15	2P: $135-$190
12/1-12/15	2P: $110-$145

Condominium **Location:** Just e of SR A1A, 0.8 mi n of jct SR 520. 300 Barlow Ave 32931. **Fax:** 321/868-0086. **Facility:** 66 units. 6 one-, 56 two- and 4 three-bedroom suites with kitchens. 8 stories, exterior corridors. *Bath:* combo or shower only. **Parking:** on-site. **Terms:** check-in 4 pm, 3 day cancellation notice, weekly rates available. **Amenities:** video library, voice mail, irons. **Dining:** 11 am-midnight; closed Mon, cocktails. **Pool(s):** heated outdoor. **Leisure Activities:** sauna, whirlpool, 2 lighted tennis courts, exercise room, basketball. *Fee:* game room. **Guest Services:** complimentary laundry. **Business Services:** fax (fee). **Cards:** MC, VI.

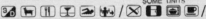

DOUBLETREE HOTEL COCOA BEACH OCEANFRONT Phone: (321)783-9222

All Year	1P: $75-$169	2P: $90-$184	XP: $15 F18

Location: SR A1A, 1 mi s of jct SR 520. 2080 N Atlantic Ave 32931. **Fax:** 321/799-3234. **Facility:** 148 units. 136 one-bedroom standard units. 12 one-bedroom suites. 6 stories, interior corridors. **Parking:** on-site. **Small-scale Hotel** **Terms:** check-in 4 pm, 2-4 night minimum stay. **Amenities:** video games (fee), dual phone lines, voice mail, irons, hair dryers. **Pool(s):** heated outdoor, wading. **Leisure Activities:** exercise room. *Fee:* game room. **Guest Services:** gift shop, valet and coin laundry. **Business Services:** conference facilities, fax (fee). **Cards:** AX, DC, DS, MC, VI.

SOME UNITS

ECONO LODGE RESORT OF COCOA BEACH Phone: (321)783-2252

All Year	1P: $69-$149

Location: 1.7 mi s of SR 520 on A1A. 1275 N Atlantic Ave 32931. **Fax:** 321/783-4485. **Facility:** 128 one-bedroom standard units, some with kitchens. 2 stories, exterior corridors. *Bath:* combo or shower only. **Parking:** on-site. **Terms:** pets (in designated rooms). **Amenities:** safes (fee). **Dining:** 11 am-2 am, cocktails. **Pool(s): Small-scale Hotel** heated outdoor. **Leisure Activities:** barbecue grills, picnic tables, pool tables, shuffleboard. **Guest Services:** valet and coin laundry. **Business Services:** meeting rooms, fax (fee). **Cards:** AX, CB, DC, DS, MC, VI. **Special Amenities:** early check-in/late check-out and preferred room (subject to availability with advanced reservations).

SOME UNITS

HAMPTON INN COCOA BEACH

Phone: (321)799-4099

AAA SAVE ▼▼◆▼▼

All Year [ECP] 1P: $99-$149 2P: $99-$149

Small-scale Hotel

Location: 0.5 mi s jct SR 520. 3425 N Atlantic Ave 32931. Fax: 321/799-4991. **Facility:** 150 one-bedroom standard units. 8 stories, interior/exterior corridors. *Bath:* combo or shower only. **Parking:** on-site. **Terms:** 7 day cancellation notice. **Amenities:** dual phone lines, voice mail, irons, hair dryers. **Pool(s):** heated outdoor. **Leisure Activities:** walkway to beach, exercise room. **Guest Services:** gift shop, valet and coin laundry. **Business Services:** meeting rooms, PC, fax. **Cards:** AX, DC, DS, MC, VI. **Special Amenities: free continental breakfast and free local telephone calls.** *(See color ad p 271)*

SOME UNITS

(S/D) (🛗) (✦M) ⬤ ⬤ ⬤ ⬤ DATA PORT ⬤ ⬤ ⬤ / ⬤

HILTON COCOA BEACH OCEANFRONT

Phone: (321)799-0003

AAA SAVE ▼▼◆▼▼

2/7-4/26	1P: $119-$169	2P: $119-$169	XP: $15	F18
12/1-2/6 & 4/27-11/30	1P: $99-$139	2P: $99-$139	XP: $15	F18

Small-scale Hotel

Location: SR A1A, 1.5 mi s of jct SR 520. 1550 N Atlantic Ave 32931. Fax: 321/799-0344. **Facility:** 296 units. 291 one-bedroom standard units. 5 one-bedroom suites ($129-$600). 7 stories, interior corridors. *Bath:* combo or shower only. **Parking:** on-site. **Terms:** check-in 4 pm, cancellation fee imposed. **Amenities:** voice mail, irons, hair dryers. **Dining:** 2 restaurants, 6:30 am-10 pm, cocktails. **Pool(s):** heated outdoor. **Leisure Activities:** beach set-up, exercise room, volleyball. *Fee:* boogie boards, surfboards, massage, game room. **Guest Services:** gift shop, valet and coin laundry. **Business Services:** conference facilities, fax (fee). **Cards:** AX, CB, DC, DS, JC, MC, VI. **Special Amenities: free newspaper.** *(See color ad below)*

SOME UNITS

(S/D) (🛗) (Y) (✦M) ⬤ ⬤ ⬤ ⬤ DATA PORT ⬤ / ⬤ ⬤ ⬤ /

FEE

HOLIDAY INN COCOA BEACH OCEANFRONT RESORT

Phone: (321)783-2271

AAA SAVE

Small-scale Hotel

All Year   1P: $120-$199   2P: $120-$199
Location: SR A1A, 1.8 mi s of jct SR 520. 1300 N Atlantic Ave 32931. Fax: 321/799-8569. **Facility:** 500 units. 458 one-bedroom standard units. 42 one-bedroom suites ($185-$300), some with kitchens. 2-3 stories, exterior corridors. *Bath:* combo or shower only. **Parking:** on-site. **Terms:** check-in 4 pm, cancellation fee imposed, small pets only ($25 deposit, $10 extra charge). **Amenities:** video games (fee), voice mail, irons, hair dryers. *Some:* CD players. **Dining:** 2 restaurants, 6:30 am-10 pm, cocktails. **Pool(s):** heated outdoor, wading. **Leisure Activities:** whirlpool, boogie/surfboards, cabanas, umbrellas, beach chairs, beach volleyball, 2 lighted tennis courts, recreation programs, playground, exercise room, shuffleboard. *Fee:* game room. **Guest Services:** gift shop, valet and coin laundry. **Business Services:** conference facilities, fax (fee). **Cards:** AX, CB, DC, DS, JC, MC, VI. **Special Amenities:** early check-in/late check-out and free newspaper. *(See color ad opposite inside back cover & below)*   SOME UNITS

HOLIDAY INN EXPRESS HOTEL & SUITES

Phone: (321)868-2525

AAA SAVE

Small-scale Hotel

2/1-4/30   1P: $109   2P: $109   XP: $10   F14
12/1-1/31 & 5/1-11/30   1P: $89   2P: $89   XP: $10   F14
Location: SR A1A, 0.7 mi n of jct SR 620. 5575 N Atlantic Ave 32931. Fax: 321/868-6302. **Facility:** 60 units. 47 one-bedroom standard units, some with whirlpools. 11 one- and 2 two-bedroom suites ($119-$129). 4 stories, interior corridors. *Bath:* combo or shower only. **Parking:** on-site. **Terms:** [ECP] meal plan available. **Amenities:** dual phone lines, voice mail, irons, hair dryers. **Pool(s):** heated outdoor. **Leisure Activities:** whirlpool, limited exercise equipment. **Guest Services:** valet and coin laundry. **Business Services:** meeting rooms, business center. **Cards:** AX, CB, DC, DS, JC, MC, VI. **Special Amenities:** early check-in/late check-out and free continental breakfast. *(See color ad opposite inside back cover)*   SOME UNITS

THE INN AT COCOA BEACH-BED & BREAKFAST

Phone: (321)799-3460

Small-scale Hotel

All Year [ECP]   1P: $135-$250   2P: $135-$250   XP: $10
Location: Just n of SR 520 (Extension); just e of SR A1A. 4300 Ocean Beach Blvd 32931. Fax: 321/784-8632. **Facility:** Designated smoking area. 50 one-bedroom standard units, some with whirlpools. 2-4 stories, interior/exterior corridors. **Parking:** on-site. **Terms:** age restrictions may apply, 7 day cancellation notice. **Amenities:** video library. *Some:* safes, hair dryers. **Pool(s):** outdoor. **Leisure Activities:** steamroom, bicycles, shuffleboard. *Fee:* massage. **Guest Services:** gift shop, complimentary evening beverages, valet laundry. **Business Services:** meeting rooms. *Fee:* administrative services, fax. **Cards:** AX, DS, MC, VI.   SOME UNITS

LUNA SEA BED & BREAKFAST

Phone: (321)783-0500

🔲 SAVE

All Year   1P: $69-$95   2P: $69-$95   XP: $6   F12

▼▼▼ **Location:** 0.7 mi s of SR 520 on SR A1A. 3185 N Atlantic Ave 32931. Fax: 321/784-6515. **Facility:** 44 units. 42 one-bedroom standard units, some with efficiencies. 2 one-bedroom suites. 2 stories, exterior corridors.

Motel   **Parking:** on-site. **Terms:** 7 day cancellation notice-fee imposed. **Amenities:** hair dryers. **Pool(s):** heated outdoor. **Leisure Activities:** picnic area. **Guest Services:** coin laundry. **Cards:** AX, CB, DC, DS, MC, VI. **Special Amenities: free continental breakfast.** *(See color ad p 273)*

SOME UNITS

OCEAN SUITE HOTEL

Phone: (321)784-4343

🔲 SAVE

All Year   1P: $89-$159   2P: $89-$159   XP: $10   F12

▼▼▼ **Location:** Just n of SR 520; just e of SR A1A. 5500 Ocean Beach Blvd 32931. Fax: 321/783-6514. **Facility:** 50 one-bedroom suites. 5 stories, interior corridors. *Bath:* meal

Motel   plan available. **Amenities:** voice mail. **Pool(s):** heated outdoor. **Guest Services:** valet and coin laundry. **Business Services:** meeting rooms, fax (fee). **Cards:** AX, DC, DS, MC, VI. **Special Amenities: free newspaper and free room upgrade (subject to availability with advanced reservations).**

SOME UNITS

QUALITY SUITES COCOA BEACH

Phone: (321)783-6868

SAVE

All Year [BP]   1P: $69-$109   2P: $69-$109

▼▼▼ **Location:** SR A1A, 0.3 mi s of jct SR 520. 120 Flagler Ln 32931. Fax: 321/783-6784. **Facility:** 48 one-bedroom suites. 5 stories, exterior corridors. *Bath:* combo or shower only. **Parking:** on-site. **Terms:** cancellation fee imposed. **Amenities:** voice mail, irons, hair dryers. **Leisure Activities:** whirlpool. **Guest Services:** valet

Small-scale Hotel   laundry. **Business Services:** meeting rooms, fax (fee). **Cards:** AX, CB, DC, DS, JC, MC, VI.

SOME UNITS

THE RESORT ON COCOA BEACH

Phone: (321)783-4000

[AAA] [SAVE]
▼▼▼

Condominium

	1P: $210-$310
2/12-9/5	
12/1-2/11	1P: $165-$235
9/6-11/30	1P: $130-$220

Location: SR A1A, 2 mi s of jct SR 520. 1600 N Atlantic Ave 32931. **Fax:** 321/799-0272. **Facility:** 124 two-bedroom suites with kitchens. 8 stories, exterior corridors. **Parking:** on-site. **Terms:** check-in 4 pm. **Amenities:** video library (fee), voice mail, irons, hair dryers. **Dining:** 11 am-9:30 pm. **Pool(s):** heated outdoor. **Leisure Activities:** sauna, whirlpool, water sprite for kids, 2 lighted tennis courts, recreation programs, exercise room, basketball. **Fee:** beach furniture, large kids area, movie theater, sand volleyball, game room. **Guest Services:** gift shop, complimentary laundry. **Cards:** AX, DC, DS, MC, VI.

SOUTH BEACH INN

Phone: 321/784-3333

▼▼▼ ▼▼▼
Motel

	1P: $80-$150	2P: $80-$150	XP: $15	F13
1/16-4/30				
5/1-9/10	1P: $70-$140	2P: $70-$140	XP: $15	F13
9/11-11/30	1P: $70-$130	2P: $70-$130	XP: $15	F13
12/1-1/15	1P: $60-$130	2P: $60-$130	XP: $15	F13

Location: SR A1A northbound, 5 mi s of jct SR 520 at Indian Village Tr, 1.5 mi n of Patrick AFB. 1701 S Atlantic Ave 32931. **Fax:** 321/784-9486. **Facility:** 16 units. 14 one-bedroom standard units with kitchens. 2 two-bedroom suites with kitchens. 2 stories, exterior corridors. **Parking:** on-site. **Terms:** 2-4 night minimum stay - seasonal, 10 day cancellation notice, small pets only ($50 deposit, $15 extra charge). **Guest Services:** coin laundry. **Business Services:** fax (fee). **Cards:** AX, DC, DS, MC, VI.

SURF STUDIO BEACH RESORT

Phone: 321/783-7100

▼▼▼ ▼▼
Motel

	1P: $90-$160	2P: $90-$160	XP: $15	F10
1/16-9/30				
12/1-1/15 & 10/1-11/30	1P: $70-$110	2P: $70-$110	XP: $15	F10

Location: SR A1A northbound, 5 mi s of jct SR 520 at Francis St, 1.3 mi n of Partrick AFB. 1801 S Atlantic Ave 32931. **Fax:** 321/783-2695. **Facility:** 11 units. 4 one-bedroom standard units, some with efficiencies. 7 one-bedroom suites with kitchens. 1 story, exterior corridors. **Bath:** combo or shower only. **Parking:** on-site. **Terms:** 7 day cancellation notice-fee imposed, pets ($20 extra charge). **Amenities:** voice mail. **Pool(s):** heated outdoor. **Leisure Activities:** bicycles. **Guest Services:** coin laundry. **Cards:** AX, DC, DS, MC, VI.

WAKULLA SUITES

Phone: (321)783-2230

[AAA] [SAVE]
▼▼▼ ▼▼
Motel

	1P: $145-$170	2P: $145-$170	XP: $10	F18
2/1-5/1				
12/1-1/31 & 5/2-11/30	1P: $99-$135	2P: $99-$135	XP: $10	F18

Location: SR A1A, 0.5 mi s of jct SR 520. 3550 N Atlantic Ave 32931. **Fax:** 321/783-0980. **Facility:** 116 two-bedroom suites with kitchens. 2 stories, exterior corridors. **Parking:** on-site. **Terms:** check-in 4 pm, 7 day cancellation notice, weekly rates available. **Amenities:** voice mail. *Some:* irons. **Pool(s):** heated outdoor, wading. **Leisure Activities:** barbecue grills, oceanside deck, shuffleboard. **Guest Services:** valet and coin laundry. **Business Services:** fax (fee). **Cards:** AX, CB, DC, DS, MC, VI.

――――――― *The following lodging was either not evaluated or did not* ―――――――
meet AAA rating requirements but is listed for your information only.

HOLIDAY INN EXPRESS

Phone: 321/868-2525

[fyi]
Motel

| All Year | 1P: $69-$129 | 2P: $69-$129 | XP: $5 | F18 |

Too new to rate, opening scheduled for December 2002. **Location:** I-95, exit 201 (SR 520). 301 Tucker Ln 32926. **Fax:** 321/868-6302. **Amenities:** coffeemakers, microwaves, refrigerators, pool. **Cards:** AX, CB, DC, DS, JC, MC, VI.

――――――― **WHERE TO DINE** ―――――――

ALMA'S SEAFOOD & ITALIAN RESTAURANT

Dinner: $7-$19   **Phone:** 321/783-1981

[AAA]
▼▼ ▼▼
Italian

Location: On SR A1A southbound; 2.5 mi s of jct SR 520. 306 N Orlando Ave 32931. **Hours:** 5 pm-10 pm. Closed major holidays; also Super Bowl Sun. **Reservations:** suggested. **Features:** Family-owned since 1963, the bistro emphasizes seafood and Italian cuisine. An ample selection of appetizers and salads provide a good start to any meal. The wine list offers international selections. There is live entertainment on Friday and Saturday. Casual dress; cocktails. **Parking:** on-site. **Cards:** AX, CB, DC, DS, MC, VI.

BERNARD'S SURF

Dinner: $17-$30   **Phone:** 321/783-2401

▼▼ ▼▼
Steak & Seafood

Location: SR A1A northbound, 2.3 mi s of jct SR 520 at Minutemen Cswy. 2 S Atlantic Ave 32931. **Hours:** 4 pm-11 pm. Closed: 12/25. **Reservations:** suggested. **Features:** This family-owned restaurant has been a Cocoa Beach favorite since 1948. Excellent steak and market-fresh seafood is served in a relaxed, fine-dining atmosphere. A lengthy wine list and a very nice variety of appetizers make happy hour a celebration. Casual dress; cocktails. **Parking:** on-site. **Cards:** AX, CB, DC, DS, MC, VI.

HEIDELBERG RESTAURANT

Lunch: $6-$11   **Dinner:** $16-$21   **Phone:** 321/783-6806

▼▼ ▼▼
German

Location: SR A1A, 3 mi s of jct SR 520. 7 N Orlando Ave 32931. **Hours:** 10 am-10 pm, Sun from 5 pm. Closed: 7/4, 11/27, 12/25; also Mon. **Reservations:** suggested; weekends. **Features:** Such specialties as goulash, stroganoff and luscious Viennese pastries make up the decidedly German and Austrian menu in the romantic restaurant. European decor enhances the cozy, classical feel. A pianist performs on Friday and Saturday evenings. Casual dress; cocktails; entertainment. **Parking:** street. **Cards:** AX, MC, VI.

THE MANGO TREE RESTAURANT

Dinner: $13-$39   **Phone:** 321/799-0513

▼▼▼ ▼▼
Continental

Location: SR A1A northbound, 2.5 mi s of jct SR 520. 118 N Atlantic Ave 32931. **Hours:** 6 pm-10 pm. Closed: 1/1, 12/25; also Mon. **Reservations:** suggested. **Features:** Several cozy areas—from an elegantly formal dining room to the tropically decorated garden terrace, complete with graceful swans all lend to the intimate plantation-home ambience of the restaurant. Attractive presentation is a trademark of every dish. Semi-formal attire; cocktails; entertainment. **Parking:** on-site. **Cards:** AX, MC, VI.

PUNJAB INDIAN CUISINE   Lunch: $5-$14   Dinner: $8-$14   Phone: 321/799-4696
◆◆◆◆   **Location:** Just e of SR 520 and A1A; in White Rose Shopping Center. 285 W Cocoa Beach Cswy 32931.
                      Hours: 11:30 am-2 & 5-10 pm, Sun from 5 pm. Closed major holidays. **Reservations:** accepted.
Indian   **Features:** A Northern influence is evident in the excellent menu variety, which includes breads, lassi and
                      kulfi. Favorites include shrimp curry and tandoori chicken and lamb as well as seafood and vegetarian
dishes. Textured walls and subdued lighting set the mood. Casual dress; beer & wine only. **Parking:** on-site. **Cards:** AX, DS,
MC, VI.
⊠

ROBERTO'S LITTLE HAVANA RESTAURANT   Lunch: $7-$11   Dinner: $7-$11   Phone: 321/784-1868
◆◆◆◆   **Location:** SR A1A southbound, 2.7 mi s of jct SR 520. 26 N Orlando Ave 33931. **Hours:** 6 am-3 & 5-9 pm, Fri &
                      Sat-10 pm. Closed: Mon nights & 2 weeks in July. **Reservations:** accepted. **Features:** The unpretentious
Cuban   downtown eatery serves up a delicious variety of Cuban dishes, such as yucca, plantain, French-bread
                      Cuban sandwiches and beans with rice, as well as beef, chicken and pork entrees. Locals often drop by
for breakfast. Casual dress; beer & wine only. **Parking:** on-site. **Cards:** AX, DS, MC, VI.
⊠

YEN YEN CHINESE RESTAURANT   Lunch: $5-$9   Dinner: $8-$16   Phone: 321/783-9512
🔺🔺🔺   **Location:** On SR A1A. 2 N Atlantic Ave 32931. **Hours:** 11:30 am-10 pm, Fri-11 pm, Sat noon-11 pm, Sun
                      noon-10 pm. Closed: one week in summer (call ahead 7/5-7/31). **Reservations:** suggested.
◆◆◆◆   **Features:** Delicate sauces and exotic seasonings flavor such entrees as Shelly's chicken and the
                      signature snow white prawn. Comfortable and quiet, the atmosphere borrows from the discrete cultures of
Chinese   Europe and Asia to create a distinct and elegant feel. Casual dress; cocktails. **Parking:** on-site.
                      Cards: AX, DC, MC, VI.
🍸 ⊠

COCONUT GROVE —*See Miami-Miami Beach p. 544.*

CONCH KEY —*See The Florida Keys p. 320.*

CORAL GABLES —*See Miami-Miami Beach p. 546.*

CORAL SPRINGS —*See Fort Lauderdale p. 389.*

CORTEZ pop. 4,491

——— WHERE TO STAY ———

——— *The following lodging was either not evaluated or did not* ———
meet AAA rating requirements but is listed for your information only.

CHARLIE'S COTTAGES   Phone: 941/794-5980
[fyi]   Not evaluated. **Location:** Just s of jct SR 684 (Cortez Rd), enter via 125th St W. 4512 124th St Ct W 34215 (PO Box
                671). Facilities, services, and decor characterize a basic property.

CRESCENT BEACH pop. 985

——— WHERE TO STAY ———

BEACHER'S LODGE   Phone: (904)471-8849
🔺🔺 [SAVE]   2/2-9/2   1P: $99-$189   2P: $99-$189
                12/1-2/1 & 9/3-11/30   1P: $79-$139   2P: $79-$139
◆◆ ◆◆   **Location:** Just s of jct SR 206. 6970 A1A South 32080. Fax: 904/471-3002. **Facility:** 90 one-bedroom standard
                units. 4 stories, exterior corridors. **Parking:** on-site. **Terms:** weekly rates available, small pets only ($15 fee,
Small-scale Hotel in designated units). **Amenities:** voice mail. *Some:* irons, hair dryers. **Pool(s):** heated outdoor. **Guest Serv-**
                ices: coin laundry. **Business Services:** meeting rooms, fax. **Cards:** AX, DS, MC, VI. **Special Amenities:**
free local telephone calls.
                                                                                   SOME UNITS
                                        🆂 🐾 ⊪ ⊵ DATA⁄PORT 🔋 🖥 💻 / ⊠ VCR

CRESCENT CITY pop. 1,776

——— WHERE TO STAY ———

LAKE VIEW MOTEL   Phone: 386/698-1090
◆◆ ◆◆   All Year   1P: $48-$75   2P: $55-$80   XP: $5   F8
                Location: 1 mi n on US 17. 1004 N Summit St 32112. Fax: 386/698-4616. **Facility:** 19 one-bedroom standard
Motel   units, some with efficiencies (no utensils). 1 story, exterior corridors. *Bath:* combo or shower only. **Parking:**
                on-site. **Terms:** cancellation fee imposed, weekly rates available, small pets only ($25 deposit). **Pool(s):** out-
door. **Business Services:** fax (fee). **Cards:** AX, DC, DS, MC, VI.
                                                                                   SOME UNITS
                                        🐾 ⊪ ⊵ / ⊠ 🔋 🖥 💻 /

CRESTVIEW pop. 14,766

——— WHERE TO STAY ———

COMFORT INN   Phone: (850)423-1200
[SAVE]   3/1-8/31 [ECP]   1P: $70-$80   2P: $70-$80   XP: $8
                9/1-11/30 [ECP]   1P: $65-$70   2P: $65-$75   XP: $8
◆◆◆◆   12/1-2/28 [ECP]   1P: $65-$70   2P: $65-$70   XP: $8
                Location: I-10, exit 56, just s. 4040 S Ferdon Blvd 32536. Fax: 850/423-1210. **Facility:** 50 one-bedroom standard
Small-scale Hotel units, some with whirlpools. 2 stories, exterior corridors. **Parking:** on-site. **Terms:** package plans.
                Amenities: *Some:* irons, hair dryers. **Pool(s):** outdoor. **Business Services:** fax (fee). **Cards:** AX, CB, DC,
DS, JC, MC, VI.
                                                                                   SOME UNITS
                                        🆂 ⊪ ⊵ 🎥 DATA⁄PORT / ⊠ 🔋 🖥 💻 /

ECONO LODGE

SAVE

Motel

All Year   1P: $42-$50   2P: $46-$60
Phone: (850)682-6255   XP: $6   F12
Location: I-10, exit 56, 0.3 mi n. 3101 S Ferdon Blvd 32536 (PO Box 1466). Fax: 850/682-7500. **Facility:** 84 one-bedroom standard units. 2 stories, exterior corridors. **Parking:** on-site. **Business Services:** fax (fee). **Cards:** AX, CB, DS, MC, VI.

SOME UNITS

HAMPTON INN

SAVE

Small-scale Hotel

All Year [ECP]   1P: $60-$70
Phone: (850)689-2378
Location: I-10, exit 56. 3709 S Ferdon Blvd 32536. Fax: 850/689-4465. **Facility:** 70 one-bedroom standard units. 3 stories, exterior corridors. *Bath:* combo or shower only. **Parking:** on-site. **Amenities:** voice mail, irons, hair dryers. **Pool(s):** outdoor. **Leisure Activities:** whirlpool. **Guest Services:** coin laundry. **Business Services:** meeting rooms, fax. **Cards:** AX, DC, DS, MC, VI.

SOME UNITS

HOLIDAY INN

Small-scale Hotel

All Year   1P: $56-$75
Phone: (850)682-6111   XP: $5   F17
Location: I-10, exit 56, 0.5 mi s. 4050 S Ferdon Blvd 32536 (PO Box 1358). Fax: 850/689-1189. **Facility:** 119 one-bedroom standard units. 2 stories, exterior corridors. *Bath:* combo or shower only. **Parking:** on-site. **Terms:** [ECP] meal plan available, small pets only ($25 fee). **Amenities:** voice mail, irons, hair dryers. **Pool(s):** outdoor. **Leisure Activities:** exercise room. **Guest Services:** valet and coin laundry. **Business Services:** meeting rooms, fax (fee). **Cards:** AX, CB, DC, DS, JC, MC, VI. *(See color ad opposite inside back cover)*

SOME UNITS

FEE

JAMESON INN

Small-scale Hotel

All Year [ECP]   1P: $52-$67   2P: $55-$70
Phone: 850/683-1778   XP: $3   F17
Location: I-10, exit 56, just s. 151 Cracker Barrel Dr 32536. Fax: 850/683-1779. **Facility:** 55 units. 53 one-bedroom standard units. 2 one-bedroom suites. 3 stories, interior corridors. *Bath:* combo or shower only. **Parking:** on-site. **Terms:** $3 service charge. **Amenities:** voice mail, irons. *Some:* hair dryers. **Pool(s):** outdoor. **Leisure Activities:** exercise room. **Guest Services:** valet laundry. **Business Services:** meeting rooms, fax. **Cards:** AX, CB, DC, DS, MC, VI.

SOME UNITS

FEE

Look for a SAVE Place to Stay!

SUPER 8 MOTEL
Phone: (850)682-9649

Motel

All Year   1P: $38-$58   2P: $43-$63
                                                XP: $5   F12
Location: I-10, exit 56, 0.3 mi s. 3925 S Ferdon Blvd 32539. Fax: 850/682-9649. **Facility:** 63 one-bedroom standard units. 2 stories, exterior corridors. **Parking:** on-site. **Terms:** weekly rates available, [CP] meal plan available, pets ($5 fee). **Amenities:** *Some:* hair dryers. **Business Services:** fax (fee). **Cards:** AX, DC, DS, MC, VI. **Special Amenities:** free continental breakfast and free local telephone calls.

SOME UNITS

CROSS CITY pop. 1,775

——— WHERE TO STAY ———

CARRIAGE INN
Phone: (352)498-0001

Motel

All Year   1P: $34-$40   2P: $39-$49   D12
Location: 0.5 mi s on US 19, 27A and 98. 280 E Main (US 19/98/27A) 32628 (PO Box 1360). Fax: 352/498-5054. **Facility:** 25 one-bedroom standard units. 2 stories, exterior corridors. **Parking:** on-site. **Terms:** pets ($4 extra charge). **Pool(s):** outdoor. **Guest Services:** airport transportation-Cross City Airport. **Business Services:** fax. **Cards:** AX, DC, DS, MC, VI. **Special Amenities:** free local telephone calls and preferred room (subject to availability with advanced reservations).

SOME UNITS

CRYSTAL RIVER pop. 3,485

——— WHERE TO STAY ———

BEST WESTERN CRYSTAL RIVER RESORT
Phone: (352)795-3171

11/14-11/30	1P: $89-$114	2P: $96-$121	XP: $5 F18
12/1-4/26	1P: $86-$111	2P: $91-$116	XP: $5 F18
4/27-11/13	1P: $74-$95	2P: $79-$100	XP: $5 F18

Resort
Small-scale Hotel

Location: On US 19/98, 0.8 mi n of jct SR 44. 614 NW Hwy 19 34428. Fax: 352/795-3179. **Facility:** 114 one-bedroom standard units. 2 stories, exterior corridors. *Bath:* combo or shower only. **Parking:** on-site. **Terms:** check-in 4 pm, weekly rates available, small pets only ($3 extra charge). **Amenities:** safes, irons, hair dryers. **Pool(s):** outdoor. **Leisure Activities:** whirlpool, rental boats, boat dock, fishing, dive shop. *Fee:* scuba diving, snorkeling, diving instruction. **Guest Services:** gift shop, coin laundry. **Business Services:** meeting rooms, fax (fee). **Cards:** AX, CB, DC, DS, MC, VI.

SOME UNITS

FEE

PLANTATION INN & GOLF RESORT
Phone: (352)795-4211

1/1-4/30	1P: $110-$165	2P: $110-$165	XP: $15 F16
10/1-11/30	1P: $109-$149	2P: $109-$149	XP: $15 F16
5/1-9/30	1P: $95-$145	2P: $95-$145	XP: $15 F16
12/1-12/31	1P: $99-$139	2P: $99-$139	XP: $15 F16

Resort
Small-scale Hotel

Location: On CR 44, 0.5 mi w of jct US 19/98. 9301 W Fort Island Tr 34429. Fax: 352/795-1156. **Facility:** On King's Bay. 144 units. 142 one-bedroom standard units. 2 one-bedroom suites. 2 stories, interior/exterior corridors. *Bath:* combo or shower only. **Parking:** on-site. **Amenities:** voice mail, irons, hair dryers. *Some:* video games (fee). **Dining:** 6-11 am, 11:30-2 & 5:30-10 pm, Sunday brunch, cocktails. **Pool(s):** heated outdoor. **Leisure Activities:** whirlpool, rental boats, rental canoes, marina, fishing, driving range, pro shop, croquet, horseshoes, shuffleboard, volleyball. *Fee:* scuba diving, snorkeling, pontoon, golf-27 holes, 2 lighted tennis courts, tennis instruction. **Guest Services:** valet and coin laundry. **Business Services:** conference facilities, fax (fee). **Cards:** AX, DC, DS, MC, VI.

SOME UNITS

FEE

——— WHERE TO DINE ———

CHARLIE'S FISH HOUSE
Lunch: $3-$15   **Dinner:** $3-$15   **Phone:** 352/795-2468

Seafood

Location: US 19, just n of jct SR 44. 224 US 19 NW 34228. **Hours:** 11 am-9 pm. Closed: 4/20, 11/27, 12/25; also 12/24 for dinner. **Features:** Japanese cuisine is prepared table-side by strikingly fast chefs with a flare for showmanship. A good place to meet new people. The hibachi tables have different parties seated together. Order the chicken, filet and shrimp combo for a spicy feast. Casual dress; beer & wine only. **Parking:** on-site. **Cards:** AX, DS, MC, VI.

CUDJOE KEY —See The Florida Keys p. 320.

CUTLER RIDGE —See Miami-Miami Beach p. 548.

DADE CITY —See Tampa Bay p. 915.

DANIA BEACH —See Fort Lauderdale p. 390.

DAVENPORT —See Orlando p. 676.

DAVIE —See Fort Lauderdale p. 391.

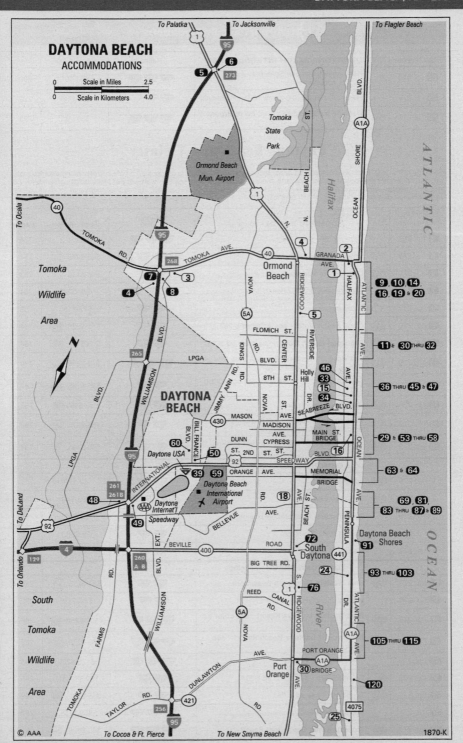

DAYTONA BEACH
ACCOMMODATIONS

✈ Airport Accommodations

Spotter/Map Page Number	OA	DAYTONA BEACH INTERNATIONAL	Diamond Rating	Rate Range High Season	Listing Page
59 / p. 279		Hampton Inn Daytona Speedway-Airport, 0.6 mi n of airport terminal	▽▽▽	$84-$94	290
39 / p. 279		Hilton Garden Inn, 0.6 mi nw of airport terminal	▽▽▽	$89-$139	290
50 / p. 279	AAA	Ramada Inn Speedway, 1 mi nw of airport terminal	▽▽▽	$89 SAVE	293

Daytona Beach and Vicinity

This index helps you "spot" where approved accommodations and restaurants are located on the corresponding detailed maps. Lodging rate ranges are for comparison only and show the property's high season; rates are per night, unless only weekly (W) rates are available. Restaurant rate range is for dinner, unless only lunch (L) is served. Turn to the listing page for more detailed rate information and consult display ads for special promotions.

Spotter/Map Page Number	OA	ORMOND BEACH - Lodgings	Diamond Rating	Rate Range High Season	Listing Page
4 / p. 279		Jameson Inn	▽▽▽	$52-$70	754
5 / p. 279	AAA	Days Inn Ormond Beach I-95	▽▽	$45-$240 SAVE	754
6 / p. 279	AAA	Comfort Inn Interstate	▽▽	$66-$186 SAVE	753
7 / p. 279		Hampton Inn Ormond Beach	▽▽▽	$79-$235	754
8 / p. 279		Sleep Inn	▽▽	$72-$186	755
9 / p. 279	AAA	Coral Beach Motel - see color ad p 287	▽▽	$55-$325 SAVE	754
10 / p. 279	AAA	Driftwood Beach Motel - see color ad p 287	▽▽	$45-$165 SAVE	754
11 / p. 279	AAA	The Cove On Ormond Beach A Club Navigo Resort - see color ad p 694	▽▽▽	$49-$299 SAVE	754
14 / p. 279	AAA	Comfort Inn On The Beach - see color ad p 288	▽▽	$85-$185 SAVE	753
16 / p. 279	AAA	Symphony Beach Club	▽▽	$59-$95 SAVE	755
19 / p. 279	AAA	Best Western Mainsail Inn and Suites - see color ad p 288	▽▽	$85-$275 SAVE	753
20 / p. 279	AAA	Econo Lodge on the Beach - see color ad p 288	▽▽	$70-$145 SAVE	754
		ORMOND BEACH - Restaurants			
1 / p. 279	AAA	Julian's	▽▽	$9-$20	755
2 / p. 279	AAA	La Crepe En Haut	▽▽▽	$23-$40	755
3 / p. 279		Royal Dynasty Restaurant & Lounge	▽	$8-$17	755
4 / p. 279		English Rose Tea Room	▽▽	$5-$9(L)	755
5 / p. 279		Mario's	▽▽	$9-$17	755
		DAYTONA BEACH - Lodgings			
29 / p. 279	AAA	Best Western Mayan Inn Beachfront	▽▽	$84-$215 SAVE	286
30 / p. 279		Howard Johnson Ocean Front Resort	▽▽	$54-$239	290
31 / p. 279	AAA	Best Western LaPlaya Resort - see color ad p 284	▽▽▽	$102-$260 SAVE	286
32 / p. 279	AAA	Beachcomer Daytona Beach Resort - see color ad p 284	▽▽▽	$89-$239 SAVE	283
33 / p. 279		The Villa Bed & Breakfast	▽▽▽	$125-$250	295
34 / p. 279	AAA	Travelers Inn - see color ad p 294	▽▽	$39-$89 SAVE	295
36 / p. 279	AAA	Aruba Inn - see ad p 283	▽▽	$35-$200 SAVE	283
37 / p. 279		Comfort Inn & Suites - see color ad p 288	▽▽▽	$69-$159	287
38 / p. 279	AAA	Tropical Winds Oceanfront Resort	▽▽▽	$49-$129 SAVE	295

Spotter/Map Page Number	OA	DAYTONA BEACH - Lodgings (continued)	Diamond Rating	Rate Range High Season	Listing Page
39 / p. 279		Hilton Garden Inn	◇◇◇	$89-$139	290
40 / p. 279	AAA	Ocean Villa Motel - see color ad p 293	◇◇	$59-$229 SAVE	292
41 / p. 279	AAA	Del-Aire Motel	◇◇	$83-$108 SAVE	290
42 / p. 279	AAA	Ocean Sands Beach Resort	◇	$69-$249 SAVE	292
44 / p. 279	AAA	Capri Motel - see color ad p 293	◇	$59-$229 SAVE	286
45 / p. 279	AAA	Holiday Inn Hotel & Suites Oceanfront - see color ad p 288, opposite inside back cover	◇◇◇	$79-$300 SAVE	290
46 / p. 279	AAA	Casa Marina Motel - see color ad p 293	◇	$49-$269 SAVE	287
47 / p. 279	AAA	The Plaza Resort & Spa - see color ad p 284	◇◇◇	$109-$499 SAVE	293
48 / p. 279	AAA	Days Inn Speedway	◇	$109-$249 SAVE	287
49 / p. 279	AAA	La Quinta Inn	◇◇	$55-$95 SAVE	292
50 / p. 279	AAA	Ramada Inn Speedway	◇◇◇	$89 SAVE	293
53 / p. 279	AAA	Breakers Beach Oceanfront Motel - see color ad p 286	◇◇	$52-$105 SAVE	286
54 / p. 279	AAA	Radisson Resort - see color ad p 284	◇◇◇	$169-$400 SAVE	293
55 / p. 279	AAA	Adam's Mark Resort - see color ad p 283	◇◇◇	$125-$215 SAVE	283
56 / p. 279	AAA	Esquire Beach Motel	◇	$73-$170 SAVE	290
57 / p. 279		Ocean Walk Resort	◇◇◇	$199-$359	292
58 / p. 279	AAA	Super 8-Oceanfront	◇◇	$79-$99 SAVE	294
59 / p. 279		Hampton Inn Daytona Speedway-Airport	◇◇◇	$84-$94	290
60 / p. 279		Suburban Lodge	◇◇	$45-$59	294
63 / p. 279	AAA	Travelodge Ocean Jewels Resort - see color ad p 294	◇◇◇	$79-$129 SAVE	295
64 / p. 279	AAA	Inn on the Beach - see color ad p 291	◇◇◇	$137-$157 SAVE	290
69 / p. 279	AAA	Nautilus Inn	◇◇◇	$129-$162 SAVE	292
72 / p. 279	AAA	Scottish Inns	◇	$39-$185 SAVE	294
		DAYTONA BEACH - Restaurants			
15 / p. 279	AAA	Riccardo's Italian Restaurant	◇◇	$9-$19	295
16 / p. 279		Starlite Diner	◇	$4-$8	295
18 / p. 279	AAA	Hungarian Village Restaurant	◇◇	$10-$16	295
		SOUTH DAYTONA - Lodgings			
76 / p. 279	AAA	Sun Ranch Motor Lodge	◇	$35-$140 SAVE	833
		DAYTONA BEACH SHORES - Lodgings			
81 / p. 279	AAA	Bahama House - see color ad p 297	◇◇◇	$136-$189 SAVE	296
83 / p. 279	AAA	Old Salty's Inn - see color ad p 294	◇◇◇	$56-$99 SAVE	302
84 / p. 279	AAA	Flamingo Inn	◇◇	$199-$398 SAVE	300
86 / p. 279		Atlantic Waves Motel	◇◇	$55-$185	296
87 / p. 279	AAA	Treasure Island Resort - see color ad p 284	◇◇◇	$149-$279 SAVE	306
89 / p. 279	AAA	Key West Village - see color ad p 302	◇◇	$89-$149 SAVE	302
91 / p. 279	AAA	Perry's Ocean-Edge Resort - see color ad p 304	◇◇◇	$61-$144 SAVE	304
93 / p. 279	AAA	Pelican Shoals Motel & Cottages	◇◇	$41-$120 SAVE	303
94 / p. 279	AAA	Hawaiian Inn - see color ad p 301	◇◇	$69-$129 SAVE	301

Spotter/Map Page Number	OA	DAYTONA BEACH SHORES - Lodgings (continued)	Diamond Rating	Rate Range High Season	Listing Page
95 / p. 279	AAA	Sun Viking Lodge - see color ad starting on p 285	◈◈◈	$79-$299 SAVE	306
96 / p. 279	AAA	Shoreline All Suites Inn - see color ad starting on p 285	◈◈	$69-$159 SAVE	306
97 / p. 279	AAA	Acapulco Hotel & Resort - see color ad p 284	◈◈◈	$149-$259 SAVE	296
98 / p. 279	AAA	Super 8 Daytona Sands	◈	$42-$99 SAVE	306
99 / p. 279	AAA	Hilton Daytona Beach Oceanfront Resort - see color ad p 301	◈◈◈	$149-$399 SAVE	302
100 / p. 279	AAA	Quality Inn Ocean Palms - see color ad p 304	◈◈◈	$85-$175 SAVE	305
102 / p. 279	AAA	Best Western-Aku Tiki Inn - see color ad p 298	◈◈◈	$95-$210 SAVE	298
103 / p. 279	AAA	Tropical Manor Motel - see color ad p 305	◈◈◈	$70-$125 SAVE	306
105 / p. 279	AAA	Atlantic Ocean Palm Inn - see color ad p 296	◈◈	$60-$90 SAVE	296
106 / p. 279	AAA	Daytona Surfside Inn & Suites - see color ad p 299	◈◈◈	$119-$149 SAVE	300
107 / p. 279	AAA	SeaGarden Resort - see color ad p 305	◈◈	$85-$95 SAVE	305
108 / p. 279	AAA	Hampton Inn Oceanfront - see color ad p 300	◈◈◈	$114-$299 SAVE	301
109 / p. 279	AAA	Holiday Inn Daytona Beach Shores - see color ad opposite inside back cover, p 291	◈◈◈	$89-$129 SAVE	302
110 / p. 279	AAA	Beachside Motel - see color ad p 297	◈◈◈	$119-$139 SAVE	298
111 / p. 279	AAA	Palm Plaza Oceanfront Resort - see color ad p 303	◈◈◈	$119-$149 SAVE	302
112 / p. 279	AAA	Beach House Oceanfront Motel	◈◈	$48-$79 SAVE	297
114 / p. 279	AAA	Dream Inn	◈◈	$79-$189 SAVE	300
115 / p. 279	AAA	Days Inn Oceanfront South Tropical Seas	◈◈	$49-$129 SAVE	299
120 / p. 279	AAA	Colonial Palms Inn Oceanfront	◈◈	$79-$105 SAVE	298
		DAYTONA BEACH SHORES - Restaurants			
24 / p. 279	AAA	China-American Garden	◈◈	$7-$14	306
25 / p. 279		Boondocks	◈	$5-$15	306
		PORT ORANGE - Restaurant			
30 / p. 279		Aunt Catfish's On The River	◈◈	$9-$29	781

Look For Savings

When you pick up a AAA TourBook® guide, look for establishments that display a bright red AAA logo, SAVE icon, and Diamond rating in their listing. These Official Appointment establishments place a high value on the patronage they receive from AAA members. And, by offering members great room rates*, they are willing to go the extra mile to get your business.

So, when you turn to the AAA TourBook guide to make your travel plans, look for the establishments that will give you the special treatment you deserve.

*See TourBook Navigator section, page 14, for complete details.

DAYTONA BEACH pop. 64,112   (See map p. 279; index p. 280)

──── WHERE TO STAY ────

ADAM'S MARK RESORT

(AAA) (SAVE)
▼▼▼▼

Phone: (386)254-8200 **55**

	1P	2P	XP	
1/31-5/1	1P: $125-$215	2P: $125-$215	XP: $25	F17
12/1-1/30 & 5/2-11/30	1P: $115-$195	2P: $115-$195	XP: $25	F17

Location: On SR A1A, 0.5 mi n of US 92. Located opposite the convention center. 100 N Atlantic Ave 32118. Fax: 386/253-0275. **Facility:** 743 units. 742 one-bedroom standard units. 1 one-bedroom suite ($175-$1600) **Large-scale Hotel** with whirlpool. 11-16 stories, interior corridors. *Bath:* combo or shower only. **Parking:** on-site (fee) and valet. **Terms:** check-in 4 pm, cancellation fee imposed, package plans. **Amenities:** video library (fee). *Some:* video games (fee), voice mail, irons, hair dryers. **Dining:** 7 am-11 pm, cocktails. **Pool(s):** heated indoor/outdoor, 2 wading, lap. **Leisure Activities:** sauna, whirlpools, steamroom, playground, exercise room, volleyball. *Fee:* tanning, massage, game room. **Guest Services:** gift shop, valet and coin laundry. **Business Services:** conference facilities, business center. **Cards:** AX, CB, DC, DS, MC, VI. **Special Amenities:** early check-in/late check-out and preferred room (subject to availability with advanced reservations). *(See color ad below)*

SOME UNITS

🅂🄳 🍴 🍽 🖥 ♿ 🚐 ⊗ / 🅰🄲 📺 (DATA PORT) 🖥 / FEE

ARUBA INN

(AAA) (SAVE)
▼▼▼

Motel

Phone: (386)253-5643 **36**

	1P	2P	XP	
All Year	1P: $35-$200	2P: $35-$200	XP: $10	F15

Location: On SR A1A, 1.5 mi n of jct US 92. 1254 N Atlantic Ave 32118. Fax: 386/248-1279. **Facility:** 32 one-bedroom standard units, some with efficiencies. 2 stories, exterior corridors. **Parking:** on-site. **Terms:** 15 day cancellation notice-fee imposed, weekly rates available, small pets only. **Pool(s):** heated outdoor. **Leisure Activities:** shuffleboard. **Guest Services:** coin laundry. **Cards:** AX, DS, MC, VI. *(See ad below)*

SOME UNITS

🐾 🍴 🚐 / 🖥 🖥 /

BEACHCOMER DAYTONA BEACH RESORT

(AAA) (SAVE)
▼▼▼

Small-scale Hotel

Phone: (386)252-8513 **32**

	1P	2P	XP	
1/31-4/20 [BP]	1P: $89-$239	2P: $89-$239	XP: $10	F18
4/21-9/1 [BP]	1P: $79-$169	2P: $79-$169	XP: $10	F18
12/1-1/30 & 9/2-11/30 [BP]	1P: $59-$09	2P: $59-$69	XP: $10	F18

Location: On SR A1A, 2.8 mi n of jct US 92. 2000 N Atlantic Ave 32118. Fax: 386/252-7400. **Facility:** 174 one-bedroom standard units, some with efficiencies or kitchens. 7 stories, interior/exterior corridors. *Bath:* combo or shower only. **Parking:** on-site. **Terms:** 7 day cancellation notice-fee imposed. **Amenities:** voice mail, safes (fee). **Dining:** 7 am-1 pm. **Pool(s):** heated outdoor, wading. **Leisure Activities:** whirlpool, recreation programs, shuffleboard. *Fee:* game room. **Guest Services:** gift shop, coin laundry. **Business Services:** meeting rooms. **Cards:** AX, DC, DS, MC, VI. *(See color ad p 284)*

SOME UNITS

🍴 🖥 🚐 ⊗ 🎥 (DATA PORT) 🖥 / ⊗ 🖥 /

Imagine ... Strolling along a tranquil seaside
where gentle waves caress silky
white sands. Nestled amid swaying
palms, you'll discover coastal
pleasures including sunning,
surfing, sailing, sports fishing and
championship golf. Explore our beautiful beach. Swim in our
sparkling oceanside pools. Ride our 60 foot waterslide.
Exercise in our Nautilus fitness room. Entertain your family
with our guest recreation program, or just
relax in our hot tub and sauna.

... *a place where you
are always welcome.*

Sun Viking Lodge
"A Unique Family Resort"
800-815-2508
sunviking.com
386-252-6252 · FAX 386-252-5463
DAYTONA BEACH SHORES, FLORIDA

(See map p. 279)

BEST WESTERN LAPLAYA RESORT　　　　　　　　　　　Phone: (386)672-0990　**31**
AAA SAVE
| 1/31-9/1 | 1P: $102-$260 | 2P: $102-$260 | XP: $10 | F19 |
| 12/1-1/30 & 9/2-11/30 | 1P: $84-$144 | 2P: $84-$144 | XP: $10 | F19 |

Location: On SR A1A, 3.3 mi n of jct US 92. 2500 N Atlantic Ave 32118. **Fax:** 386/677-0982. **Facility:** 239 units.
Small-scale Hotel 204 one-bedroom standard units, some with efficiencies. 35 one-bedroom suites ($159-$364) with efficiencies. 10 stories, exterior corridors. *Bath:* combo or shower only. **Parking:** on-site. **Terms:** check-in 4 pm, weekly rates available, [BP] meal plan available, package plans. **Amenities:** voice mail, safes (fee), irons, hair dryers. **Dining:** 7 am-1:30 pm, Sunday champagne brunch. **Pool(s):** heated outdoor, heated indoor, wading. **Leisure Activities:** saunas, whirlpools, steamrooms, recreation programs in season, exercise room, shuffleboard. *Fee:* game room. **Guest Services:** valet and coin laundry. **Business Services:** meeting rooms. **Cards:** AX, CB, DC, DS, MC, VI. **Special Amenities:** free room upgrade and preferred room (each subject to availability with advanced reservations). *(See color ad p 284)*

BEST WESTERN MAYAN INN BEACHFRONT　　　　　　　　Phone: (386)252-2378　**29**
AAA SAVE
| 2/1-11/30 [ECP] | 1P: $84-$215 | 2P: $84-$215 | XP: $10 | F17 |
| 12/1-1/31 [ECP] | 1P: $84-$104 | 2P: $84-$104 | XP: $10 | F17 |

Location: Jct US 92 and SR A1A, just n, just e, then just n. 103 S Ocean Ave 32118. **Fax:** 386/252-8670. **Facility:** 112 one-bedroom standard units, some with efficiencies and/or whirlpools. 8 stories, interior/exterior
Small-scale Hotel corridors. *Bath:* combo or shower only. **Parking:** on-site. **Terms:** package plans. **Amenities:** voice mail, safes (fee), irons, hair dryers. **Pool(s):** heated outdoor, wading. **Leisure Activities:** *Fee:* game room. **Guest Services:** coin laundry. **Cards:** AX, CB, DC, DS, MC, VI. **Special Amenities:** early check-in/late check-out and free continental breakfast.

SOME UNITS

BREAKERS BEACH OCEANFRONT MOTEL　　　　　　　　　Phone: (386)252-0863　**53**
AAA SAVE
5/1-9/4		2P: $52-$105	XP: $10	F15
1/30-4/30		2P: $73-$95	XP: $10	F15
9/5-11/30		2P: $52-$95		
12/1-1/29		2P: $52-$72	XP: $10	F15

Motel　**Location:** Located near the pier and boardwalk. 27 S Ocean Ave 32118-4363. **Fax:** 386/238-1247. **Facility:** 23 units. 22 one-bedroom standard units, some with efficiencies. 1 one-bedroom suite ($104-$134) with kitchen. 2 stories (no elevator), exterior corridors. *Bath:* combo or shower only. **Parking:** on-site. **Terms:** 30 day cancellation notice-fee imposed, weekly rates available, small pets only ($10 extra charge). **Pool(s):** heated outdoor. **Leisure Activities:** picnic area with gas grills. **Guest Services:** coin laundry. **Cards:** AX, CB, DC, DS, MC, VI. **Special Amenities:** free newspaper and preferred room (subject to availability with advanced reservations). *(See color ad below)*

CAPRI MOTEL　　　　　　　　　　　　　　　　　　　Phone: (386)252-2555　**44**
AAA SAVE
2/7-8/16	1P: $59-$229	2P: $59-$229	XP: $10	F17
8/17-11/30	1P: $55-$159	2P: $55-$159	XP: $6	F17
12/1-2/6	1P: $49-$129	2P: $49-$129	XP: $6	F17

Motel　**Location:** On SR A1A, 1.5 mi n of jct US 92. Located on the beach. 832 N Atlantic Ave 32118. **Fax:** 386/255-7378. **Facility:** 24 units. 23 one-bedroom standard units, some with efficiencies or kitchens. 1 one-bedroom suite with kitchen. 1-2 stories, exterior corridors. **Parking:** on-site. **Terms:** 7 day cancellation notice. **Amenities:** *Fee:* video library, safes. **Pool(s):** outdoor, heated outdoor. **Leisure Activities:** waterslide. *Fee:* game room. **Guest Services:** coin laundry. **Cards:** AX, CB, DC, DS, MC, VI. **Special Amenities:** free newspaper. *(See color ad p 293)*

SOME UNITS

FEE

(See map p. 279)

CASA MARINA MOTEL

Phone: (386)252-4644 **46**

2/7-8/16	1P: $49-$269	2P: $49-$269	XP: $10	F17
8/17-11/30	1P: $49-$139	2P: $49-$139	XP: $6	F17
12/1-2/6	1P: $39-$99	2P: $39-$99	XP: $6	F17

Motel

Location: On SR A1A, 1.5 mi n of jct US 92. Located opposite the beach. 837 N Atlantic Ave 32118. Fax: 386/255-7378. **Facility:** 13 one-bedroom standard units, some with efficiencies or kitchens. 1-2 stories, interior/exterior corridors. *Bath:* combo or shower only. **Parking:** on-site. **Terms:** 7 day cancellation notice. **Amenities:** *Fee:* video library, safes. **Leisure Activities:** off-site recreational facility privileges and beach access. **Cards:** AX, CB, DC, DS, MC, VI. **Special Amenities:** free newspaper. *(See color ad p 293)*

SOME UNITS

COMFORT INN & SUITES

Phone: (386)255-5491 **37**

10/14-11/30 [ECP]	1P: $69-$159	2P: $69-$159	XP: $10	F18
2/7-6/28 [ECP]	1P: $89-$149	2P: $89-$149	XP: $10	F18
12/1-2/6 & 6/29-10/13 [ECP]	1P: $79-$139	2P: $79-$139	XP: $10	F18

Motel

Location: On SR A1A, 1.3 mi n of jct US 92. 730 N Atlantic Ave 32118. Fax: 386/252-7188. **Facility:** 97 units. 85 one-bedroom standard units, some with efficiencies. 12 one-bedroom suites ($99-$259), some with efficiencies and/or whirlpools. 5 stories, interior corridors. *Bath:* combo or shower only. **Parking:** on-site. **Terms:** 30 day cancellation notice. **Amenities:** dual phone lines, voice mail, irons, hair dryers. **Pool(s):** outdoor, wading. **Guest Services:** valet and coin laundry. **Business Services:** fax. **Cards:** AX, DC, DS, MC, VI. *(See color ad p 288)*

SOME UNITS

DAYS INN SPEEDWAY

Phone: (386)255-0541 **48**

2/1-3/28	1P: $109-$249	2P: $109-$249	XP: $10	F18
12/1-1/31 & 3/29-11/30	1P: $49-$79	2P: $49-$79	XP: $10	F18

Motel

Location: I-95, exit 261B southbound; exit 261 northbound, just w on US 92. 2900 W International Speedway Blvd 32124. Fax: 386/253-1468. **Facility:** 170 one-bedroom standard units. 2 stories (no elevator), exterior corridors. **Parking:** on-site. **Terms:** 7 day cancellation notice, pets ($10 fee). **Dining:** 6 am-11 pm. **Pool(s):** outdoor. **Guest Services:** coin laundry. **Cards:** AX, CB, DC, DS, MC, VI. **Special Amenities:** early check-in/late check-out and free newspaper.

SOME UNITS

(See map p. 279)

DEL-AIRE MOTEL   Phone: (386)252-2563   41

CAD SAVE

3/2-9/2		2P: $83-$108	XP: $8	F12
2/1-3/1		2P: $70-$90	XP: $8	F12
12/1-1/31 & 9/3-11/30		2P: $55-$75	XP: $8	F12

Motel   **Location:** On SR A1A, 1.3 mi n of jct US 92. Located on the beach. 744 N Atlantic Ave 32118. Fax: 386/252-4866. **Facility:** 20 units. 19 one-bedroom standard units, some with efficiencies or kitchens. 1 one-bedroom suite ($70-$150) with kitchen. 2 stories, exterior corridors. **Parking:** on-site. **Terms:** 7 day cancellation notice-fee imposed. **Amenities:** *Some:* safes (fee). **Pool(s):** heated outdoor. **Leisure Activities:** playground. **Cards:** AX, DC, DS, MC, VI. **Special Amenities: early check-in/late check-out and free local telephone calls.**

SOME UNITS

ESQUIRE BEACH MOTEL   Phone: 386/255-3601   56

CAD SAVE

2/14-4/23	1P: $73-$110	2P: $98-$170	XP: $10	F12
4/24-8/25	1P: $48-$73	2P: $58-$88	XP: $10	F12
12/1-2/13	1P: $38-$48	2P: $53-$63	XP: $10	F12
8/26-11/30	1P: $38-$48	2P: $43-$53	XP: $10	F12

Motel   **Location:** On SR A1A, 0.8 mi n of US 92. 422 N Atlantic Ave 32118. Fax: 386/255-2166. **Facility:** 68 one-bedroom standard units, some with efficiencies. 2-3 stories, exterior corridors. **Bath:** combo or shower only. **Parking:** on-site. **Amenities:** safes (fee). *Some:* dual phone lines. **Pool(s):** heated outdoor. **Guest Services:** coin laundry.

SOME UNITS

HAMPTON INN DAYTONA SPEEDWAY-AIRPORT   Phone: (386)257-4030   59

SAVE

All Year [ECP]   1P: $84   2P: $94

Small-scale Hotel   **Location:** I-95, exit 261 northbound; exit 261A southbound, 2.1 mi e on US 92. Located adjacent to Daytona International Speedway. 1715 W International Speedway Blvd 32114. Fax: 386/257-5721. **Facility:** 121 one-bedroom standard units. 4 stories, interior corridors. **Parking:** on-site. **Terms:** 7 day cancellation notice, [CP] meal plan available. **Amenities:** voice mail, irons, hair dryers. **Pool(s):** outdoor. **Leisure Activities:** whirlpool. **Guest Services:** valet laundry, area transportation. **Business Services:** meeting rooms. **Cards:** AX, CB, DC, DS, JC, MC, VI.

SOME UNITS

FEE

HILTON GARDEN INN   Phone: (386)944-4000   39

SAVE

All Year   1P: $89-$139   2P: $89-$139

Small-scale Hotel   **Location:** I-95, exit 261A, 2 mi e, then just s. Located next to Daytona International Speedway. 189 Midway Ave 32114. Fax: 386/944-4001. **Facility:** 115 units. 101 one-bedroom standard units, some with whirlpools. 14 one-bedroom suites, some with whirlpools. 5 stories, interior corridors. **Bath:** combo or shower only. **Parking:** on-site. **Terms:** check-in 4 pm. **Amenities:** video games, high-speed Internet, dual phone lines, voice mail, irons, hair dryers. **Pool(s):** outdoor. **Leisure Activities:** whirlpool, exercise room. **Guest Services:** sundries, coin laundry. **Business Services:** meeting rooms, business center. **Cards:** AX, CB, DC, DS, MC, VI.

SOME UNITS

HOLIDAY INN HOTEL & SUITES OCEANFRONT   Phone: (386)255-5494   45

CAD SAVE

All Year   1P: $79-$300   XP: $10   F17

Small-scale Hotel   **Location:** On SR A1A, 1.3 mi n of US 92. 930 N Atlantic Ave 32118. Fax: 386/255-5495. **Facility:** 123 units. 103 one-bedroom standard units, some with whirlpools. 20 one-bedroom suites. 6 stories, interior/exterior corridors. **Bath:** combo or shower only. **Parking:** on-site. **Terms:** 14 day cancellation notice. **Amenities:** dual phone lines, voice mail, safes, irons, hair dryers. **Dining:** 6:30 am-8 pm. **Pool(s):** heated outdoor. **Leisure Activities:** exercise room. **Guest Services:** gift shop, valet and coin laundry. **Business Services:** meeting rooms, fax. **Cards:** AX, CB, DC, DS, MC, VI. *(See color ads starting on p 288 & opposite inside back cover)*

SOME UNITS

HOWARD JOHNSON OCEAN FRONT RESORT   Phone: (386)672-1440   30

All Year   1P: $54-$239   2P: $54-$239   XP: $12   F17

Small-scale Hotel   **Location:** On SR A1A, 3.3 mi n of jct US 92. 2560 N Atlantic Ave 32118. Fax: 386/677-8811. **Facility:** 143 one-bedroom standard units, some with efficiencies or kitchens. 4-8 stories, interior/exterior corridors. **Bath:** combo or shower only. **Parking:** on-site. **Terms:** 5 day cancellation notice, weekly rates available. **Amenities:** *Fee:* high-speed Internet, safes. **Pool(s):** heated outdoor, wading. **Leisure Activities:** whirlpool. *Fee:* game room. **Guest Services:** coin laundry. **Cards:** AX, DC, DS, MC, VI.

SOME UNITS

INN ON THE BEACH   Phone: (386)255-0921   64

CAD SAVE

1/31-4/26 [CP]	1P: $137-$157	2P: $137-$157	XP: $10	F18
4/27-8/16 [CP]	1P: $87-$137	2P: $87-$137	XP: $10	F18
12/1-1/30 & 8/17-11/30 [CP]	1P: $87-$107	2P: $87-$107	XP: $10	F18

Small-scale Hotel   **Location:** On SR A1A, 1.3 mi s of jct US 92. 1615 S Atlantic Ave 32118. Fax: 386/255-3849. **Facility:** 195 units. 174 one-bedroom standard units, some with kitchens and/or whirlpools. 21 one-bedroom suites ($117-$287) with kitchens. 7 stories, exterior corridors. **Bath:** combo or shower only. **Parking:** on-site. **Terms:** check-in 4 pm, 3 day cancellation notice. **Amenities:** video library (fee), voice mail, hair dryers. **Dining:** 9 am-9 pm, cocktails. **Pool(s):** heated outdoor, wading. **Leisure Activities:** sauna, whirlpool, putting green, recreation programs, exercise room, shuffleboard. *Fee:* game room. **Guest Services:** coin laundry. **Business Services:** meeting rooms, fax (fee). **Cards:** AX, CB, DC, DS, MC, VI. **Special Amenities: free continental breakfast and free local telephone calls.** *(See color ad p 291)*

SOME UNITS

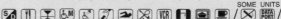

(See map p. 279)

LA QUINTA INN   Phone: (386)255-7412   **49**

AAA SAVE   Motel

All Year	1P: $59-$89	2P: $55-$95

Location: I-95, exit 261 northbound; exit 261B southbound, just e. Located in a commercial area. 2725 W International Speedway Blvd 32114. Fax: 386/255-5350. **Facility:** 143 units. 142 one-bedroom standard units. 1 one-bedroom suite. 2 stories (no elevator), interior corridors. *Bath:* combo or shower only. **Parking:** on-site. **Terms:** [ECP] meal plan available, small pets only. **Amenities:** voice mail, irons, hair dryers. **Fee:** video library, video games. **Pool(s):** outdoor, wading. **Guest Services:** coin laundry. **Business Services:** meeting rooms. **Cards:** AX, CB, DC, DS, JC, MC, VI. **Special Amenities:** free continental breakfast and free local telephone calls.

SOME UNITS

NAUTILUS INN   Phone: (386)254-8600   **69**

AAA SAVE

6/6-8/9 [CP]	1P: $129-$162	2P: $129-$162	XP: $11 F17
1/31-6/5 [CP]	1P: $119-$145	2P: $119-$145	XP: $11 F17
8/10-11/30 [CP]	1P: $109-$129	2P: $109-$129	XP: $11 F17
12/1-1/30 [CP]	1P: $97-$115	2P: $97-$115	XP: $11 F17

Small-scale Hotel **Location:** On SR A1A, 1.5 mi s of jct US 92. 1515 S Atlantic Ave 32118. Fax: 386/254-8427. **Facility:** Smoke free premises. 99 one-bedroom standard units, some with efficiencies. 10 stories, interior corridors. **Parking:** on-site. **Terms:** 10 day cancellation notice. **Amenities:** safes. **Pool(s):** heated outdoor. **Leisure Activities:** whirlpool, recreation programs. **Guest Services:** complimentary evening beverages, coin laundry. **Cards:** AX, MC, VI. **Special Amenities:** free continental breakfast.

SOME UNITS

OCEAN SANDS BEACH RESORT   Phone: (386)255-1131   **42**

AAA SAVE

1/31-4/27	2P: $69-$249	XP: $10 F18
4/28-8/17	2P: $69-$199	XP: $10 F18
8/18-11/30	2P: $59-$149	XP: $5 F18
12/1-1/30	2P: $49-$59	XP: $5 F18

Small-scale Hotel **Location:** On SR A1A, 1.8 mi n of US 92. 1024 N Atlantic Ave 32118. Fax: 386/255-5670. **Facility:** 94 units. 92 one-bedroom standard units, some with efficiencies. 2 one-bedroom suites ($149-$450) with kitchens and whirlpools. 8 stories, interior corridors. **Parking:** on-site. **Amenities:** irons. **Fee:** video library, safes. **Pool(s):** outdoor, heated indoor. **Leisure Activities:** shuffleboard. **Guest Services:** coin laundry. **Business Services:** meeting rooms, fax (fee). **Cards:** AX, DC, MC, VI.

SOME UNITS

OCEAN VILLA MOTEL   Phone: (386)252-4644   **40**

AAA SAVE   Motel

2/7-8/16	1P: $59-$229	2P: $59-$229	XP: $10 F17
8/17-11/30	1P: $55-$159	2P: $55-$159	XP: $6 F17
12/1-2/6	1P: $49-$129	2P: $49-$129	XP: $6 F17

Location: On SR A1A, 1.5 mi n of jct US 92. Located on the beach. 828 N Atlantic Ave 32118. Fax: 386/255-7378. **Facility:** 38 units. 33 one-bedroom standard units, some with efficiencies or kitchens. 5 one-bedroom suites ($99-$379) with kitchens. 2 stories, exterior corridors. *Bath:* combo or shower only. **Parking:** on-site. **Terms:** 7 day cancellation notice. **Amenities:** Fee: video library, safes. **Pool(s):** outdoor, heated outdoor, wading. **Leisure Activities:** waterslide. *Fee:* game room. **Guest Services:** coin laundry. **Cards:** AX, CB, DC, DS, MC, VI. **Special Amenities:** free newspaper. *(See color ad p 293)*

SOME UNITS

FEE

OCEAN WALK RESORT   Phone: (386)323-4800   **57**

Resort Condominium

2/11-5/1	1P: $199	2P: $359
5/2-8/31	1P: $169	2P: $309
12/1-2/10 & 9/1-11/30	1P: $129	2P: $219

Location: On SR A1A, 0.6 mi n of US 92. 300 N Atlantic Ave 32118. Fax: 386/323-4810. **Facility:** 120 units. 25 one-bedroom standard units with efficiencies. 73 one- and 22 two-bedroom suites, some with efficiencies, kitchens and/or whirlpools. 19 stories, interior corridors. *Bath:* combo or shower only. **Parking:** on-site. **Terms:** check-in 4 pm, 3 day cancellation notice, weekly rates available. **Amenities:** video library (fee), voice mail, safes, irons, hair dryers. *Some:* CD players. **Pool(s):** heated outdoor, heated indoor. **Leisure Activities:** whirlpool, waterslide, lifeguard on duty, putting green, recreation programs, exercise room. *Fee:* game room. **Guest Services:** gift shop, complimentary laundry, area transportation (fee). **Business Services:** conference facilities. *Fee:* administrative services, fax. **Cards:** AX, CB, DC, DS, JC, MC, VI.

SOME UNITS

FEE

LOOK FOR THE RED

*N*ext time you pore over a AAA TourBook® guide in search of a lodging establishment, take note of the vibrant red AAA logo, icon, and SAVE Diamond rating just under a select group of property names! These Official Appointment properties place a high value on the business they receive from dedicated AAA travelers and offer members great room rates*.

* See TourBook Navigator section, page 14, for complete details.

(See map p. 279)

THE PLAZA RESORT & SPA

Phone: (386)255-4471  47

AAA SAVE

1/31-5/22	1P: $109-$499	2P: $109-$499	XP: $15 F17
5/23-8/16	1P: $169-$349	2P: $169-$349	XP: $15 F17
8/17-11/30	1P: $99-$209	2P: $99-$209	XP: $15 F17
12/1-1/30	1P: $99-$169	2P: $99-$169	XP: $15 F17

Large-scale Hotel Location: On SR A1A, 1 mi n of US 92. 600 N Atlantic Ave 32118. Fax: 386/238-7984. **Facility:** 320 units. 315 one-bedroom standard units, some with whirlpools. 5 one-bedroom suites. 14 stories, interior corridors. *Bath:* combo or shower only. **Parking:** on-site (fee). **Terms:** check-in 4 pm, 7 day cancellation notice, $2 service charge. **Amenities:** dual phone lines, voice mail, safes (fee), irons, hair dryers. **Dining:** 2 restaurants, 7 am-10 pm, cocktails, nightclub. **Pool(s):** heated outdoor. **Leisure Activities:** whirlpools, putting green, recreation programs in season, exercise room, spa, sports court. **Guest Services:** gift shop, valet and coin laundry. **Business Services:** conference facilities. *Fee:* administrative services, fax. **Cards:** AX, CB, DC, DS, JC, MC, VI. *(See color ad p 284)*

SOME UNITS

RADISSON RESORT

Phone: (386)239-9800 54

AAA SAVE

1/31-3/31	1P: $169-$400	2P: $169-$400	XP: $10 F17
4/1-8/16	1P: $99-$389	2P: $99-$389	XP: $10 F17
8/17-11/30	1P: $99-$300	2P: $99-$300	XP: $10 F17
12/1-1/30	1P: $89-$159	2P: $89-$159	XP: $10 F17

Small-scale Hotel Location: SR A1A, 1 mi n of jct SR 90. Located on oceanfront. 640 N Atlantic Ave 32118. Fax: 386/253-0735. **Facility:** 206 one-bedroom standard units. 11 stories, interior corridors. *Bath:* combo or shower only. **Parking:** valet. **Terms:** check-in 4 pm, cancellation fee imposed, $7 service charge, small pets only ($50 extra charge). **Amenities:** voice mail, safes, irons, hair dryers. *Fee:* video library, video games. **Dining:** 6:30 am-10 pm, cocktails. **Pool(s):** heated outdoor, wading. **Leisure Activities:** exercise room. *Fee:* game room. **Guest Services:** gift shop, valet and coin laundry. **Business Services:** meeting rooms, fax (fee). **Cards:** AX, CB, DC, DS, JC, MC, VI. *(See color ad p 284)*

SOME UNITS

RAMADA INN SPEEDWAY

Phone: (386)255-2422 50

AAA SAVE

1/1-4/12	1P: $89	2P: $89
12/1-12/31 & 4/13-11/30	1P: $79	2P: $79

Small-scale Hotel **Location:** I-95, exit 261A southbound; exit 261 northbound, 2 mi e on US 92. Located across from Daytona International Speedway. 1798 W International Speedway Blvd 32114. Fax: 386/253-1749. **Facility:** 127 one-bedroom standard units. 2 stories, exterior corridors. *Bath:* combo or shower only. **Parking:** on-site. **Terms:** pets ($25 extra charge). **Amenities:** voice mail, safes, irons, hair dryers. **Dining:** 6:30 am-1 am, cocktails. **Pool(s):** outdoor. **Guest Services:** valet laundry, area transportation-within 3 mi. **Business Services:** meeting rooms. **Cards:** AX, CB, DC, DS, JC, MC, VI. **Special Amenities:** free local telephone calls.

SOME UNITS

FEE

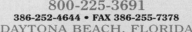

(See map p. 279)

SCOTTISH INNS

				Phone: (386)258-5742	72
1/1-4/30	1P: $39-$145	2P: $48-$185	XP: $8		F8
7/1-11/30	1P: $39-$145	2P: $46-$165	XP: $8		F8
5/1-6/30	1P: $35-$89	2P: $39-$99	XP: $8		F8
12/1-12/31	1P: $35-$55	2P: $39-$68	XP: $8		F8

Motel **Location:** I-95, exit 260A, 2.5 mi e on SR 400, just n on US 1. 1515 S Ridgewood Ave 32114. Fax: 386/253-7635. **Facility:** Designated smoking area. 20 one-bedroom standard units. 1 story, exterior corridors. **Parking:** on-site. **Terms:** 15 day cancellation notice-fee imposed, small pets only ($8 fee). **Pool(s):** outdoor. **Cards:** AX, CB, DC, DS, MC, VI.

SOME UNITS

FEE

SUBURBAN LODGE

			Phone: (386)274-4200	60
All Year	1P: $45-$55	2P: $49-$59		

Motel **Location:** I-95, exit 261 northbound; exit 261A southbound, 2 mi e, then just n. 220 Bill France Blvd 32114. Fax: 386/274-3383. **Facility:** 135 one-bedroom standard units with efficiencies. 3 stories, exterior corridors. *Bath:* combo or shower only. **Parking:** on-site. **Terms:** 3 day cancellation notice. **Amenities:** voice mail. **Pool(s):** heated outdoor. **Guest Services:** coin laundry. **Business Services:** meeting rooms. **Cards:** AX, DS, MC, VI. *(See color ad p 596)*

SOME UNITS

FEE

SUPER 8-OCEANFRONT

				Phone: (386)253-0666	58
6/1-8/16	1P: $79-$99	2P: $79-$99	XP: $10		F12
3/1-5/31	1P: $59-$89	2P: $59-$89	XP: $10		F12
8/17-11/30	1P: $49-$69	2P: $49-$69	XP: $10		F12
12/1-2/28	1P: $39-$59	2P: $39-$59	XP: $10		F12

Motel **Location:** Jct US 92 and SR A1A; n, just e, then n. 133 S Ocean Ave 32118. Fax: 386/239-0858. **Facility:** 76 units. 74 one-bedroom standard units, some with efficiencies. 2 one-bedroom suites ($169-$375) with whirlpools. 2 stories (no elevator), exterior corridors. *Bath:* combo or shower only. **Parking:** on-site. **Terms:** 30 day cancellation notice, [BP] meal plan available. **Amenities:** safes (fee). **Pool(s):** outdoor. **Guest Services:** coin laundry. **Business Services:** meeting rooms. **Cards:** AX, DC, DS, MC, VI. **Special Amenities:** free continental breakfast.

SOME UNITS

FEE

(See map p. 279)

TRAVELERS INN

AAA **SAVE**

Motel

2/2-5/1 & 6/2-11/30	1P: $39-$69	2P: $49-$89
12/1-2/1 & 5/2-6/1	1P: $29-$59	2P: $39-$79

Phone: (386)253-3501

XP: $10   F12
XP: $10   F12

Location: On SR A1A, 1 mi n of US 92. 735 N Atlantic Ave 32118. Fax: 386/441-5977. **Facility:** 21 one-bedroom standard units, some with kitchens. 1 story, exterior corridors. *Bath:* combo or shower only. **Parking:** on-site. **Terms:** 30 day cancellation notice, [CP] meal plan available. **Amenities:** hair dryers. **Pool(s):** heated outdoor. **Leisure Activities:** beach bikes. **Guest Services:** coin laundry. **Cards:** AX, DS, MC, VI.

(See color ad p 294)

SOME UNITS

TRAVELODGE OCEAN JEWELS RESORT

AAA **SAVE**

Condominium

1/31-4/12	1P: $79-$129	2P: $79-$129
4/13-8/31	1P: $69-$119	2P: $69-$119
12/1-1/30 & 9/1-11/30	1P: $59-$79	2P: $59-$79

Phone: (386)252-2581

XP: $10   F18
XP: $10   F18
XP: $10   F18

Location: On SR A1A, 0.6 mi s of jct US 92. Located ocean side. 935 S Atlantic Ave 32118. Fax: 386/257-3608. **Facility:** 135 units. 134 one-bedroom standard units with efficiencies. 1 two-bedroom suite ($79-$199) with kitchen. 2-6 stories, exterior corridors. **Parking:** on-site. **Terms:** cancellation fee imposed, weekly rates available. **Amenities:** voice mail. **Dining:** 7 am-midnight. **Pool(s):** outdoor, heated outdoor, wading. **Leisure Activities:** barbecue grills, picnic tables, exercise room. **Guest Services:** coin laundry. **Business Services:** meeting rooms. **Cards:** AX, CB, DC, DS, MC, VI. **Special Amenities:** free newspaper and preferred room (subject to availability with advanced reservations).

(See color ad p 294)

SOME UNITS

TROPICAL WINDS OCEANFRONT RESORT

AAA **SAVE**

Small-scale Hotel

All Year	1P: $49-$129	2P: $49-$129

Phone: 386-258-1016

XP: $10   F16

Location: On SR A1A, 2 mi n of jct US 92. 1398 N Atlantic Ave 32118. Fax: 386/255-6462. **Facility:** 94 units. 92 one-bedroom standard units, some with efficiencies. 2 one-bedroom suites ($129-$369) with kitchens. 8 stories, interior corridors. **Parking:** on-site. **Terms:** weekly rates available. **Amenities:** hair dryers. **Dining:** 7 am-2 pm. **Pool(s):** outdoor, heated indoor. **Leisure Activities:** shuffleboard. *Fee:* game room. **Guest Services:** coin laundry. **Cards:** AX, CB, DC, DS, MC, VI.

SOME UNITS

THE VILLA BED & BREAKFAST

Bed & Breakfast

All Year	1P: $125-$250	2P: $125-$250

Phone: (386)248-2020 33

Location: On SR A1A, 1 mi n from jct US 92, just w on Seabreeze Blvd, then 0.4 mi n. 801 N Peninsula Dr 32118. Fax: 386/248-2020. **Facility:** Flower gardens and a tiled patio accent this 1920s Spanish Revival mansion on two acres of manicured grounds fronted by a gated entry. Smoke free premises. 4 one-bedroom standard units. 2 stories (no elevator), interior corridors. **Parking:** on-site. **Terms:** age restrictions may apply, 7 day cancellation notice-fee imposed, [ECP] meal plan available, no pets allowed (owner's pets on premises). **Amenities:** video library, hair dryers. *Some:* CD players. **Pool(s):** outdoor. **Leisure Activities:** whirlpool. **Cards:** AX, MC, VI.

SOME UNITS

———— WHERE TO DINE ————

HUNGARIAN VILLAGE RESTAURANT

AAA

Hungarian

Dinner: $10-$16   **Phone: 386-226-0115** 18

Location: On US 1, 0.5 mi s of jct US 92. 424 S Ridgewood Ave 32114. **Hours:** 4:30 pm-9:30 pm. Closed: 12/25; also Sun & Mon. **Reservations:** accepted. **Features:** Authentic Hungarian specialties include stuffed cabbage, goulash, Wiener schnitzel and pork with potatoes served hot on "the Wooden Plate." The cozy atmosphere gives this restaurant a homey touch. Smoke free premises. Casual dress; cocktails. **Parking:** on-site. **Cards:** DS, MC, VI.

RICCARDO'S ITALIAN RESTAURANT

AAA

Italian

MC, VI.

Dinner: $9-$19   **Phone: 386-253-3035** 15

Location: SR A1A, 1 mi n of jct US 92, just w. 610 Glenview Blvd 32118. **Hours:** 5 pm-10 pm; closing hours may vary. Closed: 11/27, 12/24, 12/25. **Reservations:** suggested. **Features:** Lace tablecloths add a touch of formality to the casual setting, which caters to families and candlelight diners alike. Since the early 1970s, the family owners have offered homemade pasta, sourdough bread and ice cream. Sauces are made from scratch, and family-style salad and antipasto are served with each main course. Fresh seafood and veal cut from whole legs on premises are specialties. Casual dress; cocktails. **Parking:** on-site. **Cards:** AX,

STARLITE DINER

American

Cards: MC, VI.

Lunch: $4-$6   **Dinner: $4-$8**   **Phone: 386-255-9555** 16

Location: On SR A1A, 0.8 mi n of US 92. 401 N Atlantic Ave 32118. **Hours:** 7 am-9 pm, Fri & Sat-10 pm. Closed: 12/25. **Features:** This '60s-era jukebox joint is the place to go for comfort food and lots of it. Mom's meatloaf, juicy burgers, homemade cakes and pies, and decadent fountain creations might not do much for your waistline, but they'll work wonders for your state of mind. Casual dress. **Parking:** on-site.

The following restaurant has not been evaluated by AAA but is listed for your information only.

SHELLS GREAT CASUAL SEAFOOD

fyi

Phone: 386-258-0007

Not evaluated. **Location:** On SR A1A, just n of US 92. 202 S Atlantic Ave 32118. **Features:** Shellfish and pasta, a few chicken and one steak item served in a very casual, informal setting with bare table tops by servers in jeans and brightly colored tropical shirts.

DAYTONA BEACH SHORES pop. 4,299   (See map p. 279; index p. 281)

──────── WHERE TO STAY ────────

ACAPULCO HOTEL & RESORT
AAA **SAVE** Phone: (386)761-2210 **97**

| | 2/8-8/17 | 1P: $149-$259 | 2P: $149-$259 | XP: $10 | F13 |
| | 12/1-2/7 & 8/18-11/30 | 1P: $119-$149 | 2P: $119-$149 | XP: $10 | F13 |

Small-scale Hotel **Location:** On SR A1A, 2.8 mi s of jct US 92. 2505 S Atlantic Ave 32118. Fax: 386/761-2216. **Facility:** 133 one-bedroom standard units, some with efficiencies. 8 stories, interior corridors. *Bath:* combo or shower only. **Parking:** on-site. **Terms:** 7 day cancellation notice-fee imposed. **Amenities:** voice mail, safes (fee), hair dryers. **Dining:** 7 am-1:30 pm, cocktails. **Pool(s):** heated outdoor, wading. **Leisure Activities:** whirlpools, recreation programs, shuffleboard. **Guest Services:** gift shop, coin laundry. **Business Services:** fax. **Cards:** AX, CB, DC, DS, MC, VI. *(See color ad p 284)*

SOME UNITS

ATLANTIC OCEAN PALM INN
AAA **SAVE** Phone: 386/761-8450 **105**

| | 2/1-8/31 | 1P: $60-$90 | 2P: $60-$90 | XP: $10 | F12 |
| | 12/1-1/31 & 9/1-11/30 | 1P: $35-$65 | 2P: $35-$65 | XP: $10 | F12 |

Motel **Location:** On SR A1A, 5 mi s of jct US 92. 3247 S Atlantic Ave 32118. Fax: 386/304-3079. **Facility:** 50 one-bedroom standard units, some with efficiencies. 3 stories, exterior corridors. **Parking:** on-site. **Terms:** 30 day cancellation notice-fee imposed, weekly rates available, small pets only ($15 fee, in designated units). **Amenities:** hair dryers. **Pool(s):** heated outdoor. **Leisure Activities:** sun deck, shuffleboard. **Guest Services:** coin laundry. **Business Services:** fax (fee). **Cards:** AX, DS, MC, VI. *(See color ad below)*

SOME UNITS

ATLANTIC WAVES MOTEL
  Phone: 386/253-7186 **86**

	2/6-5/1	1P: $55-$175	2P: $65-$185	XP: $10	F
	5/2-8/31	1P: $35-$155	2P: $45-$165	XP: $10	F
Motel	9/1-11/30	1P: $35-$100	2P: $45-$110	XP: $10	F
	12/1-2/5	1P: $35-$65	2P: $45-$75	XP: $10	F

Location: On SR A1A, 1.5 mi s of jct US 92. 1925 S Atlantic Ave 32118. Fax: 386/252-3779. **Facility:** 22 one-bedroom standard units, some with efficiencies. 2 stories, exterior corridors. **Parking:** on-site. **Terms:** 60 day cancellation notice, weekly rates available. **Amenities:** safes (fee). **Pool(s):** heated outdoor. **Guest Services:** coin laundry. **Business Services:** fax. **Cards:** AX, DS, MC, VI.

BAHAMA HOUSE
AAA **SAVE** Phone: (386)248-2001 **81**

	12/1-4/26 [ECP]	1P: $136-$189	2P: $136-$189	XP: $10	F18
	5/30-8/16 [ECP]	1P: $174	2P: $174	XP: $10	F18
	4/27-5/29 & 8/17-11/30 [ECP]	1P: $136	2P: $136	XP: $10	F18

Small-scale Hotel **Location:** SR A1A, 1.5 mi s of jct US 92. 2001 S Atlantic Ave 32118. Fax: 386/248-0991. **Facility:** 95 units. 93 one-bedroom standard units, some with efficiencies. 2 one-bedroom suites with efficiencies. 10 stories, interior corridors. **Parking:** on-site. **Terms:** 7 day cancellation notice. **Amenities:** voice mail, safes, irons, hair dryers. **Pool(s):** heated outdoor. **Leisure Activities:** whirlpool, recreation programs. **Guest Services:** complimentary evening beverages, coin laundry. **Business Services:** fax (fee). **Cards:** AX, DC, DS, MC, VI. **Special Amenities:** free continental breakfast and free newspaper. *(See color ad p 297)*

SOME UNITS

(See map p. 279)

BEACH HOUSE OCEANFRONT MOTEL

Motel

All Year | 1P: $48 | 2P: $79 | XP: $10
Phone: (386)788-7107 [112]

Location: On SR A1A, 0.5 mi n of Port Orange Bridge. 3221 S Atlantic Ave 32118. Fax: 386/760-3672. **Facility:** 14 one-bedroom standard units, some with efficiencies. 1 story, exterior corridors. *Bath:* combo or shower only. **Parking:** on-site. **Terms:** 30 day cancellation notice-fee imposed, weekly rates available. **Amenities:** irons, hair dryers. **Pool(s):** heated outdoor. **Leisure Activities:** whirlpool. **Guest Services:** coin laundry. **Cards:** AX, DS, MC, VI. **Special Amenities:** free local telephone calls and free newspaper.

SOME UNITS

(See map p. 279)

BEACHSIDE MOTEL
Phone: (386)788-5569 110

1/31-8/31 [ECP]	1P: $119-$139	2P: $119-$139
12/1-1/30 [ECP]	1P: $79-$109	2P: $79-$109
9/1-11/30 [ECP]	1P: $79-$99	2P: $79-$99

Location: On SR A1A, 5.3 mi s of US 92, 0.3 mi n of Port Orange Bridge. 3309 S Atlantic Ave 32118. **Small-scale Hotel** Fax: 386/271-0000. **Facility:** Smoke free premises. 31 one-bedroom standard units with efficiencies. 5 stories, interior corridors. **Parking:** on-site. **Terms:** 10 day cancellation notice, weekly rates available, package plans. **Pool(s):** heated outdoor. **Leisure Activities:** whirlpool. *Fee:* game room. **Guest Services:** valet and coin laundry. **Business Services:** meeting rooms, fax (fee). **Cards:** AX, CB, DC, DS, MC, VI. **Special Amenities:** early check-in/late check-out and free continental breakfast. *(See color ad p 297)*

BEST WESTERN-AKU TIKI INN
Phone: (386)252-9631 102

4/14-8/15	1P: $95-$210	2P: $95-$210	XP: $10	F12
3/11-4/13	1P: $70-$210	2P: $70-$210	XP: $10	F12
12/1-3/10	1P: $60-$210	2P: $60-$210	XP: $10	F12
8/16-11/30	1P: $60-$150	2P: $60-$150	XP: $10	F12

Small-scale Hotel Location: On SR A1A, 2.2 mi s of jct US 92. 2225 S Atlantic Ave 32118. Fax: 386/252-1198. **Facility:** 132 one-bedroom standard units, some with efficiencies. 5 stories, interior corridors. **Parking:** on-site. **Terms:** 7 day cancellation notice. **Amenities:** voice mail, irons, hair dryers. **Dining:** 7 am-10 pm, cocktails. **Pool(s):** heated outdoor, wading. **Leisure Activities:** shuffleboard. *Fee:* game room. **Guest Services:** gift shop, coin laundry. **Cards:** AX, CB, DC, DS, MC, VI. *(See color ad below)*

SOME UNITS

COLONIAL PALMS INN OCEANFRONT
Phone: (386)767-9261 120

12/21-4/26 & 5/23-8/16	1P: $79-$105	2P: $79-$105	XP: $10	F16
4/27-5/22 & 8/17-11/30	1P: $65-$86	2P: $65-$86	XP: $10	F16

Location: I-95, exit Port Orange, 6 mi e to Atlantic Ave, then 0.8 mi s. 3801 S Atlantic Ave 32118. Fax: 386/767-0390. **Motel** **Facility:** 13 one-bedroom standard units, some with efficiencies. 1 story, exterior corridors. *Bath:* shower only. **Parking:** on-site. **Terms:** open 12/21-11/30, 14 day cancellation notice-fee imposed. **Amenities:** voice mail. **Pool(s):** heated outdoor. **Leisure Activities:** whirlpool, bicycles, shuffleboard. **Guest Services:** coin laundry. **Business Services:** fax. **Cards:** DS, MC, VI. **Special Amenities:** free newspaper and free room upgrade (subject to availability with advanced reservations).

(See map p. 279)

DAYS INN OCEANFRONT SOUTH TROPICAL SEAS

AAA **SAVE**

◆◆ ◆◆

Small-scale Hotel

All Year   1P: $49-$129   2P: $49-$129   XP: $10

Phone: (386)767-8737   **115**

F16

Location: On SR A1A, just n of Port Orange Bridge, 5.8 mi s of US 92. 3357 S Atlantic Ave 32118. Fax: 386/756-9612. **Facility:** 75 one-bedroom standard units, some with efficiencies. 7 stories, interior corridors. **Parking:** on-site. **Amenities:** hair dryers. **Pool(s):** heated outdoor. **Leisure Activities:** whirlpool, shuffleboard. *Fee:* game room. **Guest Services:** coin laundry. **Business Services:** fax. **Cards:** AX, CB, DC, DS, MC, VI. **Special Amenities:** free newspaper.

SOME UNITS

⎙ ⎙ ⎙ ⎙ ⎙ ⎙ / ⎙ ⎙ /

(See map p. 279)

DAYTONA SURFSIDE INN & SUITES   Phone: (386)788-1000   [106]

AAA [SAVE]   3/1-8/9   1P: $119-$149   2P: $119-$149   XP: $10   F17
             8/10-11/30   1P: $79-$109   2P: $79-$109   F17
▼▼▼▼▼ 12/1-2/28   1P: $79-$109   2P: $79-$109   XP: $10   F17

Location: On SR A1A, 4.5 mi s of jct US 92. 3125 S Atlantic Ave 32118. Fax: 386/756-9906. **Facility:** 118 units. 112
Small-scale Hotel one-bedroom standard units, some with efficiencies or kitchens. 6 two-bedroom suites ($129-$319) with efficiencies. 7 stories, exterior corridors. *Bath:* combo or shower only. **Parking:** on-site. **Terms:** 3 day cancellation notice-fee imposed, [BP], [CP] & [MAP] meal plans available. **Amenities:** high-speed Internet, voice mail, safes, irons, hair
dryers. **Dining:** 7 am-1 & 5-9 pm, cocktails, entertainment. **Pool(s):** heated outdoor, wading. **Leisure Activities:** whirlpool, exercise room, game room. **Guest Services:** gift shop, valet and coin laundry. **Business Services:** meeting rooms, fax (fee).
Cards: AX, CB, DC, DS, MC, VI. **Special Amenities:** free local telephone calls and free newspaper. *(See color ad p 299)*

SOME UNITS
[S▲] [¶] [Y] [&M] [E▲] [≈] [X] [DATA PORT] / [X] [🛏] [📺] [💻] /

DREAM INN   Phone: (386)767-2821   [114]

AAA [SAVE]   All Year   1P: $79-$189   2P: $79-$189   XP: $15
             Location: On SR A1A, 0.5 mi n of Port Orange Bridge. 3217 S Atlantic Ave 32118. Fax: 386/767-7778. **Facility:** 26
▼▼ one-bedroom standard units, some with efficiencies and/or whirlpools. 2 stories, exterior corridors. *Bath:*
Motel combo or shower only. **Parking:** on-site. **Terms:** 30 day cancellation notice-fee imposed. **Amenities:** voice
mail, safes, hair dryers. **Pool(s):** heated outdoor. **Leisure Activities:** shuffleboard. *Fee:* boogie boards,
beach chairs. **Guest Services:** coin laundry. **Cards:** AX, DS, MC, VI.

SOME UNITS
[S▲] [¶+] [≈] [DATA PORT] [🛏] [📺] [💻] / [X] /

FLAMINGO INN   Phone: (386)252-1412   [84]

AAA [SAVE]   2/1-4/21   1P: $199-$398   2P: $199-$398   XP: $30   F12
             6/1-9/6   1P: $89-$198   2P: $89-$198   XP: $20   F12
▼▼ 1/1-1/31 & 4/22-5/31   1P: $69-$149   2P: $69-$149   XP: $20   F12
             Location: SR A1A, 1.8 mi s of jct US 92. 2011 S Atlantic Ave 32118. Fax: 386/252-1412. **Facility:** 27 one-bedroom
Small-scale Hotel standard units, some with efficiencies. 3 stories (no elevator), exterior corridors. **Parking:** on-site.
Terms: open 1/1-9/6, 30 day cancellation notice-fee imposed. **Amenities:** safes (fee), hair dryers. **Pool(s):**
heated outdoor. **Leisure Activities:** volleyball. **Guest Services:** coin laundry. **Business Services:** fax (fee). **Cards:** MC, VI.

SOME UNITS
[S▲] [¶+] [≈] [🛏] / [📺] [💻] /

(See map p. 279)

HAMPTON INN OCEANFRONT

Phone: (386)767-8533

1/30-3/10 [ECP]	1P: $114-$289	2P: $124-$299	
3/11-8/16 [ECP]	1P: $124-$259	2P: $134-$269	
8/17-11/30 [ECP]	1P: $74-$164	2P: $84-$189	
12/1-1/29 [ECP]	1P: $74-$114	2P: $84-$124	

Small-scale Hotel **Location:** On SR A1A; 4.5 mi s of jct US 92. 3135 S Atlantic Ave 32118. Fax: 386/788-1609. **Facility:** 114 one-bedroom standard units. 8 stories, interior/exterior corridors. *Bath:* combo or shower only. **Parking:** on-site. **Terms:** check-in 4 pm, 3 day cancellation notice. **Amenities:** voice mail, irons, hair dryers. **Pool(s):** heated outdoor. **Leisure Activities:** whirlpool, volleyball. **Guest Services:** valet and coin laundry. **Business Services:** fax (fee). **Cards:** AX, CB, DC, DS, MC, VI. **Special Amenities:** free continental breakfast and free local telephone calls. *(See color ad p 300)*

SOME UNITS

HAWAIIAN INN

Phone: (386)255-5411

2/1-8/15	1P: $69-$129	2P: $69-$129	XP: $10 F17
8/16-11/30	1P: $69-$119	2P: $69-$119	XP: $10 F17
12/1-1/31	1P: $69-$109	2P: $69-$109	XP: $10 F17

Condominium **Location:** On SR A1A, 2.3 mi s of jct US 92. 2301 S Atlantic Ave 32118. Fax: 386/253-1209. **Facility:** Designated smoking area. 208 units. 167 one-bedroom standard units with efficiencies. 38 one- and 3 two-bedroom suites ($89-$239) with kitchens. 5 stories, interior/exterior corridors. *Bath:* combo or shower only. **Parking:** on-site. **Terms:** 3 day cancellation notice, weekly rates available. **Amenities:** *Some:* hair dryers. **Dining:** 7 am-2 & 5-10 pm, cocktails, entertainment. **Pool(s):** heated outdoor, heated indoor, wading. **Leisure Activities:** miniature golf, shuffleboard. **Guest Services:** gift shop, valet and coin laundry. **Business Services:** meeting rooms, fax (fee). **Cards:** AX, CB, DC, DS, MC, VI. *(See color ad below)*

SOME UNITS

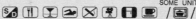

(See map p. 279)

HILTON DAYTONA BEACH OCEANFRONT RESORT

Phone: (386)767-7350 **99**

AAA SAVE

1/30-8/16	1P: $149-$399	2P: $149-$399	XP: $15 F18
8/17-11/30	1P: $99-$329	2P: $99-$329	XP: $15 F18
12/1-1/29	1P: $99-$169	2P: $99-$169	XP: $15 F18

Location: On SR A1A, 3.2 mi s of jct US 92. 2637 S Atlantic Ave 32118. Fax: 386/760-3651. **Facility:** 214 one-
Large-scale Hotel bedroom standard units, some with whirlpools. 11 stories, interior corridors. *Bath:* combo or shower only.
Parking: on-site. **Terms:** 3 day cancellation notice-fee imposed. **Amenities:** dual phone lines, voice mail,
safes (fee), irons, hair dryers. **Dining:** 7 am-10 pm, Fri & Sat-11 pm, cocktails. **Pool(s):** heated outdoor, wading. **Leisure Activi-
ties:** whirlpool, tennis privileges, exercise room. *Fee:* massage, game room. **Guest Services:** gift shop, valet and coin laundry.
Business Services: meeting rooms, fax. **Cards:** AX, CB, DC, DS, JC, MC, VI. **Special Amenities:** free newspaper.
(See color ad p 301)

SOME UNITS

HOLIDAY INN DAYTONA BEACH SHORES

Phone: (386)761-2050 **109**

AAA SAVE

12/1-3/31 & 6/6-9/4	1P: $89-$129	2P: $89-$129	XP: $10 F
4/1-6/5 & 9/5-11/30	1P: $79-$119	2P: $79-$119	XP: $10 F

Location: On SR A1A, 5 mi s of jct US 92. 3209 S Atlantic Ave 32118. Fax: 386/761-3922. **Facility:** 193 units. 190
one-bedroom standard units. 3 one-bedroom suites. 8 stories, interior corridors. **Parking:** on-site. **Terms:** 30
Small-scale Hotel day cancellation notice, weekly rates available. **Amenities:** safes (fee), irons, hair dryers. **Dining:** 7 am-11
& 5:30-8:30 pm seasonally, cocktails. **Pool(s):** heated outdoor, wading. **Leisure Activities:** exercise room.
Fee: game room. **Guest Services:** gift shop, valet and coin laundry. **Business Services:** meeting rooms, fax. **Cards:** AX, CB,
DC, DS, JC, MC, VI. **Special Amenities: free newspaper and free room upgrade (subject to availability with advanced
reservations).** *(See color ad opposite inside back cover & p 291)*

SOME UNITS

KEY WEST VILLAGE

Phone: (386)255-5394 **89**

AAA SAVE

2/13-8/31	1P: $89-$149	2P: $89-$149	XP: $15 F12
12/1-2/12 & 9/1-11/30	1P: $59-$119	2P: $59-$119	XP: $15 F12

Location: On SR A1A, 1 mi s from jct US 92, then n. 1901 S Atlantic Ave 32118. Fax: 386/258-7327. **Facility:** 19
units. 3 one-bedroom standard units. 16 one-bedroom suites with kitchens. 2 stories, exterior corridors.
Motel **Parking:** on-site. **Terms:** 30 day cancellation notice-fee imposed. **Amenities:** hair dryers. **Pool(s):** heated
outdoor. **Guest Services:** coin laundry. **Business Services:** fax (fee). **Cards:** CB, DC, DS, MC, VI.
(See color ad below)

SOME UNITS

OLD SALTY'S INN

Phone: 386-252-8090 **83**

AAA SAVE

All Year [ECP]		2P: $56-$99	XP: $30 F12

Location: On SR A1A, 1.4 mi s of US 92. 1921 S Atlantic Ave 32118. Fax: 386/947-9980. **Facility:** 18 units. 16
one-bedroom standard units, some with kitchens. 2 one-bedroom suites ($99-$150) with kitchens. 2 stories,
Motel exterior corridors. *Bath:* some combo or shower only. **Parking:** on-site. **Terms:** 30 day cancellation notice-fee
imposed, weekly rates available. **Amenities:** hair dryers. **Pool(s):** heated outdoor. **Leisure Activities:** beach
bikes, sun deck, barbecue grills. **Guest Services:** coin laundry. **Business Services:** fax. **Cards:** AX, CB,
DC, DS, JC, MC, VI. *(See color ad p 294)*

SOME UNITS

PALM PLAZA OCEANFRONT RESORT

Phone: (386)767-1711 **111**

AAA SAVE

1/31-8/31 [ECP]	1P: $119-$149	2P: $119-$149	
12/1-1/30 & 9/1-11/30 [ECP]	1P: $79-$109	2P: $79-$109	

Location: On SR A1A, 5.3 mi s of US 92, 0.3 mi n of Port Orange Bridge. 3301 S Atlantic Ave 32118-6308.
Fax: 386/756-8394. **Facility:** 98 units. 88 one-bedroom standard units with efficiencies. 10 one-bedroom
Small-scale Hotel suites ($109-$259) with efficiencies. 12 stories, exterior corridors. **Parking:** on-site. **Terms:** 10 day cancellation notice, weekly rates available, package plans. **Amenities:** safes (fee). **Pool(s):** heated outdoor, wading.
Leisure Activities: whirlpool. *Fee:* game room. **Guest Services:** valet and coin laundry. **Business Services:** meeting rooms,
fax (fee). **Cards:** AX, CB, DC, DS, MC, VI. **Special Amenities: early check-in/late check-out and free continental breakfast.** *(See color ad p 303)*

SOME UNITS

Unique tropical newly renovated suites directly on the ocean with lush garden & heated pool.
Call Toll Free   1 (800) 207-5420   www.daytonabeachsuites.com

(See map p. 279)

PELICAN SHOALS MOTEL & COTTAGES

AAA SAVE

▼▼▼ ▼▼▼

Motel

Phone: (386)253-7962   [93]

2/2-8/4	1P: $41-$120		2P: $41-$120	XP: $10	F18
12/1-2/1 & 8/5-9/2	1P: $31-$90		2P: $31-$90	XP: $10	F18
9/3-11/30	1P: $30-$70		2P: $30-$70	XP: $10	F18

Location: On SR A1A, 2.5 mi s of US 92. 2407 S Atlantic Ave 32118. Fax: 386/258-0973. **Facility:** 24 units. 19 one-bedroom standard units, some with efficiencies and/or whirlpools. 5 cottages ($49-$110). 1-2 stories, exterior corridors. *Bath:* combo or shower only. **Parking:** on-site. **Terms:** 21 day cancellation notice-fee imposed. **Amenities:** *Some:* CD players. **Pool(s):** heated outdoor. **Leisure Activities:** barbecue grills, basketball, shuffleboard. **Guest Services:** coin laundry. **Business Services:** fax. **Cards:** AX, MC, VI. **Special Amenities:** free newspaper.

SOME UNITS

[S_D] [📶] [🏊] [✕] [🎬] [🔲] [💻] / [VCR] [📷] /

(See map p. 279)

PERRY'S OCEAN-EDGE RESORT   Phone: (386)255-0581   91

12/1-8/17	1P: $61-$144	2P: $61-$144	XP: $15 F17
8/18-11/30	1P: $63-$108	2P: $63-$108	XP: $15 F17

Location: On SR A1A, 2 mi s of jct US 92. 2209 S Atlantic Ave 32118. **Fax:** 386/258-7315. **Facility:** 204 one-bedroom standard units, some with kitchens. 2-6 stories, interior/exterior corridors. **Parking:** on-site.
Small-scale Hotel Terms: check-in 4 pm, 3 day cancellation notice, [CP] meal plan available. **Amenities:** voice mail. *Fee:* video library, safes. *Some:* hair dryers. **Dining:** 7 am-2 pm. **Pool(s):** 2 outdoor, heated indoor, wading. **Leisure Activities:** whirlpool, putting green, recreation programs, bocci, lawn games, tetherball, playground, exercise room, basketball, horseshoes, shuffleboard, volleyball, game room. **Guest Services:** gift shop, valet and coin laundry. **Business Services:** meeting rooms, PC, fax (fee), **Cards:** AX, CB, DC, DS, MC, VI. Affiliated with Best Value Inn Brand Membership.
(See color ad below)

SOME UNITS

Welcome Home.

We treat our guests like family.

Spacious ocean front accommodations. Tropical indoor garden with heated pool and spa.
Complimentary homemade donuts and coffee served each morning.
Two outdoor pools surrounded by lush green lawns.
Shuffleboard. Putting green. Volleyball. Children's play area.
Customized golf packages.

2209 South Atlantic Avenue • Daytona Beach, Florida 32118
(386) 255-0581 or Toll Free 1-800-447-0002 (USA & Canada)
internet: perrysoceanedge.com   Rated since 1980

Perry's OCEAN-EDGE RESORT DAYTONA BEACH

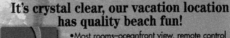

(See map p. 279)

QUALITY INN OCEAN PALMS

Phone: (386)255-0476 **100**

2/1-8/31 [ECP]	1P: $85-$175	2P: $85-$175	XP: $10	F18
9/1-11/30 [ECP]	1P: $75-$145	2P: $75-$145	XP: $10	F18
12/1-1/31 [ECP]	1P: $65-$120	2P: $65-$120	XP: $10	F18

Location: On SR A1A, 2.5 mi s of jct US 92. 2323 S Atlantic Ave 32118. Fax: 386/255-3376. **Facility:** 110 one-bedroom standard units, some with efficiencies or kitchens. 6 stories, exterior corridors. **Bath:** combo or shower only. **Parking:** on-site. **Terms:** package plans, small pets only ($10 extra charge). **Amenities:** voice mail, irons, hair dryers. **Pool(s):** heated outdoor, wading. **Leisure Activities:** Fee: game room. **Guest Services:** valet and coin laundry. **Business Services:** meeting rooms, fax (fee). **Cards:** AX, CB, DC, DS, MC, VI. **Special Amenities:** free continental breakfast and free local telephone calls. *(See color ad p 304)*

Small-scale Hotel

SOME UNITS

SEAGARDEN RESORT

Phone: (386)761-2335 **107**

6/11-9/1	1P: $85-$95	2P: $85-$95	XP: $10	F15
12/1-6/10 & 9/2-11/30	1P: $70-$85	2P: $70-$85	XP: $10	F15

Location: On SR A1A, 5 mi s of jct US 92. 3161 S Atlantic Ave 32118. Fax: 386/756-6676. **Facility:** 144 one-bedroom standard units, some with efficiencies. 10 stories, interior/exterior corridors. **Parking:** on-site. **Terms:** 2-7 night minimum stay - seasonal, 7 day cancellation notice. **Amenities:** safes (fee). **Pool(s):** heated outdoor, heated indoor, wading. **Leisure Activities:** whirlpool, exercise room. **Guest Services:** coin laundry. **Business Services:** meeting rooms, fax. **Cards:** AX, CB, DC, DS, MC, VI. **Special Amenities:** free continental breakfast. *(See color ad below)*

Small-scale Hotel

SOME UNITS

(See map p. 279)

SHORELINE ALL SUITES INN
AAA SAVE

Phone: (386)252-1692 **96**

	4/27-9/1 [CP]	2P: $69-$159	XP: $10	F12
	1/31-4/26 [CP]	2P: $79-$149	XP: $10	F12
	12/1-1/30 & 9/2-11/30 [CP]	2P: $59-$109	XP: $10	F12

Location: On SR A1A, 2.8 mi s of jct US 92. 2435 S Atlantic Ave 32118. Fax: 386/322-7068. **Facility:** 17 units. 13 **Small-scale Hotel** one- and 4 two-bedroom suites with kitchens. 1-2 stories, exterior corridors. *Bath:* combo or shower only. **Parking:** on-site. **Terms:** 30 day cancellation notice, package plans - weekends. **Amenities:** video library. **Pool(s):** heated outdoor. **Leisure Activities:** sun deck, barbecue grills, shuffleboard, volleyball. **Guest Services:** coin laundry. **Business Services:** fax. **Cards:** AX, DS, MC, VI. **Special Amenities:** early check-in/late check-out and free room upgrade (subject to availability with advanced reservations). *(See color ad starting on p 285)*

SOME UNITS
[icons]

SUN VIKING LODGE
AAA SAVE

Phone: (386)252-6252 **95**

	2/7-8/16	1P: $79-$299	2P: $79-$299	XP: $15	F17
	8/17-11/30	1P: $69-$179	2P: $69-$179	XP: $10	F17
	12/1-2/6	1P: $69-$169	2P: $69-$169	XP: $10	F17

Location: On SR A1A, 2.5 mi s of jct US 92. 2411 S Atlantic Ave 32118. Fax: 386/252-5463. **Facility:** 91 units. 69 **Small-scale Hotel** one-bedroom standard units, some with efficiencies. 22 one-bedroom suites ($99-$399) with kitchens. 2-8 stories, interior/exterior corridors. **Parking:** on-site. **Terms:** check-in 5 pm, 7 day cancellation notice. **Amenities:** *Fee:* video library, safes. **Dining:** 7:30 am-2:30 pm. **Pool(s):** heated outdoor, heated indoor, wading. **Leisure Activities:** sauna, whirlpool, waterslide, beach volleyball, recreation programs, playground, exercise room, basketball, shuffleboard. *Fee:* game room. **Guest Services:** coin laundry. **Business Services:** meeting rooms, fax (fee). **Cards:** AX, CB, DC, DS, MC, VI. **Special Amenities:** free newspaper. *(See color ad starting on p 285)*

SOME UNITS
[icons] FEE

SUPER 8 DAYTONA SANDS
AAA SAVE

Phone: (386)767-2551 **98**

| | All Year | 1P: $42-$89 | 2P: $49-$99 | XP: $6 | F12 |

Location: On SR A1A, 2.8 mi s of jct US 92. 2523 S Atlantic Ave 32118 (1300 N Ponce de Leon Blvd, ST. AUGUSTINE, 32084). Fax: 386/322-4847. **Facility:** 40 one-bedroom standard units, some with efficiencies. 3 stories (no el-**Motel** evator), exterior corridors. **Parking:** on-site. **Terms:** cancellation fee imposed. **Amenities:** safes (fee). **Pool(s):** outdoor. **Business Services:** fax. **Cards:** AX, DC, DS, MC, VI.

SOME UNITS
[icons]

TREASURE ISLAND RESORT
AAA SAVE

Phone: (386)255-8371 **87**

	1/16-4/13	1P: $149-$279	2P: $149-$279	XP: $10	F17
	4/14-8/16	1P: $89-$249	2P: $89-$249	XP: $10	F17
	12/1-1/15	1P: $79-$149	2P: $79-$149	XP: $10	F17
	8/17-11/30	1P: $69-$149	2P: $69-$149	XP: $10	F17

Large-scale Hotel **Location:** On SR A1A, 1.8 mi s of jct US 92. 2025 S Atlantic Ave 32118. Fax: 386/255-4984. **Facility:** 232 units. 228 one-bedroom standard units, some with efficiencies. 4 one-bedroom suites with kitchens. 11 stories, interior/exterior corridors. **Parking:** on-site. **Terms:** check-in 4 pm, 7 day cancellation notice-fee imposed. **Amenities:** voice mail, safes (fee), irons, hair dryers. **Dining:** 7 am-2 & 5-9:30 pm, cocktails, entertainment. **Pool(s):** outdoor, heated outdoor, wading. **Leisure Activities:** whirlpools, recreation programs, exercise room privileges. *Fee:* game room. **Guest Services:** gift shop, valet and coin laundry. **Business Services:** meeting rooms, fax. **Cards:** AX, CB, DC, DS, MC, VI. *(See color ad p 284)*

SOME UNITS
[icons]

TROPICAL MANOR MOTEL
AAA SAVE

Phone: 386/252-4920 **103**

| | 2/1-8/31 | 2P: $70-$125 | XP: $7 |
| | 12/1-1/31 & 9/1-11/30 | 2P: $55-$105 | XP: $7 |

Location: On SR A1A, 2.2 mi s of jct US 92. 2237 S Atlantic Ave 32118. Fax: 386/258-9415. **Facility:** 36 units. 16 one-bedroom standard units, some with efficiencies. 20 one-bedroom suites with kitchens. 1-2 stories, ex-**Motel** terior corridors. *Bath:* combo or shower only. **Parking:** on-site. **Terms:** 14 day cancellation notice, weekly rates available. **Pool(s):** heated outdoor, wading. **Leisure Activities:** pavillion with grill, shuffleboard. **Guest Services:** coin laundry. **Business Services:** fax. **Cards:** AX, CB, DC, DS, MC, VI. *(See color ad p 305)*

SOME UNITS
[icons]

—— **WHERE TO DINE** ——

BOONDOCKS
Seafood

Lunch: $5-$15 Dinner: $5-$15 Phone: 386/760-9001 **25**

Location: 1.3 mi s of Dunlawton Ave. 3948 S Peninsula Dr 32127. **Hours:** 11 am-10 pm. **Features:** Near a marina on the Halifax River, the restaurant offers casual outdoor dining and good views. Fresh seafood stands out on a menu that also includes tasty burgers, chowders and salads. The spot is a favorite with locals and tourists alike. Casual dress; cocktails. **Parking:** on-site. **Cards:** DS, MC, VI.

[icons]

CHINA-AMERICAN GARDEN
AAA
Chinese

Lunch: $4-$5 Dinner: $7-$14 Phone: 386/788-6269 **24**

Location: On SR A1A, 2.8 mi s of jct US 92; in Pappas Plaza Shopping Center. 2516 S Atlantic Ave 32118. **Hours:** 11:30 am-2 & 5-10 pm, Fri-11 pm, Sat 4 pm-11 pm, Sun 5 pm-10 pm. Closed: 12/1-12/25. **Reservations:** accepted. **Features:** The hot and sour soup rates high on the list of favorites. This is casual family dining specializing in Cantonese with some Szechuan and Mandarin dishes. Thai cuisine is also served. Casual dress; cocktails. **Parking:** on-site. **Cards:** AX, MC, VI.

[icons]

DEBARY pop. 15,559

------ WHERE TO STAY ------

HAMPTON INN DEBARY/DELTONA **Phone:** (386)668-5758
SAVE
Small-scale Hotel
All Year [ECP]   1P: $79-$89   2P: $89-$99
Location: I-4, exit 108, just nw. 308 Sunrise Blvd 32713. Fax: 386/668-1284. **Facility:** 76 one-bedroom standard units, some with whirlpools. 3 stories, interior corridors. *Bath:* combo or shower only. **Parking:** on-site. **Terms:** 30 day cancellation notice. **Amenities:** voice mail, irons, hair dryers. **Pool(s):** outdoor. **Leisure Activities:** whirlpool, exercise room. **Guest Services:** coin laundry. **Business Services:** fax (fee). **Cards:** AX, DC, DS, MC, VI.

SOME UNITS

DEERFIELD BEACH —*See Fort Lauderdale p. 392.*

DE FUNIAK SPRINGS pop. 5,089

------ WHERE TO STAY ------

BEST WESTERN CROSSROADS INN **Phone:** (850)892-5111
SAVE
Small-scale Hotel
All Year [ECP]   1P: $50-$79   2P: $59-$79   XP: $5   F17
Location: I-10, exit 85, just s. Located in a rural, quiet area. 2343 Freeport Rd 32435 (PO Box 852). Fax: 850/892-2439. **Facility:** 100 one-bedroom standard units. 2 stories, interior/exterior corridors. **Parking:** on-site. **Terms:** [BP] meal plan available. **Amenities:** irons, hair dryers. **Pool(s):** outdoor. **Business Services:** meeting rooms, fax (fee). **Cards:** AX, CB, DC, DS, JC, MC, VI.

SOME UNITS

DAYS INN **Phone:** (850)892-6115
AAA SAVE
Small-scale Hotel
2/16-6/30   1P: $55   2P: $75
7/1-11/30   1P: $50   2P: $65
12/1-2/15   1P: $50   2P: $55   XP: $5   F16
Location: I-10, exit 85, just n. 472 Hugh Adams Rd 32433. Fax: 850/892-0707. **Facility:** 58 one-bedroom standard units. 1 story, exterior corridors. **Parking:** on-site. **Terms:** 7 day cancellation notice, weekly rates available, pets ($10 extra charge). **Amenities:** hair dryers. **Pool(s):** outdoor. **Business Services:** fax. **Cards:** AX, DC, DS, MC, VI. **Special Amenities:** free continental breakfast and free local telephone calls.

SOME UNITS

HOTEL DE FUNIAK-CHAUTAUQUA DINING ROOM **Phone:** (850)892-4383
Small-scale Hotel
All Year   1P: $70-$90   2P: $80-$100   F6
Location: On US 90; center. 400 E Nelson 32433. Fax: 850/892-5346. **Facility:** Smoke free premises. 11 units. 9 one-bedroom standard units. 2 one-bedroom suites ($90-$100). 2 stories, interior/exterior corridors. *Bath:* combo or shower only. **Parking:** street. **Terms:** cancellation fee imposed, weekly rates available, [BP] meal plan available, package plans. **Business Services:** meeting rooms, fax. **Cards:** AX, DS, MC, VI.

ASK

RAMADA LIMITED **Phone:** (850)892-3125
Small-scale Hotel
All Year [ECP]   1P: $45-$65   2P: $55-$75   XP: $8   F18
Location: I-10, exit 85, just n. 90 Business Park Rd 32433. Fax: 850/892-5072. **Facility:** 55 one-bedroom standard units. 1 story, exterior corridors. **Parking:** on-site. **Terms:** weekly rates available. **Amenities:** voice mail. **Business Services:** fax (fee). **Cards:** AX, CB, DC, DS, MC, VI.

SOME UNITS
ASK

DELAND pop. 24,904

------ WHERE TO STAY ------

BEST INN UNIVERSITY **Phone:** (386)734-5711
AAA SAVE
Motel
All Year   1P: $59-$175   2P: $59-$175
Location: US 17, 0.9 mi n of jct SR 44. Located next to Stetson University. 644 N Woodland Blvd 32720. Fax: 386/734-5716. **Facility:** 57 one-bedroom standard units. 2 stories. *Bath:* combo or shower only. **Parking:** on-site. **Terms:** [CP] meal plan available, pets ($10 extra charge). **Pool(s):** outdoor. **Leisure Activities:** limited exercise equipment. **Business Services:** meeting rooms, fax. **Cards:** AX, DC, MC, VI. **Special Amenities:** free continental breakfast and free local telephone calls.

SOME UNITS

COMFORT INN & SUITES **Phone:** (386)736-3100
AAA SAVE
Motel
2/1-4/30 [CP]   1P: $95-$225   2P: $95-$225
12/1-1/31 [CP]   1P: $65-$175   2P: $65-$175
5/1-9/30 [CP]   1P: $65-$150   2P: $65-$150
10/1-11/30 [CP]   1P: $65-$125   2P: $65-$125
Location: 0.5 mi ne on US 92 at jct US 17. 400 E International Speedway Blvd 32724. Fax: 386/740-0570. **Facility:** 68 one-bedroom standard units, some with whirlpools. 3 stories, interior corridors. *Bath:* combo or shower only. **Parking:** on-site. **Amenities:** voice mail, irons, hair dryers. **Pool(s):** outdoor. **Leisure Activities:** whirlpool. **Guest Services:** coin laundry. **Business Services:** meeting rooms, fax (fee). **Cards:** AX, DC, DS, MC, VI. **Special Amenities:** free continental breakfast and free local telephone calls.

SOME UNITS

HOLIDAY INN

(AAA) (SAVE)

▽▽▽▽

Small-scale Hotel

1/1-3/31	1P: $99-$129	2P: $99-$129	XP: $10	F18
12/1-12/31 & 4/1-11/30	1P: $69-$99	2P: $69-$99	XP: $10	F18

Phone: (386)738-5200

Location: 0.3 mi ne on US 92 from jct US 17. 350 E International Speedway Blvd 32724. **Fax:** 386/734-7552. **Facility:** 148 units. 137 one-bedroom standard units. 11 one-bedroom suites. 6 stories, interior corridors. *Bath:* combo or shower only. **Parking:** on-site. **Terms:** check-in 4 pm, cancellation fee imposed, pets ($10 extra charge). **Amenities:** voice mail, irons, hair dryers. **Dining:** 7 am-2 & 5:30-9 pm, cocktails. **Pool(s):** heated outdoor. **Leisure Activities:** whirlpool, exercise room. **Guest Services:** valet and coin laundry. **Business Services:** conference facilities, fax. **Cards:** AX, CB, DC, DS, MC, VI. **Special Amenities:** early check-in/late check-out and free room upgrade (subject to availability with advanced reservations). *(See color ad opposite inside back cover)*

SOME UNITS

🆂 🐕 🍽 🍴 👤 🐬 📷 🖪ᴬᵀᴬ 💻 / ✕ 🗄 📺 /

HONTOON LANDING RESORT & MARINA

(AAA) (SAVE)

▽▽▽▽

Motel

All Year   1P: $75-$195   2P: $75-$195   XP: $10

Phone: (386)734-2474

Location: US 17-92, 2.1 mi w on SR 44, 1.9 mi sw on CR 4110 (Old New York), then 3.4 mi s on CR 4125 (Hontoon Rd). 2317 River Ridge Rd 32720. **Fax:** 386/738-9743. **Facility:** 18 units. 15 one-bedroom standard units, some with kitchens. 2 one- and 1 two-bedroom suites ($135-$195) with kitchens, some with whirlpools. 1-2 stories, exterior corridors. *Bath:* combo or shower only. **Parking:** on-site. **Terms:** 30 day cancellation notice-fee imposed. **Amenities:** voice mail. *Some:* irons. **Pool(s):** outdoor. **Leisure Activities:** rental boats, fishing, gas grills. *Fee:* marina, fishing boats, houseboats, pontoon boats. **Guest Services:** gift shop. **Cards:** DS, MC, VI. **Special Amenities:** free local telephone calls and preferred room (subject to availability with advanced reservations).

SOME UNITS

🐬 ✕ 🗄 / 📼 📺 💻 /

──────── **WHERE TO DINE** ────────

CHRISTO'S & ELENI'S

(AAA)

▽

Italian

Lunch: $5-$7   **Dinner:** $7-$11   **Phone:** 386/734-5705

Location: 0.3 mi w of jct SR 5A and New York Ave. 803 W New York Ave 32720. **Hours:** 11 am-9 pm, Fri-10 pm, Sat from 4 pm. Closed major holidays; also Sun. **Features:** This relaxed family restaurant features homemade pastas, sauces and desserts. Menu choices include veal and seafood dishes. Both the shrimp Rafaelo and the seafood plate give a rich taste of butter and herbs. On Monday nights the owner's wife sings, accompanied by a keyboarder. Casual dress; beer & wine only. **Parking:** on-site. **Cards:** DS, MC, VI.

✕

THE ORIGINAL HOLIDAY HOUSE

▽▽▽

American

Lunch: $9   **Dinner:** $10   **Phone:** 386/734-6319

Location: US 17, 0.8 mi n of jct SR 44. 704 N Woodland Blvd 32720. **Hours:** 11 am-9 pm. Closed: 12/24 for dinner. **Features:** Informal dining in a homey setting features signature items like carved lamb, turkey, roast beef and ham. An excellent selection of homemade desserts like the triple-layer chocolate cake and peach cobbler round out this comfort-food buffet. Casual dress. **Parking:** on-site. **Cards:** DS, MC, VI.

🄼 ✕

PONDO'S

▽▽

American

Dinner: $10-$21   **Phone:** 386/734-1995

Location: 3 mi w on SR 44, just s. 1915 Old New York Ave 32720. **Hours:** 5 pm-9 pm, Fri & Sat-10 pm. Closed: 12/25; also Mon. **Reservations:** suggested. **Features:** This secluded two-story house exudes a country inn ambience. Homemade dressings and herbs plucked from the on-site garden provide for delicious salads. Attentive servers bring well-prepared entrees of seafood, beef, veal, lamb and duck. Casual dress; cocktails. **Parking:** on-site. **Cards:** AX, MC, VI.

🍴 ✕

DE LEON SPRINGS pop. 2,358

──────── **WHERE TO DINE** ────────

KARLING'S INN

▽▽

American

Dinner: $14-$24   **Phone:** 386/985-5535

Location: On US 17, 5 mi n of jct US 92. 4640 N US 17 32130. **Hours:** 5 pm-9 pm. Closed: 12/25; also Sun & Mon. **Reservations:** suggested. **Features:** The simple Tudor-style building, in an out-of-the-way location, is well worth visiting for its attentive service, European country setting and pleasingly presented Continental dishes. The house specialty is duck in a dark bing cherry sauce. Smoke free premises. Casual dress; beer & wine only. **Parking:** on-site. **Cards:** MC, VI.

✕

DELRAY BEACH pop. 60,020

──────── **WHERE TO STAY** ────────

BUDGET INN

(AAA) (SAVE)

▽▽

Motel

12/15-4/15	1P: $79	2P: $89	XP: $10	F12
12/1-12/14 & 4/16-11/30	1P: $49	2P: $59	XP: $10	F12

Phone: 561/276-8961

Location: US 1, 1.8 mi n of jct SR 806 (Atlantic Ave). Located in a quiet area. 2500 N Federal Hwy 33483. **Fax:** 561/276-1455. **Facility:** 17 one-bedroom standard units. 1 story, exterior corridors. *Bath:* shower only. **Parking:** on-site. **Terms:** 3 day cancellation notice-fee imposed. **Pool(s):** outdoor. **Cards:** AX, DS, MC, VI. **Special Amenities:** free local telephone calls.

SOME UNITS

🆂 🍴 🐬 🗄 / ✕ 📺 /

THE COLONY HOTEL & CABANA CLUB

Phone: (561)276-4123

12/1-4/20	1P: $189-$259	2P: $189-$259	XP: $10	F13
4/21-11/30	1P: $99	2P: $189	XP: $10	F13

Location: On SR 806 at jct US 1 northbound; center. 525 E Atlantic Ave 33447. Fax: 561/276-0123. **Facility:** Smoke free premises. 70 units. 49 one- and 21 two-bedroom standard units. 3 stories, interior corridors. *Bath:* combo or shower only. **Parking:** on-site. **Terms:** 3 day cancellation notice-fee imposed, [CP] meal plan available, pets ($20 extra charge). **Amenities:** voice mail, irons, hair dryers. **Dining:** cocktails, entertainment. **Pool(s):** saltwater. **Leisure Activities:** recreation programs, limited exercise equipment. **Guest Services:** gift shop, valet and coin laundry. **Business Services:** meeting rooms, fax (fee). **Cards:** AX, MC, VI. **Special Amenities: free continental breakfast.**

Historic Small-scale Hotel

MARRIOTT DELRAY BEACH

Phone: 561/274-3200

1/1-4/30	1P: $237-$254
5/1-9/30	1P: $135-$161
12/1-12/23 & 10/1-11/30	1P: $161

Location: SR A1A Atlantic Ave. 10 N Ocean Blvd 33483. Fax: 561/274-3202. **Facility:** 268 units. 264 one-bedroom standard units. 4 one-bedroom suites. 6 stories, interior/exterior corridors. *Bath:* combo or shower only. **Parking:** on-site and valet. **Terms:** open 12/1-12/23 & 1/1-11/30, check-in 4 pm, cancellation fee imposed. **Amenities:** high-speed Internet (fee), dual phone lines, voice mail, safes, honor bars, irons, hair dryers. **Pool(s):** heated outdoor. **Leisure Activities:** whirlpool, exercise room. *Fee:* massage. **Guest Services:** gift shop, valet laundry. **Business Services:** meeting rooms, business center. **Cards:** AX, DC, DS, JC, MC, VI.

Small-scale Hotel

PARLIAMENT INN

Phone: (561)276-6245

2/1-3/31	2P: $125-$250	XP: $15	F12
12/1-1/31 & 4/1-4/30	2P: $90-$165	XP: $15	F12
5/1-11/30	2P: $55-$105	XP: $15	F12

Location: I-95, exit 52A (Atlantic Ave/SR 806 E), 1.9 mi e to SR A1A, then w. 1236 George Bush Blvd 33483. Fax: 561/274-3939. **Facility:** 7 units. 2 one-bedroom standard units with efficiencies. 5 one-bedroom suites with kitchens. 1 story, exterior corridors. *Bath:* combo or shower only. **Parking:** on-site. **Terms:** 3 night minimum stay, age restrictions may apply, cancellation fee imposed. **Amenities:** irons. **Pool(s):** heated outdoor. **Guest Services:** coin laundry.

Motel

SEAGATE HOTEL & BEACH CLUB

Phone: (561)276-2421

12/20-4/30	1P: $195-$756	2P: $204-$756	XP: $10	F18
12/1-12/19	1P: $190-$756	2P: $199-$756	XP: $10	F18
5/1-11/30	1P: $104-$338	2P: $114-$338	XP: $10	F18

Location: SR A1A, 0.5 mi s of jct SR 806 (Atlantic Ave). 400 S Ocean Blvd 33483. Fax: 561/243-4714. **Facility:** 70 units. 11 one-bedroom standard units with efficiencies. 51 one-, 7 two- and 1 three-bedroom suites ($104-$756) with kitchens. 2-3 stories, exterior corridors. *Bath:* combo or shower only. **Parking:** on-site. **Terms:** check-in 4 pm, cancellation fee imposed, [MAP] meal plan available, 15% service charge. **Amenities:** video games, voice mail, safes, irons, hair dryers. **Dining:** guests only 11:30 am-2:30 & 6-9:30 pm, cocktails. **Pool(s):** 2 heated outdoor. **Leisure Activities:** rental paddleboats, guided kayak tours. *Fee:* sailboats, windsurfing, water sports. **Guest Services:** coin laundry. **Business Services:** meeting rooms. **Cards:** AX, CB, DC, DS, MC, VI. **Special Amenities: free newspaper and free room upgrade (subject to availability with advanced reservations).**

Small-scale Hotel

WRIGHT BY THE SEA

Phone: (561)278-3355

2/1-3/31	1P: $201-$375	2P: $201-$375	XP: $30
12/1-1/31	1P: $135-$335	2P: $135-$335	XP: $30
4/1-4/30	1P: $160-$320	2P: $160-$320	XP: $30
5/1-11/30	1P: $101-$235	2P: $101-$235	XP: $30

Location: SR A1A, just s of jct Linton Blvd. 1901 S Ocean Blvd 33483. Fax: 561/278-2871. **Facility:** Designated smoking area. 28 units. 4 one-bedroom standard units with kitchens. 22 one- and 2 two-bedroom suites with kitchens. 2 stories (no elevator), exterior corridors. *Bath:* combo or shower only. **Parking:** on-site. **Terms:** 2 night minimum stay - weekends, 14 day cancellation notice-fee imposed, weekly rates available, package plans. **Amenities:** voice mail, irons, hair dryers. *Some:* CD players. **Pool(s):** heated outdoor. **Leisure Activities:** barbecue grills, horseshoes, shuffleboard. **Guest Services:** coin laundry. **Cards:** AX, CB, DC, DS, MC, VI.

Motel

WHERE TO DINE

32 EAST

Dinner: $18-$26

Phone: 561/276-7868

Location: I-95, exit 52A, 1 mi e, just e of Swinton Ave. 32 E Atlantic Ave 33444. **Hours:** 5:30 pm-10 pm, Fri & Sat-11 pm. Closed: 12/25; also 1/2 & Super Bowl Sun. **Reservations:** required. **Features:** Fresh local and regional seafood and produce go into preparations of contemporary American cuisine, complemented by a fantastic wine list. The upbeat atmosphere and comfortable dining room make this restaurant a fun place to eat. Dressy casual; cocktails. **Parking:** valet. **Cards:** AX, DS, MC, VI.

American

PINEAPPLE GRILLE

Lunch: $6-$9   **Dinner:** $12-$25   **Phone:** 561/265-1368

Location: US 1, 0.3 mi e on George Bush Blvd; SR A1A, 0.4 mi w on George Bush Blvd; in the Palm Trail Plaza. 800 Palm Tr 33483. **Hours:** 11:30 am-2:30 & 5:30-11 pm, Sun 9 am-2:30 & 5:30-10 pm. Closed: 4/20, 12/25. **Reservations:** suggested. **Features:** Look no further to taste the cuisine of the islands. The Trinidadian chef reveals his secrets in seafood and meat entrees. Also on the menu are brick-oven pizzas and burgers for the kids. The dining room's atmosphere evokes a beachfront feel. Dressy casual; cocktails; entertainment. **Parking:** on-site. **Cards:** AX, MC, VI.

Caribbean

DELTONA pop. 69,543

──── WHERE TO STAY ────

BEST WESTERN DELTONA INN
Phone: (386)860-3000

AAA SAVE
▼▼▼
Motel

All Year   1P: $59-$99   2P: $69-$109

Location: I-4, exit 108, just ne. 481 Deltona Blvd 32725. Fax: 386/860-2687. **Facility:** 130 units. 129 one-bedroom standard units. 1 one-bedroom suite ($89-$125). 2 stories, exterior corridors. **Parking:** on-site. **Amenities:** voice mail, irons, hair dryers. **Dining:** 6:30 am-2 & 4:30-9:30 pm, cocktails. **Pool(s):** outdoor. **Business Services:** meeting rooms, fax (fee). **Cards:** AX, CB, DC, DS, MC, VI.

SOME UNITS

[S✆] [🍴] [Ⓨ] [🅿] [🏊] [🎞] [DATA PORT] [💻] / [✕] [VCR] [🔌] [🖨] /

DESTIN pop. 11,119

──── WHERE TO STAY ────

BAY CLUB OF SANDESTIN
Phone: (850)837-8866

AAA SAVE
▼▼▼
Condominium

3/1-10/31	1P: $150-$225	2P: $150-$225
11/1-11/30	1P: $100-$195	2P: $100-$195
12/1-2/28	1P: $90-$175	2P: $90-$175

Location: Next to Conference Centre Bayside. 120 N Sandestin Blvd 32550. Fax: 850/654-9188. **Facility:** 44 one-bedroom standard units, some with whirlpools. 6 stories, interior corridors. **Parking:** on-site. **Terms:** 2-3 night minimum stay - weekends, age restrictions may apply, 3 day cancellation notice. **Amenities:** voice mail, irons, hair dryers. **Pool(s):** 4 outdoor, 3 wading. **Leisure Activities:** saunas, whirlpools, rental boats, fishing, recreation programs, jogging. *Fee:* sailboats, marina, waterskiing, charter fishing, jet skis, golf-72 holes, 18 tennis courts (4 lighted), bicycles, massage. **Guest Services:** complimentary laundry. **Business Services:** meeting rooms, PC, fax (fee). **Cards:** AX, DS, MC, VI.

[🍴+] [Ⓨ] [🏊] [🛁] [✕] [VCR] [🎞] [DATA PORT] [🔌] [🖨] [💻]
      FEE

BEACHSIDE INN
Phone: (850)337-8900

▼▼ ▼▼
Small-scale Hotel

5/23-8/7 [CP]	1P: $149	2P: $149
3/1-5/22 [CP]	1P: $119	2P: $119
8/8-11/30 [CP]	1P: $75-$109	2P: $75-$109
12/1-2/28 [CP]	1P: $75	2P: $75

Location: 1 mi s of US 98. 2931 Scenic Hwy 98 32541. Fax: 850/650-9012. **Facility:** 20 one-bedroom standard units. 2 stories, exterior corridors. *Bath:* combo or shower only. **Parking:** on-site. **Terms:** weekly rates available. **Amenities:** voice mail, irons, hair dryers. **Pool(s):** heated outdoor. **Leisure Activities:** whirlpool. **Business Services:** fax. **Cards:** AX, DC, MC, VI.

SOME UNITS

[A$K] [S✆] [🍴] [🖥] [🏊] [DATA PORT] [🔌] [🖨] [💻] / [✕] /

BEST WESTERN SUMMERPLACE INN
Phone: 850/650-8003

AAA SAVE
▼▼ ▼▼▼

6/1-8/15	1P: $109-$199	2P: $109-$199	XP: $10	F17
3/1-5/31	1P: $79-$139	2P: $79-$139	XP: $10	F17
8/16-11/30	1P: $49-$129	2P: $49-$129	XP: $10	F17
12/1-2/28	1P: $49-$89	2P: $49-$89	XP: $10	F17

Small-scale Hotel **Location:** US 98, 2.2 mi e. 14047 Emerald Coast Pkwy 32541. Fax: 850/650-8004. **Facility:** 72 units. 70 one-bedroom standard units, some with whirlpools. 2 one-bedroom suites. 2 stories, interior corridors. *Bath:* combo or shower only. **Parking:** on-site. **Terms:** [ECP] meal plan available. **Amenities:** voice mail, irons, hair dryers. **Pool(s):** small outdoor, heated indoor. **Leisure Activities:** whirlpool, limited exercise equipment. **Guest Services:** valet and coin laundry. **Business Services:** meeting rooms, fax (fee). **Cards:** AX, CB, DC, DS, MC, VI. **Special Amenities:** early check-in/late check-out and free continental breakfast.

SOME UNITS

[🍴+] [🖥] [🏊] [🎞] [DATA PORT] [🔌] [💻] / [✕] [🖨] /

COMFORT INN
Phone: (850)654-8611

SAVE
▼▼ ▼▼▼
Small-scale Hotel

5/26-9/3 [CP]	1P: $109-$189	2P: $109-$189		
3/1-5/25 [CP]	1P: $89-$149	2P: $89-$149		
9/4-11/30 [CP]	1P: $69-$89	2P: $69-$89		
12/1-2/28 [CP]	1P: $69-$89	2P: $69-$89	XP: $10	F18

Location: US 98, 1.9 mi e. 19001 Emerald Coast Pkwy 32541. Fax: 850/654-8815. **Facility:** 100 units. 87 one-bedroom standard units. 13 one-bedroom suites, some with whirlpools. 4 stories, interior corridors. *Bath:* combo or shower only. **Parking:** on-site. **Terms:** check-in 4 pm. **Amenities:** dual phone lines, voice mail, irons, hair dryers. **Pool(s):** outdoor, heated indoor. **Leisure Activities:** exercise room. **Guest Services:** gift shop, valet and coin laundry. **Business Services:** meeting rooms, fax (fee). **Cards:** AX, CB, DC, DS, MC, VI.

SOME UNITS

[S✆] [🍴+] [🖥] [🏊] [🎞] [DATA PORT] [🔌] [🖨] [💻] / [✕] /

COUNTRY INN & SUITES BY CARLSON
Phone: (850)650-9191

▼▼▼ ▼▼
Small-scale Hotel

5/23-9/1	1P: $125-$185
3/1-5/22	1P: $115-$185
9/2-11/30	1P: $89-$185
12/1-2/28	1P: $79-$185

Location: US 98. Located behind the TGIF Restaurant. 4415 Commons Dr E 32541. Fax: 850/654-1802. **Facility:** 83 units. 45 one-bedroom standard units. 38 one-bedroom suites. 3 stories, interior corridors. *Bath:* combo or shower only. **Parking:** on-site. **Terms:** 2-3 night minimum stay - seasonal, cancellation fee imposed, [ECP] meal plan available. **Amenities:** high-speed Internet, voice mail, irons, hair dryers. **Pool(s):** heated outdoor. **Leisure Activities:** whirlpool. **Guest Services:** valet and coin laundry. **Business Services:** meeting rooms, fax. **Cards:** AX, CB, DC, DS, MC, VI. *(See color ad p 613)*

SOME UNITS

[A$K] [S✆] [🍴+] [🖥] [🅿] [🏊] [VCR] [🎞] [DATA PORT] [💻] / [✕] [🔌] [🖨] /

EMBASSY SUITES HOTEL

SAVE ▽▼▽▼▽
Large-scale Hotel

Phone: (850)337-7000

All Year [BP] 1P: $99-$329 2P: $99-$329 XP: $15 F18
Location: 8 mi e of the bridge, just w. 570 Scenic Gulf Dr 32550. Fax: 850/337-7080. **Facility:** 155 one-bedroom standard units, some with whirlpools. 4 stories, interior corridors. *Bath:* combo or shower only. **Parking:** on-site. **Terms:** 3 day cancellation notice, package plans - seasonal. **Amenities:** video games, high-speed Internet, dual phone lines, voice mail, safes, irons, hair dryers. **Pool(s):** heated indoor. **Leisure Activities:** whirlpool, exercise room. **Guest Services:** gift shop, complimentary evening beverages, valet and coin laundry, area transportation. **Business Services:** conference facilities, fax (fee). **Cards:** AX, CB, DC, DS, MC, VI.

SOME UNITS
⬛ 🍽 🍸 🛥 🎥 📠 🔌 📱 🖥 /✕/

HAMPTON INN

SAVE ▽▼▽▼▽
Small-scale Hotel

Phone: 850/654-2677

5/26-9/3 [CP] 1P: $129-$189 2P: $129-$189
3/1-5/25 [CP] 1P: $89-$149 2P: $99-$169
12/1-2/28 & 9/4-11/30 [CP] 1P: $69-$89 2P: $69-$89
Location: US 98, 1 mi e. 1625 Hwy 98 E 32541. Fax: 850/654-0745. **Facility:** 104 units. 89 one-bedroom standard units. 15 one-bedroom suites, some with efficiencies. 2 stories, exterior corridors. *Bath:* combo or shower only. **Parking:** on-site. **Terms:** check-in 4 pm. **Amenities:** voice mail, irons, hair dryers. **Pool(s):** heated outdoor. **Leisure Activities:** whirlpool, sports court. **Guest Services:** valet and coin laundry. **Business Services:** meeting rooms, fax.

SOME UNITS
🍽 🚰 🛥 🎥 🔌 📱 🖥 /✕/

HILTON SANDESTIN BEACH, GOLF RESORT

AAA **SAVE** ▽▼▽▼▽
Resort
Large-scale Hotel

Phone: (850)267-9500

5/16-8/19 1P: $265-$415 2P: $265-$415 XP: $20 F18
3/14-5/15 1P: $220-$375 2P: $220-$375 XP: $20 F18
8/20-11/30 1P: $175-$315 2P: $175-$315 XP: $10 F18
12/1-3/13 1P: $170-$300 2P: $170-$300 XP: $10 F18
Location: 10 mi e at Sandestin. 4000 Sandestin Blvd S 32550. Fax: 850/267-3076. **Facility:** Gulf view. 598 units. 574 one-bedroom standard units. 24 one-bedroom suites ($200-$515), some with whirlpools. 15 stories, interior corridors. *Bath:* combo or shower only. **Terms:** check-in 4 pm, 7 day cancellation notice-fee imposed. **Amenities:** video library (fee), dual phone lines, voice mail, safes, honor bars, irons, hair dryers. *Some:* high-speed Internet. **Dining:** 2 restaurants, 7 am-11 pm, cocktails, also, Seagar's Prime Steaks and Seafood, see separate listing, entertainment. **Pool(s):** 2 heated outdoor, heated indoor, wading. **Leisure Activities:** saunas, whirlpools, recreation programs in season, spa, volleyball. *Fee:* sailboats, marina, scuba diving, snorkeling, charter fishing, kayak, golf-73 holes, 16 tennis courts (2 lighted), bicycles, game room. **Guest Services:** gift shop, valet and coin laundry, area transportation. **Business Services:** conference facilities, business center. **Cards:** AX, CB, DC, DS, MC, VI.

SOME UNITS
⬛ 🍽 24🕐 🍸 🛥 ✕ VCR 🎥 🔌 📱 🖥 /✕/

HOLIDAY INN OF DESTIN

Phone: (850)837-6181

Small-scale Hotel

3/7-9/2	1P: $160-$225	2P: $160-$225
9/3-11/30	1P: $85-$125	2P: $85-$125
12/1-3/6	1P: $80-$120	2P: $80-$120

XP: $10   F18

Location: 2.2 mi e of bridge on US 98. 1020 Hwy 98 E 32541 (PO Box 577). Fax: 850/837-1523. **Facility:** 233 one-bedroom standard units. 9 stories, interior corridors. *Bath:* combo or shower only. **Parking:** on-site. **Terms:** 3 day cancellation notice. **Amenities:** voice mail, safes, irons, hair dryers. **Pool(s):** outdoor, heated indoor, wading. **Leisure Activities:** sauna, whirlpool, recreation programs in season, exercise room. *Fee:* game room. **Guest Services:** gift shop, valet laundry. **Business Services:** meeting rooms, fax (fee). **Cards:** AX, DC, DS, MC, VI. *(See color ad opposite inside back cover)*

SOME UNITS
🆂🅳 🍽 📺 🅶Ⓜ 🎬 🐾 ➡ ✕ 🎥 [DATA PORT] 💻 /✕/

SANDESTIN GOLF AND BEACH RESORT

Phone: (850)267-8000

Resort
Large-scale Hotel

5/23-8/9	1P: $155-$790	2P: $155-$790
2/28-5/22	1P: $125-$510	2P: $125-$510
8/10-11/30	1P: $125-$465	2P: $125-$465
12/1-2/27	1P: $85-$360	2P: $85-$360

Location: 10 mi e on US 98. 9300 Hwy 98 W 32550. Fax: 850/267-8221. **Facility:** The resort borders the golf course and offers conventional hotel units as well as two- and three-bedroom housekeeping villas facing the gulf or bay. 755 one-bedroom standard units, some with whirlpools. 22 stories, interior/exterior corridors. **Parking:** check-in 4 pm, age restrictions may apply, 14 day cancellation notice. **Amenities:** dual phone lines, voice mail, irons. *Some:* hair dryers. **Dining:** Elephant Walk, see separate listing. **Pool(s):** 9 outdoor, 3 heated outdoor, 3 wading. **Leisure Activities:** saunas, whirlpools, rental boats, fishing, recreation programs, bicycles, jogging, playground, spa, basketball. *Fee:* sailboats, marina, charter fishing, golf-72 holes, 20 tennis courts (2 lighted). **Guest Services:** gift shop, valet and coin laundry, area transportation. **Business Services:** conference facilities, fax (fee). **Cards:** AX, CB, DC, DS, MC, VI. *(See color ad p 311)*

SOME UNITS
🅰🆂🅺 🆂🅳 🍽 📺 🎬 🅶 ➡ ➕ ✕ [VCR] [DATA PORT] 🔲 💻 /✕ 🖼/

SLEEP INN

Phone: (850)654-7022

[SAVE]

Small-scale Hotel

5/16-9/7 [CP]	1P: $100	2P: $100
3/1-5/15 [CP]	1P: $90	2P: $90
9/8-11/30 [CP]	1P: $74	2P: $74
12/1-2/28 [CP]	1P: $62	2P: $62

XP: $8   F18
XP: $8   F18
XP: $8   F18
XP: $8   F18

Location: US 98, 8 mi e of bridge. 10775 W Emerald Coast Pkwy 32541. Fax: 850/654-7022. **Facility:** 77 units. 75 one-bedroom standard units. 2 one-bedroom suites ($135-$150). 2 stories, interior corridors. *Bath:* combo or shower only. **Parking:** on-site. **Amenities:** safes (fee). *Some:* irons, hair dryers. **Pool(s):** outdoor. **Guest Services:** coin laundry. **Business Services:** meeting rooms, fax. **Cards:** AX, DC, DS, MC, VI.

SOME UNITS
🆂🅳 🍽➕ ➡ [DATA PORT] /✕ 🔲 🖼 💻/

SUNDESTIN BEACH RESORT

Phone: 850/837-7093

Condominium

All Year   1P: $95-$396

Location: 2.1 mi w of bridge. 1040 Hwy 98 E 32541. Fax: 850/837-7093. **Facility:** 250 units. 200 one- and 45 two-bedroom standard units. 5 three-bedroom suites ($95-$396). 18 stories, interior/exterior corridors. **Parking:** on-site. **Terms:** 3 night minimum stay, 30 day cancellation notice-fee imposed, weekly rates available, package plans. **Amenities:** voice mail, safes, irons. **Pool(s):** outdoor, heated indoor. **Leisure Activities:** whirlpools, recreation programs in summer, shuffleboard. *Fee:* paddleboats. **Guest Services:** gift shop, coin laundry. **Business Services:** meeting rooms, fax (fee). **Cards:** AX, DS, MC, VI.

SOME UNITS
🅰🆂🅺 🍽 ➡ ➕ ✕ [VCR] 🎥 🔲 🖼 💻 /✕/
FEE

TOPS'L BEACH & RACQUET RESORT

Phone: (850)337-1682

Resort
Condominium

All Year   2P: $166-$593

Location: 10.2 mi e on US 98. 9011 Hwy 98 W 32550. Fax: 850/267-9168. **Facility:** 310 units. 31 one- and 232 two-bedroom standard units. 37 three-bedroom suites. 10 vacation homes. 1-15 stories, interior/exterior corridors. **Parking:** on-site. **Terms:** 14 day cancellation notice-fee imposed, weekly rates available, package plans. **Amenities:** voice mail, safes, irons. **Pool(s):** outdoor, 4 heated outdoor, heated indoor/outdoor. **Leisure Activities:** saunas, whirlpools, steamroom, sailboats, putting green, 14 tennis courts (12 lighted), racquetball court, recreation programs, hiking trails, exercise room, basketball, shuffleboard, volleyball, game room. *Fee:* massage. **Guest Services:** gift shop, complimentary laundry, area transportation. **Business Services:** meeting rooms, fax (fee). **Cards:** AX, MC, VI.

🅰🆂🅺 🍽 ➡ ✕ [VCR] 🎥 [DATA PORT] 🔲 💻

The following lodging was either not evaluated or did not meet AAA rating requirements but is listed for your information only.

HOLIDAY INN EXPRESS HOTEL & SUITES

Phone: 850/654-9383

[fyi]

Motel

5/24-9/2 [ECP]	1P: $130-$169	2P: $140-$179	XP: $10 F18
3/2-5/23 [ECP]	1P: $111-$140	2P: $121-$150	XP: $10 F18
9/3-11/30 [ECP]	1P: $69-$95	2P: $79-$105	XP: $10 F18
12/1-3/1 [ECP]	1P: $59-$95	2P: $59-$105	XP: $10 F18

Too new to rate. **Location:** Corner of Hutchinson St and US 98. 108 Hutchinson St 32541. Fax: 850/654-9348. **Amenities:** pets, coffeemakers, microwaves, refrigerators, pool. **Terms:** 7 day cancellation notice. **Cards:** AX, DC, DS, MC, VI.

WHERE TO DINE

CHAN'S MARKET CAFE

Specialty

Lunch: $5-$13   **Dinner:** $6-$19   **Phone:** 850/837-1334

Location: 10 mi e of Destin; at the Market at Sandestin. 9375 Emerald Coast Pkwy 32550. **Hours:** 11 am-9 pm; to 10 pm in summer. Closed: 11/27, 12/25. **Features:** It's hard to believe this charming setting is just off the main highway. It offers both inside and outside dining with a good selection of deli items and signature sandwiches. The gourmet deli and bakery that are part of this establishment entice you to try not only the local seafood but also the selection of meats and freshly baked breads. At breakfast, linger over freshly brewed coffee, pancakes, biscuits, eggs and sausage while overlooking the duck pond. Casual dress; cocktails. **Parking:** on-site. **Cards:** AX, DS, MC, VI.

✕

THE CRAB TRAP

Seafood

Lunch: $6-$19 **Dinner:** $8-$20 **Phone:** 850/654-2722
Location: US 98; at James Lee Park. 3500 Old Hwy 98. **Hours:** 11 am-10:30 pm; to 8 pm in winter. Closed: 12/25. **Features:** Some tables and booths at this beachside restaurant afford good views. Among the inexpensive offerings are seafood specialties and sandwiches. Casual dress; cocktails. **Parking:** on-site. **Cards:** AX, CB, DC, DS, MC, VI.

DESTIN DINER

American

Lunch: $4-$6 **Dinner:** $5-$8 **Phone:** 850/654-5843
Location: US 98, 0.8 mi e. 1083 Hwy 98 E 32541. **Hours:** 6 am-10 pm; hours may vary in winter. Closed: 12/25. **Features:** The nostalgic, charming diner offers simple home cooking with '50s-era hospitality. Casual dress. **Parking:** on-site. **Cards:** DS, MC, VI.

ELEPHANT WALK

Seafood

Dinner: $25-$41 **Phone:** 850/267-4800
Location: 10 mi e on US 98; in Sandestin Golf and Beach Resort. 9300 Hwy 98 W 32541. **Hours:** 6 pm-10 pm. **Reservations:** suggested. **Features:** Experience the Asian exotica of Sri Lanka on the Gulf of Mexico in this restaurant based on the film "Elephant Walk." Among the more unusual fare featured on an ever-changing menu are the macadamia fried shrimp, Key lime cannoli and grouper Elizabeth. Smoke free premises. Casual dress; cocktails. **Parking:** on-site. **Cards:** AX, DC, DS, MC, VI.

GRAFFITI

Mediterranean

Dinner: $9-$20 **Phone:** 850/654-2764
Location: US 98, 2.9 mi w of bridge. 707 E Hwy 98 32541. **Hours:** 5 pm-9 pm, Fri & Sat-10 pm. Closed major holidays. **Features:** The walls and ceiling are adorned with an eclectic collection of artwork that keeps guests occupied between courses. This place is one of the locals' best-kept secrets. Smoke free premises. Casual dress; beer & wine only. **Parking:** on-site. **Cards:** MC, VI.

THE LIGHTHOUSE

Seafood

Dinner: $10-$21 **Phone:** 850/654-2828
Location: 2 mi e on US 98; in Shoreline Village Plaza. 878 Hwy 98 E 32541. **Hours:** 4:30 pm-8:30 pm. Closed: 11/27, 12/25. **Features:** Bring your whole family and enjoy the relaxed atmosphere. An extensive menu offers a wide selection with an emphasis on seafood. An authentic Key lime pie offers a taste of the tropics. Casual dress; cocktails. **Parking:** on-site. **Cards:** AX, DC, DS, MC, VI.

MCGUIRE'S IRISH PUB & BREWERY

Steak House

Lunch: $8-$12 **Dinner:** $12-$22 **Phone:** 850/650-0000
Location: On US 98, at east end of Destin Pass Bridge. 33 US 98 E 32541. **Hours:** 11 am-2 am. Closed: 11/27, 12/25. **Features:** A pleasant experience, this restaurant features steaks, seafood and tasty, oversized burgers. Sing along to nostalgic music or watch the action on the gulf and bay from an open upper deck. Homemade bread and butter pudding makes a delicious treat. Casual dress; cocktails; entertainment. **Parking:** on-site. **Cards:** AX, DC, DS, MC, VI.

Hungry? Look for the RED AAA Logo

*N*ext time you look through a AAA TourBook® guide in search of a place to dine, take note of the bright red AAA logo just under a select group of restaurant names! These Official Appointment restaurants place a high value on the business they receive from dedicated AAA travelers.

As a member, you already turn to TourBooks for quality travel information. Now look for restaurants that display the bright red AAA logo in their listing for dining experiences you'll long remember!

RUTHERFORDS 465 RESTAURANT

American

Dinner: $20-$40   Phone: 850/337-8888

Location: 0.7 mi e of Mid Bay Bridge. 4460 Legendary Dr, Suite 400 32541. **Hours:** 11 am-2 & 6-10 pm, Sat from 6 pm, Sun 10:30 am-2 pm. Closed: Mon. **Reservations:** suggested. **Features:** Nestled in the far corner of a country club, the fine-dining establishment traverses American, Pan Asian and French fusion cuisine. Selections such as the jasmine lobster appetizer, Chilean sea bass entree and berries Rutherford dessert wake up the nostrils and tickle the palate. The award-winning wine list is likely to impress even elite wine connoisseurs. Dressy casual; cocktails. **Parking:** on-site. **Cards:** AX, DS, MC, VI.

SAKURA ORIENTAL CUISINE AND SUSHI BAR

Chinese

Lunch: $5-$16   Dinner: $10-$16   Phone: 850/654-5818

Location: In downtown Destin K-Mart Shopping Center. 763 Hwy 98 E 32541. **Hours:** 11 am-2:30 & 5-9:30 pm, Fri-10 pm, Sat 5 pm-10 pm. Closed major holidays; also 12/24 & Sun. **Features:** A limited menu enables the casual and intimate restaurant to focus on a small assortment of tasty dishes, including sushi. Especially good are the piquant sweet and sour soup and a shrimp and beef dish served in a spicy brown sauce. Casual dress; beer & wine only. **Parking:** on-site. **Cards:** AX, CB, DC, MC, VI.

SEAGAR'S PRIME STEAKS AND SEAFOOD

Steak & Seafood

Dinner: $21-$34   Phone: 850/267-9500

Location: 10 mi e at Sandestin; in Hilton Sandestin Beach, Golf Resort. 4000 Sandestin Blvd S 32541. **Hours:** 6 pm-10 pm, Fri & Sat-11 pm. Closed: 11/27, 12/25. **Reservations:** suggested. **Features:** A sophisticated setting features lavish appointments and an upscale dress code. An open kitchen offers prime steaks and seafood with an innovative use of fresh ingredients. A separate lounge with a cigar steward is perfect for after-dinner relaxation. Dressy casual; cocktails; entertainment. **Parking:** valet. **Cards:** AX, CB, DC, DS, MC, VI.

THE VERANDA RESTAURANT AT HENDERSON PARK INN

American

Lunch: $5-$9   Dinner: $18-$23   Phone: 850/654-0404

Location: Dead end at east end of state park. 2700 Scenic Hwy 98 E 32541. **Hours:** 7 am-10 & 11:30-2 pm, Tues-Sat also 6 pm-9 pm. Closed: Sun & Mon. **Reservations:** suggested. **Features:** A beachfront view completes the lovely setting of porch swings and rocking chairs. Skillful use of local seafood and vegetables displays a Louisiana influence. Breakfast is by reservation only, with a daily lunch buffet and Sunday brunch also featured. Smoke free premises. Dressy casual; cocktails. **Parking:** on-site. **Cards:** AX, DS, MC, VI.

The following restaurants have not been evaluated by AAA but are listed for your information only.

CUVEE BEACH

Phone: 850/650-8900

Not evaluated. **Location:** 36120 Emerald Coast Pkwy 32541. **Features:** Serving wine country cuisine which designs meals to enhance the wine experience. Variety of choices include steak, seafood, poultry and pasta.

PANCAKE CREPERIE & BAKERY

Phone: 850/654-9999

Not evaluated. **Location:** 11225 Hwy 98 W 32541. **Features:** This creperie serves pancakes of every variety with a multitude of toppings to choose from. The sandwiches are made on freshly baked bread and croissants, pastries and baguettes are also available.

DUNEDIN —See Tampa Bay p. 916.

ELKTON (See map p. 785; index p. 787)

--- WHERE TO STAY ---

COMFORT INN ST. AUGUSTINE

Small-scale Hotel

Phone: (904)829-3435   [65]

2/12-8/31 [ECP]	1P: $69-$129	2P: $69-$129
12/1-2/11 & 9/1-11/30 [ECP]	1P: $59-$99	2P: $59-$99

Location: I-95, exit 311, just w. 2625 SR 207 32033. Fax: 904/824-1558. **Facility:** 62 one-bedroom standard units. 2 stories, exterior corridors. **Parking:** on-site. **Terms:** 1-4 night minimum stay, 5 day cancellation notice-fee imposed, pets ($10 extra charge). **Amenities:** *Some:* irons, hair dryers. **Pool(s):** outdoor. **Business Services:** fax (fee). **Cards:** AX, CB, DC, DS, MC, VI. **Special Amenities:** free continental breakfast and free local telephone calls.

SOME UNITS

ELLENTON pop. 3,142 (See map p. 812; index p. 815)

--- WHERE TO STAY ---

HAMPTON INN

Motel

Phone: (941)721-4000   [97]

2/1-4/30 [ECP]	1P: $89-$109	2P: $109-$129
10/1-11/30 [ECP]	1P: $89-$99	2P: $99-$119
12/1-1/31 [ECP]	1P: $89-$99	2P: $89-$109
5/1-9/30 [ECP]	1P: $79-$89	2P: $89-$109

Location: I-75, exit 224, just n on US 301, just w on 60th Ave E. 5810 20th Court E 34222. Fax: 941/721-4100. **Facility:** 116 one-bedroom standard units, some with whirlpools. 5 stories, interior corridors. *Bath:* combo or shower only. **Parking:** on-site. **Terms:** cancellation fee imposed. **Amenities:** video games, dual phone lines, voice mail, irons, hair dryers. **Pool(s):** heated outdoor. **Guest Services:** coin laundry. **Business Services:** meeting rooms, fax (fee). **Cards:** AX, CB, DC, DS, MC, VI.

SOME UNITS

(See map p. 812)

RAMADA LIMITED-ELLENTON   **Phone:** (941)729-8505 96
♦♦♦♦ ♦♦♦♦ 1/25-4/15 [CP]   1P: $90-$110   2P: $90-$110
▼▼ ▼▼   12/1-1/24 [CP]   1P: $80-$90   2P: $80-$90
Motel   4/16-11/30 [CP]   1P: $70-$90   2P: $70-$90
Location: I-75, exit 224, 0.3 mi s on US 301, just w on 51st Ave E, then just n. 5218 17th St E 34222.
Fax: 941/729-1110. **Facility:** 73 units. 62 one-bedroom standard units. 11 one-bedroom suites with efficiencies and whirlpools. 2 stories, exterior corridors. **Parking:** on-site. **Terms:** 7 day cancellation notice, small pets only ($10 extra charge). **Amenities:** voice mail, safes (fee), irons, hair dryers. **Pool(s):** heated outdoor. **Leisure Activities:** whirlpool. **Guest Services:** coin laundry. **Business Services:** meeting rooms, fax. **Cards:** AX, DC, DS, MC, VI.
SOME UNITS
(ASK) (S⊠) (🐾) (🍴➕) (➡) (🎥) (DATA PORT) (🖥) / (✕) (🛢) (📠) /

SLEEP INN & SUITES   **Phone:** (941)721-4933 99
SAVE   1/21-4/30 [ECP]   1P: $105   2P: $110   XP: $5   F18
           12/1-1/20 [ECP]   1P: $85   2P: $90   XP: $5   F18
♦♦♦♦ ♦♦♦♦ 11/1-11/30 [ECP]   1P: $70   2P: $75   XP: $5   F18
▼▼ ▼▼   5/1-10/31 [ECP]   1P: $55   2P: $60   XP: $5   F18
Motel   **Location:** I-75, exit 224, just n on US 301, just e on 19th St E, just s. 5605 18th St E 34222. Fax: 941/721-4934.
           Facility: 67 units. 59 one-bedroom standard units, some with whirlpools. 8 one-bedroom suites ($90-$140).
4 stories. *Bath:* combo or shower only. **Parking:** on-site. **Terms:** pets ($5 extra charge). **Amenities:** dual phone lines, voice mail, irons, hair dryers. **Pool(s):** heated outdoor. **Leisure Activities:** exercise room. **Guest Services:** coin laundry. **Business Services:** meeting rooms, fax (fee). **Cards:** AX, CB, DC, DS, JC, MC, VI.
SOME UNITS
(S⊠) (🐾) (🍴➕) (♿M) (🔳) (➡) (🎥) (DATA PORT) (🖥) / (✕) (🛢) (📠) /

——— *The following lodging was either not evaluated or did not* ———
meet AAA rating requirements but is listed for your information only.

SHONEY'S INN LAKESIDE   **Phone:** 941/729-0600
(fyi)   Did not meet all AAA rating requirements for property operations at time of last evaluation. **Location:** I-75, exit
Motel   224, 0.3 mi w on US 301, just n on 51st Ave E, just w. 4915 17th St E 34222. Facilities, services, and decor characterize
            a mid-range property.

——— **WHERE TO DINE** ———

CRAB TRAP II   **Lunch:** $6-$16   **Dinner:** $9-$30   **Phone:** 941/729-7777 46
♦♦♦♦ ♦♦♦♦ **Location:** I-75, exit 224, 0.4 mi s on US 301, just w on 51st Ave, then s. 4815 Memphis Rd 34222. **Hours:** 11:30
▼▼ ▼▼   am-9 pm, Fri & Sat-10 pm. Closed: 11/27, 12/25. **Features:** The bustling and rustic shanty overlooking a
Seafood   small pond and bird refuge is noted for quality seafood as well as such exotic temptations as kangaroo,
           buffalo, alligator, ostrich and barbecued wild pig. Wood carvings, mounted wildlife and pictures add effect
to the rustic spot. Casual dress; cocktails. **Parking:** on-site. **Cards:** DS, MC, VI.   (🍽) (✕)

JOHNNY LEVEROCK'S SEAFOOD HOUSE   **Lunch:** $8-$21   **Dinner:** $9-$21   **Phone:** 941/723-0677 47
♦♦♦♦ ♦♦♦♦ **Location:** I-75, exit 224, just n on US 301, just e on 19th St Se, then just s. 5317 19th St E 34222. **Hours:** 11:30
▼▼ ▼▼   am-10 pm. **Features:** Patrons enjoy the nautical theme and tasty seafood at this popular dining spot,
Seafood   established in 1948. The menu offers selections from onion-roasted salmon to a delicious seafood platter.
           The decor comprises fishing memorabilia and pictures of the restaurant's namesake, Johnny Leverock.
Casual dress; cocktails. **Parking:** on-site. **Cards:** AX, DC, DS, MC, VI.   (🍽) (✕)

Stop!
Savings Ahead

When you see the red (SAVE) icon next to lodging listings in this book, you know these establishments offer great room rates to AAA members!

So, as you're turning the pages, remember to stop when you see (SAVE).
It's your guarantee of savings.

ENGLEWOOD pop. 16,196

———— WHERE TO STAY ————

PALM MANOR CONDOMINIUMS
Phone: (941)474-3700

▼▼▼◆◆
Condominium

12/15-11/30 Wkly	1P: $695	
12/1-12/14 Wkly	1P: $455	

Location: CR 775, just w of jct SR 776. Commercial Area. 1531 Placida Rd 34223. Fax: 941/475-5366. **Facility:** 30 two-bedroom standard units with kitchens. 2 stories (no elevator), exterior corridors. **Parking:** on-site. **Terms:** 3 night minimum stay, 30 day cancellation notice-fee imposed. **Amenities:** irons. *Some:* hair dryers. **Pool(s):** heated outdoor. **Leisure Activities:** tennis court, horseshoes, shuffleboard. **Guest Services:** complimentary laundry. **Cards:** DS, MC, VI.

SOME UNITS
(ASK) (S🌣) (🏊) (✕) (DATA PORT) (🔒) (🖥) (💳) / (✕) (VCR)
FEE

SEAFARER BEACH RESORT
Phone: 941/474-4388

◆◆◆ (SAVE)
▼▼▼◆◆
Motel

2/1-4/30	1P: $125-$181	2P: $125-$181	XP: $12
12/11-1/2	1P: $111-$152	2P: $111-$152	XP: $12
1/3-1/31	1P: $96-$125	2P: $96-$125	XP: $12
5/1-11/30	1P: $77-$111	2P: $77-$111	XP: $12

Location: I-75, exit 193, on Manasota Key, 5 mi s on Jacaranda Blvd, 1.5 mi s on SR 776, 1.7 mi w on Manasota Beach Rd, then just s. Located in a remote area. 8520 Manasota Key Rd 34223 (1903 W 8th St PMB 111, ERIE, PA, 16505). Fax: 941/474-4388. **Facility:** Designated smoking area. 9 one-bedroom standard units, some with efficiencies or kitchens. 1 story, exterior corridors. *Bath:* combo or shower only. **Parking:** on-site. **Terms:** 30 day cancellation notice, weekly rates available. **Pool(s):** heated outdoor. **Leisure Activities:** fishing, table tennis. **Guest Services:** coin laundry. **Cards:** AX, DC, DS, MC, VI. **Special Amenities:** free local telephone calls and preferred room (subject to availability with advanced reservations).

(🏊) (✕) (🐾) (DATA PORT) (🔒) (🖥) (💳)

———— WHERE TO DINE ————

PRIME TIME STEAK & SPIRITS
Dinner: $6-$20
Phone: 941/697-7799

▼▼
American

Location: On CR 775, 4.2 mi w of jct SR 776; in Rotonda Plaza. 5855 Placida Rd, Suite 100 34224. **Hours:** 4 pm-10:30 pm, Fri & Sat-11:30 pm, Sun 11 am-10:30 pm. **Closed:** 11/27, 12/25. **Features:** A Southwestern aura punctuates this restaurant, where the menu dabbles in seafood, Mexican dishes, pasta, steak and poultry, all prepared from scratch. Watch romantic sunsets over Lemon Bay, or slip into the sports-themed bar for a livelier experience. Casual dress; cocktails. **Parking:** on-site. **Cards:** AX, DS, MC, VI.

(🍽) (✕)

EVERGLADES CITY pop. 479

———— WHERE TO DINE ————

THE OYSTER HOUSE RESTAURANT
Lunch: $5-$20
Dinner: $5-$20
Phone: 239/695-2073

◆◆◆
▼▼▼
Seafood

Location: 3 mi s on SR 29 (Chokoloskee Cswy). 901 Copeland Ave 34139. **Hours:** 11 am-10 pm. **Closed:** 11/27, 12/25. **Reservations:** suggested; 1/1-4/30. **Features:** Serving seasonal offerings of fresh local seafood, alligator, frog legs and stone crab claws. This rustic restaurant feels like old Florida, with stuffed wildlife and maritime decor. The bright and airy dining room looks out over the Gulf of Mexico. Casual dress; cocktails; entertainment. **Parking:** on-site. **Cards:** MC, VI.

(🍽) (✕)

FERN PARK —See Orlando p. 677.

FLAGLER BEACH pop. 4,954

———— WHERE TO STAY ————

BEACH FRONT MOTEL
Phone: (386)439-0089

◆◆◆ (SAVE)
▼▼▼◆◆
Motel

2/2-9/1	1P: $53-$58	2P: $53-$58	XP: $5	F18
9/2-11/30	1P: $49-$54	2P: $49-$54	XP: $5	F18
12/1-2/1	1P: $45-$49	2P: $45-$49	XP: $5	F18

Location: On SR A1A, 1 mi s of SR 100. 1544 S A1A 32136. Fax: 386/439-0083. **Facility:** 20 one-bedroom standard units, some with efficiencies. 2 stories, exterior corridors. **Parking:** on-site. **Terms:** weekly rates available, pets ($15 fee, dogs only). **Leisure Activities:** jogging. **Business Services:** fax. **Cards:** AX, DS, MC, VI. **Special Amenities:** early check-in/late check-out and free local telephone calls.

SOME UNITS
(S🌣) (🐾) (🍴) (🔒) / (✕) (💳)

FLAGLER BEACH MOTEL & RENTALS
Phone: 386/439-7717

▼
Motel

2/1-10/1	1P: $55	2P: $55	XP: $10	F10
12/1-1/31 & 10/2-11/30	1P: $50	2P: $50	XP: $10	F10

Location: On SR A1A, 1.5 mi s of SR 100. 1820 S Ocean Shore Blvd 32136. Fax: 386/439-7717. **Facility:** Designated smoking area. 23 units. 22 one-bedroom standard units with efficiencies. 1 one-bedroom suite. 1 story, exterior corridors. *Bath:* combo or shower only. **Parking:** on-site. **Terms:** 7 day cancellation notice. **Pool(s):** outdoor. **Cards:** DS, MC, VI.

(🍴) (🏊) (🐾) (🔒) (🖥) (💳) / (✕) /

SHIRE HOUSE BED AND BREAKFAST
Phone: (386)445-8877

▼▼▼◆◆
Bed & Breakfast

All Year	1P: $100-$250	2P: $100-$250	XP: $20	D15

Location: On SR A1A, 4.6 mi n of SR 100. 3398 N Oceanshore Blvd 32136. Fax: 386/446-5585. **Facility:** Across the street from the ocean, this modern building offers double whirlpool tubs and wet bars in every unit. Smoke free premises. 5 one-bedroom standard units. 2 stories, interior corridors. **Parking:** on-site. **Terms:** 7 day cancellation notice-fee imposed, [BP] meal plan available. **Pool(s):** heated outdoor. **Guest Services:** complimentary evening beverages, complimentary laundry. **Cards:** DS, MC, VI.

(🐾) (✕) (🍴) (🔒) (💳)

TOPAZ MOTEL

AAA SAVE
◆◆ ◆◆

Small-scale Hotel

Phone: (386)439-3301

All Year   1P: $55-$175   2P: $55-$175   XP: $10   F12
Location: On SR A1A, 0.5 mi s of SR 100. 1224 S Oceanshore Blvd 32136. Fax: 386/439-3942. **Facility:** 58 one-bedroom standard units, some with efficiencies and/or whirlpools. 2 stories, interior/exterior corridors. *Bath:* combo or shower only. **Parking:** on-site, winter plug-ins. **Terms:** 3-4 night minimum stay - seasonal, 14 day cancellation notice, pets ($11 fee, dogs only). **Amenities:** video library, voice mail. **Pool(s):** outdoor. **Guest Services:** coin laundry. **Business Services:** meeting rooms, fax. **Cards:** AX, DS, MC, VI.

SOME UNITS

🐕 ⏩ / ✕ VCR 🔲 🖥 📟 /

THE WHITE ORCHID OCEANFRONT INN

◆◆◆◆◆◆

Bed & Breakfast

Phone: 386/439-4944

All Year   1P: $109-$209   2P: $109-$209   XP: $45
Location: On SR A1A, 0.5 mi s of SR 100. 1104 S Oceanshore Blvd 32136. Fax: 386/439-4946. **Facility:** Featuring a main house and a carriage house decorated in Art Deco style, this property is across the street from the ocean. Smoke free premises. 10 one-bedroom standard units, some with whirlpools. 2 stories, interior/exterior corridors. *Bath:* combo or shower only. **Parking:** on-site. **Terms:** age restrictions may apply, 10 day cancellation notice-fee imposed, [BP] meal plan available. **Pool(s):** outdoor, heated outdoor. **Leisure Activities:** whirlpool, bicycles, spa. **Guest Services:** gift shop. **Business Services:** fax. **Cards:** AX, DS, MC, VI.

🛎 ⏩ ✕ ✕ 📹 🔲

──────── **WHERE TO DINE** ────────

KINGS OCEANSHORE RESTAURANT

◆◆ ◆◆

Seafood

Lunch: $5-$8   Dinner: $8-$14   Phone: 386/439-0380
Location: On SR A1A, just s of SR 100. 208 S Oceanshore Blvd 32136. **Hours:** 8 am-9 pm, Sun-Wed to 3 pm. Closed: 1/1, 11/27, 12/25. **Reservations:** accepted. **Features:** Directly across from the ocean, you'll find fresh seafood served in a casual, friendly atmosphere. Smoke free premises. beer & wine only. **Parking:** on-site. **Cards:** MC, VI.

✕

FLORAL CITY pop. 4,989

──────── **WHERE TO STAY** ────────

MOONRISE RESORT

◆◆ ◆◆

Cottage

Phone: 352/726-2553

All Year   1P: $50-$75   2P: $50-$75   XP: $5
Location: Just e on CR 48, 1.5 mi n on Old Floral City Rd. 8801 E Moonrise Ln, Lot 18 34436. Fax: 352/726-2553. **Facility:** 10 units. 9 one- and 1 two-bedroom standard units with kitchens. 1 story, exterior corridors. *Bath:* combo or shower only. **Parking:** on-site. **Terms:** 14 day cancellation notice, weekly rates available, pets ($20 fee). **Leisure Activities:** boat dock, fishing, shuffleboard. *Fee:* boats, canoes, paddleboats. **Guest Services:** coin laundry. **Business Services:** fax.

🛎 ✕ 🅩 🔲 🖥 📟

FLORIDA CITY —*See Miami-Miami Beach p. 548.*

Destination Florida Keys

*T*hey've been called a string of pearls, draped across a sweep of turquoise water.

*T*hat's only half the truth. Fact is, these Keys are many things to many people. From sport-fishers' gold mine to scuba divers' sunken treasure, they offer a pirate's chest full of activities for all.

Seven Mile Bridge, Pigeon Key. With a seascape this stunning, who needs a big-city skyline? (See mention page 64)

Psychedelic Scooter, Key West. This shades-of-the-'60s scooter illustrates the chilled-out attitude of residents of the Keys.

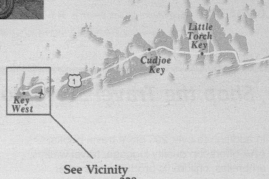

See Vicinity
map page 329

*P*laces included in this AAA Destination Area:

Cudjoe Key................320
Islamorada.................320
Key Colony Beach.......323
Key Largo...................323
Key West....................333
Little Torch Key..........352
Long Key....................352
Marathon....................353

Duval Street, Key West.
This main-drag mecca amuses
by day and mesmerizes by
night. (See mention page 66)

9336

Key
Largo

Islamorada

1

Long Key

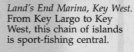

Key Colony
Beach

Marathon

Florida Keys

Land's End Marina, Key West.
From Key Largo to Key
West, this chain of islands
is sport-fishing central.

Mallory Square, Key West.
This unconventional, yet
eye-catching display at-
tempts to entice visitors
to take a sponge home.
(See mention page 60)

The Florida Keys

CONCH KEY

------ **WHERE TO STAY** ------

------ *The following lodging was either not evaluated or did not* ------
meet AAA rating requirements but is listed for your information only.

CONCH KEY COTTAGES   **Phone:** 305/289-1377
[fyi]   Did not meet all AAA rating requirements for. **Location:** US 1 at MM 62.3 (oceanside). 62250 Overseas Hwy 33050.
Cottage   Facilities, services, and decor characterize a mid-range property.

CUDJOE KEY pop. 1,695

------ **WHERE TO DINE** ------

CUDJOE LANDING   **Dinner:** $11-$21   **Phone:** 305/745-9999
♦♦♦ ♦♦♦   **Location:** From US 1, MM 21, 0.5 mi s; in Cudjoe Gardens. 457 Drost Dr 33042. **Hours:** 6 pm-10 pm. Closed:
          10/1-10/21 & Mon 6/1-10/31. **Reservations:** accepted. **Features:** Settle down in the relaxed tropical
Italian   setting with an outdoor patio overlooking the waterway. Two fireplaces and fresh flowers convey a cozy,
          warm mood. Old World style entrees of seafood and pasta are prepared from the freshest ingredients.
Casual dress; beer & wine only. **Parking:** on-site. **Cards:** AX, CB, DC, DS, MC, VI.   ⊞ ⊠

ISLAMORADA pop. 6,846

------ **WHERE TO STAY** ------

CHEECA LODGE & SPA   **Phone:** (305)664-4651
▽▽▽▽   12/1-4/27   2P: $159-$1675   XP: $30   F16
          4/28-11/30   2P: $129-$1225   XP: $30   F16
Resort   **Location:** On US 1 at MM 82. Located in a quiet area. 81801 Overseas Hwy 33036 (PO Box 527). Fax: 305/664-2893.
Large-scale Hotel **Facility:** A notable feature of this luxurious beach resort is its ocean pier. Designated smoking area. 203
          units. 140 one-bedroom standard units. 63 one-bedroom suites with kitchens. 2-4 stories, interior/exterior cor-
ridors. *Bath:* combo or shower only. **Parking:** on-site and valet. **Terms:** check-in 4 pm, 2-5 night minimum stay, cancellation fee
imposed. **Amenities:** video library, CD players, dual phone lines, voice mail, honor bars, irons, hair dryers. **Dining:** Atlantic's
Edge, see separate listing. **Pool(s):** 2 heated outdoor, wading. **Leisure Activities:** whirlpools, steamrooms, rental paddleboats,
boat dock, snorkeling, fishing, golf-9 holes, recreation programs, playground, spa. *Fee:* boats, sailboats, windsurfing, scuba
diving, charter fishing, 6 lighted tennis courts, bicycles. **Guest Services:** gift shop, valet laundry, area transportation. **Business
Services:** meeting rooms, business center. **Cards:** AX, CB, DC, DS, JC, MC, VI. *(See color ad p 321)*

                                                                          SOME UNITS

ASK ✈ ⊞ ⊠ ⌂ ⊠ ⊠ VCR DATA PORT ⊟ ⊟ / ⊟ /
FEE

EL CAPITAN AT HOLIDAY ISLE   Phone: (305)664-2711

| | 12/26-5/4 | 1P: $155-$290 | 2P: $155-$290 | XP: $15 | F18 |
| | 12/1-12/25 & 5/5-11/30 | 1P: $115-$240 | 2P: $115-$240 | XP: $10 | F18 |

Motel   **Location:** US 1, MM 84.5. Remote location. 84001 Overseas Hwy 33036. Fax: 305/664-2703. **Facility:** 14 units. 1 one- and 2 two-bedroom standard units with efficiencies. 5 one-bedroom suites with efficiencies. 1 story, exterior corridors. **Bath:** combo or shower only. **Parking:** on-site. **Terms:** check-in 3:30 pm, 2-3 night minimum stay - weekends, 3 day cancellation notice. **Amenities:** voice mail, safes (fee), hair dryers. **Leisure Activities:** fishing. **Fee:** charter fishing. **Business Services:** fax (fee). **Cards:** AX, CB, DC, DS, MC, VI.

SOME UNITS

HAMPTON INN & SUITES   Phone: (305)664-0073

SAVE	2/7-4/20 [ECP]	1P: $229-$379	2P: $229-$379
	12/1-12/31 [ECP]	1P: $139-$379	2P: $139-$379
	1/1-2/6 [ECP]	1P: $169-$299	2P: $169-$299
	4/21-11/30 [ECP]	1P: $139-$299	2P: $139-$299

Small-scale Hotel   **Location:** US 1 at MM 80. 80001 Overseas Hwy 33036. Fax: 305/664-0807. **Facility:** 79 units. 20 one-bedroom standard units. 37 one- and 22 two-bedroom suites with efficiencies. 5 stories, interior corridors. **Bath:** combo or shower only. **Parking:** on-site. **Terms:** 3 day cancellation notice-fee imposed. **Amenities:** video games, voice mail, safes, irons, hair dryers. **Pool(s):** heated outdoor. **Leisure Activities:** whirlpool, rental paddleboats, fishing, playground, exercise room, shuffleboard. **Fee:** boats, canoes, windsurfing, boat dock, scuba diving, snorkeling, charter fishing, bicycles, massage. **Guest Services:** gift shop, coin laundry. **Business Services:** fax (fee). **Cards:** AX, CB, DC, DS, MC, VI.

SOME UNITS

PELICAN COVE RESORT   Phone: (305)664-4435

	12/25-4/30	1P: $185-$225	2P: $185-$225	XP: $20	F16
	5/1-8/31	1P: $135-$155	2P: $135-$155	XP: $20	F16
	12/1-12/24 & 9/1-11/30	1P: $115-$135	2P: $115-$135	XP: $20	F16

Motel   **Location:** US 1, MM 84.5. Located behind the Theater of the Sea. 84457 Old Overseas Hwy 33036 (PO Box 633). Fax: 305/664-5134. **Facility:** 63 units. 54 one-bedroom standard units, some with efficiencies. 9 one-bedroom suites ($245-$695) with kitchens and whirlpools. 3 stories, exterior corridors. **Parking:** on-site. **Terms:** check-in 4 pm, 2 night minimum stay - weekends, 5 day cancellation notice-fee imposed, [CP] meal plan available. **Amenities:** voice mail, irons, hair dryers. **Pool(s):** heated outdoor. **Leisure Activities:** whirlpool, fishing, tennis court. **Fee:** boats, canoes, boat dock, snorkeling, charter fishing. **Guest Services:** valet laundry. **Business Services:** meeting rooms, fax (fee). **Cards:** AX, CB, DC, DS, MC, VI.

SOME UNITS

SANDS OF ISLAMORADA   Phone: (305)664-2791

| AAA SAVE | 12/1-9/4 | 1P: $130-$260 | 2P: $130-$260 | XP: $15 |
| | 9/5-11/30 | 1P: $105-$225 | 2P: $105-$225 | XP: $15 |

Motel   **Location:** US 1, MM 80. 80051 Overseas Hwy 33036 (412 Shore Dr E, OLDSMAR, 34677). Fax: 305/664-2886. **Facility:** 9 units. 8 one-bedroom standard units, some with efficiencies. 1 one-bedroom suite with efficiency. 1-2 stories, exterior corridors. **Bath:** combo or shower only. **Parking:** on-site. **Terms:** 2 night minimum stay, 3 day cancellation notice-fee imposed, pets ($15 extra charge). **Amenities:** video library, voice mail, hair dryers. **Pool(s):** outdoor. **Leisure Activities:** whirlpool, barbecue grill. **Fee:** boat dock. **Business Services:** fax (fee). **Cards:** MC, VI.

SOME UNITS

─────── *The following lodgings were either not evaluated or did not* ───────
meet AAA rating requirements but are listed for your information only.

CASA MORADA   Phone: 305/664-0044

[fyi]   Did not meet all AAA rating requirements for locking devices in some guest rooms at time of last evaluation on 10/31/2001. **Location:** MM 82.2 (Madeira Rd); Bayside. 136 Madeira Rd 33036. Facilities, services, and decor characterize a mid-range property.
Small-scale Hotel

CHESAPEAKE RESORT   Phone: 305/664-4662

[fyi]   Did not meet all AAA rating requirements for locking devices in some guest rooms at time of last evaluation. **Location:** US 1 (oceanside) MM 83.5. 83409 Overseas Hwy 33036 (PO Box 909). Facilities, services, and decor characterize a mid-range property.
Small-scale Hotel

WHITE GATE COURT   Phone: 305/664-4136

[fyi]   Not evaluated. **Location:** US 1, just s of MM 77, south side of the road. 76010 Overseas Hwy 33036. Facilities, services, and decor characterize a basic property.

─────── **WHERE TO DINE** ───────

ATLANTIC'S EDGE   Dinner: $16-$52   Phone: 305/664-4651

Location: On US 1 at MM 82; in Cheeca Lodge & Spa. 81801 Overseas Hwy 33036. **Hours:** 6 pm-10 pm. **Reservations:** suggested. **Features:** "Barefoot elegance" is the motto at comfortable yet elegant Atlantic's, where local seafood specialties dominate the menu. Atlantic Ocean views capture diners' attention while a pianist provides background music. This place satisfies those out celebrating a special occasion or those taking in an occasional treat. The menu is varied, and servers are friendly. Dressy casual; cocktails. **Parking:** on-site. **Cards:** AX, CB, DC, DS, MC, VI.
Regional American

GANIM'S ISLAMORADA RESTAURANT AND BAKERY   Lunch: $3-$6   Phone: 305/664-8363

Location: US 1, MM 81.6 (gulfside). 81620 Overseas Hwy 33036. **Hours:** 6 am-2 pm. Closed: 12/25. **Features:** Locals line up for hours to partake of the famous breakfasts at this diner-style restaurant and bakery. beer & wine only. **Parking:** on-site. **Cards:** AX, DS, MC, VI.
American

ISLAMORADA FISH COMPANY　　　Lunch: $7-$12　　　Dinner: $7-$24　　　Phone: 305/664-9271

Seafood

Location: On US 1 at MM 81.5. 81532 Overseas Hwy 33036. **Hours:** 11 am-10 pm. Closed: 11/27, 12/25. **Features:** On the waterfront, the restaurant offers the freshest seafood. The dining room has no walls, which makes for outstanding views of the gulf, mangroves and sunset from every table. Casual dress; cocktails. **Parking:** on-site. **Cards:** AX, DS, MC, VI.

MARKER 88 RESTAURANT　　　　　　Dinner: $17-$30　　　　　　Phone: 305/852-9315

Seafood

Location: US 1, MM 88 33036. **Hours:** 5 pm-11 pm. Closed: 11/27, 12/25; also Mon. **Reservations:** suggested. **Features:** An elaborate menu offers local seafood specials. The dining room overlooks Florida Bay. Both the soup and salad are very good. Try the yellowtail rangoon for a tropical twist. The service is pleasant and very professional. Casual dress; cocktails. **Parking:** on-site. **Cards:** AX, DC, DS, MC, VI.

SQUID ROW RESTAURANT　　　　Lunch: $4-$7　　　Dinner: $9-$19　　　Phone: 305/664-9865

Steak & Seafood

Location: On US 1 and MM 81.9. 81901 Overseas Hwy 33036. **Hours:** 11:30 am-9:30 pm, Fri & Sat-10 pm. Closed: 11/27, 12/25. **Reservations:** suggested; for dinner. **Features:** A wide range of fresh seafood, steak, chicken and pasta is prepared to order. Bouillabaisse is a house specialty; dessert, bread and dressing are made on the premises. A tasty grilled fish sandwich with french fries provides a satisfying lunch for those on the go. Screened patio dining is also available. Casual dress; cocktails. **Parking:** on-site. **Cards:** AX, CB, DC, DS, MC, VI.

KEY COLONY BEACH pop. 788

———— **WHERE TO STAY** ————

CONTINENTAL INN　　　　　　　　　　　　　　　　　　　　　Phone: 305/289-0101

12/22-4/7	1P: $125	2P: $125	XP: $10	F5
4/8-11/30	1P: $110	2P: $110	XP: $10	F5
12/1-12/21	1P: $99	2P: $99	XP: $10	F5

Condominium

Location: 1.2 mi sw from jct US 1 and Sadowski Cswy (MM 53.8), 1121 W Ocean Dr 33051 (PO Box 510209). Fax: 305/743-8150. **Facility:** 42 units, 41 one-bedroom standard units with kitchens. 1 two-bedroom suite with kitchen, 2 stories (no elevator), exterior corridors. *Bath:* combo or shower only. **Parking:** on-site. **Terms:** cancellation fee imposed. **Amenities:** *Some:* irons. **Pool(s):** heated outdoor. **Leisure Activities:** barbecue area, tiki huts, recreational room, shuffleboard. **Guest Services:** coin laundry. **Business Services:** fax (fee). **Cards:** AX, DS, MC, VI. **Special Amenities: free local telephone calls.**

SOME UNITS

KEY LARGO pop. 11,886

———— **WHERE TO STAY** ————

BAY BREEZE MOTEL　　　　　　　　　　　　　　　　　　　Phone: 305/852-5248

7/15-9/15	1P: $129-$179	2P: $129-$179	XP: $25
4/16-7/14 & 9/16-11/30	1P: $119-$169	2P: $119-$169	XP: $25
12/1-4/15	1P: $99-$149	2P: $99-$149	XP: $25

Motel

Location: 7.5 mi s from center of town, at MM 92.5. Located in a quiet area. 160 Sterling Rd 33070. Fax: 305/852-5758. **Facility:** 17 units. 11 one-bedroom standard units with efficiencies. 6 cottages ($149-$250). 2 stories, exterior corridors. *Bath:* combo or shower only. **Parking:** on-site. **Terms:** 30 day cancellation notice-fee imposed, $25 service charge. **Amenities:** video library (fee). **Pool(s):** heated outdoor. **Leisure Activities:** boating, paddleboats, boat dock. **Business Services:** fax (fee). **Cards:** MC, VI.

SOME UNITS

FEE

BAYSIDE RESORT　　　　　　　　　　　　　　　　　　　Phone: (305)451-4450

12/1-5/26 [CP]	1P: $89-$179
11/13-11/30 [CP]	1P: $89-$169
5/27-11/12 [CP]	1P: $89-$129

Small-scale Hotel

Location: US 1 at MM 99.5. 99490 Overseas Hwy 33037 (PO Box 1050). Fax: 305/451-9650. **Facility:** 56 units. 54 one-bedroom standard units. 2 one-bedroom suites ($189-$299) with efficiencies. 2-3 stories, exterior corridors. **Parking:** on-site. **Terms:** 3 day cancellation notice. **Amenities:** *Some:* safes, hair dryers. **Dining:** noon-3 pm & 5-11 pm, Sat & Sun from 5 pm, wine/beer only. **Pool(s):** small heated outdoor. **Leisure Activities:** fishing, volleyball. **Guest Services:** gift shop. **Business Services:** fax (fee). **Cards:** AX, DC, DS, MC, VI. **Special Amenities: free continental breakfast and free local telephone calls.** *(See color ad p 324)*

SOME UNITS

FEE

BEST WESTERN SUITES/KEY LARGO　　　　　　　　　　Phone: (305)451-5081

2/1-4/30 [CP]	1P: $149-$179	2P: $149-$179	XP: $10	F16
5/1-11/30 [CP]	1P: $119-$139	2P: $119-$139	XP: $10	F16
12/1-1/31 [CP]	1P: $119-$129	2P: $119-$129	XP: $10	F16

Condominium

Location: 0.3 mi e of US 1 at MM 100. 201 Ocean Dr 33037. Fax: 305/451-4173. **Facility:** 40 one-bedroom suites with kitchens. 2 stories, exterior corridors. **Parking:** on-site. **Terms:** 14 day cancellation notice. **Amenities:** irons, hair dryers. **Pool(s):** outdoor. **Leisure Activities:** fishing. *Fee:* scuba diving, snorkeling, charter fishing. **Guest Services:** coin laundry. **Business Services:** fax (fee). **Cards:** AX, DC, DS, MC, VI. **Special Amenities: free continental breakfast.**

SOME UNITS

HOLIDAY INN RESORT　　　　　　　　　　　　　　　　　　　　　　　**Phone:** (305)451-2121

All Year　　　　　　　　1P: $89-$199　　　　2P: $89-$199

Location: US 1, at MM 100. 99701 Overseas Hwy 33037. Fax: 305/451-5592. **Facility:** 132 one-bedroom stan-
Large-scale Hotel　dard units. 2 stories, interior/exterior corridors. **Parking:** on-site. **Terms:** cancellation fee imposed.
Amenities: voice mail, irons, hair dryers. **Pool(s):** 2 heated outdoor. **Leisure Activities:** whirlpool, fishing,
playground, exercise room. *Fee:* marina, scuba diving, snorkeling, charter fishing. **Guest Services:** gift shop, coin laundry. **Business Services:** meeting rooms, fax (fee). **Cards:** AX, DC, DS, MC, VI. *(See color ad below & opposite inside back cover)*

SOME UNITS

(ASK) (S/D) ⎡⎤ ⍍ ⟫ ⛱ ⛤ (DATA PORT) 🛏 ▣ / ✕ /

HOWARD JOHNSON RESORT KEY LARGO　　　　　　　　　　　　　　　**Phone:** (305)451-1400

12/24-4/27	1P: $155-$215	2P: $155-$215	XP: $10	F17
4/28-11/30	1P: $125-$165	2P: $125-$165	XP: $10	F17
12/1-12/23	1P: $115-$165	2P: $115-$165	XP: $10	F17

Location: US 1, at MM 102 (Bayside). 10245 Overseas Hwy 33037 (PO Box 1024). Fax: 305/451-3953. **Facility:** 100
Small-scale Hotel　one-bedroom standard units. 2 stories, interior corridors. *Bath:* combo or shower only. **Parking:** on-site.
Terms: package plans, pets ($10 extra charge). *Amenities:* safes (fee). *Some:* irons, hair dryers. **Pool(s):**
heated outdoor. **Leisure Activities:** rental canoes, boat dock. *Fee:* boats, scuba diving, snorkeling. **Guest Services:** valet and
coin laundry. **Business Services:** meeting rooms, fax (fee). **Cards:** AX, DC, DS, MC, VI. **Special Amenities:** free local telephone calls. *(See color ad p 325)*

SOME UNITS

(S/D) 🛏 ⍍ ⛤ (&M) (&) ⟫ ⛱ ✕ (DATA PORT) ▣ / ✕ 🛏 ▤ /

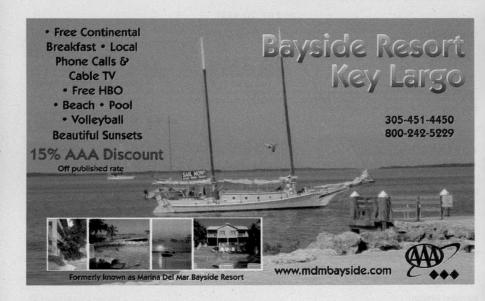

MARINA DEL MAR RESORT & MARINA   **Phone: 305/451-4107**

All Year   1P: $89-$199

Small-scale Hotel

Location: US 1 at MM 100. Located adjacent to Holiday Inn via Laguna Ave. 527 Caribbean Dr 33037. Fax: 305/451-1891. **Facility:** 76 units. 63 one-bedroom standard units, some with efficiencies and/or whirlpools. 8 one-, 4 two- and 1 three-bedroom suites with kitchens and whirlpools. 2-4 stories, exterior corridors. **Parking:** on-site. **Terms:** cancellation fee imposed, [ECP] meal plan available. **Amenities:** irons, hair dryers. **Dining:** Coconuts Restaurant & Lounge, see separate listing. **Pool(s):** heated outdoor. **Leisure Activities:** whirlpool, 2 lighted tennis courts, exercise room. **Fee:** marina, scuba diving, snorkeling, fishing, charter fishing. **Guest Services:** gift shop, coin laundry. **Business Services:** meeting rooms, fax (fee). **Cards:** AX, DC, DS, MC, VI. *(See color ad 326)*

SOME UNITS

MARRIOTT KEY LARGO BAY BEACH RESORT   **Phone: (305)453-0000**

SAVE	12/20-4/30	1P: $259-$329	2P: $259-$329	XP: $20	F18
	5/1-5/31	1P: $199-$299	2P: $199-$299	XP: $20	F18
	6/1-11/30	1P: $199-$259	2P: $199-$259	XP: $20	F18
	12/1-12/19	1P: $179-$229	2P: $179-$229	XP: $20	F18

Resort
Large-scale Hotel

Location: US 1 at MM 103.8. 103800 Overseas Hwy 33037. Fax: 305/453-0093. **Facility:** The resort features tropical-themed guest rooms and suites on extensive grounds which overlook the bay. 153 units. 133 one-bedroom standard units, some with efficiencies and/or whirlpools. 20 two-bedroom suites ($349-$1500) with kitchens, some with whirlpools. 4 stories, exterior corridors. **Parking:** on-site. **Terms:** 3 day cancellation notice-fee imposed. **Amenities:** voice mail, safes, honor bars, irons, hair dryers. **Pool(s):** heated outdoor. **Leisure Activities:** whirlpool, rental boats, rental canoes, rental paddleboats, fishing, miniature golf, tennis court, recreation programs, jogging, exercise room, basketball, shuffleboard, volleyball. **Fee:** marina, scuba diving, snorkeling, charter fishing, bicycles. **Guest Services:** gift shop, valet and coin laundry. **Business Services:** conference facilities, fax (fee). **Cards:** AX, DC, DS, MC, VI. *(See color ad p 324 & below)*

SOME UNITS

RAMADA LIMITED RESORT AND MARINA

Phone: (305)451-3939

| | 12/1-4/30 | 1P: $139-$169 | 2P: $139-$169 | XP: $10 | F18 |
| | 5/1-11/30 | 1P: $89-$129 | 2P: $89-$129 | XP: $10 | F18 |

Small-scale Hotel   **Location:** US 1, at MM 100. 99751 Overseas Hwy 33037. Fax: 305/453-0222. **Facility:** 92 units. 89 one-bedroom standard units. 3 one-bedroom suites with whirlpools. 4 stories, interior corridors. **Parking:** on-site. **Terms:** cancellation fee imposed, [CP] & [ECP] meal plans available. **Amenities:** voice mail, irons, hair dryers. **Pool(s):** heated outdoor. **Leisure Activities:** whirlpool, rental boats. *Fee:* marina, scuba diving, snorkeling, fishing, charter fishing. **Guest Services:** valet and coin laundry. **Business Services:** meeting rooms, fax (fee). **Cards:** AX, DC, DS, MC, VI.
(See color ad p 324 & below)

SOME UNITS

ROCK REEF RESORT
Phone: 305/852-2401

	12/15-4/26	1P: $109-$149	2P: $109-$149	XP: $15	D14
	4/27-9/15	1P: $95-$130	2P: $95-$130	XP: $15	D14
	12/1-12/14 & 9/16-11/30	1P: $88-$119	2P: $88-$119	XP: $15	D14

Motel   **Location:** On US 1 (southbound) at MM 98. 97850 Overseas Hwy 33037 (PO Box 73). Fax: 305/852-5355. **Facility:** 21 units. 12 one- and 3 two-bedroom standard units, some with efficiencies. 3 one- and 1 two-bedroom suites ($140-$240), some with efficiencies or kitchens. 2 cabins. 1-2 stories, exterior corridors. *Bath:* combo or shower only. **Parking:** on-site. **Terms:** 2-7 night minimum stay - weekends, 21 day cancellation notice-fee imposed, weekly rates available. **Leisure Activities:** whirlpool, paddleboats, boat dock, fishing, fishing pier, barbecue area, tetherball, tropical gardens, shuffleboard. **Guest Services:** coin laundry. **Business Services:** fax (fee). **Cards:** AX, DS, MC, VI. **Special Amenities:** free local telephone calls and free room upgrade (subject to availability with advanced reservations).

SOME UNITS

THE WESTIN BEACH RESORT, KEY LARGO

Phone: (305)852-5553

	12/26-4/26	1P: $189-$319	2P: $189-$319	XP: $20	F17
	4/27-11/30	1P: $169-$319	2P: $169-$319	XP: $20	F17
	12/1-12/25	1P: $149-$239	2P: $149-$239	XP: $20	F17

Location: US 1 southbound Carriageway at MM 97, overlooking Florida Bay. 97000 S Overseas Hwy 33037.
Resort Fax: 305/852-8669. **Facility:** Within a hammock of hardwood trees along the gulf, the hotel offers some
Large-scale Hotel water-view rooms. 200 one-bedroom standard units, some with whirlpools. 4 stories, exterior corridors. *Bath:* combo or shower only. **Parking:** on-site (fee) and valet. **Terms:** 1-7 night minimum stay - seasonal, $7 service charge. **Amenities:** video games, high-speed Internet, voice mail, honor bars, irons, hair dryers. *Some:* safes. **Dining:** 4 restaurants, 6:30 am-11 pm, cocktails. **Pool(s):** 2 heated outdoor. **Leisure Activities:** sauna, whirlpool, rental paddleboats, rental sailboats, boat dock, fishing, jet skis, kayaks, parasailing, 2 lighted tennis courts, jogging, exercise room. **Fee:** windsurfing, charter fishing, massage, game room. **Guest Services:** gift shop, valet laundry, beauty salon. **Business Services:** conference facilities, business center. **Cards:** AX, CB, DC, DS, JC, MC, VI. **Special Amenities:** free local telephone calls and free newspaper. *(See color ad p 326 & p 5)*

SOME UNITS

The following lodging was either not evaluated or did not meet AAA rating requirements but is listed for your information only.

KONA KAI RESORT

Phone: 305/852-7200

(fyi) Did not meet all AAA rating requirements for property operations at time of last evaluation on 10/31/2001.
Location: US 1, MM 97.8 (bayside). 97802 S Overseas Hwy 33037. Facilities, services, and decor characterize a mid-
Small-scale Hotel range property.

WHERE TO DINE

BALLYHOO'S HISTORIC SEAFOOD GRILLE

Lunch: $7-$22   **Dinner:** $7-$22   **Phone:** 305/852-0822

Location: US 1, at MM 97.8 (in the median). MM 97.8 33037. **Hours:** 11 am-10 pm. Closed: 11/27, 12/25.
Reservations: accepted. **Features:** This 1930s conch house is where the locals dine. Main draws are the
Seafood relaxed ambience and the abundance of tasty seafood. Locally caught yellowtail snapper prepared in a variety of ways is a highlight on a menu that also includes shrimp, scallops and stone crab in season. Delicious homemade Key lime pie makes for a perfect ending. beer & wine only. **Parking:** on-site. **Cards:** AX, MC, VI.

BAYSIDE GRILL

Lunch: $6-$10   **Dinner:** $8-$23   **Phone:** 305/451-3380

Location: On US 1 and MM 99.5. 99530 Overseas Hwy 33037. **Features:** Offering Caribbean-style dishes with local seafood and steaks, this popular spot also features a lovely sunset view of Florida Bay. A very good wine list and a wide selection of imported beers will help
American you choose just the right beverage for your meal. Casual dress; cocktails. **Parking:** on-site. **Cards:** AX, MC, VI.

Look for the Signs Along the Way

When selecting a place to dine while traveling, look for Official Appointment restaurants that display the AAA Approved sign. It's the only sign you need to be assured of an enjoyable dining experience.

As a member, you already know the AAA sign indicates quality establishments. So, when you don't have advance dining reservations, look for the AAA Approved sign along the way, for a meal you'll long remember!

CAFE LARGO
Italian
Dinner: $8-$23 **Phone:** 305/451-4885
Location: US 1, MM 99.5. 99530 Overseas Hwy 33037. **Hours:** 4:30 pm-11 pm. Closed: 11/27, 12/25. **Features:** Fresh local seafood, certified steak, pasta dishes and other Italian specialties are well complemented by a very good wine list and extensive selections of imported beer. Soup is homemade and changes daily at this spot, perfect for a quick meal. Casual dress; cocktails. **Parking:** on-site. **Cards:** AX, MC, VI.

COCONUTS RESTAURANT & LOUNGE
Steak & Seafood
Lunch: $5-$7 **Dinner:** $9-$15 **Phone:** 305/453-9794
Location: US 1 at MM 100; in Marina Del Mar Resort & Marina. 528 Caribbean Dr 33037-1050. **Hours:** 11 am-10 pm. **Features:** No need to dress up for this casual restaurant with a wooden deck overlooking the marina. Watch the yachts dock for lunch and enjoy a delicious meal with consistent service. The stuffed shrimp with crab meat is accompanied by summer squash and zucchini. Casual dress; cocktails; entertainment. **Parking:** on-site. **Cards:** AX, DC, MC, VI.

THE FISH HOUSE RESTAURANT & SEAFOOD MARKET
Seafood
Lunch: $4-$10 **Dinner:** $9-$25 **Phone:** 305/451-4665
Location: US 1 at MM 102.4. 102401 Overseas Hwy 33037. **Hours:** 11:30 am-10 pm. Closed: 11/27; also 12/25 for lunch, 9/9-10/2. **Features:** Small but always bustling, the restaurant boasts ample portions of seafood, such as pan-sauteed fish, as well as shrimp and lobster specials that change daily. The wait staff is energetic, and the meringue-topped Key lime pie is a tempting treat. Casual dress; beer & wine only. **Parking:** on-site. **Cards:** AX, DC, DS, MC, VI.

FRANK KEYS CAFE
Regional American
Dinner: $12-$28 **Phone:** 305/453-0310
Location: US 1 at MM 100.2. 100211 Overseas Hwy 33037. **Hours:** 5 pm-10 pm. Closed: Mon & Tues. **Reservations:** accepted. **Features:** Look beyond the trees to find this Victorian-style, Caribbean home. The wrap-around porch invites alfresco dining in casual attire. Imaginatively prepared cuisine with Continental touches features fresh seafood, pasta and daily chefs specials. Dressy casual; beer & wine only. **Parking:** on-site. **Cards:** AX, MC, VI.

GANIM'S - KEY LARGO
American
Lunch: $3-$8 **Phone:** 305/451-2895
Location: US 1, MM 99.6. 99696 Overseas Hwy 33037. **Hours:** 6 am-2 pm. **Features:** Whether it's breakfast, lunch or dinner, diners find generous portions of diner-style comfort food at this roadside restaurant. beer & wine only. **Parking:** on-site. **Cards:** AX, DS, MC, VI.

GANIM'S RESTAURANT-PENNEKAMP
American
Lunch: $5-$8 **Dinner:** $8-$11 **Phone:** 305/451-3337
Location: US 1, MM 102.2. 102250 Overseas Hwy 33037. **Hours:** 6 am-9 pm, Sun-2 pm. Closed: 12/25. **Features:** Whether it's breakfast, lunch or dinner, diners find generous portions of diner-style comfort food at this roadside restaurant. beer & wine only. **Parking:** on-site. **Cards:** AX, DS, MC, VI.

GANIM'S STEAK & RIBS
American
Lunch: $6-$14 **Dinner:** $6-$14 **Phone:** 305/451-0900
Location: On US 1 at MM 102.5. 102570 Overseas Hwy 33037. **Hours:** 11 am-9 pm. Closed: 11/27, 12/25. **Features:** This family-oriented spot is decked out with a rustic western motif. Efficient servers bring you traditional barbecue favorites like charbroiled steak, chicken, seafood, ribs and homemade baked beans. Try the onion rings for a delicious treat. Casual dress; beer & wine only. **Parking:** on-site. **Cards:** AX, DS, MC, VI.

SNOOKS BAYSIDE
American
Lunch: $5-$8 **Dinner:** $15-$22 **Phone:** 305/453-3799
Location: Just off US 1 at MM 99.9; between Marina del Mar Bayside and Largo Honda. 99470 Overseas Hwy 33037. **Hours:** 11:30 am-10 pm, Sun from-10 am. **Reservations:** accepted. **Features:** Choose either the terrace or an attractive dining room overlooking Florida Bay. Featuring seafood, steak, veal and chicken, the cuisine is fresh and served by a capable staff. Select tastefully arranged dessert choices brought to you on a silver tray. An extensive wine list is available. Casual dress; cocktails; entertainment. **Parking:** on-site. **Cards:** AX, DC, DS, MC, VI.

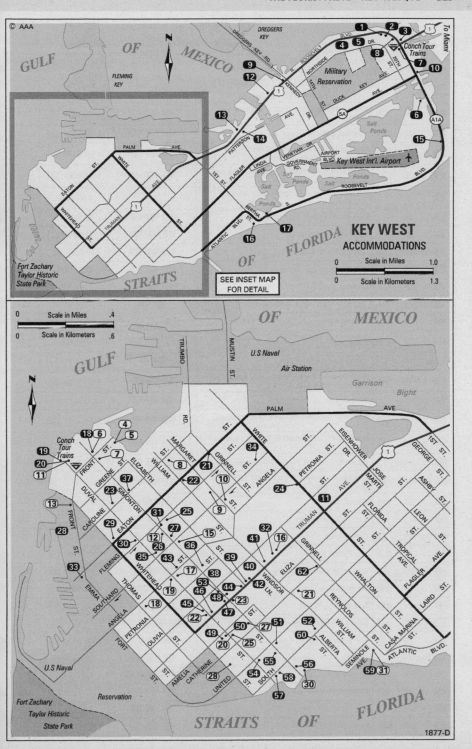

KEY WEST
ACCOMMODATIONS

SEE INSET MAP FOR DETAIL

1877-D

Key West

This index helps you "spot" where approved accommodations and restaurants are located on the corresponding detailed maps. Lodging rate ranges are for comparison only and show the property's high season; rates are per night, unless only weekly (W) rates are available. Restaurant rate range is for dinner, unless only lunch (L) is served. Turn to the listing page for more detailed rate information and consult display ads for special promotions.

Spotter/Map Page Number	OA	KEY WEST - Lodgings	Diamond Rating	Rate Range High Season	Listing Page
1 / p. 329	AAA	**Radisson Hotel Key West** - see color ad p 346	▽▽▽	$169-$299 SAVE	347
2 / p. 329	AAA	**Comfort Inn** - see color ad p 338	▽▽▽	$129-$309 SAVE	338
3 / p. 329	AAA	**Holiday Inn-Beachside Key West** - see color ad opposite inside back cover	▽▽▽	$129-$199 SAVE	342
4 / p. 329	AAA	**Courtyard by Marriott Key West** - see color ad p 339	▽▽▽	$159-$249 SAVE	339
5 / p. 329		Travelodge Key West Hotel - see color ad p 324, p 348	fyi	$129-$189	349
6 / p. 329		Grand Key Resort - see color ad p 341	▽▽▽	$139-$325	341
7 / p. 329		Days Inn-Key West	▽▽▽	$165-$350	340
8 / p. 329	AAA	**Quality Inn & Suites** - see color ad p 346	▽▽▽	$99-$359 SAVE	346
9 / p. 329		Courtyard by Marriott-Key West Waterfront	▽▽▽	$209-$269	339
10 / p. 329		Coconut Mallory Resort & Marina	▽▽▽	$250-$450	337
11 / p. 329		Travelers Palm Inn & Guesthouses	▽▽	$118-$228	347
12 / p. 329	AAA	**Hampton Inn** - see color ad p 342	▽▽▽	$139-$209 SAVE	342
13 / p. 329		Banana Bay Resort-Key West - see color ad p 340	▽▽▽	$150-$250	334
14 / p. 329		Fairfield Inn by Marriott	▽▽	$152-$242	341
15 / p. 329	AAA	**Best Western Key Ambassador Resort Inn** - see color ad p 336	▽▽▽	$139-$239 SAVE	334
16 / p. 329		1800 Atlantic Condominiums	▽▽▽	$300-$550	333
17 / p. 329	AAA	**Sheraton Suites-Key West** - see color ad p 347	▽▽▽	$169-$359 SAVE	347
18 / p. 329	AAA	**Hyatt Key West Resort & Marina** - see ad p 343	▽▽▽	$319 SAVE	343
19 / p. 329		Ocean Key Resort, A Noble House Resort	▽▽▽	$239-$899	345
20 / p. 329	AAA	**Pier House Resort & Caribbean Spa** - see color ad p 346	▽▽▽	$290-$1800 SAVE	345
21 / p. 329	AAA	**Westwinds**	▽▽	$90-$170 SAVE	348
22 / p. 329		Island City House Hotel	▽▽▽	$175-$315	343
23 / p. 329		Curry Mansion Inn	▽▽▽	$180-$325	339
24 / p. 329	AAA	**The Palms Hotel**	▽▽	$150-$250 SAVE	345
25 / p. 329	AAA	**Ambrosia Too At Fleming St**	▽▽▽	$169-$489 SAVE	333
26 / p. 329	AAA	**Heron House**	▽▽▽▽	$189-$369 SAVE	342
27 / p. 329	AAA	**The Watson House**	▽▽▽	$140-$400 SAVE	348
28 / p. 329	AAA	**Hilton Key West Resort & Marina**	▽▽▽▽	$299-$529 SAVE	342
29 / p. 329	AAA	**The Banyan Resort** - see color ad p 334	▽▽▽	$200-$400 SAVE	334
30 / p. 329		Crowne Plaza Hotel and Resort La Concha	▽▽▽	$99-$329	339
31 / p. 329		The Marquesa Hotel	▽▽▽▽	$270-$405	345
32 / p. 329	AAA	**Lightbourn Inn** - see color ad p 344	▽▽▽	$178-$278 SAVE	345
33 / p. 329		The Weatherstation Inn	▽▽▽	$195-$315	348
34 / p. 329	AAA	**Frances St Bottle Inn**	▽▽▽	$139-$189 SAVE	341

Spotter/Map Page Number	OA	**KEY WEST** - Lodgings (continued)	Diamond Rating	Rate Range High Season	Listing Page
35 / p. 329	AAA	Pegasus International Hotel	◇◇	$99-$599 SAVE	345
36 / p. 329	AAA	Courtney's Place Historic Cottages & Inn	◇◇	$115-$325 SAVE	338
37 / p. 329	AAA	Cypress House Bed & Breakfast	◇◇◇	$135-$350 SAVE	340
38 / p. 329		The Paradise Inn	◇◇◇	$270-$545	345
39 / p. 329	AAA	Chelsea House - see color ad p 337	◇◇◇	$150-$245 SAVE	337
40 / p. 329	AAA	The Colony Exclusive Cottages - see ad p 337	◇◇◇	$1555(W) SAVE	338
41 / p. 329	AAA	La Pensione	◇◇◇	$178-$198 SAVE	344
42 / p. 329	AAA	Key Lime Inn - see color ad p 343	◇◇◇	$139-$255 SAVE	344
43 / p. 329	AAA	Duval Inn	◇◇◇	$109-$398 SAVE	341
44 / p. 329	AAA	The Conch House Heritage Inn	◇◇◇	$148-$228 SAVE	338
45 / p. 329	AAA	Andrews Inn	◇◇◇	$179-$189 SAVE	334
46 / p. 329		Duval House - see color ad p 340	◇◇◇	$170-$335	340
47 / p. 329		Center Court Historic Inn & Cottages	◇◇◇	$148-$368	336
48 / p. 329		Key West Villas Resort	◇◇◇	$150-$175	344
49 / p. 329	AAA	La Casa de Luces	◇◇	$169-$269 SAVE	344
50 / p. 329		The Cuban Club Suites	◇◇◇	$169-$599	339
51 / p. 329	AAA	Best Western Hibiscus Motel - see color ad p 335	◇◇◇	$259-$359 SAVE	334
52 / p. 329	AAA	Alexander Palms Court	◇◇	$110-$280 SAVE	333
53 / p. 329		The Courtyard	◇◇	$139-$529	338
54 / p. 329		Southernmost Hotel in the USA - see color ad p 333	◇◇◇	$145-$250	347
55 / p. 329	AAA	Blue Marlin Motel - see color ad p 335	◇◇◇	$199-$299 SAVE	335
56 / p. 329	AAA	Wyndham Reach Resort	◇◇◇	$299 SAVE	349
57 / p. 329		La Mer & Dewey House - see color ad p 333	◇◇◇	$220-$350	344
58 / p. 329		Southernmost on the Beach - see color ad p 333	◇◇◇	$194-$310	347
59 / p. 329	AAA	Wyndham Casa Marina Resort	◇◇◇	$309 SAVE	348
60 / p. 329	AAA	Blue Skies Inn	◇◇◇	$169-$209 SAVE	336
62 / p. 329		The Grand	◇◇	$128-$148	341
		KEY WEST - Restaurants			
4 / p. 329		Alonzo's Oyster House	◇◇	$14-$24	349
5 / p. 329		A & B Lobster House	◇◇◇	$22-$39	349
6 / p. 329		Nicola Seafood	◇◇◇	$22-$29	351
7 / p. 329		Bagatelle Restaurant	◇◇	$15-$25	349
8 / p. 329		Pepe's Cafe	◇	$10-$20	351
9 / p. 329		Michael's	◇◇◇	$15-$29	351
10 / p. 329	AAA	Mangia Mangia	◇◇	$9-$15	351
11 / p. 329	AAA	One Duval	◇◇◇◇	$25-$36	351
12 / p. 329		Cafe Marquesa	◇◇◇◇	$23-$32	350
13 / p. 329		Latitudes Beach Cafe	◇◇◇	$18-$35	350
15 / p. 329		Antonia's Restaurant	◇◇◇	$12-$23	349

Spotter/Map Page Number	OA	**KEY WEST** - Restaurants (continued)	Diamond Rating	Rate Range High Season	Listing Page
⑯ / p. 329		Kyushu	▼▼	$12-$18	350
⑰ / p. 329		Camille's	▼▼	$11-$22	350
⑱ / p. 329		Blue Heaven	▼▼	$10-$24	350
⑲ / p. 329		Mangoes Restaurant	▼▼▼	$11-$22	351
⑳ / p. 329		Alice's at La Te Da	▼▼▼	$13-$28	349
㉑ / p. 329		El Siboney	▼	$6-$14	350
㉒ / p. 329		Croissants de France	▼▼	$5-$9(L)	350
㉓ / p. 329		Cafe des Artistes	▼▼▼▼	$23-$44	350
㉕ / p. 329		Square One Restaurant	▼▼▼	$15-$30	352
㉗ / p. 329		Abbondanza Italian Restaurant	▼▼	$9-$17	349
㉘ / p. 329		Banana Cafe	▼▼	$8-$24	349
㉚ / p. 329		Louie's Backyard	▼▼▼	$24-$38	350
㉛ / p. 329		Flagler's Restaurant & Lounge	▼▼▼	$17-$38	350

May I Take Your Order Please?

When you look through a AAA TourBook® guide in search of a place to dine while traveling, **look for restaurants that advertise**. These establishments are committed to increasing their AAA patronage, and are willing to go the extra mile to capture your attention ... and your appetite!

KEY WEST pop. 25,478   (See map p. 329; index p. 330)

-------- WHERE TO STAY --------

1800 ATLANTIC CONDOMINIUMS

| | | | Phone: (305)294-8877 | 16 |

12/21-1/5   2P: $300-$550
1/6-4/26   2P: $275-$500
12/1-12/20 & 4/27-11/30   2P: $175-$400

Condominium   **Location:** Jct US 1 and SR A1A, 3.1 mi on SR A1A. Located in a small shopping center. 1800 Atlantic Blvd 33040 (1716 N Roosevelt Blvd). Fax: 305/294-7356. **Facility:** 55 units. 3 one-, 48 two- and 4 three-bedroom suites with kitchens and whirlpools. 4 stories, interior/exterior corridors. **Parking:** on-site. **Terms:** check-in 4 pm, 2-3 night minimum stay - seasonal, 14 day cancellation notice-fee imposed, weekly rates available. **Amenities:** voice mail, irons. *Some:* CD players. **Pool(s):** heated outdoor. **Leisure Activities:** whirlpool, 3 lighted tennis courts, racquetball courts, recreation programs. **Guest Services:** complimentary laundry. **Business Services:** meeting rooms. **Cards:** AX, DC, DS, MC, VI.

SOME UNITS

ALEXANDER PALMS COURT

| | | | Phone: (305)296-6413 | 52 |

12/24-5/15 [ECP]   1P: $110-$280   2P: $110-$280   XP: $15   F18
12/1-12/23 & 5/16-11/30 [ECP]   1P: $85-$210   2P: $85-$210   XP: $15   F18

Motel   **Location:** Just n of Duval St. 715 South St 33040. Fax: 305/292-3975. **Facility:** 11 units. 6 one-bedroom standard units, some with efficiencies. 5 one-bedroom suites ($150-$280) with kitchens. 1 story, exterior corridors. *Bath:* combo or shower only. **Parking:** on-site. **Terms:** 14 day cancellation notice, weekly rates available, package plans - 5/1-12/1. **Pool(s):** heated outdoor. **Leisure Activities:** whirlpool. **Cards:** MC, VI.
Special Amenities: free continental breakfast and free local telephone calls.

SOME UNITS

AMBROSIA TOO AT FLEMING ST

| | | | Phone: (305)296-9838 | 25 |

12/15-4/30 [ECP]   1P: $169-$489   2P: $169-$489   XP: $20   F4
12/1-12/14 & 5/1-11/30 [ECP]   1P: $120-$315   2P: $120-$315   XP: $20   F4

Bed & Breakfast   **Location:** Just n of Simonton St. Located in Old Town. 622 Fleming St 33040. Fax: 305/296-2425. **Facility:** Spacious rooms and a tropical setting characterize this property which is close to the center of town. Designated smoking area. 12 units. 6 one-bedroom standard units. 5 one- and 1 two-bedroom suites ($175-$279), some with kitchens. 2-4 stories, exterior corridors. *Bath:* some combo or shower only. **Parking:** on-site. **Terms:** 3 night minimum stay - weekends, 30 day cancellation notice-fee imposed, small pets only ($25 fee). **Amenities:** voice mail, irons, hair dryers. **Pool(s):** small heated outdoor, lap. **Cards:** AX, DS, MC, VI. **Special Amenities: free continental breakfast and free local telephone calls.**

SOME UNITS

(See map p. 329)

ANDREWS INN　　　　　　　　　　　　　　　　　　　　　　　　　**Phone: 305/294-7730**　㊺

AAA SAVE

▼▼▼▼

Bed & Breakfast

12/21-4/30 [ECP]	1P: $179-$189	2P: $179-$189	XP: $20
5/1-5/31 [ECP]	1P: $139-$149	2P: $139-$149	XP: $20
12/1-12/20 & 6/1-11/30 [ECP]	1P: $119-$129	2P: $119-$129	XP: $20

Location: Just s of Duval St, between US 1 and Olivia St. Located in Old Town. 0 Whalton Ln 33040. **Fax:** 305/294-0021. **Facility:** Quiet location, tranquil pool setting. Designated smoking area. 6 one-bedroom standard units. 1-2 stories (no elevator), exterior corridors. **Parking:** on-site. **Terms:** 2 night minimum stay - weekends, 14 day cancellation notice, no pets allowed (owner's pets on premises). **Pool(s):** small heated outdoor. **Leisure Activities:** Fee: bicycles. **Cards:** AX, DC, MC, VI. **Special Amenities: free continental breakfast and free local telephone calls.**

【¶+】【⇌】【✕】【🐾】

BANANA BAY RESORT-KEY WEST　　　　　　　　　　　　　　　**Phone: (305)296-6925**　⑬

▼▼▼　▼▼▼

Motel

12/22-4/26 [ECP]	1P: $150-$250	2P: $150-$250	XP: $15
4/27-11/30 [ECP]	1P: $105-$175	2P: $105-$175	XP: $15
12/1-12/21 [ECP]	1P: $95-$125	2P: $95-$125	XP: $15

Location: On US 1, 1 mi s of entrance to island. 2319 N Roosevelt Blvd 33040. Fax: 305/296-2004. **Facility:** 48 units. 34 one-bedroom standard units, some with efficiencies. 14 one-bedroom suites ($150-$275), some with efficiencies or kitchens. 2 stories (no elevator), interior corridors. **Parking:** on-site. **Terms:** age restrictions may apply, 7 day cancellation notice-fee imposed, package plans. **Amenities:** voice mail, irons, hair dryers. **Pool(s):** outdoor. **Leisure Activities:** whirlpool, scuba diving, snorkeling, fishing, exercise room. Fee: boat dock, charter fishing. **Guest Services:** gift shop, coin laundry. **Business Services:** meeting rooms, fax (fee). **Cards:** AX, CB, DC, DS, JC, MC, VI. *(See color ad p 340)*

SOME UNITS

【ASK】【¶+】【⇌】【✕】【🐾】【DATA PORT】【🛏】【💻】【✕】【🖼】

THE BANYAN RESORT　　　　　　　　　　　　　　　　　　　　**Phone: (305)296-7786**　㉙

AAA SAVE

▼▼▼ ▼▼▼

Small-scale Hotel

12/15-5/1	1P: $200-$400	2P: $200-$400	XP: $20
12/1-12/14 & 5/2-11/30	1P: $150-$300	2P: $150-$300	XP: $20

Location: Just s of Duval St. Located in Old Town. 323 Whitehead St 33040. Fax: 305/294-1107. **Facility:** 38 units. 5 one-bedroom standard units with kitchens. 28 one- and 5 two-bedroom suites with kitchens. 2-3 stories (no elevator), interior/exterior corridors. Bath: combo or shower only. **Parking:** on-site (fee). **Terms:** check-in 4 pm, 3 night minimum stay - seasonal, weekends, age restrictions may apply, 14 day cancellation notice. **Amenities:** voice mail, safes, irons. **Pool(s):** outdoor, heated outdoor. **Leisure Activities:** whirlpool, barbecue areas. Fee: bicycles. **Guest Services:** valet and coin laundry. **Business Services:** fax (fee). **Cards:** AX, DC, MC, VI. *(See color ad below)*

SOME UNITS

【¶+】【⇌】【✕】【🛏】【🖼】【💻】【VCR】

BEST WESTERN HIBISCUS MOTEL　　　　　　　　　　　　　　**Phone: (305)294-3763**　㊿

AAA SAVE

▼▼▼ ▼▼▼

Motel

12/25-1/4 [ECP]	1P: $259-$359	2P: $259-$359	
1/5-3/31 [ECP]	1P: $159-$299	2P: $159-$299	
4/1-11/30 [ECP]	1P: $99-$179	2P: $99-$179	
12/1-12/24 [ECP]	1P: $99-$159	2P: $99-$159	

Location: Corner of United and Simonton sts. Located in Old Town. 1313 Simonton St 33040-0552. Fax: 305/293-9243. **Facility:** 61 one-bedroom standard units. 2 stories (no elevator), exterior corridors. Bath: combo or shower only. **Parking:** on-site. **Terms:** 2-7 night minimum stay - seasonal, 3 day cancellation notice-fee imposed. **Amenities:** safes, irons, hair dryers. **Pool(s):** heated outdoor. **Leisure Activities:** whirlpool, scooters. Fee: bicycles. **Guest Services:** valet and coin laundry. **Cards:** AX, DC, DS, MC, VI. **Special Amenities: free continental breakfast.** *(See color ad p 335)*

SOME UNITS

【¶+】【♿】【🔊】【⇌】【✕】【🐾】【DATA PORT】【🛏】【💻】【🖼】

BEST WESTERN KEY AMBASSADOR RESORT INN　　　　　　**Phone: 305/296-3500**　⑮

AAA SAVE

▼▼▼ ▼▼▼

Motel

12/1-1/27	1P: $139-$239	2P: $139-$239	XP: $10	F12
5/27-11/30	1P: $89-$239	2P: $89-$239	XP: $10	F12
1/28-3/31	1P: $169-$219	2P: $169-$219	XP: $15	F12
4/1-5/26	1P: $109-$189	2P: $109-$189	XP: $10	F12

Location: On SR A1A, 1 mi s of jct US 1. Located in New Town. 3755 S Roosevelt Blvd 33040. Fax: 305/296-9961. **Facility:** 100 one-bedroom standard units. 2 stories (no elevator), exterior corridors. Bath: combo or shower only. **Parking:** on-site. **Terms:** 3 day cancellation notice-fee imposed. **Amenities:** voice mail, irons, hair dryers. **Pool(s):** heated outdoor. **Leisure Activities:** barbecue/picnic area, outdoor fitness center, shuffleboard. **Guest Services:** coin laundry. **Business Services:** fax (fee). **Cards:** AX, CB, DC, DS, MC, VI. **Special Amenities: free continental breakfast and free newspaper.** *(See color ad p 336)*

【🖼】【⇌】【🐾】【DATA PORT】【🛏】【💻】

See map p. 329)

BLUE MARLIN MOTEL   Phone: (305)294-2585

12/25-3/31 [CP]	1P: $199-$299	2P: $199-$299
4/1-5/31 [CP]	1P: $99-$139	2P: $99-$139
12/1-12/24 & 6/1-11/30 [CP]	1P: $89-$129	2P: $89-$129

Motel

Location: Just s of US 1 (Truman Ave). Located in Old Town. 1320 Simonton St 33040. Fax: 305/296-1209. **Facility:** 53 one-bedroom standard units, some with efficiencies. 2 stories (no elevator), exterior corridors. **Parking:** on-site. **Terms:** cancellation fee imposed. **Pool(s):** heated outdoor. **Guest Services:** valet and coin laundry. **Cards:** AX, CB, DC, DS, MC, VI. **Special Amenities:** free continental breakfast. *(See color ad below)*

(See map p. 329)

BLUE SKIES INN

Phone: (305)295-9464 [60]

AAA SAVE
WWW

Historic Bed
& Breakfast

12/1-3/31 [ECP]	1P: $169-$209	2P: $169-$209	XP: $20
4/1-4/30 [ECP]	1P: $129-$179	2P: $129-$179	XP: $20
5/1-5/31 [ECP]	1P: $109-$149	2P: $109-$149	XP: $20
6/1-11/30 [ECP]	1P: $89-$139	2P: $89-$139	XP: $20

Location: From Truman Ave, e on Duval St, turn left onto South St, just a few blks. 630 South St 33040. Fax: 305/294-9110. **Facility:** Convenient to attractions and shopping, Blue Skies Inn is a Conch house shaded by large trees and featuring colorfully decorated, spacious rooms. 5 one-bedroom standard units. 2 stories (no elevator), exterior corridors. *Bath:* combo or shower only. **Parking:** street. **Terms:** 14 day cancellation notice-fee imposed, weekly rates available, no pets allowed (owner's pets on premises). **Amenities:** hair dryers. **Leisure Activities:** whirlpool. **Guest Services:** complimentary evening beverages. **Cards:** AX, DS, MC, VI. **Special Amenities:** free continental breakfast and preferred room (subject to availability with advanced reservations).

SOME UNITS

🅂 🕪 🎥 🎁 📺 / 🖨 /

CENTER COURT HISTORIC INN & COTTAGES

Phone: (305)296-9292 [47]

WWW

Bed & Breakfast

12/15-4/30	1P: $148-$368	2P: $148-$368	XP: $15
12/1-12/14 & 5/1-11/30	1P: $98-$298	2P: $98-$298	XP: $15

Location: 0.5 mi n of jct US 1, between Duval and Simonton sts. Located in Old Town. 915 Center St 33040. Fax: 305/294-4104. **Facility:** Just off Truman Street, this property is in a quiet area yet close to shops and eateries; rooms feature Caribbean-style decor. Designated smoking area. 7 one-bedroom standard units, some with efficiencies, kitchens and/or whirlpools. 1-2 stories (no elevator), interior/exterior corridors. *Bath:* combo or shower only. **Parking:** street. **Terms:** 3 night minimum stay - weekends, age restrictions may apply, 30 day cancellation notice-fee imposed, weekly rates available, [ECP] meal plan available, pets ($10 extra charge). **Amenities:** CD players, safes, irons, hair dryers. **Pool(s):** 2 outdoor. **Leisure Activities:** whirlpool, limited exercise equipment. **Guest Services:** valet laundry. **Cards:** AX, DS, MC, VI.

SOME UNITS

🐕 🕪 🏊 ⊗ / 📼 🎁 🖨 /

(See map p. 329)

CHELSEA HOUSE

				Phone: (305)296-2211	**39**
AAA SAVE	12/21-3/31 [ECP]	1P: $150-$245	2P: $150-$245	XP: $20	
▼▼▼	12/1-12/20 [ECP]	1P: $130-$199	2P: $130-$199	XP: $20	
	4/1-5/31 [ECP]	1P: $94-$150	2P: $94-$150	XP: $10	
	6/1-11/30 [ECP]	1P: $85-$135	2P: $85-$135	XP: $10	

Historic Bed & Breakfast

Location: At the corner of Elizabeth St and Truman Ave. 707 Truman Ave 33040. Fax: 305/296-4822. **Facility:** Close to shopping, restaurants and the historic district, this property includes two 1870 Victorian homes surrounded by lush tropical foliage. Smoke free premises. 21 one-bedroom standard units, some with kitchens. 2 stories (no elevator), interior/exterior corridors. *Bath:* combo or shower only. **Parking:** on-site. **Terms:** 2 night minimum stay - weekends, age restrictions may apply. 10 day cancellation notice-fee imposed, small pets only ($10 extra charge). **Amenities:** safes. **Pool(s):** heated outdoor. **Cards:** AX, DC, DS, MC, VI. **Special Amenities:** free continental breakfast and free local telephone calls. *(See color ad below)*

SOME UNITS

🚭 🐾 🍴 🏊 ✕ 🛜 / VCR 📺 💻 /
FEE

COCONUT MALLORY RESORT & MARINA

				Phone: (305)292-0017	**10**
▼▼▼	1/1-4/30	1P: $250-$450	2P: $250-$450		
	12/1-12/31 & 6/1-11/30	1P: $175-$450	2P: $175-$450		
Condominium	5/1-5/31	1P: $200-$250	2P: $200-$250		

Facility: On SR A1A, 0.3 mi s at Flagler and Roosevelt Blvd. 1445 S Roosevelt Blvd 33040. Fax: 305/292-5698. **Facility:** 30 two-bedroom suites with kitchens. 3 stories, exterior corridors. **Parking:** on-site. **Terms:** check-in 4 pm, 3 day cancellation notice-fee imposed. **Amenities:** video library (fee), voice mail, safes. **Pool(s):** 2 outdoor. **Leisure Activities:** fishing. **Guest Services:** coin laundry. **Cards:** AX, MC, VI.

SOME UNITS

ASK S🄳 🏊 VCR 🛜 📺 / ✕ /

(See map p. 329)

THE COLONY EXCLUSIVE COTTAGES
Phone: 305/294-6691   40

(AAA) [SAVE]
◆◆◆◆

Cottage

12/21-4/20 Wkly	2P: $1555	XP: $175
12/1-12/20 & 4/21-11/30 Wkly	2P: $1050	XP: $175

Location: 3 blks n of Duval St. Located in Old Town. 714 Olivia St 33040-6552. Fax: 305/294-0402. **Facility:** 9 cottages. 1-2 stories (no elevator), exterior corridors. **Parking:** on-site. **Terms:** 7 night minimum stay, 21 day cancellation notice. **Amenities:** voice mail, safes, irons, hair dryers. **Pool(s):** heated outdoor. **Cards:** MC, VI. *(See ad p 337)*

🍴 🏊 📼 🎦 📶 🖥 💻

COMFORT INN
Phone: (305)294-3773   2

(AAA) [SAVE]
◆◆◆◆

Motel

12/1-12/31	1P: $129-$309	2P: $129-$309	XP: $10 F18
2/14-5/26	1P: $179-$209	2P: $179-$209	XP: $10 F18
1/1-2/13	1P: $119-$199	2P: $119-$199	XP: $10 F18
5/27-11/30	1P: $99-$149	2P: $99-$149	XP: $10 F18

Location: On US 1. Located in New Town. 3824 N Roosevelt Blvd 33040-6552. Fax: 305/294-5739. **Facility:** 100 one-bedroom standard units. 2 stories (no elevator), exterior corridors. *Bath:* combo or shower only. **Parking:** on-site. **Terms:** cancellation fee imposed, [CP] meal plan available. **Amenities:** voice mail, safes (fee). *Some:* irons, hair dryers. **Pool(s):** outdoor. **Guest Services:** coin laundry. **Business Services:** fax (fee). **Cards:** AX, CB, DC, DS, MC, VI. **Special Amenities:** free continental breakfast. *(See color ad below)*

SOME UNITS

🅂🄳 🍴 ⏸ 📷 🏊 🎦 📶 / ✕ 🖥 💻 /
FEE

THE CONCH HOUSE HERITAGE INN
Phone: (305)293-0020   44

(AAA) [SAVE]
◆◆◆

Classic Historic
Bed & Breakfast

12/21-4/30 [ECP]	2P: $148-$228	XP: $15
5/1-5/31 [ECP]	2P: $108-$168	XP: $15
6/1-11/30	2P: $98-$158	
12/1-12/20 [ECP]	2P: $98-$158	XP: $15

Location: On US 1, just n of Duval St. Located in Old Town. 625 Truman Ave 33040. Fax: 305/293-8447. **Facility:** A wraparound porch adds character to this centrally located Conch house featuring spacious rooms and some antique furnishings. Smoke free premises. 8 one-bedroom standard units. 2 stories (no elevator), interior/exterior corridors. *Bath:* combo or shower only. **Parking:** on-site. **Terms:** 2 night minimum stay - weekends, age restrictions may apply, 15 day cancellation notice-fee imposed. **Pool(s):** outdoor. **Business Services:** fax (fee). **Cards:** AX, DS, MC, VI. **Special Amenities:** free continental breakfast and free local telephone calls.

🅂🄳 🍴 ⏸M 🏊 ✕

COURTNEY'S PLACE HISTORIC COTTAGES & INN
Phone: (305)294-3480   36

(AAA) [SAVE]
◆◆

Historic Cottage

12/22-4/30	2P: $115-$325	XP: $20 F12
12/1-12/21 & 5/1-11/30	2P: $75-$225	XP: $20 F12

Location: Just e from jct Petronia and Simonton sts. Located in Old Town. 720 Whitmarsh Ln 33040-6552. Fax: 305/294-7019. **Facility:** 16 units. 10 one-bedroom standard units, some with efficiencies. 6 one-bedroom suites with kitchens. 2 stories (no elevator), exterior corridors. *Bath:* combo or shower only. **Parking:** on-site. **Terms:** 2-3 night minimum stay - weekends & advanced reservations, 21 day cancellation notice-fee imposed, [CP] meal plan available, pets (owner's pets on premises). **Amenities:** irons. **Pool(s):** small outdoor. **Leisure Activities:** barbecue grills. *Fee:* bicycles. **Guest Services:** valet laundry. **Cards:** AX, DS, MC, VI. **Special Amenities:** free continental breakfast and free local telephone calls.

🐾 ⏸ 🏊 📶 🖥 💻

THE COURTYARD
Phone: (305)296-1148   53

◆◆

Historic Cottage

12/1-4/18	1P: $139-$529	2P: $139-$529	XP: $20
4/19-5/31 & 10/18-11/30	1P: $109-$279	2P: $109-$279	XP: $20
6/1-10/17	1P: $89-$229	2P: $89-$229	XP: $20

Location: Just w of US 1 (Truman Blvd). Located in Old Town. 910 Simonton St 33040. Fax: 305/292-7924. **Facility:** 6 cottages ($109-$529). 1 story, exterior corridors. *Bath:* combo or shower only. **Parking:** street. **Terms:** 2 night minimum stay - weekends. **Business Services:** fax (fee). **Cards:** AX, CB, DC, MC, VI.

SOME UNITS

[ASK] 🅂🄳 🍴 🎦 🖥 💻 / 🖥 /

(See map p. 329)

COURTYARD BY MARRIOTT KEY WEST　　　　　　　　　　**Phone:** (305)294-5541　④
[AAA] [SAVE]　12/1-4/30　　　　1P: $159-$249
▼▼▼▼　10/1-11/30　　　1P: $159-$199
　　　5/1-7/31　　　　1P: $129-$199
　　　8/1-9/30　　　　1P: $109-$179
Small-scale Hotel **Location:** On US 1. Located in New Town. 3420 N Roosevelt Blvd 33040. Fax: 305/294-7932. **Facility:** 105 one-bedroom standard units, some with efficiencies. 2 stories (no elevator), interior/exterior corridors. *Bath:* combo or shower only. **Parking:** on-site. **Amenities:** dual phone lines, voice mail, safes, irons, hair dryers. **Dining:** 6:30 am-3 pm, cocktails. **Pool(s):** heated outdoor. **Leisure Activities:** whirlpool, exercise room. **Guest Services:** valet and coin laundry. **Business Services:** meeting rooms, fax (fee). **Cards:** AX, DC, DS, MC, VI. **Special Amenities:** early check-in/late check-out and free newspaper. *(See color ad below)*

SOME UNITS

⊠🍽🍸🛗🏊🎥📶💻 /⊠🔲🖥 /
　　　　　　　　　　　　　　　FEE

COURTYARD BY MARRIOTT-KEY WEST WATERFRONT　　**Phone:** (305)296-6595　⑨
[SAVE]　12/28-4/15　　　　1P: $209-$259　　2P: $219-$269　　XP: $10　　F18
▼▼▼▼　12/1-12/27 & 4/16-11/30　1P: $119-$149　　2P: $129-$159　　XP: $10　　F18
　　Location: On US 1, 1 mi w of jct A1A. Located in New Town. 3041 N Roosevelt Blvd 33040. Fax: 305/296-8351.
　　Facility: 67 units. 43 one-bedroom standard units. 24 one-bedroom suites ($179-$499), some with efficien-
Small-scale Hotel cies and/or whirlpools. 3 stories, interior/exterior corridors. *Bath:* combo or shower only. **Parking:** on-site.
　　Terms: [BP] & [MAP] meal plans available. **Amenities:** dual phone lines, voice mail, irons, hair dryers.
Pool(s): heated outdoor. **Leisure Activities:** whirlpool, exercise room. **Guest Services:** valet and coin laundry, area transportation (fee). **Business Services:** meeting rooms, fax (fee). **Cards:** AX, DC, DS, MC, VI.

SOME UNITS

⊠🍽🍸🛗🏊🎥📶💻 /⊠🔲🖥 /

CROWNE PLAZA HOTEL AND RESORT LA CONCHA　　　**Phone:** (305)296-2991　㉚
▼▼▼　All Year　　　1P: $99-$329　　　2P: $99-$329
　　Location: Corner of Duval and Fleming sts. Located in Old Town. 430 Duval St 33040. Fax: 305/294-3283.
Large-scale Hotel **Facility:** 160 units. 158 one-bedroom standard units. 2 one-bedroom suites ($189-$489). 4-7 stories, interior
　　corridors. **Parking:** on-site (fee). **Terms:** check-in 4 pm, 3 day cancellation notice-fee imposed.
Amenities: video games (fee), dual phone lines, voice mail, irons, hair dryers. **Leisure Activities:** exercise room. *Fee:* bicycles.
Guest Services: gift shop, valet laundry. **Business Services:** meeting rooms, fax (fee). **Cards:** AX, DC, DS, MC, VI.

SOME UNITS

🍽24↑🍸🎥📶💻 /⊠🔲/

THE CUBAN CLUB SUITES　　　　　　　　　　　**Phone:** (305)296-0465　㊿
▼▼▼　All Year [CP]　　1P: $169-$599　　2P: $169-$599　　XP: $10　　F14
　　Location: Corner of Duval and Amelia sts. Located in Old Town. 1108 Duval St 33040 (422 Amelia St).
Motel　Fax: 305/292-7665. **Facility:** 5 units. 3 one- and 2 two-bedroom suites with kitchens. 2 stories (no elevator),
　　interior corridors. **Parking:** on-site. **Terms:** off-site registration, 2 night minimum stay - weekends, 14 day
cancellation notice-fee imposed, small pets only ($200 deposit). **Amenities:** irons. **Guest Services:** complimentary laundry.
Business Services: fax (fee). **Cards:** AX, MC, VI.

SOME UNITS

[ASK]⊠🛏🛗👥🎥🔲🖥 /⊠/
　　　　　　FEE

CURRY MANSION INN　　　　　　　　　　　　**Phone:** (305)294-5349　㉓
▼▼▼　1/16-4/16 [BP]　　1P: $180-$325　　2P: $180-$325　　XP: $50　　F
　　12/1-1/15 & 4/17-11/30 [BP]　1P: $145-$245　　2P: $145-$245　　XP: $50　　F
Historic Bed **Location:** Just n of jct Duval St. Located in Old Town. 511 Caroline St 33040-6604. Fax: 305/294-4093. **Facility:** Tall
& Breakfast trees surround this historic mansion built in the late 1800s; room decor ranges from period antiques to wicker
　　and tropical colors. Smoke free premises. 28 one-bedroom standard units, some with whirlpools. 2 stories
(no elevator), interior/exterior corridors. *Bath:* combo or shower only. **Parking:** on-site. **Terms:** 2 night minimum stay - with Saturday stayover, 14 day cancellation notice-fee imposed, small pets only. **Amenities:** irons, hair dryers. **Pool(s):** heated outdoor.
Leisure Activities: whirlpools. **Guest Services:** complimentary evening beverages, valet and coin laundry. **Business Services:**
meeting rooms, fax (fee). **Cards:** AX, DC, DS, MC, VI.

🛏👥🏊⊠🎥🔲

(See map p. 329)

CYPRESS HOUSE BED & BREAKFAST

AAA **SAVE**

▼▼▼▼

Historic Bed
& Breakfast

Phone: (305)294-6969 37

12/21-4/30 [ECP]	1P: $135-$350	2P: $135-$350	XP: $20
12/1-12/20 & 5/1-11/30 [ECP]	1P: $99-$300	2P: $99-$300	XP: $20

Location: At corner of Caroline and Simonton sts. 601 Caroline St 33040. Fax: 305/296-1174. **Facility:** A Bahamian-style house dating from 1888, this B&B offers spacious rooms decorated with some period antiques. 15 units. 14 one-bedroom standard units. 1 one-bedroom suite ($165-$350) with efficiency. 3 stories (no elevator), interior/exterior corridors. *Bath:* some shared or private, shower only. **Parking:** on-site. **Terms:** 3 night minimum stay - 5 night 12/15-4/30, age restrictions may apply, 14 day cancellation notice-fee imposed, no pets allowed (owner's pets on premises). **Amenities:** voice mail. **Pool(s):** small heated outdoor. **Leisure Activities:** bicycles. **Guest Services:** complimentary evening beverages. **Cards:** AX, DS, MC, VI. **Special Amenities:** free continental breakfast and free room upgrade (subject to availability with advanced reservations).

SOME UNITS

[icons] / ⊠ 📷 💻 /

DAYS INN-KEY WEST

SAVE

▼▼▼

Motel

Phone: (305)294-3742 7

12/25-4/1	1P: $165-$350	2P: $165-$350	
12/1-12/24 & 4/2-11/30	1P: $99-$175	2P: $99-$175	

Location: Just e of jct US 1 and SR A1A. 3852 N Roosevelt Blvd 33040. Fax: 305/296-7260. **Facility:** 133 units. 115 one-bedroom standard units. 18 one-bedroom suites. 2 stories, exterior corridors. *Bath:* combo or shower only. **Parking:** on-site. **Terms:** check-in 4 pm, 3 day cancellation notice. **Amenities:** dual phone lines, voice mail, safes, honor bars, hair dryers. **Pool(s):** heated outdoor. **Guest Services:** coin laundry. **Business Services:** fax (fee). **Cards:** AX, CB, DC, DS, JC, MC, VI.

SOME UNITS

[icons] / ⊠ 📷 💻 /

DUVAL HOUSE

▼▼▼

Historic Bed
& Breakfast

Phone: (305)294-1666 46

12/25-4/30	1P: $170-$335	2P: $170-$335	XP: $20
5/1-11/30	1P: $115-$275	2P: $115-$275	XP: $20
12/1-12/24	1P: $115-$205	2P: $115-$205	XP: $20

Location: Just n of jct Truman and Duval sts. Located in Old Town. 815 Duval St 33040. Fax: 305/292-1701. **Facility:** This property includes 7 Conch houses surrounded by a lush tropical courtyard; room sizes vary. Designated smoking area. 28 units. 26 one- and 1 two-bedroom standard units, some with efficiencies. 1 one-bedroom suite ($175-$335) with kitchen. 2 stories (no elevator), exterior corridors. *Bath:* combo or shower only. **Parking:** on-site. **Terms:** 2 night minimum stay - weekends, age restrictions may apply, 7 day cancellation notice-fee imposed, [ECP] meal plan available. **Amenities:** voice mail, hair dryers. **Pool(s):** outdoor. **Business Services:** fax (fee). **Cards:** AX, DC, DS, JC, MC, VI. *(See color ad below)*

SOME UNITS

[ASK] [icons] / 🖥 💻 /

(See map p. 329)

DUVAL INN

AAA SAVE

▼▼▼▼

Historic Bed
& Breakfast

Phone: (305)295-9531 43

12/25-4/30	1P: $109-$398	2P: $109-$398	XP: $15 F17
12/1-12/24 & 5/1-11/30	1P: $79-$169	2P: $79-$169	XP: $15 F17

Location: From Truman Ave (US 1), 0.3 mi w on Simmonton St, then just s. 511 Angela St 33040. **Fax:** 305/295-9525. **Facility:** Two conch houses located just off Duval Street. Cozy rooms nicely furnished and decorated. Designated smoking area. 7 one-bedroom standard units, some with efficiencies. 2 stories (no elevator), interior corridors. **Bath:** combo or shower only. **Parking:** on-site. **Terms:** 2 night minimum stay - weekends, 14 day cancellation notice-fee imposed. **Amenities:** voice mail, hair dryers. *Some:* irons. **Pool(s):** small heated outdoor. **Leisure Activities:** Fee: bicycles. **Business Services:** fax (fee). **Cards:** AX, DC, MC, VI.

SOME UNITS

🍽️ 🛋️ ✖️ / 🖥️ 💻 /

FAIRFIELD INN BY MARRIOTT

SAVE

▼▼ ▼▼

Motel

Phone: (305)296-5700 14

2/1-4/30	2P: $152-$242
1/1-1/31	2P: $125-$197
12/1-12/31	2P: $98-$197
5/1-11/30	2P: $98-$135

Location: On US 1, 1 mi s of entrance to island. 2400 N Roosevelt Blvd 33040. **Fax:** 305/292-9840. **Facility:** 132 units. 100 one-bedroom standard units. 32 one-bedroom suites, some with efficiencies. 2 stories, exterior corridors. **Bath:** combo or shower only. **Parking:** on-site. **Terms:** [ECP] meal plan available. **Amenities:** video games (fee), irons. *Some:* hair dryers. **Pool(s):** 2 heated outdoor. **Leisure Activities:** Fee: bicycles. **Guest Services:** valet and coin laundry. **Business Services:** fax (fee). **Cards:** AX, DC, DS, MC, VI.

SOME UNITS

💲 🍽️ 📶 📐 🛋️ 🎥 DATA PORT / ✖️ 🖥️ 💻 /

FRANCES ST BOTTLE INN

AAA SAVE

▼▼ ▼▼

Historic Bed
& Breakfast

Phone: (305)294-8530 34

12/20-4/30 [ECP]	1P: $139-$189	2P: $139-$189	XP: $20 F12
12/1-12/19 & 5/1-11/30 [ECP]	1P: $89-$149	2P: $89-$149	XP: $20 F12

Location: From US 1/Roosevelt Blvd, right onto White St, then left onto Southard St; at corner of Frances and Southard sts. Located in a residential area. 535 Frances St 33040. **Fax:** 305/294-1628. **Facility:** Palm trees shade a courtyard hot tub and Caribbean colors decorate the guest rooms at this property not far from shopping. Designated smoking area. 8 one-bedroom standard units. 2 stories (no elevator), interior corridors. **Bath:** combo or shower only. **Parking:** street. **Terms:** 2 night minimum stay - weekends, 14 day cancellation notice-fee imposed, small pets only ($25 fee). **Amenities:** *Some:* CD players. **Leisure Activities:** hot tub. **Cards:** AX, MC, VI. **Special Amenities:** free continental breakfast and free local telephone calls.

SOME UNITS

🛏️ 🍽️ ✖️ 🅿️ / 📼 🖥️ /

THE GRAND

▼▼ ▼▼

Historic Bed
& Breakfast

Phone: (305)294-0590 62

12/16-4/30	1P: $128-$148	2P: $128-$148	XP: $25
5/1-11/30	1P: $108-$128	2P: $108-$128	XP: $25
12/1-12/15	1P: $98-$118	2P: $98-$118	XP: $25

Location: From Truman Ave (US 1), just e on Grinnell St; between Virginia and Catherine sts. 1116 Grinnell St 33040. **Fax:** 305/294-0477. **Facility:** Designated smoking area. 7 units. 3 one-bedroom standard units. 4 one-bedroom suites ($138-$208) with efficiencies. 2 stories (no elevator), exterior corridors. **Bath:** combo or shower only. **Parking:** on-site. **Terms:** 2-3 night minimum stay - seasonal and weekends, 14 day cancellation notice-fee imposed, [CP] meal plan available, no pets allowed (owner's pets on premises). **Cards:** AX, DS, MC, VI.

SOME UNITS

ASK 🍽️ ✖️ 🖥️ / 🖥️ 💻 /

GRAND KEY RESORT

▼▼ ▼▼

Large-scale Hotel

Phone: (305)293-1818 6

12/1-12/31 & 4/27-11/30	1P: $139-$325	2P: $139-$325	XP: $10 F18
2/14-4/26	1P: $179-$279	2P: $179-$279	XP: $10 F18
1/1-2/13	1P: $139-$199	2P: $139-$199	XP: $10 F18

Location: From US 1, 0.5 mi s on SR A1A. Located in a quiet area. 3990 S Roosevelt Blvd 33040. **Fax:** 305/296-6962. **Facility:** 216 units. 208 one-bedroom standard units, some with whirlpools. 6 one- and 2 two-bedroom suites ($199-$685), some with whirlpools. 4 stories, interior corridors. **Bath:** combo or shower only. **Parking:** on-site. **Terms:** check-in 4 pm, 3 day cancellation notice-fee imposed. **Amenities:** video games (fee), high-speed Internet, dual phone lines, voice mail, safes, honor bars, irons, hair dryers. *Some:* CD players. **Pool(s):** heated outdoor. **Leisure Activities:** whirlpool, exercise room. *Fee:* scuba diving, snorkeling, fishing, massage. **Guest Services:** gift shop, valet and coin laundry, area transportation (fee). **Business Services:** meeting rooms, fax (fee). **Cards:** AX, CB, DC, DS, JC, MC, VI. *(See color ad below)*

SOME UNITS

ASK 💲 ➕ 🍽️ 🍸 🏋️ ♿ 📶 🛋️ ✖️ 🎥 DATA PORT 💻 / ✖️ 🖥️ /

(See map p. 329)

HAMPTON INN　　　　　　　　　　　　　　　　　　　　　　　Phone: (305)294-2917　🔟2

AAA SAVE

▼▼▼▼

Motel

12/26-2/13 [ECP]	1P: $139-$209	2P: $139-$209
2/14-4/20 [ECP]	1P: $159-$204	2P: $159-$204
4/21-11/30 [ECP]	1P: $94-$159	2P: $94-$159
12/1-12/25 [ECP]	1P: $89-$124	2P: $89-$124

Location: On US 1, 1.5 mi w of jct SR A1A. Located on the gulf side. 2801 N Roosevelt Blvd 33040. Fax: 305/296-0221. **Facility:** 159 one-bedroom standard units. 2 stories, exterior corridors. *Bath:* combo or shower only. **Parking:** on-site. **Amenities:** voice mail, safes, irons, hair dryers. **Pool(s):** heated outdoor. **Leisure Activities:** whirlpool. *Fee:* jet skiing, parasailing, scooters, bicycles. **Guest Services:** gift shop, coin laundry. **Business Services:** meeting rooms, fax. **Cards:** AX, CB, DC, DS, MC, VI. **Special Amenities:** free continental breakfast and free local telephone calls. *(See color ad below)*

SOME UNITS
[icons] / FEE

HERON HOUSE　　　　　　　　　　　　　　　　　　　　　　Phone: (305)294-9227　2️⃣6

AAA SAVE

▼▼▼▼ ▼▼▼▼

Bed & Breakfast

12/1-4/30 [ECP]	1P: $189-$369	2P: $189-$369　XP: $25
5/1-5/31 & 10/20-11/30 [ECP]	1P: $149-$319	2P: $149-$319　XP: $25
6/1-10/19 [ECP]	1P: $119-$239	2P: $119-$239　XP: $25

Location: From Truman Ave, w on Simonton St, near corner of Fleming St. Located in Old Town. 512 Simonton St 33040. Fax: 305/294-5692. **Facility:** Island-style touches enhance the contemporary decor of guest rooms at this property made up of four Conch houses dating from 1856. Designated smoking area. 23 one-bedroom standard units, some with whirlpools. 2 stories, exterior corridors. *Bath:* combo or shower only. **Parking:** on-site (fee) and street. **Terms:** 2 night minimum stay, age restrictions may apply, 30 day cancellation notice, 14 day off season-fee imposed. **Amenities:** voice mail, safes, irons, hair dryers. **Pool(s):** heated outdoor. **Leisure Activities:** sun deck. **Guest Services:** complimentary evening beverages. **Business Services:** fax. **Cards:** AX, CB, DC, MC, VI. **Special Amenities:** free continental breakfast and free newspaper.

SOME UNITS
[icons] /

HILTON KEY WEST RESORT & MARINA　　　　　　　　　　Phone: (305)294-4000　2️⃣8

AAA SAVE

▼▼▼▼

Resort
Large-scale Hotel

1/1-4/26	1P: $299-$529	2P: $299-$529	XP: $20　F18
4/27-5/25	1P: $189-$529	2P: $189-$529	XP: $20　F18
5/26-11/30	1P: $165-$529	2P: $165-$529	XP: $20　F18
12/1-12/31	1P: $165-$469	2P: $165-$469	XP: $20　F18

Location: Adjacent to Mallory Square. Located in Old Town. 245 Front St 33040. Fax: 305/294-4086. **Facility:** This Key West/Caribbean-style property features large guest rooms, many with balconies; a walking bridge connects to the Mallory Square Dock. 178 units. 146 one-bedroom standard units. 14 one- and 18 two-bedroom suites ($409-$959), some with whirlpools. 3-4 stories, interior/exterior corridors. *Bath:* combo or shower only. **Parking:** on-site (fee) and valet. **Terms:** check-in 4 pm, cancellation fee imposed. **Amenities:** *Some:* CD players, dual phone lines. **Dining:** 5 restaurants, 7 am-11 pm, cocktails, also, Latitudes Beach Cafe, see separate listing, entertainment. **Pool(s):** 2 heated outdoor. **Leisure Activities:** whirlpools, launch shuttle to island beach, recreation programs, casino cruises, exercise room. *Fee:* boats, marina, scuba diving, snorkeling, charter fishing, jet ski, parasailing, waverunners, massage. **Guest Services:** gift shop, valet laundry. **Business Services:** conference facilities, business center. **Cards:** AX, CB, DC, DS, JC, MC, VI. **Special Amenities:** free newspaper and preferred room (subject to availability with advanced reservations).

SOME UNITS
[icons] /

HOLIDAY INN-BEACHSIDE KEY WEST　　　　　　　　　Phone: (305)294-2571　🔟3

AAA SAVE

▼▼▼▼

Motel

12/1-4/16	1P: $129-$199	2P: $129-$199	XP: $10　F15
4/17-11/30	1P: $99-$149	2P: $99-$149	XP: $10　F15

Location: On entering island, jct US 1 and SR A1A. 3841 N Roosevelt Blvd 33040-6552. Fax: 305/292-7252. **Facility:** 222 one-bedroom standard units. 2-4 stories, exterior corridors. *Bath:* combo or shower only. **Parking:** on-site. **Terms:** [AP] meal plan available. **Amenities:** voice mail, safes (fee), irons, hair dryers. **Pool(s):** heated outdoor. **Leisure Activities:** whirlpool, rental boats, rental paddleboats, 50 ft fishing pier, jet ski rental, sun kats, kayaks. *Fee:* scuba diving, snorkeling, bicycles. **Guest Services:** gift shop, valet and coin laundry. **Business Services:** meeting rooms. **Cards:** AX, CB, DC, DS, JC, MC, VI. **Special Amenities:** early check-in/late check-out and free room upgrade (subject to availability with advanced reservations). *(See color ad opposite inside back cover)*

SOME UNITS
[icons] / FEE

(See map p. 329)

HYATT KEY WEST RESORT & MARINA

Phone: (305)296-9900   [18]

12/1-4/15	1P: $319	2P: $319	XP: $45	F18
4/16-8/31	1P: $252	2P: $252	XP: $45	F18
9/1-11/30	1P: $215	2P: $215	XP: $45	F18

Location: Simonton and Front sts, just n of Mallory Square. Located in Old Town. 601 Front St 33040.
Small-scale Hotel Fax: 305/292-1038. **Facility:** 120 units. 118 one-bedroom standard units, some with whirlpools. 2 one-bedroom suites. 5 stories, exterior corridors. *Bath:* combo or shower only. **Parking:** on-site (fee) and valet.
Terms: check-in 4 pm, 3 day cancellation notice-fee imposed. **Amenities:** dual phone lines, voice mail, safes, honor bars, irons, hair dryers. *Some:* CD players. **Dining:** Nicola Seafood, see separate listing. **Pool(s):** heated outdoor. **Leisure Activities:** whirlpool, exercise room. *Fee:* boats, boat dock, scuba diving, snorkeling, charter fishing, scuba & sunset cruises, snorkeling & scuba instruction, waverunners, parasailing, charter sailing, bicycles, massage. **Guest Services:** gift shop, valet laundry. **Business Services:** meeting rooms, fax (fee). **Cards:** AX, CB, DC, DS, JC, MC, VI. *(See ad below)*

SOME UNITS

[icons] / [icons] /
FEE   FEE

ISLAND CITY HOUSE HOTEL

Phone: (305)294-5702   [22]

12/21-4/30 [ECP]	2P: $175-$315	XP: $20	F12
5/1-5/31 [ECP]	2P: $145-$275	XP: $20	F12
12/1-12/20 & 6/1-11/30 [ECP]	2P: $115-$210	XP: $20	F12

Historic Bed & Breakfast   **Location:** Just e of Duval St. Located in Old Town. 411 William St 33040. Fax: 305/294-1289. **Facility:** The property includes a tropical courtyard, two Victorian homes dating from 1880 and a replica of a cigar factory. Designated smoking area. 24 units. 20 one- and 4 two-bedroom suites with kitchens. 2-3 stories (no elevator), interior/exterior corridors. **Parking:** street. **Terms:** 2 night minimum stay - weekends & in season, 14 day cancellation notice-fee imposed. **Amenities:** video library (fee), voice mail, hair dryers. *Some:* irons. **Pool(s):** heated outdoor. **Leisure Activities:** whirlpool. *Fee:* bicycles. **Cards:** AX, DC, DS, JC, MC, VI.

SOME UNITS

[icons] / [icons] /

(See map p. 329)

KEY LIME INN
🔺🔺🔺 SAVE
🔻🔻🔻🔻
Historic Bed
& Breakfast

Phone: (305)294-5229 **42**

12/20-4/21 [CP]	1P: $139-$255	2P: $139-$255	
4/22-11/30 [CP]	1P: $109-$159	2P: $109-$159	
12/1-12/19 [CP]	1P: $99-$149	2P: $99-$149	

Location: On US 1, just n of Duval St. 725 Truman Ave 33040. Fax: 305/294-9623. **Facility:** This Bahamian-style inn offers cottage-like rooms, some poolside with private outdoor sitting areas overlooking quiet, tree-shaded grounds. Designated smoking area. 37 one-bedroom standard units. 1-2 stories (no elevator), exterior corridors. *Bath:* shower only. **Parking:** on-site. **Terms:** 2 night minimum stay - weekends, 7 day cancellation notice. **Amenities:** safes. *Some:* irons, hair dryers. **Pool(s):** outdoor. **Leisure Activities:** Fee: bicycles. **Cards:** AX, DC, MC, VI. **Special Amenities:** free continental breakfast. *(See color ad p 343)*

SOME UNITS
🍴 🏊 ✕ 📠 / 🔋 💻

KEY WEST VILLAS RESORT
🔻🔻🔻🔻
Motel

Phone: (305)294-4427 **48**
All Year   2P: $150-$175   XP: $15   F12
Location: Just w of Duval St, off Truman Ave. 921 Center St 33040. Fax: 305/292-9044. **Facility:** 12 one-bedroom suites with kitchens, some with whirlpools. 2 stories, exterior corridors. **Parking:** street. **Terms:** 14 day cancellation notice-fee imposed, package plans. **Amenities:** irons, hair dryers. *Some:* CD players. **Leisure Activities:** whirlpool. *Fee:* bicycles. **Guest Services:** complimentary laundry. **Cards:** AX, DS, MC, VI.

SOME UNITS
ASK 🍴 VCR 📺 🔋 🛎 💻 / ✕ 📠 /

LA CASA DE LUCES
🔺🔺🔺 SAVE
🔻🔻
Historic Bed
& Breakfast

Phone: (305)296-3993 **49**

12/1-4/30 [CP]	1P: $169-$269	2P: $169-$269	XP: $10	F14
11/1-11/30 [CP]	1P: $129-$179	2P: $129-$179	XP: $10	F14
5/1-10/31 [CP]	1P: $99-$129	2P: $99-$129	XP: $10	F14

Location: Truman Ave, e on Duval St, then just s. 422 Amelia St 33040. Fax: 305/292-7665. **Facility:** 8 one-bedroom standard units, some with efficiencies and/or whirlpools. 2 stories (no elevator), exterior corridors. *Bath:* shared or private, combo or shower only. **Parking:** on-site. **Terms:** 2 night minimum stay - weekends, 14 day cancellation notice-fee imposed. **Cards:** AX, MC, VI. **Special Amenities:** early check-in/late check-out and free continental breakfast.

SOME UNITS
🛏 🍴 📺 / 🛎 /

LA MER & DEWEY HOUSE
🔻🔻🔻🔻
Classic Historic
Bed & Breakfast

Phone: (305)296-5611 **57**

12/25-4/26	1P: $220-$350	2P: $220-$350	XP: $25
4/27-5/25	1P: $165-$290	2P: $165-$290	XP: $20
5/26-11/30	1P: $140-$270	2P: $140-$270	XP: $15
12/1-12/24	1P: $130-$250	2P: $130-$250	XP: $15

Location: South St below Simonton St. Located in Old Town. 504-506 South St 33040. Fax: 305/294-2108. **Facility:** This property's two buildings face the beach and allow views of the sunrise; shops and restaurants are nearby. 19 one-bedroom standard units, some with efficiencies and/or whirlpools. 2 stories (no elevator), interior/exterior corridors. **Parking:** on-site. **Terms:** age restrictions may apply, 10 day cancellation notice. **Amenities:** voice mail, safes, honor bars, irons, hair dryers. **Leisure Activities:** whirlpool. **Guest Services:** valet laundry. **Business Services:** fax (fee). **Cards:** AX, MC, VI. *(See color ad p 333)*

SOME UNITS
🍴 🍸 📠 💻 / ✕ 🔋 🛎 /

LA PENSIONE
🔺🔺🔺 SAVE
🔻🔻🔻🔻
Historic Bed
& Breakfast

Phone: 305/292-9923 **41**

12/26-5/15 [ECP]	1P: $178-$198	2P: $178-$198	XP: $25
12/1-12/25 & 5/16-11/30 [ECP]	1P: $108-$138	2P: $108-$138	XP: $15

Location: On US 1, just n of Duval St. Located in Old Town. 809 Truman Ave 33040. Fax: 305/296-6509. **Facility:** Dating from 1891, this house has Classical architecture and spacious, tastefully appointed rooms. Designated smoking area. 9 one-bedroom standard units. 2 stories (no elevator), interior/exterior corridors. *Bath:* combo or shower only. **Parking:** on-site. **Terms:** age restrictions may apply, 7 day cancellation notice-fee imposed. **Pool(s):** small outdoor. **Business Services:** fax (fee). **Cards:** AX, CB, DC, DS, MC, VI. **Special Amenities:** free continental breakfast and free local telephone calls.

🛏 🍴 🏊 ✕ 📺

(See map p. 329)

LIGHTBOURN INN

AAA SAVE

Historic Bed & Breakfast

			Phone: (305)296-5152 32
1/2-4/15 [ECP]	1P: $178	2P: $278	XP: $25
12/1-1/1 & 4/16-5/31 [ECP]	1P: $128	2P: $278	XP: $25
6/1-11/30 [ECP]	1P: $98	2P: $278	XP: $25

Location: US 1, just n of Duval St. 907 Truman Ave 33040. Fax: 305/294-9490. **Facility:** This 1903 Queen Anne-style inn is furnished with antiques as well as artifacts from the owners' extensive travels. Designated smoking area. 10 one-bedroom standard units. 2 stories (no elevator); interior/exterior corridors. *Bath:* shower only. **Parking:** on-site. **Terms:** age restrictions may apply, 14 day cancellation notice-fee imposed. **Amenities:** voice mail. **Pool(s):** heated outdoor. **Business Services:** fax (fee). **Cards:** AX, CB, DC, DS, MC, VI.
(See color ad p 344)

THE MARQUESA HOTEL

Classic Historic Small-scale Hotel

			Phone: (305)292-1919 31
12/20-4/20	1P: $270-$405	2P: $270-$405	XP: $25
5/28-11/30	1P: $245-$395	2P: $245-$395	XP: $25
4/21-5/27	1P: $245-$345	2P: $245-$345	XP: $25
12/1-12/19	1P: $195-$345	2P: $195-$345	XP: $25

Location: Jct Simonton and Fleming sts. Located in Old Town. 600 Fleming St 33040. Fax: 305/294-2121. **Facility:** Several varieties of orchids grow in the garden of this service-oriented hotel occupying a restored 1884 house. 27 units. 25 one-bedroom standard units. 2 one-bedroom suites ($240-$405). 1-3 stories (no elevator); interior/exterior corridors. **Parking:** on-site. **Terms:** age restrictions may apply, 10 day cancellation notice. **Amenities:** voice mail, safes, irons, hair dryers. **Dining:** Cafe Marquesa, see separate listing. **Pool(s):** outdoor, heated outdoor. **Leisure Activities:** Fee: bicycles. **Guest Services:** valet laundry. **Business Services:** fax (fee). **Cards:** AX, DC, MC, VI.

SOME UNITS

OCEAN KEY RESORT, A NOBLE HOUSE RESORT

Large-scale Hotel

			Phone: (305)296-7701 19
All Year	1P: $239-$899	2P: $239-$899	XP: $35 F

Location: At Mallory Square. Located in Old Town. Zero Duval St 33040. Fax: 305/292-7685. **Facility:** 100 units. 55 one-bedroom standard units, some with whirlpools. 33 one- and two-bedroom suites ($379-$899), some with kitchens and/or whirlpools. 4 stories, exterior corridors. *Bath:* combo or shower only. **Parking:** valet. **Terms:** check-in 4 pm, 2 night minimum stay - weekends, 5 day cancellation notice. **Amenities:** CD players, voice mail, irons, hair dryers. **Pool(s):** heated outdoor. **Leisure Activities:** fishing. *Fee:* charter fishing. **Guest Services:** gift shop, valet laundry. **Business Services:** meeting rooms, fax (fee). **Cards:** AX, CB, DC, DS, MC, VI.

SOME UNITS

THE PALMS HOTEL

AAA SAVE

Historic Bed & Breakfast

			Phone: (305)294-3146 24
12/21-4/30	1P: $150	2P: $175-$250	XP: $20 F18
12/1-12/20 & 5/1-11/30	1P: $95	2P: $110-$175	XP: $10 F18

Location: Just w of Truman. 820 White St 33040. Fax: 305/294-8463. **Facility:** 30 units. 27 one-bedroom standard units. 3 one-bedroom suites, some with efficiencies or kitchens. 2 stories (no elevator); exterior corridors. *Bath:* some shared or private, combo or shower only. **Parking:** street. **Terms:** 14 day cancellation notice-fee imposed, [ECP] meal plan available, small pets only. **Pool(s):** heated outdoor. **Leisure Activities:** sun deck, pool table, exercise room. *Fee:* bicycles. **Cards:** AX, DS, MC, VI. **Special Amenities:** free continental breakfast.

THE PARADISE INN

Bed & Breakfast

			Phone: (305)293-8007 38
12/1-4/18 [ECP]	1P: $270-$375	2P: $270-$545	XP: $25
4/19-5/31 & 10/18-11/30 [ECP]	1P: $210-$290	2P: $210-$415	XP: $25
6/1-10/17 [ECP]	1P: $175-$265	2P: $175-$355	XP: $25

Location: US 1 (Truman Ave), just n. 819 Simonton St 33040. Fax: 305/293-0807. **Facility:** These elegantly contemporary rooms, suites and cottages are set on lush grounds in the heart of Old Town; on-site parking is available. Designated smoking area. 18 units. 8 one-bedroom standard units. 7 one-bedroom suites ($175-$350). 3 cottages ($265-$545) with whirlpools. 1-2 stories (no elevator); exterior corridors. **Parking:** on-site. **Terms:** 3 night minimum stay - weekends, 10 day cancellation notice. **Amenities:** CD players, voice mail, safes, irons, hair dryers. **Pool(s):** small heated outdoor. **Leisure Activities:** whirlpool. **Guest Services:** valet laundry. **Business Services:** fax (fee). **Cards:** AX, DC, DS, MC, VI.

PEGASUS INTERNATIONAL HOTEL

AAA SAVE

Small-scale Hotel

			Phone: (305)294-9323 35
1/1-11/30	1P: $99-$599	2P: $119-$599	XP: $20 F12
12/1-12/31	1P: $89-$599	2P: $89-$599	XP: $20 F12

Location: Corner of Duval and Southard sts. Located in Old Town. 501 Southard St 33040. Fax: 305/294-4741. **Facility:** 25 one-bedroom standard units. 3 stories, interior/exterior corridors. *Bath:* shower only. **Parking:** on-site. **Terms:** 14 day cancellation notice-fee imposed. **Amenities:** hair dryers. **Pool(s):** heated outdoor. **Leisure Activities:** whirlpool, sun deck. **Guest Services:** valet laundry. **Cards:** AX, DC, DS, MC, VI. **Special Amenities:** early check-in/late check-out and free room upgrade (subject to availability with advanced reservations).

SOME UNITS

PIER HOUSE RESORT & CARIBBEAN SPA

AAA SAVE

Large-scale Hotel

			Phone: (305)296-4600 20
12/25-4/20	1P: $290-$1800	2P: $290-$1800	XP: $35 F17
4/21-5/17	1P: $245-$1585	2P: $245-$1585	XP: $35 F17
5/18-11/30	1P: $200-$1400	2P: $200-$1400	
12/1-12/24	1P: $200-$1400	2P: $200-$1400	XP: $35 F17

Location: On the gulf at the foot of Duval St. Located in Old Town. One Duval St 33040. Fax: 305/296-7568. **Facility:** 142 units. 126 one-bedroom standard units. 13 one- and 3 two-bedroom suites ($355-$1800). 2-5 stories, interior/exterior corridors. *Bath:* combo or shower only. **Parking:** on-site. **Terms:** check-in 4 pm, 2-3 night minimum stay - weekends, 7 day cancellation notice. **Amenities:** video games (fee), voice mail, honor bars, irons, hair dryers. *Some:* CD players. **Dining:** 3 restaurants, 7:30 am-midnight, cocktails, also, One Duval, see separate listing, entertainment. **Pool(s):** heated outdoor. **Leisure Activities:** whirlpools, spa. *Fee:* motor scooters, bicycles. **Guest Services:** valet laundry, beauty salon. **Business Services:** meeting rooms. **Cards:** AX, CB, DC, DS, MC, VI. **Special Amenities:** free newspaper. *(See color ad p 346)*

SOME UNITS

(See map p. 329)

QUALITY INN & SUITES

AAA SAVE

5/1-11/30 [ECP]	1P: $99-$359	2P: $99-$359	XP: $20	F17
1/1-4/30 [ECP]	1P: $159-$219	2P: $159-$219	XP: $20	F17
12/1-12/31 [ECP]	1P: $119-$159	2P: $119-$159	XP: $20	F17

Phone: (305)294-6681 **8**

Location: On entering island, jct US 1 and SR A1A. 3850 N Roosevelt Blvd 33040. Fax: 305/294-5618. **Facility:** 147 Small-scale Hotel units. 145 one-bedroom standard units. 2 one-bedroom suites. 2-3 stories, exterior corridors. *Bath:* combo or shower only. **Parking:** on-site. **Terms:** package plans. **Amenities:** video games (fee), dual phone lines, voice mail, irons, hair dryers. **Dining:** 7 am-11 pm, Fri & Sat-midnight. **Pool(s):** heated outdoor. **Leisure Activities:** whirlpool, mopeds, exercise room. *Fee:* bicycles. **Guest Services:** gift shop, valet and coin laundry. **Business Services:** fax (fee). **Cards:** AX, CB, DC, DS, MC, VI. **Special Amenities:** free continental breakfast and free local telephone calls. *(See color ad below)*

SOME UNITS

(See map p. 329)

RADISSON HOTEL KEY WEST

Phone: (305)294-5511 **①**

AAA [SAVE]

3/1-3/31	1P: $169-$299	2P: $169-$299	XP: $50 F17
12/1-2/28 & 4/1-11/30	1P: $99-$299	2P: $99-$299	XP: $10 F17

Location: On US 1. Located in New Town. 3820 N Roosevelt Blvd 33040-6552. Fax: 305/296-1939. **Facility:** 145 units. 141 one-bedroom standard units. 4 one-bedroom suites ($219-$499). 6 stories, exterior corridors. *Bath:* combo or shower only. **Parking:** on-site. **Terms:** cancellation fee imposed. **Amenities:** voice mail, safes (fee), irons, hair dryers. **Dining:** 24 hours. **Pool(s):** heated outdoor. **Leisure Activities:** sun deck, exercise room. **Guest Services:** valet and coin laundry. **Cards:** AX, CB, DC, DS, JC, MC, VI. **Special Amenities: free local telephone calls and free room upgrade (subject to availability with advanced reservations).** *(See color ad p 346)*

Small-scale Hotel

SOME UNITS

SHERATON SUITES-KEY WEST

Phone: (305)292-9800 **⑰**

AAA [SAVE]

12/23-4/30	1P: $169-$359	2P: $169-$359	XP: $15 F17
12/1-12/22 & 5/1-11/30	1P: $159-$299	2P: $159-$299	XP: $15 F17

Location: Jct US 1 and SR A1A, 3 mi s. Located at Smathers Beach. 2001 S Roosevelt Blvd 33040. Fax: 305/294-6009. **Facility:** 180 one-bedroom suites, some with whirlpools. 4 stories, interior/exterior corridors. *Bath:* combo or shower only. **Parking:** on-site. **Terms:** 3 day cancellation notice-fee imposed, [AP] meal plan available. **Amenities:** dual phone lines, voice mail, honor bars, irons, hair dryers. *Fee:* video games, safes. **Dining:** 7 am-10 pm, cocktails. **Pool(s):** heated outdoor. **Leisure Activities:** whirlpool, exercise room. *Fee:* bicycles. **Guest Services:** gift shop, valet and coin laundry, area transportation-downtown. **Business Services:** meeting rooms. **Cards:** AX, DC, MC, VI. **Special Amenities: free newspaper.** *(See color ad below)*

Large-scale Hotel

SOME UNITS

SOUTHERNMOST HOTEL IN THE USA

Phone: (305)296-6577 **⑭**

12/25-4/26	1P: $145-$250	2P: $145-$250	XP: $25 F17
4/27-5/25	1P: $115-$180	2P: $115-$180	XP: $10 F17
12/1-12/24 & 5/26-11/30	1P: $95-$180	2P: $95-$180	XP: $10 F17

Location: Jct Duval and United sts. Located in Old Town. 1319 Duval St 33040. Fax: 305/294-3380. **Facility:** 127 one-bedroom standard units, some with efficiencies. 2-3 stories, exterior corridors. **Parking:** on-site. **Terms:** 2-5 night minimum stay - weekends, 5 day cancellation notice. **Amenities:** voice mail, safes, irons, hair dryers. **Pool(s):** 2 heated outdoor. **Leisure Activities:** whirlpool. *Fee:* bicycles. **Guest Services:** gift shop, coin laundry. **Business Services:** meeting rooms, fax (fee). **Cards:** AX, MC, VI. *(See color ad p 333)*

Motel

SOME UNITS
FEE

SOUTHERNMOST ON THE BEACH

Phone: (305)296-5611 **⑱**

12/25-4/26	1P: $194-$310	2P: $194-$310	XP: $15 F17
4/27-5/25	1P: $149-$270	2P: $149-$270	XP: $10 F17
12/1-12/24 & 5/26-11/30	1P: $129-$250	2P: $129-$250	XP: $10 F17

Location: South St below Simonton St. Located in Old Town. 508 South St 33040. Fax: 305/294-2108. **Facility:** 47 one-bedroom standard units, some with efficiencies. 2 stories (no elevator), exterior corridors. *Bath:* combo or shower only. **Parking:** on-site. **Terms:** 2-5 night minimum stay - weekends, 10 day cancellation notice. **Amenities:** voice mail, safes, irons, hair dryers. **Pool(s):** outdoor. **Leisure Activities:** *Fee:* scuba diving, bicycles. **Guest Services:** gift shop, coin laundry. **Business Services:** fax (fee). **Cards:** AX, MC, VI. *(See color ad p 333)*

Motel

SOME UNITS

TRAVELERS PALM INN & GUESTHOUSES

Phone: (305)294-9560 **⑪**

12/1-4/30 [ECP]	1P: $118-$228	2P: $118-$228	XP: $15 F
5/1-11/30 [ECP]	1P: $78-$178	2P: $78-$178	XP: $15 F

Location: US 1 (Truman Ave), just n. Located in Old Town. 915 Center St 33040. Fax: 305/294-4104. **Facility:** Designated smoking area. 9 units. 7 one-bedroom standard units, some with efficiencies. 1 one- and 1 two-bedroom suites ($138-$178) with kitchens. 2 stories (no elevator), exterior corridors. *Bath:* combo or shower only. **Parking:** street. **Terms:** 2-7 night minimum stay - weekends, 30 day cancellation notice-fee imposed. **Amenities:** hair dryers. *Some:* CD players. **Pool(s):** small heated outdoor. **Leisure Activities:** *Fee:* bicycles. **Guest Services:** complimentary laundry. **Business Services:** fax (fee). **Cards:** AX, DS, MC, VI.

Historic Bed & Breakfast

SOME UNITS

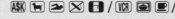
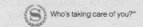

(See map p. 329)

THE WATSON HOUSE

AAA SAVE

Historic Bed & Breakfast

	1P: $140-$400	2P: $140-$400
12/1-4/30	1P: $140-$400	2P: $140-$400
8/1-11/30	1P: $125-$400	2P: $125-$400
5/1-7/31	1P: $125-$300	2P: $125-$300

Phone: (305)294-6712 27

Location: Just s of Mallory Square. Located in Old Town. 525 Simonton St 33040. Fax: 305/294-7501. **Facility:** Watson House is in the historic district and features cabana-style units as well as second-floor suites. Designated smoking area. 3 units. 1 one-bedroom standard unit. 2 one-bedroom suites with kitchens. 1-2 stories, exterior corridors. *Bath:* combo or shower only. **Parking:** on-site and street. **Terms:** 2 night minimum stay, age restrictions may apply, 14 day cancellation notice-fee imposed, [CP] meal plan available. **Amenities:** irons, hair dryers. **Pool(s):** heated outdoor. **Leisure Activities:** whirlpool. **Cards:** AX, MC, VI. **Special Amenities:** free continental breakfast and free local telephone calls.

SOME UNITS

THE WEATHERSTATION INN

Classic Historic Bed & Breakfast

	1P: $195-$315	2P: $195-$315	XP: $20
12/20-4/30	1P: $195-$315	2P: $195-$315	XP: $20
12/1-12/19 & 5/1-11/30	1P: $150-$215	2P: $150-$215	XP: $20

Phone: (305)294-7277 33

Location: US 1/Truman Ave to Whitehead St, turn right, then left onto Southard St. Located in the Truman Annex Complex. 57 Front St 33040. Fax: 305/294-0544. **Facility:** A stately white building, the inn sits on picket-fence-enclosed grounds containing a variety of tropical trees and flowering plants. Smoke free premises. 8 one-bedroom standard units. 2 stories (no elevator), interior corridors. *Bath:* shower only. **Parking:** on-site. **Terms:** 2 night minimum stay - weekends, age restrictions may apply, 15 day cancellation notice-fee imposed. **Amenities:** video library, voice mail, hair dryers. **Pool(s):** heated outdoor. **Guest Services:** valet laundry. **Cards:** AX, CB, DC, DS, JC, MC, VI.

WESTWINDS

AAA SAVE

Bed & Breakfast

		2P: $90-$170	XP: $20
12/20-4/30		2P: $90-$170	XP: $20
12/1-12/19 & 5/1-11/30		2P: $70-$120	XP: $20

Phone: 305/296-4440 21

Location: Just n of Duval St; near historic seaport. Located in Old Town. 914 Eaton St 33040. Fax: 305/293-0931. **Facility:** 22 units. 20 one-bedroom standard units. 2 one-bedroom suites, some with kitchens. 1-2 stories (no elevator), interior/exterior corridors. *Bath:* combo or shower only. **Parking:** street. **Terms:** age restrictions may apply, 14 day cancellation notice-fee imposed, [CP] meal plan available, no pets allowed (owner's pets on premises). **Amenities:** *Some:* hair dryers. **Pool(s):** outdoor, heated outdoor. **Guest Services:** coin laundry. **Business Services:** meeting rooms. **Cards:** DS, MC, VI. **Special Amenities:** free continental breakfast.

SOME UNITS

WYNDHAM CASA MARINA RESORT

AAA SAVE

Historic Large-scale Hotel

	1P: $309	2P: $309	XP: $20	F17
12/1-4/21	1P: $309	2P: $309	XP: $20	F17
4/22-5/31	1P: $259	2P: $259	XP: $20	F17
10/19-11/30	1P: $239	2P: $239	XP: $20	F17
6/1-10/18	1P: $189	2P: $189	XP: $20	F17

Phone: (305)296-3535 59

Location: 4 mi s on Flagler (CR 5A) from jct SR A1A. 1500 Reynolds St 33040-6552. Fax: 305/296-4633. **Facility:** 311 units. 242 one-bedroom standard units. 64 one- and 5 two-bedroom suites. 3-4 stories, interior/exterior corridors. *Bath:* combo or shower only. **Parking:** on-site. **Terms:** check-in 4 pm, 10 day cancellation notice-fee imposed. **Amenities:** dual phone lines, voice mail, safes, honor bars, irons, hair dryers. *Fee:* video games, high-speed Internet. *Some:* CD players. **Dining:** Flagler's Restaurant & Lounge, see separate listing, entertainment. **Pool(s):** 2 heated outdoor. **Leisure Activities:** sauna, whirlpool, fishing, pier, 3 lighted tennis courts, recreation programs, exercise room, horseshoes, volleyball. *Fee:* windsurfing, waterskiing, scuba diving, snorkeling, charter fishing, waverunners, catamaran, golf privileges, mopeds, parasailing, bicycles, massage. **Guest Services:** gift shop, valet laundry. *Fee:* scuba instruction. **Business Services:** conference facilities, business center. **Cards:** AX, DC, MC, VI.

SOME UNITS

(See map p. 329)

WYNDHAM REACH RESORT
Phone: (305)296-5000   56

AAA [SAVE]
▽▽▽▽

12/1-4/21	1P: $299	2P: $299	XP: $20	F17
4/22-5/31	1P: $249	2P: $249	XP: $20	F17
10/19-11/30	1P: $229	2P: $229	XP: $20	F17
6/1-10/18	1P: $179	2P: $179	XP: $20	F17

Large-scale Hotel **Location:** Just s of jct Truman Ave and Simonton St. 1435 Simonton St 33040. Fax: 305/296-2830. **Facility:** 150 units. 71 one-bedroom standard units. 79 one-bedroom suites. 4-5 stories, exterior corridors. **Bath:** combo or shower only. **Parking:** on-site. **Terms:** check-in 4 pm, 10 day cancellation notice-fee imposed. **Amenities:** dual phone lines, voice mail, safes, honor bars, irons, hair dryers. *Fee:* video games, high-speed Internet. *Some:* CD players. **Dining:** 7 am-10 pm, Fri & Sat-11 pm, cocktails. **Pool(s):** heated outdoor. **Leisure Activities:** sauna, whirlpool, rental paddleboats, rental sailboats, snorkeling, fishing, recreation programs, exercise room, massage, horseshoes, volleyball. *Fee:* canoes, windsurfing, scuba diving, charter fishing, waverunners. **Guest Services:** gift shop, valet laundry, scuba instruction. **Business Services:** meeting rooms, business center. **Cards:** AX, DC, MC, VI.

SOME UNITS

[icons] 🅂🄳 ✈ 🍴 🍸 🛗 🎣 🏊 ✖ 🎥 DATA PORT ☕ / ✖ /

--------- *The following lodging was either not evaluated or did not* ---------
meet AAA rating requirements but is listed for your information only.

TRAVELODGE KEY WEST HOTEL
Phone: (305)296-7593   5

[fyi]

12/24-4/30	1P: $129-$189	2P: $129-$189	XP: $10	F19
12/1-12/23 & 5/1-11/30	1P: $79-$129	2P: $79-$129	XP: $10	F19

Small-scale Hotel Under major renovation, scheduled to be completed October 2002. **Last rated:** ▽▽▽ **Location:** On US 1. Located in New Town. 3444 N Roosevelt Blvd 33040. Fax: 305/294-5246. **Facility:** 64 units. 32 one-bedroom standard units. 24 one-, 3 two- and 5 three-bedroom suites ($129-$529) with kitchens. 4 stories, exterior corridors. **Parking:** on-site. **Amenities:** voice mail, irons. *Some:* safes, hair dryers. **Pool(s):** heated outdoor. **Leisure Activities:** whirlpool. **Business Services:** fax (fee). **Cards:** AX, DC, DS, JC, MC, VI. *(See color ad p 324 & p 348)*

SOME UNITS

[icons] [ASK] 🅂🄳 🍴 🏊 🎥 DATA PORT ☕ / ✖ 🛏 📷 /

--------- **WHERE TO DINE** ---------

A & B LOBSTER HOUSE
Dinner: $22-$39   Phone: 305/294-5880   5

▽▽▽

Steak & Seafood

Location: From Duval St, just n. 700 Front St 33040. **Hours:** 6 pm-11 pm. **Closed:** 12/25. **Reservations:** accepted. **Features:** Located just off the harbor docks, this restaurant is elevated in order to present a wonderful view. Fresh seafood at its best is available in a tablecloth atmosphere. cocktails. **Parking:** on-site. **Cards:** MC, VI.

🍸 ✖

ABBONDANZA ITALIAN RESTAURANT
Dinner: $9-$17   Phone: 305/292-1199   27

▽▽ ▽▽

Italian

Location: At corner of Louise and Simonton sts. 1208 Simonton St 33040. **Hours:** 5 pm-11 pm. **Features:** The restaurant's name means "lots of food"—and appropriately so. Well-prepared entrees are made with local seafood, pasta and flavorful sauces. The ambience and decor are fresh and inviting. Casual dress; cocktails. **Parking:** street. **Cards:** MC, VI.

🍸 ✖

ALICE'S AT LA TE DA
Dinner: $13-$28   Phone: 305/296-6706   20

▽▽▽▽

Northern New World

Location: Corner of Duval and Catherine sts; in the historic La Te Da Guest House. 1125 Duval St 33040. **Hours:** 8:30 am-2:30 & 6-11 pm, Sun from 10:30 am. **Closed:** Mon. **Reservations:** suggested. **Features:** New World fusion cuisine captures the flavors of the Caribbean, Asia and the American Southwest, with great use of fresh local seafood, meat and tropical fruits. Dine outdoors under the stars or inside with the signed Picasso lithographs. Dressy casual; cocktails; entertainment. **Parking:** street. **Cards:** AX, DS, MC, VI.

🍸 ✖

ALONZO'S OYSTER HOUSE
Lunch: $8-$13   **Dinner:** $14-$24   Phone: 305/294-5880   4

▽▽▽ ▽▽▽

Seafood

Location: From Duval St, just n; at the end of Front St. 700 Front St 33040. **Hours:** 11 am-11 pm. **Features:** This restaurant is located on the water, and offers the freshest of seafood. The dining room offers great views of the harbor and the boats. The decor resembles the casualness of a dockside eatery. Casual dress; cocktails. **Parking:** on-site. **Cards:** MC, VI.

🅖Ⓜ ✖

ANTONIA'S RESTAURANT
Dinner: $12-$23   Phone: 305/294-6565   15

▽▽▽ ▽▽▽

Regional Italian

Location: In Old Town. 615 Duval St 33040. **Hours:** 6 pm-11 pm; from 6:30 pm in summer. **Closed:** 11/27. **Reservations:** suggested. **Features:** Regional Italian food features homemade pasta, fresh seafood, veal, beef and lamb. Innovative presentations, warm surroundings and an extensive wine list make this a place for special occasions. A complimentary cookie plate will satisfy your sweet tooth. Dressy casual; cocktails. **Parking:** street. **Cards:** AX, DC, MC, VI.

✖

BAGATELLE RESTAURANT
Lunch: $7-$13   **Dinner:** $15-$25   Phone: 305/296-6609   7

▽▽ ▽▽

Regional American

Location: Downtown. 115 Duval St 33040. **Hours:** 11:30 am-3 & 5-11 pm. **Closed:** 9/1. **Reservations:** suggested. **Features:** An inviting wraparound porch makes this 1884 sea captain's revival home a great location for leisurely dining. Seafood specialties are featured with other traditional entrees. Casual dress; cocktails. **Parking:** street. **Cards:** AX, DS, MC, VI.

🍸 ✖

BANANA CAFE
Lunch: $6-$10   **Dinner:** $8-$24   Phone: 305/294-7227   28

▽▽▽ ▽▽▽

French

Location: In Old Town; just s of jct US 1. 1211 Duval St 33040. **Hours:** 8 am-3 & 7-11 pm. **Closed:** Mon & Tues for dinner & 9/1-9/30. **Features:** A charming, casual restaurant, it offers a variety of dishes you may enjoy on the covered patio or in the outdoor dining area. The shredded tuna sandwich with spinach leaves, capers and a hard-boiled egg is a fresh twist on the traditional lunch entree. Casual dress; beer & wine only. **Parking:** street. **Cards:** AX, DC, DS, MC, VI.

(See map p. 329)

BLUE HEAVEN
American
Lunch: $5-$12 **Dinner:** $10-$24 **Phone:** 305/296-8666 [18]
Location: Just s of Duval, corner of Petronia and Thomas sts. 729 Thomas St 33040. **Hours:** 8 am-11:30, noon-3 & 6-10:30 pm. Closed: 9/9-10/15. **Features:** The Caribbean-influenced menu features seafood and a popular Sunday brunch with lobster Benedict and shrimp in grits. Roosters run around the converted barn house; a rooster graveyard is the resting place of prize cockfighters from the early 1900s. Casual dress; cocktails. **Parking:** street. **Cards:** DS, MC, VI.

CAFE DES ARTISTES
French
Dinner: $23-$44 **Phone:** 305/294-7100 [23]
Location: Corner Truman Ave and Simonton St. 1007 Simonton St 33040-6552. **Hours:** 6 pm-11 pm. **Reservations:** suggested. **Features:** Dine on the cafe-terrasse or in the intimate indoor dining room. Local seafood entrees are creatively prepared and presented with a tropical French flair, like the snail appetizer served in a puff pastry with goat cheese and bits of red bell pepper. Dressy casual; cocktails. **Parking:** street. **Cards:** AX, MC, VI.

CAFE MARQUESA
Northern American
Dinner: $23-$32 **Phone:** 305/292-1244 [12]
Location: In Old Town; jct Simonton and Fleming sts; in The Marquesa Hotel. 1202 Simonton St 33040. **Hours:** 6 pm-11 pm; from 7 pm 6/1-11/1. **Reservations:** suggested. **Features:** Featuring "Contemporary American" a cross-cultural blend of food from the Americas, Asia and the Caribbean, the changing menu includes meat and fresh seafood presented with artistic skill and preparation. Attentive service adds to the cozy atmosphere. Smoke free premises. Dressy casual; cocktails. **Parking:** street. **Cards:** AX, DC, MC, VI.

CAMILLE'S
American
Lunch: $6-$13 **Dinner:** $11-$22 **Phone:** 305/296-4811 [17]
Location: In Old Town; just s of US 1 (Truman Ave). 703 Simonton St 33040. **Hours:** 8 am-3 & 6-10 pm. **Features:** Resembling a roadside diner, this funky, Key West-style eatery projects a casual atmosphere with modest tables and counter seating. Breakfast is the most popular meal, with an assortment of sandwiches, seafood and beef entrees served later in the day. Casual dress; cocktails. **Parking:** on-site. **Cards:** AX, DS, MC, VI.

CROISSANTS DE FRANCE
French
Lunch: $5-$9 **Phone:** 305/294-2624 [22]
Location: In Old Town. 816 Duval St 33040. **Hours:** 7:30 am-3 pm. Closed: Wed. **Features:** Gazpacho, brioche, quiche and assorted croissants are among the popular, light offerings of the tropical, outdoor cafe. Fountains and plants add to the European character. An adjacent bakery stays open in the evenings for take-out customers. Casual dress; beer & wine only. **Parking:** street. **Cards:** AX, DC, MC, VI.

EL SIBONEY
Cuban
Dinner: $6-$14 **Phone:** 305/296-4184 [21]
Location: Just s of US 1; corner of Margaret and Catherine sts. 900 Catherine St 33040. **Hours:** 11 am-9:30 pm. Closed major holidays; also Sun. **Features:** Casual and family-oriented, the energetic restaurant is decorated with original Cuban paintings. The roast pork, shrimp paella, grilled chicken breast and the signature Siboney steak are menu favorites. Large windows make for excellent people-watching. beer & wine only. **Parking:** on-site.

FLAGLER'S RESTAURANT & LOUNGE
Steak & Seafood
Lunch: $8-$12 **Dinner:** $17-$38 **Phone:** 305/296-3535 [31]
Location: 4 mi s on Flagler (CR 5A) from jct SR A1A; in Wyndham Casa Marina Resort. 1500 Reynolds St 33040. **Hours:** 7 am-11:30, noon-2:30 & 6-10:30 pm, Sun 11 am-2 & 6-10 pm. **Reservations:** suggested. **Features:** A pleasant, comfortable setting overlooks a pool and the beach. This place is known for its aged steak and fresh seafood. The cooked-to-order steak is smothered in a delicious onion butter, and the Cuban creme brulee perfectly ends a great meal. Dressy casual; cocktails; entertainment. **Parking:** on-site. **Cards:** AX, CB, DC, DS, JC, MC, VI.

KYUSHU
Ethnic
Lunch: $7-$12 **Dinner:** $12-$18 **Phone:** 305/294-2995 [16]
Location: In Old Town; on US 1. 921 Truman Ave 33040. **Hours:** noon-2:30 & 5:30-10:30 pm, Sat & Sun from 5:30 pm. **Reservations:** suggested. **Features:** Attentive and friendly service at the sushi bar and in the tatami rooms make for a pleasant visit. The sushi is fresh and presented with a touch of class. Order the fried pork loin cooked with an egg splash and served on a bed of rice with sauteed onions. Casual dress; cocktails. **Parking:** on-site. **Cards:** AX, CB, DC, DS, MC, VI.

LATITUDES BEACH CAFE
Seafood
Lunch: $9-$18 **Dinner:** $18-$35 **Phone:** 305/292-5394 [13]
Location: In Old Town; adjacent to Mallory Square; in Hilton Key West Resort & Marina. 245 Front St 33040. **Hours:** 7 am-10 pm; you must pick up your boat tickets at the hotel concierge's desk; boat leaves on bottom of the half hour. **Reservations:** required. **Features:** On an island 500 yards from downtown, the breezy restaurant focuses on seafood but also offers other selections. Because there are no walls, this eatery closes during inclement weather. The fresh air and views are invigorating. Dressy casual; cocktails. **Parking:** on-site (fee). **Cards:** AX, CB, DC, DS, JC, MC, VI.

LOUIE'S BACKYARD
Regional American
Lunch: $10-$15 **Dinner:** $24-$38 **Phone:** 305/294-1061 [30]
Location: Just s of Truman Ave via Simonton to South St, just e to Vernon, then s. 700 Waddell Ave 33040. **Hours:** 11:30 am-3 & 6:30-10:30 pm. Closed: 9/5-9/17; 9/18-9/30 lunch only. **Reservations:** suggested. **Features:** The charming 1908 Victorian house features hardwood floors and a facade with many windows. Outdoor decks on both floors offer great views of the ocean. Beautifully prepared fish and steaks and an excellent wine list make the restaurant notable. Dressy casual; cocktails. **Parking:** street. **Cards:** AX, DC, MC, VI.

(See map p. 329)

MANGIA MANGIA

Italian

Dinner: $9-$15   Phone: 305/294-2469   ⑩

Location: Just n of US 1; corner of Margaret and Southard sts. 900 Southard St 33040. **Hours:** 5:30 pm-10 pm. Closed major holidays; also Super Bowl Sun. **Features:** Rigatoni with jumbo shrimp, fresh pasta and homemade tiramisu encourage you to "eat eat" at the casual, small restaurant. Palms, plants and herbs envelop the outdoor garden. Caribbean decor is the theme inside. Casual dress; beer & wine only. **Parking:** street. **Cards:** AX, MC, VI.   ✕

MANGOES RESTAURANT

Ethnic

Lunch: $5-$12   Dinner: $11-$22   Phone: 305/292-4606   ⑲

Location: In Old Town; at Angela St. 700 Duval St 33040. **Hours:** 11:30 am-11 pm. Closed: 9/3 - 9/17. **Reservations:** suggested. **Features:** In the heart of Key West, the restaurant lets diners eat or nurse a libation under the stars in the courtyard or linger over dinner in a romantic dining room with soft diverse lighting and original artwork. Preparations of meat and fresh local seafood creatively fuse American and Caribbean styles. Casual dress; cocktails. **Parking:** street. **Cards:** AX, DC, DS, MC, VI.   ✕

MICHAEL'S

Steak & Seafood

Dinner: $15-$29   Phone: 305/295-1300   ⑨

Location: Just n of US 1; at corner of Margaret and Southard sts. 532 Margaret St 33040. **Hours:** 5:30 pm-11 pm. Closed: 9/21-10/4. **Reservations:** suggested. **Features:** The restaurant exudes a garden atmosphere with help from large umbrellas and a focal-point fountain. The cozy dining room incorporates a mural by Maurizio Mancioli. Prime beef and local seafood feature heavily on the menu. Casual dress; cocktails. **Parking:** street. **Cards:** AX, MC, VI.   🍸 ✕

NICOLA SEAFOOD

East Seafood

Lunch: $8-$14   Dinner: $22-$29   Phone: 305/296-9900   ⑥

Location: In Old Town; Simonton and Front sts, just n of Mallory Square; in Hyatt Key West Resort & Marina. 601 Front St 33040. **Hours:** 7 am-3 & 6-10 pm. **Reservations:** suggested. **Features:** Have a drink and enjoy an excellent sunset view on the gulf with indoor or terrace dining. Seafood is the house specialty with local fresh fish, lobster and crab cakes. cocktails. **Parking:** on-site. **Cards:** AX, CB, DC, DS, JC, MC, VI.   🍸 ✕

ONE DUVAL

Regional
American

Dinner: $25-$36   Phone: 305/296-4600   ⑪

Location: On the gulf at the foot of Duval St; in Pier House Resort & Caribbean Spa. One Duval St 33040. **Hours:** 6 pm-10:30 pm. **Reservations:** suggested. **Features:** A stylish waterfront dining room also features a patio for viewing the activity in Mallory Square. Market-fresh seafood and a conch chowder that will give you a taste of the Keys are offered with other excellent choices like spinach salad and veal. Dressy casual; cocktails; entertainment. **Parking:** on-site. **Cards:** AX, CB, DC, DS, JC, MC, VI.   🍸 ✕

PEPE'S CAFE

American

Lunch: $5-$9   Dinner: $10-$20   Phone: 305/294-7192   ⑧

Location: Just e of Duval St. 806 Caroline St 33040. **Hours:** 6:30 am-4 & 5:30-10:30 pm. **Features:** The oldest restaurant in Key West, it features pleasant service and picnic-style seating on a patio shaded by blooming bougainvillea. Feast on homemade meals like meatloaf with mashed potatoes and an authentic, onion-and-sausage-filled black bean soup. Casual dress; cocktails. **Parking:** street. **Cards:** DS, MC, VI.   ✕

(See map p. 329)

SQUARE ONE RESTAURANT   **Dinner:** $15-$30   **Phone:** 305/296-4300   ㉕
▼▼▼▼   **Location:** At Duval Square. 1075 Duval St 33040. **Hours:** 6 pm-10:30 pm. **Reservations:** suggested.
American   **Features:** Expect creative steak and seafood entrees-such as grilled filet mignon, New Zealand rack of lamb and sauteed sea scallops-in this intimate restaurant. The tropical courtyard is illuminated at night. For dessert, try Key lime pie or creme brulee. Dressy casual; cocktails; entertainment. **Parking:** on-site.
Cards: AX, DS, MC, VI.   ✕

The following restaurants have not been evaluated by AAA
but are listed for your information only.

LA TRATTORIA   **Phone:** 305/296-1075
[fyi]   Not evaluated. **Location:** 524 Duval St 33040. **Features:** Located on Duval Street, this cozy place offers many house speciality Italian dishes as well as traditional favorites.

SEVEN FISH   **Phone:** 305/296-2777
[fyi]   Not evaluated. **Location:** 632 Olive St 33040. **Features:** A very little restaurant that offers big food featuring fresh seafoods and meats prepared in their own style. Reservations are a must to get a table.

SHULA'S ON THE BEACH   **Phone:** 305/296-6144
[fyi]   Not evaluated. **Location:** Just s of Truman Ave and Simonton St; in Wyndham Reach Resort. 1435 Simonton St 33040. **Features:** Certified black Angus steaks, as well as lobster and other seafood selections, are served in large portions at this place, which affords ocean views.   ☖

LITTLE TORCH KEY

──────── WHERE TO STAY ────────

LITTLE PALM ISLAND RESORT & SPA   **Phone:** (305)872-2524
(AAA) [SAVE]   12/1-3/31   1P: $795-$1995   2P: $795-$1995
▼▼▼ ▼▼▼▼   4/1-6/30 & 10/1-11/30   1P: $795-$1895   2P: $795-$1895
                7/1-9/30   1P: $695-$1795   2P: $695-$1795
Resort   **Location:** Shore Station on US 1 at MM 28.5, jct Pirate Rd, 10 minute launch ride to island leaving hourly. Located in a
Small-scale Hotel   remote area. 28500 Overseas Hwy 33042. Fax: 305/872-4843. **Facility:** 5.5 acres of lush foliage welcomes you to an island hideaway. Enjoy a thatched bungalow-style suite decorated with opulent furnishings. Designated smoking area. 30 one-bedroom standard units with whirlpools. 1 story, exterior corridors. **Parking:** on-site.
Terms: 2 night minimum stay - for Fri/Sat arrival, age restrictions may apply, 14 day cancellation notice-fee imposed, [AP] & [MAP] meal plans available, 18% service charge. **Amenities:** video library, safes, honor bars, irons, hair dryers. **Dining:** The Dining Room at Little Palm Island, see separate listing. **Pool(s):** heated outdoor. **Leisure Activities:** rental boats, canoeing, paddleboats, sailboats, windsurfing, snorkeling, fishing, water bikes, kayaks, jogging, exercise room. *Fee:* marina, scuba diving, charter fishing, fishing guides, seaplane tours, Eco tours, sailing charters, back country charters, massage. **Guest Services:** gift shop, valet laundry. *Fee:* airport transportation-by seaplane & limo, area transportation. **Cards:** AX, CB, DC, DS, MC, VI.
Special Amenities: free newspaper.
                                                                                     SOME UNITS
                ✈ 📶 🍽 � ✕ ✕ [DATA PORT] ☎ 🖥 / 📺 [VCR] /
                FEE   FEE

──────── WHERE TO DINE ────────

THE DINING ROOM AT LITTLE PALM ISLAND   **Lunch:** $14-$24   **Dinner:** $26-$41   **Phone:** 305/872-2551
▼▼▼ ▼▼▼▼   **Location:** Shore Station on US 1 at MM 28.5, jct Pirate Rd, 10 minute launch ride to island leaving hourly; in Little
Nouvelle   Palm Island Resort & Spa. 28500 Overseas Hwy 33042. **Hours:** 7:30-10 am, 11:30-2:30 & 6:30-10 pm.
Continental   **Reservations:** required. **Features:** Florida and French regional dishes are featured with a nouvelle presentation. Outdoor tables and a lengthy wine list are available. You must be at least 16 years old. Dressy casual; cocktails. **Parking:** on-site. **Cards:** AX, CB, DC, DS, MC, VI.   ☖ ✕

LONG KEY

──────── WHERE TO STAY ────────

LIME TREE BAY RESORT   **Phone:** (305)664-4740
(AAA) [SAVE]   12/20-4/15   1P: $102-$235   2P: $102-$235   XP: $10   F8
                4/16-9/1   1P: $89-$215   2P: $89-$215   XP: $10   F8
▼▼ ▼▼   12/1-12/19 & 9/2-11/30   1P: $72-$200   2P: $72-$200   XP: $10   F8
Motel   **Location:** US 1, at MM 68.5. 68500 Overseas Hwy 33001 (PO Box 839). Fax: 305/664-0750. **Facility:** 29 units. 25 one- and 2 two-bedroom standard units, some with efficiencies or kitchens. 2 one-bedroom suites with efficiencies. 1-2 stories (no elevator), exterior corridors. **Bath:** combo or shower only. **Parking:** on-site.
Terms: 15 day cancellation notice, [AP] meal plan available. **Amenities:** voice mail. **Pool(s):** outdoor. **Leisure Activities:** whirlpool, rental boats, fishing, tennis court. *Fee:* sailboats, wave runners. **Cards:** AX, DC, DS, MC, VI. **Special Amenities:** free local telephone calls and free room upgrade (subject to availability with advanced reservations). *(See color ad p 320)*
                                                                                     SOME UNITS
                [S/D] 🍽 ➲ ✕ 🐾 [DATA PORT] / 🛏 🖥 🖥 /

MARATHON pop. 10,255

—— **WHERE TO STAY** ——

BANANA BAY RESORT-MARATHON KEY
Phone: (305)743-3500

12/22-4/26 [ECP]	1P: $115-$215	2P: $115-$215	XP: $15	F5
4/27-11/30 [ECP]	1P: $85-$165	2P: $85-$165	XP: $15	F5
12/1-12/21 [ECP]	1P: $85-$105	2P: $85-$105	XP: $15	F5

Small-scale Hotel **Location:** On US 1; gulfside at MM 49.5. 4590 Overseas Hwy 33050. Fax: 305/743-2670. **Facility:** 61 one-bedroom standard units. 2 stories, interior corridors. **Parking:** on-site. **Terms:** 7 day cancellation notice, package plans. **Amenities:** voice mail, irons, hair dryers. **Pool(s):** outdoor. **Leisure Activities:** whirlpool, rental sailboats, fishing, 2 tennis courts, exercise room, horseshoes. *Fee:* boats, windsurfing, marina, scuba diving, snorkeling, charter fishing. **Guest Services:** gift shop, coin laundry. **Business Services:** meeting rooms, fax (fee). **Cards:** AX, CB, DC, DS, JC, MC, VI. *(See color ad p 340)*

SOME UNITS

(ASK) (¶) (Ŧ) (➔) (⊠) (DATA PORT) (▤) / (▣) (◨) /

COCOPLUM BEACH & TENNIS CLUB
Phone: (305) 743-0240

12/20-4/25	2P: $225-$425
4/26-8/31	2P: $225-$350
9/1-11/30	2P: $175-$300
12/1-12/19	2P: $150-$260

Vacation Home **Location:** Off US 1 at MM 54.5, then 1.5 mi. 109 Coco Plum Dr 33050. Fax: 305/743-9351. **Facility:** 20 vacation homes ($150-$425), some with pools. 2 stories, exterior corridors. **Parking:** on-site. **Terms:** 3 night minimum stay, 14 day cancellation notice-fee imposed. **Amenities:** voice mail, hair dryers. **Leisure Activities:** whirlpool, tennis court, barbecue and picnic area, hammocks, tiki huts. **Guest Services:** complimentary laundry. **Business Services:** fax (fee). **Cards:** AX, MC, VI. **Special Amenities:** free local telephone calls and free room upgrade (subject to availability with advanced reservations).

(SD) (➔) (⊠) (VCR) (▣) (DATA PORT) (▤) (◨) (▣)

CORAL LAGOON RESORT & MARINA
Phone: 305/289-0121

12/21-4/20	1P: $85-$160	2P: $85-$160	XP: $10	F3
4/21-9/6	1P: $95-$135	2P: $95-$135	XP: $10	F3
12/1-12/20	1P: $70-$135	2P: $70-$135	XP: $10	F3
9/7-11/30	1P: $70-$110	2P: $70-$110	XP: $10	F3

Cottage **Location:** On US 1, MM 53.5 oceanside. 12399 Overseas Hwy 33050. Fax: 305/289-0195. **Facility:** 18 units. 17 one-bedroom standard units with efficiencies. 1 two-bedroom suite with kitchen. 1 story, exterior corridors. *Bath:* combo or shower only. **Parking:** on-site. **Terms:** 3-7 night minimum stay - seasonal, 30 day cancellation notice-fee imposed. **Amenities:** video library (fee), safes, hair dryers. **Pool(s):** outdoor. **Leisure Activities:** boat dock, fishing, tennis court. *Fee:* charter fishing, diving tours & instruction, snorkeling trips. **Guest Services:** coin laundry. **Business Services:** fax (fee). **Cards:** AX, DS, MC, VI. **Special Amenities:** free local telephone calls.

(¶) (➔) (⊠) (VCR) (▤) (◨) (▣)

FLAMINGO INN
Phone: 305/289-1478

12/20-4/26	1P: $79-$89	2P: $79-$89	XP: $10	F7
4/27-9/6	1P: $69-$79	2P: $69-$79	XP: $10	F7
12/1-12/19 & 9/7-11/30	1P: $50-$62	2P: $50-$62	XP: $5	F7

Motel **Location:** On Grassy Key, on US 1, MM 59.5. 59299 Overseas Hwy 33050. Fax: 305/743-4399. **Facility:** 10 units. 6 one-bedroom standard units. 3 one- and 1 two-bedroom suites with kitchens. 1-2 stories, exterior corridors. *Bath:* combo or shower only. **Parking:** on-site. **Terms:** 7 day cancellation notice-fee imposed. **Pool(s):** outdoor. **Leisure Activities:** barbecue facilities. **Cards:** MC, VI.

SOME UNITS

(➔) (▣) (▣) / (▤) (◨) /

HAMPTON INN & SUITES
Phone: (305)743-9009

12/23-4/14 [ECP]	1P: $189-$289	2P: $199-$299	
4/15-9/1 [ECP]	1P: $109-$199	2P: $119-$209	
12/1-12/22 & 9/2-11/30 [ECP]	1P: $79-$179	2P: $89-$189	

Small-scale Hotel **Location:** US 1, at MM 48 (gulfside). 1688 Overseas Hwy 33050. Fax: 305/743-3835. **Facility:** 79 units. 55 one-bedroom standard units. 24 one-bedroom suites with efficiencies. 3 stories, interior corridors. *Bath:* combo or shower only. **Parking:** on-site. **Terms:** 3 day cancellation notice. **Amenities:** voice mail, irons, hair dryers. **Pool(s):** heated outdoor. **Leisure Activities:** whirlpool, fishing, exercise room. *Fee:* boats, canoes, boat dock, scuba diving, snorkeling, charter fishing, bicycles. **Guest Services:** sundries, coin laundry. **Business Services:** meeting rooms, fax (fee). **Cards:** AX, DC, DS, MC, VI. *(See color ad below)*

SOME UNITS

(SD) (¶) (ĠM) (ĠＭ) (⚲) (➔) (⊠) (▣) (DATA PORT) (▣) / (⊠) (◨) (▣) /

HAWK'S CAY RESORT

Phone: (305)743-7000

AAA SAVE

12/26-4/14	1P: $240-$465	XP: $25	F16
12/1-12/25 & 4/15-11/30	1P: $200-$325	XP: $25	F16

Location: On Duck Key, 0.5 mi s of US 1. Located in a remote area. MM 61 33050 (MM 61, DUCK KEY). Fax: 305/743-0641. **Facility:** Though this property offers conference facilities and a corporate team-building program, its atmosphere is casual and family oriented. 412 units. 177 one-bedroom standard units. 230 two- and 5 three-bedroom suites ($445-$1100) with kitchens. 2-5 stories, interior/exterior corridors. **Parking:** on-site. **Terms:** check-in 4 pm, 7 day cancellation notice-fee imposed. **Amenities:** video library, voice mail, irons, hair dryers. **Dining:** 4 restaurants, 7 am-11 pm, cocktails. **Pool(s):** outdoor, 3 heated outdoor, wading. **Leisure Activities:** sauna, whirlpools, steamroom, fishing, putting green, 8 tennis courts (2 lighted), recreation programs, ecology tours, kayak trips, sunset cruise, playground, exercise room, sports court. *Fee:* boats, waterskiing, scuba diving, snorkeling, charter fishing, diving trip & scuba instruction, parasailing, massage. **Guest Services:** gift shop, valet and coin laundry, airport transportation-Marathon Airport, area transportation-golf courses, fly fishing & sailing school. **Business Services:** conference facilities, business center. **Cards:** AX, DC, DS, MC, VI. *(See color ad below)*

Resort
Large-scale Hotel

SOME UNITS

HOLIDAY INN & MARINA, FLORIDA KEYS

Phone: (305)289-0222

All Year	2P: $99-$189	XP: $10	F17

Location: On US 1, at MM 54. 13201 Overseas Hwy 33050. Fax: 305/743-5460. **Facility:** 134 one-bedroom standard units. 2 stories, exterior corridors. *Bath:* combo or shower only. **Parking:** on-site. **Terms:** check-in 4 pm, [BP] & [MAP] meal plans available. **Amenities:** dual phone lines, voice mail, safes, honor bars, irons, hair dryers. **Pool(s):** heated outdoor, wading. **Leisure Activities:** fishing, exercise room. *Fee:* boats, scuba diving, snorkeling, charter fishing. **Guest Services:** gift shop, coin laundry. **Business Services:** meeting rooms, fax (fee). **Cards:** AX, CB, DC, DS, MC, VI. *(See color ad opposite inside back cover)*

Small-scale Hotel

SOME UNITS

ROYAL HAWAIIAN MOTEL/BOTEL

Phone: (305)743-7500

AAA SAVE

2/1-4/15	1P: $105-$115	2P: $105-$115	XP: $10	F3
12/1-1/31	1P: $79-$115	2P: $79-$115	XP: $10	F3
4/16-9/5	1P: $69-$115	2P: $69-$115	XP: $10	F3
9/6-11/30	1P: $59-$79	2P: $59-$79	XP: $10	F3

Motel

Location: US 1 at MM 53, gulfside. 12020 Overseas Hwy 33050. Fax: 305/743-0577. **Facility:** 8 one-bedroom standard units, some with efficiencies. 1 story, exterior corridors. *Bath:* shower only. **Parking:** on-site. **Terms:** 7 day cancellation notice-fee imposed. **Pool(s):** small outdoor. **Leisure Activities:** boat dock, fishing. **Cards:** AX, DS, MC, VI. **Special Amenities:** free local telephone calls.

20% off published rates for AAA members

connect with
florida's caribbean island™
at www.hawkscay.com
mile marker 61, duck key

Hawk's Cay Resort
The Heart Of The Florida Keys

1·888·809·7305

Based on availability.

──────── **WHERE TO DINE** ────────

ANNETTE'S LOBSTER & STEAKHOUSE   **Lunch:** $6-$11   **Dinner:** $10-$26   **Phone:** 305/743-5516
◈◈ ◈◈   **Location:** 3660 Overseas Hwy 33050. **Hours:** 11 am-9:30 pm, Fri & Sat-10 pm. **Reservations:** accepted.
          Features: Diners who are looking to taste and experience the seafood of coastal Florida will find it at this
Steak & Seafood   bustling roadside restaurant. Casual dress; cocktails. **Parking:** on-site. **Cards:** AX, MC, VI.
⊠

THE QUAY MARATHON   **Lunch:** $4-$15   **Dinner:** $12-$35   **Phone:** 305/289-1810
◈◈ ◈◈   **Location:** US 1 at MM 54. 12650 Overseas Hwy 33050. **Hours:** 11 am-10 pm, Fri & Sat-11 pm.
          Reservations: suggested; in season. **Features:** Relaxing gulf views enhance the mellow experience for
Steak & Seafood   diners who unwind in the cozy dining room as well as those who opt for the breezy patio. The woodwork
          and decor suggest a nautical theme. Prime rib, dolphin, alligator, swordfish and homemade cheesecake
are among tasty offerings. Casual dress; cocktails. **Parking:** on-site. **Cards:** AX, CB, DC, DS, MC, VI.
⊠

This ends listings for The Florida Keys.
The following page resumes the alphabetical listings of
cities in Florida.

Destination Ft. Lauderdale
pop. 152,397

*C*anals, lagoons, rivers, the Atlantic Ocean and the Intracoastal Waterway-Fort Lauderdale is literally shaped by various bodies of H_2O.

*C*ruise ships depart its port for Caribbean destinations, divers snorkel in crystal blue waters, waterfront cafes prepare feasts of locally caught seafood, sailboats and yachts mingle in marinas and a floating taxi takes you from here to there.

The beach at Fort Lauderdale.
Palm trees line Fort Lauderdale's beachfront promenade.

Las Olas Riverfront Marketplace, Fort Lauderdale.
Eateries, nightclubs and shops entice visitors to this plaza on the waterfront. (See mention page 76)

Deerfield Beach

Hillsboro Beach

Coral Springs

Lighthouse Point

Margate

Pompano Beach

North Lauderdale

Tamarac

Lauderdale-by-the-Sea

Lauderhill

Sunrise

Fort Lauderdale

Plantation

Weston

Davie

Dania Beach

Hollywood

Hallandale Beach

Pembroke Pines

Miramar

Convention Center, Fort Lauderdale.
A sculpture of a soaring sailfish leaps from the fountain plaza of the Broward County Convention Center.

See Vicinity map page 357

Heron Bay golf course, Coral Springs.
Scores of courses beckon pros and duffers alike to chase birdies.

*P*laces included in this AAA Destination City:

Coral Springs........389	Lauderdale-By-The-Sea.....................400	Pembroke Pines......404
Dania Beach..........390		Plantation..............405
Davie....................391	Lauderhill.............402	Pompano Beach......407
Deerfield Beach......392	Lighthouse Point....402	Sunrise.................410
Hallandale Beach....394	Margate.................402	Tamarac................412
Hillsboro Beach......396	Miramar................403	Weston.................413
Hollywood.............396	North Lauderdale...404	

FORT
LAUDERDALE
HOLLYWOOD
ACCOMMODATIONS

✈ Airport Accommodations

Spotter/Map Page Number	OA	FORT LAUDERDALE-HOLLYWOOD INT'L	Diamond Rating	Rate Range High Season	Listing Page
84 / p. 357		Hilton Fort Lauderdale Airport, 2 mi sw of airport entrance	▼▼▼	$129-$159	390
82 / p. 357		Sheraton Fort Lauderdale Airport Hotel, 2 mi sw of airport entrance	▼▼▼	$169	390
83 / p. 357	AAA	SpringHill Suites by Marriott Fort Lauderdale Airport, 3 mi s of entrance	▼▼▼	$134-$149 SAVE	390
53 / p. 357	AAA	AmeriSuites (Fort Lauderdale/17th Street), 2.6 mi n of entrance	▼▼▼	$125 SAVE	364
52 / p. 357	AAA	Best Western Marina Inn & Yacht Harbor, 3.2 mi n of entrance	▼▼▼	$149-$179 SAVE	365
42 / p. 357	AAA	Best Western-Oceanside Inn, 4 mi n of entrance	▼▼▼	$149-$199 SAVE	366
55 / p. 357		Comfort Suites Airport & Cruise Port, 1.8 mi n of entrance	▼▼▼	$89-$199	370
54 / p. 357		Embassy Suites-Fort Lauderdale, 2.3 mi n of entrance	▼▼▼	$179-$299	371
47 / p. 357	AAA	Fort Lauderdale Marina Marriott, 2.9 mi n of entrance	▼▼▼	$159-$299 SAVE	372
56 / p. 357		Hampton Inn Fort Lauderdale Airport North, 3.5 mi n of entrance	▼▼▼	$129-$149	373
28 / p. 357		Holiday Inn Express Port Everglades Cruise & Convention Center, 2.5 mi n of entrance	▼▼▼	$149-$169	374
48 / p. 357	AAA	Hyatt Regency Pier Sixty Six, 3.2 mi n of entrance	▼▼▼▼	$109-$309 SAVE	375
49 / p. 357	AAA	Marriott's Harbor Beach Resort & Spa, 4 mi n of entrance	▼▼▼▼	$199-$469 SAVE	378
45 / p. 357	AAA	Renaissance Fort Lauderdale Hotel, 2.6 mi n of entrance	▼▼▼▼	$229-$279 SAVE	381
41 / p. 357	AAA	Sheraton Yankee Clipper Beach Hotel, 4 mi n of entrance	▼▼▼	$249-$299 SAVE	383
126 / p. 357	AAA	Comfort Inn-Ft. Lauderdale/Hollywood Airport, 3 mi s of entrance	▼▼▼	$99-$139 SAVE	396
129 / p. 357		Days Inn Fort Lauderdale/Hollywood Airport South, 4 mi n of entrance	▼▼▼	$69-$159	396
125 / p. 357	AAA	Hampton Inn & Suites-Ft Lauderdale/Hollywood Airport, 3 mi s of entrance	▼▼▼	$139-$159 SAVE	397
130 / p. 357	AAA	Holiday Inn Fort Lauderdale/Hollywood Airport, 4 mi s of entrance	▼▼▼	$179-$249 SAVE	397
131 / p. 357		La Quinta Inn & Suites, 4 mi s of entrance	▼▼▼	$119-$155	397

Fort Lauderdale/Hollywood and Vicinity

This index helps you "spot" where approved accommodations and restaurants are located on the corresponding detailed maps. Lodging rate ranges are for comparison only and show the property's high season; rates are per night, unless only weekly (W) rates are available. Restaurant rate range is for dinner, unless only lunch (L) is served. Turn to the listing page for more detailed rate information and consult display ads for special promotions.

Spotter/Map Page Number	OA	FORT LAUDERDALE - Lodgings	Diamond Rating	Rate Range High Season	Listing Page
1 / p. 357	AAA	La Quinta Inn-Cypress Creek - see color ad p 377	▼▼▼	$79-$115 SAVE	377
2 / p. 357		Sheraton Suites Cypress Creek - see color ad p 5	▼▼▼	$289	383
3 / p. 357	AAA	Fort Lauderdale Marriott North - see ad p 372	▼▼▼	$169-$239 SAVE	372
4 / p. 357	AAA	Hampton Inn	▼▼▼	$89-$129 SAVE	373
5 / p. 357		The Westin, Fort Lauderdale - see color ad p 5	▼▼▼	$199-$299	384
6 / p. 357	AAA	Fairfield Inn by Marriott-Ft Lauderdale North	▼▼▼	$115-$125 SAVE	372

Spotter/Map Page Number	OA	FORT LAUDERDALE - Lodgings (continued)	Diamond Rating	Rate Range High Season	Listing Page
7 / p. 357		TownePlace Suites by Marriott - see color ad p 381	◆◆◆	$49-$159	384
8 / p. 357		Courtyard by Marriott, Fort Lauderdale East - see ad p 369	◆◆◆	$139-$189	370
9 / p. 357	AAA	Red Roof Inn	◆◆	$59-$89 SAVE	380
10 / p. 357	AAA	Best Inn - see color ad p 366	◆◆	$59-$119 SAVE	364
11 / p. 357		Days Inn-Fort Lauderdale/Oakland Park	◆◆	$59-$85	370
12 / p. 357		Holiday Inn Fort Lauderdale I-95 - see color ad opposite inside back cover	◆◆◆	$85-$110	374
13 / p. 357		Ramada Plaza Beach Resort - see color ad p 380	◆◆◆	$169-$209	380
14 / p. 357		Holiday Inn Express	◆◆◆	$99-$119	374
15 / p. 357	AAA	Oakland Park Inn	◆◆	$89-$109 SAVE	378
16 / p. 357	AAA	Ireland's Inn Beach Resort - see color ad p 375	◆◆◆	$169-$299 SAVE	375
17 / p. 357	AAA	Best Western Pelican Beach Resort - see color ad p 368	◆◆◆	$160-$340 SAVE	367
19 / p. 357	AAA	Ocean Hacienda Inn - see color ad p 379	◆◆	$99-$195 SAVE	379
21 / p. 357	AAA	Holiday Inn Ft. Lauderdale Beach - see color ad p 374, opposite inside back cover	◆◆◆	$180-$210 SAVE	374
22 / p. 357		The Doubletree Guest Suites/Galleria/Intracoastal Waterway - see color ad p 371	◆◆◆	$126-$189	371
23 / p. 357		Birch Patio Motel	◆◆	$50-$105	369
25 / p. 357	AAA	By-Eddy Apartment Motel	◆◆	$45-$73 SAVE	370
27 / p. 357		Three Suns Inn	◆◆	$82-$126	384
28 / p. 357		Holiday Inn Express Port Everglades Cruise & Convention Center	◆◆◆	$149-$169	374
29 / p. 357	AAA	Sea Chateau Resort Motel	◆	$70-$150 SAVE	382
30 / p. 357		Hampton Inn Fort Lauderdale City Center	◆◆◆	$119-$149	373
32 / p. 357	AAA	Royal Saxon Apartments	◆◆	$75-$150 SAVE	381
33 / p. 357		Ramada Sea Club Resort	◆◆	$109	380
34 / p. 357	AAA	Ft. Lauderdale Waterfront Inns Beach Resort	◆◆	$130-$187 SAVE	373
35 / p. 357	AAA	Sheraton Yankee Trader Beach Hotel	◆◆◆	$249-$299 SAVE	383
36 / p. 357	AAA	Days Inn Bahia Cabana Beach Resort & Marina	◆◆	$140 SAVE	370
37 / p. 357		Doubletree Oceanfront Hotel	◆◆◆	$139-$219	371
38 / p. 357	AAA	Riverside Hotel - see color ad p 382	◆◆◆	$179-$289 SAVE	381
39 / p. 357	AAA	Radisson Bahia Mar Beach Resort	◆◆◆	$152-$216 SAVE	379
40 / p. 357	AAA	Nina Lee/Imperial House Motel	◆	$79-$129 SAVE	378
41 / p. 357	AAA	Sheraton Yankee Clipper Beach Hotel	◆◆	$249-$299 SAVE	383
42 / p. 357	AAA	Best Western-Oceanside Inn - see color ad p 367	◆◆◆	$149-$199 SAVE	366
43 / p. 357		Ft. Lauderdale Waterfront Inns Las Olas Isle Resort	◆◆	$110-$155	373
44 / p. 357	AAA	Best Western Fort Lauderdale Inn	◆◆◆	$89-$139 SAVE	364
45 / p. 357	AAA	Renaissance Fort Lauderdale Hotel - see ad p 381	◆◆◆◆	$229-$279 SAVE	381
46 / p. 357		Ocean Holiday Motel	◆◆	$65-$150	379

Spotter/Map Page Number	OA	**FORT LAUDERDALE - Lodgings (continued)**	Diamond Rating	Rate Range High Season	Listing Page
47 / p. 357	AAA	Fort Lauderdale Marina Marriott - see ad p 372	▽▽▽	$159-$299 SAVE	372
48 / p. 357	AAA	Hyatt Regency Pier Sixty Six - see color ad p 376	▽▽/▽▽	$109-$309 SAVE	375
49 / p. 357	AAA	Marriott's Harbor Beach Resort & Spa	▽▽▽▽	$199-$469 SAVE	378
50 / p. 357	AAA	Lago Mar Resort & Club	▽▽▽▽	$215-$560 SAVE	377
51 / p. 357	AAA	Flying Cloud Motel	▽▽	$72-$115 SAVE	372
52 / p. 357	AAA	Best Western Marina Inn & Yacht Harbor - see color ad p 366	▽▽▽	$149-$179 SAVE	365
53 / p. 357	AAA	AmeriSuites (Fort Lauderdale/17th Street) - see color ad p 378	▽▽▽	$125 SAVE	364
54 / p. 357		Embassy Suites-Fort Lauderdale	▽▽▽	$179-$299	371
55 / p. 357		Comfort Suites Airport & Cruise Port - see ad p 370	▽▽▽	$89-$199	370
56 / p. 357		Hampton Inn Fort Lauderdale Airport North	▽▽▽	$129-$149	373
57 / p. 357		Motel 6 - 55	▽	$59-$75	378
58 / p. 357	AAA	Tropi Rock Resort	▽▽▽	$85-$98 SAVE	384
59 / p. 357	AAA	Eighteenth Street Inn	▽▽▽	$125-$175 SAVE	371
60 / p. 357	AAA	Best Western Rolling Hills Resort - see color ad p 369	▽▽▽	$109-$134 SAVE	369
		FORT LAUDERDALE - Restaurants			
2 / p. 357		Sea Watch Restaurant	▽▽	$15-$31	387
3 / p. 357		Mai-Kai Restaurant	▽▽	$16-$30	387
4 / p. 357		Gibby's	▽▽	$14-$28	386
6 / p. 357		Charley's Crab	▽▽▽	$12-$34	386
7 / p. 357		Big Louie's Italian Restaurant	▽	$5-$13	385
8 / p. 357		La Ferme	▽▽▽	$20-$35	386
9 / p. 357		Buca de Beppo	▽▽	$14-$23	385
10 / p. 357		Big Louie's Italian Restaurant	▽	$4-$14	385
13 / p. 357		Jackson's Steakhouse	▽▽▽	$16-$36	386
14 / p. 357		Himmarshee Bar & Grille	▽▽▽	$13-$25	386
16 / p. 357		The River House	▽▽▽	$12-$28	387
17 / p. 357	AAA	TarponBend Food & Tackle	▽▽	$6-$18	388
21 / p. 357	AAA	Shirttail Charlie's Restaurant	▽▽	$10-$20	387
22 / p. 357		California Cafe	▽▽▽	$10-$28	385
23 / p. 357		The Ambry	▽▽	$14-$30	385
27 / p. 357		Bimini Boatyard	▽▽	$6-$22	385
29 / p. 357		3030 Ocean	▽▽▽	$20-$32	385
30 / p. 357	AAA	Darrel & Oliver's Bistro 17 - see ad p 381	▽▽▽	$27-$35	386
32 / p. 357		By Word of Mouth	▽▽▽	$20-$30	385
35 / p. 357	AAA	Skinny's Yogurt, Cafe and Bakery	▽	$4-$8	387
36 / p. 357		Canyon Southwest Cafe	▽▽▽	$13-$25	385
37 / p. 357		Casablanca Cafe	▽▽	$11-$17	385

Spotter/Map Page Number	OA	FORT LAUDERDALE - Restaurants (continued)	Diamond Rating	Rate Range High Season	Listing Page
46 / p. 357	AAA	Eduardo de San Angel	◆◆◆	$15-$22	386
49 / p. 357		Food Lovers American Cafe	◆◆	$11-$18	386
55 / p. 357	AAA	The Grill Room on Las Olas - see color ad p 382	◆◆◆◆	$20-$40	386
58 / p. 357		Las Vegas	◆◆	$9-$12	386
59 / p. 357	AAA	La Tavernetta-The Italian Bistro by the Water	◆◆◆	$15-$24	387
68 / p. 357		Mark's Las Olas	◆◆◆◆	$17-$36	387
71 / p. 357	AAA	Primavera Restaurant	◆◆◆	$20-$35	387
72 / p. 357	AAA	Rainbow Palace	◆◆◆◆	$19-$40	387
75 / p. 357		Royal India	◆◆	$9-$16	387
81 / p. 357		Tropical Acres	◆◆	$11-$16	388
82 / p. 357		Yesterday's	◆◆◆	$12-$29	388
LAUDERDALE-BY-THE-SEA - Lodgings					
61 / p. 357	AAA	Holiday Inn-Lauderdale-By-The-Sea North Beach - see color ad opposite inside back cover	◆◆	$159 SAVE	400
62 / p. 357	AAA	A Little Inn By The Sea - see color ad p 377	◆◆◆	$119-$318 SAVE	400
63 / p. 357	AAA	Clarion Lauderdale Beach Resort - see color ad p 401	◆◆◆	$129-$219 SAVE	400
65 / p. 357	AAA	Courtyard Villa On The Ocean - see color ad p 400	◆◆◆	$169-$259 SAVE	400
66 / p. 357	AAA	The Pier Point Resort	◆◆	$110-$199 SAVE	401
67 / p. 357	AAA	Sea Spray Inn	◆◆	$98-$185 SAVE	402
68 / p. 357		Blue Seas Courtyard	◆◆	$99-$120	400
69 / p. 357	AAA	Tropic Seas Resort - see color ad p 383	◆◆	$150-$220 SAVE	402
LAUDERDALE-BY-THE-SEA - Restaurant					
90 / p. 357		Aruba Beach Cafe	◆◆	$5-$11	402
SUNRISE - Lodgings					
70 / p. 357	AAA	Wellesley Inn & Suites (Sunrise) - see color ad p 365	◆◆◆	$99-$109 SAVE	411
73 / p. 357		Crowne Plaza Hotel and Resort Sawgrass - Ft. Lauderdale/Sunrise	◆◆◆	$139-$155	410
74 / p. 357	AAA	Baymont Inn & Suites Sunrise at Sawgrass - see color ad p 411	◆◆◆	$79-$99 SAVE	410
75 / p. 357	AAA	Hilton Fort Lauderdale Sunrise	◆◆◆	$89-$109 SAVE	411
SUNRISE - Restaurants					
105 / p. 357		La Stella South	◆◆	$13-$25	411
109 / p. 357		Rio Vista Isle Cafe	◆◆	$11-$25	412
113 / p. 357		Legal Sea Foods	◆◆	$14-$30	411
114 / p. 357		Emerald Coast	◆◆	$17	411
DANIA BEACH - Lodgings					
80 / p. 357	AAA	Luckey's Motel	◆◆	$69-$149 SAVE	390
82 / p. 357		Sheraton Fort Lauderdale Airport Hotel - see color ad p 5	◆◆◆	$169	390
83 / p. 357	AAA	SpringHill Suites by Marriott Fort Lauderdale Airport	◆◆◆	$134-$149 SAVE	390
84 / p. 357		Hilton Fort Lauderdale Airport	◆◆◆	$129-$159	390

Spotter/Map Page Number	OA	DANIA BEACH - Restaurants	Diamond Rating	Rate Range High Season	Listing Page
(121) / p. 357		Le Petit Cafe	◆◆	$14-$17	391
(122) / p. 357		Islamorada Fish Company	◆◆	$5-$20	391
		NORTH LAUDERDALE - Lodgings			
(90) / p. 357		Courtyard by Marriott Fort Lauderdale North	◆◆◆	$99-$159	404
		TAMARAC - Lodgings			
(101) / p. 357	◆◆◆	Hampton Inn, Commercial Blvd	◆◆◆	$119-$129 SAVE	413
(102) / p. 357	◆◆◆	Wellesley Inn (Ft. Lauderdale/Tamarac) - see color ad p 365	◆◆	$79-$120 SAVE	413
(103) / p. 357		Homestead Studio Suites Hotel-Ft Lauderdale/Tamarac	◆◆	$75-$99	413
(104) / p. 357	◆◆◆	Comfort Inn	◆◆◆	$89-$119 SAVE	412
(105) / p. 357	◆◆◆	Baymont Inn & Suites Ft. Lauderdale/Tamarac - see color ad p 412	◆◆	$69-$89 SAVE	412
(107) / p. 357		Comfort Suites Sawgrass	◆◆◆	$109-$139	413
		PLANTATION - Lodgings			
(114) / p. 357		Residence Inn by Marriott-Plantation	◆◆◆	$115-$135	406
(115) / p. 357		La Quinta Inn & Suites - see color ad p 377	◆◆◆	$89-$135	406
(116) / p. 357	◆◆◆	Wellesley Inn & Suites (Plantation) - see color ad p 365	◆◆◆	$89-$119 SAVE	406
(119) / p. 357	◆◆◆	Hampton Inn Plantation	◆◆◆	$99-$159 SAVE	405
(120) / p. 357	◆◆◆	Sheraton Suites-Plantation - see color ad p 5	◆◆◆	$289-$329 SAVE	406
(121) / p. 357		Staybridge Suites by Holiday Inn Ft Lauderdale-Plantation	◆◆◆	$109-$179	406
(122) / p. 357		Courtyard by Marriott - see ad p 369	◆◆◆	$149-$159	405
(123) / p. 357	◆◆◆	AmeriSuites (Ft. Lauderdale/Plantation) - see color ad p 378	◆◆◆	$89-$149 SAVE	405
(124) / p. 357	◆◆◆	Holiday Inn Plantation/Sawgrass - see color ad p 405, opposite inside back cover	◆◆◆	$119 SAVE	406
		PLANTATION - Restaurants			
(131) / p. 357		Brasserie Max	◆◆	$8-$17	407
(133) / p. 357		Takeyama	◆◆	$10-$30	407
		HOLLYWOOD - Lodgings			
(125) / p. 357	◆◆◆	Hampton Inn & Suites-Ft Lauderdale/Hollywood Airport - see color ad p 373	◆◆◆	$139-$159 SAVE	397
(126) / p. 357	◆◆◆	Comfort Inn-Ft. Lauderdale/Hollywood Airport - see color ad p 396	◆◆◆	$99-$139 SAVE	396
(127) / p. 357		The Westin Diplomat Resort & Spa - see color ad p 5	◆◆◆◆	$289-$449	399
(128) / p. 357	◆◆◆	Ramada Inn Hollywood Beach Resort - see color ad p 398	◆◆	$159-$189 SAVE	398
(129) / p. 357		Days Inn Fort Lauderdale/Hollywood Airport South	◆◆◆	$69-$159	396
(130) / p. 357	◆◆◆	Holiday Inn Fort Lauderdale/Hollywood Airport - see color ad opposite inside back cover	◆◆◆	$179-$249 SAVE	397
(131) / p. 357		La Quinta Inn & Suites - see color ad p 377	◆◆◆	$119-$155	397
(132) / p. 357	◆◆◆	Econo Lodge	◆◆	$69-$99 SAVE	397
(133) / p. 357		Howard Johnson Plaza Resort Hollywood Beach	◆◆	$89-$129	397
(134) / p. 357	◆◆◆	Shell Motel - see ad p 398	◆◆	$45-$79 SAVE	399
(135) / p. 357	◆◆◆	Richards Motel - see ad p 398	◆	$49-$74 SAVE	399

Spotter/Map Page Number	OA	HOLLYWOOD - Lodgings (continued)	Diamond Rating	Rate Range High Season	Listing Page
136 / p. 357	AAA	**Greenbriar Beach Club**	◆◆	$119-$209 [SAVE]	397
137 / p. 357		California Dream Inn	◆◆	$139-$189	396
138 / p. 357	AAA	**Holiday Inn Hollywood Beach - see color ad opposite inside back cover**	◆◆◆	$139-$289 [SAVE]	397
139 / p. 357		The Ambassador Resort & Corporate Center	◆◆◆	$109-$129	396
		HOLLYWOOD - Restaurants			
141 / p. 357		Martha's on the Intracoastal	◆◆◆	$15-$29	399
142 / p. 357		Giorgio's Grill	◆◆◆	$10-$28	399
143 / p. 357		Hollywood Prime	◆◆◆◆	$24-$42	399
		HALLANDALE BEACH - Lodgings			
149 / p. 357		Hallandale Resort Motel	◆	$45-$85	395
150 / p. 357	AAA	**Best Western Hallandale Beach**	◆◆	$79-$199 [SAVE]	394
154 / p. 357	AAA	**The Diplomat Country Club & Spa - see color ad p 5**	◆◆◆◆	$309-$379 [SAVE]	395
		HALLANDALE BEACH - Restaurant			
144 / p. 357		The Royal Palm Room	◆◆◆	$16-$28	395
		MIRAMAR - Lodgings			
160 / p. 357		Wingate Inn	◆◆◆	$109-$129	404
161 / p. 357	AAA	**Hilton Garden Inn Ft. Lauderdale SW/Miramar - see color ad p 403**	◆◆◆	$139-$159 [SAVE]	403
		LAUDERHILL - Restaurant			
146 / p. 357		Crab House Seafood Restaurant	◆◆	$12-$21	402

FORT LAUDERDALE pop. 152,397   (See map p. 357; index p. 358)

—— WHERE TO STAY ——

AMERISUITES (FORT LAUDERDALE/17TH STREET)

AAA **SAVE** ❖❖❖❖

Small-scale Hotel

Phone: (954)763-7670   **53**

12/1-12/31 & 10/1-11/30	1P: $125	2P: $125	XP: $10	F
1/1-5/10	1P: $152		XP: $10	F
5/11-9/30	1P: $107		XP: $10	F

Location: SR A1A/17th St Cswy, just s. 1851 SE Tenth Ave 33316. Fax: 954/763-6269. **Facility:** 128 one-bedroom standard units. 6 stories, interior corridors. *Bath:* combo or shower only. **Parking:** on-site. **Terms:** [CP] meal plan available. **Amenities:** video games (fee), voice mail, irons, hair dryers. *Some:* dual phone lines. **Pool(s):** heated outdoor. **Leisure Activities:** exercise room. **Guest Services:** valet and coin laundry, area transportation-Port Everglades. **Business Services:** meeting rooms, business center. **Cards:** AX, DC, DS, JC, MC, VI. **Special Amenities: free continental breakfast and free newspaper.** *(See color ad p 378)*

SOME UNITS

 🅢🄳 ✈ 🐕 🍽️ ⛎ ❌ 🌀 🏊 📼 🎥 📠 🛜 🔲 ☕ /❌/

BEST INN

AAA **SAVE** ❖❖❖❖

Motel

Phone: (954)563-3400   **10**

| 12/1-4/15 [ECP] | 1P: $59-$119 | 2P: $69-$119 |
| 4/16-11/30 [ECP] | 1P: $39-$79 | 2P: $49-$79 |

Location: SR A1A, 1.1 mi s of Commercial Blvd (SR 870). 3711 N Ocean Blvd 33308. Fax: 954/563-6633. **Facility:** 66 one-bedroom standard units. 4 stories, exterior corridors. **Parking:** on-site. **Amenities:** safes (fee). **Dining:** noon-1 am, cocktails. **Pool(s):** heated outdoor. **Guest Services:** coin laundry. **Business Services:** fax (fee). **Cards:** AX, CB, DC, DS, JC, MC, VI. **Special Amenities: free continental breakfast and free newspaper.** *(See color ad p 366)*

SOME UNITS

🅢🄳 🍽️ 🏊 📠 🔲 ☕ /❌/

BEST WESTERN FORT LAUDERDALE INN

AAA **SAVE** ❖❖❖❖

Motel

Phone: (954)462-7005   **44**

| 12/1-4/30 [ECP] | 1P: $89-$139 | 2P: $89-$139 | XP: $10 | F18 |
| 5/1-11/30 [ECP] | 1P: $69-$109 | 2P: $69-$109 | XP: $10 | F18 |

Location: I-95, exit 25 (SR 84), 0.7 mi e. 1221 SR 84 33315. Fax: 954/462-5949. **Facility:** 50 one-bedroom standard units. 2 stories, interior corridors. *Bath:* combo or shower only. **Parking:** on-site. **Amenities:** voice mail, irons, hair dryers. **Pool(s):** heated outdoor. **Guest Services:** airport transportation-Fort Lauderdale-Hollywood International Airport, area transportation-Port Everglades, Convention Center. **Business Services:** meeting rooms, fax (fee). **Cards:** AX, CB, DC, DS, JC, MC, VI. **Special Amenities: free continental breakfast and free newspaper.**

SOME UNITS

🅢🄳 ✈ 🍽️ 🌀 🏊 📼 🎥 📠 🔲 ☕ /❌/

(See map p. 357)

BEST WESTERN MARINA INN & YACHT HARBOR　　　　　　　　　　　　　　　**Phone:** (954)525-3484　[52]

ⒶⒶⒶ [SAVE]	2/1-5/27	1P: $149-$179	2P: $149-$179	XP: $10	F12
▽▽▽▽▽	10/16-11/30	1P: $119-$169	2P: $119-$169	XP: $10	F12
	12/1-1/31	1P: $119-$149	2P: $119-$149	XP: $10	F12
	5/28-10/15	1P: $89-$99	2P: $89-$99	XP: $10	F12

Small-scale Hotel **Location:** SR A1A, 1.2 mi e of US 1. 2150 SE 17th St Cswy 33316. Fax: 954/764-2915. **Facility:** 166 one-bedroom standard units. 4 stories, exterior corridors. *Bath:* combo or shower only. **Parking:** on-site. **Terms:** 3 day cancellation notice-fee imposed, [CP] meal plan available. **Amenities:** voice mail, safes, irons, hair dryers. **Dining:** 7 am-10 pm, cocktails, entertainment. **Pool(s):** heated outdoor. **Leisure Activities:** whirlpool, putting green. *Fee:* marina. **Guest Services:** coin laundry, airport transportation-Fort Lauderdale-Hollywood International Airport, area transportation-Port Everglades, Convention Center. **Business Services:** meeting rooms, fax (fee). **Cards:** AX, DC, DS, MC, VI. **Special Amenities:** free continental breakfast and free newspaper. *(See color ad p 366)*

SOME UNITS

[icons] 🆂ⅅ ⊞ 🍴 🍽 ⊘ ⊒ ⊠ DATA PORT ▣ / ⊠ 🅱 🖨 /
FEE

(See map p. 357)

BEST WESTERN-OCEANSIDE INN   Phone: (954)525-8115   **42**

12/26-4/30 [ECP]	1P: $149-$199	2P: $149-$199	XP: $10 F12
10/1-11/30 [ECP]	1P: $129-$169	2P: $129-$169	XP: $10 F12
12/1-12/25 [ECP]	1P: $129-$149	2P: $129-$149	XP: $10 F12
5/1-9/30 [ECP]	1P: $89-$129	2P: $89-$129	XP: $10 F12

Small-scale Hotel **Location:** SR A1A, just s of Bahia Mar Marina. 1180 Seabreeze Blvd 33316. Fax: 954/527-0957. **Facility:** 101 units. 100 one-bedroom standard units. 1 one-bedroom suite ($159-$229). 5 stories, interior corridors. **Parking:** on-site. **Terms:** 3 day cancellation notice. **Amenities:** voice mail, safes (fee), irons, hair dryers. **Dining:** 7 am-3 pm. **Pool(s):** heated outdoor. **Leisure Activities:** sun deck. **Guest Services:** valet and coin laundry. **Business Services:** meeting rooms. **Cards:** AX, CB, DC, DS, JC, MC, VI. **Special Amenities:** free continental breakfast and free room upgrade (subject to availability with advanced reservations). *(See color ad p 367)*

SOME UNITS

(See map p. 357)

BEST WESTERN PELICAN BEACH RESORT

Motel

2/1-5/5 [ECP]	1P: $160-$340	2P: $160-$340	XP: $10	F12
12/22-1/31 [ECP]	1P: $150-$325	2P: $150-$325	XP: $10	F12
12/1-12/21 & 5/6-11/30 [ECP]	1P: $110-$250	2P: $110-$250	XP: $10	F12

Phone: (954)568-9431 **17**

Location: SR A1A, 0.8 mi s of SR 816 (Oakland Park Blvd). 2000 N Atlantic Blvd 33305. Fax: 954/565-2622. **Facility:** 25 units. 13 one-bedroom standard units, some with efficiencies. 12 one-bedroom suites. 6 stories, exterior corridors. **Parking:** on-site. **Terms:** 14 day cancellation notice-fee imposed. **Amenities:** voice mail, safes, irons, hair dryers. **Pool(s):** heated outdoor. **Guest Services:** sundries, valet and coin laundry. **Business Services:** fax (fee). **Cards:** AX, DS, MC, VI. **Special Amenities:** free continental breakfast. *(See color ad p 368)*

SOME UNITS

Nothing!

Between YOU and the BEACH!

No Florida vacation is complete without a stay on your own 500 feet of private sandy beach directly on the Gleaming Atlantic Ocean. Throw in a splash of oceanfront fun, sun, and family owned hospitality - that's the Best Western Pelican Beach Resort.

Stay With Us Now!
Or Watch for the Opening
of the New Best Western
Grand Pelican Beach
Resort - Spring 2003!

BEST WESTERN
Pelican Beach Resort

Best Western

THE WORLD'S LARGEST
HOTEL CHAIN

2000 N Atlantic Boulevard, Fort Lauderdale, Florida 33305
www.pelicanbeach.com   Email: info@pelicanbeach.com
Toll Free US & Canada (800) 525-6232

(See map p. 357)

BEST WESTERN ROLLING HILLS RESORT

Phone: (954)475-0400   60

12/21-4/15 [ECP]	1P: $109-$134	2P: $109-$134	XP: $10	F12
4/16-11/30 [ECP]	1P: $94-$119	2P: $94-$119	XP: $10	F12
12/1-12/20 [ECP]	1P: $89-$114	2P: $89-$114	XP: $10	F12

Location: I-595, exit 5, 1.5 mi s, then just w on SW 36th St. 3501 W Rolling Hills Cir 33328. Fax: 954/474-9967.
Small-scale Hotel Facility: 215 units. 207 one-bedroom standard units. 8 one-bedroom suites ($154-$174). 7 stories, interior corridors. *Bath:* combo or shower only. **Parking:** on-site. **Terms:** 3 day cancellation notice-fee imposed.
Amenities: voice mail, irons, hair dryers. *Some:* safes. **Dining:** 7 am-10 pm, cocktails. **Pool(s):** heated outdoor. **Leisure Activities:** whirlpool, golf privileges, 4 lighted tennis courts, exercise room, basketball. **Guest Services:** valet and coin laundry, airport transportation-Fort Lauderdale-Hollywood International Airport, area transportation-within 5 mi. **Business Services:** meeting rooms, fax (fee). **Cards:** AX, CB, DC, DS, JC, MC, VI. **Special Amenities:** free continental breakfast and free room upgrade **(subject to availability with advanced reservations).** *(See color ad below)*

SOME UNITS

FEE

BIRCH PATIO MOTEL

Phone: 954/563-9540   23

12/16-4/15	1P: $50-$105	2P: $50-$105	XP: $10	F12
12/1-12/15 & 4/16-11/30	1P: $35-$60	2P: $35-$65	XP: $5	F12

Motel

Location: 0.4 mi s on SR A1A from jct SR 838 (Sunrise Blvd), w on Aurumar St. 617 N Birch Rd 33304.
Fax: 954/563-4037. **Facility:** Designated smoking area. 20 units. 5 one-bedroom standard units. 15 one-bedroom suites, some with efficiencies or kitchens. 1-2 stories (no elevator), exterior corridors. *Bath:* combo or shower only.
Parking: on-site. **Terms:** 14 day cancellation notice, small pets only ($50 deposit, $10 extra charge). **Pool(s):** heated outdoor.
Leisure Activities: shuffleboard. **Guest Services:** coin laundry. **Cards:** MC, VI.

SOME UNITS

(See map p. 357)

BY-EDDY APARTMENT MOTEL   **Phone:** (954)764-7555
 All Year   1P: $45-$73   2P: $45-$73   XP: $8   F12
Location: 0.6 mi w of US 1 and SR 838 (Sunrise Blvd). 1021 NE 13th Ave 33304. Fax: 954/764-7577. **Facility:** 16 one-bedroom standard units, some with efficiencies or kitchens. 2 stories, exterior corridors. **Parking:** on-site. **Terms:** 3 night minimum stay, 30 day cancellation notice-fee imposed. **Pool(s):** heated outdoor. **Leisure Activities:** barbecue grills, picnic tables. **Guest Services:** coin laundry. **Cards:** MC, VI.

Motel

SOME UNITS

COMFORT SUITES AIRPORT & CRUISE PORT   **Phone:** (954)767-8700 [55]
12/21-5/8 [ECP]   1P: $89-$199   2P: $89-$199   XP: $10   F18
12/1-12/20 & 5/9-11/30 [ECP] 1P: $69-$149   2P: $69-$149   XP: $10   F18
Location: US 1, 0.5 mi s of jct SR A1A. 1800 S Federal Hwy 33316. Fax: 954/767-8629. **Facility:** 111 units. 102 one-bedroom standard units. 9 one-bedroom suites. 7 stories, interior corridors. **Parking:** on-site.
Small-scale Hotel **Terms:** cancellation fee imposed. **Amenities:** voice mail, irons, hair dryers. **Pool(s):** heated outdoor. **Guest Services:** valet laundry, area transportation. **Business Services:** meeting rooms, fax (fee). **Cards:** AX, CB, DC, DS, JC, MC, VI. *(See ad below)*

SOME UNITS

COURTYARD BY MARRIOTT, FORT LAUDERDALE EAST   **Phone:** (954)771-8100 [8]
1/12-5/11   1P: $139-$189
12/1-1/11   1P: $99-$139
10/5-11/30   1P: $109-$129
5/12-10/4   1P: $99-$119
Small-scale Hotel **Location:** US 1, at jct SR 870 and Commercial Blvd. 5001 N Federal Hwy 33308. Fax: 954/776-7980. **Facility:** 104 units. 100 one-bedroom standard units. 4 one-bedroom suites. 5 stories, interior corridors. *Bath:* combo or shower only. **Parking:** on-site. **Terms:** [BP] meal plan available, package plans, 15% service charge. **Amenities:** dual phone lines, voice mail, safes, irons, hair dryers. **Pool(s):** heated outdoor. **Leisure Activities:** whirlpool, exercise room. **Guest Services:** valet and coin laundry. **Business Services:** meeting rooms, fax (fee). **Cards:** AX, DC, DS, JC, MC, VI. *(See ad p 369)*

SOME UNITS

DAYS INN BAHIA CABANA BEACH RESORT & MARINA   **Phone:** (954)524-1555 [36]
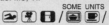 12/20-4/12   1P: $140   2P: $140   XP: $10   F12
12/1-12/19 & 4/13-11/30   1P: $70   2P: $70   XP: $5   F12
Location: On SR A1A; 0.7 mi s of jct Las Olas Blvd. 3001 Harbor Dr (A1A) 33316. Fax: 954/764-5951. **Facility:** 70 units. 62 one-bedroom standard units, some with efficiencies. 7 one- and 1 two-bedroom suites ($120-$190)
Motel with kitchens. 2-6 stories (no elevator), exterior corridors. *Bath:* combo or shower only. **Parking:** on-site. **Terms:** cancellation fee imposed. **Amenities:** voice mail, safes, hair dryers. **Dining:** 7 am-11 pm, cocktails, entertainment. **Pool(s):** 2 heated outdoor. **Leisure Activities:** saunas, whirlpool. **Fee:** boat dock, game room. **Guest Services:** gift shop. **Business Services:** fax (fee). **Cards:** AX, DC, DS, MC, VI.

SOME UNITS

DAYS INN-FORT LAUDERDALE/OAKLAND PARK   **Phone:** (954)484-9290 [11]
2/1-4/15 [CP]   1P: $59-$85   2P: $59-$85   XP: $10   F17
12/1-1/31 [CP]   1P: $49-$75   2P: $49-$75   XP: $10   F17
4/16-11/30 [CP]   1P: $49-$65   2P: $49-$65   XP: $10   F17
Location: I-95, exit 31, just w on SR 816 (Oakland Park Blvd). 1595 W Oakland Park Blvd 33311. Fax: 954/485-9025.
Motel **Facility:** 144 one-bedroom standard units. 5 stories, exterior corridors. **Parking:** on-site. **Terms:** weekly rates available. **Amenities:** safes (fee), hair dryers. **Pool(s):** outdoor. **Guest Services:** coin laundry. **Business Services:** fax (fee). **Cards:** AX, CB, DC, DS, MC, VI.

SOME UNITS

(See map p. 357)

THE DOUBLETREE GUEST SUITES/GALLERIA/INTRACOASTAL WATERWAY   Phone: (954)565-3800   22

SAVE

	1/1-4/30	1P: $126-$189	2P: $126-$189	XP: $10	F16
	12/1-12/31 & 10/1-11/30	1P: $108-$152	2P: $108-$152	XP: $10	F16
	5/1-9/30	1P: $72-$109	2P: $72-$109	XP: $10	F16

Small-scale Hotel

Location: Intracoastal Bridge on SR 838 (Sunrise Blvd), 3 blks w of jct SR A1A. 2670 E Sunrise Blvd 33304. **Fax:** 954/561-0387. **Facility:** 229 units. 207 one-bedroom standard units with kitchens. 22 two-bedroom suites with kitchens. 14 stories, interior corridors. **Parking:** on-site (fee) and valet. **Terms:** 3 day cancellation notice, pets ($15 extra charge). **Amenities:** dual phone lines, voice mail, honor bars, irons, hair dryers. **Pool(s):** heated outdoor. **Leisure Activities:** saunas, whirlpool, boat dock, exercise room. **Guest Services:** valet and coin laundry. **Business Services:** meeting rooms, business center. **Cards:** AX, CB, DC, DS, JC, MC, VI. *(See color ad below)*

SOME UNITS

(icons) / X /

DOUBLETREE OCEANFRONT HOTEL   Phone: (954)524-8733   37

SAVE

	1/1-5/4	1P: $139-$219	2P: $139-$219	XP: $20	F18
	12/1-12/31	1P: $99-$219	2P: $99-$219	XP: $20	F18
	5/5-11/30	1P: $79-$169	2P: $79-$169	XP: $20	F18

Large-scale Hotel

Location: SR A1A, just s of Las Olas Blvd. 440 Seabreeze Blvd 33316. **Fax:** 954/467-7489. **Facility:** 230 units. 224 one-bedroom standard units, some with whirlpools. 6 one-bedroom suites with whirlpools. 12 stories, interior corridors. *Bath:* combo or shower only. **Parking:** valet. **Terms:** cancellation fee imposed, [BP], [CP], [ECP] & [MAP] meal plans available. **Amenities:** voice mail, irons, hair dryers. **Pool(s):** heated outdoor. **Leisure Activities:** whirlpool, exercise room. **Guest Services:** valet laundry. **Business Services:** meeting rooms, fax (fee). **Cards:** AX, CB, DC, DS, MC, VI.

SOME UNITS

(icons) / X /
FEE

EIGHTEENTH STREET INN   Phone: (954)467-7841   59

AAA SAVE

| | 12/1-4/30 & 11/1-11/30 [ECP] | 1P: $125-$165 | 2P: $135-$175 | XP: $10 | F6 |
| | 5/1-10/31 [ECP] | 1P: $100-$140 | 2P: $110-$150 | XP: $10 | F6 |

Bed & Breakfast

Location: I-95, exit 25 (SR 84 E), 1.9 mi e on SR 84 to US 1, 0.4 mi n, just e. 712 SE 18th St 33316. **Fax:** 954/467-0309. **Facility:** Each guest room is decorated in a different theme at this inn enhanced by tropical pool-area plantings. Designated smoking area. 7 units. 4 one-bedroom standard units. 3 one-bedroom suites. 1 story, exterior corridors. **Parking:** on-site. **Terms:** age restrictions may apply, 14 day cancellation notice, weekly rates available, [CP] meal plan available, small pets only ($25 deposit). **Amenities:** voice mail. *Some:* fax, irons, hair dryers. **Pool(s):** heated outdoor. **Leisure Activities:** barbecue grills. **Guest Services:** complimentary evening beverages. **Cards:** AX, MC, VI. **Special Amenities:** free local telephone calls and preferred room (subject to availability with advanced reservations).

SOME UNITS

(icons) / VCR /

EMBASSY SUITES-FORT LAUDERDALE   Phone: (954)527-2700   54

SAVE

	10/1-11/30 [BP]	1P: $179-$299	2P: $179-$299	XP: $10	F17
	12/20-5/10 [BP]	1P: $229-$269	2P: $229-$269	XP: $10	F17
	12/1-12/19 [BP]	1P: $179-$269	2P: $179-$269	XP: $10	F17
	5/11-9/30 [BP]	1P: $109-$169	2P: $109-$169	XP: $10	F17

Large-scale Hotel

Location: On SR A1A, just e of jct US 1. 1100 SE 17th St Cswy 33316. **Fax:** 954/760-7202. **Facility:** 358 one-bedroom suites. 12 stories, interior corridors. *Bath:* combo or shower only. **Parking:** on-site (fee). **Terms:** cancellation fee imposed. **Amenities:** video games (fee), dual phone lines, voice mail, irons, hair dryers. **Pool(s):** heated outdoor. **Leisure Activities:** sauna, whirlpool, steamroom, exercise room. **Guest Services:** gift shop, complimentary evening beverages, valet and coin laundry, area transportation. **Business Services:** conference facilities, business center. **Cards:** AX, DC, DS, MC, VI.

SOME UNITS

(icons) / X /

(See map p. 357)

FAIRFIELD INN BY MARRIOTT-FT LAUDERDALE NORTH   Phone: (954)491-2500   [6]

AAA SAVE

▼▼▼▼

Motel

12/1-4/15	1P: $115-$125	2P: $115-$125
4/16-11/30	1P: $54-$59	2P: $54-$59

Location: 0.5 mi n on Federal Hwy (US 1) from Commercial Blvd (SR 870). 5727 N Federal Hwy 33308. Fax: 954/491-7945. **Facility:** 162 one-bedroom standard units. 2 stories (no elevator), exterior corridors. **Bath:** combo or shower only. **Parking:** on-site. **Terms:** [CP] meal plan available. **Amenities:** video games (fee), voice mail, irons. **Pool(s):** heated outdoor. **Leisure Activities:** whirlpool, exercise room. **Guest Services:** valet and coin laundry. **Business Services:** meeting rooms. **Cards:** CB, DC, DS, JC, MC, VI. **Special Amenities:** free continental breakfast and free local telephone calls.

SOME UNITS
⑤ 🏠 ⏱ &M ⚕ 🔲 ➤ 🎦 DATA PORT / ✕ 🗎 📷 /
FEE FEE

FLYING CLOUD MOTEL   Phone: (954)563-7062   [51]

AAA SAVE

▼▼▼▼

Motel

2/1-4/15	1P: $72-$115	2P: $72-$115	XP: $10	F12
12/1-1/4	1P: $72-$105	2P: $72-$105	XP: $10	F12
1/5-1/31	1P: $62-$95	2P: $62-$95	XP: $10	F12
4/16-11/30	1P: $37-$70	2P: $37-$70	XP: $8	F12

Location: Just w of SR A1A; between Terramar and Rio Mar sts, 0.5 mi s of Sunrise Blvd. 533 Orton Ave 33304. Fax: 954/561-2767. **Facility:** 10 one-bedroom standard units, some with efficiencies. 2 stories (no elevator), exterior corridors. **Bath:** combo or shower only. **Parking:** on-site. **Terms:** 14 day cancellation notice-fee imposed. **Pool(s):** heated outdoor. **Guest Services:** coin laundry. **Cards:** AX, DC, MC, VI.

SOME UNITS
➤ 🗎 / 📷 /

FORT LAUDERDALE MARINA MARRIOTT   Phone: (954)463-4000   [47]

AAA SAVE

▼▼▼▼

Large-scale Hotel

12/1-3/20	1P: $159-$289	2P: $169-$299
10/3-11/30	1P: $139-$279	2P: $149-$289
3/21-5/22	1P: $139-$249	2P: $149-$259
5/23-10/2	1P: $99-$229	2P: $109-$239

Location: SR A1A, 1 mi e of jct US 1. 1881 SE 17th St 33316. Fax: 954/527-6705. **Facility:** 580 units. 570 one-bedroom standard units. 10 one-bedroom suites ($299-$699). 3-14 stories, interior corridors. **Bath:** combo or shower only. **Parking:** on-site and valet. **Terms:** check-in 4 pm, [BP] meal plan available, package plans - weekends. **Amenities:** voice mail, safes, honor bars, irons, hair dryers. **Dining:** 6:30 am-11 pm, cocktails. **Pool(s):** heated outdoor. **Leisure Activities:** saunas, whirlpool, exercise room. Fee: marina, charter fishing, massage. **Guest Services:** gift shop, valet and coin laundry, area transportation-beach. **Business Services:** conference facilities, business center. **Cards:** AX, DS, MC, VI. **Special Amenities:** free newspaper. (See ad below)

SOME UNITS
⑤ 🏠 Y 🍴 🔲 ➤ ✕ 🎦 DATA PORT ☕ / ✕ 🗎 /

FORT LAUDERDALE MARRIOTT NORTH   Phone: (954)771-0440   [3]

AAA SAVE

▼▼▼▼

Large-scale Hotel

1/11-4/20	1P: $169-$239	2P: $169-$239
10/1-11/30	1P: $129-$159	2P: $129-$159
12/1-1/10 & 4/21-9/30	1P: $109-$149	2P: $109-$149

Location: I-95, exit 33B, just nw, 0.5 mi n of jct Cypress Creek Rd. 6650 N Andrews Ave 33309. Fax: 954/772-9834. **Facility:** 315 units. 311 one-bedroom standard units. 4 one-bedroom suites. 16 stories, interior corridors. **Bath:** combo or shower only. **Parking:** on-site and valet. **Terms:** cancellation fee imposed, 18% service charge, small pets only ($250 fee). **Amenities:** dual phone lines, voice mail, safes, irons, hair dryers. Fee: video games, high-speed Internet. Some: honor bars. **Dining:** 6:30 am-10 pm, cocktails. **Pool(s):** heated outdoor. **Leisure Activities:** sauna, whirlpool, exercise room. **Guest Services:** gift shop, valet and coin laundry, area transportation-beach. **Business Services:** conference facilities, business center. **Cards:** AX, CB, DC, DS, JC, MC, VI. **Special Amenities:** early check-in/late check-out and free newspaper. (See ad below)

SOME UNITS
⑤ 🐾 🍴 24T Y 🔲 ➤ ✕ 🎦 DATA PORT ☕ / ✕ VCR 🗎 📷 /

(See map p. 357)

FT. LAUDERDALE WATERFRONT INNS BEACH RESORT

Phone: (954)564-4341 34

	1P:	2P:	XP:	
(AAA) **[SAVE]** 12/15-5/14 [CP]	1P: $130-$187	2P: $130-$187	XP: $10	F13
12/1-12/14 & 5/15-11/30 [CP]	1P: $85-$115	2P: $85-$115	XP: $10	F13

Location: 0.5 mi s of Sunrise Blvd, on SR A1A; at corner of Atlantic Blvd and Viramar. 521 Fort Lauderdale Beach Blvd 33304. Fax: 954/565-9564. **Facility:** Designated smoking area. 60 units. 48 one-bedroom standard units, some with efficiencies. 11 one- and 1 two-bedroom suites with kitchens. 3 stories (no elevator), exterior corridors. *Bath:* combo or shower only. **Parking:** on-site. **Terms:** 3 day cancellation notice-fee imposed.

Motel

Amenities: voice mail. **Pool(s):** heated outdoor. **Leisure Activities:** barbecue grills, shuffleboard. *Fee:* bicycles. **Guest Services:** coin laundry. **Cards:** AX, CB, DC, DS, MC, VI. **Special Amenities: free continental breakfast and free newspaper.**

SOME UNITS

FT. LAUDERDALE WATERFRONT INNS LAS OLAS ISLE RESORT

Phone: (954)527-0026 43

	1P:	2P:	XP:	
12/15-5/14 [CP]	1P: $110-$155	2P: $110-$155	XP: $10	F13
12/1-12/14 & 5/15-11/30 [CP]	1P: $82-$105	2P: $82-$105	XP: $10	F13

Motel

Location: 1 mi e of US 1 on Las Olas Blvd to Isle of Venice, then just n. Located in a quiet area. 91 Isle of Venice 33301. Fax: 954/527-1732. **Facility:** 52 units. 24 one-bedroom standard units, some with efficiencies. 28 one-bedroom suites with kitchens. 2-7 stories (no elevator), exterior corridors. *Bath:* combo or shower only. **Parking:** on-site. **Terms:** 3 day cancellation notice-fee imposed, small pets only ($60 fee, $200 deposit). **Amenities:** voice mail. **Pool(s):** 2 heated outdoor. **Leisure Activities:** *Fee:* boat dock. **Guest Services:** coin laundry. **Business Services:** fax (fee). **Cards:** AX, CB, DC, DS, MC, VI.

SOME UNITS
FEE

HAMPTON INN

Phone: (954)776-7677 4

	1P:	2P:	XP:	
(AAA) **[SAVE]** 12/1-4/1	1P: $89-$129	2P: $89-$129	XP: $10	F18
4/2-11/30	1P: $79-$129	2P: $79-$129	XP: $10	F18

Location: I-95, exit 33, 0.5 mi e. 720 E Cypress Creek Rd 33334. Fax: 954/776-0805. **Facility:** 122 one-bedroom standard units. 4 stories, interior corridors. *Bath:* combo or shower only. **Parking:** on-site. **Terms:** 7 day cancellation notice-fee imposed, [ECP] meal plan available. **Amenities:** voice mail, irons, hair dryers. **Pool(s):** outdoor. **Leisure Activities:** whirlpool, exercise room. **Guest Services:** valet laundry. **Business Services:** meeting rooms, fax (fee). **Cards:** AX, CB, DC, DS, JC, MC, VI. **Special Amenities: free continental breakfast and free local telephone calls.**

Small-scale Hotel

SOME UNITS
FEE FEE

HAMPTON INN FORT LAUDERDALE AIRPORT NORTH

Phone: (954)524-9900 56

	1P:	2P:	XP:	
[SAVE] 1/1-4/20 [ECP]	1P: $129-$149	2P: $129-$149	XP: $10	F17
12/1-12/31 & 10/1-11/30 [ECP]	1P: $109-$129	2P: $109-$129	XP: $10	F17
4/21-9/30 [ECP]	1P: $89-$109	2P: $89-$109	XP: $10	F17

Location: I-95, exit 25 (SR 84), 0.7 mi e to SW 12th Ave, just n. Located in a quiet location. 2301 SW 12th Ave 33315. Fax: 954/524-5155. **Facility:** 109 one-bedroom standard units. 5 stories, interior corridors. *Bath:* combo or shower only. **Parking:** on-site. **Terms:** small pets only. **Amenities:** dual phone lines, voice mail, irons, hair dryers. **Pool(s):** heated outdoor. **Leisure Activities:** limited exercise equipment. **Guest Services:** sundries, valet laundry, area transportation. **Business Services:** meeting rooms, fax (fee). **Cards:** AX, DC, DS, MC, VI.

Small-scale Hotel

SOME UNITS

HAMPTON INN FORT LAUDERDALE CITY CENTER

Phone: (954)924-2700 30

	1P:	2P:	XP:	
[SAVE] 12/1-4/15 [ECP]	1P: $119-$149	2P: $119-$149	XP: $10	F12
4/16-11/30 [ECP]	1P: $99-$129	2P: $99-$129	XP: $10	F12

Location: Broward Blvd (SR 842) just n; entrance on NE 3rd St. Located just north of the historic district. 250 N Andrews Ave 33301. Fax: 954/924-2717. **Facility:** 156 one-bedroom standard units. 11 stories, interior corridors. *Bath:* combo or shower only. **Parking:** on-site. **Amenities:** video games (fee), high-speed Internet, dual phone lines, voice mail, safes, irons, hair dryers. **Pool(s):** heated outdoor. **Leisure Activities:** whirlpool, exercise room. **Guest Services:** sundries, valet and coin laundry. **Business Services:** meeting rooms, business center. **Cards:** AX, DC, DS, MC, VI.

Small-scale Hotel

SOME UNITS

(See map p. 357)

HOLIDAY INN EXPRESS
Phone: (954)566-4301   **14**

	12/23-4/1	1P: $99-$119	2P: $99-$119	XP: $10	F16
	4/2-11/30	1P: $79-$109	2P: $79-$109	XP: $10	F16
Motel	12/1-12/22	1P: $69-$89	2P: $69-$89	XP: $10	F16

Location: US 1, just n of jct SR 816 (Oakland Park Blvd). 3355 N Federal Hwy 33306. Fax: 954/565-1472. **Facility:** 144 one-bedroom standard units. 2 stories (no elevator), exterior corridors. *Bath:* combo or shower only. **Parking:** on-site. **Terms:** weekly rates available. **Amenities:** video games (fee), irons, hair dryers. **Pool(s):** heated outdoor. **Guest Services:** valet and coin laundry. **Business Services:** meeting rooms, fax (fee). **Cards:** AX, CB, DC, DS, MC, VI.

SOME UNITS (ASK) (SO) (TI+) (&) (A) (B) (B) (B) / (X) (B) / FEE

HOLIDAY INN EXPRESS PORT EVERGLADES CRUISE & CONVENTION CENTER
Phone: (954)728-2577   **28**

	12/21-3/31 & 9/2-11/30	1P: $149-$169	2P: $149-$169	XP: $10	F18
	4/1-9/1	1P: $109-$129	2P: $109-$129	XP: $10	F18
Small-scale Hotel	12/1-12/20	1P: $99-$119	2P: $99-$119	XP: $10	F18

Location: SR A1A, 1 mi e of US 1. 1500 SE 17th St Cswy 33316. Fax: 954/728-2591. **Facility:** 78 one-bedroom standard units. 5 stories, interior corridors. *Bath:* combo or shower only. **Parking:** on-site. **Terms:** 30 day cancellation notice, [ECP] meal plan available. **Amenities:** voice mail, irons, hair dryers. **Guest Services:** valet laundry, area transportation. **Business Services:** meeting rooms, fax (fee). **Cards:** AX, CB, DC, DS, JC, MC, VI.

SOME UNITS (ASK) (SO) (+) (TI+) (&M) (&) (A) (B) (B) / (X) (B) / FEE

HOLIDAY INN FT. LAUDERDALE BEACH
Phone: (954)563-5961   **21**

(AAA) (SAVE)	12/26-4/20	1P: $180-$210	2P: $180-$210	XP: $10	F
	10/1-11/30 ·	1P: $130-$160	2P: $130-$160	XP: $10	F
	12/1-12/25 & 4/21-9/30	1P: $110-$140	2P: $110-$140	XP: $10	F

Location: SR A1A, jct SR 838 (E Sunrise Blvd). 999 Ft. Lauderdale Beach Blvd 33304. Fax: 954/564-5261. **Large-scale Hotel** **Facility:** 240 units. 236 one-bedroom standard units. 4 one-bedroom suites. 12 stories, interior corridors. *Bath:* combo or shower only. **Parking:** on-site (fee). **Terms:** cancellation fee imposed. **Amenities:** voice mail, safes, irons, hair dryers. **Dining:** 7 am-10 pm, cocktails. **Pool(s):** heated outdoor. **Leisure Activities:** exercise room. **Guest Services:** valet laundry. **Business Services:** meeting rooms, business center. **Cards:** AX, CB, DC, DS, MC, VI. **Special Amenities:** early check-in/late check-out and preferred room (subject to availability with advanced reservations). *(See color ad below & opposite inside back cover)*

SOME UNITS (SO) (TI) (Y) (&) (A) (B) (B) (B) (B) / (X) /

HOLIDAY INN FORT LAUDERDALE I-95
Phone: (954)776-4880   **12**

| | 12/1-4/15 | 1P: $85-$110 | 2P: $85-$110 | XP: $10 | F12 |
| | 4/16-11/30 | 1P: $55-$69 | 2P: $55-$69 | XP: $10 | F12 |

Location: I-95, exit 32, jct Commercial Blvd and Powerline Rd. 4900 Powerline Rd 33309. Fax: 954/776-1261. **Small-scale Hotel** **Facility:** 190 one-bedroom standard units. 5 stories, exterior corridors. *Bath:* combo or shower only. **Parking:** on-site. **Terms:** weekly rates available, package plans - weekends. **Amenities:** voice mail, safes, irons, hair dryers. *Some:* dual phone lines. **Pool(s):** heated outdoor. **Leisure Activities:** exercise room. **Guest Services:** valet and coin laundry, area transportation (fee). **Business Services:** meeting rooms, fax (fee). **Cards:** AX, CB, DC, DS, JC, MC, VI. *(See color ad opposite inside back cover)*

SOME UNITS (ASK) (SO) (+) (TI) (Y) (&) (A) (B) (B) (B) / (X) (B) (B) /

(See map p. 357)

HYATT REGENCY PIER SIXTY SIX
Phone: (954)525-6666 **48**

AAA SAVE	All Year	1P: $109-$309	2P: $109-$309	XP: $30	F18

Location: SR A1A, 1.3 mi e of jct US 1. 2301 SE 17th St Cswy 33316. Fax: 954/728-3541. **Facility:** On the Intracoastal Waterway, the hotel features tropical foliage, a large deck and a pool with a waterfall. 388 units. 380 one-bedroom standard units. 8 one-bedroom suites, some with whirlpools. 2-17 stories, interior/exterior corridors. **Large-scale Hotel** *Bath:* combo or shower only. **Parking:** on-site (fee) and valet. **Terms:** check-in 4 pm, 3 day cancellation notice-fee imposed, [BP] meal plan available. **Amenities:** high-speed Internet (fee), dual phone lines, voice mail, safes, honor bars, irons, hair dryers. *Some:* CD players, fax. **Dining:** 4 restaurants, 6:30 am-11 pm, cocktails, also, California Cafe, see separate listing, nightclub, entertainment. **Pool(s):** 2 heated outdoor. **Leisure Activities:** whirlpool, rental boats, fishing, golf privileges, salon, spa. *Fee:* sauna, marina, scuba diving, snorkeling, charter fishing, 2 lighted tennis courts. **Guest Services:** gift shop, valet laundry, area transportation-beach. *Fee:* scuba instruction. **Business Services:** conference facilities, business center. **Cards:** AX, CB, DC, DS, JC, MC, VI. *(See color ad p 376)*

SOME UNITS

⟨icons⟩

IRELAND'S INN BEACH RESORT
Phone: 954/565-6661 **16**

AAA SAVE	2/1-3/31	1P: $169-$299	2P: $169-$299	XP: $15	F16
	12/1-1/31	1P: $159-$299	2P: $159-$299	XP: $15	F16
	11/2-11/30	1P: $159-$289	2P: $159-$289	XP: $15	F16
	4/1-11/1	1P: $119-$229	2P: $119-$229	XP: $15	F16

Small-scale Hotel Location: 0.8 mi s of Oakland Park Blvd/SR 816, then just e of SR A1A. 2220 N Atlantic Blvd 33305. Fax: 954/565-8893. **Facility:** 60 units. 50 one-bedroom standard units. 10 one-bedroom suites, some with efficiencies and/or whirlpools. 3-7 stories, exterior corridors. *Bath:* combo or shower only. **Parking:** on-site. **Terms:** 3 day cancellation notice. **Amenities:** voice mail, safes, irons, hair dryers. **Dining:** 7:30 am-10 pm, entertainment. **Pool(s):** 2 heated outdoor. **Guest Services:** gift shop, valet laundry. **Business Services:** meeting rooms, fax (fee). **Cards:** AX, MC, VI. *(See color ad below)*

SOME UNITS

⟨icons⟩

(See map p. 357)

LAGO MAR RESORT & CLUB

	12/15-4/30	1P: $215-$560	2P: $215-$560	**Phone:** (754)523-6511	XP: $10
	10/25-11/30	1P: $145-$285	2P: $145-$285	XP: $10	F
	12/1-12/14	1P: $135-$275	2P: $135-$275	XP: $10	F
	5/1-10/24	1P: $130-$240	2P: $130-$240	XP: $10	F

Large-scale Hotel **Location:** Just e of SR A1A; 0.5 mi ne of 17th St Cswy Bridge to Mayan Dr, to Ocean Dr, then s to Grace, e to S Ocean Ln, then just n. 1700 S Ocean Ln 33316. Fax: 954/524-6627. **Facility:** A mosaic floor mural adds interest to the lobby of this hotel, which faces the beach on one side and a lake on the other. 212 units. 52 one-bedroom standard units. 142 one- and 18 two-bedroom suites, some with kitchens. 3-5 stories, interior/exterior corridors. **Bath:** combo or shower only. **Parking:** on-site and valet. **Terms:** check-in 4 pm, 7 day cancellation notice-fee imposed, [AP], [BP], [CP] & [ECP] meal plans available, package plans - seasonal. **Amenities:** video games (fee), voice mail, safes, irons, hair dryers. *Some:* dual phone lines. **Dining:** 4 restaurants, 7:30 am-10 pm, cocktails, entertainment. **Pool(s):** 2 heated outdoor. **Leisure Activities:** miniature golf, recreation programs, playground, exercise room, spa, shuffleboard, volleyball. *Fee:* 4 tennis courts, game room. **Guest Services:** gift shop. *Fee:* tennis instruction. **Business Services:** conference facilities, business center. **Cards:** AX, DC, MC, VI. **Special Amenities:** free newspaper.

SOME UNITS

LA QUINTA INN-CYPRESS CREEK

	12/1-4/7	1P: $79-$109	2P: $85-$115	**Phone:** (954)491-7666
	4/8-11/30	1P: $59-$79	2P: $65-$85	

Location: I-95, exit 33 southbound; 0.8 mi; exit 33B northbound at Powerline Rd. 999 W Cypress Creek Rd 33309. Fax: 954/491-7669. **Facility:** 145 one-bedroom standard units. 4 stories, interior corridors. **Parking:** on-site. **Small-scale Hotel** **Terms:** [ECP] meal plan available, small pets only. **Amenities:** video games (fee), dual phone lines, voice mail, irons, hair dryers. **Pool(s):** outdoor. **Leisure Activities:** whirlpool, exercise room. **Guest Services:** valet and coin laundry. **Business Services:** meeting rooms, fax (fee). **Cards:** AX, CB, DC, DS, JC, MC, VI. **Special Amenities:** free continental breakfast and free local telephone calls. *(See color ad below)*

SOME UNITS

FEE

(See map p. 357)

MARRIOTT'S HARBOR BEACH RESORT & SPA

Phone: (954)525-4000 [49]

⟨AAA⟩ [SAVE]
◆◆◆◆

9/16-11/30	1P: $199-$469	2P: $199-$469
12/1-4/23	1P: $269-$459	2P: $269-$459
4/24-5/27	1P: $269-$379	2P: $269-$379
5/28-9/15	1P: $169-$299	2P: $169-$299

Resort Large-scale Hotel **Location:** E of SR A1A, s of Bahia Mar Marina. 3030 Holiday Dr 33316. Fax: 954/766-6152. **Facility:** A private beach, a full luxury spa, a large tropical pool and spacious rooms add appeal to this property. 637 units. 602 one-bedroom standard units. 35 one-bedroom suites, some with whirlpools. 15 stories, interior corridors. *Bath:* combo or shower only. **Parking:** on-site. **Terms:** check-in 4 pm. **Amenities:** video games, high-speed Internet, voice mail, safes, honor bars, irons, hair dryers. *Some:* CD players, dual phone lines, fax. **Dining:** 3 restaurants, 6 am-midnight, cocktails, entertainment. **Pool(s):** heated outdoor. **Leisure Activities:** saunas, whirlpools, fishing, private beach charter sailing, recreation programs, spa, volleyball, game room. *Fee:* windsurfing, waterskiing, scuba diving, snorkeling, jet skis, sunfish, parasailing, golf privileges, 5 tennis courts, bicycles. **Guest Services:** gift shop, valet and coin laundry, area transportation-within 5-10 mi. *Fee:* tennis instruction. **Business Services:** conference facilities, business center. **Cards:** AX, DC, DS, MC, VI.

SOME UNITS

⊞ 🕿 ⊤ 🖥 🕮 ➰ 🛁 ✕ 🖫 🗚 ▣ / ✕ 📼 🖪 /

MOTEL 6 - 55

Phone: 954/760-7999 [57]

◆◆◆

1/16-4/19	1P: $59-$69	2P: $65-$75	XP: $3	F17
12/1-1/15	1P: $55-$65	2P: $61-$71	XP: $3	F17
4/20-11/30	1P: $45-$55	2P: $51-$61	XP: $3	F17

Small-scale Hotel **Location:** I-95, exit 25 (SR 84 E), just e, then U-turn at light. 1801 SR 84 33315. Fax: 954/832-0653. **Facility:** 106 one-bedroom standard units. 2 stories (no elevator), interior corridors. *Bath:* shower only. **Parking:** on-site. **Pool(s):** heated outdoor. **Guest Services:** coin laundry. **Cards:** AX, CB, DC, DS, MC, VI.

SOME UNITS

🖫 🐾 ⊞ 🕮 ➰ 📺 🗚 / ✕ /

NINA LEE/IMPERIAL HOUSE MOTEL

Phone: (954)524-1568 [40]

⟨AAA⟩ [SAVE]
◆

12/22-4/19	1P: $79-$129	2P: $79-$129	XP: $12	F17
12/1-12/21 & 4/20-11/30	1P: $49-$109	2P: $49-$109	XP: $9	F17

Motel **Location:** 0.3 mi s of Bahia Mar Marina; just w of SR A1A. Located near Bahia Marina. 3048 Harbor Dr 33316. Fax: 954/763-2931. **Facility:** 26 units. 14 one-bedroom standard units, some with efficiencies. 8 one- and 4 two-bedroom suites ($99-$149) with kitchens. 2 stories (no elevator), exterior corridors. *Bath:* combo or shower only. **Parking:** on-site. **Terms:** cancellation fee imposed. **Pool(s):** heated outdoor. **Leisure Activities:** recreation privileges at Sheraton Yankee Clipper Beach Hotel. **Cards:** AX, DC, DS, MC, VI.

🖫 ⊞ ➰ 🖪 🖪 ▣

OAKLAND PARK INN

Phone: (954)565-4601 [15]

⟨AAA⟩ [SAVE]
◆◆◆

2/9-4/16			F16
12/1-2/8 & 10/24-11/30	2P: $89-$109	XP: $10	F16
4/17-10/23	2P: $69-$89	XP: $10	F16
	2P: $59-$79	XP: $10	

Motel **Location:** US 1, just s of jct SR 816, Oakland Park Blvd. 3001 N Federal Hwy 33306. Fax: 954/565-0384. **Facility:** 106 one-bedroom standard units, some with efficiencies and/or whirlpools. 3 stories, exterior corridors. **Parking:** on-site. **Terms:** cancellation fee imposed. **Amenities:** video library (fee). *Some:* safes. **Pool(s):** heated outdoor. **Leisure Activities:** *Fee:* game room. **Guest Services:** coin laundry. **Business Services:** meeting rooms, fax (fee). **Cards:** AX, DC, DS, MC, VI. **Special Amenities:** early check-in/late check-out and free continental breakfast.

SOME UNITS

🖫 ⊞ ➰ 🗚 ▣ / ✕ 📼 🖪 /

FEE

(See map p. 357)

OCEAN HACIENDA INN Phone: (954)564-7800 ⓫

12/1-5/31	1P: $99-$195	2P: $99-$195	XP: $10	F12
6/1-11/30	1P: $65-$129	2P: $65-$129	XP: $10	F12

Motel

Location: On SR A1A, 1 mi n of SR 838 (Sunrise Blvd). 1924 N Fort Lauderdale Beach Blvd 33305. Fax: 954/396-9971. **Facility:** 39 units. 32 one-bedroom standard units, some with efficiencies. 6 one- and 1 two-bedroom suites ($89-$250), some with efficiencies. 3 stories, exterior corridors. *Bath:* combo or shower only. **Parking:** on-site. **Terms:** weekly rates available, [CP] meal plan available. **Pool(s):** heated outdoor. **Guest Services:** coin laundry. **Cards:** AX, CB, DC, DS, MC, VI. **Special Amenities:** early check-in/late check-out and free continental breakfast. *(See color ad below)*

SOME UNITS

OCEAN HOLIDAY MOTEL Phone: (954)761-9933 ⓰

12/16-4/15	1P: $65-$140	2P: $75-$150	XP: $10	F10
12/1-12/15 & 4/16-11/30	1P: $45-$99	2P: $55-$109	XP: $10	F10

Motel

Location: SR A1A, between Seville and Alhambra sts. 205 N Atlantic Blvd 33304. Fax: 954/761-9933. **Facility:** 18 one-bedroom standard units. 3 stories. *Bath:* combo or shower only. **Parking:** on-site. **Terms:** 7 day cancellation notice-fee imposed, weekly rates available, package plans. **Business Services:** fax (fee). **Cards:** AX, DS, MC, VI.

SOME UNITS

RADISSON BAHIA MAR BEACH RESORT Phone: (954)764-2233 ⓳

12/26-4/30	1P: $152-$206	2P: $162-$216		
12/1-12/25	1P: $130-$166	2P: $140-$176	XP: $10	F16
6/1-11/30	1P: $99-$166	2P: $109-$176		
5/1-5/31	1P: $94-$125	2P: $104-$135		

Large-scale Hotel **Location:** SR A1A, 0.5 mi s of Las Olas Blvd. 801 Seabreeze Blvd 33316. Fax: 954/523-5424. **Facility:** 296 units. 294 one-bedroom standard units. 2 one-bedroom suites ($600-$1000). 4-16 stories, interior corridors. *Bath:* combo or shower only. **Parking:** on-site (fee). **Terms:** 3 day cancellation notice-fee imposed, 15% service charge. **Amenities:** voice mail, safes, honor bars, irons, hair dryers. **Dining:** 3 restaurants, 6:30 am-10:30 pm, cocktails. **Pool(s):** heated outdoor. **Leisure Activities:** 4 lighted tennis courts, exercise room. *Fee:* marina, scuba diving, snorkeling, fishing, charter fishing, golf course privileges, massage. **Guest Services:** gift shop, valet and coin laundry, water taxi stop. *Fee:* PADI dive instruction. **Business Services:** meeting rooms, administrative services (fee), fax. **Cards:** AX, CB, DC, DS, JC, MC, VI. *(See color ad p 384)*

SOME UNITS

FEE

(See map p. 357)

RAMADA PLAZA BEACH RESORT   Phone: (954)565-6611   [13]

	12/24-4/21	1P: $169-$209	2P: $169-$209	XP: $10	F12
	4/22-6/1	1P: $139-$179	2P: $139-$179	XP: $10	F12
Large-scale Hotel	12/1-12/23	1P: $129-$169	2P: $129-$169	XP: $10	F12
	6/2-11/30	1P: $99-$169	2P: $99-$169	XP: $10	F12

Location: Just e of SR A1A, 0.5 mi n of jct SR 816 (Oakland Park Blvd). 4060 Galt Ocean Dr 33308-6597. Fax: 954/564-7730. **Facility:** 225 units. 210 one-bedroom standard units. 15 one-bedroom suites ($169-$599) with efficiencies. 9 stories, interior corridors. **Parking:** valet. **Terms:** check-in 4 pm, 3 day cancellation notice-fee imposed. **Amenities:** high-speed Internet, voice mail, safes (fee), irons, hair dryers. **Pool(s):** heated outdoor. **Leisure Activities:** whirlpool, rental sailboats, exercise room. *Fee:* scuba diving, snorkeling. **Guest Services:** gift shop, valet and coin laundry. **Business Services:** meeting rooms, fax (fee). **Cards:** AX, DC, DS, MC, VI. *(See color ad below)*

SOME UNITS

(ASK) (S/D) (▯) (Y) (✂) (🖉) (🚤) (✗) (DATA PORT) (🔌) (🖥) (🖥) / (✗) /

RAMADA SEA CLUB RESORT   Phone: (954)564-3211   [33]

	12/16-4/15	1P: $109	2P: $109	XP: $10	F12
	12/1-12/15	1P: $95	2P: $95	XP: $10	F12
Small-scale Hotel	4/16-11/30	1P: $69	2P: $69	XP: $10	F12

Location: On SR A1A, 0.4 mi s of Sunrise Blvd (SR 838). 619 N Ft Lauderdale Beach Blvd 33304. Fax: 954/561-1252. **Facility:** 99 units. 98 one-bedroom standard units. 1 one-bedroom suite. 3-6 stories, interior/exterior corridors. *Bath:* combo or shower only. **Parking:** on-site. **Terms:** cancellation fee imposed, 15% service charge. **Amenities:** voice mail, safes (fee), irons, hair dryers. **Pool(s):** outdoor. **Guest Services:** gift shop, valet and coin laundry. **Business Services:** meeting rooms, fax (fee). **Cards:** AX, CB, DC, DS, JC, MC, VI.

SOME UNITS

(ASK) (S/D) (▯) (Y) (🚤) (🎦) (DATA PORT) (🔌) (🖥) / (✗) (🖥) /

RED ROOF INN   Phone: (954)776-6333   [9]

(AAA) (SAVE)

	12/15-4/19	1P: $59-$84	2P: $64-$89	XP: $5	F18
	9/27-11/30	1P: $49-$69	2P: $54-$74	XP: $5	F18
	4/20-9/26	1P: $46-$66	2P: $51-$71	XP: $5	F18
	12/1-12/14	1P: $49-$61	2P: $54-$66	XP: $5	F18

Small-scale Hotel **Location:** I-95, exit 32, just sw of jct Commercial Blvd. 4800 Powerline Rd 33309. Fax: 954/776-3648. **Facility:** 104 one-bedroom standard units. 4 stories, interior corridors. *Bath:* combo or shower only. **Parking:** on-site. **Terms:** small pets only. **Amenities:** video games (fee), voice mail. **Pool(s):** heated outdoor. **Guest Services:** coin laundry. **Cards:** AX, CB, DC, DS, MC, VI. **Special Amenities:** free local telephone calls and free newspaper.

SOME UNITS

(🛏) (▯▯) (✂) (🖉) (🚤) (🎦) (DATA PORT) / (✗) /

(See map p. 357)

RENAISSANCE FORT LAUDERDALE HOTEL
Phone: (954)626-1700 **45**

12/1-4/15	1P: $229-$279	2P: $229-$279
10/1-11/30	1P: $149-$199	2P: $149-$199
4/16-9/30	1P: $119-$189	2P: $119-$189

Location: SR A1A, just e of US 1. 1617 SE 17th St Cswy 33316. Fax: 954/626-1717. **Facility:** Near the beach, air-port and seaport, this hotel boasts a stylishly decorated lobby and finely appointed rooms. 233 units. 229 one-bedroom standard units, some with whirlpools. 4 one-bedroom suites ($169-$419). 12 stories, interior corridors. **Bath:** combo or shower only. **Parking:** valet. **Terms:** 11% service charge. **Amenities:** video games (fee), dual phone lines, voice mail, safes, honor bars, irons, hair dryers. **Dining:** 6-10:30 am, 11:30-2:30 & 6-10:30 pm, Fri & Sat-11 pm, cocktails, also, Darrel & Oliver's Bistro 17, see separate listing. **Pool(s):** heated outdoor. **Leisure Activities:** whirlpool, exercise room. **Guest Services:** valet laundry, airport transportation-Fort Lauderdale-Hollywood International Airport, area transportation-within 2 mi. **Business Services:** meeting rooms, business center. **Cards:** AX, DC, DS, MC, VI. **Special Amenities:** free news-paper. *(See ad below)* Large-scale Hotel

SOME UNITS
 / /

RIVERSIDE HOTEL
Phone: (954)467-0671 **38**

12/21-4/21	1P: $179-$289	2P: $179-$289	XP: $15	F16
12/1-12/20 & 10/1-11/30	1P: $149-$259	2P: $149-$259	XP: $10	F16
4/22-9/30	1P: $119-$229	2P: $119-$229	XP: $10	F16

Location: 2 mi w of SR A1A; at jct US 1 Underpass, main entrance on SE 4th St. Located in a fashionable historic dis-trict. 620 E Las Olas Blvd 33301. Fax: 954/462-2148. **Facility:** 216 units. 206 one-bedroom standard units. 10 one-bedroom suites ($199-$599), some with whirlpools. 3-12 stories, interior corridors. **Bath:** combo or shower only. **Parking:** on-site and valet. **Amenities:** video games (fee), dual phone lines, voice mail, irons, hair dryers. *Some:* high-speed Internet (fee). **Dining:** 2 restaurants, 7 am-11:30 pm, cocktails, also, The Grill Room on Las Olas, see separate listing. **Pool(s):** heated outdoor. **Leisure Activities:** Fee: boat dock. **Guest Services:** gift shop, valet laundry. **Business Services:** meeting rooms, business center. **Cards:** AX, DC, MC, VI. **Special Amenities:** free newspaper and free room upgrade (subject to availability with advanced reservations). *(See color ad p 382)* Classic Historic Small-scale Hotel

SOME UNITS
 / /

ROYAL SAXON APARTMENTS
Phone: 954/566-7424 **32**

12/16-4/14	1P: $75-$150	2P: $75-$150	XP: $10	F12
12/1-12/15 & 4/15-11/30	1P: $45-$100	2P: $45-$100	XP: $10	F12

Location: Just w of SR A1A; 0.5 mi s of SR 838 (Sunrise Blvd) at corner of Breakers Ave and Terranar St. 551 Breakers Ave 33304. Fax: 954/566-8305. **Facility:** 15 units. 2 one-bedroom standard units with efficiencies. 13 one-bedroom suites ($65-$150) with kitchens. 2 stories, exterior corridors. **Parking:** on-site. **Terms:** age restric-tions may apply, 21 day cancellation notice, small pets only ($100 deposit). **Pool(s):** heated outdoor. **Leisure Activities:** barbecue grills. **Guest Services:** coin laundry. **Cards:** DS, MC, VI. Motel

(See map p. 357)

SEA CHATEAU RESORT MOTEL

AAA [SAVE]

Motel

	1P: $70-$150	2P: $70-$150	**Phone:** (954)566-8331	[29]
All Year			XP: $10	D12

Location: 2 blks w of SR A1A, 0.5 mi s of SR 838 (Sunrise Blvd). 555 N Birch Rd & Terramar St 33304. Fax: 954/564-2411. **Facility:** 19 one-bedroom standard units, some with efficiencies. 2 stories, exterior corridors. **Parking:** on-site. **Terms:** age restrictions may apply, 10 day cancellation notice, weekly rates available. **Pool(s):** outdoor. **Special Amenities:** early check-in/late check-out and free local telephone calls.

SOME UNITS

[S/D] [≈] [CTV] / [📞] / FEE

(See map p. 357)

SHERATON SUITES CYPRESS CREEK

Phone: **(954)772-5400** **2**

1/1-3/31	1P: $289	2P: $289	XP: $10	F18
12/1-12/31 & 4/1-5/26	1P: $279	2P: $279	XP: $10	F18
5/27-11/30	1P: $199	2P: $199	XP: $10	F18

Large-scale Hotel **Location:** I-95, exit 33B (Cypress Creek Rd), just w. 555 NW 62nd St 33309. Fax: 954/772-5490. **Facility:** 253 one-bedroom suites. 8 stories, interior corridors. *Bath:* combo or shower only. **Parking:** on-site and valet. **Terms:** cancellation fee imposed. **Amenities:** video games (fee), dual phone lines, voice mail, irons, hair dryers. *Some:* fax. **Pool(s):** heated outdoor. **Leisure Activities:** sauna, whirlpool, exercise room. **Guest Services:** gift shop, valet and coin laundry, area transportation. **Business Services:** meeting rooms, fax (fee). **Cards:** AX, DC, DS, MC, VI. *(See color ad p 5)*

SOME UNITS

(ASK) (SD) (YI) (Y) (🖊) (🏊) (✗) (🎥) (DATA PORT) (🔌) (🍴) (💻) / (✗) (VCR) /
FEE

SHERATON YANKEE CLIPPER BEACH HOTEL

(AAA) (SAVE)

Phone: **(954)524-5551** **41**

12/1-4/19	1P: $249-$299	2P: $249-$299	XP: $20	F17
4/20-5/31 & 10/3-11/30	1P: $189-$269	2P: $189-$269	XP: $20	F17
6/1-10/2	1P: $139-$199	2P: $139-$199	XP: $20	F17

Location: SR A1A, just s of Bahia Mar Marina. Located near Bahia Marina. 1140 Seabreeze Blvd (A1A) 33316. Large-scale Hotel Fax: 954/523-5376. **Facility:** 501 units. 493 one-bedroom standard units. 8 one-bedroom suites ($369-$759) with whirlpools. 5-11 stories, interior/exterior corridors. *Bath:* combo or shower only. **Parking:** valet. **Terms:** cancellation fee imposed. **Amenities:** dual phone lines, voice mail, safes, irons, hair dryers. **Dining:** 2 restaurants, 6 am-11 pm, cocktails, entertainment. **Pool(s):** 2 heated outdoor. **Leisure Activities:** waverunners, parasailing, putting green, recreation programs, beach volleyball, exercise room, sports court, basketball, shuffleboard. **Guest Services:** gift shop, valet and coin laundry. **Business Services:** meeting rooms, business center. **Cards:** AX, DC, DS, MC, VI.

SOME UNITS

(SD) (YI) (Y) (🔥M) (🖊) (🏊) (✗) (🎥) (DATA PORT) (💻) / (✗) (🍴) /
FEE

SHERATON YANKEE TRADER BEACH HOTEL

(AAA) (SAVE)

Phone: **(954)467-1111** **35**

12/1-4/19	1P: $249-$299	2P: $249-$299	XP: $20	F17
4/20-5/31 & 10/3-11/30	1P: $189-$269	2P: $189-$269	XP: $20	F17
6/1-10/2	1P: $139-$199	2P: $139-$199	XP: $20	F17

Location: SR A1A, 0.8 mi s of Sunrise Blvd. Located across from the beach. 321 N Fort Lauderdale Beach Blvd, A1A Large-scale Hotel 33304. Fax: 954/462-2342. **Facility:** 460 units. 445 one-bedroom standard units. 15 one-bedroom suites ($369-$759). 14-15 stories, interior corridors. *Bath:* combo or shower only. **Parking:** on-site (fee) and valet. **Terms:** cancellation fee imposed. **Amenities:** dual phone lines, voice mail, safes, irons, hair dryers. **Dining:** 2 restaurants, 6 am-11 pm, cocktails, entertainment. **Pool(s):** 2 heated outdoor. **Leisure Activities:** 2 tennis courts, exercise room, sports court. **Guest Services:** gift shop, valet and coin laundry. **Business Services:** conference facilities, business center. **Cards:** AX, DC, DS, MC, VI.

SOME UNITS

(SD) (YI) (Y) (🔥M) (🖊) (🖊) (🏊) (✗) (🎥) (DATA PORT) (💻) / (✗) (🍴) /
FEE

(See map p. 357)

THREE SUNS INN

| | 12/1-4/15 | 1P: $82-$126 | 2P: $82-$126 | XP: $10 | F12 |
| | 4/16-11/30 | 1P: $50-$89 | 2P: $50-$89 | XP: $10 | F12 |

Phone: (954)563-7926 ㉗

Motel
Location: On SR A1A, 6 blks s of Sunrise Blvd, west corner of Breakers Ave and Windamar St. 3016 Windamar St 33304. Fax: 954/563-7988. **Facility:** 19 units. 12 one-bedroom standard units, some with efficiencies. 6 one- and 1 two-bedroom suites with kitchens. 3 stories (no elevator), exterior corridors. **Parking:** on-site. **Terms:** 15 day cancellation notice-fee imposed, weekly rates available. **Amenities:** *Some:* safes (fee). **Pool(s):** heated outdoor. **Leisure Activities:** Fee: bicycles. **Guest Services:** coin laundry. **Cards:** AX, CB, DC, DS, JC, MC, VI.

SOME UNITS

TOWNEPLACE SUITES BY MARRIOTT

SAVE

| | 4/28-11/30 | 1P: $49-$139 | 2P: $89-$159 |
| | 12/1-4/27 | 1P: $89-$139 | 2P: $89-$139 |

Phone: (954)484-2214 ❼

Small-scale Hotel
Location: I-95, exit 33 (Cypress Creek Rd/SR 811), 2.7 mi w, then 0.5 mi s on NW 31st St. 3100 Prospect Rd 33309. Fax: 954/484-4533. **Facility:** 95 units. 69 one-bedroom standard units with efficiencies. 4 one- and 22 two-bedroom suites with kitchens. 2-3 stories, interior corridors. **Bath:** combo or shower only. **Parking:** on-site. **Terms:** 5 night minimum stay - in season, [ECP] meal plan available, small pets only ($70 fee). **Amenities:** video games (fee), dual phone lines, voice mail, irons, hair dryers. **Pool(s):** small heated outdoor. **Leisure Activities:** limited exercise equipment. **Guest Services:** valet and coin laundry. **Business Services:** fax (fee). **Cards:** AX, DC, DS, JC, MC, VI. *(See color ad p 381)*

SOME UNITS

TROPI ROCK RESORT

AAA SAVE

| | 12/15-5/10 | | 2P: $85-$98 | XP: $10 | F12 |
| | 12/1-12/14 & 5/11-11/30 | | 2P: $65-$80 | XP: $10 | F12 |

Phone: 954/564-0523 ㊹

Motel
Location: 0.3 mi s of jct SR 838 (Sunrise Blvd) on SR A1A, then just right. 2900 Belmar St 33304. Fax: 954/564-1313. **Facility:** 30 one-bedroom standard units, some with efficiencies or kitchens. 3 stories, exterior corridors. **Parking:** on-site. **Terms:** 15 day cancellation notice-fee imposed, weekly rates available. **Amenities:** voice mail, hair dryers. *Some:* CD players. **Pool(s):** heated outdoor. **Leisure Activities:** rooftop sun deck, 2 tennis courts, barbecue grills, exercise room, shuffleboard. **Guest Services:** coin laundry. **Cards:** AX, DC, DS, MC, VI.

SOME UNITS

THE WESTIN, FORT LAUDERDALE

	12/1-3/31	1P: $199-$299	2P: $199-$299	XP: $20	F17
	9/30-11/30	1P: $189-$289	2P: $189-$289	XP: $20	F17
	4/1-5/26	1P: $179-$279	2P: $179-$279	XP: $20	F17
	5/27-9/29	1P: $169-$269	2P: $169-$269	XP: $20	F17

Phone: 954/772-1331 ❺

Large-scale Hotel
Location: I-95, exit 33, just e. Located in Radice Corporate Park. 400 Corporate Dr 33334-3642. Fax: 954/491-9087. **Facility:** 293 units. 291 one-bedroom standard units. 2 one-bedroom suites. 14 stories, interior corridors. **Bath:** combo or shower only. **Parking:** on-site and valet. **Terms:** cancellation fee imposed, small pets only. **Amenities:** dual phone lines, voice mail, safes, honor bars, irons, hair dryers. *Fee:* video games, high-speed Internet. **Pool(s):** heated outdoor. **Leisure Activities:** saunas, whirlpool, jogging, exercise room, sports court. **Guest Services:** gift shop, valet laundry, area transportation. **Business Services:** conference facilities, business center. **Cards:** AX, CB, DC, JC, MC, VI. *(See color ad p 5)*

SOME UNITS
FEE

The following lodging was either not evaluated or did not meet AAA rating requirements but is listed for your information only.

MARRIOTT'S BEACHPLACE TOWERS

fyi

Phone: 954/525-4440

Not evaluated. Location: 21 S Fort Lauderdale Beach Blvd 33316. Facilities, services, and decor characterize a mid-range property.

(See map p. 357)

───── **WHERE TO DINE** ─────

3030 OCEAN   **Dinner:** $20-$32   **Phone:** 954/525-4000   **29**
▼▼▼▼ **Location:** E of SR A1A, s of Bahia Mar Marina; in Marriott's Harbor Beach Resort & Spa. 3030 Holiday Dr 33316.
Hours: 6 pm-10:30 pm. **Reservations:** suggested. **Features:** Besides an upbeat, sophisticated ambience,
the restaurant's claim to fame is an innovative menu that changes monthly. Fresh local and regional
Continental seafood is always at the top of the menu, and highlights include lobster, prawns and various fish
selections. Other temptations include grilled Kansas City strip steak and rack of lamb. The chef delights diners with creative
and detailed presentations. cocktails. **Parking:** on-site. **Cards:** AX, CB, DC, DS, JC, MC, VI.
❌

THE AMBRY   **Lunch:** $9-$14   **Dinner:** $14-$30   **Phone:** 954/771-7342   **23**
▼▼▼ **Location:** Just e of Federal Hwy US 1. 3016 E Commercial Blvd 33308. **Hours:** 11:30 am-2 & 5-10 pm, Sat from
5 pm. Closed: Sun & 9/15-10/1. **Reservations:** suggested. **Features:** Such classics as sauerbraten and
Regional German Wiener schnitzel make up the tasty Teutonic fare at the intimate restaurant, which also caters to the more
timid with steak and seafood selections. Dark, windowless dining areas and cordial servers set a cozy
mood. Dressy casual; cocktails. **Parking:** on-site. **Cards:** AX, DC, MC, VI.
❌

BIG LOUIE'S ITALIAN RESTAURANT   **Lunch:** $4-$13   **Dinner:** $5-$13   **Phone:** 954/467-1166   **7**
▼ **Location:** Jct US 1; in Gateway Shopping Center. 1990 E Sunrise Blvd 33304. **Hours:** 11 am-1 am, Sun from
noon. Closed: 11/27. **Features:** Servers have to hustle in this bustling atmosphere, but they keep on
Italian smiling as they deliver oversized sandwiches and copious portions of homemade pasta. You won't find any
sissy pizza in this joint; if it isn't huge, it isn't worth it. Casual dress; beer & wine only. **Parking:** on-site.
Cards: AX, DC, DS, MC, VI.
❌

BIG LOUIE'S ITALIAN RESTAURANT   **Lunch:** $4-$14   **Dinner:** $4-$14   **Phone:** 954/771-2288   **10**
▼ **Location:** Commercial Blvd at NE 20th Ave, just w of jct US 1. 2103 E Commercial Blvd 33308. **Hours:** 11
am-midnight, Fri & Sat-1 am, Sun noon-midnight. Closed: 11/27. **Features:** You can find no-frills dining at
Italian this small, family-oriented restaurant which offers oversized sandwiches, made-to-order pizzas and an
extensive list of homemade pastas. One visit and you'll know why Big Louie's is a local favorite. Casual
dress; beer & wine only. **Parking:** on-site. **Cards:** AX, DC, MC, VI.

BIMINI BOATYARD   **Lunch:** $6-$12   **Dinner:** $6-$22   **Phone:** 954/525-7400   **27**
▼▼ **Location:** SR A1A, 0.8 mi e of jct US 1. 1555 SE 17th St Cswy 33316. **Hours:** 11:30 am-10 pm, Thurs-Sat to 11
pm, Sun-10 pm. Closed: 12/25. **Reservations:** accepted. **Features:** A relaxing, casual atmosphere makes
American dining in this waterfront eatery a great get-away-from-it-all experience. The menu includes gourmet pizzas,
sandwiches and salads as well as pasta, seafood, meat and poultry dishes. The Sunday brunch is a
special treat. Dressy casual; cocktails. **Parking:** on-site and valet. **Cards:** AX, DC, DS, MC, VI.
♿M ❌

BUCA DE BEPPO   **Dinner:** $14-$23   **Phone:** 954/229-0922   **9**
▼▼ **Location:** Commercial Blvd (SR 870), 0.8 mi n; in Imperial Square Shopping Center. 5975 N Federal Hwy 33308.
Hours: 5 pm-10 pm, Fri & Sat-11 pm, Sun noon-9 pm. Closed: 11/27, 12/25. **Reservations:** suggested.
South Italian **Features:** A fun place to eat, the restaurant offers family-style—which translates to "huge"—portions. The
various dining rooms display an eclectic collection of more than 2,500 pictures of Italy, figurines related to
the country and famous, as well as not-so-famous, natives. Casual dress; cocktails. **Parking:** on-site. **Cards:** AX, CB, DC, DS,
JC, MC, VI.
♿M 🍸 ❌

BY WORD OF MOUTH   **Lunch:** $8-$15   **Dinner:** $20-$30   **Phone:** 954/564-3663   **32**
▼▼▼▼ **Location:** I-95, exit 31A northbound; exit 31 southbound, 2.5 mi to Old Dixie Hwy, 0.4 mi n to NE 34th Ct
to NE 12th Ave, just s on NE 12th Ave, then on left. 3200 NE 12th Ave 33334. **Hours:** 11 am-3 & 5-close, Mon &
American Tues-3 pm. Closed: 11/27, 12/25; also Sun. **Reservations:** suggested. **Features:** The deli case displays a
show-and-tell of the day's dishes, described in detail by the wait staff. The flavorful main courses represent
a variety of several cuisines; desserts are as fancy as the setting is simple. Service is efficient and hospitable. Smoke free
premises. Dressy casual; beer & wine only. **Parking:** on-site. **Cards:** AX, DC, DS, MC, VI.
❌

CALIFORNIA CAFE   **Lunch:** $9-$15   **Dinner:** $10-$28   **Phone:** 954/728-3500   **22**
▼▼▼▼ **Location:** SR A1A, 1.3 mi e of jct US 1; in Hyatt Regency Pier Sixty Six. 2301 SE 17th St Cswy 33316.
Hours: 11:30 am-3:30 & 5:30-10 pm, Fri & Sat-10:30 pm, Sun 11 am-3 & 5:30-10 pm.
Regional American **Reservations:** suggested. **Features:** An upbeat dining room overlooks the Intracoastal Waterway and
marina. Start with the spicy black bean soup, then move on to innovative California entrees with hints of
the Caribbean. The macadamia crusted yellowtail snapper is served over orzo pasta. Dressy casual; cocktails; entertainment.
Parking: on-site. **Cards:** AX, CB, DC, DS, JC, MC, VI.
🍸 ❌

CANYON SOUTHWEST CAFE   **Dinner:** $13-$25   **Phone:** 954/765-1950   **36**
▼▼▼ **Location:** Just w of jct US 1 (Federal Hwy) and 19th Ave. 1818 E Sunrise Blvd 33304. **Hours:** 5:30 pm-11 pm, Fri
& Sat-midnight. Closed: 11/27, 12/25. **Reservations:** suggested. **Features:** Fabulous green chilies are
Southwest used in many dishes on this eclectic menu. You'll also find an unusual group of Southwestern dishes with
American some Asian touches. The decor is very warm and Southwestern, and the service will fulfill your every need.
Dressy casual; cocktails. **Parking:** street. **Cards:** AX, DC, DS, MC, VI.
🍸 ❌

CASABLANCA CAFE   **Lunch:** $7-$13   **Dinner:** $11-$17   **Phone:** 954/764-3500   **37**
▼▼▼ **Location:** At Alhambra St and Atlantic Blvd. 3049 Alhambra St 33305. **Hours:** 11:30 am-11 pm, Fri & Sat-11:30
pm. **Features:** An extraordinary menu combines influences from the cuisines of Morocco, Mexico, Japan,
International Italy, Spain, Cuba, the Caribbean and even Louisiana Cajun country. Fresh, authentic ingredients and a
chic Moroccan setting make this a truly exotic experience. Casual dress; cocktails; entertainment. **Parking:**
on-site (fee). **Cards:** AX, CB, DC, DS, MC, VI.
♿M

(See map p. 357)

CHARLEY'S CRAB

▼▼▼

Seafood

Lunch: $6-$17   **Dinner:** $12-$34   **Phone:** 954/561-4800   Ⓖ
Location: Off SR A1A, just s of jct Oakland Park Blvd via NE 30th St. 3000 NE 32nd Ave 33308. **Hours:** 11:30 am-10 pm, Fri & Sat-11 pm, Sun from 11 am. **Reservations:** suggested. **Features:** A knowledgeable wait staff can reel off the characteristics of the tantalizing array of dishes on the restaurant's menu. On the Intracoastal Waterway, the eatery features cozy, indoor dining as well as a comfortable, breezy terrace. Dressy casual; cocktails. **Parking:** valet. **Cards:** AX, DC, DS, MC, VI.

DARREL & OLIVER'S BISTRO 17

ⒶⒶⒶ

▼▼▼ ▼▼▼

Regional
American

Dinner: $27-$35   **Phone:** 954/626-1701   ㉚
Location: SR A1A, just e of US 1; in Renaissance Fort Lauderdale Hotel. 1617 17th St Cswy 33316. **Hours:** 6-10:30 am, 11:30-2:30 & 6-10 pm, Fri & Sat-11 pm. **Reservations:** suggested. **Features:** The cozy restaurant offers a balanced menu of meat and fresh seafood dishes that blend exciting flavors. Cuisines of many regions combine to make up the regional Floridian taste. An extensive list of wines by the bottle or glass complements the menu. Smoke free premises. Dressy casual; cocktails. **Parking:** valet. **Cards:** AX, CB, DC, DS, JC, MC, VI. *(See ad p 381)*

EDUARDO DE SAN ANGEL

ⒶⒶⒶ

▼▼▼ ▼▼▼

Mexican

Lunch: $8-$12   **Dinner:** $15-$22   **Phone:** 954/772-4731   ㊻
Location: Just e of US Federal Hwy. 2822 E Commercial Blvd 33308. **Hours:** 5:30 pm-10 pm. Closed: Sun & 6/1-6/13. **Reservations:** required. **Features:** Not your typical Mexican cuisine, the fare on this restaurant's menu includes masterfully presented gourmet specialties. The surroundings are sophisticated. beer & wine only. **Parking:** on-site. **Cards:** AX, DC, MC, VI.

FOOD LOVERS AMERICAN CAFE

◆◆ ◆◆

American

Dinner: $11-$18   **Phone:** 954/566-9606   ㊾
Location: 1576 E Oakland Park Blvd 33334. **Hours:** 5:30 pm-9:30 pm, Fri & Sat-10:30 pm. Closed: Sun & Mon. **Reservations:** suggested; weekends. **Features:** Excellent fare with a French flair is the norm in this polished, yet homey, atmosphere. Although the menu comprises primarily seafood, meat and poultry dishes, it also boasts a multicultural flavor, with such entrees as Hungarian goulash over linguine. Dressy casual; beer & wine only. **Parking:** on-site. **Cards:** DS, MC, VI.

GIBBY'S

▼▼▼

Steak & Seafood

Lunch: $13   **Dinner:** $14-$28   **Phone:** 954/565-2929   Ⓓ
Location: I-95, exit 31A northbound; exit 31 southbound, 1.5 mi e, just s of Oakland Park Blvd (SR 816). 2900 NE 12 Terr 33334. **Hours:** 5 pm-10 pm. **Reservations:** suggested. **Features:** A mouth-watering menu features such entrees as prime-aged steak, rack of lamb, stone crab and live Maine lobster as well as homemade pastries and straight-from-the-oven cracked wheat bread. The country-club-style dining rooms offer relaxed comfort. Dressy casual; cocktails. **Parking:** valet. **Cards:** AX, DC, DS, MC, VI.

THE GRILL ROOM ON LAS OLAS

ⒶⒶⒶ

▼▼▼ ▼▼▼

Continental

Dinner: $20-$40   **Phone:** 954/467-2555   ㊻
Location: 2 mi w of SR A1A; at jct US 1 Underpass, main entrance on SE 4th St; in Riverside Hotel. 620 E Las Olas Blvd 33301. **Hours:** 6 pm-11 pm. Closed: Sun & Mon. **Reservations:** suggested. **Features:** Excellent preparations feature aged meat and fresh fish and are served in a contemporary dining room. Cordial servers ably explain exquisitely presented dishes. Diners can consult an extensive wine list to find the right bottle to complement their meal. Dressy casual; cocktails; entertainment. **Parking:** valet. **Cards:** AX, CB, DC, MC, VI. *(See color ad p 382)*

HIMMARSHEE BAR & GRILLE

▼▼▼

American

Lunch: $5-$10   **Dinner:** $13-$25   **Phone:** 954/764-5154   ⑭
Location: From W Broward Blvd, s on Nugent Ave/SW 3rd Ave, then just e. 210 SW 2nd St 33301. **Hours:** 11:30 am-2:30 & 6-10:30 pm, Fri & Sat-11:30 pm, Sun 6 pm-10 pm. Closed: 12/25; also 5/24. **Reservations:** suggested. **Features:** The chef calls his creations "eclectic American cuisine" because they borrow from Mediterranean, Asian, Italian and European influences. Only the freshest seafood, meat and poultry are used in the innovative preparations. Be sure to save room for the sinful desserts. The dining room has great color with changing local art, and tables also are available on the sidewalk. Entertainment is offered weekends at the great bar on the second floor. Dressy casual; cocktails. **Parking:** valet. **Cards:** AX, MC, VI.

JACKSON'S STEAKHOUSE

▼▼▼

Steak House

Dinner: $16-$36   **Phone:** 954/522-4450   ⑬
Location: Just w of S Federal Hwy/US 1. 450 E Las Olas Blvd 33301. **Hours:** 5 pm-10:30 pm. **Reservations:** suggested. **Features:** In the trendy heart of the city, the restaurant gives the impression of a private club to diners who step inside. Such touches as wood-paneled walls, a beamed ceiling, lots of artwork and adequate brightness characterize the dining room. Menu selections of fine meat and fresh seafood are well-paired with choices from the extensive wine list. Dressy casual; cocktails; entertainment. **Parking:** valet. **Cards:** AX, CB, DC, DS, MC, VI.

LA FERME

▼▼▼

French

Dinner: $20-$35   **Phone:** 954/764-0987   Ⓗ
Location: US 1, just w of jct Sunrise Blvd and Federal Hwy at NE 16th Ave. 1601 E Sunrise Blvd 33304. **Hours:** Open 12/1-9/1 & 10/1-11/30; 5:30 pm-10 pm. Closed: Mon. **Reservations:** suggested. **Features:** Intricate and flavorful dishes are served in a charming, elegant atmosphere characterized by dim lighting, fresh flowers and candles. The restaurant is popular with the theater-going crowd. cocktails. **Parking:** on-site. **Cards:** AX, MC, VI.

LAS VEGAS

▼▼ ▼▼

Cuban

Lunch: $6-$8   **Dinner:** $9-$12   **Phone:** 954/564-1370   ㊻
Location: I-95, exit 31A northbound, exit 31, then 3.2 mi e, just w of SR A1A and intracoastal bridge. 2807 E Oakland Park Blvd 33306. **Hours:** 11 am-10 pm, Fri-Sun to 11 pm. Closed: 12/25. **Reservations:** accepted. **Features:** Authentic Cuban food, music and decor contribute to the restaurant's atmosphere. Popular standbys grilled chicken and roast pork co-exist with more sophisticated dishes, such as Argentine-style grilled flank steak, to create a tasty and diverse menu. beer & wine only. **Parking:** street. **Cards:** AX, DC, DS, MC, VI.

(See map p. 357)

LA TAVERNETTA-THE ITALIAN BISTRO BY THE WATER   Dinner: $15-$24   Phone: 954/463-2566   (59)
Location: Just s of Sunrise Blvd, between the Galleria and jct US 1 (Federal Hwy). 926 NE 20th Ave 33304.
Hours: Open 12/1-8/31 & 10/1-11/30; 5:30 pm-10:30 pm, Sun 5 pm-10 pm in season. Closed: 11/27,
12/25; also Mon 6/1-6/30 & 10/1-11/30. **Reservations:** suggested. **Features:** A water taxi stop on the
Middle River, this restaurant offers an intimate, bistro-style dining room as well as a large, open-air terrace
that gives breathtaking views. The owner/chef uses the freshest ingredients to prepare fine, classic cuisine.
Northern
Italian
Dressy casual; beer & wine only. **Parking:** street. **Cards:** AX, CB, DC, DS, MC, VI.

MAI-KAI RESTAURANT   Dinner: $16-$30   Phone: 954/563-3272   (3)
Location: US 1, 0.3 mi n of jct SR 816 (Oakland Park Blvd). 3599 N Federal Hwy 33308. **Hours:** 5 pm-10:30 pm,
Fri & Sat-midnight. **Reservations:** required. **Features:** A bright, exotic atmosphere spices up the
restaurant, noted for its lobster Bora Bora, filet mignon and Mandarin pressed duck. Pay a cover charge to
Chinese
enjoy the Polynesian revue, or instead opt to sit in a secluded, romantic dining room or on the patio.
Dressy casual; cocktails; entertainment. **Parking:** on-site (fee) and valet. **Cards:** AX, DC, DS, MC, VI.

MARK'S LAS OLAS   Lunch: $7-$18   Dinner: $17-$36   Phone: 954/463-1000   (68)
Location: E of US 1, on south side of street. 1032 E Las Olas Blvd 33301. **Hours:** 11:30 am-2:30 & 6:30-10 pm,
Fri-11 pm, Sat 6 pm-11 pm, Sun 6 pm-10 pm; dinner hours vary in winter. Closed: 11/27, 12/25.
American
Reservations: suggested. **Features:** Located in the heart of shopping and dining district, New Florida
fusion cuisine is showcased by a South Florida celebrity chef. Open kitchen design sets off the dining
room's Art Deco accents. There is an extensive wine list and bustling ambience at this popular spot. Dressy casual; cocktails.
Parking: valet. **Cards:** AX, DC, MC, VI.

PRIMAVERA RESTAURANT   Dinner: $20-$35   Phone: 954/564-6363   (71)
Location: I-95, exit 31A northbound; exit 31 southbound, 1.5 mi e. 830 E Oakland Park Blvd 33334. **Hours:** 5:30
pm-10:30 pm. Closed: 4/20, 12/25; also Mon. **Reservations:** suggested. **Features:** In addition to
homemade pasta and dessert, there is a wide variety of seafood and meat that makes for difficult
Northern
Italian
decisions. The owner visits each table keeping diners happy. Dressy casual; cocktails; entertainment.
Parking: on-site. **Cards:** AX, DC, DS, MC, VI.

RAINBOW PALACE   Lunch: $8-$14   Dinner: $19-$40   Phone: 954/565-5652   (72)
Location: 0.5 mi s of US 1. 2787 E Oakland Park Blvd 33306. **Hours:** 5 pm-10 pm, Fri & Sat-11 pm, Thurs & Fri
also noon-3 pm. Closed: 7/4, 11/27. **Reservations:** suggested. **Features:** Gourmet selections in a plush
setting include nine vegetarian offerings. Start with an exquisite mushroom appetizer with portobellos,
Chinese
shiitakes and buttons in a light scallion sauce. An extensive wine list is available. Gentlemen's jackets are
suggested. Dressy casual; cocktails. **Parking:** on-site. **Cards:** AX, CB, DC, DS, MC, VI.

THE RIVER HOUSE   Historic   Dinner: $12-$28   Phone: 954/525-7661   (16)
Location: From W Broward Blvd, 0.3 mi s on Nugent Ave/SW 3rd Ave. 301 SW 3rd Ave 33301. **Hours:** 5:30 pm-11
pm, Sun 11:30 am-3 & 5:30-10 pm. Closed: 5/26, 12/25. **Reservations:** suggested. **Features:** Built in
1903, the riverfront restaurant lures diners to sit under the canopy of trees and stars to eat and watch the
American
passing boats. Seating also is offered indoors and on the porch. On the menu are New American
preparations of fresh seafood, meat and poultry. Dressy casual; cocktails. **Parking:** valet. **Cards:** AX, MC, VI.

ROYAL INDIA   Dinner: $9-$16   Phone: 954/964-0071   (75)
Location: I-95, exit 23 (Griffin Rd), 2 mi w. 3801 Griffin Rd 33312. **Hours:** 5 pm-10:30 pm, Sat & Sun noon-3 pm.
Reservations: suggested; on weekends. **Features:** The user-friendly menu adeptly describes the savory
dishes on this varied menu. If the tangy and heady roasting doesn't add enough flavor to your entree, you
Indian
can sample from a sizable assortment of chutneys and other relishes to achieve the taste you favor.
Dressy casual; beer & wine only. **Parking:** on-site. **Cards:** AX, DC, DS, MC, VI.

SEA WATCH RESTAURANT   Lunch: $6-$18   Dinner: $15-$31   Phone: 954/781-2200   (2)
Location: SR A1A, 1 mi n of jct SR 870 (Commercial Blvd). 6002 N Ocean Blvd 33308. **Hours:** 11:30 am-3:30 &
5-10 pm. Closed: 12/25. **Reservations:** accepted. **Features:** Several dining rooms in this nautically
decorated restaurant give diners beautiful views of the beach and ocean. Widely varied entrees are served
Steak House
by a friendly, attentive wait staff. Dressy casual; cocktails. **Parking:** valet. **Cards:** AX, CB, DS, MC, VI.

SHIRTTAIL CHARLIE'S RESTAURANT   Dinner: $10-$20   Phone: 954/463-3474   (21)
Location: On south bank of the New River, just sw of Andrews Ave, via SW 5th St; downtown. 400 SW 3rd Ave
33315. **Hours:** 5:30 pm-10 pm. Closed: 11/27, 12/25; also Mon 9/1-11/23. **Reservations:** accepted.
Features: Overlooking the scenic New River, the restaurant lets you unwind while enjoying fried alligator
and stuffed yellowtail snapper. Indoor and outdoor dining both lend the same tropical experience. After
Seafood
eating, take advantage of a complimentary boat ride. Casual dress; cocktails. **Parking:** on-site. **Cards:** AX,
DC, DS, MC, VI.

SKINNY'S YOGURT, CAFE AND BAKERY   Lunch: $4-$8   Dinner: $4-$8   Phone: 954/568-5054   (35)
Location: I-95, exit Sunrise Blvd E, 2 mi n on US Hwy 1. 1756 N Federal Hwy 33305. **Hours:** 11 am-11 pm, Fri &
Sat-midnight. **Reservations:** suggested; groups over 15. **Features:** Subs, smoothies and ice cream are
the order of the day at this diner-style deli and bakery. The huge self-serve soft ice cream station lets
customers choose from decadent chocolate or sumptuous strawberry. Those avoiding carbohydrates will
Deli/Subs/
Sandwiches
find a variety of options catered to them. Smoke free premises. **Parking:** on-site. **Cards:** MC, VI.

(See map p. 357)

TARPONBEND FOOD & TACKLE   **Lunch:** $6-$9   **Dinner:** $6-$18   **Phone:** 954/523-3233   ⑰
Location: From W Broward Blvd, s on Nugent Ave/SW 3rd Ave, then just e. 200 SW 2nd St 33301. **Hours:** 11:30 am-12:30 am. Closed: 5/26, 11/27, 12/25. **Features:** On the corner of the street, the fun, friendly restaurant has sidewalk tables and a dining room bedecked in fishing memorabilia, including tackle and scores of pictures. The menu features fish, burgers, chicken and pasta. Entertainment is offered Thursday through Sunday. Casual dress; cocktails. **Parking:** valet and street. **Cards:** AX, MC, VI.
Seafood

TROPICAL ACRES   Classic   **Dinner:** $11-$16   **Phone:** 954/989-2500   ⑧①
Location: I-95, exit 23 (Griffin Rd), 0.3 mi w. 2500 Griffin Rd 33312. **Hours:** 4:30 pm-10 pm, Sun 3 pm-9 pm. Closed: 12/24, 12/25. **Reservations:** accepted. **Features:** Family-owned since 1949, the popular restaurant serves cuts of meat on sizzling skillets plucked straight out of the fireplace grill. The menu also lists 40 other tempting entrees. Cozy banquet facilities make the place a top choice for private parties. Dressy casual; cocktails. **Parking:** on-site and street. **Cards:** AX, DS, MC, VI.
Steak & Seafood

YESTERDAY'S   **Dinner:** $12-$29   **Phone:** 954/561-4400   ⑧②
Location: By the Intracoastal Waterway. 3001 E Oakland Park Blvd. **Hours:** 4:30 pm 11 pm, Fri & Sat-midnight. **Reservations:** required. **Features:** Consistently good food mixes classics with Caribbean, Cajun and Latin favorites. An Art Deco design enhances the vast, multi-level dining room. The lighting is done with moon shapes. The menu is very diverse. Dressy casual; cocktails; entertainment. **Parking:** valet. **Cards:** AX, DC, MC, VI.
Regional American

-------- **The following restaurants have not been evaluated by AAA** --------
but are listed for your information only.

BLACK ORCHID CAFE   **Phone:** 954/561-9398
[fyi]   Not evaluated. **Location:** 2985 N Ocean Blvd 33308. **Features:** This eatery is cozy and features French, American and Continental fare with some exotic wild game entrees.

CARLOS & PEPE'S   **Phone:** 954/467-7192
[fyi]   Not evaluated. **Location:** Just e of US 1 (Federal Hwy). 1302 SE 17th St 33316. **Features:** The atmosphere is casual and child-friendly. Fresh chips and salsa are served alongside Mexican favorites.

DAN MARINO'S TOWN TAVERN   **Phone:** 954/522-1313
[fyi]   Not evaluated. **Location:** 300 SW 1st Ave 33301. **Features:** Football memorabilia decorates the casual restaurant, which offers pasta, burgers, sandwiches, seafood and ribs.

FLANIGAN'S SEAFOOD BAR & GRILL   **Phone:** 954/493-5329
[fyi]   Not evaluated. **Location:** 1479 E Commercial Blvd 33334. **Features:** The family-friendly restaurant is known for its baby back ribs, burgers and seafood.

FLANIGAN'S SEAFOOD BAR & GRILL   **Phone:** 954/267-4877
[fyi]   Not evaluated. **Location:** 1721 N Andrews Blvd. **Features:** The family-friendly restaurant is known for its baby back ribs, burgers and seafood.

THE SAMBA ROOM   **Phone:** 954/468-2000
[fyi]   Not evaluated. **Location:** 350 E Las Olas Blvd 33301. **Features:** Located in the heart of Fort Lauderdales trendy Las Olas Blvd. It features affordable Latin Fusion entrees or meats and seafoods.

The Fort Lauderdale Vicinity

CORAL SPRINGS pop. 117,549

———— WHERE TO STAY ————

CORAL SPRINGS MARRIOTT AT HERON BAY

(AAA) [SAVE]
◆◆◆

Phone: (954)753-5598

12/1-4/20	1P: $149-$229	2P: $149-$229	XP: $10 F17
10/1-11/30	1P: $149	2P: $169	XP: $10 F17
4/21-9/30	1P: $129-$149	2P: $129-$149	XP: $10 F17

Large-scale Hotel
Location: Sawgrass Expwy/SR 869, exit Coral Ridge Dr N, 0.3 mi, then left onto Heron Bay Blvd, then first right. 11775 Heron Bay Blvd 33076. Fax: 954/753-2888. **Facility:** Designated smoking area. 224 units. 217 one-bedroom standard units. 7 one-bedroom suites ($199-$309). 7 stories, interior corridors. *Bath:* combo or shower only. **Parking:** on-site. **Terms:** package plans, small pets only ($100 fee). **Amenities:** voice mail, irons, hair dryers. *Fee:* video games, high-speed Internet. *Some:* dual phone lines. **Dining:** 7 am-10 pm, cocktails. **Pool(s):** heated outdoor. **Leisure Activities:** sauna, whirlpool, exercise room. *Fee:* golf-18 holes, golf instruction, game room. **Guest Services:** gift shop, valet and coin laundry, area transportation-within 5 mi. **Business Services:** meeting rooms. **Cards:** AX, CB, DC, DS, MC, VI. **Special Amenities:** free newspaper. *(See color ad below)*

SOME UNITS

COURTYARD BY MARRIOTT CORAL SPRINGS

[SAVE]
◆◆◆

Phone: (954)227-1300

12/21-4/30	1P: $119-$164
12/1-12/20	1P: $99-$164
5/1-5/31	1P: $89-$134
6/1-11/30	1P: $79-$99

Small-scale Hotel
Location: Atlantic Blvd (SR 869), just s on University Dr, then w on NW 6th Ct. Located behind McDonalds. 620 N University Dr 33071. Fax: 954/227-1500. **Facility:** 110 units. 106 one-bedroom standard units. 4 one-bedroom suites ($124-$164). 4 stories, interior corridors. *Bath:* combo or shower only. **Parking:** on-site. **Terms:** [BP] meal plan available, $7 service charge. **Amenities:** dual phone lines, voice mail, irons, hair dryers. **Pool(s):** heated outdoor. **Leisure Activities:** whirlpool, exercise room. **Guest Services:** valet and coin laundry. **Business Services:** meeting rooms, business center. **Cards:** AX, DC, DS, JC, MC, VI.

SOME UNITS

LA QUINTA INN

[SAVE]
◆◆◆

Phone: (954)753-9000

12/1-4/7	1P: $89-$119	2P: $95-$125
4/8-11/30	1P: $69-$89	2P: $75-$95

Small-scale Hotel
Location: SR 817, just n of jct Sample Rd (SR 834). 3701 University Dr 33065. Fax: 954/755-4012. **Facility:** 121 units. 118 one-bedroom standard units. 3 one-bedroom suites. 5 stories, interior corridors. *Bath:* combo or shower only. **Parking:** on-site. **Terms:** [ECP] meal plan available, small pets only. **Amenities:** video games, voice mail, irons, hair dryers. **Pool(s):** heated outdoor. **Guest Services:** coin laundry. **Business Services:** meeting rooms, fax (fee). **Cards:** AX, CB, DC, DS, JC, MC, VI. *(See color ad p 377)*

SOME UNITS

FEE FEE

WELLESLEY INN (CORAL SPRINGS)

(AAA) [SAVE]
◆◆◆

Phone: (954)344-2200

12/1-4/20 [ECP]	1P: $99-$119	2P: $99-$119	XP: $10 F18
4/21-11/30 [ECP]	1P: $65-$85	2P: $65-$85	XP: $10 F18

Small-scale Hotel
Location: SR 817, just s of jct Sample Rd (SR 834). 3100 N University Dr 33065. Fax: 954/344-7885. **Facility:** 104 units. 102 one-bedroom standard units. 2 one-bedroom suites. 4 stories, interior corridors. *Bath:* combo or shower only. **Parking:** on-site. **Terms:** small pets only. **Amenities:** video games, high-speed Internet (fee), voice mail, irons, hair dryers. *Some:* dual phone lines. **Pool(s):** heated outdoor. **Guest Services:** valet laundry. **Cards:** AX, CB, DC, DS, MC, VI. **Special Amenities:** free continental breakfast and free newspaper. *(See color ad p 365)*

SOME UNITS

FEE FEE

——— WHERE TO DINE ———

BIG BEAR BREWING COMPANY
▼▼▼▼ / ▼▼▼▼
American

Lunch: $7-$12 **Dinner:** $10-$22 **Phone:** 954/341-5545
Location: From Atlantic Blvd (SR 814), 0.9 mi n. 1800 University Dr 33065. **Hours:** 11:30 am-10 pm, Fri & Sat-11:30 pm, Sun 11 am-10 pm. Closed: 11/27, 12/25. **Reservations:** accepted; weekdays. **Features:** Dark, wood-paneled walls and large pictures contribute to the warm setting. Beers are made on the premises, as evidenced in the brew tanks at the entrance. Entrees—including chops, steaks, ribs and seafood—are served in plentiful portions. Casual dress; cocktails. **Parking:** on-site. **Cards:** AX, DC, DS, MC, VI. &M ✕

CHOWDER'S
▼▼▼▼
Continental

Dinner: $17-$29 **Phone:** 954/753-7374
Location: SR 817 (University Dr); 0.5 mi n of jct SR 814 (Atlantic Blvd). 1460 N University Dr 33065. **Hours:** 5 pm-10:30 pm, Fri & Sat-11:30 pm. **Reservations:** suggested. **Features:** Attractive modern dining rooms are an inviting place for diners to sit down to the restaurant's hearty portions. Continental touches are employed in the preparation of beef, veal, poultry and fresh seafood, including the signature homemade chowder. End the night with a cake or a tableside-prepared dessert selection for two. Dressy casual; cocktails; entertainment. **Parking:** valet. **Cards:** AX, CB, DC, DS, MC, VI. ⊥ ✕

RUNYON'S
▼▼▼▼
American

Lunch: $5-$15 **Dinner:** $15-$25 **Phone:** 954/752-2333
Location: On SR 834 (Sample Rd), 0.5 mi w of jct SR 817 (University Dr). 9810 W Sample Rd 33065. **Hours:** 11:30 am-2:30 & 4-10:30 pm, Fri-11 pm, Sat 4 pm-11 pm, Sun 4 pm-10 pm. Closed major holidays. **Reservations:** suggested. **Features:** Dining rooms are decorated with recognizable black-and-white photographs and autographed pictures of celebrities who have been seen here. On the menu are well-prepared steaks, chops and seafood. Casual dress; cocktails. **Parking:** on-site. **Cards:** AX, DC, DS, MC, VI. ⊥ ✕

DANIA BEACH pop. 20,061 (See map p. 357; index p. 361)

——— WHERE TO STAY ———

HILTON FORT LAUDERDALE AIRPORT **Phone:** (954)920-3300 **[84]**

SAVE	12/1-4/19	1P: $129-$159	2P: $129-$159	XP: $10	F18
▼▼▼▼	4/20-5/31 & 10/1-11/30	1P: $129	2P: $129	XP: $10	F18
	6/1-9/30	1P: $89	2P: $89	XP: $10	F18

Large-scale Hotel **Location:** I-95, exit 23. 1870 Griffin Rd 33004. Fax: 954/920-3348. **Facility:** 388 units. 383 one-bedroom standard units. 5 one-bedroom suites. 2-8 stories, interior/exterior corridors. *Bath:* combo or shower only. **Fee:** video games, high-speed Internet. **Parking:** on-site. **Amenities:** dual phone lines, voice mail, irons, hair dryers. **Pool(s):** heated outdoor. **Leisure Activities:** whirlpool, 2 lighted tennis courts, exercise room. **Fee:** massage. **Guest Services:** gift shop, valet laundry. **Business Services:** meeting rooms, business center. **Cards:** AX, CB, DC, DS, JC, MC, VI.
SOME UNITS
S⊘ ✈ ⑪ ⊥ 🖉 🛇 &M ⊘ 🖉 ⊅ ✕ 🐾 DATA/PORT ▣ / ✕ 🔒 /
FEE

LUCKEY'S MOTEL **Phone:** (954)925-5500 **[80]**

AAA SAVE	12/15-4/15	1P: $69-$149	2P: $69-$149	XP: $10	F
▼▼	12/1-12/14 & 4/16-11/30	1P: $59-$69	2P: $59-$69	XP: $10	F

Motel **Location:** US 1, 0.5 mi n of jct Sterling Rd, 0.5 mi s of jct Griffin Rd. Located in the heart of Dania Beach's city center. 205 N Federal Hwy 33004. Fax: 954/424-9825. **Facility:** 15 one-bedroom standard units, some with efficiencies. 1 story, exterior corridors. *Bath:* shower only. **Parking:** on-site. **Amenities:** irons, hair dryers. **Guest Services:** coin laundry. **Cards:** AX, DS, MC, VI.
SOME UNITS
S⊘ ⑪ VCR 🐾 🔒 🖆 / ✕ /

SHERATON FORT LAUDERDALE AIRPORT HOTEL **Phone:** (954)920-3500 **[82]**

▼▼▼▼	12/1-4/13	1P: $169	2P: $169	XP: $10	F16
	4/14-5/22 & 10/1-11/30	1P: $139	2P: $139	XP: $10	F16
Large-scale Hotel	5/23-9/30	1P: $119	2P: $119	XP: $10	F16

Location: I-95, exit 23. Adjoins the Design Center of the Americas. 1825 Griffin Rd 33004. Fax: 954/920-3571. **Facility:** 250 units. 246 one-bedroom standard units. 4 one-bedroom suites ($349). 12 stories, interior corridors. *Bath:* combo or shower only. **Parking:** on-site (fee). **Terms:** pets ($50 extra charge). **Amenities:** dual phone lines, voice mail, irons, hair dryers. *Some:* fax. **Pool(s):** heated outdoor. **Leisure Activities:** saunas, whirlpool, 2 lighted tennis courts, exercise room. **Guest Services:** gift shop, valet laundry, area transportation. **Business Services:** meeting rooms, business center. **Cards:** AX, DC, DS, MC, VI. *(See color ad p 5)*
SOME UNITS
ASK ✈ 🐾 ⑪ ⊥ &M &️ 🖉 ⊅ ✕ 🐾 DATA/PORT ▣ / ✕ 🔒 /
FEE

SPRINGHILL SUITES BY MARRIOTT FORT LAUDERDALE AIRPORT **Phone:** 954/920-9696 **[83]**

AAA SAVE	1/16-4/20	1P: $134-$149	2P: $134-$149	
	1/1-1/15	1P: $116-$129	2P: $116-$129	
▼▼▼▼	12/1-12/31 & 4/21-11/30	1P: $85-$94	2P: $85-$94	

Small-scale Hotel **Location:** I-95, exit 22 (Stirling Rd), just e. 151 SW 18th Ct 33004. Fax: 954/929-3577. **Facility:** 168 one-bedroom standard units. 7 stories, interior corridors. *Bath:* combo or shower only. **Parking:** on-site. **Terms:** [CP] meal plan available, 11% service charge. **Amenities:** dual phone lines, voice mail, irons, hair dryers. **Pool(s):** heated outdoor. **Leisure Activities:** whirlpool, exercise room. **Guest Services:** valet and coin laundry, airport transportation-Fort Lauderdale-Hollywood International Airport, area transportation-Port Everglades. **Business Services:** meeting rooms, business center. **Cards:** AX, DC, DS, MC, VI. **Special Amenities:** free continental breakfast and free local telephone calls.
SOME UNITS
S⊘ ✈ ⑪ &M &️ 🖉 ⊅ 🐾 DATA/PORT 🔒 🖆 🖆 / ✕ /

(See map p. 357)

──── **WHERE TO DINE** ────

ISLAMORADA FISH COMPANY   Lunch: $5-$20   Dinner: $5-$20   Phone: 954/927-7737   122
▼▼ ▼▼   **Location:** I-95, exit 23, w on Griffin Rd (SR 818) to Anglers Ave, then s; in Bass Pro Shop Outdoor World. 220
Seafood   Gulfstream Way 33004. **Hours:** 11 am-10 pm. **Closed:** 12/25. **Features:** An aquatic tank sits in the middle of
the dining room, where you can dine on selections of local seafood. The casual atmosphere spills over to
the outdoor porch, which overlooks the man-made lake. Families are welcomed. Casual dress; cocktails.
Parking: on-site. **Cards:** AX, DS, VI.

LE PETIT CAFE   Lunch: $6-$8   Dinner: $14-$17   Phone: 954/967-9912   121
▼▼ ▼▼   **Location:** I-95, exit 23, 1.4 mi w. 3308 Griffin Rd 33004. **Hours:** 11:30 am-2:30 & 4:30-10 pm, Sat & Sun from
French   4:30 pm. **Closed:** Mon. **Features:** Familiar classics dominate the menu in this spiffy creperie.
Hearts-of-palm salad, frog legs, beef bourguignonne and, of course, many crepe choices are served in a
quietly charming atmosphere featuring the music of Edith Paif. Don't leave without dessert. Dressy casual;
wine only. **Parking:** on-site. **Cards:** AX, MC, VI.

DAVIE pop. 75,720

──── **WHERE TO STAY** ────

COMFORT SUITES DAVIE   Phone: (954)585-7071
AAA SAVE   12/15-4/14 [ECP]   1P: $109-$169   2P: $109-$169   XP: $10   F18
4/15-11/30 [ECP]   1P: $89-$129   2P: $89-$129   XP: $10   F18
▼▼▼▼▼   12/1-12/14 [ECP]   1P: $89-$109   2P: $89-$109   XP: $10   F18
Small-scale Hotel   **Location:** I-595, exit 7, just s. 2540 Davie Rd 33317. Fax: 954/585-8201. **Facility:** 77 units. 74 one-bedroom standard units. 3 one-bedroom suites ($129-$199). 5 stories, interior corridors. Bath: combo or shower only.
Parking: on-site. **Terms:** 3 day cancellation notice. **Amenities:** video games (fee), dual phone lines, voice
mail, irons, hair dryers. **Leisure Activities:** whirlpool, exercise room. **Guest Services:** valet and coin laundry, airport
transportation-Fort Lauderdale-Hollywood International Airport, area transportation-cruise port, within 5 mi. **Business Services:**
meeting rooms, business center. **Cards:** AX, DC, DS, JC, MC, VI. **Special Amenities: free continental breakfast and free
local telephone calls.**
SOME UNITS

HOMESTEAD STUDIO SUITES HOTEL-PLANTATION/DAVIE   Phone: (954)476-1211
▼▼ ▼▼   12/22-4/30   1P: $90   2P: $105   XP: $5   F18
12/1-12/21 & 5/1-11/30   1P: $59   2P: $69   XP: $5   F18
Motel   **Location:** I-595, exit University Dr/SR 817, to SR 84 E, then 0.3 mi. 7550 SR 84 E 33317. Fax: 954/476-0026.
Facility: 125 one-bedroom standard units with efficiencies. 2 stories, exterior corridors. Bath: combo or
shower only. **Parking:** on-site. **Terms:** cancellation fee imposed, small pets only ($85 fee). **Amenities:** voice mail, irons. **Guest
Services:** coin laundry. **Cards:** AX, CB, DC, DS, JC, MC, VI.
SOME UNITS

──── **WHERE TO DINE** ────

ARMADILLO CAFE   Dinner: $15-$30   Phone: 954/791-4866
▼▼ ▼▼   **Location:** I-595, exit 5, 1.5 mi s on University Dr (SR 817); in University Plaza. 3400 S University Dr 33314. **Hours:** 5
Southwest   pm-10 pm, Fri & Sat-11 pm. Closed major holidays. **Reservations:** suggested. **Features:** The restaurant's
American   delicious meat and seafood entrees are prepared with a Southwestern flair. Chilis are used to enhance, but
not overwhelm, the flavor of foods. The wine list complements the menu nicely. Smoke free premises.
Dressy casual; cocktails. **Parking:** on-site. **Cards:** AX, DC, MC, VI.

BUCA DE BEPPO   Dinner: $14-$23   Phone: 954/577-3287
▼▼ ▼▼   **Location:** I-595, exit 5, 1.5 mi s; in Rolling Hills Plaza. 3355 S University Dr 33328. **Hours:** 5 pm-10 pm, Fri &
South Italian   Sat-11 pm, Sun noon-9 pm. **Closed:** 11/27, 12/25. **Reservations:** suggested. **Features:** A fun place to eat,
the restaurant offers family-style—which translates to "huge"—portions. The various dining rooms display
an eclectic collection of more than 2,500 pictures of Italy, figurines related to the country and famous, as
well as not-so-famous, natives. Casual dress; cocktails. **Parking:** on-site. **Cards:** AX, CB, DC, DS, JC, MC, VI.

DAVIE ALE HOUSE   Lunch: $5-$11   Dinner: $6-$11   Phone: 954/236-0062
▼▼   **Location:** I-95, exit 5, just s. 2080 University Dr 33324. **Hours:** 11 am-2 am, Thurs-Sat to 3 am. **Closed:** 11/27.
American   **Features:** Munch on huge onion rings or cheese fries and revel in the lively sports bar atmosphere. A
menu of fun favorites includes burgers, steak, chicken, pasta and a nice raw bar. Wash it all down with one
DS, MC, VI.   of an extensive list of draft and bottled beers. Casual dress; cocktails. **Parking:** on-site. **Cards:** AX, DC,

GERONIMOS' CASUAL GOURMET GRILL & BAR   Lunch: $7-$9   Dinner: $8-$15   Phone: 954/474-9992
▼▼ ▼▼   **Location:** On SR 817 (University Dr), 1.5 mi s of jct SR 84; in University Park Plaza. 3528 S University Dr 33328.
American   **Hours:** 11:30 am-4 am, Sat & Sun from 5 pm. Closed major holidays. **Features:** A creative menu featuring
California and international dishes with fresh ingredients brings repeat business to this eatery. The
atmosphere is simple and casual. Sample the black bean soup or order the grilled swordfish topped with
sun-dried tomato salsa. Casual dress; cocktails; entertainment. **Parking:** on-site. **Cards:** AX, MC, VI.

DEERFIELD BEACH pop. 64,583

——— WHERE TO STAY ———

COMFORT INN-OCEANSIDE
Phone: (954)428-0650

(AAA) (SAVE)
▽▽▽▽
Motel

12/1-4/15 [ECP]	1P: $99-$150	2P: $99-$150	XP: $10	F16
4/16-11/30 [ECP]	1P: $89-$120	2P: $89-$120	XP: $10	F16

Location: SR A1A, at jct SR 810 (Hillsboro Blvd). 50 SE 20th Ave 33441. Fax: 954/427-2666. **Facility:** 69 one-bedroom standard units. 6 stories, interior corridors. *Bath:* combo or shower only. **Parking:** on-site. **Amenities:** voice mail, irons, hair dryers. *Fee:* video games, safes. **Pool(s):** outdoor, wading. **Guest Services:** valet and coin laundry. **Business Services:** meeting rooms, fax (fee). **Cards:** AX, CB, DC, DS, MC, VI. **Special Amenities:** free continental breakfast and free local telephone calls.

COMFORT SUITES
Phone: (954)570-8887

(AAA) (SAVE)
▽▽▽▽
Motel

12/1-3/31	1P: $79-$109	2P: $79-$109
4/1-11/30	1P: $55-$99	2P: $55-$99

Location: I-95, exit 41, jct SW 10th St to SW 12th Ave, then s. Newport Center. 1040 E Newport Center Dr 33442. Fax: 954/428-7638. **Facility:** 101 one-bedroom standard units. 4 stories, exterior corridors. **Parking:** on-site. **Terms:** pets ($25 fee). **Amenities:** voice mail, irons. *Fee:* video games, safes. *Some:* hair dryers. **Pool(s):** heated outdoor. **Leisure Activities:** whirlpool. **Guest Services:** valet and coin laundry. **Business Services:** fax (fee). **Special Amenities:** early check-in/late check-out. *(See color ad p 364)*

EMBASSY SUITES-DEERFIELD BEACH RESORT
Phone: (954)426-0478

(AAA) (SAVE)
▽▽▽▽
Large-scale Hotel

1/1-4/25	1P: $254-$444	2P: $254-$444	XP: $20	F18
12/1-12/31	1P: $244-$424	2P: $249-$424	XP: $20	F18
10/1-11/30	1P: $170-$299	2P: $170-$299	XP: $20	F18
4/26-9/30	1P: $134-$254	2P: $134-$254	XP: $20	F18

Location: SR A1A, 0.5 mi s of jct SR 810 (Hillsboro Blvd). 950 SE 20th Ave 33441. Fax: 954/360-0539. **Facility:** 244 one-bedroom suites. 7 stories, interior corridors. *Bath:* combo or shower only. **Parking:** on-site (fee) and valet. **Terms:** 3 day cancellation notice-fee imposed, [BP] meal plan available. **Amenities:** dual phone lines, voice mail, irons, hair dryers. *Fee:* video games, safes. **Dining:** 11 am-11 pm, cocktails, entertainment. **Pool(s):** heated outdoor. **Leisure Activities:** whirlpool, recreation programs, exercise room. *Fee:* snorkeling, game room. **Guest Services:** gift shop, complimentary evening beverages, valet and coin laundry. **Business Services:** meeting rooms. **Cards:** AX, CB, DC, DS, JC, MC, VI. **Special Amenities:** free continental breakfast and free newspaper.

HAMPTON INN
Phone: 954/481-1221

▽▽▽
Small-scale Hotel

Property failed to provide current rates

Location: I-95, exit 42A, just e. Located in the Hillsboro Center. 660 W Hillsboro Blvd 33441. Fax: 954/481-3432. **Facility:** 106 units. 98 one-bedroom standard units. 8 one-bedroom suites. 4 stories, interior corridors. *Bath:* combo or shower only. **Parking:** on-site. **Amenities:** video games, high-speed Internet, dual phone lines, voice mail, irons, hair dryers. **Pool(s):** heated outdoor. **Leisure Activities:** exercise room. **Guest Services:** sundries, valet and coin laundry. **Business Services:** meeting rooms, business center.

HILTON DEERFIELD BEACH/BOCA RATON
Phone: (954)427-7700

(AAA) (SAVE)
▽▽▽▽
Large-scale Hotel

1/8-3/31	1P: $139-$199	2P: $139-$199	XP: $20	F18
12/1-1/7 & 10/1-11/30	1P: $109-$179	2P: $109-$179	XP: $20	F18
4/1-9/30	1P: $99-$159	2P: $99-$159	XP: $20	F18

Location: I-95, exit 42A southbound, just e on Hillsboro Blvd; exit 37A northbound. 100 Fairway Dr 33441. Fax: 954/427-2308. **Facility:** 221 units. 216 one-bedroom standard units. 5 one-bedroom suites ($175-$450). 8 stories, interior corridors. *Bath:* combo or shower only. **Parking:** on-site. **Terms:** cancellation fee imposed. **Amenities:** high-speed Internet (fee), dual phone lines, voice mail, safes, irons, hair dryers. **Dining:** 6:30 am-10 pm, cocktails. **Pool(s):** heated outdoor. **Leisure Activities:** whirlpool, exercise room. **Guest Services:** gift shop, valet laundry, area transportation-within 5 mi. **Business Services:** meeting rooms, fax (fee). **Cards:** AX, CB, DC, DS, JC, MC, VI.

HOWARD JOHNSON PLAZA RESORT HOTEL
Phone: (954)428-2850

▽▽▽
Small-scale Hotel

12/21-4/26	1P: $175-$195	2P: $185-$205	XP: $10	F18
4/27-11/30	1P: $115-$135	2P: $125-$145	XP: $10	F18
12/1-12/20	1P: $109-$129	2P: $119-$139	XP: $10	F18

Location: SR A1A, just n of jct SR 810 (Hillsboro Blvd). 2096 NE 2nd St 33441. Fax: 954/480-9639. **Facility:** 177 units. 175 one-bedroom standard units. 2 one-bedroom suites. 8 stories, interior corridors. *Bath:* combo or shower only. **Parking:** on-site. **Terms:** cancellation fee imposed, package plans. **Amenities:** safes (fee), hair dryers. **Pool(s):** heated outdoor. **Leisure Activities:** *Fee:* game room. **Guest Services:** gift shop, valet laundry. **Business Services:** meeting rooms, fax (fee). **Cards:** AX, CB, DC, DS, JC, MC, VI.

LA QUINTA INN
Phone: (954)421-1004

(AAA) (SAVE)
▽▽▽▽
Motel

1/14-4/7	1P: $89-$109	2P: $95-$115
12/1-1/13	1P: $69-$89	2P: $75-$95
4/8-11/30	1P: $59-$79	2P: $65-$85

Location: I-95, exit 42A, 0.3 mi e on SR 810. 351 W Hillsboro Blvd 33441-1801. Fax: 954/427-8069. **Facility:** 128 one-bedroom standard units. 3 stories, exterior corridors. **Parking:** on-site. **Terms:** [ECP] meal plan available, small pets only. **Amenities:** video games (fee), voice mail, irons, hair dryers. **Pool(s):** heated outdoor. **Guest Services:** valet and coin laundry. **Business Services:** meeting rooms. **Cards:** AX, CB, DC, DS, JC, MC, VI. **Special Amenities:** free continental breakfast and free local telephone calls. *(See color ad p 377)*

CARRIAGE HOUSE RESORT MOTEL

(AAA) (SAVE)
♦♦♦ ♦♦♦
Motel

Phone: (954)427-7670

2/1-3/14	1P: $105-$195	2P: $105-$195	XP: $12 F6
3/15-4/5	1P: $88-$195	2P: $88-$195	XP: $12 F6
12/1-1/31	1P: $88-$140	2P: $88-$140	XP: $12 F6
4/6-11/30	1P: $54-$95	2P: $54-$95	XP: $12 F6

Location: SR A1A, just s of jct SR 810 (Hillsboro Blvd). 250 S Ocean Blvd 33441. Fax: 954/428-4790. **Facility:** 30 units. 19 one-bedroom standard units, some with efficiencies. 10 one- and 1 two-bedroom suites with kitchens. 2 stories (no elevator), exterior corridors. *Bath:* combo or shower only. **Parking:** on-site. **Terms:** 40 day cancellation notice. **Amenities:** voice mail, safes (fee). **Pool(s):** heated outdoor. **Guest Services:** coin laundry. **Cards:** AX, DC, DS, MC, VI.

SOME UNITS

OCEAN TERRACE SUITES

♦♦♦ ♦♦♦
Condominium

Phone: (954)427-8400

1/15-3/31	2P: $214-$509	XP: $10
12/1-1/14	2P: $129-$459	XP: $10
4/1-4/30	2P: $149-$349	XP: $10
5/1-11/30	2P: $113-$313	XP: $10

Location: Just e of jct SR A1A and 810 (Hillsboro Blvd). 2080 E Hillsboro Blvd 33441. Fax: 954/427-0555. **Facility:** 27 units. 1 one-bedroom standard unit with efficiency. 24 one- and 2 three-bedroom suites with kitchens. 4 stories, exterior corridors. **Parking:** on-site. **Terms:** 30 day cancellation notice-fee imposed, weekly rates available. **Amenities:** voice mail, irons, hair dryers. **Pool(s):** heated outdoor. **Guest Services:** coin laundry. **Cards:** AX, DC, DS, MC, VI.

SOME UNITS

PANTHER MOTEL & APARTMENTS

♦♦♦ ♦♦♦
Motel

Phone: 954/427-0700

1/16-4/1 Wkly	1P: $366-$595	2P: $366-$595	XP: $10 F18
12/1-1/15 Wkly	1P: $310-$477	2P: $310-$477	XP: $10 F18
5/2-11/30 Wkly	1P: $210-$299	2P: $210-$299	XP: $10 F18
4/2-5/1 Wkly	1P: $250-$344		XP: $10 F18

Location: SR A1A, 0.5 mi s of jct SR 810 (Hillsboro Blvd). 715 S A1A 33441. Fax: 954/481-2389. **Facility:** 20 units. 16 one-bedroom standard units with efficiencies. 4 one-bedroom suites with kitchens. 2 stories (no elevator), exterior corridors. **Parking:** on-site. **Terms:** age restrictions may apply, 45 day cancellation notice, daily & monthly rates available. **Amenities:** safes. **Pool(s):** heated outdoor. **Leisure Activities:** shuffleboard. **Guest Services:** coin laundry. **Cards:** MC, VI.

QUALITY SUITES & COMFORT SUITES

(AAA) (SAVE)
♦♦♦ ♦♦♦
Small-scale Hotel

Phone: (954)570-8888

1/27-3/31	1P: $135-$145	2P: $145-$155	XP: $10 F17
1/1-1/26	1P: $119-$129	2P: $129-$139	XP: $10 F17
12/1-12/31	1P: $95-$105	2P: $105-$115	XP: $10 F17
4/1-11/30	1P: $85-$95	2P: $95-$105	XP: $10 F17

Location: I-95, exit 41, SW 10th St to SW 12th Ave, then s. 1050 E Newport Center Dr 33442. Fax: 954/570-5346. **Facility:** 107 one-bedroom suites. 5 stories, exterior corridors. **Parking:** on-site. **Amenities:** voice mail, irons, hair dryers. *Fee:* video games, safes. **Dining:** 6:30-9:30 am, 11-2 & 5-9 pm, Sat & Sun 7-10 am. **Pool(s):** heated outdoor. **Leisure Activities:** whirlpool, jogging, limited exercise equipment. **Guest Services:** gift shop, complimentary evening beverages, valet and coin laundry. **Business Services:** meeting rooms. **Cards:** AX, DC, DS, MC, VI. **Special Amenities:** early check-in/late check-out. *(See color ad p 364)*

SOME UNITS

RAMADA INN DEERFIELD BEACH EAST

(AAA) (SAVE)
♦♦♦ ♦♦♦
Motel

Phone: (954)421-5000

12/31-4/15	1P: $59-$65	2P: $99-$110	XP: $10 F16
12/1-12/30 & 4/16-11/30	1P: $45-$55	2P: $65-$75	XP: $10 F16

Location: On US 1, 1.3 mi s of jct SR 810 (Hillsboro Blvd). 1401 S Federal Hwy 33441. Fax: 954/426-2811. **Facility:** 107 units. 106 one-bedroom standard units, some with efficiencies. 1 one-bedroom suite ($99-$150). 2 stories, interior/exterior corridors. **Parking:** on-site. **Terms:** weekly rates available, pets ($10 extra charge, in limited units). **Amenities:** voice mail, irons, hair dryers. **Dining:** 7 am-10 pm, cocktails. **Pool(s):** heated outdoor. **Guest Services:** coin laundry, beauty salon. **Business Services:** meeting rooms. **Cards:** AX, CB, DC, DS, MC, VI. **Special Amenities:** early check-in/late check-out and preferred room (subject to availability with advanced reservations).

SOME UNITS

FEE

RETTGER RESORTS BEACH CLUB

♦♦♦ ♦♦♦
Motel

Phone: (954)427-7900

12/15-4/15 [CP]	1P: $109-$249	2P: $109-$249	XP: $10 F12
12/1-12/14 & 4/16-11/30 [CP]	1P: $59-$169	2P: $59-$169	XP: $10 F12

Location: Just n on SR A1A from SR 810 (Hillsboro Blvd) to 20th Tr. 100 NE 20th Tr 33441. Fax: 954/427-7978. **Facility:** Smoke free premises. 18 units. 16 one-bedroom standard units. 2 one-bedroom suites ($249-$249) with kitchens and whirlpools. 2 stories (no elevator), exterior corridors. **Parking:** on-site. **Terms:** cancellation fee imposed. **Amenities:** dual phone lines, voice mail. **Pool(s):** heated outdoor. **Cards:** AX, CB, DC, DS, MC, VI.

SOME UNITS

SHORE ROAD INN

♦♦♦ ♦♦♦
Motel

Phone: (954)427-8820

1/21-4/1	2P: $100-$130	XP: $12
12/1-1/20	2P: $86-$120	XP: $12
4/2-5/1	2P: $75-$105	XP: $12
5/2-11/30	2P: $58-$90	XP: $12

Location: SR A1A, just s of jct SR 810 (Hillsboro Blvd). 460 S A1A 33441. Fax: 954/427-4881. **Facility:** 18 units. 12 one-bedroom standard units, some with efficiencies. 6 one-bedroom suites with kitchens. 2 stories (no elevator), exterior corridors. *Bath:* combo or shower only. **Parking:** on-site. **Terms:** age restrictions may apply, 45 day cancellation notice-fee imposed. **Amenities:** video library, voice mail. *Some:* irons. **Pool(s):** heated outdoor. **Guest Services:** coin laundry. **Cards:** AX, DC, DS, MC, VI.

SOME UNITS

TROPIC ISLE BEACH RESORT

Phone: (954)427-1000

AAA [SAVE]

1/16-3/31 Wkly	1P: $545-$746	2P: $545-$746	XP: $56	F12
12/1-1/15 Wkly	1P: $293-$616	2P: $293-$616	XP: $56	F12
4/1-4/22 Wkly	1P: $392-$533	2P: $392-$533	XP: $56	F12
4/23-11/30 Wkly	1P: $293-$410	2P: $293-$410	XP: $56	F12

Motel **Location:** SR A1A, 0.3 mi s of jct SR 810 (Hillsboro Blvd). 370 S A1A 33441. Fax: 954/429-9754. **Facility:** 15 units. 13 one-bedroom standard units with efficiencies. 2 one-bedroom suites with kitchens. 2 stories, exterior corridors. *Bath:* combo or shower only. **Parking:** on-site. **Terms:** 30 day cancellation notice. **Amenities:** voice mail, safes. **Pool(s):** heated outdoor. **Guest Services:** coin laundry. **Cards:** DC, MC, VI. **Special Amenities: early check-in/late check-out and preferred room (subject to availability with advanced reservations).**

WELLESLEY INN & SUITES (DEERFIELD BEACH)

Phone: (954)428-0661

AAA [SAVE]

12/1-4/21	1P: $99	XP: $10	F18
4/22-11/30	1P: $65	XP: $10	F18

Location: I-95, exit 42A, just w on SR 810 (Hillsboro Blvd), then just s. 100 12th Ave SW 33442. Fax: 954/427-6701. **Facility:** 79 units. 75 one-bedroom standard units. 4 one-bedroom suites. 4 stories, interior corridors. *Bath:* Small-scale Hotel combo or shower only. **Parking:** on-site. **Terms:** cancellation fee imposed, weekly rates available, [ECP] meal plan available, small pets only. **Amenities:** voice mail, irons, hair dryers. *Fee:* video games, high-speed Internet. **Pool(s):** heated outdoor. **Guest Services:** coin laundry. **Cards:** AX, DC, DS, MC. **Special Amenities: free continental breakfast and free newspaper.** *(See color ad p 365)*

SOME UNITS
FEE

────── WHERE TO DINE ──────

BROOKS RESTAURANT

Dinner: $20-$27   **Phone:** 954/427-9302

Continental

Location: US 1, 0.5 mi s of jct SR 810 (Hillsboro Blvd). 500 S Federal Hwy 33441. **Hours:** 6 pm-10 pm. Closed: 12/25; also Mon & Tues 5/8-11/25. **Reservations:** suggested. **Features:** Although patrons normally come here dressed up, they can feel comfortable amid the subdued, attractive decor. Generous portions of well-prepared entrees are presented in an inviting manner. Smoke free premises. Semi-formal attire;
cocktails. **Parking:** on-site and valet. **Cards:** AX, CB, DC, MC, VI.

CAFE CLAUDE

Lunch: $8-$14   **Dinner:** $15-$25   **Phone:** 954/421-7337

French

Location: 0.5 mi e of jct US 1; in Cove Plaza off Hillsboro Blvd. 1544 SE 3rd Ct 33441. **Hours:** 11:30 am-2 & 5:15-10 pm, Sat & Sun from 5:15 pm. Closed: Mon. **Reservations:** suggested. **Features:** Claude Pottier, the French owner and chef, prepares authentic French cuisine in a nice, casual atmosphere. Each entree has visual appeal with decoratively carved vegetables accented with sauce. The homemade desserts top
off the superb presentation. Semi-formal attire; cocktails. **Parking:** on-site. **Cards:** AX, MC, VI.

CARAFIELLO'S

Dinner: $11-$24   **Phone:** 954/421-2481

Italian

Location: US 1, 1 mi s of jct SR 810 (Hillsboro Blvd); at SE 10th St. 949 S Federal Hwy 33441. **Hours:** 5 pm-11 pm. Closed: Tues 8/1-9/30. **Reservations:** suggested. **Features:** The owner/chef of this cozy mom-and-pop operation prepares tasty dishes such as gnocchi, spinach-stuffed breast of chicken, seafood and a delectable assortment of homemade desserts. You can get Continental cuisine here, too. Casual
dress; beer & wine only. **Parking:** on-site. **Cards:** AX, DS, MC, VI.

PAL'S CHARLEY'S CRAB

Lunch: $6-$14   **Dinner:** $12-$26   **Phone:** 954/427-4000

Seafood

Location: On Intracoastal Waterway, just off Hillsboro Blvd, 0.5 mi e of jct US 1; in Cove Plaza. 1755 SE 3rd Ct 33441. **Hours:** 11:30 am-3:30 & 4-10 pm. **Reservations:** suggested. **Features:** A well-established restaurant, it overlooks the scenic Intracoastal Waterway. A wide variety of delicious seafood dishes are served along with featured pasta specials. Start with the spicy black bean soup and order a fresh catch
from Florida waters. cocktails; entertainment. **Parking:** valet. **Cards:** AX, DC, DS, MC, VI.

─── *The following restaurant has not been evaluated by AAA* ───
but is listed for your information only.

FLANIGAN'S SEAFOOD BAR & GRILL

Phone: 954/427-9304

[fyi] Not evaluated. **Location:** 2041 NE 2nd St. **Features:** The family-friendly restaurant is known for its baby back ribs, burgers and seafood.

HALLANDALE BEACH   (See map p. 357; index p. 363)

────── WHERE TO STAY ──────

BEST WESTERN HALLANDALE BEACH

Phone: (954)456-8333   [150]

AAA [SAVE]

12/20-3/31 [ECP]	1P: $79-$199	2P: $79-$199	XP: $6	F15
12/1-12/19 [ECP]	1P: $79-$129	2P: $79-$129	XP: $6	F15
4/1-11/30 [ECP]	1P: $59-$99	2P: $59-$99	XP: $6	F15

Location: On Hallandale Beach Blvd at jct I-95, exit 18. 101 Ansin Blvd 33009. Fax: 954/455-0324. **Facility:** 100 Small-scale Hotel one-bedroom standard units. 5 stories, interior corridors. *Bath:* combo or shower only. **Parking:** on-site. **Terms:** 2-3 night minimum stay - seasonal, [CP] meal plan available, package plans - seasonal. **Amenities:** voice mail, irons, hair dryers. **Pool(s):** outdoor. **Leisure Activities:** exercise room. **Guest Services:** valet and coin laundry. **Business Services:** meeting rooms. **Cards:** AX, CB, DC, DS, JC, MC, VI. **Special Amenities: free continental breakfast and free newspaper.**

SOME UNITS

(See map p. 357)

THE DIPLOMAT COUNTRY CLUB & SPA   Phone: (954)883-4000   `154`

12/16-4/21	1P: $309-$379	2P: $309-$379	XP: $25 F18
10/1-11/30	1P: $239-$319	2P: $239-$319	XP: $25 F18
12/1-12/15	1P: $209-$309	2P: $209-$309	
4/22-9/30	1P: $209-$309	2P: $209-$309	XP: $25 F18

Resort
Small-scale Hotel

Location: I-95, exit 18 (SR 858/Hallandale Beach Blvd), 2.3 mi e, then 0.4 mi n from SR A1A, 0.5 mi w, then 0.4 mi n. 501 Diplomat Pkwy 33009. Fax: 954/883-4009. **Facility:** Located just off the waterway and surrounded by a golf course on beautiful grounds. The rooms are large and beautifully decorated and furnished. Designated smoking area. 60 units. 54 one-bedroom standard units. 6 one-bedroom suites ($600-$700). 4 stories, interior corridors. **Parking:** valet. **Terms:** 3 day cancellation notice-fee imposed, package plans, $12 service charge. **Amenities:** CD players, dual phone lines, voice mail, fax, safes, honor bars, irons, hair dryers. *Fee:* video games, high-speed Internet. **Dining:** 2 restaurants, 6:30 am-10 pm, also, The Royal Palm Room, see separate listing, entertainment. **Pool(s):** 2 heated outdoor. **Leisure Activities:** saunas, whirlpools, steamrooms, fishing, 10 tennis courts (6 lighted), spa. *Fee:* boat dock, charter fishing, golf-18 holes, golf & tennis instruction. **Guest Services:** gift shop, valet laundry. **Business Services:** meeting rooms, administrative services. **Cards:** AX, CB, DC, DS, JC, MC, VI. **Special Amenities:** free newspaper and preferred room (subject to availability with advanced reservations).** *(See color ad p 5)*

SOME UNITS

Sᴅ ⫿⫿ 24ᵀ 🖥 📶 🏊 🐾 ✕ 🐕 DATA PORT / ✕ VCR /

HALLANDALE RESORT MOTEL   Phone: (954)456-3024   `149`

12/1-3/31	1P: $45-$85	2P: $45-$85	XP: $7 F12
4/1-11/30	1P: $45-$55	2P: $45-$55	XP: $5 F12

Motel

Location: I-95, exit 19 (Pembroke Rd/SR 824), 1.5 mi e to US 1, 0.3 mi s to NE 7th St, then just left. 703 NE 7th St 33009. Fax: 954/457-3843. **Facility:** 23 units. 22 one-bedroom standard units, some with efficiencies. 1 one-bedroom suite with kitchen. 1 story, exterior corridors. *Bath:* combo or shower only. **Terms:** 3-7 night minimum stay - seasonal, 30 day cancellation notice-fee imposed. **Amenities:** voice mail. **Pool(s):** heated outdoor. **Leisure Activities:** whirlpool, horseshoes, shuffleboard. **Guest Services:** coin laundry. **Business Services:** fax (fee). **Cards:** MC, VI.

ASK 🏊 ✕ 🐕 DATA PORT 🔌 📷 💻

---

*The following lodging was either not evaluated or did not
meet AAA rating requirements but is listed for your information only.*

HAMPTON INN HALLANDALE BEACH/AVENTURA   Phone: 954/874-1111

[fyi]	12/1-3/31	1P: $119-$139	2P: $119-$139
	10/1-11/30	1P: $109-$139	2P: $109-$139
Motel	4/1-9/30	1P: $89-$109	2P: $89-$109

Too new to rate, opening scheduled for November 2002. **Location:** I-95, exit Hallandale Beach Blvd, e to Biscayne Blvd, then s. 1000 S Federal Hwy 33009. Fax: 954/874-1112. **Amenities:** coffeemakers, pool. **Terms:** cancellation fee imposed. **Cards:** AX, CB, DC, DS, JC, MC, VI.

——— **WHERE TO DINE** ———

THE ROYAL PALM ROOM   **Dinner:** $16-$28   Phone: 954/883-4000   `144`

Location: I-95, exit 18 (SR 858/Hallandale Beach Blvd), 2.3 mi e, then 0.4 mi n from SR A1A; in The Diplomat Country Club & Spa. 501 Diplomat Pkwy 33009. **Hours:** 5 pm-10 pm. Closed: Sun. **Reservations:** suggested. **Features:** This restaurant presents the diner with a classic room featuring wood accents and art work. The large chairs will give you a feel of royalty. The menu has local seafoods and is accented with great steaks and chops. Dressy casual; cocktails; entertainment. **Parking:** valet. **Cards:** AX, DC, MC, VI.

Continental

♿M ✕

——— *The following restaurant has not been evaluated by AAA
but is listed for your information only.* ———

FLANIGAN'S SEAFOOD BAR & GRILL   Phone: 954/458-2566

[fyi]   Not evaluated. **Location:** 4 N Federal Hwy 33009. **Features:** The family-friendly restaurant is known for its baby back ribs, burgers and seafood.

HILLSBORO BEACH pop. 2,163

------ WHERE TO STAY ------

ROYAL FLAMINGO VILLAS
▼▼▼▼
| | 12/1-4/30 | 1P: $140-$195 | 2P: $175-$245 | XP: $10 | F12 |
| | 5/1-11/30 | 1P: $85-$140 | 2P: $100-$155 | XP: $10 | F12 |

Phone: (954)427-0660

Condominium   **Location:** SR A1A, 0.8 mi s of jct SR 810 (Hillsboro Blvd). 1225 Hillsboro Mile 33062. Fax: 954/427-6110. **Facility:** 40 cottages. 1 story, exterior corridors. **Parking:** on-site. **Terms:** check-in 4 pm, 45 day cancellation notice. **Amenities:** voice mail, irons. **Pool(s):** heated outdoor. **Leisure Activities:** putting green, shuffleboard. **Guest Services:** coin laundry. **Cards:** DS, MC, VI.

(ASK) (S⊘) (≈) (VCR) (✳) (⊟) (⊞) (▭)

HOLLYWOOD pop. 139,357 (See map p. 357; index p. 362)

------ WHERE TO STAY ------

THE AMBASSADOR RESORT & CORPORATE CENTER   Phone: (954)458-1900   **139**
▼▼▼
	12/20-4/30	1P: $109-$129	2P: $109-$129	XP: $10	F18
	5/1-9/99	1P: $79-$99	2P: $79-$99	XP: $10	F18
	12/1-12/19	1P: $69-$89	2P: $69-$89	XP: $10	F18

Large-scale Hotel   **Location:** SR A1A, at jct SR 858 (Hallandale Beach Blvd). 4000 S Ocean Dr 33019. Fax: 954/455-9829. **Facility:** 307 units. 302 one-bedroom standard units. 5 one-bedroom suites, some with kitchens (no utensils). 10 stories, interior corridors. *Bath:* combo or shower only. **Parking:** on-site (fee) and valet. **Terms:** 3 day cancellation notice-fee imposed, [BP], [CP] & [ECP] meal plans available. **Amenities:** voice mail, safes. *Some:* irons, hair dryers. **Pool(s):** heated outdoor, wading. **Leisure Activities:** whirlpool, 2 tennis courts, exercise room, shuffleboard. *Fee:* massage. **Guest Services:** gift shop, valet and coin laundry. **Business Services:** meeting rooms. **Cards:** AX, CB, DC, DS, JC, MC, VI.

SOME UNITS

(ASK) (S⊘) (¶◀) (Y) (⟨) (⊘) (≈) (✕) (✳) (DATA PORT) (▭) / (✕) (⊟) (⊞) /

CALIFORNIA DREAM INN   Phone: 954/923-2100   **137**
▼▼▼ ▼▼▼
| | 12/1-4/30 | 1P: $139-$189 | 2P: $139-$189 | XP: $25 | |
| | 5/1-11/30 | 1P: $99-$149 | 2P: $99-$149 | XP: $25 | |

Motel   **Location:** Just s of Dania Beach Blvd/SR A1A, then e. 300 Walnut St 33019. Fax: 954/923-3222. **Facility:** 14 units. 8 one-bedroom standard units with efficiencies. 6 one-bedroom suites ($189-$250) with kitchens. 1-2 stories, exterior corridors. *Bath:* combo or shower only. **Parking:** on-site. **Terms:** cancellation fee imposed, weekly rates available, small pets only ($20 fee, in designated units). **Cards:** AX, CB, DC, DS, MC, VI.

SOME UNITS

(ASK) (🐾) (¶↑) (⊟) / (VCR) (⊞) (▭) /

COMFORT INN-FT. LAUDERDALE/HOLLYWOOD AIRPORT   Phone: (954)922-1600   **126**
(AAA) (SAVE)
▼▼▼▼
	12/20-4/30 [BP]	1P: $99-$139	2P: $99-$139	XP: $10	F17
	10/1-11/30 [BP]	1P: $89-$139	2P: $89-$139	XP: $10	F17
	12/1-12/19 & 5/1-9/30 [BP]	1P: $79-$99	2P: $79-$99	XP: $10	F17

Motel   **Location:** I-95, exit 22, just e, 2 mi s of airport. 2520 Stirling Rd 33020. Fax: 954/923-5363. **Facility:** 190 one-bedroom standard units. 4 stories, exterior corridors. *Bath:* combo or shower only. **Parking:** on-site. **Terms:** pets ($25 extra charge). **Amenities:** video games (fee), voice mail, safes, irons, hair dryers. *Some:* dual phone lines. **Pool(s):** heated outdoor. **Leisure Activities:** barbecue grills, exercise room. **Guest Services:** valet and coin laundry, airport transportation-Fort Lauderdale-Hollywood International Airport, area transportation-within 5 mi & Port Everglades Convention Center. **Business Services:** meeting rooms, business center. **Cards:** AX, CB, DC, DS, JC, MC, VI.
(See color ad below)

SOME UNITS

(S⊘) (✈) (🐾) (¶↑) (Y) (⌖M) (⟨) (⊘) (≈) (✳) (DATA PORT) (⊟) (⊞) (▭) / (✕) /

DAYS INN FORT LAUDERDALE/HOLLYWOOD AIRPORT SOUTH   Phone: (954)923-7300   **129**
(SAVE)
| | 12/1-4/15 [ECP] | 1P: $69-$159 | 2P: $69-$159 | | |
▼▼▼▼ | 4/16-11/30 [ECP] | 1P: $59-$129 | 2P: $59-$129 | | |

Small-scale Hotel   **Location:** I-95, exit 21, just nw on SR 822 (Sheriden St). 2601 N 29th Ave 33020. Fax: 954/921-6706. **Facility:** 114 one-bedroom standard units. 7 stories, interior corridors. **Parking:** on-site. **Terms:** 3 day cancellation notice, small pets only ($10 extra charge). **Amenities:** voice mail, irons, hair dryers. **Pool(s):** outdoor. **Leisure Activities:** whirlpool, exercise room. **Guest Services:** valet and coin laundry, area transportation (fee). **Business Services:** meeting rooms, fax (fee). **Cards:** AX, CB, DC, DS, MC, VI.

SOME UNITS

(✈) (🐾) (¶↑) (⊘) (≈) (✳) (DATA PORT) / (✕) (⊟) (⊞) (▭) /
FEE

(See map p. 357)

ECONO LODGE

⬥⬥⬥ SAVE
▽▽▽ ▽▽

Motel

Phone: (954)920-3001   [132]

| 12/16-4/15 [CP] | 1P: $69-$99 | 2P: $69-$99 | XP: $10 | F17 |
| 12/1-12/15 & 4/16-11/30 [CP] | 1P: $49-$69 | 2P: $49-$69 | XP: $10 | F17 |

Location: 1 mi n on US 1 from Hollywood Blvd (SR 820), then e. 1725 Taft St 33020. Fax: 954/923-7294. **Facility:** 34 one-bedroom standard units. 2 stories, exterior corridors. *Bath:* combo or shower only. **Parking:** on-site. **Terms:** 24 day cancellation notice-fee imposed. **Amenities:** hair dryers. **Pool(s):** heated outdoor. **Cards:** AX, DC, DS, MC, VI. **Special Amenities:** free continental breakfast and free local telephone calls.

SOME UNITS

GREENBRIAR BEACH CLUB

⬥⬥⬥ SAVE
▽▽▽ ▽▽

Condominium

Phone: (954)922-2606   [136]

| 12/16-4/15 [ECP] | 2P: $119-$209 | XP: $15 | F12 |
| 12/1-12/15 & 4/16-11/30 [ECP] | 2P: $84-$189 | XP: $15 | F12 |

Location: Hollywood Blvd, 0.8 mi s on SR A1A/Ocean Blvd to Iris Terrace, turn left to S Surf Rd, then just n. 1900 S Surf Rd 33019. Fax: 954/923-0897. **Facility:** 47 units. 37 one-bedroom standard units with kitchens. 10 one-bedroom suites ($129-$209) with kitchens. 2-3 stories (no elevator), exterior corridors. **Parking:** on-site. **Terms:** 30 day cancellation notice, weekly rates available. **Amenities:** voice mail, hair dryers. **Pool(s):** heated outdoor. **Guest Services:** coin laundry. **Business Services:** meeting rooms. **Cards:** AX, DC, DS, MC, VI. **Special Amenities:** free continental breakfast.

HAMPTON INN & SUITES-FT LAUDERDALE/HOLLYWOOD AIRPORT

⬥⬥⬥ SAVE
▽▽▽ ▽▽

Small-scale Hotel

Phone: (954)922-0011   [125]

1/1-4/26 [ECP]	1P: $139-$159	2P: $139-$159	XP: $10	F18
12/1-12/31 & 9/29-11/30 [ECP]	1P: $109-$129	2P: $109-$129	XP: $10	F18
4/27-9/28 [ECP]	1P: $89-$109	2P: $89-$109	XP: $10	F18

Location: I-95, exit 22, just e, 2 mi s of airport. 2500 Stirling Rd 33020. Fax: 954/929-7118. **Facility:** 104 units. 53 one-bedroom standard units. 51 one-bedroom suites ($109-$269) with efficiencies. 5 stories, interior corridors. *Bath:* combo or shower only. **Parking:** on-site. **Amenities:** video games (fee), dual phone lines, voice mail, irons, hair dryers. **Pool(s):** small heated outdoor. **Guest Services:** sundries, complimentary evening beverages: Tues & Wed, valet and coin laundry, airport transportation-Fort Lauderdale-Hollywood International Airport, area transportation-within 5 mi & Port Everglades Convention Center. **Business Services:** meeting rooms, business center. **Cards:** AX, CB, DC, DS, JC, MC, VI. **Special Amenities:** free continental breakfast and free local telephone calls. *(See color ad p 373)*

SOME UNITS

HOLIDAY INN FORT LAUDERDALE/HOLLYWOOD AIRPORT

⬥⬥⬥ SAVE
▽▽▽ ▽▽

Small-scale Hotel

Phone: (954)925-9100   [130]

1/1-4/15	1P: $179-$249	2P: $179-$249
4/16-11/30	1P: $135-$179	2P: $135-$179
12/1-12/31	1P: $129-$169	2P: $129-$169

Location: I-95, exit 21, just w on SR 822 (Sheridan St). 2905 Sheridan St 33020. Fax: 954/925-5512. **Facility:** 150 units. 146 one-bedroom standard units. 4 one-bedroom suites ($149-$349). 6 stories, interior corridors. *Bath:* combo or shower only. **Parking:** on-site. **Amenities:** dual phone lines, voice mail, irons, hair dryers. **Dining:** 6:30 am-11 & 5-10 pm, cocktails. **Pool(s):** heated outdoor. **Leisure Activities:** whirlpool, exercise room. **Guest Services:** valet and coin laundry, area transportation (fee)-Port Everglades. **Business Services:** meeting rooms, business center. **Cards:** AX, CB, DC, DS, JC, MC, VI. **Special Amenities:** free newspaper and free room upgrade (subject to availability with advanced reservations). *(See color ad opposite inside back cover)*

SOME UNITS

HOLIDAY INN HOLLYWOOD BEACH

⬥⬥⬥ SAVE
▽▽▽ ▽▽

Small-scale Hotel

Phone: (954)923-8700   [138]

| 12/21-4/30 | 1P: $139-$289 | 2P: $139-$289 | XP: $10 | F19 |
| 12/1-12/20 & 5/1-11/30 | 1P: $89-$189 | 2P: $89-$189 | XP: $10 | F19 |

Location: SR A1A, 0.5 mi n of jct SR 858 (Hallandale Beach Blvd). 2711 S Ocean Dr 33019. Fax: 954/923-7059. **Facility:** 201 one-bedroom standard units. 2-5 stories, interior corridors. *Bath:* combo or shower only. **Parking:** valet. **Terms:** check-in 4 pm, 3 day cancellation notice-fee imposed, 11% service charge. **Amenities:** voice mail, safes, irons, hair dryers. **Dining:** 7 am-10 pm, cocktails. **Pool(s):** heated outdoor. **Leisure Activities:** recreation programs, exercise room, shuffleboard. **Guest Services:** gift shop, valet and coin laundry. **Business Services:** meeting rooms, fax (fee). **Cards:** AX, CB, DC, DS, MC, VI. **Special Amenities:** free local telephone calls and free room upgrade (subject to availability with advanced reservations). *(See color ad opposite inside back cover)*

SOME UNITS

FEE

HOWARD JOHNSON PLAZA RESORT HOLLYWOOD BEACH

▽▽▽ ▽▽

Small-scale Hotel

Phone: (954)925-1411   [133]

12/1-12/25 [CP]	1P: $89-$119	2P: $99-$129
12/26-4/20 [CP]	1P: $105-$124	2P: $105-$124
4/21-11/30 [CP]	1P: $89-$108	2P: $89-$108

Location: SR A1A, 1 mi n of jct SR 820 (Hollywood Blvd). 2501 N Ocean Dr 33019. Fax: 954/921-5565. **Facility:** 242 one-bedroom standard units. 11 stories, interior corridors. **Parking:** on-site. **Terms:** 3 day cancellation notice-fee imposed. **Amenities:** voice mail, safes (fee), irons, hair dryers. **Pool(s):** heated outdoor, wading. **Business Services:** meeting rooms, fax (fee). **Cards:** AX, DC, DS, MC, VI.

SOME UNITS

FEE FEE

LA QUINTA INN & SUITES

SAVE
▽▽▽ ▽▽

Small-scale Hotel

Phone: (954)922-2295   [131]

| 12/26-4/7 | 1P: $119-$149 | 2P: $125-$155 |
| 12/1-12/25 & 4/8-11/30 | 1P: $75-$95 | 2P: $81-$101 |

Location: I-95, exit 21 (Sheridan St/SR 822), just e to Oakwood, then just left. 2620 N 26th Ave 33020. Fax: 954/922-2995. **Facility:** 131 units. 125 one-bedroom standard units. 6 one-bedroom suites. 6 stories, interior corridors. *Bath:* combo or shower only. **Parking:** on-site. **Terms:** [ECP] meal plan available, small pets only. **Amenities:** video games (fee), voice mail, irons, hair dryers. *Some:* dual phone lines. **Pool(s):** heated outdoor. **Leisure Activities:** whirlpool, fishing, exercise room. **Guest Services:** valet and coin laundry, area transportation. **Business Services:** meeting rooms, fax (fee). **Cards:** AX, CB, DC, DS, JC, MC, VI. *(See color ad p 377)*

SOME UNITS

(See map p. 357)

RAMADA INN HOLLYWOOD BEACH RESORT

AAA (SAVE)   12/22-4/17 [CP]   1P: $159-$189   2P: $159-$189   XP: $15   128
▼▼ ▼▼   12/1-12/21 & 4/18-11/30 [CP]   1P: $99-$125   2P: $99-$125   XP: $15   F18
                                                                                                      F18
Location: At jct of Hollywood Blvd (SR 820) and N Ocean Dr (SR A1A). 101 N Ocean Dr 33019. Fax: 954/920-9480.
Facility: 220 units. 190 one-bedroom standard units with efficiencies. 30 one-bedroom suites with kitchens.
Large-scale Hotel some with whirlpools. 8 stories, interior corridors. *Bath:* combo or shower only. **Parking:** on-site (fee) and
valet. **Terms:** check-in 4 pm, cancellation fee imposed. **Amenities:** voice mail, safes, irons, hair dryers.
Dining: 2 restaurants, 7 am-10 pm, cocktails. **Pool(s):** heated outdoor, wading. **Leisure Activities:** whirlpool, exercise room.
Fee: bicycles, massage, game room. **Guest Services:** valet and coin laundry. **Business Services:** meeting rooms, fax (fee).
Special Amenities: free continental breakfast and free newspaper. *(See color ad below)*
                                                                                              Phone: (954)921-0990

SOME UNITS

🅂🄳 🍴 🍸 🏊 ⊠ 🖥 🖧 🖨 / ⊠ /

(See map p. 357)

RICHARDS MOTEL   Phone: 954/921-6418   135
(AAA) (SAVE)

	1/26-3/31	1P: $49-$74	2P: $59-$74	XP: $10	F12
	12/1-1/9	1P: $36-$74	2P: $39-$74	XP: $10	F12
	1/10-1/25	1P: $39-$64	2P: $49-$64	XP: $10	F12
	4/1-11/30	1P: $36-$64	2P: $39-$64	XP: $10	F12

Motel   **Location:** US 1, 0.7 mi s of Hollywood Circle, 0.3 mi n of jct Pembroke Rd. 1219 S Federal Hwy 33020. Fax: 954/925-1797. **Facility:** 24 units. 17 one-bedroom standard units, some with efficiencies. 7 one-bedroom suites with efficiencies. 1-2 stories (no elevator), exterior corridors. *Bath:* combo or shower only. **Parking:** on-site. **Terms:** 30 day cancellation notice-fee imposed, weekly rates available. **Pool(s):** heated outdoor. **Guest Services:** coin laundry. **Business Services:** fax (fee). **Cards:** AX, CB, DC, DS, MC, VI. **Special Amenities:** free newspaper and free room upgrade (subject to availability with advanced reservations). *(See ad p 398)*

SOME UNITS

SHELL MOTEL   Phone: (954)923-8085   134
(AAA) (SAVE)

	12/1-4/30	1P: $45-$75	2P: $49-$79	XP: $10	D5
	10/1-11/30	1P: $40-$70	2P: $45-$75	XP: $10	D5
	5/1-9/30	1P: $39-$49	2P: $39-$59	XP: $10	D5

Motel   **Location:** US 1, 0.7 mi s of Hollywood Circle, 0.3 mi n of jct Pembroke Rd. 1201 S Federal Hwy 33020. Fax: 954/925-8750. **Facility:** 35 one-bedroom standard units, some with efficiencies or kitchens. 1 story, exterior corridors. *Bath:* combo or shower only. **Parking:** on-site. **Terms:** 30 day cancellation notice-fee imposed, weekly rates available, package plans - extended stays. **Pool(s):** heated outdoor. **Leisure Activities:** shuffleboard. **Guest Services:** coin laundry. **Business Services:** fax (fee). **Cards:** AX, DS, MC, VI. *(See ad p 398)*

SOME UNITS

THE WESTIN DIPLOMAT RESORT & SPA   Phone: (954)602-6000   127

	12/1-4/21	1P: $289-$449	2P: $309-$449	XP: $25	F18
	4/22-9/30	1P: $229-$369	2P: $229-$369	XP: $25	F18
	10/1-11/30	1P: $239-$319	2P: $239-$319	XP: $25	F18

Large-scale Hotel   **Location:** Just n on S Ocean Dr (SR A1A) from Hallendale Beach Blvd (SR 858). 3555 S Ocean Dr 33019. Fax: 954/602-7000. **Facility:** This beachfront resort impresses guests with its large lobby, two-level pool and spacious, luxuriously appointed rooms. 998 units. 902 one-bedroom standard units. 94 one- and 2 two-bedroom suites ($475-$6000), some with whirlpools. 36 stories, interior corridors. *Bath:* combo or shower only. **Parking:** on-site (fee) and valet. **Terms:** 3 day cancellation notice. **Amenities:** video games (fee), dual phone lines, voice mail, safes, honor bars, irons, hair dryers. *Some:* CD players, fax. **Dining:** Hollywood Prime, see separate listing. **Pool(s):** 2 heated outdoor. **Leisure Activities:** whirlpools, fishing, 10 tennis courts (6 lighted), recreation programs, exercise room, spa. *Fee:* boat dock, charter fishing, golf-18 holes. **Guest Services:** gift shop, valet laundry, area transportation. **Business Services:** conference facilities, business center. **Cards:** AX, CB, DC, DS, JC, MC, VI. *(See color ad p 5)*

SOME UNITS
FEE   FEE

—— WHERE TO DINE ——

GIORGIO'S GRILL   **Dinner:** $10-$28   Phone: 954/929-7030   142
     Location: SR A1A, just n of Hollywood Blvd (SR 820). 606 N Ocean Dr 33019. **Hours:** 4 pm-11 pm. **Reservations:** accepted. **Features:** On the Intracoastal Waterway, the restaurant invites diners to relax indoors or on the outdoor patio. Seafood is the specialty on a menu that also includes Mediterranean entrees of pasta, pizza, beef and chicken. Dressy casual; cocktails. **Parking:** on-site (fee) and valet.
Italian
Cards: AX, DS, MC, VI.

HOLLYWOOD PRIME   **Dinner:** $24-$42   Phone: 954/602-6000   143
     Location: Just n on S Ocean Dr (SR A1A) from Hallendale Beach Blvd (SR 858); in The Westin Diplomat Resort & Spa. 3555 S Ocean Dr 33019. **Hours:** 5:30 pm-11 pm. Closed: Sun & Mon. **Reservations:** suggested.
Steak House   **Features:** Contributing to the traditional steakhouse decor are white linens and leather chairs. Many wine choices are suited to the succulent dry-aged steaks and fresh seafood. Smoke free premises. Dressy casual; cocktails. **Parking:** valet. **Cards:** AX, CB, DC, DS, JC, MC, VI.

MARTHA'S ON THE INTRACOASTAL   **Lunch:** $6-$12   **Dinner:** $15-$29   Phone: 954/923-5444   141
     Location: Between Dania Beach Blvd Bridge and Sheridan St, just s. 6024 N Ocean Dr 33019. **Hours:** 11:30 am-11 pm, Fri & Sat-midnight. **Reservations:** suggested. **Features:** An island feel tinges the cuisine and decor of this waterfront eatery. The views are outstanding. Seafood dazzlers dominate the first plates, and the main plates are equally enticing and innovative. Fresh seafood is always available. Dressy casual; cocktails; entertainment. **Parking:** valet. **Cards:** AX, DC, DS, MC, VI.
American

The following restaurant has not been evaluated by AAA
but is listed for your information only.

FLANIGAN'S SEAFOOD BAR & GRILL   Phone: 954/964-3793
(fyi)   Not evaluated. **Location:** 2505 N University Dr. **Features:** The family-friendly restaurant is known for its baby back ribs, burgers and seafood.

LAUDERDALE-BY-THE-SEA pop. 2,563   (See map p. 357; index p. 361)

------ WHERE TO STAY ------

A LITTLE INN BY THE SEA   Phone: (954)772-2450   **62**
AAA [SAVE]
◆◆◆◆◆   12/16-4/30 [ECP]   1P: $119-$318   2P: $119-$318   XP: $10   F12
         12/1-12/15 & 5/1-11/30 [ECP] 1P: $79-$248   2P: $79-$248   XP: $10   F12
         Location: Just e of SR A1A, 0.4 mi n of SR 870 (Commercial Blvd). 4546 El Mar Dr 33308. Fax: 954/938-9354.
Motel   **Facility:** 29 one-bedroom standard units, some with efficiencies or kitchens. 2-3 stories (no elevator),
            interior/exterior corridors. **Parking:** on-site. **Terms:** 30 day cancellation notice. **Amenities:** voice mail, safes
            (fee). **Pool(s):** heated outdoor. **Leisure Activities:** barbecue grill, rooftop sun deck, bicycles. **Cards:** AX, DC,
DS, MC, VI. **Special Amenities:** free continental breakfast and free newspaper. *(See color ad p 377)*

SOME UNITS
[icons]

BLUE SEAS COURTYARD   Phone: 954/772-3336   **68**
◆◆◆◆   1/20-3/31   1P: $99-$120   2P: $99-$120   XP: $10   D12
        4/1-4/30   1P: $74-$120   2P: $74-$120   XP: $10   D12
Motel 12/1-1/19   1P: $95-$115   2P: $95-$115   XP: $10   D12
        5/1-11/30   1P: $65-$90   2P: $65-$90   XP: $10   D12
Location: 0.5 mi n of Commercial Blvd/SR 870. 4525 El Mar Dr 33308. Fax: 954/772-6337. **Facility:** Designated smoking area. 12 one-
bedroom standard units, some with efficiencies. 2 stories (no elevator), exterior corridors. *Bath:* combo or shower only. **Parking:**
on-site. **Terms:** age restrictions may apply, 30 day cancellation notice. **Pool(s):** heated outdoor. **Cards:** MC, VI.

SOME UNITS
[icons]

CLARION LAUDERDALE BEACH RESORT   Phone: (954)776-5660   **63**
AAA [SAVE]
◆◆◆◆   12/20-4/26   1P: $129-$219   2P: $129-$219   XP: $10   F17
        12/1-12/19 & 4/27-11/30 1P: $79-$119   2P: $79-$119   XP: $10   F17
        Location: SR A1A, 0.5 mi n of SR 870 (Commercial Blvd). 4660 N Ocean Dr 33308. Fax: 954/776-4689.
        Facility: 179 units. 162 one-bedroom standard units. 17 one-bedroom suites with kitchens. 3-5 stories,
Small-scale Hotel interior/exterior corridors. *Bath:* combo or shower only. **Parking:** on-site. **Terms:** cancellation fee imposed,
        $3 service charge. **Amenities:** dual phone lines, voice mail, safes, irons, hair dryers. **Dining:** 7 am-9:30 pm,
cocktails. **Pool(s):** 2 heated outdoor, wading. **Leisure Activities:** exercise room, shuffleboard, volleyball. **Guest Services:** valet
and coin laundry. **Business Services:** meeting rooms, fax (fee). **Cards:** AX, CB, DC, DS, MC, VI. *(See color ad p 401)*

SOME UNITS
[icons]

COURTYARD VILLA ON THE OCEAN   Phone: (954)776-1164   **65**
AAA [SAVE]
◆◆◆◆   12/19-4/25   1P: $169-$259   2P: $169-$259   XP: $15   F5
        12/1-12/18 & 4/26-11/30 1P: $109-$159   2P: $109-$159   XP: $15   F5
◆◆◆◆   **Location:** From Commerical Blvd (SR 870), just s. 4312 El Mar Dr 33308. Fax: 954/491-0768. **Facility:** Designated
        smoking area. 8 one-bedroom standard units. 2 stories (no elevator), exterior corridors. *Bath:* shower only.
Motel   **Parking:** on-site. **Terms:** age restrictions may apply, 30 day cancellation notice, weekly rates available, [BP]
        meal plan available, package plans, pets ($200 deposit with restrictions). **Amenities:** video library, voice
mail, irons, hair dryers. **Pool(s):** heated outdoor. **Leisure Activities:** scuba diving, snorkeling, beach towels, sun deck, tennis
court, barbecue grills, bicycles. **Cards:** AX, MC, VI. **Special Amenities:** free newspaper and preferred room (subject to availability with advanced reservations). *(See color ad below)*

SOME UNITS
[icons]

HOLIDAY INN-LAUDERDALE-BY-THE-SEA NORTH BEACH   Phone: (954)776-1212   **61**
AAA [SAVE]
◆◆◆◆   12/21-4/20   1P: $159   2P: $159   XP: $10   F17
        12/1-12/20 & 4/21-11/30 1P: $99   2P: $99   XP: $10   F17
        Location: SR A1A, just s of jct SR 870 (Commercial Blvd). 4116 N Ocean Dr 33308. Fax: 954/776-1411. **Facility:** 186
        one-bedroom standard units. 5 stories, exterior corridors. *Bath:* combo or shower only. **Parking:** on-site.
Small-scale Hotel **Terms:** 3 day cancellation notice-fee imposed. **Amenities:** voice mail, irons, hair dryers. *Some:* safes.
        Dining: 6 am-10 pm, cocktails. **Pool(s):** heated outdoor. **Leisure Activities:** exercise room. **Fee:** scuba
diving, snorkeling. **Guest Services:** gift shop, valet and coin laundry. **Business Services:** meeting rooms, fax (fee). **Cards:** AX,
DC, DS, MC, VI. *(See color ad opposite inside back cover)*

SOME UNITS
[icons]

(See map p. 357)

THE PIER POINT RESORT

Phone: (954)776-5121   66

◆◆◆ SAVE
▼▼ ▼▼

12/23-4/15	1P: $110-$179	2P: $120-$199
12/1-12/22 & 4/16-11/30	1P: $59-$125	2P: $69-$139

Location: From Commerical Blvd (SR 870), just s. 4320 El Mar Dr 33308. Fax: 954/491-9084. **Facility:** 100 units. 63 one-bedroom standard units, some with efficiencies. 37 one-bedroom suites with kitchens. 3-8 stories,

Small-scale Hotel exterior corridors. *Bath:* combo or shower only. **Parking:** on-site. **Terms:** cancellation fee imposed, small pets only ($50). **Amenities:** voice mail, safes (fee), hair dryers. *Some:* irons. **Pool(s):** outdoor, 2 heated outdoor.

Leisure Activities: barbecue grills, volleyball. *Fee:* bicycles. **Guest Services:** gift shop, coin laundry. **Business Services:** fax (fee).

SOME UNITS

⬛ 🐕 📶 🏊 ✖ 📷 DATA PORT 🖥 / ✖ VCR 📼 /

The Perfect Oceanfront Location on the
Greater Fort Lauderdale Beach at a Perfect Price
for AAA Members Only!

The **CLARION LAUDERDALE BEACH RESORT** just completed its $3,000,000 renovation of all sleeping rooms, efficiencies and 1-bedroom apartments and construction of our new signature restaurant, Damon's Grill & Clubhouse plus our new beachside/poolside tiki bar and grill, Damon's Beach Bar.

All rooms offer:

microwave oven • refrigerator • coffee maker • hair dryer • iron & ironing board • dataport • voice mail • in-room safe
remote-controlled color cable TV • AM/FM clock radio • plus either a full balcony, french balcony or patio

When making reservations please ask for the LTA rate

Toll-Free 1-800-327-5919
or (954) 776-5660
fax (954) 776-4689
reservations@clarionbeachresort.com

Clarion Resort

Rated AAA 3-Diamond
4660 N. Ocean Drive
Lauderdale by the Sea, FL 33308
www.clarionbeachresort.com

*$59 October 1 through December 19, 2002; $99 December 20, 2002 through April 26, 2003; $59 April 27, 2003 through December 18, 2003. Rates are per standard room per night on a single or double occupancy subject to availability, Florida state sales tax and a $2.50 per room per night Resort Surcharge; additional adult $10 each plus tax and resort surcharge. Upgrades to our Beach Building or Suites Building available.

(See map p. 357)

SEA SPRAY INN   Phone: (954)776-1311   67

12/15-4/13	1P: $98-$185	2P: $98-$185	XP: $10 F12
4/14-11/30	1P: $75-$160	2P: $75-$160	XP: $10 F12
12/1-12/14	1P: $70-$150	2P: $70-$150	XP: $10 F12

Motel   **Location:** From Commercial Blvd/SR 870, just s. 4245 El Mar Dr 33308. Fax: 954/772-3178. **Facility:** 6 units. 3 one-bedroom standard units with kitchens. 3 one-bedroom suites with kitchens. 3 stories (no elevator), exterior corridors. *Bath:* combo or shower only. **Parking:** on-site. **Terms:** 21 day cancellation notice. **Amenities:** voice mail, irons, hair dryers. *Some:* DVD players, safes. **Cards:** MC, VI. **Special Amenities: free local telephone calls and preferred room (subject to availability with advanced reservations).**

SOME UNITS

TROPIC SEAS RESORT   Phone: (954)772-2555   69

2/1-4/30	1P: $150-$220	XP: $10 F12
12/17-1/31	1P: $145-$200	XP: $10 F12
5/1-11/30	1P: $95-$160	XP: $15 F12
12/1-12/16	1P: $90-$155	XP: $10 F12

Motel   **Location:** Just e of SR A1A, 0.5 mi n of jct SR 870 (Commercial Blvd). 4616 El Mar Dr 33308. Fax: 954/771-5711. **Facility:** 16 units. 9 one-bedroom standard units, some with efficiencies. 7 one-bedroom suites with kitchens. 2 stories (no elevator), exterior corridors. **Parking:** on-site. **Terms:** 15 day cancellation notice-fee imposed, [CP] meal plan available. **Amenities:** voice mail. **Pool(s):** heated outdoor. **Leisure Activities:** barbecue grills. **Guest Services:** coin laundry. **Cards:** AX, DS, MC, VI. **Special Amenities: free continental breakfast and free newspaper.** *(See color ad p 383)*

SOME UNITS

——— **WHERE TO DINE** ———

ARUBA BEACH CAFE   **Lunch:** $3-$13   **Dinner:** $5-$11   Phone: 954-776-0001   90

Caribbean   **Location:** Just e of SR A1A. 1 E Commercial Blvd 33308. **Hours:** 11 am-11 pm. **Reservations:** accepted. **Features:** A casual, fun place to eat, the restaurant affords a panoramic view of the beach and offers fresh seafood items and meat entrees, some of which reflect an island twist. Casual dress; cocktails. **Parking:** on-site. **Cards:** AX, DC, DS, MC, VI.

LAUDERHILL pop. 57,585   (See map p. 357; index p. 363)

——— **WHERE TO DINE** ———

CRAB HOUSE SEAFOOD RESTAURANT   **Lunch:** $5-$10   **Dinner:** $12-$21   Phone: 954/749-2722   146

Seafood   **Location:** SR 817 (University Dr), 1 mi s of Commercial Blvd at NW 44th St. 4402 N University Dr 33351. **Hours:** 11:30 am-10:15 pm, Fri & Sat-11:15 pm. **Reservations:** accepted. **Features:** In a warehouse-style building, this popular, casual restaurant is decorated in a nautical theme. Fresh seafood, including several varieties of crab, is the menu staple. Hungry patrons should head for the all-you-can-eat shellfish and salad bar. Casual dress; cocktails. **Parking:** on-site. **Cards:** AX, CB, DC, DS, MC, VI.

LIGHTHOUSE POINT pop. 10,767

——— **WHERE TO DINE** ———

CAP'S PLACE-ISLAND RESTAURANT & BAR   Historic   **Dinner:** $13-$25   Phone: 954/941-0418

Seafood   **Location:** Just n on US 1 from jct Copans Rd, 1.1 mi e and n via NE 24th St, follow signs to Cap's Dock for short boat ride to the island. 2765 NE 28th #2 Ct 33064. **Hours:** 5:30 pm-10 pm, Fri & Sat-11 pm. Closed: 11/27, 12/24, 12/25; also Super Bowl Sun. **Reservations:** suggested. **Features:** Operating out of a building that once was a gambling casino, the restaurant sits on an island in the Intracoastal Waterway and has been a source of rich history since 1929. Grouper chowder, hearts of palm salad and fresh broiled fish are menu favorites. Casual dress; cocktails. **Parking:** on-site. **Cards:** AX, MC, VI.

FIFTH AVENUE GRILL   **Lunch:** $6-$15   **Dinner:** $18-$40   Phone: 954/782-4433

Steak House   **Location:** On US 1 (Federal Hwy), 1.1 mi n of Sample Rd. 4650 N Federal Hwy 33064. **Hours:** 11:30 am-4 & 5-10 pm, Fri & Sat-11 pm. Closed: Super Bowl Sun. **Reservations:** accepted. **Features:** An award-winning wine list complements flame-broiled steak and chops, as well as fresh seafood preparations. The dining room is cozy and inviting. Dressy casual; cocktails; entertainment. **Parking:** on-site and valet. **Cards:** AX, DC, MC, VI.

LE BISTRO   **Dinner:** $15-$28   Phone: 954/946-9240

French   **Location:** From Sample Rd, just n; in Main St Plaza. 4626 N Federal Hwy 33064. **Hours:** 5 pm-10 pm. Closed: 1/1, 12/25; also Mon in summer. **Reservations:** suggested. **Features:** Classic cuisine is served in generous portions at this small, quaint eatery. Great attention is given to every detail from preparation to presentation, from service to atmosphere. Smoke free premises. beer & wine only. **Parking:** on-site.
Cards: MC, VI.

MARGATE pop. 53,909

——— **WHERE TO DINE** ———

JASMINE THAI   **Lunch:** $6-$13   **Dinner:** $10-$19   Phone: 954/979-5530

Thai   **Location:** Atlantic Blvd (SR 814), 0.7 mi n on SR 7 and US 441, then just e on Coconut Creek Pkwy; in Cocogate Plaza. 5103 Coconut Creek Pkwy 33063. **Hours:** 11 am-3 & 4:30-10 pm, Sat & Sun from 4:30 pm. Closed: 4/20, 7/4, 11/27; also Super Bowl Sun. **Reservations:** accepted. **Features:** Fresh, carefully prepared cuisine such as snapper with chili garlic sauce, roast duckling, panang curry and tornado chicken is served by a friendly wait staff. A quaint bridge and large pictures in the small, comfortable setting convey an Oriental feel. Casual dress; beer & wine only. **Parking:** on-site. **Cards:** AX, CB, DC, DS, MC, VI.

MIRAMAR pop. 72,739   (See map p. 357; index p. 363)

─────── **WHERE TO STAY** ───────

HILTON GARDEN INN FT. LAUDERDALE SW/MIRAMAR Phone: (954)438-7700 **161**

| | 12/20-4/14 | 1P: $139-$149 | 2P: $149-$159 | XP: $10 | F16 |
| | 12/1-12/19 & 4/15-11/30 | 1P: $119-$129 | 2P: $129-$139 | XP: $10 | F16 |

Location: I-75, exit 7A, e to SW 145 Ave, then n. 14501 SW 29th St 33027. Fax: 954/392-8606. **Facility:** 149 one-bedroom standard units. 5 stories, interior corridors. *Bath:* combo or shower only. **Parking:** on-site. **Terms:** 2
Small-scale Hotel night minimum stay, 11% service charge. **Amenities:** video games (fee), high-speed Internet, dual phone lines, voice mail, irons, hair dryers. **Dining:** 6:30-10 am, 11-2 & 5-10 pm, cocktails. **Pool(s):** heated outdoor.
Leisure Activities: limited exercise equipment. **Guest Services:** sundries, valet and coin laundry. **Business Services:** meeting rooms, business center. **Cards:** AX, CB, DC, DS, JC, MC, VI. **Special Amenities:** free newspaper and preferred room (subject to availability with advanced reservations). *(See color ad below)*

SOME UNITS

(See map p. 357)

WINGATE INN   Phone: (954)441-0122   160
12/1-4/15 [ECP]   1P: $109-$129   2P: $109-$129   XP: $10   F12
4/16-11/30 [ECP]   1P: $89-$109   2P: $89-$109   XP: $10   F12
Small-scale Hotel   **Location:** I-75, exit 9B, just e to SW 148th Ave to Huntington Corporate Park. 2800 SW 149th Ave 33027.
Fax: 954/441-0328. **Facility:** 100 one-bedroom standard units. 4 stories, interior corridors. *Bath:* combo or
shower only. **Parking:** on-site. **Amenities:** video games (fee), high-speed Internet, dual phone lines, voice mail, safes, irons, hair
dryers. **Pool(s):** outdoor. **Leisure Activities:** whirlpool, exercise room. **Guest Services:** valet and coin laundry. **Business Services:** meeting rooms, business center. **Cards:** AX, DC, DS, MC, VI.

SOME UNITS
(ASK) (S/D) (𝖳𝖨+) (🎨) (∅) (➤) (⊛) (DATA PORT) (🖥) (🖨) (🖵) /(✕)/

NORTH LAUDERDALE pop. 26,500 (See map p. 357; index p. 362)

──── WHERE TO STAY ────

COURTYARD BY MARRIOTT FORT LAUDERDALE NORTH   Phone: (954)772-7770   90
SAVE   12/1-4/30   1P: $99-$149   2P: $109-$159   XP: $10   F18
5/1-11/30   1P: $59-$109   2P: $59-$109   XP: $10   F18
Small-scale Hotel   **Location:** I-95, exit 33B, 2.3 mi w. Located at the Fort Lauderdale Executive Airport. 2440 W Cypress Creek Rd 33309.
Fax: 954/772-4780. **Facility:** 136 units. 131 one-bedroom standard units. 5 one-bedroom suites ($109-$169).
4 stories, interior corridors. *Bath:* combo or shower only. **Parking:** on-site. **Amenities:** dual phone lines, voice
mail, irons, hair dryers. **Pool(s):** heated outdoor. **Leisure Activities:** whirlpool, exercise room. **Guest Services:** valet and coin laundry. **Business Services:** meeting rooms, fax (fee). **Cards:** AX, CB, DC, DS, JC, MC, VI.

SOME UNITS
(S/D) (𝖳𝖨) (Y) (∅) (➤) (⊛) (DATA PORT) (🖵) /(✕) (🖥) (🖨)/

PEMBROKE PINES pop. 137,427

──── WHERE TO STAY ────

GRAND PALMS GOLF & COUNTRY CLUB RESORT   Phone: (954)431-8800
12/21-4/15 [CP]   1P: $158   2P: $158   XP: $10   F16
12/1-12/20 & 4/16-11/30 [CP]   1P: $125   2P: $125   XP: $10   F16
Resort   **Location:** SR 820, 0.4 mi w of jct I-75, exit 9B (Pines Blvd). 110 Grand Palms Dr 33027. Fax: 954/435-5988.
Small-scale Hotel   **Facility:** The resort's lush landscaping and numerous recreational offerings give it the ambience of a retreat.
137 units. 101 one-bedroom standard units. 36 one-bedroom suites ($143-$238). 2 stories (no elevator), ex-
terior corridors. **Parking:** on-site and valet. **Terms:** 12 day cancellation notice. **Amenities:** voice mail, irons, hair dryers. *Some:*
dual phone lines. **Pool(s):** outdoor. **Leisure Activities:** saunas, jogging, exercise room. *Fee:* golf-27 holes, 6 lighted tennis
courts. **Guest Services:** valet and coin laundry, area transportation (fee). **Business Services:** meeting rooms, business center.
Cards: AX, CB, DC, DS, MC, VI. *(See color ad below)*

SOME UNITS
(ASK) (S/D) (✈) (𝖳𝖨) (Y) (🏊) (✕) (⊛) (DATA PORT) (🖵) /(✕) (VCR) (🖥) (🖨)/
          FEE   FEE

HAMPTON INN PEMBROKE PINES   Phone: (954)441-4242
SAVE   12/1-4/15 [ECP]   1P: $119-$149   2P: $119-$149   XP: $10   F12
4/16-11/30 [ECP]   1P: $99-$129   2P: $99-$129   XP: $10   F12
Small-scale Hotel   **Location:** I-75, exit 11A, 0.4 mi e on Sheridan St (SR 822) to NW 146th Ave, then 0.4 mi s. 1900 NW 150 Ave 33028.
Fax: 954/441-1118. **Facility:** 107 one-bedroom standard units, some with whirlpools. 5 stories, interior corri-
dors. *Bath:* combo or shower only. **Parking:** on-site. **Amenities:** video games, voice mail, irons, hair dryers.
Pool(s): outdoor. **Leisure Activities:** whirlpool, exercise room. **Guest Services:** valet and coin laundry.
Business Services: meeting rooms, fax (fee). **Cards:** AX, DC, DS, MC, VI.

SOME UNITS
(S/D) (𝖳𝖨+) (♿M) (∅) (➤) (⊛) (DATA PORT) (🖵) /(✕) (🖥) (🖨)/

──── WHERE TO DINE ────

THE ROASTED PEPPER ITALIAN SEAFOOD & GRILL   **Lunch:** $5-$9   **Dinner:** $10-$20   **Phone:** 954/450-8800
Location: I-75, exit 9A, 4.4 mi e; in The Roasted Pepper Pine Plaza Center. 9893 Pines Blvd 33024. **Hours:** 11:30
am-9:30 pm, Fri-11 pm, Sat 2 pm-11 pm, Sun 2 pm-9:30 pm. Closed major holidays. **Features:** This busy
Italian   family restaurant serves traditional favorites like brick-oven pizza. When the singer takes a break, the
servers dance and sing to keep the beat going. A neat, entertaining place to go for generous portions of
authentic Italian food. Casual dress; cocktails; entertainment. **Parking:** on-site. **Cards:** AX, DS, MC, VI.   (Y) (✕)

——— *The following restaurant has not been evaluated by AAA* ———
but is listed for your information only.

BAHAMA BREEZE

[fyi]

Phone: 954/450-6450

Not evaluated. **Location:** 11000 Pines Blvd 33025. **Features:** The atmosphere is tropical and the foods feature that of the islands with both meats, pastas and fresh seafoods.

PLANTATION pop. 66,700   (See map p. 357; index p. 362)

——— **WHERE TO STAY** ———

AMERISUITES (FT. LAUDERDALE/PLANTATION)

(AAA) [SAVE]
▼▼▼▼

Phone: (954)370-2220   [123]

12/1-4/15 [ECP]	1P: $89-$149	2P: $89-$149	XP: $10
4/16-11/30 [ECP]	1P: $79-$119	2P: $79-$119	XP: $10

Location: I-595, exit 4 (Pine Island Rd). 1.3 mi n. Located behind the Westside Corporate Center. 8530 W Broward Blvd 33324. Fax: 954/370-2272. **Facility:** 128 one-bedroom standard units. 6 stories, interior corridors. *Bath:* **Small-scale Hotel** combo or shower only. **Parking:** on-site. **Terms:** cancellation fee imposed, small pets only ($10 extra charge). **Amenities:** voice mail, irons, hair dryers. *Fee:* video games, high-speed Internet. *Some:* dual phone lines. **Pool(s):** heated outdoor. **Leisure Activities:** exercise room. **Guest Services:** valet and coin laundry, area transportation-within 5 mi. **Business Services:** meeting rooms, business center. **Cards:** AX, CB, DC, DS, MC, VI. **Special Amenities:** free continental breakfast and free newspaper. *(See color ad p 378)*

SOME UNITS

[S/D] [🐾] [🍴] [ᴹ] [🅿] [⟲] [➤] [VCR] [🎞] [DATA PORT] [🖥] [🍽] [💻] /[✕]/

COURTYARD BY MARRIOTT

[SAVE]
▼▼▼▼

Phone: (954)475-1100   [122]

1/1-4/30	1P: $149-$159
12/1-12/31 & 10/1-11/30	1P: $109-$139
5/1-9/30	1P: $99-$129

Location: Just w of University Dr (SR 817); 0.5 mi sw of Broward Blvd (SR 842). Located next to the Broward Mall. 7780 **Small-scale Hotel** SW 6th St 33324. Fax: 954/424-8402. **Facility:** 149 units. 138 one-bedroom standard units. 11 one bedroom suites. 3 stories, interior corridors. *Bath:* combo or shower only. **Parking:** on-site. **Terms:** [BP] & [CP] meal plans available, package plans, 10% service charge. **Amenities:** high-speed Internet (fee), voice mail, irons, hair dryers. **Pool(s):** heated outdoor. **Leisure Activities:** whirlpool, exercise room. **Guest Services:** valet and coin laundry. **Business Services:** meeting rooms, fax (fee). **Cards:** AX, CB, DC, DS, JC, MC, VI. *(See ad p 369)*

SOME UNITS

[S/D] [🍴] [ᴹ] [🅿] [⟲] [➤] [🎞] [DATA PORT] [💻] /[✕] [🍽]/

HAMPTON INN PLANTATION

(AAA) [SAVE]
▼▼▼▼

Phone: (954)382-4500   [119]

12/22-4/15 [ECP]	1P: $99-$149	2P: $109-$159
12/1-12/21 & 4/16-11/30 [ECP]	1P: $79-$109	2P: $89-$119

Location: Just w of University Dr (SR 817); 0.5 mi sw of Broward Blvd. Located next to the Broward Mall. 7801 SW 6th St 33324. Fax: 954/382-4510. **Facility:** 128 one-bedroom standard units. 5 stories, interior corridors. *Bath:* **Small-scale Hotel** combo or shower only. **Parking:** on-site. **Amenities:** high-speed Internet (fee), dual phone lines, voice mail, irons, hair dryers. **Pool(s):** heated outdoor. **Leisure Activities:** whirlpool, exercise room. **Guest Services:** valet and coin laundry, area transportation-within 10 mi. **Business Services:** meeting rooms, fax. **Cards:** AX, DC, DS, JC, MC, VI. **Special Amenities:** free continental breakfast and free local telephone calls.

SOME UNITS

[S/D] [🍴] [ᴹ] [🅿] [⟲] [➤] [🎞] [DATA PORT] [💻] /[✕] [VCR] [🖥] [🍽]/

(See map p. 357)

HOLIDAY INN PLANTATION/SAWGRASS   Phone: (954)472-5600   124

(AAA) [SAVE]
▼▼▼▼

12/26-4/30	2P: $119
12/1-12/25	2P: $89
10/1-11/30	2P: $79
5/1-9/30	2P: $69

Small-scale Hotel **Location:** SR 817, just s of jct SR 838 (Sunrise Blvd). 1711 N University Dr 33322. Fax: 954/370-3201. **Facility:** 335 units. 319 one-bedroom standard units. 16 one-bedroom suites. 2-5 stories, interior/exterior corridors. *Bath:* combo or shower only. **Parking:** on-site. **Terms:** cancellation fee imposed, small pets only. **Amenities:** video games (fee), dual phone lines, voice mail, irons, hair dryers. **Dining:** 6 am-11 pm, Fri & Sat-midnight, cocktails. **Pool(s):** heated outdoor. **Leisure Activities:** exercise room. **Guest Services:** valet and coin laundry, area transportation-within 5 mi. **Business Services:** meeting rooms, fax (fee). **Cards:** AX, CB, DC, DS, MC, VI. **Special Amenities: free newspaper and free room upgrade (subject to availability with advanced reservations).** *(See color ad p 405 & opposite inside back cover)*

SOME UNITS

[icons] FEE

LA QUINTA INN & SUITES   Phone: (954)476-6047   115

[SAVE]
▼▼▼▼
Small-scale Hotel

| All Year | 1P: $89-$129 | 2P: $95-$135 |

Location: I-595, exit 5 (University Dr/SR 817 N), just w. Located in Crossroad Office Park. 8101 Peters Rd 33324. Fax: 954/476-6547. **Facility:** 131 units. 127 one-bedroom standard units. 4 one-bedroom suites. 4 stories, interior corridors. *Bath:* combo or shower only. **Parking:** on-site. **Terms:** [ECP] meal plan available, small pets only ($50 deposit). **Amenities:** video games (fee), voice mail, irons, hair dryers. *Some:* dual phone lines. **Pool(s):** heated outdoor. **Leisure Activities:** whirlpool, exercise room. **Guest Services:** valet and coin laundry. **Business Services:** meeting rooms, fax (fee). **Cards:** AX, CB, DC, DS, JC, MC, VI. *(See color ad p 377)*

SOME UNITS

[icons]

RESIDENCE INN BY MARRIOTT-PLANTATION   Phone: (954)723-0300   114

[SAVE]
▼▼▼▼
Small-scale Hotel

| 12/26-4/30 [ECP] | 1P: $115-$135 | 2P: $115-$135 |
| 12/1-12/25 & 5/1-11/30 [ECP] | 1P: $99-$109 | 2P: $99-$109 |

Location: University Dr (SR 817), just n of jct Broward Blvd (SR 842). 130 N University Dr 33324. Fax: 954/474-7385. **Facility:** 138 units. 34 one-bedroom standard units with kitchens. 74 one- and 30 two-bedroom suites with kitchens. 1-4 stories, interior corridors. *Bath:* combo or shower only. **Parking:** on-site. **Terms:** small pets only ($150-$200 extra charge). **Amenities:** video games (fee), dual phone lines, voice mail, irons, hair dryers. **Pool(s):** heated outdoor. **Leisure Activities:** whirlpool, exercise room, sports court. **Guest Services:** complimentary evening beverages: Mon-Thurs, valet and coin laundry. **Business Services:** meeting rooms, fax (fee). **Cards:** AX, CB, DC, DS, JC, MC, VI.

SOME UNITS

[icons]

SHERATON SUITES-PLANTATION   Phone: (954)424-3300   120

(AAA) [SAVE]
▼▼▼▼

1/1-5/22	1P: $289-$329	2P: $289-$329	XP: $20	F18
12/1-12/31	1P: $271-$311	2P: $271-$311	XP: $20	F18
10/15-11/30	1P: $269-$309	2P: $269-$309	XP: $20	F18
5/23-10/14	1P: $239-$279	2P: $239-$279	XP: $20	F18

Large-scale Hotel **Location:** On SR 817 (University Dr), 0.3 mi n of jct SR 842 (Broward Blvd). Located at Fashion Mall. 311 N University Dr 33324. Fax: 954/452-8887. **Facility:** 263 one-bedroom suites, some with whirlpools. 9 stories, interior corridors. *Bath:* combo or shower only. **Parking:** on-site. **Terms:** cancellation fee imposed. **Amenities:** video games (fee), dual phone lines, voice mail, honor bars, irons, hair dryers. *Some:* fax. **Dining:** 6:30 am-2:30 & 5:30-10:30 pm, Sat & Sun from 7 am, cocktails. **Pool(s):** heated outdoor. **Leisure Activities:** sauna, whirlpool, exercise room. **Guest Services:** valet laundry, airport transportation (fee)-Fort Lauderdale Airport. **Business Services:** meeting rooms. *Fee:* PC, fax. **Cards:** AX, CB, DC, DS, JC, MC, VI. **Special Amenities: early check-in/late check-out and free newspaper.** *(See color ad p 5)*

SOME UNITS

[icons] FEE

STAYBRIDGE SUITES BY HOLIDAY INN FT LAUDERDALE-PLANTATION   Phone: (954)577-9696   121

▼▼▼▼
Small-scale Hotel

| 12/1-4/14 [BP] | 1P: $109-$179 |
| 4/15-11/30 [BP] | 1P: $99-$149 |

Location: I-595, exit 4, 1.7 mi n on Pine Island Rd. 410 N Pine Island Rd 33324. Fax: 954/577-9648. **Facility:** 141 units. 61 one-bedroom standard units with efficiencies. 49 one- and 31 two-bedroom suites with kitchens. 4 stories, interior corridors. *Bath:* combo or shower only. **Parking:** on-site. **Terms:** 5 day cancellation notice, small pets only ($75 fee). **Amenities:** dual phone lines, voice mail, irons, hair dryers. *Fee:* video library, high-speed Internet. **Pool(s):** heated outdoor. **Leisure Activities:** exercise room, sports court. **Guest Services:** sundries, complimentary laundry. **Business Services:** meeting rooms, business center. **Cards:** AX, CB, DC, DS, JC, MC, VI.

SOME UNITS

[icons]

WELLESLEY INN & SUITES (PLANTATION)   Phone: (954)473-8257   116

(AAA) [SAVE]
▼▼▼▼

| 12/16-3/31 | 1P: $89 | 2P: $119 | XP: $10 | F17 |
| 12/1-12/15 & 4/1-11/30 | 1P: $59 | 2P: $79 | XP: $10 | F17 |

Location: 0.3 mi w of University Dr (SR 817); 0.5 mi sw of jct Broward Blvd (SR 842). Located next to the Broward Mall. 7901 SW 6th St 33324. Fax: 954/473-9804. **Facility:** 105 units. 92 one-bedroom standard units. 13 one-bedroom suites. 4 stories, interior corridors. *Bath:* combo or shower only. **Parking:** on-site. **Terms:** [ECP] meal plan available, small pets only ($10 extra charge). **Amenities:** voice mail, irons, hair dryers. *Fee:* video games, high-speed Internet. *Some:* dual phone lines. **Pool(s):** heated outdoor. **Guest Services:** valet laundry. **Business Services:** fax (fee). **Cards:** AX, CB, DC, DS, JC, MC, VI. **Special Amenities: free continental breakfast and free newspaper.** *(See color ad p 365)*

SOME UNITS

[icons]

(See map p. 357)

——— The following lodging was either not evaluated or did not ———
meet AAA rating requirements but is listed for your information only.

RENAISSANCE FT. LAUDERDALE/PLANTATION HOTEL

				Phone: 954/472-2252
[fyi]	12/1-4/15	1P: $119-$159	2P: $119-$159	XP: $20
	4/16-6/27	1P: $99-$129	2P: $99-$129	XP: $20
Motel	6/28-11/30	1P: $89-$109	2P: $89-$109	XP: $20

Too new to rate, opening scheduled for October 2002. **Location:** I-95, to exit I-595 w to Pine Island Rd, just n. 1230 Pine Island Rd 33324. **Fax:** 954/472-2295. **Amenities:** coffeemakers, pool. **Cards:** AX, CB, DC, DS, JC, MC, VI.

——— **WHERE TO DINE** ———

BRASSERIE MAX | **Lunch:** $5-$13 | **Dinner:** $8-$17 | **Phone:** 954/424-8000 | [131]

▼▼ ▼▼
American

Location: I-95, exit Broward Blvd; in Fashion Mall. 321 N University Dr 33324. **Hours:** 11:30 am-10 pm, Fri & Sat-11 pm, Sun-9 pm. **Closed:** 11/27, 12/25. **Reservations:** suggested; 6 or more. **Features:** The fashionable bistro sets the mood with soft lighting, a grand piano and cozy wooden booths. Entrees include nut-crusted dolphin with spicy sweet potato sauce. The almond basket makes a memorable dessert. On Sunday, diners can build their own omelets until 1 p.m. Casual dress; cocktails. **Parking:** on-site. **Cards:** AX, MC, VI. [X]

TAKEYAMA | **Lunch:** $7-$12 | **Dinner:** $10-$30 | **Phone:** 954/792-0350 | [133]

▼▼▼ ▼▼▼
Japanese

Location: Just n of Broward Blvd at NW 69th Ave and Cypress Rd; in Cypress Square Center. 6920 Cypress Rd 33317. **Hours:** 11:30 am-2 & 5:30-9:30 pm, Fri & Sat-10 pm. **Closed:** Mon. **Reservations:** suggested; on weekends. **Features:** This sushi bar presents a variety of dishes that could be considered edible works of art. The Takeyama inside-out roll has a unique stone crab filling. Vegetarian sushi is offered with sukiyaki, teriyaki and tempura dishes. Try the unusual pizza sushi. Dressy casual; beer & wine only. **Parking:** on-site. **Cards:** AX, MC, VI.

POMPANO BEACH pop. 78,191

——— **WHERE TO STAY** ———

BEST WESTERN BEACHCOMBER RESORT & VILLAS

				Phone: (954)941-7830	
(AAA) [SAVE]	2/1-4/30	1P: $155-$250	2P: $155-$250	XP: $10	F17
	12/1-1/31	1P: $147-$250	2P: $147-$250	XP: $10	F17
▼▼▼ ▼▼▼	10/1-11/30	1P: $101-$250	2P: $101-$250	XP: $10	F17
	5/1-9/30	1P: $99-$250	2P: $99-$250	XP: $10	F17

Small-scale Hotel Location: SR A1A, 0.5 mi s of jct SR 814 (Atlantic Blvd). 1200 S Ocean Blvd 33062. **Fax:** 954/942-7680. **Facility:** 143 units. 139 one-bedroom standard units, some with efficiencies. 4 two-bedroom suites ($195-$250) with kitchens. 1-8 stories, interior/exterior corridors. *Bath:* combo or shower only. **Parking:** on-site. **Terms:** 11% service charge. **Amenities:** video games (fee), voice mail, safes, irons, hair dryers. **Dining:** 7 am-3 & 5-9 pm, cocktails. **Pool(s):** outdoor, heated outdoor. **Leisure Activities:** putting green, playground, shuffleboard, volleyball. **Guest Services:** gift shop, coin laundry. **Business Services:** meeting rooms, fax (fee). **Cards:** AX, CB, DC, DS, MC, VI. SOME UNITS

(icons)

CROTON ARMS APARTMENTS/MOTEL

				Phone: (954)941-1766	
▼▼ ▼▼	12/19-3/31	1P: $60-$100	2P: $60-$100	XP: $10	F5
	12/1-12/18 & 11/1-11/30	1P: $40-$65	2P: $40-$65	XP: $10	F5
Motel	4/1-10/31	1P: $39-$60	2P: $39-$60	XP: $10	F5

Location: Just w of SR A1A, 1.3 mi n of jct SR 814 (Atlantic Blvd). Located in a quiet area. 3237 NE 11th St 33062. **Fax:** 954/941-1775. **Facility:** 20 units. 3 one-bedroom standard units with efficiencies. 17 one-bedroom suites with kitchens. 1-2 stories (no elevator), exterior corridors. *Bath:* combo or shower only. **Parking:** on-site. **Terms:** 3 night minimum stay, 60 day cancellation notice-fee imposed, weekly rates available. **Pool(s):** heated outdoor. **Leisure Activities:** whirlpool, shuffleboard. **Guest Services:** coin laundry. **Cards:** DC, MC, VI. SOME UNITS

(icons)

DOLPHIN APARTMENT MOTEL

				Phone: (954)941-7373	
(AAA) [SAVE]	2/1-3/31	1P: $70-$103	2P: $70-$103	XP: $8	F10
	12/1-1/31	1P: $60-$93	2P: $60-$93	XP: $8	F10
▼▼ ▼▼	4/1-4/30	1P: $45-$75	2P: $45-$75	XP: $8	F10
Motel	5/1-11/30	1P: $40-$65	2P: $40-$65	XP: $8	F10

Location: 0.8 mi n on SR A1A from jct SR 814 (Atlantic Blvd), just w. 3215 NE 7th St 33062. **Fax:** 954/941-7388. **Facility:** 20 units. 17 one-bedroom standard units, some with efficiencies or kitchens. 3 one-bedroom suites with kitchens. 2 stories, exterior corridors. **Parking:** on-site. **Terms:** 30 day cancellation notice. **Amenities:** voice mail. *Some:* CD players. **Pool(s):** heated outdoor. **Leisure Activities:** barbecue grill, bicycles, shuffleboard. **Guest Services:** coin laundry. **Cards:** MC, VI.

(icons)

FAIRFIELD ROYAL VISTA

			Phone: 954/233-7500
▼▼▼ ▼▼▼	All Year	1P: $99-$199	2P: $129-$299

Condominium **Location:** Atlantic Blvd (SR 814), 0.6 mi s on S Ocean Blvd (SR A1A). 1110 S Ocean Blvd 33062. **Fax:** 954/233-7513. **Facility:** 95 units. 33 one- and 62 two-bedroom suites with kitchens and whirlpools. 6-9 stories, interior corridors. **Parking:** on-site. **Terms:** check-in 4 pm. **Amenities:** video library (fee), CD players, voice mail, safes, irons. **Pool(s):** 2 heated outdoor, wading. **Leisure Activities:** fishing, horseshoes, volleyball. *Fee:* sailboats, game room. **Guest Services:** complimentary laundry. **Business Services:** fax (fee).

(icons)

HOLIDAY INN POMPANO BEACH
Phone: (954)781-1300

Small-scale Hotel

12/26-4/30	1P: $155-$195	2P: $155-$195	XP: $10	F19
5/1-11/30	1P: $110-$160	2P: $110-$160	XP: $10	F19
12/1-12/25	1P: $105-$145	2P: $105-$145	XP: $10	F19

Location: Just e of SR A1A at Atlantic Blvd. 9 N Pompano Beach Blvd 33062. Fax: 954/782-5585. **Facility:** 103 units. 96 one-bedroom standard units. 7 one-bedroom suites ($160-$195). 8 stories, interior corridors. *Bath:* combo or shower only. **Parking:** on-site. **Terms:** cancellation fee imposed. **Amenities:** video games (fee), dual phone lines, voice mail, irons, hair dryers. **Pool(s):** heated outdoor. **Leisure Activities:** exercise room. **Guest Services:** valet and coin laundry. **Business Services:** meeting rooms, fax (fee). **Cards:** AX, CB, DC, DS, JC, MC, VI. *(See color ad below)*

SOME UNITS

OCEAN BEACH RESORT
Phone: 954/941-7300

Motel

12/1-4/21	1P: $105-$155	2P: $105-$155	XP: $10	F18
4/22-5/31 & 10/1-11/30	1P: $89-$139	2P: $89-$139	XP: $10	F18
6/1-9/30	1P: $79-$129	2P: $79-$129	XP: $10	F18

Location: SR A1A, 0.8 mi s of jct SR A1A (Atlantic Blvd). 1350 S Ocean Blvd 33062. Fax: 954/941-7300. **Facility:** 133 units. 113 one-bedroom standard units, some with efficiencies. 20 one-bedroom suites ($109-$225) with kitchens. 1-3 stories, exterior corridors. *Bath:* combo or shower only. **Parking:** on-site. **Terms:** 2 night minimum stay - weekends, cancellation fee imposed. **Amenities:** irons, hair dryers. **Pool(s):** 2 heated outdoor. **Leisure Activities:** putting green, 3 tennis courts. *Fee:* boat dock. **Guest Services:** valet and coin laundry. **Business Services:** meeting rooms, fax (fee). **Cards:** AX, DC, DS, MC, VI.

SOME UNITS

OCEAN POINT RESORT
Phone: 954/782-5300

Small-scale Hotel

12/15-4/15 [CP]	1P: $109	2P: $109
12/1-12/14 & 4/16-11/30 [CP]	1P: $79	2P: $79

Location: On SR A1A, 1.3 mi n of jct SR 814 (Atlantic Blvd). 1208 N Ocean Blvd 33062. Fax: 954/946-1853. **Facility:** 94 one-bedroom standard units. 9 stories, interior corridors. **Parking:** on-site. **Terms:** 3 day cancellation notice-fee imposed, [ECP] meal plan available. **Amenities:** voice mail, irons, hair dryers. **Pool(s):** heated outdoor. **Leisure Activities:** exercise room, shuffleboard. *Fee:* massage. **Guest Services:** gift shop, valet and coin laundry. **Business Services:** meeting rooms, business center. **Cards:** AX, DS, MC, VI.

SOME UNITS

PALM-AIRE RESORT & SPA
Phone: (954)972-3300

Resort Condominium

All Year	1P: $99-$269	2P: $99-$269

Location: I-95, exit 36, 1 mi w on SR 814 (Atlantic Blvd), 0.4 mi s on Powerline Rd. 2601 Palm Aire Dr N 33069. Fax: 954/968-2711. **Facility:** The resort offers supervised spa facilities; transportation while on the grounds; and large, nicely decorated rooms, some overlooking a golf course. 301 units. 15 one-bedroom standard units with efficiencies. 70 one-, 213 two- and 3 three-bedroom suites with kitchens, some with whirlpools. 10-13 stories, interior corridors. **Parking:** on-site. **Terms:** check-in 4 pm, cancellation fee imposed. **Amenities:** video library (fee), CD players, voice mail, irons. *Some:* hair dryers. **Pool(s):** 3 heated outdoor. **Leisure Activities:** sauna, whirlpools, spa, volleyball. *Fee:* golf-90 holes, 37 tennis courts (30 lighted), game room. **Guest Services:** complimentary laundry. **Business Services:** fax (fee). **Cards:** AX, DC, DS, MC, VI.

SOME UNITS

RONNY DEE MOTEL
Phone: (954)943-3020

Motel

2/1-3/31	1P: $65-$80	2P: $65-$80	XP: $7	F4
12/1-1/7	1P: $52-$70	2P: $52-$70	XP: $7	F4
1/8-1/31	1P: $49-$65	2P: $49-$65	XP: $7	F4
4/1-11/30	1P: $35-$41	2P: $35-$41	XP: $5	F4

Location: SR A1A, just s of jct SR 814 (Atlantic Blvd). 717 S Ocean Blvd 33062. Fax: 954/783-5112. **Facility:** Designated smoking area. 31 one-bedroom standard units, some with efficiencies or kitchens. 1-2 stories (no elevator), exterior corridors. *Bath:* combo or shower only. **Parking:** on-site. **Terms:** 21 day cancellation notice-fee imposed, weekly rates available. **Pool(s):** heated outdoor. **Leisure Activities:** barbecue grills, shuffleboard. **Guest Services:** coin laundry. **Cards:** MC, VI. **Special Amenities:** free room upgrade and preferred room (each subject to availability with advanced reservations).

SANTA BARBARA RESORT AND YACHT CLUB   **Phone: 954/941-5566**

▼▼◇◇▼   All Year   2P: $99-$299
                     Location: Atlantic Blvd (SR 814), 0.7 mi s on S Ocean Blvd (SR A1A). 1301 S Ocean Blvd 33062. **Fax:** 954/941-3010.
Condominium   **Facility:** 90 units. 36 one-bedroom standard units with efficiencies and whirlpools. 36 one- and 18 two-
                     bedroom suites with kitchens and whirlpools. 10 stories, interior corridors. **Parking:** on-site. **Terms:** check-in
4 pm, 3 day cancellation notice-fee imposed, weekly rates available. **Amenities:** video library (fee), CD players, voice mail, irons.
Pool(s): heated outdoor. **Leisure Activities:** whirlpool, fishing. *Fee:* charter fishing, game room. **Guest Services:** coin laundry.
Business Services: fax (fee). **Cards:** AX, DC, MC, VI.

SEA CASTLE RESORT INN   **Phone: (954)941-2570**

(AAA) [SAVE]   12/1-4/15 [CP]   1P: $99-$149   2P: $99-$149   XP: $12   F12
                     4/16-11/30 [CP]   1P: $48-$94   2P: $48-$94   XP: $7   F12
▼▼▼ ▼▼▼   **Location:** SR A1A, 1 mi n of jct SR 814 (Atlantic Blvd). 730 N Ocean Blvd 33062. **Fax:** 954/941-3150. **Facility:** 40
Motel   one-bedroom standard units, some with efficiencies. 2 stories (no elevator), exterior corridors. **Parking:** on-
                     site. **Terms:** weekly rates available, pets ($15 extra charge, in designated units). **Amenities:** voice mail.
                     Pool(s): heated outdoor. **Leisure Activities:** barbecue grill. **Guest Services:** coin laundry. **Cards:** AX, CB,
DC, MC, VI.
                                                                                                       SOME UNITS

SEA GARDENS BEACH & TENNIS RESORT   **Phone: (954)943-6200**

▼▼◇◇▼   12/1-4/15   2P: $259-$389 XP: $10   F
                     10/1-11/30   2P: $159-$259
Condominium   4/16-9/30   2P: $109-$159
                     Location: Atlantic Blvd (SR 814), 0.7 mi n on SR A1A. 615 N Ocean Blvd 33062. **Fax:** 954/783-0047. **Facility:** 217
units. 54 one-bedroom standard units with efficiencies. 58 one- and 105 two-bedroom suites with kitchens and whirlpools. 1-10
stories, interior/exterior corridors. **Parking:** on-site. **Terms:** check-in 4 pm, 3 night minimum stay, 3 day cancellation notice-fee
imposed. **Amenities:** video library (fee), CD players, voice mail, irons. **Pool(s):** outdoor, 3 heated outdoor. **Leisure Activities:** whirlpools, fishing, 7 lighted tennis courts, bicycles, exercise room, shuffleboard, volleyball. *Fee:* sailboats, windsurfing,
scuba diving, snorkeling, game room. **Guest Services:** coin laundry. **Business Services:** meeting rooms, fax (fee). **Cards:** AX,
DC, MC, VI.

SUPER 8 MOTEL   **Phone: (954)943-3500**

(AAA) [SAVE]   2/1-4/15 [CP]   1P: $69-$89   2P: $69-$89   XP: $5   F16
                     12/1-11/30 [CP]   1P: $49-$79   2P: $49-$79   XP: $5   F16
▼▼▼ ▼▼▼   4/16-11/30 [CP]   1P: $49-$59   2P: $49-$59   XP: $5   F16
                     Location: Just e of US 1 and NE 10th St; 0.8 mi n from Atlantic Blvd. 2300 NE 10th St 33063. **Fax:** 954/943-3500.
Small-scale Hotel   **Facility:** 60 one-bedroom standard units. 2 stories, interior corridors. **Parking:** on-site. **Terms:** 3 day cancel-
                     lation notice. **Pool(s):** small outdoor. **Business Services:** fax (fee). **Cards:** AX, CB, DC, DS, MC, VI.
                                                                                                       SOME UNITS

SURF SIDE MOTEL   **Phone: 954/942-5507**

(AAA) [SAVE]   12/1-4/15   1P: $85-$95   2P: $89-$99   XP: $10
                     4/16-4/30   1P: $55-$70   2P: $59-$75   XP: $10
▼▼▼   5/1-11/30   1P: $49-$65   2P: $55-$75   XP: $10
                     Location: I-95, exit 36A, Atlantic Blvd E to SR A1A, just s. 710 S Ocean Blvd 33062. **Fax:** 954/785-9713. **Facility:** 35
Motel   units. 31 one-bedroom standard units, some with kitchens. 4 one-bedroom suites with kitchens. 2 stories, ex-
                     terior corridors. *Bath:* combo or shower only. **Parking:** on-site. **Terms:** 21 day cancellation notice.
Amenities: voice mail. **Pool(s):** heated outdoor. **Leisure Activities:** barbecue grills, shuffleboard. **Guest Services:** coin laundry.
Business Services: fax (fee). **Cards:** AX, DC, DS, MC, VI.
                                                                                                       SOME UNITS

TRADERS OCEAN RESORT   **Phone: 954/941-8400**

▼▼ ▼▼   Property failed to provide current rates
                     Location: SR A1A, 1.5 mi s of jct SR 814 (Atlantic Blvd). 1600 S Ocean Blvd 33062. **Fax:** 954/941-1024. **Facility:** 93
Motel   units. 84 one-bedroom standard units, some with efficiencies. 9 one-bedroom suites with kitchens. 3 stories,
                     exterior corridors. **Parking:** on-site. **Amenities:** voice mail, safes (fee). **Pool(s):** heated outdoor. **Leisure Ac-
tivities:** shuffleboard, volleyball. **Guest Services:** coin laundry. **Cards:** AX, CB, DC, DS, MC, VI.
                                                                                                       SOME UNITS

VILLAMAR INN   **Phone: (954)941-3530**

(AAA) [SAVE]   12/19-4/19   1P: $89-$149   2P: $89-$149   XP: $10   D10
                     12/1-12/18 & 4/20-11/30   1P: $48-$94   2P: $48-$94   XP: $10   D10
▼▼▼ ▼▼▼   **Location:** SR A1A, 1 mi n of jct SR 814 (Atlantic Blvd). 740 N Ocean Blvd 33062. **Fax:** 954/782-2778. **Facility:** 18
Motel   one-bedroom standard units, some with kitchens. 1-2 stories (no elevator), exterior corridors. **Parking:** on-
                     site. **Terms:** 30 day cancellation notice. **Amenities:** safes (fee). **Pool(s):** heated outdoor. **Leisure Activi-
                     ties:** putting green, shuffleboard. **Guest Services:** coin laundry. **Cards:** MC, VI. **Special Amenities:** early
check-in/late check-out and preferred room (subject to availability with advanced reservations).
                                                                                                       SOME UNITS

WELLESLEY INN & SUITES (FT. LAUDERDALE/CYPRESS CREEK)   Phone: (954)783-1050

(AAA) (SAVE)

1/1-4/21	1P: $114-$200	2P: $114-$200	XP: $10	F18
4/22-11/30	1P: $84-$170	2P: $84-$170	XP: $5	F18
12/1-12/31	1P: $79-$165	2P: $79-$165	XP: $5	F18

Location: I-95, exit 33B (Cypress Creek Rd) to Andrews Ave, just s, then turn left onto McNab St. 1401 SW 15th St
Small-scale Hotel 33069. Fax: 954/783-1610. **Facility:** 130 units. 110 one-bedroom standard units with kitchens. 20 one-bedroom suites with efficiencies. 3 stories, interior corridors. *Bath:* combo or shower only. **Parking:** on-site.
Terms: weekly rates available, [CP] meal plan available, small pets only. **Amenities:** dual phone lines, voice mail, irons, hair dryers. **Fee:** video games, high-speed Internet. **Pool(s):** heated outdoor. **Leisure Activities:** limited exercise equipment. **Guest Services:** valet and coin laundry. **Cards:** AX, CB, DC, DS, JC, MC, VI. **Special Amenities:** free continental breakfast and free newspaper. *(See color ad p 365)*

SOME UNITS

——— WHERE TO DINE ———

CHEZ PORKY'S   Lunch: $5-$16   Dinner: $7-$19   Phone: 954/946-5590

American
Location: Atlantic Blvd (SR 820), 0.6 mi s on Old Dixie Hwy, then 0.3 mi e; in Robert Thomas Plaza. 105 SW Sixth St 33060. **Hours:** 11 am-9:30 pm, Sat & Sun 4:30 pm-10 pm. Closed major holidays. **Reservations:** suggested; weekends. **Features:** Hard to find friendlier folks than at this Louisiana kitchen and barbecue. Baby back ribs, chicken and Cajun seafood dishes are served with your choice of two delicious side dishes. This restaurant is worth any wait, so sit back and relax for a spell. Casual dress; beer & wine only. **Parking:** on-site. **Cards:** AX, MC, VI.

DARREL & OLIVER'S CAFE MAXX   Dinner: $16-$38   Phone: 954/782-0606

(AAA)

Regional
American
Location: SR 814, Atlantic Blvd, 0.3 mi e of jct US 1. 2601 E Atlantic Blvd at NE 26th St 33062. **Hours:** 5:30 pm-11 pm, Sun-10 pm. Closed: 7/4; also Super Bowl Sun. **Reservations:** suggested. **Features:** A cafe ambience contributes to the casually elegant experience diners have come to expect here. Innovatively prepared and presented dishes, which incorporate the freshest of ingredients, are well-complemented by an award-winning wine list. Dressy casual; beer & wine only. **Parking:** valet. **Cards:** AX, DC, DS, MC, VI.

NICKEL'S   Lunch: $7-$13   Dinner: $7-$13   Phone: 954/942-7030

American
Location: I-95, exit 38A southbound; exit 38 northbound (Copans Rd), 2.1 mi e, then just n. 2341 N Federal Hwy 33060. **Hours:** 7 am-11 pm, Fri & Sat-1 am. **Features:** Lots of pictures of '50s-era stars and entertainers decorate the nostalgic diner. The menu revolves around such simple, wholesome selections as meatloaf, overstuffed sandwiches, burgers, miniature pizzas and tall desserts. Fun and upbeat, this place caters to families. Casual dress; cocktails. **Parking:** on-site. **Cards:** AX, CB, DC, DS, MC, VI.

SUNFISH GRILL   Dinner: $18-$30   Phone: 954/788-2434

American
Location: Just e of US 1, just over the Intracoastal Bridge on the north side; in a small shopping complex. 2771 E Atlantic Blvd 33062. **Hours:** 5:30 pm-9:30 pm, Fri & Sat-10:30 pm; Tues-Sat 5:30 pm-9:30 pm 5/1-12/31. Closed major holidays. **Reservations:** suggested. **Features:** Chef Anthony Sindaco calls his artistic creations "contemporary American seafood," but he also prepares some meat dishes. Aromas from the open kitchen are enticing, and desserts are worth the splurge. The lengthy wine list includes hard-to-find selections as well as the traditionals. The decor is eclectic. Smoke free premises. Dressy casual; beer & wine only. **Parking:** on-site. **Cards:** AX, CB, DC, DS, JC, MC, VI.

VESUVIO'S RESTAURANT   Dinner: $12-$28   Phone: 954/941-1594

Italian
Location: 2715 E Atlantic Blvd 33062. **Hours:** 5:30 pm-11 pm. Closed: 7/1-7/31 & Mon 5/1-12/25. **Reservations:** suggested. **Features:** You'll have to wait for the made-to-order entrees, but every second will be worth it. The many offerings of veal, chicken, beef, vegetables and seafood are just delicious. Cozy and crowded at the same time, the restaurant boasts a friendly wait staff. cocktails. **Parking:** on-site. **Cards:** AX, CB, DC, DS, MC, VI.

SUNRISE pop. 85,779   (See map p. 357; index p. 361)

——— WHERE TO STAY ———

BAYMONT INN & SUITES SUNRISE AT SAWGRASS   Phone: (954)846-1200   74

(AAA) (SAVE)

All Year [ECP]	1P: $79-$99	2P: $79-$99

Location: SW 136th Ave, 0.3 mi n of jct I-595, exit 1A and SR 84; 0.5 mi e of jct I-75 and Sawgrass Expwy. Adjoins the Blockbuster Family Entertainment Park. 13651 NW 2nd St 33325. Fax: 954/845-0100. **Facility:** 101 units. 98 one-bedroom standard units. 3 one-bedroom suites ($69-$149). 4 stories, interior corridors. *Bath:* combo or shower only. **Parking:** on-site. **Terms:** small pets only. **Amenities:** video games, voice mail, irons, hair dryers. **Pool(s):** heated outdoor. **Leisure Activities:** exercise room. **Guest Services:** valet and coin laundry.
Small-scale Hotel
Business Services: meeting rooms, fax (fee). **Cards:** AX, CB, DC, DS, MC, VI. **Special Amenities:** free continental breakfast and free newspaper. *(See color ad p 411)*

SOME UNITS

CROWNE PLAZA HOTEL AND RESORT SAWGRASS - FT. LAUDERDALE/SUNRISE   Phone: (954)851-1020   73

1/1-4/15	1P: $139-$155
12/1-12/31 & 4/16-11/30	1P: $99-$149

Large-scale Hotel
Location: I-75 to Sawgrass Expwy N, exit Sunrise Blvd E, then 1 mi. Located across from Sawgrass Mills. 13400 W Sunrise Blvd 33323. Fax: 954/851-0500. **Facility:** 250 units. 236 one-bedroom standard units. 14 one-bedroom suites, some with whirlpools. 10 stories, interior corridors. *Bath:* combo or shower only. **Parking:** on-site. **Terms:** [BP] & [CP] meal plans available, 19% service charge. **Amenities:** dual phone lines, voice mail, safes, irons, hair dryers. **Fee:** video games, high-speed Internet. *Some:* DVD players. **Pool(s):** heated outdoor. **Leisure Activities:** whirlpool, exercise room. **Guest Services:** gift shop, valet and coin laundry, area transportation. **Business Services:** meeting rooms, business center. **Cards:** AX, DC, DS, MC, VI.

SOME UNITS

FEE

(See map p. 357)

HILTON FORT LAUDERDALE SUNRISE

Phone: (954)748-7000   [75]

12/1-3/31	1P: $89-$109	2P: $89-$109
4/1-11/30	1P: $69-$109	2P: $69-$109

Location: University Dr (SR 817), just s of jct Oakland Park Blvd. 3003 N University Dr 33322. Fax: 954/572-0799. **Facility:** 297 units. 200 one-bedroom standard units. 97 one-bedroom suites ($89-$169). 6 stories, interior

Small-scale Hotel corridors. *Bath:* combo or shower only. **Parking:** on-site. **Amenities:** dual phone lines, voice mail, honor bars, irons, hair dryers. **Dining:** 7 am-10 pm, cocktails. **Pool(s):** heated outdoor. **Leisure Activities:** sauna, whirlpool, exercise room. **Guest Services:** gift shop, valet laundry, area transportation-local shopping malls. **Business Services:** meeting rooms, business center. **Cards:** AX, DC, DS, MC, VI. **Special Amenities:** free newspaper.

SOME UNITS

WELLESLEY INN & SUITES (SUNRISE)

Phone: (954)845-9929   [70]

1/1-3/31 [ECP]	1P: $99-$109	2P: $99-$109	XP: $10	F18
12/1-12/31 & 4/1-11/30 [ECP]	1P: $79-$99	2P: $79-$99	XP: $10	F18

Location: SW 136th Ave, 0.3 mi n of jct I-595, exit 1A and SR 84; 0.5 mi e of jct I-75 and Sawgrass Expwy. Adjoins the Blockbuster Family Entertainment Park. 13600 NW 2nd St 33325. Fax: 954/845-9996. **Facility:** 104 one-bedroom

Small-scale Hotel standard units. 4 stories, interior corridors. *Bath:* combo or shower only. **Parking:** on-site. **Terms:** small pets only. **Amenities:** video games, high-speed Internet, voice mail, irons, hair dryers. **Pool(s):** heated outdoor.

Guest Services: valet and coin laundry. **Business Services:** meeting rooms, fax (fee). **Cards:** AX, CB, DC, DS, JC, MC, VI. **Special Amenities:** free continental breakfast and free newspaper. *(See color ad p 365)*

SOME UNITS

-------- WHERE TO DINE --------

EMERALD COAST

Lunch: $8   Dinner: $17   Phone: 954/572-3822   [114]

Chinese

Location: Sawgrass Expwy on Commercial Blvd (SR 870), then 0.9 mi s; in the Gold's Plaza. 4519 N Pine Island Rd 33351. **Hours:** 11:30 am-2:30 & 4-9 pm, Fri-10:30 pm, Sat 4:30 pm-10:30 pm, Sun noon-2:30 & 4-9:30 pm. **Reservations:** accepted. **Features:** The Chinese buffet lays out more than 100 tasty food items on several different island stations. Most favorites are represented, as are such choices as crab legs, carved prime rib and sushi rolls. Save room for dessert, as you'll have plenty of selections from which to choose. Casual dress; cocktails. **Parking:** on-site. **Cards:** AX, DC, MC, VI.

LA STELLA SOUTH

Dinner: $13-$25   Phone: 954/748-4788   [105]

Italian

Location: At Springtree and University Dr; in Country Club Plaza. 3801 N University Dr 33351. **Hours:** 5 pm-10 pm. Closed: 11/27, 12/25; also Mon & Tues in summer. **Reservations:** suggested. **Features:** This old-fashioned restaurant presents dishes of veal, chicken, seafood and fish, including the distinctive fish marechiara. Photographs of such celebrities as Jackie Gleason and Natalie Cole decorate the walls of the pleasant, dimly lit dining room. beer & wine only. **Parking:** on-site. **Cards:** AX, DC, DS, MC, VI.

LEGAL SEA FOODS

Lunch: $5-$13   Dinner: $14-$30   Phone: 954/846-9011   [113]

Seafood

Location: Sawgrass Expwy/SR 869, exit 1 (Sunrise Blvd and SR 838), 1 mi e to Sawgrass Mills Mall. 2602 Sawgrass Mills Center 33323. **Hours:** 11:30 am-10 pm, Fri & Sat-11 pm, Sun noon-10 pm. Closed: 11/27, 12/25. **Features:** Step into the unusual and sophisticated dining room at The Oasis at Sawgrass for a taste of fresh seafood with an emphasis on New England. The wine list includes a good selection of complementary vintages. Dressy casual; cocktails. **Parking:** on-site. **Cards:** AX, MC, VI.

(See map p. 357)

RIO VISTA ISLE CAFE **Dinner:** $11-$25 **Phone:** 954/749-8118 109
♦♦♦ **Location:** Just w of University Blvd; in Lincoln Park West Shopping Plaza. 7836 NW 44th St 33351. **Hours:** 5 pm-10
pm, Sat & Sun from 4:30 pm. Closed: Mon, also Tues in summer. **Reservations:** suggested.
American **Features:** Tucked away in a small shopping plaza, the upscale, intimate restaurant offers a seasonally
changing menu and don't-miss specials. Another must: one of the excellent desserts. beer & wine only.
Parking: on-site. **Cards:** DS, MC, VI. ✕

The following restaurant has not been evaluated by AAA
but is listed for your information only.

RAINFOREST CAFE **Phone:** 954/851-1015
fyi Not evaluated. **Location:** Sawgrass Expwy/SR 869, exit 1 to Sawgrass Mills Mall. 12801 Sunrise Blvd 33323.
Features: The dining room has robotic animals from the rain forest as well as a simulated tropical storm
and many large aquariums. The menu lists kid-friendly choices as well as those catering to adults.

TAMARAC pop. 55,588 (See map p. 357; index p. 362)

——— WHERE TO STAY ———

BAYMONT INN & SUITES FT. LAUDERDALE/TAMARAC **Phone:** (954)485-7900 105
AAA SAVE All Year [ECP] 1P: $69-$89 2P: $69-$89
♦♦♦ **Location:** On SR 870 (Commercial Blvd), 0.8 mi e of Florida Tpke, exit 62, just e of jct SR 7 and US 441. 3800 W Com-
mercial Blvd 33309. Fax: 954/733-5469. **Facility:** 98 units. 95 one-bedroom standard units. 3 one-bedroom
suites. 3 stories, interior corridors. **Parking:** on-site. **Terms:** 3 day cancellation notice, small pets only ($50
Small-scale Hotel deposit). **Amenities:** video games (fee), voice mail, irons, hair dryers. **Pool(s):** small outdoor. **Guest Services:** valet and coin laundry. **Business Services:** meeting rooms. **Cards:** AX, CB, DC, DS, MC, VI.
Special Amenities: free continental breakfast and free newspaper. *(See color ad below)*

SOME UNITS
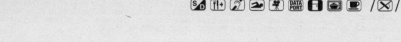

COMFORT INN **Phone:** (954)315-2900 104
AAA SAVE 12/16-4/15 [ECP] 1P: $89-$119 2P: $89-$119 XP: $10 F17
♦♦♦ 12/1-12/15 & 4/16-11/30 [ECP] 1P: $69-$99 2P: $69-$99 XP: $10 F17
Location: SR 870 (Commercial Blvd), 0.9 mi e of Florida Tpke, exit 62; 0.3 mi e of jct SR 7 and US 441. 3551 W Com-
mercial Blvd 33309. Fax: 954/733-1557. **Facility:** 70 one-bedroom standard units, some with whirlpools. 3 sto-
Small-scale Hotel ries, interior corridors. *Bath:* combo or shower only. **Parking:** on-site. **Terms:** cancellation fee imposed.
Amenities: dual phone lines, voice mail, safes (fee), irons, hair dryers. **Pool(s):** small heated outdoor.
Leisure Activities: whirlpool, exercise room. **Guest Services:** valet and coin laundry. **Business Services:** meeting rooms, fax
(fee). **Cards:** AX, CB, DC, DS, JC, MC, VI. **Special Amenities:** free continental breakfast and free local telephone calls.

SOME UNITS

(See map p. 357)

COMFORT SUITES SAWGRASS   Phone: (954)343-1322   [107]

[SAVE]	1/1-5/1	1P: $109-$139	2P: $109-$139	XP: $10	F12
	12/1-12/31	1P: $99-$129	2P: $99-$129	XP: $10	F12
▼▼▼◆	5/2-11/30	1P: $79-$109	2P: $79-$109	XP: $10	F12

Small-scale Hotel   **Location:** Sawgrass Expwy, exit 3, 2.1 mi e. 8301 W Commercial Blvd 33351. Fax: 954/343-1360. **Facility:** 80 units. 76 one-bedroom standard units. 4 one-bedroom suites with whirlpools. 4 stories, interior corridors. *Bath:* combo or shower only. **Parking:** on-site. **Terms:** [ECP] meal plan available. **Amenities:** dual phone lines, voice mail, safes (fee), irons, hair dryers. **Pool(s):** small heated outdoor. **Leisure Activities:** whirlpool, limited exercise equipment. **Guest Services:** valet and coin laundry. **Business Services:** meeting rooms, business center. **Cards:** AX, DC, DS, MC, VI.
SOME UNITS
[icons] / [X] /

HAMPTON INN, COMMERCIAL BLVD   Phone: (954)735-7575   [101]

[AAA] [SAVE]	2/1-2/28 [ECP]	1P: $119-$129	2P: $119-$129
	3/1-3/31 [ECP]	1P: $99-$119	2P: $99-$119
▼▼▼▼	12/1-1/31 [ECP]	1P: $79-$99	2P: $79-$99
	4/1-11/30 [ECP]	1P: $69-$89	2P: $69-$89

Small-scale Hotel   **Location:** On SR 870; Florida Tpke, just e to NW 47th Terrace, just w of SR 7/US 441. 4499 W Commercial Blvd 33319. Fax: 954/735-7330. **Facility:** 81 one-bedroom standard units. 3 stories, interior corridors. *Bath:* combo or shower only. **Parking:** on-site. **Terms:** check-in 4 pm. **Amenities:** dual phone lines, voice mail, irons, hair dryers. **Pool(s):** small heated outdoor. **Leisure Activities:** whirlpool, limited exercise equipment. **Business Services:** meeting rooms, fax (fee). **Cards:** AX, CB, DC, DS, JC, MC, VI. **Special Amenities:** free continental breakfast and free local telephone calls.
SOME UNITS
[icons] / [X] /

HOMESTEAD STUDIO SUITES HOTEL-FT LAUDERDALE/TAMARAC   Phone: 954/733-6644   [103]

▼▼ ▼▼	1/15-4/15	1P: $75	2P: $99	XP: $5
	12/1-1/14 & 4/16-11/30	1P: $55	2P: $69	XP: $5

Motel   **Location:** SR 870 (Commercial Blvd), 0.7 mi e of Florida Tpke, exit 62, then just e of jct SR 870 and US 441. 3873 W Commercial Blvd 33309. Fax: 954/733-9301. **Facility:** 145 one-bedroom standard units with kitchens. 2 stories (no elevator), exterior corridors. *Bath:* combo or shower only. **Parking:** on-site. **Terms:** cancellation fee imposed, pets ($75 fee). **Amenities:** voice mail, irons. **Guest Services:** coin laundry. **Cards:** AX, CB, DC, DS, JC, MC, VI.
SOME UNITS
[icons] / [X] /

WELLESLEY INN (FT. LAUDERDALE/TAMARAC)   Phone: (954)484-6909   [102]

[AAA] [SAVE]	12/17-4/15	1P: $79-$120	2P: $79-$120
	12/1-12/16 & 4/16-11/30	1P: $69-$79	2P: $69-$79
▼▼ ▼▼			

Small-scale Hotel   **Location:** SR 7 and US 441, just n of jct SR 870 (Commercial Blvd); 0.5 mi e of Florida Tpke, exit 62. 5070 N SR 7 33319. Fax: 954/731-2374. **Facility:** 100 units. 94 one-bedroom standard units. 6 one-bedroom suites. 4 stories, interior corridors. *Bath:* combo or shower only. **Parking:** on-site. **Terms:** small pets only ($10 fee). **Amenities:** video games (fee), voice mail, irons, hair dryers. **Pool(s):** heated outdoor. **Guest Services:** coin laundry. **Business Services:** fax (fee). **Cards:** AX, CB, DC, DS, MC, VI. **Special Amenities:** free continental breakfast and free newspaper. *(See color ad p 365)*
SOME UNITS
[icons] / [X] [icon] /

──────── **WHERE TO DINE** ────────

──────── *The following restaurant has not been evaluated by AAA* ────────
but is listed for your information only.

FLANIGAN'S SEAFOOD BAR & GRILL   Phone: 954/733-0514
[fyi]   Not evaluated. **Location:** 5450 N SR 7 33319. **Features:** The family-friendly restaurant is known for its baby back ribs, burgers and seafood.

WESTON pop. 49,286

──────── **WHERE TO STAY** ────────

AMERISUITES (FT. LAUDERDALE/WESTON)   Phone: (954)659-1555

[AAA] [SAVE]	12/26-4/15 & 10/1-11/30 [ECP]	1P: $109-$139	2P: $109-$139	XP: $10	F18
	12/1-12/25 [ECP]	1P: $89-$109	2P: $89-$109	XP: $10	F18
▼▼▼▼	4/16-9/30 [ECP]	1P: $79-$99	2P: $79-$99	XP: $10	F18

Small-scale Hotel   **Location:** I-75, exit 15, 0.5 mi w on Arvida Pkwy to Weston Rd, then n to N Commerce Pkwy, then just e. 2201 N Commerce Pkwy 33326. Fax: 954/659-1191. **Facility:** 128 one-bedroom standard units. 6 stories, interior corridors. *Bath:* combo or shower only. **Parking:** on-site. **Terms:** small pets only. **Amenities:** video games (fee), dual phone lines, voice mail, irons, hair dryers. **Pool(s):** small heated outdoor. **Leisure Activities:** limited exercise equipment. **Guest Services:** valet and coin laundry. **Business Services:** meeting rooms, fax (fee). **Cards:** AX, CB, DC, DS, JC, MC, VI.
(See color ad p 378)
SOME UNITS
[icons] / [X] [VCR] /

COURTYARD BY MARRIOTT WESTON   Phone: (954)343-2225

[SAVE]	12/1-3/31	1P: $79-$139	2P: $79-$139
	4/1-11/30	1P: $69-$129	2P: $69-$129
▼▼▼▼			

Small-scale Hotel   **Location:** I-75, exit 15 (Arvida Pkwy E) to Weston Rd, n to Commerce Pkwy, then just e. 2000 N Commerce Pkwy 33326. Fax: 954/343-2277. **Facility:** 174 units. 171 one-bedroom standard units. 3 one-bedroom suites. 6 stories, interior corridors. *Bath:* combo or shower only. **Parking:** on-site. **Terms:** [BP] meal plan available, package plans. **Amenities:** video games (fee), dual phone lines, voice mail, irons, hair dryers. *Some:* high-speed Internet (fee). **Pool(s):** heated outdoor. **Leisure Activities:** whirlpool, exercise room. **Guest Services:** sundries, valet and coin laundry. **Business Services:** meeting rooms, business center. **Cards:** AX, CB, DC, DS, JC, MC, VI. *(See ad p 369)*
SOME UNITS
[icons] / [X] [icon] /

RESIDENCE INN BY MARRIOTT WESTON

[SAVE]

▼▼▼▼

Small-scale Hotel

12/1-4/20 [BP]   1P: $159-$279
4/21-11/30 [BP]   1P: $109-$179

Phone: (954)659-8585

Location: I-75, exit 15 (Arvida Pkwy E) to Weston Rd, then just s. 2605 Weston Rd 33331. Fax: 954/659-3130. **Facility:** 100 units. 50 one-bedroom standard units with kitchens. 34 one- and 16 two-bedroom suites with kitchens. 3 stories, interior corridors. **Parking:** on-site. **Terms:** small pets only ($10 fee, $75 deposit). **Amenities:** dual phone lines, voice mail, irons, hair dryers. **Pool(s):** small heated outdoor. **Leisure Activities:** whirlpool, limited exercise equipment, sports court. **Guest Services:** sundries, valet and coin laundry. **Business Services:** meeting rooms, fax (fee). **Cards:** AX, CB, DC, DS, JC, MC, VI.

SOME UNITS

[S/D] [🛏] [❢] [⊇] [✕] [🎦] [DATA PORT] [🖥] [🖨] [🖵] / [✕] /

TOWNEPLACE SUITES BY MARRIOTT WESTON

[SAVE]

▼▼▼▼

Small-scale Hotel

12/1-4/20   1P: $119-$199
4/21-11/30   1P: $89-$139

Phone: (954)659-2234

Location: I-75, exit 15, 1 mi e on Arvida Pkwy to Bonaventure Blvd, n to Three Village Rd, then w. Located across the street from Weston Town Center. 1545 Three Village Rd 33326. Fax: 954/659-2282. **Facility:** 95 units. 69 one-bedroom standard units with kitchens. 4 one- and 22 two-bedroom suites with kitchens. 2-3 stories, interior corridors. *Bath:* combo or shower only. **Parking:** on-site. **Terms:** small pets only ($10 extra charge, $75 deposit). **Amenities:** dual phone lines, voice mail, irons, hair dryers. **Pool(s):** small heated outdoor. **Leisure Activities:** limited exercise equipment. **Guest Services:** valet and coin laundry. **Business Services:** fax (fee). **Cards:** AX, CB, DC, DS, JC, MC, VI.

SOME UNITS

[S/D] [🛏] [❢] [⊇] [🎦] [DATA PORT] [🖥] [🖨] [🖵] / [✕] /

WYNDHAM BONAVENTURE RESORT & SPA

[AAA] [SAVE]

▼▼▼▼

Resort

Large-scale Hotel

1/1-4/12   1P: $199   2P: $199   XP: $20   F12
12/1-12/31 & 10/1-11/30 1P: $169   2P: $169   XP: $20   F12
4/13-9/30   1P: $115   2P: $115   XP: $20   F12

Phone: (954)389-3300

Location: SR 84 and I-595; 11 mi w of turnpike, exit 54 at Bonaventure; westbound I-595, exit 1A (SW 136th Ave) to Bonaventure Blvd. 250 Racquet Club Rd 33326 (250 Racquet Club Rd, FORT LAUDERDALE). Fax: 954/384-1416. **Facility:** The resort offers full-service, European-style spa facilities; a waterfall pool area is surrounded by tropical trees and plants. 496 units. 389 one-bedroom standard units. 87 one- and 20 two-bedroom suites ($145-$250), some with whirlpools. 4 stories, exterior corridors. *Bath:* combo or shower only. **Parking:** on-site and valet. **Terms:** check-in 4 pm, cancellation fee imposed. **Amenities:** voice mail, honor bars, irons, hair dryers. **Dining:** 3 restaurants, 7 am-10 pm, cocktails, entertainment. **Pool(s):** 5 heated outdoor. **Leisure Activities:** saunas, whirlpools, recreation programs, jogging, playground, spa. *Fee:* golf-36 holes, golf instruction, 15 lighted tennis courts, racquetball courts, tennis instructions. **Guest Services:** gift shop, valet laundry, area transportation-within 5 mi. **Business Services:** conference facilities, business center. **Cards:** AX, DC, MC, VI.

SOME UNITS

[S/D] [➕] [❢] [🍸] [⛳] [🏊] [⊇] [🏊] [✕] [🎦] [DATA PORT] [🖵] / [✕] [VCR] [🖥] /
FEE   FEE

This ends listings for the Fort Lauderdale Vicinity.
The following page resumes the alphabetical listings of
cities in Florida.

FORT MYERS pop. 48,208—*See also FORT MYERS BEACH & NORTH FORT MYERS.*

------ **WHERE TO STAY** ------

BEST WESTERN AIRPORT INN

SAVE ▼▼▼ **Small-scale Hotel**

Phone: (239)561-7000

All Year — 1P: $59-$159 — 2P: $59-$159 — XP: $5 — F18

Location: I-75, exit 131, 0.6 mi w. 8955 Daniels Pkwy 33912. Fax: 239/561-5963. **Facility:** 106 units. 91 one-bedroom standard units. 15 one-bedroom suites, some with kitchens and/or whirlpools. 4 stories, interior corridors. *Bath:* combo or shower only. **Parking:** on-site. **Terms:** 3 day cancellation notice, [ECP] meal plan available, pets ($10 extra charge). **Amenities:** voice mail, safes (fee), irons, hair dryers. **Pool(s):** outdoor. **Leisure Activities:** whirlpool, exercise room. **Guest Services:** valet and coin laundry. **Business Services:** meeting rooms, fax (fee). **Cards:** AX, CB, DC, DS, JC, MC, VI.

SOME UNITS

🄢 ✈ 🛏 🍽 🐕 ➤ 🏋 🔌 🖥 ▤ 💻 / ✕ /

BEST WESTERN SPRINGS RESORT

Phone: (239)267-7900

AAA **SAVE** ▼▼▼ ▼▼▼ **Motel**

2/1-3/31	1P: $107-$116	2P: $107-$116
4/1-4/30	1P: $80-$90	2P: $80-$90
12/1-1/31	1P: $75-$85	2P: $75-$85
5/1-11/30	1P: $57-$74	2P: $57-$74

Location: On US 41 at jct Constitution Blvd. 18051 S Tamiami Tr 33908. Fax: 239/267-9763. **Facility:** 40 one-bedroom standard units. 2 stories, exterior corridors. **Parking:** on-site. **Terms:** check-in 4 pm, weekly rates available, pets ($8 extra charge). **Amenities:** safes (fee), irons, hair dryers. **Dining:** 6 am-9 pm, wine/beer only. **Pool(s):** outdoor. **Leisure Activities:** warm mineral springs bathing pool. **Guest Services:** valet and coin laundry. **Business Services:** meeting rooms, fax (fee). **Cards:** AX, CB, DC, DS, MC, VI. **Special Amenities:** early check-in/late check-out and free newspaper.

SOME UNITS

🄢 🛏 🍽 ➤ 🏋 🔌 💻 / ✕ 🖥 ▤ /

COMFORT INN

AAA **SAVE**

WWW

Motel

				Phone: (239)936-3993
2/11-4/15 [ECP]	1P: $129-$189	2P: $129-$189	XP: $10	F12
12/1-2/10 [ECP]	1P: $79-$139	2P: $79-$139	XP: $10	F12
4/16-11/30 [ECP]	1P: $69-$99	2P: $69-$99	XP: $10	F12

Location: On US 41, 1.5 mi n of jct Daniels Pkwy. 11501 S Cleveland Ave 33907. Fax: 239/936-7234. **Facility:** 80 one-bedroom standard units. 2 stories, exterior corridors. **Parking:** on-site. **Amenities:** voice mail, hair dryers. *Some:* irons. **Pool(s):** outdoor. **Business Services:** meeting rooms, fax (fee). **Cards:** AX, DC, DS, MC, VI. **Special Amenities:** free continental breakfast and free local telephone calls.

SOME UNITS

COMFORT INN-FT. MYERS

SAVE

WWW

Small-scale Hotel

			Phone: (239)694-9200
12/1-4/15 [CP]	1P: $121-$141	2P: $121-$141	
4/16-11/30 [CP]	1P: $80-$90	2P: $80-$90	

Location: I-75, exit 141, just e on SR 80, then just s on Orange River Blvd. 4171 Boatways Rd 33905. Fax: 239/690-0180. **Facility:** 61 one-bedroom standard units. 3 stories, interior corridors. *Bath:* combo or shower only. **Parking:** on-site. **Terms:** pets ($10 extra charge). **Amenities:** *Some:* irons, hair dryers. **Pool(s):** heated outdoor. **Leisure Activities:** whirlpool. **Guest Services:** valet and coin laundry. **Business Services:** meeting rooms, fax (fee). **Cards:** AX, DS, JC, MC, VI.

SOME UNITS

COMFORT SUITES AIRPORT/UNIVERSITY

AAA **SAVE**

WWW

Motel

				Phone: (239)768-0005
1/16-3/31 [ECP]	1P: $139-$179	2P: $139-$179	XP: $10	F18
12/16-1/15 [ECP]	1P: $90-$109	2P: $90-$109	XP: $10	F18
12/1-12/15 & 4/1-11/30 [ECP]	1P: $70-$90	2P: $70-$90	XP: $10	F18

Location: I-75, exit 131, just w. 13651A Indian Paint Ln 33912. Fax: 239/768-5458. **Facility:** 65 units. 64 one-bedroom standard units, some with whirlpools. 1 one-bedroom suite. 2 stories, interior corridors. *Bath:* combo or shower only. **Parking:** on-site. **Terms:** 2 night minimum stay - weekends, package plans, pets ($10 extra charge). **Amenities:** video library, voice mail, safes (fee), irons, hair dryers. **Pool(s):** heated outdoor. **Leisure Activities:** whirlpool, exercise room. **Guest Services:** complimentary evening beverages, valet and coin laundry. **Business Services:** meeting rooms, fax. **Cards:** AX, CB, DC, DS, JC, MC, VI. **Special Amenities:** free continental breakfast and free local telephone calls.

SOME UNITS

COUNTRY INN & SUITES BY CARLSON SANIBEL-GATEWAY

AAA **SAVE**

WWW

Small-scale Hotel

				Phone: (239)454-9292
2/1-4/20 [CP]	1P: $179	2P: $189	XP: $10	F18
12/1-1/31 [CP]	1P: $99	2P: $109	XP: $10	F18
4/21-11/30 [CP]	1P: $79	2P: $89	XP: $10	F18

Location: At jct McGregor Blvd; in Shell Point. 13901 Shell Point Plaza 33908. Fax: 239/454-9159. **Facility:** 112 units. 74 one-bedroom standard units. 38 one-bedroom suites ($89-$209), some with kitchens. 4 stories, interior corridors. *Bath:* combo or shower only. **Parking:** on-site. **Terms:** cancellation fee imposed, package plans, pets ($100 fee). **Amenities:** dual phone lines, voice mail, irons, hair dryers. **Pool(s):** heated outdoor. **Leisure Activities:** exercise room. *Fee:* golf club privileges. **Guest Services:** sundries, valet and coin laundry. **Business Services:** meeting rooms, fax. **Cards:** AX, DC, DS, JC, MC, VI. **Special Amenities:** free continental breakfast and free newspaper. *(See color ad p 613)*

SOME UNITS

FEE FEE

COUNTRY INN & SUITES FT MYERS-AIRPORT

WWW

Small-scale Hotel

				Phone: (239)454-0040
2/1-4/15	1P: $129	2P: $134	XP: $5	F12
1/1-1/31	1P: $99	2P: $104	XP: $5	F12
12/1-12/31	1P: $89	2P: $94	XP: $5	F12
4/16-11/30	1P: $69	2P: $74	XP: $5	F12

Location: I-75, exit 131, just w on Daniels Pkwy, then just n on Danport Blvd. 9401 Market Place Rd 33912. Fax: 239/454-6006. **Facility:** Smoke free premises. 85 units. 65 one-bedroom standard units. 20 one-bedroom suites ($109-$149). 4 stories, interior corridors. *Bath:* combo or shower only. **Parking:** on-site. **Terms:** [ECP] meal plan available. **Amenities:** video games (fee), high-speed Internet, dual phone lines, voice mail, irons, hair dryers. **Pool(s):** heated outdoor. **Leisure Activities:** whirlpool, exercise room. **Guest Services:** valet and coin laundry, area transportation. **Business Services:** meeting rooms, business center. **Cards:** AX, CB, DC, DS, MC. *(See color ad p 613)*

SOME UNITS

COURTYARD BY MARRIOTT

SAVE

Phone: (239)275-8600

1/6-4/15	1P: $110-$179
12/1-1/5	1P: $89-$135
4/16-11/30	1P: $89-$120

Small-scale Hotel **Location:** I-75, exit 136, 3.5 mi w on SR 884. 4455 Metro Pkwy 33916. Fax: 239/275-7087. **Facility:** 149 units. 137 one-bedroom standard units. 12 one-bedroom suites. 3 stories, interior corridors. *Bath:* combo or shower only. **Parking:** on-site. **Amenities:** high-speed Internet, voice mail, irons, hair dryers. **Pool(s):** heated outdoor. **Leisure Activities:** whirlpool, exercise room. **Guest Services:** valet and coin laundry. **Business Services:** meeting rooms, fax. **Cards:** AX, CB, DC, DS, JC, MC, VI. *(See ad p 416)*

SOME UNITS

DAYS INN FORT MYERS SOUTH

AAA SAVE

Phone: (239)936-1311

3/1-4/15 [ECP]	1P: $109-$129	2P: $119-$139	XP: $10	F18
2/1-2/28 [ECP]	1P: $79-$99	2P: $89-$109	XP: $10	F18
12/1-1/31 [ECP]	1P: $69-$89	2P: $79-$99	XP: $10	F18
4/16-11/30 [ECP]	1P: $49-$59	2P: $59-$69	XP: $10	F18

Motel **Location:** On US 41 at jct Beacon Manor Dr. 11435 S Cleveland Ave 33907. Fax: 239/936-7076. **Facility:** 121 one-bedroom standard units. 3 stories, exterior corridors. **Parking:** on-site. **Terms:** 15 day cancellation notice, weekly rates available. **Amenities:** safes (fee), hair dryers. **Pool(s):** outdoor. **Guest Services:** coin laundry. **Business Services:** fax. **Cards:** AX, CB, DC, DS, MC, VI. **Special Amenities:** free continental breakfast and free local telephone calls.

SOME UNITS

FAIRFIELD INN BY MARRIOTT

SAVE

Phone: (239)437-5600

1/20-4/30 [ECP]	1P: $119	2P: $119
12/23-1/19 [ECP]	1P: $89	2P: $89
12/1-12/22 & 5/1-11/30 [ECP]	1P: $69	2P: $69

Small-scale Hotel **Location:** On US 41, just s of jct Daniels Pkwy. Located in Cypress Lake Center. 7090 Cypress Terrace 33907. Fax: 239/437-5616. **Facility:** 104 one-bedroom standard units, some with whirlpools. 3 stories, interior corridors. *Bath:* combo or shower only. **Parking:** on-site. **Amenities:** voice mail, irons, hair dryers. **Pool(s):** heated outdoor. **Leisure Activities:** whirlpool. **Guest Services:** valet laundry. **Business Services:** fax. **Cards:** AX, DC, DS, MC, VI. *(See ad below)*

SOME UNITS

FEE

HAMPTON INN-FT MYERS AIRPORT

AAA SAVE

Phone: (239)768-2525

1/11-4/20 [ECP]	1P: $119-$189	2P: $129-$199	XP: $10	F18
12/1-1/10 [ECP]	1P: $89-$109	2P: $99-$119	XP: $10	F18
10/1-11/30 [ECP]	1P: $89-$99	2P: $99-$109	XP: $10	F18
4/21-9/30 [ECP]	1P: $79-$89	2P: $89-$99	XP: $10	F18

Small-scale Hotel **Location:** I-75, exit 131, just w on Daniels Pkwy, then just n on Danport Blvd. 9241 Marketplace Rd 33912. Fax: 239/768-6049. **Facility:** 87 one-bedroom standard units, some with efficiencies (no utensils). 3 stories, interior corridors. *Bath:* combo or shower only. **Parking:** on-site. **Terms:** 7 day cancellation notice. **Amenities:** irons, hair dryers. **Pool(s):** outdoor. **Leisure Activities:** exercise room. **Guest Services:** valet laundry. **Business Services:** meeting rooms, fax. **Cards:** AX, CB, DC, DS, MC, VI. **Special Amenities:** free continental breakfast and free local telephone calls.

SOME UNITS

HAWTHORN SUITES FT MYERS-AIRPORT

Phone: (239)454-6363

1/16-5/1 [BP]	1P: $99	2P: $99	XP: $10	F18
12/1-1/15 [BP]	1P: $79	2P: $79		
5/2-11/30 [BP]	1P: $79	2P: $79	XP: $10	F18

Small-scale Hotel **Location:** 1.3 mi w of US 41 at jct McGregor Blvd; in Southpointe Commons. 9200 College Pkwy 33919. Fax: 239/454-4329. **Facility:** 100 units. 30 one-bedroom standard units. 70 one-bedroom suites with kitchens. 5 stories, interior corridors. *Bath:* combo or shower only. **Parking:** on-site. **Terms:** pets ($50 extra charge). **Amenities:** video library (fee), high-speed Internet, dual phone lines, voice mail, safes, irons, hair dryers. **Pool(s):** heated outdoor. **Leisure Activities:** whirlpool. **Guest Services:** complimentary evening beverages: Mon-Thurs, valet and coin laundry. **Business Services:** meeting rooms, business center. **Cards:** AX, CB, DC, MC, VI. *(See color ad p 418)*

SOME UNITS

FEE

HILTON GARDEN INN

[SAVE]

[WW WW]

Small-scale Hotel

	1P: $109-$209	2P: $109-$209	XP: $10	F18
2/1-4/21	1P: $99-$169	2P: $99-$169	XP: $10	F18
12/1-1/31	1P: $79-$129	2P: $79-$129	XP: $10	F18
4/22-11/30				

Phone: (239)790-3500

Location: I-75, exit 131, 5.5 mi w, 1 mi n on Summerlin. Located in a commercial area. 12600 University Dr 33907. **Fax:** 239/790-3501. **Facility:** 126 one-bedroom standard units. 5 stories, interior corridors. **Bath:** combo or shower only. **Parking:** on-site. **Terms:** cancellation fee imposed, package plans - seasonal. **Amenities:** video games, high-speed Internet, dual phone lines, voice mail, irons, hair dryers. **Pool(s):** heated outdoor. **Leisure Activities:** whirlpool, exercise room. **Guest Services:** valet and coin laundry. **Business Services:** meeting rooms, business center. **Cards:** AX, DC, DS, MC, VI.

SOME UNITS

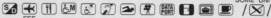
FEE

HOLIDAY INN RIVERWALK

[AAA] [SAVE]

[WW WW]

Small-scale Hotel

	1P: $159-$199	2P: $159-$199	XP: $10	F18
2/16-4/20	1P: $129-$179	2P: $129-$179	XP: $10	F18
1/19-2/15	1P: $99-$159	2P: $99-$159	XP: $10	F18
4/21-11/30	1P: $89-$159	2P: $89-$159	XP: $10	F18
12/1-1/18				

Phone: (239)334-3434

Location: 1 mi sw of Caloosahatehee River Bridge (US 41). Located on the riverfront. 2220 W First St 33901. **Fax:** 239/334-3844. **Facility:** 146 units. 138 one-bedroom standard units, some with whirlpools. 8 one-bedroom suites ($199) with whirlpools. 3 stories, interior/exterior corridors. **Bath:** combo or shower only. **Parking:** on-site. **Terms:** cancellation fee imposed. **Amenities:** voice mail, safes, irons, hair dryers. **Dining:** 7 am-10 pm, Fri & Sat-11 pm, cocktails. **Pool(s):** outdoor, wading. **Leisure Activities:** boat dock, fishing, slips for guest use, water volleyball, lending library, ping pong, playground, exercise room, basketball. **Guest Services:** valet and coin laundry. **Business Services:** meeting rooms, business center. **Cards:** AX, CB, DC, DS, MC, VI. **Special Amenities:** free local telephone calls and free newspaper. *(See color ad opposite inside back cover)*

SOME UNITS

HOLIDAY INN SELECT FT. MYERS AIRPORT AREA

[WW WW]

Large-scale Hotel

	1P: $169-$189	2P: $169-$189	XP: $10	F
1/20-4/20	1P: $149-$169	2P: $149-$169	XP: $10	F
12/1-1/19	1P: $129-$149	2P: $129-$149	XP: $10	F
4/21-6/1	1P: $119-$149	2P: $119-$149	XP: $10	F
6/2-11/30				

Phone: (239)482-2900

Location: Jct Daniels Pkwy. Located in the Bell Tower Shops. 13051 Bell Tower Dr 33907. **Fax:** 239/482-4668. **Facility:** 227 one-bedroom standard units. 5 stories, interior corridors. **Parking:** on-site. **Terms:** [BP] meal plan available. **Amenities:** dual phone lines, voice mail, irons, hair dryers. **Pool(s):** heated outdoor. **Leisure Activities:** jogging, exercise room. **Guest Services:** valet and coin laundry, area transportation. **Business Services:** conference facilities, business center. **Cards:** AX, CB, DC, DS, JC, MC, VI. *(See color ad below & opposite inside back cover)*

SOME UNITS

FEE

HOMEWOOD SUITES BY HILTON-FT. MYERS

Phone: (239)275-6000

	1/20-4/20 [ECP]	1P: $149-$239	2P: $149-$239	XP: $5	F18
	4/21-6/1 [ECP]	1P: $129-$179	2P: $129-$179	XP: $5	F18
	12/1-1/19 [ECP]	1P: $129-$149	2P: $129-$149	XP: $5	F18
	6/2-11/30 [ECP]	1P: $109-$149	2P: $109-$149	XP: $5	F18

Small-scale Hotel **Location:** Just e of jct US 41. Located in Bell Tower Shops. 5255 Big Pine Way 33907. Fax: 239/275-6601. **Facility:** 130 one-bedroom suites with kitchens. 3 stories, interior corridors. *Bath:* combo or shower only. **Parking:** on-site. **Amenities:** video library (fee), dual phone lines, voice mail, irons, hair dryers. **Pool(s):** heated outdoor. **Leisure Activities:** whirlpool, exercise room. **Guest Services:** gift shop, complimentary evening beverages: Mon-Thurs, valet and coin laundry, area transportation. **Business Services:** meeting rooms, business center. **Cards:** AX, CB, DC, DS, JC, MC, VI. *(See color ad below)*

SOME UNITS

HOWARD JOHNSON-FORT MYERS

Phone: (239)936-3229

	12/20-4/20	1P: $85-$125	2P: $89-$129	XP: $6	F17
	12/1-12/19 & 4/21-11/30	1P: $65-$95	2P: $69-$99	XP: $6	F17

Motel **Location:** On US 41, just s of jct N Airport Rd. 4811 Cleveland Ave 33907. Fax: 239/939-0424. **Facility:** 116 units. 111 one-bedroom standard units. 5 one-bedroom suites. 2 stories, exterior corridors. *Bath:* combo or shower only. **Parking:** on-site. **Terms:** check-in 4 pm, weekly rates available, package plans - weekends, pets ($25 extra charge). **Amenities:** safes (fee). *Some:* hair dryers. **Pool(s):** outdoor. **Leisure Activities:** exercise room. **Guest Services:** coin laundry. **Business Services:** meeting rooms, fax (fee). **Cards:** AX, CB, DC, DS, JC, MC, VI. **Special Amenities:** free newspaper and free room upgrade (subject to availability with advanced reservations). *(See color ad below)*

SOME UNITS

LA QUINTA INN

Phone: (239)275-3300

	2/1-4/7	1P: $109-$129	2P: $115-$135	
	12/1-1/31	1P: $79-$99	2P: $85-$105	
	4/8-11/30	1P: $49-$79	2P: $55-$85	

Motel **Location:** On US 41, just s of jct N Airport Rd. 4850 S Cleveland Ave 33907-1320. Fax: 239/275-6661. **Facility:** 129 units. 128 one-bedroom standard units. 1 one-bedroom suite. 2 stories, exterior corridors. *Bath:* combo or shower only. **Parking:** on-site. **Terms:** [ECP] meal plan available, small pets only. **Amenities:** video games, voice mail, irons, hair dryers. *Some:* fax. **Pool(s):** heated outdoor. **Guest Services:** coin laundry. **Business Services:** meeting rooms, fax. **Cards:** AX, CB, DC, DS, JC, MC, VI. **Special Amenities:** free continental breakfast and free local telephone calls.

SOME UNITS

FEE   FEE FEE

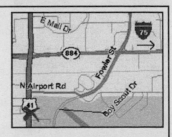

QUALITY HOTEL HISTORIC DISTRICT

Phone: (239)332-3232

2/16-4/20	1P: $110-$155	2P: $110-$155	XP: $10	F18
12/31-2/15	1P: $59-$110	2P: $59-$110	XP: $10	F18
4/21-11/30	1P: $55-$95	2P: $55-$95	XP: $10	F18
12/1-12/30	1P: $53-$95	2P: $53-$95	XP: $10	F18

Small-scale Hotel Location: On US 41, just n. 2431 Cleveland Ave 33901. Fax: 239/332-0590. **Facility:** 124 one-bedroom standard units. 4 stories, interior corridors. *Bath:* combo or shower only. **Parking:** on-site. **Terms:** cancellation fee imposed. **Amenities:** irons, hair dryers. *Some:* safes (fee). **Dining:** 7 am-10 pm, cocktails. **Pool(s):** outdoor. **Leisure Activities:** exercise room. **Guest Services:** valet and coin laundry. **Business Services:** meeting rooms, fax. **Cards:** AX, CB, DC, DS, MC, VI.

SOME UNITS

RADISSON INN FORT MYERS

Phone: (239)936-4300

2/1-4/29	1P: $109-$149	2P: $109-$149	
12/21-1/31	1P: $99-$129	2P: $99-$129	
12/1-12/20	1P: $59-$89	2P: $59-$89	
4/30-11/30	1P: $59-$79	2P: $59-$79	

Large-scale Hotel Location: US 41, 0.8 mi n of jct Daniels Pkwy. Located in a commercial area. 12635 Cleveland Ave 33907. Fax: 239/936-2058. **Facility:** 192 units. 181 one-bedroom standard units. 11 one-bedroom suites. 2-5 stories, interior/exterior corridors. *Bath:* combo or shower only. **Parking:** on-site. **Terms:** cancellation fee imposed. **Amenities:** dual phone lines, voice mail, irons, hair dryers. **Dining:** 6:30 am-10 pm; seasonal entertainment, cocktails, nightclub. **Pool(s):** heated outdoor. **Leisure Activities:** exercise room, volleyball. **Guest Services:** valet and coin laundry, airport transportation-Southwest Regional Airport. **Business Services:** conference facilities. **Cards:** AX, DC, DS, MC, VI. **Special Amenities:** free newspaper and preferred room (subject to availability with advanced reservations). *(See color ad below)*

SOME UNITS

RADISSON INN SANIBEL GATEWAY

Phone: (239)466-1200

2/1-4/26	1P: $139-$210	2P: $139-$210	XP: $10	F16
12/1-1/1	1P: $79-$210	2P: $79-$210	XP: $10	F16
1/2-1/31	1P: $89-$139	2P: $89-$139	XP: $10	F16
4/27-11/30	1P: $79-$109	2P: $79-$109	XP: $10	F16

Motel Location: I-75, exit 131, 3 mi e of Sanibel Cswy on SR 869. Located in a commercial area. 20091 Summerlin Rd SW 33908. Fax: 239/466-3797. **Facility:** 158 one-bedroom standard units, some with whirlpools. 3 stories, exterior corridors. *Bath:* combo or shower only. **Parking:** on-site. **Terms:** cancellation fee imposed, pets ($25 extra charge). **Amenities:** video games, voice mail, irons, hair dryers. **Dining:** 6:30 am-10 pm, Sat & Sun from 7 am, cocktails. **Pool(s):** heated outdoor. **Leisure Activities:** whirlpool, ping pong. **Guest Services:** valet and coin laundry. **Business Services:** meeting rooms. **Cards:** AX, CB, DC, DS, MC, VI. **Special Amenities:** free newspaper.

SOME UNITS
FEE

RESIDENCE INN BY MARRIOTT

Phone: (239)936-0110

1/12-4/25 [BP]	1P: $159-$165	2P: $159-$165	
12/1-1/11 [BP]	1P: $114-$119	2P: $114-$119	
9/1-11/30 [BP]	1P: $109-$115	2P: $109-$115	
4/26-8/31 [BP]	1P: $99-$105	2P: $99-$105	

Small-scale Hotel Location: I-75, exit 136, 3.5 mi w on SR 884. 2960 Colonial Blvd 33912. Fax: 239/936-4144. **Facility:** 78 units. 66 one- and 12 two-bedroom standard units with kitchens. 3 stories, interior corridors. **Parking:** on-site. **Terms:** 2-14 night minimum stay - seasonal, pets ($125 fee). **Amenities:** voice mail, irons, hair dryers. **Pool(s):** heated outdoor. **Leisure Activities:** whirlpool, exercise room, sports court. **Guest Services:** valet and coin laundry. **Business Services:** meeting rooms, fax (fee). **Cards:** AX, DC, DS, MC, VI.

SOME UNITS
FEE

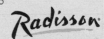

SANIBEL HARBOUR RESORT & SPA

(AAA) [SAVE]
▼▼▼ ▼▼▼

12/22-4/30	1P: $299-$2000	2P: $299-$2000	XP: $20 F17
11/1-10/31	1P: $189-$2000	2P: $189-$2000	XP: $20 F17
5/1-10/31	1P: $159-$1600	2P: $159-$1600	XP: $20 F17
12/1-12/21	1P: $189-$1400	2P: $189-$1400	XP: $20 F17

Phone: (239)466-4000

Resort
Large-scale Hotel

Location: I-75, exit 131; at Sanibel Island Cswy entrance overlooking San Carlos Bay, enter at Punta Rassa Rd. 17260 Harbour Pointe Dr 33908. Fax: 239/466-6050. **Facility:** Water-view balconies grace all of the upscale hotel rooms and condo units at this resort on 80 unspoiled acres overlooking the Intracoastal Waterway. 408 units. 343 one- and 65 two-bedroom standard units. 3-12 stories, interior/exterior corridors. **Parking:** on-site. **Terms:** 2-7 night minimum stay - seasonal, 7 day cancellation notice-fee imposed, [AP] & [MAP] meal plans available, $12 service charge. **Amenities:** video library, video games, high-speed Internet, voice mail, irons, hair dryers. *Some:* CD players, honor bars. **Dining:** 4 restaurants, 6:30 am-midnight, cocktails, also, Chez Le Bear, see separate listing, entertainment. **Pool(s):** 5 heated outdoor, heated indoor. **Leisure Activities:** whirlpools, rental boats, rental canoes, fishing, racquetball courts, recreation programs, dinner cruises, jogging, spa. *Fee:* sailboats, marina, charter fishing, kayaks, fishing pier, golf privileges, 9 lighted tennis courts, tennis instruction. **Guest Services:** gift shop, valet laundry, area transportation-Sanibel Island. **Business Services:** conference facilities, business center. **Cards:** AX, CB, DC, DS, MC, VI. **Special Amenities:** free local telephone calls and free newspaper. *(See color ad p 806)*

SOME UNITS

SHELL POINT GUEST HOUSE

(AAA) [SAVE]
▼▼▼ ▼▼▼

12/1-4/30	1P: $101	2P: $110	XP: $6 F18
5/1-11/30	1P: $53	2P: $53	XP: $6 F18

Phone: (239)466-1111

Small-scale Hotel

Location: 1.3 mi ne of Sanibel Cswy; 2 mi nw of jct McGregor Blvd; in Shell Point Village. Located in a Christian retirement community complex. 15040 Shell Point Blvd 33908. Fax: 239/466-2266. **Facility:** 36 one-bedroom standard units. 2 stories, exterior corridors. **Parking:** on-site. **Dining:** 7-10 am, 11:30-2 & 4-6:30 pm, Sun 7-10 am, 11:15-2 & 4-6 pm. **Pool(s):** heated outdoor. **Leisure Activities:** putting green, 2 lighted tennis courts, exercise room. **Guest Services:** gift shop, coin laundry. **Business Services:** meeting rooms. **Cards:** MC, VI.

SOME UNITS

SLEEP INN AIRPORT/UNIVERSITY

(AAA) [SAVE]
▼▼▼ ▼▼

12/15-4/14	1P: $89-$169	2P: $94-$174	XP: $5 F12
12/1-12/14 & 4/15-11/30	1P: $59-$109	2P: $64-$114	XP: $5 F12

Phone: (239)561-1117

Motel

Location: I-75, exit 131, just w. 13651B Indian Paint Ln 33912. Fax: 239/768-0377. **Facility:** 50 one-bedroom standard units. 2 stories, interior corridors. *Bath:* shower only. **Parking:** on-site. **Terms:** [CP] meal plan available, pets ($10 extra charge). **Amenities:** voice mail, safes (fee). *Some:* irons, hair dryers. **Pool(s):** heated outdoor. **Leisure Activities:** whirlpool. **Business Services:** fax. **Cards:** AX, CB, DC, DS, JC, MC, VI.

SOME UNITS

SUPER 8 MOTEL

▼▼ ▼▼

2/10-4/15 [ECP]	1P: $99-$129	2P: $99-$129	XP: $6 F12
12/1-2/9 [ECP]	1P: $55-$75	2P: $55-$75	XP: $6 F12
4/16-11/30 [ECP]	1P: $50-$65	2P: $50-$65	XP: $6 F12

Phone: (239)275-3500

Small-scale Hotel

Location: I-75, exit 136, 4 mi w on SR 884. 2717 Colonial Blvd 33907. Fax: 239/275-5426. **Facility:** 123 units. 122 one-bedroom standard units. 1 one-bedroom suite with kitchen. 4 stories, exterior corridors. **Parking:** on-site. **Terms:** pets ($25 extra charge). **Amenities:** voice mail, irons, hair dryers. **Pool(s):** outdoor. **Guest Services:** valet laundry. **Business Services:** fax (fee). **Cards:** AX, DC, DS, MC, VI.

SOME UNITS

TA KI-KI RIVERFRONT INN

▼▼

12/16-4/15	1P: $79-$95	2P: $79-$95	XP: $5
4/16-11/30	1P: $46-$56	2P: $46-$56	XP: $5
12/1-12/15	1P: $44-$55	2P: $44-$55	XP: $5

Phone: (239)334-2135

Motel

Location: I-75, exit 141, 4.5 mi w on SR 80. 2631 First St 33916. Fax: 239/332-1879. **Facility:** 23 one-bedroom standard units, some with efficiencies or kitchens. 1 story, exterior corridors. **Parking:** on-site. **Terms:** 4 night minimum stay - kitchen and efficiency units, 7 day cancellation notice. **Amenities:** *Some:* irons. **Pool(s):** heated outdoor. **Leisure Activities:** boat dock, fishing. **Business Services:** fax. **Cards:** AX, DC, DS, MC, VI.

SOME UNITS

WELLESLEY INN & SUITES

(AAA) [SAVE]
▼▼▼ ▼▼▼

2/1-4/20 [ECP]	1P: $84-$114	2P: $84-$114	XP: $10 F12
12/24-1/31 [ECP]	1P: $74-$94	2P: $74-$94	XP: $10 F12
4/21-11/30	1P: $54-$84	2P: $54-$84	F12
12/1-12/23 [ECP]	1P: $54-$75	2P: $54-$75	XP: $5 F12

Phone: (239)278-3949

Small-scale Hotel

Location: I-75, exit 136, 3.7 mi w on SR 884. 4400 Ford St Extension 33916. Fax: 239/278-3670. **Facility:** 105 units. 92 one-bedroom standard units. 13 one-bedroom suites ($84-$144). 4 stories, interior corridors. *Bath:* combo or shower only. **Parking:** on-site. **Terms:** cancellation fee imposed, weekly rates available, package plans. **Amenities:** video games, high-speed Internet, voice mail, irons, hair dryers. *Some:* dual phone lines. **Pool(s):** heated outdoor. **Guest Services:** coin laundry. **Business Services:** fax. **Cards:** AX, CB, DC, DS, MC, VI. **Special Amenities:** free continental breakfast and free newspaper. *(See color ad p 415)*

SOME UNITS

WINYAH HOTEL & SUITES
▼▼▼ ▼▼▼
Motel

Phone: (239)332-2048

	1P	2P	XP	
2/14-4/26 [ECP]	1P: $125-$225	2P: $135-$225	XP: $10	F18
12/21-2/13 [ECP]	1P: $95-$195	2P: $105-$195	XP: $10	F18
4/27-11/30 [ECP]	1P: $75-$185	2P: $85-$185	XP: $10	F18
12/1-12/20 [ECP]	1P: $65-$185	2P: $75-$185	XP: $10	F18

Location: Just w of US 41; center of downtown. 2038 W 1st St 33901. Fax: 239/332-2058. **Facility:** 26 units. 14 one-bedroom standard units. 10 one- and 2 two-bedroom suites with efficiencies. 77 units. 72 one-bedroom standard units. 5 one-bedroom suites ($119-$199) with efficiencies. **Features:** 2 stories (no elevator), exterior corridors. *Bath:* some combo or shower only. **Parking:** on-site. **Amenities:** voice mail, irons, hair dryers. **Pool(s):** outdoor. **Leisure Activities:** fishing. *Fee:* marina. **Guest Services:** complimentary laundry. **Business Services:** meeting rooms. **Cards:** AX, DS, MC, VI.

SOME UNITS

WYNSTAR INN & SUITES
▼▼▼▼▼
Small-scale Hotel

Phone: (239)791-5000

	1P	2P	XP	
2/1-4/20	1P: $119-$199	2P: $119-$199	XP: $5	F17
12/1-1/31	1P: $89-$159	2P: $89-$159	XP: $5	F17
4/21-5/31	1P: $79-$129	2P: $79-$129	XP: $5	F17
6/1-11/30	1P: $69-$119	2P: $69-$119	XP: $5	F17

Location: I-75, exit 131, just e. Located in a commercial area. 10150 Daniels Pkwy 33913. Fax: 239/791-5001. **Facility:** Smoke free premises. 77 units. 72 one-bedroom standard units. 5 one-bedroom suites ($119-$199) with efficiencies. 3 stories, interior corridors. *Bath:* combo or shower only. **Parking:** on-site. **Terms:** [BP] meal plan available, pets ($100 deposit in designated units, $10 extra charge). **Amenities:** voice mail, irons, hair dryers. *Some:* dual phone lines. **Pool(s):** heated outdoor. **Leisure Activities:** exercise room. *Fee:* game room. **Guest Services:** valet and coin laundry. **Business Services:** meeting rooms. **Cards:** AX, DC, DS, MC, VI.

SOME UNITS
FEE

WHERE TO DINE

CHEZ LE BEAR
ⒶⒶⒶ
▼▼▼▼▼▼
American

Dinner: $28-$42

Phone: 239/466-2136

Location: I-75, exit 131; at Sanibel Island Cswy entrance overlooking San Carlos Bay, enter at Punta Rassa Rd; in Sanibel Harbour Resort & Spa. 17260 S Harbour Pointe Dr 33908. **Hours:** 6 pm-10 pm. Closed: Sun & Mon. **Reservations:** suggested. **Features:** In the elegant Sanibel Harbour Resort and Spa, the upscale restaurant employs delightful staff members who are eager to ensure a memorable dining experience. The chef prepares each dish with individual creativity and delicious flavor. Guests may find fresh ahi tuna, braised mallard duck or filet mignon on the varied menu. The pastry chef creates incredible desserts, most notably a sinful chocolate souffle. Smoke free premises. Dressy casual; cocktails; entertainment. **Parking:** on-site. **Cards:** AX, CB, DC, DS, MC, VI.

LIGHTHOUSE RESTAURANT & BAR
▼▼ ▼▼
American
JC, MC, VI.

Lunch: $10-$24   **Dinner:** $10-$24

Phone: 239/489-0770

Location: Just n of jct McGregor Blvd; at Port Sanibel Marina. 14301 Port Lomfort Rd 33908. **Hours:** 11 am-10 pm, Fri & Sat-11 pm. **Features:** Diners can enjoy fresh seafood, aged prime beef or a rich pasta dish while enjoying a breathtaking sunset view from the restaurant's waterfront locale. From January through May, the Sunday brunch is a popular attraction. Casual dress; cocktails. **Parking:** on-site. **Cards:** AX, CB, DC, DS,

PRAWNBROKER
▼▼ ▼▼
Seafood

Dinner: $14-$20

Phone: 239/489-2226

Location: At jct Cypress Lake Dr; 2.6 mi w of US 41. 13451-16 McGregor Blvd 33919. **Hours:** 4 pm-10 pm, Sun-9 pm. Closed: 11/27; also Super Bowl Sun. **Reservations:** suggested. **Features:** The intimate restaurant is a prime spot for moderately upscale dining. Although there are numerous steak and pasta selections, seafood is the specialty, and such dishes as crunchy grouper won't disappoint. The two dining rooms overlook lush tropical gardens. Smoke free premises. Casual dress; cocktails. **Parking:** on-site. **Cards:** AX, MC, VI.

THE VERANDA
▼▼▼
American

Lunch: $6-$10   **Dinner:** $20-$28

Phone: 239/332-2065

Location: Center; corner Second at Broadway, across from City Hall. 2122 Second St 33901. **Hours:** 11 am-2:30 & 5:30-10 pm, Sat from 5:30 pm. Closed: 1/1, 12/25; also Sun. **Reservations:** suggested. **Features:** A restored house built circa 1900 boasts a brick courtyard and koi pond. Choose from an interesting selection of local seafood, beef, lamb, veal, pasta and chicken. Finish your meal with an outstanding Key lime pie. Casual dress; cocktails; entertainment. **Parking:** on-site and street. **Cards:** AX, MC, VI.

FORT MYERS BEACH pop. 6,561—*See also FORT MYERS.*

WHERE TO STAY

BAY TO BEACH RESORTS
▼▼▼▼
Condominium

Phone: (239)463-5846

12/21-4/25	1P: $200-$390	2P: $200-$390
4/26-5/30	1P: $200-$270	2P: $200-$270
5/31-11/30	1P: $165-$240	2P: $165-$240
12/1-12/20	1P: $165-$225	2P: $165-$225

Location: 0.5 mi n of Matanzas Pass Bridge. 740 Estero Blvd 33931. Fax: 239/463-5846. **Facility:** Designated smoking area. 14 units. 2 one- and 12 two-bedroom suites with kitchens, some with whirlpools. 5 stories, exterior corridors. **Parking:** on-site. **Terms:** 3-7 night minimum stay - seasonal, 30 day cancellation notice, weekly rates available, package plans. **Amenities:** irons. **Pool(s):** heated outdoor. **Leisure Activities:** fishing. **Guest Services:** gift shop, complimentary laundry. **Business Services:** fax (fee). **Cards:** MC, VI.

SOME UNITS
FEE

BEACH CLUB I

AAA SAVE
▽▽ ▽▽
Condominium

Phone: 239/463-2882

All Year Wkly   1P: $675-$1295   2P: $895-$1545
Location: 0.6 mi n of jct Matanzas Pass Bridge. 326 Estero Blvd 33931. **Fax:** 239/463-4244. **Facility:** 15 units. 5 one- and 10 two-bedroom suites with kitchens. 6 stories, exterior corridors. **Parking:** on-site. **Terms:** 30 day cancellation notice-fee imposed, daily rates available. **Amenities:** safes, irons. **Pool(s):** heated outdoor. **Leisure Activities:** gazebo and barbecue grill area, shuffleboard, volleyball. *Fee:* massage. **Guest Services:** coin laundry. **Business Services:** fax. **Cards:** AX, MC, VI.

SOME UNITS
🍴 🏊 ✕ 📠DATA 🔌 🖥 / VCR / FEE

BEST WESTERN BEACH RESORT

AAA SAVE
▽▽ ▽▽
Small-scale Hotel

Phone: (239)463-6000

2/2-4/20	1P: $219-$239	2P: $219-$239	XP: $10	F17
12/1-2/1	1P: $109-$229	2P: $109-$229	XP: $10	F17
4/21-9/1	1P: $149-$169	2P: $149-$169	XP: $10	F17
9/2-11/30	1P: $109	2P: $109	XP: $10	F17

Location: 0.4 mi n of Matanzas Pass Bridge. 684 Estero Blvd 33931. **Fax:** 239/463-3013. **Facility:** 75 units. 69 one-bedroom standard units. 2 one- and 4 two-bedroom suites ($189-$369) with kitchens. 5 stories, exterior corridors. *Bath:* combo or shower only. **Parking:** on-site. **Terms:** 7 day cancellation notice, [CP] meal plan available, small pets only ($10 extra charge). **Amenities:** safes, irons, hair dryers. **Pool(s):** heated outdoor. **Leisure Activities:** rental sailboats, playground, shuffleboard, volleyball. *Fee:* jet skis, parasailing, cabanas. **Guest Services:** coin laundry. **Business Services:** fax (fee). **Cards:** AX, CB, DC, DS, MC, VI. **Special Amenities: free continental breakfast and free newspaper.**

SOME UNITS
SD 🛏 🍴 ⛵ 🚭 🏊 ✕ 📠DATA 🔌 🖥 /✕/

CARIBBEAN BEACH CLUB

AAA SAVE
▽▽ ▽▽
Condominium

Phone: 239/463-6111

1/5-1/25 Wkly		2P: $690-$765
12/1-1/4 & 1/26-4/5 Wkly	1P: $900-$1100	
4/6-11/30 Wkly	1P: $615-$800	

Location: 5.1 mi s of Matanzas Pass Bridge. 7600 Estero Blvd 33931. **Fax:** 239/463-9579. **Facility:** 44 units. 3 one-bedroom standard units with efficiencies. 40 one- and 1 two-bedroom suites with kitchens. 2-3 stories (no elevator), exterior corridors. *Bath:* combo or shower only. **Parking:** on-site. **Terms:** 30 day cancellation notice-fee imposed. **Amenities:** *Some:* irons. **Pool(s):** heated outdoor. **Leisure Activities:** whirlpool, boating, boat dock, fishing, bicycles, horseshoes, shuffleboard, volleyball. **Guest Services:** complimentary laundry. **Business Services:** meeting rooms, fax (fee). **Cards:** AX, MC, VI.

SOME UNITS
🍴 🚭 ⛵ 🛁 ✕ 📠DATA 🔌 🖥 / VCR / FEE   FEE

CASA PLAYA HOTEL

AAA SAVE
▽▽▽▽
Motel

Phone: (239)765-0510

1/16-4/30 & 11/16-11/30	1P: $165-$250	2P: $165-$250	XP: $20	F6
12/1-1/15	1P: $125-$175	2P: $125-$175	XP: $20	F6
5/1-11/15	1P: $85-$135	2P: $85-$135	XP: $20	F6

Location: 0.5 mi n of Matanzas Pass Bridge via 5th St. 510 Estero Blvd 33931. **Fax:** 239/765-0514. **Facility:** Designated smoking area. 35 units. 21 one-bedroom standard units with efficiencies. 14 one-bedroom suites with kitchens. 8 stories, exterior corridors. **Parking:** on-site. **Terms:** 30 day cancellation notice, weekly rates available, package plans - seasonal, pets ($10-$15 extra charge). **Amenities:** voice mail, irons. **Pool(s):** heated outdoor. **Leisure Activities:** gas grill. **Guest Services:** coin laundry. **Business Services:** PC, fax. **Cards:** AX, DC, DS, MC, VI.

SD 🛏 🍴 ⛵ ✕ 📠DATA 🔌 🖥 🖥

DIAMOND HEAD ALL SUITE BEACH RESORT

AAA SAVE
▽▽ ▽▽
Large-scale Hotel

Phone: (239)765-7654

2/7-4/26	1P: $265-$320	2P: $265-$320	XP: $10	F17
12/1-1/1	1P: $158-$285	2P: $158-$285	XP: $10	F17
1/2-2/6	1P: $209-$229	2P: $209-$229	XP: $10	F17
4/27-11/30	1P: $165-$210	2P: $165-$210	XP: $10	F17

Location: 0.8 mi s of Matanzas Pass Bridge. 2000 Estero Blvd 33931. **Fax:** 239/765-1694. **Facility:** 124 one-bedroom suites with kitchens. 12 stories, interior/exterior corridors. *Bath:* combo or shower only. **Parking:** on-site. **Terms:** 3 day cancellation notice-fee imposed. **Amenities:** voice mail, irons, hair dryers. *Some:* dual phone lines. **Dining:** 7:30 am-10 pm, cocktails. **Pool(s):** heated outdoor. **Leisure Activities:** whirlpools, recreation programs, exercise room. *Fee:* parasailing, cabanas, waverunners, massage. **Guest Services:** coin laundry. **Business Services:** conference facilities, fax (fee). **Cards:** AX, DS, MC, VI. **Special Amenities: free newspaper.** *(See color ad starting on p 424)*

SOME UNITS
SD 🍴 🍸 🚭 🛡 🔒M 🛁 ⛵ ✕ 🏊 📠DATA 🔌 🖥 🖥 /✕/

{Reality Check} IT DOESN'T REALLY MATTER WHERE YOU STAY ON FORT MYERS BEACH.

OR DOES IT?

{DiamondHead} Beach Resort	{GullWing} Beach Resort	{Pointe Estero} Beach Resort	{Holiday Inn} Beach Resort	{Santa Maria} Harbour Resort	{The GrandView} On Lovers Key
One bedroom suites.	One, two and three bedroom suites.	One and two bedroom suites.	Spacious guestrooms.	One, two and three bedroom suites.	One bedroom suites.
Efficiency kitchens.	Suites up to 2,125 square feet.	Fully appointed kitchens.	Mangrove Bay Café.	Fully appointed kitchens.	Fully appointed kitchens.
Chloës restaurant & lounge.	Fully appointed kitchens.	Jacuzzi in every suite.	Tiki Poolside bar & grille.	Washer/dryer.	Adjacent to Lovers Key state park.
Cabaña's beach bar.	Jacuzzi in every suite.	Washer/dryer.	Watersports.	Barbecue grills & gazebo.	Watersports & activities.
Watersports & activities.	Activity programs.	Tennis court.	Beach volleyball.	Activity programs.	Barbecue grills.
	Tennis court.	Activity programs.			

SUNSTREAM
Hotels & Resorts

888-702-0782
www.sunstream.com
{Fort Myers Beach and Naples}

THE GRANDVIEW ALL-SUITE RESORT

Phone: (239)765-4422

(AAA) [SAVE]

2/7-4/26	1P: $175-$235	2P: $175-$235	XP: $10	F18
12/1-1/1	1P: $99-$235	2P: $99-$235	XP: $10	F18
1/2-2/6	1P: $119-$175	2P: $119-$175	XP: $10	F18
4/27-11/30	1P: $100-$135	2P: $100-$135	XP: $10	F18

Condominium **Location:** 6 mi s of Matanzas Pass Bridge. 8701 Estero Blvd 33931. Fax: 239/765-4499. **Facility:** 50 one-bedroom suites with kitchens. 14 stories, interior corridors. **Parking:** on-site. **Terms:** 2 night minimum stay - weekends, 7 day cancellation notice. **Amenities:** voice mail, irons. **Pool(s):** heated outdoor. **Leisure Activities:** rental boats, rental canoes, rental sailboats, fishing. *Fee:* jet boats, nature cruises, shelling trips, kayaks. **Guest Services:** coin laundry. **Business Services:** meeting rooms, fax (fee). **Cards:** AX, DS, MC, VI. *(See color ad starting on p 424)*

GUESTHOUSE INTERNATIONAL INN MARINER'S LODGE AND MARINA

Phone: (239)466-9700

(AAA) [SAVE]

12/18-4/22	1P: $90-$135	2P: $90-$135	XP: $10	F16
12/1-12/17 & 4/23-11/30	1P: $60-$70	2P: $60-$70	XP: $5	F16

Motel **Location:** 1.5 mi e of Matanzas Pass Bridge, on SR 865. 17990 San Carlos Blvd 33931. Fax: 239/466-6116. **Facility:** 34 units. 32 one-bedroom standard units. 2 one-bedroom suites with kitchens. 1-2 stories, exterior corridors. *Bath:* combo or shower only. **Parking:** on-site. **Terms:** 3 day cancellation notice, weekly rates available. **Pool(s):** heated outdoor. **Leisure Activities:** whirlpool, fishing. *Fee:* boat dock, bicycles. **Guest Services:** coin laundry. **Cards:** AX, CB, DC, DS, MC, VI. **Special Amenities:** early check-in/late check-out and free room upgrade (subject to availability with advanced reservations).

SOME UNITS

GULFVIEW MANOR

Phone: (239)463-4446

(AAA) [SAVE]

2/1-4/25	1P: $159-$259	2P: $169-$269	XP: $10
12/21-1/31	1P: $139-$209	2P: $149-$219	XP: $10
4/26-11/30	1P: $89-$179	2P: $99-$189	XP: $10
12/1-12/20	1P: $79-$169	2P: $89-$179	XP: $10

Small-scale Hotel **Location:** 4.2 mi se of Matanzas Pass Bridge. 6530 Estero Blvd 33931. Fax: 239/463-7634. **Facility:** 33 units. 28 one- and 5 two-bedroom suites with kitchens. 6 stories, exterior corridors. **Parking:** on-site. **Terms:** 30 day cancellation notice-fee imposed, weekly rates available. **Pool(s):** heated outdoor. **Leisure Activities:** rental boats, fishing, barbecue grills. *Fee:* cabanas, diving, parasailing. **Guest Services:** coin laundry. **Cards:** DS, MC, VI. **Special Amenities:** free room upgrade and preferred room (each subject to availability with advanced reservations). *(See color ad p 423)*

SOME UNITS

FEE

GULL WING BEACH RESORT

Phone: (239)765-4300

(AAA) [SAVE]

2/7-4/26	1P: $330-$460	2P: $330-$460	
12/1-1/1	1P: $190-$460	2P: $190-$460	
1/2-2/6	1P: $250-$380	2P: $250-$380	
4/27-11/30	1P: $190-$280	2P: $190-$280	

Condominium **Location:** 4.5 mi se of Matanzas Pass Bridge. 6620 Estero Rd 33931. Fax: 239/765-4646. **Facility:** Designated smoking area. 66 units. 22 two- and 44 three-bedroom suites with kitchens and whirlpools. 12 stories, interior corridors. *Bath:* combo or shower only. **Parking:** on-site. **Terms:** 2-7 night minimum stay - seasonal & weekends, 14 day cancellation notice. **Amenities:** video library (fee), DVD players, dual phone lines, voice mail, irons. **Pool(s):** heated outdoor. **Leisure Activities:** whirlpool, tennis court, recreation programs, exercise room, volleyball. *Fee:* cabanas, massage. **Guest Services:** gift shop, complimentary laundry. **Business Services:** meeting rooms, business center. **Cards:** AX, DS, MC, VI. *(See color ad starting on p 424)*

SOME UNITS

FEE

HAMPTON INN & SUITES

Phone: (239)437-8888

[SAVE]

2/1-4/30 [ECP]	1P: $119-$149
12/1-1/31 [ECP]	1P: $69-$89
5/1-11/30 [ECP]	1P: $69-$79

Motel **Location:** Just w of jct San Carlos Blvd. 11281 Summerlin Square Rd 33931. Fax: 239/437-8889. **Facility:** 120 units. 78 one-bedroom standard units. 42 one-bedroom suites ($89-$189) with kitchens. 4 stories, interior corridors. *Bath:* combo or shower only. **Parking:** on-site. **Terms:** cancellation fee imposed. **Amenities:** video games, dual phone lines, voice mail, irons, hair dryers. **Pool(s):** heated outdoor. **Leisure Activities:** exercise room. **Guest Services:** gift shop. **Business Services:** meeting rooms, PC, fax. **Cards:** AX, DC, DS, MC, VI.

SOME UNITS

HOLIDAY INN

Phone: (239)463-5711

(AAA) (SAVE)

	12/1-1/1	1P: $105-$470	2P: $105-$470
	2/7-4/26	1P: $225-$440	2P: $225-$440
	1/2-2/6	1P: $145-$360	2P: $145-$360
	4/27-11/30	1P: $125-$260	2P: $125-$260

Small-scale Hotel **Location:** 4.3 mi se of Matanzas Pass Bridge. 6890 Estero Blvd 33931. Fax: 239/463-7038. **Facility:** 103 units. 101 one-bedroom standard units. 2 one-bedroom suites with kitchens. 2 stories, exterior corridors. *Bath:* combo or shower only. **Parking:** on-site. **Terms:** [BP] meal plan available. **Amenities:** voice mail, safes (fee), irons, hair dryers. **Dining:** 7 am-11 & noon-9 pm, cocktails, entertainment. **Pool(s):** heated outdoor. **Leisure Activities:** exercise room, shuffleboard, volleyball. *Fee:* cabanas, parasailing, waverunners. **Guest Services:** coin laundry. **Business Services:** meeting rooms, fax (fee). **Cards:** AX, DS, VI. **Special Amenities: free newspaper and free room upgrade (subject to availability with advanced reservations).** *(See color ad starting on p 424 & opposite inside back cover)*

SOME UNITS

[icons]

ISLAND HOUSE MOTEL

Phone: (239)463-9282

	12/15-5/1	1P: $119-$139	2P: $119-$139	XP: $15
	12/1-12/14 & 5/2-11/30	1P: $59-$79	2P: $59-$79	XP: $15

Motel **Location:** 0.4 mi n of Matanzas Pass Bridge. 701 Estero Blvd 33931. Fax: 239/463-2080. **Facility:** Designated smoking area. 5 one-bedroom suites with kitchens. 1 story, exterior corridors. **Parking:** on-site. **Terms:** 30 day cancellation notice. **Amenities:** irons. **Pool(s):** heated outdoor. **Leisure Activities:** boat dock, bicycles. **Guest Services:** coin laundry. **Business Services:** fax (fee). **Cards:** MC, VI.

[icons]

LIGHTHOUSE RESORT INN & SUITES

Phone: 239/463-9392

	2/8-4/20	1P: $105-$250	2P: $105-$250	XP: $15	F
	1/3-2/7	1P: $72-$185	2P: $72-$185	XP: $15	F
	12/1-1/2 & 4/21-11/30	1P: $49-$100	2P: $49-$100	XP: $15	F

Small-scale Hotel **Location:** Jct of SR 865 and 5th St; at south end of Matanzas Pass Bridge. 1051 5th St 33931. Fax: 239/765-5297. **Facility:** Designated smoking area. 72 units. 35 one-bedroom standard units, some with efficiencies. 35 one- and 2 two-bedroom suites, some with efficiencies or kitchens. 2-3 stories, exterior corridors. *Bath:* combo or shower only. **Parking:** on-site. **Terms:** 7 day cancellation notice-fee imposed. **Amenities:** hair dryers. *Some:* high-speed Internet. **Pool(s):** 2 heated outdoor. **Leisure Activities:** playground, basketball, shuffleboard. *Fee:* game room. **Guest Services:** gift shop, coin laundry. **Business Services:** fax (fee). **Cards:** AX, DS, MC, VI. *(See color ad p 426)*

SOME UNITS

[icons] FEE

LOVERS KEY BEACH CLUB & RESORT

Phone: (239)765-1040

(AAA) (SAVE)

	2/1-4/26 [ECP]	1P: $195-$300	2P: $195-$300	XP: $10	F16
	12/20-1/31 [ECP]	1P: $145-$225	2P: $145-$225	XP: $10	F16
	4/27-11/30 [ECP]	1P: $120-$200	2P: $120-$200	XP: $10	F16
	12/1-12/19 [ECP]	1P: $110-$190	2P: $110-$190	XP: $10	F16

Condominium **Location:** 6 mi s of Matanzas Pass Bridge. 8771 Estero Blvd 33931. Fax: 239/765-1055. **Facility:** 85 one-bedroom suites with kitchens, some with whirlpools. 13 stories, interior corridors. *Bath:* combo or shower only. **Parking:** on-site. **Terms:** 3 day cancellation notice. **Amenities:** video games, high-speed Internet, voice mail, safes, irons, hair dryers. **Dining:** 7:30 am-9 pm, cocktails. **Pool(s):** heated outdoor. **Leisure Activities:** whirlpool, exercise room. *Fee:* jet boats, kayaks, nature cruises. **Guest Services:** coin laundry. **Business Services:** meeting rooms, fax (fee). **Cards:** AX, DS, MC, VI. **Special Amenities: free continental breakfast and free local telephone calls.** *(See color ad p 426)*

SOME UNITS

[icons]

OUTRIGGER BEACH RESORT

Phone: (239)463-3131

	12/1-12/31 & 2/8-4/19	1P: $115-$215	2P: $115-$215	XP: $10	F12
	1/1-2/7	1P: $100-$185	2P: $100-$185	XP: $10	F12
	4/20-11/30	1P: $85-$150	2P: $85-$150	XP: $10	F12

Motel **Location:** 4 mi s of Matanzas Pass Bridge. 6200 Estero Blvd 33931-1281. Fax: 239/463-6577. **Facility:** 144 units. 143 one-bedroom standard units, some with efficiencies. 1 one-bedroom suite with kitchen. 2-4 stories (no elevator), exterior corridors. *Bath:* combo or shower only. **Parking:** on-site. **Terms:** check-in 4 pm, 3 day cancellation notice. **Amenities:** safes, hair dryers. *Some:* irons. **Pool(s):** heated outdoor. **Leisure Activities:** recreation programs, exercise room. *Fee:* bicycles. **Guest Services:** gift shop, coin laundry. **Business Services:** meeting rooms, fax (fee). **Cards:** AX, MC, VI. *(See color ad p 426)*

SOME UNITS

[icons]

PALM TERRACE APTS. RESORT

Phone: 239/765-5783

	12/20-4/20	1P: $89-$132	2P: $89-$132	XP: $10	F8
	12/1-12/19 & 4/21-11/30	1P: $49-$81	2P: $49-$81	XP: $10	F8

Motel **Location:** 1.7 mi s of Matanzas Pass Bridge. 3333 Estero Blvd 33931. Fax: 239/765-5783. **Facility:** Designated smoking area. 9 units. 1 one-bedroom standard unit with efficiency. 4 one- and 4 two-bedroom suites with kitchens. 2 stories, exterior corridors. **Parking:** on-site. **Terms:** 3 night minimum stay, 21 day cancellation notice-fee imposed. **Amenities:** irons. *Some:* hair dryers. **Pool(s):** heated outdoor. **Leisure Activities:** shuffleboard. **Guest Services:** coin laundry. **Business Services:** fax (fee). **Cards:** AX, DS, MC, VI.

[icons]

POINTE ESTERO RESORT HOTEL

Phone: (239)765-1155

(AAA) (SAVE)

	2/7-4/26	1P: $265-$475	2P: $265-$475
	12/1-1/1	1P: $145-$445	2P: $145-$445
	1/2-2/6	1P: $195-$395	2P: $195-$395
	4/27-11/30	1P: $150-$295	2P: $150-$295

Condominium **Location:** 4.5 mi se of Matanzas Pass Bridge. 6640 Estero Blvd 33931. Fax: 239/765-0657. **Facility:** 59 two-bedroom suites with kitchens and whirlpools. 16 stories, interior corridors. **Parking:** on-site. **Terms:** 2-7 night minimum stay - weekends, seasonal, 14 day cancellation notice. **Amenities:** video library (fee), voice mail, irons, hair dryers. **Pool(s):** heated outdoor. **Leisure Activities:** whirlpool, lighted tennis court, recreation programs, barbecue grills, exercise room, volleyball. **Guest Services:** gift shop, complimentary laundry. **Cards:** AX, DS, MC, VI. *(See color ad starting on p 424)*

[icons]

SANDPIPER GULF RESORT
Phone: (239)463-5721

AAA SAVE

| 12/23-4/30 | 1P: $141-$195 | 2P: $149-$195 | XP: $8 | F12 |
| 12/1-12/22 & 5/1-11/30 | 1P: $79-$107 | 2P: $79-$107 | XP: $8 | F12 |

Location: 3.1 mi s of Matanzas Pass Bridge. 5550 Estero Blvd 33931. Fax: 239/765-0039. **Facility:** Designated smoking area. 63 one-bedroom standard units with kitchens. 2-5 stories, interior/exterior corridors. **Parking: Small-scale Hotel** on-site. **Terms:** 14 day cancellation notice, weekly rates available, package plans - seasonal. **Amenities:** hair dryers. *Some:* irons. **Pool(s):** 2 heated outdoor. **Leisure Activities:** whirlpool, barbecue grills, shuffleboard. *Fee:* jet skis, parasailing, bicycles. **Guest Services:** gift shop, coin laundry. **Business Services:** fax (fee). **Cards:** AX, DS, MC, VI.

SANTA MARIA RESORT
Phone: (239)765-6700

AAA SAVE

2/7-4/26	1P: $180-$309	2P: $180-$309
12/1-1/1	1P: $109-$309	2P: $109-$309
1/2-2/6	1P: $135-$235	2P: $135-$235
4/27-11/30	1P: $115-$209	2P: $115-$209

Condominium **Location:** 5 mi s of Matanzas Pass Bridge. 7317 Estero Blvd 33931. Fax: 239/765-6909. **Facility:** Designated smoking area. 50 units. 2 one-, 46 two- and 2 three-bedroom suites with kitchens. 4 stories, exterior corridors. **Parking:** on-site. **Terms:** 2-7 night minimum stay - weekends, age restrictions may apply, 14 day cancellation notice. **Amenities:** voice mail, irons. *Some:* hair dryers. **Pool(s):** heated outdoor. **Leisure Activities:** sauna, whirlpools, fishing, recreation programs, barbecue grills. *Fee:* boat dock. **Guest Services:** gift shop, complimentary laundry. **Business Services:** fax (fee). **Cards:** AX, DS, MC, VI. **Special Amenities:** free room upgrade (subject to availability with advanced reservations). *(See color ad starting on p 424)*

SILVER SANDS VILLAS
Phone: 239/463-6554

2/1-4/30	1P: $127-$167	2P: $127-$167	XP: $15
12/1-1/31	1P: $107-$147	2P: $107-$147	XP: $15
5/1-11/30	1P: $75-$95	2P: $75-$95	XP: $15

Small-scale Hotel **Location:** Just s of Matanzas Pass Bridge. 1207 Estero Blvd 33931. Fax: 239/463-2260. **Facility:** Designated smoking area. 20 units. 3 one-bedroom standard units with efficiencies. 13 one- and 4 two-bedroom suites with kitchens. 2 stories, exterior corridors. *Bath:* combo or shower only. **Parking:** on-site. **Terms:** age restrictions may apply, 21 day cancellation notice, small pets only ($100 fee). **Amenities:** video library. *Some:* irons, hair dryers. **Pool(s):** heated outdoor. **Guest Services:** coin laundry. **Business Services:** PC, fax. **Cards:** AX, MC, VI.

SOME UNITS

SUN DECK RESORT
Phone: (239)463-1842

| 1/15-4/15 | 1P: $79-$189 | 2P: $79-$189 | XP: $10 | F6 |
| 12/1-1/14 & 4/16-11/30 | 1P: $49-$149 | 2P: $49-$149 | XP: $10 | F6 |

Motel **Location:** Just s of Matanzas Pass Bridge. 1051 Third St 33931. Fax: 239/463-9823. **Facility:** Designated smoking area. 7 units. 5 one-bedroom standard units, some with efficiencies or kitchens. 2 two-bedroom suites ($124-$318) with kitchens. 3 stories, exterior corridors. **Parking:** on-site. **Terms:** cancellation fee imposed, pets ($60 fee). **Cards:** MC, VI.

TROPICAL INN RESORT MOTEL
Phone: 239/463-3124

AAA SAVE

| All Year | 2P: $69-$279 | XP: $10 | F5 |

Location: 3 mi s of Matanzas Pass Bridge. 5210 Estero Blvd 33931. Fax: 239/463-0417. **Facility:** 31 units. 28 one-bedroom standard units with kitchens. 1 one- and 2 three-bedroom suites ($198-$455) with kitchens. 3 stories (no elevator), exterior corridors. *Bath:* combo or shower only. **Parking:** on-site. **Terms:** 15 day **Condominium** cancellation notice, weekly rates available. **Amenities:** *Some:* irons, hair dryers. **Pool(s):** heated outdoor. **Leisure Activities:** gas barbecue. **Guest Services:** coin laundry. **Business Services:** fax. **Cards:** AX, DC, DS, MC, VI.

SOME UNITS

The following lodgings were either not evaluated or did not meet AAA rating requirements but are listed for your information only.

BEST WESTERN PINK SHELL BEACH RESORT
Phone: (239)463-6181

AAA SAVE

fyi

12/1-1/4 & 2/1-4/22	1P: $259-$475	2P: $259-$475	XP: $20	F16
4/23-11/30	1P: $165-$329	2P: $165-$329	XP: $20	F16
1/5-1/31	1P: $155-$319	2P: $155-$319	XP: $20	F16

Resort Under major renovation, scheduled to be completed September 2003. Last rated: ▽▽▽ **Location:** 0.7 mi n **Condominium** of jct Matanzas Pass Bridge. 275 Estero Blvd 33931. Fax: 239/463-1229. **Facility:** Designated smoking area. 235 units. 60 one-bedroom standard units with efficiencies. 95 one- and 80 two-bedroom suites with kitchens. 2-9 stories, exterior corridors. *Bath:* combo or shower only. **Parking:** on-site. **Terms:** check-in 4 pm, 14 day cancellation notice-fee imposed, package plans - seasonal. **Amenities:** high-speed Internet, voice mail, safes, irons, hair dryers. **Dining:** 3 restaurants, 7:30 am-9 pm, wine/beer only. **Pool(s):** 4 heated outdoor, wading. **Leisure Activities:** whirlpools, rental boats, rental paddleboats, rental sailboats, fishing, 2 tennis courts, recreation programs, playground, exercise room, shuffleboard, volleyball. *Fee:* windsurfing, boat dock, excursion boats, parasailing, waverunners, bicycles, massage. **Guest Services:** gift shop, valet and coin laundry. **Business Services:** meeting rooms, business center. **Cards:** AX, CB, DC, DS, MC, VI. **Special Amenities:** free local telephone calls and free newspaper. *(See color ad p 429)*

THE CAPER BEACH CLUB
Phone: 239/463-1423

fyi

Not evaluated. **Location:** 1.2 mi s of Matanzas Pass Bridge. 2800 Estero Blvd 33931. Facilities, services, and decor characterize a mid-range property.

CASA MARINA AT BAY BEACH
Phone: 239/765-6400

fyi

Not evaluated. **Location:** 4.7 mi s of Matanzas Pass Bridge. 7401 Estero Blvd 33931. Facilities, services, and decor characterize a mid-range property.

LIGHTHOUSE INN RESORT
[fyi]   Not evaluated. **Location:** 3.2 mi s of Matanzas Pass Bridge. 5580 Estero Blvd 33931. Facilities, services, and decor characterize a mid-range property.
Phone: 239/463-4414

POINTE SOUTH CONDOMINIUM
[fyi]   Not evaluated. **Location:** 2.7 mi s of Matanzas Pass Bridge. 5000 Estero Blvd 33931. Facilities, services, and decor characterize a mid-range property.
Phone: 239/463-4009

THE SANDARAC
[fyi]   Not evaluated. **Location:** 4.7 mi s of Matanzas Pass Bridge. 6666 Estero Blvd 33931. Facilities, services, and decor characterize a mid-range property.
Phone: 239/463-6080

SEAWATCH ON THE BEACH RESORT
[fyi]   Not evaluated. **Location:** 4.3 mi s of the Matanzas Pass Bridge. 6550 Estero Blvd 33931. Facilities, services, and decor characterize a mid-range property.
Phone: 239/463-4469

SMUGGLER'S COVE CONDOMINIUM
[fyi]   Not evaluated. **Location:** 2.6 mi s of Matanzas Pass Bridge. 5100 Estero Blvd 33931. Facilities, services, and decor characterize a mid-range property.
Phone: 239/463-4128

WATERSIDE AT BAY BEACH
[fyi]   Not evaluated. **Location:** 4.7 mi s of Matanzas Pass Bridge. 7401 Estero Blvd 33931. Facilities, services, and decor characterize a mid-range property.
Phone: 239/765-6400

--- **WHERE TO DINE** ---

ANTHONY'S ON THE GULF
Italian
Lunch: $9-$21   **Dinner:** $11-$21   **Phone:** 239/463-2600
Location: On SR 865, 2 mi s of Matanzas Pass Bridge. 3040 Estero Blvd 33931. **Hours:** 11:30 am-10 pm, Fri & Sat-11 pm. **Features:** Picturesque beach views and a tropical decor await diners at this casual gulf-shore restaurant. The menu dips into both American and Italian cuisine to assemble enticing dishes, such as baked stuffed mushrooms, buffalo shrimp and manicotti with sausage. Also available is standard fare—pizza, burgers and sandwiches. Casual dress; cocktails. **Parking:** on-site. **Cards:** AX, DS, MC, VI.

THE BEACHED WHALE
Seafood
Lunch: $7-$20   **Dinner:** $7-$20   **Phone:** 239/463-5505
Location: 0.5 mi s of Matanzas Pass Bridge. 1249 Estero Blvd 33931. **Hours:** 11 am-2 am. **Features:** Set just across from the beach and within walking distance of many shops and beach sights is this popular little restaurant. Guests enjoy the rustic charm and fresh seafood offerings. Casual dress; cocktails. **Parking:** on-site. **Cards:** MC, VI.

THE FISH MONGER
Seafood
Dinner: $10-$18   **Phone:** 239/765-5544
Location: Just n of Matanzas Pass Bridge. 19030 San Carlos Blvd 33931. **Hours:** 4 pm-10 pm. Closed major holidays. **Reservations:** accepted. **Features:** The casual, family-friendly seafood restaurant specializes in fresh fish brought in by a local fleet. The menu includes grouper, snapper, mahi mahi, tuna, tilefish, cobia, amberjack, salmon, swordfish and Pompano catfish, as well as New York steak, ribs and chicken. Diners can have their fresh catch cooked on the premises. Casual dress; cocktails. **Parking:** on-site. **Cards:** MC, VI.

JOHNNY LEVEROCK'S SEAFOOD HOUSE
Seafood
Lunch: $8-$20   **Dinner:** $8-$20   **Phone:** 239/267-2334
Location: SR 865, 1.2 mi e of Matanzas Pass Bridge. 18100 San Carlos Blvd 33931. **Hours:** 11 am-9 pm, Fri & Sat-10 pm. **Features:** The popular seafood restaurant is nautically decorated, and many tables offer a pleasant view of the dock area. Seafood prevails on the varied menu. Fried shrimp is a popular choice. Casual dress; cocktails. **Parking:** on-site. **Cards:** MC, VI.

LOGGERHEAD'S
American
Lunch: $6-$11   **Dinner:** $9-$18   **Phone:** 239/463-4644
Location: 4.5 mi se of Matanzas Pass Bridge; in Villa Santini Plaza. 7205 Estero Blvd B 33931. **Hours:** 11 am-10 pm. Closed: 1/1, 11/27, 12/25. **Features:** Popular with the local crowd, this casual restaurant specializes in seafood but also offers a wide range of comfort foods, including burgers, sandwiches, soups and salads. Casual dress; cocktails. **Parking:** on-site. **Cards:** AX, DS, MC, VI.

MUNCH BOX
American
Parking: on-site.
Lunch: $5-$11   **Phone:** 239/463-1889
Location: On SR 865, 3.8 mi s of Matanzas Pass Bridge. 6101 Estero Blvd 33931. **Hours:** 8 am-6 pm, Sun-1 pm. Closed major holidays; also Mon. **Features:** Families on a budget will favor the meat-and-potatoes fare and child-friendly atmosphere of this comfortable mom-and-pop restaurant. It serves such home-style staples as omelets, hash browns, sandwiches, meatloaf and pot roast. Casual dress; beer & wine only.

THE REEF RESTAURANT
Seafood
Lunch: $7-$20   **Dinner:** $7-$20   **Phone:** 239/463-4181
Location: 0.6 mi s of Matanzas Pass Bridge. 2601 Estero Blvd 33931. **Hours:** 11 am-10 pm. **Features:** Set just across the street from the busy beach area, the rustic restaurant exudes nautical charm. Casual servers present a menu of such seafood favorites as frog legs and lobster tails. Other choices include steaks and fried chicken. Casual dress; cocktails. **Parking:** on-site. **Cards:** AX, MC, VI.

SQUIGGY'S 50'S DINER
American
Lunch: $5-$10   **Dinner:** $5-$10   **Phone:** 239/463-6262
Location: 0.4 mi s of Matanzas Pass Bridge; in Key Estero Shop. 1661 Estero Blvd 33931. **Hours:** 11 am-10 pm. **Features:** Take a step into the past in the '50s-style diner setting. Waitresses uniformed in nostalgic cheering regalia present menu choices of burgers and sandwiches, in addition to the requisite floats and ice cream sundaes. Casual dress. **Parking:** on-site. **Cards:** MC, VI.

FORT PIERCE pop. 37,516

——— WHERE TO STAY ———

DAYS INN
Small-scale Hotel
Phone: (772)466-4066

2/1-4/20	1P: $79-$89	2P: $79-$89	XP: $5	F17
1/1-1/31	1P: $69-$79	2P: $69-$79	XP: $5	F17
12/1-12/31 & 4/21-11/30	1P: $59-$69	2P: $59-$69	XP: $5	F17

Location: I-95, exit 129. 6651 Darter Ct 34945. Fax: 772/468-3260. **Facility:** 125 one-bedroom standard units. 2 stories, exterior corridors. **Parking:** on-site. **Terms:** 14 day cancellation notice, small pets only ($10 extra charge). **Amenities:** safes (fee), irons, hair dryers. **Pool(s):** heated outdoor. **Guest Services:** coin laundry. **Business Services:** meeting rooms, fax (fee). **Cards:** AX, DC, DS, MC, VI.
SOME UNITS

DAYS INN HUTCHINSON ISLAND
Motel
Phone: (772)461-8737

12/15-4/15 [CP]	1P: $95-$135	2P: $95-$135	XP: $10	F17
12/1-12/14 & 4/16-11/30 [CP]	1P: $69-$95	2P: $69-$95	XP: $10	F17

Location: SR A1A southbound, Hutchinson Island, 2.5 mi e of jct US 1. 1920 Seaway Dr 34949. Fax: 772/460-2218. **Facility:** 36 one-bedroom standard units, some with kitchens. 1 story, interior/exterior corridors. **Parking:** on-site. **Amenities:** dual phone lines, voice mail, safes (fee), hair dryers. **Pool(s):** heated outdoor. **Leisure Activities:** fishing, private fishing pier, picnic areas with barbecue grills. **Guest Services:** coin laundry. **Business Services:** fax (fee). **Cards:** AX, CB, DC, DS, MC, VI. **Special Amenities:** free continental breakfast and free newspaper.
SOME UNITS

DOCKSIDE HARBORLIGHT RESORT
Phone: (772)468-3555

(AAA) [SAVE]

| | 12/15-4/14 [CP] | 1P: $99-$130 | 2P: $99-$130 | XP: $10 | F16 |
| | 12/1-12/14 & 4/15-11/30 [CP] | 1P: $69-$99 | 2P: $69-$99 | XP: $10 | F16 |

Small-scale Hotel

Location: SR A1A southbound, 2 mi e of jct US 1. 1160 Seaway Dr 34949. Fax: 772/489-9848. **Facility:** 20 one-bedroom standard units, some with kitchens. 2 stories, exterior corridors. **Parking:** on-site. **Terms:** 2 night minimum stay - weekends, 3 day cancellation notice, package plans. **Amenities:** voice mail. **Pool(s):** heated outdoor. **Leisure Activities:** whirlpool, rental boats, fishing, fishing piers. *Fee:* boat dock. **Guest Services:** coin laundry. **Business Services:** meeting rooms, fax (fee). **Cards:** AX, CB, DC, DS, MC, VI. **Special Amenities:** free continental breakfast and preferred room (subject to availability with advanced reservations).

SOME UNITS

🅂🄳 🏷 🐾 ⊗ 📷 [DATA PORT] 🖥 🖨 🖥 /⊗/

ECONO LODGE
Phone: (772)461-2323

(AAA) [SAVE]

| | 1/1-4/30 [CP] | 1P: $79-$89 | 2P: $89-$99 | XP: $5 | F18 |
| | 12/1-12/31 & 5/1-11/30 [CP] | 1P: $69-$79 | 2P: $79-$89 | XP: $5 | F18 |

Small-scale Hotel

Location: US 1, 1.3 mi s of jct SR 70. 3236 US 1 S 34982. Fax: 772/464-5151. **Facility:** 60 one-bedroom standard units, some with kitchens and/or whirlpools. 2 stories, exterior corridors. *Bath:* combo or shower only. **Parking:** on-site. **Terms:** 2-3 night minimum stay - seasonal, weekly rates available. **Amenities:** *Some:* irons, hair dryers. **Pool(s):** outdoor. **Leisure Activities:** whirlpool. **Guest Services:** valet and coin laundry. **Business Services:** fax (fee). **Cards:** AX, DC, DS, MC, VI. **Special Amenities:** free continental breakfast and free newspaper.

SOME UNITS

🅂🄳 🏷 🚼 📶 🐾 📷 [DATA PORT] 🖥 /⊗ 🖨 🖥/

HAMPTON INN
Phone: (772)460-9855

[SAVE]

| | 12/16-4/30 | 1P: $80-$89 | 2P: $80-$89 | |
| | 12/1-12/15 & 5/1-11/30 | 1P: $76-$79 | 2P: $76-$79 | |

Small-scale Hotel

Location: I-95, exit 129, 0.4 mi w on SR 70; 0.3 mi e of Florida Tpke, exit 152. 2831 Reynolds Dr 34945. Fax: 772/465-7117. **Facility:** 72 one-bedroom standard units. 2 stories, exterior corridors. *Bath:* combo or shower only. **Parking:** on-site. **Terms:** [ECP] meal plan available. **Amenities:** high-speed Internet, dual phone lines, voice mail, irons, hair dryers. **Guest Services:** valet laundry. **Business Services:** fax (fee). **Cards:** AX, CB, DC, DS, MC, VI.

SOME UNITS

🅂🄳 🚼 📶 📷 🐾 [DATA PORT] 🖥 /⊗/

HOLIDAY INN EXPRESS
Phone: (772)464-5000

	1/16-4/20	1P: $99-$109	2P: $99-$109	XP: $10	F18
	10/1-11/30	1P: $79-$89	2P: $79-$89	XP: $10	F18
	12/1-1/15 & 4/21-9/30	1P: $69-$79	2P: $69-$79	XP: $10	F18

Small-scale Hotel

Location: I-95, exit 129, 0.7 mi w on SR 70; at Florida Tpke, exit 152. 7151 Okeechobee Rd 34945. Fax: 772/461-9573. **Facility:** 100 one-bedroom standard units. 2 stories, exterior corridors. *Bath:* combo or shower only. **Parking:** on-site. **Terms:** [CP] & [ECP] meal plans available, small pets only ($15 deposit). **Amenities:** voice mail, irons, hair dryers. *Some:* dual phone lines. **Pool(s):** outdoor, wading. **Guest Services:** valet and coin laundry. **Business Services:** meeting rooms, fax (fee). **Cards:** AX, CB, DC, DS, MC, VI.

SOME UNITS

(A$K) 🅂🄳 🐾 🚼 🔥M 📶 📷 🐾 📷 [DATA PORT] 🖥 /⊗/

HOLIDAY INN EXPRESS HOTEL & SUITES
Phone: (772)595-0711

	2/23-4/26 [ECP]	1P: $104	2P: $104	XP: $10	F18
	4/27-11/30 [ECP]	1P: $77	2P: $77	XP: $10	F18
	12/1-2/22 [ECP]	1P: $75	2P: $75	XP: $10	F18

Small-scale Hotel

Location: SR A1A southbound, Hutchinson Island, 2 mi e of jct US 1. 1230 Seaway Dr 34949. Fax: 772/595-0712. **Facility:** 70 one-bedroom standard units. 4 stories, interior corridors. *Bath:* combo or shower only. **Parking:** on-site. **Amenities:** dual phone lines, voice mail, safes, irons, hair dryers. **Pool(s):** heated outdoor. **Leisure Activities:** whirlpool, boat dock, fishing. **Guest Services:** gift shop, valet and coin laundry. **Business Services:** fax (fee). **Cards:** AX, CB, DC, DS, MC, VI.

SOME UNITS

(A$K) 🅂🄳 🔥M 📶 🐾 ⊗ [DATA PORT] 🖥 /⊗ 🖨 🖥/

RADISSON BEACH RESORT NORTH HUTCHINSON ISLAND
Phone: (772)465-5544

(AAA) [SAVE]

| | 12/20-4/26 | 1P: $129-$229 | 2P: $129-$229 | XP: $10 | F18 |
| | 12/1-12/19 & 4/27-11/30 | 1P: $89-$149 | 2P: $89-$149 | XP: $10 | F18 |

Small-scale Hotel

Location: SR A1A northbound, 2.3 mi e of US 1. 2600 North A1A 34949. Fax: 772/465-5540. **Facility:** 149 units. 146 one-bedroom standard units. 3 two-bedroom suites ($169-$329) with whirlpools. 4 stories, interior corridors. *Bath:* combo or shower only. **Parking:** on-site. **Terms:** cancellation fee imposed. **Amenities:** video games, irons, hair dryers. **Dining:** 2 restaurants, 6:30 am-11 pm, cocktails. **Pool(s):** heated outdoor. **Leisure Activities:** snorkeling, fishing, tennis court, boogie boards, sand volleyball, exercise room, shuffleboard. *Fee:* bicycles, massage. **Guest Services:** gift shop, valet and coin laundry, area transportation-within 10 mi. **Business Services:** conference facilities. *Fee:* administrative services, fax. **Cards:** AX, CB, DC, DS, MC, VI. **Special Amenities:** free newspaper.

SOME UNITS

🅂🄳 🚼 🍽 🔥M 📶 🐾 ⊗ 📷 [DATA PORT] 🖥 /⊗ 🖨/
FEE

ROYAL INN
Phone: 772/464-0405

(AAA) [SAVE]

| | 1/15-4/15 | 1P: $59-$89 | 2P: $69-$89 | XP: $10 | F12 |
| | 12/1-1/14 & 4/16-11/30 | 1P: $39-$59 | 2P: $49-$69 | XP: $10 | F12 |

Motel

Location: 2.5 mi e on SR A1A, southbound to Hernando St, just s. 222 Hernando St 34949. Fax: 772/464-0405. **Facility:** 18 one-bedroom standard units. 3 stories, exterior corridors. **Parking:** on-site. **Terms:** weekly rates available, pets ($25 fee). **Guest Services:** coin laundry. **Special Amenities:** free local telephone calls and preferred room (subject to availability with advanced reservations).

SOME UNITS

🐾 🖨 🖥 /⊗/

SLEEP INN

Phone: (772)595-6080

(AAA) (SAVE)

All Year   1P: $50-$95   2P: $55-$100   XP: $10   F18

Location: I-95, exit 129, just w. 2715 Crossroad Pkwy 34945. **Fax:** 772/595-6070. **Facility:** 66 one-bedroom standard units. 4 stories, interior corridors. *Bath:* combo or shower only. **Parking:** on-site. **Terms:** [ECP] meal plan available. **Amenities:** voice mail, hair dryers. **Leisure Activities:** exercise room. **Guest Services:** coin

Small-scale Hotel laundry. **Business Services:** meeting rooms, fax (fee). **Cards:** AX, CB, DC, DS, MC, VI. **Special Amenities: free continental breakfast and free local telephone calls.**

SOME UNITS

(icons)

VILLA NINA ISLAND INN

Phone: 772/467-8673

All Year   2P: $140-$240

Cottage

Location: SR A1A (North Hutchinson Island), 4 mi ne of jct US 1. Located across the street from beach. 3851 N A1A 34949. **Facility:** Smoke free premises. 5 units. 3 one-bedroom standard units. 2 one-bedroom suites. 1 story, exterior corridors. *Bath:* combo or shower only. **Parking:** on-site. **Terms:** check-in 4 pm, 2 night minimum stay - weekends, age restrictions may apply, 21 day cancellation notice-fee imposed, weekly rates available. **Amenities:** hair dryers. *Some:* voice mail. **Pool(s):** heated outdoor. **Leisure Activities:** Fee: canoes, snorkeling, bicycles. **Guest Services:** coin laundry. **Cards:** DS, MC, VI.

(icons)

------ **WHERE TO DINE** ------

KRISTI'S ON THE OCEAN

Lunch: $7-$18   **Dinner:** $13-$26   **Phone:** 772/465-4200

Continental

Location: On SR A1A, S Hutchinson Island; 4.7 mi se of jct US 1; in Ocean Village Residential Complex. 2400 S Ocean Dr 34949. **Hours:** Open 12/1-8/26 & 9/27-11/30; 11:30 am-2:30 & 5-9 pm, Fri-9:30 pm. Closed: Mon 5/1-12/31. **Reservations:** suggested. **Features:** The songs of Nat King Cole combined with lovely ocean views set the mood for a romantic evening out. Share the chateaubriand for two, delicious roasted tenderloin with grilled vegetables; or keep the coco shrimp in calypso sauce all to yourself. Casual dress; cocktails; entertainment. **Parking:** on-site. **Cards:** AX, DS, MC, VI.

(icons)

MANGROVE MATTIES

Lunch: $7-$15   **Dinner:** $12-$19   **Phone:** 772/466-1044

Seafood

Location: SR A1A southbound; 2.3 mi e of jct US 1. 1640 Seaway Dr 34949. **Hours:** 11:30 am-10 pm. Closed: 12/25. **Reservations:** suggested. **Features:** Feast on fresh seafood on an open air terrace only 20 feet from the inlet. To continuously offer a good variety, the menu changes daily and features such dishes as crab and shrimp Alfredo and coco shrimp. Be sure to save room for homemade Key lime pie. Casual dress; cocktails. **Parking:** on-site. **Cards:** AX, DC, DS, MC, VI.

(icons)

------ *The following restaurants have not been evaluated by AAA* ------
but are listed for your information only.

MAX & MEGS

Phone: 772/467-0065

(fyi)

Not evaluated. **Location:** 122 N 2nd St 34949. **Features:** A favorite place for burgers and steaks.

MERVIS CAFE & GRILLE

Phone: 772/462-6600

(fyi)

Not evaluated. **Location:** 402 S 5th St 34949. **Features:** Enjoy a memorable Cuban sandwich and after-meal espresso on the outdoor patio.

PINE APPLE JOES

Phone: 772/465-6930

(fyi)

Not evaluated. **Location:** 6297 N US 1 34949. **Features:** Located in Historic Downtown area, chowders, fresh seafood and sandwiches are just a few local favorites.

FORT WALTON BEACH pop. 19,973

------ **WHERE TO STAY** ------

BEST WESTERN FORT WALTON BEACHFRONT HOTEL

Phone: (850)243-9444

(AAA) (SAVE)

3/16-9/3	1P: $149-$189	2P: $149-$289	XP: $10	F12
2/16-3/15	1P: $99-$129	2P: $99-$129	XP: $10	F12
9/4-11/30	1P: $79-$129	2P: $79-$129	XP: $10	F12
12/1-2/15	1P: $79-$99	2P: $79-$99	XP: $10	F12

Small-scale Hotel **Location:** US 98, just sw on Okaloosa Island. 380 Santa Rosa Blvd 32548. **Fax:** 850/243-5465. **Facility:** 100 onebedroom standard units, some with whirlpools. 6 stories, interior/exterior corridors. *Bath:* combo or shower only. **Parking:** on-site. **Terms:** 2-3 night minimum stay - seasonal & weekends, age restrictions may apply, [ECP] meal plan available. **Amenities:** voice mail, irons, hair dryers. **Pool(s):** heated outdoor. **Leisure Activities:** recreation programs. *Fee:* kayak, catamaran, parasailing. **Guest Services:** valet and coin laundry. **Business Services:** meeting rooms, fax. **Cards:** AX, DC, DS, MC, VI. **Special Amenities: free continental breakfast.**

SOME UNITS

(icons)

CAYO GRANDE SUITES

Phone: (850)862-9888

5/1-8/31 [BP]	1P: $85-$180	2P: $85-$180
3/1-4/30 [BP]	1P: $75-$150	2P: $75-$150
9/1-11/30 [BP]	1P: $75-$130	2P: $75-$130
12/1-2/28 [BP]	1P: $69-$115	2P: $69-$115

Small-scale Hotel **Location:** US 98, n on SR 393, w and n on SR 189, 1.6 mi to Racetrack Rd, then 0.9 mi e. 214 Racetrack Rd 32547. **Fax:** 850/862-7467. **Facility:** 103 one-bedroom standard units, some with whirlpools. 6 stories, interior/exterior corridors. **Parking:** on-site. **Terms:** cancellation fee imposed. **Amenities:** voice mail, irons, hair dryers. *Some:* video games, honor bars. **Pool(s):** 3 outdoor. **Leisure Activities:** saunas, putting green, tennis court, exercise room. **Guest Services:** valet and coin laundry. **Business Services:** meeting rooms, fax (fee). **Cards:** AX, DC, DS, MC, VI.

SOME UNITS

(icons)

ECONO LODGE

SAVE

Motel

All Year [CP]   1P: $42-$115   2P: $42-$115   Phone: 850/243-7123
XP: $10   F18

Location: US 98, at northeast end of bridge; eastbound take south service road under bridge. 1284 Marler Ave 32548. **Fax:** 850/243-7109. **Facility:** 59 one-bedroom standard units. 2 stories, interior/exterior corridors. *Bath:* combo or shower only. **Parking:** on-site. **Leisure Activities:** fishing. **Guest Services:** coin laundry. **Business Services:** fax (fee). **Cards:** AX, DC, DS, MC, VI.

SOME UNITS

FOUR POINTS HOTEL SHERATON

Large-scale Hotel

			Phone: (850)243-8116	
5/22-8/16	1P: $140-$185	2P: $140-$185	XP: $10	D18
3/14-5/21 & 8/17-11/30	1P: $120-$145	2P: $120-$145	XP: $10	D18
12/1-3/13	1P: $95-$115	2P: $95-$115	XP: $10	D18

Location: US 98, 0.7 mi e. 1325 Miracle Strip Pkwy 32548. **Fax:** 850/244-3064. **Facility:** 216 one-bedroom standard units, some with whirlpools. 7 stories, interior/exterior corridors. *Bath:* combo or shower only. **Parking:** on-site. **Terms:** age restrictions may apply, cancellation fee imposed, [BP] meal plan available, 17% service charge. **Amenities:** video games, high-speed Internet, voice mail, irons, hair dryers. *Some:* dual phone lines. **Pool(s):** outdoor, heated outdoor. **Leisure Activities:** whirlpools, exercise room, volleyball. **Guest Services:** gift shop, valet and coin laundry. **Business Services:** meeting rooms, fax (fee). **Cards:** AX, CB, DC, DS, MC, VI.

SOME UNITS

HAMPTON INN FORT WALTON BEACH

AAA SAVE

Small-scale Hotel

		Phone: (850)301-0906
5/31-8/20	1P: $149-$169	
3/30-5/30	1P: $109-$129	
12/1-3/29 & 8/21-11/30	1P: $65-$85	

Location: Just w of US 98. 1112 Santa Rosa Blvd 32548. **Fax:** 850/244-2531. **Facility:** 100 one-bedroom standard units. 2 stories, interior corridors. *Bath:* combo or shower only. **Parking:** on-site. **Terms:** check-in 4 pm, cancellation fee imposed. **Amenities:** video games, voice mail, irons, hair dryers. **Pool(s):** outdoor. **Business Services:** fax (fee). **Cards:** AX, DS, MC, VI. **Special Amenities:** free continental breakfast and free local telephone calls.

SOME UNITS

HOLIDAY INN SUNSPREE RESORT

AAA SAVE

Resort
Large-scale Hotel

			Phone: (850)244-8686	
3/7-10/3	1P: $89-$229	2P: $89-$299	XP: $10	F18
12/1-3/6 & 10/4-11/30	1P: $79-$199	2P: $79-$199	XP: $10	F18

Location: 1 mi sw of US 98. 573 Santa Rosa Blvd 32548. **Fax:** 850/244-5926. **Facility:** Some buildings lack elevators. 195 units. 151 one-bedroom standard units. 44 one-bedroom suites with kitchens. 3-7 stories, interior/exterior corridors. *Bath:* combo or shower only. **Parking:** on-site. **Terms:** 2-3 night minimum stay - seasonal. **Amenities:** dual phone lines, voice mail, safes, irons, hair dryers. *Some:* video games. **Dining:** 7 am-11 & 4:30-10 pm; lunch served in season. **Pool(s):** 2 heated outdoor. **Leisure Activities:** whirlpool, recreation programs, exercise room. **Fee:** game room. **Guest Services:** valet and coin laundry. **Business Services:** meeting rooms, fax. **Cards:** AX, CB, DC, DS, MC, VI. *(See color ad below)*

SOME UNITS

FEE

MARINA MOTEL & EFFICIENCIES

AAA SAVE

Motel

			Phone: (850)244-1129	
5/2-9/6	1P: $78-$95	2P: $78-$95	XP: $10	F16
3/2-5/1	1P: $61-$75	2P: $61-$75	XP: $10	F16
9/7-11/30	1P: $61-$69	2P: $61-$69	XP: $10	F16
12/1-3/1	1P: $49-$59	2P: $49-$59	XP: $10	F16

Location: 1 mi e on US 98. 1345 Miracle Strip Pkwy E 32548. **Fax:** 850/243-6063. **Facility:** 38 one-bedroom standard units, some with kitchens. 1-2 stories, interior/exterior corridors. *Bath:* combo or shower only. **Parking:** on-site. **Terms:** 3 day cancellation notice, weekly rates available, [CP] meal plan available, pets ($50 deposit, $9 extra charge). **Amenities:** irons. **Pool(s):** outdoor. **Leisure Activities:** Fee: boat dock, fishing, charter fishing. **Guest Services:** coin laundry. **Business Services:** fax (fee). **Cards:** AX, CB, DC, DS, MC, VI. **Special Amenities:** free continental breakfast.

SOME UNITS

RADISSON BEACH RESORT FT. WALTON BEACH

Phone: (850)243-9181

AAA (SAVE)

5/2-8/10	1P: $134	2P: $144	XP: $10	F16
3/1-5/1 & 8/11-11/30	1P: $107	2P: $117	XP: $10	F16
12/1-2/28	1P: $80	2P: $90	XP: $10	F16

Large-scale Hotel **Location:** US 98, just s. 1110 Santa Rosa Blvd 32548. Fax: 850/664-7652. **Facility:** 287 units. 261 one-bedroom standard units. 26 one-bedroom suites. 7 stories, interior/exterior corridors. **Parking:** on-site. **Terms:** check-in 4 pm, 3 day cancellation notice-fee imposed. **Amenities:** video games, voice mail, irons, hair dryers. **Dining:** 2 restaurants, 6 am-11 pm, cocktails. **Pool(s):** outdoor, heated outdoor, wading. **Leisure Activities:** 2 lighted tennis courts, exercise room. **Guest Services:** gift shop, valet and coin laundry. **Business Services:** conference facilities, fax (fee). **Cards:** AX, DC, DS, MC, VI.

SOME UNITS

⬛ 🍽 🍷 ☕ 🎦 DATA PORT 💻 / ✕ 📱 📠 /
FEE FEE

RAMADA PLAZA BEACH RESORT

Phone: (850)243-9161

5/2-8/31	1P: $130-$185	2P: $130-$185	XP: $10	F18
9/1-11/30 [CP]	1P: $105-$145	2P: $105-$145	XP: $10	F18
3/7-5/1	1P: $105-$145	2P: $105-$145	XP: $10	F18
12/1-3/6 [CP]	1P: $80-$95	2P: $80-$95	XP: $5	F18

Large-scale Hotel **Location:** US 98, 1 mi w. 1500 Miracle Strip Pkwy SE 32548. Fax: 850/243-2391. **Facility:** 335 units. 317 one-bedroom standard units. 18 one-bedroom suites ($150-$360). 6 stories, interior/exterior corridors. **Parking:** on-site. **Terms:** 3 day cancellation notice. **Amenities:** video games, voice mail, safes, irons, hair dryers. **Pool(s):** outdoor, heated outdoor, wading. **Leisure Activities:** whirlpool, exercise room. **Guest Services:** gift shop, valet and coin laundry. **Business Services:** conference facilities, fax (fee). **Cards:** AX, CB, DC, DS, JC, MC, VI.

SOME UNITS

(ASK) ⬛ 🍽 🍷 ☕ 🎦 DATA PORT 📱 💻 / ✕ 📠 /

The following lodgings were either not evaluated or did not
meet AAA rating requirements but are listed for your information only.

EMERALD ISLE CLUB
Phone: 850-244-2534

(fyi)

Condominium

Did not meet all AAA rating requirements for bathrooms at time of last evaluation on 12/13/2001. **Location:** 1.7 mi w of US 98. 770 Sundial Ct 32548. Facilities, services, and decor characterize a mid-range property.

SEA OATS RESORT CONDOMINIUMS
Phone: 850-244-5200

(fyi)

Condominium

Did not meet all AAA rating requirements for. **Location:** 0.5 mi w of US 98. 1114 Santa Rosa Blvd 32548. Facilities, services, and decor characterize a mid-range property.

SUMMERLIN
Phone: 850-244-5200

(fyi)

Condominium

Did not meet all AAA rating requirements for bathrooms at time of last evaluation on 12/13/2001. **Location:** 1.7 mi w of US 98. 774 Sundial Ct 32548. Facilities, services, and decor characterize a mid-range property.

—— WHERE TO DINE ——

OLD BAY STEAMER
Dinner: $6-$23 **Phone:** 850/664-2795

Seafood

Location: US 98, just s. 104 Santa Rosa Blvd 32548. **Hours:** 4 pm-10 pm. Closed: 1/1, 4/20. **Features:** What more can guests ask for than a warm, welcoming atmosphere and fresh, tasty food? A new location hasn't changed this restaurant's good reputation. Casual dress; cocktails. **Parking:** on-site. **Cards:** AX, CB, DC, DS, JC, MC, VI.

✕

PANDORA'S STEAK HOUSE
Dinner: $13-$22 **Phone:** 850/244-8669

Steak House

Location: US 98, just s. 1120B Santa Rosa Blvd 32548. **Hours:** 5 pm-10 pm, Fri & Sat-10:30 pm. Closed: 11/27, 12/24, 12/25; also Mon 9/1-5/25. **Reservations:** accepted. **Features:** On Okaloosa Island, the restaurant specializes in moderately priced preparations of seafood and steak. Casual dress; cocktails; entertainment. **Parking:** on-site. **Cards:** AX, DC, DS, MC, VI.

✕

PRANZO ITALIAN RISTORANTE
Dinner: $8-$22 **Phone:** 850/244-9955

Italian

Location: US 98, just n. 1225 Santa Rosa Blvd 32548. **Hours:** 5 pm-10 pm. Closed major holidays; also Sun. **Reservations:** accepted. **Features:** The restaurant nurtures a traditional Italian atmosphere, with cozy booths and subdued lighting. Couple this with authentic cuisine, and diners are transported to Italy and its family-oriented culture. Portions are ample and desserts delicious. Casual dress; cocktails. **Parking:** on-site. **Cards:** AX, DS, MC, VI.

✕

GAINESVILLE pop. 95,447

—— WHERE TO STAY ——

BAYMONT INN & SUITES-GAINESVILLE
Phone: (352)376-0004

AAA (SAVE)

All Year [ECP]	1P: $74-$154	2P: $79-$159	XP: $5	F18

Small-scale Hotel **Location:** I-75, exit 384, just w. Located behind Cracker Barrel Restaurant. 3905 SW 43rd St 32608. Fax: 352/376-1979. **Facility:** 115 units. 111 one-bedroom standard units, some with whirlpools. 4 one-bedroom suites with whirlpools, some with kitchens. 4 stories, interior corridors. **Bath:** combo or shower only. **Parking:** on-site. **Terms:** weekly rates available, small pets only ($10 fee, in designated units). **Amenities:** video games, dual phone lines, voice mail, irons, hair dryers. **Pool(s):** heated outdoor. **Leisure Activities:** exercise room. **Guest Services:** valet and coin laundry. **Business Services:** meeting rooms, fax. **Cards:** AX, DC, DS, MC, VI. **Special Amenities:** free continental breakfast and free newspaper.

SOME UNITS

⬛ 🛏 🍽 ♿ ☕ 🎦 DATA PORT 💻 / ✕ 📱 📠 /

BEST WESTERN GATEWAY GRAND

SAVE

▽▽▽▽▽

Small-scale Hotel

Phone: (352)331-3336

All Year [ECP]   1P: $79   2P: $79
Location: I-75, exit 390, just n of SR 222, just w. 4200 NW 97th Blvd 32606. Fax: 352/331-3337. **Facility:** 152 units. 151 one-bedroom standard units. 1 two-bedroom suite ($99). 3 stories, interior corridors. *Bath:* some combo or shower only. **Parking:** on-site. **Terms:** check-in 4 pm, small pets only ($15 extra charge). **Amenities:** video games, voice mail, irons, hair dryers. **Pool(s):** outdoor. **Leisure Activities:** whirlpool, exercise room. *Fee:* massage. **Guest Services:** valet and coin laundry. **Business Services:** conference facilities, fax. **Cards:** AX, CB, DC, DS, MC, VI. *(See color ad below)*

SOME UNITS

CABOT LODGE

▽▽▽▽▽

Small-scale Hotel

Phone: (352)375-2400
XP: $18   F18

All Year   1P: $80-$95   2P: $87-$102
Location: I-75, exit 384, just e on SR 24. 3726 SW 40th Blvd 32608. Fax: 352/335-2321. **Facility:** 208 one-bedroom standard units. 3 stories, interior corridors. **Parking:** on-site. **Terms:** [ECP] meal plan available. **Amenities:** voice mail, irons, hair dryers. **Pool(s):** outdoor. **Leisure Activities:** exercise room. **Guest Services:** complimentary evening beverages, valet laundry. **Business Services:** meeting rooms, business center. **Cards:** AX, CB, DC, DS, MC, VI.

SOME UNITS

COMFORT INN

AAA SAVE

▽▽▽▽

Small-scale Hotel

Phone: (352)373-6500
XP: $6   F18

All Year [ECP]   1P: $50-$115   2P: $56-$125
Location: I-75, exit 382, 2 mi ne on SR 331, then 1 mi n on US 441. 2435 SW 13th St 32608. Fax: 352/224-3311. **Facility:** 60 one-bedroom standard units, some with kitchens and/or whirlpools. 2 stories, exterior corridors. *Bath:* combo or shower only. **Parking:** on-site. **Terms:** 3 day cancellation notice. **Amenities:** *Some:* irons, hair dryers. **Pool(s):** outdoor. **Leisure Activities:** whirlpool. **Guest Services:** fax (fee). **Cards:** AX, CB, DC, DS, JC, MC, VI. **Special Amenities:** free continental breakfast.

SOME UNITS

COMFORT INN WEST
Phone: (352)264-1771

AAA SAVE ▽▽▽▽ / All Year [ECP] 1P: $69-$109 2P: $69-$109 XP: $5 F18
Location: I-75, exit 384, just e, then just n. 3440 SW 40th Blvd 32608. Fax: 352/264-9996. **Facility:** 83 units. 78 one-bedroom standard units, some with whirlpools. 5 one-bedroom suites ($89-$119), some with whirlpools. 4 stories, interior corridors. *Bath:* combo or shower only. **Parking:** on-site. **Terms:** pets ($10 extra charge).
Small-scale Hotel **Amenities:** voice mail, irons, hair dryers. **Pool(s):** small outdoor. **Leisure Activities:** exercise room. **Guest Services:** valet and coin laundry. **Business Services:** meeting rooms, fax (fee). **Cards:** AX, CB, DC, DS, JC, MC, VI. **Special Amenities: free continental breakfast and free local telephone calls.**

SOME UNITS
[icons] / [icons] / VCR FEE

COURTYARD BY MARRIOTT
Phone: 352/335-9100

SAVE ▽▽▽ / All Year 1P: $93
Location: I-75, exit 384, just e on SR 24. 3700 SW 42nd St 32608. Fax: 352/335-1502. **Facility:** 81 units. 78 one-bedroom standard units. 3 one-bedroom suites ($139). 3 stories, interior corridors. *Bath:* combo or shower only. **Parking:** on-site. **Terms:** [BP] meal plan available. **Amenities:** voice mail, irons, hair dryers. **Pool(s):** Small-scale Hotel heated outdoor. **Leisure Activities:** whirlpool, exercise room. **Guest Services:** valet and coin laundry. **Business Services:** meeting rooms, fax. **Cards:** AX, DC, DS, MC, VI.

SOME UNITS
[icons] / [icons]

DOUBLETREE HOTEL & CONFERENCE CENTER, U.F.
Phone: (352)371-3600

SAVE ▽▽▽ / All Year 1P: $99-$209 2P: $99-$209 XP: $15 F18
Location: I-75, exit 384, 0.9 mi e on SR 24, then 0.7 mi n on SR 121. Located in the University of Florida. 1714 SW 34th St 32607. Fax: 352/371-0306. **Facility:** 246 units. 245 one-bedroom standard units. 1 one-bedroom suite. 7 stories, interior corridors. *Bath:* combo or shower only. **Parking:** on-site. **Terms:** check-in 4 pm, cancellation Large-scale Hotel fee imposed, 20% service charge. **Amenities:** video games, high-speed Internet, dual phone lines, voice mail, irons, hair dryers. **Pool(s):** outdoor. **Leisure Activities:** whirlpool, exercise room. **Guest Services:** valet laundry. **Business Services:** meeting rooms, business center. **Cards:** AX, DC, DS, MC, VI.

SOME UNITS
[icons] / [icons] FEE

EXTENDED STAY AMERICA
Phone: (352)375-0073

▽▽▽ / All Year 1P: $55-$60 2P: $60-$65 XP: $5 F4
Location: I-75, exit 384, just e. 3600 SW 42nd St 32608. Fax: 352/375-0960. **Facility:** 120 one-bedroom standard Small-scale Hotel units with efficiencies. 3 stories, exterior corridors. *Bath:* combo or shower only. **Parking:** on-site. **Terms:** weekly rates available. **Amenities:** voice mail. **Guest Services:** coin laundry. **Business Services:** fax (fee). **Cards:** AX, CB, DC, DS, MC, VI.

SOME UNITS
[icons] / [icons]

FAIRFIELD INN

Small-scale Hotel

Phone: (352)332-8292

All Year [ECP]   1P: $49-$149   2P: $49-$149
Location: I-75, exit 387, just w on SR 26 to 75th St, just s to NW 4th Blvd, then e. 6901 NW 4th Blvd 32607. Fax: 352/332-8292. **Facility:** 135 one-bedroom standard units. 3 stories, interior/exterior corridors. **Parking:** on-site. **Amenities:** irons, hair dryers. **Pool(s):** heated outdoor. **Guest Services:** valet laundry. **Business Services:** fax (fee). **Cards:** AX, DC, DS, MC, VI.

SOME UNITS

HAMPTON INN

Small-scale Hotel

Phone: (352)371-4171

All Year [ECP]   1P: $80-$159   2P: $85-$159
Location: I-75, exit 384, just se. 4225 SW 40th Blvd 32608. Fax: 352/371-4234. **Facility:** 105 units. 96 one-bedroom standard units. 9 one-bedroom suites with whirlpools. 4 stories, interior/exterior corridors. *Bath:* combo or shower only. **Parking:** on-site. **Amenities:** voice mail, irons, hair dryers. **Pool(s):** heated outdoor. **Leisure Activities:** exercise room. **Guest Services:** valet laundry. **Business Services:** meeting rooms, fax (fee). **Cards:** AX, CB, DC, DS, MC, VI.

SOME UNITS

HOLIDAY INN UNIVERSITY CENTER

Small-scale Hotel

Phone: (352)376-1661

All Year   1P: $89   2P: $89
Location: Jct US 441/SR 24; downtown. Located adjacent to the University of Florida. 1250 W University Ave 32601. Fax: 352/336-8717. **Facility:** 166 one-bedroom standard units. 6 stories, interior corridors. *Bath:* combo or shower only. **Parking:** on-site. **Terms:** 3 day cancellation notice. **Amenities:** high-speed Internet, voice mail, irons, hair dryers. **Dining:** 24 hours. **Pool(s):** outdoor. **Leisure Activities:** exercise room. **Guest Services:** valet laundry, area transportation-hospital. **Business Services:** meeting rooms, fax. **Cards:** AX, CB, DC, DS, MC. **Special Amenities:** free newspaper and free room upgrade (subject to availability with advanced reservations).
(See color ad opposite inside back cover)

SOME UNITS

HOLIDAY INN-WEST

Small-scale Hotel

Phone: (352)332-7500

All Year   1P: $82-$109   2P: $82-$109
Location: I-75, exit 387, just w. 7417 NW 8th Ave 32605. Fax: 352/332-0487. **Facility:** 276 units. 273 one-bedroom standard units. 2 one-bedroom suites. 2 stories, exterior corridors. **Parking:** on-site. **Terms:** cancellation fee imposed. **Amenities:** video games, high-speed Internet, voice mail, irons, hair dryers. **Dining:** 6 am-2 & 5-10 pm; Comedy Club, cocktails. **Pool(s):** outdoor, heated outdoor, wading. **Leisure Activities:** exercise room. **Guest Services:** valet and coin laundry, area transportation-hospital. **Business Services:** conference facilities, fax (fee). **Cards:** AX, CB, DC, DS, MC, VI. *(See color ad p 436 & opposite inside back cover)*

SOME UNITS

LA QUINTA INN

Small-scale Hotel

Phone: (352)332-6466

All Year   1P: $60-$86   2P: $66-$92   XP: $6   F18
Location: I-75, exit 387, just e, then just n. Located behind the Red Lobster Restaurant. 920 NW 69th Terrace 32605. Fax: 352/332-7074. **Facility:** 135 units. 134 one-bedroom standard units. 1 one-bedroom suite ($109-$179) with kitchen. 3-4 stories, exterior corridors. **Parking:** on-site. **Terms:** [ECP] meal plan available, small pets only. **Amenities:** video games, voice mail, irons, hair dryers. **Pool(s):** heated outdoor. **Guest Services:** valet laundry. **Business Services:** meeting rooms, fax. **Cards:** AX, CB, DC, DS, JC, MC, VI. **Special Amenities:** free continental breakfast and free local telephone calls.

SOME UNITS
FEE

RED ROOF INN-GAINESVILLE

Phone: (352)336-3311

AAA [SAVE]

WWW

Small-scale Hotel

All Year .... 1P: $39-$49 .... 2P: $45-$55 .... XP: $6 .... F18
Location: I-75, exit 384, just e. 3500 SW 42nd St 32608. Fax: 352/336-7855. **Facility:** 129 units. 125 one-bedroom standard units. 4 one-bedroom suites ($62-$74). 4 stories, interior corridors. **Bath:** combo or shower only. **Parking:** on-site. **Amenities:** voice mail. **Pool(s):** heated outdoor. **Guest Services:** coin laundry. **Business Services:** fax. **Cards:** AX, CB, DC, DS, MC, VI. **Special Amenities:** free local telephone calls and free newspaper.

SOME UNITS

 🛏 🛗 🅼 🚫 🎦 🏊 🐾 🍴 DATA PORT / ✕ 🗄 🖥 /

SHERATON GAINESVILLE

Phone: (352)377-4000

WWWW

Small-scale Hotel

All Year .... 1P: $99-$209 ...... 2P: $99-$209 ...... XP: $10 ...... F17
Location: I-75, exit 382, 2 mi ne on SR 331, 0.8 mi n on US 441. 2900 SW 13th St 32608. Fax: 352/377-7766. **Facility:** 197 units. 191 one-bedroom standard units. 6 one-bedroom suites ($119-$289). 4 stories, interior corridors. **Bath:** combo or shower only. **Parking:** on-site. **Terms:** cancellation fee imposed, [BP] & [CP] meal plans available, package plans. **Amenities:** video games, dual phone lines, voice mail, irons, hair dryers. *Some:* fax. **Pool(s):** outdoor. **Leisure Activities:** recreation programs, exercise room. **Guest Services:** valet and coin laundry, area transportation. **Business Services:** conference facilities, fax (fee). **Cards:** AX, DC, DS, MC, VI. *(See color ad p 437 & p 5)*

SOME UNITS

[ASK] 🆂🄳 📶 🍴 🍸 🅼 🎦 🐾 🍴 DATA PORT 🖥 / ✕ [VCR] 🗄 🖥 /
            FEE   FEE FEE

SUPER 8 OF GAINESVILLE

Phone: (352)372-3654

AAA [SAVE]

WWW

Motel

All Year .... 1P: $40-$125 ...... 2P: $45-$130 ...... XP: $5 ...... F11
Location: I-75, exit 382, 2 mi e on SR 331, then 1.1 mi n on US 441. 2000 SW 13th St 32608. Fax: 352/335-7936. **Facility:** 41 one-bedroom standard units. 2 stories, exterior corridors. **Parking:** on-site. **Terms:** 7 day cancellation notice-fee imposed, [CP] meal plan available. **Business Services:** fax. **Cards:** AX, DC, DS, MC, VI. **Special Amenities:** free continental breakfast and free newspaper.

SOME UNITS

🆂🄳 🛗 🍴 DATA PORT / ✕ 🗄 🖥 /

SWEETWATER BRANCH INN BED & BREAKFAST

Phone: (352)373-6760

AAA [SAVE]

WWWW

Bed & Breakfast

All Year [BP] .... 2P: $90-$165 ...... XP: $20 ...... F3
Location: 1.3 mi e of the University on SR 26; 7.3 mi e of I-75, exit 387. Located in a light business, residential area. 625 E University Ave 32601. Fax: 352/371-3771. **Facility:** On landscaped grounds close to the center of town, this B&B is actually two 1895 houses, each with guest rooms decorated in period. Designated smoking area. 13 units. 9 one-bedroom standard units, some with whirlpools. 3 one-bedroom suites. 1 cottage. 2-3 stories (no elevator), interior corridors. **Parking:** on-site. **Terms:** 2 night minimum stay, 7 day cancellation notice-fee imposed, weekly rates available. **Amenities:** voice mail, irons, hair dryers. *Some:* CD players. **Dining:** 11:30 am-2 pm. **Guest Services:** complimentary evening beverages. **Business Services:** meeting rooms, fax. **Cards:** AX, MC, VI.

SOME UNITS

🍴 🅼 ✕ DATA PORT / [VCR] 🗄 🖥 🖥 /
      FEE

─────── WHERE TO DINE ───────

AMELIA'S

WW

Italian

Lunch: $9-$15 .... **Dinner:** $9-$19 .... **Phone:** 352-373-1919
Location: Just s on SR 329, just e; in Sun Centre Mall; entrance thru courtyard. 235 S Main St 32601. **Hours:** 11:30 am-2:30 & 5-10 pm, Fri-11 pm, Sat 5 pm-11 pm, Sun 5 pm-9 pm. Closed major holidays; also Mon-Wed for lunch. **Reservations:** suggested; weekends. **Features:** In the historic district behind Hippodrome Theatre is this restaurant with two cozy dining rooms. A large, covered patio runs the width of the restaurant and is accessed from the courtyard around the theater. Olive oil complements the warm loaf of Italian bread and crisp, green salad. Chicken, veal and fish, prepared in a variety of Italian and other European ways, are available. Servers are friendly. Smoke free premises. Casual dress; cocktails. **Parking:** street. **Cards:** AX, DC, MC, VI.

✕

GATOR GREATS

WW

American

Lunch: $11-$17 .... **Dinner:** $11-$17 .... **Phone:** 352-378-5494
Location: Downtown. 201 SE 2nd Ave, Suite 102 32601. **Hours:** 11 am-10 pm, Fri & Sat-midnight. Closed: 11/27, 12/25; also Sun & Mon for dinner. **Features:** This casual restaurant features walls adorned with memorabilia from past University of Florida sports figures. There are a number of televisions throughout the restaurant and lounge for sports viewing. The menu features beef, seafood and pasta. There are also numerous salad choices or simply try the salad bar. Casual dress; cocktails. **Parking:** street. **Cards:** AX, CB, DC, DS, JC, MC, VI.

🍸

MILDRED'S BIG CITY FOOD

AAA

WWW

American

Lunch: $6-$8 .... **Dinner:** $13-$29 .... **Phone:** 352-371-1711
Location: I-75, exit 387, 3 mi e on SR 26; at west end of Westgate Regency Shopping Center. 3445 W University Ave 32607. **Hours:** 11 am-9 pm, Fri & Sat-10 pm. Closed: 11/27, 12/25; also Sun. **Reservations:** suggested; for dinner. **Features:** By day, this place is a coffee shop serving estate coffees with unusual sandwiches, hummus, roast tomato and more standard fare. By night, it's a trendy bistro with sophisticated fare. Alligator fritters and roast butternut and scallop bisque lead to a baby green salad with blue cheese and spiced walnuts. Entrees include pecan-crusted chicken with brandied sweet potatoes, as well as varied beef, lamb and seafood choices. To ensure freshness, the menu changes almost daily. Smoke free premises. Casual dress; cocktails. **Parking:** on-site. **Cards:** AX, DS, MC, VI.

🍸 ✕

POMODORO CAFE

WW

Italian

Lunch: $5-$9 .... **Dinner:** $7-$16 .... **Phone:** 352-380-9886
Location: I-75, exit 390, just e. 9200 NW 39th Ave 32606. **Hours:** 11 am-10 pm, Sun-9 pm. Closed: 11/27, 12/25. **Features:** Colorful murals adorn the walls and help create a lively, festive feeling. The menu is steeped in Italian tradition, with offerings of bruschetta, cappellini Francesco and tiramisu. Smoke free premises. Casual dress; beer & wine only. **Parking:** on-site. **Cards:** AX, DC, DS, MC, VI.

✕

THE SOVEREIGN RESTAURANT **Dinner:** $18-$27 **Phone:** 352/378-6307
Continental
Location: Just e of SR 329. 12 SE 2nd Ave 32601. **Hours:** 5:30 pm-10 pm, Fri & Sat-11 pm. Closed major holidays; also Sun & middle 2 weeks of Aug. **Reservations:** suggested. **Features:** Just east of Main Street in a converted turn-of-the-20th-century carriage house, this restaurant almost has become a Gainesville institution. The menu borrows from Europe in style of preparation. Specialties are aged beef and veal on a menu that also includes lamb, chicken, fish and seafood dishes, as well as a few vegetarian choices and even some game. Service has some formal touches but is friendly and not at all stuffy. The owner/chef has been in this location since 1976. Dressy casual; cocktails. **Parking:** street. **Cards:** AX, CB, DC, DS, MC, VI.

STEVE'S CAFE AMERICAIN **Dinner:** $15-$26 **Phone:** 352/377-9337
American
Location: Just w of Main St (SR 329) on SR 26. 12 W University Ave 32601. **Hours:** 5 pm-10 pm. Closed major holidays. **Reservations:** accepted. **Features:** In a storefront at the center of downtown, the restaurant is convenient to theater and other nightlife, just a short distance from the University of Florida campus. The kitchen—in the center of the dining room—hides nothing. As the name implies, the food is American with preparation styles borrowed from the classic French. The menu changes seasonally. Desserts, including ice creams, are made on site and are worth saving room for. Prix fixe menus are also available. Smoke free premises. Casual dress; cocktails. **Parking:** street. **Cards:** AX, DC, DS, MC, VI.

GREEN COVE SPRINGS —*See Jacksonville p. 469.*

GULF BREEZE pop. 5,665

—— WHERE TO DINE ——

THE CREAMERY CAFE **Lunch:** $5-$7 **Dinner:** $6-$11 **Phone:** 850/932-1525
Regional German
Location: US 98; at Gulf Breeze Shopping Center. 348 Gulf Breeze Pkwy 32561. **Hours:** 8 am-9 pm. Closed: 11/27, 12/25. **Features:** Stop on the way to or from the coast at this family run cafe. As the name so aptly describes, creamy delicious ice cream is a must at this delightful eatery. This is not their only feature; lunch and dinner selections include German and Gulf Coast style soup, sandwiches and entrees. A complimentary glass of wine is served with a dinner entree. Smoke free premises. Casual dress; beer only. **Parking:** on-site. **Cards:** AX, DS, MC, VI.

HAINES CITY pop. 13,174

──────── **WHERE TO STAY** ────────

BEST WESTERN LAKE HAMILTON   Phone: (863)421-6929

ⒶⒶⒶ SAVE	2/10-4/20	1P: $79-$94	2P: $79-$94	XP: $3	F14
	6/23-11/30	1P: $62-$87	2P: $62-$87	XP: $3	F14
▽▽▽	12/1-2/9	1P: $65-$80	2P: $65-$80	XP: $3	F14
Motel	4/21-6/22	1P: $57-$72	2P: $57-$72	XP: $3	F14

Location: On US 27, just s of jct SR 544, 2 mi s of jct US 17-92. 605 B Moore Rd 33844. Fax: 863/422-0409. **Facility:** 50 units. 46 one-bedroom standard units. 4 one-bedroom suites ($80-$94). 1 story, exterior corridors. **Parking:** on-site. **Terms:** [ECP] meal plan available, pets ($5 extra charge). **Amenities:** irons, hair dryers. **Pool(s):** heated outdoor. **Leisure Activities:** lighted tennis court, shuffleboard. **Guest Services:** coin laundry. **Business Services:** meeting rooms, fax (fee). **Cards:** AX, CB, DC, DS, JC, MC, VI. **Special Amenities:** free continental breakfast and free newspaper.

SOME UNITS
🆂🅳 🐶 ♿M 🍴 🎦 DATA PORT 📺 / ⊠ 📶 🛎 / FEE FEE

HOWARD JOHNSON INN   Phone: (863)422-8621

ⒶⒶⒶ SAVE	All Year	1P: $49-$59	2P: $49-$59

▽▽▽ ▽▽
Motel

Location: US 27, 1.8 mi s of jct US 17-92. 33224 Hwy 27 S 33844. Fax: 863/421-4745. **Facility:** 120 one-bedroom standard units. 2 stories, exterior corridors. **Parking:** on-site. **Terms:** cancellation fee imposed, pets ($10 extra charge). **Dining:** 6:30 am-9 pm, cocktails. **Pool(s):** outdoor. **Guest Services:** coin laundry. **Business Services:** meeting rooms, fax (fee). **Cards:** AX, CB, DC, DS, JC, MC, VI. **Special Amenities:** early check-in/late check-out and free newspaper.

SOME UNITS
🆂🅳 🐶 🍴 🍸 🎦 🛎 📺 / ⊠ ✕

HALLANDALE BEACH —See Fort Lauderdale p. 394.

HAVANA pop. 1,713

──────── **WHERE TO DINE** ────────

NICHOLSON FARMHOUSE Historic   **Dinner:** $10-$26   Phone: 850/539-5931

▽▽ ▽▽
Steak House

Location: SR 12, 3.5 mi w of US 27. 200 Coca Cola Ave, SR 12 32333. **Hours:** 4 pm-10 pm. Closed major holidays; also Sun & Mon. **Reservations:** suggested. **Features:** This complex of five historic houses on 40 rustic acres is an unusual location in which to enjoy monstrous portions of quality beef, well-aged and cooked to order. Down-to-earth servers are attentive and friendly. Save room for strawberry shortcake. Casual dress. **Parking:** on-site. **Cards:** AX, DS, MC, VI.

⊠

HEATHROW —See Orlando p. 677.

HERNANDO pop. 8,253

──────── **WHERE TO STAY** ────────

BEST WESTERN CITRUS HILLS LODGE   Phone: (352)527-0015

SAVE	12/1-4/30 & 10/2-11/30 [CP]	1P: $88-$98	2P: $88-$98	XP: $7	F17
	5/1-10/1 [CP]	1P: $78-$88	2P: $78-$88	XP: $7	F17

▽▽▽ ▽▽
Small-scale Hotel

Location: CR 486 at jct Citrus Hills Blvd, 3.3 mi w of US 41. 350 E Norvell Bryant Hwy 34442. Fax: 352/527-2360. **Facility:** 50 one-bedroom standard units, some with whirlpools. 2 stories, exterior corridors. **Parking:** on-site. **Terms:** small pets only ($10 extra charge). **Amenities:** voice mail, irons, hair dryers. **Pool(s):** heated outdoor. **Leisure Activities:** Fee: massage. **Guest Services:** coin laundry. **Business Services:** meeting rooms, fax (fee). **Cards:** AX, DC, DS, MC, VI.

SOME UNITS
🆂🅳 🐶 🍴 ♿M 🎦 📺 / ⊠ 📶 🛎 /

──────── **WHERE TO DINE** ────────

ANDRE'S OF CITRUS HILLS   **Lunch:** $6-$10   **Dinner:** $12-$20   Phone: 352/746-6855

▽▽▽ ▽▽
American

Location: 1 mi s of CR 486 on Citrus Hills Blvd; 3.3 mi w of US 441; at Citrus Hills Country Club. 505 E Hartford St 34442. **Hours:** 11:30 am-9 pm, Fri-9:30 pm, Sat & Sun noon-9:30 pm. Closed: 12/24, 12/25. **Reservations:** accepted. **Features:** This country club restaurant offers informal dining overlooking a golf course. House specialties include baked prime rib, ostrich and seafood FraDiablo. Peruse the "Wall of Fame" featuring George Bush. Dressy casual; cocktails. **Parking:** on-site. **Cards:** AX, DC, DS, MC, VI.

♿M 🍸 ⊠

HIALEAH —See Miami-Miami Beach p. 550.

HIGHLAND BEACH pop. 3,775

──────── **WHERE TO STAY** ────────

HOLIDAY INN-HIGHLAND BEACH   Phone: (561)278-6241

▽▽▽ ▽	All Year	1P: $99-$279	2P: $99-$279

Small-scale Hotel

Location: SR A1A, 1 mi s of Linton Blvd. 2809 S Ocean Blvd 33487. Fax: 561/278-7133. **Facility:** 115 units. 112 one-bedroom standard units. 3 one-bedroom suites. 3-6 stories, interior/exterior corridors. **Bath:** combo or shower only. **Parking:** on-site. **Terms:** check-in 4 pm, cancellation fee imposed. **Amenities:** dual phone lines, voice mail, safes, irons, hair dryers. **Pool(s):** heated outdoor, wading. **Leisure Activities:** whirlpool, exercise room. **Guest Services:** gift shop, valet and coin laundry. **Business Services:** meeting rooms, fax (fee). **Cards:** AX, DC, DS, MC, VI.
(See color ad opposite inside back cover & p 249)

SOME UNITS
ⒶⓈⓀ 🆂🅳 🍴 🍸 ♿M 🐶 🎦 DATA PORT 📺 / ⊠ 📶 🛎 /

HIGH SPRINGS pop. 3,863

———— WHERE TO STAY ————

GRADY HOUSE BED AND BREAKFAST
Phone: (386)454-2206

Historic Bed & Breakfast

All Year [BP]   1P: $85-$125   2P: $85-$125   XP: $15
Location: 0.5 mi n on US 27. 420 NW 1st Ave 32643 (PO Box 205, 32655). Fax: 386/454-3486. **Facility:** Built in 1917, this B&B is decorated with an extensive collection of reproduction and original artwork. Designated smoking area. 5 units. 1 one-bedroom standard unit. 4 one-bedroom suites. 2 stories, interior corridors. *Bath:* combo or shower only. **Parking:** on-site. **Terms:** age restrictions may apply, 7 day cancellation notice-fee imposed, weekly rates available. **Cards:** AX, DS, MC, VI.

THE RUSTIC INN BED & BREAKFAST
Phone: (386)454-1223

Motel

3/1-10/31 [ECP]   1P: $79-$119   2P: $79-$119   XP: $15
12/1-2/28 & 11/1-11/30 [ECP]   1P: $69-$89   2P: $69-$89   XP: $15
Location: 2.1 mi s on US 27/41. 3105 S Main St 32643. Fax: 386/454-1225. **Facility:** Designated smoking area. 6 one-bedroom standard units. 1 story, exterior corridors. **Parking:** on-site. **Terms:** 7 day cancellation notice-fee imposed, weekly rates available. **Amenities:** video library. **Pool(s):** outdoor. **Cards:** MC, VI.

SOME UNITS

———— WHERE TO DINE ————

THE GREAT OUTDOORS TRADING
COMPANY & CAFE   Historic   **Lunch:** $6-$13   **Dinner:** $6-$15   **Phone:** 386/454-2900

American

Location: On US 27/41; center. 65 N Main St 32643. **Hours:** 10 am-8:30 pm, Fri-9:30 pm, Sat 9 am-9:30 pm, Sun 9 am-8:30 pm. **Closed:** 12/25. **Features:** The trading company and cafe are in the restored center of a small historic town in two buildings that once were the 1895 opera house and a 1915 barber shop. Antique and art shops line this section of Main Street. Down-home cooking features the likes of wok magic, Szechuan eggplant and New York strip steak. A variety of sandwiches, salads and soups also are provided. Finish with one of the many desserts or one of the numerous espresso drinks. Smoke free premises. Casual dress; beer & wine only. **Parking:** on-site. **Cards:** AX, DC, DS, MC, VI.

HILLSBORO BEACH —See Fort Lauderdale p. 396.

HOLIDAY —See Tampa Bay p. 917.

HOLLYWOOD —See Fort Lauderdale p. 396.

HOLMES BEACH pop. 4,966   (See map p. 812; index p. 815)

———— WHERE TO STAY ————

THE BEACH INN
Phone: (941)778-9597   84

Motel

12/17-5/1 [CP]   2P: $129-$209   XP: $25   F
12/1-12/16 & 5/2-11/30 [CP]   2P: $99-$149   XP: $25   F
Location: On CR 789, 1.5 mi n of jct SR 64. Located in a residential area. 101 66th St 34217. Fax: 941/778-8303. **Facility:** Smoke free premises. 24 units. 14 one-bedroom standard units, some with whirlpools. 10 one-bedroom suites with kitchens. 1-2 stories (no elevator), exterior corridors. *Bath:* combo or shower only. **Parking:** on-site. **Terms:** 2 night minimum stay - weekends, 14 day cancellation notice. **Amenities:** video library, voice mail, irons, hair dryers. **Pool(s):** 2 heated outdoor. **Guest Services:** coin laundry. **Cards:** MC, VI. **Special Amenities:** free continental breakfast.

SOME UNITS

HARRINGTON HOUSE BEACHFRONT BED & BREAKFAST
Phone: (941)778-5444   85

Bed & Breakfast

5/1-11/30 [BP]   2P: $139-$349   XP: $25
12/17-4/30 [BP]   2P: $189-$329   XP: $25
12/1-12/16 [BP]   2P: $139-$329   XP: $25
Location: On CR 789, 1.2 mi n of jct SR 64. Residential area. 5626 Gulf Dr 34217. Fax: 941/778-0527. **Facility:** Made from indigenous coquina, this 1925 B&B fronting on the gulf features individually decorated rooms, some with fireplaces. Designated smoking area. 19 units. 15 one-bedroom standard units, some with whirlpools. 1 one- and 2 two-bedroom suites. 1 cottage. 1-3 stories (no elevator), interior/exterior corridors. *Bath:* combo or shower only. **Parking:** on-site. **Terms:** 2 night minimum stay - weekends, age restrictions may apply, 14 day cancellation notice. **Amenities:** video library, voice mail, irons, hair dryers. **Pool(s):** heated outdoor. **Leisure Activities:** sea kayaks, bicycles. **Guest Services:** gift shop. **Cards:** AX, MC, VI.

SOME UNITS

———— WHERE TO DINE ————

BEACH BISTRO
Dinner: $22-$24   **Phone:** 941/778-6444   43

American

Location: CR 789, 1.5 mi n of jct SR 64. 6600 Gulf Dr 34217. **Hours:** 5:30 pm-9:30 pm, Fri & Sat-10 pm. **Closed:** 11/27, 12/25; also 1/19. **Reservations:** suggested. **Features:** The award-winning, beachfront restaurant is noted for its creative appetizers, main dishes and desserts. Smoke free premises. Casual dress; cocktails. **Parking:** on-site. **Cards:** AX, CB, DC, DS, MC, VI.

OOH LA LA!
Lunch: $5-$15   **Dinner:** $18-$27   **Phone:** 941/778-5320   44

French

Location: Just off Gulf Dr; in Island Shopping Center. 5406 Marina Dr 34217. **Hours:** 11 am-2:30 & 5:30-9:30 pm, Sun from 8 am. **Closed:** 12/25; also Mon & Tues. **Features:** Located in an older strip mall setting, this small but quaint bistro-type setting with its French flair for decor, offers a friendly, welcoming staff ready to serve such items as veal, salmon, lamb, duck, venison, omelets and croissants all freshly prepared by the owner/chef. Try the potato-crusted grouper with its rich variety of spices and a wonderful gravy blend. Wine is available with top California selections. Smoke free premises. Casual dress; beer & wine only. **Parking:** on-site. **Cards:** MC, VI.

HOMESTEAD —See Miami-Miami Beach p. 551.

HOMOSASSA pop. 2,294

——— WHERE TO STAY ———

THE LAST RESORT
Phone: 352/628-7117
▼▼ ▼▼ All Year   1P: $100   2P: $100   XP: $10   F10
Cottage
Location: 2.5 mi w of US 19/98. 10738 W Halls River Rd 34448. **Facility:** 6 cottages ($100). 1 story, exterior corridors. **Parking:** on-site. **Terms:** 7 day cancellation notice-fee imposed. **Leisure Activities:** boat dock, fishing. **Guest Services:** coin laundry. **Business Services:** fax. **Cards:** MC, VI.

——— WHERE TO DINE ———

K C CRUMP RESTAURANT   **Lunch: $7-$12**   **Dinner: $11-$22**   **Phone: 352/628-1500**
▼▼ ▼▼ **Location:** 3.5 mi w of US 19 via CR 490A. 11210 W Halls River Rd 34448. **Hours:** 3 pm-11 pm, Sun from 11 am.
Seafood   Closed: 12/25; also Mon. **Reservations:** suggested. **Features:** A converted 19th-century fishing lodge set on the scenic Homosassa River, this popular lunch and dinner spot features fresh local shrimp, seafood and steak choices. Savor the tender filet served with a baked potato and fresh vegetables. Casual dress; cocktails. **Parking:** on-site. **Cards:** MC, VI.

HOWEY-IN-THE-HILLS —See Orlando p. 677.

INDIALANTIC pop. 2,944—See also MELBOURNE.

——— WHERE TO STAY ———

GUESTHOUSE INTERNATIONAL INN
Phone: (321)779-9994
AAA SAVE   12/1-4/30 [CP]   1P: $59-$149   2P: $69-$149   XP: $10   F12
▼▼ ▼▼ 5/1-11/30 [CP]   1P: $49-$99   2P: $59-$99   XP: $10   F12
Motel   **Location:** 0.4 mi s of SR 518 (Eau Gallie Cswy). 2900 N A1A Hwy 32903. Fax: 321/779-3933. **Facility:** 26 one-bedroom standard units, some with efficiencies. 2 stories, exterior corridors. *Bath:* some shared or private. **Parking:** on-site. **Terms:** 7 day cancellation notice-fee imposed, small pets only ($10 extra charge). **Amenities:** hair dryers. *Some:* irons. **Dining:** 11 am-9 pm, Fri & Sat-11 pm. **Pool(s):** small outdoor. **Leisure Activities:** whirlpool. **Guest Services:** coin laundry. **Business Services:** fax (fee). **Cards:** AX, DC, DS, MC, VI.
SOME UNITS

HILTON MELBOURNE BEACH OCEANFRONT
Phone: 321/777-5000
SAVE   2/1-5/31   1P: $119-$199   2P: $129-$209   XP: $10   F18
   12/1-1/31 & 6/1-11/30   1P: $99-$179   2P: $109-$189   XP: $10   F18
▼▼ ▼▼ ▼ **Location:** N SR A1A, 3 mi n of jct US 192. 3003 N SR A1A 32903. Fax: 321/777-3713. **Facility:** 118 one-bedroom
Small-scale Hotel   standard units. 11 stories, interior corridors. **Parking:** on-site. **Terms:** cancellation fee imposed, package plans, pets ($25 deposit, $10 extra charge). **Amenities:** dual phone lines, voice mail, irons, hair dryers. **Pool(s):** heated outdoor. **Leisure Activities:** whirlpool, exercise room, volleyball. **Guest Services:** gift shop, valet laundry. **Business Services:** conference facilities, PC, fax (fee). **Cards:** AX, CB, DC, DS, JC, MC, VI.
(See color ad p 498)
SOME UNITS

HOLIDAY INN MELBOURNE OCEANFRONT
Phone: (321)777-4100
AAA SAVE   1/31-4/19   1P: $109-$179   2P: $109-$179   XP: $10   F17
▼▼ ▼▼ ▼ 12/1-1/30 & 4/20-11/30   1P: $99-$169   2P: $99-$169   XP: $10   F17
   Location: SR A1A, 2.3 mi n of jct US 192. 2605 N SR A1A 32903. Fax: 321/773-6132. **Facility:** 295 units. 283
Small-scale Hotel   one-bedroom standard units. 12 one-bedroom suites ($189-$229). 5-8 stories, interior/exterior corridors. **Parking:** on-site. **Terms:** check-in 4 pm. **Amenities:** voice mail, irons, hair dryers. **Dining:** 6:30 am-2 & 5-10 pm, cocktails. **Pool(s):** heated outdoor. **Leisure Activities:** whirlpool, 2 tennis courts, exercise room, volleyball. *Fee:* charter fishing. **Guest Services:** gift shop, valet and coin laundry. **Business Services:** conference facilities, fax (fee). **Cards:** AX, CB, DC, DS, MC, VI. **(See color ad opposite inside back cover)**
SOME UNITS

MELBOURNE QUALITY SUITES OCEANFRONT HOTEL
Phone: (321)723-4222
SAVE   2/1-4/30 [ECP]   1P: $119-$199   2P: $129-$199   XP: $10   F18
   5/1-8/31 [ECP]   1P: $109-$149   2P: $119-$159   XP: $10   F18
▼▼ ▼▼ ▼ 12/1-1/31 & 9/1-11/30 [ECP]   1P: $109-$139   2P: $119-$149   XP: $10   F18
Small-scale Hotel   **Location:** SR A1A, 1.5 mi n of jct US 192. 1665 N SR A1A 32903. Fax: 321/768-2438. **Facility:** 208 one-bedroom suites. 9 stories, exterior corridors. **Parking:** on-site. **Terms:** small pets only ($25 fee, $10 extra charge). **Amenities:** voice mail, safes, irons, hair dryers. *Fee:* video games, high-speed Internet. **Pool(s):** heated outdoor. **Leisure Activities:** whirlpool. *Fee:* game room. **Guest Services:** gift shop, valet and coin laundry. **Business Services:** meeting rooms, fax. **Cards:** AX, CB, DC, DS, JC, MC, VI. **(See color ad p 498)**
SOME UNITS

OCEANFRONT COTTAGES

Phone: 321/725-8474

| | 12/11-9/9 | 1P: $120 | 2P: $145 | XP: $15 |
| | 12/1-12/10 & 9/10-11/30 | 1P: $99 | 2P: $125 | XP: $15 |

Cottage

Location: Just s of east end of US 192. 612 Wavecrest Ave 32903. Fax: 208/723-2067. **Facility:** Designated smoking area. 4 cottages. 2 stories, exterior corridors. *Bath:* combo or shower only. **Parking:** on-site. **Terms:** age restrictions may apply, 30 day cancellation notice-fee imposed, weekly rates available, small pets only ($15 extra charge). **Amenities:** irons, hair dryers. **Pool(s):** small outdoor. **Guest Services:** coin laundry. **Cards:** MC, VI.

RADISSON SUITE HOTEL OCEANFRONT

Phone: (321)773-9260

	1/1-4/13	1P: $169-$269	2P: $169-$269	XP: $10	F
	4/14-11/30	1P: $159-$259	2P: $159-$259	XP: $10	F
	12/1-12/31	1P: $150-$215	2P: $150-$215	XP: $10	F

Small-scale Hotel

Location: 3.2 mi n of jct US 192. 3101 N Hwy A1A 32903. Fax: 321/777-3190. **Facility:** 168 units. 30 one-bedroom standard units with whirlpools. 138 one-bedroom suites. 16 stories, exterior corridors. **Parking:** on-site. **Terms:** check-in 4 pm, cancellation fee imposed. **Amenities:** video games (fee), voice mail, safes, irons, hair dryers. **Dining:** 7 am-10 pm, cocktails. **Pool(s):** heated outdoor. **Leisure Activities:** whirlpools. *Fee:* jet ski. **Guest Services:** valet and coin laundry. **Business Services:** conference facilities, fax (fee). **Cards:** AX, DC, DS, MC, VI. **Special Amenities:** free newspaper and free room upgrade (subject to availability with advanced reservations).

SOME UNITS

THE TUCKAWAY SHORES RESORT

Phone: (321)723-3355

	2/1-4/30	1P: $93-$102	2P: $93-$102	XP: $9
	12/15-1/31	1P: $75-$90	2P: $75-$90	XP: $9
	5/1-11/30	1P: $80-$85	2P: $80-$85	XP: $9
	12/1-12/14	1P: $70-$80	2P: $70-$80	XP: $9

Motel

Location: SR A1A, 0.8 mi s of jct US 192. 1441 S Miramar Ave (A1A) 32903. Fax: 321/727-1441. **Facility:** 31 one-bedroom suites with efficiencies. 3 stories (no elevator), exterior corridors. **Parking:** on-site. **Terms:** 7 day cancellation notice. **Pool(s):** outdoor. **Guest Services:** coin laundry. **Business Services:** meeting rooms, fax. **Cards:** AX, DS, MC, VI.

------ WHERE TO DINE ------

SKEWERS

Lunch: $4-$8   Dinner: $8-$17   Phone: 321/727-8944

Lebanese

Location: On SR 192, just w of SR A1A; center. 144 Fifth Ave. **Hours:** 11 am-4 & 5-9:30 pm. Closed: 1/1, 11/27, 12/25; also Sun. **Features:** The restaurant's authentic Middle Eastern atmosphere is enhanced by nightly belly-dancing performances via satellite from Lebanon. The menu blends delicious classic Middle East and Lebanese cuisine with some Continental items. Knafeh is an outstanding choice for dessert. Casual dress; beer & wine only. **Parking:** on-site. **Cards:** AX, DC, DS, MC, VI.

VILLA PALMA RISTORANTE

Lunch: $7-$12   Dinner: $11-$19   Phone: 321/951-0051

Italian

Location: 0.3 mi n of US 192; in Indialantic Shopping Plaza. 874 N Hwy A1A 32903. **Hours:** 11:30 am-2 & 5-10 pm, Fri-10:30 pm, Sat 5 pm-10:30 pm, Sun 5 pm-10 pm. Closed: 11/27, 12/25. **Reservations:** suggested. **Features:** The owner/chef makes pasta from scratch. For a treat, try shrimp parmigiana. Entrees include preparations of beef, chicken, veal and seafood. Casual dress; cocktails. **Parking:** on-site. **Cards:** AX, DC, DS, MC, VI.

INDIAN HARBOUR BEACH pop. 8,152

------ WHERE TO STAY ------

TRAVELODGE

Phone: 321/773-0325

| | 1/1-5/31 | 1P: $59 | | XP: $5 | F18 |
| | 12/1-12/31 & 6/1-11/30 | 1P: $49 | | XP: $5 | F18 |

Motel

Location: I-95, exit 183, 8 mi e, 1 mi n on SR 513. 1894 S Patrick Dr 32937. Fax: 321/773-0320. **Facility:** 79 one-bedroom standard units, some with efficiencies (no utensils). 2 stories, interior corridors. *Bath:* combo or shower only. **Parking:** on-site. **Terms:** 3 day cancellation notice, weekly rates available, [ECP] meal plan available, small pets only ($20 extra charge). **Amenities:** safes (fee). *Some:* hair dryers. **Pool(s):** outdoor. **Leisure Activities:** boat dock, fishing, 4 lighted tennis courts. *Fee:* game room. **Business Services:** meeting rooms, fax (fee). **Cards:** AX, CB, DC, DS, MC, VI.

SOME UNITS

INDIAN ROCKS BEACH — See Tampa Bay p. 917.

INDIAN SHORES — See Tampa Bay p. 918.

INDIANTOWN pop. 5,588

------ WHERE TO STAY ------

SEMINOLE INN

Phone: (772)597-3777

| | All Year [CP] | 1P: $65-$95 | 2P: $65-$95 | XP: $10 | F17 |

Country Inn

Location: On SR 710. 15885 SW Warfield Blvd 34956 (PO Box 1818). Fax: 772/597-2883. **Facility:** Dating from 1926 but featuring modern baths, this inn offers a quiet retreat in the heart of citrus country. 23 one-bedroom standard units. 2 stories, interior corridors. **Parking:** on-site. **Terms:** cancellation fee imposed, weekly rates available. **Amenities:** hair dryers. **Pool(s):** outdoor. **Business Services:** meeting rooms, fax. **Cards:** AX, DS, MC, VI.

SOME UNITS

INVERNESS pop. 6,789

------- WHERE TO STAY -------

THE CROWN HOTEL
Phone: (352)344-5555

12/1-4/30 & 10/1-11/30 [ECP]   1P: $65-$179   2P: $65-$179   XP: $20   F12
5/1-9/30 [ECP]   1P: $44-$129   2P: $44-$129   XP: $20   F12

Country Inn   **Location:** Just n of jct US 41/SR 44; center. 109 N Seminole Ave 34450. Fax: 352/726-4040. **Facility:** 34 units. 33 one-bedroom standard units. 1 one-bedroom suite ($129-$179). 3 stories, interior corridors. *Bath:* combo or shower only. **Parking:** on-site. **Terms:** weekly rates available, package plans - weekends, small pets only ($10 extra charge). **Pool(s):** outdoor. **Guest Services:** gift shop. **Business Services:** meeting rooms, fax (fee). **Cards:** AX, MC, VI.

SOME UNITS

ASK SÒ ⌷ ⌻ ⌙ ⊅ DATA PORT / ⊠ /

VAN DER VALK INVERNESS
Phone: (352)637-1140

12/1-4/30 & 10/1-11/30   1P: $166-$217   2P: $166-$217
5/1-9/30   1P: $157-$208   2P: $157-$208

Vacation Home   **Location:** 1.5 mi n on US 41. 4555 E Windmill Dr 34453. Fax: 352/637-2552. **Facility:** 52 vacation homes with pools. 1 story. **Parking:** on-site. **Terms:** check-in 4 pm, 28 day cancellation notice, [CP] & [MAP] meal plans available, 15% service charge. **Amenities:** irons, hair dryers. **Guest Services:** complimentary laundry, area transportation (fee). **Business Services:** meeting rooms. **Cards:** AX, DC, DS, MC, VI. **Special Amenities: free local telephone calls and preferred room (subject to availability with advanced reservations).**

SOME UNITS

⊅ / ⊠ /

------- WHERE TO DINE -------

COACH'S PUB & EATERY   **Lunch:** $10-$18   **Dinner:** $10-$18   **Phone:** 352-344-3333

Location: Downtown; adjacent to courthouse. 114 W Main St 34450. **Hours:** 11 am-11:30 pm, Fri & Sat-2 am,
American   Sun noon-10 pm. **Features:** Racing car hoods and college and professional sports banners highlight an entire wall in this sports bar-themed restaurant. Try the pub fare featuring sandwiches, salads and chili. Extensive selection of 40 drafts and 70 bottled beers are available. Casual dress; cocktails. **Parking:** on-site. **Cards:** MC, VI.

ISLAMORADA —*See The Florida Keys p. 320.*

Destination Jacksonville
pop. 735,617

*T*he principal city of Florida's First Coast, Jacksonville is no longer known just as a banking and insurance center.

*I*ts nearby beaches are meccas for sun worshipers. The PGA thought so much of the area it established its tour headquarters here. And architecture buffs revel in the Victorian atmosphere of Amelia Island.

Jacksonville Landing.
This downtown marketplace features shops, riverfront eateries and a water taxi to the Riverwalk. (See mention page 94)

Jacksonville's skyline.
Pleasure craft bob in this marina on the St. Johns River, which runs through downtown Jacksonville, Florida's River City by the Sea.

Jacksonville Jaguars.
Legions of fans flock to Alltell Stadium for the excitement and thrill of NFL action.

See Vicinity map page 446

Horse and carriage, Fernandina Beach on Amelia Island.
After browsing the galleries and shops along Centre Street, a perfect way to see the town's Victorian district is from a fringed-top surrey.

*P*laces included in this AAA Destination City:

Amelia Island	466	Neptune Beach	472
Atlantic Beach	468	Orange Park	473
Baldwin	469	Ponte Vedra Beach	475
Green Cove Springs	469	Yulee	477
Jacksonville Beach	470		

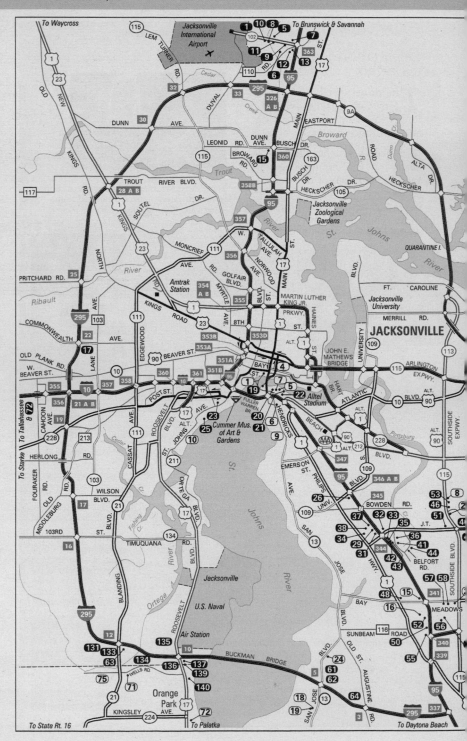

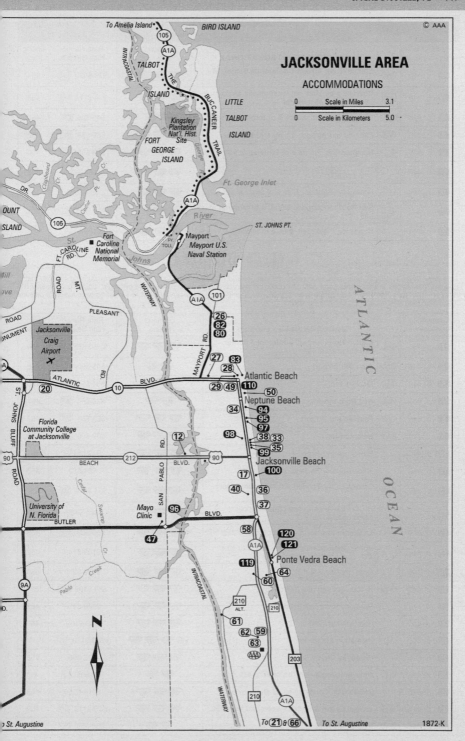

JACKSONVILLE AREA

ACCOMMODATIONS

© AAA

Scale in Miles   0 — 3.1
Scale in Kilometers   0 — 5.0

1872-K

✈ Airport Accommodations

Spotter/Map Page Number	OA	JACKSONVILLE INTERNATIONAL	Diamond Rating	Rate Range High Season	Listing Page
❶ / p. 446	AAA	Clarion Hotel Airport Conference Center, at terminal	◊◊◊	$79-$129 SAVE	454
⓬ / p. 446	AAA	Courtyard by Marriott Jacksonville Airport I-95, 2.5 mi e of terminal	◊◊◊	$94-$114 SAVE	455
❺ / p. 446	AAA	Days Inn Airport, 2.3 mi e of terminal at I-95	◊◊	$45-$95 SAVE	455
❽ / p. 446	AAA	Fairfield Inn Airport, 2.1 mi e of terminal	◊◊◊	$69-$89 SAVE	456
❾ / p. 446	AAA	Hampton Inn, 2.3 mi e of terminal at I-95	◊◊	$89-$95 SAVE	456
⓫ / p. 446		Hilton Garden Inn Jacksonville Airport, 2.2 mi e of terminal	◊◊◊	$64-$89	456
⓭ / p. 446		Holiday Inn Airport, 2.5 mi e of terminal at I-95	◊◊◊	$84-$103	457
❼ / p. 446	AAA	Red Roof Inn-Airport, 2.5 mi e of terminal at I-95	◊◊	$39-$54 SAVE	461
❿ / p. 446		Residence Inn-Airport, 2 mi e of terminal	◊◊◊	$129-$159	461

Jacksonville Area

This index helps you "spot" where approved accommodations and restaurants are located on the corresponding detailed maps. Lodging rate ranges are for comparison only and show the property's high season; rates are per night, unless only weekly (W) rates are available. Restaurant rate range is for dinner, unless only lunch (L) is served. Turn to the listing page for more detailed rate information and consult display ads for special promotions.

Spotter/Map Page Number	OA	JACKSONVILLE - Lodgings	Diamond Rating	Rate Range High Season	Listing Page
❶ / p. 446	AAA	Clarion Hotel Airport Conference Center - see color ad p 454	◊◊◊	$79-$129 SAVE	454
❺ / p. 446	AAA	Days Inn Airport	◊◊	$45-$95 SAVE	455
❻ / p. 446	AAA	Masters Inn	◊◊	$34-$51 SAVE	460
❼ / p. 446	AAA	Red Roof Inn-Airport	◊◊	$39-$54 SAVE	461
❽ / p. 446	AAA	Fairfield Inn Airport	◊◊◊	$69-$89 SAVE	456
❾ / p. 446	AAA	Hampton Inn	◊◊◊	$89-$95 SAVE	456
❿ / p. 446		Residence Inn-Airport	◊◊◊	$129-$159	461
⓫ / p. 446		Hilton Garden Inn Jacksonville Airport	◊◊◊	$64-$89	456
⓬ / p. 446	AAA	Courtyard by Marriott Jacksonville Airport I-95	◊◊◊	$94-$114 SAVE	455
⓭ / p. 446		Holiday Inn Airport - see color ad opposite inside back cover	◊◊◊	$84-$103	457
⓯ / p. 446	AAA	La Quinta Inn-North - see color ad p 459	◊◊◊	$60-$83 SAVE	459
⓱ / p. 446		Holiday Inn-Commonwealth - see color ad p 457, opposite inside back cover	◊◊◊	$109-$149	457
⓳ / p. 446		Omni Jacksonville Hotel	◊◊◊	$199-$209	460
⓴ / p. 446	AAA	Hilton Jacksonville Riverfront	◊◊◊	$69-$199 SAVE	456
㉑ / p. 446		Radisson Riverwalk Hotel	◊◊◊	$149-$159	461
㉒ / p. 446		Hampton Inn Central	◊◊◊	$99-$159	456
㉓ / p. 446	AAA	Plantation Manor Inn	◊◊◊◊	$130-$180 SAVE	460
㉕ / p. 446		House On Cherry Street	◊◊◊	$85-$95	458
㉖ / p. 446	AAA	Days Inn South - see color ad p 455	◊◊	$55-$95 SAVE	455
㉙ / p. 446		Jacksonville Courtyard at J T Butler Blvd	◊◊◊	$114-$159	458
㉛ / p. 446	AAA	La Quinta Inn & Suites - see color ad p 459	◊◊◊	$76-$112 SAVE	459
㉜ / p. 446	AAA	Inns of America	◊◊	$56-$59 SAVE	458

Spotter/Map Page Number	OA	JACKSONVILLE - Lodgings (continued)	Diamond Rating	Rate Range High Season	Listing Page
33 / p. 446	AAA	Quality Hotel Southpoint - see color ad p 452	▽▽▽	$59-$169 SAVE	460
34 / p. 446	AAA	Masters Inn JTB	▽▽	$34-$51 SAVE	460
35 / p. 446		Jacksonville Marriott Hotel	▽▽▽	$149-$198	459
36 / p. 446	AAA	Holiday Inn Express Hotel and Suites - see color ad p 457	▽▽▽	$55-$159 SAVE	458
37 / p. 446	AAA	Red Roof Inn	▽▽	$46-$59 SAVE	461
38 / p. 446	AAA	Wingate Inn/Southside - see color ad p 453	▽▽▽	$59-$189 SAVE	463
40 / p. 446		Homestead Studio Suites Hotel-Jacksonville/Southside	▽▽	$45-$60	458
41 / p. 446	AAA	MainStay Suites-Jacksonville - see color ad p 452	▽▽▽	$50-$119 SAVE	459
42 / p. 446	AAA	Hampton Inn Jacksonville I-95 South	▽▽▽	$89 SAVE	456
43 / p. 446	AAA	Southpoint Hotel	▽▽▽	$49-$99 SAVE	462
44 / p. 446		Candlewood Suites	▽▽▽	$59	452
45 / p. 446		Residence Inn by Marriott	▽▽▽	$89-$119	462
46 / p. 446		Hilton Garden Inn Deerwood Park	▽▽▽	$69-$139	456
47 / p. 446		Courtyard by Marriott - see ad p 455	▽▽▽	$60-$115	455
48 / p. 446		Homewood Suites by Hilton	▽▽▽	$119-$124	458
50 / p. 446	AAA	La Quinta Inn-Baymeadows - see color ad p 459	▽▽▽	$66-$103 SAVE	459
51 / p. 446	AAA	Wellesley Inn & Suites (Jacksonville/Deerwood Park) - see color ad p 453	▽▽▽	$79-$89 SAVE	463
52 / p. 446		Comfort Suites Baymeadows - see color ad p 454	▽▽▽	$55	454
53 / p. 446	AAA	SpringHill Suites by Marriott Jacksonville Deerwood Park	▽▽▽	$69-$109 SAVE	462
54 / p. 446	AAA	AmeriSuites (Jacksonville/Baymeadows) - see color ad p 460	▽▽▽	$95-$105 SAVE	452
55 / p. 446		Residence Inn by Marriott	▽▽▽	$79-$140	461
56 / p. 446		Holiday Inn Baymeadows - see color ad opposite inside back cover	▽▽▽	$59-$89	457
57 / p. 446		Homestead Studio Suites Hotel-Jacksonville/Baymeadows	▽▽▽	$49-$69	458
58 / p. 446		Embassy Suites Hotel	▽▽▽	$89-$169	456
61 / p. 446	AAA	Baymont Inn & Suites Jacksonville - see color ad p 453	▽▽	$64-$74 SAVE	452
62 / p. 446		Ramada Inn Conference Center - see color ad p 461	▽▽▽	$78-$83	461
63 / p. 446	AAA	Country Inn & Suites - see color ad p 613	▽▽▽	$69-$99 SAVE	454
64 / p. 446		Holiday Inn Express Hotel & Suites	▽▽▽	$75-$95	458
		JACKSONVILLE - Restaurants			
1 / p. 446		Juliette's	▽▽▽	$17-$32	464
4 / p. 446		River City Brewing Company	▽▽	$14-$25	464
5 / p. 446		Crawdaddy's	▽▽	$15-$22	463
6 / p. 446	AAA	Matthew's	▽▽▽▽	$20-$60	464
7 / p. 446		Wine Cellar	▽▽▽	$19-$29	465
8 / p. 446		Johnny Leverock's Seafood House	▽▽	$8-$16	463
9 / p. 446		Wilfried's 24 Miramar	▽▽▽	$20-$28	465

Spotter/Map Page Number	OA	JACKSONVILLE - Restaurants (continued)	Diamond Rating	Rate Range High Season	Listing Page
⑩ / p. 446		Biscotti's Espresso Cafe	▽▽	$10-$30	463
⑫ / p. 446		Marker 32	▽▽▽	$18-$45	464
⑮ / p. 446		Bombay Bicycle Club	▽▽	$7-$13	463
⑯ / p. 446	◈◈◈	**Pagoda Chinese Restaurant**	▽▽	$8-$19	464
⑰ / p. 446		Thai Room	▽▽	$4-$14	465
⑱ / p. 446		Mandarin Dragon	▽▽	$6-$12	464
⑲ / p. 446		The Tree Steak House	▽▽	$14-$30	465
⑳ / p. 446		Pattaya Thai Restaurant	▽▽	$6-$18	464
㉑ / p. 446		Clark's Fish Camp	▽	$5-$14	463
㉒ / p. 446		Joseph's Italian Restaurant	▽	$7-$15	464
㉓ / p. 446		Seven Bridges Grille & Brewery	▽▽	$8-$17	464
㉔ / p. 446		Rosalia's Italian Cafe	▽	$9-$20	464
		BALDWIN - Lodgings			
㊒ / p. 446	◈◈◈	**Best Western Inn Baldwin**	▽▽	$49-$99 SAVE	469
		ATLANTIC BEACH - Lodgings			
㊐ / p. 446	◈◈◈	**Best Western Mayport Inn & Suites**	▽▽▽	$79-$130 SAVE	468
㊒ / p. 446	◈◈◈	**Comfort Inn Mayport**	▽▽▽	$79-$109 SAVE	469
㊓ / p. 446	◈◈◈	**Sea Turtle Inn - see color ad p 471**	▽▽▽	$109-$219 SAVE	469
		ATLANTIC BEACH - Restaurants			
㉖ / p. 446		Mayport Gardens Chinese Restaurant	▽	$4-$7	469
㉗ / p. 446		Sergio's Northern Italian & Continental Cuisine	▽▽	$11-$20	469
㉘ / p. 446		Ragtime Tavern & Seafood Grill	▽▽	$10-$20	469
㉙ / p. 446		Sticky Fingers Restaurant & Bar	▽	$5-$15	469
		JACKSONVILLE BEACH - Lodgings			
㊚ / p. 446		Pelican Path B & B by the Sea	▽▽▽	$95-$165	471
㊜ / p. 446	◈◈◈	**Holiday Inn SunSpree Resort - see color ad p 471, opposite inside back cover**	▽▽▽	$89-$159 SAVE	471
㊝ / p. 446	◈◈◈	**Hampton Inn Ponte Vedra at Jacksonville Beach - see color ad p 476**	▽▽▽	$89-$98 SAVE	470
㊞ / p. 446	◈◈◈	**Comfort Inn Oceanfront - see color ad p 470**	▽▽▽	$99-$169 SAVE	470
㊟ / p. 446	◈◈◈	**Surfside Inn**	▽▽	$69-$149 SAVE	471
㊠ / p. 446	◈◈◈	**Best Western Oceanfront**	▽▽▽	$89-$179 SAVE	470
⑩⑩ / p. 446	◈◈◈	**Days Inn Oceanfront Resort**	▽▽	$105-$160 SAVE	470
		JACKSONVILLE BEACH - Restaurants			
㉝ / p. 446		Dolphin Depot	▽▽	$19-$35	472
㉞ / p. 446		Billy's	▽▽	$5-$15	472
㉟ / p. 446		Ichiban Japanese Steak House	▽▽	$8-$15	472
㊱ / p. 446		Pagoda Chinese	▽▽	$5-$12	472
㊲ / p. 446		Uli's European Restaurant	▽▽	$15-$28	472
㊳ / p. 446	◈◈◈	**First Street Grille**	▽▽	$15-$20	472
㊵ / p. 446		Ellen's Kitchen	▽	$4-$12(L)	472

Spotter/Map Page Number	OA	NEPTUNE BEACH - Lodgings	Diamond Rating	Rate Range High Season	Listing Page
110 / p. 446		Sea Horse Oceanfront Inn	◈◈	$99-$225	472
		NEPTUNE BEACH - Restaurants			
49 / p. 446		Sun Dog Diner	◈◈	$7-$12	473
50 / p. 446		Mezza Luna Vagabondo Ristorante	◈◈	$10-$19	473
		PONTE VEDRA BEACH - Lodgings			
119 / p. 446	AAA	Country Inn & Suites By Carlson-Jacksonville at Ponte Vedra - see color ad p 613	◈◈◈	$215-$300 SAVE	475
120 / p. 446	AAA	Ponte Vedra Inn and Club	◈◈◈◈◈	$350-$600 SAVE	476
121 / p. 446	AAA	Lodge and Club at Ponte Vedra Beach	◈◈◈◈	$350-$450 SAVE	476
		PONTE VEDRA BEACH - Restaurants			
58 / p. 446		J J's Cuisine & Wine	◈◈	$14-$30	476
59 / p. 446	AAA	Sawgrass Grille & The Tavern	◈◈	$13-$18	477
60 / p. 446		Gio's Cafe	◈◈◈	$18-$40	476
61 / p. 446		Lulu's Waterfront Grill	◈	$12-$18	477
62 / p. 446		Restaurant Medure	◈◈◈	$18-$28	477
63 / p. 446		Santioni's of Sawgrass	◈◈	$9-$17	477
64 / p. 446		Players Cafe	◈	$4-$6(L)	477
66 / p. 446		Barbara Jean's	◈	$8-$16	476
		ORANGE PARK - Lodgings			
131 / p. 446		Hampton Inn-Orange Park - see ad p 474	◈◈◈	$69-$89	474
133 / p. 446	AAA	Red Roof Inn-South	◈◈	$39-$55 SAVE	475
134 / p. 446	AAA	La Quinta Inn-Jacksonville/Orange Park - see color ad p 459	◈◈◈	$66-$83 SAVE	474
135 / p. 446	AAA	Best Western Hotel and Suites - see color ad p 473	◈◈◈	$69-$89 SAVE	473
136 / p. 446		Holiday Inn-Orange Park - see color ad opposite inside back cover	◈◈◈	$89-$99	474
137 / p. 446		Days Inn	◈◈	$59-$79	474
139 / p. 446		Fairfield Inn by Marriott	◈◈◈	$74-$84	474
140 / p. 446	AAA	Comfort Inn - see color ad p 473	◈◈◈	$71-$91 SAVE	474
		ORANGE PARK - Restaurants			
71 / p. 446		Venezia's Italian Restaurant	◈	$7-$15	475
72 / p. 446	AAA	Sarnelli's Ristorante	◈◈	$11-$25	475
75 / p. 446		The Hilltop	◈◈	$10-$23	475

JACKSONVILLE pop. 735,617 (See map p. 446; index p. 448)

──── WHERE TO STAY ────

AMERISUITES (JACKSONVILLE/BAYMEADOWS)   Phone: (904)737-4477   54
All Year   1P: $95-$105   2P: $95-$105   XP: $10   F17
Location: I-95, exit 341, just e. 8277 Western Way Cir 32256. **Fax:** 904/739-1649. **Facility:** 112 one-bedroom standard units, some with whirlpools. 6 stories, interior corridors. *Bath:* combo or shower only. **Parking:** on-site. **Terms:** [ECP] meal plan available, small pets only. **Amenities:** high-speed Internet (fee), voice mail, irons, hair dryers. *Some:* dual phone lines. **Pool(s):** heated outdoor. **Leisure Activities:** exercise room. **Guest Services:** valet and coin laundry. **Business Services:** meeting rooms, business center. **Cards:** AX, CB, DC, DS, JC, MC, VI. **Special Amenities:** free continental breakfast and free newspaper. *(See color ad p 460)*
Small-scale Hotel

SOME UNITS

BAYMONT INN & SUITES JACKSONVILLE   Phone: (904)268-9999   61
All Year [ECP]   1P: $64-$74   2P: $64-$74
Location: I-295, exit 5A northbound; exit 5 southbound at SR 13. 3199 Hartley Rd 32257. **Fax:** 904/268-9611. **Facility:** 99 units. 96 one-bedroom standard units. 3 one-bedroom suites ($69-$89), some with kitchens. 3 stories, interior corridors. **Terms:** small pets only. **Amenities:** video games, voice mail, irons, hair dryers. **Pool(s):** outdoor. **Guest Services:** valet and coin laundry. **Business Services:** fax. **Cards:** AX, CB, DC, DS, MC, VI. **Special Amenities:** free continental breakfast and free newspaper.
Small-scale Hotel
(See color ad p 453)

SOME UNITS

CANDLEWOOD SUITES   Phone: (904)296-7785   44
All Year   1P: $59
Location: I-95, exit 344, e to Belfort Rd, just s on southwest corner. 4990 Belfort Rd 32256. **Fax:** 904/296-9281. **Facility:** 111 units. 87 one-bedroom standard units with efficiencies. 24 one-bedroom suites with efficiencies. 3 stories, interior corridors. *Bath:* combo or shower only. **Parking:** on-site. **Terms:** weekly rates available, pets ($100 deposit). **Amenities:** video library, CD players, dual phone lines, voice mail, irons, hair dryers. **Leisure Activities:** exercise room. **Guest Services:** complimentary laundry. **Business Services:** fax. **Cards:** AX, CB, DC, DS, JC, MC, VI.
Small-scale Hotel

SOME UNITS

(See map p. 446)

CLARION HOTEL AIRPORT CONFERENCE CENTER Phone: (904)741-1997

All Year 1P: $79 2P: $129 XP: $10 F18
Location: I-95, exit 363. Located at the airport. 2101 Dixie Clipper Rd 32218. Fax: 904/741-5520. **Facility:** 200 units. 196 one-bedroom standard units. 4 one-bedroom suites ($139-$299) with whirlpools. 6 stories, interior/exterior corridors. *Bath:* combo or shower only. **Parking:** on-site. **Terms:** 4 day cancellation notice-fee imposed, [BP] meal plan available. **Amenities:** video games, dual phone lines, voice mail, irons, hair dryers. **Dining:** 2 restaurants, 11 am-11 pm. **Pool(s):** outdoor. **Leisure Activities:** whirlpool, exercise room, game room. **Guest Services:** gift shop, valet and coin laundry, airport transportation-Jacksonville International Airport. **Business Services:** conference facilities, business center. **Cards:** AX, CB, DC, DS, JC, MC, VI. **Special Amenities:** free local telephone calls and free newspaper. *(See color ad below)*

Large-scale Hotel

SOME UNITS

FEE

COMFORT SUITES BAYMEADOWS Phone: 904/739-1155 52

All Year [ECP] 1P: $55
Location: I-95, exit 341, sw off Baymeadows Rd. 8333 Dix Ellis Tr 32256. Fax: 904/731-0752. **Facility:** 127 units. 109 one-bedroom standard units. 18 one-bedroom suites. 3 stories, exterior corridors. *Bath:* combo or shower only. **Parking:** on-site. **Terms:** cancellation fee imposed. **Amenities:** voice mail, irons, hair dryers. **Pool(s):** outdoor. **Leisure Activities:** whirlpool, exercise room. **Guest Services:** complimentary evening beverages: Mon-Thurs, valet and coin laundry. **Business Services:** meeting rooms. **Cards:** AX, DC, DS, MC, VI. *(See color ad below)*

Motel

MC, VI.

SOME UNITS

COUNTRY INN & SUITES Phone: (904)772-7771 63

All Year 1P: $69-$89 2P: $79-$99 XP: $10 F
Location: I-295, exit 12, just s. 5945 Youngerman Cir E 32244. Fax: 904/772-7071. **Facility:** 61 units. 50 one-bedroom standard units. 11 one-bedroom suites ($90-$129), some with whirlpools. 3 stories, interior corridors. *Bath:* combo or shower only. **Parking:** on-site. **Terms:** 21 day cancellation notice-fee imposed, [ECP] meal plan available. **Amenities:** high-speed Internet, voice mail, irons, hair dryers. **Pool(s):** outdoor. **Leisure Activities:** exercise room. **Guest Services:** coin laundry. **Business Services:** meeting rooms. **Fee:** PC, fax. **Cards:** AX, CB, DC, DS, MC, VI. **Special Amenities:** free continental breakfast and free newspaper. *(See color ad p 613)*

Small-scale Hotel

SOME UNITS

FEE

(See map p. 446)

COURTYARD BY MARRIOTT

Small-scale Hotel

Phone: (904)223-1700   **47**

All Year   1P: $60-$115
Location: Just n of JT Butler Blvd. Located across from Mayo Clinic. 4600 San Pablo Rd 32224. Fax: 904/223-1026.
Facility: 146 units. 134 one-bedroom standard units. 12 one-bedroom suites. 3 stories, interior corridors.
Bath: combo or shower only. **Parking:** on-site. **Amenities:** voice mail, irons, hair dryers. **Pool(s):** outdoor.
Leisure Activities: whirlpool, exercise room. **Guest Services:** valet and coin laundry, area transportation.
Business Services: meeting rooms, fax. **Cards:** AX, CB, DC, DS, MC, VI. *(See ad below)*

SOME UNITS

COURTYARD BY MARRIOTT JACKSONVILLE AIRPORT I-95

Small-scale Hotel

Phone: 904-741-1122   **12**

All Year   1P: $94-$114
Location: I-95, exit 363, just sw of Airport Blvd. 14668 Duval Rd 32218 (PO Box 18369, 32229). Fax: 904/741-0929.
Facility: 81 units. 78 one-bedroom standard units. 3 one-bedroom suites ($144-$165), some with whirlpools.
3 stories, interior corridors. *Bath:* combo or shower only. **Parking:** on-site. **Terms:** [BP] meal plan available,
18% service charge. **Amenities:** dual phone lines, voice mail, irons, hair dryers. **Dining:** 6-10 am, Sat & Sun
7-11 am. **Pool(s):** outdoor. **Leisure Activities:** whirlpool, exercise room. **Guest Services:** valet and coin
laundry. **Business Services:** meeting rooms, fax. **Cards:** AX, DC, DS, MC, VI.

SOME UNITS

DAYS INN AIRPORT

Small-scale Hotel

Phone: (904)741-4000   **5**
                                                                        F12
All Year   1P: $45-$95   2P: $49-$95   XP: $6
Location: I-95, exit 363, just w. 1181 Airport Rd 32218. Fax: 904/741-0609. **Facility:** 62 one-bedroom standard
units. 2 stories, exterior corridors. **Parking:** on-site. **Terms:** [CP] meal plan available. **Amenities:** voice mail,
hair dryers. **Pool(s):** outdoor. **Guest Services:** coin laundry, airport transportation-Jacksonville International
Airport. **Business Services:** fax. **Cards:** AX, CB, DC, DS, JC, MC, VI. **Special Amenities:** free continental
breakfast and free newspaper.

SOME UNITS

DAYS INN SOUTH

Small-scale Hotel

Phone: (904)733-3890   **26**
                                                                        F10
All Year [ECP]   1P: $55-$95   2P: $55-$95   XP: $10
Location: I-95, exit 346B southbound; exit 345 northbound. 5649 Cagle Rd 32216. Fax: 904/636-9841. **Facility:** 120
one-bedroom standard units. 2 stories, exterior corridors. *Bath:* combo or shower only. **Parking:** on-site.
Terms: 3 day cancellation notice. **Amenities:** hair dryers. *Some:* irons. **Pool(s):** outdoor. **Leisure Activi-
ties:** exercise room. **Business Services:** meeting rooms, fax. **Cards:** AX, CB, DC, DS, MC, VI.
Special Amenities: free continental breakfast and free local telephone calls. *(See color ad below)*

SOME UNITS

(See map p. 446)

EMBASSY SUITES HOTEL

SAVE

Small-scale Hotel

Phone: (904)731-3555 58

All Year [BP] 1P: $89-$169 2P: $89-$169 XP: $10 F12
Location: I-95, exit 341, 0.5 mi e. 9300 Baymeadows Rd 32256. Fax: 904/731-4972. **Facility:** 277 one-bedroom standard units. 7 stories, interior corridors. *Bath:* combo or shower only. **Parking:** on-site. **Terms:** cancellation fee imposed, package plans. **Amenities:** voice mail, irons, hair dryers. *Some:* dual phone lines. **Pool(s):** heated indoor. **Leisure Activities:** sauna, whirlpool, exercise room. **Guest Services:** gift shop, complimentary evening beverages, valet and coin laundry, area transportation. **Business Services:** conference facilities, business center. **Cards:** AX, DC, DS, MC, VI.

SOME UNITS

FAIRFIELD INN AIRPORT

SAVE

Small-scale Hotel

Phone: (904)741-3500 8

All Year [ECP] 1P: $69-$89 2P: $69-$89
Location: I-95, exit 363B, 0.3 mi w. 1300 Airport Rd 32218. Fax: 904/741-3600. **Facility:** 107 one-bedroom standard units, some with whirlpools. 3 stories, interior corridors. *Bath:* combo or shower only. **Parking:** on-site. **Amenities:** voice mail, irons, hair dryers. **Pool(s):** heated indoor. **Leisure Activities:** whirlpool, exercise room. **Guest Services:** valet laundry. **Business Services:** meeting rooms, fax. **Cards:** AX, DC, DS, MC, VI. **Special Amenities:** early check-in/late check-out and free continental breakfast.

SOME UNITS

HAMPTON INN

SAVE

Motel

Phone: (904)741-4980 9

All Year 1P: $89-$95
Location: I-95, exit 363, jct Airport Rd. Gated property. 1170 Airport Entrance Rd 32218. Fax: 904/741-4186. **Facility:** 113 one-bedroom standard units. 2 stories, exterior corridors. *Bath:* combo or shower only. **Parking:** on-site. **Terms:** [ECP] meal plan available. **Amenities:** video games, voice mail, irons, hair dryers. **Pool(s):** outdoor. **Guest Services:** coin laundry. **Business Services:** meeting rooms, fax. **Cards:** AX, CB, DC, DS, JC, MC, VI.

SOME UNITS

HAMPTON INN CENTRAL

SAVE

Small-scale Hotel

Phone: (904)396-7770 22

All Year [ECP] 1P: $99-$159
Location: South side of Main St Bridge. 1331 Prudential Dr 32207. Fax: 904/396-8044. **Facility:** 118 one-bedroom standard units, some with whirlpools. 5 stories, interior corridors. *Bath:* combo or shower only. **Parking:** on-site. **Amenities:** video games, dual phone lines, voice mail, irons, hair dryers. **Pool(s):** outdoor. **Guest Services:** sundries, valet laundry. **Business Services:** meeting rooms, fax. **Cards:** AX, DC, DS, MC.

SOME UNITS

HAMPTON INN JACKSONVILLE I-95 SOUTH

SAVE

Small-scale Hotel

Phone: (904)281-0443 42

All Year [ECP] 1P: $89 2P: $89
Location: I-95, exit 344, just e, then just s. 4690 Salisbury Rd 32256. Fax: 904/281-0144. **Facility:** 128 one-bedroom standard units. 4 stories, interior corridors. **Parking:** on-site. **Amenities:** video games, dual phone lines, voice mail, irons, hair dryers. **Pool(s):** outdoor. **Leisure Activities:** exercise room. **Guest Services:** valet laundry. **Business Services:** meeting rooms, PC, fax. **Cards:** AX, CB, DC, DS, MC, VI. **Special Amenities:** early check-in/late check-out and free continental breakfast.

SOME UNITS

HILTON GARDEN INN DEERWOOD PARK

SAVE

Small-scale Hotel

Phone: (904)997-6600 46

3/23-11/30 1P: $69-$139 2P: $69-$139
12/1-3/22 1P: $69-$129 2P: $69-$129
Location: I-95, exit 344, e on JT Butler Blvd, 2.5 mi to SR 115 (Southside Blvd N), 0.8 mi n to Gate Pkwy, just e. 9745 Gate Pkwy Dr N 32246. Fax: 904/997-6601. **Facility:** 119 units. 118 one-bedroom standard units. 1 one-bedroom suite ($89-$259). 5 stories, interior corridors. *Bath:* combo or shower only. **Parking:** on-site. **Amenities:** video games, high-speed Internet (fee), dual phone lines, voice mail, irons, hair dryers. **Pool(s):** outdoor. **Leisure Activities:** whirlpool, exercise room. **Guest Services:** valet and coin laundry, area transportation. **Business Services:** meeting rooms, business center. **Cards:** AX, CB, DC, DS, JC, MC, VI.

SOME UNITS

HILTON GARDEN INN JACKSONVILLE AIRPORT

SAVE

Small-scale Hotel

Phone: (904)421-2700 11

All Year 1P: $64-$89 2P: $64-$89 XP: $10 F18
Location: I-95, exit 363B, just w. 13505 Ranch Rd 32218. Fax: 904/421-2701. **Facility:** 111 units. 102 one-bedroom standard units, some with whirlpools. 9 one-bedroom suites ($119-$139), some with whirlpools. 5 stories, interior corridors. *Bath:* combo or shower only. **Parking:** on-site. **Terms:** check-in 4 pm, cancellation fee imposed, [BP], [CP] & [ECP] meal plans available, 18% service charge. **Amenities:** video games, dual phone lines, voice mail, irons, hair dryers. *Some:* high-speed Internet. **Pool(s):** outdoor. **Leisure Activities:** whirlpool, exercise room. **Business Services:** business center. **Cards:** AX, CB, DC, DS, JC, MC, VI.

SOME UNITS

HILTON JACKSONVILLE RIVERFRONT

SAVE

Large-scale Hotel

Phone: (904)398-8800 20

All Year 1P: $69-$199 2P: $69-$199 XP: $10 F18
Location: On south bank of river; center. 1201 Riverplace Blvd 32207. Fax: 904/398-9170. **Facility:** 292 one-bedroom standard units. 8 stories, interior corridors. *Bath:* combo or shower only. **Parking:** on-site (fee). **Terms:** check-in 4 pm, cancellation fee imposed, weekly rates available. **Amenities:** video games, voice mail, irons, hair dryers. *Some:* dual phone lines. **Dining:** 2 restaurants, 6 am-11 pm, cocktails. **Pool(s):** heated outdoor. **Leisure Activities:** whirlpool. *Fee:* charter fishing. **Guest Services:** gift shop, valet laundry, area transportation-within 1 mi. **Business Services:** conference facilities, business center. **Cards:** AX, CB, DC, DS, JC, MC, VI. **Special Amenities:** free local telephone calls.

SOME UNITS

FEE

(See map p. 446)

HOLIDAY INN AIRPORT   Phone: (904)741-4404   **13**
▼▼〰▼▼ All Year   1P: $84   2P: $103
Small-scale Hotel **Location:** I-95, exit 363, just w. 14670 Duval Rd 32218 (PO Drawer 18409, 32229-0409). Fax: 904/741-4907.
Facility: 489 one-bedroom standard units. 2-6 stories, interior/exterior corridors. *Bath:* combo or shower only.
Parking: on-site. **Terms:** pets (not permitted on concierge floors). **Amenities:** dual phone lines, voice mail,
safes, irons, hair dryers. **Pool(s):** outdoor, heated indoor/outdoor, wading. **Leisure Activities:** 2 lighted tennis courts, exercise
room. **Guest Services:** gift shop, valet and coin laundry. **Business Services:** conference facilities, PC, fax. **Cards:** AX, CB, DC,
DS, JC, MC, VI. *(See color ad opposite inside back cover)*

SOME UNITS

ASK ⬛ ⬛ 🛏 🍽 🍸 🖥 📷 🏊 🎥 📠 💻 / ✖ 🔲 /

HOLIDAY INN BAYMEADOWS   Phone: (904)737-1700   **56**
▼▼〰▼▼ All Year   1P: $59-$89   2P: $59-$89
Small-scale Hotel **Location:** I-95, exit 341, 0.3 mi e. 9150 Baymeadows Rd 32256. Fax: 904/737-0207. **Facility:** 240 units. 232 one-
bedroom standard units. 8 one-bedroom suites ($79-$119). 2-4 stories, interior/exterior corridors. **Parking:**
on-site. **Terms:** package plans, small pets only ($35 fee). **Amenities:** voice mail, irons, hair dryers. **Pool(s):**
outdoor. **Guest Services:** valet and coin laundry. **Business Services:** meeting rooms, fax. **Cards:** AX, CB, DC, DS, MC, VI.
(See color ad opposite inside back cover)

SOME UNITS

ASK ⬛ 🛏 🍽 🍸 📷 🏊 🎣 🎥 📠 💻 / ✖ VCR 🔲 🖨 /
                                          FEE

HOLIDAY INN-COMMONWEALTH   Phone: (904)781-6000   **17**
▼▼〰▼▼ 12/29-1/1   1P: $109-$149   2P: $109-$149   XP: $10   F18
         1/2-11/30   1P: $59-$89   2P: $69-$99   XP: $10   F18
         12/1-12/28   1P: $59-$79   2P: $59-$89   XP: $10   F18
Small-scale Hotel **Location:** I-295, exit 22, southeast corner. 6802 Commonwealth Ave 32254. Fax: 904/781-2784. **Facility:** 178 one-
bedroom standard units. 2 stories, interior/exterior corridors. **Parking:** on-site. **Amenities:** voice mail, irons, hair dryers. **Pool(s):**
heated indoor. **Leisure Activities:** saunas, whirlpool, exercise room. **Guest Services:** valet and coin laundry. **Business Services:** meeting rooms, fax. **Cards:** AX, CB, DC, DS, JC, MC, VI. *(See color ad below & opposite inside back cover)*

SOME UNITS

ASK ⬛ 🍽 🍸 📷 🏊 ✖ 🎥 📠 💻 / ✖ 🔲 🖨 /

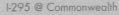

(See map p. 446)

HOLIDAY INN EXPRESS HOTEL AND SUITES
Phone: (904)332-9500 36

(AAA) (SAVE)

All Year [ECP]   1P: $55-$109   2P: $59-$159   XP: $8   F15
Location: I-95, exit 344, just e, then s. 4675 Salisbury Rd 32256. Fax: 904/332-9222. **Facility:** 88 one-bedroom standard units. 4 stories, interior corridors. *Bath:* combo or shower only. **Parking:** on-site. **Terms:** small pets only ($10 fee). **Amenities:** voice mail, irons, hair dryers. *Some:* dual phone lines. **Pool(s):** outdoor. **Leisure**

Small-scale Hotel **Activities:** exercise room. **Guest Services:** valet and coin laundry. **Business Services:** meeting rooms, fax. **Cards:** AX, CB, DC, DS, MC, VI. **Special Amenities: free continental breakfast and free local telephone calls.** *(See color ad p 457)*

SOME UNITS

HOLIDAY INN EXPRESS HOTEL & SUITES
Phone: (904)899-9000 64

All Year   1P: $75-$95   2P: $75-$95   XP: $10   F12
Location: I-295, exit 3, just n. 11262 St Augustine Rd 32257. Fax: 904/899-9001. **Facility:** 80 one-bedroom stan-
Small-scale Hotel dard units. 3 stories, interior corridors. *Bath:* combo or shower only. **Parking:** on-site. **Terms:** [ECP] meal plan available. **Amenities:** high-speed Internet, dual phone lines, voice mail, irons, hair dryers. **Pool(s):**
heated outdoor. **Leisure Activities:** exercise room. **Guest Services:** valet and coin laundry. **Business Services:** fax.
Cards: AX, DC, DS, MC, VI.

SOME UNITS

HOMESTEAD STUDIO SUITES HOTEL-JACKSONVILLE/BAYMEADOWS
Phone: (904)739-1881 57

All Year   1P: $49   2P: $69   F18
Location: I-95, exit 341, just e to Western Way, then just s. 8300 Western Way 32256. Fax: 904/739-0557.
Small-scale Hotel **Facility:** 134 one-bedroom standard units. 3 stories, interior corridors. *Bath:* combo or shower only. **Parking:** on-site. **Terms:** cancellation fee imposed, pets ($75 fee). **Amenities:** voice mail, irons. *Some:* hair dryers.
Guest Services: valet and coin laundry. **Business Services:** fax. **Cards:** AX, CB, DC, DS, JC, MC, VI.

SOME UNITS

HOMESTEAD STUDIO SUITES HOTEL-JACKSONVILLE/SOUTHSIDE
Phone: (904)642-9911 40

All Year   1P: $45   2P: $60   XP: $5   F18
Location: I-95, exit 344, 3.5 mi on JT Butler Blvd to Gate Pkwy, just ne. Located in a quiet, partly residential area. 10020
Motel Skinner Lake Dr 32246. Fax: 904/642-5673. **Facility:** 132 units. 127 one-bedroom standard units with efficien-
cies. 5 one-bedroom suites ($79-$89) with efficiencies. 2 stories, exterior corridors. *Bath:* combo or shower
only. **Parking:** on-site. **Terms:** cancellation fee imposed, pets ($75 fee). **Amenities:** voice mail, irons. *Some:* dual phone lines.
Guest Services: valet and coin laundry. **Business Services:** fax. **Cards:** AX, CB, DC, DS, JC, MC, VI.

SOME UNITS

HOMEWOOD SUITES BY HILTON
Phone: (904)733-9299 48

(SAVE)

All Year   1P: $119-$124   2P: $119-$124
Location: I-95, exit 341, 0.3 mi w. 8737 Baymeadows Rd 32256. Fax: 904/448-5889. **Facility:** 116 units. 108 one-
and 8 two-bedroom standard units, some with kitchens. 2-3 stories, interior/exterior corridors. **Parking:** on-
site. **Terms:** [ECP] meal plan available, pets ($75 extra charge). **Amenities:** video games, voice mail, irons,
Small-scale Hotel hair dryers. **Pool(s):** outdoor. **Leisure Activities:** whirlpool, exercise room, sports court. **Guest Services:**
complimentary evening beverages: Mon-Thurs, valet and coin laundry. **Business Services:** meeting rooms,
business center. **Cards:** AX, CB, DC, DS, MC, VI.

SOME UNITS

HOUSE ON CHERRY STREET
Phone: (904)384-1999 25

All Year   1P: $85   2P: $95   XP: $15
Location: Just s of Riverside Ave. Located in Riverside Historic District. 1844 Cherry St 32205. Fax: 904/384-5013.
Bed & Breakfast **Facility:** This 1909 house with a large lawn on the St. Johns River is furnished with American antiques from
the Queen Anne period as well as many oriental rugs. Designated smoking area. 4 one-bedroom standard
units. 2 stories, interior corridors. *Bath:* combo or shower only. **Parking:** on-site. **Terms:** age restrictions may apply, 3 day cancellation notice-fee imposed, [CP] meal plan available, no pets allowed (owner's dog on premises). **Leisure Activities:** canoeing,
bicycles. **Guest Services:** complimentary evening beverages. **Business Services:** PC, fax. **Cards:** AX, MC, VI.

SOME UNITS

INNS OF AMERICA
Phone: (904)281-0198 32

(AAA) (SAVE)

12/1-4/15 [CP]   1P: $56-$59   2P: $56-$59   XP: $10   F18
4/16-11/30 [CP]   1P: $49-$55   2P: $49-$55   XP: $10   F18
Location: I-95, exit 344, 0.5 mi n. of jct Butler Blvd. Located in an office park. 4300 Salisbury Rd N 32216.
Motel Fax: 904/296-3580. **Facility:** 124 one-bedroom standard units. 3 stories, exterior corridors. **Parking:** on-site.
Terms: small pets only. **Pool(s):** heated outdoor. **Guest Services:** complimentary evening beverages, coin
laundry, area transportation-hospitals & Mayo Clinic. **Business Services:** fax (fee). **Cards:** AX, DS, MC, VI.
Special Amenities: free continental breakfast.

SOME UNITS

JACKSONVILLE COURTYARD AT J T BUTLER BLVD
Phone: (904)296-2828 29

(SAVE)

12/31-1/1   1P: $114-$159   2P: $114-$159
1/2-11/30   1P: $69-$114   2P: $69-$114
12/1-12/30   1P: $69-$99   2P: $69-$99
Location: I-95, exit 344, northwest corner. 4670 Lenoir Ave S 32216. Fax: 904/296-9508. **Facility:** 137 units. 132
Small-scale Hotel one-bedroom standard units. 5 one-bedroom suites ($139-$159). 5 stories, interior corridors. *Bath:* combo or
shower only. **Parking:** on-site. **Amenities:** dual phone lines, voice mail, irons, hair dryers. **Pool(s):** heated
outdoor. **Leisure Activities:** whirlpool, exercise room. **Guest Services:** valet and coin laundry. **Business Services:** meeting
rooms, fax (fee). **Cards:** AX, DC, DS, MC, VI.

SOME UNITS

(See map p. 446)

JACKSONVILLE MARRIOTT HOTEL   **Phone:** (904)296-2222   [35]

All Year   1P: $149-$188   2P: $159-$198

Location: I-95, exit 344, southeast corner off JT Butler Blvd. 4670 Salisbury Rd 32256. Fax: 904/296-7561. **Facility:** 256 units. 251 one-bedroom standard units, some with whirlpools. 5 one-bedroom suites, some with whirlpools. 9 stories, interior corridors. **Parking:** on-site. **Terms:** [AP] meal plan available, 13% service charge. **Amenities:** dual phone lines, voice mail, irons, hair dryers. **Pool(s):** heated outdoor, indoor. **Leisure Activities:** sauna, whirlpool. *Fee:* massage. **Guest Services:** gift shop, valet laundry. **Business Services:** conference facilities, business center. **Cards:** AX, DC, DS, JC, MC, VI.

Large-scale Hotel

SOME UNITS

LA QUINTA INN & SUITES   **Phone:** (904)296-0703   [31]

1/14-3/28	1P: $76-$106	2P: $82-$112	XP: $6	F18
3/29-11/30	1P: $70-$106	2P: $76-$112	XP: $6	F18
12/1-1/13	1P: $70-$100	2P: $76-$106	XP: $6	F18

Location: I-95, exit 344, northwest corner. 4686 Lenoir Ave S 32216. Fax: 904/296-0709. **Facility:** 131 units. 125 one-bedroom standard units. 6 one-bedroom suites ($119-$179). 6 stories, interior corridors. *Bath:* combo or shower only. **Parking:** on-site. **Terms:** [ECP] meal plan available. **Amenities:** video games, voice mail, irons, hair dryers. *Some:* dual phone lines. **Pool(s):** heated indoor. **Leisure Activities:** whirlpool, exercise room. **Guest Services:** valet and coin laundry. **Business Services:** meeting rooms, fax (fee). **Cards:** AX, CB, DC, DS, JC, MC, VI. **Special Amenities:** free continental breakfast and free local telephone calls. *(See color ad below)*

Small-scale Hotel

SOME UNITS

LA QUINTA INN-BAYMEADOWS   **Phone:** (904)731-9940   [50]

All Year   1P: $66-$96   2P: $73-$103   XP: $7   F18

Location: I-95, exit 341, southwest corner. 8255 Dix Ellis Tr 32256. Fax: 904/731-3854. **Facility:** 106 units. 105 one-bedroom standard units. 1 one-bedroom suite ($109-$179). 2 stories, exterior corridors. **Parking:** on-site. **Terms:** [ECP] meal plan available, small pets only. **Amenities:** video games, voice mail, irons, hair dryers. **Pool(s):** heated outdoor. **Guest Services:** valet and coin laundry. **Business Services:** fax (fee). **Cards:** AX, CB, DC, DS, JC, MC, VI. **Special Amenities:** free continental breakfast and free local telephone calls. *(See color ad below)*

Motel

SOME UNITS

LA QUINTA INN-NORTH   **Phone:** (904)751-6960   [15]

All Year   1P: $60-$76   2P: $67-$83   XP: $7   F18

Location: I-95, exit 360, southwest corner. 812 Dunn Ave 32218. Fax: 904/751-9769. **Facility:** 128 units. 126 one-bedroom standard units. 2 one-bedroom suites ($109-$179). 3 stories, exterior corridors. **Parking:** on-site. **Terms:** [ECP] meal plan available, small pets only. **Amenities:** video games, voice mail, irons, hair dryers. **Pool(s):** heated outdoor. **Guest Services:** valet and coin laundry. **Business Services:** meeting rooms, fax (fee). **Cards:** AX, CB, DC, DS, JC, MC, VI. **Special Amenities:** free continental breakfast and free local telephone calls. *(See color ad below)*

Small-scale Hotel

SOME UNITS

FEE

MAINSTAY SUITES-JACKSONVILLE   **Phone:** (904)296-0661   [41]

All Year [CP]   1P: $50-$119   2P: $50-$119

Location: I-95, exit 344, e on Butler, then just s. 4693 Salisbury Rd S 32256. Fax: 904/296-3965. **Facility:** 100 units. 78 one-bedroom standard units with efficiencies. 22 one-bedroom suites with efficiencies. 3 stories, interior corridors. *Bath:* combo or shower only. **Parking:** on-site. **Terms:** 2-4 night minimum stay - seasonal, weekly rates available, pets ($10 fee, $100 deposit). **Amenities:** video games, dual phone lines, voice mail, irons, hair dryers. **Pool(s):** outdoor. **Leisure Activities:** grill, exercise room. **Guest Services:** valet and coin laundry. **Business Services:** fax. **Cards:** AX, DC, DS, JC, MC, VI. *(See color ad p 452)*

Small-scale Hotel

SOME UNITS

(See map p. 446)

MASTERS INN
AAA SAVE
◆◆ ◆◆
Small-scale Hotel

Phone: (904)741-1133 6

All Year [CP]   1P: $34-$51   2P: $34-$51   XP: $4   F18
Location: I-95, exit 363B, just sw. 14585 Duval Rd 32218. Fax: 904/741-0121. **Facility:** 100 one-bedroom standard units. 3 stories, interior corridors. *Bath:* combo or shower only. **Parking:** on-site. **Terms:** weekly rates available, pets ($10 fee). **Business Services:** fax (fee). **Cards:** AX, CB, DC, DS, MC, VI. **Special Amenities:** free continental breakfast and free local telephone calls.

SOME UNITS

⬛ ⬛ ⬛ ⬛ ⬛ / ⬛ ⬛ ⬛ /

MASTERS INN JTB
AAA SAVE
◆◆ ◆◆
Motel

Phone: (904)281-2244 34

All Year [CP]   1P: $34-$51   2P: $34-$51   XP: $4   F18
Location: I-95, exit 344, just w. 4940 Mustang Rd 32216. Fax: 904/281-2243. **Facility:** 100 one-bedroom standard units. 3 stories, interior corridors. *Bath:* combo or shower only. **Parking:** on-site. **Terms:** weekly rates available, small pets only ($10 fee). **Business Services:** meeting rooms, fax (fee). **Cards:** AX, CB, DC, DS, MC, VI. **Special Amenities:** free continental breakfast and free local telephone calls.

SOME UNITS

⬛ ⬛ ⬛ ⬛ ⬛ ⬛ ⬛ / ⬛ ⬛ ⬛ /

OMNI JACKSONVILLE HOTEL
◆◆◆◆
Small-scale Hotel

Phone: (904)355-6664 19

12/1-5/22 & 9/8-11/30   1P: $199-$209   2P: $199-$209   XP: $10   F17
5/23-9/7   1P: $179-$189   2P: $179-$189   XP: $10   F17
Location: Corner of Pearl and Water sts; downtown. Located adjacent to The Landing. 245 Water St 32202. Fax: 904/791-4812. **Facility:** 348 units. 344 one-bedroom standard units. 4 one-bedroom suites. 15 stories, interior corridors. **Parking:** on-site. **Terms:** package plans - weekends. **Amenities:** video games, high-speed Internet (fee), dual phone lines, voice mail, honor bars, irons, hair dryers. **Dining:** Juliette's, see separate listing. **Pool(s):** heated outdoor. **Leisure Activities:** exercise room. **Guest Services:** gift shop, valet laundry, area transportation. **Business Services:** conference facilities, business center. **Cards:** AX, CB, DC, DS, MC, VI.

SOME UNITS

ASK ⬛ ⬛ ⬛ ⬛ ⬛ ⬛ ⬛ ⬛ ⬛ / ⬛ ⬛ ⬛ /
FEE   FEE

PLANTATION MANOR INN
AAA SAVE
◆◆◆ ◆◆◆
Historic Bed
& Breakfast

Phone: 904/384-4630 23

All Year   1P: $130-$160   2P: $150-$180   XP: $20
Location: Corner of Copeland and Oak sts. Located in the Riverside Historic District. 1630 Copeland St 32204. Fax: 904/387-0960. **Facility:** Doric columns add a gracious touch to the wraparound porch of this 1905 Greek Revival plantation home; fireplaces are available in some units. Smoke free premises. 9 one-bedroom standard units. 3 stories (no elevator), interior corridors. *Bath:* combo or shower only. **Parking:** on-site. **Terms:** 7 day cancellation notice-fee imposed, [BP] meal plan available. **Amenities:** irons, hair dryers. **Pool(s):** heated outdoor. **Leisure Activities:** whirlpool. **Business Services:** PC, fax. **Cards:** AX, DC, MC, VI. **Special Amenities:** free continental breakfast and free local telephone calls.

SOME UNITS

⬛ ⬛ ⬛ ⬛ / ⬛ /

QUALITY HOTEL SOUTHPOINT
AAA SAVE
◆◆◆ ◆◆◆
Large-scale Hotel

Phone: (904)281-0900 33

All Year [ECP]   1P: $59-$149   2P: $69-$169   XP: $10   F17
Location: I-95, exit 344, just e. 4660 Salisbury Rd 32256. Fax: 904/281-0417. **Facility:** 184 one-bedroom standard units. 6 stories, interior corridors. **Parking:** on-site. **Terms:** 3 day cancellation notice, weekly rates available, small pets only ($15 extra charge). **Amenities:** video games, voice mail, irons, hair dryers. **Dining:** 2 restaurants, 11 am-2 & 5-10 pm, Sun from 5 pm, cocktails. **Pool(s):** outdoor. **Leisure Activities:** sauna, exercise room. **Guest Services:** valet and coin laundry. **Business Services:** meeting rooms. **Cards:** AX, CB, DC, DS, MC, VI. **Special Amenities:** early check-in/late check-out. *(See color ad p 452)*

SOME UNITS

⬛ ⬛ ⬛ ⬛ ⬛ ⬛ ⬛ ⬛ ⬛ / ⬛ ⬛ ⬛ /

(See map p. 446)

RADISSON RIVERWALK HOTEL
Phone: (904)396-5100 21
All Year　1P: $149　2P: $159　XP: $10　F
Location: South side of the St. Johns River; downtown. Located at St. Johns Place. 1515 Prudential Dr 32207.
Large-scale Hotel　**Fax:** 904/396-8007. **Facility:** 322 units. 309 one-bedroom standard units. 13 one-bedroom suites ($189-$475), some with whirlpools. 5 stories, interior corridors. **Amenities:** video games, high-speed Internet, voice mail, irons, hair dryers. **Pool(s):** outdoor. **Leisure Activities:** 2 lighted tennis courts, exercise room. **Guest Services:** gift shop, valet laundry. **Business Services:** conference facilities, business center. **Cards:** AX, CB, DC, DS, JC, MC, VI.

SOME UNITS
ASK SD ⏴ ⏹ ⏧ ⊷ ⊛ DATA/PORT 🖥 /⊠ 🔲 /

RAMADA INN CONFERENCE CENTER
Phone: (904)268-8080 62
12/1-4/14 & 9/1-10/31 [BP]　1P: $78　2P: $83　XP: $5　F18
4/15-8/31 & 11/1-11/30 [BP]　1P: $76　2P: $81　XP: $5　F18
Small-scale Hotel　**Location:** I-295, exit 5A northbound; exit 5 southbound, just n on SR 13. 3130 Hartley Rd 32216. **Fax:** 904/262-8718. **Facility:** 152 units. 150 one-bedroom standard units. 2 one-bedroom suites ($145-$170), some with kitchens. 2 stories, exterior corridors. **Parking:** on-site. **Terms:** weekly rates available, small pets only ($100 deposit, $10-$15 extra charge). **Amenities:** voice mail, irons, hair dryers. **Pool(s):** outdoor, wading. **Guest Services:** valet and coin laundry. **Business Services:** meeting rooms, fax. **Cards:** AX, CB, DC, DS, JC, MC, VI. *(See color ad below)*

SOME UNITS
ASK SD ⏴ ⏹ ⏧ ⊘ ⊷ ⊛ 🖥 /⊠ 🔲 /
FEE

RED ROOF INN
Phone: (904)296-1006 37
AAA SAVE
All Year　1P: $46-$59　2P: $46-$59
Location: I-95, exit 344, northwest corner. 6969 Lenoir Ave E 32216. **Fax:** 904/296-1007. **Facility:** 127 units. 121 one-bedroom standard units. 6 one-bedroom suites ($64-$69). 5 stories, interior corridors. *Bath:* combo or shower only. **Parking:** on-site. **Amenities:** video games, voice mail. *Some:* dual phone lines, hair dryers.
Small-scale Hotel　**Pool(s):** heated outdoor. **Guest Services:** coin laundry. **Business Services:** fax. **Cards:** AX, CB, DC, DS, MC, VI. **Special Amenities: free local telephone calls and free newspaper.**

SOME UNITS
⏴ ⏹ ⊘ ⊷ ⊛ DATA/PORT /⊠ 🔲 📷 /

RED ROOF INN-AIRPORT
Phone: (904)741-4488 7
AAA SAVE
1/1-4/19　1P: $39-$49　2P: $44-$54　XP: $5　F18
12/1-12/31 & 4/20-11/30　1P: $36-$46　2P: $41-$51　XP: $5　F18
Location: I-95, exit 363. 14701 Airport Entrance Rd 32218. **Fax:** 904/741-4493. **Facility:** 108 one-bedroom standard units. 2 stories, exterior corridors. **Parking:** on-site. **Terms:** small pets only. **Amenities:** video games, voice mail.
Motel　**Pool(s):** heated outdoor. **Business Services:** fax. **Cards:** AX, CB, DC, DS, MC, VI. **Special Amenities: free local telephone calls and free newspaper.**

SOME UNITS
⏴ ⏹ ⊷ ⊛ DATA/PORT /⊠ /

RESIDENCE INN-AIRPORT
Phone: (904)741-6550 10
SAVE
All Year　1P: $129-$159　2P: $129-$159
Location: I-95, exit 363B, 0.3 mi w. 1310 Airport Rd 32218. **Fax:** 904/741-6677. **Facility:** 78 units. 33 one-bedroom standard units. 33 one- and 12 two-bedroom suites ($129-$159), some with efficiencies or kitchens. 3 stories, interior corridors. *Bath:* combo or shower only. **Parking:** on-site.
Small-scale Hotel　**Terms:** cancellation fee imposed, [BP] meal plan available, pets ($100 fee). **Amenities:** dual phone lines, voice mail, irons, hair dryers. **Pool(s):** heated outdoor. **Leisure Activities:** whirlpool, exercise room, sports court. **Guest Services:** valet and coin laundry. **Business Services:** meeting rooms, fax (fee). **Cards:** AX, DC, DS, MC, VI.

SOME UNITS
SD ⊕ ⏴ ⏹ ⊜M ⊘ ⊛ ⊷ ⊠ ⊛ DATA/PORT 🔲 📷 🖥 /⊠ /

RESIDENCE INN BY MARRIOTT
Phone: (904)733-8088 55
SAVE
All Year　1P: $79-$140
Location: I-95, exit 341, sw off Baymeadows Rd. 8365 Dix Ellis Tr 32256. **Fax:** 904/731-8354. **Facility:** 112 one-bedroom standard units with kitchens. 2 stories, exterior corridors. *Bath:* combo or shower only. **Parking:** on-site. **Terms:** daily rates available, [BP] meal plan available, pets ($75 cleaning fee). **Amenities:** voice mail,
Small-scale Hotel　irons, hair dryers. **Pool(s):** heated outdoor. **Leisure Activities:** whirlpools, sports court. **Guest Services:** complimentary evening beverages: Mon-Thurs, valet and coin laundry. **Business Services:** meeting rooms, fax (fee). **Cards:** AX, CB, DC, DS, JC, MC, VI.

SOME UNITS
SD ⏴ ⏹ ⊘ ⊘ ⊷ ⊕⊕ ⊛ DATA/PORT 🔲 📷 🖥 /⊠ /

(See map p. 446)

RESIDENCE INN BY MARRIOTT
Phone: (904)996-8900 **45**

All Year [BP]   1P: $89-$119   2P: $89-$119

Small-scale Hotel

Location: I-95, exit 344, 3.5 mi e on JT Butler Blvd (SR 202) to Gate Blvd, just s, then just w. 10551 Deerwood Park Blvd 32256. Fax: 904/996-8904. **Facility:** 120 units. 60 one-bedroom standard units with efficiencies. 36 one- and 24 two-bedroom suites, some with efficiencies or kitchens. 3 stories, interior corridors. *Bath:* combo or shower only. **Parking:** on-site. **Terms:** pets ($75 extra charge). **Amenities:** video games, dual phone lines, voice mail, irons, hair dryers. **Pool(s):** outdoor. **Leisure Activities:** whirlpool, exercise room, sports court. **Guest Services:** complimentary evening beverages: Mon-Thurs, valet and coin laundry. **Business Services:** meeting rooms, fax (fee). **Cards:** AX, CB, DC, DS, JC, MC, VI.

SOME UNITS

SOUTHPOINT HOTEL
Phone: (904)281-9700 **43**

All Year   1P: $49-$89   2P: $59-$99

Small-scale Hotel

Location: I-95, exit 344, just e, then just s. 4700 Salisbury Rd 32256. Fax: 904/281-1957. **Facility:** 167 units. 164 one-bedroom standard units. 3 one-bedroom suites. 6 stories, interior corridors. **Parking:** on-site. **Terms:** cancellation fee imposed. **Amenities:** irons, hair dryers. **Dining:** 6 am-11 pm. **Pool(s):** outdoor. **Leisure Activities:** whirlpool, exercise room. **Guest Services:** valet laundry. **Business Services:** meeting rooms, business center. **Cards:** AX, DC, DS, JC, MC, VI. **Special Amenities:** free continental breakfast.

SOME UNITS

SPRINGHILL SUITES BY MARRIOTT JACKSONVILLE DEERWOOD PARK
Phone: (904)997-6650 **53**

All Year   1P: $69-$109

Small-scale Hotel

Location: I-95, exit 344, 2.5 mi e, then 1 mi n on SR 115. 4385 Southside Blvd 32216. Fax: 904/997-6610. **Facility:** 102 one-bedroom standard units. 5 stories, interior corridors. *Bath:* combo or shower only. **Parking:** on-site. **Terms:** [CP] meal plan available. **Amenities:** video games, dual phone lines, voice mail, irons, hair dryers. **Pool(s):** outdoor. **Leisure Activities:** whirlpool, exercise room. **Guest Services:** valet and coin laundry, area transportation-within 5 mi. **Business Services:** meeting rooms, fax. **Cards:** AX, CB, DC, DS, MC, VI. **Special Amenities:** free continental breakfast and free local telephone calls.

SOME UNITS

(See map p. 446)

WELLESLEY INN & SUITES (JACKSONVILLE/DEERWOOD PARK)　Phone: (904)620-9008　🚺
F16

(AAA) (SAVE)　All Year [ECP]　　　1P: $79-$89　　2P: $79-$89　　XP: $10
♦♦♦　Location: I-95, exit 344, 2.5 mi e on JT Butler Blvd to Southside Blvd, just n on west side of road. 8801 Perimeter Park
Blvd 32216. Fax: 904/620-9068. **Facility:** 126 units. 123 one-bedroom standard units. 3 one-bedroom suites
($89-$109). 3 stories, interior corridors. *Bath:* combo or shower only. **Parking:** on-site. **Terms:** 5 day cancel-
Small-scale Hotel　lation notice. **Amenities:** video games, voice mail, irons, hair dryers. **Pool(s):** outdoor. **Leisure Activi-
ties:** exercise room. **Guest Services:** valet and coin laundry. **Business Services:** fax (fee). **Cards:** AX, CB,
DC, DS, MC, VI. **Special Amenities:** free continental breakfast and free newspaper. *(See color ad p 453)*

SOME UNITS

🛇📶 ⓓ 🅜 🅚 🏊 🎦 (DATA PORT) 🖥 🖨 💻 /✕/

WINGATE INN/SOUTHSIDE　　　　　　　　　　　　　Phone: (904)281-2600　🚺

(AAA) (SAVE)　All Year [ECP]　　　1P: $59-$189　　2P: $59-$189
♦♦♦　Location: I-95, exit 344, northwest corner. 4681 Lenoir Ave S 32216. Fax: 904/281-1166. **Facility:** 102 one-
bedroom standard units, some with whirlpools. 4 stories, interior corridors. *Bath:* combo or shower only.
Parking: on-site. **Amenities:** video games, high-speed Internet, dual phone lines, voice mail, safes, irons,
Small-scale Hotel　hair dryers. **Pool(s):** outdoor. **Leisure Activities:** whirlpool, exercise room. **Guest Services:** valet and coin
laundry. **Business Services:** meeting rooms, business center. **Cards:** AX, CB, DC, DS, JC, MC, VI.

(See color ad p 453)

SOME UNITS

🛇📶 🍴 🅜 🅚 🎦 🏊 🎦 (DATA PORT) 💻 /✕ 🖥 🖨/

─────── *The following lodgings were either not evaluated or did not* ───────
　　　　meet AAA rating requirements but are listed for your information only.

WINGATE INN-AIRPORT　　　　　　　　　　　　　Phone: 904/421-5000

[fyi]　All Year [ECP]　　　1P: $99-$199　　2P: $99-$199
Too new to rate. **Location:** I-95, exit 363. 1200 Airport Rd 32218. Fax: 904/421-5001. **Amenities:** microwaves,
Small-scale Hotel　refrigerators, pool. **Terms:** 7 day cancellation notioo. **Carda:** AX, CB, DC, DS, MC, VI. *(See ad p 462)*

WINGATE INN-WINDSOR PARKE　　　　　　　　　　Phone: 904/421-7000

[fyi]　All Year [ECP]　　　1P: $99-$199　　2P: $99-$199
Too new to rate. **Location:** I-95, exit 344, 7.5 mi e on SR 202, then just n on Hodges Blvd. 4791 Windsor Commons
Small-scale Hotel　Court 32224. Fax: 904/421-7001. **Amenities:** coffeemakers, microwaves, refrigerators, pool. **Terms:** 7 day
cancellation notice. **Cards:** AX, CB, DC, DS, MC, VI. *(See ad p 462)*

─────── **WHERE TO DINE** ───────

BISCOTTI'S ESPRESSO CAFE　　Lunch: $8-$20　　Dinner: $10-$30　　Phone: 904/387-2060　🔟
♦♦ ♦♦　Location: I-10, exit 360, 2 mi s on McDuff Ave, 1 mi w. 3556 St Johns Ave 32204. **Hours:** 7 am-10 pm, Mon 11
am-3 pm, Fri 7 am-midnight, Sat 8 am-midnight, Sun 8 am-3 pm. **Features:** Indoor and outdoor seating is
American　available in the relaxed neighborhood gathering spot, which overlooks the Avondale shopping district. On
the eclectic menu are pizzas, salads and hearty sandwiches, which are nicely accompanied by freshly
ground coffee, espresso and cappuccino. Desserts are decadent. Smoke free premises. Casual dress; beer & wine only.
Parking: street. **Cards:** AX, DS, MC, VI.
✕

BOMBAY BICYCLE CLUB　　　Lunch: $5-$10　　Dinner: $7-$13　　Phone: 904/737-9555　🔟
♦♦ ♦♦　Location: I-95, exit 341, northwest corner. 8909 Baymeadows Rd 32256. **Hours:** 11:30 am-1 am, Sun
noon-midnight. **Reservations:** suggested; weekends. **Features:** The busy, casual eatery is decorated with
American　bicycle memorabilia. The freshly brewed beer brings out the younger crowd for happy hour. Order the
Chinese grilled salad filled with sweet and sour chicken. Many traditional favorites like big burgers are
served. Casual dress; cocktails. **Parking:** on-site. **Cards:** AX, CB, DC, DS, MC, VI.
🍸 ✕

CLARK'S FISH CAMP　　　　　　　Dinner: $5-$14　　Phone: 904/268-3474　㉑
♦♦♦　Location: I-295, exit 3, 0.8 mi s, then 1.7 mi w. 12903 Hood Landing Rd 32217. **Hours:** 4:30 pm-9:30 pm, Fri-10
pm, Sat 11 am-10 pm, Sun 11:30 am-9 pm. Closed: 1/1, 11/27, 12/24, 12/25; also Super Bowl Sun.
Seafood　**Features:** Guests can appreciate old Florida charm at its best. The menu lists a slew of Southern
favorites, starting with New England or Minorcan clam chowder or fried gator tail. Fried, charbroiled or the
house special stuffed fish with hush puppies and cole slaw make up the core of the menu. Mounted animals surround the
relaxing indoor dining rooms, while the patio overlooks the waterway. Most meals come with choices of vegetables and salad.
Casual dress; cocktails. **Parking:** on-site. **Cards:** AX, DC, DS, MC, VI.
✕

CRAWDADDY'S　　　　　　　Lunch: $5-$10　　Dinner: $15-$22　　Phone: 904/396-3546　⑤
♦♦ ♦♦　Location: On the south side of the St John's River; at St John's Place. 1643 Prudential Dr 32207. **Hours:** 9 am-2:30
& 5-10 pm, Fri & Sat 5 pm-11 pm. **Reservations:** suggested; for dinner. **Features:** Offerings range from
Seafood　finger foods to heavy entrees at the waterfront restaurant, which replicates the rustic feel of a 1920s fish
camp. Listen to New Orleans jazz and take in the spectacular sights of the skyline and the mighty St.
Johns River. Dressy casual; cocktails. **Parking:** on-site. **Cards:** AX, DC, DS, MC, VI.
🍸 ✕

JOHNNY LEVEROCK'S SEAFOOD HOUSE　　Lunch: $7-$10　　Dinner: $8-$16　　Phone: 904/997-1111　⑧
♦♦ ♦♦　Location: I-95, exit 344 E, e on JT Butler, 2.4 mi to SR 115 (Southside Blvd N), 1 mi n. 9750 Deer Lake Ct 32246.
Hours: 11 am-10 pm, Fri & Sat-11 pm, Sun-10 pm. Closed: 11/27, 12/25. **Features:** Bright colors bring out
Seafood　the appeal of this nautical themed restaurant. Grilled mahi mahi, coconut shrimp and seafood puff pastries
adorn the menu. An automatic player piano provides background music for a festive atmosphere. Casual
dress; cocktails; entertainment. **Parking:** on-site. **Cards:** AX, DS, MC, VI.
🍸 ✕

(See map p. 446)

JOSEPH'S ITALIAN RESTAURANT   Lunch: $6-$10   Dinner: $7-$15   Phone: 904/642-3444   ㉒

Italian

Location: I-95, exit 344, 1.5 mi e; in Baymeadows Village Shopping Center. 9802 Baymeadows Rd 32216. **Hours:** 11 am-10 pm, Sun-9:30 pm. Closed major holidays. **Features:** Diners can enjoy such Italian favorites as pizza, calzones and lasagna, all cooked fresh and made to the guest's liking. Also offered are daily soup and salad specials. An easy respite for travelers, the restaurant is just minutes from I-95. Smoke free premises. Casual dress; beer & wine only. **Parking:** on-site. **Cards:** AX, DC, DS, MC, VI.

JULIETTE'S   Lunch: $4-$13   Dinner: $17-$32   Phone: 904/355-7118   ①

American

Location: Corner of Pearl and Water sts; downtown; in Omni Jacksonville Hotel. 245 Water St 32202. **Hours:** 6:30 am-10:30 pm, Fri & Sat-11 pm. **Reservations:** suggested. **Features:** The upscale bistro offers dining in an open-ceiling, high-rise atrium. The seasonally changing menu combines the flavors of America and Italy in its pasta, seafood, steak and chicken dishes. The wine list shows breadth, and the servers are knowledgeable. Dressy casual; cocktails. **Parking:** on-site. **Cards:** AX, CB, DC, DS, JC, MC, VI.

MANDARIN DRAGON   Lunch: $4-$6   Dinner: $6-$12   Phone: 904/260-4681   ⑱

Chinese

Location: SR 13, 1 mi s of jct I-295; in The Gates of Olde Mandarin Shopping Center. 11362-8 San Jose Blvd 32223. **Hours:** 11 am-9:30 pm, Fri & Sat-10 pm. Closed: 7/4, 11/27, 12/25. **Reservations:** suggested; weekends. **Features:** An Oriental motif featuring dragon decorations and exotic flowers weaves through the bi-level dining room of the restaurant. In addition to well-presented traditional dishes, you can choose from an interesting selection of Chinese beer and wine. Casual dress; beer & wine only. **Parking:** on-site. **Cards:** AX, DC, DS, MC, VI.

MARKER 32   Dinner: $18-$45   Phone: 904/223-1534   ⑫

Continental

Location: 0.5 mi w of Intracoastal Waterway Bridge. 14549 Beach Blvd 32225. **Hours:** 5:30 pm-10 pm. Closed major holidays; also Sun. **Reservations:** suggested. **Features:** Delicious, innovative dishes of polenta, grilled mahi mahi and the sinful chocolate comet attract an upscale crowd to this casual restaurant. Polished servers are knowledgeable about the menu, and the waterfront views are outstanding. Dressy casual; cocktails. **Parking:** on-site. **Cards:** AX, DC, MC, VI.

MATTHEW'S   Dinner: $20-$60   Phone: 904/396-9922   ⑥

Continental

Location: S of downtown; in historic San Marco, just s of Atlantic Blvd. 2107 Hendricks Ave 32207. **Hours:** 5:30 pm-10 pm. Closed major holidays; also Sun. **Reservations:** required. **Features:** Recognized as one of Jacksonville's premiere dining rooms, the restaurant provides a showcase in which renowned chef Matthew Medure tantalizes guests with innovative cuisine and award-winning wines. Superbly refined service reaches each intimate booth and linen-clothed table, as well as the chef's barside tasting table near the kitchen. The diverse menu blends Southern, Mediterranean and Asian influences. Reservations typically fill up well in advance. Semi-formal attire; beer & wine only. **Parking:** on-site. **Cards:** AX, DC, DS, MC, VI.

PAGODA CHINESE RESTAURANT   Lunch: $5-$7   Dinner: $8-$19   Phone: 904/731-0880   ⑯

Chinese

Location: I-95, exit 341, 0.5 mi w on SR 152. 8617 Baymeadows Rd 32256. **Hours:** 11 am-10 pm, Fri-11 pm, Sat noon-11 pm. Closed: 7/4, 11/27, 12/25; also Sun. **Features:** A family operation since the mid 1980s, the informal restaurant serves such traditional cuisine as sweet-and-sour chicken, curry chicken, fried rice and seafood with vegetables—all spiced to diners' preferences. Modern Chinese artifacts decorate the building's interior—a pagoda-like room with a beamed ceiling and 360-degree skylights. Casual dress; cocktails. **Parking:** on-site. **Cards:** AX, CB, DC, DS, MC, VI.

PATTAYA THAI RESTAURANT   Lunch: $6-$18   Dinner: $6-$18   Phone: 904/646-9506   ⑳

Thai

Location: 0.5 mi e of SR 9A (St. John's Bluff Rd); in Justin Plaza; across from Craig Airport. 10916 Atlantic Blvd 32221. **Hours:** 11 am-2 & 5-9:45 pm, Sat & Sun from 5 pm. Closed major holidays; also Mon. **Features:** The established Thai restaurant's menu includes a variety of vegetarian dishes as well as chicken, pork and beef entrees. Descriptive listings highlight spicy, hot selections and outline specific seasonings. Delicious accompaniments include chicken coconut soup and artfully presented spring rolls. Lunch specials are prepared daily. Casual dress; beer & wine only. **Parking:** on-site. **Cards:** AX, DS, MC, VI.

RIVER CITY BREWING COMPANY   Lunch: $5-$12   Dinner: $14-$25   Phone: 904/398-2299   ④

American

Location: On the south bank of the St. Johns River, just e of the Main St Bridge. 835 Museum Cir 32207. **Hours:** 11 am-3 & 5-10 pm, Fri & Sat-11 pm. Closed: 12/25. **Features:** The restaurant carries out a mood of casual elegance with white linen tablecloths and servers working in teams. The nautically themed tiered dining room offers scenic views of the city skyline, the St. Johns River and the marina. Eclectic menu choices include preparations of chicken, chops and pasta with an emphasis on local seafood. Inviting desserts are displayed on a tray. A spacious riverside deck and a brewpub are dining alternatives and a perfect setting for happy hour. Casual dress; cocktails. **Parking:** on-site. **Cards:** AX, CB, DC, DS, MC, VI.

ROSALIA'S ITALIAN CAFE   Lunch: $5-$10   Dinner: $9-$20   Phone: 904/880-3989   ㉔

Italian

Location: I-295, exit 5, just n. 10503-3 San Jose Blvd 32257. **Hours:** 11 am-9:30 pm. Closed: Sun. **Features:** Seat yourself in this storefront cafe with real Italian flair. Offers a variey of specialties, such as baked ziti. Casual dress; beer & wine only. **Parking:** on-site. **Cards:** AX, DS, MC, VI.

SEVEN BRIDGES GRILLE & BREWERY   Lunch: $7-$15   Dinner: $8-$17   Phone: 904/997-1999   ㉓

American

Location: 9735 Gate Pkwy N 32246. **Hours:** 11 am-10 pm. Closed: 11/27. **Features:** Open warehouse feel with beer vats on the second level visible from most areas of the restaurant. Unique and tasty menu selections like hazelnut encrusted chicken. Large scale desserts are homemade and worth saving room for. Casual dress; cocktails. **Parking:** on-site. **Cards:** AX, DS, MC, VI.

(See map p. 446)

THAI ROOM **Lunch:** $4-$14 **Dinner:** $4-$14 **Phone:** 904/249-8444 ⑰
Location: Corner; 13th Ave S on SR A1A. 1286 S 3rd St 32250. **Hours:** 11 am-2 & 5-9:30 pm, Fri-10:30 pm, Sat
Thai 5 pm-10:30 pm, Sun 5 pm-9:30 pm. Closed major holidays. **Features:** This is what it's like to dine in
Thailand. An attractive fountain and greenery-surrounded waterfall grace the center of the dining room,
while a thatch-like mansard roof over the bar area fosters an outdoors feeling. Begin with a light spring roll
or one of several homemade soups, then enjoy duck curry or other favorites such as prig pow, kra proa or a host of rice and
noodle selections. Dishes are spiced to diners' preference. Smoke free premises. Casual dress; cocktails. **Parking:** on-site.
Cards: AX, DC, DS, MC, VI.
⊠

THE TREE STEAK HOUSE **Dinner:** $14-$30 **Phone:** 904-262-0006 ⑲
Location: On SR 13, 1 mi s of jct I-295; in The Gates of Olde Mandarin Shopping Center. 11362-1 San Jose Blvd
32223. **Hours:** 5:30 pm-10 pm, Fri & Sat-10:30 pm, Sun-9 pm. Closed major holidays.
Steak House **Reservations:** accepted; Fri & Sat. **Features:** Brick and low lighting contribute to the rustic atmosphere of
the busy restaurant. The open-flame grill faces the dining room, and steaks are cut to order at the table.
An extensive wine list and a varied salad bar complement the entrees. Casual dress; cocktails. **Parking:** on-site. **Cards:** AX,
CB, DC, DS, MC, VI.
Ⓨ ⊠

WILFRIED'S 24 MIRAMAR **Dinner:** $20-$28 **Phone:** 904/448-2424 ⑨
Location: 3 mi s on SR 13, just n of jct San Jose Blvd. 4446 Hendricks Ave 32207. **Hours:** 5:30 pm-10 pm, Fri &
Sat-11 pm. Closed: Sun & Mon. **Reservations:** suggested. **Features:** The chef's
American innovation shines through in imaginatively prepared and presented dishes and enticing puffed-pastry
desserts. The influences of California, Asia and the Caribbean intermingle in many dishes. The dining room
has been transformed into an art gallery featuring new artists quarterly. Semi-formal attire; beer & wine only. **Parking:** on-site.
Cards: AX, CB, DC, DS, MC, VI.
⊠

WINE CELLAR **Lunch:** $7-$15 **Dinner:** $19-$29 **Phone:** 904-398-8989 ⑦
Location: I-95, exit 350A, just ne. 1314 Prudential Dr 32207. **Hours:** 11 am-2 & 5:30-10 pm, Sat from 5:30 pm.
Closed: Sun. **Reservations:** suggested. **Features:** The warm and inviting atmosphere is enhanced by
American elegant dark wood walls and large windows. Well-rounded menu with some unique selections such as
jalapeno-encrusted mahi mahi. There is an extensive wine list. Dressy casual; cocktails. **Parking:** on-site.
Cards: AX, CB, DC, DS, MC, VI.
⊠

─────── *The following restaurant has not been evaluated by AAA* ───────
but is listed for your information only.

ATLANTA BREAD COMPANY BAKERY CAFE **Phone:** 904/928-3141
[fyi] Not evaluated. **Location:** I-95, exit 344, 2.5 mi e, then 1 mi n on SR 115. 9700-5 Deer Lake Ct 32216.
Features: Specialty sandwiches on a multitude of breads and numerous soups that rotate on a daily
schedule. Salads, pastries and gourmet coffee drinks are ordered at the counters of this bright storefront cafe. Smoke free
premises.

The Jacksonville Vicinity

AMELIA ISLAND

──────── WHERE TO STAY ────────

ADDISON HOUSE   Phone: (904)277-1604
▼▼▼▼▼▼▼   All Year [BP]   1P: $109-$189   2P: $109-$189   XP: $20
Bed & Breakfast   **Location:** In Fernandina Beach; just s of Centre St, corner of Ash and S 7th sts. Located in the historic district. 614 Ash St 32034 (614 Ash St, AMELIA CITY). Fax: 904/277-8124. **Facility:** Guests are served cookies and lemonade every afternoon at this property offering lodgings in a garden house, a cottage or an 1876 Victorian house. Smoke free premises. 14 one-bedroom standard units. 2 stories, interior/exterior corridors. *Bath:* combo or shower only. **Parking:** street. **Terms:** age restrictions may apply, 7 day cancellation notice-fee imposed. **Amenities:** video library, hair dryers. *Some:* irons. **Business Services:** meeting rooms, fax (fee). **Cards:** AX, MC, VI.

SOME UNITS
〔⑪〕 ⊠ / 〔VCR〕

AMELIA ISLAND PLANTATION   Phone: (904)261-6161
AAA SAVE   All Year   1P: $200-$320   2P: $215-$335   XP: $15   F15
▼▼▼▼ ▼▼▼▼   **Location:** In Amelia City; SR A1A, 6.5 mi s of the bridge. 3000 First Coast Hwy 32034 (PO Box 3000, AMELIA CITY, 32035-3000). Fax: 904/321-5060. **Facility:** This property features secluded, wooded, waterfront grounds; accommodations range from hotel rooms to four-bedroom villas with private pools. Designated smoking area.
Resort   667 units. 249 one-bedroom standard units. 209 one-, 129 two- and 64 three-bedroom suites ($265-$405),
Large-scale Hotel   some with kitchens. 16 vacation homes. 1-8 stories, interior/exterior corridors. *Bath:* combo or shower only. **Parking:** on-site. **Terms:** check-in 4 pm, 14 day cancellation notice-fee imposed, weekly rates available, [AP] & [MAP] meal plans available, package plans - seasonal, 20% service charge. **Amenities:** voice mail, safes, irons, hair dryers. *Some:* video games, dual phone lines, honor bars. **Dining:** 9 restaurants, 6:30 am-midnight; 20% service charge, cocktails, entertainment. **Pool(s):** 21 outdoor, 2 heated outdoor, heated indoor, wading. **Leisure Activities:** saunas, whirlpools, steamrooms, rental canoes, boat dock, fishing, recreation programs, hiking trails, jogging, playground, spa, sports court. *Fee:* charter fishing, kayaks, golf-54 holes, 23 tennis courts (3 lighted), bicycles, horseback riding. **Guest Services:** gift shop, valet laundry, area transportation-Amelia Island. **Business Services:** conference facilities, business center. **Cards:** AX, DC, DS, MC, VI. **Special Amenities:** free local telephone calls. *(See color ad below)*

SOME UNITS
〔S⁄₀〕 ✈ 〔⑪〕 〔24〕 ▽ 〔⑪〕 ✍ ⊘ ⊿ ♥ ⊠ ⊠ ⛱ 〔DATA PORT〕 🖥 / 〔VCR〕 🔲 🖨 /
FEE   FEE

EVERYBODY *loves Amelia.*™

Spectacular Oceanside Golf   Home of Bausch & Lomb Championships   Family Fun in the Sun   Luxurious Accommodations

A Perfect Blend of Man-made Luxuries and Pristine Coastal Wilderness
• 1,350 acres of natural splendor • Miles of uncrowded beach • 54 holes of championship golf
• Golf School • 23 clay tennis courts • Luxury spa • New shopping village • Supervised youth programs
• Hotel & villa accommodations • Fabulous dining • Nature trails

Four Diamond Award

🐢 *Amelia Island Plantation*®   Just 29 miles from Jacksonville International Airport
FLORIDA'S PREMIER ISLAND RESORT™   **1-800-874-6878** • **www.aipfl.com**

BAILEY HOUSE

▼▼▲▲▼▼

Historic Bed & Breakfast

Phone: (904)261-5390

All Year   2P: $129-$199   XP: $25
Location: In Fernandina Beach; just s of Centre St. Located in the historic district. 28 S 7th St 32034. **Fax:** 904/321-0103. **Facility:** Stained glass, heart-pine floors, oriental rugs, ornate mantelpieces, claw-foot bathtubs and Queen Anne furnishings distinguish this Victorian home. Designated smoking area. 10 one-bedroom standard units, some with kitchens and/or whirlpools. 2 stories, interior corridors. *Bath:* combo or shower only. **Parking:** on-site. **Terms:** 2 night minimum stay - weekends, age restrictions may apply, 5 day cancellation notice-fee imposed, [BP] meal plan available, no pets allowed (owner's dog on premises). **Amenities:** irons, hair dryers. **Leisure Activities:** bicycles. **Business Services:** fax. **Cards:** AX, DS, MC, VI.

SOME UNITS

(ASK) (††→) (✕) (DATA PORT) / (🛏) (📇) (💻) /

ELIZABETH POINTE LODGE

AAA (SAVE)
▼▼▲▲▼▼

Bed & Breakfast

Phone: (904)277-4851

All Year [BP]   2P: $160-$295
Location: In Amelia City; SR A1A, just s on the ocean. 98 S Fletcher Ave 32034. **Fax:** 904/277-6500. **Facility:** This New England-style house featuring a wraparound piazza and a lobby fireplace has nautical-themed guest rooms reminiscent of Nantucket. Designated smoking area. 25 units. 24 one-bedroom standard units, some with whirlpools. 1 two-bedroom suite. 4 stories, interior/exterior corridors. **Parking:** on-site. **Terms:** 7 day cancellation notice. **Amenities:** voice mail, irons, hair dryers. **Leisure Activities:** beach accessories. *Fee:* bicycles. **Guest Services:** valet laundry. **Business Services:** meeting rooms, fax (fee). **Cards:** AX, MC, VI. **Special Amenities: free continental breakfast and free newspaper.**

SOME UNITS

(S⚡D) (24↑) (✕) (⚡) (DATA PORT) / (🛏) (📇) (💻) /

THE FAIRBANKS HOUSE

▼▼▲▲▼▼

Historic Bed & Breakfast

Phone: (904)277-0500

All Year [BP]   1P: $170-$285   2P: $170-$285   XP: $50
Location: In Fernandina Beach; just s of Centre St. Located in the historic district. 227 S 7th St 32034. **Fax:** 904/277-3103. **Facility:** This service-oriented property includes an 1885 Italianate villa and cottages; guest units are furnished with antiques and oriental rugs. Smoke free premises. 12 units. 8 one-bedroom standard units, some with whirlpools. 1 two-bedroom suite ($250-$285) with whirlpool. 3 cottages ($195-$220), some with whirlpools. 3 stories (no elevator), interior/exterior corridors. *Bath:* combo or shower only. **Parking:** on-site. **Terms:** 2 night minimum stay - weekends, age restrictions may apply, 14 day cancellation notice, package plans. **Amenities:** irons, hair dryers. **Pool(s):** outdoor. **Leisure Activities:** bicycles. **Guest Services:** complimentary evening beverages. **Business Services:** meeting rooms. **Cards:** AX, DS, MC, VI.

SOME UNITS

(††→) (➥) (✕) (⚡) (💻) / (VCR) (🛏) /

FLORIDA HOUSE INN

AAA (SAVE)
▼▼▲▲▼▼

Historic Country Inn

Phone: 904/261-3300

All Year   XP: $10   F5
Location: In Fernandina Beach; just s of Centre St. Located in the historic area. 22 S 3rd St 32034 (PO Box 688, FERNANDINA BEACH, 32035). **Fax:** 904/277-3831. **Facility:** Said to be the oldest continuously operating hotel in the state, this service-oriented inn offers a variety of room sizes, some with fireplaces. Designated smoking area. 15 units. 14 one-bedroom standard units, some with whirlpools. 1 one-bedroom suite. 2 stories (no elevator), interior/exterior corridors. *Bath:* combo or shower only. **Parking:** on-site. **Terms:** 2-3 night minimum stay - weekends, 7 day cancellation notice, [BP] meal plan available, pets ($10 extra charge, with prior approval). **Amenities:** hair dryers. *Some:* irons. **Dining:** dining room, see separate listing. **Leisure Activities:** bicycles. **Guest Services:** complimentary evening beverages. **Business Services:** meeting rooms. **Cards:** AX, DS, MC, VI. **Special Amenities: free continental breakfast and free local telephone calls.**

SOME UNITS

(🛏) (††) (⌴) (✕) / (💻) /

HAMPTON INN AMELIA ISLAND

AAA (SAVE)
▼▼▲▲▼▼

Small-scale Hotel

Phone: (904)321-1111

3/1-8/16 [ECP]	1P: $94-$149	2P: $104-$149	XP: $10	F17
8/17-11/30 [ECP]	1P: $79-$144	2P: $84-$144	XP: $10	F17
12/1-2/28 [ECP]	1P: $79-$139	2P: $84-$139	XP: $10	F17

Location: In Amelia City; just w of jct SR A1A and Sadler Rd. 2549 Sadler Rd 32034. **Fax:** 904/321-0115. **Facility:** 82 units. 77 one-bedroom standard units. 5 one-bedroom suites, some with whirlpools. 3 stories, interior corridors. *Bath:* combo or shower only. **Parking:** on-site. **Terms:** check-in 4 pm, cancellation fee imposed. **Amenities:** video games, dual phone lines, voice mail, irons, hair dryers. **Pool(s):** small outdoor. **Guest Services:** valet laundry. **Cards:** AX, CB, DC, DS, MC, VI. **Special Amenities: free continental breakfast and free local telephone calls.**

SOME UNITS

(††→) (♿M) (♿) (🔊) (➥) (🔧) (⚡) (DATA PORT) (💻) / (✕) (🛏) (📇) /

HAMPTON INN & SUITES-AMELIA ISLAND

(SAVE)
▼▼▲▲▼▼

Small-scale Hotel

Phone: (904)491-4911

All Year [ECP]   1P: $144-$179   XP: $10   F18
Location: In Fernandina Beach; I-95, exit 373 (SR A1A), 16 mi, then left on Ash St. 19 S 2nd St 32034. **Fax:** 904/491-4910. **Facility:** 122 units. 61 one-bedroom standard units, some with whirlpools. 61 one-bedroom suites, some with efficiencies and/or whirlpools. 4 stories, interior corridors. *Bath:* combo or shower only. **Parking:** on-site. **Terms:** 3 day cancellation notice. **Amenities:** dual phone lines, voice mail, irons, hair dryers. **Pool(s):** outdoor. **Leisure Activities:** exercise room. **Guest Services:** sundries, valet and coin laundry. **Business Services:** meeting rooms, business center. **Cards:** AX, DC, DS, MC, VI.

SOME UNITS

(S⚡D) (††→) (➥) (⚡) (DATA PORT) (💻) / (✕) (VCR) (🛏) (📇) /

HOYT HOUSE

▼▼▲▲▼▼

Historic Bed & Breakfast

Phone: 904/277-4300

All Year   1P: $129-$189   2P: $129-$189   XP: $40
Location: In Fernandina Beach; on Atlantic Ave/SR 200 at Centre and S 8th sts. Located in the historic district. 804 Atlantic Ave 32034. **Fax:** 904/277-9626. **Facility:** Gourmet breakfasts are served in the dining room at this 1905 Queen Anne home decorated with antiques and reproductions. Designated smoking area. 10 one-bedroom standard units, some with whirlpools. 2 stories (no elevator), interior corridors. *Bath:* combo or shower only. **Parking:** on-site. **Terms:** 2 night minimum stay - weekends 2/1-6/30, age restrictions may apply, 7 day cancellation notice-fee imposed, [BP] meal plan available, package plans, no pets allowed (owner's cat on premises). **Amenities:** irons, hair dryers. **Guest Services:** complimentary evening beverages. **Business Services:** meeting rooms. **Cards:** AX, DS, MC, VI.

SOME UNITS

(††→) (✕) (⚡) / (VCR) /

THE RITZ-CARLTON, AMELIA ISLAND

Phone: (904)277-1100

	2/13-6/28	1P: $349-$1800	2P: $349-$1800
	10/2-11/30	1P: $299-$1500	2P: $299-$1500
	12/1-2/12	1P: $289-$1500	2P: $289-$1500
	6/29-10/1	1P: $259-$1500	2P: $259-$1500

Resort
Large-scale Hotel
Location: In Summer Beach; on SR A1A. 4750 Amelia Island Pkwy 32034. Fax: 904/277-1145. **Facility:** All guest rooms have private balconies with views of the ocean at this beach front hotel featuring extensive collections of art and antiques. 449 one-bedroom standard units, some with whirlpools. 8 stories, interior corridors. **Parking:** valet. **Terms:** 7 day cancellation notice, [BP] & [CP] meal plans available, package plans. **Amenities:** dual phone lines, voice mail, safes, honor bars, irons, hair dryers. *Fee:* video games, high-speed Internet. *Some:* CD players. **Dining:** 3 restaurants, 6:30 am-10 pm, cocktails, also, The Grill, see separate listing, entertainment. **Pool(s):** small outdoor, heated outdoor, heated indoor. **Leisure Activities:** saunas, whirlpools, steamrooms, fishing, recreation programs, jogging, playground, volleyball. *Fee:* waverunners, golf-18 holes, 9 tennis courts (6 lighted), bicycles, massage. **Guest Services:** gift shop, valet laundry, area transportation (fee). **Business Services:** conference facilities, business center. **Cards:** AX, DC, DS, MC, VI. **Special Amenities:** free newspaper.

SOME UNITS

---------- **WHERE TO DINE** ----------

BEECH STREET GRILL

Dinner: $20-$28

Phone: 904/277-3662

American
Location: Corner of 8th and Beech sts; in the Fernandina Beach Historic District. 801 Beech St 32034. **Hours:** 6 pm-10 pm. Closed: 11/27, 12/25; also Super Bowl Sun. **Reservations:** suggested. **Features:** In an 1889 Victorian house that exudes a contemporary feel inside, the restaurant is known for its progressive, imaginative treatments of such fresh seafood specialties as macadamia nut-crusted grouper topped with curried citrus cream and mango chili salsa. Also offered are such savory dishes as roasted venison loin with black currant sauce and apple chipotle-glazed pork with roasted garlic. Smoke free premises. Dressy casual; cocktails. **Parking:** on-site. **Cards:** AX, DC, DS, MC, VI.

BRETT'S WATERWAY CAFE

Lunch: $8-$13

Dinner: $16-$26

Phone: 904/261-2660

American
Location: In Fernandina Beach, on the Amelia River (Intracoastal Waterway) at the end of Centre St. 1 S Front St 32034. **Hours:** 11:30 am-2:30 & 5:30-9:30 pm, Sun from 5:30 pm; to 8:30 pm in winter. Closed major holidays. **Features:** Popular for its Southern hospitality, the restaurant is noted for its excellent seafood and beef selections, a small but impressive wine list and homemade desserts. The dining rooms face the Fernandina Harbor and a marina on the Amelia River. Casual dress; cocktails. **Parking:** on-site. **Cards:** AX, MC, VI.

CENTRE STREET CAFE

Dinner: $17-$24

Phone: 904/277-6600

Danish
Location: In Amelia City; downtown historic district. 316-D Centre St 32097. **Hours:** 6 pm-9 pm. Closed: 11/27, 12/25; also Sun & Mon. **Reservations:** accepted. **Features:** Creative dishes, prepared by Danish chef/owner, are full of robust taste with a mixture of flavors. The Danish meatballs are a fun entree to enjoy. The house salad is enhanced with asparagus and delightful homemade dressings. For dessert try the coconut creme brule'. Only the freshest and finest ingredients are used. A superb wine list is enlighting and features lesser known high quality vineyards. Smoke free premises. Casual dress; beer & wine only. **Parking:** street. **Cards:** MC, VI.

CINGHIALES TUSCAN GRILL

Dinner: $14-$25

Phone: 904/277-2336

Seafood
Location: In Amelia City; just w of Intracoastal Waterway at Shave Bridge on SR A1A. 4768 Wade Pl 32034. **Hours:** 5 pm-9:30 pm, Sat-10 pm. Closed: 1/1, 11/27, 12/25; also Super Bowl Sun. **Reservations:** suggested. **Features:** Idle time away gazing out at the ebb and flow of the Intracoastal Waterway while enjoying healthy preparations of seafood, made with Italian influences. Casual, friendly service reflects Southern gentility. Casual dress; cocktails. **Parking:** on-site. **Cards:** AX, DC, DS, MC, VI.

FLORIDA HOUSE INN DINING ROOM Historic

Lunch: $7

Dinner: $12

Phone: 904/261-3300

Regional American
Location: In Fernandina Beach Historic District; just s of Centre St; in Florida House Inn. 22 S 3rd St 32034. **Hours:** 11:30 am-2:30 & 5:30-9 pm, Sun 10:30 am-2 pm. Closed: Mon. **Features:** Traditional Southern cooking is served boarding-house style all-you-care-to-eat. International beer selections from over 100 countries are available. Smoke free premises. Casual dress; cocktails. **Parking:** street. **Cards:** DS, MC, VI.

THE GRILL

Dinner: $65-$95

Phone: 904/277-1100

Regional American
Location: In Summer Beach; on SR A1A; in The Ritz-Carlton, Amelia Island. 4750 Amelia Island Pkwy 32034. **Hours:** 6:30 pm-9:30 pm. Closed: Sun & Mon. **Reservations:** suggested. **Features:** An airy, club-like dining room overlooks the Atlantic Ocean. Although the setting is formal, the service is friendly and unpretentious. Creative, international influences abound in Florida seafood, grilled meat and wild game dishes. Smoke free premises. Semi-formal attire; cocktails; entertainment. **Parking:** valet. **Cards:** AX, CB, DC, DS, JC, MC, VI.

ATLANTIC BEACH pop. 13,368 (See map p. 446; index p. 450)

---------- **WHERE TO STAY** ----------

BEST WESTERN MAYPORT INN & SUITES

Phone: (904)435-3500

All Year | 1P: $79-$130 | 2P: $79-$130 | XP: $5

F18

Small-scale Hotel
Location: 2 mi n on SR A1A; 1.4 mi s of Naval Base. 2389 Mayport Rd 32233. Fax: 904/435-2080. **Facility:** 60 units. 48 one-bedroom standard units, some with whirlpools. 12 one-bedroom suites. 2 stories, interior corridors. *Bath:* combo or shower only. **Parking:** on-site. **Terms:** [CP] meal plan available. **Amenities:** voice mail, safes, irons, hair dryers. **Pool(s):** outdoor. **Leisure Activities:** whirlpool, exercise room. **Guest Services:** valet and coin laundry. **Business Services:** fax (fee). **Cards:** AX, CB, DC, DS, JC, MC, VI. **Special Amenities:** free continental breakfast and free newspaper.

SOME UNITS

(See map p. 446)

COMFORT INN MAYPORT
AAA SAVE
All Year [ECP]   1P: $79-$109   2P: $79-$109
Phone: (904)249-0313 **82**
XP: $10 F18
Location: 2 mi n on SR A1A; 1.3 mi s of Naval Base. 2401 Mayport Rd (SR A1A) 32233. Fax: 904/241-2155.
Small-scale Hotel **Facility:** 108 one-bedroom standard units. 3 stories (no elevator), exterior corridors. **Parking:** on-site. **Amenities:** video games, irons, hair dryers. **Pool(s):** outdoor. **Leisure Activities:** exercise room. **Guest Services:** coin laundry. **Business Services:** fax (fee). **Cards:** AX, CB, DC, DS, MC, VI. **Special Amenities:** early check-in/late check-out and free continental breakfast.
SOME UNITS

SEA TURTLE INN
AAA SAVE
All Year   1P: $109-$209   2P: $119-$219
Phone: (904)249-7402 **83**
Location: End of Atlantic Blvd at ocean. 1 Ocean Blvd 32233. Fax: 904/247-1517. **Facility:** 193 units. 191 one-bedroom standard units. 2 one-bedroom suites ($249-$599). 8 stories, interior corridors. *Bath:* combo or shower only. **Parking:** on-site. **Terms:** cancellation fee imposed, package plans, 13% service charge.
Small-scale Hotel **Amenities:** dual phone lines, voice mail, irons, hair dryers. **Dining:** 6:30 am-10 pm. **Pool(s):** outdoor. **Leisure Activities:** volleyball. *Fee:* beach accessories, bicycles. **Guest Services:** gift shop, valet and coin laundry. **Business Services:** conference facilities, fax (fee). **Cards:** AX, DC, DS, MC, VI. **Special Amenities:** early check-in/late check-out and free newspaper. *(See color ad p 471)*
SOME UNITS
FEE   FEE

------- **WHERE TO DINE** -------

MAYPORT GARDENS CHINESE RESTAURANT **Lunch:** $4-$7 **Dinner:** $4-$7 **Phone:** 904/246-2102 **26**
Chinese **Location:** 3 mi n of jct Atlantic Blvd on SR A1A; s of Naval Base. 701-24 Mayport Crossing Blvd 32233. **Hours:** 11 am-9:30 pm. Closed major holidays; also Sun. **Features:** The chef/owner uses the freshest ingredients to make all your favorite traditional Chinese dishes. Although the simply decorated dining room is welcoming enough, the restaurant is more popular for its takeout menu. Casual dress. **Parking:** on-site.

RAGTIME TAVERN & SEAFOOD GRILL **Lunch:** $7-$9 **Dinner:** $10-$20 **Phone:** 904/241-7877 **28**
Seafood **Location:** Just e of SR A1A; corner of Atlantic and Ocean blvds. 207 Atlantic Blvd 32233. **Hours:** 11 am-midnight, Fri & Sat-1:30 am. Closed: 11/27, 12/25; also 2/24 for dinner. **Features:** This bustling microbrewery offers New Orleans-style grilled Cajun specialties. Three bars feature a live band on some nights. Spicy food and a lively atmosphere, along with fresh Florida vegetables like okra and corn, make this restaurant a winner. Casual dress; cocktails. **Parking:** street. **Cards:** AX, DC, DS, MC, VI.

SERGIO'S NORTHERN ITALIAN & CONTINENTAL CUISINE **Dinner:** $11-$20 **Phone:** 904/249-0101 **27**
Italian **Location:** Located in Atlantic Village Shopping Center, 1 mi e of Intracoastal Waterway Bridge. 1021 Atlantic Blvd 32233. **Hours:** 5:30 pm-10:30 pm. Closed: 12/25; also Mon. **Features:** Sergio's offers a broad selection of seafood, steak and chicken entrees, emphasizing presentation and moving away from traditional dishes. Casual dress; cocktails. **Parking:** on-site. **Cards:** AX, CB, DC, DS, MC, VI.

STICKY FINGERS RESTAURANT & BAR **Lunch:** $5-$15 **Dinner:** $5-$15 **Phone:** 904/241-7427 **29**
American **Location:** Jct SR A1A; in Shoppes of North Shore. 363-1 Atlantic Blvd 32233. **Hours:** 11 am-10 pm, Fri & Sat-11 pm. Closed: 11/27, 12/25. **Features:** Delicious ribs are the focus at this restaurant, but there's much more! Enjoy barbecue beef, chicken or pork with a selection of sauces, and be sure to leave room for a homemade dessert. The outdoor covered seating is breezy and comfortable. Entertainment is offered on weekends. Casual dress; cocktails. **Parking:** on-site. **Cards:** AX, DC, DS, MC, VI.

BALDWIN pop. 1,634 (See map p. 446; index p. 450)

------- **WHERE TO STAY** -------

BEST WESTERN INN BALDWIN
AAA SAVE
All Year [CP]   1P: $49-$94   2P: $54-$99
Phone: (904)266-9759 **72**
XP: $5 F12
Location: I-10, exit 343, just s. 1088 US 301 & I-10 32234. Fax: 904/266-9759. **Facility:** 43 one-bedroom standard units. 1 story, exterior corridors. **Parking:** on-site. **Terms:** cancellation fee imposed, pets ($8 extra charge). **Amenities:** irons, hair dryers. **Pool(s):** outdoor. **Business Services:** fax (fee). **Cards:** AX, CB, DC, DS, JC, MC, VI. **Special Amenities:** early check-in/late check-out and free continental breakfast.
Motel
SOME UNITS

GREEN COVE SPRINGS pop. 5,378

------- **WHERE TO STAY** -------

RIVER PARK INN, THE 1887 HOUSE
All Year [BP]   1P: $65-$195   2P: $65-$195
Phone: 904/284-2994
XP: $5 D18
Location: Corner of Spring; across from park. Located in the historic business district. 103 S Magnolia Ave 32043.
Bed & Breakfast **Facility:** Designated smoking area. 5 one-bedroom standard units. 2 stories, interior corridors. *Bath:* combo or shower only. **Parking:** on-site. **Terms:** check-in 4 pm, 7 day cancellation notice-fee imposed. **Amenities:** voice mail, irons, hair dryers. *Some:* CD players. **Leisure Activities:** whirlpool, bicycles. **Guest Services:** complimentary laundry, area transportation (fee). **Business Services:** fax. **Cards:** AX, DS, MC, VI.
SOME UNITS
FEE

─────── WHERE TO DINE ───────

RONNIE'S WINGS, OYSTERS & MORE   **Lunch:** $5-$15   **Dinner:** $5-$15   **Phone:** 904/284-4728
⬥⬥⬥
American
Location: Corner of Magnolia; across from park. 232 Walnut St 32043. **Hours:** 11 am-11 pm. **Features:** You'll be amazed at the many selections on the menu. Choose lighter fare from a wide selection of such appetizers as calamari, or chow down on one of the house specials of shrimp, fish or chicken. Friendly servers are eager to please. Casual dress; cocktails. **Parking:** on-site. **Cards:** AX, DS, MC, VI.

JACKSONVILLE BEACH pop. 20,990 (See map p. 446; index p. 450)

─────── WHERE TO STAY ───────

BEST WESTERN OCEANFRONT   **Phone:** (904)249-4949   99

12/1-2/28	1P: $89-$179	2P: $89-$179
3/1-9/2	1P: $99-$229	
9/3-11/30	1P: $89-$179	

Location: 0.4 mi n of Beach Blvd (US 90). 305 N 1st St 32250. **Fax:** 904/249-6040. **Facility:** 51 one-bedroom standard units, some with whirlpools. 3 stories, interior corridors. **Parking:** on-site. **Terms:** cancellation fee imposed. **Amenities:** voice mail, irons, hair dryers. **Pool(s):** heated outdoor. **Guest Services:** valet and coin laundry. **Business Services:** fax (fee). **Cards:** AX, CB, DC, DS, MC, VI. **Special Amenities:** free continental breakfast and free newspaper.

Small-scale Hotel

SOME UNITS
Sᴅ ⏍ ☎ ⛨ DATA ⛃ 🖥 ⬜ / ⊠ VCR /

COMFORT INN OCEANFRONT   **Phone:** (904)241-2311   97

3/1-9/1 [ECP]	1P: $99-$169	2P: $99-$169	XP: $10	F18
12/1-2/28 & 9/2-11/30 [ECP]	1P: $79-$139	2P: $79-$139	XP: $10	F18

Location: Just e of SR A1A; at 14th Ave N. 1515 N 1st St 32250. **Fax:** 904/249-3830. **Facility:** 177 one-bedroom standard units. 7 stories, interior corridors. *Bath:* combo or shower only. **Parking:** on-site. **Terms:** check-in 4 pm, 2 night minimum stay - seasonal, weekends, $4 service charge. **Amenities:** video games, voice mail, safes (fee), irons. *Some:* hair dryers. **Dining:** 9 am-8 pm, cocktails. **Pool(s):** heated outdoor. **Leisure Activities:** whirlpool, exercise room. **Guest Services:** gift shop, valet laundry. **Business Services:** meeting rooms, fax (fee). **Cards:** AX, CB, DC, DS, JC, MC, VI. **Special Amenities:** free continental breakfast. *(See color ad below)*

Small-scale Hotel

SOME UNITS
Sᴅ ⏍ 🍽 ☎ ⛨ DATA ⬜ / ⊠ ⛃ 🖥 /

DAYS INN OCEANFRONT RESORT   **Phone:** (904)249-7231   100

6/1-9/1	1P: $105-$160	2P: $105-$160
3/1-5/31	1P: $95-$140	2P: $95-$140
9/2-11/30	1P: $85-$140	2P: $85-$140
12/1-2/28	1P: $85-$124	2P: $85-$124

Large-scale Hotel Location: At 11th Ave S. 1031 S 1st St 32250. **Fax:** 904/249-7924. **Facility:** 154 units. 151 one-bedroom standard units. 3 one-bedroom suites ($180-$395). 1-8 stories, exterior corridors. **Parking:** on-site. **Terms:** [MAP] meal plan available, small pets only ($25 fee). **Amenities:** safes (fee), hair dryers. **Dining:** 6 am-11 & 5-9 pm, cocktails. **Pool(s):** outdoor. **Guest Services:** valet and coin laundry, area transportation-Mayo Clinic. **Business Services:** meeting rooms. **Fee:** PC, fax. **Cards:** AX, DC, DS, MC, VI. **Special Amenities:** free newspaper.

SOME UNITS
Sᴅ ⛃ ⏍ 🍽 ☎ ⛨ ⛨ DATA / ⊠ ⛃ 🖥 /
FEE   FEE FEE

HAMPTON INN PONTE VEDRA AT JACKSONVILLE BEACH   **Phone:** (904)280-9101   96

All Year   1P: $89   2P: $98
Location: Just n of JT Butler Blvd (before crossing Intercoastal Bridge), off of San Pablo Rd. 1220 Marsh Landing Pkwy 32250. **Fax:** 904/280-9101. **Facility:** 118 one-bedroom standard units, some with whirlpools. 5 stories, interior corridors. *Bath:* combo or shower only. **Parking:** on-site. **Terms:** [ECP] meal plan available. **Small-scale Hotel Amenities:** dual phone lines, voice mail, irons, hair dryers. **Pool(s):** outdoor. **Guest Services:** valet laundry. **Business Services:** meeting rooms, fax (fee). **Cards:** AX, DC, DS, MC, VI. **Special Amenities:** free continental breakfast and free newspaper. *(See color ad p 476)*

SOME UNITS
Sᴅ ⛨ ⛨ ⌨ ⛃ ⛨ DATA ⬜ / ⊠ ⛃ 🖥 /

(See map p. 446)

HOLIDAY INN SUNSPREE RESORT

Phone: (904)249-9071   [95]

AAA SAVE

3/2-8/31	1P: $89-$159	2P: $89-$159
9/1-11/30	1P: $79-$159	2P: $79-$159
12/1-3/1	1P: $69-$149	2P: $69-$149

Small-scale Hotel

Location: Just e of SR A1A; at 16th Ave N. 1617 N 1st St 32250. Fax: 904/241-4321. **Facility:** 143 units. 137 one-bedroom standard units. 6 one-bedroom suites ($119-$219). 4-7 stories, interior/exterior corridors. **Parking:** on-site. **Terms:** check-in 4 pm, 7 day cancellation notice. **Amenities:** video games, voice mail, irons, hair dryers. **Dining:** 6:30 am-11 & 5-10 pm, cocktails. **Pool(s):** outdoor. **Leisure Activities:** beach activities, recreation programs, exercise room. *Fee:* beach supplies & games, kayaks, bicycles. **Guest Services:** gift shop, valet and coin laundry, area transportation-Mayo Clinic. **Business Services:** meeting rooms, PC, fax. **Cards:** AX, CB, DC, DS, MC, VI.
(See color ad below & opposite inside back cover)

SOME UNITS

PELICAN PATH B & B BY THE SEA

Phone: (904)249-1177   [94]

2/1-10/31 [BP]	1P: $95-$165	2P: $95-$165	XP: $30
12/1-1/31 & 11/1-11/30 [BP]	1P: $80-$140	2P: $80-$140	XP: $30

Bed & Breakfast

Location: Oceanfront at 1st St. 11 N 19th Ave 32250. Fax: 904/346-5412. **Facility:** Pan dowdy is a breakfast specialty at this B&B by the ocean; two spacious guest rooms overlook the water. Smoke free premises. 4 one-bedroom standard units, some with whirlpools. 2 stories, interior corridors. **Parking:** on-site. **Terms:** age restrictions may apply, 7 day cancellation notice-fee imposed. **Amenities:** hair dryers. **Leisure Activities:** bicycles. **Guest Services:** complimentary evening beverages. **Cards:** AX, DS, MC, VI.

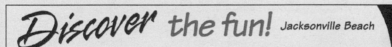

SURFSIDE INN

Phone: (904)246-1583   [98]

AAA SAVE

3/1-9/2	1P: $69-$149	2P: $69-$149	XP: $10	F16
12/1-2/28 & 9/3-11/30	1P: $59-$109	2P: $59-$109	XP: $10	F16

Motel

Location: 1.2 mi n of US 90 (Beach Blvd). 1236 N 1st St 32250. Fax: 904/241-1892. **Facility:** 32 one-bedroom standard units, some with whirlpools. 2 stories, exterior corridors. **Parking:** on-site. **Terms:** [ECP] meal plan available, pets ($15 extra charge). **Amenities:** high-speed Internet, hair dryers. **Pool(s):** heated outdoor. **Guest Services:** coin laundry. **Business Services:** fax (fee). **Cards:** AX, DC, DS, MC, VI.
Special Amenities: free continental breakfast and free local telephone calls.

SOME UNITS

(See map p. 446)

——— *The following lodging was either not evaluated or did not* ———
meet AAA rating requirements but is listed for your information only.

QUALITY SUITES OCEANFRONT   **Phone:** 904/435-3535
   [fyi]   1/31-9/8 [BP]   1P: $179-$269   2P: $179-$269   XP: $10   F16
            12/1-1/30 & 9/9-11/30 [BP]   1P: $159-$249   2P: $159-$249   XP: $10   F16
Small-scale Hotel Too new to rate. **Location:** I-95, exit 344 (JT Butler Blvd/SR 202), 10 mi e to SR A1A N (3rd St), 2 mi to US 90 E. 11 North 1st St 32250 (302 North 1st St). Fax: 904/435-3536. **Amenities:** coffeemakers, microwaves, refrigerators, pool. **Cards:** AX, CB, DC, DS, JC, MC, VI.

——— **WHERE TO DINE** ———

BILLY'S   **Lunch:** $5-$15   **Dinner:** $5-$15   **Phone:** 904/246-8099   (34)
  ♦♦ ♦♦   **Location:** Corner of SR A1A and 17th Ave N. 1728 N 3rd St 32234. **Hours:** 11 am-11 pm, Sun from noon. Closed major holidays. **Features:** Come casual and ready for a lively time. Billy's is a hopping place for food, fun
American and spirits. A great selection of domestic and imported brews complements such selections as conch fritters, mushroom caps, local fresh seafood and big burgers. Casual dress; cocktails. **Parking:** on-site.
Cards: AX, MC, VI.

DOLPHIN DEPOT   **Dinner:** $19-$35   **Phone:** 904/270-1424   (33)
  ♦♦ ♦♦   **Location:** Corner of 6th Ave N and 1st St. 704 N 1st St 32221. **Hours:** 5 pm-10 pm, Fri & Sat-11 pm, Sun-9 pm. **Features:** Preparations of eclectic Carolina coastal cuisine include lobster and variety of fish dishes.
Russian Dressy casual; cocktails. **Parking:** on-site. **Cards:** AX, DS, MC, VI.

ELLEN'S KITCHEN   **Lunch:** $4-$12   **Phone:** 904/246-1572   (40)
   ♦♦   **Location:** Pablo Plaza Shopping Center, north end. 1824 S 3rd St 32250. **Hours:** 7 am-2 pm. Closed: 11/27, 12/25. **Features:** The locals line up at this cheery diner for breakfast every day of the week. Make your
American own omelet with homemade biscuits. Eat breakfast and other fine Southern cooking all day long. The crab cake benedict is a unique offering. Servers are informed and pleasant. **Parking:** on-site. **Cards:** MC, VI.

FIRST STREET GRILLE   **Lunch:** $7-$10   **Dinner:** $15-$20   **Phone:** 904/246-6555   (38)
  (AAA)   **Location:** Just e of SR A1A; corner of N First St and 7th Ave. 807 N First St 32250. **Hours:** 11:30 am-4 & 5-10
  ♦♦ ♦♦   pm, Fri & Sat-11 pm, Sun 11 am-4 & 5-10 pm. Closed: 1/1, 11/27, 12/25. **Features:** A comfortable beach setting, it features selections from around the world. Grilled steak and seafood are offered at value prices.
American A salad of spinach, nuts and fruits topped with a raspberry vinaigrette offers a unique flavor. Outdoor dining is available. Casual dress; cocktails. **Parking:** on-site. **Cards:** AX, CB, DC, DS, MC, VI.

ICHIBAN JAPANESE STEAK HOUSE   **Dinner:** $8-$15   **Phone:** 904/247-8228   (35)
  ♦♦ ♦♦   **Location:** Jct US 90 (Beach Blvd) and SR A1A (3rd St), 0.4 mi n. 675 N 3rd St 32250. **Hours:** 5 pm-9:45 pm, Fri & Sat-10:45 pm. **Features:** Sushi, teriyaki, tempura and steak delicacies are all here at Ichiban. Combine the
Japanese casual atmosphere with attentive service and hearty portions, and you end up with an Oriental feast for the senses. Choose sushi made to order as you watch or steak, seafood and beef combinations offered by a smiling chef at spotless steak table grills. Japanese cookery with an American accent is found in entrees such as hibachi shrimp, scallops, chicken, steak and lobster. Casual dress; wine only. **Parking:** on-site. **Cards:** AX, DC, MC, VI.

PAGODA CHINESE   **Lunch:** $5-$12   **Dinner:** $5-$12   **Phone:** 904/241-0414   (36)
  ♦♦ ♦♦   **Location:** Corner of 3rd St (SR A1A), s of Beach Blvd. 223 S 9th St 32250. **Hours:** 11:30 am-10 pm, Sat 5 pm-11 pm, Sun noon-10 pm. Closed: 7/4, 11/27, 12/25. **Features:** Friendly, attentive service awaits you in this
Chinese family-owned restaurant. Choose from lots of traditional dishes, including Szechwan delights, sesame chicken, almond-pressed duck and vegetarian entrees. Casual dress; cocktails. **Parking:** on-site.
Cards: AX, DS, MC, VI.

ULI'S EUROPEAN RESTAURANT   **Lunch:** $7-$15   **Dinner:** $15-$28   **Phone:** 904/241-4969   (37)
  ♦♦ ♦♦   **Location:** Just e of 3rd St (SR A1A). 216 S 11th Ave 32224. **Hours:** 11 am-2:30 & 5-9:30 pm, Fri & Sat 5 pm-10 pm, Sun noon-9 pm. Closed: Mon. **Features:** You'll feel like you're in Germany at Uli's. The vivacious
German owner greets guests at the door with a friendly welcome. Enjoy a light lunch of crab cakes or a Reuben sandwich or heartier dinner meals of all the German favorites, including rouladen and sauerbraten. Don't
leave without trying a homemade dessert. Casual dress; beer & wine only. **Parking:** on-site. **Cards:** AX, MC, VI.

NEPTUNE BEACH pop. 7,270   (See map p. 446; index p. 451)

——— **WHERE TO STAY** ———

SEA HORSE OCEANFRONT INN   **Phone:** 904/246-2175   **110**
  ♦♦ ♦♦   All Year   1P: $99-$225   XP: $15   F18
        Location: Jct of Atlantic Blvd and 1st St. 120 Atlantic Blvd 32266. Fax: 904/246-4256. **Facility:** 38 units. 37 one-
Small-scale Hotel bedroom standard units. 1 one-bedroom suite. 3 stories, exterior corridors. *Bath:* combo or shower only. **Parking:** on-site. **Terms:** cancellation fee imposed, weekly rates available. **Pool(s):** outdoor. **Leisure Activities:** shuffleboard. **Business Services:** fax (fee). **Cards:** AX, DC, DS, MC, VI.

SOME UNITS

(See map p. 446)

——— **WHERE TO DINE** ———

MEZZA LUNA VAGABONDO RISTORANTE   **Dinner:** $10-$19   **Phone:** 904/246-5100   50
♦♦♦ ♦♦♦   **Location:** Corner shopping area of Atlantic Blvd and 1st St; adjacent to courthouse. 110 1st Ave 32266. **Hours:** 4
Italian   pm-11 pm, Fri & Sat-midnight, Sun 3 pm-11 pm. Closed major holidays; also Mon.
Reservations: suggested. **Features:** Enjoy special seafood and veal entrees and pizza made in a
wood-burning oven. A trained and knowledgeable staff make this restaurant seem like home. A scrumptious
dessert menu includes a thin, caramelized layer of creme brulee in a thick raspberry sauce. Casual dress. **Parking:** street.
Cards: AX, MC, VI.

SUN DOG DINER   **Lunch:** $7-$12   **Dinner:** $7-$12   **Phone:** 904/241-8221   49
♦♦♦ ♦♦♦   **Location:** Just e of 3rd St (SR A1A). 207 Atlantic Blvd 32233. **Hours:** 11 am-2 am, Sat & Sun from 10 am;
American   Saturday & Sunday brunch. Closed: 12/25. **Features:** An established favorite frequented by locals, this
diner has it all. Hamburgers and hot dogs share the menu with more sophisticated fare, including sesame
seared tuna and blackened NY strip. Half of the restaurant is a lively night spot with live music nightly.
Cigar connoisseurs can slip off to the Cobalt Room, which has comfy chairs and a TV. This is also a great place to sidle up to
the counter for a thick, rich milkshake. Casual dress; cocktails. **Parking:** street. **Cards:** DC, DS, MC, VI.

ORANGE PARK pop. 9,081   (See map p. 446; index p. 451)

——— **WHERE TO STAY** ———

BEST WESTERN HOTEL AND SUITES   **Phone:** (904)264-4466   135
AAA SAVE   All Year   1P: $69-$79   2P: $79-$89   XP: $10   F12
♦♦♦ ♦♦♦   **Location:** I-295, exit 10 (US 17), just nw. 4580 Collins Rd 32073. Fax: 904/264-2193. **Facility:** 105 one-bedroom
standard units. 5 stories, interior corridors. **Parking:** on-site. **Terms:** 17 day cancellation notice, [ECP] meal
Small-scale Hotel   plan available. **Amenities:** high-speed Internet, voice mail, irons, hair dryers. **Pool(s):** heated outdoor.
Leisure Activities: exercise room. **Guest Services:** valet and coin laundry. **Business Services:** meeting
rooms, fax. **Cards:** AX, CB, DC, DS, JC, MC, VI. **Special Amenities:** free continental breakfast and free
newspaper. *(See color ad below)*

SOME UNITS

(See map p. 446)

COMFORT INN   Phone: (904)264-3297   140

AAA SAVE

▼▼▼▼

Small-scale Hotel

All Year [CP]   1P: $71-$91   2P: $71-$91
Location: I-295, exit 10, just s on US 17. Located adjacent to a kennel club. 341 Park Ave 32073. Fax: 904/215-9585. **Facility:** 119 one-bedroom standard units. 2 stories, exterior corridors. **Parking:** on-site. **Terms:** pets ($25 fee). **Amenities:** irons, hair dryers. **Pool(s):** outdoor. **Leisure Activities:** tennis court. **Guest Services:** valet and coin laundry. **Business Services:** meeting rooms, fax (fee). **Cards:** AX, CB, DC, DS, MC, VI. **Special Amenities:** free continental breakfast and free local telephone calls. *(See color ad p 473)*

SOME UNITS

[icons]

DAYS INN   Phone: (904)269-8887   137

SAVE

▼▼ ▼▼

Small-scale Hotel

All Year [CP]   1P: $59-$79   2P: $59-$79
Location: I-295, exit 10, just s on US 17. 4280 Eldridge Loop 32073. Fax: 904/215-9294. **Facility:** 23 one-bedroom standard units. 3 stories (no elevator), interior corridors. **Parking:** on-site. **Terms:** pets ($25 fee). **Amenities:** hair dryers. **Guest Services:** valet laundry. **Cards:** AX, CB, DC, DS, MC, VI.

SOME UNITS

[icons]

FAIRFIELD INN BY MARRIOTT   Phone: (904)278-7442   139

SAVE

▼▼▼▼

Small-scale Hotel

All Year [ECP]   1P: $74-$84   2P: $74-$84
Location: I-295, exit 10, 0.3 mi s to Wells Rd, then w. 450 Eldridge Ave 32073. Fax: 904/278-5022. **Facility:** 83 one-bedroom standard units. 3 stories, interior corridors. *Bath:* combo or shower only. **Parking:** on-site. **Amenities:** irons. *Some:* hair dryers. **Pool(s):** outdoor. **Leisure Activities:** whirlpool, exercise room. **Guest Services:** valet laundry. **Business Services:** fax (fee). **Cards:** AX, DC, DS, MC, VI.

SOME UNITS

[icons]

HAMPTON INN-ORANGE PARK   Phone: (904)777-5313   131

SAVE

▼▼▼▼

Small-scale Hotel

All Year   1P: $69-$76   2P: $79-$89
Location: I-295, exit 12, southwest corner off SR 21. 6135 Youngerman Cir 32244. Fax: 904/778-1545. **Facility:** 121 one-bedroom standard units. 2 stories, exterior corridors. **Parking:** on-site. **Terms:** 7 day cancellation notice-fee imposed. **Amenities:** video games, voice mail, irons, hair dryers. **Pool(s):** heated outdoor. **Guest Services:** valet laundry. **Business Services:** meeting rooms, fax. **Cards:** AX, CB, DC, DS, JC, MC, VI. *(See ad below)*

SOME UNITS

[icons]

HOLIDAY INN-ORANGE PARK   Phone: (904)264-9513   138

▼▼▼▼

Small-scale Hotel

All Year   1P: $89-$99   2P: $89-$99
Location: I-295, exit 10, just s on US 17. 150 Park Ave 32073. Fax: 904/278-1575. **Facility:** 299 units. 294 one-bedroom standard units. 4 one- and 1 two-bedroom suites ($99-$199), some with whirlpools. 2 stories, exterior corridors. **Parking:** on-site. **Amenities:** video games, voice mail, irons, hair dryers. **Pool(s):** outdoor, wading. **Guest Services:** valet and coin laundry. **Business Services:** meeting rooms, fax. **Cards:** AX, CB, DC, DS, JC, MC, VI. *(See color ad opposite inside back cover)*

SOME UNITS

[icons]

LA QUINTA INN-JACKSONVILLE/ORANGE PARK   Phone: (904)778-9539   134

AAA SAVE

▼▼▼▼

Small-scale Hotel

1/15-3/29   1P: $66-$76   2P: $73-$83   XP: $7   F18
12/1-1/14 & 3/30-11/30   1P: $60-$70   2P: $67-$77   XP: $7   F18
Location: I-295, exit 12, just s on SR 21. 8555 Blanding Blvd 32244-5797. Fax: 904/779-5214. **Facility:** 122 units. 121 one-bedroom standard units. 1 one-bedroom suite ($109-$119). 2 stories, exterior corridors. **Parking:** on-site. **Terms:** [ECP] meal plan available, small pets only. **Amenities:** video games, voice mail, irons, hair dryers. **Pool(s):** outdoor. **Guest Services:** coin laundry. **Business Services:** meeting rooms, fax (fee). **Cards:** AX, CB, DC, DS, JC, MC, VI. **Special Amenities:** free continental breakfast and free local telephone calls. *(See color ad p 459)*

SOME UNITS

[icons]   FEE   FEE

(See map p. 446)

RED ROOF INN-SOUTH   Phone: (904)777-1000   133

AAA SAVE
1/31-4/19	1P: $39-$49	2P: $45-$55	XP: $6	F18
4/20-11/30	1P: $38-$49	2P: $44-$55	XP: $6	F18
12/1-1/30	1P: $37-$49	2P: $43-$55	XP: $6	F18

Motel

Location: I-295, exit 12 (SR 21). 6099 Youngerman Cir 32244. Fax: 904/777-1005. **Facility:** 108 one-bedroom standard units. 2 stories, exterior corridors. **Parking:** on-site. **Terms:** small pets only. **Amenities:** video games, voice mail. **Pool(s):** small heated outdoor. **Business Services:** fax (fee). **Cards:** AX, CB, DC, DS, MC, VI. **Special Amenities:** free local telephone calls and free newspaper.

SOME UNITS
🛏 🍴 🛁 📷 📠 / ✕ /

─────── **WHERE TO DINE** ───────

THE HILLTOP   **Dinner:** $10-$23   Phone: 904/272-5959   75

American

Location: I-295, exit 12, s on Blanding Blvd, then 0.3 mi w. 2030 Wells Rd. **Hours:** 5 pm-9 pm, Fri & Sat-10 pm. Closed major holidays; also Sun & Mon. **Features:** A prominent Orange Park landmark, the Hilltop offers gracious Southern hospitality in the charming environment of the Old South. Enjoy dinner in the stately formal dining room. Extensive wine list. Dressy casual; cocktails. **Parking:** on-site. **Cards:** AX, DC, DS, MC, VI.

🍸 ✕

SARNELLI'S RISTORANTE   **Dinner:** $11-$25   Phone: 904/269-1331   72

AAA

Italian

Location: Corner of Kingsley and US 17. 2023 Park Ave 32073. **Hours:** 5 pm-10 pm. Closed: 1/1, 11/27, 12/25; also Sun. **Reservations:** accepted. **Features:** The casual restaurant offers a menu focused on traditional Italian preparations. Smoke free premises. beer & wine only. **Parking:** on-site. **Cards:** AX, DS, MC, VI.

✕

VENEZIA'S ITALIAN RESTAURANT   **Lunch:** $5-$9   **Dinner:** $7-$15   Phone: 904/278-1989   71

Italian

Location: 1871 Wells Rd 32073. **Hours:** 11 am-2 & 5-10 pm, Sun-9 pm. Closed: 4/20, 11/27; also Wed. **Reservations:** accepted. **Features:** A trellis-type archway, statues and pillars help to create a romantic ambience reminiscent of Old Italy. Traditional menu offerings include bruschetta, assorted pasta dishes and veal preparations. Casual dress; cocktails. **Parking:** on-site. **Cards:** AX, CB, DC, DS, JC, MC, VI.

✕

PONTE VEDRA BEACH   (See map p. 446; index p. 451)

─────── **WHERE TO STAY** ───────

COUNTRY INN & SUITES BY CARLSON-JACKSONVILLE AT PONTE VEDRA   Phone: (904)280-1661   119

AAA SAVE
3/21-3/30 [ECP]	1P: $215-$300	2P: $215-$300
1/16-3/20 [ECP]	1P: $119-$179	2P: $119-$179
12/1-1/15 & 3/31-11/30 [ECP]	1P: $89-$179	2P: $89-$179

Small-scale Hotel

Location: 5 mi s of jct JT Butler Blvd on SR A1A, just e. Located in Sawgrass Village Shopping Center. 45 PGA Tour Blvd 32082. Fax: 904/280-1544. **Facility:** 127 units. 76 one-bedroom standard units, some with whirlpools. 51 one-bedroom suites. 6 stories, interior corridors. *Bath:* combo or shower only. **Parking:** on-site. **Amenities:** dual phone lines, voice mail, irons, hair dryers. **Dining:** Sawgrass Grille & The Tavern, see separate listing. **Pool(s):** heated outdoor. **Leisure Activities:** whirlpool. *Fee:* golf privileges. **Guest Services:** valet and coin laundry, area transportation-Mayo Clinic. **Business Services:** meeting rooms, fax (fee). **Cards:** AX, DC, DS, MC, VI. **Special Amenities:** free continental breakfast and free newspaper. *(See color ad p 613)*

SOME UNITS
🅂 🍴 🔧 🛁 📷 📠 💾 / ✕ 🔒 📶 /

(See map p. 446)

LODGE AND CLUB AT PONTE VEDRA BEACH

Phone: (904)273-9500   [121]

AAA SAVE

2/1-5/31	1P: $350-$450	2P: $350-$450
9/1-11/30	1P: $270-$370	2P: $270-$370
6/1-8/31	1P: $240-$340	2P: $240-$340
12/1-1/31	1P: $200-$300	2P: $200-$300

Resort
Small-scale Hotel
Location: I-95, exit 344 (JT Butler Blvd) to SR A1A, 0.5 mi n to 36th Ave, 2 mi s. 607 Ponte Vedra Blvd 32082. Fax: 904/273-0210. **Facility:** On the ocean, this service-oriented, Mediterranean-style resort offers organized activities and waterfront guest rooms with balconies and fireplaces. 66 one-bedroom standard units, some with whirlpools. 2 stories, exterior corridors. **Parking:** on-site and valet. **Terms:** check-in 4 pm, 3 day cancellation notice-fee imposed, $12 service charge. **Amenities:** dual phone lines, voice mail, safes, honor bars, irons, hair dryers. **Dining:** 7-10:30 am, 11:30-2:30 & 5:30-10 pm, guests only; 18% service charge, cocktails, entertainment. **Pool(s):** 3 heated outdoor, wading. **Leisure Activities:** saunas, whirlpools, steamrooms, recreation programs, spa. **Fee:** sailboats, charter fishing, beach kayaks, golf-90 holes, 15 tennis courts (7 lighted), bicycles. **Guest Services:** gift shop, valet laundry, area transportation-Ponte Vedra. **Business Services:** meeting rooms, PC, fax (fee). **Cards:** AX, CB, DC, DS, MC, VI. **Special Amenities:** free local telephone calls and free newspaper. Affiliated with A Preferred Hotel.

SOME UNITS
[symbols: FEE ... FEE ... / VCR]

PONTE VEDRA INN AND CLUB

Phone: (904)285-1111   [120]

AAA SAVE

3/1-5/31	1P: $350-$600	2P: $350-$600
9/1-11/30	1P: $270-$520	2P: $270-$520
12/1-2/28	1P: $200-$505	2P: $200-$505
6/1-8/31	1P: $240-$490	2P: $240-$490

Resort
Large-scale Hotel
Location: I-95, exit 344 (JT Butler Blvd) to SR A1A, 0.5 mi n to 36th Ave S, s via CR 203 and Ponte Vedra Blvd. 200 Ponte Vedra Blvd 32082-9305. Fax: 904/285-2111. **Facility:** This service-oriented beach-club resort was founded in 1927; guest rooms are waterfront with balconies or patios. 221 units. 198 one-bedroom standard units, some with whirlpools. 23 one-bedroom suites ($350-$500), some with whirlpools. 2 stories, exterior corridors. **Parking:** on-site. **Terms:** 3 day cancellation notice-fee imposed, package plans, $15 service charge. **Amenities:** dual phone lines, voice mail, safes, honor bars, irons, hair dryers. **Dining:** 3 restaurants, 7 am-10 pm; guests only, cocktails, entertainment. **Pool(s):** 2 outdoor, 2 heated outdoor, wading. **Leisure Activities:** saunas, whirlpools, steamrooms, rental paddleboats, fishing, recreation programs, aerobics room, jogging, playground. **Fee:** boats, sailboats, windsurfing, charter fishing, golf-36 holes, 15 tennis courts (7 lighted), bicycles, massage. **Guest Services:** gift shop, valet and coin laundry, area transportation-Ponte Vedra. **Business Services:** conference facilities, business center. **Cards:** AX, CB, DC, DS, MC, VI. **Special Amenities:** free local telephone calls and free newspaper.

SOME UNITS
[symbols: FEE ... FEE ... /]

———— WHERE TO DINE ————

BARBARA JEAN'S   **Dinner:** $8-$16   Phone: 904/280-7622   [66]

Regional Seafood
Location: Jct of SR A1A and CR 210A (Solano Rd), 4.6 mi w and s. 15 S Roscoe Blvd 32082. **Hours:** 11 am-9 pm, Fri & Sat-10 pm. Closed: 12/25. **Features:** Nestled in the wooded scrub alongside the intracoastal waterway, is a casual eatery serving up great crab cakes, warm breads and other Southern comfort foods. Smoke free premises. Casual dress; cocktails. **Parking:** on-site. **Cards:** AX, DS, MC, VI.

GIO'S CAFE   **Dinner:** $18-$40   Phone: 904/273-0101   [60]

Continental
Location: Center; Sawgrass Village Shopping Center. 900 Sawgrass Village 32082. **Hours:** 5:30 pm-10 pm, Fri & Sat-11 pm. Closed major holidays. **Features:** Much thought clearly goes into the preparation and presentation of such entrees as garlic-stuffed fillet and signature veal. An impressive wine list includes selections to complement any meal. The Art Deco atmosphere is energetic; the service impeccable. Casual dress; cocktails. **Parking:** street. **Cards:** AX, DC, MC, VI.

J J'S CUISINE & WINE   **Lunch:** $6-$22   **Dinner:** $14-$30   Phone: 904/273-7980   [58]

French
Location: 2 mi s of jct JT Butler Blvd; in Shoppes at Ponte Vedra. 330 A1A N, Suite 209 32082. **Hours:** 11:30 am-9:30 pm, Fri & Sat-10:30 pm. Closed major holidays. **Features:** When you enter the relaxed restaurant, you enter the streets of Paris. Browse gourmet groceries and baked goods, then dine in the cafe. Choose from quiche, soup and sandwiches for lunch, or enjoy a heartier dinner of roast loin, salmon or seared tuna. Casual dress; beer & wine only. **Parking:** on-site. **Cards:** AX, DC, DS, MC, VI.

(See map p. 446)

LULU'S WATERFRONT GRILL   **Lunch:** $7-$11   **Dinner:** $12-$18   **Phone:** 904/285-0139   61

Seafood

Location: 1 mi s. 301 N Roscoe Blvd 32082. **Hours:** 11:30 am-10 pm. Closed: 11/27, 12/25. **Features:** Dining on the screened porch of this restaurant, which resembles a clapboard house, is darn close to what old Florida is all about. Feast on shrimp jambalaya, caper-coated catch of the day and the native dessert, Key lime pie. Casual dress; cocktails. **Parking:** on-site. **Cards:** AX, MC, VI.

PLAYERS CAFE   **Lunch:** $4-$6   **Phone:** 904/273-5595   64

American

Location: 262 Solana Rd 32082. **Hours:** 6:30 am-2:30 pm. **Features:** Casual, friendly atmosphere in a coffee-shop setting. Walls are painted with amusing charicatures of people playing sports. Casual dress. **Parking:** on-site. **Cards:** MC, VI.

RESTAURANT MEDURE   **Dinner:** $18-$28   **Phone:** 904/543-3797   62

Continental

Location: 5.3 mi s of JT Butler Blvd. 818 N SR A1A 32082. **Hours:** 5:30 pm-10 pm, Sun-9 pm. Closed: 4/20, 12/25. **Reservations:** required. **Features:** This restaurant features Continental cuisine with a Mediterranean flair prepared in an exhibition-style kitchen. Select from various seafood and game in light stocks and broths. Natural wood colors and leather provide a comfortable yet upscale atmosphere. Live jazz five days a week. Smoke free premises. Dressy casual; cocktails. **Parking:** on-site. **Cards:** AX, CB, DC, DS, JC, MC, VI.

SANTIONI'S OF SAWGRASS   **Dinner:** $9-$17   **Phone:** 904/273-7272   63

Italian

Location: 1 mi n of jct SR A1A and CR 210; in Tournament Plaza Shopping Center. 832-1 A1A N 32082. **Hours:** 5 pm-10 pm, Fri & Sat-11 pm. Closed: 4/20, 11/27, 12/25. **Reservations:** suggested. **Features:** The chef/owner has prepared classic Italian fare for more than 28 years. Featured entrees on a menu of all made-to-order dishes include shrimp fra diavolo, linguine with clam sauce and gnocchi. The wine list delivers a wide selection of California selections. Pizza is available as a carryout choice. Casual dress; cocktails. **Parking:** on-site. **Cards:** AX, DS, MC, VI.

SAWGRASS GRILLE & THE TAVERN   **Lunch:** $7-$16   **Dinner:** $10-$18   **Phone:** 904/285-3133   59

American

Location: 5 mi s of jct JT Butler Blvd on SR A1A, just e; in Country Inn & Suites By Carlson-Jacksonville at Ponte Vedra. 1310 Sawgrass Village Dr 32082. **Hours:** 7 am-10 pm, Fri & Sat-11 pm. **Features:** The popular neighborhood eatery affords a relaxed and friendly atmosphere. Enjoy a large selection of finger foods or such delicacies as salmon, one of the chef's specialties. Take time to look over framed pictures taken at local golfing events. Locally owned and operated. Casual dress; cocktails. **Parking:** on-site. **Cards:** AX, DC, DS, MC, VI.

YULEE pop. 8,392

─── WHERE TO STAY ───

COMFORT INN   SAVE   **Phone:** (904)225-2600

Small-scale Hotel

2/1-7/31	1P: $95-$100	2P: $95-$100	XP: $10 F12
12/1-1/31 & 8/1-11/30	1P: $85-$95	2P: $85-$95	XP: $10 F12

Location: I-95, exit 373, just e on SR 200/A1A. 126 Sidney Pl 32097. Fax: 904/225-1966. **Facility:** 59 one-bedroom standard units, some with whirlpools. 2 stories, interior corridors. *Bath:* combo or shower only. **Parking:** on-site. **Terms:** check-in 4 pm, weekly rates available, [ECP] meal plan available. **Amenities:** irons, hair dryers. **Pool(s):** small outdoor. **Guest Services:** coin laundry.

SOME UNITS

This ends listings for the Jacksonville Vicinity.
The following page resumes the alphabetical listings of
cities in Florida.

JACKSONVILLE BEACH —*See Jacksonville p. 470.*

JENSEN BEACH pop. 11,100

———— WHERE TO STAY ————

COURTYARD BY MARRIOTT OCEANSIDE
[SAVE]
[diamond diamond diamond]
Small-scale Hotel

All Year 1P: $89-$179 2P: $89-$179 XP: $10 F18
Phone: (772)229-1000
Location: SR A1A, Hutchinson Island, 0.7 mi n of jct SR 732. 10978 S Ocean Dr 34957. Fax: 772/229-0253. **Facility:** 110 one-bedroom standard units. 8 stories, interior corridors. **Parking:** on-site. **Terms:** cancellation fee imposed. **Amenities:** voice mail, irons, hair dryers. **Pool(s):** heated outdoor. **Leisure Activities:** exercise room. **Guest Services:** valet and coin laundry. **Business Services:** meeting rooms, fax (fee). **Cards:** AX, CB, DC, DS, MC, VI. *(See color ad below)*

SOME UNITS
[amenity icons] / [amenity icons] /

HOLIDAY INN OCEANSIDE-HUTCHINSON ISLAND
(AAA) [SAVE]
[diamond diamond diamond]
Small-scale Hotel

Phone: (772)225-3000
1/26-4/27	2P: $169-$199	XP: $10	F19
12/22-1/25	2P: $139-$169	XP: $10	F19
4/28-11/30	2P: $89-$159	XP: $10	F19
12/1-12/21	2P: $89-$129	XP: $10	F19

Location: SR A1A; Hutchinson Island, 0.3 mi s of jct SR 732. 3793 NE Ocean Blvd 34957. Fax: 772/225-1956. **Facility:** 179 units. 176 one-bedroom standard units. 3 one-bedroom suites ($225-$600) with whirlpools. 5 stories, interior corridors. *Bath:* combo or shower only. **Parking:** on-site. **Terms:** check-in 4 pm. **Amenities:** video games (fee), voice mail, safes, irons, hair dryers. **Dining:** 6 am-2 & 5-10 pm, cocktails, entertainment. **Pool(s):** heated outdoor. **Leisure Activities:** fishing, 3 tennis courts (1 lighted), exercise room. *Fee:* boogie boards, massage, game room. **Guest Services:** gift shop, valet and coin laundry. **Business Services:** meeting rooms, fax (fee). **Cards:** AX, CB, DC, DS, JC, MC, VI. **Special Amenities: early check-in/late check-out and free room upgrade (subject to availability with advanced reservations).** *(See color ad opposite inside back cover)*

SOME UNITS
[amenity icons] / [amenity icons] /
FEE

HUTCHINSON INN
[diamond diamond diamond]
Motel

Phone: (772)229-2000
12/1-4/30 [ECP]	1P: $135-$275	2P: $135-$275	XP: $20
5/1-11/30	1P: $95-$175	2P: $95-$175	

Location: SR A1A, Hutchinson Island, 2.5 mi n of jct SR 732; I-95, exit 61, e to SR 76, follow signs to beach. 9750 S Ocean Dr 34957. Fax: 772/229-8875. **Facility:** Designated smoking area. 21 units. 11 one-bedroom standard units with efficiencies. 10 one-bedroom suites ($245-$345) with efficiencies. 2 stories, exterior corridors. **Parking:** on-site. **Terms:** cancellation fee imposed, no pets allowed (pets on premises). **Amenities:** irons, hair dryers. **Pool(s):** heated outdoor. **Leisure Activities:** tennis court. *Fee:* massage. **Guest Services:** gift shop, coin laundry. **Business Services:** fax (fee). **Cards:** MC, VI.

SOME UNITS
[ASK] [amenity icons] / [VCR amenity icons] [amenity icons]

RIVER PALM COTTAGES
[diamond diamond diamond]
Cottage

Phone: (772)334-0401
12/1-4/30	1P: $99-$169	2P: $139-$199	XP: $20	F10
5/1-11/30	1P: $69-$109	2P: $89-$139	XP: $10	F10

Location: On SR 707 (NE Indian River Dr), 1.4 mi s of jct SR 732 (Jensen Cswy). 2325 NE Indian River Dr 34957. Fax: 772/334-0527. **Facility:** 23 units. 4 one-bedroom standard units. 19 cottages. 1-2 stories, exterior corridors. *Bath:* combo or shower only. **Parking:** on-site. **Terms:** small pets only ($50 deposit, $10 fee). **Amenities:** voice mail, irons. **Pool(s):** heated outdoor. **Leisure Activities:** marina. **Guest Services:** coin laundry.

SOME UNITS
[ASK] [amenity icons] / [X] /

VISTANA'S BEACH CLUB
[diamond diamond diamond]
Condominium

Phone: (772)229-9200
12/22-1/7	2P: $315
1/8-11/30	2P: $285
12/1-12/21	2P: $229

Location: SR A1A, Hutchinson Island, 2 mi n of jct SR 732. 10740 S Ocean Dr 34957. Fax: 772/229-3902. **Facility:** 76 two-bedroom suites with kitchens, some with whirlpools. 9 stories, exterior corridors. **Parking:** on-site. **Terms:** check-in 4 pm, 5 day cancellation notice-fee imposed. **Amenities:** video library, irons. *Some:* hair dryers. **Pool(s):** heated outdoor. **Leisure Activities:** whirlpool, rental boats, fishing, 2 lighted tennis courts, recreation programs, playground, volleyball. *Fee:* charter fishing, bicycles, massage, game room. **Guest Services:** complimentary laundry. **Business Services:** fax (fee). **Cards:** AX, DC, MC, VI.

[ASK] [amenity icons] [VCR amenity icons]

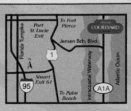

We'll take 10%* off your stay. Sorry we can't do the same for your over-packed car.

Comfort Inn

COMFORT SUITES

QUALITY

SLEEP INN

Clarion

MainStay Suites

Econo Lodge

RODEWAY INN

CHOICE HOTELS
INTERNATIONAL ®

800.228.1AAA
choicehotels.com

The Power of Being There. **Go.**

*AAA members can save 20% at many Clarion brand hotels.
©2003 Choice Hotels International, Inc.

10%* OFF
AAA Discount
without reservations.

The Power of Being There. **Go.**

RODEWAY INN

Econo Lodge

MainStay Suites

Clarion

SLEEP INN

QUALITY

COMFORT SUITES

Comfort Inn

CHOICE HOTELS INTERNATIONAL ®

Call us at 800.228.1AAA or visit us on the Web at choicehotels.com for more information and reservations.

*AAA members can save 20% at many Clarion brand hotels.
©2003 Choice Hotels International, Inc.

TourBookMark

Lodging Listing Symbols

Member Values
(see pg. 16)

- (AAA) Official Appointment
- [SAVE] Offers minimum 10% discount
- [SAVE] SYC&S chain partners
- [A$K] May offer discount
- [S_D] Offers senior discount
- [fyi] Informational listing only

Member Services

- [✈] Airport transportation
- [🐾] Pets allowed
- [🍴] Restaurant on premises
- [🍴+] Restaurant off premises (walking distance)
- [24🍴] 24-hour room service
- [🍸] Cocktail lounge
- [👶] Child care

Accessibility Features
(see pg. 20)

- [&M] Accessibility features
- [🚿] Roll-in showers
- [👂] Hearing impaired

Leisure Activities

- [🎰] Full Service Casino
- [🏊] Pool
- [💪] Health Club on premises
- [💪] Health Club off premises
- [✗] Recreational activities

In-Room Amenities

- [✗] Non-smoking rooms
- [✗] No air conditioning
- [✗] No TV
- [✗] No Cable TV
- [VCR] VCR
- [🎬] Movies
- [DATA PORT] Data port/modem line
- [☎] No telephones
- [🔲] Refrigerator
- [🔲] Microwave
- [☕] Coffee maker

Call property for detailed information about fees & restrictions relating to the lodging listing symbols.

CHOICE HOTELS
INTERNATIONAL ®

Take the road less traveled or more traveled. We're on both.

CHOICE HOTELS
INTERNATIONAL ®

800.228.1AAA
choicehotels.com

The Power of Being There. **Go**®

———— WHERE TO DINE ————

LOBSTER SHANTY   **Lunch:** $6-$11   **Dinner:** $14-$18   **Phone:** 772/334-6400
Seafood
Location: CR 707, 3 mi sw of Jensen Cswy (SR 732), 1.8 mi e of jct US 1. 999 N East Anchorage Dr 34957. **Hours:** 11:30 am-9 pm, Fri & Sat-10 pm. Closed: 12/25. **Features:** You will find a great view from an expansive porch overlooking the St Lucie River. Wonderful lobster soup and salmon in lemon sauce are specialties of this clean, comfortable eatery. Finish your meal with the Key lime pie and a robust blend of coffee. Casual dress; cocktails. **Parking:** on-site. **Cards:** AX, CB, DC, MC, VI.

JUNO BEACH pop. 3,262   (See map p. 757; index p. 760)

———— WHERE TO STAY ————

HAMPTON INN-JUNO BEACH   **Phone:** (561)626-9090   **74**
[SAVE]

| 12/1-4/21 [ECP] | 1P: $119-$199 | 2P: $129-$199 |
| 4/22-11/30 [ECP] | 1P: $69-$129 | 2P: $75-$149 |

Small-scale Hotel
Location: US 1, just s of jct Donald Ross Rd. 13801 US Hwy 1 33408. Fax: 561/624-9936. **Facility:** 88 units. 87 one-bedroom standard units, some with whirlpools. 1 one-bedroom suite. 2 stories, interior corridors. **Bath:** combo or shower only. **Parking:** on-site. **Terms:** cancellation fee imposed. **Amenities:** voice mail, irons, hair dryers. **Pool(s):** heated outdoor. **Leisure Activities:** whirlpool. **Guest Services:** valet laundry. **Business Services:** meeting rooms, fax (fee). **Cards:** AX, CB, DC, DS, MC, VI.

SOME UNITS

HOLIDAY INN EXPRESS-NORTH PALM BEACH   **Phone:** (561)622-4366   **72**

12/16-3/31 [ECP]	1P: $129-$300	2P: $129-$300	XP: $5	F19
4/1-11/30 [ECP]	1P: $59-$189	2P: $59-$189	XP: $5	F19
12/1-12/15	1P: $59-$189	2P: $59-$189	XP: $5	F19

Small-scale Hotel
Location: At jct Donald Ross Rd. 13950 US Hwy 1 33408. Fax: 561/625-5245. **Facility:** 108 units. 96 one-bedroom standard units. 12 one-bedroom suites ($89-$300). 3 stories, interior/exterior corridors. **Parking:** on-site. **Terms:** weekly rates available, pets ($25 extra charge). **Amenities:** voice mail, irons, hair dryers. **Pool(s):** outdoor. **Guest Services:** valet and coin laundry. **Business Services:** meeting rooms, fax (fee). **Cards:** AX, CB, DC, DS, JC, MC, VI.

SOME UNITS

———— WHERE TO DINE ————

CLASSICO'S ITALIAN RESTAURANT   **Dinner:** $8-$20   **Phone:** 561/622-9772   **40**
Italian
Location: US 1, just n of jct Donald Ross Rd. in Loggerhead Plaza. 14133 US Hwy 1 33408. **Hours:** 4:30 pm-10 pm, Sun 5 pm-9 pm. Closed: 11/27, 12/25. **Reservations:** suggested. **Features:** Candlelight dinners feature creative dishes of veal, chicken, pasta and seafood, all cooked to order with only fresh ingredients. The eatery is noted for its displays of movie memorabilia from the '20s through the '50s and its sinful homemade desserts. Casual dress; cocktails. **Parking:** on-site. **Cards:** AX, MC, VI.

JUPITER pop. 39,328

———— WHERE TO STAY ————

BEST WESTERN INTRACOASTAL INN   **Phone:** (561)575-2936
[AAA] [SAVE]

| 2/1-4/16 | 1P: $99-$149 | 2P: $109-$149 | XP: $10 | F17 |
| 12/1-1/31 & 4/17-11/30 | 1P: $65-$75 | 2P: $79-$85 | XP: $10 | F17 |

Small-scale Hotel
Location: 0.5 mi s of jct SR 706 (Indiantown Rd). 810 S US Hwy 1 33477. Fax: 561/575-9346. **Facility:** 53 one-bedroom standard units, some with whirlpools. 2 stories, interior corridors. **Bath:** combo or shower only. **Parking:** on-site. **Amenities:** irons, hair dryers. **Pool(s):** outdoor. **Guest Services:** coin laundry. **Business Services:** fax (fee). **Cards:** AX, CB, DC, DS, MC, VI. **Special Amenities:** free continental breakfast.

SOME UNITS

FAIRFIELD INN & SUITES BY MARRIOTT   **Phone:** (561)748-5252
[SAVE]

2/1-4/30	1P: $109-$149
1/1-1/31	1P: $99-$139
12/1-12/31 & 5/1-11/30	1P: $59-$109

Small-scale Hotel
Location: I-95, exit 87A, 0.8 mi e on SR 706 (Indiantown Rd). 6748 W Indiantown Rd 33458. Fax: 561/748-5251. **Facility:** 110 one-bedroom standard units, some with whirlpools. 4 stories, interior corridors. **Bath:** combo or shower only. **Parking:** on-site. **Amenities:** dual phone lines, voice mail, irons, hair dryers. **Some:** CD players. **Pool(s):** heated outdoor. **Leisure Activities:** whirlpool, exercise room. **Guest Services:** valet laundry. **Business Services:** fax (fee). **Cards:** AX, DC, DS, MC, VI.

SOME UNITS

THE JUPITER BEACH RESORT   **Phone:** (561)746-2511
[AAA] [SAVE]

12/1-4/30	1P: $200-$450	2P: $200-$450	XP: $25	F18
5/1-5/31 & 10/1-11/30	1P: $140-$240	2P: $140-$240	XP: $25	F18
6/1-9/30	1P: $115-$205	2P: $115-$205	XP: $25	F18

Large-scale Hotel
Location: SR A1A, 1 mi se of jct US 1; at jct SR 706 (Indiantown Rd). 5 N A1A 33477-5190. Fax: 561/744-1741. **Facility:** 153 units. 105 one-bedroom standard units. 46 one- and 2 two-bedroom suites ($450-$1200). 9 stories, interior corridors. **Parking:** on-site and valet. **Terms:** check-in 4 pm, 7 day cancellation notice, package plans - seasonal, $3 service charge. **Amenities:** high-speed Internet, voice mail, honor bars, irons, hair dryers. **Dining:** 6:30 am-10 pm, cocktails, entertainment. **Pool(s):** heated outdoor. **Leisure Activities:** lighted tennis court, exercise room, volleyball. **Fee:** scuba diving, snorkeling, boogie boards, catamarans, kayaks, seadoos. **Guest Services:** gift shop, valet and coin laundry. **Business Services:** meeting rooms, business center. **Cards:** AX, CB, DC, DS, MC, VI. **Special Amenities:** free newspaper and free room upgrade (subject to availability with advanced reservations).

SOME UNITS
FEE

WELLESLEY INN & SUITES (JUPITER)
Phone: (561)575-7201

AAA SAVE

12/1-4/30	1P: $99	XP: $10	F18
5/1-11/30	1P: $79	XP: $10	F18

Small-scale Hotel

Location: SR 706 (Indiantown Rd); 0.3 mi w of jct US 1. Located in Fisherman's Wharf Plaza. 34 Fishermans Wharf 33477. **Fax:** 561/575-1169. **Facility:** 104 units. 93 one-bedroom standard units. 11 one-bedroom suites. 3 stories, interior corridors. **Bath:** combo or shower only. **Parking:** on-site. **Terms:** cancellation fee imposed, [ECP] meal plan available, small pets only. **Amenities:** video games (fee), voice mail, hair dryers. Some: dual phone lines, safes, irons. **Pool(s):** heated outdoor. **Guest Services:** coin laundry. **Business Services:** fax (fee). **Cards:** AX, DC, DS, MC, VI. **Special Amenities:** free continental breakfast and free newspaper. (See color ad p 957)

SOME UNITS

FEE   FEE

WHERE TO DINE

CHARLEY'S CRAB
Lunch: $6-$16   **Dinner:** $15-$30   **Phone:** 561/744-4710

Seafood

Location: At jct SR A1A on southwest side of bridge; in Jupiter Harbor Complex. 1000 Hwy US 1 N 33477. **Hours:** 11:30 am-10 pm, Sun from 10:30 am. **Reservations:** suggested. **Features:** Atrium-style dining is the mode at the busy, waterfront restaurant, which offers views of the Jupiter lighthouse. The strains of jazz and calypso fill the air on weekends. Sample the crab cakes and homemade pasta, or enjoy Sunday champagne brunch. Outdoor tables are available. Casual dress; cocktails. **Parking:** on-site and valet. **Cards:** AX, CB, DC, DS, MC, VI.

KENDALL —See Miami-Miami Beach p. 551.

KEY BISCAYNE —See Miami-Miami Beach p. 552.

KEY COLONY BEACH —See The Florida Keys p. 323.

KEY LARGO —See The Florida Keys p. 323.

KEY WEST —See The Florida Keys p. 333.

KISSIMMEE —See Orlando p. 678.

LADY LAKE —See Orlando p. 714.

LAKE BUENA VISTA —See Orlando p. 714.

LAKE CITY pop. 9,980

WHERE TO STAY

BEST WESTERN INN
Phone: (386)752-3801

AAA SAVE

All Year   1P: $45-$85   2P: $50-$90   XP: $5   F17

Small-scale Hotel

Location: I-75, exit 427, just w. 3598 W US Hwy 90 32055. **Fax:** 386/755-4846. **Facility:** 80 units. 78 one-bedroom standard units. 2 one-bedroom suites. 2 stories, exterior corridors. **Parking:** on-site. **Terms:** [ECP] meal plan available, small pets only ($5 extra charge). **Amenities:** irons, hair dryers. **Pool(s):** outdoor. **Leisure Activities:** sauna, whirlpool, playground, exercise room. **Guest Services:** coin laundry. **Business Services:** meeting rooms, fax. **Cards:** AX, CB, DC, DS, JC, MC, VI. **Special Amenities:** free continental breakfast.

SOME UNITS

COMFORT INN
Phone: (386)755-1344

SAVE

All Year [ECP]   1P: $64-$95   2P: $64-$95   XP: $5   F19

Small-scale Hotel

Location: I-75, exit 427, just w. 4515 Hwy 90 W 32055 (PO Box 1985, 32056). **Fax:** 386/752-8957. **Facility:** 100 one-bedroom standard units, some with whirlpools. 2 stories, exterior corridors. **Bath:** combo or shower only. **Parking:** on-site. **Amenities:** Some: irons, hair dryers. **Pool(s):** outdoor. **Leisure Activities:** 2 lighted tennis courts, playground, basketball, shuffleboard. **Guest Services:** valet and coin laundry. **Business Services:** fax. **Cards:** AX, DC, DS, MC, VI.

SOME UNITS

FEE

COUNTRY INN & SUITES
Phone: (386)754-5944

All Year   1P: $69-$110   2P: $79-$120

Small-scale Hotel

Location: I-75, exit 427, just w. 1608 Florida Gateway Blvd 32024. **Fax:** 386/754-1557. **Facility:** 60 units. 46 one-bedroom standard units, some with whirlpools. 14 one-bedroom suites. 3 stories, interior corridors. **Bath:** combo or shower only. **Parking:** on-site. **Amenities:** dual phone lines, voice mail, irons, hair dryers. **Pool(s):** heated outdoor. **Leisure Activities:** whirlpool, exercise room. **Guest Services:** valet and coin laundry. **Business Services:** meeting rooms, fax. **Cards:** AX, CB, DC, DS, MC, VI. (See color ad p 613)

SOME UNITS

DAYS INN
Phone: (386)752-9350

AAA SAVE

All Year [CP]   1P: $45-$65   2P: $49-$65   XP: $5   F12

Small-scale Hotel

Location: I-75, exit 427, 0.3 mi e. 3144 W Hwy 90 32055. **Fax:** 386/752-9350. **Facility:** 120 one-bedroom standard units. 2 stories, exterior corridors. **Parking:** on-site. **Amenities:** hair dryers. **Pool(s):** outdoor. **Business Services:** fax. **Cards:** AX, CB, DC, DS, MC, VI. **Special Amenities:** free continental breakfast and free newspaper.

SOME UNITS

DAYS INN I-10
AAA SAVE
Small-scale Hotel

Phone: (386)758-4224
All Year [ECP]   1P: $48-$69   2P: $48-$69   XP: $4   F14
Location: I-10, exit 303, just s. US 441 32055 (Rt 16, Box 38310). Fax: 386/758-7612. **Facility:** 62 one-bedroom standard units. 2 stories, exterior corridors. **Parking:** on-site. **Terms:** small pets only ($5 extra charge). **Amenities:** hair dryers. **Pool(s):** outdoor. **Guest Services:** coin laundry. **Business Services:** PC, fax. **Special Amenities:** free continental breakfast and free local telephone calls.

SOME UNITS

DRIFTWOOD INN
AAA SAVE
Motel

Phone: (386)755-3545
All Year   1P: $30-$40   2P: $30-$40   XP: $5   D12
Location: I-75, exit 427, 0.7 mi e. 2764 W US Hwy 90 32055. Fax: 386/961-8798. **Facility:** 20 one-bedroom standard units. 1 story, exterior corridors. **Parking:** on-site. **Terms:** small pets only ($5 extra charge). **Special Amenities:** free continental breakfast.

SOME UNITS

ECONO LODGE SOUTH
AAA SAVE
Motel

Phone: 386/755-9311
All Year   1P: $39-$100   2P: $39-$100   XP: $4   F17
Location: I-75, exit 414, at US 441. Located adjacent to truck parking. (Rt 2, Box 6008, 32024). Fax: 386/755-8864. **Facility:** 59 one-bedroom standard units. 1 story, exterior corridors. **Parking:** on-site. **Terms:** 2-3 night minimum stay - seasonal, weekly rates available, [CP] meal plan available, small pets only. **Pool(s):** outdoor. **Cards:** AX, DC, DS, MC, VI. **Special Amenities:** free continental breakfast and free local telephone calls.

SOME UNITS

HAMPTON INN
AAA SAVE
Small-scale Hotel

Phone: (386)752-3419
All Year   1P: $75-$95   2P: $85-$95
Location: I-75, exit 427, just w, then 0.4 mi s. 414 SW Florida Gateway Blvd 32024. Fax: 386/758-3196. **Facility:** 60 one-bedroom standard units, some with whirlpools. 2 stories, exterior corridors. *Bath:* combo or shower only. **Parking:** on-site. **Terms:** 3 day cancellation notice, [ECP] meal plan available. **Amenities:** voice mail, irons, hair dryers. **Pool(s):** outdoor. **Leisure Activities:** whirlpool, complimentary green fees. **Guest Services:** valet laundry. **Business Services:** fax. **Cards:** AX, CB, DC, DS, MC, VI. **Special Amenities:** free continental breakfast and free local telephone calls.

SOME UNITS

FEE

HOLIDAY INN
WWW
Small-scale Hotel

Phone: (386)752-3901
All Year   1P: $69-$125   2P: $69-$125
Location: I-75, exit 427, just w. 4517 US Hwy 90 32055 (PO Box 1239, 32056). Fax: 386/754-1967. **Facility:** 227 units. 224 one-bedroom standard units. 3 one-bedroom suites. 2 stories, exterior corridors. *Bath:* combo or shower only. **Parking:** on-site. **Amenities:** voice mail, irons, hair dryers. **Pool(s):** outdoor, wading. **Leisure Activities:** 2 lighted tennis courts, playground, exercise room, basketball. **Guest Services:** valet and coin laundry. **Business Services:** meeting rooms, fax. **Cards:** AX, CB, DC, DS, JC, MC, VI. *(See color ad opposite inside back cover)*

SOME UNITS

JAMESON INN
WWW
Small-scale Hotel

Phone: 386/758-8440
All Year [ECP]   1P: $52-$67   2P: $55-$70   XP: $3   F17
Location: I-75, exit 427, just e, then s. 1393 Commerce Blvd 32025. Fax: 386/758-8166. **Facility:** 55 units. 53 one-bedroom standard units. 2 one-bedroom suites. 3 stories, interior corridors. *Bath:* combo or shower only. **Parking:** on-site. **Terms:** $3 service charge, small pets only. **Amenities:** voice mail, irons. *Some:* hair dryers. **Pool(s):** outdoor. **Leisure Activities:** exercise room. **Guest Services:** valet laundry. **Business Services:** meeting rooms, fax (fee). **Cards:** AX, CB, DC, DS, MC, VI.

SOME UNITS

RODEWAY INN
AAA SAVE
Motel

Phone: 386/755-5203
All Year   1P: $30-$40   2P: $35-$45   XP: $5   F12
Location: I-75, exit 427, just e. 1375 Commerce Blvd 32025. Fax: 386/752-4100. **Facility:** 44 one-bedroom standard units. 1 story, exterior corridors. **Parking:** on-site. **Terms:** weekly rates available, [CP] meal plan available, pets ($5 extra charge). **Guest Services:** coin laundry. **Business Services:** fax (fee). **Cards:** AX, DC, MC, VI. **Special Amenities:** free continental breakfast and preferred room (subject to availability with advanced reservations).

SOME UNITS

SCOTTISH INNS
AAA SAVE
Motel

Phone: (386)755-0230
All Year   1P: $29-$39   2P: $39-$49   XP: $5   F5
Location: I-75, exit 427, 0.6 mi e. 4450 Hwy 90 32055. Fax: 386/755-5277. **Facility:** 34 one-bedroom standard units. 1 story, exterior corridors. **Parking:** on-site. **Terms:** pets ($5-$10 extra charge). **Cards:** AX, CB, DC, DS, MC, VI. **Special Amenities:** early check-in/late check-out and free continental breakfast.

SOME UNITS

SUPER 8 MOTEL
WWW
Motel

Phone: 386/752-6450
All Year   1P: $38-$48   2P: $43-$53   XP: $5   F13
Location: I-75, exit 423, 0.3 mi w on SR 47. Located in a quiet, rural area. Rt 15, Box 3005 32024 (PO Box 7094, 32055). Fax: 386/752-6450. **Facility:** 87 one-bedroom standard units. 2 stories, exterior corridors. **Parking:** on-site. **Terms:** 7 day cancellation notice. **Pool(s):** outdoor. **Business Services:** fax. **Cards:** AX, DC, DS, MC, VI.

SOME UNITS

——— WHERE TO DINE ———

DESOTO DRUG STORE
American
Lunch: $4-$8
Phone: 386/752-9958
Location: Just n of US 90; downtown. 405 N Marion St 32055. **Hours:** 8 am-4:30 pm; to 4 pm off season. Closed major holidays; also Sat & Sun. **Features:** In the heart of the downtown antique shopping district, the authentic soda fountain entices you to come in, take a seat at the counter and sip on a frothy shake. Better yet, enjoy a scrumptious lunch of a chef specialty, such as Bordeaux chicken or steak Diane. It's worth a special trip for breakfast, when choices include pecan Belgian waffles, omelets and French toast. Smoke free premises. Casual dress. **Parking:** street. **Cards:** MC, VI. ⊠

EL POTRO
Mexican
Lunch: $5-$7
Dinner: $6-$10
Phone: 386/758-3100
Location: I-75, exit 427, 1 mi e on US 90; opposite Gleason Mall. Hwy 90 32055. **Hours:** 11 am-10 pm. Closed major holidays. **Features:** Authentic Mexican cuisine is served in semi-private booths around an open fireplace. Recipes reflect a true south-of-the-border taste. Attention to detail and professionalism go a long way here. Casual dress; cocktails. **Parking:** on-site. **Cards:** AX, MC, VI. ⊠

KEN'S BBQ
American
Lunch: $4-$8
Dinner: $4-$8
Phone: 386/752-5919
Location: 4 mi e of jct I-75. US Hwy 90 W 32056. **Hours:** 11 am-9 pm. Closed: Sun. **Features:** Locally-owned and operated for many years, Ken's is a popular Lake City institution. One visit and ya'll have to come back! Friendly efficient service is a characteristic enjoyed at all locations. The barbecue sauces go well with the pork, ribs, chicken, or beef. Most plates or dinners include a choice of baked beans and a side of cole slaw. Enjoy fresh Texas-style garlic bread with your dinner. Casual dress. **Parking:** on-site. **Cards:** AX, DS, MC, VI. ⊠

LAKE HELEN pop. 2,743

——— WHERE TO STAY ———

CLAUSER'S BED & BREAKFAST
Bed & Breakfast
Phone: (386)228-0310
All Year [BP] 1P: $85-$130 2P: $95-$140 XP: $25
Location: I-4, exit 116, 1 mi e on Main St, 0.5 mi s on CR 4139, turn left on Ohio St, right on Pleasant Rd, then right. 201 E Kicklighter Rd 32744. Fax: 386/228-0484. **Facility:** Dating from the 1890s, this two-story carriage house features a pub on the lower level and has six modern guest units; a walking path leads to a lake. Smoke free premises. 8 one-bedroom standard units, some with whirlpools. **Features:** 2 stories, interior/exterior corridors. *Bath:* combo or shower only. **Parking:** on-site. **Terms:** age restrictions may apply, 7 day cancellation notice-fee imposed, package plans - weekends, seasonal. **Amenities:** video library, hair dryers. **Leisure Activities:** whirlpool, croquet, electronic darts, lending library, walking trails, bicycles. **Guest Services:** gift shop. **Cards:** AX, DS, MC, VI. **Special Amenities:** free local telephone calls and preferred room (subject to availability with advanced reservations).

SOME UNITS
⑤🎱 Ⓨ ⊠ ⊠ / 🅦 /

LAKELAND pop. 78,452

——— WHERE TO STAY ———

AMERISUITES (LAKELAND CENTER)
Small-scale Hotel
Phone: (863)413-1122
All Year 1P: $89-$139 2P: $89-$139 XP: $10 F
Location: I-4, exit 32, 3.2 mi s on US 98, just w. Located at the Lakeland Center. 525 W Orange St 33815. Fax: 863/413-1133. **Facility:** 128 one-bedroom standard units. 6 stories, interior corridors. *Bath:* combo or shower only. **Parking:** on-site. **Terms:** cancellation fee imposed, [ECP] meal plan available, small pets only. **Amenities:** video games, voice mail, irons, hair dryers. *Some:* dual phone lines. **Pool(s):** heated outdoor. **Leisure Activities:** exercise room. **Guest Services:** coin laundry. **Business Services:** meeting rooms, fax (fee). **Cards:** AX, CB, DC, DS, JC, MC, VI. **Special Amenities:** free continental breakfast and free newspaper. *(See color ad p 485)*

SOME UNITS
⑤🎱 🐾 🔥Ⓜ 🔥 🅰 ☏ 🆅🆁 📶 📠 🖥 🖥 / ⊠ /

BAYMONT INN & SUITES LAKELAND
Small-scale Hotel
Phone: (863)815-0606
4/1-4/17 [ECP] 1P: $119-$149 2P: $119-$149
12/1-3/31 [ECP] 1P: $74-$94 2P: $74-$94
4/18-11/30 [ECP] 1P: $54-$79 2P: $54-$79
Location: I-4, exit 33; jct SR 33, just nw. 4315 Lakeland Park Dr 33809. Fax: 863/815-9711. **Facility:** 104 units. 101 one-bedroom standard units. 3 one-bedroom suites ($89-$139), some with kitchens. 4 stories, interior corridors. *Bath:* combo or shower only. **Parking:** on-site. **Terms:** small pets only ($10 fee). **Amenities:** video games, voice mail, irons, hair dryers. **Pool(s):** outdoor. **Guest Services:** coin laundry. **Business Services:** meeting rooms, fax (fee). **Cards:** AX, CB, DC, DS, MC, VI. **Special Amenities:** free continental breakfast and free newspaper. *(See color ad p 483)*

SOME UNITS
⑤🎱 🐾 🍴 🔥Ⓜ 🔥 ☏ 📶 🆆 📠 🖥 / ⊠ 📶 🖥 /

BEST WESTERN DIPLOMAT INN
Small-scale Hotel
Phone: (863)688-7972
2/1-4/30 [BP] 1P: $79-$99 2P: $79-$99 XP: $10 F16
12/26-1/31 [BP] 1P: $69-$89 2P: $69-$89 XP: $10 F16
12/1-12/25 & 5/1-11/30 [BP] 1P: $59-$79 2P: $59-$79 XP: $10 F16
Location: I-4, exit 32, just s. 3311 US 98 N 33805. Fax: 863/688-8377. **Facility:** 120 one-bedroom standard units. 2 stories, exterior corridors. **Parking:** on-site. **Terms:** weekly rates available, package plans. **Amenities:** irons, hair dryers. **Dining:** 7-9:30 am. **Pool(s):** outdoor, wading. **Guest Services:** valet and coin laundry. **Business Services:** meeting rooms, fax (fee). **Cards:** AX, DC, DS, MC, VI. **Special Amenities:** early check-in/late check-out and free newspaper.

SOME UNITS
⑤🎱 🍴 Ⓨ 📶 🆆 📠 🖥 / ⊠ 📶 🖥 /
FEE

COURTYARD BY MARRIOTT   Phone: 863/802-9000

[SAVE] All Year   1P: $79-$89
Location: I-4, exit 27, se on SR 570 (toll) to exit 5, then just n. 3725 Harden Blvd 33803. Fax: 863/802-5300.
Facility: 78 units. 75 one-bedroom standard units. 3 one-bedroom suites ($139). 3 stories, interior corridors.
Small-scale Hotel   *Bath:* combo or shower only. Parking: on-site. Terms: cancellation fee imposed. Amenities: dual phone
lines, voice mail, irons, hair dryers. Pool(s): outdoor. Leisure Activities: whirlpool, exercise room. Guest
JC, MC, VI.   Services: valet and coin laundry. Business Services: meeting rooms, fax (fee). Cards: AX, CB, DC, DS,

SOME UNITS

[icons]

ECONO LODGE   Phone: (863)688-9221

[AAA] [SAVE]   2/1-4/30   1P: $65-$75   2P: $75-$80   XP: $5   F18
               12/1-1/31   1P: $60-$65   2P: $65-$70   XP: $5   F18
               5/1-11/30   1P: $55-$60   2P: $65-$70   XP: $5   F18
Motel   Location: 2 mi e of jct US 98 and 92. 1817 E Memorial Blvd 33801. Fax: 863/687-4797. Facility: 64 one-bedroom
standard units. 2 stories, exterior corridors. Parking: on-site. Terms: weekly rates available, [ECP] meal plan
available, pets ($5 extra charge). Amenities: *Some:* irons, hair dryers. Pool(s): outdoor. Business Serv-
ices: fax (fee). Cards: AX, DC, DS, MC, VI. Special Amenities: free continental breakfast and free local telephone calls.

SOME UNITS

[icons]   FEE

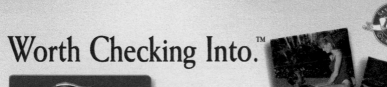

FOUR POINTS SHERATON HOTEL & SUITES

Phone: (863)647-3000

1/21-4/20 & 6/26-11/30 [CP]	1P: $149	2P: $149	XP: $10 F12
12/1-1/20 & 4/21-6/25 [CP]	1P: $129	2P: $129	XP: $10 F12

Small-scale Hotel **Location:** SR 37, 3.5 mi s of US 98 business route. 4141 S Florida Ave 33813. Fax: 863/644-0467. **Facility:** 168 units. 138 one-bedroom standard units, some with whirlpools. 30 one-bedroom suites ($164-$189) with whirlpools. 7 stories, interior corridors. *Bath:* combo or shower only. **Parking:** on-site. **Amenities:** video games (fee), dual phone lines, voice mail, irons, hair dryers. *Some:* high-speed Internet. **Pool(s):** outdoor. **Leisure Activities:** whirlpool, exercise room. **Guest Services:** valet and coin laundry. **Business Services:** conference facilities, business center. **Cards:** AX, DS, MC, VI.

SOME UNITS

(ASK) (S☐) (￦) (Y) (☐M) (☐) (☎) (☆) (DATA PORT) (☐) / (✕) (☐) (☐) /

HAMPTON INN

Phone: (863)816-2525

AAA **SAVE**

1/1-4/7 [ECP]	1P: $89-$140	2P: $99-$140
12/1-12/31 & 4/8-11/30 [ECP]	1P: $79-$89	2P: $89-$99

Small-scale Hotel **Location:** I-4, exit 33, just nw. 4420 N Socrum Loop Rd 33809. Fax: 863/816-2727. **Facility:** 70 one-bedroom standard units. 3 stories, interior corridors. *Bath:* combo or shower only. **Parking:** on-site. **Terms:** 3 day cancellation notice. **Amenities:** voice mail, irons, hair dryers. **Pool(s):** heated outdoor. **Leisure Activities:** exercise room. **Guest Services:** coin laundry. **Business Services:** meeting rooms, fax (fee). **Cards:** AX, CB, DC, DS, MC, VI. **Special Amenities:** free continental breakfast and free local telephone calls.

SOME UNITS

(S☐) (￦) (☐M) (☐) (☎) (☆) (DATA PORT) (☐) (☐) (☐) / (✕) /

HOLIDAY INN LAKELAND HOTEL & CONFERENCE CENTER

Phone: (863)688-8080

1/1-4/30	1P: $80-$89	2P: $80-$89	XP: $10 F19
12/1-12/31 & 5/1-11/30	1P: $71-$79	2P: $71-$79	XP: $10 F19

Small-scale Hotel **Location:** I-4, exit 32, just e. 3260 US Hwy 98 N 33805. Fax: 863/688-6820. **Facility:** 157 units. 156 one-bedroom standard units. 1 one-bedroom suite ($109-$119). 4 stories, interior corridors. *Bath:* combo or shower only. **Parking:** on-site. **Terms:** [AP], [BP] & [CP] meal plans available. **Amenities:** video games (fee), dual phone lines, voice mail, irons, hair dryers. **Pool(s):** outdoor. **Leisure Activities:** exercise room. *Fee:* game room. **Guest Services:** valet and coin laundry. **Business Services:** meeting rooms. *Fee:* administrative services, fax. **Cards:** AX, CB, DC, DS, JC, MC, VI.

SOME UNITS

(ASK) (S☐) (￦) (Y) (☐) (☐) (☎) (☆) (DATA PORT) (☐) / (✕) (☐) (☐) /
FEE FEE

HOLIDAY INN LAKELAND SOUTH

Phone: (863)646-5731

All Year [CP] 2P: $69

Small-scale Hotel **Location:** 3 mi s on SR 37. 3405 S Florida Ave 33803. Fax: 863/646-5215. **Facility:** 172 one-bedroom standard units. 2 stories, exterior corridors. *Bath:* combo or shower only. **Parking:** on-site. **Terms:** [MAP] meal plan available. **Amenities:** voice mail, irons, hair dryers. **Pool(s):** outdoor. **Leisure Activities:** whirlpool, exercise room. **Guest Services:** complimentary evening beverages: Mon-Fri, valet laundry. **Business Services:** meeting rooms, fax. **Cards:** AX, CB, DC, DS, JC, MC, VI. *(See color ad opposite inside back cover)*

SOME UNITS

(ASK) (S☐) (✚) (￦) (Y) (☐M) (☐) (☎) (☆) (DATA PORT) (☐) / (✕) (VCR) (☐) (☐) /
FEE FEE FEE

JAMESON INN

Phone: 863/858-9070

All Year [ECP] 1P: $52-$67 2P: $55-$70 XP: $3 F17

Small-scale Hotel **Location:** I-4, exit 33, just nw. 4375 Lakeland Park Dr 33809. Fax: 863/858-2491. **Facility:** 67 units. 65 one-bedroom standard units. 2 one-bedroom suites. 3 stories, interior corridors. *Bath:* combo or shower only. **Parking:** on-site. **Terms:** $3 service charge, small pets only. **Amenities:** dual phone lines, voice mail, irons. **Pool(s):** outdoor. **Leisure Activities:** exercise room. **Guest Services:** valet laundry. **Business Services:** meeting rooms, fax (fee). **Cards:** AX, CB, DC, DS, MC, VI.

SOME UNITS

(￦) (￦) (☐M) (☐) (☎) (☆) (DATA PORT) (☐) (☐) (☐) /

LAKELAND RESIDENCE INN BY MARRIOTT

Phone: (863)680-2323

SAVE

3/28-4/10 [ECP]	1P: $169-$300
12/1-3/27 & 4/11-11/30 [ECP]	1P: $109-$200

Small-scale Hotel **Location:** I-4, exit 27 (Polk Pkwy), se on SR 570 (toll) to exit 5, then just n. 3701 Harden Blvd 33803. Fax: 863/680-1717. **Facility:** 78 units. 33 one-bedroom standard units with kitchens. 33 one- and 12 two-bedroom suites with kitchens. 3 stories, interior corridors. *Bath:* combo or shower only. **Parking:** on-site. **Terms:** pets ($85 fee). **Amenities:** dual phone lines, voice mail, irons, hair dryers. **Pool(s):** outdoor. **Leisure Activities:** whirlpool, exercise room, sports court. **Guest Services:** valet and coin laundry. **Business Services:** meeting rooms, fax (fee). **Cards:** AX, DC, DS, MC, VI.

SOME UNITS

(S☐) (￦) (☐) (☐) (☎) (✕) (☆) (DATA PORT) (☐) (☐) (☐) / (✕) /

LA QUINTA INN & SUITES

Phone: (863)859-2866

AAA **SAVE**

2/1-4/30	1P: $89-$119	2P: $95-$125
12/1-1/31 & 5/1-11/30	1P: $59-$89	2P: $65-$95

Small-scale Hotel **Location:** I-4, exit 32, just n on US 98. 1024 Crevasse St 33809. Fax: 863/859-2956. **Facility:** 119 units. 113 one-bedroom standard units. 6 one-bedroom suites. 6 stories, interior corridors. *Bath:* combo or shower only. **Parking:** on-site. **Terms:** [ECP] meal plan available, small pets only. **Amenities:** video games, voice mail, irons, hair dryers. **Pool(s):** heated outdoor. **Leisure Activities:** whirlpool, exercise room. **Guest Services:** valet and coin laundry. **Business Services:** meeting rooms, fax (fee). **Cards:** AX, CB, DC, DS, JC, MC, VI. **Special Amenities:** free continental breakfast and free local telephone calls.

SOME UNITS

(￦) (￦) (☐M) (☐) (☎) (☆) (☆) (DATA PORT) (☐) (☐) (☐) / (✕) (☐) (☐) /

ROYALTY INN

AAA SAVE
WWW WWW
Motel

			Phone: (863)858-4481	
1/20-4/30 [ECP]	1P: $55-$85	2P: $65-$95	XP: $10	F12
12/1-1/19 [ECP]	1P: $49-$69	2P: $59-$79	XP: $10	F12
5/1-11/30 [ECP]	1P: $39-$59	2P: $49-$69	XP: $10	F12

Location: I-4, exit 32, just ne. 3425 Hwy 98 N 33809. Fax: 863/853-2514. **Facility:** 64 one-bedroom standard units. 2 stories, interior corridors. **Parking:** on-site. **Terms:** weekly rates available, small pets only ($10 extra charge). **Amenities:** voice mail, safes (fee). *Some:* hair dryers. **Pool(s):** outdoor, wading. **Leisure Activities:** exercise room. **Guest Services:** coin laundry. **Business Services:** meeting rooms. **Cards:** AX, DS, MC, VI. **Special Amenities: free continental breakfast and free newspaper.** *(See color ad below)*

SOME UNITS

SCOTTISH INNS

AAA SAVE
WW
Motel

			Phone: 863/687-2530	
2/1-4/12 [CP]	1P: $49-$59	2P: $59-$88	XP: $5	F12
1/1-1/31 [CP]	1P: $45-$49	2P: $52-$65	XP: $5	F12
4/13-11/30 [CP]	1P: $45-$49	2P: $52-$62	XP: $5	F12
12/1-12/31 [CP]	1P: $45-$49	2P: $49-$62	XP: $5	F12

Location: On US 98 business route, 0.6 mi s of jct US 92 and 98. 244 N Florida Ave 33801. Fax: 863/688-1961. **Facility:** 46 one-bedroom standard units. 2 stories, exterior corridors. *Bath:* combo or shower only. **Parking:** on-site. **Terms:** 3 day cancellation notice. **Pool(s):** outdoor. **Guest Services:** coin laundry. **Business Services:** fax (fee). **Cards:** AX, CB, DC, DS, MC, VI. **Special Amenities: free continental breakfast.**

SOME UNITS

SUBURBAN LODGE

WWW WWW
Motel

			Phone: 863/816-1700	
12/1-4/15	1P: $59-$69	2P: $69-$79	XP: $10	F18
4/16-11/30	1P: $49-$59	2P: $59-$69	XP: $10	F18

Location: I-4, exit 32, just w. 4335 Williamstown Blvd 33810. Fax: 863/816-9685. **Facility:** 138 one-bedroom standard units with kitchens. 3 stories, exterior corridors. *Bath:* combo or shower only. **Parking:** on-site. **Terms:** 14 day cancellation notice, weekly rates available. **Amenities:** voice mail. **Guest Services:** coin laundry. **Business Services:** fax (fee). **Cards:** AX, CB, DS, MC, VI. *(See color ad p 596)*

SUPER 8 MOTEL
Phone: (863)683-5961

2/1-4/30 [CP]	1P: $50-$80	2P: $55-$89	XP: $10	F12
12/1-1/31 & 5/1-11/30 [CP]	1P: $40-$65	2P: $45-$70	XP: $5	F12

Motel

Location: Just e of jct SR 33. 601 E Memorial Blvd 33801. Fax: 863/683-7723. **Facility:** 84 one-bedroom standard units. 2 stories, interior/exterior corridors. **Parking:** on-site. **Terms:** 7 day cancellation notice, small pets only ($10 extra charge). **Pool(s):** heated outdoor. **Guest Services:** coin laundry. **Business Services:** meeting rooms, fax (fee). **Cards:** AX, CB, DC, DS, MC, VI. **Special Amenities: free continental breakfast and preferred room (subject to availability with advanced reservations).**

SOME UNITS

FEE   FEE

WELLESLEY INN & SUITES (LAKELAND)
Phone: (863)859-0100

3/26-4/10	1P: $145	2P: $145	XP: $10	F17
12/1-3/25 & 4/11-11/30	1P: $65-$75	2P: $65-$75	XP: $10	F17

Small-scale Hotel

Location: I-4, exit 32, just nw. Located at the Lakeland Square Mall. 3520 Hwy US 98 N 33809. Fax: 863/859-0106. **Facility:** 106 one-bedroom standard units. 6 stories, interior corridors. *Bath:* combo or shower only. **Parking:** on-site. **Terms:** [CP] & [ECP] meal plans available, small pets only. **Amenities:** video games, voice mail, irons, hair dryers. **Pool(s):** heated outdoor. **Guest Services:** coin laundry. **Business Services:** meeting rooms, fax (fee). **Cards:** AX, CB, DC, DS, JC, MC, VI. **Special Amenities: free continental breakfast and free newspaper.** *(See color ad p 483)*

SOME UNITS

FEE

─────── **WHERE TO DINE** ───────

PAN YE'S CHINESE RESTAURANT
Lunch: $4-$10   **Dinner:** $4-$10   **Phone:** 863/686-2052

Chinese

Location: I-4, exit 32, 2.8 mi s to jct US 92, then 0.4 mi e. 743 E Memorial Blvd 33801. **Hours:** 11 am-9 pm. Closed: 7/4, 11/27, 12/25; also Mon. **Features:** Reliable, Americanized Chinese fare is served by a friendly family. The house specials include pork, poultry, beef and seafood combinations. Egg rolls, fried rice and many other tasty entrees can be sampled at the buffet from 11 am-2:30 pm. Casual dress; beer & wine only. **Parking:** on-site. **Cards:** AX, DS, MC, VI.

LAKE MARY — *See Orlando p. 740.*

LAKE PARK pop. 8,721   (See map p. 757; index p. 760)

─────── **WHERE TO DINE** ───────

CAFE DU PARK
Dinner: $16-$26
Phone: 561/845-0529   (58)

French

Location: US 1, 1.3 mi n of jct SR A1A (Blue Heron Blvd). 612 N Federal Hwy 33403. **Hours:** Open 12/1-8/31 & 10/15-11/30; 5:30 pm-10 pm. Closed: Sun. **Reservations:** suggested. **Features:** Several cozy dining rooms in a former private home offer an intimate experience. The owner-chef prepares the cuisine with a Continental touch, and the severs are attentive and friendly. Try the snails wrapped in phyllo pastry with a white wine sauce. Semi-formal attire; beer & wine only. **Parking:** on-site. **Cards:** AX, MC, VI.

LAKE PLACID pop. 1,668

─────── **WHERE TO STAY** ───────

LAKE BLUE RESORT
Phone: 863/465-3371

All Year   2P: $65-$75   XP: $5   F10

Cottage

Location: 1.5 mi n on US 27, 0.3 mi e, follow signs. Located in a quiet area. 735 S Lakeview Rd 33852. Fax: 863/465-3371. **Facility:** Designated smoking area. 18 cottages. 1 story, exterior corridors. *Bath:* shower only. **Parking:** on-site. **Terms:** 3 night minimum stay - weekends 5/31-9/4, 14 day cancellation notice, weekly rates available. **Pool(s):** heated outdoor. **Leisure Activities:** boat dock, fishing, shuffleboard, volleyball. **Guest Services:** coin laundry. **Business Services:** fax (fee). **Cards:** MC, VI.

LAKE WALES pop. 10,194

――――― **WHERE TO STAY** ―――――

CHALET SUZANNE COUNTRY INN & RESTAURANT   Phone: (863)676-6011
(AAA) (SAVE)   All Year [BP]   1P: $169-$229   2P: $169-$229   XP: $12
▼▼▼   **Location:** CR 17A, 1.5 mi e of jct SR 17. 3800 Chalet Suzanne Dr 33859. Fax: 863/676-1814. **Facility:** Approached
            via wrought iron gates and a winding, palm-lined drive, the inn is nestled on 100 acres with a private lake,
            formal gardens and a gazebo. 30 units. 29 one-bedroom standard units, some with kitchens (no utensils)
Historic   and/or whirlpools. 1 one-bedroom suite with whirlpool. 1-2 stories, exterior corridors. *Bath:* combo or shower
Country Inn only. **Parking:** on-site. **Terms:** 3 day cancellation notice-fee imposed, package plans - seasonal.
            Amenities: hair dryers. **Dining:** restaurant, see separate listing. **Pool(s):** outdoor. **Leisure Activi-**
ties: ceramics studio. **Guest Services:** gift shop, valet laundry. **Business Services:** meeting rooms, fax (fee). **Cards:** AX, CB,
DC, DS, MC, VI. **Special Amenities: free local telephone calls and free room upgrade (subject to availability with advanced reservations).**   SOME UNITS

[🍽] [♿] [🖨] [🏊] / [VCR] [🛗] [📶] /

GREEN GABLES INN   Phone: (863)676-2511
(AAA) (SAVE)   2/7-4/19   1P: $73-$83   2P: $73-$83
            12/1-12/31   1P: $48-$68   2P: $48-$68
▼▼▼   1/1-2/6   1P: $52-$62   2P: $52-$62
            4/20-11/30   1P: $48-$58   2P: $48-$58
Motel   **Location:** 2 mi n jct US 60. 21380 Hwy 27 33859. Fax: 863/676-3140. **Facility:** 56 one-bedroom standard units.
            1 story, exterior corridors. **Parking:** on-site. **Terms:** cancellation fee imposed. **Amenities:** video library (fee),
hair dryers. **Pool(s):** heated outdoor. **Leisure Activities:** fishing, sun deck, miniature golf, 2 lighted tennis courts, picnic area with
grill, exercise room, basketball. **Guest Services:** coin laundry. **Business Services:** meeting rooms, fax (fee). **Cards:** AX, CB,
DC, DS, MC, VI. **Special Amenities: free local telephone calls and free newspaper.** *(See color ad below)*
                                                                                    SOME UNITS

[S/D] [🍽+] [🏊] [✕] [DATA PORT] [📶] / [✕] [VCR] [🛗] /
                                                                              FEE   FEE

THE GV TILLMAN HOUSE BED & BREAKFAST   Phone: (863)676-5409
▼▼▼   All Year [ECP]   2P: $85-$130   XP: $15
            Location: Just e of US 17, then 0.3 mi n of Central Ave. Located in a quiet, residential area. 301 E Sessoms Ave 33853.
Bed & Breakfast Fax: 863/676-5499. **Facility:** Set on high ground under sprawling, moss-draped oaks, this B&B features col-
            umned verandas overlooking a lawn and a small lake. Designated smoking area. 5 units. 4 one- and 1 two-
bedroom standard units. 2 stories, interior corridors. *Bath:* combo or shower only. **Parking:** on-site. **Terms:** age restrictions may
apply, 7 day cancellation notice, weekly rates available, package plans. **Amenities:** video library. **Cards:** AX, MC, VI.
                                                                                    SOME UNITS

[ASK] [✕] [🖥] / [VCR] [DATA PORT] /

――――― **WHERE TO DINE** ―――――

CHALET SUZANNE RESTAURANT Country Inn   **Lunch:** $19-$46   **Dinner:** $59-$79   Phone: 863/676-6011
(AAA)   **Location:** CR 17A, 1.5 mi e of jct SR 17; in Chalet Suzanne Country Inn & Restaurant. 3800 Chalet Suzanne Dr
▼▼▼   33859. **Hours:** 8 am-8 pm, Fri & Sat-9 pm. **Reservations:** suggested. **Features:** Quaint ambience is the
            overwhelming appeal of this multilevel, lakefront restaurant. Decorated with antiques and memorabilia,
American   each dining room has its own individual charm. Six-course inclusive dinners feature cuisine with a
            Continental flair. Dressy casual; cocktails. **Parking:** on-site. **Cards:** AX, CB, DC, DS, MC, VI.   [🍸] [✕]

LEKARICA RESTAURANT Country Inn   **Lunch:** $6-$12   **Dinner:** $13-$25   Phone: 863/676-8281
▼▼▼   **Location:** From SR 60, 1.8 mi s on US 27, 0.8 mi e on CR 17B, 0.7 mi s on SR 17, then 1 mi e. 1650 S Highland
            Park Dr 33853. **Hours:** 11 am-2 & 6-9 pm, Sun-2 pm. Closed: 1/1; also Mon. **Reservations:** accepted.
American   **Features:** In a refurbished lakeside house, the charming "old Florida" restaurant serves imaginative food in
            a setting that is casual at lunch and more formal at dinner. Entrees include veal, chicken, New Zealand
lamb, steak, pasta and seafood. The signature dessert is a chocolate replica of the Bok Tower, filled with the mousse of the
day. Smoke free premises. Casual dress; cocktails. **Parking:** on-site. **Cards:** AX, DS, MC, VI.   [🍸] [✕]

LAKE WORTH pop. 35,133   (See map p. 757; index p. 760)

─────── WHERE TO STAY ───────

HOLIDAY INN WEST PALM BEACH-TURNPIKE   **Phone:** (561)968-5000   [79]
▼▼▲▲▲▲▼▼   1/17-4/5   1P: $115-$119   2P: $115-$119   XP: $6   F19
           12/20-1/16   1P: $99-$104   2P: $99-$104   XP: $6   F19
Small-scale Hotel 12/1-12/19 & 4/6-11/30 1P: $84-$89   2P: $84-$89   XP: $6   F19
           Location: SR 802, just e of Florida Tpke, exit 93. 7859 Lake Worth Rd 33467. **Fax:** 561/968-2451. **Facility:** 114 one-bedroom standard units. 2 stories (no elevator), interior/exterior corridors. **Parking:** on-site. **Amenities:** high-speed Internet (fee), dual phone lines, voice mail, irons, hair dryers. **Pool(s):** heated outdoor. **Leisure Activities:** tennis court. **Guest Services:** coin laundry. **Business Services:** meeting rooms, fax (fee). **Cards:** AX, CB, DC, DS, JC, MC, VI.
(See color ad opposite inside back cover)
SOME UNITS
[ASK] [S/D] [†] [Y] [⌂] [⇔] [✚] [DATA PORT] [▭] / [✕] [⊟] /
FEE

LAGO MOTOR INN   **Phone:** 561/585-5246   [84]
[AAA] [SAVE] All Year   1P: $50-$72   XP: $10   F10
▲▲▲▲ ▲▲▲▲ **Location:** I-95, exit 63, 0.7 mi e, then just s on US 1; US 1, just s of jct 6th Ave S. 714 S Dixie Hwy 33460.
Motel   Fax: 561/547-2001. **Facility:** 17 one-bedroom standard units, some with efficiencies. 2 stories (no elevator), exterior corridors. **Parking:** on-site. **Terms:** 7 day cancellation notice, pets ($9 extra charge). **Pool(s):** outdoor. **Guest Services:** coin laundry. **Business Services:** fax (fee). **Cards:** MC, VI.
SOME UNITS
[⇤] [⇔] [⊟] / [✕] /

MARTINIQUE MOTOR LODGE   **Phone:** 561/585-2502   [82]
[AAA] [SAVE] 12/1-5/1   1P: $65-$75   2P: $75-$95   XP: $15   F7
▲▲▲▲   5/2-11/30   1P: $45-$55   2P: $55-$65   XP: $10   F7
Motel   **Location:** I-95, exit 63, 0.5 mi e on 6th Ave S, just s. 801 S Dixie Hwy 33460. **Facility:** 19 one-bedroom standard units, some with efficiencies or kitchens. 1-2 stories (no elevator), exterior corridors. *Bath:* combo or shower only. **Parking:** on-site. **Terms:** 7 day cancellation notice-fee imposed, small pets only ($20 deposit, $7 extra charge). **Cards:** AX, MC, VI.
SOME UNITS
[S/D] [⇤] [⊟] / [▣] /

NEW SUN GATE MOTEL   **Phone:** (561)588-8110   [83]
[AAA] [SAVE] 12/1-4/15   1P: $55-$75   2P: $59-$79   XP: $5   F14
▲▲▲▲ ▲▲▲▲ 4/16-5/31 & 10/1-11/30 1P: $36-$56   2P: $41-$61   XP: $5   F14
Motel   6/1-9/30   1P: $34-$56   2P: $39-$61   XP: $5   F14
           Location: I-95, exit 63, 1 mi e on 6th Ave S, just s. 901 S Federal Hwy 33460. **Fax:** 561/588-8041. **Facility:** 36 units. 33 one-bedroom standard units, some with efficiencies. 1 one- and two-bedroom suites ($59-$89), some with kitchens. 2 stories (no elevator), exterior corridors. **Bath:** combo or shower only. **Parking:** on-site. **Terms:** 14 day cancellation notice, 7 day off season, $2 service charge. **Dining:** 8 am-8 pm, Mon-2 pm 10/1-5/31. **Pool(s):** outdoor. **Leisure Activities:** barbecue grills. *Fee:* sauna. **Guest Services:** coin laundry. **Cards:** DC, DS, MC, VI.
SOME UNITS
[S/D] [†] [⇔] [⊡] / [✕] [⊠] [⊞] [⊟] [▣] [▭] /

PARADOR OF THE PALM BEACHES   **Phone:** (561)540-1443   [85]
▼▼▲▲▲▲▼▼   12/1-4/30   1P: $125-$150   2P: $125-$150   XP: $10
           5/1-11/30   1P: $75-$100   2P: $75-$100   XP: $10
Bed & Breakfast **Location:** I-95, exit 63, 1 mi e on 6th Ave S, then 0.5 mi s on SR 5 (Federal Hwy). 1000 S Federal Hwy 33460. **Fax:** 561/547-1243. **Facility:** Two tropical courtyards and spacious accommodations with hand-painted furniture contribute to this mainland hotel's small-island feel. 7 units. 5 one-bedroom standard units. 2 one-bedroom suites. 1 story, interior/exterior corridors. **Parking:** on-site. **Terms:** check-in 4 pm, 14 day cancellation notice-fee imposed, [BP] meal plan available, small pets only (owner's pets on premises). **Amenities:** hair dryers. **Leisure Activities:** bicycles. **Guest Services:** coin laundry. **Business Services:** meeting rooms, fax (fee). **Cards:** AX, MC, VI.
SOME UNITS
[ASK] [S/D] [⇤] [†⦁] [⊘] [⊟] [▣] [▭] / [✕] /

SABAL PALM HOUSE B & B INN   **Phone:** (561)582-1090   [81]
[AAA] [SAVE] 12/15-4/14   2P: $100-$180
▼▼▲▲▲▲▼▼   12/1-12/14 & 4/15-11/30   2P: $75-$150
           Location: Just n of SR 802 at west side of Intracoastal Bridge. 109 N Golfview Rd 33460. **Fax:** 561/582-0933.
Historic Bed **Facility:** Guest rooms named after famous artists and decorated with their work add an unusual touch to this
& Breakfast B&B located along the Intracoastal Waterway. 7 units. 6 one-bedroom standard units, some with whirlpools.
           1 one-bedroom suite with whirlpool. 2 stories, interior/exterior corridors. *Bath:* combo or shower only.
           Parking: street. **Terms:** age restrictions may apply, cancellation fee imposed. **Amenities:** CD players, safes, irons, hair dryers. **Cards:** AX, DS, MC, VI.
[†⦁] [✕] [⊠]

WHITE MANOR MOTEL   **Phone:** (561)582-7437   [86]
▲▲▲▲   2/1-4/15 Wkly   1P: $375   2P: $375   XP: $10   F
           12/1-1/31 & 4/16-11/30 Wkly 1P: $250   2P: $250   XP: $10   F
Motel   **Location:** I-95, exit 63, 1 mi e, 0.8 mi s on SR 5 (Federal Hwy). Located in a quiet area. 1618 S Federal Hwy 33460 (PO Box 427). **Fax:** 561/533-0427. **Facility:** 15 one-bedroom standard units, some with kitchens. 1-2 stories, exterior corridors. *Bath:* combo or shower only. **Parking:** on-site. **Terms:** 14 day cancellation notice-fee imposed, daily rates available, pets ($10-$25 extra charge). **Pool(s):** outdoor. **Guest Services:** coin laundry. **Cards:** MC, VI.
[ASK] [S/D] [⇤] [⇔] [DATA PORT] [⊟]

(See map p. 757)

WHERE TO DINE

BOHEMIAN GARDEN RESTAURANT — **Dinner:** $8-$21 — **Phone:** 561/968-4111 ㊹

(AAA) ♦♦ Steak & Seafood

Location: SR 802, 1 mi w of jct Military Tr. 5450 Lake Worth Rd 33463. **Hours:** 4:30 pm-10 pm, Sun 4 pm-9 pm. **Reservations:** suggested; in season. **Features:** Old World charm can be found in this 53-year-old restaurant with paneled walls and oil paintings of Bohemia. An extensive menu offers chicken, beef and local seafood. The warm spinach salad will help nourish you as well as satisfy your taste buds. Casual dress; cocktails. **Parking:** on-site. **Cards:** AX, CB, DC, DS, MC, VI.

🍸 ⊠

The following restaurants have not been evaluated by AAA but are listed for your information only.

FLANIGAN'S SEAFOOD BAR & GRILL — **Phone:** 561/964-4666

[fyi] Not evaluated. **Location:** 2401 10th Ave N. **Features:** The family-friendly restaurant is known for its baby back ribs, burgers and seafood.

JOHN G'S — **Phone:** 561/585-9860

[fyi] Not evaluated. **Location:** 10 S Ocean Blvd. **Features:** Open for breakfast and lunch. Casual dining with ocean view. Inexpensive.

LANTANA pop. 9,437 (See map p. 757; index p. 760)

WHERE TO STAY

BEST WESTERN INN OF AMERICA — **Phone:** (561)588-0456 (111)

(AAA) [SAVE] ♦♦♦ Small-scale Hotel

All Year [ECP]	1P: $69-$120	2P: $69-$120	XP: $5	F18

Location: I-95, exit 60 (Hypoluxo Rd), just e, then just s. 7051 Seacrest Blvd 33462. Fax: 561/585-0607. **Facility:** 92 one-bedroom standard units. 4 stories, interior corridors. *Bath:* combo or shower only. **Parking:** on-site. **Amenities:** safes (fee), irons, hair dryers. **Pool(s):** heated outdoor. **Guest Services:** coin laundry. **Business Services:** fax (fee). **Cards:** AX, DC, DS, MC, VI. **Special Amenities: early check-in/late check-out and free continental breakfast.**

SOME UNITS

S/D 🍴 ♿M ♿ 👂 🏊 🎥 DATA PORT ☕ / ⊠ ▮ ▣ /

COMFORT INN-LANTANA/BOYNTON BEACH — **Phone:** (561)582-7878 (110)

(AAA) [SAVE] ♦♦♦ Small-scale Hotel

12/1-3/31 [BP]	1P: $75-$129	2P: $75-$129
10/1-11/30 [BP]	1P: $59-$99	2P: $59-$99
4/1-9/30 [BP]	1P: $52-$89	2P: $52-$89

Location: I-95, exit 60, 0.3 mi e. 1221 Hypoluxo Rd 33462. Fax: 561/582-8878. **Facility:** 60 units. 58 one-bedroom standard units, some with whirlpools. 2 one-bedroom suites ($75-$199) with whirlpools. 3 stories, interior corridors. *Bath:* combo or shower only. **Parking:** on-site. **Terms:** weekly rates available. **Amenities:** voice mail, safes, hair dryers. **Pool(s):** small heated outdoor. **Leisure Activities:** exercise room. **Guest Services:** coin laundry. **Business Services:** meeting rooms, fax (fee). **Cards:** AX, CB, DC, DS, MC, VI. **Special Amenities: free continental breakfast and free local telephone calls.** ***(See ad p 255)***

SOME UNITS

S/D 🍴 ♿ 👂 🏊 🎥 DATA PORT ☕ / ⊠ ▮ ▣ /

WHERE TO DINE

ANCHOR INN RESTAURANT — **Dinner:** $14-$26 — **Phone:** 561/965-4794 (55)

♦♦ Steak House

Location: I-95, exit 60, 0.5 mi w. 2810 Hypoluxo Rd 33462. **Hours:** 5 pm-9:30 pm. Closed: 11/27, 12/25. **Reservations:** accepted. **Features:** Long established in the area, the comfortable, casual lakefront restaurant offers a menu featuring such seafood dishes as shrimp scampi and broiled salmon. Other offerings include steak, chicken and chops. Casual dress; cocktails. **Parking:** on-site. **Cards:** AX, MC, VI.

🍸 ⊠

LARGO —*See Tampa Bay p. 920.*

LAUDERDALE-BY-THE-SEA —*See Fort Lauderdale p. 400.*

LAUDERHILL —*See Fort Lauderdale p. 402.*

LEESBURG —*See Orlando p. 742.*

LEHIGH ACRES pop. 33,430

WHERE TO STAY

ADMIRAL LEHIGH GOLF RESORT & SPA — **Phone:** (239)369-2121

(AAA) [SAVE] ♦♦ Small-scale Hotel

1/19-3/31	1P: $105-$115	2P: $105-$115	XP: $6	F
12/1-1/18	1P: $79-$95	2P: $79-$95	XP: $6	F
10/1-11/30	1P: $79-$89	2P: $79-$89	XP: $6	F
4/1-9/30	1P: $69-$89	2P: $69-$89	XP: $6	F

Location: 2.5 mi n on CR 884. 225 E Joel Blvd 33972. Fax: 239/368-1660. **Facility:** 131 one-bedroom standard units. 2 stories, exterior corridors. *Bath:* combo or shower only. **Parking:** on-site. **Terms:** cancellation fee imposed, package plans. **Amenities:** voice mail, hair dryers. *Some:* irons. **Dining:** 4 restaurants, 6:30 am-9 pm, cocktails, entertainment. **Pool(s):** heated outdoor. **Leisure Activities:** saunas, steamrooms, miniature golf, lighted driving range, 2 pro shops, aerobics, jogging, sports court, basketball, shuffleboard. *Fee:* golf-36 holes, golf lessons & demonstration, tanning bed, massage. **Guest Services:** coin laundry, beauty salon. **Business Services:** conference facilities, business center. **Cards:** AX, CB, DC, DS, MC, VI. ***(See color ad p 415)***

SOME UNITS

🍴 🍸 🚶 ♿ 👂 🏊 🏋 ✂ 🎥 DATA PORT ☕ / ⊠ ▮ ▣ /

FEE FEE

LEHIGH RESORT CLUB

Phone: (239)368-2022

AAA SAVE
▼▼ ▼▼
Condominium

12/1-4/11 & 11/1-11/30 Wkly   1P: $575-$700   2P: $575-$700
4/12-10/31 Wkly   1P: $395-$525   2P: $395-$525
Location: 2.5 mi n on CR 884. 231 Joel Blvd 33972. Fax: 239/368-5088. **Facility:** 20 one-bedroom suites, some with efficiencies or kitchens. 2 stories, exterior corridors. **Parking:** on-site. **Terms:** 3 night minimum stay, 3 day cancellation notice-fee imposed. **Amenities:** video library (fee), voice mail, irons. *Some:* hair dryers. **Pool(s):** heated outdoor, wading. **Leisure Activities:** whirlpool, miniature golf, golf cage, 4 lighted tennis courts, racquetball courts, recreation programs, gazebo picnic area, ping pong, playground, exercise room, basketball, horseshoes, shuffleboard, volleyball. *Fee:* fishing & Everglades trips, golf priviliges, game room. **Guest Services:** complimentary laundry. **Business Services:** fax. **Cards:** MC, VI.

SOME UNITS

[🍴] [🏊] [✕] [DATA PORT] [🛏] [📷] [📺] / [VCR] / FEE

─────── **WHERE TO DINE** ───────

INSIDE RESTAURANT AND TOUCAN BAR

Dinner: $12-$26   **Phone:** 239/369-2500

AAA
▼▼ ▼▼
German

Location: 2.8 mi n at jct Joel Blvd. 2305 Lakeview Dr 33972. **Hours:** 4 pm-10 pm. Closed: Mon & 9/1-9/30. **Reservations:** suggested. **Features:** Set on Lake Camille, the German-themed and decorated restaurant presents a menu with such specialties as bratwurst, sauerbraten, Wiener schnitzel, venison goulash and veal stew. An international favorite is grilled duck breast served in gooseberry sauce with gnocchi and red cabbage. Casual dress; cocktails. **Parking:** on-site. **Cards:** AX, DC, MC, VI.

LIGHTHOUSE POINT —See Fort Lauderdale p. 402.

LITTLE TORCH KEY —See The Florida Keys p. 352.

LIVE OAK pop. 6,300

─────── **WHERE TO STAY** ───────

ECONO LODGE

Phone: (386)362-7459

AAA SAVE
▼▼ ▼▼
Small-scale Hotel

All Year   1P: $47-$85   2P: $52-$90   F18
Location: I-10, exit 283, just s on US 129. 6811 N US 129 & I-10 32060 (PO Box 820, 32064). Fax: 386/364-6598. **Facility:** 52 one-bedroom standard units, some with whirlpools. 2 stories, exterior corridors. **Parking:** on-site. **Terms:** 3 day cancellation notice, [CP] meal plan available, pets ($10-$20 extra charge). **Amenities:** *Some:* hair dryers. **Pool(s):** outdoor. **Leisure Activities:** whirlpool, picnic table. **Guest Services:** coin laundry. **Business Services:** meeting rooms, fax (fee). **Cards:** AX, CB, DC, DS, MC, VI. **Special Amenities:** free continental breakfast.

SOME UNITS

[S/D] [🐾] [🍴] [🏊] [❄] / [✕] [🛏] [📷] [📺]

HOLIDAY INN EXPRESS

Phone: (386)362-2600

AAA SAVE
▼▼ ◆ ▼▼
Small-scale Hotel

All Year [ECP]   1P: $69-$149   2P: $69-$149   XP: $10   F19
Location: I-10, exit 283, just s. 6694 US 129 N 32060. Fax: 386/362-4300. **Facility:** 68 one-bedroom standard units. 3 stories, interior corridors. *Bath:* combo or shower only. **Parking:** on-site. **Amenities:** high-speed Internet, dual phone lines, voice mail, irons, hair dryers. **Pool(s):** outdoor. **Leisure Activities:** whirlpool, exercise room. **Guest Services:** valet and coin laundry. **Business Services:** meeting rooms, fax. **Cards:** AX, CB, DC, DS, JC, MC, VI. **Special Amenities:** free continental breakfast and free local telephone calls.

SOME UNITS

[S/D] [🏊] [❄] [DATA PORT] [📺] / [✕] [🛏] [📷]

SUWANNEE RIVER BEST WESTERN INN

Phone: (386)362-6000

AAA SAVE
▼▼ ▼▼
Small-scale Hotel

All Year   1P: $40-$130   2P: $40-$130   XP: $5   F12
Location: I-10, exit 283, 0.3 mi s. 6819 US 129 N 32060. Fax: 386/364-1308. **Facility:** 64 one-bedroom standard units. 2 stories, exterior corridors. **Parking:** on-site. **Terms:** 7 day cancellation notice, [CP] meal plan available, small pets only ($5 extra charge). **Amenities:** voice mail, irons, hair dryers. **Pool(s):** outdoor. **Guest Services:** coin laundry. **Business Services:** fax (fee). **Cards:** AX, CB, DC, DS, JC, MC, VI. **Special Amenities:** early check-in/late check-out and free continental breakfast.

SOME UNITS

[S/D] [🐾] [🍴] [🏊] [❄] [📺] / [✕] [🛏] [📷]

LONGBOAT KEY pop. 7,603   (See map p. 812; index p. 815)

─────── **WHERE TO STAY** ───────

THE COLONY BEACH & TENNIS RESORT

Phone: (941)383-6464   **[67]**

▼▼ ▼▼ ▼▼
Condominium

2/9-4/29   1P: $395-$515   2P: $395-$675   XP: $20   F18
12/1-2/8   1P: $275-$515   2P: $275-$675   XP: $20   F18
10/1-11/30   1P: $275-$395   2P: $275-$460   XP: $20   F18
4/30-9/30   1P: $195-$395   2P: $195-$395   XP: $20   F18
Location: On SR 789, 2 mi n of New Pass Bridge. 1620 Gulf of Mexico Dr 34228. Fax: 941/383-7549. **Facility:** 234 units. 125 one- and 109 two-bedroom suites with kitchens and whirlpools. 3-6 stories, interior/exterior corridors. *Bath:* combo or shower only. **Parking:** on-site. **Terms:** check-in 4 pm, 15 day cancellation notice, [MAP] meal plan available, $50 service charge. **Amenities:** video library, voice mail, safes, irons, hair dryers. **Dining:** The Colony Restaurant, see separate listing. **Pool(s):** heated outdoor. **Leisure Activities:** saunas, whirlpools, steamrooms, fishing, 21 tennis courts (2 lighted), recreation programs, playground, spa. *Fee:* sailboats, snorkeling, bicycles, personal fitness training. **Guest Services:** gift shop, valet and coin laundry, area transportation (fee). **Business Services:** conference facilities, business center. **Cards:** AX, DC, DS, MC, VI.

SOME UNITS

[ASK] [♿] [🍴] [🍸] [📶] [👨‍🦽] [🏊] [♨] [✕] [❄] [DATA PORT] [🛏] [📷] [📺] / [VCR] / FEE

(See map p. 812)

DIPLOMAT RESORT

Phone: 941/383-3791 66

Property failed to provide current rates

Condominium

Location: On SR 789, 3.7 mi n of New Pass Bridge. 3155 Gulf of Mexico Dr 34228. Fax: 941/383-0983. **Facility:** 50 units. 48 one- and 2 two-bedroom suites with kitchens. 2 stories, exterior corridors. **Parking:** on-site. **Amenities:** voice mail. *Some:* irons, hair dryers. **Pool(s):** heated outdoor. **Leisure Activities:** fishing. **Guest Services:** coin laundry. **Business Services:** fax (fee). **Cards:** DS, MC, VI.

HARBOUR VILLA CLUB

Phone: (941)383-9544 60

1/1-4/30 Wkly	1P: $1895	2P: $1895	XP: $20
11/1-11/30 Wkly	1P: $1335	2P: $1335	
12/1-12/31 Wkly	1P: $1335	2P: $1335	XP: $20
5/1-10/31 Wkly	1P: $975	2P: $975	

Condominium **Location:** 4 mi s of jct SR 684, just e of SR 789. 615 Dream Island Rd 34228. Fax: 941/383-8028. **Facility:** 14 two-bedroom suites with kitchens and whirlpools. 3 stories, exterior corridors. **Parking:** on-site. **Terms:** check-in 4 pm, 7 night minimum stay, 21 day cancellation notice-fee imposed, 9% service charge. **Amenities:** voice mail, irons. *Some:* CD players. **Pool(s):** heated outdoor. **Leisure Activities:** whirlpool, fishing, 4 tennis courts (2 lighted), barbecue grills. *Fee:* marina. **Guest Services:** complimentary laundry. **Business Services:** fax. **Cards:** AX, MC, VI. **Special Amenities:** preferred room (subject to availability with advanced reservations).

SOME UNITS

(See map p. 812)

HILTON LONGBOAT KEY BEACHFRONT RESORT
Phone: (941)383-2451 — 64

(AAA) (SAVE)
◆◆◆◆ ◆◆◆

12/1-12/31 & 1/13-4/30	1P: $210-$345	2P: $210-$345	XP: $25	F18
1/1-1/12	1P: $185-$290	2P: $185-$290	XP: $25	F18
5/1-11/30	1P: $155-$260	2P: $155-$260	XP: $25	F18

Location: On SR 789, 6.2 mi n of New Pass Bridge. 4711 Gulf of Mexico Dr 34228. Fax: 941/383-7979. **Facility:** 102 **Small-scale Hotel** one-bedroom standard units, some with efficiencies (no utensils). 5 stories, interior/exterior corridors. *Bath:* combo or shower only. **Parking:** on-site. **Terms:** 7 day cancellation notice-fee imposed. **Amenities:** voice mail, safes, honor bars, irons, hair dryers. **Dining:** 7 am-10 pm, cocktails. **Pool(s):** heated outdoor. **Leisure Activities:** rental boats, rental sailboats, recreation programs in summer, volleyball. *Fee:* cabanas, hobie cats, aqua cycle, water bikes, bicycles. **Guest Services:** gift shop, valet laundry, area transportation-St. Armands Circle Shops. **Business Services:** conference facilities, fax. **Cards:** AX, DC, DS, JC, MC, VI. *(See color ad p 491)*

SOME UNITS / FEE

HOLIDAY INN HOTEL & SUITES
Phone: (941)383-3771 — 62

(AAA) (SAVE)
◆◆◆◆ ◆◆◆

2/1-4/30	1P: $229-$399	2P: $229-$399	XP: $15	F18
12/1-1/31	1P: $199-$399	2P: $199-$399	XP: $15	F18
5/1-11/30	1P: $169-$289	2P: $169-$289	XP: $15	F18

Location: On SR 789, 6.5 mi n of New Pass Bridge. 4949 Gulf of Mexico Dr 34228. Fax: 941/383-7871. **Facility:** The **Resort** gulf locale enhances this property's appeal and its well known "Holidome," a tropically decorated area. Many **Large-scale Hotel** recreational facilities are on-site. 146 units. 121 one-bedroom standard units. 25 one-bedroom suites, some with efficiencies and/or whirlpools. 2-3 stories, interior/exterior corridors. *Bath:* combo or shower only. **Parking:** on-site. **Terms:** check-in 3:30 pm, 3 day cancellation notice-fee imposed. **Amenities:** video games, voice mail, safes, irons, hair dryers. *Some:* CD players, dual phone lines. **Dining:** 3 restaurants, 6:30 am-10 pm, cocktails. **Pool(s):** heated outdoor, heated indoor, wading. **Leisure Activities:** saunas, whirlpool, rental paddleboats, fishing, putting green, 4 lighted tennis courts, billiards, ping pong, exercise room, shuffleboard, volleyball. *Fee:* sailboats, cabanas, aqua cycles, boogie boards, hobie cats, kayaks, bicycles, massage, game room. **Guest Services:** gift shop, valet and coin laundry. **Business Services:** conference facilities, fax (fee). **Cards:** AX, CB, DC, DS, MC, VI. *(See color ad opposite inside back cover)*

SOME UNITS

THE RESORT AT LONGBOAT KEY CLUB
Phone: (941)383-8821 — 69

(AAA) (SAVE)
◆◆◆◆ ◆◆◆◆

12/1-4/30	1P: $295-$1150	2P: $295-$1150	XP: $15	F17
5/1-5/31 & 10/1-11/30	1P: $305-$575	2P: $305-$575	XP: $15	F17
6/1-9/30	1P: $190-$550	2P: $190-$550	XP: $15	F17

Location: SR 789, just n of New Pass Bridge. 301 Gulf of Mexico Dr 34228. Fax: 941/383-0359. **Facility:** All units **Resort** at this gulfside resort have a private balcony and most have a washer and dryer; a harborside complex is **Condominium** north of the main property. 229 units. 155 one-bedroom standard units, some with efficiencies. 23 one- and 51 two-bedroom suites with kitchens. 4-10 stories, exterior corridors. **Parking:** on-site. **Terms:** 14 day cancellation notice-fee imposed, package plans. **Amenities:** video games, CD players, high-speed Internet (fee), dual phone lines, voice mail, safes, honor bars, irons, hair dryers. **Dining:** 5 restaurants, 7 am-midnight, cocktails, entertainment. **Pool(s):** heated outdoor. **Leisure Activities:** whirlpool, snorkeling, recreation programs, kids club aerobics class, beach volleyball, yoga, pilates, library, bicycles, jogging, playground, basketball. *Fee:* canoes, paddleboats, hobie cats, kayaks, golf-45 holes, golf lessons, 38 tennis courts (6 lighted), adult tennis clinic, massage. **Guest Services:** sundries, valet and coin laundry, area transportation-within 5 mi, golf & tennis pro shops. **Business Services:** conference facilities, business center. **Cards:** AX, DC, MC, VI. **Special Amenities:** free local telephone calls and free newspaper. *(See ad p 491)*

SOME UNITS
FEE

RIVIERA BEACH RESORT
Phone: 941/383-2552 — 61

◆◆◆ ◆◆◆

2/1-5/3	1P: $170
12/24-1/31	1P: $150
12/1-12/23 & 5/4-11/30	1P: $120

Motel
Location: On SR 684 (Cortez Rd). 5451 Gulf of Mexico Dr 34228. Fax: 941/383-2245. **Facility:** 9 units. 7 one- and 2 two-bedroom standard units with kitchens. 1 story, exterior corridors. **Parking:** on-site. **Terms:** 4-7 night minimum stay, 30 day cancellation notice-fee imposed, small pets only ($100 deposit, $10 extra charge). **Amenities:** *Some:* irons, hair dryers. **Pool(s):** heated outdoor. **Leisure Activities:** whirlpool, shuffleboard. **Guest Services:** coin laundry. **Business Services:** fax. **Cards:** AX, MC, VI.

TURTLE CRAWL INN
Phone: (941)383-3788 — 65

◆◆◆ ◆◆◆

1/1-4/30	1P: $175-$357	2P: $175-$357	XP: $15	F5
12/1-12/31 & 5/1-11/30	1P: $110-$325	2P: $110-$325	XP: $15	F5

Motel
Location: On SR 789, 5.5 mi n of New Pass Bridge. 4235 Gulf of Mexico Dr 34228. **Facility:** Designated smoking area. 29 units. 26 one- and 3 two-bedroom standard units with kitchens. 5 stories, exterior corridors. **Parking:** on-site. **Terms:** 1-3 night minimum stay - seasonal, 60 day cancellation notice-fee imposed, weekly rates available. **Pool(s):** heated outdoor. **Leisure Activities:** putting green, shuffleboard. **Guest Services:** coin laundry. **Business Services:** fax (fee). **Cards:** DS, MC, VI.

———— WHERE TO DINE ————

CAFE ON THE BAY
Lunch: $12-$18   Dinner: $15-$26   Phone: 941/383-0440 — 30

◆◆◆ ◆◆◆

American
Location: Gulf of Mexico Dr; just e on Bay Isles Pkwy, then just s; in The Moorings. 2630 Harbourside Dr 34228. **Hours:** 11 am-3 & 5:30-9 pm, Sat 8:30 am-3 & 5:30-10 pm, Sun 9 am-3 & 5:30-9 pm. **Reservations:** accepted. **Features:** You may come by car or come by boat to this waterside eatery and then relax to enjoy the freshest ingredients combined into attractive and hearty dishes. Casual dress; cocktails. **Parking:** on-site. **Cards:** AX, DC, DS, MC, VI.

(See map p. 812)

THE COLONY RESTAURANT   Lunch: $9-$16   Dinner: $20-$38   Phone: 941/383-5558   ④⓪
▼▼▼▼   **Location:** On SR 789, 2 mi n of New Pass Bridge; in The Colony Beach & Tennis Resort. 1620 Gulf of Mexico Dr
American   34228. **Hours:** 7 am-10 pm. **Reservations:** suggested. **Features:** Adjacent to the sparkling gulf, the restaurant boasts an original, lavish menu of contemporary Continental dishes and an extensive wine list. Fresh seafood is always popular. Live entertainment contributes to the dining experience. Dressy casual; cocktails. **Parking:** valet. **Cards:** AX, DC, DS, MC, VI.

EUPHEMIA HAYE   Dinner: $20-$38   Phone: 941/383-3633   ㉞
▼▼▼   **Location:** On SR 789, 7.8 mi n of New Pass Bridge. 5540 Gulf of Mexico Dr 34228. **Hours:** 5 pm-10 pm, Fri &
   Sat-10:30 pm; hours vary off season. Haye Loft dessert lounge 6 pm-11 pm. Closed: 9/3-9/30.
Continental   **Reservations:** suggested. **Features:** The eclectic and creative menu features such delicacies as roast duckling served over stuffing with a seasonal fruit sauce. The clean, comfortable dining room, tasty food and thoughtful service should want diners to mark their maps for the next trip to town. Smoke free premises. Casual dress; cocktails; entertainment. **Parking:** on-site. **Cards:** CB, DC, DS, MC, VI.

HARRY'S CONTINENTAL KITCHENS   Lunch: $7-$19   Dinner: $19-$32   Phone: 941/383-0777   ㉟
▼▼▼ ▼▼▼   **Location:** Just e of SR 789; 4.7 mi s of jct SR 684 (Cortez Rd). 525 St Judes Dr 34228. **Hours:** 11 am-2:30 &
   5-9:30 pm, Sun 10 am-3 & 5-9:30 pm; call for off season hours. Closed: 12/25. **Reservations:** suggested.
Continental   **Features:** Pleasant, professional service and an innovative menu with fresh herbs, homemade soups and delectable desserts make this quaint, tropical eatery perfect for a gourmet seafood meal. The entire dining area is designated as non-smoking. Smoke free premises. Casual dress; cocktails. **Parking:** on-site. **Cards:** AX, MC, VI.

LYNCHES LANDING BAR & GRILL   Lunch: $7-$27   Dinner: $7-$27   Phone: 941/383-0791   ㊳
(AAA)   **Location:** On SR 789, 5 mi n of New Pass Bridge. 4000 Gulf of Mexico Dr 34228. **Hours:** 11:30 am-midnight.
▼▼▼   Closed: 11/27, 12/25; also 6/1-6/14, 9/6-10/1 & Sun off season. **Reservations:** suggested; in season.
   Features: An Irish theme carries through the energetic restaurant, which offers open-air dining overlooking the Gulf of Mexico. Although Irish food is the primary draw, the Key lime pie is outstanding. After eating,
Irish   walk off a few calories on the beach just across the road and enjoy a beautiful sunset. Casual dress; cocktails. **Parking:** on-site. **Cards:** AX, CB, DC, DS, MC, VI.

MAUREEN RESTAURANT & MARTINI BAR   Dinner: $17-$25   Phone: 941/383-7774   ㉟
▼▼▼   **Location:** On SR 789, 7 mi n of New Pass Bridge; in Centre Shops. 5350 Gulf of Mexico Dr 34228. **Hours:** 5:30
   pm-10 pm. Closed: Mon & Tues. **Features:** A trendy decor incorporates melon-colored walls with
Continental   interesting artwork, and sets the right mood for adult fine dining. Creatively prepared and displayed entrees including seafood, lamb, and steak, feature carpaccio and a fabulous bouillabaisse. Dressy casual; cocktails. **Parking:** on-site. **Cards:** AX, DC, DS, MC, VI.

POSEIDON OCEAN HARVEST RESTAURANT   Dinner: $18-$31   Phone: 941/383-2500   ㊳
▼▼▼   **Location:** On SR 789, 4 mi n of New Pass Bridge. 3454 Gulf of Mexico Dr 34228. **Hours:** 5:30 pm-10 pm. Closed:
   1/1. **Reservations:** suggested. **Features:** You will find fine dining in a scenic locale on Sarasota Bay.
Seafood   Order the shrimp cocktail for an appetizer and try the colorfully presented swordfish as an entree. Attentive servers make you feel immediately welcome and comfortable. Casual dress; cocktails. **Parking:** on-site.
Cards: AX, CB, DC, DS, MC, VI.

LONG KEY —*See The Florida Keys p. 352.*

LONGWOOD —*See Orlando p. 743.*

LOXAHATCHEE

————— **WHERE TO STAY** —————

SOUTHERN PALM BED & BREAKFAST   Phone: (561)790-1413

▼▼▼	1/1-5/15	1P: $125	2P: $125	XP: $10 F
	12/1-12/31	1P: $99	2P: $99	XP: $10 F
Bed & Breakfast	5/16-11/30	1P: $63	2P: $63	XP: $10 F

   Location: SR 7, 4.4 mi w on Southern Blvd, SR 90/S US 441 to D Rd, then left on Collection Canal Rd, just right on C Rd. 15130 Southern Palm Way 33470. Fax: 561/791-3035. **Facility:** A small pond can be seen from all rooms and balconies of this B&B in a quiet, country setting; furnishings include a variety of antiques. Smoke free premises. 6 one-bedroom standard units. 2 stories (no elevator), interior/exterior corridors. **Parking:** on-site. **Terms:** 3 night minimum stay, age restrictions may apply, 7 day cancellation notice-fee imposed, [ECP] meal plan available. **Amenities:** hair dryers. *Some:* CD players. **Guest Services:** coin laundry. **Cards:** AX, DS, MC.

MACCLENNY pop. 4,459

————— **WHERE TO STAY** —————

ECONO LODGE   Phone: (904)259-3000
(AAA) (SAVE)   All Year   1P: $47-$85   2P: $52-$85   XP: $5   F18
▼▼ ▼▼   **Location:** I-10, exit 335, just s of jct SR 121. I-10 & SR 121 32063 (PO Box 425). Fax: 904/259-4418. **Facility:** 53
Motel   one-bedroom standard units, some with whirlpools. 2 stories, exterior corridors. **Parking:** on-site. **Terms:** small pets only. **Pool(s):** outdoor. **Leisure Activities:** whirlpool. **Guest Services:** coin laundry. **Business Services:** meeting rooms, fax (fee). **Cards:** AX, CB, DC, DS, MC, VI. **Special Amenities:** free continental breakfast.

SOME UNITS

MADEIRA BEACH —*See Tampa Bay p. 920.*

MADISON pop. 3,061

------ WHERE TO STAY ------

HOLIDAY INN EXPRESS-I-10 MADISON
All Year   1P: $75-$95   2P: $75-$95   XP: $5   F18
Phone: (850)973-2020
Location: I-10, exit 258, just n. Rt 5 Box 3200 32340. **Fax:** 850/973-3366. **Facility:** 60 one-bedroom standard
Small-scale Hotel units, some with whirlpools. 3 stories, interior corridors. *Bath:* combo or shower only. **Parking:** on-site.
Terms: [ECP] meal plan available. **Amenities:** irons, hair dryers. **Pool(s):** outdoor. **Guest Services:** valet
and coin laundry. **Business Services:** meeting rooms, fax (fee). **Cards:** AX, CB, DC, DS, JC, MC, VI.

SOME UNITS

MAITLAND —See Orlando p. 744.

MANALAPAN pop. 321 (See map p. 757; index p. 760)

------ WHERE TO STAY ------

THE RITZ-CARLTON, PALM BEACH
12/15-5/1   1P: $395-$875   2P: $395-$875
Phone: (561)533-6000   [94]
12/1-12/14   1P: $295-$405   2P: $295-$405
5/2-11/30   1P: $225-$395   2P: $225-$395
Location: On SR A1A, 9 mi s of Palm Beach. 100 S Ocean Blvd 33462. **Fax:** 561/588-4202. **Facility:** The Ritz-
Large-scale Hotel Carlton's elegant ocean- or garden-view rooms all feature either a balcony or patio. 270 units. 215 one-
bedroom standard units. 55 one-bedroom suites ($725-$5000), some with whirlpools. 5-6 stories, interior
corridors. **Parking:** on-site (fee) and valet. **Terms:** cancellation fee imposed, [BP] meal plan available. **Amenities:** CD players,
dual phone lines, voice mail, safes, honor bars, irons, hair dryers. *Fee:* video games, high-speed Internet. *Some:* DVD players,
fax. **Dining:** 2 restaurants, 6:30 am-11 pm; to midnight in season, cocktails, also, The Grill, see separate listing, entertainment.
Pool(s): heated outdoor. **Leisure Activities:** saunas, whirlpool, steamrooms, rental sailboats, snorkeling, recreation programs,
bicycles, exercise room, spa, basketball, volleyball. *Fee:* scuba diving, charter fishing, jet skis, scuba instruction, parasailing, golf
privilges, 6 tennis courts, tennis instruction. **Guest Services:** gift shop, valet laundry, area transportation (fee)-within 9 mi, beauty
salon. **Business Services:** conference facilities, business center. **Cards:** AX, CB, DC, DS, MC, VI. **Special Amenities:** free
newspaper.

SOME UNITS

------ WHERE TO DINE ------

THE GRILL
Dinner: $20-$38   **Phone:** 561/533-6000   [51]
Location: On SR A1A, 9 mi s of Palm Beach; in The Ritz-Carlton, Palm Beach. 100 S Ocean Blvd 33462. **Hours:** 6
Steak & Seafood pm-10 pm. Closed: Sun & Mon. **Features:** An elegant club-like setting with warm wood tones and original
oil paintings features professional service, fresh seafood and aged beef. A nice tureen presentation of the
vichyssoise and a wonderful roasted rack of lamb are menu signatures. Semi-formal attire; cocktails;
entertainment. **Parking:** valet. **Cards:** AX, CB, DC, DS, JC, MC, VI.

MARATHON —See The Florida Keys p. 353.

MARCO ISLAND pop. 14,879

------ WHERE TO STAY ------

HILTON MARCO ISLAND BEACH RESORT
12/24-4/30   1P: $239-$379   2P: $239-$379   XP: $25   F18
Phone: (239)394-5000
12/1-12/23   1P: $199-$379   2P: $199-$379   XP: $25   F18
5/1-5/31   1P: $179-$299   2P: $179-$299   XP: $25   F18
6/1-11/30   1P: $139-$299   2P: $139-$299   XP: $25   F18
Resort **Location:** I-75, exit 101, 1 mi s of SR 92. 560 S Collier Blvd 34145. **Fax:** 239/394-5251. **Facility:** The re-
Large-scale Hotel sort offers large rooms with balconies, elegant public areas and such recreational opportunities as jet skiing
and parasailing. 297 units. 271 one-bedroom standard units. 26 one-bedroom suites, some with whirlpools.
11 stories, interior corridors. *Bath:* combo or shower only. **Parking:** on-site and valet. **Terms:** 7 day cancellation notice-fee imposed, $9 service charge. **Amenities:** video games (fee), voice mail, safes, honor bars, irons, hair dryers. *Some:* high-speed In-
ternet (fee). **Dining:** 2 restaurants, 11 am-5 pm, cocktails, also, Sandcastles, see separate listing, entertainment. **Pool(s):** heated
outdoor. **Leisure Activities:** sauna, whirlpool, recreation programs. *Fee:* sailboats, windsurfing, waterskiing, charter fishing, parasailing, sea kayaks, waverunners, 3 lighted tennis courts, massage, game room. **Guest Services:** gift shop, complimentary
evening beverages: Mon, valet laundry. **Business Services:** conference facilities, business center. **Special Amenities:** free
local telephone calls and free newspaper.

SOME UNITS

MARCO ISLAND MARRIOTT RESORT, GOLF CLUB & SPA
Phone: 239/394-2511
12/26-5/3 & 9/28-11/30   1P: $275-$385   2P: $275-$385
5/4-9/27   1P: $255-$385   2P: $255-$385
12/1-12/25   1P: $190-$260   2P: $190-$260
Location: I-75, exit 101, 0.5 mi s of SR 92. 400 S Collier Blvd (SR 951) 34145. **Fax:** 239/642-2672. **Facility:** Bou-
Resort tiques and large rooms with balconies are features at this beachfront facility overlooking the gulf. 735 units.
Large-scale Hotel 673 one-bedroom standard units. 32 one- and 30 two-bedroom suites ($550-$2500), some with whirlpools.
11 stories, interior corridors. *Bath:* combo or shower only. **Parking:** on-site and valet. **Terms:** check-in 4 pm,
1-5 night minimum stay, 7 day cancellation notice-fee imposed, package plans - seasonal. **Amenities:** voice mail, safes, honor
bars, irons, hair dryers. *Fee:* video games, high-speed Internet. **Dining:** 6 restaurants, 7 am-midnight, cocktails, entertainment.
Pool(s): outdoor, 2 heated outdoor, wading. **Leisure Activities:** whirlpool, rental sailboats, tennis & golf instruction, recreation
programs, playground, exercise room, spa. *Fee:* charter fishing, parasailing, waverunners, golf-18 holes, miniature golf, 16 tennis
courts (4 lighted), bicycles. **Guest Services:** gift shop, valet and coin laundry, area transportation (fee). **Business Services:**
conference facilities, business center. **Cards:** AX, CB, DC, DS, JC, MC, VI.

SOME UNITS

RADISSON SUITE BEACH RESORT ON MARCO ISLAND　　　Phone: (239)394-4100

(AAA) (SAVE) ▽▽▽▽	12/21-4/19	1P: $229-$469	2P: $229-$469	XP: $10	F
	4/20-5/25	1P: $139-$279	2P: $139-$279	XP: $10	F
	5/26-11/30	1P: $109-$279	2P: $109-$279	XP: $10	F
	12/1-12/20	1P: $105-$275	2P: $105-$275	XP: $10	F

Large-scale Hotel Location: I-75, exit 101, 1 mi s of SR 92. 600 S Collier Blvd (SR 951) 34145. Fax: 239/394-0419. **Facility:** 268 units. 59 one-bedroom standard units. 163 one- and 46 two-bedroom suites with kitchens, some with whirlpools. 14 stories, exterior corridors. *Bath:* combo or shower only. **Parking:** on-site and valet. **Terms:** check-in 4 pm, 3 day cancellation notice, $9 service charge. **Amenities:** high-speed Internet (fee), voice mail, safes, irons, hair dryers. **Dining:** 2 restaurants, 7 am-11 pm, cocktails. **Pool(s):** heated outdoor. **Leisure Activities:** whirlpool, lighted tennis court, recreation programs, exercise room, basketball, volleyball. *Fee:* sailboats, windsurfing, waterskiing, parasailing, waverunners, bicycles. **Guest Services:** gift shop, coin laundry. **Business Services:** conference facilities, business center. **Cards:** AX, CB, DC, DS, MC, VI. **Special Amenities:** free local telephone calls and free newspaper. *(See color ad below)*

SOME UNITS

(icons) / (icons) FEE

THE SURF CLUB OF MARCO　　　Phone: 239/642-5800

(SAVE) ▽▽▽▽	2/1-4/25 Wkly	1P: $2100-$2310
	12/1-1/3 Wkly	1P: $1295-$2275
	1/4-1/31 Wkly	1P: $1435-$1715
Condominium	4/26-11/30 Wkly	1P: $1400-$1540

Location: I-75, exit 101, 0.9 mi s of SR 92. 540 S Collier Blvd (SR 951) 34145. Fax: 239/642-7245. **Facility:** 44 two-bedroom suites with kitchens. 8 stories, exterior corridors. **Parking:** on-site. **Terms:** 30 day cancellation notice, daily rates available, 2% service charge. **Amenities:** safes, irons, hair dryers. **Pool(s):** heated outdoor. **Leisure Activities:** whirlpool, 3 tennis courts. **Guest Services:** gift shop, coin laundry. **Business Services:** meeting rooms, fax (fee). **Cards:** AX, DS, MC, VI. *(See color ad p 805)*

(icons)

——— WHERE TO DINE ———

ARTURO'S ITALIAN RESTAURANT　　Dinner: $10-$23　　Phone: 239/642-0550

▽▽▽ Italian

Location: Just n of SR 951. 844 Bald Eagle Dr 34145. **Hours:** 5 pm-9:30 pm. Closed: 4/20, 11/27, 12/25; also 6/1-6/28. **Reservations:** suggested. **Features:** Casual, comfortable dining is what to expect at this bustling restaurant. Such well-prepared traditional dishes as bruscetta and the signature mozzarella and prociutto stuffed pork chop boast a flavorful taste and colorful presentation. Casual dress; beer & wine only. **Parking:** on-site. **Cards:** MC, VI.

(icons)

BAVARIAN INN　　Dinner: $10-$20　　Phone: 239/394-7233

▽▽ German

Location: 1.1 mi se of SR 92; just off Collier Blvd. 960 Winterberry Dr 34145. **Hours:** 4:30 pm-11 pm. Closed: 12/24 & Mon 5/1-10/30. **Reservations:** suggested; 11/1-4/30. **Features:** Large portions of wholesome food are offered at reasonable prices in a casual Bavarian-style setting. The German-American cuisine includes prime rib, steak and seafood selections, as well as unique appetizers like hot, delicious pretzel bread. Casual dress; cocktails. **Parking:** on-site. **Cards:** AX, CB, DC, DS, MC, VI.

(icons)

KONRAD'S SEAFOOD & GRILLE ROOM　　Lunch: $8-$11　　Dinner: $13-$35　　Phone: 239/642-3332

▽▽ Steak & Seafood

Location: 1 mi s of SR 92; in Mission Plaza. 599 S Collier Blvd 34145. **Hours:** 5 pm-10 pm. Closed: 12/24, 12/25; also Super Bowl Sun. **Reservations:** suggested. **Features:** A slightly upscale ambience hangs in the air at this neoclassically decorated restaurant. The flavorful oak-grilled salmon is popular, as is the marinated flank steak with stuffed shrimp, plum tomatoes and cilantro. Jazz musicians perform seasonally. Dressy casual; cocktails. **Parking:** on-site. **Cards:** AX, DC, DS, MC, VI.

(icons)

MAREKS COLLIER HOUSE RESTAURANT   Historic   **Dinner:** $19-$27   **Phone:** 239/642-9948
(AAA)
             Location: 1.2 mi n of SR 951. 1121 Bald Eagle Dr 34145. **Hours:** Open 12/1-7/31 & 9/25-11/30; 5:30 pm-9:30
🔻🔻🔻   pm. Closed: Sun 9/25-12/30. **Reservations:** suggested. **Features:** In restored historic home of Capt. Bill
             Collier, this intimate restaurant has three dining areas: a main room, cozy library and quaint veranda. The
Continental chef prepares imaginative gourmet fare, such as Maine lobster, Thermidor, lamb and duckling. Smoke free
             premises. Dressy casual; beer & wine only. **Parking:** on-site. **Cards:** AX, DC, DS, MC, VI.
                                                                                                            ⊠

SANDCASTLES   **Dinner:** $18-$26   **Phone:** 239/394-5000
🔻🔻🔻   **Location:** I-75, exit 101, 1 mi s of SR 92; in Marco Island Hilton Beach Resort. 560 S Collier Blvd 33415. **Hours:** 5
             pm-10 pm. Closed: Sun-Thurs 5/1-12/22. **Reservations:** suggested. **Features:** This intimate and classy
American   restaurant is known for fine dining with many upscale specialties, including entrees of beef, veal, lamb and
             seafood. A good selection of decadent desserts; creme brulee, strawberry shortcake or Milky Way pie tame
the sweet tooth. Dressy casual; cocktails; entertainment. **Parking:** street. **Cards:** AX, DC, DS, JC, MC, VI.
                                                                                                      🍸 ⊠

THE SNOOK INN   **Lunch:** $8-$10   **Dinner:** $8-$20   **Phone:** 239/394-3313
🔻   **Location:** SR 951, 2.5 mi n. 1215 Bald Eagle Dr 34145. **Hours:** 11 am-10 pm. Closed major holidays.
             Features: Enjoy a drink at the bar while you take in a view of the Marco River. A casual nautical theme
Seafood   includes a large aquarium and tabletops inset with sand, shells and faux pieces of eight. The menu offers
             an abundance of fresh seafood, steak, sandwiches and appetizers. Casual dress; cocktails; entertainment.
Parking: on-site. **Cards:** AX, DC, DS, MC, VI.
                                                                                                      🍸 ⊠

VERDI'S - AN AMERICAN BISTRO   **Dinner:** $17-$28   **Phone:** 239/394-5533
🔻🔻🔻   **Location:** From jct SR 951 and Bald Eagle Dr, 1 mi s; in Sand Dollar Plaza. 241 N Collier Blvd 34145. **Hours:** Open
             12/1-7/31 & 10/1-11/30; 5:30 pm-9:30 pm; 6 pm-9:30 pm 5/1-7/31. Closed: 4/20, 12/25; also Sun; also Mon
American   6/1-7/31. **Reservations:** suggested. **Features:** Created with imagination and detail, the chef's fresh
             seafood and meat and pasta entrees are complemented by choices off the wine list. The dining room
decor evokes a cozy feel. Smoke free premises. Dressy casual; beer & wine only. **Parking:** on-site. **Cards:** DC, DS, MC, VI.
                                                                                                            ⊠

MARGATE —*See Fort Lauderdale p. 402.*

MARIANNA pop. 6,230

——— WHERE TO STAY ———

BEST WESTERN MARIANNA INN   **Phone:** (850)526-5666
(AAA) [SAVE]   All Year [ECP]   1P: $49-$59   2P: $59-$79   XP: $5   F18
🔻🔻🔻   **Location:** I-10, exit 142, 0.3 mi s. 2086 Hwy 71 S 32448 (PO Box 980, 32447). Fax: 850/482-2287. **Facility:** 80 one-
             bedroom standard units. 2 stories, exterior corridors. **Parking:** on-site. **Terms:** small pets only ($5 extra
             charge, in smoking units). **Amenities:** irons, hair dryers. **Pool(s):** outdoor. **Guest Services:** coin laundry.
Small-scale Hotel **Business Services:** fax. **Cards:** AX, CB, DC, DS, MC, VI. **Special Amenities:** early check-in/late
             check-out and free continental breakfast.
                                                                                             SOME UNITS
                               [S🅳] [🛏] [🍴] [🏊] [🐾] [📺] /[⊠][📶][🖼] /

COMFORT INN   **Phone:** (850)526-5600
(AAA) [SAVE]   6/1-11/30   1P: $69-$99   2P: $69-$99   XP: $7   F17
             3/1-4/5   1P: $69-$89   2P: $69-$89   XP: $7   F17
🔻🔻🔻   12/1-2/28 & 4/6-5/31   1P: $59-$69   2P: $59-$69   XP: $7   F17
Small-scale Hotel **Location:** I-10, exit 142, just n. 2175 Hwy 71 S 32448. Fax: 850/482-7899. **Facility:** 80 one-bedroom standard
             units. 2 stories, exterior corridors. **Parking:** on-site. **Terms:** [CP] meal plan available, pets ($7-$12 extra
             charge. **Amenities:** Some: irons, hair dryers. **Pool(s):** outdoor. **Guest Services:** coin laundry. **Business
Services:** fax (fee). **Cards:** AX, CB, DC, DS, MC, VI. **Special Amenities:** free continental breakfast and free local telephone
calls.
                                                                                             SOME UNITS
                               [S🅳] [🐴] [🍴] [🏊] [🐾] [DATA PORT] [📺] /[⊠][📶][🖼] /

HAMPTON INN   **Phone:** (850)526-1006
[SAVE]   All Year [ECP]   1P: $69-$84   2P: $72-$89
             Location: I-10, exit 142, just nw. 2185 Hwy 71 S 32448 (PO Box 698, 32447). Fax: 850/526-1824. **Facility:** 70 one-
🔻🔻🔻   bedroom standard units. 2 stories, exterior corridors. *Bath:* combo or shower only. **Parking:** on-site.
             Terms: daily rates available. **Amenities:** voice mail, irons. **Pool(s):** outdoor. **Guest Services:** coin laundry.
Small-scale Hotel **Business Services:** fax (fee). **Cards:** AX, CB, DC, DS, JC, MC, VI.
                                                                                             SOME UNITS
                               [S🅳] [🍴] [🏊] [🐾] [📺] [DATA PORT] [📶][🖼] [📺] /[⊠] /
                                                 FEE

HINSON HOUSE BED & BREAKFAST   **Phone:** 850/526-1500
🔻🔻🔻   All Year   1P: $55-$85   2P: $55-$85   XP: $7   F10
             Location: Just w of downtown center. 4338 Lafayette St 32446. Fax: 850/482-4449. **Facility:** It's Christmas all year
Bed & Breakfast at this service-oriented property where the holiday decorations never come down; guests may access a
             stocked refrigerator. Designated smoking area. 5 one-bedroom standard units. 2 stories, interior/exterior cor-
ridors. **Parking:** on-site. **Terms:** check-in 4 pm, cancellation fee imposed, [BP] meal plan available. **Cards:** AX, DS, MC, VI.
                                             [ASK] [S🅳] [🔛] [🍴] [⊠] [🐾]

MICROTEL INN & SUITES   **Phone:** (850)526-5005
🔻🔻🔻 🔻🔻 All Year [ECP]   1P: $61-$69   2P: $61-$69   XP: $5   F16
             Location: I-10, exit 142, just n. 4959 White Tail Dr 32448. Fax: 850/526-5003. **Facility:** 64 one-bedroom standard
Small-scale Hotel units, some with whirlpools. 3 stories, interior corridors. *Bath:* combo or shower only. **Parking:** on-site.
             Terms: weekly rates available. **Pool(s):** outdoor. **Business Services:** fax. **Cards:** AX, DC, DS, MC, VI.
                                                                                             SOME UNITS
                    [ASK] [S🅳] [🍴] [🌙] [♿] [🐾] [🐾] [DATA PORT] /[⊠][📶][🖼][📺] /

------ **WHERE TO DINE** ------

RED CANYON GRILL   **Dinner:** $8-$15   **Phone:** 850/482-4256
♦♦♦ ♦♦♦   **Location:** 2.5 mi n of jct SR 90 on SR 166 N; across from Florida Caverns. 3297 Caverns Rd 32446. **Hours:** 5 pm-9
Southwestern   pm, Fri & Sat-9:30 pm. Closed major holidays; also Sun & Mon. **Reservations:** accepted. **Features:** The
                restaurant carries off its Southwestern theme with a large antler chandelier and assorted artifacts hanging
                on the walls. Such dishes as fajitas, mesquite grilled shrimp, pasta with grilled vegetables, and corn soup
are well-presented and flavorful. Casual dress; beer & wine only. **Parking:** on-site. **Cards:** AX, MC, VI.
                                                                                                     ⊡ ☒

TONY'S RESTAURANT   **Lunch:** $3-$15   **Dinner:** $3-$16   **Phone:** 850/482-2232
♦   **Location:** I-10, exit 136, just w on US 90. 4133 Lafayette St 32448. **Hours:** 11 am-9 pm, Sat 4 pm-10 pm.
          Closed major holidays; also Sun. **Features:** Expect long lines at this popular family-owned and
Italian   family-friendly eatery. The atmosphere, red booths and soft rock music piped through speakers, is as
          comfortable and familiar as the basic, tasty fare of such dishes as chicken parmesan and spaghetti.
Casual dress; beer only. **Parking:** on-site. **Cards:** AX, CB, DC, MC, VI.
                                                                                                     ☒

MELBOURNE pop. 71,382—*See also INDIALANTIC, MELBOURNE BEACH & WEST MELBOURNE.*

OA	✈ Airport Accommodations			
	MELBOURNE INTERNATIONAL	Diamond Rating	Rate Range High Season	Listing Page
AAA	Hilton Melbourne Airport, 0.5 mi se of airport	▼▼▼	$79-$169 SAVE	498

------ **WHERE TO STAY** ------

BAYMONT INN & SUITES MELBOURNE   **Phone:** (321)242-9400
AAA SAVE   2/1-3/31 [ECP]   1P: $89-$94   2P: $89-$94
            12/21-1/31 [ECP]   1P: $74-$79   2P: $74-$79
▼▼▼▼   12/1-12/20 & 4/1-11/30 [ECP] 1P: $69   2P: $69
            Location: I-95, exit 191 (SR 709), just w. 7200 George T Edwards Dr 32940. **Fax:** 321/242-9440. **Facility:** 102 units.
Small-scale Hotel 99 one-bedroom standard units. 3 one-bedroom suites ($94-$109). 4 stories, interior corridors. *Bath:* combo
            or shower only. **Parking:** on-site. **Amenities:** video games (fee), voice mail, irons, hair dryers. *Some:* dual
phone lines. **Pool(s):** heated outdoor. **Guest Services:** valet and coin laundry. **Business Services:** meeting rooms, fax (fee).
Cards: AX, CB, DC, DS, MC, VI. **Special Amenities:** free continental breakfast and free newspaper. *(See color ad below)*
                                                                                          SOME UNITS
            ⟨S⟩ 🐕 ⊞ ⊞+ 🔥 🎿 🏊 🎥 DATA PORT ⊡ / ☒ 🗄 🖼 /

BEST WESTERN HARBORVIEW   **Phone:** 321/724-4422
AAA SAVE   All Year   1P: $69-$79   2P: $69-$79
            Location: 1 mi n of SR 192 on US 1, at jct Nasa Blvd. 964 S Harbor City Blvd 32901. **Fax:** 321/951-9974.
▼▼▼   **Facility:** 122 units. 119 one-bedroom standard units. 3 one-bedroom suites ($129). 6 stories, interior corri-
            dors. **Parking:** on-site. **Terms:** cancellation fee imposed, small pets only ($10 extra charge).
Small-scale Hotel **Amenities:** *Some:* irons, hair dryers. **Dining:** 8 am-10 pm, cocktails. **Pool(s):** outdoor. **Leisure Activities:**
            Fee: game room. **Guest Services:** coin laundry, area transportation-within 6 mi. **Business Services:**
meeting rooms, fax (fee).
                                                                                          SOME UNITS
            ⟨S⟩ ⊞ 🐕 ⊞ ⊡ 🔥 🎿 🏊 ⊞+ DATA PORT ⊡ / ☒ 🗄 🖼 /
                                                                                          FEE FEE

COURTYARD BY MARRIOTT
AAA SAVE
1/2-5/5   1P: $104-$129
5/6-11/30   1P: $89-$109
12/1-1/1   1P: $84-$104
Phone: (321)724-6400

Small-scale Hotel
Location: I-95, exit 180, 3 mi e on US 192. 2101 W New Haven Ave 32904. **Fax:** 321/984-4006. **Facility:** 146 units. 134 one-bedroom standard units. 12 one-bedroom suites ($124-$149). 3 stories, interior corridors. *Bath:* combo or shower only. **Parking:** on-site. **Terms:** [BP] meal plan available. **Amenities:** dual phone lines, voice mail, irons, hair dryers. **Dining:** 6-10 am, Sat & Sun from 7 am. **Pool(s):** heated outdoor. **Leisure Activities:** whirlpool, exercise room. **Guest Services:** valet and coin laundry. **Business Services:** meeting rooms, fax (fee). **Cards:** AX, DC, DS, MC, VI. **Special Amenities:** free newspaper and free room upgrade (subject to availability with advanced reservations).

SOME UNITS

CRANE CREEK INN WATERFRONT BED & BREAKFAST
All Year [ECP]   1P: $75-$150   2P: $75-$150   XP: $15
Phone: (321)768-6416

Bed & Breakfast
Location: Jct US 192, just s on Babcock, then 0.9 mi e. 907 E Melbourne Ave 32901. **Fax:** 321/726-1645. **Facility:** Guests may arrive by car or boat at this Key West-style guest house on a creek navigable to the Intracoastal Waterway. Smoke free premises. 5 one-bedroom standard units, some with efficiencies and/or whirlpools. 2 stories, interior/exterior corridors. *Bath:* combo or shower only. **Parking:** on-site. **Terms:** 2 night minimum stay - weekends, age restrictions may apply, 14 day cancellation notice-fee imposed, weekly rates available, package plans, pets ($10 extra charge, dogs only). **Amenities:** hair dryers. **Pool(s):** heated outdoor. **Leisure Activities:** whirlpool, canoeing, paddleboats, boat dock, fishing, bicycles. **Business Services:** fax. **Cards:** AX, CB, DC, MC, VI.

SOME UNITS

HILTON MELBOURNE AIRPORT
AAA SAVE
1/16-11/30   1P: $79-$169   2P: $79-$169
12/1-1/15   1P: $79-$169   2P: $79-$169   XP: $10   F18
Phone: (321)768-0200

Small-scale Hotel
Location: 1 mi w of US 1, 0.8 mi n of US 192. 200 Rialto Pl 32901. **Fax:** 321/984-2528. **Facility:** 237 one-bedroom standard units, some with whirlpools. 8 stories, interior corridors. *Bath:* combo or shower only. **Parking:** on-site. **Terms:** pets ($50 fee). **Amenities:** dual phone lines, voice mail, irons, hair dryers. *Fee:* video games, high-speed Internet. **Dining:** 6:30 am-midnight, Sat & Sun 7 am-10 pm, cocktails. **Pool(s):** heated outdoor. **Leisure Activities:** whirlpool, lighted tennis court, exercise room. *Fee:* massage. **Guest Services:** gift shop, valet and coin laundry, area transportation-within 5 mi. **Business Services:** conference facilities, fax. **Cards:** AX, CB, DC, DS, JC, MC, VI. **Special Amenities:** free newspaper and free room upgrade (subject to availability with advanced reservations).

SOME UNITS
FEE FEE

IMPERIAL'S HOTEL & CONFERENCE CENTER
AAA SAVE
2/7-5/3   1P: $79-$119   2P: $79-$119   XP: $10   F18
12/1-2/6 & 5/4-11/30   1P: $69-$89   2P: $69-$89   XP: $10   F18
Phone: (321)255-0077

Small-scale Hotel
Location: I-95, exit 191 (SR 509). 8298 N Wickham Rd 32940. **Fax:** 321/259-9633. **Facility:** 127 units. 126 one-bedroom standard units. 1 one-bedroom suite ($89-$149). 5 stories, interior corridors. **Parking:** on-site. **Amenities:** video games (fee), voice mail, irons, hair dryers. *Some:* dual phone lines, fax. **Dining:** 6:30 am-10 pm, cocktails. **Pool(s):** outdoor. **Guest Services:** valet and coin laundry. **Business Services:** conference facilities, fax (fee). **Cards:** AX, CB, DC, DS, MC, VI. **Special Amenities:** free newspaper and free room upgrade (subject to availability with advanced reservations).

SOME UNITS

RAMADA INN
Motel

Phone: (321)723-5320

6/6-8/17	1P: $150-$163	2P: $150-$163	XP: $10	F16
3/21-6/5	1P: $100-$128	2P: $100-$128	XP: $10	F16
8/18-11/30	1P: $54-$128	2P: $54-$128	XP: $10	F16
12/1-3/20	1P: $54-$80	2P: $54-$80	XP: $10	F16

Location: US 1, 1.7 mi n of US 192. 420 S Harbor City Blvd 32901. Fax: 321/724-0581. **Facility:** 100 one-bedroom standard units. 2 stories, exterior corridors. *Bath:* combo or shower only. **Parking:** on-site. **Terms:** cancellation fee imposed, [BP] meal plan available, pets ($25 extra charge). **Amenities:** irons, hair dryers. **Pool(s):** outdoor. **Leisure Activities:** exercise room. **Guest Services:** valet and coin laundry. **Business Services:** meeting rooms, fax (fee). **Cards:** AX, CB, DC, DS, JC, MC, VI.

SOME UNITS
(ASK) (S/D) ⟨bed⟩ ⟨fork⟩ ⟨Y⟩ ⟨⟩ ⟨⟩ (DATA PORT) ⟨⟩ / ⟨X⟩ ⟨⟩ ⟨⟩ /

SUPER 8
(AAA) (SAVE)
Motel

Phone: (321)723-4430

1/1-3/31	1P: $55-$65	2P: $55-$65	XP: $6	F
12/1-12/31 & 4/1-11/30	1P: $46-$56	2P: $46-$56	XP: $6	F

Location: I-95, exit 180, 7 mi e to US 1 on SR 192, then 0.5 mi n. 1515 S Harbor City Blvd 32901. Fax: 321/723-4312. **Facility:** 56 one-bedroom standard units. 2 stories, interior corridors. *Bath:* combo or shower only. **Parking:** on-site. **Terms:** weekly rates available, [CP] meal plan available, small pets only ($20 deposit). **Guest Services:** coin laundry. **Cards:** AX, DC, DS, MC, VI. **Special Amenities:** early check-in/late check-out and free continental breakfast.

SOME UNITS
(S/D) ⟨bed⟩ ⟨⟩ ⟨M⟩ ⟨⟩ ⟨⟩ (DATA PORT) / ⟨X⟩ ⟨⟩ ⟨⟩ /

———— **WHERE TO DINE** ————

CONCHY JOE'S SEAFOOD RESTAURANT
Seafood

Lunch: $5-$12   Dinner: $10-$25   Phone: 321/253-3131

Location: 0.3 mi e of US 1 via Eau Gallie Blvd, north side of the causeway. 1477 Pineapple Ave 32935. **Hours:** 11:30 am-2:30 & 4-10 pm. Closed: 11/27, 12/25; also 12/24 for dinner. **Features:** Deep-fried alligator, conch salad and grouper marsala are specialties in the nautically themed restaurant, on the site of the 1925 Oleander's Hotel. Photographs and memorabilia are displayed throughout the casual, riverfront establishment. Casual dress; cocktails; entertainment. **Parking:** on-site. **Cards:** AX, DS, MC, VI.

⟨Y⟩ ⟨X⟩

MELBOURNE BEACH pop. 3,335—*See also MELBOURNE.*

———— **WHERE TO DINE** ————

CAFE COCONUT COVE
Continental

Dinner: $12-$23   Phone: 321/727-3133

Location: On SR A1A, 6.8 mi s of jct US 192. 4210 S SR A1A 32951. **Hours:** 5 pm-9 pm. Closed: 12/25; also Sun, Mon & 9/1-9/30. **Features:** Diners can enjoy beautiful sunsets from a cozy dining room that overlooks the Indian River. Hearty German cuisine is prepared by the chef/owner, who extends a warm welcome to his guests. Favorites include spatzle, bratwurst and schnitzel. Smoke free premises. Casual dress; beer & wine only. **Parking:** on-site. **Cards:** DC, MC, VI.

⟨X⟩

DJON'S CHOP HOUSE
French

Dinner: $20-$40   Phone: 321/722-2737

Location: 2.5 mi s of jct US 192 and SR A1A, 0.5 mi w. 522 Ocean Ave 32951. **Hours:** 5 pm-11 pm. Closed: Sun. **Reservations:** suggested. **Features:** This inn was started under the 1842 Homestead Act and used by steamboat crews. The unusual tile stove came from Europe. On the menu are a good variety of dishes, including escargots, salad, crab cakes, chicken, veal, filet, rack of lamb and desserts flambeed tableside. Wine is stored in a temperature-controlled cellar. Casual dress; cocktails; entertainment. **Parking:** street. **Cards:** AX, CB, DC, DS, MC, VI.

⟨Y⟩ ⟨X⟩

MERRITT ISLAND pop. 36,090

———— **WHERE TO STAY** ————

CLARION HOTEL-KENNEDY SPACE CENTER AREA
(AAA) (SAVE)
Small-scale Hotel

Phone: (321)452-7711

2/13-4/30	1P: $85-$149	2P: $85-$149	XP: $10	F18
12/1-2/12 & 5/1-11/30	1P: $79-$139	2P: $79-$139	XP: $10	F18

Location: On SR 520, 0.3 mi e of SR 3. 260 E Merritt Island Causeway (SR 520) 32952. Fax: 321/452-9462. **Facility:** 128 one-bedroom standard units. 2 stories, exterior corridors. **Parking:** on-site. **Terms:** 3 day cancellation notice, [ECP] meal plan available. **Amenities:** voice mail, safes, irons, hair dryers. **Dining:** 11 am-2 am, cocktails, nightclub. **Pool(s):** outdoor. **Leisure Activities:** tennis court, exercise room. **Guest Services:** valet laundry. **Business Services:** meeting rooms, business center. **Cards:** AX, CB, DC, DS, JC, MC, VI.
(See color ad p 270)

SOME UNITS
(S/D) ⟨fork⟩ ⟨Y⟩ ⟨⟩ ⟨⟩ ⟨⟩ (DATA PORT) ⟨⟩ / ⟨X⟩ ⟨⟩ ⟨⟩ /

Destination Miami-Miami Beach

pop. 362,470

Pioneering Julia Tuttle convinced millionaire Henry Flagler to extend his railroad farther south, and the rest has been history.

Now a cosmopolitan metropolis and a leader in the world of global commerce, Miami and the Beaches also are internationally known as a vacation paradise where cultures, both pop and ethnic, blend under a bright, tropical sun.

Art Deco District, Miami Beach. The bold outlines, geometric and zigzag shapes, rounded corners and pastel colors of these Art Deco buildings are as striking today as they were in their 1920s and '30s heyday. (See mention page 117)

See Vicinity maps pages 502 and 504

Fishing boat, Greater Miami. With a bay, a river and an ocean, fishing excursions are a popular pastime.

Maximo Gomez Park in Little Havana, Miami. Chess players ponder their moves before a mural backdrop.

Homestead

Florida City

Places included in this AAA Destination City:

Aventura...............543	Hialeah..................550	North Bay Village......556
Bal Harbour............543	Homestead...............551	North Miami............557
Coconut Grove..........544	Kendall.................551	North Miami Beach...557
Coral Gables...........546	Key Biscayne............552	South Miami.............557
Cutler Ridge...........548	Miami Lakes.............553	Sunny Isles.............558
Florida City...........548	Miami Springs..........554	Surfside................559

Aventura

Sunny Isles

Miami
Lakes

North Miami

North
Miami Beach

Bal Harbour

North Bay Village

Hialeah

Miami
Springs

Surfside

South
Miami

Coconut Grove

Coral
Gables

Key Biscayne

Kendall

Miami

Cutler
Ridge

Alfresco Dining,
Greater Miami.
Sunshine and
warm, gentle
breezes entice
diners to shun
walls and roofs.

The Miami Heat,
American Airlines
Arena, Miami.
If this was a
capacity crowd,
19,600 pairs of eyes
were focused on
this shot.
(See mention
page 118)

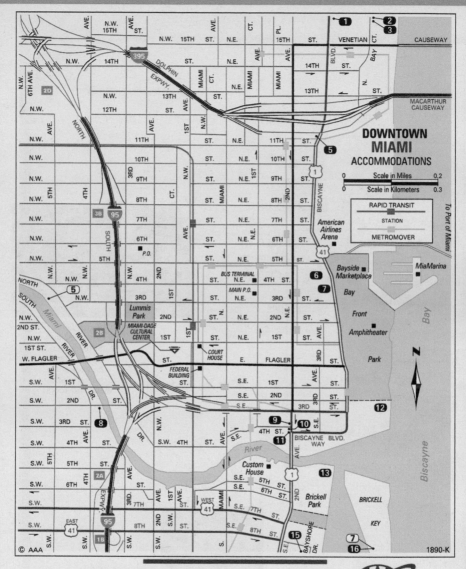

DOWNTOWN MIAMI ACCOMMODATIONS

Scale in Miles   0   0.2
Scale in Kilometers   0   0.3

RAPID TRANSIT
STATION
METROMOVER

1890-K

© AAA

Downtown Miami

This index helps you "spot" where approved accommodations and restaurants are located on the corresponding detailed maps. Lodging rate ranges are for comparison only and show the property's high season; rates are per night, unless only weekly (W) rates are available. Restaurant rate range is for dinner, unless only lunch (L) is served. Turn to the listing page for more detailed rate information and consult display ads for special promotions.

Spotter/Map Page Number	OA	**DOWNTOWN MIAMI - Lodgings**	Diamond Rating	Rate Range High Season	Listing Page
1 / p. 502		Renaissance Miami Biscayne Bay Hotel	◆◆◆	$169-$189	517
2 / p. 502		Doubletree Grand-Biscayne Bay	◆◆◆	$98-$289	515
3 / p. 502	AAA	**Biscayne Bay Marriott Hotel**	◆◆◆	$189-$219 SAVE	514
5 / p. 502	AAA	**Howard Johnson Hotel-Downtown/Port of Miami**	◆◆◆	$89-$119 SAVE	515
6 / p. 502	AAA	**Best Western-Marina Park Hotel - see color ad p 514**	◆◆◆	$99-$149 SAVE	513
7 / p. 502		Everglades Hotel	◆◆	$99-$109	515
8 / p. 502		Miami River Inn	◆◆	$99-$169	516
9 / p. 502	AAA	**Courtyard by Marriott-Miami Downtown**	◆◆	$89-$199 SAVE	515
10 / p. 502		Clarion Hotel & Suites	◆◆◆	$99-$139	515
11 / p. 502	AAA	**Hyatt Regency Miami - see ad p 516**	◆◆◆◆	$120-$250 SAVE	516
12 / p. 502		Hotel Inter-Continental Miami	◆◆◆◆	$179-$329	515
13 / p. 502		Sheraton Biscayne Bay Hotel	◆◆◆	$204-$279	517
15 / p. 502	AAA	**Fortune House Hotel**	◆◆◆	$250-$300 SAVE	515
16 / p. 502		Mandarin Oriental, Miami	◆◆◆◆◆	$575-$775	516
		DOWNTOWN MIAMI - Restaurants			
5 / p. 502		Joe's Seafood Restaurant	◆◆	$12-$20	517
7 / p. 502		Azul	◆◆◆◆	$28-$35	517

UP-CLOSE, CASUAL, PERSONAL

Our style of small-ship cruising means that whatever the destination, you're capturing the travel experience as no other means can provide. Gain insight from local guides, and our on-board Naturalist-Interpretive Guide. Get up-close to whales and wildlife, and navigate narrow waterways totally inaccessible to larger ships.

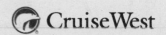 CruiseWest

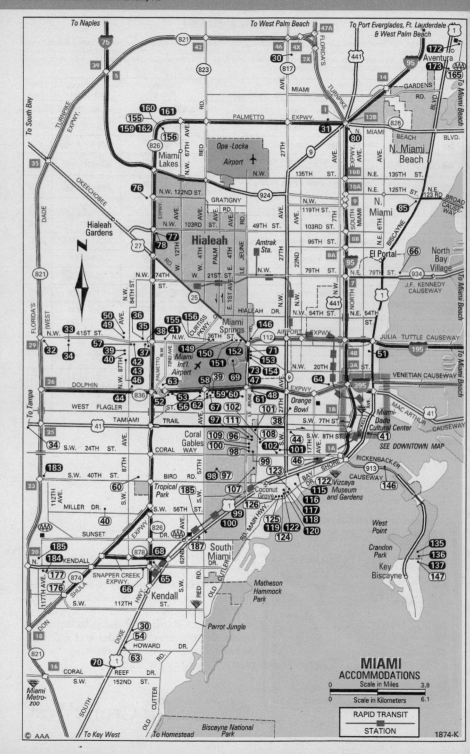

MIAMI
ACCOMMODATIONS

Scale in Miles
0   3.8

Scale in Kilometers
0   6.1

RAPID TRANSIT

STATION

1874-K

✈ Airport Accommodations

Spotter/Map Page Number	OA	MIAMI INTERNATIONAL	Diamond Rating	Rate Range High Season	Listing Page
37 / p. 504	AAA	AmeriSuites (Miami/Airport West), 4.9 mi nw of entrance	◆◆◆	$129-$159 SAVE	517
39 / p. 504		Candlewood Suites Miami Airport West, 4.5 mi nw of entrance	◆◆◆	$109-$169	518
36 / p. 504		Courtyard by Marriott-Miami Airport West/Doral Area, 4.8 mi nw of entrance	◆◆◆	$129-$149	518
47 / p. 504	AAA	Courtyard Miami Airport South, 0.8 mi s of entrance	◆◆◆	$139-$159 SAVE	518
60 / p. 504		Crowne Plaza Hotel and Resort Miami International Airport, 1 mi s of entrance	◆◆◆	Failed to provide	519
63 / p. 504	AAA	Days Inn Miami International Airport Hotel, 4.3 mi sw of terminal	◆◆◆	$69-$109 SAVE	519
50 / p. 504		Doral Golf Resort and Spa, 4.8 mi nw of entrance	◆◆◆◆	$349-$999	519
58 / p. 504		Doubletree Club Miami Airport Hotel, 2.5 mi sw of entrance	◆◆◆	$99-$189	520
71 / p. 504		Embassy Suites Miami International Airport, 0.8 mi n of airport entrance	◆◆◆	$129-$199	520
35 / p. 504		Fairfield Inn by Marriott-Miami West/Doral Area, 4.8 mi nw of entrance	◆◆◆	$84-$89	520
48 / p. 504		Fairfield Inn Miami Airport South, 0.8 mi s of entrance	◆◆◆	$99-$119	520
62 / p. 504		Hampton Inn & Suites-Miami Airport, 2.5 mi sw of entrance	◆◆◆	$109-$159	520
38 / p. 504		Hampton Inn-Miami Airport West, 4.8 mi nw of entrance	◆◆◆	$119-$129	521
59 / p. 504		Hilton Miami Airport, 2.5 mi sw of airport entrance	◆◆◆◆	$69-$199	521
43 / p. 504		Holiday Inn-Miami Airport West, 5.1 mi nw of entrance	◆◆◆	$129-$169	521
53 / p. 504		Homestead Studio Suites Hotel-Miami/Airport/Blue Lagoon, 2 mi s of entrance	◆◆	$79-$109	521
40 / p. 504		Homestead Studio Suites Hotel-Miami/Airport/Doral, 5.1 mi nw	◆◆	$79-$99	521
67 / p. 504		Homewood Suites by Hilton-Miami Blue Lagoon, 2.5 mi sw of airport entrance	◆◆◆	$143-$188	522
46 / p. 504		La Quinta Inn & Suites, 5.1 mi nw	◆◆◆	$89-$125	522
41 / p. 504		La Quinta Inn Miami Airport North, 4.5 mi nw of entrance	◆◆◆	$89-$125	522
61 / p. 504		Miami Airport Marriott, 0.8 mi s of entrance	◆◆◆	$139-$199	522
69 / p. 504		Miami International Airport Hotel, in the terminal	◆◆	$129-$199	522
52 / p. 504	AAA	Radisson Mart Plaza Hotel, 4 mi sw of terminal	◆◆◆	$139 SAVE	523
49 / p. 504		The Spa at Doral, 4.8 mi nw of entrance	◆◆◆◆	$559-$1349	523
57 / p. 504		Staybridge Suites Miami-Airport West, 5.1 mi sw of entrance	◆◆◆	$139-$179	524
56 / p. 504	AAA	Summerfield Suites by Wyndham-Miami Airport, 2.5 mi sw of entrance	◆◆◆	$99-$168 SAVE	524
42 / p. 504	AAA	Wellesley Inn & Suites, 4.9 mi nw of entrance	◆◆◆	$89-$99 SAVE	524
73 / p. 504	AAA	Wyndham Miami Airport, 0.3 mi e of entrance	◆◆◆	$185-$205 SAVE	524
151 / p. 504	AAA	Airways Inn & Suites, 2 mi nw of entrance	◆◆	$45-$79 SAVE	554
153 / p. 504	AAA	Baymont Inn & Suites Miami-Airport, 0.8 mi n of entrance	◆◆◆	$84-$114 SAVE	554

Spotter/Map Page Number	OA	MIAMI INTERNATIONAL (continued)	Diamond Rating	Rate Range High Season	Listing Page
149 / p. 504	(AAA)	Comfort Inn & Suites-Miami International Airport, 2 mi nw of entrance	◆◆◆	$99-$169 [SAVE]	554
152 / p. 504		Days Inn Miami Airport North, 2 mi nw of entrance	◆◆	$69-$119	555
150 / p. 504	(AAA)	Holiday Inn Express Miami International Airport, 2 mi nw of entrance	◆◆◆	$119-$159 [SAVE]	555
146 / p. 504		Holiday Inn-Miami International Airport-North, 0.5 mi n of entrance	◆◆◆	$104	556
156 / p. 504	(AAA)	MainStay Suites-Miami Airport, 2 mi nw of entrance	◆◆◆	$124 [SAVE]	556
155 / p. 504	(AAA)	Sleep Inn-Miami Airport, 2 mi nw of entrance	◆◆	$99-$109 [SAVE]	556

Miami

This index helps you "spot" where approved accommodations and restaurants are located on the corresponding detailed maps. Lodging rate ranges are for comparison only and show the property's high season; rates are per night, unless only weekly (W) rates are available. Restaurant rate range is for dinner, unless only lunch (L) is served. Turn to the listing page for more detailed rate information and consult display ads for special promotions.

Spotter/Map Page Number	OA	MIAMI - Lodgings	Diamond Rating	Rate Range High Season	Listing Page
30 / p. 504		Holiday Inn-Calder/Pro Player Stadium - see color ad opposite inside back cover	◆◆◆	$99-$129	521
31 / p. 504	(AAA)	El Palacio Resort Hotel & Suites	◆◆◆	$70 [SAVE]	520
32 / p. 504		Hampton Inn & Suites	◆◆◆	$104-$119	520
33 / p. 504	(AAA)	Baymont Inn & Suites Miami West	◆◆◆	$89-$109 [SAVE]	518
34 / p. 504	(AAA)	TownePlace Suites by Marriott	◆◆◆	$69-$109 [SAVE]	524
35 / p. 504		Fairfield Inn by Marriott-Miami West/Doral Area	◆◆◆	$84-$89	520
36 / p. 504		Courtyard by Marriott-Miami Airport West/Doral Area - see ad p 519	◆◆◆	$129-$149	518
37 / p. 504	(AAA)	AmeriSuites (Miami/Airport West) - see color ad p 516	◆◆◆	$129-$159 [SAVE]	517
38 / p. 504		Hampton Inn-Miami Airport West	◆◆◆	$119-$129	521
39 / p. 504		Candlewood Suites Miami Airport West	◆◆◆	$109-$169	518
40 / p. 504		Homestead Studio Suites Hotel-Miami/Airport/Doral	◆◆	$79-$99	521
41 / p. 504		La Quinta Inn Miami Airport North	◆◆◆	$89-$125	522
42 / p. 504	(AAA)	Wellesley Inn & Suites - see color ad p 514	◆◆◆	$89-$99 [SAVE]	524
43 / p. 504		Holiday Inn-Miami Airport West - see color ad opposite inside back cover	◆◆◆	$129-$169	521
44 / p. 504		Residence Inn Miami Airport by Marriott	◆◆◆	$149-$229	523
46 / p. 504		La Quinta Inn & Suites	◆◆◆	$89-$125	522
47 / p. 504	(AAA)	Courtyard Miami Airport South - see ad p 519	◆◆◆	$139-$159 [SAVE]	518
48 / p. 504		Fairfield Inn Miami Airport South	◆◆◆	$99-$119	520
49 / p. 504		The Spa at Doral	◆◆◆◆	$559-$1349	523
50 / p. 504		Doral Golf Resort and Spa	◆◆◆◆	$349-$999	519
51 / p. 504		Super 8 Motel	◆◆	$60-$120	524
52 / p. 504	(AAA)	Radisson Mart Plaza Hotel	◆◆◆	$139 [SAVE]	523
53 / p. 504		Homestead Studio Suites Hotel-Miami/Airport/Blue Lagoon	◆◆	$79-$109	521
56 / p. 504	(AAA)	Summerfield Suites by Wyndham-Miami Airport	◆◆◆	$99-$168 [SAVE]	524

Spotter/Map Page Number	OA	MIAMI - Lodgings (continued)	Diamond Rating	Rate Range High Season	Listing Page
57 / p. 504		Staybridge Suites Miami-Airport West	◆◆◆	$139-$179	524
58 / p. 504		Doubletree Club Miami Airport Hotel	◆◆◆	$99-$189	520
59 / p. 504		Hilton Miami Airport	◆◆◆◆	$69-$199	521
60 / p. 504		Crowne Plaza Hotel and Resort Miami International Airport	◆◆◆	Failed to provide	519
61 / p. 504		Miami Airport Marriott	◆◆◆	$139-$199	522
62 / p. 504		Hampton Inn & Suites-Miami Airport	◆◆◆	$109-$159	520
63 / p. 504	AAA	**Days Inn Miami International Airport Hotel**	◆◆◆	$69-$109 SAVE	519
64 / p. 504	AAA	**Days Inn Civic Center/Medical Center**	◆◆	$69-$89 SAVE	519
65 / p. 504	AAA	**Miami Dadeland Marriott**	◆◆◆	$189-$219 SAVE	522
66 / p. 504		Ramada Limited South Miami Dadeland	◆◆	$94-$119	523
67 / p. 504		Homewood Suites by Hilton-Miami Blue Lagoon	◆◆◆	$143-$188	522
68 / p. 504		Hampton Inn Miami/Dadeland	◆◆◆	$89-$119	521
69 / p. 504		Miami International Airport Hotel	◆◆	$129-$199	522
70 / p. 504	AAA	**Quality Inn-South - see color ad p 523**	◆◆◆	$79-$135 SAVE	523
71 / p. 504		Embassy Suites Miami International Airport	◆◆◆	$129-$199	520
73 / p. 504	AAA	**Wyndham Miami Airport**	◆◆◆	$185-$205 SAVE	524
		MIAMI - Restaurants			
30 / p. 504		Anacapri	◆◆	$10-$18	525
34 / p. 504		Cami's Seafood & Pasta	◆	$5-$15	525
38 / p. 504		Islas Canarias Restaurant	◆	$4-$18	525
39 / p. 504		94th Aero Squadron	◆◆	$15-$24	525
40 / p. 504		The Fish House	◆◆	$10-$20	525
41 / p. 504		Giacomo Restaurant	◆	$7-$19	525
44 / p. 504		Casa Juancho Restaurant	◆◆	$14-$29	525
46 / p. 504		Old Lisbon Restaurant	◆◆	$14-$47	526
54 / p. 504		Tani Thai Restaurant	◆◆	$9-$20	526
60 / p. 504		Tropical Chinese Restaurant	◆◆	$10-$30	526
63 / p. 504		Fleming: A Taste of Denmark	◆◆◆	$11-$23	525
66 / p. 504		Mike Gordon Seafood Restaurant	◆◆	$12-$25	525
		HIALEAH - Lodgings			
76 / p. 504		Holiday Inn Express Hotel & Suites - see color ad opposite inside back cover	◆◆◆	$89	550
77 / p. 504	AAA	**Days Inn Miami Lakes/Westland Mall - see ad p 550**	◆◆	$69-$79 SAVE	550
78 / p. 504	AAA	**Ramada Inn-Miami Airport North - see ad p 550**	◆◆	$79 SAVE	550
		NORTH MIAMI - Lodgings			
80 / p. 504		Howard Johnson North Miami	◆◆◆	$69-$89	557
85 / p. 504	AAA	**Holiday Inn North Miami - see color ad opposite inside back cover**	◆◆◆	$89 SAVE	557
		CORAL GABLES - Lodgings			
97 / p. 504		Holiday Inn Coral Gables Business District - see color ad opposite inside back cover	◆◆◆	$169	546

Spotter/Map Page Number	OA	CORAL GABLES - Lodgings (continued)	Diamond Rating	Rate Range High Season	Listing Page
98 / p. 504		The Biltmore Hotel Coral Gables	▽▽▽▽	$372	546
99 / p. 504	◬	Riviera Court Motel - see color ad p 546	▽▽	$79-$93 [SAVE]	547
100 / p. 504		Holiday Inn University of Miami - see color ad opposite inside back cover	▽▽▽	$119-$169	546
101 / p. 504	◬	Hyatt Regency Coral Gables	▽▽▽▽	$135-$289 [SAVE]	546
102 / p. 504		Omni Colonnade Hotel	▽▽▽▽	$329-$359	547
		CORAL GABLES - Restaurants			
96 / p. 504		Ammo	▽▽▽	$18-$35	547
97 / p. 504		Le Palme d'Or	▽▽▽▽	$20-$40	548
98 / p. 504		Exedra Restaurant	▽▽▽	$14-$30	547
99 / p. 504		Ortanique on the Mile	▽▽▽	$15-$30	548
100 / p. 504		Francesco Restaurant	▽▽	$13-$21	547
101 / p. 504		Mylos Restaurant & Bar	▽▽	$10-$25	548
102 / p. 504		NORMAN'S	▽▽▽▽	$26-$39	548
107 / p. 504		Christy's	▽▽▽	$17-$32	547
108 / p. 504		Restaurant St. Michel	▽▽▽	$15-$33	548
109 / p. 504		Caffe Abbracci	▽▽▽▽	$14-$28	547
111 / p. 504		Le Festival	▽▽▽	$16-$27	547
		COCONUT GROVE - Lodgings			
115 / p. 504		Hampton Inn-Coconut Grove/Coral Gables	▽▽▽	$129-$179	544
116 / p. 504		The Doubletree Hotel at Coconut Grove	▽▽▽	$115-$155	544
117 / p. 504	◬	Wyndham Grand Bay-Coconut Grove	▽▽▽▽	$264-$284 [SAVE]	545
118 / p. 504	◬	The Mutiny Hotel	▽▽▽	$189-$1000 [SAVE]	544
119 / p. 504	◬	Mayfair House Hotel	▽▽▽▽	$269-$800 [SAVE]	544
120 / p. 504		Residence Inn by Marriott	▽▽▽	$129-$149	544
122 / p. 504		Sonesta Hotel & Suites Coconut Grove	▽▽▽	$175	545
		COCONUT GROVE - Restaurants			
122 / p. 504		Baleen	▽▽▽▽	$19-$40	545
123 / p. 504		Bici Ristorante	▽▽▽▽	$14-$36	545
124 / p. 504		Mezzanotte In The Grove	▽▽	$12-$24	546
125 / p. 504		Mayfair Grill	▽▽▽	$20-$40	545
126 / p. 504		Cafe' Tu Tu Tango	▽▽	$5-$9	545
		KEY BISCAYNE - Lodgings			
135 / p. 504		Silver Sands Beach Resort	▽▽	$169-$349	552
136 / p. 504	◬	Sonesta Beach Resort Key Biscayne - see color ad p 552	▽▽▽	$320-$450 [SAVE]	553
137 / p. 504		The Ritz-Carlton, Key Biscayne	▽▽▽▽	$395-$690	552
		KEY BISCAYNE - Restaurants			
146 / p. 504	◬	Rusty Pelican	▽▽	$16-$30	553
147 / p. 504		Aria	▽▽▽	$26-$42	553
		MIAMI SPRINGS - Lodgings			
146 / p. 504		Holiday Inn-Miami International Airport-North - see color ad opposite inside back cover, p 555	▽▽▽	$104	556

Spotter/Map Page Number	OA	MIAMI SPRINGS - Lodgings (continued)	Diamond Rating	Rate Range High Season	Listing Page
149 / p. 504	AAA	Comfort Inn & Suites-Miami International Airport - see color ad p 513	◆◆◆	$99-$169 SAVE	554
150 / p. 504	AAA	Holiday Inn Express Miami International Airport	◆◆◆	$119-$159 SAVE	555
151 / p. 504	AAA	Airways Inn & Suites - see color ad p 528	◆◆	$45-$79 SAVE	554
152 / p. 504		Days Inn Miami Airport North	◆◆	$69-$119	555
153 / p. 504	AAA	Baymont Inn & Suites Miami-Airport - see color ad p 555	◆◆◆	$84-$114 SAVE	554
154 / p. 504	AAA	Red Roof Inn Miami Airport	◆◆◆	$74-$84 SAVE	556
155 / p. 504	AAA	Sleep Inn-Miami Airport - see color ad p 513	◆◆	$99-$109 SAVE	556
156 / p. 504	AAA	MainStay Suites-Miami Airport	◆◆◆	$124 SAVE	556
		MIAMI LAKES - Lodgings			
159 / p. 504		TownePlace Suites by Marriott	◆◆◆	$89-$119	554
160 / p. 504		Don Shula's Hotel & Golf Club	◆◆◆	$164-$175	553
161 / p. 504		Courtyard by Marriott-Miami Lakes Area - see ad p 519	◆◆◆	$129-$149	553
162 / p. 504	AAA	Wellesley Inn (Miami Lakes) - see color ad p 514	◆◆	$84 SAVE	554
		MIAMI LAKES - Restaurants			
155 / p. 504		Shula's Steakhouse	◆◆◆	$18-$50	554
156 / p. 504		Shula's Steak 2	◆◆	$6-$20	554
		AVENTURA - Lodgings			
172 / p. 504		Turnberry Isle Resort & Club	◆◆◆◆	$405-$4200	543
173 / p. 504		Courtyard by Marriott Aventura Mall	◆◆◆	$159-$179	543
		AVENTURA - Restaurant			
165 / p. 504		Chef Allen's	◆◆◆◆	$26-$38	543
		KENDALL - Lodgings			
183 / p. 504	AAA	Comfort Suites Miami/Kendall - see color ad p 518	◆◆◆	$107-$125 SAVE	551
184 / p. 504	AAA	AmeriSuites (Miami/Kendall) - see color ad p 516	◆◆	$115-$129 SAVE	551
185 / p. 504	AAA	Wellesley Inn (Miami/Kendall) - see color ad p 514	◆◆◆	$69-$189 SAVE	552
		KENDALL - Restaurants			
176 / p. 504		Gil Capa's Bistro	◆◆	$7-$14	552
177 / p. 504		PastaBilities	◆◆	$12-$18	552
		SOUTH MIAMI - Restaurants			
185 / p. 504		El Manara	◆◆	$10-$16	557
187 / p. 504		Khoury's	◆◆	$11-$23	557

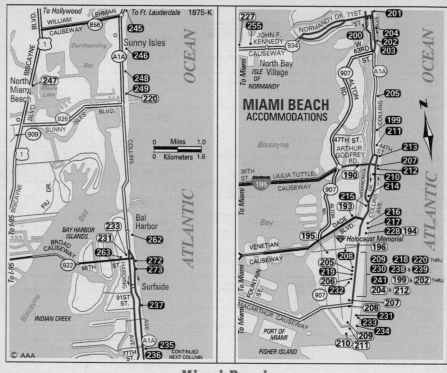

Miami Beach

This index helps you "spot" where approved accommodations and restaurants are located on the corresponding detailed maps. Lodging rate ranges are for comparison only and show the property's high season; rates are per night, unless only weekly (W) rates are available. Restaurant rate range is for dinner, unless only lunch (L) is served. Turn to the listing page for more detailed rate information and consult display ads for special promotions.

Spotter/Map Page Number	OA	MIAMI BEACH - Lodgings	Diamond Rating	Rate Range High Season	Listing Page
199 / above		Eden Roc A Renaissance Resort & Spa	▽▽▽	$240-$280	532
200 / above	AAA	Holiday Inn Indian Creek - see color ad p 533, opposite inside back cover	▽▽▽	$89-$159 [SAVE]	532
201 / above	AAA	Crystal Beach Suites & Health Club - see color ad p 529	▽▽▽	$144-$245 [SAVE]	529
202 / above	AAA	The New Casablanca On the Ocean - see color ad p 536	◆◆	$147-$187 [SAVE]	535
203 / above	AAA	Comfort Inn On the Beach - see color ad p 529	▽▽▽	$125-$165 [SAVE]	529
204 / above	AAA	Radisson Deauville Resort Miami Beach - see ad p 538	▽▽▽	$229-$299 [SAVE]	536
205 / above	AAA	Wyndham Miami Beach Resort	▽▽▽	$199-$230 [SAVE]	540
207 / above	AAA	Fairfield Inn & Suites, Miami Beach	▽▽▽	$115-$165 [SAVE]	532
208 / above		The Marlin	▽▽▽	$325-$415	535
209 / above		Hilton Grand Vacations Club at South Beach	▽▽▽	$225-$275	532
210 / above	AAA	Capri Miami Beach Condo Hotel by Signum Resorts	▽▽▽	$147-$248 [SAVE]	527
211 / above		Fontainebleau Hilton Resort	▽▽▽	$259-$489	532
212 / above	AAA	Ramada Inn Miami Beach	▽▽	$140-$155 [SAVE]	538
213 / above		Courtyard by Marriott - see color ad p 530	▽▽▽	$179-$209	529

Spotter/Map Page Number	OA	MIAMI BEACH - Lodgings (continued)	Diamond Rating	Rate Range High Season	Listing Page
214 / p. 510	AAA	The Indian Creek Hotel - see color ad p 537	◆◆◆	$140-$160 SAVE	533
215 / p. 510		Abbey Hotel	◆◆◆	$159-$249	526
216 / p. 510	AAA	Holiday Inn South Beach Resort - see color ad p 534, opposite inside back cover	◆◆◆	$189 SAVE	533
217 / p. 510	AAA	Days Inn Art Deco/Convention Center	◆◆	$139-$169 SAVE	530
218 / p. 510		Riande Continental Hotel	◆◆	$140	538
219 / p. 510		Fairwind Hotel & Suites	◆◆	$75-$140	532
220 / p. 510		Doubletree Surfcomber Hotel	◆◆◆	$129-$189	531
221 / p. 510		Tudor Hotel & Suites	◆◆◆	$184-$605	539
222 / p. 510	AAA	Shelborne Beach Resort-South Beach - see color ad p 539	◆◆◆	$185-$450 SAVE	539
223 / p. 510	AAA	Loews Miami Beach Hotel - see color ad p 535	◆◆◆◆	$299-$449 SAVE	534
224 / p. 510	AAA	The Hotel	◆◆◆	$275-$325 SAVE	533
225 / p. 510	AAA	Casa Grande Hotel	◆◆◆	$250-$1500 SAVE	527
226 / p. 510	AAA	Edison Hotel South Beach	◆◆	$175-$330 SAVE	532
227 / p. 510		Cavalier	◆◆◆	$79-$129	527
228 / p. 510	AAA	The Shore Club South Beach	◆◆◆◆	$395-$895 SAVE	539
229 / p. 510		The Tides Hotel	◆◆◆◆	$525-$3000	539
230 / p. 510		Breakwater Hotel - see color ad p 527	◆◆	$149-$249	527
231 / p. 510		Ocean Five Hotel - see color ad p 537	◆◆◆	$175-$325	535
232 / p. 510		The Blue Moon	◆◆◆◆	$235-$265	527
233 / p. 510		Savoy Hotel	◆◆◆	$310-$710	538
234 / p. 510		Century Hotel	◆◆◆	$190	528
235 / p. 510	AAA	Days Inn North Beach - see color ad p 531	◆◆	$80-$90 SAVE	530
236 / p. 510	AAA	Ocean Surf Hotel - see color ad p 537	◆◆	$99-$169 SAVE	536
237 / p. 510	AAA	Dezerland Beach Resort & Spa - see color ad p 531	◆◆◆	$109 SAVE	530
238 / p. 510		President Hotel	◆◆◆	$160-$690	536
239 / p. 510		The Kent	◆◆◆	$145-$350	533
241 / p. 510		Hotel Ocean	◆◆◆	$200-$600	533
		MIAMI BEACH - Restaurants			
190 / p. 510	AAA	Crystal Cafe	◆◆◆◆	$13-$25	541
193 / p. 510		Mama Vieja Restaurant	◆	$7-$18	541
194 / p. 510		Nobu at The Shore Club South Beach	◆◆◆	$25-$40	541
195 / p. 510		Pacific Time	◆◆◆	$17-$32	541
196 / p. 510		Yuca Restaurant	◆◆◆	$6-$40	542
199 / p. 510		Gaucho Room	◆◆◆◆	$25-$40	541
202 / p. 510		Les Deux Fontaines	◆◆	$9-$31	541
203 / p. 510		Twelve Twenty	◆◆◆	$20-$35	542
204 / p. 510		Mezzaluna, South Beach	◆◆◆	$10-$24	541
205 / p. 510		Mark's South Beach	◆◆◆◆	$18-$30	541
206 / p. 510		Astor Place Bar & Grill	◆◆◆	$7-$35	540

Spotter/Map Page Number	OA	MIAMI BEACH - Restaurants (continued)	Diamond Rating	Rate Range High Season	Listing Page
207 / p. 510		Shiva	◇◇	$8-$18	542
208 / p. 510		China Grill	◇◇◇	$21-$35	540
209 / p. 510		Nemo Restaurant	◇◇◇	$18-$28	541
210 / p. 510		Smith & Wollensky Steak & Chop House	◇◇◇	$22-$38	542
211 / p. 510		Joe's Stone Crab Restaurant	◇◇	$5-$60	541
212 / p. 510		Wish	◇◇◇◇	$20-$33	542
		SUNNY ISLES - Lodgings			
245 / p. 510	ⒶⒶⒶ	**Marco Polo Ramada Plaza Beach Resort -** see color ad p 538	◇◇◇	$155-$285 ⓈⒶⓋⒺ	558
246 / p. 510	ⒶⒶⒶ	**Suez Ocean Front Resort**	◇◇	$95-$135 ⓈⒶⓋⒺ	558
248 / p. 510	ⒶⒶⒶ	**Monaco Oceanfront Resort**	◇◇	$88-$119 ⓈⒶⓋⒺ	558
249 / p. 510	ⒶⒶⒶ	**Newport Beachside Hotel & Resort**	◇◇◇	$129-$199 ⓈⒶⓋⒺ	558
		SUNNY ISLES - Restaurant			
220 / p. 510		The World Famous Newport Pub	◇◇	$9-$30	558
		NORTH BAY VILLAGE - Lodgings			
255 / p. 510	ⒶⒶⒶ	**Best Western on the Bay Inn & Marina -** see color ad p 528	◇◇	$74-$114 ⓈⒶⓋⒺ	556
		NORTH BAY VILLAGE - Restaurant			
227 / p. 510		The Crab House Seafood Restaurant	◇◇	$11-$39	556
		BAL HARBOUR - Lodgings			
262 / p. 510	ⒶⒶⒶ	Sheraton Bal Harbour Beach Resort - see color ad p 5	◇◇◇◇	$429-$619	543
263 / p. 510		Bay Harbor Inn and Suites	◇◇◇	$129-$189	543
		BAL HARBOUR - Restaurants			
231 / p. 510		Bal Harbour Bistro	◇◇	$9-$25	544
233 / p. 510		Carpaccio	◇◇	$14-$21	544
		SURFSIDE - Lodgings			
272 / p. 510	ⒶⒶⒶ	**Best Western Oceanfront Resort -** see color ad p 526	◇◇◇	$119-$139 ⓈⒶⓋⒺ	559
273 / p. 510	ⒶⒶⒶ	**Beekman Hotel-Suites on the Ocean**	◇◇◇	$112-$206 ⓈⒶⓋⒺ	559
		NORTH MIAMI BEACH - Restaurant			
247 / p. 510		Tuna's Waterfront Grille	◇◇	$15-$28	557

DOWNTOWN MIAMI (See map p. 502; index p. 503)

──────── WHERE TO STAY ────────

BEST WESTERN-MARINA PARK HOTEL

AAA SAVE

▼▼▼▼

			Phone: (305)371-4400	**6**
1/1-3/31	1P: $99	2P: $149	XP: $10	F17
4/1-11/30	1P: $89	2P: $109	XP: $10	F17
12/1-12/31	1P: $89	2P: $99	XP: $10	F17

Location: On US 1; facing Port of Miami. Located across from the Bayside Marketplace. 340 Biscayne Blvd 33132. **Large-scale Hotel** Fax: 305/372-2862. **Facility:** 200 units. 193 one-bedroom standard units. 7 one-bedroom suites ($169-$179). 10 stories, interior corridors. *Bath:* combo or shower only. **Parking:** on-site (fee). **Amenities:** voice mail, safes, irons, hair dryers. *Some:* dual phone lines. **Dining:** 6:30 am-10:30 pm, cocktails. **Pool(s):** outdoor. **Leisure Activities:** Fee: game room. **Guest Services:** gift shop, valet laundry. **Business Services:** meeting rooms, business center. **Cards:** AX, CB, DC, DS, JC, MC, VI. **Special Amenities:** early check-in/late check-out and free continental breakfast. *(See color ad p 514)*

SOME UNITS

🅂🄳 📶 🍴 🍸 📺 ♿ 🏊 🐾 📷 [DATA PORT] ▣ /✕🔒/

(See map p. 502)

BISCAYNE BAY MARRIOTT HOTEL   Phone: (305)374-3900   ③

(AAA) (SAVE)	12/26-5/26	1P: $189-$219	2P: $189-$219
▼▼▼	12/1-12/25	1P: $169-$219	2P: $169-$219
	9/28-11/30	1P: $159-$189	2P: $159-$189
	5/27-9/27	1P: $129-$159	2P: $129-$159

Large-scale Hotel Location: Just e of US 1 (Biscayne Blvd) at 15th St. 1633 N Bayshore Dr 33132. Fax: 305/375-0597. **Facility:** 601 units. 597 one-bedroom standard units. 4 one-bedroom suites. 31 stories, interior corridors. *Bath:* combo or shower only. **Parking:** on-site (fee) and valet. **Terms:** cancellation fee imposed. **Amenities:** dual phone lines, voice mail, honor bars, irons, hair dryers. *Fee:* high-speed Internet, safes. **Dining:** 2 restaurants, 6:30 am-11 pm, cocktails. **Pool(s):** heated outdoor. **Leisure Activities:** whirlpool, rental boats, exercise room. *Fee:* marina, charter fishing. **Guest Services:** gift shop, valet and coin laundry. **Business Services:** conference facilities, business center. **Cards:** AX, DC, DS, MC, VI. **Special Amenities:** early check-in/late check-out and free newspaper.

SOME UNITS

[icons] ⑤Ⓓ 🍽 ♉ ⓛM 🐾 🚣 ⊠ ⊠ DATA PORT ▣ / ⊠ 🔊 /

(See map p. 502)

CLARION HOTEL & SUITES
Phone: (305)374-5100   **10**

SAVE

▼▼▼ ▼▼▼
Small-scale Hotel

12/1-4/15	1P: $99-$139	2P: $99-$139	XP: $10 F16
4/16-11/30	1P: $89-$109	2P: $89-$109	XP: $10 F16

Location: I-95, exit 2C, just e. 100 SE 4th St 33131. Fax: 305/381-9826. **Facility:** 149 units. 119 one-bedroom standard units. 30 one-bedroom suites. 16 stories, interior corridors. *Bath:* combo or shower only. **Parking:** valet. **Amenities:** video games (fee), voice mail, irons, hair dryers. **Pool(s):** outdoor. **Leisure Activities:** exercise room. **Guest Services:** valet laundry. **Business Services:** meeting rooms, fax (fee). **Cards:** AX, CB, DC, DS, JC, MC, VI.

SOME UNITS

COURTYARD BY MARRIOTT-MIAMI DOWNTOWN
Phone: (305)374-3000   **9**

AAA SAVE

▼▼▼ ▼▼▼
Small-scale Hotel

All Year   1P: $89-$199

Location: Just s of Flagler St on US 1 and 41, 0.8 mi e of I-95, exit 2A. Adjoins the convention center. 200 SE 2nd Ave 33131. Fax: 305/358-4061. **Facility:** 258 units. 256 one-bedroom standard units. 2 one-bedroom suites. 13 stories, interior corridors. **Parking:** valet (fee). **Terms:** check-in 4 pm, cancellation fee imposed, [AP] meal plan available, package plans, small pets only ($100 deposit). **Amenities:** voice mail, safes, irons, hair dryers. *Some:* video games (fee). **Dining:** 7 am-1 & 5-9 pm, cocktails. **Pool(s):** outdoor. **Leisure Activities:** exercise room. **Guest Services:** coin laundry. **Business Services:** meeting rooms, fax (fee). **Cards:** AX, DC, DS, MC, VI. **Special Amenities:** free newspaper.

SOME UNITS
FEE

DOUBLETREE GRAND-BISCAYNE BAY
Phone: (305)372-0313   **2**

SAVE

▼▼▼ ▼▼▼
Small-scale Hotel

1/1-3/31	1P: $98-$289	2P: $98-$289	XP: $10 F
12/1-12/31 & 4/1-11/30	1P: $80-$189	2P: $80-$189	XP: $10 F

Location: Just e of US 1 (Biscayne Blvd) at 15th St. 1717 N Bayshore Dr 33132. Fax: 305/372-9455. **Facility:** 220 units. 152 one-bedroom standard units. 40 one- and 28 two-bedroom suites with kitchens. 10 stories, interior corridors. **Parking:** valet. **Terms:** 18% service charge. **Amenities:** high-speed Internet (fee), voice mail, irons, hair dryers. *Some:* video games (fee), dual phone lines, safes, honor bars. **Pool(s):** heated outdoor. **Leisure Activities:** sauna, whirlpool, rental boats. *Fee:* marina. **Guest Services:** gift shop, valet and coin laundry. **Business Services:** meeting rooms, fax (fee). **Cards:** AX, DC, DS, MC, VI.

SOME UNITS

EVERGLADES HOTEL
Phone: (305)379-5461   **7**

▼▼▼ ▼▼▼
Large-scale Hotel

All Year   1P: $99-$109   2P: $99-$109   XP: $10   F14

Location: On US 1 at 3rd St. Located across from the Bayside Marketplace. 244 Biscayne Blvd 33132. Fax: 305/577-8390. **Facility:** 376 units. 296 one-bedroom standard units. 80 one-bedroom suites ($125-$135). 17 stories, interior corridors. **Parking:** valet. **Terms:** [AP] meal plan available, 15% service charge. **Amenities:** irons, hair dryers. **Pool(s):** heated outdoor. **Guest Services:** gift shop, valet laundry. **Business Services:** meeting rooms, fax (fee). **Cards:** AX, DC, DS, MC, VI.

SOME UNITS
FEE

FORTUNE HOUSE HOTEL
Phone: (305)349-5200   **15**

AAA SAVE

▼▼▼ ▼▼▼
Large-scale Hotel

12/1-4/30	1P: $250-$300	2P: $250-$300
5/1-11/30	1P: $190-$230	2P: $190-$230

Location: At US 1/Brickell Ave and SE 14th Terrace, just e. Located in the banking district. 185 SE 14th Terrace 33131. Fax: 305/349-5221. **Facility:** 175 units. 91 one- and 84 two-bedroom suites ($190-$250) with kitchens. 6-29 stories, interior corridors. **Parking:** valet. **Terms:** cancellation fee imposed, weekly rates available, package plans - seasonal & weekend, 15% service charge. **Amenities:** CD players, dual phone lines, voice mail, fax, honor bars, irons, hair dryers. *Fee:* video games, high-speed Internet. **Dining:** 7 am-11 pm. **Pool(s):** heated outdoor. **Leisure Activities:** sauna, whirlpool, steamroom, barbecue grill at pool area. *Fee:* massage. **Business Services:** meeting rooms. *Fee:* PC, fax. **Cards:** AX, CB, DC, MC, VI. **Special Amenities:** early check-in/late check-out and free newspaper.

SOME UNITS
FEE

HOTEL INTER-CONTINENTAL MIAMI
Phone: (305)577-1000   **12**

▼▼▼ ▼▼▼

12/1-4/30 & 10/1-11/30	1P: $179-$329	2P: $179-$329	XP: $30 F18
5/1-9/30	1P: $129-$249	2P: $129-$249	XP: $30 F18

Large-scale Hotel

Location: On the bay, at Biscayne Blvd and Chopin Plaza. 100 Chopin Plaza 33131. Fax: 305/577-0384. **Facility:** A striking sculpture dominates the large, colorful lobby of this hotel complex overlooking Biscayne Bay; many rooms offer city views. 641 units. 606 one-bedroom standard units. 34 one- and 1 two-bedroom suites ($349-$549), some with whirlpools. 34 stories, interior corridors. *Bath:* combo or shower only. **Parking:** valet. **Terms:** check-in 4 pm, cancellation fee imposed, [BP] meal plan available. **Amenities:** CD players, dual phone lines, voice mail, safes, honor bars, irons, hair dryers. *Fee:* video games, high-speed Internet. *Some:* DVD players (fee), fax. **Pool(s):** heated outdoor. **Leisure Activities:** jogging. *Fee:* massage. **Guest Services:** gift shop, valet laundry. **Business Services:** conference facilities, business center. **Cards:** AX, CB, DC, DS, JC, MC, VI.

SOME UNITS
FEE

HOWARD JOHNSON HOTEL-DOWNTOWN/PORT OF MIAMI
Phone: (305)358-3080   **5**

AAA SAVE

▼▼▼ ▼▼▼
Small-scale Hotel

12/1-3/31	1P: $89-$99	2P: $99-$119	XP: $10 F18
4/1-11/30	1P: $65-$89	2P: $69-$99	XP: $10 F18

Location: On US 1; at jct I-395. Located across from the entrance of Port of Miami. 1100 Biscayne Blvd 33132. Fax: 305/358-8631. **Facility:** 115 one-bedroom standard units. 7 stories, interior corridors. *Bath:* some combo or shower only. **Parking:** on-site (fee). **Amenities:** video games (fee), voice mail. *Some:* irons, hair dryers. **Pool(s):** outdoor. **Guest Services:** coin laundry, area transportation-Port of Miami. **Business Services:** meeting rooms. **Cards:** AX, CB, DC, DS, JC, MC, VI. **Special Amenities:** free continental breakfast and free newspaper.

SOME UNITS

(See map p. 502)

HYATT REGENCY MIAMI

(AAA) (SAVE)   All Year   1P: $120-$250   2P: $120-$250   Phone: (305)358-1234   **11**
XP: $25   F18
▼▼▼/▼▼▼   **Location:** Corner of SE 4th St and SE Second Ave. Located next to the convention center. 400 SE Second Ave 33131-2107. Fax: 305/358-0529. **Facility:** All accommodations in this contemporary hotel have balconies offering views of the city. 587 units. 575 one-bedroom standard units. 12 one-bedroom suites. 24 stories; interior cor-
Large-scale Hotel ridors. *Bath:* combo or shower only. **Parking:** valet. **Terms:** cancellation fee imposed. **Amenities:** dual phone lines, voice mail, safes, irons, hair dryers. *Some:* CD players, fax. **Dining:** 2 restaurants, 7 am-10 pm, cock-tails. **Pool(s):** heated outdoor. **Leisure Activities:** exercise room. *Fee:* massage. **Guest Services:** gift shop, valet laundry, air-port transportation (fee)-shuttle. **Business Services:** conference facilities, business center. **Cards:** AX, CB, DC, DS, JC, MC, VI. *(See ad below)*

SOME UNITS
[🚭] [🍴] [✈] [🔥M] [📺] [🏋] [🏊] [🎣] [DATA PORT] [💻] / [✕] [🛗] /
FEE

MANDARIN ORIENTAL, MIAMI
▼▼▼◆▼▼▼   12/1-3/31   1P: $575-$750   2P: $600-$775   Phone: (305)913-8288   **16**
XP: $25   F13
4/1-5/31 & 10/1-11/30   1P: $520-$700   2P: $550-$725   XP: $25   F13
6/1-9/30   1P: $420-$600   2P: $450-$625   XP: $25   F13
Large-scale Hotel **Location:** US 1 (Brickell Ave), just e on SE 8th St (Brickell Key Dr). 500 Brickell Key Dr 33131. Fax: 305/913-8300.
Facility: Many of the spacious, lavishly decorated rooms at this stunning hotel feature balconies offering great views of Biscayne Bay and the skyline. 329 units. 298 one-bedroom standard units. 31 one-bedroom suites ($1250-$5250), some with kitchens. 17 stories, interior corridors. *Bath:* some combo or shower only. **Parking:** valet. **Terms:** cancellation fee imposed, small pets only ($200 deposit). **Amenities:** high-speed Internet (fee), dual phone lines, voice mail, safes, honor bars, irons, hair dryers. *Some:* DVD players, CD players. **Dining:** Azul, see separate listing. **Pool(s):** heated outdoor. **Leisure Activities:** saunas, whirlpool, steamrooms, jogging, massage. **Guest Services:** gift shop, valet laundry, area transportation. **Business Services:** conference facilities, business center. **Cards:** AX, CB, DC, DS, MC, VI.

SOME UNITS
[🚭] [🛏] [🍴] [24] [✈] [🏢] [🔥M] [📺] [🏊] [🎣] [🏋] [✕] [📺] [DATA PORT] / [✕] [VCR] [🛗] [🖥] /
FEE

MIAMI RIVER INN
▼▼▼   12/16-3/15   1P: $99-$169   2P: $99-$169   Phone: (305)325-0045   **8**
XP: $15   F12
▼▼▼ ▼▼▼   12/1-12/15 & 3/16-6/30   1P: $89-$109   2P: $89-$109   XP: $15   F12
Bed & Breakfast   7/1-11/30   1P: $69-$99   2P: $69-$99   XP: $15   F12
Location: I-95, exit 1B (SW 7th St), just w to SW 5th Ave, just n to SW 2nd St, then e. 118 SW South River Dr 33130.
Fax: 305/325-9227. **Facility:** Smoke free premises. 40 one-bedroom standard units. 2-3 stories (no elevator); interior/exterior corridors. *Bath:* shared or private, combo, shower or tub only. **Parking:** on-site. **Terms:** cancellation fee imposed, [CP] meal plan available, small pets only ($25 extra charge, with reservation). **Pool(s):** outdoor. **Leisure Activities:** whirlpool. **Guest Services:** coin laundry. **Business Services:** meeting rooms. **Cards:** AX, CB, DC, DS, MC, VI.

[ASK] [🛏] [🍴] [🏊] [✕]

(See map p. 502)

RENAISSANCE MIAMI BISCAYNE BAY HOTEL
[SAVE]

			Phone: (305)374-0000
12/1-5/26	1P: $169-$189	2P: $169-$189	
9/28-11/30	1P: $149-$169	2P: $149-$169	
5/27-9/27	1P: $119-$159	2P: $119-$159	

Location: US 1, 1 mi n of Flagler St. 1601 Biscayne Blvd 33132. Fax: 305/714-3811. **Facility:** 528 one-bedroom Large-scale Hotel standard units. 20 stories, interior corridors. *Bath:* combo or shower only. **Parking:** valet. **Amenities:** dual phone lines, voice mail, irons, hair dryers. *Fee:* video games, safes. **Pool(s):** heated outdoor. **Leisure Activities:** sauna, exercise room. **Guest Services:** gift shop, valet laundry. **Business Services:** conference facilities, business center. **Cards:** AX, DC, DS, MC, VI.

SOME UNITS

SHERATON BISCAYNE BAY HOTEL

			Phone: (305)373-6000
1/1-3/31	1P: $204-$269	2P: $214-$279	XP: $10	F18
4/1-9/30	1P: $139-$210	2P: $149-$220	XP: $10	F18
10/1-11/30	1P: $169-$204	2P: $179-$214	XP: $10	F18
12/1-12/31	1P: $159-$194	2P: $169-$204	XP: $10	F18

Location: 0.5 mi s on US 1. 495 Brickell Ave 33131. Fax: 305/374-2279. **Facility:** 598 units. 586 one-bedroom standard units. 12 one-bedroom suites ($239-$379). 17 stories, interior corridors. *Bath:* combo or shower only. **Parking:** on-site (fee) and valet. **Terms:** cancellation fee imposed. **Amenities:** dual phone lines, voice mail, irons, hair dryers. *Fee:* video games, high-speed Internet. *Some:* fax. **Pool(s):** heated outdoor. **Leisure Activities:** exercise room. **Guest Services:** gift shop, valet laundry. **Business Services:** conference facilities, business center. **Cards:** AX, CB, DC, DS, MC, VI.

SOME UNITS
FEE

─── *The following lodging was either not evaluated or did not* ───
meet AAA rating requirements but is listed for your information only.

RESIDENCE INN BY MARRIOTT-MIAMI DOWNTOWN/BRICKELL   Phone: 786/425-0428
[fyi]

Under construction, scheduled to open January 2003. **Location:** I-95, exit 2A, s on SE 4th St, then e. 300 Biscayne Blvd Way 33131. Fax: 786/425-2077. **Planned Amenities:** 142 units, coffeemakers, microwaves, refrigerators, Small-scale Hotel pool.

─── **WHERE TO DINE** ───

AZUL   Lunch: $11-$28   Dinner: $28-$35   Phone: 305/913-8288   7

New World
Location: US 1 (Brickell Ave), just e on SE 8th St (Brickell Key Dr); in Mandarin Oriental, Miami. 500 Brickell Key Dr 33131. **Hours:** noon-3 & 7-11 pm, Sat from 7 pm. Closed: Sun. **Reservations:** required. **Features:** Located in the Mandarin Oriental, Miami, the atmosphere is soft, the view is of the city's skyline and bayfront, and the cuisine is a blend of Asian styles using the freshest of ingredients. Dressy casual; cocktails. **Parking:** valet. **Cards:** AX, DC, MC, VI.

JOE'S SEAFOOD RESTAURANT   Lunch: $7-$14   Dinner: $12-$20   Phone: 305/381-9329   5

Seafood
Location: 0.8 mi w of I-95 on Miami River; corner of 9th St and North River Dr. 400 NW North River Dr 33128. **Hours:** 11 am-10 pm, Fri & Sat-11 pm. Closed: 12/24 for dinner. **Reservations:** accepted. **Features:** The casual, bustling restaurant serves fish caught from its own fleet as well as appetizing preparations of stone crab, shrimp, scallops and lobster. An open-air terrace offers sunny, yet breezy, dining and the occasional glimpse of a celebrity yacht. Smoke free premises. Casual dress; cocktails. **Parking:** on-site. **Cards:** AX, CB, DC, MC, VI.

─── *The following restaurants have not been evaluated by AAA* ───
but are listed for your information only.

CAPITAL GRILLE   Phone: 305/374-4500
[fyi]

Not evaluated. **Location:** 444 Brickell Ave. **Features:** Popular steakhouse; rich and scrumptious desserts. Expensive.

JAPENGO   Phone: 305/679-3055
[fyi]

Not evaluated. **Location:** In Hyatt Regency Miami. 400 SE 2nd Ave. **Features:** A large mural of downtown Hong Kong decorates one wall in the dining room. Soft lighting enhances the mood. Food emphasizing the flavors of the Orient is artfully presented.

MIAMI pop. 352,470   (See map p. 504; index p. 506)

─── **WHERE TO STAY** ───

AMERISUITES (MIAMI/AIRPORT WEST)

			Phone: (305)718-8292
12/1-4/20 [ECP]	1P: $129-$159	2P: $129-$159	XP: $10	F18
9/29-11/30 [ECP]	1P: $89-$129	2P: $89-$129	XP: $10	F18
4/21-9/28 [ECP]	1P: $84-$109	2P: $84-$109	XP: $10	F18

Location: 0.4 mi w on NW 36th St from jct SR 826 (Palmetto Expwy). 3655 NW 82nd Ave 33166. Fax: 305/718-8295. Small-scale Hotel **Facility:** 126 one-bedroom standard units. 6 stories, interior corridors. *Bath:* combo or shower only. **Parking:** on-site. **Terms:** small pets only. **Amenities:** voice mail, irons, hair dryers. *Fee:* video games, high-speed Internet. *Some:* dual phone lines. **Pool(s):** heated outdoor. **Leisure Activities:** exercise room. **Guest Services:** valet and coin laundry, airport transportation-Miami International Airport. **Business Services:** meeting rooms, business center. **Cards:** AX, DC, DS, MC, VI. **Special Amenities:** free continental breakfast and free newspaper. *(See color ad p 516)*

SOME UNITS

(See map p. 504)

BAYMONT INN & SUITES MIAMI WEST

Phone: (305)640-9896 33

12/1-4/15	2P: $89-$109	XP: $10
4/16-6/15 & 9/16-11/30	2P: $79	XP: $10
6/16-9/15	2P: $69	XP: $10

Location: Florida Tpke, exit 29, 1.2 mi e to 107th Ave, then right. 3805 NW 107th Ave 33178. Fax: 305/640-0608. **Small-scale Hotel Facility:** 92 units. 84 one-bedroom standard units. 8 one-bedroom suites ($99-$139). 4 stories, interior corridors. *Bath:* combo or shower only. **Parking:** on-site. **Amenities:** video games (fee), voice mail, irons, hair dryers. *Some:* high-speed Internet, dual phone lines, safes. **Pool(s):** outdoor. **Guest Services:** valet and coin laundry. **Business Services:** meeting rooms, fax (fee). **Cards:** AX, CB, DC, DS, MC, VI. **Special Amenities:** free continental breakfast and free newspaper.

SOME UNITS

CANDLEWOOD SUITES MIAMI AIRPORT WEST

Phone: (305)591-9099 39

12/1-4/30	1P: $109-$169	2P: $109-$169	XP: $10 F17
5/1-11/30	1P: $89-$149	2P: $89-$149	XP: $10 F17

Small-scale Hotel Location: SR 836 (Palmetto Expwy), exit NW 87th Ave N, just n on NW 87th Ave. 8855 NW 27th St 33172. Fax: 305/591-4117. **Facility:** 128 units. 104 one-bedroom standard units with efficiencies. 24 one-bedroom suites with kitchens. 3 stories, interior corridors. *Bath:* combo or shower only. **Parking:** on-site. **Terms:** small pets only ($100 fee). **Amenities:** video library, CD players, dual phone lines, voice mail, irons, hair dryers. **Leisure Activities:** exercise room. **Guest Services:** valet and coin laundry. **Cards:** AX, CB, DC, DS, JC, MC, VI.

SOME UNITS

COURTYARD BY MARRIOTT-MIAMI AIRPORT WEST/DORAL AREA

Phone: (305)477-8118 36

12/1-4/5	1P: $129-$149	2P: $129-$149
4/6-7/5 & 9/28-11/30	1P: $109-$129	2P: $109-$129
7/6-9/27	1P: $99-$119	2P: $99-$119

Location: Jct SR 826 (Palmetto Expwy), exit NW 36th St. 3929 NW 79th Ave 33166. Fax: 305/599-9363. **Small-scale Hotel Facility:** 145 units. 133 one-bedroom standard units. 12 one-bedroom suites ($119-$169). 4 stories, interior corridors. *Bath:* combo or shower only. **Parking:** on-site. **Terms:** check-in 4 pm, [AP] meal plan available. **Amenities:** high-speed Internet (fee), dual phone lines, voice mail, safes, irons, hair dryers. **Pool(s):** heated outdoor. **Leisure Activities:** whirlpool, exercise room. **Guest Services:** valet and coin laundry, area transportation. **Business Services:** meeting rooms. **Cards:** AX, CB, DC, DS, JC, MC, VI. *(See ad p 519)*

SOME UNITS

COURTYARD MIAMI AIRPORT SOUTH

Phone: (305)642-8200 47

1/13-4/30	1P: $139-$159	2P: $139-$159
10/1-11/30	1P: $129-$149	2P: $129-$149
5/1-9/30	1P: $109-$129	2P: $109-$129
12/1-1/12	1P: $89-$109	2P: $89-$109

Small-scale Hotel Location: Se of jct SR 836 (Dolphin Expwy). 1201 NW LeJeune Rd 33126. Fax: 305/644-1168. **Facility:** 125 units. 124 one-bedroom standard units. 1 one-bedroom suite ($139-$200). 5 stories, interior corridors. *Bath:* combo or shower only. **Parking:** on-site (fee). **Terms:** check-in 4 pm. **Amenities:** high-speed Internet (fee), dual phone lines, voice mail, irons, hair dryers. **Dining:** 2 restaurants, 6:30 am-1 am. **Pool(s):** heated outdoor. **Leisure Activities:** whirlpools, 8 tennis courts (6 lighted), jogging, exercise room, basketball, volleyball. **Fee:** game room. **Guest Services:** valet and coin laundry, airport transportation-Miami International Airport. **Cards:** AX, CB, DC, DS, MC, VI. *(See ad p 519)*

SOME UNITS

(See map p. 504)

CROWNE PLAZA HOTEL AND RESORT MIAMI INTERNATIONAL AIRPORT   **Phone:** 305/446-9000 60
▼▼▽▼▽▼   Property failed to provide current rates
Location: 1 mi s of terminal entrance, just s of jct SR 836, Dolphin Expwy. 950 NW Le Jeune Rd 33126.
Large-scale Hotel Fax: 305/441-0729. **Facility:** 304 one-bedroom standard units. 6 stories, interior corridors. **Parking:** on-site.
Terms: small pets only. **Amenities:** voice mail, irons, hair dryers. *Some:* dual phone lines. **Pool(s):** outdoor.
Leisure Activities: saunas, whirlpool, exercise room. **Guest Services:** gift shop, valet and coin laundry. **Business Services:**
meeting rooms, business center. **Cards:** AX, CB, DC, DS, JC, MC, VI.

SOME UNITS

⊞ ✈ 🐾 🍴 🍸 🔊M 🛋 🏊 ⊠ 🎳 DATA PORT 💻 / ⊠ 🖥 FEE

DAYS INN CIVIC CENTER/MEDICAL CENTER   **Phone:** (305)324-0200 64
AAA SAVE   11/1-11/30   1P: $69-$89   XP: $5   F5
    12/1-10/31   1P: $49-$69   XP: $5   F5
▼▽▼▽ ▼▽▼▽   **Location:** Just ne of jct NW 12th Ave and SR 836 (Dolphin Expwy); exit NW 14th St westbound. Located adjacent to the
Motel hospital district. 1050 NW 14th St 33136. Fax: 305/545-8482. **Facility:** 208 one-bedroom standard units, some
with efficiencies. 5 stories, exterior corridors. *Bath:* combo or shower only. **Parking:** on-site. **Terms:** cancellation fee imposed, [BP] meal plans available. **Amenities:** voice mail,
safes (fee), hair dryers. **Dining:** 6 am-10 pm. **Pool(s):** outdoor. **Leisure Activities:** exercise room. **Guest Services:** gift shop,
coin laundry, area transportation-Port of Miami & hospital. **Business Services:** fax (fee). **Cards:** AX, DC, DS, MC, VI.
Special Amenities: free newspaper and free room upgrade (subject to availability with advanced reservations).

SOME UNITS

S🅓 ✈ 🍴 🛋 🏊 🎳 DATA PORT / ⊠ 🖥 💻 /

DAYS INN MIAMI INTERNATIONAL AIRPORT HOTEL   **Phone:** (305)261-4230 63
AAA SAVE   12/1-3/31   1P: $69-$89   2P: $89-$109   XP: $10   F12
    4/1-11/30   1P: $59-$79   2P: $69-$89   XP: $10   F12
▼▽▼▽ ▼▽▼▽   **Location:** Just n of Milam Dairy Rd and NW 11th St off SR 836. 7250 NW 11th St 33126. Fax: 305/264-9685.
Facility: 103 one-bedroom standard units. 4 stories, interior corridors. **Parking:** on-site. **Terms:** cancellation
Small-scale Hotel fee imposed, [MAP] meal plan available. **Amenities:** voice mail, safes (fee), irons, hair dryers. **Dining:** 7:30
am-10 & 11-10 pm, Fri & Sat-3 am, Sun 7-11:30 am, cocktails. **Pool(s):** outdoor. **Leisure Activities:** exer-
cise room. **Guest Services:** coin laundry, airport transportation-Miami International Airport, area transportation-Port of Miami.
Business Services: business center. **Cards:** AX, CB, DC, DS, JC, MC, VI. **Special Amenities:** free newspaper and free room
upgrade (subject to availability with advanced reservations).

SOME UNITS

S🅓 ✈ 🍴 🍸 🛋 🏊 🎳 DATA PORT / ⊠ 🖥 💻 /

DORAL GOLF RESORT AND SPA   **Phone:** (305)592-2000 50
▼▽▼▽ ▼▽▼▽   12/1-4/13   1P: $349-$999   2P: $349-$999
    4/14-5/21   1P: $269-$789   2P: $269-$788
    9/8-11/30   1P: $259-$759   2P: $259-$759
Resort   5/22-9/7   1P: $155-$480   2P: $155-$480
Large-scale Hotel **Location:** 1 mi w of jct SR 826 (Palmetto Expwy) at jct NW 36th St and NW 87th Ave; entrance on NW 87th Ave. 4400
NW 87th Ave 33178. **Facility:** The property offers many rooms with balconies, some overlooking the golf
course; admission to an adjacent European spa facility is available. 646 units. 581 one-bedroom standard units. 50 one- and 15
two-bedroom suites, some with whirlpools. 3-4 stories, interior corridors. **Parking:** on-site and valet. **Terms:** check-in 4 pm, 3
day cancellation notice-fee imposed, package plans - seasonal, $15 service charge. **Amenities:** CD players, dual phone lines,
voice mail, safes, honor bars, irons, hair dryers. *Fee:* video games, high-speed Internet. *Some:* fax. **Pool(s):** 2 heated outdoor,
wading. **Leisure Activities:** whirlpool, waterslide, fishing, recreation programs, jogging, playground, spa, sports court, basketball, volleyball, game room. *Fee:* charter fishing, golf-90 holes, 12 tennis courts (6 lighted), bicycles. **Guest Services:** valet
laundry. **Business Services:** conference facilities, business center. **Cards:** AX, DC, DS, JC, MC, VI.

SOME UNITS

ASK S🅓 ✈ 🍴 🍸 🎰 🛋 🏊 🚲 ⊠ 🎳 DATA PORT 💻 / ⊠ 🖥 /
FEE   FEE

(See map p. 504)

DOUBLETREE CLUB MIAMI AIRPORT HOTEL

Phone: (305)266-0000   **58**

SAVE

12/1-4/15	1P: $99-$189	2P: $99-$189	XP: $10	F12
10/1-11/30	1P: $99-$139	2P: $99-$139	XP: $10	F12
4/16-9/30	1P: $69-$119	2P: $69-$119	XP: $10	F12

Small-scale Hotel

Location: 2.5 mi sw of airport entrance on Red Rd and jct SR 836 (Dolphin Expwy). 1101 NW 57th Ave 33126. **Fax:** 305/266-9179. **Facility:** 266 one-bedroom standard units. 10 stories, interior corridors. **Parking:** on-site. **Terms:** [BP] meal plan available, package plans. **Amenities:** voice mail, irons, hair dryers. **Pool(s):** outdoor, wading. **Guest Services:** valet and coin laundry. **Business Services:** meeting rooms, business center. **Cards:** AX, CB, DC, DS, MC, VI.

SOME UNITS

🖥️ ✈️ 🍴 🍸 🔌 🏊 📶 DATAPORT 💻 / ✖️ VCR 📠 📷 /
FEE

EL PALACIO RESORT HOTEL & SUITES

Phone: (305)624-8401   **31**

AAA **SAVE**

All Year	2P: $70

Small-scale Hotel

Location: I-95, exit 12, w on SR 826 (Palmetto Expwy), then n. 16805 NW 12th Ave 33169. **Fax:** 305/625-0022. **Facility:** 104 units. 99 one-bedroom standard units, some with whirlpools. 5 one-bedroom suites ($189) with whirlpools. 4 stories, interior corridors. **Parking:** on-site. **Terms:** cancellation fee imposed, weekly rates available, $7 service charge. **Amenities:** voice mail, safes (fee), hair dryers. *Some:* irons. **Dining:** 8 am-10 pm, cocktails. **Pool(s):** outdoor. **Leisure Activities:** exercise room. **Guest Services:** airport transportation-Miami International Airport, area transportation-within 5 mi. **Business Services:** meeting rooms, fax (fee). **Cards:** AX, MC, VI.

SOME UNITS

🖥️ ✈️ 🍴 🍸 📶 📺 DATAPORT 💻 / ✖️ /

EMBASSY SUITES MIAMI INTERNATIONAL AIRPORT

Phone: (305)634-5000   **71**

SAVE

1/1-4/30 [BP]	1P: $129-$199	2P: $129-$199	XP: $10	F18
10/1-11/30 [BP]	1P: $159-$189	2P: $159-$189		
12/1-12/31 [BP]	1P: $159-$189	2P: $159-$189	XP: $10	F18
5/1-9/30 [BP]	1P: $109-$159	2P: $109-$159	XP: $10	F18

Large-scale Hotel **Location:** Jct SR 112 and 953 (LeJeune Rd); entrance on South River Dr. 3974 NW South River Dr 33142. **Fax:** 305/635-9499. **Facility:** 316 one-bedroom suites. 10 stories, interior corridors. *Bath:* combo or shower only. **Parking:** on-site (fee). **Terms:** package plans - seasonal & weekends. **Amenities:** video games (fee), dual phone lines, voice mail, irons, hair dryers. **Pool(s):** heated outdoor. **Leisure Activities:** whirlpool, exercise room. **Guest Services:** gift shop, complimentary evening beverages, valet and coin laundry. **Business Services:** meeting rooms, fax. **Cards:** AX, CB, DC, DS, JC, MC, VI.

SOME UNITS

✈️ 🍴 🍸 🛗 📶 📺 DATAPORT 📠 📷 💻 / ✖️ VCR /

FAIRFIELD INN BY MARRIOTT-MIAMI WEST/DORAL AREA

Phone: (305)599-5200   **35**

SAVE

1/16-4/15	1P: $84-$89
12/1-1/15	1P: $80-$84
4/16-9/30	1P: $51-$56

Motel

Location: NW 36th St, w at jct SR 826 (Palmetto Expwy). 3959 NW 79th Ave 33166. **Fax:** 305/436-2935. **Facility:** 135 one-bedroom standard units. 3 stories, interior/exterior corridors. **Parking:** on-site. **Terms:** 5 day cancellation notice. **Amenities:** irons, hair dryers. **Pool(s):** heated outdoor. **Guest Services:** valet laundry. **Business Services:** fax (fee). **Cards:** AX, CB, DC, DS, JC, MC, VI.

SOME UNITS

🖥️ ✈️ 🍴 📶 🏊 📺 DATAPORT / ✖️ 📠 📷 /

FAIRFIELD INN MIAMI AIRPORT SOUTH

Phone: 305/643-0055   **48**

SAVE

1/15-4/30	1P: $99-$119	2P: $99-$119	XP: $10	F
5/1-11/30	1P: $79-$99	2P: $79-$99	XP: $10	F
12/1-1/14	1P: $69-$85	2P: $69-$85	XP: $10	F

Motel

Location: Se of jct SR 836 (Palmetto Expwy) and NW LeJune Rd. 1201 NW LeJune Rd 33126. **Fax:** 305/649-3997. **Facility:** 281 one-bedroom standard units. 3 stories, exterior corridors. *Bath:* combo or shower only. **Parking:** on-site (fee). **Terms:** cancellation fee imposed, [ECP] meal plan available. **Amenities:** voice mail, irons, hair dryers. **Pool(s):** heated outdoor. **Leisure Activities:** whirlpools, exercise room, basketball, volleyball. **Fee:** 8 tennis courts (6 lighted), game room. **Guest Services:** valet and coin laundry. **Cards:** AX, CB, DC, DS, JC, MC, VI.

SOME UNITS

✈️ 🍴 🍸 🛗 📶 🏊 ✖️ 📺 DATAPORT / ✖️ VCR /
FEE

HAMPTON INN & SUITES

Phone: (305)500-9300   **32**

SAVE

12/1-5/1	1P: $104	2P: $119
5/2-11/30	1P: $89	2P: $109

Small-scale Hotel

Location: Florida Tpke, exit 29 (NW 41st St). 11600 NW 41st St 33178. **Fax:** 305/500-9400. **Facility:** 121 units. 77 one-bedroom standard units. 44 one-bedroom suites ($129-$159) with efficiencies. 6 stories, interior corridors. *Bath:* combo or shower only. **Parking:** on-site. **Terms:** [ECP] meal plan available. **Amenities:** dual phone lines, voice mail, safes, irons, hair dryers. *Fee:* video games, high-speed Internet. **Pool(s):** outdoor. **Leisure Activities:** limited exercise equipment. **Guest Services:** sundries, valet and coin laundry, area transportation. **Business Services:** meeting rooms, business center. **Cards:** AX, CB, DC, DS, MC, VI.

SOME UNITS

🖥️ ✈️ 🍴 🛗 🅖🅜 🛗 📶 🏊 📺 DATAPORT 💻 / ✖️ VCR 📠 📷 /

HAMPTON INN & SUITES-MIAMI AIRPORT

Phone: (305)262-5400   **62**

SAVE

1/5-4/12 [ECP]	1P: $109-$149	2P: $119-$159
12/1-1/4 & 4/13-11/30 [ECP]	1P: $79-$119	2P: $89-$129

Small-scale Hotel

Location: SR 836 (Dolphin Expwy), exit Rael Rd/57th Ave S, just s of NW 7th St. 777 NW 57th Ave 33126. **Fax:** 305/262-5488. **Facility:** 147 units. 110 one-bedroom standard units. 37 one-bedroom suites ($119-$169) with kitchens. 11 stories, interior corridors. *Bath:* combo or shower only. **Parking:** on-site. **Amenities:** video games (fee), dual phone lines, voice mail, safes, irons, hair dryers. *Some:* high-speed Internet. **Pool(s):** outdoor. **Leisure Activities:** whirlpool, exercise room. **Guest Services:** valet and coin laundry, area transportation. **Business Services:** meeting rooms, business center. **Cards:** AX, CB, DC, DS, JC, MC, VI.

SOME UNITS

🖥️ ✈️ 🍴 🛗 🅖🅜 🛗 📶 🏊 📺 DATAPORT 💻 / ✖️ VCR 📠 📷 /
FEE FEE

(See map p. 504)

HAMPTON INN-MIAMI AIRPORT WEST
Phone: (305)513-0777 [38]

SAVE

Small-scale Hotel

1/1-3/31 [ECP]	1P: $119	2P: $129	XP: $10	F18
4/1-11/30 [ECP]	1P: $109	2P: $119	XP: $10	F18
12/1-12/31 [ECP]	1P: $87	2P: $97	XP: $10	F18

Location: SR 826 (Palmetto Expwy), exit NW 36th St, just s of jct NW 58th St, exit s. Located in Boykin Center. 3620 NW 79th Ave 33166. **Fax:** 305/513-9019. **Facility:** 127 one-bedroom standard units. 6 stories, interior corridors. *Bath:* combo or shower only. **Parking:** on-site. **Terms:** 3 day cancellation notice, pets ($25 extra charge). **Amenities:** voice mail, irons, hair dryers. *Fee:* video games, high-speed Internet. **Pool(s):** heated outdoor. **Leisure Activities:** exercise room. **Guest Services:** valet and coin laundry, area transportation. **Business Services:** meeting rooms, business center. **Cards:** AX, DC, DS, MC, VI.

SOME UNITS

HAMPTON INN MIAMI/DADELAND
Phone: (305)269-0072 [68]

SAVE

Small-scale Hotel

12/1-4/15 [CP]	1P: $89-$109	2P: $99-$119
9/15-11/30 [CP]	1P: $79-$89	2P: $89-$99
4/16-9/14 [CP]	1P: $69-$79	2P: $79-$89

Location: I-95, exit 1A, off US 1 (Dixie Hwy) and SW 80th St, just w. Located next to Dadeland Mall. 8200 SW 70th Ave 33143. **Fax:** 305/269-1060. **Facility:** 131 one-bedroom standard units. 5 stories, interior corridors. *Bath:* combo or shower only. **Parking:** on-site. **Terms:** 15 day cancellation notice. **Amenities:** high-speed Internet, dual phone lines, voice mail, irons, hair dryers. *Fee:* video library, video games. **Pool(s):** heated outdoor. **Leisure Activities:** whirlpool, limited exercise equipment. **Guest Services:** area transportation. **Business Services:** meeting rooms, business center. **Cards:** AX, CB, DC, DS, MC, VI.

SOME UNITS

HILTON MIAMI AIRPORT
Phone: (305)262-1000 [59]

SAVE

Large-scale Hotel

All Year	1P: $69-$199	2P: $69-$199	XP: $25 F18

Location: Se of jct SR 836 (Dolphin Expwy), exit Red Rd, 0.7 mi e. 5101 Blue Lagoon Dr 33126. **Fax:** 305/267-0038. **Facility:** On a peninsula overlooking a lagoon, the hotel offers many units with water views; all feature desks. 500 units. 430 one-bedroom standard units. 70 one-bedroom suites. 14 stories, interior corridors. *Bath:* combo or shower only. **Parking:** on-site (fee) and valet. **Amenities:** dual phone lines, voice mail, honor bars, irons, hair dryers. *Fee:* video games, high-speed Internet. *Some:* fax. **Pool(s):** heated outdoor. **Leisure Activities:** saunas, whirlpool, boat dock, fishing, 2 tennis courts (1 lighted), jogging, exercise room, basketball. **Guest Services:** gift shop, valet laundry, area transportation. **Business Services:** conference facilities, business center. **Cards:** AX, CB, DC, DS, JC, MC, VI.

SOME UNITS

HOLIDAY INN-CALDER/PRO PLAYER STADIUM
Phone: (305)621-5801 [30]

Small-scale Hotel

12/1-3/31	1P: $99-$129	2P: $99-$129	XP: $10	F17
9/1-11/30	1P: $89-$99	2P: $89-$99	XP: $10	F17
4/1-8/31	1P: $79-$89	2P: $79-$89	XP: $10	F17

Location: SR 852 at jct SR 817 and Florida Tpke, exit 47; from the south exit 4 X. Located next to the racetrack. 21485 NW 27th Ave 33056. **Fax:** 305/624-8202. **Facility:** Designated smoking area. 214 one-bedroom standard units. 9 stories, interior corridors. **Parking:** on-site. **Amenities:** voice mail, irons, hair dryers. **Pool(s):** heated outdoor. **Leisure Activities:** exercise room. *Fee:* game room. **Guest Services:** gift shop, valet and coin laundry. **Business Services:** meeting rooms, fax (fee). **Cards:** AX, CB, DS, MC, VI. *(See color ad opposite inside back cover)*

SOME UNITS

HOLIDAY INN-MIAMI AIRPORT WEST
Phone: (305)500-9000 [43]

Small-scale Hotel

2/8-3/8	1P: $129-$169
12/1-2/7 & 3/9-4/15	1P: $119-$159
4/16-11/30	1P: $109-$149

Location: SR 826 (Palmetto Expwy), exit NW 58th and NW 36th sts, then 0.6 mi s. 3255 NW 87th Ave 33172. **Fax:** 305/500-9500. **Facility:** 120 units. 115 one-bedroom standard units. 5 one-bedroom suites ($149-$189). 6 stories, interior corridors. *Bath:* combo or shower only. **Parking:** on-site. **Terms:** package plans. **Amenities:** dual phone lines, voice mail, safes, honor bars, irons, hair dryers. *Fee:* video games, high-speed Internet. **Pool(s):** heated outdoor. **Leisure Activities:** exercise room, basketball. **Guest Services:** valet and coin laundry, area transportation. **Business Services:** meeting rooms, business center. **Cards:** AX, CB, DC, DS, JC, MC, VI. *(See color ad opposite inside back cover)*

SOME UNITS

HOMESTEAD STUDIO SUITES HOTEL-MIAMI/AIRPORT/BLUE LAGOON
Phone: (305)260-0085 [53]

Motel

1/11-4/1	1P: $79	2P: $109	XP: $5 F18
12/1-1/10 & 4/2-11/30	1P: $59	2P: $79	XP: $5 F18

Location: SR 836 (Dolphin Expwy), exit Milam Dairy Rd S, 0.3 mi e. Located in Blue Lagoon Office Park. 6605 NW 7th St 33126. **Fax:** 305/260-0042. **Facility:** 149 one-bedroom standard units with efficiencies. 2 stories, exterior corridors. *Bath:* combo or shower only. **Parking:** on-site. **Terms:** cancellation fee imposed, small pets only ($75 fee). **Amenities:** voice mail, irons. **Guest Services:** valet and coin laundry. **Cards:** AX, CB, DC, DS, JC, MC, VI.

SOME UNITS

HOMESTEAD STUDIO SUITES HOTEL-MIAMI/AIRPORT/DORAL
Phone: (305)436-1811 [40]

Motel

1/15-4/15	1P: $79	2P: $79	XP: $5 F18
12/1-1/14 & 4/16-11/30	1P: $59	2P: $79	XP: $5 F18

Location: SR 826 (Palmetto Expwy), 0.8 mi w on NW 36th St, then s on 87th St, 0.6 mi on right. Located in Westpoint Office Park. 8720 NW 33rd St 33172. **Fax:** 305/436-1864. **Facility:** 149 one-bedroom standard units with efficiencies. 2 stories, exterior corridors. *Bath:* combo or shower only. **Parking:** on-site. **Terms:** cancellation fee imposed, pets ($75). **Amenities:** voice mail, irons. **Guest Services:** coin laundry. **Business Services:** fax (fee). **Cards:** AX, CB, DC, DS, JC, MC, VI.

SOME UNITS

(See map p. 504)

HOMEWOOD SUITES BY HILTON-MIAMI BLUE LAGOON
Phone: (305)261-3335   67

SAVE

1/1-4/30	1P: $143-$188	2P: $143-$188
12/1-12/31 & 5/1-11/30	1P: $125-$170	2P: $125-$170

Small-scale Hotel

Location: Se of jct SR 836 (Dolphin Expwy), exit Red Rd. 5500 Blue Lagoon Dr 33126. Fax: 305/261-1223. **Facility:** 159 units. 134 one- and 25 two-bedroom suites with efficiencies. 7 stories, interior corridors. *Bath:* combo or shower only. **Parking:** on-site. **Terms:** cancellation fee imposed, [ECP] meal plan available, small pets only ($10-$100 fee, $20 extra charge). **Amenities:** dual phone lines, voice mail, safes (fee), irons, hair dryers. **Pool(s):** heated outdoor. **Leisure Activities:** whirlpool, fishing, exercise room, sports court. **Guest Services:** complimentary evening beverages: Mon-Thurs, valet and coin laundry, area transportation. **Business Services:** meeting rooms, business center. **Cards:** AX, DC, DS, MC, VI.

SOME UNITS

LA QUINTA INN & SUITES
Phone: (305)436-0830   46

SAVE

12/26-4/7	1P: $89-$119	2P: $95-$125
12/1-12/25 & 4/8-11/30	1P: $69-$89	2P: $75-$95

Small-scale Hotel

Location: SR 836 (Dolphin Expwy), just n on 87th NW Ave. 8730 NW 27th St 33172. Fax: 305/436-0840. **Facility:** 143 units. 137 one-bedroom standard units. 6 one-bedroom suites. 6 stories, interior corridors. *Bath:* combo or shower only. **Parking:** on-site. **Terms:** [ECP] meal plan available, small pets only. **Amenities:** video games (fee), voice mail, irons, hair dryers. *Some:* dual phone lines. **Pool(s):** heated outdoor. **Leisure Activities:** whirlpool, exercise room. **Business Services:** meeting rooms. **Cards:** AX, CB, DC, DS, JC, MC, VI.

SOME UNITS

LA QUINTA INN MIAMI AIRPORT NORTH
Phone: (305)599-9902   41

SAVE

12/26-4/7	1P: $89-$119	2P: $95-$125
4/8-11/30	1P: $59-$89	2P: $65-$95
12/1-12/25	1P: $59-$79	2P: $65-$85

Motel

Location: Just e of jct SR 826 (Palmetto Expwy). 7401 NW 36th St 33166. Fax: 305/594-0552. **Facility:** 165 one-bedroom standard units. 3 stories, exterior corridors. **Parking:** on-site. **Terms:** [ECP] meal plan available, small pets only. **Amenities:** video games (fee), voice mail, irons, hair dryers. **Pool(s):** outdoor. **Guest Services:** valet and coin laundry. **Business Services:** meeting rooms. **Cards:** AX, CB, DC, DS, JC, MC, VI.

SOME UNITS

MIAMI AIRPORT MARRIOTT
Phone: 305/649-5000   61

SAVE

1/13-4/30	1P: $139-$199	2P: $139-$199
10/1-11/30	1P: $130-$169	2P: $130-$169
5/1-9/30	1P: $109-$149	2P: $109-$149
12/1-1/12	1P: $100-$149	2P: $100-$149

Large-scale Hotel

Location: Se of jct SR 836 and NW Le Jeune Rd. 1201 NW Le Jeune Rd 33126. Fax: 305/642-3369. **Facility:** 366 units. 361 one-bedroom standard units. 5 one-bedroom suites. 10 stories, interior corridors. *Bath:* combo or shower only. **Parking:** on-site (fee). **Terms:** check-in 4 pm. **Amenities:** high-speed Internet (fee), dual phone lines, voice mail, irons, hair dryers. **Pool(s):** heated outdoor. **Leisure Activities:** whirlpools, 8 tennis courts (6 lighted), jogging, exercise room, basketball, volleyball. *Fee:* game room. **Guest Services:** gift shop, valet and coin laundry, area transportation. **Business Services:** conference facilities, business center. **Cards:** AX, DC, DS, MC, VI.

SOME UNITS

MIAMI DADELAND MARRIOTT
Phone: (305)670-1035   65

AAA **SAVE**

12/1-3/31	1P: $189-$219
4/1-5/31	1P: $169-$199
6/1-9/30	1P: $144-$169

Large-scale Hotel

Location: SR 826 (Palmetto Expwy), exit Kendall Dr E 2 blks. 9090 S Dadeland Blvd 33156. Fax: 305/670-7540. **Facility:** 302 units. 300 one-bedroom standard units. 2 one-bedroom suites ($350-$700). 24 stories, interior corridors. *Bath:* combo or shower only. **Parking:** on-site (fee) and valet. **Terms:** check-in 4 pm, cancellation fee imposed. **Amenities:** video games, dual phone lines, voice mail, honor bars, irons, hair dryers. *Fee:* high-speed Internet, safes. **Dining:** 2 restaurants, 6:30 am-2:30 & 4:30-11 pm, cocktails. **Pool(s):** heated outdoor. **Leisure Activities:** whirlpool, exercise room. **Guest Services:** gift shop, valet laundry, airport transportation-Miami International Airport, area transportation-within 3 mi. **Business Services:** conference facilities, business center. **Cards:** AX, CB, DC, DS, JC, MC, VI.

SOME UNITS

MIAMI INTERNATIONAL AIRPORT HOTEL
Phone: (305)72608100   69

12/16-4/15	1P: $129-$179	2P: $149-$199	XP: $20	F12
12/1-12/15 & 4/16-11/30	1P: $115-$165	2P: $135-$185	XP: $10	F12

Large-scale Hotel

Location: NW 20th St and Le Jeune Rd. Located in the center of the airport terminal on the second level. NW 20th St & Le Jeune Rd, Concourse E 33299 (PO Box 997510). Fax: 305/869-1233. **Facility:** 260 units. 259 one-bedroom standard units. 1 one-bedroom suite with whirlpool. 7 stories, interior corridors. **Parking:** on-site (fee). **Amenities:** voice mail, hair dryers. **Pool(s):** heated outdoor. **Leisure Activities:** sauna, whirlpool, steamroom, racquetball court, exercise room. **Guest Services:** gift shop, valet laundry. **Business Services:** meeting rooms, business center. **Cards:** AX, CB, DC, DS, JC, MC, VI.

SOME UNITS

FEE

(See map p. 504)

QUALITY INN-SOUTH

Phone: (305)251-2000   **70**

AAA SAVE
🔻🔻🔻

Motel

12/20-4/26	1P: $79-$135	2P: $79-$135	XP: $5 F18
4/27-11/30	1P: $74-$135	2P: $74-$135	XP: $5 F18
12/1-12/19	1P: $74-$95	2P: $74-$95	XP: $5 F18

Location: US 1 at SW 145th St. 14501 S Dixie Hwy (US 1) 33176. Fax: 305/235-2225. **Facility:** Designated smoking area. 100 one-bedroom standard units. 2 stories (no elevator), exterior corridors. **Parking:** on-site. **Terms:** weekly rates available, small pets only. **Amenities:** dual phone lines. *Some:* irons, hair dryers. **Dining:** 6:30 am-10 pm, Fri & Sat-11 pm, cocktails. **Pool(s):** heated outdoor. **Leisure Activities:** Fee: game room. **Guest Services:** coin laundry. **Business Services:** meeting rooms, fax (fee). **Cards:** AX, CB, DC, DS, JC, MC, VI. **Special Amenities:** free newspaper and free room upgrade (subject to availability with advanced reservations). *(See color ad below)*

SOME UNITS
🆂🄳 🐾 🍴 🍸 📷 🏊 🐾 📷 DATA PORT 💻 / ⊠ 📱 🖥 /

RADISSON MART PLAZA HOTEL

Phone: (305)261-3800   **52**

AAA SAVE
🔻🔻🔻

Large-scale Hotel

12/1-4/10	1P: $139	2P: $139	XP: $20 F17
10/1-11/30	1P: $129	2P: $129	XP: $20 F17
4/11-9/30	1P: $99	2P: $99	XP: $20 F17

Location: At Milam Dairy Rd off SR 836 (Dolphin Expwy). Located adjacent to the Merchandise Mart Complex. 711 NW 72nd Ave 33126. Fax: 305/261-7665. **Facility:** 334 units. 331 one-bedroom standard units, some with whirl-pools. 3 one-bedroom suites ($219-$499). 12 stories, interior corridors. *Bath:* combo or shower only. **Parking:** on-site (fee). **Terms:** cancellation fee imposed. **Amenities:** dual phone lines, voice mail, irons, hair dryers. *Some:* CD players, honor bars. **Dining:** 6 am-11 pm, cocktails, entertainment. **Pool(s):** heated outdoor. **Leisure Activities:** saunas, whirlpool, racquetball courts, exercise room. **Guest Services:** gift shop, valet laundry, airport transportation Miami International Airport. **Business Services:** conference facilities, business center. **Cards:** AX, DC, DS, MC, VI. **Special Amenities:** early check-in/late check-out and free newspaper.

SOME UNITS
🆂🄳 ✈ 🍴 🍸 📷 🏊 ⊠ 📷 DATA PORT 💻 / ⊠ 📱 /

RAMADA LIMITED SOUTH MIAMI DADELAND

Phone: (305)595-6000   **66**

🔻🔻🔻

Small-scale Hotel

12/1-4/20 [ECP]	1P: $94-$114	2P: $98-$119	XP: $10 F
4/21-11/30 [ECP]	1P: $69-$99	2P: $73-$104	XP: $10 F

Location: SR 826 (Palmetto Expwy), exit Kendall Dr, just w. 7600 N Kendall Dr 33156. Fax: 305/279-6988. **Facility:** 122 one-bedroom standard units. 6 stories, interior corridors. **Parking:** on-site. **Amenities:** high-speed Internet, voice mail, irons, hair dryers. **Pool(s):** outdoor. **Business Services:** meeting rooms, fax (fee). **Cards:** AX, CB, DC, DS, JC, MC, VI.

SOME UNITS
ASK 🍴 📷 🏊 ⊠ 📷 DATA PORT 💻 / ⊠ /

RESIDENCE INN MIAMI AIRPORT BY MARRIOTT

Phone: (305)591-2211   **44**

SAVE
🔻🔻🔻

Motel

12/1-4/15 [BP]	1P: $149-$189	2P: $179-$229	
4/16-11/30 [BP]	1P: $89-$129	2P: $119-$169	

Location: SR 836 (Dolphin Expwy), exit 87th Ave NW, just n to NW 82nd Ave, then e. 1212 NW 82nd Ave 33126. Fax: 305/591-0902. **Facility:** 112 units. 64 one-bedroom standard units with kitchens. 48 one-bedroom suites with kitchens. 3 stories, exterior corridors. **Parking:** on-site. **Terms:** small pets only ($60 fee, $6 extra charge). **Amenities:** voice mail, irons, hair dryers. **Pool(s):** small outdoor. **Leisure Activities:** whirlpool, sports court, basketball. **Business Services:** meeting rooms, fax (fee). **Cards:** AX, CB, DC, DS, JC, MC, VI.

SOME UNITS
🆂🄳 🐾 🍴 📷 🏊 ➕ ⊠ 📷 DATA PORT 📱 🖥 💻 / ⊠ /

THE SPA AT DORAL

Phone: (305)593-6030   **49**

🔻🔻 🔻🔻

Resort
Small-scale Hotel

12/1-4/13	1P: $559-$1349	2P: $559-$1349	
4/14-5/21	1P: $425-$979	2P: $425-$979	
9/8-11/30	1P: $405-$955	2P: $405-$955	
5/22-9/7	1P: $250-$550	2P: $250-$550	

Location: 1.3 mi w of jct SR 826 (Palmetto Expwy); on NW 36th St. Located on the grounds of the Doral Golf Resort. 8755 NW 36th St 33178. Fax: 305/591-9268. **Facility:** This property features spacious and luxurious rooms decorated with soft colors and world class spa. Designated smoking area. 48 one-bedroom standard units with whirlpools. 3 stories, interior corridors. **Parking:** on-site and valet. **Terms:** age restrictions may apply, 3 day cancellation notice-fee imposed, package plans - seasonal, $15 service charge. **Amenities:** CD players, dual phone lines, voice mail, safes, honor bars, irons, hair dryers. *Fee:* video games, high-speed Internet. **Some:** fax. **Pool(s):** 2 outdoor, heated indoor. **Leisure Activities:** saunas, whirlpool, steamrooms, waterslide, fishing, jogging, spa. *Fee:* charter fishing, golf-90 holes, 12 tennis courts (6 lighted), bicycles. **Guest Services:** gift shop, valet laundry. **Business Services:** meeting rooms, business center. **Cards:** AX, CB, DC, DS, JC, MC, VI.

ASK 🆂🄳 ✈ 🍴 🏊 ➕ ⊠ ⊠ 📷 DATA PORT 📱 💻
FEE

(See map p. 504)

STAYBRIDGE SUITES MIAMI-AIRPORT WEST
Phone: (305)500-9100 57

	2/8-3/8 [ECP]	1P: $139-$179
	12/1-2/7 & 3/9-4/15 [ECP]	1P: $129-$169
Small-scale Hotel	4/16-11/30 [ECP]	1P: $119-$159

Location: SR 826 (Palmetto Expwy), exit NW 58th and 36th sts, then 0.6 mi s. 3265 NW 87th Ave 33172. Fax: 305/500-9200. **Facility:** 96 units. 56 one-bedroom standard units with efficiencies. 40 one-bedroom suites with kitchens. 8 stories, interior corridors. *Bath:* combo or shower only. **Parking:** on-site. **Amenities:** dual phone lines, voice mail, irons, hair dryers. *Fee:* video library, video games, high-speed Internet. **Pool(s):** outdoor. **Leisure Activities:** exercise room, basketball. **Guest Services:** valet and coin laundry, area transportation. **Business Services:** meeting rooms, business center. **Cards:** AX, CB, DC, DS, JC, MC, VI.

SOME UNITS
(ASK) (S/D) [+] [T/+] (D) (~) (VCR) (*) (DATA/PORT) [H] (=) (⌐) /(X)/

SUMMERFIELD SUITES BY WYNDHAM-MIAMI AIRPORT
Phone: (305)269-1922 56

| (AAA) (SAVE) | 12/1-4/30 & 9/29-11/30 [ECP] | 1P: $99-$168 | 2P: $99-$168 | XP: $20 | F18 |
| | 5/1-9/28 [ECP] | 1P: $99-$149 | 2P: $99-$149 | XP: $20 | F18 |

Location: 2.5 mi sw of airport entrance; se of jct SR 836 (Dolphin Expwy), exit Red Rd, just w. 5710 Blue Lagoon Dr 33126. Fax: 305/269-1925. **Facility:** 156 units. 99 one- and 57 two-bedroom suites ($99-$168) with kitchens. **Small-scale Hotel** 3 stories, interior corridors. *Bath:* combo or shower only. **Parking:** on-site. **Terms:** cancellation fee imposed, pets ($200 fee). **Amenities:** dual phone lines, voice mail, safes, irons, hair dryers. *Fee:* video library, high-speed Internet. **Pool(s):** heated outdoor. **Leisure Activities:** whirlpool, barbecue grills, limited exercise equipment. **Guest Services:** complimentary evening beverages: Mon-Thurs, valet and coin laundry, airport transportation-Miami International Airport, area transportation-within 3 mi. **Business Services:** meeting rooms, fax (fee). **Cards:** AX, DC, MC, VI.

SOME UNITS
(S/D) [+] (☎) [T/+] (&M) (&) (D) (~) (X) (VCR) (*) (DATA/PORT) [H] (=) (⌐) /(X)/

SUPER 8 MOTEL
Phone: (305)573-7700 51

| | 12/1-4/30 | 1P: $60-$100 | 2P: $70-$120 | XP: $5 | F12 |
| Motel | 5/1-11/30 | 1P: $50-$70 | 2P: $55-$75 | XP: $5 | F12 |

Location: I-95, exit US 1/Biscayne Blvd, just s. 3400 Biscayne Blvd 33137. Fax: 305/573-7706. **Facility:** 49 one-bedroom standard units. 2 stories (no elevator), exterior corridors. **Parking:** on-site. **Terms:** cancellation fee imposed. **Pool(s):** outdoor. **Guest Services:** coin laundry. **Business Services:** fax (fee). **Cards:** AX, DC, DS, JC, MC, VI.

SOME UNITS
(ASK) (S/D) [T/+] (~) (*) (DATA/PORT) /(X)/ [H] /

TOWNEPLACE SUITES BY MARRIOTT
Phone: (305)718-4144 34

| (AAA) (SAVE) | 12/1-3/31 | 1P: $69-$109 |
| | 4/1-11/30 | 1P: $59-$99 |

Location: Florida Tpke, exit 29, 1.2 mi e to 107th Ave, just s on 107th Ave. Located in an office park. 10505 NW 36th St 33178. Fax: 305/718-4480. **Facility:** 95 units. 63 one-bedroom standard units with efficiencies. 6 one- and **Small-scale Hotel** 26 two-bedroom suites with kitchens. 2-4 stories, interior corridors. *Bath:* combo or shower only. **Parking:** on-site. **Terms:** pets ($125 extra charge). **Amenities:** dual phone lines, voice mail, irons. **Pool(s):** small outdoor. **Leisure Activities:** barbecue grill, limited exercise equipment. **Guest Services:** valet and coin laundry. **Business Services:** fax (fee). **Cards:** AX, DC, DS, JC, MC, VI. **Special Amenities:** free local telephone calls and free newspaper.

SOME UNITS
(S/D) (☎) [T/+] (D) (~) (*) (DATA/PORT) [H] (=) (⌐) /(X)/

WELLESLEY INN & SUITES
Phone: (305)592-4799 42

(AAA) (SAVE)	2/14-4/15 [ECP]	1P: $89-$99	2P: $89-$99	XP: $10	F18
	12/1-2/13 [ECP]	1P: $72-$79	2P: $72-$79	XP: $10	F18
	4/16-11/30 [ECP]	1P: $69	2P: $69	XP: $10	F18

Location: 0.8 mi w of jct SR 826 (Palmetto Expwy). 8436 NW 36th St 33166. Fax: 305/471-8461. **Facility:** 106 units. **Small-scale Hotel** 93 one-bedroom standard units. 13 one-bedroom suites ($89-$129). 4 stories, interior corridors. **Parking:** on-site. **Amenities:** voice mail, irons, hair dryers. *Fee:* video games, high-speed Internet. **Pool(s):** heated outdoor. **Guest Services:** valet and coin laundry. **Business Services:** meeting rooms, fax (fee). **Cards:** AX, CB, DC, DS, MC, VI. **Special Amenities:** free continental breakfast and free newspaper. *(See color ad p 514)*

SOME UNITS
(S/D) [T/+] (D) (~) (*) (DATA/PORT) [H] (=) (⌐) /(X)/

WYNDHAM MIAMI AIRPORT
Phone: (305)871-3800 73

(AAA) (SAVE)	9/29-11/30	1P: $185-$195	2P: $195-$205	XP: $10	F12
	1/1-3/30	1P: $149-$189	2P: $159-$199	XP: $10	F12
	12/1-12/31	1P: $165-$175	2P: $175-$185	XP: $10	F12
	3/31-9/28	1P: $135-$155	2P: $145-$165	XP: $10	F12

Large-scale Hotel Location: Le Jeune Rd, 0.3 mi e on NW 25th St, then s on NW 39th Ave, to end of street. 3900 NW 21st St 33142. Fax: 305/871-0447. **Facility:** 408 units. 402 one-bedroom standard units. 6 one-bedroom suites ($300-$900). 10 stories, interior corridors. **Parking:** on-site (fee) and valet. **Terms:** cancellation fee imposed. **Amenities:** dual phone lines, voice mail, irons, hair dryers. *Some:* CD players, fax. **Dining:** 6-10:30 am, 11:30-2:30 & 5:30- 10 pm, cocktails. **Pool(s):** heated outdoor. **Leisure Activities:** saunas, whirlpool, 3 lighted tennis courts, exercise room. *Fee:* golf-18 holes, golf instruction. **Guest Services:** gift shop, valet laundry, airport transportation-Miami International Airport. **Business Services:** meeting rooms, business center. **Cards:** AX, DC, MC, VI.

SOME UNITS
(S/D) [+] (☎) [T/] (24↑) (Y) (⛐) (D) (~) (X) (*) (DATA/PORT) (⌐) /(X) [H] /

The following lodgings were either not evaluated or did not
meet AAA rating requirements but are listed for your information only.

AMERISUITES (MIAMI/BLUE LAGOON)
Phone: 305-265-0144

| [fyi] | 1/1-4/15 [ECP] | 1P: $109-$129 | 2P: $119-$139 | XP: $10 | F18 |
| | 12/1-12/31 & 4/16-11/30 [ECP] | 1P: $89-$109 | 2P: $99-$119 | XP: $10 | F18 |

Small-scale Hotel Too new to rate, opening scheduled for July 2002. **Location:** SR 836, exit NW 72nd Ave S. 6700 NW 7th St 33126. Fax: 305/265-6213. **Amenities:** pets, coffeemakers, microwaves, refrigerators, pool. **Cards:** AX, CB, DS, JC, MC, VI.

(See map p. 504)

INTER-CONTINENTAL MIAMI AIRPORT   **Phone:** 305/468-1400
[fyi]   Not evaluated. **Location:** From SR 836 (Dolphin Expwy), 1 mi n. 2505 NW 87th Ave 33172. Facilities, services, and decor characterize an upscale property.

J W MARRIOTT HOTEL   **Phone:** 305/374-1224
[fyi]   Not evaluated. **Location:** On US 1. 1111 Brickell Ave 33131. Facilities, services, and decor characterize an upscale property.

——— **WHERE TO DINE** ———

94TH AERO SQUADRON   **Lunch:** $6-$11   **Dinner:** $15-$24   **Phone:** 305/261-4220   (39)
▼▼ ▼▼   **Location:** E from SR 836, exit Red Rd; U-turn at light from SR 836 W, exit Red Rd. 1395 NW 57th Ave 33126.
American   **Hours:** 11 am-11 pm, Fri & Sat-midnight, Sun 10 am-10:30 pm. **Reservations:** accepted. **Features:** Fans of flying appreciate this replica of a World War II French farmhouse for its runway views and for the headsets that let users get an earful of talk from the tower. The prime rib of beef, filet mignon and upside-down apple walnut cake are favorites. cocktails. **Parking:** on-site. **Cards:** AX, DC, DS, MC, VI.   [Y] [X]

ANACAPRI   **Lunch:** $6-$9   **Dinner:** $10-$18   **Phone:** 305/232-8001   (30)
▼▼   **Location:** Just n of SW 128th and US 1 (S Dixie Hwy); in Southpark Centre. 12669 S Dixie Hwy 33156. **Hours:** 1:30
Italian   am-2:30 & 5-10:30 pm, Fri & Sat-11:30 pm, Sun 9:00 pm. Closed major holidays; also Tues. **Reservations:** suggested; after 6:30 pm. **Features:** The friendly neighborhood restaurant brings all the favorite Italian dishes—from A to Z—to Miami. A cozy atmosphere tops it all off the right way. This place's market, with some menu favorites, is just a few steps away. Smoke free premises. Semi-formal attire; beer & wine only. **Parking:** on-site.   [X]

CAMI'S SEAFOOD & PASTA   **Lunch:** $4-$10   **Dinner:** $5-$15   **Phone:** 305/223-2911   (34)
▼▼   **Location:** Just e of SW 122nd Ave. 12170 SW 8th St 33184. **Hours:** 11:30 am-10:30 pm, Fri & Sat-11:30 pm.
Seafood   Closed: 11/27. **Features:** Here you will find fresh seafood served fast. Menu highlights include a shrimp pasta in cream sauce and stone crabs when in season. If you have a taste for garlic, choose penne pasta with spinach and shrimp. For dessert, try the local favorite, Key lime pie. Casual dress; beer & wine only. **Parking:** on-site. **Cards:** AX, DC, DS, MC, VI.   [X]

CASA JUANCHO RESTAURANT   **Lunch:** $10-$29   **Dinner:** $14-$29   **Phone:** 305/642-2452   (44)
▼▼ ▼▼   **Location:** Just e of jct SW 8th St and SW 25th Ave. 2436 SW 8th St 33135. **Hours:** noon-midnight, Fri & Sat-1
Ethnic   am. Closed: 12/24. **Reservations:** suggested. **Features:** Freshly prepared dishes of authentic Spanish cuisine are served in a tranquil garden setting with lush plants and the rush of a waterfall. Choose from a display case of live lobsters and iced red snapper, or try the shrimp sauteed in olive oil and garlic. Dressy casual; cocktails. **Parking:** valet and street. **Cards:** AX, DC, DS, MC, VI.   [Y] [X]

THE FISH HOUSE   **Lunch:** $6-$8   **Dinner:** $10-$20   **Phone:** 305/595-8453   (40)
▼▼ ▼▼   **Location:** 2.3 mi w of 56th St, exit SR 826 (Palmetto Expwy); in Miller Road Plaza. 10000 SW 56th St 33165.
Seafood   **Hours:** 11 am-10 pm, Sat-11 pm. **Features:** This family-oriented restaurant features an adjacent seafood market. Wonderfully fresh and flavorful snapper, mahi mahi and salmon are the best entrees. Try a fried blue crab sandwich with coleslaw and perhaps the savory fish soup on the side. Casual dress; beer & wine only. **Parking:** on-site. **Cards:** AX, DC, DS, MC, VI.   [X]

FLEMING: A TASTE OF DENMARK   **Dinner:** $11-$23   **Phone:** 305/232-6444   (63)
▼▼▼▼   **Location:** Jct US 1, just e. 8511 SW 136th St 33156. **Hours:** Open 12/1-8/1 & 9/1-11/30; 5:30 pm-10:30 pm.
Danish   Closed: Mon. **Reservations:** suggested. **Features:** Salmon, duck and pan-seared sea bass over couscous are among the extensive menu offerings of this intimate, family-owned restaurant. Artifacts, copper pots and displays of antiques add authenticity to the Scandinavian aura. Smoke free premises. Dressy casual; cocktails. **Parking:** on-site. **Cards:** AX, MC, VI.   [&M] [Y] [X]

GIACOMO RESTAURANT   **Lunch:** $6-$10   **Dinner:** $7-$19   **Phone:** 305/379-1525   (41)
▼▼   **Location:** Just w of S Miami Ave; across from Capital Bank. 1060 Brickell Ave 33131. **Hours:** 11 am-11 pm.
Italian   Closed: 1/1, 12/25. **Reservations:** accepted. **Features:** This innovative eatery is the marriage a sushi bar and an Italian ristorante. The entrees include warm panini sandwiches, sublime crepes with ricotta and pink sauce, and skewered shrimp with garlic. Please note, there is a fee for parking at lunch. Dressy casual; cocktails. **Parking:** on-site. **Cards:** AX, MC, VI.   [X]

ISLAS CANARIAS RESTAURANT **Lunch:** $4-$16   **Dinner:** $4-$18   **Phone:** 305/649-0440   (38)
▼▼   **Location:** Just n of Flagler St. 285 NW 27th Ave 33125. **Hours:** 7 am-11 pm, Sun from 8 am. **Features:** A
English   casual deli and diner located in Miami's "Little Havana" features authentic Cuban dishes. Decorated with an abundance of locally painted pictures of Cuba, the dining room is the perfect backdrop for well-prepared food and efficient service. Casual dress; beer & wine only. **Parking:** on-site. **Cards:** AX, MC, VI.

MIKE GORDON SEAFOOD RESTAURANT   **Lunch:** $6-$14   **Dinner:** $12-$25   **Phone:** 305/751-4429   (66)
▼▼   **Location:** At west end of 79th St Cswy; 1 mi e of jct US 1. 1201 NE 79th St 33138. **Hours:** noon-10 pm. Closed:
Seafood   11/27. **Reservations:** accepted. **Features:** Gaze out over the water and watch the pelicans at this established restaurant on the shore of Biscayne Bay. Sumptuous seafood, such as pan-fried grouper and Caribbean grilled dolphin, is the centerpiece of the menu. Expect a rustic, casual atmosphere. cocktails. **Parking:** valet. **Cards:** AX, DC, DS, MC, VI.   [Y] [X]

(See map p. 504)

OLD LISBON RESTAURANT **Lunch:** $9-$16 **Dinner:** $14-$47 **Phone:** 305/854-0039 46
Location: Jct SW 17th Ave and 24th St. 1698 SW 22 St 33145. **Hours:** noon-11 pm. **Reservations:** suggested; weekends. **Features:** Take a joyous journey to Portugal without a passport! This quaint neighborhood eatery serves appetizers like fresh octopus salad; entrees like codfish served five ways, Alentejana-style clams and grilled sardines; and, of course, decadent desserts. Dressy casual; cocktails. **Parking:** on-site.
Portuguese
Cards: AX, DC, DS, MC, VI.

TANI THAI RESTAURANT **Lunch:** $6-$10 **Dinner:** $9-$20 **Phone:** 305/253-3583 54
Location: US 1 (S Dixie Hwy). 12269 S Dixie Hwy 33156. **Hours:** 11:30 am-3 & 5-10:30 pm, Fri & Sat-11 pm, Sun 5 pm-10 pm. **Closed:** 11/27. **Reservations:** accepted. **Features:** Peculiarly named dishes, such as Gang Dang and Cocky Bob, belie the sophisticated dishes for which the restaurant is known. Check out the pad ha pow with pork, a savory brown sauce with basil and pepper-flavored juicy white meat pork.
Thai
beer & wine only. **Parking:** on-site. **Cards:** AX, MC, VI.

TROPICAL CHINESE RESTAURANT **Lunch:** $7-$15 **Dinner:** $10-$30 **Phone:** 305/262-7576 60
Location: From SR 826 (Palmetto Expwy), just w. 7991 Bird Rd 33155. **Hours:** 11:30 am-10:30 pm, Fri-11:30 pm, Sat 11 am-11:30 pm, Sun 10:30 am-10 pm. **Reservations:** accepted. **Features:** In a small shopping plaza, this restaurant surprises diners with its menu. Authentic Hong Kong-style cooking is characterized by innovative preparation. Casual dress; cocktails. **Parking:** on-site. **Cards:** AX, DC, DS, MC, VI.
Chinese

——— *The following restaurants have not been evaluated by AAA* ———
but are listed for your information only.

BUBBA GUMP SHRIMP CO **Phone:** 305/379-8866
fyi Not evaluated. **Location:** 401 S Biscayne Blvd 33132. **Features:** Just like the movie shrimp with............and prepared many ways too. You will find burgers and pastas also.

P. F. CHANG'S **Phone:** 305/234-2338
fyi Not evaluated. **Location:** US 1 (Dixie Hwy); in the Falls Shopping Center. 8888 SW 136th St 33176. **Features:** This Oriental bistro features cuisine from 5 Chinese regions in a fun and upbeat atmosphere.

MIAMI BEACH pop. 87,933 (See map p. 510; index p. 510)

——— **WHERE TO STAY** ———

ABBEY HOTEL **Phone:** (305)531-0031 215

	12/27-5/31	1P: $159-$249	2P: $159-$249	XP: $10
	12/1-12/26 & 8/26-11/30	1P: $129-$199	2P: $129-$199	XP: $10
	6/1-8/25	1P: $109-$159	2P: $109-$159	XP: $10

Classic Historic **Location:** Collins Ave, just w. 300 21st St 33139. **Fax:** 305/672-1663. **Facility:** 50 one-bedroom standard units. 3
Small-scale Hotel stories, interior corridors. *Bath:* shower only. **Parking:** on-site (fee). **Terms:** pets ($150 deposit).
Amenities: CD players, dual phone lines, voice mail, safes, honor bars, irons, hair dryers. **Guest Services:** valet laundry.
Cards: AX, CB, DC, DS, MC, VI.

SOME UNITS

(See map p. 510)

THE BLUE MOON

Phone: (305)673-2262 **232**

12/26-4/15	1P: $235-$265	2P: $235-$265
12/1-12/25 & 4/16-11/30	1P: $175-$195	2P: $175-$195

Classic Small-scale Hotel

Location: On SR A1A (Collins Ave) between 9th and 10th sts. Located in the Art Deco District. 944 Collins Ave 33139. Fax: 305/534-5399. **Facility:** The Blue Moon has guest rooms decorated in vivid colors; a small pool and deck are at the back of the property. 75 units. 72 one-bedroom standard units. 3 one-bedroom suites ($425-$525). 2-3 stories, interior corridors. *Bath:* combo or shower only. **Parking:** on-site (fee) and valet. **Terms:** 3 day cancellation notice-fee imposed. **Amenities:** CD players, dual phone lines, voice mail, safes, honor bars, irons, hair dryers. **Pool(s):** small heated outdoor. **Leisure Activities:** whirlpool. **Guest Services:** valet laundry. **Business Services:** meeting rooms, fax (fee). **Cards:** AX, CB, DC, DS, MC, VI.

SOME UNITS
(ASK) 🏊 🛗 📺 DATA/PORT 💻 / ⊠ /
FEE

BREAKWATER HOTEL

Phone: (305)532-1220 **230**

12/1-4/14	1P: $149-$249	2P: $149-$249	XP: $10	F12
4/15-11/30	1P: $139-$239	2P: $139-$239	XP: $10	F12

Motel

Location: E of SR A1A; between 9th and 10th sts. 940 Ocean Dr 33139. Fax: 305/532-4451. **Facility:** 59 units. 58 one-bedroom standard units. 1 one-bedroom suite. 22 one-, 4 stories, interior corridors. **Parking:** valet. **Terms:** 3 day cancellation notice, small pets only. **Amenities:** voice mail, safes (fee). *Some:* hair dryers. **Guest Services:** valet laundry. **Business Services:** meeting rooms, fax (fee). **Cards:** AX, CB, DC, DS, JC, MC, VI. *(See color ad below)*

SOME UNITS
(ASK) 🖥 🛏 🍴 🍽 🛗 📺 DATA/PORT / ⊠ /
FEE

CAPRI MIAMI BEACH CONDO HOTEL BY SIGNUM RESORTS

Phone: (305)532-6777 **210**

(AAA) (SAVE)

12/1-4/14 & 11/16-11/30	1P: $147-$248	2P: $147-$248	XP: $10	F
4/15-11/15	1P: $147-$184	2P: $147-$184	XP: $10	F

Small-scale Hotel

Location: On SR A1A; at 30th St. Located in a quiet area. 3010 Collins Ave 33140. Fax: 305/532-3030. **Facility:** 57 one-bedroom suites with kitchens. 7 stories, interior corridors. **Parking:** valet. **Terms:** [CP] & [ECP] meal plans available. **Amenities:** voice mail, honor bars, hair dryers. **Dining:** 7-10 am. **Pool(s):** outdoor. **Leisure Activities:** sauna, exercise room. **Business Services:** business center. **Cards:** AX, CB, DC, DS, MC, VI.

SOME UNITS
🍴 🍽 🏊 📺 DATA/PORT 🖥 📠 / ⊠ /

CASA GRANDE HOTEL

Phone: (305)672-7003 **225**

(AAA) (SAVE)

12/1-5/31 & 10/1-11/30	2P: $250-$1500
6/1-9/30	2P: $195-$950

Small-scale Hotel

Location: E of SR A1A (Collins Ave) and 8th Ave. 834 Ocean Dr 33139. Fax: 305/673-3669. **Facility:** 34 units. 9 one-bedroom standard units with kitchens. 22 one-, 2 two- and 1 three-bedroom suites ($195-$1500) with kitchens. 5 stories, interior corridors. *Bath:* combo or shower only. **Parking:** valet. **Terms:** 3 day cancellation notice-fee imposed. **Amenities:** video library (fee), CD players, dual phone lines, voice mail, safes, honor bars, irons, hair dryers. **Dining:** Mezzaluna, South Beach, see separate listing. **Guest Services:** valet laundry. **Business Services:** meeting rooms. **Cards:** AX, DC, DS, MC, VI. **Special Amenities:** free newspaper and free room upgrade (subject to availability with advanced reservations).

🖥 🍴 🍽 ♿ 🌐 🛗 VCR 📺 DATA/PORT 🖥 📠 💻
FEE

CAVALIER

Phone: (305)604-5000 **227**

12/1-12/14	1P: $79-$129
12/15-4/15	1P: $119
4/16-11/30	1P: $89

Classic Small-scale Hotel

Location: E of SR A1A (Collins Ave) and 13th Ave. 1320 Ocean Dr 33139. Fax: 305/531-5543. **Facility:** 45 units. 42 one-bedroom standard units. 3 one-bedroom suites. 3 stories, interior corridors. *Bath:* combo or shower only. **Parking:** valet. **Terms:** 3 day cancellation notice-fee imposed, weekly rates available, package plans - seasonal. **Amenities:** video library (fee), CD players, dual phone lines, voice mail, safes, honor bars, irons, hair dryers. **Guest Services:** valet laundry. **Business Services:** meeting rooms. **Cards:** AX, DC, DS, MC, VI.

SOME UNITS
(ASK) 🍴 🌐 🛗 VCR DATA/PORT / 💻 /
FEE

(See map p. 510)

CENTURY HOTEL

	12/1-3/31	1P: $190	2P: $190
	4/1-5/31	1P: $145	2P: $145
Small-scale Hotel	6/1-11/30	1P: $115	2P: $115

Phone: (305)674-8855

Location: Just e of SR A1A (Collins Ave), just s of 2nd St. 140 Ocean Dr 33139. Fax: 305/538-5733. **Facility:** 31 one-bedroom standard units. 2 stories, interior corridors. *Bath:* shower only. **Parking:** on-site (fee). **Terms:** 2 night minimum stay - seasonal with Saturday stayover, 3 day cancellation notice-fee imposed, [CP] meal plan available, small pets only ($250 deposit, $30 extra charge). **Amenities:** CD players, dual phone lines, voice mail, safes, honor bars, hair dryers. **Guest Services:** valet laundry. **Cards:** AX, CB, DC, DS, MC, VI.

(See map p. 510)

COMFORT INN ON THE BEACH

AAA SAVE

12/20-4/20	1P: $125-$155	2P: $135-$165	XP: $10	F21
12/1-12/19 & 4/21-11/30	1P: $95-$105	2P: $105-$125	XP: $10	F21

Phone: (305)868-1200   203

Location: SR A1A/Collins Ave at 63rd St. 6261 Collins Ave 33140. Fax: 305/868-3003. **Facility:** 153 one-bedroom standard units. 9 stories, interior corridors. *Bath:* combo or shower only. **Parking:** valet. **Terms:** 2-4 night **Small-scale Hotel** minimum stay, [CP] meal plan available, small pets only ($25 fee). **Amenities:** voice mail, irons, hair dryers. *Fee:* video games, safes. **Pool(s):** outdoor. **Leisure Activities:** exercise room. **Guest Services:** valet and coin laundry. **Business Services:** meeting rooms, fax (fee). **Cards:** AX, CB, DC, DS, MC, VI. *(See color ad below)*

SOME UNITS

COURTYARD BY MARRIOTT

SAVE

12/1-5/2	1P: $179-$209	2P: $179-$209	XP: $15	F17
5/3-7/1	1P: $89-$119	2P: $89-$119	XP: $15	F17
10/1-11/30	1P: $85-$119	2P: $89-$119	XP: $15	F17
7/2-9/30	1P: $79-$109	2P: $79-$109	XP: $15	F17

Phone: (305)531-3232   213

Classic
Large-scale Hotel

Location: On SR A1A, jct of Collins Ave and 43rd St. 4385 Collins Ave 33140. Fax: 305/531-1077. **Facility:** 105 units. 100 one-bedroom standard units. 5 one-bedroom suites ($119-$259). 7 stories, interior corridors. *Bath:* combo or shower only. **Parking:** valet. **Terms:** cancellation fee imposed. **Amenities:** voice mail, irons, hair dryers. **Pool(s):** heated outdoor. **Leisure Activities:** whirlpool. **Guest Services:** valet laundry. **Business Services:** meeting rooms, fax (fee). **Cards:** AX, DC, DS, MC, VI. *(See color ad p 530)*

SOME UNITS

FEE   FEE

CRYSTAL BEACH SUITES & HEALTH CLUB

AAA SAVE

All Year [CP]   2P: $144-$245

Phone: (305)865-9555   201

Location: SR A1A at 71st St E. 6985 Collins Ave 33141-3205. Fax: 305/866-3514. **Facility:** 84 one-bedroom standard units with efficiencies. 4 stories, interior corridors. *Bath:* combo or shower only. **Parking:** valet. **Small-scale Hotel** **Terms:** check-in 4 pm. **Amenities:** video library (fee), voice mail, irons, hair dryers. **Pool(s):** outdoor. **Leisure Activities:** sauna, whirlpool, steamroom. *Fee:* massage. **Guest Services:** coin laundry. **Business Services:** meeting rooms, fax (fee). **Cards:** AX, DC, DS, JC, MC, VI. **Special Amenities:** free continental breakfast. *(See color ad below)*

SOME UNITS

(See map p. 510)

DAYS INN ART DECO/CONVENTION CENTER   Phone: (305)538-6631   **217**

| | 12/23-4/1 | 1P: $139-$149 | 2P: $159-$169 | XP: $10 | F17 |
| | 12/1-12/22 & 4/2-11/30 | 1P: $99-$129 | 2P: $99-$129 | XP: $10 | F17 |

Location: SR A1A (Collins Ave) at 21st St. 100 21st St 33139. Fax: 305/674-0954. **Facility:** 172 one-bedroom standard units. 7 stories, interior/exterior corridors. *Bath:* combo or shower only. **Parking:** on-site (fee) and **Large-scale Hotel** valet. **Terms:** small pets only ($50 deposit). **Amenities:** safes (fee), irons, hair dryers. **Dining:** 7-11 am, Sat & Sun-noon. **Pool(s):** outdoor. **Guest Services:** gift shop, valet and coin laundry. **Cards:** AX, CB, DC, DS, JC, MC, VI.

SOME UNITS
FEE

DAYS INN NORTH BEACH   Phone: (305)866-1631   **235**

| | 12/20-4/20 [BP] | 1P: $80-$89 | 2P: $80-$90 | XP: $7 | F12 |
| | 12/1-12/19 & 4/21-11/30 [BP] | 1P: $59-$69 | 2P: $59-$69 | XP: $7 | F12 |

Location: SR A1A/Collins Ave and 75th St, just e on 75th St, then a right turn. 7450 Ocean Terrace 33141. Fax: 305/868-4617. **Facility:** 92 one-bedroom standard units. 7 stories, interior corridors. *Bath:* combo or **Small-scale Hotel** shower only. **Parking:** on-site (fee). **Amenities:** voice mail, safes (fee), irons, hair dryers. **Dining:** 7-9:30 am. **Pool(s):** outdoor. **Leisure Activities:** Fee: game room. **Guest Services:** coin laundry. **Business Services:** fax (fee). **Cards:** AX, CB, DC, DS, JC, MC, VI. **Special Amenities:** free newspaper and free room upgrade (subject to availability with advanced reservations). *(See color ad p 531)*

SOME UNITS

DEZERLAND BEACH RESORT & SPA   Phone: (305)865-6661   **237**

	2/1-3/9	1P: $109	2P: $109
	12/24-1/31	1P: $99	2P: $99
	12/1-12/23 & 3/10-11/30	1P: $89	2P: $89

Location: SR 922 (Broad Cswy/96th St), just s on Harding Ave, then e on 87th St. 8701 Collins Ave 33154. **Large-scale Hotel** Fax: 305/866-2630. **Facility:** 225 units. 223 one-bedroom standard units, some with efficiencies. 2 one-bedroom suites with kitchens. 10 stories, interior corridors. **Parking:** on-site (fee). **Terms:** cancellation fee imposed, [BP] meal plan available. **Amenities:** voice mail, safes (fee), hair dryers. **Dining:** 7 am-10 pm, cocktails. **Pool(s):** outdoor. **Leisure Activities:** sauna, whirlpool, steamroom, spa, volleyball. *Fee:* miniature golf, beach water sports activities. **Guest Services:** area transportation-within 5 mi. **Business Services:** meeting rooms, fax (fee). **Cards:** AX, DC, DS, MC, VI. **Special Amenities:** free newspaper and free room upgrade (subject to availability with advanced reservations). *(See color ad p 531)*

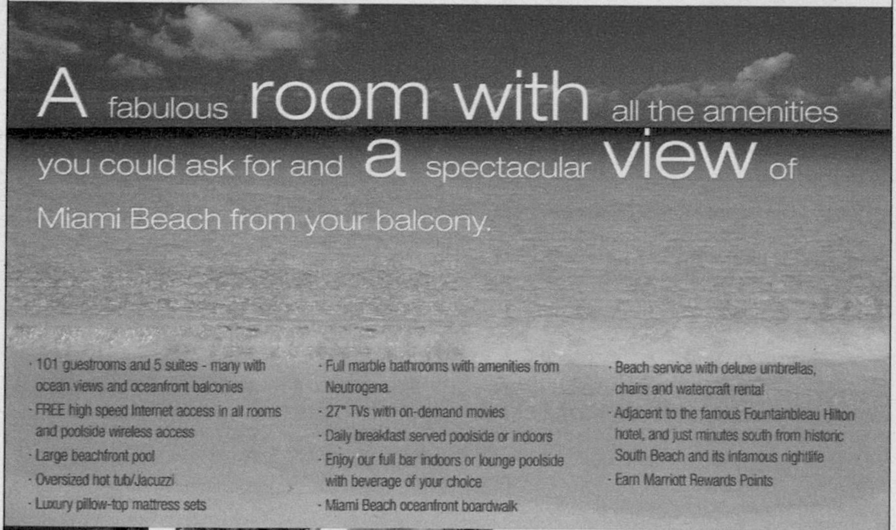

SOME UNITS
FEE

(See map p. 510)

DOUBLETREE SURFCOMBER HOTEL

SAVE
Classic
Small-scale Hotel

Phone: (305)532-7715 **220**

All Year   1P: $129-$189   2P: $129-$189
Location: On SR A1A (Collins Ave) at Collins and 17th aves. 1717 Collins Ave 33139. Fax: 305/532-7280.
Facility: 184 units. 180 one-bedroom standard units. 4 one-bedroom suites. 3 stories, interior corridors.
Bath: combo or shower only. **Parking:** valet. **Terms:** 3 day cancellation notice, package plans.
Amenities: video games (fee), dual phone lines, voice mail, irons, hair dryers. *Some:* CD players. **Pool(s):** heated outdoor. **Guest Services:** valet laundry. **Business Services:** meeting rooms. **Cards:** AX, CB, DC, MC, VI.

SOME UNITS

🍴 🍷 ⟨ 🐾 🏊 🎦 DATA⁄PORT 🖥 / ✕ 🔒 / FEE

(See map p. 510)

EDEN ROC A RENAISSANCE RESORT & SPA
Phone: (305)531-0000 · 199

[SAVE]

12/1-4/30	1P: $240-$280	2P: $240-$280
10/1-11/30	1P: $210-$250	2P: $210-$250
5/1-9/30	1P: $160-$200	2P: $160-$200

Location: SR A1A (Collins Ave), just n of 41st St. 4525 Collins Ave 33140. Fax: 305/674-5555. **Facility:** 349 units.
Large-scale Hotel 347 one-bedroom standard units, some with kitchens and/or whirlpools. 2 one-bedroom suites ($320-$2500), some with kitchens and/or whirlpools. 13 stories, interior corridors. *Bath:* combo or shower only. **Parking:** valet. **Terms:** 3 day cancellation notice, small pets only. **Amenities:** video games (fee), dual phone lines, voice mail, safes, irons, hair dryers. *Some:* honor bars. **Pool(s):** heated outdoor. **Leisure Activities:** saunas, steamrooms, rental boats, racquetball court, hiking trails, jogging, spa, basketball, volleyball. *Fee:* game room. **Guest Services:** gift shop, valet laundry. **Business Services:** meeting rooms, business center. **Cards:** AX, CB, DC, DS, JC, MC, VI.

SOME UNITS

EDISON HOTEL SOUTH BEACH
Phone: (305)531-2744 · 226

[AAA] [SAVE]

12/1-5/31 & 11/1-11/30	1P: $175-$330	2P: $175-$330	XP: $25	F12
6/1-10/31	1P: $125-$280	2P: $125-$280	XP: $25	F12

Location: At corner of 10th St and Ocean Dr. 960 Ocean Dr 33139. Fax: 305/672-4153. **Facility:** 60 one-bedroom standard units. 6 stories, interior corridors. *Bath:* combo or shower only. **Parking:** valet. **Amenities:** irons,
Small-scale Hotel hair dryers. **Dining:** 9 am-3:30 am. **Pool(s):** outdoor. **Guest Services:** valet laundry. **Business Services:** fax (fee). **Cards:** AX, DC, DS, JC, MC, VI. **Special Amenities: free room upgrade (subject to availability with advanced reservations).**

SOME UNITS

FAIRFIELD INN & SUITES, MIAMI BEACH
Phone: (305)673-3337 · 207

[AAA] [SAVE]

12/1-4/15 [CP]	1P: $115-$165	2P: $115-$165	XP: $10	F
4/16-11/30 [CP]	1P: $85-$155	2P: $85-$155	XP: $10	F

Location: Jct SR A1A (Collins Ave) and 40th St. 4101 Collins Ave 33140. Fax: 305/673-3660. **Facility:** 186 units. 168 one-bedroom standard units. 18 one-bedroom suites ($175-$260). 8 stories, interior corridors. *Bath:*
Small-scale Hotel combo or shower only. **Parking:** valet. **Terms:** cancellation fee imposed. **Amenities:** video games (fee), voice mail, safes, irons, hair dryers. **Pool(s):** heated outdoor. **Leisure Activities:** limited exercise equipment. *Fee:* beach services. **Guest Services:** valet and coin laundry. **Business Services:** meeting rooms, business center. **Cards:** AX, CB, DC, DS, JC, MC, VI. **Special Amenities: free continental breakfast and free local telephone calls.**

SOME UNITS

FAIRWIND HOTEL & SUITES
Phone: (305)531-0050 · 219

12/1-4/14	1P: $75-$140	2P: $75-$140	XP: $10	F18
4/15-11/30	1P: $75-$125	2P: $75-$125	XP: $10	F18

Classic **Location:** On SR A1A at 10th St. 1000 Collins Ave 33139. Fax: 305/531-0565. **Facility:** 83 one-bedroom standard
Small-scale Hotel units, some with kitchens. 1-3 stories, interior corridors. *Bath:* combo or shower only. **Parking:** valet. **Amenities:** voice mail, safes (fee). *Some:* hair dryers. **Business Services:** meeting rooms, business center.
Cards: AX, CB, DC, DS, MC, VI.

SOME UNITS

FONTAINEBLEAU HILTON RESORT
Phone: (305)538-2000 · 211

[SAVE]

All Year	1P: $259-$459	2P: $289-$489	XP: $30	F18

Location: On SR A1A. 4441 Collins Ave 33140. Fax: 305/535-3241. **Facility:** 1206 units. 1146 one-bedroom standard units. 40 one- and 20 two-bedroom suites ($579-$1795), some with whirlpools. 8-17 stories, interior corridors. *Bath:* combo or shower only. **Parking:** valet. **Terms:** 5 day cancellation notice, small pets only.
Large-scale Hotel **Amenities:** dual phone lines, voice mail, safes (fee), honor bars, irons, hair dryers. *Some:* high-speed Internet (fee), fax. **Pool(s):** heated outdoor, saltwater. **Leisure Activities:** saunas, whirlpools, steamrooms, waterslide, rental boats, rental paddleboats, recreation programs, spa. *Fee:* sailboats, windsurfing, charter fishing, 7 lighted tennis courts. **Guest Services:** gift shop, valet laundry. **Business Services:** conference facilities, business center. **Cards:** AX, DC, DS, MC.

SOME UNITS

HILTON GRAND VACATIONS CLUB AT SOUTH BEACH
Phone: (305)604-8225 · 209

[SAVE]

All Year	1P: $225-$275

Location: Just e of SR A1A (Collins Ave) and 14th St. 1430 Ocean Dr 33139. Fax: 305/604-8223. **Facility:** 78 units. 63 one-bedroom standard units with kitchens, some with whirlpools. 4 one- and 11 two-bedroom suites ($225-$275) with efficiencies, some with whirlpools. 4 stories, interior corridors. **Parking:** valet.
Small-scale Hotel **Terms:** check-in 4 pm, 3 day cancellation notice-fee imposed. **Amenities:** video library (fee), CD players, dual phone lines, voice mail, safes, irons, hair dryers. **Leisure Activities:** whirlpools, steamroom, exercise room. *Fee:* massage. **Guest Services:** complimentary laundry. **Business Services:** meeting rooms, fax (fee). **Cards:** AX, DC, DS, MC, VI.

HOLIDAY INN INDIAN CREEK
Phone: (305)865-2565 · 200

[AAA] [SAVE]

12/1-4/15	1P: $89-$159
4/16-11/30	1P: $79-$109

Location: 2 mi n of Julia Tuttle Cswy, I-195 on SR A1A southbound. 6060 Indian Creek Dr 33140. Fax: 305/865-2506. **Facility:** 82 units. 80 one-bedroom standard units. 2 one-bedroom suites. 15 stories, interior corridors. *Bath:*
Small-scale Hotel combo or shower only. **Parking:** valet. **Terms:** [MAP] meal plan available. **Amenities:** video games (fee), voice mail, irons, hair dryers. **Dining:** 6:30 am-10:30 & 6-9 pm, cocktails. **Pool(s):** outdoor. **Leisure Activities:** whirlpool, exercise room. **Guest Services:** valet and coin laundry. **Business Services:** meeting rooms, fax (fee). **Cards:** AX, CB, DC, DS, JC, MC, VI. *(See color ad p 533 & opposite inside back cover)*

SOME UNITS

(See map p. 510)

HOLIDAY INN SOUTH BEACH RESORT

Phone: (305)779-3200 216

AAA **SAVE** ▼▼▼ 12/28-4/20 1P: $189
12/1-12/27 & 4/21-11/30 1P: $149

Location: SR A1A, at 22nd St. 2201 Collins Ave 33139. **Fax:** 305/532-1403. **Facility:** 355 units. 353 one-bedroom standard units. 2 one-bedroom suites. 3-12 stories, interior/exterior corridors. *Bath:* combo or shower only. **Large-scale Hotel Parking:** on-site. **Terms:** check-in 4 pm, cancellation fee imposed, package plans, 15% service charge. **Amenities:** high-speed Internet (fee), dual phone lines, voice mail, safes, irons, hair dryers. **Dining:** 2 restaurants, 7 am-11 & 6-11 pm, cocktails. **Pool(s):** heated outdoor. **Leisure Activities:** whirlpool, 2 lighted tennis courts, exercise room, volleyball. *Fee:* jet skis, catamarans, parasailing, game room. **Guest Services:** gift shop, valet and coin laundry. **Cards:** AX, DC, DS, MC, VI. **Special Amenities: free local telephone calls.**
(See color ad p 534 & opposite inside back cover)

SOME UNITS / FEE

THE HOTEL

Phone: (305)531-2222 224

AAA **SAVE** ▼▼▼ ▼▼▼ 12/1-4/30 1P: $275-$325
5/1-11/30 1P: $255-$295

Location: On SR A1A (Collins Ave) and 8th St. 801 Collins Ave 33139. **Fax:** 305/531-3222. **Facility:** Fashion designer Todd Oldham is credited with selecting the finishes and furnishings in the lobby and guest rooms of **Classic** this Art Deco-area property. 53 units. 49 one-bedroom standard units. 4 one-bedroom suites with whirlpools. **Small-scale Hotel** 4 stories, interior corridors. *Bath:* combo or shower only. **Parking:** on-site (fee) and valet. **Terms:** 2-4 night minimum stay - weekends, 3 day cancellation notice-fee imposed, package plans - seasonal. **Amenities:** CD players, dual phone lines, voice mail, safes, honor bars, hair dryers. *Fee:* video library, high-speed Internet. *Some:* irons. **Dining:** Wish, see separate listing. **Pool(s):** heated outdoor. **Leisure Activities:** exercise room. *Fee:* massage. **Guest Services:** gift shop, valet laundry. **Business Services:** meeting rooms. *Fee:* administrative services, fax. **Cards:** AX, DC, MC, VI. **Special Amenities: free newspaper and free room upgrade (subject to availability with advanced reservations).**

HOTEL OCEAN

Phone: (305)672-2579 241

▼▼▼ 12/1-5/31 & 11/15-11/30 [CP] 1P: $200-$600 2P: $200-$600 XP: $49 F12
6/1-11/14 [CP] 1P: $179-$515 2P: $179-$515 XP: $49 F12

Small-scale Hotel Location: E of jct SR A1A (Collins Ave) and 12th St. Located in the heart of the Art Deco District. 1230 Ocean Dr 33139. **Fax:** 305/672-7665. **Facility:** 27 units. 13 one-bedroom standard units. 14 one-bedroom suites, some with whirlpools. 5 stories, interior corridors. *Bath:* combo or shower only. **Parking:** valet. **Terms:** 2-3 night minimum stay - weekends, 3 day cancellation notice, [AP] meal plan available, 17% service charge. **Amenities:** CD players, dual phone lines, voice mail, safes, irons, hair dryers. **Dining:** Les Deux Fontaines, see separate listing. **Guest Services:** valet laundry. **Business Services:** meeting rooms, fax (fee). **Cards:** AX, CB, DC, DS, JC, MC, VI.

SOME UNITS / FEE

THE INDIAN CREEK HOTEL

Phone: (305)531-2727 214

AAA **SAVE** ▼▼▼ 12/1-4/30 & 10/1-11/30 [CP] 1P: $140-$160 XP: $25 D3
5/1-9/30 [CP] 1P: $80-$100 XP: $25 D3

Location: SR A1A southbound, at 28th St, just w of Collins Ave. 2727 Indian Creek Dr 33140. **Fax:** 305/531-5651. **Facility:** 61 one-bedroom standard units. 3 stories, interior corridors. **Parking:** street. **Terms:** cancel- **Small-scale Hotel** lation notice. **Amenities:** voice mail, irons, hair dryers. *Some:* CD players. **Dining:** 7 am-11 & 6-11 pm, Sun-11 am, wine/beer only. **Pool(s):** outdoor. **Guest Services:** valet laundry. **Business Services:** meeting rooms. **Cards:** AX, CB, DC, DS, JC, MC, VI. **Special Amenities: free continental breakfast and free newspaper.**
(See color ad p 537)

SOME UNITS / FEE

THE KENT

Phone: (305)604-5068 239

▼▼▼ 12/1-5/31 & 10/1-11/30 [CP] 1P: $145-$350 2P: $145-$350 XP: $25 F12
6/1-9/30 [CP] 1P: $130-$160 2P: $130-$160 XP: $25 F12

Classic **Location:** On SR A1A, at Collins Ave and 11th St. Located one block from the beach. 1131 Collins Ave 33139. **Small-scale Hotel Fax:** 305/531-0720. **Facility:** 54 units. 53 one-bedroom standard units, some with whirlpools. 1 one-bedroom suite ($175-$350) with whirlpool. 3 stories, interior corridors. **Parking:** on-site and valet. **Terms:** 3 day cancellation notice-fee imposed. **Amenities:** video library (fee), CD players, voice mail, safes, honor bars, irons, hair dryers. *Some:* DVD players. **Guest Services:** valet laundry. **Business Services:** meeting rooms, PC, fax (fee). **Cards:** AX, DC, DS, MC, VI.

FEE

(See map p. 510)

LOEWS MIAMI BEACH HOTEL

Phone: (305)604-1601 223

(AAA) (SAVE)	12/1-4/30	1P: $299-$449	2P: $299-$449	XP: $30 F17
	5/1-5/31 & 9/15-11/30	1P: $249-$399	2P: $249-$399	XP: $30 F17
▼▼▼ ▼▼▼	6/1-9/14	1P: $199-$329	2P: $199-$329	XP: $30 F17

Location: On SR A1A, at Collins and 16th aves. 1601 Collins Ave 33139. Fax: 305/604-3999. **Facility:** This water-
Large-scale Hotel front hotel in the Art Deco area features two buildings on grounds enhanced by tropical trees and fountains;
a lobby has shops and eateries. 790 units. 724 one-bedroom standard units. 57 one- and 9 two-bedroom
suites ($500-$5000). 9-18 stories, interior corridors. *Bath:* combo or shower only. **Parking:** valet. **Terms:** check-in 4 pm, 3 day
cancellation notice-fee imposed, small pets only. **Amenities:** high-speed Internet (fee), dual phone lines, voice mail, safes, honor
bars, irons, hair dryers. *Some:* CD players, fax. **Dining:** 5 restaurants, 7 am-10 pm, Fri & Sat-11 pm, cocktails, also, Gaucho
Room, see separate listing, entertainment. **Pool(s):** heated outdoor, wading. **Leisure Activities:** saunas, whirlpools, spa. *Fee:*
water sports on the beach, children's programs. **Guest Services:** gift shop, valet and coin laundry. **Business Services:** conference facilities, business center. **Cards:** AX, DC, DS, MC, VI. *(See color ad p 535)*

SOME UNITS

FEE   FEE

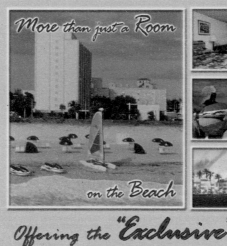

(See map p. 510)

THE MARLIN   Phone: (305)604-5063 [208]

▼▼▼   12/1-5/31 & 10/1-11/30   1P: $325-$415   2P: $325-$415
       6/1-9/30   1P: $210-$315   2P: $210-$315
Small-scale Hotel   **Location:** On SR A1A, at Collins Ave and 12th St. 1200 Collins Ave 33139. Fax: 305/673-9609. **Facility:** 11 one-bedroom standard units with efficiencies. 3 stories, interior corridors. **Parking:** valet. **Terms:** check-in 4 pm, 3 day cancellation notice-fee imposed, pets ($25 extra charge, small dogs only). **Amenities:** video library (fee), CD players, dual phone lines, voice mail, safes, honor bars, irons, hair dryers. **Leisure Activities:** Fee: massage. **Guest Services:** valet laundry. **Business Services:** fax (fee). **Cards:** AX, DC, MC, VI.

🛏 🍴 24🕐 ▼ ⊘ 🖬 VCR 🦮 DATA PORT 🔋 🖥 💻
                                          FEE

THE NEW CASABLANCA ON THE OCEAN   Phone: (305)868-0010 [202]

AAA SAVE   12/15-4/14 [CP]   1P: $147-$187   2P: $147-$187   XP: $4   F18
▼▼ ▼▼   12/1-12/14 & 4/15-11/30 [CP] 1P: $107-$137   2P: $107-$137   XP: $4   F18
           Location: SR A1A (Collins Ave), just n of 63rd St. 6345 Collins Ave 33141. Fax: 305/865-7111. **Facility:** 150 units. 146 one-bedroom standard units with kitchens. 1 one- and 3 two-bedroom suites ($198-$333) with kitchens.
Large-scale Hotel 10 stories, interior corridors. **Dining:** 7 am-10 pm, cocktails. **Pool(s):** heated outdoor. **Leisure Activities:** exercise room. **Guest Services:** gift shop, valet and coin laundry. **Business Services:** meeting rooms. **Cards:** AX, CB, DC, DS, MC, VI.
(See color ad p 536)

SOME UNITS
S🄳 🍴 ⊘ 🏊 🦮 🔋 🖥 💻 /✕ DATA PORT /

OCEAN FIVE HOTEL   Phone: (305)532-7093 [231]

▼▼▼   12/20-5/31 [CP]   1P: $175-$325   2P: $175-$325   XP: $10   F12
       12/1-12/19 & 6/1-11/30 [CP]   1P: $125-$225   2P: $125-$225   XP: $10   F12
Small-scale Hotel   **Location:** Just e of SR A1A (Collins Ave); between 4th and 5th sts. 436 Ocean Dr 33139. Fax: 305/534-7353. **Facility:** 56 units. 52 one-bedroom standard units. 4 one-bedroom suites ($225-$325), some with kitchens. 2-3 stories, interior corridors. **Bath:** shower only. **Parking:** valet. **Terms:** 3 day cancellation notice-fee imposed. **Amenities:** CD players, voice mail, safes, honor bars, irons, hair dryers. *Some:* high-speed Internet, dual phone lines. **Leisure Activities:** jogging. **Guest Services:** valet laundry. **Business Services:** fax (fee). **Cards:** AX, CB, DC, DS, MC, VI. *(See color ad p 537)*

SOME UNITS
A🅂K S🄳 ➕ 🍴 ▼ 🦮 DATA PORT /✕/
                          FEE

(See map p. 510)

OCEAN SURF HOTEL

Phone: (305)866-1648   236

	12/20-4/13 [CP]	1P: $99-$169	2P: $99-$169	XP: $6	F12
	4/14-11/30 [CP]	1P: $74-$139	2P: $74-$139	XP: $6	F12
	12/1-12/19 [CP]	1P: $69-$139	2P: $69-$139	XP: $6	F12

Location: Collins Ave and 75th St, just e on 75th St, then a right turn. 7436 Ocean Terrace 33141. Fax: 305/866-1649. **Small-scale Hotel Facility:** 49 one-bedroom standard units. 4 stories, interior corridors. *Bath:* combo or shower only. **Parking:** on-site (fee). **Terms:** cancellation fee imposed, weekly rates available. **Amenities:** safes (fee), hair dryers. **Guest Services:** valet laundry. **Cards:** AX, DC, DS, JC, MC, VI. **Special Amenities:** free continental breakfast and preferred room (subject to availability with advanced reservations). *(See color ad p 537)*

SOME UNITS

PRESIDENT HOTEL

Phone: (305)538-2882   238

| | 12/1-4/15 | 1P: $160-$690 | 2P: $160-$690 | XP: $15 | F18 |
| | 4/16-11/30 | 1P: $115-$480 | 2P: $115-$480 | XP: $15 | F18 |

Classic Small-scale Hotel

Location: On SR A1A/Collins Ave, just s of Espanola Way. 1423 Collins Ave 33139. Fax: 305/604-0350. **Facility:** 64 one-bedroom standard units. 4 stories, interior corridors. *Bath:* combo or shower only. **Parking:** valet. **Terms:** 3 day cancellation notice. **Amenities:** voice mail, safes. *Some:* hair dryers. **Pool(s):** outdoor. **Guest Services:** valet laundry. **Business Services:** meeting rooms, fax (fee). **Cards:** AX, DC, DS, MC, VI.

SOME UNITS

RADISSON DEAUVILLE RESORT MIAMI BEACH

Phone: (305)865-8511   204

| | All Year | 1P: $229-$299 | 2P: $229-$299 | XP: $20 | F15 |

Location: SR A1A at 67th St. 6701 Collins Ave 33141. Fax: 305/865-8154. **Facility:** 485 units. 472 one-bedroom standard units. 13 one-bedroom suites, some with whirlpools. 17 stories, interior corridors. *Bath:* combo or shower only. **Parking:** **Large-scale Hotel** (fee), voice mail, safes, irons, hair dryers. **Dining:** 6 am-10:30 pm, cocktails. **Pool(s):** heated outdoor. **Leisure Activities:** whirlpool, parasailing, waverunners, 3 tennis courts, exercise room, spa, basketball, horseshoes, shuffleboard, volleyball. *Fee:* scuba diving, snorkeling, charter fishing, game room. **Guest Services:** gift shop, valet and coin laundry. **Business Services:** meeting rooms, business center. **Cards:** AX, CB, DC, DS, JC, MC, VI. **Special Amenities:** free newspaper. *(See ad p 538)*

SOME UNITS

(See map p. 510)

RAMADA INN MIAMI BEACH   Phone: (305)531-5771

	1/20-2/28	1P: $140-$155	2P: $140-$155	XP: $10	F12
	3/1-3/31	1P: $135-$150	2P: $135-$150	XP: $10	F12
	12/1-1/19	1P: $89-$150	2P: $89-$150	XP: $10	F12
	4/1-11/30	1P: $80-$119	2P: $89-$119	XP: $10	F12

Large-scale Hotel Location: On SR A1A (Collins Ave), at Collins Ave and 40th St. 4041 Collins Ave 33140. **Fax:** 305/538-3568. **Facility:** 251 one-bedroom standard units. 16 stories, interior corridors. **Parking:** valet. **Amenities:** voice mail, safes (fee). **Dining:** 7 am-3 & 5:30-10 pm, cocktails. **Pool(s):** heated outdoor. **Leisure Activities:** playground, exercise room. **Fee:** water sports equipment. **Guest Services:** gift shop, valet and coin laundry. **Business Services:** meeting rooms, fax (fee). **Cards:** AX, CB, DC, DS, MC, VI.

SOME UNITS

RIANDE CONTINENTAL HOTEL   Phone: (305)531-3503

	12/31-3/31	1P: $140	2P: $140	XP: $5	F
	4/1-11/30	1P: $120	2P: $120		F
	12/1-12/30	1P: $120	2P: $120	XP: $5	F

Large-scale Hotel Location: On SR A1A (Collins Ave), just n of 18th St. 1825 Collins Ave 33139. **Fax:** 305/531-5602. **Facility:** 247 one-bedroom standard units. 8 stories, interior corridors. **Parking:** valet. **Terms:** 3 day cancellation notice-fee imposed, [ECP] meal plan available, package plans. **Amenities:** voice mail, safes (fee), hair dryers. **Some:** honor bars. **Pool(s):** outdoor. **Guest Services:** gift shop, valet laundry. **Business Services:** meeting rooms, fax (fee). **Cards:** AX, DC, MC, VI.

SOME UNITS

SAVOY HOTEL   Phone: (305)532-0200

	10/1-11/30	1P: $310-$710	2P: $310-$710	XP: $15	F16
	1/1-4/30	1P: $300-$700	2P: $300-$700	XP: $15	F16
	12/1-12/31	1P: $250-$550	2P: $250-$550	XP: $15	F16
	5/1-9/30	1P: $200-$500	2P: $200-$500	XP: $15	F16

Small-scale Hotel Location: E of SR A1A. 425 Ocean Dr 33139. **Fax:** 305/534-7436. **Facility:** 74 units. 23 one-bedroom standard units, some with efficiencies. 40 one- and 11 two-bedroom suites, some with efficiencies. 2-3 stories, interior corridors. **Bath:** combo or shower only. **Parking:** on-site (fee). **Terms:** check-in 4 pm, 3 day cancellation notice-fee imposed. **Amenities:** dual phone lines, voice mail, safes, irons, hair dryers. **Some:** CD players. **Pool(s):** 2 heated outdoor. **Leisure Activities:** exercise room. **Guest Services:** valet laundry. **Business Services:** meeting rooms, fax (fee). **Cards:** AX, DC, MC, VI.

SOME UNITS

(See map p. 510)

SHELBORNE BEACH RESORT-SOUTH BEACH

Phone: (305)531-1271 222

AAA **SAVE**

12/1-5/31 & 9/15-11/30	1P: $185-$450	2P: $185-$450	XP: $10 F13
6/1-9/14	1P: $145-$450	2P: $145-$450	XP: $10 F13

Large-scale Hotel
Location: SR A1A at 18th St. 1801 Collins Ave 33139. **Fax:** 305/531-2206. **Facility:** 200 units. 191 one-bedroom standard units. 1 one- and 8 two-bedroom suites ($475-$2800) with kitchens, some with whirlpools. 2-16 stories, interior corridors. *Bath:* combo or shower only. **Parking:** valet. **Terms:** 3 day cancellation notice-fee imposed, $3 service charge. **Amenities:** voice mail, safes (fee), hair dryers. *Some:* CD players. **Dining:** 7 am-11 pm, Fri & Sat-midnight, cocktails, nightclub. **Pool(s):** heated outdoor. **Leisure Activities:** sauna, whirlpools, exercise room, volleyball. **Guest Services:** valet and coin laundry. **Business Services:** conference facilities, fax (fee). **Cards:** AX, DC, DS, MC, VI. *(See color ad below)*

THE SHORE CLUB SOUTH BEACH

Phone: (305)695-3100 228

AAA **SAVE**

12/26-11/30	1P: $395-$895	2P: $395-$895
12/1-12/25	1P: $295-$795	2P: $295-$795

Large-scale Hotel
Location: On SR A1A (Collins Ave), just s of 20th St. 1901 Collins Ave 33139. **Fax:** 305/695-3299. **Facility:** Though designed with a minimalist modern look, guest rooms at this oceanfront hotel offer comfort and elegance. 324 units. 266 one-bedroom standard units. 58 one-bedroom suites ($3000), some with whirlpools. 2-20 stories, interior corridors. **Parking:** valet. **Terms:** 7 day cancellation notice-fee imposed, small pets only ($100 fee). **Amenities:** CD players, dual phone lines, voice mail, fax, safes, honor bars, irons, hair dryers. *Fee:* video games, high-speed Internet. *Some:* DVD players. **Dining:** 3 restaurants, 7 am-1 am, also, Nobu at The Shore Club South Beach, see separate listing, nightclub. **Pool(s):** 2 heated outdoor. **Leisure Activities:** whirlpool, exercise room, spa, volleyball. *Fee:* bicycles. **Guest Services:** gift shop, valet laundry. **Business Services:** meeting rooms, administrative services, PC (fee). **Cards:** AX, DC, MC, VI.

THE TIDES HOTEL

Phone: (305)604-5070 229

12/26-5/31	1P: $525-$3000	2P: $525-$3000
12/1-12/25 & 10/1-11/30	1P: $475-$3000	2P: $475-$3000
6/1-9/30	1P: $395-$3000	2P: $395-$3000

Small-scale Hotel
Location: E of jct SR A1A (Collins Ave) and 12th St. 1220 Ocean Dr 33139. **Fax:** 305/604-5180. **Facility:** A restored Art Deco-style hotel, The Tides features a large lobby reminiscent of the 1900s; all guest rooms face the ocean. 45 units. 42 one-bedroom standard units. 3 one-bedroom suites ($1500-$3000) with whirlpools. 10 stories, interior corridors. **Parking:** valet. **Terms:** check-in 4 pm, 3 day cancellation notice-fee imposed, pets ($25 extra charge, small dogs only). **Amenities:** video library (fee), CD players, dual phone lines, voice mail, safes, honor bars, irons, hair dryers. *Some:* DVD players, fax. **Dining:** Twelve Twenty, see separate listing. **Pool(s):** heated outdoor. **Guest Services:** gift shop, valet laundry. **Business Services:** meeting rooms. *Fee:* PC, fax. **Cards:** AX, DC, DS, MC, VI.

TUDOR HOTEL & SUITES

Phone: 305/534-2934 221

12/16-4/15	1P: $189-$605	2P: $184-$605	XP: $20 F12
4/16-11/30	1P: $179-$545	2P: $179-$545	XP: $20 F12
12/1-12/15	1P: $169-$525	2P: $169-$525	XP: $20 F12

Classic **Small-scale Hotel**
Location: On SR A1A (Collins Ave) at 11th Ave. 1111 Collins Ave 33139. **Fax:** 305/531-1874. **Facility:** 107 units. 98 one-bedroom standard units. 7 one- and 2 two-bedroom suites ($365-$605) with efficiencies. 3-4 stories, interior corridors. **Parking:** valet. **Terms:** 3 day cancellation notice-fee imposed. **Amenities:** voice mail, irons, hair dryers. **Leisure Activities:** exercise room. **Guest Services:** valet and coin laundry. **Business Services:** meeting rooms, fax (fee). **Cards:** AX, CB, DC, DS, MC, VI.

(See map p. 510)

WYNDHAM MIAMI BEACH RESORT

Phone: (305)532-3600 205

AAA SAVE	10/1-11/30	1P: $199-$230	2P: $199-$230	XP: $20	F17
	1/1-5/31	1P: $198-$230	2P: $198-$230	XP: $20	F17
▽▽▽▽	12/1-12/31	1P: $189-$219	2P: $189-$219	XP: $20	F17
	6/1-9/30	1P: $125-$155	2P: $125-$155	XP: $20	F17

Large-scale Hotel Location: On SR A1A; 0.5 mi n of jct Arthur Godfrey Rd. 4833 Collins Ave 33141. Fax: 305/534-7409. **Facility:** 424 units. 404 one-bedroom standard units. 20 one-bedroom suites, some with whirlpools. 18 stories, interior corridors. *Bath:* combo or shower only. **Parking:** on-site (fee) and valet. **Terms:** 3 day cancellation notice-fee imposed. **Amenities:** dual phone lines, voice mail, honor bars, irons, hair dryers. *Fee:* video games, high-speed Internet. **Dining:** 2 restaurants, 6:30 am-1:30 am; 20% service charge, cocktails. **Pool(s):** heated outdoor. **Leisure Activities:** saunas, steamrooms, lighted tennis court, jogging, exercise room. *Fee:* paddleboats, sailboats, windsurfing, boat dock, waterskiing, scuba diving, snorkeling, charter fishing, jet skis, scuba instruction, massage. **Guest Services:** gift shop, valet laundry. **Business Services:** conference facilities, business center. **Cards:** AX, DC, MC, VI.

SOME UNITS

[icons] FEE

The following lodgings were either not evaluated or did not meet AAA rating requirements but are listed for your information only.

CARDOZO HOTEL SOUTH BEACH

Phone: 305/535-6500

[fyi] Not evaluated. **Location:** From SR A1A (Collins Ave), e on 13th St. 1300 Ocean Blvd 33139. Facilities, services, and decor characterize an upscale property.

COURTYARD BY MARRIOTT, MIAMI SOUTH BEACH

Phone: 305/604-8887

[fyi]	12/27-4/20	1P: $190-$220
Motel	12/1-12/26	1P: $170-$200
	6/2-11/30	1P: $120-$200
	4/21-6/1	1P: $150-$180

Too new to rate, opening scheduled for July 2002. **Location:** I-95, exit 2D (395 E), over MacArthur Cswy. 1530 Washington Ave 33139. Fax: 305/604-8868. **Amenities:** coffeemakers, pool. **Cards:** AX, CB, DC, DS, JC, MC, VI. *(See ad p 519)*

DELANO HOTEL

Phone: 305/672-2000

[fyi] Not evaluated. **Location:** On SR A1A (Collins Ave) at 16th St. 1685 Collins Ave 33139. Facilities, services, and decor characterize an upscale property.

HOTEL ASTOR

Phone: 305/531-8081

[fyi] Not evaluated. **Location:** From MacArthur Cswy/US 41 to 5th St, then n. 956 Washington Ave 33139. Facilities, services, and decor characterize an upscale property.

MARRIOTT MIAMI BEACH

Phone: 305/536-7700

[fyi] Not evaluated. **Location:** Just e of SR A1A (Collins Ave), then just s of 2nd St. 161 Ocean Dr 33139. Facilities, services, and decor characterize an upscale property.

THE NATIONAL HOTEL

Phone: 305/532-2311

[fyi] Not evaluated. **Location:** On SR A1A (Collins Ave) and 16th St. 1677 Collins Ave 33139. Facilities, services, and decor characterize a mid-range property.

THE RITZ-CARLTON, SOUTH BEACH

Phone: 786/276-4000

[fyi] Under construction, scheduled to open June 2003. **Location:** At jct SR A1A (Collins Ave) and Lincoln Rd. 1 Lincoln Rd 33139. Fax: 786/276-4100. **Planned Amenities:** 375 units, restaurant, pool, exercise facilities.

Large-scale Hotel

——— WHERE TO DINE ———

ASTOR PLACE BAR & GRILL

Lunch: $7-$20 Dinner: $7-$35 Phone: 305/672-7217 206

▽▽▽▽

American

Location: Washington Ave & 10th St. 956 Washington Ave 33139. **Hours:** 11:30 am-2:30 & 7-11 pm, Fri-midnight, Sat 7 pm-midnight, Sun noon-2:30 & 7-11 pm. **Reservations:** suggested. **Features:** Featuring new Florida cuisine with fresh seafood, meat and poultry, all dishes are flavorful and excellently presented in a bustling modern dining room. Savor barbecued wasabi tuna fillet served on a bed of rice with cashews and shrimp. Dressy casual; cocktails. **Parking:** valet. **Cards:** AX, MC, VI.

CHINA GRILL

Lunch: $21-$35 Dinner: $21-$35 Phone: 305/534-2211 208

▽▽▽▽

Asian

Location: Corner of 5th St and Washington Ave. 404 Washington Ave 33139. **Hours:** 11:45 am-midnight, Fri & Sat 6 pm-1 am, Sun 6 pm-midnight. **Reservations:** suggested. **Features:** Bustling and never boring, this clublike spot is the "see-and-be-seen" place for sake, vodka and ample portions of dramatically prepared delights such as porterhouse lobster. Just eyeing the sinful desserts is likely to stretch your waistband. Dressy casual; cocktails. **Parking:** valet. **Cards:** AX, DC, MC, VI.

(See map p. 510)

CRYSTAL CAFE

Continental

Dinner: $13-$25   Phone: 305/673-8266   (190)
Location: Just e of Chase Ave. 726 Arthur Godfrey Rd 33140. **Hours:** 5 pm-10 pm, Fri & Sat-11 pm. Closed: Mon. **Reservations:** suggested. **Features:** Cozy romantic dining room with soft indirect lighting and good use of mirrors. One of the specialties is the osso bucco that is done with a French flair. A large menu offers a variety of meat, seafood and pasta entrees. A nice wine list compliments this menu. Several half bottles are also available. Dressy casual; beer & wine only. **Parking:** on-site. **Cards:** AX, DS, MC, VI.

GAUCHO ROOM
Steak House

Dinner: $25-$40   Phone: 305/604-1601   (199)
Location: On SR A1A, at Collins and 16th aves; in Loews Miami Beach Hotel. 1601 Collins Ave 33139. **Hours:** 6:30 pm-midnight. Closed: Mon. **Reservations:** suggested. **Features:** Pictures depicting scenes of Argentina and its Gauchos surround the large, warm dining room. Booths are upholstered in pony-style fabrics, and saddles serve as decor focal points. Both Argentinean and American meats are featured beside dishes of seafood and pasta. The wine list incorporates selections from both north and south of the equator. Dressy casual; cocktails; entertainment. **Parking:** on-site and valet. **Cards:** AX, CB, DC, DS, MC, VI.

JOE'S STONE CRAB RESTAURANT   Classic
Seafood

Lunch: $5-$60   Dinner: $5-$60   Phone: 305/673-0365   (211)
Location: 6 blks s of SR A1A. 11 Washington Ave 33139. **Hours:** Open 12/1-5/15 & 10/15-11/30; 11:30 am-2 & 5-10 pm, Fri & Sat-11 pm, Sun 4 pm-10 pm. Closed: 11/27. **Features:** As the restaurant's name implies, the stone crab is mighty popular here. But then again, so is the homemade Key lime pie. Owned by the same family since the early 1900s, the popular eatery offers generous portions of delectable food. cocktails. **Parking:** on-site and valet. **Cards:** AX, DC, DS, MC, VI.

LES DEUX FONTAINES
Seafood

Lunch: $7-$31   Dinner: $9-$31   Phone: 305/672-7878   (202)
Location: E of jct SR A1A (Collins Ave) and 12th St; in Hotel Ocean. 1230 Ocean Dr 33139. **Hours:** 7:30 am-11:30 pm, Fri & Sat-1 am. **Reservations:** suggested. **Features:** Bouillabaisse is the specialty at the moderately upscale restaurant, where diners also can sample well-prepared seafood and meat entrees. Meals can be enjoyed outside on the sidewalk or patio, or inside in one of the cozy dining rooms. Dressy casual; cocktails. **Parking:** on-site (fee) and valet. **Cards:** AX, CB, DC, DS, JC, MC, VI.

MAMA VIEJA RESTAURANT
Colombian

Lunch: $5-$9   Dinner: $7-$18   Phone: 305/538-2400   (193)
Location: Just w of Collins Ave (SR A1A). 235 23rd St 33139. **Hours:** noon-11 pm, Fri & Sat-midnight. Closed: 12/25; also Sun. **Reservations:** accepted. **Features:** A warm, family atmosphere embraces diners in this little slice of Colombia. The architecture and decor combine to reflect the roots of South America, as do the well-prepared dishes of seafood, pasta and steaks, such as the bandeja paisa. Casual dress; cocktails; entertainment. **Parking:** street. **Cards:** AX, CB, DC, DS, MC, VI.

MARK'S SOUTH BEACH
New World

Dinner: $18-$30   Phone: 305/604-9050   (205)
Location: SR A1A, corner of 11th St and Collins Ave; in Nash Hotel. 1120 Collins Ave 33136. **Hours:** 7 pm-11 pm, Fri & Sat-midnight. **Reservations:** suggested. **Features:** Worldly influences, techniques and ingredients lend flavor to dishes of new American cuisine. Excellent preparation and presentation characterize meat, seafood and pasta entrees. The atmosphere is stylish and sophisticated both in the dining room and in the terrace area near the pools. Dressy casual; cocktails. **Parking:** valet. **Cards:** AX, DC, MC, VI.

MEZZALUNA, SOUTH BEACH
Italian

Lunch: $15-$16   Dinner: $10-$24   Phone: 305/674-1330   (204)
Location: E of SR A1A (Collins Ave) and 8th Ave; in Casa Grande Hotel. 834 Ocean Dr 33139. **Hours:** 8 am-midnight, Fri & Sat-1 am. **Reservations:** suggested. **Features:** Authentic Italian cuisine served in a setting replete with Italian tiles and hand-painted pottery give this bustling bistro a Mediterranean flair. Fresh tomatoes top the complimentary bruscetta appetizer, which is almost a meal by itself. Dressy casual; cocktails. **Parking:** valet. **Cards:** AX, DC, MC, VI.

NEMO RESTAURANT
New World

Lunch: $8-$14   Dinner: $18-$28   Phone: 305/532-4550   (209)
Location: I-95 S to SR 395 E to MacArthur Cswy (5th St), s on Collins Ave, w onto 1st St; jct 1st and Collins Ave. 100 Collins Ave 33139. **Hours:** noon-3 & 7-midnight, Sun 11 am-3 & 6-11 pm. Closed: 8/1-8/31. **Reservations:** suggested. **Features:** Trendy and distinctive, the eatery features Asian-influenced dishes prepared with the utmost care and expertise. A nice wine list invites diners to peruse. cocktails. **Parking:** valet and street. **Cards:** AX, MC, VI.

NOBU AT THE SHORE CLUB SOUTH BEACH
Japanese

Dinner: $25-$40   Phone: 305/695-3100   (194)
Location: On SR A1A (Collins Ave), just s of 20th St; in The Shore Club South Beach. 1901 Collins Ave 33139. **Hours:** 6 pm-1 am. **Features:** The trendy, upbeat spot treats diners' taste buds to modern Japanese cuisine. The chef's Peruvian influence infuses well-prepared dishes. In addition to an extensive wine list, the restaurant offers a selection of sake. Dressy casual; cocktails. **Parking:** valet. **Cards:** AX, CB, DC, DS, JC, MC, VI.

PACIFIC TIME
Asian

Dinner: $17-$32   Phone: 305/534-5979   (195)
Location: Between Jefferson and Michigan aves; in Lincoln Road Pedestrian Mall. 915 Lincoln Rd 33139. **Hours:** 6 pm-11 pm, Fri & Sat-midnight. Closed: 11/27, 12/25. **Reservations:** suggested. **Features:** California Pacific Rim cuisine is served in a bustling environment. The chef, who is a master of seafood preparation, presents superb entrees in an attractive, artful and innovative way. Casual dress; cocktails. **Parking:** street. **Cards:** AX, MC, VI.

(See map p. 510)

SHIVA

Indian
MC, VI.

Dinner: $8-$18   **Phone:** 305/534-3700   (207)
Location: SR A1A (Collins Ave), just w. 630 Sixth St 33139. **Hours:** 6 pm-11 pm, Sun 5:30 pm-10:30 pm. Closed: 12/25. **Reservations:** suggested; weekends. **Features:** An unassuming exterior opens to a quiet, intimate restaurant with diffused lighting. Traditional Indian food is prepared with skill and reverence for the Eastern trinity of body, mind and spirit. Casual dress; beer & wine only. **Parking:** street. **Cards:** AX,

SMITH & WOLLENSKY STEAK & CHOP HOUSE   **Lunch:** $19-$23   **Dinner:** $22-$38   **Phone:** 305/673-2800   (210)

Traditional Steak House

Location: At Washington Ave and Biscayne St; behind tall condo building; in South Pointe Park. 1 Washington Ave 33139. **Hours:** noon-1:30 am. **Reservations:** suggested. **Features:** At the tip of South Beach and the entrance to Port Miami, the restaurant offers a menu of aged prime beef, prepared to order, prime rib, chops and fresh fish—all served with ample side dishes. The friendly, comfortable place provides a large, award-winning wine list. Dressy casual; cocktails. **Parking:** valet. **Cards:** AX, DC, DS, MC, VI.

TWELVE TWENTY

Provincial American

Dinner: $20-$35   **Phone:** 305/604-5000   (203)
Location: E of jct SR A1A (Collins Ave) and 12th St; in The Tides Hotel. 1220 Ocean Dr 33139. **Hours:** 7 pm-midnight. **Reservations:** suggested. **Features:** Light French cuisine is prepared with a Mediterranean flair. Distinctive presentations use fresh seafood and meat. The bar area is neat and comfortable. Dressy casual; cocktails; entertainment. **Parking:** valet and street. **Cards:** AX, DC, DS, MC, VI.

WISH

Northern American

Lunch: $6-$13   **Dinner:** $20-$33   **Phone:** 305/674-9474   (212)
Location: On SR A1A (Collins Ave) and 8th St; in The Hotel. 801 Collins Ave 33139. **Hours:** 7 am-3 & 6-11 pm, Fri-Sun to midnight. **Reservations:** suggested. **Features:** American fusion dishes meld Asian, Southwestern, Italian and French influences. The menu includes beef, poultry, fresh fish and some vegetarian appetizers and entrees. Desserts are both beautiful and sweetly satisfying. An Art Deco flair punctuates the dining room and bar. The outside dining area features a large fountain and is almost completely enclosed by foliage. Dressy casual; cocktails. **Parking:** valet. **Cards:** AX, CB, DC, DS, MC, VI.

YUCA RESTAURANT

Cuban

Lunch: $5-$14   **Dinner:** $6-$40   **Phone:** 305/532-9822   (196)
Location: In the Lincoln Road Pedestrian Mall. 501 Lincoln Rd 33139. **Hours:** noon-3 & 6-11 pm, Fri & Sat-midnight, Sun-10 pm. Closed: 1/1, 11/27, 12/25. **Reservations:** accepted. **Features:** Expect cutting-edge Cuban entrees with a more global appeal. Gourmet items such as plantain-coated dolphin, black bean soup, and yuca filled with a wild mushroom picadillo will stir the palate. Try the dessert of coconut custard served in the shell. Dressy casual; cocktails. **Parking:** on-site. **Cards:** AX, DC, MC, VI.

The following restaurants have not been evaluated by AAA but are listed for your information only.

BARABOO   **Phone:** 305/867-4242
(fyi)   Not evaluated. **Location:** 7300 Ocean Terr 33154. **Features:** A circus atmosphere featuring French and Italian influenced entrees. The location is so close to the ocean you can feel the breeze.

THE SAMBA ROOM   **Phone:** 305/672-6223
(fyi)   Not evaluated. **Location:** 1501 Collins Ave 33139. **Features:** Located in the heart of the Art Deco District offers affordable Latin Fusion entrees of meats and seafoods. Stay later and enjoy the night club, and
Samba.

TUSCAN STEAK   **Phone:** 305/534-2233
(fyi)   Not evaluated. **Location:** 433 Washington Ave. **Features:** Creative, upscale Italian cuisine. Casual, yet upscale ambience. Expensive.

The Miami-Miami Beach Vicinity

AVENTURA   pop. 25,267   (See map p. 504; index p. 509)

——— WHERE TO STAY ———

COURTYARD BY MARRIOTT AVENTURA MALL   Phone: (305)937-0805   173

SAVE

▼▼▼▼

Small-scale Hotel

12/1-12/20, 1/3-4/30 & 10/1-11/30	1P: $159-$179	2P: $159-$179
5/1-9/30	1P: $99-$139	2P: $99-$139

Location: Just e of US 1 (Biscayne Blvd) at NE 191st and 28th Ave, just se of SR 856. 2825 NE 191 St 33180. Fax: 305/937-0806. **Facility:** 166 units. 161 one-bedroom standard units, some with whirlpools. 5 one-bedroom suites ($299-$309). 5 stories, interior corridors. *Bath:* combo or shower only. **Parking:** on-site. **Terms:** open 12/1-12/20 & 1/3-11/30, cancellation fee imposed, package plans. **Amenities:** dual phone lines, voice mail, irons, hair dryers. **Pool(s):** heated outdoor. **Leisure Activities:** whirlpool, exercise room. **Guest Services:** valet and coin laundry. **Business Services:** meeting rooms, fax (fee). **Cards:** AX, DC, DS, JC, MC, VI.

SOME UNITS

[icons]   FEE   FEE

TURNBERRY ISLE RESORT & CLUB   Phone: 305/932-6200   172

▼▼▼▼ ▼▼▼▼

Resort
Large-scale Hotel

12/20-4/12	1P: $405-$4200	2P: $405-$4200	XP: $50	F12
4/13-5/17	1P: $285-$4200	2P: $285-$4200	XP: $50	F12
12/1-12/19	1P: $275-$4200	2P: $275-$4200	XP: $50	F12
5/18-11/30	1P: $175-$4200	2P: $175-$4200	XP: $50	F12

Location: 0.5 mi w of SR A1A via SR 856; from US 1 at NE 199th St and Biscayne Blvd. 19999 W Country Club Dr 33180. Fax: 305/933-6554. **Facility:** A gate marks the entrance to this service-oriented, Mediterranean-style resort offering golf, tennis and fine dining. 392 units. 366 one-bedroom standard units, some with whirlpools. 26 one-bedroom suites with whirlpools, some with kitchens. 5-7 stories, interior/exterior corridors. **Parking:** valet. **Terms:** check-in 4 pm, 3 day cancellation notice-fee imposed, [BP] & [CP] meal plans available, $8 service charge. **Amenities:** video games (fee), high-speed Internet, dual phone lines, voice mail, fax, safes, honor bars, irons, hair dryers. *Some:* CD players. **Pool(s):** 3 heated outdoor. **Leisure Activities:** saunas, whirlpools, steamrooms, rental sailboats, recreation programs, jogging, spa. *Fee:* windsurfing, marina, charter fishing, golf-36 holes, 20 tennis courts (18 lighted). **Guest Services:** gift shop, valet laundry, area transportation. **Business Services:** conference facilities, business center. **Cards:** AX, CB, DC, DS, JC, MC, VI.

SOME UNITS

[icons]

——— WHERE TO DINE ———

CHEF ALLEN'S   **Dinner:** $26-$38   Phone: 305/935-2900   165

▼▼▼▼ ▼▼▼▼

American

Location: Just e of US 1 (Biscayne Blvd) at NE 191st St and NE 28th Ave, just se of jct SR 856. 19088 NE 29th Ave 33180. **Hours:** 6 pm-10:30 pm, Fri & Sat-11 pm. Closed: 7/4; also Super Bowl Sun. **Reservations:** suggested. **Features:** Innovative New World cuisine is excellently presented in an Art Deco dining room. Watch the cook whip up your meal through the glass-enclosed "al vista" kitchen. A very extensive wine list and professional service add the finishing touch to a great meal. Dressy casual; cocktails. **Parking:** valet. **Cards:** AX, DC, MC, VI.

[icon]

BAL HARBOUR   pop. 3,305   (See map p. 510; index p. 512)

——— WHERE TO STAY ———

BAY HARBOR INN AND SUITES   Phone: (305)868-4141   263

▼▼▼

Small-scale Hotel

12/1-3/31 & 10/1-11/30 [ECP]	1P: $129-$189	2P: $129-$189
4/1-9/30 [ECP]	1P: $89-$139	2P: $89-$139

Location: Just s of SR A1A. 9660 E Bay Harbor Dr 33154. Fax: 305/867-9094. **Facility:** Designated smoking area. 45 units. 21 one-bedroom standard units. 24 one-bedroom suites. 2 stories (no elevator), interior/exterior corridors. **Parking:** valet. **Terms:** cancellation fee imposed, [AP], [BP] & [CP] meal plans available, package plans, 18% service charge. **Amenities:** dual phone lines, voice mail, safes, honor bars, irons, hair dryers. **Pool(s):** heated outdoor. **Leisure Activities:** fishing. *Fee:* boat dock. **Guest Services:** sundries, valet laundry. **Business Services:** meeting rooms, business center. **Cards:** AX, MC, VI.

SOME UNITS

[icons]

SHERATON BAL HARBOUR BEACH RESORT   Phone: (305)865-7511   262

▼▼▼ ▼▼▼

Large-scale Hotel

12/16-4/21	1P: $429-$619	2P: $429-$619	XP: $25	F18
6/6-11/30	1P: $259-$519	2P: $259-$519	XP: $25	F18
12/1-12/15 & 4/22-6/5	1P: $349-$499	2P: $349-$499	XP: $25	F18

Location: On SR A1A, just n on SR 922. 9701 Collins Ave 33154. Fax: 305/864-2601. **Facility:** Tropical trees, flowering plants and a waterfall pool enhance the manicured grounds of this resort offering on-site shopping. 659 units. 616 one-bedroom standard units. 26 one-, 16 two- and 1 three-bedroom suites ($675-$2000), some with whirlpools. 8-16 stories, interior corridors. *Bath:* combo or shower only. **Parking:** valet. **Terms:** 3 day cancellation notice-fee imposed, $12 service charge. **Amenities:** video games (fee), dual phone lines, voice mail, safes, honor bars, irons, hair dryers. *Some:* CD players, high-speed Internet (fee), fax. **Pool(s):** 2 heated outdoor, wading. **Leisure Activities:** sauna, whirlpools, waterslide, rental paddleboats, 2 lighted tennis courts, jogging, spa. *Fee:* sailboats, windsurfing, scuba diving, snorkeling, charter fishing. **Guest Services:** gift shop, valet laundry. **Business Services:** conference facilities, business center. **Cards:** AX, CB, DC, DS, JC, MC, VI.
(See color ad p 5)

SOME UNITS

[icons]   FEE   FEE

(See map p. 510)

——— **WHERE TO DINE** ———

BAL HARBOUR BISTRO   **Lunch:** $9-$25   **Dinner:** $9-$25   **Phone:** 305/861-4544   231
▼▼▼   **Location:** On SR A1A, just n of SR 922; in Bal Harbour Shops next to Sak's. 9700 Collins Ave 33154. **Hours:** 9
am-10 pm. Closed: 11/27, 12/25. **Reservations:** accepted. **Features:** Located in the Bal Harbour Mall, the
Continental   restaurant is surrounded by designer shops. Some of the tables are out in the mall with a canopy of trees
and the sky, while inside the restaurant provides a bistro feel. A diverse menu with light fare, from salads
and sandwiches to fresh seafoods, pastas, and meat items. Dressy casual; cocktails; entertainment. **Parking:** on-site (fee).
Cards: AX, DC, MC, VI.

🍽 ✕

CARPACCIO   **Lunch:** $8-$15   **Dinner:** $14-$21   **Phone:** 305/867-7777   233
▼▼▼   **Location:** On SR A1A, just n of SR 922; in Bal Harbour Shops. 9700 Collins Ave 33154. **Hours:** 11:30 am-11 pm.
Closed: 11/27, 12/25. **Reservations:** suggested; dinner. **Features:** Diners can eat inside the cozy bistro or
Italian   outside, where people-watching is a popular pastime. Foods are fresh and feature local seafood and pasta.
Meat items, too, are prepared with an Italian flair. Casual dress; cocktails. **Parking:** on-site (fee).
Cards: AX, DC, MC, VI.

🍽 ✕

COCONUT GROVE (See map p. 504; index p. 508)

——— **WHERE TO STAY** ———

THE DOUBLETREE HOTEL AT COCONUT GROVE   **Phone:** (305)858-2500   116
SAVE   2/1-3/31   1P: $115-$155   2P: $115-$155   XP: $10   F18
12/1-1/31   1P: $80-$110   2P: $80-$110   XP: $10   F18
4/1-11/30   1P: $80-$110   XP: $10   F18
▼▼▼▼   **Location:** Faces the marina. 2649 S Bayshore Dr 33133. Fax: 305/858-5776. **Facility:** 192 units. 173 one-
Small-scale Hotel   bedroom standard units. 19 one-bedroom suites ($120-$180). 20 stories, interior corridors. *Bath:* combo or
shower only. **Parking:** on-site (fee). **Terms:** cancellation fee imposed, [CP] meal plan available, 18% service
charge. **Amenities:** dual phone lines, voice mail, irons, hair dryers. **Pool(s):** heated outdoor. **Leisure Activities:** 2 lighted tennis
courts, exercise room. **Guest Services:** valet laundry, area transportation. **Business Services:** meeting rooms, fax (fee).
Cards: AX, CB, DC, DS, JC, MC, VI.

SOME UNITS
🅂 🍴 🍽 📠 🏊 🎦 📶 💻 / ✕ 🔌 🖥 /

HAMPTON INN-COCONUT GROVE/CORAL GABLES   **Phone:** (305)448-2800   115
SAVE   1/1-3/31   1P: $129-$169   2P: $139-$179   XP: $10   F18
12/1-12/31 & 4/1-11/30 [ECP]   1P: $79-$99   2P: $89-$109   XP: $10   F18
▼▼▼   **Location:** Just e of US 1. 2800 SW 28th Terrace 33133. Fax: 305/442-8655. **Facility:** 135 one-bedroom standard
Small-scale Hotel   units. 6 stories, interior corridors. *Bath:* combo or shower only. **Parking:** on-site. **Terms:** 3 day cancellation
notice, weekly rates available. **Amenities:** video games (fee), voice mail, irons, hair dryers. **Pool(s):** outdoor.
Leisure Activities: whirlpool, exercise room. **Guest Services:** valet and coin laundry. **Business Services:**
meeting rooms, fax (fee). **Cards:** AX, CB, DC, DS, MC, VI.

SOME UNITS
🅂 🍴 ♿ 🅼 🔌 🎦 🏊 📶 💻 / ✕ 🎞 🖥 /
FEE

MAYFAIR HOUSE HOTEL   **Phone:** (305)441-0000   119
AAA SAVE   12/27-4/15   1P: $269-$800   2P: $269-$800   XP: $35   F12
12/1-12/26 & 10/1-11/30   1P: $249-$800   2P: $249-$800   XP: $35   F12
▼▼▼▼   4/16-9/30   1P: $199-$800   2P: $199-$800   XP: $35   F12
Location: At Florida Ave and Virginia St; center. Adjoins May Fair Shops. 3000 Florida Ave 33133. Fax: 305/447-9173.
Small-scale Hotel   **Facility:** Tiled fountains enhance this hotel built around a ground-floor shopping mall; suites feature individu-
alized decor. 179 units. 153 one-bedroom standard units. 26 one-bedroom suites. 5 stories, interior/exterior
corridors. *Bath:* combo or shower only. **Parking:** valet. **Terms:** check-in 4 pm, cancellation fee imposed, small pets only ($200
deposit). **Amenities:** CD players, dual phone lines, voice mail, honor bars, irons, hair dryers. *Fee:* video games, high-speed Internet. **Dining:** Mayfair Grill, see separate listing, entertainment. **Pool(s):** wading. **Leisure Activities:** sauna, bi-level whirlpool.
Fee: massage. **Guest Services:** valet laundry. **Business Services:** conference facilities, business center. **Cards:** AX, DC, DS,
MC, VI.

SOME UNITS
🅂 🐾 🍴 🍽 🔌 🎦 📶 ✕ 🎞 📶 / ✕ /
FEE

THE MUTINY HOTEL   **Phone:** (305)441-2100   118
AAA SAVE   12/1-3/31   1P: $189-$1000   2P: $189-$1000
4/1-6/15 & 10/1-11/30   1P: $169-$1000   2P: $169-$1000
▼▼▼   6/16-9/30   1P: $129-$1000   2P: $129-$1000
Location: 2951 S Bayshore Dr 33133. Fax: 305/441-2822. **Facility:** Designated smoking area. 120 units. 106
Small-scale Hotel   one- and 14 two-bedroom suites with kitchens, some with whirlpools. 12 stories, interior corridors. **Parking:**
valet. **Terms:** cancellation fee imposed. **Amenities:** video library (fee), CD players, dual phone lines, voice
mail, safes, irons, hair dryers. **Dining:** 7 am-11 pm, Fri & Sat-midnight. **Pool(s):** heated outdoor. **Leisure Activities:** sauna,
whirlpool, steamroom, exercise room. *Fee:* bicycles. **Guest Services:** valet and coin laundry. **Business Services:** meeting
rooms, fax (fee). **Cards:** AX, DC, DS, MC, VI. **Special Amenities:** free newspaper.

SOME UNITS
🅂 🍴 🍽 📠 🏊 ✕ 🎞 📶 🖥 🔌 💻 / ✕ /

RESIDENCE INN BY MARRIOTT   **Phone:** (305)285-9303   120
SAVE   12/1-3/31 & 10/1-11/30 [BP]   1P: $129-$149   2P: $129-$149
4/1-9/30 [BP]   1P: $99-$109   2P: $99-$109
▼▼▼▼   **Location:** From S Bayshore Dr, w on SW 27th Ave/Cornelia Dr, then s. Located in Coco Walk and May Fair Shops. 2835
Motel   Tigertail Ave 33133. Fax: 305/285-9672. **Facility:** 140 units. 32 one-bedroom standard units with kitchens. 67
one- and 41 two-bedroom suites with kitchens, 1-5 stories, exterior corridors. *Bath:* combo or shower only.
Parking: on-site (fee). **Terms:** small pets only ($75 deposit, $10 extra charge). **Amenities:** dual phone lines,
voice mail, irons, hair dryers. **Pool(s):** 2 heated outdoor. **Leisure Activities:** exercise room. **Guest Services:** complimentary
evening beverages: Mon-Thurs, valet and coin laundry. **Business Services:** meeting rooms, fax (fee). **Cards:** AX, CB, DC, DS,
JC, MC, VI.

SOME UNITS
🅂 🐾 🍴 🏊 🎦 📶 🔌 🖥 💻 / ✕ /

(See map p. 504)

SONESTA HOTEL & SUITES COCONUT GROVE   Phone: (305)529-2828

12/22-4/30	1P: $175	2P: $175
10/1-11/30	1P: $173	2P: $173
12/1-12/21	1P: $165	2P: $165
5/1-9/30	1P: $152	2P: $152

Large-scale Hotel

Location: Just w of S Bayshore Dr, just e of jct Main Hwy and Grand Ave. Located in Coco Walk and May Fair Shops. 2889 McFarlane Rd 33133. Fax: 305/529-2008. **Facility:** 220 units. 174 one-bedroom standard units, some with kitchens. 38 one- and 8 two-bedroom suites ($195-$315) with kitchens, some with whirlpools. 23 stories, interior corridors. *Bath:* combo or shower only. **Parking:** valet. **Terms:** 3 day cancellation notice, package plans. **Amenities:** CD players, high-speed Internet (fee), dual phone lines, voice mail, safes, honor bars, irons, hair dryers. **Pool(s):** small heated outdoor. **Leisure Activities:** sauna, whirlpool, steamroom, exercise room. **Guest Services:** valet laundry. **Business Services:** meeting rooms, business center. **Cards:** AX, DC, DS, JC, MC, VI.

SOME UNITS
(ASK) + (YI) (Y) (≋) (X) (VCR) (Ϊ) (DATA PORT) (▣) / (X) (▤) (▥) /
FEE

WYNDHAM GRAND BAY-COCONUT GROVE   Phone: (305)858-9600

(AAA) (SAVE)

10/1-11/30	1P: $264-$284	2P: $264-$284
12/1-4/15	1P: $234-$279	2P: $234-$279
4/16-5/31	1P: $204-$254	2P: $204-$254
6/1-9/30	1P: $204-$224	2P: $204-$224

Small-scale Hotel **Location:** On Water Front Dr. Faces Dinner Key Marina. 2669 S Bayshore Dr 33133. Fax: 305/858-7998. **Facility:** Flowering plants cascading over each balcony form a striking accent at this hotel where many rooms offer a view of the bay. 177 units. 156 one-bedroom standard units. 21 one-bedroom suites ($249-$984), some with whirlpools. 12 stories, interior corridors. *Bath:* some combo or shower only. **Parking:** valet. **Terms:** cancellation fee imposed. **Amenities:** CD players, dual phone lines, voice mail, fax, safes, honor bars, irons, hair dryers. *Fee:* video games, high-speed Internet. **Dining:** 6:30 am-11:30, noon-3:30 & 5-11 pm, also, Bici Ristorante, see separate listing, entertainment. **Pool(s):** heated outdoor. **Leisure Activities:** saunas, whirlpool, beach privileges at Key Biscayne Resort, exercise room. *Fee:* massage. **Guest Services:** gift shop, valet laundry, area transportation-within 5 mi. **Business Services:** conference facilities, business center. **Cards:** AX, DC, MC, VI.

SOME UNITS
(S▮) (YI) (24) (Y) (&M) (✎) (≋) (X) (Ϊ) (DATA PORT) (▣) / (X) (VCR) /
FEE

—— The following lodging was either not evaluated or did not ——
meet AAA rating requirements but is listed for your information only.

THE RITZ-CARLTON, COCONUT GROVE   Phone: 305/644-4680

(fyi)

12/20-4/27	1P: $375-$650	2P: $375-$650	XP: $30	F12
9/29-11/30	1P: $305-$560	2P: $305-$560	XP: $30	F12
12/1-12/19	1P: $245-$540	2P: $245-$540	XP: $30	F12
4/28-9/28	1P: $255-$475	2P: $255-$475	XP: $30	F12

Small-scale Hotel

Too new to rate, opening scheduled for August 2002. **Location:** From Bayshore Dr, just w. 3300 SW 27th Ave 33133. Fax: 305/644-4681. **Amenities:** 115 units, restaurant, pool, exercise facilities. **Terms:** 14 day cancellation notice. **Cards:** AX, DC, DS, MC, VI.

—— WHERE TO DINE ——

BALEEN   Lunch: $9-$18   Dinner: $19-$40   Phone: 305/857-5007

Location: From Bayshore Dr, e on Fair Isle across bridge to Grove Isle; in Grove Isle Resort. 4 Grove Isle 33133. **Hours:** 7 am-3 & 6-11 pm. **Reservations:** suggested. **Features:** The romantic restaurant offers two seating areas: outside tables that afford beautiful views of the bay and the stars and a classic inside room that exudes a golden glow. The food—thoughtfully prepared and artfully presented—will not disappoint.

Seafood

The diverse menu incorporates plenty of seafood choices and land foods. Dressy casual; cocktails; entertainment. **Parking:** valet. **Cards:** AX, DC, DS, MC, VI.
(&M) (Y) (X)

BICI RISTORANTE   Lunch: $9-$16   Dinner: $14-$36   Phone: 305/860-0960

Location: On Water Front Dr; faces Dinner Key Marina; in Wyndham Grand Bay-Coconut Grove. 2669 S Bayshore Dr 33133. **Hours:** 7-11 am, 11:30-3 & 6-10:30 pm, Fri & Sat-11:30 pm, Sunday brunch 11 am-3 pm. **Reservations:** suggested. **Features:** Savor traditional Italian cuisine in a romantic setting, whether on the terrace overlooking the courtyard or in the softly illuminated dining room. Subtle strains of jazz flow from

Italian

the lounge to set the mood. Pasta is fresh and thoughtfully prepared, and meats and fresh seafood are delicious choices. An excellent wine list complements the dishes. Dressy casual; cocktails; entertainment. **Parking:** valet. **Cards:** AX, DC, MC, VI.
(&M) (Y) (X)

CAFE' TU TU TANGO   Lunch: $4-$8   Dinner: $5-$9   Phone: 305/529-2222

Location: At the corner of Grand Ave, Virginia St and McFarlane Rd; at Coco Walk. 3015 Grand Ave #215 33133. **Hours:** 11:30 am-midnight, Thurs-1 am, Fri & Sat-2 am. **Features:** Food and art combine at this cafe. Creations by local painters adorn the walls and guests may watch artists work while enjoying selections off

International

the tapas-style menu. Casual dress; cocktails. **Parking:** on-site (fee). **Cards:** AX, DC, MC, VI.
(Y) (X)

MAYFAIR GRILL   Lunch: $10-$25   Dinner: $20-$40   Phone: 305/441-0000

Location: At Florida Ave and Virginia St; center; in Mayfair House Hotel. 3000 Florida Ave 33133. **Hours:** 7 am-11 pm. **Reservations:** suggested. **Features:** The wait staff does a superb job of making you feel comfortable in the elegant restaurant. International flavors punctuate such artfully prepared dishes as yellowtail snapper

American

with citrus sauce. Dressy casual; cocktails. **Parking:** valet. **Cards:** AX, CB, DC, DS, MC, VI.
(Y) (X)

(See map p. 504)

MEZZANOTTE IN THE GROVE   **Lunch:** $9-$15   **Dinner:** $12-$24   **Phone:** 305/448-7677   (124)

Italian

Location: Adjacent Mayfair Shops at Mary and Florida sts; center. 3390 Mary St 33133. **Hours:** noon-3 & 6-midnight, Sat & Sun from 6 pm. **Reservations:** suggested. **Features:** A popular, upscale bistro, it serves pizza, pasta, grilled meat and fish all cooked to perfection. An impressive seafood salad comes with shrimp and squid on a bed of arugula. Veal-stuffed tortellini smothered in cheese sauce makes a delightful entree. Dressy casual; cocktails. **Parking:** on-site (fee). **Cards:** AX, DC, DS, MC, VI.

CORAL GABLES pop. 42,249 (See map p. 504; index p. 507)

——— WHERE TO STAY ———

THE BILTMORE HOTEL CORAL GABLES   **Phone:** (305)445-1926 (98)

12/1-4/30 & 10/1-11/30	1P: $372	2P: $372	XP: $20	F18
5/1-9/30	1P: $234	2P: $234	XP: $20	F18

Classic Historic
Large-scale Hotel

Location: 1 mi w of Le Jeune Rd. Located in a residential area. 1200 Anastasia Ave 33134. Fax: 305/913-3159. **Facility:** This 1920s-era hotel with Spanish Revival architecture and Moorish and Italian accents features hand-painted fresco ceilings in the lobby. 278 units. 241 one-bedroom standard units. 35 one-, 1 two- and three-bedroom suites ($389-$459), some with whirlpools. 2-15 stories, interior corridors. **Parking:** on-site and valet. **Terms:** cancellation fee imposed. **Amenities:** video games (fee), high-speed Internet, dual phone lines, voice mail, safes, honor bars, irons, hair dryers. *Some:* CD players. **Dining:** Le Palme d'Or, see separate listing. **Pool(s):** heated outdoor. **Leisure Activities:** saunas, steamrooms, jogging, spa. *Fee:* golf-18 holes, 10 lighted tennis courts, bicycles. **Guest Services:** gift shop, valet laundry, area transportation. **Business Services:** conference facilities, business center. **Cards:** AX, DC, DS, MC, VI.

SOME UNITS

HOLIDAY INN CORAL GABLES BUSINESS DISTRICT   **Phone:** (305)443-2301 (97)

1/1-4/15	1P: $169	2P: $169	XP: $10	F
10/1-11/30	1P: $149	2P: $149	XP: $10	F
12/1-12/31 & 4/16-9/30	1P: $139	2P: $139	XP: $10	F

Large-scale Hotel

Location: On SR 953 (Le Jeune Rd), 0.8 mi s of jct US 41. 2051 Le Jeune Rd 33134. Fax: 305/446-6827. **Facility:** 168 one-bedroom standard units. 6 stories, interior corridors. *Bath:* combo or shower only. **Parking:** on-site (fee). **Amenities:** voice mail, irons, hair dryers. **Pool(s):** outdoor. **Guest Services:** valet and coin laundry. **Business Services:** meeting rooms, fax (fee). **Cards:** AX, DC, DS, MC, VI. *(See color ad opposite inside back cover)*

SOME UNITS

HOLIDAY INN UNIVERSITY OF MIAMI   **Phone:** (305)667-5611 (100)

12/1-4/15	1P: $119-$169	2P: $119-$169
4/16-11/30	1P: $109-$119	2P: $109-$119

Small-scale Hotel

Location: US 1. Faces the University of Miami campus. 1350 S Dixie Hwy 33146. Fax: 305/669-3153. **Facility:** 155 one-bedroom standard units. 3 stories, interior corridors. *Bath:* combo or shower only. **Parking:** on-site. **Terms:** cancellation fee imposed, weekly rates available, [BP], [CP], [ECP] & [MAP] meal plans available, 18% service charge. **Amenities:** video games (fee), high-speed Internet, dual phone lines, voice mail, irons, hair dryers. **Pool(s):** outdoor. **Leisure Activities:** exercise room. **Guest Services:** valet and coin laundry. **Business Services:** meeting rooms, business center. **Cards:** AX, DC, DS, JC, MC, VI. *(See color ad opposite inside back cover)*

SOME UNITS

HYATT REGENCY CORAL GABLES   **Phone:** (305)441-1234 (101)

12/1-6/15 & 9/16-11/30	1P: $135-$289	2P: $135-$289	XP: $25	F18
6/16-9/15	1P: $120-$235	2P: $120-$235	XP: $25	F18

Large-scale Hotel

Location: At Alhambra Plaza and Douglas Rd; downtown. 50 Alhambra Plaza 33134. Fax: 305/441-0520. **Facility:** Offering large rooms, some with balconies, the Hyatt Regency Coral Gables is decorated in a Spanish style. 242 units. 231 one-bedroom standard units. 11 one-bedroom suites, some with whirlpools. 14 stories, interior corridors. *Bath:* combo or shower only. **Parking:** on-site (fee) and valet. **Terms:** cancellation fee imposed. **Amenities:** dual phone lines, voice mail, safes, honor bars, irons, hair dryers. *Some:* CD players. **Dining:** 6 am-3 & 6-11 pm, cocktails, nightclub. **Pool(s):** heated outdoor. **Leisure Activities:** saunas, whirlpool, steamrooms, exercise room. **Guest Services:** gift shop, valet laundry. **Business Services:** conference facilities, business center. **Cards:** AX, CB, DC, DS, JC, MC, VI.

SOME UNITS

(See map p. 504)

OMNI COLONNADE HOTEL　　　　　　　　　　　　　　　　Phone: (305)441-2600　[102]

▼▼▼▼ ▼▼▼▼　12/1-4/14 & 10/1-11/30　　1P: $329-$359　　2P: $329-$359
　　　　　　　4/15-6/15　　　　　　　　1P: $279-$309　　2P: $279-$309
Large-scale Hotel　6/16-9/30　　　　　　　　1P: $229-$249　　2P: $229-$249
　　　　　　　Location: At Aragon Ave and Ponce de Leon Blvd; downtown. 180 Aragon Ave 33134. Fax: 305/445-3929.
Facility: Pink and green marble, mahogany trim and hand-blown glass chandeliers impart a luxurious feel to this hotel built around a restored 1926 rotunda. 157 units. 140 one-bedroom standard units. 17 one-bedroom suites ($229-$450). 7 stories, interior corridors. **Parking:** on-site and valet. **Terms:** package plans. **Amenities:** dual phone lines, voice mail, fax, honor bars, irons, hair dryers. *Some:* CD players, safes. **Pool(s):** heated outdoor. **Leisure Activities:** whirlpool, exercise room. **Guest Services:** gift shop, valet laundry. **Business Services:** conference facilities, business center. **Cards:** AX, CB, DC, DS, MC, VI.

SOME UNITS

(A$K) (S⌀) (¶¶) (24¶) (Y) (⌀) (⊸) (※) (DATA PORT) (▣) /(✕)/

RIVIERA COURT MOTEL　　　　　　　　　　　　　　　　Phone: (305)665-3528　[99]

(AAA) (SAVE)　12/21-4/15 [CP]　　　1P: $79-$93　　2P: $79-$93　　XP: $5　　F12
▼▼▼▼　　　 4/16-11/30 [CP]　　 1P: $72-$84　　2P: $72-$84　　XP: $5　　F12
▼▼▼▼　　　 12/1-12/20 [CP]　　 1P: $68-$80　　2P: $68-$80　　XP: $5　　F12
Motel　　　**Location:** US 1, just s of jct SR 953 (LeJeune Rd). 5100 Riviera Dr 33146. Fax: 305/667-8993. **Facility:** 31 one-bedroom standard units, some with efficiencies. 2 stories (no elevator), exterior corridors. *Bath:* combo or shower only. **Parking:** on-site. **Terms:** 7 day cancellation notice-fee imposed. **Amenities:** voice mail.
Pool(s): heated outdoor. **Cards:** AX, CB, DC, DS, MC, VI. **Special Amenities: free room upgrade and preferred room (each subject to availability with advanced reservations).** *(See color ad p 546)*

SOME UNITS

(S⌀) (⊸) (DATA PORT) /(▤) (▣) (▣)/

———— WHERE TO DINE ————

AMMO　　　　　　**Lunch:** $10-$20　　　**Dinner:** $18-$35　　　**Phone:** 305/444-3357　[96]
▼▼▼ ▼▼▼　　**Location:** Just n of Alhambra Plaza; just n of Coral Gables Elementary School. 1915 Ponce de Leon Blvd 33134.
　　　　　　Hours: noon-3 & 6-11 pm, Sat from 6 pm. Sun 6 pm-10 pm. **Reservations:** suggested. **Features:** The
Nouvelle　　setting is cozy, with large local art pieces on tall, white walls and pedestals with vases and palm ferns. The
International　food explodes with flavors typically found in Mediterranean and South American cuisine. The chef's artistic
　　　　　　preparations are based on fresh spices, herbs, meat, seafood and pasta. Smoke free premises. Dressy
casual; beer & wine only. **Parking:** street. **Cards:** AX, DC, DS, MC, VI.　　　　　　　　　　(✕)

CAFFE ABBRACCI　　　**Lunch:** $9-$15　　　**Dinner:** $14-$28　　　**Phone:** 305/441-0700　[109]
▼▼▼▼ ▼▼▼▼　**Location:** At Aragon Ave and Salzedo, just e of Le Jeune Rd; downtown. 318 Aragon Ave 33134. **Hours:** 11:30
　　　　　　am-3 & 6-11:30 pm, Fri-midnight, Sat 6 pm-midnight, Sun 6 pm-11:30 pm. **Reservations:** suggested.
Northern　　**Features:** Exquisitely prepared Venetian specialties are served in an elegant yet casually decorated dining
Italian　　　room with a wonderful, fun ambience. The owner supervises the entire operation so rest assured you will
　　　　　　enjoy a well-prepared, delicious dinner. Dressy casual; cocktails. **Parking:** valet. **Cards:** AX, CB, DC,
MC, VI.　　　　　　　　　　　　　　　　　　　　　　　　　　　　(Y) (✕)

CHRISTY'S　　　　　**Lunch:** $9-$13　　　**Dinner:** $17-$32　　　**Phone:** 305/446-1400　[107]
▼▼▼▼　　　**Location:** Corner of Ponce de Leon Blvd and Malaga; downtown. 3101 Ponce de Leon Blvd 33134. **Hours:** 11:30
　　　　　　am-10 pm, Fri-11 pm, Sat 5 pm-11 pm, Sun from 5 pm. **Reservations:** suggested. **Features:** This classic
Steak House　steakhouse features dry-aged prime rib and other beef specialties. Red walls with mahogany trim and
　　　　　　brass wall sconces add to the gentlemen's club atmosphere. Nicknamed "The Powerhouse," it is an
excellent meeting place for professionals. Semi-formal attire; cocktails. **Parking:** on-site. **Cards:** AX, DC, DS, MC, VI.
　　　　　　　　　　　　　　　　　　　　　　　　　　　　　　　(✕)

EXEDRA RESTAURANT　　　**Lunch:** $10-$17　　**Dinner:** $14-$30　　**Phone:** 305/445-5858　[98]
▼▼▼▼　　　**Location:** Corner of Le Jeune Rd and Giralda Ave. 394 Giralda Ave 33134. **Hours:** noon-3 & 6-11 pm, Sat & Sun
　　　　　　from 6 pm. Closed: 11/27. **Reservations:** suggested; weekends. **Features:** Original artwork spices up the
Italian　　　decor of this Italian restaurant. Only quality ingredients go into truffled lamb, pan-cooked corvina with
　　　　　　nut-sweet garlic, and veal medallions with wild mushrooms. Pasta and risotto are the specialties of the
house. Dressy casual; cocktails. **Parking:** on-site. **Cards:** AX, DC, DS, MC, VI.　　　　(✕)

FRANCESCO RESTAURANT　　**Lunch:** $6-$12　　**Dinner:** $13-$21　　**Phone:** 305/446-3364　[100]
▼▼▼ ▼▼▼　**Location:** 325 Alcazar Ave 33134. **Hours:** noon-3 & 6-10 pm, Sat 6 pm-11 pm, Sun 1 pm-6 pm. Closed: 7/4;
　　　　　　also 12/24; also Mon. **Reservations:** accepted. **Features:** Good fun and beer by the liter are two
German　　trademarks of the lively restaurant, site of two festivals a year. Another is delightful food: smoked pork,
　　　　　　bratwurst mit kraut, veal schnitzel, salmon in Riesling cream sauce and, of course, spaetzle. Dressy
casual; beer & wine only. **Parking:** street. **Cards:** AX, DC, MC, VI.　　　　　　　　　(✕)

LE FESTIVAL　　　　**Lunch:** $9-$15　　　**Dinner:** $16-$27　　　**Phone:** 305/442-8545　[111]
▼▼▼▼　　　**Location:** Between Ponce de Leon and Le Juene Rd, at Alcazar Ave and Salzedo St; downtown. 2120 Salzedo St
　　　　　　33134. **Hours:** 11 am-3 & 6-11 pm, Sat 6 pm-10:30 pm. Closed: 5/26, 9/1; also Sun.
French　　　**Reservations:** suggested; weekends. **Features:** This restaurant features a blend of the freshest of
　　　　　　ingredients with a French style, and a tropical flavor added for good measure. The dining room has soft
lighting with a blend of pastel accents. Dressy casual; cocktails. **Parking:** street. **Cards:** AX, DC, DS, MC, VI.　(✕)

(See map p. 504)

LE PALME D'OR   **Dinner:** $20-$40   **Phone:** 305/445-1926 ⑨⑦
▼▼▼ ▼▼▼ **Location:** 1 mi w of Le Jeune Rd; in The Biltmore Hotel Coral Gables. 1200 Anastasia Ave 33134. **Hours:** 6 pm-10 pm, Fri & Sat-11 pm. Closed: Sun & Mon. **Reservations:** required. **Features:** Chef Phillip Ruiz and his
French   staff prepared excellent "modern French cuisine." His creations are distinctive and the flavors memorable from the first course to the last. Attentive servers move through the elegant dining room. Dressy casual; cocktails; entertainment. **Parking:** on-site and valet. **Cards:** AX, CB, DC, DS, MC, VI.
⌖M ⍊ ☒

MYLOS RESTAURANT & BAR   **Lunch:** $6-$10   **Dinner:** $10-$25   **Phone:** 305/461-0403 ⑩①
▼▼▼ ▼▼▼ **Location:** Corner of Antilla and Ponce de Leon Blvd. 1111 Ponce de Leon Blvd 33134. **Hours:** 11 am-3 & 6-11 pm, Fri & Sat-midnight. **Reservations:** suggested; weekends. **Features:** Appetizers and entrees like
Greek   taramosalata, stuffed vine leaves, octopus and moussaka gives you an authentic taste of Greece. Also offered are grilled whole snapper, Greek sausage, whole lobster, steak, lamb chops and shrimp. Dressy casual; cocktails; entertainment. **Parking:** street. **Cards:** AX, MC, VI.
⍊ ☒

NORMAN'S   **Dinner:** $26-$39   **Phone:** 305/446-6767 ⑩②
▼▼▼ ▼▼▼ **Location:** 3 blks s of Miracle Mile, just w of Douglas Rd. 21 Almeria Ave 33134. **Hours:** 6 pm-10 pm, Fri & Sat-11 pm. Closed major holidays; also Sun. **Reservations:** suggested. **Features:** New World cuisine blends
Regional New   cooking styles from Latin American, Caribbean and Asian cultures. Enjoy a Vietnamese spring roll stuffed
World   with tuna, carrots and cabbage while relaxing in a Spanish-style decor complete with wrought iron fixtures. Dressy casual; cocktails. **Parking:** valet. **Cards:** AX, CB, DC, MC, VI.
☒

ORTANIQUE ON THE MILE   **Lunch:** $6-$15   **Dinner:** $15-$30   **Phone:** 305/446-7710 ⑨⑨
▼▼▼ ▼▼▼ **Location:** Between Le Jeune Rd and Ponce de Leon Blvd; next to the theatre. 278 Miracle Mile 33134. **Hours:** 11:30 am-2:30 & 6-10 pm, Wed-Fri to 11 pm, Sat 6 pm-11 pm, Sun 5:30 pm-9:30 pm. Closed major holidays.
Caribbean   **Reservations:** suggested. **Features:** It's like eating in a Jamaican courtyard, as terraces with draped curtains and warm colors make the atmosphere. Preparations of new world Caribbean cuisine are spiced to varying degrees. Seafood and meat entrees are flavorful and artfully presented. Dressy casual; cocktails. **Parking:** valet. **Cards:** AX, DC, MC, VI.
⌖M ⍊ ☒

RESTAURANT ST. MICHEL   **Lunch:** $7-$20   **Dinner:** $15-$33   **Phone:** 305/446-6572 ⑩⑧
▼▼▼ ▼▼▼ **Location:** At Alcazar Ave and Ponce de Leon Blvd; downtown. 162 Alcazar Ave 33134. **Hours:** 7 am-9:30 & 11-10:30 pm, Fri-11:30 pm, Sat 11 am-11:30 pm, Sun 11 am-10:30 pm. **Reservations:** suggested.
American   **Features:** Art deco and European influences intermingle in the intimate dining room of the 1926 hotel. Glowing pink lights and fancy chandeliers contribute to an air of romance. Savor the Maryland crab cakes and the yellowtail snapper with tropical fruit salsa. cocktails; entertainment. **Parking:** street. **Cards:** AX, DC, MC, VI.
☒

──────── *The following restaurants have not been evaluated by AAA* ────────
but are listed for your information only.

BARROW   **Phone:** 305/774-1934
fyi   Not evaluated. **Location:** 1630 Ponce de Leon Blvd 33134. **Features:** Brazilian is the cuisine type but done with a Nouvelle touch featuring meats and seafood entrees. And they say leave room for dessert too.

THE HEIGHTS   **Phone:** 305/461-1774
fyi   Not evaluated. **Location:** Just s of The Miracle Mile. 2530 Ponce de Leon Blvd. **Features:** Creative blending of Southwest and Asian cuisine. Excellent combinations of flavors and ingredients; expensive.

PASCAL'S ON PONCE   **Phone:** 305/444-2024
fyi   Not evaluated. **Location:** Just s of the Miracle Mile. 2611 Ponce de Leon Blvd 33134. **Features:** Chef Oudin puts his own twist on French cuisine in a cozy bistrolike setting.

CUTLER RIDGE pop. 24,781

──────── WHERE TO STAY ────────

BAYMONT INN & SUITES MIAMI-CUTLER RIDGE   **Phone:** (305)278-0001
Ⓐ SAVE 1/1-4/15 [ECP]   1P: $74-$89   2P: $74-$89
12/1-12/31 & 4/16-11/30 [ECP]   1P: $69-$89   2P: $69-$89
▼▼▼ ▼▼ **Location:** Florida Tpke, exit 12 (US 1), northwest corner. 10821 Caribbean Blvd 33189. Fax: 305/278-0222.
Facility: This hotel offers spacious rooms and proximity to several shopping malls. Designated smoking area.
Resort   103 units. 100 one-bedroom standard units. 3 one-bedroom suites ($104-$135). 4 stories, interior corridors.
Small-scale Hotel Bath: combo or shower only. **Parking:** on-site. **Terms:** small pets only ($50 deposit). **Amenities:** video games (fee), voice mail, irons, hair dryers. **Pool(s):** outdoor. **Guest Services:** valet and coin laundry. **Business Services:** fax (fee). **Cards:** AX, CB, DC, DS, MC, VI. **Special Amenities: free continental breakfast and free newspaper.** *(See color ad p 555)*
SOME UNITS
🎲 🛉 🐾 🎙 ⌖M 🎛 🖩 🕳 🐕 ᴰᴬᵀᴬ 🖥 / ☒ 🔒 📷 /

FLORIDA CITY pop. 7,843

──────── WHERE TO STAY ────────

BEST WESTERN GATEWAY TO THE KEYS   **Phone:** (305)246-5100
Ⓐ SAVE All Year   1P: $75-$259   2P: $75-$259   XP: $10   F16
▼▼▼ ▼▼▼ **Location:** On US 1, 0.8 mi s of Florida Tpke terminus. 411 S Krome Ave 33034. Fax: 305/242-0056. **Facility:** Smoke
free premises. 114 one-bedroom standard units. 2 stories (no elevator), exterior corridors. Bath: combo or
Motel   shower only. **Parking:** on-site. **Terms:** 30 day cancellation notice, [ECP] meal plan available. **Amenities:** voice mail, irons, hair dryers. **Pool(s):** outdoor. **Leisure Activities:** whirlpool. **Guest Services:** coin laundry. **Business Services:** meeting rooms, fax (fee). **Cards:** AX, CB, DC, DS, MC, VI. **Special Amenities: free continental breakfast and free newspaper.**
🎙 ⌖M 🎛 🖩 🕳 ☒ 🐕 ᴰᴬᵀᴬ 🔒 📷 🖥

COMFORT INN

SAVE

▼▼▼▼

Motel

Phone: (305)248-4009

| 12/26-3/31 [CP] | 1P: $54-$189 | 2P: $54-$189 | XP: $10 | F15 |
| 12/1-12/25 & 4/1-11/30 [CP] | 1P: $40-$89 | 2P: $40-$89 | XP: $5 | F15 |

Location: On US 1, 0.8 mi s of Florida Tpke terminus. 333 SE 1st Ave 33034. Fax: 305/248-7935. **Facility:** 123 one-bedroom standard units. 2 stories (no elevator), interior/exterior corridors. *Bath:* combo or shower only. **Parking:** on-site. **Terms:** cancellation fee imposed. **Amenities:** voice mail, safes (fee), irons, hair dryers. **Pool(s):** outdoor. **Guest Services:** coin laundry. **Cards:** AX, CB, DC, DS, MC, VI.

SOME UNITS

〔S⌀〕〔†i†〕〔🌀〕〔🔜〕〔📷〕〔DATA PORT〕〔🖥〕〔📧〕〔📺〕〔🖥〕 /〔✕〕/

CORAL ROC MOTEL

AAA **SAVE**

▼▼▼▼

Motel

Phone: (305)246-2888

12/24-3/31 [CP]	1P: $39-$89	2P: $44-$99	XP: $5	F12
12/1-12/23	1P: $30-$69	2P: $32-$79	XP: $5	F12
4/1-11/30	1P: $30-$54	2P: $32-$69	XP: $5	F12

Location: On SR 997; just w of US 1, 0.5 mi s of Homestead. 1100 N Krome Ave 33034. Fax: 305/242-1580. **Facility:** 17 one-bedroom standard units, some with efficiencies (no utensils). 1 story, exterior corridors. **Parking:** on-site. **Terms:** 3 day cancellation notice, weekly rates available, small pets only ($50 deposit). **Pool(s):** small outdoor. **Guest Services:** coin laundry. **Cards:** AX, DS, MC, VI. **Special Amenities: free local telephone calls and preferred room (subject to availability with advanced reservations).**

SOME UNITS

〔S⌀〕〔🐾〕〔†i†〕〔🔜〕〔📷〕〔🖥〕 /〔✕〕/

ECONO LODGE

AAA **SAVE**

▼▼▼▼

Motel

Phone: (305)248-9300

12/23-4/30	1P: $50-$155	2P: $55-$155	XP: $10	F10
5/1-11/30	1P: $40-$155	2P: $45-$155	XP: $7	F10
12/1-12/22	1P: $40-$75	2P: $45-$80	XP: $7	F10

Location: US 1 at Florida Tpke, exit 1. 553 NE 1st Ave 33034. Fax: 305/245-2753. **Facility:** 42 one-bedroom standard units. 2 stories, interior corridors. *Bath:* combo or shower only. **Parking:** on-site. **Terms:** cancellation fee imposed. **Amenities:** hair dryers. **Pool(s):** small outdoor. **Guest Services:** valet and coin laundry. **Business Services:** meeting rooms. **Cards:** AX, DC, DS, MC, VI.

SOME UNITS

〔S⌀〕〔†i†〕〔🍳〕〔🔜〕〔DATA PORT〕〔🖥〕/〔✕〕〔📧〕〔📺〕/

HAMPTON INN

SAVE

▼▼▼▼

Motel

Phone: 305/247-8833

| 12/1-4/15 [CP] | 1P: $94-$104 | 2P: $104-$122 |
| 4/16-11/30 | 1P: $65-$99 | 2P: $70-$75 |

Location: On US 1, 0.3 mi s of Florida Tpke terminus. 124 E Palm Dr 33034. Fax: 305/247-6456. **Facility:** 123 one-bedroom standard units. 2 stories (no elevator), exterior corridors. **Parking:** on-site. **Terms:** small pets only. **Amenities:** high-speed Internet, voice mail, irons, hair dryers. **Pool(s):** outdoor. **Guest Services:** valet laundry. **Cards:** AX, CB, DC, DS, MC, VI.

SOME UNITS

〔🐾〕〔†i†〕〔🌀〕〔🔜〕〔📷〕〔DATA PORT〕〔🖥〕/〔✕〕〔📧〕〔📺〕/

KNIGHTS INN

AAA **SAVE**

▼▼▼▼

Motel

Phone: (305)247-6633

1/1-3/31 [CP]	1P: $69-$119	2P: $69-$119	XP: $10	F12
12/1-12/31 [CP]	1P: $39-$99	2P: $39-$119	XP: $10	F12
4/1-11/30 [CP]	1P: $39-$59	2P: $39-$59	XP: $10	F12

Location: US 1, just n of Florida Tpke terminus, exit 1. 1223 NE 1st Ave (US Hwy 1) 33034. Fax: 305/247-7515. **Facility:** 48 units. 40 one-bedroom standard units. 8 one-bedroom suites. 1-2 stories (no elevator), exterior corridors. **Parking:** on-site. **Pool(s):** outdoor. **Guest Services:** coin laundry. **Cards:** AX, DC, DS, MC, VI.

SOME UNITS

〔S⌀〕〔🌀〕〔🔜〕〔📷〕〔🖥〕/〔✕〕〔📺〕/

RODEWAY INN

AAA **SAVE**

▼▼▼▼

Motel

Phone: (305)248-2741

1/1-3/31 [CP]	1P: $69-$119	2P: $69-$119	XP: $10	D12
12/1-12/31 [CP]	1P: $39-$99	2P: $39-$119	XP: $10	D12
4/1-11/30 [CP]	1P: $39-$69	2P: $39-$69	XP: $10	D12

Location: SR 997, just w of US 1, 0.5 mi s of Homestead. 815 N Krome Ave 33034. **Facility:** 45 one-bedroom standard units. 1 story, exterior corridors. **Parking:** on-site. **Pool(s):** outdoor. **Guest Services:** coin laundry. **Cards:** AX, DC, DS, MC, VI.

SOME UNITS

〔S⌀〕〔†i†〕〔🔜〕〔📷〕〔DATA PORT〕〔🖥〕/〔✕〕〔📺〕〔🖥〕/

SUPER 8 MOTEL

AAA **SAVE**

▼▼▼▼

Motel

Phone: (305)245-0311

12/1-1/2	1P: $40-$79	2P: $40-$79	XP: $5	F16
2/1-3/31	1P: $79	2P: $79	XP: $5	F16
1/3-1/31	1P: $59	2P: $59	XP: $5	F16
4/1-11/30	1P: $40	2P: $40	XP: $5	F16

Location: SR 997, just w of US 1, 0.5 mi s of Homestead. 1202 N Krome Ave 33034. Fax: 305/247-9136. **Facility:** 52 one-bedroom standard units. 1 story, exterior corridors. **Parking:** on-site. **Terms:** cancellation fee imposed. **Pool(s):** small outdoor. **Guest Services:** coin laundry. **Cards:** AX, DC, DS, MC, VI. **Special Amenities: early check-in/late check-out and free room upgrade (subject to availability with advanced reservations).**

SOME UNITS

〔S⌀〕〔†i†〕〔🌀〕〔🔜〕〔📷〕〔DATA PORT〕/〔✕〕〔🖥〕/

TRAVELODGE

▼▼▼▼

Motel

Phone: (305)248-9777

| 12/26-3/31 [CP] | 1P: $52-$179 | 2P: $52-$179 | XP: $10 | F10 |
| 12/1-12/25 & 4/1-11/30 [CP] | 1P: $38-$79 | 2P: $38-$89 | XP: $10 | F10 |

Location: On US 1, just s of Florida Tpke terminus. 409 SE 1st Ave 33034. Fax: 305/248-9750. **Facility:** 88 one-bedroom standard units. 1 story, exterior corridors. *Bath:* combo or shower only. **Parking:** on-site. **Terms:** cancellation fee imposed. **Amenities:** voice mail, safes (fee), irons, hair dryers. **Pool(s):** small outdoor. **Guest Services:** coin laundry. **Cards:** AX, CB, DC, DS, MC, VI.

SOME UNITS

〔ASK〕〔S⌀〕〔†i†〕〔🍳〕〔🔜〕〔📷〕〔DATA PORT〕〔🖥〕〔📧〕〔📺〕〔🖥〕 /〔✕〕/

──── WHERE TO DINE ────

CAPRI RESTAURANT   **Lunch:** $5-$8   **Dinner:** $7-$10   **Phone:** 305/247-1542
▼▼ ▼▼   **Location:** On SR 997, just w of US 1. 935 N Krome Ave 33030. **Hours:** 11 am-10 pm, Fri & Sat-11 pm. Closed: 12/25; also Sun. **Reservations:** accepted. **Features:** Fair prices and Italian favorites highlight this menu.
Italian   Fresh local seafood and pasta dishes are served in a pair of dining rooms, one casual and one semi-formal. Dark wood paneled walls and red and white tablecloths set the ambience for this meal. Casual dress; cocktails. **Parking:** on-site. **Cards:** AX, MC, VI.   ⓨ Ⓧ

MUTINEER RESTAURANT   **Lunch:** $5-$20   **Dinner:** $12-$22   **Phone:** 305/245-3377
ⒶⒶⒶ   **Location:** On US 1, 0.3 mi s of Florida Tpke terminus. 11 SE 1 st Ave 33034. **Hours:** 11 am-10 pm.
▼▼ ▼▼   **Features:** Wooden beams, nautical artifacts and a theme that revolves around pirate boats all set the tone in this cozy restaurant. The stuffed grouper filled with crabmeat, broiled and coated in sauce is a menu favorite. A band performs on weekends. Casual dress; cocktails. **Parking:** on-site. **Cards:** AX, DC, DS, Steak & Seafood MC, VI.   ⓨ Ⓧ

HIALEAH pop. 226,419   (See map p. 504; index p. 507)

──── WHERE TO STAY ────

DAYS INN MIAMI LAKES/WESTLAND MALL   **Phone:** (305)823-2121   77
ⒶⒶⒶ Ⓢ ⒶⓋⒺ   All Year [CP]   1P: $69-$79   2P: $69-$79
▼▼ ▼▼   **Location:** SR 826 (Palmetto Expwy), exit NW 103rd St, just e. 1950 W 49th St 33012. Fax: 305/362-4562. **Facility:** 83 one-bedroom standard units. 4 stories, interior corridors. *Bath:* combo or shower only. **Parking:** on-site. **Terms:** small pets only ($25 fee). **Amenities:** voice mail, safes (fee), irons, hair dryers. **Leisure Ac-**
Small-scale Hotel **tivities:** pool privileges. **Guest Services:** valet laundry, airport transportation-Miami International Airport, area transportation-Port of Miami. **Business Services:** fax (fee). **Cards:** AX, MC, VI. **Special Amenities:** early check-in/late check-out and free continental breakfast. *(See below)*   SOME UNITS
Ⓢ🄳 ⬥+⟞ 🛏 🕮+ 🎥 🄳🄰🅃🄰🄿🄾🅁🅃 🖥 / Ⓧ 🎴 🖼 /

HOLIDAY INN EXPRESS HOTEL & SUITES   **Phone:** (305)362-7777   76
▼▼ ▼▼   All Year [ECP]   1P: $89   2P: $89   XP: $10   F18
Location: Jct SR 826 (Palmetto Expwy) and NW 122nd St, exit NW 138th and W 68th sts, then w on NW 122nd St. 6650 W 20th Ave 33016. Fax: 305/826-8107. **Facility:** 144 units. 80 one-bedroom standard units. 64 one-bedroom Small-scale Hotel suites ($99-$119), some with whirlpools. 5 stories, interior corridors. **Parking:** on-site. **Amenities:** video games (fee), dual phone lines, voice mail, irons, hair dryers. **Pool(s):** heated outdoor. **Leisure Activities:** exercise room. **Guest Services:** valet and coin laundry. **Business Services:** meeting rooms, business center. **Cards:** AX, DC, DS, MC, VI. *(See color ad opposite inside back cover)*   SOME UNITS
ⒶⓈⓀ Ⓢ🄳 🄳 🏊 🎥 🄳🄰🅃🄰🄿🄾🅁🅃 🖥 / Ⓧ 🎴 🖼 /

RAMADA INN-MIAMI AIRPORT NORTH   **Phone:** (305)823-2000   78
ⒶⒶⒶ Ⓢ ⒶⓋⒺ   12/1-4/15 & 10/16-11/30 [CP]   1P: $79
▼▼ ▼▼   4/16-8/15 [CP]   1P: $69
8/16-10/15 [CP]   1P: $59
Location: SR 826 (Palmetto Expwy), exit NW 103rd St, just e. 1950 W 49th St 33012. Fax: 305/362-4562. **Parking:** Small-scale Hotel **Facility:** 171 one-bedroom standard units. 4 stories, interior corridors. *Bath:* combo or shower only. **Parking:** on-site. **Terms:** cancellation fee imposed, [AP], [BP], [ECP] & [MAP] meal plans available, package plans - weekends, small pets only ($25 extra charge). **Amenities:** voice mail, safes (fee), irons, hair dryers. **Dining:** 6 am-2 & 5-10 pm, cocktails. **Pool(s):** outdoor, wading. **Guest Services:** gift shop, valet and coin laundry, airport transportation-Miami International Airport, area transportation-Port of Miami. **Business Services:** meeting rooms, fax (fee). **Cards:** AX, DC, DS, JC, MC, VI. **Special Amenities:** early check-in/late check-out and free continental breakfast. *(See below)*   SOME UNITS
Ⓢ🄳 ⬥+⟞ 🛏 🍽 ⓨ 🄳 🏊 🎥 🄳🄰🅃🄰🄿🄾🅁🅃 🖥 / Ⓧ 🎴 🖼 /
FEE

(See map p. 504)

—— WHERE TO DINE ——

—— *The following restaurant has not been evaluated by AAA* ——
but is listed for your information only.

FLANIGAN'S SEAFOOD BAR & GRILL   **Phone:** 305/821-0993
[fyi]   Not evaluated. **Location:** 1550 W 84th St. **Features:** The family-friendly restaurant is known for its baby back
           ribs, burgers and seafood.

HOMESTEAD pop. 31,909

—— WHERE TO STAY ——

DAYS INN HOMESTEAD   **Phone:** (305)245-1260
[SAVE]   12/1-4/15 [ECP]   1P: $65-$75   2P: $99-$109   XP: $10   F14
            4/16-11/30 [ECP]   1P: $52-$60   2P: $60-$70   XP: $7   F14
Motel   **Location:** US 1, 1.2 mi n of Florida Tpke, at jct 320 SW and US 1. Located at the edge of the business district. 51 S
            Homestead Blvd 33030. Fax: 305/247-0939. **Facility:** 109 one-bedroom standard units. 2 stories, exterior cor-
            ridors. **Parking:** on-site. **Terms:** 3 day cancellation notice-fee imposed, pets ($7 extra charge).
            Amenities: safes (fee), hair dryers. **Pool(s):** outdoor. **Guest Services:** valet and coin laundry. **Business**
Services: fax (fee). **Cards:** AX, CB, DC, DS, JC, MC, VI.
                                                                                         SOME UNITS

EVERGLADES MOTEL   **Phone:** (305)247-4117
[AAA] [SAVE] 12/24-3/31 [CP]   1P: $39-$68   2P: $44-$88   XP: $5   F12
              12/1-12/23 & 4/1-11/30   1P: $29-$45   2P: $32-$49   XP: $5   F12
Motel   **Location:** Just w of US 1; between Lucy and 6th sts; on SR 997, 0.5 mi s of center of town. 605 S Krome Ave 33030.
            Facility: 14 one-bedroom standard units. 1 story, exterior corridors. *Bath:* combo or shower only. **Parking:**
            on-site. **Terms:** 3 day cancellation notice, weekly rates available, small pets only ($5 fee). **Pool(s):** small
            outdoor. **Guest Services:** coin laundry. **Cards:** AX, DS, MC, VI. **Special Amenities:** free local telephone
calls and preferred room (subject to availability with advanced reservations).
                                                                                         SOME UNITS
                                                                                              FEE

REDLAND HOTEL "AN HISTORIC INN"   **Phone:** (305)246-1904
            12/1-5/31 & 11/1-11/30   1P: $89-$125   2P: $89-$125
            6/1-10/31   1P: $69-$99   2P: $69-$99
Historic   **Location:** Florida Tpke, exit 2, 1.9 mi w on Camel Dr, then 0.6 mi s. 5 S Flagler Ave 33030. Fax: 305/246-9600.
Small-scale Hotel **Facility:** Designated smoking area. 13 one-bedroom standard units. 2 stories (no elevator), interior corridors.
            Bath: shower only. **Parking:** on-site. **Amenities:** high-speed Internet, irons. **Guest Services:** valet laundry.
Business Services: meeting rooms, fax (fee). **Cards:** AX, DC, DS, MC, VI.

—— WHERE TO DINE ——

EL TORO TACO   **Lunch:** $4-$9   **Dinner:** $7-$11   **Phone:** 305/245-8182
            Location: Corner of Mowry Dr and SW 177 Ave. 1 S Krome Ave 33030. **Hours:** 10 am-9 pm, Fri-10 pm.
Mexican   **Features:** Enchiladas, burritos and fajitas are served up mild style in this warm and cozy family-owned
            restaurant, where everything is made from scratch. Take in the fresh air in the outdoor courtyard or dine
            inside. You're welcome to brown bag your own beer. Casual dress. **Parking:** street. **Cards:** DS, MC, VI.

KENDALL pop. 75,226 (See map p. 504; index p. 509)

—— WHERE TO STAY ——

AMERISUITES (MIAMI/KENDALL)   **Phone:** (305)279-8688   [184]
[AAA] [SAVE] 12/1-4/16   1P: $115-$129   XP: $10   F
              4/17-11/30   1P: $109-$115   XP: $10   F
            Location: Florida Tpke, exit 20 (SW 88th Kendall Dr), just e on SR 94, 0.3 mi s. Located across from a shopping mall.
Small-scale Hotel 11520 SW 88th St 33176. Fax: 305/279-7907. **Facility:** 67 one-bedroom suites. 5 stories, interior corridors.
            Bath: combo or shower only. **Parking:** on-site. **Terms:** 2-7 night minimum stay, [ECP] meal plan available,
            small pets only. **Amenities:** voice mail, irons, hair dryers. *Some:* dual phone lines. **Pool(s):** heated outdoor.
Guest Services: valet and coin laundry. **Business Services:** meeting rooms, business center. **Cards:** AX, DC, DS, MC, VI.
Special Amenities: free continental breakfast and free newspaper. *(See color ad p 516)*
                                                                                         SOME UNITS

COMFORT SUITES MIAMI/KENDALL   **Phone:** (305)220-3901   [183]
[AAA] [SAVE] 12/1-4/15 [ECP]   1P: $107-$116   2P: $116-$125   XP: $10   F18
              10/1-11/30 [ECP]   1P: $98-$107   2P: $107-$116   XP: $10   F18
              4/16-5/31 [ECP]   1P: $89-$98   2P: $98-$107   XP: $10   F18
              6/1-9/30 [ECP]   1P: $80-$98   2P: $89-$98   XP: $10   F18
Small-scale Hotel **Location:** Florida Tpke, exit 23 to SW 40th St, or SW 117th Ave, n to entrance. 3901 SW 117th Ave 33175.
            Fax: 305/221-1348. **Facility:** 132 units. 128 one-bedroom standard units. 4 one-bedroom suites with whirl-
            pools. 5 stories, interior corridors. *Bath:* combo or shower only. **Parking:** on-site. **Terms:** cancellation fee imposed.
            Amenities: dual phone lines, voice mail, irons, hair dryers. **Pool(s):** heated outdoor. **Leisure Activities:** whirlpool, exercise
            room. **Guest Services:** valet and coin laundry. **Business Services:** meeting rooms, business center. **Cards:** AX, DC, DS,
            MC, VI. **Special Amenities: free continental breakfast and free local telephone calls.** *(See color ad p 518)*
                                                                                         SOME UNITS

(See map p. 504)

WELLESLEY INN (MIAMI/KENDALL)   Phone: (305)270-0359   185
AAA SAVE   All Year   1P: $69-$179   2P: $69-$189   XP: $10   F18
▼▼▼▼   **Location:** Florida Tpke, exit 20, SW 88th (Kendall Dr), 0.3 mi e on SR 94, 0.3 mi n on SW 117 Ave. Adjoins Town and Country Mall. 11750 Mills Dr 33183. Fax: 305/270-1334. **Facility:** 106 units. 103 one-bedroom standard units. 3 one-bedroom suites. 4 stories, interior corridors. *Bath:* combo or shower only. **Parking:** on-site. **Terms:** [CP] meal plan available, small pets only. **Amenities:** voice mail, irons, hair dryers. *Fee:* video games, high-speed Internet. *Some:* dual phone lines. **Pool(s):** heated outdoor. **Guest Services:** valet laundry. **Business Services:** fax (fee). **Cards:** AX, CB, DC, DS, JC, MC, VI. **Special Amenities:** free continental breakfast and free newspaper.
Small-scale Hotel
(See color ad p 514)

SOME UNITS

──── WHERE TO DINE ────

GIL CAPA'S BISTRO   **Lunch:** $5-$6   **Dinner:** $7-$14   **Phone:** 305/273-1102   176
▼▼▼   **Location:** Jct SW 113th Pl and SW 107th St. 10712 SW 113th Pl 33176. **Hours:** 11:30 am-2 & 5:30-10 pm, Sat from 5:30 pm, Sun 5 pm-8:30 pm. Closed major holidays; also Mon. **Reservations:** suggested.
Italian   **Features:** Health-conscious diners take note: You can enjoy low-fat adaptations of old-style, Southern Italian dishes like sausage with peppers, eggplant parmigiana, steak pizzaiola, veal marsala and lasagna in this small, cozy neighborhood eatery. Dressy casual; beer & wine only. **Parking:** on-site. **Cards:** AX, DC, DS, MC, VI.

PASTABILITIES   **Lunch:** $5-$9   **Dinner:** $12-$18   **Phone:** 305/598-9868   177
▼▼▼   **Location:** Jct of 117th Ave and Kendall Dr; in the "Crossroads" Shopping Center; just e of Florida Tpke (SR 821), exit 20. 11652 N Kendall Dr 33176. **Hours:** 11 am-10 pm, Fri & Sat-11 pm. Closed major holidays; also Mon.
Italian   **Reservations:** accepted. **Features:** The small, family-run restaurant is noted for delicious food prepared with twists of creative inspiration. Among the many house specialties made with fresh ingredients are a spinach linguine with mint sauce and salads with homemade dressings. Casual dress; beer & wine only. **Parking:** on-site. **Cards:** AX, DC, DS, MC, VI.

KEY BISCAYNE pop. 10,507   (See map p. 504; index p. 508)

──── WHERE TO STAY ────

THE RITZ-CARLTON, KEY BISCAYNE   Phone: (305)365-4500   137
▼▼▼▼ ▼▼▼▼   12/20-4/19   1P: $395-$690   2P: $395-$690
   9/28-11/30   1P: $325-$565   2P: $325-$565
Resort   12/1-12/19   1P: $315-$555   2P: $315-$555
Large-scale Hotel   4/20-9/27   1P: $255-$525   2P: $255-$525
Location: Crandon Blvd, just e. 455 Grand Bay Dr 33149. Fax: 305/365-4505. **Facility:** In a quiet location just steps away from the Atlantic Ocean, this hotel features soft colors and fine appointments in each room. 402 units. 325 one-bedroom standard units, some with efficiencies. 44 one- and 33 two-bedroom suites ($450-$3500), some with kitchens and/or whirlpools. 14 stories, interior corridors. *Bath:* combo or shower only. **Parking:** valet. **Amenities:** CD players, dual phone lines, voice mail, safes, honor bars, irons, hair dryers. *Fee:* video games, high-speed Internet. *Some:* DVD players. **Dining:** Aria, see separate listing. **Pool(s):** 2 heated outdoor, wading. **Leisure Activities:** whirlpools, exercise room, spa, sports court, basketball, volleyball. *Fee:* 12 lighted tennis courts, bicycles, game room. **Guest Services:** gift shop, valet laundry, area transportation. **Business Services:** conference facilities, business center. **Cards:** AX, DC, DS, MC, VI.

SOME UNITS

SILVER SANDS BEACH RESORT   Phone: (305)361-5441   135
▼▼ ▼▼   12/1-4/24   1P: $169-$349   2P: $169-$349   XP: $30   F17
   4/25-11/30   1P: $129-$309   2P: $129-$309
Motel   **Location:** 0.3 mi e of Crandon Blvd via East Dr. Located in a quiet area. 301 Ocean Dr 33149. Fax: 305/361-5477. **Facility:** 56 units. 52 one-bedroom standard units. 4 one-bedroom suites. 1 story, exterior corridors. *Bath:* combo or shower only. **Parking:** on-site. **Terms:** 3 day cancellation notice. **Amenities:** voice mail, hair dryers. **Pool(s):** heated outdoor. **Guest Services:** coin laundry. **Cards:** AX, DC, MC, VI.

SOME UNITS

(See map p. 504)

SONESTA BEACH RESORT KEY BISCAYNE
Phone: (305)361-2021   136

	12/1-5/31	1P: $320-$450	2P: $320-$450	XP: $35	F17
	10/1-11/30	1P: $250-$370	2P: $250-$370	XP: $35	F17
	6/1-9/30	1P: $200-$300	2P: $200-$300	XP: $35	F17

Location: 0.3 mi e of Crandon Blvd via East Dr. Located in a quiet area. 350 Ocean Dr 33149. Fax: 305/361-3096.
Resort   **Facility:** Water views are abundant at this hotel where tropical trees and flowering plants lend an island am-
Large-scale Hotel   bience. 292 units. 280 one-bedroom standard units. 8 one- and 4 two-bedroom suites ($450-$1500). 8 stories, interior corridors. *Bath:* combo or shower only. **Parking:** on-site and valet. **Terms:** 2-3 night minimum
stay - seasonal, 3 day cancellation notice-fee imposed, package plans - seasonal. **Amenities:** CD players, dual phone lines,
voice mail, safes, honor bars, irons, hair dryers. *Fee:* video games, high-speed Internet. **Dining:** 3 restaurants, 7 am-midnight;
19% service charge, cocktails, entertainment. **Pool(s):** heated outdoor. **Leisure Activities:** saunas, whirlpools, steamroom, 9
tennis courts (3 lighted), recreation programs, playground, spa, sports court. *Fee:* sailboats, windsurfing, charter fishing, tour
boat, windsurfing instruction, tennis instruction, bicycles. **Guest Services:** gift shop, valet laundry, area transportation-Key Biscayne. **Business Services:** conference facilities, business center. **Cards:** AX, CB, DC, DS, JC, MC, VI. *(See color ad p 552)*

SOME UNITS

—— **WHERE TO DINE** ——

ARIA
Dinner: $26-$42   **Phone:** 305/365-4500   147

Location: Crandon Blvd, just e; in The Ritz-Carlton, Key Biscayne. 455 Grand Bay Dr 33149. **Hours:** 6:30 am-11
pm; Sunday Brunch. **Reservations:** suggested. **Features:** The chef's seafood and meat courses blend the
Mediterranean   Mediterranean and American styles of cuisines. Adding to the subtle atmosphere are tables offering a view
of the courtyard or open kitchen area. Semi-formal attire; cocktails; entertainment. **Parking:** valet.
Cards: AX, CB, DC, DS, JC, MC, VI.

RUSTY PELICAN
Lunch: $5-$12   **Dinner:** $16-$30   **Phone:** 305/361-3818   146

Location: At end of bridge, entrance via marina. 3201 Rickenbacker Cswy 33149. **Hours:** 11:30 am-4 & 5-11 pm,
Fri & Sat-midnight, Sun 10:30 am-3 & 5-11 pm. **Reservations:** suggested. **Features:** The nautically
appointed family restaurant offers views of the bay and downtown area. Attractive dining rooms, gracious
Seafood   service and a varied menu with many fresh seafood entrees are highlights. Valet parking is available after
5 p.m. cocktails. **Parking:** valet. **Cards:** AX, CB, DC, DS, MC, VI.

—— *The following restaurant has not been evaluated by AAA* ——
but is listed for your information only.

LINDA B STEAK HOUSE
Phone: 305/361-1111

[fyi]   Not evaluated. **Location:** On SR 913, about middle of the island. 320 Crandon Blvd 33149. **Features:** Angus beef,
fresh seafood and pasta. A wonderful wine list; all in an elegant dining room.

MIAMI LAKES pop. 22,676   (See map p. 504; index p. 509)

—— **WHERE TO STAY** ——

COURTYARD BY MARRIOTT-MIAMI LAKES AREA
Phone: 305/556-6665   161

	12/1-4/15	1P: $129-$149	2P: $129-$149
	4/16-7/5 & 9/28-11/30	1P: $109-$129	2P: $109-$129
	7/6-9/27	1P: $99-$119	2P: $99-$119

Location: Nw on service road; at jct SR 826 (Palmetto Expwy), exit 154th St. 15700 NW 77th Ct 33016.
Small-scale Hotel   Fax: 305/556-0282. **Facility:** 151 units. 139 one-bedroom standard units. 12 one-bedroom suites. 4 stories,
interior corridors. *Bath:* combo or shower only. **Parking:** on-site. **Terms:** [BP] meal plan available.
Amenities: high-speed Internet (fee), dual phone lines, voice mail, irons, hair dryers. **Pool(s):** heated outdoor. **Leisure Activi-
ties:** whirlpool, exercise room. **Guest Services:** valet and coin laundry. **Business Services:** meeting rooms, fax (fee).
Cards: AX, DC, DS, MC, VI. *(See ad p 519)*

SOME UNITS

DON SHULA'S HOTEL & GOLF CLUB
Phone: (305)821-1150   160

	1/1-4/30	1P: $164-$175	2P: $164-$175	XP: $10	F12
	10/1-11/30	1P: $139-$149	2P: $139-$149	XP: $10	F12
	12/1-12/31	1P: $139-$145	2P: $139-$145	XP: $10	F12
	5/1-9/30	1P: $124-$135	2P: $124-$135	XP: $10	F12

Location: NW 154th St at jct SR 826 (Palmetto Expwy). 6842 Main St 33014-2097. Fax: 305/820-8094. **Facility:** Vintage photographs add interest to the decor of this upscale resort where accommodations range from country-club style to contemporary. 282 units. 262 one-bedroom standard units. 20 one-bedroom suites. 2-3 stories, interior corridors. **Parking:** on-site
(fee) and valet. **Terms:** cancellation fee imposed, package plans. **Amenities:** video games (fee), voice mail, irons, hair dryers.
Dining: Shula's Steakhouse, Shula's Steak 2, see separate listing. **Pool(s):** 2 outdoor. **Leisure Activities:** sauna, whirlpool,
golf-18 holes, 9 tennis courts (Fee: 9 lighted), jogging. *Fee:* racquetball courts, massage. **Guest Services:** gift shop, valet
laundry, area transportation. **Business Services:** conference facilities, business center. **Cards:** AX, CB, DC, MC, VI.

SOME UNITS

(See map p. 504)

TOWNEPLACE SUITES BY MARRIOTT   **Phone:** (305)512-9191   [159]

[SAVE]   12/1-3/31   1P: $89-$119   2P: $89-$119
          4/1-11/30   1P: $79-$109   2P: $79-$109

▼▼▼▼   **Location:** SR 826 (Palmetto Expwy), exit 154th St, 0.4 mi w. 8079 NW 154th St 33016. Fax: 305/512-1284.
Small-scale Hotel **Facility:** 95 units. 69 one-bedroom standard units with kitchens. 4 one- and 22 two-bedroom suites with
          kitchens. 2-3 stories, interior corridors. *Bath:* combo or shower only. **Parking:** on-site. **Terms:** 3 day cancel-
          lation notice, pets ($100 fee). **Amenities:** dual phone lines, voice mail, irons, hair dryers. **Pool(s):** outdoor.
Leisure Activities: limited exercise equipment. **Guest Services:** valet and coin laundry. **Business Services:** fax. **Cards:** AX,
CB, DC, DS, JC, MC, VI.

SOME UNITS

[icons] / [X] [VCR] /

WELLESLEY INN (MIAMI LAKES)   **Phone:** (305)821-8274   [162]

[AAA] [SAVE]   12/1-4/15 [CP]   1P: $84   XP: $10   F18
               4/16-11/30 [CP]   1P: $75   XP: $10   F18

▼▼▼ ▼▼   **Location:** Jct SR 826 (Palmetto Expwy), just w. 7925 NW 154th St 33016. Fax: 305/828-2257. **Facility:** 100 units.
Motel   95 one-bedroom standard units. 5 one-bedroom suites. 4 stories, interior corridors. *Bath:* combo or shower
               only. **Parking:** on-site. **Terms:** cancellation fee imposed, small pets only ($10 extra charge).
          Amenities: video games (fee), voice mail, irons, hair dryers. **Pool(s):** heated outdoor. **Guest Services:** valet
and coin laundry. **Business Services:** fax (fee). **Cards:** AX, CB, DC, DS, MC, VI. **Special Amenities: free continental breakfast and free newspaper.** *(See color ad p 514)*

SOME UNITS

[icons] / [X] [icons] /
FEE   FEE

——— **WHERE TO DINE** ———

SHULA'S STEAK 2   **Lunch:** $6-$20   **Dinner:** $6-$20   **Phone:** 305-820-8047   [156]
▼▼▼ ▼▼   **Location:** NW 154th St at jct SR 826 (Palmetto Expwy); in Don Shula's Hotel & Golf Club. 6842 Main St 33014.
American   **Hours:** 6:30 am-10:30 & 11:30-midnight, Sun 6:30-10 am, 10:30-2:30 & 3 pm-midnight.
               Reservations: suggested. **Features:** Energy swells on game nights at this lively steakhouse, which is
               packed with authentic sports memorabilia. There's nothing better on the menu than the succulent steaks,
which are hearty and prepared to diners' specifications. Casual dress; cocktails; entertainment. **Parking:** on-site and valet.
Cards: AX, DC, MC, VI.

[Y] [X]

SHULA'S STEAKHOUSE   **Lunch:** $8-$24   **Dinner:** $18-$50   **Phone:** 305-820-8102   [155]
▼▼▼ ▼▼   **Location:** NW 154th St at jct SR 826 (Palmetto Expwy); in Don Shula's Hotel & Golf Club. 7601 NW 154th St 33014.
Steak House   **Hours:** 11:30 am-2:30 & 6-11 pm. Closed: weekends for lunch. **Reservations:** suggested.
               Features: Comfortable and clublike, the dining room is decorated with Dolphins football memorabilia.
               Finish off the 48-ounce porterhouse steak and be recognized on a plaque. The lamb chops and seafood
are good, too, as is the to-die-for seven-layer chocolate cake. The dinner menu is also available at lunch. Dressy casual;
cocktails. **Parking:** on-site and valet. **Cards:** AX, CB, DC, MC, VI.

[icons] [Y] [X]

MIAMI SPRINGS pop. 13,712   (See map p. 504; index p. 508)

——— **WHERE TO STAY** ———

AIRWAYS INN & SUITES   **Phone:** (305)883-4700   [151]

[AAA] [SAVE]   12/1-3/15   1P: $45-$79   2P: $45-$79   XP: $5   F12
               8/1-11/30   1P: $45-$69   2P: $45-$69   XP: $5   F12
▼▼▼ ▼▼   3/16-7/31   1P: $43-$62   2P: $43-$62   XP: $5   F12
Motel   **Location:** Between Le Jeune Rd and SR 826 (Palmetto Expwy). 5001 NW 36th St 33166. Fax: 305/888-8072.
               Facility: 116 one-bedroom standard units. 2 stories (no elevator), interior/exterior corridors. *Bath:* some
               combo or shower only. **Parking:** on-site. **Terms:** weekly rates available, [CP] meal plan available, small pets
only ($25 fee). **Amenities:** voice mail, safes (fee). **Dining:** 11 am-3 am, cocktails. **Pool(s):** heated outdoor. **Guest Services:**
valet and coin laundry, airport transportation-Miami International Airport, area transportation-Port of Miami. **Business Services:**
fax (fee). **Cards:** AX, CB, DC, DS, MC, VI. *(See color ad p 528)*

SOME UNITS

[icons] / [X] [icons] /
FEE   FEE

BAYMONT INN & SUITES MIAMI-AIRPORT   **Phone:** (305)871-1777   [153]

[AAA] [SAVE]   12/1-2/16 [ECP]   1P: $84-$114   2P: $84-$114
               2/17-4/15 [ECP]   1P: $84-$104   2P: $84-$104
▼▼▼ ▼▼   4/16-11/30 [ECP]   1P: $79-$84   2P: $79-$84
               Location: SR 953 (Le Jeune Rd) at jct SR 112. 3501 NW Le Jeune Rd 33142. Fax: 305/871-8080. **Facility:** 145
Small-scale Hotel units. 140 one-bedroom standard units. 5 one-bedroom suites ($124-$154). 4 stories, interior corridors. *Bath:*
               combo or shower only. **Parking:** on-site. **Terms:** small pets only. **Amenities:** dual phone lines, voice mail,
irons, hair dryers. *Fee:* video games, high-speed Internet. **Pool(s):** outdoor. **Guest Services:** valet and coin laundry, airport
transportation-Miami International Airport. **Business Services:** meeting rooms, fax (fee). **Cards:** AX, CB, DC, DS, MC, VI.
Special Amenities: free continental breakfast and free newspaper. *(See color ad p 555)*

SOME UNITS

[icons] / [X] [icons] /

COMFORT INN & SUITES-MIAMI INTERNATIONAL AIRPORT   **Phone:** (305)871-6000   [149]

[AAA] [SAVE]   12/1-4/30 [ECP]   1P: $99-$159   2P: $109-$169   XP: $10   F18
               5/1-11/30 [ECP]   1P: $79-$109   2P: $89-$119   XP: $10   F18
▼▼▼▼   **Location:** Between Le Jeune Rd and SR 826 (Palmetto Expwy). 5301 NW 36th St 33166. Fax: 305/871-4971.
               Facility: 274 units. 259 one-bedroom standard units. 15 one-bedroom suites ($129-$189). 7-11
Small-scale Hotel stories, interior corridors. *Bath:* combo or shower only. **Parking:** on-site. **Terms:** [CP] meal plan available, $1
               service charge, small pets only ($25 fee). **Amenities:** voice mail, irons, hair dryers. *Fee:* video games, safes.
Pool(s): heated outdoor. **Leisure Activities:** tennis court, racquetball court, exercise room, basketball, volleyball. *Fee:* golf privi-
leges. **Guest Services:** gift shop, valet and coin laundry, airport transportation-Miami International Airport, area transportation
(fee)-Port of Miami. **Business Services:** meeting rooms, business center. **Cards:** AX, CB, DC, DS, JC, MC, VI.
Special Amenities: early check-in/late check-out. *(See color ad p 513)*

SOME UNITS

[icons] / [X] [icons] [icons] /

(See map p. 504)

DAYS INN MIAMI AIRPORT NORTH

Small-scale Hotel

Phone: (305)888-3661   **152**

	1P: $69-$109	2P: $79-$119	XP: $10	F
12/1-3/31 & 11/1-11/30				
4/1-10/31	1P: $59-$99	2P: $69-$109	XP: $10	F

Location: Between Le Juene Rd and SR 826 (Palmetto Expwy). 4767 NW 36th St 33166. Fax: 305/887-1194. **Facility:** 145 one-bedroom standard units. 1-2 stories (no elevator), interior/exterior corridors. *Bath:* combo or shower only. **Parking:** on-site. **Amenities:** voice mail, hair dryers. *Some:* irons. **Pool(s):** outdoor. **Guest Services:** coin laundry, area transportation. **Business Services:** fax (fee). **Cards:** AX, CB, DC, DS, JC, MC, VI.

SOME UNITS

HOLIDAY INN EXPRESS MIAMI INTERNATIONAL AIRPORT
Small-scale Hotel

Phone: (305)887-2153   **150**

| 1/1-3/31 | 1P: $119-$149 | 2P: $129-$159 | XP: $10 | F18 |
| 12/1-12/31 & 4/1-11/30 | 1P: $99-$129 | 2P: $109-$139 | XP: $10 | F18 |

Location: Between Le Jeune Rd and SR 826 (Palmetto Expwy). 5125 NW 36th St 33166. Fax: 305/887-3559. **Facility:** 110 one-bedroom standard units. 6 stories, interior corridors. *Bath:* combo or shower only. **Parking:** on-site. **Terms:** cancellation fee imposed, [CP] meal plan available, small pets only ($25 fee). **Amenities:** voice mail, irons, hair dryers. *Fee:* video games, safes. **Guest Services:** valet and coin laundry, airport transportation-Miami International Airport, area transportation (fee)-Port of Miami. **Business Services:** fax (fee). **Cards:** AX, CB, DC, DS, MC, VI.

SOME UNITS

(See map p. 504)

HOLIDAY INN-MIAMI INTERNATIONAL AIRPORT-NORTH   Phone: (305)885-1941   146
▼▼▼   12/1-4/15   1P: $104   2P: $104   XP: $10   F19
          4/16-11/30   1P: $71-$81   2P: $71-$81   XP: $10   F19
Small-scale Hotel **Location:** Le Jeune Rd, at jct NW 36th St and SR 112. 1111 S Royal Poinciana Blvd 33166. Fax: 305/884-1881. **Facility:** 219 one-bedroom standard units. 9 stories, interior corridors. **Parking:** on-site. **Terms:** cancellation fee imposed. **Amenities:** voice mail, irons, hair dryers. **Pool(s):** outdoor. **Leisure Activities:** exercise room. **Guest Services:** gift shop, valet and coin laundry, area transportation. **Business Services:** meeting rooms, fax (fee). **Cards:** AX, CB, DC, DS, JC, MC, VI. *(See color ad opposite inside back cover & p 555)*

SOME UNITS

ASK SD ⊞ ⊠ ¶¶ 🍸 🐾 🏊 🚝 📷 DATA PORT ▣ / ✕ VCR 🛗 /
                                                                              FEE FEE

MAINSTAY SUITES-MIAMI AIRPORT   Phone: (305)870-0448   156
AAA SAVE   12/1-4/1   1P: $124   2P: $124   XP: $10   F17
▼▼▼▼   4/2-11/30   1P: $109   2P: $119   XP: $10   F17
Location: I-95 to SR 112 W, exit NW 36th St, then w, right on Palmetto Dr, then w; behind Clarion Hotel; between Le Jeune Rd and SR 826 (Palmetto Expwy). 101 Fairway Dr 33166. Fax: 305/871-5044. **Facility:** 102 units. 81 one-
Small-scale Hotel bedroom standard units with efficiencies. 21 one-bedroom suites with efficiencies. 3 stories, interior corridors. *Bath:* combo or shower only. **Parking:** on-site. **Terms:** small pets only ($100 deposit). **Amenities:** video games (fee), dual phone lines, voice mail, irons, hair dryers. **Pool(s):** outdoor. **Leisure Activities:** 2 tennis courts (1 lighted), barbecue grills, limited exercise equipment, volleyball. **Guest Services:** valet and coin laundry, airport transportation-Miami International Airport, area transportation (fee)-Port of Miami. **Business Services:** fax (fee). **Cards:** AX, CB, DC, DS, MC, VI.

SOME UNITS

SD ⊞ 🐾 ¶¶ 🐾 🏊 ✕ 📷 DATA PORT 🛗 🗄 ▣ / ✕ /

RED ROOF INN MIAMI AIRPORT   Phone: (305)871-4221   154
AAA SAVE   1/1-4/19   1P: $74-$79   2P: $79-$84   XP: $5   F18
▼▼▼   4/20-11/30   1P: $59-$79   2P: $64-$84   XP: $5   F18
          12/1-12/31   1P: $54-$79   2P: $59-$84   XP: $5   F18
Small-scale Hotel **Location:** On SR 953 at jct SR 112; 0.5 mi n of airport entrance. 3401 NW LeJeune Rd 33142. Fax: 305/871-3933. **Facility:** 201 units. 200 one-bedroom standard units. 1 one-bedroom suite. 4-5 stories, interior corridors. *Bath:* combo or shower only. **Parking:** on-site. **Terms:** small pets only. **Amenities:** voice mail. **Pool(s):** outdoor. **Guest Services:** valet and coin laundry, airport transportation-Miami International Airport, area transportation-Port of Miami. **Business Services:** meeting rooms. **Cards:** AX, CB, DC, DS, MC, VI. **Special Amenities:** free local telephone calls and free newspaper.

SOME UNITS

⊞ 🐾 ¶¶ 🐾 🏊 📷 DATA PORT / ✕ /

SLEEP INN-MIAMI AIRPORT   Phone: (305)871-7553   155
AAA SAVE   1/1-4/27 [CP]   1P: $99-$109   2P: $99-$109
          12/1-12/31 [CP]   1P: $79-$89   2P: $79-$89
▼▼ ▼▼   11/1-11/30 [CP]   1P: $89   2P: $89
Small-scale Hotel **Location:** I-95 to SR 112 W, exit NW 36th St, then w, right on Palmetto Dr, then w; between Le Jeune Rd and SR 826 (Palmetto Expwy). Located behind Clarion Hotel. 105 Fairway Dr 33166. Fax: 305/871-5441. **Facility:** 119 one-bedroom standard units. 3 stories, interior corridors. *Bath:* shower only. **Parking:** on-site. **Terms:** small pets only ($25 fee). **Amenities:** voice mail, irons, hair dryers. *Fee:* video games, safes. **Pool(s):** heated outdoor. **Leisure Activities:** lighted tennis court, barbecue grills, volleyball. **Guest Services:** valet and coin laundry, airport transportation-Miami International Airport, area transportation (fee)-Port of Miami. **Business Services:** fax (fee). **Cards:** AX, DC, DS, JC, MC, VI. **Special Amenities:** early check-in/late check-out. *(See color ad p 513)*

SOME UNITS

SD ⊞ 🐾 ¶¶ 🐾 🏊 ⊞ ✕ 📷 DATA PORT / ✕ 🛗 🗄 ▣ /
                                                              FEE FEE

NORTH BAY VILLAGE pop. 6,733   (See map p. 510; index p. 512)

———— WHERE TO STAY ————

BEST WESTERN ON THE BAY INN & MARINA   Phone: (305)865-7100   255
AAA SAVE   12/21-2/18 [CP]   1P: $74-$114   2P: $74-$114   XP: $5   F12
▼▼ ▼▼   12/1-12/20 & 2/19-11/30 [CP]   1P: $64-$104   2P: $69-$109   XP: $5   F12
Location: 2 mi w of SR A1A (Collins Ave). 1819 79th St Cswy 33141. Fax: 305/868-3483. **Facility:** 116 one-bedroom standard units. 5 stories, exterior corridors. **Parking:** on-site. **Terms:** 3 day cancellation notice.
Small-scale Hotel **Amenities:** voice mail, safes, irons, hair dryers. **Dining:** 11 am-1 am, cocktails. **Pool(s):** heated outdoor. **Leisure Activities:** Fee: boat dock. **Guest Services:** coin laundry. **Business Services:** meeting rooms, fax (fee). **Cards:** AX, CB, DC, DS, JC, MC, VI. **Special Amenities:** free continental breakfast. *(See color ad p 528)*

SOME UNITS

SD ¶¶ 🍸 🐾 🏊 📷 DATA PORT ▣ / ✕ 🛗 🗄 /

———— WHERE TO DINE ————

THE CRAB HOUSE SEAFOOD RESTAURANT   **Lunch:** $7-$11   **Dinner:** $11-$39   **Phone:** 305/868-7085   227
▼▼▼ ▼▼▼   **Location:** 2.1 mi w of SR A1A (Collins Ave). 1551 79th St Cswy 33141. **Hours:** 11:30 am-11:15 pm, Fri &
Seafood   Sat-midnight. **Closed:** 11/27. **Features:** The atmosphere is boisterous and fun amid the hanging fish, crabs and plants that contribute to an unmistakable nautical feel. The all-you-can-eat seafood bar is always a popular choice, but don't rule out the Alaskan trio and several varieties of shrimp. Casual dress; cocktails.
Parking: on-site. **Cards:** AX, CB, DC, DS, MC, VI.

♿M 🍸 ✕

NORTH MIAMI pop. 59,880 (See map p. 504; index p. 507)

—————— WHERE TO STAY ——————

HOLIDAY INN NORTH MIAMI Phone: (305)891-7350 85

(AAA) (SAVE)
♦♦♦♦

12/1-4/15 1P: $89 2P: $89
4/16-11/30 1P: $79 2P: $79

Location: I-95, exit 10A, 2.8 mi e; on US 1 at NE 125th St and jct Broad Cswy. 12210 Biscayne Blvd 33181. Fax: 305/891-6322. **Facility:** 98 one-bedroom standard units. 5 stories, interior corridors. *Bath:* combo or Small-scale Hotel shower only. **Parking:** on-site. **Amenities:** video games (fee), voice mail, irons, hair dryers. **Dining:** 7 am-10 pm, Fri & Sat-11 pm, cocktails. **Pool(s):** outdoor, wading. **Guest Services:** valet laundry. **Business Services:** ices: meeting rooms, fax (fee). **Cards:** AX, DC, DS, MC, VI. *(See color ad opposite inside back cover)*

SOME UNITS

[icons] (S/D) (♦) (Y) (♦) (≈) (♦) (DATA PORT) (♦) / (X) (♦) /
FEE FEE

HOWARD JOHNSON NORTH MIAMI Phone: (305)945-2621 80

♦♦♦

All Year 1P: $69-$89 2P: $69-$89

Location: I-95, exit 12 (SR 826); just e of Florida Tpke terminus and Palmetto Expwy. 16500 NW 2nd Ave 33169. Small-scale Hotel Fax: 305/945-3317. **Facility:** 142 one-bedroom standard units. 2-4 stories, interior/exterior corridors. **Parking:** on-site. **Terms:** check-in 4 pm, weekly rates available. **Amenities:** voice mail, safes (fee). *Some:* irons, hair dryers. **Pool(s):** outdoor. **Leisure Activities:** exercise room. **Guest Services:** coin laundry. **Business Services:** meeting rooms, fax (fee). **Cards:** AX, CB, DC, DS, MC, VI.

SOME UNITS

[icons] (ASK) (S/D) (♦) (Y) (≈) (♦) (DATA PORT) (♦) (♦) (♦) / (X) /

NORTH MIAMI BEACH pop. 40,786 (See map p. 510; index p. 512)

—————— WHERE TO DINE ——————

TUNA'S WATERFRONT GRILLE Lunch: $8-$16 Dinner: $15-$28 Phone: 305/945-2567 247

♦♦♦

Location: 0.6 mi n of SR 826. 17201 Biscayne Blvd 33160. **Hours:** 11:30 am-2 am. **Reservations:** suggested. **Features:** Dock your boat and enjoy live Maine lobster and an assortment of fresh seafood. Each meal Seafood starts with a bowl of coleslaw in a honey mustard dressing. Pleasant service and an on-site seafood market make this dockside dining experience special. Casual dress; cocktails. **Parking:** on-site. **Cards:** AX, DC, DS, MC, VI.

(Y) (X)

SOUTH MIAMI pop. 10,741 (See map p. 504; index p. 509)

—————— WHERE TO DINE ——————

EL MANARA Lunch: $6-$13 Dinner: $10-$16 Phone: 305/665-3374 185

♦♦

Location: Just e of Dixie Hwy/US 1. 5811 Sunset Dr 33143. **Hours:** noon-2:30 & 6-9:45 pm, Fri & Sat 6 pm-10:30 pm. Closed: Sun. **Reservations:** suggested; weekends. **Features:** This Middle Eastern kitchen Lebanese promises to make fresh tabbouleh twice daily. Other specialties include baba ghanouj, humus and stuffed, mint-scented, meatless grape leaves. Enjoy tasty, tender, aromatic meals in a setting of white-linen elegance. Smoke free premises. Casual dress; beer & wine only. **Parking:** on-site (fee) and street. **Cards:** AX, MC, VI.

(X)

KHOURY'S Lunch: $4-$12 Dinner: $11-$23 Phone: 305/662-7707 187

♦♦

Location: Just e off US 1. 5887 SW 73rd St 33143. **Hours:** 11 am-10 pm, Fri & Sat-11 pm, Sun from 1 pm. Lebanese **Features:** This family-owned establishment is a great spot for authentic Lebanese cuisine prepared with the freshest ingredients. Baba ghanouj, crusty falafel, skewered lamb grilled over charcoal and kafta kebab are among the wonderfully executed and delicious choices. Casual dress; beer & wine only. **Parking:** on-site. **Cards:** AX, DC, MC, VI.

(X)

SUNNY ISLES pop. 15,315   (See map p. 510; index p. 512)

———— WHERE TO STAY ————

MARCO POLO RAMADA PLAZA BEACH RESORT
Phone: (305)932-2233   245

(AAA) (SAVE)   12/21-4/5 [CP]   1P: $155-$285   2P: $155-$285   XP: $10   F
   12/1-12/20 & 4/6-11/30   1P: $89-$189   2P: $89-$189   XP: $10   F

▼▼▼▼   **Location:** SR A1A at 192nd St. 19201 Collins Ave 33160 (19201 Collins Ave, NORTH MIAMI BEACH). Fax: 305/935-5009. **Facility:** 330 units. 324 one-bedroom standard units. 6 one-bedroom suites. 12 stories.
Small-scale Hotel interior corridors. **Parking:** valet. **Terms:** 3 day cancellation notice-fee imposed, [BP] meal plan available, package plans. **Amenities:** voice mail, safes, irons, hair dryers. **Dining:** 7 am-10:30 pm, cocktails. **Pool(s):** heated outdoor, wading. **Leisure Activities:** sauna, steamroom, pool table, table tennis, exercise room, spa, basketball, shuffleboard, volleyball. **Guest Services:** gift shop, valet and coin laundry. **Business Services:** meeting rooms, business center. **Cards:** AX, DC, MC, VI. **Special Amenities: free continental breakfast and free newspaper.** *(See color ad p 538)*

SOME UNITS

MONACO OCEANFRONT RESORT
Phone: (305)932-2100   248

(AAA) (SAVE)   12/1-1/5 & 2/1-4/15   1P: $88-$119   2P: $88-$119   XP: $10   F18
   1/6-1/31   1P: $76-$96   2P: $76-$96   XP: $10   F18
▼▼▼ ▼▼▼   4/16-11/30   1P: $63-$85   2P: $63-$85   XP: $10   F18

   Location: SR A1A at 175th St. 17501 Collins Ave 33160. Fax: 305/931-5519. **Facility:** 113 units. 112 one-bedroom
Small-scale Hotel standard units. 1 one-bedroom suite. 2 stories (no elevator), interior/exterior corridors. **Parking:** on-site. **Terms:** 3 day cancellation notice-fee imposed. **Amenities:** hair dryers. **Dining:** 7 am-2 & 5-10 pm, cocktails, entertainment. **Pool(s):** heated outdoor, wading. **Leisure Activities:** recreation programs, horseshoes, shuffleboard. *Fee:* game room. **Guest Services:** coin laundry. **Cards:** AX, DC, DS, JC, MC, VI.

SOME UNITS

NEWPORT BEACHSIDE HOTEL & RESORT
Phone: (305)949-1300   249

(AAA) (SAVE)   2/1-2/28   1P: $129-$189   2P: $139-$199   XP: $10   F18
   12/1-1/31 & 3/1-11/30   1P: $109-$169   2P: $119-$179   XP: $10   F18

▼▼▼ ▼▼▼   **Location:** SR A1A, at jct SR 826 and Sunny Isles Blvd. 16701 Collins Ave 33160. Fax: 305/956-2733. **Facility:** 300 units. 78 one-bedroom standard units, some with whirlpools. 138 one- and 84 two-bedroom suites ($199-
Large-scale Hotel $279) with whirlpools. 12 stories, interior corridors. *Bath:* combo or shower only. **Parking:** on-site and valet. **Terms:** cancellation fee imposed, [BP] & [MAP] meal plans available, small pets only. **Amenities:** voice mail, safes, irons, hair dryers. **Dining:** 4 restaurants, 7 am-2 am, cocktails, also, The World Famous Newport Pub, see separate listing. **Pool(s):** heated outdoor, wading. **Leisure Activities:** whirlpool, fishing, fishing pier, recreation programs, playground, exercise room, volleyball. *Fee:* scuba diving, snorkeling, charter fishing, banana boat rides, jet boat, wave runners, massage, game room. **Guest Services:** gift shop, coin laundry. **Business Services:** meeting rooms, fax (fee). **Cards:** AX, CB, DC, DS, MC, VI. **Special Amenities: free newspaper and free room upgrade (subject to availability with advanced reservations).**

SOME UNITS

FEE

SUEZ OCEAN FRONT RESORT
Phone: (305)932-0661   246

(AAA) (SAVE)   12/21-4/15   1P: $95-$135   2P: $95-$135
   12/1-12/20 & 4/16-11/30   1P: $70-$125   2P: $70-$125
▼▼▼ ▼▼▼   **Location:** SR A1A at 182nd St. 18215 Collins Ave 33160. Fax: 305/937-0058. **Facility:** 196 one-bedroom standard units, some with whirlpools. 2 stories (no elevator), exterior corridors. *Bath:* combo or shower only. **Parking:**
Small-scale Hotel on-site. **Amenities:** irons, hair dryers. **Dining:** 7:30 am-6 pm, cocktails, entertainment. **Pool(s):** outdoor, heated outdoor, wading. **Leisure Activities:** saunas, lighted tennis court, playground, limited exercise equipment, shuffleboard, volleyball. **Guest Services:** coin laundry. **Business Services:** fax (fee). **Cards:** AX, DC, MC, VI.

SOME UNITS

———— *The following lodgings were either not evaluated or did not* ————
meet AAA rating requirements but are listed for your information only.

HOMEWOOD SUITES BY HILTON MIAMI BEACH
Phone: 305/932-8900

[fyi]   11/14-11/30 [ECP]   2P: $399-$599   XP: $10   F12
   12/1-4/15 [ECP]   2P: $389-$589   XP: $10   F12
Motel   4/16-11/13 [ECP]   2P: $199-$399   XP: $10   F12
Too new to rate. **Location:** I-95, exit 16. 18100 N Bay Rd 33160. Fax: 305/932-5800. **Amenities:** coffeemakers, microwaves, refrigerators, pool. **Cards:** AX, DC, MC, VI.

TRUMP INTERNATIONAL SONESTA BEACH RESORT
Phone: 305/692-5200

[fyi]   12/1-4/30   1P: $295-$495   XP: $35   F17
   9/16-11/30   1P: $225-$375   XP: $35   F17
Motel   5/1-9/15   1P: $185-$335   XP: $35   F17
Too new to rate, opening scheduled for October 2002. **Location:** On SR A1A between SR 856 and 826. 18101 Collins Ave 33160. Fax: 305/692-5111. **Amenities:** coffeemakers, microwaves, refrigerators, pool, water sports, tennis. **Terms:** 3 day cancellation notice-fee imposed. 20% service charge. **Cards:** AX, CB, DC, DS, JC, MC, VI.

———— WHERE TO DINE ————

THE WORLD FAMOUS NEWPORT PUB
Dinner: $9-$30   **Phone: 305/949-1300**   220

▼▼▼ ▼▼▼   **Location:** SR A1A, at jct SR 826 and Sunny Isles Blvd; in Newport Beachside Hotel & Resort. 16701 Collins Ave 33160. **Hours:** 6 pm-10:30 pm. Closed: Mon. **Reservations:** suggested; weekends. Here you will find aged
Steak House beef and fresh fish cooked slowly on an open hearth over hard woods and charcoal. French onion soup would be a nice start to a satisfying meal. Good, attentive service and hearty portions make this a worthwhile experience. Casual dress; cocktails. **Parking:** on-site (fee) and valet. **Cards:** AX, CB, DC, DS, JC, MC, VI.

SURFSIDE pop. 4,909 (See map p. 510; index p. 512)

———— WHERE TO STAY ————

BEEKMAN HOTEL-SUITES ON THE OCEAN
Phone: (305)861-4801 273

AAA SAVE

5/1-11/30	1P: $112-$206	2P: $112-$206
12/1-4/30	1P: $124	2P: $124

Location: On SR A1A (Collins Ave), just s of SR 922. 9499 Collins Ave 33154. Fax: 305/865-5971. **Facility:** 125 units. 26 one-bedroom standard units with kitchens. 79 one- and 20 two-bedroom suites ($450-$800) with

Small-scale Hotel kitchens. 12 stories. **Parking:** on-site (fee). **Terms:** 3 day cancellation notice, weekly rates available, [CP] & [ECP] meal plans available. **Amenities:** voice mail, safes (fee), hair dryers. **Dining:** 7:30 am-8 pm, wine/beer only. **Pool(s):** heated outdoor. **Leisure Activities:** whirlpool. **Guest Services:** coin laundry. **Business Services:** meeting rooms, fax (fee). **Cards:** AX, CB, DC, MC, VI.

SOME UNITS

🅂D 🍽 🏊 📷 DATA PORT 🔌 📠 / ✕ VCR / FEE

BEST WESTERN OCEANFRONT RESORT
Phone: (305)864-2232 272

AAA SAVE

12/1-4/28	1P: $119-$139	2P: $119-$139	XP: $10 F
6/15-9/10	1P: $109-$139	2P: $109-$139	XP: $10 F
4/29-6/14 & 9/11-11/30	1P: $89-$119	2P: $89-$119	XP: $10 F

Motel **Location:** On SR A1A (Collins Ave), just s of SR 922. 9365 Collins Ave 33154. Fax: 305/864-3045. **Facility:** 100 units. 40 one-bedroom standard units with kitchens. 60 one-bedroom suites with kitchens. 3 stories (no elevator), exterior corridors. *Bath:* combo or shower only. **Parking:** on-site. **Terms:** weekly rates available, [ECP] meal plan available. **Amenities:** irons, hair dryers. **Pool(s):** heated outdoor, indoor. **Guest Services:** valet laundry. **Business Services:** fax (fee). **Cards:** AX, CB, DC, MC, VI. **Special Amenities:** free continental breakfast and free room upgrade (subject to availability with advanced reservations). *(See color ad p 526)*

SOME UNITS

🅂D 🍽 🅰 🎣 🏊 📷 DATA PORT 🔌 📠 💻 / ✕ /

This ends listings for the Miami-Miami Beach Vicinity.
The following page resumes the alphabetical listings of cities in Florida.

MIAMI LAKES —See Miami-Miami Beach p. 553.

MIAMI SPRINGS —See Miami-Miami Beach p. 554.

MICANOPY pop. 653

——— WHERE TO STAY ———

HERLONG MANSION BED & BREAKFAST INN
Historic Bed & Breakfast
All Year   1P: $99-$189
Phone: (352)466-3322
XP: $20
Location: Just n on US 441; downtown. 402 NE Cholokka Blvd 32667 (PO Box 667). **Facility:** Built in the Cracker style in 1840 and later converted to Greek Revival, this manor features high ceilings, mahogany inlaid floors and oak woodwork. Designated smoking area. 11 units. 9 one-bedroom standard units. 2 cottages. 3 stories (no elevator), interior/exterior corridors. *Bath:* combo or shower only. **Parking:** on-site. **Terms:** 7 day cancellation notice-fee imposed, [BP] & [CP] meal plans available, small pets only (cottages only, with prior approval). **Amenities:** *Some:* CD players, irons, hair dryers. **Leisure Activities:** bicycles. **Business Services:** meeting rooms, fax. **Cards:** MC, VI.

SOME UNITS

MIDWAY pop. 1,446

——— WHERE TO STAY ———

HOWARD JOHNSON EXPRESS INN
Motel
All Year   1P: $69-$79   2P: $99-$109
Phone: (850)574-8888
Location: I-10, exit 192, just n. 56 Fortune Blvd 32343. Fax: 850/574-5011. **Facility:** 49 one-bedroom standard units, some with whirlpools. 2 stories, exterior corridors. *Bath:* combo or shower only. **Parking:** on-site. **Terms:** 3 day cancellation notice, daily rates available. **Amenities:** irons, hair dryers. **Leisure Activities:** exercise room. **Business Services:** fax (fee). **Cards:** AX, CB, DC, DS, MC, VI.

SOME UNITS

MILTON pop. 7,200

——— WHERE TO STAY ———

HOLIDAY INN EXPRESS HOTEL & SUITES
Small-scale Hotel
3/1-9/30   1P: $79-$89   2P: $79-$89   XP: $8   F
12/1-2/28 & 10/1-11/30   1P: $69-$79   2P: $69-$79   XP: $8   F
Phone: (850)626-9060
Location: I-10, exit 31, just n. 8510 Keshav Taylor Dr 32583. Fax: 850/626-8989. **Facility:** 64 units. 63 one-bedroom standard units, some with whirlpools. 1 one-bedroom suite ($89-$149) with whirlpool. 3 stories, interior corridors. *Bath:* combo or shower only. **Parking:** on-site. **Terms:** [ECP] meal plan available. **Amenities:** dual phone lines, voice mail, irons, hair dryers. **Pool(s):** outdoor. **Leisure Activities:** exercise room. **Guest Services:** coin laundry. **Business Services:** meeting rooms, fax. **Cards:** AX, DC, DS, JC, MC, VI.

SOME UNITS
FEE

——— WHERE TO DINE ———

THE CUTTING BOARD
Steak & Seafood
Lunch: $5-$8   **Dinner:** $10-$16   **Phone:** 850/623-2929
Location: 0.5 mi n of CR 90. 5365 Stewart St 32570. **Hours:** 11 am-8:30 pm, Fri & Sat-9:30 pm. Closed: 12/25; also Sun. **Features:** The casual, no-frills restaurant is well worth the trip into town for its tasty steak and seafood. Great home cooking and a hometown atmosphere contribute to this spot's popularity. Casual dress; beer only. **Parking:** on-site. **Cards:** AX, DS, MC, VI.

MIRAMAR —See Fort Lauderdale p. 403.

MONTICELLO pop. 2,533

——— WHERE TO STAY ———

PALMER PLACE B&B
Historic Bed & Breakfast
Property failed to provide current rates
Phone: 850/997-5519
Location: Jct US 90 and 19, 0.4 mi w of downtown, just s on Hickory St. 625 W Palmer Mill Rd 32344 (PO Box 507, 32345). Fax: 850/997-2863. **Facility:** Furnished with mahogany antiques, this antebellum home dating from 1836 offers good-sized rooms, many with two beds. Smoke free premises. 5 one-bedroom standard units, some with whirlpools. 2 stories, interior corridors. **Parking:** on-site. **Terms:** check-in 4 pm. **Amenities:** irons. **Guest Services:** complimentary evening beverages. **Business Services:** fax. **Cards:** AX, MC, VI.

SOME UNITS

SUPER 8 MOTEL
Motel
All Year   1P: $46-$51   2P: $51-$56
Phone: (850)997-8888
XP: $5
F12
Location: I-10, exit 225, just s on US 19. Located adjacent to antique mall. Rt 1, Box 164-E 32336 (Rt 1, Box 3329-F, MADISON, 32340). Fax: 850/997-9614. **Facility:** 52 one-bedroom standard units. 2 stories, exterior corridors. **Parking:** on-site. **Terms:** weekly rates available. **Pool(s):** outdoor. **Guest Services:** coin laundry. **Business Services:** fax (fee). **Cards:** AX, CB, DC, DS, MC, VI.

SOME UNITS

------ WHERE TO DINE ------

THE COURTYARD CAFE   **Lunch:** $2-$6   **Phone:** 850/997-1990
◆◆◆   **Location:** Corner of US 19, just n of US 90; center. 110 E Dogwood 32345. **Hours:** 6 am-2 pm. Closed major
American   holidays. **Features:** In historic downtown Monticello, the friendly restaurant is near antique shops. Enjoy
           the famous buttermilk biscuits with breakfast omelets or take a look at the lunch buffet, which offers such
           favorites as shepherd's pie and fried chicken with salads, fruit and desserts. Service is efficient. Casual
dress. **Parking:** on-site.   ☒

MOUNT DORA —*See Orlando p. 745.*

MULBERRY pop. 3,230

------ WHERE TO STAY ------

SUPER 8 MOTEL-MULBERRY   **Phone:** (863)425-2500
◆◆◆ [SAVE]   All Year [ECP]   1P: $60-$95   XP: $5   F12
           Location: On SR 60, 1.4 mi e of jct SR 37. 2525 SR 60 E 33860. Fax: 863/869-9354. **Facility:** 64 one-bedroom
◆◆◆◆   standard units, some with efficiencies (no utensils) and/or whirlpools. 2 stories, interior corridors. *Bath:*
Motel   combo or shower only. **Parking:** on-site. **Terms:** 3 day cancellation notice-fee imposed, weekly rates avail-
           able. **Pool(s):** small outdoor. **Leisure Activities:** limited exercise equipment. **Business Services:** meeting
           rooms, fax (fee). **Cards:** AX, DC, DS, MC, VI. **Special Amenities: free continental breakfast and free
local telephone calls.**

SOME UNITS
[icons] ⑤Ⓓ ⊘ 🏊 🎥 [DATA PORT] / ☒ 🖥 📺 /

NAPLES pop. 20,976

------ WHERE TO STAY ------

BAYMONT INN & SUITES NAPLES   **Phone:** (239)352-8400
◆◆◆ [SAVE]   1/21-3/31 [ECP]   1P: $79-$99   2P: $79-$99
           12/1-1/20 [ECP]   1P: $54-$64   2P: $54-$64
◆◆◆ ◆◆◆   4/1-11/30 [ECP]   1P: $49-$64   2P: $49-$64
Small-scale Hotel **Location:** I-75, exit 101, just w. 185 Bedzel Circle 34104. Fax: 239/352-8401. **Facility:** 103 units. 100 one-
           bedroom standard units. 3 one-bedroom suites ($119-$129). 4 stories, interior corridors. *Bath:* combo or
           shower only. **Parking:** on-site. **Terms:** small pets only (in smoking units). **Amenities:** video games (fee),
voice mail, irons, hair dryers. **Pool(s):** heated outdoor. **Guest Services:** valet and coin laundry. **Cards:** AX, CB, DC, DS, MC, VI.
Special Amenities: free continental breakfast and free newspaper. *(See color ad p 562)*

SOME UNITS
[icons] ⑤Ⓓ 🛏 🍴 ♿M 🚭 ⊘ 🏊 🎥 [DATA PORT] 🖥 / ☒ 🖥 📺 /
FEE FEE

BEST WESTERN NAPLES INN & SUITES

Phone: (239)261-1148

12/24-3/31 [CP]	1P: $99-$219	2P: $99-$219	XP: $10	F
4/1-4/20 [CP]	1P: $99-$149	2P: $99-$149	XP: $10	F
12/1-12/23 & 4/21-11/30 [CP]	1P: $59-$119	2P: $59-$119	XP: $10	F

Motel **Location:** I-75, exit 107, w on SR 896 to US 41, 2.5 mi s on US 41; corner of US 41 and Mooringline Dr. 2329 9th St N 34103. Fax: 239/262-4684. **Facility:** 110 units. 80 one-bedroom standard units. 24 one- and 6 two-bedroom suites with kitchens. 2-4 stories, exterior corridors. **Parking:** on-site. **Terms:** 3 day cancellation notice-fee imposed. **Amenities:** video library, high-speed Internet, voice mail, safes, irons, hair dryers. **Dining:** Chardonnay, see separate listing. **Pool(s):** 2 heated outdoor. **Leisure Activities:** whirlpools, miniature golf. **Guest Services:** coin laundry. **Cards:** AX, DC, DS, MC, VI. **Special Amenities:** free continental breakfast. *(See color ad p 563)*

SOME UNITS

BEST WESTERN NAPLES PLAZA

Phone: (239)643-6655

2/1-4/15 [ECP]	1P: $109	2P: $109
12/21-1/31 [ECP]	1P: $99	2P: $99
12/1-12/20 & 4/16-11/30 [ECP]	1P: $59	2P: $59

Small-scale Hotel **Location:** I-75, exit 107, just w. 6400 Dudley Dr 34105. Fax: 239/643-4063. **Facility:** 241 units. 210 one-bedroom standard units, some with efficiencies or kitchens. 31 one-bedroom suites ($149-$259) with kitchens. 4 stories, interior corridors. **Parking:** on-site. **Terms:** package plans - seasonal. **Amenities:** voice mail, irons, hair dryers. **Pool(s):** heated outdoor. **Leisure Activities:** whirlpool. **Guest Services:** valet and coin laundry. **Business Services:** meeting rooms, fax (fee). **Cards:** AX, CB, DC, DS, MC, VI.

SOME UNITS

CHARTER CLUB RESORT ON NAPLES BAY

Phone: (239)261-5559

12/21-4/25	2P: $279-$369
4/26-11/30	2P: $159-$189
12/1-12/20	2P: $149-$169

Condominium **Location:** I-75, exit 101, at 10th St on the bay. 1000 10th Ave S 34102. Fax: 239/261-6782. **Facility:** 33 two-bedroom suites with kitchens. 3 stories (no elevator), exterior corridors. **Parking:** on-site. **Terms:** check-in 4 pm, 30 day cancellation notice-fee imposed. **Amenities:** video library (fee), DVD players, voice mail, irons, hair dryers. **Pool(s):** heated outdoor, wading. **Leisure Activities:** whirlpool, boat dock, fishing, recreation programs, bicycles. *Fee:* boats, sailboats. **Guest Services:** complimentary laundry. **Business Services:** fax (fee). **Cards:** AX, DS, MC, VI.

CLARION INN & SUITES

Phone: (239)649-5500

1/24-4/21 [ECP]	1P: $155-$225	2P: $155-$225	XP: $10	F18
12/1-1/23 [ECP]	1P: $92-$152	2P: $92-$152	XP: $10	F18
4/22-11/30 [ECP]	1P: $65-$105	2P: $65-$105	XP: $10	F18

Small-scale Hotel **Location:** I-75, exit 107, 3.5 mi n on US 41, just n of Park Shore Dr. 4055 Tamiami Tr N 34103. Fax: 239/430-0422. **Facility:** 99 units. 63 one-bedroom standard units. 36 one-bedroom suites. 5 stories, interior corridors. *Bath:* combo or shower only. **Parking:** on-site. **Amenities:** video library (fee), voice mail, safes, irons, hair dryers. **Pool(s):** heated outdoor. **Leisure Activities:** whirlpool, exercise room. **Guest Services:** valet and coin laundry. **Business Services:** meeting rooms, business center. **Cards:** AX, CB, DC, DS, JC, MC, VI.

SOME UNITS

COMFORT INN & MARINA-DOWNTOWN ON THE BAY

Phone: (239)649-5800

	2/1-4/13 [ECP]	1P: $140-$250	2P: $140-$250	XP: $10	F18
	12/1-1/31 [ECP]	1P: $100-$250	2P: $100-$250	XP: $10	F18
	4/14-11/30 [ECP]	1P: $66-$100	2P: $66-$100	XP: $10	F18

Location: I-75, exit 101, jct US 41 and Goodlette Frank Rd (SR 864). Located in Bayfront area. 1221 5th Ave S 34102.
Small-scale Hotel Fax: 239/649-0523. **Facility:** 101 one-bedroom standard units. 4 stories, interior corridors. **Parking:** on-site. **Amenities:** voice mail, irons, hair dryers. **Dining:** 2 restaurants, 11 am-9 pm, cocktails. **Pool(s):** heated outdoor. **Leisure Activities:** whirlpool, rental boats. *Fee:* charter fishing. **Guest Services:** coin laundry. **Business Services:** fax (fee). **Cards:** AX, CB, DC, DS, JC, MC, VI. **Special Amenities:** free continental breakfast and free local telephone calls. *(See color ad p 564)*

SOME UNITS

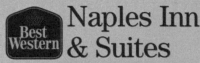

Naples Inn & Suites

Naples In-Town Resort

2329 9th Street North, Naples, FL 34103
US 41 at Mooring Line Drive
www.bestwesternnaples.com

★ 2 jacuzzi spas & 2 heated pools-
   ionized and ozonated

★ 7 waterfalls & ponds with rare, exotic,
   Japanese Koi fish

★ *1/4 mile to Gulf beaches*

★ Free high speed T1 Internet access
   plus computers

AAA 15-30% discount off published rates with this ad!

Based on availability. Must mention ad when booking reservations.

★ National award winning tropical landscaping
   with bronze and marble sculptures gardens

★ Ten restaurants within walking distance &
   across the street from the new one million
   sq. ft. mall

★ **Complimentary deluxe continental
   breakfast–poolside**

★ All rooms and mini suites have refrigerators,
   microwaves, safes and in-room coffee

★ Private balconies and patios overlooking
   both tropical pools and gardens

★ 27" remote televisions with free HBO, Disney
   and 70 channel cable TV

★ Two TV's and two VCR's in all mini suites and
   one/two bedroom condo units (32" TV's)

★ Member of the Naples Fitness Center

★ **Free movies–over 350 video library**

★ One and two bedroom condos with full kitchens
   Available nightly and weekly

★ Hair dryers, iron and ironing board in
   every room

★ 3 Guest laundry rooms with 6 washers
   and dryers

★ Chardonnay restaurant and lounge

★ Facials, massage, spa treatments available

★ 6 minutes West of I-75, exit 16

★ Covered parking

★ Multilingual staff

★ **10% commission paid promptly**

Toll Free: (800) 243-1148 Direct: (239) 261-1148 Fax: (239) 262-4684

COMFORT INN & SUITES

SAVE

▼◇◇◇▼
Small-scale Hotel

2/1-4/15 [ECP]	1P: $89-$164	2P: $89-$164	**Phone: (239)353-9500**
12/22-1/31 [ECP]	1P: $68-$129	2P: $68-$129	
12/1-12/21 & 4/16-11/30 [ECP]	1P: $49-$99	2P: $49-$99	

Location: I-75, exit 101, just w. 3860 Tollgate Blvd 34114. Fax: 239/353-0035. **Facility:** 198 one-bedroom standard units, some with efficiencies. 4 stories, interior/exterior corridors. *Bath:* combo or shower only. **Parking:** on-site. **Terms:** check-in 4 pm, [CP] meal plan available. **Amenities:** irons, hair dryers. **Pool(s):** heated outdoor. **Leisure Activities:** whirlpool. *Fee:* game room. **Guest Services:** gift shop, valet and coin laundry. **Business Services:** meeting rooms, fax (fee). **Cards:** AX, CB, DC, DS, JC, MC, VI.

SOME UNITS

🅢 🅓 🍴 🍸 👤 📷 🏊 DATA PORT 🛏 🖥 / ✕ 🛏 📺

COURTYARD BY MARRIOTT

SAVE

▼◇◇◇▼
Motel

All Year	1P: $59-$159	2P: $59-$159	**Phone: (239)434-8700**
			XP: $10 F18

Location: I-75, exit 107, 3.8 mi w on SR 896 (Pine Ridge Rd), then 1.8 mi s on US 41 (Tamiami Tr). Located in a quiet area. 3250 Tamiami Tr N (US 41) 34103. Fax: 239/434-7787. **Facility:** 102 units. 98 one-bedroom standard units. 4 one-bedroom suites. 4 stories, interior corridors. *Bath:* combo or shower only. **Parking:** on-site. **Terms:** cancellation fee imposed, [BP] meal plan available. **Amenities:** voice mail, irons, hair dryers. *Some:* dual phone lines. **Pool(s):** heated outdoor. **Leisure Activities:** whirlpool, exercise room. **Guest Services:** valet and coin laundry. **Business Services:** meeting rooms, fax (fee). **Cards:** AX, DC, DS, MC, VI.

SOME UNITS

🅢 🅓 🍴 🏋 👤 🏊 📹 DATA PORT ☕ / ✕ 🛏 🖥 /

DOUBLETREE GUEST SUITES NAPLES

SAVE

	1P: $89-$145	2P: $99-$155	XP: $10	F18
12/1-3/31 & 11/1-11/30 [CP]				
4/1-10/31 [CP]	1P: $59-$69	2P: $69-$79	XP: $10	F18

Phone: 239/593-8733

Small-scale Hotel

Location: I-75, exit 111, 3.3 mi w on Naples-Immokalee Rd to US 41, just n. 12200 Tamiami Tr N 34110. **Fax:** 239/593-8734. **Facility:** 101 one-bedroom suites, some with whirlpools. 3 stories, interior corridors. *Bath:* combo or shower only. **Parking:** on-site. **Terms:** 30 day cancellation notice, 9% service charge. **Amenities:** video games (fee), dual phone lines, voice mail, irons, hair dryers. **Pool(s):** heated outdoor. **Leisure Activities:** whirlpool, exercise room. **Guest Services:** gift shop, valet laundry. **Business Services:** meeting rooms, business center. **Cards:** AX, DC, DS, JC, MC, VI. *(See color ad below)*   SOME UNITS

EDGEWATER BEACH HOTEL

(AAA) SAVE

	1P: $345-$1500	2P: $345-$1500
12/1-4/23		
4/24-5/26 & 10/3-11/30	1P: $195-$895	2P: $195-$895
5/27-10/2	1P: $165-$795	2P: $165-$795

Phone: (239)403-2000

Large-scale Hotel

Location: I-75, exit 107, 5 mi w on Pine Ridge Rd, then 2.3 mi s on US 41. 1901 Gulf Shore Blvd N 34102. **Fax:** 239/403-2100. **Facility:** This waterfront hotel offers one- and two-bedroom units with living rooms, some featuring balconies and individual exterior entrances. 126 units. 97 one- and 29 two-bedroom suites. 4-7 stories, interior/exterior corridors. *Bath:* combo or shower only. **Parking:** on-site and valet. **Terms:** 7 day cancellation notice-fee imposed. **Amenities:** video games (fee), voice mail, safes, irons, hair dryers. *Some:* fax. **Dining:** 7 am-2 & 6-10 pm, Fri & Sat-11 pm; hotel guests only, cocktails. **Pool(s):** heated outdoor. **Leisure Activities:** rental sailboats, tennis privileges, exercise room. *Fee:* windsurfing, golf-18 holes, bicycles, massage. **Guest Services:** gift shop, valet laundry. **Business Services:** meeting rooms, fax. **Cards:** AX, DC, DS, MC, VI. **Special Amenities:** free newspaper.   SOME UNITS

THE FAIRWAYS RESORT

(AAA) SAVE

	1P: $95-$175	2P: $95-$175	XP: $10	F16
12/21-4/15				
12/1-12/20 & 4/16-11/30	1P: $50-$100	2P: $50-$100	XP: $10	F16

Phone: (239)597-8181

Motel

Location: I-75, exit 111, 2.2 mi w on CR 846. 103 Palm River Blvd 34110. **Fax:** 239/597-5413. **Facility:** 46 units. 45 one-bedroom standard units, some with kitchens. 1 two-bedroom suite with kitchen. 2 stories (no elevator), exterior corridors. **Parking:** on-site. **Terms:** 3 day cancellation notice, in season-fee imposed, [CP] meal plan available. **Amenities:** *Some:* Irons, hair dryers. **Pool(s):** heated outdoor. **Leisure Activities:** whirlpool, barbecue gas grills, pavilion, shuffleboard. **Guest Services:** coin laundry. **Business Services:** meeting rooms, fax (fee). **Cards:** AX, DC, MC, VI. **Special Amenities:** free continental breakfast and free local telephone calls.   SOME UNITS

HAMPTON INN

SAVE

	1P: $129-$159
1/1-4/26	
10/6-11/30	1P: $69-$139
12/1-12/31	1P: $79-$99
4/27-10/5	1P: $69-$99

Phone: 239/261-8000

Motel

Location: I-75, exit 107, 3.8 mi w on SR 896 (Pine Ridge Rd), then 1.8 mi s on US 41 (Tamiami Tr). 3210 Tamiami Tr N (US 41) 34103. **Fax:** 239/261-7802. **Facility:** 107 units. 105 one-bedroom standard units. 2 one-bedroom suites. 4 stories, interior corridors. **Parking:** on-site. **Terms:** 7 day cancellation notice, [ECP] meal plan available, package plans - off season. **Amenities:** voice mail, irons, hair dryers. **Pool(s):** heated outdoor. **Guest Services:** valet laundry. **Business Services:** meeting rooms, fax (fee). **Cards:** AX, CB, DC, DS, MC, VI.   SOME UNITS

HAMPTON INN-NAPLES I-75 Phone: (239)596-1299

(AAA) (SAVE)

	12/21-4/15	1P: $79-$149	2P: $79-$149
	4/16-11/30	1P: $53-$89	2P: $53-$89
	12/1-12/20	1P: $53-$69	2P: $53-$69

Location: I-75, exit 111, just ne. 2630 Northbrooke Plaza Dr 34119. Fax: 239/596-0808. Facility: 91 one-bedroom **Small-scale Hotel** standard units. 3 stories, interior corridors. Bath: combo or shower only. Parking: on-site. Terms: cancellation fee imposed, [CP] meal plan available. Amenities: dual phone lines, voice mail, irons, hair dryers. Fee: video games, high-speed Internet. Pool(s): heated outdoor. Guest Services: valet laundry. Business Services: meeting rooms, fax (fee). Cards: AX, DC, DS, MC, VI. Special Amenities: free continental breakfast and free local telephone calls. (See color ad below)

SOME UNITS

THE HAWTHORN SUITES OF NAPLES Phone: (239)593-1300

(AAA) (SAVE)

	1/15-4/22	1P: $154-$204	2P: $154-$204
	12/1-1/14	1P: $119-$165	2P: $119-$165
	11/1-11/30	1P: $99-$145	2P: $99-$145
	4/23-10/31	1P: $89-$114	2P: $89-$114

Small-scale Hotel Location: I-75, exit 107, 0.7 mi w. 3557 Pine Ridge Rd 34109. Fax: 239/593-1301. Facility: 82 units. 40 one-bedroom standard units with efficiencies. 30 one- and 12 two-bedroom suites ($89-$204) with kitchens. 3 stories, interior corridors. Bath: combo or shower only. Parking: on-site. Terms: weekly rates available, small pets only ($125 fee). Amenities: video library (fee), dual phone lines, voice mail, irons, hair dryers. Pool(s): heated outdoor. Leisure Activities: whirlpool, putting green, barbecue grill, exercise room, basketball. Guest Services: sundries, complimentary evening beverages: Mon-Thurs, valet and coin laundry. Business Services: meeting rooms, administrative services, fax (fee). Cards: AX, CB, DC, DS, MC, VI. Special Amenities: free continental breakfast and free local telephone calls. (See color ad below)

SOME UNITS

HILTON NAPLES & TOWERS

AAA **SAVE**
♦♦♦ ♦♦♦

Large-scale Hotel

Phone: (239)430-4900

2/1-3/31	1P: $119-$249	2P: $119-$249	XP: $10	F25
12/1-1/31	1P: $109-$199	2P: $109-$199	XP: $10	F25
4/1-11/30	1P: $99-$179	2P: $99-$179	XP: $10	F25

Location: US 41, just sw of jct Pine Ridge Rd. 5111 Tamiami Tr 34103. Fax: 239/430-4901. **Facility:** Large pillars, ironwork and Mediterranean-style archways enhance the lobby of this upscale property. 191 units. 180 one-bedroom standard units. 9 one- and 2 two-bedroom suites. 4 stories, interior corridors. *Bath:* combo or shower only. **Parking:** on-site and valet. **Terms:** package plans. **Amenities:** high-speed Internet (fee), dual phone lines, voice mail, irons, hair dryers. **Dining:** 6:30-11 am, 11:30-2:30 & 5:30-11 pm, Sun 5 pm-10 pm, cocktails, also, Shula's Steak House, see separate listing. **Pool(s):** heated outdoor. **Leisure Activities:** whirlpool, bicycles, exercise room. **Guest Services:** gift shop, valet laundry, area transportation-within 5 mi. **Business Services:** conference facilities, business center. **Cards:** AX, DC, DS, MC, VI. **Special Amenities:** free local telephone calls and free room upgrade (subject to availability with advanced reservations). *(See color ad below)*

SOME UNITS

🆂🅳 ✈ 🍴 24 🍽 👤🅼 📶 ⊘ 🏊 ⊠ 🎥 🖥 🛜 🖳 /⊠🖥 /

HOLIDAY INN

AAA **SAVE**
♦♦♦ ♦♦♦

Motel

Phone: (239)263-3434

1/17-3/29	1P: $119-$149	2P: $119-$149
3/30-4/26	1P: $89-$109	2P: $89-$109
12/1-1/16	1P: $69-$109	2P: $69-$109
4/27-11/30	1P: $69-$85	2P: $69-$85

Location: I-75, exit 107, 1.5 mi n on US 41. 1100 Tamiami Tr N 34102. Fax: 239/261-3809. **Facility:** 137 one-bedroom standard units. 2 stories, exterior corridors. **Parking:** on-site. **Terms:** cancellation fee imposed, weekly rates available, [AP], [BP], [CP] & [MAP] meal plans available, small pets only ($20 fee). **Amenities:** voice mail, irons, hair dryers. **Dining:** 7 am-10 & 5-10 pm, Fri & Sat-midnight, cocktails. **Pool(s):** heated outdoor. **Leisure Activities:** exercise room. **Guest Services:** valet laundry. **Business Services:** meeting rooms, fax (fee). **Cards:** AX, CB, DC, DS, JC, MC, VI. **Special Amenities:** free local telephone calls. *(See color ad opposite inside back cover & below)*

SOME UNITS

🆂🅳 🐾 🍴 🍽 🦢 🎥 🛜 🖳 /⊠🖥 /

FEE

HOLIDAY INN EXPRESS

Phone: (239)348-1700

Small-scale Hotel

| 12/22-4/13 [CP] | 1P: $85-$130 | 2P: $85-$130 |
| 12/1-12/21 & 4/14-11/30 [CP] | 1P: $50-$65 | 2P: $50-$65 |

Location: I-75, exit 101, just s to Davis, just e. 3837 Toll Gate Blvd 34114. Fax: 239/348-1704. **Facility:** 68 units. 64 one-bedroom standard units. 4 one-bedroom suites with efficiencies. 3 stories, interior corridors. *Bath:* combo or shower only. **Parking:** on-site. **Amenities:** voice mail, irons, hair dryers. **Pool(s):** heated outdoor. **Leisure Activities:** whirlpool. **Guest Services:** coin laundry. **Business Services:** meeting rooms, fax (fee). **Cards:** AX, DC, DS, MC, VI.

SOME UNITS

(ASK) (S/D) (&) (graphic) (graphic) (graphic) (DATA PORT) / (X) (VCR) (graphic) (graphic) (graphic) /

INN AT PELICAN BAY

Phone: (239)597-8777

Small-scale Hotel

12/1-3/31 [ECP]	1P: $175-$285	2P: $175-$285	XP: $20	F16
4/1-5/31 [ECP]	1P: $100-$225	2P: $100-$225	XP: $20	F16
10/1-11/30 [ECP]	1P: $100-$150	2P: $100-$150	XP: $20	F16
6/1-9/30 [ECP]	1P: $70-$110	2P: $70-$110	XP: $20	F16

Location: North end of town, just w of jct US 41, 0.7 mi e of Vanderbilt Beach. 800 Vanderbilt Beach Rd 34108. Fax: 239/597-8012. **Facility:** Designated smoking area. 100 one-bedroom standard units, some with whirlpools. 6 stories, interior corridors. *Bath:* combo or shower only. **Parking:** on-site. **Terms:** 3 day cancellation notice, package plans. **Amenities:** video games (fee), voice mail, safes, irons, hair dryers. **Pool(s):** heated outdoor. **Leisure Activities:** whirlpool, exercise room. *Fee:* massage. **Guest Services:** valet laundry. **Business Services:** meeting rooms, fax (fee). **Cards:** AX, DC, DS, MC, VI. *(See color ad below)*

SOME UNITS

(ASK) (S/D) (graphic) (&) (graphic) (X) (X) (graphic) (DATA PORT) (graphic) / (graphic) /

INN BY THE SEA

Phone: (239)649-4124

Bed & Breakfast

| 12/14-4/18 [ECP] | 1P: $149-$169 | 2P: $149-$169 |
| 12/1-12/13 & 4/19-11/30 [ECP] | 1P: $94-$104 | 2P: $94-$104 |

Location: I-75, exit 101, corner of 11th Ave S and 3rd St S. 287 Eleventh Ave S 34102-7022. Fax: 239/434-2842. **Facility:** This sunny, 1937 guest house features polished-pine floors and rooms themed to area islands; the staff speaks several languages. Smoke free premises. 6 units. 5 one-bedroom standard units. 1 cottage ($125-$200). 2 stories, interior corridors. *Bath:* some combo or shower only. **Parking:** on-site. **Terms:** age restrictions may apply. **Leisure Activities:** bicycles. **Cards:** AX, CB, DC, DS, MC, VI.

SOME UNITS

(graphic) (X) / (graphic) (graphic) /

THE INN ON FIFTH

Small-scale Hotel

12/1-4/19 [ECP]	1P: $250	2P: $250	XP: $10 F15
10/1-11/30 [ECP]	1P: $170	2P: $170	XP: $10 F15
4/20-9/30 [ECP]	1P: $130	2P: $130	XP: $10 F15

Phone: (239)403-8777

Location: Just w of jct US 41; downtown. 699 5th Ave S 34102. Fax: 239/403-8778. **Facility:** 87 units. 83 one-bedroom standard units. 4 one-bedroom suites ($400) with whirlpools. 3 stories, interior corridors. *Bath:* some combo or shower only. **Parking:** valet. **Terms:** 3 day cancellation notice-fee imposed. **Amenities:** dual phone lines, voice mail, safes, irons, hair dryers. **Pool(s):** heated outdoor. **Leisure Activities:** whirlpool, exercise room, spa, beauty salon. **Guest Services:** valet laundry. **Business Services:** meeting rooms, fax (fee). **Cards:** AX, DC, DS, MC, VI. *(See color ad p 568)*

SOME UNITS

FEE

LAPLAYA BEACH & GOLF RESORT

Resort
Large-scale Hotel

1/10-4/24	1P: $379-$499	2P: $379-$499	XP: $30 F16
4/25-10/2	1P: $179-$329	2P: $179-$329	XP: $30 F16
12/1-1/9	1P: $259-$309	2P: $259-$309	XP: $30 F16
10/3-11/30	1P: $269-$329	2P: $269-$329	XP: $30 F16

Phone: (239)597-3123

Location: North end of town; from US 41, 1.3 mi w on Vanderbilt Beach Rd (SR 862), 0.5 mi n. 9891 Gulf Shore Dr 34108. Fax: 239/597-1672. **Facility:** Tropical elegance describes this resort, with its white sandy beaches and lushly landscaped pool areas; guest rooms are well appointed. 189 units. 180 one-bedroom standard units, some with whirlpools. 9 one-bedroom suites ($399-$899), some with whirlpools. 1-15 stories, interior/exterior corridors. *Bath:* combo or shower only. **Parking:** valet. **Terms:** check-in 4 pm, 7 day cancellation notice-fee imposed. **Amenities:** CD players, dual phone lines, voice mail, safes, honor bars, irons, hair dryers. **Dining:** 2 restaurants, 6:30 am-10 pm, Fri & Sat-11 pm, cocktails, also, Baleen, see separate listing. **Pool(s):** heated outdoor, 3 small heated outdoor. **Leisure Activities:** rental paddleboats, boat dock, catamaran, kayaks, parasailing, waverunners, recreation programs, spa. *Fee:* sailboats, golf-18 holes, bicycles. **Guest Services:** gift shop, valet laundry. **Business Services:** conference facilities, business center. **Cards:** AX, CB, DC, DS, MC, VI. **Special Amenities:** free local telephone calls and free newspaper. *(See color ad below)*

SOME UNITS

THE NAPLES BEACH HOTEL & GOLF CLUB
Phone: (239)261-2222

	1P: $235-$410	2P: $235-$410	XP: $15	F18
12/1-4/20	1P: $235-$410	2P: $235-$410	XP: $15	F18
4/21-5/26 & 9/29-11/30	1P: $165-$320	2P: $165-$320	XP: $15	F18
5/27-9/28	1P: $135-$240	2P: $135-$240	XP: $15	F18

Resort
Large-scale Hotel

Location: I-75, exit 101, 1 mi n via US 41, 0.7 mi w on 7th Ave N. 851 Gulf Shore Blvd N 34102. **Facility:** Photographs by local artists decorate guest rooms in this traditional destination resort; a private orchid collection includes some 5,000 plants. 318 units. 277 one-bedroom standard units. 41 one-bedroom suites ($250-$550). 2-9 stories, interior/exterior corridors. **Parking:** on-site and valet. **Terms:** check-in 4 pm, 8 day cancellation notice-fee imposed, [MAP] meal plan available, package plans. **Amenities:** voice mail, safes, irons, hair dryers. **Dining:** 5 restaurants, 7 am-midnight, cocktails, entertainment. **Pool(s):** outdoor. **Leisure Activities:** rental paddleboats, recreation programs, exercise room, spa. *Fee:* sailboats, windsurfing, golf-18 holes, 6 tennis courts, bicycles. **Guest Services:** gift shop, valet laundry. **Business Services:** conference facilities, business center. **Cards:** AX, DC, DS, MC, VI. **Special Amenities:** free newspaper. *(See color ad p 569)*

SOME UNITS

NAPLES GRAND INN DOWNTOWN
Phone: (239)261-3500

	1P: $119-$189	2P: $119-$189	XP: $10
1/15-4/16	1P: $119-$189	2P: $119-$189	XP: $10
12/1-1/14	1P: $89-$129	2P: $89-$129	XP: $10
4/17-11/30	1P: $79-$119	2P: $79-$119	XP: $10

Small-scale Hotel

Location: I-75, exit 101, 1 mi s on SR 84. 1785 5th Ave S 34102. Fax: 239/732-0019. **Facility:** 125 units. 109 one-bedroom standard units. 16 one-bedroom suites. 4 stories, interior corridors. *Bath:* combo or shower only. **Parking:** on-site. **Terms:** 7 day cancellation notice, [ECP] meal plan available. **Amenities:** video games (fee), dual phone lines, voice mail, safes, irons, hair dryers. **Pool(s):** heated outdoor. **Leisure Activities:** exercise room. **Guest Services:** valet laundry. **Business Services:** meeting rooms, fax (fee). **Cards:** AX, DC, DS, MC, VI.

SOME UNITS

PARK SHORE RESORT
Phone: (239)263-2222

		2P: $185-$225	XP: $10	F18
2/7-4/26		2P: $185-$225	XP: $10	F18
12/1-1/1		2P: $80-$216	XP: $10	F18
1/2-2/6		2P: $147-$176	XP: $10	F18
4/27-11/30		2P: $86-$113	XP: $10	F18

Condominium

Location: I-75, exit 107, just w of jct US 41 via Island Club Loop. 600 Neapolitan Way 34103. Fax: 239/263-0946. **Facility:** 103 units. 36 one- and 67 two-bedroom suites with kitchens. 2-4 stories, exterior corridors. **Parking:** on-site. **Terms:** 3 day cancellation notice. **Amenities:** voice mail, irons, hair dryers. **Dining:** 11:30 am-9 pm, cocktails. **Pool(s):** heated outdoor. **Leisure Activities:** whirlpool, sun deck, 4 tennis courts, racquetball courts, recreation programs, gas barbecue grills, picnic table & gazebo area, basketball, shuffleboard, volleyball. **Guest Services:** valet and coin laundry, area transportation-beach. **Business Services:** meeting rooms, fax (fee). **Cards:** AX, DC, DS, MC, VI. *(See color ad below & starting on p 424)*

QUALITY INN & SUITES GOLF RESORT

Phone: (239)455-1010

SAVE

	2/1-3/31	1P: $129	2P: $129
	4/1-11/30	1P: $79-$89	2P: $79-$89
	12/25-1/31	1P: $89	2P: $89
	12/1-12/24	1P: $79	2P: $79

Small-scale Hotel **Location:** I-75, exit 101, 1.6 mi n via SR 951 (Isle of Capri Rd). 4100 Golden Gate Pkwy 34116. Fax: 239/455-4038. **Facility:** 153 units. 121 one-bedroom standard units, some with efficiencies. 24 one- and 8 two-bedroom suites ($125-$325) with kitchens, some with whirlpools. 2-4 stories, interior/exterior corridors. **Parking:** on-site. **Terms:** cancellation fee imposed, [AP], [BP], [CP] & [MAP] meal plans available, package plans. **Amenities:** irons, hair dryers. **Pool(s):** heated outdoor. **Leisure Activities:** whirlpool, 2 lighted tennis courts. *Fee:* golf-18 holes. **Guest Services:** valet laundry. **Business Services:** meeting rooms, fax (fee). **Cards:** AX, CB, DC, DS, JC, MC, VI.

SOME UNITS

QUALITY INN-GULFCOAST

Phone: (239)261-6046

SAVE

	1/16-4/30	1P: $110	2P: $140	XP: $5	F18
	12/16-1/15	1P: $100	2P: $130	XP: $5	F18
	12/1-12/15 & 5/1-11/30	1P: $45	2P: $70	XP: $5	F18

Small-scale Hotel **Location:** I-75, exit 107, 2.5 mi n on US 41; between 26th Ave N and Harbour Dr. 2555 Tamiami Tr N (US 41) 34103. Fax: 239/261-5742. **Facility:** 105 one-bedroom standard units. 2 stories (no elevator), exterior corridors. **Parking:** on-site. **Terms:** [CP] meal plan available, package plans. **Amenities:** voice mail, safes (fee), irons, hair dryers. **Pool(s):** heated outdoor. **Leisure Activities:** shuffleboard. **Guest Services:** valet and coin laundry. **Business Services:** meeting rooms, fax (fee). **Cards:** AX, CB, DC, DS, JC, MC, VI. *(See ad below)*

SOME UNITS

RED ROOF INN

Phone: (239)774-3117

AAA SAVE

	1/1-4/19	1P: $84-$89	2P: $84-$89	XP: $5	F18
	12/22-12/31	1P: $69-$79	2P: $69-$79	XP: $5	F18
	4/20-11/30	1P: $45-$55	2P: $45-$55	XP: $5	F18
	12/1-12/21	1P: $41-$49	2P: $41-$49	XP: $5	F18

Motel **Location:** I-75, exit 101 (SR 84), just e of jct US 41. 1925 Davis Blvd 34104. Fax: 239/775-5333. **Facility:** 157 units. 127 one-bedroom standard units. 30 one-bedroom suites ($65-$129) with kitchens. 3 stories, exterior corridors. *Bath:* combo or shower only. **Parking:** on-site. **Terms:** small pets only. **Amenities:** video games (fee), voice mail. **Pool(s):** heated outdoor. **Leisure Activities:** whirlpool, barbecue grills, picnic tables. **Guest Services:** coin laundry. **Business Services:** fax (fee). **Cards:** AX, CB, DC, DS, MC, VI. **Special Amenities:** free local telephone calls and free newspaper.

SOME UNITS

THE REGISTRY RESORT   Phone: (239)597-3232

(AAA) [SAVE]   12/1-4/26 [CP]   1P: $285-$829   2P: $285-$829   XP: $25   F17
               4/27-5/23   1P: $319-$649   2P: $319-$649   XP: $25   F17
▼▼▼▼ ▼▼▼▼   10/4-11/30   1P: $309-$639   2P: $309-$639   XP: $25   F17
               5/24-10/3   1P: $179-$379   2P: $179-$379   XP: $25   F17

Resort   **Location:** I-75, exit 107, north end of town; 0.5 mi w of US 41 via CR 896 (Pine Ridge/Seagate Blvd). 475 Seagate Dr
Large-scale Hotel 34103. Fax: 239/597-3147. **Facility:** Italian marble adds a luxurious touch to the public areas of this high-rise; a trolley carries guests over a protected mangrove lagoon to the beach. 474 units. 395 one-bedroom standard units. 79 one-bedroom suites ($229-$829), some with whirlpools. 1-18 stories, interior/exterior corridors. *Bath:* combo or shower only. **Parking:** valet. **Terms:** 14 day cancellation notice-fee imposed, package plans. **Amenities:** dual phone lines, voice mail, safes, honor bars, irons, hair dryers. *Some:* CD players. **Dining:** 6 restaurants, 7 am-11 pm, Sunday brunch, cocktails, also, Lafite, see separate listing, nightclub, entertainment. **Pool(s):** 5 heated outdoor. **Leisure Activities:** whirlpools, rental sailboats, fishing, golf clinic, golf concierge/master & golf privileges, recreation programs, access to nature preserve, basketball. **Fee:** canoes, windsurfing, aqua bikes, catamarans, sea kayaks, golf-18 holes, 15 tennis courts (5 lighted), bicycles, massage. **Guest Services:** gift shop, valet laundry, area transportation (fee). **Business Services:** conference facilities, business center. **Cards:** AX, DC, DS, MC, VI. **Special Amenities:** free continental breakfast. *(See color ad below)*

SOME UNITS
[S/D] [✈] [¶¶] [24¹] [Y] [♨] [♿M] [♨] [♪] [⇆] [♨] [✕] [DATA PORT] [▯] / [✕] [VCR] [▯] [▦] /
FEE   FEE   FEE   FEE

RESIDENCE INN BY MARRIOTT, NAPLES   Phone: (239)659-1300

[SAVE]   2/1-4/30 [BP]   1P: $159-$269   2P: $159-$269
          12/1-1/31 [BP]   1P: $109-$269   2P: $109-$269
▼▼▼ ▼▼▼   5/1-11/30 [BP]   1P: $59-$109   2P: $59-$109

Motel   **Location:** I-75, exit 107, 3.8 mi w on SR 896 (Pine Ridge Rd), then just s on US 41 (Tamiami Tr). 4075 Tamiami Tr N 34103. Fax: 239/659-2300. **Facility:** 120 units. 39 one-bedroom standard units with efficiencies. 52 one- and 29 two-bedroom suites with kitchens. 3 stories, interior corridors. *Bath:* combo or shower only. **Parking:** onsite. **Terms:** pets ($85 fee, $3 extra charge). **Amenities:** dual phone lines, voice mail, irons, hair dryers. **Pool(s):** heated outdoor. **Leisure Activities:** whirlpool, exercise room, sports court. **Guest Services:** complimentary evening beverages: Mon-Thurs, valet and coin laundry, area transportation. **Business Services:** meeting rooms, fax (fee). **Cards:** AX, CB, DC, DS, JC, MC, VI.

SOME UNITS
[S/D] [♨] [¶¶+] [♿M] [♨] [♪] [⇆] [✕] [♥] [DATA PORT] [▯] [▦] [▯] / [✕] [VCR] /

THE RITZ-CARLTON GOLF RESORT

Phone: (239)593-2000

12/25-4/13	1P: $399-$3529	2P: $399-$3529	XP: $25	F18
12/1-12/24 & 4/14-5/18	1P: $269-$2349	2P: $269-$2349	XP: $25	F18
5/19-11/30	1P: $189-$2199	2P: $189-$2199	XP: $25	F18

Large-scale Hotel **Location:** I-75, exit 111 (CR 846/Immokalee Rd), 1.6 mi e to Airport-Pulling Rd, then 1.3 mi s, then left. 2600 Tiburon Dr 34109. Fax: 239/593-6691. **Facility:** Luxurious rooms, great service and 36 holes of golf are among the many assets of this resort. 275 units. 236 one-bedroom standard units. 38 one- and 1 two-bedroom suites, some with whirlpools. 7 stories, interior corridors. *Bath:* combo or shower only. **Parking:** valet. **Terms:** check-in 4 pm, 7 day cancellation notice, small pets only (in designated units). **Amenities:** *Some:* DVD players, fax. **Dining:** Lemonia, see separate listing. **Pool(s):** heated outdoor. **Leisure Activities:** sauna, whirlpool, steamroom, spa. *Fee:* golf-36 holes, 4 lighted tennis courts, bicycles. **Guest Services:** gift shop, valet laundry, area transportation. **Business Services:** conference facilities, business center. **Cards:** AX, MC, VI.

THE RITZ-CARLTON, NAPLES

Phone: (239)598-3300

12/26-5/3	1P: $479-$4048
12/1-12/25	1P: $369-$3439
5/4-11/30	1P: $339-$3000

Resort **Location:** From US 41, 1.3 mi w on CR 846 (Vanderbilt Beach Rd). 280 Vanderbilt Beach Rd 34108. Large-scale Hotel Fax: 239/598-6690. **Facility:** Artwork and antiques add Old World elegance to the public areas of this hotel on the gulf; many guest rooms have water views and some have balconies. 463 units. 431 one-bedroom standard units. 32 one-bedroom suites ($579-$1778). 13 stories, interior corridors. *Bath:* combo, shower or tub only. **Parking:** valet. **Terms:** check-in 4 pm, 7 day cancellation notice-fee imposed. **Amenities:** video games, CD players, high-speed Internet, dual phone lines, voice mail, safes, honor bars, irons, hair dryers. **Dining:** 6 restaurants, 6:30 am-10 pm, cocktails, also, The Grill, The Dining Room, see separate listing, nightclub, entertainment. **Pool(s):** 2 heated outdoor. **Leisure Activities:** saunas, whirlpools, steamrooms, seasonal beach pavilion, pro shop, recreation programs, aerobics, billiards, jogging, spa. *Fee:* sailboats, fishing, charter fishing, boogie boards, catamarans, kayaks, jet skis, suncats, golf-36 holes, golf instruction, 4 lighted tennis courts, tennis instruction, bicycles. **Guest Services:** gift shop, valet laundry, area transportation (fee), jewelry store, car rental agency. **Business Services:** conference facilities, business center. **Cards:** AX, CB, DC, MC, VI.

SOME UNITS

STAYBRIDGE SUITES BY HOLIDAY INN

Phone: (239)643-8002

All Year   1P: $75-$229

Location: I-75, exit 107, w on Pine Ridge Rd to US 41 (Tamiami Tr), turn left. 4805 Tamiami Tr N 34103. Small-scale Hotel Fax: 239/643-8009. **Facility:** 122 units. 50 one-bedroom standard units with efficiencies. 64 one- and 8 two-bedroom suites with efficiencies. 4 stories, interior corridors. *Bath:* combo or shower only. **Parking:** on-site. **Terms:** 3 day cancellation notice, [ECP] meal plan available, pets ($25 fee, $10 extra charge). **Amenities:** dual phone lines, voice mail, irons, hair dryers. *Fee:* video library, high-speed Internet. **Pool(s):** heated outdoor. **Leisure Activities:** whirlpool, exercise room. **Guest Services:** sundries, complimentary evening beverages: Tues-Thurs, complimentary laundry. **Business Services:** meeting rooms, business center. **Cards:** AX, DC, DS, MC, VI.

SOME UNITS

STONEY'S COURTYARD INN

Phone: (239)261-3870

1/26-4/15 [CP]	1P: $95-$110	2P: $95-$110	XP: $10
12/1-1/25 [CP]	1P: $50-$100	2P: $50-$100	XP: $10
4/16-11/30 [CP]	1P: $50-$70	2P: $50-$70	XP: $10

Motel **Location:** I-75, exit 107, US 41, just s of Harbor Dr. 2630 9th St N 34103. Fax: 239/261-4932. **Facility:** 76 units. 72 one-bedroom standard units. 4 one-bedroom suites ($80-$130). 2 stories (no elevator), exterior corridors. **Parking:** on-site. **Amenities:** voice mail. *Some:* safes. **Pool(s):** heated outdoor. **Leisure Activities:** exercise room, shuffleboard. **Guest Services:** coin laundry. **Special Amenities:** free continental breakfast and free local telephone calls.

SOME UNITS
FEE FEE

TRIANON OLD NAPLES

Phone: 239/435-9600

▼▼▼▼	12/1-12/31	1P: $105-$295	XP: $10	F18
	1/1-1/31	1P: $150-$260	XP: $10	F18
Small-scale Hotel	2/1-4/15	1P: $180-$195	XP: $10	F18
	4/16-11/30	1P: $90-$145	XP: $10	F18

Location: Just s of jct US 41; downtown. Located in Old Naples area. 955 7th Ave S 34102. Fax: 239/261-0025. **Facility:** 58 units. 55 one-bedroom standard units. 3 one-bedroom suites ($145-$290). 3 stories, interior corridors. *Bath:* combo or shower only. **Parking:** on-site. **Terms:** cancellation fee imposed, [CP] & [ECP] meal plans available. **Amenities:** dual phone lines, voice mail, safes, irons, hair dryers. **Pool(s):** heated outdoor. **Guest Services:** valet laundry. **Business Services:** meeting rooms, fax (fee). **Cards:** AX, DC, DS, MC, VI. *(See color ad p 573)*

SOME UNITS

VANDERBILT BEACH RESORT

Phone: 239/597-3144

▼▼ ▼▼	2/1-4/30	1P: $154-$290	2P: $154-$290	XP: $10	F4
	12/1-1/31	1P: $79-$290	2P: $79-$290	XP: $10	F4
Motel	5/1-11/30	1P: $84-$180	2P: $84-$180	XP: $10	F4

Location: I-75, exit 111, north end of town; 1.5 mi w of US 41 via Vanderbilt Beach Rd (SR 862), just n. 9225 Gulfshore Dr N 34108. Fax: 239/597-2199. **Facility:** 66 units. 32 one-bedroom standard units, some with efficiencies. 20 one- and 14 two-bedroom suites, some with efficiencies or kitchens. 1-4 stories, exterior corridors. **Parking:** on-site. **Terms:** 14 day cancellation notice-fee imposed, weekly rates available. **Pool(s):** heated outdoor. **Leisure Activities:** boat dock, tennis court. **Guest Services:** coin laundry. **Cards:** AX, MC, VI.

SOME UNITS

VANDERBILT INN NAPLES

Phone: (239)597-3151

▼▼▼▼	2/1-4/30	1P: $205-$350	2P: $205-$350	XP: $10	F18
	12/1-1/31 & 5/1-5/31	1P: $145-$325	2P: $145-$325	XP: $10	F18
Motel	6/1-11/30	1P: $110-$220	2P: $110-$220	XP: $10	F18

Location: I-75, exit 111, north end of town; 1.5 mi w of US 41 via SR 846 (111th Ave). Located next to Delnor-Wiggins Pass State Recreation Area. 11000 Gulfshore Dr N 34108. Fax: 239/597-3099. **Facility:** 147 one-bedroom standard units, some with efficiencies. 2 stories (no elevator), exterior corridors. **Parking:** on-site. **Terms:** 3 day cancellation notice. **Amenities:** voice mail, safes, hair dryers. *Some:* irons. **Pool(s):** heated outdoor. **Leisure Activities:** whirlpool, rental boats, rental sailboats. *Fee:* windsurfing. **Guest Services:** gift shop, coin laundry. **Business Services:** meeting rooms, business center. **Cards:** AX, CB, DS, JC, MC, VI. *(See color ad below)*

SOME UNITS

WELLESLEY INN (NAPLES)

Phone: (239)793-4646

◬◬◬ SAVE	12/20-4/19 [ECP]	1P: $107	2P: $107	XP: $10	F18
	12/1-12/19 & 4/20-11/30 [ECP]	1P: $71	2P: $71	XP: $10	F18
▼▼ ▼▼					

Location: I-75, exit 101, 1 mi s on US 41 at jct SR 84. 1555 5th Ave S 34102. Fax: 239/793-5248. **Facility:** 104 one-bedroom standard units. 3 stories, interior corridors. *Bath:* combo or shower only. **Parking:** on-site. **Small-scale Hotel Terms:** pets ($10 extra charge). **Amenities:** video games (fee), voice mail, irons, hair dryers. **Pool(s):** heated outdoor. **Guest Services:** valet laundry. **Business Services:** fax (fee). **Cards:** AX, CB, DC, DS, MC, VI. **Special Amenities:** free continental breakfast and free newspaper. *(See color ad p 561)*

SOME UNITS

——— *The following lodgings were either not evaluated or did not* ———
meet AAA rating requirements but are listed for your information only.

THE CLUB AT NAPLES CAY   Phone: 239/262-4242
[fyi]   Not evaluated. **Location:** 40 Seagate Dr 34103. Facilities, services, and decor characterize a mid-range property.

WESTSHORE AT NAPLES CAY   Phone: 850/337-1682
[fyi]   Not evaluated. **Location:** 50 Seagate Dr 34103. Facilities, services, and decor characterize a mid-range property.

——— **WHERE TO DINE** ———

BALEEN   **Lunch:** $8-$18   **Dinner:** $27-$32   Phone: 239/597-3123
▼▲▼▲ ▼▲▼▲ **Location:** North end of town; from US 41, 1.3 mi w on Vanderbilt Beach Rd (SR 862), 0.5 mi n; in LaPlaya Beach &
Golf Resort. 9891 Gulf Shore Dr 34108. **Hours:** 6:30 am-10 pm, Fri & Sat-11 pm. **Reservations:** suggested.
Regional Seafood **Features:** The room offers two settings: the formal inside, where the atmosphere is casually elegant, and
the cozy patio, where sunset views are breathtaking. The chef labels the food as "eclectic seafood house."
Pacific Rim accents punctuate fresh seafood and aged meats. Dressy casual; cocktails; entertainment. **Parking:** valet.
Cards: AX, CB, DC, DS, JC, MC, VI. *(See color ad p 569)*   [Y] [X]

BAYSIDE-A SEAFOOD GRILL & BAR   **Lunch:** $7-$12   **Dinner:** $16-$25   Phone: 239/649-5552
(AAA)   **Location:** 1 mi w of US 41 via Park Shore Dr; in Village on Venetian Bay, southwest corner. 4270 Gulfshore Blvd N
34103. **Hours:** 11:30 am-11 pm. **Reservations:** suggested. **Features:** Live piano music by Chuck Jobes
▼▲▼▲ ▼▲▼ and a fine view of the bay both enhance the experience at this Mediterranean-flavored restaurant. The first
Seafood   floor is casual, while the more formal second floor affords lovely water views. International cuisine includes
well-prepared seafood and pasta. Valet parking for dinner is offered in winter. Casual dress; cocktails;
entertainment. **Parking:** on-site. **Cards:** AX, DC, DS, MC, VI.   [Y] [X]

BHA! BHA! A PERSIAN BISTRO   **Lunch:** $7-$15   **Dinner:** $14-$23   Phone: 239/594-5557
▼▲▼▲ ▼▲▼ **Location:** Corner of US 41 and Vanderbilt Beach Rd; in Pavillion Shopping Center. 847 Vanderbilt Beach Rd 34108.
Hours: 11:30 am-3 & 5-10 pm, Sun-9 pm. Closed: 1/1, 11/27, 12/25; also Mon. **Features:** Bordered by
Persian   shops, this dining oasis offers both indoor and outdoor seating. Diners can feast on such creatively
prepared delights as fresh seafood couscous or paella, mango-grilled shrimp and succulent lamb, beef or
chicken dishes. Save room for dessert with Turkish coffee. Smoke free premises. Casual dress; beer & wine only. **Parking:**
on-site. **Cards:** AX, MC, VI.   [X]

THE BOATHOUSE   **Lunch:** $7-$17   **Dinner:** $10-$24   Phone: 239/643-2235
(AAA)   **Location:** SR 41 S to 9th St S. 990 Broad Ave S 34102. **Hours:** 11:30 am-10 pm. Closed major holidays.
Features: Right at the water's edge close to downtown, the casual, nautically themed restaurant offers
▼▲▼▲ ▼▲▼ incredible waterfront views. The lively and fun atmosphere—created in part by an outer appearance that
American   resembles an old-time ship's store—has wide appeal. Casual dress; cocktails. **Parking:** on-site.
Cards: AX, DS, MC, VI.   [X]

CAMPIELLO RISTORANTE Historic   **Lunch:** $9-$14   **Dinner:** $16-$29   Phone: 239/435-1166
▼▲▼▲ ▼▲▼ **Location:** In historic district; jct 12th Ave S and Broad Ave. 1177 3rd St S 34102. **Hours:** 11:30 am-2:30 & 5:30-10
pm, Fri & Sat-11 pm, Sun from noon. Closed: 11/27, 12/25. **Reservations:** required. **Features:** Sitting
Northern   outside in the courtyard or in the open-air-like dining room, diners are tempted by thoughtfully prepared
Italian   offerings of Northern Italian cuisine. Dressy casual; cocktails; entertainment. **Parking:** street. **Cards:** AX,
DS, MC, VI.   [Y] [X]

CHARDONNAY   **Dinner:** $19-$32   Phone: 239/261-1744
▼▲▼▲ ▼▲▼ **Location:** I-75, exit 107, w on SR 896 to US 41, 2.5 mi s on US 41; corner of US 41 and Mooringline Dr; in Best
Western Naples Inn & Suites. 2331 Tamiami Tr N (US 41) 34103. **Hours:** 5:30 pm-10 pm. Closed: 1/1; also Sun
French   5/1-12/15 & 8/1-8/31. **Reservations:** suggested. **Features:** Lovely country French decor characterizes this
spacious restaurant, which offers several dining sections with decorative lighting and frosted-glass dividers.
Creatively prepared and presented entrees include such delights as duck pate, escargot, salmon mousse, fillet of sole, red
snapper and prime cuts of meat. For dessert, savor the sumptuous creme brulee or souffle. There is a portico for rainy days.
Dressy casual; cocktails. **Parking:** valet. **Cards:** AX, DC, MC, VI.   [Y] [X]

DA RU MA   **Dinner:** $17-$35   Phone: 239/591-1200
▼▲▼▲ ▼▲ **Location:** 1 mi w of US 41 on CR 862 (Vanderbilt Beach Rd). 241 Center St N 34108. **Hours:** 5 pm-10 pm.
Closed: 11/27; also Super Bowl Sun. **Reservations:** suggested. **Features:** With hibachi-style steak and
Japanese   seafood, and fresh sushi, this restaurant appeals to those looking for a more adventurous dining
experience. Fresh, flavorful ingredients and artistic compositions lend themselves perfectly to the exotic
delicacies offered. Casual dress; cocktails; entertainment. **Parking:** on-site. **Cards:** AX, DS, MC, VI.
                                                                                           [Y] [X]

THE DINING ROOM   **Dinner:** $65-$80   Phone: 239/598-6644
▼▲▼▲ ▼▲▼▲ **Location:** From US 41, 1.3 mi w on CR 862 (Vanderbilt Beach Rd); in The Ritz-Carlton, Naples. 280 Vanderbilt Beach
Rd 34108. **Hours:** 6 pm-10 pm, Sun also 10:30 am-2:30 pm. Closed: Sun & Mon for dinner 7/1-8/31.
Continental   **Reservations:** suggested. **Features:** This is beautifully staged, classic dining with a gracious ambience
that is rarely found. Appreciate skilled preparation of fresh seafood and other specialties; peruse the
outstanding international wine list; and enjoy outdoor dining when weather permits. Smoke free premises. Semi-formal attire;
cocktails; entertainment. **Parking:** valet. **Cards:** AX, CB, DC, DS, JC, MC, VI.   [X]

DOCK AT CRAYTON COVE

Seafood

Lunch: $5-$20   **Dinner:** $5-$20   **Phone:** 239/263-9940
Location: 8th St S to 12th Ave S, e to bay. 845 12th Ave S at Naples Bay 34102. **Hours:** 11 am-midnight. Closed: 12/24, 12/25; also 11/22 for lunch. **Features:** Diners can whet their appetites with gentle breezes and a splendid postcard view of City Dock and Naples Bay, then indulge with creative, Caribbean-style preparations, such as fresh Bahamian conch fritters, or the simple yet tasty fish and chips, burgers or sandwiches. The raw bar is a nice option from 3 pm to 6 pm. Casual dress; cocktails. **Parking:** on-site. **Cards:** AX, DS, MC, VI.

THE ENGLISH PUB

English

Lunch: $7-$11   **Dinner:** $10-$16   **Phone:** 239/774-2408
Location: I-75, exit 101, 1.5 mi s on US 41 to Commercial Dr, then e. 2408 Linwood Ave 34112. **Hours:** 11 am-9:30 pm, Sat from noon. Closed major holidays; also Sun. **Features:** Authentic English pub food—fish 'n' chips, steak and kidney pie, bangers and mash, and shepherd's pie—is served in a nice, Tudor-style dining room. A wide selection of British beers on tap is available for washing down a hearty meal. Dining may end at 9:30 pm, but the pub stays open until midnight weekdays and 2 am weekends. Casual dress; beer & wine only. **Parking:** on-site. **Cards:** AX, DC, DS, MC, VI.

FERNANDEZ DE BULL

Cuban

Lunch: $4-$7   **Dinner:** $7-$16   **Phone:** 239/263-2996
Location: 4.5 mi n on US 41; across from Tanglewood AAA office; in Bank of Naples Financial Center. 4951 N Tamiami Tr (US 41) 34103. **Hours:** 11 am-2:30 & 5-9:30 pm, Sat & Sun from 5 pm. Closed major holidays; also Sun 5/1-11/30. **Reservations:** suggested. **Features:** Decorated in a homey Spanish style, this eatery provides a relaxed atmosphere in which diners can enjoy a variety of fresh, well-prepared dishes, such as baked chicken marinated in sour oranges, garlic, oregano and lemon juice. Early bird specials are available December through March. Casual dress; beer & wine only. **Parking:** on-site. **Cards:** MC, VI.

THE FIFTH AVE DELI & BAKERY

American

Lunch: $4-$8   **Phone:** 239/262-4106
Location: Center. 467 5th Ave S 34102. **Hours:** 11 am-3 pm. Closed: Sun 5/1-10/31. **Features:** This deli and bakery, with a small service counter, offers great sandwiches, salads and soups, as well as delightful pastries. Diners can savor their lunch in the park across the street or eat at one of the sidewalk tables. The chicken salad sandwich and Key lime pie make a tasty pair. Smoke free premises. Casual dress; beer only. **Parking:** on-site. **Cards:** AX, MC, VI.

FIRST WATCH

American

Lunch: $4-$7   **Phone:** 239/434-0005
Location: 2.3 mi n on US 41, 1.2 mi sw via Mooringline Dr. 1400 Gulfshore Blvd N 34102. **Hours:** 7 am-2:30 pm. Closed: 11/27, 12/25. **Features:** This incredibly popular diner offers breakfast, brunch and lunch. Fresh air in the courtyard dining area makes the eggs, omelets, pancakes, waffles, soups and salads that much more inviting. Smoke free premises. Casual dress. **Parking:** on-site. **Cards:** AX, DS, MC, VI.

THE GRILL

American

Dinner: $22-$39   **Phone:** 239/598-6644
Location: From US 41, 1.3 mi w on CR 846 (Vanderbilt Beach Rd); in The Ritz-Carlton, Naples. 280 Vanderbilt Beach Rd 34108. **Hours:** 6 pm-10 pm. **Reservations:** suggested. **Features:** Intimate, formal dining in a peaceful, club-like atmosphere is enhanced by warm wood, original art and rich fabrics. A variety of steak and seafood is artfully presented and meticulously prepared. Choose the perfect vintage from a comprehensive wine list. Semi-formal attire; cocktails; entertainment. **Parking:** on-site. **Cards:** AX, CB, DC, DS, JC, MC, VI.

LAFITE

Continental

Dinner: $27-$40   **Phone:** 239/597-3232
Location: I-75, exit 107, north end of town; 0.5 mi w of US 41 via CR 896 (Pine Ridge/Seagate Blvd); in The Registry Resort. 475 Seagate Dr 34103. **Hours:** 6 pm-10 pm, Fri & Sat-11 pm. Closed: Sun & Mon. **Reservations:** suggested. **Features:** In a vintage setting, this upscale restaurant offers formal dining at tables or plush booths. The chef creates a wonderful array of delicious items, including fine steaks and seafood, as well as some internationally influenced game dishes. Fine wines add the finishing touch to these flavorful creations. Smoke free premises. Formal attire; cocktails. **Parking:** valet. **Cards:** AX, DC, DS, JC, MC, VI.

LEMONIA

Regional Italian

Dinner: $20-$37   **Phone:** 239/593-2000
Location: I-75, exit 111 (CR 846/Immokalee Rd), 1.6 mi e to Airport-Pulling Rd, then 1.3 mi s, then left; in The Ritz-Carlton Golf Resort. 2600 Tiburon Dr 34109. **Hours:** 6:30 am-10 pm. **Reservations:** suggested. **Features:** The atmosphere is soft, the food is Italian, and the service is smooth. From the rotunda in the center of the room, the dining area spreads out onto the patio, which affords views of the golf course. The foods have wonderful aromas and flavors. Dressy casual; cocktails; entertainment. **Parking:** valet. **Cards:** AX, CB, DC, DS, JC, MC, VI.

MICHELBOB'S

American

Lunch: $5-$13   **Dinner:** $8-$16   **Phone:** 239/643-2877
Location: I-75, exit 107, 2 mi w on Pine Ridge Rd (SR 896), 4 mi s on Airport-Pulling Rd (CR 31). 371 Airport Rd N 34104. **Hours:** 11 am-9 pm, Sat from 4 pm. Closed: 11/27; also May 6/1-10/31, Sun. **Features:** Return to the 50s in this comfortable family dining room decorated with period memorabilia. The menu offers basic ribs and chicken selections with fries, coleslaw and homemade baked beans. Friendly and attentive service makes this a popular stop. Smoke free premises. Casual dress; cocktails. **Parking:** on-site. **Cards:** AX, DC, DS, MC, VI.

PACIFIC 41 RESTAURANT & LOUNGE

American

Lunch: $6-$8   **Dinner:** $10-$20   **Phone:** 239/649-5858
Location: I-75, exit 101 (US 41), just s of Central Ave; in Naples Hotel & Suites. 173 9th St S (US 41) 34102. **Hours:** 8 am-9:30 pm. Closed: 5/29. **Reservations:** accepted. **Features:** This spacious, casual eatery features a varied menu selection including prime rib, filet mignon, turkey breast and fresh seafood. The colorful nautical theme and cheerful atmosphere make this a pleasant, family-oriented experience. Casual dress; cocktails. **Parking:** on-site. **Cards:** AX, DC, DS, MC, VI.

PIPPIN'S
▼▼ ▼▼
Steak & Seafood

Dinner: $10-$20

Phone: 239/262-2880

Location: 1.5 mi n on US 41 (Tamiami Tr). 1390 9th St N 34102. **Hours:** 4:30 pm-10 pm, Fri & Sat-10:30 pm. Closed: 11/27; also 6/8; also Super Bowl Sun. **Reservations:** suggested. **Features:** A casual interior design features a huge saltwater aquarium as the centerpiece. A friendly and efficient staff serves up tasty meals like a generously portioned yellow-fin tuna cooked to taste. A modest dessert selection is offered for meal's end. Casual dress; cocktails. **Parking:** on-site. **Cards:** AX, CB, DC, DS, MC, VI.
🍸 ✕

RIDGWAY BAR & GRILL
(AAA)
▼▼ ▼▼
Continental

Lunch: $8-$14

Dinner: $14-$28

Phone: 239/262-5500

Location: On 13th Ave; between 2nd and 3rd sts s. 1300 3rd St S 34102. **Hours:** 11:30 am-2:30 & 5:30-9:30 pm, Fri & Sat-10 pm. **Reservations:** suggested. **Features:** In Old Naples, this spacious restaurant blends Italian, Mediterranean, American and Asian cuisine. Guests can sit inside or outside on the patio, which is a prime spot for people-watching in the exclusive shopping area. Lump crab cakes and fresh peach-berry cobbler shouldn't be missed. Casual dress; cocktails; entertainment. **Parking:** on-site. **Cards:** AX, DC, DS, MC, VI.
♿M 🍸 ✕

RISTORANTE CIAO
▼▼▼
Northern Italian

Dinner: $18-$30

Phone: 239/263-3889

Location: Just w of US 41. 835 4th Ave S 34102. **Hours:** Open 12/1-6/10 & 9/1-11/30; 5:30 pm-10 pm. Closed: 4/20, 11/27; also 7/1-8/31 & Super Bowl Sun. **Reservations:** suggested. **Features:** European elegance is in the details: from Italian tenor music to fresh roses on the tables. The owner/chef creates lush preparations such as fettuccine Ciao with lobster and mushrooms in a rich cream sauce over pasta. Servers provide knowledgeable and competent assistance, but the style remains relaxed. Try the chef's evening specials. Smoke free premises. Dressy casual; beer & wine only. **Parking:** on-site. **Cards:** AX, DC, DS, MC, VI.
✕

RIVERWALK FISH & ALE HOUSE
(AAA)
▼▼ ▼▼
Seafood

Lunch: $8-$22

Dinner: $8-$22

Phone: 239/263-2734

Location: Jct US 41 and Goodlett Rd; at Tin City. 1200 5th Ave S 34102. **Hours:** 11 am-11 pm. Closed: 11/27, 12/25. **Features:** In historic Tin City, this bustling, open-air restaurant offers waterfront dining with a rustic nautical theme. Casual attire is the order of the day. Well-prepared seafood—such as flavorful, filling grouper and chips—is the specialty. Casual dress; cocktails. **Parking:** on-site. **Cards:** AX, DS, MC, VI.
🍸 🐕 ✕

ST. GEORGE & THE DRAGON
▼▼▼
Steak & Seafood

Lunch: $6-$17

Dinner: $16-$30

Phone: 239/262-6546

Location: On US 41; downtown. 936 5th Ave S 34102. **Hours:** 11 am-10 pm, Sun 5 pm-9 pm. Closed: 12/25; also Sun 4/1-12/31. **Features:** Family-operated since 1969, this local favorite presents a menu featuring fresh seafood, prime steak and the ever-popular fish and chips. Dining sections are decorated in a delightful nautical theme with soft lighting, hand-carved beams and brass accents. Semi-formal attire; cocktails. **Parking:** on-site. **Cards:** AX, DC, MC, VI.
🍸 ✕

SEAWITCH RESTAURANT & LOUNGE
▼▼ ▼▼
Seafood

Lunch: $6-$10

Dinner: $14-$22

Phone: 239/566-1514

Location: North end of town, 1.5 mi w of US 41 via Vanderbilt Beach Dr (SR 862), just n on Gulfshore Dr, then just e. 179 Southbay Dr 34108. **Hours:** 11:30 am-2:30 & 5-9:30 pm, Sat & Sun from 5 pm. Closed major holidays; also Super Bowl Sun. **Features:** A laid-back dining experience is what diners can expect at this waterfront restaurant. Whether grilled, baked, fried or blackened, the yellowtail snapper rarely misses the mark. A few meat items are offered for landlubbers. Casual dress; cocktails. **Parking:** on-site. **Cards:** AX, DS, MC, VI.
🍸 ✕

SHULA'S STEAK HOUSE
▼▼▼
Steak & Seafood

Lunch: $9-$18

Dinner: $14-$30

Phone: 239/430-4999

Location: US 41, just sw of jct Pine Ridge Rd; in Hilton Naples & Towers. 5111 Tamiami Tr 34103. **Hours:** 11:30 am-2 & 5:30-11 pm. **Reservations:** accepted. **Features:** Pictures of "the coach" and his team adorn the dining room walls. Representative of steakhouse fare are hearty Angus steaks and large lobsters and other seafood offerings. Dressy casual; cocktails. **Parking:** on-site. **Cards:** AX, DS, MC, VI.
(See color ad p 567)
🍸 ✕

SYRAH
▼▼ ▼▼
New World

Dinner: $18-$27

Phone: 239/417-9724

Location: Jct 5th Ave S and Tamiami Tr (US 41), just e on 5th, then s. 475 Bayfront Pl 34102. **Hours:** 5 pm-10 pm. Closed: 11/27, 12/25. **Reservations:** suggested. **Features:** The exciting restaurant has so much to offer, including a menu of New World entrees that incorporate interesting tastes and combinations. The comprehensive wine list includes some hard-to-find bottles as well as by-the-glass selections. Dressy casual; cocktails. **Parking:** valet. **Cards:** AX, CB, DC, DS, JC, MC, VI.
♿M 🍸 ✕

TOMMY BAHAMA'S
▼▼ ▼▼
Caribbean

Lunch: $8-$9

Dinner: $14-$21

Phone: 239/643-6889

Location: In historic district; at jct 12th Ave S. 1220 3rd St S 34102. **Hours:** 11 am-midnight. Closed: 11/27, 12/25. **Features:** A tropical Bahamian theme punctuates this upbeat restaurant in the heart of Old Naples. Live music and a large outdoor patio help set the stage for a relaxed, fun time. A creative menu, large portions and colorful, Caribbean-influenced presentations complete the picture. Casual dress; cocktails. **Parking:** on-site. **Cards:** AX, MC, VI.
🍸 ✕

The following restaurant has not been evaluated by AAA but is listed for your information only.

WIGGINS ITALIAN BRICK OVEN & BAR
[fyi]

Phone: 239/566-9473

Not evaluated. **Location:** On US 41 N, 1 mi n of Wiggins Pass Rd; in the Audubon Shops. 15495 Tamiami Tr N 34110. **Features:** Enjoy a variety of Brick Oven pizzas as well as pasta dishes. The atmosphere is casual and has that neighborhood feel to it.

NAVARRE

──────── **WHERE TO STAY** ────────

BEST WESTERN NAVARRE   **Phone:** (850)939-9400
⁂ SAVE   5/1-9/6 [ECP]   1P: $79-$109   2P: $85-$115   XP: $6   F18
            9/7-11/14 [ECP]   1P: $59-$89   2P: $65-$95   XP: $6   F18
⁂⁂⁂   12/1-4/30 & 11/15-11/30 [ECP] 1P: $49-$79   2P: $55-$85   XP: $6   F18
Small-scale Hotel **Location:** US 98, just e on bridge. 8697 Navarre Pkwy 32566. Fax: 850/939-4040. **Facility:** 69 one-bedroom standard units. 3 stories, exterior corridors. **Parking:** on-site. **Amenities:** irons, hair dryers. **Pool(s):** heated outdoor. **Leisure Activities:** fishing. **Guest Services:** coin laundry. **Business Services:** meeting rooms, fax. **Cards:** AX, CB, DC, DS, JC, MC, VI. **Special Amenities: free continental breakfast and free newspaper.**

SOME UNITS

COMFORT INN & CONFERENCE CENTER   **Phone:** (850)939-1761
⁂ SAVE   5/24-9/1 [ECP]   1P: $89-$129   2P: $89-$129   XP: $8   F18
            3/1-5/23 [ECP]   1P: $69-$89   2P: $69-$89   XP: $8   F18
⁂⁂⁂   12/1-2/28 & 9/2-11/30 [ECP] 1P: $59-$79   2P: $59-$79   XP: $8   F18
Small-scale Hotel **Location:** US 98, 0.3 mi e of Navarre Bridge. 8700 Navarre Pkwy 32566. Fax: 850/939-2084. **Facility:** 63 one-bedroom standard units. 2 stories, exterior corridors. **Parking:** on-site. **Terms:** 3 day cancellation notice-fee imposed, pets ($10 extra charge). **Amenities:** *Some:* irons, hair dryers. **Pool(s):** outdoor. **Guest Services:** coin laundry. **Business Services:** conference facilities, fax (fee). **Cards:** AX, CB, DC, DS, JC, MC, VI. **Special Amenities: free continental breakfast and free local telephone calls.**

SOME UNITS

──────── **WHERE TO DINE** ────────

COWBOY'S STEAK HOUSE   **Lunch:** $5-$10   **Dinner:** $9-$24   **Phone:** 850/939-0502
⁂   **Location:** US 98, e of Navarre Bridge. 8673 Navarre Pkwy 32566. **Hours:** 10:30 am-2 & 4:30-9 pm, Sat & Sun
American   10:30 am-9 pm. Closed: 11/27, 12/24, 12/25. **Features:** At the water's edge on the sound, the popular family steakhouse boasts a Western decor. Barbecue is a menu specialty. Prices are moderate. Casual dress; beer & wine only. **Parking:** on-site. **Cards:** AX, DC, DS, MC, VI.

NAVARRE BEACH

──────── **WHERE TO STAY** ────────

HOLIDAY INN   **Phone:** (850)939-2321
⁂⁂⁂   5/25-9/7   1P: $135-$175   2P: $135-$175   XP: $10   F18
            3/1-5/24   1P: $95-$130   2P: $95-$130   XP: $10   F18
Small-scale Hotel   9/8-11/30   1P: $95-$120   2P: $95-$120   XP: $10   F18
            12/1-2/28   1P: $80-$110   2P: $80-$110   XP: $10   F18
Location: On SR 399, 0.6 mi s of bridge. 8375 Gulf Blvd 32566. Fax: 850/939-4768. **Facility:** 253 one-bedroom standard units. 2-3 stories, interior/exterior corridors. **Parking:** on-site. **Terms:** 2-3 night minimum stay - seasonal weekends, 3 day cancellation notice. **Amenities:** voice mail, safes, irons, hair dryers. **Pool(s):** outdoor, heated indoor. **Leisure Activities:** whirlpools, recreation programs, exercise room. *Fee:* game room. **Guest Services:** gift shop, valet and coin laundry. **Business Services:** meeting rooms, fax (fee). **Cards:** AX, CB, DC, DS, JC, MC, VI. *(See color ad opposite inside back cover)*

SOME UNITS

NEPTUNE BEACH —*See Jacksonville p. 472.*

NEW PORT RICHEY —*See Tampa Bay p. 922.*

NEW SMYRNA BEACH pop. 20,048

──────── **WHERE TO STAY** ────────

BUENA VISTA INN AND APARTMENTS   **Phone:** 386/428-5565
⁂   12/16-11/30   2P: $80   XP: $12   F12
            12/1-12/15   2P: $72   XP: $12   F12
Motel   **Location:** 2 mi e on Business 44, at west end of North Cswy bridge. 500 N Causeway 32169. Fax: 386/428-5565. **Facility:** Designated smoking area. 8 units. 3 one-bedroom standard units. 5 one-bedroom suites with kitchens. 1 story, exterior corridors. *Bath:* combo or shower only. **Parking:** on-site. **Terms:** 14 day cancellation notice-fee imposed, weekly rates available, small pets only ($5 extra charge). **Amenities:** video library. *Some:* irons. **Leisure Activities:** boat dock. **Guest Services:** coin laundry. **Cards:** MC, VI.

SOME UNITS

COASTAL WATERS INN   **Phone:** (386)428-3800
⁂⁂ ⁂⁂   All Year   2P: $75-$220   XP: $9   F12
            Location: SR A1A; 3.4 mi s of SR 44. 3509 S Atlantic Ave 32169. Fax: 386/423-5002. **Facility:** 40 units. 8 one-
Small-scale Hotel bedroom standard units. 32 one-bedroom suites with kitchens. 2-3 stories (no elevator), exterior corridors. *Bath:* combo or shower only. **Parking:** on-site. **Terms:** 2 night minimum stay - weekends, 96 day cancellation notice-fee imposed, weekly rates available. **Pool(s):** heated outdoor, wading. **Business Services:** fax (fee). **Cards:** DS, MC, VI.

SOME UNITS

NIGHT SWAN INTRACOASTAL BED & BREAKFAST

Phone: (386)423-4940

(AAA) [SAVE] ▼▼▼▼

Bed & Breakfast

All Year [BP]   1P: $90-$175   2P: $90-$175   XP: $20   F6
Location: West side of Intracoastal Waterway; just s of SR 44 bridge. 512 S Riverside Dr 32168. Fax: 386/427-2814. **Facility:** Offering a private dock for boat access, this early 1900s home imbued with Old-Florida character overlooks the Indian River. Smoke free premises. 15 units. 10 one-bedroom standard units, some with whirl-pools. 3 one-bedroom suites with whirlpools. 2 cabins. 2-3 stories (no elevator), interior/exterior corridors. *Bath:* combo or shower only. **Parking:** on-site. **Terms:** 3 day cancellation notice-fee imposed. **Amenities:** *Some:* irons, hair dryers. **Leisure Activities:** boat dock. **Guest Services:** complimentary laundry, area transportation-local marinas. **Business Services:** meeting rooms, PC, fax (fee). **Cards:** AX, DC, DS, MC, VI. **Special Amenities: early check-in/late check-out and free local telephone use.**

SOME UNITS
[S/D] [&] [X] [*] / [VCR] [■] [▣] [▦] /

RIVERVIEW HOTEL

Phone: (386)428-5858

(AAA) [SAVE] ▼▼▼▼

Country Inn

All Year [ECP]   1P: $90-$200   2P: $90-$200   XP: $10   D
Location: East end of North Cswy Bridge. 103 Flagler Ave 32169. Fax: 386/423-8927. **Facility:** This restored 1885 building on the Intracoastal Waterway with easy access to a dock features natural-tone wood on the walls, ceilings and floors. 19 units. 17 one-bedroom standard units. 1 one-bedroom suite. 1 cottage. 3 stories (no elevator), interior/exterior corridors. *Bath:* combo or shower only. **Amenities:** safes, irons. **Dining:** Riverview Restaurant, see separate listing. **Pool(s):** heated outdoor. **Leisure Activities:** boat dock, bicycles. **Guest Services:** gift shop, valet laundry. **Business Services:** fax (fee). **Cards:** AX, CB, DC, DS, MC, VI. **Special Amenities: free continental breakfast and free newspaper.**

SOME UNITS
[S/D] [¶] [≈] [*] [DATA PORT] / [VCR] [■] [▣] [▦] /

SMYRNA MOTEL

Phone: 386/428-2495

(AAA) [SAVE] ▼

Motel

12/1-4/30   1P: $45-$55   2P: $55-$75   XP: $10   D5
5/1-11/30   1P: $40-$50   2P: $45-$55   XP: $10   D5
Location: 1.2 mi n on US 1. 1050 N Dixie Frwy 32168. **Facility:** 10 one-bedroom standard units. 1 story, exterior corridors. *Bath:* shower only. **Parking:** on-site. **Terms:** 14 day cancellation notice. **Cards:** AX, DS, MC, VI.

SOME UNITS
[¶→] [*] [■] / [X] /

The following lodging was either not evaluated or did not meet AAA rating requirements but is listed for your information only.

HOLIDAY INN HOTEL & SUITES

Phone: (386)426-0020

(AAA) [SAVE] [fyi]

Small-scale Hotel

All Year   1P: $129-$149   2P: $325-$350   XP: $10   F18
Under major renovation, scheduled to be completed June 2002. **Last rated:** ▼▼▼ **Location:** SR A1A, s of SR 44. 1401 S Atlantic Ave 32169. Fax: 386/423-3977. **Facility:** 102 units. 20 one-bedroom standard units with efficiencies. 76 one- and 6 two-bedroom suites with kitchens. 8 stories, interior corridors. *Bath:* combo or shower only. **Parking:** on-site. **Terms:** check-in 4 pm, 30 day cancellation notice. **Amenities:** dual phone lines, voice mail, irons, hair dryers. **Dining:** 7 am-11 & 5-8 pm, wine/beer only. **Pool(s):** outdoor. **Guest Services:** valet and coin laundry. **Business Services:** fax. **Cards:** AX, CB, DC, DS, JC, MC, VI. **Special Amenities: early check-in/late check-out and free local telephone calls.** *(See color ad opposite inside back cover)*

SOME UNITS
[S/D] [¶] [≈] [*] [DATA PORT] [■] [▦] / [X] [VCR] [▦] /

WHERE TO DINE

CHASES

Lunch: $6-$9   **Dinner:** $10-$18   **Phone:** 386/423-8787

▼ Steak & Seafood

Location: SR A1A, 3.3 mi s of SR 44. 3401 S Atlantic Blvd 32169. **Hours:** 11 am-10 pm. Closed: 12/25. **Features:** A scenic oceanfront location offers both indoor and outdoor dining. The menu is traditional fare which includes tasty burgers, homemade soup, creative salads and seafood or landlubber entrees. Casual dress; cocktails; entertainment. **Parking:** on-site. **Cards:** AX, DS, MC, VI.

[Y] [X]

JB'S FISH CAMP

Lunch: $9-$20   **Dinner:** $9-$20   **Phone:** 386/427-5747

▼ Seafood

Location: SR A1A, 8.5 mi s of SR 44 on the Indian River. 859 Pompano Ave 32169. **Hours:** 11:30 am-9:30 pm, Fri & Sat-10:30 pm. Closed: 11/27, 12/25. **Features:** A docking place for hopeful fishermen, this rustic, Florida-style structure resembles an old shack but offers delicious local oysters and fresh river clams right off the boat. A popular local spot, it is perfect for a good meal after a day at the beach. Casual dress; cocktails. **Parking:** on-site. **Cards:** AX, DS, MC, VI.

[X]

NORWOOD'S SEAFOOD RESTAURANT

Lunch: $6-$9   **Dinner:** $6-$29   **Phone:** 386/428-4621

▼▼ Seafood

Location: SR 44, 1 mi e of Intracoastal Waterway Bridge. 400 2nd Ave 32169. **Hours:** 11:30 am-9:30 pm. Closed: 12/25. **Features:** Ease into this very popular, very comfortable restaurant. Early bird specials offer the best bargain, with a variety of fresh seafood and beef dishes and an extensive wine list. Try the coconut shrimp served with a tangy, sweet-and-sour sauce. Casual dress; cocktails. **Parking:** on-site. **Cards:** AX, DC, DS, MC, VI.

[X]

PATIO RESTAURANT

Lunch: $4-$6   **Dinner:** $7-$16   **Phone:** 386/423-8355

▼▼ American

Location: On US 1; downtown. 626 N Dixie Frwy 32168. **Hours:** 11 am-2:30 & 4:30-9 pm. Closed: 12/25; also Sun. **Reservations:** suggested. **Features:** Step into a quaint, romantic world of classical music, wrought iron gates and gardens of night-blooming jasmine. Gourmet dining in an intimate setting showcases an award-winning menu with seafood, a lovely vegetarian entree and a portobello-stuffed filet. Smoke free premises. Casual dress; beer & wine only. **Parking:** on-site. **Cards:** AX, CB, DC, DS, MC, VI.

[X]

RIVERVIEW RESTAURANT **Lunch:** $5-$7 **Dinner:** $14-$23 Phone: 386/428-1865
▼▼▼ **Location:** East end of North Cswy Bridge; in Riverview Hotel. 101 Flagler Ave 32169. **Hours:** 11 am-2:30 & 4:30-10 pm, Sun 10:30 am-3 & 5-10 pm. Closed: 12/25; also Super Bowl Sun. **Reservations:** suggested.
Seafood **Features:** Located in a restored brick building, guests enjoy riverview dining from an inside window or the under cover deck dining. The creative menu offers fresh fish and shellfish, pasta and chicken. A pastry chef prepares sinful desserts. Casual dress; cocktails. **Parking:** on-site. **Cards:** AX, DC, DS, MC, VI. ✕

NICEVILLE pop. 11,684

——— WHERE TO STAY ———

HAMPTON INN AT BLUEWATER BAY Phone: (850)897-4675

	3/2-9/2 [ECP]	1P: $80-$86	2P: $86-$92	XP: $6	F18
SAVE	12/1-3/1 & 9/3-11/30 [ECP]	1P: $75-$81	2P: $80-$86	XP: $6	F18

▼▼▼ **Location:** 2 mi e on SR 20. 4400 Ansley Dr 32578. Fax: 850/897-4837. **Facility:** 56 one-bedroom standard units. 3 stories, interior corridors. *Bath:* combo or shower only. **Parking:** on-site. **Terms:** 14 day cancellation notice. **Amenities:** dual phone lines, voice mail, irons, hair dryers. **Pool(s):** outdoor. **Leisure Activities:** exercise room. **Guest Services:** valet laundry. **Business Services:** fax (fee). **Cards:** AX, CB, DC, DS, MC, VI.
Small-scale Hotel

SOME UNITS
🆂🅳 🏊 📷 🗄️ 💻 / ✕ 🛅 🖥️ /

HOLIDAY INN EXPRESS Phone: (850)678-9131
▼▼▼ All Year [ECP] 1P: $83 2P: $83 XP: $10 F
Location: SR 85, just se on jct SR 20. 106 Bayshore Dr 32578. Fax: 850/678-9272. **Facility:** 89 one-bedroom standard units. 2 stories, interior corridors. *Bath:* combo or shower only. **Parking:** on-site. **Terms:** pets ($50 deposit). **Amenities:** dual phone lines, voice mail, irons, hair dryers. **Pool(s):** outdoor. **Guest Services:** valet laundry. **Business Services:** meeting rooms, fax (fee). **Cards:** AX, DC, DS, JC, MC, VI.
Small-scale Hotel

SOME UNITS
ASK 🆂🅳 🐾 🍴 🎱 🏊 📶 📷 🗄️ 🛅 🖥️ 💻 / ✕ /

——— WHERE TO DINE ———

GIUSEPPI'S WHARF RESTAURANT & MARINA **Lunch:** $7-$12 **Dinner:** $10-$19 Phone: 850/678-4229
▼▼ **Location:** US 85, just se on jct US 20, then 0.8 mi se. 821 Bayshore Dr 32578. **Hours:** 11 am-9 pm; to 10 pm in summer. Closed: 11/27, 12/25. **Reservations:** accepted. **Features:** Surprisingly, this attractive wharfside
Seafood setting was once known as Boggy Bayou, an early fishing village. The name was changed to Niceville, and a friendlier bunch of residents you couldn't hope to meet. Although seafood dominates and live Maine lobster is steaming once a week, landlubbers are also catered to. Enjoy views of boats and the bay from the lounge, the outdoor tiki bar and the upper-floor deck. Casual dress; cocktails; entertainment. **Parking:** on-site. **Cards:** AX, CB, DC, DS, MC, VI. 🍸 ✕

NOKOMIS pop. 3,334

——— WHERE TO STAY ———

LAUREL VILLA MOTEL Phone: 941/484-3656
◆◆ ◆◆ 12/20-5/1 1P: $50-$65 2P: $60-$70 XP: $6 F10
  12/1-12/19 & 5/2-11/30 1P: $40-$46 2P: $46-$50 XP: $6 F10
Motel **Location:** I-75, exit 200, 3 mi sw on SR 681, just s on US 41. 1409 N Tamiami Tr 34275. Fax: 941/488-7444. **Facility:** 11 one-bedroom standard units with efficiencies. 1 story, exterior corridors. *Bath:* shower only.
Parking: on-site. **Terms:** 30 day cancellation notice-fee imposed, weekly rates available. **Amenities:** *Some:* irons, hair dryers. **Pool(s):** outdoor. **Leisure Activities:** putting green, bicycles. **Guest Services:** coin laundry. **Cards:** DS, MC, VI.

SOME UNITS
🍴 🏊 🛅 🖥️ / ✕ 🗄️ /

——— WHERE TO DINE ———

PELICAN ALLEY **Lunch:** $8-$10 **Dinner:** $8-$20 Phone: 941/485-1893
▼▼ ▼▼ **Location:** US 41, 1 mi w on Albee Rd at the south bridge to Casey Key. 1009 W Albee Rd 34275. **Hours:** 11:30 am-10 pm. Closed: 4/20, 11/27, 12/25; also Tues 5/15-11/2 & 9/8-9/20. **Features:** Cozy and casual, the
Seafood restaurant is a popular place to watch traffic on the Intracoastal Waterway. The big draw here is fresh seafood, including the chowder for which this place is known. It is delectably flavored with substantial chunks of seafood. Casual dress; cocktails. **Parking:** on-site. **Cards:** AX, CB, DC, DS, MC, VI. ✕

NORTH BAY VILLAGE —See Miami-Miami Beach p. 556.

NORTH FORT MYERS pop. 40,214—See also FORT MYERS.

——— WHERE TO STAY ———

CACTUS MOTEL Phone: 239/995-2456
◆◆◆ SAVE 12/1-4/30 2P: $69-$99 XP: $15 F12
  5/1-11/30 2P: $49-$65 XP: $10 F12
▼▼ **Location:** On US Business 41, just s of jct Bayshore Pine Island Rd. 1677 N Tamiami Tr (Bus 41) 33903. **Facility:** 12 one-bedroom standard units, some with kitchens. 1 story, exterior corridors. **Parking:** on-site. **Terms:** 30 day
Motel cancellation notice-fee imposed, weekly rates available. **Amenities:** voice mail. *Some:* irons, hair dryers.
Leisure Activities: gas barbecue grill area with covered seating, shuffleboard. **Cards:** DS, MC, VI.
Special Amenities: early check-in/late check-out and free local telephone calls.

SOME UNITS
🍴 / ✕ 🛅 🖥️ /

ECONO LODGE
Phone: (239)995-0571

[AAA] [SAVE]
2/2-3/24	1P: $89-$125	2P: $99-$125	XP: $5	F18
3/25-11/30	1P: $49-$69	2P: $59-$99	XP: $5	F18
12/1-2/1	1P: $59-$85	2P: $75-$95	XP: $5	F18

[diamond] [diamond]

Motel   **Location:** On US 41, 1.1 mi n of Caloosahatchee Bridge. 13301 N Cleveland Ave 33903. Fax: 239/995-9143. **Facility:** 48 one-bedroom standard units. 2 stories, exterior corridors. **Parking:** on-site. **Terms:** 14 day cancellation notice, [CP] meal plan available, small pets only ($5 extra charge). **Amenities:** *Some:* irons, hair dryers. **Pool(s):** heated outdoor. **Guest Services:** coin laundry. **Cards:** AX, CB, DC, DS, MC, VI. **Special Amenities:** free continental breakfast.

SOME UNITS

[icons]

HOWARD JOHNSON EXPRESS INN
Phone: (239)656-4000

[AAA] [SAVE]
All Year	1P: $49-$119	2P: $59-$129	XP: $5	F

[diamond][diamond][diamond]

Motel   **Location:** On US 41, 1 mi n of Caloosahatchee Bridge. 13000 N Cleveland Ave 33903. Fax: 239/656-1612. **Facility:** 121 one-bedroom standard units. 2 stories, exterior corridors. **Parking:** on-site. **Terms:** cancellation fee imposed, weekly rates available, [ECP] meal plan available. **Amenities:** safes (fee), irons. *Some:* hair dryers. **Pool(s):** outdoor. **Guest Services:** valet and coin laundry. **Business Services:** meeting rooms, fax (fee). **Cards:** AX, DC, DS, MC, VI. **Special Amenities:** free continental breakfast and free local telephone calls.

SOME UNITS

[icons]   FEE   FEE FEE

──────── **WHERE TO DINE** ────────

LAND & SEA FAMILY RESTAURANT   **Lunch:** $4-$13   **Dinner:** $4-$13   **Phone:** 239/656-3030

[diamond]   **Location:** On US 41, just n of Caloosahatchee Bridge. 13121 Cleveland Ave 33903. **Hours:** 6 am-10 pm. **Features:** A big favorite with the over-60 crowd, the large family diner serves a great selection of comfort foods, such as fried catfish, chicken fingers, mashed potatoes and country-fried steak. Expect good value and ample portions at reasonable prices. Casual dress; cocktails. **Parking:** on-site. **Cards:** AX, CB, DC,

American

DS, MC, VI.

[icon]

NORTH LAUDERDALE —*See Fort Lauderdale p. 404.*

NORTH MIAMI —*See Miami-Miami Beach p. 557.*

NORTH MIAMI BEACH —*See Miami-Miami Beach p. 557.*

NORTH PALM BEACH pop. 12,064   (See map p. 757; index p. 759)—*See also PALM BEACH.*

──────── **WHERE TO STAY** ────────

THE WATERFORD HOTEL & CONFERENCE CENTER
Phone: (561)624-7186   [43]

[AAA] [SAVE]
12/1-4/30 [ECP]	1P: $139-$399	2P: $139-$399	XP: $10	F18
5/1-11/30 [ECP]	1P: $109-$299	2P: $109-$299	XP: $10	F18

[diamond][diamond][diamond]   **Location:** US 1, just s of jct PGA Blvd (SR 786) and SR A1A. 11360 US Hwy 1 33408. Fax: 561/622-4258. **Facility:** 90 units. 87 one-bedroom standard units. 2 one- and 1 two-bedroom suites with whirlpools, some Small-scale Hotel with kitchens. 4 stories, interior corridors. **Parking:** on-site. **Terms:** cancellation fee imposed. **Amenities:** dual phone lines, voice mail, irons, hair dryers. *Some:* safes. **Dining:** 7 am-9 pm, cocktails. **Pool(s):** heated outdoor. **Leisure Activities:** exercise room. **Guest Services:** valet laundry. **Business Services:** meeting rooms, business center. **Cards:** AX, DC, DS, MC, VI. **Special Amenities:** free continental breakfast and free room upgrade (subject to availability with advanced reservations).

SOME UNITS

[icons]   FEE FEE

NORTH PORT pop. 22,797

──────── **WHERE TO DINE** ────────

OLDE WORLD RESTAURANT & LOUNGE   **Lunch:** $5-$18   **Dinner:** $5-$18   **Phone:** 941/426-1155

[AAA]   **Location:** On US 41, just s of North Port Blvd; center. 14415 S Tamiami Tr 34287. **Hours:** 7 am-10 pm. Closed: 1/1, 12/25. **Reservations:** suggested. **Features:** Friendly and casual, the relaxed restaurant boasts a bubbly service staff and all-day breakfast. Browse the varied menu for burgers, filet mignon, stuffed flounder and the three-layer chocolate fantasy, which incorporates seven decadent types of chocolate.

[diamond][diamond]

American   Casual dress; cocktails. **Parking:** on-site. **Cards:** AX, DS, MC, VI.

[icons]

NORTH REDINGTON BEACH —*See Tampa Bay p. 923.*

OCALA pop. 45,943

──────── **WHERE TO STAY** ────────

BEST WESTERN OCALA PARK CENTRE
Phone: (352)237-4848

[AAA] [SAVE]
All Year [ECP]	1P: $62-$89	2P: $62-$89	XP: $7	F17

[diamond][diamond]   **Location:** I-75, exit 350, just w on SR 200. Located in Park Centre. 3701 SW 38th Ave 34474. Fax: 352/237-2281. **Facility:** 139 units. 138 one-bedroom standard units. 1 one-bedroom suite ($101-$152) with kitchen. 4 stories, interior corridors. **Parking:** on-site. **Amenities:** irons, hair dryers. **Pool(s):** heated outdoor. **Leisure Ac-** Small-scale Hotel **tivities:** whirlpool. **Guest Services:** coin laundry. **Business Services:** meeting rooms, fax. **Cards:** AX, DC, DS, MC, VI.

SOME UNITS

BUDGET HOST INN

Phone: (352)732-6940

12/1-4/14 [CP]	1P: $42-$62	2P: $52-$72	XP: $10	F12
4/15-11/30 [CP]	1P: $35-$55	2P: $45-$65	XP: $10	F12

Location: I-75, exit 354, 0.3 mi n on US 27. 4013 NW Blitchton Rd 34482. Fax: 352/629-8048. **Facility:** 21 one-bedroom standard units. 1 story, exterior corridors. *Bath:* combo or shower only. **Parking:** on-site. **Terms:** weekly rates available, $3 service charge, pets ($4-$6 extra charge). **Business Services:** fax (fee). **Cards:** AX, DS, MC, VI. **Special Amenities:** early check-in/late check-out and free continental breakfast. *(See color ad p 244)*

SOME UNITS

COMFORT INN

Phone: (352)629-8850

12/26-4/7 [ECP]	1P: $75-$100	2P: $80-$120	XP: $5	F18
12/1-12/25 & 4/8-11/30 [ECP]	1P: $55-$60	2P: $60-$70	XP: $5	F18

Location: I-75, exit 352, just w on SR 40. 4040 W Silver Springs Blvd 34482. Fax: 352/732-0831. **Facility:** 132 units. 128 one-bedroom standard units. 4 one-bedroom suites ($85-$125), some with whirlpools. 2 stories, exterior corridors. **Parking:** on-site. **Terms:** small pets only ($5 extra charge). **Amenities:** hair dryers. *Some:* irons. **Dining:** 6 am-9 pm, Sat & Sun from 7 am. **Pool(s):** outdoor. **Guest Services:** coin laundry. **Business Services:** meeting rooms, fax (fee). **Cards:** AX, CB, DC, DS, JC, MC, VI. **Special Amenities:** free continental breakfast and free local telephone calls.

SOME UNITS
FEE FEE

COURTYARD BY MARRIOTT

Phone: (352)237-8000

1/1-4/30	1P: $89-$106	2P: $89-$106
12/1-12/31 & 5/1-11/30	1P: $79-$106	2P: $79-$106

Location: I-75, exit 350, just w on SR 200. Located in Park Centre. 3712 SW 38th Ave 34474. Fax: 352/237-0580. **Facility:** 175 units. 167 one-bedroom standard units. 8 one-bedroom suites ($150-$200), some with whirlpools. 3 stories, interior corridors. *Bath:* combo or shower only. **Parking:** on-site. **Terms:** [BP] & [CP] meal plans available. **Amenities:** video games, voice mail, irons, hair dryers. **Dining:** 6:30 am-10:30 & 4-10 pm, cocktails. **Pool(s):** heated outdoor. **Leisure Activities:** whirlpool, exercise room. **Guest Services:** valet and coin laundry. **Business Services:** meeting rooms, fax. **Cards:** AX, DC, DS, MC, VI. *(See color ad p 584)*

SOME UNITS
FEE

DAYS INN

Phone: (352)629-7041

All Year	1P: $50-$60	2P: $55-$80	XP: $5	F17

Location: I-75, exit 354, just n on US 27. 3811 NW Bonnie Heath Blvd 34482. Fax: 352/629-1026. **Facility:** 65 one-bedroom standard units, some with whirlpools. 2 stories, interior/exterior corridors. **Parking:** on-site. **Terms:** 14 day cancellation notice, pets ($5 extra charge). **Amenities:** hair dryers. **Pool(s):** outdoor. **Leisure Activities:** playground. **Guest Services:** coin laundry. **Business Services:** fax. **Cards:** AX, CB, DC, DS, JC, MC, VI. **Special Amenities:** free local telephone calls and free newspaper.

SOME UNITS

FAIRFIELD INN BY MARRIOTT

Phone: (352)861-8400

12/26-4/30 [ECP]	1P: $71-$98	2P: $71-$98
12/1-12/25 & 5/1-11/30 [ECP]	1P: $65-$93	2P: $65-$93

Location: I-75, exit 350, just w on SR 200. 4101 SW 38th Ct 34474. Fax: 352/861-8401. **Facility:** 97 one-bedroom standard units. 3 stories, interior corridors. *Bath:* combo or shower only. **Parking:** on-site. **Amenities:** dual phone lines, voice mail, irons. *Some:* hair dryers. **Pool(s):** heated outdoor. **Leisure Activities:** whirlpool, exercise room. **Guest Services:** valet and coin laundry. **Business Services:** fax. **Cards:** AX, DC, DS, MC, VI. **Special Amenities:** free continental breakfast and free local telephone calls.

SOME UNITS

HAMPTON INN OCALA

Phone: (352)854-3200

All Year [ECP]	1P: $89-$159	2P: $94-$159

Location: I-75, exit 350, 0.4 mi e on SR 200. 3434 SW College Rd 34474. Fax: 352/854-5633. **Facility:** 152 units. 148 one-bedroom standard units, some with whirlpools. 4 one-bedroom suites. 3 stories, exterior corridors. **Parking:** on-site. **Amenities:** voice mail, irons, hair dryers. **Pool(s):** heated outdoor. **Guest Services:** valet and coin laundry. **Business Services:** meeting rooms, fax. **Cards:** AX, CB, DC, DS, MC, VI.

SOME UNITS
FEE

HILTON OCALA

Phone: (352)854-1400

All Year [BP]	1P: $79-$139	2P: $79-$139

Location: I-75, exit 350, 0.3 mi e on SR 200. 3600 SW 36th Ave 34474. Fax: 352/854-4010. **Facility:** 197 units. 192 one-bedroom standard units. 5 one-bedroom suites ($199-$349), some with whirlpools. 9 stories, interior corridors. **Parking:** on-site. **Terms:** cancellation fee imposed, package plans, small pets only. **Amenities:** voice mail, irons, hair dryers. **Dining:** Arthur's, see separate listing. **Pool(s):** heated outdoor. **Leisure Activities:** whirlpool, 2 lighted tennis courts, exercise room, volleyball. **Guest Services:** valet laundry. **Business Services:** meeting rooms, business center. **Cards:** AX, CB, DC, DS, JC, MC, VI. *(See color ad p 583)*

SOME UNITS

HOLIDAY INN EXPRESS

Phone: 352/629-7300

1/1-6/30 [ECP]	1P: $95	2P: $95
12/1-12/31 & 7/1-11/30 [ECP]	1P: $75	2P: $75

Location: 0.8 mi s on US 27, 301 and 441, just s of SR 200. 1212 S Pine Ave 34474. Fax: 352/629-3331. **Facility:** 55 one-bedroom standard units, some with whirlpools. 3 stories, interior corridors. *Bath:* combo or shower only. **Parking:** on-site. **Amenities:** dual phone lines, voice mail, irons, hair dryers. **Pool(s):** outdoor. **Guest Services:** valet and coin laundry. **Business Services:** meeting rooms, fax. **Cards:** AX, DC, DS, MC, VI. *(See color ad opposite inside back cover)*

SOME UNITS

HOLIDAY INN OCALA

Phone: (352)629-0381

1/31-3/31	1P: $85-$130
4/1-5/2	1P: $85-$114
5/3-11/30	1P: $82-$114
12/1-1/30	1P: $79-$85

Small-scale Hotel

Location: I-75, exit 352, just e on SR 40. 3621 W Silver Springs Blvd 34475. **Fax:** 352/629-8813. **Facility:** 269 one-bedroom standard units. 2 stories, exterior corridors. **Parking:** on-site. **Terms:** small pets only ($20 fee). **Amenities:** irons, hair dryers. **Pool(s):** outdoor, wading. **Leisure Activities:** exercise room. **Guest Services:** coin laundry. **Business Services:** meeting rooms, fax. **Cards:** AX, CB, DC, DS, MC, VI. *(See color ad opposite inside back cover)*

SOME UNITS

(A$K) (S/D) (🐕) (🍴) (Y) (🏊) (🛎️) (DATA PORT) (💻) / (✕) (🔒) (📷) /

FEE   FEE

HOWARD JOHNSON INN

Phone: (352)629-7021

2/2-3/17	1P: $50-$150	2P: $60-$200	XP: $10 F14
12/1-2/1 & 3/18-11/30	1P: $40-$80	2P: $50-$125	XP: $10 F14

Motel

Location: I-75, exit 354, just w. 3951 NW Blitchton Rd 34482. **Fax:** 352/629-0510. **Facility:** 125 one-bedroom standard units, some with whirlpools. 3 stories (no elevator), exterior corridors. **Parking:** on-site. **Terms:** cancellation fee imposed, [BP] meal plan available, $6 service charge, pets ($10 extra charge). **Amenities:** high-speed Internet, voice mail. **Pool(s):** heated outdoor. **Leisure Activities:** miniature golf. **Guest Services:** coin laundry. **Business Services:** meeting rooms, fax. **Cards:** AX, DC, DS, MC, VI. **Special Amenities:** early check-in/late check-out and free newspaper. *(See color ad below)*

SOME UNITS

(S/D) (🐕) (🛎️) (📷) (DATA PORT) (💻) / (✕) (🔒) /

LA QUINTA INN & SUITES

Phone: (352)861-1137

All Year	1P: $79-$119

Small-scale Hotel

Location: I-75, exit 350, just e on SR 200. 3530 SW 36th Ave 34474. **Fax:** 352/861-1157. **Facility:** 117 units. 111 one-bedroom standard units. 6 one-bedroom suites. 6 stories, interior corridors. *Bath:* combo or shower only. **Parking:** on-site. **Terms:** [ECP] meal plan available, small pets only. **Amenities:** video games, voice mail, irons, hair dryers. **Pool(s):** heated outdoor. **Leisure Activities:** whirlpool, exercise room. **Guest Services:** valet and coin laundry. **Business Services:** meeting rooms, business center. **Cards:** AX, CB, DC, DS, JC, MC, VI.

SOME UNITS

(🛏️) (🍴) (🔬) (🅕) (📶) (🛎️) (📷) (DATA PORT) (💻) / (✕) (🔒) (📷) /

QUALITY INN

Phone: (352)732-2300

AAA SAVE

	1/31-3/31	1P: $45-$80	2P: $49-$175	XP: $10	F16
	12/1-1/30	1P: $30-$75	2P: $49-$125	XP: $10	F16
	4/1-11/30	1P: $38-$75	2P: $48-$125	XP: $10	F16

Location: I-75, exit 354, just e. 3767 NW Blitchon Rd 34475. Fax: 352/351-0153. **Facility:** 119 one-bedroom stan-

Small-scale Hotel dard units. 2 stories, exterior corridors. **Parking:** on-site. **Terms:** weekly rates available, [CP] meal plan available, small pets only ($9 extra charge). **Amenities:** irons, hair dryers. **Pool(s):** outdoor. **Guest Services:** coin laundry. **Business Services:** fax (fee). **Cards:** AX, CB, DC, DS, MC, VI. **Special Amenities:** free continental breakfast and free local telephone calls.

SOME UNITS

SEVEN SISTERS INN

Phone: (352)867-1170

| | All Year | 1P: $129-$269 | 2P: $129-$269 | XP: $50 | |

Historic Bed & Breakfast

Location: Just s of jct SR 40 on SE Winona Ave. Located in a residential area in the downtown historic district. 820 SE Fort King St 34471. Fax: 352/867-5266. **Facility:** Built in 1888 in the Queen Anne style, this home offers rooms of varied shapes and sizes furnished with canopied or wrought iron beds. Designated smoking area. 14 units. 11 one- and 2 two-bedroom standard units, some with whirlpools. 1 one-bedroom suite ($189-$269). 3 stories (no elevator), interior corridors. *Bath:* combo or shower only. **Parking:** on-site. **Terms:** 2-4 night minimum stay - seasonal & weekends, age restrictions may apply, 7 day cancellation notice-fee imposed, [BP] meal plan available, package plans - seasonal & weekends. **Amenities:** video library (fee), CD players, hair dryers. *Some:* irons. **Leisure Activities:** bicycles. **Guest Services:** gift shop, complimentary evening beverages. **Business Services:** meeting rooms, fax. **Cards:** AX, DC, MC, VI.

SOME UNITS

FEE

STEINBRENNER'S RAMADA INN & CONFERENCE CENTER

Phone: (352)732-3131

AAA SAVE

| | 12/1-3/31 | | 2P: $69-$135 | XP: $10 | F18 |
| | 4/1-11/30 | | 2P: $59-$89 | XP: $10 | F18 |

Location: I-75, exit 354, just w. 3810 NW Bonnie Heath Blvd 34482. Fax: 352/732-3821. **Facility:** 124 units. 123 one-bedroom standard units. 1 one-bedroom suite. 2 stories, exterior corridors. *Bath:* combo or shower only.

Small-scale Hotel **Parking:** on-site. **Terms:** cancellation fee imposed, [AP] meal plan available, 6% service charge, pets ($25 fee). **Amenities:** voice mail, irons, hair dryers. **Dining:** 6:30 am-10 pm, cocktails. **Pool(s):** heated outdoor. **Leisure Activities:** whirlpool, playground, exercise room. **Guest Services:** valet and coin laundry. **Business Services:** meeting rooms, fax. **Cards:** AX, DC, DS, MC, VI. *(See color ad below)*

SOME UNITS

FEE FEE

The following lodging was either not evaluated or did not meet AAA rating requirements but is listed for your information only.

COUNTRY INN & SUITES
Phone: 352/237-0715
[fyi]
Motel
1/1-4/30 [ECP]   1P: $79-$159   2P: $105-$165
12/1-12/31 & 5/1-11/30 [ECP]   1P: $79-$139   2P: $85-$145
Too new to rate. **Location:** I-75, exit 350. 3720 SW College Rd 34474. **Fax:** 352/237-3615. **Amenities:** coffee-makers, microwaves, refrigerators, pool. **Cards:** AX, CB, DC, DS, MC, VI. *(See color ad p 613)*

--- **WHERE TO DINE** ---

AMRIT PALACE INDIAN RESTAURANT   **Lunch:** $7-$18   **Dinner:** $10-$18   **Phone:** 352/873-8500
▼▼ ▼▼
Indian
Location: I-75, exit 350, 1.6 mi ne on SR 200. 2635 SW College Rd 34474. **Hours:** 11:30 am-9:30 pm, Fri & Sat-10:30 pm, Sun & Mon 5 pm-9:30 pm. **Features:** This restaurant offers a wide range of traditional Indian preparations, including chutney, achar, curry, lamb, chicken, seafood, biryani rice, vegetarian specialties and several specialty breads. Many items are cooked in a tandoor oven. Casual dress; beer & wine only. **Parking:** on-site. **Cards:** AX, MC, VI.

ARTHUR'S   **Lunch:** $6-$8   **Dinner:** $14-$27   **Phone:** 352/854-1400
▼▼ ▼▼
Regional Steak & Seafood
Location: I-75, exit 350, 0.3 mi e on SR 200; in Hilton Ocala. 3600 SW 36th Ave 34474. **Hours:** 4:30 am-10 pm. **Reservations:** suggested; in winter. **Features:** Noted for lobster bisque, the menu also offers tempting steak dishes. the grouper, covered in an herbed nut crust, gives new a twist to an old theme. Large windows overlook a courtyard, and fine linen tablecloths and napkins add an air of sophistication. Casual dress; cocktails. **Parking:** on-site. **Cards:** AX, CB, DC, DS, MC, VI.

BELLA LUNA CAFE   **Lunch:** $5-$9   **Dinner:** $9-$20   **Phone:** 352/237-9155
ⒶⒶⒶ
▼▼ ▼▼ ▼▼
Italian
Location: I-75, exit 350, 0.4 mi e on SR 200. 3425 SW College Rd 34474. **Hours:** 11 am-10 pm, Fri & Sat 3 pm-11 pm. Closed: 11/27, 12/25. **Reservations:** suggested; weekends. **Features:** Fine dining in an elegant, romantic setting boasts an excellent variety of entrees with unique combinations certain to inspire a return visit. The chicken and spinach served on a bed of pasta is generously portioned as well as flavorful. Dressy casual; cocktails. **Parking:** valet. **Cards:** AX, DC, DS, MC, VI.

CARMICHAEL'S RESTAURANT   **Lunch:** $6-$11   **Dinner:** $8-$15   **Phone:** 352/622-3636
▼▼ ▼▼
American
Location: On SR 40, 3 mi e of jct US 27/301/441. 3105 NE Silver Springs Blvd 34470. **Hours:** 6:30 am-8:30 pm. **Reservations:** suggested. **Features:** An array of made-from-scratch specialties are the attraction in this dining room. Friendly and attentive servers welcome you to a warm, wood-accented interior. Choose from a good selection of well-prepared fish, meat, chicken and pasta dishes. Smoke free premises. Casual dress; cocktails. **Parking:** on-site. **Cards:** AX, MC, VI.

HARRY'S SEAFOOD BAR & GRILLE   **Lunch:** $5-$7   **Dinner:** $5-$18   **Phone:** 352/840-0900
American
Location: Just e on SR 40 from jct US 27/301/441. 24 SE First Ave 34471. **Hours:** 11 am-10 pm, Wed-Sat to 11 pm, Sun-9 pm. **Closed:** 11/27, 12/25. **Features:** Expect tasty, well-presented food in a bustling, laid-back atmosphere. the menu features great variety highlighted with a few Cajun choices. Peruse the ample appetizer section or order a meal of steak, chicken or seafood. Casual dress; cocktails. **Parking:** on-site.
Cards: AX, DC, DS, MC, VI.

HUCKLEBERRY FINN'S RESTAURANT & COUNTRY STORE   **Lunch:** $5-$7   **Dinner:** $8-$15   **Phone:** 352/402-0776
Southern
Location: I-75, exit 354, just w. 3821 NW Blitchton Rd 34482. **Hours:** 7 am-9 pm. **Closed** major holidays. **Features:** Good selection of homestyle food at a good price. Quaint gift shop at entrance. Smoke free premises. Casual dress. **Parking:** on-site. **Cards:** AX, CB, DC, DS, MC, VI.

OCOEE —See Orlando p. 746.

OKEECHOBEE pop. 5,376

——— WHERE TO STAY ———

BUDGET INN   **Phone:** (863)763-3185
Motel

	1P: $59-$79	2P: $59-$99	XP: $10
1/1-4/14			
12/1-12/31	1P: $49-$69	2P: $49-$79	XP: $10
4/15-11/30	1P: $39-$69	2P: $49-$69	XP: $10

Location: US 98 and 441, just s of jct SR 70. 201 S Parrott Ave (US 441) 34974. Fax: 863/763-3185. **Facility:** 24 one-bedroom standard units. 1 story, exterior corridors. *Bath:* combo or shower only. **Parking:** on-site. **Terms:** cancellation fee imposed, [CP] meal plan available, small pets only ($10 extra charge). **Pool(s):** outdoor. **Business Services:** fax (fee). **Cards:** AX, DS, MC, VI. **Special Amenities:** free continental breakfast and preferred room (subject to availability with advanced reservations).

SOME UNITS

ECONOMY INN   **Phone:** 863/763-1148
Motel

| 12/16-4/15 | 1P: $45-$65 | 2P: $59-$79 | XP: $10 | F12 |
| 12/1-12/15 & 4/16-11/30 | 1P: $35-$50 | 2P: $40-$55 | XP: $5 | F12 |

Location: US 441, 0.3 mi n of jct SR 70. 507 N Parrott Ave (US 441) 34972. Fax: 863/763-1149. **Facility:** 24 one-bedroom standard units. 1 story, exterior corridors. *Bath:* shower only. **Parking:** on-site. **Terms:** small pets only ($5 extra charge). **Business Services:** fax (fee). **Cards:** AX, DS, MC, VI. **Special Amenities:** free local telephone calls and preferred room (subject to availability with advanced reservations).

SOME UNITS

HOLIDAY INN EXPRESS   **Phone:** (863)357-3529
Small-scale Hotel

| 1/1-4/15 | 2P: $95-$175 | XP: $5 | F18 |
| 12/1-12/31 & 4/16-11/30 | 2P: $65-$125 | XP: $5 | F18 |

Location: US 98 and 441, 3 mi s of jct SR 70, 0.3 mi n of Lake Okeechobee and jct SR 78. 3975 Hwy 441 S 34974. Fax: 863/357-3529. **Facility:** 43 one-bedroom standard units, some with whirlpools. 2 stories, exterior corridors. **Parking:** on-site. **Terms:** cancellation fee imposed, [ECP] meal plan available, small pets only ($10 extra charge). **Amenities:** irons, hair dryers. **Pool(s):** outdoor. **Guest Services:** valet and coin laundry. **Business Services:** fax (fee). **Cards:** AX, DC, DS, MC, VI.

SOME UNITS

——— WHERE TO DINE ———

LIGHTSEY'S RESTAURANT   **Lunch:** $5-$7   **Dinner:** $8-$17   **Phone:** 863/763-4276
Seafood
Location: SR 78, 4.5 mi sw of jct US 98 and 441; in Okeetanti Recreational Area. 10435 Hwy 78 W 34974. **Hours:** 11 am-9 pm, Fri & Sat-10 pm, Sun-8 pm. **Closed:** 4/20, 11/27, 12/24, 12/25. **Features:** Within Okeetanti Park, the restaurant gleans its character from the many fish tanks, animal mounts and huge bay windows that overlook the marina. Cooter fritters (turtle), catnips (catfish), alligator and frog legs are among the down-to-earth selections. Casual dress; cocktails. **Parking:** on-site. **Cards:** DS, MC, VI.

OLDSMAR —See Tampa Bay p. 924.

OLD TOWN

——— WHERE TO STAY ———

SUWANEE GABLES MOTEL   **Phone:** 352/542-7752
Motel

| All Year | 1P: $60-$68 | 2P: $75-$85 | XP: $10 | D6 |

Location: US 19, 98 and 27A; 2 mi s of jct SR 349. HC 3 Box 208 32680. Fax: 352/542-9212. **Facility:** 22 units. 18 one-bedroom standard units. 1 one-bedroom suite ($170-$180). 3 cottages ($275-$300). 1 story, exterior corridors. **Parking:** on-site. **Terms:** 3-5 night minimum stay - weekends, 14 day cancellation notice-fee imposed, small pets only ($8 extra charge). **Pool(s):** outdoor. **Leisure Activities:** Fee: boat dock. **Guest Services:** coin laundry. **Cards:** AX, DC, MC, VI. **Special Amenities:** preferred room (subject to availability with advanced reservations).

SOME UNITS

FEE   FEE

ORANGE CITY pop. 6,604

――― **WHERE TO STAY** ―――

COMFORT INN
AAA SAVE
WWWW
Motel

Phone: (386)775-7444

All Year [ECP] 1P: $59-$200 2P: $59-$200 XP: $7 F18
Location: I-4, exit 114, 2.8 mi w on SR 472, 2 mi s on US 17-92. Located in a commercial area. 445 S Volusia Ave 32763. Fax: 386/775-9887. **Facility:** 60 one-bedroom standard units. 2 stories, exterior corridors. **Parking:** on-site. **Terms:** 30 day cancellation notice-fee imposed. **Amenities:** *Some:* irons, hair dryers. **Pool(s):** outdoor. **Business Services:** fax (fee). **Cards:** AX, CB, DC, DS, JC, MC, VI. **Special Amenities:** free continental breakfast and free newspaper.

SOME UNITS

 / FEE FEE

DAYS INN
AAA SAVE
WWW
Motel

Phone: (386)775-4522

12/1-3/31 1P: $60-$250 2P: $60-$250 XP: $10 F16
4/1-7/31 1P: $60-$170 2P: $60-$170 XP: $10 F16
8/1-11/30 1P: $60-$150 2P: $60-$150 XP: $10 F16
Location: I-4, exit 114, 2.8 mi w on SR 472, 0.3 mi s on US 17-92. 2501 N Volusia Ave 32763. Fax: 386/775-0919. **Facility:** Designated smoking area. 37 one-bedroom standard units, some with efficiencies (utensils extra charge). 1-2 stories, exterior corridors. **Parking:** on-site. **Terms:** 14 day cancellation notice, weekly rates available, [CP] meal plan available. **Amenities:** irons, hair dryers. **Pool(s):** outdoor. **Leisure Activities:** barbecue pit. **Cards:** AX, CB, DS, JC, MC, VI. **Special Amenities:** free continental breakfast and free newspaper.

SOME UNITS

ORANGE PARK —*See Jacksonville p. 473.*

Destination Orlando
pop. 185,951

Airboating, Greater Orlando Area.
Shallow water and a desire for speed have made airboats a popular way to visit the less-dry regions of Central Florida.

*T*here's much more to Orlando than theme parks. Mother Nature has blessed central Florida with an abundance of sunshine—and locals love to take advantage of it.

*R*ecreational opportunities abound—frolicking in the waters of a nearby lake or river, hiking or bicycling along plentiful trails, golfing at one of the area's plush resorts. Still, others maintain that sufficient exercise can be obtained by walking from store to store.

Biking, Orlando.
Sunny days encourage biking—but be prepared for summer and fall late-afternoon showers.

Lady Lake

441

Leesburg   *Tavares*

Howey-
In-The-
Hills

Winter
Garden

Clermont

27

Walt
Disney
World
Resort

4

See Downtown map page 598

*P*laces included in this AAA Destination City:

Altamonte Springs.....671	Lake Mary................740
Apopka....................673	Leesburg...................742
Casselberry...............674	Longwood.................743
Celebration..............675	Maitland..................744
Clermont..................675	Mount Dora.............745
Davenport................676	Ocoee.....................746
Fern Park................677	Oviedo....................747
Heathrow.................677	St. Cloud.................747
Howey-In-The-Hills...677	Sanford...................747
Kissimmee...............678	Tavares...................749
Lady Lake................714	Winter Garden..........749
Lake Buena Vista.......714	Winter Park.............750

Swan boats in Lake Eola Park, Orlando.
How do you get this Ugly Duckling
back to shore? Pedal, pedal, pedal.
(See listing page 142)

See Vicinity map page 590

*Harry P. Leu
Gardens, Orlando.*
Resting in the shade among
ornamental grasses and
foliage seems a good idea
on humid summer afternoons.
(See listing page 142)

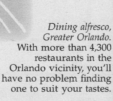

*Dining alfresco,
Greater Orlando.*
With more than 4,300
restaurants in the
Orlando vicinity, you'll
have no problem finding
one to suit your tastes.

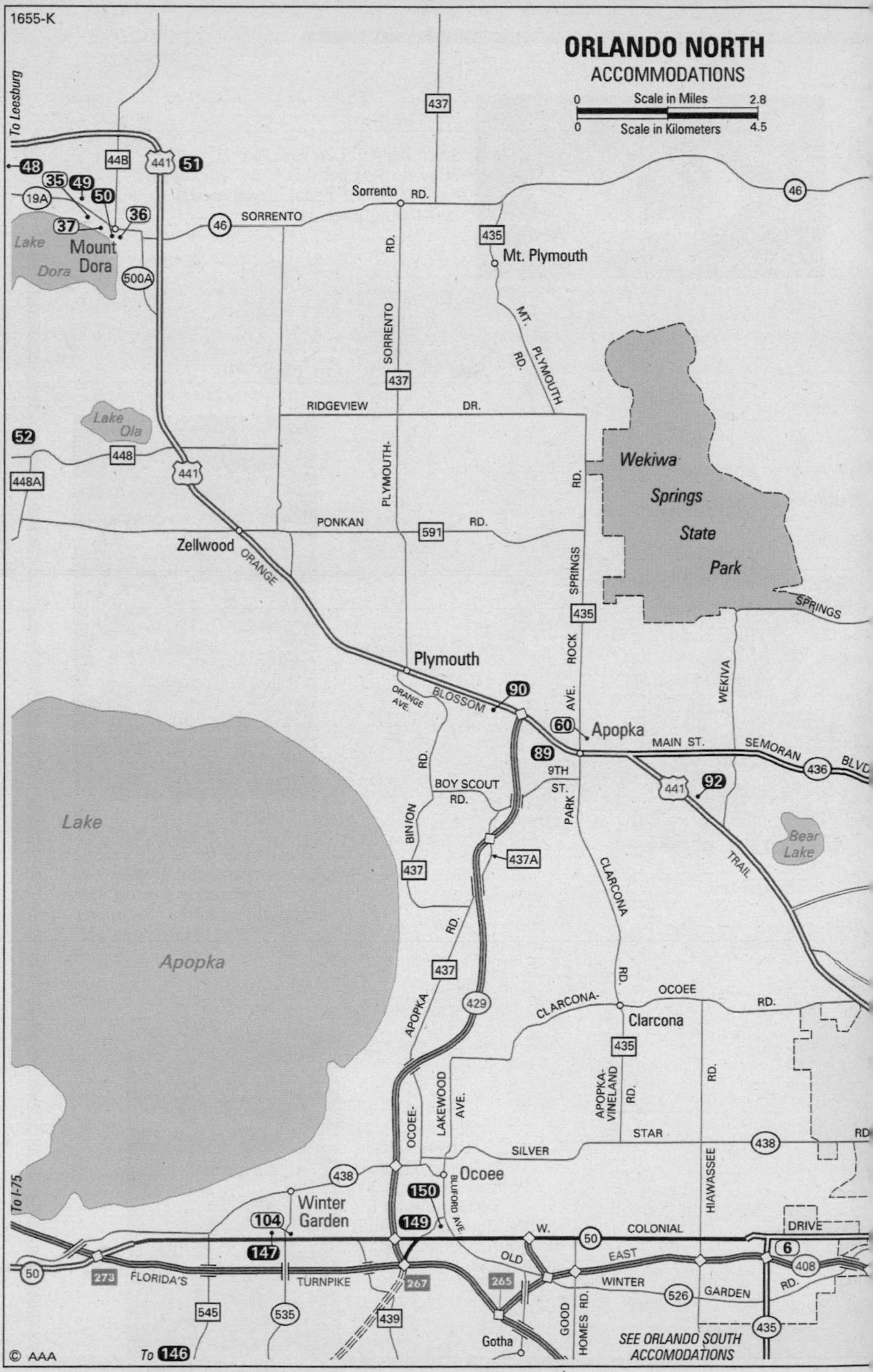

1655-K

ORLANDO NORTH
ACCOMMODATIONS

Scale in Miles
0   2.8

Scale in Kilometers
0   4.5

To Leesburg

437

46

48   **44B**   **441**   **51**

35   **49**

19A   **50**

37   **36**

Sorrento   RD.

SORRENTO   **46**

435

Mt. Plymouth

Mount Dora

500A

Lake Dora

SORRENTO   RD.

MT. PLYMOUTH   RD.

Wekiwa

52

Lake Ola

448

441

448A

RIDGEVIEW   DR.

437

Springs

State

Park

PLYMOUTH-

PONKAN   RD.

591

Zellwood

ORANGE

SPRINGS   AVE.

435

SPRINGS

ROCK

Plymouth

BLOSSOM

ORANGE AVE.

90

WEKIVA

60   Apopka

MAIN ST.

SEMORAN   BLVD.

89

9TH ST.

441

436

92

BOY SCOUT RD.

PARK   AVE.

TRAIL

Bear Lake

BINION   RD.

437

437A

CLARCONA

Lake

Apopka

RD.

437

429

CLARCONA-

OCOEE   RD.

Clarcona

435

APOPKA   RD.

LAKEWOOD AVE.

OCOEE   AVE.

APOPKA-VINELAND RD.

RD.

STAR

438

RD

SILVER

HIAWASSEE

438

BLUFORD AVE.

Ocoee

150

W.   COLONIAL   DRIVE

104   Winter Garden

149

50

EAST

6

147

OLD

WINTER

408

50   **273**   FLORIDA'S   TURNPIKE

267

265

GOOD HOMES RD.

GARDEN   RD.

526

435

545   **535**

439

Gotha

© AAA   To **146**

SEE ORLANDO SOUTH ACCOMODATIONS

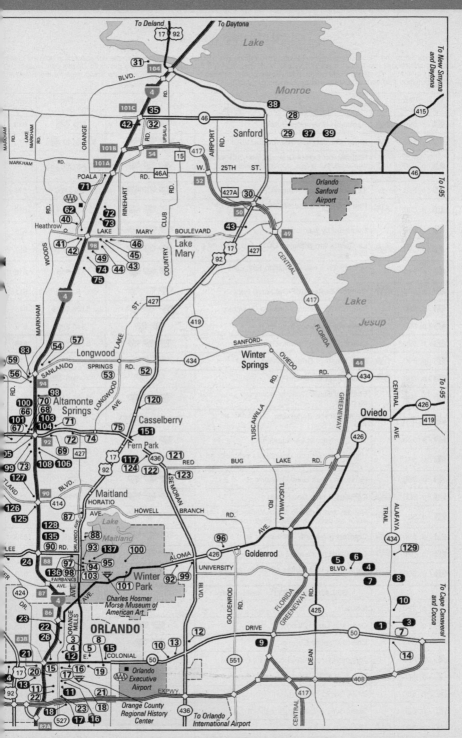

Orlando North

This index helps you "spot" where approved accommodations and restaurants are located on the corresponding detailed maps. Lodging rate ranges are for comparison only and show the property's high season; rates are per night, unless only weekly (W) rates are available. Restaurant rate range is for dinner, unless only lunch (L) is served. Turn to the listing page for more detailed rate information and consult display ads for special promotions.

Spotter/Map Page Number	OA	ORLANDO NORTH - Lodgings	Diamond Rating	Rate Range High Season	Listing Page
1 / p. 590	AAA	Radisson University Hotel	◆◆◆	$99 SAVE	618
3 / p. 590	AAA	Hilton Garden Inn Orlando East/UCF	◆◆◆	$70-$140 SAVE	615
4 / p. 590	AAA	Holiday Inn Select-Orlando East-UCF Area - see color ad p 616, opposite inside back cover	◆◆◆	$99-$129 SAVE	616
5 / p. 590		Residence Inn by Marriott/Orlando East	◆◆◆	$99-$169	618
6 / p. 590	AAA	Hampton Inn & Suites/Orlando East-UCF Area	◆◆◆	$99-$109 SAVE	615
7 / p. 590		Courtyard by Marriott UCF	◆◆◆	$119	614
8 / p. 590	AAA	La Quinta Inn & Suites UCF - see color ad p 652	◆◆◆	$79-$125 SAVE	617
9 / p. 590		Holiday Inn Express-Orlando East - see color ad p 616	◆◆◆	$75-$85	615
10 / p. 590	AAA	Comfort Suites UCF-Research Park	◆◆◆	$99-$179 SAVE	613
11 / p. 590		Four Points Sheraton Orlando Downtown	◆◆◆	$109-$149	615
12 / p. 590		Travelodge Orlando Downtown	◆◆	$45-$85	618
13 / p. 590		Orlando Marriott Downtown	◆◆◆	$149-$190	618
14 / p. 590	AAA	Best Western Orlando West	◆◆	$69-$125 SAVE	612
15 / p. 590	AAA	Travelodge Colonial Plaza	◆◆	$49-$65 SAVE	618
16 / p. 590		Embassy Suites Orlando Downtown - see color ad p 614	◆◆◆	$125-$161	614
17 / p. 590	AAA	Westin Grand Bohemian - see color ad p 636	◆◆◆◆	$189-$259 SAVE	619
18 / p. 590		The Courtyard at Lake Lucerne	◆◆◆	$89-$215	614
21 / p. 590		Holiday Inn Orlando Downtown - see color ad opposite inside back cover	◆◆◆	$84-$119	616
22 / p. 590		Radisson Plaza Hotel Orlando	◆◆◆	$70	618
23 / p. 590	AAA	Comfort Suites Downtown	◆◆◆	$79-$119 SAVE	613
24 / p. 590	AAA	Holiday Inn Orlando North-Winter Park - see color ad opposite inside back cover, p 616	◆◆◆	$79-$129 SAVE	616
25 / p. 590	AAA	Comfort Inn-North - see color ad p 612	◆◆◆	$79-$125 SAVE	613
26 / p. 590	AAA	Courtyard by Marriott Downtown	◆◆◆	$119-$139 SAVE	614
27 / p. 590	AAA	Wellesley Inn & Suites (Orlando/Maitland) - see color ad p 612	◆◆◆	$79-$89 SAVE	618
		ORLANDO NORTH - Restaurants			
3 / p. 590		Misuzu	◆	$6-$24	620
4 / p. 590		Gargi's at Lake Ivanhoe	◆◆	$10-$22	619
5 / p. 590		Chan's Chinese Cuisine	◆◆	$7-$28	619
6 / p. 590		Johnny Rivers Smokehouse and BBQ Co	◆◆	$9-$16	620
7 / p. 590		Michael's Italian Restaurant	◆◆	$9-$20	620
8 / p. 590		BAJA Burrito Kitchen	◆	$4-$8	619
10 / p. 590		Straub's Fine Seafood Restaurant	◆◆	$12-$25	620
11 / p. 590	AAA	Manuel's on the 28th	◆◆◆◆	$28-$36	620

Spotter/Map Page Number	OA	ORLANDO NORTH - Restaurants (continued)	Diamond Rating	Rate Range High Season	Listing Page
12 / p. 590		High Tide Harry's	◆◆	$4-$30	619
13 / p. 590	AAA	**Hot Dog Heaven**	◆	$2-$6	619
14 / p. 590		Panera Bread	◆	$3-$6	620
15 / p. 590		Pebbles Downtown	◆◆	$6-$19	620
16 / p. 590		Louis' Downtown	◆◆◆	$16-$35	620
17 / p. 590		Metro Espresso Pizza Cafe	◆	$15	620
18 / p. 590		Sushi Hatsu	◆◆	$9-$19	621
19 / p. 590		Dexter's of Thornton Park	◆◆	$5-$20	619
20 / p. 590		The Globe	◆◆	$8-$12	619
21 / p. 590	AAA	**Lee's Lakeside Restaurant**	◆◆	$19-$29	620
22 / p. 590		Amigos Original Tex-Mex Restaurant	◆◆	$7-$12	619
23 / p. 590	AAA	**The Boheme**	◆◆◆◆	$20-$32	619
		SANFORD - Lodgings			
35 / p. 590	AAA	**Comfort Inn & Suites North Orlando - see color ad p 747**	◆◆◆	$89-$109 SAVE	747
37 / p. 590	AAA	**The Higgins House Bed & Breakfast**	◆◆◆	$85-$165 SAVE	747
38 / p. 590		Best Western Marina Hotel & Conference Center	◆◆	$69-$79	747
39 / p. 590		Rose Cottage Inn	◆◆◆	$50-$145	748
42 / p. 590	AAA	**SpringHill Suites by Marriott**	◆◆◆	$79-$160 SAVE	748
43 / p. 590	AAA	**Holiday Inn Express-Sanford/Lake Mary**	◆◆◆	$145-$175 SAVE	748
		SANFORD - Restaurants			
28 / p. 590	AAA	**Morgan's Gourmet Cafe**	◆◆	$8-$16	748
29 / p. 590		Da Vinci, A Dining Place	◆◆	$14-$18	748
30 / p. 590		Sergio's Italian Restaurant	◆◆	$5-$15	748
31 / p. 590		Otter's Riverside Restaurant	◆◆	$9-$25	748
32 / p. 590		Joe's Crab Shack	◆	$9-$25	748
		MOUNT DORA - Lodgings			
48 / p. 590	AAA	**Comfort Inn and Suites**	◆◆◆	$68-$95 SAVE	745
49 / p. 590		Darst Victorian Manor	◆◆◆	$135-$230	745
50 / p. 590	AAA	**The Lakeside Inn**	◆◆	$125-$235 SAVE	746
51 / p. 590		Hampton Inn	◆◆◆	$70-$85	745
52 / p. 590		The Emerald Hill Inn	◆◆◆	$95-$175	745
		MOUNT DORA - Restaurants			
35 / p. 590	AAA	**The Gables Restaurant**	◆◆	$15-$25	746
36 / p. 590		The Goblin Market Restaurant	◆◆◆	$18-$27	746
37 / p. 590		Palm Tree Grill	◆◆	$10-$22	746
		HEATHROW - Lodgings			
62 / p. 590	AAA	**Courtyard by Marriott**	◆◆◆	$119-$179 SAVE	677
		HEATHROW - Restaurants			
40 / p. 590	AAA	**Luigino's Pasta & Steak House**	◆◆◆	$11-$30	677
41 / p. 590		Panera Bread Co	◆	$5-$7	677

Spotter/Map Page Number	OA	HEATHROW - Restaurants (continued)	Diamond Rating	Rate Range High Season	Listing Page
42 / p. 590		Stonewood Tavern & Grill	◆◆◆	$10-$25	677
		LAKE MARY - Lodgings			
71 / p. 590	AAA	Orlando Marriott Lake Mary - see color ad p 741	◆◆◆	$99-$199 SAVE	741
72 / p. 590	AAA	Hilton Garden Inn Lake Mary	◆◆◆	$129 SAVE	740
73 / p. 590	AAA	Homewood Suites by Hilton - see color ad p 740	◆◆◆	$99-$139 SAVE	740
74 / p. 590	AAA	MainStay Suites Hotel - see color ad p 741	◆◆◆	$129-$135 SAVE	741
75 / p. 590		La Quinta Inn & Suites - see color ad p 652	◆◆◆	$79-$125	740
		LAKE MARY - Restaurants			
43 / p. 590		Tony's Original Wings & Grill	◆	$4-$11	742
44 / p. 590		Chengs	◆◆	$6-$25	741
45 / p. 590		Caffe Positano	◆◆	$6-$18	741
46 / p. 590		Golden China Buffet	◆◆	$11-$13	742
49 / p. 590		Toojay's Original Gourmet Deli	◆◆	$5-$10	742
		LONGWOOD - Lodgings			
83 / p. 590		Ramada Inn North-Orlando	◆◆	$89-$109	743
		LONGWOOD - Restaurants			
51 / p. 590		First Watch	◆	$6-$8(L)	744
52 / p. 590		Enzo's Restaurant On The Lake	◆◆◆	$20-$38	743
53 / p. 590		The Taboule Factory	◆	$3-$5	744
54 / p. 590	AAA	Peter Scott's	◆◆◆◆	$20-$34	744
56 / p. 590		Pebbles Restaurant	◆◆	$8-$20	744
57 / p. 590		Chicago Hot Dog Co	◆	$2-$7	743
58 / p. 590		Melting Pot	◆◆	$10-$25	744
59 / p. 590	AAA	Imperial Dynasty	◆◆	$6-$26	744
		APOPKA - Lodgings			
89 / p. 590		Days Inn	◆◆	$49-$99	673
90 / p. 590	AAA	Crosby's Motor Inn	◆◆◆	$60-$100 SAVE	673
92 / p. 590	AAA	Howard Johnson Express Inn	◆◆	$63-$104 SAVE	674
		APOPKA - Restaurant			
60 / p. 590		Catfish Place of Apopka	◆◆	$7-$16	674
		ALTAMONTE SPRINGS - Lodgings			
98 / p. 590		Candlewood Suites	◆◆◆	$69-$109	671
99 / p. 590		Quality Inn	◆◆	$55-$95	672
100 / p. 590		Residence Inn by Marriott	◆◆◆	$119-$169	672
101 / p. 590	AAA	Hampton Inn	◆◆◆	$83-$149 SAVE	671
102 / p. 590		SpringHill Suites by Marriott Orlando/Altamonte Springs	◆◆◆	$99	672
103 / p. 590	AAA	Best Western Altamonte Springs	◆◆◆	$79 SAVE	671
104 / p. 590	AAA	Embassy Suites Orlando North - see color ad p 615	◆◆◆	$129-$229 SAVE	671
105 / p. 590	AAA	Holiday Inn of Altamonte Springs - see color ad opposite inside back cover	◆◆◆	$69 SAVE	671

Spotter/Map Page Number	OA	ALTAMONTE SPRINGS - Lodgings (continued)	Diamond Rating	Rate Range High Season	Listing Page
106 / p. 590		Homestead Studio Suites Hotel-Orlando/Altamonte Springs	◆◆◆	$59-$79	671
107 / p. 590		La Quinta Inn-Orlando North - see color ad p 652	◆◆◆	$59-$95	672
108 / p. 590		Hilton Orlando/Altamonte Springs	◆◆◆	$69-$125	671
		ALTAMONTE SPRINGS - Restaurants			
65 / p. 590		Baja Burrito Kitchen	◆	$4-$8	672
66 / p. 590	AAA	**Bangkok Restaurant**	◆◆	$7-$12	673
67 / p. 590		Amigos	◆◆	$7-$12	672
68 / p. 590		Kohinoor Indian Restaurant	◆◆	$8-$17	673
69 / p. 590		Eastern Pearl Chinese Restaurant	◆◆◆	$7-$28	673
70 / p. 590		First Watch	◆◆	$5-$7(L)	673
71 / p. 590		Bahama Breeze	◆◆	$7-$19	672
72 / p. 590		Straub's Fine Seafood Restaurant	◆◆	$12-$22	673
73 / p. 590	AAA	**Maison & Jardin**	◆◆◆◆	$20-$35	673
74 / p. 590		Panera Bread	◆	$3-$6	673
75 / p. 590	AAA	**Amira's**	◆	$5-$11	672
		FERN PARK - Lodgings			
117 / p. 590	AAA	**Comfort Inn-Fern Park**	◆◆◆	$79-$89 SAVE	677
		MAITLAND - Lodgings			
125 / p. 590		Homewood Suites Orlando North	◆◆◆	$139-$189	744
126 / p. 590		Courtyard by Marriott Orlando/Maitland	◆◆◆	$59-$149	744
127 / p. 590		Sheraton Orlando North Hotel	◆◆◆	$79-$99	744
128 / p. 590		Thurston House	◆◆◆	$140-$170	745
		MAITLAND - Restaurants			
87 / p. 590	AAA	**Antonio's La Fiamma Ristorante**	◆◆◆	$13-$30	745
88 / p. 590	AAA	**Chef Arthur's Nicole St Pierre Restaurant**	◆◆◆	$16-$27	745
		WINTER PARK - Lodgings			
135 / p. 590		Fairfield Inn-Winter Park	◆◆	$69-$79	750
136 / p. 590	AAA	**GuestHouse International**	◆◆	$46-$60 SAVE	750
137 / p. 590	AAA	**Best Western Mt. Vernon Inn - see ad p 750**	◆◆◆	$95-$125 SAVE	750
		WINTER PARK - Restaurants			
90 / p. 590		Bubbalou's Bodacious Bar-b-que	◆	$4-$10	751
92 / p. 590		Pebbles of Winter Park	◆◆	$7-$20	751
93 / p. 590		Siam Garden	◆◆	$10-$18	752
94 / p. 590		P. F. Chang's China Bistro	◆◆	$5-$13	751
95 / p. 590		Cheesecake Factory	◆◆	$8-$25	751
96 / p. 590		Alfonzo's Fine Italian Cuisine	◆◆	$8-$19	751
97 / p. 590		BlackFin	◆◆◆	$16-$30	751
98 / p. 590		Dexter's of Winter Park	◆◆◆	$6-$22	751
99 / p. 590		Amigos	◆◆	$7-$12	751
100 / p. 590		Park Plaza Gardens	◆◆◆	$16-$30	751

Spotter/Map Page Number	OA	WINTER PARK - Restaurants (continued)	Diamond Rating	Rate Range High Season	Listing Page
101 / p. 590		Brazilian Pavilion	◈◈	$11-$25	751
103 / p. 590		Trastevere Ristorante	◈◈	$7-$22	752
		WINTER GARDEN - Lodgings			
146 / p. 590		Orange County National Golf Center and Lodge	◈◈◈	$95	750
147 / p. 590	AAA	Best Value Inn Orlando West - see color ad p 749	◈◈	$79-$89 SAVE	749
		WINTER GARDEN - Restaurant			
104 / p. 590		Taquitos Jalisco	◈◈	$5-$14	750
		OCOEE - Lodgings			
149 / p. 590		Red Roof Inn Orlando West	◈◈	$61-$76	746
150 / p. 590		Best Western Turnpike West-Orlando	◈◈◈	$79-$89	746
		CASSELBERRY - Lodgings			
151 / p. 590		Suburban Lodge	◈◈	$199-$279	674
		CASSELBERRY - Restaurants			
120 / p. 590		Whiskey Creek Steakhouse	◈	$8-$18	674
121 / p. 590		Rolando's Cuban Restaurant	◈◈	$7-$18	674
122 / p. 590		Aladdin's Cafe	◈	$14	674
123 / p. 590		Colorado Fondue Company	◈◈	$8-$15	674
124 / p. 590		Cypriana Restaurant	◈◈	$8-$15	674
		OVIEDO - Restaurant			
129 / p. 590		Amigos Original Tex-Mex Restaurant	◈◈	$7-$12	747

Precautions Can Save A Vacation!

*T*ravelers are faced with the task of protecting themselves while in a strange environment. Although there is no way to guarantee absolute protection from crime, the experts–law enforcement officials–advise travelers to take a proactive approach to securing their property and ensuring their safety.

☑ Make sure the hotel desk clerk does not announce your room number; if he/she does, quietly request a new room assignment.

☑ Ask front desk personnel which areas of town to avoid and what, if any, special precautions should be taken when driving a rental car (some criminals target tourists driving rental cars).

☑ Never open the door to a stranger; use the peephole and request identification. If you are still unsure, call the front desk to verify the identity of the person and the purpose of his/her visit.

☑ Carry money separately from credit cards or use a "fanny pack." Carry your purse close to your body and your wallet in an inside coat or front trouser pocket. Never leave luggage unattended, and use your business address, if possible, on luggage tags.

☑ Beware of distractions staged by would-be scam artists, especially groups of children that surround you, or a stranger who accidentally spills something on you. They may be lifting your wallet.

☑ If using an automatic teller machine (ATM), choose one in a well-lit area with plenty of foot traffic, such as one at a grocery store. Law enforcement officials suggest that machines inside establishments are generally safer to use.

☑ Use room safes or safety deposit boxes provided by the hotel. Store all valuables out of sight, even when you are in the room.

☑ Law enforcement agencies consider card-key (electronic) door locks the most secure.

© AAA

SEE ORLANDO NORTH
ACCOMMODATIONS

Gotha

ORLANDO SOUTH
ACCOMMODATIONS

Scale in Miles   2.8
Scale in Kilometers   4.5

Windermere

Lake
Butler

CONROY   RD.

SEE INSET MAP
FOR DETAIL

Dr.
Phillips

Lake
Tibet

Lake
Sheen

Lake
Mable

Lake
Buena Vista

Magic
Kingdom

Walt
Disney
World
Resort

Epcot

Disney/MGM
Studios

Animal
Kingdom

Celebration

To Ocala

IRLO   BRONSON

OSCEOLA

IRLO

SEE INSET MAP
FOR DETAIL

To Lake Wales

To Tampa,
St. Petersburg

To Davenport, 590 THRU 593 THRU 595 & 600

Celebration

W. IRLO BRONSON MEM. HWY.
ACCOMMODATIONS

Walt Disney
World
Resort

OSCEOLA

SOUTHERN

Celebration

Scale in Miles   1.4
Scale in Kilometers   2.3

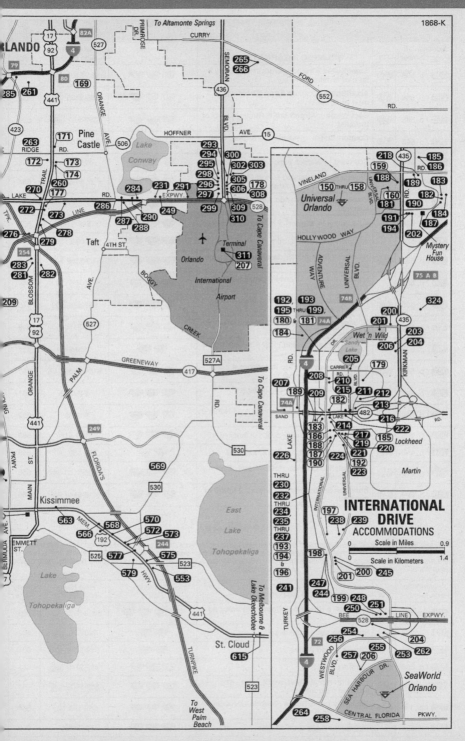

1868-K

✈ Airport Accommodations

Spotter/Map Page Number	OA	ORLANDO INTERNATIONAL	Diamond Rating	Rate Range High Season	Listing Page
309 / p. 598	AAA	AmeriSuites (Orlando Airport/Northeast), 2 mi n of terminal	▼▼▼	$85-$135 [SAVE]	623
296 / p. 598	AAA	AmeriSuites (Orlando Airport/Northwest), 2 mi n of terminal	▼▼▼	$85-$135 [SAVE]	623
288 / p. 598	AAA	Best Western Airport Inn & Suites, 4.5 nw of terminal	▼▼▼	$66-$90 [SAVE]	626
291 / p. 598	AAA	Comfort Suites - Orlando Int. Airport, 2 mi nw of terminal	▼▼▼	$99-$109 [SAVE]	631
299 / p. 598		Courtyard by Marriott Airport, 2 mi n of terminal	▼▼▼	$119-$139	632
294 / p. 598		Crowne Plaza Hotel and Resort Orlando Airport, 2.5 mi n of terminal	▼▼▼	$159-$169	634
302 / p. 598	AAA	Embassy Suites Orlando Airport, 2 mi n of terminal	▼▼▼	$109-$209 [SAVE]	635
303 / p. 598		Fairfield Inn by Marriott, 2 mi n of terminal	▼▼▼	$99-$149	638
293 / p. 598		Hampton Inn Airport, 2 mi n of terminal	▼▼▼	$109-$139	641
305 / p. 598	AAA	Hawthorn Suites Orlando Airport, 2 mi n of terminal	▼▼▼	$69-$109 [SAVE]	643
306 / p. 598		Hilton Garden Inn Orlando International Airport, 2 mi n of terminal	▼▼▼	$104-$134	644
287 / p. 598	AAA	Holiday Inn Express Orlando Airport West, 4 mi nw of terminal	▼▼▼	$59-$89 [SAVE]	645
300 / p. 598	AAA	Holiday Inn Select Orlando International Airport, 2 mi n of terminal	▼▼▼	$130-$150 [SAVE]	649
290 / p. 598		Howard Johnson Resort Hotel & Suites, 4 mi w of terminal	▼▼	$60-$75	651
311 / p. 598	AAA	Hyatt Regency Orlando International Airport, at the terminal	▼▼▼	$105-$255 [SAVE]	651
231 / p. 598		La Quinta Inn Airport West, 3.5 mi w of terminal	▼▼▼	$49-$96	651
297 / p. 598		La Quinta Inn & Suites Orlando Airport North, 2 mi n of terminal	▼▼▼	$59-$95	652
308 / p. 598		Orlando Airport Marriott, 2 mi n of terminal	▼▼▼	$149-$169	653
284 / p. 598	AAA	Quality Inn Airport, 3 mi w of terminal	▼▼	$59-$99 [SAVE]	653
295 / p. 598	AAA	Renaissance Orlando Hotel-Airport, 2 mi n of terminal	▼▼▼	$126-$153 [SAVE]	658
310 / p. 598	AAA	Sheraton Suites Orlando Airport, 2 mi ne of terminal	▼▼▼	$119-$149 [SAVE]	660

Orlando South

This index helps you "spot" where approved accommodations and restaurants are located on the corresponding detailed maps. Lodging rate ranges are for comparison only and show the property's high season; rates are per night, unless only weekly (W) rates are available. Restaurant rate range is for dinner, unless only lunch (L) is served. Turn to the listing page for more detailed rate information and consult display ads for special promotions.

Spotter/Map Page Number	OA	ORLANDO SOUTH - Lodgings	Diamond Rating	Rate Range High Season	Listing Page
181 / p. 598	AAA	Universal's Hard Rock Hotel - see color ad starting on p 150	▼▼▼▼	$229-$379 [SAVE]	663
182 / p. 598	AAA	Suburban Lodge-Universal	▼▼	$40-$70 [SAVE]	662
183 / p. 598	AAA	Sleep Inn and Suites	▼▼	$59-$139 [SAVE]	661
184 / p. 598	AAA	Comfort Suites	▼▼▼	$69-$149 [SAVE]	631
185 / p. 598	AAA	Hampton Inn at Universal Studios - see color ad card insert	▼▼▼	$59-$109 [SAVE]	641
186 / p. 598	AAA	Wellesley Inn & Suites (Orlando/Universal) - see color ad p 612	▼▼▼	$69-$99 [SAVE]	664
187 / p. 598		Red Roof Inn Universal Studios	▼▼▼	$49-$69	658

Spotter/Map Page Number	OA	ORLANDO SOUTH - Lodgings (continued)	Diamond Rating	Rate Range High Season	Listing Page
188 / p. 598	AAA	Universal's Portofino Bay Hotel - see color ad starting on p 150	◈◈◈◈	$279-$359 [SAVE]	664
189 / p. 598	AAA	Best Western Universal Inn - see ad p 627	◈◈◈	$59-$69 [SAVE]	627
190 / p. 598	AAA	Radisson Hotel Orlando at the entrance to Universal Orlando - see color ad p 657	◈◈◈	$169-$209 [SAVE]	656
191 / p. 598	AAA	Holiday Inn & Suites At Universal Orlando - see color ad p 646, opposite inside back cover	◈◈◈	$79-$159 [SAVE]	645
192 / p. 598	AAA	Holiday Inn-International Drive Resort - see color ad opposite inside back cover, p 648	◈◈◈	$69-$129 [SAVE]	648
193 / p. 598		Rodeway Inn International - see color ad p 655	◈◈	$50-$80	659
194 / p. 598	AAA	Days Inn East of Universal	◈◈	$49-$99 [SAVE]	634
195 / p. 598		Quality Inn International - see color ad p 655	◈◈	$50-$80	653
196 / p. 598	AAA	Howard Johnson Inn-International Drive	◈◈	$60-$100 [SAVE]	649
197 / p. 598	AAA	Best Western Movieland - see color ad p 628	◈◈◈	$65-$125 [SAVE]	627
198 / p. 598		Holiday Inn Express International Drive	◈◈◈	$100-$120	645
199 / p. 598		Travelodge International Drive	◈◈	$49-$69	663
200 / p. 598		Sheraton Studio City Hotel - see color ad p 636	◈◈◈	$89-$169	660
201 / p. 598		Ramada Inn at International Drive	◈◈◈	$49-$89	658
202 / p. 598		Delta Orlando Resort	◈◈	$49-$89	634
203 / p. 598	AAA	Clarion Hotel Universal - see color ad p 629	◈◈◈	$69-$109 [SAVE]	629
204 / p. 598		Hampton Inn-South of Universal Studios - see color ad p 624	◈◈◈	$79-$139	642
205 / p. 598	AAA	The Enclave Suites at Orlando - see color ad p 637	◈◈◈	$119-$159 [SAVE]	637
206 / p. 598		Howard Johnson Plaza Resort Universal Gateway - see color ad p 650	◈◈	$55-$109	650
207 / p. 598	AAA	Days Inn Orlando Lakeside - see color ad p 635	◈◈	$39-$99 [SAVE]	634
208 / p. 598	AAA	Fairfield Inn & Suites by Marriott-International Cove - see ad p 638	◈◈◈	$79-$99 [SAVE]	638
209 / p. 598		Comfort Inn International - see ad p 631	◈◈◈	$69-$129	631
210 / p. 598	AAA	Quality Suites Universal Orlando - see color ad starting on p 656	◈◈◈	$69-$119 [SAVE]	655
211 / p. 598	AAA	Hawthorn Suites Universal Orlando - see color ad p 643	◈◈◈	$79-$129 [SAVE]	644
212 / p. 598		Country Inn & Suites International Drive - see color ad p 613	◈◈◈	$79-$129	632
213 / p. 598		Hampton Inn Sand Lake - see color ad p 624	◈◈◈	$79-$139	641
214 / p. 598	AAA	Wyndham Orlando Resort	◈◈◈	$156 [SAVE]	665
215 / p. 598	AAA	Microtel Inn & Suites	◈◈	$59-$99 [SAVE]	653
216 / p. 598	AAA	Residence Inn by Marriott-Orlando International Dr	◈◈◈	$129-$179 [SAVE]	659
217 / p. 598		SpringHill Suites by Marriott International Drive Area/Orlando Conv Ctr - see color ad p 624	◈◈◈	$119-$149	661
218 / p. 598	AAA	Fairfield Inn & Suites at Universal Studios Orlando - see color ad card insert	◈◈◈	$79-$99 [SAVE]	638
219 / p. 598		Doubletree Castle Hotel - see color ad p 636	◈◈◈	$79-$169	634
220 / p. 598	AAA	La Quinta Inn & Suites - see color ad p 652	◈◈◈	$79-$125 [SAVE]	652
221 / p. 598		Homewood Suites by Hilton - see color ad p 649	◈◈◈	$99-$149	649

Spotter/Map Page Number	OA	**ORLANDO SOUTH** - Lodgings (continued)	Diamond Rating	Rate Range High Season	Listing Page
222 / p. 598	AAA	**Holiday Inn Hotel & Suites/Orlando/Orange County Convention Center** - see color ad card insert, opposite inside back cover	▼▼▼	$109-$129 SAVE	648
223 / p. 598		Sierra Suites Hotel-Pointe Orlando - see color ad p 735	▼▼▼	$79-$139	661
224 / p. 598	AAA	**AmeriSuites (Orlando/Convention Center)** - see color ad p 617	▼▼▼	$85 SAVE	623
226 / p. 598	AAA	**Comfort Suites Orlando** - see color ad p 632	▼▼	$60-$90 SAVE	631
227 / p. 598	AAA	**Summerfield Suites by Wyndham-Orlando/International Drive** - see color ad p 662	▼▼▼	$89-$289 SAVE	662
228 / p. 598	AAA	**Masters Inn International Drive**	▼▼	$41-$69 SAVE	653
229 / p. 598		Courtyard by Marriott, International Drive - see ad p 633	▼▼▼	$109-$149	633
230 / p. 598	AAA	**Embassy Suites International Drive/Jamaican Ct**	▼▼▼	$149-$179 SAVE	635
231 / p. 598		La Quinta Inn Airport West - see color ad p 652	▼▼▼	$49-$96	651
232 / p. 598	AAA	**La Quinta Inn-Orlando International Drive** - see color ad p 652	▼▼▼	$65-$101 SAVE	652
233 / p. 598	AAA	**Radisson Barcelo Resort** - see color ad p 657	▼▼▼	$77-$110 SAVE	655
234 / p. 598	AAA	**Best Western Plaza International** - see color ad p 628	▼▼▼	$65-$125 SAVE	627
235 / p. 598		Embassy Suites Hotel Orlando International Dr/Convention Center - see color ad p 728	▼▼▼	$129-$229	635
236 / p. 598		Quality Inn-Plaza - see color ad p 655	▼▼	$39-$99	655
237 / p. 598		Fairfield Inn by Marriott-International Drive	▼▼▼	$69-$129	638
238 / p. 598		Hampton Inn-Convention Center	▼▼▼	$62-$90	641
239 / p. 598		Residence Inn by Marriott Orlando Convention Center - see color ad p 624	▼▼▼	$119-$199	659
241 / p. 598	AAA	**Westgate Lakes Resort**	▼▼▼	$158-$302 SAVE	665
242 / p. 598		Marriott Residence Inn Lake Buena Vista North - see color ad p 732	▼▼▼	$119-$199	652
244 / p. 598		Rosen Centre Hotel	▼▼▼	$245-$325	659
245 / p. 598	AAA	**The Peabody Orlando**	▼▼▼▼	$390-$480 SAVE	653
247 / p. 598		Rosen PLaza	▼▼▼	$265	660
248 / p. 598	AAA	**Howard Johnson Plaza Hotel & Suites/International Dr South** - see color ad p 650	▼▼▼	$49-$99 SAVE	650
249 / p. 598	AAA	**Travelodge Hotel-Orlando International Airport**	▼▼▼	$49 SAVE	663
250 / p. 598	AAA	**Red Roof Inn Convention Center**	▼▼	$39-$89 SAVE	658
251 / p. 598	AAA	**Days Inn-Convention Center/North of Sea World**	▼▼	$109-$129 SAVE	634
253 / p. 598	AAA	**Sleep Inn-Convention Center**	▼▼	$45-$79 SAVE	661
254 / p. 598		Hawthorn Suites Orlando - see color ad p 642	▼▼▼	$95-$189	642
255 / p. 598		Sheraton World Resort - see color ad p 660	▼▼▼	$139-$279	661
256 / p. 598	AAA	**Hilton Garden Inn Orlando at SeaWorld International Center** - see color ad p 644	▼▼▼	$79-$129 SAVE	644
257 / p. 598	AAA	**Renaissance Orlando Resort at SeaWorld**	▼▼▼▼	$157-$199 SAVE	659
258 / p. 598		Hilton Grand Vacations Club	▼▼▼	$179	644
259 / p. 598	AAA	**AmeriSuites (Orlando/Universal)** - see color ad p 617	▼▼▼	$99 SAVE	626

Spotter/Map Page Number	OA	ORLANDO SOUTH - Lodgings (continued)	Diamond Rating	Rate Range High Season	Listing Page
260 / p. 598		Howard Johnson Florida Mall	◆◆	$74	649
261 / p. 598		Club Orlando	◆◆	$118-$198	631
262 / p. 598	AAA	**Travelodge Orlando Convention Center -** see color ad p 663	◆◆	$78-$98 SAVE	663
263 / p. 598		The Seasons Resort	◆◆◆	$178-$258	660
264 / p. 598		Residence Inn by Marriott Sea World International Center	◆◆◆	$129-$229	659
265 / p. 598		Ventura Resort Rentals-Kissimmee	◆◆◆	$110-$185	664
266 / p. 598		Ventura Resort Rentals Orlando	◆◆◆	$651-$924(W)	664
267 / p. 598	AAA	**Wellesley Inn & Suites (Orlando/Southpark)** - see color ad p 612	◆◆◆	$69-$89 SAVE	664
269 / p. 598		Homestead Studio Suites Hotel-Orlando/South	◆◆◆	$53-$58	649
270 / p. 598	AAA	**Travelodge Hotel At Florida Mall**	◆◆	$59-$79 SAVE	662
272 / p. 598		Best Western-Florida Mall - see color ad p 627	◆◆	$49-$89	626
273 / p. 598	AAA	**Adam's Mark Orlando**	◆◆◆	$119-$219 SAVE	621
276 / p. 598	AAA	**Holiday Inn Express Florida Mall**	◆◆◆	$70-$100 SAVE	645
278 / p. 598	AAA	**Hampton Inn-Florida Mall** - see color ad card insert	◆◆◆	$69-$89 SAVE	641
279 / p. 598		Fairfield Inn by Marriott-Orlando South	◆◆	$64	641
281 / p. 598	AAA	**Baymont Inn & Suites Orlando South** - see color ad p 626	◆◆◆	$59-$79 SAVE	626
282 / p. 598	AAA	**Holiday Homes of Orlando** - see color ad p 645	◆◆◆	$129-$269 SAVE	645
283 / p. 598	AAA	**Suburban Lodge of Orlando South Florida Mall**	◆◆	$219-$260 SAVE	661
284 / p. 598	AAA	**Quality Inn Airport**	◆◆	$59-$99 SAVE	653
285 / p. 598		Days Inn North of Universal	◆◆	$39-$79	634
286 / p. 598	AAA	**Sleep Inn & Suites Orlando International Airport**	◆◆	$69-$89 SAVE	661
287 / p. 598	AAA	**Holiday Inn Express Orlando Airport West -** see color ad p 647	◆◆◆	$59-$89 SAVE	645
288 / p. 598	AAA	**Best Western Airport Inn & Suites**	◆◆◆	$66-$90 SAVE	626
290 / p. 598		Howard Johnson Resort Hotel & Suites	◆◆	$60-$75	651
291 / p. 598	AAA	**Comfort Suites - Orlando Int. Airport -** see color ad card insert	◆◆◆	$99-$109 SAVE	631
293 / p. 598		Hampton Inn Airport - see color ad p 624	◆◆◆	$109-$139	641
294 / p. 598		Crowne Plaza Hotel and Resort Orlando Airport	◆◆◆	$159-$169	634
295 / p. 598	AAA	**Renaissance Orlando Hotel-Airport**	◆◆◆	$126-$153 SAVE	658
296 / p. 598	AAA	**AmeriSuites (Orlando Airport/Northwest) -** see color ad p 617	◆◆◆	$85-$135 SAVE	623
297 / p. 598		La Quinta Inn & Suites Orlando Airport North - see color ad p 652	◆◆◆	$59-$95	652
298 / p. 598		Country Inn & Suites By Carlson-Orlando International Airport - see color ad p 613	◆◆◆	$89-$129	632
299 / p. 598		Courtyard by Marriott Airport - see ad p 633	◆◆◆	$119-$139	632
300 / p. 598	AAA	**Holiday Inn Select Orlando International Airport** - see color ad opposite inside back cover, p 648	◆◆◆	$130-$150 SAVE	649
302 / p. 598	AAA	**Embassy Suites Orlando Airport** - see color ad p 637	◆◆◆	$109-$209 SAVE	635
303 / p. 598		Fairfield Inn by Marriott	◆◆◆	$99-$149	638

Spotter/Map Page Number	OA	**ORLANDO SOUTH** - Lodgings (continued)	Diamond Rating	Rate Range High Season	Listing Page
305 / p. 598	AAA	Hawthorn Suites Orlando Airport - see color ad p 642	◆◆◆	$69-$109 [SAVE]	643
306 / p. 598		Hilton Garden Inn Orlando International Airport - see color ad p 624	◆◆◆	$104-$134	644
308 / p. 598		Orlando Airport Marriott	◆◆◆	$149-$169	653
309 / p. 598	AAA	AmeriSuites (Orlando Airport/Northeast) - see color ad p 617	◆◆◆	$85-$135 [SAVE]	623
310 / p. 598	AAA	Sheraton Suites Orlando Airport	◆◆◆	$119-$149 [SAVE]	660
311 / p. 598	AAA	Hyatt Regency Orlando International Airport - see color ad p 651	◆◆◆	$105-$255 [SAVE]	651
313 / p. 598		The Villas of Grand Cypress	◆◆◆◆	$415-$2000	664
314 / p. 598	AAA	Ramada Inn All Suites at International Drive Center - see color ad p 658	◆◆◆	$129 [SAVE]	657
315 / p. 598		Sheraton's Vistana Villages - see color ad p 5	◆◆◆	$370-$440	660
316 / p. 598	AAA	Parc Corniche Condominium Suite Hotel	◆◆◆	$89-$129 [SAVE]	653
317 / p. 598	AAA	Crowne Plaza Hotel and Resort Orlando - see color ad p 633	◆◆◆	$119-$299 [SAVE]	633
320 / p. 598	AAA	Fairfield Inn at Marriott Village - see color ad p 717	◆◆◆	$69-$119 [SAVE]	638
322 / p. 598	AAA	Hawthorn Suites Hotel - see color ad card insert	◆◆◆	$129-$149 [SAVE]	642
324 / p. 598		Fairfield Orlando International Resort Club	◆◆	$100-$165	641
		ORLANDO SOUTH - Restaurants			
150 / p. 598		Emeril's Restaurant Orlando	◆◆◆	$20-$34	668
151 / p. 598		Jimmy Buffett's Margaritaville	◆◆	$8-$20	668
152 / p. 598		Latin Quarter	◆◆	$13-$30	669
153 / p. 598	AAA	NASCAR Cafe	◆◆	$7-$18	669
154 / p. 598		Bob Marley-A Tribute to Freedom	◆◆	$4-$11	666
155 / p. 598		Motown Cafe	◆◆	$8-$20	669
156 / p. 598		Pastamore'	◆◆	$9-$22	669
158 / p. 598		Pat O'Brien's	◆	$8-$12	669
159 / p. 598		Delfino Riviera	◆◆◆◆	$27-$38	667
160 / p. 598		Palm Restaurant	◆◆◆	$15-$34	669
168 / p. 598		BAJA Burrito Kitchen	◆	$4-$9	666
169 / p. 598		Le Coq au Vin	◆◆◆	$15-$24	669
171 / p. 598		Gain's German Restaurant	◆◆	$10-$21	668
172 / p. 598		Amigos	◆◆	$8-$15	666
173 / p. 598		Charley's Steak House	◆◆◆	$12-$28	667
174 / p. 598		Larry's Cedar River Seafood	◆◆	$9-$16	669
175 / p. 598		Chatham's Place	◆◆◆	$20-$38	667
176 / p. 598		Roy's	◆◆◆	$20-$28	670
177 / p. 598		Boston Lobster Feast	◆	$16-$30	667
178 / p. 598		Murphy's Chop House	◆◆◆	$19-$29	669
179 / p. 598	AAA	Siam Orchid	◆◆◆	$10-$18	670
180 / p. 598		Wild Jack's Steaks & BBQ	◆◆	$10-$22	670
181 / p. 598		Shamiana	◆	$9-$15	670

Spotter/Map Page Number	OA	ORLANDO SOUTH - Restaurants (continued)	Diamond Rating	Rate Range High Season	Listing Page
182 / p. 598		Fishbones	◆◆	$13-$40	668
183 / p. 598		Italianni's Restaurant	◆◆	$9-$20	668
184 / p. 598		A Taste of Japan	◆◆	$11-$25	666
185 / p. 598		Charley's Steak House	◆◆	$13-$35	667
186 / p. 598		Bergamo's Italian Restaurant	◆◆◆	$15-$39	666
187 / p. 598		Vito's Chop House	◆◆◆	$14-$33	670
188 / p. 598		Cafe Tu Tu Tango	◆◆	$4-$9	667
189 / p. 598		1-6-8 Restaurant	◆◆	$6-$22	666
190 / p. 598		Charlie's Lobster House	◆◆	$16-$40	667
192 / p. 598		The Butcher Shop Steak House	◆◆	$16-$30	667
193 / p. 598		Race Rock Restaurant	◆◆	$6-$17	670
194 / p. 598		Ran-Getsu of Tokyo	◆◆	$14-$34	670
196 / p. 598		Ming Court	◆◆◆	$12-$33	669
197 / p. 598		Bahama Breeze	◆◆	$8-$19	666
198 / p. 598		Everglades	◆◆◆	$17-$30	668
199 / p. 598	◬	**Jack's Place**	◆◆◆	$16-$28	668
200 / p. 598		Capriccio	◆◆◆	$12-$25	667
201 / p. 598		Dux	◆◆◆◆	$20-$40	668
204 / p. 598	◬	**Ciao Italia Ristorante Italiano**	◆◆◆	$15-$30	667
206 / p. 598		Atlantis	◆◆◆◆	$27-$35	666
207 / p. 598		Hemisphere	◆◆◆	$17-$28	668
208 / p. 598		The Black Swan	◆◆◆◆	$25-$40	666
209 / p. 598		La Piaza	◆◆	$7-$16	668
		LAKE BUENA VISTA - Lodgings			
345 / p. 598	◬	**Disney's Grand Floridian Resort & Spa** - see color ad starting on p 721	◆◆◆◆	$329-$815	725
346 / p. 598	◬	**Disney's Polynesian Resort** - see color ad starting on p 721	◆◆◆	$299-$650	725
347 / p. 598	◬	**Disney's Fort Wilderness Resort** - see color ad starting on p 721	◆◆◆	$224-$314	720
348 / p. 598	◬	**Disney's Wilderness Lodge & Villas** - see color ad starting on p 721	◆◆◆	$194-$920	726
349 / p. 598	◬	**Disney's Contemporary Resort** - see color ad starting on p 721	◆◆◆	$234-$525	720
350 / p. 598	◬	**Grosvenor Resort at Walt Disney World Resort** - see color ad p 729	◆◆◆	$110-$145 SAVE	728
351 / p. 598		PerriHouse Bed & Breakfast Inn	◆◆◆	$89-$149	731
352 / p. 598	◬	**Hampton Inn Lake Buena Vista** - see color ad card insert	◆◆◆	$109 SAVE	728
355 / p. 598	◬	**Disney's Port Orleans-Riverside Resort** - see color ad starting on p 721	◆◆◆	$133-$219	725
357 / p. 598	◬	**Disney's Port Orleans-French Quarter Resort** - see color ad starting on p 721	◆◆◆	$133-$219	725
358 / p. 598	◬	**Disney's Old Key West Resort** - see color ad starting on p 721	◆◆◆	$249-$755	725
361 / p. 598	◬	**Doubletree Club Hotel Lake Buena Vista** - see color ad p 726	◆◆◆	$79-$169 SAVE	726
362 / p. 598	◬	**Sheraton Safari Hotel** - see color ad p 733	◆◆◆	$135-$205 SAVE	733

Spotter/Map Page Number	OA	**LAKE BUENA VISTA -** Lodgings (continued)	Diamond Rating	Rate Range High Season	Listing Page
364 / p. 598	AAA	Summerfield Suites by Wyndham-Orlando/Lake Buena Vista - see color ad p 662	◆◆◆	$89-$289 SAVE	735
365 / p. 598	AAA	Westgate Blue Tree Resort	◆◆◆	$109-$239 SAVE	736
367 / p. 598	AAA	Homewood Suites Hotel By Hilton-Lake Buena Vista - see color ad card insert	◆◆◆	$99-$159 SAVE	730
368 / p. 598	AAA	Courtyard by Marriott Lake Buena Vista Vista Centre - see color ad p 718	◆◆◆	$79-$129 SAVE	718
370 / p. 598		Sierra Suites Hotel-Lake Buena Vista - see color ad p 735	◆◆◆	$79-$139	735
371 / p. 598	AAA	Days Inn Lake Buena Vista Hotel - see color ad p 718	◆◆	$85-$178 SAVE	719
373 / p. 598	AAA	Embassy Suites Hotel-Lake Buena Vista Resort - see color ad p 728	◆◆◆	$169-$299 SAVE	727
374 / p. 598		Comfort Inn Lake Buena Vista - see color ad p 655	◆◆	$39-$99	715
376 / p. 598	AAA	Radisson Inn Lake Buena Vista	◆◆◆	$89-$159 SAVE	733
377 / p. 598	AAA	RIU Orlando Hotel - see color ad p 734	◆◆◆	$89-$125 SAVE	733
379 / p. 598	AAA	Disney's Yacht & Beach Club Resorts - see color ad starting on p 721	◆◆◆◆	$289-$990	726
380 / p. 598	AAA	Walt Disney World Swan and Dolphin	◆◆◆◆	$385-$3100 SAVE	736
382 / p. 598	AAA	Disney's Coronado Springs Resort - see color ad starting on p 721	◆◆◆	$133-$219	720
383 / p. 598	AAA	Wyndham Palace Resort & Spa	◆◆◆	$219-$249 SAVE	736
385 / p. 598	AAA	Disney's BoardWalk Resort - see color ad starting on p 721	◆◆◆	$289-$990	720
386 / p. 598	AAA	Disney's Caribbean Beach Resort - see color ad starting on p 721	◆◆◆	$133-$219	720
388 / p. 598	AAA	Courtyard by Marriott-in the Walt Disney World Resort - see color ad p 717	◆◆◆	$139-$159 SAVE	716
390 / p. 598	AAA	Hyatt Regency Grand Cypress - see color ad p 731	◆◆◆◆	$109-$365 SAVE	731
391 / p. 598		Country Inn & Suites By Carlson - see color ad p 613, p 716, p 715, p 681, p 629	◆◆◆	$99-$149	716
392 / p. 598	AAA	Best Western Lake Buena Vista Resort Hotel in the Walt Disney World Resorts	◆◆◆	$109-$169 SAVE	714
394 / p. 598		Doubletree Guest Suites in the Walt Disney World Resort - see color ad p 727	◆◆◆	$159-$249	727
395 / p. 598	AAA	Hotel Royal Plaza in the Disney World Resort - see color ad p 730	◆◆◆	$79-$199 SAVE	731
396 / p. 598	AAA	Courtyard by Marriott at Marriott Village - see color ad p 717 & p 633	◆◆◆	$79-$129 SAVE	716
397 / p. 598	AAA	SpringHill Suites at The Marriott Village - see color ad p 717	◆◆◆	$89-$149 SAVE	735
398 / p. 598	AAA	Hilton in the Walt Disney World Resort	◆◆◆◆	$99-$325 SAVE	728
399 / p. 598	AAA	Holiday Inn-SunSpree Resort-Lake Buena Vista - see color ad p 730, opposite inside back cover	◆◆◆	$89-$129 SAVE	730
401 / p. 598	AAA	Caribe Royale Resort Suites & Villas	◆◆◆	$119-$229 SAVE	715
402 / p. 598		Embassy Vacation Resort Grand Beach	◆◆◆	$159-$269	727
404 / p. 598	AAA	Buena Vista Suites - see color ad p 715	◆◆◆	$159-$179 SAVE	714
406 / p. 598	AAA	Bryan's Spanish Cove - see color ad p 694, p 640	◆◆◆	$149-$219 SAVE	714
407 / p. 598		Sheraton's Vistana Resort - see color ad p 5	◆◆◆	$380-$450	735
409 / p. 598	AAA	Orlando World Center Marriott Resort & Convention Center	◆◆◆◆	$249-$349 SAVE	731

Spotter/Map Page Number	OA	LAKE BUENA VISTA - Lodgings (continued)	Diamond Rating	Rate Range High Season	Listing Page
410 / p. 598	AAA	Holiday Inn Family Suites Resort Lake Buena Vista - see color ad p 729, opposite inside back cover	◆◆◆	$129-$169 SAVE	729
412 / p. 598	AAA	Disney's All Star Sports - see color ad starting on p 721	◆◆◆	$77-$124	719
414 / p. 598	AAA	Disney's All Star Music - see color ad starting on p 721	◆◆◆	$77-$124	719
416 / p. 598	AAA	Disney's All Star Movies Resort - see color ad starting on p 721	◆◆◆	$77-$124	719
417 / p. 598	AAA	Disney's Animal Kingdom Lodge - see color ad starting on p 721	◆◆◆	$204-$595	719
		LAKE BUENA VISTA - Restaurants			
213 / p. 598		Cinderella's Royal Table	◆◆	$19-$26	737
216 / p. 598		The Crystal Palace	◆	$10-$20	737
217 / p. 598		Liberty Tree Tavern	◆◆	$10-$20	737
219 / p. 598		The Plaza Restaurant	◆	$8-$10	738
220 / p. 598		Tony's Town Square Restaurant	◆◆	$17-$22	738
221 / p. 598		Citricos	◆◆◆	$25-$40	737
222 / p. 598		Narcoosee's	◆◆	$21-$32	738
223 / p. 598		Victoria & Albert's	◆◆◆◆◆	$85-$100	739
224 / p. 598		California Grill	◆◆◆	$20-$30	737
225 / p. 598		Artist Point	◆◆◆	$17-$28	736
226 / p. 598		Crab House Seafood Restaurant	◆◆	$14-$25	737
227 / p. 598		Boatwright's Dining Hall	◆◆	$11-$18	736
228 / p. 598		New York China Buffet	◆	$5-$12	738
229 / p. 598		Arthur's 27	◆◆◆◆	$31-$39	736
230 / p. 598		Finn's Grill	◆◆	$19-$26	737
231 / p. 598		Fulton's Crab House	◆◆	$15-$42	737
232 / p. 598		Bongos Cuban Cafe	◆◆	$12-$24	736
233 / p. 598		Yachtsman's Steak House	◆◆◆	$22-$32	739
234 / p. 598		Pebbles/Lake Buena Vista	◆◆	$11-$26	738
235 / p. 598		Portobello Yacht Club	◆◆	$15-$30	738
236 / p. 598		Palio	◆◆	$19-$33	738
237 / p. 598		Restaurant Marrakesh	◆◆	$16-$25	738
238 / p. 598		Flying Fish Cafe	◆◆◆	$18-$26	737
239 / p. 598		Rain Forest Cafe	◆	$14-$23	738
240 / p. 598		Spoodles	◆◆	$18-$29	738
241 / p. 598		Jiko	◆◆◆◆	$18-$30	737
		KISSIMMEE - Lodgings			
440 / p. 598	AAA	Liki Tiki Village A Club Navigo Resort - see color ad p 694, p 640	◆◆◆	$99-$369 SAVE	695
441 / p. 598		Orange Lake Resort & Country Club	◆◆◆	$105-$325	698
443 / p. 598	AAA	Orbit One Vacation Villas - see color ad p 694, p 640	◆◆◆	$139-$199 SAVE	698
444 / p. 598	AAA	Days Inn - see color ad p 684	◆◆	$30-$150 SAVE	683

Spotter/Map Page Number	OA	KISSIMMEE - Lodgings (continued)	Diamond Rating	Rate Range High Season	Listing Page
445 / p. 598	AAA	Holiday Inn Maingate West - see color ad opposite inside back cover	◆◆◆	$49-$109 SAVE	689
446 / p. 598	AAA	Ramada Inn Resort Maingate	◆◆◆	$79-$129 SAVE	702
448 / p. 598	AAA	Knights Inn-Maingate - see color ad p 680	◆	$42-$99 SAVE	695
450 / p. 598	AAA	AmeriHost Resort	◆◆◆	$79-$99 SAVE	678
452 / p. 598	AAA	Renaissance WorldGate Hotel - see ad p 704	◆◆◆	$119-$189	703
453 / p. 598	AAA	Clarion Maingate - see color ad p 681	◆◆◆	$79-$109 SAVE	681
455 / p. 598	AAA	Hampton Inn Main Gate West - see color ad card insert	◆◆◆	$59-$89 SAVE	688
456 / p. 598	AAA	La Quinta Inn Lakeside - see color ad p 696	◆◆◆	$108-$188 SAVE	695
457 / p. 598	AAA	Quality Inn Main Gate West - see color ad p 701	◆◆	$49-$79 SAVE	700
458 / p. 598	AAA	Sweetwater-Bright Star Resorts & Condominiums - see color ad p 639, p 640, p 178, p 686, p 707	◆◆◆	$79-$119 SAVE	707
459 / p. 598		Motel 6 - #0436	◆	$37-$53	698
460 / p. 598	AAA	Comfort Inn-Maingate West - see color ad p 682	◆◆◆	$30-$140 SAVE	681
461 / p. 598		Wyndham Palms-Absolute Premier Vacation Homes	◆◆◆	$155-$235	709
462 / p. 598		Wyndham Palms-Regent Vacations & Management	◆◆◆	$79-$289	713
463 / p. 598	AAA	Howard Johnson Maingate Resort West - see color ad p 693	◆◆	$39-$62 SAVE	693
464 / p. 598	AAA	Sleep Inn Maingate - see color ad p 705	◆◆	$49-$89 SAVE	704
465 / p. 598		Rolling Hills-Regent Vacations & Management	◆◆◆	$79-$289	704
466 / p. 598	AAA	Travelodge Hotel Maingate	◆◆	$45-$59 SAVE	707
467 / p. 598	AAA	Lindfields Reserve	◆◆◆	$245-$333 SAVE	695
469 / p. 598		The Villages at Mango Key	◆◆◆	$125-$175	709
470 / p. 598		Indian Creek-Absolute Premier Vacation Homes	◆◆◆	$155-$235	694
471 / p. 598	AAA	Comfort Suites MainGate Resort - see color ad p 683	◆◆◆	$63-$150 SAVE	682
472 / p. 598	AAA	Super 8 Motel Maingate	◆◆	$35-$55 SAVE	706
473 / p. 598	AAA	Masters Inn-Main Gate	◆◆	$39-$59 SAVE	698
474 / p. 598	AAA	Westgate Towers/Westgate Vacation Villas	◆◆◆	$158-$302 SAVE	709
475 / p. 598	AAA	Orlando's Key Vacation Homes	◆◆◆	$95-$250 SAVE	699
476 / p. 598		Indian Creek-Regent Vacations & Management	◆◆◆	$79-$289	694
477 / p. 598		Wyndham Palms Resort - see color ad p 713	◆◆◆	$225-$409	713
478 / p. 598		Indian Point-Absolute Premier Vacation Homes	◆◆◆	$155-$235	694
479 / p. 598	AAA	Ramada Plaza Hotel and Inn Gateway - see color ad p 702	◆◆◆	$59-$99 SAVE	703
480 / p. 598		Indian Ridge Oaks-Absolute Premier Vacation Homes	◆◆◆	$155-$235	694
481 / p. 598	AAA	Holiday Inn-Nikki Bird Resort-Maingate - see color ad opposite inside back cover, p 690	◆◆◆	$59-$99 SAVE	689
482 / p. 598	AAA	Hyatt Orlando - see color ad p 651	◆◆◆	$85-$175 SAVE	693
483 / p. 598		Econo Lodge Maingate Resort	◆◆	$49-$59	685
484 / p. 598		Hampton Inn-Maingate East - see color ad p 646	◆◆◆	$69-$109	688

Spotter/Map Page Number	OA	KISSIMMEE - Lodgings (continued)	Diamond Rating	Rate Range High Season	Listing Page
485 / p. 598		Homewood Suites by Hilton - see color ad p 646	▽▽▽	$129-$199	691
487 / p. 598	AAA	Radisson Resort Parkway - see color ad p 701	▽▽▽	$89-$109 SAVE	702
488 / p. 598	AAA	Parkway International - see color ad p 694	▽▽▽	$135-$219 SAVE	699
490 / p. 598	AAA	Park Inn & Suites Orlando Maingate East - see color ad p 699	▽▽	$79-$99 SAVE	699
491 / p. 598	AAA	Howard Johnson Maingate East - see color ad p 628	▽▽	$47-$100 SAVE	693
493 / p. 598	AAA	Super 8 Motel Maingate - see color ad p 706	▽▽	$49-$69 SAVE	706
495 / p. 598	AAA	Quality Suites Maingate East - see color ad p 688	▽▽▽	$89-$199 SAVE	701
496 / p. 598	AAA	Tropical Palms Resort - see color ad starting on p 710	▽▽	$59-$109 SAVE	709
497 / p. 598	AAA	Comfort Suites Maingate East - see color ad p 682	▽▽▽	$75-$250 SAVE	682
499 / p. 598	AAA	Days Suites/Main Gate East of Walt Disney World Resort - see color ad p 685	▽▽	$69-$189 SAVE	683
500 / p. 598		Holiday Inn Hotel & Suites Main Gate East - see color ad opposite inside back cover	▽▽▽	$99-$139	689
502 / p. 598		Motel 6 - #0464	▽	$37-$53	698
503 / p. 598	AAA	Travelodge Hotel Main Gate East	▽▽	$39-$69 SAVE	708
504 / p. 598		Fairfield Orlando at Cypress Palms	▽▽▽	$125-$185	685
505 / p. 598	AAA	Best Western-Eastgate - see color ad p 678	▽▽	$49-$158 SAVE	678
506 / p. 598	AAA	Masters Inn-Kissimmee	▽▽	$35-$49 SAVE	698
507 / p. 598	AAA	Magic Castle Inn & Suites Maingate - see color ad p 697	▽	$40-$53 SAVE	697
509 / p. 598	AAA	AmeriSuites at Calypso Cay - see color ad p 617	▽▽▽	$69-$149 SAVE	678
510 / p. 598	AAA	Howard Johnson Enchantedland Resort Hotel	▽▽▽	$50-$80 SAVE	691
511 / p. 598	AAA	Fantasy World Club Villas - see color ad p 686	▽▽▽	$165-$195 SAVE	686
513 / p. 598	AAA	Red Roof Inn	▽	$40-$50 SAVE	703
514 / p. 598	AAA	Holiday Villas - see color ad p 690	▽▽▽	$159-$269 SAVE	690
516 / p. 598		DoubleTree Resort Orlando Villas at Maingate - see color ad p 727	▽▽▽	$129-$179	683
517 / p. 598	AAA	Golden Link Motel	▽▽	$29-$59 SAVE	687
518 / p. 598	AAA	Baymont Inn	▽▽	$54-$94 SAVE	678
519 / p. 598		Wonderland Inn	▽▽▽	$69-$159	709
520 / p. 598	AAA	Travelodge Suites Kissimmee East Gate Orange - see ad p 647 & color ad p 708	▽▽	$69-$129 SAVE	709
521 / p. 598	AAA	Star Island Resort & Club - see color ad p 679	▽▽▽	$127-$285 SAVE	705
523 / p. 598	AAA	Clarion Suites Resort World - see color ad p 679	▽▽▽	$89-$225 SAVE	681
525 / p. 598	AAA	Royal Oaks of Kissimmee	▽▽▽	$109-$143 SAVE	704
526 / p. 598	AAA	Sun Inn & Suites	▽▽	$32-$89 SAVE	706
527 / p. 598		Quality Inn Lake Cecile - see color ad p 700	▽▽▽	$39-$89	699
529 / p. 598	AAA	Ramada Inn Resort Eastgate	▽▽	$49-$79 SAVE	702
533 / p. 598	AAA	Howard Johnson Express Inn & Suites Lakefront Park - see color ad p 692	▽	$59-$119 SAVE	691
534 / p. 598	AAA	Record (Parkside) Inn & Suites - see ad p 703	▽▽	$32-$59 SAVE	703

Spotter/Map Page Number	OA	KISSIMMEE - Lodgings (continued)	Diamond Rating	Rate Range High Season	Listing Page
535 / p. 598		Country Inn & Suites - see color ad p 613	▽▽▽	$69-$149	682
536 / p. 598		Alhambra Resort	▽▽▽	$100	678
538 / p. 598	AAA	**Travelodge Suites Maingate** - see color ad p 680	▽▽	$45-$99 SAVE	709
539 / p. 598	AAA	**Lake Cecile Suites & Resort Hotel**	▽▽▽	$99-$139 SAVE	695
540 / p. 598	AAA	**Super 8 Motel Lakeside**	▽▽	$39-$69 SAVE	706
543 / p. 598	AAA	**Four Winds Motel**	▽▽	$49-$69 SAVE	687
546 / p. 598		Four Points Sheraton Orlando Kissimmee	▽▽▽	$98	687
547 / p. 598	AAA	**Royal Palms-Bright Star Resorts & Condominiums** - see color ad p 639, p 640, p 178, p 686, p 707	▽▽▽	$79-$119 SAVE	704
548 / p. 598		Oak Plantation - see color ad p 5	▽▽▽	$149-$219	698
549 / p. 598	AAA	**Super 8 Motel Suites**	▽▽	$39-$69 SAVE	707
550 / p. 598		Sun Set Lakes-Absolute Premier Vacation Homes	▽▽▽	$155-$235	706
551 / p. 598	AAA	**Holiday Inn Kissimmee Downtown** - see color ad opposite inside back cover & ad p 689	▽▽▽	$70-$90 SAVE	689
552 / p. 598	AAA	**Summerfield Condo Resort**	▽▽▽	$99-$149 SAVE	705
553 / p. 598	AAA	**Ritz Express Inn & Suites**	▽▽	$40-$70 SAVE	704
557 / p. 598		Econo Lodge Maingate East - see color ad p 700	▽▽	$39-$69	683
558 / p. 598	AAA	**Howard Johnson Express Inn Parkside**	▽▽	$39-$99 SAVE	691
559 / p. 598	AAA	**Magic Castle Inn & Suites Eastgate** - see color ad p 697	▽	$37-$50 SAVE	696
563 / p. 598	AAA	**Flamingo Inn** - see color ad p 679	▽▽	$29-$39 SAVE	686
566 / p. 598	AAA	**Stadium Inn & Suites**	▽▽	$60 SAVE	705
568 / p. 598		Quality Inn Conference Center	▽▽	$49-$59	699
569 / p. 598		Lago Vista Resort	▽▽	$75-$129	695
570 / p. 598		The Kingstonian Hotels & Resorts	▽▽	$56-$99	695
572 / p. 598	AAA	**Holiday Inn Express**	▽▽▽	$70-$99 SAVE	688
573 / p. 598		Days Inn-Kissimmee	▽	$45-$129	683
575 / p. 598	AAA	**Howard Johnson Hotel** - see ad p 691	▽▽	$40-$89 SAVE	691
577 / p. 598	AAA	**Best Western-Kissimmee** - see color ad p 680	▽▽	$42-$99 SAVE	679
579 / p. 598	AAA	**Riviera Motel**	▽	$27-$38 SAVE	704
580 / p. 598		Espirit-Absolute Premier Vacation Homes	▽▽▽	$155-$235	685
581 / p. 598		Greater Groves-Absolute Premier Vacation Homes	▽▽▽	$155-$235	688
		KISSIMMEE - Restaurants			
242 / p. 598		Key W. Kool's Open Pit Grill	▽▽	$8-$28	714
243 / p. 598		Giordano's	▽	$7-$11	713
245 / p. 598	AAA	**Twin Dragons Restaurant**	▽▽	$6-$17	714
247 / p. 598		Pacino's Italian Ristorante	▽▽	$10-$23	714
		DAVENPORT - Lodgings			
590 / p. 598	AAA	**Best Western Central Florida**	▽▽▽	$99-$125 SAVE	676
591 / p. 598		Ramada Inn Southgate	▽▽	$89	676

Spotter/Map Page Number	OA	DAVENPORT - Lodgings (continued)	Diamond Rating	Rate Range High Season	Listing Page
593 / p. 598	AAA	Reunion Inn	◈◈	$60-$80 SAVE	676
594 / p. 598		Holiday Inn Express Hotel & Suites	◈◈◈	$59-$99	676
595 / p. 598		Hampton Inn Orlando-S of Walt Disney Resort	◈◈◈	$69-$119	676
598 / p. 598	AAA	Prestige Vacation Homes - see color ad p 639, p 654, p 640, p 178, p 686	◈◈◈	$139-$309 SAVE	676
600 / p. 598	AAA	Super 8 Motel Maingate South	◈◈	$39-$120 SAVE	676
602 / p. 598	AAA	Villas at Polo Park	◈◈	$69-$159 SAVE	677
		ST. CLOUD - Lodgings			
615 / p. 598	AAA	Budget Inn of St Cloud	◈◈	$35-$45 SAVE	747

 Do you know the facts?

AAA publishes the Digest of Motor Laws to assist traveling motorists. Filled with facts and information, this one-of-a-kind compilation includes a comprehensive description of the laws that govern motor vehicle registration and operation in the United States and Canada. This sixty-eighth edition guide has a new, easy-to-read format with graphics, state-by-state tax summary tables and detailed information on occupant protection laws, driver licensing laws, automated enforcement laws and motor vehicle fees and taxes.

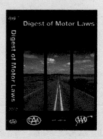

You can easily locate various licensing and motor laws governing the states in which you are traveling. In addition to vehicle registration and operation laws, the Digest contains information and facts about alcohol laws, traffic safety laws and more.

Call your local club or 1-877-AAA-BOOK to obtain a copy of the Digest.

The book retails for $13.95.

ORLANDO NORTH (See map p. 590; index p. 592)

─────── WHERE TO STAY ───────

BEST WESTERN ORLANDO WEST
Phone: (407)841-8600 **14**

12/24-4/29	2P: $69-$125	XP: $10	F12
4/30-10/31	2P: $59-$99	XP: $10	F12
12/1-12/23 & 11/1-11/30	2P: $49-$79	XP: $10	F12

Location: I-4, exit 84, 1.5 mi w on SR 50, 0.4 mi e of SR 423. Located on busy highway. 2014 W Colonial Dr 32804.
Small-scale Hotel **Fax:** 407/843-7080. **Facility:** 110 one-bedroom standard units, some with efficiencies. 2 stories, interior corridors. *Bath:* combo or shower only. **Parking:** on-site. **Terms:** cancellation fee imposed, [BP] & [MAP] meal plans available, small pets only ($25 deposit, $5 extra charge). **Amenities:** voice mail, safes (fee), irons, hair dryers. **Dining:** 7 am-2:30 pm, Sat-1:30 pm, Sun 7 am-noon. **Pool(s):** outdoor. **Guest Services:** valet and coin laundry. **Business Services:** meeting rooms, fax (fee). **Cards:** AX, DC, DS, MC, VI.

SOME UNITS FEE FEE

(See map p. 590)

COMFORT INN-NORTH

Phone: (407)629-4000   [25]

12/24-4/22 [CP]	1P: $79-$125	2P: $79-$125
4/23-11/30 [CP]	1P: $65-$69	2P: $65-$75
12/1-12/23 [CP]	1P: $59-$69	2P: $59-$75

Location: I-4, exit 88, 0.4 mi w on SR 423. 830 Lee Rd 32810. Fax: 407/645-2809. **Facility:** 145 one-bedroom
Small-scale Hotel standard units. 5 stories, interior corridors. **Parking:** on-site. **Terms:** cancellation fee imposed, [ECP] meal plan available, package plans, small pets only ($25 fee, $10 extra charge). **Amenities:** video games, voice mail, safes (fee), irons, hair dryers. **Pool(s):** heated outdoor. **Leisure Activities:** sauna, whirlpool. Fee: game room. **Guest Services:** coin laundry. **Business Services:** meeting rooms. **Cards:** AX, DS, MC, VI. **Special Amenities:** free continental breakfast and free local telephone calls. (See color ad p 612)

SOME UNITS

COMFORT SUITES DOWNTOWN

Phone: (407)228-4007   [23]

12/1-4/30 [ECP]	1P: $79-$119	2P: $79-$119
5/1-11/30 [ECP]	1P: $69-$109	2P: $69-$109

Location: I-4, exit 85, just e on Princeton, then just n. 2416 N Orange Ave 32804. Fax: 407/228-3820. **Facility:** 78
Small-scale Hotel whirlpools. 3 stories, interior corridors. Bath: combo or shower only. **Parking:** on-site. **Terms:** check-in 4 pm, 3 day cancellation notice, package plans - weekends. **Amenities:** voice mail, hair dryers. Some: irons. **Pool(s):** heated outdoor. **Leisure Activities:** whirlpool. **Guest Services:** coin laundry, area transportation-Florida Hospital. **Business Services:** meeting rooms, fax (fee). **Cards:** AX, CB, DC, DS, MC, VI. **Special Amenities:** free continental breakfast and free local telephone calls.

SOME UNITS
FEE

COMFORT SUITES UCF-RESEARCH PARK

Phone: (407)737-7303   [10]

1/31-4/15 [ECP]	1P: $99-$179	2P: $99-$179	XP: $10	F12
4/16-10/16 [ECP]	1P: $79-$139	2P: $79-$139	XP: $10	F12
12/1-1/30 [ECP]	1P: $79-$129	2P: $79-$129	XP: $10	F12
10/17-11/30 [ECP]	1P: $69-$129	2P: $69-$129	XP: $10	F12

Small-scale Hotel **Location:** On SR 434 (Alafaya Tr); 1.6 mi n of SR 408, exit 21; 0.4 mi n of SR 50. 12101 Challenger Pkwy 32826. Fax: 407/737-7304. **Facility:** 70 one-bedroom standard units, some with whirlpools. 3 stories, interior corridors. Bath: combo or shower only. **Parking:** on-site. **Terms:** cancellation fee imposed. **Amenities:** dual phone lines, voice mail, irons, hair dryers. **Pool(s):** outdoor. **Leisure Activities:** exercise room. **Guest Services:** valet and coin laundry. **Business Services:** meeting rooms, business center. **Cards:** AX, DC, DS, MC, VI. **Special Amenities:** free continental breakfast and free local telephone calls.

SOME UNITS

(See map p. 590)

THE COURTYARD AT LAKE LUCERNE
Phone: (407)648-5188 **18**
All Year [ECP]   1P: $89-$215   2P: $89-$215   XP: $15   F12
Historic Country Inn **Location:** At end of Orange Ave off-ramp eastbound (East-West Expwy); I-4, exit Anderson St, 0.5 mi e to Delany, then 0.5 mi s. 211 N Lucerne Cir 32801. Fax: 407/246-1368. **Facility:** The Courtyard at Lake Lucerne is a collection of four buildings from varied architectural periods, each furnished accordingly. 30 units. 15 one-bedroom standard units, some with whirlpools. 15 one-bedroom suites. 2-3 stories, interior/exterior corridors. *Bath:* combo or shower only. **Parking:** on-site. **Amenities:** *Some:* hair dryers. **Guest Services:** complimentary evening beverages. **Business Services:** meeting rooms, fax (fee). **Cards:** AX, CB, DC, MC, VI.

SOME UNITS

COURTYARD BY MARRIOTT DOWNTOWN
Phone: (407)996-1000 **26**
9/16-11/30   1P: $119-$139   2P: $119-$139   XP: $10   F18
12/31-3/31   1P: $109-$129   2P: $109-$129   XP: $10   F18
12/1-12/30 & 4/1-9/15   1P: $89-$109   2P: $89-$109   XP: $10   F18
Small-scale Hotel **Location:** I-4, exit 83B, just e; just n of SR 50 (Colonial Dr). 730 N Magnolia Ave 32803. Fax: 407/996-1001. **Facility:** 200 units. 189 one-bedroom standard units, some with whirlpools. 11 one-bedroom suites. 6 stories, interior corridors. *Bath:* combo or shower only. **Parking:** dual phone lines, voice mail, irons, hair dryers. **Dining:** 6:30-10:30 am, Sat & Sun 7-11 am. **Pool(s):** outdoor. **Leisure Activities:** whirlpool, exercise room. **Guest Services:** complimentary laundry. **Business Services:** meeting rooms, fax (fee). **Cards:** AX, CB, DC, DS, JC, MC, VI.

SOME UNITS

COURTYARD BY MARRIOTT UCF
Phone: 407/277-7676 **7**
All Year   1P: $119   2P: $119
Small-scale Hotel **Location:** On University Blvd, 2.2 mi e of SR 417, exit 32A, just w of SR 434 (Alafaya Tr). Located at Collegiate Square. 12000 Collegiate Way 32817. Fax: 407/277-5710. **Facility:** 123 units. 119 one-bedroom standard units. 4 one-bedroom suites ($139). 4 stories, interior corridors. *Bath:* combo or shower only. **Parking:** on-site. **Terms:** [BP] & [CP] meal plans available. **Amenities:** high-speed Internet (fee), voice mail, irons, hair dryers. **Pool(s):** heated outdoor. **Leisure Activities:** whirlpool, exercise room. **Guest Services:** valet and coin laundry. **Business Services:** meeting rooms, PC, fax (fee). **Cards:** AX, DC, DS, JC, MC, VI.

SOME UNITS

EMBASSY SUITES ORLANDO DOWNTOWN
Phone: (407)841-1000 **16**
1/5-4/17   1P: $125-$161   2P: $125-$161   XP: $15   F18
9/7-11/30   1P: $116-$161   2P: $116-$161   XP: $15   F18
12/1-1/4   1P: $116-$152   2P: $116-$152   XP: $15   F18
4/18-9/6   1P: $107-$152   2P: $107-$152   XP: $15   F18
Small-scale Hotel **Location:** I-4, exit 82C, 0.3 mi e on Anderson, then 0.3 mi n on Rosalind. 191 E Pine St 32801. Fax: 407/841-0010. **Facility:** 167 one-bedroom suites, some with whirlpools. 7 stories, interior corridors. *Bath:* combo or shower only. **Parking:** valet. **Terms:** check-in 4 pm, cancellation fee imposed, [BP] meal plan available. **Amenities:** video games, dual phone lines, voice mail, irons, hair dryers. **Pool(s):** heated outdoor. **Leisure Activities:** whirlpool, exercise room. **Guest Services:** gift shop, complimentary evening beverages, valet and coin laundry. **Business Services:** conference facilities, business center. **Cards:** AX, CB, DC, DS, MC, VI. *(See color ad below)*

(See map p. 590)

FOUR POINTS SHERATON ORLANDO DOWNTOWN

			Phone: 407/841-3220	11
1/6-3/28 [BP]	1P: $109-$149	2P: $109-$149	XP: $10	F18
9/16-11/30 [BP]	1P: $99-$139	2P: $99-$139	XP: $10	F18
12/1-1/5 & 3/29-9/15 [BP]	1P: $89-$119	2P: $89-$119	XP: $10	F18

Small-scale Hotel   **Location:** I-4, exit 83A (Robinson St) eastbound; exit US 17-92 and SR 50 westbound, s on Orange Ave to Washington St, then just e. 151 E Washington St Ave 32801. Fax: 407/648-4758. **Facility:** 250 units. 206 one-bedroom standard units. 44 one-bedroom suites, some with whirlpools. 5 stories, interior/exterior corridors. *Bath:* combo or shower only. **Parking:** valet. **Terms:** package plans. **Amenities:** high-speed Internet, dual phone lines, voice mail, irons, hair dryers. *Fee:* video games, safes. **Pool(s):** heated outdoor. **Leisure Activities:** exercise room. **Guest Services:** gift shop, valet laundry. **Business Services:** conference facilities, business center. **Cards:** AX, CB, DC, DS, JC, MC, VI.

SOME UNITS

HAMPTON INN & SUITES/ORLANDO EAST-UCF AREA

Phone: (407)282-0029   6

All Year [ECP]   1P: $99-$109

Location: 2.2 mi e of SR 417 on University Blvd, then just n. Located in Quadrangle Office Park. 3450 Quadrangle Blvd 32817. Fax: 407/206-3001. **Facility:** 110 units. 76 one-bedroom standard units. 34 one-bedroom suites ($129) with efficiencies. 3 stories, interior corridors. *Bath:* shower only. **Parking:** on-site. **Terms:** 14 day cancellation notice. **Amenities:** dual phone lines, voice mail, irons, hair dryers. *Some:* CD players. **Pool(s):** heated outdoor. **Leisure Activities:** whirlpool, exercise room. **Guest Services:** complimentary evening beverages: Mon-Thurs, valet and coin laundry. **Business Services:** meeting rooms, fax (fee). **Cards:** AX, CB, DC, DS, MC, VI.

Motel

SOME UNITS

HILTON GARDEN INN ORLANDO EAST/UCF

Phone: (407)992-5000   3

All Year   1P: $70-$140   2P: $70-$140   F18

Location: Just n of SR 50; 1.4 mi n of SR 408 (East-West Expwy). 1959 N Alafaya Tr 32826. Fax: 407/992-7000. **Facility:** 122 units. 116 one-bedroom standard units. 6 one-bedroom suites. 3 stories, interior corridors. *Bath:* combo or shower only. **Parking:** on-site. **Terms:** 3 day cancellation notice, [BP], [CP] & [ECP] meal plans available, 18% service charge. **Amenities:** video games (fee), dual phone lines, voice mail, irons, hair dryers. **Dining:** 6 am-11 & 5-10 pm, wine/beer only. **Pool(s):** heated outdoor. **Leisure Activities:** whirlpool, exercise room. **Guest Services:** valet and coin laundry. **Business Services:** meeting rooms, business center. **Cards:** AX, CB, DC, DS, JC, MC, VI.

Small-scale Hotel

SOME UNITS

HOLIDAY INN EXPRESS-ORLANDO EAST

Phone: (407)282-3900   9

All Year   1P: $75-$85

Location: SR 417, exit Colonial Dr (SR 50), just w. 8750 E Colonial Dr 32817. Fax: 407/282-0416. **Facility:** 118 one-bedroom standard units. 2 stories, exterior corridors. **Parking:** on-site. **Terms:** [ECP] meal plan available. **Amenities:** voice mail, irons, hair dryers. **Pool(s):** outdoor. **Leisure Activities:** whirlpool. **Guest Services:** valet and coin laundry. **Business Services:** meeting rooms, fax. **Cards:** AX, CB, DC, DS, JC, MC, VI. *(See color ad p 616)*

Motel

SOME UNITS

(See map p. 590)

HOLIDAY INN ORLANDO DOWNTOWN
Phone: (407)996-0100 21
All Year   1P: $84-$109   2P: $89-$119
Location: I-4, exit 84, just w on SR 50. 304 W Colonial Dr 32801. Fax: 407/996-0103. **Facility:** 276 units. 275 one-bedroom standard units. 1 two-bedroom suite with whirlpool. 14 stories, interior corridors. *Bath:* combo or
Small-scale Hotel   shower only. **Parking:** on-site. **Terms:** cancellation fee imposed. **Amenities:** video games (fee), voice mail, safes, irons, hair dryers. *Some:* CD players. **Pool(s):** heated outdoor. **Leisure Activities:** exercise room. **Guest Services:** gift shop, valet and coin laundry. **Business Services:** meeting rooms, fax. **Cards:** AX, DC, DS, JC, MC, VI.
(See color ad opposite inside back cover)

SOME UNITS
[ASK] [S♦] [¶¶] [Y] [⅙M] [⊡] [∅] [⇌] [※] [DATA PORT] [▣] / [✕] [VCR] [⊟] [▥] /

HOLIDAY INN ORLANDO NORTH-WINTER PARK
Phone: (407)645-5600 24
All Year [MAP]   1P: $79-$129   2P: $79-$129   XP: $5   F18
Location: I-4, exit 88 (Lee Rd), just w on SR 438. 626 Lee Rd 32810. Fax: 407/740-7912. **Facility:** 200 one-bedroom standard units, some with whirlpools. 5 stories, interior corridors. *Bath:* combo or shower only.
Parking: on-site. **Terms:** 3 day cancellation notice-fee imposed, [BP] meal plan available. **Amenities:** dual
Small-scale Hotel phone lines, voice mail, irons, hair dryers. *Some:* high-speed Internet (fee). **Dining:** 6:30 am-11 & 4-10 pm, cocktails, nightclub. **Pool(s):** outdoor. **Leisure Activities:** exercise room. **Guest Services:** gift shop, valet and coin laundry. **Business Services:** meeting rooms, business center. **Cards:** AX, CB, DC, DS, MC, VI. **Special Amenities:** free newspaper and preferred room (subject to availability with advanced reservations).
(See color ad opposite inside back cover & below)

SOME UNITS
[S♦] [¶¶] [Y] [⅙] [∅] [⇌] [※] [DATA PORT] [▣] / [✕] [⊟] [▥] /
FEE FEE

HOLIDAY INN SELECT-ORLANDO EAST-UCF AREA
Phone: (407)275-9000 4
All Year   1P: $99-$129
Location: 2.4 mi e of SR 417 on University Blvd, then just n. 12125 High Tech Ave 32817. Fax: 407/381-0019.
Facility: 246 one-bedroom standard units. 6 stories, interior corridors. **Parking:** on-site. **Amenities:** *Some:* CD players, dual phone lines, fax. **Dining:** 6:30 am-11 pm, cocktails. **Pool(s):** outdoor. **Leisure Activi-
Small-scale Hotel ties:** sauna, whirlpool, jogging, exercise room, volleyball. **Guest Services:** valet laundry, area transportation-within 5 mi. **Business Services:** meeting rooms, business center. **Cards:** AX, CB, DC, DS, JC, MC, VI.
Special Amenities: free newspaper and preferred room (subject to availability with advanced reservations).
(See color ad below & opposite inside back cover)

SOME UNITS
[S♦] [⊞] [¶¶] [Y] [∅] [⇌] [✕] [※] [DATA PORT] [▣] / [✕] [VCR] [⊟] [▥] /
FEE   FEE FEE

(See map p. 590)

LA QUINTA INN & SUITES UCF
🔺🔺🔺 SAVE   All Year   1P: $79-$119   2P: $85-$125   **Phone:** (407)737-6075   🔟

Location: Just se of jct University Blvd and SR 434 (Alafaya Tr). 11805 Research Pkwy 32826. **Fax:** 407/737-7562. **Facility:** 130 units. 123 one-bedroom standard units. 7 one-bedroom suites. 6 stories, interior corridors. *Bath:* combo or shower only. **Parking:** on-site. **Terms:** check-in 4 pm, [ECP] meal plan available, small pets only.

Small-scale Hotel **Amenities:** video games (fee), voice mail, irons, hair dryers. *Some:* dual phone lines. **Pool(s):** heated outdoor. **Leisure Activities:** whirlpool, exercise room. **Guest Services:** valet and coin laundry. **Business Services:** meeting rooms, fax (fee). **Cards:** AX, CB, DC, DS, JC, MC, VI. **Special Amenities:** free continental breakfast and free local telephone calls. *(See color ad p 652)*

SOME UNITS

🐕 ♿M 🛗 📶 🏊 📺 📠 DATA/PORT 🍽 / ⊠ 🔌 🖨 /

(See map p. 590)

ORLANDO MARRIOTT DOWNTOWN
Phone: (407)843-6664 🔳13

SAVE	9/16-11/30	1P: $149-$190	2P: $149-$190	XP: $10	F18
	12/31-4/30	1P: $139-$190	2P: $139-$190	XP: $10	F18
	5/1-9/15	1P: $129-$170	2P: $129-$170	XP: $10	F18
	12/1-12/30	1P: $119-$160	2P: $119-$160	XP: $10	F18

Small-scale Hotel **Location:** I-4, exit 84 (Colonial Dr) westbound; exit 40 (Robinson St) eastbound, just w at jct Livingston and Hughey sts. Located opposite T.D. Waterhouse Centre & Bob Carr Arts Center. 400 W Livingston St 32801. **Fax:** 407/648-5414. **Facility:** 290 units. 282 one-bedroom standard units. 8 one-bedroom suites, some with whirlpools. 15 stories, interior corridors. **Parking:** on-site (fee) and valet. **Amenities:** high-speed Internet (fee), dual phone lines, voice mail, irons, hair dryers. **Pool(s):** heated outdoor. **Leisure Activities:** whirlpool, exercise room. **Guest Services:** gift shop, valet laundry. **Business Services:** conference facilities, business center. **Cards:** AX, CB, DC, DS, JC, MC, VI.

SOME UNITS 🅂🄳 📶 ▥ 🍽 ⓜ ⊘ 🔌 🎬 📠 ▤ / ✕ 🛈 / FEE

RADISSON PLAZA HOTEL ORLANDO
Phone: (407)425-4455 🔳22

	All Year	1P: $70	2P: $70	XP: $15	F17

Small-scale Hotel **Location:** I-4, exit Ivanhoe Blvd. 60 Ivanhoe Blvd 32804. **Fax:** 407/843-0262. **Facility:** 337 one-bedroom standard units, some with whirlpools. 15 stories, interior corridors. **Parking:** on-site (fee) and valet. **Amenities:** dual phone lines, voice mail, irons, hair dryers. *Some:* honor bars. **Pool(s):** heated outdoor. **Leisure Activities:** whirlpool, 2 lighted tennis courts, exercise room, basketball. *Fee:* massage. **Guest Services:** gift shop, valet laundry. **Business Services:** meeting rooms, business center. **Cards:** AX, DC, DS, MC, VI.

SOME UNITS 📶 24 ▥ ⊘ 🔌 ✕ 📠 ▤ / ✕ 🛈 /

RADISSON UNIVERSITY HOTEL
Phone: 407/658-9008 🔳1

AAA SAVE	2/1-4/30	1P: $99	2P: $99	XP: $10	F12
	12/1-1/31 & 5/1-11/30	1P: $79	2P: $79	XP: $10	F12

Small-scale Hotel **Location:** 1 mi n of East-West Expwy (SR 408) on Alafaya Tr, 0.3 mi n of SR 50, 3.8 mi e of jct SR 50 and Central Florida Greenway (SR 417). 1724 Alafaya Tr 32826. **Fax:** 407/381-5456. **Facility:** 149 one-bedroom standard units. 7 stories, interior corridors. *Bath:* combo or shower only. **Parking:** on-site. **Terms:** cancellation fee imposed, [AP] & [BP] meal plans available. **Amenities:** video games (fee), dual phone lines, voice mail, irons, hair dryers. **Dining:** 6:30 am-1:30 & 5-10 pm, cocktails. **Pool(s):** outdoor. **Leisure Activities:** exercise room. **Guest Services:** valet laundry, area transportation-within 5 mi. **Business Services:** meeting rooms, fax (fee). **Cards:** AX, CB, DC, DS, JC, MC, VI. **Special Amenities:** free newspaper.

SOME UNITS 📶 ⊘ 🔌 🎬 📠 ▤ / ✕ 🛈 🖨 /

RESIDENCE INN BY MARRIOTT/ORLANDO EAST
Phone: (407)513-9000 🔳5

SAVE	All Year [BP]	1P: $99-$169	2P: $99-$169		

Small-scale Hotel **Location:** SR 417, exit 37A, 1.5 mi e. 11651 University Blvd 32817. **Fax:** 407/513-9001. **Facility:** 99 units. 36 one-bedroom standard units with kitchens. 39 one- and 24 two-bedroom suites with kitchens. 4 stories, interior corridors. *Bath:* combo or shower only. **Parking:** on-site. **Terms:** cancellation fee imposed, pets ($20 extra charge). **Amenities:** dual phone lines, voice mail, irons, hair dryers. **Pool(s):** heated outdoor. **Leisure Activities:** whirlpool, exercise room, sports court. **Guest Services:** complimentary evening beverages: Mon-Thurs, valet and coin laundry. **Business Services:** meeting rooms, fax (fee). **Cards:** AX, DC, DS, MC, VI.

SOME UNITS 🅂🄳 🐾 ⊘ 🔌 ✕ 🎬 📠 🛈 🖨 ▤ / ✕ /

TRAVELODGE COLONIAL PLAZA
Phone: 407/894-2741 🔳15

AAA SAVE	All Year [ECP]	1P: $49-$65	2P: $49-$65	XP: $5	F18

Small-scale Hotel **Location:** I-4, exit 83B/84, 2 mi e on SR 50. 2801 E Colonial Dr 32803. **Fax:** 407/896-9858. **Facility:** 227 one-bedroom standard units. 2 stories, exterior corridors. *Bath:* combo or shower only. **Parking:** on-site. **Terms:** check-in 4 pm. **Amenities:** safes (fee), irons, hair dryers. **Pool(s):** heated outdoor. **Leisure Activities:** whirlpool. **Guest Services:** coin laundry. **Business Services:** meeting rooms. **Cards:** AX, CB, DC, DS, JC, MC, VI. **Special Amenities:** free continental breakfast.

SOME UNITS ⊘ 🔌 📠 🛈 ▤ / ✕ /

TRAVELODGE ORLANDO DOWNTOWN
Phone: (407)423-1671 🔳12

	All Year	1P: $45-$85	2P: $45-$85	XP: $5	F18

Motel **Location:** Corner of Magnolia, Rosalind aves and Livingston St. 409 N Magnolia Ave 32801. **Fax:** 407/423-1523. **Facility:** 75 units. 74 one-bedroom standard units. 1 one-bedroom suite. 2 stories, interior/exterior corridors. *Bath:* combo or shower only. **Parking:** on-site. **Terms:** pets ($10 extra charge). **Amenities:** safes (fee). **Pool(s):** outdoor. **Guest Services:** coin laundry. **Cards:** AX, CB, DC, DS, JC, MC, VI.

SOME UNITS A$K 🅂🄳 🐾 📶 ⊘ 🔌 📠 ▤ / ✕ 🛈 🖨 /

WELLESLEY INN & SUITES (ORLANDO/MAITLAND)
Phone: (407)659-0066 🔳27

AAA SAVE	All Year	1P: $79-$89			

Small-scale Hotel **Location:** I-4, exit 90, 1 mi w. 1951 Summit Tower Blvd 32810. **Fax:** 407/659-0067. **Facility:** 135 units. 103 one-bedroom standard units with efficiencies. 32 one-bedroom suites with efficiencies. 3 stories, interior corridors. *Bath:* combo or shower only. **Parking:** on-site. **Terms:** cancellation fee imposed, small pets only. **Amenities:** high-speed Internet (fee), dual phone lines, voice mail, irons, hair dryers. **Pool(s):** heated outdoor. **Leisure Activities:** exercise room. **Guest Services:** valet and coin laundry. **Business Services:** meeting rooms, fax. **Cards:** AX, CB, DC, DS, JC, MC, VI. **Special Amenities:** free continental breakfast and free newspaper. *(See color ad p 612)*

SOME UNITS 🅂🄳 🐾 ⓜ ⊘ 🔌 ✕ 📠 🛈 🖨 ▤ / ✕ /

(See map p. 590)

WESTIN GRAND BOHEMIAN   Phone: (407)313-9000   [17]
AAA [SAVE]   All Year   1P: $189-$259   2P: $189-$259
▼▼▼ ▼▼▼   **Location:** Downtown. 325 S Orange Ave 32801. Fax: 407/313-9001. **Facility:** In addition to a rare Imperial Grand
             Bosendorfer piano, the hotel showcases many classic and contemporary works of art. 250 units. 214 one-
Small-scale Hotel bedroom standard units. 36 one-bedroom suites ($289-$359), some with whirlpools. 14 stories, interior cor-
             ridors. *Bath:* combo or shower only. **Parking:** on-site (fee) and valet. **Terms:** cancellation fee imposed.
             Amenities: CD players, dual phone lines, voice mail, safes, honor bars, irons, hair dryers. *Fee:* video games,
high-speed Internet. **Dining:** 6 am-10:30 pm, Fri & Sat-11:30 pm, cocktails, also, The Boheme, see separate listing. **Pool(s):**
heated outdoor. **Leisure Activities:** whirlpool, exercise room. *Fee:* massage. **Guest Services:** gift shop, valet laundry. **Business
Services:** conference facilities, business center. **Cards:** AX, CB, DC, DS, MC, VI. **Special Amenities:** free newspaper.
(See color ad p 636)
                                                                                         SOME UNITS

[icons: $⊘] [ⅱ] [24⌐] [Y] [&M] [&] [⌐] [⇌] [✕] [✦] [DATA PORT] [▣] / [✕] /

──────── **WHERE TO DINE** ────────

AMIGOS ORIGINAL TEX-MEX RESTAURANT   Lunch: $6-$7   Dinner: $7-$12   Phone: 407/999-4885   [22]
▼▼▼ ▼▼▼   **Location:** I-4, exit 83, just e. 25 W Church St 32801. **Hours:** 11 am-9:30 pm, Fri-2 am, Sat 4 pm-2 am. Closed:
             4/20, 11/27, 12/25; also Sun. **Features:** The staff moves at a bustling pace to deliver oversized burritos
Tex-Mex   and platefuls of tacos. Casual surroundings and Tex-Mex dishes are popular with the whole family. Order
             the fajitas for a sizzling, hot sensation. Casual dress; cocktails. **Parking:** on-site (fee). **Cards:** AX, DC,
MC, VI.
                                                                                         [Y] [✕]

BAJA BURRITO KITCHEN   Lunch: $4-$8   Dinner: $4-$8   Phone: 407/895-6112   [8]
▼▼▼   **Location:** Just s of SR 50; 2 mi e of I-4, exit 83B; in Colonial Market Center. 2716 E Colonial Dr 32803. **Hours:** 11
             am-10 pm, Sun 11:30 am-9 pm. Closed: 4/20, 11/27, 12/25. **Features:** This fast-food shop located in a
American   shopping complex serves good, freshly prepared Tex-Mex dishes. A salsa bar offers a variety of tasty
             toppings from fresh tomatoes to hot habanero salsa and chopped cilantro. Enjoy a nice made-to-order
meal served up fast. Smoke free premises. Casual dress; beer & wine only. **Parking:** on-site.
                                                                                         [✕]

THE BOHEME   Lunch: $8-$16   Dinner: $20-$32   Phone: 407/313-9000   [23]
AAA   **Location:** Downtown, in Westin Grand Bohemian. 325 S Orange Ave 32801. **Hours:** 6 am-10 pm, Fri & Sat-11:30
             pm. **Reservations:** suggested. **Features:** In the Westin Grand Bohemian, the restaurant lists mildly
▼▼▼ ▼▼▼   eclectic and diverse selections on its menu. Nouvelle American cuisine reflects French and Pacific Rim
             influences. Casual dress; cocktails. **Parking:** on-site (fee) and valet. **Cards:** AX, DC, DS, MC, VI.
Continental
                                                                                         [&M] [Y]

CHAN'S CHINESE CUISINE   Lunch: $4-$6   Dinner: $7-$28   Phone: 407/896-0093   [5]
▼▼▼   **Location:** I-4, exit 83B, 1.5 mi e on SR 50. 1901 E Colonial Dr 32803. **Hours:** 10 am-11 pm. **Features:** Feast on
             a far-ranging menu of dim sum and Hong Kong-style dinners. Delectable dishes include fried chicken with
Chinese   ginger sauce and stir-fried jumbo shrimp with honey walnut sauce. Traditional Chinese paintings and curios
             create a serene setting. Casual dress; cocktails. **Parking:** on-site. **Cards:** AX, MC, VI.
                                                                                         [✕]

DEXTER'S OF THORNTON PARK   Lunch: $5-$12   Dinner: $5-$20   Phone: 407/648-2777   [19]
▼▼▼   **Location:** I-4, exit Robinson St, 0.7 mi e on Robinson, just s on Eola, then just e; 0.3 mi e of Lake Eola Park. 808 E
             Washington St 32801. **Hours:** 11 am-10 pm, Sun-9 pm. Closed major holidays. **Features:** This eclectic
Nouvelle American neighborhood meeting place serves a variety of creative soups, pastas, salads and entrees. Some may be
             content to have a glass of wine and a platter of gourmet cheese with fresh bread and fruit, but don't stop
there. The food is wonderful. Casual dress; beer & wine only. **Parking:** on-site. **Cards:** AX, DC, DS, MC, VI.

GARGI'S AT LAKE IVANHOE   Lunch: $5-$9   Dinner: $10-$22   Phone: 407/894-7907   [4]
▼▼▼   **Location:** I-4, exit 85 (Princeton St), 0.8 mi se. 1421 N Orange Ave 32804. **Hours:** 11:30 am-2 & 6-10 pm, Sun 5
             pm-9 pm. Closed major holidays. **Reservations:** accepted. **Features:** Good cuisine is served in a small,
Italian   intimate restaurant that maintains the feel of a New York-style neighborhood eatery. A busy lunch crowd
             from nearby downtown keeps this place hopping. Wonderful eggplant and a rich cheesecake are menu
highlights. Smoke free premises. Casual dress; beer & wine only. **Parking:** street. **Cards:** AX, DC, MC, VI.
                                                                                         [✕]

THE GLOBE   Lunch: $6-$10   Dinner: $8-$12   Phone: 407/849-9904   [20]
▼▼▼   **Location:** Between Orange and Garland aves; downtown. 25 Wall Street Ct 32801. **Hours:** 11 am-2 am, Sat-3 am.
             Reservations: accepted. **Features:** This tragically hip and trendy eatery is just off Heritage Square Park
American   and is open from breakfast through the late night hours. The menu features unique twists on classic dishes
             from around the globe. cocktails. **Parking:** on-site. **Cards:** AX, DS, MC, VI.

HIGH TIDE HARRY'S   Lunch: $5-$10   Dinner: $4-$30   Phone: 407/273-4422   [12]
▼▼▼   **Location:** Just n on SR 436 from jct SR 50. 925 N Semoran Blvd 32807. **Hours:** 11 am-10 pm, Fri & Sat-11 pm.
             Closed: 11/27, 12/25. **Features:** This laid-back eatery features a fishing motif. Quality seafood includes
Seafood   all-you-can-eat dinner specials Sun-Thurs. Expect simple presentation at affordable prices. An excellent
             selection of microbrewed beer is offered with two-for-one specials on Wednesday nights. Casual dress;
cocktails. **Parking:** on-site. **Cards:** AX, CB, DC, DS, JC, MC, VI.
                                                                                         [✕]

HOT DOG HEAVEN   Lunch: $2-$6   Dinner: $2-$6   Phone: 407/282-5746   [13]
AAA   **Location:** SR 50, just w of jct SR 436. 5355 E Colonial Dr 32807. **Hours:** 11 am-6 pm. Closed major holidays.
             Features: Authentic Chicago hot dogs and hand-dipped ice cream are served in a pristine '50s-style
▼   cafeteria. Pile on the sauerkraut or choose a chili-cheese combo. A lunch-time favorite, it offers outside
             seating when crowded. Look for the landmark hot dog sign. Smoke free premises. Casual dress. **Parking:**
American   on-site.
                                                                                         [✕]

(See map p. 590)

JOHNNY RIVERS SMOKEHOUSE AND BBQ CO   **Lunch:** $6-$8   **Dinner:** $9-$16   **Phone:** 407/293-5803   ⑥

Steak House

Location: I-4, exit 84 (SR 50), 4.4 mi w, just e of SR 435. 5370 W Colonial Dr 32808. **Hours:** 11 am-9:30 pm, Fri & Sat-10:30 pm, Sun noon-9:30 pm. **Closed:** 11/27, 12/25. **Reservations:** accepted. **Features:** Not the average smokehouse. There are etched glass dividers and booths with denim covered backs. The food is creative and down-home with specialties like smoked pork, baby back ribs and bourbon oysters. Don't miss the Hershey Bar bread pudding. Casual dress; cocktails. **Parking:** on-site. **Cards:** AX, DC, DS, MC, VI.   ⓎⓍ

LEE'S LAKESIDE RESTAURANT   **Dinner:** $19-$29   **Phone:** 407/841-1565   ㉑

American

Location: On Lake Eola at Central Blvd and Osceola Ave. 431 E Central Blvd 32801. **Hours:** 4 pm-11 pm, Sunday brunch 11 am-2 pm. **Reservations:** suggested. **Features:** From large bay windows, look out at the Lake Eola fountain and the downtown skyline. Tasty and well-presented dishes, such as tenderloin stuffed with crabmeat and pina colada muffins, and attentive service are trademarks of the elegant restaurant. Patio dining is available. Casual dress; cocktails; entertainment. **Parking:** on-site. **Cards:** AX, CB, DC, DS, MC, VI.   ⓎⓍ

LOUIS' DOWNTOWN   **Dinner:** $16-$35   **Phone:** 407/648-4688   ⑯

Continental

Location: Downtown. 116 W Church St 32801. **Hours:** 2 pm-midnight. **Closed:** Sun & Mon. **Reservations:** suggested. **Features:** This long-time local favorite has a new location. The New Orleans inspired cuisine remains steadfast featuring fried green tomatoes that never tasted so good! For intimate dining, reserve a table in the wine cellar. Casual dress; cocktails. **Parking:** on-site (fee). **Cards:** AX, DC, DS, MC, VI.   ⓎⓍ

MANUEL'S ON THE 28TH   **Dinner:** $28-$36   **Phone:** 407/246-6580   ⑪

International

Location: Orange Ave and E Livingston; on the 28th floor of the Bank of America Bldg. 390 N Orange Ave, Suite 2800 32801. **Hours:** 6 pm-10 pm. **Closed:** 11/27, 12/25; also Sun & Mon. **Reservations:** suggested. **Features:** A candlelit setting on the 28th floor offers unparalleled views of downtown. The seasonally changing menu lists memorable dishes prepared with an international flair. While the chef specializes in the use of exotic meats, the fare also includes tamer selections. The signature duck confit appetizer is a perennial favorite. Smoke free premises. Semi-formal attire; cocktails. **Parking:** on-site (fee). **Cards:** AX, DC, DS, MC, VI.   Ⓧ

METRO ESPRESSO PIZZA CAFE   **Lunch:** $5   **Dinner:** $15   **Phone:** 407/422-5282   ⑰

Italian

Location: At Central Blvd and Osceola Ave. 417 E Central Blvd 32801. **Hours:** 11 am-9 pm. **Closed:** 1/1, 11/27, 12/25; also Sun. **Features:** Minutes from Lake Eola in the trendy downtown area, the cafe presents a menu of made-to-order food, including specialty pizzas, sandwiches and salads. Diners can take a few minutes out of their day to enjoy the relaxing atmosphere. Smoke free premises. Casual dress. **Parking:** street. **Cards:** AX, MC, VI.   Ⓧ

MICHAEL'S ITALIAN RESTAURANT   **Lunch:** $7-$10   **Dinner:** $9-$20   **Phone:** 407/273-3631   ⑦

Italian

Location: 4 mi e of Eastern Beltway (SR 417). 12309 E Colonial Dr 32826. **Hours:** 11 am-10 pm, Fri-11 pm, Sun 4:30 pm-9:30 pm. **Features:** Located in a busy commercial area, this restaurant features traditional Italian favorites that are made to order. A variety of menu offerings to please everyone in your family. Casual dress; beer & wine only. **Parking:** on-site. **Cards:** AX, DC, MC, VI.   Ⓧ

MISUZU   **Lunch:** $6-$8   **Dinner:** $6-$24   **Phone:** 407/895-8396   ③

Japanese

Location: I-4, exit 85 (Princeton St), 0.5 mi se. 1905 N Orange Ave 32804. **Hours:** 11:30 am-2:30 & 5:30-9 pm, Fri-10 pm, Sat 5:30 pm-10 pm. **Closed** major holidays; also Sun & Mon. **Features:** Tucked among antique shops, the storefront eatery presents a menu of everything from finger foods to full meals. Also offered is an excellent variety of sushi and sashimi. Diners who are unsure about what to order can request samples. The menu lends itself to grazing. Simple appointments and a laid-back, casual atmosphere provide for an experience totally devoid of pretense. Smoke free premises. Casual dress; beer & wine only. **Parking:** street. **Cards:** AX, DC, DS, MC, VI.   Ⓧ

PANERA BREAD   **Lunch:** $3-$6   **Dinner:** $3-$6   **Phone:** 407/737-3011   ⑭

American

Location: 0.3 mi s of jct Colonial Dr and SR 434. 473 N Alafaya Tr 32828. **Hours:** 6:30 am-9:30 pm, Sun 7 am-8:30 pm. **Closed:** 12/25. **Features:** Diners order and pick up their soup, salad or "upscale" sandwich at the counter in this casual eatery and bakery, a popular place for a quick bite during or after shopping or a weekend outing with the family. Simple, comfortable tables are offered for eating in, but carry out is another option. Smoke free premises. Casual dress. **Parking:** on-site. **Cards:** AX, MC, VI.   ⒼⓂ Ⓧ

PEBBLES DOWNTOWN   **Lunch:** $6-$9   **Dinner:** $6-$19   **Phone:** 407/839-0892   ⑮

American

Location: Just w of Orange Ave; center. 17 W Church St 32801. **Hours:** 11 am-10 pm, Fri-11:30 pm, Sat 5 pm-11:30 pm. **Closed:** 5/26, 11/27, 12/25; also Sun. **Reservations:** accepted. **Features:** The distinctive decor of this informal, upbeat restaurant is highlighted by a ceiling covered with carved ship figureheads. A broad menu includes herb-crusted chicken, grilled pork tenderloin with citrus sauce, scallops in puff pastry and grilled mahi tuna. Casual dress; cocktails. **Parking:** no self-parking. **Cards:** AX, DC, DS, MC, VI.   Ⓧ

STRAUB'S FINE SEAFOOD RESTAURANT   **Dinner:** $12-$25   **Phone:** 407/273-9330   ⑩

Seafood

Location: I-4, exit 83B, 3.8 mi e on SR 50. 5101 E Colonial Dr 32803. **Hours:** 4:30 pm-10 pm, Sun-9 pm. **Closed:** 11/27, 12/25. **Reservations:** suggested. **Features:** Here you will find seafood prepared in a wide range of styles: traditional, blackened, broiled, baked or mesquite-grilled. The salmon is marinated in Straub's own special sauce. You may also choose pasta dishes and a limited selection of beef and chicken. Smoke free premises. Casual dress; cocktails. **Parking:** on-site. **Cards:** AX, CB, DC, DS, MC, VI.   ⓎⓍ

(See map p. 590)

SUSHI HATSU
♥♥♥ ♥♥♥
Ethnic

Lunch: $6-$9   **Dinner:** $9-$19   **Phone:** 407/422-1551   (18)
Location: Between Magnolia and Orange aves. 24 E Washington St 32801. **Hours:** 11 am-2:30 & 5-10 pm, Fri & Sat-11 pm. Closed: 1/1, 11/27, 12/25; also Sun. **Reservations:** accepted; Mon-Fri. **Features:** A few Korean dishes are found among sushi and other Japanese items on the menu. Try the bibimbap — small chunks of beef, shredded vegetables and a fried egg, drizzled with a spicy sauce and served over rice. Quick and helpful service makes dinner easy. Casual dress; beer & wine only. **Parking:** on-site. **Cards:** AX, DC, MC, VI.   ☒

--------- *The following restaurants have not been evaluated by AAA* ---------
but are listed for your information only.

ATHENINAN GARDEN CAFE   **Phone:** 407/898-2151
[fyi]   Not evaluated. **Location:** 2918 N Orange Ave 32804. **Features:** A diamond in the rough. Owners warmly welcome you with service and very tasty well prepared food, including stuffed grape leaves and appetizers of lamb; combo is great value.

LITTLE SAIGON   **Phone:** 407/423-8539
[fyi]   Not evaluated. **Location:** 1106 E Colonial Dr 32801. **Features:** Vietnamese cuisine. Large menu selection of traditional items and other interesting offerings. Inexpensive.

WHITE WOLF CAFE   **Phone:** 407/895-5590
[fyi]   Not evaluated. **Location:** 1829 N Orange Ave. **Features:** American cuisine, plus a few international specialties. Eclectic, casual surroundings; furnished with many antiques.

ORLANDO SOUTH   (See map p. 598; index p. 600)

--------- **WHERE TO STAY** ---------

ADAM'S MARK ORLANDO   **Phone:** (407)859-1500   (273)
(AAA) [SAVE]

1/1-4/15	1P: $119-$199	2P: $139-$219	XP: $20	F17
9/15-11/30	1P: $109-$189	2P: $129-$209	XP: $20	F17
4/16-9/14	1P: $99-$119	2P: $119-$199	XP: $20	F17
12/1-12/31	1P: $89-$169	2P: $109-$189	XP: $20	F17

Large-scale Hotel **Location:** Just s of jct Sand Lake Rd and S Orange Blossom Tr. Located at the south end of the Florida Mall. 1500 Sand Lake Rd 32809. Fax: 407/855-1585. **Facility:** 510 units. 505 one-bedroom standard units. 5 one-bedroom suites, some with whirlpools. 11 stories, interior corridors. *Bath:* combo or shower only. **Parking:** on-site and valet. **Terms:** package plans. **Amenities:** video games (fee), voice mail, irons, hair dryers. **Dining:** 6 am-11 pm, cocktails. **Pool(s):** heated outdoor. **Leisure Activities:** sauna, whirlpool, exercise room. **Guest Services:** gift shop, valet laundry. **Business Services:** conference facilities, business center. **Cards:** AX, CB, DC, DS, JC, MC, VI. **Special Amenities:** early check-in/late check-out and preferred room (subject to availability with advanced reservations).   SOME UNITS

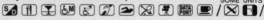

"If we stayed at Travelodge, I wouldn't have to get a job to pay for our vacation."

AAA Members
Save 10-20%*

When you stay at any of the 18 Travelodge® hotels in Florida, there are lots of things to look forward to... paying a lot for your stay isn't one of them. With our friendly staff, comfortable rooms and amenities like an in-room coffee maker, we let you take a vacation from high prices.

Travelodge®

For reservations
www.travelodge.com
800-578-7878
Ask for plan code S3A

(See map p. 598)

AMERISUITES (ORLANDO AIRPORT/NORTHEAST)
Phone: (407)240-3939   **309**
AAA SAVE   All Year [ECP]   1P: $85-$135   2P: $85-$135   XP: $10   F
◆◆◆   **Location:** SR 528 (Bee Line Expwy), exit 11, 0.5 mi n on SR 436, just e on TG Lee Blvd, then just s. 7500 Augusta National Dr 32822. Fax: 407/240-3920. **Facility:** 128 one-bedroom standard units. 4 stories, interior corridors. *Bath:* combo or shower only. **Parking:** on-site. **Terms:** 3 night minimum stay - seasonal, 3 day cancellation
Small-scale Hotel   notice-fee imposed, small pets only. **Amenities:** voice mail, irons, hair dryers. *Fee:* video games, high-speed Internet. *Some:* dual phone lines. **Pool(s):** heated outdoor. **Leisure Activities:** exercise room. **Guest Serv-**
ices: complimentary evening beverages: Wed, valet and coin laundry. **Business Services:** meeting rooms, business center.
Cards: AX, CB, DC, DS, JC, MC, VI. **Special Amenities: free continental breakfast and free newspaper.**
(See color ad p 617)

SOME UNITS

AMERISUITES (ORLANDO AIRPORT/NORTHWEST)
Phone: (407)816-7800   **296**
AAA SAVE   All Year [ECP]   1P: $85-$135   2P: $85-$135   XP: $10   F17
◆◆◆   **Location:** SR 528 (Bee Line Expwy), exit 11, 0.5 mi n on SR 436, just w. 5435 Forbes Pl 32812. Fax: 407/816-0050.
Facility: 135 one-bedroom standard units. 6 stories, interior corridors. *Bath:* combo or shower only. **Parking:**
on-site. **Terms:** 3 night minimum stay - seasonal, 3 day cancellation notice-fee imposed, small pets only. **Pool(s):**
Small-scale Hotel   **Amenities:** dual phone lines, voice mail, irons, hair dryers. *Fee:* video games, high-speed Internet. **Pool(s):**
heated outdoor. **Leisure Activities:** exercise room. **Guest Services:** valet and coin laundry, area
transportation-within 2 mi. **Business Services:** meeting rooms, fax (fee). **Cards:** AX, CB, DC, DS, MC, VI. **Special Amenities:**
free continental breakfast and free newspaper. *(See color ad p 617)*

SOME UNITS

AMERISUITES (ORLANDO/CONVENTION CENTER)
Phone: (407)370-4720   **224**
AAA SAVE   All Year   1P: $85   2P: $85   XP: $10
◆◆◆   **Location:** I-4, exit 74A, just e, then 0.7 mi s of SR 482 (Sand Lake Rd). 8741 International Dr 32819.
Fax: 407/370-4721. **Facility:** 152 one-bedroom standard units. 7 stories, interior corridors. *Bath:* combo or
shower only. **Parking:** on-site. **Terms:** 3 day cancellation notice-fee imposed, [ECP] meal plan available.
Small-scale Hotel   **Amenities:** voice mail, irons, hair dryers. *Fee:* video games, high-speed Internet. *Some:* dual phone lines.
Pool(s): heated outdoor. **Leisure Activities:** exercise room. **Guest Services:** valet and coin laundry, area
transportation-major attractions. **Business Services:** meeting rooms, business center. **Cards:** AX, CB, DC, DS, JC, MC, VI.
Special Amenities: free continental breakfast and free newspaper. *(See color ad p 617)*

SOME UNITS

(See map p. 598)

AMERISUITES (ORLANDO/UNIVERSAL) **Phone: (407)351-0627** 259
   🔷 SAVE   12/23-1/7 [ECP]   1P: $99   XP: $10   F18
                 12/1-12/22 & 1/8-8/15 [ECP]   1P: $89   XP: $10   F18
   🔷🔷🔷   8/16-11/30 [ECP]   1P: $79   XP: $10   F18
Location: I-4, exit 75B, 0.6 mi ne. 5895 Caravan Ct 32819. Fax: 407/351-3317. **Facility:** 151 one-bedroom standard units. 7 stories, interior corridors. *Bath:* combo or shower only. **Parking:** on-site. **Terms:** cancellation fee imposed, small pets only. **Amenities:** video games, voice mail, irons, hair dryers. *Some:* dual phone lines. **Pool(s):** heated outdoor. **Leisure Activities:** exercise room. **Guest Services:** valet and coin laundry, airport transportation (fee)- Orlando International Airport, area transportation-major attractions. **Business Services:** meeting rooms, fax (fee). **Cards:** AX, CB, DC, DS, JC, MC, VI. **Special Amenities:** free continental breakfast and free newspaper. *(See color ad p 617)*

SOME UNITS

 /🗙/

BAYMONT INN & SUITES ORLANDO SOUTH **Phone: (407)240-0500** 281
   🔷 SAVE   All Year [ECP]   1P: $59-$79   2P: $59-$79
Location: US 17-92 and 441, just s of SR 528 (Bee Line Expwy), off Florida Tpke, exit 254. 2051 Consulate Dr 32837. Fax: 407/240-5194. **Facility:** 126 units. 122 one-bedroom standard units. 4 one-bedroom suites ($99-$119), some with efficiencies (no utensils) and/or whirlpools. 3 stories, interior corridors. **Parking:** on-site. **Terms:** small pets only ($50 deposit). **Amenities:** video games (fee), voice mail, irons, hair dryers. **Pool(s):** outdoor. **Guest Services:** valet and coin laundry. **Business Services:** meeting rooms, fax (fee). **Cards:** AX, CB, DC, DS, MC, VI. **Special Amenities:** free continental breakfast and free newspaper. *(See color ad below)*

SOME UNITS

/🗙/

BEST WESTERN AIRPORT INN & SUITES **Phone: 407/581-2800** 288
   🔷 SAVE   All Year   1P: $66-$90   2P: $66-$90   F18
Location: SR 528 (Bee Line Expwy), exit 8, just w on McCoy Rd. 1850 McCoy Rd 32809 (8101 Aircenter Ct, ORLANDO). Fax: 407/581-2810. **Facility:** 95 one-bedroom standard units. 5 stories, interior corridors. *Bath:* combo or shower only. **Parking:** on-site. **Terms:** 7 day cancellation notice, [ECP] meal plan available. **Amenities:** safes (fee), irons, hair dryers. **Pool(s):** outdoor. **Leisure Activities:** exercise room. **Guest Services:** coin laundry, area transportation (fee). **Business Services:** fax (fee). **Cards:** AX, CB, DC, DS, JC, MC, VI. **Special Amenities:** free continental breakfast and free room upgrade (subject to availability with advanced reservations).

SOME UNITS

/🗙/

BEST WESTERN-FLORIDA MALL **Phone: (407)855-6060** 272
   SAVE   All Year   1P: $49-$89   2P: $49-$89   XP: $10   F16
Location: US 17-92 and 441, 0.5 mi s of jct SR 482 (Sand Lake Rd), 0.8 mi n of Florida Tpke, exit 254. Located adjacent to a shopping mall. 8421 S Orange Blossom Tr 32809. Fax: 407/859-5132. **Facility:** 204 one-bedroom standard units. 2 stories, exterior corridors. **Parking:** on-site. **Terms:** check-in 4 pm, [MAP] meal plan available. **Amenities:** safes (fee), hair dryers. **Pool(s):** heated outdoor. **Leisure Activities:** playground. *Fee:* game room. **Guest Services:** gift shop, valet and coin laundry, area transportation. **Business Services:** meeting rooms. **Cards:** AX, CB, DC, DS, MC, VI. *(See color ad p 627)*

SOME UNITS

/🗙/
FEE FEE

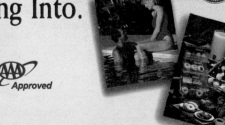

(See map p. 598)

BEST WESTERN MOVIELAND

Phone: (407)351-3900 `197`

(AAA) (SAVE)

Motel

All Year — 1P: $65-$125 — 2P: $65-$125 — XP: $10 — F17
Location: I-4, exit 74A, 1.5 mi n of SR 482 (Sand Lake Rd). Located across from Wet-N-Wild. 6233 International Dr 32819. Fax: 407/363-5119. **Facility:** 261 units. 258 one-bedroom standard units. 3 one-bedroom suites. 4 stories, interior corridors. *Bath:* some combo or shower only. **Parking:** on-site. **Terms:** cancellation fee imposed, $3 service charge. **Amenities:** voice mail, safes (fee), irons, hair dryers. **Dining:** 7:30 am-11 pm. **Pool(s):** heated outdoor. **Leisure Activities:** Fee: game room. **Guest Services:** gift shop, valet and coin laundry, area transportation-Universal & Sea World. **Business Services:** meeting rooms, fax. **Cards:** AX, CB, DC, DS, MC, VI. **Special Amenities:** early check-in/late check-out. *(See color ad p 628)*

SOME UNITS

FEE

BEST WESTERN PLAZA INTERNATIONAL

Phone: (407)345-8195 `234`

(AAA) (SAVE)

Small-scale Hotel

All Year — 1P: $65-$125 — 2P: $65-$125 — XP: $10 — F17
Location: I-4, exit 74A, just e on SR 482 (Sand Lake Rd), then 0.8 mi s. 8738 International Dr 32819. Fax: 407/345-0417. **Facility:** 671 units. 567 one-bedroom standard units, some with efficiencies and/or whirlpools. 104 one-bedroom suites. 4 stories, interior/exterior corridors. *Bath:* some combo or shower only. **Parking:** on-site. **Terms:** check-in 4 pm, cancellation fee imposed, $3 service charge. **Amenities:** voice mail, irons. *Fee:* video games, safes. **Dining:** 8 am-11 pm. **Pool(s):** heated outdoor, wading. **Leisure Activities:** whirlpool. *Fee:* game room. **Guest Services:** gift shop, valet and coin laundry, area transportation-major attractions. **Business Services:** fax (fee). **Cards:** AX, CB, DC, DS, MC, VI. **Special Amenities:** early check-in/late check-out and free room upgrade (subject to availability with advanced reservations). *(See color ad p 628)*

SOME UNITS

BEST WESTERN UNIVERSAL INN

Phone: (407)226-9119 `189`

(AAA) (SAVE)

Small-scale Hotel

12/1-3/31 & 5/23-9/2 — 1P: $59-$69 — 2P: $59-$69
4/1-5/22 & 9/3-11/30 — 1P: $49-$59 — 2P: $49-$59
Location: I-4, exit 75B, 0.5 mi n, then just e. 5618 Vineland Rd 32819. Fax: 407/370-2448. **Facility:** 70 one-bedroom standard units. 3 stories, interior corridors. *Bath:* combo or shower only. **Parking:** on-site. **Terms:** cancellation fee imposed, weekly rates available, [ECP] meal plan available. **Amenities:** safes (fee), irons, hair dryers. **Pool(s):** outdoor. **Guest Services:** coin laundry. **Business Services:** fax (fee). **Cards:** AX, DC, DS, MC, VI. **Special Amenities:** early check-in/late check-out and free continental breakfast. *(See ad below)*

SOME UNITS

(See map p. 598)

CLARION HOTEL UNIVERSAL   **Phone:** (407)351-5009   [203]

 (SAVE) All Year   1P: $69-$109   2P: $69-$109
Location: I-4, exit 75A, just e of International Dr. Located adjacent to Wet-N-Wild. 7299 Universal Blvd 32819.
Fax: 407/352-7277. **Facility:** 298 one-bedroom standard units. 7-8 stories, interior corridors. *Bath:* combo or
shower only. **Parking:** on-site. **Terms:** check-in 4 pm, cancellation fee imposed. **Amenities:** voice mail, irons,
Large-scale Hotel hair dryers. *Fee:* video games, safes. **Dining:** 2 restaurants, 7 am-11 & 5-10 pm, cocktails. **Pool(s):** heated
outdoor. **Leisure Activities:** whirlpools, lighted tennis court, basketball. *Fee:* game room. **Guest Services:**
valet and coin laundry, area transportation-selected attractions. **Business Services:** meeting rooms, fax (fee). **Cards:** AX, CB,
DC, DS, MC, VI. **Special Amenities: preferred room (subject to availability with advanced reservations).**
(See color ad below)
                                                                            SOME UNITS

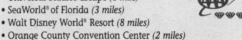

(See map p. 598)

CLUB ORLANDO   **Phone:** 407/855-9551   261

All Year   2P: $118-$198

Location: I-4, exit 79, 1.6 mi s on SR 423, 0.7 mi e on Americana Blvd, then 0.3 mi n. Located in a residential area. 5305 San Antonio St 32839. Fax: 407/438-3664. **Facility:** 28 units. 27 one- and 1 two-bedroom suites with kitchens

Condominium   and whirlpools. 2 stories, exterior corridors. **Parking:** on-site. **Terms:** check-in 4 pm, 14 day cancellation notice, weekly rates available. **Amenities:** safes, irons, hair dryers. **Pool(s):** heated outdoor. **Leisure Activities:** tennis court, playground. **Guest Services:** coin laundry. **Cards:** AX, DC, DS, MC, VI.

ASK SD 🚫 🛇 VCR 📻 DATA/PORT 🖥 🖨 💻

COMFORT INN INTERNATIONAL   **Phone:** (407)313-4000   209

SAVE   **All Year [ECP]**   1P: $69-$129   2P: $69-$129

Location: I-4, exit 74A, just e on Sand Lake Rd, then just s. 8134 International Dr 32819. Fax: 407/313-4001.
Facility: 112 one-bedroom standard units. 6 stories, interior corridors. *Bath:* combo or shower only. **Parking:**

Small-scale Hotel   on-site. **Terms:** cancellation fee imposed, $3 service charge. **Amenities:** high-speed Internet (fee), voice mail, safes, irons, hair dryers. **Pool(s):** outdoor. **Guest Services:** gift shop, valet and coin laundry, area transportation. **Business Services:** fax (fee). **Cards:** AX, CB, DC, DS, JC, MC, VI. *(See ad below)*

SOME UNITS

SD 🍽 🛗M 📻 🚫 🛇 🛎 📻 DATA/PORT 🖥 / ✕ 🖨 💻 /

COMFORT SUITES   **Phone:** (407)363-1967   184

AAA SAVE   **All Year [ECP]**   1P: $69-$149   2P: $69-$149

Location: I-4, exit 75B, 1 mi n on SR 435 (Kirkman Rd), then e. 5617 Major Blvd 32819. Fax: 407/363-6873.
Facility: 101 one-bedroom standard units. 4 stories, interior corridors. *Bath:* combo or shower only. **Parking:**

Small-scale Hotel   on-site. **Terms:** 3 day cancellation notice-fee imposed, weekly rates available, [CP] meal plan available. **Amenities:** voice mail, irons, hair dryers. **Pool(s):** heated outdoor. **Leisure Activities:** whirlpool, exercise room. **Guest Services:** valet and coin laundry. **Business Services:** meeting rooms, fax (fee). **Cards:** AX, CB, DC, DS, MC, VI. **Special Amenities: free continental breakfast and free local telephone calls.**

SD 🛗M 📻 🛇 🛎 📻 DATA/PORT 🖥 🖨 💻

COMFORT SUITES ORLANDO   **Phone:** (407)351-5050   226

AAA SAVE   **All Year [ECP]**   1P: $60-$90   2P: $60-$90

Location: I-4, exit 74A, just w on Sand Lake Rd, then 1.5 mi s. 9350 Turkey Lake Rd 32819. Fax: 407/363-7953.
Facility: 214 one-bedroom standard units. 3 stories, exterior corridors. *Bath:* combo or shower only. **Parking:**

Small-scale Hotel   on-site. **Terms:** package plans. **Amenities:** voice mail, irons. *Fee:* video games, safes. *Some:* hair dryers. **Dining:** cocktails. **Pool(s):** heated outdoor, wading. **Leisure Activities:** whirlpool, game room. **Guest Services:** gift shop, valet and coin laundry, area transportation-major attractions. **Business Services:** fax (fee). **Cards:** AX, CB, DC, DS, JC, MC, VI. **Special Amenities: free continental breakfast and free newspaper.** *(See color ad p 632)*

SOME UNITS

SD 🛗M 📻 🚫 🛇 🛎 📻 🖥 🖨 💻 / ✕ DATA/PORT /

COMFORT SUITES - ORLANDO INT. AIRPORT   **Phone:** (407)581-7900   291

AAA SAVE   2/11-4/30 [ECP]   1P: $99-$109   2P: $99-$109   XP: $10

12/1-2/10 & 10/1-11/30 [ECP]   1P: $79-$109   2P: $79-$109

Motel   5/1-9/30 [ECP]   1P: $69-$109   2P: $69-$109

Location: SR 528 (Bee Line Expwy), exit 9, just n. 7900 Conway Rd 32812. Fax: 407/581-7901. **Facility:** Designated smoking area. 107 one-bedroom standard units, some with efficiencies. 4 stories, interior corridors. *Bath:* combo or shower only. **Parking:** on-site. **Terms:** cancellation fee imposed, $2 service charge. **Amenities:** voice mail, irons, hair dryers. **Pool(s):** outdoor. **Leisure Activities:** limited exercise equipment. **Guest Services:** valet laundry. **Business Services:** meeting rooms, business center. **Cards:** AX, DC, DS, MC, VI. **Special Amenities: free continental breakfast and free local telephone calls.** *(See color ad card insert)*

SOME UNITS

SD 🚬 🛗M 📻 🛇 🛎 📻 DATA/PORT 🖥 🖨 💻 / ✕ /

(See map p. 598)

COUNTRY INN & SUITES BY CARLSON-ORLANDO INTERNATIONAL AIRPORT   **Phone:** (407)856-8896   298
All Year [CP]   1P: $89-$129   2P: $89-$129   XP: $10   F16
Location: SR 528 (Bee Line Expwy), exit 11, 0.6 mi n on SR 436, then just w. 5440 Forbes Pl 32812.
Small-scale Hotel   Fax: 407/856-7456. **Facility:** 136 units. 120 one-bedroom standard units, some with whirlpools. 16 one-bedroom suites. 6 stories, interior corridors. *Bath:* combo or shower only. **Parking:** on-site. **Amenities:** voice mail, irons, hair dryers. **Pool(s):** heated outdoor. **Leisure Activities:** whirlpool, exercise room. **Guest Services:** valet and coin laundry. **Business Services:** meeting rooms, fax (fee). **Cards:** AX, DC, DS, MC, VI. *(See color ad p 613)*

SOME UNITS
(ASK) (S𝐷) (⤒) (¶↑) (🏊) (✦) (DATA PORT) (💻) / (✕) (🔌) (🖥) /

COUNTRY INN & SUITES INTERNATIONAL DRIVE   **Phone:** (407)313-4200   212
All Year [ECP]   1P: $79-$129   2P: $79-$129   XP: $5   F17
Location: I-4, exit 74A (Sand Lake Rd), just e, then just n. 7701 Universal Blvd 32819. Fax: 407/313-4201.
Small-scale Hotel   **Facility:** 170 units. 122 one-bedroom standard units, some with whirlpools. 48 one-bedroom suites. 5 stories, interior corridors. *Bath:* combo or shower only. **Parking:** on-site. **Amenities:** voice mail, safes, irons, hair dryers. **Pool(s):** outdoor. **Leisure Activities:** exercise room. *Fee:* game room. **Guest Services:** valet and coin laundry, area transportation. **Business Services:** meeting rooms, fax (fee). **Cards:** AX, DC, DS, MC, VI. *(See color ad p 613)*

SOME UNITS
(ASK) (S𝐷) (¶↑) (&M) (✦) (📞) (🏊) (✦) (DATA PORT) (💻) / (✕) (🔌) (🖥) /

COURTYARD BY MARRIOTT AIRPORT   **Phone:** (407)240-7200   299
[SAVE]   1/8-5/23 & 9/10-11/30   1P: $119-$139   2P: $119-$139
12/1-1/7 & 5/24-9/9   1P: $99-$129   2P: $99-$129
Location: SR 436, 0.3 mi n of SR 528 (Bee Line Expwy). 7155 N Frontage Rd 32812. Fax: 407/240-8962.
Small-scale Hotel   **Facility:** 149 units. 137 one-bedroom standard units. 12 one-bedroom suites. 3 stories, interior corridors. *Bath:* combo or shower only. **Parking:** on-site. **Amenities:** high-speed Internet (fee), dual phone lines, voice mail, irons, hair dryers. **Pool(s):** heated outdoor. **Leisure Activities:** whirlpool, exercise room. **Guest Services:** valet and coin laundry. **Business Services:** meeting rooms, fax (fee). **Cards:** AX, CB, DC, DS, JC, MC, VI.
(See ad p 633)

SOME UNITS
(S𝐷) (⤒) (¶↑) (&M) (✦) (📞) (🏊) (✦) (DATA PORT) (💻) / (✕) (🔌) (🖥) /

(See map p. 598)

COURTYARD BY MARRIOTT, INTERNATIONAL DRIVE   Phone: (407)351-2244   229

	1/10-4/30 & 9/5-11/30	1P: $109-$149	2P: $109-$149
	12/1-1/9 & 5/1-9/4	1P: $89-$119	2P: $89-$119

Small-scale Hotel   **Location:** I-4, exit 74A, just e on Sand Lake Rd, then just s on International Dr. 8600 Austrian Ct 32819. **Fax:** 407/351-3306. **Facility:** 151 units. 140 one-bedroom standard units. 11 one-bedroom suites. 4 stories. interior corridors. *Bath:* combo or shower only. **Parking:** on-site. **Terms:** [BP] meal plan available. **Amenities:** high-speed Internet (fee), dual phone lines, voice mail, safes, irons, hair dryers. **Pool(s):** heated outdoor. **Leisure Activities:** whirlpool, exercise room. **Guest Services:** valet and coin laundry, area transportation. **Business Services:** meeting rooms, fax (fee). **Cards:** AX, DC, DS, MC, VI. *(See ad below)*

SOME UNITS
🅂 📶 ⛍ 📺 🅢 🅼 🏊 🍽 📠 🖥 / ✕ 🛗 📠 /

CROWNE PLAZA HOTEL AND RESORT ORLANDO   Phone: (407)239-1222   317

AAA SAVE   All Year   1P: $119-$299

Small-scale Hotel   **Location:** I-4, exit 72, just e on SR 528 (Bee Line Expwy) to exit 1, then 2.7 mi s. 12000 International Dr 32821. **Fax:** 407/239-1190. **Facility:** 140 units. 58 one-bedroom standard units. 82 one-bedroom suites ($189-$299) with efficiencies. 5 stories, exterior corridors. *Bath:* combo or shower only. **Parking:** on-site. **Terms:** 3 day cancellation notice, weekly rates available, [BP] meal plan available, package plans, $5 service charge. **Amenities:** video games, CD players, voice mail, safes, irons, hair dryers. **Dining:** 6:30 am-10 pm, cocktails. **Pool(s):** 2 heated outdoor, wading. **Leisure Activities:** whirlpools, 2 tennis courts, playground, exercise room, volleyball. *Fee:* massage, game room. **Guest Services:** gift shop, valet and coin laundry, area transportation-selected attractions. **Business Services:** meeting rooms, fax (fee). **Cards:** AX, CB, DC, DS, JC, MC, VI. *(See color ad below)*

SOME UNITS
🅂 ⛍ 🍽 🅼 🅢 🏊 ✕ 📠 🖥 🛗 / ✕ 📼 /

(See map p. 598)

CROWNE PLAZA HOTEL AND RESORT ORLANDO AIRPORT   Phone: (407)856-0100 [294]

	1/1-3/31	1P: $159-$169	2P: $159-$169	XP: $10	F10
	12/1-12/31 & 10/1-11/30	1P: $139-$159	2P: $139-$159	XP: $10	F10
Large-scale Hotel	4/1-9/30	1P: $129-$149	2P: $129-$149	XP: $10	F10

Location: SR 528 (Bee Line Expwy), exit 11, 0.8 mi n on SR 436, just w. 5555 Hazeltine National Dr 32812. Fax: 407/855-7991. **Facility:** 347 units. 337 one-bedroom standard units. 10 one-bedroom suites ($189-$359). 10 stories, interior corridors. *Bath:* combo or shower only. **Parking:** on-site. **Terms:** 7 day cancellation notice, [BP] & [CP] meal plans available. **Amenities:** voice mail, irons, hair dryers. **Pool(s):** heated outdoor. **Leisure Activities:** whirlpool, exercise room. **Guest Services:** gift shop, valet laundry. **Business Services:** conference facilities, business center. **Cards:** AX, CB, DC, DS, MC, VI.

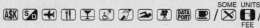

DAYS INN-CONVENTION CENTER/NORTH OF SEA WORLD   Phone: (407)352-8700 [251]

| | All Year | 1P: $109-$129 | 2P: $109-$129 |

Location: I-4, exit 72, just e to International Dr; Bee Line Expwy (SR 528), exit 1, then just n. 9990 International Dr 32819. Fax: 407/363-3965. **Facility:** 220 one-bedroom standard units. 4 stories, exterior corridors. *Bath:* combo or shower only. **Parking:** on-site. **Terms:** check-in 4 pm, cancellation fee imposed. **Amenities:** voice mail, safes, hair dryers. **Dining:** 6 am-11 pm, wine/beer only. **Pool(s):** outdoor. **Leisure Activities:** playground. **Guest Services:** valet and coin laundry. **Business Services:** fax (fee). **Cards:** AX, CB, DC, DS, MC, VI. **Special Amenities:** early check-in/late check-out and free newspaper.

DAYS INN EAST OF UNIVERSAL   Phone: (407)351-3800 [194]

| | All Year | 1P: $49-$99 | 2P: $49-$99 | XP: $10 | F18 |

Location: I-4, exit 75B, 0.5 mi n on SR 435 (Kirkman Rd), then just e. 5827 Caravan Ct 32819. Fax: 407/363-0907. **Facility:** 262 one-bedroom standard units. 2 stories, exterior corridors. *Bath:* combo or shower only. **Parking:** on-site. **Terms:** check-in 4 pm, 3 day cancellation notice, $2 service charge, pets ($10 extra charge). **Amenities:** voice mail, hair dryers. **Pool(s):** heated outdoor, wading. **Leisure Activities:** Fee: game room. **Guest Services:** gift shop, coin laundry, area transportation-Disney. **Business Services:** meeting rooms, fax (fee). **Cards:** AX, CB, DC, DS, JC, MC, VI.

DAYS INN NORTH OF UNIVERSAL   Phone: 407/841-3731 [285]

| | All Year | 1P: $39-$79 | 2P: $39-$79 |

Location: I-4, exit 79, just e. 2500 W 33rd St 32839. Fax: 407/841-0642. **Facility:** 200 one-bedroom standard units. 4 stories, exterior corridors. *Bath:* combo or shower only. **Parking:** on-site. **Terms:** $2 service charge, pets ($8 extra charge). **Amenities:** irons, hair dryers. **Pool(s):** outdoor. **Guest Services:** valet and coin laundry. **Business Services:** fax (fee). **Cards:** AX, CB, DC, DS, MC, VI.

DAYS INN ORLANDO LAKESIDE   Phone: (407)351-1900 [207]

| | All Year | 1P: $39-$99 | 2P: $39-$99 | XP: $10 | F17 |

Location: I-4, exit 74A, just w. 7335 Sand Lake Rd 32819. Fax: 407/352-2690. **Facility:** 695 units. 671 one-bedroom standard units. 24 one-bedroom suites ($55-$110). 2-3 stories, exterior corridors. *Bath:* combo or shower only. **Parking:** on-site. **Terms:** check-in 4 pm, 3 day cancellation notice, weekly rates available, small pets only ($20 fee, $10 extra charge). **Amenities:** voice mail, safes, hair dryers. **Dining:** 6:30-11 am. **Pool(s):** 2 outdoor, heated outdoor. **Leisure Activities:** picnic area with grills, playground, volleyball. *Fee:* game room. **Guest Services:** gift shop, valet and coin laundry. **Business Services:** fax (fee). **Cards:** AX, CB, DC, DS, JC, MC, VI. **Special Amenities:** free newspaper and free room upgrade (subject to availability with advanced reservations). *(See color ad p 635)*

DELTA ORLANDO RESORT   Phone: (407)351-3340 [202]

| | All Year | 1P: $49-$89 | 2P: $49-$89 | XP: $10 | F |

Location: I-4, exit 75B, w on Kirkman Rd, then n. 5715 Major Blvd 32819. Fax: 407/351-5117. **Facility:** 800 units. 792 one-bedroom standard units. 8 one-bedroom suites, some with whirlpools. 4 stories, interior corridors. *Bath:* combo or shower only. **Parking:** on-site. **Terms:** check-in 4 pm, cancellation fee imposed. **Amenities:** video games (fee), safes, irons, hair dryers. **Pool(s):** 3 heated outdoor. **Leisure Activities:** whirlpools, miniature golf, 2 lighted tennis courts, playground, basketball, volleyball. *Fee:* game room. **Guest Services:** coin laundry. **Business Services:** conference facilities, fax (fee). **Cards:** AX, DC, DS, MC, VI.

DOUBLETREE CASTLE HOTEL   Phone: (407)345-1511 [219]

| | All Year | 1P: $79-$169 | 2P: $79-$169 | XP: $10 | F18 |

Location: I-4, exit 74A, 1 mi se, just e of International Dr, 0.5 mi s of SR 483 (Sand Lake Rd). 8629 International Dr 32819. Fax: 407/248-8181. **Facility:** 216 one-bedroom standard units. 9 stories, interior corridors. *Bath:* combo or shower only. **Parking:** on-site. **Terms:** check-in 4 pm, 3 day cancellation notice-fee imposed, $3 service charge. **Amenities:** video games (fee), voice mail, safes, irons, hair dryers. **Dining:** Cafe Tu Tu Tango, Vito's Chop House, see separate listing. **Pool(s):** heated outdoor. **Leisure Activities:** whirlpool, exercise room. *Fee:* game room. **Guest Services:** gift shop, valet and coin laundry, area transportation. **Business Services:** meeting rooms, fax (fee). **Cards:** AX, CB, DC, DS, JC, MC, VI. *(See color ad p 636)*

(See map p. 598)

EMBASSY SUITES HOTEL ORLANDO INTERNATIONAL DR/CONVENTION CENTER **Phone: (407)352-1400** 235
[SAVE] All Year 1P: $129-$229 2P: $129-$229 XP: $10 F17
Location: I-4, exit 74A, just e on Sand Lake Rd, then just s. 8978 International Dr 32819. Fax: 407/363-1120. **Facility:** 244 units. 243 one- and 1 two-bedroom suites ($129-$229). 8 stories, interior corridors. *Bath:* combo or shower only. **Parking:** on-site. **Terms:** check-in 4 pm, 3 day cancellation notice-fee imposed, [BP]
Large-scale Hotel meal plan available. **Amenities:** voice mail, irons, hair dryers. *Some:* CD players. **Pool(s):** heated outdoor, heated indoor, wading. **Leisure Activities:** sauna, whirlpools, steamroom, exercise room. *Fee:* game room.
Guest Services: gift shop, complimentary evening beverages, valet and coin laundry, area transportation. **Business Services:** meeting rooms, fax (fee). **Cards:** AX, CB, DC, DS, JC, MC, VI. *(See color ad p 728)*
SOME UNITS

[icons]

EMBASSY SUITES INTERNATIONAL DRIVE/JAMAICAN CT **Phone: (407)345-8250** 230
[AAA] [SAVE] All Year [BP] 1P: $149-$159 2P: $169-$179 XP: $10 F18
Location: I-4, exit 74A, just e on Sand Lake Rd, then just s on International Dr. 8250 Jamaican Ct 32819. Fax: 407/352-1463. **Facility:** 246 one-bedroom suites. 8 stories, interior corridors. *Bath:* combo or shower only. **Parking:** on-site. **Terms:** 3 day cancellation notice-fee imposed, 11% service charge. **Amenities:** dual
Small-scale Hotel phone lines, voice mail, safes, irons, hair dryers. **Pool(s):** indoor/outdoor. **Leisure Activities:** sauna, whirlpool, exercise room. *Fee:* game room. **Guest Services:** gift shop, complimentary evening beverages, valet and coin laundry, area transportation-major attractions. **Business Services:** meeting rooms, fax (fee). **Cards:** AX, CB, DC, DS, MC, VI. **Special Amenities: free continental breakfast and free newspaper.**
SOME UNITS

[icons]

EMBASSY SUITES ORLANDO AIRPORT **Phone: (407)888-9339** 302
[AAA] [SAVE] 1/1-4/30 [BP] 1P: $109-$209 2P: $109-$209 XP: $15 F18
12/1-12/31 & 10/1-11/30 [BP] 1P: $109-$179 2P: $109-$179 XP: $15 F18
5/1-9/30 [BP] 1P: $99-$179 2P: $99-$179 XP: $15 F18
Location: SR 528 (Bee Line Expwy), exit 11, 0.5 mi n on SR 436, just e. 5835 TG Lee Blvd 32822. Fax: 407/856-5956.
Small-scale Hotel **Facility:** Designated smoking area. 174 one-bedroom suites. 7 stories, interior corridors. *Bath:* combo or shower only. **Parking:** on-site. **Terms:** check-in 4 pm, cancellation fee imposed, package plans - weekends.
Amenities: video games (fee), dual phone lines, voice mail, irons, hair dryers. **Dining:** 6:30 am-11 pm. **Pool(s):** heated outdoor.
Leisure Activities: whirlpool, exercise room. **Guest Services:** gift shop, complimentary evening beverages, valet and coin laundry. **Business Services:** meeting rooms, fax (fee). **Cards:** AX, DC, DS, MC, VI. **Special Amenities: free newspaper.**
(See color ad p 637)
SOME UNITS

[icons] FEE

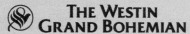

(See map p. 598)

THE ENCLAVE SUITES AT ORLANDO

Phone: (407)351-1155   (205)

12/1-12/31 [CP]	1P: $119-$159
7/1-8/31 [CP]	1P: $109-$159
1/1-6/30 & 9/1-11/30 [CP]	1P: $109-$149

Condominium

Location: I-4, exit 74A, just e on SR 482 (Sand Lake Rd), 0.6 mi n on International Dr, then just e. 6165 Carrier Dr 32819. **Fax:** 407/351-2001. **Facility:** 321 units. 155 one-bedroom standard units. 166 two-bedroom suites ($179-$219). 10 stories, interior corridors. **Parking:** on-site. **Terms:** 3 day cancellation notice-fee imposed, package plans - seasonal. **Amenities:** voice mail, safes (fee), irons, hair dryers. **Dining:** 7 am-midnight. **Pool(s):** outdoor, heated outdoor, heated indoor, 2 wading. **Leisure Activities:** whirlpools, lighted tennis court, playground, exercise room. *Fee:* game room. **Guest Services:** gift shop, valet and coin laundry, airport transportation (fee)-Orlando International and Sanford Airports, area transportation-major attractions. **Business Services:** conference facilities, fax. **Cards:** AX, DC, MC, VI. **Special Amenities:** free continental breakfast and free local telephone calls. *(See color ad below)*

SOME UNITS

FEE

(See map p. 598)

FAIRFIELD INN & SUITES AT UNIVERSAL STUDIOS ORLANDO Phone: 407/581-5600 **218**
(AAA) [SAVE] All Year [CP] 1P: $79-$99 2P: $79-$99
Location: I-4, exit 75B, 1 mi n on SR 435 (Kirkman Rd), then just e. 5614 Vineland Rd 32819. Fax: 407/581-5601. **Facility:** 116 one-bedroom standard units. 6 stories, interior corridors. *Bath:* combo or shower only. **Parking:** on-site. **Amenities:** voice mail, irons, hair dryers. *Some:* dual phone lines. **Pool(s):** outdoor. **Leisure Activi-**
Small-scale Hotel **ties:** whirlpool, exercise room. **Guest Services:** valet and coin laundry, area transportation (fee)-major attractions. **Business Services:** fax (fee). **Cards:** AX, CB, DC, DS, MC, VI. **Special Amenities:** free continental breakfast and free local telephone calls. *(See color ad card insert)*

SOME UNITS
[icons] FEE

FAIRFIELD INN & SUITES BY MARRIOTT-INTERNATIONAL COVE Phone: (407)351-7000 **208**
(AAA) [SAVE] All Year [CP] 1P: $79-$99 2P: $79-$99
Location: I-4, exit 74A (Sand Lake Rd), just e, then left. 7495 Canada Ave 32819. Fax: 407/351-0052. **Facility:** 200 one-bedroom standard units. 5 stories, interior corridors. *Bath:* combo or shower only. **Parking:** on-site. **Amenities:** voice mail, irons, hair dryers. *Some:* CD players. **Pool(s):** heated outdoor. **Leisure Activi-**
Small-scale Hotel **ties:** whirlpool, exercise room. *Fee:* game room. **Guest Services:** valet and coin laundry, area transportation-major attractions. **Cards:** AX, CB, DC, DS, MC, VI. **Special Amenities:** free continental breakfast and free local telephone calls. *(See ad below)*

SOME UNITS
[icons]

FAIRFIELD INN AT MARRIOTT VILLAGE Phone: (407)938-9001 **320**
(AAA) [SAVE] All Year 1P: $69-$119 2P: $69-$119
Location: I-4, exit 68, e on SR 535 to Vineland Ave. 8615 Vineland Ave 32821. Fax: 407/938-9002. **Facility:** 388 one-bedroom standard units. 5 stories, interior corridors. *Bath:* combo or shower only. **Parking:** on-site. **Terms:** [AP] & [CP] meal plans available, package plans - seasonal, weekends. **Amenities:** video games
Small-scale Hotel (fee), voice mail, irons, hair dryers. **Pool(s):** heated outdoor. **Leisure Activities:** whirlpool, exercise room. *Fee:* game room. **Guest Services:** valet and coin laundry, area transportation-major attractions. **Business Services:** fax (fee). **Cards:** AX, DC, DS, MC, VI. **Special Amenities:** free continental breakfast and free local telephone calls. *(See color ad p 717)*

SOME UNITS
[icons] FEE

FAIRFIELD INN BY MARRIOTT Phone: (407)888-2666 **303**
[SAVE] 6/16-11/30 [ECP] 1P: $99-$139 2P: $109-$149
2/10-4/27 [ECP] 1P: $99-$119 2P: $109-$129
4/28-6/15 [ECP] 1P: $89-$109 2P: $99-$119
12/1-2/9 [ECP] 1P: $69-$79 2P: $74-$104
Small-scale Hotel **Location:** SR 528 (Bee Line Expwy), exit 11, 0.5 mi n on SR 436, just e. 7100 Augusta National Dr 32822. Fax: 407/888-8464. **Facility:** 139 one-bedroom standard units, some with whirlpools. 4 stories, interior corridors. *Bath:* combo or shower only. **Parking:** on-site. **Amenities:** high-speed Internet (fee), irons, hair dryers. **Pool(s):** heated outdoor. **Leisure Activities:** whirlpool, exercise room. **Guest Services:** valet and coin laundry. **Business Services:** meeting rooms, fax (fee). **Cards:** AX, CB, DC, DS, MC, VI.

SOME UNITS
[icons]

FAIRFIELD INN BY MARRIOTT-INTERNATIONAL DRIVE Phone: (407)363-1944 **237**
[SAVE] All Year [ECP] 1P: $69-$129 2P: $69-$129
Location: I-4, exit 74A, then just e on Sand Lake Rd, then just s on International Dr. 8342 Jamaican Ct 32819. Fax: 407/363-1944. **Facility:** 135 one-bedroom standard units. 3 stories, interior/exterior corridors. **Parking:** on-site. **Terms:** cancellation fee imposed. **Amenities:** safes, irons. *Some:* hair dryers. **Pool(s):** heated out-
Small-scale Hotel door. **Guest Services:** valet laundry. **Business Services:** fax (fee). **Cards:** AX, CB, DC, DS, MC, VI.

SOME UNITS
[icons]

(See map p. 598)

FAIRFIELD INN BY MARRIOTT-ORLANDO SOUTH

Motel

Phone: (407)240-8400 **279**

All Year 1P: $64
Location: Just e of Landstreet Rd and S Orange Blossom Tr; from Florida Tpke, exit 254, just n. 1850 Landstreet Rd 32809. Fax: 407/240-8400. **Facility:** 132 one-bedroom standard units. 3 stories, interior/exterior corridors. *Bath:* combo or shower only. **Parking:** on-site. **Terms:** cancellation fee imposed, [CP] meal plan available. **Amenities:** irons, hair dryers. **Pool(s):** heated outdoor. **Guest Services:** valet laundry. **Business Services:** fax (fee). **Cards:** AX, DC, DS, MC, VI.
SOME UNITS

FAIRFIELD ORLANDO INTERNATIONAL RESORT CLUB
Condominium

Phone: (407)351-2641 **324**

12/1-1/4 1P: $100-$165
3/9-9/6 1P: $165
1/5-3/8 & 9/7-11/30 1P: $100
Location: I-4, exit 75A, just s on Universal Blvd, then 0.3 mi e on International Blvd. 5353 Del Verde Way 32819. Fax: 407/352-2994. **Facility:** 63 two-bedroom suites with kitchens. 2 stories, exterior corridors. **Parking:** on-site. **Terms:** check-in 4 pm. **Amenities:** video library (fee), voice mail, irons, hair dryers. **Pool(s):** heated outdoor. **Leisure Activities:** lighted tennis court, exercise room, basketball, shuffleboard. **Business Services:** fax (fee). **Cards:** AX, MC, VI.

HAMPTON INN AIRPORT
Small-scale Hotel

Phone: (407)888-2995 **293**

2/10-4/27 [ECP] 1P: $109-$139 2P: $109-$139
6/16-11/30 [ECP] 1P: $99-$119 2P: $109-$129
4/28-6/15 [ECP] 1P: $89-$109 2P: $99-$119
12/1-2/9 [ECP] 1P: $89-$109 2P: $89-$109
Location: SR 528 (Bee Line Expwy) exit 11, 0.5 mi n on SR 436, just e. 5767 TG Lee Blvd 32822. Fax: 407/888-2418. **Facility:** 124 one-bedroom standard units. 7 stories, interior corridors. *Bath:* combo or shower only. **Parking:** on-site. **Amenities:** high-speed Internet (fee), voice mail, irons, hair dryers. **Pool(s):** outdoor. **Leisure Activities:** limited exercise equipment. **Guest Services:** valet and coin laundry. **Business Services:** meeting rooms, fax (fee). **Cards:** AX, CB, DC, DS, MC, VI. *(See color ad p 624)*
SOME UNITS

HAMPTON INN AT UNIVERSAL STUDIOS
Small-scale Hotel

Phone: (407)351-6716 **185**

All Year 1P: $59-$109 2P: $69-$109
Location: I-4, exit 75B, 1 mi n on SR 435 (Kirkman Rd), just e. 5621 Windhover Dr 32819. Fax: 407/363-1711. **Facility:** 120 one-bedroom standard units. 5 stories, interior corridors. *Bath:* combo or shower only. **Parking:** on-site. **Terms:** check-in 4 pm, cancellation fee imposed, [ECP] meal plan available. **Amenities:** irons, hair dryers. **Pool(s):** heated outdoor. **Guest Services:** valet laundry. **Business Services:** meeting rooms, fax. **Cards:** AX, CB, DC, DS, MC, VI. **Special Amenities:** free continental breakfast and free local telephone calls. *(See color ad card insert)*
SOME UNITS
FEE FEE

HAMPTON INN-CONVENTION CENTER
Small-scale Hotel

Phone: (407)354-4447 **238**

All Year [ECP] 1P: $62-$90 2P: $62-$90
Location: I-4, exit 74A, 0.5 mi e on SR 482 (Sand Lake Rd), then 0.9 mi s. 8900 Universal Blvd 32819. Fax: 407/354-3031. **Facility:** Designated smoking area. 170 one-bedroom standard units. 7 stories, interior corridors. *Bath:* combo or shower only. **Parking:** on-site. **Terms:** cancellation fee imposed. **Amenities:** video games (fee), dual phone lines, voice mail, irons. **Pool(s):** heated outdoor. **Leisure Activities:** exercise room. **Guest Services:** valet laundry. **Business Services:** meeting rooms, fax. **Cards:** AX, CB, DC, DS, JC, MC, VI.
SOME UNITS

HAMPTON INN-FLORIDA MALL
Small-scale Hotel

Phone: (407)859-4100 **278**

All Year [ECP] 1P: $69-$89 2P: $79-$89
Location: On US 17-92 and 441, 0.5 mi n of Florida Tpke, exit 254. 8601 S Orange Blossom Tr 32809. Fax: 407/240-4736. **Facility:** 128 one-bedroom standard units. 2 stories, interior corridors. *Bath:* combo or shower only. **Parking:** on-site. **Terms:** package plans - weekends. **Amenities:** dual phone lines, voice mail, irons, hair dryers. **Pool(s):** outdoor. **Guest Services:** valet and coin laundry. **Business Services:** meeting rooms, fax. **Cards:** AX, CB, DC, DS, MC, VI. **Special Amenities:** free continental breakfast and free local telephone calls. *(See color ad card insert)*
SOME UNITS
FEE FEE

HAMPTON INN SAND LAKE
Small-scale Hotel

Phone: (407)363-7886 **213**

2/10-4/27 & 6/16-11/30 [ECP] 1P: $79-$129 2P: $89-$139
12/1-2/9 & 4/28-6/15 [ECP] 1P: $69-$109 2P: $79-$119
Location: I-4, exit 74A, 0.3 mi e on SR 482, at Universal Blvd. 6101 Sand Lake Rd 32819. Fax: 407/345-0670. **Facility:** 334 one-bedroom standard units. 4 stories, interior corridors. *Bath:* combo or shower only. **Parking:** on-site. **Amenities:** high-speed Internet (fee), voice mail, irons, hair dryers. **Pool(s):** outdoor, wading. **Leisure Activities:** exercise room. *Fee:* game room. **Guest Services:** gift shop, valet and coin laundry, area transportation. **Business Services:** meeting rooms, fax (fee). **Cards:** AX, CB, DC, DS, MC, VI. *(See color ad p 624)*
SOME UNITS

(See map p. 598)

HAMPTON INN-SOUTH OF UNIVERSAL STUDIOS **Phone:** (407)345-1112 [204]

[SAVE]

| | 2/10-4/27 & 6/16-11/30 [ECP] | 1P: $79-$129 | 2P: $89-$139 |
| | 12/1-2/9 & 4/28-6/15 [ECP] | 1P: $69-$109 | 2P: $79-$119 |

Location: I-4, exit 75B, 0.8 mi s on SR 435. 7110 S Kirkman Rd 32819. **Fax:** 407/352-6591. **Facility:** 170 units. 169 one-bedroom standard units, some with whirlpools. 1 one-bedroom suite. 8 stories, interior corridors. *Bath:* Small-scale Hotel combo or shower only. **Parking:** on-site. **Amenities:** high-speed Internet, voice mail, irons, hair dryers. **Pool(s):** outdoor, wading. **Leisure Activities:** exercise room. *Fee:* game room. **Guest Services:** gift shop, valet and coin laundry, area transportation. **Business Services:** meeting rooms, fax (fee). **Cards:** AX, CB, DC, DS, MC, VI.
(See color ad p 624)

SOME UNITS

[S🆓] [🛎📶] [🚹M] [⚙] [🅿] [🏊] [🎬] [DATA PORT] [🔌] [🍴] [📺] /[❌]/

HAWTHORN SUITES HOTEL **Phone:** (407)597-5000 [322]

[AAA] [SAVE]

	6/13-8/9 [BP]	1P: $129-$149	2P: $129-$149
	2/7-6/12 [BP]	1P: $109-$149	2P: $109-$149
	12/1-2/6 & 8/10-11/30 [BP]	1P: $89-$129	2P: $89-$129

Location: I-4, exit 68, 0.6 mi n on SR 535, 0.8 mi e. 8303 Palm Pkwy 32836. **Fax:** 407/597-6000. **Facility:** 120 units. Small-scale Hotel 8 one-bedroom standard units. 112 one-bedroom suites with kitchens. 5 stories, interior corridors. *Bath:* combo or shower only. **Parking:** on-site. **Terms:** cancellation fee imposed. **Amenities:** video games, voice mail, irons, hair dryers. **Pool(s):** outdoor. **Leisure Activities:** whirlpool, exercise room, basketball. **Guest Services:** gift shop, complimentary evening beverages: Mon, Tues & Thurs, valet and coin laundry, area transportation-Disney. **Business Services:** meeting rooms, fax (fee). **Cards:** AX, CB, DC, DS, MC, VI. *(See color ad card insert)*

SOME UNITS

[S🆓] [🛎📶] [⚙] [🅿] [🏊] [❌] [🎬] [DATA PORT] /[❌] [🔌] [🍴] [📺] /

HAWTHORN SUITES ORLANDO **Phone:** (407)351-6600 [254]

All Year [BP] 1P: $95-$189 2P: $95-$189

Location: I-4, exit 72, just e on SR 528 (Bee Line Expwy) to exit 1, then just s. 6435 Westwood Blvd 32821. Small-scale Hotel **Facility:** 150 units. 30 one-bedroom standard units. 120 one-bedroom suites with kitchens. 5 stories, interior corridors. **Parking:** on-site. **Terms:** check-in 4 pm, cancellation fee imposed. **Amenities:** video library (fee), video games, voice mail, irons, hair dryers. **Pool(s):** heated outdoor, wading. **Leisure Activities:** whirlpool, playground, exercise room. *Fee:* game room. **Guest Services:** valet and coin laundry, area transportation. **Business Services:** meeting rooms, fax (fee). **Cards:** AX, DC, DS, MC, VI. *(See color ad below)*

SOME UNITS

[ASK] [S🆓] [🛎📶] [⚙] [🏊] [❌] [VCR] [🎬] [DATA PORT] [🔌] [🍴] [📺] /[❌]/

(See map p. 598)

HAWTHORN SUITES ORLANDO AIRPORT   **Phone:** (407)438-2121   305

(AAA) SAVE   All Year [BP]   1P: $69-$109   2P: $69-$109

▼▼◆▼◆▼▼   **Location:** SR 528 (Bee Line Expwy), exit 11, 0.5 mi n on SR 436, just e, then just s. 7450 Augusta National Dr 32822.
         Fax: 407/438-2275. **Facility:** 135 units. 129 one- and 6 two-bedroom suites, some with efficiencies or
Small-scale Hotel   kitchens. 3 stories, interior corridors. *Bath:* combo or shower only. **Parking:** on-site. **Terms:** pets ($50 extra
         charge). **Amenities:** CD players, high-speed Internet, dual phone lines, voice mail, fax, safes, irons, hair
dryers. **Pool(s):** heated outdoor. **Leisure Activities:** whirlpool, exercise room, basketball, volleyball. *Fee:*
game room. **Guest Services:** complimentary evening beverages, valet and coin laundry, area transportation-within 3 mi. **Business Services:** meeting rooms, business center. **Cards:** AX, CB, DC, DS, JC, MC, VI. **Special Amenities:** free continental
breakfast and free local telephone calls. *(See color ad p 642)*

SOME UNITS

[icons row] S/D ⊞ 🛏 ⏮ ⌕M ⊠ ⊘ ⊠ VCR ⊠ DATA/PORT ⊟ ⊡ ⊟ /⊠/

(See map p. 598)

HAWTHORN SUITES UNIVERSAL ORLANDO

Phone: (407)581-2151

[211]

AAA [SAVE]

All Year [BP]

1P: $79-$129   2P: $79-$129

Location: Just e of jct Sand Lake Rd and International Dr. 7601 Canada Dr 32819. Fax: 407/581-2152. **Facility:** 143 units. 133 one- and 10 two-bedroom suites with kitchens. 6 stories, interior corridors. *Bath:* combo or shower only. **Parking:** on-site. **Amenities:** CD players, dual phone lines, voice mail, safes, irons, hair dryers. **Small-scale Hotel** **Pool(s):** heated outdoor. **Leisure Activities:** whirlpool, gas grills, exercise room, sports court. *Fee:* game room. **Guest Services:** complimentary evening beverages, valet and coin laundry, area transportation-major attractions. **Business Services:** meeting rooms, fax (fee). **Cards:** AX, CB, DC, DS, JC, MC, VI. **Special Amenities:** free continental breakfast and free local telephone calls. *(See color ad p 643)*

SOME UNITS

(icons) / (icon) /

HILTON GARDEN INN ORLANDO AT SEAWORLD INTERNATIONAL CENTER

Phone: (407)354-1500

[256]

AAA [SAVE]

All Year

1P: $79-$129   2P: $79-$129   XP: $10   F18

Location: I-4, exit 72, 1 mi e to International Dr, 0.4 mi w. 6850 Westwood Blvd 32821. Fax: 407/354-1528. **Facility:** 233 units. 226 one-bedroom standard units. 7 one-bedroom suites. 8 stories, interior corridors. *Bath:* combo or shower only. **Parking:** on-site. **Terms:** check-in 4 pm, cancellation fee imposed. **Amenities:** video **Small-scale Hotel** games (fee), dual phone lines, voice mail, irons, hair dryers. **Dining:** 6:30 am-1 & 5-10 pm, cocktails. **Pool(s):** heated outdoor. **Leisure Activities:** whirlpool, exercise room. **Guest Services:** valet and coin laundry, area transportation-Disney. **Business Services:** meeting rooms, business center. **Cards:** AX, CB, DC, DS, MC, VI. *(See color ad below)*

SOME UNITS

(icons) / (icon) /

HILTON GARDEN INN ORLANDO INTERNATIONAL AIRPORT

Phone: (407)240-3725

[306]

[SAVE]

2/10-4/27   1P: $104-$124   2P: $114-$134
6/16-11/30   1P: $99-$119   2P: $109-$129
12/1-2/9 & 4/28-6/15   1P: $89-$114   2P: $99-$124

Location: SR 528, exit 11, 0.5 mi n on SR 436, just e, then just s (Bee Line Expwy). 7300 Augusta National Dr 32822. **Small-scale Hotel** Fax: 407/240-3825. **Facility:** 132 units. 129 one-bedroom standard units, some with whirlpools. 3 one-bedroom suites ($109-$149). 4 stories, interior corridors. *Bath:* combo or shower only. **Parking:** on-site. **Amenities:** dual phone lines, voice mail, irons, hair dryers. *Fee:* video games, high-speed Internet. **Pool(s):** heated outdoor, wading. **Leisure Activities:** exercise room. **Guest Services:** valet and coin laundry. **Business Services:** meeting rooms, business center. **Cards:** AX, CB, DC, DS, MC, VI. *(See color ad p 624)*

SOME UNITS

(icons) / (icon) /

HILTON GRAND VACATIONS CLUB

Phone: (407)239-0100

[258]

[SAVE]

12/1-4/30   1P: $179   2P: $179
5/1-11/30   1P: $169   2P: $169

Location: I-4, exit 72, just s on International Dr, 1 mi w on Sea Harbour Dr; Bee Line Expwy (SR 528), exit 1, s to Sea Harbour Dr. 6924 Grand Vacations Way 32821. Fax: 407/239-0200. **Facility:** 420 units. 207 one-bedroom standard units. 165 two- and 48 three-bedroom suites ($229-$329). 1-6 stories, exterior corridors. *Bath:* combo or shower only. **Parking:** on-site. **Terms:** check-in 4 pm, 3 day cancellation notice. **Amenities:** video library, voice mail, irons, hair dryers. *Some:* CD players. **Pool(s):** outdoor, 2 heated outdoor, 2 wading. **Leisure Activities:** whirlpools, putting green, recreation programs, playground, exercise room, shuffleboard. *Fee:* massage. **Guest Services:** gift shop, complimentary laundry, area transportation. **Business Services:** fax (fee). **Cards:** AX, CB, DC, DS, JC, VI.

SOME UNITS

(icons) / (icon) /

(See map p. 598)

HOLIDAY HOMES OF ORLANDO
Phone: (407)240-5527 **282**

(AAA) (SAVE)
◈◈◈◈

Condominium

1/5-8/31	1P: $129-$269	2P: $129-$269
12/1-1/4 & 9/1-11/30	1P: $99-$269	2P: $99-$269

Location: 0.5 mi s of jct Florida Tpke, exit 254, then e on Taft-Vineland. Located in Cypress Park Plaza Business Park. 9521 S Orange Blossom Tr-118A 32837. **Fax:** 407/240-5530. **Facility:** 100 units. 15 two- and 85 three-bedroom suites. 2 stories, exterior corridors. **Parking:** on-site. **Terms:** check-in 4 pm, 30 day cancellation notice-fee imposed, weekly rates available. **Amenities:** irons. **Leisure Activities:** Fee: golf-18 holes. **Guest Services:** complimentary laundry. **Business Services:** fax (fee). **Cards:** MC, VI. **Special Amenities:** free room upgrade and preferred room (each subject to availability with advanced reservations). *(See color ad below)*

SOME UNITS

[$ᴅ] [⬭] [VCR] [✦] [🖥] [⬜] [⬜] / [✕] /

HOLIDAY INN & SUITES AT UNIVERSAL ORLANDO
Phone: (407)351-3333 **191**

(AAA) (SAVE)
◈◈◈

Small-scale Hotel

All Year	1P: $79-$159

Location: I-4, exit 75B, 0.5 mi n on SR 435 (Kirkman Rd). 5905 S Kirkman Rd 32819. **Fax:** 407/351-3577. **Facility:** 390 units. 257 one-bedroom standard units. 94 one- and 39 two-bedroom suites ($129-$299). 10 stories, interior corridors. *Bath:* combo or shower only. **Parking:** on-site. **Terms:** check-in 4 pm, package plans, pets ($50 fee). **Amenities:** video games, voice mail, irons, hair dryers. *Some:* dual phone lines, safes (fee). **Dining:** 6:30 am-11 pm, cocktails. **Pool(s):** heated outdoor, wading. **Leisure Activities:** exercise room. *Fee:* game room. **Guest Services:** gift shop, valet and coin laundry, area transportation-selected attractions. **Business Services:** meeting rooms, business center. **Cards:** AX, DC, DS, JC, VI. **Special Amenities:** free newspaper. *(See color ad p 646 & opposite inside back cover)*

SOME UNITS

[$ᴅ] [⬭] [🍴] [⬩ᴹ] [♿] [⬭] [✦] [🖥] / [✕] [🖥] [⬜] /

HOLIDAY INN EXPRESS FLORIDA MALL
Phone: (407)851-8200 **276**

(AAA) (SAVE)
◈◈◈

Small-scale Hotel

All Year [ECP]	1P: $70-$100	2P: $70-$100	XP: $10
			F12

Location: Florida Tpke, exit 254, then just n. 8820 S Orange Blossom Tr 32809. **Fax:** 407/855-7153. **Facility:** 162 units. 137 one-bedroom standard units. 25 one-bedroom suites ($90-$130). 2 stories, interior corridors. *Bath:* combo or shower only. **Parking:** on-site. **Terms:** 1-3 night minimum stay - seasonal, package plans - seasonal & weekends. **Amenities:** dual phone lines, voice mail, irons, hair dryers. **Pool(s):** outdoor, wading. **Leisure Activities:** exercise room. **Guest Services:** coin laundry, area transportation-major attractions. **Cards:** AX, DC, DS, MC, VI. **Special Amenities:** free continental breakfast and free local telephone calls.

SOME UNITS

[$ᴅ] [🍴] [⬩ᴹ] [♿] [⬭] [✦] [⬜] [🖥] [🖥] / [✕] [⬜] /

HOLIDAY INN EXPRESS INTERNATIONAL DRIVE
Phone: (407)351-4430 **198**

◈◈◈

Motel

12/1-1/2 & 6/12-8/17 [ECP]	1P: $100-$120	2P: $100-$120
1/3-6/11 & 8/18-11/30 [ECP]	1P: $90-$110	2P: $90-$110

Location: I-4, exit 74A, just e on Sand Lake Rd, then 0.7 mi n. 6323 International Dr 32819. **Fax:** 407/345-0742. **Facility:** 218 one-bedroom standard units. 2 stories, interior corridors. *Bath:* combo or shower only. **Parking:** on-site. **Terms:** check-in 4 pm, $3 service charge, small pets only ($75 fee). **Amenities:** video games (fee), safes, irons, hair dryers. **Pool(s):** heated outdoor. **Leisure Activities:** Fee: game room. **Guest Services:** valet and coin laundry, area transportation. **Business Services:** fax (fee). **Cards:** AX, CB, DC, DS, JC, MC, VI.

SOME UNITS

[ASK] [$ᴅ] [⬭] [🍴] [⬩ᴹ] [♿] [⬭] [✦] [🖥] / [✕] [⬜] [🖥] [⬜] /

HOLIDAY INN EXPRESS ORLANDO AIRPORT WEST
Phone: (407)851-1113 **287**

(AAA) (SAVE)
◈◈◈

Motel

All Year [ECP]	1P: $59-$89	2P: $59-$89

Location: SR 482, just w of jct SR 528 (Bee Line Expwy). 1853 McCoy Rd 32809. **Fax:** 407/438-5883. **Facility:** 168 units. 114 one-bedroom standard units. 54 one-bedroom suites ($69-$99). 3 stories, interior/exterior corridors. *Bath:* combo or shower only. **Parking:** on-site. **Amenities:** voice mail, irons, hair dryers. *Some:* CD players, dual phone lines, safes. **Pool(s):** outdoor. **Leisure Activities:** whirlpool. **Guest Services:** complimentary evening beverages, valet and coin laundry. **Business Services:** meeting rooms, business center. **Cards:** AX, CB, DC, DS, JC, MC, VI. **Special Amenities:** free continental breakfast and free local telephone calls. *(See color ad p 647)*

SOME UNITS

[$ᴅ] [✦] [🍴] [♿] [🖥] [⬭] [✦] [🖥] [⬜] / [✕] [VCR] [🖥] [⬜] /

(See map p. 598)

HOLIDAY INN HOTEL & SUITES/ORLANDO/ORANGE COUNTY

CONVENTION CENTER   **Phone:** (407)581-9001   222

(AAA) (SAVE) All Year   1P: $109-$129   2P: $109-$129

▼▼▼▼ **Location:** I-4, exit 74A, 0.5 mi e on SR 482 (Sand Lake Rd), then just s; exit 29A westbound. 8214 Universal Blvd 32819. Fax: 407/581-9002. **Facility:** 150 units. 115 one-bedroom standard units. 35 one-bedroom suites with kitchens. 6 stories, interior corridors. *Bath:* combo or shower only. **Parking:** on-site. **Terms:** [MAP] meal plan

Small-scale Hotel available, 6% service charge. **Amenities:** dual phone lines, voice mail, irons, hair dryers. **Dining:** 6 am-9:30 & 5-10 pm, cocktails. **Pool(s):** outdoor. **Leisure Activities:** whirlpool, exercise room. **Guest Services:** gift shop, valet and coin laundry, area transportation (fee). **Business Services:** meeting rooms, business center. **Cards:** AX, DC, DS, MC, VI. **Special Amenities:** early check-in/late check-out and free newspaper.
(See color ad card insert & opposite inside back cover)

SOME UNITS

[icons] FEE /✕/

HOLIDAY INN-INTERNATIONAL DRIVE RESORT   **Phone:** (407)351-3500   192

(AAA) (SAVE) All Year   1P: $69-$129

▼▼▼▼ **Location:** I-4, exit 74A, just e on Sand Lake Rd, then 0.5 mi n. 6515 International Dr 32819. Fax: 407/351-5727. **Facility:** 652 units. 646 one-bedroom standard units. 6 one-bedroom suites, some with efficiencies (no uten-

Motel sils). 2-12 stories, interior/exterior corridors. *Bath:* combo or shower only. **Parking:** on-site. **Terms:** check-in 4 pm, pets ($25 fee, $75 deposit). **Amenities:** voice mail, safes, irons, hair dryers. *Some:* fax. **Dining:** 2 restaurants, 6:30 am-11 pm, cocktails. **Pool(s):** heated outdoor, wading. **Leisure Activities:** whirlpool, playground, exercise room, shuffleboard, volleyball. **Guest Services:** gift shop, valet and coin laundry, area transportation-major attractions. **Business Services:** conference facilities, business center. **Cards:** AX, CB, DC, DS, JC, MC, VI. **Special Amenities:** early check-in/late check-out and free newspaper. *(See color ad opposite inside back cover & below)*

SOME UNITS

[icons] /✕/

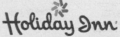

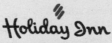

(See map p. 598)

HOLIDAY INN SELECT ORLANDO INTERNATIONAL AIRPORT

Phone: (407)851-6400 **300**

(AAA) [SAVE]

1/1-3/31	1P: $130-$150	2P: $130-$150
9/1-11/30	1P: $110-130	2P: $110-130
12/1-12/31	1P: $100-$110	2P: $100-$110
4/1-8/31	1P: $90-$110	2P: $90-$110

Small-scale Hotel Location: SR 528 (Bee Line Expwy), exit 11, 0.5 mi n on SR 436, just e. 5750 TG Lee Blvd 32822. **Fax:** 407/354-3421. **Facility:** 288 one-bedroom standard units. 7 stories, interior corridors. *Bath:* combo or shower only. **Parking:** on-site. **Terms:** check-in 4 pm, [BP] & [CP] meal plans available. **Amenities:** voice mail, irons, hair dryers. *Some:* fax. **Dining:** 6-10:30 am, 11:30-2 & 6-10 pm, Sat & Sun from 7 am, cocktails. **Pool(s):** heated outdoor. **Leisure Activities:** saunas, whirlpool, 2 lighted tennis courts, exercise room, basketball, volleyball. **Guest Services:** gift shop, valet and coin laundry. **Business Services:** conference facilities, business center. **Cards:** AX, CB, DC, DS, MC, VI. **Special Amenities:** free newspaper.
(See color ad opposite inside back cover & p 648)

SOME UNITS

🛰 🕂 🍴 🍸 🔊ᴹ 🛦 🔊 🏊 ✂ 🐾 ᴅᴬᵀᴬᴾᴼᴿᵀ 🖳 / 🗙 🖳 / FEE FEE

HOMESTEAD STUDIO SUITES HOTEL-ORLANDO/SOUTH

Phone: (407)352-5577 **269**

All Year	1P: $53	2P: $58	XP: $5 F18

Motel

Location: Just sw of jct SR 423 (John Young Pkwy) and 482 (Sand Lake Rd). 4101 Equity Row 32819. **Fax:** 407/352-2029. **Facility:** 135 one-bedroom standard units with efficiencies. 3 stories, interior corridors. *Bath:* combo or shower only. **Parking:** on-site. **Terms:** cancellation fee imposed, pets ($75 fee). **Amenities:** voice mail, irons. **Guest Services:** valet and coin laundry. **Cards:** AX, CB, DC, DS, JC, MC, VI.

SOME UNITS

[ASK] 🛰 🐾 🔊ᴹ 🛦 🔊 🕂 📹 ᴅᴬᵀᴬᴾᴼᴿᵀ 🖳 🖳 🖳 / 🗙 /

HOMEWOOD SUITES BY HILTON

Phone: (407)248-2232 **221**

[SAVE]

All Year [ECP] 1P: $99-$149

Location: I-4, exit 74A, just e on SR 482 (Sand Lake Rd), then 0.5 mi s. 8745 International Dr 32819. **Fax:** 407/248-6552. **Facility:** 252 units. 231 one- and 21 two-bedroom suites with efficiencies. 6 stories, interior corridors. *Bath:* combo or shower only. **Parking:** on-site. **Terms:** check-in 4 pm, cancellation fee imposed. **Amenities:** dual phone lines, voice mail, irons, hair dryers. *Fee:* video games, safes. **Pool(s):** heated outdoor. **Leisure Activities:** whirlpool, exercise room. **Guest Services:** complimentary evening beverages: Mon-Thurs, valet and coin laundry, area transportation. **Business Services:** meeting rooms, business center. **Cards:** AX, CB, DC, DS, MC, VI. *(See color ad below)*

Small-scale Hotel

SOME UNITS

🛰 🍴 🔊ᴹ 🛦 🔊 🏊 📹 ᴅᴬᵀᴬᴾᴼᴿᵀ 🖳 🖳 🖳 / 🗙 /

HOWARD JOHNSON FLORIDA MALL

Phone: (407)851-4300 **260**

12/1-3/31 & 6/1-8/31	1P: $74
4/1-5/31 & 9/1-11/30	1P: $69

Motel

Location: On US 17-92 and 441; 3.5 mi s of I-4, exit 80; 1 mi n of jct SR 482 and Sand Lake Rd. 7101 S Orange Blossom Tr 32809. **Fax:** 407/859-6723. **Facility:** 162 one-bedroom standard units. 2 stories, interior/exterior corridors. **Parking:** on-site. **Terms:** check-in 4 pm, [CP] meal plan available. **Amenities:** high-speed Internet, voice mail. *Some:* hair dryers. **Pool(s):** outdoor, wading. **Guest Services:** valet and coin laundry. **Business Services:** meeting rooms, fax (fee). **Cards:** AX, CB, DC, DS, MC, VI.

SOME UNITS

[ASK] 🛰 🍴 🔊 🏊 📹 ᴅᴬᵀᴬᴾᴼᴿᵀ 🖳 / 🗙 /

HOWARD JOHNSON INN-INTERNATIONAL DRIVE

Phone: (407)351-2900 **196**

(AAA) [SAVE]

All Year 1P: $60-$100 2P: $60-$100

Location: I-4, exit 74A, just e on Sand Lake Rd, then 0.4 mi n. 6603 International Dr 32819. **Fax:** 407/352-2738. **Facility:** 173 one-bedroom standard units. 3 stories, exterior corridors. **Parking:** on-site. **Terms:** [BP] meal plan available, $2 service charge. **Amenities:** safes, hair dryers. **Pool(s):** outdoor, wading. **Leisure Activi-ties:** exercise room, game room. **Guest Services:** valet and coin laundry, area transportation-major attractions. **Business Services:** fax (fee). **Cards:** AX, DC, DS, MC, VI. **Special Amenities:** free newspaper and free room upgrade (subject to availability with advanced reservations).

Small-scale Hotel

SOME UNITS

🛰 🏊 🖳 / 🗙 🕂 /

(See map p. 598)

HOWARD JOHNSON PLAZA HOTEL & SUITES/INTERNATIONAL DR SOUTH Phone: (407)351-5100 248

AAA SAVE All Year [CP] 1P: $49-$99 2P: $49-$99 XP: $6 F18
Location: I-4, exit 72, just e to International Dr; Bee Line Expwy (SR 528), exit 1, then just n. 9956 Hawaiian Ct 32819. Fax: 407/352-7188. **Facility:** 223 units. 175 one-bedroom standard units, some with whirlpools. 48 one-bedroom suites ($79-$119). 2 stories, interior corridors. *Bath:* combo or shower only. **Parking:** on-site.
Small-scale Hotel **Terms:** check-in 4 pm. **Amenities:** voice mail. *Fee:* video games, safes. *Some:* irons, hair dryers. **Pool(s):** outdoor. **Leisure Activities:** whirlpool, exercise room. **Guest Services:** valet and coin laundry, area transportation-major attractions. **Business Services:** meeting rooms. **Cards:** AX, CB, DC, DS, MC, VI. **Special Amenities:** free continental breakfast and free newspaper. *(See color ad below)*

SOME UNITS

HOWARD JOHNSON PLAZA RESORT UNIVERSAL GATEWAY Phone: (407)351-2000 206

All Year 1P: $55-$109 2P: $55-$109 XP: $10 F18
Location: I-4, exit 75A, 0.8 mi s on SR 435. 7050 S Kirkman Rd 32819. Fax: 407/363-1835. **Facility:** 356 one-
Small-scale Hotel bedroom standard units. 2 stories, interior corridors. *Bath:* combo or shower only. **Parking:** on-site. **Terms:** 3 day cancellation notice-fee imposed, [MAP] meal plan available, pets ($75 fee). **Amenities:** voice mail, safes (fee). **Pool(s):** outdoor, heated outdoor, wading. **Leisure Activities:** playground, shuffleboard. *Fee:* game room. **Guest Services:** gift shop, valet and coin laundry, area transportation. **Business Services:** conference facilities. **Cards:** AX, DC, DS, MC, VI. *(See color ad below)*

SOME UNITS

FEE

(See map p. 598)

HOWARD JOHNSON RESORT HOTEL & SUITES   **Phone:** (407)581-5000   [290]
▼▼▼▼▼   12/20-4/20   1P: $60-$75   2P: $60-$75
         12/1-12/19 & 4/21-11/30   1P: $50-$70   2P: $50-$70
Motel   **Location:** SR 528 (Bee Line Expwy), exit 8, just nw. 2323 McCoy Rd 32809. Fax: 407/581-5001. **Facility:** 270 one-bedroom standard units. 3 stories, exterior corridors. *Bath:* combo or shower only. **Parking:** on-site.
Terms: check-in 4 pm. **Amenities:** voice mail, safes (fee), hair dryers. *Some:* dual phone lines, irons. **Pool(s):** heated outdoor. **Leisure Activities:** putting green, exercise room. **Guest Services:** valet laundry. **Business Services:** fax (fee). **Cards:** AX, CB, DC, DS, MC, VI.

SOME UNITS

(ASK) (S/D) (✈) (†|†) (&) (🍽) (DATA PORT) (📶) / (✕) (📦) (🍳) /

HYATT REGENCY ORLANDO INTERNATIONAL AIRPORT   **Phone:** (407)825-1234   [311]
(AAA) (SAVE)   All Year   1P: $105-$255   2P: $105-$255   XP: $25   F18
▼▼▼▼▼   **Location:** At the Orlando International Airport (Terminal A). 9300 Airport Blvd 32827. Fax: 407/856-1672. **Facility:** 446 units. 431 one-bedroom standard units. 15 one-bedroom suites, some with whirlpools. 10 stories, interior corridors. *Bath:* combo or shower only. **Terms:** check-in 4 pm,
Small-scale Hotel   cancellation fee imposed. **Amenities:** video games (fee), voice mail, irons, hair dryers. *Some:* CD players, dual phone lines. **Dining:** 2 restaurants, 6:30 am-12:30 am, cocktails, also, Hemisphere, see separate listing.
Leisure Activities: jogging, exercise room, spa. *Fee:* game room. **Guest Services:** gift shop, valet laundry. **Business Services:** conference facilities, business center. **Cards:** AX, CB, DC, DS, JC, MC, VI. *(See color ad below)*

SOME UNITS

(†|†) (24†) (🍸) (&|M) (🌀) (✕) (🐾) (DATA PORT) (📶) / (✕) (VCR) (🍳) (🍳) /

LA QUINTA INN AIRPORT WEST   **Phone:** (407)857-9215   [231]
(SAVE)   All Year   1P: $49-$89   2P: $55-$96
▼▼▼▼▼   **Location:** Bee Line Expwy (SR 528), exit 9 (Trade Port), via McCoy Rd. 7931 Daetwyler Dr 32812. Fax: 407/857-0877. **Facility:** 130 one-bedroom standard units. 3 stories, exterior corridors. *Bath:* combo or shower only. **Parking:**
Small-scale Hotel   on-site. **Terms:** [ECP] meal plan available. **Amenities:** video games (fee), voice mail, irons, hair dryers. **Pool(s):** heated outdoor. **Guest Services:** coin laundry, area transportation. **Business Services:** meeting rooms, fax (fee). **Cards:** AX, CB, DC, DS, JC, MC, VI. *(See color ad p 652)*

(✈) (🐾) (†|†) (🌀) (🍽) (DATA PORT) (📶)

(See map p. 598)

LA QUINTA INN & SUITES
Phone: (407)345-1365 ⬤220

AAA SAVE

▽▽✕△▽

Small-scale Hotel

All Year   1P: $79-$119   2P: $85-$125
Location: I-4, exit 74A, 0.5 mi e on SR 482 (Sand Lake Rd), then 0.5 mi s. 8504 Universal Blvd 32819.
Fax: 407/345-5586. **Facility:** 184 units. 169 one-bedroom standard units. 15 one-bedroom suites. 7 stories,
interior corridors. *Bath:* combo or shower only. **Parking:** on-site. **Terms:** [ECP] meal plan available, small
pets only. **Amenities:** video games, voice mail, irons, hair dryers. **Pool(s):** heated outdoor. **Leisure Activities:** whirlpool, exercise room. **Guest Services:** coin laundry, area transportation-Universal Studios, Seaworld. **Business Services:** meeting rooms, fax (fee). **Cards:** AX, CB, DC, DS, JC, MC, VI. **Special Amenities:** free continental
breakfast and free local telephone calls. *(See color ad below)*

SOME UNITS

[icons] / [icons]

LA QUINTA INN & SUITES ORLANDO AIRPORT NORTH
Phone: (407)240-5000 ⬤297

SAVE

▽▽✕△▽

Small-scale Hotel

All Year   1P: $59-$89   2P: $65-$95
Location: SR 528 (Bee Line Expwy), exit 11, 0.5 mi n on SR 436, just w. 7160 N Frontage Rd 32812.
Fax: 407/240-5261. **Facility:** 148 units. 143 one-bedroom standard units. 5 one-bedroom suites. 5 stories,
interior corridors. *Bath:* combo or shower only. **Parking:** on-site. **Terms:** [ECP] meal plan available, small
pets only. **Amenities:** video games (fee), dual phone lines, voice mail, irons, hair dryers. **Pool(s):** heated
outdoor. **Leisure Activities:** whirlpool, exercise room. **Guest Services:** valet and coin laundry. **Business
Services:** meeting rooms, fax (fee). **Cards:** AX, CB, DC, DS, JC, MC, VI. *(See color ad below)*

SOME UNITS

[icons] / [icons]

LA QUINTA INN-ORLANDO INTERNATIONAL DRIVE
Phone: (407)351-1660 ⬤232

AAA SAVE

▽▽✕△▽

Small-scale Hotel

All Year   1P: $65-$95   2P: $71-$101
Location: I-4, exit 74A, just e on Sand Lake Rd, then just s on International Dr. 8300 Jamaican Ct 32819.
Fax: 407/351-9264. **Facility:** 200 one-bedroom standard units. 4 stories, exterior corridors. *Bath:* combo or
shower only. **Parking:** on-site. **Terms:** [ECP] meal plan available, small pets only. **Amenities:** video games,
voice mail, irons, hair dryers. **Pool(s):** heated outdoor, wading. **Leisure Activities:** whirlpool, putting green.
Fee: game room. **Guest Services:** valet and coin laundry. **Business Services:** fax (fee). **Cards:** AX, CB,
DC, DS, JC, MC, VI. **Special Amenities:** free continental breakfast and free local telephone calls. *(See color ad below)*

SOME UNITS

[icons] / [icons]

MARRIOTT RESIDENCE INN LAKE BUENA VISTA NORTH
Phone: (407)465-0075 ⬤242

SAVE

▽▽✕△▽

Small-scale Hotel

2/10-4/27 [BP]   1P: $119-$189   2P: $129-$199
6/16-11/30 [BP]   1P: $129-$149   2P: $139-$189
12/1-2/9 [BP]   1P: $99-$169   2P: $109-$189
4/28-6/15 [BP]   1P: $89-$129   2P: $99-$149
Location: I-4, exit 68, n to SR 535 E. 11450 Marabella Palms Ct 32836. Fax: 407/465-0050. **Facility:** 210 units. 128
one- and 82 two-bedroom suites with kitchens. 5 stories, interior corridors. *Bath:* combo or shower only.
Parking: on-site. **Terms:** pets ($150 fee). **Amenities:** dual phone lines, voice mail, irons, hair dryers. **Pool(s):** heated outdoor.
Leisure Activities: whirlpool, exercise room, sports court. **Guest Services:** complimentary evening beverages: Mon-Thurs, valet
and coin laundry, area transportation. **Business Services:** meeting rooms, business center. **Cards:** AX, CB, DC, DS, MC, VI.
(See color ad p 732)

SOME UNITS

[icons] / [icons]

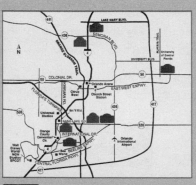

(See map p. 598)

MASTERS INN INTERNATIONAL DRIVE　Phone: (407)345-1172　228
(AAA) (SAVE)　All Year [CP]　1P: $41-$69　2P: $41-$69　XP: $4　F18
Location: I-4, exit 74A, e on Sand Lake Rd, then just s on International Dr. 8222 Jamaican Ct 32819.
Fax: 407/352-2801. Facility: 120 one-bedroom standard units. 4 stories, exterior corridors. Parking: on-site.
Terms: check-in 4 pm, small pets only ($20 fee). Amenities: voice mail, safes (fee). Pool(s): heated out-
Small-scale Hotel　door. Guest Services: valet and coin laundry, area transportation (fee). Business Services: fax (fee).
Cards: AX, CB, DC, DS, MC, VI. Special Amenities: free continental breakfast and free local telephone
calls.

SOME UNITS
(SD) (FEE) (🐕) (📷) (🍳) (📺) (DATA PORT) / (✕) (🛗) (📠) /
　　　FEE　　　　　　　　　　　　　　　　　　　　　　　FEE FEE

MICROTEL INN & SUITES　Phone: (407)226-9887　215
(AAA) (SAVE)　All Year　1P: $59-$99　2P: $59-$99
Location: I-4, exit 74A, just e on Sand Lake Rd (SR 82), then n. 7531 Canada Ave 32819. Fax: 407/226-9877.
Facility: 130 one-bedroom standard units. 3 stories, interior corridors. Bath: combo or shower only. Parking:
on-site. Terms: 5 day cancellation notice, $1 service charge. Amenities: safes (fee). Pool(s): outdoor.
Small-scale Hotel　Guest Services: valet laundry, area transportation-Universal & Sea World. Business Services: fax (fee).
Cards: AX, CB, DC, DS, MC, VI. Special Amenities: free continental breakfast and free local telephone
calls.

SOME UNITS
(SD) (🛏) (📺) (DATA PORT) / (✕) (🛗) (📠) (📟) /

ORLANDO AIRPORT MARRIOTT　Phone: (407)851-9000　308
(SAVE)　1/1-5/24　1P: $149-$169　2P: $149-$169
10/1-11/30　1P: $139-$159　2P: $139-$159
12/1-12/31　1P: $139-$149　2P: $139-$149
5/25-9/30　1P: $109-$129　2P: $109-$129
Large-scale Hotel　Location: SR 528 (Bee Line Expwy), exit 11, 0.5 mi n on SR 436, just e, then s. 7499 Augusta National Dr 32822.
Fax: 407/857-6211. Facility: 484 one-bedroom standard units. 9 stories, interior corridors. Bath: combo or
shower only. Parking: on-site and valet. Amenities: dual phone lines, voice mail, irons, hair dryers. Dining: Murphy's Chop
House, see separate listing. Pool(s): heated indoor/outdoor, wading. Leisure Activities: saunas, whirlpool, 2 lighted tennis
courts, basketball. Fee: massage. Guest Services: gift shop, valet and coin laundry. Business Services: conference facilities,
business center. Cards: AX, DC, DS, MC, VI.

SOME UNITS
(SD) (FEE) (🍴) (🍽) (🏋) (🎣) (📺) (🛗) (✕) (📺) (DATA PORT) (📟) / (✕) (🛗) /

PARC CORNICHE CONDOMINIUM SUITE HOTEL　Phone: (407)239-7100　316
(AAA) (SAVE)　All Year [ECP]　1P: $89-$109　2P: $109-$129
Location: I-4, exit 72, just e on Bee Line Expwy (SR 528) to exit 1, then 1.7 mi s on International Dr. Located in a quiet
area. (6300 Parc Corniche Dr, ORLANDO, 32821). Fax: 407/239-8501. Facility: Designated smoking area. 210
units. 90 one- and 120 two-bedroom suites with kitchens. 3 stories, exterior corridors. Parking: on-site.
Condominium　Terms: check-in 4 pm, 3 day cancellation notice-fee imposed. Amenities: voice mail, safes, irons. Dining: 5
pm-10 pm, cocktails. Pool(s): heated outdoor, wading. Leisure Activities: whirlpool, playground. Fee: golf
privileges, game room. Guest Services: gift shop, valet and coin laundry, area transportation-some attractions. Business Services: meeting rooms, fax (fee). Cards: AX, CB, DC, DS, MC, VI. Special Amenities: early check-in/late check-out and free
continental breakfast.

(SD) (🍴) (🍽) (🏋) (🎣) (✕) (📺) (DATA PORT) (🛗) (📠) (📟) /

THE PEABODY ORLANDO　Phone: (407)352-4000　245
(AAA) (SAVE)　1/1-11/30　1P: $390-$480　2P: $390-$480　XP: $15　F18
12/1-12/31　1P: $380-$470　2P: $380-$470　XP: $15　F18
Location: 0.5 mi n of SR 528 (Bee Line Expwy). Located opposite the Orange County Convention Center. 9801 International Dr 32819. Fax: 407/351-9177. Facility: This service-oriented hotel featuring marble-accented public
Large-scale Hotel　spaces is known for the resident ducks that parade twice daily through its lobby. 891 units. 872 one-bedroom
standard units. 19 one-bedroom suites, some with whirlpools. 27 stories, interior corridors. Bath: combo or
shower only. Parking: on-site (fee) and valet. Terms: 3 day cancellation notice-fee imposed, 12% service charge.
Amenities: video games (fee), dual phone lines, voice mail, honor bars, irons, hair dryers. Some: CD players. Dining: 3 restaurants, 24 hours, cocktails, also, Capriccio, Dux, see separate listing, entertainment. Pool(s): heated outdoor, wading. Leisure
Activities: saunas, whirlpools, steamrooms, 4 lighted tennis courts. Fee: aerobics, tanning bed, massage, game room. Guest
Services: gift shop, valet laundry, area transportation (fee)-Disney, beauty salon. Fee: swim & pro shop, tennis instruction, personal trainer. Business Services: conference facilities, business center. Cards: AX, DC, DS, JC, MC, VI. Special Amenities:
free newspaper. Affiliated with A Preferred Hotel.

SOME UNITS
(SD) (FEE) (🍴) (24T) (🍽) (🏋) (&M) (🎣) (🍳) (🛗) (✕) (📺) (DATA PORT) / (✕) (🛗) (📠) /
　　FEE　　　　　　　　　　　　　　　　　　　　　　　　　FEE　　　　　　　FEE FEE

QUALITY INN AIRPORT　Phone: (407)856-4663　284
(AAA) (SAVE)　2/1-4/15 [CP]　1P: $59-$99　2P: $65-$99
12/20-1/31 [CP]　1P: $55-$85　2P: $59-$89
4/16-11/30 [CP]　1P: $45-$65　2P: $49-$65
12/1-12/19 [CP]　1P: $45-$55　2P: $49-$59
Motel　Location: SR 482, at jct SR 528 (Bee Line Expwy). 2601 McCoy Rd 32809. Fax: 407/857-0933. Facility: 98 one-
bedroom standard units. 2 stories, exterior corridors. Parking: on-site. Terms: cancellation fee imposed.
Amenities: safes (fee), irons, hair dryers. Pool(s): outdoor. Guest Services: complimentary evening beverages: Mon-Sat, coin
laundry. Business Services: fax (fee). Cards: AX, CB, DC, DS, JC, MC, VI. Special Amenities: free continental breakfast
and free local telephone calls.

SOME UNITS
(SD) (📷) (🍳) (📺) (DATA PORT) (🛗) (📠) (📟) / (✕) /

QUALITY INN INTERNATIONAL　Phone: (407)996-1600　195
(SAVE)　All Year　1P: $50-$80
Location: I-4, exit 74A, just e on Sand Lake Rd, then just n. 7600 International Dr 32819. Fax: 407/996-5328.
Facility: 728 one-bedroom standard units. 2-6 stories, exterior corridors. Bath: combo or shower only.
Parking: on-site. Terms: cancellation fee imposed, pets ($6 extra charge). Amenities: voice mail, safes, hair
Small-scale Hotel　dryers. Pool(s): 2 heated outdoor, wading. Leisure Activities: Fee: game room. Guest Services: gift shop,
valet and coin laundry, area transportation (fee). Business Services: business center. Cards: AX, CB, DC,
DS, JC, MC, VI. (See color ad p 655)

SOME UNITS
(SD) (🛏) (🍴) (🍽) (&M) (🎣) (🍳) (🍳) (📺) (🛗) (📠) (📟) / (✕) (DATA PORT) /

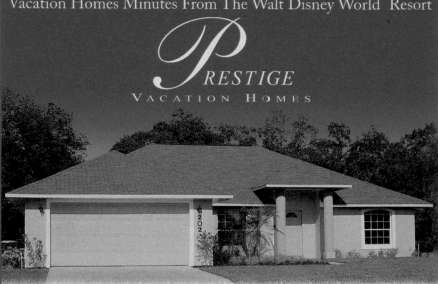

(See map p. 598)

QUALITY INN-PLAZA

Motel

Phone: (407)996-8585 236

All Year   1P: $39-$99   2P: $39-$99   XP: $5   F18
Location: I-4, exit 74A, just e on SR 482 (Sand Lake Rd), then 1 mi s. 9000 International Dr 32819. Fax: 407/996-6839. **Facility:** 1020 one-bedroom standard units. 4-10 stories, exterior corridors. *Bath:* combo or shower only. **Parking:** on-site. **Terms:** cancellation fee imposed, pets ($10 extra charge). **Amenities:** voice mail, safes, hair dryers. *Some:* irons. **Pool(s):** outdoor, 2 heated outdoor. **Leisure Activities:** playground. *Fee:* game room. **Guest Services:** gift shop, valet and coin laundry, area transportation (fee). **Business Services:** business center. **Cards:** AX, CB, DC, DS, JC, MC, VI. *(See color ad below)*

SOME UNITS

QUALITY SUITES UNIVERSAL ORLANDO
Small-scale Hotel

Phone: (407)363-0332 210

All Year [BP]   1P: $69-$119   2P: $69-$119
Location: I-4, exit 74A, just e on Sand Lake Rd, then just n. 7400 Canada Ave 32819. Fax: 407/352-2598. **Facility:** 154 one-bedroom suites. 7 stories, exterior corridors. **Parking:** on-site. **Amenities:** safes, irons, hair dryers. **Pool(s):** heated outdoor. **Leisure Activities:** whirlpool, playground, exercise room. *Fee:* game room. **Guest Services:** gift shop, complimentary evening beverages, valet and coin laundry, area transportation-major attractions. **Business Services:** meeting rooms, fax (fee). **Cards:** AX, CB, DC, DS, JC, MC, VI. **Special Amenities:** free continental breakfast and free newspaper. *(See color ad starting on p 656)*

SOME UNITS

RADISSON BARCELO RESORT
Small-scale Hotel

Phone: (407)345-0505 233

12/1-2/28 & 8/16-11/30   1P: $77-$110   2P: $77-$110
3/1-8/15   1P: $69-$110   2P: $69-$110
Location: I-4, exit 74A, just e on Sand Lake Rd, then just s. 8444 International Dr 32819. Fax: 407/581-2022. **Facility:** 522 one-bedroom standard units. 5-7 stories, interior/exterior corridors. *Bath:* combo or shower only. **Parking:** on-site. **Terms:** check-in 4 pm, 3 day cancellation notice. **Amenities:** voice mail, safes, irons, hair dryers. *Some:* video games (fee), dual phone lines. **Dining:** 2 restaurants, 6:30 am-10 pm, cocktails. **Pool(s):** heated outdoor. **Leisure Activities:** whirlpool, lighted tennis court, sand volleyball, bocci, playground, horseshoes. **Guest Services:** gift shop, valet and coin laundry, area transportation-major attractions. **Business Services:** meeting rooms. *Fee:* administrative services, fax. **Cards:** AX, CB, DC, DS, JC, MC, VI. **Special Amenities:** free newspaper and preferred room (subject to availability with advanced reservations).** *(See color ad p 657)*

SOME UNITS

(See map p. 598)

RADISSON HOTEL ORLANDO AT THE ENTRANCE TO UNIVERSAL ORLANDO   Phone: (407)351-1000   190
All Year   1P: $169-$209   2P: $169-$209   XP: $10   F18
Location: I-4, exit 75B, 0.7 mi n on SR 435 (Kirkman Rd). Located opposite the main entrance to Universal Studios. 5780 Major Blvd 32819. Fax: 407/363-0106. **Facility:** 742 units. 738 one-bedroom standard units. 4 two-bedroom suites. 18 stories, interior corridors. *Bath:* combo or shower only. **Parking:** on-site. **Terms:** check-in 4 pm, 3 day cancellation notice. **Amenities:** voice mail, irons, hair dryers. *Fee:* video games, high-speed Internet, safes. *Some:* CD players. **Dining:** 2 restaurants, 6 am-2 am, cocktails. **Pool(s):** heated outdoor, wading. **Leisure Activities:** whirlpool, playground, exercise room. **Guest Services:** gift shop, valet and coin laundry, airport transportation (fee)-Orlando International Airport, area transportation-Universal Studios. **Business Services:** conference facilities, business center. **Cards:** AX, CB, DC, DS, MC, VI. **Special Amenities:** free newspaper and preferred room (subject to availability with advanced reservations). *(See color ad p 657)*

Small-scale Hotel

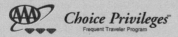

(See map p. 598)

RAMADA INN ALL SUITES AT INTERNATIONAL DRIVE CENTER Phone: (407)239-0707

All Year 1P: $129

Small-scale Hotel **Location:** I-4, exit 72, just e on SR 528 (Bee Line Expwy) to exit 1 (International Dr), just s to Westwood Blvd, then 2.5 mi sw. 6800 Villa de Costa Dr 32821. Fax: 407/239-8243. **Facility:** 105 two-bedroom suites with kitchens. 2-3 stories (no elevator), exterior corridors. **Parking:** on-site. **Terms:** check-in 4 pm, cancellation fee imposed, $2 service charge, pets ($10 extra charge). **Amenities:** voice mail, safes, irons, hair dryers. **Dining:** 11 am-10 pm in season, wine/beer only. **Pool(s):** 4 heated outdoor. **Leisure Activities:** whirlpools, sand volleyball, outside exercise course, exercise room, basketball. *Fee:* bicycles. **Guest Services:** gift shop, valet and coin laundry, area transportation-selected attractions. **Business Services:** meeting rooms, fax (fee). **Cards:** AX, DC, DS, MC, VI. **Special Amenities:** free continental breakfast. *(See color ad p 658)* SOME UNITS

(See map p. 598)

RAMADA INN AT INTERNATIONAL DRIVE
▼▼▼▼
Small-scale Hotel

Phone: (407)351-4410 [201]

All Year   1P: $49-$79   2P: $59-$89
Location: I-4, exit 75A, just s on Kirkland Rd, then just w. 5858 International Dr 32819. Fax: 407/351-2481.
Facility: 265 units. 252 one-bedroom standard units. 13 one-bedroom suites. 2-4 stories, exterior corridors.
Bath: combo or shower only. **Parking:** on-site. **Terms:** check-in 4 pm, cancellation fee imposed.
Amenities: voice mail, safes (fee). **Pool(s):** outdoor. **Leisure Activities:** Fee: game room. **Guest Services:** gift shop, coin laundry, area transportation. **Business Services:** fax (fee). **Cards:** AX, CB, DC, DS, MC, VI.

SOME UNITS
(ASK) (S/D) (↑↓+) (↓) (🅟) (🐕) (🚗) (DATA PORT) / (✕) (🔒) (📶)

RED ROOF INN CONVENTION CENTER
(AAA) (SAVE)
▼▼▼▼
Motel

Phone: (407)352-1507 [250]
    F18

All Year   1P: $39-$89   2P: $39-$89   XP: $5
Location: I-4, exit 72, 0.9 mi e on Bee Line Expwy (SR 528) to exit 1, then just n. 9922 Hawaiian Ct 32819.
Fax: 407/352-5550. **Facility:** 134 one-bedroom standard units. 2 stories, exterior corridors. *Bath:* combo or shower only. **Parking:** on-site. **Amenities:** video games (fee), voice mail. **Pool(s):** small outdoor. **Leisure Activities:** whirlpool. **Guest Services:** valet and coin laundry. **Business Services:** fax (fee). **Cards:** AX, CB, DC, DS, MC, VI. **Special Amenities: free local telephone calls and free newspaper.**

SOME UNITS
(🛁) (↑↓+) (&M) (🐕) (🚗) (📺) (DATA PORT) / (✕) (🔒) (📶)

RED ROOF INN UNIVERSAL STUDIOS
▼▼▼▼
Small-scale Hotel

Phone: 407/313-3100 [187]

All Year [CP]   1P: $49-$69   2P: $49-$69
Location: I-4, exit 75B, just n, then just e. 5621 Major Blvd 32819. Fax: 407/313-3131. **Facility:** 80 one-bedroom standard units. 3 stories, interior corridors. *Bath:* combo or shower only. **Parking:** on-site. **Pool(s):** outdoor. **Guest Services:** coin laundry. **Business Services:** fax. **Cards:** AX, DC, DS, MC, VI.

SOME UNITS
(ASK) (S/D) (🐕) (&M) (🐕) (🚗) (📺) (DATA PORT) / (✕) /

RENAISSANCE ORLANDO HOTEL-AIRPORT
(AAA) (SAVE)
▼▼▼▼
Large-scale Hotel

Phone: (407)240-1000 [295]

1/7-4/17   1P: $126-$153   2P: $126-$153
12/1-1/6 & 4/18-5/22   1P: $108-$135   2P: $108-$135
5/23-11/30   1P: $81-$108   2P: $81-$108
Location: SR 436; just n of SR 528 (Bee Line Expwy). 5445 Forbes Pl 32812. Fax: 407/240-1005. **Facility:** 298 units. 297 one-bedroom standard units. 1 one-bedroom suite. 9 stories, interior corridors. *Bath:* combo or shower only. **Parking:** on-site and valet. **Terms:** cancellation fee imposed. **Amenities:** dual phone lines, voice mail, irons, hair dryers. *Fee:* video games, high-speed Internet. **Dining:** 6:30 am-10 pm, cocktails. **Pool(s):** heated outdoor. **Leisure Activities:** sauna, whirlpool, exercise room. *Fee:* massage. **Guest Services:** gift shop, valet laundry. **Business Services:** conference facilities, business center. **Cards:** AX, CB, DC, DS, MC, VI. **Special Amenities: free newspaper.**

SOME UNITS
(S/D) (✈) (↑↓) (24↑) (↓) (&M) (🐕) (🚗) (✕) (📺) (💻) / (✕) (🔒) (📶) /

(See map p. 598)

RENAISSANCE ORLANDO RESORT AT SEAWORLD
Phone: (407)351-5555 — 257
12/1-1/13 & 10/2-11/30 — 1P: $157-$199
1/14-5/23 — 1P: $129-$157
5/24-10/1 — 1P: $99-$115
Location: I-4, exit 72, just e on Central Florida Pkwy, 0.3 mi n or 0.7 mi w of International Dr. Faces Sea World. 6677
Large-scale Hotel Sea Harbor Dr 32821-8092. Fax: 407/351-9991. **Facility:** The atrium lobby of this convention hotel features an aviary and a waterfall pond stocked with fish. 778 units. 777 one-bedroom standard units. 1 one-bedroom suite with whirlpool. 10 stories, interior corridors. *Bath:* combo or shower only. **Parking:** on-site and valet. **Terms:** 3 day cancellation notice, small pets only ($100 fee). **Amenities:** dual phone lines, voice mail, safes, honor bars, irons, hair dryers. *Fee:* video games, high-speed Internet. **Dining:** 3 restaurants, 6 am-11 pm, cocktails, also, Atlantis, see separate listing, entertainment. **Pool(s):** heated outdoor, wading. **Leisure Activities:** sauna, whirlpools, steamroom, 4 lighted tennis courts, jogging, playground, basketball, volleyball. *Fee:* golf privileges, tennis instruction & equipment, massage, game room. **Guest Services:** gift shop, valet and coin laundry, area transportation (fee)-major attractions, beauty salon. **Business Services:** conference facilities, business center. **Cards:** AX, CB, DC, DS, JC, MC, VI.

RESIDENCE INN BY MARRIOTT ORLANDO CONVENTION CENTER
Phone: (407)226-0288 — 239
2/10-4/27 [BP] — 1P: $119-$189 — 2P: $129-$199
6/16-11/30 [BP] — 1P: $129-$149 — 2P: $139-$189
12/1-2/9 [BP] — 1P: $99-$169 — 2P: $109-$189
4/28-6/15 [BP] — 1P: $89-$129 — 2P: $99-$149
Small-scale Hotel **Location:** I-4, exit 74A, 0.5 mi e on SR 482 (Sand Lake Rd), then 0.8 mi s. 8800 Universal Blvd 32819. Fax: 407/226-9979. **Facility:** 124 units. 31 one-bedroom standard units, some with efficiencies or kitchens. 59 one- and 34 two-bedroom suites, some with efficiencies or kitchens. 5 stories, interior corridors. *Bath:* combo or shower only. **Parking:** on-site. **Terms:** check-in 4 pm, small pets only ($75 fee, $75 deposit). **Amenities:** high-speed Internet (fee), dual phone lines, voice mail, irons, hair dryers. **Pool(s):** heated outdoor. **Leisure Activities:** whirlpool, exercise room, sports court. **Guest Services:** complimentary evening beverages: Mon-Thurs, valet and coin laundry, area transportation. **Business Services:** meeting rooms, fax (fee). **Cards:** AX, CB, DC, DS, MC, VI. *(See color ads starting on p 624)*

RESIDENCE INN BY MARRIOTT-ORLANDO INTERNATIONAL DR
Phone: (407)345-0117 — 216
12/1-4/18 [BP] — 1P: $129-$179 — 2P: $129-$179
4/19-11/30 [BP] — 1P: $119-$169 — 2P: $119-$169
Location: I-4, exit 74A, just e on Sand Lake Rd (SR 482). 7975 Canada Ave 32819. Fax: 407/352-2689. **Facility:** 176 units. 132 one-bedroom standard units with kitchens. 44 two-bedroom suites with kitchens. 2 stories, exterior Small-scale Hotel corridors. *Bath:* combo or shower only. **Parking:** on-site. **Terms:** check-in 4 pm, $1 service charge, small pets only ($50 fee, $50 extra charge). **Amenities:** voice mail, safes, irons, hair dryers. *Some:* video games, CD players. **Pool(s):** heated outdoor. **Leisure Activities:** whirlpool, poolside gas grills, exercise room, sports court, volleyball. **Guest Services:** complimentary evening beverages: Mon-Thurs, valet and coin laundry, area transportation-Disney. **Business Services:** meeting rooms, fax (fee). **Cards:** AX, CB, DC, DS, JC, MC, VI.

RESIDENCE INN BY MARRIOTT SEA WORLD INTERNATIONAL CENTER
Phone: (407)313-3600 — 264
1/1-4/4 & 9/6-11/30 — 1P: $129-$229 — 2P: $129-$229
12/1-12/31 & 4/5-9/5 — 1P: $119-$229 — 2P: $119-$229
Location: I-4, exit 72. 11000 Westwood Blvd 32821. Fax: 407/313-3611. **Facility:** 350 units. 154 one-bedroom standard units with kitchens. 143 one- and 53 two-bedroom suites ($119-$229) with kitchens. 6 stories, interior corridors. *Bath:* combo or shower only. **Parking:** on-site. **Terms:** check-in 4 pm, cancellation fee imposed, pets ($150 fee). **Amenities:** video games (fee), dual phone lines, voice mail, irons, hair dryers. **Pool(s):** heated outdoor. **Leisure Activities:** whirlpool, playground, exercise room, sports court. *Fee:* game room. **Guest Services:** gift shop, valet and coin laundry, area transportation. **Business Services:** meeting rooms, fax (fee). **Cards:** AX, CB, DC, DS, JC, MC, VI.

RODEWAY INN INTERNATIONAL
Phone: (407)996-4444 — 193
All Year — 1P: $50-$80 — 2P: $50-$80
Location: I-4, exit 74A, just e on Sand Lake Rd, then 0.7 mi n. 6327 International Dr 32819. Fax: 407/996-5806. **Facility:** 315 one-bedroom standard units. 4-9 stories, interior/exterior corridors. *Bath:* combo or shower only. **Parking:** on-site. **Terms:** $2 service charge, pets ($5 extra charge). **Amenities:** video library (fee), voice mail, safes. **Pool(s):** heated outdoor. **Leisure Activities:** *Fee:* game room. **Guest Services:** gift shop, valet and coin laundry, area transportation (fee). **Business Services:** fax. **Cards:** AX, CB, DC, DS, MC, VI.
Motel
(See color ad p 655)

ROSEN CENTRE HOTEL
Phone: (407)996-9840 — 244
All Year — 1P: $245-$325 — 2P: $245-$325 — XP: $20 — F18
Location: I-4, exit 72, just e on SR 528 (Bee Line Expwy) to exit 1 (International Dr), then just n. Located next to the convention center. 9840 International Dr 32819. Fax: 407/996-3169. **Facility:** 1334 one-bedroom standard units, some with whirlpools. 24 stories, interior corridors. *Bath:* combo or shower only. **Parking:** on-site. **Terms:** 5 day cancellation notice-fee imposed, 12% service charge. **Amenities:** voice mail, safes, irons, hair dryers. *Some:* CD players. **Dining:** Everglades, see separate listing. **Pool(s):** heated outdoor, wading. **Leisure Activities:** whirlpools. *Fee:* 2 lighted tennis courts, massage. **Guest Services:** gift shop, valet and coin laundry, area transportation (fee). **Business Services:** conference facilities, business center. **Cards:** AX, CB, DC, DS, JC, MC, VI.

(See map p. 598)

ROSEN PLAZA
Phone: (407)996-9700 [247]

Small-scale Hotel

1/16-6/23 & 9/10-11/30	1P: $265	2P: $265	XP: $20	F18
12/1-1/15	1P: $175	2P: $175	XP: $20	F18
6/24-9/9	1P: $145	2P: $145	XP: $20	F18

Location: I-4, exit 72, just n; from Bee Line Expwy (SR 528), exit 1, then just n. 9700 International Dr 32819. Fax: 407/354-5774. **Facility:** 800 units. 786 one-bedroom standard units. 14 one-bedroom suites ($390-$1130). 14 stories, interior corridors. *Bath:* combo, shower or tub only. **Parking:** on-site. **Terms:** 5 day cancellation notice-fee imposed. **Amenities:** video games, voice mail, safes, irons, hair dryers. **Dining:** Jack's Place, see separate listing. **Pool(s):** heated outdoor. **Leisure Activities:** whirlpool, exercise room. *Fee:* game room. **Guest Services:** gift shop, valet and coin laundry, area transportation (fee). **Business Services:** conference facilities, business center. **Cards:** AX, CB, DC, DS, JC, MC, VI.

SOME UNITS
(ASK) (SD) (FEE) (♦) (↑↓) (♀) (&M) (☞) (➔) (✕) (▦) (DATA PORT) (▭) / (✕) (♦) / FEE FEE

THE SEASONS RESORT
Phone: 407/851-2278 [263]

Condominium

All Year	2P: $178-$258

Location: I-4, exit 79, 2.6 mi s on SR 423 (John Young Pkwy), 0.3 mi e on Oak Ridge Rd, then just n. 5736 S Texas Ave 32839. Fax: 407/438-1362. **Facility:** 24 two-bedroom standard units with kitchens. 2 stories, exterior corridors. **Parking:** on-site. **Terms:** check-in 4 pm, 14 day cancellation notice, weekly rates available. **Amenities:** video library (fee), safes, irons, hair dryers. **Pool(s):** heated outdoor, wading. **Leisure Activities:** sauna, whirlpool, 2 lighted tennis courts, racquetball court, playground, exercise room. *Fee:* game room. **Guest Services:** complimentary laundry. **Cards:** AX, DC, DS, MC, VI.

(➔) (✕) (VCR) (♦) (♦) (▭)

SHERATON STUDIO CITY HOTEL
Phone: (407)351-2100 [200]

Small-scale Hotel

12/25-4/26	1P: $89-$169	2P: $89-$169	XP: $20	F18
4/27-11/30	1P: $79-$149	2P: $79-$149	XP: $20	F18
12/1-12/24	1P: $79-$99	2P: $79-$99	XP: $20	F18

Location: I-4, exit 75A, just w of SR 435. 5905 International Dr 32819. Fax: 407/248-0266. **Facility:** 302 one-bedroom standard units. 21 stories, interior corridors. *Bath:* combo or shower only. **Parking:** on-site. **Terms:** 3 day cancellation notice-fee imposed, [AP], [BP], [CP] & [ECP] meal plans available, $4 service charge. **Amenities:** video games, voice mail, safes, irons, hair dryers. *Some:* fax. **Pool(s):** heated outdoor, wading. **Leisure Activities:** whirlpool, exercise room. *Fee:* massage, game room. **Guest Services:** gift shop, valet and coin laundry, area transportation. **Business Services:** conference facilities, business center. **Cards:** AX, DC, DS, MC, VI. *(See color ad p 636)*

SOME UNITS
(ASK) (SD) (↑↓) (♀) (➔) (✕) (♦) (DATA PORT) (▭) / (✕) (♦) (▭) /

SHERATON SUITES ORLANDO AIRPORT
Phone: (407)240-5555 [310]

(AAA) (SAVE)

Small-scale Hotel

1/1-4/30	1P: $119-$149	2P: $119-$149	XP: $10	F18
12/1-12/31 & 5/1-11/30	1P: $89-$119	2P: $89-$119	XP: $10	F18

Location: 2 mi n of airport terminal; via SR 436 and TG Lee Blvd. 7550 Augusta National Dr 32822. Fax: 407/240-1300. **Facility:** 150 one-bedroom suites. 3 stories, interior corridors. *Bath:* combo or shower only. **Parking:** on-site. **Terms:** cancellation fee imposed. **Amenities:** high-speed Internet (fee), dual phone lines, voice mail, irons, hair dryers. *Some:* fax. **Dining:** 6:30 am-10 pm, cocktails. **Pool(s):** heated indoor/outdoor. **Leisure Activities:** whirlpool, exercise room. **Guest Services:** gift shop, valet and coin laundry, area transportation-within 3 mi. **Business Services:** meeting rooms, fax (fee). **Cards:** AX, DC, DS, MC, VI. **Special Amenities:** free newspaper.

SOME UNITS
(SD) (♦) (↑↓) (♀) (&M) (☞) (☞) (➔) (♦) (DATA PORT) (♦) (▭) (▭) / (✕) /

SHERATON'S VISTANA VILLAGES
Phone: (407)238-5000 [315]

Condominium

12/22-1/7	2P: $370-$440
1/8-11/30	2P: $239-$325
12/1-12/21	2P: $229-$309

Location: Between SR 535 and Central Florida Pkwy. 12401 International Dr 32821. Fax: 407/238-5005. **Facility:** 360 units. 150 one- and 210 two-bedroom suites with kitchens and whirlpools. 5 stories, exterior corridors. *Bath:* combo or shower only. **Parking:** on-site. **Terms:** check-in 4 pm, 3 day cancellation notice-fee imposed. **Amenities:** video library (fee), voice mail, safes, irons, hair dryers. *Some:* CD players. **Pool(s):** 2 heated outdoor. **Leisure Activities:** sauna, whirlpools, steamroom, 2 tennis courts, recreation programs, exercise room, basketball, shuffleboard, volleyball. *Fee:* massage, game room. **Guest Services:** complimentary laundry, area transportation, convenience shop. **Business Services:** fax (fee). **Cards:** AX, DC, MC, VI. *(See color ad p 5)*

(ASK) (SD) (FEE) (♦) (↑↓) (♀) (☞) (➔) (✕) (VCR) (♦) (DATA PORT) (♦) (▭) (▭)

(See map p. 598)

SHERATON WORLD RESORT
Phone: (407)352-1100 [255]
All Year   1P: $139-$259   2P: $159-$279   XP: $20   F12
Location: I-4, exit 72, just s on International Dr; Bee Line Expwy (SR 528), exit 1, just e. 10100 International Dr 32821.
Large-scale Hotel   **Fax:** 407/352-3679. **Facility:** 1102 one-bedroom standard units. 3-16 stories, interior/exterior corridors. *Bath:* some combo or shower only. **Parking:** on-site (fee) and valet. **Terms:** 3 day cancellation notice-fee imposed, $6 service charge. **Amenities:** video games, dual phone lines, voice mail, safes, irons, hair dryers. *Some:* fax. **Pool(s):** 3 heated outdoor, 2 wading. **Leisure Activities:** whirlpool, miniature golf, playground, exercise room. *Fee:* massage, game room. **Guest Services:** gift shop, valet and coin laundry, area transportation. **Business Services:** conference facilities, business center. **Cards:** AX, CB, DC, DS, JC, MC. *(See color ad p 660)*

SOME UNITS

(ASK) (S/D) (TI) (Y) (&M) (☆) (☏) (🏊) (✕) (🎥) (DATA PORT) (🔒) (💻) / (✕) (📷)

SIERRA SUITES HOTEL-POINTE ORLANDO
Phone: (407)903-1500 [223]
All Year [ECP]   1P: $79-$139   2P: $79-$139
Location: I-4, exit 74A, 0.5 mi e on SR 482 (Sand Lake Rd), then 0.7 mi s. 8750 Universal Blvd 32819.
Small-scale Hotel   **Fax:** 407/903-1555. **Facility:** 137 one-bedroom standard units with efficiencies. 3 stories, interior corridors. **Parking:** on-site. **Terms:** check-in 4 pm, 3 day cancellation notice. **Amenities:** dual phone lines, voice mail, irons, hair dryers. *Fee:* video library, high-speed Internet, safes. **Pool(s):** heated outdoor. **Leisure Activities:** whirlpool, exercise room. *Fee:* game room. **Guest Services:** valet and coin laundry, area transportation. **Cards:** AX, CB, DC, JC, MC, VI.
(See color ad p 735)

SOME UNITS

(ASK) (S/D) (TI+) (&M) (☆) (☏) (🏊) (✕) (VCR) (🎥) (DATA PORT) (🔒) (💻) / (✕) /

SLEEP INN AND SUITES
Phone: (407)363-1333 [183]
All Year [ECP]   1P: $59-$139   2P: $59-$139
Location: I-4, exit 75B, just n, then just e. 5605 Major Blvd 32819. Fax: 407/363-4510. **Facility:** 196 one-bedroom standard units. 11 stories, interior corridors. *Bath:* combo or shower only. **Parking:** on-site. **Terms:** 3 day cancellation notice-fee imposed, 1% service charge. **Amenities:** video games (fee), voice mail. *Some:* irons,
Small-scale Hotel   hair dryers. **Pool(s):** heated outdoor. **Leisure Activities:** exercise room. *Fee:* game room. **Guest Services:** valet and coin laundry, area transportation-Universal Studios. **Business Services:** meeting rooms, fax (fee).
Cards: AX, CB, DC, DS, JC, MC, VI. **Special Amenities:** free continental breakfast and free local telephone calls.

SOME UNITS

(S/D) (🏊) (🎥) (DATA PORT) / (✕) (🔒) (💻) /

SLEEP INN & SUITES ORLANDO INTERNATIONAL AIRPORT
Phone: (407)855-4447 [286]
1/22-4/15 [ECP]   1P: $69-$89   2P: $69-$89
4/16-8/7 [ECP]   1P: $59-$79   2P: $59-$79
12/1-1/21 [ECP]   1P: $59-$69   2P: $59-$69
8/8-11/30 [ECP]   1P: $49-$69   2P: $49-$69
Small-scale Hotel   **Location:** SR 528 (Beeline Expwy), exit 8, just w. 1700 McCoy Rd 32809. Fax: 407/856-9350. **Facility:** 74 one-bedroom standard units, some with whirlpools. 3 stories, interior corridors. *Bath:* combo or shower only. **Parking:** on-site. **Amenities:** voice mail, safes (fee), irons, hair dryers. **Pool(s):** outdoor. **Leisure Activities:** whirlpool, limited exercise equipment. **Guest Services:** valet and coin laundry. **Business Services:** fax (fee). **Cards:** AX, DC, DS, MC, VI.
Special Amenities: free continental breakfast and free local telephone calls.

SOME UNITS

(S/D) (🔒) (TI+) (☏) (🏊) (🎥) (DATA PORT) / (✕) (🔒) (💻) /

SLEEP INN-CONVENTION CENTER
Phone: (407)313-4100 [253]
All Year [CP]   1P: $45-$79   2P: $45-$79
Location: I-4, exit 72, just e on SR 538 to exit 1 (International Dr), just s, then just w. 6301 Westwood Blvd 32821. Fax: 407/313-4101. **Facility:** 94 one-bedroom standard units. 4 stories, interior corridors. *Bath:* combo or shower only. **Parking:** on-site. **Amenities:** safes, irons, hair dryers. **Pool(s):** outdoor. **Guest Services:** valet
Small-scale Hotel   and coin laundry, area transportation-Disney. **Business Services:** fax. **Cards:** AX, CB, DC, DS, JC, MC, VI.
Special Amenities: free continental breakfast and free local telephone calls.

SOME UNITS

(S/D) (TI+) (&M) (☆) (☏) (🏊) (🎥) (DATA PORT) / (✕) /

SPRINGHILL SUITES BY MARRIOTT INTERNATIONAL
DRIVE AREA/ORLANDO CONV CTR
Phone: (407)345-9073 [217]
2/10-4/27 & 6/16-11/30 [ECP]   1P: $119-$139   2P: $129-$149
12/1-2/9 [ECP]   1P: $89-$119   2P: $99-$129
4/28-6/15 [ECP]   1P: $79-$119   2P: $89-$129
Small-scale Hotel   **Location:** I-4, exit 74A, 0.5 mi e on SR 482 (Sand Lake Rd), then 0.8 mi s. 8840 Universal Blvd 32819. Fax: 407/345-9075. **Facility:** 167 one-bedroom standard units. 7 stories, interior corridors. *Bath:* combo or shower only. **Parking:** on-site. **Amenities:** high-speed Internet (fee), dual phone lines, voice mail, irons, hair dryers. **Pool(s):** heated outdoor, wading. **Leisure Activities:** exercise room. *Fee:* game room. **Guest Services:** valet and coin laundry, area transportation. **Business Services:** business center. **Cards:** AX, CB, DC, DS, MC, VI.
(See color ads starting on p 624)

SOME UNITS

(S/D) (TI+) (&M) (☆) (☏) (🏊) (🎥) (DATA PORT) (🔒) (💻) / (✕) /

SUBURBAN LODGE OF ORLANDO SOUTH FLORIDA MALL
Phone: (407)251-1110 [283]
All Year   1P: $219-$260   XP: $10   F17
Location: Just s of SR 528 (Bee Line Expwy), exit 4; just w of US 17-92 and 441, just s of Florida Tpke, exit 244. 9435 Delegates Dr 32837. Fax: 407/855-3625. **Facility:** 144 one-bedroom standard units with efficiencies. 3 stories, exterior corridors. *Bath:* combo or shower only. **Parking:** on-site. **Terms:** weekly rates available.
Motel   **Amenities:** voice mail. *Some:* irons. **Pool(s):** heated outdoor. **Guest Services:** coin laundry. **Business Services:** fax (fee). **Cards:** AX, DC, DS, MC, VI. *(See color ad p 596)*

(S/D) (TI+) (☆) (🏊) (🎥) (DATA PORT) (🔒) (💻) (📷)

(See map p. 598)

SUBURBAN LODGE-UNIVERSAL

Phone: (407)313-2000 182

⬥⬥⬥ (SAVE) ▼▼ ▼▼
All Year   1P: $40-$70   2P: $40-$70   XP: $10   F17
Location: I-4, exit 75B, just n, then just e. 5615 Major Blvd 32819. Fax: 407/313-2010. **Facility:** 149 one-bedroom standard units with efficiencies. 3 stories, exterior corridors. *Bath:* combo or shower only. **Parking:** on-site. **Terms:** cancellation fee imposed, weekly rates available, package plans - seasonal & weekends.
Small-scale Hotel   **Amenities:** voice mail. **Pool(s):** heated outdoor. **Guest Services:** coin laundry. **Cards:** AX, CB, DC, DS, MC, VI. **Special Amenities:** early check-in/late check-out and free room upgrade (subject to availability with advanced reservations).** *(See color ad p 596)*

SOME UNITS
(S)(D)(🛎)(&)(🛏)(⬥)(📷)(DATA PORT)(🔌)(📺)(💻) /(X)/

SUMMERFIELD SUITES BY WYNDHAM-ORLANDO/INTERNATIONAL DRIVE

Phone: (407)352-2400 227

⬥⬥⬥ (SAVE) ▼▼▼ ⬥⬥⬥▼
12/1-4/26 & 6/21-8/15 [ECP]   1P: $89-$289   2P: $89-$289
4/27-6/20 & 8/16-11/30 [ECP]   1P: $79-$269   2P: $79-$269
Location: I-4, exit 74A, just e on Sand Lake Rd, then just s. 8480 International Dr 32819. Fax: 407/352-4631. **Facility:** 146 units. 42 one- and 104 two-bedroom suites ($79-$289) with kitchens. 5 stories, exterior corri-
Small-scale Hotel   dors. **Parking:** on-site. **Terms:** check-in 4 pm, 3 day cancellation notice-fee imposed. **Amenities:** voice mail, safes, irons, hair dryers. *Fee:* video library, high-speed Internet. *Some:* dual phone lines. **Pool(s):** heated outdoor, wading. **Leisure Activities:** whirlpool, exercise room. *Fee:* game room. **Guest Services:** gift shop, valet and coin laundry, area transportation (fee)-major attractions. **Business Services:** meeting rooms, fax (fee). **Cards:** AX, DC, MC, VI. *(See color ad below)*

SOME UNITS
(S)(D)(🔷)(🛎)(🍽)(📶)(⬥)(X)(VCR)(📷)(DATA PORT)(🔌)(📺)(💻) /(X)/
     FEE

TRAVELODGE HOTEL AT FLORIDA MALL

Phone: (407)859-7900 270

⬥⬥⬥ (SAVE) ▼▼ ▼▼
All Year   1P: $59-$79   2P: $59-$79   XP: $10   F18
Location: Corner of Sand Lake Rd and S Orange Blossom Tr. 7900 S Orange Blossom Tr 32809. Fax: 407/859-7442. **Facility:** 121 one-bedroom standard units. 2 stories, exterior corridors. *Bath:* combo or shower only. **Parking:** on-site. **Terms:** cancellation fee imposed. **Amenities:** irons, hair dryers. **Pool(s):** outdoor, wading. **Leisure Activities:** exercise room. **Guest Services:** valet and coin laundry. **Business Services:** meeting rooms. Small-scale Hotel   **Cards:** AX, DC, DS, MC, VI. **Special Amenities:** early check-in/late check-out and free local telephone calls.

SOME UNITS
(S)(D)(🛎)(🍽)(&)(📶)(⬥)(📷)(DATA PORT)(🔌)(📺)(💻) /(X)/

(See map p. 598)

TRAVELODGE HOTEL-ORLANDO INTERNATIONAL AIRPORT
Phone: (407)859-2711   249

(AAA) (SAVE)
▼▼ ▼▼▼

All Year   1P: $49
Location: On SR 528 (Bee Line Expwy), exit 9, just w. 3835 McCoy Rd 32812. Fax: 407/859-0380. **Facility:** 332 one-bedroom standard units. 2-4 stories, interior/exterior corridors. *Bath:* combo or shower only. **Parking:** on-site. **Amenities:** dual phone lines, voice mail, safes, irons, hair dryers. **Dining:** 6-10 am, 11-2 & 5-10 pm,

Small-scale Hotel cocktails, entertainment. **Pool(s):** heated outdoor, wading. **Leisure Activities:** whirlpool, exercise room. **Guest Services:** gift shop, valet and coin laundry, area transportation-Florida Mall. **Business Services:** meeting rooms, fax (fee). **Cards:** AX, MC. **Special Amenities:** early check-in/late check-out and free newspaper.

SOME UNITS

[icons] SO / X /

TRAVELODGE INTERNATIONAL DRIVE
Phone: (407)345-8880   199

▼▼ ▼▼▼

All Year [CP]   1P: $49-$69   2P: $49-$69
Location: I-4, exit 74A, e on Sand Lake Rd to International Dr, 2 mi n, then just w. 5859 American Way 32819.

Small-scale Hotel Fax: 407/363-9366. **Facility:** 192 one-bedroom standard units. 4 stories, exterior corridors. **Parking:** on-site. **Terms:** cancellation fee imposed, weekly rates available, $2 service charge. **Amenities:** voice mail, safes (fee). **Pool(s):** heated outdoor. **Leisure Activities:** Fee: game room. **Guest Services:** gift shop, valet and coin laundry, area transportation. **Business Services:** fax (fee). **Cards:** AX, CB, DC, DS, MC, VI.

SOME UNITS

[icons] ASK SO / X VCR / FEE FEE

TRAVELODGE ORLANDO CONVENTION CENTER
Phone: (407)345-8000   262

(AAA) (SAVE)
▼▼ ▼▼

All Year [CP]   1P: $78-$98   2P: $78-$98
Location: I-4, exit 72, just e on SR 538 to exit 1 (International Dr), just s, then just w. 6263 Westwood Blvd 32821. Fax: 407/345-1508. **Facility:** 144 one-bedroom standard units. 3 stories, exterior corridors. **Parking:** on-site. **Amenities:** voice mail. **Pool(s):** 2 small outdoor. **Leisure Activities:** game room.

Small-scale Hotel **Guest Services:** coin laundry, airport transportation (fee)-Orlando International Airport, area transportation-major attractions. **Business Services:** meeting rooms, business center. **Cards:** AX, DS, MC, VI.

Special Amenities: free continental breakfast. *(See color ad below)*

SOME UNITS

[icons] SO / X / FEE FEE

UNIVERSAL'S HARD ROCK HOTEL
Phone: (407)503-2000   181

(AAA) (SAVE)
▼▼▼ ▼▼

1/2-4/23	1P: $229-$379	2P: $229-$379	XP: $25 F18
12/1-1/1	1P: $199-$345	2P: $199-$345	XP: $25 F18
4/24-8/31	1P: $229-$339	2P: $229-$339	XP: $25 F18
9/1-11/30	1P: $209-$319	2P: $209-$319	XP: $25 F18

Large-scale Hotel **Location:** I-4, exit 75A. 5800 Universal Blvd 32819 (1000 Universal Studios Plaza, ORLANDO). Fax: 407/503-2010. **Facility:** Lush landscaping surrounds this hotel designed in a California-Mission style. 650 units. 630 one-bedroom standard units. 20 one-bedroom suites, some with whirlpools. 7 stories, interior corridors. *Bath:* combo or shower only. **Parking:** on-site (fee) and valet. **Terms:** check-in 4 pm, 5 day cancellation notice-fee imposed. **Amenities:** CD players, dual phone lines, voice mail, safes, honor bars, irons, hair dryers. *Fee:* video games, high-speed Internet. *Some:* DVD players (fee), fax. **Dining:** 3 restaurants, 6:30 am-11 pm, cocktails, also, Palm Restaurant, see separate listing. **Pool(s):** heated outdoor, wading. **Leisure Activities:** whirlpools, waterslide, recreation programs, jogging, playground, exercise room, shuffleboard, volleyball. *Fee:* scooters, massage, game room. **Guest Services:** gift shop, valet and coin laundry, area transportation-Universal Studios. **Business Services:** conference facilities, business center. **Cards:** AX, CB, DC, DS, JC, MC, VI. Affiliated with Loews Hotels. *(See color ad starting on p 150)*

SOME UNITS

[icons] SO / X VCR / FEE FEE FEE

(See map p. 598)

UNIVERSAL'S PORTOFINO BAY HOTEL
Phone: (407)503-1000   [188]

(AAA) [SAVE]

▼▼▼▼ ▼▼▼▼

1/2-4/23	1P: $279-$359	2P: $279-$359	XP: $25	F18
12/1-1/1	1P: $249-$359	2P: $249-$359	XP: $25	F18
4/24-8/31	1P: $279-$339	2P: $279-$339	XP: $25	F18
9/1-11/30	1P: $259-$299	2P: $259-$299	XP: $25	F18

Large-scale Hotel **Location:** I-4, exit 75B, 0.5 mi n on SR 435 (Kirkman Rd), then just w via Vineland Rd; at Universal Studios. 5601 Universal Blvd 32819 (1000 Universal Studios Plaza, ORLANDO). Fax: 407/503-1010. **Facility:** Styled after a small town on the Italian Riviera, the property includes a miniature bay, gardens, piazzas and several pools. 750 units. 706 one-bedroom standard units. 44 one-bedroom suites, some with whirlpools. 6 stories, interior corridors. *Bath:* combo or shower only. **Parking:** on-site. **Terms:** check-in 4 pm, 5 day cancellation notice-fee imposed. **Amenities:** video games (fee), dual phone lines, voice mail, safes, honor bars, irons, hair dryers. *Some:* CD players, fax. **Dining:** 4 restaurants, 6 am-midnight, cocktails, also, Delfino Riviera, see separate listing, entertainment. **Pool(s):** 3 heated outdoor, wading. **Leisure Activities:** whirlpools, waterslide, recreation programs, bocci, playground, spa. *Fee:* game room. **Guest Services:** gift shop, complimentary evening beverages, valet laundry, area transportation-Universal attractions, beauty salon. **Business Services:** conference facilities, business center. **Cards:** AX, CB, DC, DS, JC, MC, VI. Affiliated with Loews Hotels. *(See color ad starting on p 150)*

SOME UNITS

[icons] FEE ... FEE ... DATA PORT ... /✕ VCR 🅿 📠/

VENTURA RESORT RENTALS-KISSIMMEE
Phone: (407)273-8770   [265]

▼▼▼▼

All Year   1P: $110-$185   2P: $110-$185
Location: 0.6 mi e of SR 436. 5946 Curry Ford Rd 32822. Fax: 407/658-6530. **Facility:** 79 units. 7 two- and 22
Condominium   three-bedroom suites with kitchens. 50 vacation homes ($128-$215). 1-2 stories, exterior corridors. **Parking:** on-site. **Terms:** 3 night minimum stay, cancellation fee imposed, weekly rates available, small pets only ($200 deposit, $100 extra charge). **Amenities:** irons. *Some:* DVD players (fee), CD players. **Pool(s):** 56 outdoor. **Guest Services:** complimentary laundry. **Business Services:** fax (fee). **Cards:** AX, MC, VI.

SOME UNITS

[icons] ASK ... /VCR/ FEE

VENTURA RESORT RENTALS ORLANDO
Phone: (407)273-8770   [266]

▼▼▼▼

All Year Wkly   2P: $651-$924
Location: 0.6 mi e of SR 436. Located in a gated area. 5946 Curry Ford Rd 32822. Fax: 407/658-6530. **Facility:** 167
Condominium   units. 25 one-, 77 two- and 25 three-bedroom suites. 40 vacation homes ($924-$1193). 1-2 stories, exterior corridors. **Parking:** on-site. **Terms:** 5-7 night minimum stay, cancellation fee imposed, daily rates available, small pets only ($200 deposit, $100 extra charge). **Amenities:** irons. *Some:* DVD players (fee). **Pool(s):** 6 outdoor. **Leisure Activities:** 4 lighted tennis courts, playground, basketball, shuffleboard. **Guest Services:** complimentary laundry. **Business Services:** fax (fee). **Cards:** AX, DS, MC, VI.

SOME UNITS

[icons] ASK ... /VCR/ FEE

THE VILLAS OF GRAND CYPRESS
Phone: (407)239-4700   [313]

▼▼▼ ▼▼▼

1/1-5/12	1P: $415-$485	2P: $515-$2000
10/1-11/30	1P: $310-$470	2P: $610-$1450
12/1-12/31	1P: $300-$460	2P: $600-$1440
5/13-9/30	1P: $225-$375	2P: $440-$990

Large-scale Hotel

Location: I-4, exit 68, 2.3 mi nw on SR 535. 1 N Jacaranda 32836. Fax: 407/239-7219. **Facility:** This golf course property offers extensive recreational facilities; some guest rooms include fireplaces. 121 units. 73 one-bedroom standard units, some with whirlpools. 23 one- and 25 two-bedroom suites with kitchens, some with whirlpools. 2 stories, exterior corridors. **Parking:** on-site. **Terms:** check-in 4 pm, 3 day cancellation notice-fee imposed. **Amenities:** video library, CD players, dual phone lines, voice mail, safes, honor bars, irons, hair dryers. **Dining:** The Black Swan, see separate listing. **Pool(s):** heated outdoor. **Leisure Activities:** whirlpools, paddleboats, 12 tennis courts (3 lighted), recreation programs, bicycles, jogging, playground. *Fee:* golf-45 holes, massage. **Guest Services:** gift shop, valet laundry, area transportation. **Business Services:** meeting rooms, business center. **Cards:** AX, CB, DC, DS, JC, MC, VI.

SOME UNITS

[icons] ... /✕ 📠/

WELLESLEY INN & SUITES (ORLANDO/SOUTHPARK)
Phone: (407)248-8010   [267]

(AAA) [SAVE]

▼▼▼▼

All Year   1P: $69-$89   2P: $69-$89
Location: Just sw of jct of SR 423 (John Young Pkwy) and 482 (Sand Lake Rd). 8687 Commodity Cir 32819. Fax: 407/248-9940. **Facility:** 138 units. 129 one-bedroom standard units with efficiencies. 9 one-bedroom suites with efficiencies. 3 stories, interior corridors. *Bath:* combo or shower only. **Parking:** on-site. **Small-scale Hotel** **Terms:** [ECP] meal plan available, small pets only. **Amenities:** dual phone lines, voice mail, irons, hair dryers. *Fee:* video games, high-speed Internet. **Pool(s):** outdoor. **Leisure Activities:** exercise room. **Guest Services:** valet and coin laundry. **Business Services:** meeting rooms, fax. **Cards:** AX, CB, DC, DS, JC, MC, VI. **Special Amenities:** free continental breakfast and free newspaper. *(See color ad p 612)*

SOME UNITS

[icons] ... /✕ VCR/ FEE

WELLESLEY INN & SUITES (ORLANDO/UNIVERSAL)
Phone: (407)370-5100   [186]

(AAA) [SAVE]

▼▼▼ ▼▼▼

All Year   1P: $69-$99   2P: $69-$99   XP: $10   F17
Location: I-4, exit 75B, 1 mi n on SR 435 (Kirkman Rd), just e. 5635 Windhover Dr 32819. Fax: 407/370-2026. **Facility:** 104 units. 93 one-bedroom standard units. 11 one-bedroom suites. 4 stories, interior corridors. *Bath:* combo or shower only. **Parking:** on-site. **Terms:** [ECP] meal plan available, small pets only. **Small-scale Hotel** **Amenities:** voice mail, hair dryers. *Fee:* video games, high-speed Internet, safes. *Some:* irons. **Pool(s):** heated outdoor. **Guest Services:** valet and coin laundry, area transportation-major attractions. **Business Services:** fax (fee). **Cards:** AX, DS, JC, MC, VI. **Special Amenities:** free continental breakfast and free newspaper. *(See color ad p 612)*

SOME UNITS

[icons] ... /✕ VCR/

(See map p. 598)

WESTGATE LAKES RESORT
Phone: (407)345-0000   241

AAA SAVE

▽▽◇◇▽

Condominium

5/25-9/9	1P: $158-$302	2P: $158-$302
12/1-5/24 & 9/10-11/30	1P: $110-$238	2P: $110-$238

Location: I-4, exit 74A, 0.3 mi w on Sand Lake Rd (SR 482), 2.5 mi s. 10000 Turkey Lake Rd 32819 (2601 Professional Pkwy, OCOEE, 34761). Fax: 407/355-2980. **Facility:** 1540 units. 500 one-, 500 two- and 540 three-bedroom suites ($110-$366), some with kitchens and/or whirlpools. 6 stories, exterior corridors. **Parking:** on-site. **Terms:** check-in 4 pm, 14 day cancellation notice-fee imposed. **Amenities:** CD players, voice mail, safes. *Some:* irons, hair dryers. **Dining:** 2 restaurants, 6:30 am-11 pm, Sun-Thurs to 10 pm, cocktails. **Pool(s):** 6 heated outdoor, 6 wading. **Leisure Activities:** whirlpools, rental paddleboats, boat dock, fishing, lighted tennis court, recreation programs, sand volleyball, jogging, playground, spa, basketball, shuffleboard. *Fee:* bicycles. **Guest Services:** gift shop, coin laundry. **Business Services:** fax (fee). **Cards:** AX, DC, DS, MC, VI.

🆂🅳 🍴 🍸 ⛳ 🎣 🏊 ➕ ⚒ ✕ VCR 🎥 📶 🖥 💻

WYNDHAM ORLANDO RESORT
Phone: (407)351-2420   214

AAA SAVE

▽▽◇◇▽

Large-scale Hotel

12/1-12/31 & 1/19-11/30	1P: $156	2P: $156	XP: $10	F17
1/1-1/18	1P: $116	2P: $116	XP: $10	F17

Location: I-4, exit 74A, just e at Sand Lake Rd (SR 482). 8001 International Dr 32819. Fax: 407/345-5611. **Facility:** 1052 units. 1046 one-bedroom standard units. 6 one-bedroom suites ($146-$186), some with whirl-pools. 2 stories, interior/exterior corridors. *Bath:* combo or shower only. **Parking:** on-site. **Terms:** check-in 4 pm, 3 day cancellation notice-fee imposed, small pets only ($50 extra charge). **Amenities:** dual phone lines, voice mail, safes, irons, hair dryers. *Fee:* video games, high-speed Internet. **Dining:** 3 restaurants, 6:30 am-midnight, cocktails. **Pool(s):** 3 heated outdoor, 2 wading. **Leisure Activities:** saunas, whirlpool, steamrooms, 4 lighted tennis courts, recreation programs, sand volleyball, jogging, playground, basketball, volleyball. *Fee:* massage, game room. **Guest Services:** gift shop, valet and coin laundry, area transportation-major attractions. **Business Services:** conference facilities, business center. **Cards:** AX, DC, MC, VI.

SOME UNITS

🆂🅳 🐕 🍴 🍸 🖥M ♿ 🎣 🏊 ➕ ⚒ 🎥 DATA PORT 💻 / ✕ 📶 🖥 /

FEE   FEE

─── *The following lodgings were either not evaluated or did not* ───
meet AAA rating requirements but are listed for your information only.

CROWNE PLAZA HOTEL AND RESORT UNIVERSAL
Phone: 407/355-0550

fyi

Small-scale Hotel

All Year   1P: $109-$189   2P: $109-$189
Too new to rate. **Location:** I-4, exit 74A. 7800 Universal Blvd 32819. Fax: 407/355-0504. **Amenities:** 400 units, restaurant, coffeemakers, refrigerators, pool. **Terms:** check-in 4 pm, 3 day cancellation notice-fee imposed. **Cards:** AX, DC, DS, MC, VI. *(See color ad below)*

HORIZONS BY MARRIOTT AT ORLANDO
Phone: 407/465-6100

fyi

Not evaluated. **Location:** 7102 Grand Horizons Blvd 32821. Facilities, services, and decor characterize a mid-range property.

MARRIOTT'S CYPRESS HARBOUR
Phone: 407/238-1300

fyi

Not evaluated. **Location:** 11251 Harbour Villa Rd 32821. Facilities, services, and decor characterize a mid-range property.

MARRIOTT'S GRANDE VISTA
Phone: 407/238-7676

fyi

Not evaluated. **Location:** 5925 Avenida Vista 32821. Facilities, services, and decor characterize a mid-range property.

MARRIOTT'S PALMS VILLAS
Phone: 407/238-6200

fyi

Not evaluated. **Location:** 8404 Vacation Way 32821. Facilities, services, and decor characterize a mid-range property.

THE RITZ-CARLTON, ORLANDO
Phone: 407/529-2255

fyi

Large-scale Hotel

Under construction, scheduled to open July 2003. **Location:** 3000 Central Florida Pkwy 32837. **Planned Amenities:** 400 units.

(See map p. 598)

UNIVERSAL'S ROYAL PACIFIC RESORT

[fyi]	1/2-4/23	1P: $199-$399	2P: $199-$399	XP: $25	F18
	12/1-1/1	1P: $159-$299	2P: $159-$299	XP: $25	F18
Large-scale Hotel	4/24-8/31	1P: $199-$279	2P: $199-$279	XP: $25	F18
	9/1-11/30	1P: $179-$259	2P: $179-$259	XP: $25	F18

Too new to rate. **Location:** I-4, exit 75A. 6312 Hollywood Way 32819. **Fax:** 407/503-3010. **Amenities:** 1000 units, pets, restaurant, coffeemakers, microwaves, refrigerators, pool. **Terms:** check-in 4 pm, 5 day cancellation notice-fee imposed. **Cards:** AX, CB, DC, DS, JC, MC, VI. *(See color ad starting on p 150)*

Phone: 407/503-3000

─────── WHERE TO DINE ───────

1-6-8 RESTAURANT   **Lunch:** $5-$9   **Dinner:** $6-$22   **Phone:** 407/363-1688   (189)
Chinese   **Location:** I-4, exit 74A, just w on Sand Lake Rd (SR 482), then just n on Turkey Lake Rd; in Bayhill Shopping Center. 7721 Turkey Lake Rd 32819. **Hours:** 11:30 am-10 pm, Fri & Sat-10:30 pm. **Closed:** 11/27, 12/25. **Features:** More than 40 daily lunch specials featuring Mandarin and Szechuan cuisine attract the local business crowd. Spotless and clean with pleasant, congenial service, this dining room, located in a small shopping mall, displays lovely decorator touches. Casual dress; beer & wine only. **Parking:** on-site. **Cards:** AX, MC, VI.

AMIGOS   **Lunch:** $6-$8   **Dinner:** $8-$15   **Phone:** 407/857-3144   (172)
Mexican   **Location:** I-4, exit 80, 2 mi s. 6036 S Orange Blossom Tr 32809. **Hours:** 11 am-9:30 pm, Fri & Sat-10 pm, Sun-9 pm. Closed major holidays. **Features:** A lively crowd keeps the staff moving at a bustling pace to deliver oversized burritos and platefuls of tacos. Casual surroundings and popular Tex-Mex dishes are sure to please the whole family. Order the fajitas for a sizzling, hot sensation. Casual dress; cocktails. **Parking:** on-site. **Cards:** AX, MC, VI.

A TASTE OF JAPAN   **Lunch:** $8-$25   **Dinner:** $11-$25   **Phone:** 407/363-0360   (184)
Japanese   **Location:** I-4, exit 74A, 0.5 mi nw; in Bayhill Shopping Center. 7637 Turkey Lake Rd 32819. **Hours:** 11:30-2 pm & 5:30-10 pm, Sat from 5:30. **Closed:** Sun. **Features:** Nightly karaoke performances set the mood in this cozy restaurant, where the menu includes sushi, sashimi, noodles, rice, meat and seafood. If you're in the mood to walk a little on the wild side, ask for the separate Japanese menu. Casual dress; beer & wine only. **Parking:** on-site. **Cards:** AX, MC, VI.

ATLANTIS   **Dinner:** $27-$35   **Phone:** 407/351-5555   (206)
Seafood   **Location:** I-4, exit 72, just e on Central Florida Pkwy, 0.3 mi n or 0.7 mi w of International Dr; in Renaissance Orlando Resort at SeaWorld. 6677 Sea Harbor Dr 32821-8092. **Hours:** 6 pm-10 pm. Closed major holidays; also Sun. **Reservations:** suggested. **Features:** Relax in a lovely formal setting complete with crystal chandeliers and hand-painted murals. Fresh, expertly prepared seafood is offered along with lamb and filet mignon. Savor a glass of wine from a very select list. Resort-casual attire is accepted. Dressy casual; cocktails. **Parking:** on-site and valet. **Cards:** AX, CB, DC, DS, JC, MC, VI.

BAHAMA BREEZE   **Dinner:** $8-$19   **Phone:** 407/248-2499   (197)
Caribbean   **Location:** I-4, exit 74A (Sand Lake Rd), 1 mi s. 8849 International Dr 32817. **Hours:** 4 pm-1 am, Fri & Sat-1:30 am. **Closed:** 11/27, 12/25. **Features:** Move to an island beat at this popular restaurant featuring Caribbean fare in a tropical decor. Many favorites are offered, including a jerk chicken that gives you a spicy taste of Jamaica. Visit the on-site gift shop for a little after-dinner browsing. Casual dress; cocktails; entertainment. **Parking:** on-site and valet. **Cards:** AX, DC, DS, MC, VI.

BAJA BURRITO KITCHEN   **Lunch:** $4-$9   **Dinner:** $4-$9   **Phone:** 407/299-5001   (168)
Mexican   **Location:** On west side of SR 435, 1.3 mi n of I-4, exit 75, 2.1 mi n of International Dr; in Kirkman Oaks Center. 4642 S Kirkman Rd 32811. **Hours:** 11 am-10 pm, Sun 11:30 am-9 pm. **Closed:** 4/20, 11/27, 12/25. **Features:** Fresh Tex-Mex favorites are prepared hot and fast. Sample a host of toppings at the salsa bar, from fresh tomatoes to very hot habanero salsa and chopped cilantro. Enjoy casual, no-fuss, paper plate dining and savor a nice made-to-order meal. Smoke free premises. Casual dress; beer & wine only. **Parking:** on-site.

BERGAMO'S ITALIAN RESTAURANT   **Dinner:** $15-$39   **Phone:** 407/352-3805   (186)
Italian   **Location:** I-4, exit 74A, just e on Sand Lake Rd, then 0.5 mi s; on west side of Mercado Shopping Village. 8445 International Dr 32819. **Hours:** 6 pm-10 pm. **Closed:** 11/27, 12/25. **Reservations:** suggested. **Features:** Although the elegent decor might lead you to believe this place is haughty and stiff, you'll quickly notice a more casual and bustling atmosphere pervades. Accomplished vocalists, the servers take turns belting out opera and Broadway tunes at the mic. Casual dress; cocktails; entertainment. **Parking:** on-site. **Cards:** AX, DC, DS, MC, VI.

THE BLACK SWAN   **Dinner:** $25-$40   **Phone:** 407/239-1999   (208)
Continental   **Location:** I-4, exit 68, 2.3 mi nw on SR 535; in The Villas of Grand Cypress. 1 North Jacaranda 32819. **Hours:** 6 pm-10 pm. **Reservations:** suggested. **Features:** Piano music plays while an extensive menu is served in a multi-level dining room that overlooks an emerald green golf course. The seared tuna is peppered, sliced thin and tied with orange rind to a tower of scallions. A 16% service charge will be assessed. Smoke free premises. Semi-formal attire; cocktails; entertainment. **Parking:** on-site. **Cards:** AX, CB, DC, DS, JC, MC, VI.

BOB MARLEY-A TRIBUTE TO FREEDOM   **Lunch:** $4-$11   **Dinner:** $4-$11   **Phone:** 407/224-2262   (154)
Jamaican   **Location:** I-4, exit 74B; in Universal Studios CityWalk. Universal Studios 32835. **Hours:** 4 pm-2 am. **Features:** Located in Citywalk this themed restaurant not only features light Jamaican fare but also memoribilia from the legendary musicians life. Continuious concerts are shown on numerous televisions scattered throughout the restaurant. Casual dress; cocktails. **Parking:** on-site (fee). **Cards:** AX, DS, MC, VI.

(See map p. 598)

BOSTON LOBSTER FEAST   **Dinner:** $16-$30   **Phone:** 407/438-0607   177
Seafood
Location: Se of jct SR 482 (Sand Lake Rd) and US 17-92/441. 8204 Crystal Clear Ln 32809. **Hours:** 4 pm-10 pm, Sat & Sun from 2 pm. **Features:** Famished after a day of shopping at the Florida Mall? This casual, all-you-can-eat Maine lobster buffet may be just what you need. Lobster, crab, beef, salad and soup are among the many selections served in an inventive, nautical atmosphere. Casual dress; cocktails. **Parking:** on-site. **Cards:** AX, DC, DS, MC, VI.

THE BUTCHER SHOP STEAK HOUSE   **Dinner:** $16-$30   **Phone:** 407/363-9727   192
Steak House
Location: I-4, exit 74A, just e on Sand Lake Rd, then 0.5 mi s; in Mercado Shopping Village. 8445 International Dr, S-140 32819. **Hours:** 5 pm-10 pm, Fri & Sat-11 pm. **Closed:** 11/27, 12/25. **Reservations:** suggested. **Features:** Richly appointed dining rooms decked out in mahogany are the setting for surprisingly informal dining. The menu is primarily charcoal-broiled steak and prime rib ranging in size from an 8-oz filet to a 32-oz bone-in rib. A cook-your-own option is featured. Casual dress; cocktails. **Parking:** on-site. **Cards:** AX, CB, DC, DS, JC, MC, VI.

CAFE TU TU TANGO   **Lunch:** $4-$9   **Dinner:** $4-$9   **Phone:** 407/248-2222   188
International
Location: I-4, exit 74A, 1 mi se, just e of International Dr, 0.5 mi s of SR 483 (Sand Lake Rd); in Doubletree Castle Hotel. 8625 International Dr 32819. **Hours:** 11:30 am-11 pm, Fri & Sat-midnight. **Closed:** 11/27, 12/25. **Features:** A multiethnic menu that reaches into different parts of the world offers a broad variety of exclusively appetizer-sized dishes. Creativity and flair shows in such specialties as Cajun chicken egg rolls, Barcelona stir-fry and tenderloin skewers. View the works of local artists on display throughout the restaurant. Casual dress; cocktails; entertainment. **Parking:** on-site. **Cards:** AX, DC, DS, MC, VI.

CAPRICCIO   **Dinner:** $12-$25   **Phone:** 407/345-4540   200
Northern Italian
Location: 0.5 mi n of SR 528 (Bee Line Expwy); opposite Orange County Convention Center; in The Peabody Orlando. 9801 International Dr 32819. **Hours:** 6 pm-11 pm, Sun also 11 am-2 pm. **Closed:** Mon. **Reservations:** suggested. **Features:** Buzzing with a bustling atmosphere, this upscale, casual eatery features an exhibition kitchen with a wood-burning pizza oven. Sunday champagne brunch is popular and offers an abundance of hearty, delicious choices. Choose from a well-rounded wine list. Smoke free premises. Dressy casual; cocktails. **Parking:** on-site and valet. **Cards:** AX, CB, DC, DS, JC, MC, VI.

CHARLEY'S STEAK HOUSE   **Dinner:** $13-$35   **Phone:** 407/363-0228   185
Steak House
Location: I-4, exit 74A, just e on SR 482 (Sand Lake Rd), then 0.3 mi s. 8255 International Dr 32819. **Hours:** 5 pm-10:30 pm, Fri & Sat-11 pm. **Closed:** 11/27, 12/25. **Reservations:** suggested. **Features:** Charlie's specializes in steak, chicken and seafood grilled over an open-flame. Five dining rooms with an antique look are available. Peruse the extensive wine list to find the perfect complement to the 20-oz filet mignon or the 52-oz porterhouse steak. Casual dress; cocktails. **Parking:** on-site. **Cards:** AX, MC, VI.

CHARLEY'S STEAK HOUSE   **Dinner:** $12-$28   **Phone:** 407/851-7130   173
Steak House
Location: US 17-92 and 441, 3.0 mi s of jct I-4, exit 80. 6107 S Orange Blossom Tr 32809. **Hours:** 4:30 pm-10:30 pm, Fri & Sat-11:30 pm. **Closed:** 11/27, 12/25. **Reservations:** suggested. **Features:** Specializing in aged steak, chops and chicken grilled over an open flame of oak and orange woods, the casually elegant restaurant offers ample portions and an impressive wine list. Desserts are huge in taste and size, a great value, and enough for two. Dressy casual; cocktails. **Parking:** on-site. **Cards:** AX, MC, VI.

CHARLIE'S LOBSTER HOUSE   **Dinner:** $16-$40   **Phone:** 407/352-6929   190
Seafood
Location: I-4, exit 74A, just e on Sand Lake Rd, then just s; in Mercado Shopping Village. 8445 International Dr 122 32819. **Hours:** 6 pm-10 pm. **Closed:** 11/27, 12/25. **Reservations:** suggested. **Features:** New England and fresh Florida seafood are featured along with black Angus beef in this bustling, lively restaurant. This is the place for smothering fresh lobster in melted butter and feasting on delicious side dishes like mashed potatoes and vegetables. Casual dress; cocktails. **Parking:** on-site. **Cards:** AX, DC, DS, MC, VI.

CHATHAM'S PLACE   **Dinner:** $20-$38   **Phone:** 407/345-2992   175
Continental
Location: I-4, exit 74A, 0.5 mi w; opposite Market Place Shopping Ctr. 7575 Dr Phillips Blvd 32819. **Hours:** 5:30 pm-10 pm. **Closed:** major holidays. **Reservations:** suggested. **Features:** Relaxed elegance is evoked in the small, intimate dining room where live music is performed nightly and the refined menu boasts a selection of entrees ranging from rack of lamb to fresh black grouper with a pecan butter crust. Smoke free premises. Dressy casual; cocktails; entertainment. **Parking:** on-site. **Cards:** AX, DC, DS, MC, VI.

CIAO ITALIA RISTORANTE ITALIANO   **Dinner:** $15-$30   **Phone:** 407/354-0770   204
Italian
Location: Bee Line Expwy (SR 528), exit 1, just e; in International Towne Center. 6149 Westwood Blvd 32821. **Hours:** 5 pm-midnight. **Features:** This Italian bistro is located within a strip mall. Their walls have decorative tiles, the dishes are prepared using the freshest of ingredients, and the friendly wait staff is happy to offer suggestions. cocktails. **Parking:** on-site. **Cards:** AX, DC, DS, MC, VI.

DELFINO RIVIERA   **Dinner:** $27-$38   **Phone:** 407/503-1415   159
Northern Italian
Location: I-4, exit 75B, 0.5 mi n on SR 435 (Kirkman Rd), then just w via Vineland Rd; at Universal Studios; in Universal's Portofino Bay Hotel. 5601 Universal Blvd 32819. **Hours:** 6 pm-10 pm. **Closed:** Sun & Mon. **Reservations:** suggested. **Features:** The quiet, upscale restaurant is known for wonderful food and a cozy, romantic setting. Its menu, service and decor combine to successfully capture the concept of credibly representing life on the Italian Riviera. Appetizers are delightful, intriguing entrees are excellent, and desserts are truly artful presentations of decadence. The crowning touch is a roving musician, who makes your dining experience one to remember. Reservations should be made well in advance. Smoke free premises. Dressy casual; cocktails; entertainment. **Parking:** on-site and valet. **Cards:** AX, CB, DC, DS, JC, MC, VI.

(See map p. 598)

DUX
♥♥♥♥ **Dinner:** $20-$40 **Phone:** 407/345-4540 [201]
Location: 0.5 mi n of SR 528 (Bee Line Expwy); opposite Orange County Convention Center; in The Peabody Orlando. 9801 International Dr 32819. **Hours:** 6 pm-10 pm, Fri & Sat-11 pm. Closed: Sun & 8/1-8/31.
Continental **Reservations:** suggested. **Features:** An intimate, elegant dining room and refined service set the scene for traditional cuisine with a creative, international spin. The menu changes seasonally and features dishes like skewered beef in a spicy, tangy sauce. Gentlemen's jackets are suggested. Smoke free premises. Semi-formal attire; cocktails. **Parking:** on-site. **Cards:** AX, CB, DC, DS, JC, MC, VI.

EMERIL'S RESTAURANT ORLANDO **Lunch:** $18-$22 **Dinner:** $20-$34 **Phone:** 407/224-2424 [150]
♥♥♥ **Location:** In Universal Studios CityWalk. 6000 Universal Blvd, S-702 32819. **Hours:** 11:30 am-2 & 5:30-10 pm, Fri & Sat-11 pm. **Reservations:** suggested. **Features:** You will find a wonderful mix of Old World, Louisiana
Creole cooking with the style of today's modern kitchen. From oven-baked pizza to rack of lamb to ham crusted snapper, all dishes are fabulously well-prepared and graciously served in a New Vogue setting. Dressy casual; cocktails. **Parking:** on-site (fee) and valet. **Cards:** AX, CB, DC, DS, JC, MC, VI.

EVERGLADES **Dinner:** $17-$30 **Phone:** 407/996-9840 [198]
♥♥♥ **Location:** I-4, exit 72, just e on SR 528 (Bee Line Expwy) to exit 1 (International Dr), then just n; in Rosen Centre Hotel. 9840 International Dr 32819. **Hours:** 5:30 pm-11 pm. **Reservations:** suggested. **Features:** Diners here
Regional American can unwind in an artfully created atmosphere among images of the flora and fauna of Florida. Flashes of color and motion coming from the large aquarium entice patrons to relax. On the adventurous menu are such choices as Alligator Bay chowder, sauteed wild boar medallions, venison pepper steak and tenderloin of buffalo. Those who prefer to stay closer to home can opt for one of the many fresh seafood or beef entrees. An 18% gratuity is added automatically to the bill. Casual dress; cocktails. **Parking:** on-site. **Cards:** AX, DC, DS, JC, MC, VI.

FISHBONES **Dinner:** $13-$40 **Phone:** 407/352-0135 [182]
♥♥♥ **Location:** I-4, exit 74A, 0.3 mi e on SR 482. 6707 Sand Lake Rd 32819. **Hours:** 5 pm-10:30 pm, Fri & Sat-11 pm. Closed: 11/27, 12/25. **Reservations:** suggested. **Features:** Nine dining rooms cast off a nautical
Seafood personality, with plenty of wood, fishing poles and a big saltwater fish tank. Fresh fish cooked over an open citrus and oak flame, pan-seared sesame tuna and crab-stuffed filet mignon are all good choices. Casual dress; cocktails. **Parking:** on-site. **Cards:** AX, MC, VI.

GAIN'S GERMAN RESTAURANT **Lunch:** $7-$8 **Dinner:** $10-$21 **Phone:** 407/438-8997 [171]
♥♥♥ **Location:** I-4, exit 80, 1.8 mi s; on US 17-92 and 441. 5731 S Orange Blossom Tr 32809. **Hours:** 11:30 am-2:30 & 4:30-10 pm, Fri & Sat-11 pm, Sun 4:30 pm-10 pm. Closed: 11/27, 12/24, 12/25; also Mon.
German **Reservations:** suggested; Fri & Sat. **Features:** Featuring authentic German cuisine and a homey decor, the pleasant little restaurant also serves a good selection of German draft and bottled beer. Casual dress; beer & wine only. **Parking:** on-site. **Cards:** AX, DC, DS, MC, VI.

HEMISPHERE **Dinner:** $17-$28 **Phone:** 407/825-1234 [207]
♥♥♥ **Location:** At the Orlando International Airport (Terminal A); in Hyatt Regency Orlando International Airport. 9300 Airport Blvd 32827. **Hours:** 6:30 am-11 & 5:30-10 pm, Sat 7 am-3 & 5:30-10 pm, Sun 8 am-1 pm.
Continental **Reservations:** suggested. **Features:** Watch planes depart while enjoying a delightful meal in this rich, airy 9th floor dining room overlooking a terminal and runway. A tasteful decor and delicious food are the strong points. Be sure to make a reservation as this restaurant is quite popular. Casual dress; cocktails. **Parking:** valet. **Cards:** AX, CB, DC, DS, JC, MC, VI.

ITALIANNI'S RESTAURANT **Lunch:** $7-$14 **Dinner:** $9-$20 **Phone:** 407/345-8884 [183]
♥♥♥ **Location:** I-4, exit 74A, just e on Sand Lake Rd, then 0.3 mi s. 8148 International Dr 32819. **Hours:** 11:30 am-11 pm. Closed: 11/27. **Reservations:** accepted. **Features:** An imaginative chef prepares a good variety of
Italian dishes with distinctive flavor. Pizza, pasta, chicken and seafood, such as shrimp fried diablo, are served along with daily specials and wonderful dessert, most notably a chocolate black raspberry cake. Casual dress; cocktails. **Parking:** on-site. **Cards:** AX, CB, DC, DS, MC, VI.

JACK'S PLACE **Dinner:** $16-$28 **Phone:** 407/996-9700 [199]
AAA **Location:** I-4, exit 72, just n; from Bee Line Expwy (SR 528), exit 1, then just n; in Rosen Plaza. 9700 International Dr 32819. **Hours:** 5:30 pm-11 pm. **Reservations:** suggested. **Features:** A casually elegant decor features a
♥♥♥ collection of autographed celebrity caricatures. Excellent cuisine is skillfully prepared, and offered along with list of daily specials. Please note, a service charge of 18% is automatically added to the check.
Steak & Seafood Casual dress; cocktails. **Parking:** on-site. **Cards:** AX, DC, DS, JC, MC, VI.

JIMMY BUFFETT'S MARGARITAVILLE **Lunch:** $5-$10 **Dinner:** $8-$20 **Phone:** 407/224-2155 [151]
♥♥♥ **Location:** In Universal Studios CityWalk. 6000 Universal Blvd, S-704 32819. **Hours:** 11 am-2 am. **Features:** Kick back with a margarita and feast on cheeseburgers in paradise. Island trinkets and twinkling lights decorate
American a two-story dining room where favorite Buffett tunes are played to set the perfect lazy-day-at-the-beach mood. A must for devoted parrotheads. Casual dress; cocktails; entertainment. **Parking:** on-site (fee).
Cards: AX, DC, DS, MC, VI.

LA PIAZA **Lunch:** $5-$7 **Dinner:** $7-$16 **Phone:** 407/855-1170 [209]
♥♥♥ **Location:** Central Florida Greenway (SR 417), exit 10, 1 mi s on John Young Pkwy; in Colonial Hunter Creek Promenade shopping mall. 4060 Town Center 32837. **Hours:** 11:30 am-9:30 pm, Fri & Sat-10:30 pm. Closed
Italian major holidays; also Mon. **Reservations:** accepted. **Features:** Decorated to resemble the patio of an Italian villa, this restaurant offers delicious food and gracious service. The menu features reliable Italian fare, such as pizza, pasta and sandwiches. Simple food preparations make this a pleasant place for lunch or a casual supper. cocktails. **Parking:** on-site. **Cards:** AX, DS, MC, VI.

(See map p. 598)

LARRY'S CEDAR RIVER SEAFOOD   **Lunch:** $6-$11   **Dinner:** $9-$16   **Phone:** 407/858-0525   (174)
Seafood
Location: US 17-92 and 441, 2 mi s of Florida Tpke, exit 254; 3 mi s of I-4. 7101 S Orange Blossom Tr 32809. **Hours:** 4 pm-9:30 pm, Fri & Sat-10:30 pm, Sun noon-9:30 pm. Closed major holidays; also Mon. **Reservations:** suggested. **Features:** Combining the styles of New England and the South, the restaurant is notable for nicely prepared fresh seafood served grilled, fried, broiled, sauteed or blackened. A raw bar entices adventurous palates. If it's not too hot, pay a visit to the patio. Casual dress; cocktails. **Parking:** on-site. **Cards:** AX, DC, DS, MC, VI.

LATIN QUARTER   **Lunch:** $7-$25   **Dinner:** $13-$30   **Phone:** 407/363-5922   (152)
Latino
Location: I-4, exit 74B; in Universal Studios CityWalk. Universal/City Walk S-606 32835. **Hours:** 5 pm-11 pm, Fri-Sun from noon. **Features:** Contributing to the elegant, lively and earthy decor are colorful mosaic tile, strobe lighting and fine table settings. Menu items are light, creative and artistic, combining distinct flavorings with pork, lamb, chicken and beef. This place is great for a good meal and all-night dancing. Casual dress; cocktails. **Parking:** on-site (fee). **Cards:** AX, DC, DS, MC, VI.

LE COQ AU VIN   **Lunch:** $11-$14   **Dinner:** $15-$24   **Phone:** 407/851-6980   (169)
French
Location: I-4, exit 81A, 2.3 mi se. 4800 S Orange Ave 32806. **Hours:** 11:30 am-2 & 5:30-10 pm, Sat from 5:30 pm, Sun 5 pm-9 pm. Closed: 1/1, 11/27, 12/25; also Mon. **Reservations:** suggested. **Features:** The simple setting is reminiscent of a cozy, country cottage. While the candlelight dinner setting appears elegant, the local clientele has come to expect a refined, but more casual, dining experience. The menu provides an interesting blend of country and cosmopolitan fare. Favorites include escargot, onion and herb-seasoned rack of lamb, coq au vin, duck a L'Orange and creme brulee with seasonal berries. Light eaters can request half portions of all entrees. Smoke free premises. Casual dress; beer & wine only. **Parking:** on-site. **Cards:** AX, DC, DS, MC, VI.

MING COURT   **Lunch:** $5-$10   **Dinner:** $12-$33   **Phone:** 407/351-9988   (196)
Chinese
Location: 0.8 mi n of SR 528 (Bee Line Expwy); 1 mi s of SR 482 (Sand Lake Rd). 9188 International Dr 32819. **Hours:** 11 am-2:30 & 4:30-11:30 pm. **Reservations:** suggested. **Features:** A 250-foot dragon will greet you as you enter the courtyard of this elegant Oriental restaurant. Gourmet regional specialties served in split-level dining rooms have a nouvelle flair, including the Szechuan Flaming Wok, sushi bar and daily Dim Sum lunch. Casual dress; cocktails; entertainment. **Parking:** on-site. **Cards:** AX, DC, DS, MC, VI.

MOTOWN CAFE   **Lunch:** $6-$11   **Dinner:** $8-$20   **Phone:** 407/224-2500   (155)
American
Location: In Universal Studios CityWalk. 6000 Universal Blvd, S-735 32819. **Hours:** 11 am-2 am. **Features:** Enjoy the best of Motown at this Universal Studios attraction, a clean, classy number with great music and lots of favorite finger foods. An eager staff makes the presentation fun. A gift shop and nightly entertainment add to the Motown experience. Casual dress; cocktails. **Parking:** on-site (fee). **Cards:** AX, DS, JC, MC, VI.

MURPHY'S CHOP HOUSE   **Dinner:** $19-$29   **Phone:** 407/851-9000   (178)
Steak House
Location: SR 528 (Bee Line Expwy), exit 11, 0.5 mi n on SR 436, just e, then s; in Orlando Airport Marriott. 7499 Augusta National Dr 32822. **Hours:** 5 pm-10 pm. Closed: Sun. **Reservations:** suggested. **Features:** This mainly Chicago-style chop house also offers seafood dishes such as tuna fillet coated with sesame seeds or horseradish-encrusted red snapper. In the center of a mid-rise hotel just north of Orlando International Airport, the setting is classic, complete with hardwood floors and brass accents. Smoke free premises. Casual dress; cocktails. **Parking:** valet. **Cards:** AX, DC, DS, JC, MC, VI.

NASCAR CAFE   **Lunch:** $7-$18   **Dinner:** $7-$18   **Phone:** 407/224-7223   (153)
American
Location: I-4, exit 74B; in Universal Studios CityWalk. 6000 Universal CityWalk 32819. **Hours:** 11 am-10 pm. **Features:** Cars displayed out front are only the beginning of this auto racing adventure. Forget dieting! The portions of burgers, steaks, barbecue ribs and chicken are huge. A gift shop and arcade games make this more than your usual burger joint. Casual dress; cocktails. **Parking:** on-site (fee). **Cards:** AX, DC, DS, MC, VI.

PALM RESTAURANT   **Lunch:** $12-$25   **Dinner:** $15-$34   **Phone:** 407/503-7256   (160)
American
Location: I-4, exit 75A; in Universal's Hard Rock Hotel. 5800 Universal Blvd 32819. **Hours:** 11:30 am-11 pm, Sat 5 pm-11 pm, Sun 5 pm-10 pm. **Reservations:** suggested. **Features:** At this classic, bustling steakhouse, diners are treated to superb steaks and chops in flavorful and ample cuts, along with a variety of pasta, poultry and seafood dishes. Dressy casual; cocktails. **Parking:** valet. **Cards:** AX, CB, DC, MC, VI.

PASTAMORE'   **Lunch:** $6-$13   **Dinner:** $9-$22   **Phone:** 407/224-2244   (156)
Italian
Location: In Universal Studios CityWalk. 6000 Universal Blvd, S-700 32819. **Hours:** 7 am-1 & 5-10:30 pm, Fri & Sat-midnight. **Features:** One of Universal Studio's favorites, it offers wonderful pastries and coffee served in a sidewalk cafe or inside a spacious dining room. A menu of veal, chicken, pizza and homemade pasta is highlighted by cheese-covered tomatoes soaked in oil and basil. Casual dress; cocktails. **Parking:** on-site (fee). **Cards:** AX, CB, DC, DS, JC, MC, VI.

PAT O'BRIEN'S   **Lunch:** $8-$12   **Dinner:** $8-$12   **Phone:** 407/224-2961   (158)
Creole
Location: In Universal Studios CityWalk. 6000 Universal Blvd, S-723 32819. **Hours:** 3 pm-2 am. **Reservations:** accepted. **Features:** This exact replica of the famous New Orleans bar offers nightly entertainment, a courtyard and three bars. A clean-cut staff delivers dishes mixed with spicy Cajun and Creole specialties. Don't miss the better-than-Grandma's creamy bread pudding. Casual dress; cocktails; entertainment. **Parking:** on-site (fee). **Cards:** AX, DS, MC, VI.

(See map p. 598)

RACE ROCK RESTAURANT　　**Lunch:** $6-$17　　**Dinner:** $6-$17　　**Phone:** 407/248-9876　　(193)

American

Location: I-4, exit 74A (Sand Lake Rd), 1 mi s. 8986 International Dr 32819. **Hours:** 11:30 am-10:30 pm, Fri & Sat-11:30. Closed: 12/25. **Features:** This loud and lively racing-themed restaurant displays an impressive collection of authentic racing memorabilia. Tasty offerings include burgers, sandwiches, pasta and some gourmet items. Fast, friendly service makes this a favorable pit stop. Casual dress; cocktails. **Parking:** on-site. **Cards:** AX, DC, DS, MC, VI.

RAN-GETSU OF TOKYO　　**Dinner:** $14-$34　　**Phone:** 407/345-0044　　(194)

Japanese

Location: I-4, exit 74A, 0.3 mi s of SR 482 (Sand Lake Rd), just se. 8400 International Dr 32819. **Hours:** 5 pm-11:30 pm. **Reservations:** suggested. **Features:** Located near local attractions, Ran-Getsu serves authentic Japanese cuisine in a nice, cozy setting. Order from the sushi bar, or try the Shabu-Shabu, a sirloin and vegetable dinner for two cooked right at the table. Traditional drum shows on weekends. Smoke free premises. Casual dress; cocktails. **Parking:** on-site. **Cards:** AX, DC, DS, JC, MC, VI.

ROY'S　　**Dinner:** $20-$28　　**Phone:** 407/352-4844　　(176)

Seafood

Location: I-4, exit 74A, 0.8 mi w. 7760 W Sand Lake Rd 32819. **Hours:** 5:30-10 pm, Fri & Sat-10:30 pm. Closed: 11/27, 12/25. **Reservations:** accepted. **Features:** From greetings of "aloha" to departing, guests enjoy a warm, satisfying dining experience. The open surroundings blend traditional concepts with wood accents to create a comfortable, casual setting. Well-trained, friendly staff are knowledgeable and skilled in attending to guests' needs. The menu changes daily, always offering a varied selection of Hawaiian and Pacific seafood, highlighted by highly creative sauces. Smoke free premises. Dressy casual. **Parking:** on-site and valet. **Cards:** AX, DC, DS, MC, VI.

SHAMIANA　　**Lunch:** $4-$9　　**Dinner:** $9-$15　　**Phone:** 407/354-1160　　(181)

East Indian

Location: I-4, exit 74A (Sand Lake Rd), just n on International Dr; in small shopping plaza. 7040 International Dr 32819. **Hours:** 11:30 am-2:30 & 5-11 pm, Sat from 5 pm. Closed: 7/4, 11/27; also 12/25. **Reservations:** suggested. **Features:** A far-ranging menu offers popular East Indian fare as well as Tandoori selections. Spicy flavors can be adjusted to suit the tastes of the uninitiated. Vegetarian dishes are available, and a wonderful flat bread is served with the meal. beer & wine only. **Parking:** on-site. **Cards:** AX, DC, DS, MC, VI.

SIAM ORCHID　　**Dinner:** $10-$18　　**Phone:** 407/351-0821　　(179)

Thai

Location: I-4, exit 74A, 0.5 mi e on SR 482 (Sand Lake Rd), 0.3 mi n. 7575 Universal Blvd 32819. **Hours:** 11 am-2 & 5-11 pm, Sat & Sun from 5 pm. Closed major holidays. **Reservations:** suggested; weekends. **Features:** Fine khundoke or Thai-style dining can be enjoyed in a subdued, relaxing atmosphere. The focus is on Thai and other Oriental specialties, including Pad Thai pot pie filled with rice, noodles, vegetables, shrimp and crab meat. Another classic dish is whole snapper. Casual dress; cocktails. **Parking:** on-site. **Cards:** AX, CB, DS, MC, VI.

VITO'S CHOP HOUSE　　**Dinner:** $14-$33　　**Phone:** 407/354-2467　　(187)

Steak House

Location: I-4, exit 74A, 1 mi se, just e of International Dr, then 0.5 mi s of SR 483 (Sand Lake Rd); in Doubletree Castle Hotel. 8633 International Dr 32821. **Hours:** 5 pm-10:30 pm, Fri & Sat-11 pm. Closed: 11/27, 12/25. **Reservations:** accepted. **Features:** Decorated in a comfortably masculine style, the classy operation reflects touches of Tuscany. Ample portions of doubly thick veal chops, tender all the way through, are nicely complemented by an expansive wine list. For dessert, pucker up for the luscious key lime pie. Dressy casual; cocktails. **Parking:** on-site. **Cards:** AX, MC, VI.

WILD JACK'S STEAKS & BBQ　　**Dinner:** $10-$22　　**Phone:** 407/352-4407　　(180)

American

Location: 0.3 mi n of Sandlake Rd (SR 482); 0.5 mi ne of I-4, exit 74A. 7364 International Dr 32819. **Hours:** 4 pm-10 pm, Fri & Sat-10:30 pm. **Reservations:** accepted. **Features:** Antler-rack chandeliers, exposed beam ceilings and simulated animal hide seats evoke the rustic air of the Old West. Servers in jeans and plaid shirts or deputy uniforms and badges serve such dishes as a well-seasoned chili-crusted New York strip. Casual dress; cocktails. **Parking:** on-site. **Cards:** AX, CB, DC, DS, MC, VI.

The following restaurants have not been evaluated by AAA but are listed for your information only.

CHRISTINI'S　　**Phone:** 407/345-8770

(fyi) Not evaluated. **Location:** I-4, exit 74A, 0.5 mi w; in Marketplace Shopping Center. 7600 Dr Phillips Blvd 32819. **Features:** Famous for their 26 ounce veal chop, Christini's also makes their own fresh pasta. Menu selections include shrimp diablo, veal with four cheeses and calamari. Italian art and a strolling accordionist add charm to a friendly, though bustling atmosphere.

CITYJAZZ　　**Phone:** 407/224-2189

(fyi) Not evaluated. **Location:** I-4, exit 74B; in Universal Studios CityWalk. Universal Studios. **Features:** Best jazz Orlando has to offer! Light menu offers appetizers, drinks, coffees and cigars. Open nightly.

N.Y.P.D. PIZZA & DELICATESSEN　　**Phone:** 407/872-6973

(fyi) Not evaluated. **Location:** Center. 373 N Orange Ave 32801. **Features:** Traditional Italian favorites; pizza, pasta and salads that are popular at any time of the day.

TIMPANO ITALIAN CHOP HOUSE　　**Phone:** 407/248-0429

(fyi) Not evaluated. **Location:** I-4, exit 74A, just w. 7488 W Sand Lake Rd 32819. **Features:** Chicken, chops and veal prepared with Italian flare and seasoned to perfection are highlights on this unique menu.

The Orlando Vicinity

ALTAMONTE SPRINGS pop. 41,200 (See map p. 590; index p. 594)

------ WHERE TO STAY ------

BEST WESTERN ALTAMONTE SPRINGS
Phone: (407)862-8200 [103]
AAA SAVE
All Year [ECP]   1P: $79   2P: $79
Location: I-4, exit 92, just nw. 150 Douglas Ave 32714. Fax: 407/862-5750. **Facility:** 144 one-bedroom standard units. 3 stories, exterior corridors. *Bath:* combo or shower only. **Parking:** on-site. **Amenities:** voice mail, irons, hair dryers. **Pool(s):** outdoor. **Leisure Activities:** exercise room. **Guest Services:** valet and coin Small-scale Hotel laundry. **Business Services:** meeting rooms. **Cards:** AX, CB, DC, DS, MC, VI. **Special Amenities:** early check-in/late check-out and free continental breakfast.
SOME UNITS

CANDLEWOOD SUITES
Phone: (407)767-5757 [98]
All Year   1P: $69-$109   2P: $69-$109
Location: I-4, exit 92, just w to Douglas Ave, 0.8 mi n to Central Pkwy, just e. 644 Raymond Ave 32701. Small-scale Hotel Fax: 407/767-0097. **Facility:** 122 units. 98 one-bedroom standard units with efficiencies. 24 one-bedroom suites with efficiencies. 3 stories, interior corridors. *Bath:* combo or shower only. **Parking:** on-site. **Amenities:** video library, CD players, dual phone lines, voice mail, irons, hair dryers. **Pool(s):** heated outdoor. **Leisure Activities:** exercise room. **Guest Services:** complimentary laundry. **Business Services:** fax. **Cards:** AX, CB, DC, DS, JC, MC, VI.
SOME UNITS

EMBASSY SUITES ORLANDO NORTH
Phone: (407)834-2400 [104]
AAA SAVE
1/1-11/30 [BP]   1P: $129-$229   2P: $129-$229   XP: $15   F
12/1-12/31 [BP]   1P: $99-$149   2P: $99-$149   XP: $15   F
Location: I-4, exit 92, 0.3 mi e on SR 436, just n on North Lake Blvd. 225 E Altamonte Dr 32701. Fax: 407/834-2117. Small-scale Hotel site. **Terms:** cancellation fee imposed, pets ($15 fee). **Amenities:** dual phone lines, voice mail, irons, hair dryers. **Dining:** 6:30 am-9 & 11-10 pm, Sat & Sun 7 am-10:30 & 11-10 pm, cocktails. **Pool(s):** heated indoor. **Leisure Activities:** sauna, whirlpool, steamroom, exercise room. **Guest Services:** gift shop, complimentary evening beverages, valet and coin laundry, area transportation-within 5 mi. **Business Services:** conference facilities, business center. **Cards:** AX, CB, DC, DS, MC, VI. **Special Amenities:** free continental breakfast and free newspaper. *(See color ad p 615)*
SOME UNITS

HAMPTON INN
Phone: (407)869-9000 [101]
AAA SAVE
All Year   1P: $83-$149
Location: I-4, exit 92, just nw. 151 N Douglas Ave 32714. Fax: 407/869-9870. **Facility:** 210 one-bedroom standard units. 2 stories, exterior corridors. *Bath:* combo or shower only. **Parking:** on-site. **Terms:** [ECP] meal plan available, pets ($60 extra charge). **Amenities:** video games (fee), voice mail, irons, hair dryers. **Pool(s):** Small-scale Hotel heated outdoor. **Leisure Activities:** whirlpool, exercise room. **Guest Services:** valet and coin laundry. **Business Services:** meeting rooms, business center. **Cards:** AX, DC, DS, MC, VI. **Special Amenities:** free continental breakfast and free local telephone calls.
SOME UNITS

HILTON ORLANDO/ALTAMONTE SPRINGS
Phone: (407)830-1985 [108]
SAVE
All Year   1P: $69-$125   2P: $69-$125   XP: $10   F
Location: I-4, exit 92, just e on SR 436, then 0.5 mi s. 350 S North Lake Blvd 32715. Fax: 407/331-2911. **Facility:** 322 units. 317 one-bedroom standard units. 5 one-bedroom suites ($295-$500). 3 stories, interior corridors. *Bath:* combo or shower only. **Parking:** on-site. **Amenities:** dual phone lines, voice mail, irons, hair dryers. *Some:* high-speed Internet (fee). **Pool(s):** heated outdoor. **Leisure Activities:** whirlpool, exercise Small-scale Hotel room. **Guest Services:** gift shop, valet laundry, area transportation. **Business Services:** conference facilities, administrative services (fee), fax. **Cards:** AX, CB, DC, DS, MC, VI. *(See ad p 611)*
SOME UNITS
FEE

HOLIDAY INN OF ALTAMONTE SPRINGS
Phone: (407)862-4455 [105]
AAA SAVE
All Year   1P: $69   2P: $69
Location: I-4, exit 92, just sw. 230 W Hwy 436 32714. Fax: 407/682-5982. **Facility:** 263 one-bedroom standard units, some with whirlpools. 3-4 stories, interior/exterior corridors. *Bath:* combo or shower only. **Parking:** on-site. **Terms:** check-in 4 pm. **Amenities:** video games, high-speed Internet, voice mail, irons, hair dryers. Small-scale Hotel **Dining:** 6 am-2 & 5-10 pm, cocktails. **Pool(s):** outdoor. **Leisure Activities:** exercise room. **Guest Services:** valet and coin laundry, area transportation-within 5 mi. **Business Services:** conference facilities, fax (fee). **Special Amenities:** free newspaper and free room upgrade (subject to availability with advanced reservations). *See color ad opposite inside back cover)*
SOME UNITS

HOMESTEAD STUDIO SUITES HOTEL-ORLANDO/ALTAMONTE SPRINGS
Phone: (407)332-9300 [106]
All Year   1P: $59   2P: $79   XP: $5   F18
Location: I-4, exit 92, just e, then 0.3 mi s. 302 S North Lake Blvd 32701. Fax: 407/332-9330. **Facility:** 135 one-bedroom standard units with efficiencies. 3 stories, interior corridors. *Bath:* combo or shower only. **Parking:** Small-scale Hotel on-site. **Terms:** cancellation fee imposed, pets ($75 extra charge). **Amenities:** voice mail, irons. **Guest Services:** valet and coin laundry. **Cards:** AX, CB, DC, DS, JC, MC, VI.
SOME UNITS

(See map p. 590)

LA QUINTA INN-ORLANDO NORTH

Phone: (407)788-1411 `107`

[SAVE]
[diamond diamond diamond]
Small-scale Hotel

All Year
Location: I-4, exit 92, 0.3 mi w, just s of SR 436. 150 S Westmonte Dr 32714. Fax: 407/788-6472. **Facility:** 115 one-bedroom standard units. 2 stories, exterior corridors. *Bath:* combo or shower only. **Parking:** on-site. **Terms:** [ECP] meal plan available, small pets only. **Amenities:** video games (fee), voice mail, irons, hair dryers. **Pool(s):** heated outdoor. **Guest Services:** valet laundry. **Business Services:** meeting rooms, fax (fee). **Cards:** AX, CB, DC, DS, JC, MC, VI. *(See color ad p 652)*

| 1P: $59-$89 | 2P: $65-$95 |

SOME UNITS

QUALITY INN

Phone: (407)862-2800 `99`

[SAVE]
[diamond diamond diamond]
Small-scale Hotel

12/1-2/10 [ECP]	1P: $55-$95	2P: $55-$95	XP: $10	F13
2/11-4/30 [ECP]	1P: $60-$90	2P: $60-$90	XP: $10	F13
10/1-11/30 [ECP]	1P: $55-$85	2P: $55-$85	XP: $10	F13
5/1-9/30 [ECP]	1P: $50-$80	2P: $50-$80	XP: $10	F13

Location: I-4, exit 92, just s. 235 S Wymore Rd 32714. Fax: 407/862-7982. **Facility:** 167 units. 157 one-bedroom standard units. 10 one-bedroom suites ($80-$110) with kitchens (no utensils). 3 stories, exterior corridors. *Bath:* combo or shower only. **Parking:** on-site. **Amenities:** irons, hair dryers. *Some:* safes (fee). **Pool(s):** outdoor. **Leisure Activities:** playground. **Guest Services:** valet laundry. **Business Services:** fax. **Cards:** AX, DC, DS, MC, VI.

SOME UNITS

RESIDENCE INN BY MARRIOTT

Phone: (407)788-7991 `100`

[SAVE]
[diamond diamond diamond]
Small-scale Hotel

10/1-11/30 [ECP]	1P: $119-$169	2P: $119-$169
12/1-3/31 [ECP]	1P: $109-$159	2P: $109-$159
4/1-9/30 [ECP]	1P: $99-$149	2P: $99-$149

Location: I-4, exit 92, just w on SR 436, just n. 270 Douglas Ave 32714. Fax: 407/869-5468. **Facility:** 128 units. 96 one-bedroom standard units with kitchens. 32 two-bedroom suites with kitchens. 2 stories, exterior corridors. *Bath:* combo or shower only. **Parking:** on-site. **Terms:** cancellation fee imposed, pets ($150 fee, $5 extra charge). **Amenities:** voice mail, irons, hair dryers. **Pool(s):** heated outdoor. **Leisure Activities:** whirlpools, sports court. **Guest Services:** complimentary evening beverages: Mon-Thurs, valet and coin laundry. **Business Services:** meeting rooms, fax (fee). **Cards:** AX, CB, DC, DS, JC, MC, VI.

SOME UNITS

SPRINGHILL SUITES BY MARRIOTT ORLANDO/ALTAMONTE SPRINGS

Phone: (407)865-6400 `102`

[SAVE]
[diamond diamond diamond]
Small-scale Hotel

All Year [ECP]   1P: $99
Location: I-4, exit 92, just w. 205 W Hwy 436 32714. Fax: 407/865-6773. **Facility:** 91 one-bedroom standard units. 4 stories, interior corridors. *Bath:* combo or shower only. **Parking:** on-site. **Amenities:** dual phone lines, voice mail, irons, hair dryers. **Pool(s):** heated indoor. **Leisure Activities:** whirlpool, exercise room. **Guest Services:** valet and coin laundry. **Business Services:** meeting rooms. **Cards:** AX, DC, DS, MC, VI.

SOME UNITS

─── **WHERE TO DINE** ───

AMIGOS

[diamond diamond] [diamond diamond]
Tex-Mex

Lunch: $6-$8   **Dinner:** $7-$12   **Phone:** 407/774-4334 `67`
Location: I-4, exit 92, 0.5 mi w, just n of SR 436. 120 N Westmonte Dr 32714. **Hours:** 11 am-9:30 pm, Fri & Sat-10 pm, Sun-9 pm. Closed major holidays. **Features:** Very popular on weekends, this Tex-Mex style of dining is enjoyed in an establishment decorated with license plates and Mexican curios. Your favorite Tex-Mex entrees overflow the plates, so grab a pitcher of margaritas, and settle down to a hearty meal. Casual dress; cocktails. **Parking:** on-site. **Cards:** AX, DC, MC, VI.

AMIRA'S

[AAA]
[diamond diamond]
Kosher

Lunch: $5-$8   **Dinner:** $5-$11   **Phone:** 407/831-0999 `75`
Location: Between CR 427 and US 17-92; on SR 436. 1349 E Altamonte Dr 32701. **Hours:** 11 am-8:30 pm, Fri-5 pm. Closed: All Jewish holidays, Passover week, Sat & Mon. **Features:** This New York-style kosher deli with an adjoining market serves a wide range of deli sandwiches, plus specialties such as falafel, hummus, chopped liver and stuffed cabbage rolls. Although the decor is plain, the food more than makes up for it. Amira's is popular enough with the locals that servers are likely to call many patrons by name. Smoke free premises. Casual dress; beer & wine only. **Parking:** on-site. **Cards:** AX, DS, MC, VI.

BAHAMA BREEZE

[diamond diamond] [diamond diamond]
Caribbean

Dinner: $7-$19   **Phone:** 407/831-2929 `71`
Location: I-4, exit 92, 1.5 mi e. 499 E Altamonte Dr 32701. **Hours:** 4 pm-1:30 am, Mon & Tues-midnight, Sun noon-midnight. Closed: 11/27, 12/25. **Features:** Capturing the sights, sounds and sensations of the Caribbean, Bahama Breeze caters to those seeking an exciting evening out. In addition to delicious food such as fresh mahi-mahi and Key lime pie, there is a full bar, retail shop and live entertainment. Casual dress; cocktails; entertainment. **Parking:** on-site. **Cards:** AX, CB, DC, DS, MC, VI.

BAJA BURRITO KITCHEN

[diamond diamond]
Mexican

Lunch: $4-$8   **Dinner:** $4-$8   **Phone:** 407/788-2252 `65`
Location: 1 mi n of jct SR 434 and 436; in Jamestown Place Mall. 931 N SR 434, Suite 1145 32714. **Hours:** 11 am-10 pm, Sun 11:30 am-9 pm. Closed: 11/27, 12/25. **Features:** A salsa bar offers an impressive array of fresh choices, from basic chopped tomatoes to very hot habanero salsa. Fast, walk-up counter service provides good food made to order at this friendly shop tucked into a strip mall. Casual dress; beer & wine only. **Parking:** on-site.

(See map p. 590)

BANGKOK RESTAURANT   Lunch: $4-$7   Dinner: $7-$12   Phone: 407/788-2685   66

Thai

Location: I-4, exit 92, just w, then just n of jct SR 436 and Douglas Ave. 260 Douglas Ave 32714. **Hours:** 11:30 am-3 & 5-11 pm. Closed: Sun. **Features:** Reasonably priced Thai cuisine is colorfully presented and may be ordered in hot, spicy or mild varieties. The menu is varied, offering beef, pork, chicken, seafood and vegetables in authentic preparations. In keeping with the Thai tradition of hospitality, service is friendly and attentive. Convenient to commercial areas, the location is a plus. Casual dress; cocktails. **Parking:** on-site. **Cards:** AX, DS, MC, VI.   ✖

EASTERN PEARL CHINESE RESTAURANT   Lunch: $5-$28   Dinner: $7-$28   Phone: 407/339-8877   69

Chinese

Location: I-4, exit 92, 0.7 mi e on SR 436. 478 E Altamont Dr, Suite 102 32701. **Hours:** 11:30 am-2:30 & 4:30-9:30 pm, Mon-9 pm, Fri-10 pm, Sat noon-10 pm, Sun noon-9 pm. Closed: 11/27. **Reservations:** suggested. **Features:** Imaginative, superbly prepared food is presented in a busy, yet refined, atmosphere. A distinctive wall fountain enhances a feel of tranquility. Smoke free premises. Dressy casual; cocktails. **Parking:** on-site. **Cards:** AX, MC, VI.   ✖

FIRST WATCH   Lunch: $5-$7   Phone: 407/682-2315   70

American

Location: I-4, exit 92, just nw; in Ethan Allen Plaza. 419 W SR 436 32714. **Hours:** 7 am-2:30 pm. Closed: 11/27, 12/25. **Features:** This eatery serves breakfast and lunch, from traditional eggs and omelets to waffles and crepes. Pancakes fill the entire plate and are topped with fresh fruits and syrup. Great salad, soups and sandwiches are featured to satisfy the busy lunch crowd. Smoke free premises. Casual dress. **Parking:** on-site. **Cards:** AX, DS, MC, VI.   ✖

KOHINOOR INDIAN RESTAURANT   Lunch: $7   Dinner: $8-$17   Phone: 407/788-6004   68

Indian

Location: I-4, exit 92, 0.3 mi w; in Ethan Allen Plaza. 249 W SR 436 32714. **Hours:** 11:30 am-2:30 & 5-10 pm, Fri & Sat-11 pm. Closed: Mon. **Reservations:** accepted. **Features:** Partake of expertly prepared Indian cuisine made with fine ingredients and fresh spices. The mixed tandoori platter offers a chance to sample all the meats cooked in the tandor oven. Freshly made mango ice cream for dessert makes this a worthy venture. Korma dishes are the specialty. Dressy casual; beer & wine only. **Parking:** on-site. **Cards:** AX, DS, MC, VI.

MAISON & JARDIN   Dinner: $20-$35   Phone: 407/862-4410   73

Continental

Location: I-4, exit 92, just w on SR 436, then 0.5 mi s. 430 S Wymore Rd 32714. **Hours:** 6 pm-10 pm. Closed major holidays; also Sun & Mon. **Reservations:** suggested. **Features:** Expect an elegant, candlelit meal in a secluded Mediterranean villa and service that caters to your every whim. A variety of fresh seafood, prime beef, veal, lamb and wild game is prepared with a French-Continental flair. The wine list is extensive. Semi-formal attire; cocktails. **Parking:** on-site. **Cards:** AX, CB, DC, DS, MC, VI.   ▯ ✖

PANERA BREAD   Lunch: $3-$6   Dinner: $3-$6   Phone: 407/332-7600   74

American

Location: I-4, exit 92, 1.3 mi e. 696 E Altamonte Dr 32701. **Hours:** 6:30 am-9:30 pm, Sun 7 am-8:30 pm. Closed: 12/25. **Features:** Diners order and pick up their soup, salad or "upscale" sandwich at the counter in this casual eatery and bakery, a popular place for a quick bite during or after shopping or a weekend outing with the family. Simple, comfortable tables are offered for eating in, but carry out is another option. Smoke free premises. Casual dress. **Parking:** on-site. **Cards:** AX, MC, VI.   M ✖

STRAUB'S FINE SEAFOOD RESTAURANT   Dinner: $12-$22   Phone: 407/831-2250   72

Seafood

Location: I-4, exit 92, 0.8 mi e on SR 436. 512 E Altamonte Dr 32701. **Hours:** 4:30 pm-10 pm. Closed major holidays. **Reservations:** suggested. **Features:** Mesquite-grilled and Cajun seafood entrees are highlights on a menu that offers a wide selection of fresh seasonal seafood. Beef, chicken and pasta dishes also are available. Service is friendly and efficient, and the ambience is casual. Smoke free premises. Casual dress; cocktails. **Parking:** on-site. **Cards:** AX, DC, DS, MC, VI.   ✖

APOPKA pop. 26,642   (See map p. 590; index p. 594)

—— WHERE TO STAY ——

CROSBY'S MOTOR INN   Phone: (407)886-3220   90

Motel

	1P: $60-$90	2P: $70-$100	XP: $10	F18
12/1-5/14 & 10/1-11/30				
5/15-9/30	1P: $50-$60	2P: $60-$90	XP: $10	F18

Location: 1.8 mi nw on US 441. Located in a rural area. 1440 W Orange Blossom Tr/Hwy 441 32712. Fax: 407/886-7458. **Facility:** 61 one-bedroom standard units, some with kitchens and/or whirlpools. 2 stories, exterior corridors. *Bath:* combo or tub only. **Parking:** on-site. **Terms:** 2 night minimum stay, 7 day cancellation notice, small pets only ($10 extra charge). **Pool(s):** outdoor. **Guest Services:** complimentary laundry. **Cards:** AX, MC, VI.

SOME UNITS

⬛ 🐾 ✈ 📠 / ✖ VCR 🔋 ▭ /

DAYS INN   Phone: (407)880-3800   89

Motel

2/1-4/15 [CP]	1P: $49-$99	2P: $49-$99
12/1-1/31 [CP]	1P: $39-$89	2P: $39-$89
4/16-11/30 [CP]	1P: $39-$59	2P: $39-$59

Location: On US 441, 0.5 mi w of Park Ave. 228 W Main St 32703. Fax: 407/884-0690. **Facility:** 59 one-bedroom standard units. 2 stories, exterior corridors. **Parking:** on-site. **Terms:** weekly rates available. **Amenities:** irons, hair dryers. **Pool(s):** small outdoor. **Business Services:** fax (fee). **Cards:** AX, CB, DC, DS, MC, VI.

SOME UNITS

⬛ ✈ 🏋 / ✖ 🔋 📷 /

(See map p. 590)

HOWARD JOHNSON EXPRESS INN   Phone: (407)886-1010 [92]
  (AAA) (SAVE)   All Year   1P: $63-$99   2P: $69-$104   XP: $5   F12
  ♦♦ ♦♦   **Location:** On US 441; 1.5 mi s of jct SR 436. 1317 S Orange Blossom Tr 32703. Fax: 407/886-1010. **Facility:** 32
         one-bedroom standard units. 2 stories, exterior corridors. *Bath:* combo or shower only. **Parking:** on-site.
  Motel **Terms:** 3 day cancellation notice-fee imposed, [CP] meal plan available. **Pool(s):** small outdoor. **Business
         Services:** fax (fee). **Cards:** AX, DC, DS, MC, VI. **Special Amenities:** early check-in/late check-out and
         free local telephone calls.

                                                                    SOME UNITS
         [SD] [&] [➔] [✦] [DATA PORT] [▯] / [✕] [🛏] [🖳] /

──────── **WHERE TO DINE** ────────

CATFISH PLACE OF APOPKA   **Lunch:** $5-$8   **Dinner:** $7-$16   Phone: 407/889-7980   [60]
  ♦♦ ♦♦   **Location:** US 441 and Forest Ave; across from Chamber of Commerce. 311 S Forest Ave 32703. **Hours:** 11 am-9
         pm, Fri & Sat-10 pm. **Features:** Sample crispy fried catfish at this aptly named, fish camp-style favorite. A
  Steak & Seafood simple menu features well-seasoned, boneless or fingerling catfish, chunky clam chowder, creamy
         coleslaw and crunchy hush puppies. Take out dinners are available. Casual dress; beer & wine only.
  Parking: on-site. **Cards:** DS, MC, VI.
                                                                                          [✕]

CASSELBERRY pop. 22,629   (See map p. 590; index p. 596)

──────── **WHERE TO STAY** ────────

SUBURBAN LODGE   Phone: (407)265-7699 [151]
  ♦♦♦♦ ♦♦   All Year   1P: $199-$269   2P: $210-$279   XP: $20   F
         Location: Just e of jct SR 436 and US 17-92. 210 N Oxford Rd 32707. Fax: 407/265-0291. **Facility:** 144 one-
  Small-scale Hotel bedroom standard units with efficiencies. 3 stories, exterior corridors. *Bath:* combo or shower only. **Parking:**
         on-site. **Terms:** weekly rates available. **Guest Services:** coin laundry. **Business Services:** fax (fee).
  Cards: AX, DC, DS, MC, VI. *(See color ad p 596)*

                                                                    SOME UNITS
         [ASK] [SD] [&] [✍] [✦] [DATA PORT] [🛏] [🖳] / [✕] /

──────── **WHERE TO DINE** ────────

ALADDIN'S CAFE   **Lunch:** $9   **Dinner:** $14   Phone: 407/331-0488   [122]
  ♦♦   **Location:** SR 436, 1 mi se of US 17-92. 1015 E Semoran Blvd 32707. **Hours:** 11:30 am-10 pm, Sat 4
       pm-11 pm. Closed major holidays; also Sun. **Reservations:** suggested. **Features:** Freshly made kabobs
  Ethnic with rice, tabbouleh, falafel and baklava are among the samplings of traditional Middle Eastern cuisine,
       primarily of the Lebanese persuasion, served at this small and cozy restaurant. The dinner buffet is
  especially popular. Casual dress. **Parking:** on-site. **Cards:** AX, DC, DS, MC, VI.
                                                                                          [✕]

COLORADO FONDUE COMPANY   **Dinner:** $8-$15   Phone: 407/767-8232   [123]
  ♦♦ ♦♦   **Location:** SR 436 and Red Bug Lake Rd; in Goodings Plaza. 1016 E Semoran Blvd 32707. **Hours:** 5:30 pm-9:30
         pm, Fri & Sat-10 pm, Sun 5 pm-9 pm. Closed: 1/1, 11/27, 12/25. **Reservations:** suggested.
  American **Features:** Touches such as grapevine-shaped wine racks set a romantic tone in the fondue restaurant.
         Raw meat, seafood and vegetables are laid before diners, who then cook them at the table in hot liquids or
  on a hot rock. Those who are new to this style of dining should try the combination platter, a good introduction to the variety of
  methods and results. Dressy casual; beer & wine only. **Parking:** on-site. **Cards:** AX, DC, DS, MC, VI.
                                                                                       [Y] [✕]

CYPRIANA RESTAURANT   **Lunch:** $6-$11   **Dinner:** $8-$15   Phone: 407/834-8088   [124]
  ♦♦ ♦♦   **Location:** SR 436, just n of Red Bug Lake Rd. 505 Semoran Blvd 32707. **Hours:** 11 am-10 pm. Closed: 7/4,
         11/27, 12/25; also Sun. **Reservations:** accepted. **Features:** The traditional moussaka of potatoes and
  Greek eggplant layered with meat sauce is a wonderful example of the good, authentic Greek food in this bustling
         atmosphere. Also on the menu are combination dinners and gyros. Tables and seating can be a bit
  crowded. Casual dress; beer & wine only. **Parking:** on-site. **Cards:** AX, DS, MC, VI.
                                                                                          [✕]

ROLANDO'S CUBAN RESTAURANT   **Lunch:** $4-$6   **Dinner:** $7-$18   Phone: 407/767-9677   [121]
  ♦♦ ♦♦   **Location:** SR 436, 1.3 mi se of US 17-92. 870 N Semoran Blvd 32707. **Hours:** 11 am-3 & 5-9:30 pm, Fri-10 pm,
         Sat noon-10 pm, Sun noon-8:30 pm. Closed: 1/1, 11/27, 12/25. **Features:** Simple textured walls and basic
  Cuban decor belie the sumptuous offerings of this casual establishment. Try the Cuban sandwich or picadillo for
         lunch, or take advantage of an extensive dinner menu that tempts with tamales, fried eggplant and sweet
  plantains. Smoke free premises. Casual dress; beer & wine only. **Parking:** on-site. **Cards:** AX, DC, DS, MC, VI.
                                                                                          [✕]

WHISKEY CREEK STEAKHOUSE   **Lunch:** $5-$10   **Dinner:** $8-$18   Phone: 407/834-3385   [120]
  ♦♦   **Location:** US 17-92, 1.5 mi n of SR 436. 3385 US 17-92 (Orlando Ave) 32707. **Hours:** 11 am-10 pm, Fri & Sat-11
       pm, Sun noon-9 pm. Closed: 11/27, 12/25. **Features:** Quality and a bit of creativity can be found in the
  Steak House preparation of oak-fired prime rib, smoked "loaded" chicken, and a colossal onion bloom served with a
       spicy horseradish sauce. A friendly, pleasant atmosphere and good service make this a popular spot.
  Casual dress; cocktails. **Parking:** on-site. **Cards:** AX, DC, DS, MC, VI.
                                                                                       [Y] [✕]

CELEBRATION pop. 2,736

――――― **WHERE TO STAY** ―――――

CELEBRATION HOTEL
Phone: (407)566-6000

12/1-4/30 & 10/1-11/30	1P: $169-$299	2P: $169-$299	XP: $20	F17
5/1-9/30	1P: $149-$199	2P: $149-$199	XP: $20	F17

Small-scale Hotel **Location:** I-4, exit 64A, 0.8 mi w to Celebration Ave, s to Village Center, off Front St. 700 Bloom St 34747. **Fax:** 407/566-6001. **Facility:** 115 units. 109 one-bedroom standard units. 6 one-bedroom suites ($269-$399). 3 stories, interior corridors. *Bath:* combo or shower only. **Parking:** on-site (fee). **Terms:** check-in 4 pm, 3 day cancellation notice-fee imposed, $5 service charge. **Amenities:** video games, high-speed Internet, dual phone lines, voice mail, safes, irons, hair dryers. **Pool(s):** heated outdoor. **Leisure Activities:** whirlpool, exercise room. *Fee:* massage. **Guest Services:** valet laundry, area transportation. **Business Services:** meeting rooms, fax (fee). **Cards:** AX, CB, DC, DS, MC, VI.
(See color ad p 636)

SOME UNITS

(ASK) 🚿 🍴 🍸 🔊M 📶 📷 🔄 ✕ 🎥 ⬛ 💻 / ✕ 🔋 🖥 /
FEE

――――― **WHERE TO DINE** ―――――

CAFE D'ANTONIO   **Lunch:** $7-$13   **Dinner:** $10-$27   **Phone:** 407/566-2233

Regional Italian **Location:** I-4, exit 64A, 0.7 mi e on US 192, then 1.3 mi s on Celebration Ave; 1 blk e of Celebration Ave at corner of Front and Market sts. 691 Front St, Suite 110 34747. **Hours:** 11:30 am-3 & 5-10 pm, Sat 11:30 am-10 pm, Sun 11:30 am-9 pm. Closed: 1/1, 11/27, 12/25. **Reservations:** suggested. **Features:** On the ground floor of a building in the heart of downtown, the cafe overlooks the water. Diners can eat indoors or al fresco on the front veranda or in the side alley. Both outdoor areas are covered, and the veranda can be enclosed with vinyl curtains in inclement weather. Many Disney employees frequent at lunchtime. Fresh ingredients are used in the preparation of multiregional Italian cuisine, and some meals are prepared in a wood-fired oven. Smoke free premises. Casual dress; cocktails. **Parking:** street. **Cards:** AX, DC, DS, MC, VI.

🔊M ✕

CLERMONT pop. 9,333

――――― **WHERE TO STAY** ―――――

AWARD VACATION HOMES-GREATER GROVES
Phone: (352)243-8669

(AAA) (SAVE) All Year   1P: $135-$215   2P: $135-$215

Vacation Home **Location:** Jct US 192 and 27, 2 mi n; in Greater Groves Subdivision. 2303 Hamlin Tr 34711. **Fax:** 352/241-0960. **Facility:** 31 vacation homes with pools. 1 story, exterior corridors. **Parking:** on-site. **Terms:** check-in 4 pm, 31 day cancellation notice-fee imposed, weekly rates available. **Amenities:** voice mail, irons, hair dryers. **Leisure Activities:** whirlpools, community recreation area. **Guest Services:** complimentary laundry. **Business Services:** fax (fee). **Cards:** AX, DS, MC, VI. **Special Amenities:** early check-in/late check-out and free local telephone calls. *(See color ad p 623)*

🔊 🔄 ✕ 🎥 🔋 🖥 💻

AWARD VACATION HOMES-ORANGE TREE
Phone: (352)243-8669

All Year   2P: $135-$215

Vacation Home **Location:** Jct US 192 and 27, 2 mi n; in Greater Groves Subdivision. 2303 Hamlin Tr 34711. **Fax:** 352/241-0960. **Facility:** 25 vacation homes ($135-$215) with pools. 1 story, exterior corridors. **Parking:** on-site. **Terms:** check-in 4 pm, 31 day cancellation notice-fee imposed, weekly rates available. **Amenities:** voice mail, irons, hair dryers. **Leisure Activities:** whirlpools. **Guest Services:** complimentary laundry. **Business Services:** fax (fee). **Cards:** AX, DS, MC, VI.

(ASK) 🔊 🔄 ✕ 🎥 🔋 🖥 💻

FLORIDA DESTINATIONS, INC.-HIGHLANDS RESERVE
Phone: (863)424-3300

All Year   1P: $85-$185   2P: $85-$185

Vacation Home **Location:** On US 192, 1 mi e of US 27. 9230 US Hwy 192 34711. **Fax:** 863/424-6681. **Facility:** 200 vacation homes ($85-$185) with pools. 1 story, exterior corridors. **Parking:** on-site. **Terms:** check-in 4 pm, 3 night minimum stay, 14 day cancellation notice-fee imposed, pets ($150 fee, $100 deposit). **Amenities:** video library (fee), voice mail, safes, irons, hair dryers. *Some:* CD players. **Leisure Activities:** playground, basketball, volleyball. *Fee:* golf-18 holes. **Guest Services:** complimentary laundry. **Business Services:** fax (fee). **Cards:** AX, DS, MC, VI.

SOME UNITS

(ASK) 🔊 🐾 🔄 ✕ 🎥 🔋 🖥 💻 / (VCR) /
FEE

HOLIDAY INN EXPRESS
Phone: (352)243-7878

All Year [ECP]   1P: $90-$100   2P: $90-$100

Small-scale Hotel **Location:** Just s of SR 50. 1810 S US Hwy 27 34711. **Fax:** 352/243-7882. **Facility:** 70 units. 69 one-bedroom standard units, some with whirlpools. 1 one-bedroom suite ($110-$150) with kitchen (no utensils). 3 stories, interior corridors. *Bath:* combo or shower only. **Parking:** on-site. **Amenities:** dual phone lines, voice mail, irons, hair dryers. **Pool(s):** outdoor. **Guest Services:** valet and coin laundry. **Business Services:** meeting rooms, fax (fee). **Cards:** AX, DC, DS, MC, VI.

SOME UNITS

(ASK) 🔊 🍴 🔊M 📶 📷 🔄 ⬛ / ✕ 🔋 🖥 💻 /

HOLIDAY INN EXPRESS & SUITES WEST OF THEME PARKS
Phone: 407/239-8315

All Year [ECP]   1P: $69-$179   2P: $69-$179

Small-scale Hotel **Location:** I-4, exit 64B, 7.2 mi w on US 192; 0.5 mi e jct US 27. 105 Summer Bay Blvd 34711. **Fax:** 407/239-8297. **Facility:** 155 one-bedroom standard units. 4 stories, interior corridors. *Bath:* combo or shower only. **Parking:** on-site. **Terms:** cancellation fee imposed. **Amenities:** dual phone lines, voice mail, irons, hair dryers. **Pool(s):** heated outdoor. **Leisure Activities:** exercise room. **Guest Services:** gift shop, valet and coin laundry, area transportation (fee). **Business Services:** meeting rooms, business center. **Cards:** AX, CB, DC, DS, MC, VI.

SOME UNITS

(ASK) 🍴 🔄 ✕ ⬛ 💻 / 🔋 🖥 /

MULBERRY INN B&B

Phone: (352)242-0670

◆◆ ◆◆
Country Inn

All Year [CP]   1P: $70-$90   2P: $75-$95
Location: 1.6 mi w of US 27 on SR 50, 0.3 mi n on 8th St, just w. 915 W Montrose St 34711. Fax: 352/242-9898. **Facility:** Smoke free premises. 5 units. 3 one-bedroom standard units. 2 one-bedroom suites. 2 stories, interior/exterior corridors. **Parking:** on-site. **Terms:** check-in 4 pm, age restrictions may apply, cancellation fee imposed, weekly rates available. **Amenities:** hair dryers. *Some:* irons. **Business Services:** meeting rooms. **Cards:** AX, CB, DS, MC.

SOME UNITS
(ASK) (†1) (✕) (🕿) / (📺) (VCR) /

DAVENPORT pop. 1,924 (See map p. 598; index p. 610)

——— WHERE TO STAY ———

BEST WESTERN CENTRAL FLORIDA

Phone: 863/424-2596   590

(AAA) (SAVE)

12/26-1/1	1P: $99-$125	2P: $99-$125	XP: $6	F18
1/2-8/17	1P: $59-$85	2P: $59-$85	XP: $6	F18
12/1-12/25	1P: $54-$79	2P: $54-$79	XP: $6	F18
8/18-11/30	1P: $54-$69	2P: $54-$69	XP: $6	F18

◆◆◆ ◆◆

Small-scale Hotel Location: I-4, exit 55, just s on US 27. 2425 Frontage Rd 33837. Fax: 863/420-8717. **Facility:** 113 one-bedroom standard units. 2 stories, exterior corridors. **Parking:** on-site. **Terms:** [CP] meal plan available, small pets only ($10 extra charge). **Amenities:** irons, hair dryers. **Pool(s):** heated outdoor. **Leisure Activities:** whirlpool. **Guest Services:** gift shop, coin laundry. **Business Services:** fax (fee). **Cards:** AX, DC, DS, MC, VI. **Special Amenities:** free continental breakfast and free newspaper.

SOME UNITS
(S🄳) (🐾) (†1→) (&M) (🎞) (🛬) (🎥) (DATA PORT) (💻) / (✕) (🔒) (🖼) /
FEE FEE

HAMPTON INN ORLANDO-S OF WALT DISNEY RESORT

Phone: (863)420-9898   595

(SAVE)

◆◆◆ ◆◆
Small-scale Hotel

All Year [ECP]   1P: $69-$109   2P: $79-$119
Location: I-4, exit 55, just nw. 5530 US Hwy 27 N 33837. Fax: 863/420-9797. **Facility:** 83 one-bedroom standard units. 5 stories, interior corridors. *Bath:* combo or shower only. **Parking:** on-site. **Terms:** small pets only ($25 minimum fee, in smoking units, $10 extra charge). **Amenities:** voice mail, irons, hair dryers. **Pool(s):** heated outdoor. **Leisure Activities:** whirlpool, exercise room. **Guest Services:** coin laundry. **Business Services:** meeting rooms, fax (fee). **Cards:** AX, DC, DS, MC, VI.

SOME UNITS
(S🄳) (🐾) (†1→) (&M) (✦) (🎞) (🛬) (🎥) (DATA PORT) (💻) / (✕) (🔒) /
FEE

HOLIDAY INN EXPRESS HOTEL & SUITES

Phone: (863)424-2120   594

◆◆◆ ◆◆

12/1-4/6 [ECP]	1P: $59-$99	2P: $59-$99	XP: $10	F18
6/30-8/24 [ECP]	1P: $69-$89	2P: $69-$89	XP: $10	F18
4/7-6/29 & 8/25-11/30 [ECP]	1P: $49-$69	2P: $49-$69	XP: $10	F18

Small-scale Hotel Location: I-4, exit 55, just s. 43824 US Hwy 27 33837. Fax: 863/424-5317. **Facility:** 104 one-bedroom standard units. 2 stories, interior corridors. *Bath:* combo or shower only. **Parking:** on-site. **Amenities:** safes, irons, hair dryers. **Pool(s):** heated outdoor, wading. **Guest Services:** valet and coin laundry. **Business Services:** meeting rooms. **Cards:** AX, CB, DC, JC, MC, VI.

SOME UNITS
(ASK) (S🄳) (🛬) (🎥) (DATA PORT) / (✕) (🔒) (🖼) (💻)

PRESTIGE VACATION HOMES

Phone: (863)424-7400   598

(AAA) (SAVE)

◆◆◆ ◆◆
Vacation Home

All Year   1P: $139-$309
Location: I-4, exit 58, 1.5 mi e on CR 532, then 1 mi s on CR 545, 1.2 mi e on CR 54. Located in a residential area. 101 Thousand Oaks Blvd 33896. Fax: 863/424-7500. **Facility:** 68 vacation homes. 1 story, exterior corridors. **Parking:** on-site. **Terms:** check-in 4 pm, 3-7 night minimum stay - seasonal, cancellation fee imposed, $2 service charge. **Amenities:** voice mail, safes, irons, hair dryers. **Guest Services:** complimentary laundry. **Business Services:** fax (fee). **Cards:** AX, DS, MC, VI. **Special Amenities:** free local telephone calls.
(See color ad p 639, p 654, p 640, p 178 & p 686)

(S🄳) (VCR) (🎥) (DATA PORT) (🔒) (🖼) (💻)

RAMADA INN SOUTHGATE

Phone: (863)424-2511   591

◆◆◆ ◆◆
Small-scale Hotel

5/16-8/15   1P: $89
12/1-5/15 & 8/16-11/30   1P: $59
Location: I-4, exit 55, just w. 5414 Hwy 27 N 33837. Fax: 863/424-3889. **Facility:** 153 units. 145 one-bedroom standard units. 8 one-bedroom suites. 5 stories, exterior corridors. **Parking:** on-site. **Terms:** cancellation fee imposed, weekly rates available, small pets only ($15 deposit). **Amenities:** voice mail, irons, hair dryers. **Pool(s):** outdoor. **Leisure Activities:** playground, basketball, volleyball. *Fee:* game room. **Guest Services:** valet and coin laundry. **Business Services:** meeting rooms, fax (fee). **Cards:** AX, CB, DC, DS, MC, VI.

SOME UNITS
(ASK) (S🄳) (🐾) (†1) (🍸) (🎞) (🛬) (✕) (🎥) (DATA PORT) (💻) / (✕) (🔒) (🖼)

REUNION INN

Phone: 863/424-2811   593

(AAA) (SAVE)

◆◆◆ ◆◆
Small-scale Hotel

All Year   1P: $60-$80
Location: I-4, exit 55, just w. 44089 US 27 33897. Fax: 863/424-1723. **Facility:** 150 one-bedroom standard units. 3 stories, exterior corridors. **Parking:** on-site. **Terms:** small pets only ($25 minimum fee, $10 extra charge). **Amenities:** *Some:* hair dryers. **Pool(s):** outdoor. **Guest Services:** coin laundry. **Business Services:** meeting rooms, fax (fee). **Cards:** AX, CB, DC, JC, MC, VI. **Special Amenities:** free local telephone calls and free newspaper.

SOME UNITS
(S🄳) (†1) (†1→) (🛬) (🎥) / (✕) (🔒) (💻)

SUPER 8 MOTEL MAINGATE SOUTH

Phone: (863)420-8888   600

(AAA) (SAVE)

◆◆◆ ◆◆
Motel

All Year   1P: $39-$120   2P: $39-$120
Location: I-4, exit 55, 0.5 mi n. 5620 US Hwy 27 N 33837. Fax: 863/424-6602. **Facility:** 154 one-bedroom standard units. 2 stories, exterior corridors. *Bath:* combo or shower only. **Parking:** on-site. **Terms:** [CP] meal plan available, pets ($10 extra charge). **Amenities:** hair dryers. **Pool(s):** heated outdoor. **Guest Services:** coin laundry. **Cards:** AX, CB, DC, DS, MC, VI. **Special Amenities:** early check-in/late check-out and free continental breakfast.

SOME UNITS

FEE FEE

(See map p. 598)

VILLAS AT POLO PARK   Phone: (863)420-3838   602

AAA SAVE

VVVV

Condominium

All Year   1P: $69-$159
Location: 0.5 mi s of US 192. 12727 US 27 N 33837. **Fax:** 863/420-3877. **Facility:** Designated smoking area. 48 units. 24 two- and 24 three-bedroom suites with kitchens. 2 stories, exterior corridors. **Parking:** on-site. **Terms:** check-in 4 pm, 4 night minimum stay, cancellation fee imposed, weekly rates available, pets ($75 fee). **Amenities:** video library, safes (fee), irons, hair dryers. **Pool(s):** heated outdoor. **Leisure Activities:** whirlpool, barbecue area, playground, exercise room, basketball, volleyball. *Fee:* golf privileges, game room. **Guest Services:** complimentary laundry. **Business Services:** meeting rooms, fax. **Cards:** AX, DC, JC, MC, VI. **Special Amenities: free local telephone calls.**

FERN PARK pop. 8,318   (See map p. 590; index p. 595)

──── WHERE TO STAY ────

COMFORT INN–FERN PARK   Phone: (407)339-3333   117

AAA SAVE

VVVV

Small-scale Hotel

2/13-3/10	1P: $79-$89	2P: $79-$89	XP: $6	F10
12/1-2/12 & 3/11-11/30	1P: $54	2P: $54	XP: $6	F10

Location: I-4, exit 92, 3 mi e on SR 436, then 0.8 mi e. 8245 S Hwy 17-92 32730. **Fax:** 407/332-6659. **Facility:** 75 one-bedroom standard units, some with whirlpools. 4 stories, exterior corridors. **Parking:** on-site. **Terms:** 3 night minimum stay - seasonal, [CP] meal plan available. **Amenities:** hair dryers. *Some:* irons. **Pool(s):** outdoor. **Leisure Activities:** whirlpool. **Cards:** AX, CB, DC, DS, JC, MC, VI. **Special Amenities: free continental breakfast and free newspaper.**

SOME UNITS

HEATHROW pop. 4,068   (See map p. 590; index p. 593)

──── WHERE TO STAY ────

COURTYARD BY MARRIOTT   Phone: (407)444-1000   62

AAA SAVE

VVVV

Small-scale Hotel

All Year   1P: $119-$179
Location: I-4, exit 98, just nw. 135 International Pkwy 32746. **Fax:** 407/444-5921. **Facility:** 83 units. 77 one-bedroom standard units. 6 one-bedroom suites ($139-$189). 3 stories, interior corridors. *Bath:* combo or shower only. **Parking:** on-site. **Terms:** weekly rates available, [BP] meal plan available. **Amenities:** voice mail, irons, hair dryers. **Dining:** 6:30-10 am, Sat & Sun-11 am. **Pool(s):** heated outdoor. **Leisure Activities:** whirlpool, exercise room. **Guest Services:** valet and coin laundry. **Business Services:** meeting rooms, business center. **Cards:** AX, CB, DC, DS, MC, VI. **Special Amenities: early check-in/late check out and free newspaper.**

SOME UNITS

──── WHERE TO DINE ────

LUIGINO'S PASTA & STEAK HOUSE   Lunch: $7-$16   Dinner: $11-$30   Phone: 407/333-2847   40

AAA

VVVV

Italian

Location: I-4, exit 98, 0.5 mi w; in Heathrow Shops. 120 International Pkwy, #140 32746. **Hours:** 11:30 am-9:30 pm, Fri-10:30 pm, Sat 4:30 pm-10:30 pm, Sun 4:30 pm-9:30 pm. **Closed:** 11/27, 12/25. **Reservations:** suggested. **Features:** Located in a fairly upscale shopping plaza, this restaurant offers two distinctly different dining rooms. One offers excellent views of the adjacent private golf course while the other offers a dark, masculine setting. While the menu is predominantly Italian, there is also a selection of high-quality Midwestern steaks. Make sure to start off your dining experience with the bruschetta with a nice variety of pasta and entrée selections, everyone will find something they enjoy. Dressy casual; cocktails. **Parking:** valet. **Cards:** AX, DC, DS, MC, VI.

PANERA BREAD CO   Lunch: $5-$7   Dinner: $5-$7   Phone: 407/804-8340   41

VVV

American

Location: I-4, exit 98, just w. 1210 International Pkwy 32746. **Hours:** 6:30 am-9:30 pm, Sun-8:30 pm. **Closed:** 11/27, 12/25. **Features:** In a shopping area, the restaurant is a great place for healthy sandwiches and homemade soups served in a large bread bowl. Numerous varieties of freshly baked breads and bagels make this a popular stop for breakfast. Outdoor seating is available. Smoke free premises. Casual dress. **Parking:** on-site. **Cards:** AX, MC, VI.

STONEWOOD TAVERN & GRILL   Dinner: $10-$25   Phone: 407/333-3292   42

VVV

Steak & Seafood

Location: I-4, exit 98, just w. 1210 International Pkwy S 32746. **Hours:** 4 pm-10:30 pm, Fri & Sat-11:30 pm, Sun-10 pm. **Closed:** 11/27, 12/25. **Features:** Enjoy an array of well-prepared dishes, including filet mignon, rack of lamb and grilled scallops. The dining room is comfortably appointed, with the decor reflecting a beautiful use of stone, wood and earth tones. Servers are knowledgeable and attentive. Casual dress; cocktails. **Parking:** on-site. **Cards:** AX, CB, DC, DS, MC, VI.

HOWEY-IN-THE-HILLS pop. 956

──── WHERE TO STAY ────

MISSION INN GOLF & TENNIS RESORT   Phone: (352)324-3101

VVVV

Resort
Large-scale Hotel

1/4-3/31	1P: $230-$260	2P: $230-$260	XP: $15	F16
4/1-9/7	1P: $130-$230	2P: $130-$230	XP: $15	F16
9/8-11/30	1P: $185-$210	2P: $185-$210	XP: $15	F16
12/1-1/3	1P: $180-$205	2P: $180-$205	XP: $15	F16

Location: On CR 48 at jct SR 19. Located in a quiet, rural area. 10400 CR 48 34737. **Fax:** 352/324-2636. **Facility:** Set on lush grounds, the resort offers private, screened patios or balconies with most rooms. 203 units. 180 one-bedroom standard units. 8 one-, 8 two- and 7 three-bedroom suites, some with kitchens and/or whirlpools. 2-4 stories, interior/exterior corridors. **Parking:** on-site. **Terms:** check-in 4 pm, 15 day cancellation notice-fee imposed. **Amenities:** voice mail, irons, hair dryers. **Pool(s):** outdoor, heated outdoor. **Leisure Activities:** whirlpools, rental boats, jogging, playground, exercise room. *Fee:* sailboats, marina, golf-36 holes, 8 tennis courts (6 lighted), bicycles, massage. **Guest Services:** gift shop, valet and coin laundry, area transportation (fee). **Business Services:** meeting rooms, business center. **Cards:** AX, MC, VI.

SOME UNITS

KISSIMMEE pop. 47,814   (See map p. 598; index p. 607)

———— WHERE TO STAY ————

ALHAMBRA RESORT
Phone: 407/933-0700 536

All Year   2P: $100

Location: 13 mi s on Poinciana Blvd from jct of US 192, then 1 mi w. 500 E Cypress Pkwy 34759. Fax: 407/870-5412.

Small-scale Hotel   **Facility:** 112 units. 56 one-bedroom standard units. 56 one-bedroom suites ($100-$160) with kitchens. 2 stories, exterior corridors. **Parking:** on-site. **Terms:** check-in 4 pm, 14 day cancellation notice, package plans. **Amenities:** voice mail, irons. **Pool(s):** heated outdoor, wading. **Leisure Activities:** 4 lighted tennis courts, jogging, playground, shuffleboard. *Fee:* golf-18 holes. **Business Services:** meeting rooms. **Cards:** AX, DS, MC, VI.

ⒶⓈⓀ 📶 🔒 ➰ ✕ 🎥 🚪 🔲 💻

AMERIHOST RESORT
ⒶⒶⒶ SAVE
Phone: (407)396-6000 450

All Year   1P: $79-$99   2P: $79-$99   XP: $10   F17

Location: I-4, exit 64B, 2.4 mi w on US 192; 1.3 mi w of Disney World main gate. 7491 W Irlo Bronson Memorial Hwy 34747. Fax: 407/396-7393. **Facility:** 442 one-bedroom standard units. 4 stories, interior corridors. **Parking:** on-site. **Terms:** 3 day cancellation notice-fee imposed. **Amenities:** video games, voice mail, safes, irons.

Small-scale Hotel   *Some:* hair dryers. **Dining:** 7 am-midnight, cocktails, entertainment. **Pool(s):** heated outdoor, heated indoor. **Leisure Activities:** whirlpool, recreation programs, exercise room. **Guest Services:** gift shop, valet and coin laundry, area transportation-Disney. **Cards:** AX, CB, DC, DS, MC, VI. **Special Amenities: free local telephone calls and free room upgrade (subject to availability with advanced reservations).**

SOME UNITS

⬛ 🍴 🛏 ➰ ✕ 🎥 🔌 🔲 💻 /✕/

AMERISUITES AT CALYPSO CAY
ⒶⒶⒶ SAVE
Phone: (407)997-1300 509

6/8-8/23 [ECP]   1P: $69-$149   2P: $69-$149   XP: $10   F18
12/1-4/26 [ECP]   1P: $59-$149   2P: $59-$149   XP: $10   F18
4/27-6/7 & 8/24-11/30 [ECP]   1P: $59-$109   2P: $59-$109   XP: $10   F18

Location: I-4, exit 68, 3 mi s on SR 535, just s of Osceola Pkwy and just n of US 192. 4991 Calypso Cay Way 34746.

Small-scale Hotel   Fax: 407/997-1301. **Facility:** 151 one-bedroom standard units. 6 stories, interior corridors. *Bath:* combo or shower only. **Parking:** on-site. **Terms:** check-in 4 pm, pets ($25 fee). **Amenities:** video games (fee), dual phone lines, voice mail, irons, hair dryers. **Pool(s):** heated outdoor. **Leisure Activities:** whirlpool, miniature golf, exercise room. **Guest Services:** gift shop, valet and coin laundry, area transportation-attractions. **Business Services:** meeting rooms. **Cards:** AX, CB, DC, DS, JC, MC, VI. **Special Amenities: free continental breakfast and free newspaper.**
(See color ad p 617)

SOME UNITS

⬛ 🐕 ♿ 🛋 🔒 ➰ ✕ 🎥 🔌 🔲 💻 /✕/

BAYMONT INN
ⒶⒶⒶ SAVE
Phone: (407)787-3555 518

1/1-4/30 [ECP]   1P: $54-$84   2P: $64-$94   XP: $10   F16
12/1-12/31 & 5/1-11/30 [ECP]   1P: $54-$74   2P: $59-$79   XP: $10   F16

Location: I-4, exit 64A, 2 mi e on US 192. 5196 W Irlo Bronson Hwy 34746. Fax: 407/787-0700. **Facility:** 64 one-bedroom standard units, some with whirlpools. 4 stories, interior corridors. *Bath:* combo or shower only.

Motel   **Parking:** on-site. **Terms:** check-in 4 pm. **Amenities:** dual phone lines, voice mail, irons, hair dryers. *Fee:* video library, video games. **Pool(s):** outdoor. **Leisure Activities:** whirlpool. **Guest Services:** valet and coin laundry. **Cards:** AX, CB, DC, DS, JC, MC, VI. **Special Amenities: free continental breakfast and free newspaper.**

SOME UNITS

⬛ ♿ 🛋 🔒 ➰ 🎥 🔌 💻 /✕ 🔲 /

BEST WESTERN-EASTGATE
ⒶⒶⒶ SAVE
Phone: (407)396-0707 505

12/1-1/1   1P: $49-$158   2P: $49-$158
1/2-8/16   1P: $49-$98   2P: $49-$98
8/17-11/30   1P: $42-$89   2P: $42-$89

Location: I-4, exit 64A, 2 mi e on US 192. 5565 W Irlo Bronson Memorial Hwy 34746. Fax: 407/396-6644.

Small-scale Hotel   **Facility:** 403 one-bedroom standard units. 5 stories, exterior corridors. **Parking:** on-site. **Terms:** check-in 4 pm, pets ($15 extra charge, in limited units). **Amenities:** safes (fee). *Some:* irons, hair dryers. **Dining:** 7-11 am, Fri & Sat also 5:30 pm-10 pm, wine/beer only. **Pool(s):** heated outdoor. **Leisure Activities:** whirlpool, 2 lighted tennis courts, playground. *Fee:* game room. **Guest Services:** gift shop, area transportation-Disney. **Cards:** AX, CB, DC, DS, JC, MC, VI.
(See color ad below)

SOME UNITS

⬛ 🛏 🍴 🔒 ➰ ✕ 🔌 /✕ 🔲 💻 /
FEE

(See map p. 598)

BEST WESTERN-KISSIMMEE   Phone: (407)846-2221   577

All Year   1P: $42-$99   2P: $42-$99

Location: US 192 and 441 at Florida Tpke, exit 244. 2261 E Irlo Bronson Memorial Hwy 34744. Fax: 407/846-1095. **Facility:** 282 one-bedroom standard units, some with efficiencies. 2-3 stories, exterior corridors. *Bath:* combo or shower only. **Parking:** on-site. **Terms:** cancellation fee imposed, $2 service charge. **Amenities:** voice mail, safes (fee), hair dryers. *Some:* irons. **Dining:** 7 am-11 pm. **Pool(s):** heated outdoor. **Leisure Activities:** playground, basketball, volleyball. *Fee:* game room. **Guest Services:** gift shop, coin laundry, area transportation-Disney. **Business Services:** meeting rooms. **Cards:** AX, CB, DC, DS, MC, VI. **Special Amenities:** early check-in/late check-out and free room upgrade (subject to availability with advanced reservations). *(See color ad p 680)*

Small-scale Hotel

(See map p. 598)

CLARION MAINGATE
Phone: (407)396-4000   **453**

All Year   1P: $79-$109   2P: $79-$109

Location: I-4, exit 64B, 2.9 mi w on US 192, 1.7 mi w of Disney World main gate. 7675 W Irlo Bronson Memorial Hwy 34747. Fax: 407/396-0714. **Facility:** 198 one-bedroom standard units. 5 stories, interior corridors. *Bath:* combo or shower only. **Parking:** on-site. **Terms:** cancellation fee imposed, [BP] meal plan available.

Small-scale Hotel   **Amenities:** voice mail, safes (fee), irons, hair dryers. **Dining:** 6:30-11 am. **Pool(s):** heated outdoor, wading. **Leisure Activities:** whirlpool, exercise room. *Fee:* game room. **Guest Services:** gift shop, valet and coin laundry, area transportation-Disney. **Business Services:** meeting rooms, business center. **Cards:** AX, CB, DC, DS, MC, VI. **Special Amenities: early check-in/late check-out and free newspaper.** *(See color ad below)*

SOME UNITS

CLARION SUITES RESORT WORLD
Phone: (407)997-5000   **523**

All Year   1P: $89-$225   2P: $89-$225

Location: I-4, exit 64A, 2.8 mi e on US 192, then just s; between MM 10 and 11. Gated property. 2800 N Poinciana Blvd 34746. Fax: 407/997-5225. **Facility:** 311 units. 226 one- and 85 two-bedroom suites, some with kitchens and/or whirlpools. 2-3 stories, exterior corridors. **Parking:** on-site. **Terms:** check-in 4 pm, cancellation fee imposed, weekly rates available, 12% service charge. **Amenities:** video library (fee), voice mail, safes.

Small-scale Hotel   *Some:* irons, hair dryers. **Pool(s):** outdoor, 3 heated outdoor, wading. **Leisure Activities:** saunas, whirlpools, 6 tennis courts (4 lighted), racquetball courts, recreation programs, recreation area in spa section, bicycles, exercise room, basketball, shuffleboard, volleyball. *Fee:* game room. **Guest Services:** gift shop, complimentary laundry, area transportation (fee)-Disney. **Business Services:** meeting rooms. **Cards:** AX, CB, DC, DS, JC, MC, VI. *(See color ad p 679)*

COMFORT INN-MAINGATE WEST
Phone: (863)424-8420   **460**

All Year   1P: $30-$140   2P: $30-$140   XP: $5   F12

Location: I-4, exit 64B, 7.3 mi w on US 192; 0.7 mi e of jct US 27. 9330 W Hwy 192 34711 (PO Box 691484, ORLANDO, 32869). Fax: 863/424-9670. **Facility:** Smoke free premises. 73 one-bedroom standard units. 2 stories, exterior corridors. *Bath:* combo or shower only. **Parking:** on-site. **Terms:** check-in 4 pm, [ECP] meal plan available. **Amenities:** voice mail. *Some:* hair dryers. **Pool(s):** outdoor. **Cards:** AX, DC, DS, MC, VI.

Motel   **Special Amenities: free continental breakfast and free local telephone calls.** *(See color ad p 682)*

SOME UNITS

(See map p. 598)

COMFORT SUITES MAINGATE EAST Phone: (407)397-7848 **497**
AAA SAVE 2/11-8/23 [ECP] 1P: $75-$250 2P: $75-$250 XP: $10 F21
WWW 12/1-2/10 & 8/24-11/30 [ECP] 1P: $65-$250 2P: $65-$250 XP: $10 F21
Location: I-4, exit 64A, 1.7 mi e on US 192, then just s. 2775 Florida Plaza Blvd 34746. Fax: 407/396-7045. **Facility:** 198 one-bedroom standard units, some with whirlpools. 7 stories, interior corridors. *Bath:* combo or
Small-scale Hotel shower only. **Parking:** on-site. **Terms:** $2 service charge. **Amenities:** dual phone lines, voice mail, safes, irons, hair dryers. **Pool(s):** heated outdoor, wading. **Leisure Activities:** whirlpool, exercise room. *Fee:* game room. **Guest Services:** gift shop, valet and coin laundry, area transportation-major attractions. **Business Services:** meeting rooms, business center. **Cards:** AX, CB, DC, DS, JC, MC, VI. **Special Amenities: free continental breakfast and free news-paper.** *(See color ad below)*

SOME UNITS

/ X /

COMFORT SUITES MAINGATE RESORT Phone: (407)390-9888 **471**
AAA SAVE 12/21-11/30 [ECP] 1P: $63-$150 2P: $63-$150
WWW 12/1-12/20 [ECP] 1P: $63-$99 2P: $63-$99
Location: I-4, exit 64B, 3.5 mi w on US 192. 7888 W Irlo Bronson Hwy 34747. Fax: 407/390-0981. **Facility:** 150
Motel units. 149 one-bedroom standard units. 1 one-bedroom suite with efficiency and whirlpool. 3 stories, exterior corridors. *Bath:* combo or shower only. **Parking:** on-site. **Terms:** check-in 4 pm. **Amenities:** voice mail, safes (fee), hair dryers. *Some:* irons. **Pool(s):** heated outdoor, wading. **Leisure Activities:** whirlpool. *Fee:* game room. **Guest Services:** gift shop, valet and coin laundry, area transportation-major attractions. **Business Services:** meeting rooms. **Cards:** AX, CB, DC, DS, MC, VI. **Special Amenities: free continental breakfast and free newspaper.**
(See color ad p 683)

SOME UNITS
/ X /

COUNTRY INN & SUITES Phone: (407)997-1400 **535**
WWW 6/8-8/23 [ECP] 1P: $69-$149 2P: $69-$149 XP: $10 F18
12/1-4/26 [ECP] 1P: $59-$149 2P: $59-$149 XP: $10 F18
Small-scale Hotel 4/27-6/7 & 8/24-11/30 [ECP] 1P: $59-$109 2P: $59-$109 XP: $10 F18
Location: I-4, exit 68, 3 mi s on SR 535, just s of Osceola Pkwy, just n of US 192. 5001 Calypso Cay Way 34746.
Fax: 407/997-1401. **Facility:** 162 units. 114 one-bedroom standard units. 48 one-bedroom suites. 7 stories, interior corridors. *Bath:* combo or shower only. **Parking:** on-site. **Terms:** check-in 4 pm, pets ($25 fee). **Amenities:** video games (fee), dual phone lines, voice mail, irons, hair dryers. **Pool(s):** heated outdoor. **Leisure Activities:** whirlpool, miniature golf, exercise room. *Fee:* massage, game room. **Guest Services:** sundries, valet laundry, area transportation. **Cards:** AX, CB, DC, DS, JC, MC, VI.
(See color ad p 613)

SOME UNITS
/ X /

(See map p. 598)

DAYS INN

Phone: (407)846-4714 **444**

🔷 SAVE | All Year [CP] | 1P: $30-$150 | 2P: $35-$150 | XP: $10 | F17
♦♦♦♦

Motel

Location: US 192, 3 mi w of jct US 17-92. 4104 W Irlo Bronson Memorial Hwy 34741. Fax: 407/932-2699. **Facility:** 174 one-bedroom standard units. 3 stories, exterior corridors. **Parking:** on-site. **Terms:** cancellation fee imposed, package plans. **Amenities:** hair dryers. **Pool(s):** heated outdoor. **Leisure Activities:** Fee: game room. **Guest Services:** coin laundry, area transportation-Disney. **Business Services:** fax (fee). **Cards:** AX, CB, DC, DS, MC, VI. **Special Amenities:** free continental breakfast and free newspaper.

(See color ad p 684)

SOME UNITS

🔲 🛏 🔈 ⤢ 📷 / ✕ 🗄 📖 /

DAYS INN-KISSIMMEE

Phone: (407)846-7136 **573**

SAVE | All Year | 1P: $45-$129 | 2P: $45-$129 | XP: $10 | F17
♦♦

Small-scale Hotel

Location: Florida Tpke, exit 244, 0.8 mi w on US 192. 2095 E Irlo Bronson Memorial Hwy 34744. Fax: 407/846-8423. **Facility:** 118 one-bedroom standard units. 2 stories (no elevator), exterior corridors. **Parking:** on-site. **Terms:** 3 day cancellation notice, pets ($50 deposit). **Amenities:** safes (fee). **Pool(s):** outdoor. **Guest Services:** coin laundry. **Cards:** AX, DC, DS, MC, VI.

SOME UNITS

🔲 🛏 🛎 ⤢ 📷 / ✕ 🗄 📖 /
FEE FEE

DAYS SUITES/MAIN GATE EAST OF WALT DISNEY WORLD RESORT

Phone: (407)396-7900 **499**

🔷 SAVE | All Year | 1P: $69-$189 | 2P: $69-$189
♦♦ ♦♦

Small-scale Hotel

Location: I-4, exit 64A, 1.5 mi e on US 192. 5820 W Irlo Bronson Memorial Hwy 34746. Fax: 407/396-0940. **Facility:** 603 units. 8 one-bedroom standard units. 587 one- and 8 two-bedroom suites with efficiencies (utensils extra charge). 2 stories, exterior corridors. **Bath:** combo or shower only. **Parking:** on-site. **Terms:** check-in 4 pm, 3 day cancellation notice-fee imposed, $3 service charge. **Amenities:** video games, voice mail, safes (fee), hair dryers. **Pool(s):** outdoor, 2 heated outdoor. **Leisure Activities:** Fee: game room. **Guest Services:** coin laundry, area transportation-Disney. **Cards:** AX, CB, DC, DS, MC, VI. **Special Amenities:** free newspaper and preferred room (subject to availability with advanced reservations).** *(See color ad p 685)*

SOME UNITS

🔲 🛏 🔈 🦽 🔈 🛎 ⤢ 📷 🔌 🗄 📖 💻 / ✕ /

DOUBLETREE RESORT ORLANDO VILLAS AT MAINGATE

Phone: (407)397-0555 **516**

SAVE | 12/1-4/30 & 6/20-8/16 | 1P: $129-$169 | 2P: $139-$179 | XP: $10 | F18
♦♦♦ ♦♦♦ | 8/17-11/30 | 1P: $119-$139 | 2P: $129-$149 | XP: $10 | F18
| 5/1-6/19 | 1P: $109-$129 | 2P: $119-$139 | XP: $10 | F18

Small-scale Hotel

Location: On US 192 at MM 12, 4.8 mi w of jct US 17-92 and 441; 0.5 mi e of jct SR 535. 4787 W Irlo Bronson Memorial Hwy 34746. Fax: 407/397-0553. **Facility:** 150 units. 20 one-, 80 two- and 50 three-bedroom suites with kitchens. 2 stories (no elevator), exterior corridors. **Parking:** on-site. **Terms:** 3 day cancellation notice-fee imposed. **Amenities:** voice mail, irons, hair dryers. **Pool(s):** heated outdoor, wading. **Leisure Activities:** whirlpool, lighted tennis court, playground, exercise room, basketball. *Fee:* game room. **Guest Services:** gift shop, coin laundry, area transportation (fee). **Business Services:** meeting rooms, PC (fee). **Cards:** AX, CB, DC, DS, MC, VI. *(See color ad p 727)*

SOME UNITS

🔲 🛎 ⤢ ✕ 📷 🔌 🗄 📖 💻 / ✕ /

ECONO LODGE MAINGATE EAST

Phone: (407)870-7374 **557**

SAVE | All Year | 1P: $39-$69
♦♦ ♦♦

Motel

Location: US 192, 2.8 mi w of jct US 17-92 and 441. 4156 W Vine St 34741. Fax: 407/870-2154. **Facility:** 130 one-bedroom standard units. 3 stories, exterior corridors. **Parking:** on-site. **Terms:** cancellation fee imposed. **Amenities:** irons, hair dryers. *Some:* safes (fee). **Pool(s):** outdoor. **Guest Services:** gift shop, coin laundry. **Cards:** AX, DC, DS, MC, VI. *(See color ad p 700)*

SOME UNITS

🔲 🔈 ⤢ 📷 🔌 💻 / ✕ 🗄 📖 /
FEE FEE

(See map p. 598)

ECONO LODGE MAINGATE RESORT

Phone: (407)396-2000   483

	1P: $49-$59	2P: $49-$59
6/13-8/16	1P: $49-$59	2P: $49-$59
4/27-6/12	1P: $39-$59	2P: $39-$59
12/1-4/26 & 8/17-11/30	1P: $31-$49	2P: $31-$49

Small-scale Hotel **Location:** I-4, exit 64B, 2.4 mi w, 1 mi w of Disney main gate. 7514 W Hwy 192 34747. Fax: 407/396-1295. **Facility:** 445 units. 444 one-bedroom standard units. 1 one-bedroom suite with kitchen. 2 stories, exterior corridors. *Bath:* combo or shower only. **Parking:** on-site. **Terms:** check-in 4 pm, small pets only ($50 fee, $25 deposit). **Pool(s):** heated outdoor, wading. **Leisure Activities:** whirlpool. *Fee:* game room. **Guest Services:** gift shop, coin laundry, area transportation. **Business Services:** meeting rooms, fax (fee). **Cards:** AX, CB, DC, DS, MC, VI.

ESPIRIT-ABSOLUTE PREMIER VACATION HOMES

Phone: (407)396-2401   580

12/1-4/5	2P: $155-$235
6/22-8/30	2P: $155-$215
4/6-6/21 & 8/31-11/30	2P: $120-$185

Vacation Home **Location:** I-4, exit 68, 2.5 mi e on SR 535 (Apopka-Vineland Rd). 3160 Vineland Rd, Suite 1 34746. Fax: 407/396-0113. **Facility:** 23 vacation homes with pools. 1 story, exterior corridors. **Parking:** on-site. **Terms:** off-site registration, check-in 4 pm, 1-4 night minimum stay, 31 day cancellation notice-fee imposed, small pets only ($150 fee, in select homes). **Amenities:** irons, hair dryers. **Guest Services:** complimentary laundry. **Business Services:** fax (fee). **Cards:** AX, DS, MC, VI.

FAIRFIELD ORLANDO AT CYPRESS PALMS

Phone: 407/397-1600   504

All Year   1P: $125-$185

Condominium **Location:** I-4, exit 64A, 3 mi e, then s on Scott Blvd. 5324 Fairfield Lake Dr 34746 (8669 Commodity Cir, Suite 300, ORLANDO, 32819). Fax: 407/397-9167. **Facility:** 366 units. 244 one- and 122 two-bedroom suites, some with efficiencies, kitchens and/or whirlpools. 3-5 stories, exterior corridors. *Bath:* combo or shower only. **Parking:** on-site. **Terms:** check-in 4 pm. **Amenities:** video library, CD players, voice mail, irons. **Pool(s):** 2 heated outdoor. **Leisure Activities:** whirlpools, playground, exercise room, horseshoes. *Fee:* game room. **Guest Services:** complimentary laundry, area transportation (fee). **Cards:** AX, CB, DS, MC, VI.

(See map p. 598)

FANTASY WORLD CLUB VILLAS

Phone: (407)396-1808   **511**

AAA SAVE

All Year   1P: $165   2P: $195

WWWW

Location: I-4, exit 64A, 3.5 mi e on US 192 and just n; at MM 11. 5005 Kyngs Heath Rd 34746. Fax: 407/396-6737. **Facility:** Designated smoking area. 334 two-bedroom suites with kitchens, some with whirlpools. 2-4 stories, exterior corridors. **Parking:** on-site. **Terms:** check-in 4 pm, cancellation fee imposed, small pets only ($30 extra charge). **Amenities:** video library (fee), voice mail, irons, hair dryers. *Some:* safes. **Pool(s):** 2 outdoor, heated outdoor. **Leisure Activities:** whirlpool, 5 lighted tennis courts, playground, basketball, volleyball. *Fee:* game room. **Guest Services:** coin laundry, area transportation-major attractions. **Cards:** AX, DC, DS, MC, VI. *(See color ad below)*

Condominium

tennis equipment,
MC, VI. *(See color ad below)*

SOME UNITS

🅢🅓 🛏 🍽 🏊 ✕ VCR 🎬 DATA PORT 🛗 ▦ ▭ /✕/

FLAMINGO INN

Phone: (407)846-1935   **563**

AAA SAVE

All Year   1P: $29-$39   2P: $29-$39

WWW

Location: 0.3 mi e of jct US 441 and 192, on US 192. 801 E Vine St 34744. Fax: 407/846-7225. **Facility:** 40 one-bedroom standard units. 2 stories (no elevator), exterior corridors. **Parking:** on-site. **Terms:** 3 day cancellation notice, weekly rates available, small pets only ($8 extra charge). **Pool(s):** outdoor. **Cards:** AX, DS, MC, VI. **Special Amenities:** early check-in/late check-out and free room upgrade (subject to availability with advanced reservations). *(See color ad p 679)*

Motel

SOME UNITS

🅢🅓 🛏 🏊 🎬 DATA PORT 🛗 ▦ /✕/

(See map p. 598)

FOUR POINTS SHERATON ORLANDO KISSIMMEE

Phone: (407)870-2000   546

	12/1-1/3	1P: $98	2P: $98	XP: $10	F18
	1/4-11/30	1P: $62	2P: $62	XP: $10	F18

Small-scale Hotel   **Location:** I-4, exit 64A, 7 mi e on US 192. 4018 W Vine St 34741. Fax: 407/870-2010. **Facility:** 221 one-bedroom standard units. 3-5 stories, exterior corridors. **Parking:** on-site. **Amenities:** dual phone lines, voice mail, safes, irons, hair dryers. **Pool(s):** heated outdoor, wading. **Leisure Activities:** whirlpool, exercise room. **Guest Services:** gift shop, valet and coin laundry, area transportation. **Business Services:** meeting rooms. **Cards:** AX, DC, DS, MC, VI.

SOME UNITS

ASK SD ❲❙❙❳ ❲Y❳ 🏊 🎦 DATA PORT 💻 / ✕ 📶 📠 / FEE

FOUR WINDS MOTEL

Phone: (407)396-4011   543

❲❲❲ SAVE❳	12/20-4/30	1P: $49-$55	2P: $55-$69		
	5/1-9/3	1P: $35-$45	2P: $39-$49	XP: $10	F12
◆◆ ◆◆	12/1-12/19 & 9/4-11/30	1P: $30-$35	2P: $35-$39	XP: $10	F12

Motel   **Location:** US 192, 3.8 mi w of jct US 17-92 and 441, 1.3 mi e of SR 535. 4596 W Irlo Bronson Memorial Hwy 34746. Fax: 407/239-8976. **Facility:** 48 one-bedroom standard units. 2 stories (no elevator), exterior corridors. **Parking:** on-site. **Terms:** 2-3 night minimum stay - seasonal, 3 day cancellation notice, 1% service charge. **Amenities:** safes (fee). **Pool(s):** outdoor. **Cards:** AX, DC, DS, MC, VI. **Special Amenities:** early check-in/late check-out and free room upgrade (subject to availability with advanced reservations).

SOME UNITS

SD ❲❙❙❳ 🏊 🎦 / ✕ 📶 📠 / FEE FEE

GOLDEN LINK MOTEL

Phone: (407)396-0555   517

❲❲❲ SAVE❳	12/1-4/26	1P: $29-$59	2P: $29-$59	XP: $3	D18
	6/13-8/23	1P: $32-$49	2P: $32-$49	XP: $3	D18
◆◆ ◆◆	4/27-6/12 & 8/24-11/30	1P: $29-$39	2P: $29-$39	XP: $2	D18

Motel   **Location:** I-4, exit 64A, 3.7 mi e on US 192; jct SR 535. 4914 W Irlo Bronson Memorial Hwy (Hwy 192) 34746. Fax: 407/396-6531. **Facility:** 84 one-bedroom standard units. 2 stories (no elevator), exterior corridors. *Bath:* combo or shower only. **Parking:** on-site. **Amenities:** safes (fee). **Pool(s):** heated outdoor. **Leisure Activities:** Fee: waterskiing, jet skis. **Guest Services:** coin laundry. **Cards:** AX, DS, MC, VI.

SOME UNITS

❲❙❙❳ 🏊 🎦 / ✕ 📶 📠 / FEE FEE

(See map p. 598)

GREATER GROVES-ABSOLUTE PREMIER VACATION HOMES

Phone: (407)396-2401   581

Vacation Home

12/1-4/5	2P: $155-$235
6/22-8/30	2P: $155-$215
4/6-6/21 & 8/31-11/30	2P: $120-$185

Location: I-4, exit 68, 2.5 mi e on SR 535 (Apopka-Vineland Rd). 3160 Vineland Rd, Suite 1 34746. Fax: 407/396-0113. **Facility:** 25 vacation homes with pools. 1 story, exterior corridors. **Parking:** on-site. **Terms:** off-site registration, check-in 4 pm, 1-4 night minimum stay, 31 day cancellation notice-fee imposed, small pets only ($150 fee, in select homes). **Amenities:** irons, hair dryers. **Guest Services:** complimentary laundry. **Business Services:** fax (fee). **Cards:** AX, DS, MC, VI.

HAMPTON INN-MAINGATE EAST

SAVE

Phone: (407)396-8484   484

Small-scale Hotel

All Year [ECP]   1P: $69-$109   2P: $69-$109

Location: I-4, exit 64A, 0.3 mi e on US 192, 0.5 mi n. 3104 Parkway Blvd 34747. Fax: 407/396-7344. **Facility:** 163 one-bedroom standard units. 4 stories, interior corridors. **Parking:** on-site. **Terms:** cancellation fee imposed. **Amenities:** voice mail, safes (fee), irons. *Some:* hair dryers. **Pool(s):** heated outdoor. **Leisure Activities:** exercise room privileges, sports court. **Guest Services:** coin laundry, area transportation. **Cards:** AX, CB, DC, DS, MC, VI. *(See color ad p 646)*

SOME UNITS
FEE   FEE

HAMPTON INN MAIN GATE WEST

AAA SAVE

Phone: (407)396-6300   455

Small-scale Hotel

5/2-11/30 [ECP]	1P: $59-$89	2P: $69-$89
12/1-12/22 [ECP]	1P: $64-$69	2P: $64-$79
12/23-5/1 [ECP]	1P: $54-$64	2P: $64-$74

Location: I-4, exit 64B, 2.5 mi w on US 192. 3000 Main Gate Ln 34747. Fax: 407/396-8989. **Facility:** 118 one-bedroom standard units. 5 stories, interior corridors. *Bath:* combo or shower only. **Parking:** on-site. **Terms:** cancellation fee imposed. **Amenities:** dual phone lines, voice mail, irons, hair dryers. **Pool(s):** outdoor. **Guest Services:** valet laundry, area transportation-Disney. **Special Amenities:** free continental breakfast and free local telephone calls. *(See color ad card insert)*

SOME UNITS

HOLIDAY INN EXPRESS

AAA SAVE

Phone: (407)846-4646   572

Small-scale Hotel

All Year [ECP]   1P: $70-$99

Location: US 192 and 441 at Florida Tpke, exit 244, 0.5 mi w. 2145 E Irlo Bronson Memorial Hwy 34744. Fax: 407/932-2467. **Facility:** 146 one-bedroom standard units. 2 stories (no elevator), exterior corridors. *Bath:* combo or shower only. **Parking:** on-site. **Amenities:** voice mail, safes, irons, hair dryers. **Pool(s):** outdoor. **Guest Services:** valet and coin laundry, area transportation-Disney. **Business Services:** meeting rooms. **Cards:** AX, CB, DC, DS, JC, MC, VI. **Special Amenities:** early check-in/late check-out and free continental breakfast.

SOME UNITS

(See map p. 598)

HOLIDAY INN HOTEL & SUITES MAIN GATE EAST

Phone: (407)396-4488 (500)

Small-scale Hotel

12/20-1/4	1P: $99-$139	2P: $99-$139
1/5-8/16	1P: $79-$119	2P: $79-$119
12/1-12/19 & 8/17-11/30	1P: $59-$89	2P: $59-$89

Location: I-4, exit 64A (US 192); between MM 9 and 10. 5678 W Irlo Bronson Memorial Hwy 34746. Fax: 407/396-8915. **Facility:** 614 one-bedroom standard units, some with whirlpools. 2 stories, exterior corridors. *Bath:* combo or shower only. **Parking:** on-site. **Terms:** check-in 4 pm, cancellation fee imposed. **Amenities:** video library (fee), voice mail, irons, hair dryers. *Some:* video games, CD players. **Pool(s):** 2 heated outdoor, wading. **Leisure Activities:** whirlpools, 2 lighted tennis courts, recreation programs, playground, exercise room, basketball, volleyball. *Fee:* game room. **Guest Services:** gift shop, valet and coin laundry, area transportation. **Business Services:** meeting rooms. **Cards:** AX, CB, DC, DS, JC, MC, VI. *(See color ad opposite inside back cover)*

SOME UNITS

HOLIDAY INN KISSIMMEE DOWNTOWN

Phone: (407)846-2713 (551)

Small-scale Hotel

All Year   1P: $70-$90   2P: $70-$90

Location: I-4, exit 64A, 8 mi e on US 192; 1.4 mi w of jct US 17-92 and 441. 2009 W Vine St 34741. Fax: 407/846-8695. **Facility:** 200 one-bedroom standard units. 3-4 stories, exterior corridors. *Bath:* combo or shower only. **Parking:** on-site. **Terms:** check-in 4 pm, pets ($8 extra charge). **Amenities:** voice mail, safes, irons, hair dryers. **Dining:** 7 am-11 pm, cocktails. **Pool(s):** outdoor, heated outdoor, wading. **Leisure Activities:** whirlpool, lighted tennis court, sun deck, playground, exercise room. *Fee:* game room. **Guest Services:** gift shop, valet and coin laundry, area transportation (fee). **Business Services:** meeting rooms. **Cards:** AX, DS, MC, VI. **Special Amenities:** early check-in/late check-out and free newspaper. *(See color ad opposite inside back cover & ad below)*

SOME UNITS

FEE FEE

HOLIDAY INN MAINGATE WEST

Phone: (407)396-1100 (445)

Small-scale Hotel

All Year [BP]   1P: $49-$109   2P: $49-$109   XP: $10   F18

Location: I-4, exit 64B, 2.9 mi w on US 192, then just n; 1 mi w of Disney World main gate access road. 7601 Black Lake Rd 34747. Fax: 407/396-0689. **Facility:** 295 one-bedroom standard units. 6 stories, exterior corridors. *Bath:* combo or shower only. **Parking:** on-site. **Terms:** check-in 4 pm, cancellation fee imposed, [AP] meal plan available, 15% service charge, small pets only ($50 fee, $25 deposit). **Amenities:** safes (fee), irons, hair dryers. *Some:* video games, CD players. **Dining:** 2 restaurants, 7 am-11 & 5-10 pm, cocktails. **Pool(s):** heated outdoor, wading. **Leisure Activities:** exercise room, volleyball. *Fee:* game room. **Guest Services:** gift shop, valet and coin laundry, area transportation-Disney. **Business Services:** meeting rooms. **Cards:** AX, CB, DC, DS, JC, MC, VI. **Special Amenities:** free room upgrade and preferred room (each subject to availability with advanced reservations). *(See color ad opposite inside back cover)*

SOME UNITS

FEE

HOLIDAY INN-NIKKI BIRD RESORT-MAINGATE

Phone: (407)396-7300 (481)

Motel

All Year   1P: $59-$99

Location: I-4, exit 64B, 2.3 mi w on US 192; 1 mi w of Disney World main gate. 7300 W Irlo Bronson Memorial Hwy 34747. Fax: 407/396-7555. **Facility:** 530 one-bedroom standard units. 2 stories, exterior corridors. *Bath:* combo or shower only. **Parking:** on-site. **Terms:** check-in 4 pm. **Amenities:** video games, voice mail, safes, irons, hair dryers. *Some:* CD players. **Dining:** 2 restaurants, 6:30 am-11 pm, cocktails. **Pool(s):** 3 heated outdoor, 2 wading. **Leisure Activities:** whirlpools, 3 lighted tennis courts, recreation programs, playground, exercise room, basketball, horseshoes, volleyball. **Guest Services:** gift shop, valet and coin laundry, area transportation-Disney. **Business Services:** meeting rooms, fax. **Cards:** AX, CB, DC, DS, JC, MC, VI. **Special Amenities:** early check-in/late check-out and free newspaper. *(See color ad opposite inside back cover & p 690)*

SOME UNITS

FEE

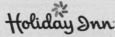

(See map p. 598)

HOLIDAY VILLAS

Phone: (407)397-0700   514

	12/1-1/3	1P: $159-$249	2P: $169-$269
	1/4-8/22	1P: $159-$189	2P: $169-$199
	8/23-11/30	1P: $159-$179	2P: $169-$189

Condominium

Location: I-4, exit 64A, 2.8 mi e on US 192; northwest corner of jct US 192 and SR 535; between MM 11 and 12. Located adjacent to the International Promenade Shopping Plaza. 2928 Vineland Rd 34746. Fax: 407/397-0566. **Facility:** 255 units. 100 two- and 155 three-bedroom suites with kitchens. 2 stories, exterior corridors. **Parking:** on-site. **Terms:** check-in 4 pm, 3 day cancellation notice-fee imposed, package plans. **Amenities:** irons. *Fee:* video library, safes. **Pool(s):** heated outdoor. **Leisure Activities:** sauna, whirlpool, lighted tennis court, exercise room. **Cards:** AX, DS, MC, VI. *(See color ad below)*

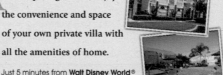
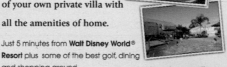

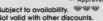
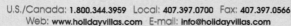

(See map p. 598)

HOMEWOOD SUITES BY HILTON
Phone: (407)396-2229   485
SAVE
▼▼▼▼ All Year [ECP]   1P: $129-$199   2P: $129-$199
Location: I-4, exit 64A, 0.3 mi e on US 192, 0.5 mi n. 3100 Parkway Blvd 34747. Fax: 407/396-4833. **Facility:** 156
Small-scale Hotel units. 147 one- and 9 two-bedroom suites ($129-$199) with efficiencies. 2-3 stories, interior/exterior corridors.
Parking: on-site. **Terms:** cancellation fee imposed, pets ($250 deposit, $75 extra charge). **Amenities:** video
games, voice mail, safes (fee), irons, hair dryers. **Pool(s):** heated outdoor, wading. **Leisure Activities:** whirl-
pool, playground, exercise room, sports court, basketball. *Fee:* game room. **Guest Services:** gift shop, com-
plimentary evening beverages: Mon-Thurs, valet and coin laundry, area transportation. **Business Services:** meeting rooms.
Cards: AX, CB, DC, DS, MC, VI. *(See color ad p 646)*
SOME UNITS
🅂🄳 🐕 🛋 🗙 🎥 DATA PORT 🖥 📺 📼 / 🗙 /

HOWARD JOHNSON ENCHANTEDLAND RESORT HOTEL
Phone: (407)396-4343   510
AAA SAVE
▼▼▼ All Year   2P: $50-$80
Location: I-4, exit 64A, 3.2 mi e on US 192. 4985 W Irlo Bronson Memorial Hwy 34746. Fax: 407/396-8998.
Facility: 160 one-bedroom standard units, some with whirlpools. 2 stories, exterior corridors. *Bath:* combo or
shower only. **Parking:** on-site. **Amenities:** video library, voice mail, safes
Small-scale Hotel (fee). *Some:* irons, hair dryers. **Dining:** 7-11 am. **Pool(s):** heated outdoor. **Leisure Activities:** whirlpool. *Fee:*
Children's Adventure Club, game room. **Guest Services:** sundries, valet and coin laundry, area
transportation-major attractions. **Cards:** AX, CB, DC, DS, JC, MC, VI. **Special Amenities: early check-in/late check-out and
free newspaper.**
SOME UNITS
🅂🄳 🍽 🖏 🛋 🗙 🎥 DATA PORT 🖥 / 🗙 VCR 🖥 🖼 /

HOWARD JOHNSON EXPRESS INN & SUITES LAKEFRONT PARK
Phone: (407)396-4762   533
AAA SAVE
12/21-8/23 [CP]   1P: $59-$119   2P: $59-$119   XP: $5   F12
▼▼ 12/1-12/20 & 8/24-11/30 [CP]   1P: $39-$79   2P: $39-$79   XP: $5   F12
Location: I-4, exit 64A, 3.9 mi e on US 192; jct SR 535, just e. 4836 W Irlo Bronson Memorial Hwy 34746.
Fax: 407/396-4866. **Facility:** 131 units. 89 one-bedroom standard units, some with whirlpools. 42 one-
Small-scale Hotel bedroom suites ($79-$139) with kitchens. 2 stories, exterior corridors. *Bath:* combo or shower only. **Parking:**
on-site. **Amenities:** safes (fee). **Pool(s):** heated outdoor, wading. **Leisure Activities:** whirlpool, boat dock,
fishing, covered picnic pavilion, playground. *Fee:* jet skis. **Guest Services:** coin laundry, area transportation-Disney. **Cards:** AX,
CB, DC, DS, MC, VI. **Special Amenities: free continental breakfast.** *(See color ad p 692)*
SOME UNITS
🅂🄳 🖏 🛋 🗙 DATA PORT 🖥 / 🗙 🖥 /

HOWARD JOHNSON EXPRESS INN PARKSIDE
Phone: (407)396-7100   558
AAA SAVE
12/1-4/12 [ECP]   1P: $39-$69   2P: $49-$99
▼▼ ▼▼ 6/20-8/16 [ECP]   1P: $39-$59   2P: $49-$99
4/13-6/19 & 8/17-11/30 [ECP]   1P: $29-$39   2P: $39-$59
Location: I-4, exit 64A (US 192), 3.5 mi w of jct US 17-92 and 441. 4311 W Hwy 192 34746-6315. Fax: 407/239-2636.
Small-scale Hotel **Facility:** 172 one-bedroom standard units. 2-3 stories, exterior corridors. **Parking:** on-site. **Terms:** check-in
4 pm, small pets only ($20 deposit, $10 extra charge). **Pool(s):** heated outdoor, wading. **Guest Services:**
coin laundry. **Business Services:** meeting rooms, fax (fee). **Cards:** AX, CB, DC, DS, MC, VI. **Special Amenities: free conti-
nental breakfast and preferred room (subject to availability with advanced reservations).**
SOME UNITS
🅂🄳 🐕 🛋 🎥 DATA PORT 🖥 / 🗙 🖥 🖼 /

HOWARD JOHNSON HOTEL
Phone: (407)846-4900   575
AAA SAVE
▼▼ ▼▼ All Year   1P: $40-$89   2P: $40-$89   XP: $10   F
Location: On US 192 and 441; Florida Tpke, exit 244, just e. 2323 E Irlo Bronson Memorial Hwy 34744.
Fax: 407/994-0188. **Facility:** 194 one-bedroom standard units. 2 stories (no elevator), interior corridors.
Bath: combo or shower only. **Parking:** on-site. **Terms:** check-in 4 pm, cancellation fee imposed, [AP] meal
Small-scale Hotel plan available, pets ($10 extra charge). **Amenities:** *Some:* safes (fee), irons, hair dryers. **Dining:** 6:30 am-9
pm, cocktails. **Pool(s):** outdoor. **Leisure Activities:** *Fee:* game room. **Guest Services:** gift shop, coin
laundry, area transportation-Disney. **Cards:** AX, CB, DC, DS, MC, VI. **Special Amenities: free local telephone calls and free
room upgrade (subject to availability with advanced reservations).** *(See ad below)*
SOME UNITS
🅂🄳 🐕 🍽 🍸 🖏 🎵 🛋 🖥 / 🗙 DATA PORT 🖥 🖼 /
FEE   FEE FEE

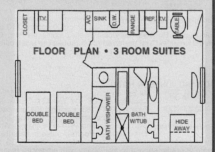

(See map p. 598)

HOWARD JOHNSON MAINGATE EAST　　　　　　　　　Phone: (407)396-1748　**491**
AAA SAVE　　All Year　　　　　　1P: $47-$100　　2P: $47-$100　　XP: $10　　　F17
♦♦♦♦ ♦♦♦♦　Location: I-4, exit 64A, 1 mi e on US 192 at MM 9. 6051 W Irlo Bronson Memorial Hwy 34747. Fax: 407/396-4835.
　　　　　Facility: 567 units. 559 one-bedroom standard units, some with efficiencies, kitchens and/or whirlpools. 8
　　　　　one-bedroom suites. 2-3 stories, interior/exterior corridors. *Bath:* combo or shower only. **Parking:** on-site.
Small-scale Hotel **Terms:** check-in 4 pm, cancellation fee imposed, $3 service charge. **Amenities:** video games, voice mail,
safes (fee). **Pool(s):** 2 heated outdoor, wading. **Leisure Activities:** whirlpool. *Fee:* game room. **Guest Serv-**
ices: gift shop, coin laundry, area transportation-Disney. **Business Services:** meeting rooms. **Cards:** AX, CB, DC, DS, MC, VI.
Special Amenities: free newspaper and free room upgrade (subject to availability with advanced reservations).
(See color ad p 628)

SOME UNITS
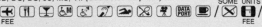

HOWARD JOHNSON MAINGATE RESORT WEST　　　　　Phone: (407)396-4500　**463**
AAA SAVE　　All Year　　　　　　1P: $39-$62　　2P: $39-$62
♦♦♦♦ ♦♦♦♦　Location: I-4, exit 64B, 5.6 mi w on SR 192. 8660 W Irlo Bronson Memorial Hwy 34747. Fax: 407/396-8045.
　　　　　Facility: 435 units. 434 one-bedroom standard units. 1 one-bedroom suite. 2 stories, exterior corridors.
Motel　　**Parking:** on-site. **Amenities:** voice mail, safes (fee). *Some:* irons, hair dryers. **Dining:** 2 restaurants, 7
am-10 pm, cocktails. **Pool(s):** 2 outdoor, heated outdoor, wading. **Leisure Activities:** whirlpool, 2 lighted
tennis courts, playground, exercise room, basketball, shuffleboard, volleyball. *Fee:* game room. **Guest Serv-**
ices: gift shop, valet and coin laundry, area transportation-Disney. **Business Services:** meeting rooms, fax. **Cards:** AX, DC, DS,
MC, VI. **Special Amenities: early check-in/late check-out and preferred room (subject to availability with advanced res-**
ervations). *(See color ad below)*

SOME UNITS

FEE

HYATT ORLANDO　　　　　　　　　　　　　　　Phone: (407)396-1234　**482**
AAA SAVE　　12/1-4/30 & 10/1-11/30　1P: $85-$175　　2P: $85-$175　　XP: $25　　F18
♦♦♦♦ ♦♦♦♦ ♦♦♦♦　5/1-9/30　　　　　1P: $79-$145　　2P: $79-$145　　XP: $25　　F18
　　　　　Location: I-4, exit 64A, just e on US 192, just n on Parkway Blvd, then just w. 6375 W Irlo Bronson Memorial Hwy 34747.
Large-scale Hotel　Fax: 407/396-5090. **Facility:** 922 one-bedroom standard units, some with whirlpools. 2 stories, interior corridors. *Bath:* combo or shower only. **Parking:** on-site. **Terms:** check-in 4 pm, cancellation fee imposed.
　　　　　Amenities: video games (fee), voice mail, safes, irons, hair dryers. **Dining:** 3 restaurants, 6 am-1 am, cocktails. **Pool(s):** 4 heated outdoor, 4 wading. **Leisure Activities:** whirlpools, 3 lighted tennis courts, fitness trail, playground, exercise room. *Fee:* game room. **Guest Services:** gift shop, coin laundry, area transportation (fee)-Disney. **Business Services:**
conference facilities, business center. **Cards:** AX, CB, DC, DS, JC, MC, VI. *(See color ad p 651)*

SOME UNITS
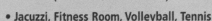
FEE　　　　　　　　　　　　　　　　　　　　　　　　　　　　　FEE

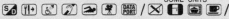

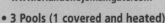
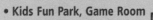

(See map p. 598)

INDIAN CREEK-ABSOLUTE PREMIER VACATION HOMES　　　　Phone: (407)396-2401　　470
Vacation Home
12/1-4/5		2P: $155-$235
6/22-8/30		2P: $150-$215
4/6-6/21 & 8/31-11/30		2P: $120-$185

Location: I-4, exit 68, 2.5 mi e on SR 535 (Apopka-Vineland Rd). 3160 Vineland Rd, Suite 1 34746. Fax: 407/396-0113. **Facility:** 19 vacation homes with pools. Exterior corridors. **Parking:** on-site. **Terms:** off-site registration, check-in 4 pm, 1-4 night minimum stay, 31 day cancellation notice, small pets only ($150 fee, in select homes). **Amenities:** irons, hair dryers. **Guest Services:** complimentary laundry. **Business Services:** fax (fee). **Cards:** AX, DS, MC, VI.

ASK SD 🐾 🗔 ⇌ ✕ DATA⧸PORT 🖥 🖨 🖵

INDIAN CREEK-REGENT VACATIONS & MANAGEMENT　　　　Phone: (407)397-9868　　476
Vacation Home
12/1-2/28	1P: $79-$289	2P: $79-$289
3/1-6/13 & 10/1-11/30	1P: $79-$259	2P: $79-$259
6/14-9/30	1P: $79-$249	2P: $79-$249

Location: I-4, exit 64B, 3.1 mi w on US 192. 7801 W Irlo Bronson Hwy 34747. Fax: 407/397-7881. **Facility:** 8 vacation homes with pools. Exterior corridors. **Parking:** on-site. **Terms:** off-site registration, check-in 4 pm, 60 day cancellation notice-fee imposed, weekly rates available. **Amenities:** irons, hair dryers. **Guest Services:** complimentary laundry. **Business Services:** fax (fee). **Cards:** AX, DS, MC, VI.

ASK SD ⇌ ✕ 🖥 🖨 🖵

INDIAN POINT-ABSOLUTE PREMIER VACATION HOMES　　　　Phone: 407/396-2401　　478
Vacation Home
12/1-4/5		2P: $155-$235
6/22-8/30		2P: $155-$215
4/6-6/21 & 8/31-11/30		2P: $120-$185

Location: I-4, exit 68, 2.5 mi e on SR 535 (Apopka-Vineland Rd). 3160 Vineland Rd, Suite 1 34746. Fax: 407/396-0113. **Facility:** 11 vacation homes with pools. 1 story, exterior corridors. **Parking:** on-site. **Terms:** off-site registration, check-in 4 pm, 1-4 night minimum stay, 31 day cancellation notice-fee imposed, small pets only ($150 fee, in select homes). **Amenities:** irons, hair dryers. **Guest Services:** complimentary laundry. **Business Services:** fax (fee). **Cards:** AX, DS, MC, VI.

🐾 ⇌ ✕ DATA⧸PORT 🖥 🖨 🖵

INDIAN RIDGE OAKS-ABSOLUTE PREMIER VACATION HOMES　　　　Phone: (407)396-2401　　480
Vacation Home
12/1-4/5		2P: $155-$235
6/22-8/30		2P: $155-$215
4/6-6/21 & 8/31-11/30		2P: $120-$185

Location: I-4, exit 68, 2.5 mi e on SR 535 (Apopka-Vineland Rd). 3160 Vineland Rd, Suite 1 34746. Fax: 407/396-0113. **Facility:** 70 vacation homes with pools. Exterior corridors. **Parking:** on-site. **Terms:** off-site registration, check-in 4 pm, 1-4 night minimum stay, 31 day cancellation notice-fee imposed, small pets only ($150 fee, in select homes). **Amenities:** irons, hair dryers. **Guest Services:** complimentary laundry. **Business Services:** fax (fee). **Cards:** AX, DS, MC, VI.

ASK SD 🐾 ⇌ ✕ DATA⧸PORT 🖥 🖨 🖵

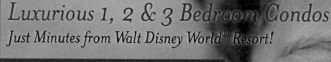

(See map p. 598)

THE KINGSTONIAN HOTELS & RESORTS   Phone: (407)846-1530   **570**

All Year   1P: $56-$99   2P: $56-$99
Location: Florida Tpke, exit 244, 0.3 mi w on US 192, just n. 201 Simpson Rd 34744. Fax: 407/846-2162.
Small-scale Hotel   Facility: 198 one-bedroom standard units. 4 stories, exterior corridors. Parking: on-site. Terms: cancellation fee imposed, [CP] meal plan available, small pets only ($5 extra charge, $50 deposit). Amenities: voice
mail, safes (fee). Pool(s): heated outdoor. Leisure Activities: Fee: game room. Guest Services: gift shop, coin laundry, area
transportation. Business Services: meeting rooms. Cards: AX, CB, DC, DS, MC, VI.

SOME UNITS
FEE FEE

KNIGHTS INN-MAINGATE   Phone: (407)396-4200   **448**

All Year [CP]   1P: $42-$99   2P: $42-$99
Location: I-4, exit 64B, 2.3 mi w on US 192; 1 mi w of Disney World main gate. 7475 W Irlo Bronson Memorial Hwy
34746. Fax: 407/396-8838. Facility: 120 units. 119 one-bedroom standard units, some with efficiencies (no
Motel   utensils). 1 one-bedroom suite with kitchen. 1 story, exterior corridors. Parking: on-site. Terms: cancellation
fee imposed, $2 service charge. Amenities: voice mail, safes (fee). Pool(s): heated outdoor. Guest Serv-
ices: coin laundry. Cards: AX, CB, DC, MC, VI. Special Amenities: early check-in/late check-out and free
continental breakfast. *(See color ad p 680)*

SOME UNITS

LAGO VISTA RESORT   Phone: 407/348-5246   **569**

All Year   1P: $75-$129   2P: $75-$129
Location: Florida Tpke, exit 244, 0.3 mi w on US 192, 1.3 mi n on Simpson Rd, 1.7 mi n on Boggy Creek Rd, then 0.4
mi w. 180 Royal Palm Dr 34743. Fax: 407/348-5083. Facility: 40 two-bedroom suites with kitchens. 2 stories (no
Condominium   elevator), exterior corridors. Parking: on-site. Terms: check-in 4 pm, 3 night minimum stay, 14 day cancellation notice-fee imposed. Amenities: video library (fee), voice mail. Pool(s): heated outdoor. Leisure Activities: sauna, playground, exercise room, shuffleboard, volleyball. Cards: AX, DS, MC, VI.

SOME UNITS
FEE

LAKE CECILE SUITES & RESORT HOTEL   Phone: (407)396-2056   **539**

All Year   1P: $99-$139
Location: I-4, exit 64A, 4 mi e on US 192; 4.8 mi w of jct US 17-92 and 441. 4786 W Irlo Bronson Memorial Hwy 34746.
Fax: 407/396-2000. Facility: 160 units. 120 one- and 40 two-bedroom suites with kitchens. 2 stories, exterior
corridors. Parking: on-site. Terms: check-in 4 pm, 2 night minimum stay, [CP] meal plan available.
Small-scale Hotel   Amenities: safes (fee), irons, hair dryers. Pool(s): heated outdoor. Leisure Activities: whirlpool, boat dock,
fishing, recreational dock, small picnic area with grills, playground, sports court, basketball. Fee: waterskiing,
game room. Guest Services: coin laundry, area transportation-Disney. Business Services: PC (fee). Cards: AX, DC, DS,
MC, VI. Special Amenities: early check-in/late check-out and free continental breakfast.

SOME UNITS

LA QUINTA INN LAKESIDE   Phone: (407)396-2222   **456**

12/1-12/31   1P: $108-$188   XP: $10   F18
2/7-8/9   1P: $128-$148   XP: $10   F18
1/1-2/6 & 8/10-11/30   1P: $108-$128   XP: $10   F18
Location: I-4, exit 64B westbound on US 192; exit 64A eastbound, 3 mi w; 1.8 mi w of Disney World main gate. Located
Large-scale Hotel   opposite Splendid China Theme Park. 7769 W Irlo Bronson Memorial Hwy 34747-1750. Fax: 407/396-7087.
Facility: 651 one-bedroom standard units. 2 stories, exterior corridors. Bath: combo or shower only. Parking:
on-site. Terms: check-in 4 pm, cancellation fee imposed. Amenities: video games, voice mail, safes (fee), irons, hair dryers.
Dining: 2 restaurants, 6 am-11:30 & 5-11 pm, cocktails. Pool(s): 3 heated outdoor, 2 wading. Leisure Activities: 4 lighted tennis
courts, recreation programs, playground, exercise room. Fee: miniature golf, game room. Guest Services: gift shop, valet and
coin laundry, area transportation-major attractions. Business Services: meeting rooms. Cards: AX, CB, DC, DS, MC, VI.
Special Amenities: free local telephone calls and free newspaper. *(See color ad p 696)*

SOME UNITS

LIKI TIKI VILLAGE A CLUB NAVIGO RESORT   Phone: (407)239-5000   **440**

All Year   1P: $99-$369   2P: $99-$369
Location: I-4, exit 64B, 7 mi w on US 192; 1 mi e of jct US 27. 17777 Bali Blvd 34787 (17777 Bali Blvd, WINTER GAR-
DEN). Fax: 407/857-2698. Facility: 458 units. 175 one-, 175 two- and 108 three-bedroom suites ($99-$369)
Condominium   with kitchens, some with whirlpools. 2-5 stories, exterior corridors. Parking: on-site. Terms: check-in 4 pm,
15 day cancellation notice-fee imposed. Amenities: voice mail, safes, irons, hair dryers. Some: CD players.
Pool(s): 2 heated outdoor. Leisure Activities: saunas, whirlpools, waterslide, paddleboats, fishing, lagoon
water island, wave pool, water volleyball, 2 lighted tennis courts, bicycles, playground, exercise room, fitness trail, basketball,
volleyball. Fee: game room. Guest Services: gift shop, complimentary laundry, area transportation (fee)-Disney. Business Services: meeting rooms. Special Amenities: free local telephone calls and preferred room (subject to availability with advanced reservations). *(See color ad p 694)*

FEE

LINDFIELDS RESERVE   Phone: (407)396-2262   **467**

All Year   1P: $245-$333   2P: $245-$333
Location: I-4, exit 64B, 6 mi w on SR 192, then just s; 2 mi e of US 27. 7799 Styles Blvd 34747. Fax: 407/396-1588.
Facility: 16 three-bedroom suites with kitchens. 1-2 stories, exterior corridors. Parking: on-site.
Terms: check-in 4 pm, 4 night minimum stay, 30 day cancellation notice. Amenities: CD players, voice mail,
Condominium   irons, hair dryers. Leisure Activities: whirlpool, heating extra charge, lighted tennis court. Guest Services:
complimentary laundry. Cards: AX, CB, DC, DS, MC, VI.

(See map p. 598)

MAGIC CASTLE INN & SUITES EASTGATE

			Phone: (407)396-1212	559
6/13-8/16 [ECP]	1P: $37-$44	2P: $43-$50	XP: $4	F17
12/1-4/26 [ECP]	1P: $26-$44	2P: $32-$50	XP: $4	F17
4/27-6/12 & 8/17-11/30 [ECP]	1P: $26-$36	2P: $32-$42	XP: $4	F17

ⒶⒶⒶ (SAVE) ▼▼▼

Motel

Location: 4.5 mi w of US 17-92 and 441; 6.5 mi e of Disney/Epcot entrance. 4559 W Hwy 192 34746. **Fax:** 407/396-7926. **Facility:** 114 one-bedroom standard units. 2 stories (no elevator), exterior corridors. **Parking:** on-site. **Terms:** cancellation fee imposed, small pets only ($25 deposit, $6 extra charge). **Amenities:** safes (fee). **Pool(s):** outdoor. **Leisure Activities:** playground. **Guest Services:** coin laundry, area transportation-Disney. **Cards:** AX, DS, MC, VI. **Special Amenities:** early check-in/late check-out and free continental breakfast. *(See color ad p 697)*

SOME UNITS

ⓢⒹ 🐾 ➥ 📷 DATA PORT 🅿 / ⊠ 📠 📧 /
FEE

(See map p. 598)

MAGIC CASTLE INN & SUITES MAINGATE

AAA SAVE

	6/13-8/16 [ECP]	1P: $40-$47	2P: $46-$53	XP: $4	F17
	12/1-4/26 [ECP]	1P: $29-$47	2P: $35-$53	XP: $4	F17
	4/27-6/12 & 8/17-11/30 [ECP]	1P: $29-$39	2P: $35-$45	XP: $4	F17

Phone: (407)396-2212 **507**

Location: I-4, exit 64A, 3.2 mi e on US 192; between MM 10 and 11. 5055 W Irlo Bronson Memorial Hwy 34746. **Small-scale Hotel** Fax: 407/396-0253. **Facility:** 107 one-bedroom standard units. 3 stories, exterior corridors. **Parking:** on-site. **Terms:** cancellation fee imposed, pets ($25 deposit, $6 extra charge). **Amenities:** safes (fee). *Some:* hair dryers. **Pool(s):** outdoor. **Leisure Activities:** picnic tables & grills, playground. **Guest Services:** coin laundry. **Cards:** AX, DS, MC, VI. **Special Amenities:** early check-in/late check-out and free continental breakfast. *(See color ad below)*

SOME UNITS

(See map p. 598)

MASTERS INN-KISSIMMEE

AAA **SAVE**
◆◆ ◆◆
Motel

Phone: (407)396-4020 506

All Year   1P: $35-$49   2P: $35-$49
Location: I-4, exit 25, 2.5 mi e on US 192. 5367 W Irlo Bronson Hwy 34746. Fax: 407/396-5450. **Facility:** 188 units. 182 one-bedroom standard units. 6 one-bedroom suites. 2 stories, exterior corridors. **Parking:** on-site. **Terms:** check-in 4 pm, [CP] meal plan available, small pets only ($5-$10 extra charge). **Amenities:** safes (fee). **Pool(s):** heated outdoor. **Guest Services:** coin laundry. **Cards:** AX, CB, DC, DS, MC, VI. **Special Amenities: free continental breakfast and free local telephone calls.**

SOME UNITS
[icons]

MASTERS INN-MAIN GATE

AAA **SAVE**
◆◆ ◆◆
Small-scale Hotel

Phone: (407)396-7743 473

All Year [CP]   1P: $39-$59   2P: $39-$59   XP: $4   F18
Location: I-4, exit 25, 2.5 mi w on US 192; 1 mi w of Disney World main gate. 2945 Entry Point Blvd 34747. Fax: 407/396-6307. **Facility:** 116 one-bedroom standard units. 3 stories, exterior corridors. **Parking:** on-site. **Terms:** check-in 4 pm, small pets only ($10 fee). **Amenities:** safes (fee). **Pool(s):** heated outdoor. **Guest Services:** coin laundry. **Cards:** AX, CB, DC, DS, MC, VI. **Special Amenities: free continental breakfast and free local telephone calls.**

SOME UNITS
[icons]
FEE

MOTEL 6 - #0436

◆◆◆◆
Small-scale Hotel

Phone: 407/396-6422 459

6/12-8/16	1P: $37-$47	2P: $43-$53	XP: $3	F17
1/23-6/11 & 8/17-11/30	1P: $35-$45	2P: $41-$51	XP: $3	F17
12/1-1/22	1P: $33-$43	2P: $39-$49	XP: $3	F17

Location: I-4, exit 64B, 1.3 mi w on US 192. 7455 W Irlo Bronson Hwy 34747. Fax: 407/396-0720. **Facility:** 148 one-bedroom standard units. 2 stories, exterior corridors. *Bath:* combo or shower only. **Parking:** on-site. **Pool(s):** heated outdoor. **Guest Services:** coin laundry. **Cards:** AX, CB, DC, DS, MC, VI.

SOME UNITS
[icons]

MOTEL 6 - #0464

◆◆◆◆
Motel

Phone: 407/396-6333 502

6/12-8/16	1P: $37-$47	2P: $43-$53	XP: $3	F17
1/23-6/11 & 8/17-11/30	1P: $35-$45	2P: $41-$51	XP: $3	F17
12/1-1/22	1P: $33-$43	2P: $39-$49	XP: $3	F17

Location: I-4, exit 64A, 2 mi e. 5731 W Hwy 192 34746. Fax: 407/396-7715. **Facility:** 347 one-bedroom standard units. 2 stories, exterior corridors. *Bath:* combo or shower only. **Parking:** on-site. **Terms:** small pets only. **Pool(s):** 2 heated outdoor. **Guest Services:** coin laundry. **Cards:** AX, CB, DC, DS, MC, VI.

SOME UNITS
[icons]

OAK PLANTATION

◆◆◆◆
Condominium

Phone: (407)847-8200 548

12/22-1/7	2P: $149-$219
1/8-11/30	2P: $105-$165
12/1-12/21	2P: $109-$149

Location: Just n of jct SR 192 and Hoagland Blvd. Located in a gated community. 4090 Enchanted Oaks Cir 34741. Fax: 407/847-7948. **Facility:** 242 units. 167 one- and 75 two-bedroom suites with kitchens. 2-3 stories (no elevator), exterior corridors. **Parking:** on-site. **Terms:** check-in 4 pm, 3 day cancellation notice-fee imposed. **Amenities:** video library (fee), voice mail, safes, irons, hair dryers. **Pool(s):** 2 heated outdoor, wading. **Leisure Activities:** whirlpool, lighted tennis court, jogging, playground, exercise room, basketball. *Fee:* game room. **Guest Services:** complimentary laundry, area transportation (fee), car wash station. **Business Services:** fax (fee). **Cards:** AX, DC, MC, VI. *(See color ad p 5)*

SOME UNITS
[icons]

ORANGE LAKE RESORT & COUNTRY CLUB

◆◆◆◆
Resort
Small-scale Hotel

Phone: (407)239-0000 441

All Year   2P: $105-$325
Location: I-4, exit 64B, 5 mi w on SR 192; 3.5 mi e of US 27. 8505 W Irlo Bronson Memorial Hwy 34747. Fax: 407/239-5119. **Facility:** This 1,200-unit time-share complex on manicured grounds includes single-room efficiencies and two- and three-bedroom villas and mid-rise units. 105 units. 25 one-bedroom standard units. 65 two- and 15 three-bedroom suites with kitchens, some with whirlpools. 1-6 stories, interior/exterior corridors. **Parking:** on-site. **Terms:** check-in 4 pm, 2 night minimum stay, 14 day cancellation notice. **Amenities:** video library (fee), voice mail, irons. **Pool(s):** 5 heated outdoor, 2 wading. **Leisure Activities:** whirlpools, rental boats, rental canoes, rental paddleboats, 12 lighted tennis courts, racquetball courts, recreation programs, playground, exercise room, basketball, shuffleboard, volleyball. *Fee:* waterskiing, fishing, golf-90 holes, game room. **Guest Services:** gift shop, complimentary laundry, area transportation (fee). **Business Services:** meeting rooms. **Cards:** AX, CB, DC, MC, VI.

SOME UNITS
[icons]
FEE

ORBIT ONE VACATION VILLAS

AAA **SAVE**
◆◆◆◆
Condominium

Phone: (407)396-1300 443

All Year   1P: $139-$199   2P: $139-$199
Location: I-4, exit 64B, 2.5 mi w on US 192. 2950 Entry Point Blvd 34741. Fax: 407/857-2698. **Facility:** 116 two-bedroom suites with kitchens and whirlpools. 2-3 stories (no elevator), exterior corridors. **Parking:** on-site. **Terms:** check-in 4 pm, 15 day cancellation notice-fee imposed. **Amenities:** video library (fee), voice mail, safes, irons, hair dryers. **Pool(s):** 2 heated outdoor, wading. **Leisure Activities:** sauna, whirlpool, putting green, 2 lighted tennis courts, racquetball court, playground, exercise room, basketball, horseshoes, shuffleboard, volleyball. *Fee:* game room. **Guest Services:** complimentary laundry. **Cards:** AX, DC, DS, MC, VI. **Special Amenities: free local telephone calls and preferred room (subject to availability with advanced reservations).** *(See color ad p 694)*

[icons]

(See map p. 598)

ORLANDO'S KEY VACATION HOMES Phone: (407)997-7789 **475**

(AAA) (SAVE)

▼▼▼

Vacation Home

12/1-1/5 & 6/16-8/31	1P: $95-$250	2P: $95-$250
1/6-6/15 & 9/1-11/30	1P: $90-$220	2P: $90-$220

Location: I-4, exit 64B, 3 mi w to Formosa Gardens Blvd, 0.8 mi s. Located in a residential area. 7802 W Irlo Bronson Hwy 34747. Fax: 407/997-2742. **Facility:** Designated smoking area. 40 vacation homes, some with pools. 1-2 stories, exterior corridors. **Parking:** on-site. **Terms:** check-in 4 pm, cancellation fee imposed. **Amenities:** safes, irons. *Some:* CD players. **Leisure Activities:** whirlpools. **Guest Services:** complimentary laundry. **Business Services:** fax (fee). **Cards:** AX, MC, VI. **Special Amenities: free local telephone calls.**

⬛ 🏊 ✕ VCR DATA/PORT 🛏 🍽 ☕

PARK INN & SUITES ORLANDO MAINGATE EAST Phone: (407)396-6100 **490**

(AAA) (SAVE)

▼▼ ▼▼

Small-scale Hotel

12/1-12/31 & 2/1-8/15 [ECP]	1P: $79-$99	2P: $79-$99
1/1-1/31 [ECP]	1P: $69-$89	2P: $69-$89
8/16-11/30 [ECP]	1P: $69-$79	2P: $69-$79

Location: I-4, exit 64A, 1 mi e on US 192; between MM 8 and 9. Located next to a water park. 6075 W Irlo Bronson Memorial Hwy 34747. Fax: 407/396-6965. **Facility:** 176 units. 160 one-bedroom standard units, some with efficiencies. 16 one-bedroom suites ($125-$145). 4 stories, exterior corridors. *Bath:* combo or shower only. **Parking:** on-site. **Terms:** check-in 4 pm, cancellation fee imposed, pets ($10 fee). **Amenities:** voice mail, safes (fee), irons, hair dryers. **Dining:** 6 am-midnight. **Pool(s):** heated outdoor. **Leisure Activities:** whirlpool, playground. *Fee:* game room. **Guest Services:** gift shop, coin laundry, area transportation (fee)-Disney. **Cards:** AX, DC, DS, MC, VI. **Special Amenities: free continental breakfast and free newspaper.** Affiliated with Park Plaza International Hotels. *(See color ad below)*

SOME UNITS
⬛ 🛏 🍴 ♿ 🏊 📺 ✕ 🎾 DATA/PORT 🛏 🍽 / ✕ ☕ /

PARKWAY INTERNATIONAL Phone: (407)396-6600 **488**

(AAA) (SAVE)

▼▼▼

Condominium

All Year   1P: $135-$219   2P: $135-$219

Location: I-4, exit 64A, 0.3 mi e on US 192, just n. 6200 Safari Tr 34746. Fax: 407/396-6165. **Facility:** 144 two-bedroom suites ($135-$219) with kitchens and whirlpools. 3 stories (no elevator), exterior corridors. **Parking:** on-site. **Terms:** check-in 4 pm, 15 day cancellation notice-fee imposed. **Amenities:** video library (fee), voice mail, safes, irons, hair dryers. *Some:* CD players. **Pool(s):** heated outdoor, wading. **Leisure Activities:** whirlpool, lighted tennis court, recreation programs, playground, basketball, shuffleboard. *Fee:* game room. **Guest Services:** complimentary laundry, area transportation (fee)-Disney. **Cards:** AX, DC, DS, MC, VI. **Special Amenities: free local telephone calls and preferred room (subject to availability with advanced reservations).** *(See color ad p 694)*

⬛ 🅿️ 🏊 ✕ VCR DATA/PORT 🛏 🍽 ☕
FEE

QUALITY INN CONFERENCE CENTER Phone: (407)846-4545 **568**

(SAVE)

▼▼ ▼▼

Small-scale Hotel

12/21-1/3	1P: $49-$59
4/4-11/30	1P: $44-$59
1/4-4/3	1P: $39-$59
12/1-12/20	1P: $38-$49

Location: Florida Tpke, exit 244, 1 mi w on US 192. 2050 E Irlo Bronson Memorial Hwy 34744. Fax: 407/932-2268. **Facility:** 152 one-bedroom standard units. 2 stories (no elevator), exterior corridors. *Bath:* combo or shower only. **Parking:** on-site. **Terms:** check-in 4 pm, 3 day cancellation notice, [BP] meal plan available, package plans - seasonal. **Amenities:** voice mail. *Some:* irons, hair dryers. **Pool(s):** outdoor. **Leisure Activities:** 2 lighted tennis courts, playground, exercise room. *Fee:* game room. **Guest Services:** coin laundry, area transportation. **Business Services:** meeting rooms. **Cards:** AX, CB, DC, DS, JC, MC, VI.

SOME UNITS
⬛ ♿ 🏊 ✕ 🎾 DATA/PORT ☕ / ✕ 🛏 🍽 /

QUALITY INN LAKE CECILE Phone: (407)396-4455 **527**

(SAVE)

▼▼▼▼

Small-scale Hotel

All Year   1P: $39-$89

Location: I-4, exit 64A, 3.6 mi e on US 192; at jct SR 535. 4944 W Irlo Bronson Memorial Hwy 34746. Fax: 407/396-4182. **Facility:** 222 one-bedroom standard units. 5 stories, interior corridors. **Parking:** on-site. **Terms:** cancellation fee imposed. **Amenities:** irons, hair dryers. *Fee:* video games, safes. **Pool(s):** outdoor. **Leisure Activities:** *Fee:* waterskiing, fishing. **Guest Services:** sundries, coin laundry, area transportation. **Cards:** AX, DC, DS, MC, VI. *(See color ad p 700)*

SOME UNITS
⬛ 🍴 🏊 🎾 DATA/PORT ☕ / ✕ 🛏 🍽 /
FEE FEE

(See map p. 598)

QUALITY INN MAIN GATE WEST   Phone: (407)396-1828   457

△△△ SAVE   12/21-4/25 & 6/16-11/30   1P: $49-$59   2P: $52-$79   XP: $10   F16
♦♦ ♦♦   12/1-12/20 & 4/26-6/15   1P: $37-$47   2P: $39-$49   XP: $5   F16
Location: I-4, exit 64B, 3 mi w on US 192; 2 mi w of Disney World main gate. Located opposite Splendid China Theme
Park and shopping. 7785 W Irlo Bronson Memorial Hwy 34747. Fax: 407/396-1305. **Facility:** 198 one-bedroom
Small-scale Hotel standard units, some with efficiencies (utensils extra charge). 3 stories, exterior corridors. *Bath:* combo or
shower only. **Parking:** on-site. **Terms:** 14 day cancellation notice-fee imposed, [CP] meal plan available.
Amenities: safes. *Some:* irons, hair dryers. **Pool(s):** heated outdoor. **Leisure Activities:** playground. *Fee:* game room. **Guest
Services:** gift shop, coin laundry, area transportation-Disney. **Cards:** AX, DC, DS, MC, VI. **Special Amenities:** free continental
breakfast and free local telephone calls. *(See color ad p 701)*

SOME UNITS

[S⃝] [📶] [🛗M] [🚫] [📡] [⤢] [🎥] [DATA PORT] [☕] / [✕] [🔌] [🔲] /
                                                                    FEE FEE

Just 4 miles from the Walt Disney World® Resort!

- Bus service available to Walt Disney World if you arrive without a car
- In-room coffee, hairdryer, iron & ironing board
- Lakeside swimming pool
- Beautiful white sandy beach
- Jet skiing/water skiing
- Group rates available
- Disney Multi-Day passes available through guest services

Call your AAA Travel Counselor or the hotel direct at

800-864-4855

Lake Cecile

QUALITY INN
BY CHOICE HOTELS

www.qualityinnlakececile.com

4944 W. Irlo Bronson Memorial Hwy.
(East of Mile Marker 11) Kissimmee, FL 34746
Phone: (407) 396-4455 Fax: (407) 396-4182

···**10-20% OFF PUBLISHED RATES**···

Just 7 miles from the Walt Disney World® Resort!

- Complimentary in-room coffee, hairdryer and iron & ironing board
- Swimming pool
- Free HBO, ESPN and Disney Channel/AM-FM radio
- Group rates available

Call your AAA Travel Counselor or the hotel direct at

800-337-8479

Econo Lodge
BY CHOICE HOTELS

Maingate East

Easy Access to All Central Florida Attractions!

4156 West Vine Street (East of Mile Marker 15) Kissimmee, FL 34741
www.econolodgemaingateeast.com Phone: (407) 870-7374 Fax: (407) 870-2154

(See map p. 598)

QUALITY SUITES MAINGATE EAST

 Phone: (407)396-8040

	12/1-4/26 [ECP]	1P: $89-$199	2P: $89-$199
	6/13-8/23 [ECP]	1P: $99-$179	2P: $99-$179
	8/24-11/30 [ECP]	1P: $89-$169	2P: $89-$169
	4/27-6/12 [ECP]	1P: $89-$159	2P: $89-$159

Small-scale Hotel **Location:** I-4, exit 64A, 1 mi e on US 192. 5876 W Irlo Bronson Memorial Hwy 34746. Fax: 407/396-6766. **Facility:** 225 units. 113 one- and 112 two-bedroom suites with efficiencies. 5 stories, exterior corridors. *Bath:* combo or shower only. **Parking:** on-site. **Terms:** check-in 4 pm, 3 day cancellation notice-fee imposed. **Amenities:** video games, voice mail, safes (fee), irons, hair dryers. **Pool(s):** heated outdoor, wading. **Leisure Activities:** whirlpool, playground. *Fee:* game room. **Guest Services:** gift shop, complimentary evening beverages, coin laundry, area transportation-Disney. **Cards:** AX, CB, DC, DS, MC, VI. **Special Amenities:** free continental breakfast and free local telephone calls. *(See color ad p 688)*

SOME UNITS

(See map p. 598)

RADISSON RESORT PARKWAY

Phone: (407)396-7000 [487]

(AAA) (SAVE) — All Year [BP]   1P: $89-$109   2P: $89-$109   XP: $10   F18

◆◆◆◆

Location: I-4, exit 64A, 0.3 mi e on US 192, then just n. 2900 Parkway Blvd 34747. **Fax:** 407/396-6792. **Facility:** 718 one-bedroom standard units. 3-8 stories, interior corridors. *Bath:* combo or shower only. **Parking:** on-site. **Terms:** check-in 4 pm. **Amenities:** video games, voice mail, safes, honor bars, irons, hair dryers. **Dining:** 2 restaurants, 6:30 am-12:30 am, cocktails. **Pool(s):** outdoor, heated outdoor, wading. **Leisure Activities:** sauna, waterslide, 2 lighted tennis courts, playground, exercise room, volleyball. *Fee:* game room. **Guest Services:** gift shop, valet and coin laundry, area transportation-major attractions. **Business Services:** conference facilities, business center. **Cards:** AX, CB, DC, DS, JC, MC, VI. *(See color ad p 701)*

Large-scale Hotel

SOME UNITS

[S/D] [✈]FEE [ℍ] [Y] [ᏩM] [🖉] [⇌] [✕] [🎥] [DATA PORT] [🖥] / [✕] [🔒] / FEE

RAMADA INN RESORT EASTGATE

Phone: (407)396-1111 [529]

(AAA) (SAVE) — All Year   1P: $49-$79   2P: $49-$79

◆◆◆

Location: I-4, exit 64A, 2.8 mi e on US 192. 5150 W Irlo Bronson Memorial Hwy 34746. **Fax:** 407/396-1607. **Facility:** 402 one-bedroom standard units, some with efficiencies. 4-10 stories, interior corridors. *Bath:* combo or shower only. **Parking:** on-site. **Amenities:** video games, voice mail, safes (fee), irons, hair dryers. **Dining:** 6 am-11 & 5-10 pm, cocktails. **Pool(s):** heated outdoor, wading. **Leisure Activities:** whirlpool, 2 lighted tennis courts, playground, basketball, shuffleboard. *Fee:* game room. **Guest Services:** gift shop, valet and coin laundry, area transportation-Disney. **Business Services:** meeting rooms. **Cards:** AX, CB, DC, DS, MC, VI. **Special Amenities:** free continental breakfast and free newspaper.

Small-scale Hotel

SOME UNITS

[S/D] [🐾] [ℍ] [Y] [ᏩM] [🖉] [⇌] [✕] [🎥] [DATA PORT] [🖥] / [✕] [🔒] [🖾] /

RAMADA INN RESORT MAINGATE

Phone: (407)396-4466 [446]

(AAA) (SAVE)

◆◆◆

12/20-1/4	1P: $79-$129	2P: $79-$129	XP: $10 F18
1/5-6/13	1P: $69-$109	2P: $69-$109	XP: $10 F18
6/14-11/30	1P: $49-$109	2P: $49-$109	XP: $10 F18
12/1-12/19	1P: $45-$65	2P: $45-$65	XP: $10 F18

Motel

Location: I-4, exit 64B, 2.3 mi w on US 192, 1 mi w of Disney World access road. 2950 Reedy Creek Blvd 34747. **Fax:** 407/396-6418. **Facility:** 391 units. 388 one-bedroom standard units. 2 one- and 1 two-bedroom suites. 2 stories, exterior corridors. *Bath:* combo or shower only. **Parking:** on-site. **Terms:** check-in 4 pm, $3 service charge. **Amenities:** video games, voice mail, safes (fee), irons, hair dryers. **Dining:** 2 restaurants, 7 am-2 & 5-10 pm, cocktails. **Pool(s):** 2 heated outdoor, wading. **Leisure Activities:** lighted tennis court, exercise room, basketball. *Fee:* game room. **Guest Services:** gift shop, valet and coin laundry, area transportation-Disney. **Business Services:** meeting rooms. **Cards:** AX, CB, DC, DS, MC, VI.

SOME UNITS

[S/D] [✈]FEE [ℍ] [Y] [ᏩM] [⚙] [🖉] [⇌] [✕] [🎥] [DATA PORT] [🖥] / [✕] [🔒] [🖾] / FEE

(See map p. 598)

RAMADA PLAZA HOTEL AND INN GATEWAY
Phone: (407)396-4400   **479**

🔺🔺🔺 (AAA) (SAVE)

Location: I-4, exit 64B, 2.3 mi w on US 192; 1 mi w of Disney World main gate. 7470 W Irlo Bronson Memorial Hwy 34747. Fax: 407/397-4481. **Facility:** 500 one-bedroom standard units. 2-8 stories, interior/exterior corridors. *Bath:* combo or shower only. **Parking:** on-site. **Terms:** check-in 4 pm, cancellation fee imposed, [BP] meal plan available, 18% service charge, small pets only ($25 fee). **Amenities:** voice mail, safes (fee). *Some:* irons, hair dryers. **Dining:** 2 restaurants, 7 am-midnight, cocktails. **Pool(s):** outdoor, heated outdoor. **Leisure Activities:** putting green, exercise room, basketball, shuffleboard. *Fee:* game room. **Guest Services:** gift shop, valet and coin laundry, area transportation-major attractions. **Business Services:** meeting rooms, business center. **Cards:** AX, CB, DC, DS, MC, VI. **Special Amenities:** free local telephone calls and free room upgrade (subject to availability with advanced reservations). *(See color ad p 702)*

All Year   1P: $59-$99   2P: $59-$99

Large-scale Hotel

SOME UNITS

[icons]

RECORD (PARKSIDE) INN & SUITES
Phone: (407)396-8400   **534**

🔺🔺🔺 (AAA) (SAVE)

Motel

6/27-8/16 [CP]	1P: $32-$44	2P: $35-$59	XP: $10	D12
12/1-4/26 [CP]	1P: $26-$49	2P: $32-$59	XP: $10	D12
4/27-6/26 [CP]	1P: $26-$39	2P: $29-$42	XP: $5	D12
8/17-11/30 [CP]	1P: $26-$36	2P: $29-$39	XP: $5	D12

Location: US 192, 4.2 mi w of jct US 17-92 and 441. 4651 W Irlo Bronson Memorial Hwy 34746. Fax: 407/396-8415. **Facility:** 57 one-bedroom standard units, some with efficiencies. 1-2 stories, exterior corridors. **Parking:** on-site. **Terms:** 5 day cancellation notice. **Amenities:** hair dryers. **Pool(s):** heated outdoor. **Leisure Activities:** picnic grill area. **Guest Services:** coin laundry. **Cards:** AX, DC, DS, JC, MC, VI. **Special Amenities:** early check-in/late check-out and preferred room (subject to availability with advanced reservations). *(See ad below)*

SOME UNITS

[icons]

RED ROOF INN
Phone: (407)396-0065   **513**

🔺 (AAA) (SAVE)

Motel

All Year   1P: $40-$50   2P: $50

Location: I-4, exit 64A, 3.6 mi e on US 192; at jct SR 535. 4970 Kyngs Heath Rd 34746. Fax: 407/396-0245. **Facility:** 102 one-bedroom standard units. 3 stories, exterior corridors. **Parking:** on-site. **Terms:** weekly rates available, [CP] meal plan available. **Amenities:** video games (fee), voice mail, hair dryers. **Pool(s):** heated outdoor. **Leisure Activities:** whirlpool. *Fee:* game room. **Guest Services:** coin laundry, area transportation-Disney. **Cards:** AX, DS, MC, VI.

SOME UNITS

[icons]

RENAISSANCE WORLDGATE HOTEL
Phone: (407)396-1400   **452**

🔺🔺🔺 (AAA) (SAVE)

Large-scale Hotel

12/1-1/3	1P: $119-$189	2P: $119-$189
1/4-8/25	1P: $139-$179	2P: $139-$179
8/26-11/30	1P: $139-$159	2P: $139-$159

Location: US 192, 2.8 mi w of I-4, 1 mi w of Disney World main gate access road. 3011 Maingate Ln 34747. Fax: 407/396-0660. **Facility:** 577 one-bedroom standard units. 7 stories, interior corridors. *Bath:* combo or shower only. **Parking:** on-site. **Terms:** check-in 4 pm, package plans. **Amenities:** video library (fee), video games, dual phone lines, voice mail, safes, irons, hair dryers. **Dining:** 7 am-midnight, cocktails. **Pool(s):** 2 heated outdoor, wading. **Leisure Activities:** whirlpool, 2 lighted tennis courts, recreation programs, playground, exercise room, basketball. *Fee:* game room. **Guest Services:** gift shop, valet and coin laundry, area transportation-Disney. **Business Services:** conference facilities, business center. **Cards:** AX, CB, DC, DS, MC, VI. *(See ad p 704)*

SOME UNITS

[icons]

(See map p. 598)

RITZ EXPRESS INN & SUITES Phone: 407/933-2400 [553]
AAA SAVE 3/16-11/30 [CP] 1P: $40-$70 2P: $50-$70 XP: $10 F12
12/1-3/15 [CP] 1P: $30-$60 2P: $40-$70 XP: $10 F12
Location: I-4, exit 64A on US 192, 1.5 mi w of jct US 17/92/441. 2407 W Irlo Bronson Memorial Hwy 34741. Fax: 407/933-1474. **Facility:** 131 one-bedroom standard units, some with efficiencies. 2 stories (no elevator), exterior corridors. **Parking:** on-site. **Terms:** $3 service charge. **Amenities:** high-speed Internet, voice mail, safes. **Pool(s):** outdoor. **Leisure Activities:** exercise room. *Fee:* game room. **Guest Services:** valet and coin laundry, area transportation (fee)-major attactions. **Business Services:** meeting rooms, fax. **Cards:** AX, CB, DC, DS, JC, MC, VI. **Special Amenities:** early check-in/late check-out and free continental breakfast.
Motel

SOME UNITS
[icons] / [icons] / FEE

RIVIERA MOTEL Phone: (407)847-9494 [579]
AAA SAVE All Year 1P: $27-$38 2P: $27-$38
Location: US 192 and 441 at Florida Tpke, exit 244. 2248 E Irlo Bronson Memorial Hwy 34744. **Facility:** 28 one-bedroom standard units. 2 stories (no elevator), exterior corridors. *Bath:* combo or shower only. **Parking:** on-site. **Terms:** 3 day cancellation notice, weekly rates available. **Pool(s):** outdoor. **Cards:** AX, DS, MC, VI.
Motel

[icons]

ROLLING HILLS-REGENT VACATIONS & MANAGEMENT Phone: (407)397-9868 [465]
12/1-2/28 1P: $79-$289
3/1-6/13 & 10/1-11/30 1P: $79-$259
6/14-9/30 1P: $79-$249
Vacation Home Location: I-4, exit 64B, 3.1 mi w on US 192. 7801 W Irlo Bronson Hwy 34747. Fax: 407/397-7881. **Facility:** 7 vacation homes with pools. Exterior corridors. **Parking:** on-site. **Terms:** off-site registration, check-in 4 pm, 60 day cancellation notice-fee imposed, package plans. **Amenities:** irons, hair dryers. **Guest Services:** complimentary laundry. **Business Services:** fax (fee). **Cards:** AX, DC, MC, VI.

[icons]

ROYAL OAKS OF KISSIMMEE Phone: (407)390-8200 [525]
AAA SAVE All Year 1P: $109-$143
Location: I-4, exit 64A, 3.1 mi e on US 192. 5075 W Irlo Bronson Hwy 34746. Fax: 407/390-0718. **Facility:** 55 three-bedroom suites with kitchens. 2 stories, exterior corridors. *Bath:* combo or shower only. **Parking:** on-site. **Terms:** check-in 4 pm, 3 night minimum stay, 14 day cancellation notice-fee imposed, small pets only ($50 extra charge). **Amenities:** irons. **Pool(s):** heated outdoor. **Leisure Activities:** whirlpool, barbecue grills, picnic tables, playground. **Guest Services:** complimentary laundry. **Cards:** DS, MC, VI. **Special Amenities:** free local telephone calls.
Condominium

[icons]

ROYAL PALMS-BRIGHT STAR RESORTS & CONDOMINIUMS Phone: (407)397-1700 [547]
AAA SAVE All Year 2P: $79-$119
Location: I-4, exit 64A, 5.7 mi e. 4533 W Irlo Bronson Hwy 34746. Fax: 407/397-1100. **Facility:** 9 three-bedroom suites with kitchens. Exterior corridors. **Parking:** on-site. **Terms:** check-in 4 pm, cancellation fee imposed. **Amenities:** irons, hair dryers. **Pool(s):** 2 heated outdoor. **Leisure Activities:** community recreation facility. **Guest Services:** complimentary laundry. **Business Services:** fax (fee). **Cards:** AX, DS, MC, VI. **Special Amenities:** free local telephone calls. *(See color ad p 639, p 640, p 178, p 686 & p 707)*
Condominium

[icons]

SLEEP INN MAINGATE Phone: (407)396-1600 [464]
AAA SAVE All Year 1P: $49-$89 2P: $59-$89
Location: On US 192, 2.7 mi e of jct US 27; I-4, exit 64B, 5.3 mi w. 8536 W Irlo Bronson Memorial Hwy 34747. Fax: 407/396-1971. **Facility:** Smoke free premises. 104 one-bedroom standard units. 3 stories, interior corridors. *Bath:* combo or shower only. **Parking:** on-site. **Terms:** [CP] meal plan available. **Amenities:** safes (fee), hair dryers. **Pool(s):** outdoor. **Guest Services:** coin laundry, area transportation-Disney. **Cards:** AX, CB, DC, DS, JC, MC, VI. **Special Amenities:** early check-in/late check-out and free continental breakfast. *(See color ad p 705)*
Small-scale Hotel

[icons]

(See map p. 598)

STADIUM INN & SUITES
Phone: (407)846-7814 566
AAA SAVE
All Year 1P: $60 2P: $60
Location: Florida Tpke, exit 244, 1 mi w on US 192. 2039 E Irlo Bronson Memorial Hwy 34744. Fax: 407/846-1863.
Facility: 112 one-bedroom standard units, some with efficiencies. 2 stories (no elevator), interior corridors.
Parking: on-site. **Terms:** pets ($5 extra charge). **Pool(s):** heated outdoor. **Leisure Activities:** whirlpool.
Small-scale Hotel **Guest Services:** coin laundry. **Business Services:** meeting rooms. **Cards:** AX, CB, DC, DS, MC, VI.

SOME UNITS
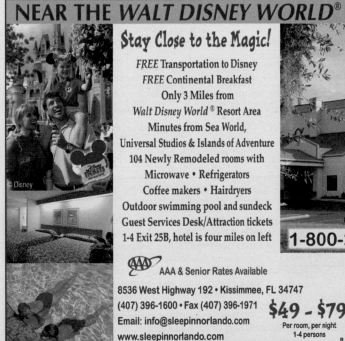

STAR ISLAND RESORT & CLUB
Phone: (407)997-8000 521
AAA SAVE
All Year 1P: $127-$285 2P: $127-$285
Location: I-4, exit 64A, 3.5 mi e on US 192, 0.5 mi s at MM 11. Gated property. 5000 Avenue of the Stars 34746.
Fax: 407/997-5252. **Facility:** Landscaped grounds complete the Mediterranean-style design of this golf,
tennis and spa resort buffered by a gated entry. 364 two-bedroom suites with kitchens and whirlpools. 3-6
Resort stories, exterior corridors. *Bath:* combo or shower only. **Parking:** on-site. **Terms:** check-in 4 pm, cancellation
Large-scale Hotel fee imposed, weekly rates available. **Amenities:** video library (fee), voice mail, safes, irons, hair dryers.
Pool(s): 2 heated outdoor. **Leisure Activities:** saunas, whirlpools, steamrooms, driving range, golf pro, 10
tennis courts (Fee: 10 lighted), recreation programs, bicycles, playground, spa, sports court. *Fee:* paddleboats, jet ski, putting
green, stadium tennis courts with instruction & equipment, game room. **Guest Services:** gift shop, valet and coin laundry.
Cards: AX, CB, DC, DS, MC, VI. **Special Amenities:** free newspaper. *(See color ad p 679)*

SUMMERFIELD CONDO RESORT
Phone: (407)847-7222 552
AAA SAVE
12/1-3/31 & 4/21-11/30 1P: $99-$149 2P: $99-$149
4/1-4/20 1P: $139 2P: $149
Location: SR 423 (John Young Pkwy), 0.8 mi n of US 192; Florida Tpke, exit 249, 2.5 mi w, 1.7 mi s. Located in a resi-
dential area. 2422 Summerfield Way 34741. Fax: 407/847-6774. **Facility:** 37 two-bedroom suites with kitchens. 2
Condominium stories (no elevator), exterior corridors. **Parking:** on-site. **Terms:** 3 night minimum stay, 15 day cancellation
notice-fee imposed, pets ($25-$100 extra charge). **Amenities:** irons, hair dryers. **Pool(s):** heated outdoor.
Leisure Activities: whirlpool, gazebo with grill, playground. **Guest Services:** complimentary laundry. **Cards:** AX, DS, MC, VI.
Special Amenities: free local telephone calls.

SOME UNITS

(See map p. 598)

SUN INN & SUITES
Phone: (407)396-2673 526

12/1-4/18	1P: $32-$65	2P: $35-$89	XP: $10
6/20-8/20	1P: $32-$55	2P: $35-$59	XP: $10
4/19-6/19 & 8/21-11/30	1P: $29-$35	2P: $34-$40	XP: $10

Motel
Location: I-4, exit 64A, 3.3 mi e on US 192. 5020 W Hwy 192 34746. Fax: 407/396-0878. **Facility:** 106 one-bedroom standard units. 2 stories (no elevator), exterior corridors. **Parking:** on-site. **Terms:** 2-3 night minimum stay, 3 day cancellation notice, [CP] meal plan available. **Amenities:** hair dryers. **Pool(s):** outdoor. **Guest Services:** coin laundry. **Cards:** AX, DC, DS, MC, VI. **Special Amenities:** free continental breakfast and free room upgrade (subject to availability with advanced reservations).

SOME UNITS

SUN SET LAKES-ABSOLUTE PREMIER VACATION HOMES
Phone: (407)396-2401 550

12/1-4/5	2P: $155-$235
6/22-8/30	2P: $155-$215
4/6-6/21 & 8/31-11/30	2P: $120-$185

Vacation Home
Location: I-4, exit 68, 2.5 mi e on SR 535 (Apopka-Vineland Rd). 3160 Vineland Rd, Suite 1 34746. Fax: 407/396-0113. **Facility:** 13 vacation homes with pools. Exterior corridors. **Parking:** on-site. **Terms:** off-site registration, check-in 4 pm, 1-4 night minimum stay, 31 day cancellation notice-fee imposed, small pets only ($150 fee, in select homes). **Amenities:** irons, hair dryers. **Guest Services:** complimentary laundry. **Business Services:** fax (fee). **Cards:** AX, DS, MC, VI.

SUPER 8 MOTEL LAKESIDE
Phone: (407)396-1144 540

12/1-1/2	1P: $39-$69	2P: $39-$69	XP: $5	F12
6/14-11/30	1P: $32-$69	2P: $32-$69	XP: $5	F12
1/3-6/13	1P: $29-$69	2P: $29-$69	XP: $5	F12

Motel
Location: I-4, exit 64A, 3.8 mi e on US 192; jct SR 535, just e. 4880 W Irlo Bronson Memorial Hwy 34746. Fax: 407/396-4389. **Facility:** 126 one-bedroom standard units, some with efficiencies. Exterior corridors. **Parking:** on-site. **Terms:** [CP] meal plan available. **Amenities:** safes (fee). **Pool(s):** outdoor. **Guest Services:** coin laundry. **Cards:** AX, CB, DC, DS, MC, VI.

SOME UNITS
FEE FEE

SUPER 8 MOTEL MAINGATE
Phone: (407)396-8883 493

3/1-4/30 [CP]	1P: $49-$69	2P: $49-$69	XP: $5	F12
5/1-8/15 [CP]	1P: $39-$59	2P: $39-$59	XP: $5	F12
12/1-2/28 [CP]	1P: $35-$59	2P: $35-$59	XP: $5	F12
8/16-11/30 [CP]	1P: $35-$55	2P: $35-$55	XP: $5	F12

Motel
Location: I-4, exit 64A (US 192), 1.5 mi e. 5875 W Irlo Bronson Hwy 34746. Fax: 407/396-8907. **Facility:** 60 one-bedroom standard units. 2 stories, exterior corridors. **Parking:** on-site. **Terms:** cancellation fee imposed, small pets only ($25 fee). **Pool(s):** outdoor. **Guest Services:** coin laundry. **Business Services:** fax (fee). **Cards:** AX, DS, JC, MC, VI. **Special Amenities:** free continental breakfast. *(See color ad below)*

SOME UNITS

SUPER 8 MOTEL MAINGATE
Phone: (407)396-7500 472

All Year [CP]	1P: $35-$55	2P: $35-$55

Location: I-4, exit 64B, 2.7 mi w on US 192. 7571 W Irlo Bronson Memorial Hwy 34747. Fax: 407/396-7497. **Facility:** 281 units. 279 one- and 2 two-bedroom standard units. 2 stories, exterior corridors. *Bath:* combo or shower only. **Parking:** on-site. **Amenities:** voice mail. *Some:* hair dryers. **Pool(s):** outdoor. **Leisure Activi-**
Motel **ties:** gazebo at garden rooms, sun deck, playground. **Guest Services:** gift shop, valet and coin laundry, area transportation-Disney. **Cards:** AX, CB, DC, DS, MC, VI. **Special Amenities:** free continental breakfast and free local telephone calls.

SOME UNITS
FEE

(See map p. 598)

SUPER 8 MOTEL SUITES Phone: (407)847-6121 **549**

AAA SAVE

12/1-1/2	1P: $39-$69	2P: $39-$69	XP: $5	F12
6/14-11/30	1P: $32-$69	2P: $32-$69	XP: $5	F12
1/3-6/13	1P: $29-$69	2P: $29-$69	XP: $5	F12

Motel

Location: I-4, exit 64A, 8 mi e on US 192, 1.3 mi w of jct US 17-92 and 441. 1815 W Vine St 34741. Fax: 407/847-0728. **Facility:** 123 units. 83 one-bedroom standard units. 40 two-bedroom suites with efficiencies. 2 stories (no elevator), exterior corridors. **Parking:** on-site. **Terms:** [CP] meal plan available. **Pool(s):** outdoor. **Cards:** AX, CB, DC, DS, MC, VI. **Special Amenities:** early check-in/late check-out and free continental breakfast.

SOME UNITS
FEE

SWEETWATER-BRIGHT STAR RESORTS & CONDOMINIUMS Phone: (407)397-1700 **458**

AAA SAVE

All Year 2P: $79-$119

Location: I-4, exit 64A, 5.7 mi e. 4533 W Irlo Bronson Memorial Hwy 34746. Fax: 407/397-1100. **Facility:** Designated smoking area. 11 units. 2 one- and 9 three-bedroom suites with kitchens. 1-2 stories, exterior corridors.

Condominium

Parking: on-site. **Terms:** check-in 4 pm, cancellation fee imposed. **Amenities:** irons. **Pool(s):** 2 heated outdoor. **Leisure Activities:** community recreation center, exercise room. **Guest Services:** complimentary laundry. **Business Services:** fax (fee). **Cards:** AX, DS, MC, VI.

(See color ad p 639, p 640, p 178, p 686 & below)

TRAVELODGE HOTEL MAINGATE Phone: (407)396-0100 **466**

AAA SAVE

All Year 1P: $45-$59 2P: $45-$59

Location: US 192, 5.5 mi w of jct I-4, 2.5 mi e of US 27. 8600 W Irlo Bronson Memorial Hwy 34747.

Motel

Fax: 407/396-6718. **Facility:** 298 one-bedroom standard units. 2 stories, exterior corridors. **Parking:** on-site. **Terms:** cancellation fee imposed, $2 service charge. **Amenities:** safes (fee), hair dryers. **Dining:** 7 am-10:30 & 7-10 pm. **Pool(s):** outdoor, wading. **Leisure Activities:** basketball. **Guest Services:** gift shop, coin laundry, area transportation-Disney. **Cards:** AX, DC, DS, MC, VI. **Special Amenities:** early check-in/late check-out and preferred room (subject to availability with advanced reservations).

SOME UNITS
FEE FEE

(See map p. 598)

TRAVELODGE HOTEL MAIN GATE EAST   Phone: (407)396-4222   503

AAA **SAVE**   All Year   1P: $39-$69   2P: $39-$69
♦♦ ♦♦   **Location:** I-4, exit 64A (US 192), 2 mi e. 5711 W Irlo Bronson Memorial Hwy 34746. Fax: 407/396-0570. **Facility:** 446
one-bedroom standard units, some with whirlpools. 8 stories, interior corridors. **Parking:** on-site.
Small-scale Hotel   **Terms:** check-in 4 pm, $3 service charge, small pets only ($50 extra charge). **Amenities:** voice mail, safes
(fee), irons, hair dryers. **Dining:** 6 am-11 pm. **Pool(s):** heated outdoor, wading. **Leisure Activities:** saunas,
whirlpool, volleyball. *Fee:* game room. **Guest Services:** gift shop, valet and coin laundry, area transportation-
Disney. **Business Services:** meeting rooms. **Cards:** AX, CB, DC, DS, MC, VI. **Special Amenities:** free continental breakfast
and free newspaper.

SOME UNITS

🚐🕭🐾🍸🏊⊗🎯 | 🖥️💻 / ⊠📱📺 /

(See map p. 598)

TRAVELODGE SUITES KISSIMMEE EAST GATE ORANGE
Phone: (407)396-7666   **520**

🔺🔺 [SAVE]
🔻🔻🔻 🔻🔻🔻

12/21-8/23 [CP]	1P: $69-$129	2P: $69-$129	XP: $5 F12
12/1-12/20 & 8/24-11/30 [CP]	1P: $49-$89	2P: $49-$89	XP: $5 F12

Location: I-4, exit 64A, 2.5 mi e on US 192; between MM 10 and 11. 5399 W Irlo Bronson Memorial Hwy 34746. Fax: 407/396-0696. **Facility:** 158 units. 156 one-bedroom standard units, some with whirlpools. 2 two-**Small-scale Hotel** bedroom suites with kitchens, some with whirlpools. 2 stories, exterior corridors. *Bath:* combo or shower only. **Parking:** on-site. **Amenities:** safes. **Pool(s):** heated outdoor, wading. **Leisure Activities:** whirlpool, playground. *Fee:* game room. **Guest Services:** coin laundry, area transportation-Disney. **Business Services:** fax (fee). **Cards:** AX, CB, DC, DS, MC, VI. **Special Amenities: free continental breakfast.** *(See ad p 647 & color ad p 708)*

TRAVELODGE SUITES MAINGATE
Phone: (407)396-1780   **538**

🔺🔺 [SAVE]
🔻🔻🔻 🔻🔻🔻
Motel

All Year [CP]	1P: $45-$99	2P: $45-$99

Location: I-4, exit 64A, 4.8 mi e on US 192, 1.3 mi e of SR 535. 4694 W Irlo Bronson Memorial Hwy 34746. Fax: 407/396-1448. **Facility:** 134 one-bedroom standard units. 2 stories (no elevator), exterior corridors. **Parking:** on-site. **Terms:** cancellation fee imposed, $2 service charge. **Amenities:** safes (fee). **Pool(s):** heated outdoor. **Guest Services:** coin laundry, area transportation-Disney. **Cards:** AX, CB, DC, MC, VI. **Special Amenities: early check-in/late check-out and free continental breakfast.** *(See color ad p 680)*

SOME UNITS

TROPICAL PALMS RESORT
Phone: (407)396-4595   **496**

🔺🔺 [SAVE]
🔻🔻🔻 🔻🔻🔻
Cabin

All Year	2P: $59-$109

Location: I-4, exit 64A, 1.2 mi e on US 192, 0.5 mi s at MM 9. 2650 Holiday Tr 34746. Fax: 407/396-8938. **Facility:** 144 units. 40 one-bedroom standard units with efficiencies. 10 one- and 94 two-bedroom suites, some with efficiencies or kitchens. 1 story, exterior corridors. **Parking:** on-site. **Terms:** check-in 4 pm, 3 night minimum stay - seasonal, weekends, 7 day cancellation notice. **Pool(s):** heated outdoor, wading. **Leisure Activities:** fishing, playground, basketball, horseshoes, shuffleboard, volleyball. **Guest Services:** gift shop, coin laundry, area transportation (fee)-Disney. **Cards:** AX, DS, MC, VI. *(See color ad starting on p 710)*

THE VILLAGES AT MANGO KEY
Phone: (407)397-2211   **469**

🔻🔻🔻🔻
Condominium

All Year	2P: $125-$175

Location: I-4, exit 64B, 5.9 mi w on US 192, then just s, 2 mi e of US 27; 4.5 mi w of Disney World main gate access road. Quiet location. 3201 Lindfields Blvd 34747. Fax: 407/397-2789. **Facility:** 33 units. 28 two- and 5 three-bedroom suites with kitchens. 2 stories, exterior corridors. **Parking:** on-site. **Terms:** check-in 4 pm, 3 night minimum stay. **Amenities:** irons, hair dryers. *Fee:* video library, safes. *Some:* CD players. **Pool(s):** heated outdoor. **Leisure Activities:** whirlpool, playground. **Guest Services:** complimentary laundry. **Cards:** AX, DS, MC, VI.

WESTGATE TOWERS/WESTGATE VACATION VILLAS
Phone: (407)355-1105   **474**

🔺🔺 [SAVE]
🔻🔻🔻 🔻🔻🔻
Condominium

5/25-9/9	1P: $158-$302	2P: $158-$302
12/1-5/24 & 9/10-11/30	1P: $110-$238	2P: $110-$238

Location: I-4, exit 64B, 2.5 mi w on SR 192, at jct SR 545; 1 mi w of Disney World main gate. 7600 W Irlo Bronson Memorial Hwy 34747 (2601 Professional Pkwy, OCOEE, 34761). Fax: 407/355-2980. **Facility:** 1000 units. 118 one- and 882 two-bedroom suites ($110-$366) with kitchens, some with whirlpools. 3-5 stories, interior corridors. **Parking:** on-site. **Terms:** check-in 4 pm, 14 day cancellation notice-fee imposed. **Amenities:** video library (fee), voice mail, safes, irons, hair dryers. **Dining:** 2 restaurants, 7 am-11 pm. **Pool(s):** 16 heated outdoor, 16 wading. **Leisure Activities:** whirlpool, paddleboats, 4 lighted tennis courts, recreation programs, bicycles, exercise room, basketball, horseshoes, shuffleboard, volleyball. *Fee:* snowmobiling, game room. **Guest Services:** gift shop, complimentary laundry, area transportation (fee)-Major Attractions. **Cards:** AX, DC, DS, MC, VI.

FEE

WONDERLAND INN
Phone: (407)847-2477   **519**

🔻🔻🔻🔻
Bed & Breakfast

12/1-4/30 & 9/16-11/30 [ECP]	1P: $69-$159	2P: $69-$159
5/1-9/15 [ECP]	1P: $49-$139	2P: $49-$139

Location: US 192, 3 mi s on US 17-92 (John Young Pkwy/Bermuda Ave). 3601 S Orange Blossom Tr 34741. Fax: 407/847-4099. **Facility:** Within driving distance of local attractions, this inn is close to shopping yet set apart from the bustling tourist corridor. Designated smoking area. 11 one-bedroom standard units, some with efficiencies and/or whirlpools. 1 story, exterior corridors. *Bath:* combo or shower only. **Parking:** on-site. **Terms:** cancellation fee imposed, package plans. **Amenities:** voice mail, hair dryers. **Leisure Activities:** *Fee:* massage. **Guest Services:** complimentary evening beverages. **Cards:** AX, DC, DS, MC, VI.

SOME UNITS

WYNDHAM PALMS-ABSOLUTE PREMIER VACATION HOMES
Phone: (407)396-2401   **461**

🔻🔻🔻🔻
Vacation Home

12/1-4/5	2P: $155-$235
6/22-8/30	2P: $155-$215
4/6-6/21 & 8/31-11/30	2P: $120-$185

Location: I-4, exit 68, 2.5 mi e on SR 535 (Apopka-Vineland Rd). 3160 Vineland Rd, Suite 1 34746. Fax: 407/396-0113. **Facility:** 8 vacation homes with pools. Exterior corridors. **Parking:** on-site. **Terms:** off-site registration, check-in 4 pm, 1-4 night minimum stay, 31 day cancellation notice-fee imposed, small pets only ($150 fee, in select homes). **Amenities:** irons, hair dryers. **Guest Services:** complimentary laundry. **Business Services:** fax (fee). **Cards:** AX, DS, MC, VI.

Tropical Palms FunResort

BORDERING WALT DISNEY WORLD® Resort

2 Bedroom & Studio Models

- Sleep up to 4 adults and 4 children
- Fully equipped kitchen with range, refrigerator, microwave, dishwasher
- Living room and dining area
- TV and A/C
- Sleeping loft for kids
- Deck with picnic table and chairs

CLOSET | TV | CLO-SET | DOUBLE
SLEEPING LOFT ABOVE
LIVING ROOM
QUEEN | KITCHEN | BATH
SOFA BED

2 Bedroom Model

The octopus water slide at the Marine Activity Pool

*D*iscover
All of Florida in One Extraordinary Place.

The New Gaylord Palms™ Resort in Kissimmee-St. Cloud, Florida

You can discover all you love about Florida at the new Gaylord Palms.™
From the historic, old-world charm of St. Augustine and the festive island
spirit of Key West to the mysteries of the Everglades, everything you want
is right here. Including the total indulgence of our Canyon Ranch SpaClub℠
at Gaylord Palms™ and unique shopping in exclusive boutiques. Award-
winning golf and La Petite Academy® Kids Station℠. And tantalizing regional
dining in a variety of signature restaurants. Just five minutes away from
WALT DISNEY WORLD® Resort.

For special AAA rates, call 407-586-2000.

GAYLORD PALMS™
RESORT & CONVENTION CENTER
Florida

Created With You In Mind

For reservations or more information,
visit us at **www.gaylordhotels.com**
or call **407-586-2000**.

6000 W. Osceola Parkway, Kissimmee, FL 34746

(See map p. 598)

WYNDHAM PALMS-REGENT VACATIONS & MANAGEMENT   Phone: (407)397-9868   462

12/1-2/28	1P: $79-$289	2P: $79-$289
3/1-6/13 & 10/1-11/30	1P: $79-$259	2P: $79-$259
6/14-9/30	1P: $79-$249	2P: $79-$249

Vacation Home   **Location:** I-4, exit 64B, 3.1 mi w on US 192. 7801 W Irlo Bronson Hwy 34747. Fax: 407/397-7881. **Facility:** 10 units. 2 three-bedroom suites with kitchens. 8 vacation homes. 1 story, exterior corridors. **Parking:** on-site. **Terms:** off-site registration, check-in 4 pm, 60 day cancellation notice-fee imposed. **Amenities:** irons, hair dryers. **Guest Services:** complimentary laundry. **Business Services:** fax (fee). **Cards:** AX, DS, MC, VI.

WYNDHAM PALMS RESORT   Phone: (407)396-1311   477

12/1-4/5 & 5/25-11/30	1P: $225-$275	2P: $319-$409
4/6-5/24	1P: $158-$193	2P: $224-$287

Condominium   **Location:** I-4, exit 64B, 2.4 mi w on US 192, then 1.2 mi s on Old Lake Wilson Rd. Rural area. 7900 Palms Pkwy 34747. Fax: 407/390-1765. **Facility:** 360 units. 194 one- and 166 two-bedroom suites with whirlpools, some with efficiencies or kitchens. 3-4 stories, exterior corridors. **Parking:** on-site. **Terms:** check-in 4 pm, cancellation fee imposed. **Amenities:** video library (fee), voice mail, safes, irons. **Pool(s):** 3 heated outdoor, 2 wading. **Leisure Activities:** miniature golf, 2 lighted tennis courts, recreation programs, bicycles, playground, basketball. *Fee:* golf-18 holes, game room. **Guest Services:** gift shop, complimentary laundry, area transportation (fee). **Cards:** AX, DC, DS, MC, VI. *(See color ad below)*

---

*The following lodgings were either not evaluated or did not
meet AAA rating requirements but are listed for your information only.*

GAYLORD PALMS RESORT   Phone: 407/586-0000

[fyi]   All Year   1P: $239-$279   2P: $239-$279   XP: $20   F17
Too new to rate. **Location:** SR 417, exit 3 (Osceola Pkwy); I-4 to exit 65 (Osceola Pkwy), just e. 3200 International Dr
Large-scale Hotel   34746. Fax: 407/586-0199. **Amenities:** 1406 units, restaurant, coffeemakers, refrigerators, pool, golf.
Terms: 3 day cancellation notice-fee imposed. $10 service charge. **Cards:** AX, CB, DC, DS, JC, MC, VI.
(See color ad p 712)

LA QUINTA INN & SUITES ORLANDO MAINGATE AT CALYPSO CAY   Phone: 407/997-1700

[fyi]   Under construction, scheduled to open April 2003. **Location:** I-4, exit 68, s on SR 535, just e. 3484 Polynesian Isle
Motel   Blvd 34746. Fax: 407/997-1700. **Planned Amenities:** pets, coffeemakers, microwaves, refrigerators, pool.

WHERE TO DINE

GIORDANO'S   Lunch: $6-$8   Dinner: $7-$11   Phone: 407/397-0044   243

Location: I-4, exit 64, 3.5 mi w on US 192; in Formosa Garden Shopping Center. 7866 W Irlo Bronson Hwy 34747.
Italian   **Hours:** 11 am-midnight. **Features:** Chicago-style stuffed pizza is the specialty of the house with home delivery an option. A friendly, casual atmosphere with traditional Italian dishes is offered here. Feast on the pizza, but don't skip dessert at this family-oriented restaurant. Casual dress; cocktails. **Parking:** on-site.
Cards: AX, CB, DC, MC, VI.

(See map p. 598)

KEY W. KOOL'S OPEN PIT GRILL   **Lunch:** $8-$28   **Dinner:** $8-$28   **Phone:** 407/396-1166   (242)
Steak House

Location: I-4, exit 64, 2.8 mi w on US 192. 7725 W US 192 34746. **Hours:** 4 pm-11 pm. **Reservations:** suggested; after 8 pm. **Features:** After waiting in hot lines at the attractions, cool off in this casual, comfortable eatery that specializes in steak and seafood. Start with a fresh salad, then choose from a host of grilled items. The dessert tray tempts with a variety of confections. Casual dress; cocktails. **Parking:** on-site. **Cards:** AX, DC, DS, MC, VI.

PACINO'S ITALIAN RISTORANTE   **Dinner:** $10-$23   **Phone:** 407/396-8022   (247)
Italian

Location: I-4, exit 64A, 1.7 mi e on US 192; just e of MM 9. 5795 W Hwy 192 34746. **Hours:** 5-11 pm. **Reservations:** accepted. **Features:** Owned and operated by an Italian family, the red-brick trattoria features hard-cut steaks, individual pizzas and southern Italian selections prepared with homemade pasta. Casual dress; cocktails. **Parking:** on-site. **Cards:** AX, DC, DS, MC, VI.

TWIN DRAGONS RESTAURANT   **Lunch:** $6-$17   **Dinner:** $6-$17   **Phone:** 407/846-6161   (245)
Regional Chinese

Location: US 192, 2.5 mi w of jct US 17-92 and 441, e of MM 15. 4002 W Vine St 34741. **Hours:** 11 am-11 pm, Sat & Sun from noon. Closed: 11/27. **Reservations:** suggested. **Features:** Traditional Cantonese and Szechwan dishes make up the menu at the family-oriented restaurant. A weekday lunch buffet is popular. The Asian feel begins at the entrance, where a footbridge crosses a goldfish pond, and carries on throughout the dining area. Casual dress; cocktails. **Parking:** on-site. **Cards:** AX, DC, DS, MC, VI.

LADY LAKE pop. 11,828

———— **WHERE TO STAY** ————

SHAMROCK THISTLE & CROWN   **Phone:** (352)821-1887

	1P	2P	XP
10/4-11/30 [BP]	1P: $80-$180	2P: $90-$199	XP: $15
1/1-4/28 [BP]	1P: $80-$180	2P: $90-$195	XP: $15
12/1-12/31 [BP]	1P: $75-$180	2P: $85-$195	XP: $15
4/29-10/3 [BP]	1P: $75-$170	2P: $85-$185	XP: $15

Bed & Breakfast

Location: From US 27/441, 2.8 mi e. 12971 SE CR 42 32195 (PO Box 624, WEIRSDALE). Fax: 352/821-1886. **Facility:** Some rooms with fireplace. Home built in 1887. Smoke free premises. 7 units. 6 one-bedroom standard units, some with whirlpools. 1 cottage ($139-$195) with whirlpool. 3 stories, interior corridors. *Bath:* combo or shower only. **Parking:** on-site. **Terms:** 2 night minimum stay - weekends 10/1-4/30, age restrictions may apply, 7 day cancellation notice-fee imposed. **Amenities:** irons, hair dryers. *Some:* CD players. **Business Services:** fax (fee). **Cards:** AX, DS, MC, VI.

SOME UNITS

LAKE BUENA VISTA pop. 16   (See map p. 598; index p. 605)

———— **WHERE TO STAY** ————

BEST WESTERN LAKE BUENA VISTA RESORT HOTEL IN THE WALT DISNEY WORLD RESORTS   **Phone:** (407)828-2424   (392)
Small-scale Hotel

All Year   1P: $109   2P: $169

Location: I-4, exit 68. 2000 Hotel Plaza Blvd 32830 (PO Box 22205). Fax: 407/828-8933. **Facility:** 325 units. 321 one-bedroom standard units. 4 one-bedroom suites ($299-$399) with whirlpools. 18 stories, interior corridors. **Parking:** on-site. **Terms:** [BP] meal plan available. **Amenities:** video games (fee), voice mail, safes, irons, hair dryers. **Dining:** 2 restaurants, 7 am-11 pm, cocktails. **Pool(s):** heated outdoor, wading. **Leisure Activities:** golf & tennis privileges, playground. *Fee:* game room. **Guest Services:** gift shop, valet and coin laundry, area transportation-Disney. **Business Services:** meeting rooms, fax (fee). **Cards:** AX, CB, DC, DS, JC, MC, VI. **Special Amenities:** free newspaper.

SOME UNITS

BRYAN'S SPANISH COVE   **Phone:** (407)239-4222   (406)
Condominium

All Year   1P: $149-$219   2P: $149-$219

Location: I-4, exit 68, 1 mi s on SR 535. 13875 SR 535 32821. Fax: 407/239-1886. **Facility:** 44 two-bedroom suites ($149-$219) with kitchens and whirlpools. 2 stories, exterior corridors. **Parking:** on-site. **Terms:** check-in 4 pm, 15 day cancellation notice-fee imposed. **Amenities:** video library (fee), voice mail, safes, irons, hair dryers. **Pool(s):** small heated outdoor. **Leisure Activities:** whirlpool, boating, canoeing, paddleboats, boat dock, fishing, playground. *Fee:* waterskiing, water ski instruction, innertube rides, jet skis. **Guest Services:** complimentary laundry. **Special Amenities:** free local telephone calls and preferred room (subject to availability with advanced reservations).** *(See color ad p 694)*

BUENA VISTA SUITES   **Phone:** (407)239-8588   (404)
Small-scale Hotel

12/20-1/4 [BP]	1P: $159-$179	2P: $159-$179
1/5-7/31 [BP]	1P: $119-$159	2P: $119-$159
12/1-12/19 & 8/1-11/30 [BP]	1P: $109-$129	2P: $109-$129

Location: I-4, exit 67, 1.3 mi e; at jct SR 535 and 536. 8203 World Center Dr 32821. Fax: 407/239-1401. **Facility:** 280 one-bedroom suites, some with whirlpools. 7 stories, interior corridors. *Bath:* combo or shower only. **Parking:** on-site. **Terms:** cancellation fee imposed, package plans. **Amenities:** video games, voice mail, safes (fee), irons, hair dryers. **Pool(s):** heated outdoor. **Leisure Activities:** whirlpool, 2 lighted tennis courts, exercise room. *Fee:* game room. **Guest Services:** gift shop, valet and coin laundry, area transportation-Disney attractions. **Business Services:** meeting rooms, fax (fee). **Cards:** AX, CB, DC, DS, JC, MC, VI. **Special Amenities:** free continental breakfast and free newspaper. *(See color ad p 715)*

SOME UNITS

FEE

(See map p. 598)

CARIBE ROYALE RESORT SUITES & VILLAS   Phone: (407)238-8000   401

 SAVE

12/1-1/4   1P: $119-$229
1/5-5/21 & 10/1-11/30   1P: $149-$209
5/22-9/30   1P: $119-$169

Location: I-4, exit 68, 1.2 mi s on SR 535, 0.3 mi e. 8101 World Center Dr 32830. Fax: 407/238-8050. **Facility:** 1338 units. 1218 one- and 120 two-bedroom suites ($229-$329), some with kitchens. 4-10 stories, interior/exterior corridors. *Bath:* combo or shower only. **Parking:** on-site. **Terms:** 3 day cancellation notice-fee imposed. **Amenities:** video games, voice mail, irons, hair dryers. *Fee:* video library, safes. *Some:* CD players, high-speed Internet, honor bars. **Dining:** 2 restaurants, 6 am-midnight, cocktails. **Pool(s):** 2 heated outdoor, wading. **Leisure Activities:** whirlpools, waterslide, 2 lighted tennis courts, playground, exercise room, weight training room. *Fee:* game room. **Guest Services:** gift shop, valet and coin laundry, area transportation. **Business Services:** conference facilities, business center. **Cards:** AX, DC, DS, JC, MC, VI. **Special Amenities:** free newspaper.

Large-scale Hotel

SOME UNITS

🚐 🍴 24 📺 🔲 🅼 🛗 ⊘ 🏊 ✕ 📷 DATA PORT 🖥 🖨 / ✕ VCR 🔋 /

COMFORT INN LAKE BUENA VISTA   Phone: (407)996-7300   374

SAVE

All Year   1P: $39-$99

Location: I-4, exit 68, 0.6 mi n on SR 535, 0.5 mi e. 8442 Palm Pkwy 32836. Fax: 407/996-7301. **Facility:** 640 one-bedroom standard units. 5 stories, exterior corridors. *Bath:* combo or shower only. **Parking:** on-site. **Terms:** $3 service charge, small pets only ($6 fee). **Amenities:** voice mail, safes. *Some:* irons, hair dryers. **Pool(s):** 2 heated outdoor. **Leisure Activities:** playground. *Fee:* game room. **Guest Services:** gift shop, valet and coin laundry, area transportation. **Cards:** AX, CB, DC, DS, MC, VI. *(See color ad p 655)*

Small-scale Hotel

SOME UNITS

🚐 🐾 🍴 📺 🅼 🛗 ⊘ 🏊 📷 🔋 🖥 🖨 / ✕ VCR /

(See map p. 598)

COUNTRY INN & SUITES BY CARLSON   **Phone:** (407)239-1115   391

Small-scale Hotel

	2/10-4/27 & 6/16-11/30 [ECP]	1P: $99-$139	2P: $109-$149
	4/28-6/15 [ECP]	1P: $79-$129	2P: $89-$139
	12/1-2/9 [ECP]	1P: $79-$119	2P: $89-$129

Location: I-4, exit 68, 0.6 mi n. 12191 S Apopka-Vineland Rd 32836. Fax: 407/239-8882. **Facility:** 170 units. 160 one-bedroom standard units, some with whirlpools. 10 one-bedroom suites ($109-$149). 5 stories, interior corridors. *Bath:* combo or shower only. **Parking:** on-site. **Amenities:** video library, high-speed Internet, voice mail, irons, hair dryers. *Some:* video games. **Pool(s):** heated outdoor. **Leisure Activities:** exercise room. *Fee:* game room. **Guest Services:** gift shop, valet and coin laundry, area transportation. **Business Services:** meeting rooms. **Cards:** AX, CB, DC, DS, MC, VI.
(See color ad p 613, below, p 715, p 681 & p 629)

SOME UNITS

[ASK] [S/D] [I↑] [&M] [icon] [icon] [icon] [icon] [DATA PORT] [icon] [icon] [icon] / [⊠] [VCR] /

COURTYARD BY MARRIOTT AT MARRIOTT VILLAGE   **Phone:** (407)938-9001   396

[AAA] [SAVE]

Large-scale Hotel

All Year   1P: $79-$129

Location: I-4, exit 68, just e on 535 to Vineland Ave, then n. 8623 Vineland Ave 32821. Fax: 407/938-9002. **Facility:** 312 one-bedroom standard units, some with whirlpools. 5 stories, interior corridors. *Bath:* combo or shower only. **Parking:** on-site. **Terms:** [AP] & [BP] meal plans available, package plans - seasonal, weekends. **Amenities:** video games, dual phone lines, voice mail, irons, hair dryers. **Dining:** 6 am-11 pm. **Pool(s):** outdoor, heated indoor, heated indoor/outdoor. **Leisure Activities:** whirlpools, exercise room. **Guest Services:** gift shop, valet and coin laundry, area transportation-major attractions. **Business Services:** conference facilities, business center. **Cards:** AX, DC, DS, MC, VI. **Special Amenities:** early check-in/late check-out and free newspaper.
(See color ad p 717 & ad p 633)

SOME UNITS

[S/D] [I↑] [Y] [icon] [icon] [DATA PORT] [icon] [icon] / [⊠] [icon] /

COURTYARD BY MARRIOTT-IN THE WALT DISNEY WORLD RESORT   **Phone:** (407)828-8888   388

[AAA] [SAVE]

Large-scale Hotel

	12/1-4/27	1P: $139-$159	2P: $139-$159
	4/28-8/15 & 10/1-11/30	1P: $109-$139	2P: $109-$139
	8/16-9/30	1P: $99-$119	2P: $99-$119

Location: I-4, exit 68, just n. 1805 Hotel Plaza Blvd 32830 (PO Box 22204). Fax: 407/827-4623. **Facility:** 323 one-bedroom standard units. 6-14 stories, interior corridors. *Bath:* combo or shower only. **Parking:** on-site. **Terms:** check-in 4 pm, 3 day cancellation notice-fee imposed. **Amenities:** video games, high-speed Internet (fee), voice mail, safes, irons, hair dryers. **Dining:** 2 restaurants, 6:30 am-midnight, cocktails. **Pool(s):** 2 heated outdoor, wading. **Leisure Activities:** whirlpool, playground, exercise room. *Fee:* game room. **Guest Services:** gift shop, valet and coin laundry, area transportation-major attractions. **Business Services:** meeting rooms. **Cards:** AX, DC, DS, MC, VI. **Special Amenities:** free newspaper. *(See color ad p 717)*

SOME UNITS

[S/D] [+] [I↑] [Y] [&M] [icon] [icon] [icon] [⊠] [icon] [DATA PORT] [icon] / [⊠] [icon] /
FEE   FEE

(See map p. 598)

COURTYARD BY MARRIOTT LAKE BUENA VISTA

@ VISTA CENTRE   Phone: (407)239-6900   368

AAA SAVE   All Year   1P: $79-$129
WWWW   **Location:** I-4, exit 68, 0.6 mi n on SR 535, 0.3 mi e. 8501 Palm Pkwy 32830 (PO Box 22527). Fax: 407/239-1287.
Facility: 308 units. 222 one-bedroom standard units. 86 one-bedroom suites ($99-$149). 3 stories, interior/exterior corridors. *Bath:* combo or shower only. **Parking:** on-site. **Terms:** check-in 4 pm, cancellation
Small-scale Hotel   fee imposed. **Amenities:** dual phone lines, voice mail, safes, irons, hair dryers. **Dining:** 6:30-11 am. **Pool(s):** 2 heated outdoor, wading. **Leisure Activities:** whirlpool, playground, exercise room, shuffleboard. *Fee:* game room. **Guest Services:** gift shop, valet and coin laundry, area transportation-Disney. **Business Services:** meeting rooms, business center. **Cards:** AX, DC, DS, MC, VI. *(See color ad below)*

SOME UNITS

(See map p. 598)

DAYS INN LAKE BUENA VISTA HOTEL
Phone: (407)239-4441 371

(AAA) [SAVE]
▼▼ ▼▼

12/1-12/31	1P: $85-$168	2P: $85-$178
2/7-4/30	1P: $85-$132	2P: $85-$142
1/1-2/6 & 5/1-11/30	1P: $65-$118	2P: $65-$128

Small-scale Hotel
Location: I-4, exit 68, just n. 12799 Apopka-Vineland Rd 32836. Fax: 407/239-0325. **Facility:** 203 one-bedroom standard units. 8 stories, interior corridors. *Bath:* combo or shower only. **Parking:** on-site. **Amenities:** video library, voice mail, hair dryers. **Pool(s):** outdoor. **Leisure Activities:** playground. *Fee:* game room. **Guest Services:** gift shop, valet and coin laundry, area transportation-Disney. **Cards:** AX, CB, DC, DS, JC, MC, VI. **Special Amenities:** free newspaper and free room upgrade (subject to availability with advanced reservations). *(See color ad p 718)*

SOME UNITS
[S⚡] [♿] [📞] [🏊] [🎥] / [✕] [VCR] [🅱] /

DISNEY'S ALL STAR MOVIES RESORT
Phone: (407)939-7000 416

(AAA)
▼▼▼ ▼▼

12/1-12/31	1P: $77-$124	2P: $77-$124	XP: $10	F17
2/13-8/23	1P: $99-$119	2P: $99-$119	XP: $10	F17
8/24-11/30	1P: $77-$109	2P: $77-$109	XP: $10	F17
1/1-2/12	1P: $77-$87	2P: $77-$87	XP: $10	F17

Resort
Large-scale Hotel
Location: I-4, exit 64B, 1.3 mi w on US 192, 1 mi n on World Dr; just w of Disney World main gate access road. 1991 W Buena Vista Dr 32830-1000 (PO Box 10,000). Fax: 407/939-7111. **Facility:** From talking toys to spotted dogs, themes in each of this resort's buildings are based on Disney movies. Designated smoking area. 1920 one-bedroom standard units. 3 stories, exterior corridors. *Bath:* some combo or shower only. **Parking:** on-site. **Terms:** check-in 4 pm, 5 day cancellation notice-fee imposed. **Amenities:** voice mail, safes. **Dining:** 6:30 am-midnight. **Pool(s):** 2 heated outdoor, wading. **Leisure Activities:** playground. *Fee:* game room. **Guest Services:** gift shop, coin laundry, area transportation-within Disney complex. **Business Services:** fax (fee). **Cards:** AX, DC, DS, JC, MC, VI. *(See color ad starting on p 721)*

SOME UNITS
[✈]FEE [🍴] [🍸] [🛗] [⚒M] [♿] [📞] [🏊] [DATA PORT] [🅱]FEE / [✕] /

DISNEY'S ALL STAR MUSIC
Phone: (407)939-6000 414

(AAA)
▼▼▼ ▼▼

12/1-12/31	1P: $77-$124	2P: $77-$124	XP: $10	F17
2/13-8/23	1P: $99-$119	2P: $99-$119	XP: $10	F17
8/24-11/30	1P: $77-$109	2P: $77-$109	XP: $10	F17
1/1-2/12	1P: $77-$87	2P: $77-$87	XP: $10	F17

Resort
Large-scale Hotel
Location: Just w of Disney World main gate access road (World Dr); 1 mi n of US 192. 1801 W Buena Vista Dr 32830-1000 (PO Box 10,000). Fax: 407/939-7222. **Facility:** Music is the theme and images of standout performers are everywhere at this property dedicated to lyrics and legends. 1920 one-bedroom standard units. 3 stories, exterior corridors. *Bath:* combo or shower only. **Parking:** on-site. **Terms:** 5 day cancellation notice-fee imposed. **Amenities:** voice mail, safes. **Dining:** 6:30 am-midnight. **Pool(s):** 2 heated outdoor, wading. **Leisure Activities:** playground. *Fee:* game room. **Guest Services:** gift shop, valet and coin laundry, area transportation-within Disney complex. **Business Services:** fax. **Cards:** AX, DC, DS, JC, MC, VI. *(See color ad starting on p 721)*

SOME UNITS
[✈]FEE [🍴] [🍸] [🛗] [♿] [⚒M] [📞] [🏊] [DATA PORT] / [✕] [🅱] /

DISNEY'S ALL STAR SPORTS
Phone: (407)939-5000 412

(AAA)
▼▼ ▼▼

12/1-12/31	1P: $77-$124	2P: $77-$124	XP: $10	F17
2/13-8/23	1P: $99-$119	2P: $99-$119	XP: $10	F17
8/24-11/30	1P: $77-$109	2P: $77-$109	XP: $10	F17
1/1-2/12	1P: $77-$87	2P: $77-$87	XP: $10	F17

Resort
Large-scale Hotel
Location: Just w of Disney World main gate access road (World Dr); 1 mi n of US 192. 1701 W Buena Vista Dr 32830-1000 (PO Box 10,000). Fax: 407/939-7333. **Facility:** Larger-than-life sports icons decorate stairways, vending areas and courtyards at this athletics-themed property. 1920 one-bedroom standard units. 3 stories, exterior corridors. *Bath:* combo or shower only. **Parking:** on-site. **Terms:** 5 day cancellation notice-fee imposed. **Amenities:** voice mail, safes. **Dining:** 6:30 am-midnight. **Pool(s):** 2 heated outdoor, wading. **Leisure Activities:** playground. *Fee:* game room. **Guest Services:** gift shop, valet and coin laundry, area transportation-within Disney complex. **Cards:** AX, DC, DS, JC, MC, VI. *(See color ad starting on p 721)*

SOME UNITS
[✈]FEE [🍴] [🍸] [🛗] [⚒M] [♿] [📞] [🏊] [DATA PORT] / [✕] [🅱] /FEE

DISNEY'S ANIMAL KINGDOM LODGE
Phone: (407)938-3000 417

(AAA)
▼▼▼ ▼▼

12/1-12/31	1P: $204-$595	2P: $204-$595	XP: $25	F17
2/13-7/3	1P: $239-$545	2P: $239-$545	XP: $25	F17
7/4-11/30	1P: $199-$480	2P: $199-$480	XP: $25	F17
1/1-2/12	1P: $199-$425	2P: $199-$425	XP: $25	F17

Resort
Large-scale Hotel
Location: N of US 192 on World Dr, follow signs. 2901 Osceola Pkwy 32830. Fax: 407/938-4799. **Facility:** 1293 units. 1274 one-bedroom standard units. 5 one- and 14 two-bedroom suites ($620-$2455), some with whirlpools. 5 stories, interior corridors. *Bath:* combo or shower only. **Parking:** on-site and valet. **Terms:** 5 day cancellation notice-fee imposed. **Amenities:** voice mail, safes, irons, hair dryers. *Some:* DVD players, CD players, dual phone lines. **Dining:** 3 restaurants, 6 am-midnight, cocktails, also, Jiko, see separate listing. **Pool(s):** heated outdoor, wading. **Leisure Activities:** saunas, whirlpools, steamrooms, waterslide, playground. *Fee:* exercise room, massage, game room. **Guest Services:** gift shop, valet and coin laundry, area transportation-within Disney complex. **Cards:** AX, DC, DS, JC, MC, VI. *(See color ad starting on p 721)*

SOME UNITS
[✈]FEE [🍴] [🍸] [🛗] [⚒M] [♿] [📞] [🏊] [✕] [DATA PORT] / [✕] [🅱] [🖥] [💻] /

(See map p. 598)

DISNEY'S BOARDWALK RESORT
Phone: (407)939-5100 385

12/1-12/31	1P: $289-$990	2P: $289-$990	XP: $25	F17
2/13-7/3	1P: $329-$890	2P: $329-$890	XP: $25	F17
7/4-11/30	1P: $289-$705	2P: $289-$705	XP: $25	F17
1/1-2/12	1P: $289-$545	2P: $289-$545	XP: $25	F17

Resort
Large-scale Hotel
Location: 0.5 mi e of Disney World main gate access road, 2 mi n of US 192. 2101 N Epcot Resorts Blvd 32830 (PO Box 10,000). Fax: 407/939-5150. **Facility:** Inn or villa units are available at this resort where the fixtures, furniture and finishes reflect the styles of the 1920s and '30s. 893 units. 373 one-bedroom standard units. 513 one- and 7 three-bedroom suites ($1065-$2275), some with kitchens and/or whirlpools. 2-5 stories, interior/exterior corridors. *Bath:* combo or shower only. **Parking:** on-site and valet. **Terms:** 5 day cancellation notice-fee imposed. **Amenities:** voice mail, safes, irons, hair dryers. *Some:* dual phone lines. **Dining:** 4 restaurants, 7 am-midnight, cocktails, also, Flying Fish Cafe, Spoodles, see separate listing. **Pool(s):** 3 heated outdoor, wading. **Leisure Activities:** sauna, whirlpools, 2 lighted tennis courts, jogging, playground. *Fee:* bicycles, massage, game room. **Guest Services:** gift shop, coin laundry, airport transportation (fee)-Orlando International Airport, area transportation-within Disney complex. **Business Services:** conference facilities, business center. **Cards:** AX, DC, DS, JC, MC, VI. *(See color ad starting on p 721)*
SOME UNITS

DISNEY'S CARIBBEAN BEACH RESORT
Phone: (407)934-3400 386

12/1-12/31	1P: $133-$219	2P: $133-$219	XP: $15	F17
2/13-8/23	1P: $144-$194	2P: $144-$194	XP: $15	F17
8/24-11/30	1P: $133-$159	2P: $133-$159	XP: $15	F17
1/1-2/12	1P: $133-$148	2P: $133-$148	XP: $15	F17

Resort
Large-scale Hotel
Location: I-4, exit 67, 1.5 mi e of Disney World main gate access road, 2 mi n of US 192; off Buena Vista Dr, 1 mi w of Typhoon Lagoon. 900 Cayman Way 32830 (PO Box 10,000). Fax: 407/934-3288. **Facility:** The resort's five complexes are each named after a Caribbean island. Designated smoking area. 2112 one-bedroom standard units. 2 stories, exterior corridors. *Bath:* combo or shower only. **Parking:** on-site. **Terms:** 5 day cancellation notice-fee imposed. **Amenities:** voice mail, safes. **Dining:** 6 am-midnight, cocktails. **Pool(s):** 7 heated outdoor, wading. **Leisure Activities:** whirlpool, boating, rental paddleboats, rental sailboats, marina, children's recreation island, jogging, playground. *Fee:* waterskiing, pontoon boats, water mice, bicycles, game room. **Guest Services:** gift shop, valet and coin laundry, area transportation-within Disney complex. **Cards:** AX, DC, DS, JC, MC, VI. *(See color ad starting on p 721)*
SOME UNITS

DISNEY'S CONTEMPORARY RESORT
Phone: (407)824-1000 349

12/1-12/31	1P: $234-$525	2P: $234-$525	XP: $25	F17
2/13-7/3	1P: $264-$505	2P: $264-$505	XP: $25	F17
7/4-11/30	1P: $239-$435	2P: $239-$435	XP: $25	F17
1/1-2/12	1P: $239-$395	2P: $239-$395	XP: $25	F17

Resort
Large-scale Hotel
Location: I-4, exit 26B, follow signs to Disney's Magic Kingdom. Located in Disney World. 4600 N World Dr 32830 (PO Box 10,000). Fax: 407/824-3539. **Facility:** A soaring structure, the resort features a monorail line traversing the building; public areas and guest rooms have contemporary decor. Designated smoking area. 1008 units. 997 one-bedroom standard units. 6 one- and 5 two-bedroom suites ($755-$2335). 3-15 stories, interior corridors. *Bath:* combo or shower only. **Parking:** on-site and valet. **Terms:** 5 day cancellation notice-fee imposed, no pets allowed (kennel available). **Amenities:** voice mail, safes, irons, hair dryers. *Some:* CD players, fax. **Dining:** 5 restaurants, 7 am-midnight, cocktails, also, California Grill, see separate listing. **Pool(s):** 2 heated outdoor. **Leisure Activities:** sauna, whirlpools, waterslide, rental boats, rental sailboats, recreation programs, jogging, playground, basketball, volleyball. *Fee:* waterskiing, parasailing, water mice, golf-99 holes, 6 lighted tennis courts, tennis instruction, tanning facility, massage, game room. **Guest Services:** gift shop, valet and coin laundry, area transportation-within Disney complex. *Fee:* beauty salon. **Business Services:** conference facilities, business center. **Cards:** AX, DC, DS, JC, MC, VI. *(See color ad starting on p 721)*
SOME UNITS

DISNEY'S CORONADO SPRINGS RESORT
Phone: (407)939-1000 382

12/1-12/31	1P: $133-$219	2P: $133-$219	XP: $15	F17
2/13-8/23	1P: $144-$194	2P: $144-$194	XP: $15	F17
8/24-11/30	1P: $133-$159	2P: $133-$159	XP: $15	F17
1/1-2/12	1P: $133-$148	2P: $133-$148	XP: $15	F17

Resort
Large-scale Hotel
Location: I-4, exit 67, just nw, follow signs to Disney's Animal Kingdom Park. 1000 W Buena Vista Blvd 32830 (PO Box 10,000). Fax: 407/939-1001. **Facility:** Water activities, as well as dining and shopping, provide diversions at this resort where landscaping and decor set a Southwestern theme. Designated smoking area. 1921 units. 1875 one-bedroom standard units. 46 one-bedroom suites ($266-$1080), some with whirlpools. 2-4 stories, exterior corridors. *Bath:* combo or shower only. **Parking:** on-site. **Terms:** 5 day cancellation notice-fee imposed. **Amenities:** voice mail, safes, irons, hair dryers. *Some:* fax. **Dining:** 7 am-11 pm, cocktails. **Pool(s):** 4 heated outdoor, wading. **Leisure Activities:** sauna, whirlpool, waterslide, rental paddleboats, playground, volleyball. *Fee:* pontoon boats, surrey bikes, water mice, massage, game room. **Guest Services:** gift shop, valet and coin laundry, area transportation-within Disney complex. **Business Services:** conference facilities, business center. **Cards:** AX, DC, DS, JC, MC, VI. *(See color ad starting on p 721)*
SOME UNITS

DISNEY'S FORT WILDERNESS RESORT
Phone: (407)824-2900 347

12/1-12/31	1P: $224-$314	2P: $224-$314
2/13-7/3	1P: $269-$299	2P: $269-$299
7/4-11/30	1P: $229-$269	2P: $229-$269
1/1-2/12	1P: $229	2P: $229

Cabin
Location: Off US 192. Located in Disney World. 4510 N Fort Wilderness Tr 32830-1000. Fax: 407/824-3508. **Facility:** 409 cabins. 1 story, exterior corridors. *Bath:* combo or shower only. **Parking:** on-site. **Terms:** 5 day cancellation notice-fee imposed. **Amenities:** voice mail, safes, irons, hair dryers. **Dining:** 7:30 am-11, noon-3:30 & 4:30-10 pm. **Pool(s):** 2 heated outdoor, wading. **Leisure Activities:** rental canoes, rental paddleboats, fishing, 2 lighted tennis courts, recreation programs, hay rides, nightly campfire & Disney movie, petting farm, tetherball, sand volleyball, jogging, playground, basketball, horseshoes, shuffleboard. *Fee:* fishing equipment, tennis, bicycles, horseback riding, game room. **Guest Services:** valet and coin laundry, area transportation-within Disney complex. **Business Services:** fax (fee). **Cards:** AX, DC, DS, JC, MC, VI. *(See color ad starting on p 721)*
SOME UNITS

Walt Disney World®

CHOOSING YOUR

DISNEY RESORT

When you stay at a selected Disney Resort, the magic doesn't end with the Theme Parks – you experience it every single moment of your stay. Smile all vacation long in delightful wonderlands only Disney could dream up. Disney Resorts come in four varieties to fit any taste and budget.

Disney's Value Resorts
The most affordable way to enjoy Disney magic! Adorned with whimsical, larger-than-life icons, these Resorts are big on everything but price.

Disney's Home Away From Home Resorts
Enjoy all the comforts of home, including fully equipped kitchens or kitchenettes and separate bedrooms for up to twelve Guests.

Disney's Moderate Resorts
The perfect combination of magical Disney theming, value and amenities including incredible pools, plus family restaurants and food courts.

Disney's Deluxe Resorts
These magnificent Resorts are famed for the highest level of attentive personal service and meticulous detail.

DISNEY RESORTS

Disney's Grand Floridian Resort & Spa
Deluxe Resort

Enjoy the ultimate in Disney luxury set in an exquisite world of Victorian grandeur, from the stunning lobby to the meticulously detailed Guest rooms.

Disney's Wilderness Lodge
Deluxe Resort

Inspired by great lodges of the American Northwest, the towering lobby of this Resort is rimmed with authentic totem poles.

Disney's Polynesian Resort
Deluxe Resort

Enjoy a South Seas fantasy featuring lush, tranquil beauty along a sandy beach, marina and waterfall pool. The monorail's just a whisper away.

Disney's Coronado Springs Resort
Moderate Resort

The enchantment of Mexico and the American Southwest comes to life with vibrant colors and even a Mayan pyramid-themed swimming area.

Disney's Animal Kingdom Lodge
Deluxe Resort

An awe-inspiring African paradise where most rooms feature private balconies overlooking a vast wildlife reserve where exotic animals roam.

Disney's All-Star Music Resort
Value Resort

With giant icons and cleverly themed pools, music is the magic at this Resort.

Disney's Contemporary Resort
Deluxe Resort

A true Disney masterpiece of powerful, dramatic design. Sleek monorails glide smoothly through the 14-story tower and over the garden wings.

Disney's Fort Wilderness Resort & Campground
Home Away From Home Resort

Disney's Fort Wilderness Campground is a camper's paradise, complete with all the luxuries of home. RV and tent camping available.

Disney's Port Orleans Resort
Moderate Resort

The charm of the South and allure of the French Quarter come together along a rippling river.

Disney's Caribbean Beach Resort
Moderate Resort

With five islands of colorful tropical fun along a sparkling lake, this Resort is as lively as it is relaxing.

Disney's Old Key West Resort
Home Away From Home Resort

Experience the tropical ambience of a Key West resort, surrounded with swaying palms and winding waterways.

See the accommodations listings in this section for more information on Disney Resorts.

Disney's Value Resorts
1. Disney's All-Star Sports Resort
2. Disney's All-Star Music Resort
3. Disney's All-Star Movies Resort

Disney's Moderate Resorts
4. Disney's Caribbean Beach Resort
5. Disney's Coronado Springs Resort
6. Disney's Port Orleans Resort – Riverside
7. Disney's Port Orleans Resort – French Quarter

Disney's Deluxe Resorts
8. Disney's Grand Floridian Resort & Spa
9. Disney's Contemporary Resort
10. Disney's Polynesian Resort
11. Disney's Wilderness Lodge
12. Disney's Yacht Club Resort
13. Disney's Beach Club Resort
14. Disney's BoardWalk Inn
15. Disney's Animal Kingdom Lodge

Disney's Home Away From Home Resorts
16. Disney's Old Key West Resort
17. Disney's BoardWalk Villas
18. The Villas at Disney's Wilderness Lodge
19. Disney's Fort Wilderness Resort & Campground

DISNEY RESORT BENEFITS

There's nothing like a stay at a Disney Resort. Guests enjoy these exclusive benefits along the way:

- **Disney's Famous Guest Service**
Relax. We'll help you with everything from dining and show reservations to delivering purchases directly to your Resort.

- **Disney Transportation**
Whether it's by monorail, ferryboat, motor coach or tram, we'll whisk you anywhere in our World and have you there in minutes!

- **A Magical Send-off from Your Disney Pals**
The Disney characters arrive on select mornings to start your day off with magic!

- **A Relaxing Disney Break**
Take the kids back to your Resort in the afternoon for a swim or quick nap. Rest up, then return to the Parks for even more fun!

- **A Whole World of Recreation**
Enjoy championship golf courses, tennis, marinas, health clubs, horseback riding and so much more.

AAA Vacations® Packages Put It All Together!

Enjoying all the Disney magic is easy. You can save on select Disney Resort accommodations with the AAA Disney *Magic Moments®* savings plan or other special AAA Vacations® packages. Packages include a Disney Resort stay, Disney's *Ultimate Park Hopper* Tickets, and exclusive AAA benefits. To book, simply call or visit your local AAA Travel office. They can help with all your travel needs.

AAA Vacations® Walt Disney World benefits include:

- **AAA Vacations® Diamond Card** entitles you to special savings on meals, merchandise and recreation at select Disney locations.

- **AAA VIP Lounge** in the *Magic Kingdom®* Park. It's like having a private club in the middle of the magic. What a great place to unwind and enjoy a beverage.

- **Preferred Parking** in special AAA spaces is available at all four *Walt Disney World* Theme Parks (some block-out dates apply).

- **Preferred viewing** for selected Theme Park fireworks and parades (selected packages only). See your AAA Travel professional for details.

Call your AAA Travel office today and make your Disney dreams come true!

(See map p. 598)

DISNEY'S GRAND FLORIDIAN RESORT & SPA

Phone: (407)824-3000 345

12/1-12/31	1P: $329-$815	2P: $329-$815	XP: $25	F17
2/13-7/3	1P: $384-$755	2P: $384-$755	XP: $25	F17
7/4-11/30	1P: $339-$670	2P: $339-$670	XP: $25	F17
1/1-2/12	1P: $339-$595	2P: $339-$595	XP: $25	F17

Resort
Large-scale Hotel **Location:** 8 mi nw of jct I-4 and US 192. 4401 Grand Floridian Way 32830 (PO Box 10,000). Fax: 407/824-3186. **Facility:** Cypress and magnolia trees and manicured lawns surround white, frame buildings at this resort which merges Victorian and old-Florida styles. 876 units. 852 one-bedroom standard units. 8 one- and 16 two-bedroom suites ($835-$2375) with whirlpools. 4-5 stories, interior corridors. *Bath:* combo or shower only. **Parking:** on-site and valet. **Terms:** 5 day cancellation notice-fee imposed, no pets allowed (kennel on property). **Amenities:** video library, voice mail, safes, honor bars, irons, hair dryers. *Some:* CD players. **Dining:** 5 restaurants, 24 hours, cocktails, also, Victoria & Albert's, Citricos, Narcoosee's, see separate listing, entertainment. **Pool(s):** heated outdoor, small heated outdoor. **Leisure Activities:** saunas, whirlpools, rental boats, rental sailboats, recreation programs, croquet, jogging, playground, spa, volleyball. *Fee:* charter fishing, pontoon boats, yacht, golf-99 holes, 2 lighted tennis courts, tennis instruction, game room. **Guest Services:** gift shop, valet and coin laundry, area transportation-within Disney complex. **Business Services:** conference facilities, business center. **Cards:** AX, DC, DS, JC, MC, VI. *(See color ad starting on p 721)*

SOME UNITS

DISNEY'S OLD KEY WEST RESORT

Phone: (407)827-7700 358

12/1-12/31	1P: $249-$755	2P: $249-$755
2/13-7/3	1P: $284-$680	2P: $284-$680
7/4-11/30	1P: $254-$560	2P: $254-$560
1/1-2/12	1P: $254-$479	2P: $254-$479

Condominium **Location:** I-4, exit 67, 2 mi nw on SR 536 and Bennet Creek Pkwy. 1510 N Cove Rd 32830 (PO Box 10,000). Fax: 407/827-1192. **Facility:** 761 units. 230 one-bedroom standard units. 230 one-, 274 two- and 27 three-bedroom suites ($1015-$1410) with kitchens and whirlpools. 2-3 stories (no elevator), exterior corridors. *Bath:* some combo or shower only. **Parking:** on-site. **Terms:** check-in 4 pm, 5 day cancellation notice-fee imposed. **Amenities:** video library (fee), voice mail, irons, hair dryers. *Some:* safes. **Dining:** 7:30 am-10:30 & 11-11 pm, cocktails. **Pool(s):** 4 heated outdoor, wading. **Leisure Activities:** sauna, whirlpools, rental boats, rental paddleboats, 2 tennis courts (1 lighted), recreation programs, jogging, playground, exercise room, basketball, shuffleboard, volleyball. *Fee:* canopy boats, pontoon boats, tennis equipment, bicycles, massage, game room. **Guest Services:** gift shop, complimentary laundry, area transportation-within Disney complex. **Cards:** AX, DC, DS, JC, MC, VI. *(See color ad starting on p 721)*

SOME UNITS

DISNEY'S POLYNESIAN RESORT

Phone: (407)824-2000 346

12/1-12/31	1P: $299-$650	2P: $299-$650	XP: $25	F17
2/13-7/3	1P: $344-$605	2P: $344-$605	XP: $25	F17
7/4-11/30	1P: $299-$525	2P: $299-$525	XP: $25	F17
1/1-2/12	1P: $299-$470	2P: $299-$470	XP: $25	F17

Resort
Large-scale Hotel **Location:** I-4, exit 67, nw and follow signs to Disney's Magic Kingdom. Located in Disney World. 1600 Seven Seas Dr 32830 (PO Box 10,000). Fax: 407/824-3174. **Facility:** A lagoon anchors this sprawling 11-building complex that's just a monorail ride away from attractions. Designated smoking area. 847 units. 842 one-bedroom standard units. 1 one- and 4 two-bedroom suites ($480-$2430). 2-3 stories, interior corridors. *Bath:* combo or shower only. **Parking:** on-site and valet. **Terms:** 5 day cancellation notice-fee imposed. **Amenities:** voice mail, safes, irons, hair dryers. *Some:* CD players. **Dining:** 3 restaurants, 6:30 am-11 pm, cocktails. **Pool(s):** heated outdoor, wading. **Leisure Activities:** waterslide, rental boats, rental sailboats, racquetball court, recreation programs, 1.5 mi paved walking trail. *Fee:* waterskiing, fishing, charter fishing, pontoon boats, specialty cruises, water mice, golf-99 holes, bicycles, massage, game room. **Guest Services:** gift shop, valet and coin laundry, area transportation-within Disney complex. **Business Services:** meeting rooms. **Cards:** AX, DC, DS, JC, MC, VI. *(See color ad starting on p 721)*

SOME UNITS

DISNEY'S PORT ORLEANS-FRENCH QUARTER RESORT

Phone: (407)934-5000 357

12/1-12/31	1P: $133-$219	2P: $133-$219	XP: $15	F17
2/13-8/23	1P: $144-$194	2P: $144-$194	XP: $15	F17
8/24-11/30	1P: $133-$159	2P: $133-$159	XP: $15	F17
1/1-2/12	1P: $133-$148	2P: $133-$148	XP: $15	F17

Resort
Large-scale Hotel **Location:** I-4, exit 67, 2.3 mi nw on SR 536 and Bennet Creek Pkwy. 2201 Orleans Dr 32830 (PO Box 10,000). Fax: 407/934-5353. **Facility:** Pale-colored stucco and black wrought iron adorn this French Quarter-themed resort; rooms overlook landscaped courtyards, the pool area or a river. 1008 one-bedroom standard units. 3 stories, exterior corridors. *Bath:* combo or shower only. **Parking:** on-site. **Terms:** 5 day cancellation notice-fee imposed. **Amenities:** voice mail, safes. **Pool(s):** heated outdoor, wading. **Leisure Activities:** whirlpool, waterslide, rental boats, boat transportation to Marketplace, Pleasure Island & Downtown Disney, playground. *Fee:* bicycles. **Guest Services:** gift shop, coin laundry, area transportation-within Disney complex. **Business Services:** fax (fee). **Cards:** AX, DC, DS, JC, MC, VI. *(See color ad starting on p 721)*

SOME UNITS

DISNEY'S PORT ORLEANS-RIVERSIDE RESORT

Phone: (407)934-6000 355

12/1-12/31	1P: $133-$219	2P: $133-$219	XP: $15	F17
2/13-8/23	1P: $144-$194	2P: $144-$194	XP: $15	F17
8/24-11/30	1P: $133-$159	2P: $133-$159	XP: $15	F17
1/1-2/12	1P: $133-$148	2P: $133-$148	XP: $15	F17

Resort
Large-scale Hotel **Location:** I-4, exit 67, just nw, follow signs to Downtown Disney. 1251 Riverside Dr 32830 (PO Box 10,000). Fax: 407/934-5777. **Facility:** A gated entry buffers this antebellum-style resort's 350 acres of manicured grounds; a canal system provides boat transportation to attractions. Designated smoking area. 2048 one-bedroom standard units. 2-3 stories, exterior corridors. *Bath:* combo or shower only. **Parking:** on-site. **Terms:** 5 day cancellation notice-fee imposed. **Amenities:** voice mail, safes. **Dining:** 6 am-midnight, cocktails, also, Boatwright's Dining Hall, see separate listing, entertainment. **Pool(s):** 7 heated outdoor, wading. **Leisure Activities:** whirlpool, waterslide, rental paddleboats, playground. *Fee:* bicycles, game room. **Guest Services:** gift shop, valet and coin laundry, area transportation-within Disney complex. **Business Services:** fax (fee). **Cards:** AX, DC, DS, JC, MC, VI. *(See color ad starting on p 721)*

SOME UNITS

(See map p. 598)

DISNEY'S WILDERNESS LODGE & VILLAS

Phone: (407)824-3200 **348**

12/1-12/31	1P: $194-$920	2P: $194-$920	XP: $25	F17
2/13-7/3	1P: $239-$890	2P: $239-$890	XP: $25	F17
7/4-11/30	1P: $199-$670	2P: $199-$670	XP: $25	F17
1/1-2/12	1P: $199-$535	2P: $199-$535	XP: $25	F17

Resort
Large-scale Hotel
Location: Located in Walt Disney World Resort. 901 W Timberline Dr 32830 (PO Box 10,000). Fax: 407/824-3232. **Facility:** Set on the edge of a forest of cypress and slash pine, this rustic lodge is fashioned after an inn at Yellowstone National Park. 908 units. 765 one-bedroom standard units, some with whirlpools. 99 one- and 44 two-bedroom suites ($700-$1120), some with whirlpools. 5-7 stories, interior corridors. *Bath:* combo or shower only. **Parking:** on-site (fee) and valet. **Terms:** 5 day cancellation notice-fee imposed. **Amenities:** voice mail, hair dryers. *Some:* CD players, safes, irons. **Dining:** 2 restaurants, 7 am-midnight, cocktails, also, Artist Point, see separate listing. **Pool(s):** 2 heated outdoor, wading. **Leisure Activities:** whirlpools, waterslide, rental boats, rental canoes, rental sailboats, recreation programs, hiking trails, jogging, playground, volleyball. *Fee:* marina, waterskiing, fishing, float boats, water sprites, bicycles, massage, game room. **Guest Services:** gift shop, coin laundry, area transportation-within Disney complex. **Business Services:** meeting rooms, fax (fee). **Cards:** AX, DC, DS, JC, MC, VI. *(See color ad starting on p 721)*

SOME UNITS

DISNEY'S YACHT & BEACH CLUB RESORTS

Phone: (407)934-7000 **379**

12/1-12/31	1P: $289-$990	2P: $289-$990	XP: $25	F17
2/13-7/3	1P: $329-$890	2P: $329-$890	XP: $25	F17
7/4-11/30	1P: $289-$705	2P: $289-$705	XP: $25	F17
1/1-2/12	1P: $289-$545	2P: $289-$545	XP: $25	F17

Resort
Large-scale Hotel
Location: I-4, exit 67, follow signs to Disney's Epcot Park. 1700 Epcot Resorts Blvd 32830 (PO Box 10,000). Fax: 407/934-3450. **Facility:** The resort sports a New England yachting theme and includes a lagoon-style pool featuring various water and sand activity areas. Designated smoking area. 1196 units. 1169 one-bedroom standard units. 10 one- and 17 two-bedroom suites ($480-$2220), some with whirlpools. 5 stories, interior corridors. *Bath:* combo or shower only. **Parking:** on-site. **Terms:** 5 day cancellation notice-fee imposed. **Amenities:** voice mail, safes, honor bars, irons, hair dryers. *Some:* CD players. **Dining:** 2 restaurants, 7-11 am, 11:30-2:30 & 4:30-10 pm, cocktails, also, Yachtsman's Steak House, see separate listing. **Pool(s):** 3 heated outdoor, wading. **Leisure Activities:** sauna, whirlpools, waterslide, rental boats, lighted tennis court, tennis equipment, recreation programs, croquet, jogging, playground, volleyball. *Fee:* fishing, "breathless" boat rides, floaters for pool, pontoon boats, water mice, massage, game room. **Guest Services:** gift shop, valet and coin laundry, area transportation-within Disney complex, beauty salon. **Business Services:** conference facilities. **Cards:** AX, DC, DS, JC, MC, VI. *(See color ad starting on p 721)*

SOME UNITS

DOUBLETREE CLUB HOTEL LAKE BUENA VISTA

Phone: (407)239-4646 **361**

All Year	1P: $79-$169	2P: $79-$169	XP: $10	F18

Small-scale Hotel
Location: I-4, exit 68, 0.4 mi n on SR 535. Located in a busy commercial frontage district. 12490 Apopka-Vineland Rd 32836. Fax: 407/239-8469. **Facility:** 246 units. 242 one-bedroom standard units. 4 one-bedroom suites. 7 stories, interior corridors. *Bath:* combo or shower only. **Parking:** on-site. **Terms:** check-in 4 pm, cancellation fee imposed. **Amenities:** dual phone lines, voice mail, irons, hair dryers. *Fee:* video games, safes. **Dining:** 6 am-11 pm, cocktails. **Pool(s):** heated outdoor, wading. **Leisure Activities:** whirlpool, exercise room. *Fee:* game room. **Guest Services:** gift shop, valet and coin laundry, area transportation. **Business Services:** meeting rooms, business center. **Cards:** AX, CB, DC, DS, JC, MC, VI. **Special Amenities:** free newspaper. *(See color ad below)*

SOME UNITS

(See map p. 598)

DOUBLETREE GUEST SUITES IN THE WALT DISNEY WORLD RESORT   Phone: (407)934-1000   394

	1/1-4/26	1P: $159-$249	2P: $159-$249	XP: $20	F17
	12/1-12/31	1P: $129-$249	2P: $129-$249	XP: $20	F17
	10/3-11/30	1P: $149-$229	2P: $149-$229	XP: $20	F17
	4/27-10/2	1P: $129-$199	2P: $129-$199	XP: $20	F17

Small-scale Hotel   **Location:** I-4, exit 68. Located in Disney World Village. 2305 Hotel Plaza Blvd 32830. Fax: 407/934-1015. **Facility:** 229 units. 224 one- and 5 two-bedroom suites. 7 stories, interior corridors. **Parking:** on-site. **Terms:** check-in 4 pm, 3 day cancellation notice-fee imposed, [BP] meal plan available, package plans, $26 service charge. **Amenities:** voice mail, irons, hair dryers. *Fee:* video games, safes. **Pool(s):** heated outdoor, wading. **Leisure Activities:** whirlpool, 2 lighted tennis courts, playground, exercise room, volleyball. *Fee:* game room. **Guest Services:** sundries, valet and coin laundry, area transportation. **Business Services:** meeting rooms. **Cards:** AX, CB, DC, DS, MC, VI. *(See color ad below)*

SOME UNITS

EMBASSY SUITES HOTEL-LAKE BUENA VISTA RESORT   Phone: (407)239-1144   373

	12/17-1/3 [BP]	1P: $169-$299	2P: $169-$299	XP: $15	F17
	1/4-4/30 [BP]	1P: $149-$249	2P: $149-$249	XP: $15	F17
	5/1-11/30 [BP]	1P: $119-$249	2P: $119-$249	XP: $15	F17
	12/1-12/16 [BP]	1P: $109-$199	2P: $109-$199	XP: $15	F17

Small-scale Hotel   **Location:** I-4, exit 68, 0.6 mi n on SR 535, then 1 mi e Palm Pkwy, then just se. 8100 Lake Ave 32836. Fax: 407/239-1718. **Facility:** 333 one-bedroom suites. 5-6 stories, interior/exterior corridors. *Bath:* combo or shower only. **Parking:** on-site and valet. **Terms:** check-in 4 pm, 3 day cancellation notice-fee imposed, package plans. **Amenities:** video games (fee), dual phone lines, voice mail, safes, irons, hair dryers. **Dining:** 11 am-10 pm, cocktails. **Pool(s):** heated indoor/outdoor, wading. **Leisure Activities:** sauna, whirlpool, lighted tennis court, jogging, playground, exercise room, basketball, volleyball. *Fee:* game room. **Guest Services:** gift shop, complimentary evening beverages, valet and coin laundry, area transportation-Disney. **Business Services:** meeting rooms. **Cards:** AX, CB, DC, DS, JC, MC, VI. **Special Amenities:** free continental breakfast and free newspaper. *(See color ad p 728)*

SOME UNITS

FEE

EMBASSY VACATION RESORT GRAND BEACH   Phone: (407)238-2500   402

	6/22-11/30	1P: $159-$269	2P: $159-$269
	2/2-5/3	1P: $149-$199	2P: $149-$199
	5/4-6/21	1P: $139-$189	2P: $139-$189
	12/1-2/1	1P: $79-$179	2P: $79-$179

Small-scale Hotel   **Location:** I-4, exit 68, 1.1 mi s. 8317 Lake Bryan Beach Blvd 32821. Fax: 407/238-1825. **Facility:** 210 units. 30 one- and 180 three-bedroom suites, some with efficiencies, kitchens and/or whirlpools. 5 stories, interior corridors. **Parking:** on-site. **Terms:** check-in 4 pm, 3 day cancellation notice-fee imposed. **Amenities:** voice mail, irons, hair dryers. **Pool(s):** outdoor, wading. **Leisure Activities:** whirlpool, boating, canoeing, paddleboats, putting green, exercise room. *Fee:* game room. **Guest Services:** sundries, complimentary laundry. **Cards:** AX, CB, DC, DS, MC, VI.

(See map p. 598)

GROSVENOR RESORT AT WALT DISNEY WORLD RESORT

Phone: (407)828-4444 350

2/13-4/24	1P: $110-$145	2P: $110-$145	XP: $15 F18
12/26-2/12	1P: $95-$145	2P: $95-$145	XP: $15 F18
4/25-11/30	1P: $95-$115	2P: $95-$115	XP: $15 F18
12/1-12/25	1P: $69-$99	2P: $69-$99	XP: $15 F18

Large-scale Hotel Location: I-4, exit 68. Located opposite Disney Marketplace. 1850 Hotel Plaza Blvd 32830. Fax: 407/828-8192. **Facility:** 626 one-bedroom standard units. 5-19 stories, interior/exterior corridors. *Bath:* combo or shower only. **Parking:** on-site. **Terms:** 5 day cancellation notice-fee imposed, package plans, 5% service charge. **Amenities:** voice mail, irons, hair dryers. *Fee:* video library, safes. **Dining:** 2 restaurants, 6 am-10:30 & 5-11:30 pm, cocktails. **Pool(s):** 2 heated outdoor, wading. **Leisure Activities:** whirlpool, 2 lighted tennis courts, playground, exercise room, sports court, shuffleboard, volleyball. *Fee:* tennis equipment. **Guest Services:** gift shop, valet and coin laundry, area transportation-Disney. **Business Services:** conference facilities, business center. **Cards:** AX, CB, DC, JC, MC, VI. *(See color ad p 729)*

SOME UNITS

[icons]

HAMPTON INN LAKE BUENA VISTA

Phone: (407)465-8150 352

All Year   1P: $109   2P: $109

Location: I-4, exit 68, 0.6 mi n on SR 535, 0.6 mi e. 8150 Palm Pkwy 32836. Fax: 407/465-0150. **Facility:** 147 one-bedroom standard units. 5 stories, interior corridors. *Bath:* combo or shower only. **Parking:** on-site. **Terms:** [ECP] meal plan available. **Amenities:** dual phone lines, voice mail, irons, hair dryers. **Pool(s):** small **Small-scale Hotel** outdoor. **Leisure Activities:** whirlpool, exercise room. **Guest Services:** valet laundry, area transportation-Disney. **Cards:** AX, DC, DS, MC, VI. **Special Amenities: free continental breakfast and free local telephone calls.** *(See color ad card insert)*

SOME UNITS

[icons]

HILTON IN THE WALT DISNEY WORLD RESORT

Phone: (407)827-4000 398

All Year   1P: $99-$325   2P: $99-$325   XP: $20   F18

Location: I-4, exit SR 535. 1751 Hotel Plaza Blvd 32830 (PO Box 22781). Fax: 407/827-6369. **Facility:** Extensive facilites. 814 units. 813 one-bedroom standard units. 1 two-bedroom suite with efficiency. 10 stories, interior corridors. *Bath:* combo or shower only. **Parking:** on-site. **Terms:** 5 day cancellation notice-fee imposed. **Large-scale Hotel Amenities:** video games, dual phone lines, voice mail, honor bars, irons, hair dryers. *Some:* DVD players, CD players, high-speed Internet. **Dining:** 4 restaurants, 7:30 am-2 am, cocktails, also, Finn's Grill, see separate listing, entertainment. **Pool(s):** 2 heated outdoor, wading. **Leisure Activities:** sauna, whirlpools, recreation programs. **Guest Services:** gift shop, valet and coin laundry, area transportation-Disney. **Business Services:** conference facilities, business center. **Cards:** AX, CB, DC, DS, JC, MC, VI.

SOME UNITS

[icons] FEE   FEE FEE

(See map p. 598)

HOLIDAY INN FAMILY SUITES RESORT LAKE BUENA VISTA   Phone: (407)387-5437   `410`

AAA SAVE	4/28-8/31 [BP]	1P: $129-$169	2P: $129-$169
	12/22-4/27 [BP]	1P: $129-$159	2P: $129-$159
	9/1-11/30 [BP]	1P: $109-$129	2P: $109-$129
	12/1-12/21 [BP]	1P: $109-$119	2P: $109-$119

Small-scale Hotel **Location:** I-4, exit 67, 0.5 mi e on SR 536. 14500 Continental Gateway 32821. Fax: 407/387-1489. **Facility:** 800 units. 326 one- and 474 two-bedroom suites, some with whirlpools. 6 stories, exterior corridors. *Bath:* combo or shower only. **Parking:** on-site. **Terms:** check-in 4 pm. **Amenities:** video library (fee), dual phone lines, voice mail, safes, irons, hair dryers. *Some:* video games, CD players. **Dining:** 7 am-midnight. **Pool(s):** 2 heated outdoor, wading. **Leisure Activities:** whirlpools, recreation programs, kiddie train ride tour, playground, exercise room, shuffleboard. *Fee:* game room. **Guest Services:** gift shop, valet and coin laundry, area transportation-Disney. **Business Services:** business center. **Cards:** AX, CB, DC, DS, JC, MC, VI. **Special Amenities:** free room upgrade (subject to availability with advanced reservations). *(See color ad below & opposite inside back cover)*   SOME UNITS

[icons]

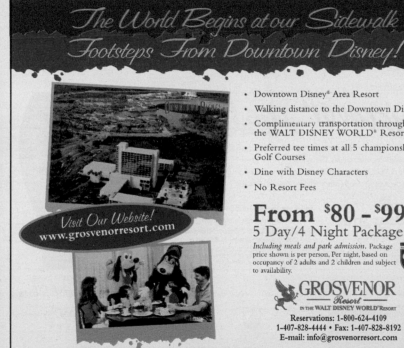

(See map p. 598)

HOLIDAY INN-SUNSPREE RESORT-LAKE BUENA VISTA

Phone: (407)239-4500 [399]

2/10-4/26	1P: $89-$129	2P: $99-$129	XP: $10 F17
4/27-11/30	1P: $79-$129	2P: $89-$129	XP: $10 F17
12/1-2/9	1P: $79-$99	2P: $89-$109	XP: $10 F17

Location: I-4, exit 68, 0.3 mi se. 13351 SR 535 32821. Fax: 407/239-8463. **Facility:** 507 one-bedroom standard **Large-scale Hotel** units. 6 stories, exterior corridors. *Bath:* combo or shower only. **Parking:** on-site. **Terms:** small pets only ($25 deposit). **Amenities:** video library (fee), voice mail, safes, irons, hair dryers. *Some:* video games, CD players. **Dining:** 7 am-11 pm, cocktails. **Pool(s):** heated outdoor, wading. **Leisure Activities:** whirlpools, recreation programs, family movie theater, playground, exercise room, basketball. *Fee:* game room. **Guest Services:** gift shop, valet and coin laundry, area transportation-Disney. **Business Services:** PC. **Cards:** AX, CB, DC, DS, JC, MC, VI.
(See color ad below & opposite inside back cover)

SOME UNITS

HOMEWOOD SUITES HOTEL BY HILTON-LAKE BUENA VISTA

Phone: (407)465-8200 [367]

All Year [BP] 1P: $99 2P: $159

Location: I-4, exit 68, 0.6 mi n on SR 535, 0.5 mi e. 8200 Palm Pkwy 32836. Fax: 407/465-0200. **Facility:** 123 units. 120 one- and 3 two-bedroom suites with kitchens. 4 stories, interior corridors. *Bath:* combo or shower only. **Parking:** on-site. **Terms:** cancellation fee imposed. **Amenities:** dual phone lines, voice mail, irons, hair **Small-scale Hotel** dryers. **Pool(s):** outdoor. **Leisure Activities:** whirlpool, jogging, exercise room. *Fee:* game room. **Guest Services:** gift shop, complimentary evening beverages: Mon-Thurs, valet and coin laundry, area transportation-Disney. **Business Services:** meeting rooms. **Cards:** AX, CB, DC, DS, MC, VI. **Special Amenities:** free continental breakfast. *(See color ad card insert)*

SOME UNITS

FEE

(See map p. 598)

HOTEL ROYAL PLAZA IN THE DISNEY WORLD RESORT
Phone: (407)828-2828 **395** F17

AAA SAVE

All Year 1P: $79 2P: $199 XP: $20

Location: Sw jct I-4 and SR 535. Located in Disney World Village. 1905 Hotel Plaza Blvd 32830. **Fax:** 407/827-6338. **Facility:** 394 units. 371 one-bedroom standard units, some with whirlpools. 23 one-bedroom suites with whirlpools. 2-16 stories, interior corridors. *Bath:* combo or shower only. **Parking:** on-site and valet. Large-scale Hotel **Terms:** check-in 4 pm, 3 day cancellation notice-fee imposed. **Amenities:** video games (fee), voice mail, safes, honor bars, irons, hair dryers. *Some:* dual phone lines. **Dining:** 6:30 am-11 pm, cocktails. **Pool(s):** heated outdoor. **Leisure Activities:** whirlpool, 4 lighted tennis courts, exercise room. **Guest Services:** gift shop, valet and coin laundry, area transportation-Disney parks. **Business Services:** meeting rooms, business center. **Cards:** AX, DC, DS, MC, VI. *(See color ad p 730)*

SOME UNITS

HYATT REGENCY GRAND CYPRESS
Phone: (407)239-1234 **390**

AAA SAVE

12/1-5/31 & 9/3-11/30 1P: $109-$365 2P: $109-$365
6/1-9/2 1P: $159-$315 2P: $159-$315

Location: I-4, exit 68, just w on CR 535; near entrance to Walt Disney World Village. 1 Grand Cypress Blvd 32836. **Fax:** 407/239-3800. **Facility:** Dramatic atrium lobby. Very fine facilities. Extensive landscaped grounds on private lake. 750 units. 745 one-bedroom standard units. 5 one-bedroom suites. 18 stories, interior corridors. Large-scale Hotel **Parking:** on-site and valet. **Terms:** check-in 4 pm, 3 day cancellation notice-fee imposed, $10 service charge. **Amenities:** video games, voice mail, safes, honor bars, irons, hair dryers. **Dining:** 3 restaurants, 6:30 am-10 pm, cocktails, entertainment. **Pool(s):** 2 outdoor, heated outdoor. **Leisure Activities:** saunas, whirlpools, rental boats, rental canoes, rental paddleboats, rental sailboats, racquetball courts, recreation programs, playground, basketball, volleyball. *Fee:* golf-45 holes, 12 tennis courts (5 lighted), bicycles, horseback riding, game room. **Guest Services:** gift shop, valet laundry. **Business Services:** conference facilities, business center. **Cards:** AX, CB, DC, DS, JC, MC, VI. *(See color ad below)*

SOME UNITS

ORLANDO WORLD CENTER MARRIOTT RESORT & CONVENTION CENTER
Phone: (407)239-4200 **409**

AAA SAVE

1/1-4/30 1P: $249-$349 2P: $249-$349
9/15-11/30 1P: $239-$339 2P: $239-$339
5/1-9/14 1P: $189-$289 2P: $189-$289
12/1-12/31 1P: $199-$239 2P: $199-$239

Resort **Location:** I-4, exit 67, 0.5 mi e on SR 536. 8701 World Center Dr 32821. **Fax:** 407/238-8777. **Facility:** A full-service Large-scale Hotel spa is a highlight at this hotel, which features expansive grounds and a range of accommodations spread over several sections. 2000 units. 1954 one-bedroom standard units, some with whirlpools. 46 one-bedroom suites. 28 stories, interior corridors. *Bath:* combo or shower only. **Parking:** on-site and valet. **Terms:** check-in 4 pm, cancellation fee imposed. **Amenities:** dual phone lines, voice mail, safes, honor bars, irons, hair dryers. *Fee:* video library, high-speed Internet. **Dining:** 7 restaurants, 6:30 am-10 pm, cocktails, entertainment. **Pool(s):** 3 heated outdoor, heated indoor, 2 wading. **Leisure Activities:** saunas, whirlpools, steamrooms, 4 lighted tennis courts, recreation programs, playground, exercise room, spa, sports court, volleyball. *Fee:* golf-18 holes, golf and tennis instruction & equipment, game room. **Guest Services:** gift shop, valet and coin laundry, area transportation (fee)-major attractions. **Business Services:** conference facilities, business center. **Cards:** AX, DC, DS, MC, VI.

SOME UNITS

PERRIHOUSE BED & BREAKFAST INN
Phone: (407)876-4830 **351** D12

All Year [ECP] 1P: $89-$138 2P: $99-$149 XP: $10

Location: I-4, exit 68, 3.4 mi n on SR 535. Located adjacent to the Grand Cypress Equestrian Center. 10417 Vista Oaks Bed & Breakfast Ct 32836. **Fax:** 407/876-0241. **Facility:** A natural setting is the backdrop for this modern home where each guest unit has an exterior entrance as well as a doorway to the common area. Smoke free premises. 8 one-bedroom standard units. 1 story, interior/exterior corridors. **Parking:** on-site. **Terms:** 2 night minimum stay - weekends, 3 day cancellation notice, [CP] meal plan available. **Amenities:** CD players. **Pool(s):** outdoor. **Leisure Activities:** whirlpool. **Guest Services:** coin laundry. **Cards:** AX, CB, DC, DS, MC, VI.

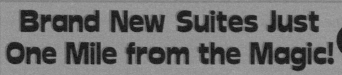

(See map p. 598)

RADISSON INN LAKE BUENA VISTA
Phone: (407)239-8400 376
(AAA) (SAVE) All Year   1P: $89-$159
Location: I-4, exit 68, 0.5 mi n on CR 535, then 0.3 mi e. 8686 Palm Pkwy 32836. Fax: 407/239-8025. **Facility:** 200 one-bedroom standard units. 7 stories, interior corridors. **Parking:** on-site. **Terms:** cancellation fee imposed. **Amenities:** video library (fee), irons, hair dryers. **Dining:** 6:30 am-10 pm, cocktails. **Pool(s):** heated outdoor.
Large-scale Hotel **Leisure Activities:** whirlpool, waterslide, playground, exercise room. *Fee:* game room. **Guest Services:** gift shop, valet laundry, area transportation-Disney. **Business Services:** meeting rooms, fax (fee). **Cards:** AX, DC, DS, MC, VI.

SOME UNITS
⊛ ⓔ ⓨ ⊘ ⊜ ⊠ ⊞ ⊟ / ⊗ ⊟ /

RIU ORLANDO HOTEL
Phone: (407)239-8500 377
(AAA) (SAVE) All Year   1P: $89-$125   2P: $89-$125   XP: $10   F12
Location: I-4, exit 68, 0.6 mi n on SR 535, then just e. 8688 Palm Pkwy 32836. Fax: 407/239-8591. **Facility:** 167 units. 164 one-bedroom standard units. 3 one-bedroom suites. 6 stories, interior corridors. **Parking:** on-site.
Terms: cancellation fee imposed. **Amenities:** honor bars, irons, hair dryers. *Fee:* video games, safes.
Small-scale Hotel **Dining:** 7-10 am. **Pool(s):** heated outdoor. **Leisure Activities:** whirlpool. **Guest Services:** gift shop, valet and coin laundry, area transportation-major attractions. **Business Services:** meeting rooms, PC (fee).
Cards: AX, DC, DS, MC, VI. *(See color ad p 734)*

SOME UNITS
⊛ ⓔ ⊜ ⊞ ⊟ ⊟ / ⊗ ⊟ /
FEE

SHERATON SAFARI HOTEL
Phone: (407)239-0444 362
(AAA) (SAVE) 2/13-4/24   1P: $135-$205   2P: $135-$205
10/1-11/30   1P: $125-$195   2P: $125-$195
12/1-2/12   1P: $115-$175   2P: $115-$175
4/25-9/30   1P: $105-$165   2P: $105-$165
Small-scale Hotel **Location:** I-4, exit 68, 0.5 mi n on SR 535. 12205 Apopka-Vineland Rd 32836. Fax: 407/239-1778. **Facility:** 489 units. 395 one-bedroom standard units. 94 one-bedroom suites ($145-$245), some with efficiencies. 6 stories, interior/exterior corridors. *Bath:* combo or shower only. **Parking:** on-site. **Terms:** check-in 4 pm, 3 day cancellation notice-fee imposed. **Amenities:** dual phone lines, voice mail, irons, hair dryers. *Fee:* video games, high-speed Internet, safes. **Dining:** 2 restaurants, 6:30 am-10 pm, cocktails. **Pool(s):** heated outdoor, wading. **Leisure Activities:** whirlpool, waterslide, playground, exercise room. *Fee:* game room. **Guest Services:** gift shop, valet and coin laundry, area transportation-Disney. **Business Services:** conference facilities, business center. **Cards:** AX, DC, MC, VI. **Special Amenities:** free newspaper and preferred room (subject to availability with advanced reservations). *(See color ad below)*

SOME UNITS
⊛ ⓔ ⓨ ⊛ ⊛ ⊘ ⊜ ⊠ ⊞ ⊟ ⊟ / ⊗ ⊟ ⊟ /

(See map p. 598)

SHERATON'S VISTANA RESORT
Phone: (407)239-3100 **407**

12/22-1/7	2P: $380-$450
1/8-11/30	2P: $249-$335
12/1-12/21	2P: $239-$319

Condominium

Location: I-4, exit 68, 0.6 mi s. 8800 Vistana Center Dr 32821. Fax: 407/239-3541. **Facility:** Designated smoking area. 200 units. 100 one- and 100 two-bedroom suites with kitchens, some with whirlpools. 3-5 stories, exterior corridors. *Bath:* combo or shower only. **Parking:** on-site. **Terms:** check-in 4 pm, 5 day cancellation notice-fee imposed, package plans. **Amenities:** video library (fee), voice mail, irons, hair dryers. *Some:* CD players. **Pool(s):** 7 heated outdoor, 6 wading. **Leisure Activities:** saunas, whirlpools, steamrooms, 13 lighted tennis courts, recreation programs, jogging, playground, basketball, shuffleboard. *Fee:* miniature golf, bicycles, massage, game room. **Guest Services:** gift shop, complimentary laundry, area transportation. **Business Services:** business center. **Cards:** AX, DC, MC, VI. *(See color ad p 5)*

SIERRA SUITES HOTEL-LAKE BUENA VISTA
Phone: (407)239-4300 **370**

All Year [ECP]   1P: $79-$139   2P: $79-$139

Motel

Location: I-4, exit 68, 0.6 mi n on SR 535, then 0.7 mi e. 8100 Palm Pkwy 32836 (8100 Palm Pkwy, ORLANDO). Fax: 407/239-4446. **Facility:** 124 one-bedroom standard units with efficiencies. 3 stories, interior corridors. **Parking:** on-site. **Terms:** check-in 4 pm, 3 day cancellation notice. **Amenities:** dual phone lines, voice mail, irons, hair dryers. *Fee:* video library, high-speed Internet, safes. **Pool(s):** heated outdoor. **Leisure Activities:** whirlpool, exercise room. *Fee:* game room. **Guest Services:** valet and coin laundry, area transportation. **Cards:** AX, CB, DC, JC, MC, VI. *(See color ad below)*

SOME UNITS

SPRINGHILL SUITES AT THE MARRIOTT VILLAGE
Phone: (407)938-9001 **397**

All Year   1P: $89-$149   2P: $89-$149

Small-scale Hotel

Location: I-4, exit 68, just e, then n on SR 535. 8623 Vineland Ave 32821. Fax: 407/938-9002. **Facility:** 400 one-bedroom suites. 5 stories, interior corridors. *Bath:* combo or shower only. **Parking:** on-site. **Terms:** [AP] & [CP] meal plans available, package plans - seasonal, weekends. **Amenities:** video games, voice mail, irons, hair dryers. **Pool(s):** heated outdoor. **Leisure Activities:** whirlpool, exercise room. **Guest Services:** valet and coin laundry, area transportation-major attractions. **Cards:** AX, DC, DS, MC. **Special Amenities:** free continental breakfast and free local telephone calls. *(See color ad p 717)*

SOME UNITS

SUMMERFIELD SUITES BY WYNDHAM-ORLANDO/LAKE BUENA VISTA
Phone: (407)238-0777 **364**

12/1-4/26 & 6/21-8/15 [ECP]	1P: $89-$289	2P: $89-$289
4/27-6/20 & 8/16-11/30 [ECP]	1P: $79-$269	2P: $79-$269

Small-scale Hotel

Location: I-4, exit 68, 0.8 mi n. 8751 Suiteside Dr 32836. Fax: 407/238-2640. **Facility:** 150 units. 47 one- and 103 two-bedroom suites ($79-$289), some with efficiencies or kitchens. 3 stories (no elevator), interior/exterior corridors. *Bath:* combo or shower only. **Parking:** on-site. **Terms:** check-in 4 pm, 3 day cancellation notice-fee imposed. **Amenities:** voice mail, irons, hair dryers. *Fee:* video library, high-speed Internet, safes. *Some:* dual phone lines. **Dining:** 7 am-10:30 pm, wine/beer only. **Pool(s):** heated outdoor, wading. **Leisure Activities:** whirlpool, exercise room. *Fee:* game room. **Guest Services:** gift shop, valet and coin laundry, area transportation-Disney. **Business Services:** meeting rooms. **Cards:** AX, DC, MC, VI. *(See color ad p 662)*

SOME UNITS

(See map p. 598)

WALT DISNEY WORLD SWAN AND DOLPHIN

Phone: (407)934-3000 [380]

(AAA) [SAVE]
▼▼▼ ▼▼▼

Resort
Large-scale Hotel

| | 1/16-4/30 | 1P: $385-$3100 | 2P: $385-$3100 | XP: $25 | F18 |
| | 12/1-1/15 & 5/1-11/30 | 1P: $345-$3100 | 2P: $345-$3100 | XP: $25 | F18 |

Location: I-4, exit 67, follow Epcot Resort area signs; 0.3 mi e of Walt Disney World Resort main gate access road, 2 mi n of US 192. 1500 Epcot Resorts Blvd 32830 (PO Box 22786). Fax: 407/934-4884. **Facility:** The hotel complex, which includes a glass pyramid surrounded by pastel masonry buildings, offers numerous restaurants and meeting facilities. 2267 units. 2090 one-bedroom standard units. 177 one-bedroom suites ($425-$3100), some with whirlpools. 12-20 stories, interior corridors. **Bath:** combo or shower only. **Parking:** on-site (fee) and valet. **Terms:** 5 day cancellation notice-fee imposed, [AP], [BP], [CP] & [ECP] meal plans available, $8 service charge. **Amenities:** video library (fee), video games, dual phone lines, voice mail, safes, honor bars, irons, hair dryers. *Some:* CD players, fax. **Dining:** 11 restaurants, 24 hours, cocktails, also, Palio, see separate listing, entertainment. **Pool(s):** 4 heated outdoor, 2 wading. **Leisure Activities:** saunas, whirlpools, waterslide, rental paddleboats, 4 lighted tennis courts, recreation programs, jogging, playground, exercise room, volleyball. *Fee:* miniature golf, tennis instruction, massage, game room. **Guest Services:** gift shop, valet and coin laundry, area transportation-Disney. **Business Services:** conference facilities, business center. **Cards:** AX, CB, DC, DS, JC, MC, VI.

SOME UNITS

[icons] 🛏️ FEE 🍴 24h 🎦 🛗 ♿M 🔒 📷 🏊 ⚔ 📺 DATAPORT 💻 / ⊠ 📼 📠 🖥️ /

WESTGATE BLUE TREE RESORT

Phone: (407)238-6000 [365]

(AAA) [SAVE]
▼▼▼ ▼▼▼

Condominium

| All Year | 1P: $109-$239 | 2P: $109-$239 |

Location: I-4, exit 68, 0.5 mi n on SR 535, just n on Apopka-Vineland, then just e on Vining's Way Blvd. 12007 Cypress Run Dr 32836. Fax: 407/239-2649. **Facility:** 394 units. 104 one- and 290 two-bedroom suites with kitchens, some with whirlpools. 2-3 stories (no elevator), exterior corridors. **Parking:** on-site. **Terms:** check-in 4 pm, 2-3 night minimum stay - weekends, 14 day cancellation notice-fee imposed. **Amenities:** video library (fee), voice mail, irons. **Pool(s):** 2 outdoor, 2 heated outdoor, wading. **Leisure Activities:** whirlpools, miniature golf, lighted tennis court, recreation programs, ping pong, sand volleyball, exercise room, basketball, horseshoes, shuffleboard. *Fee:* game room. **Guest Services:** coin laundry. **Cards:** AX, DS, MC, VI.

🔒 📷 🏊 ⊠ 📼 📺 📠 🖥️

WYNDHAM PALACE RESORT & SPA

Phone: (407)827-2727 [383]

(AAA) [SAVE]
▼▼▼ ▼▼▼

Large-scale Hotel

	12/1-4/30 & 9/14-11/30	1P: $219-$249	2P: $219-$249	XP: $20	F17
	5/1-5/22	1P: $199	2P: $199	XP: $20	F17
	5/23-9/13	1P: $159	2P: $159	XP: $20	F17

Location: I-4, exit 68, 0.3 mi n on SR 535 to Hotel Plaza Blvd (Walt Disney World Resort), then 0.7 mi. 1900 Buena Vista Dr 32830. Fax: 407/827-6034. **Facility:** 1013 units. 885 one-bedroom standard units, some with whirlpools. 128 one-bedroom suites ($239-$329), some with whirlpools. 6-27 stories, interior corridors. **Bath:** combo or shower only. **Parking:** on-site and valet. **Terms:** 3 day cancellation notice-fee imposed. **Amenities:** video games, dual phone lines, voice mail, safes, honor bars, irons, hair dryers. *Some:* CD players. **Dining:** 3 restaurants, 6 am-11 pm, cocktails, also, Arthur's 27, see separate listing, nightclub, entertainment. **Pool(s):** 3 heated outdoor, wading. **Leisure Activities:** saunas, whirlpools, 3 lighted tennis courts, recreation programs, arcade, sand volleyball, spa. **Guest Services:** gift shop, valet and coin laundry, airport transportation (fee)-shuttle, area transportation-within Disney complex. **Business Services:** conference facilities, business center. **Cards:** AX, MC, VI.

SOME UNITS

[icons] 🛏️ FEE 🍴 24h 🎦 🛗 ♿M 🔒 📷 🏊 🛜 ⊠ 📺 DATAPORT 💻 / ⊠ 📠 🖥️ FEE

——— WHERE TO DINE ———

ARTHUR'S 27

Dinner: $31-$39   Phone: 407/827-3450 [229]

▼▼▼ ▼▼▼

Continental

Location: I-4, exit 68, 0.3 mi n on SR 535 to Hotel Plaza Blvd (Walt Disney World Resort), then 0.7 mi; in Wyndham Palace Resort & Spa. 1900 Buena Vista Dr 32830. **Hours:** 6 pm-10 pm. **Reservations:** required. **Features:** On the 27th floor, this sophisticated dining room affords a dramatic view of Walt Disney World while offering a unique culinary experience. Expect creative, artistic presentation and exceptional service. Executive chef Theresa Connors exquisitely combines specialty and exotic ingredients in phenomenally savory dishes. Smoke free premises. Semi-formal attire; cocktails; entertainment. **Parking:** on-site. **Cards:** AX, DC, DS, MC, VI.

♿M 🍷 ⊠

ARTIST POINT

Dinner: $17-$28   Phone: 407/824-3200 [225]

▼▼▼

Regional American

Location: In Walt Disney World Resort; in Disney's Wilderness Lodge & Villas. 901 W Timberline Dr 32830. **Hours:** 5:30 pm-10 pm. **Reservations:** suggested. **Features:** Bring the kids to the character breakfast and enjoy folksy service in a lodge setting. A selection of Northwestern steak and seafood favorites and vegetarian dishes are cooked over an open hardwood fire. Fresh ingredients and homemade desserts make this a delicious find. Smoke free premises. Casual dress; cocktails. **Parking:** valet. **Cards:** AX, DC, DS, JC, MC, VI.

♿M 🍷 ⊠

BOATWRIGHT'S DINING HALL

Dinner: $11-$18   Phone: 407/934-5422 [227]

▼▼▼ ▼▼▼

South American

Location: I-4, exit 67, just nw, follow signs to Downtown Disney; in Disney's Port Orleans-Riverside Resort. 1251 Dixie Dr 32830. **Hours:** 7 am-11:30 & 5-10 pm. **Reservations:** suggested. **Features:** Traditional and unique American, Southern and Cajun specialties are offered in Dixie Landing's restored boat building warehouse along the Sassagoula River. Boat transportation to and from Downtown Disney and Pleasure Island is available. Smoke free premises. Casual dress; cocktails; entertainment. **Parking:** on-site. **Cards:** AX, DC, DS, MC, VI.

♿M 🍷 ⊠

BONGOS CUBAN CAFE

Lunch: $9-$18   **Dinner:** $12-$24   Phone: 407/828-0999 [232]

▼▼▼

Cuban

DC, DS, MC, VI.

Location: In Downtown Disney. 1498 E Buena Vista Dr 32830. **Hours:** 11 am-11 pm. **Features:** In an old Havana setting, the restaurant displays the flair of traditionally Cuban South Beach. On the menu is an enticing mix of soups and sandwiches as well as chicken, pork and beef preparations. A favorite is the churrasco, a skirt steak marinated in a Cuban sauce. Casual dress; cocktails. **Parking:** on-site. **Cards:** AX,

♿M 🍷 ⊠

(See map p. 598)

CALIFORNIA GRILL
Dinner: $20-$30   Phone: 407/824-1576   224

Regional American

Location: I-4, exit 26B, follow signs to Disney's Magic Kingdom; in Disney's Contemporary Resort. 4600 W World Dr 32830. **Hours:** 5:30 pm-10 pm. **Reservations:** suggested. **Features:** This is a full service, fine dining restaurant appealing to adults, particularly those with an appetite for innovative concepts in food. The menu is revised weekly but it consistently offers sophisticated, cutting edge California dishes with Pacific Rim influences throughout. House specialties include flatbread appetizers baked in a brick oven, sushi, sashimi and some vegetarian dishes. The wine list is primarily California vintages. Smoke free premises. Casual dress; cocktails. **Parking:** on-site. **Cards:** AX, DC, DS, JC, MC, VI.

CINDERELLA'S ROYAL TABLE
Lunch: $11-$16   Dinner: $19-$26   Phone: 407/939-3463   213

American

Location: In Walt Disney World's Magic Kingdom. **Hours:** 8-10 am, 11:30-2:55 & 4-9 pm; closing hours may vary. **Reservations:** required. **Features:** Diners can experience the grandeur of royalty from a setting inside the legendary Cinderella's castle. The menu features prime rib, beef pie, roast chicken, barbecue and other comfort foods. Particularly popular for its Disney character breakfast, the eatery is a favorite dining spot in the Magic Kingdom. Smoke free premises. Casual dress. **Parking:** on-site (fee). **Cards:** AX, DS, MC, VI.

CITRICOS
Dinner: $25-$40   Phone: 407/939-3463   221

Nouvelle French

Location: 8 mi nw of jct I-4 and US 192; in Disney's Grand Floridian Resort & Spa. 4401 Grand Floridian Way 32830. **Hours:** 5:30 pm-10 pm. **Reservations:** accepted. **Features:** Wonderful open kitchen with fusion of French and Mediterranean styles of cooking and decor, soft lighting and warm service top off the evening. Entrees range from seafood to roast leg of lamb and duck. A chef's vegetarian special and wine pairing is available. Smoke free premises. Dressy casual; cocktails. **Parking:** on-site. **Cards:** AX, CB, DC, DS, JC, MC, VI.

CRAB HOUSE SEAFOOD RESTAURANT
Lunch: $9-$22   Dinner: $14-$25   Phone: 407/239-1888   226

Seafood

Location: I-4, exit 68, 0.5 mi n; in Vista Center off SR 535. 8496 Palm Pkwy 32836. **Hours:** 11:30 am-11 pm, Sun from 1 pm. **Features:** Featuring casual family dining amid a nautical decor, this is the place for an abundance of crab and other seafood choices. For a fresh taste of the ocean, try the shrimp scampi with rice pilaf. A self-serve salad bar completes a delicious meal. Casual dress; cocktails. **Parking:** on-site. **Cards:** AX, CB, DC, DS, JC, MC, VI.

THE CRYSTAL PALACE
Lunch: $9-$17   Dinner: $10-$20   Phone: 407/939-3463   216

American

Location: In Walt Disney World's Magic Kingdom. **Hours:** 8:05-10:30 am, 11:30-2:45 & 4-9 pm; closing hours may vary. **Features:** Left of Main Street USA, this stunning, beautifully designed glass palace features a family-oriented all-you-can-eat buffet. Salad, pasta and dessert bars compliment entree selections of freshly roasted and carved meat. Disney characters appear. Smoke free premises. Casual dress. **Parking:** on-site (fee). **Cards:** AX, DC, DS, JC, MC, VI.

FINN'S GRILL
Dinner: $19-$26   Phone: 407/827-3838   230

American

Location: I-4, exit SR 535; in Hilton in the Walt Disney World Resort. 1751 Hotel Plaza Blvd 32830. **Hours:** 5:30 pm-11 pm. **Features:** Kick back in an upbeat Key West atmosphere, and choose from a variety of seafood, black Angus steak, pasta and salad choices served by a professional staff. The hearty, spicy Cajun gumbo shouldn't be missed. Come in on Saturday for the excellent seafood buffet. Casual dress; cocktails. **Parking:** valet. **Cards:** AX, CB, DC, DS, JC, MC, VI.

FLYING FISH CAFE
Dinner: $18-$26   Phone: 407/939-2359   238

Seafood

Location: 0.5 mi e of Disney World main gate access road, 2 mi n of US 192; in Disney's BoardWalk Resort. 2101 N Epcot Resorts Blvd 32830. **Hours:** 5:30 pm-10 pm, Fri & Sat-10:30 pm. **Reservations:** suggested. **Features:** Casual dining in an eclectic decor offers fresh, seasonal specialties served from a cutting-edge open kitchen. The lobster appetizer is creatively produced. Stroll around the boardwalk after dinner to walk off those extra calories from dessert. Smoke free premises. Casual dress; cocktails. **Parking:** valet. **Cards:** AX, MC, VI.

FULTON'S CRAB HOUSE
Lunch: $11-$17   Dinner: $15-$42   Phone: 407/934-2628   231

Seafood

Location: Downtown Disney; between Pleasure Island and Disney Village Marketplace. 1670 Buena Vista Dr 32830. **Hours:** 11:30 am-4 & 5-11 pm. **Reservations:** accepted; priority seat. **Features:** Exceptionally fresh and expertly prepared seafood is the highlight of a menu that changes daily. Alaskan king crab is a house specialty. If you experience a wait, you can enjoy a drink and savor the appetizers outside on the patio deck. Smoke free premises. Casual dress; cocktails. **Parking:** valet. **Cards:** AX, DC, DS, MC, VI.

JIKO
Dinner: $18-$30   Phone: 407/938-3000   241

African

Location: N of US 192 on World Dr, follow signs; in Disney's Animal Kingdom Lodge. 2901 Osceola Pkwy 32820. **Hours:** 5:30 pm-11 pm. **Reservations:** suggested. **Features:** As African music plays in the background, a polished and knowledgeable staff attends to guests' dining needs. A highly skilled culinary staff prepares impressive and colorful offerings. The restaurant defines its food as traditional African dishes with influences from other cultures to create a cuisine described as New African. Smoke free premises. Casual dress; cocktails. **Parking:** on-site. **Cards:** AX, DS, MC, VI.

LIBERTY TREE TAVERN
Lunch: $10-$15   Dinner: $10-$20   Phone: 407/939-3463   217

American

Location: In Walt Disney World's Magic Kingdom. **Hours:** 11:30 am-3 & 4-9 pm; closing hours may vary. **Reservations:** suggested. **Features:** This colonial style eatery, located in Liberty Square features nightly Disney character dinners. Menu is fixed price offering a hearty selection of regal foods including salad, entree and beverage. Fresh baked desserts are extra. Smoke free premises. Casual dress. **Parking:** on-site (fee). **Cards:** AX, DS, MC, VI.

(See map p. 598)

NARCOOSEE'S
▼▼▼
Spanish
Dinner: $21-$32 **Phone:** 407/939-3463 ②②②
Location: 8 mi nw of jct I-4 and US 192; in Disney's Grand Floridian Resort & Spa. 4401 Grand Floridian Way 32830. **Hours:** 5 pm-10 pm. **Reservations:** accepted. **Features:** In a lovely location on the water, the octagonal building is notable for its rotunda depicting a sea mural as well as innovative samplings of grilled salmon, tuna, chops and filets. The wine list is matched daily, and desserts should never be overlooked. Smoke free premises. Casual dress; cocktails. **Parking:** valet. **Cards:** AX, CB, DC, DS, JC, MC, VI.

NEW YORK CHINA BUFFET
▼
Chinese
Lunch: $5-$11 **Dinner:** $5-$12 **Phone:** 407/238-9198 ②②⑧
Location: I-4, exit 68, 0.7 mi n. 12173 S Apopka-Vineland Rd 32836. **Hours:** 11 am-midnight, Sun from noon. **Features:** In a small shopping plaza, the restaurant lays out more than 200 items on its extensive buffet. Although most choices are of Chinese cuisine, other Japanese and American selections can be sampled, as can Mongolian barbecue and sushi bar creations. Casual dress. **Parking:** on-site. **Cards:** AX, CB, DC, DS, JC, MC, VI.

PALIO
▼▼▼▼
Northern Italian
Dinner: $19-$33 **Phone:** 407/934-1610 ②③⑥
Location: I-4, exit 67, follow Epcot Resort area signs; 0.3 mi e of Walt Disney World Resort main gate access road, 2 mi n of US 192; in Walt Disney World Swan and Dolphin. 1200 Epcot Resorts Blvd 32830-2786. **Hours:** 6 pm-11 pm. **Reservations:** suggested. **Features:** Dinner at this full service, fine dining restaurant starts with tempting antipasto including carpaccio, bruschetta, and porcini risotto. The restaurant also serves a variety of seafood, veal and pasta entrees. Hearty Northern Italian dishes are the backbone of the menu: osso buco with saffron risotto, piccata alla Milanese and a beef filet with polenta and shallots. The decor is taken from the Palio Horse Race in Siena and includes colorful flags from the city. Smoke free premises. Casual dress; cocktails; entertainment. **Parking:** valet. **Cards:** AX, DC, DS, JC, MC, VI.

PEBBLES/LAKE BUENA VISTA
▼▼▼
American
Lunch: $8-$22 **Dinner:** $11-$26 **Phone:** 407/827-1111 ②③④
Location: I-4, exit 68 (SR 535), 0.3 mi n; in Crossroads Shopping Center. 12551 SR 535 32836. **Hours:** 11 am-11 pm, Fri-midnight, Sat noon-midnight, Sun noon-11 pm. **Closed:** 11/27, 12/25. **Features:** This is a casual gourmet dining adventure. The homemade soups and salads are fresh and spicy. Well-seasoned seafood, duck, lamb, beef and pasta specialties round out this menu. A tiki bar and patio provide a nice setting for outdoor dining. Casual dress; cocktails. **Parking:** on-site. **Cards:** AX, CB, DC, DS, MC, VI.

THE PLAZA RESTAURANT
▼▼▼
American
Lunch: $8-$10 **Dinner:** $8-$10 **Phone:** 407/939-3463 ②①⑨
Location: In Walt Disney World's Magic Kingdom. 32830. **Hours:** 11 am-9 pm, hours vary with park closing. **Reservations:** suggested. **Features:** This old-time southern soda fountain is located to the right of Mainstreet USA in the heart of the Magic Kingdom. The menu offers burgers, fries, deli sandwiches and sundaes. Reservations are suggested for both lunch and dinner. Smoke free premises. Casual dress. **Parking:** on-site (fee). **Cards:** AX, DS, MC, VI.

PORTOBELLO YACHT CLUB
▼▼ ▼▼
Regional Italian
Lunch: $8-$10 **Dinner:** $15-$30 **Phone:** 407/934-8888 ②③⑤
Location: At Downtown Disney. 1650 E Buena Vista Dr 32830. **Hours:** 11:30 am-11 pm. **Features:** The lively, inviting atmosphere is perfect for tourists in the Lake Buena Vista area. The chef presents special creations nightly featuring fresh seafood. The dining room affords a lovely lakeside view, or enjoy it with fresh air on the outdoor deck. Casual dress; cocktails. **Parking:** on-site. **Cards:** AX, CB, DC, DS, JC, MC, VI.

RAIN FOREST CAFE
▼
American
Lunch: $12-$15 **Dinner:** $14-$23 **Phone:** 407/827-8500 ②③⑨
Location: In Disney Marketplace. 1800 E Buena Vista Dr 32830. **Hours:** 11:30 am-11 pm, Fri & Sat-midnight. **Reservations:** accepted. **Features:** A lively atmosphere of a simulated rain forest with dripping water, plants, trees, birds, elephants and fish tanks will keep the kids busy, then comes the storm! Finger food, pasta, frozen drinks and great dessert are offered. Smoke free premises. Casual dress; cocktails. **Parking:** on-site. **Cards:** AX, CB, DC, DS, MC, VI.

RESTAURANT MARRAKESH
▼▼▼
Moroccan
Lunch: $10-$15 **Dinner:** $16-$25 **Phone:** 407/939-3463 ②③⑦
Location: In Walt Disney World's Epcot; Morocco Pavilion. **Hours:** noon-4 & 4:30-9 pm; closing hours vary with park closing. **Features:** Enjoy Moroccan cuisine in a recreation of a royal palace with mosaic tile work and inlaid ceilings. Selections include couscous and shish-kabob. Belly dancers and musicians perform regularly throughout the day. Smoke free premises. Casual dress; cocktails. **Parking:** on-site (fee). **Cards:** AX, DC, DS, JC, MC, VI.

SPOODLES
▼▼ ▼▼
Mediterranean
Dinner: $18-$29 **Phone:** 407/939-3463 ②④⓪
Location: 0.5 mi e of Disney World main gate access road, 2 mi n of US 192; in Disney's BoardWalk Resort. 2101 N Epcot Resorts Blvd 32830. **Hours:** 7:30 am-11 & 5-10 pm. **Reservations:** accepted. **Features:** Mediterranean fare is the highlight of the menu at this fast-paced eatery. Affable and knowledgeable servers present a variety of creative pasta dishes, as well as chicken and seafood preparations. The wine bar is a nice spot in which to unwind. Smoke free premises. Casual dress; cocktails. **Parking:** valet. **Cards:** AX, DC, DS, JC, MC, VI.

TONY'S TOWN SQUARE RESTAURANT
▼▼▼
Italian
Lunch: $10-$15 **Dinner:** $17-$22 **Phone:** 407/939-3463 ②②⓪
Location: In Walt Disney World's Magic Kingdom. **Hours:** 8:30 am-10:45, noon-3 & 4-9 pm; closing hours may vary. **Reservations:** suggested. **Features:** A first stop on Mainstreet USA, this popular outtake from Disney's Lady and the Tramp offers an Italian-influenced menu including large portions of pasta, salad, panini and various specialty entrees. Indoor and outdoor patio dining available. Smoke free premises. Casual dress. **Parking:** on-site (fee). **Cards:** AX, DS, MC, VI.

(See map p. 598)

VICTORIA & ALBERT'S   **Dinner:** $85-$100   **Phone:** 407/939-3463   223

▼▼▼ ▼▼▼ ▼▼▼   **Location:** 8 mi nw of jct I-4 and US 192; in Disney's Grand Floridian Resort & Spa. 4401 Grand Floridian Way 32830. **Hours:** seatings at 7 pm & 9 pm; at 7 pm Sun-Fri 6/15-9/15. **Reservations:** required. **Features:** Hidden within the Grand Floridian Resort, this is Disney's best restaurant. Intimate surroundings complement personalized service from your attendants, Victoria and Albert. The dinner menu offers an ever-changing six-course culinary adventure. The chef creates meticulous and incredibly delicious world-class contemporary cuisine, reflecting both American and International influences. The coffee presentation is extraordinary and the souffles are to die for. Smoke free premises. Formal attire; cocktails; entertainment. **Parking:** on-site and valet. **Cards:** AX, CB, DC, DS, JC, MC, VI.

Continental

YACHTSMAN'S STEAK HOUSE   **Dinner:** $22-$32   **Phone:** 407/934-3356   233

▼▼▼   **Location:** I-4, exit 67, follow signs to Disney's Epcot Park; in Disney's Yacht & Beach Club Resorts. 1700 Epcot Resorts Blvd 32830. **Hours:** 5:30 pm-10 pm. **Reservations:** suggested. **Features:** A spacious wood-beamed dining room is the setting for guests to enjoy choice, dry-aged steaks cut daily and cooked over a wood-burning grill. Various fresh seafood selections, lighter creative vegetarian menu offerings and a creative assortment of unique dessert creations are also offered. Smoke free premises. Casual dress; cocktails. **Parking:** on-site and valet. **Cards:** AX, DC, DS, JC, MC, VI.

Steak House

The following restaurants have not been evaluated by AAA but are listed for your information only.

AKERSHUS   **Phone:** 407/939-3463

[fyi]   Not evaluated. **Location:** In Walt Disney World's Epcot Center. Norway, World Showcase. **Features:** 40 plus item selection of Scandinavian cuisine, including seafood and smoked meat. The restaurant is modeled after a medieval Norwegian castle.

ALFREDO'S   **Phone:** 407/939-3463

[fyi]   Not evaluated. **Location:** In Walt Disney World's Epcot Center. Italy, World Showcase. **Features:** Dark and rich decor accents the Italian piazza murals. Traditional Italian cuisine; selection of Italian wines.

BIERGARTEN   **Phone:** 407/939-3463

[fyi]   Not evaluated. **Location:** In Walt Disney World's Epcot Center. Germany, World Showcase. **Features:** All-you-can-eat buffet featuring assorted sausage, cabbage, spaetzle, strudel, etc.

BOULANGERIE PATISSERIE   **Phone:** 407/939-3463

[fyi]   Not evaluated. **Location:** In Walt Disney World's Epcot Center. France, World Showcase. **Features:** Counter service. Specialties include French pastry, quiche and coffee.

CHEFS DE FRANCE   **Phone:** 407/939-3463

[fyi]   Not evaluated. **Location:** In Walt Disney World's Epcot Center. France, World Showcase. **Features:** Creative menu of French cuisine, served in a more formal surrounding. Varied wine selections; exceptional pastries and desserts.

THE CORAL REEF   **Phone:** 407/939-3463

[fyi]   Not evaluated. **Location:** In Walt Disney World's Epcot Center. Living Seas, Future World. **Features:** Seafood offerings; menu varies seasonally. Tiered dining room offers view of the marine life tank.

THE GARDEN GRILL   **Phone:** 407/939-3463

[fyi]   Not evaluated. **Location:** In Walt Disney World's Epcot Center. The Land, Future World. **Features:** Character meals at breakfast and lunch. Dining room revolves through scenes in nature. Meals served family style, with some vegetables grown on-site.

HOLLYWOOD AND VINE CAFE OF STARS   **Phone:** 407/939-3463

[fyi]   Not evaluated. **Location:** In Walt Disney World's, MGM Studios. **Features:** Recreates a 40's-50's diner, with stainless steel and deco touches. Serve yourself buffet offering traditional American fare. Moderately priced.

THE HOLLYWOOD BROWN DERBY   **Phone:** 407/939-3463

[fyi]   Not evaluated. **Location:** In Walt Disney World's, MGM Studios. Hollywood Blvd. **Features:** Recreation of the original Brown Derby, including caricatures of stars. American cuisine. Moderately priced.

LE CELLIER STEAK HOUSE   **Phone:** 407/939-3463

[fyi]   Not evaluated. **Location:** In Walt Disney World's Epcot Center. Canada, World Showcase. **Features:** "Canadian" foods served in the wine cellar (lower level) of a replica of a Canadian national historic hotel.

MAMA MELROSE'S   **Phone:** 407/939-3463

[fyi]   Not evaluated. **Location:** In Walt Disney World'S MGM Studios. **Features:** Recreating the look of a neighborhood restaurant. Traditional pasta selections and seafood specialties. Moderately priced.

MITSUKOSHI TEPPANYAKI   **Phone:** 407/939-3463

[fyi]   Not evaluated. **Location:** In Walt Disney World's Epcot Center. Japan, World Showcase. **Features:** Grilled meat, seafood and chicken prepared at your teppanyaki table. Be entertained as you watch your chef prepare your meal. Touches of traditional Japanese decor. Sushi available.

NINE DRAGONS   **Phone:** 407/939-3463

[fyi]   Not evaluated. **Location:** In Walt Disney World's Epcot Center. China, World Showcase. **Features:** Menu selections include Mandarin, Cantonese and Szechuan items. Dining room rich in Oriental decor.

PRIME TIME CAFE   **Phone:** 407/939-3463

[fyi]   Not evaluated. **Location:** In Walt Disney World's MGM Studios. **Features:** Fun atmosphere. Decor reminiscent of a 50's TV sitcom kitchen. Home-type specialties and soda fountain drinks. Moderately priced.

(See map p. 598)

ROSE AND CROWN
Phone: 407/939-3463

[fyi] Not evaluated. **Location:** In Walt Disney World's Epcot Center. UK, World Showcase. **Features:** Limited menu selection of traditional English pub fare. Selections of British beer and ale. Rustic dining room and outdoor patio seating.

SAN ANGEL INN
Phone: 407/939-3463

[fyi] Not evaluated. **Location:** In Walt Disney World's Epcot Center. Mexico, World Showcase. **Features:** Selection of traditional Mexican offerings with some creative combinations. Standard, commercial type Mexican decor; dim lighting.

SCI-FI DINE-IN THEATRE
Phone: 407/939-3463

[fyi] Not evaluated. **Location:** In Walt Disney World's MGM Studios. Backlot. **Features:** Dine in a 50's style replica car at the drive-in theater while watching clips of sci-fi films. Traditional American menu selections. Moderate prices.

LAKE MARY pop. 11,458   (See map p. 590; index p. 594)

——— WHERE TO STAY ———

HILTON GARDEN INN LAKE MARY
Phone: (407)531-9900   72

(AAA) [SAVE] All Year   1P: $129   2P: $129
Location: I-4, exit 98, just ne via Lake Mary Blvd and Primera. 705 Currency Cir 32746. Fax: 407/531-1144. **Facility:** 123 units. 122 one-bedroom standard units, some with whirlpools. 1 one-bedroom suite ($169-$225) with whirlpool. 3 stories, interior corridors. *Bath:* combo or shower only. **Parking:** on-site. **Amenities:** dual Small-scale Hotel phone lines, voice mail, irons, hair dryers. *Fee:* video games, high-speed Internet. **Pool(s):** heated outdoor. **Leisure Activities:** whirlpool, exercise room. **Guest Services:** valet and coin laundry. **Business Services:** meeting rooms, business center. **Cards:** AX, CB, DC, DS, JC, MC, VI. **Special Amenities:** free newspaper and preferred room **(subject to availability with advanced reservations).**

SOME UNITS

[icons] /⊠/

HOMEWOOD SUITES BY HILTON
Phone: (407)805-9111   73

(AAA) [SAVE] All Year   1P: $99-$139   2P: $99-$139
Location: I-4, exit 98, just ne via Lake Mary Blvd and Primera. 755 Currency Cir 32746. Fax: 407/805-0236. **Facility:** 112 units. 105 one- and 7 two-bedroom suites ($159-$169) with kitchens. 5 stories, interior corridors. *Bath:* combo or shower only. **Parking:** on-site. **Terms:** cancellation fee imposed, [BP] meal plan availSmall-scale Hotel able. **Amenities:** video games (fee), dual phone lines, voice mail, irons, hair dryers. **Pool(s):** outdoor. **Leisure Activities:** exercise room. **Guest Services:** sundries, complimentary evening beverages: Mon-Thurs, valet and coin laundry. **Business Services:** meeting rooms, business center. **Cards:** AX, CB, DC, DS, MC, VI. **Special Amenities:** free continental breakfast and free newspaper. *(See color ad below)*

SOME UNITS

[icons] /⊠ [VCR] /
FEE

LA QUINTA INN & SUITES
Phone: (407)805-9901   75

[SAVE] All Year   1P: $79-$119   2P: $85-$125
Location: I-4, exit 98, just se via Lake Mary Blvd. 1060 Greenwood Blvd 32746. Fax: 407/805-9968. **Facility:** 128 units. 123 one-bedroom standard units. 5 one-bedroom suites. 5 stories, interior corridors. *Bath:* combo or Small-scale Hotel shower only. **Parking:** on-site. **Terms:** [ECP] meal plan available, small pets only. **Amenities:** video games (fee), voice mail, irons, hair dryers. **Pool(s):** heated outdoor. **Leisure Activities:** whirlpool, exercise room. **Guest Services:** valet and coin laundry, area transportation. **Business Services:** meeting rooms, fax. **Cards:** AX, CB, DC, DS, JC, MC, VI. *(See color ad p 652)*

SOME UNITS

[icons] /⊠ [icons] /

(See map p. 590)

MAINSTAY SUITES HOTEL

[AAA] [SAVE]
♦♦♦♦

Phone: (407)829-2332   **74**

1/17-4/30   1P: $129-$135
12/1-1/16 & 5/1-11/30   1P: $109-$129

Location: I-4, exit 98, 0.5 mi s on Lake Emma Rd; in Commerce Park. 1040 Greenwood Blvd 32746. **Fax:** 407/829-4436. **Facility:** 100 units. 76 one-bedroom standard units with efficiencies. 24 one-bedroom **Small-scale Hotel** suites with efficiencies. 3 stories, interior corridors. *Bath:* combo or shower only. **Parking:** on-site. **Terms:** cancellation fee imposed, weekly rates available, [CP] meal plan available, small pets only ($100 deposit, $5-$10 extra charge). **Amenities:** video games (fee), voice mail, irons, hair dryers. **Pool(s):** outdoor. **Leisure Activities:** gas grill, exercise room. **Guest Services:** complimentary evening beverages: Mon-Wed, valet and coin laundry. **Business Services:** fax. **Cards:** AX, CB, DC, DS, JC, MC, VI. *(See color ad below)*

SOME UNITS

[icons] /✕/

ORLANDO MARRIOTT LAKE MARY

[AAA] [SAVE]
♦♦♦♦

Phone: (407)995-1100   **71**

All Year   1P: $99-$199   2P: $99-$199

Location: I-4, exit 101A, just w. 1501 International Pkwy 32746. **Fax:** 407/995-1150. **Facility:** 304 units. 299 one-bedroom standard units. 5 one-bedroom suites. 10 stories, interior corridors. *Bath:* combo or shower only. **Parking:** on-site. **Amenities:** high-speed Internet, dual phone lines, voice mail, irons, hair dryers. **Small-scale Hotel** **Dining:** 6:30 am-11 pm, cocktails. **Pool(s):** heated outdoor. **Leisure Activities:** whirlpool, exercise room. **Guest Services:** gift shop, valet and coin laundry. **Business Services:** conference facilities, business center. **Cards:** AX, CB, DC, DS, JC, MC, VI. **Special Amenities:** free newspaper. *(See color ad below)*

SOME UNITS

[icons] /✕/

──────── **WHERE TO DINE** ────────

CAFFE POSITANO

♦♦♦
Italian

Lunch: $6-$18   **Dinner:** $6-$18   **Phone:** 407/833-9377   **45**

Location: I-4, exit 98, just e; in Lake Mary Center. 3837 Lake Emma Rd 32746. **Hours:** 11 am-10 pm, Fri & Sat-11 pm, Sun from noon. **Closed:** 11/27, 12/25. **Features:** This modest Italian eatery is tucked away in Lake Mary Center. Order cautiously as the chef serves up large portions of contemporary homemade fare. If you are feeling full, try the dessert sampler serving four to five people at a real value. Subs, pizza and calzones are also available. Casual dress; cocktails. **Parking:** on-site. **Cards:** AX, CB, DC, DS, JC, MC, VI.

[✕]

CHENGS

♦♦♦
Chinese

Lunch: $5-$7   **Dinner:** $6-$25   **Phone:** 407/333-0099   **44**

Location: I-4, exit 98, 0.5 mi e; in Lake Mary Center. 3705 Lake Emma Rd 32746. **Hours:** 11 am-10 pm, Fri-11 pm, Sat noon-10 pm. Closed major holidays. **Features:** Cantonese, Mandarin, Szechuan and Hunan are all offered at this modest, informal restaurant. You will find many delicious selections at the popular lunch buffet served every weekday, or taste such specialties as Rainbow Delight or General Teau chicken. Casual dress; beer & wine only. **Parking:** on-site. **Cards:** AX, DC, MC, VI.

[✕]

(See map p. 590)

GOLDEN CHINA BUFFET **Lunch:** $6-$13 **Dinner:** $11-$13 **Phone:** 407/321-5858 46
Chinese
Location: I-4, exit 98 (Lake Mary Blvd), 1 mi e. 4225 W Lake Mary Blvd 32746. **Hours:** 11 am-10:30 pm, Fri & Sat-11 pm. Closed major holidays. **Reservations:** accepted. **Features:** Known for abundant food at a reasonable price, the buffet features more than 100 Chinese and traditional American selections. In a busy shopping plaza, this place is almost always packed for lunch. Casual dress. **Parking:** on-site.
Cards: MC, VI.

TONY'S ORIGINAL WINGS & GRILL **Lunch:** $4-$11 **Dinner:** $4-$11 **Phone:** 407/333-4656 43
American
Location: I-4, exit 98, just e; in Lake Mary Center. 3689 Lake Emma Rd 32746. **Hours:** 11 am-9:30 pm, Thurs-Sat-10:30 pm. Closed major holidays. **Features:** No-nonsense wings and things make up the restaurant's menu. The mood is fast and friendly. Homemade French fries with the customary malt vinegar are featured with draft beer, sandwiches and sports on the TV. Casual dress; cocktails. **Parking:** on-site.
Cards: AX, DS, MC, VI.

TOOJAY'S ORIGINAL GOURMET DELI **Lunch:** $5-$10 **Dinner:** $5-$10 **Phone:** 407/833-0848 49
American
Location: I-4, exit 98, just e to Lake Emma Rd, then just s. 3577 Lake Emma Rd 32746. **Hours:** 8 am-9 pm. Closed: 11/27, 12/25. **Features:** The quick-serve delicatessen offers take-out or dine-in options. A large display case showcases homemade salads and desserts. Diners also can choose from a large selection of sandwiches and entrees. Smoke free premises. cocktails. **Parking:** on-site. **Cards:** AX, CB, DC, DS, JC, MC, VI.

The following restaurant has not been evaluated by AAA but is listed for your information only.

OSAKA JAPANESE STEAK HOUSE **Phone:** 407/333-2419
fyi
Not evaluated. **Location:** I-4, exit 98, just e, then n; in Lake Mary Center. 3847 Lake Emma Rd 32746. **Features:** A professional chef prepares tableside Japanese favorites while entertaining everyone seated around him.

LEESBURG pop. 15,956

--- **WHERE TO STAY** ---

DAYS INN LEESBURG **Phone:** (352)787-3131
1/1-3/31 [CP]	1P: $54-$69	2P: $54-$89	XP: $5	F14
12/1-12/31 [CP]	1P: $49-$59	2P: $49-$65	XP: $5	F14
4/1-11/30 [CP]	1P: $39-$59	2P: $44-$59	XP: $5	F14

Small-scale Hotel
Location: US 441, 0.5 mi s of jct US 27. 1115 W North Blvd 34748. Fax: 352/365-1497. **Facility:** 61 one-bedroom standard units, some with efficiencies (no utensils). 2 stories, exterior corridors. **Parking:** on-site. **Amenities:** hair dryers. **Pool(s):** heated outdoor. **Guest Services:** coin laundry. **Cards:** AX, DC, DS, MC, VI.
Special Amenities: free local telephone calls and free newspaper. (See color ad below)
SOME UNITS

GUESTHOUSE INTERNATIONAL INN & SUITES
Phone: (352)787-1210

[AAA] [SAVE]

Small-scale Hotel

All Year [ECP]   1P: $44-$84   2P: $44-$84
Location: Jct US 27 and 441. 1308 N 14th St 34748. Fax: 352/365-0163. **Facility:** 114 units. 105 one-bedroom standard units. 9 one-bedroom suites ($88). 2 stories, exterior corridors. **Parking:** on-site. **Terms:** weekly rates available, small pets only ($5-$10 fee). **Amenities:** voice mail, safes (fee). **Pool(s):** heated outdoor. **Guest Services:** coin laundry. **Business Services:** meeting rooms, fax. **Cards:** AX, DC, DS, MC, VI.

SOME UNITS

MICROTEL INN & SUITES
Phone: (352)315-1234

[AAA] [SAVE]

Small-scale Hotel

1/1-3/31 [CP]	1P: $59-$69	2P: $59-$69	XP: $5	F16
4/1-11/30 [CP]	1P: $54-$64	2P: $54-$64	XP: $5	F16
12/1-12/31 [CP]	1P: $49-$59	2P: $49-$59	XP: $5	F16

Location: 4 mi e of US 27. 9700 US Hwy 441 34788. Fax: 352/315-1027. **Facility:** 81 one-bedroom standard units. 3 stories, interior corridors. *Bath:* combo or shower only. **Parking:** on-site. **Amenities:** dual phone lines. **Pool(s):** outdoor. **Business Services:** meeting rooms, fax. **Cards:** AX, DC, DS, MC, VI. **Special Amenities:** free continental breakfast and free local telephone calls.

SOME UNITS

SLEEP INN
Phone: (352)326-9002

[AAA] [SAVE]

Small-scale Hotel

12/1-4/30	1P: $80	2P: $80	XP: $10	F15
5/1-11/30	1P: $70	2P: $70	XP: $10	F15

Location: On US 27 N. 2476 N Citrus Blvd, Hwy 27 34748. Fax: 352/326-8668. **Facility:** 66 one-bedroom standard units. 4 stories, interior corridors. *Bath:* combo or shower only. **Parking:** on-site. **Terms:** [ECP] meal plan available. **Amenities:** high-speed Internet, dual phone lines, voice mail, hair dryers. **Leisure Activities:** exercise room. **Guest Services:** coin laundry. **Business Services:** meeting rooms, fax. **Cards:** AX, CB, DC, DS, JC, MC, VI. **Special Amenities:** free continental breakfast and free local telephone calls.

SOME UNITS

SUPER 8 MOTEL
Phone: (352)787-6363

Small-scale Hotel

12/25-4/15 [CP]	1P: $50-$90	2P: $50-$90	XP: $5	F17
12/1-12/24 [CP]	1P: $45-$65	2P: $50-$75	XP: $5	F17
4/16-11/30 [CP]	1P: $40-$60	2P: $45-$65	XP: $5	F17

Location: Jct US 27 and 441. 1392 North Blvd W 34748. Fax: 352/787-6363. **Facility:** 52 one-bedroom standard units. 3 stories, interior corridors. **Parking:** on-site. **Terms:** small pets only ($5 fee). **Amenities:** safes (fee). **Pool(s):** heated outdoor. **Business Services:** fax (fee). **Cards:** AX, CB, DC, DS, JC, MC, VI.

SOME UNITS
FEE   FEE

——— WHERE TO DINE ———

VIC'S EMBERS
American

Dinner: $12-$22   Phone: 352/728-8989
Location: On US 441, 4.4 mi se of jct US 27. 7940 US 441 34788. **Hours:** 4:30 pm-10 pm, Fri & Sat-11 pm, Sun 11:30 am-2 & 4-9:30 pm. Closed major holidays. **Features:** This casual, somewhat elegant eatery boasts a pleasant atmosphere and some tableside preparations. Watch the planes fly into Leesburg Airport and order the Polynesian salmon heaped with vegetables and garlic mashed potatoes. Casual dress; cocktails; entertainment. **Parking:** valet. **Cards:** MC, VI.

LONGWOOD pop. 13,745   (See map p. 590; index p. 594)

——— WHERE TO STAY ———

RAMADA INN NORTH-ORLANDO
Phone: (407)862-4000   [83]

Small-scale Hotel

2/2-4/1	1P: $89-$109	2P: $89-$109	XP: $10	F18
12/1-2/1 & 4/2-11/30	1P: $69-$99	2P: $69-$99	XP: $10	F18

Location: I-4, exit 94, just nw. 2025 W SR 434 32779. Fax: 407/862-3530. **Facility:** 193 units. 192 one-bedroom standard units. 1 one-bedroom suite ($159-$259). 2 stories, exterior corridors. *Bath:* combo or shower only. **Parking:** on-site. **Terms:** check-in 4 pm, [AP], [BP], [CP] & [ECP] meal plans available. **Amenities:** high-speed Internet, voice mail, irons, hair dryers. **Pool(s):** outdoor. **Leisure Activities:** exercise room. **Guest Services:** valet and coin laundry. **Business Services:** meeting rooms, business center. **Cards:** AX, CB, DC, DS, JC, MC, VI.

SOME UNITS

——— WHERE TO DINE ———

CHICAGO HOT DOG CO
American

Lunch: $2-$7   Dinner: $2-$7   Phone: 407/331-8591   [57]
Location: I-4, exit 94, 1.5 mi e. 1155 W SR 434 32750. **Hours:** 11 am-6 pm. Closed major holidays. **Features:** In a busy shopping plaza, the eatery caters to the hot dog enthusiast. Vienna hot dogs, polish sausage and corn dogs are just a few of the menu staples. A buffet is also available. Smoke free premises. Casual dress. **Parking:** on-site.

ENZO'S RESTAURANT ON THE LAKE
Italian

Dinner: $20-$38   Phone: 407/834-9872   [52]
Location: 0.5 mi s of SR 434. 1130 S Hwy 17-92 32750. **Hours:** 6 pm-11 pm. Closed: 1/1, 12/25; also Sun. **Reservations:** suggested. **Features:** Elegant trattoria ambience is found in a converted house on Lake Fairy. Go early for the sunsets since dinner is a very busy time. Excellent house pastas, fresh veal and fish specialties are served with finesse. The tiramisu is rich with flavor. Dressy casual; cocktails. **Parking:** on-site and valet. **Cards:** AX, DC, DS, MC, VI.

(See map p. 590)

FIRST WATCH   **Lunch:** $6-$8   **Phone:** 407/774-1830   51
▽▽▽   **Location:** I-4, exit 94, 2 mi w; in Albertsons Shopping Plaza. 2425 W SR 434 32779. **Hours:** 7 am-2:30 pm.
Closed: 11/27, 12/25. **Features:** One of a dozen like it in Florida, it serves breakfast, brunch and lunch
American   with traditional omelets, pancakes, waffles and crepes. Great salads and sandwiches are accompanied by
fresh fruits and muffins. Attentive and accurate service brings patrons back. Smoke free premises. Casual
dress; cocktails. **Parking:** on-site. **Cards:** AX, DS, MC, VI.   ⊠

IMPERIAL DYNASTY   **Lunch:** $6-$9   **Dinner:** $6-$26   **Phone:** 407/786-2266   59
AAA   **Location:** I-4, exit 94, just w. 2045 W SR 434 32779. **Hours:** 11 am-9:30 pm, Fri & Sat-10:30 pm, Sun from
noon. **Reservations:** accepted. **Features:** Traditional sure-to-please favorites—preparations of beef,
▽▽ ▽▽   chicken, fish, pork and vegetables—are served at the eatery. Dishes are prepared with minimal salt and no
Chinese   MSG. Casual dress; cocktails. **Parking:** on-site. **Cards:** AX, DS, MC, VI.   ⊥ ⊠

MELTING POT   **Dinner:** $10-$25   **Phone:** 407/862-8773   58
▽▽▽ ▽▽   **Location:** I-4, exit 94, 2 mi w; in Albertson's Shopping Plaza. 145 Wekiva Springs Rd 32779. **Hours:** 5:30 pm-10
pm, Fri & Sat-11 pm. Closed major holidays. **Reservations:** suggested. **Features:** The moderately upscale
American   restaurant is known for tableside fondue preparations. Combination platters allow for a variety of meats,
seafood and poultry to be cooked using different oils and batters. White- or dark-chocolate fondue is a
treat on various fruits and cake. Casual dress; cocktails. **Parking:** on-site. **Cards:** AX, CB, DC, DS, JC, MC, VI.
                                                                                                              ⊠

PEBBLES RESTAURANT   **Lunch:** $7-$15   **Dinner:** $8-$20   **Phone:** 407/774-7111   56
▽▽▽ ▽▽   **Location:** I-4, exit 94, 0.3 mi w on SR 434. 2110 W SR 434 32779. **Hours:** 11 am-10 pm, Fri & Sat-11 pm.
Closed: 11/27, 12/25. **Reservations:** accepted. **Features:** This informal, tropical restaurant features fresh
American   fish, lamb and duck. The black-pepper-crusted filet is flavorful and well-presented. Unique salads can be
accompanied by tapas for a complete meal. Fresh, homemade soups and desserts make this a favorite.
Casual dress; cocktails. **Parking:** on-site. **Cards:** AX, DC, DS, MC, VI.   ⊥ ⊠

PETER SCOTT'S   **Dinner:** $20-$34   **Phone:** 407/834-4477   54
AAA   **Location:** I-4, exit 94, 0.3 mi ne; in Longwood Village Shoppes. 1811 W SR 434 32750. **Hours:** 6 pm-1 am. Closed
major holidays; also Sun & Mon. **Reservations:** suggested. **Features:** Dance to jazz and swing, and
▽▽▽ ▽▽▽   delight in fine, candlelit dining in a formal setting. The menu offers a nice variety of poultry, fish, veal and
beef. Private rooms and a lengthy wine list create a special mood. Smoking is permitted in the lounge only.
Continental   Semi-formal attire; cocktails; entertainment. **Parking:** on-site. **Cards:** AX, CB, DC, DS, MC, VI.   ⊥ ⊠

THE TABOULE FACTORY   **Lunch:** $3-$5   **Dinner:** $3-$5   **Phone:** 407/831-5781   53
▽▽▽   **Location:** At jct SR 434 and 427, 1 mi s; across from Lyman High School. 830 S CR 427, Suite 262 32750. **Hours:** 6
am-9 pm, Sat from 9 am, Sun-8 pm. Closed major holidays. **Features:** The working taboule factory is
American   known for wholesome meals at factory prices. The "good-for-you" menu reflects many trendy selections,
such as falafel, hummus, panini, couscous and, of course, taboule. Homemade smoothies and family
meals are other favorites. Smoke free premises. Casual dress. **Parking:** on-site. **Cards:** AX, MC, VI.   ⊠

MAITLAND pop. 12,019   (See map p. 590; index p. 595)

——— **WHERE TO STAY** ———

COURTYARD BY MARRIOTT ORLANDO/MAITLAND   **Phone:** (407)659-9100   126
[SAVE]   All Year   1P: $59-$149
Location: I-4, exit 90B, 0.5 mi w, just s on Keller Rd, then just w. 1750 Pembrook Dr 32810. Fax: 407/659-9101.
▽▽▽▽   **Facility:** 112 units. 108 one-bedroom standard units, some with whirlpools. 4 one-bedroom suites. 4 stories,
interior corridors. *Bath:* combo or shower only. **Parking:** on-site. **Amenities:** dual phone lines, voice mail,
Small-scale Hotel   irons, hair dryers. **Pool(s):** heated outdoor. **Leisure Activities:** whirlpool, exercise room. **Guest Services:**
valet and coin laundry. **Business Services:** meeting rooms, PC, fax. **Cards:** AX, DC, DS, MC, VI.
                                                                                                SOME UNITS
🅂🄳 🍴 ⊥ 🅰M 🄴 🕾 🏊 ☒ 〔DATA PORT〕 💻 / ⊠ 📠 🖼 /

HOMEWOOD SUITES ORLANDO NORTH   **Phone:** (407)875-8777   125
[SAVE]   All Year [ECP]   1P: $139-$189   2P: $139-$189
Location: I-4, exit 90 (Maitland Ave), just w, then just s on Lake Destiny. 290 Southhall Ln 32751. Fax: 407/875-8812.
▽▽▽▽   **Facility:** 143 units. 138 one- and 5 two-bedroom suites with efficiencies. 6 stories, interior corridors. *Bath:*
combo or shower only. **Parking:** on-site. **Terms:** check-in 4 pm, cancellation fee imposed, pets ($75 fee).
Small-scale Hotel   **Amenities:** video games (fee), high-speed Internet, dual phone lines, voice mail, irons, hair dryers. **Pool(s):**
outdoor. **Leisure Activities:** exercise room. **Guest Services:** complimentary evening beverages: Mon-Thurs,
valet and coin laundry, area transportation. **Business Services:** meeting rooms, business center. **Cards:** AX, CB, DC, DS,
MC, VI.   SOME UNITS
🅂🄳 🐾 🍴 🅰M 🄴 🕾 🏊 〔VCR〕 ☒ 〔DATA PORT〕 🖼 🖼 💻 / ⊠ /

SHERATON ORLANDO NORTH HOTEL   **Phone:** (407)660-9000   127
▽▽▽▽   2/1-4/15   1P: $79-$99   2P: $79-$99   XP: $10   F16
12/1-1/31 & 4/16-11/30   1P: $69-$89   2P: $69-$89   XP: $10   F16
Small-scale Hotel   **Location:** I-4, exit 90, just w on SR 414 (Maitland Blvd). 600 N Lake Destiny Dr 32751. Fax: 407/660-9008.
Facility: 394 one-bedroom standard units. 6 stories, interior corridors. **Amenities:** dual phone lines, voice
mail, irons, hair dryers. *Fee:* video games, high-speed Internet. *Some:* fax. **Pool(s):** heated outdoor. **Leisure Activities:** lighted
tennis court. *Fee:* exercise room. **Guest Services:** gift shop, valet laundry, area transportation. **Business Services:** conference
facilities, business center. **Cards:** AX, CB, DC, DS, MC, VI.   SOME UNITS
〔ASK〕 🅂🄳 🍴 ⊥ 🕾 🏊 ☒ 〔DATA PORT〕 💻 / ⊠ 🖼 /

(See map p. 590)

THURSTON HOUSE
Bed & Breakfast
All Year   1P: $140-$170   2P: $140-$170   **Phone: (407)539-1911**   128
Location: 0.5 mi w of US 17-92. 851 Lake Ave 32751. Fax: 407/539-0365. **Facility:** A swing and rocking chairs invite lingering on the screened porch of this 1885 Queen Anne house; a parlor has cable TV and a fireplace. Designated smoking area. 4 one-bedroom standard units. 2 stories, interior corridors. *Bath:* combo or shower only. **Parking:** on-site. **Terms:** 2-3 night minimum stay - seasonal weekends, age restrictions may apply, 5 day cancellation notice, [BP] & [ECP] meal plans available. **Amenities:** video library, CD players, voice mail, irons, hair dryers. **Guest Services:** complimentary evening beverages. **Cards:** AX, MC, VI.
SOME UNITS
(ASK) (S☐) (X) (DATA PORT) / (VCR) /

──────── **WHERE TO DINE** ────────

ANTONIO'S LA FIAMMA RISTORANTE   **Lunch:** $6-$13   **Dinner:** $13-$30   **Phone:** 407/645-5523   87
Italian
Location: On US 17-92, 1.3 mi n of jct SR 423 (Lee Rd). 611 S Orlando Ave 32751. **Hours:** 11:30 am-2:30 & 5-10 pm, Sat from 5 pm. Closed major holidays; also Sun. **Reservations:** suggested. **Features:** The second floor dining room of the energetic and elegant restaurant overlooks Lake Lily. Wood-fired ovens contribute to the rich flavors of gourmet creations of chicken, fish and beef. Be sure to try their version of that classic dessert, tiramisu. The first-floor delicatessen has a feel all its own. Dressy casual; cocktails. **Parking:** on-site. **Cards:** AX, CB, DS, MC, VI.
(Y) (X)

CHEF ARTHUR'S NICOLE ST PIERRE RESTAURANT   **Lunch:** $8-$17   **Dinner:** $16-$27   **Phone:** 407/647-7575   88
Continental
Location: US 17-92, 0.5 mi n of jct SR 423 (Lee Rd). 1300 S Orlando Ave 32751. **Hours:** 11:30 am-2:30 & 5:30-10 pm, Fri & Sat-11 pm. Closed: 1/1, 12/25; also Sun. **Reservations:** suggested. **Features:** The elegant bistro is set in a private park with well-aged oak trees, brilliant flowers and ponds. Imaginative dishes, such as grilled lamb chops and key lime strawberry tarts, show the innovation of the chef. The wine list is extensive. Dressy casual; cocktails. **Parking:** on-site. **Cards:** AX, CB, DC, DS, MC, VI.
(Y) (X)

──────── *The following restaurant has not been evaluated by AAA* ────────
but is listed for your information only.

ANTONIO'S CAFE
fyi
    Phone: 407/645-5523
Not evaluated. **Location:** On US 17-92, 1.3 mi n of jct SR 423 (Lee Rd). 611 S Orlando Ave 32751. **Features:** An alternative to the formal restaurant on the second floor, this cafe serves fresh made-to-order Italian favorites in a casual atmosphere.

MOUNT DORA pop. 9,418   (See map p. 590; index p. 593)

──────── **WHERE TO STAY** ────────

COMFORT INN AND SUITES
Small-scale Hotel
        Phone: (352)383-3400   48

12/20-4/20	1P: $68-$85	2P: $72-$95	XP: $5	F18
12/1-12/19 & 4/21-11/30	1P: $60-$80	2P: $68-$88	XP: $5	F18

Location: Just s of southern jct SR 19. 16630 Hwy 441 W 32757. Fax: 352/383-8499. **Facility:** 89 one-bedroom standard units, some with efficiencies and/or whirlpools. 2 stories, exterior corridors. *Bath:* combo or shower only. **Parking:** on-site. **Terms:** [ECP] meal plan available. **Amenities:** hair dryers. *Some:* irons. **Pool(s):** outdoor. **Leisure Activities:** whirlpool. **Guest Services:** coin laundry. **Business Services:** fax (fee). **Cards:** AX, DC, DS, MC, VI. **Special Amenities:** free continental breakfast and free local telephone calls.
SOME UNITS
(S☐) (¶↑) (♿) (⇌) (✦) (DATA PORT) (◫) (▭) / (X) /

DARST VICTORIAN MANOR
Bed & Breakfast
        Phone: (352)383-4050   49

12/1-5/31 & 10/1-11/30 [BP]	1P: $135-$220	2P: $145-$230	XP: $25	
6/1-9/30 [BP]	1P: $125-$210	2P: $135-$220	XP: $25	

Location: 0.3 mi w on CR 441 (old US 441). 495 Old Hwy 441 32757. Fax: 352/383-7653. **Facility:** This reproduction of a late-1800s, Queen Anne-style home overlooks Lake Dora; check-in time is 3-6 p.m. Smoke free premises. 5 units. 3 one-bedroom standard units. 2 one-bedroom suites ($185-$230). 3 stories (no elevator), interior corridors. *Bath:* combo or shower only. **Parking:** on-site. **Terms:** 2 night minimum stay - weekends, age restrictions may apply, 7 day cancellation notice-fee imposed. **Amenities:** irons, hair dryers. **Leisure Activities:** whirlpool. *Fee:* massage. **Cards:** AX, DS, MC, VI.
(♿) (X) (☎)

THE EMERALD HILL INN
Bed & Breakfast
        Phone: 352/383-2777   52
All Year [BP]   1P: $95-$175   2P: $95-$175   XP: $25
Location: Jct US 441 and CR 448 (Sadler Ave), 2.5 mi w on CR 448, 0.5 mi n on E Jem Rd, then n. 27751 Lake Jem Rd 32757. Fax: 928/396-4763. **Facility:** Alligators are occasionally spotted on the banks of the lake fronting this 1941 limestone-block house on two acres. Smoke free premises. 4 units. 3 one-bedroom standard units. 1 one-bedroom suite ($225). 1 story, interior corridors. *Bath:* combo or shower only. **Parking:** on-site. **Terms:** age restrictions may apply, 14 day cancellation notice, weekly rates available. **Amenities:** *Some:* irons. **Cards:** DS, MC, VI.
(X) (VCR) (☎)

HAMPTON INN
SAVE
Small-scale Hotel
        Phone: (352)383-4267   51
All Year [ECP]   1P: $70-$80   2P: $75-$85   XP: $10   F12
Location: 2.6 mi n of jct SR 46 and US 441. 19700 US Hwy 441 32757. Fax: 352/383-4114. **Facility:** 62 one-bedroom standard units. 2 stories, interior corridors. *Bath:* combo or shower only. **Parking:** on-site. **Terms:** 3 day cancellation notice. **Amenities:** dual phone lines, voice mail, irons, hair dryers. **Pool(s):** outdoor. **Leisure Activities:** whirlpool, exercise room. **Guest Services:** coin laundry. **Business Services:** meeting rooms, fax (fee). **Cards:** AX, DC, DS, MC, VI.
SOME UNITS
(S☐) (♿) (⇌) (✦) (DATA PORT) (◫) (▭) (▱) / (X) /

(See map p. 590)

THE LAKESIDE INN   Phone: (352)383-4101   50

AAA SAVE
12/1-4/30 & 9/16-11/30	1P: $125-$235	2P: $125-$235	XP: $15 F18
5/1-6/15	1P: $115-$235	2P: $115-$235	XP: $15 F18
6/16-9/15	1P: $105-$235	2P: $105-$235	XP: $15 F18

Location: Just s from downtown. 100 N Alexander St 32757. Fax: 352/735-2642. **Facility:** 89 units. 73 one-
Small-scale Hotel   bedroom standard units. 16 one-bedroom suites. 2-3 stories (no elevator), interior corridors. *Bath:* combo or
shower only. **Parking:** on-site. **Terms:** 3 day cancellation notice-fee imposed, package plans - seasonal.
Amenities: *Some:* irons, hair dryers. **Dining:** 7-9:30 am, 11-2:30 & 5-9 pm, Fri & Sat-9:30 pm; Sunday brunch, cocktails.
Pool(s): outdoor. **Leisure Activities:** boat dock, fishing, 2 lighted tennis courts. *Fee:* canoes, bicycles. **Business Services:**
meeting rooms, fax (fee). **Cards:** AX, DC, DS, MC, VI.

SOME UNITS

🍴 🍸 🏊 ✕ / ✕ 🔌 /

----- **WHERE TO DINE** -----

THE GABLES RESTAURANT   **Lunch:** $6-$12   **Dinner:** $15-$25   Phone: 352/383-8993   35

AAA
Location: Just s of old US 441; opposite Chamber of Commerce. 322 N Alexander St 32757. **Hours:** 11 am-2:30 &
5-8:30 pm. Closed: 1/1, 12/25. **Reservations:** suggested. **Features:** A country garden setting includes
limited dining on the front porch. International offerings feature beef, poultry and seafood selections.
Consistent servers bring dishes like turkey chili made with fresh vegetables and a rich peanut butter pie.
American   Casual dress; cocktails. **Parking:** on-site. **Cards:** AX, DS, JC, MC, VI.

🍸 ✕

THE GOBLIN MARKET RESTAURANT   **Lunch:** $7-$9   **Dinner:** $18-$27   Phone: 352/735-0059   36

Location: On the alley between 4th and 5th aves. 330 Dora Drawdy Ln 32757. **Hours:** 11 am-3 & 5-9 pm, Fri &
Sat-10 pm. Closed major holidays; also Mon; 9/16-9/22. **Reservations:** suggested. **Features:** After a day
American   visiting the town's antique shops, diners can gather with their friends to relax in the peaceful intimacy of
this centrally located, "back alley" restaurant. Offered is a selection of well-prepared and artfully presented
dishes, including entrees of beef, pork, lamb, poultry and seafood. The Chesapeake Bay crab cakes are a popular starter. An
often-requested entree is a signature dish: potato-crusted black grouper. Dressy casual; cocktails. **Parking:** street. **Cards:** AX,
DS, MC, VI.

✕

PALM TREE GRILL   **Lunch:** $6-$10   **Dinner:** $10-$22   Phone: 352/735-1936   37

Location: Center of downtown. 351 N Donnelly 32757. **Hours:** Closed major holidays. **Features:** Near shops in
the historic downtown area, the restaurant serves traditional favorites in a patio-type setting. The menu
Italian   includes a nice selection of seafood and beef dishes. Smoke free premises. Casual dress; cocktails.
Parking: street. **Cards:** AX, CB, DC, DS, JC, MC, VI.

✕

----- *The following restaurants have not been evaluated by AAA*
but are listed for your information only. -----

FROSTY MUG   Phone: 352/383-1696

fyi   Not evaluated. **Location:** Downtown. 411 N Donnelly 32757. **Features:** Located in downtown area, this eatery
serves sandwiches and salads and refreshing beverages.

PARK BENCH RESTAURANT   Phone: 352/383-7004

fyi   Not evaluated. **Location:** Center of downtown. 116 E 5th St 32757. **Features:** This downtown eatery features
delicious seafood, beef and chicken entrees served in a wonderfully relaxing atmosphere.

SHIRAZ BISTRO   Phone: 352/735-5227

fyi   Not evaluated. **Location:** Center of downtown. 301 N Baker St, #106 32757. **Features:** Wonderful variety of
beef, poultry & seafood selections.

WINDSOR ROSE TEA ROOM & GARDEN   Phone: 352/735-2551

fyi   Not evaluated. **Location:** Center of downtown. 144 W 4th Ave 32757. **Features:** Traditional English tea served
in beautifully maintained garden setting.

OCOEE pop. 24,391   (See map p. 590; index p. 596)

----- **WHERE TO STAY** -----

BEST WESTERN TURNPIKE WEST-ORLANDO   Phone: (407)656-5050   150

SAVE   All Year   1P: $79-$89
Location: I-4, exit 84, 10 mi w on SR 50, 0.5 mi e of Florida Tpke, exit 267B. 10945 W Colonial Dr 34761.
Fax: 407/877-9346. **Facility:** 169 one-bedroom standard units. 2-3 stories, exterior corridors. **Parking:** on-
site. **Amenities:** video games (fee), voice mail, irons, hair dryers. **Pool(s):** outdoor. **Leisure Activi-**
Small-scale Hotel   **ties:** whirlpool. **Guest Services:** valet and coin laundry. **Business Services:** meeting rooms, fax.
Cards: AX, MC, VI.

SOME UNITS

S/D 🍴 🍸 🖥 🏊 📷 DATA PORT 💻 / ✕ 🔌 /
FEE

RED ROOF INN ORLANDO WEST   Phone: 407/347-0140   149

1/2-11/30	1P: $61-$71	2P: $66-$76
12/1-1/1	1P: $55-$60	2P: $61-$66

Small-scale Hotel   **Location:** I-4, exit 84, 10 mi w on SR 50; 0.6 mi e of Florida Tpke, exit 267. 11241 W Colonial Dr 34761 (10945 W Colonial Dr). Fax: 407/347-0149. **Facility:** 83 one-bedroom standard units. 3 stories, interior corridors. *Bath:*
combo or shower only. **Parking:** on-site. **Terms:** 3 night minimum stay - seasonal, 7 day cancellation notice. **Amenities:** voice
mail. **Pool(s):** small heated outdoor. **Guest Services:** coin laundry. **Business Services:** meeting rooms, fax (fee). **Cards:** AX,
DC, DS, MC, VI.

SOME UNITS

ASK 🐾 📷 🏊 📷 DATA PORT / ✕ 🔌 📺 /

OVIEDO pop. 26,316 (See map p. 590; index p. 596)

——— WHERE TO DINE ———

AMIGOS ORIGINAL TEX-MEX RESTAURANT   **Lunch:** $5-$7   **Dinner:** $7-$12   **Phone:** 407/359-1333   129
▼▼▼ ▼▼▼   **Location:** 0.5 mi n of jct University Blvd. 4250 Alafaya Tr 32765. **Hours:** 11 am-9:30 pm, Fri & Sat-10 pm, Sun
Tex-Mex   11 am-9 pm. **Features:** In a strip mall not too far from the University of Central Florida, the restaurant
presents a menu of simple and straightforward Tex-Mex dishes at reasonable prices. Casual dress;
cocktails. **Parking:** on-site. **Cards:** AX, CB, DC, MC, VI.

ST. CLOUD pop. 20,074 (See map p. 598; index p. 611)

——— WHERE TO STAY ———

BUDGET INN OF ST CLOUD   **Phone:** (407)892-2858   615
AAA SAVE   All Year   1P: $35-$45   2P: $35-$45   XP: $5   F9
▼▼▼ ▼▼▼   **Location:** US 192, 0.5 mi e of The Water Tower, 2 mi w of jct CR 15. 602 13th St 34769. **Fax:** 407/892-8063.
Motel   **Facility:** 17 one-bedroom standard units, some with kitchens. 1 story, exterior corridors. *Bath:* combo or
shower only. **Parking:** on-site. **Terms:** 3 day cancellation notice, small pets only. **Amenities:** hair dryers.
Cards: AX, DC, MC, VI. **Special Amenities:** early check-in/late check-out and free room upgrade (subject to availability with advanced reservations).
SOME UNITS

SANFORD pop. 38,291 (See map p. 590; index p. 593)

——— WHERE TO STAY ———

BEST WESTERN MARINA HOTEL & CONFERENCE CENTER   **Phone:** (407)323-1910   38
SAVE   12/1-4/15 & 11/15-11/30 [ECP]   1P: $69-$79   2P: $69-$79
   4/16-11/14 [ECP]   1P: $59-$69   2P: $59-$69
▼▼▼ ▼▼▼   **Location:** I-4, exit 101C, 4.8 mi e. 530 N Palmetto Ave 32771. **Fax:** 407/321-3442. **Facility:** 96 one-bedroom stan-
Motel   dard units. 2 stories, exterior corridors. **Parking:** on-site. **Terms:** check-in 4 pm, small pets only ($20 extra
charge). **Amenities:** voice mail, irons, hair dryers. **Pool(s):** outdoor. **Leisure Activities:** marina. **Guest Services:** valet and coin laundry. **Business Services:** meeting rooms, fax. **Cards:** AX, CB, DC, DS, MC, VI.
SOME UNITS

COMFORT INN & SUITES NORTH ORLANDO   **Phone:** (407)585-1590   35
AAA SAVE   1/12-11/30 [ECP]   1P: $89-$109   2P: $89-$109   XP: $5   F18
   12/1-1/11 [ECP]   1P: $84-$104   2P: $84-$104   XP: $5   F18
▼▼▼ ▼▼▼   **Location:** I-4, exit 101C, just ne. 590 Ava Ct 32771. **Fax:** 407/585-1599. **Facility:** 108 units. 105 one-bedroom
Small-scale Hotel   standard units. 3 one-bedroom suites ($90-$149) with efficiencies. 4 stories, interior corridors. *Bath:* combo
or shower only. **Parking:** on-site. **Amenities:** high-speed Internet (fee), dual phone lines, voice mail, irons,
hair dryers. **Pool(s):** outdoor. **Leisure Activities:** exercise room. **Guest Services:** valet laundry. **Business
Services:** meeting rooms, business center. **Cards:** AX, CB, DC, DS, MC, VI. **Special Amenities:** free continental breakfast
and free room upgrade (subject to availability with advanced reservations). *(See color ad below)*
SOME UNITS

THE HIGGINS HOUSE BED & BREAKFAST   **Phone:** (407)324-9238   37
AAA SAVE   All Year [ECP]   1P: $85-$90   2P: $100-$165   XP: $15   D8
   Location: Just s of 1st St. Located in historic district. 420 S Oak Ave 32771. **Fax:** 407/324-5060. **Facility:** Built circa
▼▼▼ ▼▼▼   1894, this small historic inn has been restored; its Victorian ambience provides for a peaceful stay just 5 min-
Bed & Breakfast   utes from I-4. Smoke free premises. 4 units. 3 one-bedroom standard units. 1 one-bedroom suite. 1-2 sto-
ries, interior/exterior corridors. *Bath:* combo or tub only. **Parking:** street. **Terms:** 5 day cancellation notice.
Leisure Activities: whirlpool, bicycles. **Guest Services:** complimentary evening beverages. **Business Services:** fax. **Cards:** AX, DS, MC, VI. **Special Amenities:** free continental breakfast and free local telephone calls.
SOME UNITS

(See map p. 590)

HOLIDAY INN EXPRESS-SANFORD/LAKE MARY　　　　　　　Phone: (407)320-0845　**43**

[AAA] [SAVE]　2/11-3/10 [ECP]　　　1P: $145-$175　　2P: $145-$175　　XP: $10　　　F18
　　　　3/11-11/30 [ECP]　　1P: $85-$175　　2P: $85-$175　　XP: $10　　　F18
▽▽▽▽　12/1-2/10 [ECP]　　1P: $85-$110　　2P: $85-$110　　XP: $10　　　F18
Motel　　**Location:** I-4, exit 98, e on Lake Mary Blvd, then 0.5 mi n on US 17-92. 3401 S Orlando Dr 32773. Fax: 407/328-6306. **Facility:** 72 units. 69 one-bedroom standard units, some with whirlpools. 3 one-bedroom suites ($110-$175) with whirlpools. 4 stories, interior corridors. *Bath:* combo or shower only. **Parking:** on-site. **Amenities:** dual phone lines, voice mail, irons, hair dryers. **Guest Services:** valet laundry. **Business Services:** meeting rooms, fax. **Cards:** AX, DC, DS, MC, VI. **Special Amenities: free continental breakfast and free local telephone calls.**

SOME UNITS

⬛ ⬛ ⬛ ⬛ ⬛ ⬛ ⬛ / ⬛ ⬛ ⬛ ⬛ /

ROSE COTTAGE INN　　　　　　　　　　　　　　　　Phone: (407)323-9448　**39**

▽▽▽▽　All Year [ECP]　　　　1P: $50-$135　　2P: $65-$145
　　　　Location: From 1st St, 0.8 mi s on Park Ave; downtown. 1301 Park Ave 32771. Fax: 407/323-9448. **Facility:** Designated smoking area. 4 one-bedroom standard units, some with whirlpools. 2 stories (no elevator), interior corridors. **Parking:** on-site. **Terms:** 3-4 night minimum stay, cancellation fee imposed, weekly rates available, [AP], [BP], [CP] & [MAP] meal plans available, 15% service charge, small pets only. **Amenities:** video library, hair dryers. **Guest Services:** gift shop, coin laundry. **Business Services:** fax (fee). **Cards:** AX, DC, MC, VI.

Bed & Breakfast

SOME UNITS

⬛ ⬛ ⬛ ⬛ ⬛ ⬛ ⬛ / ⬛ ⬛ /

SPRINGHILL SUITES BY MARRIOTT　　　　　　　　　Phone: (407)995-1000　**42**

[AAA] [SAVE]　All Year [ECP]　　　1P: $79-$160　　　　　XP: $8
　　　　Location: I-4, exit 101C, just se. Located in a commercial area. 201 N Towne Rd 32771. Fax: 407/995-5921.
▽▽▽▽　**Facility:** 105 one-bedroom standard units, some with whirlpools. 5 stories, interior corridors. *Bath:* combo or shower only. **Parking:** on-site. **Amenities:** dual phone lines, voice mail, irons, hair dryers. **Pool(s):** heated outdoor. **Leisure Activities:** whirlpool, exercise room. **Guest Services:** valet and coin laundry. **Business Services:** meeting rooms, business center. **Cards:** AX, CB, DC, DS, MC, VI.

Small-scale Hotel

SOME UNITS

⬛ ⬛ ⬛ ⬛ ⬛ ⬛ ⬛ ⬛ ⬛ ⬛ / ⬛ /

────── **WHERE TO DINE** ──────

DA VINCI, A DINING PLACE　　**Lunch:** $5-$8　　**Dinner:** $14-$18　　**Phone:** 407/323-1388　**29**
▽▽ ▽▽▽▽　**Location:** I-4, exit 101, 5 mi e on SR 46, jct US 17-92, just e on 1st St. 107 Magnolia Ave 32771. **Hours:** 11:30 am-2 & 5:30-10 pm. Closed major holidays; also Sun & Mon. **Reservations:** suggested. **Features:** Near a Italian　shopping area in the historic downtown district, the restaurant serves large portions to ensure diners don't walk away hungry. Combinations of seafood, meat and pasta are creatively prepared to please the taste buds, and desserts should not be forgotten. Casual dress; cocktails. **Parking:** street. **Cards:** AX, MC, VI.
⬛

JOE'S CRAB SHACK　　　　　**Lunch:** $7-$9　　**Dinner:** $9-$25　　**Phone:** 407/323-0934　**32**
▽▽▽▽　**Location:** I-4, exit 104, just e. 4659 W First St 32771. **Hours:** 11 am-10 pm, Fri & Sat-11 pm. Closed: 11/27, 12/25. **Features:** Just off the interstate, the whimsically decorated restaurant is a fun place to enjoy Seafood　seafood favorites. A playground for the kids can be found out back. Casual dress; cocktails. **Parking:** on-site. **Cards:** AX, CB, DC, DS, JC, MC, VI.
⬛

MORGAN'S GOURMET CAFE　　**Lunch:** $5-$8　　**Dinner:** $8-$16　　**Phone:** 407/688-4745　**28**
[AAA]　**Location:** Historic downtown area. 112 E First St 32771. **Hours:** 11 am-3 pm, Thurs-Sat to 10 pm. Closed major holidays; also Sun. **Features:** Step into yesteryear at this neighborhood cafe. A pressed-tin ceiling and ▽▽ ▽▽　ornate antique wood bar grace the small dining area, where one can enjoy a small delight of Asian American　potstickers or a substantial meal of chicken piccata. The owner/chef receives rave reviews for his desserts, including the blueberry pie. Casual dress; cocktails. **Parking:** street. **Cards:** AX, CB, DC, DS, JC, MC, VI.
⬛

OTTER'S RIVERSIDE RESTAURANT　**Lunch:** $6-$9　　**Dinner:** $9-$25　　**Phone:** 407/323-3991　**31**
▽▽ ▽▽　**Location:** I-4, exit 104; in the "Port of Sanford". 4380 Carraway Pl 32771. **Hours:** 11 am-3 pm, Sun 11 am-10 pm. Closed: 11/27, 12/25. **Features:** At this very popular spot, you may dine on an enclosed patio while Steak & Seafood　the kids splash and play in the swimming pool. A view of the marina sets the mood for feasting on all-you-can-eat crab legs, or partake of the champagne brunch buffet on Sundays. Casual dress; cocktails. **Parking:** on-site. **Cards:** AX, CB, DC, DS, MC, VI.
⬛ ⬛

SERGIO'S ITALIAN RESTAURANT　　**Lunch:** $5-$8　　**Dinner:** $5-$15　　**Phone:** 407/323-4040　**30**
▽▽ ▽▽　**Location:** 0.5 mi n of Airport Blvd on US 17-92. 2895 Orlando Dr 32773. **Hours:** 11 am-10 pm. Closed: 11/27, 12/25; also Sun. **Reservations:** accepted. **Features:** On the restaurant's menu is a traditional selection of Italian　well-prepared and moderately priced items. Families are welcomed in the straightforward and relaxed environment. Tables are well-spaced, with the nonsmoking area far removed and partitioned from the lounge. Casual dress; cocktails. **Parking:** on-site. **Cards:** AX, CB, DC, DS, MC, VI.
⬛ ⬛ ⬛

TAVARES pop. 9,700

———— WHERE TO STAY ————

BUDGET INN
AAA [SAVE]
◆◆◆
Motel

Phone: (352)343-4666

10/1-11/30	1P: $60-$65	2P: $68-$74	XP: $6	F10
1/1-4/30	1P: $55-$62	2P: $64-$74	XP: $6	F10
12/1-12/31	1P: $40-$44	2P: $48-$52	XP: $6	F10
5/1-9/30	1P: $40-$45	2P: $46-$52	XP: $6	F10

Location: On US 441, 0.3 mi e of jct SR 19 S. 101 W Burleigh Blvd 32778-2498. Fax: 352/742-2717. **Facility:** 40 one-bedroom standard units, some with efficiencies. 2 stories, exterior corridors. **Parking:** on-site. **Terms:** 14 day cancellation notice, small pets only ($8 fee). **Pool(s):** outdoor. **Cards:** AX, DS, MC, VI.

SOME UNITS

INN ON THE GREEN
AAA [SAVE]
◆◆◆◆
Motel

Phone: (352)343-6373

12/1-12/14	1P: $79-$135	2P: $79-$135		F
4/16-11/30	1P: $79-$135	2P: $79-$135	XP: $6	F
12/15-4/15	1P: $65-$99	2P: $65-$99	XP: $6	F

Location: On US 441, 1 mi e of jct SR 19. 700 E Burleigh Blvd 32778. Fax: 352/343-7216. **Facility:** 77 units. 70 one-bedroom standard units, some with efficiencies (utensils extra charge). 6 one- and 1 two-bedroom suites ($99-$135), some with kitchens (utensils extra charge). 2 stories, exterior corridors. **Parking:** on-site. **Terms:** [ECP] meal plan available, small pets only ($5 extra charge). **Amenities:** voice mail. *Some:* irons, hair dryers. **Pool(s):** outdoor. **Leisure Activities:** putting green, driving range,, picnic area, barbecue grills, shuffleboard. *Fee:* golf instruction. **Guest Services:** coin laundry. **Business Services:** meeting rooms, fax (fee). **Cards:** AX, DC, DS, MC, VI. **Special Amenities:** free continental breakfast and free local telephone calls.

SOME UNITS

———— WHERE TO DINE ————

AMIGOS ORIGINAL TEX-MEX RESTAURANT
◆◆◆
Tex-Mex

Lunch: $5-$12   Dinner: $7-$12   Phone: 352/253-1045

Location: SR 436 N to US 441 N; approximately 20 mi to Tavares. 901 Lakeshore Blvd 32778. **Hours:** 11 am-9 pm, Fri & Sat-10 pm. **Closed:** 1/1, 11/27, 12/25. **Features:** The staff moves at a bustling pace to deliver oversized burritos and platefuls of tacos. Casual surroundings and popular Tex-Mex dishes are offered for the whole family. Dine indoors or on the outdoor deck, with a good view of the lake. Casual dress; cocktails. **Parking:** on-site. **Cards:** AX, DC, MC, VI.

DEAD RIVER VIC'S
◆◆◆
Steak & Seafood

Lunch: $7-$10   Dinner: $7-$20   Phone: 352/742-5000

Location: On US 441, 2 mi w of SR 19. 3351 W Burleigh Blvd 32778. **Hours:** 11 am-11 pm. **Features:** Golf carts will ferry you from the parking lot to this lovely, waterfront restaurant with outdoor seating, a gift shop and boat slips. Fresh seafood, chicken and ribs are featured, and the banana muffin with caramel ice cream will make your mouth water. Casual dress; cocktails. **Parking:** on-site. **Cards:** AX, DS, MC, VI.

WINTER GARDEN pop. 14,351   (See map p. 590; index p. 596)

———— WHERE TO STAY ————

BEST VALUE INN ORLANDO WEST
AAA [SAVE]
◆◆◆
Motel

Phone: (407)654-1188   [147]

6/27-8/16	1P: $79-$89	2P: $79-$89	XP: $5	F12
12/21-6/26	1P: $69-$89	2P: $69-$89	XP: $5	F12
12/1-12/20 & 8/17-11/30	1P: $69-$79	2P: $69-$79	XP: $5	F12

Location: SR 50, just e of jct CR 535. 13603 W Colonial Dr 34787. Fax: 407/654-0140. **Facility:** 102 one-bedroom standard units, some with efficiencies (utensil deposit required). 2 stories, exterior corridors. **Parking:** on-site. **Dining:** 6 am-11 pm, cocktails. **Pool(s):** heated outdoor. **Leisure Activities:** *Fee:* exercise room. **Guest Services:** valet and coin laundry. **Business Services:** meeting rooms, fax (fee). **Cards:** AX, DC, DS, MC, VI. **Special Amenities:** early check-in/late check-out and free room upgrade (subject to availability with advanced reservations). *(See color ad below)*

SOME UNITS

FEE   FEE

(See map p. 590)

ORANGE COUNTY NATIONAL GOLF CENTER AND LODGE   Phone: (407)656-2626   146

▼▼▼▼▼   1/14-3/31 [ECP]   1P: $95   2P: $95

            4/1-11/30 [ECP]   1P: $75   2P: $75

Motel   12/1-1/13 [ECP]   1P: $70   2P: $70

            Location: From US 192, 6.8 mi n on CR 545. 16301 Phil Ritson Way 34787. Fax: 407/656-4045. **Facility:** 46 one-bedroom standard units. 1 story, exterior corridors. *Bath:* some combo or shower only. **Parking:** on-site. **Terms:** 3 day cancellation notice, [CP] meal plan available, 11% service charge. **Leisure Activities:** Fee: golf-45 holes. **Guest Services:** gift shop. **Business Services:** meeting rooms, fax (fee). **Cards:** AX, DC, MC, VI.

SOME UNITS

(A$K) (🍴) (♿) (📺) (DATA PORT) (📟) / (✖) /

──────── **WHERE TO DINE** ────────

TAQUITOS JALISCO   **Lunch:** $3-$9   **Dinner:** $5-$14   **Phone:** 407/654-0363   104

▼▼▼ ▼▼▼ **Location:** In Tri-City Shopping Center. 1041 S Dillard St 34787. **Hours:** 11 am-9 pm, Fri-10 pm, Sat-9:30 pm.

            Closed: 11/27; also Mon. **Reservations:** accepted. **Features:** A friendly staff serves up cuisine with fresh

Mexican   ingredients, lots of heat and lots of flavor. Entrees are presented with a colorful flair and prepared from authentic recipes. A modest place with only a few tables and chairs, it is important to arrive early. Smoke free premises. Casual dress; beer & wine only. **Parking:** on-site. **Cards:** AX, DS, MC, VI.

(✖)

WINTER PARK pop. 24,090   (See map p. 590; index p. 595)

──────── **WHERE TO STAY** ────────

BEST WESTERN MT. VERNON INN   Phone: (407)647-1166   137

(AAA) (SAVE) All Year   1P: $95-$125   2P: $95-$125

▼▼▼ ▼▼▼ **Location:** I-4, exit 87 (Fairbanks Ave), 1 mi e, then 0.3 mi n on US 17-92. Located opposite the Winter Park Civic Center. 110 S Orlando Ave 32789-3698. Fax: 407/647-8011. **Facility:** 144 one-bedroom standard units. 2 stories, interior/exterior corridors. *Bath:* combo or shower only. **Parking:** on-site. **Amenities:** voice mail, irons, hair

Small-scale Hotel   dryers. *Some:* dual phone lines. **Dining:** 7 am-2 pm, entertainment. **Pool(s):** outdoor. **Leisure Activities:** jogging. *Fee:* tennis privileges. **Guest Services:** valet laundry. **Business Services:** conference facilities, fax. **Cards:** AX, CB, DC, DS, JC, MC, VI. **Special Amenities: free newspaper and preferred room (subject to availability with advanced reservations).** *(See ad below)*

SOME UNITS

(S/D) (🍴) (🍸) (♿) (🏋) (🏊) (📺) (DATA PORT) / (✖) (🛗) /

FAIRFIELD INN-WINTER PARK   Phone: (407)539-1955   135

(SAVE) 1/1-4/30   1P: $69-$79   2P: $69-$79

            5/1-11/30   1P: $55-$59   2P: $55-$59

▼▼▼ ▼▼▼ 12/1-12/31   1P: $55   2P: $55

            Location: I-4, exit 88, just ne. 951 Wymore Rd 32789. Fax: 407/539-0705. **Facility:** 135 one-bedroom standard

Small-scale Hotel   units. 3 stories, interior/exterior corridors. **Parking:** on-site. **Amenities:** voice mail, irons. **Pool(s):** heated outdoor. **Guest Services:** valet laundry. **Business Services:** meeting rooms, fax (fee). **Cards:** AX, CB, DC, DS, MC, VI.

SOME UNITS

(S/D) (♿M) (🏋) (🏊) (♿) (📺) (DATA PORT) / (✖) (🛗) /

GUESTHOUSE INTERNATIONAL   Phone: (407)644-8000   136

(AAA) (SAVE) All Year   1P: $46-$56   2P: $50-$60

▼▼ ▼▼ **Location:** I-4, exit 88, 1 mi e on Lee Rd, then just s. 901 N Orlando Ave 32789. Fax: 407/644-0032. **Facility:** 102

Motel   one-bedroom standard units. 2 stories, exterior corridors. [AP] & [CP] meal plans available. **Amenities:** *Some:* irons, hair dryers. **Pool(s):** outdoor. **Guest Services:** coin laundry. **Business Services:** fax (fee). **Cards:** AX, DC, MC, VI.

SOME UNITS

(S/D) (🍴) (🏊) (📺) (DATA PORT) / (✖) (🛗) (📠) (📟) /

(See map p. 590)

──────── WHERE TO DINE ────────

ALFONZO'S FINE ITALIAN CUISINE   Lunch: $5-$7   Dinner: $8-$19   Phone: 407/657-0101   96
▼▼▼ ▼▼▼
Italian   **Location:** 7325 Aloma Ave 32792. **Hours:** 11 am-9:15 pm, Sun 4 pm-8:45 pm. Closed major holidays; also Mon. **Reservations:** accepted. **Features:** In an unpretentious setting on a busy avenue, this spot is popular with locals on the weekends and offers a typical array of Italian-American food. For those craving pizza, there is a good selection. Casual dress; beer & wine only. **Parking:** on-site. **Cards:** AX, DC, DS,
MC, VI.

AMIGOS   Lunch: $5-$12   Dinner: $7-$12   Phone: 407/657-8111   99
▼▼▼ ▼▼▼
Tex-Mex   **Location:** Jct Aloma Ave and SR 436; just sw. 494 N Semoran Blvd 32792. **Hours:** 11 am-9:30 pm, Fri & Sat-10 pm, Sun-9 pm. Closed major holidays. **Features:** The staff moves at a bustling pace to deliver oversized burritos and platefuls of tacos. Casual surroundings and popular Tex-Mex dishes are offered for the whole family. Order the fajitas for a sizzling, hot sensation. Casual dress; cocktails. **Parking:** on-site. **Cards:** AX,
DC, MC, VI.
⊗

BLACKFIN   Dinner: $16-$30   Phone: 407/691-4653   97
▼▼▼▼▼
Seafood   **Location:** I-4, exit 88, 1 mi e on Lee Rd, then 0.5 mi s; in Winter Park Village. 460 N Orlando Ave, Suite 122 32789. **Hours:** 5 pm-10 pm, Fri & Sat-11 pm. Closed: 4/20. **Reservations:** suggested. **Features:** The menu changes daily, reflecting the available fresh seafood purchased at a local market each morning. The formal look to the decor belies the casual comfort enjoyed at this locally popular restaurant. Knowledgeable wait staff lead diners through the selection of the day's creation. Casual dress; cocktails. **Parking:** on-site and valet. **Cards:** AX,
DC, DS, MC, VI.
⊤ ⊗

BRAZILIAN PAVILION   Lunch: $8-$11   Dinner: $11-$25   Phone: 407/740-7440   101
▼▼▼ ▼▼▼
Brazilian   **Location:** Just w of Rollins College and jct of Park and Fairbanks aves. 140 W Fairbanks Ave 32789. **Hours:** 11:30 am-3 & 5:30-11 pm. Closed: Sun. **Reservations:** accepted. **Features:** Authentic, gourmet Brazilian cuisine includes feijoada, churrasco steak and fresh fish dishes, all generously seasoned and served in simple elegance. Arrive early for lunch to beat the crowd. Casual dress; beer & wine only. **Parking:** on-site.
Cards: AX, CB, DC, MC, VI.
⊗

BUBBALOU'S BODACIOUS BAR-B-QUE   Lunch: $4-$10   Dinner: $4-$10   Phone: 407/628-1212   90
▼▼▼▼
Barbecue   **Location:** I-4, exit 88, 0.5 mi e. 14/1 Lee Rd 32789. **Hours:** 10 am-9:30 pm, Fri-10:30 pm. Closed: 11/27, 12/25; also Sun. **Features:** Barbecue sandwiches and meats. Limited inside dining. Counter service. Inexpensive. Casual dress. **Parking:** on-site. **Cards:** AX, DS, MC, VI.
₭ ⊗

CHEESECAKE FACTORY   Lunch: $8-$25   Dinner: $8-$25   Phone: 407/644-4220   95
▼▼▼ ▼▼▼
American   **Location:** Just e of US 17-92, just s of jct US 17-92 and Lee Rd; in Winter Park Village Shops. 520 N Orlando Ave #110 32789. **Hours:** 11 am-11:30 pm, Fri & Sat-12:30 am, Sun 10 am-11 pm. Closed: 11/27, 12/25. **Features:** In a busy shopping plaza, the eatery is most-noted for its large portions and varieties of homemade cheesecake. The menu's many pages list numerous types of cuisines. Casual dress; cocktails.
Parking: on-site. **Cards:** AX, CB, DC, DS, JC, MC, VI.
⊤ ⊗

DEXTER'S OF WINTER PARK   Lunch: $5-$12   Dinner: $6-$22   Phone: 407/629-1150   98
▼▼▼ ▼▼▼
American   **Location:** I-4, exit 87, 0.7 mi e on Fairbanks Ave, 0.3 mi n to Morse Blvd, just e to Pennsylvania Ave, then just s. 558 W New England Ave 32789. **Hours:** 11 am-11 pm, Thurs-Sat to midnight. Closed major holidays. **Features:** Located just three blocks off prominent Park Avenue, this eatery features a rotating art collection hung on every wall. Many wine connoisseurs frequent this establishment for the interesting selection of wines available. The food is trendy yet simple. Eggplant pie and stuffed meatloaf are local favorites. Smoke free premises. Casual dress; beer & wine only. **Parking:** on-site. **Cards:** AX, CB, DC, DS, MC, VI.
₭ ⊗

PARK PLAZA GARDENS   Lunch: $6-$12   Dinner: $16-$30   Phone: 407/645-2475   100
▼▼▼ ▼▼▼
Continental   **Location:** Center; at jct Park Ave S and New England Ave. 319 Park Ave S 32789. **Hours:** 11:30 am-2:30 & 6-10 pm, Fri & Sat-11 pm, Sun 11 am-3 pm. Closed: 1/1, 7/4, 12/25; also Mon. **Reservations:** suggested. **Features:** A glass-enclosed garden filled with lush plants brings the outdoors indoors. You will find impeccable service with great attention to detail. Beef, seafood and pork are featured with lighter fair available in the lounge between lunch and dinner. Semi-formal attire; cocktails. **Parking:** street. **Cards:** AX, CB, DC, DS,
MC, VI.
⊤ ⊗

PEBBLES OF WINTER PARK   Lunch: $7-$20   Dinner: $7-$20   Phone: 407/678-7001   92
▼▼▼ ▼▼▼
American   **Location:** SR 436, 0.3 mi w. 2516 Aloma Ave 32792. **Hours:** 11 am-10 pm, Fri & Sat-11 pm, Sun from 11:30 am. Closed major holidays. **Features:** The festive eatery has an island theme and a menu to complement. Salads, as well as seafood, beef and poultry dishes, are prepared with distinctive seasonings and presented in creative ways. Diners should save room for one of the delicious desserts. Casual dress; cocktails. **Parking:** on-site. **Cards:** AX, DS, MC, VI.
⊤ ⊗

P. F. CHANG'S CHINA BISTRO   Lunch: $5-$13   Dinner: $5-$13   Phone: 407/622-0188   94
▼▼▼ ▼▼▼
Chinese   **Location:** Just e of US 17-92; just s of jct US 17-92 and Lee Rd; in Winter Park Village Shops. 436 N Orlando Ave 32789. **Hours:** 11 am-11 pm, Fri & Sat-midnight, Sun-10 pm. Closed: 11/27, 12/25. **Features:** In a busy shopping area, the eatery nurtures a wonderful atmosphere for dining. Dim lighting enhances the warm gold and wood tones that surround the dining room. Chinese favorites are served with flair. Smoke free premises. Casual dress; cocktails. **Parking:** on-site. **Cards:** AX, CB, DC, DS, JC, MC, VI.
₤M ⊗

(See map p. 590)

SIAM GARDEN

Thai

Lunch: $8-$11	**Dinner:** $10-$18	**Phone:** 407/599-7443 (93)

Location: Just e of US 17-92; across from Winter Park Mall. 1111 Webster Ave 32789. **Hours:** 11 am-2:30 & 5-10 pm, Sat from 5 pm, Sun 4 pm-9 pm. Closed: 11/27, 12/25. **Features:** Full-bodied and flavorful soups are a wonderful lead in to such preparations as savory Pad Thai, a mixture of flat noodles stir-fried with shrimp, scallions, egg and paprika. Casual dress; beer & wine only. **Parking:** on-site. **Cards:** AX, DS, MC, VI. ☒

TRASTEVERE RISTORANTE   **Lunch:** $7-$11   **Dinner:** $7-$22   **Phone:** 407/628-1277   (103)
Italian
Location: Just n of SR 426 (Fairbanks Ave) on US 17-92; 0.5 mi s of SR 423 (Lee Rd). 400 S Orlando Ave 32789. **Hours:** 11:30 am-2:30 & 5:30-10 pm; Sat-Mon from 5:30 pm. Closed: 5/26, 12/25. **Reservations:** suggested. **Features:** Charm and character bathe this quiet, romantic restaurant, which in some areas has the unmistakable feel of a wine cellar. Veal and seafood specialties are prepared with a touch of richness; pasta dishes can be ordered in half or full portions. Smoke free premises. Casual dress; beer & wine only. **Parking:** on-site. **Cards:** AX, DS, MC, VI. ☒

The following restaurant has not been evaluated by AAA but is listed for your information only.

FUJI SUSHI   **Phone:** 407/645-1299
[fyi]   Not evaluated. **Location:** 1449 Lee Rd 32789. **Features:** Strictly Japanese, no blending of Chinese influences, very large extensive menu. Sashimi and sushi are expertly done by chefs in main dining room. Combination dinners are a good choice here.

This ends listings for the Orlando Vicinity.
The following page resumes the alphabetical listings of cities in Florida.

ORMOND BEACH pop. 36,301   (See map p. 279; index p. 280)

──────── WHERE TO STAY ────────

BEST WESTERN MAINSAIL INN AND SUITES

Phone: 386-677-2131   **19**

(AAA) (SAVE)

12/1-3/9 [CP]	1P: $85-$275	2P: $85-$275	XP: $10 F18
3/10-5/25 [CP]	1P: $75-$250	2P: $75-$250	XP: $10 F18
5/26-11/30 [CP]	1P: $75-$200	2P: $75-$200	XP: $10 F18

Motel   **Location:** SR A1A, 0.5 mi s of SR 40. 281 S Atlantic Ave 32176. Fax: 386/676-0323. **Facility:** 42 units. 33 one-bedroom standard units, some with efficiencies or kitchens. 7 one- and 2 two-bedroom suites, some with kitchens and/or whirlpools. 4 stories, interior/exterior corridors. *Bath:* combo or shower only. **Parking:** on-site. **Terms:** 3 day cancellation notice-fee imposed. **Amenities:** voice mail, safes, irons, hair dryers. **Pool(s):** heated outdoor, wading. **Guest Services:** valet and coin laundry. **Business Services:** fax (fee). **Cards:** AX, DC, DS, MC, VI. **Special Amenities:** free continental breakfast. *(See color ad p 288)*

SOME UNITS

COMFORT INN INTERSTATE

Phone: (386)672-8621   **6**

(AAA) (SAVE)

2/1-4/30 [ECP]	1P: $66-$186	2P: $66-$186	XP: $6 F18
5/1-8/31 [ECP]	1P: $60-$186	2P: $60-$186	XP: $6 F18
9/1-11/30 [ECP]	1P: $53-$161	2P: $53-$161	XP: $6 F18
12/1-1/31 [ECP]	1P: $53-$106	2P: $53-$106	XP: $6 F18

Small-scale Hotel   **Location:** I-95, exit 273, just e. 1567 N US 1 32174. Fax: 386/677-9107. **Facility:** 75 one-bedroom standard units. 2 stories, exterior corridors. **Parking:** on-site. **Terms:** cancellation fee imposed, [CP] meal plan available. **Amenities:** hair dryers. *Some:* irons. **Pool(s):** outdoor. **Guest Services:** coin laundry. **Business Services:** fax (fee). **Cards:** AX, CB, DC, DS, JC, MC, VI. **Special Amenities: free continental breakfast and free local telephone calls.**

SOME UNITS

COMFORT INN ON THE BEACH

Phone: (386)677-8550   **14**

(AAA) (SAVE)

12/1-3/11 [CP]	1P: $85-$185	2P: $85-$185	XP: $10 F18
9/3-11/30 [CP]	1P: $75-$170	2P: $75-$170	XP: $10 F18
3/12-7/7 [CP]	1P: $90-$100	2P: $90-$100	XP: $10 F18
7/8-9/2 [CP]	1P: $85-$95	2P: $85-$95	XP: $10 F18

Motel   **Location:** On SR A1A, 1 mi s of jct SR 40. 507 S Atlantic Ave 32176. Fax: 386/673-6260. **Facility:** 47 units. 44 one-bedroom standard units, some with efficiencies. 3 one-bedroom suites with efficiencies. 4 stories, exterior corridors. **Parking:** on-site. **Terms:** 10 day cancellation notice-fee imposed, weekly rates available, small pets only ($10 extra charge). **Amenities:** voice mail, safes (fee), irons, hair dryers. **Pool(s):** heated outdoor, wading. **Business Services:** fax (fee). **Cards:** AX, DS, MC, VI. **Special Amenities: free continental breakfast and free newspaper.** *(See color ads starting on p 288)*

SOME UNITS

(See map p. 279)

CORAL BEACH MOTEL

Phone: 386/677-4712 **9**

AAA SAVE					
	2/28-5/31	1P: $55-$325	2P: $55-$325	XP: $10	F17
	12/1-2/27	1P: $45-$320	2P: $45-$320	XP: $10	F17
	6/1-8/31	1P: $50-$315	2P: $50-$315	XP: $10	F17
	9/1-11/30	1P: $45-$235	2P: $45-$235	XP: $10	F17

Small-scale Hotel Location: On SR A1A, 1.5 mi s of SR 40. 711 S Atlantic Ave 32176. **Fax:** 386/523-1000. **Facility:** 97 units. 78 one- and 17 two-bedroom standard units, some efficiencies. 2 two-bedroom suites with efficiencies. 7 stories, interior/exterior corridors. **Parking:** on-site. **Terms:** 2-7 night minimum stay - weekends, 14 day cancellation notice-fee imposed. **Amenities:** safes (fee), hair dryers. **Pool(s):** outdoor, heated indoor. **Leisure Activities:** shuffleboard. *Fee:* game room. **Guest Services:** coin laundry. **Business Services:** fax (fee). **Cards:** AX, MC, VI. **Special Amenities:** free local telephone calls. *(See color ad p 287)*

SOME UNITS

THE COVE ON ORMOND BEACH A CLUB NAVIGO RESORT

Phone: (386)677-1446 **11**

AAA SAVE

Condominium

All Year 1P: $49-$299 2P: $49-$299 **Location:** Just s of jct SR 40. 145 S Atlantic 32176. **Fax:** 386/677-2834. **Facility:** 54 units. 6 one-bedroom standard units with efficiencies. 30 one- and 18 two-bedroom units ($49-$299) with efficiencies. 7 stories, interior corridors. *Bath:* combo or shower only. **Parking:** on-site. **Terms:** check-in 4 pm, 15 day cancellation notice-fee imposed. **Amenities:** voice mail, irons, hair dryers. **Pool(s):** heated outdoor. **Leisure Activities:** playground, exercise room. **Guest Services:** coin laundry. **Business Services:** meeting rooms, fax. **Special Amenities:** free local telephone calls and preferred room (subject to availability with advanced reservations). *(See color ad p 694)*

SOME UNITS

DAYS INN ORMOND BEACH I-95

Phone: 386/672-7341 **5**

AAA SAVE

Small-scale Hotel

All Year [ECP] 1P: $45-$240 2P: $45-$240 XP: $10 F18 **Location:** I-95, exit 273, just nw on US 1. 1608 N US 1 & I-95 32174. **Fax:** 386/672-3717. **Facility:** 72 one-bedroom standard units. 2 stories, exterior corridors. **Parking:** on-site. **Terms:** 3 day cancellation notice-fee imposed, weekly rates available, small pets only ($5 extra charge). **Amenities:** hair dryers. **Pool(s):** outdoor. **Guest Services:** coin laundry. **Business Services:** fax (fee). **Cards:** AX, DS, MC, VI. **Special Amenities:** free continental breakfast and preferred room (subject to availability with advanced reservations).

SOME UNITS

DRIFTWOOD BEACH MOTEL

Phone: (386)677-1331 **10**

AAA SAVE

Motel

All Year 1P: $45-$165 2P: $45-$165 XP: $7 F14 **Location:** On SR A1A, 1.5 mi s of jct SR 40. 657 S Atlantic Ave 32176. **Fax:** 386/677-0625. **Facility:** 44 units. 38 one-bedroom standard units, some with efficiencies. 4 one- and 2 two-bedroom suites ($70-$350) with efficiencies. 2-3 stories (no elevator), exterior corridors. *Bath:* combo or shower only. **Terms:** 14 day cancellation notice, weekly rates available, small pets only ($20 extra charge). **Pool(s):** heated outdoor. **Leisure Activities:** shuffleboard. **Guest Services:** coin laundry. **Business Services:** fax (fee). **Cards:** DS, MC, VI. **Special Amenities:** free newspaper and preferred room (subject to availability with advanced reservations). *(See color ad p 287)*

SOME UNITS

ECONO LODGE ON THE BEACH

Phone: (386)672-2651 **20**

AAA SAVE					
	12/1-3/11	1P: $70-$145	2P: $70-$145	XP: $10	F17
	9/3-11/30	1P: $65-$145	2P: $65-$145		
	3/12-7/7	1P: $80-$95	2P: $80-$95	XP: $10	F17
	7/8-9/2	1P: $75-$85	2P: $75-$85	XP: $10	F17

Motel **Location:** SR A1A, 0.5 mi s of SR 40. 295 S Atlantic Ave 32176. **Fax:** 386/672-2651. **Facility:** 57 one-bedroom standard units, some with efficiencies. 4 stories, exterior corridors. **Parking:** on-site. **Terms:** 10 day cancellation notice, weekly rates available. **Pool(s):** heated outdoor, wading. **Guest Services:** coin laundry. **Business Services:** fax. **Cards:** AX, DC, DS, MC, VI. *(See color ads starting on p 288)*

SOME UNITS

HAMPTON INN ORMOND BEACH

Phone: (386)677-9999 **7**

SAVE

Small-scale Hotel

All Year [ECP] 1P: $79 2P: $235 **Location:** I-95, exit 268, just w. 155 Interchange Blvd 32174. **Fax:** 386/677-0663. **Facility:** 84 one-bedroom standard units, some with whirlpools. 4 stories, interior corridors. *Bath:* combo or shower only. **Parking:** on-site. **Terms:** check-in 4 pm. **Amenities:** voice mail, irons, hair dryers. **Pool(s):** outdoor. **Leisure Activities:** exercise room. **Guest Services:** coin laundry. **Business Services:** meeting rooms. **Cards:** AX, CB, DC, DS, JC, MC, VI.

SOME UNITS

JAMESON INN

Phone: 386/672-3675 **4**

Small-scale Hotel

All Year [ECP] 1P: $52-$67 2P: $55-$70 XP: $3 F17 **Location:** I-95, exit 268, just w, then just s. 175 Interchange Blvd 32174. **Fax:** 386/672-0453. **Facility:** 67 units. 65 one-bedroom standard units. 2 one-bedroom suites. 3 stories, interior corridors. *Bath:* combo or shower only. **Parking:** on-site. **Terms:** small pets only. **Amenities:** *Some:* voice mail, irons. **Pool(s):** outdoor. **Leisure Activities:** exercise room. **Guest Services:** valet laundry. **Business Services:** meeting rooms, fax. **Cards:** AX, CB, DC, DS, MC, VI.

SOME UNITS

(See map p. 279)

SLEEP INN
[SAVE]

Phone: (386)673-6030   **8**

12/1-7/7 [ECP]	1P: $72-$186	2P: $72-$186	XP: $5	F18
7/8-11/30 [ECP]	1P: $70-$102	2P: $70-$105	XP: $5	F18

Small-scale Hotel

Location: I-95, exit 268, just e. 170 Williamson Blvd 32174. Fax: 386/673-7017. **Facility:** 83 one-bedroom standard units. 3 stories, interior corridors. *Bath:* shower only. **Parking:** on-site. **Amenities:** *Some:* irons, hair dryers. **Pool(s):** outdoor. **Guest Services:** coin laundry. **Business Services:** fax (fee). **Cards:** AX, CB, DC, DS, JC, MC, VI.

SOME UNITS

🆔 ⏸️ ♿M ♿ ⌨️ ➿ 📺 [DATA PORT] / ✕ 🍴 🖥️ /

SYMPHONY BEACH CLUB
(AAA) [SAVE]

Phone: 386/672-7373   **16**

2/1-8/31	1P: $59-$95	2P: $59-$95	XP: $10	F16
9/1-11/30	1P: $54-$95	2P: $54-$95	XP: $10	F16
12/1-1/31	1P: $54-$90	2P: $54-$90	XP: $10	F16

Condominium

Location: SR A1A, 0.8 mi s of jct SR 40. 453 S Atlantic Ave 32176. Fax: 386/673-1174. **Facility:** 30 units. 28 one-bedroom standard units with efficiencies. 2 one-bedroom suites with efficiencies. 4 stories, exterior corridors. **Parking:** on-site. **Terms:** 14 day cancellation notice-fee imposed, weekly rates available, [CP] meal plan available, package plans. **Pool(s):** heated outdoor. **Guest Services:** coin laundry. **Business Services:** fax. **Cards:** DS, MC, VI.

SOME UNITS

🆔 ⏸️ ➿ 🍴 🖥️ / ✕ /

——————— **WHERE TO DINE** ———————

ENGLISH ROSE TEA ROOM

Lunch: $5-$9   Phone: 386/672-7673   **4**

English

Location: SR A1A, 1.3 mi n on SR 40. 49 W Granada Blvd (Rt 40) 32174. **Hours:** 9 am-3 pm. Closed: Sun. **Features:** British and vegetarian foods are among the breakfast, lunch and afternoon tea items served at the cozy tea room. Smoke free premises. Casual dress. **Parking:** on-site. **Cards:** MC, VI.

✕

JULIAN'S
(AAA)

Dinner: $9-$20   Phone: 386/677-6767   **1**

American

Location: On SR A1A, just s of SR 40. 88 S Atlantic Ave 32176. **Hours:** 4 pm-11 pm. **Features:** Vintage decor in a Polynesian motif sets a tropical feel in the casual restaurant. A wall mural of a Hawaiian village brightens the sunken bar. The cordial and knowledgeable wait staff adeptly describe the menu offerings, such as grilled salmon. Casual dress; cocktails; entertainment. **Parking:** on-site. **Cards:** AX, CB, DC, DS, MC, VI.

✕

LA CREPE EN HAUT
(AAA)

Lunch: $8-$12   Dinner: $23-$40   Phone: 386/673-1999   **2**

French

Location: SR 40, just w of se SR A1A. 142 E Granada Blvd 32176. **Hours:** 11:30 am-2:30 & 5:30-10 pm, Sat & Sun from 5:30 pm. Closed major holidays; also Mon. **Reservations:** suggested. **Features:** Expect fine French cuisine offered in a charming dining room. A polished wait staff gives personalized service and extends a warm invitation for a return visit. Excellent veal smothered in a fabulous sauce is colorfully presented with crisp vegetables. Semi-formal attire; cocktails. **Parking:** on-site. **Cards:** AX, MC, VI.

✕

MARIO'S

Dinner: $9-$17   Phone: 386/677-2711   **5**

Traditional Italian

Location: US 1. 521 S Yonge St 32176. **Hours:** 4:30 pm-10 pm. Closed: 11/27, 12/25. **Features:** Moderately priced lunch and dinner selections tend toward the traditional at this family-owned Italian restaurant. The menu includes a tasty choice of pastas, salads, pizzas, lasagna and seafood. The atmosphere is casual and comfortable. Casual dress; cocktails. **Parking:** on-site. **Cards:** AX, MC, VI.

Ⓨ ✕

ROYAL DYNASTY RESTAURANT & LOUNGE

Lunch: $5-$8   Dinner: $8-$17   Phone: 386/676-2266   **3**

Chinese

Location: Jct Williamson Blvd and SR 40. 1482 W Granada Blvd 32174. **Hours:** 11 am-9:30 pm, Fri & Sat-10:30 pm. **Features:** Delectable moo shu chicken is prepared right at your table. Lunch combination plates as well as an a la carte menu feature a very good variety of traditional Chinese entrees. Clean and neat service with quality table settings are nice touches. Casual dress; cocktails. **Parking:** on-site. **Cards:** AX, DS, MC, VI.

Ⓨ

——————— *The following restaurant has not been evaluated by AAA* ———————
but is listed for your information only.

GENOVESE'S ITALIAN CAFE
[fyi]

Phone: 904/677-3222

Not evaluated. **Location:** 183 E Granada Blvd 32176. **Features:** This small, casual, family-style Italian restaurant offers a variety of subs, salads, pizza and pasta dishes. Carry out also available.

OSPREY pop. 4,143

——————— **WHERE TO STAY** ———————

RAMADA INN-SARASOTA SOUTH
(AAA) [SAVE]

Phone: (941)966-2121   **125**

12/24-3/31 [ECP]	1P: $100-$120	2P: $100-$120
4/1-5/31 [ECP]	1P: $69-$79	2P: $69-$79
12/1-12/23 [ECP]	1P: $60-$70	2P: $60-$70
6/1-11/30 [ECP]	1P: $50-$60	2P: $50-$60

Motel

Location: On US 41, 1.8 mi n of jct SR 681. 1660 S Tamiami Tr 34229. Fax: 941/966-1124. **Facility:** 136 units. 128 one-bedroom standard units. 8 one-bedroom suites ($80-$140), some with kitchens. 2 stories, interior/exterior corridors. **Parking:** on-site. **Terms:** pets ($25 fee, in designated units). **Amenities:** voice mail, irons, hair dryers. **Dining:** 11 am-1 & 5-10 pm. **Pool(s):** heated outdoor. **Leisure Activities:** exercise room. **Guest Services:** valet and coin laundry. **Business Services:** meeting rooms, fax. **Cards:** AX, DC, DS, MC, VI. **Special Amenities:** early check-in/late check-out and free continental breakfast.

SOME UNITS

🆔 🐕 ⏸️ ➿ 📺 [DATA PORT] 🖥️ / ✕ 🍴 🖥️ /

OVIEDO —See Orlando p. 747.

PALATKA pop. 10,033—See also EAST PALATKA.

——— WHERE TO STAY ———

HOLIDAY INN-RIVERFRONT
▼▼▼▼ All Year   1P: $64-$99   Phone: (386)328-3481
Location: At foot of St. John's River Bridge on US 17. 201 N First St 32177. Fax: 386/329-9907. **Facility:** 130 one-bedroom standard units. 2 stories, exterior corridors. **Parking:** on-site. **Terms:** [AP] meal plan available, package plans. **Amenities:** voice mail, irons, hair dryers. **Pool(s):** outdoor. **Leisure Activities:** marina, fishing, exercise room. **Guest Services:** valet and coin laundry. **Business Services:** meeting rooms, fax (fee). **Cards:** AX, DC, DS, MC, VI. *(See color ad opposite inside back cover)*

Small-scale Hotel

SOME UNITS

(ASK) (S🅓) (🍽) (⅄) (🏊) (☒) (🎥) (DATA PORT) (🖥) / (⊠) (📠) / FEE

PALM BAY pop. 79,413

——— WHERE TO STAY ———

JAMESON INN
▼▼▼▼ All Year [ECP]   1P: $52-$67   2P: $55-$70   XP: $3   F17
Location: I-95, exit 176. 890 Palm Bay Rd 32905. Fax: 321/768-1759. **Facility:** 67 units. 65 one-bedroom standard units. 2 one-bedroom suites. 3 stories, interior corridors. *Bath:* combo or shower only. **Parking:** on-site. **Terms:** $3 service charge, small pets only. **Amenities:** voice mail, irons. **Pool(s):** outdoor. **Leisure Activities:** exercise room. **Business Services:** meeting rooms. **Cards:** AX, CB, DC, DS, MC, VI.

Small-scale Hotel

SOME UNITS

(🐕) (🅼) (🛗) (🍽) (🏊) (🎥) (DATA PORT) / (⊠) (📠) (🖥) /

RAMADA PLAZA HOTEL
▼▼▼▼
2/1-2/28	1P: $79	2P: $79	XP: $7	F17
1/2-1/31	1P: $69	2P: $69	XP: $7	F17
12/1-1/1 & 3/1-11/30	1P: $64	2P: $64	XP: $7	F17

Small-scale Hotel
Phone: (321)723-8181

Location: I-95, exit 176, 2.1 mi e. 1881 Palm Bay Rd NE 32905. Fax: 321/727-7390. **Facility:** 122 units. 120 one-bedroom standard units. 2 one-bedroom suites. 4 stories, interior corridors. **Parking:** on-site. **Amenities:** voice mail, irons, hair dryers. **Pool(s):** outdoor, indoor. **Leisure Activities:** exercise room. **Guest Services:** coin laundry. **Business Services:** conference facilities, business center. **Cards:** AX, DC, DS, MC, VI.

SOME UNITS

(ASK) (S🅓) (🛗) (🎥) (🏊) (🎥) (DATA PORT) (🖥) / (⊠) (VCR) (📠) (🖥) / FEE

——— WHERE TO DINE ———

THE CROW'S NEST   Lunch: $5-$10   Dinner: $8-$26   Phone: 321/725-4020
▼▼▼ **Location:** Just e off US 1, 1.3 mi n of jct SR 514 on the river. 3450 Gran Ave 32905. **Hours:** 11:30 am-9 pm, Fri & Sat-10 pm, Sun noon-9 pm. **Reservations:** suggested. **Features:** Look out over the Indian River marina, where you may catch an occasional glimpse of a dolphin or manatee. Steaks, shrimp New Orleans and herb-crusted salmon are tasty entrees; the hot fudge brownie sundae is a tempting topper. Casual dress; cocktails. **Parking:** on-site. **Cards:** AX, DS, MC, VI.

Seafood

(⅄) (⊠)

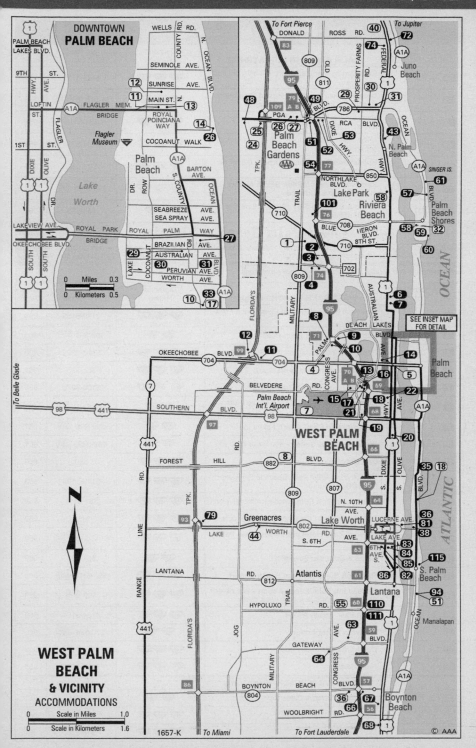

DOWNTOWN
PALM BEACH

WEST PALM
BEACH
& VICINITY
ACCOMMODATIONS

1657-K
© AAA

✈ Airport Accommodations

Spotter/Map Page Number	OA	PALM BEACH INTERNATIONAL	Diamond Rating	Rate Range High Season	Listing Page
21 / p. 757		Courtyard by Marriott Airport, 0.8 mi n of airport entrance	◆◆◆	$129-$159	958
15 / p. 757	AAA	**Crowne Plaza Hotel and Resort West Palm Beach, 0.3 mi n of airport entrance**	◆◆◆	$143-$161 SAVE	958
13 / p. 757		Hampton Inn West Palm Beach/International Airport, 0.5 mi ne of airport entrance	◆◆◆	$81-$116	958
19 / p. 757		Hilton Palm Beach Airport, 0.8 mi s of airport entrance	◆◆◆	$134-$154	959
18 / p. 757	AAA	**Holiday Inn Palm Beach Airport, 0.8 mi ne of airport entrance**	◆◆◆	$99 SAVE	959
17 / p. 757	AAA	**Radisson Suite Inn Palm Beach Airport, 0.8 mi n of airport entrance**	◆◆◆	$98-$116 SAVE	960
16 / p. 757		Studio 6 Extended Stay #6026, 0.8 mi n of airport entrance	◆◆	$54-$83	960

West Palm Beach & Vicinity

This index helps you "spot" where approved accommodations and restaurants are located on the corresponding detailed maps. Lodging rate ranges are for comparison only and show the property's high season; rates are per night, unless only weekly (W) rates are available. Restaurant rate range is for dinner, unless only lunch (L) is served. Turn to the listing page for more detailed rate information and consult display ads for special promotions.

Spotter/Map Page Number	OA	WEST PALM BEACH - Lodgings	Diamond Rating	Rate Range High Season	Listing Page
2 / p. 757		Courtyard by Marriott-West Palm Beach - see ad p 247	◆◆◆	$139-$159	958
3 / p. 757	AAA	**Red Roof Inn-West Palm Beach**	◆◆	$69-$94 SAVE	960
4 / p. 757		Residence Inn by Marriott West Palm Beach	◆◆◆	$120-$229	960
6 / p. 757		Tropical Gardens Bed & Breakfast	◆◆◆	$85-$95	961
7 / p. 757		Hibiscus House Bed & Breakfast	◆◆◆	$100-$270	958
8 / p. 757	AAA	**Comfort Inn-on Palm Beach Lakes - see color ad p 957**	◆◆	$89-$119 SAVE	957
9 / p. 757	AAA	**Best Western Palm Beach Lakes Inn**	◆◆	$94-$96 SAVE	957
10 / p. 757	AAA	**Wellesley Inn & Suites - see color ad p 957**	◆◆	$89-$129 SAVE	961
11 / p. 757		La Quinta Inn	◆◆◆	$80	960
12 / p. 757		Hampton Inn West Palm Beach at Emerald Dunes Golf Course	◆◆◆	$149-$189	958
13 / p. 757		Hampton Inn West Palm Beach/International Airport	◆◆◆	$81-$116	958
14 / p. 757		Sheraton Hotel at CityPlace - see color ad p 5	◆◆◆	$155	960
15 / p. 757	AAA	**Crowne Plaza Hotel and Resort West Palm Beach**	◆◆◆	$143-$161 SAVE	958
16 / p. 757		Studio 6 Extended Stay #6026	◆◆	$54-$83	960
17 / p. 757	AAA	**Radisson Suite Inn Palm Beach Airport**	◆◆◆	$98-$116 SAVE	960
18 / p. 757	AAA	**Holiday Inn Palm Beach Airport - see color ad p 959, opposite inside back cover**	◆◆◆	$99 SAVE	959
19 / p. 757		Hilton Palm Beach Airport	◆◆◆	$134-$154	959
20 / p. 757	AAA	**Parkview Motor Lodge**	◆◆	$70-$88 SAVE	960
21 / p. 757		Courtyard by Marriott Airport	◆◆◆	$129-$159	958
22 / p. 757		Hotel Biba	◆◆◆	$109-$179	959
		WEST PALM BEACH - Restaurants			
1 / p. 757		Great Texas Land & Cattle Co.	◆◆	$9-$23	961
4 / p. 757		Rain Dancer Steak House	◆◆◆	$15-$30	961
5 / p. 757		Mark's City Place	◆◆◆	$18-$30	961

Spotter/Map Page Number	OA	WEST PALM BEACH - Restaurants (continued)	Diamond Rating	Rate Range High Season	Listing Page
7 / p. 757		391st Bomb Group	◈◈	$12-$29	961
8 / p. 757		Orchids of Siam	◈◈	$10-$18	961
		PALM BEACH - Lodgings			
26 / p. 757	AAA	**The Breakers**	◈◈◈◈◈	$445-$845 SAVE	761
27 / p. 757		Heart of Palm Beach Hotel	◈◈◈	$199-$329	762
29 / p. 757		Plaza Inn	◈◈◈	$205-$275	762
30 / p. 757	AAA	**The Chesterfield Hotel**	◈◈◈	$225-$1500 SAVE	761
31 / p. 757	AAA	**Palm Beach Historic Inn**	◈◈◈	$150-$325 SAVE	762
33 / p. 757		The Colony	◈◈◈	$305-$1200	761
35 / p. 757	AAA	**The Four Seasons Resort, Palm Beach**	◈◈◈◈◈	$395-$725	762
36 / p. 757		Palm Beach Hilton Oceanfront Resort - see color ad p 761	◈◈◈	$219-$549	762
38 / p. 757		Marriott Fairfield Inn & Suites	◈◈◈	$119-$189	762
		PALM BEACH - Restaurants			
10 / p. 757		Polo	◈◈	$16-$33	763
11 / p. 757	AAA	**Testa's Restaurant**	◈◈	$12-$25	763
12 / p. 757		Echo	◈◈◈	$18-$28	763
13 / p. 757		Chuck & Harold's	◈◈	$14-$34	763
14 / p. 757	AAA	**L'Escalier**	◈◈◈◈	$32-$40	763
17 / p. 757		Charley's Crab	◈◈◈	$16-$38	763
18 / p. 757	AAA	**The Restaurant at The Four Seasons**	◈◈◈◈◈	$29-$36	763
		NORTH PALM BEACH - Lodgings			
43 / p. 757	AAA	**The Waterford Hotel & Conference Center**	◈◈◈	$139-$399 SAVE	581
		PALM BEACH GARDENS - Lodgings			
48 / p. 757	AAA	**PGA National Resort & Spa**	◈◈◈◈	$279-$379 SAVE	765
49 / p. 757	AAA	**Doubletree Hotel In The Gardens - see color ad p 764**	◈◈◈	$149 SAVE	763
51 / p. 757		Embassy Suites Hotel	◈◈◈	$139-$249	764
52 / p. 757	AAA	**Palm Beach Gardens Marriott**	◈◈◈	$89-$199 SAVE	764
53 / p. 757		Hampton Inn	◈◈◈	$149-$189	764
54 / p. 757	AAA	**Inns of America**	◈◈	$89-$119 SAVE	764
		PALM BEACH GARDENS - Restaurants			
24 / p. 757		Shula's Steak House	◈◈◈	$30-$50	765
25 / p. 757		Ebisu Japanese Restaurant	◈◈	$12-$20	765
26 / p. 757		Cafe Chardonnay	◈◈◈	$17-$32	765
27 / p. 757		Paddy Mac's	◈◈	$9-$19	765
29 / p. 757		No Anchovies! Neighborhood Pastaria	◈◈	$9-$17	765
30 / p. 757		The River House	◈◈◈	$17-$40	765
31 / p. 757		Fathom	◈◈◈	$17-$30	765
		PALM BEACH SHORES - Lodgings			
57 / p. 757	AAA	**Crowne Plaza Oceanfront North Palm Beach Hotel**	◈◈◈	$299-$329 SAVE	766
58 / p. 757		Sailfish Marina & Resort	◈◈	$69-$149	767
59 / p. 757	AAA	**Radisson Palm Beach Shores Resort and Vacation Villas**	◈◈◈	$269-$369 SAVE	766

Spotter/Map Page Number	OA	PALM BEACH SHORES - Lodgings (continued)	Diamond Rating	Rate Range High Season	Listing Page
60 / p. 757	AAA	Best Western Seaspray Inn - see ad p 766	◆◆	$110-$180 [SAVE]	766
61 / p. 757	AAA	Hilton Singer Island Oceanfront Resort - see color ad p 959	◆◆◆	$179-$279 [SAVE]	766
		PALM BEACH SHORES - Restaurant			
32 / p. 757		Sailfish Waterfront Dining	◆◆	$11-$27	767
		BOYNTON BEACH - Lodgings			
63 / p. 757		Hampton Inn & Suites Boynton Beach	◆◆◆	$129-$209	256
64 / p. 757		Holiday Inn-Catalina - see color ad opposite inside back cover	◆◆◆	$69-$149	256
66 / p. 757	AAA	Holiday Inn Express I-95 - see color ad p 256	◆◆	$117 [SAVE]	256
67 / p. 757		Boynton Motel	◆	$65-$80	255
68 / p. 757	AAA	Atlantic Lodge	◆◆	$66-$80 [SAVE]	255
		BOYNTON BEACH - Restaurant			
36 / p. 757	AAA	Mama Jennie's Italian Restaurant	◆	$8-$15	256
		JUNO BEACH - Lodgings			
72 / p. 757		Holiday Inn Express-North Palm Beach	◆◆◆	$129-$300	479
74 / p. 757		Hampton Inn-Juno Beach	◆◆◆	$119-$199	479
		JUNO BEACH - Restaurant			
40 / p. 757		Classico's Italian Restaurant	◆◆	$8-$20	479
		LAKE WORTH - Lodgings			
79 / p. 757		Holiday Inn West Palm Beach-Turnpike - see color ad opposite inside back cover	◆◆◆	$115-$119	488
81 / p. 757	AAA	Sabal Palm House B & B Inn	◆◆◆◆	$100-$180 [SAVE]	488
82 / p. 757	AAA	Martinique Motor Lodge	◆	$65-$95 [SAVE]	488
83 / p. 757	AAA	New Sun Gate Motel	◆◆	$55-$79 [SAVE]	488
84 / p. 757	AAA	Lago Motor Inn	◆◆	$50-$72 [SAVE]	488
85 / p. 757		Parador of the Palm Beaches	◆◆◆	$125-$150	488
86 / p. 757		White Manor Motel	◆	$375(W)	488
		LAKE WORTH - Restaurant			
44 / p. 757	AAA	Bohemian Garden Restaurant	◆◆	$8-$21	489
		MANALAPAN - Lodgings			
94 / p. 757	AAA	The Ritz-Carlton, Palm Beach	◆◆◆◆◆	$395-$875 [SAVE]	494
		MANALAPAN - Restaurant			
51 / p. 757		The Grill	◆◆◆◆	$20-$38	494
		RIVIERA BEACH - Lodgings			
101 / p. 757		Super 8 Motel West Palm Beach/Riviera Beach	◆◆	$69-$89	784
		LANTANA - Lodgings			
110 / p. 757	AAA	Comfort Inn-Lantana/Boynton Beach - see ad p 255	◆◆◆	$75-$129 [SAVE]	489
111 / p. 757	AAA	Best Western Inn of America	◆◆◆	$69-$120 [SAVE]	489
		LANTANA - Restaurant			
55 / p. 757		Anchor Inn Restaurant	◆◆	$14-$26	489
		SOUTH PALM BEACH - Lodgings			
115 / p. 757		Palm Beach Hawaiian Ocean Inn	◆◆	$150	834
		LAKE PARK - Restaurant			
58 / p. 757		Cafe du Park	◆◆◆	$16-$26	486

PALM BEACH pop. 10,468   (See map p. 757; index p. 759)—
See also NORTH PALM BEACH, PALM BEACH GARDENS, PALM BEACH SHORES, SOUTH PALM BEACH & WEST PALM BEACH.

———— WHERE TO STAY ————

THE BREAKERS
Phone: (561)655-6611 26

11/1-11/30	1P: $445-$845	2P: $445-$845	XP: $50 F16
12/1-5/17	1P: $435-$835	2P: $435-$835	XP: $50 F16
5/18-10/31	1P: $275-$490	2P: $275-$490	XP: $50 F16

Location: On SR A1A, 0.3 mi s of jct Royal Poinciana Way. One South County Rd 33480. Fax: 561/659-8403.
Resort **Facility:** Fine hardwoods enhance the guest rooms of this service-oriented, Italian villa-style hotel built in
Large-scale Hotel 1896 by Henry Flagler. 560 units. 515 one-bedroom standard units. 45 one-bedroom suites ($505-$4000), some with whirlpools. 5-9 stories, interior corridors. **Bath:** some combo or shower only. **Parking:** on-site (fee) and valet. **Terms:** check-in 4 pm, cancellation fee imposed, [AP], [BP] & [MAP] meal plans available, 20% service charge. **Amenities:** video games (fee), CD players, dual phone lines, voice mail, safes, honor bars, irons, hair dryers. **Dining:** 6 restaurants, 7 am-10 pm; afternoon tea 12/15-4/15, cocktails, also, L'Escalier, see separate listing, entertainment. **Pool(s):** 3 heated outdoor, wading. **Leisure Activities:** whirlpool, pool & beach cabana, recreation programs, playground, spa. *Fee:* scuba diving, snorkeling, charter fishing, golf-36 holes, 10 lighted tennis courts, bicycles. **Guest Services:** gift shop, valet laundry, area transportation (fee)-within 20 mi, barber shop, beauty salon. *Fee:* golf & tennis instruciion. **Business Services:** conference facilities, business center. **Cards:** AX, CB, DC, DS, MC, VI. Affiliated with A Preferred Hotel.

SOME UNITS

THE CHESTERFIELD HOTEL
Phone: (561)659-5800 30

12/1-4/30	1P: $225-$1500	XP: $15 F16
5/1-5/31 & 9/29-11/30	1P: $139-$610	XP: $15 F16
6/1-9/28	1P: $99-$500	XP: $15 F16

Location: Just w of SR A1A; at Australian Ave and Cocoanut Row. 363 Cocoanut Row 33480. Fax: 561/659-6707.
Historic **Facility:** 55 units. 44 one-bedroom standard units. 10 one- and 1 two-bedroom suites ($185-$1500). 4 sto-
Small-scale Hotel ries, interior corridors. **Parking:** valet. **Terms:** 3 day cancellation notice-fee imposed, pets ($50 deposit). **Amenities:** video library, dual phone lines, voice mail, safes, irons, hair dryers. *Some:* CD players, honor bars. **Dining:** 7-10:30 am, 11:30-2:30 & 6-1 am, cocktails, entertainment. **Pool(s):** heated outdoor. **Leisure Activities:** whirlpool. *Fee:* massage. **Guest Services:** valet laundry. **Business Services:** meeting rooms, PC, fax (fee). **Cards:** AX, CB, DC, DS, MC, VI. **Special Amenities:** free local telephone calls and free newspaper.

SOME UNITS

THE COLONY
Phone: (561)655-5430 33

12/1-4/30	1P: $305-$1200	2P: $305-$1200	XP: $25 F17
5/1-5/31 & 10/16-11/30	1P: $160-$800	2P: $160-$800	XP: $25 F17
6/1-10/15	1P: $130-$650	2P: $130-$650	XP: $25 F17

Small-scale Hotel **Location:** SR A1A, just s of Worth Ave. 155 Hammon Ave 33480. Fax: 561/659-8104. **Facility:** 90 units. 73 one-bedroom standard units. 14 one- and 3 two-bedroom suites ($385-$1200), some with kitchens. 6 stories, interior corridors. **Parking:** on-site (fee) and valet. **Terms:** check-in 4 pm, 3 day cancellation notice, package plans - seasonal. **Amenities:** voice mail, irons, hair dryers. *Some:* safes. **Dining:** Polo, see separate listing. **Pool(s):** 2 heated outdoor. **Leisure Activities:** whirlpool. *Fee:* bicycles, massage. **Guest Services:** valet laundry. **Business Services:** meeting rooms, business center. **Cards:** AX, CB, DC, DS, JC, MC, VI.

SOME UNITS

(See map p. 757)

THE FOUR SEASONS RESORT, PALM BEACH

Phone: (561)582-2800 | 35

All Year | 1P: $395-$725 | 2P: $395-$725 | XP: $30 | F17

Location: SR A1A, 0.3 mi n of jct SR 802. 2800 S Ocean Blvd 33480. Fax: 561/547-1374. **Facility:** An on-site spa, private beach and fine dining contribute an elegant ambience to this waterfront property. 210 units. 198 one-bedroom standard units. 8 one- and 4 two-bedroom suites ($1750-$3000). 4 stories, interior corridors. *Bath:*

Large-scale Hotel combo or shower only. **Parking:** on-site (fee) and valet. **Terms:** check-in 4 pm, 7 day cancellation notice-fee imposed, small pets only. **Amenities:** video library, CD players, dual phone lines, voice mail, safes, honor bars, irons, hair dryers. *Fee:* video games, high-speed Internet. *Some:* fax. **Dining:** 2 restaurants, 7 am-10 pm, Fri & Sat-11 pm, cocktails, also, The Restaurant at The Four Seasons, see separate listing, entertainment. **Pool(s):** heated outdoor. **Leisure Activities:** saunas, whirlpools, steamrooms, jogging, spa. *Fee:* sailboats, windsurfing, boggie boards, jet skis, kayaks, 3 tennis courts, bicycles. **Guest Services:** gift shop, valet laundry, area transportation. *Fee:* tennis instruction, pro shop, aerobics, beauty salon. **Business Services:** conference facilities, business center. **Cards:** AX, CB, DC, DS, JC, MC, VI. **Special Amenities: free newspaper.**

SOME UNITS

HEART OF PALM BEACH HOTEL

Phone: (561)655-5600 | 27

12/15-4/30 | 1P: $199-$329 | 2P: $199-$329 | XP: $15 | F18
12/1-12/14 & 5/1-11/30 | 1P: $99-$159 | 2P: $99-$159 | XP: $15 | F18

Small-scale Hotel **Location:** Just e of SR A1A; center. 160 Royal Palm Way 33480. Fax: 561/832-1201. **Facility:** 88 one-bedroom standard units. 2-3 stories, interior corridors. **Parking:** on-site. **Terms:** 3 day cancellation notice, package plans, 18% service charge, small pets only. **Amenities:** high-speed Internet (fee), voice mail, irons, hair dryers. **Pool(s):** heated outdoor. **Leisure Activities:** Fee: bicycles. **Guest Services:** valet laundry. **Business Services:** meeting rooms, fax (fee). **Cards:** AX, DC, MC, VI.

SOME UNITS

FEE

MARRIOTT FAIRFIELD INN & SUITES

Phone: (561)582-2585 | 38

12/9-4/27 [ECP] | 1P: $119-$189 | 2P: $119-$189
12/1-12/8 & 4/28-11/30 [ECP] | 1P: $79-$149 | 2P: $79-$149

Small-scale Hotel **Location:** On SR A1A; at jct SR 802. 2870 S Ocean Blvd 33480. Fax: 561/582-7189. **Facility:** 98 one-bedroom standard units. 3 stories, interior corridors. *Bath:* combo or shower only. **Parking:** on-site. **Terms:** cancellation fee imposed. **Amenities:** voice mail, irons, hair dryers. *Some:* CD players. **Pool(s):** outdoor. **Leisure Activities:** whirlpool, exercise room. **Guest Services:** valet and coin laundry. **Business Services:** meeting rooms, fax (fee). **Cards:** AX, CB, DC, DS, JC, MC, VI.

SOME UNITS

PALM BEACH HISTORIC INN

Phone: (561)832-4009 | 31

12/15-4/30 [CP] | 1P: $150-$325 | 2P: $150-$325
12/1-12/14 & 5/1-11/30 [CP] | 1P: $85-$150 | 2P: $85-$150

Historic Bed & Breakfast **Location:** On SR A1A at Chilian Ave, just n of Worth Ave; center. 365 S County Rd 33480. Fax: 561/832-6255. **Facility:** All guest rooms are on the second floor of this 1921 inn, which includes smoke-free public areas and some on-site parking. 13 units. 9 one-bedroom standard units. 4 one-bedroom suites ($150-$325). 2 stories (no elevator), interior corridors. **Parking:** on-site (fee) and street. **Terms:** 7 day cancellation notice-fee imposed. **Amenities:** video library, voice mail, irons, hair dryers. **Business Services:** fax (fee). **Cards:** AX, CB, DC, DS, JC, MC, VI. **Special Amenities: free continental breakfast and free room upgrade (subject to availability with advanced reservations).**

FEE

PALM BEACH HILTON OCEANFRONT RESORT

Phone: (561)586-6542 | 36

12/26-4/30 | 1P: $219-$549 | 2P: $219-$549 | XP: $15 | F18
12/1-12/25 & 10/1-11/30 | 1P: $159-$329 | 2P: $159-$329 | XP: $15 | F18
5/1-9/30 | 1P: $139-$310 | 2P: $139-$310 | XP: $15 | F18

Small-scale Hotel **Location:** SR A1A; just n of jct SR 802. 2842 S Ocean Blvd 33480. Fax: 561/585-7499. **Facility:** 134 units. 132 one-bedroom standard units. 2 one-bedroom suites ($250-$1150) with whirlpools. 5 stories, interior corridors. **Parking:** valet. **Terms:** check-in 4 pm, 10 day cancellation notice-fee imposed. **Amenities:** voice mail, honor bars, irons, hair dryers. *Some:* CD players. **Pool(s):** heated outdoor. **Leisure Activities:** whirlpool. *Fee:* sailboats, massage. **Guest Services:** gift shop, valet laundry. **Business Services:** meeting rooms. *Fee:* PC, fax. **Cards:** AX, DC, DS, MC, VI. *(See color ad p 761)*

SOME UNITS

FEE

PLAZA INN

Phone: (561)832-8666 | 29

12/18-4/30 [CP] | 1P: $205-$275 | 2P: $235-$275 | XP: $15 | F12
12/1-12/17 & 5/1-10/31 [CP] | 1P: $115-$145 | 2P: $135-$160 | XP: $15 | F12
11/1-11/30 | 1P: $115-$145 | 2P: $135-$160 | XP: $15 | F12

Historic Small-scale Hotel **Location:** At Brazilian Ave and SR A1A (S County Rd); center. 215 Brazilian Ave 33480. Fax: 561/835-8776. **Facility:** 47 units. 44 one-bedroom standard units. 3 one-bedroom suites ($205-$395). 3 stories, interior corridors. *Bath:* combo or shower only. **Parking:** on-site. **Terms:** 7 day cancellation notice, 3 day 5/1-12/17-fee imposed, package plans - 5/1-9/30, small pets only. **Amenities:** dual phone lines, voice mail. *Some:* DVD players. **Pool(s):** heated outdoor. **Leisure Activities:** whirlpool. **Guest Services:** valet laundry. **Cards:** AX, MC, VI.

SOME UNITS

FEE

The following lodging was either not evaluated or did not meet AAA rating requirements but is listed for your information only.

BRAZILIAN COURT HOTEL

Phone: 561/655-7740

[fyi] Not evaluated. **Location:** From Royal Palm Way (SR 204), s on Cocoanut Row, 2 blks to Australian Ave, then just e; at corner of Hibiscus and Australian aves. 301 Australian Ave 33480. Facilities, services, and decor characterize an upscale property.

(See map p. 757)

──────── WHERE TO DINE ────────

CHARLEY'S CRAB   **Lunch:** $9-$19   **Dinner:** $16-$38   **Phone:** 561/659-1500   ⑰
▽▽▽▽   **Location:** Across from ocean; 0.4 mi s of Royal Palm Way. 456 S Ocean Blvd 33480. **Hours:** 11:30 am-10 pm, Fri & Sat-10 pm, Sun 10:30 am-2:30 & 4:30-10 pm. **Reservations:** suggested; for dinner. **Features:** A snappy chipotle pepper sauce adds intrigue to the spring roll stuffed with crab, alfalfa sprouts and bamboo shoots.
Seafood   A knowledgeable staff helps you select from an extensive menu of fresh seafood. Enjoy cozy ambience with an ocean view from the bar. Dressy casual; cocktails; entertainment. **Parking:** valet. **Cards:** AX, CB, DC, DS, MC, VI.

🍸 ✕

CHUCK & HAROLD'S   **Lunch:** $5-$16   **Dinner:** $14-$34   **Phone:** 561/659-1440   ⑬
▽▽ ▽▽   **Location:** 0.3 mi e of Flager Memorial Bridge on SR A1A. 207 Royal Poinciana Way 33480. **Hours:** 7:30 am-1 am. **Reservations:** suggested. **Features:** Diners here will experience comfort whether they eat inside or at the tables on the sidewalk. The daily-changing menu offers a variety of fresh seafood dishes prepared in many
American   ways, as well as non-seafood selections. cocktails; entertainment. **Parking:** street. **Cards:** AX, DC, DS, MC, VI.

🍸 ✕

ECHO   **Dinner:** $18-$28   **Phone:** 561/802-4222   ⑫
▽▽▽▽   **Location:** SR A1A/Royal Poinciana Way, just n to Sunrise Ave, then just e. 230 Sunrise Ave 33480. **Hours:** 5:30 pm-9:30 pm, Fri & Sat-10:30 pm. Closed: 1/1, 12/25; also Sun & Mon 4/1-12/24.
Pacific Rim   **Reservations:** suggested. **Features:** The sophisticated restaurant serves a medley of Oriental cuisines in an upbeat and trendy dining room. Dressy casual; cocktails. **Parking:** valet. **Cards:** AX, CB, DC, DS, JC, MC, VI.

⬛M 🍸 ✕

L'ESCALIER   **Dinner:** $32-$40   **Phone:** 561/655-6611   ⑭
◈◈   **Location:** On SR A1A, 0.3 mi s of jct Royal Poinciana Way; in The Breakers. One S County Rd 33480. **Hours:** 6 pm-10 pm. Closed: Sun & Mon. **Reservations:** suggested. **Features:** In The Breakers Resort, the richly
▽▽◈◈▽▽   decorated dining room displays detailed workmanship, including a handcrafted fresco on the 30-foot-high ceiling. Modern French cuisine is prepared with fresh ingredients and artfully presented to enhance a
French   sumptuous dining occasion. Try the chef's daily presentation of foie gras, followed by a roasted rack and grilled saddle of lamb. Diners looking for a special treat should splurge on the nightly tasting menu, Save room for a sensational dessert. Semi-formal attire; cocktails; entertainment. **Parking:** valet. **Cards:** AX, CB, DC, DS, MC, VI.

🍸 ✕

POLO   **Lunch:** $8-$14   **Dinner:** $16-$33   **Phone:** 561/655-5430   ⑩
▽▽ ▽▽   **Location:** SR A1A, just s of Worth Ave; in The Colony. 155 Hammon Ave 33480. **Hours:** 7 am-10 pm. Closed: Sun 4/1-11/30. **Reservations:** suggested. **Features:** In the classic retro hotel dining room, the staff shows that
American   service is as important as the flavorful food. Lunch is always a popular choice on sunny days, when most diners sit poolside at linen-draped tables shaded by wide umbrellas. Key lime pie is a specialty of the house. Casual dress; cocktails. **Parking:** valet. **Cards:** AX, CB, DC, DS, MC, VI.

🍸 ✕

THE RESTAURANT AT THE FOUR SEASONS   **Dinner:** $29-$36   **Phone:** 561/533-3750   ⑱
◈◈   **Location:** SR A1A, 0.3 mi n of jct SR 802; in The Four Seasons Resort, Palm Beach. 2800 S Ocean Blvd 33480. **Hours:** 6 pm-10 pm. Closed: Mon; Tues 5/1-11/15. **Reservations:** suggested. Guests are in for a treat at
▽▽◈◈▽▽   this top-notch establishment. Dining is an all-around pleasurable experience—from the wait staff's casually elegant service approach to the tranquil, oceanfront setting to the striking grounds views from the cozy
Regional   dining area. The chef transforms ingredients, based on what is seasonally and regionally available, into
American   sumptuous, mouthwatering dishes. Examples include yellowtail snapper, sea bass or tender lamb. Decadent desserts put an exclamation mark on the meal. Smoke free premises. Semi-formal attire; cocktails; entertainment. **Parking:** valet. **Cards:** AX, CB, DC, DS, MC, VI.

⬛M 🍸 ✕

TESTA'S RESTAURANT   **Lunch:** $7-$12   **Dinner:** $12-$25   **Phone:** 561/832-0992   ⑪
◈◈   **Location:** 0.3 mi e of Flagler Memorial Bridge on SR A1A. 221 Royal Poinciana Way 33480. **Hours:** 7 am-10 pm. Closed: 11/27. **Reservations:** accepted. **Features:** Under the same family ownership for more than 80
▽▽ ▽▽   years, the eatery promises consistency. Seafood, steak and Italian dishes are offered; guests may choose to dine in the dining room, on a sidewalk terrace or on an open-air patio. Dressy casual; cocktails.
Steak & Seafood   **Parking:** on-site. **Cards:** AX, CB, DC, DS, MC, VI.

🍸 ✕

PALM BEACH GARDENS pop. 35,058   (See map p. 757; index p. 759)—*See also PALM BEACH.*

──────── WHERE TO STAY ────────

DOUBLETREE HOTEL IN THE GARDENS   **Phone:** (561)622-2260   ㊾
◈◈◈ SAVE   2/1-4/10   1P: $149   2P: $149   XP: $15   F
    12/1-1/31 & 9/1-11/30   1P: $109   2P: $109   XP: $15   F
▽▽▽▽   4/11-8/31   1P: $99   2P: $99   XP: $15   F
    Location: Just w from Florida Tpke, exit 109, 1.8 mi e. 4431 PGA Blvd 33410. Fax: 561/624-1043. **Facility:** 280
Large-scale Hotel   units. 277 one-bedroom standard units. 3 one-bedroom suites. 6 stories, interior corridors. **Bath:** combo or shower only. **Parking:** on-site. **Terms:** cancellation fee imposed, [BP] meal plan available, package plans.
Amenities: video games (fee), dual phone lines, voice mail, irons, hair dryers. **Dining:** 6:30 am-11 pm, cocktails. **Pool(s):** heated outdoor. **Leisure Activities:** whirlpool, exercise room. **Guest Services:** area transportation-Gardens Mall. **Business Services:** meeting rooms, business center. **Cards:** AX, CB, DC, DS, MC, VI. **Special Amenities:** free newspaper and preferred room **(subject to availability with advanced reservations).** *(See color ad p 764)*   SOME UNITS

Ⓢ🅳 🍴 🍸 ⬛M ♿ 🕒 ➤ 🐾 🌐 🔲 ▣ / ✕ 🖼 /

(See map p. 757)

EMBASSY SUITES HOTEL   Phone: (561)622-1000 [51]

SAVE

1/1-4/15 [BP]	1P: $139-$249	2P: $139-$249	XP: $10	F18
12/1-12/31 [BP]	1P: $109-$169	2P: $109-$169	XP: $10	F18
4/16-11/30 [BP]	1P: $99-$149	2P: $99-$149	XP: $10	F18

Small-scale Hotel **Location:** I-95, exit 79AB, 1.8 mi e of Florida Tpke, exit 109. 4350 PGA Blvd 33410. **Fax:** 561/626-6254. **Facility:** 160 one-bedroom suites, some with whirlpools. 10 stories, interior corridors. *Bath:* combo or shower only. **Parking:** on-site. **Amenities:** dual phone lines, voice mail, irons, hair dryers. **Pool(s):** heated outdoor. **Leisure Activities:** sauna, whirlpool, tennis court, jogging, exercise room. **Guest Services:** gift shop, complimentary evening beverages, valet and coin laundry, area transportation. **Business Services:** meeting rooms, fax (fee). **Cards:** AX, CB, DC, DS, MC, VI.

SOME UNITS

HAMPTON INN   Phone: (561)625-8880 [53]

SAVE

1/6-3/30	1P: $149-$179	2P: $159-$189	
12/1-1/5	1P: $109-$129	2P: $119-$139	
3/31-5/31	1P: $99-$119	2P: $109-$129	
6/1-11/30	1P: $79-$109	2P: $89-$119	

Small-scale Hotel **Location:** I-95, exit 79AB, just se of PGA Blvd, 2 mi e of Florida Tpke, exit 109. 4001 RCA Blvd 33410. **Fax:** 561/625-6766. **Facility:** 116 units. 113 one-bedroom standard units. 3 one-bedroom suites with kitchens. 4 stories, interior corridors. *Bath:* combo or shower only. **Parking:** on-site. **Terms:** cancellation fee imposed, [CP] meal plan available. **Amenities:** video games (fee), dual phone lines, voice mail, irons, hair dryers. **Pool(s):** heated outdoor. **Guest Services:** complimentary evening beverages: Mon-Thurs, valet and coin laundry. **Business Services:** meeting rooms, fax (fee). **Cards:** AX, CB, DC, DS, MC, VI.

SOME UNITS

INNS OF AMERICA   Phone: (561)626-4918 [54]

(AAA) SAVE

1/16-4/30 [CP]	1P: $89-$119		XP: $10	F12
12/1-1/15 [CP]	1P: $69-$79		XP: $10	F12
5/1-11/30 [CP]	1P: $59-$69		XP: $10	F12

Motel **Location:** I-95, exit 77. 4123 Northlake Blvd 33410. **Fax:** 561/626-8790. **Facility:** 95 one-bedroom standard units. 3 stories, exterior corridors. **Parking:** on-site. **Pool(s):** heated outdoor. **Guest Services:** coin laundry. **Business Services:** fax (fee). **Cards:** AX, DS, MC, VI. **Special Amenities:** free continental breakfast and free local telephone calls.

SOME UNITS

PALM BEACH GARDENS MARRIOTT   Phone: (561)622-8888 [52]

(AAA) SAVE

12/1-3/28	1P: $89-$199	2P: $89-$199	
3/29-5/23 & 9/27-11/30	1P: $89-$129	2P: $89-$129	
5/24-9/26	1P: $76-$109	2P: $76-$109	

Large-scale Hotel **Location:** I-95, exit 79AB, just se of PGA Blvd, 2 mi e of Florida Tpke, exit 109. 4000 RCA Blvd 33410. **Fax:** 561/622-0052. **Facility:** 279 one-bedroom standard units. 11 stories, interior corridors. *Bath:* combo or shower only. **Parking:** on-site. **Terms:** check-in 4 pm. **Amenities:** high-speed Internet (fee), voice mail, irons, hair dryers. **Dining:** 6:30 am-2 & 5-10 pm, cocktails, nightclub. **Pool(s):** heated outdoor. **Leisure Activities:** sauna, whirlpool, steamroom, exercise room. **Guest Services:** gift shop, valet and coin laundry, area transportation-Gardens Mall. **Business Services:** conference facilities, business center. **Special Amenities:** early check-in/late check-out and free newspaper.

SOME UNITS

FEE

(See map p. 757)

PGA NATIONAL RESORT & SPA

(AAA) (SAVE)
▼▼▼▼ ▼▼▼▼

			Phone: (561)627-2000	**48**
1/1-5/10	1P: $279-$379	2P: $279-$379	XP: $15	F18
12/1-12/31	1P: $189-$229	2P: $189-$229	XP: $15	F18
10/1-11/30	1P: $189-$219	2P: $189-$219	XP: $15	F18
5/11-9/30	1P: $109-$159	2P: $109-$159	XP: $15	F18

Resort
Large-scale Hotel
Location: I-95, exit 79AB, 2 mi w; Florida Tpke, exit 109, just w. Located at PGA National. 400 Ave of the Champions 33418. Fax: 561/622-0261. **Facility:** Two mineral pools are part of this lakefront property's European-style spa; a balcony lounging area overlooks a swimming pool and the golf course. 339 units. 333 one-bedroom standard units. 6 one-bedroom suites ($489-$1500). 3-4 stories, interior corridors. *Bath:* combo or shower only. **Parking:** on-site and valet. **Terms:** cancellation fee imposed, $5 service charge. **Amenities:** dual phone lines, voice mail, safes, honor bars, irons, hair dryers. **Dining:** 3 restaurants, 6:30 am-midnight; 18% service charge, cocktails, also, Shula's Steak House, see separate listing, entertainment. **Pool(s):** 2 outdoor, heated outdoor, wading, lap. **Leisure Activities:** saunas, whirlpools, fishing, golf-90 holes, jogging, spa. *Fee:* sailboats, 19 tennis courts (10 lighted), golf & tennis instruction, croquet & instruction, bicycles. **Guest Services:** gift shop, valet laundry, area transportation (fee)-within 8 mi. **Business Services:** conference facilities, business center. **Cards:** AX, DC, DS, JC, MC, VI. **Special Amenities:** free local telephone calls and free newspaper.

SOME UNITS

⊁ ⊓ ☷ ♨ ⊘ ⇆ ✈ ⊠ ✦ 〔DATA PORT〕 / ⊠ 〔VCR〕 ⊟ /
FEE   FEE

────── **WHERE TO DINE** ──────

CAFE CHARDONNAY

▼▼▼▼
American

Lunch: $6-$12   **Dinner:** $17-$32   **Phone:** 561/627-2662   **26**
Location: I-95, exit 79AB, 0.3 mi w; jct PGA Blvd and Military Tr; in Garden Square Shoppes. 4533 PGA Blvd 33418. **Hours:** 11:30 am-2:30 - & 5:30-10 pm, Sat & Sun from 5:30 pm. Closed: 11/27, 12/25. **Reservations:** suggested. **Features:** For an inventive meal, step into this bright, colorful, bi-level dining room. The house speciality is macadamia nut crusted yellowtail snapper. An efficient team provides good service and sets the tone for an enjoyable evening out. Dressy casual; beer & wine only. **Parking:** on-site. **Cards:** AX, CB, MC, VI.
⊠

EBISU JAPANESE RESTAURANT

▼▼▼ ▼▼
Japanese

Lunch: $7-$10   **Dinner:** $12-$20   **Phone:** 561/622-4495   **25**
Location: Just w of jct Florida Tpke, exit 102 (PGA Blvd); 1.7 mi w of jct I-95, exit 57; in Shoppes on the Green Shopping Center. 7100 Fairway Dr 33418. **Hours:** 11:30 am-2 & 5:30-10 pm, Fri-10:30 pm, Sat 5:30 pm 10:30 pm. Closed: 7/4, 11/27, 12/25; also Sun. **Reservations:** accepted. **Features:** Beautifully presented, authentic Japanese cuisine features several styles of preparation, including sushi and sashimi. A traditional dining room offers both Western and Japanese seating. The owner/chef sends out pickled bean sprouts as an appetizer. Casual dress; beer & wine only. **Parking:** on-site. **Cards:** AX, MC, VI.
⊠

FATHOM

▼▼▼▼
Seafood

Dinner: $17-$30   **Phone:** 561/626-8788   **31**
Location: I-95, exit 79AB, 2.3 mi e on PGA Blvd, then just n. 11611 Ellison Wilson Rd 33408. **Hours:** 5:30 pm-9:30 pm. Fri & Sat-10:30 pm. Closed: 12/25. **Reservations:** suggested. **Features:** Fresh fish from both the Atlantic and Pacific oceans are prepared with Pacific Rim and traditional influences. Also on the menu are New American meat preparations. Despite its large size, the dining room sustains a cozy feel, in part due to the subtle lighting. The patio overlooks the Intracoastal Waterway. Dressy casual; cocktails. **Parking:** on-site and valet. **Cards:** AX, CB, DC, DS, JC, MC, VI.
〔&M〕 ☷ ⊠

NO ANCHOVIES! NEIGHBORHOOD PASTARIA

▼▼▼ ▼▼
Italian

Lunch: $5-$8   **Dinner:** $9-$17   **Phone:** 561/622-7855   **29**
Location: 0.5 mi w of jct US 1; at Prosperity Farms Rd; in PGA Plaza. 2650 PGA Blvd 33410. **Hours:** 11:30 am-2:30 & 5-10 pm, Fri & Sat-10:30 pm, Sun 5 pm-10 pm. Closed: 11/27, 12/25; also 1/1 for lunch. **Features:** The name is a solemn promise. An open kitchen adds to the lively ambience of this modern pastaria. Some of the specialty pasta dishes are prepared in a wood-burning oven along with tasty pizzas. This is a great value on family favorites. Casual dress; cocktails. **Parking:** on-site. **Cards:** AX, DC, MC, VI.
☷ ⊠

PADDY MAC'S

▼▼▼ ▼▼
Irish

Lunch: $6-$9   **Dinner:** $9-$19   **Phone:** 561/691-4366   **27**
Location: Jct Military Tr and PGA Blvd; at north end of Garden Square Shoppes; 0.3 mi w of jct I-95, exit 57. 10971 N Military Tr 33418. **Hours:** 11:30 am-3 & 4:30-10 pm, Sun from 4:30 pm. Closed: 5/26, 11/27, 12/25. **Reservations:** accepted; 5/1-12/1. **Features:** Log fireplaces, Irish paintings and a wood bar evoke the aura of a Dublin pub. Casual and noisy, the restaurant serves up such entrees as salmon with citrus butter and chicken with apple-honey stuffing. Entertainers perform on Friday and Saturday nights. Casual dress; cocktails. **Parking:** on-site. **Cards:** AX, DC, DS, MC, VI.
☷ ⊠

THE RIVER HOUSE

▼▼▼ ▼▼
Steak & Seafood

Dinner: $17-$40   **Phone:** 561/694-1188   **30**
Location: 0.5 mi w of jct US 1; at Soverel Harbour. 2373 PGA Blvd 33410. **Hours:** 5 pm-10 pm, Fri & Sat-10:30 pm. Closed: 11/27, 12/25. **Reservations:** required; Fri & Sat. **Features:** Bustling and warm, the atmosphere of the restaurant lends itself to a pleasant dining experience. Lots of windows offer views of the Intracoastal Waterway. A sweet fresh fruit chutney accompanies the yellowtail snapper and Chilean sea bass which is topped with macadamia nuts. Another favorite is the 25 ounce prime rib on the bone. Dressy casual; cocktails. **Parking:** valet. **Cards:** AX, DC, DS, MC, VI.
☷ ⊠

SHULA'S STEAK HOUSE

▼▼▼ ▼▼
Steak House

Dinner: $30-$50   **Phone:** 561/627-4852   **24**
Location: I-95, exit 79AB, 2 mi w; Florida Tpke, exit 109, just w; in PGA National Resort & Spa. 400 Ave of the Champions 33418. **Hours:** 6 pm-10 pm. **Reservations:** suggested. **Features:** Miami's honored football coach filled his dining room with rich wood and Dolphin memorabilia. Extra large lobsters and Angus beef will please the heartiest of appetites. Menu options are listed on a football along with a fine selection of delicious wines. Dressy casual; cocktails. **Parking:** on-site and valet. **Cards:** AX, CB, DC, DS, JC, MC, VI.
⊠

PALM BEACH SHORES pop. 1,269   (See map p. 757; index p. 759)—See also PALM BEACH.

──────── WHERE TO STAY ────────

BEST WESTERN SEASPRAY INN
Phone: (561)844-0233   60

AAA SAVE

	1P:	2P:	XP:	
12/1-12/31 & 2/10-3/31	1P: $110-$180	2P: $120-$180	XP: $10	F18
1/1-2/9	1P: $100-$150	2P: $110-$150	XP: $10	F18
4/1-11/30	1P: $60-$116	2P: $70-$116	XP: $10	F18

Small-scale Hotel   **Location:** On Singer Island; 0.5 mi s of SR A1A. 123 S Ocean Ave 33404. Fax: 561/844-9885. **Facility:** 50 one-bedroom standard units. 4 stories, interior corridors. **Parking:** on-site. **Terms:** 14 day cancellation notice, pets ($15 extra charge). **Amenities:** safes (fee), irons, hair dryers. **Dining:** 8 am-2:30 & 5:30-9:30 pm, cocktails, entertainment. **Pool(s):** heated outdoor. **Guest Services:** valet laundry. **Business Services:** fax (fee). **Cards:** AX, CB, DC, DS, MC, VI. **Special Amenities:** free room upgrade (subject to availability with advanced reservations). *(See ad below)*

SOME UNITS

... FEE FEE

CROWNE PLAZA OCEANFRONT NORTH PALM BEACH HOTEL
Phone: (561)842-6171   57

AAA SAVE

	1P:	2P:	XP:	
12/22-5/5	1P: $299-$329	2P: $299-$329	XP: $15	F17
5/6-6/1	1P: $209-$239	2P: $209-$239	XP: $15	F17
6/2-11/30	1P: $179-$239	2P: $179-$239	XP: $15	F17
12/1-12/21	1P: $169-$199	2P: $169-$199	XP: $15	F17

Large-scale Hotel   **Location:** 1.8 mi e, n on SR A1A from jct US 1. 3200 N Ocean Dr 33404. Fax: 561/848-6842. **Facility:** 193 units. 186 one-bedroom standard units. 7 one-bedroom suites. 9 stories, interior corridors. *Bath:* combo or shower only. **Parking:** on-site (fee). **Terms:** check-in 4 pm, 3 day cancellation notice-fee imposed. **Amenities:** video games (fee), dual phone lines, voice mail, safes, irons, hair dryers. *Some:* fax. **Dining:** 6:30 am-10 pm, cocktails. **Pool(s):** heated outdoor. **Leisure Activities:** whirlpool, recreation programs, exercise room. *Fee:* scuba diving, snorkeling, cabana supplies, jet ski, bicycles, massage. **Guest Services:** gift shop, valet and coin laundry. **Business Services:** meeting rooms, business center. **Cards:** AX, CB, DC, DS, JC, MC, VI.

SOME UNITS

HILTON SINGER ISLAND OCEANFRONT RESORT
Phone: (561)848-3888   61

AAA SAVE

	1P:	2P:	XP:	
12/1-4/30	1P: $179-$279	2P: $179-$279	XP: $15	F18
5/1-11/30	1P: $119-$179	2P: $119-$179	XP: $15	F18

Large-scale Hotel   **Location:** On Singer Island; 1.8 mi n and e on SR A1A from jct US 1. 3700 N Ocean Dr 33404 (3700 N Ocean Dr, SINGER ISLAND). Fax: 561/848-4299. **Facility:** 223 one-bedroom standard units. 8 stories, interior corridors. *Bath:* combo or shower only. **Parking:** on-site. **Terms:** check-in 4 pm, cancellation fee imposed. **Amenities:** video games (fee), voice mail, irons, hair dryers. **Dining:** 6:30 am-10 pm, cocktails. **Pool(s):** heated outdoor, wading. **Leisure Activities:** whirlpool, snorkeling, boogie boards, cabanas, water cycles, recreation programs, exercise room, volleyball. *Fee:* beach water sports, bicycles, massage. **Guest Services:** gift shop, valet and coin laundry. **Business Services:** meeting rooms, business center. **Cards:** AX, DC, DS, MC, VI. **Special Amenities:** free newspaper. *(See color ad p 959)*

SOME UNITS

RADISSON PALM BEACH SHORES RESORT AND VACATION VILLAS
Phone: (561)863-4000   59

AAA SAVE

12/21-5/1	1P: $269-$369	2P: $269-$369	
12/1-12/20 & 5/2-11/30	1P: $169-$180	2P: $169-$180	

Small-scale Hotel   **Location:** On Singer Island; 0.3 mi s of SR A1A. 181 Ocean Ave 33404. Fax: 561/845-3245. **Facility:** 219 units. 211 one- and 8 two-bedroom suites. 6 stories, interior corridors. **Parking:** on-site. **Terms:** check-in 4 pm, cancellation fee imposed. **Amenities:** voice mail, irons, hair dryers. *Fee:* video games, high-speed Internet, safes. **Dining:** 6:30 am-10 pm, cocktails. **Pool(s):** heated outdoor. **Leisure Activities:** whirlpool, snorkeling, recreation programs, exercise room. *Fee:* windsurfing, catamaran, jet skis, surfboards, massage. **Guest Services:** gift shop, valet and coin laundry. **Business Services:** fax (fee). **Cards:** AX, CB, DC, DS, JC, MC, VI.

SOME UNITS

(See map p. 757)

SAILFISH MARINA & RESORT   **Phone:** (561)844-1724   🔲58

All Year   1P: $69-$149

Motel   **Location:** US 1, 1 mi e, then 0.4 mi s. 98 Lake Dr 33404 (PO Box 10848, 33419). Fax: 561/848-9684. **Facility:** 26 units. 18 one-bedroom standard units, some with efficiencies. 8 one-bedroom suites ($109-$179) with kitchens. 1 story, exterior corridors. *Bath:* shower only. **Parking:** on-site. **Terms:** 3 day cancellation notice, weekly rates available, [BP] meal plan available, pets ($10 extra charge). **Dining:** Sailfish Waterfront Dining, see separate listing. **Pool(s):** heated outdoor. **Leisure Activities:** rental boats, fishing. *Fee:* sailboats, marina, charter fishing, bicycles. **Guest Services:** gift shop, coin laundry. **Business Services:** meeting rooms. **Cards:** AX, MC, VI.

SOME UNITS

(ASK) (SⓈⒹ) (🛏) (🍴) (🍸) (🌊) (✕) (🎞) (💻) / (✕) (🔋) (🖥) /

--------- *The following lodging was either not evaluated or did not* ---------
meet AAA rating requirements but is listed for your information only.

MARRIOTT'S OCEAN POINTE   **Phone:** 561/882-3000

(fyi)   Not evaluated. **Location:** 71 Ocean Ave 33404. Facilities, services, and decor characterize a mid-range property.

--------- WHERE TO DINE ---------

SAILFISH WATERFRONT DINING   **Lunch:** $6-$10   **Dinner:** $11-$27   **Phone:** 561/842-8449   🔲32

Location: US 1, 1 mi e, then 0.4 mi s; in Sailfish Marina & Resort. 98 Lake Dr 33404. **Hours:** 7 am-10 pm, Mon-2 pm. **Features:** Fresh seafood and meat dishes are prepared with a special twist. The open air dining room, overlooking the water, promotes the tropical feel. Casual dress; cocktails. **Parking:** on-site and valet. **Cards:** AX, MC, VI.

Seafood

(🍸M) (🍸) (✕)

PALM COAST pop. 32,732

--------- WHERE TO STAY ---------

HAMPTON INN   **Phone:** 386/446-4457

(AAA) (SAVE)   2/1-4/30   1P: $64-$239   2P: $69-$239

5/1-11/30   1P: $64-$169   2P: $69-$169

12/1-1/31   1P: $64-$99   2P: $69-$99

Small-scale Hotel   **Location:** I-95, exit 289, 0.5 mi se via Old Kings Rd. Located in Kingswood Center. 5 Kingswood Dr 32137. Fax: 386/445-1438. **Facility:** 50 one-bedroom standard units. 2 stories, exterior corridors. **Parking:** on-site. **Terms:** 3 day cancellation notice, [ECP] meal plan available. **Amenities:** voice mail, irons. **Pool(s):** heated outdoor. **Leisure Activities:** whirlpool. **Business Services:** fax. **Cards:** AX, CB, DC, DS, MC, VI. **Special Amenities:** free continental breakfast and free local telephone calls.

SOME UNITS

(SⓈⒹ) (🍴) (🌊) (🐾) (📶) (💻) / (✕) /

HOLIDAY INN EXPRESS HOTEL & SUITES   **Phone:** (386)439-3939

2/7-2/16   1P: $109-$239   2P: $109-$239   XP: $5   F18

2/17-11/30   1P: $69-$169   2P: $74-$174   XP: $5   F18

Small-scale Hotel   12/1-2/6   1P: $64-$89   2P: $69-$94   XP: $5   F18

Location: I-95, exit 284 (SR 100), just se. 200 Flagler Plaza Dr 32137. Fax: 386/439-4300. **Facility:** 81 one-bedroom standard units. 3 stories, interior corridors. *Bath:* combo or shower only. **Parking:** on-site. **Terms:** 7 day cancellation notice, [ECP] meal plan available, package plans - seasonal. **Amenities:** dual phone lines, voice mail, irons, hair dryers. **Pool(s):** outdoor. **Leisure Activities:** whirlpool. **Guest Services:** valet and coin laundry. **Business Services:** meeting rooms, fax. **Cards:** AX, CB, DC, DS, JC, MC, VI.

SOME UNITS

(ASK) (SⓈⒹ) (🍴) (🎞) (📷) (🌊) (📶) (📡) / (✕) (🔋) (🖥) (💻) /

MICROTEL INN & SUITES   **Phone:** (386)445-8976

All Year [CP]   1P: $49-$159   2P: $49-$159   XP: $10   F18

Small-scale Hotel   **Location:** I-95, exit 289, just e, then just s. 16 Kingswood Dr 32137. Fax: 386/445-8977. **Facility:** 82 one-bedroom standard units. 3 stories, interior corridors. *Bath:* combo or shower only. **Parking:** on-site. **Terms:** small pets only ($25 fee). **Amenities:** safes (fee). *Some:* irons, hair dryers. **Pool(s):** small outdoor. **Guest Services:** coin laundry. **Business Services:** fax (fee). **Cards:** AX, CB, DC, DS, JC, MC, VI.

SOME UNITS

(ASK) (SⓈⒹ) (🛏) (🍴) (🍸M) (🎞) (🌊) (📶) (📷) / (✕) (🔋) (🖥) (💻) /

PALM COAST RESORT
Phone: (386)445-3000
All Year 1P: $89-$365 2P: $89-$365 XP: $25 F16
Location: I-95, exit 289, 2 mi e. 300 Clubhouse Dr 32137-9985. Fax: 386/445-2947. **Facility:** 154 one-bedroom
Small-scale Hotel standard units. 3 stories (no elevator), exterior corridors. **Parking:** on-site. **Terms:** 3 day cancellation notice-fee imposed, [BP] & [CP] meal plans available. **Amenities:** video games, voice mail, safes, irons, hair dryers. *Some:* honor bars. **Pool(s):** 3 outdoor. **Leisure Activities:** whirlpool, rental boats, rental canoes, fishing, 18 lighted tennis courts, recreation programs, hiking trails, jogging, playground, exercise room. *Fee:* marina, golf-90 holes, racquetball courts, bicycles. **Guest Services:** gift shop, valet and coin laundry. **Business Services:** conference facilities, fax. **Cards:** AX, DC, DS, MC, VI. *(See color ad p 767)*

SOME UNITS
ASK SD ⊓ Y ≈ X ⚡ DATA/PORT ⊞ /X/

PALM COAST VILLAS
Phone: (386)445-3525
AAA SAVE All Year 1P: $49-$135 2P: $49-$135 XP: $5 F13
Location: I-95, exit 289, 2.8 mi e to SR A1A, 1.8 mi n. 5454 N Oceanshore Blvd 32137. Fax: 386/445-3525.
Motel **Facility:** 22 units. 21 one- and 1 two-bedroom standard units, some with efficiencies. 2 stories, exterior corridors. *Bath:* combo or shower only. **Parking:** on-site. **Terms:** weekly rates available, small pets only (in designated units). **Amenities:** video library (fee), voice mail. *Some:* hair dryers. **Pool(s):** outdoor. **Leisure Activities:** Fee: bicycles. **Guest Services:** coin laundry. **Business Services:** fax (fee). **Cards:** DC, MC, VI.

SOME UNITS
SD ⊶ ≈ ⊟ ⊞ /X VCR ⊞ /
FEE

SLEEP INN
Phone: (386)446-8180
SAVE 2/9-3/31 [CP] 1P: $65-$154 2P: $65-$154 XP: $5 F16
4/1-7/9 [CP] 1P: $65-$119 2P: $65-$119 XP: $5 F16
12/1-2/8 [CP] 1P: $65-$85 2P: $65-$85 XP: $5 F16
7/10-11/30 [CP] 1P: $65-$75 2P: $65-$75 XP: $5 F16
Small-scale Hotel **Location:** I-95, exit 289, 0.5 mi se via Old Kings Rd. Located in Kingswood Center. 10 Kingswood Dr 32137. Fax: 386/446-4004. **Facility:** 78 one-bedroom standard units. 3 stories, interior corridors. *Bath:* shower only. **Parking:** on-site. **Amenities:** *Some:* irons, hair dryers. **Pool(s):** outdoor. **Leisure Activities:** whirlpool. **Guest Services:** coin laundry. **Business Services:** meeting rooms, fax (fee). **Cards:** AX, CB, DC, DS, JC, MC, VI.

SOME UNITS
SD ⊓ GM ⇦ ≈ ⚡ DATA/PORT /X ⊟ ⊞ /

——— **WHERE TO DINE** ———

THE MEETING PLACE **Lunch:** $6-$8 **Dinner:** $9-$15 **Phone:** 386/445-1310
Location: I-95, exit 289, 0.5 mi e; in Palm Harbor Shopping Village. 278 Palm Coast Pkwy 32137. **Hours:** 11 am-3
American & 4-9 pm, Wed-Sat to 10 pm. Closed major holidays. **Features:** A relaxed, casual atmosphere, popular with the local business crowd, offers the chance to enjoy flavorful entrees like the traditional Reuben sandwich served with a New York deli-style pickle. An organized staff expertly attends to your needs.
Casual dress; cocktails. **Parking:** on-site. **Cards:** CB, DC, DS, MC, VI.
Y X

PALMETTO pop. 12,571 (See map p. 812; index p. 816)

——— **WHERE TO DINE** ———

CRAB TRAP 1 **Lunch:** $5-$14 **Dinner:** $10-$40 **Phone:** 941/722-6255 62
Location: I-75, exit 224, 3 mi w on US 301, 2.3 mi n; I-275, exit 2, just s. 5611 US 19 34221. **Hours:** 11:30 am-9
Seafood pm, Fri & Sat-10 pm. Closed: 11/27, 12/25. **Features:** Stone crabs, three-crab soup and other rural Florida dishes are served in a very rustic setting. Among the more daring selections are the gator and wild boar. Frog legs, scalloped bananas, conch fritters and fresh lobster are all prepared from scratch. Casual dress; cocktails. **Parking:** on-site. **Cards:** DS, MC, VI.
Y X

PALM HARBOR —*See Tampa Bay p. 924.*

PANAMA CITY pop. 36,417

——— **WHERE TO STAY** ———

BEST WESTERN SUITES
Phone: (850)784-7700
AAA SAVE 3/1-9/7 1P: $70-$100 2P: $76-$106 XP: $6 F
12/1-2/28 & 9/8-11/30 1P: $50-$80 2P: $56-$65 XP: $6 F
Location: US 98, 1.5 mi ne on US 231, just w on SR 368. 1035 E 23rd St 32405. Fax: 850/763-9095. **Facility:** 50
Small-scale Hotel one-bedroom standard units, some with whirlpools. 2 stories, interior corridors. *Bath:* combo or shower only. **Parking:** on-site. **Terms:** 3 day cancellation notice, [ECP] meal plan available. **Amenities:** irons, hair dryers. **Pool(s):** outdoor. **Leisure Activities:** exercise room. **Guest Services:** valet laundry. **Business Services:** meeting rooms, fax. **Cards:** AX, CB, DC, DS, MC, VI. **Special Amenities:** free continental breakfast and free room upgrade (subject to availability with advanced reservations).

SOME UNITS
SD G ≈ ⚡ DATA/PORT ⊟ ⊞ ⊞ /X/

COMFORT INN & CONFERENCE CENTER
Phone: (850)769-6969
AAA SAVE 2/16-9/1 1P: $87-$110 2P: $89-$110 XP: $6 F18
12/1-2/15 & 9/2-11/30 1P: $59-$65 2P: $59-$65 XP: $6 F18
Location: SR 368, just w of jct US 231. 1013 E 23rd St 32405. Fax: 850/763-4353. **Facility:** 105 one-bedroom
Small-scale Hotel standard units. 2 stories, exterior corridors. **Parking:** on-site. **Terms:** [ECP] meal plan available, package plans. **Amenities:** voice mail, irons, hair dryers. **Pool(s):** heated outdoor. **Leisure Activities:** exercise room. **Guest Services:** complimentary evening beverages: Mon-Thurs, coin laundry. **Business Services:** conference facilities, fax (fee). **Cards:** AX, CB, DC, DS, JC, MC, VI. **Special Amenities:** free continental breakfast and free local telephone calls.

SOME UNITS
SD ≈ ⚡ DATA/PORT ⊞ /X ⊟ ⊞ /

COMFORT INN AND SUITES

Phone: 850/763-0101

SAVE

2/26-9/5	1P: $95-$105	2P: $105-$115	XP: $10	F12
12/1-2/25 & 9/6-11/30	1P: $75-$85	2P: $85-$95	XP: $10	F12

▽▽▽▽

Small-scale Hotel

Location: 4 mi w of jct SR 231. 4128 W US 98 32401. Fax: 850/763-4234. **Facility:** 40 one-bedroom standard units, some with whirlpools. 2 stories, exterior corridors. **Parking:** on-site. **Terms:** 3 day cancellation notice, [ECP] meal plan available. **Amenities:** irons, hair dryers. **Pool(s):** outdoor. **Business Services:** fax (fee). **Cards:** AX, DC, DS, MC, VI.

SOME UNITS

COUNTRY INN & SUITES BY CARLSON PANAMA CITY

Phone: (850)913-0074

AAA **SAVE**

3/1-9/6	1P: $95-$135	2P: $95-$135	XP: $5	F15
9/7-11/30	1P: $95-$125	2P: $95-$125	XP: $5	F15
12/1-2/28	1P: $85-$125	2P: $85-$125	XP: $5	F15

▽▽▽▽

Small-scale Hotel

Location: 0.5 mi w of US 231, just s of 23rd St. 2203 Harrison Ave 32405. Fax: 850/913-9970. **Facility:** 53 units. 47 one-bedroom standard units. 6 one-bedroom suites ($85-$125), some with whirlpools. 2 stories, interior corridors. *Bath:* combo or shower only. **Parking:** on-site. **Terms:** [BP] & [CP] meal plans available. **Amenities:** irons, hair dryers. **Pool(s):** outdoor. **Leisure Activities:** exercise room. **Guest Services:** valet laundry. **Business Services:** meeting rooms, fax. **Cards:** AX, CB, DC, DS, MC, VI. **Special Amenities:** free continental breakfast and free newspaper. *(See color ad p 613)*

SOME UNITS

DAYS INN & SUITES

Phone: (850)769-7400

SAVE

12/1-9/6 [CP]	1P: $80-$150	2P: $80-$150	XP: $10	F16
9/7-11/30 [CP]	1P: $50-$110	2P: $50-$110	XP: $10	F16

▽▽▽▽

Small-scale Hotel

Location: US 98 E, 2 mi e of jct US 98 E and Transmitter Rd. 435 N Tyndall Pkwy 32404. Fax: 850/769-9558. **Facility:** 52 one-bedroom standard units, some with whirlpools. 2 stories, interior corridors. *Bath:* combo or shower only. **Parking:** on-site. **Amenities:** voice mail, hair dryers. *Some:* irons. **Pool(s):** outdoor. **Business Services:** fax (fee). **Cards:** AX, CB, DC, DS, JC, MC, VI.

SOME UNITS

DAYS INN BAYSIDE

Phone: (850)763-4622

AAA **SAVE**

5/16-9/30	1P: $66-$99	2P: $73-$106	XP: $7	F12
3/1-5/15	1P: $62-$92	2P: $69-$99	XP: $7	F12
12/1-2/28 & 10/1-11/30	1P: $49-$79	2P: $56-$63	XP: $7	F12

▽▽ ▽▽

Small-scale Hotel

Location: Business US 98, 0.5 mi w of jct US 231. 711 W Beach Dr 32401. Fax: 850/747-9522. **Facility:** 100 units. 99 one-bedroom standard units. 1 one-bedroom suite ($129-$189). 2 stories, exterior corridors. **Parking:** on-site. **Terms:** weekly rates available, small pets only ($10 extra charge). **Amenities:** hair dryers. **Dining:** 6 am-11 & 5-9 pm, Sat from 7 am; Sun & Mon 7 am-noon off season, cocktails. **Pool(s):** outdoor. **Leisure Activities:** playground, volleyball. **Guest Services:** valet and coin laundry. **Business Services:** meeting rooms, fax (fee). **Cards:** AX, DC, DS, MC, VI. **Special Amenities:** free local telephone calls and preferred room (subject to availability with advanced reservations).

SOME UNITS

HOLIDAY INN SELECT

Phone: (850)769-0000

▽▽▽▽

3/1-11/30	1P: $92-$102	XP: $10	F18
12/1-2/28	1P: $89-$99	XP: $10	F18

Small-scale Hotel

Location: SR 77, just n of jct US 231. 2001 N Cove Blvd 32405. Fax: 850/763-3828. **Facility:** 173 one-bedroom standard units. 6 stories, interior corridors. **Parking:** on-site. **Terms:** [BP], [CP], [ECP] & [MAP] meal plans available. **Amenities:** voice mail, irons, hair dryers. **Pool(s):** heated indoor. **Leisure Activities:** saunas, whirlpool, jogging, exercise room. **Guest Services:** valet and coin laundry. **Business Services:** meeting rooms. **Cards:** AX, CB, DC, DS, JC, MC, VI. *(See color ad opposite inside back cover)*

SOME UNITS

HOWARD JOHNSON INN

Phone: (850)785-0222

▽▽▽ ▽▽

2/28-11/30	1P: $69	2P: $76	XP: $5	F17
12/1-2/27	1P: $62	2P: $76	XP: $5	F17

Small-scale Hotel

Location: On US 98, 0.8 mi e of Hathaway Bridge. 4601 W Hwy 98 32401. Fax: 850/769-3472. **Facility:** 80 one-bedroom standard units. 1-3 stories (no elevator), interior/exterior corridors. **Parking:** on-site. **Terms:** 14 day cancellation notice, weekly rates available, [BP] meal plan available, small pets only ($25 fee). **Amenities:** irons, hair dryers. **Pool(s):** outdoor. **Leisure Activities:** boat dock. **Business Services:** meeting rooms, fax. **Cards:** AX, DC, DS, MC, VI.

SOME UNITS

LA QUINTA INN & SUITES

Phone: (850)914-0022

AAA **SAVE**

2/1-9/3	1P: $90-$106	2P: $97-$113	XP: $7	F18
12/1-1/31 & 9/4-11/30	1P: $80-$96	2P: $87-$103	XP: $7	F18

▽▽▽▽

Small-scale Hotel

Location: Jct US 231 and CR 390A. 1030 E 23rd St 32405. Fax: 850/914-0027. **Facility:** 119 units. 113 one-bedroom standard units. 6 one-bedroom suites ($119-$179). 6 stories, interior corridors. *Bath:* combo or shower only. **Parking:** on-site. **Terms:** [ECP] meal plan available, small pets only. **Amenities:** video games, voice mail, irons, hair dryers. **Pool(s):** heated outdoor. **Leisure Activities:** whirlpool, exercise room. **Guest Services:** coin laundry. **Business Services:** meeting rooms, fax (fee). **Cards:** AX, CB, DC, DS, JC, MC, VI. **Special Amenities:** free continental breakfast and free local telephone calls.

SOME UNITS

SLEEP INN

Phone: (850)763-7777

SAVE

3/1-9/5	1P: $69-$89	2P: $69-$89	XP: $10	F12
12/1-2/28 & 9/6-11/30	1P: $59-$79	2P: $59-$79	XP: $10	F12

▽▽ ▽▽

Small-scale Hotel

Location: US 98, 0.5 mi e of Hathaway Bridge. 5126 W Hwy 98 32401. Fax: 850/785-9545. **Facility:** 83 one-bedroom standard units. 2 stories, interior corridors. *Bath:* shower only. **Parking:** on-site. **Terms:** 3 day cancellation notice, [AP] meal plan available. **Amenities:** *Some:* washing machines, hair dryers. **Pool(s):** outdoor. **Business Services:** meeting rooms, fax (fee). **Cards:** AX, CB, DC, DS, JC, MC, VI.

SOME UNITS

SUPER 8 MOTEL
Phone: (850)784-1988

Motel

3/1-11/30	1P: $50-$80	2P: $50-$80	XP: $5	F
12/1-2/28	1P: $40-$50	2P: $40-$50	XP: $5	F

Location: Just n of jct US 98. 207 Hwy 231 N 32405. Fax: 850/763-9154. **Facility:** 63 one-bedroom standard units. 2 stories, interior/exterior corridors. **Parking:** on-site. **Terms:** small pets only ($10 extra charge).
Amenities: safes. **Pool(s):** outdoor. **Business Services:** fax (fee). **Cards:** AX, CB, DC, MC, VI.

SOME UNITS

──────── **WHERE TO DINE** ────────

CANOPIES
Dinner: $15-$27
Phone: 850/872-8444

Continental

Location: 1 mi e of bridge on US 98. 4423 W Hwy 98 32401. **Hours:** 5 pm-10 pm. Closed: 11/27, 12/25. **Reservations:** suggested. **Features:** Upscale decor with black and white color scheme, featuring black cloth napkins. Signature dessert of white creme brule is excellent. Sophisticated wine selections. Dressy casual. **Parking:** on-site. **Cards:** AX, DC, DS, MC, VI.

FERRUCCI RISTORANTE
Lunch: $6-$8
Dinner: $9-$20
Phone: 850/913-9131

Italian

Location: Downtown. 301 Harrison Ave 32401. **Hours:** 11 am-2 & 5-9:30 pm, Sat from 5 pm. Closed major holidays; also Sun & Mon, 2 weeks in Sept. **Reservations:** suggested. **Features:** In a quaint, downtown location, the restaurant offers a sophisticated dining experience that appeals to locals and tourists alike. Dressy casual; cocktails. **Parking:** on-site. **Cards:** AX, CB, DC, DS, JC, MC, VI.

HOUSE OF CHAN
Dinner: $6-$16
Phone: 850/769-9404

Chinese

Location: 1 mi e of bridge on US 98. 4425 W Hwy 98 32401. **Hours:** 4 pm-11 pm, Fri & Sat-midnight. Closed: 11/27. **Features:** Chinese entrees are the focus with a few American offerings. Enjoy the bay view and order from the cart rolled out of an immaculate kitchen by the friendly wait staff. Five soups and numerous entrees make this tempting menu difficult to choose from. Casual dress; cocktails. **Parking:** on-site. **Cards:** AX, DS, MC, VI.

SAVELLI'S
Lunch: $5-$9
Dinner: $6-$17
Phone: 850/236-1288

Italian

Location: 8406 Front Beach Rd 32407. **Hours:** 11 am-10 pm, Sun-8:30 pm. Closed: 11/27, 12/25. **Reservations:** accepted. **Features:** On the menu are specialty pizzas and traditional pasta dishes. The cafe-style setting is casually comfortable. Casual dress; cocktails. **Parking:** on-site. **Cards:** AX, CB, DC, DS, JC, MC, VI.

UNCLE ERNIE'S BAYFRONT GRILL & BREWHOUSE
Lunch: $6-$10
Dinner: $12-$22
Phone: 850/763-8427

Seafood

Location: US 98 S, 0.5 mi w on US 98 Business (Beck St), then just e on 12th Ave. 1151 Bayview Ave 32401. **Hours:** 11 am-10:30 pm. Closed major holidays; also Sun. **Features:** Specializing in inexpensive to moderately priced steaks, seafood and pasta, the restaurant affords nice views of the bay, particularly from the patio. Varied beers are made in the on-premises brewery. Casual dress; cocktails. **Parking:** street. **Cards:** AX, MC, VI.

PANAMA CITY BEACH pop. 7,671

──────── **WHERE TO STAY** ────────

ANDY'S MOTEL
Phone: 850/230-8999

Motel

5/24-9/5	1P: $95-$115	2P: $105-$115	XP: $5	F18
2/15-5/23	1P: $80-$98	2P: $88-$98	XP: $5	F18
12/1-2/14 & 9/6-11/30	1P: $60-$75	2P: $65-$75	XP: $5	F18

Location: US 98A, 1.5 mi s on Joan Ave, then 0.5 mi e. 8101 W Surf Dr 32408. Fax: 850/230-3723. **Facility:** 25 one-bedroom standard units. 3 stories, exterior corridors. **Bath:** combo or shower only. **Parking:** on-site. **Terms:** 7 day cancellation notice. **Pool(s):** heated outdoor. **Guest Services:** coin laundry. **Business Services:** fax. **Cards:** AX, MC, VI.

BEACHCOMBER BY THE SEA
Phone: (850)233-3600

5/23-8/9	1P: $129-$229	2P: $129-$229	XP: $10	F17
3/1-5/22	1P: $89-$169	2P: $89-$169	XP: $10	F17
8/10-11/30	1P: $49-$129	2P: $49-$129	XP: $10	F17
12/1-2/28	1P: $59-$119	2P: $59-$119	XP: $10	F17

Small-scale Hotel **Location:** Jct SR 79 and US 98. 17101 Front Beach Rd 32413. Fax: 850/233-3622. **Facility:** 96 one-bedroom standard units, some with kitchens and/or whirlpools. 8 stories, exterior corridors. **Bath:** combo or shower only. **Parking:** on-site. **Terms:** check-in 4 pm, cancellation fee imposed, weekly rates available. **Amenities:** irons, hair dryers. **Pool(s):** heated outdoor. **Leisure Activities:** whirlpool. **Fee:** water sports and lounge chairs, game room. **Guest Services:** coin laundry. **Business Services:** meeting rooms, fax (fee). **Cards:** AX, DS, MC, VI. **Special Amenities:** free continental breakfast and free newspaper. *(See color ad p 771)*

SOME UNITS

BEACH TOWER RESORT MOTEL
Phone: 850/235-0089

Motel

3/1-4/22	1P: $115-$145	2P: $115-$145	
4/23-9/4	1P: $94-$129	2P: $94-$129	
12/1-2/28 & 9/5-11/30	1P: $42-$60	2P: $42-$60	

Location: US 98, exit D, just e. 12001 Front Beach Rd 32407 (PO Box 9227, 32417). Fax: 850/235-2025. **Facility:** 48 one-bedroom standard units. 7 stories, exterior corridors. **Parking:** on-site. **Terms:** check-in 4 pm, 10 day cancellation notice-fee imposed. **Pool(s):** heated outdoor. **Business Services:** fax. **Cards:** AX, DC, DS, MC, VI.

SOME UNITS

BEST WESTERN CASA LOMA

	2/24-9/9	1P: $89-$169	2P: $89-$169	XP: $10	F12
SAVE	9/10-10/31	1P: $89-$109	2P: $89-$109	XP: $10	F12
	11/1-11/30	1P: $69-$99	2P: $69-$99	XP: $10	F12
◆◆◆ ◆◆◆	12/1-2/23	1P: $69-$89	2P: $69-$89	XP: $10	F12

Phone: (850)234-1100

Motel **Location:** US 98A, 3.2 mi sw of jct CR 392. 13615 Front Beach Rd 32413 (PO Box 18049, 32407). **Fax:** 850/234-0864. **Facility:** 101 one-bedroom standard units, some with kitchens. 3 stories (no elevator), exterior corridors. **Bath:** combo or shower only. **Parking:** on-site. **Terms:** check-in 4 pm, 3 day cancellation notice-fee imposed, weekly rates available. **Amenities:** irons, hair dryers. **Pool(s):** heated outdoor. **Business Services:** fax. **Cards:** AX, DC, DS, MC, VI.

SOME UNITS
(icons)

DAYS INN

◆◆◆ SAVE	3/1-4/15	1P: $169-$229	2P: $169-$229
	4/16-9/2	1P: $139-$189	2P: $139-$189
◆◆◆ ◆◆◆	9/3-11/30	1P: $59-$89	2P: $59-$89
	12/1-2/28	1P: $59-$79	2P: $59-$79

Phone: (850)233-3333

Small-scale Hotel Location: US 98A, 2.5 mi sw of jct CR 392. 12818 Front Beach Rd 32407. **Fax:** 850/233-9568. **Facility:** 188 one-bedroom standard units, some with kitchens. 7 stories, exterior corridors. **Parking:** on-site. **Terms:** check-in 4 pm, 3 day cancellation notice, [ECP] meal plan available. **Amenities:** voice mail, irons, hair dryers. **Pool(s):** outdoor. **Leisure Activities:** whirlpool. **Business Services:** fax (fee). **Cards:** AX, CB, DC, DS, MC, VI. **Special Amenities: free continental breakfast and free newspaper.**

SOME UNITS
(icons)

EDGEWATER BEACH RESORT

Property failed to provide current rates

Phone: 850/235-4044

Condominium **Location:** US 98A, 1.3 mi sw of jct CR 392. 11212 Front Beach Rd 32407. **Fax:** 850/233-7591. **Facility:** 510 one-bedroom standard units. 2-12 stories, exterior corridors. **Parking:** on-site. **Terms:** check-in 4 pm, no pets allowed (owner's pets on premises). **Amenities:** voice mail, irons, hair dryers. **Pool(s):** outdoor, 10 heated outdoor. **Leisure Activities:** whirlpools, rental sailboats, recreation programs, spa, shuffleboard. **Fee:** charter fishing, golf-36 holes, 11 tennis courts (6 lighted), game room. **Guest Services:** gift shop, complimentary laundry. **Business Services:** conference facilities. **Cards:** AX, DC, DS, MC, VI. **(See color ad p 772)**

SOME UNITS
(icons) FEE FEE

HAMPTON INN AT BAY POINT

SAVE	1/1-2/28	1P: $79-$189	2P: $79-$189	XP: $10	F17
	12/1-12/31	1P: $95-$179	2P: $95-$179	XP: $10	F17
◆◆◆ ◆◆◆	3/1-11/30	1P: $69-$179	2P: $69-$179	XP: $10	F17

Phone: (850)236-8988

Small-scale Hotel Location: On US 98, 0.5 mi w of bridge, 2.5 mi s on CR 3031. 2909 Thomas Dr 32408. **Fax:** 850/236-1157. **Facility:** 89 units. 85 one-bedroom standard units. 4 one-bedroom suites ($179-$209) with whirlpools. 3 stories, interior corridors. **Bath:** combo or shower only. **Parking:** on-site. **Terms:** 7 day cancellation notice, [ECP] meal plan available. **Amenities:** dual phone lines, voice mail, irons, hair dryers. **Pool(s):** heated outdoor. **Leisure Activities:** whirlpool, exercise room. **Guest Services:** valet laundry. **Business Services:** meeting rooms, fax (fee). **Cards:** AX, CB, DC, DS, MC, VI.

SOME UNITS
(icons)

HOLIDAY INN SUNSPREE RESORT

Phone: (850)234-1111

AAA SAVE ▼▼▼	2/16-4/20	1P: $189-$199	2P: $189-$199	XP: $25	F12
	5/13-11/30	1P: $129-$189	2P: $129-$189	XP: $15	F12
	4/21-5/12	1P: $119-$179	2P: $119-$179	XP: $15	F12
	12/1-2/15	1P: $89-$109	2P: $89-$109	XP: $15	F12

Large-scale Hotel Location: US 98A, 1.1 mi w of jct CR 392. 11127 Front Beach Rd 32407. Fax: 850/235-1907. **Facility:** 341 units. 338 one-bedroom standard units. 2 one- and 1 two-bedroom suites ($500-$1000) with whirlpools. 15 stories, exterior corridors. **Parking:** on-site. **Terms:** check-in 4 pm, 3 day cancellation notice-fee imposed, [BP] meal plan available. **Amenities:** voice mail, safes, irons, hair dryers. **Dining:** 6:30 am-11 & 5-10 pm; grill service for lunch in season; seasonal entertainment, cocktails. **Pool(s):** heated outdoor. **Leisure Activities:** sauna, whirlpools, steamroom, recreation programs, exercise room. *Fee:* scuba diving, snorkeling, beach watersports, golf-18 holes, 9 hole par 3, lighted driving range. **Guest Services:** gift shop, valet and coin laundry. **Business Services:** meeting rooms, fax. **Cards:** AX, DC, DS, MC, VI.
(See color ad below & opposite inside back cover)

SOME UNITS

🍽 ⛱ 🏊 ✕ 🐾 DATA PORT 🛏 ☕ 📺 / ✕ VCR /

MARRIOTT'S BAY POINT RESORT VILLAGE

Phone: (850)236-6000

SAVE ▼▼▼ Resort	2/21-4/26	1P: $209-$259	2P: $209-$259	XP: $20	F17
	4/27-9/6	1P: $159-$209	2P: $159-$209	XP: $20	F17
	12/1-2/20 & 9/7-11/30	1P: $139-$189	2P: $139-$189	XP: $20	F17

Large-scale Hotel Location: On US 98, 0.5 mi w of bridge, 2 mi s on CR 3031, 1.8 mi e on Magnolia Beach Rd, follow signs. 4200 Marriott Dr 32408. Fax: 850/236-6153. **Facility:** A bay and a wildlife sanctuary provide pleasant views from the guest rooms at this 1,100-acre resort; every unit has a patio or balcony. 356 units. 278 one-bedroom standard units. 78 one-bedroom suites ($179-$299), some with whirlpools. 5 stories, interior/exterior corridors. **Parking:** on-site. **Terms:** check-in 4 pm, 10 day cancellation notice-fee imposed, [BP] meal plan available. **Amenities:** dual phone lines, voice mail, irons, hair dryers. *Some:* video games. **Pool(s):** 3 heated outdoor, heated indoor, wading. **Leisure Activities:** whirlpools, rental boats, rental sailboats, fishing, recreation programs, playground, exercise room, volleyball. *Fee:* windsurfing, marina, waterskiing, scuba diving, snorkeling, charter fishing, golf-36 holes, 4 lighted tennis courts, bicycles, massage. **Guest Services:** gift shop, valet laundry, area transportation. *Fee:* sailing instruction. **Business Services:** conference facilities, business center. **Cards:** AX, CB, DC, DS, MC, VI.

SOME UNITS

S/D FEE ✈ 🍽 🍷 🎿 ✕ 🐾 DATA PORT 🛏 📺 / ✕ VCR 🛏 /

MOONSPINNER CONDOMINIUM

Phone: 850/234-8900

5/31-8/12	1P: $215-$350	2P: $215-$350
3/16-5/30	1P: $155-$250	2P: $155-$250
8/13-11/30	1P: $130-$200	2P: $130-$200
12/1-3/15	1P: $120-$150	2P: $120-$150

Condominium

Location: Jct US 98, 3.5 mi s on CR 3031, then e. 4425 Thomas Dr 32408. **Fax:** 850/233-0719. **Facility:** 121 units. 90 two- and 31 three-bedroom suites ($205-$345). 8 stories, exterior corridors. **Parking:** on-site. **Terms:** age restrictions may apply, 14 day cancellation notice-fee imposed, weekly rates available, no pets allowed (owner's pets on premises). **Amenities:** *Some:* CD players. **Pool(s):** heated outdoor, wading. **Leisure Activities:** whirlpool, 2 lighted tennis courts, exercise room, basketball, shuffleboard, volleyball. *Fee:* game room. **Guest Services:** complimentary laundry. **Business Services:** meeting rooms, fax (fee). **Cards:** MC, VI.

SOME UNITS

OSPREY RESORT MOTEL

Phone: 850/234-0303

3/1-9/2	1P: $73-$175	2P: $73-$175	XP: $10	F17
12/1-2/28	1P: $60-$124	2P: $60-$124	XP: $10	F17
9/3-11/30	1P: $60-$124		XP: $10	F17

Motel

Location: 2 mi e of jct SR 79 and US 98. 15801 Front Beach Rd 32413. **Fax:** 850/234-0303. **Facility:** 70 one-bedroom standard units with kitchens. 6 stories, exterior corridors. **Parking:** on-site. **Terms:** 3-7 night minimum stay - seasonal, 14 day cancellation notice-fee imposed. **Amenities:** irons, hair dryers. **Pool(s):** heated outdoor. **Leisure Activities:** whirlpool. **Guest Services:** coin laundry. **Business Services:** fax (fee). **Cards:** AX, DS, MC, VI.

PANAMA CITY RESORT & CLUB

Phone: (850)235-2002

3/1-9/10	2P: $92-$125
12/1-2/28 & 9/11-11/30	2P: $50-$64

Condominium

Location: 0.3 mi e of jct SR 79 and US 98. 16709 Front Beach Rd 32413. **Fax:** 850/235-2900. **Facility:** 40 units. 29 one-bedroom standard units with kitchens. 11 one-bedroom suites with kitchens. 4 stories, exterior corridors. **Parking:** on-site. **Terms:** 2 night minimum stay, 14 day cancellation notice, weekly rates available. **Amenities:** irons. **Pool(s):** heated outdoor. **Leisure Activities:** whirlpool, volleyball. **Guest Services:** complimentary laundry. **Business Services:** fax (fee). **Cards:** AX, DS, MC, VI.

RAMADA LIMITED

Phone: 850/234-1700

3/1-4/15	1P: $169-$199	2P: $169-$199
4/16-9/2	1P: $139-$169	2P: $139-$169
9/3-11/30	1P: $59-$79	2P: $59-$79
12/1-2/28	1P: $59-$69	2P: $59-$69

Small-scale Hotel **Location:** US 98, 2.7 mi sw of jct CR 392. 12907 Front Beach Rd 32407. **Fax:** 850/235-2700. **Facility:** 147 one-bedroom standard units. 4 stories, exterior corridors. *Bath:* combo or shower only. **Parking:** on-site. **Terms:** check-in 4 pm, 3 day cancellation notice, [ECP] meal plan available. **Amenities:** voice mail, irons, hair dryers. **Pool(s):** outdoor, heated outdoor. **Leisure Activities:** whirlpool, game room. **Guest Services:** coin laundry. **Business Services:** meeting rooms, fax (fee). **Cards:** AX, CB, DC, DS, MC, VI.

SOME UNITS

SUNSET INN

Phone: 850/234-7370

5/23-9/1	1P: $70-$130	2P: $75-$140	XP: $5	F17
3/1-5/22	1P: $66-$105	2P: $70-$125	XP: $5	F17
12/1-2/28 & 9/2-11/30	1P: $50-$90	2P: $55-$95	XP: $15	F17

Motel

Location: US 98A, 1.5 mi s on Joan Ave, then 0.5 mi e. 8109 Surf Dr 32408. **Fax:** 850/234-7370. **Facility:** 62 one-bedroom standard units, some with kitchens. 2 stories, exterior corridors. *Bath:* combo or shower only. **Parking:** on-site. **Terms:** 7 day cancellation notice. **Pool(s):** heated outdoor. **Guest Services:** coin laundry. **Business Services:** fax. **Cards:** AX, DC, MC, VI.

The following lodging was either not evaluated or did not meet AAA rating requirements but is listed for your information only.

MARRIOTT'S LEGEND'S EDGE

Phone: 850/236-4200

[fyi] Not evaluated. **Location:** 4000 Marriott Dr 32411. Facilities, services, and decor characterize a mid-range property.

——— WHERE TO DINE ———

30 DEGREE BLUE

Dinner: $17-$26 **Phone: 850/236-1115**

Location: 0.5 mi w of bridge on US 98, 2 mi s on CR 3031, 1.5 mi e on Magnolia Beach Rd, follow signs. 3900 Marriott Dr, Suite G 32408. **Hours:** 5:30 pm-9 pm, Fri & Sat-10 pm. **Closed:** 12/25; also Sun & Mon.

New World **Reservations:** suggested. **Features:** Guests can dine comfortably while gazing out at the bay. Although the menu changes regularly, it always includes the chef's distinctive creations, such as crab mango salad, coconut-encrusted fish and the exquisite coconut creme brulee dessert. Knowledgeable staff members help with wine selections. Dressy casual; cocktails. **Parking:** on-site. **Cards:** AX, DS, MC, VI.

ALL AMERICAN DINER

Lunch: $4-$11 **Dinner: $4-$11** **Phone: 850/235-2443**

Location: 10590 Front Beach Rd 32407. **Hours:** 24 hours. **Closed:** 11/27, 12/25. **Features:** '50s style diner. Inexpensive. Casual dress. **Parking:** on-site.

American

BOAR'S HEAD RESTAURANT

Dinner: $14-$26

Phone: 850/234-6628

Steak & Seafood

Location: 0.3 mi w of jct SR 79, on US 98. 17290 Front Beach Rd 32413. **Hours:** 4:30 pm-9 pm, Fri & Sat-10 pm. Closed: 11/27; also 12/20-12/27. **Features:** This quiet, rustic spot offers many seafood and steak entrees, and appeals to those who recognize good value. The eager-to-please staff aims for professional service. Try fried shrimp served with sweet potatoes, green beans, and a scrumptious dessert. Casual dress; cocktails. **Parking:** on-site. **Cards:** AX, DC, DS, MC, VI.

HAMILTON'S RESTAURANT

Dinner: $11-$19

Phone: 850/234-1255

Seafood

Location: Jct Thomas Dr. 5711 N Lagoon Dr 32408. **Hours:** 5 pm-10 pm. **Features:** Taste the zesty flavor of feta cheese in the shrimp Christo entree or the decadent chocolate sweetness of mud pie while you gaze out over the scenic lagoon. Hardwood floors and stained glass windows help to give the restaurant a romantic feel. Casual dress; cocktails. **Parking:** on-site. **Cards:** AX, DS, MC, VI.

PEMBROKE PINES —See Fort Lauderdale p. 404.

PENSACOLA pop. 56,255

—— WHERE TO STAY ——

BEST WESTERN VILLAGE INN

Phone: (850)479-1099

Small-scale Hotel

All Year [ECP]   1P: $59-$72   2P: $59-$72   XP: $5   F12

Location: I-10, exit 13, 0.8 mi n. Located across from West Florida Hospital. 8240 N Davis Hwy 32514. Fax: 850/479-9320. **Facility:** 142 one-bedroom standard units. 3 stories, interior/exterior corridors. *Bath:* combo or shower only. **Parking:** on-site. **Terms:** weekly rates available. **Amenities:** irons, hair dryers. **Pool(s):** outdoor. **Guest Services:** valet laundry. **Business Services:** meeting rooms. **Cards:** AX, CB, DC, DS, JC, MC, VI. **Special Amenities:** free continental breakfast.

SOME UNITS

COMFORT INN-NAS CORRY

Phone: (850)455-3233

Small-scale Hotel

All Year   1P: $60-$70   2P: $60-$70   XP: $6   F18

Location: Just n of jct US 98 and SR 292. Located at entrance to Corry Field. 3 New Warrington Rd 32506. Fax: 850/453-3445. **Facility:** 101 one-bedroom standard units. 2-3 stories (no elevator), exterior corridors. **Parking:** on-site. **Terms:** check-in 4 pm, cancellation fee imposed, pets ($25 fee). **Amenities:** voice mail. *Some:* irons, hair dryers. **Dining:** entertainment. **Pool(s):** outdoor. **Guest Services:** valet and coin laundry. **Business Services:** meeting rooms, fax. **Cards:** AX, CB, DC, DS, JC, MC, VI. **Special Amenities:** free continental breakfast and free newspaper.

SOME UNITS

COURTYARD BY MARRIOTT

Phone: (850)857-7744

Small-scale Hotel

5/2-10/1	1P: $74-$94	2P: $74-$94
10/2-11/30	1P: $59-$94	2P: $59-$94
3/16-5/1	1P: $54-$94	2P: $54-$94
12/1-3/15	1P: $54-$92	2P: $54-$92

Location: I-10, exit 13, 0.5 mi s, just w. 451 Creighton Rd 32504. Fax: 850/857-0904. **Facility:** 90 units. 87 one-bedroom standard units, some with whirlpools. 3 one-bedroom suites ($129-$149) with whirlpools. 3 stories, interior corridors. *Bath:* combo or shower only. **Parking:** on-site. **Amenities:** voice mail, irons, hair dryers. **Pool(s):** heated outdoor. **Leisure Activities:** whirlpool, exercise room. **Guest Services:** valet and coin laundry. **Business Services:** meeting rooms, fax. **Cards:** AX, CB, DC, DS, MC, VI.

SOME UNITS

CROWNE PLAZA HOTEL AND RESORT PENSACOLA GRAND

Phone: (850)433-3336

Large-scale Hotel

All Year   1P: $125-$150   2P: $135-$160   XP: $10   F18

Location: Jct I-110 and US 98. 200 E Gregory St 32501. Fax: 850/432-7572. **Facility:** 212 units. 203 one-bedroom standard units. 8 one- and 1 two-bedroom suites ($250-$408), some with whirlpools. 15 stories, interior corridors. **Parking:** on-site. **Terms:** 3 day cancellation notice, small pets only ($50 fee). **Amenities:** voice mail, irons, hair dryers. **Dining:** 1912 The Restaurant, see separate listing. **Pool(s):** heated outdoor. **Leisure Activities:** exercise room. **Guest Services:** gift shop, valet laundry. **Business Services:** conference facilities, business center. **Cards:** AX, DC, DS, MC, VI.

SOME UNITS

DAYS INN NORTH

Phone: 850/476-9090

Small-scale Hotel

5/1-7/31	1P: $49-$69	2P: $54-$79	XP: $9 F15
8/1-11/30	1P: $39-$69	2P: $49-$69	XP: $9 F15
12/1-4/30	1P: $39-$59	2P: $49-$69	XP: $9 F15

Location: I-10, exit 10A, 0.3 mi s on US 29. 7051 Pensacola Blvd 32505. Fax: 850/476-9090. **Facility:** 80 one-bedroom standard units. 2 stories, interior corridors. **Parking:** on-site. **Terms:** pets ($10 extra charge). **Amenities:** safes, hair dryers. **Pool(s):** outdoor. **Leisure Activities:** exercise room. **Guest Services:** coin laundry. **Business Services:** fax. **Cards:** AX, CB, DC, DS, JC, MC, VI. **Special Amenities:** free local telephone calls and free newspaper.

SOME UNITS

FAIRFIELD INN BY MARRIOTT

Phone: (850)484-8001

Small-scale Hotel

All Year [CP]   1P: $69   2P: $69

Location: I-10, exit 13, just s. 7325 N Davis Hwy 32514. Fax: 850/484-6008. **Facility:** 63 one-bedroom standard units. 3 stories, interior corridors. *Bath:* combo or shower only. **Parking:** on-site. **Amenities:** irons, hair dryers. **Pool(s):** heated indoor. **Guest Services:** valet laundry. **Business Services:** fax. **Cards:** AX, DC, DS, MC, VI.

SOME UNITS

HAMPTON INN UNIVERSITY MALL

Phone: (850)477-3333

AAA SAVE

All Year [ECP]   1P: $59-$85   2P: $69-$85

Location: I-10, exit 13, just s. Located at entrance to the University Mall. 7330 Plantation Rd 32504. Fax: 850/477-8163. **Facility:** 122 one-bedroom standard units. 3 stories, exterior corridors. **Parking:** on-site. **Amenities:** voice mail, irons, hair dryers. **Leisure Activities:** pool privileges. **Guest Services:** valet laundry. Small-scale Hotel **Business Services:** meeting rooms, fax (fee). **Cards:** AX, CB, DC, DS, JC, MC, VI.

SOME UNITS

HOLIDAY INN EXPRESS

Phone: (850)476-7200

AAA SAVE

All Year   1P: $59-$79

Location: I-10, exit 10, 1.3 mi s on US 29. Located at Car City. 6501 Pensacola Blvd 32505. Fax: 850/476-1277. **Facility:** 214 one-bedroom standard units. 3 stories, exterior corridors. *Bath:* combo or shower only. **Parking:** on-site. **Terms:** cancellation fee imposed, [ECP] meal plan available. **Amenities:** voice mail, irons, hair Small-scale Hotel dryers. **Pool(s):** outdoor. **Leisure Activities:** exercise room. **Guest Services:** valet and coin laundry, airport transportation-Pensacola Airport. **Business Services:** meeting rooms, fax. **Cards:** AX, DC, DS, MC, VI.

SOME UNITS

HOLIDAY INN-UNIVERSITY MALL

Phone: 850/474-0100

AAA SAVE

All Year   1P: $68   2P: $68

Location: I-10, exit 13, just s of University Mall entrance. 7200 Plantation Rd 32504. Fax: 850/477-9821. **Facility:** 152 one-bedroom standard units. 2 stories, exterior corridors. *Bath:* combo or shower only. **Parking:** on-site. **Terms:** pets ($25 fee). **Amenities:** video games, voice mail, irons, hair dryers. **Dining:** 6 am-11 & Small-scale Hotel 5-10 pm, Sun-9 pm, cocktails, entertainment. **Pool(s):** outdoor. **Guest Services:** valet and coin laundry. **Business Services:** meeting rooms, fax (fee). **Cards:** AX, DC, DS, MC, VI.

(See color ad opposite inside back cover)

SOME UNITS

HOSPITALITY INN

Phone: (850)477-2333

5/1-9/5   1P: $60   2P: $60
12/1-4/30 & 9/6-11/30   1P: $55   2P: $55

Small-scale Hotel **Location:** I-10, exit 10A, 0.5 mi s on US 29. 6900 Pensacola Blvd 32505. Fax: 850/479-3575. **Facility:** 124 units. 121 one-bedroom standard units. 3 one-bedroom suites. 1 story, interior/exterior corridors. **Parking:** on-site. **Terms:** check-in 4 pm, weekly rates available, [ECP] meal plan available, pets ($25 fee, in limited units). **Amenities:** *Some:* hair dryers. **Pool(s):** outdoor. **Leisure Activities:** exercise room. **Guest Services:** valet and coin laundry. **Business Services:** meeting rooms, fax (fee). **Cards:** AX, DC, DS, MC, VI.

SOME UNITS
FEE

LA QUINTA INN

Phone: (850)474-0411

AAA SAVE

All Year   1P: $59-$89   2P: $65-$95

Location: I-10, exit 13, just n. 7750 N Davis Hwy 32514-7557. Fax: 850/474-1521. **Facility:** 130 units. 128 one-bedroom standard units. 2 one-bedroom suites. 3 stories, exterior corridors. *Bath:* combo or shower only. **Parking:** on-site. **Terms:** [ECP] meal plan available, small pets only. **Amenities:** video games, voice mail, irons, hair dryers. **Pool(s):** outdoor. **Guest Services:** coin laundry. **Business Services:** fax (fee). **Cards:** AX, CB, DC, DS, JC, MC, VI. **Special Amenities:** free continental breakfast and free local telephone calls.

SOME UNITS

MICROTEL INN & SUITES

Phone: (850)941-8902

All Year [ECP]   1P: $49-$89   2P: $49-$89   XP: $6   F18

Location: I-10, exit 7, just s. 8001 Lavelle Way 32526. Fax: 850/941-8906. **Facility:** 71 one-bedroom standard units. 2 stories, interior corridors. *Bath:* combo or shower only. **Parking:** on-site. **Terms:** cancellation fee imposed. **Amenities:** safes (fee). **Guest Services:** valet laundry. **Business Services:** meeting rooms, fax (fee). **Cards:** AX, CB, DC, DS, MC, VI.

SOME UNITS
FEE

RAMADA INN BAYVIEW

Phone: (850)477-7155

3/1-8/31   1P: $79-$89   2P: $79-$89
12/1-2/28   1P: $69   2P: $69
9/1-11/30   1P: $69   2P: $69

Location: I-10, exit 17, just sw on US 90. 7601 Scenic Hwy 32504. Fax: 850/477-7155. **Facility:** 150 units. 140 Small-scale Hotel one-bedroom standard units. 10 one-bedroom suites ($85-$105). 2 stories, interior corridors. **Parking:** on-site. **Terms:** small pets only ($25 fee). **Amenities:** video games, voice mail, irons, hair dryers. **Dining:** 6 am-1 & 5:30-9 pm, Fri & Sat-10 pm, cocktails, entertainment. **Pool(s):** outdoor. **Leisure Activities:** exercise room. **Guest Services:** valet and coin laundry. **Business Services:** meeting rooms, fax (fee). **Cards:** AX, CB, DC, DS, MC, VI. **Special Amenities:** free local telephone calls.

SOME UNITS

RAMADA INN NORTH

Phone: (850)477-0711

AAA SAVE

All Year   1P: $62   2P: $74   XP: $8   F18

Location: I-10, exit 10, 1.2 mi s on US 29. Located at Car City. 6550 N Pensacola Blvd 32505. Fax: 850/479-1977. **Facility:** 106 units. 103 one-bedroom standard units. 3 one-bedroom suites with whirlpools. 2 stories, exterior corridors. **Parking:** on-site. **Terms:** [ECP] meal plan available, pets ($25-$50 fee). **Amenities:** voice mail, irons, hair dryers. **Dining:** 11 am-10 pm, cocktails. **Pool(s):** outdoor. **Guest Services:** coin laundry. **Business Services:** meeting rooms, fax (fee). **Cards:** AX, CB, DC, DS, JC, MC, VI. **Special Amenities:** free continental breakfast and free local telephone calls.

SOME UNITS

RAMADA LIMITED

Phone: (850)944-0333

Small-scale Hotel

All Year 1P: $49-$79 2P: $55-$85 XP: $6 F18
Location: I-10, exit 7, just s. 8060 Lavalle Way 32526. Fax: 850/941-1961. **Facility:** 92 one-bedroom standard units. 2 stories, exterior corridors. **Parking:** on-site. **Terms:** [ECP] meal plan available, small pets only ($25 fee, in designated units). **Amenities:** safes (fee), irons, hair dryers. **Pool(s):** outdoor. **Guest Services:** valet and coin laundry. **Business Services:** meeting rooms, fax (fee). **Cards:** AX, CB, DC, DS, MC, VI.

SOME UNITS

RED ROOF INN

Phone: (850)476-7960

Motel

free newspaper.

5/11-9/6 1P: $39-$56 2P: $45-$62 XP: $6 F18
12/1-5/10 & 9/7-11/30 1P: $36-$54 2P: $42-$60 XP: $6 F18
Location: I-10, exit 13, just s. Located at entrance to the University Mall. 7340 Plantation Rd 32504. Fax: 850/477-3399. **Facility:** 108 one-bedroom standard units. 2 stories, exterior corridors. **Parking:** on-site. **Terms:** small pets only. **Amenities:** video games, voice mail. **Guest Services:** valet laundry. **Business Services:** fax (fee). **Cards:** AX, CB, DC, DS, MC, VI. **Special Amenities:** free local telephone calls and

SOME UNITS

RESIDENCE INN BY MARRIOTT

Phone: (850)479-1000

Small-scale Hotel

All Year 1P: $99 2P: $145
Location: I-10, exit 13, just s. Located at entrance to the University Mall. 7230 Plantation Rd 32504. Fax: 850/479-4706. **Facility:** 64 one-bedroom standard units. 2 stories, exterior corridors. **Terms:** weekly rates available, [ECP] meal plan available. **Amenities:** voice mail, irons, hair dryers. **Pool(s):** outdoor. **Leisure Activities:** whirlpool, sports court. **Guest Services:** valet and coin laundry. **Business Services:** meeting rooms, fax. **Cards:** AX, CB, DC, DS, MC, VI.

SOME UNITS
FEE

SLEEP INN

Phone: (850)941-0908

Small-scale Hotel

All Year [CP] 1P: $56-$80 2P: $56-$80 XP: $5 F18
Location: I-10, exit 7, just s. 2591 Wilde Lake Blvd 32526. Fax: 850/941-0760. **Facility:** 77 one-bedroom standard units. 3 stories, interior corridors. *Bath:* combo or shower only. **Parking:** on-site. **Amenities:** *Some:* irons, hair dryers. **Pool(s):** outdoor. **Guest Services:** coin laundry. **Business Services:** meeting rooms, fax (fee). **Cards:** AX, CB, DC, DS, JC, MC, VI.

SOME UNITS

TRAVELODGE INN & SUITES

Phone: (850)454-0280

Small-scale Hotel

All Year 1P: $89 XP: $6 F18
Location: Just n of jct US 98 and SR 292. 4 New Warrington Rd 32506. Fax: 850/454-0250. **Facility:** 71 units. 48 one-bedroom standard units with efficiencies. 23 one-bedroom suites ($89) with efficiencies. 3 stories, interior corridors. *Bath:* combo or shower only. **Parking:** on-site. **Terms:** 3 day cancellation notice, [CP] meal plan available, pets ($20 fee). **Amenities:** dual phone lines, voice mail, safes, irons, hair dryers. **Pool(s):** heated outdoor. **Leisure Activities:** exercise room. **Guest Services:** valet and coin laundry, area transportation. **Business Services:** meeting rooms, PC, fax. **Cards:** AX, DC, DS, MC, VI.

SOME UNITS

TRAVELODGE INN & SUITES

Phone: (850)473-0222

Small-scale Hotel

All Year 1P: $69-$89 2P: $69-$89 XP: $4 F18
Location: I-10, exit 10A, just s on US 29. 6950 Pensacola Blvd 32505. Fax: 850/475-9358. **Facility:** 60 one-bedroom standard units. 2 stories, interior corridors. *Bath:* combo or shower only. **Parking:** on-site. **Terms:** 3 day cancellation notice, [CP] meal plan available. **Amenities:** irons, hair dryers. *Some:* video games. **Pool(s):** outdoor. **Guest Services:** valet and coin laundry. **Business Services:** fax. **Cards:** AX, CB, DC, DS, MC, VI.

SOME UNITS

—— WHERE TO DINE ——

1912 THE RESTAURANT

Lunch: $6-$7 Dinner: $11-$19 Phone: 850/433-3336

Regional American

Location: Jct I-110 and US 98; in Crowne Plaza Pensacola Grand. 200 E Gregory St 32501. **Hours:** 6:30 am-2 & 5:30-10 pm, Fri & Sat-11 pm, Sun-2 pm. Closed: 12/25. **Reservations:** suggested. **Features:** Inside a historic 1912 train depot, this casual restaurant is decorated throughout with period antiques. Although most people visit to sample from a good variety of fresh seafood specialties, you'll find other tasty entrees, such as seared chicken. Smoke free premises. Casual dress; cocktails. **Parking:** on-site. **Cards:** AX, DC, DS, MC, VI.

COFFEE CUP

Lunch: $5-$7 Phone: 850/432-7060

American

Location: 520 E Cervantes St 32501. **Hours:** 6 am-2 pm. Closed: 11/27, 12/25; also Sun. **Features:** The traditional diner offers inexpensive breakfast fare at a reasonable price. Smoke free premises. Casual dress. **Parking:** on-site. **Cards:** AX, CB, DC, DS, MC, VI.

JAMIE'S FRENCH RESTAURANT

Lunch: $8-$9 Dinner: $18-$22 Phone: 850/434-2911

French

Location: Downtown historic district. 424 E Zarragossa St 32501. **Hours:** 11:30 am-2:30 & 5:30-9 pm, Fri & Sat-10 pm. Closed: Mon. **Reservations:** accepted. **Features:** In an 1884 cottage, the restaurant offers a menu of Provencal-style French cuisine with an award-winning wine list. Dressy casual. **Parking:** on-site. **Cards:** AX, MC, VI.

JERRY'S CAJUN CAFE   Lunch: $6-$19   Dinner: $6-$19   Phone: 850/484-6962
▼▼ ▼▼   **Location:** 1.3 mi e on Airport Blvd, then 1 mi n. 6205 N 9th Ave 32504. **Hours:** 11 am-8:30 pm, Fri & Sat-9:30
          pm. Closed major holidays; also Sun. **Features:** A bright, cheery New Orleans-style setting and authentic
Cajun   Cajun cuisine combine to satisfy diners. Louisiana specialties such as gumbo, jambalaya, etouffee,
          muffulettas and po'boys round out the menu. Dishes are seasoned mild or spicy, depending on the guest's
preference. Casual dress; beer & wine only. **Parking:** on-site. **Cards:** AX, DS, MC, VI.

MCGUIRE'S IRISH PUB   Lunch: $7-$11   Dinner: $9-$25   Phone: 850/433-6789
(AAA)   **Location:** 0.3 mi e of civic center; downtown. 600 E Gregory St 32501. **Hours:** 11 am-2 am. Closed: 12/25.
          Features: Here is a pleasant surprise in a unique wine cellar atmosphere. After a hearty welcome from the
▼▼ ▼▼   staff, start with a chicken, bean and corn eggroll in a delicious avocado sauce; then feast on steak,
          seafood and an exceptional variety of large hamburgers. Casual dress; cocktails; entertainment. **Parking:**
Steak House   on-site. **Cards:** AX, DC, DS, MC, VI.   Ⓨ Ⓧ

MESQUITE CHARLIE'S STEAKS & SEAFOOD   Lunch: $4-$6   Dinner: $8-$16   Phone: 850/434-0498
▼▼ ▼▼   **Location:** I-110, exit 5, 1.5 mi w on Brent Ln, 0.8 mi n. 5901 North W St 32505. **Hours:** 11 am-10 pm, Fri & Sat-11
          pm. Closed: 11/27, 12/25. **Reservations:** accepted. **Features:** Round up the family and head to this
Steak & Seafood   casual restaurant, where the flavor of the West is evident in everything from the charcoal-grilled steaks to
          the late 1900s decor. Seafood is also a must. Cattle and deer heads, antiques and bronze sculptures
convey the mood. Casual dress; cocktails. **Parking:** on-site. **Cards:** AX, DS, MC, VI.
                                                                                          Ⓧ

THE OYSTER BAR   Lunch: $5-$23   Dinner: $6-$23   Phone: 850/455-3925
▼▼ ▼▼   **Location:** 3.5 mi w on US 98. 709 N Navy Blvd 32507. **Hours:** 11 am-10 pm, Fri & Sat-11 pm. Closed major
          holidays; also Tues. **Features:** The attractive, well-coordinated decor, which revolves around the sea,
Seafood   enhances your experience in this large and busy restaurant. Seasonal ingredients give the New
          Orleans-style seafood gumbo a snappy kick. The extensive menu also features steaks. Casual dress; beer
& wine only. **Parking:** on-site. **Cards:** AX, DC, DS, MC, VI.   Ⓨ Ⓧ

THE SCREAMING COYOTE   Lunch: $5-$10   Dinner: $5-$10   Phone: 850/435-9002
▼▼▼   **Location:** Corner of Gregory; downtown. 196 N Palafox 32501. **Hours:** 11 am-9:30 pm, Fri & Sat-11 pm. Closed:
          11/27, 12/25; also Sun. **Features:** For a taste of the hot stuff to keep you screaming, try this fun and
Mexican   friendly Mexican-style eatery. The salsa bar's eight toppings range from mild to tongue-searing, and beers
          deliver a refreshing twist of lime. Spicy Cajun crawfish and crabmeat stand out on the menu of
made-from-scratch Latino dishes with modest prices. Vegetarians aren't left out in the cold. Smoke free premises. Casual
dress; beer & wine only. **Parking:** street. **Cards:** AX, DS, MC, VI.   Ⓧ

SKOPELOS ON THE BAY   Lunch: $6-$12   Dinner: $14-$23   Phone: 850/432-6565
▼▼▼ ▼   **Location:** US 90/Scenic Hwy, continuing e from Cervantes. 670 Scenic Hwy 32503. **Hours:** 5 pm-10:30 pm, Fri
          also 11:30 am-2:30 pm. Closed: 12/25; also Sun & Mon. **Reservations:** suggested. **Features:** Fresh
Seafood   vegetables and seafood are well-prepared and served to you in this bayfront dining room. Local patrons
          rave about the seafood, lamb, steak and veal choices including the tender roasted lamb accompanied by a
traditional green jelly. Casual dress; cocktails. **Parking:** on-site. **Cards:** AX, DS, MC, VI.   Ⓨ Ⓧ

——————— *The following restaurants have not been evaluated by AAA* ———————
                 but are listed for your information only.

JACKSON'S   Phone: 850/469-9898
[fyi]   Not evaluated. **Location:** Downtown. 400 S Palafox. **Features:** This historic downtown restaurant provides a
          selection of prime aged meats, fresh local and Pan-American seafood. Also an extensive selection of wine.

LOU MICHAEL'S   Phone: 850/470-9191
[fyi]   Not evaluated. **Location:** Downtown. 25 S Palafox Pl. **Features:** Relaxing supper club atmosphere with live
          entertainment.

PENSACOLA BEACH

——————— **WHERE TO STAY** ———————

BEACHSIDE RESORT & CONFERENCE CENTER   Phone: (850)932-5331

(AAA) [SAVE]	5/16-8/15	1P: $109-$399	2P: $109-$399	XP: $10	F18
	3/1-5/15	1P: $89-$249	2P: $89-$249	XP: $10	F18
▼▼(▼▼)▼	12/1-2/28 & 8/16-11/30	1P: $69-$209	2P: $69-$209	XP: $10	F18

Small-scale Hotel   **Location:** SR 399, just e of traffic light. 14 Via De Luna Dr 32561. Fax: 850/932-3011. **Facility:** 100 one-bedroom
standard units. 4 stories, interior corridors. *Bath:* combo or shower only. **Parking:** on-site. **Terms:** check-in 4
pm, weekly rates available, small pets only ($50 deposit). **Amenities:** irons, hair dryers. **Dining:** 6:30 am-10
pm, cocktails. **Pool(s):** heated outdoor, wading. **Guest Services:** valet and coin laundry. **Business Services:** conference facilities. **Cards:** AX, CB, DC, DS, JC, MC, VI. **Special Amenities:** free newspaper. *(See color ad p 778)*

                                                                        SOME UNITS
Ⓢ🅳 🐾 🍴 Ⓨ Ⓚ 🏊 📶 ✈ 📠 🛗 🖨 💻 / Ⓧ 🆅🅲🆁 /

BEST WESTERN RESORT   Phone: (850)934-3300

(AAA) [SAVE]	5/2-9/2 [ECP]	1P: $155-$195	2P: $155-$195	XP: $10	F17
	3/1-5/1 [ECP]	1P: $125-$135	2P: $125-$135	XP: $10	F17
▼▼▼	9/3-11/30 [ECP]	1P: $90-$125	2P: $90-$125	XP: $10	F17
	12/1-2/28 [ECP]	1P: $80-$90	2P: $80-$90	XP: $10	F17

Small-scale Hotel   **Location:** 0.5 mi e on SR 399. 16 Via De Luna 32561. Fax: 850/934-9780. **Facility:** 123 one-bedroom standard
units. 3 stories, exterior corridors. **Parking:** on-site. **Terms:** 7 day cancellation notice. **Amenities:** voice mail,
irons, hair dryers. **Pool(s):** 2 outdoor. **Leisure Activities:** playground, volleyball. **Guest Services:** valet and coin laundry. **Business Services:** meeting rooms, fax. **Cards:** AX, CB, DC, DS, JC, MC, VI. **Special Amenities:** free continental breakfast and
free room upgrade (subject to availability with advanced reservations).

                                                                        SOME UNITS
Ⓢ🅳 🛗 ✈ 📠 🛗 🖨 💻 / Ⓧ /

CLARION SUITES RESORT & CONVENTION CENTER
Phone: (850)932-4300

AAA SAVE

Small-scale Hotel

	1P: $139-$189	2P: $139-$189	XP: $10	F18
5/16-9/1 [ECP]	1P: $139-$189	2P: $139-$189	XP: $10	F18
3/1-5/15 [ECP]	1P: $109-$149	2P: $109-$149	XP: $10	F18
12/1-2/28 & 9/2-11/30 [ECP]	1P: $84-$129	2P: $84-$129	XP: $10	F18

Location: On SR 399, just e. 20 Via De Luna 32561. **Fax:** 850/934-9112. **Facility:** 86 one-bedroom standard units. 2 stories, exterior corridors. *Bath:* combo or shower only. **Parking:** on-site. **Terms:** 3 day cancellation notice-fee imposed. **Amenities:** irons, hair dryers. **Pool(s):** outdoor. **Guest Services:** valet and coin laundry. **Business Services:** meeting rooms, fax (fee). **Cards:** AX, CB, DC, DS, JC, MC, VI. **Special Amenities:** free continental breakfast.

SOME UNITS

COMFORT INN PENSACOLA BEACH
Phone: (850)934-5400

SAVE

Small-scale Hotel

5/24-10/27 [CP]	1P: $100-$180	2P: $100-$180	XP: $10	F18
2/1-5/23 [CP]	1P: $80-$110	2P: $80-$110	XP: $10	F18
10/28-11/30 [CP]	1P: $60-$90	2P: $60-$90	XP: $10	F18
12/1-1/31 [CP]	1P: $60-$80	2P: $60-$80	XP: $10	F18

Location: Just off SR 399. 40 Fort Pickens Rd 32561. **Fax:** 850/932-7210. **Facility:** 100 one-bedroom standard units. 4 stories, exterior corridors. *Bath:* combo or shower only. **Parking:** on-site. **Terms:** cancellation fee imposed. **Amenities:** voice mail, hair dryers. *Some:* irons. **Pool(s):** outdoor. **Guest Services:** valet and coin laundry. **Business Services:** meeting rooms, fax. **Cards:** AX, DC, DS, MC, VI.

SOME UNITS

HAMPTON INN PENSACOLA BEACH
Phone: (850)932-6800

SAVE

Small-scale Hotel

	1P: $149-$189	2P: $149-$189
5/15-8/31 [ECP]	1P: $149-$189	2P: $149-$189
3/1-5/14 [ECP]	1P: $119-$149	2P: $119-$149
9/1-11/30 [ECP]	1P: $109-$139	2P: $109-$139
12/1-2/28 [ECP]	1P: $79-$99	2P: $89-$109

Location: SR 399; center. Two Via DeLuna 32561. **Fax:** 850/932-6833. **Facility:** 181 units. 180 one-bedroom standard units. 1 one-bedroom suite. 4 stories, interior corridors. *Bath:* combo or shower only. **Parking:** on-site. **Terms:** check-in 4 pm, 3 day cancellation notice-fee imposed. **Amenities:** voice mail, irons, hair dryers. **Pool(s):** 2 heated outdoor. **Leisure Activities:** rental paddleboats, recreation programs, exercise room. **Guest Services:** gift shop, valet and coin laundry. **Business Services:** meeting rooms, fax (fee). **Cards:** AX, CB, DC, DS, MC, VI.

SOME UNITS

——— *The following lodgings were either not evaluated or did not* ———
meet AAA rating requirements but are listed for your information only.

HILTON GARDEN INN
Phone: 866/916-2999
(fyi) Under construction, scheduled to open March 2003. **Location:** I-10, exit 12. 12 Via De Luna Dr 32561.
Fax: 850/934-0891. **Planned Amenities:** pool. *(See color ad p 778)*
Motel

SPRINGHILL SUITES
Phone: 850/932-6000
(fyi) 5/16-9/1 [CP] 2P: $164-$384
3/1-5/15 [CP] 2P: $139-$351
Small-scale Hotel 9/2-11/30 [CP] 2P: $120-$340
12/1-2/28 [CP] 2P: $79-$279
Too new to rate. **Location:** On SR 399, 0.3 mi e. 24 Via De Luna 32561. Fax: 850/932-6050. **Amenities:** coffeemakers, microwaves, refrigerators, pool. **Terms:** 3 day cancellation notice-fee imposed. **Cards:** AX, DC, DS, MC, VI.

——— **WHERE TO DINE** ———

FLOUNDERS CHOWDER & ALE HOUSE **Lunch:** $6-$14 **Dinner:** $6-$21 **Phone:** 850/932-2003
(AAA) **Location:** Just e of Quietwater Beach Boardwalk. 800 Quietwater Beach Rd 32561. **Hours:** 11 am-2 am. Closed:
11/27, 12/25. **Features:** On Santa Rosa Sound, the restaurant is known for its friendly service and
generous portions of such dishes as blackened tuna, stuffed flounder and eye-watering barbecue shrimp.
The three-layer Key lime pie will leave you with serious pucker power. Casual dress; cocktails;
Steak & Seafood entertainment. **Parking:** on-site. **Cards:** AX, CB, DC, DS, MC, VI. ▢▢

JUBILEE RESTAURANT **Dinner:** $9-$23 **Phone:** 850/934-3108
(AAA) **Location:** On Quietwater Beach Boardwalk. 400 Quietwater Beach Rd 32561. **Hours:** 6 pm-10 pm, Sun 9 am-2
pm. Closed: 11/27, 12/25. **Reservations:** suggested. **Features:** View the stunning sunset on Santa Rosa
Sound as you dine on absolutely delicious entrees like New York strip poivre crusted with black
peppercorns, red wine and brandy in a creamy mushroom sauce. A superb chocolate creme caramel
Seafood brings a sweet ending. Casual dress; cocktails. **Parking:** on-site. **Cards:** AX, DC, DS, MC, VI. ▢▢

PEG LEG PETE'S OYSTER BAR **Lunch:** $6-$14 **Dinner:** $10-$45 **Phone:** 850/932-4139
Location: US 98, 1.5 mi w. 1010 Fort Pickens Rd 32561. **Hours:** 11 am-midnight. Closed: 11/27, 12/24, 12/25.
Features: Plastic serving baskets do not detract from the enjoyment of this tasty cuisine. Cajun influences
can be found in the seafood, steak and pasta entrees. A shrimp po'boy overflows with an ample portion of
Seafood shrimp on a big, fresh bun. Casual dress; cocktails. **Parking:** on-site. **Cards:** AX, DS, MC, VI. ▢

PERRY pop. 6,847

——— **WHERE TO STAY** ———

BEST BUDGET INN
Phone: (850)584-6231
(AAA) (SAVE) All Year [ECP] 1P: $38 2P: $43 XP: $5 F16
Location: US 19 and 98, 0.4 mi s jct US 221. 2220 US 19 S 32348. Fax: 850/584-3700. **Facility:** 61 one-bedroom
standard units. 2 stories, exterior corridors. **Parking:** on-site. **Terms:** pets ($3 extra charge). **Pool(s):** out-
door. **Guest Services:** valet laundry. **Business Services:** fax (fee). **Cards:** AX, CB, DC, DS, MC, VI.
Motel SOME UNITS
⬛ 🛏 🍴 🏊 📷 / ⊠ 🖳 /

THE CHAPARRAL INN
Phone: 850/584-2441
(AAA) (SAVE) All Year 1P: $38-$42 2P: $42-$45 XP: $5 F12
Location: US 19 and 98, 0.3 mi s of jct US 221. 2159 S Byron Butler Pkwy 32347. Fax: 850/838-1747. **Facility:** 24
one-bedroom standard units. 1 story, exterior corridors. **Parking:** on-site. **Pool(s):** outdoor. **Business Serv-**
ices: fax (fee). **Cards:** AX, DS, MC, VI.
Motel SOME UNITS
⬛ 🍴 🏊 / ⊠ /

HAMPTON INN
Phone: (850)223-3000
(SAVE) All Year 1P: $66-$76 2P: $74-$84
Location: 1 mi s of jct US 221 and 19 (Byron Butler Pkwy). 2399 S Byron Butler Pkwy 32348 (PO Box 111).
Fax: 850/223-2622. **Facility:** 60 one-bedroom standard units, some with whirlpools. 3 stories, interior corri-
dors. *Bath:* combo or shower only. **Parking:** on-site. **Amenities:** voice mail, irons, hair dryers. **Pool(s):** out-
Small-scale Hotel door. **Leisure Activities:** exercise room. **Guest Services:** valet and coin laundry. **Business Services:**
meeting rooms, business center. **Cards:** AX, CB, DC, DS, MC, VI.
SOME UNITS
⬛ 🍴 ♿ ♿ 🏊 📷 🖳 ☕ / ⬛ /

——— **WHERE TO DINE** ———

POUNCEY'S RESTAURANT **Lunch:** $4-$6 **Dinner:** $8-$12 **Phone:** 850/584-9942
Location: US 19 and 98, 0.3 mi s of jct US 221. 2186 S Byron Butler Pkwy 32347. **Hours:** 6 am-10 pm. Closed:
11/27, 12/25. **Features:** Simple but scrumptious describes the menu offerings at this family-style diner.
Walk in, seat yourself and enjoy everything from BLT sandwiches and seafood specials to fresh vegetables
American and chocolate meringue pie. The dishes leave your taste buds satisfied. Casual dress. **Parking:** on-site.
⊠

PINELLAS PARK —*See Tampa Bay p. 925.*

PLANTATION —*See Fort Lauderdale p. 405.*

PLANT CITY —See Tampa Bay p. 926.

POMPANO BEACH —See Fort Lauderdale p. 407.

PONCE INLET pop. 2,513

──────── WHERE TO DINE ────────

INLET HARBOR MARINA & RESTAURANT　　　　**Lunch:** $6-$9　　　**Dinner:** $9-$23　　**Phone:** 386/767-3266
（AAA）
Location: 0.5 mi w of S Atlantic Ave, 4.8 mi s of jct Dunlawton. 133 Inlet Harbor Rd 32127. **Hours:** 11 am-10 pm.
Closed: 12/25. **Features:** It's hard to say what's most notable at this waterfront restaurant: the scenic
views of birds, boats and the nearby sandbar or the savory flavors that go into the many steak, chicken
and seafood dishes. Dine on the deck for maximum ambience. Casual dress; cocktails; entertainment.
American　　**Parking:** on-site. **Cards:** AX, DS, MC, VI.

PONTE VEDRA BEACH —See Jacksonville p. 475.

PORT CHARLOTTE pop. 46,451

──────── WHERE TO STAY ────────

DAYS INN OF PORT CHARLOTTE　　　　　　　　　　　　　　　　　　**Phone:** (941)627-8900

SAVE	2/11-3/31	1P: $82-$99	2P: $87-$119	XP: $5	F18
	12/26-2/10	1P: $52-$84	2P: $57-$89	XP: $5	F18
	12/1-12/25 & 4/1-11/30	1P: $42-$59	2P: $47-$69	XP: $5	F18

Location: On US 41, just s of jct Toledo Blade Blvd. 1941 Tamiami Tr 33948. Fax: 941/743-8503. **Facility:** 126 one-
Small-scale Hotel　bedroom standard units. 3 stories, exterior corridors. **Parking:** on-site. **Terms:** small pets only.
Amenities: irons, hair dryers. **Pool(s):** heated outdoor. **Leisure Activities:** exercise room. **Guest Services:**
valet and coin laundry. **Business Services:** meeting rooms, fax. **Cards:** AX, DC, DS, MC, VI.
SOME UNITS

HAMPTON INN　　　　　　　　　　　　　　　　　　　　　　　　**Phone:** (941)627-5600

SAVE	2/11-3/31	1P: $99-$129	2P: $109-$139	
	12/26-2/10	1P: $84-$119	2P: $94-$129	
	12/1-12/25 & 4/1-11/30	1P: $74-$94	2P: $79-$99	

Location: I-75, exit 170, just e on Kings Hwy, then just s. 24480 Sand Hill Blvd 33983. Fax: 941/627-6883.
Small-scale Hotel　**Facility:** 73 one-bedroom standard units. 3 stories, interior corridors. **Parking:** on-site. **Amenities:** voice
mail, irons, hair dryers. **Pool(s):** heated outdoor. **Guest Services:** coin laundry. **Business Services:** fax.
Cards: AX, CB, DC, DS, MC, VI.
SOME UNITS
FEE

HOLIDAY INN EXPRESS HOTEL & SUITES　　　　　　　　　　　　**Phone:** (941)764-0056

	2/10-4/10 [ECP]	1P: $114-$169	2P: $114-$169	XP: $5	F18
	12/27-2/9 [ECP]	1P: $94-$124	2P: $99-$124	XP: $5	F18
Small-scale Hotel	12/1-12/26 & 4/11-11/30 [ECP]	1P: $74-$99	2P: $74-$99	XP: $5	F18

Location: I-75, exit 170, just e on Kings Hwy, then just s. 24440 Sandhill Blvd 33983. Fax: 941/613-1380. **Facility:** 69
units. 51 one-bedroom standard units. 18 one-bedroom suites. 3 stories, interior corridors. *Bath:* combo or shower only. **Parking:**
on-site. **Amenities:** high-speed Internet, dual phone lines, voice mail, irons, hair dryers. **Pool(s):** heated outdoor. **Guest Services:** coin laundry. **Business Services:** meeting rooms, fax. **Cards:** AX, DC, DS, MC, VI.
SOME UNITS
FEE

PORT CHARLOTTE MOTEL　　　　　　　　　　　　　　　　　　　**Phone:** (941)625-4177

	1/1-4/1		2P: $85	XP: $10	F12
	12/1-12/31		2P: $65	XP: $10	F12
Motel	4/2-4/30	1P: $55	2P: $55	XP: $10	F12
	5/1-11/30	1P: $45		XP: $10	F12

Location: On US 41, just s of jct Harbor Blvd. 3491 Tamiami Tr 33952. Fax: 941/624-5591. **Facility:** 52 one-bedroom standard units,
some with efficiencies. 2 stories, exterior corridors. **Parking:** on-site. **Terms:** cancellation fee imposed, weekly rates available.
Pool(s): heated outdoor, wading. **Leisure Activities:** whirlpool, boat dock, fishing, shuffleboard. **Guest Services:** coin laundry.
Business Services: fax. **Cards:** AX, DC, MC, VI.
SOME UNITS

──────── *The following lodging was either not evaluated or did not* ────────
meet AAA rating requirements but is listed for your information only.

AMERICINN LODGE & SUITES　　　　　　　　　　　　　　　　　　**Phone:** 763/421-2335

[fyi]	1/1-4/30 [ECP]	1P: $95-$200	2P: $95-$200	XP: $6	F12
	12/1-12/31 & 5/1-8/31 [ECP]	1P: $80-$150	2P: $80-$150	XP: $6	F12
Motel	9/1-11/30 [ECP]	1P: $70-$150	2P: $70-$150	XP: $6	F12

Too new to rate, opening scheduled for December 2002. **Location:** I-75, exit 170, just w. 812 Kings Hwy 33980.
Amenities: coffeemakers, microwaves, refrigerators, pool. **Cards:** AX, DC, DS, MC, VI.

------ **WHERE TO DINE** ------

CAP'N & THE COWBOY **Lunch:** $6-$11   **Dinner:** $11-$22   **Phone:** 941/743-3969
▼▼ ▼▼ **Location:** I-75, exit 170, 1.6 mi w on Kings Hwy (SR 769); in Maple Leaf Plaza. 2200 Kings Hwy, Unit 3N 33980.
Hours: 11 am-9 pm, Fri & Sat-10 pm. Closed major holidays; also Mon. **Features:** A favorite spot of the
Steak & Seafood locals, this laid-back restaurant has a menu of such tasty dishes as coconut fried shrimp, fresh grouper,
yellowfin tuna and a signature filet topped with Jack Daniels, mushrooms, onions and Monterey Jack
cheese. Casual dress; cocktails. **Parking:** on-site. **Cards:** AX, DC, DS, MC, VI.

PORT ORANGE pop. 45,823   (See map p. 279; index p. 282)

------ **WHERE TO DINE** ------

AUNT CATFISH'S ON THE RIVER **Lunch:** $7-$15   **Dinner:** $9-$29   **Phone:** 386/767-4768   ㉚
▼▼ ▼▼ **Location:** On SR A1A, just e of US 1; on the Intracoastal Waterway at west end of Port Orange Bridge Cswy
(Dunlawton Ave). 4009 Halifax Dr 32127. **Hours:** 11:30 am-9:30 pm, Fri & Sat-10 pm, Sun 9 am-9 pm. Closed:
American 12/25. **Reservations:** suggested. **Features:** Southern hospitality, a waterfront view and a down-home
menu complete with grits and catfish can be found at this bustling, casual eatery. Fresh local seafood,
chicken, steak, ribs and an extensive salad bar make any wait during peak hours worthwhile. cocktails. **Parking:** on-site.
Cards: AX, DS, MC, VI.

PORT RICHEY —See Tampa Bay p. 927.

PORT ST. LUCIE pop. 88,769

------ **WHERE TO STAY** ------

BEST WESTERN PORT ST. LUCIE SUITES   **Phone:** (772)878-7600
(AAA) (SAVE) 2/1-3/31 [ECP]   1P: $79-$129   2P: $79-$129   XP: $5   F18
1/1-1/31 [ECP]   1P: $79-$119   2P: $79-$119   XP: $5   F18
▼▼▼▼ 12/1-12/31 & 4/1-11/30 [ECP]   1P: $55-$89   2P: $55-$89   XP: $5   F18
Motel   **Location:** 0.5 mi s of Prima Vista Blvd, at Spanish Lakes Blvd. 7900 S US 1 34952. Fax: 772/340-0422. **Facility:** 98
one-bedroom standard units. 2 stories, exterior corridors. **Parking:** on-site. **Terms:** weekly rates available,
package plans - weekends & seasonal. **Amenities:** video games (fee), irons, hair dryers. **Pool(s):** heated
outdoor. **Leisure Activities:** whirlpool. **Guest Services:** coin laundry. **Business Services:** meeting rooms, fax (fee). **Cards:** AX,
CB, DC, DS, MC, VI. **Special Amenities: free continental breakfast and free room upgrade (subject to availability with advanced reservations).**

SOME UNITS
[icons]

HAMPTON INN & SUITES PORT ST. LUCIE   **Phone:** (772)878-5900
(SAVE) 12/16-4/15 [ECP]   1P: $109-$149   2P: $109-$149
4/16-11/30 [ECP]   1P: $84-$104   2P: $84-$104
▼▼▼ 12/1-12/15 [ECP]   1P: $79-$99   2P: $79-$99
Small-scale Hotel **Location:** I-95, exit 121, just e. 155 Peacock Blvd 34986. Fax: 772/878-9338. **Facility:** 73 one-bedroom standard
units, some with whirlpools. 4 stories, interior corridors. *Bath:* combo or shower only. **Parking:** on-site.
Amenities: dual phone lines, voice mail, irons, hair dryers. *Fee:* video games, high-speed Internet. **Pool(s):**
outdoor. **Leisure Activities:** whirlpool, exercise room. **Guest Services:** gift shop, valet and coin laundry. **Business Services:**
meeting rooms, business center. **Cards:** AX, DC, DS, MC, VI.

SOME UNITS
[icons]

HOLIDAY INN-PORT ST LUCIE   **Phone:** (772)337-2200
▼▼▼ 12/31-4/5   1P: $149-$169   2P: $149-$169   XP: $10   F18
12/1-12/30 & 4/6-11/30   1P: $79-$99   2P: $79-$99   XP: $10   F18
Small-scale Hotel **Location:** US 1, 0.5 mi n of jct SR 716, Port St Lucie Blvd. 10120 S Federal Hwy, Rt 1 34952. Fax: 772/335-7872.
Facility: 142 units. 70 one-bedroom standard units. 72 one-bedroom suites ($129-$200), some with whirl-
pools. 5 stories, interior corridors. **Parking:** on-site. **Amenities:** voice mail, irons, hair dryers. **Pool(s):** heated outdoor. **Leisure
Activities:** whirlpool, exercise room. **Guest Services:** valet and coin laundry. **Business Services:** meeting rooms, fax (fee).
(See color ad opposite inside back cover)

SOME UNITS
[icons]   FEE

MAINSTAY SUITES AT PGA VILLAGE

Phone: (772)460-8882

	1/1-4/15 [CP]	2P: $93-$120	
	12/1-12/31 [CP]	2P: $75-$95	
Small-scale Hotel	4/16-11/30 [CP]	2P: $68-$80	

Location: I-95, exit 121, just w. 8501 Champions Way 34953. Fax: 772/460-8301. **Facility:** 80 units. 68 one-bedroom standard units, some with kitchens. 12 one-bedroom suites with kitchens. 2 stories, interior corridors. *Bath:* combo or shower only. **Parking:** on-site. **Terms:** weekly rates available. **Amenities:** dual phone lines, voice mail, irons. **Pool(s):** outdoor. **Guest Services:** coin laundry. **Business Services:** meeting rooms, fax (fee). **Cards:** AX, CB, DC, DS, MC, VI.

SOME UNITS
(ASK) (SD) (accessibility) (pool) (DATA PORT) (fridge) (microwave) / (X) (computer) /

SHERATON'S PGA VACATION RESORT

Phone: (772)460-5700

	12/1-12/31	1P: $279-$379	2P: $279-$379
	1/1-4/30 & 9/28-11/30	1P: $219-$299	2P: $219-$299
Condominium	5/1-9/27	1P: $189-$265	2P: $189-$265

Location: I-95, exit 121, just w. 8702 Champions Way 34986. Fax: 772/460-5705. **Facility:** 42 units. 24 one- and 18 two-bedroom suites with kitchens, some with whirlpools. 3 stories, exterior corridors. **Parking:** check-in 4 pm. **Terms:** check-in 4 pm, 3 day cancellation notice-fee imposed. **Amenities:** voice mail, safes, irons, hair dryers. *Some:* CD players. **Pool(s):** heated outdoor, wading. **Leisure Activities:** whirlpool, playground. **Guest Services:** complimentary laundry. **Business Services:** fax (fee). **Cards:** AX, DC, MC, VI. *(See color ad p 5)*

(ASK) (SD) (restaurant) (accessibility) (pool) (VCR) (microwave) (DATA PORT) (fridge) (computer)

SPRINGHILL SUITES

Phone: (772)871-2929

SAVE

	2/15-3/31	1P: $129	2P: $129
	12/1-2/14	1P: $89	2P: $89
Small-scale Hotel	4/1-11/30	1P: $84	2P: $84

Location: I-95, exit 121, just e on St. Lucie West Blvd, then just n on Peacock Blvd. 2000 NW Courtyard Cir 34986. Fax: 772/871-0016. **Facility:** 105 one-bedroom standard units. 4 stories, interior corridors. *Bath:* combo or shower only. **Parking:** on-site. **Terms:** [ECP] meal plan available. **Amenities:** dual phone lines, voice mail, irons, hair dryers. **Pool(s):** heated outdoor. **Leisure Activities:** whirlpool, exercise room. **Guest Services:** valet and coin laundry. **Business Services:** meeting rooms, administrative services. **Cards:** AX, DC, DS, MC, VI. *(See ad p 781)*

SOME UNITS
(SD) (accessibility) (pool) (microwave) (DATA PORT) (fridge) (computer) / (X) /

──────── **WHERE TO DINE** ────────

LE BRITTANY

Dinner: $12-$25
Phone: 772/871-2231

Continental

Location: At jct US 1 and Prima Vista Blvd; in St. Lucie Shopping Center. 899A Prima Vista Blvd 34952. **Hours:** Open 12/1-8/31 & 10/1-11/30; 4:30 pm-9 pm. Closed: Mon & Tues. **Reservations:** suggested. **Features:** Fine home-style cooking with a French flair is what you'll get in this cozy restaurant. The chef/owner whips up tasty offerings, such as beef and vegetable soup and the scrumptious duck, served with chutney and a carrot-broccoli medley. Casual dress; beer & wine only. **Parking:** on-site. **Cards:** MC, VI.

PUNTA GORDA pop. 14,344

──────── **WHERE TO STAY** ────────

BEST WESTERN WATERFRONT INN

Phone: (941)639-1165

	2/1-4/22	1P: $97-$148	2P: $97-$148	XP: $10	F16
	12/1-12/31	1P: $69-$117	2P: $69-$117	XP: $10	F16
	4/23-11/30	1P: $69-$109	2P: $69-$109	XP: $10	F16
	1/1-1/31	1P: $92-$107	2P: $92-$107	XP: $10	F16

Small-scale Hotel **Location:** On US 41; just s of Peace River Bridge. 300 Retta Esplanade 33950. Fax: 941/639-8116. **Facility:** 183 units. 179 one-bedroom standard units. 4 one-bedroom suites ($120-$375) with efficiencies and whirlpools. 2-5 stories, interior corridors. **Parking:** on-site. **Terms:** check-in 4 pm, 10% service charge, pets ($25 extra charge). **Amenities:** voice mail, irons, hair dryers. *Some:* CD players. **Dining:** 6:30 am-9 pm, cocktails. **Pool(s):** heated outdoor. **Leisure Activities:** whirlpool, boat dock, fishing, exercise room. **Guest Services:** gift shop, valet and coin laundry. **Business Services:** meeting rooms, business center. **Cards:** AX, DC, DS, JC, MC, VI. *(See color ad p 783)*

SOME UNITS
(SD) (pets) (restaurant) (dining) (pool) (X) (microwave) (DATA PORT) (computer) / (X) (VCR) (fridge) (microwave) /
FEE FEE FEE

GILCHRIST BED & BREAKFAST INN

Phone: 941/575-4129

	12/1-4/30 [ECP]	1P: $95-$105	2P: $95-$105	XP: $10	F17
Bed & Breakfast	5/1-11/30 [ECP]	1P: $75-$85	2P: $75-$85		

Location: 0.5 mi w on Marion Ave, just n. Located in a residential area. 115 Gilchrist St 33950. Fax: 941/575-6041. **Facility:** Smoke free premises. 3 one-bedroom standard units, some with kitchens. 1 story, interior/exterior corridors. *Bath:* combo or shower only. **Parking:** on-site. **Terms:** 2 night minimum stay, 5 day cancellation notice-fee imposed. **Amenities:** irons, hair dryers. **Leisure Activities:** whirlpool, bicycles. **Business Services:** meeting rooms. **Cards:** AX, DS, MC, VI.

SOME UNITS
(X) (microwave) / (W) (fridge) (microwave) (computer)

HOLIDAY INN HARBORSIDE

Phone: (941)639-2167

	12/1-4/15	1P: $99-$189	2P: $99-$189	XP: $10	F17
	4/16-11/30	1P: $69-$109	2P: $69-$109	XP: $10	F17

Location: On US 41; at Peace River Bridge. 33 Tamiami Tr 33950. Fax: 941/639-1707. **Facility:** 100 units. 97 one-bedroom standard units. 3 one-bedroom suites ($99-$299) with kitchens. 2 stories, interior corridors. *Bath:* **Small-scale Hotel** combo or shower only. **Parking:** on-site. **Terms:** cancellation fee imposed, weekly rates available, package plans - weekends, small pets only ($25-$40 extra charge). **Amenities:** high-speed Internet, dual phone lines, voice mail, irons, hair dryers. **Dining:** 7 am-9:30 pm, cocktails. **Pool(s):** heated outdoor. **Leisure Activities:** marina, fishing, exercise room. **Guest Services:** coin laundry. **Business Services:** meeting rooms, fax. **Cards:** AX, DC, DS, JC, MC, VI. **Special Amenities:** free local telephone calls. *(See color ad p 783 & opposite inside back cover)*

SOME UNITS
(SD) (pets) (restaurant) (dining) (pool) (accessibility) (pool) (X) (microwave) (DATA PORT) (computer) / (X) (fridge) (microwave)
FEE FEE

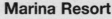

MARINA INN

▼▼ ▼▼

| | 12/1-4/30 | 1P: $150-$195 | 2P: $150-$195 | XP: $10 | F12 |
| | 5/1-11/30 | 1P: $89-$99 | 2P: $89-$99 | XP: $10 | F12 |

Condominium **Location:** I-75, exit 161, 11.2 mi w on CR 768/765 (Burnt Store Rd). Located in the Burnt Store Marina and Country Club; gated area. 3160 Matecumbe Key Rd 33955. Fax: 941/575-2363. **Facility:** 36 units. 34 one- and 2 two-bedroom suites ($195-$275) with kitchens. 3 stories, interior corridors. **Parking:** on-site. **Terms:** 3 day cancellation notice-fee imposed. **Amenities:** irons. *Some:* CD players, hair dryers. **Pool(s):** heated outdoor. **Leisure Activities:** sauna, rental boats, marina, fishing. *Fee:* charter fishing, golf-27 holes, 4 lighted tennis courts, bicycles. **Guest Services:** gift shop, coin laundry. **Business Services:** meeting rooms, fax. **Cards:** AX, DS, MC, VI.

SOME UNITS
ASK S/D ❚❶+ ☎ ⌂ FEE ☒ 🛢 🖳 / ☒ / VCR /

———— **WHERE TO DINE** ————

CAPTAIN'S TABLE **Lunch:** $7-$11 **Dinner:** $17-$30 **Phone:** 941/637-1177

▼▼ ▼▼ **Location:** In Fisherman's Village; 1.5 mi w off Marion Ave. 1200 W Retta Esplanade 33951-1289. **Hours:** 11 am-9 pm, Fri & Sat-10 pm. Closed: 1/1. **Features:** A lovely, scenic view of Charlotte Harbor and plenty of fresh Seafood seafood bring in the locals. The fisherman's platter spills over with whitefish, shrimp, mussels, scallops and fried rice. A lunch and dinner buffet offers seafood and nice crisp salads. Casual dress; cocktails. **Parking:** on-site. **Cards:** AX, DS, MC, VI.

🍸 ☒

SALTY'S HARBORSIDE RESTAURANT **Lunch:** $10-$15 **Dinner:** $14-$37 **Phone:** 941/639-3650

▼▼ ▼▼ **Location:** I-75, exit 161, 11.2 mi w on CR 768/765 (Burnt Store Marina and Country Club. 5000 Burnt Store Rd 33955. **Hours:** 11:30 am-9 pm, Sun-3 pm. Closed: Mon. **Features:** A beautiful harbor view of American many luxurious boats and yachts is a strong point at this restaurant set back within the grounds of a popular country club. Although service is casual, the chef puts together well-prepared dishes marked by beautiful presentation. Chicken marsala is a delight. A limited menu is available in the lounge from 3 pm to 5 pm. Casual dress; cocktails. **Parking:** on-site. **Cards:** AX, DS, MC, VI.

🍸 ☒

QUINCY pop. 6,982

———— **WHERE TO STAY** ————

ALLISON HOUSE INN **Phone:** 850/875-2511

▼▼▼ ▼▼ **All Year [ECP]** 1P: $75-$90 2P: $105-$120 XP: $15 F12

Historic Bed **Location:** Just e of town center. Located in historic district. 215 N Madison St 32351. Fax: 850/875-2511. & Breakfast **Facility:** Granola and biscotti are among the homemade foods served to guests at this 1843 Greek Revival home. Smoke free premises. 6 one-bedroom standard units. 2 stories, interior corridors. *Bath:* combo or shower only. **Parking:** on-site. **Terms:** 14 day cancellation notice-fee imposed, [BP] meal plan available, small pets only (owner's pet on premises). **Amenities:** hair dryers. **Leisure Activities:** bicycles. **Business Services:** fax. **Cards:** AX, DS, MC.

ASK 🛏 ☒ DATA PORT

MCFARLIN HOUSE BED & BREAKFAST INN **Phone:** 850/875-2526

▼▼▼ ▼▼ **All Year [BP]** 1P: $85-$175 XP: $20

Historic Bed **Location:** Corner of King and Love sts. Located in historic district. 305 E King St 32351. Fax: 850/627-4703. & Breakfast **Facility:** 1895 Queen Ann Victorian. Designated smoking area. 9 one-bedroom standard units, some with whirlpools. 4 stories (no elevator), interior corridors. *Bath:* combo or shower only. **Parking:** on-site. **Terms:** check-in 4 pm, 14 day cancellation notice-fee imposed. **Guest Services:** area transportation. **Business Services:** fax. **Cards:** AX, DS, MC, VI.

SOME UNITS
✈ ☒ DATA PORT / VCR /

REDINGTON BEACH —See Tampa Bay p. 928.

REDINGTON SHORES —See Tampa Bay p. 928.

RIVERVIEW (HILLSBOROUGH COUNTY) —See Tampa Bay p. 928.

RIVIERA BEACH pop. 29,884 (See map p. 757; index p. 760)

———— **WHERE TO STAY** ————

SUPER 8 MOTEL WEST PALM BEACH/RIVIERA BEACH **Phone:** (561)848-1188 [101]

▼▼ ▼▼

	2/1-4/15 [CP]	1P: $69-$89	2P: $69-$89	XP: $5	F16
Motel	12/1-1/31 [CP]	1P: $49-$79	2P: $49-$79	XP: $5	F16
	4/16-11/30 [CP]	1P: $49-$69	2P: $49-$69	XP: $5	F16

Location: I-95, exit 76, just w on SR 708. 4112 W Blue Heron Blvd 33404. Fax: 561/848-4583. **Facility:** 100 one-bedroom standard units. 2 stories (no elevator), exterior corridors. **Parking:** on-site. **Terms:** 3 day cancellation notice. **Amenities:** *Some:* hair dryers. **Pool(s):** outdoor. **Guest Services:** coin laundry. **Business Services:** fax (fee). **Cards:** AX, CB, DC, DS, MC, VI.

SOME UNITS
ASK S/D ❚❶+ ☎ ⛱ / ☒ DATA PORT 🛢 🖳 🖳 /

RUSKIN —See Tampa Bay p. 928.

SAFETY HARBOR —See Tampa Bay p. 930.

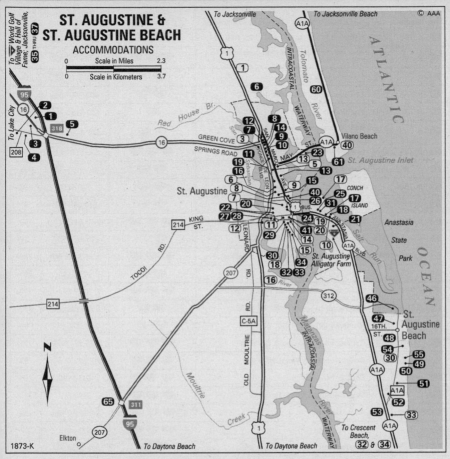

St. Augustine & St. Augustine Beach

This index helps you "spot" where approved accommodations and restaurants are located on the corresponding detailed maps. Lodging rate ranges are for comparison only and show the property's high season; rates are per night, unless only weekly (W) rates are available. Restaurant rate range is for dinner, unless only lunch (L) is served. Turn to the listing page for more detailed rate information and consult display ads for special promotions.

Spotter/Map Page Number	OA	ST. AUGUSTINE - Lodgings	Diamond Rating	Rate Range High Season	Listing Page
1 / above		Days Inn-West	◆◆	$44-$150	792
2 / above	AAA	Hampton Inn St. Augustine Outlet Center	◆◆◆	$69-$109 SAVE	792
3 / above	AAA	Ramada Limited	◆◆	$49-$169 SAVE	796
4 / above	AAA	Best Western Inn - see color ad p 790	◆◆	$49-$89 SAVE	790
5 / above	AAA	Holiday Inn Express	◆◆◆	$69-$189 SAVE	794
6 / above	AAA	Ponce de Leon Hotel and Golf Resort	◆◆◆	$89-$169 SAVE	796
7 / above	AAA	Days Inn Historic	◆◆	$46-$89 SAVE	792
8 / above	AAA	Alhambra Inn - see color ad p 788	◆◆	$69-$175 SAVE	788
9 / above	AAA	Merida Motel	◆◆	$39-$99 SAVE	795

Spotter/Map Page Number	OA	ST. AUGUSTINE - Lodgings (continued)	Diamond Rating	Rate Range High Season	Listing Page
🔟 / p. 785	AAA	Hampton Inn Historic - see color ad p 793	◆◆◆	$65-$175 SAVE	792
🈕 / p. 785	AAA	Best Western Historical Inn - see color ad p 793	◆◆◆	$59-$150 SAVE	789
🈔 / p. 785	AAA	Travelodge & Suites	◆◆	$54-$110 SAVE	798
🈓 / p. 785	AAA	La Quinta Inn - see color ad p 794	◆◆	$69-$150 SAVE	795
🈖 / p. 785	AAA	Thriftlodge	◆	$40-$160 SAVE	798
🈗 / p. 785	AAA	Best Western Spanish Quarters Inn - see color ad p 793	◆◆	$69-$139 SAVE	790
🈘 / p. 785	AAA	Holiday Inn Hotel & Suites-Historic	◆◆◆	$99-$139 SAVE	794
🈙 / p. 785	AAA	Lion Inn	◆◆	$50-$175 SAVE	795
🈚 / p. 785		Conch House Marina Resort	◆◆	$70-$250	792
🈛 / p. 785	AAA	Scottish Inns	◆◆	$40-$89 SAVE	797
🈜 / p. 785	AAA	Casa de Suenos Bed & Breakfast	◆◆◆	$175-$225 SAVE	790
🈝 / p. 785	AAA	Sleep Inn - see color ad p 797	◆◆	$75-$150 SAVE	797
🈞 / p. 785	AAA	Alexander Homestead Bed & Breakfast	◆◆◆	$115-$195 SAVE	788
🈟 / p. 785		The Inn At Camachee Harbor	◆◆	$79-$149	794
🈠 / p. 785	AAA	Casa de la Paz Bayfront Bed & Breakfast	◆◆◆	$130-$275 SAVE	790
🈡 / p. 785	AAA	Edgewater Inn - see color ad p 792	◆◆	$69-$139 SAVE	792
🈢 / p. 785	AAA	Monterey Inn - see color ad p 795	◆◆	$45-$150 SAVE	796
🈣 / p. 785	AAA	Centennial House Bed & Breakfast	◆◆◆	$115-$245 SAVE	791
🈤 / p. 785	AAA	Cedar House Inn Victorian B & B	◆◆◆	$124-$209 SAVE	791
🈥 / p. 785		Old City House Inn & Restaurant	◆◆◆	$85-$195	796
🈦 / p. 785		Casa De Solana Bed & Breakfast Inn	◆◆◆	$99-$219	790
🈧 / p. 785	AAA	Anastasia Inn	◆◆◆	$45-$150 SAVE	789
🈨 / p. 785		St. Francis Inn	◆◆◆	$99-$219	797
🈩 / p. 785	AAA	Bayfront Inn - see color ad p 789	◆◆	$69-$159 SAVE	789
🈪 / p. 785		Bayfront Westcott House	◆◆◆	$95-$279	789
🈫 / p. 785	AAA	Comfort Suites	◆◆◆	$74-$129 SAVE	791
🈬 / p. 785		Sheraton's Vistana Resort at World Golf Village - see color ad p 5	◆◆◆	$165-$249	797
🈭 / p. 785	AAA	World Golf Village Renaissance Resort - see color ad p 798	◆◆◆	$169-$269 SAVE	798
🈮 / p. 785		Castle Garden Bed & Breakfast	◆◆	$65-$199	791
🈯 / p. 785		Casa Monica Hotel - see color ad p 791	◆◆◆◆	$169-$269	791
		ST. AUGUSTINE - Restaurants			
① / p. 785		King's Head British Pub	◆	$4-$12	800
③ / p. 785		Marty's Seafood & Steak House	◆	$6-$15	800
⑤ / p. 785	AAA	Raintree Restaurant	◆◆◆	$15-$29	800
⑥ / p. 785		Barnacle Bill's Seafood House	◆	$9-$16	799
⑦ / p. 785		Columbia Restaurant	◆◆	$12-$30	799
⑧ / p. 785		Tavern on the Bay	◆	$8-$17	800
⑨ / p. 785		Le Pavillon	◆◆	$14-$22	800
⑩ / p. 785	AAA	Gypsy Cab Co	◆◆	$11-$17	799

Spotter/Map Page Number	OA	ST. AUGUSTINE - Restaurants (continued)	Diamond Rating	Rate Range High Season	Listing Page
11 / p. 785		Cafe Alcazar	◆◆	$7-$10(L)	799
12 / p. 785	AAA	Theos' Restaurant	◆	$4-$7(L)	800
13 / p. 785		Cortesse's Bistro & Flamingo Room	◆◆	$11-$20	799
14 / p. 785		Denoel French Pastry Shop	◆	$5-$7(L)	799
15 / p. 785		Azalea's Cafe	◆	$4-$10(L)	799
16 / p. 785	AAA	Creekside Dinery	◆	$6-$16	799
17 / p. 785		The Conch House Restaurant and Lounge	◆◆	$13-$23	799
18 / p. 785		White Lion Restaurant	◆◆	$6-$18	800
19 / p. 785		95 Cordova	◆◆◆	$14-$25	799
20 / p. 785		A1A Ale Works Brewery and Restaurant	◆◆	$10-$19	799
		ST. AUGUSTINE BEACH - Lodgings			
46 / p. 785	AAA	Super 8	◆◆	$59-$119 SAVE	802
47 / p. 785	AAA	Days Inn-St. Augustine Beach - see color ad p 793	◆◆◆	$69-$150 SAVE	802
48 / p. 785		Hilton Garden Inn-St. Augustine Beach	◆◆◆	$89-$139	802
49 / p. 785	AAA	La Fiesta Ocean Inn & Suites - see color ad p 801, p 794	◆◆	$85-$259 SAVE	802
50 / p. 785	AAA	Holiday Inn-St Augustine Beach - see color ad opposite inside back cover, p 801	◆◆◆	$110-$130 SAVE	802
51 / p. 785		Ramada Limited, at the Beach	◆◆	$59-$210	802
52 / p. 785	AAA	Comfort Inn at St. Augustine Beach	◆◆	$42-$79 SAVE	800
53 / p. 785	AAA	Best Western Ocean Inn	◆◆	$69-$159 SAVE	800
54 / p. 785		Hampton Inn-St. Augustine Beach	◆◆◆	$69-$249	802
55 / p. 785		Coquina Gables Oceanfront B&B	◆◆◆	$139-$219	801
		ST. AUGUSTINE BEACH - Restaurants			
30 / p. 785		Aruanno's Italian Restaurant	◆◆	$10-$18	803
32 / p. 785	AAA	Greenstreet's	◆	$3-$10(L)	803
33 / p. 785	AAA	The World Famous Oasis Restaurant & Deck	◆	$4-$14	803
34 / p. 785	AAA	Saltwater Cowboys	◆◆	$9-$18	803
		VILANO BEACH - Lodgings			
60 / p. 785	AAA	Ocean Sands Beach Inn - see color ad p 796	◆◆	$69-$99 SAVE	954
61 / p. 785		Hampton Inn Oceanside	◆◆◆	$139-$259	954
		VILANO BEACH - Restaurant			
40 / p. 785	AAA	Fiddler's Green	◆◆	$12-$25	955
		ELKTON - Lodgings			
65 / p. 785	AAA	Comfort Inn St. Augustine	◆◆	$69-$129 SAVE	314

ST. AUGUSTINE pop. 11,592   (See map p. 785; index p. 785)

———— WHERE TO STAY ————

ALEXANDER HOMESTEAD BED & BREAKFAST Phone: (904)826-4147 [22]

All Year 1P: $115-$195 2P: $115-$195 XP: $15

Location: Just s of Orange St; center. 14 Sevilla St 32084. Fax: 904/823-9503. **Facility:** This Victorian home built in 1888 is decorated with antiques and features wood-burning fireplaces in two guest rooms. Smoke free premises. 4 one-bedroom standard units, some with whirlpools. 2 stories, interior corridors. **Parking:** on-site. **Terms:** 2 night minimum stay - weekends, age restrictions may apply, 7 day cancellation notice-fee imposed, [BP] meal plan available, no pets allowed (owner's pet on premises). **Amenities:** hair dryers. **Leisure Activities:** bicycles. **Business Services:** fax. **Cards:** AX, DS, MC, VI. **Special Amenities:** free local telephone calls and free newspaper.

Historic Bed & Breakfast

ALHAMBRA INN Phone: (904)824-2883 [8]

2/1-4/30	1P: $69-$75	2P: $69-$175	XP: $10	F18
5/1-8/31	1P: $59-$175	2P: $59-$175	XP: $6	F18
12/1-1/31	1P: $49-$125	2P: $49-$125	XP: $6	F18
9/1-11/30	1P: $49-$99	2P: $49-$99	XP: $6	F18

Small-scale Hotel **Location:** Jct US 1 and SR 16. 2700 N Ponce de Leon Blvd 32084. Fax: 904/825-0976. **Facility:** 77 one-bedroom standard units, some with whirlpools. 2 stories, exterior corridors. *Bath:* combo or shower only. **Parking:** on-site. **Terms:** check-in 4 pm. **Amenities:** video library (fee), irons, hair dryers. **Dining:** 6 am-10 pm. **Pool(s):** outdoor. **Leisure Activities:** whirlpool. **Guest Services:** gift shop, area transportation. **Business Services:** fax. **Cards:** AX, CB, DC, DS, MC, VI. **Special Amenities:** free local telephone calls and free room upgrade (subject to availability with advanced reservations). *(See color ad below)*

SOME UNITS / FEE

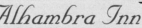

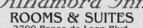

(See map p. 785)

ANASTASIA INN
AAA SAVE
Motel

All Year [CP]   1P: $45-$150   2P: $45-$150   **Phone: 904/825-2879** **31**
                                                  XP: $5
Location: SR A1A, 0.3 mi s of Bridge of Lions. 218 Anastasia Blvd 32080. Fax: 904/825-2724. **Facility:** 23 one-bedroom standard units. 2 stories, exterior corridors. *Bath:* combo or shower only. **Parking:** on-site. **Terms:** 3 day cancellation notice-fee imposed. **Amenities:** voice mail. **Pool(s):** small heated outdoor. **Business Services:** fax. **Cards:** AX, DS, MC, VI. **Special Amenities:** free continental breakfast and free local telephone calls.

SOME UNITS

BAYFRONT INN
AAA SAVE
Motel

All Year   1P: $69-$159   2P: $69-$159   **Phone: (904)824-1681** **33**
                                                  XP: $8
Location: Just s of SR A1A and Bridge of Lions; center. Located in quiet historic district. 138 Avenida Menendez 32084. Fax: 904/829-8721. **Facility:** Designated smoking area. 39 units. 38 one-bedroom standard units. 1 two-bedroom suite ($99-$225). 1-2 stories, exterior corridors. *Bath:* combo or shower only. **Parking:** on-site. **Terms:** 3 day cancellation notice, [CP] meal plan available. **Amenities:** voice mail, irons, hair dryers. **Pool(s):** small outdoor. **Leisure Activities:** whirlpool. **Business Services:** fax (fee). **Cards:** AX, DC, MC, VI.
Special Amenities: free local telephone calls and free newspaper. *(See color ad below)*

BAYFRONT WESTCOTT HOUSE
Historic Bed
& Breakfast

All Year [BP]   2P: $95-$279   **Phone: (904)824-4301** **34**
                                                                       D
Location: 1 blk s of the Bridge of Lions. 146 Avenida Menendez 32084-5049. Fax: 904/824-1502. **Facility:** Across the street from Matanzas Bay, this property dating from 1890 offers views of the water in a Victorian-style setting. Designated smoking area. 9 one-bedroom standard units, some with whirlpools. 2 stories, interior/exterior corridors. *Bath:* combo or shower only. **Parking:** street. **Terms:** 3 night minimum stay - weekends, age restrictions may apply, 7 day cancellation notice-fee imposed, package plans, $1 service charge. **Amenities:** hair dryers. **Leisure Activities:** bicycles. **Business Services:** fax. **Cards:** AX, DS, MC, VI.

BEST WESTERN HISTORICAL INN
AAA SAVE
Small-scale Hotel

2/2-9/1 [ECP]   1P: $59-$150   2P: $59-$150   **Phone: (904)829-9088** **11**
                                                  XP: $10   F18
12/1-2/1 & 9/2-11/30 [ECP]   1P: $49-$99   2P: $49-$99   XP: $10   F18
Location: 0.5 mi s of jct SR 16 and US 1, 6 blks n from historic district. 2010 N Ponce de Leon Blvd 32084. Fax: 904/829-0629. **Facility:** 40 units. 38 one-bedroom standard units. 2 two-bedroom suites ($99-$299). 2 stories, exterior corridors. **Parking:** on-site. **Amenities:** *Some:* irons, hair dryers. **Pool(s):** outdoor. **Leisure Activities:** whirlpool. *Fee:* historical tours. **Guest Services:** coin laundry. **Business Services:** fax. **Cards:** AX, CB, DC, DS, JC, MC, VI. **Special Amenities:** free continental breakfast. *(See color ad p 793)*

SOME UNITS

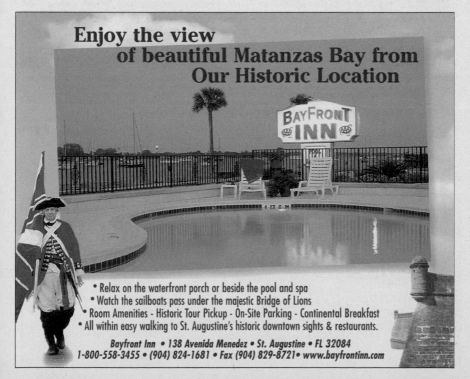

(See map p. 785)

BEST WESTERN INN   Phone: (904)829-1999   **4**
[AAA] [SAVE]
All Year   1P: $49-$79   2P: $55-$89   XP: $6   F12
▼▼ ▼▼▼ **Location:** I-95, exit 318, southwest corner. 2445 SR 16 32092. Fax: 904/829-0660. **Facility:** 120 one-bedroom standard units. 2 stories, exterior corridors. *Bath:* combo or shower only. **Parking:** on-site. **Terms:** cancellation fee imposed, pets ($6 extra charge). **Amenities:** safes, irons, hair dryers. **Pool(s):** outdoor. **Guest Serv-**
Small-scale Hotel **ices:** coin laundry. **Business Services:** fax. **Cards:** AX, CB, DC, DS, JC, MC, VI. **Special Amenities: early check-in/late check-out and free continental breakfast.** *(See color ad below)*

SOME UNITS
[S/D] [☎] [♦] [≈] [▭] / [✕] /

BEST WESTERN SPANISH QUARTERS INN   Phone: (904)824-4457   **15**
[AAA] [SAVE]
2/1-5/31 [ECP]   1P: $69-$139   2P: $69-$139
6/1-8/31 [ECP]   1P: $69-$119   2P: $69-$119
▼▼ ▼▼▼ 12/1-1/31 & 9/1-11/30 [ECP]   1P: $59-$99   2P: $59-$99
Location: Just w of San Marcos Ave. Located across from visitor's center. 6 Castillo Dr 32084. Fax: 904/829-8330.
Small-scale Hotel **Facility:** 40 one-bedroom standard units. 2 stories, exterior corridors. **Parking:** on-site. **Amenities:** irons, hair dryers. **Pool(s):** outdoor. **Leisure Activities:** whirlpool. **Business Services:** fax. **Cards:** AX, CB, DC, DS, JC, MC, VI. **Special Amenities: free continental breakfast.** *(See color ad p 793)*

SOME UNITS
[S/D] [☎] [≈] [DATA PORT] [▭] / [✕] [■] [▣] /

CASA DE LA PAZ BAYFRONT BED & BREAKFAST   Phone: 904/829-2915   **24**
[AAA] [SAVE]
All Year   2P: $130-$275   XP: $35
▼▼▼▼▼ **Location:** 0.3 mi n of Bridge of Lions on SR A1A. 22 Avenida Menendez 32084. Fax: 904/824-6269. **Facility:** A fireplace adds a warm touch to one guest room of this Mediterranean-style home overlooking Matanzas Bay.
Historic Bed Smoke free premises. 7 one-bedroom standard units, some with whirlpools. 3 stories (no elevator),
& Breakfast interior/exterior corridors. *Bath:* combo or shower only. **Parking:** on-site. **Terms:** 2-4 night minimum stay - weekends, age restrictions may apply, 7 day cancellation notice-fee imposed, [BP] meal plan available. **Amenities:** hair dryers. **Guest Services:** complimentary evening beverages. **Business Services:** fax.
Cards: AX, DC, DS, MC, VI. **Special Amenities: early check-in/late check-out and free local telephone calls.**

SOME UNITS
[S/D] [☎] [✕] / [▯] /

CASA DE SOLANA BED & BREAKFAST INN   Phone: (904)824-3555   **30**
▼▼▼▼▼
All Year [BP]   1P: $99-$219   2P: $99-$219   XP: $15
Location: Aviles St at Cadiz St. Located in historic district. 21 Aviles St 32084. Fax: 904/824-3316. **Facility:** This
Historic Bed Spanish Colonial house overlooking a courtyard features sleeping quarters and a parlor in most units. Smoke
& Breakfast free premises. 10 one-bedroom standard units. 3 stories (no elevator), interior corridors. **Parking:** street. **Terms:** age restrictions may apply, 7 day cancellation notice-fee imposed. **Amenities:** voice mail, irons, hair dryers. **Leisure Activities:** bicycles. **Business Services:** fax. **Cards:** AX, DC, DS, MC, VI.

SOME UNITS
[ASK] [✕] / [■] /

CASA DE SUENOS BED & BREAKFAST   Phone: (904)824-0887   **20**
[AAA] [SAVE]
All Year [BP]   2P: $175-$225   XP: $25   D17
▼▼▼▼▼ **Location:** Corner of Saragossa St; center. 20 Cordova St 32084. Fax: 904/824-6102. **Facility:** Tastefully decorated units; some with fireplace. Smoke free premises. 5 one-bedroom standard units, some with whirlpools. 2 stories, interior/exterior corridors. *Bath:* combo or shower only. **Parking:** on-site. **Terms:** age restrictions may
Bed & Breakfast apply, 14 day cancellation notice-fee imposed. **Amenities:** hair dryers. **Guest Services:** complimentary evening beverages. **Business Services:** meeting rooms, fax. **Cards:** DS, MC, VI.

SOME UNITS
[☎] [&M] [▯] [✕] [VCR] [DATA PORT] / [■] /

(See map p. 785)

CASA MONICA HOTEL
Phone: (904)827-1888　[41]
▼▼▼▼ ▼▼▼▼　12/1-5/25 & 8/29-11/30　1P: $169-$269　2P: $169-$269　XP: $25　F17
　　　　5/26-8/28　1P: $159-$259　2P: $159-$259　XP: $25　F17
Historic　**Location:** Downtown. Located across 'from Lightner Museum and Flagler College. 95 Cordova St 32084.
Large-scale Hotel　Fax: 904/819-6065. **Facility:** The hotel, built in 1888, offers cozy guest units with Spanish-style furnishings.
138 units. 126 one-bedroom standard units. 12 one-bedroom suites ($399-$1999), some with whirlpools. 5
stories, interior corridors. *Bath:* combo or shower only. **Parking:** valet and street. **Terms:** check-in 4 pm, 3 day cancellation
notice-fee imposed, package plans - seasonal, $5 service charge. **Amenities:** video games, dual phone lines, voice mail, safes,
irons, hair dryers. **Dining:** 95 Cordova, see separate listing. **Pool(s):** heated outdoor. **Leisure Activities:** whirlpool, exercise
room. *Fee:* bicycles. **Guest Services:** gift shop, valet laundry, area transportation. **Business Services:** meeting rooms, business
center. **Cards:** AX, DC, DS, MC, VI. *(See color ad below)*

SOME UNITS

(ASK) (S🅓) (➡) (🍴) (🍸) (🏊) (✂) (📽) (DATA PORT) (💻) / (✕) (🔒) (📠) /

CASTLE GARDEN BED & BREAKFAST
Phone: (904)829-3839　[40]
▼▼ ▼▼　All Year [BP]　1P: $65-$199　2P: $79-$199　XP: $20　F4
Historic Bed　**Location:** Downtown center. Located opposite Ripley's Believe It or Not Museum. 15 Shenandoah St 32084.
& Breakfast　Fax: 904/829-9049. **Facility:** Smoke free premises. 6 one-bedroom standard units, some with whirlpools. 2
stories, interior corridors. *Bath:* combo or shower only. **Parking:** on-site. **Terms:** 2 night minimum stay -
weekends, age restrictions may apply, 7 day cancellation notice-fee imposed, package plans - seasonal.
Leisure Activities: bicycles. **Business Services:** PC, fax. **Cards:** AX, DS, MC, VI.

SOME UNITS

(ASK) (S🅓) (➡) (✕) / (🆆) (VCR) (DATA PORT) /
　　　　FEE

CEDAR HOUSE INN VICTORIAN B & B
Phone: (904)829-0079　[28]
(AAA) (SAVE)　All Year　1P: $124-$209　XP: $35
▼▼ ▼▼　**Location:** Just w of Lightner Museum; just s of King St via Granada. 79 Cedar St 32084-4311. Fax: 904/825-0916.
Historic Bed　**Facility:** 1893 Victorian home in historic district. Smoke free premises. 6 one-bedroom standard units, some
& Breakfast　with whirlpools. 2 stories, interior/exterior corridors. **Parking:** on-site. **Terms:** 2-3 night minimum stay - week-
ends, age restrictions may apply, 14 day cancellation notice-fee imposed, [BP] meal plan available, package
plans. **Amenities:** voice mail, irons, hair dryers. **Leisure Activities:** whirlpool, bicycles. **Guest Services:**
complimentary evening beverages. **Business Services:** business center. **Cards:** AX, DS, MC, VI.
Special Amenities: free local telephone calls.

SOME UNITS

(➡) (🍴) (✕) (DATA PORT) / (VCR) (🔒) /

CENTENNIAL HOUSE BED & BREAKFAST
Phone: 904/810-2218　[27]
(AAA) (SAVE)　All Year [BP]　1P: $115-$245　2P: $115-$245
▼▼ ▼▼　**Location:** Corner of Saragossa and Cordova sts. Located in historic district. 26 Cordova St 32084. Fax: 904/810-1930.
Facility: Fireplaces enhance the ambience of some of this upscale B&B's comfortable accommodations.
Smoke free premises. 7 one-bedroom standard units, some with whirlpools. 2 stories, interior/exterior corri-
Bed & Breakfast　dors. *Bath:* combo or shower only. **Parking:** on-site. **Terms:** 2 night minimum stay - weekends, 7 day can-
cellation notice-fee imposed. **Amenities:** video library, hair dryers. **Guest Services:** complimentary evening
beverages. **Business Services:** fax. **Cards:** AX, DS, MC, VI. **Special Amenities:** early check-in/late check-out and free local
telephone calls.

(S🅓) (🦽) (✕) (📽)

COMFORT SUITES
Phone: (904)940-9500　[35]
(AAA) (SAVE)　2/1-3/31 [ECP]　1P: $74-$129　2P: $74-$129　XP: $10　F18
▼▼ ▼▼　12/1-1/31 & 4/1-11/30 [ECP]　1P: $69-$99　2P: $69-$99　XP: $10　F18
Small-scale Hotel　**Location:** I-95, exit 323, just e, then just s. 475 Commerce Lake Dr 32095. Fax: 904/940-9600. **Facility:** 162 units.
160 one-bedroom standard units, some with whirlpools. 2 one-bedroom suites. 6 stories, interior/exterior corridors.
Bath: combo or shower only. **Parking:** on-site. **Amenities:** video games, voice mail, hair dryers. *Fee:* high-
speed Internet, safes. *Some:* irons. **Pool(s):** heated outdoor, indoor. **Leisure Activities:** whirlpool, golf privileges, exercise room. **Guest Services:** sundries, valet and coin laundry. **Business Services:** meeting rooms, fax (fee).
Cards: AX, CB, DC, DS, JC, MC, VI.

SOME UNITS

(S🅓) (🍴) (🍸) (🦽) (🏊) (📽) (DATA PORT) (🔒) (📠) (💻) / (✕) /

(See map p. 785)

CONCH HOUSE MARINA RESORT
Phone: 904/829-8646 [18]
▼▼▼ ▼▼▼
All Year — 1P: $70-$250 — 2P: $70-$250 — XP: $10 — F12
Location: 1 mi s of Bridge of Lions on SR A1A, then 0.3 mi n. 57 Comares Ave 32084. Fax: 904/829-5414.
Small-scale Hotel — **Facility:** 17 units. 14 one-bedroom standard units. 3 two-bedroom suites ($125-$250). 1 story, exterior corridors. **Bath:** combo or shower only. **Parking:** on-site. **Terms:** 7 day cancellation notice, pets ($50 fee).
Dining: The Conch House Restaurant and Lounge, see separate listing. **Pool(s):** outdoor. **Leisure Activities:** fishing. **Fee:** boats, sailboats, windsurfing, marina, scuba diving, charter fishing. **Guest Services:** gift shop, coin laundry. **Business Services:** fax. **Cards:** AX, DC, DS, MC, VI.

SOME UNITS

🖼🍴🏊♿❌☎ / 🖥🖥🖥🖥 /

DAYS INN HISTORIC
Phone: (904)829-6581 [7]
AAA SAVE
All Year — 1P: $46-$84 — 2P: $51-$89 — XP: $5 — F12
Location: US 1 at SR 16. Located in historic district; next to sightseeing-tram departure. 2800 N Ponce de Leon Blvd
▼▼▼ ▼▼▼ 32084. Fax: 904/824-0135. **Facility:** 124 one-bedroom standard units. 2 stories, exterior corridors. **Parking:**
Small-scale Hotel **Amenities:** hair dryers. *Some:* irons. **Dining:** 6-11:30 am. **Pool(s):** outdoor. **Leisure Activities:** gazebo & picnic tables in large, shaded lawn area. **Guest Services:** sundries, coin laundry, airport transportation-St. Augustine Airport. **Business Services:** fax (fee). **Cards:** AX, CB, DC, DS, JC, MC, VI. **Special Amenities:** free newspaper and preferred room (subject to availability with advanced reservations).

SOME UNITS

🆓🔧🖼🍴🚳🏊♿📺🖧 / ❌🖥🖥 /
FEE

DAYS INN-WEST
Phone: (904)824-4341 [1]
SAVE
All Year — 1P: $44-$150 — 2P: $49-$150
Location: I-95, exit 318, northwest corner. Located adjacent to outlet mall. 2560 SR 16 32092. Fax: 904/824-1158.
▼▼▼ ▼▼▼ **Facility:** 120 one-bedroom standard units. 2 stories, exterior corridors. **Parking:** on-site. **Terms:** small pets
only ($10 extra charge). **Amenities:** hair dryers. **Pool(s):** outdoor. **Guest Services:** coin laundry. **Business**
Small-scale Hotel **Services:** fax (fee). **Cards:** AX, DC, DS, MC, VI.

SOME UNITS

🆓🖼🍴🏊📺🖥 / ❌🖧 🖥🖥 /

EDGEWATER INN
Phone: (904)825-2697 [25]
AAA SAVE
All Year — 1P: $69-$139 — 2P: $69-$139 — XP: $8
Location: SR A1A, just s of Bridge of Lions. 2 St. Augustine Blvd 32080. Fax: 904/824-0436. **Facility:** 20 one-
▼▼ ▼▼ bedroom standard units. 1 story, exterior corridors. **Bath:** combo or shower only. **Parking:** on-site.
Motel **Terms:** cancellation fee imposed, [CP] meal plan available. **Amenities:** voice mail, hair dryers. **Pool(s):** outdoor. **Business Services:** fax (fee). **Cards:** AX, DS, MC, VI. **Special Amenities:** free local telephone calls and free newspaper. *(See color ad below)*

🏊❌🖧

HAMPTON INN HISTORIC
Phone: (904)829-1996 [10]
AAA SAVE
2/2-9/1 [ECP] — 1P: $65-$175 — 2P: $75-$175 — XP: $10 — F18
12/1-2/1 & 9/2-11/30 [ECP] — 1P: $59-$149 — 2P: $69-$169 — XP: $10 — F18
▼▼▼ ▼▼▼ **Location:** I-95, exit 318, 7 mi e on SR 16, just s on US 1, n of downtown. 2050 N Ponce De Leon Blvd 32084.
Fax: 904/829-1988. **Facility:** 52 one-bedroom standard units, some with whirlpools. 3 stories, interior corri-
Small-scale Hotel dors. **Bath:** combo or shower only. **Parking:** on-site. **Amenities:** voice mail, irons, hair dryers. **Pool(s):** outdoor. **Leisure Activities:** whirlpool. **Business Services:** fax. **Cards:** AX, CB, DC, DS, MC, VI.
Special Amenities: free continental breakfast and free local telephone calls. *(See color ad p 793)*

SOME UNITS

🆓🔧⬛🚳🏊📺🖧🖥 / ❌🖥🖥 /

HAMPTON INN ST. AUGUSTINE OUTLET CENTER
Phone: (904)824-4422 [2]
AAA SAVE
All Year [ECP] — 1P: $69-$99 — 2P: $79-$109
Location: I-95, exit 318, just w on CR 208, then s. 2525 CR 208 32092. Fax: 904/824-4400. **Facility:** 67 one-
▼▼▼ ▼▼▼ bedroom standard units. 4 stories, interior corridors. **Bath:** combo or shower only. **Parking:** on-site.
Terms: [CP] meal plan available. **Amenities:** voice mail, irons. **Pool(s):** outdoor. **Leisure Activities:** whirl-
Small-scale Hotel pool. **Guest Services:** coin laundry. **Business Services:** fax. **Cards:** AX, CB, DC, DS, MC, VI.
Special Amenities: free continental breakfast and free local telephone calls.

SOME UNITS

🆓🍴♿⬛🏊📺🖧🖥 / ❌ /

(See map p. 785)

HOLIDAY INN EXPRESS   Phone: (904)823-8636   **5**
[AAA] [SAVE]   2/1-8/31   1P: $69-$189   2P: $69-$189   XP: $6   F15
               12/1-1/31 & 9/1-11/30   1P: $59-$189   2P: $59-$189   XP: $6   F15
▼▼▼▼▼   **Location:** I-95, exit 318, just e. 2310 SR 16 32095. Fax: 904/823-8728. **Facility:** 50 one-bedroom standard units,
         some with whirlpools. 2 stories, exterior corridors. **Parking:** on-site. **Amenities:** irons, hair dryers. **Pool(s):**
Small-scale Hotel outdoor. **Guest Services:** valet and coin laundry. **Business Services:** meeting rooms, fax (fee). **Cards:** AX,
         CB, DC, DS, JC, MC, VI.
                                                                                    SOME UNITS
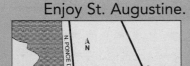

HOLIDAY INN HOTEL & SUITES-HISTORIC   Phone: 904/494-2100   **16**
[AAA] [SAVE]   3/1-8/28   1P: $99-$139
               12/1-2/28 & 8/29-11/30   1P: $89-$129
▼▼▼▼▼   **Location:** 0.7 mi s of jct SR 16. 1302 N Ponce de Leon Blvd 32084. Fax: 904/494-2101. **Facility:** 121 units. 99
         one-bedroom standard units, some with whirlpools. 22 one-bedroom suites. 4 stories, interior corridors. *Bath:*
Small-scale Hotel combo or shower only. **Parking:** on-site. **Terms:** check-in 4 pm, cancellation fee imposed. **Amenities:** voice
mail, irons, hair dryers. **Dining:** 7 am-11 & 5-10 pm, wine/beer only. **Pool(s):** outdoor. **Leisure Activi-**
ties: whirlpool, exercise room. **Guest Services:** valet and coin laundry. **Business Services:** meeting rooms, fax (fee).
Cards: AX, CB, DC, DS, JC, MC, VI. **Special Amenities:** free local telephone calls and free newspaper.
(See color ad p 801)
                                                                                    SOME UNITS

THE INN AT CAMACHEE HARBOR   Phone: (904)825-0003   **23**
▼▼▼ ▼▼▼   All Year [CP]   1P: $79-$149   2P: $79-$149   XP: $15   D12
         Location: On the Intracoastal Waterway at west side of Usine Bridge, 1 mi e of jct N SR A1A and San Marco Blvd. 201
Small-scale Hotel Yacht Club Dr 32084. Fax: 904/825-0048. **Facility:** 19 one-bedroom standard units, some with whirlpools. 2
         stories, interior/exterior corridors. **Parking:** on-site. **Terms:** cancellation fee imposed. **Leisure Activities:**
Fee: sailboats, boat dock, fishing, charter fishing. **Guest Services:** area transportation (fee). **Business Services:** meeting
rooms, fax (fee). **Cards:** AX, MC, VI.
                                                                                    SOME UNITS

(See map p. 785)

LA QUINTA INN

　　(AAA) (SAVE)

(diamond)(diamond)

Small-scale Hotel

Phone: (904)824-3383　**13**

2/7-9/1	1P: $69-$140	2P: $69-$150
9/2-11/30	1P: $59-$79	2P: $69-$89
12/1-2/6	1P: $59-$79	2P: $69-$89　XP: $6　F12

Location: US 1, 1 mi n. 1300 Ponce de Leon Blvd 32084. Fax: 904/829-0668. **Facility:** 102 one-bedroom standard units. 2 stories, exterior corridors. *Bath:* combo or shower only. **Parking:** on-site. **Terms:** cancellation fee imposed, [CP] meal plan available, pets ($25 extra charge, small dogs only). **Amenities:** voice mail, safes (fee), irons, hair dryers. **Dining:** 24 hours, cocktails. **Pool(s):** outdoor. **Leisure Activities:** exercise room. *Fee:* game room. **Guest Services:** valet and coin laundry. **Business Services:** meeting rooms, fax (fee). **Cards:** AX, CB, DC, DS, JC, MC, VI. **Special Amenities: free continental breakfast and free local telephone calls.** *(See color ad p 794)*

SOME UNITS

(S)(D) (icons) DATA PORT (icons) / (X) (icons) /

LION INN

(AAA) (SAVE)

(diamond)(diamond)

Motel

Phone: (904)824-2831　**17**

All Year　　1P: $50-$175　　2P: $50-$175
Location: 1 mi s of Bridge of Lions. 420 Anastasia Blvd 32084. Fax: 904/824-2831. **Facility:** 36 one-bedroom standard units. 1 story, exterior corridors. *Bath:* combo or shower only. **Parking:** on-site. **Pool(s):** outdoor. **Cards:** AX, DS, MC, VI.

SOME UNITS

(S)(D) (icons) / (X) /

MERIDA MOTEL

(AAA) (SAVE)

(diamond)(diamond)

Motel

Phone: (904)825-2398　**9**

All Year　　1P: $39-$89　　2P: $44-$99　XP: $5　D12
Location: Just s of jct US 1 and SR 16. 2150 N Ponce De Leon Blvd 32084. Fax: 904/824-7822. **Facility:** 18 one-bedroom standard units, some with kitchens and/or whirlpools. 2 stories, exterior corridors. **Parking:** on-site. **Amenities:** *Some:* hair dryers. **Pool(s):** outdoor. **Business Services:** fax. **Cards:** AX, DS, MC, VI. **Special Amenities: early check-in/late check-out and preferred room (subject to availability with advanced reservations).**

SOME UNITS

(S)(D) (icons) / (X) (icons) /

(See map p. 785)

MONTEREY INN
Phone: 904/824-4482 26 F

AAA SAVE

All Year   1P: $45-$150   2P: $49-$150   XP: $10

Location: US 1 business route and SR A1A; center. Located in the historic district. 16 Avenida Menendez 32084. Fax: 904/829-8854. **Facility:** Smoke free premises. 59 one-bedroom standard units. 2 stories, exterior corridors. *Bath:* combo or shower only. **Parking:** on-site. **Terms:** 2-3 night minimum stay - weekends, cancellation fee imposed. **Amenities:** voice mail, hair dryers. **Dining:** 7 am-9 pm. **Pool(s):** outdoor. **Business Services:** fax. **Cards:** AX, DC, DS, MC, VI. *(See color ad p 795)*

Small-scale Hotel

SOME UNITS

🍴 🛢 🐟 ✕ 🖥 / 🛢 🖥 /
FEE

OLD CITY HOUSE INN & RESTAURANT
Phone: 904/826-0113 29

All Year   2P: $85-$195   XP: $25

Bed & Breakfast

Location: Center. Located across from the Lightner Museum. 115 Cordova St 32084. Fax: 904/826-3294. **Facility:** In the Spanish historic district, this 19th-century building offers comfortably decorated guest rooms with an old-world feel. Designated smoking area. 7 one-bedroom standard units, some with whirlpools. 2 stories, exterior corridors. *Bath:* combo or shower only. **Parking:** on-site. **Terms:** 2 night minimum stay - weekends, age restrictions may apply, 7 day cancellation notice-fee imposed. **Leisure Activities:** bicycles. **Guest Services:** complimentary evening beverages: Fri & Sat. **Business Services:** fax. **Cards:** AX, DC, DS, MC, VI.

SOME UNITS

🍴 🍸 ✕ / VCR /

PONCE DE LEON HOTEL AND GOLF RESORT
Phone: (904)824-2821 6

AAA SAVE

1/11-5/31	1P: $89-$169	2P: $89-$169	XP: $15 F16
12/1-1/10 & 10/1-11/30	1P: $79-$159	2P: $79-$159	XP: $15 F16
6/1-9/30	1P: $59-$139	2P: $59-$139	XP: $15 F16

Small-scale Hotel

Location: 3 mi n on US 1. 4000 US 1 N 32095. Fax: 904/824-8254. **Facility:** 193 units. 185 one-bedroom standard units. 8 one-bedroom suites ($129-$299). 1-4 stories, interior/exterior corridors. *Bath:* combo or shower only. **Parking:** on-site. **Terms:** 3 day cancellation notice-fee imposed, package plans. **Amenities:** voice mail, irons, hair dryers. **Dining:** 6:30 am-2:30 & 5-9 pm, Fri & Sat-10 pm, cocktails. **Pool(s):** outdoor. **Leisure Activities:** whirlpool, putting green, golf pro shop, 6 tennis courts, jogging. *Fee:* golf-18 holes. **Guest Services:** valet and coin laundry. **Business Services:** conference facilities, fax (fee). **Cards:** AX, CB, DC, DS, JC, MC, VI.

SOME UNITS

🅢 🍴 24 🍸 🛢 🐕 🐟 ✕ 🖥 🖳 / ✕ 🛢 🖥 /

RAMADA LIMITED
Phone: (904)829-5643 3

AAA SAVE

2/12-7/6 [CP]	1P: $49-$169	2P: $49-$169	
7/7-11/30 [CP]	1P: $49-$99	2P: $49-$99	
12/1-2/11 [CP]	1P: $59-$79	2P: $59-$79	

Small-scale Hotel

Location: I-95, exit 318, just w. 2535 SR 16 32092. Fax: 904/829-0804. **Facility:** 140 units. 139 one-bedroom standard units. 1 one-bedroom suite ($79-$189). 2 stories, exterior corridors. **Parking:** on-site. **Terms:** small pets only ($15 extra charge). **Amenities:** voice mail, safes, irons, hair dryers. **Pool(s):** outdoor, wading. **Guest Services:** coin laundry. **Cards:** AX, CB, DC, DS, MC, VI. **Special Amenities:** free continental breakfast and free local telephone calls.

SOME UNITS

🅢 🍴+ 🐟 🎥 🖥 / ✕ VCR 🛢 🖥 /
FEE

(See map p. 785)

ST. FRANCIS INN

▽▽▽▽

Historic Bed
& Breakfast

All Year [BP]   1P: $99-$219   2P: $99-$219

Phone: **(904)824-6068**   🟦32

XP: $15

Location: Just s. Located in the historic district. 279 St George St 32084. Fax: 904/810-5525. **Facility:** This inn dating to the late 1700s features a courtyard with tropical plants. Smoke free premises. 17 units. 13 one-bedroom standard units, some with whirlpools. 4 one-bedroom suites ($149-$219), some with whirlpools. 3 stories (no elevator), interior/exterior corridors. **Bath:** combo or shower only. **Parking:** on-site. **Terms:** age restrictions may apply, 7 day cancellation notice-fee imposed, package plans. **Amenities:** irons, hair dryers. **Pool(s):** small outdoor. **Leisure Activities:** bicycles. **Guest Services:** complimentary evening beverages. **Business Services:** fax. **Cards:** AX, DC, DS, MC, VI.

SOME UNITS

(ASK) (S/D) (🏊) (✕) / (VCR) (DATA PORT) (🛏) (📠) (📺) /

SCOTTISH INNS

(AAA) (SAVE)

▽▽▽ ▽▽▽

Motel

2/1-8/31   1P: $40-$89   2P: $45-$89

12/1-1/31 & 9/1-11/30   1P: $35-$89   2P: $40-$89

Phone: **(904)824-2871**   🟦19

XP: $7   F18

XP: $7   F18

Location: Old Mission and San Marco aves; center. Located across from Mission of Nombre De Dios; on route of train. 110 San Marco Ave 32084. Fax: 904/826-4149. **Facility:** 27 one-bedroom standard units. 1-2 stories, exterior corridors. **Parking:** on-site. **Terms:** small pets only ($5 extra charge). **Pool(s):** outdoor. **Business Services:** fax. **Special Amenities:** free local telephone calls and free newspaper.

SOME UNITS

(S/D) (🛏) (🏊) (📺) / (✕) /

SHERATON'S VISTANA RESORT AT WORLD GOLF VILLAGE

▽▽▽▽

Condominium

12/1-2/28   1P: $165-$249   2P: $165-$249

3/1-4/26   1P: $179-$239   2P: $179-$239

9/30-11/30   1P: $169-$219   2P: $169-$219

4/27-9/29   1P: $129-$179   2P: $129-$179

Phone: **(904)940-2000**   🟦36

Location: I-95, exit 323, just w to WGV Blvd, 1.3 mi n, just s. 100 Front Nine Dr 32092. Fax: 904/940-0741. **Facility:** 134 one-bedroom standard units. 5 stories, exterior corridors. **Bath:** combo or shower only. **Parking:** on-site. **Terms:** check-in 4 pm, 3 day cancellation notice-fee imposed. **Amenities:** voice mail, safes, irons, hair dryers. **Pool(s):** heated outdoor. **Leisure Activities:** whirlpool, 2 lighted tennis courts, recreation programs, playground, exercise room, basketball, volleyball. **Fee:** charter fishing, golf-36 holes, game room. **Guest Services:** complimentary laundry. **Business Services:** fax (fee). **Cards:** AX, DC, MC, VI.
(See color ad p 5)

(ASK) (S/D) (♿) (🏊) (✕) (VCR) (📺) (DATA PORT) (🛏) (📠) (📺)

SLEEP INN

(AAA) (SAVE)

▽▽▽ ▽▽▽

Small-scale Hotel

6/1-9/8   1P: $75-$150   2P: $75-$150

2/7-5/31   1P: $65-$150   2P: $65-$150

9/9-11/30   1P: $48-$95   2P: $48-$95

12/1-2/6   1P: $45-$95   2P: $45-$95

Phone: **(904)825-4535**   🟦21

XP: $7   F16

XP: $7   F16

XP: $7   F16

Location: 1.3 mi s of Bridge of Lions on SR A1A. 601 Anastasia Blvd 32084. Fax: 904/829-8963. **Facility:** 50 one-bedroom standard units. 2 stories, interior corridors. **Bath:** combo or shower only. **Parking:** on-site. **Terms:** check-in 4 pm, [CP] meal plan available. **Amenities:** irons, hair dryers. **Pool(s):** outdoor. **Leisure Activities:** whirlpool. **Business Services:** meeting rooms, fax. **Cards:** AX, DC, DS, MC, VI. **Special Amenities:** free continental breakfast and free local telephone calls. *(See color ad below)*

SOME UNITS

(S/D) (♿) (🏊) (📺) (DATA PORT) / (✕) (🛏) (📠) (📺) /

(See map p. 785)

THRIFTLODGE

Motel

				Phone: (904)824-1341	**14**
	2/1-9/10	1P: $40-$160	2P: $42-$160	XP: $5	F12
	12/1-1/31 & 9/11-11/30	1P: $35-$120	2P: $40-$120	XP: $5	F12

Location: Just s of jct US 1 and SR 16. 2500 N Ponce de Leon Blvd 32084. Fax: 904/823-9850. **Facility:** 31 one-bedroom standard units. 2 stories, exterior corridors. **Parking:** on-site. **Terms:** cancellation fee imposed. **Pool(s):** small outdoor. **Business Services:** fax. **Cards:** AX, CB, DC, DS, JC, MC, VI. **Special Amenities:** early check-in/late check-out and preferred room (subject to availability with advanced reservations).

SOME UNITS

TRAVELODGE & SUITES

Small-scale Hotel

				Phone: (904)829-3850	**12**
	All Year [CP]	1P: $54-$90	2P: $56-$110	XP: $5	

Location: City Center; 2 mi n, just off US 1. 290 San Marco Ave 32084. Fax: 904/829-0313. **Facility:** 30 one-bedroom standard units, some with whirlpools. 2 stories, exterior corridors. **Parking:** on-site. **Amenities:** irons, hair dryers. **Pool(s):** outdoor. **Guest Services:** coin laundry, airport transportation-St. Augustine Airport, area transportation-sightseeing trains. **Business Services:** fax. **Cards:** AX, CB, DC, MC, VI. **Special Amenities:** free continental breakfast and free newspaper.

SOME UNITS

WORLD GOLF VILLAGE RENAISSANCE RESORT

Large-scale Hotel

				Phone: (904)940-8000	**37**
	2/9-5/8	1P: $169-$269	2P: $169-$269	XP: $15	F17
	10/12-11/30	1P: $139-$219	2P: $139-$219	XP: $15	F17
	12/1-2/8 & 5/9-10/11	1P: $119-$189	2P: $119-$189	XP: $15	F17

Location: I-95, exit 323, just w, then 2 mi follow signs. 500 S Legacy Tr 32092. Fax: 904/940-8008. **Facility:** 301 units. 269 one-bedroom standard units. 32 one-bedroom suites, some with whirlpools. 9 stories, interior corridors. **Bath:** combo or shower only. **Parking:** valet. **Terms:** check-in 4 pm, 3 day cancellation notice, $10 service charge. **Amenities:** video games, high-speed Internet, dual phone lines, voice mail, irons, hair dryers. **Dining:** 6 am-midnight. **Pool(s):** heated outdoor. **Leisure Activities:** sauna, whirlpool, beach club, 2 lighted tennis courts, billiards, playground, exercise room, basketball, volleyball. *Fee:* golf-36 holes, golf simulator, bicycles, massage, game room. **Guest Services:** gift shop, valet and coin laundry, area transportation-within 20 mi. **Business Services:** conference facilities, business center. **Cards:** AX, DC, DS, JC, MC, VI. **Special Amenities:** free newspaper. *(See color ad below)*

SOME UNITS

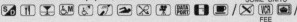

FEE

(See map p. 785)

──────── **WHERE TO DINE** ────────

95 CORDOVA   Historic   **Lunch:** $5-$12   **Dinner:** $14-$25   **Phone:** 904/827-1887   ⑲
▼▼▼▼
American
Location: Downtown; across from Lightner Museum and Flagler College; in Casa Monica Hotel. 95 Cordova St 32084. **Hours:** 6:45-10 am, 11-2:30 & 5-10 pm. **Reservations:** suggested. **Features:** Enjoy a special experience in the newly renovated Casa Monica Hotel, which dates to 1888. An intriguing wine list with many selections by the glass accompanies an enticing menu of steak, seafood and chicken entrees. Salmon is popular, as is the tangy Key lime pie. Dressy casual; cocktails. **Parking:** valet. **Cards:** AX, DC, DS, JC, MC, VI.

A1A ALE WORKS BREWERY AND RESTAURANT   **Lunch:** $6-$9   **Dinner:** $10-$19   **Phone:** 904/829-2977   ⑳
▼▼▼ ▼▼▼
Caribbean
Location: Corner of Avenida Menendez; downtown. 1 King St 32084. **Hours:** 11 am-10:30 pm, Fri & Sat-11:30 pm. Closed: 11/27, 12/25; also 12/24 for dinner. **Features:** The second-floor restaurant overlooks the bay and the Bridge of Lions. Examples of New World cuisine include seafood paella and island cavatappi pasta. The brews are renowned. For a quick bite, migrate to the lengthy list of appetizers, which includes calamari, boniachos or "hommus.". Casual dress; cocktails. **Parking:** street. **Cards:** AX, DC, DS, MC, VI.   ✕

AZALEA'S CAFE   **Lunch:** $4-$10   **Phone:** 904/824-6465   ⑮
▼▼▼
Continental
Location: Historic district, s of King St. 4 Aviles St 32084. **Hours:** 10 am-4 pm, Sat & Sun from 9 am. Closed: 12/25. **Features:** Watch the horses trot by and enjoy a cozy, friendly cafe with indoor and outdoor seating. The owner/chef has drawn up a health-conscious menu with a host of vegetable selections. Breakfast is served all day, and the desserts are made right in the kitchen. Casual dress; beer & wine only. **Parking:** street. **Cards:** MC, VI.   ✕

BARNACLE BILL'S SEAFOOD HOUSE   **Lunch:** $6-$8   **Dinner:** $9-$16   **Phone:** 904/824-3663   ⑥
▼▼▼
Seafood
Location: Across from visitor's information center. 14 Castillo Dr 32084. **Hours:** 11 am-9 pm. Closed: 11/27, 12/25. **Features:** A St. Augustine tradition since 1981. Lines can be long at this popular laid back restaurant. Enjoy Minorcan clam chowder, Florida gator tail, catfish and grits, or the ever popular shrimp dinner. A good selection of steak and chicken is available for the landlubber. Casual dress; cocktails. **Parking:** on-site. **Cards:** AX, CB, DC, DS, MC, VI.   ✕

CAFE ALCAZAR   Historic   **Lunch:** $7-$10   **Phone:** 904/824-7813   ⑪
▼▼▼ ▼▼▼
Continental
Location: In Lightner Museum Complex. 25 Granada St 32084. **Hours:** 11:30 am-3 pm. Closed: 1/1, 11/27, 12/25; also Sun & Mon. **Features:** In the deep end of what was once a huge swimming pool, the elegant cafe exudes a quaint ambience that makes it an ideal place to take your mom. Creativity characterizes the entrees. Top one off with warm oatmeal cookies coated with ice cream. Smoke free premises. Casual dress; beer & wine only. **Parking:** street. **Cards:** MC, VI.   ✕

COLUMBIA RESTAURANT   **Lunch:** $7-$15   **Dinner:** $12-$30   **Phone:** 904/824-3341   ⑦
▼▼▼ ▼▼▼
Ethnic
Location: St. George St at Hypolita St; center. 98 St George St 32084. **Hours:** 11 am-4 & 4:30-10 pm, Fri & Sat-10 pm, Sun 11 am-3 & 3:30-9 pm. **Reservations:** suggested; for dinner. **Features:** Hearty portions of Cuban and Spanish specialties can be found in this bustling tourist destination in the historical district of St. Augustine. An informal atmosphere includes a violin trio to set the mood, and the outdoor lounge is a popular gathering spot. Parking is limited. cocktails. **Parking:** on-site. **Cards:** AX, CB, DC, DS, MC, VI.   ⍉ ✕

THE CONCH HOUSE RESTAURANT AND LOUNGE   **Lunch:** $5-$11   **Dinner:** $13-$23   **Phone:** 904/829-8646   ⑰
▼▼▼ ▼▼▼
Seafood
Location: 1 mi s of Bridge of Lions on SR A1A, then 0.3 mi n; in Conch House Marina Resort. 57 Comares Ave 32080. **Hours:** 8 am-9 pm, Fri & Sat-10 pm. Closed: 12/25. **Features:** Palm-thatched dining huts give diners unusual vantage points from which to gaze out over the Intracoastal Waterway. A Caribbean influence is evident in many dishes, which are presented with colorful garnishes. The tangy Key lime pie is homemade. Casual dress; cocktails. **Parking:** on-site. **Cards:** AX, MC, VI.   ⍉ ✕

CORTESSE'S BISTRO & FLAMINGO ROOM   Historic   **Lunch:** $5-$10   **Dinner:** $11-$20   **Phone:** 904/825-6775   ⑬
▼▼▼ ▼▼▼
Continental
Location: Corner of San Marco and San Carlos; in historic district. 172 San Marco 32084. **Hours:** 11 am-9:30 pm, Fri & Sat-10 pm. Closed: 12/25. **Reservations:** suggested; weekends. **Features:** Such culinary treats as sauteed veal with crabmeat are dished up in the late-19th-century house. The Flamingo Room, a martini bar features local musicians, jazz and '40s contemporary music. Works by local artists enliven the walls of the restaurant. Smoking is permitted in the Flamingo Room. Smoke free premises. Casual dress; cocktails. **Parking:** on-site. **Cards:** AX, DS, MC, VI.   ✕

CREEKSIDE DINERY   **Dinner:** $6-$16   **Phone:** 904/829-6113   ⑯
ⓐⓐⓐ
▼▼▼
Seafood
Location: Just e of US 1, just n of jct SR 312. 160 Nix Boatyard Rd 32084. **Hours:** 5 pm-10 pm, 11/1-2/28 to 9 pm, Fri & Sat-10 pm. Closed: 11/27, 12/25. **Features:** Settle into a rocking chair and relax in this quaint, Southern-style atmosphere complete with a jasmine-entwined, columned porch under sheltering oaks and magnolias. Well-chosen spices enliven entrees served with sweet potato compote and Indian corn. Casual dress; cocktails. **Parking:** on-site. **Cards:** AX, DC, DS, MC, VI.   ✕

DENOEL FRENCH PASTRY SHOP   **Lunch:** $5-$7   **Phone:** 904/829-3974   ⑭
▼▼▼
French
Location: In historic district; just s of the plaza. 212 Charlotte St 32084. **Hours:** 10 am-5 pm. Closed major holidays; also Mon & Tues. **Features:** A local favorite since 1966, this nifty, out-of-the-way place features a bakery that's the real reason to visit. Scrumptious croissants and wonderful pastries are all baked right on the premises. Sandwiches, soups, and salads are also a lunch-time treat. Casual dress. **Parking:** street.

GYPSY CAB CO   **Lunch:** $6-$10   **Dinner:** $11-$17   **Phone:** 904/824-8244   ⑩
ⓐⓐⓐ
▼▼▼ ▼▼▼
Ethnic
Location: SR A1A, 1 mi s of the Bridge of Lions. 828 Anastasia Blvd 32084. **Hours:** 11 am-4 & 4:30-10 pm, Fri-11 pm, Sat 11 am-11 pm, Sun 10:30 am-10 pm. Closed: 7/4, 12/25. **Features:** A casual atmosphere with an eclectic decor. The "surprise" menu changes daily, reflecting cuisine from around the world served up in hearty portions. Mainstays include black bean soup and Key lime and peanut butter pies. Come early for specials. Casual dress; cocktails. **Parking:** on-site. **Cards:** AX, DC, DS, MC, VI.   ✕

(See map p. 785)

KING'S HEAD BRITISH PUB　　　　　**Lunch:** $4-$12　　　**Dinner:** $4-$12　　　**Phone:** 904/823-9787　　①
　　Location: 6 mi n. 6460 Hwy 1 N 32084. **Hours:** 11:30 am-1 am. Closed: 11/27, 12/25; also Mon.
English
　　Features: Owned and operated by an English chef, the authentic British pub delivers a wide selection of beers and hearty food. Enjoy Scotch egg, bangers and mash, Cornish pastry or fish and chips. British keepsakes line the walls of the friendly restaurant. Casual dress; cocktails. **Parking:** on-site. **Cards:** AX, DC, DS, MC, VI.

LE PAVILLON　　　　　**Lunch:** $5-$10　　　**Dinner:** $14-$22　　　**Phone:** 904/824-6202　　⑨
Continental
　　Location: 0.8 mi n on SR A1A, just n of Mulberry St. 45 San Marco Ave 32084. **Hours:** 11:30 am-2:30 & 5-10 pm. **Reservations:** suggested; weekends. **Features:** Antiques and fresh flowers set the stage for quiet, intimate dining in an old-style house. A varied menu offers selections ranging from light dining, more robust entrees like the marinated rack of lamb. Tiramisu is a house specialty. Smoke free premises. Dressy casual; cocktails. **Parking:** on-site. **Cards:** CB, DC, DS, MC, VI.
Ⓧ

MARTY'S SEAFOOD & STEAK HOUSE　　**Lunch:** $4-$10　　**Dinner:** $6-$15　　**Phone:** 904/829-8679　　③
American
　　Location: Southwest corner US 1 N and SR 16. 2703 Ponce De Leon Blvd 32085. **Hours:** 4 pm-9 pm, Fri-Sun from 11:30 am. Closed: 12/25; also 12/7-12/13. **Features:** A different fresh-baked bread is offered each day, and seafood selections like the half lobster stuffed with crab meat are enjoyed in a nautical antique decor. If you can save room, indulge in the Key lime pie. A well-trained staff keeps the pace smooth. Casual dress; cocktails. **Parking:** on-site. **Cards:** MC, VI.
Ⓧ

RAINTREE RESTAURANT　　　　　**Dinner:** $15-$29　　　**Phone:** 904/824-7211　　⑤
Continental
　　Location: 1 mi n of Bridge of Lions. 102 San Marco Ave 32084. **Hours:** 5 pm-9:30 pm, Sat-10 pm; from 6 pm in summer. Closed: 12/25. **Reservations:** suggested. **Features:** A rambling Victorian home with brick courtyards, an aviary and antiques provides the setting for outstanding, creative selections like the lamb chop in a potato basket accompanied by mini zucchini and yellow squash. Be sure to save room for dessert. Casual dress; cocktails. **Parking:** on-site. **Cards:** AX, MC, VI.
Ⓨ Ⓧ

TAVERN ON THE BAY　　　　　**Lunch:** $5-$17　　　**Dinner:** $8-$17　　　**Phone:** 904/810-1919　　⑧
American

Cards: MC, VI.
　　Location: On bayfront; in historic downtown area. 20 Avenida Menendez 32221. **Hours:** 11:30 am-9 pm, Sat-10 pm. **Features:** Diners can engage in people- or whale-watching at this bayfront establishment. Such menu offerings as gourmet burgers and seafood all are labeled with creative names from jolly old England. The house is famous for its many appetizers, particularly spicy chicken wings. Casual dress. **Parking:** street.
Ⓧ

THEOS' RESTAURANT　　　　　**Lunch:** $4-$7　　　　**Phone:** 904/824-5022　　⑫
American
　　Location: From jct US 1 and King St, just e. 169 King St 32084. **Hours:** 6:30 am-3 pm, Sat 6:30 am-2 pm. Closed: 11/27, 12/24, 12/25; also Sun. **Features:** A small, attractive spot that is popular with locals, the decor reflects St. Augustine's rich history, with vintage photos and paintings by local artists. Generous portions of pastitso (Greek lasagna) and homemade bread are highlights of a varied menu. Smoke free premises. Casual dress; beer & wine only. **Parking:** on-site. **Cards:** AX, DS, MC, VI.
Ⓧ

WHITE LION RESTAURANT　　　　**Lunch:** $4-$8　　　**Dinner:** $6-$18　　　**Phone:** 904/829-2388　　⑱
American
　　Location: Historic district across street from fort; center. 20 Cuna St 32084. **Hours:** 11 am-9 pm, Sat 11:30 am-10 pm, Sun 11 am-10 pm. Closed: 11/27, 12/25. **Features:** Located in the historic district, White Lion offers indoor and outdoor dining in the tradition of old English taverns. The menu spotlights grilled, blackened and fried seafood, and desserts like Key Lime pie. Florida folk music is featured on weekends. Casual dress; cocktails. **Parking:** street. **Cards:** MC, VI.
Ⓧ

ST. AUGUSTINE BEACH pop. 4,683　(See map p. 785; index p. 787)

─── **WHERE TO STAY** ───

BEST WESTERN OCEAN INN　　　　　　　　　**Phone:** (904)471-8010　　53
Small-scale Hotel

2/7-9/7	1P: $69-$159	2P: $69-$159	XP: $6	F17
12/1-2/6 & 9/8-11/30	1P: $59-$109	2P: $59-$109	XP: $6	F17

　　Location: 2 mi s of jct SR 312. 3955 A1A S 32080. Fax: 904/460-9124. **Facility:** 34 units. 33 one-bedroom standard units. 1 one-bedroom suite with whirlpool. 2 stories, exterior corridors. **Parking:** on-site. **Amenities:** irons, hair dryers. **Pool(s):** heated outdoor. **Guest Services:** coin laundry. **Business Services:** fax (fee). **Special Amenities:** early check-in/late check-out and free continental breakfast.
SOME UNITS

COMFORT INN AT ST. AUGUSTINE BEACH　　　　　　**Phone:** (904)471-1414　　52
Small-scale Hotel

12/1-1/23 & 9/6-11/30	1P: $42-$69	2P: $47-$79	XP: $5	F14
1/24-9/5	1P: $52-$129		XP: $5	F14

　　Location: 1.6 mi s of jct SR 312 and A1A, on Business Rt A1A. 901 A1A Beach Blvd 32080. Fax: 904/461-9659. **Facility:** 70 one-bedroom standard units, some with whirlpools. 3 stories, exterior corridors. **Parking:** on-site. **Terms:** [ECP] meal plan available. **Amenities:** voice mail. Some: irons, hair dryers. **Pool(s):** heated outdoor. **Leisure Activities:** whirlpool. **Guest Services:** coin laundry. **Business Services:** fax (fee). **Cards:** AX, CB, DC, DS, MC, VI. **Special Amenities:** free continental breakfast and free local telephone calls.
SOME UNITS

(See map p. 785)

COQUINA GABLES OCEANFRONT B&B   **Phone:** (904)461-8727   **55**
~~~~~~   All Year [BP]   1P: $139-$219   2P: $139-$219   XP: $30
Bed & Breakfast   **Location:** From jct CR 312 and SR A1A, 1 mi e. 1 F St 32080. **Facility:** Enjoy breakfast upstairs with a breath-taking ocean view. The gathering area has elegant wood accents and a safari style decor. Some rooms are not located in the main house, but have a warm, "cottage" feel to them. Smoke free premises. 6 one-bedroom standard units. 2 stories, interior/exterior corridors. *Bath:* combo or shower only. **Parking:** on-site. **Terms:** 2 night minimum stay - weekends, age restrictions may apply, 7 day cancellation notice. **Pool(s):** outdoor. **Leisure Activities:** whirlpool, bicycles. **Business Services:** fax. **Cards:** AX, MC, VI.

SOME UNITS

(ASK) (SD) 🏊 ⊠ ☎ / 🏧 🍴 🖥 /

(See map p. 785)

DAYS INN-ST. AUGUSTINE BEACH

Phone: (904)461-9990 **47**

2/1-3/31 [ECP]	1P: $69-$150	2P: $69-$150	XP: $10	F18
4/1-9/3 [ECP]	1P: $59-$150	2P: $59-$150	XP: $10	F18
9/4-11/30 [ECP]	1P: $49-$130	2P: $49-$130	XP: $10	F18
12/1-1/31 [ECP]	1P: $49-$99	2P: $49-$99	XP: $10	F18

Small-scale Hotel **Location:** 1.3 mi s of SR 312 and A1A, on Business Rt A1A. 541 A1A Beach Blvd 32084. Fax: 904/471-4774. **Facility:** 50 units. 48 one-bedroom standard units. 2 one-bedroom suites ($99-$200) with whirlpools. 2 stories, exterior corridors. **Parking:** on-site. **Amenities:** hair dryers. **Pool(s):** outdoor. **Leisure Activities:** whirlpool. *Fee:* exercise room. **Guest Services:** coin laundry. **Business Services:** fax. **Cards:** AX, CB, DC, DS, MC, VI. **Special Amenities:** free continental breakfast and free local telephone calls. *(See color ad p 793)*

SOME UNITS

HAMPTON INN-ST. AUGUSTINE BEACH

Phone: (904)471-4000 **54**

All Year [ECP]   1P: $69-$239   2P: $79-$249

Small-scale Hotel **Location:** 1.3 mi s of jct SR 312 and A1A on Business Rt A1A. 430 A1A Beach Blvd 32080. Fax: 904/471-4888. **Facility:** 100 one-bedroom standard units, some with whirlpools. 4 stories, interior corridors. *Bath:* combo or shower only. **Parking:** on-site. **Terms:** 3 day cancellation notice. **Amenities:** video games, dual phone lines, voice mail, irons, hair dryers. **Pool(s):** outdoor. **Leisure Activities:** whirlpool, exercise room, volleyball. **Guest Services:** coin laundry. **Business Services:** meeting rooms, business center. **Cards:** AX, CB, DC, DS, JC, MC, VI.

SOME UNITS

HILTON GARDEN INN-ST. AUGUSTINE BEACH

Phone: (904)471-5559 **48**

1/31-8/31	1P: $89-$139
9/1-11/30	1P: $79-$119
12/1-11/30	1P: $79-$109

Small-scale Hotel **Location:** Jct CR 312 and SR A1A, 1.2 mi e. 401 A1A Beach Blvd 32084. Fax: 904/471-7146. **Facility:** 83 units. 81 one-bedroom standard units, some with whirlpools. 2 one-bedroom suites ($104-$199) with whirlpools. 3 stories, interior corridors. *Bath:* combo or shower only. **Parking:** on-site. **Terms:** [BP] & [ECP] meal plans available. **Amenities:** video games, high-speed Internet, dual phone lines, voice mail, irons, hair dryers. **Pool(s):** outdoor. **Leisure Activities:** exercise room. **Guest Services:** sundries, coin laundry. **Business Services:** meeting rooms, business center. **Cards:** AX, DC, DS, MC, VI.

SOME UNITS

HOLIDAY INN-ST AUGUSTINE BEACH

Phone: (904)471-2555 **50**

4/1-8/31	1P: $110-$130	2P: $110-$130
2/13-3/31	1P: $99-$119	2P: $99-$119
12/1-2/12 & 9/1-11/30	1P: $89-$109	2P: $89-$109

Small-scale Hotel **Location:** 1.8 mi s of jct SR 312 and A1A, on Business Rt A1A. 860 A1A Beach Blvd 32080. Fax: 904/461-8450. **Facility:** 151 one-bedroom standard units. 5 stories, interior/exterior corridors. *Bath:* combo or shower only. **Parking:** on-site. **Terms:** [BP] meal plan available, small pets only ($10 extra charge). **Amenities:** voice mail, irons, hair dryers. **Dining:** 7 am-11:30 & 5-10 pm, Sun 7 am-noon & 5-10 pm, cocktails. **Pool(s):** outdoor. **Leisure Activities:** exercise room. **Guest Services:** valet and coin laundry. **Business Services:** meeting rooms, fax. **Cards:** AX, CB, DS, MC, VI. **Special Amenities:** free newspaper. *(See color ad opposite inside back cover)*

SOME UNITS
FEE

LA FIESTA OCEAN INN & SUITES

Phone: (904)471-2220 **49**

2/9-9/7 [CP]	1P: $85-$259	2P: $85-$259	XP: $10	F12
12/1-2/8 & 9/8-11/30 [CP]	1P: $65-$299	2P: $65-$299	XP: $10	F12

Motel **Location:** 1.7 mi s of jct SR 312 and A1A, on Business Rt A1A. 810 A1A Beach Blvd 32080. Fax: 904/471-0186. **Facility:** 44 units. 38 one-bedroom standard units. 6 one-bedroom suites ($179-$259), some with whirlpools. 2 stories, exterior corridors. *Bath:* combo or shower only. **Parking:** on-site. **Terms:** 7 day cancellation notice. **Amenities:** *Some:* hair dryers. **Pool(s):** outdoor. **Leisure Activities:** Fee: miniature golf. **Guest Services:** coin laundry. **Business Services:** fax (fee). **Cards:** AX, CB, DC, DS, MC, VI. **Special Amenities:** free continental breakfast. *(See color ad p 801 & p 794)*

SOME UNITS

RAMADA LIMITED, AT THE BEACH

Phone: (904)471-1440 **51**

All Year [ECP]   1P: $59-$210   XP: $5   F17

Small-scale Hotel **Location:** 2 mi s of jct SR 312 and A1A, on Business Rt A1A. 894 A1A Beach Blvd 32084. Fax: 904/471-2922. **Facility:** 38 one-bedroom standard units, some with whirlpools. 3 stories, interior corridors. *Bath:* combo or shower only. **Parking:** on-site. **Amenities:** voice mail, irons, hair dryers. **Pool(s):** outdoor. **Guest Services:** coin laundry. **Business Services:** fax. **Cards:** AX, CB, DC, DS, MC, VI.

SOME UNITS

SUPER 8

Phone: (904)471-2330 **46**

2/12-8/31 [CP]	1P: $59-$109	2P: $69-$119	XP: $10	F18
12/1-2/11 & 9/1-11/30 [CP]	1P: $49-$79	2P: $59-$89	XP: $10	F18

Small-scale Hotel **Location:** 1 mi s of jct SR 312 and A1A, on Business Rt A1A. 311 A1A Beach Blvd 32080. Fax: 904/471-1018. **Facility:** 50 one-bedroom standard units. 2 stories, exterior corridors. **Parking:** on-site. **Terms:** [BP] meal plan available. **Pool(s):** outdoor. **Leisure Activities:** whirlpool. **Guest Services:** coin laundry. **Business Services:** fax (fee). **Cards:** AX, CB, DC, DS, JC, MC, VI. **Special Amenities:** free continental breakfast and free local telephone calls.

SOME UNITS

(See map p. 785)

———— **WHERE TO DINE** ————

ARUANNO'S ITALIAN RESTAURANT   **Dinner:** $10-$18   **Phone:** 904/471-9373   ㉚

Italian
Location: S of jct of SR 312 and A1A, on Business Rt A1A. 105 D St 32084. **Hours:** 5 pm-10 pm. Closed major holidays; also Sun. **Reservations:** suggested. **Features:** A family operation that aims to please, this restaurant lets you enjoy all the Italian classics, as well as steak, rack of lamb and nightly pasta specials. Don't leave without trying a homemade dessert. Casual dress; beer & wine only. **Parking:** on-site.
Cards: AX, DC, MC, VI.

GREENSTREET'S   **Lunch:** $3-$10   **Phone:** 904/471-5573   ㉜
American
Location: 1.4 mi n of SR 206. 5545 A1A S 32080. **Hours:** 7:30 am-3:30 pm. Closed: 12/25. **Features:** Join the local crowd as they flock here for hearty breakfasts and linger in the friendly atmosphere over lunch. A large selection of omelets and pancakes grace the menu. Enjoy the famous homemade pies for dessert. **Parking:** on-site.

SALTWATER COWBOYS   **Dinner:** $9-$18   **Phone:** 386/471-2332   ㉞
Regional American
Location: At the western end of Dondanville Rd; off SR A1A, 0.8 mi s of southern jct SR 3. 299 Dondanville Rd 32080. **Hours:** 5 pm-9 pm; to 10 pm 3/1-9/30. Closed major holidays. **Features:** Travel down a dirt road to a saltwater marsh to find this quaint, waterfront restaurant. A casual atmosphere recaptures the charm of Old Florida, with a menu offering seafood, rib and chicken dishes. Casual dress; cocktails. **Parking:** on-site. **Cards:** AX, DS, MC, VI.

THE WORLD FAMOUS OASIS RESTAURANT & DECK   **Lunch:** $4-$14 **Dinner:** $4-$14 **Phone:** 904/471-3424 ㉝
Seafood
Location: 0.3 mi s of jct SR A1A at Ocean Trace Rd. 4000 A1A S 32095. **Hours:** 6:30 am-midnight. Closed: 11/27, 12/25; also 11/30-12/16. **Features:** Bustling, friendly neighborhood spot. Join the locals for a breakfast of omelettes or a salad for lunch. Daily dinner specials feature steak, chicken or fish. The open air deck is a great place to unwind after a day on the beach. Casual dress; cocktails; entertainment. **Parking:** on-site. **Cards:** AX, DC, DS, MC, VI.

ST. CLOUD —See Orlando p. 747.

ST. MARKS pop. 272

———— **WHERE TO STAY** ————

SWEET MAGNOLIA INN   **Phone:** 850/925-7670
All Year [BP]   1P: $105-$125   2P: $105-$125   XP: $20
Bed & Breakfast
Location: Center on CR 363. 803 Port Leon Dr 32355 (PO Box 335). Fax: 850/925-0569. **Facility:** This bed and breakfast built in 1916, is nicely decorated with themed rooms with names like Sake, Safari and Magnolia. Most rooms have queen-sized poster beds. Designated smoking area. 7 one-bedroom standard units, some with whirlpools. 2 stories, interior corridors. *Bath:* combo or shower only. **Parking:** on-site. **Terms:** age restrictions may apply, 7 day cancellation notice-fee imposed. **Leisure Activities:** boat dock, bicycles. **Guest Services:** complimentary laundry, area transportation. **Cards:** AX, DS, MC, VI.

SOME UNITS
(ASK) 🅖 ☒ 🐾 🕿 / (VCR) /

ST. PETERSBURG —See Tampa Bay p. 863.

ST. PETE BEACH —See Tampa Bay p. 931.

SANFORD —See Orlando p. 747.

SANIBEL pop. 6,064

———— **WHERE TO STAY** ————

BEST WESTERN SANIBEL ISLAND BEACH RESORT   **Phone:** (239)472-1700

	1P	2P	XP	
2/7-4/26 [CP]	1P: $249-$439	2P: $249-$439	XP: $20	F16
12/1-2/6 [CP]	1P: $139-$439	2P: $139-$439	XP: $20	F16
4/27-5/26 [CP]	1P: $175-$295	2P: $175-$295	XP: $20	F16
5/27-11/30 [CP]	1P: $139-$289	2P: $139-$289	XP: $20	F16

Motel
Location: From causeway, 2.8 mi w on Periwinkle Way, 0.8 mi s on Tarpon Bay Rd, 1.3 mi w. 3287 W Gulf Dr 33957. Fax: 239/482-2470. **Facility:** 45 units. 42 one-bedroom standard units, some with efficiencies. 3 two-bedroom suites with kitchens. 2 stories, exterior corridors. **Parking:** on-site. **Terms:** check-in 4 pm, 14 day cancellation notice-fee imposed. **Amenities:** safes, irons, hair dryers. **Pool(s):** heated outdoor. **Leisure Activities:** fishing, tennis court, badminton, barbecue grills, croquet, picnic area, bicycles, shuffleboard. **Guest Services:** coin laundry. **Business Services:** fax (fee). **Cards:** AX, CB, DC, DS, MC, VI. **Special Amenities:** free continental breakfast and free local telephone calls.
(See color ad p 809)

SOME UNITS
🆂🅓 🎧 ⊇ ☒ 🐾 DATA PORT 🗄 🖨 🖥 / ☒ /

BRENNEN'S TARPON TALE INN

Phone: 239/472-0939

AAA **SAVE**

Motel

12/1-5/1 [CP]	2P: $129-$209	XP: $30
5/2-11/30 [CP]	2P: $79-$150	XP: $30

Location: From causeway, 0.9 mi e at jct East Gulf Dr. 367 Periwinkle Way 33957. Fax: 239/472-6202. **Facility:** Smoke free premises. 5 units. 3 one-bedroom standard units with efficiencies. 2 two-bedroom suites with kitchens. 1 story, exterior corridors. *Bath:* shower only. **Parking:** on-site. **Terms:** 45 day cancellation notice-fee imposed, weekly rates available. **Amenities:** video library. *Some:* irons, hair dryers. **Leisure Activities:** whirlpool, grill, beach chairs, small library, bicycles. **Guest Services:** coin laundry. **Business Services:** fax. **Cards:** DS, MC, VI. **Special Amenities:** early check-in/late check-out and free continental breakfast.

BUTTONWOOD COTTAGES

Phone: 239/395-9061

Motel

12/1-1/2 & 2/1-4/30	1P: $155-$230	2P: $155-$265
1/3-1/31	1P: $125-$175	2P: $125-$210
5/1-11/30	1P: $85-$150	2P: $85-$180

Location: From causeway, 1 mi e on Periwinkle Way, just n. 1234 Buttonwood Ln 33957. Fax: 239/395-2620. **Facility:** Designated smoking area. 5 cottages. 1 story, exterior corridors. *Bath:* combo or shower only. **Parking:** on-site. **Terms:** 45 day cancellation notice-fee imposed. **Amenities:** CD players, hair dryers. *Some:* irons. **Leisure Activities:** whirlpools, fishing, bicycles. **Guest Services:** complimentary laundry. **Business Services:** fax. **Cards:** AX, DS, MC, VI.

CASA YBEL RESORT

Phone: (239)472-3145

Condominium

2/7-5/31 Wkly	1P: $255-$495
12/1-2/6 Wkly	1P: $250-$375
10/25-11/30 Wkly	1P: $250-$325
6/1-10/24 Wkly	1P: $220-$275

Location: From causeway, 1.3 mi w on Periwinkle Way, 1.3 mi s on Casa Ybel. 2255 W Gulf Dr 33957. Fax: 239/472-2109. **Facility:** 114 units. 40 one- and 74 two-bedroom suites with kitchens, some with whirlpools. 2-3 stories (no elevator), exterior corridors. **Parking:** on-site. **Terms:** 2-4 night minimum stay - seasonal, 60 day cancellation notice. **Amenities:** video library (fee), voice mail, safes, irons. *Some:* hair dryers. **Pool(s):** heated outdoor, wading. **Leisure Activities:** whirlpool, rental boats, rental sailboats, 6 tennis courts, recreation programs, playground, basketball, horseshoes, shuffleboard. *Fee:* windsurfing, bicycles, massage. **Guest Services:** coin laundry. **Business Services:** meeting rooms, fax (fee). **Cards:** AX, DC, DS, MC, VI.

SOME UNITS

COLONY RESORT

Phone: (239)472-5151

AAA **SAVE**

Condominium

2/1-4/30	2P: $160-$210	XP: $15	F12
12/16-1/31	2P: $140-$175	XP: $15	F12
12/1-12/15 & 5/1-11/30	2P: $95-$145	XP: $15	F12

Location: From causeway, 1 mi e. 419 E Gulf Dr 33957. Fax: 239/472-3541. **Facility:** 44 one-bedroom suites with kitchens. 1-2 stories, exterior corridors. *Bath:* combo or shower only. **Parking:** on-site. **Terms:** 2 night minimum stay - weekends, 30 day cancellation notice, package plans. **Amenities:** *Some:* CD players. **Pool(s):** heated outdoor. **Leisure Activities:** picnic tables & grills. **Guest Services:** coin laundry. **Cards:** DS, MC, VI. **Special Amenities:** free newspaper and preferred room (subject to availability with advanced reservations).

SOME UNITS

HOLIDAY INN SANIBEL ISLAND

Phone: (239)472-4123

AAA **SAVE**

Small-scale Hotel

2/9-4/26	1P: $249-$299	2P: $249-$299
12/22-2/8	1P: $189-$229	2P: $189-$229
4/27-11/30	1P: $169-$219	2P: $169-$219
12/1-12/21	1P: $149-$199	2P: $149-$199

Location: From causeway, 0.7 mi w on Periwinkle Way, 0.5 mi s on Donax St. 1231 Middle Gulf Dr 33957. Fax: 239/472-0930. **Facility:** 98 units. 97 one-bedroom standard units, some with efficiencies. 1 one-bedroom suite with kitchen. 2 stories, exterior corridors. *Bath:* combo or shower only. **Parking:** on-site. **Terms:** [BP] meal plan available. **Amenities:** video games (fee), safes, irons, hair dryers. **Dining:** 7 am-11 & 5-10 pm, cocktails. **Pool(s):** heated outdoor. **Leisure Activities:** beach cabanas & chairs, 2 tennis courts, ping pong. *Fee:* bicycles. **Guest Services:** gift shop, valet and coin laundry. **Business Services:** meeting rooms, fax. **Cards:** AX, CB, DC, DS, MC, VI. **Special Amenities:** free local telephone calls. *(See color ad opposite inside back cover)*

SOME UNITS

HURRICANE HOUSE

Phone: (239)472-1696

Condominium

1/31-11/30 Wkly	1P: $1470-$2485
12/20-1/2 Wkly	1P: $2324
1/3-1/30 Wkly	1P: $1610
12/1-12/19 Wkly	1P: $1470

Location: From causeway, 2.8 mi w on Periwinkle Way, 0.8 mi s on Tarpon Bay Rd, 0.7 mi w. 2939 W Gulf Dr 33957. Fax: 239/472-1718. **Facility:** 15 two-bedroom suites with kitchens and whirlpools. 3 stories, exterior corridors. **Parking:** on-site. **Terms:** 3-7 night minimum stay - seasonal, 30 day cancellation notice-fee imposed, daily rates available. **Amenities:** video library (fee), irons. **Pool(s):** heated outdoor. **Leisure Activities:** whirlpools, tennis court. **Guest Services:** complimentary laundry. **Business Services:** fax (fee). **Cards:** AX, DC, DS, MC, VI. *(See color ad p 805)*

ISLAND INN

Phone: (239)472-1561

AAA **SAVE**

Historic Motel

12/1-4/23 [MAP]	1P: $135-$440	2P: $175-$440	XP: $55	D10
11/15-11/30 [MAP]	1P: $140-$370	2P: $185-$370	XP: $55	D10
4/24-11/14	1P: $95-$215	2P: $110-$210	XP: $12	D10

Location: From causeway, 2.8 mi w on Periwinkle Way, 0.8 mi s on Tarpon Bay Rd, then 1 mi w. 3111 W Gulf Dr 33957 (PO Box 659). Fax: 239/472-0051. **Facility:** 57 units. 52 one-bedroom standard units, some with efficiencies. 5 cottages. 1-2 stories, interior/exterior corridors. *Bath:* combo or shower only. **Parking:** on-site. **Terms:** 2 night minimum stay - weekends, 7 night in cottages, 14 day cancellation notice, 30 days 11/15-4/23-fee imposed. **Amenities:** voice mail. *Some:* safes, irons, hair dryers. **Dining:** 7:30 am-10 & 6-9 pm 11/15-4/23; 15% service charge public by reservation only. **Pool(s):** heated outdoor. **Leisure Activities:** 2 tennis courts, butterfly garden, croquet, outdoor ping-pong, library with piano, shuffleboard, volleyball. **Guest Services:** coin laundry. **Business Services:** fax. **Cards:** AX, DS, MC, VI. **Special Amenities:** free local telephone calls.

PELICANS ROOST

Phone: (239)472-2996

12/1-12/31 Wkly	2P: $1150-$2400
2/1-4/18 Wkly	2P: $2400
1/1-1/31 Wkly	2P: $1750
4/19-11/30 Wkly	2P: $1200-$1400

Condominium

Location: From causeway, 0.7 mi w on Periwinkle Way, 0.5 mi s. 605 Donax St 33957. Fax: 239/472-0317. **Facility:** 21 two-bedroom suites. 4 stories, exterior corridors. **Parking:** on-site. **Terms:** 7 night minimum stay, 60 day cancellation notice. **Amenities:** irons. **Pool(s):** heated outdoor. **Leisure Activities:** fishing, 2 lighted tennis courts, horseshoes, shuffleboard. **Guest Services:** complimentary laundry. *(See color ad below)*

SANIBEL ARMS WEST

Phone: (239)472-1138

2/1-4/25 Wkly	1P: $1575-$1995	2P: $1575-$1995
12/21-1/31 Wkly	1P: $1195-$1395	2P: $1195-$1395
12/1-12/20 & 4/26-11/30 Wkly	1P: $795-$1095	2P: $795-$1095

Condominium

Location: From causeway, 0.4 mi e. 827 E Gulf Dr 33957. Fax: 239/472-9688. **Facility:** 90 two-bedroom suites with kitchens. 2 stories, exterior corridors. **Parking:** on-site. **Terms:** 3 night minimum stay, 60 day cancellation notice-fee imposed. **Amenities:** video library (fee), irons. *Some:* hair dryers. **Pool(s):** heated outdoor. **Leisure Activities:** boat dock, 2 tennis courts, shuffleboard. **Guest Services:** coin laundry. **Business Services:** meeting rooms, fax (fee). **Cards:** MC, VI.

SOME UNITS

SANIBEL BEACH CLUB II

Phone: (239)472-5772

All Year Wkly   1P: $1200-$2000   2P: $1200-$2000

Condominium

Location: From causeway, 1.5 mi e. 205 Periwinkle Way 33957. Fax: 239/472-3790. **Facility:** 29 two-bedroom suites with kitchens. 3 stories (no elevator), exterior corridors. **Parking:** on-site. **Terms:** 7 night minimum stay, 30 day cancellation notice-fee imposed, $25 service charge. **Amenities:** CD players, safes, irons. *Some:* hair dryers. **Pool(s):** heated outdoor. **Leisure Activities:** tennis court, bicycles, playground, horseshoes, shuffleboard. **Guest Services:** complimentary laundry. **Business Services:** fax (fee). **Cards:** AX, MC, VI.

SANIBEL COTTAGES

Phone: 239/472-1868

1/31-11/30 Wkly	1P: $1785-$2800	
12/20-1/30 Wkly	1P: $1820	
12/1-12/19 Wkly	1P: $1750	

Condominium **Location:** From causeway, 2.8 mi on Periwinkle Way, 0.8 mi s on Tarpon Bay Rd, 0.3 mi e. 2341 W Gulf Dr 33957. **Fax:** 239/472-8711. **Facility:** 28 two-bedroom suites with kitchens and whirlpools. 3 stories (no elevator), exterior corridors. **Parking:** on-site. **Terms:** 3-7 night minimum stay - seasonal, 30 day cancellation notice, 14 day off season. **Amenities:** video library (fee), safes, irons. *Some:* hair dryers. **Pool(s):** heated outdoor. **Leisure Activities:** whirlpool, fishing, 2 tennis courts, shuffleboard, volleyball. **Guest Services:** complimentary laundry. **Business Services:** fax (fee). **Cards:** AX, DC, DS, MC, VI. *(See color ad p 805)*

THE SANIBEL INN

Phone: (239)472-3181

2/7-4/26	1P: $319-$539	2P: $319-$539	XP: $20	F16
12/1-2/6	1P: $175-$539	2P: $175-$539	XP: $20	F16
4/27-5/26	1P: $239-$309	2P: $239-$309	XP: $20	F16
5/27-11/30	1P: $175-$275	2P: $175-$275	XP: $20	F16

Small-scale Hotel Location: From causeway, just w at jct Lindgren Blvd. 937 E Gulf Dr 33957. **Fax:** 239/472-5234. **Facility:** 92 units. 48 one-bedroom standard units. 20 one- and 24 two-bedroom suites, some with kitchens. 2-3 stories, exterior corridors. *Bath:* combo or shower only. **Parking:** on-site. **Terms:** check-in 4 pm, 14 day cancellation notice-fee imposed. **Amenities:** voice mail, safes, irons, hair dryers. **Dining:** 7:30 am-11 & 5-10 pm, cocktails. **Pool(s):** heated outdoor. **Leisure Activities:** 2 tennis courts, recreation programs. *Fee:* kayaks, exercise room privileges, beach cabanas, umbrellas, barbecue grills, environmental lectures, bicycles. **Guest Services:** gift shop, valet laundry. **Business Services:** meeting rooms, fax (fee). **Cards:** AX, CB, DC, DS, MC, VI. **Special Amenities:** free newspaper. *(See color ad p 809)* SOME UNITS

SANIBEL MOORINGS

Phone: (239)472-4119

12/20-1/5	1P: $210-$355	2P: $210-$355	XP: $15
1/6-4/27	1P: $195-$355	2P: $195-$355	XP: $15
4/28-11/30	1P: $131-$260	2P: $131-$260	XP: $15
12/1-12/19	1P: $125-$248	2P: $125-$248	XP: $15

Condominium **Location:** From causeway, 0.4 mi e. 845 E Gulf Dr 33957 (PO Box 899). **Fax:** 239/472-8148. **Facility:** Designated smoking area. 110 units. 16 one-, 85 two- and 9 three-bedroom suites with kitchens. 2 stories, exterior corridors. **Parking:** on-site. **Terms:** check-in 4:30 pm, 4-7 night minimum stay - seasonal, 30 day cancellation notice-fee imposed, weekly rates available. **Amenities:** video library (fee), voice mail, irons, hair dryers. **Pool(s):** 2 heated outdoor, small heated outdoor, wading. **Leisure Activities:** canoeing, boat dock, fishing, kayaks, 2 tennis courts, horticultural tours barbecue grill area. **Guest Services:** coin laundry. **Business Services:** meeting rooms, business center. **Cards:** MC, VI. *(See color ad p 807)*

SANIBEL'S SEASIDE INN

Phone: (239)472-1400

2/7-4/26 [CP]	1P: $299-$408	2P: $299-$408	XP: $20	F16
12/1-2/6 [CP]	1P: $175-$408	2P: $175-$408	XP: $20	F16
4/27-5/26 [CP]	1P: $209-$285	2P: $209-$285	XP: $20	F16
5/27-11/30 [CP]	1P: $175-$229	2P: $175-$229	XP: $20	F16

Motel **Location:** From causeway, 0.7 mi e. 541 E Gulf Dr 33957. **Fax:** 239/481-4947. **Facility:** Designated smoking area. 32 units. 22 one-bedroom standard units. 2 one-, 1 two- and 3 three-bedroom suites with kitchens. 6 cottages. 1-2 stories, exterior corridors. *Bath:* combo or shower only. **Parking:** on-site. **Terms:** check-in 4 pm, 14 day cancellation notice-fee imposed. **Amenities:** video library, safes, irons, hair dryers. **Pool(s):** heated outdoor. **Leisure Activities:** fishing, bicycles, shuffleboard. **Guest Services:** gift shop, coin laundry. **Business Services:** fax (fee). **Cards:** AX, CB, DC, DS, MC, VI. **Special Amenities:** free continental breakfast and free newspaper. *(See color ad p 809)*

SANIBEL SIESTA CONDOMINIUM

Phone: (239)472-4117

12/1-1/3 & 2/1-4/25 Wkly	1P: $1653-$2170	2P: $1653-$2170	XP: $15	F5
1/4-1/31 Wkly	1P: $1325-$1650	2P: $1325-$1650	XP: $15	F5
4/26-11/30 Dly	1P: $140-$198	2P: $140-$198	XP: $15	F5

Condominium

Location: From causeway, 0.7 mi w on Periwinkle Way, 0.5 mi s on Donax St, just w. 1246 Fulgur St 33957. **Fax:** 239/472-6826. **Facility:** 57 two-bedroom suites with kitchens. 3 stories, exterior corridors. **Parking:** on-site. **Terms:** 3 night minimum stay, 45 day cancellation notice-fee imposed. **Amenities:** irons. *Some:* CD players, hair dryers. **Pool(s):** heated outdoor. **Leisure Activities:** fishing, 2 tennis courts, gas grills, shuffleboard. **Guest Services:** coin laundry. **Business Services:** fax (fee). **Cards:** AX, DS, MC, VI. **Special Amenities:** early check-in/late check-out and free local telephone calls.

SOME UNITS

SANIBEL'S SONG OF THE SEA, A EUROPEAN-STYLE SEASIDE INN

Phone: (239)472-2220

2/7-4/26 [CP]	1P: $329-$449	2P: $329-$449	XP: $20	F16
12/1-2/6 [CP]	1P: $165-$449	2P: $165-$449	XP: $20	F16
4/27-5/26 [CP]	1P: $229-$305	2P: $229-$305	XP: $20	F16
5/27-11/30 [CP]	1P: $165-$249	2P: $165-$249	XP: $20	F16

Motel

Location: From causeway, just e. 863 E Gulf Dr 33957. **Fax:** 239/481-4947. **Facility:** Designated smoking area. 30 units. 22 one-bedroom standard units with efficiencies. 8 one-bedroom suites with kitchens. 2 stories, exterior corridors. **Parking:** on-site. **Terms:** check-in 4 pm, 14 day cancellation notice-fee imposed. **Amenities:** video library, voice mail, safes, irons, hair dryers. **Pool(s):** heated outdoor. **Leisure Activities:** whirlpool, gas grill, bicycles, shuffleboard. *Fee:* golf privileges, tennis privileges. **Guest Services:** gift shop, valet and coin laundry. **Business Services:** fax (fee). **Cards:** AX. **Special Amenities: free continental breakfast and free newspaper.** *(See color ad p 809)*

SHALIMAR RESORT

Phone: 239/472-1353

2/1-4/30 [CP]	1P: $235-$310	2P: $235-$310	XP: $12	F12
12/1-1/31 [CP]	1P: $129-$310	2P: $129-$310	XP: $10	F12
5/1-5/31 [CP]	1P: $155-$237	2P: $155-$237	XP: $12	F12
6/1-11/30 [CP]	1P: $129-$223	2P: $129-$223	XP: $10	F12

Motel

Location: From causeway, 2.8 mi w on Periwinkle Way, 0.8 mi s on Tarpon Bay Rd, 0.5 mi w. 2823 W Gulf Dr 33957 (PO Box 389). **Fax:** 239/472-6430. **Facility:** 33 units. 18 one-bedroom standard units with kitchens. 2 two-bedroom suites with kitchens. 13 cottages. 1-2 stories, exterior corridors. **Parking:** on-site. **Terms:** 30 day cancellation notice-fee imposed, weekly & monthly rates available. **Amenities:** vidoo library, voice mail. *Some:* irons, hair dryers. **Pool(s):** heated outdoor. **Leisure Activities:** fishing, gas barbecues, basketball, shuffleboard. *Fee:* bicycles. **Guest Services:** coin laundry. **Business Services:** fax (fee). **Cards:** DS, MC, VI. **Special Amenities: free continental breakfast and free local telephone calls.** *(See color ad p 808)*

SHELL ISLAND BEACH CLUB

Phone: (239)472-4497

1/4-4/25 Wkly	2P: $1435-$2450
12/21-1/3 Wkly	2P: $2100-$2275
4/26-11/30 Wkly	2P: $1400-$1540
12/1-12/20 Wkly	2P: $1365-$1505

Condominium

Location: From causeway, 1.2 mi e. 255 Periwinkle Way 33957. **Fax:** 239/472-4218. **Facility:** 44 two-bedroom suites with kitchens. 3 stories (no elevator), exterior corridors. **Parking:** on-site. **Terms:** 3 night minimum stay - Sat-Mon, 30 day cancellation notice-fee imposed. **Amenities:** video library (fee), CD players, irons. *Some:* hair dryers. **Pool(s):** 2 heated outdoor. **Leisure Activities:** sauna, whirlpool, tennis court, bicycles, shuffleboard. **Guest Services:** gift shop, complimentary laundry. **Business Services:** meeting rooms. **Cards:** AX, DS, MC, VI. *(See color ad p 805)*

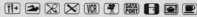

SUNDIAL BEACH RESORT

Phone: (239)472-4151

2/7-4/26	1P: $348-$749	2P: $345-$749	XP: $20	F16
12/1-2/6	1P: $175-$749	2P: $135-$749	XP: $20	F16
4/27-5/26	1P: $229-$429	2P: $229-$429	XP: $20	F16
5/27-11/30	1P: $175-$399	2P: $175-$399	XP: $20	F16

Resort Condominium

Location: From causeway, 0.7 mi w on Periwinkle Way, s on Donax St to Gulf Dr, 1 mi nw. 1451 Middle Gulf Dr 33957. **Fax:** 239/481-4947. **Facility:** This facility, fronting on a mile of beach, offers extensive activities as well as spacious one- and two-bedroom condominium units. 271 units. 122 one- and 149 two-bedroom suites with kitchens. 4 stories, exterior corridors. **Parking:** on-site. **Terms:** check-in 4 pm, 14 day cancellation notice-fee imposed. **Amenities:** video library (fee), voice mail, safes, irons, hair dryers. **Dining:** 4 restaurants, 7 am-11 pm, cocktails, also, Windows on the Water, see separate listing, entertainment. **Pool(s):** 5 heated outdoor. **Leisure Activities:** whirlpool, waterslide, fishing, 12 tennis courts (2 lighted), recreation programs, ecological center, jogging, playground, exercise room, shuffleboard, volleyball. **Fee:** sailboats, windsurfing, charter fishing, catamaran, kayak, golf privileges, tennis instruction, bicycles, massage, game room. **Guest Services:** gift shop, valet and coin laundry. **Business Services:** conference facilities, business center. **Cards:** AX, CB, DC, DS, MC, VI. **Special Amenities:** free newspaper. *(See color ad p 809)*

SOME UNITS

TORTUGA BEACH CLUB

Phone: 239/472-0400

1/31-4/24 Wkly	1P: $2625
12/1-1/2 Wkly	1P: $1645-$2555
1/3-1/30 Wkly	1P: $1820
4/25-11/30 Wkly	1P: $1645

Condominium

Location: From causeway, just w. Located in a residential area. 959 E Gulf Dr 33957. **Fax:** 239/472-6540. **Facility:** 54 one-bedroom suites with kitchens and whirlpools. 3 stories (no elevator), exterior corridors. **Parking:** on-site. **Terms:** 30 day cancellation notice, daily rates available. **Amenities:** irons. **Pool(s):** heated outdoor. **Leisure Activities:** whirlpool, 4 tennis courts, recreation programs, shuffleboard. **Guest Services:** complimentary laundry. **Cards:** AX, DS, MC, VI. *(See color ad p 805)*

WATERSIDE INN ON THE BEACH

Phone: (239)472-1345

1/2-4/27	1P: $228-$299	2P: $228-$299	XP: $20	F16
12/1-1/1	1P: $187-$269	2P: $187-$269	XP: $20	F16
4/28-5/26	1P: $149-$209	2P: $149-$209	XP: $20	F16
5/27-11/30	1P: $131-$180	2P: $131-$180	XP: $20	F16

Condominium

Location: From causeway, 2.8 mi w on Periwinkle Way, 0.8 mi s on Tarpon Bay Rd, then 1 mi w. 3033 W Gulf Dr 33957. **Fax:** 239/472-2148. **Facility:** 43 units. 14 one-bedroom standard units, some with kitchens. 13 one- and 16 two-bedroom suites ($204-$340), some with kitchens and/or whirlpools. 1-3 stories, exterior corridors. **Bath:** combo or shower only. **Parking:** on-site. **Terms:** 60 day cancellation notice, 14 day 5/27-12/18-fee imposed, small pets only (in limited units). **Amenities:** *Some:* irons, hair dryers. **Pool(s):** 2 heated outdoor. **Leisure Activities:** barbecue grills, shuffleboard. **Fee:** bicycles. **Guest Services:** coin laundry. **Business Services:** meeting rooms, fax. **Cards:** AX, DS, MC, VI.

SOME UNITS

Sanibel Island

Leave your cares on the mainland

Make your island escape today! the **Shell Islands**

Accommodations from hotel rooms to 1 & 2 bedroom units, start from*:

	1/01/03-2/06/03	2/07/03-4/26/03	4/27/03-5/26/03	5/27/03-11/30/03
Sundial-studio	$172	$276	$172	$124
Sundial -2 bdrm	$236	$431	$236	$191
Best Western Sanibel	$140	$199	$140	$108
Sanibel Inn	$191	$255	$191	$135
Seaside Inn	$167	$239	$167	$135
Song of the Sea	$199	$284	$199	$143

Call your AAA travel counselor today or

800-931-6600
www.SouthSeas.com/aaatb

*All rates are per room, per night and based on single or double occupancy, subject to availability and room type. Black out dates may apply. Valid on new reservations only. Not valid for groups or with other offers. Applicable taxes not included.

WEST WIND INN
(AAA) (SAVE)

▽▽▽▽

Motel

	12/21-4/30	1P: $252-$316	2P: $252-$316	XP: $22	F14
	5/1-11/30	1P: $154-$211	2P: $154-$211	XP: $22	F14
	12/1-12/20	1P: $147-$203	2P: $147-$203	XP: $21	F14

Phone: (239)472-1541

Location: From causeway, 2.8 mi s on Periwinkle Way, 0.8 mi s on Tarpon Bay Rd, then 1.5 mi w. 3345 W Gulf Dr 33957. **Fax:** 239/472-8134. **Facility:** 103 units. 102 one-bedroom standard units, some with kitchens. 1 one-bedroom suite ($353-$556) with kitchen. 2 stories, exterior corridors. **Parking:** on-site. **Terms:** 3 day cancellation notice, package plans - seasonal. **Amenities:** voice mail, safes, irons, hair dryers. **Dining:** 8 am-2 pm, Fri & Sat 5 pm-9 pm, cocktails. **Pool(s):** heated outdoor, wading. **Leisure Activities:** rental boats, rental sailboats, golf privileges, 2 tennis courts, tennis clinics, croquet, shuffleboard, volleyball. *Fee:* windsurfing, floats, catamarans, kayaks, bicycles. **Guest Services:** gift shop, coin laundry. **Business Services:** meeting rooms, fax (fee). **Cards:** AX, DS, MC, VI. **Special Amenities:** free local telephone calls and free newspaper.

SOME UNITS

🍽 🏊 ✕ [DATA PORT] 📶 / ✕ [VCR] 🗑 💻

The following lodging was either not evaluated or did not meet AAA rating requirements but is listed for your information only.

SANIBEL BEACH CLUB
[fyi]

Phone: 239/472-3382

Not evaluated. **Location:** From causeway, 0.7 mi w on Periwinkle Way, 0.5 mi s on Donax, just e. 626 Nerita St 33957. Facilities, services, and decor characterize a mid-range property.

──── WHERE TO DINE ────

HUNGRY HERON
▽▽▽▽

American

Lunch: $7-$19   **Dinner:** $7-$19   **Phone:** 239/395-2300

Location: From causeway, 2.4 mi w, then just n; in Palm Ridge Plaza. 2330 Palm Ridge Rd 33957. **Hours:** 11 am-9 pm, Sat & Sun from 7:30 am. Closed: 12/25. **Features:** Native Florida cuisine, crisp salads and overstuffed sandwiches bring in a loyal crowd of locals. Guests can choose from more than 250 dishes on a menu that includes several homemade desserts. Casual dress; beer & wine only. **Parking:** on-site. **Cards:** AX, CB, DC, DS, JC, MC, VI.

🍽 ✕

JEAN-PAUL'S FRENCH CORNER
▽▽▽ ▽▽▽

French

Dinner: $20-$28   **Phone:** 239/472-1493

Location: From causeway, 2.8 mi w on Periwinkle Way, just n. 708 Tarpon Bay Rd 33957. **Hours:** Open 12/15-5/1; 6 pm-10 pm. Closed: Sun. **Reservations:** suggested. **Features:** Popular with islanders, this dressy-casual restaurant tempts patrons with French favorites from escargot to chocolate mousse. The dining room is located on the first floor of a residential building. Tables are intimately spaced, so whisper your secrets. Casual dress; beer & wine only. **Parking:** on-site. **Cards:** MC, VI.

LAZY FLAMINGO SEAFOOD GRILL
▽▽▽

Seafood

Lunch: $9-$19   **Dinner:** $9-$19   **Phone:** 239/472-6939

Location: From causeway, 0.3 mi w. 1036 Periwinkle Way 33957. **Hours:** 11:30 am-1 am. Closed: 11/27, 12/25. **Features:** The fun restaurant sports rustic and tropical decor and employs a friendly service staff. Come early for a seat, as this place is popular with the islanders. The menu is seafood-oriented, with such dishes as mesquite-grilled grouper, mussels marinara and peel-and-eat shrimp. Casual dress; beer & wine only. **Parking:** on-site. **Cards:** AX, DS, MC, VI.

MAD HATTER
▽▽▽▽▽

American

Lunch: $10-$12   **Dinner:** $25-$35   **Phone:** 239/472-0033

Location: 7.5 mi n from jct Periwinkle Way and Sanibel-Captiva Rd. 6467 Sanibel-Captiva Rd 33957. **Hours:** 5 pm-9:30 pm; seasonal lunch hours. **Reservations:** suggested. **Features:** A delightful find, the small, charming dining room offers superior vantage points for viewing sunsets and local wildlife. Service is friendly, unpretentious and informative. The menu features market fresh fish and veal among dishes prepared with care and artistic presentation. Smoke free premises. Casual dress; beer & wine only. **Parking:** on-site and street. **Cards:** AX, MC, VI.

✕

PIPPIN'S BAR & GRILL
▽▽▽ ▽▽▽

American

Dinner: $13-$23   **Phone:** 239/395-2255

Location: From causeway, 1.8 mi w; in Tahitian Gardens Shopping Center. 1975 Periwinkle Way 33957. **Hours:** 4:30 pm-9:30 pm. Closed: 11/27; also Super Bowl Sun. **Features:** This restaurant ages its own beef for six to eight weeks, which along with thoughtful grilling and seasoning, makes up the rich flavor of the sirloin and other steaks. Ribs, chicken and fish also are popular in this intimate, tropical-themed eatery. Casual dress; cocktails. **Parking:** on-site. **Cards:** AX, CB, DC, DS, MC, VI.

🍽 ✕

THE SANIBEL STEAKHOUSE
▽▽▽▽▽

Steak House

Dinner: $16-$28   **Phone:** 239/472-5700

Location: From causeway, 1.2 mi w. 1473 Periwinkle Way 33957. **Hours:** 5 pm-10 pm. **Features:** Island guests in search of a fine dining experience should pay a visit to this spot, where friendly, professional service and well-prepared food contribute to the appeal. Such entrees as tasty filet mignon are nicely complemented by the wonderful desserts. Casual dress; cocktails. **Parking:** on-site. **Cards:** AX, MC, VI.

THE SEAFOOD FACTORY
▽▽▽ ▽▽▽

Seafood

Lunch: $7-$14   **Dinner:** $15-$25   **Phone:** 239/472-2323

Location: From causeway, 2.8 mi w. 2499 Periwinkle Way 33957. **Hours:** 11:30 am-10 pm. **Features:** Specializing in a wide variety of seafood; you'll enjoy hearty portions at this popular spot on the island. With it's nautical theme and friendly service, you'll be in for a treat here. Casual dress; cocktails. **Parking:** on-site. **Cards:** AX, DC, DS, MC, VI.

🍽 ✕

TRADERS STORE & CAFE
▽▽ ▽▽

American

Lunch: $7-$14   **Dinner:** $14-$26   **Phone:** 239/472-7242

Location: From causeway, 1.1 mi w. 1551 Periwinkle Way 33957. **Hours:** 11 am-10 pm. **Features:** Comprising the menu are such palatable items as grilled shrimp and chicken burritos and poached Atlantic salmon. After enjoying Chef Patnode's creations, diners can browse artifacts from around the world. Casual dress; beer & wine only. **Parking:** on-site. **Cards:** AX, DS, MC, VI.

WINDOWS ON THE WATER   **Lunch:** $7-$13   **Dinner:** $17-$25   **Phone:** 239/395-6014

▼▼▼ ▼▼▼   **Location:** From causeway, 0.7 mi w on Periwinkle Way, s on Donax St to Gulf Dr, 1 mi nw; in Sundial Beach Resort. 1451 Middle Gulf Dr 33957. **Hours:** 7:30-10:30 am, 11:30-2 & 5:30-9:30 pm, Sun 7:30-10 am, 11-2 & Regional American 5:30-9:30 pm. **Reservations:** suggested. **Features:** In Sundial Beach Resort, the restaurant has a bright, airy dining room that affords views of the Gulf of Mexico. Floridian cuisine consists of fresh local seafood seasoned with Mexican and Caribbean spices. Smoke free premises. Casual dress; cocktails; entertainment. **Parking:** on-site. **Cards:** AX, CB, DC, DS, MC, VI.

⊻ ⊠

------- *The following restaurants have not been evaluated by AAA* -------
but are listed for your information only.

CHEEBURGER CHEEBURGER   **Phone:** 239/472-6111

[fyi]   Not evaluated. **Location:** From causeway, 2.8 mi w. 2413 Periwinkle Way 33957. **Features:** Enjoy this fun establishment with its emphasis on, you guessed it- Cheeseburgers!! Add onion rings and a milk shake and you're all set!

DOLCE VITA RESTAURANT & LOUNGE   **Phone:** 239/472-5555

[fyi]   Not evaluated. **Location:** From causeway, 0.7 mi w. 1244 Periwinkle Way 33957. **Features:** With its Mediterranean flair and emphasis on variety; you'll find various dishes from around the world. Some popular choices are the linguine Saint Tropez, the penne rigate dolce vita or the pork chop Aux figs.

⊻

GILLIGAN'S-A FINE PLACE TO EAT   **Phone:** 239/472-0606

[fyi]   Not evaluated. **Location:** From causeway, 2.7 mi w. 2163 Periwinkle Way 33957. **Features:** This popular restaurant is set off of the road with a lush tropical setting. The menu is varied with a variety of seafood dishes to choose from.

THE ISLAND HOUSE RESTAURANT   **Phone:** 239/472-8311

[fyi]   Not evaluated. **Location:** 1.8 mi s on Sanibel-Captiva Rd; in Rabbit Road Center. 975 Rabbit Rd 33957. **Features:** While on your way to Captiva, stop in and try one of the island favorites such as coconut chicken or gingerbread pork. Pasta and seafood is also offered as well as home style cooking with southern fried chicken.

ISLAND PIZZA & PASTA ITALIAN RESTAURANT   **Phone:** 239/472-1581

[fyi]   Not evaluated. **Location:** From causeway, 1.7 mi w; in Island Tower Plaza. 1619 Periwinkle Way 33957. **Features:** Popular for its fabulous pizzas; this casual eatery also offers a variety of pasta, veal, meat & fish dishes as well.

JACARANDA SEAFOOD   **Phone:** 239/472-1771

[fyi]   Not evaluated. **Location:** From causeway, 0.7 mi w. 1223 Periwinkle Way 33957. **Features:** A local favorite since 1988, this restaurant offers some of the best pasta, seafood or steak dishes you'll find. Florida snapper and yellowfin tuna are popular dishes.

LAVIGNA ITALIAN RESTAURANT & GRILL   **Phone:** 239/472-5453

[fyi]   Not evaluated. **Location:** From causeway, 1.7 mi w. 1625 Periwinkle Way 33957. **Features:** This locally popular eatery offers a variety of Italian dishes which include such items as pasta, veal, poultry and meat dishes.

MATZALVNA ITALIAN KITCHEN   **Phone:** 239/472-1998

[fyi]   Not evaluated. **Location:** From causeway, 0.6 mi w. 1200 Periwinkle Way 33957. **Features:** You can't miss this popular spot set back from the road among the lush tropical foliage. You'll find an Italian themed restaurant with a varied menu offered.

MCT'S SHRIMP HOUSE & TAVERN   **Phone:** 239/472-3161

[fyi]   Not evaluated. **Location:** From causeway, 1.3 mi w. 1523 Periwinkle Way 33957. **Features:** This local favorite is popular for its many seafood offerings as well as some steak & poultry dishes.

SANIBEL BREW PUB & RESTAURANT   **Phone:** 239/395-2030

[fyi]   Not evaluated. **Location:** From causeway, 1.4 mi w. 1547 Periwinkle Way 33957. **Features:** Set off the road among the rich tropical foliage, is this locally favorite spot. Menu offerings are varied.

THE TIMBERS RESTAURANT & FISH MARKET   **Phone:** 239/395-2022

[fyi]   Not evaluated. **Location:** From causeway, 2.8 mi w on Periwinkle Way, then just n. 703 Tarpen Bay Rd 33957. **Features:** You'll find this one while on your way to Captiva or the many other island attractions. A must try with its varied menu offerings and a fresh seafood market is on site.

SANTA ROSA BEACH

------- **WHERE TO STAY** -------

A HIGHLANDS HOUSE BED & BREAKFAST   **Phone:** (850)267-0110

▼▼▼   All Year   2P: $95-$175   XP: $20   F10

Location: US 98, 2 mi s to CR 393, just e on SR 30A. 4193 W Scenic SR 30A 32459 (PO Box 1189). Bed & Breakfast   Fax: 850/267-3602. **Facility:** A large porch on the second floor of this B&B allows views of the ocean and sunsets; a boardwalk extends to the beach. Smoke free premises. 8 one-bedroom standard units, some with whirlpools. 2 stories, interior corridors. *Bath:* combo or shower only. **Parking:** on-site. **Terms:** 3 day cancellation notice-fee imposed, no pets allowed (owner's pet on premises). **Amenities:** irons. **Business Services:** fax. **Cards:** DS, MC, VI.

(A$K) 🛈 ⊠ 🅿 🖀

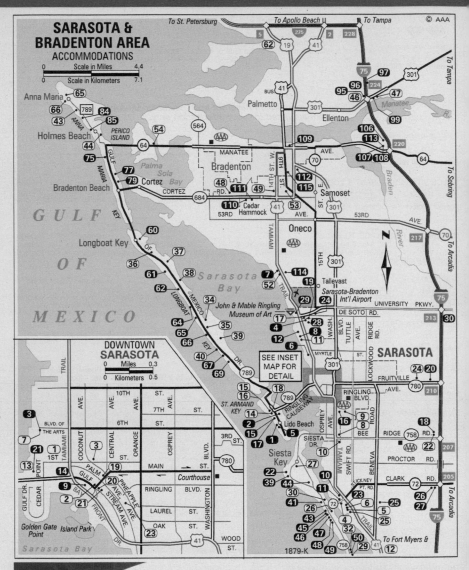

SARASOTA & BRADENTON AREA ACCOMMODATIONS

Scale in Miles 0 — 4.4
Scale in Kilometers 0 — 7.1

© AAA

To St. Petersburg
To Apollo Beach
To Tampa
To Tampa
To Sebring
To Arcadia
To Fort Myers &

GULF OF MEXICO

Anna Maria
Holmes Beach
Cortez
Bradenton Beach
Longboat Key
Palmetto
Ellenton
Bradenton
Samoset
Oneco
Tallevast
Sarasota-Bradenton Int'l Airport
John & Mable Ringling Museum of Art
SARASOTA

DOWNTOWN SARASOTA

Miles 0 — 0.3
Kilometers 0 — 0.5

SEE INSET MAP FOR DETAIL

St. Armand Key
Lido Beach
Siesta Key
Golden Gate Point
Island Park
Courthouse
Sarasota Bay

1879-K

✈ Airport Accommodations

Spotter/Map Page Number	OA	SARASOTA-BRADENTON INT'L	Diamond Rating	Rate Range High Season	Listing Page
8 / p. 812	AAA	Best Western Golden Host Resort, 1.5 mi s of airport	◆◆	$95-$120 [SAVE]	817
28 / p. 812	AAA	Days Inn-Airport, 0.5 mi s of airport	◆◆	$69-$129 [SAVE]	819
4 / p. 812		Hampton Inn Sarasota Airport, 0.5 mi s of airport	◆◆◆	$94-$109	820
7 / p. 812	AAA	Holiday Inn-Airport/Marina, 2.7 mi n of terminal	◆◆◆	$94-$259 [SAVE]	820
24 / p. 812		Sarasota/Bradenton Courtyard By Marriott, at entrance	◆◆◆	$129-$160	824
19 / p. 812	AAA	Sleep Inn, at entrance	◆◆	$59-$89 [SAVE]	825

Sarasota & Bradenton Area

This index helps you "spot" where approved accommodations and restaurants are located on the corresponding detailed maps. Lodging rate ranges are for comparison only and show the property's high season; rates are per night, unless only weekly (W) rates are available. Restaurant rate range is for dinner, unless only lunch (L) is served. Turn to the listing page for more detailed rate information and consult display ads for special promotions.

Spotter/Map Page Number	OA	SARASOTA - Lodgings	Diamond Rating	Rate Range High Season	Listing Page
1 / p. 812	AAA	The Helmsley Sandcastle Hotel - see color ad p 821	◆◆	$169-$299 [SAVE]	820
2 / p. 812	AAA	Holiday Inn-Lido Beach - see color ad p 822, opposite inside back cover	◆◆◆	$250-$280 [SAVE]	821
3 / p. 812	AAA	Hyatt Sarasota	◆◆◆	$119-$215 [SAVE]	822
4 / p. 812		Hampton Inn Sarasota Airport	◆◆◆	$94-$109	820
5 / p. 812	AAA	Half Moon Beach Club - see color ad p 820	◆◆◆	$149-$279 [SAVE]	819
6 / p. 812	AAA	Best Western Royal Palms	◆◆	$79-$119 [SAVE]	818
7 / p. 812	AAA	Holiday Inn-Airport/Marina - see color ad opposite inside back cover	◆◆◆	$94-$259 [SAVE]	820
8 / p. 812	AAA	Best Western Golden Host Resort	◆◆	$95-$120 [SAVE]	817
9 / p. 812		The Cypress, A Bed & Breakfast Inn	◆◆◆	$210-$250	819
10 / p. 812	AAA	The Calais Motel-Apartments	◆◆	$80-$105 [SAVE]	818
11 / p. 812		The Tides Inn	◆	$100-$115	826
12 / p. 812	AAA	Southland Inn	◆◆	$69-$109 [SAVE]	825
14 / p. 812		Inn By The Bay	◆◆	$69-$109	822
15 / p. 812	AAA	Radisson Lido Beach Resort - see color ad p 824	◆◆◆	$229-$549 [SAVE]	823
16 / p. 812	AAA	Best Western Midtown - see color ad p 817	◆◆	$89-$119 [SAVE]	818
17 / p. 812	AAA	Coquina on the Beach Resort - see color ad p 823	◆◆	$179-$349 [SAVE]	819
18 / p. 812		Hampton Inn I-75/Bee Ridge	◆◆◆	$129-$139	820
19 / p. 812	AAA	Sleep Inn	◆◆	$59-$89 [SAVE]	825
20 / p. 812		AmericInn Hotel & Suites - see color ad p 871	◆◆◆	$129-$189	817
21 / p. 812		The Ritz-Carlton, Sarasota	◆◆◆◆	$275-$310	824
22 / p. 812		Siesta Breeze Beachside Inn	◆◆	$149-$210	825
23 / p. 812		The Sunset Lodge Motel	◆◆	$95-$570	826
24 / p. 812		Sarasota/Bradenton Courtyard By Marriott	◆◆◆	$129-$160	824
25 / p. 812	AAA	Timberwoods Vacation Villas & Resort - see color ad p 825	◆◆	$146-$151 [SAVE]	826

Spotter/Map Page Number	OA	SARASOTA - Lodgings (continued)	Diamond Rating	Rate Range High Season	Listing Page
26 / p. 812	AAA	Ramada Limited	◇◇	$110-$139 SAVE	824
27 / p. 812	AAA	Comfort Inn	◇◇	$89-$139 SAVE	818
28 / p. 812	AAA	Days Inn-Airport	◇◇	$69-$129 SAVE	819
29 / p. 812	AAA	Super 8 Motel of Sarasota - see color ad p 825	◇◇	$45-$85 SAVE	826
30 / p. 812	AAA	Holiday Inn Lakewood Ranch - see color ad opposite inside back cover, p 821	◇◇◇	$159-$236 SAVE	821
		SARASOTA - Restaurants			
1 / p. 812		Michael's Mediterranean Grille	◇◇◇	$13-$29	827
2 / p. 812		Pino's Primi Piatti	◇◇	$12-$28	828
3 / p. 812	AAA	The Bijou Cafe	◇◇◇	$15-$24	826
4 / p. 812		Coasters Seafood Co at the Southbridge	◇◇	$14-$22	827
5 / p. 812	AAA	La Champagne Restaurant	◇◇◇	$20-$31	827
6 / p. 812		Blackboard Bistro	◇◇	$14-$19	826
7 / p. 812		Scalini	◇◇◇	$15-$32	828
8 / p. 812		Cosimo's Brick Oven	◇◇	$8-$23	827
9 / p. 812	AAA	Michael's on East	◇◇◇◇	$16-$35	828
10 / p. 812		Cafe Baci	◇◇	$11-$23	826
11 / p. 812		Cuoco Matto Ristorante	◇◇	$7-$17	827
12 / p. 812		Roessler's Restaurant	◇◇◇	$15-$31	828
13 / p. 812		Vernona	◇◇◇	$20-$45	828
14 / p. 812		Osteria Northern Italian Restaurant	◇◇◇	$12-$26	828
15 / p. 812		Columbia Restaurant	◇◇	$15-$22	827
16 / p. 812		Crab & Fin	◇◇	$12-$26	827
17 / p. 812		Cafe of the Arts	◇◇◇	$12-$36	827
18 / p. 812		Tommy Bahama's Tropical Cafe	◇◇	$15-$23	828
19 / p. 812		First Watch Restaurant	◇◇	$3-$8(L)	827
20 / p. 812		Tropical Thai Restaurant and Sushi Bar	◇◇	$6-$20	828
21 / p. 812		Patrick's Restaurant & Tavern	◇◇	$6-$19	828
22 / p. 812		Sugar & Spice	◇◇	$4-$14	828
23 / p. 812		Uva Rara Ristorante	◇◇◇	$16-$25	828
24 / p. 812		Johnny Leverock's Seafood House	◇◇	$9-$19	827
25 / p. 812		Waterfront Restaurant	◇	$12-$25	829
		SIESTA KEY - Lodgings			
39 / p. 812	AAA	Tropical Breeze Resort of Siesta Key	◇◇	$120-$350 SAVE	832
41 / p. 812	AAA	Palm Bay Club - see color ad p 823	◇◇◇	$270-$675 SAVE	831
43 / p. 812	AAA	Crescent View Beach Club Hotel - see color ad p 819	◇◇	$199-$469 SAVE	831
44 / p. 812	AAA	Sunsets on the Key	◇◇◇	$159-$249 SAVE	831
45 / p. 812	AAA	Sara Sea Inn at the Beach - see color ad p 822	◇◇◇	$159-$399 SAVE	831
46 / p. 812	AAA	Tropical Shores Beach Resort - see color ad p 817	◇◇◇	$189-$395 SAVE	832

Spotter/Map Page Number	OA	SIESTA KEY - Lodgings (continued)	Diamond Rating	Rate Range High Season	Listing Page
47 / p. 812	AAA	**Captiva Beach Resort - see color ad p 818**	◆◆	$855-$1525(W) SAVE	830
48 / p. 812	AAA	**Conclare Motel & Apartments**	◆◆	$135-$275 SAVE	831
49 / p. 812		Gulf Terrace Vacation Apartments	◆◆	$660-$1300(W)	831
50 / p. 812	AAA	**Turtle Beach Resort**	◆◆◆	$290-$390 SAVE	832
		SIESTA KEY - Restaurants			
26 / p. 812		Chez Daniel	◆◆	$16-$24	832
27 / p. 812		Village Cafe	◆	$4-$8(L)	832
29 / p. 812	AAA	**Ophelia's on the Bay**	◆◆◆	$15-$27	832
30 / p. 812		The Summerhouse Restaurant	◆◆◆	$10-$25	832
32 / p. 812	AAA	**Turtles on Little Sarasota Bay**	◆◆	$7-$21	832
		LONGBOAT KEY - Lodgings			
60 / p. 812	AAA	**Harbour Villa Club**	◆◆◆	$1895(W) SAVE	491
61 / p. 812		Riviera Beach Resort	◆◆	$170	492
62 / p. 812	AAA	**Holiday Inn Hotel & Suites - see color ad opposite inside back cover**	◆◆◆	$229-$399 SAVE	492
64 / p. 812	AAA	**Hilton Longboat Key Beachfront Resort - see color ad p 491**	◆◆◆	$210-$345 SAVE	492
65 / p. 812		Turtle Crawl Inn	◆◆	$175-$357	492
66 / p. 812		Diplomat Resort	◆◆	Failed to provide	491
67 / p. 812		The Colony Beach & Tennis Resort	◆◆◆	$395-$675	490
69 / p. 812	AAA	**The Resort at Longboat Key Club - see ad p 491**	◆◆◆◆	$295-$1150 SAVE	492
		LONGBOAT KEY - Restaurants			
30 / p. 812		Cafe on the Bay	◆◆	$15-$26	492
35 / p. 812		Maureen Restaurant & Martini Bar	◆◆◆	$17-$25	493
36 / p. 812		Euphemia Haye	◆◆◆	$20-$38	493
37 / p. 812		Harry's Continental Kitchens	◆◆	$19-$32	493
38 / p. 812	AAA	**Lynches Landing Bar & Grill**	◆◆	$7-$27	493
39 / p. 812		Poseidon Ocean Harvest Restaurant	◆◆◆	$18-$31	493
40 / p. 812		The Colony Restaurant	◆◆◆	$20-$38	493
		BRADENTON BEACH - Lodgings			
75 / p. 812		Econo Lodge Surfside - see color ad p 257	◆◆	$136-$205	259
77 / p. 812	AAA	**Tradewinds Resort**	◆◆◆	$149-$289 SAVE	259
79 / p. 812	AAA	**Tortuga Inn**	◆◆◆	$125-$319 SAVE	259
		HOLMES BEACH - Lodgings			
84 / p. 812	AAA	**The Beach Inn**	◆◆◆	$129-$209 SAVE	441
85 / p. 812	AAA	**Harrington House Beachfront Bed & Breakfast**	◆◆◆	$139-$349 SAVE	441
		HOLMES BEACH - Restaurants			
43 / p. 812		Beach Bistro	◆◆◆	$22-$24	441
44 / p. 812		OOH LA LA!	◆◆	$18-$27	441
		ELLENTON - Lodgings			
96 / p. 812		Ramada Limited-Ellenton	◆◆	$90-$110	315

Spotter/Map Page Number	OA	ELLENTON - Lodgings (continued)	Diamond Rating	Rate Range High Season	Listing Page
97 / p. 812		Hampton Inn	◆◆◆	$89-$129	314
99 / p. 812		Sleep Inn & Suites	◆◆	$105-$110	315
		ELLENTON - Restaurants			
46 / p. 812		Crab Trap II	◆◆	$9-$30	315
47 / p. 812		Johnny Leverock's Seafood House	◆◆	$9-$21	315
		BRADENTON - Lodgings			
106 / p. 812	AAA	Comfort Inn-Bradenton	◆◆◆	$90-$120 SAVE	257
107 / p. 812	AAA	Holiday Inn Express	◆◆◆	$109 SAVE	258
108 / p. 812		Days Inn I-75	◆◆	$75	257
109 / p. 812		Holiday Inn-Riverfront - see color ad opposite inside back cover	◆◆◆	$109-$169	258
110 / p. 812	AAA	Park Inn & Suites	◆◆	$114-$144 SAVE	258
111 / p. 812		Shorewalk Vacation Villas Resort	◆◆	$135	258
112 / p. 812		Quality Inn & Suites	◆◆	$65-$95	258
113 / p. 812	AAA	Econo Lodge I-75 - see color ad p 257	◆◆	$69-$99 SAVE	258
114 / p. 812	AAA	Econo Lodge Airport	◆◆	$55-$90 SAVE	257
115 / p. 812		Days Inn Bradenton	◆◆	$79-$99	257
		BRADENTON - Restaurants			
52 / p. 812	AAA	Anna Maria Oyster Bar	◆◆	$5-$25	258
53 / p. 812		Miller's Dutch Kitch'n	◆◆	$5-$14	259
54 / p. 812		Leverock's of Perico Harbor	◆◆	$9-$19	259
		PALMETTO - Restaurant			
62 / p. 812		Crab Trap 1	◆◆	$10-$40	768
		ANNA MARIA - Restaurants			
65 / p. 812		Bistro at Island's End	◆◆◆	$8-$27	244
66 / p. 812		Sandbar	◆◆	$11-$18	244

SARASOTA pop. 52,715   (See map p. 812; index p. 813)

─── WHERE TO STAY ───

AMERICINN HOTEL & SUITES   Phone: (941)342-8778

Small-scale Hotel

2/1-4/15 [ECP]	1P: $129-$189	
12/24-1/31 [ECP]	1P: $99-$179	
12/1-12/23 & 4/16-11/30 [ECP]	1P: $89-$169	

Location: I-75, exit 210, 0.4 mi w, just n on N Cattleman, then just e on Commercial Way. 5931 Fruitville Rd 34232. Fax: 941/342-8668. **Facility:** 111 units. 99 one-bedroom standard units, some with whirlpools. 12 one-bedroom suites ($129-$189), some with whirlpools. 4 stories, interior corridors. *Bath:* combo or shower only. **Parking:** on-site. **Amenities:** dual phone lines, voice mail, irons, hair dryers. **Pool(s):** heated outdoor. **Leisure Activities:** whirlpool, exercise room. **Guest Services:** valet and coin laundry. **Business Services:** meeting rooms, fax (fee). **Cards:** AX, DC, DS, MC, VI. *(See color ad p 871)*

SOME UNITS

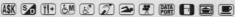

BEST WESTERN GOLDEN HOST RESORT   Phone: (941)355-5141

Motel

2/1-4/20 [ECP]	1P: $95-$120	2P: $95-$120
12/1-1/31 & 4/21-5/17 [ECP]	1P: $75-$100	2P: $75-$100
5/18-11/30 [ECP]	1P: $55-$80	2P: $55-$80

Location: On US 41, 0.6 mi s of jct University. 4675 N Tamiami Tr 34234. Fax: 941/355-9286. **Facility:** 80 one-bedroom standard units, some with efficiencies. 2 stories, exterior corridors. **Parking:** on-site. **Terms:** package plans. **Amenities:** safes, irons, hair dryers. **Pool(s):** heated outdoor. **Leisure Activities:** barbecue area, shuffleboard. **Guest Services:** coin laundry. **Business Services:** meeting rooms, fax (fee). **Cards:** AX, CB, DC, DS, MC, VI. **Special Amenities:** free continental breakfast and free room upgrade (subject to availability with advanced reservations).

SOME UNITS

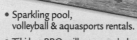

(See map p. 812)

BEST WESTERN MIDTOWN

Phone: (941)955-9841 🔢16

	2/1-4/30	1P: $89-$119	2P: $89-$119
	12/1-12/31	1P: $59-$119	2P: $59-$119
	1/1-1/31 & 5/1-11/30	1P: $59-$79	2P: $59-$79

Motel

Location: On US 41, jct Prospect St. Located just north of Sarasota Memorial Hospital. 1425 S Tamiami Tr 34239. Fax: 941/954-8948. **Facility:** 100 one-bedroom standard units. 2-3 stories, exterior corridors. **Parking:** on-site. **Terms:** cancellation fee imposed, package plans. **Amenities:** voice mail, irons, hair dryers. **Pool(s):** heated outdoor. **Leisure Activities:** barbecue area. **Guest Services:** coin laundry. **Business Services:** meeting rooms, fax (fee). **Cards:** AX, CB, DC, DS, JC, MC, VI. **Special Amenities: free continental breakfast and free newspaper.** *(See color ad p 817)*

SOME UNITS

(S) (icons) / (icons) /

BEST WESTERN ROYAL PALMS

Phone: (941)365-1342 🔢6

	2/1-4/26 [CP]	1P: $79-$119	2P: $79-$119	XP: $5	F17
	12/24-1/31 [CP]	1P: $59-$89	2P: $59-$89	XP: $5	F17
	12/1-12/23 & 4/27-11/30 [CP]	1P: $55-$79	2P: $55-$79	XP: $5	F17

Motel

Location: On US 41, 0.9 mi n of jct SR 780. 1701 N Tamiami Tr 34234. Fax: 941/955-8066. **Facility:** 37 one-bedroom standard units, some with kitchens. 1 story, exterior corridors. *Bath:* combo or shower only. **Parking:** on-site. **Terms:** 3 day cancellation notice. **Amenities:** irons, hair dryers. **Pool(s):** small heated outdoor. **Leisure Activities:** shuffleboard. **Business Services:** fax. **Cards:** AX, CB, DC, DS, MC, VI. **Special Amenities: free continental breakfast.**

SOME UNITS

(S) (icons) / (icons) /

FEE FEE

THE CALAIS MOTEL-APARTMENTS

Phone: (941)921-5797 🔢10

	1/20-4/30	1P: $80-$95	2P: $90-$105	XP: $10
	12/20-1/19	1P: $65-$72	2P: $72-$79	XP: $7
	12/1-12/19 & 5/1-11/30	1P: $54-$60	2P: $59-$65	XP: $5

Motel

Location: On SR 72, 0.3 mi sw of jct US 41. 1735 Stickney Point Rd 34231. Fax: 941/922-1284. **Facility:** 26 units. 25 one- and 1 two-bedroom standard units, some with kitchens. 2 stories, exterior corridors. **Parking:** on-site. **Terms:** 30 day cancellation notice-fee imposed, weekly & monthly rates available, pets ($5-$8 extra charge). **Amenities:** voice mail. *Some:* irons, hair dryers. **Pool(s):** heated outdoor. **Leisure Activities:** barbecue grill. **Guest Services:** coin laundry. **Business Services:** fax (fee). **Cards:** AX, DS, MC, VI. **Special Amenities: early check-in/late check-out and preferred room (subject to availability with advanced reservations).**

SOME UNITS

(S) (icons) / (icons) /

FEE

COMFORT INN

Phone: (941)921-7750 🔢27

	2/1-4/20	1P: $89-$139	2P: $89-$139	XP: $10	F12
	12/21-1/31	1P: $69-$109	2P: $69-$119	XP: $10	F12
	12/1-12/20	1P: $59-$89	2P: $69-$99	XP: $10	F12
	4/21-11/30	1P: $59-$89	2P: $59-$99	XP: $10	F12

Small-scale Hotel **Location:** I-75, exit 205, just w on SR 72. 5778 Clark Rd 34233. Fax: 941/925-2474. **Facility:** 63 one-bedroom standard units. 3 stories, interior corridors. *Bath:* combo or shower only. **Parking:** on-site. **Terms:** [CP] meal plan available, pets ($10 extra charge). **Amenities:** irons, hair dryers. **Pool(s):** heated outdoor. **Leisure Activities:** whirlpool. **Guest Services:** coin laundry. **Business Services:** meeting rooms, fax. **Cards:** AX, CB, DC, DS, MC, VI.

SOME UNITS

(S) (icons) / (icons) /

FEE

(See map p. 812)

COQUINA ON THE BEACH RESORT

ⒶⒶⒶ SAVE ◈◈ ◈◈	2/1-4/30	1P: $179-$349	2P: $179-$349
	12/1-1/2	1P: $89-$309	2P: $89-$309
	1/3-1/31	1P: $109-$269	2P: $109-$269
	5/1-11/30	1P: $89-$269	2P: $89-$269

Phone: (941)388-2141 ⓱

Small-scale Hotel Location: On St. Armands Key of Lido Beach, 0.9 mi s of St. Armands Circle. 1008 Benjamin Franklin Dr 34236. Fax: 941/388-3017. **Facility:** 34 units. 26 one-bedroom standard units with efficiencies. 7 one- and 1 two-bedroom suites with kitchens. 2 stories, exterior corridors. *Bath:* combo or shower only. **Parking:** on-site. **Terms:** 14 day cancellation notice-fee imposed, pets ($30 extra charge). **Pool(s):** heated outdoor. **Leisure Activities:** barbecues, beach loungers. **Guest Services:** coin laundry. **Business Services:** fax (fee). **Cards:** AX, DC, DS, MC, VI. *(See color ad p 823)*

SOME UNITS

🅢🅓 🛏 🍴 🏊 🎬 DATAPORT 🛗 🖥 / 🖥 /

THE CYPRESS, A BED & BREAKFAST INN

◈◈◈	12/17-4/30 [BP]	2P: $210-$250	XP: $20
	12/1-12/16 & 5/1-11/30 [BP]	2P: $150-$180	XP: $20

Phone: 941/955-4683 ⑨

Bed & Breakfast Location: Just n on Palm Ave from jct US 41; or just n on Ringling Blvd, just s on Palm Ave. 621 Gulfstream Ave S 34236. Fax: 941/906-8952. **Facility:** Guest-room themes at this B&B next to a marina and park include Victorian, Key West, floral and French elegance; a garden enhances the grounds. Designated smoking area. 4 one-bedroom standard units, some with whirlpools. 2 stories, interior corridors. *Bath:* combo or shower only. **Parking:** on-site. **Terms:** age restrictions may apply, 14 day cancellation notice-fee imposed. **Amenities:** irons, hair dryers. **Leisure Activities:** bicycles. **Guest Services:** complimentary evening beverages. **Business Services:** fax. **Cards:** AX, DC, DS, MC, VI.

SOME UNITS

🍴 ✖ ☎ / VCR /

DAYS INN-AIRPORT

ⒶⒶⒶ SAVE ◈◈ ◈◈	2/1-4/25	1P: $69-$99	2P: $79-$129	XP: $10 F12
	1/1-1/31	1P: $49-$79	2P: $59-$89	XP: $10 F12
	12/1-12/31	1P: $49-$69	2P: $59-$89	XP: $10 F12
	4/26-11/30	1P: $49-$69	2P: $59-$79	XP: $10 F12

Phone: (941)355-9721 ㉘

Motel Location: On US 41, just s of jct University Pkwy. 4900 N Tamiami Tr 34234. Fax: 941/351-7316. **Facility:** 119 one-bedroom standard units. 2 stories, exterior corridors. **Parking:** on-site. **Terms:** check-in 4 pm, cancellation fee imposed. [BP] meal plan available, pets ($10 extra charge). **Amenities:** safes (fee), hair dryers. *Some:* irons. **Dining:** 6 am 2 pm. **Pool(s):** outdoor. **Leisure Activities:** barbecue grills, playground, shuffleboard. **Guest Services:** coin laundry. **Business Services:** fax (fee). **Cards:** AX, DC, DS, MC, VI. **Special Amenities:** free continental breakfast and free newspaper.

SOME UNITS

🅢🅓 ♿ 🛏 🍴 📶 🏊 ✖ 🎬 / ✖ 🛗 🖥 🖥 /
　　　　　　　FEE　FEE

HALF MOON BEACH CLUB

ⒶⒶⒶ SAVE ◈◈ ◈◈	12/23-4/20	1P: $149-$279	2P: $149-$279	XP: $15 F17
	4/21-11/30	1P: $129-$199	2P: $129-$199	XP: $15 F17
	12/1-12/22	1P: $124-$194	2P: $124-$194	XP: $15 F17

Phone: (941)388-3694 ⑤

Small-scale Hotel Location: On St. Armands Key of Lido Beach, 1.6 mi s of St. Armands Circle. 2050 Benjamin Franklin Dr 34236. Fax: 941/388-1938. **Facility:** 84 units. 72 one-bedroom standard units, some with efficiencies. 12 one-bedroom suites ($194-$279) with efficiencies. 2 stories, interior/exterior corridors. *Bath:* combo or shower only. **Parking:** on-site. **Terms:** 2-3 night minimum stay - seasonal, weekends, 3 day cancellation notice, package plans. **Amenities:** video library (fee), voice mail, irons, hair dryers. **Dining:** 7 am-11 pm, cocktails. **Pool(s):** heated outdoor. **Leisure Activities:** Fee: bicycles. **Guest Services:** valet and coin laundry. **Business Services:** meeting rooms, PC, fax. **Cards:** AX, CB, DC, DS, MC, VI. *(See color ad p 820)*

SOME UNITS

🅢🅓 🍴 🍸 📶 🏊 🎬 DATAPORT 🛗 🖥 / ✖ VCR 🖥 /
　　　　　　　　　　　　　　　　FEE

(See map p. 812)

HAMPTON INN I-75/BEE RIDGE　　　　　　　　　　　　　Phone: (941)371-1900　[18]

[SAVE]　1/1-4/15 [CP]　　　　1P: $129-$139
　　　　12/1-12/31 & 4/16-11/30 [CP]　1P: $89-$99
▼▼▼▼　**Location:** I-75, exit 207, just w on Bee Ridge, then just n. 5995 Cattleridge Rd 34232. Fax: 941/371-0241.
Small-scale Hotel　**Facility:** 121 one-bedroom standard units. 5 stories, interior corridors. *Bath:* combo or shower only. **Parking:** on-site. **Terms:** check-in 4 pm, cancellation fee imposed, [ECP] meal plan available. **Amenities:** video games, voice mail, irons, hair dryers. **Pool(s):** heated outdoor. **Leisure Activities:** whirlpool, exercise room. **Guest Services:** valet and coin laundry. **Business Services:** meeting rooms, fax. **Cards:** AX, DC, MC, VI.

SOME UNITS
[🛇] [📶] [⚕M] [🛋] [🗇] [🛶] [⚞] [DATA PORT] [🖥] / [✕] [🖪] [🖼] /

HAMPTON INN SARASOTA AIRPORT　　　　　　　　　　Phone: 941/351-7734　[4]

[SAVE]　1/19-4/17　　　　1P: $94-$109
　　　　12/1-1/18 & 4/18-11/30　1P: $55-$81
▼▼▼▼　**Location:** US 41, just s of jct University Pkwy. 5000 N Tamiami Tr 34234. Fax: 941/351-8820. **Facility:** 97 one-
Small-scale Hotel　bedroom standard units. 3 stories, exterior corridors. **Parking:** on-site. **Amenities:** video games, voice mail, irons. *Some:* hair dryers. **Pool(s):** heated outdoor. **Leisure Activities:** exercise room. **Guest Services:** valet and coin laundry. **Business Services:** meeting rooms, fax. **Cards:** AX, DC, DS, MC, VI.

SOME UNITS
[✈] [📶] [⚕M] [🗇] [🛶] [⚞] [DATA PORT] [🖥] / [✕] [🖪] [🖼] /
　　　　　　　　　　　　　　　　　　　　　　FEE FEE

THE HELMSLEY SANDCASTLE HOTEL　　　　　　　　Phone: (941)388-2181　[1]

(AAA) [SAVE]　2/1-4/27　　1P: $169-$299　　2P: $169-$299　　XP: $10　　F18
▼▼▼▼　4/28-11/30　1P: $109-$199　　2P: $109-$199　　XP: $10　　F18
　　　　12/1-1/31　1P: $99-$199　　2P: $99-$199　　XP: $10　　F18
Small-scale Hotel　**Location:** On St. Armand's Key of Lido Beach, 1.3 mi s of St. Armand's Circle. 1540 Benjamin Franklin Dr 34236.
Fax: 941/388-2655. **Facility:** 179 units. 174 one-bedroom standard units. 5 one-bedroom suites ($399-$499) with whirlpools. 1-4 stories, exterior corridors. *Bath:* combo or shower only. **Parking:** on-site.
Amenities: safes, irons, hair dryers. **Dining:** 2 restaurants, 7 am-10 pm, cocktails, entertainment. **Pool(s):** 2 heated outdoor.
Leisure Activities: rental boats, recreation programs, table tennis, horseshoes, shuffleboard, volleyball. *Fee:* sailboats, aqua cycles, cabanas; bicycles, game room. **Guest Services:** gift shop, valet and coin laundry, area transportation-St. Armand's Circle. **Business Services:** meeting rooms, fax (fee). **Cards:** AX, CB, DC, DS, JC, MC, VI. **Special Amenities:** free newspaper. *(See color ad p 821)*

SOME UNITS
[🛇] [🍽] [⚟] [🛋] [🗇] [🛶] [✕] [DATA PORT] [🖪] / [✕] [🖼] /

HOLIDAY INN-AIRPORT/MARINA　　　　　　　　　　Phone: (941)355-2781　[7]

(AAA) [SAVE]　All Year　　　1P: $94-$259　　2P: $94-$259
▼▼▼▼　**Location:** On US 41, 2.4 mi n of jct University Pkwy. 7150 N Tamiami Tr 34243. Fax: 941/355-1605. **Facility:** 178
　　　　units. 173 one-bedroom standard units. 4 one- and 1 two-bedroom suites ($129-$259). 2 stories,
Small-scale Hotel　interior/exterior corridors. *Bath:* combo or shower only. **Parking:** on-site. **Amenities:** dual phone lines, voice mail, irons, hair dryers. **Dining:** 6:30 am-10 pm, cocktails. **Pool(s):** heated outdoor. **Leisure Activities:** exercise room. *Fee:* marina, 100 boat slips. **Guest Services:** valet and coin laundry, area transportation-within 5 mi. **Business Services:** meeting rooms, fax (fee). **Cards:** AX, CB, DC, DS, JC, MC, VI. **Special Amenities:** free room upgrade and preferred room (each subject to availability with advanced reservations).
(See color ad opposite inside back cover)

SOME UNITS
[🛇] [✈] [📶] [⚟] [🛋] [🗇] [🛶] [✕] [⚞] [DATA PORT] [🖥] / [✕] [🖪] [🖼] /
　　　　　　　　　　　　　　　　　　　　　　FEE FEE

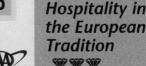

(See map p. 812)

HOLIDAY INN LAKEWOOD RANCH

Phone: (941)782-4400 30

⚫⚫⚫ SAVE	2/1-4/6	1P: $159-$236	2P: $159-$236	XP: $10	F18
	12/20-1/31	1P: $136-$220	2P: $136-$220	XP: $10	F18
▽▽▽▽	12/1-12/19 & 4/7-11/30	1P: $122-$196	2P: $122-$196	XP: $10	F18

Location: I-75, exit 213, just e. 6231 Lake Osprey Dr 34240. Fax: 941/782-4401. **Facility:** 128 one-bedroom stan-
Small-scale Hotel dard units, some with whirlpools. 5 stories, interior corridors. *Bath:* combo or shower only. **Parking:** on-site.
Terms: cancellation fee imposed, [BP] meal plan available, package plans, 18% service charge.
Amenities: video games, voice mail, irons, hair dryers. **Dining:** 6:30 am-10 pm, cocktails. **Pool(s):** heated outdoor. **Leisure Ac-
tivities:** whirlpool, exercise room. **Guest Services:** gift shop, coin laundry. **Business Services:** conference facilities, business
center. **Cards:** AX, CB, DC, DS, JC, MC, VI. **Special Amenities:** free local telephone calls and free newspaper.
(See color ad opposite inside back cover & below)

SOME UNITS

🆂🅳 🍴 🍽 🕹 👤 🏊 🎣 📠 DATA PORT 🛗 💻 / ❎ 🖼 /

HOLIDAY INN-LIDO BEACH

Phone: (941)388-5555 2

⚫⚫⚫ SAVE	12/1-12/31 & 2/1-4/30	1P: $250-$280	2P: $250-$280	XP: $10	F18
	5/1-11/30	1P: $175-$195	2P: $175-$195	XP: $10	F18
▽▽▽▽	1/1-1/31	1P: $150-$195	2P: $150-$195	XP: $10	F18

Location: On St. Armands Key of Lido Beach, 0.4 mi s of St. Armands Circle. 233 Ben Franklin Dr 34236.
Small-scale Hotel Fax: 941/388-4321. **Facility:** 135 units. 131 one-bedroom standard units. 4 one-bedroom suites with whirlpools. 7 stories, interior corridors. *Bath:* combo or shower only. **Parking:** on-site. **Terms:** 7 day cancellation
notice-fee imposed. **Amenities:** video games, voice mail, irons, hair dryers. **Dining:** 6:30 am-10 pm, cocktails. **Pool(s):** heated
outdoor. **Leisure Activities:** exercise room. *Fee:* beach chairs & umbrellas, bicycles. **Guest Services:** gift shop, valet and coin
laundry, area transportation-within 3 mi. **Business Services:** meeting rooms, PC, fax. **Cards:** AX, CB, DC, DS, JC, MC, VI.
Special Amenities: free newspaper and free room upgrade (subject to availability with advanced reservations).
(See color ad p 822 & opposite inside back cover)

SOME UNITS

🆂🅳 ✈ 🍴 🍽 🕹 📷 🏊 ❎ 🎣 DATA PORT 💻 / ❎ VCR 🛗 🖼 /
FEE FEE

(See map p. 812)

HYATT SARASOTA
AAA SAVE
◆◆◆◆◆

			Phone: 941/953-1234 [3]
1/1-4/30	1P: $119-$215	2P: $119-$215	XP: $25
12/1-12/31 & 5/1-11/30	1P: $90-$169	2P: $90-$169	XP: $25

Location: Just w of jct US 41. 1000 Blvd of the Arts 34236. **Fax:** 941/952-1987. **Facility:** 297 units. 293 one-bedroom standard units. 4 one-bedroom suites. 10 stories, interior corridors. *Bath:* combo or shower only. **Large-scale Hotel Parking:** on-site (fee). **Terms:** cancellation fee imposed. **Amenities:** voice mail, irons, hair dryers. *Some:* CD players, fax, honor bars. **Dining:** 2 restaurants, 6:30 am-midnight, cocktails. **Pool(s):** heated outdoor. **Leisure Activities:** pool table, exercise room. *Fee:* boat dock, charter fishing, cruising boats, scuba boat, massage. **Guest Services:** gift shop, valet laundry, area transportation-within 5 mi. **Business Services:** conference facilities, business center. **Cards:** AX, CB, DC, DS, JC, MC, VI.

✈ ⊷[FEE] ⊷ ⊤ ⅏M ⊠ ⊘ ⬈ ⊠ ⊠ [DATA PORT] ⊡ / ⊠ [SOME UNITS] [VCR][FEE] ⊟[FEE] ⊡[FEE] /

INN BY THE BAY
◆◆◆ ◆◆◆

		Phone: (941)365-1900 [14]
2/2-3/31		2P: $69-$109
12/1-2/1 & 4/1-11/30		2P: $39-$69

Small-scale Hotel Location: On US 41 at jct SR 789. 1 N Tamiami Tr 34236. **Fax:** 941/365-1900. **Facility:** 100 one-bedroom standard units. 6 stories, interior/exterior corridors. *Bath:* combo or shower only. **Parking:** on-site. **Terms:** cancellation fee imposed. **Amenities:** voice mail, irons, hair dryers. **Pool(s):** outdoor. **Guest Services:** valet and coin laundry. **Business Services:** meeting rooms, fax. **Cards:** AX, CB, DC, DS, MC, VI.

⊤ ⊡[24] ⅏M ⊠ ⊘ ⬈ [DATA PORT] ⊡ / ⊠ [SOME UNITS] ⊟[FEE] ⊡[FEE] /

(See map p. 812)

RADISSON LIDO BEACH RESORT

Phone: (941)388-2161   **15**

	1P: $229-$549	2P: $229-$549	XP: $15	F16
2/14-4/26	1P: $229-$549	2P: $229-$549	XP: $15	F16
12/1-2/13 & 4/27-7/3	1P: $119-$409	2P: $119-$409	XP: $15	F16
7/4-11/30	1P: $119-$339	2P: $119-$339	XP: $15	F16

Location: On St. Armands Key of Lido Beach, 0.8 mi s of St. Armands Circle. 700 Benjamin Franklin Dr 34236.
Large-scale Hotel Fax: 941/388-3175. **Facility:** 222 units. 172 one-bedroom standard units, some with efficiencies or kitchens. 30 one- and 20 two-bedroom suites ($250-$859) with kitchens. 4-12 stories, interior/exterior corridors. *Bath:* combo or shower only. **Parking:** on-site. **Terms:** check-in 4 pm, [BP] meal plan available. **Amenities:** video games, high-speed Internet, dual phone lines, voice mail, safes, irons, hair dryers. **Dining:** 2 restaurants, 6:30 am-9:30 pm, Fri & Sat-10 pm, cocktails. **Pool(s):** 2 heated outdoor. **Leisure Activities:** whirlpools, exercise room. *Fee:* sailboats, windsurfing, cabanas, jet skis, kayaks, waverunners. **Guest Services:** gift shop, valet and coin laundry, airport transportation-Sarasota/Bradenton Airport, area transportation. **Business Services:** conference facilities, business center. **Cards:** AX, DC, DS, JC, MC, VI. **Special Amenities:** free local telephone calls and free newspaper. *(See color ad p 824)*

SOME UNITS

(See map p. 812)

RAMADA LIMITED   **Phone:** (941)921-7812    ㉖

AAA SAVE

| | 12/16-4/20 | 1P: $110 | 2P: $139 |
| | 12/1-12/15 & 4/21-11/30 | 1P: $79 | 2P: $99 |

Location: I-75, exit 205, just w on SR 72. 5774 Clark Rd 34233. Fax: 941/921-1982. **Facility:** 63 one-bedroom standard units. 3 stories, interior corridors. *Bath:* combo or shower only. **Parking:** on-site. **Terms:** [CP] meal

Small-scale Hotel plan available, pets ($10 extra charge). **Amenities:** voice mail, irons, hair dryers. **Pool(s):** heated outdoor. **Leisure Activities:** whirlpool. **Guest Services:** coin laundry. **Business Services:** meeting rooms, fax.

Cards: AX, CB, DS, MC, VI. **Special Amenities:** free continental breakfast and free newspaper.

SOME UNITS / FEE

THE RITZ-CARLTON, SARASOTA   **Phone:** 941/309-2000   ㉑

	12/1-4/26	1P: $275-$310	2P: $275-$310	XP: $25	F18
	9/19-11/30	1P: $215-$240	2P: $215-$240	XP: $25	F18
Large-scale Hotel	4/27-5/25	1P: $210-$235	2P: $210-$235	XP: $25	F18
	5/26-9/18	1P: $179-$205	2P: $179-$205	XP: $25	F18

Location: I-75, exit 210, just w of jct US 41; center. 1111 Ritz-Carlton Dr 34236. Fax: 941/309-2100. **Facility:** The Ritz-Carlton, Sarasota offers first class and very luxurious accommodations. You may not be a world leader, but you will be treated like one. 266 one-bedroom standard units. 9 stories, interior corridors. **Parking:** valet, winter plug-ins (fee). **Terms:** cancellation fee imposed. **Amenities:** CD players, high-speed Internet, dual phone lines, voice mail, safes, honor bars, hair dryers. **Dining:** Vernona, see separate listing. **Pool(s):** heated outdoor. **Leisure Activities:** whirlpool, 4 lighted tennis courts, exercise room. **Guest Services:** gift shop, area transportation. **Business Services:** conference facilities, business center. **Cards:** AX, DC, DS, JC, MC, VI.

SOME UNITS

SARASOTA/BRADENTON COURTYARD BY MARRIOTT   **Phone:** 941/355-3337   ㉔

SAVE

| | 1/1-4/30 | 1P: $129-$160 | 2P: $129-$160 |
| | 12/1-12/31 & 5/1-11/30 | 1P: $69-$130 | 2P: $69-$130 |

Location: Just e of jct US 41. 850 University Pkwy 34234. Fax: 941/355-5518. **Facility:** 81 units. 78 one-bedroom standard units, some with whirlpools. 3 one-bedroom suites with efficiencies. 3 stories, interior corridors.

Small-scale Hotel *Bath:* combo or shower only. **Parking:** on-site. **Terms:** [BP] meal plan available. **Amenities:** dual phone lines, voice mail, irons, hair dryers. **Pool(s):** heated outdoor. **Leisure Activities:** whirlpool, exercise room.

Guest Services: valet and coin laundry. **Business Services:** meeting rooms, fax (fee). **Cards:** AX, CB, DC, DS, MC, VI.

SOME UNITS / FEE

(See map p. 812)

SIESTA BREEZE BEACHSIDE INN   Phone: (941)349-8088
▽▽ ▽▽▽   12/21-4/30   1P: $149-$210   2P: $149-$210   XP: $10   F14
12/1-12/20 & 5/1-11/30   1P: $119-$159   2P: $119-$159   XP: $10   F14
Small-scale Hotel   **Location:** I-75, exit 205, just w of Ocean Blvd via Avendia Messina; in Siesta Village. 94 Columbus Blvd 34242.
Fax: 941/349-8095. **Facility:** 8 units. 6 one-bedroom standard units with kitchens. 2 one-bedroom suites with
kitchens. 2 stories, exterior corridors. **Parking:** on-site. **Terms:** cancellation fee imposed. **Amenities:** safes, irons. **Leisure Activities:** whirlpool. **Cards:** AX, DC, MC, VI.

SOME UNITS

(A$K) (SD) 📷 🔒 📠 📺 / (X) /

SLEEP INN   Phone: (941)359-8558
(AAA) (SAVE)   1/1-4/30   1P: $59-$89   2P: $59-$89
5/1-11/30   1P: $52-$69   2P: $52-$69
▽▽ ▽▽▽   12/1-12/31   1P: $52-$59   2P: $52-$59   XP: $10   F16
Small-scale Hotel   **Location:** Just e of jct US 41; in Airport Business Park. 900 University Pkwy 34234. Fax: 941/359-8558. **Facility:** 80
units. 74 one-bedroom standard units. 6 one-bedroom suites. 3 stories, interior corridors. *Bath:* combo or
shower only. **Parking:** on-site. **Terms:** [CP] meal plan available, package plans. **Amenities:** safes (fee).
Some: irons, hair dryers. **Pool(s):** outdoor. **Guest Services:** valet and coin laundry. **Business Services:** meeting rooms, fax.
Cards: AX, CB, DC, DS, MC, VI. **Special Amenities: free continental breakfast and free local telephone calls.**

SOME UNITS

(SD) ✈ 🏊 📷 (DATA PORT) / (X) 🔒 📠 📺 /
FEE   FEE

SOUTHLAND INN   Phone: 941/954-5775
(AAA) (SAVE)   2/1-4/30   1P: $69-$109   2P: $69-$109   XP: $10   D12
12/1-1/31   1P: $55-$85   2P: $55-$85   XP: $10   D12
▽▽ ▽▽▽   5/1-11/30   1P: $49-$69   2P: $49-$69   XP: $10   D12
Motel   **Location:** On US 41, 1.8 mi s of jct University. 2229 N Tamiami Tr 34234. Fax: 941/364-8329. **Facility:** 30 units. 21
one-bedroom standard units, some with efficiencies. 9 one-bedroom suites with kitchens. 2 stories, exterior
corridors. *Bath:* combo or shower only. **Parking:** on-site. **Terms:** 3 day cancellation notice.
Amenities: *Some:* irons, hair dryers. **Pool(s):** outdoor. **Leisure Activities:** sun deck. **Guest Services:** coin laundry. **Business
Services:** fax (fee). **Cards:** AX, DS, MC, VI.

SOME UNITS

(SD) 🍴 🏊 / (X) (DATA PORT) 🔒 📠 /

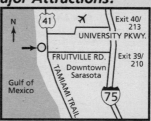

(See map p. 812)

THE SUNSET LODGE MOTEL   Phone: 941/925-1151 [23]

▼▼▼ ▼▼▼   1/16-4/30   1P: $95-$570   2P: $95-$570   XP: $8   F12
          12/1-1/15   1P: $75-$450   2P: $75-$450   XP: $8   F12
          5/1-11/30   1P: $60-$360   2P: $60-$360   XP: $8   F12
Motel   **Location:** Jct Stickney Point Rd, just s on Ave C, then just w. 1765 Dawn St 34231. Fax: 941/925-8168.
Facility: Designated smoking area. 6 one-bedroom standard units with efficiencies. 1 story, exterior corridors. *Bath:* shower only.
Parking: on-site. **Terms:** 3 day cancellation notice, weekly rates available, small pets only (in designated units). **Amenities:** hair
dryers. *Some:* irons. **Pool(s):** outdoor. **Leisure Activities:** bicycles, shuffleboard. **Guest Services:** coin laundry. **Business Services:** fax. **Cards:** AX, DC, MC, VI.

SUPER 8 MOTEL OF SARASOTA   Phone: (941)355-9326 [29]

(AAA) [SAVE] All Year   1P: $45-$85   2P: $45-$85   XP: $10
▼▼▼ ▼▼▼   **Location:** US 41, 2.3 mi n. 4309 N Tamiami Tr 34234. Fax: 941/355-5285. **Facility:** 51 units. 50 one-bedroom
          standard units. 1 one-bedroom suite. 2 stories (no elevator), exterior corridors. **Parking:** on-site.
Motel   **Terms:** [ECP] meal plan available. **Pool(s):** outdoor. **Leisure Activities:** horseshoes. **Guest Services:** coin
          laundry, airport transportation-Sarasota-Bradenton International Airport. **Cards:** AX, CB, DC, DS, JC, MC, VI.
          **Special Amenities: free continental breakfast and free room upgrade (subject to availability with ad-
vanced reservations).** *(See color ad p 825)*

SOME UNITS

THE TIDES INN   Phone: 941/924-7541 [11]

▼▼▼ ▼▼▼   1/16-4/15   1P: $100-$115   2P: $100-$115   XP: $10
          12/16-1/15   1P: $68-$80   2P: $68-$80   XP: $10
Motel   12/1-12/15 & 4/16-11/30 1P: $55-$70   2P: $55-$70   XP: $7
          Location: On SR 72, 0.3 mi sw of jct US 41. 1800 Stickney Point Rd 34231. Fax: 941/923-6445. **Facility:** 12 one-
bedroom standard units with efficiencies. 1 story, exterior corridors. *Bath:* combo or shower only. **Parking:** on-site. **Terms:** 28
day cancellation notice, in season-fee imposed. **Amenities:** *Some:* irons, hair dryers. **Pool(s):** heated outdoor. **Leisure Activities:** horseshoes, shuffleboard. *Fee:* bicycles. **Business Services:** fax (fee). **Cards:** MC, VI.

SOME UNITS

TIMBERWOODS VACATION VILLAS & RESORT   Phone: (941)923-4966 [25]

(AAA) [SAVE] 2/1-4/15   1P: $146-$151   2P: $146-$151
▼▼▼ ▼▼▼   12/1-1/5   1P: $142-$147   2P: $142-$147
          1/6-1/31 & 4/16-11/30 1P: $104-$109   2P: $104-$109
          Location: 2.2 mi s on Beneva Rd from jct SR 72 (Clark Rd). 7964 Timberwood Cir 34238. Fax: 941/924-3109.
Condominium **Facility:** 87 two-bedroom standard units with kitchens. 1 story, exterior corridors. **Parking:** on-site. **Terms:** 7
night minimum stay - 12/18-4/15, 31 day cancellation notice-fee imposed, $5 service charge.
Amenities: video library (fee), voice mail, irons, hair dryers. *Some:* DVD players (fee). **Pool(s):** heated outdoor. **Leisure Activities:** whirlpool, putting green, 2 tennis courts (1 lighted), barbecue & picnic area, clubhouse with billiard room & library, ping pong,
foosball, basketball, shuffleboard, volleyball. **Guest Services:** complimentary laundry. **Business Services:** meeting rooms, PC,
fax (fee). **Cards:** AX, DS, MC, VI. *(See color ad p 825)*

SOME UNITS

FEE

The following lodging was either not evaluated or did not
meet AAA rating requirements but is listed for your information only.

COUNTRY INN & SUITES BY CARLSON   Phone: 941/925-0631

[fyi]   2/1-4/19 [ECP]   1P: $95-$140   2P: $105-$150   XP: $10   F16
          12/25-1/31 [ECP]   1P: $65-$120   2P: $70-$130   XP: $10   F16
Motel   12/1-12/24 & 4/20-11/30 [ECP] 1P: $59-$99 2P: $65-$105   XP: $10   F16
          Too new to rate, opening scheduled for October 2002. **Location:** I-75, exit 205, 0.3 mi w. 5645 Clark Rd 34233.
Fax: 941/925-0752. **Amenities:** pets, coffeemakers, microwaves, refrigerators, pool. **Cards:** AX, CB, DC, DS, MC, VI.
(See color ad p 613)

--- **WHERE TO DINE** ---

THE BIJOU CAFE   Lunch: $8-$16   Dinner: $15-$24   Phone: 941/366-8111 [3]

(AAA)   **Location:** Between Cocoanut Ave and Pineapple; downtown. 1287 1st St 34236. **Hours:** 11:30 am-2 & 5-9:30 pm,
▼▼▼▼▼▼   Fri & Sat-10 pm. Closed major holidays; also 12/24 & Sun 5/14-12/25. **Reservations:** suggested.
          Features: In the heart of the theater and arts district, the stylish, upscale bistro draws diners in search of
Continental romance. Bijou pepper steak, pan-sizzled in a spicy hot sauce, and rack of lamb are outstanding examples
          on a winning menu. Dressy casual; cocktails. **Parking:** on-site. **Cards:** AX, CB, DC, MC, VI.

BLACKBOARD BISTRO   Dinner: $14-$19   Phone: 941/923-4511 [6]

▼▼▼ ▼▼▼   **Location:** On US 41, 0.9 mi s of jct SR 72. 7252 S Tamiami Tr 34231. **Hours:** 5 pm-9:30 pm, Fri & Sat-10 pm.
          Closed: 4/20, 11/27, 12/25; also Sun. **Reservations:** accepted. **Features:** Found in a small shopping plaza
American along busy US 41, this is a true "bistro" experience with a small dining room, friendly staff and wonderfully
          prepared dishes using the freshest ingredients. Some vegetarian dishes are on the menu which changes
seasonally. Smoke free premises. Casual dress; wine only. **Parking:** on-site. **Cards:** AX, DS, MC, VI.

CAFE BACI   Lunch: $7-$10   Dinner: $11-$23   Phone: 941/924-0963 [10]

▼▼▼ ▼▼▼   **Location:** On US 41, just s of jct Bee Ridge Rd. 4001 S Tamiami Trail 34231. **Hours:** 11:30 am-2:30 & 4:30-10
          pm, Fri-11 pm, Sat 4:30 pm-11 pm, Sun 4:30 pm-10 pm. Closed: 12/25. **Features:** Settle into a
Northern comfortable chair and relish the lovely upscale setting. Authentic Italian dishes are tastefully presented,
Italian   including the excellent shrimp cocktail loaded with huge, fresh shrimp. Also, for a hearty taste of the ocean,
          try the seafood pasta. Dressy casual; cocktails. **Parking:** on-site. **Cards:** AX, DC, DS, MC, VI.

(See map p. 812)

CAFE OF THE ARTS   **Lunch:** $7-$15   **Dinner:** $12-$36   **Phone:** 941/351-4304   ⑰
▼▼▼   **Location:** On US 41, just s of jct University. 5230 N Tamiami Tr 34234. **Hours:** 11 am-3 & 5-9 pm, Fri & Sat-9:30
French   pm, Sun 11 am-3 pm. Closed: 1/1, 12/25. **Reservations:** suggested. **Features:** Varied courses are offered
in intimate, sociable surroundings with a French theme. A wonderful concoction is a French loaf filled with seafood, ratatouille and rice in a flavorful cream sauce. Kudos to the staff for outstanding, attentive service. Casual dress; cocktails. **Parking:** on-site. **Cards:** AX, DS, MC, VI.

COASTERS SEAFOOD CO AT THE SOUTHBRIDGE   **Lunch:** $9-$17   **Dinner:** $14-$22   **Phone:** 941/925-0300   ④
▼▼ ▼▼   **Location:** On SR 72, 0.6 mi sw of jct US 41; in Boatyard Village. 1500 Stickney Pt Rd 34231. **Hours:** 11:30 am-10
Seafood   pm, Sun-9 pm. **Reservations:** suggested. **Features:** Relax and enjoy either waterfront or patio dining.
You'll find an array of health-conscious items as well as an extensive menu of pork, poultry and steak choices. The delicious grilled salmon tastes like they just plucked it from the water. Casual dress; cocktails; entertainment. **Parking:** valet. **Cards:** AX, CB, DC, DS, MC, VI.

COLUMBIA RESTAURANT   **Lunch:** $8-$14   **Dinner:** $15-$22   **Phone:** 941/388-3987   ⑮
▼▼ ▼▼   **Location:** On St. Armands Key at The Circle at St. Armands. 411 St Armands Cir 34236. **Hours:** 11 am-10 pm, Fri
Spanish   & Sat-11 pm, Sun from noon. **Reservations:** suggested; in season. **Features:** Colorful hand-painted tiles
contribute to the Spanish motif that weaves through the cozy restaurant. Such dishes as the 1905 salad in garlic dressing and the snapper Alicante brim with flavor. Diners can unwind either in the indoor dining room or on the airy patio, where they can watch the shoppers of St. Armands pass by. Casual dress; cocktails. **Parking:** street. **Cards:** AX, DC, DS, MC, VI.

COSIMO'S BRICK OVEN   **Lunch:** $8-$23   **Dinner:** $8-$23   **Phone:** 941/363-0211   ⑧
▼▼ ▼▼   **Location:** On US 41, at jct Bee Ridge Rd; in Southgate Plaza. 3501 S Tamiami Tr 201 34239. **Hours:** 11 am-10 pm,
Italian   Fri & Sat-10 pm, Sun noon-8 pm. Closed: 4/20, 11/27, 12/25. **Features:** In trendy Southgate Plaza, this
restaurant offers a comfortable dining setting. The varied menu offers such treats as wood-fired brick oven pizzas, signature pasta dishes and such hearty-appetite goodies as herb-roasted chicken and grilled veal chop. Casual dress; cocktails. **Parking:** on-site. **Cards:** AX, DC, MC, VI.

CRAB & FIN   **Lunch:** $6-$14   **Dinner:** $12-$26   **Phone:** 941/388-3964   ⑯
▼▼ ▼▼   **Location:** On St. Armands Key at The Circle at St. Armands. 420 St. Armands Cir 34236. **Hours:** 11:30 am-10 pm,
Seafood   Fri & Sat-10:30 pm, Sun noon-10 pm. Closed: 11/27, 12/25. **Reservations:** suggested; dinner.
Features: Extensive menu offerings of homemade pasta, rack of veal, domestic lamb shank and many varieties of fresh fish, flown in daily, make it difficult to narrow down a choice. Casual dress; cocktails; entertainment. **Parking:** street. **Cards:** AX, CB, DC, MC, VI.

CUOCO MATTO RISTORANTE   **Lunch:** $5-$9   **Dinner:** $7-$17   **Phone:** 941/365-0000   ⑪
▼▼ ▼▼   **Location:** On US 41, 2.1 mi s of jct University. 1603 N Tamiami Tr 34236. **Hours:** 11:30 am-11 pm. **Features:** A
Italian   bistro setting decorated with Italian scenes makes for a cozy dining experience. On the menu are varied
selections, such as pasta, pizza, fish and meat dishes. Try the excellent tuttu mare. The bread, dipped in herbal olive oil, is delicious. Casual dress; cocktails. **Parking:** on-site. **Cards:** AX, DC, DS, MC, VI.

FIRST WATCH RESTAURANT   **Lunch:** $3-$8   **Phone:** 941/954-1395   ⑲
▼▼ ▼▼   **Location:** Corner of Main and Pineapple sts; downtown. 1395 Main St 34236. **Hours:** 7 am-2:30 pm. Closed:
American   11/27, 12/25. **Features:** "Eggsellent" culinary experimentation results in such light specialties as crepes,
pancakes, omelets, sandwiches and salads. The classic Reuben is served with fried potatoes, salad and a small bowl of fresh fruit wedges. Service is friendly and attentive. Smoke free premises. Casual dress. **Parking:** street. **Cards:** AX, DS, MC, VI.

JOHNNY LEVEROCK'S SEAFOOD HOUSE   **Lunch:** $7-$19   **Dinner:** $9-$19   **Phone:** 941/342-8865   ㉔
▼▼ ▼▼   **Location:** I-75, exit 210, 0.4 mi w, just n on Cattlemen Rd, then just e on Commercial Way. 5981 Fruitville Rd 34232.
Seafood   **Hours:** 11 am-10 pm, Fri & Sat-11 pm. Closed: 11/27, 12/25. **Features:** Take in the nautical and friendly
atmosphere at this popular destination. The dining room teems with the fishing memorabilia of the restaurant's namesake, Johnny Leverock. The menu offers many palatable treats, from onion-roasted salmon to the seafood platter with its freshly caught bounty. Casual dress; cocktails. **Parking:** on-site. **Cards:** AX, DC, DS, MC, VI.

LA CHAMPAGNE RESTAURANT   **Dinner:** $20-$31   **Phone:** 941/926-8000   ⑤
🔺🔺🔺   **Location:** On Us 41, 1.3 mi s of jct SR 72. 7500 S Tamiami Tr 34231. **Hours:** 6 pm-9:30 pm. **Features:** The
professional chef/owner, who has 35 years of experience and also owns and operates two restaurants in
▼▼▼   Paris, lends a creative touch to the dishes here. Among numerous menu choices are rabbit stew
French   provencale, veal, kidney, red snapper and scallops and shrimp. Other special touches include tasty hors
d'oeuvres, a cheese tray with French varieties and sumptuous desserts. cocktails. **Parking:** on-site. **Cards:** AX, DS, MC, VI.

MICHAEL'S MEDITERRANEAN GRILLE   **Dinner:** $13-$29   **Phone:** 941/951-2467   ①
▼▼▼   **Location:** On US 41; in Sarasota Quay at jct Fruitville Rd. 214 Sarasota Quay 34236. **Hours:** 5 pm-10 pm.
Mediterranean   **Reservations:** accepted. **Features:** In the popular Sarasota Quay and overlooking the waterfront, the
accomplished staff will provide you a unique dining experience serving Italian foods with distinctive Mediterranean elements of herbs and flavor blends. Smoke free premises. Casual dress; cocktails. **Parking:** on-site. **Cards:** AX, DC, MC, VI.

(See map p. 812)

MICHAEL'S ON EAST
AAA
▽▽▽ ▽▽▽
Continental

Lunch: $8-$24   Dinner: $16-$35   Phone: 941/366-0007   ⑨
Location: On US 41; in Midtown Plaza, east entrance at jct Bahia Vista Dr. 1212 East Ave S 34239. **Hours:** 11:30 am-2 & 5:30-10 pm, Sat from 5:30, Sun from 6 pm. Closed: 1/1. **Reservations:** suggested. **Features:** Creative dishes awaken taste buds in the upscale restaurant. Spicy seafood gumbo whets diners' appetites for larger catches such as grilled salmon, attractively presented with a colorful vegetable medley. Dressy casual; cocktails. **Parking:** on-site. **Cards:** AX, DC, DS, MC, VI.   🍸 ✕

OSTERIA NORTHERN ITALIAN RESTAURANT
▽▽▽ ▽▽▽
Northern Italian

Dinner: $12-$26   Phone: 941-388-3671   ⑭
Location: Just n of jct St. Armands Cir. 29 1/2 N Blvd of Presidents 34236. **Hours:** 4:30 pm-10 pm. **Reservations:** suggested. **Features:** Photographs of northern Italy help to set the tone in the friendly restaurant, on the building's second floor. A full bar and extensive wine list complement such entrees as veal over homemade linguine and lobster with mussels, clams, shrimp and scallops. Casual dress; cocktails. **Parking:** street. **Cards:** AX, DC, DS, MC, VI.   🍸 ✕

PATRICK'S RESTAURANT & TAVERN
▽▽▽ ▽▽▽
American
Cards: AX, DC, MC, VI.

Lunch: $6-$19   Dinner: $6-$19   Phone: 941/952-1170   ㉑
Location: Downtown; in Kress International Plaza at jct Pineapple. 1400 Main St 34236. **Hours:** 11 am-midnight. Closed: 12/25. **Features:** A chicken Vesuvio that erupts with flavor is the highlight of this upscale sports bar with a nice roadside appeal. Pull in for a variety of entree choices such as steak, pasta, pizza and burgers. Fresh flowers and cloth napkins add a nice touch. Casual dress; cocktails. **Parking:** street.   🍸 ✕

PINO'S PRIMI PIATTI
▽▽ ▽▽
Italian
wine only. **Parking:** street. **Cards:** AX, CB, DC, DS, JC, MC, VI.

Lunch: $7-$13   Dinner: $12-$28   Phone: 941/955-3739   ②
Location: Jct with US 780 (Fruitville Rd), just s on US 41 (Tamiami Tr) to Gulfstream Ave, just e. 1301 Main St 34236. **Hours:** 11 am-10:30 pm, Sat-11 pm. Closed: 11/27, 12/25; also Sun. **Reservations:** suggested. **Features:** Located just across from the downtown marina, the bistro setting is the perfect foil for the eye-pleasing and flavorful dishes brought to you by the friendly staff. Smoke free premises. Casual dress;   ✕

ROESSLER'S RESTAURANT
▽▽▽ ▽▽▽
Continental
Dressy casual; cocktails. **Parking:** on-site. **Cards:** AX, DS, MC, VI.

Dinner: $15-$31   Phone: 941/966-5688   ⑫
Location: 0.8 mi s of Sarasota Square Mall, just e of jct US 41. 2033 Vamo Way 34238. **Hours:** 5 pm-10 pm. Closed: Mon 6/1-10/31. **Reservations:** suggested. **Features:** In an elegant estate setting beside an ornamental pond, the romantic restaurant offers splendid entrees of duck, veal, lamb and seafood. A raspberry-mango glaze coats the delicious almond- and pecan-crusted grouper. Service is exemplary.   🍸 ✕

SCALINI
▽▽▽ ▽▽▽
American
and valet. **Cards:** AX, DC, DS, JC, MC, VI.

Dinner: $15-$32   Phone: 941/363-2615   ⑦
Location: Just w of jct US 41; in Hyatt Sarasota. 1000 Blvd of the Arts 34236. **Hours:** 6:30 am-11 pm, Sun 10:30 am-2 pm. **Features:** On the first floor of the Hyatt, the restaurant overlooks the grounds and the waterway. Clam chowder is a wonderful start to an intimate dining experience. Follow it up with fresh salmon. For a real treat, opt for the sinful chocolate lava cake as a finishing touch. Casual dress. **Parking:** on-site (fee)   🍸

SUGAR & SPICE
▽▽ ▽▽
American
premises. Casual dress. **Parking:** on-site. **Cards:** DS, MC, VI.

Lunch: $4-$14   Dinner: $4-$14   Phone: 941/342-1649   ㉒
Location: I-75, exit 207, just w on Bee Ridge, then just s. 4000 Cattleman Rd 34233. **Hours:** 11 am-10 pm. Closed major holidays; also Sun. **Features:** Experience Amish-style cooking in a homey setting. The staff is dressed in conservative attire and dish up such good, hearty meals as fried chicken with mashed potatoes, green beans and a basket of bread. This enormously popular eatery is well worth any wait. Smoke free   ✕

TOMMY BAHAMA'S TROPICAL CAFE
▽▽ ▽▽
Caribbean
street. **Cards:** MC, VI.

Lunch: $8-$10   Dinner: $15-$23   Phone: 941/388-2888   ⑱
Location: On St. Armands Key; at The Circle of St. Armands. 300 John Ringling Blvd 34236. **Hours:** 11 am-11 pm, Fri & Sat-midnight. Closed major holidays. **Features:** Expect a wait at this extremely popular spot, but it will be well worth it. A Caribbean flair punctuates the tropically decorated dining room. Among the wonderful food choices are island pasta, boca chica chicken, Trinidad tuna, Martinique mahi, quiche, salmon and ribs. Not too hungry? Select from many salads, sandwiches and appetizers. Casual dress; cocktails. **Parking:**   🍸

TROPICAL THAI RESTAURANT AND SUSHI BAR
▽▽ ▽▽
Thai
dress; beer & wine only. **Parking:** street. **Cards:** AX, DS, MC, VI.

Lunch: $6-$7   Dinner: $6-$20   Phone: 941/364-5775   ⑳
Location: 0.5 mi e of jct US 41; downtown. 1420 Main St 34236. **Hours:** 11:30 am-3 & 4-10 pm, Fri & Sat-11 pm. Closed: 11/27; also Super Bowl Sun. **Features:** Authentic Thai cuisine is served in an intimate, nicely decorated dining room. Vegetable lovers will enjoy the sweet and sour shrimp, which is loaded with fresh vegetables and comes with a perfectly cooked bowl of rice. Service is gracious and welcoming. Casual   ✕

UVA RARA RISTORANTE
▽▽▽ ▽▽▽
Italian

Dinner: $16-$25   Phone: 941/362-9006   ㉓
Location: Just w of jct S Orange Ave and Dolphin Ln. 443 Burns Ct 34236. **Hours:** 5 pm-10 pm. **Features:** This "rare grape" is located just off the charming Burns Court and is a local favorite for inspired Italian dining. Tantalizing fresh preparations, homemade pastas and fine wine nourish an intimate experience designed for the most discriminating appetite. Dressy casual; cocktails. **Parking:** on-site. **Cards:** MC, VI.

VERNONA
▽▽▽ ▽▽▽
Continental

Dinner: $20-$45   Phone: 941/309-2008   ⑬
Location: I-75, exit 210, just w of jct US 41; center; in The Ritz-Carlton, Sarasota. 1111 Ritz-Carlton Dr 34236. **Hours:** 5 pm-11 pm. **Reservations:** suggested. **Features:** Verona features luxurious fine dining, a refined menu and a very knowledgeable staff. A large variety of bread and dessert and a distinctive European flair. Smoke free premises. Dressy casual; cocktails. **Parking:** on-site. **Cards:** AX, CB, DC, DS, JC, MC, VI.   ✕

(See map p. 812)

WATERFRONT RESTAURANT   **Dinner:** $12-$25   **Phone:** 941/921-1916 [25]
▽▽   **Location:** On US 41, 1.3 mi s of jct SR 72. 7660 S Tamiami Tr 34231. **Hours:** 4 pm-10 pm, Fri & Sat 11 pm.
                 Closed: 11/27, 12/25; also 6/1-10/1. **Features:** The casual atmosphere and pleasant views over the marina
Steak & Seafood enhance dishes like lobster, chicken teriyaki, barbecue baby back ribs and daily fresh fish. Casual dress;
                 cocktails. **Parking:** on-site. **Cards:** AX, DS, MC, VI.   ✕

──────── **The following restaurants have not been evaluated by AAA** ────────
but are listed for your information only.

HEMINGWAY'S   **Phone:** 941/388-3948
 [fyi]   Not evaluated. **Location:** On St. Armands Key at the Circle of St. Armands. 325 Ringling Blvd. **Features:** Located
                 at the popular St. Armands Circle, you'll find this casual and relaxing restaurant. The menu offers a wide
choice of appetizers, entrees and desserts. Patio dining is also available.

JORDAN'S STEAKHOUSE   **Phone:** 941/954-1332
 [fyi]   Not evaluated. **Location:** US 41 at jct Fruitville; in Sarasota Quay. 310 Sarasota Quay 34236. **Features:** Enjoy a
                 panoramic view of Sarasota Bay while dining at this restaurant known for its porterhouse, aged rib-eye,
lamb chops and 16oz. Lobster tail.   ☖

MI PUEBLO   **Phone:** 941/379-2880
 [fyi]   Not evaluated. **Location:** I-75, exit 207, 0.4 mi w at jct McIntosh Rd; in Palm Plaza. 4436 Bee Ridge Rd.
                 Features: Mexican cuisine with such offerings as fajitas, postres, chile rellenos & taquitos served in a
traditional Mexican atmosphere.

SATELLITE BEACH pop. 9,577

──────── **WHERE TO STAY** ────────

DAYS INN   **Phone:** (321)777-3552
 (AAA) [SAVE]   All Year   1P: $69-$149
▽▽ ▽▽   **Location:** 0.3 mi s of jct SR 404. 180 SR A1A 32937. Fax: 321/777-1090. **Facility:** 104 one-bedroom standard
                 units, some with whirlpools. 2 stories, exterior corridors. *Bath:* combo or shower only. **Parking:** on-site.
Motel   **Terms:** cancellation fee imposed, [CP] meal plan available, small pets only ($10 extra charge).
                 Amenities: hair dryers. **Pool(s):** heated outdoor. **Leisure Activities:** whirlpool, exercise room, shuffleboard,
                 volleyball. **Guest Services:** coin laundry. **Cards:** AX, DC, DS, MC, VI. **Special Amenities: free continental
breakfast and free newspaper.**
                                                                       SOME UNITS
                    ⑤ 🐕 [†] ⓓ 🏊 ✕ ⚡ [DATA PORT] / ✕ 🖥 📠 /

RAMADA INN OCEANFRONT RESORT HOTEL   **Phone:** (321)777-7200
 (AAA) [SAVE]   1/16-4/15   1P: $89-$169   2P: $89-$169
▽▽▽▽▽▽   12/1-1/15 & 4/16-11/30   1P: $79-$139   2P: $79-$139
                 Location: SR A1A, 2 mi s of jct SR 404. 1035 Hwy A1A 32937. Fax: 321/773-4608. **Facility:** 108 one-bedroom
Small-scale Hotel standard units, some with kitchens. 7 stories, interior corridors. **Parking:** on-site. **Terms:** cancellation fee im-
                 posed, [BP] meal plan available, 6% service charge. **Amenities:** video library (fee), dual phone lines, voice
                 mail, hair dryers. *Some:* irons. **Dining:** 6:30-10:30 am, 11-2 & 5-9 pm, Sun 9 am-1 & 5-9 pm, cocktails.
Pool(s): heated outdoor. **Leisure Activities:** lighted tennis court. **Guest Services:** valet laundry. **Business Services:** meeting
rooms, fax (fee). **Cards:** AX, DC, DS, MC, VI. **Special Amenities: early check-in/late check-out and free newspaper.**
                                                                       SOME UNITS
                 ⑤ [†] ☖ 🔈 🏊 ⚡ [DATA PORT] 🖥 / ✕ [VCR] 🖥 📠 /

──────── **WHERE TO DINE** ────────

THE DOVE RESTAURANT   **Lunch:** $6-$10   **Dinner:** $15-$30   **Phone:** 321/777-5817
▽▽ ▽▽   **Location:** 4 mi s of jct SR 404. 1790 SR A1A 32937. **Hours:** 11:30 am-2 & 5-9 pm, Fri & Sat 5 pm-10 pm,
                 Saturday brunch noon-2 pm. Closed major holidays; also Sun & 3 weeks 9/1-9/30.
Italian   **Reservations:** suggested. **Features:** Both the signature Sophia sauce (light cream) and the tangy pepper
                 sauce are favorites at this delightful Italian spot. A "doggie box" may be necessary, as traditional pasta
specialties are heaped on an oversized dish. The tuxedo-clad wait staff brings an air of formality to the otherwise casual
experience. Dressy casual; cocktails. **Parking:** on-site. **Cards:** AX, CB, DC, DS, MC, VI.
                                                                                  ☖ ✕

THE PHOENIX   **Dinner:** $17-$24   **Phone:** 321/777-8414
▽▽▽▽   **Location:** SR A1A, 3.3 mi s of jct SR 404. 1550 Hwy A1A 32937. **Hours:** 5 pm-10 pm. Closed: 12/25.
                 Reservations: suggested. **Features:** Elegant without being stuffy, the neoclassic restaurant exudes
Continental   intimacy, with dim lighting and cozy seating. Among the traditional entrees are rack of lamb with a
                 rosemary honey mustard crust, shrimp madras and calf liver with onions and apples. Semi-formal attire;
cocktails. **Parking:** on-site. **Cards:** AX, CB, DC, DS, MC, VI.
                                                                                  ☖ ✕

SEASIDE

──────── **WHERE TO STAY** ────────

JOSEPHINE'S FRENCH COUNTRY INN   **Phone:** (850)231-1940
▽▽▽▽   All Year   2P: $200-$250   XP: $30
                 Location: Jct SR 395, 0.5 mi w on SR 30A, just n on Quincy Cir. 38 Seaside Ave 32459 (PO Box 4767).
Country Inn   Fax: 850/231-2446. **Facility:** Close to boutique shops and the ocean, this property is in an area of beach
                 cottages and Victorian-replica homes. Smoke free premises. 9 one-bedroom standard units. 2 stories, inte-
rior corridors. *Bath:* combo or shower only. **Parking:** on-site. **Terms:** check-in 4 pm, 2 night minimum stay, age restrictions may
apply, 14 day cancellation notice-fee imposed, [BP] meal plan available. **Amenities:** irons. **Business Services:** meeting rooms.
Cards: DS, MC, VI.
                 [ASK] ⑤ [†] ✕ [VCR] ⚡ [DATA PORT] 🖥 📠 🖥

SEBASTIAN pop. 16,181

———— WHERE TO STAY ————

THE DAVIS HOUSE INN
▼▼ ▼▼
Motel

All Year   2P: $59-$79   XP: $10
Location: I-95, exit 156, 7.5 mi e, n on Indian River, then 1.3 mi. 607 Davis St 32958. **Fax:** 772/589-1722. **Facility:** 12 one-bedroom standard units with efficiencies. 2 stories, exterior corridors. *Bath:* combo or shower only. **Parking:** on-site. **Terms:** 14 day cancellation notice-fee imposed. **Guest Services:** coin laundry. **Business Services:** fax (fee).

Phone: 772/589-4114

KEY WEST INN AT CAPT HIRAM'S
AAA SAVE
▼▼▼▼▼

Small-scale Hotel

2/7-6/8	1P: $109	2P: $109	XP: $10	F17
12/20-2/6 & 6/9-11/30	1P: $99	2P: $99	XP: $10	F17
12/1-12/19	1P: $89	2P: $89	XP: $10	F17

Location: I-95, exit 156, 7.5 mi e, then 0.5 mi n. 1580 US 1 32958. **Fax:** 772/388-3118. **Facility:** 56 units. 51 one-bedroom standard units, some with efficiencies and/or whirlpools. 5 one-bedroom suites ($129-$149). 3 stories, interior corridors. *Bath:* combo or shower only. **Parking:** on-site. **Terms:** cancellation fee imposed, [ECP] meal plan available. **Amenities:** voice mail, irons, hair dryers. *Some:* video games, dual phone lines. **Dining:** 11:30 am-10 pm, cocktails. **Pool(s):** heated outdoor. **Leisure Activities:** Fee: marina, charter fishing, jet skis, bicycles. **Guest Services:** valet and coin laundry. **Business Services:** meeting rooms, fax (fee). **Cards:** AX, CB, DC, DS, MC, VI.

Phone: (772)388-8588

SOME UNITS

SEBRING pop. 9,667

———— WHERE TO STAY ————

INN ON THE LAKES
AAA SAVE
▼▼▼▼▼

Small-scale Hotel

1/1-4/30	1P: $75-$89	2P: $75-$89
12/1-12/31 & 5/1-11/30	1P: $69-$89	2P: $69-$89

Location: US 27, 1.5 mi n of jct SR 17. 3100 Golfview Rd 33870. **Fax:** 863/471-9400. **Facility:** 161 units. 160 one-bedroom standard units. 1 one-bedroom suite ($89-$150). 2-3 stories, interior/exterior corridors. **Parking:** on-site. **Terms:** cancellation fee imposed, weekly rates available, small pets only ($40 fee). **Amenities:** voice mail, hair dryers. **Dining:** 6:30 am-11 pm, cocktails. **Pool(s):** outdoor. **Leisure Activities:** golf privileges, exercise room. *Fee:* jet skis, massage. **Guest Services:** coin laundry. **Business Services:** meeting rooms, fax (fee). **Cards:** AX, DC, MC, VI.

Phone: (863)471-9400

SOME UNITS
FEE

QUALITY INN & SUITES CONFERENCE CENTER
AAA SAVE
▼▼▼▼▼

Small-scale Hotel

3/1-3/15	1P: $139-$290	2P: $149-$299	XP: $10	F18
12/1-2/28	1P: $99-$130	2P: $109-$140	XP: $10	F18
3/16-9/15	1P: $79-$139	2P: $89-$140	XP: $10	F18
9/16-11/30	1P: $90-$120	2P: $100-$130	XP: $10	F18

Location: On US 27, 7 mi n of jct SR 17. 6525 US 27 N 33870. **Fax:** 863/382-4793. **Facility:** 148 one-bedroom standard units. 2 stories, exterior corridors. **Parking:** on-site. **Terms:** check-in 4 pm, [BP] meal plan available, package plans, 15% service charge, pets ($25 fee). **Amenities:** safes (fee), irons. *Some:* hair dryers. **Dining:** 6:30 am-11 & 4-9 pm, cocktails. **Pool(s):** outdoor, wading. **Leisure Activities:** volleyball. **Guest Services:** coin laundry. **Business Services:** conference facilities, fax (fee). **Cards:** AX, CB, DC, DS, MC, VI. **Special Amenities:** free local telephone calls and free newspaper.

Phone: (863)385-4500

SOME UNITS
FEE   FEE

———— *The following lodging was either not evaluated or did not* ————
meet AAA rating requirements but is listed for your information only.

LAKE JACKSON GUESTHOUSE BED & BREAKFAST
fyi
Not evaluated. **Location:** I-4, From US 27, 1.3 mi e on CR 634A, 2.7 mi s. 413 Northeast Lakeview Dr 33870. Facilities, services, and decor characterize a mid-range property.

Phone: 863/385-0323

SIESTA KEY pop. 7,150 (See map p. 812; index p. 814)

———— WHERE TO STAY ————

CAPTIVA BEACH RESORT
AAA SAVE
▼▼ ▼▼
Motel

2/1-3/31 Wkly	1P: $855-$1525	2P: $855-$1525	XP: $56
12/18-1/31 & 4/1-11/30 Wkly	1P: $675-$1275	2P: $675-$1275	XP: $56
12/1-12/17 Wkly	1P: $435-$855	2P: $435-$855	XP: $56

Location: Just w of jct Midnight Pass Rd. 6772 Sara Sea Cir 34242. **Fax:** 941/349-8141. **Facility:** Designated smoking area. 20 units. 16 one-bedroom standard units with efficiencies. 2 one- and 2 two-bedroom suites with kitchens. 1 story, exterior corridors. *Bath:* combo or shower only. **Parking:** on-site. **Terms:** check-out 9:30 am, 60 day cancellation notice-fee imposed, daily rates available. **Amenities:** voice mail, hair dryers. *Some:* irons. **Leisure Activities:** pool privileges, gas grills, shuffleboard. **Guest Services:** coin laundry. **Business Services:** fax (fee). **Cards:** AX, DS, MC, VI. **Special Amenities:** early check-in/late check-out. *(See color ad p 818)*

Phone: 941/349-4131   47

SOME UNITS

(See map p. 812)

CONCLARE MOTEL & APARTMENTS
Phone: (941)349-2322 48

AAA SAVE

2/1-4/30	2P: $135-$275	XP: $10 F6
12/1-1/31	2P: $109-$240	XP: $10 F6
5/1-11/30	2P: $99-$210	XP: $10 F6

Motel

Location: Just w of jct Midnight Pass Rd. 6738 Sara Sea Cir 34242. **Fax:** 941/349-6572. **Facility:** 18 units. 16 one- and 1 two-bedroom standard units, some with efficiencies or kitchens. 1 two-bedroom suite with kitchen. 1 story, exterior corridors. *Bath:* combo or shower only. **Parking:** on-site. **Terms:** 30 day cancellation notice-fee imposed, weekly rates available. **Amenities:** *Some:* irons. **Leisure Activities:** pool privileges, gas grills, shuffleboard. *Fee:* bicycles. **Guest Services:** coin laundry. **Business Services:** fax. **Cards:** DC, MC, VI. **Special Amenities:** free local telephone calls and free room upgrade (subject to availability with advanced reservations).

SOME UNITS

CRESCENT VIEW BEACH CLUB HOTEL
Phone: (941)349-2000 43

AAA SAVE

2/1-4/27	1P: $199	2P: $469
12/26-1/31	1P: $159	2P: $429
12/1-12/25 & 4/28-11/30	1P: $199	2P: $369

Small-scale Hotel

Location: Just s of jct SR 72 (Stickney Point Rd). 6512 Midnight Pass Rd 34242. **Fax:** 941/349-9748. **Facility:** 27 units. 1 one-bedroom standard unit. 11 one- and 15 two-bedroom suites with kitchens. 2-4 stories, exterior corridors. **Parking:** on-site. **Terms:** cancellation fee imposed. **Amenities:** high-speed Internet, dual phone lines, voice mail, irons, hair dryers. **Pool(s):** heated outdoor. **Leisure Activities:** whirlpool, barbecue grill. **Guest Services:** complimentary laundry. **Business Services:** fax (fee). **Cards:** AX, DC, DS, MC, VI. **Special Amenities:** free local telephone calls and preferred room (subject to availability with advanced reservations). *(See color ad p 819)*

SOME UNITS

GULF TERRACE VACATION APARTMENTS
Phone: (941)349-4444 49

2/1-4/13 Wkly	1P: $660-$1300	2P: $660-$1300 XP: $10
12/22-1/31 Wkly	1P: $505-$975	2P: $505-$975 XP: $10
12/1-12/21 & 4/14-11/30 Wkly	1P: $375-$850	2P: $375-$850 XP: $10

Motel

Location: 0.5 mi s of jct SR 72 (Stickney Point Rd) on Midnight Pass Rd, just w. 1105 Point of Rocks Rd 34242. Fax: 941/349-4444. **Facility:** Designated smoking area. 12 one-bedroom standard units with kitchens. 2 stories, exterior corridors. **Parking:** on-site. **Terms:** 30 day cancellation notice, pets ($5-$15 extra charge, dogs only). **Amenities:** *Some:* irons, hair dryers. **Pool(s):** heated outdoor. **Leisure Activities:** shuffleboard. **Guest Services:** coin laundry. **Cards:** MC, VI.

PALM BAY CLUB
Phone: (941)349-1911 41

AAA SAVE

3/14-4/27	1P: $270-$675	2P: $270-$675 XP: $25
2/1-3/13	1P: $230-$545	2P: $230-$545 XP: $25
12/1-1/31	1P: $125-$460	2P: $125-$460 XP: $25
4/28-11/30	1P: $130-$435	2P: $130-$435 XP: $25

Condominium

Location: On SR 758, 0.8 mi n of jct SR 72 (Stickney Pt Rd). 5960 Midnight Pass Rd 34242. Fax: 941/349-1034. **Facility:** 145 units. 61 one- and 84 two-bedroom suites with kitchens. 2-3 stories, interior/exterior corridors. **Parking:** on-site. **Terms:** 3 night minimum stay, 60 day cancellation notice-fee imposed, weekly rates available. **Amenities:** high-speed Internet (fee), voice mail, irons, hair dryers. *Some:* CD players. **Pool(s):** 2 heated outdoor. **Leisure Activities:** saunas, whirlpool, marina, cabanas, fishing pier, 2 lighted tennis courts, recreation room, barbecue grills, exercise room. *Fee:* boat slips, billiards, ping pong, game room. **Guest Services:** valet and coin laundry. **Business Services:** meeting rooms, fax. **Cards:** MC, VI. *(See color ad p 823)*

SOME UNITS

SARA SEA INN AT THE BEACH
Phone: (941)349-3244 45

AAA SAVE

2/1-4/30	1P: $159-$399	2P: $159-$399 XP: $15 F12
5/1-11/30	1P: $99-$299	2P: $99-$299 XP: $15 F12
12/1-1/31	1P: $89-$289	2P: $89-$289 XP: $15 F12

Motel

Location: Just w of jct Midnight Pass Rd. 6760 Sara Sea Cir 34242. **Fax:** 941/349-4999. **Facility:** Designated smoking area. 30 units. 20 one-bedroom standard units with efficiencies. 7 one-, 2 two- and 1 three-bedroom suites ($159-$399) with kitchens. 1 story, exterior corridors. **Parking:** on-site. **Terms:** 2 night minimum stay weekends, 3 night for suites, 30 day cancellation notice-fee imposed. **Amenities:** voice mail, irons, hair dryers. *Some:* dual phone lines. **Pool(s):** heated outdoor. **Leisure Activities:** whirlpool, fishing, beach chairs, umbrellas, gas barbecue, picnic area, roller blades, scooters, shuffleboard. *Fee:* sailboats, catamaran, water bikes, kayaks, bicycles. **Guest Services:** coin laundry. **Business Services:** meeting rooms, fax. **Cards:** AX, DS, MC, VI. **Special Amenities:** free room upgrade and preferred room (each subject to availability with advanced reservations). *(See color ad p 822)*

SUNSETS ON THE KEY
Phone: 941/312-9797 44

AAA SAVE

12/21-5/14	1P: $159-$249	2P: $159-$249
12/1-12/20 & 5/15-11/30	1P: $89-$139	2P: $89-$139

Motel

Location: In Siesta Village; just w of Ocean Blvd via Avenida Messina. 5203 Avenida Navarra 34242. Fax: 941/312-9105. **Facility:** Designated smoking area. 9 units. 4 one- and 5 two-bedroom standard units, some with kitchens. 2 stories, exterior corridors. *Bath:* combo or shower only. **Parking:** on-site. **Terms:** 30 day cancellation notice-fee imposed, weekly rates available, package plans - seasonal. **Amenities:** CD players, voice mail, irons, hair dryers. **Leisure Activities:** fishing, beach chairs, umbrellas, gazebo, barbecue grill, deck/patio area. **Guest Services:** coin laundry. **Business Services:** fax. **Cards:** MC, VI. **Special Amenities:** free local telephone calls and free room upgrade (subject to availability with advanced reservations).

(See map p. 812)

TROPICAL BREEZE RESORT OF SIESTA KEY Phone: (941)349-1125 [39]
AAA [SAVE]
12/21-4/30	1P: $120-$350	2P: $120-$350	XP: $10	F14
12/1-12/20 & 5/1-11/30	1P: $69-$250	2P: $69-$250	XP: $10	F14

WWW **Location:** Just w of Ocean Blvd via Avenida Messina. Located in Siesta Village. 140 Columbus Blvd 34242.
Motel Fax: 941/349-0057. **Facility:** Designated smoking area. 44 units. 35 one- and 5 two-bedroom standard units, some with efficiencies, kitchens and/or whirlpools. 2 one- and 2 two-bedroom suites with kitchens. 1-2 stories, exterior corridors. *Bath:* combo or shower only. **Parking:** on-site. **Terms:** 14 day cancellation notice-fee imposed, weekly rates available, pets ($40 extra charge). **Amenities:** safes (fee), irons, hair dryers. **Pool(s):** 3 heated outdoor. **Leisure Activities:** whirlpools, sun deck, barbecue grills, beach chairs, yoga deck, tai chi, bicycles, shuffleboard. *Fee:* massage. **Guest Services:** coin laundry. **Business Services:** fax (fee). **Cards:** AX, DC, MC, VI. **Special Amenities:** free local telephone calls and free room upgrade (subject to availability with advanced reservations).

TROPICAL SHORES BEACH RESORT Phone: (941)349-3330 [46]
AAA [SAVE]
1/20-4/28	1P: $189-$395	2P: $189-$395	
12/1-1/19 & 4/29-11/30	1P: $99-$325	2P: $99-$325	

WWW **Location:** S of jct SR 72 on Midnight Pass Rd, just w. 6717 Sara Sea Cir 34242. Fax: 941/346-0025. **Facility:** Designated smoking area. 30 units. 24 one-bedroom standard units with efficiencies. 5 one- and 1 two-bedroom suites with kitchens, some with whirlpools. 2 stories, exterior corridors. *Bath:* combo or shower only. **Parking:** on-site. **Terms:** 21 day cancellation notice-fee imposed, weekly rates available. **Amenities:** voice mail. *Some:* irons, hair dryers. **Leisure Activities:** pool privileges, barbecue grills, shuffleboard, volleyball. **Guest Services:** coin laundry. **Business Services:** fax (fee). **Cards:** AX, DS, MC, VI. **Special Amenities:** early check-in/late check-out and free room upgrade (subject to availability with advanced reservations). *(See color ad p 817)*

TURTLE BEACH RESORT Phone: (941)349-4554 [50]
AAA [SAVE]
12/15-4/30	1P: $290	2P: $390	XP: $25	F18
12/1-12/14 & 5/1-11/30	1P: $200	2P: $300	XP: $25	F18

WWW **Location:** 2.8 mi s of jct SR 72 (Stickney Pt). 9049 Midnight Pass Rd 34242. Fax: 941/312-9034. **Facility:** Designated smoking area. 10 units. 4 one- and 6 two-bedroom standard units, some with efficiencies or kitchens. 1 story, exterior corridors. *Bath:* combo or shower only. **Parking:** on-site. **Terms:** 90 day cancellation notice-fee imposed, pets (10% surcharge). **Amenities:** hair dryers. *Some:* CD players, irons. **Pool(s):** heated outdoor. **Leisure Activities:** boating, canoeing, paddleboats, boat dock, fishing, docking fee, fishing equipment, kayak, 10 boat slips, barbecue grills, gazebo, bicycles. **Guest Services:** complimentary laundry. **Cards:** DS, MC, VI. **Special Amenities:** free local telephone calls and free newspaper.

FEE

------- WHERE TO DINE -------

CHEZ DANIEL **Lunch:** $6-$14 **Dinner:** $16-$24 Phone: 941/346-9228 [26]
WWW **Location:** On SR 758, just s of jct SR 72 (Stickney Point Rd); in Crest Plaza. 6621 Midnight Pass Rd 34242.
French **Hours:** 11:30 am-2 & 5-9 pm, Sat & Sun from 5 pm. Closed: Sun off season. **Features:** In this quaint cozy restaurant, the chef/owner prepares authentic French cuisine, such as canard a l'Orange, steak au poivre, filet mignon bordelaise and salmon grille au beurre blanc. Desserts are a treat. The staff is welcoming and French, giving pleasant service with a gracious feel. Smoke free premises. Casual dress; beer & wine only. **Parking:** on-site. **Cards:** AX, DC, MC, VI.

OPHELIA'S ON THE BAY **Dinner:** $15-$27 Phone: 941/349-2212 [29]
AAA **Location:** 2.8 mi s of jct SR 72 (Stickney Point Rd). 9105 Midnight Pass Rd 34242. **Hours:** 5 pm-10 pm. Closed 12/25. **Reservations:** suggested. **Features:** Set on Little Sarasota Bay, this intimate restaurant offers varied dishes of duckling, veal, lamb, pasta and seafood, most notably the house specialty pompano wrapped in parchment paper. The atmosphere is gracious, as are the attentive servers. Casual dress; cocktails. **Parking:** valet. **Cards:** AX, DC, DS, MC, VI.

THE SUMMERHOUSE RESTAURANT **Dinner:** $10-$25 Phone: 941/349-1100 [30]
WWW **Location:** 0.6 mi n of jct SR 72 (Stickney Pt). 6101 Midnight Pass Rd 34242. **Hours:** 5:30 pm-10 pm, Sat from 5 pm, Sun 10:30 am-2 & 5-10 pm; Sunday brunch seasonal hours. **Reservations:** suggested. **Features:** A lush, tropical landscape serves as the backdrop for this restaurant, and Continental cuisine is the menu theme. Look out over the manicured lawn from the outdoor dining deck. The abundant seasoning on the roast duck entree is spectacular. A light fare menu is available in the lounge. Dressy casual; cocktails; entertainment. **Parking:** valet. **Cards:** AX, CB, DC, DS, MC, VI.

TURTLES ON LITTLE SARASOTA BAY **Lunch:** $6-$9 **Dinner:** $7-$21 Phone: 941/346-2207 [32]
AAA **Location:** 2.7 mi s of jct Stickney Point Rd; opposite Turtle Beach. 8875 Midnight Pass Rd 34242. **Hours:** 11:30 am-10 pm. **Features:** Potato-crusted mahi mahi and snapper New Orleans are among exquisite seafood entrees at the tropical restaurant, which also serves chicken, pork and steak. Lots of windows overlook the bay for indoor dining, or enjoy the crisp air on the outdoor deck. Nightly entertainment is available in season. Casual dress; cocktails; entertainment. **Parking:** on-site. **Cards:** AX, DS, MC, VI.

VILLAGE CAFE **Lunch:** $4-$8 Phone: 941/349-2822 [27]
WWW **Location:** Center; in Siesta Village. 5133 Ocean Blvd 34242. **Hours:** 7 am-2:30 pm. Closed: 12/25. **Features:** Centrally located in a small strip mall in the village, the popular cafe is basically decorated and has a friendly wait staff. Menu options include many breakfast items, salads and sandwiches. Try the turkey club with its fresh crisp ingredients. Smoke free premises. Casual dress; beer & wine only. **Parking:** on-site. **Cards:** MC, VI.

SILVER SPRINGS

—— WHERE TO STAY ——

HOLIDAY INN-SILVER SPRINGS

All Year   1P: $65-$89   2P: $65-$89   **Phone:** (352)236-2575
XP: $6   F18

Small-scale Hotel

Location: SR 40. Located across from Silver Springs entrance. 5751 E Silver Springs Blvd 34488 (PO Box 156, 34489). **Fax:** 352/236-2575. **Facility:** 103 units. 101 one-bedroom standard units. 1 one- and 1 two-bedroom suites ($125-$195), some with whirlpools. 2 stories, exterior corridors. **Parking:** on-site. **Terms:** 15% service charge, small pets only ($50 deposit). **Amenities:** safes, irons, hair dryers. **Pool(s):** outdoor, wading. **Leisure Activities:** exercise room. **Guest Services:** valet laundry. **Business Services:** meeting rooms, fax (fee). **Cards:** AX, CB, DC, DS, JC, MC, VI.

SOME UNITS
FEE FEE

SUN PLAZA MOTEL
All Year   1P: $40-$70   2P: $40-$70   **Phone:** 352/236-2343
XP: $5

Motel

Location: SR 40 at jct CR 35. 5461 E Silver Springs Blvd 34488 (PO Box 216, 34489-0216). **Fax:** 352/236-1214. **Facility:** 47 one-bedroom standard units, some with efficiencies. 1 story, exterior corridors. *Bath:* combo or shower only. **Parking:** on-site. **Terms:** 7 day cancellation notice, weekly rates available, pets ($10 fee). **Pool(s):** outdoor. **Leisure Activities:** playground, shuffleboard. **Business Services:** fax. **Cards:** AX, DS, MC, VI. **Special Amenities: free continental breakfast.**

SOME UNITS
FEE

SOUTH DAYTONA pop. 13,177 (See map p. 279; index p. 281)

—— WHERE TO STAY ——

SUN RANCH MOTOR LODGE
4/16-11/30   1P: $35-$129   2P: $40-$140   **Phone:** (386)767-0661   76
12/1-4/15   1P: $29-$135   2P: $35-$140   XP: $5   F10
XP: $5   F10

Motel

Location: US 1, 1 mi s of SR 400. 2425 S Ridgewood Ave 32119. **Fax:** 386/761-9766. **Facility:** 22 one-bedroom standard units, some with efficiencies. 1 story, exterior corridors. *Bath:* combo or shower only. **Parking:** on-site. **Terms:** 15 day cancellation notice, weekly rates available. **Pool(s):** outdoor. **Leisure Activities:** shuffleboard. **Guest Services:** coin laundry.

SOME UNITS
FEE

SOUTH MIAMI —*See Miami-Miami Beach p. 557.*

LOOK FOR THE RED

*N*ext time you pore over a AAA TourBook® guide in search of a lodging establishment, take note of the vibrant red AAA logo, **SAVE** icon, and Diamond rating just under a select group of property names! These Official Appointment properties place a high value on the business they receive from dedicated AAA travelers and offer members great room rates*.

* See TourBook Navigator section, page 14, for complete details.

SOUTH PALM BEACH pop. 699   (See map p. 757; index p. 760)—See also PALM BEACH.

—— WHERE TO STAY ——

PALM BEACH HAWAIIAN OCEAN INN
Phone: 561/582-5631 **115**

♦♦♦ Motel

12/15-5/1	1P: $150	2P: $150	XP: $10 F18
12/1-12/14 & 5/2-11/30	1P: $90	2P: $90	XP: $10 F18

Location: On SR A1A, 1.5 mi s of jct SR 802. Located on the oceanfront. 3550 S Ocean Blvd 33480. **Fax:** 561/588-4563. **Facility:** 58 units. 50 one-bedroom standard units. 6 one- and 2 three-bedroom suites with kitchens. 2 stories (no elevator), exterior corridors. *Bath:* combo or shower only. **Parking:** on-site. **Amenities:** safes (fee), hair dryers. **Pool(s):** heated outdoor. **Guest Services:** coin laundry. **Business Services:** fax (fee). **Cards:** AX, CB, DC, DS, MC, VI.

SOME UNITS
(A$K) (S/D) (🍴) (Y) (🏊) (DATA PORT) (🖥) (🖨) / (⊠) (🖥)

SOUTH PASADENA —See Tampa Bay p. 937.

SPRING HILL pop. 69,078

—— WHERE TO STAY ——

HAMPTON INN
Phone: 352/684-5000

(SAVE)
♦♦♦ Small-scale Hotel

All Year [CP]	1P: $90-$160	2P: $95-$165 XP: $10 F18

Location: On US 19, 0.4 mi s of SR 574 (Spring Hill Rd). 1344 Commercial Way 34606. **Fax:** 352/684-5075. **Facility:** 72 one-bedroom standard units, some with whirlpools. 3 stories, interior corridors. *Bath:* combo or shower only. **Parking:** on-site. **Terms:** 3 day cancellation notice-fee imposed. **Amenities:** dual phone lines, voice mail, irons, hair dryers. **Pool(s):** outdoor. **Leisure Activities:** exercise room. **Business Services:** meeting rooms, fax. **Cards:** AX, CB, DC, DS, JC, MC, VI.

SOME UNITS
(S/D) (♿) (🏊) (🎬) (DATA PORT) (🖥) / (⊠) (🖥) /
FEE FEE

—— WHERE TO DINE ——

MICHAEL'S BISTRO
Lunch: $5-$8   Dinner: $6-$19   Phone: 352/683-8420

♦♦ Italian

Location: On US 19, 0.8 mi n of jct Spring Hill Rd (CR 574); in the Village at Timber Pines Shopping Center. 2410 Commercial Way 34608. **Hours:** 11 am-10 pm, Sat & Sun from noon. **Closed:** Mon. **Reservations:** suggested; for dinner. **Features:** Lovely touches—such as chandeliers, candlesticks, linen napkins and tablecloths—add romantic elegance to this small dining room. The outdoor cafe is an equally inviting spot to enjoy such entrees as chicken cordon bleu with roasted potatoes. Dressy casual; beer & wine only. **Parking:** on-site. **Cards:** DS, MC, VI.   (⊠)

STARKE pop. 5,593

—— WHERE TO STAY ——

BEST WESTERN MOTOR INN
Phone: (904)964-6744

(AAA) (SAVE)
♦♦♦ Small-scale Hotel

All Year [CP]	1P: $55-$65	2P: $60-$70 XP: $10 F12

Location: 1 mi n on US 301 from jct SR 100. 1290 N Temple Ave 32091. **Fax:** 904/964-3355. **Facility:** 51 one-bedroom standard units. 2 stories, exterior corridors. **Parking:** on-site. **Terms:** 30 day cancellation notice, pets ($11 extra charge). **Amenities:** irons, hair dryers. **Pool(s):** outdoor. **Business Services:** fax (fee) **Cards:** AX, CB, DC, DS, MC, VI. **Special Amenities:** free continental breakfast.

SOME UNITS
(S/D) (🛏) (🍴) (🏊) (🎬) (DATA PORT) (🖥) / (⊠) (🖥)

—— WHERE TO DINE ——

LAREDO MEXICAN RESTAURANT
Lunch: $4-$7   Dinner: $5-$10   Phone: 904/966-2323

♦♦ Southwest Mexican

Location: 0.5 mi n on US 301. 800 N Temple Ave 32091. **Hours:** 11 am-10 pm. Closed major holidays; also Sun. **Reservations:** suggested. **Features:** A must for the best food and service south of the border. Colorful flower beds and a bright, attractive decor create an inviting setting. Try the chalupa, a thick, toasty tortilla topped with hot beans, lettuce, tomato and a generous scoop of guacamole. Casual dress; cocktails. **Parking:** on-site. **Cards:** AX, DS, MC, VI.   (⊠)

STEINHATCHEE

WHERE TO STAY

STEINHATCHEE LANDING RESORT
8/16-11/30   1P: $120-$300   **Phone:** (352)498-3513

Cottage

Location: SR 51, 8 mi w of jct US 19/98. SR 51 N 32359 (PO Box 789). Fax: 352/498-2346. **Facility:** 28 units. 14 one- and 11 two-bedroom standard units. 3 three-bedroom suites. 2 stories, exterior corridors. **Parking:** on-site. **Terms:** open 8/16-11/30, check-in 4 pm, 2 night minimum stay - weekends, 14 day cancellation notice-fee imposed, pets ($100 deposit, in designated units). **Amenities:** irons, hair dryers. **Pool(s):** outdoor, heated outdoor. **Leisure Activities:** whirlpool, canoeing, boat dock, fishing, lighted tennis court, bicycles, playground, exercise room, basketball, volleyball. **Guest Services:** complimentary laundry. **Business Services:** meeting rooms, fax (fee). **Cards:** AX, DS, MC, VI.

SOME UNITS

STEINHATCHEE RIVER INN

			Phone: (352)498-4049
5/21-9/10	1P: $75-$90	2P: $75-$90	XP: $10
12/1-5/20 & 9/11-11/30	1P: $60-$70	2P: $60-$70	XP: $10

Motel

Location: Center. Located across from marina. 1111 Riverside Dr 32359 (PO Box 828). **Facility:** 17 one-bedroom standard units, some with kitchens. 2 stories, exterior corridors. **Parking:** on-site. **Terms:** 28 day cancellation notice-fee imposed, pets ($5 extra charge, small dogs only). **Pool(s):** outdoor. **Cards:** AX, DC, MC, VI.

SOME UNITS

THE SUNSET PLACE RESORT MOTEL

			Phone: 352/498-0860	
7/1-9/30	1P: $100	2P: $135	XP: $7	F6
12/1-6/30 & 10/1-11/30	1P: $75-$85	2P: $95-$105	XP: $7	F6

Small-scale Hotel

Location: SR 51, 12 mi w of jct US 98. 115 1st St SW 32359 (PO Box 975). Fax: 352/498-0840. **Facility:** 19 units. 10 one- and 9 two-bedroom standard units with kitchens. 3 stories (no elevator), exterior corridors. **Parking:** on-site. **Terms:** 3 night minimum stay - weekends, 14 day cancellation notice-fee imposed, package plans, small pets only ($10 extra charge, in designated units). **Pool(s):** outdoor. **Leisure Activities:** boat dock. Fee: boat tie-up at dock. **Business Services:** fax. **Cards:** AX, CB, DC, DS, JC, MC, VI. **Special Amenities:** early check-in/late check-out and free local telephone calls.

SOME UNITS

—————— **WHERE TO DINE** ——————

ROY'S

Spanish

Lunch: $6-$14 **Dinner:** $10-$18 **Phone:** 352/498-5000
Location: Just w of town center on gulf. Hwy 51 Jct 361 32359. **Hours:** 11 am-9 pm. **Closed:** 12/24, 12/25.
Features: A lovely gulf view and superbly prepared food explain why this restaurant has been serving for 30 years. Here you will find the tastiest shrimp in the region along with other ocean fare that is fried, broiled or steamed, and served with great hushpuppies. Casual dress. **Parking:** on-site. **Cards:** MC, VI.

STUART pop. 14,633

—————— **WHERE TO STAY** ——————

HOLIDAY INN-DOWNTOWN **Phone:** (772)287-6200

2/1-3/31 1P: $149-$230 2P: $149-$230
12/1-11/31 & 4/1-11/30 1P: $99-$170 2P: $99-$170
Small-scale Hotel **Location:** On US 1, 0.5 mi s of jct SR 76. 1209 S Federal Hwy 34994 (PO Box 566-34997). **Fax:** 772/600-2002. **Facility:** 119 units. 118 one-bedroom standard units. 1 one-bedroom suite with whirlpool. 2 stories, exterior corridors. *Bath:* combo or shower only. **Parking:** on-site. **Amenities:** video games (fee), voice mail, irons, hair dryers. **Pool(s):** heated outdoor. **Leisure Activities:** sauna, exercise room. **Guest Services:** valet and coin laundry. **Business Services:** meeting rooms, fax (fee). **Cards:** AX, DC, DS, MC, VI. *(See color ad opposite inside back cover)*

SOME UNITS
FEE

HOWARD JOHNSON HOTEL **Phone:** (772)287-3171

1/1-4/1 1P: $85-$90
4/2-11/30 1P: $60-$65
12/1-12/31 1P: $55
Location: On US 1, just s of jct SR 76. 950 S Federal Hwy 34994. **Fax:** 772/220-3594. **Facility:** Designated
Small-scale Hotel smoking area. 81 one-bedroom standard units. 2 stories, interior corridors. *Some:* irons, hair dryers. **Dining:** 11 am-8 pm, Sun from 8 am, cocktails. **Pool(s):** outdoor. **Guest Services:** valet and coin laundry. **Business Services:** meeting rooms. **Cards:** AX, CB, DC, DS, MC, VI. **Special Amenities:** free continental breakfast and free room upgrade (subject to availability with advanced reservations).

SOME UNITS
FEE

HUTCHINSON ISLAND MARRIOTT BEACH RESORT & MARINA **Phone:** (772)225-3700

1/13-4/26 1P: $199-$259 2P: $199-$259
12/1-1/12 & 4/27-6/1 1P: $159-$219 2P: $159-$219
6/2-11/30 1P: $99-$179 2P: $99-$179
Resort **Location:** 4 mi ne on SR A1A, on south end of Hutchinson Island at east end of causeway. 555 NE Ocean Blvd 34996.
Large-scale Hotel **Fax:** 772/225-0003. **Facility:** This plantation-style hotel on the river features large hotel-room units as well as waterfront housekeeping apartments with balconies. 292 units. 222 one-bedroom standard units, some with efficiencies. 58 one- and 12 two-bedroom suites ($219-$399), some with efficiencies, kitchens and/or whirlpools. 4 stories, interior/exterior corridors. *Bath:* combo or shower only. **Parking:** on-site and valet. **Terms:** 3 day cancellation notice-fee imposed, pets ($75 fee). **Amenities:** voice mail, irons, hair dryers. **Dining:** Scalawags Restaurant, see separate listing. **Pool(s):** 3 heated outdoor. **Leisure Activities:** whirlpools, fishing, recreation programs, playground, exercise room, spa, volleyball. *Fee:* marina, waterskiing, charter fishing, golf-18 holes, 18 tennis courts (5 lighted), bicycles. **Guest Services:** gift shop, valet and coin laundry, area transportation. **Business Services:** conference facilities, business center. **Cards:** AX, DC, DS, MC, VI.

FEE
SOME UNITS

PIRATE'S COVE RESORT & MARINA **Phone:** 772/287-2500

12/1-4/20 1P: $150-$175 XP: $15 F18
4/21-6/1 & 11/1-11/30 1P: $130-$150 XP: $15 F18
6/2-10/31 1P: $110-$130 XP: $15 F18
Small-scale Hotel **Location:** 0.3 mi e of SR A1A. 4307 SE Bayview St 34997. **Fax:** 772/220-2704. **Facility:** 50 one-bedroom standard units. 3-4 stories, exterior corridors. *Bath:* combo or shower only. **Amenities:** voice mail, irons, hair dryers. **Dining:** Pirate's Loft Restaurant, see separate listing, entertainment. **Pool(s):** heated outdoor. **Leisure Activities:** *Fee:* marina, fishing, charter fishing, rack storage for boats. **Guest Services:** gift shop, valet and coin laundry. **Business Services:** meeting rooms, fax (fee). **Cards:** AX, CB, DC, DS, MC, VI. **Special Amenities:** free room upgrade and preferred room (each subject to availability with advanced reservations).

SOME UNITS
FEE

PLANTATION BEACH CLUB AT INDIAN RIVER PLANTATION **Phone:** (772)225-0074

1/31-4/24 2P: $285-$320
12/1-1/2 2P: $255-$290
1/3-1/30 2P: $210-$245
Condominium 4/25-11/30 2P: $180-$230
Location: 0.5 mi se of SR A1A, via McArthur Blvd, just ne on NE Plantation Rd to NE Tradewind Lane, follow signs. Located in the Indian River Plantation Resort. 329 NE Tradewind Lane 34996. **Fax:** 772/225-6318. **Facility:** 30 units. 10 one- and 20 two-bedroom suites with kitchens and whirlpools. 1-4 stories, exterior corridors. **Parking:** on-site. **Terms:** 2 night minimum stay, 30 day cancellation notice, weekly rates available. **Amenities:** video library (fee), CD players, irons. **Pool(s):** heated outdoor. **Leisure Activities:** sauna, whirlpool, fishing, exercise room. **Guest Services:** complimentary laundry, area transportation. **Business Services:** fax (fee). **Cards:** AX, DS, MC, VI. *(See color ad p 805)*

RAMADA INN
Phone: (772)287-6900

	2/1-4/15 [ECP]	1P: $104	2P: $104	XP: $8	F18
	1/1-1/31 [ECP]	1P: $88	2P: $88	XP: $8	F18
Small-scale Hotel	4/16-11/30 [ECP]	1P: $72	2P: $72	XP: $8	F18
	12/1-12/31 [ECP]	1P: $70	2P: $70	XP: $8	F18

Location: US 1, 0.5 mi s of jct SR 76. 1200 S Federal Hwy 34994. Fax: 772/286-8188. **Facility:** 118 units. 114 one-bedroom standard units, some with whirlpools. 4 one-bedroom suites. 2 stories, exterior corridors. *Bath:* combo or shower only. **Parking:** on-site. **Terms:** check-in 4 pm, 7 day cancellation notice. **Amenities:** voice mail, irons, hair dryers. **Pool(s):** heated outdoor. **Leisure Activities:** Fee: game room. **Guest Services:** valet and coin laundry. **Business Services:** meeting rooms, fax (fee). **Cards:** AX, CB, DC, DS, MC, VI.

SOME UNITS

[ASK] [S/D] [🍴] [Y] [👤] [♪] [🏊] [🎣] [DATA PORT] [💻] / [✕] [📶] [🛄] /

SUBURBAN LODGE-STUART
Phone: (772)286-1010

	12/1-4/15	1P: $70-$100	2P: $70-$100	XP: $10	F17
	4/16-11/30	1P: $65-$75	2P: $65-$75	XP: $10	F17

Location: On US 1, 2 mi s of jct SR 76. 1900 S Federal Hwy 34994. Fax: 772/286-6488. **Facility:** 126 one-bedroom standard units with efficiencies. 3 stories, exterior corridors. *Bath:* combo or shower only. **Parking:** on-site. **Terms:** cancellation fee imposed, weekly rates available, package plans - seasonal, weekends. **Amenities:** voice mail. **Guest Services:** coin laundry. **Business Services:** fax (fee). **Cards:** AX, CB, DC, DS, MC, VI. **Special Amenities:** early check-in/late check-out and free room upgrade (subject to availability with advanced reservations). *(See color ad p 596)*

SOME UNITS

[S/D] [👤] [🎣] [DATA PORT] [🛄] [📶] [💻] / [✕] /

—— WHERE TO DINE ——

DON RAMON RESTAURANT
Lunch: $4-$7   **Dinner:** $6-$19   **Phone:** 772/221-7711

Cuban

Location: Jct of SR 76 and Monterey Rd. 2220 SE Ocean Blvd 34996. **Hours:** 11:30 am-9 pm, Fri & Sat-10 pm. **Features:** Warm ambience fills the dining room and the airy patio of the comfortable restaurant, a favorite with the locals. On the enticing menu are chicken, fish and shredded pork dishes, as well as sweet fried plantains and black beans with rice. Casual dress; cocktails. **Parking:** on-site. **Cards:** AX, DC, DS, MC, VI.

[Y] [✕]

THE FLAGLER GRILL
Dinner: $14-$25   **Phone:** 772/221-9517

Regional American

Location: Just e of US 1; in historic downtown area. 47 SW Flagler Ave 34994. **Hours:** 5 pm-9:30 pm. Closed: 1/1, 12/25. **Reservations:** suggested. **Features:** In a turn-of-the-20th-century building, the cozy, friendly restaurant is noted for excellent service and innovative cuisine. Fresh ingredients and international seasonings contribute to the food's great taste; a well-balanced wine list enhances it. Smoke free premises. Casual dress; cocktails. **Parking:** street. **Cards:** AX, DS, MC, VI.

[Y] [✕]

MARIO'S ITALIAN RESTAURANT
Dinner: $6-$15   **Phone:** 772/283-6660

Italian

Location: On US 1, 1 mi s of jct SR 76; in Federal Plaza Shops. 1924 S Federal Hwy 34994. **Hours:** 3 pm-10 pm. Closed major holidays; also Mon & 6/26-7/9. **Features:** Although the decor is plain and simple, the food is far from it. The owner/chef shares time-tested family recipes and freshly baked desserts, such as cheesecake, tiramisu and cannoli. Generous portions and a friendly staff add to the experience. Casual dress; beer & wine only. **Parking:** on-site. **Cards:** AX, MC, VI.

[✕]

PIRATE'S LOFT RESTAURANT
Lunch: $5-$12   **Dinner:** $7-$20   **Phone:** 772/223-5048

Seafood

Location: 0.3 mi e of SR A1A; in Pirate's Cove Resort & Marina. 4307 SE Bayview St 34997. **Hours:** 7:30 am-9 pm, Thurs-10 pm, Fri & Sat 7 am-10 pm, Sun 7 am-9 pm. **Reservations:** suggested. **Features:** Fish nets and nautical decorations set the mood in the restaurant, which overlooks the marina. The menu features surf and turf specials and such specialties as the seafood sampler, which includes crab cake, scallops, shrimp and the fresh catch. Casual dress; cocktails; entertainment. **Parking:** on-site. **Cards:** AX, CB, DC, DS, MC, VI.

[Y] [✕]

RIVERWALK CAFE AND RAW BAR
Lunch: $5-$9   **Dinner:** $11-$20   **Phone:** 772/221-1511

Regional American

Location: Just e of US 1; in historic downtown area, close to the river. 201 SW St Lucie Ave 34994. **Hours:** 11:30 am-2 & 5:30-9 pm, Fri & Sat-10 pm. Closed major holidays; also Sun. **Reservations:** accepted. **Features:** Although the menu changes regularly at the small, gourmet cafe, diners can always count on innovative, well-presented cuisine that samples intricate flavors from around the world. Created in the bistro style, the restaurant bustles with activity. Smoke free premises. Casual dress; beer & wine only. **Parking:** street. **Cards:** AX, DS, MC, VI.

[✕]

SCALAWAGS RESTAURANT
Dinner: $19-$29   **Phone:** 772/225-6818

American

Location: 4 mi ne on SR A1A, on south end of Hutchinson Island at east end of causeway; in Hutchinson Island Marriott Beach Resort & Marina. 555 NE Ocean Blvd 34996. **Hours:** 7 am-noon & 5-10 pm. **Reservations:** suggested. **Features:** Overlooking a marina on the Intracoastal Waterway, the breezy restaurant exudes an island feel, with many tropical plants, brass lanterns and paddle fans. Specialties include the Mediterranean crusted rack of lamb and the decadent chocolate cake. Casual dress; cocktails. **Parking:** on-site. **Cards:** AX, CB, DC, DS, MC, VI.

[Y] [✕]

THE TWISTED GRILLE
Lunch: $7-$13   **Dinner:** $9-$21   **Phone:** 772/287-1140

American

Location: At jct with Monteray Rd; in Smithfield Plaza. 2111 E Ocean Blvd 34996. **Hours:** 11:30 am-2:30 & 4:30-9:30 pm, Sat from 4:30 pm. Closed: 11/27, 12/25; also Sun. **Reservations:** suggested. **Features:** In a plaza with plenty of parking, this comfortably decorated restaurant offers a variety of contemporary American dishes, each with its own "twist." Sauteed shrimp crab cakes with Creole-spiced mustard sauce are tasty. Servings are ample. Casual dress; cocktails. **Parking:** on-site. **Cards:** AX, CB, DC, DS, MC, VI.

[✕]

——— *The following restaurant has not been evaluated by AAA* ———
but is listed for your information only.

THE ASHLEY   **Phone:** 772/221-9476
[fyi]   Not evaluated. **Location:** Jct Osceola St and St. Lucie Ave; downtown historic district. 61 SW Oceola St.
Features: In a historic, circa 1900 building, the restaurant is eclectic in menu and decor and offers dishes
at moderate prices.

SUN CITY CENTER —*See Tampa Bay p. 937.*

SUNNY ISLES —*See Miami-Miami Beach p. 558.*

SUNRISE —*See Fort Lauderdale p. 410.*

SURFSIDE —*See Miami-Miami Beach p. 559.*

TALLAHASSEE pop. 150,624

——— **WHERE TO STAY** ———

BEST WESTERN SEMINOLE INN   **Phone:** 850/656-2938
[AAA] [SAVE]   All Year   1P: $49-$120   2P: $55-$130   XP: $5   F12
◆◆◆◆   **Location:** I-10, exit 31A, just w on US 90. Located in quiet, rural surroundings. 6737 Mahan Dr 32308.
Fax: 850/656-6380. **Facility:** 60 one-bedroom standard units. 2 stories, exterior corridors. **Parking:** on-site.
Motel   **Terms:** 2 night minimum stay, cancellation fee imposed, [ECP] meal plan available, pets ($5 extra charge).
Amenities: irons, hair dryers. **Pool(s):** outdoor. **Guest Services:** coin laundry. **Business Services:** meeting
rooms, business center. **Cards:** AX, DC, DS, MC, VI. **Special Amenities:** early check-in/late check-out
and free continental breakfast.

SOME UNITS

[icons] /[X]/

CABOT LODGE-NORTH   **Phone:** (850)386-8880
◆◆◆◆   All Year [ECP]   1P: $72-$78   2P: $78-$84   XP: $6   F18
Location: I-10, exit 199, 0.3 mi s on US 27. Located in a quiet area. 2735 N Monroe St 32303. Fax: 850/386-4254.
Small-scale Hotel   **Facility:** 160 one-bedroom standard units. 2 stories, exterior corridors. **Parking:** on-site. **Amenities:** voice
mail, irons, hair dryers. **Pool(s):** outdoor. **Guest Services:** complimentary evening beverages, valet laundry.
Business Services: fax. **Cards:** AX, CB, DC, DS, MC, VI.

SOME UNITS

[ASK] [icons] /[X] [icons]

CABOT LODGE-THOMASVILLE RD

Phone: (850)386-7500

▼▼▼

Small-scale Hotel

All Year   1P: $88-$106   2P: $98-$116
Location: I-10, exit 203, 0.4 mi se. 1653 Raymond Diehl Rd 32308. Fax: 850/386-1136. **Facility:** 135 units. 134 one-bedroom standard units. 1 one-bedroom suite ($175) with whirlpool. 5 stories, interior corridors. *Bath:* combo or shower only. **Parking:** on-site. **Terms:** [ECP] meal plan available. **Amenities:** voice mail, irons, hair dryers. *Some:* dual phone lines. **Pool(s):** outdoor. **Guest Services:** coin laundry. **Business Services:** meeting rooms, fax. **Cards:** AX, CB, DC, DS, MC, VI.

SOME UNITS
(ASK) (SO) (TI+) (&M) (⊘) (≈) (⊞⁺) (⚓) (DATA PORT) / (☒) (VCR) (⊟) (⛶) (▣) /

CALHOUN STREET INN BED AND BREAKFAST

Phone: 850/425-5095

▼▼▼

Historic Bed
& Breakfast

12/1-4/29 & 9/21-11/30   1P: $65-$95   2P: $65-$95   XP: $20
Location: Corner of Calhoun and E Georgia, parking off Georgia St; downtown historic district. Located in a residential area. 525 N Calhoun St 32301. Fax: 207/863-4866. **Facility:** This 1907 Colonial Revival home is in a tree-lined area within walking distance of a park with recreational facilities. Designated smoking area. 4 one-bedroom standard units. 2 stories, interior corridors. *Bath:* combo or shower only. **Parking:** on-site. **Terms:** open 12/1-4/29 & 9/21-11/30, age restrictions may apply, [BP] meal plan available. **Amenities:** hair dryers. **Cards:** AX, DS, MC, VI. (☒)

COMFORT INN

Phone: (850)562-7200

SAVE

▼▼▼

Small-scale Hotel

All Year   1P: $49-$129   2P: $49-$149   XP: $10   F17
Location: I-10, exit 199, just n. 2727 Graves Rd 32303. Fax: 850/562-6335. **Facility:** 100 one-bedroom standard units, some with whirlpools. 3 stories, interior corridors. *Bath:* combo or shower only. **Parking:** on-site. **Terms:** 3 day cancellation notice, [ECP] meal plan available. **Amenities:** voice mail, hair dryers. **Pool(s):** outdoor. **Guest Services:** valet and coin laundry. **Business Services:** fax (fee). **Cards:** AX, CB, DC, DS, JC, MC, VI. *(See color ad p 841)*

SOME UNITS
(SO) (TI+) (⊘) (≈) (⚓) (DATA PORT) / (☒) (⊟) (▣) /

COMFORT SUITES

Phone: (850)224-3200

(AAA) SAVE

▼▼▼

Small-scale Hotel

All Year   1P: $69-$170   2P: $69-$170   XP: $10   F18
Location: 1 mi se on US 27. 1026 Apalachee Pkwy 32301. Fax: 850/224-2206. **Facility:** 64 one-bedroom standard units, some with whirlpools. 3 stories, interior corridors. *Bath:* combo or shower only. **Parking:** on-site. **Amenities:** high-speed Internet, dual phone lines, voice mail, safes, irons, hair dryers. **Pool(s):** outdoor. **Leisure Activities:** exercise room. **Guest Services:** valet and coin laundry. **Business Services:** meeting rooms, business center. **Cards:** AX, CB, DC, DS, MC, VI. **Special Amenities:** free continental breakfast and free local telephone calls.

SOME UNITS
(SO) (TI+) (&M) (⊘) (≈) (⚓) (DATA PORT) (⊟) (⛶) (▣) / (☒) /

COURTYARD BY MARRIOTT

Phone: (850)222-8822

SAVE

▼▼▼

Small-scale Hotel

1/12-5/3   1P: $129
12/1-1/11 & 8/17-11/30   1P: $99-$109
5/4-8/16   1P: $79-$99
Location: 1 mi se on US 27. 1018 Apalachee Pkwy 32301. Fax: 850/561-0354. **Facility:** 154 units. 142 one-bedroom standard units. 12 one-bedroom suites ($127-$189). 3-4 stories, interior corridors. *Bath:* combo or shower only. **Parking:** on-site. **Amenities:** dual phone lines, voice mail, irons, hair dryers. **Pool(s):** heated outdoor. **Leisure Activities:** whirlpool, exercise room. **Guest Services:** coin laundry. **Business Services:** meeting rooms, PC, fax. **Cards:** AX, CB, DC, DS, JC, MC, VI. *(See ad below)*

SOME UNITS
(TI) (Y) (≈) (⚓) (DATA PORT) (▣) / (☒) (⊟) (⛶) /

DOUBLETREE HOTEL TALLAHASSEE

Phone: (850)224-5000

SAVE

▼▼▼

Large-scale Hotel

All Year   1P: $79-$159   2P: $79-$159
Location: Jct Adams St and Park Ave; downtown. Located opposite the courthouse. 101 S Adams St 32301. Fax: 850/513-9516. **Facility:** 243 units. 236 one-bedroom standard units. 7 one-bedroom suites ($200-$275). 16 stories, interior corridors. *Bath:* combo or shower only. **Parking:** on-site. **Terms:** check-in 3:30 pm, cancellation fee imposed. **Amenities:** voice mail, irons, hair dryers. **Pool(s):** outdoor. **Guest Services:** gift shop, valet laundry. **Business Services:** meeting rooms, business center. **Cards:** AX, CB, DC, DS, JC, MC, VI.

SOME UNITS
(SO) (TI) (Y) (&M) (⊘) (≈) (⊞⁺) (⚓) (DATA PORT) (▣) / (☒) (⊟) (⛶) /
FEE

ECONO LODGE

Phone: (850)385-6155

AAA SAVE

Motel

5/1-11/30	1P: $49-$100	2P: $54-$100	XP: $5 F18
12/1-4/30	1P: $46-$100	2P: $51-$100	XP: $5 F18

Location: I-10, exit 199, 0.5 mi s. 2681 N Monroe St 32303. Fax: 850/385-6155. **Facility:** 82 one-bedroom standard units. 2 stories, exterior corridors. **Parking:** on-site. **Terms:** 3 day cancellation notice, [CP] meal plan available, small pets only ($10 fee). **Cards:** AX, CB, DC, DS, MC, VI. **Special Amenities:** free continental breakfast.

SOME UNITS
FEE FEE

FAIRFIELD INN BY MARRIOTT

Phone: (850)562-8766

SAVE

Small-scale Hotel

8/16-11/30 [CP]	1P: $79-$189	2P: $79-$189
1/1-3/31 [CP]	1P: $79-$169	2P: $79-$169
12/1-12/31 & 4/1-8/15 [CP]	1P: $69-$169	2P: $69-$169

Location: I-10, exit 199, just n. 3211 N Monroe St 32303. Fax: 850/562-2194. **Facility:** 79 one-bedroom standard units. 3 stories, interior corridors. *Bath:* combo or shower only. **Parking:** on-site. **Amenities:** irons. **Pool(s):** heated indoor. **Leisure Activities:** whirlpool, exercise room. **Guest Services:** valet laundry. **Business Services:** fax. **Cards:** AX, DC, DS, MC, VI.

SOME UNITS

GOVERNORS INN

Phone: (850)681-6855

AAA SAVE

Classic Historic
Small-scale Hotel

All Year	1P: $139-$219	2P: $149-$229	XP: $10 F12

Location: Just n of state capitol; center. 209 S Adams St 32301. Fax: 850/222-3105. **Facility:** 40 units. 39 one-bedroom standard units. 1 one-bedroom suite ($159-$229) with whirlpool. 3 stories (no elevator), interior corridors. **Terms:** cancellation fee imposed, [CP] meal plan available. **Guest Services:** complimentary evening beverages: Mon-Sat, valet laundry. **Business Services:** meeting rooms, fax (fee). **Cards:** AX, DC, DS, MC, VI. **Special Amenities:** free continental breakfast and free newspaper.

SOME UNITS

GUESTHOUSE INTERNATIONAL INN

Phone: (850)386-8286

AAA SAVE

Motel

All Year [ECP]	1P: $42-$69	2P: $47-$74	XP: $5 F18

Location: I-10, exit 199, just s. 2801 N Monroe St 32303. Fax: 850/422-1074. **Facility:** 113 one-bedroom standard units, some with whirlpools. 2 stories, exterior corridors. *Bath:* combo or shower only. **Parking:** on-site. **Terms:** pets ($10 extra charge). **Pool(s):** outdoor. **Guest Services:** valet and coin laundry. **Business Services:** meeting rooms, fax. **Cards:** AX, CB, DC, DS, MC, VI. **Special Amenities:** free continental breakfast and free local telephone calls.

SOME UNITS

HAMPTON INN

Phone: (850)562-4300

SAVE

Small-scale Hotel

All Year [ECP]	1P: $69-$89	2P: $69-$99

Location: I-10, exit 199, just n. 3210 N Monroe St 32303. Fax: 850/562-6735. **Facility:** 93 units. 92 one-bedroom standard units. 1 one-bedroom suite with whirlpool. 2 stories, exterior corridors. *Bath:* combo or shower only. **Parking:** on-site. **Amenities:** voice mail, irons. **Pool(s):** outdoor. **Guest Services:** valet laundry. **Business Services:** fax (fee). **Cards:** AX, CB, DC, DS, JC, MC, VI.

SOME UNITS
FEE

HAMPTON INN TALLAHASSEE CENTRAL

Phone: 850/309-1300

SAVE

Small-scale Hotel

5/1-11/30	1P: $99-$109	2P: $109-$119	XP: $10 F18
1/31-4/30	1P: $119	2P: $119	XP: $10 F18
12/1-1/30	1P: $99	2P: $109	XP: $10 F18

Location: US 27, 3.5 mi s. 2979 Apalachee Pkwy 32301. Fax: 850/309-0111. **Facility:** 78 one-bedroom standard units. 4 stories, interior corridors. *Bath:* combo or shower only. **Parking:** on-site. **Terms:** 7 day cancellation notice. **Amenities:** dual phone lines, voice mail, irons. **Pool(s):** heated outdoor. **Leisure Activities:** exercise room. **Guest Services:** valet laundry. **Business Services:** meeting rooms, fax (fee). **Cards:** AX, CB, DC, DS, MC, VI.

SOME UNITS

HILTON GARDEN INN TALLAHASSEE

Phone: (850)385-3553

AAA SAVE

Small-scale Hotel

All Year	1P: $99-$169	2P: $104-$174	XP: $5 F

Location: I-10, exit 203, just s. 3333 Thomasville Rd 32308. Fax: 850/385-4242. **Facility:** 99 units. 93 one-bedroom standard units. 6 one-bedroom suites. 4 stories, interior corridors. *Bath:* combo or shower only. **Parking:** on-site. **Amenities:** dual phone lines, voice mail, irons, hair dryers. **Dining:** 6:30-10 am, to 11 am weekends. **Pool(s):** outdoor. **Leisure Activities:** whirlpool, exercise room. **Guest Services:** coin laundry. **Business Services:** meeting rooms, business center. **Special Amenities:** free local telephone calls.

SOME UNITS

HOLIDAY INN CAPITAL EAST

Phone: (850)877-3171

Small-scale Hotel

All Year	1P: $80-$99	2P: $80-$99

Location: 1.3 mi se on US 27. 1355 Apalachee Pkwy 32301. Fax: 850/942-2918. **Facility:** 149 one-bedroom standard units. 4 stories, interior corridors. *Bath:* combo or shower only. **Parking:** on-site. **Amenities:** dual phone lines, voice mail, irons, hair dryers. **Pool(s):** outdoor. **Leisure Activities:** exercise room. **Guest Services:** coin laundry, area transportation. **Business Services:** conference facilities, PC, fax. **Cards:** AX, CB, DC, DS, JC, MC, VI. *(See color ad opposite inside back cover)*

SOME UNITS

HOLIDAY INN-NORTHWEST

Phone: 850/562-2000

Property failed to provide current rates

Small-scale Hotel

Location: I-10, exit 199, just n. 2714 Graves Rd 32303. Fax: 850/562-8519. **Facility:** 178 one-bedroom standard units. 2 stories, exterior corridors. **Parking:** on-site. **Amenities:** video games, voice mail, irons, hair dryers. **Pool(s):** outdoor. **Guest Services:** coin laundry. **Business Services:** meeting rooms, fax (fee). **Cards:** AX, CB, DC, DS, JC, MC, VI. *(See color ad below & opposite inside back cover)*

SOME UNITS

HOLIDAY INN SELECT DOWNTOWN CAPITAL HILL

Phone: (850)222-9555

	1P	2P	XP	
2/1-4/30	1P: $109-$149	2P: $109-$149	XP: $10	F13
9/1-11/30	1P: $99-$149	2P: $99-$149	XP: $10	F13
12/1-1/31 & 5/1-8/31	1P: $89-$129	2P: $89-$129	XP: $10	F13

Small-scale Hotel

Location: Just w of Monroe (US 27); downtown. 316 W Tennessee St 32301. Fax: 850/224-8410. **Facility:** 164 units. 153 one-bedroom standard units. 11 one-bedroom suites ($129-$199). 12 stories, interior corridors. *Bath:* combo or shower only. **Parking:** on-site. **Amenities:** video games, voice mail, irons, hair dryers. **Pool(s):** outdoor. **Guest Services:** valet laundry, area transportation. **Business Services:** conference facilities, business center. **Cards:** AX, DC, DS, MC, VI. *(See color ad opposite inside back cover)*

SOME UNITS

HOWARD JOHNSON EXPRESS INN

Phone: (850)386-5000

	1P	2P	XP	
All Year [ECP]	1P: $45-$65	2P: $45-$65	XP: $5	F16

Motel

Location: I-10, exit 199, 0.5 mi s. 2726 N Monroe St 32303. Fax: 850/386-5000. **Facility:** 51 one-bedroom standard units. 2 stories, exterior corridors. **Parking:** on-site. **Terms:** pets ($10 extra charge). **Amenities:** hair dryers. **Pool(s):** small outdoor. **Guest Services:** coin laundry. **Business Services:** fax (fee). **Cards:** AX, CB, DC, DS, MC, VI. **Special Amenities:** free continental breakfast and free local telephone calls.

SOME UNITS

LA QUINTA INN-NORTH

Phone: (850)385-7172

	1P	2P	XP
1/22-5/4	1P: $70-$75	2P: $76-$81	XP: $6
12/1-1/21 & 5/5-11/30	1P: $60-$70	2P: $66-$76	XP: $6

Small-scale Hotel

Location: I-10, exit 199, just s on US 27, east side. 2905 N Monroe St 32303-3636. Fax: 850/422-2463. **Facility:** 154 units. 153 one-bedroom standard units. 1 one-bedroom suite ($109-$179). 2-3 stories, exterior corridors. **Parking:** on-site. **Terms:** [ECP] meal plan available, small pets only. **Amenities:** video games, voice mail, irons, hair dryers. **Pool(s):** outdoor. **Leisure Activities:** picnic area. **Guest Services:** valet laundry. **Business Services:** fax (fee). **Cards:** AX, CB, DC, DS, JC, MC, VI. **Special Amenities:** free continental breakfast and free local telephone calls.

SOME UNITS

LA QUINTA INN-TALLAHASSEE SOUTH

Phone: (850)878-5099

	1P	2P
1/22-5/4	1P: $66-$86	2P: $66-$86
12/1-1/21 & 5/5-11/30	1P: $66-$76	2P: $66-$76

Small-scale Hotel

Location: 3 mi se on US 27. 2850 Apalachee Pkwy 32301-3608. Fax: 850/878-6665. **Facility:** 134 units. 133 one-bedroom standard units. 1 one-bedroom suite ($119-$179). 3-4 stories, exterior corridors. *Bath:* combo or shower only. **Parking:** on-site. **Terms:** [ECP] meal plan available, small pets only. **Amenities:** video games, voice mail, irons, hair dryers. **Pool(s):** outdoor. **Guest Services:** valet laundry. **Business Services:** fax. **Cards:** AX, CB, DC, DS, JC, MC, VI. **Special Amenities:** free continental breakfast and free local telephone calls.

SOME UNITS

MICROTEL INN & SUITES

Phone: (850)562-3800

	1P	2P
All Year [ECP]	1P: $49-$75	2P: $49-$75

Small-scale Hotel

Location: I-10, exit 199, just n. 3216 N Monroe St 32303. Fax: 850/562-8611. **Facility:** 91 one-bedroom standard units. 3 stories, interior corridors. *Bath:* combo or shower only. **Parking:** on-site. **Terms:** weekly rates available. **Amenities:** voice mail. **Guest Services:** valet laundry. **Business Services:** fax (fee). **Cards:** AX, CB, DC, DS, MC, VI.

SOME UNITS

MOTEL 6 - 420

Phone: 850/668-2600

Motel

5/22-11/30	1P: $37-$47	2P: $43-$53	XP: $3	F17
12/1-5/21	1P: $36-$46	2P: $42-$52	XP: $3	F17

Location: I-10, exit 203, just n, w on Timberlane. Located next to the Market Square Shopping Center. 1481 Timberlane Rd 32308. Fax: 850/894-3104. **Facility:** 131 one-bedroom standard units. 2 stories, exterior corridors. *Bath:* combo or shower only. **Parking:** on-site. **Terms:** small pets only. **Pool(s):** outdoor. **Guest Services:** coin laundry. **Business Services:** fax (fee). **Cards:** AX, CB, DC, DS, MC, VI.

SOME UNITS

QUALITY INN & SUITES

Phone: (850)877-4437

Small-scale Hotel

1/1-4/30 [BP]	1P: $89	2P: $89
12/1-12/31 & 5/1-11/30 [BP]	1P: $79	2P: $79

Location: 2.2 mi s on US 27. 2020 Apalachee Pkwy 32301. Fax: 850/878-9964. **Facility:** 90 units. 80 one-bedroom standard units. 10 one-bedroom suites ($119-$189), some with whirlpools. 3 stories, interior corridors. *Bath:* combo or shower only. **Parking:** on-site. **Terms:** 7 day cancellation notice-fee imposed. **Amenities:** voice mail, irons, hair dryers. **Pool(s):** outdoor. **Guest Services:** complimentary evening beverages: Mon-Thurs, valet laundry. **Business Services:** meeting rooms, business center. **Cards:** AX, DC, DS, MC, VI. **Special Amenities: free continental breakfast and free newspaper.**

SOME UNITS

RADISSON HOTEL TALLAHASSEE

Phone: (850)224-6000

Large-scale Hotel

All Year	1P: $89	2P: $89

Location: 0.5 mi n of Capitol. 415 N Monroe St 32301. Fax: 850/222-0335. **Facility:** 119 one-bedroom standard units, some with whirlpools. 7 stories, interior corridors. **Terms:** cancellation fee imposed, 10% service charge. **Amenities:** voice mail, irons, hair dryers. **Leisure Activities:** sauna, exercise room. **Guest Services:** valet laundry, area transportation. **Business Services:** meeting rooms, PC, fax. **Cards:** AX, CB, DC, DS, JC, MC, VI.

SOME UNITS

FEE

RED ROOF INN

Phone: (850)385-7884

Motel

2/2-11/30	1P: $39-$49	2P: $44-$54	XP: $5	F18
12/1-2/1	1P: $36-$46	2P: $41-$51	XP: $5	F18

Location: I-10, exit 199, just off US 27. Located behind the Cracker Barrel. 2930 Hospitality St 32303. Fax: 850/386-8896. **Facility:** 108 one-bedroom standard units. 2 stories, exterior corridors. **Parking:** on-site. **Terms:** small pets only. **Amenities:** video games, voice mail. **Business Services:** fax (fee). **Cards:** AX, CB, DC, DS, MC, VI. **Special Amenities: free local telephone calls and free newspaper.**

SOME UNITS

SUPER 8 MOTEL

Phone: (850)386-8818

Small-scale Hotel

All Year [CP]	1P: $40-$60	2P: $40-$60	XP: $5 F16

Location: I-10, exit 199, 0.4 mi s on US 27. 2702 N Monroe St 32303. Fax: 850/386-8818. **Facility:** 61 one-bedroom standard units. 3 stories, interior corridors. **Parking:** on-site. **Terms:** pets ($10 fee). **Business Services:** fax. **Cards:** AX, CB, DC, DS, MC, VI. **Special Amenities: early check-in/late check-out and free local telephone calls.**

SOME UNITS

——— WHERE TO DINE ———

ALBERT'S PROVENCE

Lunch: $10-$18   **Dinner:** $25-$50   **Phone:** 850/894-9003

French

Location: I-10, exit 203, 0.3 mi n, then w; in Market Square. 1415 Timberlane Rd 32312. **Hours:** 11:30 am-2 & 6-9:30 pm, Fri-10 pm, Sat 6 pm-10 pm. Closed major holidays; also Sun. **Reservations:** suggested. **Features:** Enjoy classic French Mediterranean cuisine in an intimate dining room with well-trained service. Hailing from France, Albert delights diners with his fabulous lobster bisque and locals rave over his crab cakes a l'aubergine. Choose from a wide variety of wine, many available by the glass. The homemade pate changes daily. Always leave room to make a selection from the dessert tray. For those wishing a more casual experience, sit at the cafe de artiste to the rear of the dining room. Casual dress; cocktails. **Parking:** on-site. **Cards:** AX, DS, MC, VI.

BARNACLE BILL'S

Lunch: $4-$8   **Dinner:** $8-$16   **Phone:** 850/385-8734

American

Location: I-10, exit 199, 2 mi s. 1830 N Monroe St 32303. **Hours:** 11 am-11 pm, Fri & Sat-midnight. Closed: 11/27, 12/24, 12/25. **Features:** A popular local gathering spot, it features Florida seafood, pasta and an oyster bar with seasonal outdoor seating. The efficient wait staff excels at keeping guests happy. A close cousin of jambalaya, the shrimp skillet is a nice mix of rice and sausage. Casual dress; cocktails. **Parking:** on-site. **Cards:** AX, DC, DS, MC, VI.

CHEZ PIERRE

Lunch: $6-$12   **Dinner:** $10-$22   **Phone:** 850/222-0936

French

Location: Corner of Thomasville Rd and 6th Ave, just e of Monroe; center. 1215 Thomasville Rd 32303. **Hours:** 11 am-10 pm, Sun 9 am-9 pm. Closed major holidays. **Reservations:** suggested. **Features:** A romantic atmosphere popular with couples, the restaurant features such intimate touches as fresh flowers, French artwork and a deck bedecked with tiny white lights. Sample from creatively presented specials or from a sinful selection of pastries. Casual dress; cocktails. **Parking:** on-site. **Cards:** AX, DC, DS, MC, VI.

LORENZO'S STUDIO AND PIANO BAR

Dinner: $12-$18   **Phone:** 850/681-3622

Italian

Location: 0.5 mi n of jct US 90 and 27. 1001 N Monroe St 32303. **Hours:** 5 pm-11 pm. Closed: 11/27, 12/25; also Mon in summer and Sun. **Features:** House specialties feature large portions of hearty, delicious American-Italian favorites. A laid-back ambience and an opportunity for outdoor dining make this place special. The dessert list includes creme brulee, chocolate mousse and rich Key lime pie. Casual dress; cocktails. **Parking:** on-site. **Cards:** MC, VI.

LUCY HO'S ORIENTAL BISTRO   **Lunch:** $6-$9   **Dinner:** $6-$20   **Phone:** 850/893-4112
Chinese
Location: I-10, exit 203, 0.3 mi n on SR 61, just e on Capitol Circle Rd; in Oak Lake Village. 1700 Halstead Blvd 5 32308. **Hours:** 11 am-10 pm. Closed major holidays. **Features:** A professional staff will gladly help you select from the many entrees featured on this Chinese-Japanese menu. Crab ragoons are delicious with huge pieces of crab prepared with a light peanut oil. Large portions and a sushi bar will please every appetite. Casual dress; cocktails. **Parking:** on-site. **Cards:** AX, DC, DS, MC, VI.

NINO - A RESTAURANT   **Dinner:** $9-$18   **Phone:** 850/878-8141
Italian
Location: 7 mi e of the Capitol Building on US 27. 6497 Apalachee Pkwy 32311. **Hours:** 5 pm-10 pm. Closed major holidays; also Sun, Mon & week of July 4th. **Reservations:** suggested; weekends. **Features:** An intimate, cozy atmosphere derives from candlelit tables, lace-curtained windows and charming, old farmhouse decor. Enjoy an excellent variety of veal and seafood entrees, as well as tasty Bavarian favorites such as Wiener Schnitzel. Dressy casual; cocktails. **Parking:** on-site. **Cards:** AX, DC, DS, MC, VI.

SILVER SLIPPER   **Dinner:** $12-$25   **Phone:** 850/386-9366
Steak & Seafood
Location: I-10, exit 199, 1.3 mi s on US 27, 0.3 mi e on John Knox, just s. 531 Scotty's Ln 32303. **Hours:** 5 pm-11 pm. Closed: 1/1, 11/27, 12/25; also Sun. **Reservations:** suggested. **Features:** The restaurant has lots of history and once was a hot spot for an impressive list of celebrity and political guests. It's still a good place to enjoy steaks and seafood and delicious baklava. Low lighting and greenery sets the table for romance. Casual dress; cocktails; entertainment. **Parking:** on-site. **Cards:** AX, CB, DC, DS, MC, VI.

TALLEVAST

—— WHERE TO STAY ——

—— *The following lodging was either not evaluated or did not* ——
meet AAA rating requirements but is listed for your information only.

COMFORT SUITES   **Phone:** 941/360-2636
Motel
2/1-5/15 [ECP]   1P: $99-$139   2P: $109-$149   XP: $10
12/1-1/31 & 5/16-11/30 [ECP]   1P: $89-$109   2P: $99-$119   XP: $10
Too new to rate, opening scheduled for August 2002. **Location:** I-75 S, exit 40, to Cooper Creek Dr. 8470 Tourist Center Dr 34201. **Fax:** 941/360-1876 **Amenities:** coffeemakers, microwaves, refrigerators, pool. **Terms:** 3 day cancellation notice-fee imposed. **Cards:** AX, DC, DS, MC, VI.

TAMARAC —*See Fort Lauderdale p. 412.*

Destination Tampa Bay including St. Petersburg, Tampa and Clearwater

Tampa pop. 303,447
St. Petersburg pop. 248,232

Sunshine Skyway Bridge, St. Petersburg. A colorful sailboard mimics the elegant lines of the graceful Sunshine Skyway Bridge. (See listing page 216)

A lthough often considered as one, Tampa, St. Petersburg, Clearwater and their neighboring beach communities are distinct entities. Taken collectively or individually, though, these cities by the bay are liberally sprinkled with enticements.

W hile Tampa is more oriented toward business and industry, St. Petersburg and Clearwater and their sister sun-dappled beaches appeal to those seeking a resort atmosphere. The worlds of work and play come together in the Tampa Bay area, and the combination is hard to beat.

See Vicinity map page 846

Tampa Bay Lightning, Tampa. Even before this NHL team came to Tampa, Florida was known as the lightning capital of the world. (See mention page 221)

P laces included in this AAA Destination Area:

Apollo Beach...............896		
Belleair Bluffs.............896		
Brandon.....................896	North Redington	
Clearwater..................899	Beach.......................923	Safety Harbor..............930
Clearwater Beach.........906	Oldsmar.....................924	St. Pete Beach............931
Dade City..................915	Palm Harbor..............924	South Pasadena..........937
Dunedin.....................916	Pinellas Park..............925	Sun City Center..........937
Holiday......................917	Plant City..................926	Tarpon Springs............938
Indian Rocks Beach.....917	Port Richey................927	Temple Terrace............939
Indian Shores.............918	Redington Beach.........928	Tierra Verde...............939
Largo........................920	Redington Shores........928	Treasure Island...........940
Madeira Beach............920	Riverview..................928	Wesley Chapel.............945
New Port Richey........922	Ruskin......................928	Zephyrhills.................946

Mothers and cub, Busch Gardens Tampa Bay.
Busch Gardens is the purrfect place for close encounters of the furred kind. (See listing page 217)

Wesley Chapel
Dade City
Zephyrhills
Temple Terrace
Plant City
Brandon
Tampa
Riverview
Apollo Beach
St. Petersburg
Sun City Center
Ruskin

See Vicinity map page 856

Fire Fountain, downtown Tampa.
Modern skyscrapers soar above a representation of the ancient elements of fire, water and earth.

Boats in Clearwater Harbor, Clearwater.
Palm trees and masts compete for a share of the horizon.

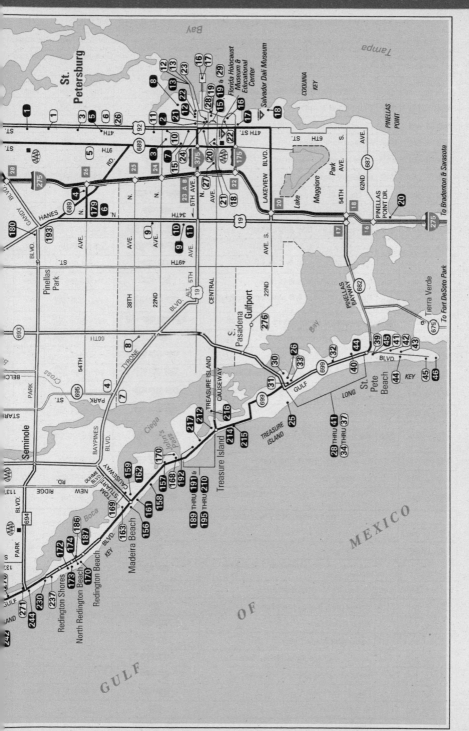

St. Petersburg, Tampa and Clearwater Area

This index helps you "spot" where approved accommodations and restaurants are located on the corresponding detailed maps. Lodging rate ranges are for comparison only and show the property's high season; rates are per night, unless only weekly (W) rates are available. Restaurant rate range is for dinner, unless only lunch (L) is served. Turn to the listing page for more detailed rate information and consult display ads for special promotions.

Spotter/Map Page Number	OA	ST. PETERSBURG - Lodgings	Diamond Rating	Rate Range High Season	Listing Page
1 / p. 846	AAA	Grant Motel & Apts	◈	$45-$60 SAVE	864
2 / p. 846		Dickens House Bed and Breakfast	◈◈◈	$120-$210	864
3 / p. 846	AAA	Terrace Park Suites	◈◈◈	$139 SAVE	867
4 / p. 846	AAA	Days Inn of St. Petersburg	◈◈	$66-$82 SAVE	864
5 / p. 846	AAA	Kentucky Motel	◈	$39-$53 SAVE	865
6 / p. 846		La Quinta Inn - see color ad p 881	◈◈◈	$59-$95	865
7 / p. 846	AAA	Empress Motel Apartments	◈◈	$49-$66 SAVE	864
8 / p. 846	AAA	Sunset Bay Inn Bed & Breakfast	◈◈◈◈	$150-$270 SAVE	867
9 / p. 846		Hampton Inn - see color ad p 864	◈◈	$109-$119	865
10 / p. 846		Comfort Inn & Suites	◈◈	$71-$91	863
11 / p. 846		Days Inn St. Pete Central	◈◈	$60-$66	864
12 / p. 846	AAA	Mansion House B & B and The Courtyard on Fifth	◈◈◈	$99-$220 SAVE	866
13 / p. 846	AAA	Renaissance Vinoy Resort & Golf Club	◈◈◈◈	$246-$319 SAVE	867
15 / p. 846	AAA	Colonial Bayfront Hotel	◈◈	$85-$160 SAVE	863
16 / p. 846		St. Petersburg Bayfront Hilton	◈◈◈	$143	867
17 / p. 846	AAA	Bayboro Inn & Hunt Room Bed & Breakfast	◈◈◈	$95-$125 SAVE	863
18 / p. 846	AAA	Bayboro House Bed & Breakfast On Old Tampa Bay	◈◈◈	$149-$229 SAVE	863
19 / p. 846	AAA	Pier Hotel	◈◈◈	$78-$188 SAVE	866
20 / p. 846	AAA	Holiday Inn SunSpree Resort Marina Cove - see color ad p 865, opposite inside back cover	◈◈◈	$109-$199 SAVE	865
21 / p. 846		Inn at the Bay Bed & Breakfast	◈◈◈	$119-$250	865
22 / p. 846		Lee Manor Inn	◈◈	$89-$139	866
23 / p. 846		Radisson Hotel and Conference Center - see ad p 866	◈◈◈	$139-$189	866
		ST. PETERSBURG - Restaurants			
1 / p. 846		Paisano's Pizza & Pasta	◈	$7-$18	869
2 / p. 846		Crab Shack	◈	$5-$14	868
3 / p. 846		Red Mesa Regional Mexican & Southwest Cuisine	◈◈	$7-$18	869
4 / p. 846		Carmelita's Mexican Restaurant	◈◈	$8-$11	868
5 / p. 846		Casual Clam Seafood Restaurant	◈	$5-$11	868
6 / p. 846		Pepin Restaurant	◈◈	$14-$30	869
7 / p. 846		Saffron's at Jungle Prada	◈◈	$10-$20	870
8 / p. 846		Arigato Japanese Steak House Restaurant	◈◈	$11-$21	867
9 / p. 846		Texas Cattle Company	◈◈	$10-$30	870
10 / p. 846		The Limey's Pub	◈◈	$9-$18	869
11 / p. 846		El Cap	◈	$3-$7	868
12 / p. 846		Marchand's Bar & Grill	◈◈◈	$11-$29	869

Spotter/Map Page Number	OA	ST. PETERSBURG - Restaurants (continued)	Diamond Rating	Rate Range High Season	Listing Page
13 / p. 846		Terrace Room	◆◆◆	$11-$29	870
15 / p. 846		4th Street Shrimp Store	◆	$4-$21	867
16 / p. 846		Cafe Lido	◆◆	$9-$18	868
17 / p. 846		Columbia Restaurant	◆◆	$14-$22	868
18 / p. 846		Ovo Cafe	◆◆◆	$9-$16	869
19 / p. 846		Moon Under Water	◆◆	$7-$17	869
20 / p. 846		The Keystone Club	◆◆	$12-$21	869
21 / p. 846		Redwoods Restaurant	◆◆◆	$17-$29	869
22 / p. 846		Jo Jo's in Citta Restaurant, Piano Bar & Lounge	◆◆	$8-$17	869
23 / p. 846		Dish Baywalk	◆◆	$13-$18	868
24 / p. 846		Gratzzi Ristorante	◆◆	$12-$26	868
26 / p. 846		Fred's Famous Bar-B-Que and Brewery	◆◆	$5-$17	868
27 / p. 846		Grand Finale	◆◆◆	$12-$22	868
28 / p. 846		The Garden-A Mediterranean Bistro	◆◆	$7-$18	868
29 / p. 846		Bertoni Italian Restaurant & Bar	◆◆	$10-$21	867
ST. PETE BEACH - Lodgings					
25 / p. 846	AAA	**Lamara Motel Apartments**	◆◆	$70-$80 [SAVE]	933
26 / p. 846	AAA	**Pasa Tiempo Bed & Breakfast**	◆◆◆	$125-$200 [SAVE]	933
28 / p. 846	AAA	**Beach Haven**	◆◆	$90-$147 [SAVE]	931
29 / p. 846	AAA	**Alden Beach Resort - see color ad p 931**	◆◆◆	$187-$274 [SAVE]	931
30 / p. 846	AAA	**Beach House Suites By The Don Cesar**	◆◆◆	$272-$419 [SAVE]	931
31 / p. 846		Travelodge St. Pete Beach - see color ad p 933	◆◆	$126-$137	936
32 / p. 846		Caprice Condominiums on St. Pete Beach	◆◆	$1075-$1450(W)	932
33 / p. 846	AAA	**Long Key Beach Resort**	◆	$122-$131 [SAVE]	933
34 / p. 846	AAA	**Best Western Beachfront Resort**	◆◆◆	$168-$208 [SAVE]	932
35 / p. 846		Howard Johnson Lodge St Pete Beach Resort Inn	◆◆	$115-$140	932
36 / p. 846	AAA	**TradeWinds Sandpiper Hotel & Suites - see color ad p 935**	◆◆◆	$159-$245 [SAVE]	934
37 / p. 846	AAA	**TradeWinds Island Grand Beach Resort - see color ad p 935**	◆◆◆◆	$209-$359 [SAVE]	934
38 / p. 846	AAA	**Plaza Beach Motel - see color ad p 943**	◆◆	$89-$120 [SAVE]	934
39 / p. 846		Holiday Inn Hotel & Suites Beachfront Resort & Conference Center - see color ad opposite inside back cover	◆◆◆	$168-$228	932
40 / p. 846	AAA	**Palm Crest Resort Motel**	◆◆	$89-$132 [SAVE]	933
41 / p. 846	AAA	**TradeWinds Sirata Beach Resort - see color ad p 935**	◆◆◆	$175-$317 [SAVE]	934
44 / p. 846		Ritz Motel	◆◆	$60-$90	934
45 / p. 846	AAA	**The Don CeSar Beach Resort & Spa**	◆◆◆◆	$282-$2245 [SAVE]	932
46 / p. 846	AAA	**Island's End Resort**	◆◆	$171-$259 [SAVE]	932
ST. PETE BEACH - Restaurants					
30 / p. 846		Johnny Leverock's on the Beach	◆◆	$7-$19	936
31 / p. 846		La Croisette Family Restaurant	◆	$4-$7(L)	936

Spotter/Map Page Number	OA	ST. PETE BEACH - Restaurants (continued)	Diamond Rating	Rate Range High Season	Listing Page
32 / p. 846		Skidder's Restaurant	◆◆	$6-$24	937
33 / p. 846		Der Eisenhut	◆◆	$9-$15	936
34 / p. 846		Aunt Heidi's Italian Restaurant	◆◆	$6-$12	936
35 / p. 846		Starlite Diner	◆	$4-$12	937
36 / p. 846		Palm Court Restaurant	◆◆◆	$16-$25	936
37 / p. 846		The Sloppy Pelican	◆	$5-$12	937
39 / p. 846		Sea Porch Cafe	◆◆◆	$9-$21	937
40 / p. 846		Silas Dent's Steakhouse	◆◆	$8-$21	937
41 / p. 846		Maritana Grille	◆◆◆◆	$20-$33	936
42 / p. 846	AAA	**Sea Critters Cafe**	◆◆	$6-$17	936
43 / p. 846	AAA	**The Wharf Seafood Restaurant**	◆◆	$5-$16	937
44 / p. 846		The Seahorse Tavern & Restaurant	◆	$5-$11(L)	936
45 / p. 846		Hurricane Seafood Restaurant	◆◆	$8-$20	936
		CLEARWATER - Lodgings			
52 / p. 846		Hampton Inn-Clearwater/St. Petersburg Airport	◆◆◆	$89-$99	901
53 / p. 846		Ramada Inn Countryside	◆◆	$79-$99	902
54 / p. 846	AAA	**Bay Queen Motel - see color ad p 906**	◆◆	$60-$80 SAVE	899
55 / p. 846	AAA	**Econo Lodge Clearwater Central**	◆◆	$72 SAVE	901
56 / p. 846	AAA	**Clearwater Central-Best Western**	◆◆	$80 SAVE	900
57 / p. 846		Super 8 of Clearwater	◆◆	$59	903
59 / p. 846		Holiday Inn Hotel & Suites Clearwater Central - see color ad opposite inside back cover	◆◆◆	$98	902
60 / p. 846		Hampton Inn Clearwater Central	◆◆◆	$81-$98	901
61 / p. 846		Days Inn-Clearwater Central	◆◆	$55-$75	900
62 / p. 846		Quality Inn Clearwater Central	◆◆◆	$69-$125	902
64 / p. 846	AAA	**Belleview Biltmore Resort & Spa - see color ad p 900**	◆◆	$159-$169 SAVE	899
65 / p. 846		Candlewood Suites Clearwater-St Petersburg	◆◆◆	$89-$129	899
66 / p. 846		Holiday Inn Express	◆◆◆	$119-$149	901
67 / p. 846		Fairfield Inn & Suites Clearwater/Bayside	◆◆◆	$94	901
69 / p. 846		Holiday Inn Select-St. Pete/Clearwater Int'l Airport - see color ad opposite inside back cover	◆◆◆	$95-$125	902
70 / p. 846	AAA	**La Quinta Inn Clearwater-Airport - see color ad p 881**	◆◆◆	$69-$105 SAVE	902
71 / p. 846		Courtyard by Marriott - see ad p 873	◆◆◆	$99-$149	900
72 / p. 846		Residence Inn by Marriott	◆◆◆	$104-$170	903
73 / p. 846		Towne Place Suites by Marriott St. Petersburg/Clearwater	◆◆◆	$79-$159	903
74 / p. 846	AAA	**Days Inn-St. Pete/Clearwater Airport - see color ad p 901**	◆◆	$79-$94 SAVE	900
76 / p. 846	AAA	**Super 8 Clearwater/St. Petersburg Airport - see color ad p 903**	◆◆	$59-$99 SAVE	903
77 / p. 846		St. Petersburg/Clearwater Fairfield Inn by Marriott	◆◆◆	$89-$119	903
78 / p. 846		Homestead Studio Suites Hotel-Tampa/Clearwater	◆◆	$69-$89	902

Spotter/Map Page Number	OA	CLEARWATER - Lodgings (continued)	Diamond Rating	Rate Range High Season	Listing Page
79 / p. 846		Homewood Suites by Hilton	◆◆◆	$169-$229	902
80 / p. 846		Wingate Inn Clearwater	◆◆◆	$89-$109	904
		CLEARWATER - Restaurants			
48 / p. 846		Sam Seltzer's Steakhouse	◆◆	$11-$21	905
49 / p. 846		Harrison's Grill & Bar	◆◆	$7-$19	904
50 / p. 846		Durango Steakhouse	◆◆	$7-$18	904
52 / p. 846		First Watch	◆◆	$5-$7(L)	904
53 / p. 846		Oriental Super Buffet	◆	$10	905
54 / p. 846		Arigato Japanese Steak House	◆◆	$11-$21	904
55 / p. 846		Antonio's Pasta Grille	◆◆	$8-$22	904
57 / p. 846		Lenny's	◆	$4-$8(L)	905
58 / p. 846		Key West Grill	◆◆	$10-$30	905
59 / p. 846		Tio Pepe Restaurante	◆◆	$11-$30	905
60 / p. 846		Alfano's Restaurant	◆◆◆	$12-$25	904
61 / p. 846		Tucson's	◆◆	$9-$27	905
63 / p. 846		Joe's Crab Shack	◆◆	$10-$25	905
65 / p. 846		Jillian's On The Lake	◆◆	$10-$23	904
66 / p. 846		Sweetwater's Restaurant	◆◆	$6-$17	905
68 / p. 846		Primo's Pasta-Ribs	◆◆	$6-$16	905
69 / p. 846		G. Bellini's Ristorante & Bar	◆◆	$11-$27	904
70 / p. 846		Carmelita's Mexican Restaurant	◆◆	$5-$11	904
73 / p. 846		Roadhouse Grill	◆◆	$7-$19	905
		CLEARWATER BEACH - Lodgings			
86 / p. 846	AAA	**East Shore Resort Apartment Motel**	◆◆	$180-$260 SAVE	908
88 / p. 846	AAA	**Koli-Bree Motel/Apt**	◆	$82 SAVE	910
89 / p. 846	AAA	**Pelican Cove Resort on the Bay**	◆◆	$55-$89 SAVE	911
90 / p. 846	AAA	**Blue Jay Motel**	◆◆	$70-$102 SAVE	907
91 / p. 846	AAA	**Island Queen Resort Motel**	◆◆	$72-$96 SAVE	910
92 / p. 846		Brightwater Inn on the Bay	◆	$65	907
93 / p. 846	AAA	**New Yorker Motel**	◆◆	$78-$100 SAVE	911
94 / p. 846	AAA	**Echo Sails Motel & Apts**	◆◆	$60-$80 SAVE	908
95 / p. 846		Tropical Breeze Motel	◆◆	$85-$95	913
96 / p. 846	AAA	**Chart House Suites on Clearwater Bay**	◆◆◆	$110-$179 SAVE	908
98 / p. 846	AAA	**Howard Johnson Express Inn**	◆◆	$79-$129 SAVE	910
99 / p. 846		Sea Captain Resort On the Bay	◆◆	Failed to provide	912
100 / p. 846	AAA	**Bel Crest Beach Resort**	◆	$102-$175 SAVE	907
104 / p. 846	AAA	**Mannings On The Bay**	◆◆	$85-$165 SAVE	910
105 / p. 846	AAA	**The Dunes Motel**	◆	$79-$181 SAVE	908
106 / p. 846	AAA	**Hilton Clearwater Beach Resort - see color ad p 909**	◆◆◆	$129-$219 SAVE	909
109 / p. 846	AAA	**Falcon Apartment Motel**	◆	$85 SAVE	909

Spotter/Map Page Number	OA	CLEARWATER BEACH - Lodgings (continued)	Diamond Rating	Rate Range High Season	Listing Page
110 / p. 846	AAA	Shephard's Beach Resort - see color ad p 913	◆◆◆	$119-$179 SAVE	913
111 / p. 846		Beachouse	◆◆	$95-$185	906
112 / p. 846	AAA	Holiday Inn SunSpree Resort & Conference Center - see color ad p 910, opposite inside back cover	◆◆◆	$149-$199 SAVE	909
115 / p. 846	AAA	Best Western Sea Stone Resort & Suites	◆◆◆	$99-$199 SAVE	907
116 / p. 846	AAA	Ramada Inn Gulfview - see color ad p 912	◆◆	$169-$209 SAVE	912
117 / p. 846	AAA	Adam's Mark Clearwater Beach Resort - see color ad p 906	◆◆◆	$165-$255 SAVE	906
118 / p. 846	AAA	Econo Lodge - see ad p 908	◆◆	$109-$159 SAVE	908
119 / p. 846	AAA	Quality Hotel On The Beach - see color ad p 911	◆◆◆	$149-$209 SAVE	911
120 / p. 846	AAA	Best Western Sea Wake Beach Resort - see color ad p 907	◆◆◆	$162-$204 SAVE	907
122 / p. 846		Travelodge Beachview Resort	◆◆	$94-$150	913
123 / p. 846	AAA	Howard Johnson Beachview Resort	◆◆	$99-$165 SAVE	910
125 / p. 846	AAA	Sheraton Sand Key Resort	◆◆◆	$160-$240 SAVE	913
126 / p. 846	AAA	Radisson Suite Resort on Sand Key - see color ad p 912	◆◆◆	$239-$339 SAVE	911
		CLEARWATER BEACH - Restaurants			
95 / p. 846		Waterfront Restaurant	◆	$7-$18	915
96 / p. 846		Cooters Raw Bar & Restaurant	◆	$6-$14	914
97 / p. 846		Frenchy's Cafe	◆	$6-$13	914
98 / p. 846		Frenchy's Rockaway Grill & Beach Club	◆◆	$6-$13	914
99 / p. 846		Bob Heilman's Beachcomber	◆◆◆	$13-$30	914
102 / p. 846		Big Ben British Restaurant & Pub	◆◆	$7-$16	914
104 / p. 846		Gondolier Pizza and Italian Restaurant	◆	$6-$19	914
109 / p. 846		Britt's Laguna Grill	◆◆	$8-$16	914
111 / p. 846		Bonsai Japanese Cuisine-Sushi Bar	◆	$9-$18	914
112 / p. 846		Seafood & Sunsets at Julie's Cafe	◆◆	$10-$30	915
113 / p. 846		Frenchy's Saltwater Cafe	◆	$6-$13	914
114 / p. 846	AAA	Shephard's Waterfront Restaurant	◆◆	$21	915
115 / p. 846		Leverock's of Clearwater Beach	◆◆	$7-$21	914
116 / p. 846		Columbia Restaurant	◆◆	$13-$20	914
		DUNEDIN - Lodgings			
130 / p. 846		Holiday Inn Express Hotel & Suites Clearwater North/Dunedin	◆◆◆	$105-$155	916
131 / p. 846	AAA	Best Western Yacht Harbor Inn & Suites - see color ad p 916	◆◆◆	$119-$139 SAVE	916
		DUNEDIN - Restaurants			
129 / p. 846		Jesse's Dockside	◆◆	$9-$21	916
130 / p. 846		Cafe Alfresco	◆◆	$15-$22	916
131 / p. 846		"Kelly's For Just About...Anything!"	◆◆	$10-$18	916
133 / p. 846		Bon Appetit Restaurant - see color ad p 916	◆◆◆	$12-$15	916
136 / p. 846		Sea Sea Riders	◆◆	$6-$16	917

Spotter/Map Page Number	OA	**INDIAN ROCKS BEACH** - Lodgings	Diamond Rating	Rate Range High Season	Listing Page
138 / p. 846		Sea Star Motel & Apartments	◇	$65-$100	918
139 / p. 846	AAA	**Anchor Court Apartments**	◇◇	$85-$111 SAVE	917
140 / p. 846		810 Gulfside	◇◇◇	$589-$2300(W)	917
141 / p. 846		Gulf Towers Resort Motel	◇◇	$497-$658(W)	917
142 / p. 846		Oaks Court Apartment I	◇	$500(W)	917
143 / p. 846		Oaks Court Apartment II	◇	$500(W)	918
144 / p. 846		West Coast Vista	◇◇◇	$1175(W)	918
145 / p. 846	AAA	**Holiday Inn Hotel & Suites-Harbourside -** see color ad opposite inside back cover	◇◇◇	$159-$449 SAVE	917
		INDIAN ROCKS BEACH - Restaurants			
146 / p. 846		Thai Pan Alley & Bamboo Beach Bar	◇	$7-$9	918
147 / p. 846		Guppy's on the Beach	◇◇	$6-$28	918
		LARGO - Lodgings			
149 / p. 846		Suburban Lodge	◇◇	$60-$85	920
		LARGO - Restaurants			
153 / p. 846		Roger's Real Pit Bar-B-Que	◇◇	$4-$17	920
155 / p. 846		The Gathering Restaurant	◇	$5-$9(L)	920
		MADEIRA BEACH - Lodgings			
156 / p. 846	AAA	**Holiday Inn Madeira Beach** - see color ad p 920, opposite inside back cover	◇◇◇	$159-$189 SAVE	920
157 / p. 846		The Lighthouse Bed & Breakfast Motel	◇◇	$85-$110	920
158 / p. 846	AAA	**Wits End Motel** - see color ad p 921	◇◇	$95-$140 SAVE	922
159 / p. 846	AAA	**Snug Harbor Inn**	◇	$39-$94 SAVE	922
161 / p. 846	AAA	**Shoreline Island Resort** - see color ad p 921	◇◇◇	$112-$252 SAVE	921
162 / p. 846	AAA	**Sea Dawn Motel**	◇	$55-$75 SAVE	921
		MADEIRA BEACH - Restaurants			
163 / p. 846	AAA	**The Apple of Madeira Beach Family Restaurant & Lounge**	◇◇	$7-$18	922
168 / p. 846		Scully's Boardwalk Grille	◇◇	$8-$21	922
169 / p. 846		Johnny Leverock's Seafood House	◇◇	$7-$21	922
170 / p. 846		Friendly Fisherman Waterfront Seafood Restaurant	◇◇	$7-$26	922
		NORTH REDINGTON BEACH - Lodgings			
170 / p. 846		Sails Resort Motel	◇◇	$80-$150	924
172 / p. 846		Far Horizons Motel	◇◇	$62-$98	923
173 / p. 846	AAA	**RamSea** - see color ad p 923	◇◇	$600-$1320(W) SAVE	923
174 / p. 846		Hilton Tampa Bay/North Redington Beach Resort	◇◇◇	$145-$350	923
		NORTH REDINGTON BEACH - Restaurant			
186 / p. 846		The Frog Pond	◇	$6-$11(L)	924
		PINELLAS PARK - Lodgings			
179 / p. 846	AAA	**Days Inn Gateway**	◇◇	$58-$65 SAVE	925
180 / p. 846	AAA	**La Quinta Inn-Pinellas Park** - see color ad p 881	◇◇◇	$74-$96 SAVE	925

Spotter/Map Page Number	OA	**PINELLAS PARK** - Restaurant	Diamond Rating	Rate Range High Season	Listing Page
193 / p. 846		Johnny Leverock's Seafood House	◆◆	$7-$21	925
		SAFETY HARBOR - Lodgings			
184 / p. 846	AAA	Safety Harbor Resort and Spa on Tampa Bay - see ad p 930	◆◆◆	$129-$209 (SAVE)	930
		SAFETY HARBOR - Restaurant			
199 / p. 846		Enver's Paradise Restaurant	◆	$4-$9	930
		REDINGTON BEACH - Lodgings			
187 / p. 846	AAA	El Morocco Resort Motel	◆	$295-$455(W) (SAVE)	928
		TREASURE ISLAND - Lodgings			
189 / p. 846	AAA	Algiers Gulf Resort	◆◆	$70-$100 (SAVE)	940
190 / p. 846	AAA	Fargo Motel	◆◆	$65-$90 (SAVE)	942
191 / p. 846	AAA	Gulf Sounds Beach Rentals	◆◆◆	$103-$114 (SAVE)	942
192 / p. 846	AAA	Jolly Roger Motel	◆◆	$65-$100 (SAVE)	943
195 / p. 846	AAA	Best Western Sea Castle Suites	◆◆	$99-$157 (SAVE)	940
196 / p. 846	AAA	Bilmar Beach Resort	◆◆◆	$145-$179 (SAVE)	940
197 / p. 846		Best Western Treasure Island - see color ad p 933	◆◆	$99-$114	940
198 / p. 846		The Twins Apartments	◆◆	$350-$370(W)	945
199 / p. 846	AAA	Ramada Inn Treasure Island	◆◆	$130-$150 (SAVE)	943
200 / p. 846		Holiday Inn-Treasure Island Beach - see color ad opposite inside back cover, p 942	◆◆◆	$119-$149	942
201 / p. 846	AAA	Buccaneer Beachfront Resort Motel - see color ad p 941	◆◆	$82-$120 (SAVE)	941
202 / p. 846		Carol Ann Condo Hotel	◆◆	$155-$195	942
205 / p. 846	AAA	The Sea Chest	◆◆	$84-$119 (SAVE)	944
207 / p. 846	AAA	Trails End Resort Motel - see color ad p 944	◆◆	$90-$125 (SAVE)	944
209 / p. 846	AAA	Thunderbird Beach Resort - see color ad p 944	◆◆	$135-$179 (SAVE)	944
210 / p. 846		Arvilla Resort Motel	◆◆	$61-$98	940
212 / p. 846		Mardi Gras Motel	◆	$45-$75	943
214 / p. 846	AAA	Page Terrace Motel - see color ad p 943	◆◆	$69-$102 (SAVE)	943
215 / p. 846		The Jefferson Motel Apts.	◆◆	$735(W)	942
216 / p. 846	AAA	Bluenose Motel	◆	$60-$80 (SAVE)	940
217 / p. 846		The Bayside Inn	◆◆	$59-$540	940
		REDINGTON SHORES - Lodgings			
230 / p. 846		San Remo Resort	◆◆	$995-$1345(W)	928
		REDINGTON SHORES - Restaurant			
237 / p. 846	AAA	The Lobster Pot	◆◆◆	$16-$46	928
		OLDSMAR - Lodgings			
235 / p. 846		Holiday Inn Express Hotel & Suites	◆◆◆	$119-$159	924
		INDIAN SHORES - Lodgings			
240 / p. 846		Sand Castle I	◆◆	$1095	918
242 / p. 846		Sand Castle III	◆◆	$1230(W)	919
243 / p. 846		Sand Castle II	◆◆	$1175(W)	919

Spotter/Map Page Number	OA	**INDIAN SHORES - Lodgings (continued)**	Diamond Rating	Rate Range High Season	Listing Page
244 / p. 846		Beach Cottage III	◈◈	$1175-$1260(W)	918
246 / p. 846		Sea Gate	◈◈	$1150(W)	919
		INDIAN SHORES - Restaurants			
265 / p. 846		The Pub Restaurant & Lounge	◈◈	$7-$17	919
267 / p. 846		The Hungry Fisherman	◈◈	$6-$23	919
269 / p. 846		Chateau Madrid	◈◈◈	$10-$21	919
270 / p. 846		Il Lido Ristorante Italiano	◈◈	$11-$21	919
271 / p. 846		Salt Rock Grill	◈◈◈	$11-$31	919
		BELLEAIR BLUFFS - Restaurant			
274 / p. 846		E & E Stakeout Grill	◈◈	$6-$19	896
		SOUTH PASADENA - Restaurant			
276 / p. 846		Horse & Jockey British Restaurant & Bar	◈◈	$7-$11	937

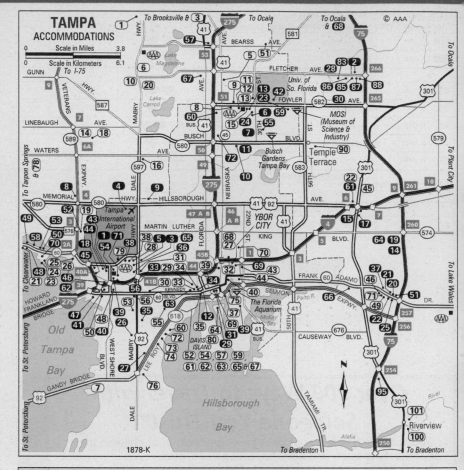

TAMPA
ACCOMMODATIONS

1878-K

✈ Airport Accommodations

Spotter/Map Page Number	OA	TAMPA INTERNATIONAL	Diamond Rating	Rate Range High Season	Listing Page
1 / p. 856	AAA	**AmeriSuites (Tampa Airport/Westshore), 2.5 mi se of terminal**	◆◆◆	$159 SAVE	870
62 / p. 856		Best Western-The Westshore Hotel, 2.5 mi n of terminal	◆◆	$99-$119	873
50 / p. 856		Chase Suite Hotel by Woodfin, 4 mi sw of airport terminal	◆◆◆	$119-$169	873
33 / p. 856		Courtyard by Marriott, 3.5 mi se of the terminal	◆◆◆	$109-$179	873
43 / p. 856		Crowne Plaza Hotel and Resort Tampa-Westshore, 3 mi se of terminal	◆◆◆	$129-$159	875
3 / p. 856		Days Inn Airport Stadium, 4 mi n of terminal	◆◆◆	$85-$129	876
49 / p. 856		Doubletree Guest Suites Tampa Bay, 4 mi sw of terminal	◆◆◆	$109-$179	876
35 / p. 856	AAA	**Econo Lodge Midtown, 5 mi se of terminal**	◆◆	$48-$85 SAVE	877
40 / p. 856		Embassy Suites Hotel-Tampa/Airport/Westshore, 3.5 mi s of terminal	◆◆◆	$169-$249	877
53 / p. 856	AAA	**Hampton Inn, 4 mi sw of terminal**	◆◆◆	$89-$129 SAVE	878
44 / p. 856	AAA	**Hampton Inn Tampa Int'l Airport - Westshore, 2.5 mi se of terminal**	◆◆◆	$89-$149 SAVE	879
38 / p. 856		Hilton Tampa Airport Westshore, 2 mi e of airport terminal	◆◆◆	$79-$159	880
58 / p. 856	AAA	**Holiday Inn Express Hotel & Suites, 4 mi sw of terminal**	◆◆◆	$89-$129 SAVE	880
4 / p. 856		Holiday Inn Express Hotel & Suites Tampa Stadium/Airport, 5.3 mi n of terminal	◆◆◆	$75-$108	880
8 / p. 856		Homestead Studio Suites Hotel-Tampa/North Airport, 4 mi w of terminal	◆◆	$89-$99	880
27 / p. 856	AAA	**Howard Johnson Express Inn & Suites, 6 mi se of terminal**	◆◆◆	$45-$65 SAVE	880
5 / p. 856	AAA	**Howard Johnson Tampa Airport/Stadium, 4.5 mi ne of terminal**	◆	$59-$64 SAVE	880
46 / p. 856	AAA	**Hyatt Regency Westshore, 3 mi w of terminal**	◆◆◆◆	$119-$280 SAVE	881
45 / p. 856	AAA	**La Quinta Inn Tampa Airport, 2.5 mi n of terminal**	◆◆◆	$99-$135 SAVE	881
71 / p. 856		Marriott-Tampa Westshore, 3 mi se of terminal	◆◆◆	$199-$209	882
47 / p. 856	AAA	**Park Plaza Tampa Airport Westshore, 3 mi s of terminal**	fyi	$129-$169 SAVE	887
48 / p. 856	AAA	**Radisson Bay Harbor Hotel, 4.3 mi w of airport terminal**	◆◆◆	$147-$157 SAVE	883
70 / p. 856		Sailport Waterfront Resort, 4.8 mi w of airport terminal	◆◆	$69-$129	884
36 / p. 856		Sheraton Suites Hotel, 3.5 mi se of terminal	◆◆◆	$189-$295	884
52 / p. 856		Tampa Airport Marriott, in terminal	◆◆◆	$215-$225	886
54 / p. 856	AAA	**Wellesley Inn & Suites (Tampa/Westshore), 3.5 mi w of terminal**	◆◆◆	$99-$109 SAVE	886
41 / p. 856	AAA	**Wyndham Westshore, 3 mi s of airport terminal**	◆◆◆	$169-$239 SAVE	887

Tampa

This index helps you "spot" where approved accommodations and restaurants are located on the corresponding detailed maps. Lodging rate ranges are for comparison only and show the property's high season; rates are per night, unless only weekly (W) rates are available. Restaurant rate range is for dinner, unless only lunch (L) is served. Turn to the listing page for more detailed rate information and consult display ads for special promotions.

Spotter/Map Page Number	OA	TAMPA - Lodgings	Diamond Rating	Rate Range High Season	Listing Page
❶ / p. 856	AAA	AmeriSuites (Tampa Airport/Westshore) - see color ad p 871	♦♦♦	$159 SAVE	870
❷ / p. 856		Courtyard by Marriott Tampa North	♦♦♦	$59-$139	874
❸ / p. 856		Days Inn Airport Stadium - see color ad p 874	♦♦♦	$85-$129	876
❹ / p. 856		Holiday Inn Express Hotel & Suites Tampa Stadium/Airport	♦♦♦	$75-$108	880
❺ / p. 856	AAA	Howard Johnson Tampa Airport/Stadium	♦	$59-$64 SAVE	880
❻ / p. 856	AAA	Doubletree Guest Suites Tampa/Busch Gardens - see color ad p 875	♦♦	$79-$116 SAVE	876
❼ / p. 856	AAA	Baymont Inn & Suites Tampa/near Busch Gardens - see color ad p 872	♦♦	$74-$94 SAVE	872
❽ / p. 856		Homestead Studio Suites Hotel-Tampa/North Airport	♦♦	$89-$99	880
❾ / p. 856		Microtel Inn & Suites	♦♦	$44-$62	882
❿ / p. 856		Value Inn	♦♦	$39-$65	886
⓫ / p. 856	AAA	Red Roof Inn	♦♦	$56-$74 SAVE	883
⓬ / p. 856		Residence Inn by Marriott	♦♦♦	$169-$189	884
⓭ / p. 856	AAA	Holiday Inn Tampa Near Busch Gardens - see color ad opposite inside back cover, p 879	♦♦♦	$109-$149 SAVE	880
⓮ / p. 856		Residence Inn by Marriott Sabal Park	♦♦♦	$129-$169	884
⓯ / p. 856	AAA	Red Roof Inn-Fairgrounds	♦♦	$59-$79 SAVE	883
⓱ / p. 856	AAA	Baymont Inn Tampa-Fairgrounds - see color ad p 872	♦♦	$79-$99 SAVE	872
⓲ / p. 856		SpringHill Suites by Marriott Tampa/Westshore - see color ad p 884	♦♦♦	$159	885
⓳ / p. 856		Crowne Plaza Hotel and Resort Tampa at Sabal Park	♦♦♦	$99-$199	874
⓴ / p. 856	AAA	Baymont Inn & Suites Tampa-Brandon - see color ad p 872	♦♦	$74-$94 SAVE	872
㉑ / p. 856		Days Inn/State Fairgrounds - see color ad p 875	♦♦	$79-$89	876
㉒ / p. 856		Fairfield Inn by Marriott-Tampa/Brandon	♦♦♦	$89-$189	878
㉓ / p. 856		Wingate Inn-USF Near Busch Gardens	♦♦♦	$99-$139	886
㉔ / p. 856	AAA	AmeriSuites (Tampa near Busch Gardens) - see color ad p 871	♦♦♦	$105-$135 SAVE	871
㉕ / p. 856		Courtyard by Marriott-Tampa/Brandon	♦♦♦	$99-$299	874
㉖ / p. 856		Tahitian Inn	♦♦♦	$99-$119	885
㉗ / p. 856	AAA	Howard Johnson Express Inn & Suites	♦♦♦	$45-$65 SAVE	880
㉘ / p. 856	AAA	Hampton Inn & Suites - see color ad p 877	♦♦♦	$105-$120 SAVE	879
㉙ / p. 856	AAA	Wyndham Harbour Island	♦♦♦	$199-$269 SAVE	887
㉚ / p. 856	AAA	Shoney's Inn - see color ad p 885	♦♦♦	$71-$83 SAVE	884
㉛ / p. 856	AAA	Hyatt Regency Tampa	♦♦♦	$105-$249 SAVE	881
㉝ / p. 856		Courtyard by Marriott - see ad p 873	♦♦♦	$109-$179	873
㉞ / p. 856		Courtyard by Marriott-Downtown Tampa	♦♦♦	$159-$179	873

Spotter/Map Page Number	OA	TAMPA - Lodgings (continued)	Diamond Rating	Rate Range High Season	Listing Page
35 / p. 856	AAA	Econo Lodge Midtown	◆◆	$48-$85 SAVE	877
36 / p. 856		Sheraton Suites Hotel - see color ad p 5	◆◆◆	$189-$295	884
37 / p. 856	AAA	Comfort Suites	◆◆◆	$104-$114 SAVE	873
38 / p. 856		Hilton Tampa Airport Westshore - see ad p 879	◆◆◆	$79-$159	880
39 / p. 856	AAA	Tampa Marriott Waterside Hotel	◆◆◆	$169-$264 SAVE	886
40 / p. 856		Embassy Suites Hotel-Tampa/Airport/Westshore	◆◆◆	$169-$249	877
41 / p. 856	AAA	Wyndham Westshore	◆◆◆	$169-$239 SAVE	887
42 / p. 856	AAA	Embassy Suites Hotel USF/Near Busch Gardens - see color ad p 877	◆◆◆	$129-$229 SAVE	877
43 / p. 856		Crowne Plaza Hotel and Resort Tampa-Westshore	◆◆◆	$129-$159	875
44 / p. 856	AAA	Hampton Inn Tampa Int'l Airport - Westshore	◆◆◆	$89-$149 SAVE	879
45 / p. 856	AAA	La Quinta Inn Tampa Airport - see color ad p 881	◆◆◆	$99-$135 SAVE	881
46 / p. 856	AAA	Hyatt Regency Westshore	◆◆◆◆	$119-$280 SAVE	881
47 / p. 856	AAA	Park Plaza Tampa Airport Westshore - see ad p 887	[fyi]	$129-$169 SAVE	887
48 / p. 856	AAA	Radisson Bay Harbor Hotel - see ad p 883	◆◆◆	$147-$157 SAVE	883
49 / p. 856		Doubletree Guest Suites Tampa Bay	◆◆◆	$109-$179	876
50 / p. 856		Chase Suite Hotel by Woodfin	◆◆◆	$119-$169	873
51 / p. 856	AAA	Red Roof Inn-Brandon	◆◆	$76-$85 SAVE	883
52 / p. 856		Tampa Airport Marriott	◆◆◆	$215-$225	886
53 / p. 856	AAA	Hampton Inn - see color ad p 878	◆◆◆	$89-$129 SAVE	878
54 / p. 856	AAA	Wellesley Inn & Suites (Tampa/Westshore) - see color ad p 863	◆◆◆	$99-$109 SAVE	886
55 / p. 856	AAA	Best Western All Suites Hotel Behind Busch Gardens - see color ad p 856	◆◆◆	$79-$129 SAVE	872
56 / p. 856	AAA	Doubletree Hotel Tampa Airport-Westshore - see color ad p 876	◆◆◆	$79-$169 SAVE	876
57 / p. 856	AAA	Quality Inn-Busch Gardens - see color ad p 882	◆◆◆	$69 SAVE	882
58 / p. 856	AAA	Holiday Inn Express Hotel & Suites - see color ad p 878	◆◆◆	$89-$129 SAVE	880
59 / p. 856	AAA	La Quinta Inn & Suites USF - see color ad p 881	◆◆◆	$89-$115 SAVE	881
60 / p. 856		Motel 6 - 483	◆◆	$39-$55	882
61 / p. 856		Motel 6 #1192	◆◆	$37-$53	882
62 / p. 856		Best Western-The Westshore Hotel	◆◆	$99-$119	873
63 / p. 856	AAA	Radisson Riverwalk Hotel Tampa	◆◆◆	$119-$219 SAVE	883
64 / p. 856	AAA	AmeriSuites (Tampa/Sabal Corp. Park) - see color ad p 871	◆◆◆	$129-$139 SAVE	871
65 / p. 856		Gram's Place BnB Guesthouses/Youth Hostel & Music	◆◆	$80-$95	878
66 / p. 856		Suburban Lodge-Brandon	◆◆	Failed to provide	885
67 / p. 856	AAA	Super 8 Motel-Tampa	◆◆	$40-$115 SAVE	885
68 / p. 856		Wingate Inn-Tampa North	◆◆◆	$129-$149	886
69 / p. 856		Hilton Garden Inn/Tampa Ybor City Historic District - see color ad p 875	◆◆◆	$99-$159	879

Spotter/Map Page Number	OA	**TAMPA** - Lodgings (continued)	Diamond Rating	Rate Range High Season	Listing Page
70 / p. 856		Sailport Waterfront Resort	◇◇	$69-$129	884
71 / p. 856		Marriott-Tampa Westshore	◇◇◇	$199-$209	882
72 / p. 856		Travelodge Hotel Near Busch Gardens - see color ad p 874	◇◇◇	$69-$89	886
		TAMPA - Restaurants			
1 / p. 856		Jasmine Thai Restaurant	◇◇	$6-$19	891
3 / p. 856		Good Fellas	◇◇	$8-$19	891
5 / p. 856		Skipper's Smokehouse Restaurant & Oyster Bar	◇	$6-$16	893
6 / p. 856		Arigato Japanese Steak House	◇◇	$10-$22	888
7 / p. 856		Jimmy Mac's Marina Restaurant	◇◇	$7-$25	891
8 / p. 856		Hops Restaurant Bar & Brewery	◇◇	$7-$17	891
9 / p. 856		Woody's Bar-B-Que	◇	$5-$14	895
10 / p. 856		Windy City Pizza	◇	$6-$19	894
11 / p. 856		First Watch	◇◇	$5-$7(L)	891
12 / p. 856		Saigon Bay Vietnamese Restaurant	◇◇	$7-$17	893
13 / p. 856		Taj Indian Cuisine	◇	$9-$17	894
14 / p. 856		Logan's Roadhouse	◇◇	$6-$19	892
15 / p. 856		Tia's Tex Mex	◇◇	$7-$15	894
16 / p. 856		Sukhothai Restaurant	◇◇	$6-$20	894
18 / p. 856		Copeland's Restaurant and Bar	◇◇	$8-$19	890
19 / p. 856		CK's Restaurant	◇◇◇	$18-$38	890
20 / p. 856		Vallarto's Restaurante Mexicano	◇◇	$6-$11	894
21 / p. 856		The Castaway	◇◇	$11-$20	889
22 / p. 856		Frontier Steak House	◇	$9-$31	891
23 / p. 856		The Rusty Pelican	◇◇◇	$18-$23	893
24 / p. 856		Crawdaddy's	◇◇	$16-$36	890
25 / p. 856		Armani's	◇◇◇◇	$23-$35	888
26 / p. 856		Oystercatchers	◇◇◇	$12-$30	893
27 / p. 856		Barley Hoppers International Alehouse & Grill	◇◇	$7-$20	888
28 / p. 856		Sam Seltzer's Steakhouse	◇◇	$10-$19	893
29 / p. 856		First Watch	◇◇	$5-$7(L)	891
30 / p. 856		Miguel's Mexican Restaurant	◇◇	$8-$15	892
31 / p. 856		Tia's Tex-Mex	◇◇	$9-$16	894
32 / p. 856		La Tropicana Cafe	◇	$5-$10(L)	892
33 / p. 856		Valencia Garden	◇◇	$10-$17	894
34 / p. 856		Cafe European	◇◇	$10-$19	888
35 / p. 856		Mise en Place	◇◇◇	$13-$23	892
36 / p. 856		Newk's Lighthouse Cafe	◇◇	$5-$12	892
37 / p. 856		Stumps Supper Club	◇◇	$10-$21	894
38 / p. 856		Roy's Restaurant	◇◇◇	$11-$35	893

Spotter/Map Page Number	OA	TAMPA - Restaurants (continued)	Diamond Rating	Rate Range High Season	Listing Page
㊴ / p. 856		Cafe Creole	◆◆	$12-$17	888
㊵ / p. 856		Tampa Bay Brewing Company	◆	$8-$20	894
㊸ / p. 856		Columbia Restaurant	◆◆	$14-$22	890
㊹ / p. 856		Ovo Cafe	◆◆	$10-$16	892
㊺ / p. 856		V.P.'s Country BBQ & Catering	◆	$5-$16	894
㊻ / p. 856		First Choice Bar-B-Que	◆	$4-$15	890
㊽ / p. 856	AAA	**Bay Cafe**	◆◆	$10-$20	888
㊾ / p. 856		Sweet Tomatoes	◆	$7	894
㊿ / p. 856		Shula's Steakhouse	◆◆◆	$17-$66	893
51 / p. 856		Remington's Steakhouse	◆◆	$9-$21	893
52 / p. 856		The Wine Exchange Bistro & Wine Bar	◆◆	$8-$10	895
53 / p. 856		Lauro Ristorante Italiano	◆◆	$12-$23	892
54 / p. 856		Samba Room	◆◆◆	$9-$25	893
55 / p. 856		Blue Gardenia	◆◆	$12-$28	888
56 / p. 856		Donatello	◆◆◆	$16-$29	890
57 / p. 856		Royal Palace Thai Restaurant	◆◆	$10-$18	893
59 / p. 856		The Cactus Club Southwestern Grill & Bar	◆◆	$7-$16	888
60 / p. 856		The Old Meeting House	◆	$4-$8	892
61 / p. 856		Ceviche'	◆◆◆	$18-$31	889
62 / p. 856		Bernini	◆◆◆	$10-$25	888
63 / p. 856		Ho Ho Windows	◆◆	$6-$12	891
64 / p. 856	AAA	**Jackson's Bistro-Bar & Sushi**	◆◆◆	$13-$21	891
65 / p. 856		42nd Street The Bistro	◆◆	$7-$18	887
67 / p. 856		Hugo's Spanish Restaurant	◆	$4-$10	891
68 / p. 856		Dish Centro Ybor	◆◆	$16	890
69 / p. 856		Lonni's Sandwiches, Etc	◆	$7-$9(L)	892
70 / p. 856		Carmine's	◆	$8-$12	889
71 / p. 856		Chillada's Fresh Mex Cantina	◆	$4-$7	889
72 / p. 856		Bern's Steak House	◆◆◆	$23-$40	888
73 / p. 856		The Colonnade	◆◆	$6-$21	890
74 / p. 856		Le Bordeaux	◆◆◆	$17-$33	892
75 / p. 856		G Elliott's Restaurante	◆◆	$13-$21	891
76 / p. 856		Caffe Paradiso	◆◆◆	$8-$24	889
78 / p. 856		Cody's Original Roadhouse	◆◆	$7-$20	890
79 / p. 856		Kahunaville	◆◆◆	$12-$19	892
80 / p. 856		Estela's Mexican Restaurant	◆	$4-$12	890
		TEMPLE TERRACE - Lodgings			
83 / p. 856		Hilton Garden Inn Tampa North	◆◆◆	$79-$129	939
85 / p. 856		Sleep Inn Temple Terrace USF Near Busch Gardens	◆◆	$70	939
86 / p. 856		Residence Inn by Marriott Tampa North	◆◆◆	$129-$169	939

Spotter/Map Page Number	OA	TEMPLE TERRACE - Lodgings (continued)	Diamond Rating	Rate Range High Season	Listing Page
87 / p. 856		Fairfield Inn Tampa North	▽▽▽	$69-$89	939
88 / p. 856		Extended Stay America	▽▽	$369-$419	939
		TEMPLE TERRACE - Restaurant			
90 / p. 856		Vallarto's Restaurante Mexicano	▽▽	$6-$11	939
		RIVERVIEW (HILLSBOROUGH COUNTY) - Lodgings			
95 / p. 856	AAA	**Bianchi Motel**	▽	$35-$65 SAVE	928
		RIVERVIEW (HILLSBOROUGH COUNTY) - Restaurants			
100 / p. 856		ABC Pizza	▽	$7-$18	928
101 / p. 856		Beef 'O' Brady's	▽	$5-$7	928

ST. PETERSBURG pop. 248,232 (See map p. 846; index p. 848)

─── WHERE TO STAY ───

BAYBORO HOUSE BED & BREAKFAST ON OLD TAMPA BAY

Phone: 727/823-4955 (18)

AAA (SAVE)
▼▼▼▼▼

Historic Bed
& Breakfast

12/1-4/30 [ECP]	1P: $149-$229	2P: $149-$229	XP: $25 F12
10/1-11/30 [ECP]	1P: $149-$209	2P: $149-$209	XP: $25 F12
5/1-9/30 [ECP]	1P: $149-$189	2P: $149-$189	XP: $25 F12

Location: I-275, exit 22, e to 4th St S, 0.5 mi s to 22nd Ave S, 0.4 mi e to Tampa Bay, 0.3 mi n. 1719 Beach Dr SE 33701. Fax: 727/822-2341. **Facility:** On Tampa Bay, this 1907 Victorian home offers individually themed units, each with a view of the bay; age restrictions are imposed in the main house. Designated smoking area. 8 units. 5 one-bedroom standard units. 2 one- and 1 two-bedroom suites, some with whirlpools. 2 stories, interior corridors. *Bath:* combo or shower only. **Parking:** on-site. **Terms:** 1-2 night minimum stay, 10 day cancellation notice-fee imposed, [CP] meal plan available. **Amenities:** video library, hair dryers. *Some:* irons. **Pool(s):** heated outdoor. **Leisure Activities:** whirlpool, fishing equipment, bicycles. **Guest Services:** complimentary evening beverages, complimentary laundry. **Business Services:** fax. **Cards:** AX, CB, DC, DS, MC, VI. **Special Amenities:** early check-in/late check-out and free room upgrade (subject to availability with advanced reservations).

SOME UNITS

BAYBORO INN & HUNT ROOM BED & BREAKFAST

Phone: 727/823-0498 (17)

AAA (SAVE)
▼▼▼▼▼

Historic Bed
& Breakfast

1/1-4/30	1P: $95	2P: $125	XP: $25 F12
12/1-12/31 & 5/1-11/30	1P: $85	2P: $110	XP: $25 F12

Location: At jct 3rd Ave S; downtown. 357 3rd St S 33701. Fax: 727/823-0498. **Facility:** This 1914 home's guest units each have a different theme, ranging from ancient Egypt to Art Deco to Key West. Designated smoking area. 4 one-bedroom standard units. 2 stories, interior corridors. *Bath:* shower only. **Parking:** street. **Terms:** age restrictions may apply, 14 day cancellation notice-fee imposed, [ECP] meal plan available, 5% service charge. **Leisure Activities:** deck, barbecue grill. **Guest Services:** complimentary evening beverages, valet laundry. **Cards:** MC, VI. **Special Amenities:** early check-in/late check-out and free local telephone calls.

COLONIAL BAYFRONT HOTEL

Phone: (727)896-6400 (15)

AAA (SAVE)
▼▼▼ ▼▼▼

Historic
Small-scale Hotel

12/1-4/30	1P: $85-$160	XP: $10 F12
10/1-11/30	1P: $85-$135	
5/1-9/30	1P: $75-$115	

Location: Just e of jct 1st St NE; downtown. 126 2nd Ave NE 33701. Fax: 727/896-0505. **Facility:** Designated smoking area. 64 one-bedroom standard units. 4 stories, interior corridors. *Bath:* combo or shower only. **Parking:** on-site. **Terms:** cancellation fee imposed, [CP] meal plan available. **Amenities:** *Some:* irons. **Leisure Activities:** reading room, exercise room. **Guest Services:** coin laundry. **Business Services:** meeting rooms, fax. **Cards:** AX, DC, DS, MC, VI. **Special Amenities:** free continental breakfast and free local telephone calls.

SOME UNITS

COMFORT INN & SUITES

Phone: (727)323-3100 (10)

(SAVE)
▼▼▼▼▼
Motel

12/1-4/1	1P: $71-$91	2P: $71-$91	XP: $7 F18
4/2-11/30	1P: $61-$81	2P: $61-$81	XP: $7 F18

Location: I-275, exit 24, 1.2 mi w on 22nd Ave N, 0.5 mi s. 1400 34th St N 33713. Fax: 727/327-5792. **Facility:** 75 units. 57 one-bedroom standard units, some with efficiencies. 18 one-bedroom suites with efficiencies. 3 stories, exterior corridors. **Parking:** on-site. **Terms:** 7 day cancellation notice, [ECP] meal plan available. **Amenities:** *Some:* irons, hair dryers. **Pool(s):** heated outdoor. **Leisure Activities:** whirlpool, exercise room. **Guest Services:** coin laundry. **Business Services:** meeting rooms, fax. **Cards:** AX, CB, DC, DS, MC, VI.

SOME UNITS

(See map p. 846)

DAYS INN OF ST. PETERSBURG

Phone: (727)522-3191 **4**

2/15-4/15	1P: $66-$76	2P: $72-$82	XP: $6 F18
12/1-2/14 & 4/16-11/30	1P: $49-$59	2P: $55-$65	XP: $6 F18

Motel

Location: I-275, exit 26 southbound; exit 26B northbound, 0.3 mi w. 2595 54th Ave N 33714. Fax: 727/527-6120. **Facility:** 155 one-bedroom standard units. 2 stories, exterior corridors. *Bath:* combo or shower only. **Parking:** on-site. **Terms:** 11% service charge, pets ($10 extra charge). **Amenities:** safes (fee), hair dryers. *Some:* irons. **Dining:** 6 am-9 pm, Sun-2 pm, cocktails. **Pool(s):** outdoor, wading. **Leisure Activities:** picnic area, gazebo, playground, shuffleboard. **Guest Services:** coin laundry. **Business Services:** meeting rooms, fax. **Cards:** AX, DC, DS, MC, VI. **Special Amenities: free newspaper and free room upgrade (subject to availability with advanced reservations).**

SOME UNITS
⎡S/D⎤ 🐾 🍴 🍸 📡 � 🗙 📺 📠 / 🗙 🔋 🖥 / FEE FEE

DAYS INN ST. PETE CENTRAL

SAVE

Phone: (727)321-2958 **11**

All Year [CP]	2P: $60-$66	XP: $7 F12

Motel

Location: I-275, exit 24, 1.2 mi w on 22nd Ave N, 1 mi s. 650 34th St N 33713. Fax: 727/327-1625. **Facility:** 28 one-bedroom standard units, some with efficiencies. 2 stories, exterior corridors. **Parking:** on-site. **Terms:** cancellation fee imposed, weekly rates available. **Amenities:** hair dryers. *Some:* irons. **Pool(s):** heated outdoor. **Leisure Activities:** whirlpool. **Guest Services:** coin laundry. **Business Services:** fax. **Cards:** AX, CB, DC, DS, JC, MC, VI.

SOME UNITS
⎡S/D⎤ 🍴 🏊 📺 📡 / 🗙 🔋 🖥 /

DICKENS HOUSE BED AND BREAKFAST

Phone: (727)822-8622 **2**

12/24-4/30	1P: $120-$210	2P: $120-$210	XP: $20
12/1-12/23	1P: $102-$178	2P: $102-$178	XP: $20
5/1-11/30	1P: $96-$170	2P: $96-$170	XP: $20

Historic Bed & Breakfast

Location: Just w of jct Beach Dr NE; downtown; in Old Northeast. 335 8th Ave NE 33701. Fax: 727/822-6312. **Facility:** Designated smoking area. 5 units. 3 one- and 2 two-bedroom standard units, some with whirlpools. 3 stories, interior corridors. **Parking:** street. **Terms:** 10 day cancellation notice-fee imposed, weekly rates available, [BP] meal plan available. **Amenities:** high-speed Internet, voice mail, irons, hair dryers. **Guest Services:** complimentary laundry. **Business Services:** fax. **Cards:** AX, DS, MC, VI.

ⒶⓈⓀ ⎡S/D⎤ 🗙 ⎡VCR⎤ 📺 🔋

EMPRESS MOTEL APARTMENTS

Phone: (727)894-0635 **7**

All Year	1P: $49-$66	2P: $52-$66 XP: $5 F16

Motel

Location: I-275, exit 24 (22nd Ave N), 1 mi e to 9th St, 0.3 mi s. 1503 9th St N 33704. Fax: 727/823-1446. **Facility:** 33 units. 29 one- and 4 two-bedroom standard units, some with efficiencies or kitchens. 2 stories, exterior corridors. **Parking:** on-site. **Terms:** 14 day cancellation notice-fee imposed, weekly rates available. **Amenities:** *Some:* irons, hair dryers. **Pool(s):** outdoor. **Leisure Activities:** barbecue grill. **Guest Services:** coin laundry. **Business Services:** fax.

SOME UNITS
⎡S/D⎤ 🍴 🏊 📺 / 🗙 🔋 🖥 /

GRANT MOTEL & APTS

Phone: 727/576-1369 **1**

12/1-4/15	1P: $45-$60	2P: $45-$60	XP: $10 D3
4/16-11/30	1P: $39-$55	2P: $39-$55	XP: $10 D3

Motel

Location: I-275, exit 32; exit 28 northbound, 0.8 mi s on US 92. 9046 4th St N 33702. Fax: 727/579-0148. **Facility:** 31 units. 23 one-bedroom standard units, some with efficiencies. 6 one- and 2 two-bedroom suites with kitchens. 1 story, exterior corridors. *Bath:* combo or shower only. **Parking:** on-site. **Terms:** 7 day cancellation notice, weekly rates available. **Amenities:** *Some:* irons, hair dryers. **Pool(s):** outdoor. **Leisure Activities:** shuffleboard. **Guest Services:** coin laundry. **Business Services:** fax (fee). **Cards:** AX, DS, MC, VI. **Special Amenities: early check-in/late check-out.**

SOME UNITS
⎡S/D⎤ 🍴 🏊 🔋 / 🗙 🖥 /

(See map p. 846)

HAMPTON INN

SAVE · ▼▼▼

Small-scale Hotel

Phone: (727)322-0770 9

12/1-4/30 [ECP]	1P: $109-$119	2P: $109-$119
5/1-11/30 [ECP]	1P: $89-$109	2P: $89-$109

Location: I-275, exit 24, 1.2 mi w on 22nd Ave N, 0.6 mi s on US 19. Located in a commercial area. 1200 34th St N 33713. Fax: 727/322-0378. **Facility:** 130 units. 126 one-bedroom standard units. 4 one-bedroom suites ($149-$169). 4 stories, interior corridors. *Bath:* combo or shower only. **Parking:** on-site. **Terms:** check-in 4 pm. **Amenities:** video games, dual phone lines, voice mail, irons, hair dryers. **Pool(s):** heated outdoor. **Leisure Activities:** whirlpool, exercise room. **Guest Services:** valet and coin laundry. **Business Services:** meeting rooms, PC, fax (fee). **Cards:** AX, CB, DC, DS, MC, VI.

SOME UNITS

HOLIDAY INN SUNSPREE RESORT MARINA COVE

AAA SAVE · ▼▼▼

Resort
Large-scale Hotel

Phone: (727)867-1151 20

2/14-4/26	1P: $109-$199	2P: $109-$199	XP: $10	F18
12/1-2/13 & 4/27-11/30	1P: $89-$154	2P: $89-$154	XP: $10	F18

Location: I-275, exit 16, just n of Sunshine Skyway Bridge, 1st frontage road exit. Located in a semi-residential area off of the interstate. 6800 Sunshine Skyway Ln 33711. Fax: 727/864-4494. **Facility:** Many recreational activities are available at this 18-acre resort on Old Tampa Bay; an on-site restaurant has a submarine theme. 156 units. 145 one-bedroom standard units. 11 one-bedroom suites ($154-$209) with efficiencies. 2 stories, interior/exterior corridors. *Bath:* combo or shower only. **Parking:** on-site. **Amenities:** video library, dual phone lines, voice mail, safes, irons, hair dryers. *Some:* video games, high-speed Internet. **Dining:** 2 restaurants, 7 am-10 pm, cocktails. **Pool(s):** outdoor, heated outdoor. **Leisure Activities:** whirlpool, fishing, 5 lighted tennis courts, recreation programs, playground, exercise room, shuffleboard, volleyball. *Fee:* sailboats, marina, charter fishing, sailing school, water bike, waverunners, tennis instruction, fishing equipment, massage, game room. **Guest Services:** gift shop, valet and coin laundry. **Business Services:** meeting rooms, PC, fax (fee). **Cards:** AX, CB, DC, DS, JC, MC, VI.
(See color ad below & opposite inside back cover)

SOME UNITS

INN AT THE BAY BED & BREAKFAST

▼▼▼

Bed & Breakfast

Phone: (727)822-1700 21

All Year [BP]	1P: $119-$250	2P: $119-$250	XP: $25	D

Location: I-275, exit 23A, just s 4th Ave NE; downtown. 126 4th Ave NE 33701. Fax: 727/896-7412. **Facility:** In-room whirlpools enhance many accommodations at this service-oriented inn, which is close to shops, restaurants and the pier. 12 one-bedroom standard units, some with whirlpools. 3 stories (no elevator), interior corridors. **Parking:** on-site. **Terms:** 14 day cancellation notice-fee imposed. **Amenities:** CD players, irons, hair dryers. **Guest Services:** complimentary evening beverages. **Business Services:** meeting rooms. **Cards:** AX, CB, DC, DS, MC, VI.

SOME UNITS

KENTUCKY MOTEL

AAA SAVE · ▼▼

Motel

Phone: (727)526-7373 5

12/1-5/5 & 11/1-11/30	1P: $39-$46	2P: $44-$53	XP: $5	F5
5/6-10/31	1P: $36-$43	2P: $40-$48	XP: $5	F5

Location: I-275, exit 26 southbound; exit 26B northbound, 1.4 mi e on 54th Ave N, 0.7 mi s on US 92. 4246 4th St N 33703. Fax: 727/526-2698. **Facility:** 10 one-bedroom standard units. 1 story, exterior corridors. *Bath:* combo or shower only. **Parking:** on-site. **Terms:** 3 day cancellation notice, weekly rates available, package plans. **Amenities:** *Some:* irons, hair dryers. **Business Services:** fax. **Cards:** AX, CB, DS, MC, VI.
Special Amenities: preferred room (subject to availability with advanced reservations).

SOME UNITS

LA QUINTA INN

SAVE · ▼▼▼

Motel

Phone: (727)527-8421 6

All Year	1P: $59-$89	2P: $65-$95

Location: I-275, exit 26, just w on 54th Ave N, just s on US 19 (34th St). 4999 34th St N 33714. Fax: 727/527-8851. **Facility:** 120 one-bedroom standard units. 2 stories, exterior corridors. *Bath:* combo or shower only. **Parking:** on-site. **Terms:** [ECP] meal plan available, small pets only. **Amenities:** video games, voice mail, irons, hair dryers. **Pool(s):** heated outdoor. **Leisure Activities:** exercise room. **Guest Services:** coin laundry. **Business Services:** meeting rooms, fax. **Cards:** AX, CB, DC, DS, JC, MC, VI. *(See color ad p 881)*

SOME UNITS
FEE   FEE

(See map p. 846)

LEE MANOR INN

Phone: (727)894-3248   22

▼▼ ▼▼

Bed & Breakfast

| 12/1-4/30 [ECP] | 1P: $89-$139 | 2P: $89-$139 |
| 5/1-11/30 [ECP] | 1P: $69-$119 | 2P: $69-$119 |

Location: At jct 4th St N; downtown. 342 3rd Ave N 33701. Fax: 727/895-8759. **Facility:** Designated smoking area. 21 one-bedroom standard units, some with efficiencies. 2 stories, interior corridors. *Bath:* combo or shower only. **Parking:** on-site. **Terms:** weekly rates available. **Amenities:** hair dryers. *Some:* irons. **Business Services:** fax. **Cards:** AX, DS, MC, VI.

SOME UNITS
(ASK) (S✦) (冬+) (冬+) (✕) (DATA PORT) (冬) (◻) / (VCR) (◻) /
FEE

MANSION HOUSE B & B AND THE COURTYARD ON FIFTH

Phone: (727)821-9391   12

(AAA) (SAVE)
▼▼▼ ▼▼▼

Historic Bed
& Breakfast

| All Year | 1P: $99 | 2P: $220 |

Location: 0.5 mi n at jct 5th Ave NE and 1st St N; downtown. 105 5th Ave NE 33701. Fax: 727/821-6906. **Facility:** This refurbished turn-of-the-20th-century home offers a picturesque garden area with both a pool and a whirlpool. Designated smoking area. 12 one-bedroom standard units. 2 stories, interior/exterior corridors. *Bath:* combo or shower only. **Parking:** on-site. **Terms:** 2 night minimum stay - weekends, cancellation fee imposed, [BP] meal plan available. **Amenities:** hair dryers. *Some:* irons. **Pool(s):** heated outdoor. **Leisure Activities:** whirlpool, 2 TV/library rooms with VCR & refrigerator, bicycles. *Fee:* boat cruises (shelling, moonlight cruise). **Guest Services:** complimentary evening beverages, valet laundry. **Business Services:** meeting rooms, PC, fax. **Cards:** AX, CB, DC, DS, MC, VI. **Special Amenities:** early check-in/late check-out.

SOME UNITS
(冬+) (🏊) (✕) (✕) (⚡) (DATA PORT) / (◻) /

PIER HOTEL

Phone: (727)822-7500   19

(AAA) (SAVE)
▼▼▼ ▼▼▼

Small-scale Hotel

| All Year [ECP] | 1P: $78-$188 | 2P: $78-$188 | XP: $10 |
| | | | F17 |

Location: At jct 3rd St N; downtown. 253 Second Ave N 33701. Fax: 727/822-0200. **Facility:** Smoke free premises. 28 units. 26 one-bedroom standard units. 2 one-bedroom suites ($118-$168). 3 stories (no elevator), interior corridors. *Bath:* combo or shower only. **Parking:** street. **Terms:** package plans - weekends. **Amenities:** high-speed Internet, voice mail, hair dryers. *Some:* irons. **Dining:** entertainment. **Guest Services:** complimentary evening beverages, valet laundry. **Business Services:** meeting rooms, fax. **Cards:** AX, CB, DC, DS, MC, VI.

SOME UNITS
(S✦) (冬+) (✕) (DATA PORT) / (◻) (◻) /

RADISSON HOTEL AND CONFERENCE CENTER

Phone: (727)572-7800   23

▼▼▼ ▼▼▼

Large-scale Hotel

1/1-4/30	1P: $139-$189	2P: $139-$189	XP: $15	F17
9/15-11/30	1P: $129-$179	2P: $129-$179	XP: $15	F17
5/1-9/14	1P: $119-$169	2P: $119-$169	XP: $15	F17
12/1-12/31	1P: $109-$129	2P: $109-$129		

Location: I-275, exit 30, 0.7 mi w on SR 686. 12600 Roosevelt Blvd 33716. Fax: 727/572-5700. **Facility:** 205 one-bedroom standard units. 9 stories, interior corridors. *Bath:* combo or shower only. **Parking:** on-site. **Terms:** 3 day cancellation notice-fee imposed, [AP], [BP], [CP] & [MAP] meal plans available, 20% service charge. **Amenities:** high-speed Internet, dual phone lines, voice mail, safes, irons, hair dryers. *Some:* CD players. **Pool(s):** heated outdoor. **Leisure Activities:** steamroom, exercise room. **Guest Services:** gift shop, coin laundry. **Business Services:** conference facilities, business center. **Cards:** AX, DS, MC, VI. *(See ad below)*

SOME UNITS
(ASK) (S✦) (✈) (⑪) (🏊) (⚡) (DATA PORT) (冬) (◻) / (✕) (◻) /

(See map p. 846)

RENAISSANCE VINOY RESORT & GOLF CLUB   **Phone:** (727)894-1000   **13**

(AAA) (SAVE)

1/10-5/22	1P: $246-$319	2P: $246-$319
12/1-1/9 & 9/26-11/30	1P: $189-$269	2P: $189-$269
5/23-9/25	1P: $151-$219	2P: $151-$219

Location: 1.8 mi e on 4th Ave, just n on Beach Dr; downtown. 501 Fifth Ave NE 33701. Fax: 727/822-2785.
Resort   **Facility:** Originally opened in 1925 as a haven for the rich and famous, this hotel has been restored and
Large-scale Hotel modernized but retains its historical grandeur. 360 units. 353 one-bedroom standard units, some with whirlpools. 7 one-bedroom suites ($289-$799). 7 stories, interior corridors. *Bath:* combo or shower only. **Parking:**
on-site and valet. **Terms:** check-in 4 pm, 3 day cancellation notice-fee imposed. **Amenities:** video games, voice mail, honor bars,
irons, hair dryers. **Dining:** 5 restaurants, 6 am-11 pm, cocktails, also, Marchand's Bar & Grill, Terrace Room, see separate listing,
entertainment. **Pool(s):** 2 heated outdoor. **Leisure Activities:** saunas, whirlpools, steamrooms, fishing, golf & tennis pro shop,
recreation programs, aerobics, hair salon, jogging, spa. **Fee:** sailboats, marina, charter fishing, sailing lessons, golf-18 holes, 12
lighted tennis courts, bicycles. **Guest Services:** gift shop, valet and coin laundry, airport transportation (fee)-Tampa Airport, area
transportation-within 5 mi. **Business Services:** conference facilities, business center. **Cards:** AX, CB, DC, DS, JC, MC, VI.

SOME UNITS

ST. PETERSBURG BAYFRONT HILTON   **Phone:** 727/894-5000   **16**

(SAVE)

1/10-5/31	1P: $143	2P: $143	XP: $10	F18
12/1-1/9 & 9/1-11/30	1P: $123	2P: $123	XP: $10	F18
6/1-8/31	1P: $83	2P: $83	XP: $10	F18

Location: Downtown. Located across from the Al Lang Stadium. 333 1st St S 33701. Fax: 727/894-7655.
Large-scale Hotel **Facility:** 333 one-bedroom standard units. 15 stories, interior corridors. *Bath:* some combo or shower only.
Parking: on-site. **Terms:** package plans, pets ($100 extra charge). **Amenities:** high-speed Internet, dual
phone lines, voice mail, irons, hair dryers. *Some:* CD players. **Pool(s):** heated outdoor. **Leisure Activities:** whirlpool. **Guest
Services:** gift shop, valet laundry, area transportation. **Business Services:** conference facilities, fax. **Cards:** AX, CB, DC, DS,
MC, VI.

SOME UNITS

SUNSET BAY INN BED & BREAKFAST   **Phone:** (727)896-6701   **8**

(AAA) (SAVE)

12/1-4/30 [BP]	1P: $150-$270	2P: $150-$270	XP: $25
10/1-11/30 [BP]	1P: $140-$260	2P: $140-$260	XP: $25
5/1-9/30 [BP]	1P: $130-$250	2P: $130-$250	XP: $25

Location: Just w of Beach Dr via 6th Ave NE, downtown. 635 Bay St NE 33701. Fax: 727/898-5311. **Facility:** This
Bed & Breakfast service-oriented inn set in a restored home dating from 1910 features tastefully decorated rooms, each with
a theme. Designated smoking area. 8 units. 7 one-bedroom standard units. 1 one-bedroom suite ($240-
$270). 3 stories (no elevator), interior/exterior corridors. **Parking:** street. **Terms:** 14 day cancellation notice-fee imposed, weekly
rates available, [ECP] meal plan available, package plans. **Amenities:** video library, CD players, dual phone lines, voice mail,
irons, hair dryers. **Leisure Activities:** bicycles. **Guest Services:** complimentary evening beverages, valet laundry. **Business
Services:** meeting rooms, fax. **Cards:** AX, DC, DS, MC, VI. **Special Amenities: early check-in/late check-out and free
newspaper.**

SOME UNITS

TERRACE PARK SUITES   **Phone:** (727)896-0071   **3**

(AAA) (SAVE)

12/15-4/30	1P: $139	2P: $139	XP: $10	F18
12/1-12/14 & 5/1-11/30	1P: $109	2P: $109	XP: $10	F18

Location: Just w of Beach Dr via 9th Ave NE; downtown. 206 9th Ave NE 33701. Fax: 727/822-1209. **Facility:** 10
Motel one-bedroom standard units with kitchens. 1 story, exterior corridors. **Parking:** on-site. **Terms:** 3 day cancellation notice-fee imposed, weekly rates available. **Amenities:** irons, hair dryers. **Cards:** AX, DS, MC, VI.

—— **WHERE TO DINE** ——

4TH STREET SHRIMP STORE   **Lunch:** $4-$21   **Dinner:** $4-$21   **Phone:** 727/822-0325   **15**

Location: 0.7 mi n at jct 10th Ave N. 1006 4th St N 33701. **Hours:** 11 am-9 pm. Closed: 4/20, 11/27, 12/25.
Features: A bright, nautical decor with colorful knickknacks will put you in the mood for fresh, delicious
Seafood seafood. An extensive menu of sandwiches, chowder, fish and shrimp is served on throwaway plates and
paper place mats for a no-fuss, no-muss meal. Casual dress; cocktails. **Parking:** on-site. **Cards:** MC, VI.

ARIGATO JAPANESE STEAK HOUSE RESTAURANT   **Dinner:** $11-$21   **Phone:** 727/343-5200   **8**

Location: Just s of jct 38th Ave N. 3600 66th St N 33710. **Hours:** 5 pm-10 pm, Sun 4 pm-9 pm. Closed: 1/1,
7/4, 11/27; also 12/24. **Reservations:** suggested. **Features:** Diners should come for the show, as
Ethnic entertaining chefs prepare Japanese specialties right at the table. The ichiban lets you sample shrimp,
chicken and filet with piquant oils and spices. This is a popular place, so expect to wait on groupings at the
hibachi table. Casual dress; cocktails. **Parking:** on-site. **Cards:** AX, CB, DC, DS, MC, VI.

BERTONI ITALIAN RESTAURANT & BAR   **Lunch:** $8-$13   **Dinner:** $10-$21   **Phone:** 727/822-5503   **29**

Location: At jct Central Ave; downtown. 16 2nd St N 33706. **Hours:** 11:30 am-2 & 5-10 pm, Sat from 5 pm.
Closed: Sun. **Features:** Downtown near the Baywalk shops, this Italian-style bistro offers a variety of tasty
Italian and pleasantly presented dishes. Favorites include such choices as sauteed Atlantic salmon, grilled beef
tenderloin and quill tube pasta with spinach. Casual dress; cocktails. **Parking:** street. **Cards:** AX, MC, VI.

(See map p. 846)

CAFE LIDO Lunch: $6-$11   Dinner: $9-$18   Phone: 727/898-5800   ⑯
Italian
MC, VI.
Location: Downtown; 1st floor of The Pier. 800 2nd Ave NE 33701. **Hours:** 11:30 am-10 pm, Fri & Sat-11 pm. **Features:** Handpainted murals by an Italian artist add to the romantic appeal of this bayfront locale. A tempting array of main dishes, such as rigatoni a la vodka and chicken parmesan, makes up a well-varied menu. Service is pleasant and prompt. Casual dress; cocktails. **Parking:** on-site (fee). **Cards:** AX, DS,

CARMELITA'S MEXICAN RESTAURANT   Lunch: $6-$10   Dinner: $8-$11   Phone: 727/545-2956   ④
Mexican
DS, MC, VI.
Location: Just s of jct 54th Ave N, 0.6 mi n of jct Tyrone Blvd. 5211 Park St N 33709. **Hours:** 11 am-9:30 pm, Fri & Sat-10 pm. Closed major holidays; also Super Bowl Sun. **Features:** A wide variety of entrees are featured like the Del Ray burrito, a good mixture of seasoned ground beef, tomatoes, onion and cheese. A live mariachi band performs on Tuesday nights. Casual dress; beer & wine only. **Parking:** on-site. **Cards:** AX,

CASUAL CLAM SEAFOOD RESTAURANT   Lunch: $5-$11   Dinner: $5-$11   Phone: 727/895-2526   ⑤
Seafood
wine only. **Parking:** on-site. **Cards:** MC, VI.
Location: I-275, exit 25, 0.9 mi e on 38th Ave N, 0.3 mi s. 3336 9th St N 33704. **Hours:** 11 am-9 pm, Thurs-Sat to 10 pm. Closed: 11/27, 12/25. **Features:** A popular neighborhood hangout, this light and airy eatery has the feel of rustic New England. Steamed clams, fish and chips, snow crab and shrimp scampi are among menu specialties. Pleasant servers in T-shirts and shorts add to the casual mood. Casual dress; beer &

COLUMBIA RESTAURANT   Lunch: $7-$10   Dinner: $14-$22   Phone: 727/822-8000   ⑰
Spanish
Parking: on-site (fee) and valet. **Cards:** AX, DC, DS, MC, VI.
Location: 4th floor of The Pier; downtown. 800 2nd Ave NE 33701. **Hours:** 11 am-10 pm, Fri & Sat-11 pm. **Reservations:** suggested. **Features:** Many of the tables afford a spectacular view of Tampa Bay and the St. Petersburg skyline. Traditional Spanish and Cuban cuisine is prepared with chicken, beef and Florida seafood. Try the pollo de arroz, baked chicken with yellow rice and pepper strips. Casual dress; cocktails.

CRAB SHACK   Lunch: $5-$14   Dinner: $5-$14   Phone: 727/576-7813   ②
Seafood
of sandwiches. Landlubbers may prefer the steak and chicken choices. Casual dress; cocktails. **Parking:** on-site. **Cards:** DS, MC, VI.
Location: 0.6 mi e of jct 4th St N. 11400 Gandy Blvd 33702. **Hours:** 11 am-9:30 pm, Fri & Sat-10:30 pm, Sun 1 pm-9:30 pm. Closed: 12/25; also Super Bowl Sun. **Features:** Just as the name suggests, a rustic crab shack setting—with picnic-table seating in the main dining room and small tables in the bar—awaits you here. Among menu selections are more than two dozen appetizers, three dozen entrees and a wide array

DISH BAYWALK   Lunch: $11-$13   Dinner: $13-$18   Phone: 727/894-5700   ㉓
American
Cards: MC, VI.
Location: Downtown; on 2nd floor of Baywalk. 192 2nd Ave N, Suite B200 33701. **Hours:** 11:30 am-9:30 pm, Fri & Sat-11 pm, Sun 10:30 am-9:30 pm. **Features:** This is a unique restaurant. Follow the tables around choosing the items that you want prepared from salad items, to sauces, to meats, to vegetables and take it to the center round where it is prepared before your eyes. Casual dress; cocktails. **Parking:** street.

EL CAP   Lunch: $3-$7   Dinner: $3-$7   Phone: 727/521-1314   ⑪
American
on-site. **Cards:** MC, VI.
Location: Jct 35th Ave N. 3500 4th St N 33704. **Hours:** 11 am-11 pm, Sun-10 pm. Closed: 11/27, 12/25. **Features:** Munch on the best burgers around at this basic sports bar where you'll also find subs, sandwiches, chili fries and jalapeno poppers. Expect good stick-to-your-ribs food served in a no-frills atmosphere. Patio dining and a carry-out window are available. Casual dress; beer & wine only. **Parking:**

FRED'S FAMOUS BAR-B-QUE AND BREWERY   Lunch: $5-$17   Dinner: $5-$17   Phone: 727/822-3733   ㉖
American
from which to choose. Casual dress; beer & wine only. **Parking:** on-site. **Cards:** AX, MC, VI.
Location: I-275, exit 26B southbound; 1.8 mi e on 54th Ave N, 1 mi s on US 92. 4351 4th St N 33703. **Hours:** 11 am-10 pm. Closed: 4/20, 11/27, 12/25. **Features:** The contemporary restaurant is a good place to go for great Southern barbecue. Beef and pork dinners, smoked chicken and hickory-grilled filet mignon or porterhouse are flavorfully prepared. Lighter appetites have plenty of sandwiches, salads and appetizers

THE GARDEN-A MEDITERRANEAN BISTRO   Lunch: $6-$8   Dinner: $7-$18   Phone: 727/896-3800   ㉘
Mediterranean
live jazz Friday and Saturday evenings. Casual dress; cocktails. **Parking:** street. **Cards:** AX, DC, MC, VI.
Location: Just e of jct 2nd St S; downtown. 217 Central Ave 33701. **Hours:** 11:30 am-10:30 pm, Fri & Sat-12:30 am. **Features:** The setting reflects the style of a bistro, with cozy indoor seating and a comfortable garden dining area. Mediterranean stylings, with bright colors and lots of plants, punctuate the surroundings. The on-site chef de cuisine prepares such wonderful entrees as fennel-crusted tuna or grilled lamb steak. Enjoy

GRAND FINALE   Dinner: $12-$22   Phone: 727/823-9921   ㉗
Continental
experience. Terrazzo floors, stylish glass bricks and hard walls create an acoustic situation that in some circumstances can be noisy. Dressy casual; cocktails. **Parking:** on-site. **Cards:** AX, DS, MC, VI.
Location: Just e of jct Central Ave at jct 11th St N. 1101 1st Ave N 33701. **Hours:** 5 pm-1 am. Closed: 11/27, 12/25; also Sun & Mon. **Features:** New American cuisine is the focus of the menu at this trendy establishment. From sashimi tuna to baby spinach and watercress salad to ginger- and scallion-encrusted salmon, a wonderful dinner awaits. Interesting Andy Warhol-style art lends to the "dining in a gallery"

GRATZZI RISTORANTE   Lunch: $8-$10   Dinner: $12-$26   Phone: 727/822-7769   ㉔
Italian
Location: Jct 2nd St N; in Baywalk; downtown. 199 2nd Ave N 33701. **Hours:** 11:30 am-10 pm, Fri & Sat-11 pm. **Features:** On the second floor of the Baywalk is this trendy and upscale dining establishment. The menu emphasizes northern Italian cuisine, including ably prepared and pleasantly presented selections of pasta, fish, meat, fowl, veal and chicken. Dressy casual; cocktails. **Parking:** on-site (fee). **Cards:** MC, VI.

(See map p. 846)

JO JO'S IN CITTA RESTAURANT, PIANO BAR & LOUNGE **Lunch:** $4-$10 **Dinner:** $8-$17 **Phone:** 727/894-0075　22
▼▼ ▼▼　**Location:** At jct 3rd St S; downtown; in Bank of America Tower. 200 Central Ave 33701. **Hours:** 11 am-10 pm, Fri &
Italian　Sat-11 pm, Sun noon-9 pm. Closed major holidays. **Features:** Hearty portions of pasta, pizza and calzones
are some of the dishes served in the fresh and modern cafe-style dining room. Guests on Friday and
Saturday evenings are treated to live entertainment. Casual dress; cocktails. **Parking:** street. **Cards:** AX,
DC, MC, VI.

THE KEYSTONE CLUB　**Dinner:** $12-$21　**Phone:** 727/822-6600　20
▼▼ ▼▼　**Location:** Just n of jct 4th St N and 3rd Ave N; center. 320 4th St N 33701. **Hours:** 4:30 pm-9 pm, Fri & Sat-10
pm. Closed major holidays; also Super Bowl Sun. **Reservations:** suggested. **Features:** This New
Steak & Seafood　York-style chop house offers a wide selection of salad, steak and fish. Try one of the specials or order the
filet mignon with mashed potatoes. House specialty is prime rib. The decor is pleasant, and prompt service
will get you back on the road in no time. Dressy casual; cocktails. **Parking:** on-site. **Cards:** AX, DC, DS, MC, VI.

THE LIMEY'S PUB　**Lunch:** $6-$7　**Dinner:** $9-$18　**Phone:** 727/895-2049　10
▼▼ ▼▼　**Location:** I-275, exit 24, 1.4 mi e on 22nd Ave N, just s. 1492 4th St N 33704. **Hours:** 11 am-2 am, Sun
noon-midnight. Closed: 11/27, 12/25. **Features:** The ambience of an English pub is pervasive in these
English　down-to-earth surroundings. Fresh air makes the deck a comfy place to dine. The beef in Guinness
pie-steak marinated in hearty beer and baked with chunks of pastry-satisfies the hungries. Cozy deck
dining and a kiddie playland are on-site. Casual dress; cocktails. **Parking:** on-site. **Cards:** AX, CB, DC, MC, VI.

MARCHAND'S BAR & GRILL　**Lunch:** $8-$15　**Dinner:** $11-$29　**Phone:** 727/894-1000　12
▼▼▼▼▼　**Location:** 1.8 mi e on 4th Ave, just n on Beach Dr; downtown; in Renaissance Vinoy Resort & Golf Club. 501 Fifth Ave
NE 33701. **Hours:** 11 am-2:30 & 5:30-10 pm. **Reservations:** suggested. **Features:** Marchand's occupies
Mediterranean　half of the original main dining room in the Vinoy, built in 1925 and restored in 1992. The hotel is a short
distance from The Pier and several museums and theaters. Much of the opulence of the original dining
room has been preserved. The menu is Mediterranean, with such specialties as seafood bouillabaisse, pan-roasted chicken
and braised lamb shank. Starters range from roasted eggplant soup to beef carpaccio. Grilled meats and fish are also
featured. Dressy casual; cocktails; entertainment. **Parking:** valet. **Cards:** AX, CB, DC, DS, JC, MC, VI.

MOON UNDER WATER　**Lunch:** $7-$9　**Dinner:** $7-$17　**Phone:** 727/896-6160　19
▼▼▼ ▼▼　**Location:** Just s of jct 4th Ave NE; downtown. 332 Beach Dr NE 33701. **Hours:** 11:30 am-11 pm, Fri & Sat-12:30
am. Closed: 11/27, 12/25. **Features:** This restaurant has the look and feel of a British pub. Lunch features
British　sandwiches and salads, with the Philly cheese steak as the standout. Tiered patio dining and excellent
service make for a pleasant meal. Casual dress; cocktails. **Parking:** street. **Cards:** AX, DC, MC, VI.

OVO CAFE　**Lunch:** $7-$14　**Dinner:** $9-$16　**Phone:** 727/895-5515　18
▼▼▼▼　**Location:** Just w of jct 5th St N; downtown. 515 Central Ave 33701. **Hours:** 11 am-10 pm, Mon-3 pm, Fri &
Sat-11 pm. Closed major holidays; also Sun. **Features:** This very trendy, upscale cafe gives the feeling of
American　a night out in New York. The chicken mushroom pirogue is marvelously tasty and artfully presented. A
polished espresso machine brews up the perfect accompaniment to a fine selection of desserts. Dressy
casual; cocktails. **Parking:** street. **Cards:** AX, DC, DS, MC, VI.

PAISANO'S PIZZA & PASTA　**Lunch:** $5-$18　**Dinner:** $7-$18　**Phone:** 727/521-2656　1
▼　**Location:** I-275, exit 26 southbound; exit 26B northbound, 1.4 mi e on 54th Ave N, 1 mi n on US 92. 6000 4th St N
Italian　33703. **Hours:** 11 am-10 pm, Fri & Sat-midnight. Closed: 11/27, 12/25. **Features:** In business since 1974,
this popular eatery is a true local favorite. It's known for its gourmet pizzas, calzones, stromboli, pasta
dishes and a tempting lunch buffet. Casual dress; cocktails. **Parking:** on-site. **Cards:** AX, DS, MC, VI.

PEPIN RESTAURANT　**Lunch:** $8-$12　**Dinner:** $14-$30　**Phone:** 727/821-3773　6
▼▼▼▼　**Location:** I-275, exit 26B southbound; exit 26 northbound, 1.8 mi e on 54th Ave N, 7 mi s on US 92. 4125 4th St N
33703. **Hours:** 11 am-10 pm, Fri-11 pm, Sat 5 pm-11 pm, Sun 5 pm-10 pm. Closed major holidays; also
Spanish　Mon. **Reservations:** suggested. **Features:** Dali and Picasso prints appeal to an artistic eye, while a
concert pianist fascinates a musical ear. The friendly restaurant serves up a splendid salad as well as
steak, seafood and dishes with a delightfully piquant Spanish influence. Casual dress; cocktails; entertainment. **Parking:**
on-site. **Cards:** AX, CB, DC, DS, MC, VI.

RED MESA REGIONAL MEXICAN & SOUTHWEST CUISINE **Lunch:** $5-$9 **Dinner:** $7-$18 **Phone:** 727/527-8728　3
▼▼ ▼▼　**Location:** I-275, exit 26, 1.4 mi e on 54th Ave N, just s. 4912 4th St N 33703. **Hours:** 11:30 am-9:30 pm, Fri-10:30
pm, Sat 5 pm-10:30 pm, Sun 5 pm-9 pm. Closed major holidays; also Super Bowl Sun. **Features:** Latin
Mexican　flavors spice up such intricate dishes as honey-marinated tuna, which is cured with sugar cane, oven
roasted and served with black bean puree and roasted potatoes. The theme carries over into the colorful
dining room as well as in the music. Smoke free premises. Casual dress; beer & wine only. **Parking:** on-site. **Cards:** AX, CB,
DC, DS, MC, VI.

REDWOODS RESTAURANT　**Dinner:** $17-$29　**Phone:** 727/896-5118　21
▼▼▼▼▼　**Location:** Just w of jct 3rd St N; downtown. 247 Central Ave 33702. **Hours:** 5:30 pm-10 pm, Fri & Sat 6:30
pm-11 pm. Closed: Sun & Mon. **Reservations:** suggested. **Features:** At the base of many menu offerings
American　is a profound Pacific Rim influence, with "lau lau" banana leaf cooking. A bakery and sushi bar are on the
premises. Casual dress; cocktails. **Parking:** street. **Cards:** AX, DS, MC, VI.

(See map p. 846)

SAFFRON'S AT JUNGLE PRADA Dinner: $10-$20 Phone: 727/345-6400 ⑦
Caribbean
Location: From jct Tyrone Blvd, 1.5 mi s. 1700 Park St N 33710. **Hours:** 5 pm-10 pm, Sun 3 pm-9 pm. Closed: 5/26. **Features:** Ample portions of Caribbean cuisine are served in a comfortable setting on the Intercoastal Waterway. Jamaican jerk chicken is colorfully displayed with plantains, cabbage and yellow rice. Casual dress; cocktails; entertainment. **Parking:** on-site and valet. **Cards:** AX, CB, DC, DS, MC, VI.

TERRACE ROOM Lunch: $7-$16 Dinner: $11-$29 Phone: 727/894-1000 ⑬
American
Location: 1.8 mi e on 4th Ave, just n on Beach Dr; downtown; in Renaissance Vinoy Resort & Golf Club. 501 Fifth Ave NE 33701. **Hours:** 6 am-3 & 5:30-10 pm. **Reservations:** suggested. **Features:** Terrace Room occupies half of the original main dining room in the Vinoy, built in 1925 and restored in 1992. Much of the opulence of the original was preserved. The menu is diverse, and the atmosphere casually elegant. Start with duck confit spring rolls, then move to a mixed greens or spinach salad. Interesting main courses include macadamia nut grouper with citrus-papaya salsa or grilled strip sirloin with blue cheese butter. Service is friendly and attentive. Dressy casual; cocktails; entertainment. **Parking:** valet. **Cards:** AX, CB, DC, DS, JC, MC, VI.

TEXAS CATTLE COMPANY Dinner: $10-$30 Phone: 727/527-3335 ⑨
Steak House
Location: I-275, exit 24, 1.2 mi w on 22nd Ave N, just n on US 19. 2600 34th St N 33713. **Hours:** 5 pm-10 pm, Fri & Sat-11 pm, Sun-9:30 pm. Closed: 11/27, 12/25. **Features:** Wood accents convey a decidedly Western aura in this rustic steakhouse. Sure, you'll find a juicy filet mignon, but the menu also includes fresh fish, chicken and tasty rock lobster. Try not to giggle when ordering the Charlie Brownie ice cream pie. Casual dress; cocktails. **Parking:** on-site. **Cards:** AX, MC, VI.

──────── *The following restaurants have not been evaluated by AAA* ────────
but are listed for your information only.

BEJING GARDEN CHINESE RESTAURANT Phone: 727/578-0972
[fyi] Not evaluated. **Location:** I-275, exit 32 southbound; exit 28 northbound, 1.2 mi n. 8901 4th St N 33701. **Features:** This restaurant is popular for it's expansive menu offering some 150 items to choose from. Typical chinese fare includes fried rice, sauteed shrimp or try the house specialty; steak kew.

CODY'S ORIGINAL ROADHOUSE Phone: 727/577-7730
[fyi] Not evaluated. **Location:** I-275, exit 32 southbound; exit 28 northbound, 1.2 mi s on US 92. 11270 4th St N 33716. **Features:** A fun, casual setting with lots of neat memorablia about is one of the draws here not to mention the filet, porterhouse and NY strip which are popular foods of choice. They also offer fresh fish such as grouper or salmon.

DAN MARINO'S TOWN TAVERN Phone: 727/822-4413
[fyi] Not evaluated. **Location:** Jct 2nd St N, in Baywalk; downtown. 121 2nd Ave N 33701. **Features:** Named for the famous Miami Dolphin's quarterback, you'll find lots of sports memorabilia at this popular spot. The menu is varied with chops, pastas, seafood, flatbread and sandwiches to choose from.

MARBO ON 4TH STREET Phone: 727/578-3080
[fyi] Not evaluated. **Location:** I-275, exit 32 southbound; exit 28 northbound, 1.2 mi s. 8123 4th St N 33702. **Features:** A popular spot for Chinese fare. The menu is extensive with some 114 items to choose from. Try anything from pork, poultry, beef, seafood or how about a combo dinner which will hit the spot!

MATTISON'S AN AMERICAN BISTRO Phone: 727/895-2200
[fyi] Not evaluated. **Location:** Jct 1st St N; in Plaza Tower Courtyard Shops; downtown. 111 2nd Ave NE 33701. **Features:** Chef Mattison prepares many delectable items at this 2nd floor bistro. Enjoy a fine meal after taking in a movie or shopping at this upscale eatery.

MIDTOWN RESTAURANT & BAR Phone: 727/502-0222
[fyi] Not evaluated. **Location:** Just s of jct Central Ave; downtown. 200 1st Ave S 33701. **Features:** Located in the heart of the city, this restaurant offers a variety of specialty sandwiches, burgers, soups and salads. They are noted for their seasoned wings.

SIAM GARDEN THAI RESTAURANT Phone: 727/822-0613
[fyi] Not evaluated. **Location:** I-275, exit 24, 1 mi e on 22nd Ave N, 1.2 mi n. 3125 9th St N 33704. **Features:** This casual eatery is known for quality Thai cuisine. There are many menu offerings from steak Thai to sizzling duckling or snapper.

TAMPA pop. 303,447 (See map p. 856; index p. 858)

──────── **WHERE TO STAY** ────────

AMERISUITES (TAMPA AIRPORT/WESTSHORE) Phone: (813)282-1037 ❶

	1P:	2P:	XP:	
12/1-4/20 [ECP]	1P: $159	2P: $159	XP: $10	F18
4/21-11/30 [ECP]	1P: $135	2P: $135	XP: $10	F18

Location: I-275, exit 40A, 0.5 mi w on Westshore; exit 20A northbound, 1 mi n on Kennedy Blvd, 1 mi w on Westshore. 4811 W Main St 33607. Fax: 813/282-1148. **Facility:** 126 one-bedroom standard units. 6 stories, interior corridors. Small-scale Hotel **Bath:** combo or shower only. **Parking:** on-site. **Terms:** small pets only. **Amenities:** voice mail, irons, hair dryers. *Some:* dual phone lines. **Pool(s):** heated outdoor. **Leisure Activities:** exercise room. **Guest Services:** valet and coin laundry. **Business Services:** meeting rooms, fax (fee). **Cards:** AX, CB, DC, DS, JC, MC, VI. **Special Amenities:** free continental breakfast and free newspaper. *(See color ad p 871)*

SOME UNITS

(See map p. 856)

AMERISUITES (TAMPA NEAR BUSCH GARDENS) Phone: (813)979-1922 [24]
AAA SAVE 12/1-3/31 1P: $105-$125 2P: $115-$135 XP: $10 F17
4/1-11/30 1P: $95-$105 2P: $99-$115 XP: $10 F17
◆◆◆◆◆ **Location:** I-275, exit 51, 1.8 mi e on SR 582, just s. 11408 N 30th St 33612-6446. Fax: 813/979-1926. **Facility:** 128 one-bedroom suites. 6 stories, interior corridors. *Bath:* combo or shower only. **Parking:** on-site. **Terms:** small Small-scale Hotel pets only (in smoking units only). **Amenities:** high-speed Internet, dual phone lines, voice mail, safes (fee), irons, hair dryers. **Pool(s):** heated outdoor. **Leisure Activities:** exercise room. **Guest Services:** valet and coin laundry. **Business Services:** meeting rooms, fax (fee). **Cards:** AX, CB, DC, DS, MC, VI. **Special Amenities:** free continental breakfast and free newspaper. *(See color ad below)*

SOME UNITS
[icons] / [X] /

AMERISUITES (TAMPA/SABAL CORP. PARK) Phone: (813)622-8557 [64]
AAA SAVE 1/1-3/31 [CP] 1P: $129-$139 2P: $129-$139 XP: $10 F18
4/1-11/30 [CP] 1P: $90-$109 2P: $99-$109 XP: $10 F18
◆◆◆◆◆ 12/1-12/31 [CP] 1P: $95-$105 2P: $95-$105 XP: $10 F18
Location: I-75, exit 260 southbound; exit 260B northbound, 0.5 mi w on SR 574, just s on Falkenburg Rd, just w. Lo-
Small-scale Hotel cated in the Sabal Corporate Center. 10007 Princess Palm Ave 33619. Fax: 813/620-4866. **Facility:** 59 units. 27 one-bedroom standard units. 32 one-bedroom suites. 2 stories, interior corridors. *Bath:* combo or shower only. **Parking:** on-site. **Terms:** small pets only. **Amenities:** video games, dual phone lines, voice mail, irons, hair dryers. **Pool(s):** heated outdoor. **Leisure Activities:** jogging, exercise room. **Guest Services:** complimentary evening beverages, valet and coin laundry. **Business Services:** meeting rooms, fax. **Cards:** AX, CB, DC, DS, MC, VI. **Special Amenities:** free continental breakfast and free newspaper. *(See color ad below)*

SOME UNITS
[icons] / [X] /

(See map p. 856)

BAYMONT INN & SUITES TAMPA-BRANDON   Phone: (813)684-4007   [20]
(AAA) [SAVE]   12/1-4/13 [ECP]   1P: $74-$94   2P: $74-$94
◆◆ ◆◆   4/14-11/30 [ECP]   1P: $59-$79   2P: $59-$79
                 Location: I-75, exit 257, just w on SR 60. 602 S Falkenburg Rd 33619. Fax: 813/681-3042. **Facility:** 100 units. 92
                 one-bedroom standard units. 6 one- and 2 two-bedroom suites. 3 stories, interior corridors. **Parking:** on-site.
Small-scale Hotel **Terms:** small pets only. **Amenities:** video games, voice mail, irons, hair dryers. *Some:* dual phone lines.
                 Pool(s): outdoor. **Guest Services:** coin laundry. **Business Services:** fax. **Cards:** AX, CB, DC, DS, MC, VI.
Special Amenities: **free continental breakfast and free newspaper.** *(See color ad below)*

SOME UNITS

[icons] FEE

BAYMONT INN & SUITES TAMPA/NEAR BUSCH GARDENS   Phone: (813)930-6900   [7]
(AAA) [SAVE]   12/1-3/31 & 5/31-9/8 [ECP]   1P: $74-$94   2P: $74-$94
◆◆◆◆   4/1-5/30 & 9/9-11/30 [ECP]   1P: $59-$79   2P: $59-$79
                 Location: I-275, exit 50, 2 mi e on SR 580, just n. 9202 N State St 33612. Fax: 813/930-0563. **Facility:** 143 units.
                 134 one-bedroom standard units. 9 one-bedroom suites ($109-$129). 3 stories, exterior corridors. **Parking:**
Small-scale Hotel on-site. **Terms:** small pets only ($10 extra charge, in smoking units). **Amenities:** video games, voice mail,
                 irons, hair dryers. **Pool(s):** outdoor. **Guest Services:** valet and coin
laundry. **Business Services:** meeting rooms, fax. **Cards:** AX, CB, DC, DS, MC, VI. Special Amenities: **free continental breakfast and free newspaper.** *(See color ad below)*

SOME UNITS

[icons]

BAYMONT INN TAMPA-FAIRGROUNDS   Phone: (813)626-0885   [17]
(AAA) [SAVE]   2/2-4/13 [ECP]   1P: $79-$99   2P: $79-$99
◆◆ ◆◆   12/1-2/1 & 4/14-11/30 [ECP]   1P: $59-$79   2P: $59-$79
                 Location: I-4, exit 6 westbound; exit 6A eastbound, just se. 4811 US 301 N 33610. Fax: 813/623-3321. **Facility:** 101
                 one-bedroom standard units. 3 stories, interior corridors. **Parking:** on-site. **Terms:** small pets only ($10 extra
Motel   charge). **Amenities:** video games, voice mail, irons, hair dryers. **Pool(s):** outdoor. **Guest Services:** coin
                 laundry. **Business Services:** fax. **Cards:** AX, CB, DC, DS, MC, VI. Special Amenities: **free continental
breakfast and free newspaper.** *(See color ad below)*

SOME UNITS

[icons]

BEST WESTERN ALL SUITES HOTEL BEHIND BUSCH GARDENS   Phone: (813)971-8930   [55]
(AAA) [SAVE]   All Year [BP]   1P: $79-$129   2P: $79-$129   XP: $10   F17
◆◆◆◆   **Location:** I-275, exit 51, 1.8 mi e on SR 582, 0.5 mi s on N 30th St. 3001 University Center Dr 33612.
                 Fax: 813/971-8935. **Facility:** 150 one-bedroom standard units. 3 stories, exterior corridors. **Parking:** on-site.
                 Terms: 2-3 night minimum stay - seasonal, weekly rates available, package plans, pets ($10 extra charge).
Small-scale Hotel **Amenities:** video library (fee), dual phone lines, voice mail, irons, hair dryers. **Dining:** 6 am-10 & 4:30-10
                 pm, cocktails. **Pool(s):** heated outdoor. **Leisure Activities:** whirlpool, sun deck, billiards, ping pong. **Guest
Services:** gift shop, valet and coin laundry. **Business Services:** meeting rooms, fax. **Cards:** AX, CB, DC, DS, MC, VI.
Special Amenities: **free continental breakfast and free newspaper.** *(See color ad p 856)*

SOME UNITS

[icons]

(See map p. 856)

BEST WESTERN-THE WESTSHORE HOTEL
Phone: (813)282-3636   62

SAVE

	1/16-4/30 [BP]	1P: $99-$109	2P: $99-$119	XP: $10	F17
	12/1-1/15 & 9/1-11/30 [BP]	1P: $79-$99	2P: $79-$109	XP: $10	F17
	5/1-8/31 [BP]	1P: $69-$89	2P: $79-$99	XP: $10	F17

Large-scale Hotel

Location: I-275, exit 40A southbound; exit 39A northbound (Kennedy Blvd), 0.8 mi w. Located in commercial area. 1200 N Westshore Blvd 33607. Fax: 813/282-0055. **Facility:** 238 units. 236 one-bedroom standard units. 2 one-bedroom suites ($99-$149). 5 stories, exterior corridors. **Parking:** on-site. **Terms:** weekly rates available, package plans. **Amenities:** voice mail, safes (fee), irons, hair dryers. **Pool(s):** outdoor. **Leisure Activities:** exercise room. **Fee:** game room. **Guest Services:** gift shop, valet and coin laundry, area transportation. **Business Services:** conference facilities, business center. **Cards:** AX, CB, DC, DS, JC, MC, VI.

SOME UNITS

🔊 ✈ 🍴 🍸 🛥 📺 DATA PORT 🖥 / ✕ 🛄 🖼 /

CHASE SUITE HOTEL BY WOODFIN
Phone: (813)281-5677   50

	12/1-4/30	1P: $119-$159	2P: $129-$169	XP: $10	F16
	5/1-11/30	1P: $109-$149	2P: $119-$159	XP: $10	F16

Motel

Location: I-275, exit 39 southbound; exit 39B northbound, 3 mi w on SR 60, just n. Located in Rocky Point Harbor. 3075 N Rocky Point Dr 33607. Fax: 813/289-0266. **Facility:** 176 units. 130 one- and 46 two-bedroom standard units with kitchens. 2 stories, exterior corridors. **Parking:** on-site. **Terms:** [ECP] meal plan available, package plans - weekends, attractions, pets ($50 fee, $5 extra charge). **Amenities:** high-speed Internet, voice mail, irons, hair dryers. **Pool(s):** heated outdoor. **Leisure Activities:** whirlpool, boat dock, fishing, sports court. **Guest Services:** complimentary evening beverages, valet and coin laundry, area transportation. **Business Services:** meeting rooms, PC, fax. **Cards:** AX, DC, DS, MC, VI.

SOME UNITS

ASK 🔊 ✈ 🐾 🍴 🚭 🛥 🏃 ✕ 📺 DATA PORT 🛄 🖼 🖥 / ✕ VCR /
FEE

COMFORT SUITES
Phone: (813)630-4444   37

AAA SAVE

	1/4-4/20 [ECP]	1P: $104	2P: $114	XP: $10	F
	12/1-1/3 & 4/21-11/30 [ECP]	1P: $80	2P: $90	XP: $10	F

Motel

Location: I-75, exit 257, 0.5 mi w on SR 60. 9932 E Adamo Dr 33619. Fax: 813/630-2093. **Facility:** 67 one-bedroom suites with whirlpools. 4 stories, interior corridors. **Parking:** on-site. **Amenities:** dual phone lines, voice mail, irons, hair dryers. **Pool(s):** heated outdoor. **Leisure Activities:** exercise room. **Guest Services:** valet and coin laundry. **Business Services:** meeting rooms, fax. **Cards:** AX, CB, DC, DS, MC, VI.
Special Amenities: free continental breakfast and free local telephone calls.

SOME UNITS

🍴 🗜 🚭 🛥 🏃 DATA PORT 🛄 🖼 🖥 / ✕ /

COURTYARD BY MARRIOTT
Phone: (813)874-0555   33

SAVE

	1/6-4/20	1P: $109-$179
	9/9-11/30	1P: $99-$169
	12/1-1/5 & 4/21-9/8	1P: $89-$149

Motel

Location: I-275, exit 41A, just s. 3805 W Cypress 33607. Fax: 813/870-0685. **Facility:** 145 units. 134 one-bedroom standard units. 11 one-bedroom suites ($169-$199). 4 stories, interior corridors. *Bath:* combo or shower only. **Parking:** on-site. **Terms:** check-in 4 pm. **Amenities:** high-speed Internet, voice mail, irons, hair dryers. **Pool(s):** heated outdoor. **Leisure Activities:** whirlpool, exercise room. **Guest Services:** valet and coin laundry, area transportation. **Business Services:** meeting rooms, business center. **Cards:** AX, CB, DC, DS, MC, VI. *(See ad below)*

SOME UNITS

🔊 ✈ 🗜 ♿ 🚭 🛥 📺 DATA PORT 🖥 / ✕ VCR 🛄 🖼 /
FEE

COURTYARD BY MARRIOTT-DOWNTOWN TAMPA
Phone: (813)229-1100   34

SAVE

	1/3-4/1	1P: $159-$179	2P: $159-$179
	12/1-1/2	1P: $139-$159	2P: $139-$159
	4/2-11/30	1P: $119-$159	2P: $119-$159

Small-scale Hotel

Location: I-275, exit 44, 0.6 mi sw via Tampa St; downtown. 102 E Cass St 33602. Fax: 813/224-9200. **Facility:** 141 units. 136 one-bedroom standard units, some with whirlpools. 5 one-bedroom suites. 6 stories, interior corridors. *Bath:* combo or shower only. **Parking:** valet. **Terms:** check-in 4 pm. **Amenities:** dual phone lines, voice mail, irons, hair dryers. **Pool(s):** heated outdoor. **Leisure Activities:** whirlpool, exercise room. **Guest Services:** valet and coin laundry. **Business Services:** meeting rooms, business center. **Cards:** AX, DC, DS, MC, VI.

SOME UNITS

🔊 🍴 🍸 🗜 ♿ 🚭 🛥 📺 DATA PORT 🖥 / ✕ 🛄 🖼 /

(See map p. 856)

COURTYARD BY MARRIOTT-TAMPA/BRANDON　　　　　　　　Phone: (813)661-9559　[25]

[SAVE]

▼▼◇▼◇▼

Motel

1/16-11/30	1P: $99-$299	2P: $99-$299
12/1-1/15	1P: $69-$149	2P: $69-$149

Location: I-75, exit 257, just w on SR 60, just s on Falkenburg Rd. 10152 Palm River Rd 33619. Fax: 813/661-4583. **Facility:** 90 units. 87 one-bedroom standard units, some with whirlpools. 3 one-bedroom suites. 3 stories, interior corridors. *Bath:* combo or shower only. **Parking:** on-site. **Terms:** [BP] meal plan available. **Amenities:** video games, high-speed Internet, dual phone lines, voice mail, irons, hair dryers. **Pool(s):** heated indoor. **Leisure Activities:** whirlpool, exercise room. **Guest Services:** valet and coin laundry. **Business Services:** meeting rooms, fax. **Cards:** AX, DC, DS, MC, VI.

SOME UNITS

[icons] [⚫] [&M] [⚫] [✈] [★] [DATA PORT] [⚫] / [✕] [⬛] [⚫] /

COURTYARD BY MARRIOTT TAMPA NORTH　　　　　　　　　　Phone: 813/978-9898　[2]

[SAVE]

▼▼◇▼◇▼

Motel

All Year　　　1P: $59-$139

Location: I-75, exit 266, 0.5 mi w on Fletcher Ave. Located at Hidden River Corporate Park. 13575 Cypress Glen Ln 33637. Fax: 813/978-1835. **Facility:** 81 units. 78 one-bedroom standard units, some with whirlpools. 3 one-bedroom suites. 3 stories, interior corridors. *Bath:* combo or shower only. **Parking:** on-site. **Terms:** package plans. **Amenities:** dual phone lines, voice mail, irons, hair dryers. **Pool(s):** heated outdoor. **Leisure Activities:** whirlpool, exercise room. **Guest Services:** valet and coin laundry. **Business Services:** meeting rooms, fax. **Cards:** AX, DC, DS, MC, VI.

SOME UNITS

[icons] [⚫] [🍴] [Y] [&M] [⚫] [✈] [★] [DATA PORT] [⚫] / [✕] [⬛] [⚫] /

CROWNE PLAZA HOTEL AND RESORT TAMPA AT SABAL PARK　　　Phone: (813)623-6363　[19]

▼▼◇▼◇▼

Large-scale Hotel

1/1-4/18	1P: $99-$189	2P: $109-$199	XP: $10	F18
8/30-11/30	1P: $89-$179	2P: $99-$179	XP: $10	F18
4/19-8/29	1P: $89-$169	2P: $99-$179	XP: $10	F18
12/1-12/31	1P: $79-$169	2P: $89-$179	XP: $10	F18

Location: I-75, exit 260 southbound; exit 260B northbound, just w. Located in the Sabal Center. 10221 Princess Palm Ave 33610. Fax: 813/621-7224. **Facility:** 269 units. 228 one-bedroom standard units. 41 one-bedroom suites ($94-$450), some with kitchens. 5 stories, interior corridors. *Bath:* combo or shower only. **Parking:** on-site. **Terms:** [BP] meal plan available. **Amenities:** video games, dual phone lines, voice mail, irons, hair dryers. **Pool(s):** heated outdoor. **Leisure Activities:** whirlpool, lighted tennis court, jogging, exercise room, basketball. **Guest Services:** gift shop, valet and coin laundry, area transportation. **Business Services:** conference facilities, business center. **Cards:** AX, CB, DC, DS, JC, MC, VI.

SOME UNITS

[ASK] [⚫] [✈] [🍴] [Y] [&M] [⚫] [✈] [✕] [★] [DATA PORT] [⚫] / [✕] [⬛] /

(See map p. 856)

CROWNE PLAZA HOTEL AND RESORT TAMPA-WESTSHORE

12/1-4/30	1P: $129-$159
10/1-11/30	1P: $119-$159
5/1-9/30	1P: $99-$139

Phone: (813)289-8200   **43**
XP: $10

Large-scale Hotel   **Location:** I-275, exit 40A southbound; exit 39A northbound, 1 mi n on Kennedy Blvd, 0.9 mi w. Located in a commercial area. 700 N Westshore Blvd 33609. Fax: 813/289-9166. **Facility:** 272 units. 266 one-bedroom standard units. 4 one- and 2 two-bedroom suites. 11 stories, interior corridors. **Bath:** combo or shower only. **Parking:** on-site and valet. **Amenities:** video games, high-speed Internet, dual phone lines, voice mail, irons, hair dryers. **Pool(s):** outdoor. **Leisure Activities:** saunas, whirlpool, exercise room. **Guest Services:** gift shop, valet laundry, area transportation. **Business Services:** meeting rooms, business center. **Cards:** AX, CB, DC, DS, MC, VI.

SOME UNITS
(ASK) (SD) (✦) (¶) (Y) (⬥) (⬦) (⬤) (⬛) (⬤) (DATA PORT) (⬜) / (✕) (⬜) /
FEE

Hilton
Garden Inn
Tampa/Ybor Historic District

1700 East 9th Avenue
Tampa, Florida 33605

(813) 769-YBOR
(877) FOR-HILTON

• 95 Guestrooms & Suites • Garden Pavilion • Two Conference Rooms • Beautiful Courtyard
• Market Place • Retail Center • Fully "Cooked-to-Order" Breakfast • Outdoor Swimming Pool
• Fully Equipped Fitness and Business Center • Self-Service Laundry • Shuttle Service

DAYS INN

9942 Adamo Dr.
Tampa, Florida 33619

(813) 623-5121
(800) 835-3297

Minutes to Florida State Fairgrounds, Brandon Town Center Mall, Downtown Tampa, Busch Gardens, Tampa Convention Center & Historic Ybor City • Sparkling Swimming Pool • Complimentary Continental Breakfast • Guest Laundry • In-Room Refrigerators

IMPACT HOTELS

Check Us Out The Web: **www.impact–hotels.com**

(See map p. 856)

DAYS INN AIRPORT STADIUM

SAVE

▼▼▼▼▼
Small-scale Hotel

Phone: (813)877-6181 **3** F17

All Year [CP]	1P: $85-$129	2P: $85-$129

XP: $10

Location: I-275, exit 41B, 0.6 mi n on US 92. Located in a commercial area. 2522 N Dale Mabry 33607. Fax: 813/875-6171. **Facility:** 296 units. 293 one-bedroom standard units. 3 one-bedroom suites. 2 stories, exterior corridors. *Bath:* combo or shower only. **Parking:** on-site. **Terms:** weekly rates available, pets ($25 extra charge). **Amenities:** voice mail, safes (fee), irons, hair dryers. **Pool(s):** outdoor, heated outdoor. **Guest Services:** valet and coin laundry. **Business Services:** meeting rooms, business center. **Cards:** AX, DC, DS, MC, VI. *(See color ad p 874)*

SOME UNITS

🔲 🖕 🐾 🍴 🅱 🍳 🛥 📷 🔌 🔲 🍽 / ✕ 💻 /

DAYS INN/STATE FAIRGROUNDS

SAVE

▼▼▼ ▼▼▼
Motel

Phone: (813)623-5121 **21**

2/1-3/31	1P: $79-$89	2P: $79-$89
1/1-1/31	1P: $64-$74	2P: $64-$74
4/1-11/30	1P: $59-$69	2P: $59-$69
12/1-12/31	1P: $54-$64	2P: $54-$64

XP: $10
XP: $10
XP: $10
XP: $10

Location: I-75, exit 257, 0.5 mi w on SR 60. 9942 Adamo Dr 33619. Fax: 813/628-4989. **Facility:** 100 units. 99 one-bedroom standard units. 1 one-bedroom suite with kitchen. 2 stories, interior corridors. **Parking:** on-site. **Terms:** [CP] meal plan available. **Amenities:** safes (fee), hair dryers. *Some:* irons. **Pool(s):** outdoor. **Guest Services:** coin laundry. **Business Services:** meeting rooms, fax. **Cards:** AX, CB, DC, DS, JC, MC, VI. *(See color ad p 875)*

SOME UNITS

🔲 🍴 🍳 🛥 🚶 🍽 / ✕ 🔌 🍽 /
FEE   FEE

DOUBLETREE GUEST SUITES TAMPA BAY

SAVE

▼▼▼▼▼
Large-scale Hotel

Phone: (813)888-8800 **49**

12/1-5/31	1P: $109-$179	2P: $109-$179
6/1-11/30	1P: $79-$149	2P: $79-$149

XP: $20   F18
XP: $20   F18

Location: I-275, exit 39 southbound; exit 39B northbound, 3 mi w on SR 60, just n. Located in Rocky Point Harbour. 3050 N Rocky Point Dr W 33607. Fax: 813/888-8743. **Facility:** 203 one-bedroom suites. 7 stories, interior corridors. **Parking:** on-site. **Terms:** cancellation fee imposed, package plans. **Amenities:** voice mail, honor bars, irons, hair dryers. *Some:* dual phone lines. **Pool(s):** heated outdoor. **Leisure Activities:** sauna, whirlpool, boat dock, jogging, exercise room. **Guest Services:** gift shop, valet and coin laundry, area transportation. **Business Services:** meeting rooms, PC, fax. **Cards:** AX, CB, DC, DS, MC, VI.

SOME UNITS

🔲 🖕 🍴 🍸 🏋 🍳 🛥 ✕ 🍽 🔌 💻 / ✕ 📼 🍽 /
FEE

DOUBLETREE GUEST SUITES TAMPA/BUSCH GARDENS

AAA **SAVE**

▼▼▼ ▼▼
Small-scale Hotel

Phone: (813)971-7690 **6**

All Year [BP]	1P: $79-$116	2P: $79-$116

XP: $10   F18

Location: I-275, exit 51, 1.8 mi e on SR 582, just s. 11310 N 30th St 33612. Fax: 813/972-5525. **Facility:** 129 one-bedroom standard units. 3 stories, exterior corridors. **Parking:** on-site. **Terms:** cancellation fee imposed. **Amenities:** video games, dual phone lines, voice mail, irons, hair dryers. **Pool(s):** heated outdoor. **Leisure Activities:** whirlpool. **Guest Services:** valet and coin laundry, area transportation-within 5 mi. **Business Services:** meeting rooms, fax. **Cards:** AX, CB, DC, DS, MC, VI. **Special Amenities:** free continental breakfast and free newspaper. *(See color ad p 875)*

SOME UNITS

🔲 🍳 🛥 🚶 🍽 🔌 🔲 🍽 💻 / ✕ /
FEE

DOUBLETREE HOTEL TAMPA AIRPORT-WESTSHORE

AAA **SAVE**

▼▼▼▼▼
Large-scale Hotel

Phone: (813)879-4800 **56**

12/1-12/28 [BP]	1P: $79-$169	2P: $79-$169
12/29-3/31 [BP]	1P: $99-$159	2P: $99-$159
4/1-11/30 [BP]	1P: $89-$159	2P: $89-$159

XP: $10   F
XP: $10   F
XP: $10   F

Location: I-275, exit 40A; exit 39B northbound, just w on Westshore, then just n. 4500 W Cypress St 33607. Fax: 813/873-2401. **Facility:** 489 one-bedroom standard units, some with kitchens. 5-10 stories, interior corridors. *Bath:* combo or shower only. **Parking:** on-site. **Terms:** 18% service charge. **Amenities:** video games, high-speed Internet, dual phone lines, voice mail, irons, hair dryers. **Dining:** 2 restaurants, 6:30 am-midnight, cocktails. **Pool(s):** heated outdoor. **Leisure Activities:** whirlpool, exercise room. **Guest Services:** gift shop, valet and coin laundry, area transportation-within 2 mi. **Business Services:** conference facilities, fax. **Cards:** AX, CB, DC, DS, MC, VI. *(See color ad below)*

SOME UNITS

🔲 🖕 🍴 🍸 🅱 🛥 ✕ 🔌 💻 / ✕ 🍴 /

(See map p. 856)

ECONO LODGE MIDTOWN
Phone: (813)254-3005   **35**

AAA SAVE
12/1-4/15   1P: $48-$75   2P: $52-$85   XP: $6   F18
4/16-11/30   1P: $45-$65   2P: $48-$70

WWWW
Location: I-275, exit 41A, 1.5 mi s. 1020 S Dale Mabry Hwy 33629. Fax: 813/253-2909. **Facility:** 74 one-bedroom
standard units. 2 stories, exterior corridors. *Bath:* combo or shower only. **Parking:** on-site. **Terms:** weekly
Motel   rates available, [ECP] meal plan available. **Amenities:** high-speed Internet, voice mail, hair dryers. *Some:*
irons. **Pool(s):** heated outdoor. **Guest Services:** coin laundry. **Business Services:** fax. **Cards:** AX, CB, DC,
DS, MC, VI. **Special Amenities: free continental breakfast and free local telephone calls.**

SOME UNITS
(🛎 ⊞ ⊞⁺ 📺 🖥 📷 🏊 🎥 DATA PORT / ✕ 🔲 🖥 💻 / FEE)

EMBASSY SUITES HOTEL-TAMPA/AIRPORT/WESTSHORE
Phone: (813)875-1555   **40**

SAVE
1/1-4/30 [BP]   1P: $169-$249   2P: $169-$249   XP: $20   F18
10/1-11/30 [BP]   1P: $159-$239   2P: $159-$239   XP: $20   F18
12/1-12/31 [BP]   1P: $139-$219   2P: $139-$219   XP: $20   F18

WWWW
5/1-9/30 [BP]   1P: $149-$209   2P: $149-$209   XP: $20   F18
Large-scale Hotel   **Location:** I-275, exit 40A southbound; exit 39A northbound, 1 mi n on Kennedy Blvd, 0.5 mi w. Located in a commercial
area. 555 N Westshore Blvd 33609. Fax: 813/287-3664. **Facility:** 221 units. 195 one- and 26 two-bedroom
suites, some with kitchens. 16 stories, interior corridors. *Bath:* combo or shower only. **Parking:** on-site and valet. **Terms:** cancellation fee imposed. **Amenities:** voice mail, honor bars, irons, hair dryers. **Dining:** Bay Cafe, see separate listing. **Pool(s):**
heated outdoor. **Leisure Activities:** saunas, whirlpool, exercise room. **Guest Services:** gift shop, complimentary evening beverages, valet and coin laundry, area transportation. **Business Services:** conference facilities, business center. **Cards:** AX, CB,
DC, DS, JC, MC, VI.

SOME UNITS
(🛎 ⊞ ⊞ 🍴 🖥 📷 🏊 ✕ 🎥 DATA PORT 🔲 💻 / ✕ 🖥 /)

EMBASSY SUITES HOTEL USF/NEAR BUSCH GARDENS
Phone: (813)977-7066   **42**

AAA SAVE
All Year [BP]   1P: $129-$229   2P: $129-$229   XP: $15   F18

WWWW
Location: I-275, exit 51, 2.2 mi e on SR 582. 3705 Spectrum Blvd 33612. Fax: 813/977-7933. **Facility:** 247 one-
bedroom suites. 8 stories, interior corridors. *Bath:* combo or shower only. **Parking:** on-site. **Terms:** cancellation fee imposed. **Amenities:** video games, high-speed Internet, dual phone lines, voice mail, irons, hair
Large-scale Hotel   dryers. **Dining:** 11 am-2 & 5-10 pm. **Pool(s):** heated outdoor. **Leisure Activities:** sauna, whirlpool, exercise
room. *Fee:* game room. **Guest Services:** gift shop, complimentary evening beverages, valet and coin
laundry, area transportation-within 5 mi. **Business Services:** conference facilities, business center. **Cards:** AX, CB, DC, DS,
MC, VI. **Special Amenities: free continental breakfast and free newspaper.** *(See color ad below)*

SOME UNITS
(🛎 ⊞ 🍴 🖥 🅜 📷 🏊 ✕ 🎥 DATA PORT 🔲 🖥 💻 / ✕ /)

(See map p. 856)

FAIRFIELD INN BY MARRIOTT-TAMPA/BRANDON   Phone: (813)661-9719   [22]

[SAVE]

	1/15-4/25	1P: $89-$189	2P: $89-$189
	12/1-1/14	1P: $79-$189	2P: $79-$189
	4/26-11/30	1P: $59-$109	2P: $59-$109

Motel   **Location:** I-75, exit 257, just w on SR 60, just s on Falkenburg Rd. 10150 Palm River Rd 33619. Fax: 813/661-0416. **Facility:** 107 one-bedroom standard units, some with whirlpools. 3 stories, interior corridors. *Bath:* combo or shower only. **Parking:** on-site. **Terms:** [ECP] meal plan available. **Amenities:** video games, irons. *Some:* hair dryers. **Pool(s):** heated outdoor. **Leisure Activities:** exercise room. **Guest Services:** valet and coin laundry. **Business Services:** fax. **Cards:** AX, DC, DS, MC, VI.

SOME UNITS
[icons] /

GRAM'S PLACE BNB GUESTHOUSES/YOUTH HOSTEL & MUSIC   Phone: (813)221-0596   [65]

| | 12/1-4/30 [CP] | 1P: $80-$95 | 2P: $80-$95 |
| | 5/1-11/30 [CP] | 1P: $65-$80 | 2P: $65-$80 |

Bed & Breakfast   **Location:** I-275, exit 46B, 0.6 mi w on E Dr Martin Luther King Jr Blvd, 0.6 mi s on N Ola Ave; at jct Plymouth St. Located in a residential area. 3109 N Ola Ave 33603. Fax: 813/221-0596. **Facility:** Designated smoking area. 7 one-bedroom standard units. 1 story, interior/exterior corridors. *Bath:* some shared or private, combo or shower only. **Parking:** on-site. **Terms:** 7 day cancellation notice-fee imposed. **Leisure Activities:** whirlpool. **Guest Services:** complimentary laundry. **Cards:** AX, MC, VI.

[ASK] [icons]

HAMPTON INN   Phone: (813)289-6262   [53]

[AAA] [SAVE]

	2/1-4/13	1P: $89-$129	2P: $89-$129
	1/1-1/31	1P: $79-$119	2P: $79-$119
	12/1-12/31 & 4/14-11/30	1P: $69-$109	2P: $69-$109

Motel   **Location:** I-275, exit 39 southbound; exit 39B northbound, 3 mi w on SR 60, just n. Located in Rocky Point Harbor. 3035 N Rocky Point Dr 33607. Fax: 813/287-9363. **Facility:** 70 one-bedroom standard units. 5 stories, interior corridors. *Bath:* combo or shower only. **Parking:** on-site. **Terms:** cancellation fee imposed. **Amenities:** video games, high-speed Internet, voice mail, irons, hair dryers. **Pool(s):** heated outdoor. **Guest Services:** valet and coin laundry, area transportation. **Business Services:** fax. **Cards:** AX, CB, DC, DS, MC, VI. **Special Amenities:** free continental breakfast and free local telephone calls. *(See color ad below)*

SOME UNITS
[icons] /

(See map p. 856)

HAMPTON INN & SUITES Phone: (813)903-6000 [28]

AAA **SAVE**
🔷🔷🔷
Motel

12/26-3/31 1P: $105-$120 2P: $105-$120
12/1-12/25 & 4/1-11/30 1P: $85-$95 2P: $85-$95
Location: I-75, exit 266, 0.8 mi w on Fletcher Ave. Located at Hidden River Corporate Park. 8210 Hidden River Pkwy 33637. Fax: 813/977-3343. **Facility:** 127 units. 89 one-bedroom standard units. 38 one-bedroom suites ($115-$139) with kitchens. 4 stories, interior corridors. *Bath:* combo or shower only. **Parking:** on-site. **Terms:** weekly rates available, [ECP] meal plan available, package plans. **Amenities:** video games, high-speed Internet (fee), dual phone lines, voice mail, irons, hair dryers. **Pool(s):** outdoor. **Leisure Activities:** exercise room. **Guest Services:** complimentary evening beverages: Mon-Thurs, valet and coin laundry. **Business Services:** meeting rooms, fax. **Cards:** AX, CB, DC, DS, MC, VI. **Special Amenities:** free continental breakfast and free local telephone calls.
(See color ad p 877)

SOME UNITS
🛎️ 📠 💺 🍳 ➳ 🎥 DATA PORT 📺 / ✖️ VCR 🍴 📷 /

HAMPTON INN TAMPA INT'L AIRPORT - WESTSHORE Phone: (813)287-0778 [44]

AAA **SAVE**
🔷🔷🔷
Small-scale Hotel

1/1-4/30 [ECP] 1P: $89-$139 2P: $99-$149
5/1-11/30 [ECP] 1P: $79-$139 2P: $89-$149
12/1-12/31 [ECP] 1P: $69-$119 2P: $79-$129
Location: I-275, exit 40A, 0.5 mi w Westshore; exit 20A northbound (Kennedy Blvd), 1 mi w on Westshore, 0.3 mi s. 4817 W Laurel St 33607. Fax: 813/287-0882. **Facility:** 134 one-bedroom standard units. 6 stories, interior corridors. **Parking:** on-site. **Amenities:** video games, high-speed Internet, voice mail, irons, hair dryers. *Some:* dual phone lines. **Pool(s):** outdoor. **Leisure Activities:** exercise room. **Guest Services:** valet laundry, area transportation-within 2 mi. **Business Services:** meeting rooms, PC, fax. **Cards:** AX, CB, DC, DS, MC, VI. **Special Amenities:** early check-in/late check-out and free continental breakfast.

SOME UNITS
🛎️ ✈️ 🍴 💺 🍳 ➳ 🎥 DATA PORT 📺 / ✖️ 🍴 📷 /

HILTON GARDEN INN/TAMPA YBOR CITY HISTORIC DISTRICT Phone: (813)769-9267 [69]

SAVE
🔷🔷🔷
Small-scale Hotel

All Year 1P: $99-$159 XP: $10 F18
Location: I-4, exit 1, just s on 21st St, just w. 1700 E 9th Ave 33605. Fax: 813/769-3299. **Facility:** 95 units. 84 one-bedroom standard units. 11 one-bedroom suites ($159-$209). 4 stories, interior corridors. *Bath:* combo or shower only. **Parking:** on-site (fee). **Terms:** 14 day cancellation notice, [BP] & [ECP] meal plans available. **Amenities:** video games, dual phone lines, voice mail, irons, hair dryers. **Pool(s):** outdoor. **Leisure Activities:** whirlpool, exercise room. **Guest Services:** valet and coin laundry, area transportation. **Business Services:** meeting rooms, business center. **Cards:** AX, CB, DC, DS, JC, MC, VI. *(See color ad p 875)*

SOME UNITS
🛎️ ✈️ 🍴 💺 🍳 ➳ 🎥 DATA PORT 🍴 📷 📺 / ✖️ /

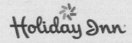

(See map p. 856)

HILTON TAMPA AIRPORT WESTSHORE
SAVE

Large-scale Hotel

Phone: (813)877-6688 **38**
All Year [CP]   1P: $79-$159   2P: $79-$159   XP: $10   F18
Location: I-275, exit 40B, 0.8 mi n. Located in a commercial area. 2225 N Lois Ave 33607. Fax: 813/879-3264. **Facility:** 238 units. 236 one-bedroom standard units. 1 one- and 1 two-bedroom suites. 12 stories, interior corridors. *Bath:* combo or shower only. **Parking:** on-site. **Amenities:** high-speed Internet, dual phone lines, voice mail, irons, hair dryers. **Pool(s):** heated outdoor. **Leisure Activities:** whirlpool, lighted tennis court, exercise room, basketball. **Guest Services:** gift shop, valet laundry, area transportation. **Cards:** AX, DC, DS, MC, VI. *(See ad p 879)*

SOME UNITS

HOLIDAY INN EXPRESS HOTEL & SUITES
(AAA) SAVE

Motel

Phone: (813)287-8585 **58**
2/1-4/13   1P: $89-$129   2P: $89-$129
1/1-1/31   1P: $79-$119   2P: $79-$119
12/1-12/31 & 4/14-11/30   1P: $69-$109   2P: $69-$109
Location: I-275, exit 39 southbound; exit 39B northbound, 3 mi w on SR 60, just n. Located in Rocky Point Harbour. 3025 N Rocky Point Dr 33607. Fax: 813/287-8484. **Facility:** 88 units. 52 one-bedroom standard units. 36 one-bedroom suites. 4 stories, interior corridors. *Bath:* combo or shower only. **Parking:** on-site. **Terms:** cancellation fee imposed. **Amenities:** dual phone lines, voice mail, irons, hair dryers. **Pool(s):** heated outdoor. **Leisure Activities:** exercise room. **Guest Services:** valet and coin laundry, area transportation-within 5 mi. **Business Services:** meeting rooms, fax. **Cards:** AX, DC, DS, JC, MC, VI. **Special Amenities:** free continental breakfast and free local telephone calls. *(See color ad p 878)*

SOME UNITS

HOLIDAY INN EXPRESS HOTEL & SUITES TAMPA STADIUM/AIRPORT

Motel

Phone: (813)877-6061 **4**
1/19-4/20 [ECP]   1P: $75-$108   2P: $75-$108
12/1-1/18 & 4/21-11/30 [ECP]   1P: $69-$103   2P: $69-$103
Location: I-275, exit 41B, 2 mi n. 4732 N Dale Mabry Hwy 33614. Fax: 813/876-1531. **Facility:** 236 units. 212 one-bedroom standard units. 24 one-bedroom suites ($89-$149), some with kitchens. 2 stories, exterior corridors. **Parking:** on-site. **Terms:** pets ($25 extra charge). **Amenities:** dual phone lines, voice mail, irons, hair dryers. **Pool(s):** outdoor. **Leisure Activities:** jogging, exercise room. **Guest Services:** valet and coin laundry, area transportation. **Business Services:** conference facilities, business center. **Cards:** AX, CB, DC, DS, MC, VI.

SOME UNITS

HOLIDAY INN TAMPA NEAR BUSCH GARDENS
(AAA) SAVE

Small-scale Hotel

Phone: (813)971-4710 **13**
12/1-4/30   1P: $109-$149   2P: $109-$149
5/1-11/30   1P: $99-$149   2P: $99-$149
Location: I-275, exit 51, 1.5 mi e on SR 582. 2701 E Fowler Ave 33612. Fax: 813/910-8038. **Facility:** 408 units. 406 one-bedroom standard units. 2 one-bedroom suites ($109-$169). 2 stories, interior/exterior corridors. *Bath:* combo or shower only. **Parking:** on-site. **Terms:** check-in 4 pm, age restrictions may apply, cancellation fee imposed, pets ($25 extra charge). **Amenities:** video games, voice mail, irons, hair dryers. *Some:* CD players. **Dining:** 6 am-11 pm, cocktails. **Pool(s):** heated outdoor, wading. **Leisure Activities:** exercise room. *Fee:* game room. **Guest Services:** gift shop, valet and coin laundry, area transportation-within 5 mi. **Business Services:** conference facilities, fax (fee). **Cards:** AX, DC, DS, MC, VI. **Special Amenities:** early check-in/late check-out and free newspaper. *(See color ad opposite inside back cover & p 879)*

SOME UNITS

FEE   FEE

HOMESTEAD STUDIO SUITES HOTEL-TAMPA/NORTH AIRPORT

Small-scale Hotel

Phone: (813)243-1913 **8**
1/15-4/15   1P: $89   2P: $99   XP: $5   F18
12/1-1/14 & 4/16-11/30   1P: $49   2P: $59   XP: $5   F18
Location: SR 589 (Veterans Expwy), exit 4, just w on SR 580. Commercial area. 5401 Beaumont Ctr Blvd 33634. Fax: 813/243-1813. **Facility:** 121 one-bedroom standard units with efficiencies. 2 stories, exterior corridors. *Bath:* some combo or shower only. **Parking:** on-site. **Terms:** cancellation fee imposed, pets ($75 extra charge). **Amenities:** voice mail, irons. **Guest Services:** valet and coin laundry. **Business Services:** fax (fee). **Cards:** AX, CB, DC, DS, JC, MC, VI.

SOME UNITS

HOWARD JOHNSON EXPRESS INN & SUITES
(AAA) SAVE

Small-scale Hotel

Phone: (813)832-4656 **27**
All Year [ECP]   1P: $45-$65   2P: $45-$65   XP: $5   F18
Location: I-275, exit 41A, 2.5 mi s. 3314 S Dale Mabry Hwy 33629. Fax: 813/832-5454. **Facility:** 80 units. 58 one-bedroom standard units, some with whirlpools. 22 one-bedroom suites ($65-$125). 2 stories, exterior corridors. *Bath:* combo or shower only. **Parking:** on-site. **Terms:** weekly rates available. **Amenities:** irons, hair dryers. **Pool(s):** heated outdoor. **Guest Services:** coin laundry. **Business Services:** meeting rooms, fax. **Special Amenities:** early check-in/late check-out and free continental breakfast.

SOME UNITS

HOWARD JOHNSON TAMPA AIRPORT/STADIUM
(AAA) SAVE

Motel

Phone: (813)875-8818 **5**
All Year   1P: $59   2P: $64   XP: $5   F18
Location: I-275, exit 41B, 0.5 mi n. 2055 N Dale Mabry Hwy 33607. Fax: 813/876-4964. **Facility:** 138 units. 135 one-bedroom standard units. 3 one-bedroom suites ($109-$120). 2 stories, exterior corridors. **Parking:** on-site. **Terms:** weekly rates available, [ECP] meal plan available, 12% service charge, pets ($25 fee). **Amenities:** voice mail, safes (fee), irons, hair dryers. **Dining:** 2 restaurants, 11:15 am-10:30 pm, Sat & Sun 2:15 pm-10 pm, cocktails. **Pool(s):** heated outdoor. **Leisure Activities:** exercise room. **Guest Services:** coin laundry, area transportation-within 6 mi (downtown & Port of Tampa also). **Business Services:** meeting rooms, fax. **Cards:** AX, CB, DC, DS, JC, MC, VI. **Special Amenities:** early check-in/late check-out and free continental breakfast.

SOME UNITS

FEE

(See map p. 856)

HYATT REGENCY TAMPA
Phone: (813)225-1234   **31**

(AAA) [SAVE]
▼▼▼

All Year   1P: $105-$249   2P: $105-$249   XP: $25   F18

Location: I-275, exit 44, 0.8 mi s on Ashley St to Jackson, just e on Tampa St S. Connects to downtown office and shopping complex. 2 Tampa City Center 33602. Fax: 813/273-0234. **Facility:** 521 units. 519 one-bedroom standard units. 2 one-bedroom suites. 17 stories, interior corridors. *Bath:* combo or shower only. **Parking:** on-site and **Large-scale Hotel** valet. **Terms:** cancellation fee imposed. **Amenities:** dual phone lines, voice mail, safes, irons, hair dryers. *Some:* CD players, fax. **Dining:** 2 restaurants, 6:30 am-11 pm, cocktails. **Pool(s):** heated outdoor. **Leisure Activities:** whirlpool, exercise room. **Guest Services:** gift shop, valet and coin laundry, airport transportation (fee)-Tampa International Airport. **Business Services:** conference facilities, business center. **Cards:** AX, CB, DC, DS, JC, MC, VI.

SOME UNITS
[🅵 ⏍ 🍴 🍸 ⬚ 🚹M 🚭 ⌗ 🏊 🎦 🖥DATA PORT ☕ / ✕ VCR 🧺 /]
FEE   FEE   FEE

HYATT REGENCY WESTSHORE
Phone: (813)874-1234   **46**

(AAA) [SAVE]
▼▼▼ ▼▼▼

All Year   1P: $119-$280   2P: $119-$280   XP: $25   F18

Location: SR 60, at east end of Courtney Campbell Cswy. Located in an upscale office park area. 6200 Courtney Campbell Cswy 33607. Fax: 813/207-6790. **Facility:** The Hyatt Regency Westshore is next to an ecologically protected salt marsh and overlooks Old Tampa Bay; rooms offer city and bay views. 445 units. 435 one-bedroom **Large-scale Hotel** standard units, some with whirlpools. 10 one-bedroom suites, some with whirlpools. 1-13 stories, interior/exterior corridors. *Bath:* combo or shower only. **Parking:** on-site and valet. **Terms:** cancellation fee imposed. **Amenities:** dual phone lines, voice mail, honor bars, irons, hair dryers. *Some:* CD players, fax, safes. **Dining:** 3 restaurants, 6:30 am-10 pm, cocktails, also, Armani's, Oystercatchers, see separate listing, entertainment. **Pool(s):** 2 heated outdoor. **Leisure Activities:** saunas, whirlpools, 2 lighted tennis courts, nature preserve, nature walk & observation deck, basketball. *Fee:* massage. **Guest Services:** gift shop, valet laundry, airport transportation-Tampa International Airport. **Business Services:** conference facilities, business center. **Cards:** AX, CB, DC, DS, JC, MC, VI.

SOME UNITS
[🅵 ⏍ 🍴 🍸 ⌂ 🚭 🏊 🎾 ✕ 🎦 🖥DATA PORT ☕ / ✕ 🧺 🍽 /]

LA QUINTA INN & SUITES USF
Phone: (813)910-7500   **59**

(AAA) [SAVE]
▼▼▼ ▼▼▼

1/20-4/6   1P: $89-$109   2P: $95-$115
12/1-1/19 & 4/7-11/30   1P: $79-$99   2P: $85-$105

Location: I-275, exit 51, 2.2 mi e on SR 582. 3701 E Fowler 33612. Fax: 813/910-7600. **Facility:** 109 units. 105 one-bedroom standard units. 4 one-bedroom suites. 4 stories, interior corridors. *Bath:* combo or shower only. **Small-scale Hotel** **Parking:** on-site. **Terms:** [ECP] meal plan available, small pets only. **Amenities:** video games, dual phone lines, voice mail, irons, hair dryers. **Pool(s):** heated outdoor. **Leisure Activities:** whirlpool, exercise room. **Guest Services:** valet and coin laundry. **Business Services:** meeting rooms, fax. **Cards:** AX, CB, DC, DS, JC, MC, VI **Special Amenities:** free continental breakfast and free local telephone calls. *(See color ad below)*

SOME UNITS
[🐾 ⏍ 🚹M 🚭 🎦 🖥DATA PORT ☕ / ✕ 🧺 🍽 /]

LA QUINTA INN TAMPA AIRPORT
Phone: (813)287-0440   **45**

(AAA) [SAVE]
▼▼▼

12/26-4/7   1P: $99-$129   2P: $105-$135
12/1-12/25 & 4/8-11/30   1P: $69-$89   2P: $75-$95

Location: I-275, exit 40A southbound; exit 39A northbound (Westshore Dr), 0.8 mi w. 4730 Spruce St 33607-1497. **Motel** Fax: 813/286-7399. **Facility:** 122 one-bedroom standard units. 2 stories, exterior corridors. **Parking:** on-site. **Terms:** [ECP] meal plan available, small pets only. **Amenities:** video games, voice mail, irons, hair dryers. **Pool(s):** heated outdoor. **Guest Services:** valet laundry. **Business Services:** meeting rooms, fax. **Cards:** AX, CB, DC, DS, JC, MC, VI. **Special Amenities:** free continental breakfast and free local telephone calls. *(See color ad below)*

SOME UNITS
[⏍ 🐾 ⏍ 🚭 🎦 🖥DATA PORT ☕ / ✕ 🧺 🍽 /]
FEE   FEE

(See map p. 856)

MARRIOTT-TAMPA WESTSHORE

Phone: (813)287-2555 **71**

[SAVE]

12/1-4/12 & 9/7-11/30	1P: $199-$209	2P: $199-$209	XP: $10	F18
4/13-9/6	1P: $189-$199	2P: $189-$199	XP: $10	F18

Location: I-275, exit 40A, just w; exit 39A northbound 1 mi n on Kennedy Blvd, 09 mi w. 1001 N Westshore Blvd 33607. Fax: 813/289-5464. **Facility:** 310 one-bedroom standard units. 13 stories, interior corridors. **Parking:** on-site.

Large-scale Hotel **Terms:** check-in 4 pm, cancellation fee imposed, 20% service charge. **Amenities:** high-speed Internet, dual phone lines, voice mail, irons, hair dryers. **Pool(s):** heated indoor/outdoor. **Leisure Activities:** saunas, whirlpool, exercise room. *Fee:* massage, personal trainer. **Guest Services:** gift shop, valet and coin laundry, area transportation. **Business Services:** business center. **Cards:** AX, CB, DC, DS, JC, MC, VI.

SOME UNITS

MICROTEL INN & SUITES

Phone: (813)739-2244 **9**

All Year [CP] 1P: $44-$53 2P: $53-$62 XP: $5 F12

Location: I-275, exit 47B, 3.3 mi w on Hillsborough Ave, just n. 5405 N Church Ave 33614. Fax: 813/739-2250.

Small-scale Hotel **Facility:** 63 one-bedroom standard units. 3 stories, interior corridors. *Bath:* combo or shower only. **Parking:** on-site. **Amenities:** voice mail, irons, hair dryers. **Pool(s):** outdoor. **Guest Services:** coin laundry. **Business Services:** meeting rooms, fax. **Cards:** AX, DS, MC, VI.

SOME UNITS
FEE

MOTEL 6 #1192

Phone: 813/628-0888 **61**

1/9-11/30	1P: $37-$47	2P: $43-$53	XP: $3	F17
12/1-1/8	1P: $35-$45	2P: $41-$51	XP: $3	F17

Motel **Location:** I-4, exit 6 westbound; exit 6B eastbound, 0.7 mi n. 6510 US 301 N 33610. Fax: 813/620-4899. **Facility:** 108 one-bedroom standard units. 3 stories, exterior corridors. *Bath:* combo or shower only. **Parking:** on-site. **Terms:** small pets only. **Pool(s):** heated outdoor. **Guest Services:** coin laundry. **Cards:** AX, CB, DC, DS, MC, VI.

SOME UNITS

MOTEL 6 - 483

Phone: 813/932-4948 **60**

2/1-4/19	1P: $39-$49	2P: $45-$55	XP: $3	F17
4/20-11/30	1P: $37-$47	2P: $43-$53	XP: $3	F17
12/1-1/31	1P: $36-$46	2P: $42-$52	XP: $3	F17

Motel **Location:** I-275, exit 51, just w on SR 582. 333 E Fowler Ave 33612. Fax: 813/931-4577. **Facility:** 150 one-bedroom standard units. 2 stories, exterior corridors. **Parking:** on-site. **Terms:** small pets only (limit 1, must be attended). **Pool(s):** outdoor. **Guest Services:** coin laundry. **Business Services:** fax. **Cards:** AX, CB, DC, DS, MC, VI.

SOME UNITS

QUALITY INN-BUSCH GARDENS

Phone: (813)961-1000 **57**

(AAA) [SAVE]

All Year 2P: $69 XP: $5 F

Location: I-275, exit 53, just w. 400 E Bearss Ave 33613. Fax: 813/961-5704. **Facility:** 155 one-bedroom standard

Motel units. 2 stories, exterior corridors. *Bath:* combo or shower only. **Parking:** on-site. **Terms:** [BP] meal plan available. **Amenities:** irons, hair dryers. **Pool(s):** outdoor, wading. **Guest Services:** coin laundry. **Business Services:** meeting rooms, fax. **Cards:** AX, DS, MC, VI. *(See color ad below)*

SOME UNITS
FEE FEE

(See map p. 856)

RADISSON BAY HARBOR HOTEL
(AAA) [SAVE]
▼▼▼▼

Phone: (813)281-8900 **48**

	1P: $147-$157	2P: $147-$157	XP: $10	F16
1/1-5/3				
12/1-12/31	1P: $119-$129	2P: $119-$129	XP: $10	F16
5/4-11/30	1P: $79-$119	2P: $79-$119	XP: $10	F16

Location: I-275, exit 39 southbound; exit 39B norhtbound, 3 mi w on SR 60. 7700 Courtney Campbell Cswy 33607. **Large-scale Hotel** Fax: 813/281-0927. **Facility:** 257 units. 252 one-bedroom standard units. 4 one- and 1 two-bedroom suites. 6 stories, interior corridors. **Bath:** combo or shower only. **Parking:** on-site. **Terms:** cancellation fee imposed. **Amenities:** video games, dual phone lines, voice mail, irons, hair dryers. *Some:* fax. **Dining:** 6:30 am-11 pm, Fri & Sat 7 am-midnight, cocktails. **Pool(s):** heated outdoor. **Leisure Activities:** boat dock, fishing, 2 lighted tennis courts, exercise room, basketball. **Guest Services:** gift shop, valet and coin laundry, area transportation-within 3 mi. **Business Services:** conference facilities, fax. **Cards:** AX, CB, DC, DS, JC, MC, VI. **Special Amenities:** free newspaper and free room upgrade (subject to availability with advanced reservations). *(See ad below)*

SOME UNITS
[icons] / [icons] VCR 🛏 📠 /
FEE FEE FEE

RADISSON RIVERWALK HOTEL TAMPA
(AAA) [SAVE]
▼▼▼▼

Phone: (813)223-2222 **63**

| 12/1-4/16 & 9/5-11/30 [CP] | 1P: $119-$219 | 2P: $119-$219 | XP: $10 | F18 |
| 4/17-9/4 [CP] | 1P: $109-$179 | 2P: $109-$179 | XP: $10 | F18 |

Location: I-275, exit 44, 0.8 mi s; downtown. 200 N Ashley Dr 33602. Fax: 813/273-0839. **Facility:** 282 units. 277 one-bedroom standard units. 5 one-bedroom suites ($235-$325). 6 stories, interior corridors. **Parking:** valet. **Large-scale Hotel Terms:** [AP], [BP], [ECP] & [MAP] meal plans available, 12% service charge. **Amenities:** video games, voice mail, irons, hair dryers. *Some:* dual phone lines. **Dining:** 2 restaurants, 6 am-10 pm, Fri & Sat-11 pm, cocktails. **Pool(s):** outdoor. **Leisure Activities:** sauna, boat dock, exercise room. *Fee:* charter fishing. **Guest Services:** gift shop, valet and coin laundry, airport transportation (fee)-Tampa International Airport, area transportation-within 1 mi. **Business Services:** conference facilities. **Cards:** AX, CB, DC, DS, JC, MC, VI. **Special Amenities:** free newspaper and free room upgrade (subject to availability with advanced reservations).

SOME UNITS
[icons] / [icons] 🛏 📠 /
FEE

RED ROOF INN
(AAA) [SAVE]
▼▼▼

Motel

Phone: (813)932-0073 **11**

2/8-4/19	1P: $56-$74	2P: $56-$74
4/20-11/30	1P: $39-$59	2P: $39-$59
12/1-2/7	1P: $39-$54	2P: $39-$54

Location: I-275, exit 50, 1.4 mi e on SR 580. 2307 E Busch Blvd 33612. Fax: 813/933-5689. **Facility:** 108 one-bedroom standard units. 2 stories, exterior corridors. **Parking:** on-site. **Terms:** small pets only. **Amenities:** video games, voice mail. *Some:* irons, hair dryers. **Pool(s):** outdoor. **Leisure Activities:** whirlpool. **Business Services:** fax. **Cards:** AX, CB, DC, DS, MC, VI. **Special Amenities:** free local telephone calls and free newspaper.

SOME UNITS
[icons] / [icons] /

RED ROOF INN-BRANDON
(AAA) [SAVE]
▼▼▼

Motel

Phone: (813)681-8484 **51**

2/1-4/20	1P: $76-$85	2P: $76-$85
1/1-1/31	1P: $62-$72	2P: $62-$72
12/1-12/31 & 4/21-11/30	1P: $47-$55	2P: $47-$55

Location: I-75, exit 257, just w to S Falkenberg Rd, just n. 10121 Horace Ave 33619. Fax: 813/681-8892. **Facility:** 120 one-bedroom standard units. 3 stories, exterior corridors. **Parking:** on-site. **Terms:** small pets only. **Amenities:** video games, voice mail. *Some:* irons, hair dryers. **Pool(s):** heated outdoor. **Guest Services:** coin laundry. **Business Services:** fax. **Cards:** AX, CB, DC, DS, MC, VI. **Special Amenities:** free local telephone calls and free newspaper.

SOME UNITS
[icons] / [icons] /

RED ROOF INN-FAIRGROUNDS
(AAA) [SAVE]
▼▼▼

Motel

Phone: (813)623-5245 **15**

| 1/10-4/19 | 1P: $59-$79 | 2P: $59-$79 |
| 12/1-1/9 & 4/20-11/30 | 1P: $39-$51 | 2P: $39-$51 |

Location: I-4, exit 7, just se. 5001 N US 301 33610. Fax: 813/623-5240. **Facility:** 108 one-bedroom standard units. 2 stories, exterior corridors. **Parking:** on-site. **Terms:** small pets only. **Amenities:** video games, voice mail. *Some:* irons, hair dryers. **Business Services:** fax. **Cards:** AX, CB, DC, DS, MC, VI. **Special Amenities:** free local telephone calls and free newspaper.

SOME UNITS
[icons] / [icons] /

(See map p. 856)

RESIDENCE INN BY MARRIOTT

Phone: (813)221-4224 🔢12

[SAVE]

♦♦♦♦

Small-scale Hotel

1/1-4/30 [ECP]	1P: $169-$189	
12/1-12/31 & 9/1-11/30 [ECP]	1P: $149-$169	
5/1-8/31 [ECP]	1P: $119-$139	

Location: I-275, exit 44, 0.5 mi sw via Tampa St; downtown. 101 E Tyler St 33602. Fax: 813/221-4228. **Facility:** 109 units. 48 one-bedroom standard units with efficiencies. 47 one- and 14 two-bedroom suites, some with kitchens. 7 stories, interior corridors. *Bath:* combo or shower only. **Parking:** on-site (fee). **Terms:** check-in 4 pm, pets ($125 fee). **Amenities:** dual phone lines, voice mail, irons, hair dryers. **Leisure Activities:** whirlpool, exercise room, sports court, basketball. **Business Services:** meeting rooms, fax (fee). **Cards:** AX, CB, DC, DS, JC, MC, VI.

SOME UNITS

🄢 🐾 🍴 ♿ ⛔ 🎥 ✕ 🎬 📟 🔌 📺 💻 / 📼 /

RESIDENCE INN BY MARRIOTT SABAL PARK

Phone: (813)627-8855 🔢14

[SAVE]

♦♦♦♦

Small-scale Hotel

1/1-3/31 [BP]	1P: $129-$169
12/1-12/31 & 4/1-11/30 [BP]	1P: $99-$139

Location: I-75, exit 260, just w. 9719 Princess Palm Ave 33619. Fax: 813/627-8899. **Facility:** 102 one-bedroom standard units. 3 stories, interior corridors. **Parking:** on-site. **Terms:** small pets only ($125). **Amenities:** voice mail, irons, hair dryers. **Pool(s):** heated outdoor. **Leisure Activities:** whirlpool, exercise room, sports court. **Business Services:** meeting rooms. **Cards:** AX, DC, DS, JC, MC, VI.

SOME UNITS

🄢 🐾 ➦ ✕ 🎬 📟 🔌 📺 💻 / ✕ 📼

SAILPORT WATERFRONT RESORT

Phone: (813)281-9599 🔢70

♦♦

Condominium

All Year [CP]	1P: $69-$129	2P: $69-$129

Location: I-275, exit 39 southbound; exit 39B northbound, SR 60 (towards Clearwater), 3 mi w to Rocky Point Dr, then 2 mi s. 2506 Rocky Point Dr 33607. Fax: 813/281-9510. **Facility:** 212 units. 189 one- and 23 two-bedroom suites with kitchens. 4 stories, interior/exterior corridors. **Parking:** on-site. **Terms:** cancellation fee imposed, weekly rates available, package plans. **Amenities:** CD players, voice mail, irons. **Pool(s):** heated outdoor. **Leisure Activities:** boat dock, fishing, lighted tennis court. **Guest Services:** gift shop, coin laundry. **Business Services:** meeting rooms. **Cards:** AX, CB, DC, JC, MC, VI.

[ASK] 🄢 🍴 ➦ ✕ 📼 🎬 📟 🔌 📺 💻

SHERATON SUITES HOTEL

Phone: (813)873-8675 🔢36

♦♦♦

Large-scale Hotel

1/1-5/6	1P: $189-$295	2P: $189-$295	XP: $10	F12
9/9-11/30	1P: $169-$275	2P: $179-$285	XP: $10	F12
5/7-9/8	1P: $159-$275	2P: $169-$285	XP: $10	F12
12/1-12/31	1P: $169-$275	2P: $179-$285	XP: $10	F12

Location: I-275, exit 40B, n to Cypress St, 0.3 mi w; exit 20B northbound. Commercial area. 4400 W Cypress St 33607. Fax: 813/877-6766. **Facility:** 260 one-bedroom suites. 8 stories, interior corridors. *Bath:* combo or shower only. **Parking:** on-site. **Terms:** 3 day cancellation notice, [AP], [BP], [CP] & [ECP] meal plans available, package plans - weekends, 20% service charge. **Amenities:** CD players, dual phone lines, voice mail, irons, hair dryers. *Some:* fax. **Pool(s):** heated indoor. **Leisure Activities:** sauna, whirlpool, exercise room. **Guest Services:** valet and coin laundry, area transportation. **Business Services:** conference facilities. **Cards:** AX, CB, DC, DS, MC, VI. *(See color ad p 5)*

SOME UNITS

[ASK] 🄢 ♿ 🍴 🍷 🎥 🔲 🎬 ➦ ✕ 🎬 📟 🔌 📺 💻 / ✕ /

SHONEY'S INN

Phone: (813)985-8525 🔢30

(AAA) [SAVE]

♦♦♦♦

Motel

12/26-4/30 [CP]	1P: $71-$77	2P: $77-$83	XP: $6	F17
12/1-12/25 & 5/1-11/30 [CP]	1P: $59-$65	2P: $65-$71	XP: $6	F17

Location: I-75, exit 265, 0.5 mi w on SR 582. 8602 Morris Bridge Rd 33617. Fax: 813/988-3552. **Facility:** 122 one-bedroom standard units. 2 stories, exterior corridors. **Parking:** on-site. **Amenities:** hair dryers. *Some:* irons. **Pool(s):** outdoor. **Guest Services:** sundries, valet laundry. **Business Services:** meeting rooms, fax. **Cards:** AX, DC, DS, MC, VI. **Special Amenities:** free continental breakfast and free local telephone calls. *(See color ad p 885)*

SOME UNITS

🄢 🍴 🔲 ➦ 🎬 📟 💻 / ✕ 🔌 📺 /

FEE FEE

(See map p. 856)

SPRINGHILL SUITES BY MARRIOTT TAMPA/WESTSHORE
Phone: (813)639-9600
SAVE
12/26-4/20   1P: $159   2P: $159
12/1-12/25 & 4/21-11/30   1P: $109-$129   2P: $109-$129
Small-scale Hotel
Location: I-275, exit 40A (Westshore Blvd) southbound; exit 39B northbound, just w on Westshore Blvd, then just n. 4835 W Cypress St 33607. Fax: 813/639-9700. **Facility:** 149 one-bedroom standard units. 6 stories, interior corridors. *Bath:* combo or shower only. **Parking:** on-site. **Terms:** [CP] meal plan available. **Amenities:** video games (fee), voice mail, irons, hair dryers. **Pool(s):** heated outdoor. **Leisure Activities:** whirlpool, exercise room. **Business Services:** meeting rooms, business center. **Cards:** AX, CB, DC, DS, MC, VI. *(See color ad p 884)*
SOME UNITS

SUBURBAN LODGE-BRANDON
Phone: 813/635-0404 66
Motel
Property failed to provide current rates
Location: I-75, exit 257, 2.3 mi w on SR 60. 8207 E Adamo Dr 33619. Fax: 813/635-0203. **Facility:** 150 one-bedroom standard units with efficiencies. 3 stories, exterior corridors. *Bath:* combo or shower only. **Parking:** on-site. **Amenities:** voice mail. *Some:* irons, hair dryers. **Guest Services:** valet and coin laundry. **Business Services:** fax. **Cards:** AX, DS, MC, VI. *(See color ad p 596)*

SUPER 8 MOTEL-TAMPA
Phone: 813/933-4545 67
AAA SAVE
All Year [CP]   1P: $40-$115   2P: $40-$115   XP: $4   F14
Motel
Location: I-275, exit 52, just w. 321 E Fletcher Ave 33612. Fax: 813/935-4118. **Facility:** 100 one-bedroom standard units, some with kitchens (no utensils). 2 stories, exterior corridors. **Parking:** on-site. **Terms:** 2-3 night minimum stay - seasonal, cancellation fee imposed, weekly rates available, [ECP] meal plan available. **Amenities:** *Some:* irons, hair dryers. **Pool(s):** outdoor. **Guest Services:** coin laundry. **Business Services:** fax. **Cards:** AX, DC, DS, MC, VI. **Special Amenities:** free continental breakfast and free newspaper.
SOME UNITS

TAHITIAN INN
Phone: (813)877-6721 26
2/1-4/10 [CP]   1P: $99-$109   2P: $109-$119   XP: $5   F18
4/11-11/30 [CP]   1P: $75-$85   2P: $85-$95   XP: $5   F18
12/1-1/31 [ECP]   1P: $69-$79   2P: $79-$89   XP: $5   F18
Motel
Location: I-275, exit 41A, 1.1 mi s. 601 S Dale Mabry Hwy 33609. Fax: 813/877-6218. **Facility:** 62 units. 58 one-bedroom standard units. 4 one-bedroom suites ($99-$149). 2 stories, exterior corridors. **Parking:** on-site. **Terms:** pets ($25 extra charge, in designated units). **Amenities:** dual phone lines, voice mail, irons, hair dryers. **Pool(s):** heated outdoor. **Guest Services:** coin laundry. **Business Services:** fax (fee). **Cards:** AX, CB, DC, DS, MC, VI.
SOME UNITS

(See map p. 856)

TAMPA AIRPORT MARRIOTT   Phone: (813)879-5151   52

[SAVE]

	1P: $215-$225	2P: $215-$225	XP: $10	F18
12/1-4/12	1P: $199-$219	2P: $199-$219	XP: $10	F18
9/7-11/30	1P: $185-$195	2P: $185-$195	XP: $10	F18
4/13-9/6				

Large-scale Hotel **Location:** I-275, exit 39 southbound; exit 39B northbound, 2 mi w on SR 60 to Tampa International Airport. Tampa International Airport 33607. Fax: 813/873-0945. **Facility:** 296 one-bedroom standard units. 8 stories, interior corridors. *Bath:* combo or shower only. **Parking:** on-site. **Terms:** cancellation fee imposed. **Amenities:** high-speed Internet, voice mail, irons, hair dryers. **Dining:** CK's Restaurant, see separate listing. **Pool(s):** heated outdoor. **Leisure Activities:** exercise room. **Guest Services:** gift shop, valet laundry. **Business Services:** conference facilities, business center. **Cards:** AX, DC, DS, JC, MC, VI.

SOME UNITS

TAMPA MARRIOTT WATERSIDE HOTEL   Phone: (813)221-4900   39

(AAA) [SAVE]

1/4-5/24	1P: $169-$264	2P: $169-$264
12/1-1/3 & 9/7-11/30	1P: $159-$219	2P: $159-$219
5/25-9/6	1P: $99-$189	2P: $99-$189

Large-scale Hotel **Location:** I-275, exit 44, 2.2 mi e on Ashley Dr to Platt/Channelside Dr, then just n; downtown. Located opposite the convention center. 700 S Florida Ave 33602. Fax: 813/221-0923. **Facility:** 717 units. 698 one-bedroom standard units. 19 one-bedroom suites, some with whirlpools. 27 stories, interior corridors. *Bath:* combo or shower only. **Parking:** valet. **Terms:** check-in 4 pm, package plans. **Amenities:** video games, high-speed Internet, dual phone lines, voice mail, safes, irons, hair dryers. **Dining:** 3 restaurants, 6 am-2 am, cocktails, entertainment. **Pool(s):** heated outdoor. **Leisure Activities:** whirlpool, boat dock, hair salon, spa. **Guest Services:** gift shop, valet and coin laundry, airport transportation (fee)-Tampa International Airport, area transportation-trolley. **Business Services:** conference facilities, business center. **Cards:** AX, CB, DC, DS, JC, MC, VI. **Special Amenities: free newspaper and free room upgrade (subject to availability with advanced reservations).**

SOME UNITS

FEE   FEE

TRAVELODGE HOTEL NEAR BUSCH GARDENS   Phone: (813)933-4011   72

2/1-4/20 [CP]	1P: $69-$89	2P: $69-$89	XP: $10	F18
4/21-11/30 [CP]	1P: $59-$89	2P: $59-$89	XP: $10	F18
12/1-1/31 [CP]	1P: $59-$79	2P: $59-$79	XP: $10	F18

Small-scale Hotel **Location:** I-275, exit 50, just e on SR 580. 820 E Busch Blvd 33612. Fax: 813/932-1784. **Facility:** 257 one-bedroom standard units. 2-4 stories, interior/exterior corridors. **Parking:** on-site. **Terms:** package plans - seasonal, weekends, pets ($25 fee). **Amenities:** safes (fee), irons, hair dryers. **Pool(s):** outdoor, heated indoor. **Leisure Activities:** whirlpools, 4 lighted tennis courts. *Fee:* game room. **Guest Services:** gift shop, valet and coin laundry. **Business Services:** conference facilities, PC, fax (fee). **Cards:** AX, CB, DC, DS, JC, MC, VI. *(See color ad p 874)*

SOME UNITS

FEE   FEE

VALUE INN   Phone: (813)933-6760   10

XP: $10

Motel   All Year | 1P: $39-$59 | 2P: $45-$65

Location: I-275, exit 50, 1.5 mi e on SR 580. 2523 E Busch Blvd 33612. Fax: 813/933-2372. **Facility:** 40 one-bedroom standard units. 2 stories, exterior corridors. **Parking:** on-site. **Pool(s):** outdoor. **Cards:** AX, CB, DC, DS, MC, VI.

SOME UNITS

WELLESLEY INN & SUITES (TAMPA/WESTSHORE)   Phone: (813)637-8990   54

(AAA) [SAVE]   All Year [ECP] | 1P: $99-$109 | 2P: $99-$109 | XP: $10 | F18

Small-scale Hotel **Location:** I-275, exit 40A southbound, 0.5 mi n; exit 39A northbound, 0.5 mi e on Kennedy Blvd, 1.3 mi n. Commercial area. 1805 N Westshore Blvd 33607. Fax: 813/637-8991. **Facility:** 133 units. 128 one-bedroom standard units with efficiencies. 5 one-bedroom suites with efficiencies. 3 stories, interior corridors. *Bath:* combo or shower only. **Parking:** on-site. **Terms:** small pets only. **Amenities:** video games, dual phone lines, voice mail, irons, hair dryers. **Pool(s):** heated outdoor. **Leisure Activities:** picnic area, exercise room. **Guest Services:** valet and coin laundry. **Business Services:** meeting rooms, fax. **Cards:** AX, CB, DC, DS, JC, MC, VI. **Special Amenities: free continental breakfast and free newspaper.** *(See color ad p 863)*

SOME UNITS

WINGATE INN-TAMPA NORTH   Phone: (813)971-7676   68

| 1/16-4/15 [BP] | 1P: $129-$149 | 2P: $129-$149 | XP: $5 | F17 |
| 12/1-1/15 & 4/16-11/30 [BP] | 1P: $99-$129 | 2P: $99-$129 | XP: $5 | F17 |

Motel   **Location:** I-75, exit 270, just n on Bruce B Downs Blvd. 17301 Dona Michelle Dr 33647. Fax: 813/910-0950. **Facility:** 85 units. 82 one-bedroom standard units. 3 one-bedroom suites ($119-$299) with whirlpools. 4 stories, interior corridors. *Bath:* combo or shower only. **Parking:** on-site. **Terms:** cancellation fee imposed. **Amenities:** video games, high-speed Internet, dual phone lines, voice mail, safes, irons, hair dryers. **Pool(s):** heated outdoor. **Leisure Activities:** whirlpool, exercise room. **Guest Services:** complimentary evening beverages: Mon-Thurs, valet and coin laundry, area transportation. **Business Services:** meeting rooms, business center. **Cards:** AX, CB, DC, DS, JC, MC, VI.

SOME UNITS

WINGATE INN-USF NEAR BUSCH GARDENS   Phone: (813)979-2828   23

1/1-4/21 [ECP]	1P: $99-$129	2P: $109-$139	XP: $5	F17
4/22-7/5 [ECP]	1P: $89-$109	2P: $94-$114	XP: $5	F17
7/6-11/30 [ECP]	1P: $79-$109	2P: $89-$114	XP: $5	F17
12/1-12/31 [ECP]	1P: $79-$109	2P: $84-$114		

Motel

Location: I-275, exit 51, 2.2 mi e on SR 582. 3751 E Fowler Ave 33612. Fax: 813/977-1818. **Facility:** 85 units. 82 one-bedroom standard units. 3 one-bedroom suites ($129-$189) with whirlpools. 4 stories, interior corridors. *Bath:* combo or shower only. **Parking:** on-site. **Terms:** pets ($40 extra charge). **Amenities:** video games, high-speed Internet, dual phone lines, voice mail, safes, irons, hair dryers. **Pool(s):** outdoor. **Leisure Activities:** whirlpool, exercise room. **Guest Services:** valet and coin laundry, area transportation. **Business Services:** meeting rooms, business center. **Cards:** AX, CB, DC, DS, JC, MC, VI.

SOME UNITS

(See map p. 856)

WYNDHAM HARBOUR ISLAND

(AAA) (SAVE)
▼▼▼▼▼

			Phone: (813)229-5000	29
1/1-4/25 & 9/27-11/30	1P: $199-$249	2P: $219-$269	XP: $20	F12
12/1-12/31	1P: $179-$229	2P: $199-$249	XP: $20	F12
4/26-9/26	1P: $149-$219	2P: $169-$239	XP: $20	F12

Location: I-275, exit 44 (Downtown East), just e, then 2 mi s via Tampa St, follow signs for the Convention Center, then **Large-scale Hotel** to Harbour Island. Located in an upscale office/commercial area. 725 S Harbour Island Blvd 33602. Fax: 813/229-5322. **Facility:** 300 units. 280 one-bedroom standard units. 20 one-bedroom suites. 12 stories, interior corridors. **Parking:** on-site and valet. **Terms:** cancellation fee imposed. **Amenities:** video games, high-speed Internet, dual phone lines, voice mail, honor bars, irons, hair dryers. *Some:* CD players. **Dining:** 6:30 am-11 pm, cocktails. **Pool(s):** heated outdoor. **Leisure Activities:** limited exercise equipment. *Fee:* boat dock, charter fishing, spa privileges. **Guest Services:** gift shop, valet laundry, airport transportation-Tampa International Airport, area transportation-within 5 mi. **Business Services:** conference facilities, PC, fax. **Cards:** AX, DC, MC, VI.

SOME UNITS
[icons] / [icons] FEE

WYNDHAM WESTSHORE

(AAA) (SAVE)
▼▼▼▼

			Phone: (813)286-4400	41
1/1-4/25	1P: $169-$219	2P: $199-$239	XP: $20	F12
9/27-11/30	1P: $129-$199	2P: $159-$219	XP: $20	F12
4/26-9/26	1P: $119-$199	2P: $139-$219	XP: $20	F12
12/1-12/31	1P: $119-$189	2P: $139-$209	XP: $20	F12

Large-scale Hotel Location: I-275, exit 40A, 0.5 mi s; jct SR 60 and Westshore Blvd. Located in a commercial area. 4860 W Kennedy Blvd 33609-2591. Fax: 813/286-4053. **Facility:** 324 one-bedroom standard units. 11 stories, interior corridors. **Parking:** on-site and valet. **Terms:** cancellation fee imposed. **Amenities:** video games, high-speed Internet, dual phone lines, voice mail, irons, hair dryers. *Some:* CD players. **Dining:** 3 restaurants, 6:30 am-11:30 pm, Fri & Sat 2 am, cocktails, also, Shula's Steakhouse, see separate listing, entertainment. **Pool(s):** heated outdoor. **Leisure Activities:** jogging, exercise room. *Fee:* massage. **Guest Services:** gift shop, valet laundry, airport transportation-Tampa International Airport, area transportation-within 3 mi. **Business Services:** conference facilities, business center. **Cards:** AX, DC, MC, VI.

SOME UNITS
[icons] / [icons] FEE

The following lodging was either not evaluated or did not meet AAA rating requirements but is listed for your information only.

PARK PLAZA TAMPA AIRPORT WESTSHORE

(AAA) (SAVE)
[fyi]

			Phone: (813)289-1950	47
1/1-4/30	1P: $129-$169	2P: $129-$169	XP: $10	F18
9/1-11/30	1P: $109-$149	2P: $109-$149	XP: $10	F18
12/1-12/31 & 5/1-8/31	1P: $99-$139	2P: $99-$139	XP: $10	F18

Large-scale Hotel Under major renovation, scheduled to be completed December 2002. **Last rated:** ▼▼ **Location:** I-275, exit 40A southbound, 0.4 mi e on Westshore, 0.5 mi s; exit 39B northbound, just e. Located in a commercial area. 5303 W Kennedy Blvd 33609. Fax: 813/282-8964. **Facility:** 248 one-bedroom standard units. 11 stories, interior/exterior corridors. **Parking:** on-site. **Terms:** pets ($20 deposit, in selected units). **Amenities:** video games, high-speed Internet, voice mail, safes (fee), hair dryers. *Some:* irons. **Dining:** 6 am-10 pm, cocktails. **Pool(s):** outdoor. **Leisure Activities:** exercise room. **Guest Services:** valet and coin laundry, airport transportation-Tampa International Airport, area transportation-within 10 mi. **Business Services:** conference facilities, fax. **Cards:** AX, DC, DS, JC, MC, VI. **Special Amenities:** free newspaper. *(See ad below)*

SOME UNITS
[icons] / [icons] FEE FEE

--- WHERE TO DINE ---

42ND STREET THE BISTRO

▼▼▼ ▼▼▼
American

Lunch: $7-$18   **Dinner:** $7-$18   **Phone:** 813/253-0042   65

Location: I-275, exit 42, 1 mi s on Armenia Ave, just e on Azeele, 0.6 mi s on Howard Ave. 516 S Howard Ave 33606. **Hours:** 11:30 am-11 pm, Tues & Wed-midnight, Thurs & Fri-1 am, Sat noon-1 am, Sun 4 pm-10 pm. **Features:** A New York Broadway theme and city library appearance give life to the trendy, upscale establishment. The well-thought-out menu offers "show stoppers," gourmet pizza, salad and a variety of flavorful entrees. Casual dress; cocktails. **Parking:** on-site. **Cards:** AX, DC, DS, MC, VI.

(See map p. 856)

ARIGATO JAPANESE STEAK HOUSE   **Dinner:** $10-$22   **Phone:** 813/960-5050   ⑥
♦♦ ♦♦   **Location:** US 92, just w of jct Fletcher Ave. 13755 N Dale Mabry Hwy 33618. **Hours:** 5 pm-10 pm, Fri & Sat-10:30
Japanese   pm. Closed major holidays; also 12/24. **Features:** Traditional floor seating lends an air of authenticity as diners enjoy the showmanship of professional tableside chefs. Expect a wait for group seating, but Japanese entrees—such as ichiban, a spicy mix of shrimp, chicken and beef—are well worth it. Casual
dress; cocktails. **Parking:** on-site. **Cards:** AX, DC, DS, MC, VI.   ⊻

ARMANI'S   **Dinner:** $23-$35   **Phone:** 813/281-9165   ㉕
♦♦♦♦♦♦   **Location:** SR 60, at east end of Courtney Campbell Cswy; in Hyatt Regency Westshore. 6200 Courtney Campbell
Northern   Cswy 33607. **Hours:** 6 pm-10 pm, Fri & Sat-11 pm. Closed: Sun. **Reservations:** required.
Italian   **Features:** Overlooking Old Tampa Bay, the romantic, upscale Italian restaurant is on the top floor of the Hyatt Regency Westshore. Veal is the house specialty. Diners can order antipasto directly from the chef or
let the waiter help. Depending on the night and the clientele, Armani's can be bustling. Service is always
prompt, and servers efficient and well-mannered. Some selections are prepared tableside. Servers are more than willing to
have valet claim checks validated. Smoke free premises. Dressy casual; cocktails; entertainment. **Parking:** on-site and valet.
Cards: AX, CB, DC, DS, JC, MC, VI.   ⊛ ⊻ ⊠

BARLEY HOPPERS INTERNATIONAL
ALEHOUSE & GRILL   **Lunch:** $7-$20   **Dinner:** $7-$20   **Phone:** 813/242-6680   ㉗
♦♦ ♦♦   **Location:** I-4, exit 1, just w at Centro Ybor; in Ybor City. 1600 E 8th Ave (E200) 33605.
American   **Hours:** 11:30 am-10 pm, Fri & Sat-11 pm, Sun-8 pm. **Features:** On the second floor of the popular Centro Ybor complex, the lively restaurant invites diners to unwind on the patio, which overlooks the complex, or in the busy dining room, where they can watch programming on TV monitors around the room.
Representative of basic fare are various sandwiches, salads, appetizers and the popular ribs. Casual dress; cocktails.
Parking: on-site (fee). **Cards:** MC, VI.   ⊠

BAY CAFE   **Lunch:** $8-$13   **Dinner:** $10-$20   **Phone:** 813/875-1555   ㊽
АAА   **Location:** I-275, exit 40A southbound; exit 39A northbound, 1 mi n on Kennedy Blvd, 0.5 mi w; in Embassy Suites
♦♦ ♦♦   Hotel-Tampa/Airport/Westshore. 555 N Westshore Blvd 33609. **Hours:** 11:30 am-2 & 5-10 pm.
American   **Reservations:** suggested; weekends. **Features:** An extensive menu offers many choices from such favorites as surf and turf to chicken and shrimp with pasta. Fresh flowers on every table and contemporary paintings contribute to the tropical theme, with mohogany wood. The atrium is a delightful dining getaway.
Casual dress; cocktails. **Parking:** on-site. **Cards:** AX, CB, DC, DS, MC, VI.   ⊻ ⊠

BERNINI   **Lunch:** $7-$18   **Dinner:** $10-$25   **Phone:** 813/248-0099   ㉖
♦♦♦   **Location:** In Ybor City; at jct 17th St. 1702 E 7th Ave 33607. **Hours:** 11:30 am-2 & 5:30-11 pm, Sat 5:30 pm-11
Italian   pm. Closed: Sun. **Features:** The casually upscale restaurant features examples of fine and innovative Italian cuisine, such as carpaccio of salmon, crispy duck with a balsamic glaze finish and Caribbean stuffed
lobster. Dessert choices are plentiful. Casual dress; cocktails. **Parking:** street. **Cards:** MC, VI.   ⊻ ⊠

BERN'S STEAK HOUSE   **Dinner:** $23-$40   **Phone:** 813/251-2421   ㉒
♦♦♦♦   **Location:** I-275, exit 42, 1 mi s on Armenia Ave, just e on Azeele, 0.8 mi s, under overpass. 1208 S Howard Ave
Steak House   33606. **Hours:** 5 pm-11 pm. Closed: 12/25. **Reservations:** suggested. **Features:** A local landmark, it is renowned for its beef entrees. Guests are invited to tour the kitchen and wine cellar before dinner. A comprehensive wine list and a separate dessert lounge make the visit enjoyable. A 12% gratuity is added
in the dining room. Dressy casual; cocktails. **Parking:** valet. **Cards:** AX, CB, DC, DS, MC, VI.   ⊻ ⊠

BLUE GARDENIA   **Dinner:** $12-$28   **Phone:** 813/250-1595   ㊼
♦♦♦♦   **Location:** I-275, exit 42, 1 mi s on Armenia, then just e. 1809 W Platt St. **Hours:** 5 pm-10 pm, Fri & Sat 6 pm-11
American   pm. Closed: Sun. **Reservations:** suggested. **Features:** Menu specialties at the eclectic trattoria include eggplant souffle cheesecake and brandy-spiked tiramisu. Don't miss the chance to try lobster Popsicles.
Smoke free premises. Casual dress; cocktails. **Parking:** on-site. **Cards:** AX, DC, DS, MC, VI.   ⊻ ⊠

THE CACTUS CLUB SOUTHWESTERN GRILL & BAR   **Lunch:** $7-$16 **Dinner:** $7-$16 **Phone:** 813/251-4089   ㊾
♦♦ ♦♦   **Location:** Jct Kennedy Blvd; in Old Hyde Park. 1601 Snow Ave 33606. **Hours:** 11 am-10:30 pm, Fri & Sat-11:30 pm,
Southwestern   Sun-10 pm. Closed: 11/27, 12/25. **Features:** Munch on sizzling fajitas at this casual eatery. Outdoor cafe-style seating is available to enjoy a wide choice of border favorites in the fresh air. At this attractive spot, service is first rate and will keep you coming back for more. Casual dress; cocktails. **Parking:** street.
Cards: AX, CB, DC, MC, VI.   ⊻ ⊠

CAFE CREOLE   **Lunch:** $6-$9   **Dinner:** $12-$17   **Phone:** 813/247-6283   ㊴
♦♦ ♦♦   **Location:** I-4, exit 1, just s to 8th Ave, 0.5 mi w to 13th St, then just n. 1330 9th Ave 33605. **Hours:** 11:30 am-10
Cajun   pm, Fri-11:30 pm, Sat 5 pm-11:30 pm. Closed major holidays; also Sun. **Features:** Why go to New Orleans when you can taste authentic Cajun and Creole cuisine in the lively historic setting of Ybor City? Feast on oysters Bienville, jambalaya and crawfish etouffe in the courtyard dining area. Wonderful service
will enhance your meal. Casual dress; cocktails. **Parking:** street. **Cards:** AX, DC, DS, MC, VI.   ⊻ ⊠

CAFE EUROPEAN   **Lunch:** $7-$8   **Dinner:** $10-$19   **Phone:** 813/254-9458   ㉞
♦♦ ♦♦   **Location:** Just s of jct Kennedy Blvd (SR 60); opposite entrance to University of Tampa. 113 Hyde Park Ave 33606.
Continental   **Hours:** 11 am-2 & 5:30-9 pm, Fri-11 pm, Sat 5:30 pm-11 pm. Closed: 4/20, 12/25; also Sun.
Reservations: suggested. **Features:** This family-operated restaurant dedicates itself to preparing
traditional foods with a European flair. Good, basic meals in a pleasant cafe setting include delicious fish
and chips served hot and fast. Kids may choose from an available children's menu. Casual dress; beer & wine only. **Parking:**
street. **Cards:** AX, MC, VI.   ⊠

(See map p. 856)

CAFFE PARADISO

Northern
Italian

Dinner: $8-$24   **Phone:** 813/835-6622   76
Location: 0.5 mi w of jct W Gandy Blvd; in St Croix's Plaza. 4205 S MacDill 33611. **Hours:** 5:30 pm-10:30 pm. Closed: Sun. **Features:** Elegant, chic and intimate, this ristorante is the place to go on special occasions. You will find traditional appetizers, whole or half orders of pasta, red snapper and veal piccata, all nicely done and expertly served by a trained and cordial staff. Smoke free premises. Dressy casual; cocktails. **Parking:** on-site. **Cards:** AX, CB, DC, DS, MC, VI.

CARMINE'S

Spanish

Lunch: $8-$12   **Dinner:** $8-$12   **Phone:** 813/248-3834   70
Location: I-4, exit 1, just s to 7th Ave, then just w; in Ybor City. 1802 7th Ave 33605. **Hours:** 11 am-10 pm, Tues-11 pm, Wed & Thurs-1 am, Fri-3 am, Sun-6 pm. **Features:** On the main drag in Ybor City, the restaurant presents an extensive menu of Cuban and Spanish fare. The atmosphere is casual, and the service is friendly. Casual dress. **Parking:** street.

THE CASTAWAY

Seafood

Lunch: $6-$12   **Dinner:** $11-$20   **Phone:** 813/281-0770   21
Location: I-275, exit 39A northbound; exit 39 southbound, 3.3 mi w on SR 60. 7720 Courtney Campbell Cswy 33607. **Hours:** 11 am-10:30 pm, Sun 9:30 am-2:30 & 5-10 pm. **Features:** Bright Caribbean decor enlivens the breezy, bayfront setting. The Thai-style whole snapper, drenched in a spicy yet sweet chili sauce and served with a head and tail, gets your taste buds jumping. The rich tiramisu settles them back down. Casual dress; cocktails. **Parking:** on-site. **Cards:** AX, CB, DC, DS, MC, VI.

CEVICHE'

Spanish

Dinner: $18-$31   **Phone:** 813/250-0203   61
Location: Jct S Howard Ave; in Soho District. 2109 Bayshore Blvd 33629. **Hours:** 5 pm-midnight. Closed: Mon. **Features:** On the menu are some 45 offerings of tapas frias or tapas calientes, as well as paella, prime New York strip and many desserts. Casual dress; cocktails. **Parking:** street. **Cards:** AX, MC, VI.

CHILLADA'S FRESH MEX CANTINA
Mexican

Lunch: $4-$7   **Dinner:** $4-$7   **Phone:** 843/571-8320   71
Location: I-75, exit 257, 0.4 mi w on SR 6; in Brandon Crossings. 10033 E Adamo Dr 33619. **Hours:** 11 am-9 pm, Fri & Sat-10 pm, Sun-6 pm. **Features:** A casual setting with some Southwest touches, enjoy a relaxing meal with Mexican offerings of anything from a vegetarian quesedilla to a fajita burrito. Casual dress; beer & wine only. **Parking:** on-site. **Cards:** MC, VI.

(See map p. 856)

CK'S RESTAURANT
Dinner: $18-$38   **Phone: 813/878-6500**   ⑲
Continental
Location: I-275, exit 39 southbound; exit 39B northbound, 2 mi w on SR 60 to Tampa International Airport; in Tampa Airport Marriott. **Hours:** 5 pm-10 pm, Fri & Sat-11 pm, Sun 10:30 am-2 & 5-10 pm. **Reservations:** suggested; weekends. **Features:** The revolving, rooftop restaurant affords panoramic views of Tampa Bay, the airport and the downtown skyline. Try a nice presentation from the raw bar, fresh fish or certified Angus steak. Casual dress; cocktails. **Parking:** on-site. **Cards:** AX, CB, DC, DS, JC, MC, VI.

CODY'S ORIGINAL ROADHOUSE
Dinner: $7-$20   **Phone: 813/855-2787**   ⑦⑧
Steak House
Location: Jct Memorial Hwy, 1.9 mi w on SR 580; in Silver Mill Plaza. 11202 W Hillsborough Ave 33635. **Hours:** 3:30 pm-10 pm, Fri & Sat-11 pm, Sun noon-10 pm. Closed: 12/25. **Features:** The use of lots of hardwoods and old nostalgic signs gives the lively restaurant a rustic roadhouse feel. The welcoming and efficient staff assists in creating a nice dining experience. On the menu are ribs, steaks, chicken, chops, burgers and sandwiches, as well as the fantastic fajitas, a real experience. Casual dress; cocktails. **Parking:** on-site. **Cards:** AX, DS, MC, VI.

THE COLONNADE
Lunch: $6-$21   **Dinner: $6-$21**   **Phone: 813/839-7558**   ⑦③
Seafood
Location: I-275, exit 41A, 4.2 mi s, 1.2 mi e on W Gandy, 1.3 mi n. 3401 Bayshore Blvd 33629. **Hours:** 11 am-10 pm, Fri & Sat-11 pm. Closed: 11/27, 12/25. **Features:** Established in 1935, the warm and friendly atmosphere makes this a comfy place to savor a meal while enjoying panoramas of downtown Tampa from across the bay. The shrimp sampler platter is a favorite, as is the delectable chocolate bourbon pecan pie. Casual dress; cocktails. **Parking:** on-site. **Cards:** AX, DC, DS, MC, VI.

COLUMBIA RESTAURANT   Historic
Lunch: $6-$15   **Dinner: $14-$22**   **Phone: 813/248-4961**   ④③
Spanish
Location: I-4, exit 1 in Ybor City; between 21st and 22nd sts. 2117 E 7th Ave 33605. **Hours:** 11 am-10 pm, Fri & Sat-11 pm, Sun noon-9 pm. **Features:** Located in Ybor City, this original Columbia Restaurant was established in 1905. Clubs and shops surround the popular tourist destination. Delicious Spanish and Cuban dishes are offered. Flamenco dancing and entertainment are offered every night except Sunday. Casual dress; cocktails; entertainment. **Parking:** on-site. **Cards:** AX, DC, DS, MC, VI.

COPELAND'S RESTAURANT AND BAR
Lunch: $7-$19   **Dinner: $8-$19**   **Phone: 813/884-8400**   ①⑧
Creole
Location: Just s of jct Linebaugh. 9210 Anderson Rd 33634. **Hours:** 11 am-10 pm. **Features:** Near a popular new shopping area, this restaurant is one of the latest offerings from the New Orleans-based restaurant and bar. This version has a trendy, modern look with a bit of an Art Deco flair punctuating the dining room. Menu offerings are extensive, with many Cajun- and Creole-style seafood and pasta dishes, chicken, prime steaks and pork. Casual dress; cocktails. **Parking:** on-site. **Cards:** AX, DC, DS, MC, VI.

CRAWDADDY'S
Dinner: $16-$36   **Phone: 813/281-0407**   ②④
American
Location: From east end of Courtney Campbell Cswy (SR 60), just s. 2500 Rocky Point Dr 33607. **Hours:** 5 pm-10 pm, Fri & Sat-11 pm. **Reservations:** suggested. **Features:** In the spirit of the roaring '20s, this feisty fish camp dishes up spicy jambalaya and smashed bourbon sweet potatoes, both of which boast a decidedly New Orleans flavor. The menu features steak, poultry and seafood. Enjoy great views of Old Tampa Bay. Casual dress; cocktails. **Parking:** on-site. **Cards:** AX, DC, DS, MC, VI.

DISH CENTRO YBOR
Lunch: $11   **Dinner: $16**   **Phone: 813/241-8300**   ⑥⑧
American
Location: I-4, exit 1, just s to 8th ave, just w to Centro Ybor; in Ybor City. 1600 E 8th Ave, Suite E202 33605. **Hours:** 11:30 am-9 pm, Fri & Sat-11 pm. **Features:** Meals are prepared before diners' eyes on the center round cooking table. After choosing ingredients from the vast assortment of meats, sauces and vegetables, patrons present their selections to the preparer. Casual dress; cocktails. **Parking:** on-site (fee). **Cards:** MC, VI.

DONATELLO
Lunch: $9-$18   **Dinner: $16-$29**   **Phone: 813/875-6660**   ⑤⑥
Northern Italian
Location: I-275, exit 23 northbound; exit 23B southbound, 0.5 mi s on SR 92 (N Dale Mabry). 232 N Dale Mabry Hwy 33609. **Hours:** 11:30 am-2:30 & 6-11 pm, Sat & Sun from 6 pm. Closed major holidays. **Reservations:** suggested. **Features:** Homemade pasta and veal specialties prepared with varied sauces are highlights on the restaurant's menu. Signature dishes include Florentine oysters and linguine lobster. Also appealing are the decadent desserts. Dressy casual; cocktails; entertainment. **Parking:** on-site and valet. **Cards:** AX, DC, DS, MC, VI.

ESTELA'S MEXICAN RESTAURANT
Lunch: $4-$12   **Dinner: $4-$12**   **Phone: 813/251-0558**   ⑧⓪
Mexican
Location: 1.6 mi s on S Hyde Park Ave from jct SR 60; on Davis Island. 209 E Davis Blvd 33606. **Hours:** 11 am-10 pm, Fri & Sat-11 pm. **Features:** The quaint, little cantina-type setting, nestled among many eclectic area shops, is reminiscent of a true Mexican eatery. Tasty choices include chimichangas, nachos, fajitas, huevos ranchero, quesadillas, poblanos and burritos. Casual dress; beer & wine only. **Parking:** on-site. **Cards:** MC, VI.

FIRST CHOICE BAR-B-QUE
Lunch: $4-$15   **Dinner: $4-$15**   **Phone: 813/621-7434**   ④⑥

American
Location: I-75, exit 257, 0.5 mi w on SR 60. 10113 Adamo Dr 33619. **Hours:** 11 am-9 pm. Closed major holidays; also Sun. **Features:** The sound of meat sizzling over an open-pit grill is a nice treat for the senses, but even nicer is the delicious Southern barbecue that perks up the taste buds. Locals flock here for succulent beef, pork, chicken, turkey, ham and sausage. Smoke free premises. Casual dress. **Parking:** on-site. **Cards:** AX, CB, DC, DS, MC, VI.

(See map p. 856)

FIRST WATCH
American
Lunch: $5-$7   **Phone:** 813/307-9006   [29]
Location: At jct Twiggs St; downtown. 520 Tampa St 33602. **Hours:** 7 am-2:30 pm. **Closed:** 11/27, 12/25. **Features:** Pancakes and crepes fill the plates and are only two types of varied breakfast entrees that make regulars out of first-time guests. Fruit and salad options for the health-conscious and sandwiches you need both hands to hold please the lunch crowd. Smoke free premises. Casual dress. **Parking:** on-site (fee). **Cards:** AX, DS, MC, VI.

FIRST WATCH
American
Lunch: $5-$7   **Phone:** 813/975-1718   [11]
Location: I-275, exit 51, 1.5 mi e on Fowler Ave (SR 582); in University Collection. 2726 E Fowler Ave 33618. **Hours:** 7 am-2:30 pm. **Closed:** 11/27, 12/25. **Features:** Smooth service and an excellent breakfast menu make this a family favorite. Hefty portions of waffles, eggs, crepes and omelets are served during the morning hours, and salad, soups and sandwiches round out the lunch menu. Healthy options are listed, too. Casual dress. **Parking:** on-site. **Cards:** DS, MC, VI.

FRONTIER STEAK HOUSE
Steak House
Dinner: $9-$31   **Phone:** 813/621-3050   [22]
Location: I-4, exit 7, 0.9 mi n on US 301, just w. 8602 E Sligh Ave 33610. **Hours:** 3 pm-10 pm, Fri & Sat-11 pm. **Features:** Don't expect quick service at the comfortable restaurant, a local favorite, but enjoy the wonderful steaks: This place is famous for the "six-pound challenge." If you're craving something less weighty, choose from chicken, chops, ribs, lobster tail and varied salads, appetizers and desserts. Casual dress; cocktails; entertainment. **Parking:** on-site. **Cards:** AX, DC, DS, MC, VI.

G ELLIOTT'S RESTAURANTE
American
Lunch: $13-$21   **Dinner:** $13-$21   **Phone:** 813/229-2489   [75]
Location: Just s of jct SR 60; in Channelside; downtown. 615 Channelside Dr 33602. **Hours:** 5 pm-11 pm, Fri-midnight, Sat 11 am midnight, Sun 11 am-10 pm. **Closed:** Mon. **Features:** Located in the popular Channelside shops and adjacent to the cruise line port, this trendy & upscale restaurant offers a varied menu with many creative choices. A friendly staff provides great service in this upbeat atmosphere. Casual dress; cocktails. **Parking:** on-site (fee). **Cards:** MC, VI.

GOOD FELLAS
American
Lunch: $8-$19   **Dinner:** $8-$19   **Phone:** 813/963-6644   [3]
Location: 2 mi e of jct Dale Mabry Hwy; at jct Plantation Blvd. 4802 Gunn Hwy 33607. **Hours:** 11 am-3 am, Sun from 11 pm. **Features:** A fun setting for casual dining, this place offers a menu with varied salads, burgers, sandwiches, soups, old-fashioned pizza and nachos. Also offered are heartier selections: New York strip, chicken and ribs, pasta and grouper. Casual dress; cocktails. **Parking:** on-site. **Cards:** AX, MC, VI

HO HO WINDOWS
Chinese
Lunch: $5-$12   **Dinner:** $6-$12   **Phone:** 813/254-9557   [63]
Location: I-275, exit 42, 1 mi s on Armenia Ave, just e on Azeele, 0.4 mi s; in Whaley's Market Place. 533 S Howard Ave 33606. **Hours:** 11:30 am-9:45 pm, Fri-10:45 pm, Sat 4 pm-10:45 pm. **Closed:** 7/4, 11/27, 12/25. **Features:** The contemporary, inviting decor welcomes you to enjoy yourself at this Oriental restaurant. The expansive menu lists at least 75 choices, such as Mandarin beef, General Tso's chicken, spicy vegetable, dragon in the nest and honey chicken. Smoke free premises. Casual dress; beer & wine only. **Parking:** on-site. **Cards:** AX, DC, DS, MC, VI.

HOPS RESTAURANT BAR & BREWERY
American
Lunch: $7-$17   **Dinner:** $7-$17   **Phone:** 813/632-0717   [8]
Location: I-275, exit 51, 0.5 mi e on SR 582. 1241 E Fowler Ave 33612. **Hours:** 11 am-11 pm, Fri & Sat-midnight, Sun-10 pm. **Closed:** 11/27, 12/25. **Features:** Although the restaurant is famous for its on-site microbrewery, its fresh-from-scratch menu items are no shrinking violets. Enjoy well-prepared filet mignon, rib-eye, pork chops, prime rib and top sirloin, as well as flavorful baby back ribs, grilled chicken, pasta dishes, burgers and sandwiches. Casual dress; cocktails. **Parking:** on-site. **Cards:** AX, DC, DS, MC, VI.

HUGO'S SPANISH RESTAURANT
Spanish
Lunch: $4-$10   **Dinner:** $4-$10   **Phone:** 813/251-2842   [67]
Location: I-275, exit 42, 1 mi s on Armenia Ave, just e on Azeele, 0.6 mi s; at jct W Morrison Ave. 931 S Howard Ave 33606. **Hours:** 11 am-9 pm, Sat from 7:30 am. **Closed:** Sun. **Features:** A fixture of the Hyde Park area since 1975, the casual restaurant is known for its Cuban sandwiches and black beans and rice. Other menu favorites include steak and chicken choices, Italian dishes and sandwiches. Casual dress; beer only. **Parking:** on-site. **Cards:** DS, MC, VI.

JACKSON'S BISTRO-BAR & SUSHI
American
Lunch: $7-$12   **Dinner:** $13-$21   **Phone:** 813/277-0339   [64]
Location: I-275, exit 44, 2 mi e on Tampa St to Harbour Island; in Knights Point. 601 S Harbour Island Blvd, Suite 100 33602. **Hours:** 11:30 am-2:30 & 5-11 pm, Sun 10:30 am-2:30 & 5-10 pm. **Features:** Set on the waterfront in a trendy complex of shops and businesses, the decidedly upscale restaurant is beautifully decorated. Trained chefs expertly prepare many enticing dishes. Dessert is a must, especially the absolutely scrumptious raspberry macadamia nut pie. Dressy casual; cocktails; entertainment. **Parking:** on-site. **Cards:** AX, DS, MC, VI.

JASMINE THAI RESTAURANT
Thai
Lunch: $6-$9   **Dinner:** $6-$19   **Phone:** 813/968-1501   [1]
Location: On US 92 at jct Fletcher Ave; in Village Center. 13248 N Dale Mabry Hwy 33618. **Hours:** 11:30 am-10:30 pm, Fri & Sat-11 pm, Sun-10 pm. **Closed:** 11/27. **Features:** Thai cuisine is served in very attractive surroundings by a pleasant wait staff. Try the duck mixed with mushroom caps, corn and broccoli and garnished with a butterfly-shaped carrot. You will find several nice touches during this excellent meal. Casual dress; beer & wine only. **Parking:** on-site. **Cards:** AX, DS, MC, VI.

JIMMY MAC'S MARINA RESTAURANT
Seafood
Lunch: $7-$25   **Dinner:** $7-$25   **Phone:** 813/839-3449   [7]
Location: At the east end of the Gandy Bridge, 0.5 mi w of jct W Shore Blvd. 5000 W Gandy Blvd 33611. **Hours:** 11 am-10 pm, Fri & Sat-11 pm. **Closed:** 11/27, 12/25. **Features:** The beautiful marina setting affords great views of boats and sunsets. Decor is nautical with lots of wood enhancements. On the extensive menu is something for everyone: appetizers, raw bar items, steamers, salads, soups, sandwiches, burgers, fresh fish, steak and chicken. Casual dress; cocktails. **Parking:** on-site. **Cards:** AX, DC, DS, MC, VI.

(See map p. 856)

KAHUNAVILLE   Lunch: $12-$19   Dinner: $12-$19   Phone: 813/348-2011   79
▽▽▽   Location: I-275, exit 40A southbound; exit 39A northbound, 0.9 mi w on Westshore Blvd; in International Plaza and
Bay Street. 2223 N Westshore Blvd 33607. Hours: 11 am-11 pm, Fri & Sat-midnight. Features: The tropical
American   jungle setting is complete with a dancing water show that diners can watch as they eat. Spectacular meals
are served in huge, colorfully presented portions. Choices center on steak, fish and pasta, while other
favorites include wraps. Casual dress; cocktails. Parking: on-site. Cards: MC, VI.
⟨Y⟩

LA TROPICANA CAFE   Lunch: $5-$10   Phone: 813/247-4040   32
▽   Location: I-4, exit 1, just s to 7th Ave, just w; in Ybor City. 1822 E 7th Ave 33605. Hours: 9 am-3 pm, Sat-2:30
pm. Closed: Sun. Features: In popular Ybor City, the restaurant offers some of the best in Cuban dishes.
Spanish   In addition to the signature Cuban sandwich, menu choices include tamales, Spanish fries and delicious
black bean soup. Casual dress. Parking: on-site.

LAURO RISTORANTE ITALIANO   Lunch: $8-$10   Dinner: $12-$23   Phone: 813/281-2100   53
▽▽   Location: I-275, exit 41A southbound, 1.5 mi w to Henderson Blvd, just s. 3915 Henderson Blvd 33629.
Hours: 11:30 am-2 & 5:30-close. Closed: 1/1; also Sun. Features: Private parties are welcome in this
Northern   quaint eatery. A wide selection of pasta, fish and meat dishes is served by a staff that is well-trained to
Italian   meet guests' needs. Fresh, crisp salads served with sliced bread will really whet your appetite. Dressy
casual; cocktails; entertainment. Parking: on-site. Cards: AX, CB, DC, DS, MC, VI.
⟨Y⟩⟨X⟩

LE BORDEAUX   Dinner: $17-$33   Phone: 813/254-4387   74
▽▽▽   Location: I-275, exit 42, 1 mi s on Armenia Ave, just e on Azeele, 1 mi s. 1502 S Howard Ave 33606. Hours: 5:30
pm-10 pm. Closed: 1/1, 12/25. Features: Cozy, romantic appointments characterize the classy bistro. The
French   menu lists freshly prepared and artfully displayed entrees, such as roast duckling, baby lamb, veal chops,
grilled sole, bouillabaisse a la Marseilles and salmon dishes. Dressy casual; cocktails; entertainment.
Parking: valet. Cards: AX, DC, MC, VI.
⟨Y⟩⟨X⟩

LOGAN'S ROADHOUSE   Dinner: $6-$19   Phone: 813/884-5229   14
▽▽   Location: Just s of jct Linebaugh. 9218 Anderson 33634. Hours: 11 am-10 pm, Fri & Sat-11 pm.
Features: Rustic effects enhance this replica of an old roadhouse. The atmosphere is relaxed, and the
Steak House   friendly staff is eager to help. Enjoy chicken, ribs, burgers, sandwiches, salads, appetizers and desserts, as
well as signature steaks, including the noteworthy porterhouse. Casual dress; cocktails. Parking: on-site.
Cards: MC, VI.
⟨Y⟩⟨X⟩

LONNI'S SANDWICHES, ETC   Lunch: $7-$9   Phone: 813/223-2333   69
▽   Location: Just n of jct Tampa St; downtown. 513 E Jackson St 33602. Hours: 9 am-4 pm. Closed major holidays;
also Sat & Sun. Features: This local favorite offers a variety of sandwiches, salads and soups in a
American   sandwich shop setting. Smoke free premises. Casual dress. Parking: street. Cards: AX, MC, VI.
⟨X⟩

MIGUEL'S MEXICAN RESTAURANT   Lunch: $8-$15   Dinner: $8-$15   Phone: 813/876-2587   30
▽▽   Location: On SR 60; at jct McDill. 3035 W Kennedy Blvd 33609. Hours: 11 am-10 pm, Fri-11 pm, Sat noon-11
pm, Sun noon-9 pm. Features: Basic decor characterizes the locally favorite Mexican restaurant, which
Mexican   offers diners a multitude of freshly prepared specialties along the lines of burritos, tacos and nachos. For a
casual meal and good food, this place won't disappoint. Casual dress; beer & wine only. Parking: on-site.
Cards: MC, VI.

MISE EN PLACE   Dinner: $13-$23   Phone: 813/254-5373   35
▽▽▽   Location: I-275, exit 44, 0.4 mi s on Ashley, 0.3 mi w on Kennedy; in Grand Central Place; opposite University of
Tampa. 442 W Kennedy Blvd 33606. Hours: 5:30 pm-10 pm, Fri & Sat-11 pm. Closed major holidays; also
American   Sun & Mon. Reservations: accepted. Features: The trendy bistro features expertly created dishes that
reflect a Mediterranean flair. The interesting grilled grouper chili with a cheese-filled pasta base is
wonderfully presented. An appealing lunch menu also is offered. Dressy casual; cocktails. Parking: street. Cards: AX, CB,
DC, DS, MC, VI.
⟨Y⟩⟨X⟩

NEWK'S LIGHTHOUSE CAFE   Lunch: $5-$12   Dinner: $5-$12   Phone: 813/307-6395   36
▽▽   Location: Just e, adjacent to The Ice Palace; downtown. 514 Channelside Dr 33602. Hours: 11 am-9 pm, Fri &
Sat-10 pm, Sun 11 am-6 pm, Mon 11 am-3 pm. Features: Before heading off to the Ice Palace, visitors
American   can stop at this casual spot for a great sandwich, gourmet pasta or fried shrimp. Desserts are tasty, too,
particularly the Mississippi mud pie. Casual dress. Parking: on-site. Cards: MC, VI.

THE OLD MEETING HOUSE   Dinner: $4-$8   Phone: 813/251-1754   60
▽▽   Location: I-275, exit 42, 1 mi s on Armenia Ave, just e on Azeele, 0.6 mi s. 901 S Howard Ave 33606. Hours: 7
am-10 pm. Closed: 12/25. Features: Established in 1947, a local favorite for its '40-'50s look, ice cream,
American   home cooked entrees and daily blue plate specials. Casual dress. Parking: on-site.
⟨X⟩

OVO CAFE   Lunch: $10-$16   Dinner: $10-$16   Phone: 813/248-6979   44
▽▽▽   Location: I-4, exit 1, just e on 21st St, then just s; in Ybor City. 1907 E 7th Ave 33607. Hours: 11 am-9 pm, Mon &
Tues-3 pm, Fri & Sat-1 am. Closed major holidays. Features: This trendy place in Ybor City attracts the
American   younger party crowd. Appetizing menu choices and many low-cal delights keep you light on your feet for
dancing all night. Opt for the white-wine barbecue pizza for a twist on traditional late-night pig-out food.
Casual dress; cocktails. Parking: street. Cards: AX, DC, DS, MC, VI.
⟨Y⟩⟨X⟩

(See map p. 856)

OYSTERCATCHERS   Lunch: $8-$12   Dinner: $12-$30   Phone: 813/281-9116   26
▼▼▼
Seafood
Location: SR 60, at east end of Courtney Campbell Cswy; in Hyatt Regency Westshore. 6200 Courtney Campbell Cswy 33607. **Hours:** 11:30 am-2:30 & 6-10 pm, Sun 10:30 am-2:45 pm. **Reservations:** suggested. **Features:** Nestled on a point that juts into Old Tampa Bay and built low among coastal shrubbery is this upscale seafood restaurant. The three-tiered dining room affords views of the bay through many bay windows. White painted furniture, bright floral prints and staff attired in tropical whites contribute to the bright openness of the restaurant. An open kitchen adds atmosphere, as well as a measure of noise. Several tables occupy an outdoor patio. Casual dress; cocktails; entertainment. **Parking:** valet. **Cards:** AX, CB, DC, DS, JC, MC, VI.

REMINGTON'S STEAKHOUSE   Dinner: $9-$21   Phone: 813/972-1646   51
▼▼▼
Steak House
Location: I-75, exit 266, 3.8 mi w on Fletcher, 0.5 mi n on Bruce B Downs, then just w. 2836 E Bearss Ave 33613. **Hours:** 4 pm-10 pm, Fri & Sat-11 pm. **Closed:** 12/25. **Features:** Diners who stroll past the attractive landscaping and enter the restaurant, which resembles a weathered barn, experience a rustic interior design that evokes the ambience of a Western town. On the varied menu are choices such as steak, ribs, chicken, pork chops and fajitas, as well as an array of appetizers, salads and desserts. Casual dress; cocktails. **Parking:** on-site. **Cards:** AX, DC, DS, MC, VI.

ROYAL PALACE THAI RESTAURANT   Lunch: $7-$18   Dinner: $10-$18   Phone: 813/258-5893   57
▼▼▼
Thai
Location: I-275, exit 42, 1 mi s on Armenia Ave, just e on Azeele, 0.7 mi s. 811 S Howard Ave 33606. **Hours:** 11:30 am-2:30 & 4:30-10:30 pm. **Closed** major holidays. **Features:** The beautifully decorated restaurant is a welcoming Thai-themed setting. The menu builds on this theme, with an extensive variety of authentic Thai cuisine and numerous chef specialties. The charming staff makes for a delightful meal. Casual dress; beer & wine only. **Parking:** on-site. **Cards:** MC, VI.

ROY'S RESTAURANT   Dinner: $11-$35   Phone: 813/873-7697   38
▼▼▼
American
Location: I-275, exit 40B, 0.9 mi n, just w. 4342 W Boy Scout Blvd 33607. **Hours:** 5:30 pm-10 pm, Fri & Sat-10:30 pm. **Features:** Aloha-style service is evident from the moment you enter the deliciously different restaurant. Innovative Hawaiian fusion cuisine includes all the classic favorites. Casual dress; cocktails. **Parking:** on-site. **Cards:** AX, DC, DS, MC, VI.

THE RUSTY PELICAN   Dinner: $18-$23   Phone: 813/281-1943   23
▼▼▼
Seafood
Location: 0.5 mi s of east end of Courtney Campbell Cswy (SR 60). 2425 Rocky Point Dr 33607. **Hours:** 5 pm-10 pm, Fri & Sat-11 pm. **Reservations:** suggested; weekends. **Features:** Tableside cooking is just one enticement at this intimate restaurant. Fireplace parlors offer Tampa Bay panoramas. Holiday brunches are special treats and beautifully prepared dessert, such as bananas foster and cherries jubilee, is a fitting final touch. Banquet facilities from 20 to 460 may be accommodated. Dressy casual; cocktails. **Parking:** on-site and valet. **Cards:** AX, DC, DS, MC, VI.

SAIGON BAY VIETNAMESE RESTAURANT   Lunch: $7-$17   Dinner: $7-$17   Phone: 813/971-0854   12
▼▼▼
Vietnamese
Location: I-275, exit 51, 1.5 mi e; in Fowler Plaza South. 2373 E Fowler Ave 33612. **Hours:** 11 am-9:30 pm, Fri & Sat-10:30 pm. **Closed:** 11/27, 12/25; also Sun. **Features:** Traditional artwork and decor characterizes this intimate Vietnamese restaurant. A lunch buffet features such tasty favorites as chicken wings, white rice, pork, fried squash and puffed sugar pastry. Or make a selection from the full menu. Casual dress; beer & wine only. **Parking:** on-site. **Cards:** AX, DS, MC, VI.

SAMBA ROOM   Lunch: $8-$20   Dinner: $9-$25   Phone: 813/254-5870   54
▼▼▼
Latino
Location: Jct N Dakota Ave; in Olde Hyde Park Village. 1610 W Swann Ave 33606. **Hours:** 11:30 am-10 pm, Fri & Sat-midnight, Sun-10 pm. **Features:** Offered in a cafe-style setting, an eclectic menu displays a distinctly European influence. Start with fried pita chips covered with feta cheese and an avocado-scallion dip; then for a moist, tender entree, select the salmon prepared in parchment paper. Casual dress; cocktails. **Parking:** on-site. **Cards:** AX, CB, DC, DS, MC, VI.

SAM SELTZER'S STEAKHOUSE   Lunch: $8-$19   Dinner: $10-$19   Phone: 813/873-7267   28
▼▼
Steak & Seafood
Location: I-275, exit 41B, 2.1 mi n. 4744 N Dale Mabry Hwy 33614. **Hours:** 11:30 am-10:30 pm, Fri-11 pm, Sat noon-11:30 pm, Sun noon-10 pm. **Closed:** 11/27, 12/25. **Reservations:** suggested. **Features:** Old family portraits and Western knickknacks adorn the wood walls of the rustic restaurant. Hearty portions of mostly steak and chicken entrees satisfy the biggest of appetites. Sam's Napoleon custard cream in a graham-cracker crust is a sweet treat. Casual dress; cocktails. **Parking:** on-site. **Cards:** AX, DC, DS, MC, VI.

SHULA'S STEAKHOUSE   Lunch: $17-$33   Dinner: $17-$66   Phone: 813/286-4366   50
▼▼▼
Steak House
Location: I-275, exit 40A, 0.5 mi s; jct SR 60 and Westshore Blvd; in Wyndham Westshore. 4860 W Kennedy Blvd 33609. **Hours:** 11:30 am-2:30 & 5:30-10:30 pm, Fri & Sat-11 pm, Sun 5:30 pm-10 pm. **Reservations:** suggested. **Features:** Although predominantly a steakhouse, the restaurant also offers fish, chicken, chops and lobster. Presentations are elegant, and the a la carte side dishes are large enough to share. For dessert, splurge on the decadent seven-layer chocolate cake. Classy decor intermingles with football memorabilia from Coach Don Shula's Dolphins in their "glory years." At dinner, the menu is printed on a football, and the theme promotes a bit of rowdiness among guests. Casual dress; cocktails; entertainment. **Parking:** valet. **Cards:** AX, CB, DC, DS, JC, MC, VI.

SKIPPER'S SMOKEHOUSE RESTAURANT & OYSTER BAR Lunch: $6-$16 Dinner: $6-$16 Phone: 813/971-0666   5
▼
Seafood
Location: I-275, exit 51, 1.6 mi n on Nebraska, just e. 910 Skipper Rd 33612. **Hours:** 11 am-midnight, Sat from noon, Sun 1 pm-10 pm. **Closed:** 12/25; also Mon. **Features:** The casual Key West-style restaurant and oyster bar serves Florida fare with Caribbean and Louisiana accents. Menu selections include alligator, crab, shrimp, wings, ribs and conch chowder. Live entertainment invigorates the atmosphere outdoors. Casual dress; beer & wine only; entertainment. **Parking:** on-site. **Cards:** MC, VI.

(See map p. 856)

STUMPS SUPPER CLUB
American
Dinner: $10-$21   **Phone:** 813/226-2261   ③⑦
Location: Just s of jct SR 60; in Channelside; downtown. 615 Channelside Dr 33602. **Hours:** 4 pm-11 pm.
Features: At the Channelside complex, the interesting dining spot treats guests to "Southern cooking and deep-fried dancing" in a replicated '50s supper club atmosphere. The menu lists such choices as fried chicken, pork chops, meatloaf and other home-style meals. Casual dress; cocktails; entertainment.
Parking: on-site (fee). **Cards:** MC, VI.

SUKHOTHAI RESTAURANT
Thai
Lunch: $5-$8   **Dinner:** $6-$20   **Phone:** 813/933-7990   ⑯
Location: I-275, exit 41B, 4.8 mi n. 8201-A N Dale Mabry Hwy 33614. **Hours:** 11 am-11 pm, Sat & Sun from 5 pm. Closed major holidays; also Super Bowl Sun. **Features:** Pictures, writings and dolls decorate the dimly lit, cozy restaurant. For the most authentic experience, journey upstairs, where you'll sit on the floor to enjoy such dishes as the spicy seafood platter or stir-fried chicken in a three-spice sauce. Casual dress; beer & wine only. **Parking:** on-site. **Cards:** AX, CB, DC, DS, MC, VI.

SWEET TOMATOES
American
Lunch: $7   **Dinner:** $7   **Phone:** 813/661-0803   ⑷⑨
Location: I-75, exit 257, 0.5 mi w on SR 60. 10017 Adamo Dr 33619. **Hours:** 11 am-9 pm, Fri & Sat-10 pm. Closed: 11/27. **Features:** The contemporary, open and airy dining room contains buffet lines with colorful displays of goodies. On one bar are salad fixings with a variety of dressings, and other lines have fresh-baked muffins and bread, soup, chili, hot pasta and dessert, including frozen yogurt. Casual dress.
Parking: on-site. **Cards:** MC, VI.

TAJ INDIAN CUISINE
Indian
Lunch: $9   **Dinner:** $9-$17   **Phone:** 813/971-8483   ⑬
Location: I-275, exit 51, 1.3 mi e; in University Collection shops. 2734B E Fowler Ave 33612. **Hours:** 11:30 am-2:30 & 5-10 pm, Sat & Sun 11:30 am-3 & 5-10 pm. Closed: 11/27, 12/25; also Mon. **Features:** Instrumental music plays in the background of this quiet, contemporary setting. Taste such specialties as pulao rice and curried chicken from the lunch buffet. The a la carte dinner menu features a good variety, including many vegetarian dishes. Smoke free premises. Casual dress; beer & wine only. **Parking:** on-site. **Cards:** AX, MC, VI.

TAMPA BAY BREWING COMPANY
American
Lunch: $6-$20   **Dinner:** $8-$20   **Phone:** 813/247-1422   ⑷⓪
Location: I-4, exit 1, 0.3 mi s on 21st, 0.6 mi w on 7th Ave, then just n. 1812 N 15th St 33605. **Hours:** 11:30 am-midnight, Wed-Sat to 2 am, Sun 1 pm-midnight. Closed: 12/25. **Features:** In lively and historic Ybor City, the popular establishment is famous for its variety of house brewed beers, all made on site. The varied menu lists many choices—from delicious fried calamari to burgers, seafood, poultry and steaks. Casual dress; cocktails. **Parking:** street. **Cards:** MC, VI.

TIA'S TEX MEX
Mexican
Lunch: $7-$15   **Dinner:** $7-$15   **Phone:** 813/972-7737   ⑮
Location: I-275, exit 51, 1.6 mi e on SR 582. 2815 Fowler Ave E 33612. **Hours:** 11 am-10 pm, Fri & Sat-11 pm. Closed: 12/25. **Features:** This cantina rocks with live entertainment on Wednesday nights, and features mesquite-grilled Tex-Mex items served with a playful, fun attitude by caring servers. Save room for dessert and indulge in the fried ice cream for a chilling taste sensation. Casual dress; cocktails. **Parking:** on-site.
Cards: AX, DC, DS, MC, VI.

TIA'S TEX-MEX
Mexican
Lunch: $6-$16   **Dinner:** $9-$16   **Phone:** 813/877-5000   ③⑴
Location: I-275, exit 41B; exit 41A northbound, just n. 1503 N Dale Mabry Hwy 33607. **Hours:** 11 am-10 pm, Fri & Sat-11 pm. Closed: 12/25. **Features:** Enjoy a wonderful meal in a festive Mexican cantina setting. Try any of the Tex-Mex classics—burritos, tacos, enchiladas, chalupas, quesadillas and fajitas—or something off the mesquite wood grill, such as delicious ribs. Platters satisfy hearty appetites, while salads are a tempting representative of lighter fare. Casual dress; cocktails. **Parking:** on-site. **Cards:** AX, DC, DS, MC, VI.

VALENCIA GARDEN
Spanish
Lunch: $6-$8   **Dinner:** $10-$17   **Phone:** 813/253-3773   ③③
Location: I-275, exit 44, 0.7 mi w on Ashley Dr, 0.5 mi s. 811 W Kennedy Blvd 33606. **Hours:** 11 am-2:30 & 5-10 pm, Sat from 5 pm. Closed major holidays; also Sun. **Reservations:** suggested; weekends. **Features:** Established in 1927, the restaurant details its vivid history in old murals, tiles and decorations. Each dining room carries its own theme, ranging from romantic to raucous. The chicken with yellow rice, garnished with red pepper, is delightfully spicy. Casual dress; cocktails. **Parking:** on-site. **Cards:** AX, DC, DS, MC, VI.

VALLARTO'S RESTAURANTE MEXICANO
Mexican
Lunch: $5-$11   **Dinner:** $6-$11   **Phone:** 813/264-7691   ⑵⓪
Location: On US 92 just s of jct Fletcher Ave. 13731-37 N Dale Mabry Hwy 33618. **Hours:** 11 am-10 pm. **Features:** Authentic Mexican cuisine served in decorative Southwestern surroundings. The menu is extensive, with at least 60 items to choose from. The burritos and taco combo platter are quite good or try the chihuahua cheese. Casual dress; beer & wine only. **Parking:** on-site. **Cards:** MC, VI.

V.P.'S COUNTRY BBQ & CATERING
American
Lunch: $5-$16   **Dinner:** $5-$16   **Phone:** 813/626-1996   ⑷⑸
Location: I-4, exit 7, 1.1 mi n on US 301. 7117 N US 301 33610. **Hours:** 10 am-8 pm. Closed: Sun. **Features:** A water wheel and pond area add to the rustic exterior of the welcoming restaurant. Seating, both inside and out, is at picnic benches and tables amid weathered furnishings. The menu offers rotisserie pie, lamb, chicken, ribs, sausage, beef, pork choices and side dishes. Casual dress; beer & wine only; entertainment. **Parking:** on-site. **Cards:** AX, MC, VI.

WINDY CITY PIZZA
American
Lunch: $6-$19   **Dinner:** $6-$19   **Phone:** 813/960-1400   ⑴⓪
Location: Jct Fletcher; in Cascades Center. 12908 N Dale Mabry Hwy 33618. **Hours:** 11:30 am-10 pm, Fri & Sat-11 pm, Sun from 4 pm. **Features:** A subtle Chicago sports theme is at the heart of the restaurant's contemporary decor. Gourmet pizza featuring over 15 toppings, garden fresh salad and hearty pasta entrees with homemade sauces are menu mainstays. Casual dress; beer & wine only. **Parking:** on-site.
Cards: AX, DS, MC, VI.

(See map p. 856)

THE WINE EXCHANGE BISTRO & WINE BAR   **Lunch:** $8-$10   **Dinner:** $8-$10   **Phone:** 813/254-9463   52
Location: At jct Snow Ave; in Old Hyde Park Village. 1611 W Swann Ave 33606. **Hours:** 11:30 am-10 pm, Fri & Sat-11 pm. Closed major holidays. **Features:** Dine among Greek ruins at this upscale, cafe-style restaurant. An Italian-influenced menu features many different dishes ranging from filet mignon served with mushrooms to traditional pasta and pizza. Smoking is allowed on the patio area only. Smoke free premises. Casual dress; beer & wine only. **Parking:** street. **Cards:** AX, CB, DC, DS, JC, MC, VI.
American

WOODY'S BAR-B-QUE   **Lunch:** $5-$14   **Dinner:** $5-$14   **Phone:** 813/978-9132   9
Location: I-275, exit 51, just e. 1120 E Fowler Ave 33612. **Hours:** 11 am-9 pm, Thurs-Sat to 10 pm. Closed: 11/27, 12/25. **Features:** Vintage movie posters and bright colors pique your senses in this rustic diner. Wood-smoked pork, beef, ribs and chicken are topped with a distinctive hickory barbecue sauce and served in record time by a khaki-clad staff. Southern style quality barbecue. Casual dress; beer & wine only. **Parking:** on-site. **Cards:** AX, DC, DS, MC, VI.
American

———— *The following restaurants have not been evaluated by AAA* ————
but are listed for your information only.

ADOBE GILA'S   **Phone:** 813/241-8588
[fyi]   Not evaluated. **Location:** I-4, exit 1, just s to 8th Ave, just w at Centro Ybor; in Ybor City. 1600 E 8th Ave 33605. **Features:** A Mexican cantina setting located at Centro Ybor. The spot is popular for its fajitas and margaritas.

BAMBOO CLUB   **Phone:** 813/353-0326
[fyi]   Not evaluated. **Location:** I-275, exit 40A southbound; exit 39A northbound, 0.9 mi w on West Shore Blvd; in International Plaza and Bay Street. 2223 N West Shore Blvd 33607.

BIG CITY TAVERN   **Phone:** 813/247-3000
[fyi]   Not evaluated. **Location:** I-4, exit 1, just s to 8th Ave, just w; at Centro Ybor; in Ybor City. 1600 E 8th Ave 33605. **Features:** For a fine dining experience, visit this spot located on the 2nd level of the popular Centro Ybor complex. Menu offerings are varied with such items as grilled tuna, pan-fried trout and roasted salmon being some of the specialties.

BILL'S SUNDOWNER   **Phone:** 813/636-8686
[fyi]   Not evaluated. **Location:** I-275, exit 40A southbound; exit 39B northbound; 0.4 mi e on Westshore Blvd; 0.4 mi s. 5401 W Kennedy Blvd 33609. **Features:** Enjoy such items as seared ahi tuna, island spiced lamb or steaks & chops just to mention a few items that will draw you to this casual restaurant.

GALLERY ECLECTIC BISTRO   **Phone:** 813/353-3838
[fyi]   Not evaluated. **Location:** I-275, exit 40A southbound; exit 39A northbound; 0.9 mi w on Westshore Blvd; in International Plaza and Bay Street. 2223 N Westshore Blvd 33607.

MIA'S   **Phone:** 813/258-9400
[fyi]   Not evaluated. **Location:** Jct Dakota; in Old Hyde Park. 1633 Snow Ave 33606. **Features:** This very trendy eatery located in the popular Old Hyde Park shopping district is quite the draw. The menu offers such creations as marinated leg of lamb and Yucatan pork.

OYSTER BAY   **Phone:** 813/885-2600
[fyi]   Not evaluated. **Location:** Just s of jct Linebaugh. 9902 Anderson Rd 33612. **Features:** Enjoy seafood and more seafood from sandwiches to platters as well as house specialties. If you love seafood; you'll find something to satisfy your appetite.

PIPO'S & SON RESTAURANT   **Phone:** 813/882-0184
[fyi]   Not evaluated. **Location:** At jct Haley Rd. 7233 W Hillsborough 33635. **Features:** Spanish cuisine—such as the specialty roast pork—is the order of the day in this family-run, cafe-style restaurant.

PREZZO   **Phone:** 813/877-7455
[fyi]   Not evaluated. **Location:** I-275, exit 40A southbound; exit 39A northbound; 0.9 mi w on Westshore Blvd; in International Plaza and Bay Street. 2223 N Westshore Blvd 33607.

PROFUSION   **Phone:** 813/353-8400
[fyi]   Not evaluated. **Location:** I-275, exit 40A southbound; exit 39A northbound; 0.9 mi w on Westshore Blvd; in International Plaza and Bay Street. 2223 W Westshore Blvd 33607.

SAMURAI BLUE SUSHI AND SAKE BAR   **Phone:** 813/242-6688
[fyi]   Not evaluated. **Location:** I-4, exit 1, just s to 8th Ave; just w at Centro Ybor; in Ybor City. 1600 E 8th Ave (L208) 33605. **Features:** Upscale restaurant located on the 2nd level at the popular Centro Ybor— this restaurant's main focus is sushi but there is also a varied menu which offers various Japanese specialties.

TUSCA BELLA PASTA HOUSE   **Phone:** 813/290-7744
[fyi]   Not evaluated. **Location:** Just s of jct Linebaugh. 9212 Anderson Rd 33612. **Features:** Upscale restaurant which offers a wide choice of Italian specialties from Tuscan wood stone pizzas to flatbread folds, to fire-roasted chicken breast.

The Tampa Vicinity

APOLLO BEACH pop. 7,444

──────── WHERE TO STAY ────────

RAMADA INN ON TAMPA BAY
Phone: (813)641-2700
(AAA) (SAVE)   2/1-4/19   1P: $75-$150   2P: $75-$150   XP: $10   F17
◆◆◆ ◆◆◆   12/1-1/31 & 4/20-11/30   1P: $60-$125   2P: $60-$125   XP: $10   F17
Motel   **Location:** I-75, exit 246, 1.8 mi w on CR 672; 1.8 mi s on US 41, 2.4 mi w on Apollo Beach Blvd. 6414 Surfside Blvd 33572. Fax: 813/645-9294. **Facility:** 102 one-bedroom standard units. 2 stories, exterior corridors. **Parking:** on-site. **Terms:** check-in 4 pm, weekly rates available, pets ($15 extra charge). **Amenities:** voice mail, safes (fee), irons, hair dryers. **Dining:** 7:30 am-10 pm, Fri & Sat-11 pm, cocktails. **Pool(s):** outdoor, heated outdoor. **Leisure Activities:** fishing, bicycles, volleyball. *Fee:* aqua trikes, jet skis, pontoon boat rides (seasonal). **Guest Services:** valet and coin laundry. **Business Services:** meeting rooms, fax (fee). **Cards:** AX, CB, DC, DS, MC, VI. **Special Amenities:** early check-in/late check-out and free newspaper.

SOME UNITS
[icons]

──────── WHERE TO DINE ────────

BEEF O'BRADY'S   **Lunch:** $5-$7   **Dinner:** $5-$7   **Phone:** 813/641-1989
◆◆◆   **Location:** I-75, exit 246, 1.8 mi w on CR 672, 1.8 mi s on US 41. 205 Apollo Beach Blvd, Suite 108 33572. **Hours:** 11 am-11 pm, Sun 12:30 pm-10 pm. **Closed:** 11/27, 12/25. **Features:** Big screen TVs keep this
American   spot hopping on game days. A bustling family sports pub that cooks up a variety of traditional burgers, sandwiches, salads and wings, it features a terrific Philly cheese steak served with french fries and a pickle spear. Casual dress; beer & wine only. **Parking:** on-site. **Cards:** AX, MC, VI.

[icons]

BELLEAIR BLUFFS pop. 2,243 (See map p. 846; index p. 855)

──────── WHERE TO DINE ────────

E & E STAKEOUT GRILL   **Lunch:** $6-$19   **Dinner:** $6-$19   **Phone:** 727/585-6399   (274)
◆◆◆   **Location:** Jct Indian Rocks Rd and West Bay; in The Plaza. 100 N Indian Rocks Rd 33770. **Hours:** 11:30 am-10 pm, Fri-10:30 pm, Sat 4 pm-10:30 pm, Sun 4 pm-10 pm. **Closed:** 7/4, 9/1, 12/25; also Super Bowl Sun.
American   **Features:** Located in strip mall of galleries and upscale boutiques, this Southwestern themed restaurant gives you the feel of New Mexico with kokopelli, the mischievous spirit, as the mascot. Choices include steak, seafood, poultry and appetizers. Dessert is a must. Casual dress; cocktails. **Parking:** on-site. **Cards:** AX, DC, DS, MC, VI.

[icons]

BRANDON pop. 77,895

──────── WHERE TO STAY ────────

BEHIND THE FENCE BED & BREAKFAST   **Phone:** (813)685-8201
◆◆◆   All Year [ECP]   1P: $59-$79   2P: $79-$89   F10
Bed & Breakfast   **Location:** I-75, exit 254, just s on US 301 (northbound); 1.5 mi s on US 301 (southbound), 2.5 mi e on Bloomingdale Ave, just n on Countryside St; at jct Viola Dr. Located in a residential area. 1400 Viola Dr 33511. **Facility:** An 1800s look is achieved at this rustic B&B through antique furnishings, vintage woodwork and even historically accurate styles of nails. Smoke free premises. 5 one-bedroom standard units. 2 stories, interior/exterior corridors. **Parking:** on-site. **Terms:** check-in 4 pm, 10 day cancellation notice-fee imposed, package plans, small pets only ($10 deposit). **Amenities:** irons. *Some:* hair dryers. **Pool(s):** outdoor. **Business Services:** meeting rooms.

SOME UNITS
[icons] FEE

BRANDON MOTOR LODGE   **Phone:** (813)689-1261
(AAA) (SAVE)   2/1-4/25   1P: $59-$69   2P: $69-$79   XP: $10   F12
◆◆◆   12/1-1/31   1P: $49-$59   2P: $59-$69   XP: $10   F12
Motel   4/26-11/30   1P: $45-$49   2P: $49-$59   XP: $10   F12
Location: I-75, exit 257, 4.1 mi e on SR 60. 906 E Brandon Blvd 33511. Fax: 813/685-0975. **Facility:** 35 one-bedroom standard units. 2 stories, exterior corridors. *Bath:* combo or shower only. **Parking:** on-site. **Amenities:** *Some:* irons, hair dryers. **Pool(s):** outdoor. **Guest Services:** coin laundry. **Business Services:** fax (fee). **Cards:** AX, DC, DS, MC, VI. **Special Amenities:** early check-in/late check-out and preferred room (subject to availability with advanced reservations).

SOME UNITS
[icons]

HOLIDAY INN EXPRESS-BRANDON   **Phone:** (813)643-3800
◆◆◆   1/13-4/18 [ECP]   1P: $99-$115   2P: $105-$125   XP: $6   F18
Motel   12/1-1/12 & 4/19-11/30 [ECP]   1P: $79-$89   2P: $85-$91   XP: $6   F18
Location: I-75, exit 257, just e to Grand Regency Blvd, just n. Located in Regency Office Park. 510 Grand Regency Blvd 33510. Fax: 813/643-5888. **Facility:** 119 units. 112 one-bedroom standard units. 7 one-bedroom suites with whirlpools. 4 stories, interior corridors. *Bath:* combo or shower only. **Parking:** on-site. **Amenities:** voice mail, irons, hair dryers. **Pool(s):** outdoor. **Leisure Activities:** exercise room. **Guest Services:** valet and coin laundry. **Business Services:** meeting rooms, fax. **Cards:** AX, CB, DC, DS, JC, MC, VI.

SOME UNITS

HOMESTEAD STUDIO SUITES HOTEL-TAMPA/BRANDON Phone: (813)643-5900

▼▼▼ 1/16-4/30 1P: $89 2P: $109 XP: $5 F18
12/1-1/15 & 5/1-11/30 1P: $59 2P: $79 XP: $5 F18

Motel **Location:** I-75, exit 257, just e on SR 60, 0.4 mi n. Located in Regency Office Park. 330 Grand Regency Blvd 33510.
Fax: 813/643-4343. **Facility:** 141 one-bedroom standard units with efficiencies. 2 stories, exterior corridors.
Bath: combo or shower only. **Parking:** on-site. **Terms:** cancellation fee imposed, pets ($75 extra charge). **Amenities:** voice mail,
irons. *Some:* hair dryers. **Guest Services:** coin laundry. **Business Services:** fax. **Cards:** AX, CB, DC, DS, JC, MC, VI.

SOME UNITS

(ASK) (S/D) (⌖) (▤◄) (⌂M) (⌖) (⌐) (⊕) (⌖) (DATA PORT) (⊟) (⌖) (⌐) / (✕) /

LA QUINTA INN & SUITES Phone: (813)643-0574

(AAA) (SAVE) 12/26-4/7 1P: $99-$119 2P: $105-$125
▼▼▼ 12/1-12/25 & 4/8-11/30 1P: $69-$89 2P: $75-$95

Location: I-75, exit 257, just e on SR 60, 0.4 mi n. Located in the Regency Office Park. 310 Grand Regency Blvd 33510.
Fax: 813/643-5408. **Facility:** 128 units. 123 one-bedroom standard units. 5 one-bedroom suites. 5 stories,
Small-scale Hotel interior corridors. *Bath:* combo or shower only. **Parking:** on-site. **Terms:** [ECP] meal plan available, small
pets only ($35 deposit). **Amenities:** video games, dual phone lines, voice mail, irons, hair dryers. **Pool(s):**
heated outdoor. **Leisure Activities:** whirlpool, exercise room. **Guest Services:** valet and coin laundry. **Business Services:**
meeting rooms, fax (fee). **Cards:** AX, CB, DC, DS, JC, MC, VI. **Special Amenities: free continental breakfast and free local
telephone calls.** *(See color ad p 881)*

SOME UNITS

(▤◄) (⌖) (⌂M) (⌖) (⌐) (⊕) (⌖) (DATA PORT) (⌐) / (✕) (⊟) (⌖) /

———— WHERE TO DINE ————

THE AMERICAN CAFE Lunch: $7-$11 Dinner: $8-$14 Phone: 813-681-8891

▼▼▼ **Location:** I-75, exit 257, just e on SR 60, then just s; in Brandon Town Center Mall. 504 Brandon Town Center 33511.
Hours: 11 am-10 pm. Closed: 11/27, 12/25. **Features:** In Brandon Town Center Mall, the restaurant offers
American a variety of tasty treats—poultry, steak and seafood dishes, as well as burgers and sandwiches. Soups and
house salads are tasty starts. It's hard to go wrong with the hearty pot roast. Casual dress; cocktails.
Parking: on-site. **Cards:** AX, DC, DS, MC, VI. (✕)

BARNACLES Lunch: $6-$17 Dinner: $6-$17 Phone: 813-653-0959

▼▼▼ **Location:** At jct Lunsten Rd. 926 Providence Rd 33511. **Hours:** 11 am-2 am, Thurs-Sat-3 am, Sun-1 am.
Features: At least 100 television sets line the walls inside and outside of the sports bar and restaurant,
Seafood and diners can keep up with nearly any sport imaginable. The extensive menu includes such house
specialties as shrimp Malibu or steak Napoleon. The pasta also is tasty. For a lighter meal, try one of the
many salads, soups, chicken sandwiches, po'boy subs or gourmet burgers. The andouille sausage sub is a good choice.
Casual dress; cocktails. **Parking:** on-site. **Cards:** AX, DC, DS, MC, VI. (✕)

BEN'S FAMILY RESTAURANT Lunch: $6-$14 Dinner: $6-$14 Phone: 813-685-5501

▼▼▼ **Location:** I-75, exit 257, 3.3 mi e on SR 60; jct Ridgewood Ave. 704 E Brandon Ave 33511. **Hours:** 7:30 am-9 pm.
Closed: Mon & Tues. **Features:** Relax in this comfortable, family style restaurant with country decor and a
American nautical touch. A variety of home cooked entrees such as steak, chicken, pork and sandwiches are
available. Try one of their many homemade desserts. Casual dress. **Parking:** on-site. **Cards:** MC, VI.

BRANDON ALE HOUSE & RAW BAR Lunch: $6-$13 Dinner: $6-$13 Phone: 813-643-0511

▼▼▼ **Location:** I-75, exit 257, 2.4 mi e on SR 60. 1817 W Brandon Blvd 33511. **Hours:** 11 am-2 am. **Features:** This
sports-themed restaurant will impress many fans with 40 TV monitors and four satellite dishes. Catch the
Seafood big game and enjoy a variety of sandwiches, pasta and seafood. Casual dress; cocktails. **Parking:** on-site.
Cards: AX, DC, DS, MC, VI. (⊤) (✕)

BRANDON BREW HOUSE Lunch: $7-$19 Dinner: $7-$19 Phone: 813-655-0511

▼▼▼ **Location:** At jct of Kings; in Oak Park Plaza. 779 W Lumsden Rd 33511. **Hours:** 11 am-3 am. **Features:** A local
favorite serving up casual fare such as burgers, sandwiches, steaks and chicken dishes. The service is
American friendly in this local eatery. A comedy club is on site offering local entertainers for a fun night out. Casual
dress; cocktails. **Parking:** on-site. **Cards:** MC, VI.

BUDDY FREDDY'S Lunch: $6-$8 Dinner: $8-$11 Phone: 813-661-6005

▼ **Location:** I-75, exit 257, 0.7 mi e on SR 60, just s. 134 S Gornto Lake Rd 33511. **Hours:** 7 am-8:30 pm, Fri &
Sat-9 pm. Closed: 4/20, 7/4, 12/25. **Features:** This is good, old-fashioned home cooking dished up in a
American country decor. An excellent lunch and dinner buffet is offered with an a la carte menu for added variety.
Bring the whole family, and take advantage of early bird specials and senior discounts. Smoke free
premises. Casual dress. **Parking:** on-site. **Cards:** AX, DS, MC, VI. (✕)

CATFISH COUNTRY Lunch: $7-$18 Dinner: $7-$18 Phone: 813-689-0246

▼▼▼ **Location:** On SR 60; jct Ridgewood Ave. 706 E Brandon Blvd 33511. **Hours:** 11 am-9 pm, Fri & Sat-10 pm,
Sun-8:30 pm. **Features:** Diners who love catfish come here. The casual, "fish shanty" atmosphere
Seafood combines with a menu of all kinds of goodies prepared with a Cajun flair. Choose from alligator, frog legs,
grouper, steaks, pasta, shrimp and, of course, catfish—all served in heaping portions. Casual dress; beer
& wine only. **Parking:** on-site. **Cards:** MC, VI. (✕)

CHOP STIX CHINESE RESTAURANT Lunch: $5-$14 Dinner: $5-$14 Phone: 813-654-5195

▼ **Location:** SR 60, just w of jct Mt Carmel. 801 E Brandon Blvd 33511. **Hours:** 11 am-9:30 pm, Fri & Sat-10 pm,
Sun noon-9 pm. **Features:** Although seating is limited in this small restaurant, the food is worth the wait
Chinese and is some of the best authentic Chinese food you'll find in these parts. The menu is extensive. Casual
dress. **Parking:** on-site. **Cards:** MC, VI.

CRABBY TOM'S OYSTER BAR & SEAFOOD RESTAURANT   **Lunch:** $7-$16   **Dinner:** $7-$16   **Phone:** 813/651-3499
Location: I-75, exit 257. 2.6 mi e on SR 60. 1414 W Brandon Blvd 33511. **Hours:** 11 am-10 pm, Fri & Sat-11 pm, Sun noon-9 pm. Closed: 4/20, 11/27, 12/25. **Features:** An eclectic sports bar with nautical touches provides an appealing menu of sandwiches, salads and seafood platters. For instance, the seafood sampler offers shrimp, scallops, oysters and clams with fries, coleslaw and homemade hushpuppies. Casual dress; cocktails. **Parking:** on-site. **Cards:** AX, DC, DS, MC, VI.
Seafood

DURANGO STEAKHOUSE   **Lunch:** $6-$10   **Dinner:** $7-$18   **Phone:** 813/681-3999
Location: Jct Providence Rd; in Brandon Town Centre South. 1995 W Lumsden Rd 33511. **Hours:** 4 pm-10 pm, Sat & Sun from 11:30 am-11 pm. Closed: 11/27, 12/25. **Features:** Ample servings of tasty food abound in this Southwestern eatery that serves a variety of oak-grilled entrees such as ribs, steak and chicken. Murals and knotty-pine hardwood floors lend a warm and distinctive ambience to the dining area. Casual dress; cocktails. **Parking:** on-site. **Cards:** AX, DC, DS, MC, VI.
Steak House

ESTELA'S MEXICAN RESTAURANT   **Lunch:** $3-$6   **Dinner:** $5-$10   **Phone:** 813/657-1421
Location: I-75, exit 257, 3 mi e on SR 60 at jct Kings Ave. 312 E Brandon Blvd 33511. **Hours:** 11 am-10 pm, Fri & Sat-11 pm. **Features:** The quaint Mexican cantina setting offers a relaxed ambience for a casual meal. The menu offers many choices, such as chimichangas, nachos, fajitas, huevos rancheros and quesadillas. Casual dress; beer & wine only. **Parking:** on-site. **Cards:** MC, VI.
Mexican

GATORZ SOUTHERN ROCK CAFE   **Lunch:** $6-$10   **Dinner:** $6-$10   **Phone:** 813/662-1557
Location: SR 60, just w of jct Bryan. 509 E Brandon Blvd 33511. **Hours:** 11 am-3 am, Sun from noon. Closed: 12/25. **Features:** Rock 'n' roll memorabilia and nostalgic knickknacks create an eye-catching decor. Sandwiches, ribs, pizza and market-fresh crab fill out a fun-food menu. Start with the fried wing appetizers with celery and dressing, and you can't go wrong. Casual dress; cocktails; entertainment. **Parking:** on-site. **Cards:** AX, DC, DS, MC, VI.
American

HAO ONE CHINESE RESTAURANT   **Lunch:** $6-$12   **Dinner:** $6-$12   **Phone:** 813/685-6381
Location: I-75, exit 257, 0.6 mi e on SR 60. 2020 W Brandon Blvd, Suite 145 33511. **Hours:** 11:30 am-3 & 4:30-10 pm. Closed: 11/27, 12/25. **Features:** Chinese food in all its variety is the focus at this relaxing, Asian-themed restaurant. The lo mein, beef and broccoli, and General Tso's chicken are particularly tasty, and an extensive buffet is available. Casual dress; beer & wine only. **Parking:** on-site. **Cards:** AX, DS, MC, VI.
Chinese

JOEY'S FAMOUS PHILLY STEAKS   **Lunch:** $6-$8   **Dinner:** $6-$8   **Phone:** 813/662-5300
Location: Jct Lumsden. 921 S Lithia Pinecrest Rd 33511. **Hours:** 10:30 am-9 pm, Fri & Sat-9:30, Sun 11 am-6 pm. Closed major holidays. **Features:** Diners who order one of the signature Philly cheese steaks are in for a delicious treat. The small eatery offers some of the best of the Northeast, with a variety of subs and sandwich offerings. Casual dress. **Parking:** on-site. **Cards:** MC, VI.
American

JO-TO JAPANESE STEAK HOUSE   **Dinner:** $12-$25   **Phone:** 813/684-0221
Location: 1.1 mi s of jct SR 60; in Lithia Square. 905 Lithia Pinecrest Rd 33511. **Hours:** 5 pm-10 pm, Fri & Sat-11 pm. Closed: 7/4, 11/27; also Super Bowl Sun. **Features:** Appreciate traditional Japanese cuisine prepared with the Teppan-yaki method of cooking. Choose from seafood, steak and chicken teriyaki or tempura dishes. Watch the cooks practice their craft table-side, or sample delicacies from the sushi bar. Casual dress; cocktails. **Parking:** on-site. **Cards:** AX, CB, DC, MC, VI.
Japanese

LATIN CAFE 2000   **Lunch:** $4-$8   **Dinner:** $8-$12   **Phone:** 813/643-9475
Location: Jct Bell Shoals Rd; in Bloomingdale Square. 829 E Bloomingdale Ave 33594. **Hours:** 7 am-10 pm. **Features:** The decor is trendy in the upscale restaurant. Breakfast options are plentiful, and the main menu offers sandwiches, meat dishes, soup, chicken, seafood, salad and dessert, all prepared with a zippy Latin flair. Smoke free premises. Casual dress; beer & wine only. **Parking:** on-site. **Cards:** MC, VI.
Spanish

LIN'S GARDEN CHINESE RESTAURANT   **Lunch:** $5-$13   **Dinner:** $5-$13   **Phone:** 813/689-6868
Location: Jct Brandon Town Center Dr; in Lake Brandon Plaza. 11237 Causeway Blvd 33511. **Hours:** 11 am-10 pm, Fri & Sat-10:30 pm, Sun noon-9:30 pm. **Features:** Dine in or take out, the small, ultra-casual restaurant specializes in more than 100 choices of "New York-style" Chinese food. Casual dress. **Parking:** on-site. **Cards:** MC, VI.
Chinese

MCHALE'S CHOPHOUSE   **Lunch:** $9-$18   **Dinner:** $10-$18   **Phone:** 813/655-0027
Location: I-75, exit 257, 2.7 mi e on SR 60. 1215 W Brandon Blvd 33511. **Hours:** 11 am-10 pm, Fri-11 pm, Sat noon-11 pm, Sun noon-9 pm. **Features:** With its relaxing and rustic setting, enjoy anything from Texas brisket to a hearty Chophouse Delmonico steak. "Barbecue with style" is their motto and the food is quite good and served in hearty portions. Casual dress; cocktails. **Parking:** on-site. **Cards:** MC, VI.
American

THE OAKS BAR & GRILL   **Lunch:** $5-$6   **Dinner:** $10-$15   **Phone:** 813/685-5257
Location: Just s of jct SR 60. 108 S Lithia-Pinecrest Rd 33511. **Hours:** 11 am-9 pm, Wed-Sat to 10 pm. Closed: 11/27, 12/25. **Features:** Touches of Key West accent the decor, and live entertainment on Fridays and Saturdays keeps the mood jovial. Enjoy fresh seafood, sandwiches and steaks, including a savory seafood gumbo with a generous helping of fish in a seasoned tomato broth. Casual dress; cocktails. **Parking:** on-site. **Cards:** AX, DS, MC, VI.
Seafood

O'BRIEN'S IRISH PUB   **Lunch:** $8-$17   **Dinner:** $8-$17   **Phone:** 813/661-9688
Location: Jct Kings; in Oak Plaza Shops. 701 W Lumsden Rd 33511. **Hours:** 11 am-3 am, Sun from noon. **Features:** A comfortable, casual setting is the scene for a wonderful Irish experience. Guests can try anything from shepherd's pie to Irish stew to bangers and mash. Casual dress; cocktails. **Parking:** on-site. **Cards:** MC, VI.
Irish

RIO BRAVO CANTINA
▼▼ ▼▼
Mexican
Lunch: $6-$14   **Dinner:** $8-$14   **Phone:** 813/655-1495
Location: Jct Providence Rd; in Lake Brandon Village. 11395 Causeway Blvd 33511. **Hours:** 11 am-10 pm, Fri & Sat-11 pm. Closed: 11/27, 12/25. **Features:** Step into the festive Mexican cantina setting, and enjoy made-from-scratch entrees. Selections include the usual favorites, such as tacos al carbon, as well as flavorful baby back ribs. Diners are encouraged to create their own combos. Casual dress; cocktails.
Parking: on-site. **Cards:** AX, DC, DS, MC, VI.

ROADHOUSE GRILL
▼▼ ▼▼
Steak House
Lunch: $7-$18   **Dinner:** $7-$18   **Phone:** 813/657-9892
Location: I-75, exit 257, 2.8 mi e on SR 60. 775 W Brandon Blvd 33511. **Hours:** 11 am-10 pm, Fri & Sat-11 pm. Closed: 11/27, 12/25. **Features:** As the name says, the restaurant gives you the feel of stepping into an old Texas roadhouse. Grab peanuts from a pail, and after you pop the nut in your mouth, toss the shell on the floor. Savory steaks are at the heart of a menu that also includes ribs, chicken and mesquite-grilled pork chops. Casual dress; cocktails. **Parking:** on-site. **Cards:** AX, DC, DS, MC, VI.

SIMPLY THAI FOR TAKE OUT ONLY
▼▼ ▼▼
Thai
Lunch: $7-$14   **Dinner:** $7-$14   **Phone:** 813/681-4470
Location: Jct Bell Shoals Rd; in Bloomingdale Square. 875 E Bloomingdale Ave 33511. **Hours:** 11:30 am-3 & 5-9 pm, Fri-9:30 pm, Sat 5 pm-9:30 pm, Sun 5 pm-9 pm. Closed: Mon. **Features:** Oriental surroundings characterize this friendly Thai establishment, which serves up an enticing array of traditional entrees. Casual dress; beer & wine only. **Parking:** on-site. **Cards:** MC, VI.

TIA'S TEX MEX
▼▼ ▼▼
Mexican
Lunch: $7-$15   **Dinner:** $7-$15   **Phone:** 813/681-7716
Location: I-75, exit 257, just e on SR 60 in; Brandon Town Center. 144 Brandon Town Center Dr 33511. **Hours:** 11 am-10 pm, Fri & Sat-11 pm. Closed: 11/27, 12/25. **Features:** Tex-Mex and mesquite-grilled dishes are served in a Mexican-style cantina setting complete with a courtyard dining area. Fresh, hearty portions mean flavorful choices with burritos, tacos, fajitas and the chalupa tortilla. Casual dress; cocktails.
Parking: on-site. **Cards:** AX, DC, DS, MC, VI.

WIZEGUYZ PIZZERIA
▼▼
Italian
Lunch: $5-$14   **Dinner:** $5-$14   **Phone:** 813/643-1200
Location: I-75, exit 257, just w on SR 60; in Regency Square. 2498 W Brandon Blvd 33511. **Hours:** 11 am-10 pm, Fri & Sat-midnight. Closed: 12/25. **Features:** The casual New York pizzeria setting is the place to go for some of the best Italian food around. Dishes are freshly prepared after you step up to the window to order. On the menu are sandwiches and pizza by the slice and by the pie, as well as such entrees as lasagna, spaghetti, baked ziti and parmesan dishes. Casual dress; beer only. **Parking:** on-site. **Cards:** MC, VI.

YOKOHAMA JAPANESE RESTAURANT SUSHI BAR
▼▼ ▼▼
Japanese
Lunch: $11-$21   **Dinner:** $11-$21   **Phone:** 813/684-3485
Location: Jct King St; in La Viva Plaza. 700 W Lumsden 33511. **Hours:** 11:30 am-2 & 5-10 pm, Fri & Sat-10:30 pm, Sun 5 pm-10 pm. **Features:** This is a cozy, intimate restaurant with a varied menu of freshly prepared, artistically decorated entrees. Try the tempura, sashimi, eel, beef, poultry, lobster, soup and various appetizers. There is also a wide variety of sushi choices. Very gracious service. Casual dress. **Parking:** on-site. **Cards:** MC, VI.

CLEARWATER pop. 108,787   (See map p. 846; index p. 850)

—— WHERE TO STAY ——

BAY QUEEN MOTEL
(AAA) (SAVE)
▼▼ ▼▼
Motel
Phone: (727)441-3295   [54]

2/1-4/6	1P: $60-$80	2P: $60-$80	XP: $5	F17
12/1-1/31 & 4/7-4/30	1P: $45-$65	2P: $45-$65	XP: $5	F17
5/1-11/30	1P: $35-$55	2P: $35-$55	XP: $5	F17

Location: On US Alt 19, just n of jct Sunset Point Rd (CR 576). 1925 Edgewater Dr 33755. **Fax:** 727/466-6186. **Facility:** 18 units. 15 one-bedroom standard units, some with efficiencies or kitchens. 3 one-bedroom units with kitchens. 2 stories, exterior corridors. *Bath:* combo or shower only. **Parking:** on-site. **Terms:** 14 day cancellation notice-fee imposed, package plans. **Amenities:** irons. *Some:* hair dryers. **Pool(s):** heated outdoor. **Leisure Activities:** barbecue grill, bicycles, shuffleboard. **Guest Services:** coin laundry. **Business Services:** PC, fax. **Cards:** AX, CB, DC, MC, VI. **Special Amenities:** free local telephone calls and free room upgrade (subject to availability with advanced reservations). *(See color ad p 906)*
SOME UNITS

BELLEVIEW BILTMORE RESORT & SPA
(AAA) (SAVE)
▼▼ ▼▼
Classic Historic
Small-scale Hotel
Phone: (727)373-3000   [64]

1/24-4/18	1P: $159-$169	2P: $159-$169	XP: $20	F18
9/26-11/30	1P: $129-$159	2P: $129-$159	XP: $20	F18
4/19-9/25	1P: $119-$149	2P: $119-$149	XP: $20	F18
12/1-1/23	1P: $129-$139	2P: $129-$139	XP: $20	F18

Location: 0.5 mi w of jct US Alt 19 (Fort Harrison). 25 Belleview Blvd 33756. **Fax:** 727/441-4173. **Facility:** 244 units. 209 one-bedroom standard units. 34 one- and 1 three-bedroom suites ($169-$950), some with kitchens. 4 stories, interior corridors. *Bath:* combo or shower only. **Parking:** on-site. **Terms:** [AP] & [BP] meal plans available. **Amenities:** voice mail, irons, hair dryers. **Dining:** 7 am-10:30 pm, cocktails. **Pool(s):** outdoor, heated indoor. **Leisure Activities:** saunas, whirlpools, boat dock, water aerobics, 4 tennis courts, aerobics, tai chi, yoga, playground, exercise room, spa, volleyball. *Fee:* golf-18 holes, bicycles, game room. **Guest Services:** gift shop, valet laundry, area transportation-beach and golf club. **Business Services:** conference facilities, business center. **Cards:** AX, CB, DC, DS, MC, VI. *(See color ad p 900)*
SOME UNITS

CANDLEWOOD SUITES CLEARWATER-ST PETERSBURG
▼▼ ▼▼ ▼▼
Small-scale Hotel
Phone: (727)573-3344   [65]

All Year	1P: $89-$109	2P: $109-$129	

Location: I-275, exit 31B southbound; exit 30 northbound, 3 mi w on SR 688, just s. 13231 49th St N 33762. **Fax:** 727/573-3074. **Facility:** 104 units. 80 one-bedroom standard units with efficiencies. 24 one-bedroom suites with kitchens. 3 stories, interior corridors. *Bath:* combo or shower only. **Parking:** on-site. **Amenities:** video library, CD players, dual phone lines, voice mail, irons, hair dryers. **Pool(s):** heated outdoor. **Leisure Activities:** exercise room. **Guest Services:** sundries, valet and coin laundry. **Business Services:** fax. **Cards:** AX, DC, DS, MC, VI.
SOME UNITS

(See map p. 846)

CLEARWATER CENTRAL-BEST WESTERN

Phone: (727)799-1565 **56**

AAA **SAVE**
▼▼▼ ▼▼

2/1-4/30 [ECP]	1P: $80	2P: $80	XP: $5 F18
12/1-1/31 & 5/1-11/30 [ECP]	1P: $65	2P: $65	XP: $5 F18

Location: US 19, just n of jct SR 60. Located in a commercial area. 21338 US 19 N 33765. Fax: 727/797-6801. **Facility:** 148 one-bedroom standard units. 2 stories (no elevator), interior corridors. **Parking:** on-site. Small-scale Hotel **Terms:** weekly rates available, package plans. **Amenities:** irons, hair dryers. **Pool(s):** heated outdoor. **Leisure Activities:** whirlpool, 2 tennis courts, picnic area with grill, horseshoes, shuffleboard, volleyball. **Guest Services:** valet and coin laundry. **Business Services:** meeting rooms. **Cards:** AX, CB, DC, DS, MC, VI. **Special Amenities:** free continental breakfast and free newspaper.

SOME UNITS

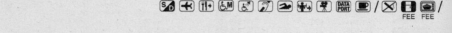

COURTYARD BY MARRIOTT

Phone: (727)572-8484 **71**

SAVE
▼▼▼ ▼▼
Motel

12/1-5/31	1P: $99-$149
6/1-11/30	1P: $79-$139

Location: I-275, exit 31B southbound; exit 30 northbound, 1.6 mi w on SR 688. Located in The Centres Office Park. 3131 Executive Dr 33762. Fax: 727/572-6991. **Facility:** 149 units. 137 one-bedroom standard units. 12 one-bedroom suites. 3 stories, interior corridors. *Bath:* combo or shower only. **Parking:** on-site. **Terms:** [BP] meal plan available. **Amenities:** high-speed Internet, voice mail, irons, hair dryers. **Pool(s):** heated outdoor. **Leisure Activities:** whirlpool, exercise room. **Guest Services:** valet and coin laundry. **Business Services:** meeting rooms, fax. **Cards:** AX, DC, DS, MC, VI. *(See ad p 873)*

SOME UNITS

DAYS INN-CLEARWATER CENTRAL

Phone: (727)799-0100 **61**

SAVE
▼▼▼ ▼▼
Motel

All Year	1P: $55-$75	2P: $55-$75 XP: $6 F12

Location: On SR 60, 0.8 mi e of jct US 19. 2940 Gulf-to-Bay Blvd 33759. Fax: 727/726-6569. **Facility:** 90 one-bedroom standard units, some with efficiencies. 2 stories, interior corridors. **Parking:** on-site. **Terms:** [CP] meal plan available. **Amenities:** hair dryers. *Some:* irons. **Pool(s):** heated outdoor. **Leisure Activities:** whirlpool, playground, shuffleboard. **Guest Services:** coin laundry. **Business Services:** meeting rooms, fax. **Cards:** AX, CB, DC, DS, JC, MC, VI.

SOME UNITS

DAYS INN-ST. PETE/CLEARWATER AIRPORT

Phone: (727)573-3334 **74**

AAA **SAVE**
▼▼▼ ▼▼

2/1-4/30 [ECP]	1P: $79-$89	2P: $84-$94	XP: $5 F18
12/1-1/31 & 5/1-11/30 [ECP]	1P: $59-$69	2P: $64-$74	XP: $5 F18

Location: I-275, exit 31B southbound; exit 30 northbound, 2 mi w on SR 688. 3910 Ulmerton Rd 33762. Fax: 727/572-4845. **Facility:** 117 one-bedroom standard units. 4 stories, interior corridors. *Bath:* combo or Small-scale Hotel shower only. **Parking:** on-site. **Terms:** 3 day cancellation notice-fee imposed. **Amenities:** video games, safes (fee), hair dryers. *Some:* irons. **Pool(s):** heated outdoor. **Guest Services:** valet and coin laundry, airport transportation-Tampa International and St. Pete/Clearwater Airports, area transportation-within 5 mi. **Business Services:** meeting rooms, fax (fee). **Cards:** AX, DC, DS, JC, MC, VI. **Special Amenities:** free continental breakfast and free room upgrade (subject to availability with advanced reservations). *(See color ad p 901)*

SOME UNITS
FEE FEE

(See map p. 846)

ECONO LODGE CLEARWATER CENTRAL

Phone: (727)799-1569 [55]

AAA SAVE

2/1-4/30	1P: $72	2P: $72	XP: $5	F18
12/1-1/31 & 5/1-11/30	1P: $55	2P: $55	XP: $5	F18

Motel. **Location:** US 19, just n of jct SR 60. Located in a commercial area. 21252 US 19 N 33765. Fax: 727/796-3165. **Facility:** 121 one-bedroom standard units. 2 stories (no elevator), exterior corridors. **Parking:** on-site. **Terms:** package plans. **Amenities:** *Some:* hair dryers. **Pool(s):** heated outdoor. **Leisure Activities:** 2 tennis courts, barbecue area, horseshoes, shuffleboard. **Guest Services:** valet and coin laundry. **Business Services:** meeting rooms. **Cards:** AX, CB, DC, DS, MC, VI. **Special Amenities:** early check-in/late check-out and free local telephone calls.

SOME UNITS

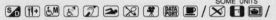

FAIRFIELD INN & SUITES CLEARWATER/BAYSIDE

Phone: (727)724-6223 [67]

SAVE

1/1-5/15 [ECP]	1P: $94
12/1-12/31 & 5/16-11/30 [ECP]	1P: $84

Small-scale Hotel **Location:** SR 60, just w of CR 611 (McMullen Booth Rd). Located in a commercial area. 3070 Gulf to Bay Blvd 33759. Fax: 727/724-3413. **Facility:** 127 one-bedroom standard units, some with whirlpools. 5 stories, interior corridors. *Bath:* combo or shower only. **Parking:** on-site. **Terms:** 3 day cancellation notice-fee imposed, 1% service charge. **Amenities:** video games, high-speed Internet, dual phone lines, voice mail, irons, hair dryers. *Some:* CD players. **Pool(s):** heated outdoor. **Leisure Activities:** whirlpool, exercise room. **Guest Services:** valet and coin laundry. **Business Services:** meeting rooms, business center. **Cards:** AX, CB, DC, DS, JC, MC, VI.

SOME UNITS

HAMPTON INN CLEARWATER CENTRAL

Phone: (727)797-8173 [60]

SAVE

2/1-3/31 [CP]	1P: $81-$98	2P: $81-$98	XP: $10	F18
4/1-4/30 [CP]	1P: $69-$83	2P: $69-$83	XP: $10	F18
12/1-11/30 [CP]	1P: $68-$83	2P: $68-$83	XP: $10	F18
5/1-11/30 [CP]	1P: $63-$76	2P: $63-$76	XP: $10	F18

Motel **Location:** On US 19, just n of jct SR 60. 21030 US 19 N 33765. Fax: 727/791-7759. **Facility:** 174 units. 158 one-bedroom standard units. 16 one-bedroom suites ($107-$150). 2 stories, exterior corridors. *Bath:* combo or shower only. **Parking:** on-site. **Terms:** check-in 4 pm, weekly rates available. **Amenities:** video games, voice mail, irons, hair dryers. **Pool(s):** heated outdoor, wading. **Leisure Activities:** sauna, whirlpool, putting green, playground, exercise room. **Guest Services:** valet and coin laundry. **Business Services:** meeting rooms, fax. **Cards:** AX, CB, DC, DS, JC, MC, VI.

SOME UNITS

HAMPTON INN-CLEARWATER/ST. PETERSBURG AIRPORT

Phone: (727)577-9200 [52]

SAVE

12/25-11/30 [ECP]	1P: $89-$99	2P: $89-$99
12/1-12/24 [ECP]	1P: $79-$84	2P: $79-$84

Motel **Location:** I-275, exit 31B southbound; exit 30 northbound, 1.8 mi w on SR 688. 3655 Hospitality at Ulmerton Rd 33762. Fax: 727/572-8931. **Facility:** 117 one-bedroom standard units. 2 stories, exterior corridors. **Parking:** on-site. **Amenities:** dual phone lines, voice mail, irons. **Pool(s):** outdoor. **Leisure Activities:** sauna, whirlpool, exercise room. **Guest Services:** complimentary evening beverages: Mon-Thurs, valet and coin laundry. **Business Services:** meeting rooms, fax. **Cards:** AX, CB, DC, DS, MC, VI.

SOME UNITS

HOLIDAY INN EXPRESS

Phone: (727)536-7275 [66]

2/1-4/20 [ECP]	1P: $119-$149	2P: $119-$149	XP: $9	F19
12/1-1/31 [ECP]	1P: $99-$129	2P: $99-$129	XP: $9	F19
4/21-11/30	1P: $99-$129	2P: $99-$129	XP: $9	F19

Motel **Location:** 0.5 mi e of jct US 19; just off Ulmerton Rd (SR 688). Located in Icot Center. 13625 Icot Blvd 33760. Fax: 727/530-3053. **Facility:** 127 units. 101 one-bedroom standard units. 26 one-bedroom suites ($129-$159), some with whirlpools. 3 stories, interior corridors. *Bath:* combo or shower only. **Parking:** on-site. **Terms:** cancellation fee imposed. **Amenities:** dual phone lines, voice mail, irons, hair dryers. **Pool(s):** heated outdoor. **Leisure Activities:** whirlpool. **Guest Services:** valet laundry. **Business Services:** meeting rooms, fax. **Cards:** AX, CB, DC, DS, JC, MC, VI.

SOME UNITS

(See map p. 846)

HOLIDAY INN HOTEL & SUITES CLEARWATER CENTRAL

Phone: (727)799-1181 59

Motel

| | 12/1-4/15 | 1P: $98 | 2P: $98 | XP: $6 | F |
| | 4/16-11/30 | 1P: $78 | 2P: $78 | XP: $6 | F |

Location: On US 19, just n of jct SR 60. 20967 US 19 N 33765. Fax: 727/712-8404. **Facility:** 148 units. 114 one-bedroom standard units, some with efficiencies. 34 one-bedroom suites ($110-$118). 3 stories, interior/exterior corridors. **Parking:** on-site. **Terms:** 7 day cancellation notice, [BP], [CP] & [MAP] meal plans available. **Amenities:** video games, voice mail, irons, hair dryers. **Pool(s):** heated outdoor, wading. **Leisure Activities:** sauna, whirlpool, playground, exercise room. **Guest Services:** valet and coin laundry. **Business Services:** meeting rooms, business center. **Cards:** AX, CB, DC, DS, JC, MC, VI. *(See color ad opposite inside back cover)*

SOME UNITS
(ASK) (SD) (†1) (Y) (⊘) (⇌) (✕) (🎬) (DATA PORT) (💻) / (✕) (VCR) (🔌) (🖨) /
FEE

HOLIDAY INN SELECT-ST. PETE/CLEARWATER INT'L AIRPORT

Phone: (727)577-9100 69

Small-scale Hotel

All Year | 1P: $95-$125

Location: I-275, exit 31B southbound; exit 30 northbound, 1.8 mi w on SR 688. 3535 Ulmerton Rd 33762. Fax: 727/573-5022. **Facility:** 173 units. 172 one-bedroom standard units. 1 one-bedroom suite. 5 stories, interior corridors. **Parking:** on-site. **Amenities:** dual phone lines, voice mail, irons, hair dryers. *Some:* CD players. **Pool(s):** heated outdoor. **Leisure Activities:** whirlpool, 2 lighted tennis courts, exercise room. *Fee:* golf-18 holes. **Guest Services:** valet and coin laundry. **Business Services:** conference facilities, business center. **Cards:** AX, DC, DS, MC, VI. *(See color ad opposite inside back cover)*

SOME UNITS
(ASK) (SD) (✈) (†1) (Y) (⊘) (⇌) (✕) (🎬) (DATA PORT) (💻) / (✕) (VCR) (🔌) (🖨) /
FEE FEE FEE

HOMESTEAD STUDIO SUITES HOTEL-TAMPA/CLEARWATER

Phone: (727)572-4800 78

Small-scale Hotel

| | 1/15-4/15 | 1P: $69 | 2P: $89 | XP: $5 | F18 |
| | 12/1-1/14 & 4/16-11/30 | 1P: $49 | 2P: $69 | XP: $5 | F18 |

Location: I-275, exit 31B southbound; exit 30 northbound, 1.5 mi w on SR 688. 2311 Ulmerton Rd 33762. Fax: 727/572-1200. **Facility:** 113 one-bedroom standard units with efficiencies. 2 stories, exterior corridors. *Bath:* combo or shower only. **Parking:** on-site. **Terms:** cancellation fee imposed, pets ($75 fee). **Amenities:** voice mail, irons. *Some:* hair dryers. **Guest Services:** fax (fee). **Business Services:** fax (fee). **Cards:** AX, CB, DC, DS, JC, MC, VI.

SOME UNITS
(ASK) (SD) (🐾) (†1+) (🔌) (⊘) (📶) (🎬) (DATA PORT) (🔌) (🖨) (💻) / (✕) /

HOMEWOOD SUITES BY HILTON

Phone: (727)573-1500 79

[SAVE]

Motel

| | 1/1-4/30 [ECP] | 1P: $169-$229 | 2P: $169-$229 | |
| | 12/1-12/31 & 5/1-11/30 [ECP] | 1P: $139-$229 | 2P: $139-$229 | |

Location: I-275, exit 31B southbound; exit 30 northbound, 1.3 mi w on SR 688. 2233 Ulmerton Rd 33762. Fax: 727/573-5950. **Facility:** 112 units. 104 one- and 8 two-bedroom suites with kitchens. 2 stories, interior corridors. *Bath:* combo or shower only. **Parking:** on-site. **Terms:** pets ($150 fee). **Amenities:** video games, voice mail, irons, hair dryers. **Pool(s):** heated outdoor. **Leisure Activities:** exercise room. **Guest Services:** sundries, valet and coin laundry. **Business Services:** meeting rooms, business center. **Cards:** AX, DC, DS, MC, VI.

SOME UNITS
(SD) (🐾) (†1+) (🅖M) (🔌) (⊘) (⇌) (VCR) (🎬) (DATA PORT) (🔌) (🖨) (💻) / (✕) /

LA QUINTA INN CLEARWATER-AIRPORT

Phone: (727)572-7222 70

(AAA) [SAVE]

Small-scale Hotel

All Year | 1P: $69-$99 | 2P: $75-$105

Location: I-275, exit 31B southbound; exit 30 northbound, 1.7 mi w on SR 688. Located in The Centres Office Park. 3301 Ulmerton Rd 33762. Fax: 727/572-0076. **Facility:** 115 one-bedroom standard units. 3 stories, interior corridors. *Bath:* combo or shower only. **Parking:** on-site. **Terms:** [ECP] meal plan available, small pets only. **Amenities:** video games, voice mail, irons, hair dryers. *Some:* dual phone lines. **Pool(s):** heated outdoor. **Leisure Activities:** sauna, whirlpool, sun deck, exercise room. **Guest Services:** valet and coin laundry, airport transportation-St. Petersburg/Clearwater Airport. **Business Services:** meeting rooms, fax (fee). **Cards:** AX, CB, DC, DS, JC, MC, VI. **Special Amenities:** free continental breakfast and free local telephone calls.** *(See color ad p 881)*

SOME UNITS
(✈) (🐾) (†1+) (🔌) (⊘) (⇌) (✕) (🎬) (DATA PORT) (🔌) (💻) / (✕) (🖨) /

QUALITY INN CLEARWATER CENTRAL

Phone: (727)799-6133 62

[SAVE]

Motel

| | 12/1-4/15 [ECP] | 1P: $69-$125 | 2P: $69-$125 | XP: $20 | F18 |
| | 4/16-11/30 [ECP] | 1P: $59-$109 | 2P: $59-$109 | XP: $20 | F18 |

Location: On US 19, just s of jct SR 60; at jct Druid. 20162 US Hwy 19 N 33764. Fax: 727/726-6564. **Facility:** 76 one-bedroom standard units, some with efficiencies. 3 stories, interior/exterior corridors. *Bath:* combo or shower only. **Parking:** on-site. **Terms:** cancellation fee imposed. **Amenities:** voice mail, irons, hair dryers. **Pool(s):** heated outdoor. **Leisure Activities:** whirlpool, exercise room. **Guest Services:** coin laundry. **Business Services:** meeting rooms, fax. **Cards:** AX, CB, DC, DS, MC, VI.

SOME UNITS
(SD) (†1+) (⊘) (⇌) (🎬) (DATA PORT) (🔌) (💻) / (✕) (🖨) /

RAMADA INN COUNTRYSIDE

Phone: (727)796-1234 53

Small-scale Hotel

| | 2/1-4/15 | 1P: $79-$99 | 2P: $79-$99 | XP: $10 | F |
| | 12/1-1/31 & 4/16-11/30 | 1P: $69-$89 | 2P: $69-$89 | XP: $10 | F |

Location: On US 19; just s of jct SR 580. Located adjacent to Countryside Mall. 26508 US 19 N 33761. Fax: 727/796-0452. **Facility:** 126 one-bedroom standard units with whirlpools, some with efficiencies (no utensils). 5 stories, interior corridors. **Parking:** on-site. **Terms:** [ECP] meal plan available, package plans, small pets only. **Amenities:** voice mail, irons, hair dryers. **Dining:** Arigato Japanese Steak House, see separate listing. **Pool(s):** outdoor. **Leisure Activities:** whirlpool, lighted tennis court. **Guest Services:** valet and coin laundry. **Business Services:** meeting rooms, fax. **Cards:** AX, CB, DC, DS, JC, MC, VI.

SOME UNITS
(ASK) (SD) (🐾) (†1) (Y) (⊘) (⇌) (📶) (🎬) (DATA PORT) (🔌) (💻) / (✕) (🔌) (🖨) /
FEE

(See map p. 846)

RESIDENCE INN BY MARRIOTT

Phone: (727)573-4444 [72]

SAVE

Motel

1/11-4/18 [ECP]	1P: $104-$170	2P: $104-$170
9/19-11/30 [ECP]	1P: $85-$155	2P: $85-$155
4/19-9/18 [ECP]	1P: $85-$135	2P: $85-$135
12/1-1/10 [ECP]	1P: $85-$126	2P: $85-$126

Location: On SR 688, 1 mi e of jct US 19. 5050 Ulmerton Rd 33760. Fax: 727/572-4446. **Facility:** 88 units. 66 one- and 22 two-bedroom suites with kitchens. 2 stories, exterior corridors. *Bath:* combo or shower only. **Parking:** on-site. **Terms:** pets ($150 fee). **Amenities:** voice mail, irons, hair dryers. **Pool(s):** heated outdoor. **Leisure Activities:** whirlpool, sports court. **Guest Services:** complimentary evening beverages: Mon-Thurs, valet and coin laundry. **Business Services:** meeting rooms, fax. **Cards:** AX, CB, DC, DS, JC, MC, VI.

SOME UNITS

ST. PETERSBURG/CLEARWATER FAIRFIELD INN BY MARRIOTT

Phone: (727)572-4400 [77]

SAVE

Motel

2/6-4/16	1P: $89-$99	2P: $109-$119
12/1-2/5 & 4/17-11/30	1P: $79-$89	2P: $89-$99

Location: I-275, exit 31B southbound; exit 30 northbound, 1.6 mi w on SR 688. Located in The Centres Office Park. 3211 Executive Dr 33762. Fax: 727/572-8500. **Facility:** 83 one-bedroom standard units. 3 stories, interior corridors. *Bath:* combo or shower only. **Parking:** on-site. **Terms:** [ECP] meal plan available. **Amenities:** irons, hair dryers. **Pool(s):** outdoor. **Leisure Activities:** whirlpool, exercise room. **Guest Services:** valet laundry. **Business Services:** PC (fee), fax. **Cards:** AX, CB, DC, DS, JC, MC, VI.

SOME UNITS

SUPER 8 CLEARWATER/ST. PETERSBURG AIRPORT

Phone: (727)572-8881 [76]

AAA SAVE

Small-scale Hotel

1/16-4/15	1P: $59-$99	2P: $59-$99	XP: $8	F12
12/1-1/15 & 4/16-11/30	1P: $45-$79	2P: $45-$79	XP: $8	F12

Location: I-275, exit 31B southbound; exit 30 northbound, 1.8 mi w on SR 688, just s. 13260 34th St N 33762. Fax: 727/572-6962. **Facility:** 75 one-bedroom standard units. 3 stories, interior corridors. **Parking:** on-site. **Terms:** 2-3 night minimum stay - seasonal, weekly rates available, [CP] meal plan available, pets ($8 extra charge). **Amenities:** safes (fee). *Some:* irons, hair dryers. **Pool(s):** heated outdoor. **Guest Services:** valet and coin laundry. **Business Services:** meeting rooms, business center. **Cards:** AX, DC, DS, MC, VI. **Special Amenities:** early check-in/late check-out and free continental breakfast. *(See color ad below)*

SOME UNITS

FEE FEE

SUPER 8 OF CLEARWATER

Phone: (727)799-2678 [57]

Motel

2/15-4/30	1P: $59	2P: $59	XP: $6	F17
12/1-2/14 & 5/1-11/30	1P: $49	2P: $49	XP: $6	F17

Location: On US 19, 1.5 mi n of jct SR 60. 22950 US 19 N 33765. Fax: 727/726-7263. **Facility:** 100 one-bedroom standard units. 3 stories (no elevator), exterior corridors. **Parking:** on-site. **Terms:** check-in 4 pm. **Amenities:** safes (fee). *Some:* irons, hair dryers. **Pool(s):** outdoor. **Guest Services:** complimentary evening beverages, coin laundry. **Business Services:** meeting rooms, fax. **Cards:** AX, DC, MC, VI.

SOME UNITS

FEE FEE

TOWNE PLACE SUITES BY MARRIOTT ST. PETERSBURG/CLEARWATER

Phone: (727)299-9229 [73]

SAVE

Small-scale Hotel

1/19-3/30	1P: $79-$139	2P: $99-$159
1/1-1/18	1P: $79-$129	2P: $95-$149
3/31-11/30	1P: $59-$109	2P: $79-$129
12/1-12/31	1P: $59-$79	2P: $79-$99

Location: I-275, exit 31B southbound; exit 30 northbound, 3 mi w on SR 688, just s. 13200 49th St N 33762. Fax: 727/299-0926. **Facility:** 95 units. 68 one-bedroom standard units, some with efficiencies or kitchens. 4 one- and 23 two-bedroom suites with kitchens. 3 stories, interior corridors. *Bath:* combo or shower only. **Parking:** on-site. **Terms:** cancellation fee imposed, pets ($75 deposit, $10 extra charge). **Amenities:** dual phone lines, voice mail, irons, hair dryers. **Pool(s):** heated outdoor. **Leisure Activities:** exercise room. **Guest Services:** valet and coin laundry. **Business Services:** business center. **Cards:** AX, CB, DC, DS, MC, VI.

SOME UNITS

(See map p. 846)

WINGATE INN CLEARWATER

▼▼▼▼   **Phone:** (727)299-9800   **80**

Small-scale Hotel

1/15-4/30 [ECP]   1P: $89-$109   2P: $89-$109
12/1-1/14 & 5/1-11/30 [ECP]   1P: $79-$99   2P: $79-$99

Location: On US 19, 2.3 mi s of jct Ulmerton Rd (SR 688). 5000 Lake Blvd 33760. Fax: 727/299-0088. **Facility:** 84 units. 81 one-bedroom standard units. 3 one-bedroom suites ($109-$130). 4 stories, interior corridors. *Bath:* combo or shower only. **Parking:** on-site. **Amenities:** video games, high-speed Internet, dual phone lines, voice mail, safes, irons, hair dryers. **Pool(s):** heated outdoor. **Leisure Activities:** whirlpool, exercise room. **Guest Services:** valet and coin laundry. **Business Services:** meeting rooms, business center. **Cards:** AX, DC, DS, MC, VI.

SOME UNITS

(ASK) 🆔 🔥 📶 🚫 🐬 📹 📠 💻 / ✕ 🚪 📠 /

───── **WHERE TO DINE** ─────

ALFANO'S RESTAURANT

▼▼▼▼   **Lunch:** $6-$10   **Dinner:** $12-$25   **Phone:** 727/584-2125   **60**

Italian

Location: On Alt US 19, 1.2 mi n of jct West Bay Dr; in Belleair Place. 1702 Clearwater-Largo Rd 33756. **Hours:** 11:30 am-2:30 & 5-10 pm, Fri & Sat-11 pm. Closed: 11/27, 12/25; also Sun. **Features:** The striking interior design is marked by gorgeous use of fabric and elements that give the room the feel of an Italian villa. Wall tapestries and artifacts are distinctive. The menu is well-rounded, with pasta and unusual dishes prepared by the trained chef. Dressy casual; cocktails; entertainment. **Parking:** on-site. **Cards:** AX, DS, MC, VI.

✕

ANTONIO'S PASTA GRILLE

▼▼▼▼   **Lunch:** $7-$10   **Dinner:** $8-$22   **Phone:** 727/572-5566   **55**

Italian

Location: I-275, exit 31B southbound; exit 30 northbound, 1.6 mi w. 2755 Ulmerton Rd 33762. **Hours:** 11 am-10 pm, Sat from 5 pm, Sun from 4 pm. **Features:** The popular restaurant offers Italian fare in a casual setting. On the menu are numerous choices, including such favorites as shrimp scampi, veal piccata, eggplant rolletini and delicious gourmet pizzas. Casual dress; cocktails. **Parking:** on-site. **Cards:** MC, VI.

ARIGATO JAPANESE STEAK HOUSE

▼▼   **Dinner:** $11-$21   **Phone:** 727/799-0202   **54**

Japanese

Location: On US 19; just s of jct SR 580; adjacent to Countryside Mall; in Ramada Inn Countryside. 26508 US 19 N 34621. **Hours:** 5 pm-10 pm, Fri & Sat-10:30 pm, Sun 4 pm-9 pm. Closed: 1/1, 7/4, 11/27; also 12/24. **Reservations:** suggested. **Features:** Japanese cuisine is prepared table-side by strikingly fast chefs with a flare for showmanship. A good place to meet new people, the hibachi tables have different parties seated together. Order the chicken, filet and shrimp combo for a spicy feast. Casual dress; cocktails. **Parking:** on-site. **Cards:** AX, DC, DS, MC, VI.

🍸 ✕

CARMELITA'S MEXICAN RESTAURANT

▼▼   **Lunch:** $5-$8   **Dinner:** $5-$11   **Phone:** 727/524-8226   **70**

Mexican

Location: At jct US 19 and SR 686; in TriCity Plaza. 5042 E Bay Dr 33764. **Hours:** 11 am-9:30 pm, Fri & Sat-10 pm. Closed major holidays. **Features:** The large, friendly restaurant serves a wide variety of authentic, made-to-order choices, ranging from grilled chicken quesadillas to a hearty taco salad. Colorful wall decorations and servers in Mexican dress contribute to the south-of-the-border feel. Casual dress; cocktails. **Parking:** on-site. **Cards:** AX, DS, MC, VI.

🍸 ✕

DURANGO STEAKHOUSE

▼▼   **Lunch:** $6-$10   **Dinner:** $7-$18   **Phone:** 727/726-7735   **50**

Steak & Seafood

Location: US 19, just n of jct SR 60 at Drew St; in Campus Walk Plaza. 2571 Drew St 33765. **Hours:** 11:30 am-10 pm, Fri & Sat-11 pm, Sun noon-9 pm. Closed: 11/27, 12/25. **Features:** A welcoming staff adds to the inviting feel of the decidedly Southwestern-themed restaurant. Oak-grilled ribs, steak and chicken melt in your mouth, while such dishes as burritos and fajitas cater to other cravings. Also on the menu are several appetizers, salads, sandwiches and desserts. Casual dress; cocktails. **Parking:** on-site. **Cards:** AX, DC, DS, MC, VI.

🍸 ✕

FIRST WATCH

▼▼▼▼   **Lunch:** $5-$7   **Phone:** 727/712-8769   **52**

American

Location: Just e on Enterprise Rd from jct US 19, just n; in Countryside Square. 2569 Village Dr 33761. **Hours:** 7 am-2:30 pm. Closed: 11/27, 12/25. **Features:** High-quality omelets practically overflow the plates, and a wide array of breakfast and lunch items including pancakes, eggs, salad and sandwiches tempt the taste buds. Clean and attractive, this is a popular spot with a short wait to be expected. Smoke free premises. Casual dress. **Parking:** on-site. **Cards:** AX, DS, MC, VI.

✕

G. BELLINI'S RISTORANTE & BAR

▼▼   **Lunch:** $5-$11   **Dinner:** $11-$27   **Phone:** 727/724-5716   **69**

Italian

Location: On CR 611 at jct Enterprise Rd; in Northwood Plaza. 2544 McMullen Booth Rd 33761. **Hours:** 11:30 am-2 & 4:30-10 pm, Fri & Sat-11 pm, Sun 4:30 pm-9 pm. Closed major holidays. **Features:** An authentic Italian eatery specializing in quality ingredients. The setting is trendy and cosmopolitan. Innovative offerings of antipasto, fresh seafood, ample portions of pasta and create-your-own pizza will bring you back a second time. Casual dress; cocktails. **Parking:** on-site. **Cards:** AX, DC, DS, MC, VI.

🍸 ✕

HARRISON'S GRILL & BAR

▼▼   **Lunch:** $7-$19   **Dinner:** $7-$19   **Phone:** 727/449-2942   **49**

American

Location: Just s of jct SR 60; downtown. 401 S Ft Harrison Ave 33756. **Hours:** 11 am-11 pm. **Features:** The interesting train section of this diner-style restaurant now has a second life as a bar area. The menu features a wide variety of sandwiches, steaks, ribs and poultry dishes. Casual dress. **Parking:** on-site. **Cards:** AX, DS, MC, VI.

JILLIAN'S ON THE LAKE

▼▼   **Lunch:** $5-$9   **Dinner:** $10-$23   **Phone:** 727/538-7776   **65**

Continental

Location: Just n of jct SR 688; in Summit Office Building at Icot Center. 13575 58th St N 33760. **Hours:** 11:30 am-2 & 4-10 pm, Fri-11 pm, Sat 5 pm-11 pm, Mon-2 pm. Closed: Sun. **Features:** On the lower level of an office complex building, the trendy bistro is casual with a touch of sophistication. Patio dining is a breezy and relaxed experience. Dressy casual; cocktails; entertainment. **Parking:** on-site. **Cards:** AX, CB, DC, DS, JC, MC, VI.

(See map p. 846)

JOE'S CRAB SHACK
Seafood
Lunch: $10-$25 **Dinner:** $10-$25 **Phone:** 727/799-8530 `63`
Location: On SR 60, just e of jct US 19. 2730 Gulf to Bay Blvd 33759. **Hours:** 11 am-10 pm. Closed: 11/27, 12/25. **Features:** Bright lights and vivid colors enhance the eclectic and festive atmosphere of this fish camp/shanty-themed restaurant. Varied menu selections include appetizers, salads, sandwiches, pasta, seafood and grilled items. The fisherman's platter is superb and the stuffed crab a plus. Casual dress; cocktails. **Parking:** on-site. **Cards:** AX, DC, DS, MC, VI.

KEY WEST GRILL
Seafood
Lunch: $6-$12 **Dinner:** $10-$30 **Phone:** 727/797-1988 `58`
Location: On US 60, just e of jct US 19. 2660 Gulf to Bay Blvd 33759. **Hours:** 11:30 am-10 pm, Fri & Sat-11 pm. Closed: 11/27, 12/25. **Features:** Partake of a variety of fresh seafood entrees served in a Key West-style setting. Start with the seafood chowder, a creamy broth with tasty chunks of seafood. The fried shrimp are large and cooked to a golden brown with beans and rice as a side dish. Casual dress; cocktails. **Parking:** on-site. **Cards:** AX, CB, DC, DS, MC, VI.

LENNY'S
American
Lunch: $4-$8 **Phone:** 727/799-0402 `57`
Location: On US 19, 0.3 mi n of SR 60. 21220 US 19 N 33765. **Hours:** 6 am-3 pm. Closed: 2 weeks in Sept. **Features:** Sensory overload is what you get in this eclectic sports diner. Memorabilia competes for your eyes; a noisy atmosphere conveys an energetic personality; and unusual specialties, such as alligator omelet, pique the attention of your nose and taste buds. Casual dress. **Parking:** on-site. **Cards:** MC, VI.

ORIENTAL SUPER BUFFET
Chinese
Lunch: $8 **Dinner:** $10 **Phone:** 727/725-2083 `53`
Location: On SR 60, just w of jct US 19. 2456 Gulf-to-Bay Blvd 33765. **Hours:** 11 am-9:30 pm, Fri & Sat-10:30 pm, Sun 11:30 am-9:30 pm. Closed: 11/27. **Features:** The popular restaurant's extensive Chinese buffet lays out more than 130 items each day, including sushi, snow crab legs, mussels, shrimp, egg rolls, salads, fruit and sweet treats from the dessert bar. Casual dress; beer & wine only. **Parking:** on-site. **Cards:** AX, DC, MC, VI.

PRIMO'S PASTA-RIBS
Italian
Lunch: $6-$16 **Dinner:** $6-$16 **Phone:** 727/573-7656 `68`
Location: I-275, exit 31B southbound; exit 30 northbound, 1.8 mi w on SR 688. 3580 Ulmerton Rd 33762. **Hours:** 11 am-1 am. **Features:** Located near the local airport and many lodgings, the casual restaurant is decorated in contemporary style with Italian touches. Pasta dishes factor heavily on a menu that also includes steak, seafood and sandwiches. Casual dress; cocktails. **Parking:** on-site. **Cards:** AX, MC, VI.

ROADHOUSE GRILL
Steak House
Monterey.
Lunch: $7-$19 **Dinner:** $7-$19 **Phone:** 727/712-3222 `73`
Location: On SR 60; at jct US 19. 2630 Gulf to Bay Blvd 33759. **Hours:** 11 am-10 pm, Fri & Sat-11 pm. Closed: 11/27, 12/25. **Features:** As guests might guess, the decor here is set around a roadhouse theme and the atmosphere is fun and relaxed. The menu is varied, with numerous choices of appetizers, salads, burgers, sandwiches, beef and chops, combination platters and such favorites as the baby back ribs and chicken Monterey. Casual dress; cocktails. **Parking:** on-site. **Cards:** AX, DC, DS, MC, VI.

SAM SELTZER'S STEAKHOUSE
Steak House
Dinner: $11-$21 **Phone:** 727/519-7267 `48`
Location: On US 19, 1.5 mi s of SR 60. 18409 US Hwy 19 N 33764. **Hours:** 4 pm-10 pm, Fri-11 pm, Sat 3:30 pm-11 pm, Sun 1 pm-10 pm. Closed: 11/27, 12/25. **Features:** Ample portions of chicken, pork and various steak choices are what make this busy chain so popular. Any wait is worthwhile for a good steak, cooked to order. Meals are accompanied by hot rolls, choice of side items and salad. Casual dress; cocktails. **Parking:** on-site. **Cards:** AX, DC, DS, MC, VI.

SWEETWATER'S RESTAURANT
Steak & Seafood
Lunch: $6-$17 **Dinner:** $6-$17 **Phone:** 727/799-0818 `66`
Location: On SR 60, 0.5 mi w of jct US 19. 2400 Gulf-to-Bay Blvd 33765. **Hours:** 11:30 am-9 pm. Closed: 12/25. **Reservations:** required. **Features:** This is a very popular, local restaurant for tour groups and buses. The varied menu offers steak, poultry, seafood, salad, appetizers and dessert. Casual dress; cocktails. **Parking:** on-site. **Cards:** AX, DS, MC, VI.

TIO PEPE RESTAURANTE
Spanish
Lunch: $6-$11 **Dinner:** $11-$30 **Phone:** 727/799-3082 `59`
Location: SR 60, 0.8 mi e of jct US 19. 2930 Gulf-to-Bay Blvd 33759. **Hours:** 11 am-2:30 & 5-11 pm, Fri-11:30 pm, Sat 5 pm-11:30 pm, Sun 4 pm-10 pm. Closed: 1/1, 11/27, 12/25; also Mon. **Reservations:** suggested. **Features:** Servers crush fruit and blend in brown sugar to make a one-of-a-kind table-side sangria. Ample portions of Spanish cuisine make for a satisfying meal. For something unique, try the pork in an apple-prune sauce; then indulge in rich chocolate mousse cake. Casual dress; cocktails. **Parking:** on-site. **Cards:** AX, MC, VI.

TUCSON'S
American
MC, VI.
Lunch: $9-$27 **Dinner:** $9-$27 **Phone:** 727/530-0637 `61`
Location: On SR 688, just e of jct US 19; in Icot Center. 13563 Icot Blvd 34620. **Hours:** 11 am-midnight, Sun noon-10 pm. Closed: 11/27, 12/25. **Features:** Oak-grilled steaks and seafood stand out on a menu that features Southwest-themed dishes such as enchiladas, chimichangas, fajitas, pasta and salad. The breezy patio has a casual bar and dining area. Casual dress; cocktails. **Parking:** on-site. **Cards:** AX, DC, DS, MC, VI.

——————— *The following restaurants have not been evaluated by AAA* ———————
but are listed for your information only.

94TH AERO SQUADRON RESTAURANT & LOUNGE **Phone:** 727/524-4155
`fyi` Not evaluated. **Location:** Just n of jct SR 686; adjacent to the Bayshore Bridge and St Peter. 94 Fairchild Dr 34622-3596. **Features:** Enjoy great prime rib, steaks, seafood, pasta or poultry as you enjoy watching the planes land at the adjacent airport. They are also popular for their Sunday brunch which offers some 100 items.

CAFE CALIFORNIA AT FEATHER SOUND

[fyi] Not evaluated. **Location:** I-275, exit 31B, 1.5 mi w. 2325 Ulmerton Rd 33762. **Features:** Known for it gourmet pizza, this trendy spot also offers such items as basil penne and filet mignon quesadillas.

Phone: 727/571-3400

JOE DUGAN'S RESTAURANT

[fyi] Not evaluated. **Location:** Just w of jct US 19 at jct Gulf to Bay. 420 Park Place Blvd. **Features:** A popular spot for casual dining; you'll find menu offerings of such casual foods as burgers, quesadillas, buffalo shrimp and barbecue ribs.

Phone: 727/796-7867

ST ANDREWS STEAKHOUSE

[fyi] Not evaluated. **Location:** On US 19, 1 mi n of jct SR 580. 29000 US 19 N 33761. **Features:** Enjoy such signature dishes as the blackberry salmon, chicken Edinborough or the blue stone pasta and finish with one of their tasty desserts.

Phone: 727/771-1515

CLEARWATER BEACH (See map p. 846; index p. 851)

———— WHERE TO STAY ————

ADAM'S MARK CLEARWATER BEACH RESORT

Phone: (727)443-5714 [117]

AAA SAVE

	1P: $165-$255	2P: $165-$255	XP: $25	F18
2/14-4/26				
4/27-11/30	1P: $125-$225	2P: $125-$225	XP: $25	F18
12/1-2/13	1P: $125-$205	2P: $125-$205	XP: $25	F18

Location: 0.5 mi s of roundabout. 430 S Gulfview Blvd 33767. Fax: 727/442-8389. **Facility:** 217 one-bedroom
Large-scale Hotel standard units. 14 stories, interior corridors. *Bath:* combo or shower only. **Parking:** on-site (fee).
Terms: check-in 4 pm, 3 day cancellation notice-fee imposed, [BP] meal plan available, package plans.
Amenities: dual phone lines, voice mail, irons, hair dryers. **Dining:** 2 restaurants, 6:30 am-11 pm, cocktails, entertainment.
Pool(s): heated outdoor, wading. **Leisure Activities:** whirlpool, fishing, recreation programs, volleyball. *Fee:* parasailing, waverunners. **Guest Services:** gift shop, valet and coin laundry, area transportation (fee)-trolley. **Business Services:** conference facilities, fax. **Cards:** AX, CB, DC, DS, MC, VI. **Special Amenities:** early check-in/late check-out and preferred room (subject to availability with advanced reservations).** *(See color ad below)*

SOME UNITS

FEE   FEE

BEACHOUSE

Phone: 727/461-4862 [111]

| 2/1-4/30 | 1P: $95-$185 | 2P: $95-$185 |
| 12/1-1/31 & 5/1-11/30 | 1P: $65-$185 | 2P: $65-$185 |

Motel **Location:** 0.5 mi s on Coronado, just n. 421 Hamden Dr 33767. **Facility:** Smoke free premises. 5 units. 3 one-bedroom standard units with efficiencies. 2 one-bedroom suites with kitchens. 1 story, exterior corridors.
Bath: combo or shower only. **Parking:** on-site. **Terms:** 30 day cancellation notice-fee imposed. **Pool(s):** heated outdoor.
Cards: MC, VI.

(See map p. 846)

BEL CREST BEACH RESORT
(AAA) (SAVE)
◆◆◆

Condominium

Phone: 727/442-4923   [100]

2/7-4/26	1P: $102-$175	2P: $102-$175	XP: $8
12/22-2/6	1P: $79-$132	2P: $79-$132	XP: $6
12/1-12/21 & 4/27-11/30	1P: $61-$117	2P: $61-$117	XP: $6

Location: 1 mi s of jct roundabout via Gulfview Blvd. 706 Bayway Blvd 33767. Fax: 727/442-7455. **Facility:** 19 units. 16 one- and 3 two-bedroom standard units with kitchens. 2 stories, exterior corridors. **Parking:** on-site. **Terms:** 3 night minimum stay - 5 night in season, age restrictions may apply, 10 day cancellation notice-fee imposed. **Amenities:** safes, irons. *Some:* hair dryers. **Pool(s):** heated outdoor. **Leisure Activities:** boat dock, fishing. **Guest Services:** coin laundry. **Business Services:** fax. **Cards:** DS, MC, VI.

SOME UNITS
[SD] [⊪] [≈] [🛢] [🖥] / [VCR] /

BEST WESTERN SEA STONE RESORT & SUITES
(AAA) (SAVE)
◆◆◆◆◆

Small-scale Hotel

Phone: (727)441-1722   [115]

2/17-4/30	1P: $99-$199	2P: $99-$199	XP: $12	F17
12/21-2/16	1P: $79-$199	2P: $79-$199	XP: $12	F17
12/1-12/20 & 5/1-11/30	1P: $59-$199	2P: $59-$199	XP: $12	F17

Location: 0.8 mi s of jct roundabout. Located on Intracoastal Waterway. 445 Hamden Dr 33767. Fax: 727/461-1680. **Facility:** 106 units. 62 one-bedroom standard units. 44 one-bedroom suites with kitchens. 6 stories, exterior corridors. **Parking:** on-site. **Terms:** check-in 4 pm, 3 day cancellation notice, [BP] meal plan available. **Amenities:** voice mail, safes, irons, hair dryers. **Dining:** 7-11 am, Sat & Sun-noon; 5 pm-10 pm seasonally, cocktails. **Pool(s):** heated outdoor. **Leisure Activities:** whirlpool, fishing, hair salon. *Fee:* boat dock, charter fishing, jet ski, parasailing, sailing lessons. **Guest Services:** valet and coin laundry. **Business Services:** meeting rooms. *Fee:* administrative services, fax. **Cards:** AX, DC, DS, JC, MC, VI. **Special Amenities:** free newspaper.

SOME UNITS
[SD] [+] [⊪] [Y] [⟨?⟩] [≈] [✕] [📷] [DATA PORT] [🛢] [🖥] / [✕] [🖥] /
FEE

BEST WESTERN SEA WAKE BEACH RESORT
(AAA) (SAVE)
◆◆◆◆

Small-scale Hotel

Phone: (727)443-7652   [120]

2/10-4/28	1P: $162-$204	2P: $162-$204	XP: $10	F18
1/1-2/9 & 4/29-11/30	1P: $116-$159	2P: $116-$159	XP: $10	F18
12/1-12/31	1P: $111-$153	2P: $111-$153	XP: $10	F18

Location: 0.9 mi s of jct SR 60 (causeway). 691 S Gulfview Blvd 33767. Fax: 727/461-2836. **Facility:** 110 one-bedroom standard units. 6 stories, interior corridors. **Parking:** on-site. **Terms:** check-in 4 pm, 3 day cancellation notice. **Amenities:** dual phone lines, voice mail, safes, irons, hair dryers. **Dining:** 7 am-3 pm, cocktails. **Pool(s):** heated outdoor. **Leisure Activities:** fishing, sun deck, recreation programs, children's activity center, playground, volleyball. **Guest Services:** valet and coin laundry. **Business Services:** meeting rooms, fax. **Cards:** AX, CB, DC, DS, MC, VI. **Special Amenities:** free newspaper. *(See color ad below)*

SOME UNITS
[SD] [⊪] [Y] [⟨?⟩] [≈] [✕] [📷] [DATA PORT] [🛢] [🖥] [🖥] / [✕] /

BLUE JAY MOTEL
(AAA) (SAVE)
◆◆◆ ◆◆

Motel

Phone: 727/446-0356   [90]

1/31-4/28	1P: $70-$102	2P: $70-$102	XP: $10
12/16-1/30	1P: $47-$82	2P: $47-$82	XP: $10
4/29-11/30	1P: $43-$78	2P: $43-$78	XP: $6
12/1-12/15	1P: $38-$60	2P: $38-$60	

Location: 0.5 mi s on Coronado Dr, 0.4 mi e. 150 Brightwater Dr 33767. Fax: 727/446-0356. **Facility:** 18 one-bedroom standard units, some with efficiencies. 2 stories, exterior corridors. **Parking:** on-site. **Terms:** 3-7 night minimum stay - weekends, seasonal, 30 day cancellation notice-fee imposed, package plans - weekends. **Pool(s):** heated outdoor. **Leisure Activities:** fishing, dock for small boats, shuffleboard. **Guest Services:** coin laundry. **Business Services:** fax. **Cards:** AX, DC, MC, VI. **Special Amenities:** free local telephone calls and free newspaper.

SOME UNITS
[SD] [+] [≈] [✕] [🛢] [🖥] / [✕] /

BRIGHTWATER INN ON THE BAY
◆

Motel

Phone: 727/441-3001   [92]

12/1-4/30	2P: $65	XP: $10	F3
5/1-11/30	2P: $50	

Location: 0.5 mi s on Coronado Dr, 0.3 mi e. 124 Brightwater Dr 33767. Fax: 727/447-7423. **Facility:** Designated smoking area. 6 units. 2 one-bedroom standard units with efficiencies. 4 one-bedroom suites ($55-$75) with kitchens. 1 story, exterior corridors. **Parking:** on-site. **Terms:** 3 night minimum stay, 31 day cancellation notice-fee imposed, small pets only ($60 deposit, $10 extra charge). **Amenities:** video library, irons. *Some:* hair dryers. **Pool(s):** small heated outdoor. **Leisure Activities:** whirlpool, boat dock, fishing, bicycles, shuffleboard. **Guest Services:** complimentary laundry. **Cards:** DS, MC, VI.

SOME UNITS
[ASK] [SD] [🐾] [≈] [✕] [✕] [🛢] [🖥] / [VCR] /

(See map p. 846)

CHART HOUSE SUITES ON CLEARWATER BAY Phone: (727)449-8007 **96**

(AAA) (SAVE)
WWW ◆◆◆ Motel

1/16-4/30	1P: $110-$179	2P: $110-$179	XP: $10	F18
12/1-1/15 & 5/1-11/30	1P: $80-$149	2P: $80-$149	XP: $10	F18

Location: 1.3 mi s of jct SR 60 (causeway) via Gulf View Blvd. 850 Bayway Blvd 33767. Fax: 727/443-6081. **Facility:** 25 units. 15 one-bedroom standard units with efficiencies. 9 one- and 1 two-bedroom suites ($149-$179) with kitchens, some with whirlpools. 4 stories, interior corridors. **Parking:** on-site. **Terms:** check-in 4 pm, 3 day cancellation notice-fee imposed, weekly rates available. **Amenities:** voice mail, irons, hair dryers. **Pool(s):** heated outdoor. **Leisure Activities:** whirlpool, marina, fishing. *Fee:* boat slips. **Guest Services:** valet and coin laundry. **Business Services:** fax. **Cards:** AX, DC, DS, MC, VI. **Special Amenities:** free local telephone calls.

THE DUNES MOTEL Phone: (727)441-4939 **105**

(AAA) (SAVE)
WWW ◆ Motel

2/16-4/17	2P: $79-$181	XP: $5	F12
12/1-2/15	2P: $58-$158	XP: $5	F12
4/18-9/4	2P: $55-$119	XP: $5	F12
9/5-11/30	2P: $50-$119	XP: $5	F12

Location: 0.5 mi s of jct SR 60 (causeway). 514 S Gulfview Blvd 33767. Fax: 727/443-0490. **Facility:** 38 one-bedroom standard units, some with efficiencies. 2 stories, interior/exterior corridors. *Bath:* combo or shower only. **Parking:** on-site. **Terms:** 10 day cancellation notice-fee imposed, weekly rates available. **Amenities:** *Some:* irons, hair dryers. **Pool(s):** heated outdoor. **Leisure Activities:** fishing, sun deck, fishing pier, barbecue grill. *Fee:* pontoon, fishing rods. **Guest Services:** coin laundry. **Business Services:** fax. **Cards:** AX, DC, MC, VI.

SOME UNITS

EAST SHORE RESORT APARTMENT MOTEL Phone: (727)442-3636 **86**

(AAA) (SAVE)
WWW WWW Motel

12/1-4/30	1P: $180-$260	2P: $180-$260	XP: $10
5/1-11/30	1P: $130-$235	2P: $130-$235	XP: $7

Location: Just n on East Shore Dr from jct SR 60 (causeway). 473 E Shore Dr 33767. Fax: 727/449-8302. **Facility:** 10 one-bedroom standard units with kitchens. 2 stories, exterior corridors. **Parking:** on-site. **Terms:** 30 day cancellation notice-fee imposed. **Amenities:** irons, hair dryers. *Some:* safes. **Pool(s):** heated outdoor. **Leisure Activities:** boat dock, fishing, cabana, floats & beach chairs, fishing poles, 2 hour mini-cruise, barbecue grill & patio area, bicycles. **Guest Services:** complimentary laundry. **Business Services:** meeting rooms, fax. **Cards:** MC, VI. **Special Amenities:** free local telephone calls.

SOME UNITS

ECHO SAILS MOTEL & APTS Phone: 727/442-6962 **94**

(AAA) (SAVE)
WWW WWW Motel

2/1-4/27	2P: $60-$80	XP: $10	D12
12/20-1/31	2P: $45-$60	XP: $10	D12
12/1-12/19 & 4/28-11/30	2P: $40-$55	XP: $8	D12

Location: 0.3 mi s of jct roundabout. 216 Hamden Dr 33767. Fax: 727/442-6962. **Facility:** 16 units. 14 one- and 2 two-bedroom standard units, some with efficiencies or kitchens. 2 stories, exterior corridors. **Parking:** on-site. **Terms:** 3 night minimum stay, 30 day cancellation notice-fee imposed, weekly rates available. **Pool(s):** heated outdoor. **Leisure Activities:** barbecue grills, shuffleboard. **Guest Services:** coin laundry. **Cards:** MC, VI. **Special Amenities:** early check-in/late check-out and free local telephone calls.

ECONO LODGE Phone: (727)446-3400 **118**

(AAA) (SAVE)
WWW WWW Small-scale Hotel

2/1-4/30	1P: $109-$159	2P: $109-$159	XP: $10	F18
12/1-1/31 & 5/1-11/30	1P: $79-$99	2P: $79-$99	XP: $10	F18

Location: 0.8 mi s of jct SR 60 (causeway). 625 S Gulfview Blvd 33767. Fax: 727/446-4615. **Facility:** 64 one-bedroom standard units with efficiencies. 5 stories, interior corridors. *Bath:* combo or shower only. **Parking:** on-site. **Terms:** 3 day cancellation notice-fee imposed. **Amenities:** voice mail, safes. *Some:* irons. **Pool(s):** heated outdoor. **Leisure Activities:** whirlpool, fishing. **Guest Services:** valet and coin laundry. **Business Services:** fax. **Cards:** AX, CB, DC, DS, JC, MC, VI. *(See ad below)*

SOME UNITS

(See map p. 846)

FALCON APARTMENT MOTEL

Phone: 727/447-8714　109

AAA SAVE

2/10-4/1	1P: $85	2P: $85	XP: $8
4/2-8/31	1P: $60	2P: $60	XP: $5
12/1-2/9	1P: $55	2P: $55	XP: $5
9/1-11/30	1P: $45	2P: $45	XP: $5

Motel

Location: 0.7 mi s of jct roundabout. 415 Coronado Dr 33767. Fax: 727/461-3735. **Facility:** 19 one-bedroom standard units, some with efficiencies. 2 stories, exterior corridors. *Bath:* combo or shower only. **Parking:** on-site. **Terms:** age restrictions may apply, 30 day cancellation notice-fee imposed. **Amenities:** hair dryers. *Some:* irons. **Pool(s):** heated outdoor. **Leisure Activities:** barbecue area, shuffleboard. **Guest Services:** coin laundry. **Business Services:** fax.

HILTON CLEARWATER BEACH RESORT

Phone: (727)461-3222　106

AAA SAVE

1/15-4/30	1P: $129-$219	2P: $129-$219
5/1-8/2	1P: $129-$189	2P: $129-$189
12/1-1/14 & 8/3-11/30	1P: $129-$169	2P: $129-$169

Large-scale Hotel

Location: Jct SR 60 (Clearwater Pass Bridge); adjacent to the "Roundabout". 400 Mandalay Ave 33767. Fax: 727/461-0610. **Facility:** 425 one-bedroom standard units. 9 stories, interior corridors. *Bath:* combo or shower only. **Parking:** on-site. **Terms:** 3 day cancellation notice-fee imposed. **Amenities:** video games, voice mail, safes, irons, hair dryers. **Dining:** 2 restaurants, 6:30 am-10 pm, cocktails, entertainment. **Pool(s):** 2 heated outdoor. **Leisure Activities:** whirlpool, recreation programs, supervised kids camp, exercise room, spa, volleyball. *Fee:* sailboats, cabanas, hydro bikes, wave runners, game room. **Guest Services:** gift shop, valet and coin laundry. **Business Services:** conference facilities, business center. **Cards:** AX, CB, DC, DS, JC, MC, VI. **Special Amenities:** free newspaper. *(See color ad below)*

HOLIDAY INN SUNSPREE RESORT & CONFERENCE CENTER

Phone: (727)447-9566　112

AAA SAVE

12/1-1/2 & 2/14-4/26	1P: $149-$199	2P: $149-$199	XP: $10	F18
1/3-2/13 & 4/27-11/30	1P: $139-$179	2P: $139-$179	XP: $10	F18

Large-scale Hotel

Location: 1 mi s at Clearwater Pass Bridge. 715 S Gulfview Blvd 33767. Fax: 727/446-4978. **Facility:** 216 units. 213 one-bedroom standard units. 3 one-bedroom suites, some with kitchens. 2-10 stories, interior/exterior corridors. *Bath:* combo or shower only. **Parking:** on-site. **Terms:** check-in 4 pm, 3 day cancellation notice-fee imposed. **Amenities:** video library, voice mail, safes, irons, hair dryers. **Dining:** 6:30 am-11 & 5-10 pm, cocktails. **Pool(s):** heated outdoor, wading. **Leisure Activities:** whirlpool, fishing, sun deck, putting green, recreation programs, activities center, lending library, playground, exercise room, shuffleboard, volleyball. *Fee:* waterskiing, jet skis, parasailing, game room. **Guest Services:** gift shop, valet and coin laundry, area transportation (fee)-trolley. **Business Services:** conference facilities. *Fee:* PC, fax. **Cards:** AX, CB, DC, MC. *(See color ad p 910 & opposite inside back cover)*

(See map p. 846)

HOWARD JOHNSON BEACHVIEW RESORT
Phase: (727)461-7695 123

AAA SAVE
◆◆◆

3/2-4/20	1P: $99-$165	2P: $99-$165	XP: $8	F16
4/21-9/9	1P: $77-$140	2P: $77-$140	XP: $8	F16
9/10-11/30	1P: $59-$109	2P: $59-$109	XP: $8	F16
12/1-3/1	1P: $74-$99	2P: $74-$99	XP: $8	F16

Small-scale Hotel Location: 0.5 mi s of jct SR 60 (causeway). 325 S Gulfview Blvd 33767. Fax: 727/442-9983. **Facility:** 60 one-bedroom standard units, some with efficiencies. 5 stories, exterior corridors. **Parking:** on-site. **Terms:** 3 day cancellation notice, [CP] meal plan available. **Amenities:** safes (fee), irons, hair dryers. **Pool(s):** heated outdoor. **Leisure Activities:** sun deck. **Guest Services:** gift shop, area transportation (fee). **Business Services:** fax (fee). **Cards:** AX, DS, MC, VI. **Special Amenities:** free local telephone calls and free newspaper.

SOME UNITS
⬛ 📶 🛶 🎥 📠 💻 / ✕ 🔋 📷 /

HOWARD JOHNSON EXPRESS INN
Phone: (727)442-6606 98

AAA SAVE
◆◆◆
Motel

All Year [CP]	1P: $79-$129	2P: $79-$129	XP: $15	F17

Location: 0.8 mi s of jct roundabout via Gulfview Blvd. 656 Bayway Blvd 33767. Fax: 727/461-0809. **Facility:** 38 one-bedroom standard units, some with efficiencies. 2 stories, exterior corridors. **Parking:** on-site. **Amenities:** high-speed Internet, safes (fee), hair dryers. *Some:* irons. **Pool(s):** heated outdoor. **Leisure Activities:** boat dock, fishing, shuffleboard. **Guest Services:** coin laundry. **Business Services:** fax. **Cards:** AX, DS, MC, VI. **Special Amenities:** early check-in/late check-out and free continental breakfast.

SOME UNITS
⬛ 📶 🛶 ✕ 💻 / ✕ 🔋 📷 /

ISLAND QUEEN RESORT MOTEL
Phone: (727)442-8068 91

AAA SAVE
◆◆◆
Motel

2/1-4/30	2P: $72-$96	XP: $10	F5
12/20-1/31	2P: $59-$74	XP: $10	F5
12/1-12/19	2P: $49-$63	XP: $5	F5
5/1-11/30	2P: $49-$63	XP: $10	F5

Location: 0.5 mi s on Coronado Dr, just e on Devon Dr, just s. 158 Brightwater Dr 33767. Fax: 727/442-2412. **Facility:** 14 one-bedroom standard units, some with efficiencies or kitchens. 2 stories, exterior corridors. *Bath:* combo or shower only. **Parking:** on-site. **Amenities:** irons. **Pool(s):** heated outdoor. **Leisure Activities:** marina, fishing, sun deck, barbecue grill, shuffleboard. **Guest Services:** coin laundry. **Business Services:** fax. **Cards:** MC, VI.

SOME UNITS
⬛ 📶 🚭 🛶 ✕ 📠 🔋 📷 / VCR /

KOLI-BREE MOTEL/APT
Phone: (727)461-6223 88

AAA SAVE
◆
Motel

2/1-4/30	1P: $82	2P: $82	XP: $10	F10
12/15-1/31	1P: $62	2P: $62	XP: $10	F10
12/1-12/14 & 5/1-11/30	1P: $56	2P: $56	XP: $10	F10

Location: Just n on Pointsettia Dr from jct SR 60 (Cswy). 440 E Shore Dr 33767. Fax: 727/298-8712. **Facility:** 10 one-bedroom standard units with kitchens. 2 stories, exterior corridors. *Bath:* combo or shower only. **Parking:** on-site. **Terms:** 2 night minimum stay, 14 day cancellation notice-fee imposed. **Amenities:** *Some:* irons, hair dryers. **Leisure Activities:** sun deck. **Business Services:** fax. **Cards:** AX, CB, DC, DS, MC, VI.

SOME UNITS
📶 🔋 📷 / ✕ /

MANNINGS ON THE BAY
Phone: (727)447-6407 104

AAA SAVE
◆◆
Motel

2/16-4/25 [CP]	1P: $85-$165	2P: $85-$165	XP: $8	F13
12/1-2/15 [CP]	1P: $60-$138	2P: $60-$138	XP: $8	F13
4/26-9/2 [CP]	1P: $58-$110	2P: $58-$110	XP: $8	F13
9/3-11/30 [CP]	1P: $54-$98	2P: $54-$98	XP: $8	F13

Location: 0.8 mi s of jct SR 60 (causeway). 530 S Gulfview Blvd 33767. Fax: 727/449-8109. **Facility:** 29 one-bedroom standard units, some with efficiencies. 2 stories, interior corridors. **Parking:** on-site. **Terms:** 14 day cancellation notice, weekly rates available. **Amenities:** *Some:* irons, hair dryers. **Pool(s):** heated outdoor. **Leisure Activities:** boat dock, fishing, sun deck, fishing equipment. *Fee:* bicycles. **Guest Services:** coin laundry. **Business Services:** business center. **Cards:** AX, DS, MC, VI. **Special Amenities:** free continental breakfast.

SOME UNITS
📶 🛶 ✕ 🔋 / ✕ 📷 /

(See map p. 846)

NEW YORKER MOTEL

AAA **SAVE** ▽▽ ▽▽
Motel

2/1-4/23	1P: $78-$100	2P: $78-$100	XP: $10
12/1-1/31 & 4/24-9/5	1P: $55-$76	2P: $55-$76	XP: $8
9/6-11/30	1P: $52	2P: $71	XP: $8

Phone: (727)446-2437 93

Location: 0.5 mi s on Coronado Dr, just e on Brightwater Dr. 332 Hamden Dr 33767. Fax: 727/446-5818. **Facility:** 15 units. 14 one- and 1 two-bedroom standard units, some with efficiencies or kitchens. 2 stories, exterior corridors. **Parking:** on-site. **Terms:** 3 night minimum stay, 30 day cancellation notice-fee imposed, weekly rates available. **Amenities:** safes. Some: irons, hair dryers. **Pool(s):** heated outdoor. **Leisure Activities:** barbecue grill. **Guest Services:** coin laundry. **Business Services:** PC, fax. **Cards:** DS, MC, VI.

SOME UNITS

⟨S/D⟩ ⟨†|†⟩ ⟨≈⟩ ⟨📷⟩ ⟨DATA PORT⟩ ⟨📱⟩ ⟨📺⟩ /⟨✕⟩/

PELICAN COVE RESORT ON THE BAY

AAA **SAVE** ▽▽ ▽▽
Motel

2/1-4/30	1P: $55-$89	2P: $55-$89	XP: $10	D16
12/15-1/31	1P: $44-$77	2P: $44-$77	XP: $10	D16
12/1-12/14 & 5/1-11/30	1P: $42-$75	2P: $42-$75	XP: $8	D16

Phone: 727/442-3735 89

Location: 0.5 mi s on Coronado Dr, just e. 125 Brightwater Dr 33767. Fax: 727/461-2541. **Facility:** 11 one-bedroom standard units, some with kitchens. 1 story, exterior corridors. Bath: combo or shower only. **Parking:** on-site. **Terms:** 3 night minimum stay, 30 day cancellation notice. **Pool(s):** heated outdoor. **Leisure Activities:** whirlpool, boat dock, fishing, barbecue grill area, tiki huts. **Guest Services:** coin laundry. **Business Services:** fax. **Cards:** AX, DS, MC, VI. **Special Amenities:** free local telephone calls and free room upgrade (subject to availability with advanced reservations).

⟨S/D⟩ ⟨≈⟩ ⟨✕⟩ ⟨📱⟩ ⟨📺⟩

QUALITY HOTEL ON THE BEACH

AAA **SAVE** ▽▽▽▽
Small-scale Hotel

2/14-4/26	1P: $149-$209	2P: $149-$209	XP: $20	F17
12/1-2/13 & 4/27-11/30	1P: $99-$159	2P: $99-$159	XP: $10	F17

Phone: (727)442-7171 119

Location: 0.8 mi s of jct SR 60 (causeway). 655 S Gulfview Blvd 33767. Fax: 727/446-7177. **Facility:** 93 one-bedroom standard units. 5 stories, interior/exterior corridors. **Parking:** on-site. **Amenities:** voice mail, safes, irons, hair dryers. **Dining:** 24 hours; seasonal entertainment, cocktails. **Pool(s):** heated outdoor. **Leisure Activities:** sun deck, playground. Fee: parasailing, waverunners, high speed powerboat. **Guest Services:** valet and coin laundry. **Business Services:** meeting rooms, fax. **Cards:** AX, CB, DC, DS, MC, VI. **Special Amenities:** free local telephone calls. (See color ad below)

SOME UNITS

⟨S/D⟩ ⟨†|†⟩ ⟨Y⟩ ⟨≈⟩ ⟨†|†⟩ ⟨📷⟩ ⟨DATA PORT⟩ ⟨📱⟩ ⟨📺⟩ ⟨📺⟩ /⟨✕⟩/
FEE

RADISSON SUITE RESORT ON SAND KEY

AAA **SAVE** ▽▽▽▽
Large-scale Hotel

2/16-4/30	1P: $239-$339	2P: $239-$339	XP: $10	F17
12/20-2/15	1P: $209-$299	2P: $209-$299	XP: $10	F17
12/1-12/19	1P: $199-$279	2P: $199-$279	XP: $10	F17
5/1-11/30	1P: $189-$279	2P: $189-$279	XP: $10	F17

Phone: (727)596-1100 126

Location: SR 699, just s of Clearwater Pass Bridge. 1201 Gulf Blvd 33767. Fax: 727/595-4292. **Facility:** 220 one-bedroom suites, some with whirlpools. 10 stories, exterior corridors. **Parking:** on-site. **Terms:** check-in 4 pm, cancellation fee imposed. **Amenities:** video games, voice mail, honor bars, irons, hair dryers. Some: CD players. **Dining:** 2 restaurants, 7 am-10 pm, cocktails, entertainment. **Pool(s):** heated outdoor, wading. **Leisure Activities:** whirlpool, fishing, recreation programs, sand & water volleyball, playground, exercise room. Fee: bicycles, massage. **Guest Services:** gift shop, valet and coin laundry, area transportation (fee)-trolley. **Business Services:** conference facilities, business center. **Cards:** AX, CB, DC, DS, JC, MC, VI. **Special Amenities:** free newspaper. (See color ad p 912)

SOME UNITS

⟨S/D⟩ ⟨†⟩ ⟨†|†⟩ ⟨Y⟩ ⟨≈⟩ ⟨🔧⟩ ⟨≈⟩ ⟨✕⟩ ⟨📷⟩ ⟨DATA PORT⟩ ⟨📺⟩ ⟨📺⟩ /⟨✕⟩/
FEE

(See map p. 846)

RAMADA INN GULFVIEW   Phone: (727)447-6461   [1]

 [SAVE]   2/14-4/30   1P: $169-$209   2P: $169-$209   XP: $10   F1
                12/1-2/13 & 5/1-11/30   1P: $149-$189   2P: $149-$189   XP: $10   F1
 Location: 0.7 mi s of jct SR 60 at jct Hamden. 521 S Gulfview Blvd 33767. Fax: 727/443-5888. **Facility:** 289 units,
                288 one-bedroom standard units, some with efficiencies (no utensils). 1 one-bedroom suite ($175-$195) with
Small-scale Hotel kitchen. 9 stories, interior corridors. *Bath:* combo or shower only. **Parking:** on-site. **Terms:** check-in 4 pm,
                day cancellation notice. **Amenities:** video games, high-speed Internet, voice mail, safes, irons, hair dryers.
Dining: 24 hours, cocktails, entertainment. **Pool(s):** heated outdoor, wading. **Leisure Activities:** sun deck, hair & nail salon.
Fee: parasailing, waverunner, game room. **Guest Services:** gift shop, valet and coin laundry. **Business Services:** meeting
rooms, administrative services, fax. **Cards:** AX, CB, DC, DS, MC, VI. *(See color ad below)*

SOME UNITS

SEA CAPTAIN RESORT ON THE BAY   Phone: 727/446-7550   [9]

 Property failed to provide current rates
                Location: Just s of jct SR 60 (causeway) via Coronado. 40 Devon Dr 33767. Fax: 727/298-0100. **Facility:** Design-
        Motel   nated smoking area. 28 units. 17 one-bedroom standard units, some with efficiencies. 11 one-bedroom suites
                with kitchens. 2 stories, exterior corridors. **Parking:** on-site. **Amenities:** hair dryers. *Some:* irons. **Pool(s):**
heated outdoor. **Leisure Activities:** whirlpool, boat dock, fishing, shuffleboard. **Guest Services:** coin laundry. **Business Serv-**
ices: fax. **Cards:** AX, DS, MC, VI.

SOME UNITS

FEE

ee map p. 846)

HEPHARD'S BEACH RESORT — Phone: 727/442-5107 — 110

AAA SAVE

2/1-4/30	1P: $119-$179	2P: $119-$179	XP: $10
5/1-11/30	1P: $109-$159	2P: $109-$159	XP: $10
12/1-1/31	1P: $89-$139	2P: $89-$139	XP: $10

Location: 1 mi s of jct SR 60 (causeway). 619 S Gulfview Blvd 33767. Fax: 727/446-4238. **Facility:** 97 units. 41 one-bedroom standard units. 53 one- and 3 two-bedroom suites ($299-$359), some with kitchens and/or whirlpools. 2-6 stories, interior/exterior corridors. *Bath:* combo or shower only. **Parking:** on-site. **Terms:** 2 ght minimum stay - weekends, 15 day cancellation notice-fee imposed. **Amenities:** video games, voice mail, safes, irons, hair ers. **Dining:** Shephard's Waterfront Restaurant, see separate listing, nightclub, entertainment. **Pool(s):** heated outdoor. isure Activities: whirlpool, exercise room. *Fee:* jet skis, game room. **Guest Services:** gift shop, valet and coin laundry. **Busi-ss Services:** meeting rooms, fax (fee). **Cards:** AX, DC, DS, MC, VI. **Special Amenities:** free newspaper and free room up-ade (subject to availability with advanced reservations). *(See color ad below)*

SOME UNITS / FEE

ERATON SAND KEY RESORT — Phone: (727)595-1611 — 125

AAA SAVE

2/1-4/30	1P: $160-$240	2P: $160-$240	XP: $10	F18
12/1-1/31 & 5/1-11/30	1P: $140-$220	2P: $140-$220	XP: $10	F18

Location: 2 mi s on SR 699, at south end of Clearwater Pass Bridge. 1160 Gulf Blvd 33767. Fax: 727/596-8488. Resort **Facility:** On a 1,000-foot-wide beach just west of the Gulf of Mexico, the resort offers bright, cheery rooms, all with patios or decks. 390 units. 375 one-bedroom standard units. 15 one-bedroom suites ($275-$450). 9 rge-scale Hotel stories, interior corridors. *Bath:* combo or shower only. **Parking:** on-site. **Terms:** package plans. **Amenities:** video library, video games, voice mail, safes, irons, hair dryers. *Some:* high-speed Internet. ning: 3 restaurants, 7 am-11 pm, Sun 7 am-noon & 6-10 pm, cocktails, entertainment. **Pool(s):** heated outdoor, wading. isure Activities: saunas, whirlpool, rental paddleboats, fishing, 3 lighted tennis courts, tennis pro, recreation programs, sand lleyball, playground. *Fee:* sailboats, windsurfing, charter fishing, cabanas, waverunners, bicycles, massage, game room. uest Services: gift shop, valet and coin laundry. **Business Services:** conference facilities, business center. **Cards:** AX, CB, , DS, JC, MC, VI.

SOME UNITS
FEE FEE FEE FEE

RAVELODGE BEACHVIEW RESORT — Phone: (727)446-8305 — 122

3/2-4/20	1P: $94-$150	2P: $94-$150	XP: $8	F16
4/21-9/9	1P: $67-$130	2P: $67-$130	XP: $8	F16
12/1-3/1	1P: $64-$99	2P: $64-$99	XP: $8	F16
9/10-11/30	1P: $49-$99	2P: $49-$99	XP: $8	F16

mall-scale Hotel

cation: 0.5 mi s of jct roundabout. 401 S Gulfview Blvd 33767. Fax: 727/447-5293. **Facility:** 53 one-bedroom standard units, some th efficiencies. 4 stories, exterior corridors. *Bath:* combo or shower only. **Parking:** on-site. **Terms:** 3 day cancellation notice, P] meal plan available. **Amenities:** safes (fee), irons, hair dryers. **Pool(s):** heated outdoor. **Cards:** AX, DS, MC, VI.

SOME UNITS /

ROPICAL BREEZE MOTEL — Phone: 727/442-6865 — 95

2/1-4/30	1P: $85-$95	2P: $85-$95	XP: $10	F5
12/1-1/31 & 5/1-9/7	1P: $60-$70	2P: $60-$70	XP: $8	F5
9/8-11/30	1P: $55-$65	2P: $55-$65	XP: $8	F5

Motel

Location: 0.5 mi s on Coronado, just e on Brightwater. 333 Hamden Dr 33767. Fax: 727/443-4371. **Facility:** 20 one-droom standard units, some with kitchens. 2 stories, exterior corridors. **Parking:** on-site. **Terms:** 30 day cancellation notice-fee posed, weekly rates available. **Amenities:** safes (fee), irons. *Some:* hair dryers. **Pool(s):** heated outdoor. **Leisure Activi-s:** boat dock, fishing, shuffleboard. **Guest Services:** coin laundry. **Business Services:** fax (fee). **Cards:** AX, DS, MC, VI.

(See map p. 846)

——— WHERE TO DINE ———

BIG BEN BRITISH RESTAURANT & PUB **Lunch:** $7-$16 **Dinner:** $7-$16 **Phone:** 727/446-8809
▼▼ ▼▼
English
Location: 1 mi s of jct SR 60 (causeway) via Gulfview Blvd; in Bay Bazaar. 731 Bayway Blvd 33767. **Hours:** am-10:30 pm. **Features:** The feel of an authentic British pub invites you to ease on in to the restaura The traditional menu delivers such favorites as Lords roast, fish and chips, Cornish pastry, bangers a mash, shepherd's pie and kidney pie. If you're feeling less adventurous, there are plenty of sandwi salad, steak, chop, dessert and side dish choices. Casual dress; beer & wine only. **Parking:** on-site. **Cards:** AX, CB, DC, C MC, VI.

BOB HEILMAN'S BEACHCOMBER **Lunch:** $5-$15 **Dinner:** $13-$30 **Phone:** 727/442-4144
▼▼▼▼
Seafood
Location: Just n of jct SR 60. 447 Mandalay Ave 33767. **Hours:** 11:30 am-midnight, Sun noon-10 p **Reservations:** suggested. **Features:** Seafood specialties head the menu with steak and chops. Grou five ways and back-to-back farm fried chicken are favorites. Meals are served in a spacious, well-light dining room beside a cozy, intimate lounge area. Excellent desserts round out the meal. Casual dre cocktails; entertainment. **Parking:** valet. **Cards:** AX, DC, DS, MC, VI.

BONSAI JAPANESE CUISINE-SUSHI BAR **Lunch:** $7-$9 **Dinner:** $9-$18 **Phone:** 727/446-9452
▼▼▼▼
Japanese
Location: 0.8 mi s of jct SR 60 (causeway). 656 S Gulfview Blvd 33767. **Hours:** 11:30 am-2:30 & 5-10 p Closed: Mon. **Features:** The surroundings are basic but comfortable. Although the main menu is limited a few entrees, the sushi choices are abundant: ikura, kappamaki, tekka maki, temaki, salmon, skin r sake, hamachi, unagi, hotategemi, ebi, saba and amaebiare. Casual dress; beer & wine only. **Parkir** on-site. **Cards:** AX, DC, DS, MC, VI.

BRITT'S LAGUNA GRILL **Lunch:** $8-$16 **Dinner:** $8-$16 **Phone:** 727/445-1755
▼▼▼▼
American
Location: Just s of jct SR 60 (causeway). 309 S Gulfview Blvd 34630. **Hours:** 11 am-11 pm. Closed: 10 **Features:** Across from the beach, the comfy restaurant affords great views of the gulf. Seating is co both indoors and on the outdoor deck. Menu choices include appetizers, salads, pasta dishes, seafo entrees, sandwiches and steaks. Casual dress; cocktails; entertainment. **Parking:** on-site. **Cards:** AX, C DS, MC, VI.

COLUMBIA RESTAURANT **Lunch:** $6-$10 **Dinner:** $13-$20 **Phone:** 727/596-8400
▼▼▼▼
Spanish
Location: SR 669, just s of Clearwater Pass Bridge. 1241 Gulf Blvd 33767. **Hours:** 11:30 am-10 p **Reservations:** suggested; evenings. **Features:** This very elegant Spanish eatery overlooks Tampa B and specializes in Cuban favorites like chicken and rice with black beans. The cigar bar and the cock bar are perfect for relaxing after a leisurely meal overseen by a gracious, professional staff. Casual dre cocktails. **Parking:** on-site. **Cards:** AX, CB, DC, DS, MC, VI.

COOTERS RAW BAR & RESTAURANT **Lunch:** $6-$14 **Dinner:** $6-$14 **Phone:** 727/462-2668
▼▼
Seafood
Location: Just n of jct SR 60 (roundabout). 423 Poinsettia Ave 33767. **Hours:** 11:30 am-10:30 pm, Fri & Sa am. **Features:** The popular local spot has the look of a rustic sea shanty. Among the many menu choic are salads, gumbo, chowder, grouper sandwiches, po'boys, burgers, New York strip, ribeye and baby ba ribs, as well as plenty of entrees from the seafood family: grouper, mahi mahi, shrimp, snow crab and cr cakes. Casual dress; cocktails. **Parking:** on-site. **Cards:** AX, MC, VI.

FRENCHY'S CAFE **Lunch:** $6-$13 **Dinner:** $6-$13 **Phone:** 727/446-3607
▼▼
Seafood
Location: 0.4 mi n on Mandalay Ave from jct SR 60 (causeway), just e. 41 Baymont St 33767. **Hours:** 11:30 am- pm, Fri & Sat-midnight, Sun from noon. Closed: 11/27, 12/25. **Features:** The beachlike establishment h a Key West theme and an appropriately laid-back atmosphere, both in the dining room and on the bree deck. On the menu are such offerings as sandwiches, burgers, appetizers and a limited selection entrees. Casual dress; beer & wine only. **Parking:** on-site. **Cards:** AX, MC, VI.

FRENCHY'S ROCKAWAY GRILL & BEACH CLUB **Lunch:** $6-$13 **Dinner:** $6-$13 **Phone:** 727/446-4844
▼▼▼▼
American
Location: Jct SR 60 (causeway), 0.4 mi n on Mandalay Ave, just w. 7 Rockaway St 33767. **Hours:** 11 am-midnig Fri & Sat-1 am. Closed: 11/27, 12/25. **Features:** A variety of salads, burgers, sandwiches and seafood w Caribbean flair is offered in a festive beachfront setting. Pleasant servers bring entrees in plastic bask with french fries and coleslaw. Try the stuffed grouper with crabmeat. Casual dress; cocktails. **Parkir** on-site. **Cards:** AX, MC, VI.

FRENCHY'S SALTWATER CAFE **Lunch:** $6-$13 **Dinner:** $6-$13 **Phone:** 727/461-6295
▼▼
Seafood
Location: Just n of jct Clearwater Pass Bridge (SR 60). 419 Poinsetta Ave 33767. **Hours:** 11 am-11 pm, Sun fr noon. Closed: 11/27, 12/25. **Features:** You'll get the feeling you're at a Key West fish camp in this cas cafe, which offers indoor and outdoor dining areas with mainly picnic table seating. Fresh catches, boi shrimp and Key lime pie are yummy. Casual dress; cocktails. **Parking:** on-site. **Cards:** AX, MC, VI.

GONDOLIER PIZZA AND ITALIAN RESTAURANT **Lunch:** $6-$19 **Dinner:** $6-$19 **Phone:** 727/441-3353
▼▼
Italian
Location: 0.9 mi s of jct SR 60 (causeway). 674 S Gulfview Blvd 34630. **Hours:** 7 am-midnight. **Features:** Italian theme and decor is pervasive in the relaxed restaurant. The pleasant wait staff eagerly serves ite from an extensive menu of some 100 specialty and standard items. Casual dress; beer & wine or **Parking:** on-site. **Cards:** AX, DS, MC, VI.

LEVEROCK'S OF CLEARWATER BEACH **Lunch:** $7-$21 **Dinner:** $7-$21 **Phone:** 727/446-5884
▼▼▼▼
Seafood
Location: North end of Clearwater Pass Bridge. 551 Gulf Blvd 33767. **Hours:** 11 am-10 pm. Closed: 11/ 12/25. **Features:** Well-established and centrally located near the end of the Clearwater Pass Bridge offers a wide range of choices such as seafood Martinique, a puffed pastry filled with shrimp and fish in creamy sauce. Hot honey wheat bread makes a nice appetizer. Casual dress; cocktails. **Parking:** on-s **Cards:** AX, DC, DS, MC, VI.

(See map p. 846)

SEAFOOD & SUNSETS AT JULIE'S CAFE   Lunch: $5-$11   Dinner: $10-$30   Phone: 727/441-2548   (112)
Location: 0.5 mi s of jct SR 60 (causeway). 351 S Gulfview Blvd 33767. Hours: 11 am-10 pm. Closed: 11/27.
Features: A tropical Key West theme punctuates the lively restaurant, which has a charming deck dining
Seafood   area directly across from the beach and gulf. While taking in a breathtaking sunset, feast on well-prepared
entrees of shellfish, fish, steak, chicken or pork, as well as surf and turf specials and several other
goodies. Casual dress; beer & wine only. Parking: on-site. Cards: AX, MC, VI.   ⊠

SHEPHARD'S WATERFRONT RESTAURANT   Lunch: $9   Dinner: $21   Phone: 727/441-6875   (114)
Location: 1 mi s of jct SR 60 (causeway); in Shephard's Beach Resort. 601 S Gulfview Blvd 33767. Hours: 8-11
am, 11:30-3 & 4-10 pm. Features: Known for its seafood and prime rib buffet, the waterfront family
restaurant offers views of the sparkling Gulf of Mexico from nearly every seat. A colorful and casual
atmosphere is enhanced by live entertainment with a Caribbean flavor. Casual dress; cocktails;
Seafood   entertainment. Parking: on-site. Cards: AX, DC, DS, MC, VI.   ⊤ ⊠

WATERFRONT RESTAURANT   Lunch: $6-$8   Dinner: $7-$18   Phone: 727/442-3684   (95)
Location: 0.5 mi n of jct Clearwater Pass Bridge (SR 60). 490 Mandalay Ave 33767. Hours: 7 am-10 pm.
Features: The basic restaurant is a good stop at any time of day. The breakfast menu is expansive, lunch
American   choices include appetizers, soups, salads, sandwiches and pasta dishes, and dinner offerings center on
steaks, pork chops, chicken, ribs and seafood. Casual dress; cocktails. Parking: on-site. Cards: AX,
DC, VI.   ⊠

DADE CITY pop. 6,188

—— WHERE TO STAY ——

RAINBOW FOUNTAIN MOTEL   Phone: 352/567-3427
(AAA) (SAVE)   12/1-4/30   1P: $40-$52   2P: $40-$56   XP: $6   D6
5/1-11/30   1P: $32-$42   2P: $32-$46   XP: $6   D6
Location: 2 mi n on US 301 and 98. 16210 N US 301 33523. Facility: 21 one-bedroom standard units. 1 story,
exterior corridors. Bath: combo or shower only. Parking: on-site. Terms: 3 day cancellation notice-fee im-
Motel   posed, weekly rates available. Pool(s): outdoor. Guest Services: coin laundry. Cards: AX, DC, MC, VI.
SOME UNITS
⑤ ☎ ✇ [DATA PORT] 🔌 / 🖥 /

—— WHERE TO DINE ——

LUNCH ON LIMOGES   Lunch: $9-$13   Phone: 352/567-5685
Location: Center; opposite the Court House in Williams Department Store. 14139 7th St 33525. Hours: 11:30
am-2:30 pm. Closed: Sun, also Mon 5/1-10/31. Reservations: suggested. Features: Located in an historic
American   department store near the courthouse, the small cafe features excellent Southern cooking with nice
touches like a basket of delectable homemade muffins. The varied menu changes daily, making fine use of
market-fresh ingredients. Smoke free premises. Casual dress. Parking: street. Cards: AX, CB, DC, DS, MC, VI.   ⊠

DUNEDIN pop. 35,691 (See map p. 846; index p. 852)

─── WHERE TO STAY ───

BEST WESTERN YACHT HARBOR INN & SUITES Phone: (727)733-4121

2/1-4/15 [ECP]	1P: $119-$139	2P: $119-$139	XP: $10
12/21-1/31 [ECP]	1P: $89-$109	2P: $89-$109	XP: $10
12/1-12/20 & 4/16-11/30 [ECP]	1P: $79-$99	2P: $79-$99	XP: $10

Motel **Location:** Jct US Alt 19 and gulf end of Main St, 0.5 mi s of SR 580. Located across from the marina. 150 Marina Pla 34698. Fax: 727/736-4365. **Facility:** Designated smoking area. 55 units. 54 one-bedroom standard units two-bedroom suite ($139-$279). 2 stories, exterior corridors. *Bath:* combo or shower only. **Parking:** on-si **Terms:** 7 day cancellation notice-fee imposed, weekly rates available. **Amenities:** voice mail, irons, hair dryers. *Some:* hor bars. **Dining:** 2 restaurants, 11:30 am-10 pm, cocktails, also, Bon Appetit Restaurant, see separate listing. **Pool(s):** heated o door. **Leisure Activities:** shuffleboard. **Guest Services:** valet laundry. **Business Services:** meeting rooms, PC, fax. **Cards:** A DC, DS, MC, VI. **Special Amenities: free continental breakfast and free newspaper.** *(See color ad below)*

SOME UN

HOLIDAY INN EXPRESS HOTEL & SUITES CLEARWATER NORTH/DUNEDIN Phone: (727)450-1200

1/16-4/15 [ECP]	1P: $105-$155	2P: $105-$155	XP: $5
12/1-1/15 & 4/16-11/30 [ECP]	1P: $85-$125	2P: $85-$125	XP: $5

Small-scale Hotel **Location:** Center. 975 Broadway (Alt 19) 34698. Fax: 727/450-1200. **Facility:** 76 one-bedroom standard units stories, interior corridors. *Bath:* combo or shower only. **Parking:** on-site. **Terms:** cancellation fee impose **Amenities:** voice mail, irons, hair dryers. **Pool(s):** heated outdoor. **Leisure Activities:** whirlpool, exercise room. **Guest Ser ices:** coin laundry. **Business Services:** meeting rooms, business center. **Cards:** AX, CB, DC, DS, JC, MC, VI.

SOME UNITS

─── WHERE TO DINE ───

BON APPETIT RESTAURANT **Lunch:** $7-$14 **Dinner:** $12-$15 Phone: 727-733-2151

Continental **Location:** Jct US Alt 19 and gulf end of Main St, 0.5 mi s of SR 580; in Best Western Yacht Harbor Inn & Suites. 1 Marina Plaza 34698. **Hours:** 11:30 am-10 pm. **Reservations:** suggested. **Features:** Overlooking t Intracoastal Waterway, the restaurant is a great spot for creative bistro cuisine. Seagoers can dock at t Best Western Yacht Harbor Inn, where this restaurant is located, and dine in the outdoor cafe. Professio service and attentiveness are key to a grand, enchanting meal. Smoke free premises. Casual dress; cocktails. **Parkir** on-site. **Cards:** AX, CB, DC, DS, MC, VI. *(See color ad below)*

CAFE ALFRESCO **Lunch:** $5-$15 **Dinner:** $15-$22 Phone: 727-736-4299

American **Location:** Just w of jct Alt US 19; downtown. 344 Main St 34698. **Hours:** 11 am-9 pm, Fri & Sat 10 am-10 p **Features:** On the menu are such dishes as penne pasta, baked brie, roast duck, sauteed fillet of sno vegetarian paella and five grilled chipolata sausages. The atmosphere is casual and friendly, and outdo dining is available. Casual dress; cocktails. **Parking:** on-site. **Cards:** AX, DC, DS, MC, VI.

JESSE'S DOCKSIDE **Lunch:** $7-$9 **Dinner:** $9-$21 Phone: 727-736-2611

Seafood **Location:** On SR 586, 0.3 mi w of Alt US 19; at west end of the Causeway Bridge. 345 Causeway Blvd 346 **Hours:** 11:30 am-10 pm, Sun-9 pm. Closed: 12/25. **Features:** Overlooking a marina, the restaurant serv ample portions of attractively garnished, tasty food, including a spicy fried alligator appetizer, seafo gumbo and fresh gulf seafood. Landlubbers and children may prefer beef, chicken and pasta dish Casual dress; cocktails. **Parking:** on-site. **Cards:** AX, DS, MC, VI.

"KELLY'S FOR JUST ABOUT...ANYTHING!" **Lunch:** $5-$12 **Dinner:** $10-$18 Phone: 727-736-5284

American **Location:** Just e of jct Alt US 19; center. 319 Main St 34698. **Hours:** 8 am-10 pm. Closed: 12/2 **Reservations:** suggested; dinner. **Features:** An eclectic menu runs the gamut from simple to sublime, w a dining room decor that is as creative as the food. Professional and attentive service follows an "anythi goes" philosophy. Try the grilled chicken sandwich for a light lunch. Smoke free premises. Casual dre beer & wine only. **Parking:** street. **Cards:** AX, DS, MC, VI.

(See map p. 846)

EA SEA RIDERS **Lunch:** $6-$16 **Dinner:** $6-$16 **Phone:** 727/734-1445 [136]
▼▼▼ **Location:** Jct Main St and US 19 Alt; center. 221 Main St 34698. **Hours:** 11:30 am-10 pm, Fri & Sat-11 pm.
American Closed: 11/27, 12/25. **Features:** Veranda and inside seating both provide for a pleasant and relaxing experience at this 1906 Florida cracker house. Flavorful coconut shrimp, sauteed chicken and mahi-mahi whet the appetite, while artwork by state denizens adds to the tropical decor. Casual dress; cocktails.
arking: on-site. **Cards:** AX, MC, VI.

OLIDAY pop. 21,904

——— WHERE TO STAY ———

EST WESTERN-TAHITIAN RESORT **Phone:** (727)937-4121
⬥⬥ SAVE	2/1-4/30	1P: $69-$99	2P: $69-$99	XP: $8	F12
	12/1-1/31	1P: $59-$89	2P: $59-$89	XP: $8	F12
▼▼ ▼▼	5/1-11/30	1P: $49-$79	2P: $49-$79	XP: $8	F12

Motel **Location:** On US 19, 3 mi n of jct SR 582, 1.5 mi s of jct SR 54. 2337 US 19 34691. **Fax:** 727/937-3806. **Facility:** 140 one-bedroom standard units, some with efficiencies. 2 stories. **Parking:** on-site. **Terms:** 3 day cancellation notice-fee imposed, weekly rates available, [BP] meal plan available, pets ($5 extra charge, designated units). **Amenities:** irons, hair dryers. **Pool(s):** heated outdoor. **Guest Services:** coin laundry. **Business Services:** meeting rooms, fax (fee). **Cards:** AX, DC, DS, MC, VI. **Special Amenities: free continental breakfast and free newspaper.**
(See color ad p 938)

SOME UNITS

INDIAN ROCKS BEACH pop. 5,072 (See map p. 846; index p. 853)

——— WHERE TO STAY ———

0 GULFSIDE **Phone:** (727)596-8063 [140]
▼▼▼ All Year Wkly 1P: $589-$2300
Motel **Location:** On SR 699, 0.4 mi n of jct SR 688, entrance to property via Beach Tr, just n of property. 810 Gulf Blvd 33785. **Fax:** 727/593-9343. **Facility:** Designated smoking area. 6 units. 2 one- and 4 two-bedroom suites with kitchens. 2 stories, exterior corridors. **Parking:** on-site. **Terms:** 7 night minimum stay, 60 day cancellation notice-fee imposed. **Amenities:** irons, hair dryers. Some: CD players. **Pool(s):** heated outdoor. **Leisure Activities:** boating, fishing, shuffleboard. **Guest Services:** coin laundry. **Business Services:** fax.

NCHOR COURT APARTMENTS **Phone:** 727/595-4449 [139]
⬥⬥ SAVE	1/1-4/30	1P: $85-$111	2P: $85-$111	XP: $20	D18
	5/1-9/8	1P: $75-$100	2P: $75-$100	XP: $20	D18
▼▼ ▼▼	12/31-12/31 & 9/9-11/30	1P: $70-$90	2P: $70-$90	XP: $20	D18

Motel **Location:** On SR 699, 0.5 mi n of jct SR 688. 940 Gulf Blvd 33785. **Fax:** 727/595-4449. **Facility:** 20 units. 4 one-bedroom standard units. 16 one-bedroom suites with kitchens. 2 stories, exterior corridors. **Parking:** on-site. **Terms:** 14 day cancellation notice. **Amenities:** Some: irons, hair dryers. **Pool(s):** heated outdoor. **Leisure Activities:** tennis privileges, patio seating on wood deck, gazebo and grill area, shuffleboard. **Guest Services:** coin laundry. **Cards:** AX, DS, MC, VI.

ULF TOWERS RESORT MOTEL **Phone:** 727/595-2563 [141]
▼▼▼▼ ▼▼▼▼	2/1-4/30 Wkly	1P: $497-$658	2P: $497-$658	XP: $10
	12/1-1/31 & 5/1-9/2 Wkly	1P: $371-$525	2P: $371-$525	XP: $10
Small-scale Hotel	9/3-11/30 Wkly	1P: $322-$469	2P: $322-$469	XP: $10

Location: On SR 699, just s of jct SR 688. 404 Gulf Blvd 33785. **Fax:** 727/595-2553. **Facility:** 45 units. 41 one-bedroom standard units with efficiencies. 4 one-bedroom suites with kitchens. 4 stories, interior corridors. **Parking:** on-site. **Terms:** 14 day cancellation notice-fee imposed. **Amenities:** voice mail, safes (fee). **Pool(s):** outdoor. **Guest Services:** sundries, coin laundry. **Cards:** AX, MC, VI.

SOME UNITS

OLIDAY INN HOTEL & SUITES-HARBOURSIDE **Phone:** (727)595-9484 [145]
⬥⬥ SAVE	12/31-4/30	1P: $159-$449	2P: $159-$449	XP: $15	F17
	12/1-12/30 & 5/1-11/30	1P: $129-$239	2P: $129-$239	XP: $15	F17
▼▼▼ ▼▼▼				

Small-scale Hotel **Location:** Just e of jct SR 699; just s of jct SR 688 (Walsingham Rd). 401 2nd St 33785. **Fax:** 727/596-4825. **Facility:** 164 units. 82 one-bedroom standard units, some with efficiencies. 82 one-bedroom suites ($199-$449) with kitchens, some with whirlpools. 3 stories, exterior corridors. Bath: combo or shower only. **Parking:** on-site. **Terms:** check-in 4 pm, 3 day cancellation notice-fee imposed, 11% service charge. **Amenities:** voice mail, irons, hair dryers. **Dining:** 2 restaurants, 7 am-11 pm, Fri & Sat-midnight, cocktails, entertainment. **Pool(s):** 2 heated outdoor. **Leisure Activities:** whirlpool, waterslide, marina, fishing, tennis court, inline skates, motor scooters, dockmaster, playground, exercise room, volleyball. Fee: boats, sailboats, windsurfing, waterskiing, charter fishing, jet skis, bicycles, game room. **Guest Services:** gift shop, valet and coin laundry. **Business Services:** meeting rooms. Fee: administrative services, fax. **Cards:** AX, CB, DC, DS, JC, MC, VI. **Special Amenities: free local telephone calls and free newspaper.**
(See color ad opposite inside back cover)

SOME UNITS

AKS COURT APARTMENT I **Phone:** (727)595-7586 [142]
▼▼▼	12/1-4/25 Wkly	1P: $500	2P: $500
	4/26-11/30 Wkly	1P: $400	2P: $400

Motel **Location:** Just s of jct SR 688. 315 First St 33785 (417 1st St). **Fax:** 727/595-4104. **Facility:** 2 two-bedroom suites with kitchens. 1 story, exterior corridors. **Parking:** on-site. **Terms:** check-in 4 pm, 3-7 night minimum stay - weekends in spring, 45 day cancellation notice-fee imposed, weekly rates available, package plans. **Business Services:** fax. **Cards:** DS, MC, VI.

(See map p. 846)

OAKS COURT APARTMENT II   Phone: (727)597-7586   🔟
△△△△△ 12/1-2/7 & 2/8-4/25 Wkly   1P: $500   2P: $500
        4/26-11/30 Wkly   1P: $400   2P: $400
Motel   **Location:** Just s of jct SR 688. 317 First St 33785 (417 1st St). Fax: 727/595-4104. **Facility:** 2 two-bedroom suit
with kitchens. 1 story, exterior corridors. **Parking:** on-site. **Terms:** check-in 4 pm, 3-7 night minimum sta
seasonal, 45 day cancellation notice-fee imposed, daily rates available, package plans. **Business Services:** fax. **Cards:** D
MC, VI.

(ASK) (S🔊) (📶▸) (VCR) (DATA PORT) 🔲 🔲

SEA STAR MOTEL & APARTMENTS   Phone: (727)596-2525   🔟
△△△△   1/1-4/30   2P: $65-$100
       12/1-12/31   2P: $60-$90
Motel 5/1-11/30   2P: $55-$75
       Location: On SR 699, 1.2 mi n of jct SR 688 (Walsingham Rd). 1805 Gulf Blvd 33785. Fax: 727/596-252
Facility: Designated smoking area. 13 units. 7 one-bedroom standard units with efficiencies. 4 one- and 1 two-bedroom suit
($410-$510) with kitchens. 1 cottage ($410-$510). 1-2 stories, exterior corridors. *Bath:* combo or shower only. **Parking:** on-si
Terms: 30 day cancellation notice, weekly rates available. **Amenities:** *Some:* irons, hair dryers. **Leisure Activities:** whirlpo
bicycles, shuffleboard. **Guest Services:** coin laundry. **Business Services:** fax. **Cards:** AX, DS, MC, VI.

(ASK) (📶▸) (⊗) (✕) (☎) 🔲 🔲

WEST COAST VISTA   Phone: (727)595-7586   🔟
△△△▽△△△   2/8-4/25 Wkly   1P: $1175   2P: $1175
          12/1-2/7 Wkly   1P: $1075   2P: $1075
Condominium 4/26-9/5 Wkly   1P: $925   2P: $925
          9/6-11/30 Wkly   1P: $850   2P: $850
Location: On SR 699, just s of jct SR 688. 24 Gulf Blvd 33785 (417 1st St). Fax: 727/595-4104. **Facility:** 4 units. 3 two- and 1 thre
bedroom suites with kitchens. 4 stories, interior corridors. **Parking:** on-site. **Terms:** check-in 4 pm, 7 night minimum stay - se
sonal, 45 day cancellation notice-fee imposed, package plans. **Pool(s):** heated outdoor. **Guest Services:** complimentary laund
Business Services: fax. **Cards:** DS, MC, VI.

SOME UNI
(ASK) (S🔊) (📶▸) (🏊) (VCR) (DATA PORT) 🔲 🔲 /(✕) /

———— **WHERE TO DINE** ————

GUPPY'S ON THE BEACH   **Lunch:** $6-$28   **Dinner:** $6-$28   Phone: 727/593-2032   🔟
△△△△ △△△△ **Location:** On SR 699, 1 mi n of jct SR 688. 1701 N Gulf Blvd 33785. **Hours:** 11:30 am-10:30 pm, Fri & Sat-
           pm. Closed: 11/27, 12/25. **Features:** Enjoy the gulf breeze with patio dining. This diner offers an excelle
Seafood   variety of seafood, steak and sandwich choices with a gorgeous sunset view. The fried shrimp is fresh a
           served with herbed wild rice and delicate vegetables. Casual dress; beer & wine only. **Parking:** on-si
Cards: AX, DC, DS, MC, VI.
                                                                                                           ⊘

THAI PAN ALLEY & BAMBOO BEACH BAR   **Lunch:** $6-$8   **Dinner:** $7-$9   Phone: 727/593-3663   🔟
△△△△   **Location:** On SR 699, 1.5 mi n of jct SR 688; in Western Plaza. 2300 Gulf Blvd 33785. **Hours:** 11 am-9 pm, Fr
       Sat-10 pm, Sun 4 pm-9 pm. Closed major holidays. **Features:** Hearty portions of rice and noodle dish
Thai   coated with sauces from mild to eye-watering spicy characterize the restaurant's cuisine. Dine inside an
       Thai decorations that lend the air of the Orient or head out to the colorful beach bar setting. beer & wi
only. **Parking:** on-site. **Cards:** DC, DS, MC, VI.
                                                                                                       (Y) ⊘

———— *The following restaurant has not been evaluated by AAA* ————
but is listed for your information only.

NADIA'S RESTAURANT & BAR   Phone: 727/596-722
(fyi) Not evaluated. **Location:** On SR 699, 1.6 mi n of jct SR 688. 2721 Gulf Blvd 33785. **Features:** This popu
       restaurant located near the gulf beach is popular for it Continental French cuisine.

INDIAN SHORES pop. 1,705   (See map p. 846; index p. 854)

———— **WHERE TO STAY** ————

BEACH COTTAGE III   Phone: (727)595-7586   2️⃣
△△△△ △△△△   2/8-4/25 Wkly   1P: $1175-$1260   2P: $1175-$1260
            12/1-2/7 Wkly   1P: $1075-$1175   2P: $1075-$1175
Condominium 4/26-9/5 Wkly   1P: $925-$975   2P: $925-$975
            9/6-11/30 Wkly   1P: $775-$875   2P: $775-$875
Location: On SR 699, 0.4 mi s of jct CR 694. 18450 Gulf Blvd 33785 (417 1st St, INDIAN ROCKS BEACH). Fax: 727/595-41(
Facility: 15 units. 1 one-, 1 two- and 13 three-bedroom suites with kitchens. 6 stories, exterior corridors. **Parking:** on-si
Terms: check-in 4 pm, 7 night minimum stay - seasonal, 45 day cancellation notice-fee imposed, package plans. **Pool(s):** heat
outdoor. **Guest Services:** complimentary laundry. **Business Services:** fax. **Cards:** DS, MC, VI.

SOME UNI
(ASK) (S🔊) (📶▸) (🏊) (VCR) 🔲 🔲 /(✕) /

SAND CASTLE I   Phone: (727)595-7586   2️⃣
△△△△ △△△△   2/8-4/25   1P: $1095   2P: $1095
            12/1-2/7   1P: $1000   2P: $1000
Condominium 4/26-9/5   1P: $850   2P: $850
            9/6-11/30   1P: $775   2P: $775
Location: On SR 699, 1.3 mi s of jct SR 688. 20000 Gulf Blvd 33785 (417 1st St, INDIAN ROCKS BEACH). Fax: 727/595-4104. **Facility**
three-bedroom suites with kitchens. 10 stories, exterior corridors. **Parking:** on-site. **Terms:** check-in 4 pm, 5-7 night minimu
stay - seasonal, 45 day cancellation notice-fee imposed, daily rates available, package plans. **Pool(s):** outdoor, heated outdo
Business Services: fax. **Cards:** DS, MC, VI.

SOME UNI
(ASK) (S🔊) (📶▸) (🏊) (VCR) 🔲 🔲 /(✕) /

(See map p. 846)

AND CASTLE II

Phone: (727)595-7586 243

♦♦♦♦ ♦♦♦♦	2/8-4/25 Wkly	1P: $1175		2P: $1175
	12/1-2/7 Wkly	1P: $1125		2P: $1125
	4/26-9/5 Wkly	1P: $925		2P: $925
Condominium	9/6-11/30 Wkly	1P: $825		2P: $825

Location: On SR 699, 1.2 mi s of jct SR 688. 20002 Gulf Blvd 33785 (417 1st St, INDIAN ROCKS BEACH). Fax: 727/595-4104. Facility: Designated smoking area. 7 three-bedroom suites with kitchens. 10 stories, exterior corridors. Parking: on-site. Terms: check-in 4 pm, 3-7 night minimum stay - seasonal, 45 day cancellation notice-fee imposed, daily rates available, package plans. Pool(s): outdoor, heated outdoor. Leisure Activities: whirlpool. Business Services: fax. Cards: DS, MC, VI.

(ASK) (S/D) (Y|+) (≈) (✕) (VCR) (DATA PORT) (☎) (➤)

AND CASTLE III

Phone: (727)595-7586 242

♦♦♦♦ ♦♦♦♦	2/8-4/25 Wkly	1P: $1230		2P: $1230
	12/1-2/7 Wkly	1P: $1150		2P: $1150
	4/26-9/5 Wkly	1P: $950		2P: $950
Condominium	9/6-11/30 Wkly	1P: $850		2P: $850

Location: On SR 699, 1.2 mi s of SR 688. 20040 Gulf Blvd 33785 (417 1st St, INDIAN ROCKS BEACH). Fax: 727/595-4104. Facility: 16 three-bedroom suites with kitchens. 6 stories, exterior corridors. Parking: on-site. Terms: check-in 4 pm, 3-7 night minimum stay - seasonal, 45 day cancellation notice-fee imposed, daily rates available, package plans. Amenities: irons. Pool(s): heated outdoor. Leisure Activities: whirlpool. Guest Services: complimentary laundry. Business Services: fax. Cards: DS, MC, VI.

SOME UNITS

(ASK) (S/D) (Y|+) (≈) (VCR) (DATA PORT) (☎) (➤) / (✕) /

EA GATE

Phone: (727)595-7586 246

♦♦♦♦ ♦♦♦♦	2/8-4/25 Wkly	1P: $1150		2P: $1150
	12/1-2/7 Wkly	1P: $1075		2P: $1075
	4/26-9/5 Wkly	1P: $900		2P: $900
Condominium	9/6-11/30 Wkly	1P: $825		2P: $825

Location: On SR 699, 2.4 mi s of jct SR 688. 19418 Gulf Blvd 33785 (417 1st St, INDIAN ROCKS BEACH). Fax: 727/595-4104. Facility: 4 three-bedroom suites with kitchens. 6 stories, exterior corridors. Parking: on-site. Terms: check-in 4 pm, 3-7 night minimum stay - seasonal, 45 day cancellation notice-fee imposed, daily rates available, package plans. Pool(s): heated outdoor. Guest Services: complimentary laundry. Business Services: fax. Cards: DS, MC, VI.

(ASK) (S/D) (Y|+) (≈) (VCR) (DATA PORT) (☎) (➤)

──────── WHERE TO DINE ────────

CHATEAU MADRID

Dinner: $10-$21   Phone: 727/596-9100 269

♦♦♦♦ ♦♦♦♦

Spanish

Location: 0.8 mi n of Park Blvd Cswy (CR 694). 19519 Gulf Blvd 33785. Hours: 4 pm-10 pm, Fri & Sat-11 pm. Reservations: suggested. Features: A friendly staff serves authentic Spanish cuisine while live entertainment performs on Fridays and Saturdays. Savor the filet mignon with bearnaise sauce for a tender and tasty steak entree. Salads large enough to share are prepared right at your table. Casual dress; cocktails. Parking: on-site. Cards: AX, DC, MC, VI.

(Y) (✕)

THE HUNGRY FISHERMAN

Lunch: $5-$23   Dinner: $6-$23   Phone: 727/595-4218 267

♦♦♦♦ ♦♦♦♦

Seafood

Location: 1.3 mi n of Park Blvd Cswy (CR 694). 19915 Gulf Blvd 33785. Hours: 11:30 am-10 pm. Closed: 11/27, 12/25. Features: This local landmark serves peel-and-eat shrimp with a unique cocktail sauce on a bed of lettuce. Try the catfish fillets for a fresh local catch. Seafood and meat specialties complete the menu choices. The service is prompt and pleasant. Casual dress; cocktails. Parking: on-site. Cards: MC, VI.

(Y) (✕)

LIDO RISTORANTE ITALIANO

Dinner: $11-$21   Phone: 727/593-0926 270

♦♦♦♦ ♦♦♦♦

Italian

Location: On SR 699, 0.4 mi n of jct Park Blvd Cswy (CR 694). 19211 Gulf Blvd 33785. Hours: 5 pm-10 pm. Closed major holidays. Features: Across the street from the gulf and on the Intracoastal Waterway, this restaurant offers a menu of Italian specialties. Casual dress; cocktails. Parking: on-site. Cards: AX, DC, DS, MC, VI.

(✕)

THE PUB RESTAURANT & LOUNGE

Lunch: $7-$17   Dinner: $7-$17   Phone: 727/595-3172 265

♦♦♦♦ ♦♦♦♦

American

Location: On SR 699, 1.2 mi s of jct SR 688 (Walsingham Rd). 20025 Gulf Blvd 33785. Hours: 11 am-midnight, Sun from noon. Closed: 11/27, 12/25. Features: The great Intracoastal Waterway location affords beautiful views of the dock from the outdoor patio as well as the cozy inside dining area. The piano bar and dance floor add to the ambience. Listed on the extensive menu are numerous steak, seafood, pasta, rib, burger and sandwich selections, as well as salads, appetizers and desserts. Casual dress; cocktails; entertainment. Parking: on-site. Cards: AX, DS, MC, VI.

(Y) (✕)

SALT ROCK GRILL

Dinner: $11-$31   Phone: 727/593-7625 271

♦♦♦♦ ♦♦♦♦

Swiss

Location: On SR 699, 0.5 mi n of jct Park Blvd Cswy (CR 694). 19325 Gulf Blvd 33785. Hours: 4 pm-10 pm, Fri & Sat-11 pm. Features: An extremely trendy and upscale setting—a remake of "Le Pompano"—awaits the diner here. Beautiful artwork and objects abound, and the decor is tastefully done. The menu offers open-pit citrus- and oak-fired steaks and seafood prepared by trained chefs. Dressy casual; cocktails. Parking: on-site. Cards: MC, VI.

(Y)

LARGO pop. 69,371 (See map p. 846; index p. 853)

-------- WHERE TO STAY --------

SUBURBAN LODGE Phone: (727)532-4800 14

1/1-4/15	1P: $60-$80	2P: $65-$85	
12/1-12/31 & 4/16-11/30	1P: $50-$70	2P: $55-$75	

Small-scale Hotel **Location:** On SR 688, just w of jct US 19. 6500 Ulmerton Rd 33771. Fax: 727/507-8527. **Facility:** 132 one-bedroo standard units with efficiencies. 3 stories, exterior corridors. *Bath:* combo or shower only. **Parking:** on-si **Terms:** weekly rates available. **Amenities:** voice mail. *Some:* irons, hair dryers. **Guest Services:** valet and coin laundry. **Bu ness Services:** fax (fee). **Cards:** AX, DS, MC, VI. *(See color ad p 596)*

SOME

-------- WHERE TO DINE --------

THE GATHERING RESTAURANT **Lunch:** $5-$9 Phone: 727/593-1600 1

American **Location:** On SR 688, 1 mi e of jct SR 699; in Sabala Plaza. 14100 Walsingham Rd 33774. **Hours:** 6 am-3 p **Features:** Bright and airy with lots of room, the restaurant offers up lighter fare, ranging from omelets a eggs Benedict to corned beef sandwiches on rye bread. The Belgian waffles are pretty tasty, too. T servers are polite and prompt. Casual dress. **Parking:** on-site.

ROGER'S REAL PIT BAR-B-QUE **Lunch:** $4-$17 **Dinner:** $4-$17 Phone: 727/586-2629 1

American **Location:** On US Alt 19, 0.8 i s of jct SR 688. 12150 Seminole Blvd 33778. **Hours:** 11 am-9 pm, Fri & Sat-9: pm. **Features:** Popular with the locals, this spot offers old-fashioned service and food in a rustic decor. I known for pit-barbecue beef, pork ribs and chicken, as well as an extensive salad bar with a variety fresh salads, vegetables and fruit. Casual dress. **Parking:** on-site. **Cards:** MC, VI.

MADEIRA BEACH pop. 4,511 (See map p. 846; index p. 853)

-------- WHERE TO STAY --------

HOLIDAY INN MADEIRA BEACH Phone: (727)392-2275 1

2/14-4/30	1P: $159-$189	2P: $159-$189	XP: $10
5/1-11/30	1P: $134-$164	2P: $134-$164	XP: $10
12/1-1/4	1P: $129-$159	2P: $129-$159	XP: $10
1/5-2/13	1P: $124-$154	2P: $124-$154	XP: $10

Small-scale Hotel **Location:** On SR 699, just n of jct Tom Stuart Cswy. 15208 Gulf Blvd 33708. Fax: 727/393-4012. **Facility:** 148 un 147 one-bedroom standard units. 1 one-bedroom suite with kitchen. 4 stories, exterior corridors. *Bath:* combo or shower only. **Parking:** on-site. **Terms:** check-in 4 pm, cancellation fee imposed. **Amenities:** video games, dual phone lin voice mail, safes, irons, hair dryers. **Dining:** 2 restaurants, 6:30 am-10 pm, cocktails. **Pool(s):** heated outdoor, wading. **Leisu Activities:** lighted tennis court, exercise room, volleyball. *Fee:* sailboats, cabana kayaks, beach chairs, game room. **Guest Se ices:** valet and coin laundry, area transportation (fee)-trolley service. **Business Services:** meeting rooms, PC, fax. **Cards:** A DC, DS, MC, VI. *(See color ad below & opposite inside back cover)*

SOME UNITS

FEE

THE LIGHTHOUSE BED & BREAKFAST MOTEL Phone: (727)391-0015 1

1/1-4/30 [BP]	1P: $85-$110	2P: $85-$110	XP: $15
12/1-12/31 & 5/1-11/30 [BP]	1P: $65-$90	2P: $65-$90	XP: $15

Motel **Location:** Just e of jct SR 699 on 134th Ave. 13355 2nd St E 33708. Fax: 727/393-7285. **Facility:** Designat smoking area. 7 one-bedroom standard units, some with efficiencies or kitchens. 2 stories, exterior corrido *Bath:* shower only. **Parking:** on-site. **Terms:** 2 night minimum stay, 14 day cancellation notice-fee imposed, pets ($5 ex charge, $50 deposit). **Amenities:** *Some:* irons. **Leisure Activities:** bicycles. **Guest Services:** coin laundry. **Cards:** AX, D MC, VI.

SOME UNI

FEE

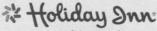

(See map p. 846)

SEA DAWN MOTEL

AAA SAVE ♦ Motel

Phone: (727)391-7500 [162]

		XP	
2/1-3/31	2P: $55-$75	XP: $8	F10
4/1-4/30	2P: $50-$65	XP: $8	F10
12/1-1/31	2P: $35-$65	XP: $8	F10
5/1-11/30	2P: $35-$50	XP: $8	F10

Location: On SR 699, 0.7 mi s of Tom Stuart Cswy. 13733 Gulf Blvd 33708. Fax: 727/391-7500. **Facility:** 8 one-bedroom standard units, some with efficiencies or kitchens. 2 stories, exterior corridors. **Parking:** on-site. **Terms:** 10 day cancellation notice-fee imposed. **Amenities:** *Some:* irons. **Pool(s):** small outdoor. **Leisure Activities:** boat dock, fishing, sun deck. **Business Services:** fax. **Cards:** MC, VI. **Special Amenities:** free local telephone calls and preferred room (subject to availability with advanced reservations).

SOME UNITS
🍴 🏊 ⊠ 🖥 / ⊠ 📷 /

SHORELINE ISLAND RESORT

AAA SAVE ♦♦♦ Small-scale Hotel

Phone: (727)397-6641 [161]

			XP
1/26-4/25	1P: $112-$252	2P: $112-$252	XP: $10
12/1-1/25	1P: $81-$188	2P: $81-$188	XP: $10
4/26-11/30	1P: $112-$152	2P: $112-$152	XP: $10

Location: On SR 699, 0.5 mi s of Tom Stuart Cswy. 14200 Gulf Blvd 33708. Fax: 727/393-9157. **Facility:** 71 units. 51 one-bedroom standard units, some with efficiencies. 16 one- and 4 two-bedroom suites with kitchens. 2-5 stories, exterior corridors. **Parking:** on-site. **Terms:** age restrictions may apply, 7 day cancellation notice. **Amenities:** video library, hair dryers. *Some:* irons. **Pool(s):** heated outdoor. **Leisure Activities:** shuffleboard. **Guest Services:** coin laundry. **Cards:** AX, DS, MC, VI. *(See color ad below)*

SOME UNITS
S/D 🍴 🏊 VCR 🐕 DATA PORT 🖥 📷 📼 / ⊠ /

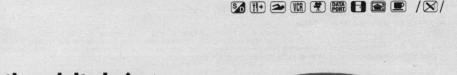

(See map p. 846)

SNUG HARBOR INN Phone: (727)395-9256 **159**
AAA SAVE   All Year   1P: $39-$94   2P: $39-$94   XP: $10   F12
Location: On SR 699, 0.9 mi s of jct Tom Stuart Cswy. 13655 Gulf Blvd 33708. Fax: 877/379-6704. **Facility:** 8 one-bedroom suites ($80-$259) with kitchens. 2 stories, exterior corridors. **Parking:** on-site. **Terms:** 14 day cancellation notice-fee imposed, weekly rates available, [CP] meal plan available, package plans.
Motel   **Amenities:** *Some:* irons, hair dryers. **Pool(s):** outdoor. **Leisure Activities:** boat dock, 6 boat slips, 120-foot deck on Boca Ciega Bay, barbecue grill. **Business Services:** fax. **Cards:** AX, DC, DS, MC, VI.
Special Amenities: free local telephone calls.

SOME UNITS
🐾 🏊 ✕ 🛢 ☕ / ✕ VCR 🖨 /

WITS END MOTEL Phone: (727)391-6739 **158**
AAA SAVE   2/1-4/28   1P: $95-$140   2P: $95-$140   XP: $8
           12/1-1/31   1P: $75-$135   2P: $75-$135   XP: $8
           4/29-9/7   1P: $75-$125   2P: $75-$125   XP: $8
           9/8-11/30   1P: $67-$115   2P: $67-$115   XP: $8
Motel   **Location:** On SR 699, 0.9 mi s of Tom Stuart Cswy. 13600 Gulf Blvd 33708. Fax: 727/392-4578. **Facility:** 30 units. 23 one- and 1 two-bedroom standard units, some with efficiencies. 6 one-bedroom suites with kitchens. 2 stories, interior/exterior corridors. **Parking:** on-site. **Terms:** 30 day cancellation notice-fee imposed. **Amenities:** *Some:* irons, hair dryers. **Pool(s):** heated outdoor. **Leisure Activities:** shuffleboard. **Business Services:** fax (fee). **Cards:** DS, MC, VI.
(See color ad p 921)

🛗 🏊 ✕ 🛢 🖨

─────── WHERE TO DINE ───────

THE APPLE OF MADEIRA BEACH FAMILY
RESTAURANT & LOUNGE   Lunch: $5-$13   Dinner: $7-$18   Phone: 727/391-1302 **163**
AAA   **Location:** Just e of jct SR 699. 100 Madeira Way 33708. **Hours:** 7 am-11 pm. **Features:** At the junction of Gulf Boulevard and a welcoming beacon to the beach, this local favorite is impossible to miss. It offers reliable preparations of fresh seafood, steaks and ribs. Casual dress. **Parking:** on-site. **Cards:** MC, VI.
American
Y

FRIENDLY FISHERMAN WATERFRONT
SEAFOOD RESTAURANT   Lunch: $7-$26   Dinner: $7-$26   Phone: 727/391-6025 **170**
Location: At John's Pass Village. 1.4 mi s of jct Madeira Cswy. 150 Johns Pass Boardwalk 33708. **Hours:** 7 am-10 pm, Fri & Sat-11 pm. Closed: 12/25. **Features:** This rustic boardwalk eatery offers an array of seafood choices. Peel-and-eat shrimp is fresh and light. You will be treated to prompt, detail-oriented service during
Seafood   your seafood meal. Enjoy the waterfront view and shop the boardwalk after dinner. Casual dress; cocktails.
Parking: on-site (fee). **Cards:** AX, MC, VI.
Y ✕

JOHNNY LEVEROCK'S SEAFOOD HOUSE   Lunch: $7-$21   Dinner: $7-$21   Phone: 727/393-0459 **169**
Location: 0.5 mi e of jct SR 699 on Tom Stuart Cswy (SR 666). 565 150th Ave 33708. **Hours:** 11 am-10 pm. Closed: 11/27, 12/25. **Features:** The crisp, clean dining rooms of this cozy restaurant overlook Boca Ciega
Steak & Seafood   Bay. Lots of wood and displays of such items as fishing rods mold a decidedly ocean-themed feeling. The New England clam chowder and onion-crusted salmon are menu favorites. Casual dress; cocktails.
Parking: on-site. **Cards:** AX, DC, DS, MC, VI.
Y ✕

SCULLY'S BOARDWALK GRILLE   Lunch: $8-$21   Dinner: $8-$21   Phone: 727/393-7749 **168**
Location: At John's Pass Village, 1.4 mi s of jct Tom Stuart Cswy. 190 Johns Pass Boardwalk 33708. **Hours:** 11 am-10 pm. **Features:** A nice view of the Intracoastal Waterway can be enjoyed at this rustic and
Seafood   comfortable sea shanty, which offers boardwalk dining and is decorated in a nautical theme. Menu choices range from seafood to sandwiches to burgers. Casual dress; beer & wine only. **Parking:** on-site.
Cards: MC, VI.

NEW PORT RICHEY pop. 16,117

─────── WHERE TO STAY ───────

BEST WESTERN NEW PORT RICHEY Phone: (727)842-6800
SAVE   1/1-4/30 [CP]   1P: $65-$85
       5/1-11/30 [CP]   1P: $62-$79
       12/1-12/31 [CP]   1P: $49-$65
Motel   **Location:** On US 19, 0.5 mi n of jct Main St. 6826 US 19 N 34652. Fax: 727/842-5072. **Facility:** 66 one-bedroom standard units, some with efficiencies. 2 stories, exterior corridors. **Parking:** on-site. **Terms:** check-in 4 pm. **Amenities:** *Some:* irons, hair dryers. **Pool(s):** heated outdoor. **Leisure Activities:** whirlpool, steamroom.
Guest Services: coin laundry. **Business Services:** meeting rooms, fax. **Cards:** AX, DC, DS, MC, VI.

SOME UNITS
SD 🛗 🏊 ✕ 📠 / ✕ 🛢 🖨 🖨 /

CLARION HOTEL Phone: (727)847-9005
AAA SAVE   1/17-5/1   1P: $79-$99   2P: $79-$99   XP: $10   F16
           12/1-1/16 & 5/2-11/30   1P: $69-$89   2P: $69-$89   XP: $10   F16
Location: On US 19; 1 mi n of jct SR 54. 5316 US Hwy 19 34652. Fax: 727/844-3360. **Facility:** 150 units. 139 one-bedroom standard units. 11 one-bedroom suites ($109-$134) with efficiencies. 2 stories, exterior corridors.
Small-scale Hotel   *Bath:* combo or shower only. **Parking:** on-site. **Amenities:** video games, dual phone lines, irons, hair dryers. **Dining:** 6:30 am-9 pm, cocktails. **Pool(s):** heated outdoor, wading. **Leisure Activities:** whirlpool, exercise room. **Guest Services:** valet and coin laundry. **Business Services:** meeting rooms, business center. **Cards:** AX, CB, DC, DS, MC, VI. **Special Amenities:** early check-in/late check-out and free local telephone calls.

SOME UNITS
SD 🍴 Y 🛗 🏊 ✕ 📠 🖨 / ✕ 🛢 🖨

ECONO LODGE

Phone: (727)845-4990

(AAA) [SAVE]

Motel

	1P: $60-$100	2P: $60-$100	XP: $10	F18
2/1-4/20 [CP]	1P: $55-$90	2P: $55-$90	XP: $10	F18
1/1-1/31 & 4/21-11/30 [CP]	1P: $50-$80	2P: $50-$80	XP: $10	F18
12/1-12/31 [CP]				

Location: 0.8 mi n of jct Main St. 7631 US 19 34652. Fax: 727/849-1424. **Facility:** 105 one-bedroom standard units, some with efficiencies. 1 story, exterior corridors. **Parking:** on-site. **Terms:** weekly rates available, package plans - weekly & monthly, small pets only ($10 extra charge). **Amenities:** Some: irons, hair dryers. **Pool(s):** heated outdoor. **Leisure Activities:** picnic and barbecue area. **Guest Services:** coin laundry. **Business Services:** fax. **Cards:** AX, CB, DC, DS, MC, VI. **Special Amenities: free continental breakfast and free local telephone calls.**

SOME UNITS

[icons]

------ WHERE TO DINE ------

CAFE GRAND

Lunch: $6-$17   **Dinner:** $9-$17   **Phone:** 727/848-7098

American

Location: Just s of Main St; downtown. 6238 Grand Blvd 34652. **Hours:** 11 am-9:30 pm, Fri-10 pm, Sat 5 pm-10 pm. Closed: 1/1, 12/25; also Sun. **Features:** In an established area of downtown, the restaurant sits opposite the theater in two storefront sections of a historic building. Operated by California transplants, the cafe uses the freshest products and ingredients, purchased daily, to create interesting pork, chicken, beef and seafood dishes. The owner's mother prepares sinful desserts. The decor is artsy and distinctive. Dressy casual; cocktails. **Parking:** on-site.

[icon]

LEVEROCKS SEAFOOD HOUSE OF NEW PORT RICHEY

Lunch: $7-$21   **Dinner:** $9-$21   **Phone:** 727/849-8000

Seafood

DS, MC, VI.

Location: On US 19, 1 mi n of jct SR 54. 4927 US 19 S 34652. **Hours:** 11 am-10 pm. Closed: 11/27, 12/25. **Features:** The nautically decorated restaurant, with large windows and multiple dining levels, affords views of the yacht basin from many flattering angles. With its own fleet of fishing boats, the restaurant boasts: "If it's fresher than Leverocks, it's still swimming.". Casual dress; cocktails. **Parking:** on-site. **Cards:** AX, DC,

[icons]

NORTH REDINGTON BEACH pop. 1,474   (See map p. 846; index p. 853)

------ WHERE TO STAY ------

FAR HORIZONS MOTEL

Phone: 727/393-8791   [172]

Condominium

| All Year | 1P: $62-$98 | 2P: $62-$98 | XP: $5 | F3 |

Location: On SR 699, 1.5 mi s of jct Park Blvd (SR 694). 17248 Gulf Blvd 33708. Fax: 727/391-3980. **Facility:** 24 one-bedroom suites with efficiencies. 2 stories, exterior corridors. **Parking:** on-site. **Terms:** 3 day cancellation notice-fee imposed, weekly rates available. **Amenities:** Some: irons, hair dryers. **Pool(s):** heated outdoor. **Leisure Activities:** shuffleboard. **Guest Services:** coin laundry. **Business Services:** fax. **Cards:** DS, MC, VI.

[icons]

HILTON TAMPA BAY/NORTH REDINGTON BEACH RESORT

Phone: (727)391-4000   [174]

[SAVE]

Large-scale Hotel

| 2/1-4/30 | 1P: $145-$350 | 2P: $145-$350 | XP: $25 | F18 |
| 12/1-1/31 & 5/1-11/30 | 1P: $115-$300 | 2P: $115-$300 | XP: $25 | F18 |

Location: On SR 699, 2 mi n of Tom Stuart Cswy. 17120 Gulf Blvd 33708. Fax: 727/397-0699. **Facility:** 125 units. 124 one-bedroom standard units. 1 one-bedroom suite. 6 stories, interior corridors. **Parking:** on-site. **Terms:** 3 day cancellation notice. **Amenities:** dual phone lines, voice mail, honor bars, irons, hair dryers. **Pool(s):** heated outdoor. **Leisure Activities:** rental boats, volleyball. Fee: sailboats, windsurfing. **Guest Services:** gift shop, valet laundry. **Business Services:** meeting rooms, fax (fee). **Cards:** AX, CB, DC, DS, MC, VI.

SOME UNITS

[icons] FEE

RAMSEA

Phone: (727)397-0441   [173]

(AAA) [SAVE]

Condominium

| All Year Wkly | 1P: $600-$1320 | 2P: $600-$1320 | | |

Location: On SR 699, 1.6 mi s of jct Park Blvd (SR 694). 17200 Gulf Blvd 33708. Fax: 727/397-8894. **Facility:** 68 units. 6 one-, 19 two- and 43 three-bedroom suites with kitchens. 6 stories, exterior corridors. **Parking:** on-site. **Terms:** check-in 4 pm, 7 night minimum stay, 30 day cancellation notice-fee imposed. **Amenities:** safes (fee), irons. **Pool(s):** heated outdoor. **Leisure Activities:** whirlpool. Fee: cabanas, aquacycles, catamaran, hobiecats, jet skis. **Guest Services:** coin laundry. **Business Services:** fax (fee). **Cards:** DS, MC, VI. **Special Amenities: free newspaper. (See color ad below)**

[icons]

(See map p. 846)

SAILS RESORT MOTEL
Phone: 727/391-6000   170

| | 2/1-4/28 | 1P: $80-$150 | 2P: $80-$150 | XP: $12 |
| | 4/29-5/31 | 1P: $60-$100 | 2P: $60-$100 | XP: $10 |
Motel | 12/1-1/31 & 6/1-11/30 | 1P: $55-$80 | 2P: $55-$80 | XP: $10 |

Location: SR 699, 2 mi n of Tom Stuart Cswy. 17004 Gulf Blvd 33708. Fax: 727/391-6000. **Facility:** 24 units. 2 one-bedroom standard units with efficiencies. 22 one-bedroom suites with kitchens. 2 stories, exterior corridors. **Parking:** on-site. **Terms:** 21 day cancellation notice-fee imposed. **Pool(s):** heated outdoor. **Leisure Activities:** shuffleboard. **Guest Services:** coin laundry. **Business Services:** fax. **Cards:** DS, MC, VI.

SOME UNITS

──────── **WHERE TO DINE** ────────

THE FROG POND
Lunch: $6-$11
Phone: 727/392-4117   186

American
Location: On SR 699, 2 mi n on Tom Stuart Cswy. 16909 Gulf Blvd 33708. **Hours:** 7 am-2 pm, Sun from 8 am. Closed: 11/27, 12/25. **Features:** The decor dabbles equally in comfortable country and bright tropical at the local-favorite restaurant. Select from a wide variety of omelets, eggs Benedict and other breakfast staples, as well as burgers, sandwiches, soups and salads. Smoke free premises. Casual dress. **Parking:** on-site. **Cards:** DS, MC, VI.

OLDSMAR pop. 11,910 (See map p. 846; index p. 854)

──────── **WHERE TO STAY** ────────

HOLIDAY INN EXPRESS HOTEL & SUITES
Phone: (813)854-5080   235

| | 12/22-4/26 [ECP] | 1P: $119-$159 | 2P: $119-$159 | XP: $10 | F |
| | 12/1-12/21 & 4/27-11/30 [ECP] | 1P: $99-$129 | 2P: $99-$129 | XP: $10 | F |

Small-scale Hotel **Location:** Just s on Memorial Hwy (SR 580). 3990 Tampa Rd 34677. Fax: 813/854-5189. **Facility:** 81 one-bedroom standard units. 4 stories, interior corridors. **Bath:** combo or shower only. **Parking:** on-site. **Amenities:** high-speed Internet, voice mail, irons, hair dryers. **Pool(s):** outdoor. **Leisure Activities:** exercise room. **Business Services:** meeting rooms. **Cards:** AX, CB, DC, DS, JC, MC, VI.

SOME UNITS

──────── *The following lodging was either not evaluated or did not* ────────
meet AAA rating requirements but is listed for your information only.

COURTYARD BY MARRIOTT TAMPA-OLDSMAR
Phone: 813/925-8887

| fyi | 2/1-4/21 | 1P: $109-$129 | 2P: $109-$129 | XP: $10 | D18 |
| | 1/1-1/31 & 4/22-11/30 | 1P: $99-$109 | 2P: $109-$119 | XP: $10 | D18 |
Motel |

Too new to rate, opening scheduled for January 2003. **Location:** I-275, exit Memorial Hwy to Hillsborough Ave (becomes Tampa Rd). 4014 Tampa Rd 34677. Fax: 813/814-7884. **Amenities:** restaurant, coffeemakers, pool. **Terms:** open 1/1-11/30, cancellation fee imposed. **Cards:** AX, CB, DC, MC, VI.

PALM HARBOR pop. 59,248

──────── **WHERE TO STAY** ────────

FOUR POINTS BY SHERATON TARPON SPRINGS
Phone: (727)942-0358

AAA SAVE	1/15-4/15	1P: $98-$150	2P: $98-$150	XP: $10	F13
	4/16-11/30	1P: $88-$130	2P: $88-$130	XP: $10	F13
	12/1-1/14	1P: $83-$125	2P: $83-$125	XP: $10	F13

Location: On US 19, 3 mi s of jct SR 582. 37611 US 19 N 34684. Fax: 727/938-9826. **Facility:** 99 units. 98 one-bedroom standard units, some with whirlpools. 1 two-bedroom suite ($196-$360) with kitchen. 4 stories, exterior corridors. **Bath:** combo or shower only. **Parking:** on-site. **Terms:** cancellation fee imposed, pets ($15 extra charge). **Amenities:** voice mail, irons, hair dryers. **Dining:** 6:30 am-10:30 pm, cocktails. **Pool(s):** heated outdoor. **Leisure Activities:** whirlpool, putting green, exercise room. *Fee:* boats, pontoon. **Guest Services:** gift shop, valet and coin laundry. **Business Services:** meeting rooms, business center. **Cards:** AX, CB, DC, DS, JC, MC, VI.

SOME UNITS
FEE FEE

KNIGHTS INN-CLEARWATER/PALM HARBOR
Phone: 727/789-2002

| | 12/1-4/30 | | 2P: $45-$110 |
| | 5/1-11/30 | | 2P: $30-$49 |
Motel |

Location: 1.8 mi n of CR 752 (Tampa Rd). 34106 US 19 N 34684. Fax: 727/784-6206. **Facility:** 114 one-bedroom standard units, some with efficiencies. 1 story, exterior corridors. **Parking:** on-site. **Terms:** weekly rates available, small pets only ($10 extra charge). **Amenities:** safes (fee). *Some:* irons, hair dryers. **Pool(s):** heated outdoor. **Guest Services:** coin laundry. **Business Services:** fax (fee). **Cards:** AX, CB, DC, DS, MC, VI.

SOME UNITS

RED ROOF INN
Phone: (727)786-2529

| AAA SAVE | 12/31-4/15 | 1P: $63-$89 | 2P: $69-$95 | XP: $6 | F18 |
| | 12/1-12/30 & 4/16-11/30 | 1P: $53-$79 | 2P: $58-$85 | XP: $6 | F18 |
Motel |

Location: On US 19, 0.4 mi s of jct Tampa Rd. 32000 US 19 N 34684. Fax: 727/786-7462. **Facility:** 100 one-bedroom standard units, some with efficiencies. 2 stories, exterior corridors. **Bath:** combo or shower only. **Parking:** on-site. **Terms:** weekly rates available. **Amenities:** voice mail. *Some:* irons. **Pool(s):** heated outdoor. **Business Services:** fax (fee). **Cards:** AX, CB, DC, DS, MC, VI.

SOME UNITS

THE WESTIN INNISBROOK RESORT

Phone: (727)942-2000

AAA SAVE

12/1-4/16	1P: $189-$325	2P: $189-$325	XP: $20 F17
9/18-11/30	1P: $169-$285	2P: $169-$285	XP: $20 F17
4/17-5/28	1P: $149-$265	2P: $149-$265	XP: $20 F17
5/29-9/17	1P: $109-$185	2P: $109-$185	XP: $20 F17

Resort Condominium   Location: On US 19, 2.8 mi s of jct SR 582. 36750 US Hwy 19 N 34684. Fax: 727/942-5576. Facility: This golf resort is a complex of 25 buildings on 1,000 manicured acres. 605 units. 129 one-bedroom standard units, some with whirlpools. 476 one-bedroom suites ($365-$549) with kitchens. 3 stories (no elevator), interior corridors. Bath: combo or shower only. Parking: on-site. Terms: 3 day cancellation notice, package plans, $10 service charge. Amenities: video games, dual phone lines, voice mail, irons, hair dryers. Some: DVD players, CD players, honor bars. Dining: 4 restaurants, 6 am-midnight, cocktails. Pool(s): 6 heated outdoor. Leisure Activities: saunas, whirlpools, waterslide, fishing, putting green, miniature golf, night driving range, 3 pro shops, recreation programs, nature walk, water volleyball & equipment, jogging, playground, horseshoes. Fee: fishing equipment, golf-72 holes, golf instruction & equipment, 11 tennis courts (7 lighted), racquetball courts, tennis instruction & equipment, bicycles, massage, basketball. Guest Services: gift shop, valet and coin laundry, area transportation-beach. Business Services: conference facilities, business center. Cards: AX, CB, DC, DS, MC, VI. (See color ad p 5)

SOME UNITS

[icons]

---------- **WHERE TO DINE** ----------

THE BLUE HERON   Dinner: $17-$28   Phone: 727/789-5176

Seafood   Location: On SR 752 (Tampa Rd), 1 mi e of jct US 19; in Shoppes at Cloverplace. 3285 Tampa Rd 34684. Hours: 5 pm-10 pm, Fri & Sat-11 pm, Sun 5 pm-9 pm. Closed major holidays. Reservations: accepted. Features: Gracious service and elegant, intimate surroundings make entree choices such as snapper, salmon, grouper, duck and chicken that much more enjoyable. All dishes are well-prepared and nicely presented with a salad of mixed greens. The creative desserts are a must. Dressy casual; cocktails. Parking: on-site. Cards: AX, DC, DS, MC, VI.

SAINT LARRY   Dinner: $12-$21   Phone: 727/786-0077

Steak & Seafood   Location: Just s of jct Alderman Rd; in the Fountains. 34980 US 19 N 34684. Hours: 5 pm-10 pm. Closed: 12/25; also Sun. Features: Reminiscent of Greenwich Village, the upscale setting features original paintings by local artists and a carpet by surrealist Salvador Dali. Large portions of certified Angus beef, fresh seafood and quality produce have pleased the local community for many years. Casual dress; cocktails. Parking: on-site. Cards: AX, DC, DS, MC, VI.

THAI NANA   Lunch: $6-$7   Dinner: $8-$19   Phone: 727/787-0189

Thai   Location: US Alt 19 at jct Alderman Rd; in Crystal Beach Plaza. 2880 Alt 19 N 34683. Hours: 11 am-3 & 4:30-10 pm, Sat from 4:30 pm, Sun 4 pm-9 pm. Closed major holidays. Features: Spicy, stir-fried dishes are the mainstay of this traditional Thai restaurant. Fresh ingredients can be found in all the entrees, especially Thai salad with peanut dressing, pad Thai noodle and panang curry. Casual dress; beer & wine only. Parking: on-site. Cards: DS, MC, VI.

PINELLAS PARK   pop. 45,658   (See map p. 846; index p. 853)

---------- **WHERE TO STAY** ----------

DAYS INN GATEWAY   Phone: (727)577-3838   179

AAA SAVE

12/25-3/31	1P: $58	2P: $65
4/1-5/31	1P: $49	2P: $54
12/1-12/24 & 6/1-11/30	1P: $45	2P: $49

Small-scale Hotel   Location: I-275, exit 28, 1.4 mi e on Gandy Blvd, then 1.3 mi n on US 19. 9359 US 19 N 33782. Fax: 727/576-3790. Facility: 154 one-bedroom standard units. 2 stories, exterior corridors. Parking: on-site. Terms: pets ($6 extra charge). Pool(s): outdoor. Leisure Activities: putting green. Guest Services: coin laundry. Business Services: meeting rooms. Cards: AX, CB, DC, DS, MC, VI. Special Amenities: early check-in/late check-out and free newspaper.

SOME UNITS

[icons]   FEE   FEE

LA QUINTA INN-PINELLAS PARK   Phone: (727)545-5611   180

AAA SAVE

12/1-4/15 [ECP]	1P: $74-$90	2P: $79-$96
4/16-11/30 [ECP]	1P: $59-$79	2P: $65-$85

Small-scale Hotel   Location: I-275, exit 28, 1.4 mi s on Gandy Blvd (SR 694), just n. 7000 US Hwy 19N 33781. Fax: 727/544-4202. Facility: 116 units. 113 one-bedroom standard units. 3 one-bedroom suites. 3 stories, interior/exterior corridors. Parking: on-site. Terms: Small pets only. Amenities: video games, voice mail, irons, hair dryers. Pool(s): heated outdoor. Guest Services: valet and coin laundry. Business Services: meeting rooms, fax. Cards: AX, CB, DC, DS, JC, MC, VI. Special Amenities: free continental breakfast and free local telephone calls. (See color ad p 881)

SOME UNITS

[icons]   FEE

---------- **WHERE TO DINE** ----------

JOHNNY LEVEROCK'S SEAFOOD HOUSE   Lunch: $7-$21   Dinner: $7-$21   Phone: 727/526-9188   193

Steak & Seafood   Location: I-275, exit 28, 1.6 mi w on Gandy Blvd (SR 694), just s on US 19. 7000 US 19 N 33781. Hours: 11 am-10 pm. Closed: 11/27, 12/25. Features: This casual and popular restaurant has an interior rustic shanty theme which teems with the memorabilia of fisherman Johnny Leverock. The crunchy texture of the onion-crusted salmon and the light, sweet taste of the molasses bread are but two of the menu's palate tempters. Casual dress; cocktails. Parking: on-site. Cards: AX, DC, DS, MC, VI.

PLANT CITY pop. 29,915

——— WHERE TO STAY ———

COMFORT INN OF PLANT CITY
SAVE
▼▼▼▼
Small-scale Hotel

	1P:	2P:	
1/1-4/20 [ECP]	1P: $65-$105	2P: $75-$115	XP: $5	F18
12/1-12/31 & 4/21-11/30 [ECP]	1P: $50-$75	2P: $60-$85	XP: $5	F18

Phone: (813)707-6000

Location: I-4, exit 22, just e. 2003 S Frontage Rd 33566. Fax: 813/707-6081. **Facility:** 61 units. 52 one-bedroom standard units. 9 one-bedroom suites ($75-$125). 3 stories, interior corridors. *Bath:* combo or shower only. **Parking:** on-site. **Terms:** package plans. **Amenities:** dual phone lines, voice mail, irons, hair dryers. **Pool(s):** heated outdoor. **Leisure Activities:** whirlpool. **Guest Services:** valet and coin laundry. **Business Services:** meeting rooms, fax. **Cards:** AX, CB, DC, DS, JC, MC, VI.

SOME UNITS

DAYS INN PLANT CITY
SAVE
▼▼▼ ▼▼▼
Motel

	1P:	2P:	
12/1-4/30	1P: $85	2P: $95	XP: $5	F
5/1-11/30	1P: $65	2P: $70	XP: $5	F

Phone: (813)752-0570

Location: I-4, exit 13A; exit 13 eastbound, just e via Frontage Rd. 301 S Frontage Rd 33566. Fax: 813/754-3422. **Facility:** 174 one-bedroom standard units. 3 stories, exterior corridors. **Parking:** on-site. **Terms:** pets ($10 extra charge). **Amenities:** hair dryers. *Some:* irons. **Pool(s):** outdoor. **Leisure Activities:** playground, shuffleboard, volleyball. *Fee:* game room. **Guest Services:** coin laundry. **Business Services:** meeting rooms, PC, fax. **Cards:** AX, DS, MC, VI.

SOME UNITS

HOLIDAY INN EXPRESS PLANT CITY
▼▼▼▼
Small-scale Hotel

	1P:
12/1-5/31 [ECP]	1P: $89-$109
9/1-11/30 [ECP]	1P: $79-$99
6/1-8/31 [ECP]	1P: $69-$89

Phone: (813)719-3800

Location: I-4, exit 22, just e. 2102 N Park Rd 33566. Fax: 813/764-8381. **Facility:** 70 units. 54 one-bedroom standard units. 16 one-bedroom suites ($99-$139). 4 stories, interior corridors. *Bath:* combo or shower only. **Parking:** on-site. **Terms:** pets ($40 extra charge). **Amenities:** dual phone lines, voice mail, safes, irons, hair dryers. **Pool(s):** outdoor. **Leisure Activities:** exercise room. **Guest Services:** valet and coin laundry. **Business Services:** meeting rooms, fax. **Cards:** AX, DC, DS, JC, MC, VI.

SOME UNITS

——— WHERE TO DINE ———

ABC PIZZA HOUSE
▼
American

Lunch: $7-$18   **Dinner:** $7-$18   **Phone:** 813/752-5146
Location: Act jct W Reynolds St. 114 N Alexander 33566. **Hours:** 11 am-11 pm, Fri & Sat-midnight. **Features:** This pizza and sub restaurant has a casual, easy decor to match its simple menu of pizzas, grinders, pasta dishes, seafood entrees, sandwiches, gyros and numerous appetizers. Casual dress; beer & wine only. **Parking:** on-site. **Cards:** MC, VI.

ALL STAR GRILL
▼▼ ▼▼
American

Lunch: $5-$16   **Dinner:** $5-$16   **Phone:** 813/719-8187
Location: Just w of jct SR 39; in Lake Walden Square. 266 W Alexander Rd 33567. **Hours:** 10:45 am-2 am, Sun-midnight. Closed: 4/20, 11/27, 12/25. **Features:** The open and airy sports-themed restaurant has large-screen TVs, many pool tables and a game room area. Although the menu is limited to a handful of entrees, it's loaded with selections of sandwiches, salads, burgers and appetizers. Casual dress; cocktails. **Parking:** on-site. **Cards:** AX, MC, VI.

BEEF O'BRADY'S
▼▼ ▼▼
American

Lunch: $5-$7   **Dinner:** $5-$7   **Phone:** 813/757-0300
Location: SR 39, at jct Alexander St; in Walten Village Shopping Center. 2418 Jim Redman Pkwy 33566. **Hours:** 11 am-11 pm, Fri & Sat-11:30 pm, Sun noon-10 pm. **Features:** Big-screen televisions keep this family sports pub hopping on game days. The bustling spot cooks up traditional burgers, sandwiches, salads and wings. It features a terrific Philadelphia cheese steak served with fries and a pickle spear. Casual dress; beer & wine only. **Parking:** on-site. **Cards:** DS, MC, VI.

BRANCH RANCH DINING ROOM
▲▲▲
▼▼ ▼▼
American

Lunch: $6-$9   **Dinner:** $7-$18   **Phone:** 813/752-1957
Location: I-4, exit 17, 0.9 mi n on Branch Forbes Rd, just e. 5121 W Thonotosassa Rd 33565. **Hours:** 11:30 am-9 pm, Sun to 8 pm. Closed: Mon, Tues & 12/18-12/25. **Features:** Southern food served family-style has been the trademark of this family restaurant since 1956. Fried green tomatoes, homemade buttermilk biscuits with orange-pineapple marmalade or strawberry preserves and Southern fried chicken complement the blackboard specials. Casual dress; cocktails. **Parking:** on-site. **Cards:** AX, DS, MC, VI.

BUDDY FREDDY'S RESTAURANT
▼▼
American

Lunch: $6-$8   **Dinner:** $8-$11   **Phone:** 813/754-5120
Location: I-4, exit 19, 0.4 mi s on SR 566. 1101 Goldfinch Dr 33566. **Hours:** 7 am-9 pm. **Features:** A congenial atmosphere fills the popular, family-operated establishment. A flexible menu of home-style food allows for easy substitutions like replacing mashed potatoes with grits. Try the catfish for a real Florida feast. Also popular is the extensive buffet. Casual dress. **Parking:** on-site. **Cards:** AX, CB, DC, DS, MC, VI.

CHANCY'S CATFISH SHACK
▼▼
Seafood

Lunch: $4-$10   **Dinner:** $7-$17   **Phone:** 813/754-3433
Location: I-4, exit 22, just n. 2509 N Park Rd 33566. **Hours:** 11 am-9 pm, Fri & Sat-10 pm. Closed: Sun & Mon. **Features:** Lines of hungry patrons eager for a taste of good, reasonably priced food snake outside the door of this family-owned local favorite. Bring your appetite: whopping portions can easily overwhelm. Try the catfish fillets or the fried seaman's platter. Casual dress; beer & wine only. **Parking:** on-site.

HENRY B'S RESTAURANT

Lunch: $5-$18 **Dinner:** $5-$18 **Phone:** 813/707-9037

American

Location: Just e of jct SR 39 on US 92; downtown. 110 E Reynolds St 33566. **Hours:** 11 am-9 pm, Fri-10 pm, Sat noon-10 pm, Sun 11 am-2 pm. Closed: 11/27, 12/25. **Features:** The use of woods and copper fixtures brings about a '30s look to this cozy restaurant. The menu lines up an assortment of choices including pizza, sandwiches, steaks, seafood, Italian favorites, pasta dishes, stir-fry, salads, appetizers and desserts. Smoke free premises. Casual dress; cocktails. **Parking:** on-site. **Cards:** AX, DS, MC, VI.

PESO'S MEXICAN RESTAURANT

Lunch: $7-$11 **Dinner:** $7-$11 **Phone:** 813/752-8841

Mexican

Location: At jct N Lemon St. 2006 W Reynolds St, Suite 1 33567. **Hours:** 11 am-9 pm. Closed: 1/1, 11/27, 12/25. **Features:** The surroundings may be simple, but the food is simply excellent. Savor burritos, flautas, fajitas, chimichangas and combination platters. Smoke free premises. Casual dress; beer & wine only. **Parking:** on-site. **Cards:** AX, DS, MC, VI.

SHANGHAI CHINESE RESTAURANT

Lunch: $6-$11 **Dinner:** $6-$11 **Phone:** 813/759-0518

Chinese

Location: On SR 39; at E Alsobrook St. 805 S Collins St 33566. **Hours:** 11 am-9 pm. **Features:** An Oriental theme weaves through the dining room of this relaxed restaurant. A Mongolian grill is central to the buffet area, a tempting alternative to the main menu. Its extensive offerings include some 80 selections. Casual dress. **Parking:** on-site. **Cards:** AX, DC, MC, VI.

SNELLGROVES

Lunch: $6-$10 **Dinner:** $6-$10 **Phone:** 813/752-3652

American

Location: On SR 39; downtown. 109 S Collins St 33566. **Hours:** 6 am-9 pm. Closed major holidays; also Sun. **Features:** Reminiscent of the early '60s, this basic restaurant offers blue-plate meals, a salad bar and such home-cooked favorites as fried chicken, liver and onions, meatloaf and pork chops. Casual dress. **Parking:** street. **Cards:** DC, MC, VI.

TIME OUT SPORTS GRILL

Lunch: $6-$11 **Dinner:** $6-$11 **Phone:** 813/759-2233

American

Location: On SR 39, just s. 1707 James L Redmond Pkwy 33566. **Hours:** 11 am-11:30 pm, Fri & Sat-2 am. **Features:** This casual sports themed restaurant offers one of the best fried catfish sandwiches that you'll find in these parts. Also popular for their buffalo wings, you'll enjoy a relaxing atmosphere, friendly service and good food while watching various sports events on any one of the numerous monitors stationed about the dining room. Casual dress; cocktails. **Parking:** on-site. **Cards:** MC, VI.

WOODY'S BARBECUE

Lunch: $5-$8 **Dinner:** $7-$16 **Phone:** 813/754-3229

American

Location: Just s of jct SR 39; in Lake Walden Square. 203 W Alexander 33566. **Hours:** 11 am-9 pm, Fri & Sat-10 pm. Closed major holidays. **Features:** Forget the formality of tablecloths, and eat with a laid-back attitude. Take in the rustic decor and enjoy down-home barbecue chicken, ribs and pork. Hearty portions are coated in a tasty sauce and served with coleslaw, baked beans and garlic toast. Casual dress; beer & wine only. **Parking:** on-site. **Cards:** AX, DS, MC, VI.

PORT RICHEY pop. 3,021

—— **WHERE TO STAY** ——

COMFORT INN

SAVE

Motel

Phone: (727)863-3336

	1P	2P	XP	
2/1-4/20 [ECP]	1P: $60-$89	2P: $60-$89	XP: $7	F18
4/21-11/30 [ECP]	1P: $52-$79	2P: $52-$79	XP: $6	F18
12/1-1/31 [ECP]	1P: $50-$79	2P: $50-$79	XP: $6	F18

Location: On US 19, just s of jct SR 52. 11810 US 19 34668. Fax: 727/863-3336. **Facility:** 98 one-bedroom standard units. 2 stories, exterior corridors. **Parking:** on-site. **Terms:** check-in 4 pm, pets ($6 extra charge). **Amenities:** Some: dual phone lines, irons, hair dryers. **Pool(s):** heated outdoor. **Guest Services:** coin laundry. **Business Services:** fax (fee). **Cards:** AX, CB, DC, DS, JC, MC, VI.

HOLIDAY INN EXPRESS HOTEL & SUITES

Small-scale Hotel

Phone: (727)869-9999

	1P
2/1-3/31	1P: $90-$140
1/1-1/31	1P: $80-$120
12/1-12/31 & 4/1-11/30	1P: $70-$110

Location: On US 19, 1 mi s of SR 52. 10826 US 19 N 34668. Fax: 727/861-0941. **Facility:** 110 units. 103 one-bedroom standard units, some with efficiencies. 7 one-bedroom suites with efficiencies. 2 stories, exterior corridors. **Bath:** combo or shower only. **Parking:** on-site. **Terms:** check-in 4 pm, [ECP] meal plan available. **Amenities:** video games, voice mail, irons, hair dryers. **Pool(s):** heated outdoor. **Leisure Activities:** whirlpool, steamroom, playground, exercise room. **Guest Services:** valet and coin laundry. **Business Services:** meeting rooms, fax. **Cards:** AX, CB, DC, DS, JC, MC, VI.

TRAVELODGE SUITES

Small-scale Hotel

Phone: (727)863-1502

	1P	2P
3/1-4/1	1P: $60-$80	2P: $60-$80
12/1-2/28 & 4/2-11/30	1P: $50-$80	2P: $50-$80

Location: US 19, just s of jct SR 52. 11736 US Hwy 19 N 34668. Fax: 727/378-0003. **Facility:** 151 one-bedroom standard units, some with kitchens. 2 stories, exterior corridors. **Parking:** on-site. **Terms:** 7 day cancellation notice, pets ($5 extra charge). **Amenities:** safes (fee), hair dryers. **Pool(s):** heated outdoor. **Guest Services:** coin laundry. **Business Services:** meeting rooms, fax. **Cards:** AX, CB, DC, DS, MC, VI.

REDINGTON BEACH pop. 1,539   (See map p. 846; index p. 854)

———— WHERE TO STAY ————

EL MOROCCO RESORT MOTEL   Phone: 727/391-1675   `187`

AAA **SAVE**   All Year Wkly   1P: $295-$455   2P: $295-$455
◆◆◆◆   **Location:** On SR 699, 1.3 mi n of Tom Stuart Cswy. 16333 Gulf Blvd 33708. Fax: 727/391-1675. **Facility:** Desig-
         nated smoking area. 18 one-bedroom standard units, some with efficiencies. 2 stories, exterior corridors.
Motel   **Parking:** on-site. **Terms:** 14 day cancellation notice-fee imposed, $25 service charge. **Amenities:** Some
         irons. **Pool(s):** outdoor. **Leisure Activities:** sun deck, shuffleboard. **Cards:** MC, VI.

SOME UNITS
🍴 🏊 ✕ 🛗 / 🖥 /

REDINGTON SHORES pop. 2,338   (See map p. 846; index p. 854)

———— WHERE TO STAY ————

SAN REMO RESORT   Phone: (727)320-9306   `230`

◆◆◆ ◆◆◆   12/15-4/30 Wkly   1P: $995-$1345   2P: $995-$1345
          5/1-8/15 Wkly   1P: $795-$1095   2P: $795-$1095
Condominium 12/1-12/14 & 8/16-11/30 Wkly 1P: $695-$895   2P: $695-$895
          Location: SR 699, 3 mi n of Pinellas Bayway. 18320 Gulf Blvd 33708. Fax: 727/320-9207. **Facility:** 35 units. 30
two- and 5 three-bedroom suites with kitchens. 7 stories, interior corridors. **Parking:** on-site. **Terms:** 3-7 night minimum stay -
seasonal, 3 day cancellation notice-fee imposed, $75 service charge, pets (small dogs only). **Amenities:** voice mail, irons, hair
dryers. **Pool(s):** heated outdoor. **Leisure Activities:** whirlpool, exercise room, volleyball. **Guest Services:** coin laundry. **Business Services:** fax. **Cards:** MC, VI.

SOME UNITS
ASK 🐾 🐕 🍴 🏊 ✕ 🖥 🛗 🖥 / ✕ /

———— WHERE TO DINE ————

THE LOBSTER POT   **Dinner:** $16-$46   Phone: 727/391-8592   `237`

AAA   **Location:** On SR 699; 1 mi s of jct Park Blvd (CR 694). 17814 Gulf Blvd 33708. **Hours:** 4:30 pm-10 pm, Fri &
◆◆◆◆◆   Sat-11 pm, Sun 4 pm-10 pm. Closed major holidays; also Super Bowl Sun. **Reservations:** suggested.
         Features: A block from the gulf, this popular restaurant offers a fine dining experience in a rustic setting
Seafood   with formal touches. Select from a wide variety of dishes including fresh seafood, lobster and steak. The
         lobster bisque is superb, and bouillabaisse Marseille is a must try. Dressy casual; cocktails. **Parking:** valet
         and street. **Cards:** AX, DC, DS, MC, VI.
                                                                                       ✕

RIVERVIEW (HILLSBOROUGH COUNTY)   (See map p. 856; index p. 862)

———— WHERE TO STAY ————

BIANCHI MOTEL   Phone: (813)677-1829   `95`
AAA **SAVE**   XP: $5   F12
◆◆◆   All Year   1P: $35-$45   2P: $40-$65
         Location: I-75, exit 254, 3.1 mi to US 301 southbound; 1.6 mi s northbound exit. 6425 US 301 S 33569.
Motel   Fax: 813/677-6550. **Facility:** 15 one-bedroom standard units, some with efficiencies. 1 story, exterior corri-
         dors. *Bath:* shower only. **Parking:** on-site. **Terms:** 14 day cancellation notice-fee imposed, package plans -
         seasonal. **Pool(s):** outdoor. **Cards:** DS, MC, VI.
                                                                              SOME UNITS
🐾 🏊 📺 🛗 / ✕ 🖥 🖵 /

———— WHERE TO DINE ————

ABC PIZZA   **Lunch:** $7-$18   **Dinner:** $7-$18   Phone: 813/677-8465   `100`
◆◆◆   **Location:** 0.5 mi n of jct Riverview Dr. 7210 SR 301 33569. **Hours:** 11 am-10 pm, Fri & Sat-11 pm. Closed:
         11/27, 12/25; also Sun. **Features:** The pizza and sub restaurant has a casual, easy decor to match its
American simple menu of pizzas, grinders, pasta dishes, seafood entrees, sandwiches, gyros and numerous
         appetizers. Casual dress; cocktails. **Parking:** on-site. **Cards:** MC, VI.

BEEF 'O' BRADY'S   **Lunch:** $5-$7   **Dinner:** $5-$7   Phone: 813/672-9464   `101`
◆◆◆   **Location:** On US 301; at jct Gibsonton Rd. 9622 US 301 S 33569. **Hours:** 11 am-11 pm, Sun noon-10 pm.
         Closed: 11/27, 12/25. **Features:** Dozens of TVs and favorite sports bar foods like burgers, sandwiches and
American wings make this a locals' hangout. Casual dining from plastic baskets is the norm, so feel free to dress
down. Try the Philly cheese steak paired with a hearty order of onion rings. Casual dress; beer & wine
only. **Parking:** on-site. **Cards:** AX, DC, DS, MC, VI.
                                                                                       🍸 ✕

RUSKIN pop. 8,321

———— WHERE TO STAY ————

BAHIA BEACH ISLAND RESORT & MARINA   Phone: (813)645-3291
AAA **SAVE**   1/1-4/30   1P: $99-$119   2P: $99-$119   XP: $10   F18
◆◆◆◆◆   5/1-9/30   1P: $89-$119   2P: $89-$119   XP: $10   F18
         12/1-12/31 & 10/1-11/30 1P: $79-$99   2P: $79-$99   XP: $10   F18
Motel   **Location:** 3.5 mi w of US 41 via Shell Point Rd, follow signs. Located in rural area on Old Tampa Bay. 611 Destiny Dr
         33570. Fax: 813/641-1589. **Facility:** 94 units. 92 one-bedroom standard units, some with efficiencies or
         kitchens. 2 one-bedroom suites with kitchens and whirlpools. 2 stories, interior/exterior corridors. *Bath:*
combo or shower only. **Parking:** on-site. **Terms:** small pets only ($25 extra charge, 1st floor smoking units). **Amenities:** voice
mail, irons, hair dryers. **Dining:** 2 restaurants, 8 am-9 pm, Fri & Sat-10 pm, cocktails, also, Tropics Restaurant, see separate
listing. **Leisure Activities:** whirlpool, fishing, fishing pier, 5 tennis courts (3 lighted), sand volleyball, helicopter pad, picnic area, playground, basketball, horseshoes, shuffleboard. *Fee:* marina
tennis club on-site,, sand volleyball, helicopter pad, picnic area, playground, basketball, horseshoes, shuffleboard. *Fee:* marina
tennis lessons. **Guest Services:** gift shop, coin laundry. **Business Services:** meeting rooms, fax (fee). **Cards:** AX, CB, DC, DS,
MC, VI.
                                                                              SOME UNITS
🐾 🐕 🍴 🍸 ♿ 🛗 📷 🏊 ✕ 📺 🖥 🛗 🖥 🖵 / ✕ /

HOLIDAY INN EXPRESS

Motel

Phone: (813)641-3437

1/27-3/31	2P: $99
12/22-1/26	2P: $89
12/1-12/21	2P: $81
4/1-11/30	2P: $79

Location: I-75, exit 240 northbound, just w at jct 33rd St SE. 3113 College Ave 33570. Fax: 813/641-3213. **Facility:** 55 one-bedroom standard units. 3 stories, interior corridors. *Bath:* combo or shower only. **Parking:** on-site. **Terms:** cancellation fee imposed, weekly rates available, [ECP] meal plan available. **Amenities:** dual phone lines, voice mail, safes, irons, hair dryers. **Pool(s):** outdoor. **Guest Services:** coin laundry. **Business Services:** meeting rooms, fax. **Cards:** AX, DS, MC, VI.

SOME UNITS

SOUTHERN COMFORT BED & BREAKFAST

Bed & Breakfast

Phone: 813/645-6361

12/1-5/1 & 11/1-11/30 [BP]	2P: $55-$95	XP: $10
5/2-10/31 [BP]	2P: $50-$85	XP: $10

Location: Jct US 41, 1.1 mi sw on 1st St, just w on 24th Ave S. Located in quiet, rural, residential area. 2409 Ravine Dr W 33570. Fax: 813/645-7375. **Facility:** This 6,800-square-foot country home shaded by large trees features a tennis court and putting green. Designated smoking area. 5 one-bedroom standard units, some with efficiencies. 1 story, interior/exterior corridors. *Bath:* combo or shower only. **Parking:** on-site. **Terms:** 2 night minimum stay, age restrictions may apply, cancellation fee imposed. **Amenities:** *Some:* irons, hair dryers. **Pool(s):** outdoor. **Leisure Activities:** sauna, whirlpool, putting green, lighted tennis court, exercise room. **Guest Services:** complimentary laundry. **Business Services:** meeting rooms, PC, fax. **Cards:** MC, VI.

SOME UNITS

———— WHERE TO DINE ————

BUDDY FREDDY'S COUNTRY BUFFET

American

Lunch: $5-$7   **Dinner:** $5-$8   **Phone:** 813/641-2241

Location: I-75, exit 240 northbound; exit 240B southbound, just w; in Sun Point. 3074 College Ave 33570. **Hours:** 11:30 am-7:30 pm. **Features:** The atmosphere is casual and contemporary in the congenial restaurant. The food is all-you-can-eat home-style cooking: fried chicken, meatloaf, liver, fresh vegetables, homemade mashed potatoes, salad bar fixings and a dessert bar with cake, pie and ice cream. Smoke free premises. Casual dress. **Parking:** on-site. **Cards:** AX, DS, MC, VI.

THE GOLDEN BUDDHA

Chinese

Lunch: $6-$15   **Dinner:** $6-$15   **Phone:** 813/645-7730

Location: 1 mi s of jct Apollo Beach Blvd. 5813 US 41 N 33570. **Hours:** 11 am-9:30 pm, Sat & Sun from noon. **Features:** Basic but welcoming and friendly service is offered at this small local favorite. The all-you-can-eat Chinese buffet is a popular attraction, but a standard menu—which includes chicken, beef, seafood and pork items—is also available. Peking duck is a favorite selection, as is General Tso's chicken in a spicy, flavorful sauce. Casual dress; cocktails. **Parking:** on-site. **Cards:** AX, DC, MC, VI.

TROPICS RESTAURANT

American

Lunch: $5-$9   **Dinner:** $11-$16   **Phone:** 813/645-3291

Location: 3.5 mi w of US 41 via Shell Point Rd, follow signs; in Bahia Beach Island Resort & Marina. 611 Destiny Dr 33570. **Hours:** 8 am-2 & 4-9 pm, Fri & Sat-10 pm, Sunday brunch 11 am- 2:30 pm. **Features:** Diners who patronize this locally favorite restaurant on Old Tampa Bay are in for a treat. This place is noted for its Wednesday and Friday night seafood buffets, its Saturday night prime rib buffet and its Sunday brunch. An a la carte menu also is available. Casual dress; cocktails. **Parking:** on-site. **Cards:** AX, DC, DS, MC, VI.

SAFETY HARBOR pop. 17,203   (See map p. 846; index p. 854)

─────── WHERE TO STAY ───────

SAFETY HARBOR RESORT AND SPA ON TAMPA BAY   Phone: (727)726-1161   184

(AAA) (SAVE)

▼▼▼▼▼

1/1-4/30	1P: $129-$209	2P: $129-$209	XP: $10 F17
12/1-12/31 & 10/1-11/30	1P: $99-$189	2P: $99-$189	XP: $10 F17
5/1-9/30	1P: $89-$179	2P: $89-$179	XP: $10 F17

Location: At jct SR 590 (Main St); downtown. 105 N Bayshore Dr 34695. Fax: 727/726-4268. **Facility:** On extensive, manicured grounds facing Tampa Bay, this property offers a spa, a fitness studio and recreational facilities. 189 units. 185 one-bedroom standard units. 4 one-bedroom suites ($250-$750) with whirlpools. 6 stories, interior corridors. *Bath:* combo or shower only. **Parking:** on-site. **Terms:** 3 day cancellation notice-fee imposed, $10 service charge, small pets only ($35 extra charge). **Amenities:** dual phone lines, voice mail, irons, hair dryers. **Dining:** 7 am-1 am, cocktails. **Pool(s):** 3 heated outdoor. **Leisure Activities:** saunas, whirlpools, steamrooms, fishing, 9 tennis courts (6 lighted), recreation programs, bicycles, playground, spa, volleyball. *Fee:* tennis & golf academy, driving range, mineral springs, salon, theater, hammock park. **Guest Services:** gift shop, valet and coin laundry, area transportation (fee). **Business Services:** conference facilities, business center. **Cards:** AX, DC, DS, MC, VI. **Special Amenities:** early check-in/late check-out and free newspaper. *(See ad below)*

Resort
Small-scale Hotel

SOME UNITS

[icons] FEE   FEE

─────── WHERE TO DINE ───────

ENVER'S PARADISE RESTAURANT   **Lunch:** $4-$9   **Dinner:** $4-$9   **Phone:** 727/725-1208   199
▼   **Location:** On SR 590 (Main St); downtown. 443 Main St 34695. **Hours:** 7 am-9 pm, Sun 7:30 am-8 pm.
American   **Features:** This family-oriented restaurant features an eclectic menu that includes sandwiches, burgers, steaks, seafood and such Greek favorites as moussaka and grape leaves. Desserts, particularly the bread and rice pudding, are a treat. Casual dress; beer & wine only. **Parking:** on-site. **Cards:** MC, VI.   [X]

ST. PETE BEACH pop. 9,929 (See map p. 846; index p. 849)

──────── WHERE TO STAY ────────

ALDEN BEACH RESORT

Phone: (727)360-7081   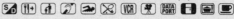29

				XP:	
AAA SAVE	2/1-4/30	1P: $187-$274	2P: $187-$274	XP: $10	F12
▼▼▼▼	5/1-8/31	1P: $135-$189	2P: $135-$189	XP: $10	F12
	12/1-1/31	1P: $125-$179	2P: $125-$179	XP: $10	F12
	9/1-11/30	1P: $119-$172	2P: $119-$172	XP: $10	F12

Resort
Small-scale Hotel
Location: SR 699, 1.7 mi n of Pinellas Bayway. 5900 Gulf Blvd 33706. Fax: 727/360-5957. **Facility:** Facing the gulf on five lushly landscaped acres, this property offers covered parking and 10 types of accommodations. 143 one-bedroom suites with kitchens. 1-6 stories, exterior corridors. **Parking:** on-site. **Terms:** check-in 4 pm, cancellation fee imposed. **Amenities:** video library (fee), voice mail, safes, irons, hair dryers. **Pool(s):** 2 heated outdoor. **Leisure Activities:** whirlpools, 2 lighted tennis courts, cookout deck with gas barbecue grills, ping pong, playground, basketball, shuffleboard, volleyball. *Fee:* sailboats, charter fishing, cabanas, kayak, water trikes, parasailing, game room. **Guest Services:** coin laundry. **Business Services:** meeting rooms, fax. **Cards:** AX, DC, DS, MC, VI. **Special Amenities:** free newspaper.
(See color ad below)

BEACH HAVEN

Phone: 727/367-8642   28

				XP:	
AAA SAVE	2/1-4/30	1P: $90-$147	2P: $90-$147	XP: $10	F3
▼▼▼	12/1-1/31	1P: $80-$122	2P: $80-$122	XP: $10	F3
	5/1-8/10	1P: $68-$110	2P: $68-$110	XP: $10	F3
	9/8-11/30	1P: $58-$95	2P: $58-$95	XP: $10	F3

Motel
Location: SR 699, 1 mi n of Pinellas Bayway. 4080 Gulf Blvd 33706. Fax: 727/360-8202. **Facility:** Designated smoking area. 18 units. 17 one- and 1 two-bedroom standard units, some with kitchens and/or whirlpools. 1 story, exterior corridors. *Bath:* combo or shower only. **Parking:** on-site. **Terms:** 3-5 night minimum stay - weekends, [CP] meal plan available. **Amenities:** video library. *Some:* irons, hair dryers. **Pool(s):** heated outdoor. **Leisure Activities:** beach deck, croquet & barbecue grills, volleyball. **Guest Services:** coin laundry. **Business Services:** fax (fee). **Cards:** AX, DS, MC, VI.

SOME UNITS

BEACH HOUSE SUITES BY THE DON CESAR

Phone: (727)363-0001   30

				XP:	
AAA SAVE	2/14-4/30	1P: $272-$419	2P: $272-$419	XP: $15	F18
▼▼▼	12/1-2/13 & 10/1-11/30	1P: $209-$345	2P: $209-$345	XP: $15	F18
	5/1-9/30	1P: $193-$324	2P: $193-$324	XP: $15	F18

Small-scale Hotel
Location: SR 699, 0.4 mi n of jct Pinellas Bayway. 3860 Gulf Blvd 33706. Fax: 727/363-5055. **Facility:** 70 one-bedroom suites with kitchens. 6 stories, exterior corridors. **Parking:** on-site. **Terms:** check-in 4 pm, 5 day cancellation notice-fee imposed, [BP] meal plan available. **Amenities:** voice mail, safes, irons, hair dryers. *Some:* CD players. **Pool(s):** heated outdoor. **Leisure Activities:** whirlpool, sun deck, hobie cats, picnic area, sand volleyball, shuffleboard. *Fee:* windsurfing, scuba diving, charter fishing, banana boat, cabanas, kayaks, sailing lessons, massage. **Guest Services:** gift shop, complimentary laundry, area transportation. **Business Services:** meeting rooms, fax.

SOME UNITS

(See map p. 846)

BEST WESTERN BEACHFRONT RESORT
Phone: (727)367-1902 〔34〕

AAA *SAVE*

2/1-4/26	1P: $168-$208	2P: $168-$208	XP: $20	F17
12/1-1/31 & 4/27-11/30	1P: $108-$188	2P: $108-$188	XP: $12	F17

Motel

Location: SR 699, 2 mi n of Pinellas Bayway. 6200 Gulf Blvd 33706. Fax: 727/367-4422. **Facility:** 102 one-bedroom standard units, some with kitchens. 2 stories, exterior corridors. **Parking:** on-site. **Terms:** check-in 4 pm, 3 day cancellation notice-fee imposed. **Amenities:** safes (fee), irons, hair dryers. **Dining:** 2 restaurants, noon-midnight, cocktails, entertainment. **Pool(s):** 2 heated outdoor. **Leisure Activities:** fishing. *Fee:* windsurfing, cabanas, catamarans, jet skis, parasailing, water bikes & instruction, game room. **Guest Services:** valet laundry. **Business Services:** fax (fee). **Cards:** AX, CB, DC, DS, JC, MC, VI. **Special Amenities: early check-in/late check-out & free room upgrade (subject to availability with advanced reservations).**

SOME UNITS

CAPRICE CONDOMINIUMS ON ST. PETE BEACH
Phone: 727/360-6199 〔32〕

2/1-4/30 Wkly	1P: $1075	2P: $1450
5/1-10/31 Wkly	1P: $800	2P: $1050
12/1-1/31 & 11/1-11/30 Wkly	1P: $725	2P: $975

Condominium

Location: Just w of Gulf Blvd (SR 699) at jct 70th Ave. 6950 Beach Plaza St 33706. Fax: 727/363-8707. **Facility:** 35 units. 10 one- and 25 two-bedroom suites with kitchens. 6 stories, exterior corridors. **Parking:** on-site. **Terms:** 3-7 night minimum stay, 30 day cancellation notice. **Amenities:** video library, voice mail, irons. *Some:* DVD players, CD players, safes, hair dryers. **Pool(s):** heated outdoor. **Leisure Activities:** exercise room, volleyball. **Guest Services:** coin laundry. **Business Services:** fax. **Cards:** AX, DS, MC, VI.

SOME UNITS

THE DON CESAR BEACH RESORT & SPA
Phone: (727)360-1881 〔45〕

AAA *SAVE*

2/14-4/30	1P: $282-$2245	2P: $282-$2245	XP: $15	F18
12/1-2/13 & 10/1-11/30	1P: $240-$1818	2P: $240-$1818	XP: $15	F18
5/1-9/30	1P: $214-$1667	2P: $214-$1667	XP: $15	F18

Resort
Large-scale Hotel

Location: On SR 699; at jct Pinellas Bayway. 3400 Gulf Blvd 33706. Fax: 727/367-6952. **Facility:** Set on the gulf, the resort boasts large, lavishly decorated public areas, rooms with a gulf view and numerous specialty boutiques. 277 units. 257 one-bedroom standard units. 18 one- and 2 two-bedroom suites ($282-$2245). 10 stories, interior corridors. *Bath:* combo or shower only. **Parking:** on-site and valet. **Terms:** check-in 4 pm, 5 day cancellation notice-fee imposed, [BP] meal plan available. **Amenities:** video games, CD players, dual phone lines, voice mail, safes, honor bars, irons, hair dryers. **Dining:** 3 restaurants, 7 am-7 pm, cocktails, also, Maritana Grille, Sea Porch Cafe, see separate listing, entertainment. **Pool(s):** 2 heated outdoor. **Leisure Activities:** sauna, whirlpools, steamroom, rental paddleboats, water aerobics, recreation programs, aerobic classes, yoga classes, playground, spa, shuffleboard, volleyball. *Fee:* sailboats, windsurfing, charter fishing, cabana, water bikes, catamarans, parasails, waverunners, golf privileges, game room. **Guest Services:** gift shop, valet and coin laundry, area transportation-golf course & charters. **Business Services:** conference facilities, business center. **Cards:** AX, CB, DC, DS, MC, VI.

SOME UNITS
FEE FEE FEE

HOLIDAY INN HOTEL & SUITES BEACHFRONT RESORT & CONFERENCE CENTER
Phone: (727)360-1811 〔39〕

1/3-4/17	1P: $168-$228	2P: $168-$228	XP: $10	F19
12/1-1/2 & 4/18-11/30	1P: $148-$228	2P: $148-$228	XP: $10	F19

Large-scale Hotel

Location: On SR 699, 1 mi n of Pinellas Bayway. 5250 Gulf Blvd 33706. Fax: 727/360-6919. **Facility:** 156 one-bedroom standard units. 11 stories, interior corridors. *Bath:* combo or shower only. **Parking:** on-site. **Terms:** check-in 4 pm, cancellation fee imposed, 11% service charge. **Amenities:** voice mail, safes, irons, hair dryers. **Pool(s):** heated outdoor. **Leisure Activities:** exercise room. *Fee:* sailboats, windsurfing, waterskiing, snorkeling, charter fishing, game room. **Guest Services:** gift shop, valet and coin laundry. **Business Services:** meeting rooms, fax (fee). **Cards:** AX, DC, DS, JC, MC, VI. **(See color ad opposite inside back cover)**

SOME UNITS
FEE

HOWARD JOHNSON LODGE ST PETE BEACH RESORT INN
Phone: (727)360-7041 〔35〕

2/1-4/30	1P: $115-$140	2P: $115-$140	XP: $10	F18
12/1-1/31 & 5/1-11/30	1P: $95-$120	2P: $95-$120	XP: $10	F18

Small-scale Hotel

Location: SR 699, 1.8 mi n of Pinellas Bayway. 6100 Gulf Blvd 33706. Fax: 727/360-8941. **Facility:** 133 units. 123 one- and 10 two-bedroom standard units, some with kitchens (no utensils) and/or whirlpools. 5 stories, interior corridors. **Parking:** on-site. **Terms:** age restrictions may apply. **Amenities:** safes (fee), irons, hair dryers. **Pool(s):** heated outdoor, wading. **Leisure Activities:** shuffleboard. *Fee:* game room. **Guest Services:** gift shop, valet and coin laundry. **Business Services:** meeting rooms. **Cards:** AX, CB, DC, DS, JC, MC, VI.

SOME UNITS

ISLAND'S END RESORT
Phone: 727/360-5023 〔46〕

AAA *SAVE*

1/1-5/31	1P: $171-$259	2P: $171-$259	XP: $15
6/1-9/14	1P: $155-$259	2P: $155-$259	XP: $15
9/15-11/30	1P: $132-$259	2P: $132-$259	XP: $15
12/1-12/31	1P: $96-$237	2P: $96-$237	XP: $15

Cottage

Location: South end of island, 2 mi s of Pinellas Bayway. Located in Pass-A-Grille section. 1 Pass-A-Grille Way 33706. Fax: 727/367-7890. **Facility:** 6 units. 5 one- and 1 three-bedroom suites with kitchens, some with whirlpools. 1 story, exterior corridors. **Parking:** on-site. **Terms:** check-in 4 pm, 14 day cancellation notice-fee imposed, [CP] meal plan available. **Amenities:** video library (fee), voice mail, safes, irons, hair dryers. **Leisure Activities:** fishing, sun deck, private fishing pier, gas barbecue grills. **Guest Services:** coin laundry. **Business Services:** fax. **Cards:** MC, VI. **Special Amenities: free continental breakfast and free local telephone calls.**

(See map p. 846)

LAMARA MOTEL APARTMENTS
Phone: (727)360-7521 25

AAA SAVE ◆◆◆◆ Motel

	1P:$70-$80	2P:$70-$80	XP:$8	F5
1/1-4/30				
12/1-12/31 & 5/1-11/30	1P:$50-$75	2P:$50-$75	XP:$8	F5

Location: Just w of Gulf Blvd (SR 699). 520 73rd Ave 33706. Fax: 727/363-0193. **Facility:** 16 one-bedroom standard units with kitchens (no utensils). 2 stories, exterior corridors. *Bath:* combo or shower only. **Parking:** on-site. **Terms:** 7 day cancellation notice, 5/1-12/31, 30 day 1/1-4/30-fee imposed, weekly rates available, small pets only. **Amenities:** *Some:* irons, hair dryers. **Pool(s):** heated outdoor. **Leisure Activities:** recreation programs, barbecue grill, playground, shuffleboard. **Guest Services:** coin laundry. **Business Services:** fax (fee). **Cards:** AX, MC, VI. **Special Amenities:** early check-in/late check-out and free local telephone calls.

SOME UNITS

LONG KEY BEACH RESORT
Phone: (727)360-1748 33

AAA SAVE ◆◆◆ Motel

2/1-4/30	1P:$122-$131	2P:$122-$131	XP:$5	F5
12/15-1/31 & 5/1-11/30	1P:$90-$104	2P:$90-$104	XP:$5	F5
12/1-12/14	1P:$69-$79	2P:$69-$79	XP:$5	F5

Location: On SR 699, 0.3 mi n of jct Pinellas Bayway. 3828 Gulf Blvd 33706. Fax: 727/360-9026. **Facility:** Designated smoking area. 16 units. 1 one-bedroom standard unit. 15 one-bedroom suites with kitchens. 1-2 stories, exterior corridors. **Parking:** on-site. **Terms:** 30 day cancellation notice. **Amenities:** hair dryers. *Some:* irons. **Pool(s):** heated outdoor. **Leisure Activities:** whirlpool, sun deck, shuffleboard. **Guest Services:** coin laundry. **Business Services:** fax. **Cards:** AX, MC, VI.

SOME UNITS

PALM CREST RESORT MOTEL
Phone: (727)360-9327 40

AAA SAVE ◆◆◆ ◆◆◆ Motel

2/1-4/30	1P:$89-$132	XP:$6	F5
5/1-11/30	1P:$64-$98	XP:$6	F5
12/20-1/31	1P:$69-$89	XP:$6	F5
12/1-12/19	1P:$61-$84	XP:$6	F5

Location: SR 699, 0.5 mi n of Pinellas Bayway. 3848 Gulf Blvd 33706. Fax: 727/367-1073. **Facility:** 18 one-bedroom standard units with efficiencies. 2 stories, exterior corridors. **Parking:** on-site. **Terms:** 2-5 night minimum stay - seasonal, weekends, 14 day cancellation notice, weekly rates available, $6 service charge. **Amenities:** *Some:* irons, hair dryers. **Pool(s):** heated outdoor. **Leisure Activities:** gas grill, shuffleboard. **Guest Services:** coin laundry. **Business Services:** fax. **Cards:** AX, DC, DS, MC, VI.

PASA TIEMPO BED & BREAKFAST
Phone: (727)367-9907 26

AAA SAVE ◆◆◆◆ Bed & Breakfast

| 12/1-5/31 & 10/1-11/30 | 1P:$125-$200 | 2P:$125-$200 | XP:$25 | |
| 6/1-9/30 | 1P:$110-$185 | 2P:$110-$185 | XP:$25 | |

Location: Jct SR 699, just e on 72nd Ave. 7141 Bay St 33706. Fax: 727/367-9906. **Facility:** On Intracoastal Waterway. Designated smoking area. 10 units. 2 one-bedroom standard units. 8 one-bedroom suites, some with kitchens and/or whirlpools. 2 stories, exterior corridors. *Bath:* combo or shower only. **Parking:** on-site. **Terms:** age restrictions may apply, 7 day cancellation notice, [ECP] meal plan available. **Amenities:** dual phone lines, voice mail, irons, hair dryers. **Pool(s):** heated outdoor. **Leisure Activities:** boat dock, patio. **Business Services:** meeting rooms, fax. **Cards:** AX, MC, VI. **Special Amenities:** free continental breakfast and free local telephone calls.

SOME UNITS

(See map p. 846)

PLAZA BEACH MOTEL
AAA [SAVE]

2/1-4/28	1P: $89-$120	2P: $89-$120	XP: $7	F4
4/29-9/3	1P: $65-$85	2P: $65-$85	XP: $7	F4
12/1-1/31	1P: $60-$80	2P: $60-$80	XP: $7	F4
9/4-11/30	1P: $55-$75	2P: $55-$75	XP: $7	F4

Phone: (727)367-2791 [38]

Motel   **Location:** SR 699, 0.7 mi n of Pinellas Bayway. 4506 Gulf Blvd 33706. Fax: 727/367-3620. **Facility:** Designated smoking area. 39 units. 37 one-bedroom standard units with kitchens. 2 one-bedroom suites ($120) with kitchens. 2 stories, exterior corridors. **Parking:** on-site. **Terms:** 14 day cancellation notice-fee imposed, weekly rates available. **Amenities:** video games, voice mail, irons, hair dryers. *Some:* DVD players (fee). **Pool(s):** heated outdoor. **Leisure Activities:** miniature golf, barbecue grill, human checker board, shuffleboard. *Fee:* cabanas, jet skis, parasailing, water bikes. **Guest Services:** coin laundry. **Business Services:** meeting rooms, PC (fee), fax. **Cards:** AX, DS, MC, VI. **Special Amenities: free local telephone calls and preferred room (subject to availability with advanced reservations).** *(See color ad p 943)*

SOME UNITS

RITZ MOTEL

12/1-4/16	1P: $60-$90	2P: $60-$90	XP: $5	F5
4/17-11/30	1P: $50-$70	2P: $50-$70	XP: $5	F5

Phone: (727)360-7642 [44]

Motel   **Location:** SR 699, 0.5 mi n of Pinellas Bayway. 4237 Gulf Blvd 33706. Fax: 727/360-7642. **Facility:** 14 one-bedroom standard units, some with efficiencies or kitchens. 2 stories, exterior corridors. *Bath:* combo or shower only. **Parking:** on-site. **Terms:** 14 day cancellation notice, small pets only. **Amenities:** voice mail, hair dryers. **Pool(s):** heated outdoor. **Leisure Activities:** boat dock, fishing. **Guest Services:** coin laundry. **Cards:** AX, DS, MC, VI.

SOME UNITS

TRADEWINDS ISLAND GRAND BEACH RESORT
AAA [SAVE]

2/1-4/30	1P: $209-$359	2P: $209-$359	XP: $15	F12
12/1-1/31 & 5/1-11/30	1P: $179-$289	2P: $179-$289	XP: $15	F12

Phone: (727)367-6461 [37]

Resort
Large-scale Hotel   **Location:** SR 699, 1 mi n of Pinellas Bayway. 5500 Gulf Blvd 33706 (PO Box 66307). Fax: 727/562-1214. **Facility:** A winding stream, complete with gondolas, circles the gulfside property, which is highlighted by a tropical courtyard. 585 units. 378 one-bedroom standard units. 158 one-, 42 two- and 7 three-bedroom suites ($229-$449), some with efficiencies or kitchens. 2-7 stories, interior/exterior corridors. *Bath:* combo or shower only. **Parking:** on-site and valet. **Terms:** check-in 4 pm, 2-7 night minimum stay - seasonal, weekends, $12 service charge. **Amenities:** video games, high-speed Internet, dual phone lines, voice mail, safes, irons, hair dryers. **Dining:** 4 restaurants, 7 am-10 pm, cocktails, also, Palm Court Restaurant, see separate listing, entertainment. **Pool(s):** 4 heated outdoor, wading. **Leisure Activities:** sauna, whirlpools, paddleboats, cabanas, putting green, golf privileges, 4 tennis courts, racquetball court, aerobic instruction, gondola rides, playground, sports court, horseshoes, volleyball. *Fee:* snorkeling, charter fishing, swimming lessons water tricycles, tennis lessons, bicycles, massage. **Guest Services:** gift shop, valet and coin laundry, area transportation, beauty salon. **Business Services:** conference facilities, business center. **Cards:** AX, CB, DC, DS, MC, VI.
(See color ad p 935)

SOME UNITS

TRADEWINDS SANDPIPER HOTEL & SUITES
AAA [SAVE]

2/1-4/30	1P: $159-$245	2P: $159-$245	XP: $15	F12
12/1-1/31 & 5/1-11/30	1P: $119-$189	2P: $119-$189	XP: $15	F12

Phone: (727)360-5551 [36]

Resort
Large-scale Hotel   **Location:** SR 699, 1.8 mi n of Pinellas Bayway. Located in commercial area. 6000 Gulf Blvd 33706. Fax: 727/562-1282. **Facility:** Trendy architecture and manicured grounds add upscale roadside appeal to this waterfront property. 159 units. 44 one-bedroom standard units. 110 one- and 5 two-bedroom suites ($179-$359) with efficiencies. 7 stories, interior/exterior corridors. *Bath:* combo or shower only. **Parking:** on-site. **Terms:** check-in 4 pm, 2-7 night minimum stay - seasonal, weekends, $12 service charge. **Amenities:** voice mail, safes, irons, hair dryers. **Dining:** 7 am-10 pm, cocktails. **Pool(s):** heated outdoor, heated indoor. **Leisure Activities:** fishing, recreation programs, exercise trainer available for appointments, shuffleboard. *Fee:* charter fishing, water bikes, cabanas, exercise room, massage. **Guest Services:** gift shop, valet and coin laundry, area transportation-among Tradewinds resorts. **Business Services:** meeting rooms, business center. **Cards:** AX, CB, DC, DS, MC, VI.
(See color ad p 935)

SOME UNITS

TRADEWINDS SIRATA BEACH RESORT
AAA [SAVE]

2/1-4/30	1P: $175-$317	2P: $175-$317	XP: $15	F12
12/1-1/31 & 5/1-11/30	1P: $145-$245	2P: $145-$245	XP: $15	F12

Phone: (727)367-5100 [41]

Resort
Large-scale Hotel   **Location:** SR 699, 1.2 mi n of Pinellas Bayway. Commercial area. 5300 Gulf Blvd 33706. Fax: 727/367-8082. **Facility:** This contemporary resort's decor includes tile and pickled woods appropriate to the beach setting; guest rooms with computers are available. 380 units. 300 one-bedroom standard units, some with kitchens. 80 one-bedroom suites ($198-$399), some with kitchens. 2-8 stories, interior/exterior corridors. *Bath:* combo or shower only. **Parking:** on-site. **Terms:** check-in 4 pm, 2-7 night minimum stay - seasonal & weekends, restrictions may apply, $12 service charge. **Amenities:** video games, voice mail, safes, irons, hair dryers. *Some:* dual phone lines. **Dining:** 2 restaurants, 7 am-10 pm, cocktails, entertainment. **Pool(s):** 3 heated outdoor. **Leisure Activities:** whirlpools, fishing, miniature golf, playground, exercise room, volleyball. *Fee:* charter fishing, aqua trikes, boat tours, cabanas, parasailing, game room. **Guest Services:** gift shop, valet and coin laundry, area transportation-among Tradewinds Resorts. **Business Services:** conference facilities, business center. **Cards:** AX, CB, DC, DS, MC, VI. *(See color ad p 935)*

SOME UNITS

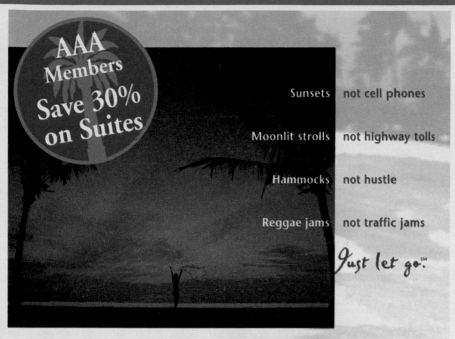

(See map p. 846)

TRAVELODGE ST. PETE BEACH   Phone: (727)367-2711   (31)

	2/21-4/27	1P: $126-$137	2P: $126-$137	XP: $6	F17
	12/1-2/20	1P: $112-$137	2P: $112-$137	XP: $6	F17
Motel	4/28-11/30	1P: $112-$122	2P: $112-$122	XP: $6	F17

Location: SR 699, 2 mi n of Pinellas Bayway. 6300 Gulf Blvd 33706. Fax: 727/367-7068. **Facility:** 200 one-bedroom standard units. 2 stories, exterior corridors. *Bath:* combo or shower only. **Parking:** on-site. **Terms:** check-in 4 pm, 3 day cancellation notice. **Amenities:** video games, safes (fee). *Some:* irons, hair dryers. **Pool(s):** heated outdoor, wading. **Leisure Activities:** shuffleboard, volleyball. *Fee:* sailboats, game room. **Guest Services:** gift shop. **Business Services:** meeting rooms, fax (fee). **Cards:** AX, CB, DC, DS, MC, VI. *(See color ad p 933)*

SOME UNITS

(ASK) (SØ) (¶¶) (Ɣ) (🛗) (🤸) (🗘) (╳) (📷) (💻) / (╳) (DATA PORT) (🔌) (📠) /

——————— WHERE TO DINE ———————

AUNT HEIDI'S ITALIAN RESTAURANT   **Lunch:** $4-$12   **Dinner:** $6-$12   **Phone:** 727/367-3448   (34)

Italian

Location: On SR 699, 2.2 mi n of Pinellas Bayway. 6340 Gulf Blvd 33706. **Hours:** 11 am-10 pm, Sat & Sun from 4 pm. Closed: 11/27, 12/25; also Super Bowl Sun. **Features:** Established in 1963, the small, family-oriented restaurant delivers personable service and a tasty selection of entrees that includes many pasta specialties as well as other yummies, such as beef stroganoff, chicken cordon bleu and a turkey club. Casual dress; beer & wine only. **Parking:** on-site.   (╳)

DER EISENHUT   **Dinner:** $9-$15   **Phone:** 727/367-6495   (33)

German

Cards: MC, VI.

Location: Just e of SR 699. 357 Corey Ave 33706. **Hours:** 4 pm-10 pm. Closed: 1/1, 12/24, 12/25; also Sun & Mon. **Features:** Relax in the cozy bistro setting and savor an excellent variety of ethnic dishes, ranging from German and French to Hungarian and Russian. European antiques, paintings, crystal chandeliers and assorted imports give this restaurant an air of authenticity. Casual dress; beer & wine only. **Parking:** street.

(Ɣ) (╳)

HURRICANE SEAFOOD RESTAURANT   **Lunch:** $8-$20   **Dinner:** $8-$20   **Phone:** 727/360-9558   (45)

Seafood

Location: On Pass-A-Grille; at jct 9th Ave. 807 Gulf Way 33706. **Hours:** 8 am-2 am. **Features:** The restaurant is a local favorite for watching beautiful sunsets from the rooftop. Dining is casual on the rustic first floor and slightly more upscale in the trendy second floor area, which becomes a popular dance bar after hours. Casual dress; cocktails; entertainment. **Parking:** on-site. **Cards:** AX, MC, VI.

(╳)

JOHNNY LEVEROCK'S ON THE BEACH   **Lunch:** $7-$19   **Dinner:** $7-$19   **Phone:** 727/367-4588   (30)

Steak & Seafood

Location: West end of St Petersburg Beach Cswy (75th Ave); on Boca Ciega Bay. 10 Corey Ave 33706. **Hours:** 11:30 am-10 pm. Closed: 11/27, 12/25. **Features:** An Old Florida decor complete with hardwood floors, antiques, nautical memorabilia and big picture windows gives the bayfront restaurant its personality. Grilled mahi coconut shrimp, fresh clam chowder and onion-crusted salmon bring the menu to life. Casual dress; cocktails. **Parking:** on-site. **Cards:** AX, DC, DS, MC, VI.

(Ɣ) (╳)

LA CROISETTE FAMILY RESTAURANT   **Lunch:** $4-$7   **Phone:** 727/360-2253   (31)

American

Cards: MC, VI.

Location: SR 699; at jct Corey Ave. 7401 Gulf Blvd 33706. **Hours:** 7 am-2 pm. Closed: 12/25. **Features:** Known locally for its extensive selection of hearty breakfasts, the local favorite establishment also serves up sandwiches and salads at lunch and numerous dinner items including French dishes and pasta preparations. The decor is basic but inviting. Casual dress; beer & wine only. **Parking:** on-site.

(╳)

MARITANA GRILLE   **Dinner:** $20-$33   **Phone:** 727/360-1882   (41)

American

Location: On SR 699; at jct Pinellas Bayway; in The Don CeSar Beach Resort & Spa. 3400 Gulf Blvd 33706. **Hours:** 5:30 pm-10 pm, Fri & Sat-11 pm. **Reservations:** suggested. **Features:** Resort-casual dining with artistic creations like swirled mashed potatoes that add charm to any plate. A private dining room and chef's table are available. For a light and tasty appetizer, try the lobster spring roll. Smoking is permitted in the bar only. Smoke free premises. Dressy casual; cocktails. **Parking:** on-site. **Cards:** AX, CB, DC, DS, MC, VI.

(♿M) (Ɣ) (╳)

PALM COURT RESTAURANT   **Lunch:** $7-$12   **Dinner:** $16-$25   **Phone:** 727/367-6461   (36)

American

Location: SR 699, 1 mi n of Pinellas Bayway; in TradeWinds Island Grand Beach Resort. 5500 Gulf Blvd 33706. **Hours:** 11:30 am-2 & 5:30-10 pm, Sun from 10 am. **Features:** A quaint atmosphere features indoor and outdoor seating amid resort surroundings. Order the seafood pasta and you will find a thick marinara sauce filled with clams, shrimp, fish, scallops and mussels. The rich raspberry cake is artistically swirled and the chocolate cake is the highlight. Smoke free premises. Casual dress; cocktails. **Parking:** on-site and valet. **Cards:** AX, CB, DC, DS, MC, VI.

(╳)

SEA CRITTERS CAFE   **Lunch:** $6-$17   **Dinner:** $6-$17   **Phone:** 727/360-3706   (42)

(AAA)

Seafood

Location: SR 699, 1 mi s of Pinellas Bayway; at jct 21st Ave. 2007 Pass-A-Grille Way 33706. **Hours:** 11:30 am-9 pm, Fri & Sat-10 pm. Closed: 12/24, 12/25; also 12/31 for dinner. **Features:** Dock your boat and bring a hearty appetite for generous portions of Key West-style food. Experience dockside dining on the Intracoastal Waterway at Vina Del Mar Bridge. The seafood platter gives a sampling of fried clams, shrimp, squid, crab cake grouper nuggets and onion rings. Casual dress; cocktails. **Parking:** on-site. **Cards:** AX, DC, MC, VI.

(Ɣ) (╳)

THE SEAHORSE TAVERN & RESTAURANT   **Lunch:** $5-$11   **Phone:** 727/360-1734   (44)

Seafood

Cards: DS, MC, VI.

Location: SR 699, 1.5 mi s of jct Pinellas Bayway. 800 Pass-A-Grille Way 33706. **Hours:** 8 am-2:30 pm. Closed: Tues. **Features:** A no-frills eatery dating back to 1937, it boasts a breezy courtyard reminiscent of Old Florida homes. Well-seasoned black beans are a signature favorite along with specialty sandwiches such as Cajun chicken and grouper served on grilled Cuban bread. Casual dress; cocktails. **Parking:** on-site.

(╳)

(See map p. 846)

SEA PORCH CAFE
▼▼▼
American
Lunch: $8-$12   **Dinner:** $9-$21   **Phone:** 727/360-1884 ㊴
Location: On SR 699; at jct Pinellas Bayway; in The Don CeSar Beach Resort & Spa. 3400 Gulf Blvd 33706. **Hours:** 7 am-11, noon-4 & 5-11 pm. **Reservations:** suggested; for dinner. **Features:** Bright and colorful, the decor of the waterfront restaurant is unmistakably tropical. Strong flavor characterizes the rosemary chicken with homemade gravy and the Key lime pie. Light, crisp breezes drift across the outdoor boardwalk. Casual dress; cocktails; entertainment. **Parking:** valet. **Cards:** AX, CB, DC, DS, MC, VI.

SILAS DENT'S STEAKHOUSE
▼▼▼
Steak House
Dinner: $8-$21   **Phone:** 727/360-6961 ㊵
Location: SR 699, 1 mi n of Pinellas Bayway; in Bayside Shores. 5501 Gulf Blvd 33706. **Hours:** 5 pm-10 pm, Fri & Sat-11 pm. **Features:** On the Intracoastal Waterway, the restaurant has an inviting patio area that overlooks the water. The original Silas Dent—the name of which ties to much history—was established in 1979, and this newer version carries on the tradition. The menu has a wide variety of salad, seafood, surf and turf fare, smokehouse items and steak. Casual dress; cocktails. **Parking:** on-site. **Cards:** MC, VI.

SKIDDER'S RESTAURANT
▼▼▼
American
Lunch: $6-$24   **Dinner:** $6-$24   **Phone:** 727/360-1029 ㉜
Location: SR 699, 1 mi n of Pinellas Bayway. 5799 Gulf Blvd 33706. **Hours:** 7 am-11 pm. **Features:** Very popular locally, the restaurant has a contemporary design and welcoming staff. On the menu are a good variety of breakfast items—omelets, waffles and croissants—as well as numerous lunch and dinner entrees, home-cooked selections and Greek specialties. Casual dress; cocktails. **Parking:** on-site. **Cards:** AX, DC, DS, MC, VI.

THE SLOPPY PELICAN
▼▼
Seafood
Lunch: $5-$12   **Dinner:** $5-$12   **Phone:** 727/367-5556 ㊲
Location: Just w of jct SR 699. 677 75th Ave 33706. **Hours:** 11 am-midnight. **Closed:** 11/27, 12/25. **Features:** Nicknamed "the Sloppy" by locals, the name is hardly a commentary on the service or food. Enjoy a relaxed setting on the water as you feast on shrimp, fresh stone crab claws, grouper, and burgers that have a backyard-barbecue flavor. Casual dress; cocktails. **Parking:** on-site. **Cards:** AX, MC, VI.

STARLITE DINER
▼▼▼
American
Lunch: $4-$12   **Dinner:** $4-$12   **Phone:** 727/363-0434 ㉟
Location: SR 699, 2.1 mi n of Pinellas Bayway. 5200 Gulf Blvd 33706. **Hours:** 7 am-8 pm, Fri & Sat-9 pm. **Closed:** 12/25. **Features:** A '50s-style diner, complete with red vinyl upholstery and vintage signs, features mainly sandwiches, but you'll find selections like pork chops, mashed potatoes and vegetables, too. So put on your poodle skirt and bobby socks and sip on a Coke float. Casual dress. **Parking:** on-site. **Cards:** MC, VI.

THE WHARF SEAFOOD RESTAURANT
🅰🅰🅰
▼▼▼
Seafood
Lunch: $5-$16   **Dinner:** $5-$16   **Phone:** 727/367-9469 ㊸
Location: SR 699, 0.9 mi s of Pinellas Bayway; in Historic Pass-A-Grille. 2001 Pass-A-Grille Way 33706. **Hours:** 11 am-11 pm. **Features:** A weathered exterior lends to the rustic appeal of the casual, nautically themed restaurant, which affords great views from its location on the Intracoastal Waterway. Dine on the deck and sample choices from the oyster bar. Seafood is the menu's primary focus. Casual dress; cocktails. **Parking:** on-site. **Cards:** MC, VI.

SOUTH PASADENA pop. 5,778   (See map p. 846; index p. 855)

------- WHERE TO DINE -------

HORSE & JOCKEY BRITISH RESTAURANT & BAR
▼▼▼
English
Lunch: $5-$7   **Dinner:** $7-$11   **Phone:** 727/345-4995 ㉜㉗㉖
Location: Just s of jct Gulfport Blvd; in Pasadena Square. 1155 Pasadena Ave S 33707. **Hours:** 11 am-11 pm, Sun-10 pm. **Closed:** 7/4, 12/25. **Features:** Fresh British specialties are served along with American favorites in pub-style surroundings. Order the fish 'n' chips in a tasty batter, bangers and mash, or cottage pie. Dine at ease with professional servers who provide knowledgeable, observant care. Casual dress; beer & wine only. **Parking:** on-site. **Cards:** DS, MC, VI.

SUN CITY CENTER

------- WHERE TO STAY -------

COMFORT INN-SUN CITY CENTER
🅰🅰🅰 SAVE
▼▼▼
Motel
Phone: (813)633-3318

	1P	2P	XP	
1/15-4/20 [ECP]	1P: $80-$90	2P: $90-$100	XP: $10	F12
12/16-1/14 [ECP]	1P: $70-$80	2P: $80-$90	XP: $10	F12
12/1-12/15 [ECP]	1P: $60-$70	2P: $70-$80	XP: $10	F12
4/21-11/30 [ECP]	1P: $50-$60	2P: $60-$70	XP: $10	F12

Location: I-75, exit 240A southbound; exit 240 northbound, 0.5 mi e on SR 674. 718 Cypress Village Blvd 33573. Fax: 813/633-2747. **Facility:** 74 units. 67 one-bedroom standard units. 7 one-bedroom suites ($100-$110) with efficiencies. 2 stories, exterior corridors. *Bath:* combo or shower only. **Parking:** on-site. **Terms:** 7 day cancellation notice. **Amenities:** irons, hair dryers. **Pool(s):** outdoor. **Leisure Activities:** whirlpool. **Guest Services:** coin laundry. **Business Services:** fax. **Cards:** AX, CB, DC, DS, MC, VI. **Special Amenities:** free continental breakfast and free local telephone calls.

SOME UNITS

SUN CITY CENTER INN
▼▼▼
Motel
Phone: (813)634-3331

	1P	2P	XP	
1/16-4/30	1P: $79	2P: $79	XP: $10	F18
12/1-1/15 & 5/1-11/30	1P: $49	2P: $49	XP: $10	F18

Location: I-75, exit 240A southbound; exit 240 northbound, 2.1 mi e on SR 674. Located in a retirement community. 809 W Pebble Beach Blvd 33573. Fax: 813/634-2053. **Facility:** 88 one-bedroom standard units. 2 stories, exterior corridors. *Bath:* combo or shower only. **Parking:** on-site. **Terms:** pets ($7.50 extra charge). **Amenities:** irons, hair dryers. **Pool(s):** outdoor. **Leisure Activities:** Fee: golf-90 holes, 6 lighted tennis courts. **Business Services:** meeting rooms, fax. **Cards:** AX, DS, MC, VI.

SOME UNITS

FEE

TARPON SPRINGS pop. 21,003

------ WHERE TO STAY ------

BAVARIAN INN   Phone: (727)939-0850
♦♦♦ ♦♦♦ 9/15-11/30 [ECP]   1P: $70-$125   2P: $70-$125   XP: $20   D12
          12/1-4/15 [ECP]   1P: $70-$95   2P: $70-$125   XP: $20   D12
Bed & Breakfast 4/16-9/14 [ECP] 1P: $60-$95   2P: $70-$125   XP: $20   D12
Location: 1 mi n of US 19, just w. 427 E Tarpon Ave 34689. Fax: 727/945-8647. **Facility:** 7 one-bedroom standard units. 2 stories (no elevator), interior corridors. *Bath:* some shared or private. **Parking:** on-site. **Terms:** 7 day cancellation notice-fee imposed, weekly rates available, package plans. **Cards:** AX, DC, MC, VI.

(ASK) (S₀) (⊠) (📶)

HOLIDAY INN HOTEL & SUITES   Phone: (727)934-5781
♦♦♦ ♦♦♦ 1/1-4/30   1P: $99-$149   2P: $99-$149   XP: $6   F19
          5/1-5/31   1P: $85-$129   2P: $85-$129   XP: $6   F19
Small-scale Hotel 12/1-12/31 & 6/1-11/30 1P: $79-$119 2P: $79-$119 XP: $6 F19
Location: On US 19, at jct Klosterman Rd. 38724 US Hwy 19 N 34689. Fax: 727/934-1755. **Facility:** 122 units. 89 one-bedroom standard units, some with efficiencies (no utensils). 33 one-bedroom suites with efficiencies (no utensils). 1-3 stories, interior/exterior corridors. *Bath:* combo or shower only. **Parking:** on-site. **Terms:** check-in 4 pm. **Amenities:** video games, voice mail, irons, hair dryers. **Pool(s):** heated outdoor. **Leisure Activities:** whirlpool, steamroom, playground, exercise room. **Guest Services:** valet and coin laundry. **Business Services:** meeting rooms, fax. **Cards:** AX, CB, DC, DS, JC, MC, VI.
(See color ad opposite inside back cover)   SOME UNITS

(ASK) (S₀) (🍴) (🍸) (🏋) (🖊) (🏊) (✕) (🎥) (DATA PORT) (▣) / (⊠) (📶) (📺) /

------ WHERE TO DINE ------

COSTA'S RESTAURANT   Lunch: $5-$14   Dinner: $5-$14   Phone: 727/938-6890
♦♦♦ ♦♦♦ **Location:** At Sponge Docks; 0.5 mi w on Dodecanese Blvd from jct Alt US 19, just s. 521 Athens St 34689.
Greek   **Hours:** 11:30 am-10 pm. Closed: 12/25. **Features:** Imagine what the sponge divers ate after a day in the sun, and you'll find these authentic Greek dishes and seafood specialties all the more intriguing. Snapper that is char-broiled and seasoned with garlic and sauteed in olive oil brings new meaning to the word "tasty.". Casual dress; beer & wine only. **Parking:** on-site. **Cards:** AX, DC, DS, MC, VI.
(⊠)

HELLA'S AUTHENTIC GREEK BAKERY & RESTAURANT   Lunch: $5-$14 Dinner: $5-$14 Phone: 727/943-2400
♦♦♦ ♦♦♦ **Location:** Center; at Sponge Docks. 785 Dodecanese Blvd 34689. **Hours:** 11 am-10 pm, Fri & Sat-11 pm.
Greek   **Features:** A family operation since 1970, Hella's offers a wide range of authentic Greek and Mediterranean fare from fFeta cheese to gyros, spanakopita, dolmades, fresh local seafood and lamb dishes. An extensive list of Greek desserts are made on the premises. Casual dress; cocktails. **Parking:** street.
Cards: AX, DC, DS, MC, VI.
(⊠)

LOUIS PAPPAS' RIVERSIDE RESTAURANT   Lunch: $8-$21   Dinner: $8-$21   Phone: 727/937-5101
♦♦♦ ♦♦♦ **Location:** US Alt 19 at Dodecanese Blvd; at Sponge Docks. 10 W Dodecanese Blvd 34689. **Hours:** 11:30 am-9 pm,
Greek   Fri & Sat-10 pm. **Features:** This popular restaurant is a landmark at the Sponge Docks. Patrons are treated to river views as they sample such Greek house specialties as the ever-popular chicken spanakopita, moussaka and kalamatakia. Casual dress; cocktails. **Parking:** on-site. **Cards:** MC, VI.
(⊠)

TASTE OF GREECE   Lunch: $5-$15   Dinner: $5-$15   Phone: 727/938-0088
♦♦♦   **Location:** Center; at the Sponge Docks. 709 Dodecanese Blvd 34689. **Hours:** 10 am-10 pm. **Features:** At the
Greek   famous Sponge Docks, a favorite tourist spot, the Greek restaurant is a comfortable retreat from shopping amid the many favorite haunts. The menu boasts such items as souvlaki, moussaka, pastitsio, dolmades, tiropite or spanakopita. The popular chicken kebab is a must. Homemade desserts are beautifully displayed and enticing. Casual dress; cocktails. **Parking:** street. **Cards:** AX, DS, MC, VI.

TEMPLE TERRACE pop. 20,918   (See map p. 856; index p. 861)

——— WHERE TO STAY ———

EXTENDED STAY AMERICA
Phone: 813/989-2264   [88]

1/1-4/30	1P: $369-$409	2P: $375-$419
12/1-12/31	1P: $259-$310	2P: $280-$309
5/1-11/30	1P: $279-$309	2P: $279-$309

Motel

Location: I-75, exit 266, just w on Fletcher Ave. 12242 Morris Bridge Rd 33637. **Fax:** 813/989-1184. **Facility:** 101 one-bedroom standard units with efficiencies. 3 stories, interior corridors. *Bath:* combo or shower only. **Parking:** on-site. **Amenities:** voice mail. *Some:* irons. **Guest Services:** coin laundry. **Business Services:** fax. **Cards:** AX, CB, DC, DS, MC, VI.

SOME UNITS

FAIRFIELD INN TAMPA NORTH
Phone: (813)989-0007   [87]

SAVE

2/5-5/15	1P: $69-$89	2P: $69-$89
12/1-2/4 & 5/16-11/30	1P: $59-$69	2P: $59-$69

Motel

Location: I-75, exit 266, just w on Fletcher Ave. 12260 Morris Bridge Rd 33637. **Fax:** 813/988-0255. **Facility:** 83 one-bedroom standard units. 3 stories, interior corridors. *Bath:* combo or shower only. **Parking:** on-site. **Terms:** [ECP] meal plan available. **Amenities:** irons. **Pool(s):** outdoor. **Leisure Activities:** whirlpool, exercise room. **Guest Services:** valet laundry. **Business Services:** fax. **Cards:** AX, CB, DC, DS, JC, MC, VI.

SOME UNITS

HILTON GARDEN INN TAMPA NORTH
Phone: (813)342-5000   [83]

SAVE

12/1-4/30	1P: $79-$119	2P: $79-$129	XP: $10 F18
5/1-11/30	1P: $69-$119	2P: $69-$119	XP: $10 F18

Small-scale Hotel

Location: I-75, exit 266, 0.6 mi w on Fletcher Ave (CR 582A), just s on Morris Bridge Rd. Located in Tampa Oaks Office Park. 600 Tampa Oaks Blvd 33637. **Fax:** 813/342-6000. **Facility:** 148 units. 126 one-bedroom standard units. 22 one-bedroom suites. 6 stories, interior corridors. *Bath:* combo or shower only. **Parking:** on-site. **Terms:** check-in 4 pm, [BP] meal plan available. **Amenities:** video games, high-speed Internet, dual phone lines, voice mail, irons, hair dryers. **Pool(s):** heated outdoor. **Leisure Activities:** whirlpool, exercise room. **Guest Services:** sundries, valet and coin laundry. **Business Services:** meeting rooms, business center. **Cards:** AX, DC, DS, MC, VI.

SOME UNITS

RESIDENCE INN BY MARRIOTT TAMPA NORTH
Phone: (813)972-4400   [86]

SAVE

All Year	1P: $129-$169

Small-scale Hotel

Location: I-75, exit 266, 1.1 mi w on Fletcher Ave (CR 582A). Located in the Telecom Tampa Park. 13420 N Telecom Pkwy 33637. **Fax:** 813/972-3376. **Facility:** 78 units. 66 one- and 12 two-bedroom suites with kitchens. 3 stories, interior corridors. *Bath:* combo or shower only. **Parking:** on-site. **Terms:** cancellation fee imposed, [BP] meal plan available, pets ($125 fee). **Amenities:** voice mail, irons, hair dryers. **Pool(s):** heated outdoor. **Leisure Activities:** whirlpool, exercise room, sports court. **Guest Services:** complimentary evening beverages, valet and coin laundry. **Business Services:** meeting rooms, fax (fee). **Cards:** AX, CB, DC, DS, JC, MC, VI.

SOME UNITS

SLEEP INN TEMPLE TERRACE USF NEAR BUSCH GARDENS
Phone: 813/988-4048   [85]

SAVE

12/28-4/14	1P: $70	2P: $70	XP: $6 F
12/1-12/27 & 4/15-11/30	1P: $60	2P: $60	XP: $6 F

Small-scale Hotel

Location: I-75, exit 266, just w on Fletcher Ave (CR 582A). 12282 Morris Bridge Rd 33637. **Fax:** 813/989-1659. **Facility:** 83 units. 81 one-bedroom standard units. 2 one-bedroom suites. 4 stories, interior corridors. *Bath:* combo or shower only. **Parking:** on-site. **Terms:** [CP] meal plan available. **Amenities:** *Some:* irons, hair dryers. **Pool(s):** heated outdoor. **Leisure Activities:** basketball. **Guest Services:** valet and coin laundry. **Business Services:** meeting rooms, fax. **Cards:** AX, CB, DC, DS, MC, VI.

SOME UNITS

——— WHERE TO DINE ———

VALLARTO'S RESTAURANTE MEXICANO
Lunch: $6-$11   **Dinner:** $6-$11   **Phone:** 813/987-2720   [90]

Mexican

Location: Just s of jct Busch Blvd. 9255 N 54th St 33617. **Hours:** 11 am-10 pm. **Features:** More than 60 preparations of authentic cuisine are served in decorative Southwestern surroundings. Chihuahua cheese is excellent with chips, and fajitas are a sizzling temptation. A colorful Mexican flair punctuates the dining room. Casual dress. **Parking:** on-site. **Cards:** MC, VI.

TIERRA VERDE pop. 3,574

——— WHERE TO DINE ———

BILLY'S STONE CRAB & STEAKHOUSE
Lunch: $8-$16   **Dinner:** $9-$20   **Phone:** 727/866-2115

Seafood

Location: 1 mi s. One Collany Rd 33715. **Hours:** 11:30 am-11 pm. **Features:** Diners can take in views of the marina while filling up on tasty seafood. Those who don't try the specialty stone crabs can choose from fried shrimp, oysters Rockefeller, gator nuggets or any of a number of other seafood favorites. For the landlubber, there are aged steaks and chicken dishes. Casual dress; cocktails. **Parking:** on-site. **Cards:** AX, MC, VI.

TREASURE ISLAND pop. 7,450 (See map p. 846; index p. 854)

——— WHERE TO STAY ———

ALGIERS GULF RESORT

AAA [SAVE] **Motel**

Phone: 727/367-3793 **189**

2/1-4/30		2P: $70-$100	XP: $8
5/1-9/10		2P: $50-$80	XP: $8
12/1-1/31 & 9/11-11/30		2P: $45-$65	XP: $8

Location: On SR 699, just n of jct Treasure Island Cswy. 11600 Gulf Blvd 33706. Fax: 727/367-6288. **Facility:** 17 one-bedroom standard units, some with kitchens. 2 stories, exterior corridors. **Parking:** on-site. **Terms:** 30 day cancellation notice-fee imposed, weekly rates available. **Amenities:** *Some:* irons. **Pool(s):** heated outdoor. **Leisure Activities:** ping pong, barbecue grill, patio area, shuffleboard. **Guest Services:** coin laundry. **Business Services:** fax. **Cards:** MC, VI. **Special Amenities: preferred room (subject to availability with advanced reservations).**

ARVILLA RESORT MOTEL

Motel

Phone: 727/360-0598 **210**

2/1-4/30	2P: $61-$98	XP: $10
12/1-1/31	2P: $51-$79	XP: $10
5/1-9/3	2P: $48-$77	XP: $10
9/4-11/30	2P: $40-$60	XP: $10

Location: SR 699, just n of jct Treasure Island Cswy. 11580 Gulf Blvd 33706. Fax: 727/363-3110. **Facility:** 15 one-bedroom standard units, some with efficiencies. 2 stories, exterior corridors. *Bath:* combo or shower only. **Parking:** on-site. **Terms:** 30 day cancellation notice-fee imposed. **Pool(s):** heated outdoor. **Leisure Activities:** shuffleboard. **Guest Services:** coin laundry. **Business Services:** fax. **Cards:** MC, VI.

SOME UNITS

THE BAYSIDE INN

Motel

Phone: (727)367-6456 **217**

2/1-4/15	1P: $59-$400	2P: $79-$540	XP: $15	D
12/1-1/31	1P: $45-$300	2P: $59-$405	XP: $15	D
4/16-11/30	1P: $35-$240	2P: $50-$330	XP: $15	D

Location: SR 699, just n of Treasure Island Cswy. 11365 Gulf Blvd 33706. Fax: 727/367-1291. **Facility:** 23 one-bedroom standard units with efficiencies. 2 stories, interior/exterior corridors. *Bath:* combo or shower only. **Parking:** on-site. **Terms:** 30 day cancellation notice, weekly rates available. **Amenities:** *Some:* irons. **Pool(s):** heated outdoor. **Leisure Activities:** boat dock, fishing, shuffleboard. **Guest Services:** coin laundry. **Cards:** DC, MC, VI.

BEST WESTERN SEA CASTLE SUITES

AAA [SAVE] **Motel**

Phone: (727)367-2704 **195**

1/10-4/30	1P: $99-$157	2P: $99-$157	XP: $5	F12
5/1-9/8	1P: $73-$146	2P: $73-$146	XP: $5	F12
9/9-11/30	1P: $66-$116	2P: $66-$116	XP: $5	F12
12/1-1/9	1P: $73-$110	2P: $73-$110	XP: $5	F12

Location: On SR 699; at jct Treasure Island Cswy. 10750 Gulf Blvd 33706. Fax: 727/360-2492. **Facility:** 41 one-bedroom standard units with kitchens. 2-3 stories (no elevator), exterior corridors. **Parking:** on-site. **Terms:** 3 day cancellation notice, weekly rates available, package plans, small pets only ($50 deposit). **Amenities:** irons, hair dryers. **Pool(s):** heated outdoor. **Leisure Activities:** fishing, barbecue grills, playground, shuffleboard. **Guest Services:** coin laundry. **Business Services:** fax (fee). **Cards:** AX, DC, DS, MC, VI.

SOME UNITS

FEE

BEST WESTERN TREASURE ISLAND

[SAVE] **Motel**

Phone: (727)360-6971 **197**

2/15-4/21	1P: $99-$114	2P: $99-$114	XP: $10	F18
1/1-2/14	1P: $90-$110	2P: $90-$110	XP: $10	F18
12/1-12/31	1P: $80-$105	2P: $80-$105	XP: $10	F18
4/22-11/30	1P: $80-$95	2P: $80-$95	XP: $10	F18

Location: On SR 699, just n of jct Treasure Island Cswy. 11125 Gulf Blvd 33706. Fax: 727/360-9014. **Facility:** 84 one-bedroom standard units. 3 stories, interior corridors. *Bath:* combo or shower only. **Parking:** on-site. **Terms:** cancellation fee imposed. **Amenities:** safes (fee). *Some:* irons, hair dryers. **Pool(s):** heated outdoor. **Leisure Activities:** boat dock, fishing, playground. **Guest Services:** valet and coin laundry. **Business Services:** meeting rooms, fax. **Cards:** AX, DC, DS, MC, VI. *(See color ad p 933)*

SOME UNITS

BILMAR BEACH RESORT

AAA [SAVE] **Large-scale Hotel**

Phone: (727)360-5531 **196**

1/31-4/26	1P: $145-$179	2P: $145-$179	XP: $10	F18
12/1-1/30	1P: $119-$169	2P: $119-$169	XP: $10	F18
4/27-9/1	1P: $121-$139	2P: $121-$139	XP: $10	F18
9/2-11/30	1P: $105-$125	2P: $105-$125	XP: $10	F18

Location: On SR 699, jct Treasure Island Cswy. 10650 Gulf Blvd 33706. Fax: 727/360-2362. **Facility:** 172 units. 165 one-bedroom standard units, some with efficiencies. 7 one-bedroom suites ($175-$400), some with kitchens. 3-8 stories, exterior corridors. **Parking:** on-site. **Terms:** 3 day cancellation notice. **Amenities:** voice mail, safes (fee), hair dryers. *Some:* irons. **Dining:** 7 am-10 pm, cocktails, entertainment. **Pool(s):** 2 heated outdoor. **Leisure Activities:** whirlpool, fishing, cabanas, sun deck, jogging, exercise room, volleyball. **Guest Services:** gift shop, valet and coin laundry. **Business Services:** conference facilities, fax (fee). **Cards:** AX, CB, DC, DS, MC, VI.

SOME UNITS

BLUENOSE MOTEL

AAA [SAVE] **Motel**

Phone: (727)360-1730 **216**

12/1-4/30	1P: $60-$80	2P: $60-$80	XP: $5	F3
5/1-11/30	1P: $50-$60	2P: $50-$60	XP: $5	F3

Location: Just e of jct SR 699 (Gulf Blvd). 292 107th Ave 33706. Fax: 727/360-1730. **Facility:** 9 units. 6 one-bedroom standard units, some with efficiencies or kitchens. 3 one-bedroom suites ($70-$90) with kitchens. 2 stories, exterior corridors. **Parking:** on-site. **Terms:** 3 night minimum stay - suites only, 8 day cancellation notice-fee imposed. **Amenities:** *Some:* irons, hair dryers. **Pool(s):** outdoor. **Leisure Activities:** boat dock, fishing, 3 slips, picnic area, barbecue grill, sun deck, shuffleboard. **Guest Services:** coin laundry. **Business Services:** fax. **Cards:** AX, DS, MC, VI. **Special Amenities: free local telephone calls.**

SOME UNITS

(See map p. 846)

BUCCANEER BEACHFRONT RESORT MOTEL   Phone: (727)367-1908 **201**

AAA SAVE	2/1-4/30	2P: $82-$120	XP: $6	F14
	12/1-1/31 & 5/1-9/7	2P: $55-$95	XP: $6	F14
◇◇◇ ◇◇◇	9/8-11/30	2P: $52-$85	XP: $6	F14

Motel

Location: SR 699, just n of Treasure Island Cswy. 10800 Gulf Blvd 33706. Fax: 727/367-4890. **Facility:** 69 units. 60 one-bedroom standard units, some with efficiencies. 8 one- and 1 two-bedroom suites ($85-$130), some with kitchens. 2 stories, exterior corridors. **Parking:** on-site. **Terms:** 2-7 night minimum stay - weekends in efficiencies, 30 day cancellation notice-fee imposed, weekly rates available. **Pool(s):** heated outdoor. **Leisure Activities:** sun deck, barbecue grills, shuffleboard, volleyball. **Fee:** game room. **Guest Services:** coin laundry. **Business Services:** meeting rooms. **Cards:** AX, DS, MC, VI. *(See color ad below)*

SOME UNITS

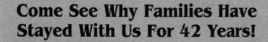

(See map p. 846)

CAROL ANN CONDO HOTEL
Phone: (727)367-1991 〔202〕
Condominium
12/15-4/30	2P: $155-$195	XP: $10
12/1-12/14 & 5/1-11/30	2P: $125-$155	XP: $10

Location: On SR 699, 0.5 mi n of Treasure Island Cswy. 11360 Gulf Blvd 33706. Fax: 727/368-0096. **Facility:** 40 units. 30 one- and 10 two-bedroom suites with kitchens. 6 stories, exterior corridors. *Bath:* combo or shower only. **Parking:** on-site. **Terms:** 4 night minimum stay, 30 day cancellation notice-fee imposed. **Amenities:** voice mail, safes, irons. *Some:* hair dryers. **Pool(s):** outdoor, heated outdoor. **Leisure Activities:** exercise room, horseshoes, shuffleboard. **Guest Services:** complimentary laundry. **Business Services:** fax (fee). **Cards:** DC, MC, VI.

SOME UNITS

FARGO MOTEL
Phone: (727)367-3166 〔190〕
Motel
2/1-4/20	1P: $65-$90	2P: $65-$90	XP: $5 D12
12/1-1/31 & 4/21-9/2	1P: $45-$65	2P: $45-$65	XP: $5 D12
9/3-11/30	1P: $40-$60	2P: $40-$60	XP: $5 D12

Location: SR 699, just n of jct Treasure Island Cswy. 10810 Gulf Blvd 33706. Fax: 727/363-3341. **Facility:** 21 one-bedroom standard units, some with kitchens. 2 stories, exterior corridors. *Bath:* combo or shower only. **Parking:** on-site. **Terms:** 28 day cancellation notice-fee imposed. **Amenities:** *Some:* irons, hair dryers. **Pool(s):** heated outdoor. **Leisure Activities:** barbecue grill area, shuffleboard. **Guest Services:** coin laundry. **Business Services:** fax. **Cards:** AX, DC, MC, VI. **Special Amenities: preferred room (subject to availability with advanced reservations).**

SOME UNITS

GULF SOUNDS BEACH RENTALS
Phone: (727)363-6114 〔191〕
Motel
1/30-4/30	1P: $103-$114	2P: $103-$114	XP: $7
12/19-1/29	1P: $79-$89	2P: $79-$89	XP: $7
12/1-12/18 & 5/1-11/30	1P: $69-$79	2P: $69-$79	XP: $7

Location: SR 699, 0.6 mi s of Johns Pass. 12240 Gulf Blvd 33706. Fax: 727/341-1037. **Facility:** 6 units. 2 one-bedroom standard units with efficiencies. 4 two-bedroom suites with kitchens. 1-2 stories, exterior corridors. **Parking:** on-site. **Terms:** 14 day cancellation notice-fee imposed, weekly rates available. **Amenities:** voice mail. *Some:* irons, hair dryers. **Leisure Activities:** gas barbecue, patio, sun deck. **Guest Services:** coin laundry. **Business Services:** fax. **Cards:** DS, MC, VI.

HOLIDAY INN-TREASURE ISLAND BEACH
Phone: (727)367-2761 〔200〕
Large-scale Hotel
2/10-4/30	1P: $119-$149	2P: $119-$149	XP: $10 F19
5/1-9/3	1P: $99-$149	2P: $99-$149	XP: $10 F19
9/4-11/30	1P: $89-$139	2P: $89-$139	XP: $10 F19
12/1-2/9	1P: $89-$129	2P: $89-$129	XP: $10 F19

Location: On SR 699, 0.8 mi n of jct Treasure Island Cswy. 11908 Gulf Blvd 33706. Fax: 727/367-9446. **Facility:** 117 one-bedroom standard units. 9 stories, interior corridors. **Parking:** check-in 4 pm, [AP], [BP] & [CP] meal plans available. **Amenities:** voice mail, irons, hair dryers. **Pool(s):** heated outdoor. **Leisure Activities:** whirlpool, exercise room. *Fee:* game room. **Guest Services:** valet and coin laundry. **Business Services:** fax (fee). **(See color ad opposite inside back cover & below)**

SOME UNITS

FEE

THE JEFFERSON MOTEL APTS.
Phone: 727/360-5826 〔215〕
Motel
2/1-4/30 Wkly	1P: $735	2P: $735	XP: $10
5/1-9/1 Wkly	1P: $532	2P: $532	XP: $10
12/1-1/31 Wkly	1P: $532	2P: $532	XP: $12
9/2-11/30 Wkly	1P: $469	2P: $469	XP: $10

Location: SR 699, 0.6 mi s of jct Treasure Island Cswy. 10116 Gulf Blvd 33706. Fax: 727/367-9396. **Facility:** 14 one-bedroom standard units with kitchens. 2-3 stories, exterior corridors. **Parking:** on-site. **Terms:** 28 day cancellation notice-fee imposed. **Amenities:** voice mail. *Some:* irons. **Pool(s):** heated outdoor. **Leisure Activities:** shuffleboard, volleyball. **Cards:** MC, VI.

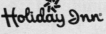

(See map p. 846)

JOLLY ROGER MOTEL

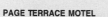 AAA SAVE

Phone: 727/360-5571 [192]

2/1-4/27	1P: $65-$100	2P: $65-$100	XP: $10 F9
12/1-1/31	1P: $50-$75	2P: $50-$75	XP: $10 F9
4/28-9/3	1P: $45-$75	2P: $45-$75	XP: $10 F9
9/4-11/30	1P: $45-$65	2P: $45-$65	XP: $10 F9

Motel   **Location:** On SR 699, 0.5 mi n of jct Treasure Island Cswy. 11525 Gulf Blvd 33706. Fax: 727/360-4475. **Facility:** 29 units. 25 one-bedroom standard units, some with efficiencies. 4 one-bedroom suites with kitchens. 2 stories, exterior corridors. *Bath:* combo or shower only. **Parking:** on-site. **Terms:** 14 day cancellation notice-fee imposed. **Amenities:** *Some:* irons, hair dryers. **Pool(s):** heated outdoor. **Leisure Activities:** boat dock, fishing, barbecue grill, patio area, shuffleboard. **Guest Services:** coin laundry. **Business Services:** fax (fee). **Cards:** MC, VI.

SOME UNITS

MARDI GRAS MOTEL

Phone: 727/367-1621 [212]

All Year	1P: $45-$75	2P: $50-$75	XP: $6 F12

Motel   **Location:** SR 699, 0.7 mi n of jct Treasure Island Cswy. 11965 Gulf Blvd 33706. Fax: 727/360-5910. **Facility:** Designated smoking area. 10 one-bedroom standard units, some with efficiencies. 2 stories, exterior corridors. **Parking:** on-site. **Pool(s):** heated outdoor.

PAGE TERRACE MOTEL

AAA SAVE

Phone: 727/367-1997 [214]

2/1-4/24	2P: $69-$102	XP: $6 F6
12/1-1/31 & 4/25-9/4	2P: $54-$80	XP: $6 F6
9/5-11/30	2P: $46-$70	XP: $6 F6

Motel   **Location:** On SR 699, just s of jct Treasure Island Cswy. 10500 Gulf Blvd 33706. Fax: 727/360-7179. **Facility:** 36 one-bedroom standard units, some with efficiencies. 3 stories (no elevator), interior/exterior corridors. **Parking:** on-site. **Terms:** 3 night minimum stay - weekends, 14 day cancellation notice-fee imposed. **Amenities:** *Some:* irons, hair dryers. **Pool(s):** heated outdoor. **Leisure Activities:** shuffleboard. **Guest Services:** coin laundry. **Business Services:** fax. **Cards:** AX, DS, MC, VI. **Special Amenities:** early check-in/late check-out and free room upgrade (subject to availability with advanced reservations). *(See color ad below)*

SOME UNITS

RAMADA INN TREASURE ISLAND

AAA SAVE

Phone: (727)360-7051 [199]

2/14-4/20	1P: $130	2P: $150	XP: $10 F17
12/1-12/19	1P: $115	2P: $135	XP: $10 F17
4/21-11/30	1P: $95	2P: $135	XP: $10 F17
12/20-2/13	1P: $105	2P: $125	XP: $10 F17

Small-scale Hotel **Location:** SR 699, 0.8 mi n of jct Treasure Island Cswy. 12000 Gulf Blvd 33706. Fax: 727/367-6641. **Facility:** 121 one-bedroom standard units, some with efficiencies. 4 stories, interior corridors. **Parking:** on-site. **Terms:** 3 day cancellation notice. **Amenities:** video library (fee), voice mail, safes. *Some:* irons, hair dryers. **Dining:** 7 am-10 pm, cocktails, entertainment. **Pool(s):** heated outdoor. **Leisure Activities:** whirlpool, pool table, playground, shuffleboard, volleyball. *Fee:* game room. **Guest Services:** gift shop, valet and coin laundry. **Business Services:** meeting rooms, fax (fee). **Cards:** AX, CB, DC, DS, MC, VI.

SOME UNITS

FEE

(See map p. 846)

THE SEA CHEST Phone: 727/360-5501 ⟨205⟩

AAA SAVE	1/18-4/30 1P: $84-$119	2P: $84-$119 XP: $6
▼▼▼ ▼▼	12/19-1/17 1P: $71-$103	2P: $71-$103 XP: $6
Motel	12/1-12/18 & 5/1-11/30 1P: $62-$88	2P: $62-$88 XP: $6

Location: SR 699, 0.5 mi n of jct Treasure Island Cswy. 11780 Gulf Blvd 33706. Fax: 727/360-8453. **Facility:** 21 one-bedroom standard units, some with kitchens. 2 stories, interior/exterior corridors. **Parking:** on-site. **Terms:** 30 day cancellation notice-fee imposed. **Amenities:** *Some:* irons, hair dryers. **Pool(s):** heated outdoor. **Leisure Activities:** gas barbecue, ping pong, picnic area, shuffleboard. **Guest Services:** coin laundry. **Cards:** AX, MC, VI.

THUNDERBIRD BEACH RESORT Phone: (727)367-1961 ⟨209⟩

AAA SAVE	2/14-4/21 1P: $135-$179	2P: $135-$179 XP: $10	F18
▼▼▼ ▼▼	4/22-9/1 1P: $95-$135	2P: $95-$135 XP: $10	F18
Motel	12/1-2/13 1P: $89-$125	2P: $89-$125 XP: $10	F18
	9/2-11/30 1P: $85-$105	2P: $85-$105 XP: $10	F18

Location: SR 699, at jct Treasure Island Cswy. 10700 Gulf Blvd 33706. Fax: 727/367-1961. **Facility:** 64 one-bedroom standard units, some with kitchens. 2-3 stories, exterior corridors. **Parking:** on-site. **Terms:** [BP] meal plan available, package plans - seasonal, $6 service charge. **Amenities:** voice mail, safes, hair dryers. *Some:* irons. **Dining:** 7 am-2 pm, cocktails. **Pool(s):** heated outdoor. **Leisure Activities:** whirlpool, volleyball. **Business Services:** meeting rooms, PC, fax. **Cards:** AX, CB, DC, DS, MC, VI. *(See color ad below)*

SOME UNITS

TRAILS END RESORT MOTEL Phone: 727/360-5541 ⟨207⟩

AAA SAVE	2/1-4/30 1P: $90-$125	2P: $90-$125 XP: $10
▼▼▼ ▼▼	12/1-1/31 & 5/1-11/30 1P: $59-$99	2P: $59-$99 XP: $10

Location: SR 699, 0.5 mi n of jct Treasure Island Cswy. 11500 Gulf Blvd 33706. Fax: 727/360-1508. **Facility:** 54 one-bedroom standard units, some with efficiencies or kitchens. 1-2 stories, exterior corridors. *Bath:* combo or shower only. **Parking:** on-site. **Terms:** 3 night minimum stay, 14 day cancellation notice-fee imposed, package plans. **Pool(s):** heated outdoor. **Leisure Activities:** fishing, shuffleboard. **Guest Services:** valet laundry. **Cards:** AX, CB, DC, DS, JC, MC, VI. *(See color ad below)*

SOME UNITS

(See map p. 846)

THE TWINS APARTMENTS   Phone: (727)360-7420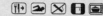

▼▼▼ ▼▼▼	2/1-4/30 Wkly	1P: $350-$370	2P: $350-$370	XP: $35	
	12/1-1/31 & 5/1-9/2 Wkly	1P: $270-$290	2P: $270-$290	XP: $35	
Motel	9/3-11/30 Wkly	1P: $250-$270	2P: $250-$270	XP: $35	

Location: SR 699, 1 mi n of Treasure Island Cswy, just s of John's Pass. 12520 Gulf Blvd 33706. Fax: 727/360-8196. **Facility:** Designated smoking area. 11 units. 8 one-bedroom standard units with kitchens. 3 three-bedroom suites ($460-$500) with kitchens. 2 stories, exterior corridors. **Parking:** on-site. **Terms:** 7-30 night minimum stay, 28 day cancellation notice. **Amenities:** irons. **Pool(s):** heated outdoor. **Leisure Activities:** shuffleboard. **Guest Services:** coin laundry.

WESLEY CHAPEL pop. 5,691

—— WHERE TO STAY ——

COMFORT INN   Phone: (813)991-4600

AAA SAVE	12/24-4/30 [ECP]	1P: $67	2P: $67	XP: $5	F18
	5/1-11/30 [ECP]	1P: $63	2P: $63	XP: $5	F18
▼▼▼▼	12/1-12/23 [ECP]	1P: $61	2P: $61	XP: $5	F18
Motel					

Location: I-75, exit 279, just w on SR 54, then just n. 5642 Oakley Blvd 33544. Fax: 813/991-7733. **Facility:** 68 units. 66 one-bedroom standard units. 2 one-bedroom suites ($125-$135). 2 stories, interior corridors. *Bath:* combo or shower only. **Parking:** on-site. **Terms:** weekly rates available. **Amenities:** *Some:* irons, hair dryers. **Pool(s):** outdoor. **Leisure Activities:** exercise room. **Guest Services:** valet and coin laundry. **Business Services:** meeting rooms, fax. **Cards:** AX, DC, DS, MC, VI. **Special Amenities:** free continental breakfast and free local telephone calls.

SOME UNITS

HOLIDAY INN EXPRESS   Phone: 813/907-1379

▼▼▼▼	1/21-3/31	1P: $89	2P: $89	XP: $5	F19
	1/1-1/20 & 4/1-11/30	1P: $69	2P: $69	XP: $5	F19
Small-scale Hotel					

Location: I-75, exit 279, just w. 27615 SR 54 W 33543. Fax: 813/907-8421. **Facility:** 82 units. 80 one-bedroom standard units. 2 one-bedroom suites ($120). 4 stories, interior corridors. *Bath:* combo or shower only. **Parking:** on-site. **Terms:** [CP] meal plan available. **Amenities:** dual phone lines, voice mail, safes, irons, hair dryers. **Pool(s):** outdoor. **Guest Services:** valet laundry. **Business Services:** meeting rooms, fax.

SOME UNITS

MASTERS INN TAMPA NORTH   Phone: (813)973-0155

AAA SAVE	All Year	1P: $40-$60	2P: $40-$60	XP: $4	F18
▼▼ ▼▼					

Location: I-75, exit 279, just w. 27807 SR 54 W 33543. Fax: 813/973-0210. **Facility:** 119 one-bedroom standard units. 2 stories, exterior corridors. **Parking:** on-site. **Terms:** [CP] meal plan available. **Dining:** 24 hours. **Pool(s):** outdoor. **Guest Services:** coin laundry. **Business Services:** meeting rooms, fax. **Cards:** AX, CB, DC, DS, MC, VI. **Special Amenities:** free local telephone calls.

Small-scale Hotel

SOME UNITS
FEE FEE

SADDLEBROOK RESORT TAMPA   Phone: (813)973-1111

AAA SAVE	1/12-5/8 [MAP]	1P: $327-$352	2P: $400-$574	
	12/1-1/11 & 10/1-11/30 [MAP]	1P: $277-$322	2P: $350-$518	
▼▼▼	5/9-9/30 [MAP]	1P: $187-$217	2P: $260-$360	

Location: I-75, exit 279, 1.2 mi e on SR 54. 5700 Saddlebrook Way 33543. Fax: 813/973-4504. **Facility:** The resort offers large, hotel-style rooms as well as clusters of suites with kitchens, all on spacious, manicured grounds. 547 units. 133 one-bedroom standard units. 160 one- and 254 two-bedroom suites ($352-$720) with kitchens, some with whirlpools. 2 stories, exterior corridors. **Parking:** on-site. **Terms:** 3 day cancellation notice-fee imposed. **Amenities:** dual phone lines, voice mail, honor bars, irons, hair dryers. **Dining:** 3 restaurants, 6 am-10:30 pm, cocktails, entertainment. **Pool(s):** 3 heated outdoor. **Leisure Activities:** saunas, whirlpools, steamrooms, fishing, recreation programs, car rental office, salon, wellness program, team building course, jogging, playground, basketball, volleyball. *Fee:* fishing equipment, golf-36 holes, practice range, golf equipment & instruction, 45 tennis courts, tennis equipment & instruction, bicycles, massage. **Guest Services:** gift shop, valet and coin laundry, area transportation (fee). **Business Services:** conference facilities, business center. **Cards:** AX, CB, DC, DS, MC, VI. **Special Amenities:** free local telephone calls and free newspaper.

Resort
Large-scale Hotel

SOME UNITS
FEE   FEE

SLEEP INN   Phone: (813)973-1665

AAA SAVE	12/1-1/15	1P: $54-$64	2P: $59-$69	XP: $5	F18
	1/16-4/30	1P: $64-$69		XP: $5	F18
▼▼ ▼▼	5/1-11/30	1P: $54-$59		XP: $5	F18

Location: I-75, exit 279, just w. 5703 Oakley Blvd 33544. Fax: 813/973-1665. **Facility:** 78 units. 77 one-bedroom standard units. 1 one-bedroom suite ($89-$109). 3 stories, interior corridors. *Bath:* shower only. **Parking:** on-site. **Terms:** 3 day cancellation notice, [CP] meal plan available. **Amenities:** voice mail. *Some:* irons, hair dryers. **Pool(s):** heated outdoor. **Guest Services:** valet and coin laundry. **Business Services:** meeting rooms, fax. **Cards:** AX, CB, DC, DS, JC, MC, VI. **Special Amenities:** free continental breakfast and free local telephone calls.

Small-scale Hotel

SOME UNITS

—— WHERE TO DINE ——

BEEF O'BRADY'S   Lunch: $5-$8   Dinner: $5-$8   Phone: 813/994-1511

▼   **Location:** I-75, exit 279, just w; in Town Centre at Wesley Chapel. 27315 SR 54 33543. **Hours:** 11 am-10 pm, Fri & Sat-11 pm, Sun noon-10 pm. Closed: 4/20, 11/27, 12/25. **Features:** This ever popular sports-themed restaurant was established in 1985. Enjoy watching a favorite sports program on one of the several monitors set about the dining room while feasting on one of their tasty sandwiches, a burger or their famous O'Brady's buffalo-style chicken wings. Casual dress; beer & wine only. **Parking:** on-site. **Cards:** AX, DS, MC, VI.

American

REMINGTON'S STEAKHOUSE　　　　**Lunch:** $6-$20　　　**Dinner:** $6-$20　　　**Phone:** 813/973-1208

Steak House

Location: I-75, exit 279, just w. 27405 SR 54 33543. **Hours:** 3 pm-10 pm, Fri & Sat-11 pm, Sun noon-10 pm.
Features: Known for their signature steaks, enjoy the cowboy theme and the rustic look to this restaurant while enjoying a hearty 16-ounce T-bone or how about a combo dish with some wonderful BBQ rotisserie chicken and ribs! Casual dress; cocktails. **Parking:** on-site. **Cards:** MC, VI.

ZEPHYRHILLS pop. 10,833

─────── **WHERE TO STAY** ───────

BEST WESTERN ZEPHYRHILLS　　　　　　　　　　　　　　　　　**Phone:** (813)782-5527

SAVE

Motel

	1P	2P	XP	
2/1-4/30 [CP]	1P: $89-$99	2P: $89-$99	XP: $5	F12
12/1-1/31 & 11/15-11/30 [CP]	1P: $69-$99	2P: $69-$99	XP: $5	F12
5/1-11/14 [CP]	1P: $59-$69	2P: $59-$69	XP: $5	F12

Location: On US 301, 0.5 mi n of jct SR 54. 5734 Gall Blvd 33542. **Fax:** 813/783-7102. **Facility:** 52 one-bedroom standard units. 2 stories, exterior corridors. **Parking:** on-site. **Amenities:** irons, hair dryers. **Pool(s):** outdoor. **Business Services:** meeting rooms, fax (fee). **Cards:** AX, CB, DC, DS, MC, VI.

SOME UNITS

─────── **WHERE TO DINE** ───────

BEEF O'BRADY'S　　　　　　**Lunch:** $5-$7　　　**Dinner:** $5-$7　　　**Phone:** 813/780-7931

American

Location: On SR 301, just n of jct CR 54; in Merchants Square. 7337 Gall Blvd 33541. **Hours:** 11 am-11 pm, Fri & Sat-11:30 pm, Sun noon-10 pm. Closed: 12/25. **Features:** Big-screen televisions keep this family sports pub hopping on game days. The bustling spot cooks up traditional burgers, sandwiches, salads and wings. It features a terrific Philadelphia cheese steak served with fries and a pickle spear. Casual dress; beer & wine only. **Parking:** on-site. **Cards:** AX, DS, MC, VI.

This ends listings for the Tampa Vicinity.
The following page resumes the alphabetical listings of cities in Florida.

TARPON SPRINGS —See Tampa Bay p. 938.

TAVARES —See Orlando p. 749.

TEMPLE TERRACE —See Tampa Bay p. 939.

TEQUESTA pop. 5,273

──────── WHERE TO STAY ────────

JUPITER WATERFRONT INN
Phone: (561)747-9085

(AAA) (SAVE)
ᐁᐁᐁᐁ
Motel

12/15-4/15		2P: $158-$219	XP: $8	F13
12/1-12/14 & 4/16-11/30		2P: $85-$117	XP: $8	F13

Location: 1.5 mi n of SR 811, on US 1. 18903 SE Federal Hwy 33469. Fax: 561/575-3374. **Facility:** 38 one-bedroom standard units, some with whirlpools. 2 stories (no elevator), exterior corridors. **Parking:** on-site. **Terms:** [CP] meal plan available. **Amenities:** hair dryers. **Pool(s):** heated outdoor. **Leisure Activities:** whirlpool, fishing. **Guest Services:** coin laundry. **Business Services:** fax (fee). **Cards:** AX, DS, MC, VI.

TIERRA VERDE —See Tampa Bay p. 939.

TITUSVILLE pop. 40,670

──────── WHERE TO STAY ────────

BEST WESTERN SPACE SHUTTLE INN
Phone: (321)269-9100

(AAA) (SAVE)
ᐁᐁᐁᐁ
Small-scale Hotel

2/1-3/31	1P: $99-$135	2P: $99-$135
1/1-1/31 & 4/1-11/30	1P: $79-$135	2P: $79-$135
12/1-12/31	1P: $75-$135	2P: $75-$135

Location: I-95, exit 215, just e on SR 50. 3455 Cheney Hwy 32780. Fax: 321/383-4674. **Facility:** 129 units. 125 one-bedroom standard units, some with whirlpools. 4 one-bedroom suites ($129-$159). 2 stories, exterior corridors. **Parking:** on-site. **Terms:** [ECP] meal plan available, small pets only ($5 extra charge). **Amenities:** irons, hair dryers. **Dining:** 11:30 am-10:30 pm. **Pool(s):** heated outdoor. **Leisure Activities:** sauna, fishing, picnic area, playground, basketball, volleyball. **Guest Services:** valet and coin laundry. **Business Services:** meeting rooms, fax (fee). **Cards:** AX, CB, DC, DS, JC, MC, VI. **Special Amenities:** early check-in/late check-out and preferred room (subject to availability with advanced reservations).

SOME UNITS

DAYS INN-KENNEDY SPACE CENTER
Phone: (321)269-4480

(AAA) (SAVE)
ᐁᐁ ᐁᐁ
Small-scale Hotel

All Year	1P: $59-$135	2P: $59-$135	XP: $6	F17

Location: I-95, exit 215 (SR 50). 3755 Cheney Hwy 32780. Fax: 321/383-0646. **Facility:** 149 one-bedroom standard units. 2 stories, exterior corridors. **Parking:** on-site. **Terms:** [BP] meal plan available, pets ($10 extra charge). **Amenities:** hair dryers. *Some:* irons. **Pool(s):** outdoor, wading. **Leisure Activities:** exercise room, shuffleboard. **Guest Services:** valet and coin laundry. **Business Services:** meeting rooms, fax (fee). **Cards:** AX, CB, DC, DS, MC, VI. **Special Amenities:** free continental breakfast and free local telephone calls. *(See color ad below)*

SOME UNITS

HOLIDAY INN RIVERFRONT-KENNEDY SPACE CENTER
Phone: (321)269-2121

ᐁᐁᐁᐁ
Small-scale Hotel

All Year	1P: $100-$130	2P: $100-$130

Location: US 1, 0.5 mi s of jct SR 50; 1.7 mi n of jct SR 405. 4951 S Washington Ave 32780. Fax: 321/267-4739. **Facility:** 117 units. 115 one-bedroom standard units. 2 one-bedroom suites. 2 stories, exterior corridors. *Bath:* combo or shower only. **Parking:** on-site. **Terms:** small pets only ($20 fee). **Amenities:** irons, hair dryers. **Pool(s):** outdoor, wading. **Leisure Activities:** fishing, exercise room, volleyball. **Guest Services:** valet and coin laundry. **Business Services:** meeting rooms, fax (fee). *(See color ad p 948 & opposite inside back cover)*

SOME UNITS

LA VISTA INN

(AAA) (SAVE)
♦♦ ♦♦
Motel

All Year   2P: $30-$175   **Phone:** (321)269-7110
Location: I-95, exit 215, just w. 3655 Cheney Hwy 32780. Fax: 321/268-6972. **Facility:** 114 one-bedroom standard units. 2 stories (no elevator), exterior corridors. **Parking:** on-site. **Terms:** weekly rates available, [CP] meal plan available, small pets only ($10 extra charge). **Amenities:** hair dryers. *Some:* safes. **Pool(s):** outdoor. **Guest Services:** coin laundry. **Business Services:** fax (fee). **Cards:** AX, DC, DS, MC, VI. **Special Amenities: free continental breakfast and free local telephone calls.** *(See color ad below)*

SOME UNITS

RAMADA INN & SUITES-KENNEDY SPACE CENTER

(AAA) (SAVE)
♦♦♦ ♦♦♦
Small-scale Hotel

Phone: (321)269-5510
| 2/13-4/19 | 1P: $99 | 2P: $109 | XP: $6 | F18 |
| 12/1-2/12 & 4/20-11/30 | 1P: $94 | 2P: $99 | XP: $6 | F18 |

Location: I-95, exit 215, just e on SR 50. 3500 Cheney Hwy 32780. Fax: 321/269-3796. **Facility:** 124 units. 96 one-bedroom standard units. 28 one-bedroom suites ($119-$129), some with efficiencies. 2 stories, interior corridors. **Parking:** on-site. **Amenities:** voice mail, irons, hair dryers. **Dining:** 24 hours, cocktails. **Pool(s):** heated outdoor. **Leisure Activities:** sauna, whirlpool, playground, exercise room. **Guest Services:** valet and coin laundry. **Business Services:** meeting rooms, fax (fee). **Cards:** AX, DC, DS, MC, VI. **Special Amenities: free local telephone calls and free newspaper.**

SOME UNITS

FEE FEE

THE RANDOLPH INN

♦♦ ♦♦
Motel

All Year [CP]   1P: $57-$64   2P: $57-$64   XP: $3   **Phone:** (321)269-5945
   F18
Location: US 1, 0.8 mi n of jct SR 50. 3810 S Washington Ave 32780. Fax: 321/269-1054. **Facility:** 105 one-bedroom standard units. 2 stories, exterior corridors. **Parking:** on-site. **Terms:** weekly rates available. **Pool(s):** outdoor. **Guest Services:** coin laundry. **Business Services:** fax (fee). **Cards:** AX, MC, VI.

SOME UNITS

———— **WHERE TO DINE** ————

DIXIE CROSSROADS

(AAA)
♦♦ ♦♦
Seafood

Lunch: $6-$10   **Dinner:** $10-$14   **Phone:** 321/268-5000
Location: I-95, exit 220, 2 mi e; 1 mi w of jct US 1. 1475 Garden St 32796. **Hours:** 11 am-10 pm. Closed: 11/27, 12/25. **Reservations:** accepted. **Features:** Stroll through the butterfly garden or stand on the bridge over the fish pond on the grounds of this large and homey family restaurant. Ample servings of such favorites as rock shrimp make up a menu of mostly seafood and steak choices. Casual dress; cocktails. **Parking:** on-site. **Cards:** AX, CB, DC, DS, MC, VI.

PAUL'S SMOKEHOUSE RESTAURANT & LOUNGE　　　**Lunch:** $6-$12　　**Dinner:** $7-$18　　**Phone:** 321/267-3663

Location: US 1, 1 mi n of jct US 50. 3665 S Washington Ave 32780. **Hours:** 11 am-3:30 & 4:30-9 pm, Fri & Sat-10 pm. Closed major holidays; also Mon. **Features:** Witness space shuttle launches from this friendly, waterfront diner on the Indian River. Served in an Early American decor, the menu leans toward barbecue with prime rib and seafood specialties. Savor the fresh and flavorful rock shrimp, a local favorite. Casual dress; cocktails. **Parking:** on-site. **Cards:** AX, CB, DC, DS, MC, VI.

Steak & Seafood

PUMPERNICKEL'S DELI　　　**Lunch:** $4-$10　　**Dinner:** $12-$17　　**Phone:** 321/268-5160

Location: I-95, exit 215, 1 mi e on SR 50; just w of US 1. 2850 S Hopkins Ave 32780. **Hours:** 8 am-9 pm, Sun-2 pm. Closed major holidays. **Features:** The authentic, German-style deli lets patrons choose from a variety of moderately priced favorites: bratwurst, weisswurst, knockwurst, potato pancakes, Wiener schnitzel and Jaeger schnitzel. A sweet tooth can be soothed with homemade pastries or desserts. Senior portions and hot lunch and dinner buffet bars are available. Casual dress; beer & wine only. **Parking:** on-site. **Cards:** AX, CB, DC, DS, MC, VI.

German

TREASURE ISLAND —See Tampa Bay p. 940.

VALRICO pop. 6,582

─────── **WHERE TO DINE** ───────

BACKBAY RESTAURANT　　　**Lunch:** $7-$16　　**Dinner:** $7-$16　　**Phone:** 813/685-7111

Location: Jct Morningside Dr. 1807 SR 60 E 33594. **Hours:** 6 am-9:30 pm, Fri & Sat-10 pm. Closed: 11/27, 12/25. **Features:** Tucked amid sheltering oaks is a family-friendly restaurant that serves tried-and-true home cooking. A standout on the menu of steak, seafood and barbecue dishes is homemade specialty sausage. The Backbay house plate overflows with seafood, gator and frog legs. Casual dress; beer only. **Parking:** on-site. **Cards:** AX, DS, MC, VI.

Steak & Seafood

WILLIE'S FISH CAMP　　　　　　　**Dinner:** $9-$16　　　　　　**Phone:** 813/571-7630

Location: Jct SR 60, 0.7 mi n on Valrico Rd, 0.3 mi w. 1912 Front St 33595. **Hours:** 4:30 pm-9:30 pm, Fri & Sat-10 pm. Closed: 11/27, 12/25; also Sun & Mon. **Features:** Willie didn't get fat sitting in the corner. He was too busy cooking up great tasting seafood, chicken, steak and ribs over an oak-burning fire. Specialties such as catfish, gator bites and frog legs fit in perfectly with the tin-roofed shanty setting. Casual dress; cocktails. **Parking:** on-site. **Cards:** MC, VI.

Seafood

WOODY'S BAR B Q　　　**Lunch:** $5-$8　　**Dinner:** $7-$16　　**Phone:** 813/689-7722

Location: On SR 60 at jct Valrico Rd; in Valrico Square. 1905 E Hwy 60 33594. **Hours:** 11 am-9 pm, Fri & Sat-10 pm. Closed: 12/25. **Features:** Rustic decor gives the casual restaurant the feel of a barbecue shack, with picnic-bench seating and replica signs on the walls. The menu delivers the expected variety of barbecue sandwiches, ribs, beef, turkey and chicken, with a tempting array of platters, salads, desserts and side dishes, too. Casual dress; beer only. **Parking:** on-site. **Cards:** AX, DS, MC, VI.

American

VENICE pop. 17,764

─────── **WHERE TO STAY** ───────

BANYAN HOUSE HISTORIC BED & BREAKFAST　　　　　　　　**Phone:** 941/484-1385

| 12/1-4/30 | 2P: $109-$139 |
| 5/1-7/1 & 10/1-11/30 | 2P: $99-$119 |

Location: 0.7 mi s of jct Venice Ave W; downtown. Located in an upscale residential area. 519 Harbor Dr S 34285. Fax: 941/484-8032. **Facility:** Each guest room has its own theme in this European-style home built in 1926 and each is decorated with Victorian-style furnishings. Smoke free premises. 5 one-bedroom standard units, some with efficiencies. **Features:** 2 stories, interior corridors. *Bath:* combo or shower only. **Parking:** on-site. **Terms:** open 12/1-7/1 & 10/1-11/30, 2 night minimum stay - weekends, age restrictions may apply, 21 day cancellation notice-fee imposed, [BP] meal plan available. **Amenities:** irons, hair dryers. **Pool(s):** heated outdoor. **Leisure Activities:** whirlpool, bicycles. **Guest Services:** coin laundry. **Business Services:** PC, fax. **Cards:** MC, VI.

Bed & Breakfast

SOME UNITS

BEST WESTERN AMBASSADOR SUITES　　　　　　　　**Phone:** (941)480-9898

2/7-4/1 [ECP]	1P: $109-$149	2P: $109-$149	XP: $10	F17
12/20-2/6 [ECP]	1P: $99-$129	2P: $99-$129	XP: $10	F17
12/1-12/19 & 4/2-11/30 [ECP]	1P: $79-$109	2P: $79-$109	XP: $10	F17

Location: I-75, exit 193, just w. 400 Commercial Ct 34292. Fax: 941/488-6692. **Facility:** 83 units. 80 one-bedroom standard units. 3 one-bedroom suites with whirlpools. 3 stories, interior corridors. *Bath:* combo or shower only. **Parking:** on-site. **Amenities:** high-speed Internet, dual phone lines, irons, hair dryers. **Pool(s):** heated outdoor. **Leisure Activities:** exercise room. **Guest Services:** coin laundry. **Business Services:** meeting rooms, fax (fee). **Cards:** AX, DC, DS, MC, VI. **Special Amenities:** free continental breakfast and free newspaper.

Small-scale Hotel

SOME UNITS

BEST WESTERN SANDBAR BEACH RESORT　　　　　　　　**Phone:** (941)488-2251

2/1-4/30	1P: $159-$319	2P: $159-$319
12/1-1/31	1P: $79-$259	2P: $79-$259
5/1-8/31	1P: $89-$179	2P: $89-$179
9/1-11/30	1P: $79-$179	2P: $79-$179

Location: On Venice Beach, just n of jct Venice Ave. 811 The Esplanade North 34285. Fax: 941/485-2894. **Facility:** 44 one-bedroom standard units, some with efficiencies or kitchens. 1-4 stories, exterior corridors. *Bath:* combo or shower only. **Parking:** on-site. **Terms:** 7 day cancellation notice-fee imposed, package plans - in summer. **Amenities:** irons, hair dryers. **Dining:** 7 am-2 pm, Sun-noon; to 11 am 5/1-1/31, wine/beer only. **Pool(s):** heated outdoor. **Leisure Activities:** fishing, sand volleyball, shuffleboard. **Guest Services:** coin laundry. **Business Services:** fax (fee). **Cards:** AX, DC, DS, MC, VI. **Special Amenities:** free newspaper. *(See color ad p 950)*

Motel

SOME UNITS

HAMPTON INN & SUITES   Phone: (941)488-5900

2/1-4/30	1P: $79-$149	2P: $79-$149
12/18-1/31	1P: $69-$129	2P: $69-$129
12/1-12/17 & 5/1-11/30	1P: $59-$109	2P: $59-$109

Location: Just e of US 41 at jct of US Business 41. 881 Venetia Bay Blvd 34292. Fax: 941/488-6746. **Facility:** 110
Small-scale Hotel units. 74 one-bedroom standard units. 36 one-bedroom suites with kitchens. 3 stories, interior corridors. *Bath:*
combo or shower only. **Parking:** on-site. **Terms:** cancellation fee imposed. **Amenities:** voice mail, irons.
Some: DVD players (fee), dual phone lines, hair dryers. **Pool(s):** heated outdoor. **Leisure Activities:** whirlpool, jogging, exercise
room. **Guest Services:** valet and coin laundry. **Business Services:** meeting rooms, fax. **Cards:** AX, CB, DC, DS, MC, VI.
(See color ad below)

INN AT THE BEACH RESORT

Phone: (941)484-8471

AAA [SAVE]

◆◆◆◆

1/31-4/26 [ECP]	1P: $189-$289	2P: $189-$289	XP: $8	F16
12/1-1/30 & 4/27-7/5 [ECP]	1P: $94-$239	2P: $94-$239	XP: $8	F16
7/6-11/30 [ECP]	1P: $99-$189	2P: $99-$189	XP: $8	F16

Small-scale Hotel

Location: On Venice Beach at jct The Esplanade. 725 W Venice Ave 34285. Fax: 941/484-0593. **Facility:** 49 units. 35 one-bedroom standard units, some with efficiencies. 10 one- and 4 two-bedroom suites ($149-$429) with kitchens. 2 stories, exterior corridors. **Parking:** on-site. **Terms:** check-in 4 pm, 10 day cancellation notice, package plans - off season. **Amenities:** voice mail, safes, irons, hair dryers. **Pool(s):** heated outdoor. **Leisure Activities:** whirlpool. **Guest Services:** coin laundry. **Business Services:** fax. **Cards:** AX, DC, DS, MC, VI. **Special Amenities:** free continental breakfast and free newspaper. *(See color ad below)*

SOME UNITS

[icons]

KON-TIKI MOTEL

Phone: (941)485-9696

AAA [SAVE]

◆◆◆

1/19-4/21		2P: $120-$750	XP: $10	F12
12/17-1/18		2P: $70-$450	XP: $10	F12
12/1-12/16 & 4/22-11/30		2P: $60-$380	XP: $10	F12

Motel

Location: On US 41 business route, just n of jct Center St. 1487 S Tamiami Tr 34285. **Facility:** 10 one-bedroom standard units with efficiencies. 1 story, exterior corridors. **Parking:** on-site. **Pool(s):** indoor/outdoor. **Cards:** DS, MC, VI.

SOME UNITS

[icons]

MOTEL 6 - 364

Phone: 941/485-8255

◆◆

1/9-4/19	1P: $59-$69	2P: $65-$75	XP: $3	F17
4/20-5/31	1P: $42-$52	2P: $48-$58	XP: $3	F17
6/1-11/30	1P: $37-$47	2P: $43-$53	XP: $3	F17
12/1-1/8	1P: $36-$46	2P: $42-$52	XP: $3	F17

Motel

Location: On US 41, just n of jct Venice Ave. 281 US 41 Bypass N 34292. Fax: 941/488-3005. **Facility:** 103 one-bedroom standard units. 2 stories, exterior corridors. *Bath:* shower only. **Parking:** on-site. **Terms:** small pets only. **Pool(s):** heated outdoor. **Guest Services:** coin laundry. **Business Services:** fax. **Cards:** AX, CB, DC, DS, MC, VI.

SOME UNITS

[icons]

QUARTERDECK RESORT CONDOMINIUMS

Phone: 941/488-0449

AAA [SAVE]

◆◆◆

12/1-4/30 Wkly	1P: $780-$1005	2P: $780-$1005	XP: $8	F5
5/1-11/30 Wkly	1P: $595-$810	2P: $595-$810	XP: $8	F5

Condominium

Location: On Venice Beach, 0.4 mi n of jct Venice Ave on The Esplanade, then just w. 1275 Tarpon Center Dr 34285. Fax: 941/485-7288. **Facility:** 30 units. 5 one- and 25 two-bedroom standard units with kitchens. 2 stories, exterior corridors. **Parking:** on-site. **Terms:** check-in 4 pm, 30 day cancellation notice, package plans. **Amenities:** video library, irons. *Some:* CD players, hair dryers. **Pool(s):** heated outdoor. **Leisure Activities:** fishing, recreation programs. **Guest Services:** valet and coin laundry. **Business Services:** fax. **Cards:** MC, VI. **Special Amenities:** free room upgrade and preferred room (each subject to availability with advanced reservations).

SOME UNITS

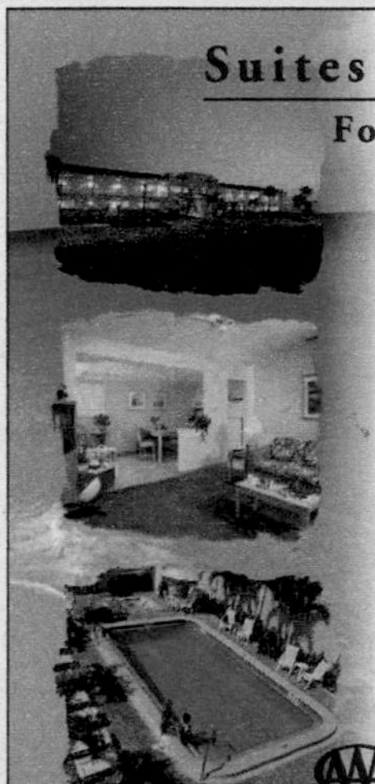

[icons]

WHERE TO DINE

THE CROW'S NEST MARINA RESTAURANT   Lunch: $5-$13   Dinner: $11-$23   Phone: 941/484-9551

AAA

▼▼▼

Seafood

Location: At S Jetty Venice Inlet, 0.9 mi w of US 41 via Venice Ave, 0.4 mi n on The Esplanade, then 0.5 mi nw. 1968 Tarpon Center Dr 34285. **Hours:** 11:30 am-3 & 5-10 pm, Sun noon-10 pm. Closed: 11/27, 12/25. **Features:** This bustling restaurant on Venice Inlet gives off a casual ambience. Rich flavors enhance the grouper Key Largo served with scallops, shrimp, crabmeat, mushrooms and hollandaise sauce and the tart Key lime pie. The wine cellar is extensive. Smoke free premises. Casual dress; cocktails. **Parking:** on-site. **Cards:** AX, DS, MC, VI.

LUNA RISTORANTE   Lunch: $7-$17   Dinner: $7-$17   Phone: 941/496-9090

▼▼

Italian

Location: On US 41; in Venice Village Shops at jct Jacaranda Blvd. 4191 S Tamiami Tr 34285. **Hours:** 11 am-9 pm, Fri & Sat-10 pm, Sun noon-9 pm. Closed major holidays. **Features:** Diners who have eaten one of the specialties here understand the popularity of this sports-themed restaurant. Hearty portions of chicken, veal, pasta and various baked dishes are loaded onto 16-inch plates. Spicy seafood marinara is full of shrimp, clams, mussels, scallops and fish. Casual dress; beer & wine only. **Parking:** on-site.

MYAKKA RIVER OYSTER BAR   Lunch: $4-$7   Dinner: $6-$14   Phone: 941/423-9616

▼▼

Seafood

Location: I-75, exit 191, 4.1 mi w on River Rd, just s on US 41; on the northwest bank of the Myakka River, enter via Myakka Dr. 121 Playmore Dr 34293. **Hours:** 11:30 am-9 pm, Fri & Sat-9:30 pm. Closed: 4/20, 11/27, 12/25. **Features:** Diners can look out onto the scenic Myakka River—home to manatees, osprey and alligators—while enjoying dishes ranging from fried seafood to steak to sandwiches. Spicy gumbo is a treat. Casual dress; cocktails. **Parking:** on-site. **Cards:** AX, DS, MC, VI.

SHARKY'S ON THE PIER   Lunch: $6-$8   Dinner: $9-$29   Phone: 941/488-1456

AAA

▼▼ ▼▼

Seafood

Location: US 41 business route, 0.5 mi w via Venice Ave, 2 mi s; at the Venice Fishing Pier. 1600 S Harbor Dr 34284. **Hours:** 11:30 am-3 & 4-10 pm. Closed: 11/27, 12/25. **Features:** Fish mounted on the walls and maritime decorations convey a fitting theme in this busy, gulf-front restaurant. Market fresh fish can be broiled, blackened, grilled or fried. Summer treats include children's crab races and calypso sundaes. Casual dress; cocktails; entertainment. **Parking:** on-site. **Cards:** AX, DS, MC, VI.

VERO BEACH pop. 20,362

WHERE TO STAY

AQUARIUS OCEAN FRONT RESORT MOTEL   Phone: 772/231-5218

AAA (SAVE)

▼▼▼

Motel

	1P:	2P:	XP:	
2/1-4/30	1P: $79-$149	2P: $79-$149	XP: $5	F11
12/1-1/31	1P: $69-$115	2P: $69-$115	XP: $5	F11
6/30-11/30	1P: $60-$99	2P: $60-$99	XP: $5	F11
5/1-6/29	1P: $55-$95	2P: $55-$95	XP: $5	F11

Location: 1.8 mi s, just e of SR A1A on south beach, just s of 17th St Causeway Bridge (E Causeway Blvd, SR 656). 1526 S Ocean Dr 32963. Fax: 772/231-5218. **Facility:** 26 one-bedroom standard units, some with kitchens. 2 stories, exterior corridors. **Parking:** on-site. **Terms:** 14 day cancellation notice, weekly rates available. **Pool(s):** heated outdoor. **Leisure Activities:** tiki huts & grills beachside, shuffleboard. **Guest Services:** coin laundry. **Business Services:** fax (fee). **Cards:** AX, DC, DS, MC, VI.

SOME UNITS

BEST WESTERN VERO BEACH   Phone: (772)567-8321

AAA (SAVE)

▼▼▼

Small-scale Hotel

	1P:	2P:	XP:	
12/15-4/19 [ECP]	1P: $69-$125	2P: $69-$125	XP: $5	F18
12/1-12/14 & 10/1-11/30 [ECP]	1P: $54-$84	2P: $54-$84	XP: $5	F18
4/20-9/30 [ECP]	1P: $49-$79	2P: $49-$79	XP: $5	F18

Location: I-95, exit 147 (SR 60), 0.5 mi e. 8797 20th St 32966. Fax: 772/569-8558. **Facility:** 114 one-bedroom standard units. 2 stories, exterior corridors. *Bath:* combo or shower only. **Parking:** on-site. **Terms:** weekly rates available. **Amenities:** irons, hair dryers. **Dining:** 11 am-9 pm, cocktails. **Pool(s):** heated outdoor, wading. **Guest Services:** coin laundry. **Business Services:** meeting rooms, fax (fee). **Cards:** AX, DC, DS, MC, VI. **Special Amenities:** free continental breakfast and free room upgrade (subject to availability with advanced reservations).

SOME UNITS

COMFORT INN   Phone: (772)569-0900

(SAVE)

▼▼▼

Small-scale Hotel

	1P:	2P:	XP:	
12/15-4/15 [ECP]	1P: $69-$109	2P: $69-$109	XP: $5	F12
12/1-12/14 & 4/16-11/30 [ECP]	1P: $59-$79	2P: $59-$79	XP: $5	F12

Location: US 1, 1.3 mi s of jct SR 60. 950 Hwy 1 32960. Fax: 772/569-5502. **Facility:** 66 one-bedroom standard units. 2 stories, exterior corridors. *Bath:* combo or shower only. **Parking:** on-site. **Terms:** 3 day cancellation notice-fee imposed. **Amenities:** *Some:* irons, hair dryers. **Pool(s):** heated outdoor. **Guest Services:** coin laundry. **Business Services:** fax (fee). **Cards:** AX, CB, DC, DS, MC, VI.

SOME UNITS

DISNEY'S VERO BEACH RESORT   Phone: (772)234-2000

AAA

▼▼▼

Resort
Large-scale Hotel

	1P:	2P:
1/1-6/4	1P: $165-$640	2P: $165-$640
12/1-12/31	1P: $160-$635	2P: $160-$635
6/5-8/23	1P: $190-$380	2P: $190-$380
8/24-11/30	1P: $165-$325	2P: $165-$325

Location: 7 mi n of Vero Beach; SR A1A, at jct CR 510; from jct I-95, exit 156, 11 mi e via CR 512 and 510. 9250 Island Grove Terrace 32963. Fax: 772/234-2030. **Facility:** Nestled among sea grass and palm trees, this Florida-themed resort offers a variety of accommodations, all with a porch or balcony. 112 one-bedroom standard units. 4 stories, interior corridors. *Bath:* combo or shower only. **Parking:** on-site. **Terms:** check-in 4 pm, 5 day cancellation notice-fee imposed. **Amenities:** voice mail, safes, irons, hair dryers. **Dining:** 2 restaurants, 7:30-11 am, 11:30-3 & 5-10 pm, cocktails, entertainment. **Pool(s):** heated outdoor. **Leisure Activities:** sauna, whirlpool, waterslide, fishing, wave runners, miniature golf, 2 lighted tennis courts, recreation programs, camp fires, lawn croquet, jogging, playground, exercise room, basketball, horseshoes, shuffleboard, volleyball. *Fee:* charter fishing, bicycles, massage, game room. **Guest Services:** gift shop, valet and coin laundry. **Business Services:** meeting rooms, business center. **Cards:** AX, DC, DS, JC, MC, VI.

SOME UNITS

HAMPTON INN VERO BEACH　　　　　　　　　　　　　　　**Phone:** (772)770-4299

SAVE

▼▼▼▼

Small-scale Hotel

All Year　　　　　　　1P: $83-$96　　　　　2P: $88-$101

Location: I-95, exit 147, just w. 9350 19th Ln 32966. Fax: 772/770-3549. **Facility:** 63 one-bedroom standard units. 3 stories, interior corridors. *Bath:* combo or shower only. **Parking:** on-site. **Terms:** [ECP] meal plan available. **Amenities:** voice mail, irons, hair dryers. **Pool(s):** outdoor. **Guest Services:** valet laundry. **Business Services:** fax (fee). **Cards:** AX, CB, DC, DS, MC, VI.

SOME UNITS

[S📶] [🐕] [📶] [🏊] [📷] [DATA PORT] [💻] / [✕] /

HOLIDAY INN EXPRESS　　　　　　　　　　　　　　　　**Phone:** (772)567-2500

▼▼▼▼

Small-scale Hotel

12/1-5/31 [ECP]　　　　1P: $99-$135

6/1-11/30 [ECP]　　　　1P: $69-$89

Location: I-95, exit 147. 9400 19th Lane 32966. Fax: 772/567-4979. **Facility:** 65 one-bedroom standard units. 3 stories, interior corridors. *Bath:* combo or shower only. **Parking:** on-site. **Terms:** 10 day cancellation notice, [CP] meal plan available. **Amenities:** irons, hair dryers. **Pool(s):** outdoor. **Leisure Activities:** exercise room. **Guest Services:** valet laundry. **Business Services:** meeting rooms, administrative services, fax (fee). **Cards:** AX, CB, DC, DS, JC, MC, VI.

SOME UNITS

[ASK] [S📶] [🍴+] [🐕] [📶] [🏊] [📷] [DATA PORT] [💻] / [✕] /

HOWARD JOHNSON EXPRESS INN　　　　　　　　　　　**Phone:** (772)778-1985

AAA SAVE

▼▼▼

Motel

2/1-4/5 [CP]　　　　　1P: $69-$99　　　　2P: $69-$99　　　XP: $8　　　F17

1/1-1/31 [CP]　　　　　1P: $59-$99　　　　2P: $59-$99　　　XP: $5　　　F17

12/1-12/31 & 4/6-11/30 [CP]　1P: $45-$55　　　2P: $45-$55　　　XP: $5　　　F17

Location: I-95, exit 147 (SR 60), just se. 1985 90th Ave 32966. Fax: 772/778-1998. **Facility:** 58 one-bedroom standard units. 2 stories, exterior corridors. **Parking:** on-site. **Pool(s):** outdoor. **Guest Services:** coin laundry. **Business Services:** fax (fee). **Cards:** AX, CB, DC, DS, MC, VI.

SOME UNITS

[S📶] [🍴+] [📶] [🏊] [📷] [💻] / [✕] [🔌] /

HOWARD JOHNSON EXPRESS INN-DOWNTOWN　　　　**Phone:** (772)567-5171

AAA SAVE

▼▼▼

Motel

1/1-4/15　　　　　　　1P: $53-$100　　　2P: $73-$100　　　XP: $8　　　F18

12/1-12/31 & 4/16-11/30　1P: $47-$100　　　2P: $47-$100　　　XP: $8　　　F18

Location: 0.3 mi s of jct SR 60. 1725 US Hwy 1 32960. Fax: 772/567-5194. **Facility:** 51 one-bedroom standard units. 2 stories, interior/exterior corridors. **Parking:** on-site. **Terms:** [CP] meal plan available. **Pool(s):** outdoor. **Business Services:** fax (fee). **Cards:** AX, DC, DS, MC, VI. **Special Amenities:** free continental breakfast and free newspaper.

SOME UNITS

[S📶] [🍴+] [📶] [🏊] [📷] [DATA PORT] [💻] / [✕] /

THE ISLANDER INN　　　　　　　　　　　　　　　　　**Phone:** 772/231-4431

AAA SAVE

▼▼▼

Motel

2/9-4/21　　　　　　　1P: $105-$120　　2P: $105-$120　　XP: $10　　F12

1/19-2/8　　　　　　　1P: $89-$109　　　2P: $89-$109　　　XP: $10　　F12

12/1-1/18　　　　　　　1P: $79-$99　　　　2P: $79-$99　　　XP: $10　　F12

4/22-11/30　　　　　　1P: $69-$95　　　　2P: $69-$95　　　XP: $10　　F12

Location: Just s of SR 60. 3101 Ocean Dr 32963. Fax: 772/231-4431. **Facility:** 16 one-bedroom standard units, some with efficiencies or kitchens. 2 stories, exterior corridors. *Bath:* combo or shower only. **Parking:** on-site. **Terms:** 14 day cancellation notice-fee imposed. **Pool(s):** outdoor. **Business Services:** fax (fee). **Cards:** AX, MC, VI.

SOME UNITS

[S📶] [🍴+] [🏊] [🔌] / [🖥] [💻] /

PALM COURT RESORT HOTEL　　　　　　　　　　　　**Phone:** (772)231-2800

▼▼▼▼

Small-scale Hotel

12/23-4/15　　　　　　1P: $169-$219　　2P: $169-$219　　XP: $10　　F16

12/1-12/22　　　　　　1P: $109-$189　　2P: $109-$189　　XP: $10　　F16

4/16-5/27　　　　　　　1P: $119-$179　　2P: $119-$179　　XP: $10　　F16

5/28-11/30　　　　　　1P: $109-$169　　2P: $109-$169　　XP: $10　　F16

Location: Just s of SR 60. 3244 Ocean Dr 32963. Fax: 772/231-3446. **Facility:** 106 units. 104 one-bedroom standard units, some with efficiencies. 2 one-bedroom suites ($179-$379) with efficiencies. 5 stories, interior corridors. *Bath:* combo or shower only. **Parking:** on-site. **Terms:** 3 day cancellation notice-fee imposed, weekly rates available, [AP] meal plan available, 20% service charge. **Amenities:** voice mail, irons, hair dryers. **Pool(s):** heated outdoor. **Leisure Activities:** exercise room. *Fee:* charter fishing. **Guest Services:** valet and coin laundry. **Business Services:** meeting rooms, fax (fee). **Cards:** AX, DC, DS, JC, MC, VI.

SOME UNITS

[ASK] [S📶] [🍴] [🍸] [⚙M] [🐕] [📶] [🏊] [📷] [DATA PORT] [💻] / [✕] [🔌] [🖥] /

FEE　FEE

THE VERO BEACH HOTEL & CLUB　　　　　　　　　　**Phone:** (772)231-5666

▼▼▼▼

Small-scale Hotel

2/1-4/15　　　　　　　1P: $279-$409　　2P: $279-$409

12/23-1/31　　　　　　1P: $259-$349　　2P: $259-$349

12/1-12/22　　　　　　1P: $209-$319　　2P: $209-$319

4/16-11/30　　　　　　1P: $149-$319　　2P: $149-$319

Location: Just n of SR 60. 3500 Ocean Dr 32963. Fax: 772/234-4866. **Facility:** 54 units. 40 one- and 14 two-bedroom standard units. 5 stories, interior/exterior corridors. **Parking:** on-site. **Terms:** 7 day cancellation notice-fee imposed, [AP] meal plan available. **Amenities:** video library (fee), voice mail, irons, hair dryers. **Pool(s):** heated outdoor, wading. **Leisure Activities:** whirlpool. **Guest Services:** valet and coin laundry. **Business Services:** meeting rooms. *Fee:* administrative services, fax. **Cards:** AX, DC, DS, JC, MC, VI.

SOME UNITS

[ASK] [S📶] [🍴] [⚙M] [📶] [🏊] [VCR] [DATA PORT] [🔌] [💻] / [✕] [🖥] /

VERO BEACH RESORT　　　　　　　　　　　　　　　　**Phone:** 772/562-9991

▼▼▼ ▼▼▼

Motel

12/1-4/15　　　　　　　1P: $62-$69　　　　2P: $62-$69

4/16-11/30　　　　　　1P: $44-$49　　　　2P: $44-$49

Location: I-95, exit 147 (SR 60), 0.5 mi e. 3500 20th St 32966. Fax: 772/562-0716. **Facility:** 211 units. 195 one-bedroom standard units. 16 one-bedroom suites ($89). 2 stories, exterior corridors. *Bath:* combo or shower only. **Parking:** on-site. **Terms:** check-in 4 pm, weekly rates available, small pets only ($5 extra charge). **Pool(s):** outdoor. **Leisure Activities:** exercise room. **Guest Services:** coin laundry. **Business Services:** meeting rooms, fax (fee). **Cards:** AX, CB, DS, MC.

SOME UNITS

[ASK] [🐕] [🍴] [📶] [🏊] [📷] [DATA PORT] / [✕] [🔌] [🖥] [💻] /

——— WHERE TO DINE ———

CAFE' DU SOIR
▼▼▼
French

Dinner: $18-$27

Phone: 772/569-4607

Location: 2 mi e of jct US 1 and SR 603 (Indian River Blvd). 21 Royal Palm Point 32960. **Hours:** 6 pm-10 pm. Closed: 1/1, 12/25. **Reservations:** suggested. **Features:** The second-floor restaurant, with a terrace that looks out onto the Indian River, is a great place for cozy, romantic dining. Attentive servers often go out of their way to make your experience memorable. Enjoy the snapper for two or the rack of lamb. Smoke free premises. Semi-formal attire; beer & wine only. **Parking:** on-site. **Cards:** AX, DC, MC, VI.

CHARLEY'S SOUTH BEACH GRILLE
▼▼▼ ▼▼▼
Steak & Seafood

Dinner: $10-$25

Phone: 772/231-6311

Location: SR A1A. 0.3 mi s of jct SR 656. 1410 Hwy A1A 32963. **Hours:** 5 pm-9:30 pm, Fri & Sat-10 pm. Closed: 11/27; also Super Bowl Sun. **Reservations:** accepted. **Features:** A popular spot for retirees, this established restaurant is known for well-prepared entrees of fresh fish, steaks, Danish ribs and chicken. The prime rib is slow-cooked and served au jus. The tropical garden setting contributes to the relaxing atmosphere. Casual dress; cocktails. **Parking:** on-site. **Cards:** AX, CB, DC, DS, MC, VI.

CHEZ YANNICK
▼▼▼ ▼▼▼
French

Dinner: $15-$29

Phone: 772/234-4115

Location: 1.8 mi s, just e of SR A1A on South Beach, just s of 17th St Causeway Bridge (E Causeway Blvd, SR 656). 1601 S Ocean Dr 32963. **Hours:** 6 pm-9:30 pm. Closed: Sun. **Reservations:** suggested. **Features:** Smart, airy dining rooms feature an on-the-ball staff circulating to deliver delicious meals. Select from a great mix of breads, and try the green salad with a most delicate raspberry dressing. For a creative main event, order the tasty veal piccata. Casual dress; cocktails; entertainment. **Parking:** on-site. **Cards:** AX, DC, MC, VI.

GUYTANO'S ITALIAN BISTRO & BAR
▼▼▼
Italian

Lunch: $6-$13   **Dinner:** $7-$19   **Phone:** 772/778-4088

Location: On SR 60; west end of Indian River Mall. 6200 20th St #394 32966. **Hours:** 11:30 am-10 pm. Closed: 11/27, 12/25. **Reservations:** accepted. **Features:** Close your eyes and savor the tastes and smells of Little Italy. All the pasta is handmade. Other specialties include calzone, sandwiches and pizza cooked in an open-flame brick oven. Veal Milanese makes a striking meal presentation. Casual dress; cocktails. **Parking:** on-site. **Cards:** AX, DC, DS, MC, VI.

LOBSTER SHANTY
▼▼▼ ▼▼
Seafood

Lunch: $6-$15   **Dinner:** $11-$22   **Phone:** 772/562-1941

Location: SR 60; 1 mi w of jct SR A1A. 1 Royal Palm Blvd 32960. **Hours:** 11:30 am-9 pm, Fri & Sat-10 pm. Closed: 11/27. **Features:** When there's a wait, you can guess the reason. Tourists and locals flock to this casual dining room overlooking the Indian River. Chicken, seafood and beef specialties are the best in town, and the salad is one of the crispiest concoctions ever. Casual dress; cocktails. **Parking:** on-site. **Cards:** AX, CB, DC, MC, VI.

OCEAN GRILL
🔴🔴🔴
▼▼ ▼▼
Steak & Seafood

Lunch: $8-$18   **Dinner:** $15-$30   **Phone:** 772/231-5409

Location: E of SR A1A, at end of SR 60. 1050 Sexton Plaza 32963. **Hours:** 11:30 am-2 & 5-10 pm; 11:30 am-2 & 5:45-10 pm 4/16-12/14. Closed: 7/4, 11/27; also Super Bowl Sun. **Features:** A dramatic oceanfront view and a rustic dining room serving great food translates to a popular, busy eatery. Broiled salmon with a particularly good dill sauce is definitely worth any wait. A courteous and knowledgeable staff attend your every need. Smoke free premises. Casual dress; cocktails. **Parking:** on-site. **Cards:** AX, CB, DC, DS, MC, VI.

TANGOS
▼▼▼
Regional American

Dinner: $18-$25

Phone: 772/231-1550

Location: Jct SR A1A and Beachland, just e to Cardinal Dr, then s to Bougainvillea, just e. 925 Bougainville Ln 32963. **Hours:** Open 12/1-8/31 & 10/1-11/30; 5:30 pm-10 pm. Closed: 11/27, 12/25; also Sun & Mon. **Reservations:** suggested. **Features:** The chef/owner's creative touch enlivens the cuisine, which include selections of prime cuts of meat, fresh seafood, pasta and breads and desserts made on the premises. Choose from a wide variety of wines, several available by the glass. Smoke free premises. Casual dress; beer & wine only. **Parking:** street. **Cards:** AX, CB, DC, DS, MC, VI.

VILANO BEACH pop. 2,533   (See map p. 785; index p. 787)

——— WHERE TO STAY ———

HAMPTON INN OCEANSIDE
[SAVE]
▼▼▼
Small-scale Hotel

Phone: (904)827-9797   61

	2/10-9/6 [ECP]	1P: $139-$259	2P: $139-$259
	9/7-11/30 [ECP]	1P: $109-$199	2P: $109-$199
	12/1-2/9 [ECP]	1P: $99-$199	2P: $99-$199

Location: Just s of Vilano Bridge, s of SR A1A. 95 Vilano Rd 32084. Fax: 904/824-1599. **Facility:** 94 one-bedroom standard units, some with whirlpools. 3 stories, interior corridors. *Bath:* combo or shower only. **Parking:** on-site. **Terms:** 2-3 night minimum stay - weekends, cancellation fee imposed. **Amenities:** video games, dual phone lines, voice mail, safes, irons, hair dryers. *Some:* fax. **Pool(s):** outdoor. **Leisure Activities:** whirlpool, exercise room. **Guest Services:** sundries, valet and coin laundry. **Business Services:** meeting rooms. **Cards:** AX, CB, DC, DS, MC, VI.

SOME UNITS

🛎️ 🔲 📶 📷 🛏️ 🏊 💻 🔌 📠 📷 📺 / ✕ /

OCEAN SANDS BEACH INN
🔴🔴🔴 [SAVE]
▼▼▼
Motel

Phone: (904)824-1112   60

| | 2/8-8/15 [CP] | 1P: $69-$99 | 2P: $69-$99 | XP: $5 | F12 |
| | 12/1-2/7 & 8/16-11/30 [CP] | 1P: $49-$79 | 2P: $49-$79 | XP: $5 | F12 |

Location: 2 mi ne at Vilano Bridge on SR A1A. Located across from beach. 3465 Coastal Hwy 32084 (3465 Coastal Hwy, ST. AUGUSTINE). Fax: 904/824-1112. **Facility:** Designated smoking area. 29 one-bedroom standard units. 2 stories, interior corridors. *Bath:* combo or shower only. **Parking:** on-site. **Terms:** 2 night minimum stay - weekends 2/15-8/15. **Amenities:** *Some:* hair dryers. **Business Services:** fax. **Cards:** AX, DS, MC, VI. **Special Amenities:** free continental breakfast and free local telephone calls. *(See color ad p 796)*

SOME UNITS

🔲 🛎️ 📶 📠 📷 📺 / ✕ /

(See map p. 785)

------ WHERE TO DINE ------

FIDDLER'S GREEN　　　　**Dinner:** $12-$25　　　　　　**Phone:** 904/824-8897　　
　　　🔷　　　**Location:** Just e of SR A1A where SR A1A turns n, 0.5 mi e of Vilano Beach Bridge. 2750 Anahma Dr 32084.
　🔻🔻🔻　**Hours:** 5 pm-10 pm. Closed: 11/27; also 12/19-12/26; also Super Bowl Sun. **Reservations:** suggested.
　　　　　　　Features: Sink into large rattan chairs and take in the lovely ocean view. Fresh local seafood is used in
　American　many of the entrees, including a creative medley of lobster, shrimp and scallops in a white cream sauce.
　　　　　　　Twice-baked potatoes make a tasty side dish. Casual dress; cocktails. **Parking:** on-site. **Cards:** AX, DC,
　　　　　　　DS, MC, VI.

WAKULLA SPRINGS

------ WHERE TO STAY ------

WAKULLA SPRINGS LODGE　　　　　　　　　　　　　　　**Phone:** (850)224-5950
　🔻🔻🔻　　All Year　　　　　　1P: $79-$99　　　　2P: $79-$99　　　　XP: $5　　　　　F12
　　　　　　　Location: At jct SR 61 and 267. Located in Wakulla Springs State Park. 550 Wakulla Park Dr 32305.
Small-scale Hotel　**Fax:** 850/561-7251. **Facility:** 27 one-bedroom standard units. 2 stories, interior corridors. **Parking:** on-site.
　　　　　　　Terms: 3 day cancellation notice. **Dining:** The Ball Room, see separate listing. **Leisure Activi-**
ties: recreation programs. **Guest Services:** gift shop. **Business Services:** meeting rooms, fax (fee). **Cards:** AX, DS, MC, VI.
　　　　　　　　　　　　　　　　　　　　　　　　　　　　　SOME UNITS

------ WHERE TO DINE ------

THE BALL ROOM　　　　　**Lunch:** $6-$12　　　　**Dinner:** $7-$16　　　　**Phone:** 850/224-5950
　🔻🔻🔻　**Location:** Jct SR 61 and 267; in Wakulla Springs State Park; in Wakulla Springs Lodge. 550 Wakulla Park Dr 32327.
　　　　　　　Hours: 7:30-10 am, 11:30-2 & 6-8 pm. Closed: 11/27; also 12/25 for dinner. **Reservations:** suggested.
Regional American　**Features:** Freshly prepared meals with a strong Southern accent, including pecan-crusted grouper, veal
　　　　　　　chops and excellent fried oysters from Apalachicola Bay, are the key to the restaurant's appeal. Gaze out
over lovely and scenic Wakulla Springs. Smoke free premises. Casual dress; beer & wine only. **Parking:** on-site. **Cards:** AX,
DS, MC, VI.

WEEKI WACHEE pop. 12

──────── WHERE TO STAY ────────

BEST WESTERN WEEKI WACHEE RESORT

Phone: (352)596-2007

AAA [SAVE]
▼▼▼▼
Motel

	1P: $69-$89	2P: $69-$89
12/21-4/30 [CP]	1P: $69-$89	2P: $69-$89
5/1-9/1 [CP]	1P: $59-$89	2P: $59-$89
12/1-12/20 & 9/2-11/30 [CP]	1P: $59-$79	2P: $59-$79

Location: On US 19; at jct SR 50 (Cortez Blvd). 6172 Commercial Way 34606. Fax: 352/596-0667. **Facility:** 122 one-bedroom standard units. 2 stories, exterior corridors. **Parking:** on-site. **Amenities:** voice mail, irons, hair dryers. **Pool(s):** outdoor, wading. **Leisure Activities:** shuffleboard. **Guest Services:** coin laundry. **Business Services:** meeting rooms, fax (fee). **Cards:** AX, CB, DC, DS, JC, MC, VI. **Special Amenities:** free continental breakfast and free newspaper. *(See color ad p 233 & p 834)*

SOME UNITS

[icons] / ⊠ /

COMFORT INN

Phone: 352/596-9000

[SAVE]
▼▼▼▼
Motel

	1P: $75-$140	2P: $75-$140	XP: $10	F18
All Year [CP]	1P: $75-$140	2P: $75-$140	XP: $10	F18

Location: On SR 50, just e of jct US 19. 9373 Cortez Blvd 34613. Fax: 352/597-4010. **Facility:** 68 one-bedroom standard units. 2 stories, exterior corridors. *Bath:* combo or shower only. **Parking:** on-site. **Terms:** 3 day cancellation notice-fee imposed, pets ($10 extra charge). **Amenities:** hair dryers. *Some:* irons. **Pool(s):** outdoor. **Leisure Activities:** exercise room. **Guest Services:** coin laundry. **Business Services:** meeting rooms, fax. **Cards:** AX, CB, DC, DS, JC, MC, VI.

SOME UNITS

[icons] / ⊠ 🛏 🖼 /
FEE FEE

──────── WHERE TO DINE ────────

NELLIE'S RESTAURANT

Lunch: $5-$7   **Dinner:** $5-$11   **Phone:** 352/596-8321

▼▼▼
American

Location: On SR 50, just e of jct US 19; in Weeki Wachee Village Shops. 6234 Commercial Way 34613. **Hours:** 6 am-9 pm. Closed major holidays. **Features:** A savory Yankee pot roast and homemade mashed potatoes are highlights of this homey eatery. Freshly-prepared dishes of poultry, steaks and seafood complete the menu. Don't leave without a piece of the coconut cream pie and a cup of coffee. Casual dress; beer & wine only. **Parking:** on-site. **Cards:** MC, VI.

⊠

WESLEY CHAPEL —See Tampa Bay p. 945.

WEST MELBOURNE pop. 9,824—See also MELBOURNE.

──────── WHERE TO STAY ────────

HAMPTON INN MELBOURNE

Phone: (321)956-6200

[SAVE]
▼▼▼▼
Small-scale Hotel

	1P: $99	2P: $109
1/1-5/15 [ECP]	1P: $99	2P: $109
5/16-11/30 [ECP]	1P: $89	2P: $99
12/1-12/31 [ECP]	1P: $89	2P: $89

Location: I-95, exit 180, just ne. 194 Dike Rd 32904. Fax: 321/956-3230. **Facility:** 66 one-bedroom standard units, some with whirlpools. 3 stories, interior corridors. *Bath:* combo or shower only. **Parking:** on-site. **Terms:** package plans. **Amenities:** voice mail, irons, hair dryers. **Pool(s):** outdoor. **Leisure Activities:** exercise room. **Guest Services:** valet and coin laundry. **Business Services:** meeting rooms, fax (fee). **Cards:** AX, CB, DC, DS, JC, MC.

SOME UNITS

[icons] / 🛏 🖼 /
FEE FEE

HOLIDAY INN EXPRESS MELBOURNE

Phone: (321)724-2050

▼▼▼▼
Small-scale Hotel

	1P: $89-$129	2P: $89-$129	XP: $10	F15
1/1-5/30 [ECP]	1P: $89-$129	2P: $89-$129	XP: $10	F15
12/1-12/31 & 5/31-11/30 [ECP]	1P: $79	2P: $79	XP: $10	F15

Location: I-95, exit 180, just e. 4510 W New Haven Ave 32904. Fax: 321/724-9882. **Facility:** 68 one-bedroom standard units. 5 stories, interior corridors. *Bath:* combo or shower only. **Parking:** on-site. **Amenities:** dual phone lines, voice mail, irons, hair dryers. **Business Services:** meeting rooms, fax (fee). **Cards:** AX, DC, DS, JC, MC, VI.

SOME UNITS

[ASK] [icons] / ⊠ /

HOWARD JOHNSON

Phone: (321)768-8877

▼▼ ▼▼
Small-scale Hotel

	1P: $69-$129	2P: $69-$129	XP: $6	F
1/16-4/30	1P: $69-$129	2P: $69-$129	XP: $6	F
5/1-11/30	1P: $59-$89	2P: $59-$89	XP: $6	F
12/1-1/15	1P: $59-$69	2P: $59-$69	XP: $6	F

Location: I-95, exit 180, just e on SR 192. 4431 W New Haven Ave 32904. Fax: 321/768-8666. **Facility:** 119 one-bedroom standard units. 2 stories, exterior corridors. *Bath:* combo or shower only. **Parking:** on-site. **Terms:** 10 day cancellation notice, small pets only ($20 extra charge). **Amenities:** safes (fee). **Pool(s):** outdoor. **Guest Services:** coin laundry. **Business Services:** meeting rooms, fax (fee). **Cards:** AX, CB, DC, DS, MC, VI.

SOME UNITS

[ASK] [icons] / ⊠ 🛏 🖼 /
FEE FEE

WESTON —See Fort Lauderdale p. 413.

WEST PALM BEACH pop. 82,103 (See map p. 757; index p. 758)—*See also PALM BEACH.*

──────── WHERE TO STAY ────────

BEST WESTERN PALM BEACH LAKES INN   Phone: (561)683-8810   **9**

1/15-4/14 [ECP]	1P: $94-$96	2P: $94-$96	XP: $10 F17
4/15-11/30 [ECP]	1P: $64-$66	2P: $64-$66	XP: $10 F17
12/1-1/14 [ECP]	1P: $61-$66	2P: $61-$66	XP: $10 F17

Location: I-95, exit 71, just e. Faces Palm Beach Mall. 1800 Palm Beach Lakes Blvd 33401. Fax: 561/697-3497.

Motel   **Facility:** 135 units. 134 one-bedroom standard units. 1 one-bedroom suite ($125-$150). 2 stories (no elevator), interior/exterior corridors. *Bath:* combo or shower only. **Parking:** on-site. **Terms:** cancellation fee imposed. **Amenities:** voice mail, irons, hair dryers. **Pool(s):** heated outdoor. **Leisure Activities:** shuffleboard. **Guest Services:** valet laundry, airport transportation-Palm Beach International Airport, area transportation-within 4 mi. **Business Services:** meeting rooms, fax (fee). **Cards:** AX, CB, DC, DS, MC, VI. **Special Amenities:** free continental breakfast and free newspaper.

SOME UNITS

FEE   FEE

COMFORT INN-ON PALM BEACH LAKES   Phone: (561)689-6100   **8**

12/1-4/15	1P: $89-$109	2P: $99-$119	XP: $10 F18
4/16-11/30	1P: $59-$89	2P: $69-$99	XP: $10 F18

Location: I-95, exit 71, just w. 1901 Palm Beach Lakes Blvd 33409. Fax: 561/686-6177. **Facility:** 162 one-bedroom standard units. 6 stories, interior corridors. **Parking:** on-site. **Terms:** [ECP] meal plan available, small pets

Small-scale Hotel   only ($25 fee, $10 extra charge). **Amenities:** voice mail, irons, hair dryers. *Fee:* video games, safes. **Pool(s):** heated outdoor. **Guest Services:** valet and coin laundry. **Business Services:** meeting rooms, fax (fee). **Cards:** AX, CB, DC, DS, JC, MC, VI. **Special Amenities:** early check-in/late check-out. *(See color ad below)*

SOME UNITS

FEE   FEE

(See map p. 757)

COURTYARD BY MARRIOTT AIRPORT
Phone: 561/207-1800 21

SAVE

Small-scale Hotel

1/12-5/3	1P: $129-$159	2P: $129-$159
12/1-1/11 & 5/4-11/30	1P: $79-$129	2P: $79-$129

Location: I-95, exit 69, 0.5 mi w on Belvedere Rd, 0.5 mi n on Australian Ave, then e. 1800 Centrepark Dr E 33401. Fax: 561/207-1818. **Facility:** 103 units. 99 one-bedroom standard units, some with whirlpools. 4 one-bedroom suites ($149-$199). 4 stories, interior corridors. *Bath:* combo or shower only. **Parking:** on-site. **Amenities:** video games (fee), dual phone lines, voice mail, irons, hair dryers. **Pool(s):** small heated outdoor. **Leisure Activities:** whirlpool, exercise room. **Guest Services:** sundries, valet and coin laundry, area transportation. **Business Services:** meeting rooms, fax (fee). **Cards:** AX, DC, DS, MC, VI.

SOME UNITS

COURTYARD BY MARRIOTT-WEST PALM BEACH
Phone: (561)640-9000 2

SAVE

Small-scale Hotel

12/31-5/31	1P: $139-$159	2P: $139-$159
12/1-12/30 & 10/1-11/30	1P: $99-$129	2P: $99-$129
6/1-9/30	1P: $89-$119	2P: $89-$119

Location: I-95, exit 74 (45th St), just w on CR 702. Located in Northpoint Corporate Park. 600 Northpoint Pkwy 33407. Fax: 561/471-0122. **Facility:** 149 units. 137 one-bedroom standard units. 12 one-bedroom suites. 3 stories, interior corridors. *Bath:* combo or shower only. **Parking:** on-site. **Terms:** check-in 4 pm, cancellation fee imposed, [BP] meal plan available. **Amenities:** high-speed Internet (fee), voice mail, irons, hair dryers. **Pool(s):** heated outdoor. **Leisure Activities:** whirlpool, exercise room. **Guest Services:** valet and coin laundry. **Business Services:** meeting rooms, fax (fee). **Cards:** AX, DC, DS, MC, VI. *(See ad p 247)*

SOME UNITS

CROWNE PLAZA HOTEL AND RESORT

WEST PALM BEACH
Phone: (561)689-6400 15

AAA SAVE

Large-scale Hotel

1/1-4/12	1P: $143-$161	2P: $143-$161	XP: $10	F17
4/13-11/30	1P: $98-$125	2P: $98-$125	XP: $10	F17
12/1-12/31	1P: $98-$107	2P: $98-$107	XP: $10	F17

Location: I-95, exit 69, 0.5 mi w at jct Australian Ave. 1601 Belvedere Rd 33406. Fax: 561/683-7150. **Facility:** 219 units. 115 one-bedroom standard units. 104 one-bedroom suites. 15 stories, interior corridors. *Bath:* combo or shower only. **Parking:** on-site and valet. **Terms:** check-in 4 pm. **Amenities:** dual phone lines, voice mail, irons, hair dryers. **Dining:** 6:30 am-2 & 5-10 pm, cocktails. **Pool(s):** heated outdoor. **Leisure Activities:** saunas, whirlpool, 2 tennis courts, exercise room. **Guest Services:** gift shop, valet laundry, airport transportation-Palm Beach International Airport, area transportation-within 5 mi. **Business Services:** meeting rooms, business center. **Cards:** AX, CB, DC, DS, MC, VI.

SOME UNITS
FEE

HAMPTON INN WEST PALM BEACH AT EMERALD

DUNES GOLF COURSE
Phone: 561/682-9990 12

SAVE

Small-scale Hotel

1/6-3/30	1P: $149-$179	2P: $159-$189
12/1-1/5	1P: $109-$129	2P: $119-$139
3/31-5/31	1P: $99-$119	2P: $109-$129
6/1-11/30	1P: $79-$109	2P: $89-$119

Location: Florida Tpke, exit 99 (SR 704/Okeechobee Blvd), then just w to Vista Pkwy. 2025 Vista Pkwy 33411. Fax: 561/682-9446. **Facility:** 110 one-bedroom standard units. 4 stories, interior corridors. *Bath:* combo or shower only. **Parking:** on-site. **Amenities:** video games (fee), high-speed Internet, dual phone lines, voice mail, irons, hair dryers. **Pool(s):** heated outdoor. **Leisure Activities:** whirlpool, limited exercise equipment. **Guest Services:** sundries, complimentary evening beverages: Mon-Thurs, valet and coin laundry. **Business Services:** meeting rooms, fax (fee). **Cards:** AX, CB, DC, DS, JC, MC, VI.

SOME UNITS

HAMPTON INN WEST PALM BEACH/INTERNATIONAL

AIRPORT
Phone: (561)471-8700 13

SAVE

Motel

1/14-4/15	1P: $81-$116
12/1-1/13	1P: $71-$116
4/16-11/30	1P: $116

Location: I-95, exit 69, 0.3 mi w. 1505 Belvedere Rd 33406. Fax: 561/689-7385. **Facility:** 135 one-bedroom standard units. 3 stories, exterior corridors. **Parking:** on-site. **Terms:** cancellation fee imposed, [ECP] meal plan available. **Amenities:** video games (fee), voice mail, irons, hair dryers. **Pool(s):** heated outdoor. **Guest Services:** valet laundry. **Business Services:** fax (fee). **Cards:** AX, DS, MC, VI.

SOME UNITS
FEE FEE

HIBISCUS HOUSE BED & BREAKFAST
Phone: (561)863-5633 7

Historic Bed & Breakfast

12/1-4/30	1P: $100-$270	2P: $100-$270
5/1-11/30	1P: $75-$180	2P: $75-$180

Location: 1.2 mi n on Flagler Dr from jct Palm Beach Lakes Blvd, 0.3 mi w. 501 30th St 33407. Fax: 561/863-5633. **Facility:** A secluded tropical garden enhances this restored home which was built for the local mayor in 1922; guest rooms have period furnishings. Smoke free premises. 5 one-bedroom standard units, some with whirlpools. 2 stories (no elevator), interior corridors. *Bath:* combo or shower only. **Parking:** on-site. **Terms:** 14 day cancellation notice-fee imposed, - off season, small pets only. **Amenities:** irons, hair dryers. **Pool(s):** small heated outdoor. **Business Services:** fax. **Cards:** AX, DC, MC, VI.

SOME UNITS

(See map p. 757)

HILTON PALM BEACH AIRPORT   Phone: (561)684-9400   **19**

	1/1-4/26	1P: $134-$144	2P: $144-$154	
	4/27-11/30	1P: $114-$124	2P: $124-$134	
	12/1-12/31	1P: $114-$124	2P: $124-$134	XP: $10 F

Location: I-95, exit 68, 0.3 mi w at jct Australian Ave and Southern Blvd. 150 Australian Ave 33406. Fax: 561/689-9421.
Large-scale Hotel Facility: 247 units. 245 one-bedroom standard units. 2 one-bedroom suites ($325-$450). 10 stories, interior corridors. *Bath:* combo or shower only. Parking: on-site and valet. Amenities: high-speed Internet (fee), dual phone lines, voice mail, safes, irons, hair dryers. Pool(s): heated outdoor. Leisure Activities: whirlpool, fishing, 2 lighted tennis courts, exercise room, volleyball. *Fee:* waterskiing. Guest Services: gift shop, valet laundry, area transportation. Business Services: conference facilities, fax (fee). Cards: AX, DC, DS, JC, MC, VI.

SOME UNITS
🛎️ ✈️ 🍴 🍸 🏊 ✖️ 🐾 [DATA PORT] 🖥️ / ✖️ 🔌 /
FEE

HOLIDAY INN PALM BEACH AIRPORT   Phone: (561)659-3880   **18**

| **AAA** | 1/1-4/21 | 1P: $99 | 2P: $99 | XP: $10   F18 |
| | 12/1-12/31 & 4/22-11/30 | 1P: $59 | 2P: $59 | |

Location: I-95, exit 69, just w. 1301 Belvedere Rd 33405 (718 Naylor Mill Rd, SALISBURY, MD, 21801). Fax: 561/655-8886. Facility: 199 one-bedroom standard units. 11 stories, interior corridors. Parking: on-site.
Large-scale Hotel Amenities: voice mail, irons, hair dryers. Dining: 7 am-2 & 5-10 pm, cocktails. Pool(s): heated outdoor. Leisure Activities: saunas, exercise room. Guest Services: valet laundry, airport transportation-Palm Beach International Airport. Business Services: meeting rooms, business center. Cards: AX, DC, DS, MC, VI. Special Amenities: free room upgrade and preferred room (each subject to availability with advanced reservations). *(See color ad below & opposite inside back cover)*

SOME UNITS
🛎️ ✈️ 🍴 🍸 🏌️ 🏊 🐾 [DATA PORT] 🖥️ / ✖️ 🔌 /

HOTEL BIBA   Phone: (561)832-0094   **22**

	12/1-4/1 [CP]	2P: $109-$179	XP: $10 F18
	9/30-11/30 [CP]	2P: $89-$139	XP: $10 F18
Classic Motel	4/2-9/29 [CP]	2P: $79-$129	XP: $10 F18

Location: I-95, exit 69, 0.8 mi e, at corner of US 1 and Olive Rd. 320 Belvedere Rd 33405. Fax: 561/833-7848. Facility: Designated smoking area. 43 units. 41 one-bedroom standard units. 2 one-bedroom suites ($149-$229). 2 stories (no elevator), interior/exterior corridors. *Bath:* combo or shower only. Parking: on-site and valet. Terms: cancellation fee imposed, weekly rates available. Amenities: CD players, voice mail, irons, hair dryers. Pool(s): outdoor, heated outdoor. Leisure Activities: *Fee:* bicycles. Business Services: meeting rooms, administrative services. Cards: AX, MC, VI.

[ASK] 🛎️ 🍴 🍸 🏊 🐾 ✖️ [DATA PORT]

(See map p. 757)

LA QUINTA INN

SAVE

▼▼▼▼▼ Motel

Phone: 561/697-3388 ⑪

All Year   1P: $80   2P: $80
Location: SR 704, at east side of Florida Tpke, exit 99. 5981 Okeechobee Blvd 33417. Fax: 561/697-2834. **Facility:** 114 one-bedroom standard units. 4 stories, exterior corridors. *Bath:* combo or shower only. **Parking:** on-site. **Terms:** [CP] meal plan available. **Amenities:** voice mail, safes (fee), irons, hair dryers. **Pool(s):** heated outdoor. **Guest Services:** valet and coin laundry. **Business Services:** fax (fee). **Cards:** AX, DC, MC, VI.

SOME UNITS

FEE

PARKVIEW MOTOR LODGE

🔺🔺🔺 **SAVE**

▼▼▼▼▼ Motel

Phone: (561)833-4644 ⑳

1/10-4/16 [CP]	1P: $70-$80	2P: $76-$88	XP: $8	F17
12/19-1/9 [CP]	1P: $60-$70	2P: $62-$74	XP: $8	F17
12/1-12/18 & 4/17-11/30 [CP]	1P: $46-$58	2P: $48-$60	XP: $8	F17

Location: On US 1, 0.5 mi s of US 908 and SR 80. Located in a commercial area. 4710 S Dixie Hwy 33405. Fax: 561/833-4644. **Facility:** 28 units. 27 one-bedroom standard units. 1 one-bedroom suite ($92-$176). 1-2 stories (no elevator), exterior corridors. *Bath:* combo or shower only. **Parking:** on-site. **Terms:** weekly rates available. **Business Services:** fax (fee). **Cards:** AX, CB, DC, DS, JC, MC, VI. **Special Amenities:** free continental breakfast and free local telephone calls.

SOME UNITS

RADISSON SUITE INN PALM BEACH AIRPORT

🔺🔺🔺 **SAVE**

▼▼▼▼▼ Small-scale Hotel

Phone: (561)689-6888 ⑰

All Year   1P: $98-$116   2P: $98-$116
Location: I-95, exit 69, 0.5 mi w on Belvedere Rd, then 0.5 mi n. 1808 Australian Ave S 33409. Fax: 561/683-5783. **Facility:** 174 units. 134 one-bedroom standard units. 40 one-bedroom suites ($128-$136). 6 stories, interior corridors. **Parking:** on-site. **Terms:** small pets only ($125 fee). **Amenities:** high-speed Internet (fee), dual phone lines, voice mail, honor bars, irons, hair dryers. **Dining:** 6:30 am-2 & 5-10 pm, Sat & Sun from 7 am, cocktails. **Pool(s):** heated outdoor. **Leisure Activities:** whirlpool, exercise room. **Guest Services:** gift shop, valet laundry, airport transportation-Palm Beach International Airport, area transportation-within 5 mi. **Business Services:** meeting rooms, business center. **Cards:** AX, CB, DC, DS, JC, MC, VI. **Special Amenities:** free newspaper.

SOME UNITS

RED ROOF INN-WEST PALM BEACH

🔺🔺🔺 **SAVE**

▼▼▼▼ Motel

Phone: (561)697-7710 ③

1/1-4/19	1P: $69-$89	2P: $74-$94	XP: $5	F18
12/1-12/31 & 4/20-11/30	1P: $43-$61	2P: $48-$66	XP: $5	F18

Location: I-95, exit 74 (45th St), just w on CR 702. Located in Metrocentre Corporate Park. 2421 Metro Center Blvd E 33407. Fax: 561/697-1728. **Facility:** 129 one-bedroom standard units. 3 stories, interior/exterior corridors. *Bath:* combo or shower only. **Parking:** on-site. **Terms:** small pets only. **Amenities:** video games (fee), voice mail. **Pool(s):** heated outdoor. **Business Services:** fax (fee). **Cards:** AX, CB, DC, DS, MC, VI. **Special Amenities:** free local telephone calls and free newspaper.

SOME UNITS
FEE   FEE

RESIDENCE INN BY MARRIOTT WEST PALM BEACH

SAVE

▼▼▼▼▼ Small-scale Hotel

Phone: (561)687-4747 ④

12/1-4/30 [ECP]	1P: $120-$179	2P: $169-$229
5/1-6/26 & 10/1-11/30 [ECP]	1P: $79-$129	2P: $135-$165
6/27-9/30 [ECP]	1P: $69-$114	2P: $109-$149

Location: I-95, exit 74, just w on 45th St. Located in Metrocentre Corporate Park. 2461 Metrocenter Blvd 33407. Fax: 561/697-3633. **Facility:** 78 units. 33 one-bedroom standard units with kitchens. 33 one- and 12 two-bedroom suites. 3 stories, interior corridors. *Bath:* combo or shower only. **Parking:** on-site. **Terms:** cancellation fee imposed, small pets only ($100 fee). **Amenities:** dual phone lines, voice mail, irons, hair dryers. **Pool(s):** heated outdoor. **Leisure Activities:** whirlpool, exercise room, sports court, basketball, volleyball. **Guest Services:** complimentary evening beverages: Mon-Thurs, valet and coin laundry. **Business Services:** meeting rooms, fax (fee). **Cards:** AX, CB, DC, DS, JC, MC, VI.

SOME UNITS

SHERATON HOTEL AT CITYPLACE

▼▼▼▼▼ Large-scale Hotel

Phone: (561)833-1234 ⑭

12/1-1/7	1P: $155	2P: $155	XP: $10	F
1/8-4/15 & 6/1-11/30	1P: $125	2P: $125	XP: $10	F
4/16-5/31	1P: $112	2P: $112	XP: $10	F

Location: I-95, exit 70A, 0.8 mi e on Okeechobee Blvd E. 630 Clearwater Park Rd 33401. Fax: 561/833-4689. **Facility:** 349 units. 335 one-bedroom standard units. 14 one-bedroom suites. 10 stories, interior corridors. **Parking:** on-site. **Amenities:** high-speed Internet (fee), dual phone lines, voice mail, irons, hair dryers. *Some:* fax. **Pool(s):** heated outdoor. **Leisure Activities:** whirlpool, 2 lighted tennis courts, exercise room. **Guest Services:** gift shop, valet laundry, area transportation. **Business Services:** conference facilities, fax (fee). **Cards:** AX, CB, DC, DS, JC, MC, VI. *(See color ad p 5)*

SOME UNITS
FEE   FEE

STUDIO 6 EXTENDED STAY #6026

▼▼▼▼ Motel

Phone: 561/640-3335 ⑯

All Year   1P: $54-$79   2P: $58-$83   XP: $4
Location: I-95, exit 69 (Belvedere Rd), w to Australian Ave, n to Centrepark Dr, then e straight ahead. 1535 Centrepark Dr N 33401. Fax: 561/640-3374. **Facility:** 137 one-bedroom standard units with kitchens. 2 stories, exterior corridors. *Bath:* combo or shower only. **Parking:** on-site. **Terms:** 7 night minimum stay, weekly rates available, small pets only ($10 extra charge). **Amenities:** voice mail, irons. **Guest Services:** coin laundry. **Business Services:** fax (fee). **Cards:** AX, CB, DC, DS, MC, VI.

SOME UNITS

(See map p. 757)

TROPICAL GARDENS BED & BREAKFAST   **Phone:** 561/848-4064   **6**

| | 12/1-5/15 | 1P: $85-$95 | 2P: $85-$95 | XP: $20 | F12 |
| | 5/16-11/30 | 1P: $75-$85 | 2P: $85-$95 | XP: $20 | F12 |

Historic Bed & Breakfast

Location: Palm Beach Lakes Blvd, 1.2 mi n on N Dixie Hwy, then just w. Located in a quiet area. 419 32nd St 33407-4809. Fax: 561/848-2422. **Facility:** Decorated in a Key West theme, this B&B features a courtyard area around the pool. Smoke free premises. 4 units. 2 one-bedroom standard units. 2 cottages ($95-$135). 1 story. *Bath:* combo or shower only. **Parking:** on-site. **Terms:** age restrictions may apply, 14 day cancellation notice-fee imposed, weekly rates available, [ECP] meal plan available, package plans. **Amenities:** *Some:* CD players, irons. **Pool(s):** small heated outdoor. **Leisure Activities:** bicycles. **Business Services:** fax. **Cards:** AX, DS, MC, VI.

SOME UNITS

(ASK) (S/D) (+) (~) (X) / (VCR) (■) (▤) (▣) /

WELLESLEY INN & SUITES   **Phone:** (561)689-8540   **10**

(AAA) (SAVE)

| | 12/1-4/19 [CP] | 1P: $89-$129 | 2P: $89-$129 |
| | 4/20-11/30 [CP] | 1P: $53-$89 | 2P: $53-$89 |

Small-scale Hotel

Location: I-95, exit 71, just w. 1910 Palm Beach Lakes Blvd 33409. Fax: 561/687-8090. **Facility:** 104 one-bedroom standard units. 6 stories, interior corridors. *Bath:* combo or shower only. **Parking:** on-site. **Terms:** cancellation fee imposed, small pets only ($50 fee). **Amenities:** voice mail, irons, hair dryers. *Fee:* video games, high-speed Internet. **Pool(s):** heated outdoor. **Guest Services:** valet and coin laundry. **Business Services:** meeting rooms, fax (fee). **Cards:** AX, CB, DC, DS, MC, VI. *(See color ad p 957)*

SOME UNITS

(S/D) (🐾) (♈) (🖐) (🛋) (🏊) (✈) (DATA PORT) (▣) / (X) (■) (▤) /
                                                          FEE FEE

──────── *The following lodging was either not evaluated or did not* ────────
meet AAA rating requirements but is listed for your information only.

ROYAL PALM HOUSE B & B   **Phone:** 561/863-9836

(fyi)   Not evaluated; management refused evaluation. **Location:** I-95, exit 74 (45th St), 2.4 mi e to Spruce Ave, then 0.7 mi s. Located in the historic district. 3215 Spruce Ave 33407. Facilities, services, and decor characterize a mid-range property.

──────── **WHERE TO DINE** ────────

391ST BOMB GROUP   **Lunch:** $4-$11   **Dinner:** $12-$29   **Phone:** 561/683-3919   **7**

American

Location: I-95, exit 68, 2 mi w on US 98. 3989 Southern Blvd 33406. **Hours:** 11:30 am-10 pm, Fri-11 pm, Sat noon-11 pm, Sun 10 am-2:30 & 4:30-10 pm. **Closed:** Sat for lunch 6/1-9/30. **Reservations:** suggested. **Features:** The runway lights of Palm Beach International Airport create a romantic mood in this dining room. World War II memorabilia decorates the walls, and there are some replica aircraft outside. Casual dress; cocktails. **Parking:** on-site. **Cards:** AX, CB, DC, DS, MC, VI.

(Y) (X)

GREAT TEXAS LAND & CATTLE CO.   **Dinner:** $9-$23   **Phone:** 561/840-1511   **1**

American

Location: SR 809 (Military Tr), 0.5 mi n of jct 45th St. 6000 N Military Tr 33407. **Hours:** 4:30 pm-9 pm, Fri & Sat-10 pm. **Closed:** 12/25. **Features:** A warm, friendly and casual atmosphere with a touch of the Old West, Great Texas offers a full menu featuring USDA choice steak, prime rib, seafood and pasta dishes. Casual dress; cocktails. **Parking:** on-site. **Cards:** AX, DS, MC, VI.

(Y) (X)

MARK'S CITY PLACE   **Dinner:** $18-$30   **Phone:** 561/514-0770   **5**

Regional American

Location: I-95, exit 70A, 1.1 mi e to Florida Ave, then n; in City Place on 2nd level. 700 S Rosemary Ave #228 33401. **Hours:** 5 pm-11 pm, Fri & Sat-midnight, Sun-10:30 pm. **Reservations:** suggested. **Features:** Decor in the busy "City Place" restaurant is soft with wrought iron accents and indirect lighting along with the wall treatments. Memorable food reflects Mark Militello's twist on fresh seafood and American favorites. Dressy casual; cocktails. **Parking:** on-site. **Cards:** AX, CB, DC, DS, JC, MC, VI.

(&M) (Y) (K) (X)

ORCHIDS OF SIAM   **Lunch:** $5-$9   **Dinner:** $10-$18   **Phone:** 561/969-2444   **8**

Thai

Location: I-95, exit 66, 1.3 mi w on Forest Hill Blvd (SR 882); jct Forest Hill Blvd and Congress Ave; in the Forest Hill Center. 3027 Forest Hill Blvd 33406. **Hours:** 11:30 am-2:30 & 4:30-10 pm, Fri-11 pm, Sat 4:30 pm-11 pm, Sun 4:30 pm-10 pm. **Closed:** 7/4; also 6/30-7/4. **Reservations:** suggested. **Features:** Lining the menu are traditional Thai favorites prepared with varying degrees of spiciness. Soft decor colors offer comfort, and one dining room nurtures a tropical feel with live orchids all around. Dressy casual; cocktails. **Parking:** on-site. **Cards:** AX, DC, MC, VI.

(Y) (X)

RAIN DANCER STEAK HOUSE   **Dinner:** $15-$30   **Phone:** 561/684-2811   **4**

Steak & Seafood

Location: I-95, exit 71, 0.8 mi w. 2300 Palm Beach Lakes Blvd, Suite 109 33409. **Hours:** 5 pm-10 pm, Fri & Sat-10:30 pm. **Closed:** 11/27, 12/25. **Features:** An Old World decor sets the tone in the cozy, rustic restaurant, where servers handle the busy tempo without missing a beat. A balanced selection of wines complement succulent top-grade steak, such as a juicy 22-ounce porterhouse. Dressy casual; cocktails. **Parking:** on-site. **Cards:** AX, CB, DC, DS, MC, VI.

(Y) (X)

──────── *The following restaurants have not been evaluated by AAA* ────────
but are listed for your information only.

CRAZY BUFFET   **Phone:** 561/616-9288

(fyi)   Not evaluated. **Location:** I-95, exit 71, just w. 2030 Palm Beach Lakes Blvd 33409. **Features:** Included among selections of Japanese and Chinese foods are many varieties of sushi. The buffet lines up many traditional Chinese favorites.

(Y)

(See map p. 757)

FLANIGAN'S SEAFOOD BAR & GRILL   **Phone:** 561/659-3129
[fyi]   Not evaluated. **Location:** 330 Southern Blvd. **Features:** The family-friendly restaurant is known for its baby
         back ribs, burgers and seafood.

LEGAL SEA FOODS   **Phone:** 561/838-9000
[fyi]   Not evaluated. **Location:** 550 S Rosemary Ave 33401. **Features:** New England style seafood has arrived,
         experience the clam chowder and the New England Clam Bake as well as other favorites.

WILLISTON pop. 2,297

——————— WHERE TO STAY ———————

WILLISTON MOTOR INN   **Phone:** 352/528-4801
         All Year   1P: $35   2P: $35
▽▽▽   **Location:** 0.5 mi n on US 27 Alternate. 606 W Noble Ave 32696. Fax: 352/528-4650. **Facility:** 44 one-bedroom
Motel   standard units, some with kitchens. 1 story, exterior corridors. *Bath:* combo or shower only. **Parking:** on-site.
         Terms: cancellation fee imposed, weekly rates available, small pets only ($6 extra charge). **Pool(s):** outdoor.
Guest Services: coin laundry. **Business Services:** fax (fee). **Cards:** AX, DC, MC, VI.
                                                                                           SOME UNITS
🏠 🍴 🏊 🛎 💻 / ✕ 📷 🖨 💻 /

WINTER GARDEN —*See Orlando p. 749.*

WINTER HAVEN pop. 26,487

——————— WHERE TO STAY ———————

BEST WESTERN ADMIRAL'S INN   **Phone:** (863)324-5950
(AAA) [SAVE]   2/14-3/31 [CP]   1P: $95-$125   2P: $95-$125   XP: $6   F17
               12/1-2/13 [CP]   1P: $77-$107   2P: $77-$107   XP: $6   F17
▽▽▽▽   4/1-11/30 [CP]   1P: $72-$102   2P: $72-$102   XP: $6   F17
               Location: SR 540, 3 mi e of jct US 17; 3.9 mi w of jct US 27. Located at entrance to Cypress Gardens. 5665 Cypress
Small-scale Hotel Gardens Blvd 33884. Fax: 863/324-2376. **Facility:** 156 units. 153 one-bedroom standard units. 3 one-bedroom
               suites, some with whirlpools. 3-5 stories, interior/exterior corridors. **Parking:** on-site. **Terms:** small pets only
($15 extra charge). **Amenities:** voice mail, irons, hair dryers. **Dining:** 5 pm-10 pm; closed Sun & Mon, cocktails, entertainment.
Pool(s): heated outdoor. **Leisure Activities:** whirlpool, exercise room. *Fee:* miniature golf. **Guest Services:** gift shop, valet and
coin laundry, beauty salon, florist. **Business Services:** meeting rooms, business center. **Cards:** AX, CB, DC, DS, JC, MC, VI.
Special Amenities: free continental breakfast. *(See ad below)*
                                                                                           SOME UNITS
🆓 🐕 🍴 📺 🏐 🏊 ✕ 🎣 💻 / ✕ 🖨 🖨 /

CYPRESS MOTEL   **Phone:** (863)324-5867
(AAA) [SAVE]   2/14-3/31   1P: $60-$70   2P: $70-$80   XP: $10   F12
               12/19-2/13   1P: $50-$60   2P: $54-$64   XP: $10   F12
▽▽   12/1-12/18 & 4/1-11/30   1P: $40-$50   2P: $49-$59   XP: $10   F12
Motel   **Location:** 1.7 mi w of US 27 on SR 540; or 2 mi e of Cypress Gardens Theme Park, then 500 yds n. 5651 Cypress Gar-
               dens Rd 33884. Fax: 863/324-9655. **Facility:** 21 one-bedroom standard units, some with efficiencies. 1 story,
               exterior corridors. *Bath:* combo or shower only. **Parking:** on-site. **Terms:** [CP] meal plan available, small pets
only ($10 fee). **Pool(s):** heated outdoor. **Leisure Activities:** playground. **Guest Services:** gift shop, coin laundry. **Cards:** AX,
DC, MC, VI. **Special Amenities: early check-in/late check-out and free continental breakfast.**
                                                                                           SOME UNITS
🆓 🐕 🏊 🛎 💻 / ✕ 🖨 🖨 /
                                                                                           FEE FEE

HAMPTON INN   **Phone:** (863)299-9251
[SAVE]   All Year   1P: $74-$150   2P: $74-$150
               Location: On SR 580, 0.3 mi e of jct US 17. 202 Cypress Gardens Blvd 33880. Fax: 863/401-9388. **Facility:** 54
▽▽▽   one-bedroom standard units. 3 stories, interior corridors. *Bath:* combo or shower only. **Parking:** on-site.
Small-scale Hotel **Terms:** [ECP] meal plan available. **Amenities:** dual phone lines, voice mail, irons, hair dryers. **Pool(s):**
               heated outdoor. **Leisure Activities:** exercise room. **Guest Services:** valet laundry. **Business Services:**
               business center. **Cards:** AX, CB, DC, DS, MC, VI.
                                                                                           SOME UNITS
🆓 🏊 🛎 💻 💻 / ✕ 🖨 /

HOLIDAY INN CYPRESS GARDENS-WINTER HAVEN

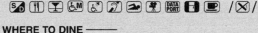

		Phone: (863)294-4451
⊕⊕⊕ SAVE	3/1-3/31	1P: $119	XP: $10	F17
	12/1-2/28 & 4/1-11/30	1P: $79	XP: $10	F17

Location: 0.8 mi s on US 17. 1150 Third St SW 33880. Fax: 863/293-9829. **Facility:** 226 one-bedroom standard units. 2 stories, exterior corridors. *Bath:* combo or shower only. **Parking:** on-site. **Amenities:** voice mail, irons, hair dryers. **Dining:** 6:30 am-2 & 4-8 pm, cocktails. **Pool(s):** heated outdoor, wading. **Leisure Activities:** golf privileges, exercise room. **Guest Services:** valet and coin laundry. **Business Services:** meeting rooms, fax (fee). **Cards:** AX, CB, DC, DS, JC, MC, VI. *(See color ad opposite inside back cover)*

Small-scale Hotel

SOME UNITS

🛎️ 🍴 🍸 🚹M ♿ 🎣 🐾 🐶 📠 🛄 ☕ /✕/

------- WHERE TO DINE -------

CHRISTY'S SUNDOWN RESTAURANT

	Lunch: $5-$10	Dinner: $12-$27	Phone: 863/293-0069

⊕⊕⊕

▼▼▼

American

Location: 0.8 mi s on US 17. 1100 3rd St 33882. **Hours:** 11 am-2 & 5-10:30 pm, Sat from 5 pm. Closed major holidays; also Sun. **Reservations:** accepted. **Features:** Although the restaurant specializes in prime rib, its menu selections also incorporate seafood, veal, pasta and chicken dishes. The quiet dining room is a favorite of major-league baseball players during spring training. Casual dress; cocktails. **Parking:** on-site. **Cards:** AX, DS, MC, VI.

🍸 ✕

WINTER PARK —See Orlando p. 750.

YULEE —See Jacksonville p. 477.

ZEPHYRHILLS —See Tampa Bay p. 946.

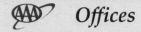 *Offices*

Cities with main offices are listed in **BOLD TYPE** and toll-free member service numbers in *ITALIC TYPE*.
All are closed Saturdays, Sundays and holidays unless otherwise indicated.

The type of service provided is designated below the name of the city where the office is located:

✚ Auto travel services, including books/maps, marked maps and on-demand Triptik maps
● Auto travel services, including books/maps, marked maps, but no on-demand Triptik maps
■ Provides books/maps only. No marked maps or on-demand Triptik maps available
▲ Travel agency services

NATIONAL OFFICE: 1000 AAA DRIVE, HEATHROW, FLORIDA 32746-5063, (407) 444-7000

FLORIDA

BELLEAIR BLUFFS—AAA AUTO CLUB SOUTH, 100 N INDIAN ROCKS RD, 33770. MON-FRI 8:30-5:30. (727) 584-7678.■▲

BOCA RATON—AAA AUTO CLUB SOUTH, 4400 N FEDERAL HWY #152, 33431. MON-FRI 8:30-5:30. (561) 395-8687.■▲

BOCA RATON—AAA AUTO CLUB SOUTH, 21073 POWERLINE RD STE 53, 33433. MON-FRI 9-5:30. (561) 477-8471.▲

BRADENTON—AAA AUTO CLUB SOUTH, 6210 MANATEE AVE W, 34209. MON-FRI 8:30-5:30. (941) 798-2221.✚▲

BRADENTON—AAA AUTO CLUB SOUTH, 6513 14TH ST W/SARABAY PL, 34207. MON-FRI 8:30-5:30. (941) 756-0606.●▲

BRANDON—AAA AUTO CLUB SOUTH, 415 W ROBERTSON ST, 33511. MON-FRI 8:30-5:30. (813) 681-5761.✚▲

CLEARWATER—AAA AUTO CLUB SOUTH, 2170 RAINBOW DR, 33765. MON-FRI 8:30-5:30. (727) 448-2600.✚▲

DAYTONA BEACH—AAA AUTO CLUB SOUTH, 2525 INTNL SPEEDWAY BLVD, 32114. MON-FRI 8:30-5:30. (386) 252-0531.✚▲

DELRAY BEACH—AAA AUTO CLUB SOUTH, 14539 MILITARY TR #A, 33484. MON-FRI 8:30-5:30. (561) 865-1400.✚▲

FORT MYERS—AAA AUTO CLUB SOUTH, 2516 COLONIAL BLVD, 33907. MON-FRI 8:30-5:30. (239) 939-6500.✚▲

FORT PIERCE—AAA AUTO CLUB SOUTH, 1971 S US HWY #1, 34950. MON-FRI 8:30-5:30. (772) 461-6972.✚▲

FORT WALTON BEACH—AAA AUTO CLUB SOUTH, SANTA ROSA MALL SUITE #16, MARY ESTHER, FL 32569. MON-FRI 8:30-5:30. (850) 244-3126.●▲

GAINESVILLE—AAA AUTO CLUB SOUTH, 1201 NW 13TH ST, 32601. MON-FRI 8:30-5:30. (352) 373-7801.✚▲

HEATHROW—AAA AUTO CLUB SOUTH, 1000 AAA DR #28, 32746. MON-FRI 8:30-5:30. (407) 444-4240.✚▲

HOLIDAY—AAA AUTO CLUB SOUTH, 4740 MILE STRETCH DR, 34690. MON-FRI 8:30-5:30. (727) 938-3794.✚▲

JACKSONVILLE—AAA AUTO CLUB SOUTH, 3718 BEACH BLVD, 32207. MON-FRI 8:30-5:30. (904) 398-0564.✚▲

MIAMI—AAA AUTO CLUB SOUTH, 7074 SW 117 AVE, 33183. MON-FRI 8:30-5:30. (305) 270-6450.✚▲

KISSIMMEE—AAA AUTO CLUB SOUTH, 204 W OAK ST, 34741. MON-FRI 8:30-5:30. (407) 944-0866.✚▲

LAKELAND—AAA AUTO CLUB SOUTH, 1457 E MEMORIAL BLVD, 33801. MON-FRI 8:30-5:30. (863) 688-7921.✚▲

LAUDERHILL—AAA AUTO CLUB SOUTH, 4800 N UNIVERSITY DR, 33351. MON-FRI 8:30-5:30. (954) 748-2700.✚▲

LEESBURG—AAA AUTO CLUB SOUTH, 1107 W NORTH BLVD #16, 34748. MON-FRI 8:30-5:30. (352) 787-8800.✚▲

MELBOURNE—AAA AUTO CLUB SOUTH, 3578 N HARBOR CITY BLVD, 32935. MON-FRI 8:30-5:30. (321) 253-9100.✚▲

MIAMI—AAA AUTO CLUB SOUTH, 20801 BISCAYNE BLVD #101, 33180. MON-FRI 8:30-5:30. (305) 682-2100.✚▲

MIAMI—AAA AUTO CLUB SOUTH, 6101 SUNSET DR SW, 33143. MON-FRI 8:30-5:30. (305) 661-6131.✚▲

NAPLES—AAA AUTO CLUB SOUTH, 5401 AIRPORT PULLING RD N, 34109. MON-FRI 8:30-5:30. (239) 594-5006.✚▲

OCALA—AAA AUTO CLUB SOUTH, 3033 SW COLLEGE RD, 34474. MON-FRI 8:30-5:30. (352) 237-6251.✚▲

ORANGE PARK—AAA AUTO CLUB SOUTH, 555 BLANDING BLVD, 32073. MON-FRI 8:30-5:30. (904) 272-2010.■▲

ORLANDO—AAA AUTO CLUB SOUTH, 4300 E COLONIAL DR, 32803. MON-FRI 8:30-5:30. (407) 894-3333.✚▲

PALM BEACH GARDENS—AAA AUTO CLUB SOUTH, 9123 N MILITARY TRL #110, 33410. MON-FRI 8:30-5:30. (561) 694-9090.✚▲

PALM HARBOR—AAA AUTO CLUB SOUTH, 32050 US HWY 19 N, 34684. MON-FRI 8:30-5:30. (727) 789-7850.✚▲

PENSACOLA—AAA AUTO CLUB SOUTH, 540 BRENT LN, 32503. MON-FRI 8:30-5:30. (850) 477-6860.✚▲

POMPANO BEACH—AAA AUTO CLUB SOUTH, 601 E ATLANTIC BLVD, 33060. MON-FRI 8:30-5:30. (954) 942-5450.✚▲

PONTE VEDRA BEACH—AAA AUTO CLUB SOUTH, 840 A1A N #180, 32082. MON-FRI 8:30-5:30. (904) 280-8181.✚▲

PORT CHARLOTTE—AAA AUTO CLUB SOUTH, 21229-A OLEAN BLVD, 33952. MON-FRI 8:30-5:30. (941) 627-1544.✚▲

PORT RICHEY—AAA AUTO CLUB SOUTH, 10532 DEVCO DR, 34668. MON-FRI 8:30-5:30. (727) 868-9523.✚▲

SARASOTA—AAA AUTO CLUB SOUTH, 3844 BEE RIDGE RD, 34233. MON-FRI 8:30-5:30. (941) 362-2220.✚▲

SARASOTA—AAA AUTO CLUB SOUTH, 258 RINGLING SHOPPING CTR, 34237. MON-FRI 8:30-5:30. (941) 362-2500.✚▲

SEMINOLE—AAA AUTO CLUB SOUTH, 9200 SEMINOLE BLVD, 33772. MON-FRI 8:30-5:30. (727) 398-3120.✚▲

SPRING HILL—AAA AUTO CLUB SOUTH, 1410 PINEHURST DR, 34606. MON-FRI 8:30-5:30. (352) 683-3446.✚▲

SAINT PETERSBURG—AAA AUTO CLUB SOUTH, 800 SECOND AVE S, 33701. MON-FRI 8:30-5:30. (727) 826-3600.✚▲

SAINT PETERSBURG—AAA AUTO CLUB SOUTH, 7787 NINTH ST N, 33702. MON-FRI 8:30-5:30. (727) 577-5282.■▲

STUART—AAA AUTO CLUB SOUTH, 1610 SE FEDERAL HWY, 34994. MON-FRI 8:30-5:30. (772) 287-5300.✚▲

TALLAHASSEE—AAA AUTO CLUB SOUTH, 1205 APALACHEE PKY, 32301. MON-FRI 8:30-5:30. (850) 878-6000.✚▲

TAMPA—AAA AUTO CLUB SOUTH, 1515 N WESTSHORE BLVD, 33607. MON-FRI 8:30-5:30. (813) 289-5000.✚▲

TAMPA—AAA AUTO CLUB SOUTH, 2335 E FOWLER AVE, 33612. MON-FRI 8:30-5:30. (813) 971-4900.✚▲

TAMPA—AAA AUTO CLUB SOUTH, 14755 N DALE MABRY, 33618. MON-FRI 8:30-5:30. (813) 963-2121.✚▲

THE VILLAGES—AAA AUTO CLUB SOUTH, 955 BICHARA BLVD, 32159. MON-FRI 8:30-5:30. (352) 753-2500.✚▲

VENICE—AAA AUTO CLUB SOUTH, 2100 S TAMIAMI TRL, 34293. MON-FRI 8:30-5:30. (941) 493-2100.✚▲

VERO BEACH—AAA AUTO CLUB SOUTH, 6650 20TH ST, 32966. MON-FRI 8:30-5:30. (772) 770-3400.■▲

WINTER HAVEN—AAA AUTO CLUB SOUTH, 601 W CENTRAL AVE, 33880. MON-FRI 8:30-5:30. (863) 293-3151.■▲

FLORIDA

DRIVING DISTANCES

100 MILES IN US

2:00 AVERAGE TIME (EXCLUDING STOPS)

© AAA

3650-K

Quality
Repair Ahead

AAA
*Approved
Auto Repair*

You can count on AAA's Approved Auto Repair providers to manage your vehicle's repair and maintenance needs. The providers meet strict standards for technician training and customer service. And, when you use an Approved Auto Repair provider, you get a 12-month/12,000-mile warranty. When you need a trusted resource for repair or maintenance services, just follow the signs.

Bed & Breakfast Lodgings Index

Some bed and breakfasts listed below might have historical significance. Those properties are also referenced in the Historical index. The indication that continental [CP] or full breakfast [BP] is included in the room rate reflects whether a property is a Bed-and-Breakfast facility.

FLORIDA
ACCOMMODATIONS

A Highlands House Bed & Breakfast ...... Santa Rosa Beach 811
Addison House ....Amelia Island 466
Alexander Homestead Bed & Breakfast...........St. Augustine 788
Allison House Inn...Quincy 784
Ambrosia Too At Fleming St .... Key West 333
Andrews Inn .... Key West 334
Arcadia's Magnolia House ....Arcadia 245
Bailey House...Amelia Island 467
Banyan House Historic Bed & Breakfast.................Venice 949
Bavarian Inn ....Tarpon Springs 938
Bayboro House Bed & Breakfast On
  Old Tampa Bay ....St. Petersburg 863
Bayboro Inn & Hunt Room Bed & Breakfast....St. Petersburg 863
Bayfront Westcott House...........................St. Augustine 789
Behind the Fence Bed & Breakfast ....Brandon 896
Blue Skies Inn .... Key West 336
Calhoun Street Inn Bed and Breakfast ....Tallahassee 839
Casa de la Paz Bayfront Bed & Breakfast ....St. Augustine 790
Casa De Solana Bed & Breakfast Inn ....St. Augustine 790
Casa de Suenos Bed & Breakfast ....St. Augustine 790
Castle Garden Bed & Breakfast......................St. Augustine 791
Cedar House Inn Victorian B & B ....St. Augustine 791
Centennial House Bed & Breakfast ....St. Augustine 791
Center Court Historic Inn & Cottages.................. Key West 336
Chelsea House .... Key West 337
Clauser's Bed & Breakfast .... Lake Helen 482
Coquina Gables Oceanfront B&B ....St. Augustine Beach 801
The Conch House Heritage Inn .... Key West 338
Crane Creek Inn Waterfront Bed & Breakfast .... Melbourne 498
Curry Mansion Inn... Key West 339
Cypress House Bed & Breakfast........................Bushnell 261
Cypress House Bed & Breakfast .... Key West 340
Darst Victorian Manor................................Mount Dora 745
Dickens House Bed and Breakfast...............St. Petersburg 864
Duval House .... Key West 340
Duval Inn .... Key West 341
Eighteenth Street Inn .... Fort Lauderdale 371
Elizabeth Pointe Lodge ....Amelia Island 467
Frances St Bottle Inn .... Key West 341
Gilchrist Bed & Breakfast Inn ....Punta Gorda 782
Grady House Bed and Breakfast.................... High Springs 441
Gram's Place BnB Guesthouses/Youth Hostel &
  Music...Tampa 878
Harrington House Beachfront Bed &
  Breakfast .... Holmes Beach 441
Herlong Mansion Bed & Breakfast Inn .... Micanopy 560
Heron House .... Key West 342
Hibiscus House Bed & Breakfast............ West Palm Beach 958
Hinson House Bed & Breakfast ....Marianna 496
House On Cherry Street................................ Jacksonville 458

Hoyt House..Amelia Island 467
Inn at the Bay Bed & Breakfast ....St. Petersburg 865
Inn by the Sea...Naples 568
Island City House Hotel .... Key West 343
Key Lime Inn .... Key West 344
La Casa de Luces.. Key West 344
La Mer & Dewey House .... Key West 344
La Pensione.. Key West 344
Lee Manor Inn ....St. Petersburg 866
Lightbourn Inn .... Key West 345
Mansion House B & B and The Courtyard
  on Fifth...St. Petersburg 866
McFarlin House Bed & Breakfast Inn......................Quincy 784
Miami River Inn............................... Downtown Miami 516
Night Swan Intracoastal Bed &
  Breakfast .... New Smyrna Beach 579
Old City House Inn & Restaurant ....St. Augustine 796
Palm Beach Bed and Breakfast .... Palm Beach 762
Palmer Place B&B ....Monticello 560
Parador of the Palm Beaches .... Lake Worth 488
Pasa Tiempo Bed & Breakfast.................St. Pete Beach 933
Pelican Path B & B by the Sea............Jacksonville Beach 471
PerriHouse Bed & Breakfast Inn ....Lake Buena Vista 731
Plantation Manor Inn...................................Jacksonville 460
River Park Inn, the 1887 House.......... Green Cove Springs 469
Rose Cottage Inn.. Sanford 748
Sabal Palm House B & B Inn .... Lake Worth 488
Seven Sisters Inn ....Ocala 584
Shamrock Thistle & Crown........................... Lady Lake 714
Shire House Bed and Breakfast.................... Flagler Beach 316
Southern Comfort Bed & Breakfast ....Ruskin 929
Southern Palm Bed & Breakfast.....................Loxahatchee 493
St. Francis Inn ....St. Augustine 797
Sunset Bay Inn Bed & Breakfast ....St. Petersburg 867
Sweet Magnolia Inn .... St. Marks 803
Sweetwater Branch Inn Bed & Breakfast..............Gainesville 438
The Cypress, A Bed & Breakfast Inn .... Sarasota 819
The Emerald Hill Inn ....Mount Dora 745
The Fairbanks House ....Amelia Island 467
The Grand.. Key West 341
The GV Tillman House Bed & Breakfast ....Lake Wales 747
The Higgins House Bed & Breakfast .... Sanford 747
The Palms Hotel.. Key West 345
The Paradise Inn .... Key West 345
The Stanford Inn...Bartow 246
The Villa Bed & Breakfast......................Daytona Beach 295
The Watson House... Key West 348
The White Orchid Oceanfront Inn .... Flagler Beach 317
Thurston Inn...Maitland 745
Travelers Palm Inn & Guesthouses.................... Key West 347
Tropical Gardens Bed & Breakfast.......... West Palm Beach 961
Westwinds .... Key West 348
Wonderland Inn..Kissimmee 709

Country Inns Index

Some of the following country inns can also be considered as bed-and-breakfast operations. The indication that continental [CP] or full breakfast [BP] is included in the room rate reflects whether a property is a Bed-and-Breakfast facility.

FLORIDA
ACCOMMODATIONS

Chalet Suzanne Country Inn & Restaurant ....Lake Wales 487
Florida House Inn.....................................Amelia Island 467
Josephine's French Country Inn..........................Seaside 829
Mulberry Inn B&B ....Clermont 676
Riverview Hotel .... New Smyrna Beach 579
Seminole Inn..Indiantown 443

The Courtyard at Lake Lucerne .... Orlando North 614
The Crown Hotel .... Inverness 444
The Gibson Inn ....Apalachicola 245

RESTAURANTS

Chalet Suzanne
  Restaurant.. Lake Wales 487
Lekarica Restaurant.....................................Lake Wales 487
The Gibson Inn ....Apalachicola 245

Historical Lodgings & Restaurants Index

Some of the following historical lodgings can also be considered as bed-and-breakfast operations. The indication that continental [CP] or full breakfast [BP] is included in the room rate reflects whether a property is a Bed-and-Breakfast facility.

FLORIDA
ACCOMMODATIONS

Abbey Hotel... Miami Beach 526
Alexander Homestead Bed & Breakfast..........St. Augustine 788
Allison House Inn...Quincy 784
Arcadia's Magnolia House ....Arcadia 245

Bailey House...Amelia Island 467
Bayboro House Bed & Breakfast On
  Old Tampa Bay ....St. Petersburg 863
Bayboro Inn & Hunt Room Bed &
  Breakfast ....St. Petersburg 863
Bayfront Westcott House............................St. Augustine 789
Belleview Biltmore Resort & Spa....................Clearwater 899

Historical Lodgings & Restaurants (cont'd)

Blue Skies Inn .... Key West 336
Calhoun Street Inn Bed and Breakfast .... Tallahassee 839
Casa de la Paz Bayfront Bed & Breakfast .... St. Augustine 790
Casa De Solana Bed & Breakfast Inn .... St. Augustine 790
Casa Monica Hotel .... St. Augustine 791
Castle Garden Bed & Breakfast .... St. Augustine 791
Cavalier .... Miami Beach 527
Cedar House Inn Victorian B & B .... St. Augustine 791
Chalet Suzanne Country Inn & Restaurant .... Lake Wales 487
Chelsea House .... Key West 337
Colonial Bayfront Hotel .... St. Petersburg 863
Courtney's Place Historic Cottages & Inn .... Key West 338
Courtyard by Marriott .... Miami Beach 529
Curry Mansion Inn .... Key West 339
Cypress House Bed & Breakfast .... Key West 340
Dickens House Bed and Breakfast .... St. Petersburg 864
Doubletree Surfcomber Hotel .... Miami Beach 531
Duval House .... Key West 340
Duval Inn .... Key West 341
Fairwind Hotel & Suites .... Miami Beach 532
Florida House Inn .... Amelia Island 467
Frances St Bottle Inn .... Key West 341
Governors Inn .... Tallahassee 840
Grady House Bed and Breakfast .... High Springs 441
Herlong Mansion Bed & Breakfast Inn .... Micanopy 560
Hibiscus House Bed & Breakfast .... West Palm Beach 958
Hotel Biba .... West Palm Beach 959
Hoyt House .... Amelia Island 467
Island City House Hotel .... Key West 343
Island Inn .... Sanibel 804
Key Lime Inn .... Key West 344
La Mer & Dewey House .... Key West 344
La Casa de Luces .... Key West 344
La Pensione .... Key West 344
Lightbourn Inn .... Key West 345
Mansion House B & B and The Courtyard
  on Fifth .... St. Petersburg 866
McFarlin House Bed & Breakfast Inn .... Quincy 784
Palm Beach Historic Inn .... Palm Beach 762
Palmer Place B&B .... Monticello 560
Plantation Manor Inn .... Jacksonville 460

Plaza Inn .... Palm Beach 762
President Hotel .... Miami Beach 536
Redland Hotel "An Historic Inn" .... Homestead 551
Riverside Hotel .... Ft. Lauderdale 381
Sabal Palm House B & B Inn .... Lake Worth 488
Seven Sisters Inn .... Ocala 584
St. Francis Inn .... St. Augustine 797
The Biltmore Hotel Coral Gables .... Coral Gables 546
The Blue Moon .... Miami Beach 527
The Chesterfield Hotel .... Palm Beach 761
The Colony Hotel & Cabana Club .... Delray Beach 309
The Courtyard .... Key West 338
The Courtyard at Lake Lucerne .... Orlando North 614
The Fairbanks House .... Amelia Island 467
The Gibson Inn .... Apalachicola 245
The Grand .... Key West 341
The Hotel .... Miami Beach 333
The Kent .... Miami Beach 533
The Palms Hotel .... Key West 345
The Watson House .... Key West 348
The Weatherstation Inn .... Key West 348
Travelers Palm Inn & Guesthouses .... Key West 347
Tropical Acres .... Ft. Lauderdale 388
Tropical Gardens Bed & Breakfast .... West Palm Beach 961
Tudor Hotel & Suites .... Miami Beach 539
Wyndham Casa Marina Resort .... Key West 348

RESTAURANTS

95 Cordova .... St. Augustine 790
Cafe Alcazar .... St. Augustine 799
Campiello Ristorante .... Naples 575
Cap's Place-Island Restaurant & Bar .... Lighthouse Point 402
Columbia Restaurant .... Tampa 890
Cortesse's Bistro & Flamingo Room .... St. Augustine 799
Florida House Inn Dining Room .... Amelia Island 468
Joe's Stone Crab Restaurant .... Miami Beach 541
La Vieille Maison .... Boca Raton 252
Mareks Collier House Restaurant .... Marco Island 496
Nicholson Farmhouse .... Havana 440
The Great Outdoors Trading
  Company & Cafe .... High Springs 441
The River House .... Fort Lauderdale 387

Resorts Index

Many establishments are located in resort areas; however, the following places have extensive on-premises recreational facilities:

FLORIDA

ACCOMMODATIONS

Alden Beach Resort .... St. Pete Beach 931
Amelia Island Plantation .... Amelia Island 466
Baymont Inn & Suites Miami-Cutler Ridge .... Cutler Ridge 548
Best Western Crystal River Resort .... Crystal River 278
Best Western Pink Shell Beach Resort .... Fort Myers Beach 428
Boca Raton Resort & Club .... Boca Raton 247
Cheeca Lodge & Spa .... Islamorada 320
Disney's All Star Movies Resort .... Lake Buena Vista 719
Disney's All Star Music .... Lake Buena Vista 719
Disney's All Star Sports .... Lake Buena Vista 719
Disney's Animal Kingdom Lodge .... Lake Buena Vista 719
Disney's BoardWalk Resort .... Lake Buena Vista 720
Disney's Caribbean Beach Resort .... Lake Buena Vista 720
Disney's Contemporary Resort .... Lake Buena Vista 720
Disney's Coronado Springs Resort .... Lake Buena Vista 720
Disney's Grand Floridian Resort & Spa ..... Lake Buena Vista 725
Disney's Polynesian Resort .... Lake Buena Vista 725
Disney's Port Orleans-French Quarter
  Resort .... Lake Buena Vista 725
Disney's Port Orleans-Riverside Resort ..... Lake Buena Vista 725
Disney's Vero Beach Resort .... Vero Beach 952
Disney's Wilderness Lodge & Villas .... Lake Buena Vista 726
Disney's Yacht & Beach Club Resorts .... Lake Buena Vista 726
Don Shula's Hotel & Golf Club .... Miami Lakes 553
Doral Golf Resort and Spa .... Miami 519
Grand Palms Golf & Country Club
  Resort .... Pembroke Pines 404
Hawk's Cay Resort .... Marathon 354
Hilton Key West Resort & Marina .... Key West 342
Hilton Marco Island Beach Resort .... Marco Island 494
Hilton Sandestin Beach, Golf Resort .... Destin 311
Holiday Inn Hotel & Suites .... Longboat Key 492
Holiday Inn SunSpree Resort .... Fort Walton Beach 433
Holiday Inn SunSpree Resort Marina
  Cove .... St. Petersburg 865
Hutchinson Island Marriott Beach Resort & Marina ...... Stuart 836
Hyatt Regency Coconut Point Resort & Spa .. Bonita Springs 254
LaPlaya Beach & Golf Resort .... Naples 569
Little Palm Island Resort & Spa .... Little Torch Key 352
Lodge and Club at Ponte Vedra
  Beach .... Ponte Vedra Beach 476
Marco Island Marriott Resort, Golf Club & Spa .. Marco Island 494

Marriott Key Largo Bay Beach Resort .... Key Largo 325
Marriott's Bay Point Resort Village .... Panama City Beach 772
Marriott's Harbor Beach Resort & Spa ...... Fort Lauderdale 378
Mission Inn Golf & Tennis Resort .... Howey-In-The-Hills 677
Ocean Walk Resort .... Daytona Beach 292
Orange Lake Resort & Country Club .... Kissimmee 698
Orlando World Center Marriott Resort & Convention
  Center .... Lake Buena Vista 731
Palm Island Resort .... Cape Haze 263
Palm-Aire Resort & Spa .... Pompano Beach 408
PGA National Resort & Spa .... Palm Beach Gardens 765
Plantation Inn & Golf Resort .... Crystal River 278
Ponte Vedra Inn and Club .... Ponte Vedra Beach 476
Renaissance Vinoy Resort & Golf Club .... St. Petersburg 867
Saddlebrook Resort Tampa .... Wesley Chapel 945
Safety Harbor Resort and Spa on
  Tampa Bay .... Safety Harbor 930
Sandestin Golf and Beach Resort .... Destin 312
Sanibel Harbour Resort & Spa .... Fort Myers 421
Sheraton Sand Key Resort .... Clearwater Beach 913
Sonesta Beach Resort Key Biscayne .... Key Biscayne 553
South Seas Resort & Yacht Harbor .... Captiva 264
Star Island Resort & Club .... Kissimmee 705
Sundial Beach Resort .... Sanibel 808
The Breakers .... Palm Beach 761
The Diplomat Country Club & Spa .... Hallandale Beach 395
The Don CeSar Beach Resort & Spa .... St. Pete Beach 932
The Inn At Boca Teeca .... Boca Raton 250
The Naples Beach Hotel & Golf Club .... Naples 570
The Registry Resort .... Naples 572
The Resort at Longboat Key Club .... Longboat Key 492
The Ritz-Carlton, Amelia Island .... Amelia Island 468
The Ritz-Carlton, Key Biscayne .... Key Biscayne 552
The Ritz-Carlton, Naples .... Naples 573
The Spa at Doral .... Miami 523
The Westin Beach Resort, Key Largo .... Key Largo 327
The Westin Innisbrook Resort .... Palm Harbor 925
Tops'l Beach & Racquet Resort .... Destin 312
TradeWinds Island Grand Beach Resort .... St. Pete Beach 934
TradeWinds Sandpiper Hotel & Suites .... St. Pete Beach 934
TradeWinds Sirata Beach Resort .... St. Pete Beach 934
Turnberry Isle Resort & Club .... Aventura 543
Walt Disney World Swan and Dolphin .... Lake Buena Vista 736
Wyndham Bonaventure Resort & Spa .... Weston 414

Points of Interest Index

AIRPORTS

ALBERT WHITTED AIRPORT....................TAMPA BAY , FL   210
FORT LAUDERDALE-HOLLYWOOD INTERNATIONAL
    AIRPORT....................................FORT LAUDERDALE, FL   72
JACKSONVILLE INTERNATIONAL AIRPORT......JACKSONVILLE, FL   90
MIAMI INTERNATIONAL AIRPORT.......MIAMI- MIAMI BEACH, FL   110
ORLANDO INTERNATIONAL AIRPORT.............ORLANDO, FL   140
ORLANDO SANFORD AIRPORT.....................ORLANDO, FL   140
THE PETER O. KNIGHT AIRPORT..................TAMPA BAY , FL   210
ST. PETERSBURG-CLEARWATER INTERNATIONAL
    AIRPORT...TAMPA BAY , FL   210
TAMPA INTERNATIONAL AIRPORT................TAMPA BAY , FL   210

AMUSEMENTS & THEME PARKS

ADVENTURE ISLAND.....................................TAMPA, FL   216
ADVENTURE LANDING..................JACKSONVILLE BEACH, FL   96
☙ BUSCH GARDENS TAMPA BAY.........................TAMPA, FL   217
CARIBBEAN GARDENS: THE ZOO IN NAPLES...........NAPLES, FL   128
DISNEY-MGM STUDIOS......................LAKE BUENA VISTA, FL   164
DISNEY'S ANIMAL KINGDOM THEME
    PARK..LAKE BUENA VISTA, FL   165
DISNEY'S BLIZZARD BEACH WATER PARK.. LAKE BUENA VISTA, FL   166
DISNEY'S TYPHOON LAGOON WATER
    PARK..LAKE BUENA VISTA, FL   166
EPCOT..LAKE BUENA VISTA, FL   168
HOLY LAND EXPERIENCE.............................ORLANDO, FL   142
ISLANDS OF ADVENTURE.............................ORLANDO, FL   149
LION COUNTRY SAFARI.....................WEST PALM BEACH, FL   233
MAGIC KINGDOM PARK.....................LAKE BUENA VISTA, FL   169
MIRACLE STRIP AMUSEMENT PARK.....PANAMA CITY BEACH, FL   183
☙ SEAWORLD ORLANDO..............................ORLANDO, FL   147
SHIPWRECK ISLAND....................PANAMA CITY BEACH, FL   183
SPLENDID CHINA.......................................KISSIMMEE, FL   162
SUN SPLASH FAMILY WATERPARK................CAPE CORAL, FL   50
UNIVERSAL ORLANDO.................................ORLANDO, FL   149
☙ UNIVERSAL STUDIOS.................................ORLANDO, FL   152
☙ WALT DISNEY WORLD RESORT............LAKE BUENA VISTA, FL   163
WATER MANIA...KISSIMMEE, FL   162
WET 'N WILD..ORLANDO, FL   153

AMPHITHEATERS

KRAVIS CENTER FOR THE PERFORMING
    ARTS...WEST PALM BEACH, FL   233
THE ZOO..GULF BREEZE, FL   86

ANTIQUES

ALHAMBRA ANTIQUES CENTER.........MIAMI- MIAMI BEACH, FL   120
IVANHOE ROW...ORLANDO, FL   156
MOUNT DORA...FL   178
NORTH ORANGE AVENUE ANTIQUES DISTRICT......ORLANDO, FL   155
OLDE TYME SHOPPE....................MIAMI- MIAMI BEACH, FL   120
PARK AVENUE...ORLANDO, FL   156

AQUARIUMS

ANN KOLB NATURE CENTER......................HOLLYWOOD, FL   78
CLEARWATER MARINE AQUARIUM.............CLEARWATER, FL   227
THE CONSERVANCY—NAPLES NATURE CENTER........NAPLES, FL   128
☙ DISCOVERY COVE.....................................ORLANDO, FL   142
☙ THE FLORIDA AQUARIUM..............................TAMPA, FL   218
HOMOSASSA SPRINGS WILDLIFE SP.....HOMOSASSA SPRINGS, FL   87
IMAGINARIUM HANDS-ON MUSEUM.............FORT MYERS, FL   80
JOHN PENNEKAMP CORAL REEF SP................KEY LARGO, FL   65
KEY WEST AQUARIUM.................................KEY WEST, FL   68
KONGER TARPON SPRINGS AQUARIUM......TARPON SPRINGS, FL   230
MIAMI SEAQUARIUM....................MIAMI- MIAMI BEACH, FL   115
MOTE AQUARIUM..SARASOTA, FL   199
PARKER MANATEE AQUARIUM...................BRADENTON, FL   49
THE PIER...ST. PETERSBURG, FL   216
☙ SEAWORLD ORLANDO..............................ORLANDO, FL   147
SOUTH FLORIDA SCIENCE MUSEUM........WEST PALM BEACH, FL   234
WELAKA NATIONAL FISH HATCHERY AQUARIUM....WELAKA, FL   233

ARCHEOLOGICAL SITES

CRYSTAL RIVER ARCHEOLOGICAL SP...........CRYSTAL RIVER, FL   52

ART GALLERIES

ALEXANDER BREST MUSEUM...................JACKSONVILLE, FL   89
☙ THE APPLETON MUSEUM OF ART.........................OCALA, FL   130
ART AND CULTURE CENTER OF HOLLYWOOD...HOLLYWOOD, FL   78
ART LEAGUE OF MANATEE COUNTY...............BRADENTON, FL   48
THE ATLANTIC CENTER FOR THE ARTS.. NEW SMYRNA BEACH, FL   130
BASS MUSEUM OF ART.................MIAMI- MIAMI BEACH, FL   112
BOCA RATON MUSEUM OF ART..................BOCA RATON, FL   47
BREVARD MUSEUM OF ART AND SCIENCE...MELBOURNE, FL   103
☙ CHARLES HOSMER MORSE MUSEUM OF
    AMERICAN ART...................................WINTER PARK, FL   180
CORNELL FINE ARTS MUSEUM....................WINTER PARK, FL   180
CULTURAL ARTS CENTER...............................DELAND, FL   55
☙ CUMMER MUSEUM OF ART & GARDENS........JACKSONVILLE, FL   93
DELAND MUSEUM OF ART.................................DELAND, FL   55
DUNCAN GALLERY OF ART.................................DELAND, FL   55
EAST MARTELLO MUSEUM AND GALLERY...........KEY WEST, FL   68
GULF COAST MUSEUM OF ART...............................LARGO, FL   229
HENRY B. PLANT MUSEUM.................................TAMPA, FL   219
INTERNATIONAL SWIMMING HALL
    OF FAME.....................................FORT LAUDERDALE, FL   71
☙ THE JOHN AND MABLE RINGLING MUSEUM OF
    ART...SARASOTA, FL   198
LAKE WALES ARTS CENTER.........................LAKE WALES, FL   101
LOWE ART MUSEUM, UNIVERSITY OF MIAMI.. CORAL GABLES, FL   125
MAITLAND ART CENTER...................................MAITLAND, FL   178
MARIE SELBY BOTANICAL GARDENS.................SARASOTA, FL   199
THE MARY BROGAN MUSEUM OF ART AND
    SCIENCE...TALLAHASSEE, FL   203
THE MENNELLO MUSEUM OF AMERICAN
    FOLK ART..ORLANDO, FL   146
MIAMI ART MUSEUM....................MIAMI- MIAMI BEACH, FL   114
MUSEUM OF ART.................................FORT LAUDERDALE, FL   71
MUSEUM OF ARTS AND SCIENCES..............DAYTONA BEACH, FL   54
MUSEUM OF CONTEMPORARY ART.....NORTH MIAMI BEACH, FL   126
MUSEUM OF FINE ARTS........................ST. PETERSBURG, FL   213

Index Legend

NB...............................national battlefield		NR...................................national river	
NBP.......................national battlefield park		NS..................................national seashore	
NC.............................national cemetery		NWR.........................national wildlife refuge	
NF..................................national forest		PHP.....................provincial historic(al) park	
NHM...................national historic(al) monument		PHS......................provincial historic(al) site	
NHP.......................national historic(al) park		PP......................................provincial park	
NHS.........................national historic(al) site		SF...state forest	
NL.............................national lakeshore		SHM.....................state historic(al) monument	
NME............................national memorial		SHP......................state historic(al) park	
NMO.............................national monument		SHS.......................state historic(al) site	
NMP.......................national military park		SME....................................state memorial	
NP....................................national park		SP...state park	
NRA.......................national recreation area		SRA..............................state recreation area	

☙ **GEM: Points of Interest Offering a *Great Experience for Members***

NORTON MUSEUM OF ART ....WEST PALM BEACH, FL 234
OLD SCHOOL SQUARE CULTURAL ARTS CENTER AND
   NHS ....DELRAY BEACH, FL 55
ORLANDO MUSEUM OF ART ....ORLANDO, FL 146
ORMOND MEMORIAL ART MUSEUM AND
   GARDENS .... ORMOND BEACH, FL 181
P. BUCKLEY MOSS GALLERY..................ST. PETERSBURG, FL 216
POLK MUSEUM OF ART.................................LAKELAND, FL 100
ST. AUGUSTINE LIGHTHOUSE AND MUSEUM .. ST. AUGUSTINE, FL 195
☞ SALVADOR DALI MUSEUM ....ST. PETERSBURG, FL 216
SAMUEL P. HARN MUSEUM OF ART................GAINESVILLE, FL 86
SELBY GALLERY.......................................SARASOTA, FL 200
SOCIETY OF THE FOUR ARTS .... PALM BEACH, FL 182
SOUTHEAST MUSEUM OF PHOTOGRAPHY..DAYTONA BEACH, FL 54
TAMPA MUSEUM OF ART ....TAMPA, FL 219
UNIVERSITY GALLERY ....GAINESVILLE, FL 86
VISUAL ARTS CENTER ....PUNTA GORDA, FL 187

ARTS & CRAFTS
CANADA FEST ....FORT LAUDERDALE, FL 76
FESTIVAL OF STATES....................................TAMPA, FL 225
FLORIDA RENAISSANCE FESTIVAL ....FORT LAUDERDALE, FL 76
FLORIDA STATE FAIR...................................TAMPA, FL 225
GASPARILLA FESTIVAL OF THE ARTS ....TAMPA, FL 225
LAS OLAS ART FAIR ....FORT LAUDERDALE, FL 76
RIVERWALK FALL ARTS SHOW ....FORT LAUDERDALE, FL 76
STEPHEN FOSTER FOLK CULTURE CENTER SP... WHITE SPRINGS, FL 235
WEST INDIAN AMERICAN DAY
   CARNIVAL ....MIAMI- MIAMI BEACH, FL 122
WINTER PARK SIDEWALK ART FESTIVAL ....ORLANDO, FL 158
YOUNG AT ART CHILDREN'S MUSEUM ....DAVIE, FL 77

ATOMIC ENERGY INSTALLATIONS & NUCLEAR PLANTS
FPL'S ENERGY ENCOUNTER ....FORT PIERCE, FL 82

AUDITORIUMS
BROWARD CENTER FOR THE PERFORMING
   ARTS ....FORT LAUDERDALE, FL 76
LAKE WALES ARTS CENTER.......................LAKE WALES, FL 101
MIAMI-DADE COUNTY AUDITORIUM ...MIAMI- MIAMI BEACH, FL 121
PHILHARMONIC CENTER FOR THE ARTS.................NAPLES, FL 127
SOCIETY OF THE FOUR ARTS ....PALM BEACH, FL 182
WAR MEMORIAL AUDITORIUM ....FORT LAUDERDALE, FL 76

BATTLEFIELDS
DADE BATTLEFIELD HISTORIC SP ....BUSHNELL, FL 50
NATURAL BRIDGE BATTLEFIELD HISTORIC SP ......WOODVILLE, FL 237
OLUSTEE BATTLEFIELD HISTORIC SP...................OLUSTEE, FL 132

BEACHES
BEN T. DAVIS BEACH....................................TAMPA, FL 222
BILL BAGGS CAPE FLORIDA SRA.........MIAMI- MIAMI BEACH, FL 120
CRANDON PARK........................MIAMI- MIAMI BEACH, FL 120
HOBE SOUND NWR ....HOBE SOUND, FL 87
PICNIC ISLAND PARK.....................................TAMPA, FL 222

BOARDWALKS
PALM ISLAND BOARDWALK.....................MOUNT DORA, FL 178

BRIDGES
SUNSHINE SKYWAY ....ST. PETERSBURG, FL 216

BUILDINGS, PUBLIC; CAPITOL; CITY HALL
FLORIDA STATE CAPITOL ....TALLAHASSEE, FL 203
THE OLD CAPITOL ....TALLAHASSEE, FL 203

CANALS
INTERCOASTAL WATERWAY ....FORT LAUDERDALE, FL 70

CARILLONS
☞ HISTORIC BOK SANCTUARY ....LAKE WALES, FL 101

CASINO AND RIVERBOAT GAMBLING
LA CRUISE CASINO......................................MAYPORT, FL 96
SUNCRUZ CASINO...................................KEY LARGO, FL 66

CAVES
FLORIDA CAVERNS SP ....MARIANNA, FL 103

CEMETERIES
CITY CEMETERY...KEY WEST, FL 66
FLORIDA NATIONAL MILITARY CEMETERY...........BUSHNELL, FL 50
HUGUENOT CEMETERY..........................ST. AUGUSTINE, FL 188
OLD MANATEE BURIAL GROUNDS ....BRADENTON, FL 49
SAN MARCOS DE APALACHE HISTORIC SP ....ST. MARKS, FL 196
TOLOMATO CEMETERY..........................ST. AUGUSTINE, FL 188

CHILDREN'S ATTRACTIONS
ADVENTURE ISLAND......................................TAMPA, FL 216
BREVARD MUSEUM OF ART AND SCIENCE ....MELBOURNE, FL 103
BREVARD ZOO ....MELBOURNE, FL 103
☞ BUSCH GARDENS TAMPA BAY ....TAMPA, FL 217
CHILDREN'S MUSEUM ....BOCA RATON, FL 47
THE CHILDREN'S MUSEUM OF THE HIGHLANDS........SEBRING, FL 200
☞ CYPRESS GARDENS ....WINTER HAVEN, FL 236
DINOSAUR WORLD ....PLANT CITY, FL 229
DISNEY-MGM STUDIOS ....LAKE BUENA VISTA, FL 164
DISNEY'S BLIZZARD BEACH WATER PARK.. LAKE BUENA VISTA, FL 166
DISNEY'S TYPHOON LAGOON
   WATER PARK ....LAKE BUENA VISTA, FL 166
EXPLORATIONS V CHILDREN'S MUSEUM ....LAKELAND, FL 100
GREAT EXPLORATIONS .... ST. PETERSBURG, FL 213
GREEN MEADOWS PETTING FARM ....KISSIMMEE, FL 162
GULFCOAST WONDER & IMAGINATION ZONE
   (G.WIZ) ....SARASOTA, FL 198
☞ I.G.F.A. FISHING HALL OF FAME & MUSEUM .... DANIA BEACH, FL 77
IMAGINARIUM HANDS-ON MUSEUM ....FORT MYERS, FL 80
ISLANDS OF ADVENTURE ....ORLANDO, FL 149
JUNIOR MUSEUM OF BAY COUNTY ....PANAMA CITY, FL 182
KID CITY: THE CHILDREN'S MUSEUM OF TAMPA.......TAMPA, FL 218
LION COUNTRY SAFARI.....................WEST PALM BEACH, FL 233
MAGIC KINGDOM PARK ....LAKE BUENA VISTA, FL 169
THE MARY BROGAN MUSEUM OF ART AND
   SCIENCE...TALLAHASSEE, FL 203
MIRACLE STRIP AMUSEMENT PARK ..... PANAMA CITY BEACH, FL 183
MUSEUM OF DISCOVERY AND SCIENCE AND BLOCKBUSTER IMAX
   THEATER ....FORT LAUDERDALE, FL 74
MUSEUMS AND NATURE CENTER OF CRANE POINT
   HAMMOCK ....MARATHON, FL 69
ORLANDO SCIENCE CENTER ....ORLANDO, FL 146
ROGERS' CHRISTMAS HOUSE VILLAGE ....BROOKSVILLE, FL 50
☞ SEAWORLD ORLANDO................................ORLANDO, FL 147
SHIPWRECK ISLAND ....PANAMA CITY BEACH, FL 183
SILVER SPRINGS WILD WATERS.........................OCALA, FL 131
SUN SPLASH FAMILY WATERPARK ....CAPE CORAL, FL 50
THE TEDDY BEAR MUSEUM OF NAPLES ....NAPLES, FL 129
T.T. WENTWORTH JR. FLORIDA STATE MUSEUM...PENSACOLA, FL 185
☞ UNIVERSAL ORLANDO................................ORLANDO, FL 149
UNIVERSAL STUDIOS...................................ORLANDO, FL 152
☞ WALT DISNEY WORLD RESORT.............LAKE BUENA VISTA, FL 163
WATER MANIA ....KISSIMMEE, FL 162
WET 'N WILD...ORLANDO, FL 153
WONDERWORKS ....ORLANDO, FL 153
YOUNG AT ART CHILDREN'S MUSEUM ....DAVIE, FL 77

CHURCHES, CATHEDRALS & BASILICAS
BETHESDA-BY-THE-SEA............................ PALM BEACH, FL 181
CATHEDRAL OF ST. AUGUSTINE .... ST. AUGUSTINE, FL 190
GREEK ORTHODOX CATHEDRAL OF
   ST. NICHOLAS.................................TARPON SPRINGS, FL 230
MEMORIAL PRESBYTERIAN CHURCH ....ST. AUGUSTINE, FL 194

CHURCHES-CHAPELS
THE AMERICAN POLICE HALL OF FAME AND
   MUSEUM ....MIAMI- MIAMI BEACH, FL 112
ANNIE PFEIFFER CHAPEL............................LAKELAND, FL 100
GULF BEACHES HISTORICAL MUSEUM ....ST. PETE BEACH, FL 230
KNOWLES MEMORIAL CHAPEL.......................ORLANDO, FL 158

CHURCHES-MISSONS
MISSION OF NOMBRE DE DIOS .... ST. AUGUSTINE, FL 194
MISSION SAN LUIS ....TALLAHASSEE, FL 203

CHURCHES-SHRINES
SHRINE OF OUR LADY OF LA LECHE ....ST. AUGUSTINE, FL 194

CHURCHES-TEMPLES & SYNAGOGUES
JEWISH MUSEUM OF FLORIDA .... MIAMI- MIAMI BEACH, FL   114

CONVENTS & MONASTERIES
ANCIENT SPANISH MONASTERY .... NORTH MIAMI BEACH, FL   126

CULTURAL CENTERS & CIVIC CENTERS
ANNIE RUSSELL THEATRE .... ORLANDO, FL   157
ART AND CULTURE CENTER OF HOLLYWOOD ... HOLLYWOOD, FL   78
THE ATLANTIC CENTER FOR THE ARTS .. NEW SMYRNA BEACH, FL   130
BOB CARR PERFORMING ARTS CENTRE .... ORLANDO, FL   157
THE CASEMENTS .... ORMOND BEACH, FL   181
CULTURAL ARTS CENTER .... DELAND, FL   55
THE DEPOT—LAKE WALES MUSEUM AND CULTURAL
CENTER .... LAKE WALES, FL   101
DR. PHILLIPS CENTER FOR THE PERFORMING ARTS .. ORLANDO, FL   158
ENZIAN THEATER .... ORLANDO, FL   157
GUSMAN CENTER FOR THE PERFORMING
ARTS .... MIAMI- MIAMI BEACH, FL   121
JOHN AND RITA LOWNDES SHAKESPEARE CENTER, . ORLANDO, FL   157
KRAVIS CENTER FOR THE PERFORMING
ARTS .... WEST PALM BEACH, FL   233
THE LAKELAND CENTER .... LAKELAND, FL   100
MIAMI-DADE CULTURAL CENTER .... MIAMI- MIAMI BEACH, FL   114
NAPLES DEPOT CIVIC AND CULTURAL CENTER .... NAPLES, FL   129
OLD SCHOOL SQUARE CULTURAL ARTS CENTER AND
NHS .... DELRAY BEACH, FL   55
ORANGE COUNTY HISTORICAL MUSEUM
THEATRE .... ORLANDO, FL   158
RICHARD B. BAUMGARDNER CENTER .... CLEARWATER, FL   227
RUTH ECKERD HALL .... CLEARWATER, FL   227
SOCIETY OF THE FOUR ARTS .... PALM BEACH, FL   182
STEPHEN FOSTER FOLK CULTURE CENTER SP ... WHITE SPRINGS, FL   235
TAMPA BAY PERFORMING ARTS CENTER .... TAMPA, FL   224
THEATRE DOWNTOWN .... ORLANDO, FL   158
UCF CIVIC THEATRE .... ORLANDO, FL   158
WALT DISNEY AMPHITHEATER AT LAKE EOLA
PARK .... ORLANDO, FL   158

EVENTS-GENERAL
CALLE OCHO .... MIAMI- MIAMI BEACH, FL   122
CHRISTMAS IN THE PARK .... ORLANDO, FL   158
GASPARILLA PIRATE FEST .... TAMPA, FL   225
GATOR BOWL NEW YEAR'S EVE STREET
FESTIVAL .... JACKSONVILLE, FL   95
SUN 'N FUN EAA FLY-IN .... LAKELAND, FL   100
SUNSETS AT PIER 60 .... CLEARWATER, FL   227

EVENTS-CARNIVAL & CIRCUSES
CARIBBEAN CARNIVAL .... MIAMI- MIAMI BEACH, FL   122
FLYING HIGH CIRCUS .... TALLAHASSEE, FL   202
WEST INDIAN AMERICAN DAY
CARNIVAL .... MIAMI- MIAMI BEACH, FL   122

EVENTS-CRAFT SHOWS
TASTE OF ART AND JAZZ .... MIAMI- MIAMI BEACH, FL   122

EVENTS-FAIRS
CAJUN/ZYDECO CRAWFISH FESTIVAL ...... FORT LAUDERDALE, FL   76
FLORIDA STATE FAIR .... TAMPA, FL   225
GREATER JACKSONVILLE AGRICULTURAL
FAIR .... JACKSONVILLE, FL   95
INTERNATIONAL FOLK FAIR .... TAMPA, FL   225
SEMINOLE TRIBAL FAIR .... FORT LAUDERDALE, FL   76

EVENTS-FESTIVALS
ART DECO WEEKEND .... MIAMI- MIAMI BEACH, FL   122
BEACHES FESTIVAL WEEKEND .... JACKSONVILLE, FL   95
BLACK HISTORY MONTH FESTIVAL .... ORLANDO, FL   158
CANADA FEST .... FORT LAUDERDALE, FL   76
CARIBBEAN CARNIVAL .... MIAMI- MIAMI BEACH, FL   122
CARNIVAL MIAMI .... MIAMI- MIAMI BEACH, FL   122
DOWNTOWN ORLANDO ARTS FESTIVAL .... ORLANDO, FL   158
EVERGLADES MUSIC AND CRAFT
FESTIVAL .... MIAMI- MIAMI BEACH, FL   122
FESTIVAL OF STATES .... TAMPA, FL   225
FLORIDA RENAISSANCE FESTIVAL .... FORT LAUDERDALE, FL   76
FLORIDA STRAWBERRY FESTIVAL .... PLANT CITY, FL   229
FORT LAUDERDALE INTERNATIONAL FILM
FESTIVAL .... FORT LAUDERDALE, FL   76

FORT LAUDERDALE SEAFOOD FESTIVAL ... FORT LAUDERDALE, FL   76
GASPARILLA FESTIVAL OF THE ARTS .... TAMPA, FL   225
HARVEST FESTIVAL .... MIAMI- MIAMI BEACH, FL   122
HOLLYWOOD JAZZ FESTIVAL .... FORT LAUDERDALE, FL   76
INTERNATIONAL FRINGE FESTIVAL .... ORLANDO, FL   158
ISLE OF EIGHT FLAGS SHRIMP FESTIVAL .. FERNANDINA BEACH, FL   95
ITALIAN RENAISSANCE FESTIVAL .... MIAMI- MIAMI BEACH, FL   122
JUNIOR ORANGE BOWL INTERNATIONAL YOUTH
FESTIVAL .... MIAMI- MIAMI BEACH, FL   122
KUUMBA FESTIVAL .... JACKSONVILLE, FL   95
LAS OLAS ART FAIR .... FORT LAUDERDALE, FL   76
MAITLAND ARTS & FINE CRAFTS FESTIVAL .... ORLANDO, FL   158
MIAMI INTERNATIONAL FILM
FESTIVAL .... MIAMI- MIAMI BEACH, FL   122
MIAMI-BAHAMAS GOOMBAY
FESTIVAL .... MIAMI- MIAMI BEACH, FL   122
MIAMI/COCONUT GROVE ART
FESTIVAL .... MIAMI- MIAMI BEACH, FL   122
MOUNT DORA ARTS FESTIVAL .... ORLANDO, FL   158
OCEAN FEST .... FORT LAUDERDALE, FL   76
ORANGE BOWL FESTIVAL .... MIAMI- MIAMI BEACH, FL   122
ORLANDO-UCF SHAKESPEARE FESTIVAL .... ORLANDO, FL   158
ROYAL POINCIANA FESTIVAL .... MIAMI- MIAMI BEACH, FL   122
SOUND ADVICE BLUES FESTIVAL .... FORT LAUDERDALE, FL   76
TASTE OF ART AND JAZZ .... MIAMI- MIAMI BEACH, FL   122
WEST INDIAN AMERICAN DAY
CARNIVAL .... MIAMI- MIAMI BEACH, FL   122
WINTER PARK SIDEWALK ART FESTIVAL .... ORLANDO, FL   158
ZELLWOOD SWEET CORN FESTIVAL .... ORLANDO, FL   158
ZORA NEALE HURSTON FESTIVAL OF ARTS AND
HUMANITIES .... ORLANDO, FL   158

EVENTS-FIESTAS
FIESTA DAY .... TAMPA, FL   225
FIESTA IN THE PARK .... ORLANDO, FL   158

EVENTS-MUSIC
BACH FESTIVAL .... ORLANDO, FL   158
CHRISTMAS IN THE PARK .... ORLANDO, FL   158
CLEARWATER JAZZ HOLIDAY .... TAMPA, FL   225
FESTIVAL CONCERT SERIES .... ORLANDO, FL   158
HOLLYWOOD JAZZ FESTIVAL .... FORT LAUDERDALE, FL   76
SOUND ADVICE BLUES FESTIVAL .... FORT LAUDERDALE, FL   76
TASTE OF ART AND JAZZ .... MIAMI- MIAMI BEACH, FL   122

EVENTS-PAGEANTS, PARADES, DAYS
ART DECO WEEKEND .... MIAMI- MIAMI BEACH, FL   122
BIG ORANGE NEW YEAR'S EVE CELEBRATION AND
PARADE .... MIAMI- MIAMI BEACH, FL   122
CARNIVAL MIAMI .... MIAMI- MIAMI BEACH, FL   122
FESTIVAL OF STATES .... TAMPA, FL   225
FIESTA DAY .... TAMPA, FL   225
GASPARILLA PIRATE FEST .... TAMPA, FL   225
GUAVAWEEN .... TAMPA, FL   225
HOLIDAY FANTASY OF LIGHTS .... FORT LAUDERDALE, FL   122
KING MANGO STRUT .... MIAMI- MIAMI BEACH, FL   122
LIGHTED BOAT PARADE .... TAMPA, FL   225
WINTERFEST BOAT PARADE .... FORT LAUDERDALE, FL   76

EVENTS-SHOWS
FIESTA IN THE PARK .... ORLANDO, FL   158
FORT LAUDERDALE AIR & SEA SHOW ...... FORT LAUDERDALE, FL   76
FORT LAUDERDALE INTERNATIONAL
BOAT SHOW .... FORT LAUDERDALE, FL   76
THE FORT LAUDERDALE SPRING
BOAT SHOW .... FORT LAUDERDALE, FL   76
MIAMI INTERNATIONAL BOAT SHOW ... MIAMI- MIAMI BEACH, FL   122
OCEAN FEST .... FORT LAUDERDALE, FL   76
RIVERWALK FALL ARTS SHOW .... FORT LAUDERDALE, FL   76
SUN 'N FUN EAA FLY-IN .... LAKELAND, FL   100
WALT DISNEY WORLD FESTIVAL OF THE MASTERS .. ORLANDO, FL   158
WINTER PARK SIDEWALK ART FESTIVAL .... ORLANDO, FL   158

EVENTS-SPORTS
12 HOURS OF SEBRING ENDURANCE RACE .... SEBRING, FL   200
BAY HILL INVITATIONAL .... ORLANDO, FL   158
CAPITAL ONE BOWL .... ORLANDO, FL   122
CELEBRITY GOLF CHAMPIONSHIP .... MIAMI- MIAMI BEACH, FL   122
DANIA JAI-ALAI .... DANIA BEACH, FL   77
DAYTONA 500 .... DAYTONA BEACH, FL   53
DISNEY'S WIDE WORLD OF SPORTS .... LAKE BUENA VISTA, FL   167

FLORIDA DERBY .... FORT LAUDERDALE, FL 76
GASPARILLA DISTANCE CLASSIC........................TAMPA, FL 225
GATE RIVER RUN.............................. JACKSONVILLE, FL 95
GATOR BOWL................................. JACKSONVILLE, FL 95
GREATER JACKSONVILLE KINGFISH
  TOURNAMENT.................................. JACKSONVILLE, FL 95
JUNIOR ORANGE BOWL INTERNATIONAL YOUTH
  FESTIVAL...................... MIAMI- MIAMI BEACH, FL 122
MARION EDWARDS JR. MEMORIAL
  RACE........................ MIAMI- MIAMI BEACH, FL 122
MIAMI GRAND PRIX................. MIAMI- MIAMI BEACH, FL 122
MID-WINTER SAILING REGATTA....... MIAMI- MIAMI BEACH, FL 122
NASCAR BUSCH SERIES MIAMI 300...... MIAMI- MIAMI BEACH, FL 122
NASCAR WINSTON CUP SERIES
  PENNZOIL 400 .... MIAMI- MIAMI BEACH, FL 122
NATIONAL CAR RENTAL GOLF CLASSIC AT WALT DISNEY
  WORLD ....ORLANDO, FL 158
OCEAN FEST .... FORT LAUDERDALE, FL 76
ORANGE BOWL .... MIAMI- MIAMI BEACH, FL 122
ORANGE BOWL 5K/10K........... MIAMI- MIAMI BEACH, FL 122
ORLANDO-SEMINOLE JAI-ALAI FRONTON............ORLANDO, FL 154
THE OUTBACK BOWL.............................TAMPA, FL 225
PEPSI 400.................................DAYTONA BEACH, FL 53
THE PLAYERS CHAMPIONSHIP................. JACKSONVILLE, FL 95
THE POMPANO FISHING RODEO .... FORT LAUDERDALE, FL 76
ROYAL CARIBBEAN CLASSIC........MIAMI- MIAMI BEACH, FL 122
ST. ANTHONY'S TAMPA BAY TRIATHLON........TAMPA, FL 225
SARASOTA SKI-A-REES.........................SARASOTA, FL 197
SWAMP BUGGY RACES ....NAPLES, FL 127
TAMPA BAY POLO CLUB................... PLANT CITY, FL 229
TARPON ROUND-UP ....TAMPA, FL 225
VERIZON CLASSIC.............................TAMPA, FL 225

EXHIBITS & COLLECTIONS-GENERAL

⇨ THE BAILEY-MATTHEWS SHELL MUSEUM..............SANIBEL, FL 196
FANTASY OF FLIGHT ....POLK CITY, FL 186
FLORIDA STATE CIVILIAN CONSERVATION CORPS
  MUSEUM ....SEBRING, FL 201
FOREST CAPITAL STATE MUSEUM.......................PERRY, FL 186
THE MUSEUM OF MAN IN THE SEA...... PANAMA CITY BEACH, FL 183
RIPLEY'S BELIEVE IT OR NOT! ORIGINAL
  MUSEUM .... ST. AUGUSTINE, FL 194
RIPLEY'S BELIEVE IT OR NOT! ORLANDO
  ODDITORIUM ....ORLANDO, FL 147
ST. AUGUSTINE LIGHTHOUSE AND
  MUSEUM .... ST. AUGUSTINE, FL 195
SOUTH FLORIDA MUSEUM OF NATURAL
  HISTORY .... DANIA BEACH, FL 77
SOUTHEAST MUSEUM OF PHOTOGRAPHY ...DAYTONA BEACH, FL 54
SPLENDID CHINA..............................KISSIMMEE, FL 162
UDT SEAL MUSEUM .... FORT PIERCE, FL 83

EXHIBITS & COLLECTIONS-ANIMALS & BIRDS

ANN KOLB NATURE CENTER......................... HOLLYWOOD, FL 78
BIG CYPRESS VISITOR
  CENTER .... BIG CYPRESS NATIONAL PRESERVE, FL 47
BRIGGS NATURE CENTER ....NAPLES, FL 128
BUTTERFLY WORLD............................ COCONUT CREEK, FL 77
CLEARWATER MARINE AQUARIUM .... CLEARWATER, FL 227
THE CONSERVANCY—NAPLES NATURE CENTER ....NAPLES, FL 128
⇨ THE FLORIDA AQUARIUM ....TAMPA, FL 218
⇨ FRED BEAR MUSEUM .... GAINESVILLE, FL 86
GREEN MEADOWS PETTING FARM ....KISSIMMEE, FL 162
GULF SPECIMEN MARINE LABORATORY .... PANACEA, FL 182
GULFARIUM.............................FORT WALTON BEACH, FL 84
JUNGLE ADVENTURES ....CHRISTMAS, FL 160
KONGER TARPON SPRINGS AQUARIUM...... TARPON SPRINGS, FL 230
LEE COUNTY MANATEE PARK................ FORT MYERS, FL 82
MANATEE OBSERVATION AND EDUCATION
  CENTER .... FORT PIERCE, FL 83
MANATEE VIEWING CENTER .... APOLLO BEACH, FL 227
MUSEUM OF SCIENCE AND SPACE TRANSIT
  PLANETARIUM........................MIAMI- MIAMI BEACH, FL 115
MUSEUMS AND NATURE CENTER OF CRANE POINT
  HAMMOCK ....MARATHON, FL 69
OCTAGON WILDLIFE SANCTUARY............. PUNTA GORDA, FL 187
PEACE RIVER WILDLIFE CENTER .... PUNTA GORDA, FL 187
PELICAN MAN'S BIRD SANCTUARY .... SARASOTA, FL 199
SAWGRASS RECREATION PARK............. FORT LAUDERDALE, FL 74
SOUTH FLORIDA MUSEUM .... BRADENTON, FL 49
SUNCOAST SEABIRD SANCTUARY .... INDIAN SHORES, FL 228

EXHIBITS & COLLECTIONS-AVIATION

AIR FORCE ARMAMENT MUSEUM.......FORT WALTON BEACH, FL 84
FANTASY OF FLIGHT ....POLK CITY, FL 186
⇨ FLORIDA AIR MUSEUM AT SUN 'N FUN .... LAKELAND, FL 100
FLYING TIGERS WARBIRD RESTORATION
  MUSEUM ....KISSIMMEE, FL 162
⇨ KENNEDY SPACE CENTER VISITOR
  COMPLEX .... KENNEDY SPACE CENTER, FL 97
⇨ NATIONAL MUSEUM OF NAVAL AVIATION ....PENSACOLA, FL 185
ST. PETERSBURG MUSEUM OF HISTORY....... ST. PETERSBURG, FL 216
⇨ U.S. ASTRONAUT HALL OF FAME.....KENNEDY SPACE CENTER, FL 99
VALIANT AIR COMMAND WARBIRD AIR
  MUSEUM .... TITUSVILLE, FL 232

EXHIBITS & COLLECTIONS-CIVIL WAR HISTORY

CIVIL WAR SOLDIERS MUSEUM....................PENSACOLA, FL 184
MUSEUM OF SCIENCE AND HISTORY.............JACKSONVILLE, FL 93
MUSEUM OF SOUTHERN HISTORY .............JACKSONVILLE, FL 93
MUSEUM OF WEAPONS AND EARLY AMERICAN
  HISTORY .... ST. AUGUSTINE, FL 194
OLUSTEE BATTLEFIELD HISTORIC SP.................. OLUSTEE, FL 132

EXHIBITS & COLLECTIONS-DOLLS & TOYS

ELLIOTT MUSEUM .... STUART, FL 201
FLORIDA HERITAGE MUSEUM .... ST. AUGUSTINE, FL 194
THE MORIKAMI MUSEUM AND JAPANESE
  GARDENS .... DELRAY BEACH, FL 55
PIONEER FLORIDA MUSEUM AND VILLAGE .... DADE CITY, FL 228
THE TEDDY BEAR MUSEUM OF NAPLES ....NAPLES, FL 129

EXHIBITS & COLLECTIONS-HISTORICAL

AMELIA ISLAND MUSEUM OF HISTORY .. FERNANDINA BEACH, FL 95
THE AMERICAN POLICE HALL OF FAME AND
  MUSEUM ....MIAMI- MIAMI BEACH, FL 112
BLACK ARCHIVES RESEARCH CENTER AND
  MUSEUM ....TALLAHASSEE, FL 203
BOCA RATON HISTORICAL SOCIETY .... BOCA RATON, FL 47
BREVARD MUSEUM OF HISTORY AND SCIENCE.........COCOA, FL 52
⇨ CASTILLO DE SAN MARCOS NMO .... ST. AUGUSTINE, FL 188
CEDAR KEY HISTORICAL SOCIETY MUSEUM ...... CEDAR KEY, FL 51
CEDAR KEY STATE MUSEUM .... CEDAR KEY, FL 51
CENTRO YBOR MUSEUM ....TAMPA, FL 217
COLLIER COUNTY MUSEUM ....NAPLES, FL 128
⇨ COLONIAL SPANISH QUARTER.............. ST. AUGUSTINE, FL 190
CONSTITUTION CONVENTION MUSEUM SP ....PORT ST. JOE, FL 187
DE SOTO NME .... FL 56
THE DEPOT—LAKE WALES MUSEUM AND CULTURAL
  CENTER .... LAKE WALES, FL 101
DUNEDIN HISTORICAL SOCIETY AND MUSEUM ......DUNEDIN, FL 228
EAST MARTELLO MUSEUM AND GALLERY ....KEY WEST, FL 68
ELLIOTT MUSEUM .... STUART, FL 201
⇨ FLAGLER MUSEUM............................ PALM BEACH, FL 182
FLAMINGO GARDENS..............................DAVIE, FL 77
FLORIDA ADVENTURE MUSEUM .... PUNTA GORDA, FL 187
FLORIDA CENTER FOR POLITICAL HISTORY AND
  GOVERNANCE ....TALLAHASSEE, FL 203
FLORIDA HERITAGE MUSEUM .... ST. AUGUSTINE, FL 194
FLORIDA HISTORY CENTER & MUSEUM .... JUPITER, FL 97
⇨ THE FLORIDA HOLOCAUST MUSEUM .... ST. PETERSBURG, FL 212
FLORIDA MUSEUM OF NATURAL HISTORY........ GAINESVILLE, FL 86
FOREST CAPITAL STATE MUSEUM ....PERRY, FL 186
FORT CHRISTMAS MUSEUM .... CHRISTMAS, FL 160
FORT MYERS HISTORICAL MUSEUM .... FORT MYERS, FL 80
GAMBLE PLANTATION HISTORIC SP AND JUDAH P. BENJAMIN
  CONFEDERATE MEMORIAL....................ELLENTON, FL 56
GILBERT'S BAR HOUSE OF REFUGE MUSEUM .... STUART, FL 201
⇨ GOVERNMENT HOUSE MUSEUM .... ST. AUGUSTINE, FL 191
GULF BEACHES HISTORICAL MUSEUM .... ST. PETE BEACH, FL 230
HALIFAX HISTORICAL SOCIETY AND
  MUSEUM ....DAYTONA BEACH, FL 54
HENRY A. DELAND HOUSE MUSEUM ....DELAND, FL 55
HENRY B. PLANT MUSEUM ....TAMPA, FL 219
HERITAGE VILLAGE ....LARGO, FL 229
HISTORIC SPANISH POINT.........................OSPREY, FL 181
HISTORICAL MUSEUM OF SOUTHERN
  FLORIDA ....MIAMI- MIAMI BEACH, FL 114
THE HOLOCAUST MEMORIAL RESOURCE AND EDUCATION
  CENTER OF CENTRAL FLORIDA .... MAITLAND, FL 178
INTERNATIONAL SWIMMING HALL OF
  FAME .... FORT LAUDERDALE, FL 71
JACKSONVILLE HISTORICAL CENTER............. JACKSONVILLE, FL 93
JOHN GORRIE MUSEUM SP ..................APALACHICOLA, FL 46

JUNIOR MUSEUM OF BAY COUNTY .... PANAMA CITY, FL   182
KEY WEST LIGHTHOUSE MUSEUM .... KEY WEST, FL   68
KINGSLEY PLANTATION .... FORT GEORGE ISLAND, FL   96
☙ LIGHTNER MUSEUM .... ST. AUGUSTINE, FL   191
MAY STRINGER HERITAGE MUSEUM .... BROOKSVILLE, FL   50
MCLARTY TREASURE MUSEUM...................... SEBASTIAN, FL   200
MEL FISHER MARITIME MUSEUM.................... KEY WEST, FL   68
MICANOPY HISTORICAL SOCIETY MUSEUM......... MICANOPY, FL   127
THE MORIKAMI MUSEUM AND JAPANESE
   GARDENS .... DELRAY BEACH, FL   55
MUSEUM OF ARTS AND SCIENCES............ DAYTONA BEACH, FL   54
MUSEUM OF COMMERCE .... PENSACOLA, FL   185
MUSEUM OF FLORIDA HISTORY .... TALLAHASSEE, FL   203
THE MUSEUM OF FLORIDA'S ARMY .... ST. AUGUSTINE, FL   191
MUSEUM OF INDUSTRY .... PENSACOLA, FL   185
MUSEUM OF SEMINOLE COUNTY HISTORY .... SANFORD, FL   179
MUSEUM OF SOUTHERN HISTORY .... JACKSONVILLE, FL   93
MUSEUM OF THE EVERGLADES .... EVERGLADES CITY, FL   56
MUSEUM OF WEAPONS AND EARLY AMERICAN
   HISTORY .... ST. AUGUSTINE, FL   194
MUSEUMS AND NATURE CENTER OF CRANE POINT
   HAMMOCK .... MARATHON, FL   69
☙ NATIONAL MUSEUM OF NAVAL AVIATION .... PENSACOLA, FL   185
NATIONAL PRESIDENTS HALL OF FAME .... CLERMONT, FL   160
THE OLD CAPITOL .... TALLAHASSEE, FL   203
OLD FORT LAUDERDALE MUSEUM OF
   HISTORY .... FORT LAUDERDALE, FL   74
THE OLD JAIL .... ST. AUGUSTINE, FL   194
OLD SCHOOL SQUARE CULTURAL ARTS CENTER AND
   NHS .... DELRAY BEACH, FL   55
☙ OLDEST HOUSE .... ST. AUGUSTINE, FL   191
OLDEST STORE MUSEUM .... ST. AUGUSTINE, FL   191
OLDEST WOODEN SCHOOLHOUSE .... ST. AUGUSTINE, FL   191
ORANGE COUNTY REGIONAL HISTORY CENTER ..... ORLANDO, FL   147
PAYNES PRAIRIE PRESERVE SP .... MICANOPY, FL   127
PEÑA-PECK HOUSE .... ST. AUGUSTINE, FL   191
PENSACOLA HISTORICAL MUSEUM............... PENSACOLA, FL   185
PIONEER FLORIDA MUSEUM AND VILLAGE ...... DADE CITY, FL   228
THE PIONEER SETTLEMENT FOR THE CREATIVE
   ARTS .... BARBERVILLE, FL   46
THE PIONEER/HERITAGE MUSEUM .... PLANT CITY, FL   229
PONCE DE LEON INLET LIGHTHOUSE .... PONCE INLET, FL   187
ST. LUCIE COUNTY HISTORICAL MUSEUM .... FORT PIERCE, FL   83
ST. PETERSBURG MUSEUM OF HISTORY .... ST. PETERSBURG, FL   216
SAN MARCOS DE APALACHE HISTORIC SP .... ST. MARKS, FL   196
THE SANFORD MUSEUM............................ SANFORD, FL   179
SANIBEL HISTORICAL VILLAGE AND MUSEUM .... SANIBEL, FL   197
SOUTH FLORIDA MUSEUM .... BRADENTON, FL   49
SPANISH MILITARY HOSPITAL .... ST. AUGUSTINE, FL   190
TALLAHASSEE MUSEUM OF HISTORY AND NATURAL
   SCIENCE....................................... TALLAHASSEE, FL   203
TAMPA BAY HISTORY CENTER .... TAMPA, FL   219
T.T. WENTWORTH JR. FLORIDA STATE MUSEUM... PENSACOLA, FL   185
☙ U.S. ASTRONAUT HALL OF FAME....... KENNEDY SPACE CENTER, FL   99
THE WOLFSONIAN-FLORIDA INTERNATIONAL
   UNIVERSITY................................ MIAMI- MIAMI BEACH, FL   117
WRECKERS' MUSEUM/OLDEST HOUSE .... KEY WEST, FL   68
YBOR CITY MUSEUM SP .... TAMPA, FL   219

EXHIBITS & COLLECTIONS-INDIAN

AH-TAH-THI-KI
   MUSEUM ..... BIG CYPRESS SEMINOLE INDIAN RESERVATION, FL   47
CEDAR KEY HISTORICAL SOCIETY MUSEUM .... CEDAR KEY, FL   51
COLLIER COUNTY MUSEUM .... NAPLES, FL   128
CRYSTAL RIVER ARCHEOLOGICAL SP .... CRYSTAL RIVER, FL   52
FLORIDA HERITAGE MUSEUM .... ST. AUGUSTINE, FL   194
FLORIDA MUSEUM OF NATURAL HISTORY....... GAINESVILLE, FL   86
FORT CHRISTMAS MUSEUM .... CHRISTMAS, FL   160
☙ FRED BEAR MUSEUM .... GAINESVILLE, FL   86
☙ GOVERNMENT HOUSE MUSEUM .... ST. AUGUSTINE, FL   191
HALIFAX HISTORICAL SOCIETY AND
   MUSEUM...................................... DAYTONA BEACH, FL   54
HISTORIC SPANISH POINT............................. OSPREY, FL   181
INDIAN TEMPLE MOUND MUSEUM ..... FORT WALTON BEACH, FL   84
MISSION SAN LUIS .... TALLAHASSEE, FL   203
MUSEUM OF SCIENCE AND HISTORY........... JACKSONVILLE, FL   93
MUSEUM OF SEMINOLE COUNTY HISTORY .... SANFORD, FL   179
MUSEUM OF WEAPONS AND EARLY
   AMERICAN HISTORY........................... ST. AUGUSTINE, FL   194
PENSACOLA HISTORICAL MUSEUM............... PENSACOLA, FL   185
PIONEER FLORIDA MUSEUM AND VILLAGE .... DADE CITY, FL   228
ST. LUCIE COUNTY HISTORICAL MUSEUM .... FORT PIERCE, FL   83
SAWGRASS RECREATION PARK............. FORT LAUDERDALE, FL   74

EXHIBITS & COLLECTIONS-MUSIC

ELLIOTT MUSEUM .... STUART, FL   201
☙ LIGHTNER MUSEUM .... ST. AUGUSTINE, FL   191
SARASOTA CLASSIC CAR MUSEUM .... SARASOTA, FL   199
STEPHEN FOSTER FOLK CULTURE CENTER SP... WHITE SPRINGS, FL   235

EXHIBITS & COLLECTIONS-RELIGIOUS ITEMS

HOLY LAND EXPERIENCE .... ORLANDO, FL   142
JEWISH MUSEUM OF FLORIDA .... MIAMI- MIAMI BEACH, FL   114

EXHIBITS & COLLECTIONS-SCIENCE

☙ THE BAILEY-MATTHEWS SHELL MUSEUM.............. SANIBEL, FL   196
BREVARD MUSEUM OF ART AND SCIENCE .... MELBOURNE, FL   103
BREVARD MUSEUM OF HISTORY AND SCIENCE .... COCOA, FL   52
THE CHILDREN'S SCIENCE CENTER .... CAPE CORAL, FL   50
THE CONSERVANCY—NAPLES NATURE CENTER .... NAPLES, FL   128
DINOSAUR WORLD .... PLANT CITY, FL   229
EPCOT.................................. LAKE BUENA VISTA, FL   168
FPL'S ENERGY ENCOUNTER...................... FORT PIERCE, FL   82
GREAT EXPLORATIONS .... ST. PETERSBURG, FL   213
GULFCOAST WONDER & IMAGINATION ZONE
   (G.WIZ) .... SARASOTA, FL   198
JOHN GORRIE MUSEUM SP .... APALACHICOLA, FL   46
☙ KENNEDY SPACE CENTER VISITOR
   COMPLEX................... KENNEDY SPACE CENTER, FL   97
THE MARY BROGAN MUSEUM OF ART AND
   SCIENCE...................................... TALLAHASSEE, FL   203
MIAMI MUSEUM OF SCIENCE........... MIAMI- MIAMI BEACH, FL   115
☙ MOSI (MUSEUM OF SCIENCE & INDUSTRY)............. TAMPA, FL   218
MULBERRY PHOSPHATE MUSEUM .... MULBERRY, FL   127
MUSEUM OF ARTS AND SCIENCES........... DAYTONA BEACH, FL   54
MUSEUM OF DISCOVERY AND SCIENCE AND BLOCKBUSTER IMAX
   THEATER .... FORT LAUDERDALE, FL   74
MUSEUM OF SCIENCE AND HISTORY .... JACKSONVILLE, FL   93
MUSEUM OF SCIENCE AND SPACE TRANSIT
   PLANETARIUM .... MIAMI- MIAMI BEACH, FL   115
ORLANDO SCIENCE CENTER .... ORLANDO, FL   146
RIVERWALK....................................... FORT LAUDERDALE, FL   74
SOUTH FLORIDA SCIENCE MUSEUM .... WEST PALM BEACH, FL   234

EXHIBITS & COLLECTIONS-SPORTS

☙ I.G.F.A. FISHING HALL OF FAME & MUSEUM .... DANIA BEACH, FL   77

EXHIBITS & COLLECTIONS-VEHICLES

BOCA RATON HISTORICAL SOCIETY .... BOCA RATON, FL   47
☙ DAYTONA USA .... DAYTONA BEACH, FL   53
ELLIOTT MUSEUM .... STUART, FL   201
E-ONE FACTORY TOURS .... OCALA, FL   131
☙ FLORIDA'S SILVER SPRINGS .... OCALA, FL   131
GARLITS' AUTO ATTRACTION .... OCALA, FL   131
KLASSIX AUTO ATTRACTION .... DAYTONA BEACH, FL   54
MUSEUM OF COMMERCE .... PENSACOLA, FL   185
THE MUSEUM OF THE CIRCUS .... SARASOTA, FL   199
OLDEST STORE MUSEUM .... ST. AUGUSTINE, FL   191
PIONEER FLORIDA MUSEUM AND VILLAGE .... DADE CITY, FL   228
SARASOTA CLASSIC CAR MUSEUM .... SARASOTA, FL   199

EXHIBITS & COLLECTIONS-WARS

AIR FORCE ARMAMENT MUSEUM....... FORT WALTON BEACH, FL   84
CAMP BLANDING MUSEUM AND MEMORIAL PARK ... STARKE, FL   201
MUSEUM OF SCIENCE AND HISTORY .... JACKSONVILLE, FL   93
MUSEUM OF SEMINOLE COUNTY HISTORY .... SANFORD, FL   179
SAN MARCOS DE APALACHE HISTORIC SP .... ST. MARKS, FL   196

EXHIBITS & COLLECTIONS-WEAPONS

AIR FORCE ARMAMENT MUSEUM....... FORT WALTON BEACH, FL   84
THE AMERICAN POLICE HALL OF FAME
   AND MUSEUM .... MIAMI- MIAMI BEACH, FL   112
☙ CASTILLO DE SAN MARCOS NMO .... ST. AUGUSTINE, FL   188
DE SOTO NME .... FL   56
FLORIDA HERITAGE MUSEUM .... ST. AUGUSTINE, FL   194
FORT ZACHARY TAYLOR HISTORIC SP............... KEY WEST, FL   67
☙ FRED BEAR MUSEUM .... GAINESVILLE, FL   86
MUSEUM OF WEAPONS AND EARLY AMERICAN
   HISTORY .... ST. AUGUSTINE, FL   194
THE OLD JAIL .... ST. AUGUSTINE, FL   194

FARMS

ECHO... FORT MYERS, FL   80
GREEN MEADOWS PETTING FARM .... KISSIMMEE, FL   162

HUNSADER FARMS .... BRADENTON, FL   48

FISH HATCHERIES

WELAKA NATIONAL FISH HATCHERY AQUARIUM .... WELAKA, FL   233

FORESTS, NATIONAL; STATE

APALACHICOLA NF .... FL   46
OCALA NF .... FL   132
OSCEOLA NF .... FL   181
WITHLACOOCHEE SF .... BUSHNELL, FL   50

FORTS & MILITARY INSTALLATIONS

CAPE CANAVERAL AIR STATION...... KENNEDY SPACE CENTER, FL   97
CASTILLO DE SAN MARCOS NMO .... ST. AUGUSTINE, FL   188
DRY TORTUGAS NP .... FL   64
EGLIN AIR FORCE BASE .... FORT WALTON BEACH, FL   84
FORT BARRANCAS .... GULF ISLANDS NS, FL   86
FORT BARRANCAS .... PENSACOLA, FL   185
FORT CAROLINE NME........................... JACKSONVILLE, FL   93
FORT CLINCH SP .... FERNANDINA BEACH, FL   95
FORT DE SOTO .... ST. PETERSBURG, FL   213
FORT FOSTER .... THONOTOSASSA, FL   231
FORT MATANZAS NMO.. FL   79
FORT PICKENS .... GULF ISLANDS NS, FL   86
FORT ZACHARY TAYLOR HISTORIC SP................ KEY WEST, FL   67
MARTELLO TOWERS .... KEY WEST, FL   68
NAVAL AIR STATION, PENSACOLA .... PENSACOLA, FL   185
REDOUBT .... GULF ISLANDS NS, FL   86
TYNDALL AIR FORCE BASE .... PANAMA CITY, FL   182

FOSSILS

ST. PETERSBURG MUSEUM OF HISTORY........ ST. PETERSBURG, FL   216

FOUNTAINS

LAKE EOLA PARK .... ORLANDO, FL   142

GARDENS

ALBIN POLASEK MUSEUM AND GARDENS .... WINTER PARK, FL   179
ALFRED B. MACLAY GARDENS SP .... TALLAHASSEE, FL   202
AUDUBON HOUSE AND TROPICAL GARDENS .... KEY WEST, FL   66
BUSCH GARDENS TAMPA BAY .... TAMPA, FL   217
BUTTERFLY WORLD........................... COCONUT CREEK, FL   77
CARIBBEAN GARDENS: THE ZOO IN NAPLES .... NAPLES, FL   128
CLUETT MEMORIAL GARDENS................... PALM BEACH, FL   181
CUMMER MUSEUM OF ART & GARDENS .... JACKSONVILLE, FL   93
CYPRESS GARDENS .... WINTER HAVEN, FL   236
EDEN STATE GARDENS AND MANSION .. POINT WASHINGTON, FL   186
EDISON-FORD WINTER ESTATES.................... FORT MYERS, FL   80
EVERGLADES WONDER GARDENS............. BONITA SPRINGS, FL   48
FAIRCHILD TROPICAL GARDEN .... CORAL GABLES, FL   125
FLAMINGO GARDENS............................... DAVIE, FL   77
FLORIDA BOTANICAL GARDENS.................... LARGO, FL   229
FRUIT AND SPICE PARK .... HOMESTEAD, FL   126
HARRY P. LEU GARDENS............................ ORLANDO, FL   142
HEATHCOTE BOTANICAL GARDENS .... FORT PIERCE, FL   83
HISTORIC BOK SANCTUARY .... LAKE WALES, FL   101
THE HOLOCAUST MEMORIAL ....MIAMI- MIAMI BEACH, FL   112
KANAPAHA BOTANICAL GARDENS............. GAINESVILLE, FL   86
KEY WEST GARDEN CENTER........................ KEY WEST, FL   68
KORESHAN SHS .... ESTERO, FL   56
MARIE SELBY BOTANICAL GARDENS .... SARASOTA, FL   199
MEAD GARDENS................................. ORLANDO, FL   155
THE MORIKAMI MUSEUM AND JAPANESE
GARDENS .... DELRAY BEACH, FL   55
MOUNTS BOTANICAL GARDEN............. WEST PALM BEACH, FL   234
OLDEST HOUSE .... ST. AUGUSTINE, FL   191
ORMOND MEMORIAL ART MUSEUM AND
GARDENS .... ORMOND BEACH, FL   181
POLK MUSEUM OF ART............................. LAKELAND, FL   100
RAVINE STATE GARDENS .... PALATKA, FL   181
SARASOTA JUNGLE GARDENS .... SARASOTA, FL   199
SOCIETY OF THE FOUR ARTS .... PALM BEACH, FL   182
SUGAR MILL BOTANICAL GARDENS .... PORT ORANGE, FL   187
SUNKEN GARDENS .... ST. PETERSBURG, FL   216
THOMAS A. EDISON'S WINTER HOME............. FORT MYERS, FL   80
VIZCAYA MUSEUM AND GARDENS....... MIAMI- MIAMI BEACH, FL   116
WASHINGTON OAKS GARDENS SP .... PALM COAST, FL   182
A WORLD OF ORCHIDS .... KISSIMMEE, FL   162
THE ZOO .... GULF BREEZE, FL   86

GENEALOGICAL INFORMATION

MUSEUM OF SOUTHERN HISTORY .... JACKSONVILLE, FL   93
PENSACOLA HISTORICAL MUSEUM................. PENSACOLA, FL   185

GEOLOGICAL FORMATIONS

DEVIL'S MILLHOPPER GEOLOGICAL SP .... GAINESVILLE, FL   84

HALLS OF FAME

THE AMERICAN POLICE HALL OF FAME
AND MUSEUM..........................MIAMI- MIAMI BEACH, FL   112
I.G.F.A. FISHING HALL OF FAME & MUSEUM .... DANIA BEACH, FL   77
INTERNATIONAL SWIMMING HALL
OF FAME.......................... FORT LAUDERDALE, FL   71
TED WILLIAMS MUSEUM AND HITTERS HALL OF
FAME .... HERNANDO, FL   86
U.S. ASTRONAUT HALL OF FAME..... KENNEDY SPACE CENTER, FL   99
WATER SKI MUSEUM AND HALL OF FAME..........POLK CITY, FL   186
WORLD GOLF VILLAGE AND HALL OF FAME... ST. AUGUSTINE, FL   195

HISTORIC BUILDINGS & HOUSES

ALFRED B. MACLAY GARDENS SP ....TALLAHASSEE, FL   202
AUDUBON HOUSE AND TROPICAL GARDENS .... KEY WEST, FL   66
THE BARNACLE SHP .... COCONUT GROVE, FL   124
BOCA RATON HISTORICAL SOCIETY .... BOCA RATON, FL   47
BONNET HOUSE MUSEUM & GARDENS .... FORT LAUDERDALE, FL   71
BRONSON-MULHOLLAND HOUSE .... PALATKA, FL   181
BURROUGHS HOME .... FORT MYERS, FL   79
CASA DE GALLEGOS .... ST. AUGUSTINE, FL   190
CASA DE GÓMEZ .... ST. AUGUSTINE, FL   190
THE CASEMENTS................................ ORMOND BEACH, FL   181
CÀ D'ZAN .... SARASOTA, FL   199
CORAL CASTLE OF FLORIDA .... HOMESTEAD, FL   126
CORAL GABLES HOUSE .... CORAL GABLES, FL   124
DE HITA/GONZÁLEZ HOUSES .... ST. AUGUSTINE, FL   190
DE MESA/SÁNCHEZ SITE .... ST. AUGUSTINE, FL   190
DONKEY MILK HOUSE MUSEUM .... KEY WEST, FL   66
DORR HOUSE .... PENSACOLA, FL   184
EDEN STATE GARDENS AND MANSION .. POINT WASHINGTON, FL   186
EDISON-FORD WINTER ESTATES................. FORT MYERS, FL   80
ERNEST HEMINGWAY HOME AND MUSEUM......... KEY WEST, FL   67
FLAGLER MUSEUM............................... PALM BEACH, FL   182
GAMBLE PLANTATION HISTORIC SP AND JUDAH P. BENJAMIN
CONFEDERATE MEMORIAL....................... ELLENTON, FL   56
GILBERT'S BAR HOUSE OF REFUGE MUSEUM .... STUART, FL   201
GOVERNOR'S MANSION ....TALLAHASSEE, FL   202
HARRY P. LEU GARDENS.......................... ORLANDO, FL   142
HENRY A. DELAND HOUSE MUSEUM.................... DELAND, FL   55
HENRY FORD WINTER HOME................... FORT MYERS, FL   80
HERITAGE VILLAGE .... LARGO, FL   229
HISTORIC OLD JAIL COMPLEX .... ST. AUGUSTINE, FL   194
HISTORIC SPANISH POINT.......................... OSPREY, FL   181
HISTORIC WATERHOUSE RESIDENCE AND CARPENTRY SHOP
MUSEUMS .... MAITLAND, FL   178
JULEE COTTAGE .... PENSACOLA, FL   185
KINGSLEY PLANTATION .... FORT GEORGE ISLAND, FL   96
THE KNOTT HOUSE MUSEUM ....TALLAHASSEE, FL   203
KORESHAN SHS .... ESTERO, FL   56
LAKE WALES ARTS CENTER........................ LAKE WALES, FL   101
LAKE WALES HISTORIC DISTRICT .... LAKE WALES, FL   101
LAVALLE HOUSE .... PENSACOLA, FL   185
LIGHTNER MUSEUM .... ST. AUGUSTINE, FL   191
LITTLE WHITE HOUSE MUSEUM .... KEY WEST, FL   68
MANATEE VILLAGE HISTORICAL PARK .... BRADENTON, FL   49
MAY STRINGER HERITAGE MUSEUM .... BROOKSVILLE, FL   50
MICANOPY HISTORICAL SOCIETY MUSEUM....... MICANOPY, FL   127
THE OLD CAPITOL ....TALLAHASSEE, FL   203
THE OLD JAIL .... ST. AUGUSTINE, FL   194
OLD SCHOOL SQUARE CULTURAL ARTS CENTER AND
NHS .... DELRAY BEACH, FL   55
OLD ST. AUGUSTINE VILLAGE .... ST. AUGUSTINE, FL   191
OLDEST HOUSE .... ST. AUGUSTINE, FL   191
OLDEST WOODEN SCHOOLHOUSE .... ST. AUGUSTINE, FL   191
PALACE SALOON .... FERNANDINA BEACH, FL   95
PEÑA-PECK HOUSE .... ST. AUGUSTINE, FL   191
PIONEER FLORIDA MUSEUM AND VILLAGE .... DADE CITY, FL   228
THE PIONEER SETTLEMENT FOR THE CREATIVE
ARTS .... BARBERVILLE, FL   46
SANIBEL HISTORICAL VILLAGE AND MUSEUM .... SANIBEL, FL   197
SPANISH MILITARY HOSPITAL .... ST. AUGUSTINE, FL   190
STEPHEN FOSTER FOLK CULTURE CENTER SP... WHITE SPRINGS, FL   235
STRANAHAN HOUSE..................... FORT LAUDERDALE, FL   74
THOMAS A. EDISON'S WINTER HOME............. FORT MYERS, FL   80

THURSBY HOUSE ....ORANGE CITY, FL 132
UNION BANK ....TALLAHASSEE, FL 202
♥ VIZCAYA MUSEUM AND GARDENS......MIAMI- MIAMI BEACH, FL 116
WRECKERS' MUSEUM/OLDEST HOUSE ....KEY WEST, FL 68
XIMENEZ-FATIO HOUSE ....ST. AUGUSTINE, FL 192

HISTORIC DOCUMENTS, MANUSCRIPTS & RARE BOOKS

BLACK ARCHIVES RESEARCH CENTER AND
MUSEUM ....TALLAHASSEE, FL 203
KARPELES MANUSCRIPT LIBRARY MUSEUM ....JACKSONVILLE, FL 93
SANIBEL HISTORICAL VILLAGE AND MUSEUM ....SANIBEL, FL 197

HISTORIC SITES

THE BARNACLE SHP ....COCONUT GROVE, FL 124
BULOW PLANTATION RUINS HISTORIC SP ....BUNNELL, FL 50
CONSTITUTION CONVENTION MUSEUM SP ....PORT ST. JOE, FL 187
DADE BATTLEFIELD HISTORIC SP ....BUSHNELL, FL 50
FORT FOSTER ................................THONOTOSASSA, FL 231
FORT ZACHARY TAYLOR HISTORIC SP................KEY WEST, FL 67
GAMBLE PLANTATION HISTORIC SP AND JUDAH P. BENJAMIN
CONFEDERATE MEMORIAL...........................ELLENTON, FL 56
INDIAN KEY HISTORIC SP ....ISLAMORADA, FL 65
KINGSLEY PLANTATION ....FORT GEORGE ISLAND, FL 96
KORESHAN SHS......................................ESTERO, FL 56
MANATEE VILLAGE HISTORICAL PARK ....BRADENTON, FL 49
MARJORIE KINNAN RAWLINGS HISTORIC SP ..... CROSS CREEK, FL 52
MISSION SAN LUIS ....TALLAHASSEE, FL 203
NATURAL BRIDGE BATTLEFIELD HISTORIC SP ....WOODVILLE, FL 237
OLD SCHOOL SQUARE CULTURAL ARTS CENTER AND
NHS ....DELRAY BEACH, FL 55
OLUSTEE BATTLEFIELD HISTORIC SP ....OLUSTEE, FL 132
PONCE DE LEÓN'S FOUNTAIN OF YOUTH NATIONAL
ARCHEOLOGICAL PARK ....ST. AUGUSTINE, FL 194
SAN MARCOS DE APALACHE HISTORIC SP ....ST. MARKS, FL 196
SUGAR MILL RUINS ....NEW SMYRNA BEACH, FL 130
YULEE SUGAR MILL RUINS
HISTORIC SP ....HOMOSASSA SPRINGS, FL 87
ZERO MILESTONE...............................ST. AUGUSTINE, FL 196

HORSE FARMS

COUNTRY DAY STABLE................................HILLIARD, FL 96
KELLY SEAHORSE RANCH.......................AMELIA ISLAND, FL 95

INDIAN MOUNDS, REMAINS & RUINS

CRYSTAL RIVER ARCHEOLOGICAL SP ....CRYSTAL RIVER, FL 52
HISTORIC SPANISH POINT...............................OSPREY, FL 181
INDIAN TEMPLE MOUND MUSEUM .....FORT WALTON BEACH, FL 84
LAKE JACKSON MOUNDS STATE ARCHAEOLOGICAL
SITE ....TALLAHASSEE, FL 203

INDIAN BURIAL GROUNDS

PONCE DE LEÓN'S FOUNTAIN OF YOUTH NATIONAL
ARCHEOLOGICAL PARK ....ST. AUGUSTINE, FL 194

INDIAN RESERVATIONS & VILLAGES

BIG CYPRESS SEMINOLE INDIAN RESERVATION ....FL 47
SAWGRASS RECREATION PARK............FORT LAUDERDALE, FL 74

INDUSTRIAL TOURS

ANGELL & PHELPS CHOCOLATE FACTORY
TOUR ....DAYTONA BEACH, FL 53
ANHEUSER-BUSCH BREWERY.....................JACKSONVILLE, FL 94
E-ONE FACTORY TOURS ....OCALA, FL 131
UNIVERSAL STUDIOS..................................ORLANDO, FL 152
WHETSTONE CHOCOLATE FACTORY ....ST. AUGUSTINE, FL 195

ISLANDS

AMELIA ISLAND...FL 95
BIG PINE KEY..FL 64
CALADESI ISLAND SP ....DUNEDIN, FL 228
CAPTIVA ISLAND....................................SANIBEL, FL 196
CEDAR KEY..FL 51
DAVIS ISLAND..TAMPA, FL 220
FORT GEORGE ISLAND.....................................FL 96
GARDEN KEY...............................DRY TORTUGAS NP, FL 64
GULF ISLANDS NS..FL 86
HONEYMOON ISLAND SRA ....DUNEDIN, FL 228
INDIAN KEY HISTORIC SP ....ISLAMORADA, FL 65
LIGNUMVITAE KEY STATE BOTANICAL SITE ......ISLAMORADA, FL 65

MARCO ISLAND..FL 102
SANIBEL ISLAND ....SANIBEL, FL 196
SINGER ISLAND ....FL 201
TORTUGAS KEYS..........................DRY TORTUGAS NP, FL 64

JAILS

THE OLD JAIL ....ST. AUGUSTINE, FL 194

LAKES, PONDS & RESERVOIRS

BLUE HOLE.......................................BIG PINE KEY, FL 64
BUTLER CHAIN OF LAKES...............................ORLANDO, FL 155
LAKE DORA ....MOUNT DORA, FL 178
LAKE EOLA...ORLANDO, FL 142
LAKE IVANHOE ....ORLANDO, FL 155
LAKE OKEECHOBEE.................................OKEECHOBEE, FL 132
LAKE SILVER ....WINTER HAVEN, FL 235
LAKE THONOTOSASSA ....TAMPA, FL 221
LAKE TOHOPEKALIGA ....ORLANDO, FL 154
LAKE UNDERHILL.....................................ORLANDO, FL 155
WINTER PARK CHAIN OF LAKES ....ORLANDO, FL 155

LIBRARIES, ARCHIVES

BLACK ARCHIVES RESEARCH CENTER AND
MUSEUM ....TALLAHASSEE, FL 203
BOCA RATON HISTORICAL SOCIETY ....BOCA RATON, FL 47
HALIFAX HISTORICAL SOCIETY AND
MUSEUM ....DAYTONA BEACH, FL 54
JACKSONVILLE HISTORICAL CENTER............JACKSONVILLE, FL 93
MAIN LIBRARY ....MIAMI- MIAMI BEACH, FL 114
OLD FORT LAUDERDALE MUSEUM
OF HISTORY ....FORT LAUDERDALE, FL 74
♥ OLDEST HOUSE ....ST. AUGUSTINE, FL 191
SOCIETY OF THE FOUR ARTS ....PALM BEACH, FL 182

LIGHTHOUSES

JUPITER INLET LIGHTHOUSE ....JUPITER, FL 97
KEY WEST LIGHTHOUSE MUSEUM ....KEY WEST, FL 68
PONCE DE LEON INLET LIGHTHOUSE ....PONCE INLET, FL 187
ST. AUGUSTINE LIGHTHOUSE AND
MUSEUM ....ST. AUGUSTINE, FL 195

MARINE ATTRACTIONS

♥ THE FLORIDA AQUARIUM ....TAMPA, FL 218
GILBERT'S BAR HOUSE OF REFUGE MUSEUM ....STUART, FL 201
GULF SPECIMEN MARINE LABORATORY ....PANACEA, FL 182
GULFARIUM.............................FORT WALTON BEACH, FL 84
HARBOR BRANCH OCEANOGRAPHIC
INSTITUTION ....FORT PIERCE, FL 83
KONGER TARPON SPRINGS AQUARIUM......TARPON SPRINGS, FL 230
MIAMI SEAQUARIUM.....................MIAMI- MIAMI BEACH, FL 115
MOTE AQUARIUM....................................SARASOTA, FL 199
THE PIER ....ST. PETERSBURG, FL 216
♥ SEAWORLD ORLANDO...................................ORLANDO, FL 147

MARKETS

DAYTONA FLEA MARKET.....................DAYTONA BEACH, FL 53
FARMERS MARKET....................................DAYTONA BEACH, FL 53
FLEA WORLD..ORLANDO, FL 157
FLORIDA CITY STATE FARMER'S MARKET ....FLORIDA CITY, FL 125
PLAZA DE LA CONSTITUCIÓN...................ST. AUGUSTINE, FL 191
WEBSTER FLEA MARKET..............................BUSHNELL, FL 50
WINTER PARK FARMER'S MARKET ....ORLANDO, FL 156

MEMORIALS

THE AMERICAN POLICE HALL OF FAME AND
MUSEUM ....MIAMI- MIAMI BEACH, FL 112
♥ ASTRONAUTS MEMORIAL SPACE
MIRROR ....KENNEDY SPACE CENTER, FL 99
CAMP BLANDING MUSEUM AND MEMORIAL PARK ... STARKE, FL 201
DE SOTO NME ....FL 56
FORT CAROLINE NME...........................JACKSONVILLE, FL 93
♥ THE HOLOCAUST MEMORIAL ....MIAMI- MIAMI BEACH, FL 112
THE HOLOCAUST MEMORIAL RESOURCE AND EDUCATION
CENTER OF CENTRAL FLORIDA ....MAITLAND, FL 178
MEDAL OF HONOR PARK.............................SEBRING, FL 200
VETERANS MEMORIAL PARK ....PENSACOLA, FL 186

MILLS

SUGAR MILL BOTANICAL GARDENS ....PORT ORANGE, FL 187

YULEE SUGAR MILL RUINS
  HISTORIC SP .... HOMOSASSA SPRINGS, FL   87

MINES & MINERALS

  GILLESPIE MUSEUM OF MINERALS .... DELAND, FL   55

MONUMENTS, GENERAL

☞ ASTRONAUTS MEMORIAL SPACE
  MIRROR.............................. KENNEDY SPACE CENTER, FL   99
  CAMP BLANDING MUSEUM AND MEMORIAL PARK ... STARKE, FL   201
  CARL FISHER MONUMENT.............. MIAMI- MIAMI BEACH, FL   112
☞ THE HOLOCAUST MEMORIAL .... MIAMI- MIAMI BEACH, FL   112
  MONUMENT OF STATES .... KISSIMMEE, FL   161
  PLAZA DE LA CONSTITUCIÓN.................. ST. AUGUSTINE, FL   191
  RIBAULT MONUMENT .... JACKSONVILLE, FL   93

MONUMENTS, NATIONAL; STATE

☞ CASTILLO DE SAN MARCOS NMO .... ST. AUGUSTINE, FL   188
  FORT MATANZAS NMO.. FL   79

MURALS & MOSAICS

  SCOTTISH RITE MASONIC TEMPLE .... LAKE WORTH, FL   102

MUSEUMS

  THE AFRICAN AMERICAN MUSEUM OF THE ARTS ..... DELAND, FL   55
  AH-TAH-THI-KI
    MUSEUM ..... BIG CYPRESS SEMINOLE INDIAN RESERVATION, FL   47
  AIR FORCE ARMAMENT MUSEUM....... FORT WALTON BEACH, FL   84
  ALBIN POLASEK MUSEUM AND GARDENS .... WINTER PARK, FL   179
  ALEXANDER BREST MUSEUM.................... JACKSONVILLE, FL   89
  AMELIA ISLAND MUSEUM OF
    HISTORY .... FERNANDINA BEACH, FL   95
  THE AMERICAN POLICE HALL OF FAME AND
    MUSEUM .... MIAMI- MIAMI BEACH, FL   112
☞ THE APPLETON MUSEUM OF ART .... OCALA, FL   130
☞ THE BAILEY-MATTHEWS SHELL MUSEUM............. SANIBEL, FL   196
  BASS MUSEUM OF ART .... MIAMI- MIAMI BEACH, FL   112
  BLACK ARCHIVES RESEARCH CENTER AND
    MUSEUM .... TALLAHASSEE, FL   203
  BOCA RATON MUSEUM OF ART................... BOCA RATON, FL   47
  BREVARD MUSEUM OF ART AND SCIENCE .... MELBOURNE, FL   103
  BREVARD MUSEUM OF HISTORY AND SCIENCE .... COCOA, FL   52
  BUTTERFLY WORLD........................... COCONUT CREEK, FL   77
  CAMP BLANDING MUSEUM AND MEMORIAL PARK ...... STARKE, FL   201
  CEDAR KEY HISTORICAL SOCIETY MUSEUM .... CEDAR KEY, FL   51
  CEDAR KEY STATE MUSEUM .... CEDAR KEY, FL   51
  CENTRO YBOR MUSEUM............................... TAMPA, FL   217
☞ CHARLES HOSMER MORSE MUSEUM OF
  AMERICAN ART.............................. WINTER PARK, FL   180
  CHILDREN'S MUSEUM .... BOCA RATON, FL   47
  THE CHILDREN'S MUSEUM OF THE HIGHLANDS........ SEBRING, FL   200
  THE CHILDREN'S SCIENCE CENTER................. CAPE CORAL, FL   50
  CIVIL WAR SOLDIERS MUSEUM .... PENSACOLA, FL   184
  CLEARWATER MARINE AQUARIUM .... CLEARWATER, FL   227
  COLLIER COUNTY MUSEUM .... NAPLES, FL   128
☞ COLONIAL SPANISH QUARTER.................. ST. AUGUSTINE, FL   190
  THE CONSERVANCY—NAPLES NATURE CENTER .... NAPLES, FL   128
  CONSTITUTION CONVENTION MUSEUM SP .... PORT ST. JOE, FL   187
  CORAL SPRINGS MUSEUM OF ART .... CORAL SPRINGS, FL   77
  CORNELL FINE ARTS MUSEUM.................... WINTER PARK, FL   180
☞ CYPRESS GARDENS .... WINTER HAVEN, FL   236
☞ DAYTONA USA .... DAYTONA BEACH, FL   53
  DELAND MUSEUM OF ART .... DELAND, FL   55
  THE DEPOT—LAKE WALES MUSEUM AND CULTURAL
    CENTER .... LAKE WALES, FL   101
  DONKEY MILK HOUSE MUSEUM .... KEY WEST, FL   66
  DUNEDIN HISTORICAL SOCIETY AND MUSEUM ...... DUNEDIN, FL   228
  EAST MARTELLO MUSEUM AND GALLERY .... KEY WEST, FL   68
  ELLIOTT MUSEUM .... STUART, FL   201
  ERNEST HEMINGWAY HOME AND MUSEUM......... KEY WEST, FL   67
  EVERGLADES WONDER GARDENS............. BONITA SPRINGS, FL   48
  EXPLORATIONS V CHILDREN'S MUSEUM .... LAKELAND, FL   100
  FANTASY OF FLIGHT................................ POLK CITY, FL   186
☞ FLAGLER MUSEUM .... PALM BEACH, FL   182
  FLAMINGO GARDENS................................. DAVIE, FL   77
  FLORIDA ADVENTURE MUSEUM .... PUNTA GORDA, FL   187
☞ FLORIDA AIR MUSEUM AT SUN 'N FUN .... LAKELAND, FL   100
  FLORIDA HERITAGE MUSEUM .... ST. AUGUSTINE, FL   194
  FLORIDA HISTORY CENTER & MUSEUM .... JUPITER, FL   97
☞ THE FLORIDA HOLOCAUST MUSEUM ... ST. PETERSBURG, FL   212
  FLORIDA INTERNATIONAL MUSEUM .... ST. PETERSBURG, FL   213

FLORIDA MUSEUM OF NATURAL HISTORY........ GAINESVILLE, FL   86
FLORIDA STATE CIVILIAN CONSERVATION CORPS
  MUSEUM .... SEBRING, FL   201
FLYING TIGERS WARBIRD RESTORATION MUSEUM . KISSIMMEE, FL   162
FOREST CAPITAL STATE MUSEUM .... PERRY, FL   186
FORT CHRISTMAS MUSEUM .... CHRISTMAS, FL   160
FORT MYERS HISTORICAL MUSEUM............... FORT MYERS, FL   80
☞ FRED BEAR MUSEUM .... GAINESVILLE, FL   86
GARLITS' AUTO ATTRACTION .... OCALA, FL   131
GILBERT'S BAR HOUSE OF REFUGE MUSEUM .... STUART, FL   201
GILLESPIE MUSEUM OF MINERALS .... DELAND, FL   55
☞ GOVERNMENT HOUSE MUSEUM .... ST. AUGUSTINE, FL   191
GREAT EXPLORATIONS .... ST. PETERSBURG, FL   213
GULF BEACHES HISTORICAL MUSEUM .... ST. PETE BEACH, FL   230
GULF COAST MUSEUM OF ART .... LARGO, FL   229
GULFCOAST WONDER & IMAGINATION ZONE
  (G.WIZ) .... SARASOTA, FL   198
HALIFAX HISTORICAL SOCIETY AND
  MUSEUM .... DAYTONA BEACH, FL   54
HENRY A. DELAND HOUSE MUSEUM................ DELAND, FL   55
HENRY B. PLANT MUSEUM .... TAMPA, FL   219
HERITAGE VILLAGE .... LARGO, FL   229
☞ HISTORIC BOK SANCTUARY .... LAKE WALES, FL   101
HISTORIC WATERHOUSE RESIDENCE AND CARPENTRY SHOP
  MUSEUMS .... MAITLAND, FL   178
HISTORICAL MUSEUM OF SOUTHERN
  FLORIDA .... MIAMI- MIAMI BEACH, FL   114
HOBE SOUND NWR .... HOBE SOUND, FL   87
THE HOLOCAUST MEMORIAL RESOURCE AND EDUCATION
  CENTER OF CENTRAL FLORIDA .... MAITLAND, FL   178
☞ I.G.F.A. FISHING HALL OF FAME & MUSEUM .... DANIA BEACH, FL   77
IMAGINARIUM HANDS-ON MUSEUM .... FORT MYERS, FL   80
INDIAN TEMPLE MOUND MUSEUM ..... FORT WALTON BEACH, FL   84
INTERNATIONAL SWIMMING HALL
  OF FAME.................................. FORT LAUDERDALE, FL   71
JACKSONVILLE HISTORICAL CENTER............. JACKSONVILLE, FL   92
JACKSONVILLE MARITIME MUSEUM .... JACKSONVILLE, FL   93
JEWISH MUSEUM OF FLORIDA .... MIAMI- MIAMI BEACH, FL   114
☞ THE JOHN AND MABLE RINGLING MUSEUM OF
  ART .... SARASOTA, FL   198
JOHN GORRIE MUSEUM SP .... APALACHICOLA, FL   46
JUNIOR MUSEUM OF BAY COUNTY .... PANAMA CITY, FL   182
KARPELES MANUSCRIPT LIBRARY MUSEUM .... JACKSONVILLE, FL   93
KEY WEST LIGHTHOUSE MUSEUM .... KEY WEST, FL   68
KEY WEST SHIPWRECK HISTOREUM .... KEY WEST, FL   68
KID CITY: THE CHILDREN'S MUSEUM OF TAMPA....... TAMPA, FL   218
KLASSIX AUTO ATTRACTION .... DAYTONA BEACH, FL   54
THE KNOTT HOUSE MUSEUM .... TALLAHASSEE, FL   203
☞ LIGHTNER MUSEUM .... ST. AUGUSTINE, FL   191
LITTLE WHITE HOUSE MUSEUM .... KEY WEST, FL   68
LOWE ART MUSEUM, UNIVERSITY OF MIAMI .. CORAL GABLES, FL   125
MARIE SELBY BOTANICAL GARDENS .... SARASOTA, FL   199
THE MARY BROGAN MUSEUM OF ART AND
  SCIENCE....................................... TALLAHASSEE, FL   203
MAY STRINGER HERITAGE MUSEUM .... BROOKSVILLE, FL   50
MCLARTY TREASURE MUSEUM....................... SEBASTIAN, FL   200
MEL FISHER MARITIME MUSEUM.................... KEY WEST, FL   68
MIAMI ART MUSEUM .... MIAMI- MIAMI BEACH, FL   114
MIAMI MUSEUM OF SCIENCE........... MIAMI- MIAMI BEACH, FL   115
MICANOPY HISTORICAL SOCIETY MUSEUM......... MICANOPY, FL   127
THE MORIKAMI MUSEUM AND JAPANESE
  GARDENS .... DELRAY BEACH, FL   55
☞ MOSI (MUSEUM OF SCIENCE & INDUSTRY)............. TAMPA, FL   218
MULBERRY PHOSPHATE MUSEUM .... MULBERRY, FL   127
MUSEUM OF ART .... FORT LAUDERDALE, FL   71
MUSEUM OF ARTS AND SCIENCES........... DAYTONA BEACH, FL   54
MUSEUM OF COMMERCE .... PENSACOLA, FL   185
MUSEUM OF CONTEMPORARY ART....... NORTH MIAMI BEACH, FL   126
MUSEUM OF DISCOVERY AND SCIENCE AND BLOCKBUSTER IMAX
  THEATER................................. FORT LAUDERDALE, FL   74
MUSEUM OF FINE ARTS....................... ST. PETERSBURG, FL   213
MUSEUM OF FLORIDA HISTORY................. TALLAHASSEE, FL   203
THE MUSEUM OF FLORIDA'S ARMY .... ST. AUGUSTINE, FL   191
MUSEUM OF INDUSTRY .... PENSACOLA, FL   185
THE MUSEUM OF MAN IN THE SEA...... PANAMA CITY BEACH, FL   183
MUSEUM OF SCIENCE AND HISTORY........... JACKSONVILLE, FL   93
MUSEUM OF SCIENCE AND SPACE TRANSIT
  PLANETARIUM......................... MIAMI- MIAMI BEACH, FL   115
MUSEUM OF SEMINOLE COUNTY HISTORY .... SANFORD, FL   179
MUSEUM OF SOUTHERN HISTORY............... JACKSONVILLE, FL   93
THE MUSEUM OF THE CIRCUS .... SARASOTA, FL   199
MUSEUM OF THE EVERGLADES .... EVERGLADES CITY, FL   56

MUSEUM OF WEAPONS AND EARLY AMERICAN
HISTORY .... ST. AUGUSTINE, FL 194
MUSEUMS AND NATURE CENTER OF CRANE POINT
HAMMOCK ....MARATHON, FL 69
▽ NATIONAL MUSEUM OF NAVAL AVIATION ....PENSACOLA, FL 185
NORTON MUSEUM OF ART.................WEST PALM BEACH, FL 234
OLD FORT LAUDERDALE MUSEUM OF
HISTORY ....FORT LAUDERDALE, FL 74
▽ OLDEST HOUSE .... ST. AUGUSTINE, FL 191
OLDEST STORE MUSEUM .... ST. AUGUSTINE, FL 191
OLUSTEE BATTLEFIELD HISTORIC SP...................OLUSTEE, FL 132
ORANGE COUNTY REGIONAL HISTORY CENTER .....ORLANDO, FL 147
ORLANDO MUSEUM OF ART ....ORLANDO, FL 146
ORLANDO SCIENCE CENTER ....ORLANDO, FL 146
ORMOND MEMORIAL ART MUSEUM AND
GARDENS ....ORMOND BEACH, FL 181
PENSACOLA HISTORICAL MUSEUM...................PENSACOLA, FL 185
PIONEER FLORIDA MUSEUM AND VILLAGE ....DADE CITY, FL 228
THE PIONEER/HERITAGE MUSEUM ....PLANT CITY, FL 229
POLK MUSEUM OF ART..............................LAKELAND, FL 100
PONCE DE LEON INLET LIGHTHOUSE ....PONCE INLET, FL 187
RIPLEY'S BELIEVE IT OR NOT! ORIGINAL
MUSEUM .... ST. AUGUSTINE, FL 194
RIPLEY'S BELIEVE IT OR NOT! ORLANDO
ODDITORIUM...ORLANDO, FL 147
ST. AUGUSTINE LIGHTHOUSE AND MUSEUM .. ST. AUGUSTINE, FL 195
ST. LUCIE COUNTY HISTORICAL MUSEUM...........FORT PIERCE, FL 83
ST. PETERSBURG MUSEUM OF HISTORY.........ST. PETERSBURG, FL 216
▽ SALVADOR DALI MUSEUM ....ST. PETERSBURG, FL 216
SAMUEL P. HARN MUSEUM OF ART...............GAINESVILLE, FL 86
THE SANFORD MUSEUM..................................SANFORD, FL 179
SANIBEL HISTORICAL VILLAGE AND MUSEUM ....SANIBEL, FL 197
SARASOTA CLASSIC CAR MUSEUM ....SARASOTA, FL 199
SOUTH FLORIDA MUSEUM ....BRADENTON, FL 49
SOUTH FLORIDA MUSEUM OF NATURAL
HISTORY .... DANIA BEACH, FL 77
SOUTH FLORIDA SCIENCE MUSEUM.........WEST PALM BEACH, FL 234
SOUTHEAST MUSEUM OF PHOTOGRAPHY...DAYTONA BEACH, FL 54
SPORTS IMMORTALS MUSEUM....................BOCA RATON, FL 48
TALLAHASSEE MUSEUM OF HISTORY AND NATURAL
SCIENCE...TALLAHASSEE, FL 203
TAMPA BAY HISTORY CENTER ....TAMPA, FL 219
TAMPA MUSEUM OF ART ....TAMPA, FL 219
TED WILLIAMS MUSEUM AND HITTERS HALL OF
FAME ....HERNANDO, FL 86
THE TEDDY BEAR MUSEUM OF NAPLES................NAPLES, FL 129
T.T. WENTWORTH JR. FLORIDA STATE MUSEUM...PENSACOLA, FL 185
UDT SEAL MUSEUM ....FORT PIERCE, FL 83
VALIANT AIR COMMAND WARBIRD AIR
MUSEUM .... TITUSVILLE, FL 232
▽ VIZCAYA MUSEUM AND GARDENS......MIAMI- MIAMI BEACH, FL 116
WATER SKI MUSEUM AND HALL OF FAME...........POLK CITY, FL 186
THE WOLFSONIAN-FLORIDA INTERNATIONAL
UNIVERSITY ....MIAMI- MIAMI BEACH, FL 117
WRECKERS' MUSEUM/OLDEST HOUSE ....KEY WEST, FL 68
YBOR CITY MUSEUM SP ....TAMPA, FL 219
YOUNG AT ART CHILDREN'S MUSEUM...................DAVIE, FL 77

MUSIC HALLS & OPERA HOUSES
FLORIDA WEST COAST SYMPHONY CENTER ....SARASOTA, FL 197
THE F.S.U. CENTER FOR THE PERFORMING ARTS....SARASOTA, FL 197
SAN CARLOS INSTITUTE................................KEY WEST, FL 66
SARASOTA OPERA HOUSE ....SARASOTA, FL 197
TIMES-UNION CENTER FOR THE PERFORMING
ARTS ....JACKSONVILLE, FL 94
VAN WEZEL PERFORMING ARTS HALL ....SARASOTA, FL 197

NATIONALITIES & ETHNIC AREAS
CHINESE...................................... CORAL GABLES, FL 124
DUTCH-SOUTH AFRICAN...................... CORAL GABLES, FL 124
FRENCH .... CORAL GABLES, FL 124
LITTLE HAVANA ....MIAMI- MIAMI BEACH, FL 117
TARPON SPRINGS ....TARPON SPRINGS, FL 230

NATURAL PHENOMENA
SPOOK HILL ....LAKE WALES, FL 101
THE SPRINGS.......................WARM MINERAL SPRINGS, FL 232

NATURE CENTERS
ANN KOLB NATURE CENTER.....................HOLLYWOOD, FL 78
BOYD HILL NATURE PARK ....ST. PETERSBURG, FL 212

BRIGGS NATURE CENTER ....NAPLES, FL 128
CALUSA NATURE CENTER AND PLANETARIUM ...FORT MYERS, FL 80
THE CONSERVANCY—NAPLES NATURE CENTER ....NAPLES, FL 128
GUMBO LIMBO NATURE CENTER.................BOCA RATON, FL 48
▽ HISTORIC BOK SANCTUARY ....LAKE WALES, FL 101
HOBE SOUND NWR...............................HOBE SOUND, FL 87
JOHN D. MACARTHUR BEACH SP.............. SINGER ISLAND, FL 201
MOCCASIN LAKE NATURE PARK: AN ENVIRONMENTAL AND
ENERGY EDUCATION CENTER ....CLEARWATER, FL 227
SANIBEL-CAPTIVA CONSERVATION FOUNDATION .....SANIBEL, FL 197
TREE HILL NATURE CENTER........................JACKSONVILLE, FL 93
▽ WASHINGTON OAKS GARDENS SP ....PALM COAST, FL 182

NATURE TRAILS
▽ ALFRED B. MACLAY GARDENS SP ....TALLAHASSEE, FL 202
ANHINGA TRAIL .... EVERGLADES NP, FL 58
ARTHUR R. MARSHALL LOXAHATCHEE NWR .. DELRAY BEACH, FL 55
BIG PINE KEY..FL 64
BREVARD MUSEUM OF HISTORY AND SCIENCE.........COCOA, FL 52
CARIBBEAN GARDENS: THE ZOO IN NAPLES ....NAPLES, FL 128
CHEKIKA .... EVERGLADES NP, FL 58
THE CONSERVANCY—NAPLES NATURE CENTER ....NAPLES, FL 128
CORKSCREW SWAMP SANCTUARY ....NAPLES, FL 128
DADE BATTLEFIELD HISTORIC SP ....BUSHNELL, FL 50
DE SOTO NME ....FL 56
EDEN OF THE EVERGLADES.................. EVERGLADES CITY, FL 56
▽ EDWARD BALL WAKULLA SPRINGS SP ....WAKULLA, FL 232
FPL'S ENERGY ENCOUNTER ....FORT PIERCE, FL 82
GAINESVILLE TO HAWTHORNE RAIL TRAIL........ GAINESVILLE, FL 84
GULF ISLANDS NS ....FL 86
GUMBO LIMBO TRAIL .... EVERGLADES NP, FL 59
▽ HIGHLANDS HAMMOCK SP..........................SEBRING, FL 201
HISTORIC SPANISH POINT............................. OSPREY, FL 181
HOBE SOUND NWR............................... HOBE SOUND, FL 87
HOMOSASSA SPRINGS WILDLIFE SP ..... HOMOSASSA SPRINGS, FL 87
J.N. "DING" DARLING NWR..........................SANIBEL, FL 197
JOHN D. MACARTHUR BEACH SP.............. SINGER ISLAND, FL 201
JOHN PENNEKAMP CORAL REEF SP .... KEY LARGO, FL 65
JUNIOR MUSEUM OF BAY COUNTY ....PANAMA CITY, FL 182
LEE COUNTY MANATEE PARK......................FORT MYERS, FL 82
LONG PINE KEY AREA .... EVERGLADES NP, FL 59
MAHOGANY HAMMOCK .... EVERGLADES NP, FL 59
MANGROVE TRAIL .... EVERGLADES NP, FL 59
MERRITT ISLAND NWR............................... TITUSVILLE, FL 232
MOCCASIN LAKE NATURE PARK: AN ENVIRONMENTAL AND
ENERGY EDUCATION CENTER ....CLEARWATER, FL 227
THE MORIKAMI MUSEUM AND JAPANESE
GARDENS .... DELRAY BEACH, FL 55
▽ MOSI (MUSEUM OF SCIENCE & INDUSTRY)............TAMPA, FL 218
MOUNTS BOTANICAL GARDEN ....WEST PALM BEACH, FL 234
MUSEUMS AND NATURE CENTER OF CRANE POINT
HAMMOCK ....MARATHON, FL 69
PALM BEACH ZOO...........................WEST PALM BEACH, FL 234
PINELANDS TRAIL.............................. EVERGLADES NP, FL 59
PINELLAS TRAIL..TAMPA, FL 222
RAVINE STATE GARDENS ....PALATKA, FL 181
SAN FELASCO HAMMOCK PRESERVE SP............ GAINESVILLE, FL 84
SARASOTA JUNGLE GARDENS ....SARASOTA, FL 199
SHARK VALLEY .... EVERGLADES NP, FL 59
SOUTH FLORIDA SCIENCE MUSEUM........WEST PALM BEACH, FL 234
TALLAHASSEE MUSEUM OF HISTORY AND NATURAL
SCIENCE...TALLAHASSEE, FL 203
TALLAHASSEE-ST. MARKS HISTORIC RAILROAD
STATE TRAIL .... ST. MARKS, FL 196
TIMUCUAN ECOLOGICAL & HISTORIC
PRESERVE .....................................JACKSONVILLE, FL 94
TREE HILL NATURE CENTER.......................JACKSONVILLE, FL 93
UNIVERSITY OF NORTH FLORIDA NATURE
PRESERVE .....................................JACKSONVILLE, FL 94
▽ WASHINGTON OAKS GARDENS SP ....PALM COAST, FL 182
WEEKI WACHEE SPRINGS WATERPARK ....WEEKI WACHEE, FL 233

OBSERVATORIES
ASTRONAUT MEMORIAL PLANETARIUM &
OBSERVATORY ....COCOA, FL 52
BUEHLER PLANETARIUM & OBSERVATORY ....DAVIE, FL 77
LEE COUNTY MANATEE PARK.......................FORT MYERS, FL 82
MANATEE OBSERVATION AND EDUCATION
CENTER ....FORT PIERCE, FL 83
MUSEUM OF SCIENCE AND SPACE TRANSIT
PLANETARIUM..........................MIAMI- MIAMI BEACH, FL 115
SOUTH FLORIDA SCIENCE MUSEUM ....WEST PALM BEACH, FL 234

PAINTINGS

GEORGE INNESS JR. PICTURES .... TARPON SPRINGS, FL   230

PARKS, CITY; STATE; PROVINCIAL

BIG TREE PARK.. SANFORD, FL   179
BILL DREGGORS PARK .... DELAND, FL   55
BLUE SPRING SP..ORANGE CITY, FL   132
BOWDITCH POINT PARK................... FORT MYERS BEACH, FL   82
BOYD HILL NATURE PARK .... ST. PETERSBURG, FL   212
CALADESI ISLAND SP ....DUNEDIN, FL   228
CARL JOHNSON PARK .... FORT MYERS BEACH, FL   82
CENTRAL PARK ....ORLANDO, FL   157
CRANDON PARK ....KEY BISCAYNE, FL   126
DELNOR-WIGGINS PASS SRA...............................NAPLES, FL   127
DEVIL'S MILLHOPPER GEOLOGICAL SP .... GAINESVILLE, FL   84
EDWARD BALL WAKULLA SPRINGS SP ....WAKULLA, FL   232
FLORIDA CAVERNS SP .... MARIANNA, FL   103
FORT CLINCH SP .... FERNANDINA BEACH, FL   95
FORT DE SOTO PARK .... ST. PETERSBURG, FL   213
FORT DE SOTO PARK ....TAMPA, FL   222
FORT PIERCE INLET SRA............................ FORT PIERCE, FL   82
FRUIT AND SPICE PARK .... HOMESTEAD, FL   126
GASTON EDWARDS PARK ....ORLANDO, FL   154
GILBERT PARK,.................................... MOUNT DORA, FL   178
HERNANDO PARK .... BROOKSVILLE, FL   49
HIGHLANDS HAMMOCK SP.............................SEBRING, FL   201
HILLSBOROUGH RIVER SP.................................TAMPA, FL   222
HOMOSASSA SPRINGS WILDLIFE SP ..... HOMOSASSA SPRINGS, FL   87
HONEYMOON ISLAND SRA ....DUNEDIN, FL   228
JOHN D. MACARTHUR BEACH SP............... SINGER ISLAND, FL   201
JOHN PENNEKAMP CORAL REEF SP .... KEY LARGO, FL   65
JONATHAN DICKINSON SP..............................JUPITER, FL   97
KRAFT AZALEA GARDENS AND PARK ....ORLANDO, FL   155
LAKE CANE/MARSHA PARK................................ORLANDO, FL   154
LAKE EOLA PARK ....ORLANDO, FL   142
LAKE FRONT PARK ....KISSIMMEE, FL   161
LAKE KISSIMMEE SP .... LAKE WALES, FL   102
LAKE LOUISA SP ....CLERMONT, FL   160
LAKE MAGGIORE PARK .... ST. PETERSBURG, FL   212
LAKE UNDERHILL PARK ....ORLANDO, FL   154
LANGFORD PARK ....ORLANDO, FL   155
LEE COUNTY MANATEE PARK...................... FORT MYERS, FL   82
LOCH HAVEN PARK......................................ORLANDO, FL   146
LOVERS KEY SP .... FORT MYERS BEACH, FL   82
LYNN HALL MEMORIAL PARK .... FORT MYERS BEACH, FL   82
MANATEE OBSERVATION AND EDUCATION
  CENTER .... FORT PIERCE, FL   83
MARJORIE PARK...TAMPA, FL   222
MATHESON HAMMOCK PARK.................. CORAL GABLES, FL   125
MEAD GARDENS ....ORLANDO, FL   155
MIRROR LAKE RECREATION PARK........................TAMPA, FL   223
MOCCASIN LAKE NATURE PARK: AN ENVIRONMENTAL AND
  ENERGY EDUCATION CENTER .... CLEARWATER, FL   227
THE MORIKAMI MUSEUM AND JAPANESE
  GARDENS .... DELRAY BEACH, FL   55
OCEANFRONT PARK ....DAYTONA BEACH, FL   53
O'LENO SP ....HIGH SPRINGS, FL   87
PALM BEACH ZOO ....WEST PALM BEACH, FL   234
PAYNES PRAIRIE PRESERVE SP .... MICANOPY, FL   127
PINEWOOD CULTURAL PARK...............................LARGO, FL   229
PONCE DE LEÓN'S FOUNTAIN OF YOUTH NATIONAL
  ARCHEOLOGICAL PARK .... ST. AUGUSTINE, FL   194
QUIET WATERS COUNTY PARK............. DEERFIELD BEACH, FL   78
RAVINE STATE GARDENS ....PALATKA, FL   181
ROCK SPRINGS AND KELLY PARK......................APOPKA, FL   160
ST. ANDREWS SRA .... PANAMA CITY BEACH, FL   183
SAN FELASCO HAMMOCK PRESERVE SP............. GAINESVILLE, FL   84
SAWGRASS RECREATION PARK........... FORT LAUDERDALE, FL   74
SEAWALK PAVILION ...............................JACKSONVILLE, FL   95
SOUTH POINTE PARK ....MIAMI- MIAMI BEACH, FL   118
STEPHEN FOSTER FOLK CULTURE CENTER SP... WHITE SPRINGS, FL   235
STRAUB PARK ....TAMPA, FL   224
TOSOHATCHEE STATE PRESERVE .... CHRISTMAS, FL   160
TURKEY LAKE PARK ....ORLANDO, FL   154
VINOY PARK ....TAMPA, FL   224
WASHINGTON OAKS GARDENS SP .... PALM COAST, FL   182
WILLIAMS PARK ....TAMPA, FL   224
YOUNG CIRCLE PARK .... HOLLYWOOD, FL   78

PARKS, NATIONAL

BIG CYPRESS NATIONAL PRESERVE........................... FL   46
BISCAYNE NP .... FL   124

CANAVERAL NATIONAL SEASHORE .... FL   50
DRY TORTUGAS NP .... FL   64
EVERGLADES NP .... FL   57
GULF ISLANDS NS .... FL   86

PIERS

COCOA BEACH PIER ....COCOA BEACH, FL   52
NAPLES PIER ....NAPLES, FL   127
THE PIER .... ST. PETERSBURG, FL   216
THE SKYWAY FISHING PIER...............................TAMPA, FL   221

PLANETARIUMS

ASTRONAUT MEMORIAL PLANETARIUM &
  OBSERVATORY ....COCOA, FL   52
BUEHLER PLANETARIUM & OBSERVATORY .... DAVIE, FL   77
CALUSA NATURE CENTER AND PLANETARIUM ... FORT MYERS, FL   80
MOSI (MUSEUM OF SCIENCE & INDUSTRY).............TAMPA, FL   218
MUSEUM OF ARTS AND SCIENCES...........DAYTONA BEACH, FL   54
MUSEUM OF SCIENCE AND HISTORY ...........JACKSONVILLE, FL   93
MUSEUM OF SCIENCE AND SPACE TRANSIT
  PLANETARIUM........................MIAMI- MIAMI BEACH, FL   115
ORLANDO SCIENCE CENTER ....ORLANDO, FL   146
PONCE DE LEÓN'S FOUNTAIN OF YOUTH NATIONAL
  ARCHEOLOGICAL PARK .... ST. AUGUSTINE, FL   194
SOUTH FLORIDA SCIENCE MUSEUM   WEST PALM BEACH, FL   234
SPACE TRANSIT PLANETARIUM.........MIAMI- MIAMI BEACH, FL   116

RACETRACKS-AUTO

DAYTONA INTERNATIONAL SPEEDWAY .....DAYTONA BEACH, FL   53
GAINESVILLE RACEWAY .... GAINESVILLE, FL   84
HIALEAH SPEEDWAY ....MIAMI- MIAMI BEACH, FL   117
HOMESTEAD-MIAMI SPEEDWAY ....MIAMI- MIAMI BEACH, FL   117
RICHARD PETTY DRIVING EXPERIENCE ..... LAKE BUENA VISTA, FL   163
SEBRING INTERNATIONAL RACEWAY ....SEBRING, FL   200

RACETRACKS-DOGS

DAYTONA BEACH KENNEL CLUB ....DAYTONA BEACH, FL   53
DERBY LANE ....TAMPA, FL   221
FLAGLER GREYHOUND TRACK ,.........MIAMI- MIAMI BEACH, FL   118
HOLLYWOOD GREYHOUND DOG TRACK HALLANDALE BEACH, FL   78
JACKSONVILLE KENNEL CLUB ....................JACKSONVILLE, FL   94
THE NAPLES-FORT MYERS GREYHOUND
  TRACK ....BONITA SPRINGS, FL   48
ORANGE PARK KENNEL CLUB ...................JACKSONVILLE, FL   94
PALM BEACH KENNEL CLUB ....WEST PALM BEACH, FL   233
PENSACOLA GREYHOUND TRACK ....PENSACOLA, FL   184
SANFORD-ORLANDO KENNEL CLUB ....ORLANDO, FL   154
SARASOTA KENNEL CLUB .... SARASOTA, FL   197
TAMPA GREYHOUND TRACK...............................TAMPA, FL   221

RACETRACKS-HORSE

CALDER RACE COURSE ....MIAMI- MIAMI BEACH, FL   118
GULFSTREAM PARK .... HALLANDALE BEACH, FL   78
POMPANO PARK RACING .... POMPANO BEACH, FL   78
TAMPA BAY DOWNS ....TAMPA, FL   221

RADIO & TV STATIONS

DISNEY-MGM STUDIOS .... LAKE BUENA VISTA, FL   164
UNIVERSAL STUDIOS...................................ORLANDO, FL   152

RAILROADS

ORLANDO & MOUNT DORA RAILWAY .... MOUNT DORA, FL   179
SEMINOLE GULF RAILWAY ....FORT MYERS, FL   82

RAILROADS-LOCOMOTIVES & CARS

THE DEPOT—LAKE WALES MUSEUM AND CULTURAL
  CENTER .... LAKE WALES, FL   101
FLAGLER MUSEUM.................................. PALM BEACH, FL   182
JUNIOR MUSEUM OF BAY COUNTY .... PANAMA CITY, FL   182
NAPLES DEPOT CIVIC AND CULTURAL CENTER..........NAPLES, FL   129
PIONEER FLORIDA MUSEUM AND VILLAGE .... DADE CITY, FL   228

RAILROADS & SKI LIFTS, CABLE; COG; INCLINE; NARROW GAUGE

GATORLAND...ORLANDO, FL   142

RANCHES

COLONEL HERRMAN'S RANCH .... BRADENTON, FL   48

J.B. STARKEY'S FLATWOODS ADVENTURES .... ODESSA, FL 229

RECREATION-SUMMER ACTIVITIES
ADVENTURES UNLIMITED .... MILTON, FL 127
APALACHICOLA NF .... FL 46
APOLLO BEACH .... CANAVERAL NATIONAL SEASHORE, FL 50
ARTHUR R. MARSHALL LOXAHATCHEE NWR .. DELRAY BEACH, FL 55
CADY WAY TRAIL...................................ORLANDO, FL 155
CANOE ESCAPE ....TAMPA, FL 222
COCOA BEACH PIER ....COCOA BEACH, FL 52
COUNTRY DAY STABLE .... HILLIARD, FL 96
DISNEY'S BLIZZARD BEACH WATER PARK .. LAKE BUENA VISTA, FL 166
DISNEY'S TYPHOON LAGOON WATER
  PARK...............................LAKE BUENA VISTA, FL 166
DRY TORTUGAS NP FERRY........................... KEY WEST, FL 67
FLORIDA KEYS NATIONAL MARINE
  SANCTUARY .... BIG PINE KEY, FL 64
FORT MYERS BEACH .... FL 82
GRAND CYPRESS RACQUET CLUB ....ORLANDO, FL 155
GULF ISLANDS NS .... FL 86
MATHESON HAMMOCK PARK................. CORAL GABLES, FL 125
O'LENO SP ....HIGH SPRINGS, FL 87
THE PIER .... ST. PETERSBURG, FL 216
PLAYALINDA BEACH....... CANAVERAL NATIONAL SEASHORE, FL 50
POINCIANA GOLF & RACQUET RESORT...............ORLANDO, FL 155
QUIET WATERS COUNTY PARK............. DEERFIELD BEACH, FL 78
RAY'S CANOE HIDEAWAY .... BRADENTON, FL 49
ST. PETERSBURG CHESS CLUB.........................TAMPA, FL 223
ST. PETERSBURG SHUFFLEBOARD CLUB ....TAMPA, FL 223
ST. PETERSBURG TENNIS CENTER ....TAMPA, FL 222
SANIBEL ISLAND .... SANIBEL, FL 196
SANTA FE CANOE OUTPOST ....HIGH SPRINGS, FL 87
SINGER ISLAND .... FL 201
TAMPA BAY SPORTING CLAYS ....TAMPA, FL 223
TREASURE ISLAND GOLF, TENNIS AND RECREATION
  CENTER ....TAMPA, FL 222
WATER MANIA ....KISSIMMEE, FL 162
WEST ORANGE TRAIL ....ORLANDO, FL 155
WET 'N WILD ....ORLANDO, FL 153

RECREATION-WINTER ACTIVITIES
ST. PETERSBURG CHESS CLUB...........................TAMPA, FL 223
TAMPA BAY SPORTING CLAYS ....TAMPA, FL 223

RELIGIOUS COLONIES
KORESHAN SHS ....ESTERO, FL 56

RESEARCH ORGANIZATIONS
HARBOR BRANCH OCEANOGRAPHIC
  INSTITUTION....................................... FORT PIERCE, FL 83

RESTORED VILLAGES & SETTLEMENTS
⌘ COLONIAL SPANISH QUARTER.................. ST. AUGUSTINE, FL 190
HISTORIC PENSACOLA VILLAGE ....PENSACOLA, FL 184
KISSIMMEE COW CAMP ....LAKE WALES, FL 102
MEDIEVAL LIFE ....KISSIMMEE, FL 162
OLD ST. AUGUSTINE VILLAGE .... ST. AUGUSTINE, FL 191

RIVERS
WEKIVA RIVER...ORLANDO, FL 155

RUINS
MUSEUMS AND NATURE CENTER OF CRANE POINT
  HAMMOCK ....MARATHON, FL 69
SUGAR MILL RUINS .... NEW SMYRNA BEACH, FL 130

SCENIC DRIVES
BAYSHORE BOULEVARD..............................TAMPA, FL 220
FLORIDA'S TURNPIKE ....KISSIMMEE, FL 161
FORT LAUDERDALE BEACH BOULEVARD... FORT LAUDERDALE, FL 70
INDIAN RIVER DRIVE .... FORT PIERCE, FL 82
MAIN AND INGRAHAM HIGHWAYS.....MIAMI- MIAMI BEACH, FL 117
OLD CUTLER ROAD ....MIAMI- MIAMI BEACH, FL 117
OVERSEAS HIGHWAY (US 1)..........................KEY WEST, FL 66
SOUTH MIAMI AVENUE..............MIAMI- MIAMI BEACH, FL 117
SR A1A...DAYTONA BEACH, FL 53
SR A1A............................... FERNANDINA BEACH, FL 95
SR A1A..................................... PALM BEACH, FL 181
TAMIAMI TRAIL (US 41).....BIG CYPRESS NATIONAL PRESERVE, FL 47

US 1 .... KEY LARGO, FL 65
US 27... OCALA, FL 130
US 98... PANAMA CITY, FL 182
US 301... OCALA, FL 130

SCHOOLS
HILLSBOROUGH COMMUNITY COLLEGE ....TAMPA, FL 222

SCHOOLS-COLLEGES & UNIVERSITIES
FLORIDA A&M UNIVERSITY.......................TALLAHASSEE, FL 202
FLORIDA SOUTHERN COLLEGE .... LAKELAND, FL 100
FLORIDA STATE UNIVERSITY.....................TALLAHASSEE, FL 202
PALM BEACH COMMUNITY COLLEGE .... LAKE WORTH, FL 102
ROLLINS COLLEGE ....WINTER PARK, FL 179
SANTA FE COMMUNITY COLLEGE ....GAINESVILLE, FL 84
STETSON UNIVERSITY.................................DELAND, FL 55
UNIVERSITY OF FLORIDA .... GAINESVILLE, FL 84
UNIVERSITY OF MIAMI .... CORAL GABLES, FL 124
UNIVERSITY OF SOUTH FLORIDA ....TAMPA, FL 219
UNIVERSITY OF TAMPA........................TAMPA, FL 219

SCHOOLS-INSTITUTES
HARBOR BRANCH OCEANOGRAPHIC
  INSTITUTION....................................... FORT PIERCE, FL 83

SELF-GUIDING TOURS
BLACK POINT WILDLIFE DRIVE......................TITUSVILLE, FL 232
BROOKSVILLE .... FL 49
CORKSCREW SWAMP SANCTUARY.....................NAPLES, FL 128
FLORIDA SOUTHERN COLLEGE .... LAKELAND, FL 100
KEY WEST .... FL 66
LAKELAND .... FL 100
PELICAN PATH ....KEY WEST, FL 66
PENSACOLA .... FL 184
QUINCY .... FL 187
STUART .... FL 201

SHIPS & BOATS
AMERICAN VICTORY MARINERS MEMORIAL & SHIP
  MUSEUM ....TAMPA, FL 217
CANOE ESCAPE .........................THONOTOSASSA, FL 231
X-PRESS TO KEY WEST ....FORT MYERS BEACH, FL 82

SHOPS, FIRMS & STORES
8TH AVENUE SHOPPING DISTRICT.............. ST. PETE BEACH, FL 230
ALHAMBRA ANTIQUES CENTER ....MIAMI- MIAMI BEACH, FL 120
ALTAMONTE MALL.............................ORLANDO, FL 156
ANGELL & PHELPS CHOCOLATE FACTORY
  TOUR ....DAYTONA BEACH, FL 53
ANTIQUE & DECORATIVE ARTS........................TAMPA, FL 223
AVENTURA MALL....................MIAMI- MIAMI BEACH, FL 120
AVENUES SHOPPING MALL .....................JACKSONVILLE, FL 94
BAL HARBOUR SHOPS ....MIAMI- MIAMI BEACH, FL 120
BASS PRO SHOPS OUTDOOR WORLD ...... DANIA BEACH, FL 77
BASS PRO SHOPS OUTDOOR WORLD............ISLAMORADA, FL 65
BASS PRO SHOPS OUTDOOR WORLD..............ORLANDO, FL 156
BAYSIDE MARKETPLACE.................MIAMI- MIAMI BEACH, FL 120
BAYWALK ....TAMPA, FL 223
BEACH DRIVE ....TAMPA, FL 223
BELL TOWER SHOPS .... FORT MYERS, FL 79
BELZ DESIGNER OUTLET CENTRE ....ORLANDO, FL 156
BELZ FACTORY OUTLET WORLD ....ORLANDO, FL 156
BELZ FACTORY OUTLET WORLD.......... ST. AUGUSTINE, FL 188
BOCA CENTER .... BOCA RATON, FL 47
BRANDON TOWNCENTER ....TAMPA, FL 223
BROWARD MALL ....FORT LAUDERDALE, FL 76
CENTRO YBOR ....TAMPA, FL 224
CHANNELSIDE ....TAMPA, FL 224
CITRUS PARK TOWN CENTER ....TAMPA, FL 223
CITYPLACE ....WEST PALM BEACH, FL 233
CITYWALK ....ORLANDO, FL 149
CLEARWATER MALL ....TAMPA, FL 223
CLEMATIS STREET ....WEST PALM BEACH, FL 233
COASTLAND CENTER ....NAPLES, FL 127
COCOWALK ....MIAMI- MIAMI BEACH, FL 121
COLLINS AVENUE ....MIAMI- MIAMI BEACH, FL 120
CORAL SQUARE MALL ....FORT LAUDERDALE, FL 76
CORDOVA MALL ....PENSACOLA, FL 184
COREY AVENUE.....................ST. PETE BEACH, FL 230
COUNTRYSIDE MALL ....CLEARWATER, FL 227

COUNTRYSIDE MALL ....TAMPA, FL 223
CROSSROADS MALL .... CLEARWATER, FL 227
CROSSROADS MALL ....TAMPA, FL 223
CROSSWINDS SHOPPING CENTER...................TAMPA, FL 223
CUTLER RIDGE MALL .... MIAMI- MIAMI BEACH, FL 120
DADELAND MALL .... MIAMI- MIAMI BEACH, FL 120
DAYTONA FLEA MARKET....................DAYTONA BEACH, FL 53
DE SOTO SQUARE MALL........................ BRADENTON, FL 48
DISNEY'S TOWN OF CELEBRATION .... ORLANDO, FL 157
DOWNTOWN DISNEY AREA .... LAKE BUENA VISTA, FL 167
DOWNTOWN DISNEY MARKETPLACE .... ORLANDO, FL 157
EAGLE RIDGE MALL................... LAKE WALES, FL 101
EDISON MALL .... FORT MYERS, FL 79
EL PRADO BOULEVARD...................TAMPA, FL 223
EUCLID AVENUE ....TAMPA, FL 223
THE FALLS................... MIAMI- MIAMI BEACH, FL 120
FASHION MALL AT PLANTATION .... FORT LAUDERDALE, FL 76
FESTIVAL FLEA MARKET MALL .... POMPANO BEACH, FL 78
FISHERMAN'S VILLAGE .... PUNTA GORDA, FL 187
FLEA WORLD.........................ORLANDO, FL 157
FLORIDA MALL ....ORLANDO, FL 156
FRANKLIN STREET MALL....................TAMPA, FL 223
GALLERIA .... FORT LAUDERDALE, FL 76
GAS PLANT ANTIQUE ARCADE ....TAMPA, FL 223
GOVERNORS SQUARE MALL.............TALLAHASSEE, FL 202
HIDDEN GARDEN ....ORLANDO, FL 156
INTERNATIONAL DRIVE......................ORLANDO, FL 156
INTERNATIONAL PLAZA ....TAMPA, FL 223
IVANHOE ROW ....ORLANDO, FL 156
JACKSONVILLE LANDING .... JACKSONVILLE, FL 94
JOHN'S PASS VILLAGE & BOARDWALK...................TAMPA, FL 224
JOHN'S PASS VILLAGE AND BOARDWALK.... MADEIRA BEACH, FL 229
KISSIMMEE MANUFACTURER'S OUTLET............ORLANDO, FL 156
LAKE WALES HISTORIC DISTRICT .... LAKE WALES, FL 101
LAKELAND SQUARE .... LAKELAND, FL 100
LARGO MALL ....LARGO, FL 229
LAS OLAS BOULEVARD .... FORT LAUDERDALE, FL 76
LINCOLN ROAD .... MIAMI- MIAMI BEACH, FL 121
MAIN STREET ....TALLAHASSEE, FL 202
THE MALL AT WELLINGTON GREEN .... WEST PALM BEACH, FL 233
MELBOURNE SQUARE MALL................. MELBOURNE, FL 103
MIAMI INTERNATIONAL MALL .... MIAMI- MIAMI BEACH, FL 120
MIRACLE MILE .... MIAMI- MIAMI BEACH, FL 121
MIROMAR OUTLETS .... FORT MYERS, FL 79
MIZNER PARK.........................BOCA RATON, FL 47
NORTH ORANGE AVENUE ANTIQUES DISTRICT ......ORLANDO, FL 155
OAKS MALL .... GAINESVILLE, FL 84
OAKWOOD PLAZA.............. FORT LAUDERDALE, FL 76
OLD HYDE PARK VILLAGE ....TAMPA, FL 224
OLD MARINE MARKETPLACE AT TIN CITY............NAPLES, FL 127
OLD TOWN .... KISSIMMEE, FL 161
OLD TOWN ....ORLANDO, FL 157
OLDE TYME SHOPPE.................. MIAMI- MIAMI BEACH, FL 120
ORANGE PARK MALL................... JACKSONVILLE, FL 94
ORLANDO FASHION SQUARE MALL .... ORLANDO, FL 156
ORLANDO PREMIUM OUTLETS ....ORLANDO, FL 156
OVIEDO MARKETPLACE ....ORLANDO, FL 156
PADDOCK MALL .... OCALA, FL 130
PALAFOX PLACE .... PENSACOLA, FL 184
PALM BEACH MALL...............WEST PALM BEACH, FL 233
PARK AVENUE ....ORLANDO, FL 156
PARK AVENUE ....WINTER PARK, FL 179
PARKSIDE MALL ....TAMPA, FL 223
PEMBROKE LAKES MALL .... FORT LAUDERDALE, FL 76
THE PIER .... ST. PETERSBURG, FL 216
THE PIER ....TAMPA, FL 224
PLANET HOLLYWOOD ....ORLANDO, FL 157
POINTE*ORLANDO ....ORLANDO, FL 157
POMPANO SQUARE MALL.................. POMPANO BEACH, FL 78
PRIME OUTLETS AT FLORIDA CITY............FLORIDA CITY, FL 125
PRIME OUTLETS AT NAPLES .... MARCO ISLAND, FL 102
PRIME OUTLETS ELLENTON ....ELLENTON, FL 56
REGENCY SQUARE .... JACKSONVILLE, FL 94
RENNINGER'S ANTIQUE CENTER................. MOUNT DORA, FL 179
ROGERS' CHRISTMAS HOUSE VILLAGE .... BROOKSVILLE, FL 50
ROYAL PALM SHOPPING PLAZA .... BOCA RATON, FL 47
ROYAL PALM SQUARE .... FORT MYERS, FL 79
ST. ARMANDS CIRCLE .... SARASOTA, FL 197
ST. AUGUSTINE OUTLET CENTER .... ST. AUGUSTINE, FL 188
SARASOTA SQUARE MALL .... SARASOTA, FL 197
SAWGRASS MILLS...............FORT LAUDERDALE, FL 76
SEMINOLE MALL ....TAMPA, FL 223
SEMINOLE TOWNE CENTER....................ORLANDO, FL 156

SEVILLE SQUARE .... PENSACOLA, FL 184
SILAS BAYSIDE MARKET ....TAMPA, FL 224
SILAS BAYSIDE SHOPPING CENTER .... ST. PETE BEACH, FL 230
SOUTH GATE MALL .... SARASOTA, FL 197
STREETS OF MAYFAIR .... MIAMI- MIAMI BEACH, FL 120
SWAP SHOP.................... FORT LAUDERDALE, FL 76
TALLAHASSEE MALL....................TALLAHASSEE, FL 202
TANGER SANIBEL FACTORY STORES............... FORT MYERS, FL 79
THIRD STREET SOUTH SHOPPING AREA ....NAPLES, FL 127
TOWN CENTER MALL .... BOCA RATON, FL 47
TYRONE SQUARE MALL ....TAMPA, FL 223
UNIVERSITY MALL .... PENSACOLA, FL 184
UNIVERSITY MALL ....TAMPA, FL 223
THE VILLAGE ON VENETIAN BAY ....NAPLES, FL 127
VOLUSIA MALL ....DAYTONA BEACH, FL 53
WAGON WHEEL FLEA MARKET ....TAMPA, FL 224
WATERSIDE SHOPS ....NAPLES, FL 127
WEST OAKS MALL ....ORLANDO, FL 156
WEST SHORE PLAZA ....TAMPA, FL 223
WESTLAND MALL................ MIAMI- MIAMI BEACH, FL 120
WORTH AVENUE .... PALM BEACH, FL 181

SIGHTSEEING-AIRCRAFT RIDES & TOURS

THE BIG RED BALLOON ....TAMPA, FL 219
BLUE WATER BALLOONS ....UKLANDO, FL 153
CRYSTAL MAGIC BALLOON COMPANY...................TAMPA, FL 220
NORTH AMERICAN TOP-GUN..... ST. AUGUSTINE, FL 194
ORANGE BLOSSOM BALLOONS.......................ORLANDO, FL 153

SIGHTSEEING TOURS

☞ CONCH TOUR TRAINS.....................................KEY WEST, FL 67
DUCK TOURS OF TAMPA BAY ....TAMPA, FL 220
FIRST CLASS COACH MARTZ GROUP....................TAMPA, FL 220
GATOR TOURS ....ORLANDO, FL 153
GHOST TOURS OF ST. AUGUSTINE....... ST. AUGUSTINE, FL 188
GRAY LINE .... ST. AUGUSTINE, FL 188
J.B. STARKEY'S FLATWOODS ADVENTURES .... ODESSA, FL 229
KELLY SEAHORSE RANCH....................AMELIA ISLAND, FL 95
MARCO ISLAND TROLLEY TOURS............... MARCO ISLAND, FL 102
NAPLES TROLLEY TOURS ....NAPLES, FL 129
OLD FORT LAUDERDALE MUSEUM OF
HISTORY .... FORT LAUDERDALE, FL 74
OLD TOWN TROLLEY ....KEY WEST, FL 68
OLD TOWN TROLLEY TOURS OF
ST. AUGUSTINE .... ST. AUGUSTINE, FL 194
ORLANDO & MOUNT DORA RAILWAY .... MOUNT DORA, FL 179
ROSEWOOD............................ GAINESVILLE, FL 84
ST. AUGUSTINE .... ST. AUGUSTINE, FL 188
SEAPLANES OF KEY WEST INC. .... DRY TORTUGAS NP, FL 64
SEMINOLE GULF RAILWAY .... FORT MYERS, FL 82
THE SHARK VALLEY TRAM TOUR.............. EVERGLADES NP, FL 59
SIGHTSEEING TRAINS .... ST. AUGUSTINE, FL 192
STEPHEN FOSTER FOLK CULTURE CENTER SP ... WHITE SPRINGS, FL 235
VANTASTIC TOURS.............................MARCO ISLAND, FL 103

SIGHTSEEING TOURS-BOATS

AQUATIC WONDERS BOAT TOURS .... KISSIMMEE, FL 161
BABCOCK WILDERNESS ADVENTURES.......... PUNTA GORDA, FL 187
BACKCOUNTRY CRUISES...................... EVERGLADES NP, FL 58
BILLIE SWAMP
SAFARI........ BIG CYPRESS SEMINOLE INDIAN RESERVATION, FL 47
BISCAYNE NATIONAL UNDERWATER PARK INC.. BISCAYNE NP, FL 124
BOGGY CREEK AIRBOAT RIDES.................. KISSIMMEE, FL 161
CAPTAIN ANDERSON CRUISES........... PANAMA CITY BEACH, FL 183
CAPTAIN DAVE'S DORA CANAL CRUISES .... TAVARES, FL 179
CAPTAIN MEMO'S PIRATE CRUISE ....CLEARWATER, FL 227
CAPTIVA CRUISES .... SANIBEL, FL 196
COLLIER-SEMINOLE SP BOAT TOURS ....NAPLES, FL 128
DISCOVERY CRUISE LINE.................... FORT LAUDERDALE, FL 75
DISCOVERY UNDERSEA TOURS ....KEY WEST, FL 67
DOLPHIN LANDINGS CHARTER BOAT
CENTER .... ST. PETE BEACH, FL 230
DOUBLE SUNSHINE ....NAPLES, FL 128
DRY TORTUGAS NP FERRY....................KEY WEST, FL 67
DUCK TOURS OF TAMPA BAY ....TAMPA, FL 220
EDEN OF THE EVERGLADES.................. EVERGLADES CITY, FL 56
☞ EDWARD BALL WAKULLA SPRINGS SP .... WAKULLA, FL 232
ENTERPRISE SAILING CHARTERS .... SARASOTA, FL 197
EVERGLADES EXCURSIONS ....NAPLES, FL 129
☞ EVERGLADES NP .... FL 57
EVERGLADES NP BOAT TOURS .... EVERGLADES CITY, FL 56
FLORIDA BAY CRUISE.......................... EVERGLADES NP, FL 58

FLORIDA COASTAL CRUISES'
MANATEE.. NEW SMYRNA BEACH, FL 130
FLORIDA'S SILVER SPRINGS .... OCALA, FL 131
HUBBARD'S SEA ADVENTURES .... MADEIRA BEACH, FL 229
J.C. SIGHTSEEING BOAT CRUISES .... FORT MYERS, FL 80
JOHN PENNEKAMP CORAL REEF SP .... KEY LARGO, FL 65
JUNGLE QUEEN RIVERBOAT CRUISE .... FORT LAUDERDALE, FL 75
KING FISHER CRUISE LINES...................... PUNTA GORDA, FL 187
THE LIBERTY FLEET OF TALL SHIPS .... KEY WEST, FL 68
LOOE KEY DIVE CENTER .... BIG PINE KEY, FL 64
LOXAHATCHEE QUEEN .... JUPITER, FL 97
MANATEE SEEKER SCENIC RIVER TOUR .... DELAND, FL 55
MYAKKA WILDLIFE TOURS .... SARASOTA, FL 199
RIVERBOAT TOURS AT THE NAV-A-GATOR .... ARCADIA, FL 46
RIVERFRONT CRUISES....................... FORT LAUDERDALE, FL 75
RIVERSHIP ROMANCE.. SANFORD, FL 179
ST. AUGUSTINE SCENIC CRUISE .... ST. AUGUSTINE, FL 188
ST. JOHNS RIVER CRUISES........................ ORANGE CITY, FL 132
ST. NICHOLAS BOAT LINE...................... TARPON SPRINGS, FL 231
SAWGRASS RECREATION PARK............. FORT LAUDERDALE, FL 74
SCENIC BOAT TOURS.................................. WINTER PARK, FL 180
SHOW QUEEN .... CLEARWATER, FL 228
STARLITE MAJESTY .... CLEARWATER, FL 228
STARLITE PRINCESS RIVERBOAT .... TAMPA, FL 220
STARS & STRIPES—KEY WEST............................ KEY WEST, FL 68
A TINY CRUISE LINE........................... DAYTONA BEACH, FL 54
TROPIC STAR OF PINE ISLAND .... BOKEELIA, FL 48
WATER TAXI .... FORT LAUDERDALE, FL 75
WEEKI WACHEE SPRINGS WATERPARK .... WEEKI WACHEE, FL 233
WILD BILL'S AIRBOAT TOURS & WILDLIFE PARK .... INVERNESS, FL 87
X-PRESS TO KEY WEST...................... FORT MYERS BEACH, FL 82

SIGHTSEEING TOURS-RAFTING & CANOEING
ADVENTURES UNLIMITED .... MILTON, FL 127

SPORTS ARENAS
ALLTEL STADIUM .... JACKSONVILLE, FL 94
AMERICAN AIRLINES ARENA .... MIAMI- MIAMI BEACH, FL 118
BROWARD COUNTY BRIAN PICCOLO
VELODROME .... FORT LAUDERDALE, FL 75
CAPITAL ONE BOWL .... ORLANDO, FL 158
CHAIN OF LAKES STADIUM..................... WINTER HAVEN, FL 235
CITRUS BOWL .... ORLANDO, FL 154
CITY OF PALMS PARK .... FORT MYERS, FL 79
DISNEY'S WIDE WORLD OF SPORTS .... LAKE BUENA VISTA, FL 167
DISNEY'S WIDE WORLD OF SPORTS .... ORLANDO, FL 153
DUNEDIN STADIUM.. DUNEDIN, FL 228
DUNEDIN STADIUM.. TAMPA, FL 221
ED SMITH SPORTS COMPLEX .... SARASOTA, FL 197
EVERBLADES ARENA...................................... FORT MYERS, FL 79
FLORIDA POWER PARK .... TAMPA, FL 220
FORT PIERCE JAI-ALAI .... FORT PIERCE, FL 82
HOLMAN STADIUM....................................... VERO BEACH, FL 232
HOMESTEAD-MIAMI MOTORSPORTS COMPLEX .. HOMESTEAD, FL 126
JACK RUSSELL MEMORIAL STADIUM............. CLEARWATER, FL 227
JACK RUSSELL MEMORIAL STADIUM.................... TAMPA, FL 221
JACKSONVILLE VETERANS MEMORIAL
COLISEUM .... JACKSONVILLE, FL 94
JOKER MARCHANT STADIUM .... LAKELAND, FL 100
LEE COUNTY SPORTS COMPLEX .... FORT MYERS, FL 79
LEGENDS FIELD .... TAMPA, FL 220
MARK LIGHT STADIUM .... MIAMI- MIAMI BEACH, FL 117
MCKECHNIE FIELD .... BRADENTON, FL 48
MIAMI JAI-ALAI FRONTON .... MIAMI- MIAMI BEACH, FL 118
NATIONAL CAR RENTAL CENTER .... FORT LAUDERDALE, FL 75
OSCEOLA COUNTY STADIUM.......................... ORLANDO, FL 153
OSCEOLA COUNTY STADIUM AND SPORTS
COMPLEX .... KISSIMMEE, FL 161
PRO PLAYER STADIUM .... MIAMI- MIAMI BEACH, FL 117
RAYMOND JAMES STADIUM .... TAMPA, FL 221
RAYMOND JAMES STADIUM .... TAMPA, FL 225
ST. PETE TIMES FORUM .... TAMPA, FL 221
T.D. WATERHOUSE CENTRE .... ORLANDO, FL 153
THOMAS J. WHITE STADIUM .... FORT PIERCE, FL 82
TROPICANA FIELD .... TAMPA, FL 220
UNIVERSITY OF CENTRAL FLORIDA ARENA .... ORLANDO, FL 154
WOLFSON PARK .... JACKSONVILLE, FL 94

SPRINGS
BLUE SPRING SP.. ORANGE CITY, FL 132
BLUE SPRINGS... HIGH SPRINGS, FL 87
EDWARD BALL WAKULLA SPRINGS SP .... WAKULLA, FL 232

FLORIDA'S SILVER SPRINGS .... OCALA, FL 131
GINNIE SPRINGS.. HIGH SPRINGS, FL 87
HOMOSASSA SPRINGS WILDLIFE SP ..... HOMOSASSA SPRINGS, FL 87
ICHETUCKNEE SPRINGS .... HIGH SPRINGS, FL 87
POE SPRINGS.. HIGH SPRINGS, FL 87
PONCE DE LEÓN'S FOUNTAIN OF YOUTH NATIONAL
ARCHEOLOGICAL PARK .... ST. AUGUSTINE, FL 194
ROCK SPRINGS AND KELLY PARK...................... APOPKA, FL 160
THE SPRINGS......................... WARM MINERAL SPRINGS, FL 232
WEEKI WACHEE SPRINGS WATERPARK .... WEEKI WACHEE, FL 233
WHITE SPRINGS................................... WHITE SPRINGS, FL 235

STATUES
ANDREW JACKSON .... PENSACOLA, FL 186
CHRIST OF THE DEEP .... KEY LARGO, FL 65

STREETS, PLAZAS, SQUARES, CITY AREAS
ART DECO DISTRICT .... MIAMI- MIAMI BEACH, FL 117
COCONUT GROVE .... MIAMI- MIAMI BEACH, FL 117
DAVIS ISLAND.. TAMPA, FL 220
EDGEWATER DRIVE... ORLANDO, FL 156
FAIRBANKS AVENUE.. ORLANDO, FL 156
INTERNATIONAL DRIVE.................................... ORLANDO, FL 156
LINCOLN ROAD .... MIAMI- MIAMI BEACH, FL 121
LITTLE HAVANA .... MIAMI- MIAMI BEACH, FL 117
PARK AVENUE .... ORLANDO, FL 156
PLAZA DE LA CONSTITUCIÓN................... ST. AUGUSTINE, FL 191
PLAZA FERDINAND VII................................... PENSACOLA, FL 186
RIVERWALK .... FORT LAUDERDALE, FL 74
SEVILLE SQUARE .... PENSACOLA, FL 184

SWAMPS
BABCOCK WILDERNESS ADVENTURES.......... PUNTA GORDA, FL 187
BIG CYPRESS NATIONAL PRESERVE................................. FL 46
CORKSCREW SWAMP SANCTUARY..................... NAPLES, FL 128
HIGHLANDS HAMMOCK SP............................... SEBRING, FL 201
PAYNES PRAIRIE PRESERVE SP......................... MICANOPY, FL 127
SAN FELASCO HAMMOCK PRESERVE SP........... GAINESVILLE, FL 84

THEATERS-BUILDINGS
AMERICAN STAGE THEATER................................ TAMPA, FL 224
BEACH THEATER.. HOLLYWOOD, FL 78
COCONUT GROVE PLAYHOUSE.......... MIAMI- MIAMI BEACH, FL 121
COLONY THEATER........................ MIAMI- MIAMI BEACH, FL 121
FLORIDA THEATER....................................... JACKSONVILLE, FL 94
THE F.S.U. CENTER FOR THE PERFORMING ARTS .... SARASOTA, FL 197
GOLDEN APPLE DINNER THEATRE.................... SARASOTA, FL 197
HIPPODROME STATE THEATRE .... GAINESVILLE, FL 84
INDIAN RIVER COMMUNITY COLLEGE MCALPHIN FINE ARTS
CENTER .... FORT PIERCE, FL 82
JACKIE GLEASON THEATER OF THE PERFORMING
ARTS........................... MIAMI- MIAMI BEACH, FL 121
KENNEDY SPACE CENTER... FL 97
KENNEDY SPACE CENTER VISITOR
COMPLEX.......................... KENNEDY SPACE CENTER, FL 97
KRAVIS CENTER FOR THE PERFORMING
ARTS.. WEST PALM BEACH, FL 233
LAKE WORTH PLAYHOUSE .... LAKE WORTH, FL 102
PARKER PLAYHOUSE .... FORT LAUDERDALE, FL 76
ST. PETERSBURG LITTLE THEATER .... TAMPA, FL 224
SEMINOLE COMMUNITY COLLEGE'S FINE ARTS
THEATRE.. ORLANDO, FL 158
SLEUTHS MYSTERY DINNER SHOWS.................. ORLANDO, FL 149
TALLAHASSEE LITTLE THEATRE.................. TALLAHASSEE, FL 202
TAMPA THEATRE .... TAMPA, FL 224
THEATRE WINTER HAVEN .... WINTER HAVEN, FL 235
TIMES-UNION CENTER FOR THE PERFORMING
ARTS .... JACKSONVILLE, FL 94
WATSON B. DUNCAN III THEATER................ LAKE WORTH, FL 102

THEATERS-PLAYS, DRAMAS & MUSICALS
3D WORLD .... ST. AUGUSTINE, FL 194
ARABIAN NIGHTS................................... KISSIMMEE, FL 161
BEACH THEATER... TAMPA, FL 224
CAPONE'S DINNER AND SHOW .... KISSIMMEE, FL 161
CAROL MORSANI HALL .... TAMPA, FL 224
FERGUSON HALL .... TAMPA, FL 224
HOLLYWOOD PLAYHOUSE .... HOLLYWOOD, FL 78
HOLY LAND EXPERIENCE .... ORLANDO, FL 142
JAEB THEATER .... TAMPA, FL 224
MAHAFFEY THEATER .... TAMPA, FL 224

MEDIEVAL TIMES DINNER AND TOURNAMENT ..... KISSIMMEE, FL 162
THE OCEAN OPRY MUSIC SHOW .... PANAMA CITY BEACH, FL 184
ORLANDO-UCF SHAKESPEARE FESTIVAL .... ORLANDO, FL 158
PIRATE'S DINNER ADVENTURE .... ORLANDO, FL 147
RUTH ECKERD HALL .... TAMPA, FL 224
SHAKESPEARE IN THE PARK .... TAMPA, FL 225
SHIMBERG PLAYHOUSE................................. TAMPA, FL 224
SKULL KINGDOM .... ORLANDO, FL 149

TOWERS

ARTHUR R. MARSHALL LOXAHATCHEE NWR .. DELRAY BEACH, FL 55
BAT TOWER.................................... SUGARLOAF KEY, FL 69
CITRUS TOWER CENTRE............................. CLERMONT, FL 160
⇥ HISTORIC BOK SANCTUARY .... LAKE WALES, FL 101
MARTELLO TOWERS .... KEY WEST, FL 68
PA-HAY-OKEE OVERLOOK.................... EVERGLADES NP, FL 59
PAYNES PRAIRIE PRESERVE SP .... MICANOPY, FL 127

TREES

BIG TREE PARK... SANFORD, FL 179
FRUIT AND SPICE PARK .... HOMESTEAD, FL 126
LIGNUMVITAE KEY STATE BOTANICAL SITE ...... ISLAMORADA, FL 65
PAYNES PRAIRIE PRESERVE SP .... MICANOPY, FL 127
THE SENATOR.. SANFORD, FL 179

VIEWS

CITRUS TOWER CENTRE............................. CLERMONT, FL 160
JOHN D. MACARTHUR BEACH SP .... SINGER ISLAND, FL 201
KEY WEST LIGHTHOUSE MUSEUM .... KEY WEST, FL 68
PA-HAY-OKEE OVERLOOK.................... EVERGLADES NP, FL 59
ST. AUGUSTINE LIGHTHOUSE AND MUSEUM .. ST. AUGUSTINE, FL 195

VISITOR CENTERS

ARTHUR R. MARSHALL LOXAHATCHEE NWR .. DELRAY BEACH, FL 55
BIG CYPRESS VISITOR
  CENTER .... BIG CYPRESS NATIONAL PRESERVE, FL 47
BIG PINE KEY.. FL 64
CONVOY POINT................................... BISCAYNE NP, FL 124
DAYTONA INTERNATIONAL SPEEDWAY ..... DAYTONA BEACH, FL 53
DE SOTO NME .... FL 56
ELLENTON .... FL 56
ERNEST COE VISITOR CENTER.................. EVERGLADES NP, FL 58
FLAMINGO VISITOR CENTER.................... EVERGLADES NP, FL 58
FLORIDA'S NATURAL GROVE HOUSE VISITOR
  CENTER .... LAKE WALES, FL 101
GREATER FORT LAUDERDALE CONVENTION AND VISITORS
  BUREAU .... FORT LAUDERDALE, FL 72
GREATER MIAMI CONVENTION AND
  VISITORS BUREAU .... MIAMI- MIAMI BEACH, FL 107
GULF COAST VISITOR CENTER .... EVERGLADES NP, FL 58
GULF ISLANDS NS....................................... FL 86
HOMESTEAD.. FL 125
⇥ KENNEDY SPACE CENTER VISITOR
  COMPLEX............................. KENNEDY SPACE CENTER, FL 97
NAPLES.. FL 127
OCKLAWAHA VISITOR CENTER...................... OCALA NF, FL 132
ORLANDO/ORANGE COUNTY CONVENTION & VISITORS
  BUREAU .... ORLANDO, FL 137
PENSACOLA.. FL 184
ROYAL PALM VISITOR CENTER .... EVERGLADES NP, FL 58
ST. AUGUSTINE .... FL 188
SANIBEL... FL 196
SUNCOAST WELCOME CENTER .... TAMPA BAY , FL 207

VISITOR INFORMATION

AMELIA ISLAND.. FL 95
APALACHICOLA.. FL 46
BOCA RATON .... FL 47
BONITA SPRINGS.. FL 48
BRADENTON .... FL 48
BROOKSVILLE .... FL 49
BUSHNELL... FL 50
CEDAR KEY .... FL 51
CLEARWATER.. FL 227
CLERMONT.. FL 160
COCOA.. FL 52
COCOA BEACH .... FL 52
CORAL GABLES .... FL 124
CRYSTAL RIVER .... FL 52
DADE CITY .... FL 228
DAYTONA BEACH .... FL 53

DELAND... FL 55
DELRAY BEACH .... FL 55
DUNEDIN .... FL 228
EVERGLADES CITY .... FL 56
FERNANDINA BEACH .... FL 95
FLORIDA CITY .... FL 125
FORT MYERS .... FL 79
FORT MYERS BEACH .... FL 82
FORT PIERCE .... FL 82
FORT WALTON BEACH.................................... FL 84
GAINESVILLE .... FL 84
GREATER FORT LAUDERDALE CHAMBER OF
  COMMERCE................................... FORT LAUDERDALE, FL 72
GULF BREEZE .... FL 86
HIGH SPRINGS .... FL 87
HOLLYWOOD .... FL 78
INDIAN ROCKS BEACH .... FL 228
ISLAMORADA .... FL 65
JACKSONVILLE AND THE BEACHES CONVENTION AND VISITORS
  BUREAU .... JACKSONVILLE, FL 90
JUPITER .... FL 97
KEY LARGO .... FL 65
KEY WEST .... FL 66
KISSIMMEE.. FL 160
LAKE WALES... FL 101
LAKE WORTH.. FL 102
LAKELAND .... FL 100
LARGO.. FL 228
LATIN CHAMBER OF COMMERCE........ MIAMI- MIAMI BEACH, FL 123
MADEIRA BEACH .... FL 229
MARCO ISLAND .... FL 102
MELBOURNE .... FL 103
MILTON .... FL 127
MOUNT DORA .... FL 178
NEW SMYRNA BEACH .... FL 129
OCALA .... FL 130
OKEECHOBEE .... FL 132
ORANGE CITY .... FL 132
ORMOND BEACH .... FL 181
PALATKA .... FL 181
PALM BEACH .... FL 181
PANAMA CITY .... FL 182
PANAMA CITY BEACH .... FL 183
PENSACOLA BEACH .... FL 186
PLANT CITY .... FL 229
POLK CITY .... FL 186
POMPANO BEACH .... FL 78
PUNTA GORDA .... FL 187
QUINCY .... FL 187
ST. PETE BEACH .... FL 230
SANFORD .... FL 179
SARASOTA .... FL 197
SEBASTIAN.. FL 200
SEBRING .... FL 200
STUART .... FL 201
TALLAHASSEE .... FL 202
TARPON SPRINGS .... FL 230
THONOTOSASSA .... FL 231
TITUSVILLE .... FL 232
VENICE .... FL 232
VERO BEACH .... FL 232
WEST PALM BEACH....................................... FL 233
WINTER HAVEN.. FL 235
WINTER PARK... FL 179

WALKING TOURS

ANGELL & PHELPS CHOCOLATE FACTORY
  TOUR .... DAYTONA BEACH, FL 53
ART DECO DISTRICT .... MIAMI- MIAMI BEACH, FL 117
BROOKSVILLE .... FL 49
COCONUT GROVE .... MIAMI- MIAMI BEACH, FL 117
KEY WEST .... FL 66
PELICAN PATH .... KEY WEST, FL 66
STETSON UNIVERSITY .... DELAND, FL 55
STUART .... FL 201

WATERFALLS

VENETIAN POOL .... CORAL GABLES, FL 124

WATER PARKS

ADVENTURE ISLAND................................ TAMPA, FL 216
ADVENTURE LANDING.............. JACKSONVILLE BEACH, FL 96

DISNEY'S BLIZZARD BEACH WATER PARK .. LAKE BUENA VISTA, FL   166
DISNEY'S TYPHOON LAGOON WATER PARK .... LAKE BUENA
VISTA, FL   166
SILVER SPRINGS WILD WATERS .... OCALA, FL   131
SUN SPLASH FAMILY WATERPARK .... CAPE CORAL, FL   50
WATER MANIA .... KISSIMMEE, FL   162
WEEKI WACHEE SPRINGS WATERPARK ....WEEKI WACHEE, FL   233
WET 'N WILD... ORLANDO, FL   153

WAX MUSEUMS
POTTER'S WAX MUSEUM....................... ST. AUGUSTINE, FL   191

WILDERNESS AREAS
BRADWELL BAY .... APALACHICOLA NF, FL   46
CANAVERAL NATIONAL SEASHORE .... FL   50
LIGNUMVITAE KEY STATE BOTANICAL SITE...... ISLAMORADA, FL   65
LOWER SUWANNEE NWR ....CHIEFLAND, FL   51
MUD SWAMP/NEW RIVER .... APALACHICOLA NF, FL   46
SAN FELASCO HAMMOCK PRESERVE SP.......... GAINESVILLE, FL   84
TIMUCUAN ECOLOGICAL AND HISTORIC
PRESERVE .... JACKSONVILLE, FL   93
⚜ WASHINGTON OAKS GARDENS SP ....PALM COAST, FL   182

WILDLIFE SANCTUARIES
ARTHUR R. MARSHALL LOXAHATCHEE NWR .. DELRAY BEACH, FL   55
BIG CYPRESS NATIONAL PRESERVE................................FL   46
BIG PINE KEY...FL   64
BISCAYNE NP ....FL   124
CORKSCREW SWAMP SANCTUARY.....................NAPLES, FL   128
⚜ EDWARD BALL WAKULLA SPRINGS SP ....WAKULLA, FL   232
FLORIDA KEYS NATIONAL MARINE
SANCTUARY ....BIG PINE KEY, FL   64
HOBE SOUND NWR .... HOBE SOUND, FL   87
JACK ISLAND...................................... FORT PIERCE, FL   82
J.N. "DING" DARLING NWR...........................SANIBEL, FL   197
MERRITT ISLAND NWR............................. TITUSVILLE, FL   232
NATIONAL KEY DEER REFUGE....................BIG PINE KEY, FL   64
PELICAN MAN'S BIRD SANCTUARY .... SARASOTA, FL   199
ROOKERY BAY..NAPLES, FL   127
ST. MARKS NWR .... ST. MARKS, FL   196
SIX MILE CYPRESS SLOUGH PRESERVE............ FORT MYERS, FL   82
SUNCOAST SEABIRD SANCTUARY ....INDIAN SHORES, FL   228
WILDLIFE ON EASY STREET ....TAMPA, FL   219
WILDLIFE SANCTUARY OF NORTHWEST
FLORIDA....................................... PENSACOLA, FL   184

WINERIES
LAKERIDGE WINERY AND VINEYARDS ....CLERMONT, FL   160
SAN SEBASTIAN WINERY .... ST. AUGUSTINE, FL   196

ZOOLOGICAL PARKS & EXHIBITS
BREVARD ZOO.. MELBOURNE, FL   103
⚜ BUSCH GARDENS TAMPA BAY ....TAMPA, FL   217
CARIBBEAN GARDENS: THE ZOO IN NAPLES ....NAPLES, FL   128
⚜ CYPRESS GARDENS ....WINTER HAVEN, FL   236
⚜ DISCOVERY COVE...................................ORLANDO, FL   142
DISNEY'S ANIMAL KINGDOM THEME
PARK.. LAKE BUENA VISTA, FL   165
EVERGLADES WONDER GARDENS............BONITA SPRINGS, FL   48
GATORLAND... ORLANDO, FL   142
HOMOSASSA SPRINGS WILDLIFE SP ..... HOMOSASSA SPRINGS, FL   87
JACKSONVILLE ZOOLOGICAL GARDENS......... JACKSONVILLE, FL   93
JUNGLE ADVENTURES .... CHRISTMAS, FL   160
JUNGLELAND ZOO .... KISSIMMEE, FL   162
LION COUNTRY SAFARI.....................WEST PALM BEACH, FL   233
LOWRY PARK ZOO..TAMPA, FL   218
⚜ MIAMI METROZOO ....MIAMI- MIAMI BEACH, FL   114
MONKEY JUNGLE ....MIAMI- MIAMI BEACH, FL   115
PALM BEACH ZOO ....WEST PALM BEACH, FL   234
⚜ PARROT JUNGLE ....MIAMI- MIAMI BEACH, FL   116
REPTILE WORLD SERPENTARIUM .... ST. CLOUD, FL   179
⚜ ST. AUGUSTINE ALLIGATOR FARM .... ST. AUGUSTINE, FL   195
SARASOTA JUNGLE GARDENS........................ SARASOTA, FL   199
WEEKI WACHEE SPRINGS WATERPARK ....WEEKI WACHEE, FL   233
WILD BILL'S AIRBOAT TOURS & WILDLIFE PARK .... INVERNESS, FL   87
THE ZOO ....GULF BREEZE, FL   86
ZOO ORLANDO AT SANFORD .... SANFORD, FL   179

ZOOLOGICAL PARKS & EXHIBITS-CHILDREN'S ZOOS
BREVARD ZOO.. MELBOURNE, FL   103
⚜ BUSCH GARDENS TAMPA BAY ....TAMPA, FL   217
CARIBBEAN GARDENS: THE ZOO IN NAPLES ....NAPLES, FL   128
⚜ FLORIDA'S SILVER SPRINGS .... OCALA, FL   131
HUNSADER FARMS .... BRADENTON, FL   48
JACKSONVILLE ZOOLOGICAL GARDENS......... JACKSONVILLE, FL   93
JUNGLELAND ZOO .... KISSIMMEE, FL   162
LOWRY PARK ZOO..TAMPA, FL   218
⚜ MIAMI METROZOO ....MIAMI- MIAMI BEACH, FL   114
PALM BEACH ZOO ....WEST PALM BEACH, FL   234
⚜ PARROT JUNGLE ....MIAMI- MIAMI BEACH, FL   116
SARASOTA JUNGLE GARDENS........................ SARASOTA, FL   199
WEEKI WACHEE SPRINGS WATERPARK ....WEEKI WACHEE, FL   233
THE ZOO ....GULF BREEZE, FL   86
ZOO ORLANDO AT SANFORD .... SANFORD, FL   179

SAVE Attraction Admission Discount Index

FLORIDA

ADVENTURE ISLAND...................................TAMPA 216
AH-TAH-THI-KI MUSEUM ....BIG CYPRESS SEMINOLE
    INDIAN RESERVATION 47
ALTAMONTE MALL .... ORLANDO 156
ARABIAN NIGHTS....................................KISSIMMEE 161
THE BAILEY-MATTHEWS SHELL
    MUSEUM..SANIBEL 196
BILLIE SWAMP
    SAFARIBIG CYPRESS SEMINOLE INDIAN RESERVATION 47
BOCA RATON MUSEUM OF ART ....BOCA RATON 47
BOGGY CREEK AIRBOAT RIDES.................. KISSIMMEE 161
BONNET HOUSE MUSEUM &
    GARDENS .... FORT LAUDERDALE 71
BREVARD ZOO ....MELBOURNE 103
BROWARD MALL ....FORT LAUDERDALE 76
BUSCH GARDENS TAMPA BAY ....TAMPA 217
CALUSA NATURE CENTER AND
    PLANETARIUM...........................FORT MYERS 80
CAPONE'S DINNER AND SHOW .... KISSIMMEE 161
CARIBBEAN GARDENS: THE ZOO IN NAPLES ......NAPLES 128
THE CHILDREN'S SCIENCE CENTER............CAPE CORAL 50
CLEARWATER MARINE AQUARIUM........CLEARWATER 227
COASTLAND CENTER ....NAPLES 127
CORAL CASTLE OF FLORIDA ....HOMESTEAD 126
CORAL SPRINGS MUSEUM OF ART .... CORAL SPRINGS 77
CYPRESS GARDENS.......................... WINTER HAVEN 236
DINOSAUR WORLD .... PLANT CITY 229
DISCOVERY UNDERSEA TOURS .... KEY WEST 67
EAST MARTELLO MUSEUM AND GALLERY .... KEY WEST 68
THE FALLS .... MIAMI- MIAMI BEACH 120
FESTIVAL FLEA MARKET MALL.........POMPANO BEACH 78
FLAMINGO GARDENS...................................DAVIE 77
FLORIDA ADVENTURE MUSEUM..............PUNTA GORDA 187
THE FLORIDA HOLOCAUST MUSEUM... ST. PETERSBURG 212
FLYING TIGERS WARBIRD RESTORATION
    MUSEUM .... KISSIMMEE 162
FORT MYERS HISTORICAL MUSEUM ....FORT MYERS 80
GALLERIA .... FORT LAUDERDALE 76
GARLITS' AUTO ATTRACTION .... OCALA 131
GATORLAND.. ORLANDO 142
GRAY LINE ....ST. AUGUSTINE 188
GREAT EXPLORATIONS...................... ST. PETERSBURG 213
GREEN MEADOWS PETTING FARM .... KISSIMMEE 162
HARBOR BRANCH OCEANOGRAPHIC
    INSTITUTION .... FORT PIERCE 83
HISTORIC PENSACOLA VILLAGE .... PENSACOLA 184
HOMOSASSA SPRINGS
    WILDLIFE SP ....HOMOSASSA SPRINGS 87
I.G.F.A. FISHING HALL OF FAME &
    MUSEUM .... DANIA BEACH 77
IMAGINARIUM HANDS-ON MUSEUM........FORT MYERS 80
INTERNATIONAL PLAZA................................TAMPA 223
ISLANDS OF ADVENTURE .... ORLANDO 149
JACKSONVILLE ZOOLOGICAL GARDENS.. JACKSONVILLE 93
JUNGLE ADVENTURES............................ CHRISTMAS 160
JUNGLELAND ZOO .... KISSIMMEE 162
KEY WEST LIGHTHOUSE MUSEUM .... KEY WEST 68
KLASSIX AUTO ATTRACTION .... DAYTONA BEACH 54
KONGER TARPON SPRINGS
    AQUARIUM..................................TARPON SPRINGS 230
THE LIBERTY FLEET OF TALL SHIPS .... KEY WEST 68
LION COUNTRY SAFARI .... WEST PALM BEACH 233
LOWE ART MUSEUM, UNIVERSITY OF
    MIAMI...CORAL GABLES 125
MARIE SELBY BOTANICAL GARDENS .... SARASOTA 199
THE MARY BROGAN MUSEUM OF ART AND
    SCIENCE .... TALLAHASSEE 203
MEDIEVAL TIMES DINNER AND
    TOURNAMENT.....................................KISSIMMEE 162
THE MENNELLO MUSEUM OF AMERICAN FOLK
    ART...ORLANDO 146

MIAMI METROZOO .... MIAMI- MIAMI BEACH 114
MIAMI SEAQUARIUM.............. MIAMI- MIAMI BEACH 115
MONKEY JUNGLE .... MIAMI- MIAMI BEACH 115
THE MORIKAMI MUSEUM AND JAPANESE
    GARDENS .... DELRAY BEACH 55
MOTE AQUARIUM .... SARASOTA 199
MUSEUM OF ART .... FORT LAUDERDALE 71
MUSEUM OF CONTEMPORARY
    ART...NORTH MIAMI BEACH 126
MUSEUM OF DISCOVERY AND SCIENCE AND
    BLOCKBUSTER IMAX THEATER .... FORT LAUDERDALE 74
MUSEUM OF FINE ARTS.................... ST. PETERSBURG 213
THE MUSEUM OF MAN IN
    THE SEA ....PANAMA CITY BEACH 183
MUSEUMS AND NATURE CENTER OF CRANE POINT
    HAMMOCK....................................MARATHON 69
OLD SCHOOL SQUARE CULTURAL ARTS CENTER
    AND NHS.................................. DELRAY BEACH 55
ORANGE BLOSSOM BALLOONS .... ORLANDO 153
ORANGE COUNTY REGIONAL HISTORY
    CENTER .... ORLANDO 147
ORLANDO PREMIUM OUTLETS .... ORLANDO 156
PEÑA-PECK HOUSE............................ST. AUGUSTINE 191
PEMBROKE LAKES MALL .... FORT LAUDERDALE 76
PIONEER FLORIDA MUSEUM AND VILLAGE .. DADE CITY 228
THE PIONEER SETTLEMENT FOR THE CREATIVE
    ARTS .... BARBERVILLE 46
REGENCY SQUARE .... JACKSONVILLE 94
RIPLEY'S BELIEVE IT OR NOT! ORIGINAL
    MUSEUM...ST. AUGUSTINE 194
RIPLEY'S BELIEVE IT OR NOT! ORLANDO
    ODDITORIUM .... ORLANDO 147
RIVERSHIP ROMANCE....................................SANFORD 179
ST. AUGUSTINE ALLIGATOR FARM ....ST. AUGUSTINE 195
ST. AUGUSTINE SCENIC CRUISE.............ST. AUGUSTINE 188
ST. PETERSBURG MUSEUM OF
    HISTORY .... ST. PETERSBURG 216
SALVADOR DALI MUSEUM................ ST. PETERSBURG 216
SAWGRASS MILLS .... FORT LAUDERDALE 76
SEAWORLD ORLANDO .... ORLANDO 147
SHOW QUEEN ....CLEARWATER 228
SKULL KINGDOM .... ORLANDO 149
SLEUTHS MYSTERY DINNER SHOWS .... ORLANDO 149
SOUTH FLORIDA MUSEUM ....BRADENTON 49
SOUTH FLORIDA MUSEUM OF NATURAL
    HISTORY .... DANIA BEACH 77
SPLENDID CHINA .... KISSIMMEE 162
SPORTS IMMORTALS MUSEUM..............BOCA RATON 48
THE SPRINGS .... WARM MINERAL SPRINGS 232
STARLITE MAJESTY......................CLEARWATER 228
STARLITE PRINCESS RIVERBOAT......................TAMPA 220
STARS & STRIPES—KEY WEST.................... KEY WEST 68
STRANAHAN HOUSE .... FORT LAUDERDALE 74
SUN SPLASH FAMILY WATERPARK .... CAPE CORAL 50
TAMPA MUSEUM OF ART ....TAMPA 219
TANGER SANIBEL FACTORY STORES ....FORT MYERS 79
UNIVERSAL STUDIOS.................................. ORLANDO 152
UNIVERSITY MALL...TAMPA 223
U.S. ASTRONAUT HALL OF
    FAME ....KENNEDY SPACE
    CENTER 99
VANTASTIC TOURS .... MARCO ISLAND 103
VIZCAYA MUSEUM AND
    GARDENS .... MIAMI- MIAMI BEACH 116
WEST OAKS MALL................................... ORLANDO 156
WEST SHORE PLAZA ....TAMPA 223
WET 'N WILD .... ORLANDO 153
THE WOLFSONIAN-FLORIDA INTERNATIONAL
    UNIVERSITY .... MIAMI- MIAMI BEACH 117
WRECKERS' MUSEUM/OLDEST HOUSE.......... KEY WEST 68
YOUNG AT ART CHILDREN'S MUSEUM.............. DAVIE 77

Comprehensive City Index

Here is an alphabetical list of all cities appearing in this TourBook® guide. Cities are presented by state/province. Page numbers under the POI column indicate where points of interest text begins. Page numbers under the L&R column indicate where lodging and restaurant listings begin.

FLORIDA	POI	L&R
ALACHUA	N/A	244
ALTAMONTE SPRINGS	N/A	671
AMELIA ISLAND	95	466
ANNA MARIA	N/A	244
APALACHICOLA	46	244
APALACHICOLA NF	46	N/A
APOLLO BEACH	227	896
APOPKA	160	673
ARCADIA	46	245
ATLANTIC BEACH	N/A	468
AVENTURA	N/A	543
AVON PARK	N/A	245
BAL HARBOUR	N/A	543
BALDWIN	N/A	469
BARBERVILLE	46	N/A
BARTOW	N/A	246
BELLE GLADE	N/A	246
BELLEAIR BLUFFS	N/A	896
BIG CYPRESS NATIONAL PRESERVE	46	N/A
BIG CYPRESS SEMINOLE INDIAN RESERVATION	47	N/A
BIG PINE KEY	64	N/A
BISCAYNE NP	124	N/A
BOCA GRANDE	N/A	246
BOCA RATON	47	246
BOKEELIA	48	N/A
BONITA SPRINGS	48	253
BOYNTON BEACH	N/A	255
BRADENTON BEACH	N/A	259
BRADENTON	48	257
BRANDON	N/A	896
BROOKSVILLE	49	260
BUNNELL	50	N/A
BUSHNELL	50	261
CANAVERAL NS	50	N/A
CAPE CANAVERAL	N/A	261
CAPE CORAL	50	262
CAPE HAZE	N/A	263
CAPTIVA	N/A	264
CARRABELLE	N/A	265
CASSELBERRY	N/A	674
CEDAR KEY	51	265
CELEBRATION	N/A	675
CHARLOTTE HARBOR	N/A	266
CHIEFLAND	51	266
CHIPLEY	N/A	266
CHRISTMAS	160	N/A
CLEARWATER	227	899
CLEARWATER BEACH	N/A	906
CLERMONT	160	675
CLEWISTON	N/A	266
COCOA BEACH	52	268
COCOA	52	267
COCONUT CREEK	77	N/A
COCONUT GROVE	124	544
CONCH KEY	N/A	320
CORAL GABLES	124	546
CORAL SPRINGS	77	389
CORTEZ	N/A	276
CRESCENT BEACH	N/A	276
CRESCENT CITY	N/A	276
CRESTVIEW	N/A	276
CROSS CITY	N/A	278
CROSS CREEK	52	N/A
CRYSTAL RIVER	52	278
CUDJOE KEY	N/A	320
CUTLER RIDGE	N/A	548
DADE CITY	228	915
DANIA BEACH	77	390
DAVENPORT	N/A	676
DAVIE	77	391
DAYTONA BEACH	53	283
DAYTONA BEACH SHORES	N/A	296
DE FUNIAK SPRINGS	N/A	307
DE LEON SPRINGS	N/A	308
DE SOTO NME	56	N/A
DEBARY	N/A	307
DEERFIELD BEACH	78	392

FLORIDA (CONT'D)	POI	L&R
DELAND	55	307
DELRAY BEACH	55	308
DELTONA	N/A	310
DESTIN	N/A	310
DOWNTOWN MIAMI	N/A	513
DRY TORTUGAS NP	64	N/A
DUNEDIN	228	916
ELKTON	N/A	314
ELLENTON	56	314
ENGLEWOOD	N/A	316
ESTERO	56	N/A
EVERGLADES CITY	56	316
EVERGLADES NP	57	N/A
FERN PARK	N/A	677
FERNANDINA BEACH	95	N/A
FLAGLER BEACH	N/A	316
FLORAL CITY	N/A	317
FLORIDA CITY	125	548
FORT GEORGE ISLAND	96	N/A
FORT LAUDERDALE	70	356
FORT MATANZAS NMO	79	N/A
FORT MYERS	79	415
FORT MYERS BEACH	82	422
FORT PIERCE	82	430
FORT WALTON BEACH	84	432
GAINESVILLE	84	434
GREEN COVE SPRINGS	N/A	469
GULF BREEZE	86	439
GULF ISLANDS NS	86	N/A
HAINES CITY	N/A	440
HALLANDALE BEACH	78	394
HAVANA	N/A	440
HEATHROW	160	677
HERNANDO	86	440
HIALEAH	N/A	550
HIGH SPRINGS	87	441
HIGHLAND BEACH	N/A	440
HILLIARD	96	N/A
HILLSBORO BEACH	N/A	396
HOBE SOUND	87	N/A
HOLIDAY	N/A	917
HOLLYWOOD	78	396
HOLMES BEACH	N/A	441
HOMESTEAD	125	551
HOMOSASSA	N/A	442
HOMOSASSA SPRINGS	87	N/A
HOWEY-IN-THE-HILLS	N/A	677
INDIALANTIC	N/A	442
INDIAN HARBOUR BEACH	N/A	443
INDIAN ROCKS BEACH	228	917
INDIAN SHORES	228	918
INDIANTOWN	N/A	443
INVERNESS	87	444
ISLAMORADA	65	320
JACKSONVILLE BEACH	96	470
JACKSONVILLE	88	445
JENSEN BEACH	N/A	478
JUNO BEACH	N/A	479
JUPITER	97	479
KENDALL	N/A	551
KENNEDY SPACE CENTER	97	N/A
KEY BISCAYNE	126	552
KEY COLONY BEACH	N/A	323
KEY LARGO	65	323
KEY WEST	66	333
KISSIMMEE	160	678
LADY LAKE	N/A	714
LAKE BUENA VISTA	163	714
LAKE CITY	N/A	480
LAKE HELEN	N/A	482
LAKE MARY	N/A	740
LAKE PARK	N/A	486
LAKE PLACID	N/A	486
LAKE WALES	101	487
LAKE WORTH	102	488
LAKELAND	100	482
LANTANA	N/A	489
LARGO	228	920

COMPREHENSIVE CITY INDEX (CONT'D)

FLORIDA (CONT'D)	POI	L&R
LAUDERDALE-BY-THE-SEA	N/A	400
LAUDERHILL	N/A	402
LEESBURG	N/A	742
LEHIGH ACRES	N/A	489
LIGHTHOUSE POINT	N/A	402
LITTLE TORCH KEY	N/A	352
LIVE OAK	N/A	490
LONG KEY	N/A	352
LONGBOAT KEY	N/A	490
LONGWOOD	N/A	743
LOXAHATCHEE	N/A	493
MACCLENNY	N/A	493
MADEIRA BEACH	229	920
MADISON	N/A	494
MAITLAND	178	744
MANALAPAN	N/A	494
MARATHON	69	353
MARCO ISLAND	102	494
MARGATE	N/A	402
MARIANNA	103	496
MAYPORT	96	N/A
MELBOURNE	103	497
MELBOURNE BEACH	N/A	499
MERRITT ISLAND	N/A	499
MIAMI-MIAMI BEACH	104	500
MIAMI	N/A	517
MIAMI BEACH	N/A	526
MIAMI LAKES	N/A	553
MIAMI SPRINGS	N/A	554
MICANOPY	127	560
MIDWAY	N/A	560
MILTON	127	560
MIRAMAR	N/A	403
MONTICELLO	N/A	560
MOUNT DORA	178	745
MULBERRY	127	561
NAPLES	127	561
NAVARRE	N/A	578
NAVARRE BEACH	N/A	578
NEPTUNE BEACH	N/A	472
NEW PORT RICHEY	N/A	922
NEW SMYRNA BEACH	129	578
NICEVILLE	N/A	580
NOKOMIS	N/A	580
NORTH BAY VILLAGE	N/A	556
NORTH FORT MYERS	N/A	580
NORTH LAUDERDALE	N/A	404
NORTH MIAMI	N/A	557
NORTH MIAMI BEACH	126	557
NORTH PALM BEACH	N/A	581
NORTH PORT	N/A	581
NORTH REDINGTON BEACH	N/A	923
OCALA	130	581
OCALA NF	132	N/A
OCOEE	N/A	746
ODESSA	229	N/A
OKEECHOBEE	132	586
OLD TOWN	N/A	586
OLDSMAR	N/A	924
OLUSTEE	132	N/A
ORANGE CITY	132	587
ORANGE PARK	N/A	473
ORLANDO	134	588
ORLANDO NORTH	N/A	612
ORLANDO SOUTH	N/A	621
ORMOND BEACH	181	753
OSCEOLA NF	181	N/A
OSPREY	181	755
OVIEDO	N/A	747
PALATKA	181	756
PALM BAY	N/A	756
PALM BEACH	181	761
PALM BEACH GARDENS	N/A	763
PALM BEACH SHORES	N/A	766
PALM COAST	182	767
PALM HARBOR	N/A	924
PALMETTO	N/A	768
PANACEA	182	N/A
PANAMA CITY	182	768
PANAMA CITY BEACH	183	770
PEMBROKE PINES	N/A	404
PENSACOLA	184	774
PENSACOLA BEACH	186	777
PERRY	186	779

FLORIDA (CONT'D)	POI	L&R
PINELLAS PARK	N/A	925
PLANT CITY	229	926
PLANTATION	N/A	405
POINT WASHINGTON	186	N/A
POLK CITY	186	N/A
POMPANO BEACH	78	407
PONCE INLET	187	780
PONTE VEDRA BEACH	N/A	475
PORT CHARLOTTE	N/A	780
PORT ORANGE	187	781
PORT RICHEY	N/A	927
PORT ST. JOE	187	N/A
PORT ST. LUCIE	N/A	781
PUNTA GORDA	187	782
QUINCY	187	784
REDINGTON BEACH	N/A	928
REDINGTON SHORES	N/A	928
RIVERVIEW	N/A	928
RIVIERA BEACH	N/A	784
RUSKIN	N/A	928
SAFETY HARBOR	N/A	930
SANFORD	179	747
SANIBEL	196	803
SANTA ROSA BEACH	N/A	811
SARASOTA	197	817
SATELLITE BEACH	N/A	829
SEASIDE	N/A	829
SEBASTIAN	200	830
SEBRING	200	830
SIESTA KEY	N/A	830
SILVER SPRINGS	N/A	833
SINGER ISLAND	201	N/A
SOUTH DAYTONA	N/A	833
SOUTH MIAMI	N/A	557
SOUTH PALM BEACH	N/A	834
SOUTH PASADENA	N/A	937
SPRING HILL	N/A	834
ST. AUGUSTINE	188	788
ST. AUGUSTINE BEACH	N/A	800
ST. CLOUD	179	747
ST. MARKS	196	803
ST. PETERSBURG	212	863
ST. PETE BEACH	230	931
STARKE	201	834
STEINHATCHEE	N/A	835
STUART	201	836
SUGARLOAF KEY	69	N/A
SUN CITY CENTER	N/A	937
SUNNY ISLES	N/A	558
SUNRISE	N/A	410
SURFSIDE	N/A	559
TALLAHASSEE	202	838
TALLEVAST	N/A	843
TAMARAC	N/A	412
TAMPA BAY	204	844
TAMPA	216	870
TARPON SPRINGS	230	938
TAVARES	179	749
TEMPLE TERRACE	N/A	939
TEQUESTA	N/A	947
THE FLORIDA KEYS	60	318
THONOTOSASSA	231	N/A
TIERRA VERDE	N/A	939
TITUSVILLE	232	947
TREASURE ISLAND	N/A	940
VALRICO	N/A	949
VENICE	232	949
VERO BEACH	232	952
VILANO BEACH	N/A	954
WAKULLA	232	N/A
WAKULLA SPRINGS	N/A	955
WARM MINERAL SPRINGS	232	N/A
WEEKI WACHEE	233	956
WELAKA	233	N/A
WESLEY CHAPEL	N/A	945
WEST MELBOURNE	N/A	956
WEST PALM BEACH	233	957
WESTON	N/A	413
WHITE SPRINGS	235	N/A
WILLISTON	N/A	962
WINTER GARDEN	N/A	749
WINTER HAVEN	235	962
WINTER PARK	179	750
WOODVILLE	237	N/A
YULEE	N/A	477
ZEPHYRHILLS	N/A	946

Photo Credit Index

The world famous Cinderella Castle in the *Magic Kingdom* ® Park at the *Walt Disney World* ® Resort
As to Disney logos, artwork and properties:
© Disney .... Cover, Title, Table of Contents

Photo Research provided in part by Image Select International, United Kingdom

TOURBOOK NAVIGATOR

Large-scale Hotel / Hotel Royal Plaza,
Lake Buena Vista, FL 22
Small-scale Hotel / Baymont Inn,
Dallas/Ft. Worth-Airport North, TX 22
Motel / Best Western Deltona Inn, Deltona, FL 22
Country Inn / Greenville Inn, Greenville, ME 22
B&B / Harbour Town Inn, Boothbay Harbor, ME 22
Condo / Sands of Kahana, Kahana, Maui, HI 22
Cabin/Cottage / Desert Rose Inn, Bluff, UT 23
Ranch / C Lazy U Ranch, Granby, CO 23
Vacation Home / ResortQuest,
Hilton Head Island, SC 23

FLORIDA

Sanibel Island / © Maxine Cass 29, 35, 241
Shells on the beach at Sanibel Island
© Maxine Cass 30
Historical Timeline
Archive Films & Photos, Inc. 32
© Corbis 33
© US Army/Airforce Website 33

The Florida Keys

Sunrise on Islamorada; and Key West pier
© Trip / J. Greenberg 60, 61, 69, 355
Mallory Market in Key West
© Trip / M. Morton 62
Southernmost Home
© Gibson Stock Photography 62
Roadside art structures in Florida Keys; and
Key West Lighthouse Museum
© Maxine Cass .... 63, Table of Contents
Christ of the Deep statue, John Pennekamp Coral Reef
State Park / © Stephen Frink / Index Stock 63
Skyline-Overseas Highway; Duval Street; Lands End
Marina, Key West; and Mallory Square sponge
market / © Trip / J. Greenberg 318, 319
Key West scooter / © Graeme Teague 318

Fort Lauderdale

Palm trees on Fort Lauderdale Beach;
and Fort Lauderdale waterway
© Trip / J. Greenberg .... 70, 73, Table of Contents
Rollerbladers on the beach
© Maxine Cass 71, 78, 414
I.G.F.A. Fishing Hall of Fame and Museum, Dania Beach;
and Peacock at Flamingo Gardens, Davie
© Graeme Teague 73
Aerial view of the skyline / © Trip / Streano / Havens .. 73
Biking at Las Olas Beach / © Maxine Cass 356
Convention Center fountain
© Trip / J. Greenberg 356

Golfing in Coral Springs / Courtesy Greater Fort
Lauderdale CVB 356
Las Olas Riverfront shopping district
© Richard Cummins / Corbis 356

Jacksonville

Riverwalk on the St. Johns River
© Gibson Stock Photography 88
Kayakers on Amelia Island
© Wendell Metzen / Index Stock 89, 96, 477
Jacksonville Landing / Visit Florida 91
Mural at Museum of Science and History
© Corbis .... 91, Table of Contents
Jacksonville Zoological Gardens
© Gibson Stock Photography 91
Fountain at Cummer Musuem of Art and Gardens
© Cummer Museum of Art 91
Jacksonville Landing / © W. Metzen
H. Armstrong Roberts 445
Skyline / Visit Florida 445
Amelia Island buggy tour / Amelia Island Tourist
Development Council 445
Jacksonville Jaguars football player
© Empics 445

Miami-Miami Beach

Ocean Drive at night
© R. Kord / H. Armstrong Roberts 104
The flamingo exhibit at Metrozoo;
Little Havana park and mural; and
Miami-Dade Cultural Center
© Gibson Stock Photography 105, 107, 108
Calle Ocho dancers at Carnival Miami
© Nik Wheeler / Corbis 106
Palm trees along the beach
© Richard Bickel / Corbis 108
Flamingo at Metrozoo / © Corbis 108
Vizcaya Museum and Gardens
© Maxine Cass 109
Killer whale show at Miami Seaquarium; and
Parrot Jungle / © Trip / E. Knight 109, 118
Metromover crossing the Miami River
© Trip / K. McClaren .... 111, Table of Contents
Aerial view of Miami's Art Deco District on Ocean Drive
© Trip / J. Greenberg 112
Sailboats on the beach / © Trip / A. Tovy 119
CocoWalk Shopping Mall / © Corbis 120
Renaissance acrobats at Vizcaya
© Gibson Stock Photography 121
Vizcaya Museum and Gardens
P. Yusefzadeh / © AAA 122
Art Deco District, South Beach
© Maxine Cass 123
Sandcastles on the beach
© Graeme Teague 126, 559
Hotels along South Beach
© Trip / J. Greenberg 500
Park chess players in Little Havana
© Gibson Stock Photography 500
Deep sea fishing boat / © Trip / J. Mason 500
Street diners / © Spectrum Colour Library 501
Miami Heat NBA basketball player © Empics 501

Photo Credit Index (cont'd)

Orlando

Orlando skyline / © International Stock
ImageState 134

Boys playing at the Orange County Regional History
Center / Courtesy Orange County
Regional History Center 135

Winter Park Farmers' Market; and Orlando Museum of
Art Orlando/Orange County CVB 136, 137

Orlando Philharmonic; Charles Hosmer Morse Museum of
American Art, Winter Park; and The Dome at
the Orange County Regional History Center
Orlando/Orange County CVB 138, 139

Universal Studios 60's rock and roll stage show
© Gibson Stock Photography 139

Disney's the Seven Dwarfs / © Trip / H. Rogers 138

I-Ride trolley along International Drive;
Sleuths Mystery Dinner Shows; Shopping on Park
Avenue, Winter Park; The Orlando Ballet;
and The Incredible Hulk Roller Coaster,
Islands of Adventure / Orlando/Orange
County CVB 141, 149, 155, 157, 180, 752

Gatorland Zoo / © Corbis 142

Dolphin at SeaWorld / © Trip / R. Belbin 147

Houston Astros spring training at Osceola County
Stadium; and Boggy Creek airboating
Kissimmee/St. Cloud CVB 153, 154

Acrobats at Splendid China
© Gibson Stock Photography 158

Airboating; Swan boat at Lake Eola; Harry P. Leu
Gardens; Dining; and Family bicycling
Orlando/Orange County CVB 588, 589

Tampa Bay

Skyline and Hillsborough River; and The Pier,
St. Petersburg / © Corbis 204, 207

Fun at the beach; and Citrus plant
St. Petersburg/Clearwater Area CVB 205, 206

Dunedin Historical Society and Museum
St. Petersburg/Clearwater Area CVB 208

The NFL's Tampa Bay Buccaneers
© Empics 208

Water ride at Busch Gardens
© Trip / G. Heath 209

Chaise lounges on beach / © Corbis 209

The Pre-History Exhibit at St. Petersburg Museum of
History / Courtesy St. Petersburg Museum
of History 209

Sunshine Skyway Bridge
© Nik Wheeler / Corbis 844

NHL's Tampa Bay Lightning Hockey player
© Empics 844

African lion at Busch Gardens Tampa Bay
© Busch Entertainment Corp. 845

Skyscrapers rise above Fire Fountain sculpture
© Corbis 845

Yachts in Clearwater Harbor
© Trip / L. Gullichsen 845

Beach trolley; St. Johns Pass Village and
Boardwalk, Madeira Beach; Golfing;
and Fun in the sun at Pier 60 / St. Petersburg/
Clearwater Area CVB 211, 220, 221, 222

Salvador Dali Museum
© Raymond Gehman / Corbis 212

Feeding the giraffes at Busch Gardens
© Dave G. Houser / Corbis ..... 216, Table of Contents

Florida Aquarium / © Trip / K. McClaren 218

Rollerblading in Tampa
Visit Florida 219

Ybor City couple; Ybor City musician; and
Sunshine Skyway Bridge, St. Petersburg
© Trip / J. Greenberg 223, 225, 231, 946

Parade of the Pirates at the Gasparilla Festival
of the Arts / © Corbis 224

Up-Close, Casual, Personal

Our style of small-ship cruising means that whatever the destination, you're capturing the travel experience as no other means can provide. Gain insight from local guides, and our on-board Naturalist-Interpretive Guide. Get up-close to whales and wildlife, and navigate narrow waterways totally inaccessible to larger ships.

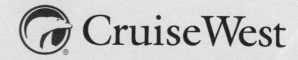

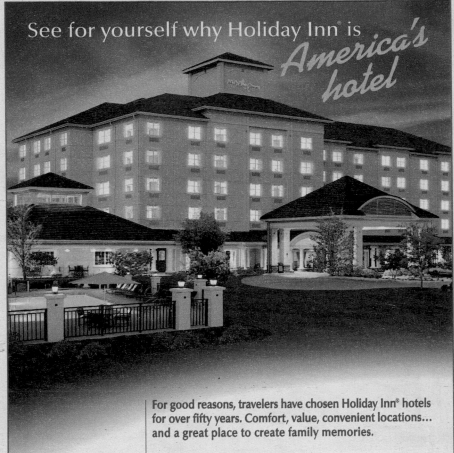

See for yourself why Holiday Inn® is *America's hotel*

For good reasons, travelers have chosen Holiday Inn® hotels for over fifty years. Comfort, value, convenient locations... and a great place to create family memories.

Here's what you can expect at every Holiday Inn hotel:*
- Kids Eat & Stay Free
- Swimming pools
- Restaurant, lounge, room service, and fitness center
- In-room amenities, including: dataport, iron/ironing board, coffeemaker, and hair dryer.

Holiday Inn hotels across the nation offer special AAA rates.

HOTELS · RESORTS

For Reservations:
Call **1-800-734-4275**,
your AAA Travel Professional
or visit **holiday-inn.com/aaa**

For more information on Holiday Inn hotels in the area you plan to visit, look for our hotel ads and "red" Official Appointment hotel listings.